WHEN YOU'RE IN NEW YORK CITY-COME VISIT OUR BRAND NEW SHOWROOM!
OPEN WEEKDAYS, 10 AM TO 5 PM: BY APPOINTMENT ONLY
FOUR COLOR COMICS
BUY
WHY YOU SHOULD CALL US BEFORE YOU SELL YOUR COLLECTION OF COMICS, ARTWORK OR MEMORABILIA:
SELL
We make it easy! No waiting for payment, No song and dance about grading. We'll come to you: Anywhere, Anytime! FOUR COLOR COMICS takes the risk out of selling. Treat yourself to an honest, straight-forward experience—Sell your collection to us and walk away with more money in your pocket and a smile on your face.
And if you're looking to buy comics, original artwork or memorabilia, give us a call first! We probably already have that elusive issue or object you've been searching for—and at a price you'll like!
CALL ROBERT ROGOVIN!
(212) 675-6990
NEW YORK SHOWROOM: 115 West 27th Street, New York, NY 10001 TEL: (212) 675-6990
Detective Comics
Action Comics
64 Pages of New CAPTAIN MARVEL Adventures
© 1995 DC COMICS
© 1995 MARVEL COMICS
THE JOKER ©1939, 1995 DC COMICS. ALL RIGHTS RESERVED
P9-DDG-799

25th Edition

BOOKS FROM 1897 - PRESENT INCLUDED
CATALOGUE & EVALUATION GUIDE - ILLUSTRATED

By
Robert M. Overstreet

SPECIAL CONTRIBUTORS TO THIS EDITION

Pat Calhoun, Joe Mannarino, Jerry Weist,
Tom Inge, Bruce Hamilton, Robert Roter

SPECIAL ADVISORS TO THIS EDITION

Bruce Hamilton • Hugh O'Kennon • Ron Pussell • Gary M. Carter • John Snyder
Terry Stroud • Michael Naiman • Steve Geppi • Gary Colabuono • James Payette
Harry Matetsky • Jerry Weist • John Verzyl • Mark Wilson • Joe Mannarino
Gary Guzzo • Robert Hall • Joe Dungan • David T. Alexander • Jon Berk
Larry Curico • Gary Dolgoff • Richard Evans • Steve Fishler • Steve Gentner
Michael Goldman • Jamie Graham • Daniel Greenhalgh • John Hauser • Bill Howard
Bill Hughes • Rob Hughes • Joseph Koch • Phil Levine • Matt Nelson • Richard Olson
Chris Pedrin • Bill Ponseti • Todd Reznik • Robert Rogovin • Rory Root
Robert Roter • Chuck Rozanski • Tony Starks • Joe Verenault • Harley Yee

AVON BOOKS NEW YORK

Serious Comic Book Collectors, Don't Miss

THE OVERSTREET COMIC BOOK GRADING GUIDE

By Robert M. Overstreet and Gary M. Carter

A Confident Collector Title from Avon Books

Important Notice. All of the information, including valuations, in this book has been compiled from the most reliable sources, and every effort has been made to eliminate errors and questionable data. Nevertheless, the possibility of error always exists in a work of such immense scope. The publisher will not be held responsible for losses which may occur in the purchase, sale, or other transaction of items because of information contained herein. Readers who feel they have discovered errors are invited to *write* and inform us so that the errors may be corrected in subsequent editions.

Cover Illustration by John Romita, Jr.

THE OVERSTREET COMIC BOOK PRICE GUIDE (25th Edition) is an original publication of Avon Books. This edition has never before appeared in book form.

AVON BOOKS
A division of
The Hearst Corporation
1350 Avenue of the Americas
New York, New York 10019

Published by arrangement with Gemstone Publishing, Inc.
Library of Congress Catalog Card Number: 94-96754
ISBN: 0-380-78210-3

First Avon Books Trade Printing: May 1995

AVON TRADEMARK REG. U.S. PAT. OFF. AND IN OTHER COUNTRIES, MARCA REGISTRADA, HECHO EN U.S.A.

Printed in the U.S.A.
10 9 8 7 6 5 4 3 2 1

TABLE OF CONTENTS

ACKNOWLEDGEMENTS

Larry Bigman (Frazetta-Williamson data); Glenn Bray (Kurtzman data); Dan Malan & Charles Heffelfinger (Classic Comics data); Gary Carter (DC data); J. B. Clifford Jr. (E. C. data); Gary Coddington (Superman data); Wilt Conine (Fawcett data); Dr. S. M. Davidson (Cupples & Leon data); Al Dellinges (Kubert data); Kevin Hancer (Tarzan data); Charles Heffelfinger and Jim Ivey (March of Comics listing); R. C. Holland and Ron Pussell (Seduction and Parade of Pleasure data); Grant Irwin (Quality data); Richard Kravitz (Kelly data); Phil Levine (giveaway data); Fred Nardelli (Frazetta data); Michelle Nolan (love comics); Mike Nolan (MLJ, Timely, Nedor data); George Olshevsky (Timely data); Don Rosa (Late 1940s to 1950s data); Richard Olson (LOA & R. F. Outcault data); Scott Pell ('50s data); Greg Robertson (National data); Mark Arnold (Harvey data); Frank Scigliano (Little Lulu data); Gene Seger (Buck Rogers data); Rick Sloane (Archie data); David R. Smith, Archivist, Walt Disney Productions (Disney data); Don and Maggie Thompson (Four Color listing); Mike Tiefenbacher & Jerry Sinkovec (Atlas and National data); Raymond True (Classic Comics data); Jim Vadeboncoeur Jr. (Williamson and Atlas data); Kim Weston (Disney and Barks data); Cat Yronwode (Spirit data); Andrew Zerbe and Gary Behymer (M. E. data).

My appreciation must also be extended to Bruce Hamilton, Jerry Weist, John Verzyl, James Payette, Robert Rotor, Ron Pussell, Joe Mannarino, Terry Stroud, Dave Anderson (OK), Gary Colabuono, Rod Dyke, Gary Guzzo, Denise Treco, Stephen Fishler, Harley Yee, John Snyder, Matt Hawkins, Lou Bank, Jeff Mariotte, Donna Sava, Maureen McTigue, Marty Stever, Gale Young, Steve Geppi, Hugh O'Kennon and Don Maris, for their support and help; to Dr. Richard Olson for grading and Yellow Kid information; to Tom Inge for his "Chronology of the American Comic Book"; to Pat Calhoun for his entertaining article; to Bill Spicer and Zetta DeVoe (Western Publishing Co.) for their contribution of data; and especially to Bill for his kind permission to reprint portions of his and Jerry Bails' America's Four Color Pastime;

Special Credit is due our talented staff for their assistance with this anniversary edition and for their help at the conventions last year; to Todd Hoffer(layout and design), Dave Noah(research and statistical data) and Tony Overstreet (technical support and layout and design) for their valuable contributions in the continuing success of the Annual Price Guide.

Finally, thanks is due to my wife Caroline Overstreet and my editor Mike Renegar for their inspiration, advice and hard work in getting this reference work to the printer on time. Thanks to everyone that placed ads in this 25th edition.

Acknowledgement is also due to the following people who have so generously contributed much needed data for this edition:

Mark Arnold
Stephen Baer
The Bag Man
Bob Bailey
Tim Barnes
Jonathan Bennett
John Binder, MD
Robert Bradley
Richard M. Brown
Robert Brown
Douglas Chambers
Raphael H. Chang
Robert N. Cherry, Jr.
Monte Cohen
David W. Cushman
Len Cutler
Sterling Dashiell
Sol Davidson
Lee De Broff
Tad Delius
Anthony F. De Maria
John Doliber
Rafael Elortequi
Brandon Finkler
Liam Foster
Chris Gage
David Gerstein
Boyd Graham
Tom Hamilton
Matthew Hawes
Peter Healy
Mark Heike
Dan Hering
Anton Hermus
Wayne E. Hinson
Carl Horak
Richard Howell
Bill Hutchison
Michael Ingersoll
Mark Jarasitis
Dave Johnson
Robert Karon
Ken Kerouac
Richard Kolkman
Dan Kurdilla
Brian Lambert
Gene Lomoriello
David Luhn
Gretel Lumley
Boyd Magers
Ron Massingill
Derek Matthews
James P. McLoughlin
Dan Mei
Harry W. Miller
Al Mindy
John Mlachnik
David W. Mote
Michael L. Murphy
John Newberry
Hugh O'Kennon
Richard D. Olson
Roland Palmer
Leo Pando
Jeff Patton
Gary Payne
Don Petterson
Rick Pilotte
Lynn Potter
Brian Powell
Ken Quattro
Jeff Rader
A. B. Randall
Michael Rhode
Bruce A. Ritzen
Hans-Jurgen Runge
Henry Scagnoli
William K. Schoch
Eugene Seger
Patrick Shaughnessy
William Shipley
Ed Spiegel
Tony Starks
John R. Stefanik
Ray Storch
Reed Stover
Steven Swenson
William Tighe
James Walls
Paul Wardle
Chris Williams
M. Wayne Williams
Ronnie W. Wise
Gary Woloszyn
Garth & Kelly Wood

INTRODUCTION

Congratulations! We at Overstreet welcome you to the hobby of comic books. This book is the most comprehensive reference work available on comics. It is also respected and used by dealers and collectors everywhere. The Overstreet price is the accepted price around the world, and we have not earned this privilege easily. Through hard work, diligence and constant contact with the market for decades, Overstreet has become the most trusted name in comics.

HOW TO USE THIS BOOK

This volume is an accurate, detailed alphabetical list of comic books and their retail values. Comic books are listed by title, regardless of company. Prices listed are shown in good, fine and near mint condition with many key books priced in an additional very fine grade. Comic books that fall in between the grades listed can be priced simply with the following procedure: Very good is half way between good and fine; very fine is half way between fine and near mint (unless a VF price is already shown). The older true mint books usually bring a premium over the near mint price. Books in fair bring 50 to 70% of the good price. Some books only show a very fine price as the highest grade. The author has not been able to determine if these particular books exist in better than very fine condition, thus the omission of a near mint price. Most comic books are listed in groups, i.e., 11-20, 21-30, 31-50, etc. The prices listed opposite these groupings represent the value of each issue in that group. More detailed information is given for individual comic books. If you are looking for a particular character, consult the first appearance indexes which will help you locate the correct title and issue. This book also contains hundreds of ads covering all aspects of this hobby. Whether you are buying or selling, the advertising sections can be of tremendous benefit to you.

COMIC BOOK VALUES LISTED

All values listed in this book are in U.S. currency and are retail prices based on (but not limited to) reports from our extensive network of experienced advisors which include convention sales, mail order, auctions, unpublished personal sales and stores. Overstreet, with several decades of market experience, has developed a unique and comprehensive system for gathering, documenting, averaging and pricing data on comic books. The end result is a true fair market value for your use. We have earned the reputation for our cautious, conservative approach to pricing comic books. You, the collector, can be assured that the prices listed in this volume are the most accurate and useful in print.

IMPORTANT NOTE: This book is not a dealer's price list, although some dealers may base their prices on the values listed. The true value of any comic book is what you are willing to pay. Prices listed herein are an indication of what collectors (not dealers) would probably pay. For one reason or another, these collectors might want certain books badly, or else need specific issues to complete their runs and so are willing to pay more.

DEALERS POSITION: Dealers are not in a position to pay the full prices listed, but work on a percentage depending largely on the amount of investment required and the quality of material offered. Usually they will pay from 20 to 70% of the list price depending on how long it will take them to sell the collection after making the investment; the higher the demand and better the condition, the more the percentage. Most dealers are faced with expenses such as advertising, travel, telephone and mailing, rent, employee salaries, plus convention costs. These costs all go in before the books are sold. The high demand books usually sell right away but there are many other titles that are difficult to sell due to low demand. Sometimes a dealer will have cost tied up in this type of matrial for several years before finally moving it. Remember, his position is that of handling, demand and overhead. Most dealers are victims of these economics.

HOW COMIC BOOKS ARE LISTED

Comic books are listed alphabetically by title. All titles are listed as if they are one word, ignoring spaces, hyphens and apostrophes. The true title of a comic book can be found listed with the publisher's information or indicia usually found at the bottom of the inside front cover. Usually, the official title are those words that are listed in all caps. Titles that appear on the front cover can vary from the official title listed inside.

Comic book titles, sequence of issues, dates of first and last issues, publishing companies, origin and special issues are listed when known. Prominent and collectible artists are also pointed out (usually in footnotes). Page counts will always include covers.

Most comic books began with a #1, but occasionally many titles began with an odd number. There is a reason for this. Publishers had to register new titles with the post office for 2nd class permits. The registration fee was expensive. To avoid this expense, many publishers would continue the numbering of new titles from old defunct titles. For instance, Weird Science #12 (1st issue) was continued from the defunct Saddle Romances #11 (the last issue). In doing this, the publishers hoped to avoid having to register new titles. However, the post office would soon discover the new title and force the publisher to pay the registration fee as well as to list the correct number. For instance, the previous title mentioned began with #12 (1st issue). Then #13 through #15 were published. The next issue became #5 after the Post Office correction. Now the sequence of published issues (see the listings) is #12-15,5-on. This created a problem in early fandom for the collector because the numbers 12-15 in this title were duplicated.

WHAT COMIC BOOKS ARE LISTED

The Guide will be listing primarily American comic books due to space limitation. Most newsstand comic books will be listed. Some variations of the regular comic book format are listed. These mainly include those pre-1933 comic strip reprint books with varying sizes usually with cardboard covers, but sometimes with hardback. As forerunners of the modern comic book format, they deserve to be listed despite their obvious differences in presentation. Other books that will be listed are giveaway comics but only those that contain known characters, work by known collectible artists, or those of special interest.

POLICY OF LISTING NEW COMIC BOOKS

The current market has experienced an explosion of publishers with hundreds of new titles appearing in black and white and color. Many of these comics are listed in this book, but not all due to space limitation. We will attempt to list complete information only on those titles that show some collector interest. The selection of titles to include is constantly being monitored by our board of advisors who work on our monthly magazine. Of course a much better coverage of recent books will be made in the monthly throughout the year. Please do not contact us to list your new comic books. Listings are determined by the marketplace. However, we are interested in receiving review copies of all new comic books published

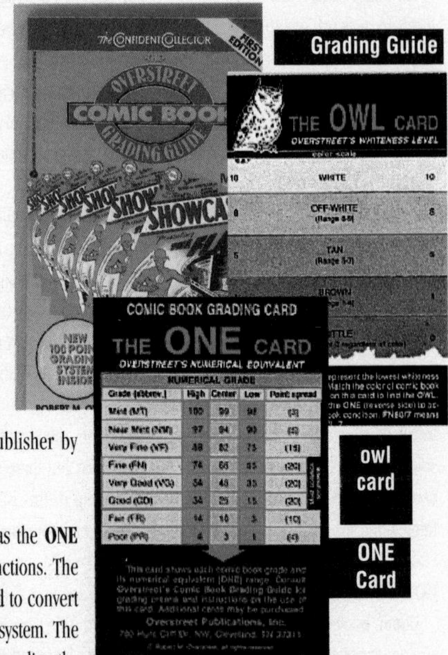

GRADING COMIC BOOKS

GET THE TOOLS

For complete, detailed information on grading and restoration, consult the Overstreet Comic Book Grading Guide. Copies are available through all normal distribution channels or can be ordered direct from the publisher by sending $12 plus $2.00 postage and handling.

The Overstreet Comic Book Grading Card, known as the **ONE** and **OWL Card** is also available. This card has two functions. The **ONE Card** (**O**verstreet's **N**umerical **E**quivalent) is used to convert grading condition terms to the new numerical grading system. The **OWL Card** (**O**verstreet's **W**hiteness **L**evel) is used for grading the whiteness of paper. The color scale on the **OWL Card** is simply placed over the interior comic book paper. The paper color is matched with the color on the card to get the **OWL** number. The **ONE/OWL Card** is available through all normal distribution channels or may be ordered direct from the publisher by sending $2.75 per card, postpaid.

HOW TO GRADE

Before a comic book's true value can be assessed, its condition or state of preservation must be determined. In all comic books, the better the condition the more desirable and valuable the book. Comic books in **MINT** condition will bring several times the price of the same book in **POOR** condition. Therefore it is very important to be able to properly grade your books. Comics should be graded from the inside out, so the following comic book areas should be examined before assigning a final grade.

Check inside pages, inside spine and covers and outside spine and covers for any tears, markings, brittleness, tape, soiling, chunks out or other defects that would affect the grade. After all the above steps have been taken, then the reader can begin to consider an overall grade for his or her book. The grading of a comic book is done by simply looking at the book and describing its condition, which may range from absolutely perfect newsstand condition (MINT) to extremely worn, dirty, and torn (POOR.)

Numerous variables influence the evaluation of a comic book's condition and all must be considered in the final evaluation. As grading is the most subjective aspect of determining a comic's value, it is very important that the grader be careful not to allow wishful thinking to influence what the eyes see. It is also very important to realize that older comics in MINT condition are extremely scarce and are rarely advertised for sale; most of the higher grade comics advertised range from VERY FINE to NEAR MINT.

GRADING DEFINITIONS

Note: This edition uses both the traditional grade abbreviations and the ONE number throughout the listings. The Overstreet Numerical Equivalent (ONE) spread range is given with each grade.

MINT (MT) (ONE 100-98): Near perfect in every way. Only the most subtle bindery or printing defects are allowed. Cover is flat with no surface wear. Cover inks are bright with high reflectivity and minimal fading. Corners are cut square and sharp. Staples are generally centered, clean with no rust. Cover is generally well centered and firmly secured to interior pages. Paper is supple and fresh. Spine is tight and flat.

NEAR MINT (NM) (ONE 97-90): Nearly perfect with only minor imperfections such as tiny corner creases or staple stress lines, a few color flecks, bindery tears, tiny impact creases or a combination of the above where the overall eye appeal is less than Mint. Only the most subtle binding and/or printing defects allowed. Cover is flat with no surface wear. Cover inks are bright with high reflectivity and minimum of fading. Corners are cut square and sharp with ever so slight blunting permitted. Staples are generally centered, clean with no rust. Cover is well centered and firmly secured to interior pages. Paper is supple and like new. Spine is tight and flat.

VERY FINE (VF) (ONE 89-75): An excellent copy with outstanding eye appeal. Sharp, bright and clean with supple pages. Cover is relatively flat with minimal surface wear beginning to show. Cover inks are generally bright with moderate to high reflectivity. Slight wear beginning to show including some minute wear at corners. Staples may show some discoloration. Spine may have a few transverse stress lines but is relatively flat. A light 1/2 inch crease is acceptible. Pages and covers can be yellowish/tannish (at the least, but not brown and will usually be off-white to white).

FINE (FN) (ONE 74-55): An exceptional, above-average copy that shows minor wear but is still relatively flat and clean with no major creasing or other serious defects. Eye appeal is somewhat reduced because of noticeable surface wear and the accumulation of smaller defects, especially on the spine and edges. A Fine condition comic book appears to have been read many times and has been handled with moderate care. Compared to a VF, cover inks are beginning to show a significant reduction in reflectivity but it is still ahighly collectible and desirable book.

VERY GOOD (VG) (ONE 54-35): The average used comic book. A comic in this grade shows moderate wear, can have a reading or center crease or a rolled spine, but has not accumulated enough total defects to reduce eye appeal to the point that it is not a desirable copy. Some discoloration, fading and even minor soiling is allowed.

No chunks can be missing but a small piece can be out at the corner or edge. Store stamps, name stamps, arrival dates, initials, etc. have no effect on this grade. Cover and interior pages can have minor tears and folds and the centerfold may be loose or detached. One or both staples might be loose, but cover is not completely detached. Common bindery and printing defects do not affect grade. Pages and inside covers may be brown but not brittle. Tape should never be used for comic book repair, however many VG condition comics have minor tape repair.

GOOD (GD) (ONE 34-15): A copy in this grade has all pages and covers, although there may be small pieces missing. Books in this grade are commonly creased, scuffed, abraded and soiled, but completely readable. Often paper quality is low but not brittle. Cover reflectivity is low and in some cases completely absent. Most collectors consider this the lowest collectible grade because comic books in lesser condition are usually incomplete and/or brittle. This grade can have a large accumulation of defects but still maintains its basic structural integrity.

FAIR (FR) (ONE 14-5): A copy in this grade has all pages and most of the covers, is soiled, ragged and unattractive. Creases and folds are prevalent and paper quality may be very low. The centerfold may be missing if it does not affect a story. Spine may be completely split its entire length. Staples may be gone, and/or cover completely detached. Corners are commonly severely rounded or absent. Coupons may be cut from front cover and/or back cover and/or interior pages. These books are mostly readable although soiling, staining, tears, markings or chunks missing may interfere with reading the complete story. Very often paper quality is low and may even be brittle around the edges but not in the central portion of the pages.

POOR (PR) (ONE 4-1): Most comic books in this grade have been sufficiently degraded to the point that there is no longer any collector value. Copies in this grade typically have pages and/or approximately 1/3 or more of the front cover missing. They may have extremely severe stains, mildew or heavy cover abrasion to the point that cover inks are indistinct/absent. They may have been defaced with paints, varnishes, glues, oil, indelible markers or dyes. Other defects often include severe rips, tears, folding and creasing. Another common defect in this grade is moderate to severe brittleness, often to the point that the comic book literally "falls apart" when examined.

DUST JACKETS

Many of the early strip reprint comics were printed in hardback with dust jackets. Books with dust jackets are worth more. The value can increase from 20 to 50 percent depending on the rarity of book. Usually, the earlier the book, the greater the percentage. Unless noted, prices listed are without dust jackets. The condition of the dust jacket should be graded independently of the book itself.

RESTORED COMICS

Our board of advisors suggests that **professionally restored comic books** are an accepted component of the comic book market, but only if the following criteria are met: 1–Must be professional work. 2–Complete disclosure of the extent and type of restoration. 3–Both parties are informed. 4–Priced accordingly depending on availability and demand. **Note:** A professionally restored book, reasonably priced, while not worth as much as the same book unrestored, will increase in value at the same rate. However, if you pay the unrestored price for a restored book, you would be paying a premium, which of course may not be a good investment.

Initial indications on sales and auction results suggests the following: Unrestored key books in Fine or better condition may prove in the future to be better investments as their availability decreases, and should not be restored to an apparent higher grade. Restoration should be concentrated on books in less than Fine condition. **Warning:** Before getting restoration done, seek advice from a professional and avoid doing it yourself.

Many rare and expensive books are being repaired and restored by professionals and amateurs alike. If the book is expensive, there is a strong likelihood that some type of repair, cleaning or restoration has been done. In most cases, after restoration, these books are not actually higher grades but are altered lower grade books. Note: Expert restoration is always preferable to amateur work and is sometimes very difficult to spot and can be easily missed when grading. In some cases, the work done is so good that it is impossible to spot.

Your Comic Books Are Dying

Save them with the Only True Archival Quality Preservation Supplies

Mylar® Sleeves (Made entirely of Mylar® type D)

Many manufacturers claim that their sleeves are archival when they are not. These inferior quality sleeves will ruin your comic books.True archival quality sleeves must meet the standards set forth by the Library of Congress and the National Archives.
BCE offers three sleeves in different weights and configurations that meet these requirements.

Genuine Acid-Free Backing Boards

Don't take a chance with boards that are so called "acid free". True archival, acid free boards must have both a minimum pH of 8.0 - 8.5 and a 3% calcium carbonate buffer throughout - not just on the surface.
BCE offers two boards in different thicknesses that meet these requirements as well as *NEW LIFE-X-TENDER™ BACKING BOARDS.*
(see next 2 pages for detailed information)

Acid-Free Boxes

Preserving comics can only be done by using true archival supplies. Skimp on one item and your entire collection could become worthless.
BCE offers five genuine acid free boxes made from the same basic archival material as our acid free backing boards, only in a heavier weight.

Independent Laboratory tests show that many preservation supply manufacturers claim their products are archival when they are not. Don't be fooled.

Call BCE today and get the preservation supplies used by the U.S. Library of Congress and the National Archives

Bill Cole Enterprises, Inc.
617-986-2653 FAX 617-986-2656

Send for your free catalog today and receive a $5.00 merchandise coupon good towards your first order

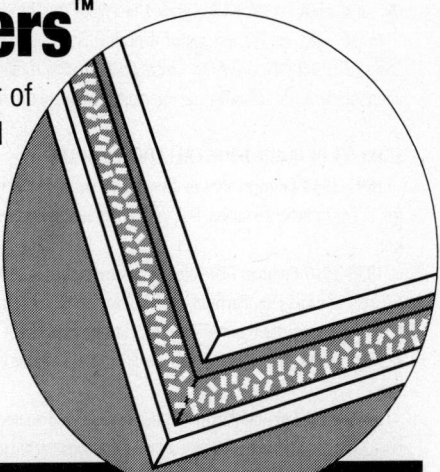

Depending upon the extent and type of restoration and the quality of what was done, you will have to decide whether the value has increased or decreased. In many cases we have observed in the market that the value has been increased on certain books that were originally in low grade before restoration where the appearance and structural integrity was greatly improved afterwards. Restoration on higher grade copies may or may not affect value depending on what is done. Of course, when a comic book is graded, everything must be taken into account in the final grade given.

To the novice grading will appear difficult at first, but as experience is gained accuracy will improve. Whenever in doubt (after using *the Overstreet Comic Book Grading Guide)*, consult with a reputable dealer or experienced collector in your area. The following grading information is given to further aid the collector:

SCARCITY OF COMIC BOOKS RELATED TO GRADE

1897-1933 Comics: Most of these books are bound with thick cardboard covers and are very rare to non-existent in fine or better condition. Due to their extreme age, paper browning is very common. Brittleness could be a problem.

1933-1940 Comics: There are many issues from this period that are very scarce in any condition, especially from the early to mid-1930s. Surviving copies of any particular issue range from a handful to several hundred. Near Mint to Mint copies are virtually non-existent with known examples of any particular issue limited to five or fewer copies. Most surviving copies are in FN-VF or less condition. Brittleness or browning of paper is fairly common and could be a problem.

1941-1952 Comics: Surviving comic books would number from less than 100 to several thousand copies of each issue. Near Mint to Mint copies are a little more common but are still relatively scarce with only a dozen or so copies in this grade existing of any particular issue. Exceptions would be recent warehouse finds of most Dell comics (6-100 copies, but usually 30 or less), and Harvey comics (1950s-1970s) surfacing. Due to low paper quality of the late 1940s and 1950s, many comics from this period are rare in Near Mint to Mint condition. Most remaining copies are VF or less. Browning of paper could be a problem.

1953-1959 Comics: As comic book sales continued to drop during the 1950s, production values were lowered resulting in cheaply printed comics. For this reason, high grade copies are extremely rare. Many Atlas and Marvel comics have chipping along the trimmed edges (Marvel chipping) which reduces even more the number of surviving high grade copies.

1960-1970 Comics: Early '60s comics are rare in Near Mint to Mint condition. Most copies of early '60s Marvels and DCs grade no higher than VF. Many early keys in NM or MT exist in numbers less than 10-20 of each. Mid- to late '60s books in high grade are more common due to the hoarding of comics that began in the mid-'60s.

1970-Present: Comics of today are common in high grade. VF to NM is the standard rather than the exception.

When you consider how few Golden and Silver Age books exist compared to the current market, you will begin to appreciate the true rarity of these early books. In many cases less than 5-10 copies exist of a particular issue in Near Mint to Mint condition, while most of the 1930s books do not exist in this grade at all.

KNOW THE BUZZ WORDS

Many of the following terms and abbreviations are used in the comic book market and are explained here: (Note: Consult the Overstreet Comic Book Grading Guide for a more detailed list of terms.)

a-Story art; **a(i)**-Story art inks; **a(p)**-Story art pencils; **a(r)**-Story art reprint.

Adult material–Contains story and/or art for "mature" readers. Re: sex, violence, strong language.

Adzine-A magazine primarily devoted to the advertising of comic books and collectibles as its first publishing priority as opposed to written articles.

Annual-A book that is published yearly.

Arrival date-Markings on a comic book cover (usually in pencil) made by either the newsstand dealer or the distributor. These markings denote the date the book was placed on the newsstand. Usually the arrival date is one to two months prior to the cover date.

Ashcan-A publisher's inhouse facsimile of a proposed new title. Most ashcans have black and white covers stapled to an existing coverless comic on the inside. Other ashcans are totally black and white.

B&W-Black and white art.

Baxter paper–A high quality, white, heavy paper used in the printing of some comic books.

Bimonthly-Published every two months.

Biweekly-Published every two weeks.

Bondage cover-Usually denotes a female in restraints.

Brittleness-The final stage of paper deterioration.

c-Cover art; **c(i)**-Cover inks;

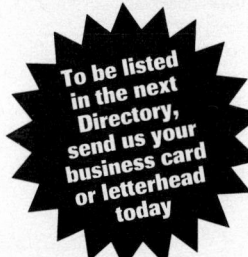

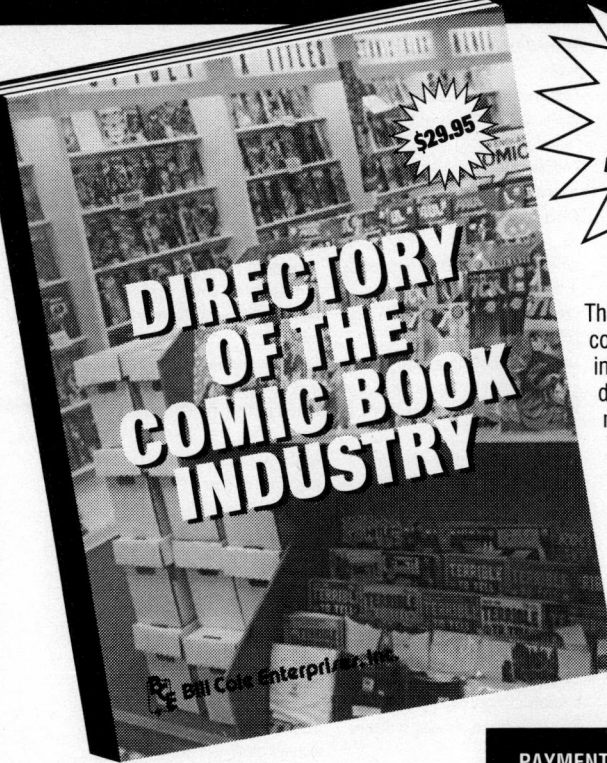

c(p)-Cover pencils; **c(r)**-Cover reprint.
Bronze Age–(1) Non-specific term not in general acceptance by collectors which denotes comics published from approximately 1970 through 1980, (2) Term which describes "the Age" of comic books after the Silver Age.
Browning –Paper aging between tanning and brittleness.
Cameo-When a character appears briefly in one or two panels.
CCA-Comics Code Authority.
CCA seal-An emblem that was placed on the cover of all CCA approved comics beginning in April-May, 1955.
Center Crease– (see Subscription Crease)
Centerfold-The two folded pages in the center of a comic at the bent ends of the staples.
CFO–Abbreviation for "Centerfold out."
Chromium cover–A special Chromium foil used on covers
Church, Edgar collection-A large high grade comic book collection discovered by Mile High Comics in Colorado (over 22,000 books).
Classic Cover–A cover cosidered by collectors to be highly desirable.
Cleaning–A process in which dirt and dust is removed.
Color Touch–A restoration process by which colored ink is used to hide color flecks, flakes and larger areas
Colorist-Artist that applies color to the black and white pen and ink art.
Comic book dealer–(1) A seller of comic books. (2) One who makes a living buying and selling comic books.
Comic book repair-When a tear, loose staple or centerfold has been mended without changing or adding to the original finish of the book. Repair may involve tape, glue or nylon gossamer and is easily detected. It is considered a defect
Comic book restoration-Any attempt, whether professional or amateur, to enhance the appearance of a comic book. These procedures may include any or all of the following techniques: Recoloring, adding missing paper, stain, ink, dirt, tape removal, whitening, pressing out wrinkles, staple replacement, trimming, re-glossing, etc. Note: Unprofessional work can lower the value of a book. In all cases, a restored book can never be worth the same as an unrestored book in the same condition.
Comics Code Authority-In 1954 the major publishers joined together and formed a committee which set up guidelines for acceptable comic contents. It was their task to approve the contents of comics before publication.
Complete Run–All issues of a given title.
Con-A Convention or public gathering of fans.
Condition–The state of preservation of a comic book.
Cosmic Aeroplane-Refers to a large collection discovered by Cosmic Aeroplane Books.
Costumed Hero–A costumed crime fighter with "developed" powers instead of "super" powers.
Coupon Cut–Comic book missing a coupon.
Cover Loose–Cover is detached from staple.
Cover Trimmed–Cover has been reduced in size through trimming.
Crease–A paper fold that occurs in comic books from misuse
Crossover–When one character appears briefly in another character's story.
Deacidification–The process of reducing acid in paper.
Debut-The first time that a character appears anywhere.
Defect–Any fault or flaw that detracts from perfection.
Denver Collection–A collection of early '40s high grade #1s bought at auction in Pennsylvania by a Denver, Colorado dealer.
Die-cut cover–When areas of a cover are cut away for special effect.
Distributor painted stripes–Color brushed or sprayed on the edges of comic book stacks as special coding by distributors (not a defect).
Double–A duplicate copy.
Double cover-An error in the binding process which results in two or more covers being bound to a single book. Multiple covers are not considered a defect.
Drug propaganda story-Where comic makes an editorial stand about drug abuse.
Drug use story-Shows the actual use of drugs: shooting, taking a trip, harmful effects, etc.
Dust Shadow–Usually an edge of a comic exposed to the gathering of dust creating a dark strip.
Embossed cover–When a pattern is pressed into the cover creating a raised area.
Eye Appeal–A term used to describe the overall appeal of a comic's apparent condition.
Fanzine-An amateur fan publication.
File Copy-A high grade comic originating from the publisher's file. Not all file copies are in pristine condition. Note: An arrival date on the cover of a comic indicates that it is not a file copy.
First app.-Same as debut.
Flashback-When a previous story is being recalled.
Foil cover–A thin metallic foil that is hot stamped on comic covers.
Four color-A printing process in which all primary colors plus black are used. Also refers to the Four Color series published by Dell.
Foxing-Tiny orange-brown spots on the cover or pages of a comic book caused by mold growth.
G. A.-Golden Age period.
Gatefold cover–A double cover folded in itself.
Genre–Categories of comic book subject matter grouped as to type.
Giveaway–Type of comic book used as a premium.
Golden Age (G.A.)-The period beginning with *Action* #1 (June, 1938) and ending with World War II in 1945.
Headlights-Protruding breasts.
Hologram cover–True 3-D holograms are prepared and affixed to comic book covers and cards for special effect.
Hot stamping–The process of pressing foil, prism paper and inks on cover stock.
i-Art inks.
Indicia-Publishers title, issue number, date, copyright and general information statement usually located on the inside front cover, facing page or inside back cover.
Infinity cover-Shows a scene that repeats itself to infinity.
Inker-Artist that does the inking.
Intro-Same as debut.
JLA-Justice League of America.
JLI-Justice League International.
JSA-Justice Society of America.
Key Issue–An important issue in a run
Lamont Larson-Refers to a large high grade collection of comics. Many of the books have Lamont or Larson written on the cover.
Linticular covers (aka flicker covers)–Images move when viewed at different

angles specially prepared and affixed to cover.

Logo-The title of a strip or comic book as it appears on the cover or title page.

LSH-Legion of Super-Heroes.

Marvel chipping-A defect that occurred during the trimming process of 1950s and 1960s Marvels which produced a ragged edge around the comic cover. Usually takes the form of a tiny chip or chips along the right hand edge of the cover.

Mile High-Refers to a large NM-Mint collection of comics originating from Denver, Colorado (Edgar Church collection).

Modern Age–Period from 1980 to the present.

Mylar ™–An inert, very hard, space age plastic used to make high quality protective bags and sleeves used for comic storage. Mylar ™ is a trademark of the DuPont Company.

nd-No date.

nn-No number.

N. Y. Legis. Comm.-New York Legislative Committee to Study the Publication of Comics (1951).

One-shot-When only one issue is published of a title, or when a series is published where each issue is a different title (i.e. Four Color Comics).

Origin-When the story of the character's creation is given.

Over Guide-When a comic book is priced at a value over Guide list.

p-Art pencils.

Painted cover–Cover taken from an actual painting instead of a line drawing.

Paper cover–Comic book cover made from the same newsprint as interior pages (self cover). These books are extremely rare in high grade.

Pedigree-A book from a famous collection, e.g. Allentown, Larson, Church/Mile High, Denver, San Francisco, Cosmic Aeroplane, etc. Note: Beware of non-pedigree collections being promoted as pedi gree books. Only outstanding high grade collections similar to those listed qualify.

Penciler-Artist that does the pencils.

Photo cover–Made from a photograph instead of a line drawing or painting.

POG–(passion orange guava)-A game that originated in Hawaii which uses small paper milk caps or discs.

POP-Parade of Pleasure, book about the censorship of comics.

Post-Code-Comic books published with the CCA seal.

Post-Golden Age-Comic books published between 1945 and 1950.

Post-Silver Age-Comic books published from 1969 to present.

Poughkeepsie-Refers to a large collection of Dell Comics' "file copies" believed to have originated from the warehouse of Western Publishing in Poughkeepsie, N.Y.

Pre-Code-Comic books published before the CCA seal.

Pre-Golden Age-Comic books published prior to *Action* #1 (June, 1938).

Pre-Hero–A term that describes the issues in a run prior to a super hero entering the run.

Pre-Silver Age-Comic books published between 1950 and *Showcase* #4 (1956).

Printing defect-A defect caused by the printing process.Examples would include paper wrinkling, miscut edges, misfolded spine, untrimmed pages, off-registered color, off-centered trimming, misfolded and misbound pages. It should be noted that these are defects that lower the grade of the book.

Prism cover–Special reflective foil material with 3-dimensional repeated designs. Used for special effect.

Provenance-When the owner of a book is known and is stated for the purpose of authenticating and documenting the history of the book. Example: A book from the Stan Lee or Forrest Ackerman collection would be an example of a value-adding provenance.

Quarterly-Published every three months (four times a year).

R or r-Reprint.

Rare-10 to 20 copies estimated to exist.

Rat Chew–Damage caused by gnawing rats or mice.

Reprint comics-Comic books that contain newspaper strip reprints.

Restoration–The fine art of repairing a comic book to look as close as possible to its original condition.

Rice paper-A thin, transparent paper commonly used by restorers to repair tears and replace small pieces on covers and pages of comic books.

Rolled Spine–A spine condition caused by folding back pages while reading.

S. A.-Silver Age.

Saddle Stitch–The staple binding of comic books.

S&K-Joe Simon and Jack Kirby (artists).

Scarce-20 to 100 copies estimated to exist.

Silver Age-Officially begins with *Showcase* #4 in 1956 and ends in 1969.

Silver proof-A black & white actual size print on thick glossy paper given to the colorist to indicate colors to the engraver.

SOTI-Seduction of the Innocent, book about the censorship of comics. Refer to listing in this Guide.

Spine-The area representing the folded and stapled part of a comic book.

Spine roll-A defect caused by improper storage which results in uneven pages and the shifting or bowing of the spine.

Splash panel-A large panel that usually appears at the front of a comic story.

Squarebound-A comic book glue-bound with a square spined cover.

Store Stamp–Store name stamped in ink on cover.

Stress lines-Light, tiny wrinkles occuring along the spine, projecting from the staples or appearing anywhere on the covers of a comic book.

Subscription crease-A center crease caused by the folding of comic books for mailing to subscribers. This is considered a defect.

Sun Shadow–See dust shadow.

Super-hero–A costumed hero crime fighter with powers beyond those of mortal man.

Super-villain–A costumed criminal with powers beyond those of mortal man.

Swipe–A panel, sequence, or story obviously borrowed from previously published material.

3-D comic-Comic art that is drawn and printed in two color layers, producing a true 3-D effect when viewed through special glasses.

3-D Effect comic-Comic art that is drawn to appear 3-D, but isn't.

Title Page–The first page showing the title of a story.

Under guide-When a comic book is priced at a value less than Guide list.

Very rare-1 to 10 copies estimated to exist.

Warehouse copy-Originating from a publisher's warehouse; similar to file copy.

X-over-When one character crosses over into another's strip.

Zine-See Fanzine.

HOW TO START COLLECTING

New comic books are available in many different kinds of stores. Grocery stores, drug stores, Wal-Mart, K-Mart, book stores, comic book stores and card and comics specialty shops are a few examples. Local flea markets and, of course, comic book conventions in your area are excellent sources for new and old comic books.

Most collectors begin by buying new issues in mint condition directly off the newsstand or from their local comic store. (Subscription copies are available from several mail-order services as well.) Each week new comics appear on the stands that are destined to become true collectors' items. The trick is to locate a store that carries a complete line of comics. In several localities this may be difficult. Most collectors frequent several magazine stands in order not to miss something they want. Even then, it pays to keep in close contact with collectors in other areas. Sooner or later, nearly every collector has to rely upon a friend in Fandom or a dealer to obtain for him an item that is unavailable locally (see ads in this book).

Before you buy any comic to add to your collection, you should carefully inspect its condition. Unlike stamps and coins, defective comics are generally not highly prized. The cover should be properly cut and printed. Remember that every blemish or sign of wear depreciates the beauty and value of your comics.

The serious collector usually buys extra copies of popular titles. He may trade these multiples for items unavailable locally (for example, foreign comics), or he may store the multiples for resale at some future date. Such speculation is, of course, a gamble. Selecting the right investment books is tricky business that requires special knowledge. With experience, the beginner will improve his buying skills. Remember, if you play the new comics market, be prepared to buy and sell fast as values rise and fall rapidly.

COLLECTING IN THE 1990s

Comic book collecting has become more fun and exciting than ever before. The stands are filled with a broad selection of every type of comic book imaginable, but look closely. There is something new about today's comic book. The inside pages are printed on slick paper that makes the colors jump. The covers are beautiful, exciting and dazzling. Most comic book companies, especially Marvel, DC, Image, Valiant, Defiant and Malibu, are placing these eye-catching specialty covers on their comic books.

Yes, the face of today's newsstand has really changed with more pizzazz and glitter than ever before. Gimmicks to encourage point of purchase sales abound. Take your pick. Holograms, prism, foil, embossed, die-cut, 3-D, posters, cards, talking covers, scratch and sniff, you name it. Check out that die-cut *Sabretooth* cover by Marvel, or that *X-Factor* #92 with the Havok hologram on the cover, or that black bagged *Superman* #75 (death issue), or even that multicolor foil *WildC.A.T.s* Trilogy cover by Image.

Polybagged comics–It is the official policy of this Guide to grade comics regardless of whether they are still sealed in their polybag or not. Sealed comics in bags are not always in mint condition and could even be damaged. The value should not suffer as long as the bag (opened) and all of its original manufactured contents are preserved and kept together.

Collecting on a budget–Collectors check out their local newsstand or comic specialty store for the latest arrivals. Hundreds of brand new comic books are displayed each week for the collector–much more than anyone can afford to purchase. Due to this, today's reader must be careful and budget his money wisely in choosing what to buy.

Trading Cards–Very popular today are the trading cards which are being offered by most publishers. Much like the baseball card market, comic cards are now offered by more and more outlets. In fact, many baseball card collectors and dealers are now collecting comic books. Because of this, today's comic book market is growing and changing faster than ever before. The card sets and rare issues are a very popular, and a very interesting, alternative to comic book collecting.

Collecting artists–Many collectors enjoy favorite artists and follow their work from issue to issue, title to title, company to company. In recent years, some artists have achieved stardom status. Autograph signings occur at all major comic conventions as well as special promotions with local stores. Fans line up by the hundreds at such events to meet these super stars. Some of the current top artists of new comics are: Todd McFarlane, Rob Liefeld, Jae Lee, Jim Lee, Joe Quesada, Whilce Portacio, Franchesco, Sam Kieth, Marc Silvestri, Dale Keown and Mark Bagley. Original artwork from these artists have been bringing record prices at auctions and from dealers' lists.

Collecting by companies–Some collectors become loyal to a particular company and only collect its titles. It is another way to specialize and collect in a market that expands faster than your pocket book.

Collecting number ones–For decades, comic enthusiasts have always collected number ones. It is yet another way to control spending and build a very interesting collection for the future. Number ones have everything going for them. Some introduce new characters. Other issues are sometimes underprinted, creating a rarity factor. A number one collection crosses many subjects, as well as companies, and makes an intriguing display.

COLLECTING BACK ISSUES

A back issue is any comic currently not available on the stands. Collectors of current titles often want to find the earlier issues in order to complete the run. Thus a back issue collector is born. Comic books have been published and collected for over 90 years. However, the earliest known comic book dealers didn't appear until the late 1930s. But today, there are hundreds of dealers that sell old comic books (See ads in this book).

Locating back issues–The first place to begin, of course, is with your collector friends who may have unwanted back issues or duplicates for sale. Look in the yellow pages to see if you have a comic book store available. If you do, they would know of other collectors in your area. Advertising in local papers could get good results. Go to regional markets and look for comic book dealers. There are many trade publications in the hobby that would put you in touch with out-of-town dealers. The Overstreet Monthly Magazine, and, of course, this Annual Guide have ads buying and selling old comic books. Some dealers publish regular price lists of old comic books for sale. Get on their mailing list.

Putting a quality collection of old comics together takes a lot of time, effort and money. Many old comics are not easy to find. Persistence and luck play a big part in acquiring needed issues. Most quality collections are put together over a long period of time by placing mail orders with dealers and other collectors.

Comics of early vintage are extremely expensive if they are purchased through a regular dealer or collector. Unless you have unlimited funds to invest in your hobby, you will find it necessary to restrict your collecting in certain ways. However you define your collection, you should be careful to set your goals well within affordable limits.

PROPER HANDLING OF COMIC BOOKS

Comic books are fragile and easy to damage. Most dealers and collectors hesitate to let anyone personally handle their rare comics. It is common courtesy to ask permission before handling another person's comic book. Most dealers would prefer to remove the comic from its bag and show it to the customer themselves. In this way, if the book is damaged, it would be the dealer's responsibility–not the customer's. Remember, the slightest crease or chip could render an otherwise Mint book to Near Mint or even Very Fine.

Consult the Overstreet Comic Book Grading Guide and learn the proper way to hold a comic book. The following steps are provided to aid the novice in the proper handling of comic books: 1. Remove the comic from its protective sleeve or bag very carefully. 2. Gently lay the comic (unopened) in the palm of your hand so that it will stay relatively flat and secure. 3. You can now leaf through the book by carefully rolling or flipping the pages with the thumb and forefinger of your other hand. Caution: Be sure the book always remains relatively flat or slightly rolled. Avoid creating stress points on the covers with your fingers and be particularly cautious in bending covers back too far on Mint books. 4. After examining the book, carefully insert it back into the bag or protective sleeve. Watch corners and edges for folds or tears as you replace the book (also watch the tape).

STORAGE OF COMIC BOOKS

In order to preserve and safeguard your comic books, it is important to restrict their exposure to harmful elements. Environmental considerations should take into account the forces of light, heat and humidity, air quality and the chemical composition of any and all items coming into direct or indirect contact with the collection. Harmful or inadequate storage methods or materials will only hasten the deterioration of the paper being stored, resulting in damage, discoloration or both.

- **Keep light levels as low as possible**

Light consists of two components - quality and quantity. Quality refers to the spectrum of light that is being emitted while quantity refers to the length of time an object is being exposed. Light damage is cumulative — that is, every time the book is exposed, some damage occurs — increased exposure means increased damage. Paper should be stored in the dark, using lights only when needed. If lights are used, fluorescence (and other types with high levels of ultraviolet radiation) should be avoided.

Ultraviolet (UV) light is strong, containing lots of energy. UV serves as a catalyst for many chemical reactions, including the formation of acid compounds and the breakdown of chemical bonds resulting in a product that is weak and brittle.

- **Lower and maintain temperature levels**

It is estimated that for every 10° F drop in temperature, paper life is doubled. Higher temperatures also promote the growth of fungus and mold. The lower the temperature, the better.

- **Maintain a steady relative humidity (rh)**

High relative humidity will aid in the breakdown of molecular bonds by promoting the formation of acidic compounds. High rh will also allow mold and bacteria to grow — possibly leading to the condition known as foxing. Paper is hygroscopic — it takes in, and gives off, moisture depending on its surroundings. This cycling between low and high levels of rh is stressful to the paper and results in its breakdown.

- **Use products designed for long-term storage**

Many storage materials commonly in use by collectors pose a danger to the collection. So called "archivally safe" bags, boards and boxes may contain additives and impurities that, given time, will degrade and attack the collection they are meant to protect. Only products designed for long-term storage are suitable - such as Mylar type "D" or lignin-free boards and boxes. Polypropylene and polyethylene bags are suitable for temporary short-term storage only as their chemical structure is not inert and with time the bags break down.

Shelving should consist of enameled metal or sealed wood surfaces, allowing any treated surfaces to dry completely (usually a month or longer). If possible, avoid using wood in the storage area, as all types of wood emit vapors that (in the presence of moisture) form acidic compounds. Store comics vertically in tailor-made boxes specifically designed for this purpose.

- **Place items away from walls and off of floors**

Items should never be placed directly on a floor, but elevated 6-10 inches allowing for the possibility of flooding. As well, never place a collection directly against a wall (especially an outside wall) as condensation can form. Condensation coupled with poor circulation will result in the growth of mold and fungus in the collection.

- **Handle with care**

Many collectors believe that a comic cannot be mint if it's been read. Comics should be handled with care, washing your hands before reading to eliminate oils from the skin. By laying the comic down on a flat surface and turning the pages slowly you can better avoid putting stress on the staples or spine.

In summary, light levels of 150 lux or lower are recommended, darkness being preferable, limiting exposure to when it's needed. Temperature levels should be maintained in a range between 68-72° F with little or no variance over the year. Relative humidity levels should be at 50%, exclusive of seasons, avoiding any rapid changes.

HOW TO SELL YOUR COMICS

If you have a collection of comics for sale, large or small, the following steps should be taken. (1) Make a detailed list of the books for sale, being careful to grade them accurately, showing any noticeable defects; i.e., torn or missing pages, centerfolds, etc. (2) Decide whether to sell or trade wholesale to a dealer all in one lump or to go through the long laborious process of advertising and selling piece by piece to collectors. Both have their advantages and disadvantages.

In selling to dealers, you will get the best price by letting everything go at once–the good with the bad–all for one price. Simply select names either from ads in this book or from some of the adzines mentioned below. Send them your list and ask for bids. The bids received will vary depending on the demand, rarity and condition of the books you have. The more in demand and better the condition, the higher the bids will be.

On the other hand, you could become a "dealer" and sell the books yourself. Order a copy of one or more of the adzines. Take note how most dealers lay out their ads. Type up your ad copy, carefully pricing each book (using the Guide as a reference). Send finished ad copy with payment to the adzine editor to be run. You will find that certain books will sell at once while others will not sell at all. The ad will probably have to be retyped, remaining books repriced, and run again. Price books according to how fast you want them to move. If you try to get top dollar, expect a much longer period of time. Otherwise, the better deal you give the collector, the faster they will move. Remember, in being your own dealer, you will have overhead expenses in postage, mailing supplies and advertising cost. Some books might even be returned for refund due to misgrading, etc.

In selling all at once to a dealer, you get instant cash, immediate profit, and eliminate the long process of running several ads to dispose of the books; but if you have patience, and a small amount of business sense, you could realize more profit selling them directly to collectors yourself.

WHERE TO BUY AND SELL

Throughout this book you will find the advertisements of many reputable dealers who sell back-issue comics magazines. If you are an inexperienced collector, be sure to compare prices before you buy. When a dealer is selected (ask for references), send him a small order (under $100) first to check out his grading accuracy, promptness in delivery, guarantees of condition advertised, and whether he will accept returns when dissatisfied. Never send cash through the mail. Send money orders or checks for your personal protection. Beware of bargains, as the items advertised sometimes do not exist but are only a fraud to get your money.

The Price Guide is indebted to everyone who placed ads in this volume, whose support has helped in curbing printing costs. Your mentioning this book when dealing with the advertisers would be greatly appreciated.

COMIC BOOK CONVENTIONS

The first comic book conventions, or cons, were originally conceived as the comic book counterpart to science fiction fandom conventions. There were many attempts to form successful national cons prior to the time of the first one that materialized, but they were all stillborn. It is interesting that after only three relatively organized years of existence, the first comic con was held. Of course, its magnitude was nowhere nearly as large as most established cons held today.

What is a comic con? As might be expected, there are comic books to be found at these gatherings. Dealers, collectors, fans, publishers, distributors, manufacturers, whatever they call themselves can be found trading, selling, and buying the adventures of their favorite characters for hours on end. Additionally most cons have guests of honor, usually professionals in the field of comic art, either writers, artists, or editors. The committees put together panels for the con attendees in which the assembled pros talk about certain areas of comics, most of the time fielding questions from the assembled audience. At cons one can usually find displays of various and sundry things, usually toys, thousands of comic books, original art, and more. There can be the showing of movies or videos. Of course there is always the chance to get together with friends at cons and just talk about comics. One also has a good opportunity to make new friends who have similar interests and with whom one can correspond after the con.

It is difficult to describe accurately what goes on at a con. The best way to find out is to go to one and see for yourself.

The largest cons are San Diego (August), Chicago (July), New York (February), Atlanta (July) and Dallas (June). For accurate dates and addresses, consult ads in this edition as well as some of the adzines. Please remember when writing for convention information to include a self addressed, stamped envelope for reply.

COVER BAR CODES FOR NEW COMIC BOOKS

Newsstand

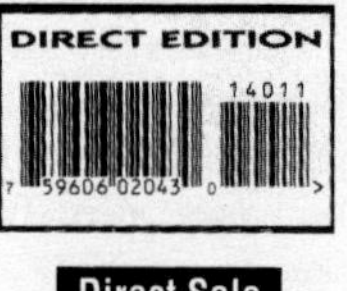

Direct Sale

Today's comic books are cover-coded for the direct sales (comic shop, newsstand, and foreign markets). They are all first printings, with the special coding being the only difference. The comics sold to the comic shops have to be coded differently, as they are sold on a no-return basis while newsstand comics are not. The Price Guide has not detected any price difference between these versions. Currently, the difference is easily detected by looking at the front cover bar code (a box located at the lower left). The bar code used to be filled in for newsstand sales and left blank or contain a character for comic shop sales. Now, as you can see above, the direct sale edition is clearly marked and both versions contain the bar code.

MARVEL REPRINTS

In recent years Marvel has reprinted some of their comics. There has been confusion in identifying the reprints from the originals. However, in 99 percent of the cases, the reprints have listed "reprint," or "2nd printing," etc. in the indicia, along with a later copyright date in some cases. Some Marvel 2nd printings will have a gold logo. The only known exceptions are a few of the movie books such as Star Wars, the Marvel Treasury Editions, and tie-in books such as G.I. Joe. These books were reprinted and not identified as reprints. The Star Wars reprints have a large diamond with no date and a blank UPC symbol on the cover. The other reprints had some cover variation such as a date missing, different colors, etc. Beginning in mid-1990, all Marvel 2nd printings have a gold logo.

Gold Key and other comics were also sold with a Whitman label. There are collectors who prefer the regular labels to Whitman, although the Price Guide does not differentiate in the price. Beginning in 1980, all comics produced by Western carried the Whitman label.

COMIC BOOK PUBLISHERS CODES– The following abbreviations are used with the cover reproductions throughout the book for copyright credit purposes. The companies they represent are listed here:

AC-(Americomics)
ACE-Ace Periodicals
ACG-American Comics Group
AJAX-Ajax-Farrell
AP-Archie Publications
ATLAS-Atlas Comics (see below)
AVON-Avon Periodicals
BP-Better Publications
C & L-Cupples & Leon
CC-Charlton Comics
CEN-Centaur Publications
CCG-Columbia Comics Group
CG-Catechetical Guild
CHES-Harry 'A' Chesler
CLDS-Classic Det. Stories
CM-Comics Magazine
DC-DC Comics, Inc.
DEF-Defiant Comics
DELL-Dell Publishing Co.
DH-Dark Horse
DMP-David McKay Publishing
DS-D. S. Publishing Co.
EAS-Eastern Color Printing Co.
EC-E. C. Comics
ECL-Eclipse Comics
ENWIL-Enwil Associates
EP-Elliott Publications
ERB-Edgar Rice Burroughs
FAW-Fawcett Publications
FC-First Comics
FF-Famous Funnies
FH-Fiction House Magazines
FOX-Fox Features Syndicate
GIL-Gilberton
GK-Gold Key
GP-Great Publications
HARV-Harvey Publications
H-B-Hanna-Barbera
HILL-Hillman Periodicals
HOKE-Holyoke Publishing Co.
IM-Image Comics
KING-King Features Syndicate
LEV-Lev Gleason Publications
MAL-Malibu Comics
ME-Magazine Enterprises
MEG-Marvel Ent. Group
MLJ-MLJ Magazines
MS-Mirage Studios
NOVP-Novelty Press
PG-Premier Group
PINE-Pines
PMI-Parents' Magazine Institute
PRIZE-Prize Publications
QUA-Quality Comics Group
REAL-Realistic Comics
RH-Rural Home
S & S-Street and Smith Publishers
SKY-Skywald Publications
STAR-Star Publications
STD-Standard Comics
STJ-St. John Publishing Co.
SUPR-Superior Comics
TC-Tower Comics
TM-Trojan Magazines
TOBY-Toby Press
TOPS-Tops Comics
UFS-United Features Syndicate
VAL-Valiant
VITL-Vital Publications
WDC-The Walt Disney Company
WEST-Western Publishing Co.
WHIT-Whitman Publishing Co.
WHW-William H. Wise
WMG-William M. Gaines (E. C.)
WP-Warren Publishing Co.
YM-Youthful Magazines
Z-D-Ziff-Davis Publishing Co.

TIMELY/MARVEL/ATLAS COMICS

"A Marvel Magazine" and "Marvel Group" was the symbol used between December 1946 and May 1947 (not used on all titles/issues during period). The Timely Comics symbol was used between July 1942 and September 1942 (not on all titles/issues during period). The round "Marvel Comic" symbol was used between February 1949 and June 1950. Early comics code symbol (star and bar) was used between April 1952 and February 1955. The Atlas globe symbol was used between December 1951 and September 1957. The M over C symbol (beginning of Marvel Comics) was used between July 1961 until the price increased to 12 cents on February 1962.

COMIC COMPANIES

The following are histories of some of the major publishers in the comic industry.

Comic books began as reprint collections of newspaper strips, given away as premiums or sales promotions. It was not until DC Comics began in 1935 that the medium assumed its present form and began its ascent to the billion-dollar-a-year industry it is today.

DC Comics sprang from the vision of the legendary Major Malcolm Wheeler-Nicholson, cavalry officer, sportsman, adventurer and pulp-fiction writer. Wheeler-Nicholson conceived the idea of commissioning original work for a line of comic books in 1934 and his company, National Allied Publications, initiated the modern comic book with the revolutionary *New Fun #1,* published in February, 1935. Thirty-six pages long with a full-color cover, it measured 10" x 15" — the size of the comic book to consist entirely of new material. Establishing many features of the modern comic book, it included humor, adventure, the first original western strip, a sports page, and the first installment of a comic book adaptation of Sir Walter Scott's Ivanhoe. It inaugurated the extended continuity story, each issue enticing readers to buy the next with "To be continued" at the end of its features.

In December, 1935, Wheeler-Nicholson published his second title, *New Comics*. Issue #1 boasted "80 pages packed and jammed with new comic features, written and drawn especially for *New Comics*— never printed before anywhere. Here is a magazine of picturized stories chock full of laughter and thrills, comic characters of every hue... adventuring heroes, detectives, aviator daredevils of today and hero supermen of the days to come"— a fair description of the book and an accurate projection of the industry it helped to create.

In 1936, Wheeler-Nicholson changed the format of his publications to the "smaller, handier size 7-1/2" x 10-1/2" that became the standard of the Golden Age comic book and, with minor trim changes and a reduced page count, remains the standard today. *New Fun* (which changed its name to *More Fun* in January) and *New Comics* quickly became the leaders in the fledgling industry, and other titles soon appeared. Wheeler-Nicholson sold his burgeoning business to his distributor and partner, Harry Donenfeld, in 1937, after creating *Detective Comics*, the first all-original comic book devoted to a single theme. *Detective Comics* was an instant success, and the company took its initials, DC, as its trademark and, later, its name.

An industry that spoke eloquently to a country still recovering from the Great Depression, comic books were to reach their Golden Age in the late 1930s with the introduction of two of DC's most significant innovations.

The first issue of DC's fourth title, *Action Comics*, introduced a new character named Superman. Created by two 19-year-olds, writer Jerome Siegel and artist Joe Shuster, Superman was the first of the costumed super-heroes who were to define the medium during the following decades, and inaugurated a new era in comic books. By the fourth issue of *Action Comics*, sales were approaching half a million copies a month, more than twice the industry average.

In May, 1939, *Detective Comics* #27 carried the first appearance of Bob Kane and Bill Finger's character, Batman, the second of the archetypal figures that comics contributed to American mythology. Unlike the Man of Steel, Batman was a normal man who deliberately developed his natural abilities in order to fight crime. He became the prototype of the more psychologically complex super-heroes that were to come.

The revolution wrought in comics with the introduction of these two figures was to inspire a host of imitators in the field, but DC continued to be the front-runner. In August, 1939, it created *Movie Comics*, the first comic to be based on current motion pictures. In January, 1940, it introduced *The Flash*, the fastest man alive, and the astral figure of *The Spectre*. *All Star Comics* #3 (Winter, 1940) inaugurated the concept of the super-hero team with the introduction of The Justice Society of America, the first assemblage of heroes in one story. Another of DC's innovations was the first youthful super-hero, Batman's sidekick Robin, the Boy Wonder, introduced in *Detective Comics* #38 in April, 1940. Wonder Woman, comics' first super-heroine, was the creation of psychologist Charles Moulton and debuted in *All Star* #8 in December, 1941.

© DC

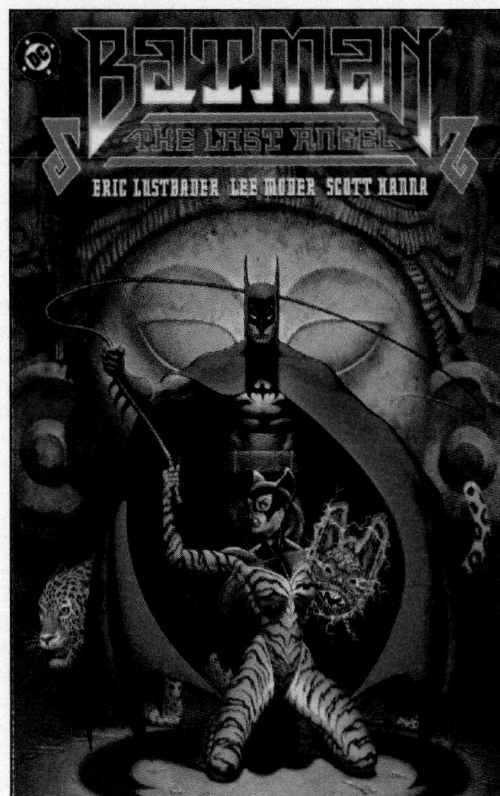

BATMAN
THE LAST ANGEL
ERIC LUSTBADER LEE MODER SCOTT HANNA

© DC

The early 1940s saw DC's already established super-heroes, male, female and juvenile, contributing their superpowers to the war effort. It also saw new characters and styles emerging. *Picture Stories from the Bible*, whose seven issues sold millions of copies in 1942 and '43, contributed part of its profits to religious groups as a public service. Those dark days also saw a much-needed return to humor with such titles as *All Funny Comics* (1943) and *Funny Stuff* (1944).

As tastes changed in the early 1950s, DC was ready. The popularity of caped super-heroes was fading (by 1954, the only survivors in the market were its own perennial Superman, Batman and Wonder Woman), and DC continued to generate new subjects. During that decade, it introduced science-fiction titles such as *Strange Adventures* (1950) and *Mystery in Space* (1951), romances such as *Girl's Romances* (1950) and *Heart Throbs* (1957), westerns such as *All Star Western* (1951), and horror titles such as *House of Mystery* (1951) and *House of Secrets* (1956). DC also licensed characters from other media, creating *Sergeant Bilko* (1957) from TV's Phil Silvers Show and initiating such popular and long-lived comic series as *Bob Hope* (1950) and *Martin and Lewis* (1952).

When the middle 1950s saw a renewal of interest in the classic super-heroes, DC remained in the forefront of the market. In creating new versions of the Golden Age super-heroes, adapted to a modern sensibility, DC revitalized the industry, and a new era dawned, today called the Silver Age. The Flash, the fastest man alive, returned in *Showcase* #4 (October 1956), and Green Lantern, who got his superpowers from an alien ring, was revived in *Showcase* #22 (October 1959). Hawkman took to the air once more in *Brave & Bold* #34 (March 1961), and a transformed Atom, always the smallest of super-heroes but now capable of actually shrinking himself, came back in *Showcase* #34 (October 1961). New characters, adapted to a new market, emerged. Supergirl, Superman's younger cousin, began to appear in adventures directed at girls in *Action Comics* #252 (May 1959).

As the renewed taste for super-heroes threatened to fade in the middle 1960s, DC remained an innovator. It created an offbeat approach to the heroic with the Teen Titans (*Brave & Bold* #54, 1964), a wry blend of traditional action-adventure and contemporary teenage humor which had many imitators. The growing taste of that generation for the supernatural prompted several other new titles, including *Witching Hour* (February 1969) and the revival of *House of Mystery* (May/June 1968). Fantasy, action and epic drama blended in a complex saga create by Jack Kirby called The Fourth World, comprising the series *New Gods* (1971), *Forever People* (1971) and *Mr. Miracle* (1972) and Kirby's run on *Jimmy Olsen*. A watershed in the history of horror comics, and one of the major events of the industry, came with the publication of the gripping and poignant Swamp Thing in *House of Secrets* #92 (June/July 1971), a now legendary series that continues to make its mark in the comics and in several other media as well.

DC entered the 1980s, and its own sixth decade, with an eye keenly attuned to the spirit of the times. In the 1980s it revived and updated the *Teen Titans*. In its 50th year, 1985, DC refreshed its entire super-hero line with a 12-issue series called *Crisis on Infinite Earths*, simplifying the complex universe it had created during the preceding half-century. The following year made comic book history. A redefined Batman appeared in Frank Miller's *Batman: The Dark Knight Returns*, an upscale four-part series which received national attention. And DC broke new ground in the fantasy and science-fiction field with Alan Moore's and Dave Gibbons' widely acclaimed *Watchmen*. The year 1987 saw the continued revitalization of DC's super-heroes with drastically transformed and modernized versions of *Superman* (January), *Wonder Woman* (February), *Justice League International* (May) and *The Flash* (June), all of which reach issue #100 in 1995.

DC titles have always been major award winners in the industry. When the Academy of Comic Book Arts and Sciences started its Alley Awards in 1961, the Board of Directors voted all ten to DC, and the *Comic Buyer's Guide* Fan Awards have regularly included DC features among its Favorite Comic Book Stories, Favorite Comic Books and other categories. Alan Moore's and Dave Gibbons' 1986 *Watchmen*, considered one of the finest artistic achievements among comic book series in the 1980s, has earned more awards than any other comic collection, including the World Science Fiction Convention's coveted Hugo. Neil Gaiman's *The Sandman* was the first comic book ever to earn national honors for fiction when it received the World Fantasy Award for Best Short Story of 1990.

As DC's art and story have remained the standard of excellence in the industry, so has its production. With the introduction of new styles and formats, editions have been made available on high-quality paper. Always an innovator in the field, DC has found a new market with its elegantly produced graphic novels — complete stories issued in self-contained volumes directed at more mature readers. It has also pioneered the American appearance of comics in trade paperback collections, and in both hard as well as soft cover. In addition to traditional newsstand distribution, its publications appear in bookstores, and with *Camelot 3000* (1982-1985), it released the first original offset series published solely for the new "direct sales" market in comic book stores. At prices ranging from $1.50 to $49.95, DC publishes comics and collections for every age and taste.

With over 900 published titles, DC Comics is the oldest publisher of comic books in America, and its *Detective Comics*, originating in March, 1937, and *Action Comics*, published since June, 1938, are the two longest-running titles in the history of the comics. The parent company has employed many corporate names during its long history. Beginning as National Allied Publications in 1935 and becoming National Allied Newspaper Syndicate the next year, it changed to National Comic Publications in 1946 and National Periodical Publications in 1961, when it became a public corporation. In 1968 it was sold to Kinney National Services, which became Warner Communications, Inc. Finally taking DC Comics as its official name in 1977, the company is now a part of Warner Bros., a division of Time Warner, the world's largest media conglomerate.

Through all of these changes, however, DC has retained a unique creative identity, and its myriad characters have consistently enjoyed recognition unsurpassed by those of any other company in the industry. Licensed in some 40 countries and translated into at least 20 languages, its characters are known and its stories followed worldwide.

DC is a vital, growing company whose innovative approach to the medium it pioneered has kept it at the cutting edge of the industry both creatively and commercially.

The growth of DC Comics in the past two decades has reflected the increased awareness of the public. The enormously successful series of four Superman movies produced from 1978 to 1987, and the 1989 and 1992 smash hits, Batman and Batman Returns, as well as the upcoming Batman Forever, dramatized the timelessness of these cultural icons and gave new depth to their characters. Other characters have also been resurrected, revamped and made relevant to contemporary readers. But DC has never rested on its laurels or depended on its distinguished backlist. It was on the cutting edge of the industry in the 1930s and '40s, and it has created new dimensions in the medium ever since. DC still addresses its wide teenage audience, but it has added product lines to attract an ever-widening range of new fans of all ages. Milestone Media, an independent company whose comics are distributed by DC, has introduced multi-cultural super-heroes in acknowledgment of today's multi-cultural audiences within the pages of such favorites as *Icon, Static* and *Blood Syndicate*; Paradox calls out to the book-buying segment of the public enticing them with the likes of the sleeper hit *The Big Book of Urban Legends*; and Vertigo is broadening the definition of the comic book to include material appreciated by older, more sophisticated readers, including more creator-owned projects like *The Invisibles* by Grant Morrison and *Preacher* by Garth Ennis and Steve Dillon while still supporting the hugely successful *The Sandman, Hellblazer* and *The Books of Magic*.

Publishing approximately 70 monthly books (including a Superman Family consisting of *Action Comics, Adventures of Superman, Steel, Superboy, Superman, Superman: Man of Steel* and the Metropolis based *Showcase* '95 and a Batman Family of books including *Batman, The Batman Adventures, Batman: Legends of the Dark Knight, Batman: Shadow of the Bat, Catwoman, Detective Comics,* and *Robin, Showcase* '93 and '94 both had a Gotham City base), various miniseries and one-shots, trade paperbacks and graphic novels, DC continues to explore and expand new techniques and styles in comics publishing.

It was 1939, comics were young, and science fiction pulp magazines publisher Martin Goodman was ready to toss his hat into the four color ring. He did so with *Marvel Comics* #1, and though his company was known as Timely Comics, that first issue would one day provide the roots of a dynasty.

During those early days, the Timely writers and artists included many who would become legend: Joe Simon, Jack Kirby, Bill Everett, Carl Burgos, and a young editorial assistant named Stan Lee. They and their peers created some of the most bizarre characters imaginable, including an artificial man who burst into flames, the half-human prince of Atlantis—flying via tiny-yet-powerful ankle wings, the Whizzer—a super speedster who got his abilities from a transfusion of mongoose blood, and the Vision-an other-dimensional hero who appeared literally in a puff of smoke. Perhaps the most famous was the star-spangled Captain America, and even he defied convention by slugging it out with Hitler and his Nazi hordes months before the U.S. entered World War II.

The Axis was the primary foe for half a decade, offering a universally-hated enemy to combat, but eventually the war ended and Timely lost much of its focus. By the 1950s, all super heroes had waned and publishers tried their hands at new venues with renewed vigor, leading to westerns, romance tales, humor/funny animal titles, and horror.

A few of the original spandex set survived, led by Captain America ("Commie Smasher" — illustrated by John Romita), the Human Torch, and the Sub-Mariner. Toward the mid-'50s, they were joined by quirky headliners the likes of the Black Knight (with classic art by Joe Maneely) and a Fu Manchu pastiche—the Yellow Claw (illustrated by Maneely, Kirby, and John Severin).

Graphic horror—in the guise of the EC Comics (among others)—brought down controversy, led to the creation of the comics code (a self-governing review board for the industry), and caused Marvel (by this time known as Atlas Comics) to come up with its own angle, under the editorial direction of Stan Lee. Hidden among the more commonplace zombie and vampire stories, offbeat monsters like "Fin Fang Foom," "Vandoom," "Groot," and "Xemnu" appeared on into the early 1960s. Lurking in *Tales of Suspense*, *Strange Tales*, *Journey into Mystery,* and *Amazing Adult Fantasy*, these stories were written by Lee and illustrated by Kirby, Steve Ditko, Don Heck, Gene Colan, and others.

These monsters indirectly led to what was to become known as The Marvel Age of Comics. Some of the more unusual tales became the prototypes for a new type of weird hero. For example, "The Man in the Ant Hill" led to the creation of Ant Man, and Xemnu debuted as the original "Hulk."

And in the wake of DC's successful Flash, Green Lantern, and Justice League of America, Lee and company turned their collaborative efforts toward the development of an entire new generation of heroes, giving birth to The Fantastic Four, The Incredible Hulk, The Amazing Spider-Man, The Mighty Thor, Dr. Strange, and The X-Men, to name a few.

These heroes once again broke the established mold by having human qualities and foibles. They took the public by storm. Comics, traditionally juvenile fare, became "hip" and Marvel Comics became a campus phenomenon. Celebrities like author Tom Wolfe and film maker Federico Fellini were seen at the Marvel offices and in the pages of the comics.

So while the '60s opened with DC as the major comic book publisher, by the end of the decade it was Marvel's ball game. Heroes began spinning off into their own new titles and striking out in new directions, such as the fantasy adventures of *Conan the Barbarian* (courtesy of Roy Thomas and Barry Windsor-Smith). The Marvel milieu began to attract many hot new creative talents including Jim Steranko, Neal Adams, Len Wein, Jim Starlin, Marv Wolfman, and Walt Simonson.

Stan Lee stepped down as Editor in Chief in 1972, with several successors: Roy Thomas, Len Wein, Marv Wolfman, Gerry Conway and Archie Goodwin. In 1977 Jim Shooter signed on, and retained the title for nine years.

Spider-Man, the Fantastic Four, the Avengers, and company continued to form the backbone of the line, but in 1975 a striking new phenomenon hit the scene. The X-Men, a concept that had enjoyed limited success, was dramatically re-vamped to form an entirely new, ethnically and ideologically mixed team of heroes. Conceived by Len Wein and Dave Cockrum, the title was handed over to neo-writer Chris Claremont and proceeded to grown into a creative force that, to this day, is one of the most powerful comics have ever seen.

Another phenomenon from this period was the "gritty" hero, who better represented the increasingly alarming crime scene of the American streets. This grimness took a variety of forms, from the street-wise military tactics of the Punisher to the macabre horrors of the Ghost Rider. Even the super hero set was impacted with the pragmatic, sometimes vicious scrapping heralded by Wolverine (in The X-Men).

Across the pond, Marvel Comics Ltd. was formed in London, at first reprinting packages featuring U.S. material, later developing their own titles like *Captain Britain* and *Doctor Who*. Many of the most successful British writers (including Alan Moore, Bernie Jaye, and Jamie Delano) and artists (like Alan Davis, Paul Neary, and Dave Gibbons) produced work for the imprint.

Spider-Man, Captain America, the Hulk, and Dr. Strange entered the network TV scene with live-action movies and series, most notably the weekly Bill Bixby Hulk series, while the Fantastic Four (minus the Human Torch) hit the Saturday morning schedule. Marvel Productions was formed in 1980, and Spider-Man and the Hulk joined the Saturday morning lineup. The studio also developed a number of third-party properties, including Jim Henson's The Muppet Babies and Fraggle Rock.

The 1980s proved an era of acceleration—within the books and on the business front. Martin Goodman had sold the company (amid little fanfare or change) to Cadence Industries in 1968, and Cadence retained the company until selling it in 1986 to New World Pictures, a movie company that hoped to develop Marvel's heroes into film properties. This marriage proved short-lived, and in 1989 Marvel was purchased by The Andrews Group, a subsidiary of MacAndrews & Forbes Group, Inc.

Within the comics, the '80s witnessed successes and failures. Success for the Uncanny X-Men led to the creation of The New Mutants, X-Factor, Wolverine, and

Excalibur, while the Spider-Man franchise (*Amazing Spider-Man, Spectacular Spider-Man, Marvel Tales*) expanded to include *Web of Spider-Man*. The web-spinner even took the plunge and married Mary Jane Watson.

The Punisher, She-Hulk, Spider-Woman, Dazzler, Moon Knight, and Alpha Flight got their own titles. New lines were tried, including the creator-owned innovation of Epic Comics, the youth-oriented Star Comics, and the abortive New Universe. Editor in Chief Jim Shooter left the company, and Tom DeFalco moved into the top office.

The pace really accelerated at the beginning of the 1990s. The million-copies-plus releases of *Spider-Man* #1 by Todd MacFarlane, *X-Men* (second series) #1 by Chris Claremont and Jim Lee, and *X-Force* #1 by Rob Liefeld and Fabian Nicieza set incredible sales records. Heroes such as The New Warriors, Darkhawk, War Machine, and Thunderstrike emerged, classic heroes like The Sub-Mariner and Daredevil underwent radical change. The world of Marvel 2099 was created.

Marvel Comics forged new ties to produce a number of high-profile series under license, reaching young girls with Mattel's *Barbie*, and other young readers with Disney's *Aladdin, Beauty and the Beast, Little Mermaid, Lion King,* and *Disney Afternoon*. Targeting a slightly older and more street-savvy audience, Nickelodeon's *Ren & Stimpy Show* and MTV's *Beavis and Butt-Head* took slots among the top-sellers.

Marvel Comics led to Marvel Entertainment Group, Inc., and under this umbrella Marvel Films has realized a dream earlier administrations could not—development of major motion pictures under the supervision of world-class talent like James Cameron (Spider-Man), Richard Donner (X-Men), Chris Columbus (Daredevil, Fantastic Four), and Ernest Dickerson (Blade), among others.

The X-Men animated series (by Saban) has helped propel the Fox Kids' Network to the top of the ratings, and Spider-Man has followed suit, produced by Marvel Films Animation. This new studio also developed the syndicated Marvel Action Hour, starring Iron Man and The Fantastic Four and sold it into more than 90 percent of the U.S. television markets.

Marvel Entertainment continues to expand many new venues, including trading cards (through Fleer Entertainment), toys (via Toy Biz), children's magazines (Welsh Publishing) and even stickers (Panini). This mainstreaming of super heroes has led to a high-profile unlike any Marvel's characters ever before enjoyed.

But it all comes back to comics. In an effort to keep core concepts supercharged, Marvel has departed radically from the traditional way in which titles are produced. With Tom DeFalco's 1994 departure, the single Editor in Chief position has been eliminated. In a structure more like that of a major book publisher, Marvel established five editors in chief, each pulled from the ranks of Marvel's executive and group editors. Each spearheads a group of titles that will receive individual mandates, resources, and marketing support aimed to increase the number of readers.

Bob Harras will act as Editor in Chief of the X-Men branch, Bob Budiansky, formerly of the high-tech Special Projects division, will be Editor in Chief of the Spider-Man titles, and Executive Editor Mark Gruenwald proved a natural as Editor in Chief of the Marvel Classic imprint (*Avengers, Iron Man, Force Works, Fantastic Four, Silver Surfer*, and the related titles). "Edge" Editor in Chief Bobbie

Chase retains the macabre *Midnight Sons* and will work with singularly stylistic New Warriors, Punisher, and Hulk books, as well as the cyber-oriented 2099 Universe. Finally, Carl Potts will coordinate the General Entertainment titles (Disney, humor, Conan) that spearhead the thrust for new audiences.

And Stan Lee, continuing his title as Marvel Comics Publisher, will return to the editorial role by forming his own West Coast imprint, Excelsior Comics.

The millennium is rushing forward at a dizzying pace, the audience is increasingly demanding and sophisticated, and there are many people who have yet to pick up a comic book. Marvel has instituted an experimental and ever-evolving structure with the goal of continuing to create the quirky, bizarre, and explosive concepts that propelled the company to the '90s.

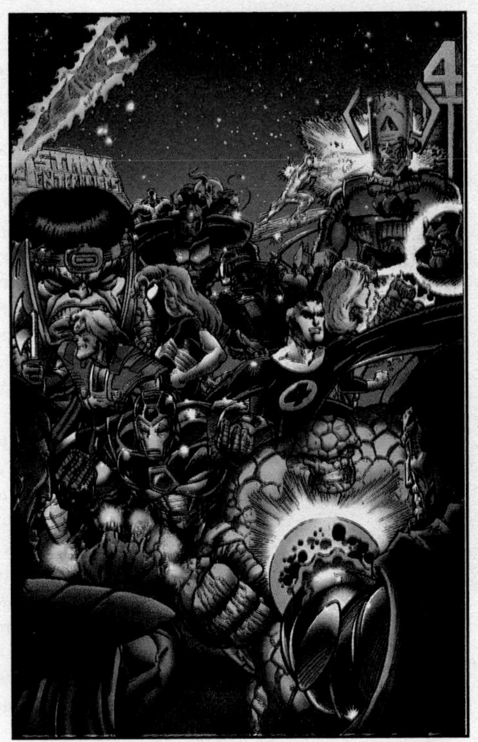

© MEG

Comic book specialty store owner Mike Richardson had a problem: there weren't enough comics in his stores that he wanted to read. So Richardson set out to create a line of comics that went beyond the superhero stereotypes that filled his store's racks. And so, in 1986, Dark Horse Comics was founded.

Richardson wanted a company atmosphere which would attract top-name talent. Competitive contracts and page rates were key to the plan, but more important was a firm commitment to maintain high-quality production values and a publishing environment unencumbered by the bureaucratic red tape which characterized the larger publishers. The writers' and artists' right to creative freedom proved to be an attractive incentive.

© 20th Cent. Fox

Today, Dark Horse is home to such well-known creators as John Byrne, Frank Miller, Art Adams, Matt Wagner, Paul Chadwick, Mike Kaluta, Bob Burden, Harlan Ellison, Andrew Vachss, Keith Giffen, Cam Kennedy, Chris Claremont, Adam Warren, Mike Baron, Steve Rude, Mike Mignola, Steven Grant, Dave Gibbons, Michael Allred, Dave Stevens, and Geof Darrow. The quality of their comic line has earned them such sought-after licenses as *Aliens, Star Wars, James Bond*, and *Predator*, and has given them entree into the film industry, which resulted in the smash success films The Mask and Timecop. But more importantly, Richardson finally has solved his greatest problem: he has a whole line of comics that he enjoys reading!

Dark Horse was founded on three basic principals: quality, diversity, and creativity. By maintaining those three basic principals during the various industry cycles in which they've published, they've kept their head above water. It would have been easier during these cycles to pander to the trends of the market, and would have served to make a quick buck for Dark Horse; but it wouldn't have served their long range goals.

Mike had already created a successful chain of comic book stores in the Portland metropolitan area selling comics which he felt were both below the artistic standards of those he had read in his youth and which suffered from an inability to grow beyond the superhero genre. If a publisher were to offer a line of comics that headed into new territories, he reasoned, the readers would gladly follow! In Dark Horse Comics, Mike has created an atmosphere that attracts the industry's very best talent. Competitive contracts and page rates were key incentives to enticing such luminaries as John Byrne and Frank Miller from Marvel and DC, but more important was Dark Horse's commitment to high quality production values and creator freedom; the bureaucratic red tape that has entangled the larger publishers has choked the creativity out their lines. But Mike Richardson has offered a "safe haven," of sorts, to the comics creative community, and his payback is a publishing schedule that stands out as the most diverse line of quality comics in the industry.

© 20th Cent. Fox

Dark Horse currently produces these titles: *Grendel Tales, Sin City, John Byrne's Next Men, Hellboy, Rascals in Paradise, The Rocketeer Adventure Magazine, The Mask, X, Star Wars: Tales of the Jedi - Dark Lords of the Sith, Martha Washington Goes To War, Babe, Aliens, Predator, Dark Horse Presents, Barb Wire Concrete: Killer Smile, Oh My Goddess!, The Tale of One Bad Rat, Madman Comics, Badger, Shattered Mirror, Johnny Dynamite,*

Medal of Honor, Flaming Carrot Comics, Shadow Empires, Aliens/Predator: Deadliest of the Species, Star Wars: The Early Adventures, Classic Star Wars, Division 13, Rebel Sword, Caravan Kids, White Like She, The Dirty Pair, Enemy, The Shadow, Instant Piano, Indiana Jones and The Iron Phoenix, and a cast of thousands!

Best-selling creator-owned comic: *Sin City: A Dame to Kill For*

Best-selling licensed comic: *Star Wars: Tales of the Jedi - Dark Lords of the Sith*

Best-selling company-owned comic: *X*

Best-selling manga: *Oh My Goddess!*

Best-selling collection: *Star Wars: Dark Empire*

© 20th Cent. Fox

Some of Dark Horses upcoming titles include: *Tarzan: The Lost Adventure, The Big Guy and Rusty the Boy Robot, Harlan Ellison's Dream Corridor, Star Wars: Dark Empire II, Nexus: Wages of Sin, Otomo's Domu, Monkeyman & O'Brien, Hellboy: Wake the Devil, The Rocketeer Adventure Magazine, Sin City: The Big Fat Kill, Droopy, Ghost in the Shell, Agents of Law, Aliens vs. Predator: Duel, Colors in Black, Spirit of Wonder, Ghost,* and *Star Wars: River of Chaos!*

Dark Horse is also responsible for other products besides comics. They produce: motion pictures (They just closed a nine picture deal!), animation (Look for *The Mask* on Saturday mornings beginning 3/95!), games (A 16 bit *Comics' Greatest World* game will hit mid-95!) novels (Did you know they have *Aliens* and *Predator* novels in bookstores everywhere?), cold-cast painted figures (Were you able to find a Bone figure?), and cold-cast model kits (Oh, man, does The Bride of Frankenstein look great!). 1995 will be their best year yet!!

© WDC

The Bruce Hamilton Company—parent to its three publishing divisions—can trace its origin to an application in 1980 to publish a hardcover book based on the oil paintings of the legendary Duck Man, comic book great Carl Barks, The Fine Art of Walt Disney's Donald Duck. The Fine Art sold out quickly at a hefty issue price of $200, won a national book award, and set the tone for the company's subsequent successes. The 30-volume hard cover Carl Barks Library quickly followed plus an energetic program to release supreme quality lithographs.

Gladstone's first newsstand comic books began to appear in 1985—all Disney issues, led by the long running flagship title, *Walt Disney's Comics & Stories. Sir Charles Barkley and the Referee Murders*—touted by some as being the first in a genre: sports fantasy—and the lavish book of Toby Press reprints of the great Otto Messmer, Felix the Cat Keeps on Walkin', have carried the Hamilton Comics emblem.

Gladstone and Hamilton Comics both intend to aggressively expand into licensed TV and movie properties in 1995, in addition to doing their own comics. Another Rainbow's activities will mostly center around the design and development of high end collectibles in such diverse mediums as bronzes, porcelains, character-related furniture, jewelry and stained glass.

© WDC

The Carl Barks Library in Color is scheduled to continue its multiple series throughout the 1990s.

Like many kids, Matt Groening began doodling in notebook margins during science class. At this young age, he often dreamed of becoming a cartoonist and drawing comics. Groening's dream would become a reality, beginning with the nationally syndicated "Life in Hell" comic strip. In 1987, he created The Simpsons, one of the most successful primetime animated show in television history. The Simpsons became a phenomenon, generating platinum record albums, video games, trading cards, and more bootleg t-shirts than could be imagined.

The worldwide popularity of The Simpsons led, in 1991, to the publication of a fan magazine called *Simpsons Illustrated*. Groening began the magazine with his longtime friends and fellow artists Steve and Cindy Vance. In 1993 this creative trio, along with Bill Morrison, produced the one-shot comic book, *Simpsons Comics & Stories*. The comic was an immediate hit, making the top ten list of enthusiast magazines. With this success, Groening made the decision to make a long term commitment to comic books and, in 1993, Bongo Comics was born.

By starting Bongo Comics, Groening fulfills one of his childhood dreams inspired by those classroom doodles. He has created a comic book company that he hopes will help to revive the humor genre.

And with the creative talents of the Vances and Morrison, Bongo produces comics filled with humor that is synonymous with The Simpsons.

Itchy & Scratchy Comics unleashes the catastrophic cat-and-mouse team from the mayhem-minded cartoon within the Simpsons TV show. *Bartman* reveals the heroic adventures of Bart Simpson, arch-enemy of evil, as he dons cape and cowl to battle bad guys. *Radioactive Man*, starring Bart's favorite super-hero, is a humorous crash course in comic book history.

Already in the works for 1995 are two new titles-*The Secret Files of Lisa Simpson* and *Krusty Comics*. Comics based on The Simpsons are only the beginning for Bongo Comics which will draw on new characters and stories invented by Groening as well as other writers and artists.

Matt Groening formed Bongo Comics Group in 1993. He serves as publisher over the four current comic book titles—*Simpsons Comics, Itchy & Scratchy Comics, Bartman, Radioactive Man*—with other titles forthcoming. Best known as creator and executive producer of the Emmy Award-winning series, The Simpsons, Groening made television history by bringing animation back to prime-time and creating an immortal nuclear family. The Simpsons remains one of the Fox network's highest rated shows and currently airs in over 70 countries around the world. Syndication of the series begins September 19, 1994.

Originally created and brought to life in 1987 for Fox's, The Tracey Ullman Show, The Simpsons was Groening's introduction into the animation world. Previously he was best known for his "Life in Hell" cartoon strip, an irreverent portrayal of broken life that debuted in 1977 and currently appears in more than 250 newspapers in the United States and Canada.

In addition to producing his weekly strip, keeping on top of the ongoing production demands of the weekly television series, and meeting regularly with the Bongo team, Groening also oversees all aspects of the licensing and merchandising of The Simpsons.

Groening's best-selling books, based on Life in Hell and The Simpsons, include Love is Hell, Work is Hell, School is Hell, The Big Book of Hell, Akbar & Jeff's Guide to Life, Love is Hell 10th Anniversary Edition, Binky's Guide to Love, The Simpson's Xmas Book, The Simpsons Rainy Day Fun Book, Making Faces With The Simpsons, Bart Simpson's Guide to Life, The Simpson's Uncensored Family Album, Cartooning With The Simpsons, *Simpsons Illustrated* magazine and *Simpsons Comics & Stories*. Stay tuned for Bongo: Year Two! Coming in 1995:

Krusty Comics: That ringmaster of riotous revelry, Krusty the Clown, runs amok in his own comic book! See Sideshow Mel, Corporal Punishment, Miss Pennycandy, and Mr. Teeny, as well as the inevitable guest appearance by a certain spiky-haired #1 fan! It's a 3-issue limited series published monthly starting in January!

The Secret Files of Lisa Simpson : Lisa, the brains of the Simpson clan, finally busts out, cuts loose, and grabs center stage for herself in this super-special one-shot comic book! It's a hilarity-packed tale of eye-popping adventure, brain-baffling intrigue, and psyche-rattling sibling rivalry, coming in April!

When the formation of Image Comics was announced in 1992, the news rocked the comic book industry to its core and set off a chain reaction that continues to be felt to this day.

Six of Marvel's most popular artists–Jim Lee, Rob Liefeld, Todd McFarlane, Jim Valentino, Erik Larsen, and Marc Silvestri–left the world's biggest, most profitable comic book company to strike out on their own, publishing their own "creator-owned" comic books. Tired of the work-for-hire system under which Marvel worked, where an artist could create a character but have no control over the fate of that character, they decided to take the risk of creating all new characters and publishing their own books.

Image was also different from other companies in that each of the founding members created his own studio and produced his own comic books. This ensured that each creator could fully own and control his characters and determine their destinies. Jim Lee called his production company WildStorm Productions, after two of the core titles in his line, *WildC.A.T.s: Covert Action Teams* and *StormWatch*.

© Jim Lee

In 1987, before there was an Image or WildStorm, Jim Lee started out at Marvel Comics after graduating from Princeton University. He illustrated such titles as *Alpha Flight* and *Punisher: War Journal*. His attention to detail and characterization revitalized the *X-Men*, catapulting that title to record sales and earning him the Comic Buyer's Guide's awards for best artist and best cover artist in 1991.

While working for Marvel, Lee and his studio mates Scott Williams and Whilce Portacio formed Homage Studios for companionship and to share expenses, so when Image came about there was already an infrastructure on which to build the new company. With the addition of Joe Chiodo as colorist and Mike Heisler as letterer, a full-fledged comic book publisher was born.

As the list of titles published by WildStorm Productions grew, the ranks of top creative talent swelled as well. WildStorm now has an impressive lineup of some of the hottest artists in the comic book business today. Jim Lee, Whilce Portacio, J. Scott Campbell, Brett Booth, Scott Clark, Travis Charest, Aron Wiesenfeld are some of the pencillers who work at WildStorm's San Diego, California studio, accompanied by equally illustrious inkers, writers, colorists, and computer color separators.

WildStorm's flagship title, *WildC.A.T.s: Covert Action Teams*, has been hugely successful, rarely dropping out of the top ten bestsellers nationally. Since its premiere on CBS TV in October, Jim Lee's *WildC.A.T.s: Covert Action Teams*, an animated series based on the comic book, has been adding a whole new segment of the population to its growing audience.

WildStorm has cracked the top ten with several other titles as well. *WetWorks* and *Team 7* both debuted in the top ten, and *Gen*^{13} overcame relatively low initial orders to become one of the hottest comic books of 1994. Overall, WildStorm's line average is consistently one of the highest in the very competitive world of comic publishing.

Some of the other popular comic books from WildStorm Productions include *StormWatch, Deathblow, Union, WildC.A.T.s Adventures,* and *Backlash*. WildStorm has also recently launched its trading card division. WildStorm Set 1, the fledgling company's first set, was the third best selling card set of its time, against stiff competition from the biggest card manufacturers in the business. WildStorm's second set, featuring the WildC.A.T.s, blew away any competition at all, emerging securely in first place.

WildStorm Productions is a forward-looking comic book publisher, with a keen eye for the marketplace and a sharp sense of what makes a quality book. Diverse enough to entertain a wide range of fans but with a standard of excellence that defines all of its publications, WildStorm and its founder, Jim Lee, intend to stay on the cutting edge of the ever-changing world of comic books.

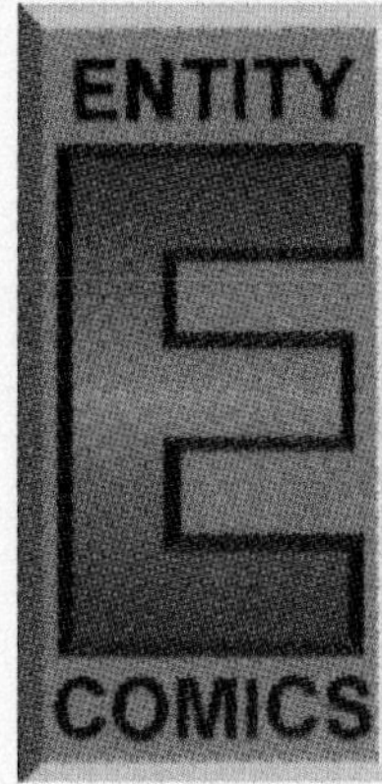

Launched in 1992 by Publishers Don and Laura Davis Chin, Express Publications, Inc. has three separate comic-book imprints. Entity Comics publishes super-hero and science fiction action titles such as *Zen Intergalactic Ninja, Aster, Manosaurs,* and *Stygmata*. Express Press publishes independent material such as the "How To Draw Comics Series" by Rich Buckler. Parody Press publishes satirical and humor comics such as *Kill Barny Again!, Hellspock*, and *Generation X-Farce*. According to *Internal Correspondence* magazine, the company has been ranked as high as #17 out of over 100 publishers. Express Publications was nominated for the 1992 Diamond Distribution Gem award for best new publisher of the year.

Current titles include: *Zen Intergalactic Ninja (color), Zen Intergalactic Ninja: Starquest, Young Zen: City Of Death, Zen Illustrated Novella Series, Stygmata, Manosaurs, Aster, Captain Nauticus & The Ocean Force.*

Best-selling current title: *Zen Intergalactic Ninja, Aster* (tie)

Upcoming projects: (From Entity Comics) *Aster #0, Adolescent Radioactive Black Belt Hamsters: Phase II, Captain Nauticus & The Ocean Force, Enchanter* novellas, Entity Comics Anthology (unnamed), *WarZone* mini-series, *Nira X: Cyberangel* mini-series, *Mutazens* mini-series, *Stygmata Yearbook* #1, *VOX* mini-series, The *All-New Zen Intergalactic Ninja, Zen-nisms: The Wit & Wisdom of Zen* #1, *Zen Adventures, Zen Starquest* trade paperback, *Zen The Hunted* trade paperback, *Zen: Tiberia's Curse* trade paperback, *Zen: Fire Upon The Earth* trade paperback, *Zen Tour Of The Universe: The Airbrush Art of Dan Cote Special* #1, *Zen Yearbook: Hazardous Duty* #1, *Zen: Immortal Combat* Novella, *Zen: Bubble Economy* Novella by Jo Duffy, *Zen Intergalactic Ninja: The Movie official adaptation*; (From Parody Press Comics) *Captain Commander, Star Blecch: Generation Gap, Parody Press Presents, Generation X-Farce, Yawn, Zen April Fool's Special '95: Zen Vs Michael Jack-Zen.*

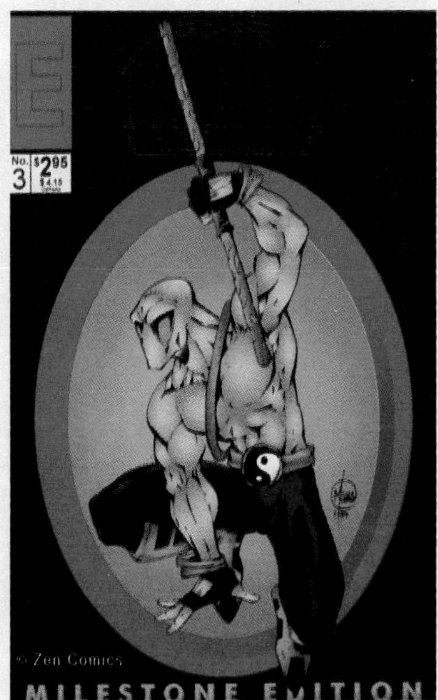

Some of Entity's hot writers and illustrators include: Ross Andru, Dell Barras, Don Chin, Hearn Cho, Dan Cote, Mike Dringenberg, Jo Duffy, Mike Esposito, Stacy Freeman, Nat Gertler, Ben Go, Raff Ienco, Oliver Isabedra, Tatsuya Ishida, Kaleb, Kevin MacKenzie, Charles Marshall, Bill Maus, Joel Orbeta, Jimmy Palmiotti, Ronnie and Narcisco Roxas, Joe Quesada, Thad Rhodes, Steve Stern, and Scooter Tidwell.

It all started with an undead teenage psychopath. And then she came. She debuted at the end of January and since then, no one can forget her. The lady's name is death, Lady Death. Her comic, *Lady Death* #1, (complete with chromium cover), continues to burn up the secondary market! The Lady has put her publisher, Chaos! Comics, on the map as perhaps the leading indy press publisher!

SUCH IS THE DESTINY, SUCH IS THE CURSE OF ...
...LADY DEATH!
AND SO MY STORY GOES.
FIN

"Our focus is to create cutting edge, mega-quality fiction," says publisher Brian Pulido. "We want to surpass readers' and retailers' expectations of what a comic book should be."

This is a lofty goal in the face of such mega-buck competition as Marvel, DC, and Image. Yet Chaos! has done just that. Chaos! has managed to carve out a solid (and substantial) reader base making horrific comics like *Evil Ernie* and horror/fantasy books like *Lady Death* that have fiercely loyal readers. It doesn't hurt that Chaos! Comics has a good on-time shipping record either.

Recently Chaos! has expanded into the super heroic genre with *Lynch Mob* and plans other heroic launches in the upcoming year. Why would this company tread into such over saturated territory?

"Standard super heroes are being done very well by the big boys," says Teven Hughes of *Lady Death* fame. "Their target audience is 12- to 18-year-olds. But who writes hero fiction for the over 18-year-old reader? We do. Don't get the wrong impression, our books are for all ages. Kids can read them for sure. But our target is the older reader, the college age reader, the reader who is sick of the same old regurgitated, super hero stuff."

To get an idea of the Chaos! to come Overstreet asked the individual creators about their books:

Roman Morales on his co-creation Lynch Mob – "They're a paramilitary fighting force from the future that get stuck in the present...with several hundred para-human villainous marauders. The Mob are cool because they are mostly borg. In this series we see the toll of repeated battles on the human body. It's not pretty. We also have fun with a lot of uniquely choreographed battles. We introduce easily over fifty characters who will play roles in the Lynch Mob mythos. This story is huge!"

Steven Hughes on his co-creation Detonator – "Our world, right here, right now. Judge aka Detonator mistakenly triggers an event that empowers people with bizarre, super human abilities with one side effect: The power appears to corrupt their minds. Detonator watches as the United States is ripped apart by these Augments. Messiah, perhaps the most powerful Augment of all, uses the power of persuasion to rally the Augments to his side – all except Detonator, who flatly refuses. Messiah isn't pleased and Detonator the hunter becomes hunted."

Leonardo Jimenez on his co-creation Killzone – "A slave that has been bred to adapt to survive any situation escapes from an intergalactic labor camp. His blood makes him near immortal and is considered the most valued prize in the galaxy. Through a freak event, the slave assumes the idenity and armor of Killzone, a renowed and notorious mercenary. He must 'adapt' to the armor and situation before he is discovered. His complications? Among others, he's immediately dispatched to assemble a strike squad and nullify the gravitational field of earth. It's not long before his fellow mercs, intergalatic bounty hunters, and enemies of the real Killzone want his blood – literally! Killzone is a full color, four issue mini-series shipping monthly starting April 1995."

Jason Jensen (Chaos! Comics senior colorist) on Lady Death - "The new Lady Death series (*Caught Between Heaven And Hell*) will remain a mystery until its release. Suffice it to say, old friends will return as enemies, Lady Death's graveyard will be transformed, and the same guys who did it before are creating it again. *Lady Death: Caught Between Heaven and Hell* is a four issue mini-series in full color starting February 1995. First issue sports a chromium cover."

The Chaos! Crew are committed to producing high quality comics that challenge the mind. Their track record so far leads most to believe they'll hold up their end of the bargain. Expect the unexpected from Chaos! Comics...originators of the "Onyx Age" of comics.

© Rob Liefeld

Extreme Studios is best characterized by its name— Extreme! Harboring some of the brightest stars in the industry today and cultivating the talent of tomorrow, Extreme Studios has made an everlasting impression on the billion dollar a year comic book industry. Former X-Force creator Rob Liefeld founded Extreme Studios and simultaneously launched Image Comics in April of '92 with the release of *Youngblood* #1—the highest selling independent title in the history of comics at that time! The impetus for the creator-owned revolution that has shaken the corporate foundation of comics to its knees, Liefeld's Extreme Studios branched out into other top selling titles, including *Bloodstrike, Brigade, Newmen, Prophet, Supreme, Team Youngblood, Troll* and *Youngblood Strikefile!* Only two years after the initial launch, the distributors list Extreme Studios as the number two family of comics. After proving the longevity of their unprecedented venture, many of the top artists and writers left their corporate counterparts to join this existing stable of creators. Some of these top industry names include Stephen Platt, Dan Panosian, Art Thibert, Chap Yaep, Dan Fraga, Marat Mychaels, Danny Miki and countless others. Perhaps the most striking difference behind the philosophy of Extreme and its industry brethren is the battle for creative freedom and the ability of its artists to control the destinies of the characters they create. Along these lines, Extreme has expanded its reach with a new imprint entitled Maximum Press. This new entity publishes comics and graphic novels outside of the traditional super-hero fare. Designed with a broad range of genres in mind, Maximum Press's initial launch assaults the senses with titles like *Warchild, Black Flag, Cybrid, Risk,* and *Battlestar Galactica*! With their vigorous involvement in a number of mass market arenas including interactive video gaming, animation, movies, television projects and music, Extreme Entertainment is prepared to ride the cutting edge of entertainment well into the next century.

© Rob Liefeld

© Rob Liefeld

®

© Big Ent.

Tekno•Comix, an imprint of BIG Entertainment [NASDAQ: BIGE], is publishing comic books based on original characters and concepts created by best-selling authors and media celebrities including: Leonard Nimoy (Spock from Star Trek), Neil Gaiman, Mickey Spillane (creator of Mike Hammer), John Jakes (author of North and South and Love and War), Anne McCaffrey (leading fantasy writer), Max Allan Collins (*Dick Tracy* writer) and Robert Silverberg (award-winning science fiction writer), as well as the late Gene Roddenberry (Star Trek creator) and Isaac Asimov.

The Tekno•Comix comic book line goes on sale in November, 1994 with Leonard Nimoy's *Primortals™*, a story of Earth's first contact with alien life; and Neil Gaiman's *Mr. Hero - The Newmatic Man™*, the adventures of a steam-powered Victorian robot; followed by Gene Roddenberry's *Lost Universe™*, a new science fiction space adventure, in December. These initial titles will be followed in 1995 by Mickey Spillane's *Mike Danger™*, which features a 1950s private eye thrown into the far future; John Jakes' *Mullkon Empire*, a multi-generational family saga set in the distant future, and Neil Gaiman's *Teknophage™*, starring the most evil villain in this or any other universe.

Some of the most talented pencilers, inkers and writers in the industry are working on Tekno•Comix line including: Rick Veitch, Bryan Talbot, Scot Eaton, James Callahan, Lawrence Watt-Evans, Kate Worley, James Vance, Mike Barreiro, Robert McLeod and Marc Sasso.

Additional product lines include: Tekno•Comix Forum, an interactive comics area on Prodigy, the country's most popular on-line service; the Tekno•Comix Official Calling Card, a collectible prepaid telephone card featuring full color artwork; and an electronic comic strip featuring Tekno•Comix characters on Bell Atlantic's digital fiber optic network. Tekno•Comix also produces a line of merchandise, including T-shirts, posters, watches, rings, frisbees and leather bomber jackets adorned with the Tekno•Comix logo.

SHADOWLINE®

Where do we go from here? If you're Image co-founder Jim Valentino, the answer is simple: anywhere and everywhere, except for the obvious. And that's why the next 12 months are going to be filled with excitement and surprises galore as Valentino's trademark ShadowHawk character undergoes some major transformations! At the same time a trio of brand new comic book projects will take readers soaring into the heights of outer space as well as the depths of the subterranean and the minds of the criminal element.

The biggest buzz out of Valentino's Shadowline, Inc. Studios centers around the upcoming inter-company crossover that will pair his dark avenger, ShadowHawk, with Harris Comics' breathtaking lady of the night, Vampirella. The two-part "Creatures of the Night" storyline, described by Valentino as "a love story dripping in blood," will explode onto the scene, fittingly enough, on Valentine's Day. Harris Comics will be releasing the first 48 page installment on February 14, with the Image-produced Book Two slated for release two weeks later.

Once a true rarity in the comic book realm, crossovers between companies have suddenly become vogue. But not all inter-company crossovers were created equal. In preparing for the marathon plotting sessions at the recent San Diego Comic Convention that helped produce the dynamic storyline for the first meeting between the two nocturnal figures, Valentino spent long hours studying past projects of this nature. By taking both the successes as well as the failures of these other inter-company undertakings into consideration, he has helped to produce a union between the companies that will be anything but run-of-the-mill!

"Two things are really going to make this stand out," the ShadowHawk creator noted. "First off I think the characters themselves interact well. They're sort of a yin and yang. They work together, they look good together, there's a lot of good contrast here between the characters. It's not the exact same character teaming up with the exact same character. They are different enough, one from the other, that they create a springboard off of each other because of their differences. Yet their similarities allow them to be taken in the context together. The other part of it is that we have a very exciting, character oriented story. This won't be your average slugfest, which isn't to say that there won't be action in the story, because there certainly will be. But the story is motivated and moved by the characters and the character interaction."

Unlike some of the previous projects that involved two companies, "Creatures of the Night" hasn't been established as a competition between Image and Harris that happens to utilize characters from each publisher. *Vengeance of Vampirella* writer Tom Sniegoski and Vampi editor Meloney Crawford Chadwick each played a pivotal role in the development of the storyline, along with Valentino and ShadowHawk editor Len Senecal. "It's a single story that has been clearly worked out," Valentino commented. "The first chapter is in the Harris book and the second chapter is in the Image book. It covers a very wide range. It is at times exciting, it is at times poignant, it is at times chilling, and I think that's what we've really got going for us. The juxtaposition of these two characters is really one of the stronger points about this whole project. These two characters just work together."

Also working in favor of this particular crossover are the numerous selling points that flow from the very chemistry of the characters themselves. "ShadowHawk and Vampirella have different audiences. We see this as bridging the two audiences. We hope to have people who have either never read a Vampirella or never read a ShadowHawk pick this up. It's a good story, it has a lot of gothic overtones along with good solid superhero action and characterization. Because it's an imaginary tale, a lot will happen within the context of this story. This book will appeal to the ShadowHawk fan, it will appeal to the Vampirella fan, it will appeal to the fan of inter-company crossovers, it will appeal to people who like to read their comics, and it will appeal to people who like superhero comics," Valentino predicts. "And it has a taste of the supernatural in it as well as a romantic element."

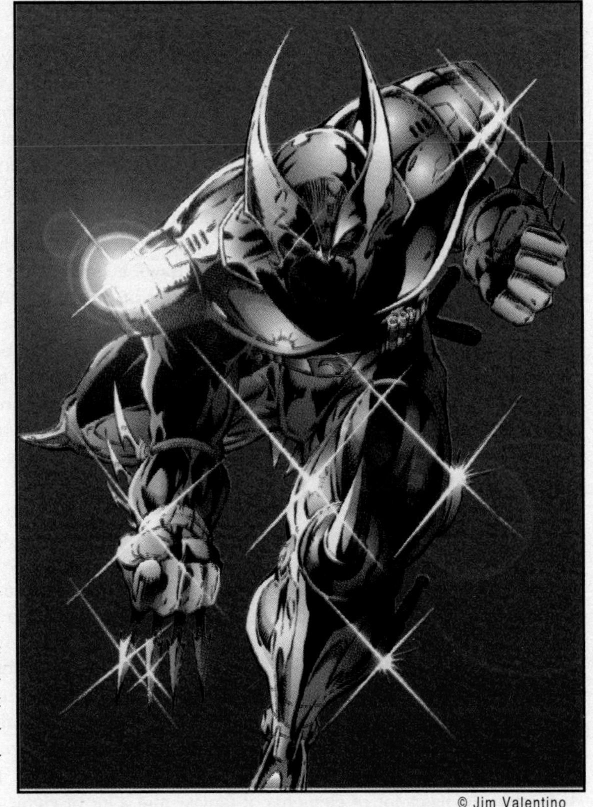
© Jim Valentino

While he was not at liberty to give away specific details about the story itself, he did reveal that "ShadowHawk will become a vampire and the question that remains after he becomes one is whether or not he and Vampirella will remain a couple or become enemies." He was, however, able to reveal some important news about the artistic end of the book. "Our version features a stunning Mark Texeira cover, and Olyoptics will be handling the color. I'm dedicating myself to making this the best work of my career!"

Along with major advertising in comic book trade magazines and papers, retailers and fans alike can expect some interesting promotional materials that will capitalize on the Valentine's Day/gothic/love story angles. In addition, the February release of the first Vampirella trading card set will include a card featuring ShadowHawk and Vampirella together. And one other important factor for comic book aficionados everywhere is Valentino's guarantee that the crossover will come out on time. "Like all books from Shadowline, it will ship on time," he stated. "We've never shipped a late book, and we don't intend to start with this one!"

The team-up with Vampirella isn't the only big news concerning Valentino's vigilante spine-breaker. A lot of things are brewing in Paul Johnstone's world during 1995, including his ultimate demise. Issue #17, which is scheduled for a March release, will bring the character's fourth major story-arc, "The Monster Within," to a close. It will also feature the long-awaited reunion between ShadowHawk and Todd McFarlane's Spawn that fans have been calling for every since the demonic one's brief appearance way back in *ShadowHawk* #2. Look for Keith Giffen's soul repossessing Trencher to join in on the "Dead Man's Party," where ShadowHawk will learn that death is not absolute, and that there are fates worse than death!

Approximately two months later, *ShadowHawk* #18 will answer the question: "Can A Hero Die?" as Valentino's version of ShadowHawk comes to a close with the death of Paul Johnstone. Gone, but certainly not forgotten, this will be followed in close proximity by the release of *The New ShadowHawk*, which will feature the writing talents of award-winning scribe Kurt Busiek. "This new ShadowHawk will not be Paul Johnstone, although who it is is going to be a mystery," Valentino commented. "We're going to let Kurt weave the same magic that he wove in *Marvels* to keep you on your toes and guessing who ShadowHawk is, who the New ShadowHawk is, why the New ShadowHawk is, and what the New ShadowHawk is doing! Kurt promises some exciting, character driven stories, and he's got a lot of great ideas that we unfortunately can't give too much away about, but it's pretty stunning stuff, so expect the best."

Busiek's red-hot talents and interesting perspectives will also be featured in the first ShadowHawk spin-off, *The Regulators*, which will take a deep and sometimes disturbing look inside the world of the super villain. What do they do on their day off? What do they do after a heist? How do they rationalize what they do, or do they? Busiek will be providing all of the answers in this series. *The Regulators* is slated for a spring or early summer release.

And while *The Regulators* will provide a view of the world from inside the mind of the criminal element, another new series, *The Others*, will take the reader all the way inside the Earth to discover a world quite unlike anything previously explored in the comic book medium. Scheduled to debut in early spring, *The Others* are no newcomers to ShadowHawk fans, who have chronicled their existence over the past few years in *ShadowHawk* #3 and #4, and most recently during their return in *ShadowHawk* #15. Talented newcomers Patrick Blaine and Jason Gorder, who were featured in *SH* #15, will be handling the penciling and inking duties, while highly respected *Vengeance of Vampirella* writer Tom Sniegoski has signed on to write the story of a race of sentient beings whose hopes of hiding from mankind have just been dashed.

"It's a different kind of book in that they're not superheroes, per se," according to Valentino. "It has a lot of elements of fantasy and a lot of elements of science fiction. It's quite different, although it also takes in a lot of action and a lot of suspense because we will be exploring a totally different world."

Different worlds are also the theme of Valentino's next solo project, *The Alliance*, which is scheduled to blast off in the summer of 1995. It is described by its creator as "a story of an invasion, and the rise of a small band of freedom fighters who will push the invasion back. It will be a very character oriented book with a strong emphasis on action."

"This will be my book, and it will be a space opera," he continued. "It will be very similar in tone and temperament to *The Guardians of the Galaxy*. It will have a lot of action, but more than that there will be a lot of character interplay, there will be a lot of changes within the characters themselves. Since they're brand new characters, everything we have is pretty much free reign and we can do whatever we want to. If that means that a character is going to die, then he's going to die. Since I've done space opera before and I kind of know my way around it and I feel pretty comfortable with it, I'm really looking forward to doing this series."

Fans of his previous work are looking forward to it as well, as this appears to be the year that Jim Valentino and Shadowline, Inc. step forward in a big way. From the grim and gritty world of *ShadowHawk* and *The Regulators* to the underground struggles of *The Others* and all the way into the vast and endless expanses of space itself with *The Alliance*, Valentino and company are truly offering something for everyone in 1995!

Valiant, a division of Acclaim Comics, published its first superhero comic book in March of 1991 when *Magnus Robot Fighter* #1 debuted. Since then, Acclaim has risen through the ranks to become one of the leading publishers of comic books. In 1993, Acclaim, then known as Voyager/Valiant, was actually the third largest comic book publisher, winning just over 10% of the market.

In 1995, Acclaim is again causing a major shake-up in the comic industry. This March, Acclaim Comics introduced two new comic imprints—imprints which promise to generate new levels of excitement for fans.

They are Windjammer and Armada. Comics published under the Valiant imprint will continue to feature action/adventure storylines with the familiar stable of Valiant heroes and villains. However, Valiant promises a new surge of energy for their line with art and storytelling by the hottest names in the comic book industry. Creators such as Bart Sears, Ron Marz, Andy Smith, and Norm Breyfogle have signed on to give Valiant a dynamic new look for 1995.

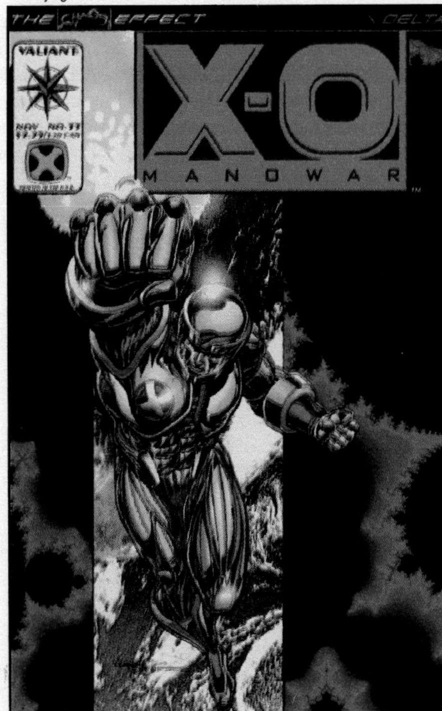

Under the Windjammer imprint, Acclaim Comics showcases creator owned projects. The premiere offerings from the Windjammer imprint will be Mike Grell's *Bar Sinister* and *Starslayer - The Director's Cut.*

Finally, Acclaim launches the Armada line in 1995 featuring adaptations of licensed properties. The first project on tap is the comic adaptation of the nation's hottest collectible card game, Magic: the Gathering. Two series based directly on the game are set to debut in early 1995. Look for adaptations of movies, television shows, games, and music under the Armada imprint throughout the year.

Since its inception, Valiant comics has been known for its dedication to editorial and artistic quality. This reputation will continue to grow during 1995 and beyond under the new banner—Acclaim.

MARVEL/TIMELY/ATLAS Publishers' Abbreviation Codes:

ACI-Animirth Comics, Inc.
AMI-Atlas Magazines, Inc.
ANC-Atlas News Co., Inc.
BPC-Bard Publishing Corp.
BFP-Broadcast Features Pubs.
CBS-Crime Bureau Stories
CLDS-Classic Detective Stories
CCC-Comic Combine Corp.
CDS-Current Detective Stories
CFI-Crime Files, Inc.
CmPI-Comedy Publications, Inc.
CmPS-Complete Photo Story
CnPC-Cornell Publishing Corp.
CPC-Chipiden Publishing Corp.
CPI-Crime Publications, Inc.
CPS-Canam Publishing Sales Corp.
CSI-Classics Syndicate, Inc.
DCI-Daring Comics, Inc.
EPC-Euclid Publishing Co.
EPI-Emgee Publications, Inc.
FCI-Fantasy Comics, Inc.
FPI-Foto Parade, Inc.
GPI-Gem Publishing, Inc.
HPC-Hercules Publishing Corp.
IPS-Interstate Publishing Corp.
JPI-Jaygee Publications, Inc.
LBI-Lion Books, Inc.
LCC-Leading Comic Corp.
LMC-Leading Magazine Corp.
MALE-Male Publishing Corp.
MAP-Miss America Publishing Corp.
MCI-Marvel Comics, Inc.
MgPC-Margood Publishing Corp.
MjMC-Marjean Magazine Corp.
MMC-Mutual Magazine Corp.
MPC-Medalion Publishing Corp.
MPI-Manvis Publications, Inc.
NPI-Newsstand Publications, Inc.
NPP-Non-Pareil Publishing Corp.
OCI-Official Comics, Inc.
OMC-Official Magazine Corp.
OPI-Olympia Publications, Inc.
PPI-Postal Publications, Inc.
PrPI-Prime Publications, Inc.
RCM-Red Circle Magazines, Inc.
SAI-Sports Actions, Inc.
SePI-Select Publications, Inc.
SnPC-Snap Publishing Co.
SPC-Select Publishing Co.
SPI-Sphere Publications, Inc.
TCI-Timely Comics, Inc.
TP-Timely Publications
20 CC-20th Century Comics Corp.
USA-U.S.A. Publications, Inc.
VPI-Vista Publications, Inc.
WFP-Western Fiction Publishing
WPI-Warwick Publications, Inc.
YAI-Young Allies, Inc.
ZPC-Zenith Publishing Co., Inc.

COMIC BOOK ARTISTS

Many of the popular artists are pointed out in the listings. When more than one artist worked on a story, their names are separated by a (/). The first name did the pencil drawings and the second the inks. When two or more artists work on a story, only the most prominent will be noted in some cases. We wish all good artists could be listed, but due to space limitation, only the most popular can. The following list of artists are considered to be either the most collected in the comic field or are historically significant and should be pointed out. Artists designated below with an (*) indicate that only their most noted work will be listed. The rest will eventually have all their work shown as the information becomes available. This list could change from year to year as new artists come into prominence.

Adams, Arthur
Adams, Neal
Bagley, Mark
Baker, Matt
Barks, Carl
Beck, C. C.
*Brunner, Frank
*Buscema, John
Byrne, John
Capullo, Greg
*Check, Sid
Cole, Jack
Cole, L. B.
Craig, Johnny
Crandall, Reed
Davis, Jack
Disbrow, Jayson
*Ditko, Steve
Eisner, Will
*Elder, Bill
Evans, George
Everett, Bill
Feldstein, Al
Fine, Lou
Foster, Harold
Fox, Matt
Frazetta, Frank
*Giffen, Keith
Golden, Michael
Gottfredson, Floyd
*Guardineer, Fred
Gustavson, Paul
*Heath, Russ
Howard, Wayne
*Infantino, Carmen
Ingels, Graham
Jones, Jeff
Kamen, Jack
Kane, Bob
*Kane, Gil
Kelly, Walt
Kieth, Sam
Kinstler, E. R.
Kirby, Jack
Krenkel, Roy
Krigstein, Bernie
Kubert, Adam & Andy
*Kubert, Joe
Kurtzman, Harvey
Lapham, Dave
Larsen, Erik
Lee, Jae
Lee, Jim
Liefeld, Rob
Manning, Russ
McFarlane, Todd
McWilliams, Al
Meskin, Mort
Mignola, Mike
Miller, Frank
Moreira, Ruben
*Morisi, Pete
*Newton, Don
Nostrand, Howard
Orlando, Joe
Pakula, Mac
*Palais, Rudy
*Perez, George
Portacio, Whilce
Powell, Bob
Quesada, Joe
Raboy, Mac
Raymond, Alex
Ravielli, Louis
*Redondo, Nestor
Rogers, Marshall
Schomburg, Alex
Sears, Bart
Siegel & Shuster
Silvestri, Marc
Simon & Kirby (S&K)
*Simonson, Walt
Smith, Barry Windsor
Smith, Paul
Stanley, John
*Starlin, Jim
Steranko, Jim
Stevens, Dave
Texeira, Mark
Thibert, Art
Torres, Angelo
Toth, Alex
Tuska, George
Ward, Bill
Williamson, Al
Woggon, Bill
Wolverton, Basil
Wood, Wallace
Wrightson, Bernie
Zeck, Mike

COMIC BOOK ARTISTS & THEIR FIRST WORK

Adams, Neal - (1 pg.) Archie's Jokebook Mag. #41, 9/59; (1st on Batman, cvr only) Detective Comics #370, 12/67; (1st Warren art) Creepy #14

Barks, Carl - (art only) Donald Duck Four Color #9, 8/42; (scripts only) Large Feature Comic #7, ca. Spring 1942

Broderick, Pat - (cover & art) Planet of Vampires #1, 2/75

Brunner, Frank - (fan club sketch) Creepy #10, 1965

Buckler, Rich - Flash Gordon #10, 11/67

Burnley, Jack - (cover & art) New York World's Fair nn, '40

Buscema, John - (1st at Marvel) Strange Tales #150, 11/66

Byrne, John - Nightmare #20, 8/74; (1st at DC) Untold Legend of the Batman #1, 7/80; (1st at Marvel) Giant-Size Dracula #5, 6/75

Capullo, Greg - (1st on X-Force) X-Force Annual #1, '92

Cole, Jack - (1 pg.) Star Comics #11, 4/38

Crandall, Reed - Hit Comics #10, 4/41

Davis, Jack - (cartoon) Tip Top Comics #32, 12/38

Ditko, Steve - (1st publ.) Black Magic V4#3, 11-12/53 (1st drawn story), Fantastic Fears #5, 1-2/54

Ellison, Harlan - (1st pro story) Weird Science-Fantasy #24, 6/54

Everett, Bill - Amazing Mystery Funnies V1#2,9/38

Fine, Lou - (1st cvr) Wonder Comics #2, 6/39; Jumbo Comics #4, 12/38

Frazetta, Frank - Tally-Ho Comics nn, 12/44

Giffen, Keith - (1 pg.) Deadly Hands of Kung-Fu #17, 11/75; (1st story) Deadly Hands of Kung-Fu #22, 4?/76; (tied w/Deadly Hands) Amazing Adventures #35, 3/76

Golden, Michael - Marvel Classics Comics #28, '77

Grell, Mike - Adventure Comics #435, 9-10/74

Ingels, Graham art at E.C. - Saddle Justice #4, Sum '48

Kaluta, Michael - Teen Confessions #59, 12/69

Kelly, Walt - New Comics #1, 12/35

Keown, Dale - Nth Man the Ultimate Ninja #8, 1/90; (1st at Marvel) Samurai #13, ?/87; (1st on Hulk) Incredible Hulk #367, 3/90

Kieth, Sam - Primer #5, 11?/83

Kirby, Jack - Jumbo Comics #1, 9/38;

Kubert, Adam/Andy/Joe art team - Sgt. Rock #422, 7/88

Kurtzman, Harvey - Tip Top Comics #36, 4/39; (1st at E.C.) Lucky Fights It Through nn, 1949

Larsen, Erik - Megaton #1, 11/83

Lee, Jae - Marvel Comics Presents #85, '91

Lee, Jim - (1st at Marvel) Alpha Flight #51, 10/87; (1st on X-Men) X-Men #248?, ?/89; (art on Punisher) - Punisher War Journal #1, 11/88

Liefeld, Rob - (1st at DC) Warlord #131, 9/88; (1st at Marvel) X-Factor #40, 4?/89; (1st full story) Megaton #8, 8/87; (inside front cover only) Megaton #5, 6/86; (art on New Mutants) New Mutants Annual #5, '89

Lim, Ron - (art on Silver Surfer) Silver Surfer Annual #1, '88

Mayer, Sheldon - New Comics #1, 12/35

McFarlane, Todd - Coyote #11, ?/85; (1st full story) All Star Squadron #47, 7/85; (1st on Hulk) Incredible Hulk #330, 4/87

Medina, Angel - (pin-up only) Megaton #3, 2/86

Miller, Frank - (1st on Batman) DC Special Series #21, Spr '80; (1st on Daredevil) Spectacular Spider-Man #27, 2/79

Newton, Don - Many Ghosts of Dr. Graves #45, 5/74

Perez, George - (1st at DC) Flash #289, 9/80; (2 pgs.) Astonishing Tales #25, 8/74

Portacio, Whilce - (1st on X-Men) X-Men #201, 1/86

Quesada, Joe - (1st on X-Factor) X-Factor Annual #7, '92

Raboy, Mac - (1st cover for Fawcett) Master Comics #21, 12/41

Romita, John - Daredevil #12, 1/66

Shuster, Joe - (cover) New Adventure Comics #16, 6/37

Siegel & Shuster - New Fun Comics #6, 10/35

Simon & Kirby - Blue Bolt #2, 7/40

Simonson, Walter - Magnus, Robot Fighter #10, 5/65

Smith, Barry - X-Men #53, 2/69

Smith, Paul - (1 pg. pin-up) King Conan #7, 9/81; (1st full story) Marvel Fanfare #1, 3/82

Steranko, Jim - Spyman #1, Sep '66; (1st at Marvel) Strange Tales #151, 12/66

Swan, Curt - Dick Cole #1, 12-1/48-49

Thomas, Roy - (scripts) Son of Vulcan #50, 1/66

Torres, Angelo - Crime Mysteries #13, 5/54

Weiss, Alan - (illo) Blue Beetle #5, 3-4/65

Williamson, Al - (1st at E.C.) Tales From the Crypt #31, 9/52; (text illos) Famous Funnies #169, 8/48

Wood, Wally - (art at E.C.) Saddle Romances #10, 1-2/50

Wrightson, Bernie - House of Mystery #179, 4/68; (1st at Marvel) Chamber of Darkness #7, 10/70; (1st cover) Web of Horror #3, 4/70; (fan club sketch) Creepy #9

Zeck, Mike - (illos) Barney and Betty Rubble #11, 2/75

KEY COMICS SOLD IN 1994

The following list of books sold were reported to Overstreet during the year and represent only a small portion of the total amount of important books that sell.

GOLD (Reported sales)

Action Comics #17 FN	$1,100
Action Comics #19 FN	$1,000
Action Comics #21 VF	$1,100
Action Comics #23 VF+	$4,200
Adventure Comics #62 FN71	$700
Adventure Comics #103 NM	$2,200
All-American #16 VG	$13,000
All-American #17 VF+(R)	$5,600
All-American #61 VF	$1,485
All Flash #1 VF84	$3,400
All Select #1 VG54	$1,700
All Star #1 FN	$3,850
Batman #1 VF78	$29,000
Batman #1 FN58(R)	$14,000
Batman #1 VG52	$9,500
Batman #1 FR+	$7,000
Batman #8 FN69	$1200
Batman #47 VF	$2,900
Batman #55 NM	$1,300
Captain America #1 VF85	$32,000
Captain America #1 VF80	$25,000
Captain America #1 FN68	$15,000
Captain America #1 VG+	$10,200
Captain America #12 VF79	$1,200
Captain America #74 FN	$2,065
Comic Cavalcade #1 VG52	$1300
Daring Mystery #4 VF+	$1,500
Detective #1 FN61	$37,500
Detective #15 VF(R)	$1,700
Detective #30 VF79	$2,800
Detective #34 VF+	$3,000
Detective #38 FN+	$15,000
Detective #38 VF+(R)	$12,000
Detective #39 VF+	$5,000
Donald Duck FC #9 NM	$5,040
Donald Duck FC #178	$675
Flash Comics #5 VF+	$3,800
Flash Comics #92 VF	$2,200
40 Big Pages of M. Mouse FN	$800
Future Comics #1 VF78	$800
Green Lantern #6 VF82	$750
Harvey Comics Library #1	$625
Human Torch #2(1) FN+	$4,000
Human Torch #2(1) VG52	$3,000
King Comics #1 VG54	$1,700
Mad #19 MT(Gaines)	$770
Marvel Comics #1 FN72	$18,250
Marvel Mystery #5 VF75	$3,500
Marvel Mystery #6 VF79	$2,100
Marvel Mystery Annual FN	$5,000
Mickey Mouse Mag. #1 FN61	$3,500
More Fun #9 VG43	$2,200
More Fun #11 VF75	$3,200
More Fun #52 VG55(R)	$10,800
More Fun #54 VF+	$9,100
More Fun #55 FN+	$2,700
More Fun #57 VF+	$3,700
Mystery Men #2 VF	$750
Mystery Men #4 VF	$600
Mystic Comics #1 FN+	$4,000
Mystic Comics #2 VF+	$3,150
N.Y. World's Fair 1939 VF+	$30,000
N.Y. World's Fair '39 VF/NM	$20,000
Sub-Mariner #1 FN70	$4,200
Superman #1 VG42(R)	$6,500
Superman #3 VF+	$7,600
Superman #4 FN68	$2,200
Superman #5 VF+	$4,200
Superman #14 NM	$2,860
Superman #71 NM	$550
Walt Disney's C&S #31 NM	$2,025
Wonder Woman #1 VF84	$11,000
Wonder Woman #1 FN+	$3,450
World's Best #1 FN72	$4,200

SILVER (Reported sales)

Amazing Fantasy #15 VF84	$17,500
Amaz. Spider-Man #1 VF87	$11,000
Amaz. Spider-Man #1 VF82	$6,500
Amaz. Spider-Man #1 FN+	$6,500
Amaz. Spider-Man #2 VF87	$2,700
Amaz.Spider-Man Ann. #1 NM	$500
Avengers #1 VF86	$1,300
Avengers #4 NM	$1,430
Avengers #4 NM90	$1,200
Batman Annual #1 NM	$770
Brave & the Bold 28 VF	$3,520
Brave & the Bold #28 VF77	$1,700
Challengers/Unknown #1 VF+	$2,000
Daredevil #1 NM92	$1,650
Fantastic Four #1 NM+	$20,250
Fantastic Four #1 VF77	$5,500
Fantastic Four #5 NM	$3,850
Fantastic Four #5 NM90	$3,500
Fantastic Four #5 NM	$2,200
Fantastic Four #6 VF+	$795
Fantastic Four #48 NM94	$1,000
Flash #105 VF80	$2,700
Flash #123 NM	$925
Green Lantern #1 VF79	$1,300
Incredible Hulk #1 NM	$15,400
Iron Man #1 VF+	$525
Jimmy Olsen #1 NM	$8,250
Journey I. Mystery #83 VF85	$2,500
Lois Lane #1 FN+	$1,150
Showcase #1 VF87	$4,000
Showcase #4 VF77	$14,000
Showcase #4 FN+	$8,700
Showcase #4 FN65	$6,000
Showcase #10 NM89	$6,500
Showcase #11 VF+	$1,600
Showcase #13 VF	$2,500
Showcase #14 FN60	$1,500
Showcase #15 VF	$1,500
Silver Surfer #4 NM	$500
Strange Tales #110 VF89	$1,600
Superman Annual #1 NM	$935
Tales of Suspense #1 VF	$1,400
Tales of Susp. #39 NM (WM)	$10,400
Tales of Suspense #39 NM91	$4,800
X-Men #1 NM90	$5,000
X-Men #1 VF+	$4,500
X-Men #1 VF83	$3,800

PEDIGREE BOOKS SOLD

Allentown (AT), Bethlehem (BH), Mile High (MH), San Francisco (SF), White Mountain (WM)

Advs. Into Terror #9 (WM)	$265
Americas Best #15 (MH)	$395
Astonishing #13 (WM)	$330
Blue Beetle #8 (MH)	$470
Captain America #1 (AT)	$82,500
Captain Marvel Advs. #26 (MH)	$550
Cyclone Comics #3 (MH)	$465
Detective #26 (AT)	$5,200
Detective #27 (MH)	$125,000
Exciting Comics #20 (MH)	$500
Fighting Yank #2 (MH)	$965
Flash Comics #1 (MH)	$100,000
Flash Annual #1 (BH)	$385
Green Hornet #2 (MH)	$1,735
Haunt of Fear #6 (WM)	$410
Mad #2 (WM)	$675
Marvel Mystery #29 (Chicago)	$990
Marvel Tales #105 (WM)	$660
Miss Fury #7 (AT)	$580
More Fun #48 (MH)	$2,750
More Fun #62 (MH)	$6,050
Mystic #13 (WM)	$300
Nickel Comics #2 (AT)	$935
Pep Comics #6 (Larson)	$580
Planet Comics #1 (Denver)	$14,500
Prize Comics #15 (MH)	$825
Red Dragon #6 (MH)	$875
Sensation #33 (AT)	$530
Showcase #9 (BH)	$10,000
Space Worlds #6 (WM)	$700
Star Spangled #22 (SF)	$1,100
Strange Worlds #9 (WM)	$310
Tales of Suspense #39 (WM)	$10,400
Vault of Horror #12 (WM)	$4,950
Wonder Woman #9 (MH)	$1,760
World's Finest #19 (AT)	$1,575

MARKET AT A GLANCE

The following is a quick reference list of selected books from the Gold and Silver Age showing last year's price, this year's price and the rate of change.

GOLDEN AGE

Title	1995 price	% change	1994 price
Action Comics #1	$125,000	38%	$90,000
Action Comics #23	3,500	100%	1,750
Adventure Comics #40	22,000	37%	16,000
All-American Comics #16	52,000	40%	37,000
All-American Comics #25	5,500	30%	4,200
All Flash #1	7,000	20%	5,800
All Star Comics #3	25,000	25%	20,000
All Winners #1	8,000	60%	5,000
Batman #1	42,000	16%	36,000
Captain America Comics #1	45,000	25%	36,000
Daredevil #1	5,500	38%	4,000
Detective Comics #1	54,000	50%	36,000
Detective Comics #27	115,000	25%	92,000
Detective Comics #33	22,000	22%	18,000
Donald Duck 4-Color #4	7,000	16%	6,000
Flash Comics #1	32,000	39%	23,000
Funnies On Parade	8,200	13%	7,200
Green Lantern #1	17,500	34%	13,000
Human Torch #1	15,000	57%	9,500
Looney Tunes #1	5,500	66%	3,000
Jumbo Comics #1	17,000	41%	12,000
Marvel Comics #1	85,000	13%	75,000
Marvel Mystery Comics #9	9,500	46%	6,500
More Fun Comics #14	12,000	33%	9,000
More Fun Comics #52	32,000	14%	28,000
New Book Of Comics #1	12,000	28%	9,400
New Comics #1	13,500	25%	10,750
New Fun Comics #6	14,250	30%	10,900
N.Y. World's Fair 1939	16,000	45%	11,000
Sensation #1	9,000	50%	6,000
Silver Streak Comics #1	6,500	35%	4,800
Silver Streak Comics #6	6,500	54%	4,200
Superman #1	80,000	14%	70,000
Walt Disney's Comics and Stories #1	10,000	42%	7,000
Whiz #1	46,000	9%	42,000
Wonder Woman #1	8,000	23%	6,500
Young Allies #1	6,200	55%	4,000

SILVER AGE

Title	1995 price	% change	1994 price
Amazing Fantasy #15	$22,000	10%	20,000
Amazing Spider-Man #1	14,500	7%	13,500
Amazing Spider-Man #1	1,100	10%	1,000
Avengers #1	1,775	5%	1,675
Brave & The Bold #28	3,300	7%	3,070
Brave & The Bold #29	1,900	8%	1,750
Brave & The Bold #34	1,450	16%	1,250
Challengers Of The Unknown #1	1,525	22%	1,250
Detective Comics #225	3,850	10%	3,500
Fantastic Four #1	13,000	8%	12,000
Fantastic Four #4	1,850	13%	1,625
Fantastic Four #5	2,000	14%	1,750
Flash #105	3,100	12%	2,750
Green Lantern #1	1,750	9%	1,600
Incredible Hulk #1	8,500	19%	7,100
Jimmy Olsen #1	2,050	20%	1,700
Journey Into Mystery #83	2,950	8%	2,730
Justice League Of America #1	2,500	13%	2,200
Lois Lane #1	1,475	22%	1,200
Showcase #4	21,000	16%	18,000
Showcase #6	2,400	11%	2,150
Showcase #8	9,750	30%	7,500
Showcase #9	4,000	29%	3,100
Showcase #14	3,500	16%	3,000
Showcase #22	3,900	18%	3,300
Tales Of Suspense #1	1,100	15%	950
Tales Of Suspense #39	3,000	17%	2,550
Tales Of The Unexpected #40	700	16%	600
Tales To Astonish #1	1,100	22%	900
Tales To Astonish #27	2,600	13%	2,300
X-Men #1	3,200	6%	3,000

OVERSTREET ADVISORS

DAVID T. ALEXANDER
David Alexander Comics
Tampa, FL

JON BERK, Attorney
President AACBC
Hartford, CT

GARY M. CARTER
Editor CBM
Coronado, CA

GARY COLABUONO
Moondog's Comicland
Elk Grove Village, IL

LARRY CURCIO
Avalon Comics
Medford, MA

GARY DOLGOFF
Gary Dolgoff Comics
Brooklyn, NY

RICHARD EVANS
Bedrock City Comics
Houston, TX

STEVE FISHLER
Metropolis Collectibles
New York, NY

STEVEN GENTNER
Golden Age Specialist
Portland, OR

MICHAEL GOLDMAN
Motor City Comics
Southfield, MI

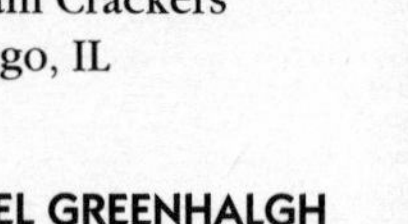

JAMIE GRAHAM
Graham Crackers
Chicago, IL

DANIEL GREENHALGH
Showcase New England
Wallingford, CT

ROBERT HALL
Collector
Harrisburg, PA

BRUCE HAMILTON
Hamilton Comics
Prescott, AZ

JOHN HAUSER
Dealer/Collector
New Berlin, WI

BILL HOWARD
Collector
San Francisco, CA

BILL HUGHES
Executive Investments
Beverly Hills, CA

ROB HUGHES
Executive Investments
Beverly Hills, CA

JOSEPH KOCH
Dealer/Collector
Brooklyn, NY

PHIL LEVINE
Dealer/Collector
Three Bridges, NJ

HARRY MATETSKY
Collector
Baldwin, NY

PETER MOROLO
Collector
Long Island, NY

MICHAEL NAIMAN
Silver Age Specialist
San Diego, CA

MATT NELSON
More Fun Comics
New Orleans, LA

RICHARD OLSON
Dealer/Collector
Slidell, LA

JIM PAYETTE
Golden Age Specialist
Bethlehem, NH

CHRIS PEDRIN
Pedrin Conservatory
Redwood City, CA

BILL PONSETI
More Fun Comics
New Orleans, LA

TODD REZNIK
Pacific Comic Exchange
Los Angeles, CA

ROBERT ROGOVIN
Four Color Comics
New York, NY

RORY ROOT
Comic Relief
Berkeley, CA

ROBERT ROTER
Pacific Comic Exchange
Los Angeles, CA

CHUCK ROZANSKI
Mile High Comics
Denver, CO

JOHN SNYDER
Diamond Int. Galleries
Timonium, MD

CRAIG SOIFER
Comic Shop Owner
Brooklyn, NY

TONY STARKS
Silver Age Specialist
Newburgh, IN

JOE VERENAULT
Golden Age Specialist
Woodbury Heights, NJ

JERRY WEIST
Sotheby's
New York, NY

HARLEY YEE
Dealer/Collector
Detroit, MI

Our thanks to these fine people and all the others for their help in providing pricing information for this edition.

ANNUAL REPORT

by Bob Overstreet

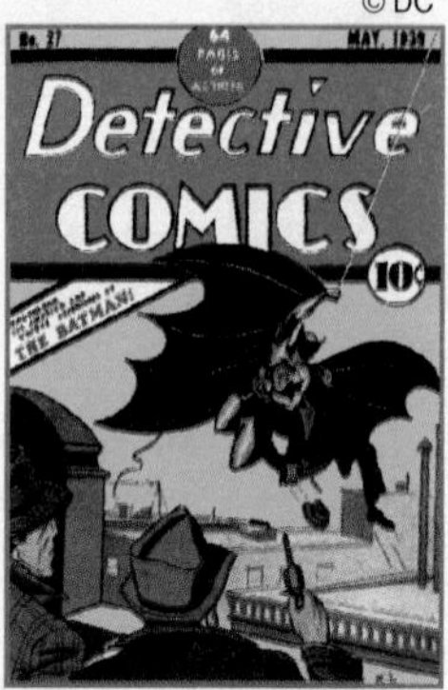

© DC

Hottest Book of 1994!! Mile High Detective #27 sells for $135,000 to a private collector!!

Prices in the comic marketplace continued to soar to new record highs, once again outpacing the national rate of economic expansion. Brisk sales in high grade Silver Age books accompanied by a strong resurgence in Golden Age books has allowed the marketplace to sustain its solid growth pattern.

Current values in the marketplace are experiencing strong upward pressure. Given the existing supply shortages, one may expect future prices to reflect this increase in demand.

GOLDEN AGE: Now the hottest area in collecting. Reported sales from dealers across the country strongly indicate a rapidly expanding market for these older books with diminishing supplies. Most DC and Timely titles are experiencing accelerated demand resulting in prices over the 1994 Guide in all grades. In fact, most Golden Age books are selling extremely well. We are seeing a resurgence of interest in Disney, L.B. Cole, SOTI books, early Archies and good girl art comics. This increased interest may be the result of collectors moving from the Silver Age boom of recent years into collecting the scarcer Golden Age material. Demand for already scarce material, coupled with fewer collections surfacing, has made it more difficult for dealers to restock needed inventory. As a result we are seeing astronomical prices for vintage books. The law of supply and demand will figure heavily in the years ahead in the Golden Age market.

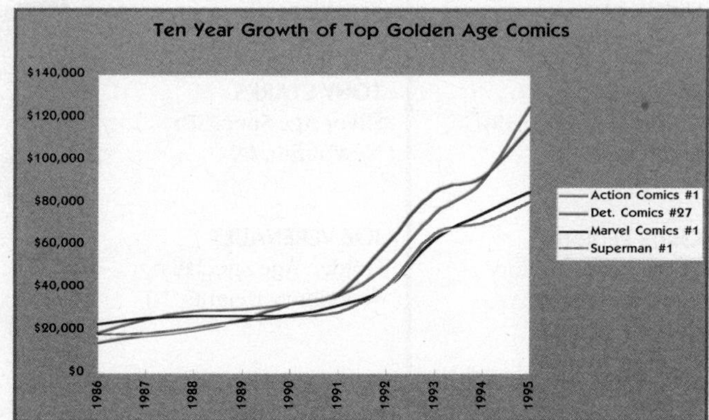

The four most valuable Golden Age books at left had relatively the same value 10 years ago. Prices began to spread in 1992.

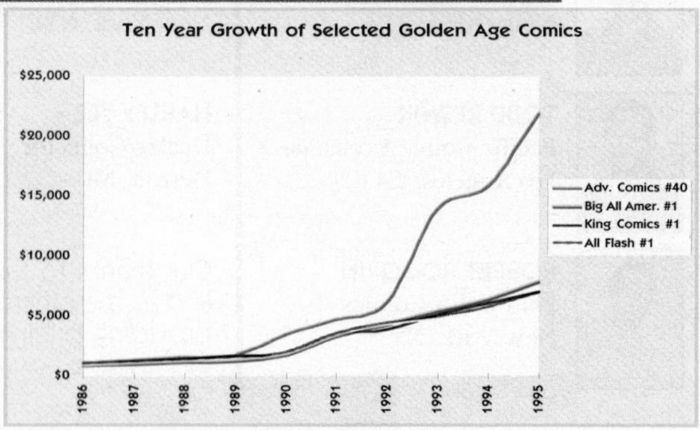

The four selected Golden Age books at right all had the same relative value 10 years ago. Note how Adventure #40 (Sandman) began its upward trend in 1989 while the other books showed slow, steady growth.

SILVER AGE: Demand in this area has become quite specialized. Most sales at prices over Guide are almost exclusively in the high grade area. Hottest Marvel title is still *Spider-Man*, followed by *Fantastic Four. Incredible Hulk* #1-6 still remain very popular. *Showcase* and key *Brave and the Bold* in high grade remain the hottest area for DC. Sales slow for VG or less copies of all but the most key of the Silver Age books. The 1990s Silver Age boom seems to be stablizing at current price levels.

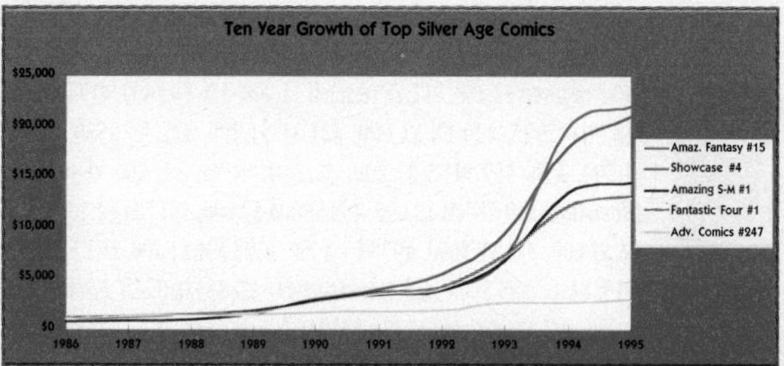

The most valuable Silver Age books 10 years ago had the same relative value. Note how Showcase #4 & Amazing Fantasy #15 have pulled away from the rest while Adventure #247 only showed a 10% per year increase since 1986.

The selected Silver Age books at left had the same relative value in 1986. Note how their values have spread over the past 10 years with Detective #225 (Martian Manhunter) beginning to accelerate in 1992. Richie Rich #1 has enjoyed only a slight increase.

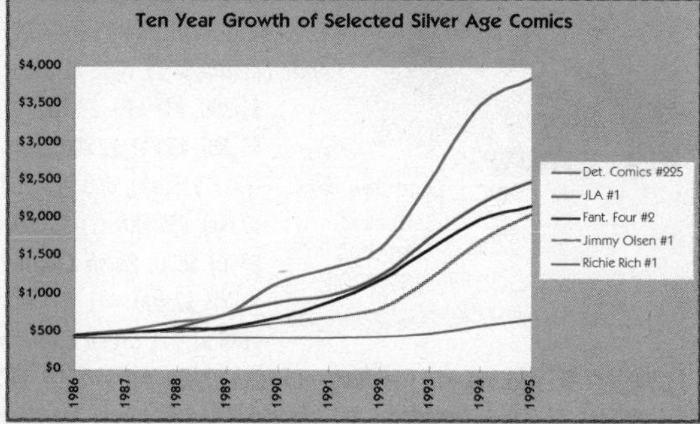

DIAMOND ACQUIRES OVERSTREET

September 2, 1994 was a big day for long time friends Steve Geppi and Bob Overstreet and the culmination of years of discussion. Geppi acquired Overstreet Publications, Inc. with all of its copyrights and intellectual properties, including this Price Guide. The merger of these two companies insures the continued success of the Overstreet family of products which has served fandom for the last 25 years. The first product under the new Gemstone Publishing umbrella will be an all-new monthly magazine, the first of many products created to better serve comic fandom. The company relocated to the Timonium, MD Gemstone headquarters and will continue to publish their products in this location.

Steve Geppi and Bob Overstreet cut the deal!

A LOOK AT SOME OF THE HOTTEST COMIC BOOK TITLES IN 1994:

1897-1920s Titles - Rare, especially in fine or better condition, with few sales reported from this period. Demand is high for the Yellow Kid, Buster Brown and other early strip characters due (in part) to the 100 year anniversary.

1930s Titles - Supply limitations once again governed the increases shown in this area of collecting. Demand far outweighed supply. DC titles were still the most requested usually selling at over-Guide prices. A *King Comics* #1 VG54 sold for $1,700.

1940s Titles - Superhero titles still led the way. Timely is now the hottest area followed closely by DC. Gleason, MLJ, Fawcett and Fox issues with Lou Fine art sold extremely well as supplies surfaced. Matt Baker, L.B. Cole, Feldstein and other good girl art books were in demand. Disney's and Warner Brother's books also showed increased demand with Donald, Mickey and Bugs Bunny leading the pack.

1950s Titles - The hot publishers were Atlas followed by DC. ACG, Charlton, EC, Avon and other horror/science fiction books sold easily as well. White Mountain books sold easily at multiples of Guide.

A Look at some selected titles in 1994:

DC - The big news for 1994 was the sale of the Mile High copy of *Flash Comics* #1 for $100,000 and the Mile High copy of *Detective Comics* #27 for a staggering $135,000!! DC is still the leader in the Golden Age market commanding the highest prices paid for comic books. All mainline superhero titles were selling for over guide list in almost all grades. The higher the grade, the higher the multiple over Guide. Key scarcer issues were of course selling at even higher percentages of Guide. Best selling are Superman, Flash, Green Lantern and their related titles. Some offbeat titles were also in high demand. Some of the sales for 1994 include: ***Action*** #10 FN/VF restored $2,250, #11 VF restored $1,000, #16 FN $800, #17 FN $1,100, #18 FN+ $925, #19 FN $1,000, #21 VF $1,100, #22 FN $550, #23 VF+ $4,200, #56, #57 VF82 $1,200; ***Action*** #'s 74, 87, 106 VF86 $1,600; ***Adventure*** #49 VF/NM $2,000, #50 VF-NM $2,000, #51 NM $2,400, #52 VF-NM $1,600, #74 VF $600, #97 VF+ $350, #103 NM $1,700, #62 FN71 $700, #113, #116 VF85 $900; ***All American*** #16 VG $13,000; ***All Flash*** #1 VF84 $3,400; ***All Star Comics*** #30 NM/MT (Guide $665) $1,320; ***Batman*** #1 FR/GD $7,000, #1 VF78 $29,000, #1 FN58(r) $14,000, VG52 $9,500, GD32 $4,500, #2 GD+ $1,200, #3 FN57 $1,600, #8 FN69 $1,200, #50 VG $200; ***Comic Cavalcade*** #1 VG52 #1 $300; ***Detective*** #1 FN $37,500, #10 FN+ $1,200, #18 VF+ $2,700, #12 VG47 $650, #26 NM (Allentown) $5,200, #30 VF $2,800, #34 VF+ $3,000, #35 VF/NM $8,600, #38 FN/VF $15,000, #38 VF+ restored $12,000, #38 VF81(Restored) $7,000, #38 FN65(r) $5,000, #39 VF/NM $5,000, #113 NM (Guide $350) $800; ***Flash Comics*** #4 VF $950, #5 VF/NM $3,800, #7 VF/NM $2,400, #41 VF/NM $400, #53 VF+ $350, #41, #80, #89 VF83 $1,900; ***Green Lantern*** #6 VF82 $750; ***More Fun*** #9 VG43 $2,200; #11 VF75 $3,200, #13 VG+ $600, #15 VG43 $1,000, #46 VF $600, #52 VG55(r) $10,800, #54 VF+ $9,100, #55 VF75(r) -$3,500, #57 VF/NM $3,700, #58 VF/NM $3,700, #78 VF/NM $900, #79 FN+ $450, #97 VF+ $400, #48 NM (Mile High), $2,750 (Guide $600), #62 NM/M (Mile High)(Guide $1,200) $6,050; ***New Adventure*** #29 VG42 $450; ***New Book of Comics*** NM (Mile High)(Guide $5,250) $8,830; **New Comics** #5, #6 GD20 $600; ***New York World's Fair*** 1940 GD $800; ***Sensation Comics*** #33 NM/MT (Allentown)(Guide $235) $530, #'s 4, 9, 17, 39 VF77 $2,500; ***Star Spangled Comics*** #22 M (San Francisco)(Guide $460) $1,100; ***Superman*** #1 VG42(r) $6,500, #2 VG $1,400, #3 VF/NM $7,600, #3 FN72 $3,200, #4 VF $2,900, #4 FN68 $2,200, #5 VF/NM $4,200, #29 VF84 $650; ***Wonder Woman*** #1 VF84 $11,000, #1 FN+ $3,450; ***World's Best*** #1 FN72 $4,200, FN68 $3,500, VG42 $1,900; ***World's Fair 1939*** VF+ $30,000, VF/NM $20,000, VG48 $2,200; ***World's Fair 1940*** FN68 $2,500; ***World's Finest Comics*** #19 NM++ (Allentown)(Guide $575) $1,575.

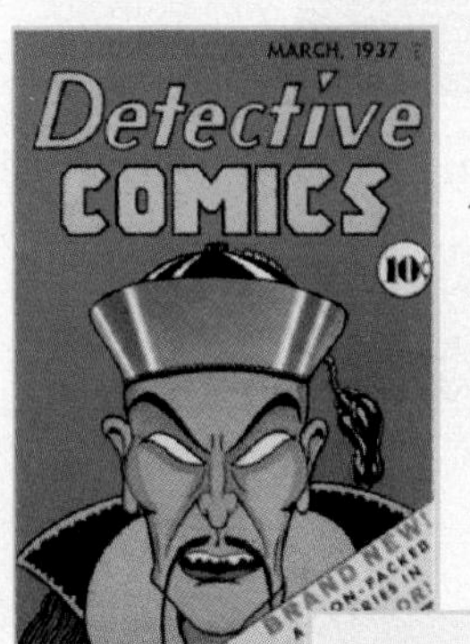

Detective #1 in Fine fetches $37,500!!

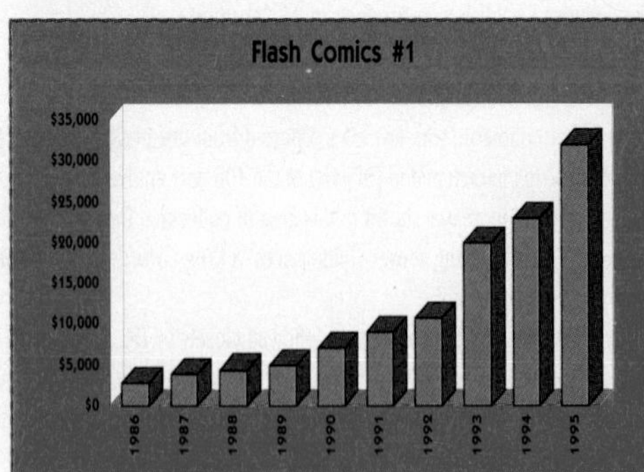

Flash Comics #1 shows a phenomenal growth in the 1990s.

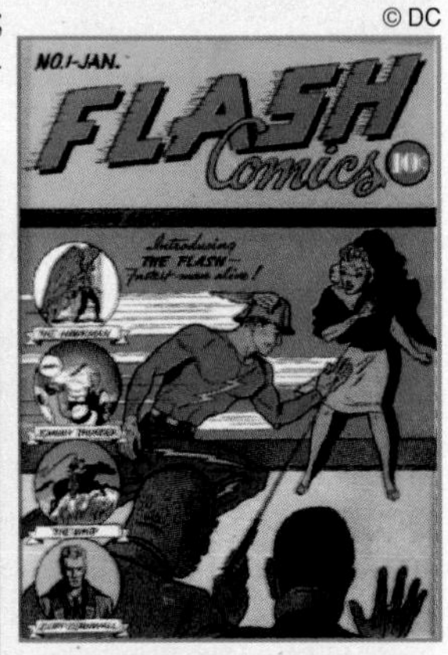

Flash Comics #1 brings $100,000!!

TIMELY - The hottest area in the comic marketplace! The Allentown copy of *Captain America Comics* #1 sold for an earth-shattering price of $82,500!! Led by Captain America, these books were selling rapidly at above current Guide levels regardless of condition! There was a large demand for Captain America, Human Torch, Sub-Mariner and their related titles in all grades. Covers by Timely's premiere cover artist, Alex Schomburg were in high demand. Dealers consistently sold out of all Timely titles very quickly. Some of this company's offbeat titles also showed increased demand. Some of the sales for 1994 include: ***All Select*** #1 VG54 $1,700; ***Captain America*** #1 VF85 $32,000 (Guide $31,000), #1 (Allentown) NM (Guide $32,000) $82,500, #1 VF80(cleaned) $25,000, FN72(r) $8,000, FN68 (cleaned) $15,000, #7 GD+ $600, #12 VF $1,200, #23 VG/FN $350, #25 VG/FN $350, #37 VF $475, #38 VF $500, #49 VF $400; ***Daring Mystery*** #4 VF+ $1500; ***Human Torch*** #2(1) VG48 -$2,700, VG52 $3,000, #8 VG35; ***Marvel Comics*** #1 FN72 $18,250; ***Marvel Mystery*** #4 VF85(r) $2,800, #5 FN69 $1,900, VF75 $3,500, #24 VG35 $600 (Guide $450), #6 VF $2,100, #19 FN74 $700 (Guide $500), #33, #40 VG83 $1,400 (Guide $800), #63, #65S VF87 $1,600 (Guide $700), *Annual* F $5,000; ***Miss Fury Comics*** #7 (Allentown) NM (Guide $350), $580; ***Mystic*** #1 FN+ $4,000, #2 VF+ $3,150, #4 VG $400; ***Namora*** #1 VF+ $770; ***Sub-Mariner*** #1 FN70 $4,200, FN65 $3,500, VG42 $1,700; ***USA*** #1 GD/VG $750, #15 VF87 $480 (Guide $300).

© MEG

Captain America #1 sells for $82,500!

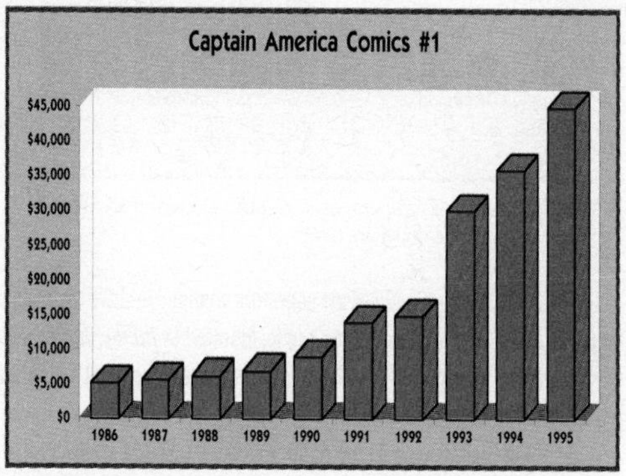

Demand for this title runs high among collectors as you can see by the above growth chart. This key issue also featured a dynamic Hitler cover adding to its collectibility.

FAWCETT - Sales of *Captain Marvel* and related titles were up. Good sales for *Captain Midnight*. Offbeat titles sell at or slightly over current Guide levels. A few selected sales are: ***Captain Marvel Adventures*** #26 (Mile High) NM (Guide $210) $550, #27 (MIle High) NM/MT (Guide $210) $605, #2 (Allentown) NM (Guide $475) $935; ***Captain Midnight*** #1 VG/FN $1200; ***Nickel Comics*** #3 (Allentown) NM (Guide $400) $825, #8 (Allentown) NM (Guide $335) $715. ***Slam Bang*** #1 VF+ $580.

DISNEY - After many years of stability, Disney books began to show considerable demand in 1994 as you will note by the increased prices in this edition. The supply of various 1930s books of this genre, as well as the early issues of *Comics & Stories,* are drying up with demand on the increase. There is still a strong demand for high grade Duck one-shots which are not available at prices near Guide. This is one of the few areas in Golden Age collecting that does need to be in higher grade to sell well. *Comics and Stories* above #100 were reported to be slow by some dealers. Some sales in 1994 include: ***40 Big pages of Mickey Mouse*** FN70 $800; ***Mickey Mouse Mag*** #1 FN61 $3,500 (Guide $2,900); ***Uncle Scrooge*** #1 NM $605.

FOX - Dealers have reported to us that they still get solid request for all Lou Fine issues. The rest of the superhero titles were also selling fairly well at above 1994 Guide levels. Offbeat titles sell at or slightly over current Guide levels. Late 1940s good girl art issues were at an all time high, especially *Phantom Lady, Blue Beetle, Rulah* and *Zoot.* Some sales in 1994 include: ***Blue Beetle*** #8 NM (Mile High)(Guide $210) $470; ***Mysterymen*** #2 VF $750, 3VG $600, 4VF $600, #25 NM (Mile High)(Guide $180) $440; ***Phantom Lady*** #17 NM $5,500.

HARVEY - Good sales reported for most 1940s titles with *Green Hornet* the most popular. Some reported sales: ***Green Hornet Comics*** #2 NM (Mile High)(Guide 650) $1,735, #12 MT (Mile High)(Guide $235) $850; ***Li'l Abner*** #63 NM (Mile High)(Guide $100) $330.

CENTAUR - Demand has reached a temporary plateau. Still an interesting publisher that will gain further, should Timely prices become too high in relation to Centaur levels. Along with Nedor, this publisher has become a poor man's Timely. Books were selling at and slightly over Guide levels. A few reported sales: ***Detective Picture Stories*** #2 GD+ $150, #4 VG $175; ***Funny Pages*** #4 VG $300.

GLEASON - Average sales at or slightly above Guide list. *Silver Streak, Daredevil* and early issues of *Boy* are some of the most popular titles from this line.

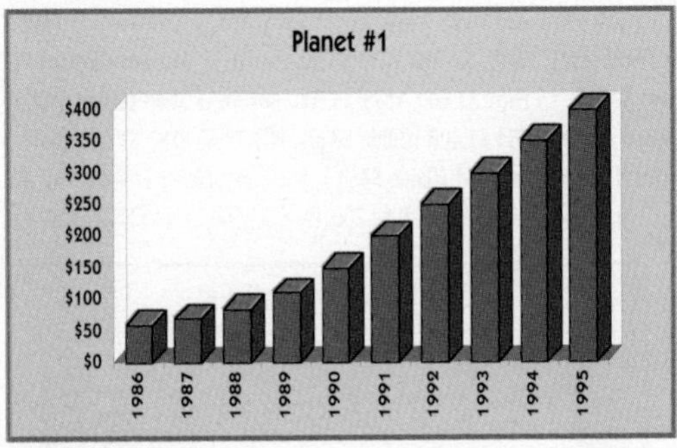

Planet Comics #1 has shown, as illustrated above, good steady growth with a price surge in 1991.

© FH

Planet Comics #1 sells for $14,500!

FICTION HOUSE - Good girl art collectors continue to drive the mainline titles of this company higher. Most popular is still *Planet* selling at and above Guide, followed by *Jumbo, Jungle, Fight, Rangers,* and *Wings*. It was reported that these titles are a steady seller with inventories moving very well within a short period of time. Early issues of *Jumbo* remained very scarce. Offbeat titles sell at slightly over current Guide levels. Some sales in 1994 include: ***Fight Comics*** #20 NM (Mile High)(Guide $170) $550; ***Planet*** #1 VF/NM (Denver) $14,500, #15 (apparent)FN restored $575, #44 VF/NM $350; ***Jumbo*** #8 VG+ $495, #9 (apparent) FN restored $550, VG+ $600.

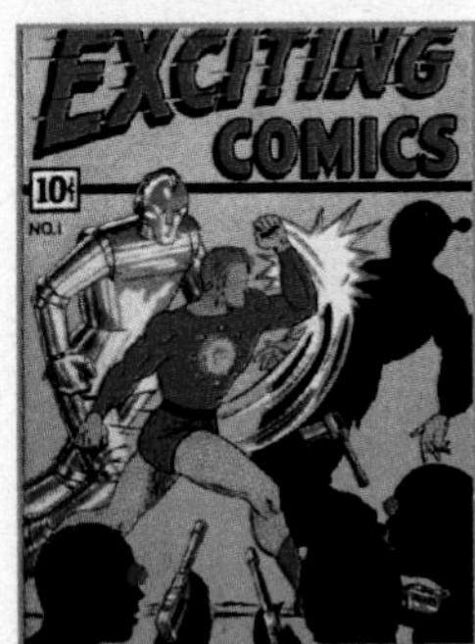

© Nedor

Exciting Comics #1 goes for $1300!

NEDOR - With the tremendous demand for Timely, this company's books with their exciting Schomburg covers were also in popular demand. ***America's Best Comics*** #15 (Mile High) NM (Guide $100) $395; ***Exciting Comics*** #1 VF/NM $1300, #2 VF/NM $600, #15(Mile High) MT (Guide 225) $880, #16 (Mile High) VF/NM (Guide $140) $330, #20 (Mile High) NM++ (Guide $140) $500, #38 (Mile High) NM+ (Guide $115) $385, #42 (Mile High) MT (Guide $160) $605, #52 (Mile High) NM++ (Guide $150) $605; ***Fighting Yank*** #2 (Mile High) NM/MT (Guide $325) $965, #3 (Mile High) NM (Guide $220) $665, #4 (Mile High) NM/MT (Guide $155) $550, #9 (Mile High) MT (Guide $120) $470, #10 (Mile High) MT (Guide $125) $550, #13 (Mile High) NM (Guide $110) $470, #14 (Mile High) NM (Guide $110) $350, #18 (Mile High) NM (Guide $120) $500, #27 (Mile High) NM/M (Guide $130) $505; ***Startling Comics*** #21 (Mile High) NM/MT (Guide $120) $500, #22 (Mile High) NM (Guide $110) $470, #23 (Mile High) NM (Guide $110) $360, #25 (Mile High) MT (Guide $110) $470, #30 (Mile High) NM/MT (Guide $110) $500, #32 (Mile High) NM/MT (Guide $110) $245, #38 (Mile High) MT (Guide $140) $660, #39 (Mile High) NM/MT (Guide $120) $580, #40 (Mile High) MT (Guide $140) $770.

QUALITY/ MLJ - Pickup in demand led by all Lou Fine titles. Very strong sales of *Blackhawk* and all related titles at and over current Guide levels. Other than *Buccaneers* and *Lady Luck* all offbeat titles were slower selling at or slightly above current Guide levels. Large increase in demand for all horror/science fiction titles. Sales at above current Guide.

Romance and western titles remain slower. Some sales in 1994 include: ***Hit Comics*** #1 FN/VF $800 (color touch); ***Jackpot*** #1 VF $950; ***Pep Comics*** #6 (Larson) VF/NM (Guide $350) $580; ***Police Comics*** #32 (Mile High) MT (Guide $225) $770, #69 (Mile High) NM (Guide $120) $300, #91 (Mile High) NM (Guide $110) $290, #98 (Mile High) NM/M (Guide $180) $470; ***Shield Wizard*** #1 VF $1,130; ***Smash Comics*** #42 (Mile High) NM (Guide $95) $240; ***Special Comics*** #1 $950.

FUNNY ANIMAL - The demand is mostly for Timely and DC titles, otherwise most other publishers enjoyed slow to average sales. Early *Looney Tunes* were scarce while Jay Ward and Hanna Barbera titles continued to be popular.

1950s TITLES - Atlas comics continued to break price records in 1994 with the pedigree White Mountain copies selling for multiples of guide. DC, ACG, Charlton and EC books led the pack for some of the best sales in 1994. Other books such as those from Avon began to show movement from an otherwise dormant state. Interest in pre-code books was also on the rise. A ***Fantastic Fears*** #5 in VG sold for $180.

ATLAS - Probably the hottest of the 1950s companies whose titles continued to break sales records throughout 1994. Some recorded sales are: ***Adventure Into Mystery*** #7 (White Mountain) NM (Guide $55) $250, #9 (White Mountain) NM (Guide $70) $265; ***Adventures Into Terror*** #10 (White Mountain) NM (Guide $70) $265; ***Astonishing*** #14 (White Mountain) NM (Guide $80) $300, #37 (White Mountain) NM (Guide $45) $250; ***Marvel Tales*** #105 (White Mountain) NM (Guide $230) $660; #106 (White Mountain) NM (Guide $190) $525, #107 (White Mountain) NM (Guide $190) $525, #113 (White Mountain) NM (Guide $125) $415, #129 (White Mountain) NM (Guide $95) $360, #137 (White Mountain) NM (Guide $60) $250; ***Journey Into Unknown Worlds*** #37 (White Mountain) NM (Guide 365) $1,210, #8 (White Mountain) NM (Guide $210) $690, #14 (White Mountain) NM (Guide $275) $770; ***Mystic*** #12 (White Mountain) NM (Guide $80) $265, #13 (White Mountain) NM (Guide $80) $300, #20 (White Mountain) NM (Guide $80) $355, #58 (White Mountain) NM (Guide $60) $225; ***Suspense*** #25 (White Mountain) NM (Guide $80) $355; ***Space Worlds*** #6 (White Mountain) NM (Guide $180) $700.

© EC

Vault of Horror #12 (#1) brings $4950!

EC - Slight pickup in demand once again. Horror and SF titles selling fairly well at and slightly above guide. *MAD* in all its titles is still the hottest selling book and quickly goes at or over Guide. ***Haunt of Fear*** #6 (White Mountain) NM (Guide $215) $410, #7 (White Mountain) NM (Guide $215) $410, #8 (White Mountain) NM (Guide $215) $410, ***MAD*** #2 (White Mountain) NM (Guide $675) $835, #19 Gaines 5/12 MT (Guide $165) $770, #s 24-59 FN $2,200, #24 FN+ $300, #26 VF+ $200, #s 60-123 VF $1,200, #s 124-328 VF $600; ***Vault of Horror*** #12 (White Mountain) VF (Guide $2,200) $4,950. Note new E.C. discovery (*Narrative Illustration*) in listing.

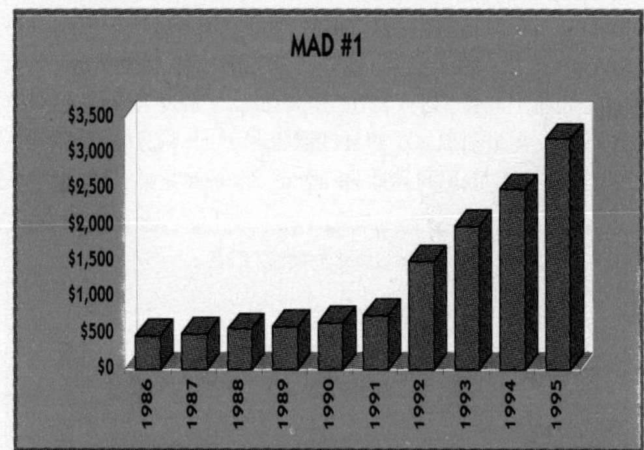

Mad #1 is still one of the hottest books from the 1950s as noted by the above chart. Note recent increase in value beginning in 1992. Where will this book be in the year 2000?

AVON - After being dormant for so many years, 1994 has shown an increase in demand for horror and science fiction titles. High grade books from the company are now always in demand, but the romance and western issues still remain slow movers. A few sales reported: ***Strange Worlds*** #9 (White Mountain) VF (Guide $120) $310.

TV/MOVIE - Brisk sales were reported, especially in most TV issues. *The Addams Family, Astro Boy, Dark Shadows, Jetsons, Munsters, Space Ghost,* and especially *Star Trek* showed steady sales. Early in the year, Dell and Gold Key titles from the 1960s surfaced from probably the last Dell warehouse. These particular titles and issues were not in earlier warehouse finds. Consequently, sales of these books were fast and at above Guide prices.

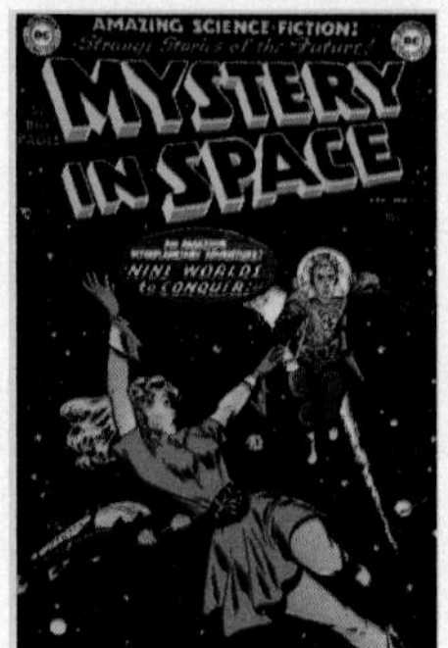

© DC

Mystery In Space #1 sells in FN for $700!

SILVER AGE DC - The growth of the Silver Age market has slowed compared to 1993's explosion. Key books in top grade still continued to bring high prices with *Brave and the Bold* and *Showcase* being the hottest titles. Sales are slow for VG or less copies of most titles except for the key numbers. Reported sales are: ***Atom*** #1 & ***Showcase*** #34 VG84 $1,100; ***Brave and the Bold*** #28 VF77 $1,700, VF75 $1,400, FN72 $1,300, FN65 $1,000, #34 VF87 $1,600, VF82 $1,300, FN72 $850; ***Challengers of Unknown*** #1 VF+ $2,000, #2 VF $650; ***Flash*** #105 VF80 $2,700, VF75 $2,000, VG48 $675; ***Flash Annual*** #1 (Bethlehem) VF/NM (Guide $280) $385; ***Green Lantern*** #1 VF79 $1,300; ***Justice League*** #1 FN62 $600; ***Mystery In Space*** #1 FN63 $700; ***Showcase*** #1 VG87 $4,000, #4 VF77 $7,000, VF77 $14,000, FN65 $7,000, FN65 $6,000, FN58 $4,500, VG52 $4,200, GD32 $1,800, GD25 $1,400, #10 NM89 $6,500, #13,14 FN74 $1,700, #13 VG $2,500, #14 FN $1,500, #15 VF $1,500, #18 FN+ $500, #22-24 FN57 $1,300; ***Strange Adventures*** #35 VF (Mile High)(Guide $185) $220; ***Superman's Girl Friend*** #1 FN/VF $1,150, #3, #9 VF86 $1,800, #9 M (Mile High)(Guide $425) $1,760.

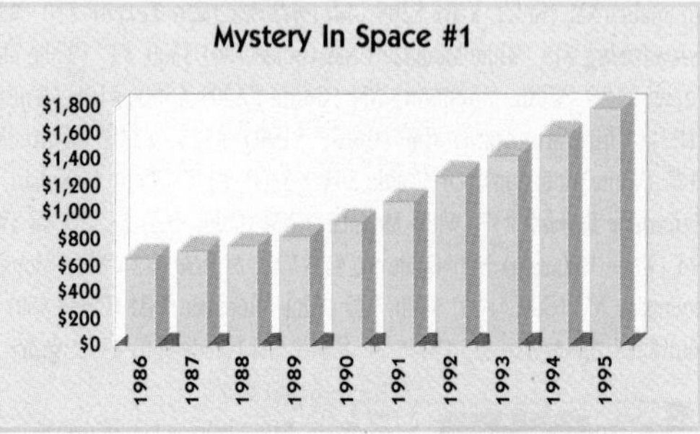

Mystery In Space #1 has shown steady growth over the past 10 years with a value of $680 in 1986 and a staggering $1800 price tag in 1994!

SILVER AGE MARVEL-With the market shifting to Golden Age, the previous year's fast rise of Silver Age prices began to slow in 1994 to levels still above Guide, but more reasonable. Key Marvels in top condition are still fetching over-Guide prices, but the lower grades have slowed to values at and below Guide. A ***Fantastic Four*** in NM sold for a record $20,250!! Reported sales are: ***Amazing Fantasy*** #15 VF84 $17,500, VF75 $7,800, FN73 $6,200, FN72 $7,000, VG54 $4100, VG35 $1,700, GD32 $1,300, GD14 $700; ***Amazing Spider Man*** #1 VF $13,750, VF87 $11,000,

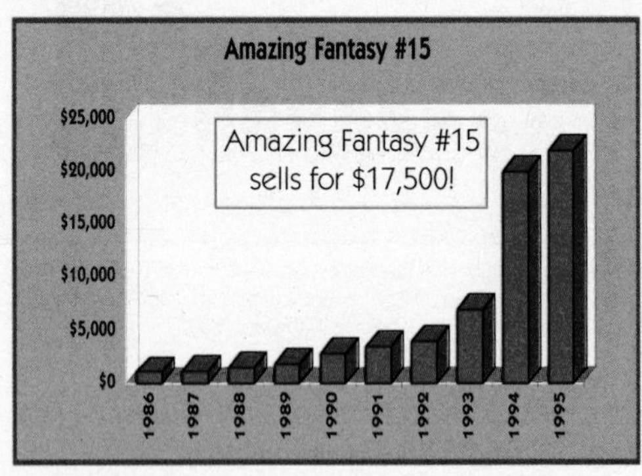

Amazing Fantasy #15 (the first app. of Spider-Man) exploded in 1994, leveling off in 1995 at $22,000.

© MEG

Hulk #1 in NM brings $15,400!!

© MEG

Tales of Suspense #39 in NM+ sells at $10,400!!

VF83 $10,000, VF82 $6,500, FN72 $3,300, FN68 $2,800, FN58 $2,200, VG45 $1,700, GD27 $900, GD22 $600, #2-10 VF86 $5,000, #3 VF88 $1450, VF85 $1,200, #11-20 VF89 $3,200, #13 NM (Guide $1,025) $2,100, #28VF $250; ***Avengers*** #1 VF86 $1,300, VF82 $900, VF79 $875, FN62 $425, VG38 $175, #4 NM90 $1200, VF85 $1,000; ***Captain Marvel*** #1 NM $150; ***Daredevil*** #1 NM92 $1,650, VF87 $1,200, VF76 $1,200, VF75 $700, FN65 $475, FN55 $375, VG45 $300; ***Fantastic Four*** #1 VF77 $5,500, FN72 $4,600, VG54 $3,500, VG49 $2,500, GD32 $1,100, GD18 $550, #4 VF80 $1,000, #5 NM90 $3,500, VF87 $2700, VF82 $2250, VF75 $1700, #48 NM94 $1,000, NM90 $750, VF87 $500, #50 FN+ $100; ***Incredible Hulk*** #1 NM (Guide $4,475) $15,400, FN72 $3,200, VG52 $1,400, VG45 $2,200, VG38 $875; ***Journey Into Mystery*** #83 VF/NM+ $2,800, #83 VF87 $3,000, VF85 $2,500, VF82 $2,200, FN72 $1,000, VG49 $550, GD28 $300; ***Silver Surfer*** #1 NM $440; ***Strange Tales*** #101 VF $550, #105 VF+ $205, #110 VF89 $1,600, VF82 $1,000, #115 NM $635, Annual #1 VF81 $500; ***Tales of Suspense*** #1 VF $1,400, #1 FN/VF $1,150, #39 (White Mountain) NM/MT (Guide $2,800) $10,400, NM91 $4,800, VF+ $2,900, VF87 $2,600, FN72 $1,350, FN58 $650, VG42 $425, #49 NM $150, #52VF+ $100; ***Tales To Astonish*** #1-26, 28-34 FN70 $2,400, #5 (White Mountain) VF/NM (Guide $215) $550, #27 VG+ $480, VG48 $400, VG38 $250, #39 VF $250, #44 VF $330; ***X-Men*** #1 NM90 $5,000, NM $4,400, VF84 $3,500, VF83 $3,800, VF80 $2,500, FN68 $1,100, VG46 $600, GD20 $200, #2 VF $970, #2-4 FN63 $1,350, #3 VF $400, #5-32, 34, 35-58, 60-64, 67-69 VF84 $4,500, #5 VF+ $265, NM $295, #6 VF+ $200, #9 NM $205.

© MEG

Fantastic Four #l sells for $20,250!!

Sotheby's Fourth Comic Book and Comic Art Auction, Spring/Summer, 1994

"The Great Golden Age Come Back"

by Jerry Weist and Roger Hill

The fourth annual Sotheby's Comic Book and Comic Art auction took place in New York City on Saturday, June 18, to a packed crowd of eager and determined collectors. Word had spread through fandom that Sotheby's had assembled its largest and most fairly estimated catalogue of Golden and Silver Age comics and artwork in its four year history. The "Mile High" comic runs of two and three years before were missing, and high grade "key" number one titles were few and far in-between. However, this auction offered very serious comics at very low estimates, and the dealer and collectors were not to be denied their chance to get a piece of the action. For the record, Sotheby's first auction totaled $1,201,695 with 76% sold, auction No. 2 sold $1,019,260 with 68 % sold, and auction No. 3 sold $1,348,462 with 81.5% of the lots sold. The fourth auction was by far the most successful with a total of $1,688,304 and 91.5% of all lots sold. Many fans and collectors have also missed the news that 48 hours after the cover lot passed at auction, the origin artwork to Superman by Joe Shuster sold to a private collector for $77,000!

The Western file copies of Dell and Gold Key comics brought results within estimates, but there were bargains to be had! Some lucky bidder walked off with a double set of Near Mint *Turok Son of Stone* Dell and Gold Key comics for $3,450. All the sets of *Mickey Mouse Magazine* from the Western file copies sold at just at or over double Guide prices. Marvel Silver Age comics all performed very well with a Very Fine copy of *Spider-Man* #1 selling for $18,400 and the Bethlehem copies for *X-Men* #1 and *Tales of Suspense* #39 selling for $4,600 and $6,900 respectively. The real interest this year was the chance that many collectors found with the offering from the Silver Age D.C. collection of Murphy Anderson. "Anderson" copies of *Strange Adventures* estimated at $1,500/$2,500 sold for $5,750, with a run of *Flash* estimated at $3,000 to $4,000 fetching $6,900 and a beautiful run of the *Atom* including the *Showcase* numbers estimated at $3,000/$4,000 selling for $4,025. Complete Silver Age runs of *Lois Lane, Jimmy Olsen, Superman, Action, World's Finest*, and *Adventure* all sold for close to their high end estimates or over... and these runs were in very mixed condition from Fair to VG+!

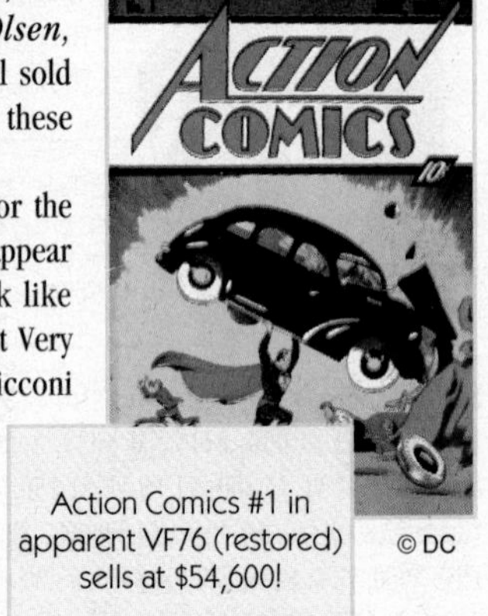

Action Comics #1 in apparent VF76 (restored) sells at $54,600!

© DC

The real explosion of buying, however, was saved for the second session when the Golden Age comics began to appear on the bidding screen. Previously at auction, a book like *Superman* #1 found few buyers; this year an apparent Very Good 48 copy of *Superman* #1 restored by Susan Cicconi estimated for $4,000/$5,000 sold for $7,760 and an unrestored copy in Very Good 41 estimated at $5,500/$7,500 sold for $14,950! What was so remarkable about the Golden Age offering were the complete runs of *Action Comics, World's Finest, Superman* and *Adventure Comics* (from 103 up). All of these comic lots sold for their high end estimate or well above, and again these runs, it must be stressed, were in mixed condition from Fair to VG+ to Fine. To round out the Superman offering, the crowd was held breathless while an apparent Very Fine 76 copy of *Action Comics* #1, restored by Susan Cicconi, sailed from its estimate of $20,000/$25,000 to final hammer price of $54,600. This price stands as a world record for a restored comic, and reflects the market's growing confidence in "key" rare titles that have minimal restoration by a master such as Ms. Cicconi. The telling final force with this particular issue of *Action* #1 was also its newer white interior pages.

Not to be outdone by his pal Superman, Batman succeeded in bringing in the bidders. The most impressive comic in the auction to all experienced dealers and collectors was lot 384, the *Detective Comics* #27, in unrestored A.C.G. Very Good plus 54 (missing the fine rating by just one point!) with interior OWL paper of 8.5. This very important comic was estimated at $25,000/$30,000 and brought a final price of $48,875! The private buyer has since been offered $65,000 for this same comic and has turned down all offers. (Who says it does not pay to buy important comics at auction!) A very heavily restored copy of *Batman* #1 with a Very Good grade 47, by Susan Cicconi, estimated at $1,500/$2,000 sold for $6,610. Another copy of *Detective Comics* #33, restored by Cicconi from the collection of Murphy Anderson, sold for above estimate at $4,890. The real heated bidding for Batman comics came from lots from the collection of Dick Sprang where mixed runs of *Detective* and *Batman* brought prices near high end and considerably over.

© DC

Detective Comics #27 in VG 54 brings $48,875!!

If the bidding on D.C. Golden Age titles surprised people, then what was to follow with Timely Comics challenged any previous records. From the collection of Murphy Anderson copies of *Captain America* #1 in A.C.G. Fine 55 estimated at $5,000/$6,000 brought in $16,100 and *Marvel Comics* #1 restored by Susan Cicconi in apparent Fine 65 and estimated at $6,000/$9,000 fetched $17,250. White-hot bidding awaited the Murphy Anderson copies of the *Captain America* runs, and copies of *Daring Mystery* #1 Fine 59 sold for $3,560, and *Marvel Mystery Comics* #2 in unrestored Fine 62 brought $5,460. Would anyone care to guess what Sotheby's could do with unrestored Fine+ runs of the great Quality comics titles or other elusive Golden Age runs? Some Golden Age comics are becoming so scarce in the market place that even the major auction houses cannot flush them out into the open! In case anyone misses the message here....."Golden Age comics in all unrestored grades are BLUE CHIP investments."

© MEG

Captain America #1 in FN 55 brings $16,100!!

Once again this year's Sotheby's auction offered a treasure trove of original art for collectors everywhere. The aura of anticipation and excitement surrounding the offering of Marvel Silver Age comic cover recreations by Jack Kirby, Dick Ayers and John Romita was unprecedented. Through a special one time only arrangement with Marvel, twenty-two classic Marvel comic cover images were offered up for sale. Here is just a sampling of the results: *Amazing Spider-Man* #1 (pencils by Kirby) $14,950, *Amazing Fantasy* #15 (Kirby) $10,925, *Journey Into Mystery* #83-(Kirby pencils/Ayers inks) $9,200 *Fantastic Four* #5 (Kirby/Ayer) $6,325, *Strange Tales* #89 (Kirby/Ayers) $5,750, and *X-Men* #1(Kirby/Ayers) $4,887.

Covers penciled and inked by Dick Ayers performed very well with the following results: *Avengers* #1 $8,050, *Strange Tales* #101, *Fantastic Four Annual* #1 and *Fantastic Four* #4 all sold for $3,737 each. *Tales to Astonish* #27 $2,875. Covers penciled and inked by John Romita realized the following prices: *Amazing Spider-Man* #39 $2,300/#50 $3,450/#53 $1,150/#54 $1,380/#64 $2,070 and #100 $3,737.

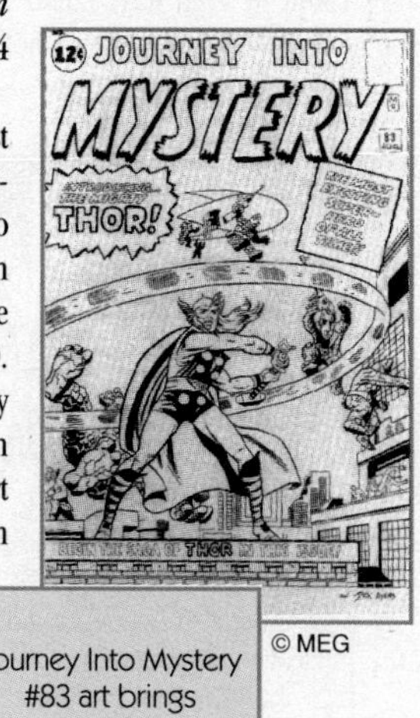

© MEG

Journey Into Mystery #83 art brings $9,200!!

Sotheby's worked very hard this year to bring a vast selection of other choice Silver Age artwork to the auction, covering both Marvel and D.C. The cover art to *Conan* #1 by Barry Smith hammered down at an incredible $13,800, followed by the complete 19 page Conan story from that same issue selling for $11,500. Two Spider-Man pages by Steve Ditko sold respectively at $2,185 and $2,587. An *Avengers* # 44 cover by John Buscema realized $2,185, and the spectacular cover art to *Iron Man and Sub-Mariner* #1 by Gene Colan fetched a whooping $6,325. Marie Severin's cover art to *The Hulk* #102 sold for $2,185. Where else but at Sotheby's could you have found prime examples of Murphy Anderson's classic D.C. Silver Age art? His fan-following and market demand for his work continues to grow consistently. Healthy prices were seen on such examples as: cover art to *Mystery in Space* #20 $2,873, *Strange Adventures* #142 $2,185,

Strange Adventures #230 $1,035. The beautiful cover to *Mystery in Space* #73 (featuring Adam Strange) orbited up to $4,600, followed by cover art to *Hawkman* #2, which flew up to an incredible hammer price of $8,050. Infantino cover recreations to *Showcase* #14 (Flash) and *Flash* #105 brought in a respectable $2,070 and $2,587 each. A beautiful Superman cover by Curt Swan and George Klein from the 1960s fetched $4,600 while the cover art to *Justice League of America* #32 sold for $2,587. Shelley Moldoff's *Batman* #156 page from the famous story titled "Robin Dies at Dawn" resulted in a final bid of $1,610, followed by a Gil Kane Atom page from his first *Showcase* appearance (#34) coming in at $1,035.

The demand for original EC artwork continues to escalate with no end in sight. Most of the EC artwork was auctioned off years ago by art-dealer Russ Cochran, and good examples of EC art returning to the market-place are seldom seen. We at Sotheby's always strive to present a nice selection of EC artwork, and this year was no exception. Al Feldstein's flying saucer cover art to *Weird Science-Fantasy* #26 flew out at $4,600, followed by Wally Wood's *Shock Suspense* #14 cover shooting up to $4,312. Of special interest to collectors was the first *Vault of Horror* introductory story from *War Against Crime* #10 by Al which fetched $3,450, and Feldstein's cover recreation in oils to *Weird Fantasy* #13 did a respectable $4,600. Also of note was a Captain Comet page by Al Williamson and Frank Frazetta that rocketed up to $2,645.

Weird Science-Fantasy #26 original art brings $4,600! © EC

As in preceding years, only Sotheby's has continually managed to bring fine examples of Golden Age artwork to the auctions. Golden Age art from the 1940s is the rarest of all comic book art to find in today's market due to the fact that most of it was long ago discarded and thrown away. Who would have thought that the covers to *Action Comics* #50 and *World's Finest* #5 (both by Fred Ray) could have survived? In a rousing round of bidding fever, the *Action* #50 and *World's Finest* #5 both sold for the amazing price of $16,100 each. Also, for the first time ever, a gorgeous cover by the talented brush man, Lou Fine, came to auction. The cover art to *Hit* #6 hammered down at $11,500.

Original newspaper strip art received wide-spread attention also in the auction. Everyone was waiting with baited breath to see what would happen on Jerry Siegel's and Joe Shuster's *Superman* daily #1. As it turned out, this very historic piece did not sell at the auction but rather the day after, for an incredible $77,000. Other original strip art made a good showing too with two *Little Nemo* Sunday pages from 1908 fetching a price of $8,625 each. A *Krazy Kat* Sunday page sold for $5,462, followed by a Kat daily for $3,450. The beautiful *Prince Valiant* Sunday pages by Hal Foster from 1940 and 1939 hammered down at $21,850 and $9,775 respectively. A *Tarzan* Sunday page by Foster from 1937 brought a bid of $2,875. Two *Thimble Theater* Sunday pages featuring Popeye by artist E.C. Segar received bids respectively of $6,037 and $4,887. A *Flash Gordon* Sunday page from

Siegel and Shuster's original art to Superman Daily #1 brings an incredible $77,000! © DC

1939 by the incomparable Alex Raymond sold for $9,775, followed by a *Buck Rogers* daily by Dick Calkins reaching a final price of $2,587. Other original strip art examples included: *Alley Oop* Sunday page from 1945 $1,035, *Barney Google* Sunday page from 1932 $3,450, *Dick Tracy* daily from 1931 $4,025 and several *Peanuts* Sunday pages which sold individually at $1,380, $2,300, and $6,325.

These are just some of the highlights of artwork that sold in this year's auction, and already great surprises are beginning to show up consigned to our next big auction in 1995.

A Flash Gordon Sunday page by Alex Raymond sells for $9,775!

The A.C.G. Committee (the committee for authenticity, certification, and grading) this year was the most balanced and harmonious in memory. Michael Naiman (Acting Chairperson), Gary Carter (Chair emeritus), Jon S. Berk, Mike Dalessandro, Bruce Edwards, James Payette, and Joe Vereneault worked with Susan Cicconi, Roger Hill, Hans Curtis, Tony Davis and Mark Nevins to make sure that this year's auction brought security and precision to the grades and descriptions in the fourth Sotheby's comic catalogue. One of the most telling compliments for this committee came from long time collector and dealer John Snyder who spent considerable time grading the *Detective Comic* #27 and during the preview commented to the consultant that his grade was TO THE NUMBER POINT the same as the A.C.G. - a Very Good 54; it was remarkable that the clarity was such that no one was tempted to move this book into the FINE grade. Precision and clarity is now a standard set by Sotheby's comic book auctions, and we owe our thanks to each member's contribution.

Sotheby's is celebrating its 250th birthday this year, and next year comics fandom will celebrate the 100th birthday of the comic art form in America. In keeping with these special events Sotheby's fifth comic book and comic art auction promised to continue its traditions of discovery, excitement, and excellence. How could Sotheby's match the offering of the Joe Shuster Superman origin daily? The answer comes from the never before known to exist original artwork of Bob Kane for the "introductory" and origin dailies to Batman from 1943! Sotheby's will offer the #2 (or B. intro daily, with the origin told) #5 and #6 (or E. and F.), and three consecutive daily *Batman* strips from 1945. For 30 years the existence of the Superman Daily by Joe Shuster was known to fandom. This introductory and origin artwork by Bob Kane where the characters Batman and Robin, the Bat-Cave, the Bat-Car, and Bat-Plane were introduced to the public for the first time in newspaper strip form represents another historic first at auction. The largest collection ever brought to auction of premium comic character rings will come to light with over 135 different premium rings just signed to this auction. High grade copies of *Detective Comics* #27, *Action Comics* #1, 3, 5, *Batman* #1-20, *Adventure* #61, *All-American*

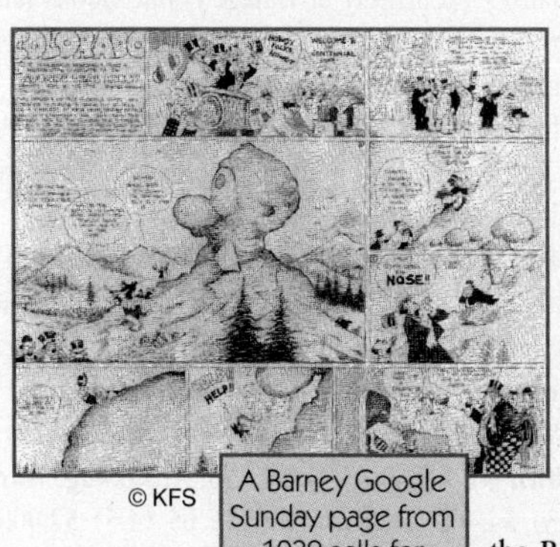

© KFS

A Barney Google Sunday page from 1932 sells for $3,450!

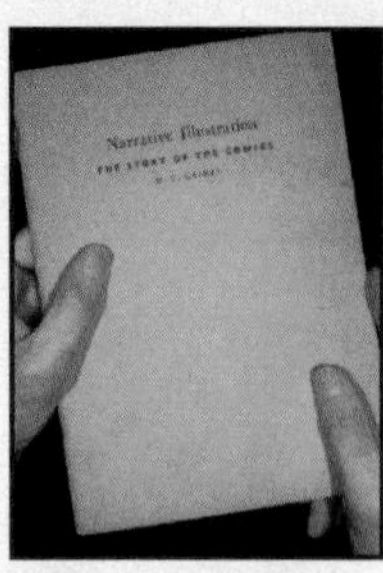

The Newly Discovered E.C. Pamplet will be offered in the 1995 Sotheby's auction!

#16, 17, *Superman* #1, 2, *Marvel Comics* #1 (unrestored in Fine+ from the collection of Roger Zelazny), *Captain America* #s 1-10 from the collection of Jack Kirby, and *All Star* #3, are already signed for our fifth auction. The important E.C. pamphlet featured in this year's Overstreet Comic Book Price Guide will be offered for sale. Very strong runs of D.C. Silver Age comics, and special Marvel Silver Age titles will test the market. Comics from the collection of Dick Ayers like *Journey Into Mystery* #1 in VF, along with a very high grade *Showcase* #4 from another private collection will ask further questions from the market place. Without question the largest ever selection of newspaper strip artwork will be brought into the fifth Sotheby's auction. From Fosdick daily *Little Abner's* to *Krazy Kat* Sundays from the collection of Bud Sagendorf, to hand colored *Tarzan* Sundays by Burne Hogarth, to rare and never before offered *Gasoline Alley* Frank King originals, to the rare Floyd Gottfredson *Mickey Mouse* dailies, and Al Taliaferro toppers for Silly Symphonies from *Mickey Mouse* Sunday pages, the listing of rare strip artwork will serve as a mirror to collector interest and celebrate the great historical richness from which the comic books began their evolution.

Besides celebrating the 100th year birthday for comics, Sotheby's plans also to acknowledge the "first fandom" that came before comics fandom with a special science fiction auction that will be held the Friday before the Saturday Comic Book auction. The largest personal collection ever brought to market by the late great Virgil Finlay will offer over 50 black and white masterful originals with over 10 classic paintings. Complete collections of *Amazing Stories* and *Astounding Stories* and an original painting from the collection of Forrest J. Ackerman will be grouped with an amazing offering of Science Fiction movie posters and first edition books that will range from E.R.B. to Robert Heinlein.

Any questions or inquires that fans or collectors have can be answered by contacting Sotheby's collectibles department at (212) 606-7424 or by calling subscriptions at 1-800-444-3709.

PACIFIC COMIC EXCHANGE INC. 1994 YEAR IN REVIEW

by Robert J. Roter

Pacific Comic Exchange, Inc. ("PCE") specializes exclusively in vintage comic books and operates in the same manner as a real estate brokerage house. Prices are negotiable between buyer and seller and all sales are documented through the PCE Monthly Listing Report.

1994 was a record year for trading at PCE. The major trend was a significant shift in interest from Silver Age to Golden Age. However, Silver Age keys in high grade continued to set record prices. Timelys were highly sought after, especially *Captain America Comics*.

Sample sales for 1994 (prices include the 10% buyers commission) are listed below. All books are reported in the Comic Grading Service of America ("CGSA") grading scale with the Page Quality (PQ) rating: ***Adventure Comics*** #103 NM 80 (4.0) $2,200; ***All Star Comics*** #1 FN 35 (4.5) $3,850; ***All Star Comics*** #8 VG 25 (5.5) $4,200; ***All Winners Comics*** #1 VF 60 (4.0) $5,500; ***All-American Comics*** #16 VG 20 (4.0) $13,000; ***Amazing Fantasy*** #15 FN35 (3.5) $4,100; ***Amazing Spider-Man*** #1 VF 60 (3.5) $7,150; ***Amazing Man Comics*** #5 (Moderate Restoration) FN 40 (3.3) $4,400; ***Batman*** #47 VF 65 (4.5) $2,900; ***Batman*** #55 NM 85 (2.5) $1,300; ***Brave and the Bold*** #28 VF 60 (5.0) $3,525; ***Captain America Comics*** Allentown Copy NM 88 (3.5) $75,000; ***Captain America Comics*** #74 FN 40 (4.0) $2,065; ***Detective Comics*** #5 VG/FN 30 (5.5) $2,420; ***Detective Comics*** #33 VG 25 (4.0) $7,150, #38 G/VG 15 (4.0) $2,800; ***Fantastic Four*** #1 NM 85 (3.0) $20,250; ***Fantastic Four*** #5 NM 85 (1.0) $3,850; ***Flash Comics*** #92 VF 60 (3.3) $2,200; ***Green***

Hornet Comics #2 Mile High copy, NM 85 (3.0) $1,735; ***Green Lantern*** #1 (GA) VG 25 (4.5) $3,000; ***House of Secrets*** #1 VF 68(4.5) $1,430; ***Incredible Hulk*** #1 NM 75 (1.0) $15,400; ***March of Comics*** #20 NM 75 (4.5) $2,500; ***Marvel Mystery Comics Annual*** #1 GD/VG 15 (4.5) $4,050; ***More Fun Comics*** #48 Mile High Copy NM 80 (2.5) $2,750; ***More Fun Comics*** #62 Mile High Copy NM/MT 90 (2.0) $6,050; ***New Book of Comics*** #2 Mile High Copy NM 80 (2.0) $8,830; ***New Comics*** #8 VF 55 (5.0) $1,650; ***New York World's Fair 1940*** VF 60 (4.5) $5,500; ***Showcase*** #13 VF/VF 63 (3.3) $3,300; ***Showcase*** #22 VF 68 (4.5) $4,675; ***Superman*** #14 NM 75 (3.3) $2,860; ***Superman's Pal Jimmy Olsen*** #1 NM 80 (3.5) $8,250; ***Tales of Suspense*** #39 White Mountain Copy NM/MT 90 (2.0) $10,400; ***Vault of Horror*** #12, White Mountain Copy VF 65 (2.5) $4,950; ***World's Best Comics*** #1 FN/VF 50 (4.5) $3,000; ***X-Men*** #1 NM 75 (4.0) $4,400.

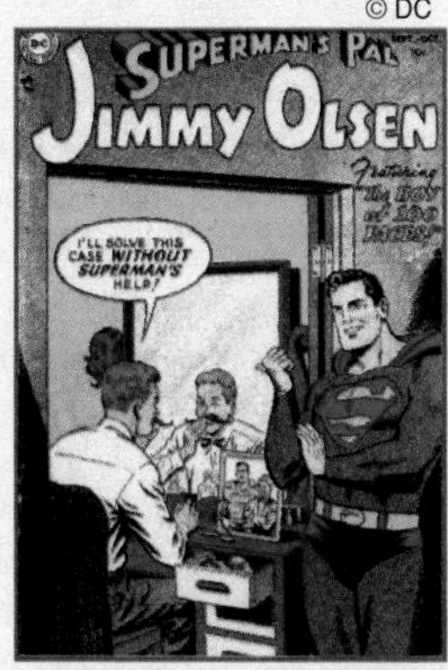

Superman's Pal Jimmy Olsen #1 NM sells "Faster than a Speeding Bullet" at $8,250

In summary, there appeared to be upward pressure on all Golden Age material during 1994. This probably was due to the gap between Silver Age and Golden Age prices narrowing in recent years. The combination of increased interest in Golden Age and its relative scarcity to Silver Age was the impetus for higher prices and increased liquidity. Investor mentality continued to drive the market. Investors were opting for keys in high grade while generally ignoring non-key books in lower or mid-grade.

CHRISTIE'S COMIC COLLECTIBLES SALE

by Joe Mannarino

Christie's Fall Comic Collectibles sale held October 29, 1994 was a huge success. The sale resulted in extraordinary prices for Golden Age comics, Silver Age art and related material.

The auction was the culmination of an unequaled weekend. The auction featured a private preview and cocktail party at Christie's East galleries that marked Frank Frazetta's first public appearance in nearly twenty years. Aside from Frazetta, the list of luminaries included living legends Joe Simon, Carmine Infantino, Mort Drucker, Creig Flessel, Angelo Torres, George Evans, Dick Ayers and a host of others. Earlier in the week the Overstreet Senior Advisors Conference was held with over 40 experts in the field attending. Diamond was kind enough to provide transportation for the attendees to the Christie's event. The auction was followed by the grand opening party for the "Frank Frazetta Fifty Year Retrospective" at the prestigious Alexander Gallery on Madison Avenue in New York. Over 600 people attended the event.

The Christie's sale was highlighted by the most comprehensive selection of Jack Kirby art ever offered at an auction. The results were astonishing; forty-six of the fifty lots of vintage Kirby Silver Age art surpassed their mean estimates. The cover lot known as "the Doomsday page" (a Kirby/Sinnott page from *Fantastic Four* #59 featuring Doctor Doom and The Silver Surfer), estimated at $2000-2500, sold for $10,350, a record price for an interior Kirby page. Two pages from *Fantastic Four* #5 sold for $5,750 and $5,520; both had been estimated at $3,000-4,000. Page 10 from *Fantastic Four* #46, one of four pages from the classic Inhumans saga, realized $4,830. This was over four times estimate, while the splash page from *Fantastic Four* #35 sold for $5,750.

Golden Age comics fared equally well. The top lot was a VF (85) *Captain America* #1 from the first Denver collection selling for $36,800. A newly discovered *Batman* #1 in VF (78), estimated at $10,000-15,000, realized $33,350. All sixty lots of Golden Age comics sold, with all but two meeting estimate, which was essentially Guide. Other Golden Age highlights included a group of *Archie Comics* that included eight of the first ten issues, estimated at $2000-2,500, realizing $6350. A *More Fun* #11 (in rarely found VF-(75)), estimated at $1000-1500, realized $3,680.

Silver Age comics remained strong with the Bethlehem *Showcase* #10 selling for $7475 (over 5X Guide). Runs of *Spider-Man, X-Men,* and *Showcase* all fared extremely well.

© MEG

The Denver Captain America #1 sold for $36,800!

Comic Art

A wide array of comic art did well. Some examples included an Alex Schomburg recreation of *USA* #10, $11,500. A six-page story from *MAD* #1 sold for $9,200. Joe Simon's recreations of *Captain America* #1 and #10 sold for $6,900 and $5,175 respectively, and Carmine Infantino's full color recreation of *Showcase* #4 sold for $4,830. A Russ Heath story from *Sea Devil* #9 realized $5,500 (2X estimate), Howard Purcell's cover art from *Sea Devils* #32 sold for $3,220 (over 3X high estimate), and four John Severin covers sold over estimate. Two classic Joe Maneely covers also sold over estimate. *MAD* continues to sizzle with Mort Drucker art faring particularly well. The cover of *MAD* Super Special #96 brought $4,830 and four lots of illustration sold.

Alex Schomburg's USA #10 recreation brings $11,500!

Comic strip art

A beautiful Hal Foster Prince Valiant Sunday sold for $10,925, an Alex Raymond 1937 Flash Gordon $8,625, and a Segar 1935 Sunday for $4,370. Hogarth, McCay, Schulz, Kelly and Davis all did very well also. A pleasant surprise of the sale were the prices realized for four sets of color Sunday proof sheets from the Superman comic strip, each page was signed by Jerry Siegel and came from the Siegel's personal collection. Prices ranged from $1,725 to $3,450, nearly four times the high estimate.

A Sunday Prince Valiant by Hal Foster sold for $10,925.

Fantasy and Sci-fi

Highlights included: the sale of Frank Frazetta's The Rider for $51,750; a Frazetta preliminary for Conan The Barbarian for $6,135; Boris Vallejo cover art to Dracula for $9,200; a Hannes Bok painting for $5,175; and sales of examples by David Wenzel, Julie Bell, Virgil Finlay, Bernie Wrightson and Ken Kelly.

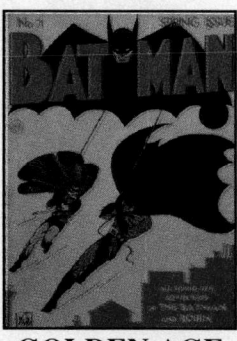

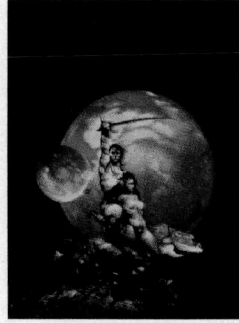

Action Comics #12 © DC

Adventure Comics #72 © DC

Adventures Into Terror #16 © MEG

Adventures of Martin & Lewis #14 © DC

Air Fighters Comics V2/#6 © HILL

All-Flash Quarterly #3 © DC

America's Best Comics #25 © STD

Animal Comics #13 © Dell

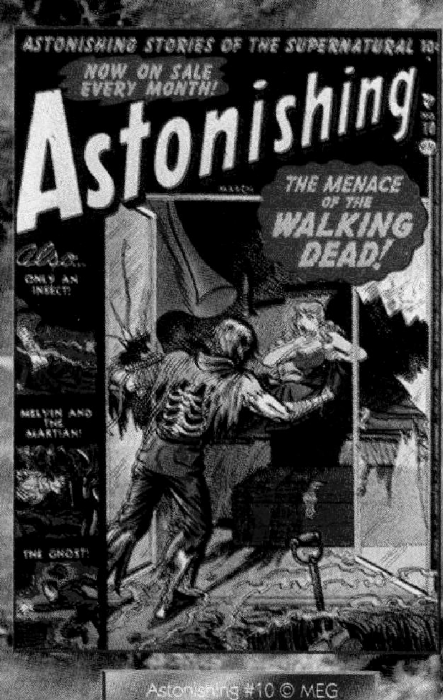

Astonishing #10 © MEG

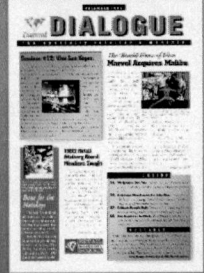

Diamond Dateline

Vital weekly reading for late-breaking comics and card industry news, shipping updates, product price changes, returnable merchandise, and more!

The Diamond Retailers Seminar

Preview new projects, listen to informative and exciting guest speakers, attend retailing workshops, talk with industry experts and Diamond personnel, and share your experience with your fellow retailers!

Open Houses

Our Spring Breaks and Fall Flings bring you publisher representatives, editorial plans, free premiums, drawings, auctions, refreshments, and fun!

PREVIEWS on Disk

Our monthly *Previews* Order Form, available in an easy-to-use program for IBM and Mac computer users!

Retail Advisory Board

Our 50-member panel of retailers from around the world provides us with valuable sell-through data and input on select Diamond policies to help us create services that benefit all retailers!

Electronic Bulletin Board System

Use your computer and modem to download the current *Previews* Order Form directly into your system, receive weekly shipping updates, and leave electronic mail for other Diamond retailers!

Reduced Ordering Uncertainty

Our full-color "Shipping Soon" list and 30-day cancellation window for late-shipping product are just two of the many ways Diamond continually strives to reduce the amount of uncertainty you face when committing your purchasing dollars!

Being the industry's leading distributor means a lot to us.

Being your distributor means **more.**

To learn **more** about Diamond and our services, contact our Customer Service Department today!

1966 Greenspring Drive,
Suite 300
Timonium, MD 21093
(410) 560-7100
Fax: (410) 560-7148

Batman #4 © DC

Black Terror #1 © STD

Bob Colt #6 © FAW

Brave And The Bold #10 © DC

Captain America's Weird Tales #74 © MEG

Captain Midnight #24 © The Wander Co.

Captain America Comics #11 © MEG

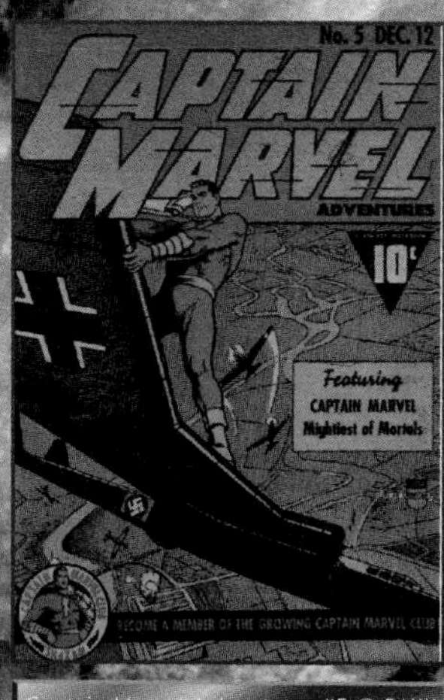

Captain Marvel Adventures #5 © FAW

DON'T GO
TO PIECES
LOOKING FOR
CHILDREN'S
COMICS...
THIS IS IT, VERONICA!
YEAH! THIS TIME IT'S WAR!
Dan DeCarlo
HENRY SCARPELLI
Archie® COMICS
THE LEADER IN
FAMILY ENTERTAINMENT
FOR OVER 54 YEARS!
COMING SOON:
ARCHIE MOVIE, ARCHIE RESTAURANTS
AND ARCHIE ON BROADWAY!!!
TM & © 1995 ARCHIE COMIC PUBLICATIONS, INC.

INVESTOR'S DATA

The following tables denote the rate of appreciation of the top Golden Age books and the top Silver Age books, as well as selected genres over the past year and the past six years (1989-1994). The retail value for a NM copy of each book in 1995 is compared to its value in 1994 and 1989. The rate of return for 1995 over 1994, and 1995 over 1989 are given. The place in rank is given for each comic by year, with its corresponding NM value. These tables can be very useful in forecasting trends in the market place. For instance, the investor might want to know which book is yielding the best dividend from one year to the next, or one might just be interested in seeing how the popularity of books changes from year to year. For instance, *Adventure Comics* #40 was in 18th place in 1994 and has increased to 14th place in 1995.

The following tables are meant as a guide to the investor. However, it should be pointed out that trends may change at anytime and that some books can meet market resistance with a slowdown in price increases, while others can develop into real comers from a presently dormant state. In the long run, if the investor sticks to the books that are appreciating steadily each year, he shouldn't go very far wrong.

TOP GOLDEN AGE BOOKS

1995 OVER 1994 GUIDE VALUES

Issue No.	1995 Rank	1995 NM Price	1994 Rank	1994 NM Price	$ Incr.	% Incr.
Action Comics #1	1	$125,000	2	$90,000	$35,000	39%
Detective Comics #27	2	$115,000	1	$92,000	$23,000	25%
Marvel Comics #1	3	$85,000	3	$75,000	$10,000	13%
Superman #1	4	$80,000	4	$70,000	$10,000	14%
Detective Comics #1	5	$54,000	8	$36,000	$18,000	50%
All-American Comics #16	6	$52,000	6	$37,000	$15,000	40%
Whiz Comics #2 (#1)	7	$46,000	5	$42,000	$4,000	9%
Captain America Comics #1	8	$45,000	9	$36,000	$9,000	25%
Batman #1	9	$42,000	7	$36,000	$6,000	16%
New Fun Comics #1	10	$40,500	10	$29,200	$11,300	38%
Flash Comics #1	11	$32,000	12	$23,000	$9,000	39%
More Fun Comics #52	12	$32,000	11	$28,000	$4,000	14%
All Star Comics #3	13	$25,000	13	$20,000	$5,000	25%
Adventure Comics #40	14	$22,000	18	$16,000	$6,000	38%
Detective Comics #33	15	$22,000	14	$18,000	$4,000	22%
Detective Comics #38	16	$21,000	15	$18,000	$3,000	16%
More Fun Comics #53	17	$20,500	16	$17,500	$3,000	17%
Captain Marvel Adventures #1	18	$19,000	17	$17,000	$2,000	12%
Green Lantern #1	19	$17,500	20	$13,000	$4,500	35%
Jumbo Comics #1	20	$17,000	24	$12,000	$5,000	42%
Detective Comics #29	21	$16,500	22	$12,500	$4,000	32%
Detective Comics #31	22	$16,000	23	$12,500	$3,500	28%
Famous Funnies-Series 1 #1	23	$16,000	19	$14,000	$2,000	14%
New York World's Fair 1939	24	$16,000	26	$11,000	$5,000	45%
Human Torch #2 (#1)	25	$15,000	33	$9,500	$5,500	58%
New Fun Comics #2	26	$15,000	21	$12,500	$2,500	20%
New Fun Comics #6	27	$14,250	27	$10,900	$3,350	31%
Detective Comics #2	28	$14,100	34	$9,430	$4,670	50%
Century Of Comics nn	29	$14,000	25	$11,900	$2,100	18%
New Comics #1	30	$13,000	28	$10,750	$2,250	21%
Adventure Comics #48	31	$12,000	40	$8,500	$3,500	41%
Amazing Man #5	32	$12,000	29	$10,500	$1,500	14%
Marvel Mystery Comics #2	33	$12,000	32	$9,500	$2,500	26%
More Fun Comics #14	34	$12,000	39	$9,000	$3,000	33%
New Book Of Comics #1	35	$12,000	35	$9,400	$2,600	28%
Famous Funnies-No. 1 #1	36	$11,500	30	$10,000	$1,500	15%
Big Book Of Fun Comics #1	37	$11,200	31	$9,750	$1,450	15%
Daring Mystery #1	38	$11,000	41	$8,000	$3,000	38%
Motion Picture Funnies Weekly #1	39	$11,000		$8,400	$2,600	31%
Sub-Mariner Comics #1	40	$11,000	48	$7,200	$3,800	53%
Comic Magazine #1	41	$10,500	36	$9,000	$1,500	17%
Detective Comics #3	42	$10,200	46	$7,400	$2,800	38%
Four Color Ser. 1 (Mickey Mouse) #16	43	$10,200	44	$7,500	$2,700	36%
Walt Disney's Comics & Stories #1	44	$10,000	49	$7,000	$3,000	43%
Wow Comics #1	45	$10,000	38	$9,000	$1,000	11%
All Star Comics #8	46	$9,500	45	$7,500	$2,000	27%
Marvel Mystery Comics #9	47	$9,500	58	$6,500	$3,000	46%
Marvel Mystery Comics #5	48	$9,000	50	$7,000	$2,000	29%

TOP GOLDEN AGE BOOKS (cont'd) Issue No.	1995 Rank	1995 NM Price	1994 Rank	1994 NM Price	$ Increase	% Increase
Mickey Mouse Magazine #1	49	$9,000	37	$9,000	$0	0%
Sensation Comics #1	50	$9,000	67	$6,000	$3,000	50%
World's Best #1	51	$9,000	52	$7,000	$2,000	29%
All-American Comics #17	52	$8,500	70	$6,000	$2,500	42%
All-American Comics #19	53	$8,500	65	$6,000	$2,500	42%
All Star Comics #1	54	$8,500	42	$7,800	$700	9%
Detective Comics #28	55	$8,500	61	$6,300	$2,200	35%
Double Action #2	56	$8,500	43	$7,500	$1,000	13%
Feature Book (Dick Tracy) nn(#1)	57	$8,500	79	$5,250	$3,250	62%
Feature Book (Popeye) nn(#1)	58	$8,500	80	$5,250	$3,250	62%
More Fun Comics #55	59	$8,500	51	$7,000	$1,500	21%
Mystic Comics #1	60	$8,500	59	$6,500	$2,000	31%
New York World's Fair 1940	61	$8,500	69	$6,000	$2,500	42%
New Fun Comics #3	62	$8,250	53	$6,750	$1,500	22%
New Fun Comics #4	63	$8,250	54	$6,750	$1,500	22%
New Fun Comics #5	64	$8,250	55	$6,750	$1,500	22%
Funnies On Parade nn	65	$8,200	47	$7,200	$1,000	14%
Action Comics #2	66	$8,000	62	$6,200	$1,800	29%
All Winners #1	67	$8,000	88	$5,000	$3,000	60%
Big All-American #1	68	$8,000	57	$6,500	$1,500	23%
Mickey Mouse Book (Bibo & Lang) 1930	69	$8,000	75	$5,500	$2,500	45%
Wonder Woman #1	70	$8,000	60	$6,500	$1,500	23%
Red Raven #1	71	$7,500	56	$6,500	$1,000	15%
Adventure Comics #61	72	$7,200	64	$6,000	$1,200	20%
King Comics #1	73	$7,200	63	$6,200	$1,000	16%
Action Comics #3	74	$7,000	82	$5,000	$2,000	40%
All Flash #1	75	$7,000	71	$5,800	$1,200	21%
Batman #2	76	$7,000	72	$5,700	$1,300	23%
Four Color Ser. 1 (Donald Duck) #4	77	$7,000	68	$6,000	$1,000	17%
Archie Comics #1	78	$6,500	73	$5,500	$1,000	18%
Captain America Comics #2	79	$6,500	84	$5,000	$1,500	30%
Famous Funnies-Carnival/Comics nn	80	$6,500	66	$6,000	$500	8%
Planet Comics #1	81	$6,500	76	$5,500	$1,000	18%
Silver Steak #1	82	$6,500	92	$4,800	$1,700	35%
Silver Steak #6	83	$6,500	101	$4,200	$2,300	55%
Superman #2	84	$6,500	86	$5,000	$1,500	30%
Adventure Comics #73	85	$6,300	81	$5,200	$1,100	21%
New Book Of Comics #2	86	$6,300	78	$5,380	$920	17%
Young Allies Comics #1	87	$6,200	109	$4,000	$2,200	55%
Adventure Comics #72	88	$6,000	96	$4,500	$1,500	33%
Four Color (Donald Duck) #9	89	$6,000	87	$5,000	$1,000	20%
Green Giant #1	90	$6,000	83	$5,000	$1,000	20%
March Of Comics (Donald Duck) nn(#4)	91	$6,000	74	$5,500	$500	9%
More Fun Comics #73	92	$6,000	85	$5,000	$1,000	20%
Special Edition Comics #1	93	$6,000	77	$5,500	$500	9%
More Fun Comics #54	94	$5,800	89	$4,800	$1,000	21%
Wonder Comics #1	95	$5,800	91	$4,800	$1,000	21%
Action Comics #7	96	$5,750	90	$4,800	$950	20%
All American Comics #18	97	$5,500	103	$4,000	$1,500	38%
All American Comics #25	98	$5,500	99	$4,200	$1,300	31%
Daredevil #1	99	$5,500	108	$4,000	$1,500	38%
More Fun Comics #101	100	$5,500	95	$4,500	$1,000	22%
USA Comics #1	101	$5,500	93	$4,600	$900	20%

Note: The above chart includes books where the highest grade in the listings is a VF price. A NM price has been estimated in each case for the purpose of this chart.

TOP SILVER AGE BOOKS
1995 OVER 1994 GUIDE VALUES

Issue No.	1995 Rank	1995 NM Price	1994 Rank	1994 NM Price	$ Incr.	% Incr.
Amazing Fantasy #15	1	$22,000	1	$20,000	$2,000	10%
Showcase #4	2	$21,000	2	$18,000	$3,000	17%
Amazing Spider-Man #1	3	$14,500	3	$13,500	$1,000	7%
Fantastic Four #1	4	$13,000	4	$12,000	$1,000	8%
Showcase #8	5	$8,775	5	$7,500	$1275	17%
Incredible Hulk #1	6	$8,500	6	$7,100	$1400	20%
Showcase #9	7	$4,000	9	$3,100	$900	29%
Showcase #22	8	$3,900	8	$3,300	$600	18%
Detective Comics #225	9	$3,850	7	$3,500	$350	10%
Showcase #14	10	$3,500	12	$3,000	$500	17%

TOP SILVER AGE BOOKS (cont'd) Issue No.	1995 Rank	1995 NM Price	1994 Rank	1994 NM Price	$ Increase	% Increase
Brave And The Bold #28	11	$3,300	10	$3,070	$230	7%
X-Men #1	12	$3,200	11	$3,000	$200	7%
Flash #105(#1)	13	$3,100	13	$2,750	$350	13%
Tales Of Suspense #39	14	$3,000	16	$2,550	$450	18%
Journey Into Mystery #83	15	$2,950	14	$2,730	$220	8%
Adventure Comics #247	16	$2,850	15	$2,600	$250	10%
Showcase #13	17	$2,700	18	$2,250	$450	20%
Tales To Astonish #27	18	$2,600	17	$2,300	$300	13%
Justice League Of America #1	19	$2,500	19	$2,200	$300	14%
Showcase #6	20	$2,400	20	$2,150	$250	12%
Adventure Comics #210	21	$2,275	21	$2,100	$175	8%
Amazing Spider-Man #2	22	$2,200	22	$2,050	$150	7%
Fantastic Four #2	23	$2,175	23	$2,000	$175	9%
Showcase #1	24	$2,100	24	$1,800	$300	17%
Superman's Pal, Jimmy Olsen #1	25	$2,050	27	$1,700	$350	21%
Fantastic Four #5	26	$2,000	25	$1,750	$250	14%
Brave And The Bold #29	27	$1,900	26	$1,750	$150	9%
Fantastic Four #4	28	$1,850	29	$1,625	$225	14%
Incredible Hulk #2	29	$1,800	30	$1,600	$200	13%
Avengers #1	30	$1,775	28	$1,675	$100	6%
Green Lantern #1	31	$1,750	31	$1,600	$150	9%
Showcase #10	32	$1,700	33	$1,450	$250	17%
Brave And The Bold #1	33	$1,600	34	$1,350	$250	16%
Brave And The Bold #30	34	$1,550	32	$1,450	$100	7%
Challengers Of The Unknown #1	35	$1,525	35	$1,350	$175	13%
Fantastic Four #3	36	$1,500	36	$1,325	$175	13%
Superman's Girl Friend, Lois Lane #1	37	$1,475	41	$1,200	$275	23%
Brave And The Bold #34	38	$1,450	38	$1,250	$200	16%
Incredible Hulk #6	39	$1,425	37	$1,300	$125	10%
Showcase #17	40	$1,400	40	$1,200	$200	17%
Batman #100	41	$1,375	44	$1,125	$250	22%
Amazing Spider-Man #3	42	$1,350	42	$1,175	$175	15%
Showcase #24	43	$1,325	43	$1,150	$175	15%
Daredevil #1	44	$1,300	39	$1,225	$75	6%
Showcase #7	45	$1,300	45	$1,125	$175	16%
Showcase #23	46	$1,300	46	$1,100	$200	18%
Tales To Astonish #35	47	$1,250	47	$1,100	$150	14%
Our Army At War #81	48	$1,225	53	$1,000	$225	23%
Showcase #12	49	$1,200	48	$1,075	$125	12%
Superman #100	50	$1,200	58	$950	$250	26%
Amazing Spider-Man #4	51	$1,175	49	$1,050	$125	12%
Showcase #11	52	$1,150	54	$1,000	$150	15%
Showcase #15	53	$1,150	60	$925	$225	24%
X-Men #2	54	$1,125	50	$1,025	$100	10%
Amazing Spider-Man #14	55	$1,100	51	$1,000	$100	10%
Mystery In Space #53	56	$1,100	57	$965	$135	14%
Tales Of Suspense #1	57	$1,100	59	$950	$150	16%
Tales To Astonish #1	58	$1,100	61	$900	$200	22%
Tales Of Suspense #40	59	$1,075	52	$1,000	$75	8%
Showcase #34	60	$1,050	55	$975	$75	8%
Incredible Hulk #3	61	$1,025	56	$975	$50	5%
Amazing Spider-Man #5	62	$960	62	$850	$110	13%
Showcase #19	63	$950	63	$850	$100	12%
Detective Comics #226	64	$900	69	$750	$150	20%
Action Comics #252	65	$875	64	$800	$75	9%
Detective Comics #233	66	$860	65	$800	$60	8%
My Greatest Adventure #1	67	$840	70	$740	$100	14%
Amazing Spider-Man #6	68	$825	68	$750	$75	10%
Incredible Hulk #4	69	$825	66	$780	$45	6%
Incredible Hulk #5	70	$825	67	$780	$45	6%
Showcase #18	71	$825	71	$720	$105	15%
Amazing Adventures #1	72	$800	79	$675	$125	19%
Brave And The Bold #2	73	$800	81	$650	$150	23%
Sugar & Spike #1	74	$800	75	$700	$100	14%
Superman's Pal, Jimmy Olsen #2	75	$800	77	$675	$125	19%
Tales Of The Unexpected #1	76	$790	76	$700	$90	13%
Action Comics #242	77	$775	72	$700	$75	11%
Fantastic Four #6	78	$775	73	$700	$75	11%
Flash #106	79	$775	74	$700	$75	11%
Strange Tales #110	80	$735	78	$675	$60	9%
Flash #123	81	$725	80	$650	$75	12%

TOP SILVER AGE BOOKS (cont'd) Issue No.	1995 Rank	1995 NM Price	1994 Rank	1994 NM Price	$ Increase	% Increase
Showcase #5	82	$715	82	$630	$85	13%
Journey Into Mystery #84	83	$700	83	$625	$75	12%
Tales Of The Unexpected #40	84	$700	86	$600	$100	17%
Showcase #35	85	$675	85	$600	$75	13%
Flash #110	86	$660	84	$600	$60	10%
Fantastic Four #48	87	$650	89	$575	$75	13%
Showcase #16	88	$650	91	$575	$75	13%
Justice League Of America #2	89	$640	87	$590	$50	8%
Adventure Comics #267	90	$625	88	$580	$45	8%
Strange Tales #101	91	$625	90	$575	$50	9%
Amazing Spider-Man #9	92	$600	92	$550	$50	9%
House Of Secrets #1	93	$600	93	$550	$50	9%
Showcase #2	94	$600	94	$530	$70	13%
World's Finest Comics #71	95	$600	103	$500	$100	20%

TOP 25 HORROR COMICS

1995 OVER 1994 AND 1989 GUIDE VALUE

Title Issue#	1995	1994	% change '94 to '95	1989	%change '89 to 95
Vault of Horror 12	$2,800	$2,500	12%	$750	273%
Tales of Terror Annual 1	$2,600	$2,400	8%	$1400	86%
Strange Tales 1	$1,675	$1,450	16%	$455	268%
Journey into Mystery 1	$1,575	$1,200	31%	$315	400%
Crypt of Terror 17	$1,400	$1,200	17%	$490	186%
Haunt of Fear 15	$1,400	$1,200	17%	$700	100%
Crime Patrol 15	$1,400	$1,150	22%	$400	250%
War Against Crime 10	$1,150	$1,000	15%	$370	211%
Tales of Terror Annual 2	$1,100	$1,000	10%	$700	57%
Tales of Suspense 1	$1,100	$950	16%	$250	340%
Tales to Astonish 1	$1,100	$900	22%	$260	323%
House of Mystery 1	$1,100	$850	29%	$280	293%
Crime Patrol 16	$900	$800	13%	$330	173%
Crypt of Terror 18	$900	$800	13%	$365	147%
Crypt of Terror 19	$900	$800	13%	$365	147%
My Greatest Adventure 1	$840	$740	14%	$250	236%
Tales of Terror Annual 3	$825	$750	10%	$490	68%
Amazing Adventures 1	$800	$675	19%	$150	433%
Tales of the Unexpected 1	$790	$700	13%	$210	276%
Adventures into the Unknown 1	$750	$625	20%	$265	183%
Eerie 1	$750	$525	43%	$245	206%
Tales From the Crypt 20	$725	$650	12%	$295	146%
Forbidden Worlds 1	$700	$600	17%	$350	100%
War Against Crime 11	$700	$600	17%	$320	119%
Vault of Horror 13	$615	$575	7%	$350	76%

TOP '50s SCIENCE FICTION COMICS

1995 OVER 1994 AND 1989 GUIDE VALUE

Title Issue#	1995	1994	% change '94 to '95	1989	% change '89 to '95
Mystery In Space 1	$1,800	$1,600	13%	$840	114%
Strange Adventures 1	$1,750	$1,500	17%	$665	163%
Showcase (Adam Strange) 17	$1,400	$1,200	17%	$260	438%
Showcase (Space Ranger) 15	$1,150	$925	24%	$100	1050%
Fawcett Movie (Man From Planet X) 15	$1,100	$1,050	5%	$1,050	5%
Weird Science-Fantasy Annual 1952	$1,100	$1,000	10%	$725	52%
Strange Adventures 9	$975	$850	15%	$490	99%
Showcase (Adam Strange) 19	$950	$850	12%	$155	513%
Journey Into Unknown Worlds 36	$900	$725	24%	$210	329%
Showcase (Adam Strange) 18	$825	$720	15%	$155	432%
Strange Adventures 2	$800	$700	14%	$315	154%
Weird Science 12	$800	$725	10%	$575	39%
Weird Fantasy 13	$775	$700	11%	$560	38%
Strange Worlds 3	$750	$560	34%	$540	39%
Mystery In Space 2	$700	$600	17%	$350	100%
Showcase (Space Ranger) 16	$650	$575	13%	$100	550%
Weird Science-Fantasy Annual 1953	$635	$575	10%	$460	38%
Mystery In Space 3	$600	$500	20%	$280	114%

TOP '50s SCI-FI BOOKS (cont'd) Title & Issue	1995 Value	1994 Value	% Change '94 to '95	1989 Value	% Change '89 to '95
Showcase (Rip Hunter) 20	$550	$500	10%	$60	817%
Space Detective 1	$550	$500	10%	$435	26%
Rocket to the Moon nn	$525	$480	9%	$385	36%
Motion Picture (When Worlds Collide) 110	$520	$485	7%	$475	9%
Strange Adventures 3	$500	$450	11%	$195	156%
Strange Adventures 4	$500	$450	11%	$195	156%
Weird Tales Of The Future 2	$500	$450	11%	$335	49%
Weird Tales Of The Future 3	$500	$450	11%	$335	49%
Weird Tales Of The Future 5	$500	$450	11%	$335	49%

TOP 25 WESTERN COMICS

1995 OVER 1994 AND 1989 GUIDE VALUE

Title Issue#	1995	1994	% change '94 to '95	1989	% change '89 to '95
Gene Autry 1	$3,200	$1,900	68%	$750	327%
Hopalong Cassidy 1	$2,950	$1,800	64%	$665	344%
Red Ryder Victory Patrol	$2,800	$2,200	27%	$245	1043%
Tom Mix 1	$1,500	$1,200	25%	$455	230%
Red Ryder Comics 1	$900	$800	13%	$560	61%
Western Picture Stories 1	$850	$750	13%	$560	52%
Gene Autry 2	$750	$525	43%	$310	142%
Tomahawk 1	$735	$650	13%	$280	163%
Roy Rogers Four Color 38	$700	$575	22%	$315	122%
Lone Ranger Large Feature Comic 7	$650	$450	44%	$350	86%
Lash LaRue Western 1	$625	$575	9%	$315	98%
Cowboy Comics 13	$600	$500	20%	$310	94%
Red Ryder Comics 3	$600	$500	20%	$350	71%
Rocky Lane Western 1	$550	$500	10%	$280	96%
Tom Mix Western 1	$550	$500	10%	$265	108%
Western Picture Stories 2	$550	$500	10%	$350	57%
Gene Autry 3	$520	$365	42%	$240	117%
Gene Autry 4	$520	$365	42%	$240	117%
Gene Autry 5	$520	$365	42%	$240	117%
Jimmy Wakely 1	$500	$400	25%	$200	150%
Lone Ranger Large Feature Comic 3	$500	$400	25%	$280	79%
Lone Ranger Feature Book 21	$500	$375	33%	$280	79%
Lone Ranger Feature Book 24	$500	$375	33%	$280	79%
Tom Mix 2	$500	$450	11%	$260	92%
Two Gun Kid 1	$500	$425	18%	$210	138%

Selected samplings from particular genres. Note the proximity of the starting points (prices) of these selected books.

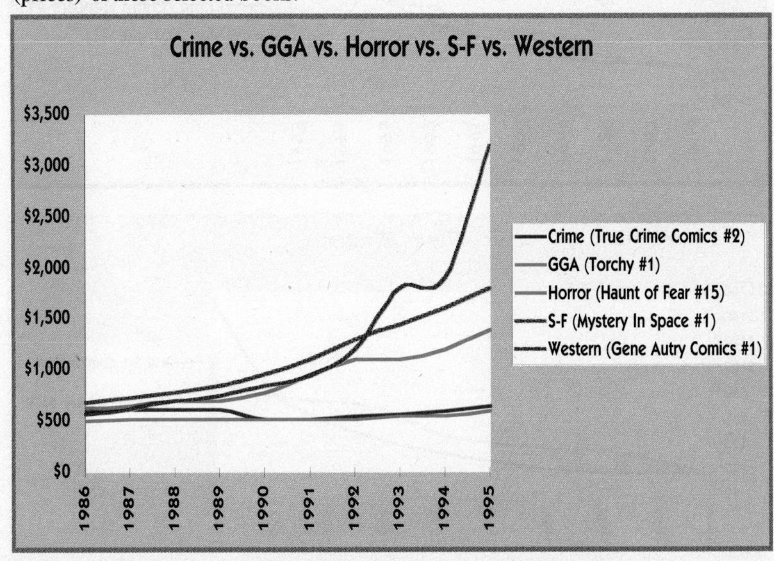

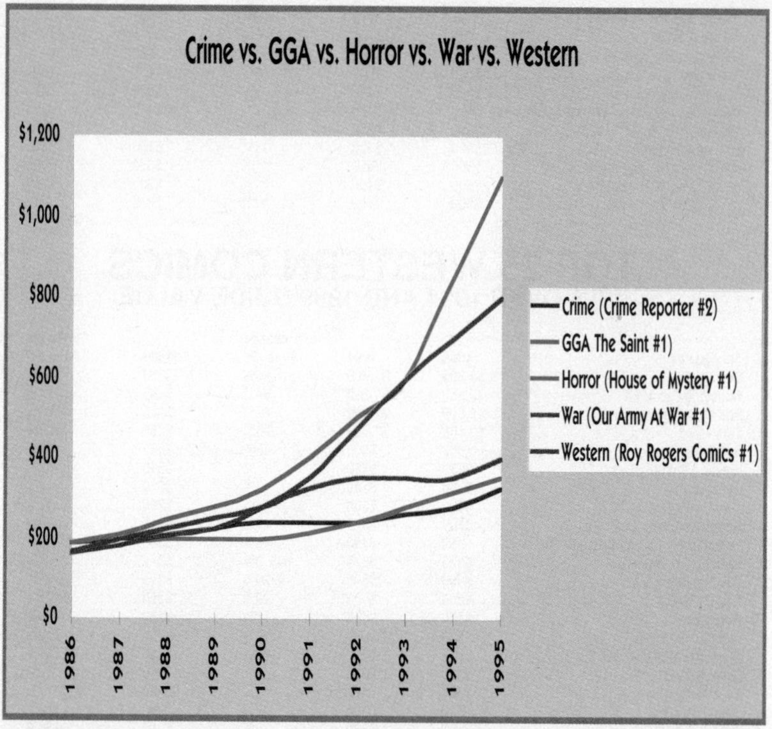

Crime vs. GGA vs. Horror vs. War vs. Western

$1,200
$1,000
$800
$600
$400
$200
$0

1986 1987 1988 1989 1990 1991 1992 1993 1994 1995

Crime (Crime Reporter #2)
GGA The Saint #1)
Horror (House of Mystery #1)
War (Our Army At War #1)
Western (Roy Rogers Comics #1)

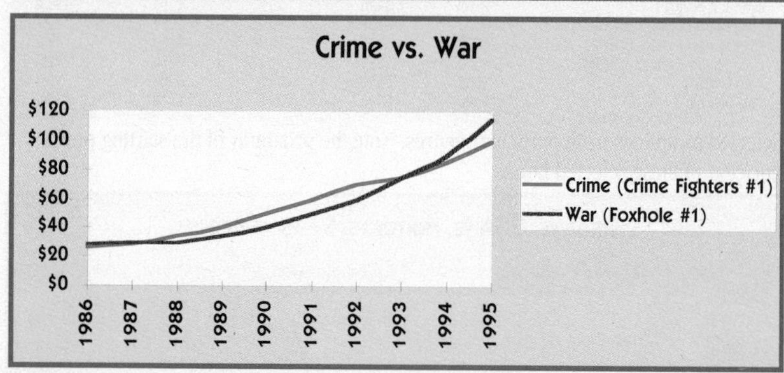

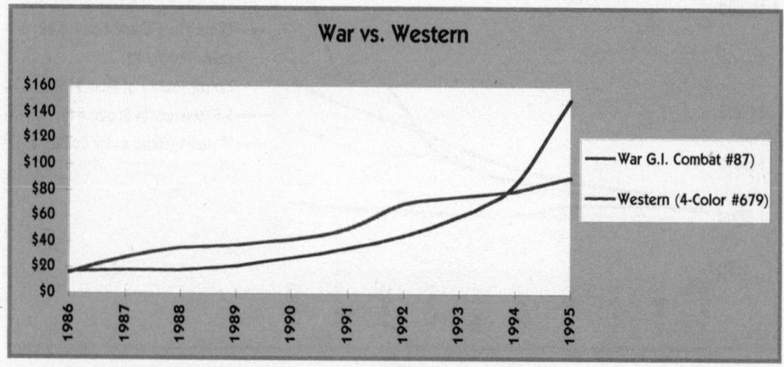

HISTORY OF COMIC BOOKS

The very first comic book was a 1933 giveaway called *Funnies On Parade.* Containing repackaged Sunday comic strips, it set the standard for many comic books to follow until DC comics published *New Fun Comics*, the first comic book to contain original material.

Since that time, thousands of every type of comic book imaginable has been published. For decades, historians, collectors and bibliofiles have tried to identify, list and document all the important, trend-setting comic books. This interesting topic continues to be debated and discussed by experts everywhere. In an attempt to answer these questions, Overstreet would like to nominate the following books to Overstreet's Hall Of Fame. The author invites your critique, comments and ideas concerning the accuracy of this list for future editions. Remember, only the very top books will be considered for inclusion.

THE OVERSTREET COMIC BOOK HALL OF FAME
(1933 - 1993)

PRE-GOLDEN AGE
1933 - May, 1938

Funnies On Parade #nn, 1933, Eastern Color (1st comic book)
Century Of Comics #nn, 1933, Eastern Color (2nd comic book, 1st 100 pgs.)
Famous Funnies-Carnival Of Comics nn, 1933, Eastern Color, (3rd comic book)
Famous Funnies-Series 1, 1934, Eastern Color, (1st 10 cent comic book)
Famous Funnies #1, 7/34, Eastern Color (1st newsstand comic book)
New Fun Comics #1, 2/35, DC (1st DC comic book)
Big Book Of Fun Comics #1, Spr/35, DC, (1st annual in comics)
New Fun Comics #6, 10/35, DC (1st siegel & Shuster work in comics)
More Fun Comics #14, 10/36, DC (1st Superman prototype at DC, 1st in color)
Detective Comics #1, 3/37, DC (1st issue of title that launched Batman)

GOLDEN AGE
June, 1938 - 1945

Action Comics #1, 6/38, DC (1st Superman and Lois Lane)
Funny Pages #V2#10, 9/38, Centaur (1st Arrow, 1st costumed hero (1st Hourman)
Jumbo Comics #1, 9/38, Fiction House (1st Sheena, 1st Fiction House comic book)
Movie Comics #1, 4/39, DC (1st movie comic)
New York World's Fair 1939, 4/39, DC (1st published Sandman story)

Detective Comics #27, 5/39, DC (1st Batman)
Wonder Comics #1, 5/39, Fox (1st Wonderman, 1st Superman imitator)
Superman #nn (#1), Summer/39, DC (1st issue, 1st hero to get his own book)
Adventure Comics #40, 7/39, DC (1st conceived Sandman story)
Marvel Comics #1, 10/39, Timely (1st newsstand Sub-Mariner, 1st Human Torch, 1st Marvel comic)
Silver Steak #1, 12/39, Lev Gleason (1st Gleason comic book, 1st Claw)
Flash Comics #1, 1/40, DC (1st Flash, Hawkman, & Johnny Thunder)
Pep Comics #1, 1/40, MLJ/Archie (1st Shield, 1st patriotic hero)
Planet Comics #1, 1/40, Fiction House (1st all science fiction comic book)
More Fun Comics #52, 2/40, DC (1st Spectre)
Whiz Comics #2 (#1), 2/40, Fawcett (1st Captain Marvel & Spy Smasher, 1st Fawcett comic book
Adventure Comics #48, 3/40, DC
More Fun Comics #53, 3/40, DC (Part II of 1st Spectre story)
Four Color Ser. 1 (Donald Duck) #4, 3?/40, (1st four color Donald Duck)
Action Comics #23, 4/40, DC (1st Lex Luthor)
Detective Comics #38, 4/40, DC (1st Robin)
Batman #1, Spring/40, DC (1st issue of DC's 2nd most important character; 1st 2 Joker stories; 1st Catwoman)
More Fun Comics #55, 5/40, DC (1st Dr. Fate)
All American Comics #16, 7/40, DC (1st Green Lantern)
Blue Bolt #3, 7/40, Fox (1st Simon & Kirby story art)
Marvel Mystery Comics #9, 7/40, Timely (1st super hero battle; key battle issue)
Red Raven #1, 8/40, Timely (Early Kirby art)
Special Edition Comics #1, 8/40, Fawcett (1st comic book devoted to Captain Marvel)
Silver Steak #6, 9/40, Lev Gleason (1st Daredevil)
Human Torch #2 (#1), Fall/40, Timely (1st issue of early Marvel star)
Walt Disney's Comics & Stories #1, 10/40, Dell (1st funny animal comic book series)
All American Comics #19, 10/40, DC (1st Atom)

All Star Comics #3, Winter/40-41, DC (1st super hero group)
Adventure Comics #72, 3/41, DC (1st Simon & Kirby Sandman)
Captain America Comics #1, 3/41, Timely (1st Captain America)
Captain Marvel Adventures #1, 3/41, Fawcett (1st issue of Fawcett's top character)
Sub-Mariner Comics #1, Spring/41, Timely (1st issue of Marvel's important character)
Adventure Comics #61, 4/41, DC (1st Starman)
All Flash #1, Summer/41, DC (1st issue of top DC character)
Daredevil #1, 7/41, Lev Gleason (1st issue of top character)
Military Comics #1, 8/41, Quality (1st Blackhawk)
Famous Funnies #100, 10/41, Eastern (1st comic book to reach 100)
Green Lantern #1, Fall/41, DC (1st issue of top DC character)
More Fun Comics #73, 11/41, DC (1st Aquaman)
Pep Comics #22, 12/41, MLJ/Archie (1st Archie)
Four Color Ser. 1 (Mickey Mouse) #16, 1941, (1st comic book devoted to Mickey Mouse)
Looney Tunes #1, Fall/41, Dell (1st Bugs Bunny, Porky Pig & Elmer Fudd in comics)
All Star Comics #8, 12-1/41-42, DC (1st Wonder Woman)
Animal Comics #1, 12-1/41-42, Dell (1st Pogo by Walt Kelly)
Sensation Comics #1, 1/42, DC (1st series to star Wonder Woman)
Crime Does Not Pay #22, 6/42, Gleason (1st Crime comic book series)
Wonder Woman #1, Summer/42, DC (1st issue of top DC character)
Four Color (Donald Duck) #9, 8/42 Dell (1st Barks story/art on Donald Duck)
Archie Comics #1, Winter/42-43, MLJ/ Archie, (1st Teenage comic)
Capt Marvel Adventures #22, 3/43, Fawcett, (Begins Mr. Mind serial)
Plastic Man #1, Summer/43, Quality (1st issue of top Quality character)
Big All-American Comic Book #1, 1944, DC, (1st annual of All-American Comics)
More Fun Comics #101, 1/2/45, DC (1st Superboy)
Molly O'Day #1, 2/45, Avon (1st Avon comic)
Terry Toones #38, 11/45, Timely (1st Mighty Mouse)

POST GOLDEN AGE
1946 - 1949

Romantic Picture Novelette #1, 1946, ME (one shot)(1st love comic theme)
All Winners #19, Fall/46, Timely (1st All Winners Squad, 1st Marvel group)
All Winners #21, Winter/46-47, Timely (2nd All Winners Squad)
Eerie #1, 1/47, Avon (1st horror comic)
Young Romance Comics #1, 9-10/47, Prize (1st romance series)
Four Color (Uncle Scrooge) #178, 12/47, Dell (1st Uncle Scrooge)
Phantom Lady #17, 4/48, Fox (Classic cover issue–good girl art)
Adventures Into The Unknown #1, Fall/48, ACG (1st horror series)
Moon Girl #5, Winter/48, EC (1st E.C. horror story)
Casper #1, 9/49, St John (1st Baby Huey)
Crime Patrol #15, 12-1/49-50, EC (1st Crypt Keeper)
War Against Crime #10, 12-1/49-50, EC (1st Vault Keeper)

PRE-SILVER AGE
1950 - Aug, 1956

Howdy Doody #1, 1/50, Dell (1st T.V. comic book)
Archie Annual #1, 1950, Archie (1st Archie annual)
Crypt Of Terror #17, 4-5/50, EC (1st issue of Crypt Keeper tales, E.C. horror)
Haunt Of Fear #15 (#1), 5-6/50, EC (1st issue of E.C. horror, trend-setting)
Weird Fantasy #13 (#1), 5-6/50, EC (1st issue of E.C. science fiction, trend-setting)
Weird Science #12 (#1), 5-6/50, EC (1st issue of E.C. science fiction, trend-setting)
Strange Tales #1, 6/51, Marvel (1st issue of top Marvel title)
Mad #1, 10-11/52, EC (1st satire comic)l
Journey Into Mystery #1, 6/52, Marvel (1st issue of top Marvel title)
Little Dot #1, 9/53, Harvey (1st Richie Rich)
Young Men #24, 12/53, Marvel (Revival of Capt. America, Human Torch & Sub-Mariner)
World's Finest Comics #71, 7-8/54, DC (1st Superman/Batman team issue)
Superman's Pal, Jimmy Olsen #1, 9-10/54, DC, (1st issue of top DC title)
My Greatest Adventure #1, 1-2/55, DC (1st issue of top DC fantasy title)
Brave And The Bold #1, 8-9/55, DC

(1st issue of top DC showcase title)
Superman #100, 9-10/55, DC (Landmark issue)
Detective Comics #225, 11/55, DC (1st Martian Manhunter)
Tales Of The Unexpected #1, 2-3/56, DC (1st issue of top DC fantasy title)
Showcase #1, 3-4/56, DC (1st issue of top DC showcase title)
Sugar & Spike #1, 4-5/56, DC (1st issue of top title by Sheldon Mayer)
Batman #100, 6/56, DC (Landmark issue)
Detective Comics #233, 7/56, DC (1st Batwoman)

SILVER AGE
Sept, 1956 - 1969

House Of Secrets #1, 11-12/56, DC (1st issue of top DC horror title)
Showcase #4, 9-10/56, DC (1st Silver Age book) (The Flash)
Showcase #6, 1-2/57, DC (1st Silver Age group) (Challengers)
Showcase #9, 7-8/57, DC (1st Lois Lane book)
Superman's Girl Friend, Lois Lane #1, 3-4/58, DC (1st issue of top character)
Adventure Comics #247, 4/58, DC (1st Legion of Superheroes)
Challengers Of The Unknown #1, 4-5/58, DC, (1st issue of 1st Silver Age group)
Showcase #15, 7-8/58, DC (1st Space Ranger)
Showcase #17, 11-12/58, DC (1st Adam Strange)
Tales Of Suspense #1, 1/59, Marvel (1st issue of top fantasy title)
Tales To Astonish #1, 1/59, Marvel (1st issue of top fantasy title)
Flash #105 (#1), 2-3/59, DC (1st issue of top DC title)
Our Army At War #81, 4/59, DC (1st Sgt. Rock)
Action Comics #252, 5/59, DC (1st Supergirl)
Showcase #20, 5-6/59, DC (1st Rip Hunter)
Double Life Of Private Strong #1, 6/59, Archie (1st Silver Age Shield, 1st Fly)
Mystery In Space #53, 8/59, DC (1st Adam Strange)
Tales Of The Unexpected #40, 8/59, DC (1st Space Ranger in own title)
Adventures of the Fly #1, 8/59, Archie (1st issue of top Archie title)
Showcase #22, 9-10/59, DC (1st Silver Age Green Lantern)
Flash #110, 12-1/59/60, DC (1st Kid Flash)
Brave And The Bold #28, 2/3/60, DC (1st Justice League of America)
Green Lantern #1, 7-8/60, DC (1st issue of top DC character)
Showcase #27, 7-8/60, DC (1st Sea Devils)
Brave And The Bold #31, 8-9/60, DC (1st Cave Carson)
Justice League Of America #1, 10-11/60, DC (1st issue of top DC title)
Showcase #30, 1-2/61, DC (1st Silver Age Aquaman)
Brave And The Bold #34, 2-3/61, DC (1st Silver Age Hawkman)
Amazing Adventures #1, 6/61, Marvel (1st Dr. Droom, the 1st Marvel-Age superhero)
Flash #123, 9/61, DC (1st G.A. Flash in Silver Age)
Showcase #34, 9-10/61, DC (1st Silver Age Atom)
Fantastic Four #1, 11/61, Marvel (1st Fantastic Four)
Amazing Adult Fantasy #7, 12/61, Marvel (1st issue of title that leads to Spider-Man)
Tales To Astonish #27, 1/62, Marvel (1st Antman)
Showcase #37, 3-4/62, DC (1st Metal Men)
Fantastic Four #4, 5/62, Marvel (1st Silver Age Sub-Mariner)
Incredible Hulk #1, 5/62, Marvel (1st Hulk)
Mystery In Space #75, 5/62, DC (Early JLA cross-over in Adam Strange story)
Fantastic Four #5, 7/62, Marvel (1st Dr. Doom)
Journey Into Mystery #83, 8/62, Marvel (1st Thor)
Amazing Fantasy #15, 8-9/62, Marvel (1st Spider-Man)
Tales To Astonish #35, 9/62, Marvel (2nd Antman, 1st in costume)
Strange Tales #101, 10/62, Marvel (1st S.A. Human Torch solo story)
Amazing Spider-Man #1, 3/63, Marvel (1st Spider-Man in own title)
Tales Of Suspense #39, 3/63, Marvel (1st Iron Man)
Strange Tales #110, 7/63, Marvel (1st Dr. Strange)
Avengers #1, 9/63, Marvel (1st Avengers)
X-Men #1, 9/63, Marvel (1st X-Men)
Mystery In Space #87, 11/63, DC (1st Hawkman in title)
Avengers #4, 3/64, Marvel (1st Silver Age Captain America)
Daredevil #1, 4/64, Marvel (1st Daredevil)
Amazing Spider-Man #14, 7/64, Marvel (1st Green Goblin)
Fantastic Four #48, 3/66, Marvel (1st Silver Surfer)

Strange Tales #135, 7/65, Marvel (Origin & 1st app. Nick Fury)

Strange Adventures #205, 10/67, DC (1st Deadman)

POST SILVER AGE
1970 - 1979

Detective Comics #400, 6/70, DC (1st Man-Bat)

Star Spangled War Stories #151, 6-7/70, DC (1st Unknown Soldier)

Superman's Pal, Jimmy Olsen #133, 10/70, DC (1st Silver Age Newsboy Legion)

Forever People #1, 2-3/71, DC (1st Forever People)

New Gods #1, 3/71, DC (1st New Gods)

Mister Miracle #1, 3/71, DC (1st Mister Miracle)

Savage Tales #1, 5/71, Marvel (1st Man-Thing)

House of Secrets #92, 6/71, DC (1st app. Swamp Thing by Bernie Wrightson)

Amazing Spider-Man #101, 10/71, Marvel (1st Morbius the Living Vampire)

Marvel Feature #1, 12/71, Marvel (Origin and 1st app. Defenders)

All Star Western #10, 2-3/72, DC (1st Jonah Hex)

Tomb of Dracula #1, 4/72, Marvel (1st app. Dracula)

Marvel Spotlight #2, 6/72, Marvel (1st app. Werewolf by Night)

Marvel Spotlight #5, 8/72, Marvel (Origin and 1st app. new Ghost Rider)

Kamandi: The Last Boy on Earth #1, 10/72, DC (Origin and 1st app. Kamandi)

Iron Man #55, 2/73, Marvel (1st. app. Thanos & Drax the Destroyer)

Marvel Spotlight #12, 10/73, Marvel (1st solo Son of Satan)

Marvel Special Edition #15, 12/73, Marvel (1st Master of Kung Fu)

Amazing Spider-Man #129, 2/74, Marvel (1st Punisher)

Astonishing Tales #25, 8/74, Marvel (1st Deathlok)

Incredible Hulk #181, 11/74, Marvel (1st app. of Wolverine) (story)

Giant Size X-Men #1, Summer/75, Marvel (1st New X-Men; intro Nightcrawler, Storm, Colossus & Thunderbird)

X-Men #94, 8/75, Marvel (New X-Men team begins)

All Star Comics #58, 1-2/76, DC (1st Power Girl)

Marvel Spotlight #32, 2/77, Marvel (1st Spider-Woman)

Black Lightning #1, 4/77, DC (1st Black Lightning)

Cerebus #1, 12/77, Aardvark-Vanaheim (1st app. Cerebus)(B&W)

MODERN AGE
1980 - PRESENT

Detective Comics #327, 5/84, DC (New Batman) (Silver Age/ Modern)

Teenage Mutant Ninja Turtles #1, pre 6/84, Mirage, (1st App. Teenage Mutant Ninja Turtles)

Amazing Spider-Man #300, 5/88, Marvel (1st venom) (full app & story)

Youngblood #1, 4/92, Image (1st Image comic)

Superman (2nd Series) #75, 1/93, DC (Death of Superman) (Huge Media Coverage)

HISTORIC FIRSTS
(First comic book of a genre, publisher, theme or type, etc.)

Aviation Comic–Wings Comics #1, 9/40

Comic Book Annual–Big Book Of Fun Comics #1, Spr, 1936

Comic Book–Funnies On Parade nn, 1933

Comic Book to go into endless reprints–Classic Comics #1, 10/41

Comic Book to kill off a super hero–Pep Comics #17, 7/41 (The Comet)

Comic Book with metallic logo–Silver Streak #1, 12/39

Comic Book with original material–New Fun Comics #1, 2/35

Costumed Hero Battle comic–Marvel Mystery #9, 7/40

Costumed Hero Comic (Strip)–Ace Comics #11, 2/38 (The Phantom)

Costumed Hero Comic (Original material)–Funny Pages V2/10 9/38 (The Arrow)(3 months after Superman)

Costumed Hero sidekick comic–Detective Comics #38, 4/40 (Robin)

Crime–Crime Does Not Pay #22, 6/42

Detective comic–Detective Picture Stories #1, 12/36

Disney Single Character comic book–Donald Duck nn, 1938

Disney Single Character comic book in color–Donald Duck 4-Color #4, 3/40

Educational theme comic–Classic Comics #1, 10/41

5 cent comic–Nickel Comics #1, 1938

15 cent comic–New York World's Fair, 1940

Flying Saucer comic–Spirit Section 9/28/47 (3 months after 1st sighting in Idaho on 6/25/47

Funny Animal Series–Walt Disney's Comics & Stories #1, 10/40

Funny Animal single character comic–Donald Duck nn, 1938

Giveaway comic–Funnies On Parade nn, 1933

Golden Age comic–Action Comics #1, 6/38

Heroine Single Theme comic–Sheena, Queen of the Jungle #1, Spr, 1942

Horror comic (one shot)–Eerie Comics #1, 1/47

Horror comic (series)–Adventures Into The Unknown #1, Fall, 1948

Jungle comic–Jumbo Comics #1, 9/38

Large Sized comic–New Fun Comics #1, 2/35

Love comic (One Shot)–Romantic Picture Novelettes #1, 1946 (Mary Worth strip-r)

Love comic (series)–Young Romance Comics #1, 10/47

Magician comic–Super Magic Comics #1, 5/41

Magician comic series–Super Magician Comics #2, 9/41

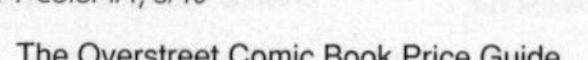

Masked Hero–Funny Pages #6, 11/36(The Clock)
Movie comic–Movie Comics #1, 4/39
Negro comic–Negro Heroes, Spr, 1947
Newsstand comic–Famous Funnies #1, 7/34
#2 in comics–Famous Funnies #2, 8/34
100 page comic–Century of Comics nn, 1933
100th issue–Famous Funnies #100, 11/43
One Shot Series–Feature Book nn, 1937
Patriotic Hero comic–Pep Comics #1, 1/40 (The Shield)
Prototype comic–The Comics Magazine #1, 5/36 (Superman)
Public Event comic–New York World's Fair 1939
Religious Theme series–Topix Comics #1, 11/42
Reprint comic–Funnies On Parade nn, 1933
Satire comic–Mad #1, 10-11/52
Science Fiction comic–Planet Comics #1, 1/40
Sidekick group comic–Young Allies #1, Sum, 1941
Silver Age Archie comic–Double Life of Private Strong #1, 6/59
Silver Age comic–Showcase #4, 9-10/56
Silver Age DC Annual–Superman Annual #1, 10/60
Silver Age Marvel Annual–Strange Tales Annual #1, 1962
Silver Age Marvel comic–Fantastic Four #1, 11/61
Single Character comic–Skippy's Own Book Of Comics, 1934
Single original character comic–Superman #1, Sum, 1939
Single Strip Reprint Character comic–Mutt and Jeff #1, Sum, 1939
Single Theme comic–Detective Picture Stories #1, 12/36
Single Theme comic, the first important–Detective Comics #1, 3/37
Single Theme Reprint Strip comic–Mutt and Jeff #1, Sum, 1939
Small-sized comic–Little Giant Comics #1, 7/38
Sports comic–Champion Comics #2, 12/39
Squarebound comic–New Book Of Comics #1, 1937
Squarebound series–World's Best #1, Spr, 1941
Super Hero comic–Action Comics #1, 6/38 (Superman)
Super Hero Team–All Star Comics #3, Wint, 1940-41
Super Heroine comic–All Star Comics #8, 11-12/41
Super Heroine comic series–Sensation Comics #1, 1/42
Superman imitator–Wonder Comics #1, 5/39 (Wonder Man)
Teen-age comic–Pep Comics #22, 12/41
Teen-age comic series–Archie Comics #1, Wint, 1942-43
10 cent comic–Famous Funnies Series 1, 3-5/34
3-D comic–Mighty Mouse 3-D #1, 9/53
T.V. comic–Howdy Doody #1, 1/50
25 cent comic–New York World's Fair, 1939
True Life comic–Sport Comics #1, 10/40
Villain cover (Fu Manchu)–Detective Comics #1, 3/37
Villain Story (Fu Manchu)–Detective Comics #17, 7/38
Villain Cover/story (Original to comics)–Silver Streak #1, 12/39 (The Claw)
War comic–War Comics #1, 5/40
Weekly comic book–The Spirit #1, 6/2/40
Western comic–Western Picture Stories #1, 2/37 & Star Ranger #1, 2/37
Western of one character–The Lone Ranger Comics nn, 1939
Western run of one character (Giveaway)–Tom Mix #1, 9/40
Western newsstand run of one character–Red Ryder Comics #1, 8/41
Western with photo cover–Roy Rogers 4-color #38, 4/44
X-Over comic–Marvel Mystery #9, 7/40

A Chronology of the Development of THE AMERICAN COMIC BOOK

By M. Thomas Inge

Precursors: The facsimile newspaper strip reprint collections constitute the earliest "comic books." The first of these was a collection of Richard Outcault's **Yellow Kid** from the Hearst New York American in March 1897. Commercial and promotional reprint collections, usually in cardboard covers, appeared through the 1920s and featured such newspaper strips as **Mutt and Jeff, Foxy Grandpa, Buster Brown**, and **Barney Google**. During 1922 a reprint magazine, **Comic Monthly**, appeared with each issue devoted to a separate strip, and from 1929 to 1930 George Delacorte published 36 issues of **The Funnies** in tabloid format with original comic pages in color, becoming the first four-color comic newsstand publication.

1933: The Ledger syndicate published a small broadside of their Sunday comics on 7" by 9" plates. Employees of Eastern Color Printing Company in New York, sales manager Harry I. Wildenberg and salesman Max C. Gaines, saw it and figured that two such plates would fit a tabloid page, which would produce a book about 7-1/2" x 10" when folded. Thus 10,000 copies of **Funnies on Parade**, containing 32 pages of Sunday newspaper reprints, was published for Proctor and Gamble to be given away as premiums. Some of the strips included were: **Joe Palooka, Mutt and Jeff, Hairbreadth Harry**, and **Reg'lar Fellas**. M. C. Gaines was very impressed with this book and convinced Eastern Color that he could sell a lot of them to such big advertisers as Milk-O-Malt, Wheatena, Kinney Shoe Stores, and others to be used as premiums and radio give-aways. So, Eastern Color printed **Famous Funnies: A Carnival of Comics**, and then **Century of Comics**, both as before, containing Sunday newspaper reprints. Mr. Gaines sold these books in quantities of 100,000 to 250,000.

1934: The give-away comics were so successful that Mr. Gaines believed that youngsters would buy comic books for ten cents like the "Big Little Books" coming out at that time. So, early in 1934, Eastern Color ran off 35,000 copies of **Famous Funnies, Series 1**, 64 pages of reprints for Dell Publishing Company to be sold for ten cents in chain stores. Since it sold out promptly on the stands, Eastern Color, in May 1934, issued **Famous Funnies** No. 1 (dated July 1934) which became, with issue No. 2 in July, the first monthly comic magazine. The title continued for over 20 years through 218 issues, reaching a circulation peak of over 400,000 copies a month. At the same time, Mr. Gaines went to the sponsors of Percy Crosby's **Skippy,** who was on the radio, and convinced them to put out a Skippy book, advertise it on the air, and give away a free copy to anyone who bought a tube of Phillip's toothpaste. Thus 500,000 copies of **Skippy's Own Book of Comics** was run off and distributed through drug stores everywhere. This was the first four-color comic book of reprints devoted to a single character.

1935: Major Malcolm Wheeler-Nicholson's National Periodical Publications issued in February a tabloid-sized comic publication called **New Fun**, which became **More Fun** after the sixth issue and was converted to the normal comic-book size after issue eight. **More Fun** was the first comic book of a standard size to publish original material, and it continued publication until 1949. **Mickey Mouse Magazine** began in the summer, to become **Walt Disney's Comics and Stories** in 1940, and combined original material with reprinted newspaper strips in most issues.

1936: In the wake of the success of **Famous Funnies**, other publishers, in conjunction with the major newspaper strip syndicates, inaugurated more reprint comic books: **Popular Comics** (News Tribune, February), **Tip Top Comics** (United Features, April), **King Comics** (King Features, April), and **The Funnies** (new series, NEA, October). Four issues of **Wow Comics**, from David McKay and Henle Publications, appeared, edited by S. M. Iger and including early art by Will Eisner, Bob Kane, and Alex Raymond. The first non-reprint comic book devoted to a single theme was **Detective Picture Stories** issued in December by The Comics Magazine Company.

1937: The second single theme title, **Western Picture Stories**, came in February from The Comics Magazine Company, and the third was **Detective Comics**, an offshoot of **More Fun**, which began in March to be published to the present. The book's initials, "D.C.," have long served to refer to National Periodical Publications, which was purchased from Major Nicholson by Harry Donenfeld late this year.

1938: "DC" copped a lion's share of the comic book market with the publication of **Action Comics** No. 1 in June which contained the first appearance of Superman by writer Jerry Siegel and artist Joe Shuster, a discovery of Max C. Gaines. The "man of steel" inaugurated the "Golden Era" in comic book history. Fiction House, a pulp publisher, entered the comic book field in September with **Jumbo Comics**, featuring Sheena, Queen of the Jungle, and appearing in oversized format for the first eight issues.

1939: The continued success of "DC" was assured in May with the publication of **Detective Comics** No. 27 containing the first episode of Batman by artist Bob Kane and writer Bill Finger. **Superman Comics** appeared in the summer. Also, during the summer, a black and white premium comic titled **Motion Picture Funnies Weekly** was published to be given away at motion picture theatres. The plan was to issue it weekly and to have continued stories so that the kids would come back week after week not to miss an episode. Four issues were planned but only one came out. This book contains the first appearance and origin of the Sub-Mariner by Bill Everett (8 pages) which was later reprinted in **Marvel Comics**. In November, the first issue of

Marvel Comics came out, featuring the Human Torch by Carl Burgos and the Sub-Mariner reprint with color added.

1940: The April issue of **Detective Comics** No. 38 introduced Robin the Boy Wonder as a sidekick to Batman, thus establishing the "Dynamic Duo" and a major precedent for later costumed heroes who would also have boy companions. **Batman Comics** began in the spring. Over 60 different comic book titles were being issued, including **Whiz Comics** begun in February by Fawcett Publications. A creation of writer Bill Parker and artist C. C. Beck, Whiz's Captain Marvel was the only superhero ever to surpass Superman in comic book sales. Drawing on their own popular pulp magazine heroes, Street and Smith Publications introduced **Shadow Comics** in March and **Doc Savage Comics** in May. A second trend was established with the summer appearance of the first issue of **All Star Comics**, which brought several superheroes together in one story and in its third issue that winter would announce the establishment of the Justice Society of America.

1941: Wonder Woman was introduced in the spring issue of **All Star Comics** No. 8, the creation of psychologist William Moulton Marston and artist Harry Peter. **Captain Marvel Adventures** began this year. By the end of 1941, over 160 titles were being published, including **Captain America** by Jack Kirby and Joe Simon, **Police Comics** with Jack Cole's Plastic Man and later Will Eisner's Spirit, **Military Comics** with Blackhawk by Eisner and Charles Cuidera, **Daredevil Comics** with the original character by Charles Biro, **Air Fighters** with Airboy also by Biro, and **Looney Tunes & Merrie Melodies** with Porky Pig, Bugs Bunny, and Elmer Fudd, reportedly created by Bob Clampett for the Leon Schlesinger Productions animated films and drawn for the comics by Chase Craig. Also, Albert Kanter's Gilberton Company initiated the **Classics Illustrated** series with The Three Musketeers.

1942: Crime Does Not Pay by editor Charles Biro and publisher Lev Gleason, devoted to factual accounts of criminals' lives, began a different trend in realistic crime stories. **Wonder Woman** appeared in the summer. John Goldwater's character Archie, drawn by Bob Montana, first published in **Pep Comics**, was given his own magazine **Archie Comics**, which has remained popular over 40 years. The first issue of **Animal Comics** contained Walt Kelly's "Albert Takes the Cake," featuring the new character of Pogo. In mid-1942, the undated Dell Four Color title, No. 9, **Donald Duck Finds Pirate Gold**, appeared with art by Carl Barks and Jack Hannah. Barks, also featured in **Walt Disney's Comics and Stories**, remained the most popular delineator of Donald Duck and later introduced his greatest creation, Uncle Scrooge, in **Christmas on Bear Mountain** (Dell Four Color No. 178). The fantasy work of George Carlson appeared in the first issue of **Jingle Jangle Comics**, one of the most imaginative titles for children ever to be published.

1945: The first issue of **Real Screen Comics** introduced the Fox and the Crow by James F. Davis, and John Stanley began drawing the **Little Lulu** comic book based on a popular feature in the **Saturday Evening Post** by Marjorie Henderson Buell from 1935 to 1944. Bill Woggon's Katy Keene appears in issue No. 5 of **Wilbur Comics** to be followed by appearances in **Laugh, Pep, Suzie** and her own comic book in 1950. The popularity of Dick Briefer's satiric version of the Frankenstein monster, originally drawn for **Prize Comics** in 1941, led to the publication of **Frankenstein Comics** by Prize publications.

1950: The son of Max C. Gaines, William M. Gaines, who earlier had inherited his father's firm Educational Comics (later Entertaining Comics), began publication of a series of well-written and masterfully drawn titles which would establish a "New Trend" in comics magazines: **Crypt of Terror** (later **Tales from the Crypt**, April), **The Vault of Horror** (April), **The Haunt of Fear** (May), **Weird Science** (May), **Weird Fantasy** (May), **Crime SuspenStories** (October), and **Two Fisted Tales** (November), the latter stunningly edited by Harvey Kurtzman.

1952: In October "E.C." published the first number of **Mad** under Kurtzman's creative editorship, thus establishing a style of humor which would inspire other publications and powerfully influence the underground comic book movement of the 1960s.

1953: All Fawcett titles featuring Captain Marvel were ceased after many years of litigation in the courts during which National Periodical Publications claimed that the super-hero was an infringement on the copyrighted Superman. In December, Captain America, Human Torch, and Sub-Mariner were revived by Atlas Comics.

1954: The appearance of Fredric Wertham's book **Seduction of the Innocent** in the spring was the culmination of a continuing war against comic books fought by those who believed they corrupted youth and debased culture. The U. S. Senate Subcommittee on Juvenile Delinquency investigated comic books and in response the major publishers banded together in October to create the Comics Code Authority and adopted, in their own words, "the most stringent code in existence for any communications media." Before the Code took effect, more than 1,000,000,000 issues of comic books were being sold annually.

1955: In an effort to avoid the Code, "E.C." launched a "New Direction" series of titles, such as **Impact, Valor, Aces High, Extra, M.D.**, and **Psychoanalysis**, none of which lasted beyond the year. **Mad** was changed into a larger magazine format with issue No. 24 in July to escape the Comics Code entirely, and "E.C." closed down its line of comic books altogether.

1956: Beginning with the Flash in **Showcase** No. 4, Julius Schwartz began a popular revival of "DC" superheroes which would lead to the "Silver Age" in comic book history.

1957: Atlas reduced the number of titles published by two-thirds, with **Journey into Mystery** and **Strange Tales** surviving, while other publishers did the same or went out of business. Atlas would survive as a part of the Marvel Comics Group.

1960: After several efforts at new satire magazines (**Trump** and **Humbug**), Harvey Kurtzman, no longer with Gaines, issued in August the first number of another abortive effort, **Help!**, where the early work of underground cartoonists Jay Lynch, Skip Williamson, Gilbert Shelton, and Robert Crumb appeared.

1961: Stan Lee edited in November the first **Fantastic Four**, featuring Mr. Fantastic, the Human Torch, the Thing, and the Invisible Girl, and inaugurated an enormously popular line of titles from Marvel Comics featuring a more contemporary style of superhero.

1962: Lee introduced **The Amazing Spider-Man** in August, with art by Steve Ditko, **The Hulk** in May and **Thor** in August, the last two produced by Dick Ayers and Jack Kirby.

1963: Marvel's **The X-Men**, with art by Jack Kirby, began a successful run in November, but the title would experience a revival and have an even more popular reception in the 1980s.

1965: James Warren issued **Creepy**, a larger black and white comic book, outside Comics Code's control, which emulated the "E.C." horror comic line. Warren's **Eerie** began in September and **Vampirella** in September 1969.

1967: Robert Crumb's **Zap** No. 1 appeared, the first underground comic book to achieve wide popularity, although the undergrounds had begun in 1962 with **Adventures of Jesus** by Foolbert Sturgeon (Frank Stack) and 1964 with **God Nose** by Jack Jackson.

1970: Editor Roy Thomas at Marvel begins **Conan the Barbarian** based on fiction by Robert E. Howard with art by Barry Smith, and Neal Adams began to draw for "DC" a series of **Green Lantern/Green Arrow** stories which would deal with relevant social issues such as racism, urban poverty, and drugs.

1972: The Swamp Thing by Berni Wrightson begins in November from "DC".

1973: In February, "DC" revived the original **Captain Marvel** with new art by C. C. Beck and reprints in the first issue of **Shazam** and in October **The Shadow** with scripts by Denny O'Neil and art by Mike Kaluta.

1974: "DC" began publication in the spring of a series of over-sized facsimile reprints of the most valued comic books of the past under the general title of "Famous First Editions," beginning with a reprint of **Action** No. 1 and including afterwards **Detective Comics** No. 27, **Sensation Comics** No. 1, **Whiz Comics** No. 2, **Batman** No. 1, **Wonder Woman** No. 1, **All-Star Comics** No. 3, **Flash Comics** No. 1, and **Superman** No. 1. Mike Friedrich, an independent publisher, released **Star★Reach** with work by Jim Starlin, Neal Adams, and Dick Giordano, with ownership of the characters and stories invested in the creators themselves.

1975: In the first collaborative effort between the two major comic book publishers of the previous decade, Marvel and "DC" produced together an over-sized comic book version of MGM's **Marvelous Wizard of Oz** in the fall, and then the following year in an unprecedented cross-over produced **Superman vs. the Amazing Spider-Man**, written by Gerry Conway, drawn by Ross Andru, and inked by Dick Giordano.

1976: Frank Brunner's Howard the Duck, who had appeared earlier in Marvel's **Fear** and **Man-Thing**, was given his own book in January, which because of distribution problems became an overnight collector's item. After decades of litigation, Jerry Siegel and Joe Shuster were given financial recompense and recognition by National Periodical Publications for their creation of Superman, after several friends of the team made a public issue of the case.

1977: Stan Lee's **Spider-Man** was given a second birth, fifteen years after his first, through a highly successful newspaper comic strip, which began syndication on January 3 with art by John Romita. This invasion of the comic strip by comic book characters continued with the appearance on June 6 of Marvel's **Howard the Duck**, with story by Steve Gerber and visuals by Gene Colan. In an unusually successful collaborative effort, Marvel began publication of the comic book adaption of the George Lucas film **Star Wars**, with script by Roy Thomas and art by Howard Chaykin, at least three months before the film was released nationally on May 25. The demand was so great that all six issues of **Star Wars** were reprinted at least seven times, and the installments were reprinted in two volumes of an over-sized Marvel Special Edition and a single paperback volume for the book trade. Dave Sim, with an issue dated December, began self-publication of his **Cerebus the Aardvark**, the success of which would help establish the independent market for non-traditional black-and-white comics.

1978: In an effort to halt declining sales, Warner Communications drastically cut back on the number of "DC" titles and overhauled its distribution process in June. The interest of the visual media in comic book characters reached a new high with the Hulk, Spider-Man, and Doctor Strange, the subjects of television shows; with various projects begun to produce film versions of Flash Gordon, Dick Tracy, Popeye, Conan, The Phantom, and Buck Rogers; and with the movement reaching an outlandish peak of publicity with the release of **Superman** in December. Two significant applications of the comic book format to traditional fiction appeared this year: **A Contract with God and Other Tenement Stories** by Will Eisner and **The Silver Surfer** by Stan Lee and Jack Kirby. Eclipse Enterprises published Don McGregor and Paul Gulacy's **Sabre**, the first graphic album produced for the direct sales market, and initiated a policy of paying royalties and granting copyrights to comic book creators. Wendy and Richard Pini's **Elfquest**, a self-publishing project begun this year, eventually became so popular that it achieved bookstore distribution. The magazine **Heavy Metal** brought to American attention the avant-garde comic book work of European artists.

1980: Publication of the November premier issue of **The New Teen Titans**, with art by George Perez and story by Marv Wolfman, brought back to widespread popularity a title originally published by "DC" in 1966.

1981: The distributor Pacific Comics began publishing titles for direct sales through comic shops with the inaugural issue of Jack Kirby's **Captain Victory and the Galactic Rangers** and offered royalties to artists and writers on the basis of sales. "DC" would do the same for regular newsstand comics in November (with payments retroactive to July 1981), and Marvel followed suit by the end of the year. The first issue of **Raw**, irregularly published by Art Spiegelman and Francoise Mouly, carried comic book art into new extremes of experimentation and innovation with work by European and American artists. With issue No. 158, Frank Miller began to write and draw Marvel's **Daredevil** and brought a vigorous style of violent action to comic book pages.

1982: The first slick format comic book in regular size appeared, **Marvel Fanfare** No. 1, with a March date. Fantagraphics Books began publication in July of **Love and Rockets** by Mario, Gilbert, and Jaime Hernandez and brought a new ethnic sensibility and sophistication in style and content to comic book narratives for adults.

1983: This year saw more comic book publishers, aside from Marvel and DC, issuing more titles than had existed in the past 40 years, most small independent publishers relying on direct sales, such as Americomics, Capital, Eagle, Eclipse, First, Pacific, and Red Circle, and with Archie, Charlton, and Whitman publishing on a limited scale. Frank Miller's mini-series **Ronin** demonstrated a striking use of sword play and martial arts typical of Japanese comic book art, and Howard Chaykin's stylish but controversial **American Flagg** appeared with an October date on its first issue.

1984: A publishing, media, film, and merchandising phenomenon began with the first issue of **Teenage Mutant Ninja Turtles** from Mirage Studios by Kevin Eastman and Peter Laird.

1985: Ohio State University's Library of Communication and Graphic Arts hosted the first major exhibition devoted to the comic book May 19 through August 2. In what was billed as an irreversible decision, the Silver Age superheroine Supergirl was killed in the seventh (October) issue of **Crisis on Infinite Earths**, a limited series intended to reorganize and simplify the DC universe on the occasion of the publisher's 50th anniversary.

1986: In recognition of its twenty-fifth anniversary, Marvel began publication of several new ongoing titles comprising Marvel's "New Universe", a self-contained fictional world. DC attracted extensive publicity and media coverage with its revisions of the character of **Superman** by John Byrne and of **Batman** in the **Dark Knight** series by Frank Miller. **Watchmen**, a limited-series graphic novel by Alan Moore and artist Dave Gibbons, began publication with a September issue from DC and Marvel's **The `Nam**, written by Vietnam veteran Doug Murray and penciled by Michael Golden, began with its December issue. DC issued guidelines in December for labelling their titles as either for mature readers or for readers of all ages; in response, many artists and writers publicly objected or threatened to resign.

1987: Art Spiegelman's **Maus: A Survivor's Tale** was nominated for the National Book Critics Circle Award in biography, the first comic book to be so honored. A celebration of Superman's fiftieth Birthday began with the opening of an exhibition on his history at the Smithsonian's Museum of American History in Washington, D.C., in June and a symposium on "The Superhero in America" in October.

1988: Superman's birthday celebration continued with a public party in New York and a CBS television special in February, a cover story in Time magazine in March (the first comic book character to appear on the cover), and an international exposition in Cleveland in June. With issue number 601 for May 24, **Action Comics** became the first modern weekly comic book, which ceased publication after 42 issues with the December 13 number. In August, DC initiated a new policy of allowing creators of new characters to retain ownership of them rather than rely solely on work-for-hire.

1989: The fiftieth anniversary of Batman was marked by the release of the film **Batman**, starring Michael Keaton as Bruce Wayne and Jack Nicholson as the Joker; it grossed more money in the weekend it opened than any other motion picture in film history to that time.

1990: The publication of a new **Classics Illustrated** series began in January from Berkley/First with adaptations of Poe's **The Raven and Other Poems** by Gahan Wilson,

Dickens' **Great Expectations** by Rick Geary, Carroll's **Through the Looking Glass** by Kyle Baker, and Melville's **Moby Dick** by Bill Sienkiewicz, with extensive media attention. The adaptation of characters to film continued with the most successful in terms of popularity and box office receipts being **Teenage Mutant Ninja Turtles** and Warren Beatty's **Dick Tracy**. In November, the engagement of Clark Kent and Lois Lane was announced in **Superman** No. 50 which brought public fanfare about the planned marriage.

1991: One of the first modern comic books to appear in the former Soviet Union was a Russian version of **Mickey Mouse** published in Moscow on May 16 in a printing of 200,000 copies which were sold out within hours. The first issue of **Bone**, written, drawn, and published by Jeff Smith, appeared with a July cover date. Issue number one of a new series of Marvel's **X-Men**, with story and art by Chris Claremont and Jim Lee, was published in October in five different editions with a print run of eight million copies, the highest number in the history of the comic book. On December 18, Sotheby's of New York held its first auction of comic book material.

1992: The opening weekend for **Batman Returns** in June was the biggest in film box office history, bringing in over 46 million dollars, exceeding the record set by **Batman** in 1989, and not to be topped until the release of **Jurassic Park** a year later. At the second Sotheby action in September, **Action Comics** No. 1 brought $82,500, a world record for a single comic book sold at auction. In November the death of Superman generated considerable media attention, with **Superman** No. 75 selling in excess of 4 million copies, the second best-selling issue in comic book history. A record number of over one hundred publishers of comic books and graphic albums issued titles this year.

1993: In April, for the first time since 1987, DC Comics surpassed Marvel in sales, primarily because of interest in the titles devoted to the return of Superman.

1994: Overproduction, changes in marketing practices, and publisher mergers and collapses triggered an apparent crisis in comic book publishing–which some have read as a sign of its influence and presence in American commerce and culture.

FOREIGN COMIC BOOKS

COLLECTING FOREIGN COMICS AND AMERICAN REPRINTS

One extremely interesting source of comics of early vintage–one which does not necessarily have to be expensive–is the foreign market. Many American strips, from both newspapers and magazines, are reprinted abroad (both in English and in other languages) months and even years after they appear in the states. By working out trade agreements with foreign collectors, one can obtain, for practically the cover price, substantial runs of a number of newspaper strips and reprints of American comic books dating back five, ten, or occasionally even twenty or more years. These reprints are often in black and white, and sometimes the reproduction is poor, but this is not always the case. In any event, this is a source of material that every serious collector should look into.

Once the collector discovers comics published in foreign lands, he often becomes fascinated with the original strips produced in these countries. Many are excellent, and have a broader range of appeal than those of American comic books.

CANADIAN REPRINTS (E.C.s: by J. B. Clifford)

Several E.C. titles were published in Canada by Superior Comics from 1949 to at least 1953. Canadian editions of the following E.C. titles are known: (Pre-Trend) *Saddle Romances, Moon Girl, A Moon A Girl...Romance, Modern Love, Saddle Justice*; (New-Trend) *Crypt of Terror, Tales*

From the Crypt, Haunt of Fear, Vault of Horror, Weird Science, Weird Fantasy, Two-Fisted Tales, Frontline Combat, and *MAD. Crime SuspenStories* was also published in Canada under the title *Weird SuspenStories* (Nos. 1-3 known). No reprints of Shock SuspenStories by Superior are known, nor have any "New Direction" reprints ever been reported. No reprints later than January 1954 are known. Canadian reprints sometimes exchanged cover and contents with adjacent numbers (e.g., a *Frontline Combat* 12 with a *Frontline Combat* No. 11 cover). They are distinguished both in cover and contents. As the interior pages are always reprinted poorly, these comics are of less value (about 1/2) than the U.S. editions; they were printed from asbestos plates made from the original plates. On some reprints, the Superior seal replaces the E.C. seal. Superior publishers took over Dynamic in 1947.

CANADIAN REPRINTS (Dells: by Ronald J. Ard)

Canadian editions of Dell comics, and presumably other lines (Fiction House, Atlas/Marvel, Superior, etc.), began in March-April, 1948 and lasted until February-March, 1951. They were a response to the great Canadian dollar crisis of 1947. Intensive development of the post-war Canadian economy was financed almost entirely by American capital. This massive import of money reached such a level that Canada was in danger of having grossly disproportionate balance of payments which could drive it into technical bankruptcy in the midst of the biggest boom in its history. The Canadian government responded by banning a long list of imports. Almost 500 separate items were involved. Alas, the consumers of approximately 499 of them were politically more formidable than the consumers of comic books.

Dell responded by publishing its titles in Canada through an arrangement with Wilson Publishing Company of Toronto. This company had not existed for a number of years and it is reasonable to assume that its sole business was the production and distribution of Dell titles in Canada. There is no doubt that they had a captive market. If you check the publication data on the U. S. editions of the period you will see the sentence "Not for sale in Canada." Canada was thus the only area of the Free World in those days technically beyond the reach of the American comic book industry.

We do not know whether French editions existed of the Dell titles put out by Wilson. The English editions were available nationwide. They were priced at 10 cents and were all 36 pages in length, at a time when their American parents were 52 pages. The covers were made of coarser paper, similar to that used in the Dell Four Color series in 1946 and 1947 and were abandoned as the more glossy cover paper became more economical. There was also a time lag of from six to eight weeks between, say, the date an American comic appeared and the date that the Canadian edition appeared.

Many Dell covers had seasonal themes and by the time the Canadian edition came out (two months later) the season was over. Wilson solved this problem by switching covers around so that the appropriate season would be reflected when the books hit the stands. Most Dell titles were published in Canada during this period including the popular Atom Bomb giveaway, *Walt Disney Comics and Stories* and the *Donald Duck* and *Mickey Mouse* Four Color one-shots. The quality of the Duck one-shots is equal to that of their American counterparts and generally bring about 30 percent less.

By 1951 the Korean War had so stimulated Canadian exports that the restrictions on comic book importation, which in any case were an offense against free trade principle, could be lifted without danger of economic collapse. Since this time Dell, as well as other companies, have been shipping direct into Canada.

CANADIAN REPRINTS (DCs: by Doug A. England)

Many DC comics were reprinted in Canada by National Comics Publications Limited and Simcoe Publishing and Distributing Co., both of Toronto, for years 1948-1950 at least. Like the Dells, these issues were 36 pages rather than the 52 pages offered in the U.S. editions, and the inscription "Published in Canada" would appear in place of "A 52 Page Magazine" or "52 Big Pages" appearing on U.S. editions. These issues contained no advertisements and some had no issue numbers.

COMIC BOOK FANDOM

THE HISTORY OF COMICS FANDOM

At this time it is possible to discern two distinct and largely unrelated movements in the history of Comics Fandom. The first of these movements began about 1953 as a response to the then popular trend-setting EC lines of comics. The first true comics fanzines of this movement were short-lived. Bob Stewart's EC FAN BULLETIN was a hectographed newsletter that ran two issues about six months apart; and Jimmy Taurasi's FANTASY COMICS, a newsletter devoted to all science-fiction comics of the period, was a monthly that ran for about six months. These were followed by other newsletters, such as Mike May's EC FAN JOURNAL, and George Jennings' EC WORLD PRESS. EC fanzines of a wider and more critical scope appeared somewhat later. Two of the finest were POTRZEBIE, the product of a number of fans, and Ron Parker's HOOHAH. Gauging from the response that POTRZEBIE received from a plug in an EC letter column, Ted White estimated the average age of EC fans to lie in the range of 9 to 13, while many EC fans were in their mid-teens. This fact was taken as discouraging to many of the fanzine editors, who had hoped to reach an older audience. Consequently, many of them gave up their efforts in behalf of Comics Fandom, especially with the demise of the EC groups, and turned their attention to science-fiction fandom with its longer tradition and older membership. While the flourish of fan activity in response to the EC comics was certainly noteworthy, it is fair to say that it never developed into a full-fledged, independent, and self-sustaining movement.

The second comics fan movement began in 1960. It was largely a response to (though it later became a stimulus for) the Second Heroic Age of Comics. Most fan historians date the Second Heroic Age from the appearance of the new *Flash* comics (numbered 105 and dated February 1959). The letter departments of Julius Schwartz (editor at National Periodicals), and later those of Stan Lee (Marvel Group) and Bill Harris (Gold Key) were most influential in bringing comics readers into Fandom. Beyond question, it was the reappearance of the costumed hero that sparked the comics fan movement of the sixties. Sparks were lit among some science-fiction fans first, when experienced fan writers, who were part of an established tradition, produced the first in a series of articles on the comics of the forties–ALL IN COLOR FOR A DIME. The series was introduced in XERO No. 1 (September 1960), a general fanzine for science-fiction fandom edited and published by Dick Lupoff.

Meanwhile, outside science-fiction fandom, Jerry Bails and Roy Thomas, two strictly comics fans of long-standing, conceived the first true comics fanzine in response to the Second Heroic Age. The fanzine, ALTER EGO, appeared in March 1961. The first several issues were widely circulated among comics fans, and were to influence profoundly the comics fan movement to follow. Unlike the earlier EC fan movement, this new movement attracted many fans in their twenties and thirties. A number of these older fans had been active collectors for years but had been largely unknown to each other. Joined by scores of new, younger fans, this group formed the nucleus of a new movement that is still growing and shows every indication of being self-sustaining. Although it has borrowed a few of the more appropriate terms coined by science-fiction fans, Comics Fandom of the Sixties was an independent if fledging movement, without, in most cases, the advantages and disadvantages of a longer tradition. What Comics Fandom did derive from science-fiction fandom it did so thanks largely to the fanzines produced by so-called double fans. The most notable of this type is COMIC ART, edited and published by Don and Maggie Thompson.

The ROCKETS BLAST COMIC COLLECTOR by G.B. Love was the first sucessful adzine in the early 1960s and was instrumental and important in the early development of the comics market. G.B. remembers beginning his fanzine THE ROCKET'S BLAST in late 1961. Only six copies of the first issue were printed and consisted of only 4 pages. Shortly thereafter Mr. Love had a letter published in MYSTERY IN SPACE, telling all about his new fanzine. His circulation began to grow. Buddy Saunders, a well known comic book store owner, designed the first ROCKET'S BLAST logo, and was an artist for this publication for many years thereafter. With issue #29 he took over THE COMICOLLECTOR fanzine from Biljo White and combined it with the ROCKET'S BLAST to from the RBCC. He remembers that the RBCC hit its highest circulation of 2500 around 1971. Many people who wrote, drew or otherwise contributed to the RBCC went on to become well known writers, artists, dealers and store-owners in the comics field.

COLLECTING STRIPS

Collecting newspaper comic strips is somewhat different than collecting magazines, although it can be equally satisfying.

Obviously, most strip collectors begin by clipping strips from their local paper, but many soon branch out to strips carried in out-of-town papers. Naturally this can become more expensive and it is often frustrating because it is easy to miss editions of out-of-town papers. Consequently, most strip collectors work out trade agreements with collectors in other cities in order to get an uninterrupted supply of the strips they want. This usually necessitates saving local strips to be used for trade purposes only.

Back issues of strips dating back several decades are also available from time to time from dealers. The prices per panel vary greatly depending on the age, condition, and demand for the strip. When the original strips are unavailable, it is sometimes possible to get photostatic copies from collectors, libraries, or newspaper morgues.

COLLECTING ORIGINAL ART

In addition to magazines and strips, some enthusiasts also collect the original art for the comics. These black and white, inked drawings are usually done on illustration paper at about 30 percent up (i.e., 30 percent larger than the original printed panels). Because original art is a one-of-a kind article, it is highly prized and often difficult to obtain.

Interest in original comic art has increased tremendously in the past several years. Many companies now return the originals to the artists who have in turn offered them for sale, usually at cons but sometimes through agents and dealers. As with any other area of collecting, rarity and demand governs value. Although the masters' works bring fine art prices, most art is available at moderate prices. Comic strips are the most popular facet with collectors, followed by comic book art. Once scarce, current and older comic book art has surfaced within the last few years. In 1974 several original painted covers of vintage comic books and coloring books turned up from Dell, Gold Key, Whitman, and Classic Comics.

The Mystery of the 12 MISSING E.C.'s

by
Bruce Hamilton

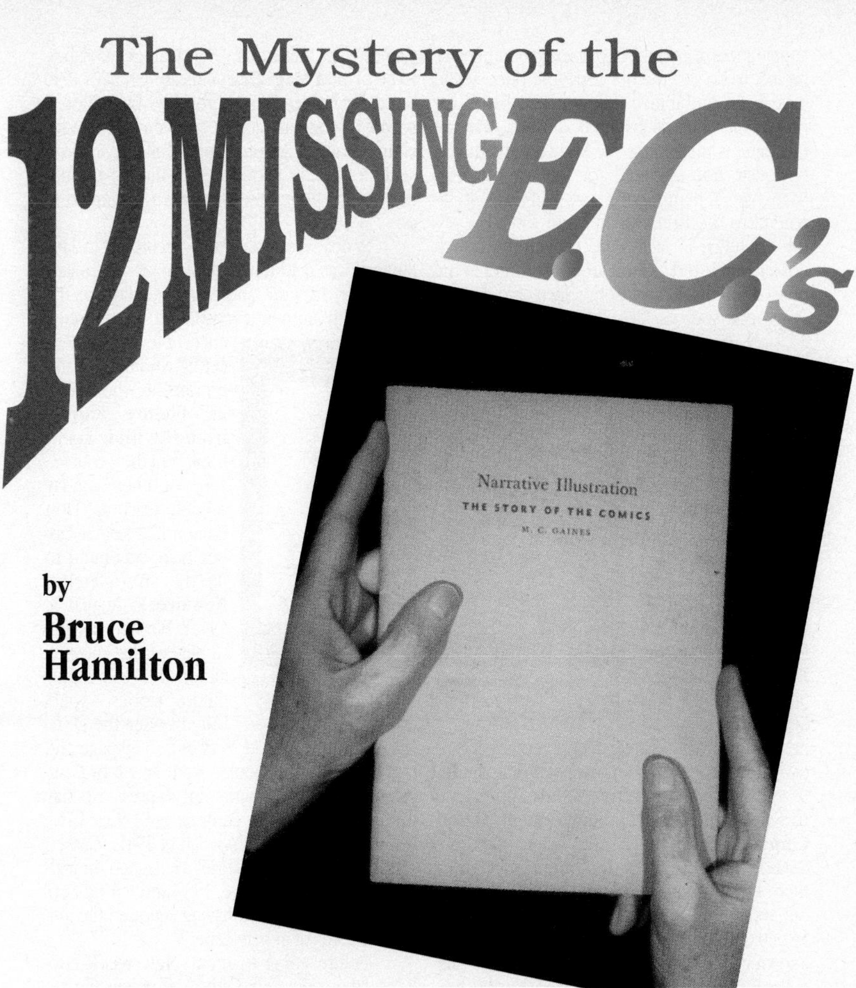

Narrative Illustration: the Story of the Comics, written and published by M. C. Gaines—"father" of the comics—is more than rare. Its discovery is exciting because it opens the door to the search for a **dozen** unheard of pre-trend, "E. C. roots" comics! It also postulates a history of comics from the pen of a man who should know.

Narrative Illustration has twelve interior pages in color, the rest a sixteen-page booklet reprinting text (with some new copy added by Gaines) that had appeared recently, as of the summer of 1942, in **Print, A Quarterly Journal of the Graphic Arts**, Volume III, No. 2.

NI has thirty-two pages including covers and is comic book size, 7¼″ x 10″. The unimposing, heavy stock cover is blank on all sides except the front. The stapled, illustrated text is on book paper with two comic sections inserted into the center. One of these is on pulp comic book paper (eight pages) and the other is a slick-paper giveaway (four pages) glued in.

The giveaway is titled, **The Minute Man Answers the Call**, written by Gaines and drawn by Sheldon "Shelly" Moldoff of Hawkman fame. Is it the first pre-trend, pre-E. C.? More about it later.

Of primary interest, though, is the eight-page center portion, which reprints "The Story of Saul, the First King of Israel," from **Picture Stories from the Bible** #1!

Questions surrounding **Narrative Illustration** begin to surface as its contents are examined. In fact, it's a **real mystery**! By all appearances it should have been an expensive project to do and the per copy unit price would have been prohibitive unless it had had a big press run, which it evidently did not. Why, to this date, is there only one known copy? It was obviously **not** intended for sale or it would have had a better cover, so who was it intended to be given away to? And why? The entire contents, in fact, were **recycled** (though not all **reprinted**). Clues are to be found in the publication itself and some facts are known from other sources.

M. C. "Charlie" Gaines may not have actually come up with the idea himself but he did publish the industry's first comic book in the format recognized today, a 1933 four-color giveaway with newspaper reprints called **Funnies on Parade**, which was soon followed by **Famous Funnies**, experimentally sold to the public for ten cents. A host of imitators began and a burgeoning industry was in force by the outbreak of World War II.

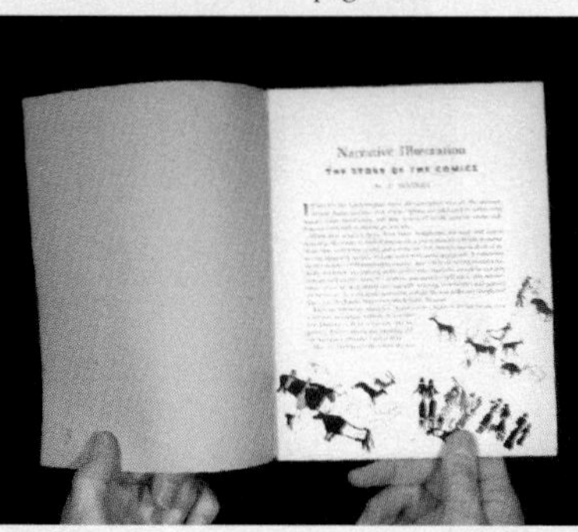
Illustrations accompanying M. C. Gaines' text on the history of comics trace back to prehistoric man's pictorial narratives.

It is well known that the first appearance of Siegel and Shuster's Superman in **Action Comics** #1 in 1938 really put comic book production into high gear (according to Gaines, there were twenty publishers in 1942 "putting out about 100 comics with a total sale of about 15,000,000" copies a month). What is less well known is that it was also M. C. Gaines who "discovered" Superman; more accurately, he was the first to **recognize** its potential and when Harry Donnenfeld of National Periodical Publications was looking for something new and sensational to head up his new **Action Comics** title, it was Gaines who suggested he contact Jerry and Joe about their caped superhero. Superman had been previously turned down by virtually every publisher in the business, including by Gaines himself (who, at the time, was only publishing reprints).

After the success of **Action Comics**, Gaines affiliated with Donnenfeld to expand the company's stable of new product under the All-American imprint, including Wonder Woman, The Flash, The Green Lantern and others.

E. C. historian, collector and friend Roger Hill provided notes from his files (that he says may have come from an interview he did with Gaines' son, William M. "Bill" Gaines publisher-to-be of **Mad Magazine**) indicating that in 1940 the elder Gaines was approached by a Sunday school teacher and author of juvenile pieces for church papers, Montgomery Mulford, to do a series of comic narratives on Biblical themes that he had either already written or wanted to do.

A deal was struck and, according to Hill, Mulford was paid ten dollars a page (a princely sum then) to write and essentially lay out the pages with authentic costumes, locale references, etc. He even received royalties on later reprints as the resulting **Picture Stories from the Bible** comic books ran their course.

Another Sunday school teacher, Don Cameron, a former Disney man, was hired to do the art (reference **Newsweek**, August 3, 1942). We have reason to believe that most or all of the Old Testament stories (published under the D. C. colophon in 1942 and 1943 in two 68-page and two 60-page comic books) were drawn by Cameron before the first one went to press! He may have begun his art as early as in 1939 or 1940, but surely no later than by fall of 1941. (Cameron's stint at Disney was brief. He signed on with the Studio on January 16, 1939 and left on September 30 of that year, having acquired the animation status of in-betweener.)

Before going to press, **Newsweek** confirms, "the comics got Catholic sanction and approval from an advisory board of prominent Protestants and Jews."

Early in 1942 Gaines/Donnenfeld put out the four-page giveaway that was tipped into **Narrative Illustration**. **The Minute Man Answers the Call** concludes with an appeal to "the men, women and children of America...(that by) working, fighting, sacrificing...liberty may live forever!" Gaines says it was produced to "help sell War Bonds and Stamps to young Americans," a choice of words that suggests it may have been mailed to subscribers of the D. C./A-A comics. This giveaway could vie to be considered the first pre-E. C. if one follows a certain chain of logic.

New readers should know that defining the beginnings of the E. C. "legend" is fuzzy business. The colophon first appeared in 1946 (and stood for Educational Comics, then Entertaining Comics), but its roots were earlier. **The Complete E. C. Checklist** by Fred von Bernewitz and Joe Vucenic (originally published in 1956, amazingly only ten years after the E. C. emblem first appeared!) boldly includes the National/All-American/D. C. comics that Gaines took with him when he sold out to Donnenfeld; that is, everything that **became** an E. C. or that had, in any way, an E. C. connection. Gaines copyrighted all the parts of **Narrative Illustration** in his own name and took them with him after the Donnenfeld split, so we believe **NI** and all its contents have legitimate, so-called E. C. roots.

Since the **Minute Man** giveaway may have been mailed out as early as in January of 1942 to comic book subscribers, maybe—someday—someone will turn up an issue of **Detective Comics** or **All American** that's still in its dated mailing envelope and—lo!—inside will be a neatly folded copy of **The Minute Man Answers the Call**!

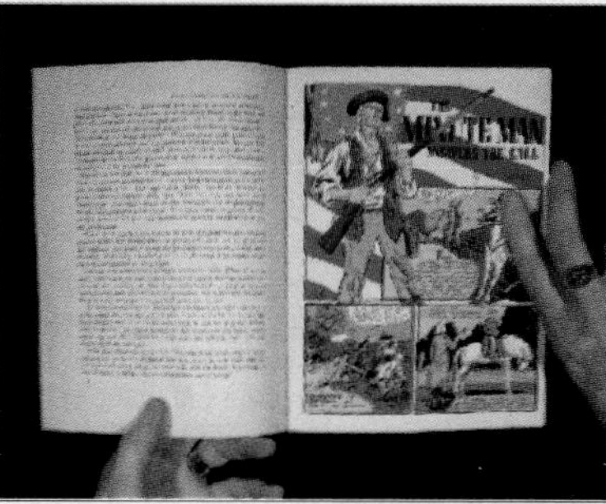

A four-page giveaway was glued in **Narrative Illustration** as the first of two comic inserts.

A mini-bio in **Narrative Illustration** mentions that M. C. Gaines was a former school principal, Army officer, advertising executive and "now President of All-American Comics, Inc." Considering his background and accomplishments and predilection for the "softer" comics he did on his own in the 1940s, it's safe to assume that Gaines was not only a patriot and a humanitarian, but a man with deep religious convictions.

He and Mulford had grander ideas concerning **Picture Stories from the Bible** than just putting out a series of comic books. Gaines wrote:

"Within the last several months an experiment has been made in the use of stories from the Bible, using the comic book colored continuity technique. A series of ten ran in a New England paper, and responses indicated such wide acceptance that a 10-cent, 64-page book, **Picture Stories from the Bible**, has lately gone on sale. One of these stories is inserted with this article."

Ten of these **Picture Stories** ran in a New England newspaper? That means that all or part of **Picture Stories from the Bible** #1 was reprint material! Sotheby's Consultant and E. C. historian/publisher of the famed **Squa Tront** fanzine, Jerry Weist, confirms that while he was with The Million Year Picnic in Boston, someone once called him up and said he had some of these Sunday section **Picture Stories**. Never having seen them, Weist confesses he had forgotten about the conversation until the appearance of **Narrative Illustration**. (This copy will be in the June, 1995 Sotheby's auction.) I have known Weist as a friend for over twenty-five years and I have a strong suspicion that he will know a lot more about these mysterious Sunday sections before this article even sees print!

Having always wondered why the Old Testament stories in the **Picture Stories from the Bible** comic books appeared in such a random order, I now believe I have reasoned out two explanations. First, greater variety could be achieved in issues 1-4 by mixing up the tales and second, by so doing, it made the Complete Old Testament Edition, in which everything was chronological, more desirable (even if you already had #'s 1-4) and, thus, it also became more **saleable**. It was published in December, 1943, contained 236 pages and sold initially for five times as much as the single issues (50¢, later upped to 65¢).

The complexity in analyzing **Narrative Illustration** is deepened by the **Picture Stories** insert and its variations. "The Story of Saul," is seven pages plus a title sheet numbered "10" with a bold, red-ink, all-caps credit line across the bottom that reads, "SUNDAY HERALD." That clue should make it easier for Hill or Weist or other researchers to find. We have part of the paper's name and we are sure the Sunday dates in question are most likely to have run during a two-and-a-half-month window between February and May, 1942.

The **Picture Stories** newspaper inserts must have all been done as eight-pagers, seven for each story plus a title. Most of the Old Testament could have been published in a twenty-six week run, and that may have been their plan. The title page proudly proclaims, "For the first time in newspaper history, stories from the Bible are pictured in colored continuity." A large drawing of an opened Bible adorns the title page of #10, along with an interior illustration and the name of the story. To the right side of the page are the words, "Copyright 1942 by M. C. Gaines" printed in red.

What is especially unusual about this insert is that it is obviously **not** an exact duplicate of what ran in either the comic book or in the **Herald**! While the stories must have appeared comic book size in the **Herald**, using the same color plates as printed for the insert, there are several odd differences.

For one, the words, "Copyrighted 1942 by M. C. Gaines, 225 Lafayette St., N. Y. C." appear as a **second** notice in black ink in the lower margin of the title page. It's extremely unlikely this double identification appeared in the **Herald** continuities. So why the duplication in **NI**?

A seven-page **Picture Stories from the Bible** insert has an odd title page added with two copyright notices, a redundant page identification at the top and a clue as to the Sunday **Herald**, a yet-to-be-identified New England newspaper.

Two, the words "THIS IS PAGE 1" appear in the top margin of the first page. Why? One would assume even the youngest reader could figure out that the title was page one, should he care.

Three, printed vertically in light blue ink on the inside gutter between pages four and five is the numeral three in a circle with the words, "Insert pins on this inside fold as indicated." There is a hyphenated fold-line drawn right down the centerfold crease. **What the**? (I ask in comic book parlance.)

Four, printed vertically along the inside margin of page eight, with a dotted (hyphenated) light blue line are the words, "'A' ② Fold along this dotted line ③ insert pins on inside fold".

To explain **all** of the reasoning behind the conclusions I've reached would take too long, some of my thinking based on a knowledge of both the publishing and the printing businesses. So let me leap to the bottom lines, to what I think really happened and why.

Again, I believe Gaines was a religious man. He badly wanted the Bible story continuities to be a success. The **Newsweek** article says that before the **Picture Stories** comic book debuted, "the colored-comic Bible idea was tested on 12- and 13-year olds." This sounds to me as though one or more of the Sunday **Herald** printings were taken to Mulford and Cameron's Sunday school classes. And, the article continues, "should the idea take hold, they will next do the New Testament and eventually may try to sell the books direct to Sunday schools as supplemental Bible teaching."

So we **know** that Gaines was highly motivated. I believe he was gilding the lily a little, though, when he spoke of "responses (that) indicated such wide acceptance." Experience has taught me that responses to publications can be deceptive: extreme enthusiasm may come from a vocal minority and sound louder than the true general acceptance. In hindsight, we also know that religious comics never have had the widespread favor many would like to see. Even **Newsweek's** article pointedly noted the candor of a 12-year-old who confessed "that if he had only one dime to spend he would buy a rip-roaring, non-biblical comic," foregoing **Picture Stories from the Bible**.

If the Sunday **Herald** experiment had been a solid success, would it not have been continued beyond the first ten weeks? I think so. Having decided to go ahead with the newsstand comic book idea—although cautiously limiting the first issue's print run to only 10,000 copies!—Gaines was still looking around for a way to pursue the Sunday newspaper format. I believe he may have reasoned (remember, he was a former advertising executive) that he had to make a strong presentation vehicle to get the attention of newspaper editors all over the country. Just to do a simple mailer risked having busy people toss them in wastebaskets!

Then: **inspiration**!

In the original article Gaines had written

for **Print**, the graphic arts quarterly journal, he told of the history of narrative illustration, dating examples back to caveman times and continuing forward to the European artisans in the 16th and 19th centuries who evolved line sketches as a way "to convey an idea and tell a story."

He continued, "this story has been documented in an exhibition by the American Institute of Graphic Arts, now touring the country. Assembled under the direction of Miss Jessie Gillespie Willing, Program Chairman (not chairperson in those days) of the Institute, the exhibition sets forth for the first time a history of narrative art from the first recorded picture-story to the comic book of the twentieth century."

That's it! **Narrative Illustration**—article **and** booklet—were done to promote this very important exhibition. The show had the support of the intelligentsia and included board members as diverse as Gerald McDonald of the New York Public Library, who was an advisory in charge of the ancient section of the exhibit.

Gaines' script suggests that the exhibit must have been phenomenal. A question that surfaces when I've talked about this exhibit to old-time collectors is why they have never heard of it! Perhaps it **is** well known and documented in some circles and we are expressing our ignorance by not knowing about it, but as long as we're sticking our collective necks out, I'll also ask, did the exhibit produce a catalog? If so, none of us have seen it, either.

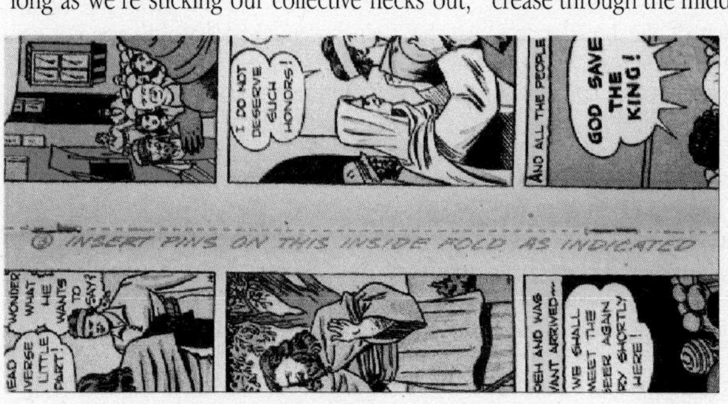

Bindery instructions in the centerfold suggest a major difference between the Sunday **Herald's** comic sections and the **Narrative Illustration** insert. The former's pages would have more likely been glued—rather than stapled—to save an unnecessary expense.

It's not unlikely to think that Gaines may have produced **Narrative Illustration** to be given away at the exhibits, whether or not with another "official" catalog. To have done that would have given the booklet a **reason** for being done that would have carried great weight as a presentation and, by extension, added extra credibility to **Picture Stories from the Bible**. His motivations may have been such he volunteered to produce the booklet for them at cost, or may have paid for it himself. We do know that he added a little text to what had run in the **Print** article to describe the inserts and tell of their origins. He may, in fact, have convinced the directors of the exhibit that it would spice up the booklet if he were to bind in these two special items, a couple of color comics. Logic counters that as President of All-American he could have come up with something featuring Wonder Woman or Hawkman, or even Superman or Batman. Though he paid tribute to all these characters in **NI**, he instead chose as examples to represent the industry a World War II War Bonds and Stamps giveaway and an unproven **Pictures Stories from the Bible** insert! Interesting. But put yourself in the Institute's position: how were you going to argue with someone like M. C. Gaines? To challenge either choice might have hinted at a lack of patriotism or of being mildly non-religious, if not sacrilegious.

Choosing the giveaway was a no-brainer, since Gaines probably had full boxes left over from the comic subscription mailings. But they had all been folded in half to insert in the mailing envelopes! The copy of the **Minute Man** propaganda piece in **Narrative Illustration** lies open, full-sized and flat (as glued in), but the crease through the middle still shows...meaning that all copies had to be opened by hand before binding them in! Translation: higher cost or fewer copies, take your choice.

Still, it was the **Picture Stories from the Bible** insert that he **really** wanted everyone to see. And he may have planned to take a few hundred extra copies—with permission, of course—to mail out to newspapers all over the country. Now here was a booklet editors wouldn't trash! As every good advertising executive knows, the number one goal of any mailer is to get it **read**. With or without a cover letter (if he did such a mailing), most recipients probably did read it. But, unfortunately, it's almost a certainty that it resulted in no more newspapers willing to book the Sunday supplements. If other papers had subscribed, I'm sure **some** would have surfaced in the collector's market.

In the meantime, what city boasted

Gaines' Sunday **Herald**? After talking to Weist, I called the **New Britain Herald**, from near Hartford, Connecticut, but they don't publish a Sunday edition. Then I called the **Boston Herald** and that paper's librarian said he thought their paper would be highly unlikely. Their presses would not have been able to have printed an insert in that type of color at that time and it would have had to have been jobbed out or preprinted elsewhere.

So let's do some more speculating.

Our unknown Sunday **Herald** canceled the run of **Picture Stories** continuities or failed to renew; in either case, it was to stop with the printing of #10. The comic book was already in the works when the idea of the booklet was born. It would be **much** too expensive to go to press with an eight-page, four-color comic just to stick into a giveaway unless the cost could be brought down enough. How, then, might that have been accomplished? To do a re-paginated overrun from the soon-to-be-released **Picture Stories from the Bible** #1 would have made no sense. Whoever the printer was, however, whether the newspaper or the same printer who did the comic books, maybe a deal was made. Whatever.

More binding and staple inserts appear in the gutter margin of the last comic page.

The printer agrees to do an overrun of the #10 continuity—"Saul"—using the same color plates. Everything that was to be in the newspaper section would also have to appear on the inserts, including the words, "SUNDAY HERALD," but that would be explained away in the article, no problem. Anything that Gaines **added** was okay because **NI** could be printed and then the extras stripped out or with a single plate change the printer could then continue for the regular newspaper run. Perfect!

Two problems remained. He didn't have his address on the insert anywhere and the people who were going to be doing the binding (maybe the printer, maybe not) had never worked with him before doing such a peculiar type of job. How could he be **absolutely sure** they wouldn't make some mistake and ruin the print run?

The simple solution to the first problem was just to add his name and address in black ink at the bottom of page one. A little redundant, perhaps, but no matter. The second problem required some careful consideration. The best way to make sure they didn't goof up the binding and stapling was to put the instructions right on the booklet itself, printed in a light blue so as to not be as noticeable to readers of **Narrative Illustration**. Not many people would see it, anyway, and probably wouldn't care if they did. After all, **NI** was just a giveaway!

So, in summation, the deal with the printer was that he would add this extra stuff—all in one color ink, black or light blue—and the printer would then run Gaines' copies first, whether a few hundred or a few thousand. When these "extras" were removed, the regular run progressed.

Now the booklet that Gaines wanted badly to do was not going to be prohibitively expensive. That problem was solved. But, sad to say for collectors today, the size of the print run or to whom it was given away, has dictated that few copies survive (one is known as this edition of the Guide goes to press).

One other question has been bugging me, too, as an aside. Why was "The Story of Saul, the First King of Israel," chosen as the **tenth** Sunday continuity? Perhaps it was for no reason, but I can think of a possibility.

If we are correct and all of the Old Testament stories were done in advance, I would think the natural inclination would have been to have published the stories in chronological order rather than arbitrarily as they came out in the comic books. Mixing them up in the comics made sense, since that added variety to the mix in each issue. But in the newspapers, one story would run each week, so why not do them in correct order? In any case, why was "Saul" tenth in the Sunday **Herald**?

"Saul" was the **sixth** seven-pager slated in the yet-to-run **Picture Stories from the Bible** #1 and was only the **second** seven-pager in **PS** #1 that was **not** a two-parter. Follow me so far? They planned to begin **PS** #1 with "Noah," a seven-pager. Following that, the comic was to have "Joseph" and "Moses," each fourteen pages in length, broken into two parts. Then came "Saul" in **PS** #1.

I think Gaines and Mulford might have concluded that continued newspaper stories (ones that took **two** Sundays to read) would not be a good idea, at least for the initial **Herald** trial run. Two-parters would reduce the number of stories that could be given to readers in ten weeks. So, why not start at the beginning with "Creation" in the Sundays and run only **complete** seven-page tales, skipping for the moment the longer stories? Where would that put "Saul," if my reasoning is correct? Well, "Saul," it turns out, is only the **eighth** short story in the Old Testament chronology. Close, but no cigar!

However...just suppose **one** two-parter was thrown into the mix—and only one—for whatever reason, perhaps to give a glimpse into future continuities, should the series continue. The first chronological long story was "Abraham," but it was written and drawn in three parts. Too long. Next came "Joseph." Fourteen pages, in two parts. Fine.

So, at the risk of additional embarrassment if I'm wrong (and there's a good chance this time we'll find out for sure), I'm going to **predict** the published sequence of the ten sections that appeared in the Sunday **Herald**, should they be unearthed (maybe it won't be all **that** embarrassing, because how many people will read this article anyway?). My predictions:

(1) "Creation," (2) "Noah," (3) "Jacob," (4) "Joseph," Part I, (5) "Joseph," Part II, (6) "Deborah," (7) "Samson," (8) "Ruth," (9) "Samuel," and (10) "Saul!" Neat as a bug in a rug, as they say.

Please, please let it not be another arbitrary mix!

Afterthoughts

I'd like to thank Bill Pearson, who dug deep into his trove of comics to find this copy of **Narrative Illustration**. He continues to amaze me with the things he's squirreled away (having been in the hobby a few years less than God). I confess he showed it to me for the first time twenty years ago, but I didn't have the eyes then to appreciate what I was seeing.

As Gladstone's publisher of the current Walt Disney traditional character comics, I couldn't help but note with interest the circulation figures Gaines quoted in **Narrative Illustration**. He said the industry put out about 100 comic books with total monthly sales of about fifteen million. (**Newsweek** claimed the number of books out at the time was 135.) The mini-bio on Gaines attributed the Superman-DC group as providing "one third of the entire monthly comic book circulation," or about five million copies sold per month. At that particular time the circulation figures of **Walt Disney's Comics & Stories** were increasing at the rate of about 100,000 every month and had reached 1,700,000 by the end of '42. The sell-through percentages were very high in those days and complete sellouts were not uncommon. The Dell Disney's still had an average of an 85% sell through ten years later. The conclusion, then, is that **Comics & Stories** alone accounted for about 10% of all the comics sold in the U.S. in 1942!

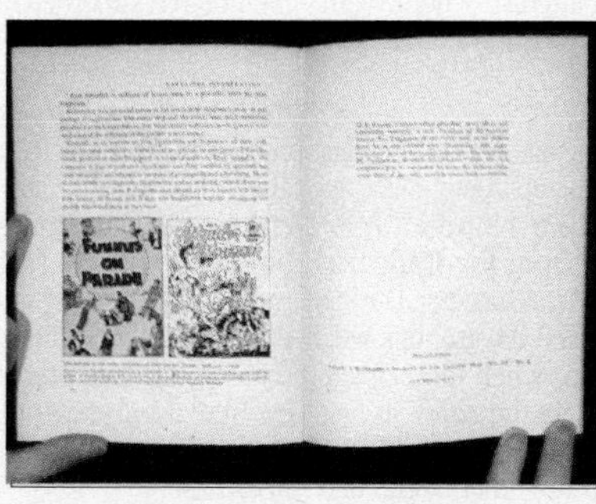

Gaines captioned his last two illustrations: "The earliest of the comic magazines in their present format—and a newcomer." In 1942 All-American Comics, Inc., had just released the first issue of **Wonder Woman**.

All the history books and their hoopla about how much **Superman** sold and the famous counter that **Captain Marvel** was the **only** title to outsell **Superman**, when it had peaked out at two million a month makes me suspect that Western Publishing's figures were ignored, as they had an independent distribution. It's something like the Top 10 television shows that are touted weekly in the press: they ignore syndication. There is no question whatsoever that **Walt Disney's Comics & Stories** is the best-selling comic book of all time, having climbed in the 1950s to between four and five million, month in and month out! The ledger copies I have from Western during the 1940s indicate so much volume on all titles they did (virtually nothing printed in quantities fewer than a half million copies) that the 15,000,000 a month figure touted by Gaines should have catapulted Dell/Western above D.C. Doesn't sound to me like there was room enough for **everyone**, according to his figures.

I got the impression from reading Gaines'

text in **Narrative Illustration** that the exhibition put on by the American Institute of Graphic Arts began with a viewing at the National Arts Club in New York before going on tour. In speaking of the cartoonists whose art was in the show, Gaines said Milton Caniff's strip, **Terry and the Pirates** "is rapidly becoming one of America's top favorites...(It) was voted the favorite by visitors" who saw it at the N.A.C. exhibit.

Tidbits from **NI**: one of the earliest comic characters–widely ignored today as politically incorrect–was **Black Berries** with "colored comic characters, (drawn for) the **World**, in 1897." ...Winsor McCay's **Dreams of a Rarebit Fiend** was the first daily strip "to go across the top of the page," just after the turn of the century! ...Dick Outcault's **Buster Brown** was the first comics "character to inspire clothes-trends." ...Cliff Sterrett's **Polly and Her Pals**, according to Gaines, was the "first girl strip." ...Clare Briggs, he added, "was the first outstanding artist of the human-interest school, with **When a Feller Needs a Friend**." Could this be a new genre?

Readers shouldn't mistakenly get the idea that because M. C. Gaines apparently failed to get newspapers to subscribe to his weekly color inserts of **Picture Stories from the Bible** that the comic books were not a success. During 1942-44 the industry doubled its size, enjoying monthly sales of 30 million. When the 52-page **PSFTB** New Testament #1 hit the stands its first printing was 450,000 copies! **Newsweek** reported in a 1944 follow-up story that Gaines had marketed more than 1,000,000 **Picture Stories** comics since the "risky" debut of 10,000 printed of the first issue in '42. And, the fully compiled, large-size Old Testament edition sold a quarter million more! Interestingly, when 52-page reprints were eventually marketed under the E. C. colophon, the stories were at last presented in chronological order. The project was abandoned after two issues, less than half complete. (#1 was forced to end with a cliffhanger, leaving "The Story of Joseph," Part II, to lead off the second issue!)

Gaines triumphed despite initial howls of complaint. **Newsweek** reported that "at first, shocked adults stigmatized them as garish, offensive, sacrilegious. Those 'horrid balloon things that come out of speakers' mouths,' they protested, should never be allowed to vulgarize scriptural characters." But he quickly prevailed, even though not in the long term. One minister said **Picture Stories** was the "only book in the church library children asked to take home to read." Since "thousands" of churches ordered them in the early '40s, one wonders why they stopped, assuming they'd want to replace ragged, worn out or lost copies. (Reorders from **anyone** has always been the bane of this business, grumbles the present-day publisher.)

Final comment: Gaines must have taken great satisfaction when he distributed $3,500 in profits to the ten denominations that were on his advisory council!

I've often wondered what M. C. Gaines would have thought about what his son, Bill, did with the Entertaining Comics line of comic books he inherited upon the elder's death in 1947. I suspect he would not have approved. There's no documentation I am aware of that has explained the reasons why father, Charlie, sold out his affiliated interest in All-American Comics, Inc., an offshoot of the Superman-DC group. Gaines' association with Harry Donnenfeld was certainly timely; some of the most memorable superhero titles were begun while they worked together.

Regardless what M. C. Gaines might have thought about the shock, crime and horror comics his son was to launch scarcely two years after the unfortunate boating accident that claimed the father's life, no blame can be placed on Bill's decisions. Falling sales will result in a publishing company's demise unless it bends to the times, and nothing that the younger Gaines did was tackled precipitously. Things sort of evolved...were experimented with—and when found successful—only then were they pursued in earnest.

Whether documented or not, M. C. Gaines' decisions to part company with Donnenfeld were probably at least partially due to what he may have determined as a disturbing trend toward violence. His own pre-trend E. C.'s certainly reflect a disdain for costumed crime fighters.

The timing of his death was almost storybook: the legendary founder dies just as his empire is crumbling and he has done all he can do...some things immensely successful, others abject failures. The reluctant son is thrown into the maelstrom and is unwilling to see his father's domain fall; he ventures into arenas where no one has gone before and in the process—perhaps even against his inclination—eclipses the fame of his father. That's heady stuff.

Charlie and Bill: we salute you both!

Choke!...Gasp!...Good lord!...Argh!... Spa fon!...Squa tront!...Eh...Eh...Eh...Eh...

A Century Of Comics

by Pat S. Calhoun

From the Stone Age to the Comics Page

Ever since the Stone Age, when drawings were made on the walls of caves, people have communicated with visual images. In ancient Egypt hieroglyphics were used as "captions" on paintings, thus combining the narrative and pictorial modes. The Greek, Roman, and Norse mythologies (primordial "superhero" stories) all used illustration to augment the epic tales of mortals and monsters. The next giant step forward was the technological revolution— specifically the printing press. As newspapers began to proliferate in Europe, the cartoon was delivered unto the masses. In America, in 1895, the New York World began a series of large panels by R. F. Outcault that took place in a wrong-side-of-the-tracks neighborhood called Hogan's Alley. Prominent in the crowd of street folk was a bald-headed boy dressed in a long nightgown. In 1896 the addition of color— yellow ink— brought all into focus by dyeing the nightshirt of Outcault's youngster. Thus was born the first great comics character, the Yellow Kid.

Color was not the only innovation the Kid pioneered. Soon the panel evolved into a strip, and the Kid began speaking— with the dialogue drawn on his shirt. A famous strip from October 1896 has a golf gag that revolves around repartee between the Kid and a parrot. That such verbal wit could reside within a comic strip came as a revelation. One of the staples of vaudeville was rapid fire dialogue between two parties, and once Outcault demonstrated the possibilities of such exchanges in strip form, the funnies got a lot funnier.

The Yellow Kid was published by William Randolph Hearst, whose newspapers were often criticized for sensationalism. Hearst's inflamma-

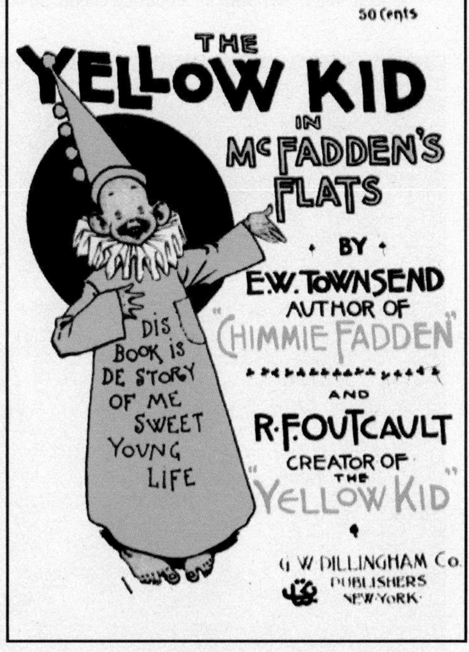

The Yellow Kid courtesy of the Bob Cook Collection.

tory rhetoric in the 1890s was a factor in starting the Spanish-American War. The Kid's nightshirt was what led to the Hearst stance being labeled "yellow journalism." And indeed, for all its innovation, the Yellow Kid was definitely representative of low-brow humor— vulgar, slapstick, and utterly delicious. Outcault went on to create another character, this time an upper-class kid, Buster Brown, who debuted in 1902. Buster Brown was one of the first strips to be reprinted in hard cover, by Cupples and Leon starting in 1906.

Rudolph Dirks began the Katzenjammer Kids in 1897, a masterfully mirthful chronicling of the war between parents and children. In 1914 Dirks left Hearst, and after a legal battle the strip split into two versions. Hearst assigned a new artist to the Katzenjammer Kids, and Dirks went over to the Pulitzer chain, where his version continued as Hans and Fritz (later known as The Captain and the Kids). In the 1940s Dirks' son John took over The Captain and the Kids, and the strip continues to amuse readers across the world.

In 1905 one of the most visually arresting and imaginative strips was begun, Windsor McCay's immortal Little Nemo in Slumberland. The young hero would undergo fantastic and exquisitely detailed adventures that would always reveal themselves as dreams in the last panel. Jim Steranko in his History of the Comics credits McCay as being the "first to utilize color for pure psychological effect." This translates into the use of color and bizarre perspectives as an almost psychedelic stimulation of the "sense of wonder." McCay also gained fame as an early animator— his Gertie the Dinosaur was one of the first screen cartoon characters.

In California, in 1907, the San Francisco Chronicle's sports cartoonist, Bud Fisher, started a strip called A. Mutt. Mutt's passion in life was playing the ponies, and the strip's schtick was jocular horse-racing tips. The strip was immediately successful, and Hearst, who published the Chronicle's rival, the Examiner, lured Fisher into his camp with a hefty raise in salary. This strip, one of the first to appear daily, grew into the enduring classic Mutt and Jeff.

Hairbreadth Harry, Happy Hooligan, more and more characters came to expand narrative potential. George Herriman's Krazy Kat began in 1910 and offered a more sophisticated form of humor— urbane, oblique, and surreal. On January 31, 1912 Hearst introduced the first ongoing daily comics page in the New York Journal, and other publishers were quick to see that such a popular page would sell papers. Many fine strips began during the 'teens: George McManus' Bringing Up Father— a wry look at matrimony and family life, E. C. Segar's Thimble Theater— which would go on to introduce Popeye in 1929, Cliff Sterrett's Polly and her Pals— which was ostensibly a "pretty girl" strip but often emerged as a beautiful exercise in abstract art, and Frank King's Gasoline Alley— where characters got a year older every year in a strip that has survived to this day. (McManus deserves special mention for his involvement in 1922 with a publishing venture, Comic Monthly, that was a prototype "comic book".)

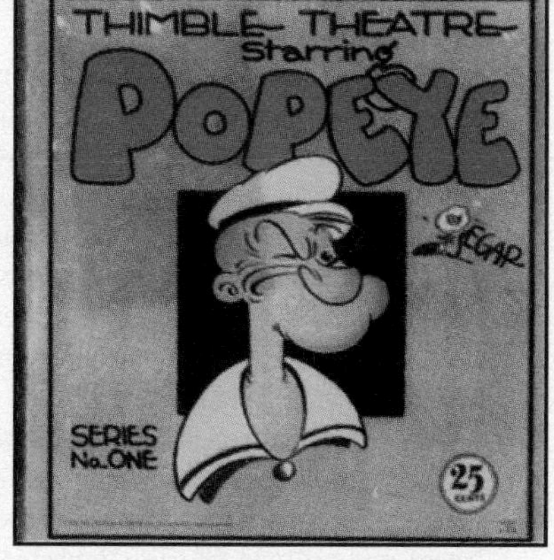

Adventure Every Day

1924 introduced Little Orphan Annie by Harold Gray, and seventy years later she is still thrilling readers every day. Roy Crane's Wash Tubbs also began in 1924, but it was the debut of Captain Easy in the strip in 1928 that gave comics its first great adventure character. In 1933 Easy got his own Sunday page, and the soldier-of-fortune fought his way through exotic locales that were depicted with superb inventiveness of layout and design.

The adventure strip really came into its own in 1929. January 7, 1929 marked the beginning of two strips, both derived from characters who had appeared in the pulps, who stood at either end of the spectrum of excitement. Tarzan of the Apes represented man in his primitive state, "unaccommodated," with only his strength, skill, and cunning to help him survive in the jungle. And Buck Rogers showed future man, a game-player in the technological wonderland of the 25th century- full of rocket-ships and ray-guns. Tarzan had a lot of momentum going for him from a whole string of novels by Edgar Rice Burroughs, and the strip was drawn by a man who became one of the true kings of adventure art— Hal Foster. Buck Rogers, whose first appearances were in *Amazing Stories*, rode the wave of science fiction, the popular genre that helped prepare the industrial age for the changes that were coming thick and fast. Escape literature would be in great demand in the next decade- for 1929 was also the year that the Depression started.

Ham Fisher's hero, boxer Joe Palooka, started scrapping in 1929 as well. Although Fisher's art wasn't outstanding, what really made this strip was the humanity. Palooka combined common sense with a respectful attitude, and the strip did a lot to upgrade the image of boxing as a sport. Joe was

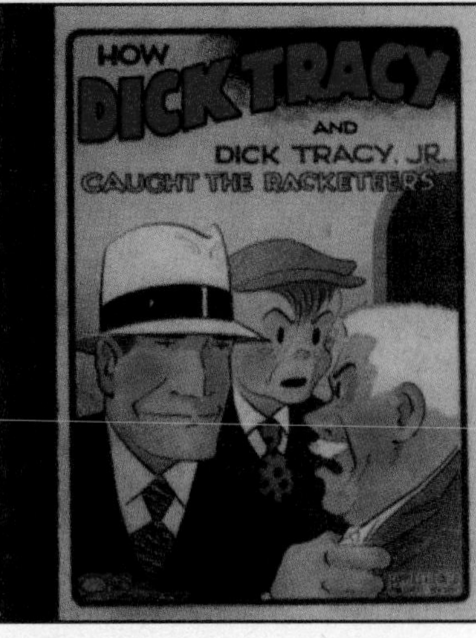

also an able campaigner for democracy and freedom during World War II.

In 1930, the classic domestic household strip began, Chic Young's Blondie. Here, "normal" American lives were shown as treasure troves of humor, and Dagwood Bumstead became an "Everyman", whose chief goals in life were a good sandwich and a nap. Also that year Walt Disney entered the comic strip business, with adventures of his big-screen superstar Mickey Mouse. The strip soon fell into the capable hands of Floyd Gottfredson, who went on to establish many of the conventions of what would come to be known as "funny animal" comics. Additionally, as strip historian Bill Blackbeard has pointed out, Mickey Mouse was also one of the great adventure strips. Another animal character who moved from cartoons to comics was Otto Messmer's Felix the Cat.

1931 was another milestone year. The first and foremost of the comic strip crime-busters burst onto the scene amidst the roar of machine guns- Chester Gould's Dick Tracy. Gould upped the ante with a realistic violence that went far beyond anything previous. People died, with bullet holes between their eyes! It was grim but glorious. As the years went on Gould proved himself to be a magnificent storyteller. Tracy survived ferocious beatings and ghastly death traps, and always, with dogged determination, triumphed in the end. This narrative verve more than made up for Gould's two-dimensional art style. The rogue's gallery of villains that Tracy faced (Itchy, the Brow, Fly-Face, the Mole, Influence, Pruneface, etc) prefigured the kind of over-the-top adversaries that the comic book super heroes would battle against.

1934 debuted three immortal strips. Comic genius Al Capp unleashed his hillbilly hero, Li'l Abner. The ultimate space-adventure strip, Flash Gordon, was written and drawn by Alex Raymond. Flash became the pinnacle of high romantic fantasy. Intricate rendering combined with a heroic vision of human existence, and the finely "feathered" forms of Flash and his lovely companion Dale Arden remain as unsurpassed archetypes. Serious storytelling received a whole new handbook of techniques with Milt Caniff's Terry and the Pirates. Inspired by his friend Noel Sickle's aviator strip, Scorchy Smith, Caniff made contributions both in drawing style and narrative that would influence countless artists. Visual shorthand was accomplished with no compromising of quality, and the stories brought a new respect for the graphic medium.

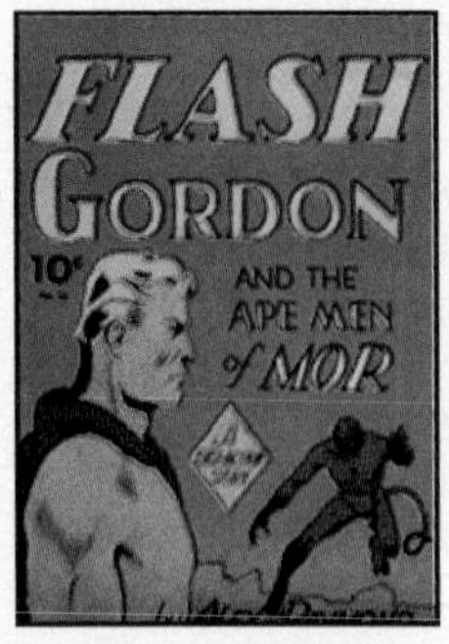

The Phantom, by Lee Falk and Ray Moore, started in 1936 and further advanced the costumed hero concept that would become so integral to the success of the comic book industry. Also in 1936 Hal Foster surrendered the Tarzan strip to another artist— Burne Hogarth. The jungle world and its loincloth-clad hero was the perfect place for Hogarth's mastery of dynamic anatomy. This was action art that leapt off the page, and in the physical combat scenes every sinew could be seen strained to the utmost. In 1937 Foster started his own strip, Prince Valiant. This medieval epic ranks as one of comics' greatest creations, and Foster's art perfectly combined realism and fantasy.

Enter the Comic Book

1937 was also the year that many Sunday pages began to shrink their format (to accommodate more advertising) and in many ways marks the beginning of the end of an artistic epoch. However, this was also when the comic book was in its apprentice stage, and here would be found a "canvas" that would open up new avenues for artistic expression. In 1933 the Eastern Color Printing Company produced some broadsides for the Philadelphia Ledger that contained Sunday pages reduced to half-size. Eastman's Harry Wildenberg came up with the idea of printing pages that size side by side on a page and folding them in half to make a booklet. This was the birth of the modern comic book. This first book made in this format was *Funnies on Parade*, published in Spring 1933. This comic reprinted popular Sunday pages, and salesman Max Gaines talked Proctor and Gamble into buying it for a promotional giveaway.

Eastern produced a second promotional comic in 1933, *Famous Funnies: A Carnival of Comics*. Gaines, on a hunch, took some copies and pasted 10¢ stickers on them, and took them to local newsstands. They sold out over the first weekend!

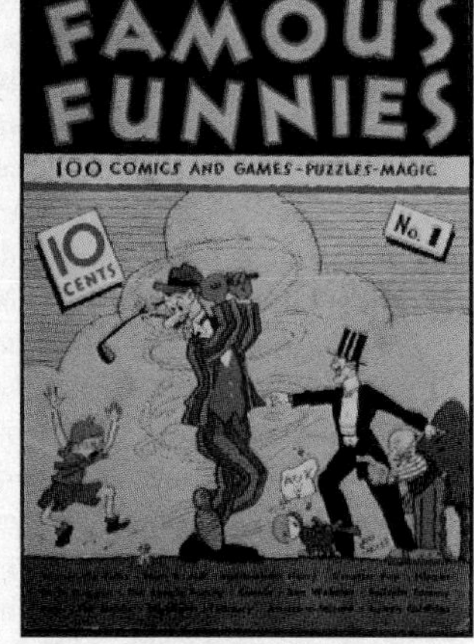

Convinced of the comic book's potential for newsstand sales, Eastern approached Dell, who had published a tabloid-size original material comic magazine (The Funnies) in 1929. Dell published *Famous Funnies* (series 1) in 1934, but remembering The Funnies' failure, distributed it only to department stores. Dell backed out after the first issue, and Eastern decided to go it on their own. *Famous Funnies #1* (series 2) was cover-dated July 1934, the first regular format monthly comic magazine. Among those appearing in the first issue were Mutt and Jeff, Hairbreadth Harry, and Tailspin Tommy. The editor and production manager was Stephen Douglas. By issue #7 the venture was becoming noticeably profitable.

Pulp writer Major Malcolm Wheeler-Nicholson was paying attention to *Famous Funnies'* sales figures and decided to try publishing a comic filled with original material rather than reprints. One virtue of this idea was that the contents wouldn't be appearing at half the size they were meant for. The Major's first effort was *New Fun Comics #1* (Feb 1935). It was tabloid size with black-and-white interior pages. Sales were not

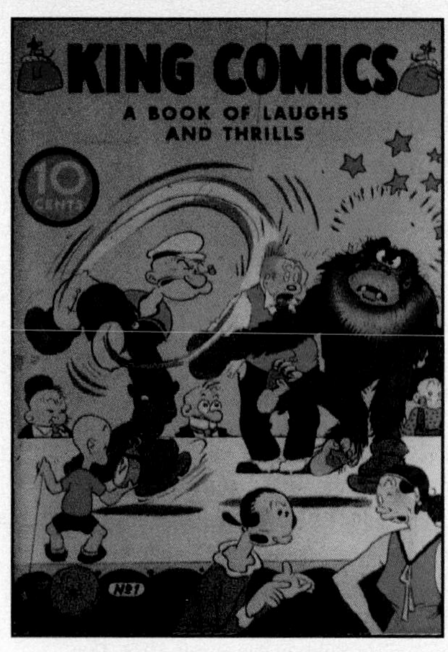

impressive, but the magazine struggled through six issues in 1935. In December Nicholson launched a companion magazine, *New Comics*, this time in "standard" comic book size (although with 80 mostly black-and-white pages).

By mid-1936 the Major's two titles (with *New Fun* renamed *More Fun*) had both evolved to standard size, with more color pages inside. Some of the features were developing as well. Federal Men by Jerry Siegel and Joe Shuster showcased a team that was obviously dedicated to this new medium. Siegel and Shuster also contributed Dr. Occult the Ghost Detective, whose look prefigured their upcoming Superman. 1936 also saw other publishers entering the field. Dell decided that comics might actually be worthwhile and began *Popular Comics #1* (Feb 1936) featuring strip reprints of Dick Tracy, Terry and the Pirates, and Gasoline Alley. David McKay started *King Comics #1* (Apr 1936) which reprinted King Features Syndicate stars Flash Gordon, Popeye, and Mandrake the Magician. United Features came out with *Tip Top Comics #1* (Apr 1936) reprinting their syndicated strips, most notably Tarzan and Li'l Abner.

In May 1936 the second company to offer original material comics debuted with *The Comics Magazine*. The publisher, Comic Magazine Company, was two of Major Nicholson's (ex-)employees, and strips included Siegel and Shuster's Dr. Occult renamed Dr. Mystic. With issue six their magazine's title changed to *Funny Pages;* this issue (Nov 1936) also introduced the Clock, comics first original masked hero. They added *Funny Picture Stories* and *Detective Picture Stories* in November 1936, the latter title laying claim to being the first "single theme" comic book title.

Dell started their second reprint title (borrowed from their 1929 failure), *The Funnies #1* (Oct 1936), with Alley Oop and Captain Easy headlining the features. Around this time Major Nicholson-still floundering financially— went into partnership with his printer, Harry Donenfield, in order to afford issuing a third title— *Detective Comics #1* (Mar 1937). The cover featured a glowering Oriental villain against a red background and a blurb stating "action-packed stories in color!" Speed Saunders, Ace Investigator, took the lead spot, with the capable Creig Flessel doing the drawing. At the back of the book Siegel and Shuster premiered Slam Bradley in a 13-page complete story- including a full-page splash panel. Not necessarily great literature— but very definitely comics, fast-moving and fun! David McKay released *Ace Comics #1* (Apr 1937), another reprint title, which offered Jungle Jim and the Phantom. Harry Chesler entered the comics publishing arena with a couple of over-sized original material titles, followed by a reprint title, *Feature Funnies #1* (Oct 1937), starring Joe Palooka and Mickey Finn.

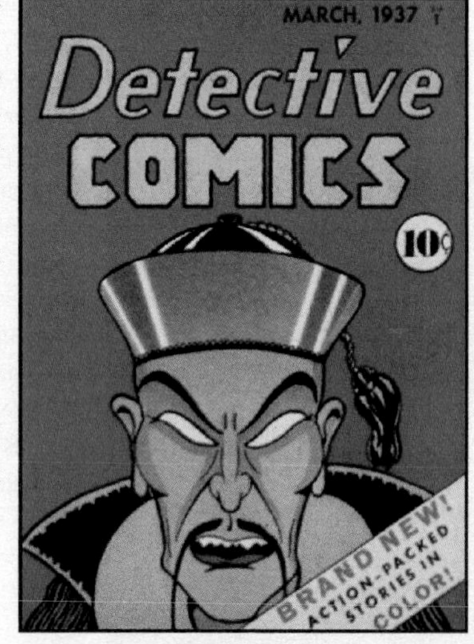

The Golden Age Begins

Even though reprint titles still far outnumbered original material comics, in 1938 something happened that changed the course of the industry. That something was Superman. Jerry Siegel and Joe Shuster had been trying to sell their super-creation as a newspaper strip for years. Young Sheldon Mayer saw the strip when they tried to peddle it to the McClure Syndicate. Mayer realized that this could be a character with great appeal. He convinced Max Gaines, who took the strip to National (now Donenfield's company as he had bought out Nicholson's interest). Editor Vincent Sullivan not only approved of the concept but had been looking in vain for a lead feature for a fourth title, to join *More Fun, Adventure* (formerly *New Comics*), and *Detective*. *Action* #1 (June 1938) started the Golden Age of comics.

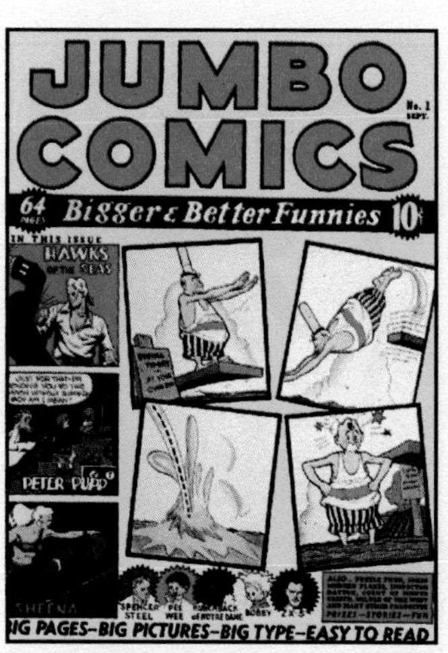

It took a few months to sink in, but newsstand surveys soon revealed that readers were clamoring for "the magazine with Superman in it." Within a year the formula would become clear: super heroes equalled super sales. Newcomer Centaur unveiled the Arrow in *Funny Pages* #10 (Sep 1938), a title they'd picked up from Chesler by way of the defunct Comic Magazine Co. And National contributed the Crimson Avenger, beginning in *Detective* #20 (Oct 1938), both, of course, a bit too soon to have been inspired by the Man of Steel. Fiction House entered the fray with *Jumbo Comics* #1 (Sept 1938), featuring Sheena, Queen of the Jungle— comics' first female superstar.

1939 was the year when publishers started trying to create costumed characters to rival Superman. In a move that assured their dominance of the field for decades, it was National who came up with another winner. Bob Kane had been asked (by editor Whitney Ellsworth) to try his hand at a super hero, and working with writer Bill Finger, the result was Batman. Premiering in *Detective* #27 (May 1939) the Caped Crusader was, in contrast to Superman, a human being of vulnerable flesh and blood. But as the origin (in *Detective* #33' Nov 1939) showed, Batman's strong suit was his determination. As a child he witnessed his parents being gunned down by a burglar and vowed to dedicate his life to fighting crime. It was this obsessive motivation that gave Batman an edge over his competition. Kane's art was cartoony but credible, capturing the darkness and violence of the urban underworld.

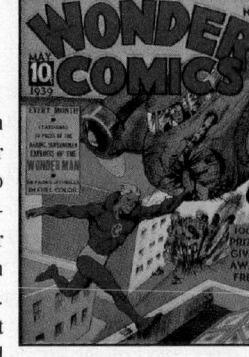

The Heroic Horde

Also dated May 1939 was *Wonder Comics* #1, the first book from a new publisher, Fox. Victor Fox had been an accountant for Donenfield, and the sales figures of National's titles inspired him to enter the comic book business. Wonder Man, the cover and lead feature of Fox's book, was wrought in Superman's image, with super strength, the ability to fly, and a colorful costume. So obviously so, in fact, that National filed a lawsuit for copyright infringement and won.

Wonder Comics #2 appeared without Wonder Man. Fox remained undaunted and with a title change to *Wonderworld Comics* #3 (July 1939) premiered the Flame, a hero armed with a flame gun, drawn by one of the best Golden Age craftsmen, Lou Fine. This was followed by *Mystery Men Comics* #1 (Aug 1939) debuting Fox's most successful super hero, the Blue Beetle. With a costume of close-fitting chain mail and a secret vitamin drink to boost his strength, Blue Beetle waged war on evildoers.

Centaur also became a spawning ground for super heroes. The Fantom of the Fair entered *Amazing Mystery Funnies* in July, the same month the Masked Marvel started in *Keen Detective Funnies*. The star of the Centaur line, Amazing Man, debuted in his own title with issue #5 (Aug 1939), created by the imaginative Bill Everett. Flanking A-Man were a host of second-bananas, including Minimidget and the Iron Skull.

National released *Superman* #1 that summer, a blockbuster that finalized the argument of original material versus newspaper reprints. They added Sandman to *Adventure* in #40 (July 1939), a gas-gun gas-mask knock-off of radio's Green Hornet. *Marvel Comics* #1 (Nov 1939), the first comic from pulp publisher Martin Goodman, featured the one-two punch of Bill Everett's Sub-Mariner and Carl Burgos' Human Torch. Goodman's company, Timely, would become one of the three biggest super hero factories. MLJ and Lev Gleason also started up in late 1939, with titles that would soon house several important heroes. Quality Comics, which had inherited *Feature Funnies* (renamed *Feature Comics*) from Chesler, introduced their first hero, Doll Man, in #27 (Dec 1939).

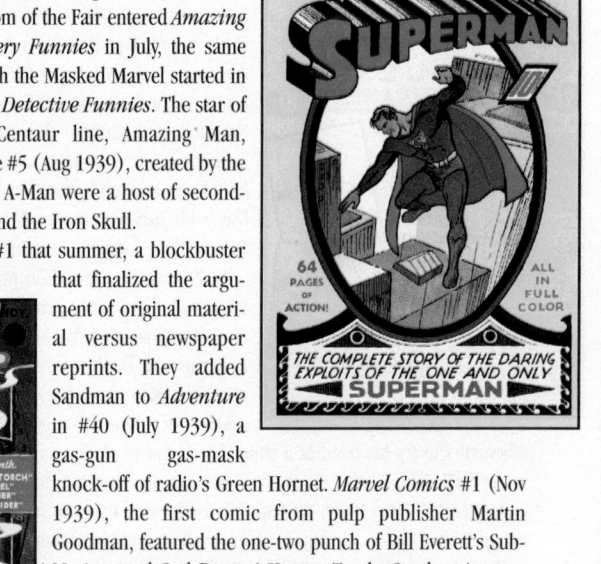

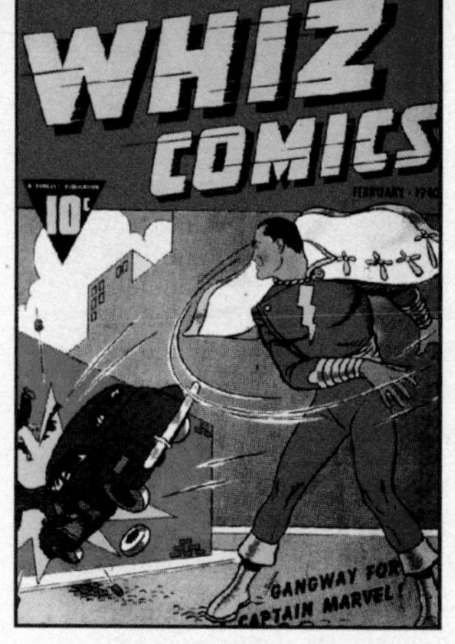

The third most important costumed character publisher, Fawcett, led off with *Whiz* #2 (Feb 1940), which featured a hero that would soon outsell even Superman. Captain Marvel was the creation of writer Bill Parker and artist C. C. Beck. Rather than the science that supplied the origins of Superman, Blue Beetle, Human Torch, and many others, Captain Marvel was a boy, Billy Batson, who was told a magic word by an old wizard. Upon uttering "Shazam," Billy changed to Captain Marvel, with the requisite powers of strength and flight. As befitted the fairy tale origin, Captain Marvel was more whimsical than his contemporaries, at times almost a satire on the superhero genre.

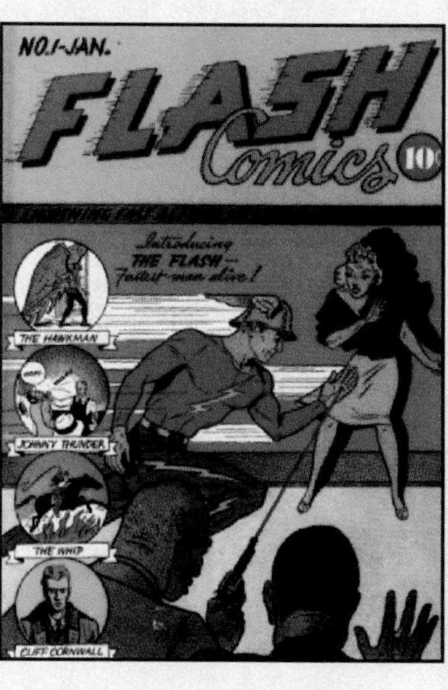

National added two more superstars to their lineup, Hawkman and the Flash, in *Flash* #1 (Jan 1940). After the first few issues the Hawkman strip was assigned to Sheldon Moldoff, and the result was some of the most elegant art of the era. National started another trend in *Detective* #38 (Apr 1940) by giving Batman a boy partner, Robin. MLJ's *Pep Comics* #1 (Jan 1940) introduced the Shield, the first red-white-and-blue hero. Month by month new publishers climbed onto the bandwagon, Better, Harvey, Prize, Columbia, Ace, and Novelty Press all were underway by mid-1940. Some of the more prolific creators were churning out heroes for three or more companies at a time: Will Eisner worked for Fox, Quality, and Fiction House, Joe Simon's characters appeared in Fox, Timely and Novelty Press publications, and Bill Everett, already cited for Centaur and Timely, also produced for Novelty and Eastern Color. In June 1940 Eisner also struck out on his own with his greatest creation, the Spirit, which appeared as the lead feature in a syndicated newspaper Sunday supplement, and was later reprinted by Quality.

After National (now known as DC- -from *Detective Comics*) installed Green Lantern in *All American* #16 (July 1940) they had enough heroes to launch another innovation. *All Star Comics* #1 (Sum 1940) collected the stars from several of the monthlies, and by issue #3 had them grouped together as a crime-fighting team, the Justice Society of America. Gardner Fox wrote a series of full-length JSA adventures, admirably juggling the assorted heroes. Fiction House got an early corner on the genre market with three entries started in 1940: *Jungle, Planet*, and *Wings*. Dell got *Walt Disney's Comics and Stories* underway in October 1940— the first funny animal title. Closing out the overview of this super year with Street and Smith's arrival into the comic book field is appropriate because this pulp publisher was responsible in the 1930s for two characters that were extremely influential to the superhero concept. In fact their first two comic book titles were four-color versions of them: *Shadow* #1 (Mar 1940) and *Doc Savage* #1 (May 1940).

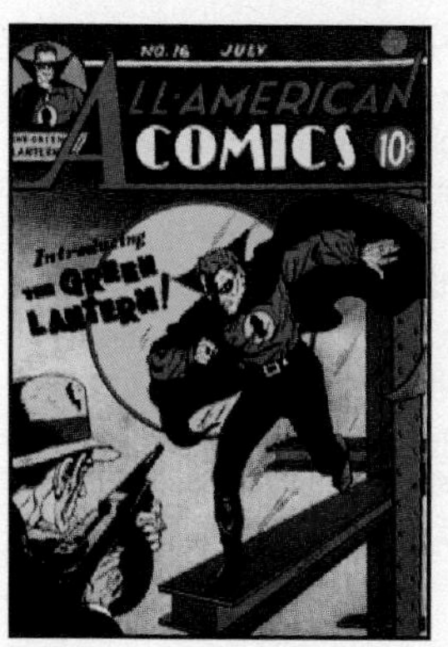

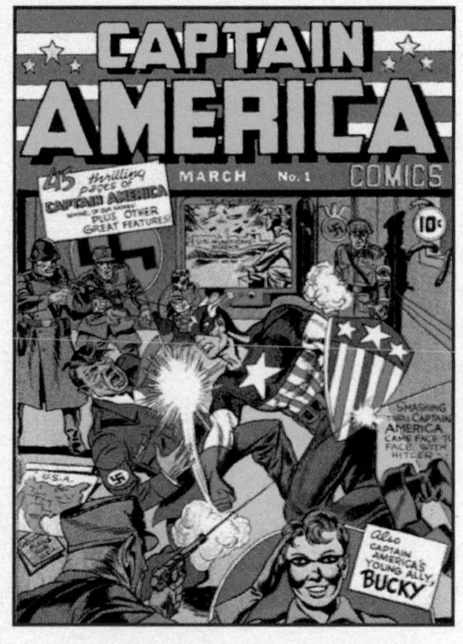

A War to Fight

Patriotic heroes had been springing up ever since the Shield's debut, one especially notable character being Quality's Uncle Sam who started in *National* #1 (July 1940). The incarnation of the famous recruiting poster, Uncle Sam materialized every time America really needed him. This handsome creation was the work of Will Eisner. War covers had also been coming on ever since early 1940, but in 1941, with the war in Europe going strong and American sentiment to get involved increasing, a flood of patriotic propaganda was unleashed. The ultimate example was Timely's Captain America, who— on the cover of #1 (Mar 1941)— was shown punching Hitler's lights out. This action masterpiece sprang from the talented team of Joe Simon and Jack Kirby, and spoke in a loud clear voice Timely's opinion of what America's role should be. Fawcett's Minute-Man (who premiered in *Master* #11 Feb 1941) also deserves mention, and perhaps Better's Fighting Yank (who bowed in *Startling* #10 Sep 1941), but most of the purely patriotic heroes shared a conceptual weakness, however well-intentioned their propaganda purpose.

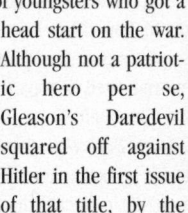

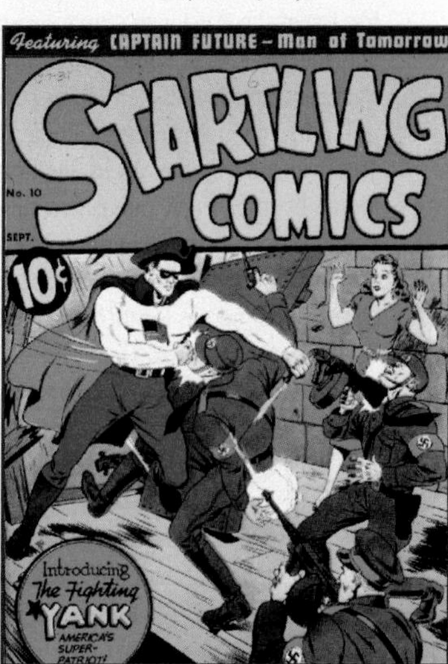

Timely's *Young Allies* #1 (Sum 1941) inaugurated the "kid gang" concept- with a group of youngsters who got a head start on the war. Although not a patriotic hero per se, Gleason's Daredevil squared off against Hitler in the first issue of that title, by the energetic Charles Biro. Interestingly, *National* #18, on the stands in late-October/early-November 1941 even had an oriental attack upon Pearl Harbor- over a month before the real thing!

Captain Marvel got his own title in January 1941, and *Whiz* #25 (Dec 1941) saw the birth of Captain Marvel Jr. Quality's *Police* #1 (Aug 1941) featured the origin and first appearance of Jack Cole's Plastic Man. Plas battled crime by twisting and stretching into all kinds of silly shapes, in another strip that satirized costume characters. That same month Quality also released *Military Comics* #1, starring the international freedom-fighting aviation team, the Blackhawks. This strip really began to soar when Reed Crandall took over the art chores.

Gilberton started their *Classics Illustrated* series in October 1941 with an adaptation of The Three Musketeers. MLJ's *Pep* #22 (Dec 1941) heralded the end of the superhero horde with the first appearance of Archie Andrews, the red-headed teenager who led the way with that company's switch from thrills to laughs. Another important humor feature debuted that same month in Dell's *Animal Comics* #1— Walt Kelly's Pogo. And at DC, *All Star* #8 (Dec 1941/Jan 1942) introduced Wonder Woman. The success of this "two-fisted Amazon" has been best described by Golden Age pundit Ron Goulart, who called it "one of the enigmas of comics history."

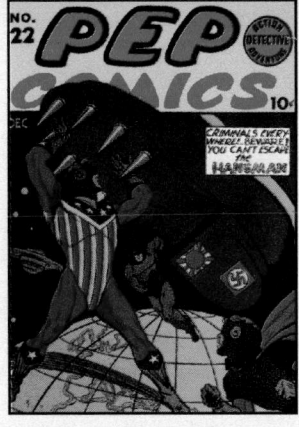

1942 was full of kids fighting both crime and Nazis (with the USA now officially at war). Gleason's *Boy Comics* #3 introduced the young Crimebuster, another product of Biro's sure storytelling skills. Simon and Kirby moved to DC and began the Newsboy Legion in *Star Spangled* #7 (Apr 1942), followed by the Boy Commandos in *Detective* #64 (Jun 1942). Another young hero was Hillman's Airboy, whose first flight was in *Air Fighters* #2 (Nov 1942). Charles Biro wrote the introductory yarn. For Gleason, Biro spearheaded a breakthrough genre book, *Crime Does Not Pay*, which began with #22 (Jun 1942).

Timely started four humor titles in 1942, and in August Dell's *Four Color* #9 featured the first Donald Duck story drawn by Carl Barks, beginning 25 years of wonderful duck tales. Archie #1 (Win 1942) gave the Riverdale gang a showcase for their enduring antics. The "funny book" trend continued in 1943 with a new publisher, the American Comics Group's (ACG) initial entries, *Giggle* and *Ha Ha* in October. And the unique talent of Basil Wolverton took center stage in Timely's *Powerhouse Pepper* #1, the strip with enough zip to make you flip.

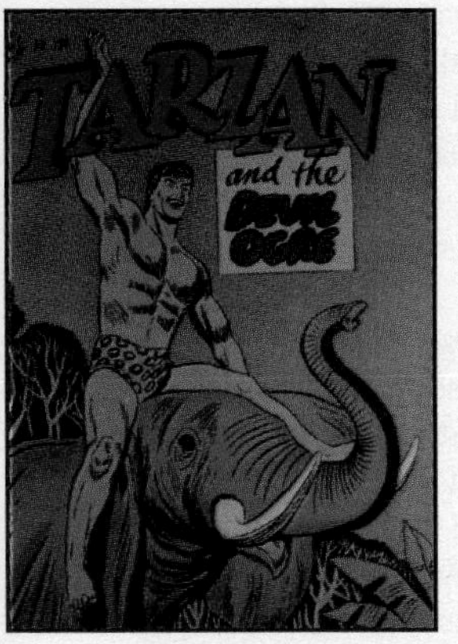

The Postwar Changeover

1944 and 1945 saw only minor innovations- like Timely's "working girl" titles— *Millie the Model* and *Nellie the Nurse*, and the awarding of his own title to Dick Briefer's Frankenstein (#1 Sum 1945) who had appeared in Prize Comics since 1940. And mention should be made of the series that began with Dell's *Four Color* #74 (June 1945)- *Little Lulu* (by John Stanley)- the greatest of the "kid" comics. Despite changing trends overall sales continued to rise, and all the returning servicemen after WW II's end made for a more adult audience. Dell latched onto a character with a broad appeal and began a long Tarzan series with *Four Color* #134 (Feb 1947). Simon and Kirby catered to the older audience with *Young Romance* #1 (Sep 1947), modeled on the popular magazine True Confessions. And as comics historian Mike Benton has noted, Fawcett's *Hopalong Cassidy* title doubled in circulation at this time. A crime wave was also starting. Timely came out with *Justice* and *Official Crime Cases*, both dated Fall 1947, and Magazine Enterprises (ME) issued *Manhunt* #1 (Oct 1947). Humor was still quite popular, and a signal event occurred in Four-Color #178 (Dec 1947), the

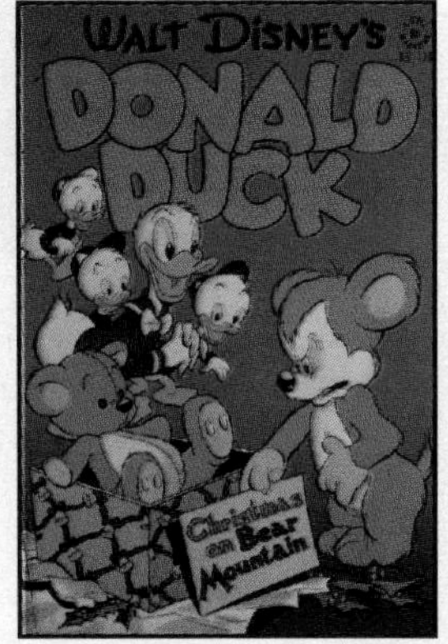

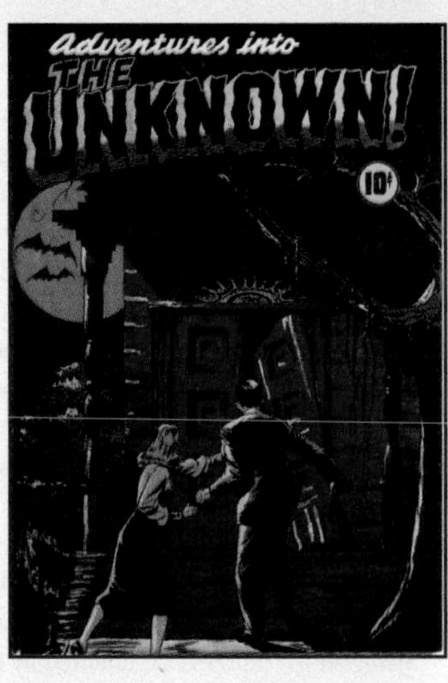

introduction of Barks' greatest creation— Uncle Scrooge. DC's Western Comics #1 (Jan-Feb 1948), Lev Gleason's *Crime and Punishment* #1 (Apr 1948), and Timely's *My Romance* #1 (Sept 1948) illustrate the rise of these three genres— the Golden Age of heroes was ending, and the genres were ready to take over.

In Fall 1948, ACG, with *Adventures Into the Unknown* #1, added another genre of utmost importance to the era- fantasy. In a move that sums up the spirit of the times, Timely (soon to become known as Atlas) took their main superhero anthology, *Marvel Mystery*— then housing the Human Torch, Sub-Mariner, and *Captain America*— and converted it to *Marvel Tales* with #93 (Aug 1949). By the early 1950s Atlas would be offering over a dozen fantasy/horror titles, including two that would go on to Silver Age fame— *Strange Tales* and *Journey Into Mystery*. Editor Stan Lee amassed a stable of freelance talent (including artists Bill Everett, Russ Heath, and Joe Maneely) that filled the Atlas books with the best four-color fantasy around. Late in 1949 EC started running some horror stories, and in 1950 unveiled a triumvirate of ghastly titles: *Crypt of Terror, Vault of Horror*, and *Haunt of Fear*. They also offered *Weird Science* and *Weird Fantasy*, but these two couldn't match the strong sales of their horror trio. Only DC kept a superhero stronghold, and they gave Superboy his own title in early 1949.

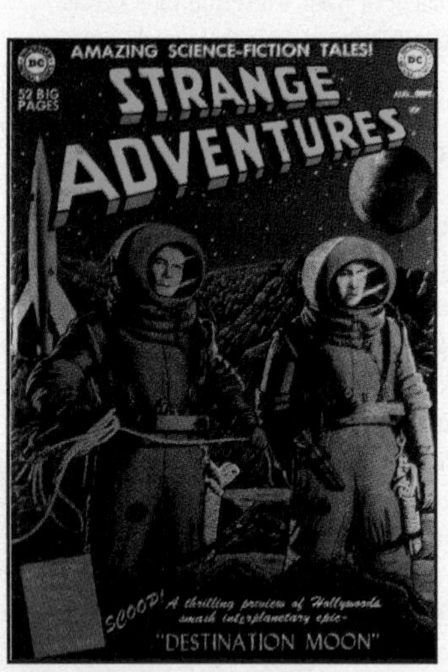

Publishers also combined genres, such as Fawcett's *Love Mystery* which ran for three issues in 1950. By far the most successful of these blendings was ME's *Ghost Rider* by Dick Ayers (#1 late-1950), which mixed superhero, western, and horror. The Korean War inspired the war comics genre, led by EC's *Two-Fisted Tales* (Nov 1950), and followed by Atlas with a bunch of titles and DC with several long-running battle books.

DC launched a couple of significant sci-fi titles— *Strange Adventures* #1 (Aug-Sep 1950) and *Mystery In Space* (#1 Apr-May 1951). Paperback publisher Avon and magazine publisher Ziff-Davis also produced some good S-F comics. ACG added a second supernatural title, *Forbidden Worlds* (#1 Jul-Aug 1951) which enjoyed a 16-year run. Frankenstein abandoned the clownish capers he'd done so enjoyably in the late-1940s to return as a full-fledged monster- still drawn by the redoubtable Dick Briefer. And EC scored another hit with *MAD* #1 (Oct-Nov 1952), Harvey Kurtzman's brainchild which began with parodies of comic strips and books. St. John started the 3-D craze in 1953, using a process developed by Joe Kubert and Norman Maurer. But the fad burned out quickly, a little over six months after it started. Better (now Standard) launched a humor series that would enjoy a long faithful following, with *Dennis the Menace* #1 (Aug 1953).

Witch Hunt!

EC published many excellent stories, and their art staff (led by Wally Wood, Jack Davis, and Graham Ingels) was superb. But they also regularly crossed the line into gratuitous gore and violence. ACG stayed pretty mild, Atlas kept within the confines of good taste, Fawcett was modest, DC steered clear of horror, but many smaller publishers followed EC's lead of mayhem and dismemberment. This led to a storm of protest from pop psychologists, P.T.A. groups, etc. that was eventually heard by the government. After a Senate Investigation demanded a clean-up, the publishers capitulated and in late 1954 adopted a code of strictures that shut down crime and horror comics.

The industry was devastated, and by 1956 sales were down by 75%, with most publishers abandoning the field. Even the companies that continued were mired in lackluster material. Atlas' fantasy titles kept on, but the heart and soul was gone.

Only Dell had refused to go with the Comics Code, relying on their own reputation for good taste, and this was when they were producing a lot of TV tie-ins and movie adaptations. (Their *Zorro* issues drawn by Alex Toth are well-remembered.) Television was, of course, also helping to erode the comics readership, as the boob tube offered more and more households cheap entertainment. The outlook for the comic book business was bleak.

Glimmers of Silver

DC still had Superman and Batman pulling for them, and editor Julius Schwartz decided to try a new tack with super heroes. What with comic readership turning over every few years, the new generation was unaware of DC's Golden Age greats. So Schwartz tried a little recycling. They took the Flash, gave him a new scientific origin and a new sleeker costume, and set him loose in Showcase #4 (Sept-Oct 1956). This was followed by a new Jack Kirby team of heroes, the Challengers of the Unknown, in *Showcase* #6 (Jan-Feb 1957). Flash appeared again in issue #8, and sales reports on #4 and #6 came in with promising results. The Challengers came back in *Showcase* #7, #11, and #12, and the Flash sped through issues #13 and #14, and by this time there was no doubt about it. Even in the greatly reduced marketplace the right material could still turn a profit. *Challengers of the Unknown #1* (Apr-May 1958) was followed by the Flash's re-entry into his own magazine (#105 Feb-Mar 1959).

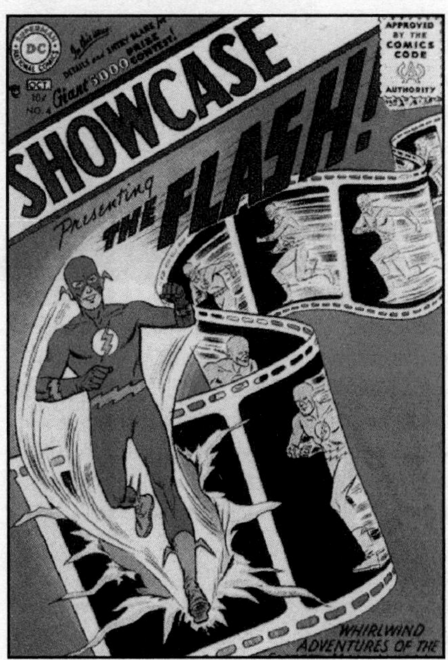

Other signs of life at DC included the introduction of the Legion of Super Heroes in *Adventure* #247 (Apr 1958), and the debuts of a couple of space heroes: *Showcase* #15 (Jul-Aug 1958) premiered Space Ranger and #17 (Nov-Dec 1958) featured Adam Strange. Both of these characters would go on to claim the cover/lead slots in DC fantasy titles.

These were the Sputnik days, and sci-fi was the rage. Even Atlas, who had almost expired in 1957, came back with a quartet of fantasy titles in early 1959. The revived *Strange Tales* and *Journey Into Mystery* were joined by *Tales To Astonish* and *Tales Of Suspense.* Soon these titles would by dominated by stories of fearsome monsters drawn by Jack Kirby, and every issue also contained a five-page fantasy gem by Stan Lee and Steve Ditko.

Showcase #22 (Sept-Oct 1959) updated Green Lantern for the new generation, again with a sci-fi origin. This led the way for *Brave and Bold* #28's Justice League of America (Feb-Mar 1960), which brought the DC heroes together for a book-length adventure. With the dawn of the new decade the Silver Age was well underway.

The three JLA tryout issues were followed by *Justice League of America* #1 (Oct-Nov 1960), and soon after that Martin Goodman— hearing of the book's success— suggested to Stan Lee that Atlas should try super heroes again. Lee's idea was a group of somewhat more fallible heroes, who squabbled and battled self-doubt as well as crime. Teaming with Jack Kirby they produced the *Fantastic Four* #1 (Nov 1961). This was followed by the *Incredible Hulk* #1 (May 1962), and the introduction of Spider-Man (with Ditko art) in *Amazing Fantasy* #15 (Aug 1962). With a name change to Marvel Comics, the transformation was complete, and these more-human heroes started to climb in popularity.

Marvel began adding heroes to their fantasy titles- Thor premiered in *Journey Into Mystery* #83 (Aug 1962). In September 1963 Marvel introduced two super-teams. The Avengers were a JLA-like compilation of various stars, but the X-Men were completely original. This band of teenage mutants had to contend with society-at-large's lack of understanding of their special abilities. Even more than fellow troubled teenager Spider-Man, the X-Men would come to represent that outcast feeling that readers identified with so easily.

Iron Man, who bowed in *Tales Of Suspense* #39 (Mar 1963) and Daredevil, who started in his own title (#1 Apr 1964), are both apt examples of Marvel's flawed hero formula: Iron Man had a bad heart which necessitated his armored apparatus and Daredevil was blind. Another part of Marvel's appeal was Stan Lee's going beyond his role as writer and editor to act as master of ceremonies for the whole line. Also in 1964, James Warren began publishing *Creepy,* a black-and-white magazine-sized comic that did not need the approval of the Comics Code. After a dormant decade the horror genre was back, with art by such greats as Frank Frazetta, Reed Crandall, and Al Williamson.

1966 was the year that the Batman TV spoof started, and DC, floundering in the face of Marvel's competition, unwisely began accenting a camp approach to their titles. From this point on Marvel would lead the Silver Age.

Rise and Fall

In 1968 Marvel went through a huge expansion. The revived Sub-Mariner and Captain America received their own titles, as did the popular Silver Surfer, who had first appeared in the *Fantastic Four*. And in 1970 they began a sword-and-sorcery series based on Robert E. Howard's classic character, Conan. But the superhero schtick was wearing thin again. Both Marvel and DC turned to fantasy anthologies, but neither company got readers excited enough to sustain the trend. Comics were having a harder time on newsstand racks, and many outlets, corner drug stores etc., stopped carrying them. In 1973 Dell quit publishing comics, leaving only DC, Marvel, Archie, Charlton, Gold Key, and Harvey, who had the bulk of the younger market with characters like Casper and Richie Rich. Times were hard again.

Long-time comics fan and convention organizer Phil Seuling got the idea of distributing comics directly to the many comic book stores across the country. Although the implementation of this idea marked another eleventh hour rescue for the industry, it also led to a restricted focus for the field. Now comics were for comics fans and not for John and Jane Q. Public.

Generation X

In summer 1975 with the *Giant Size X-Men* and *X-Men* #94 (by Len Wein and Dave Cockrum) the first signs of the new vitality emerged. This amounted to the same kind of "*Showcase* #4" revival that had sparked the Silver Age. The X-Men had been running on reprints, as lukewarm as most everything else, when this spark took hold. Wolverine, with his super sharp claws and belligerent attitude, defined the new spirit. Another up-and-coming character, the Punisher (who'd debuted in *Amazing Spider-Man* #129 Feb 1974), took the new stance even further. After his family was gunned down by the "Mob", the Punisher embarked on a no-holds-barred mission of vengeance— packing plenty of deadly hardware. The term hero should be used loosely in describing these characters. But, the times were changin', and the gritty mood of these books spoke to an audience. DC took this cue, but with more restraint, and came out with the *New Teen Titans* #1 (Nov 1980), led by high-anxiety versions of Robin, Wonder Girl, and Kid Flash. Marvel also began a successful adaptation of the Star Wars mythos, with issue #1 dated July 1977.

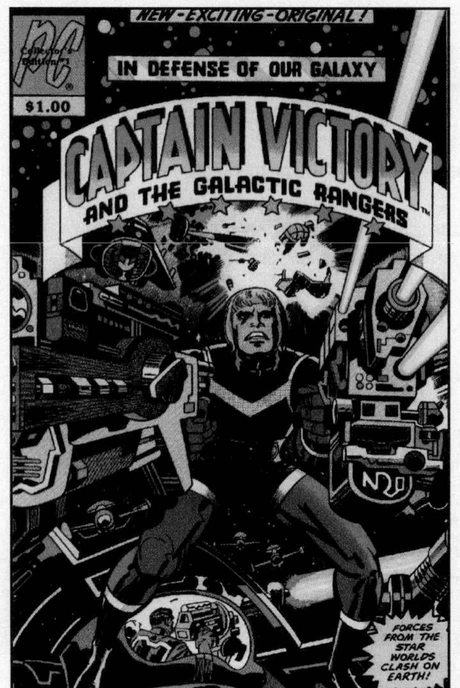

The new direct market did make it easier for small publishers to distribute their material. In November 1981 Pacific Comics released *Captain Victory and the Galactic Rangers* by Jack Kirby. Pacific followed this with *Groo* #1 (Dec 1982), featuring the hilarious misadventures of the dim barbarian by Sergio Aragones and Mark Evanier. An added virtue of Pacific's endeavor was that the comics creators would be allowed to retain ownership of their characters. This company, along with "maverick" Dave Sim's *Cerebus* (which he'd been direct marketing since 1977) paved the way for a host of independent publishers.

One of the most high-profile results of this was 1984's *Teenage Mutant Ninja Turtles* phenomenon from Mirage Studios. Cowabunga! Other major indies included Eclipse, Kitchen Sink, Comico, Warp, First, and Dark Horse. Things came full circle in 1986 when Bruce Hamilton's Gladstone obtained the rights to reprint Carl Barks' classic Donald Duck and Uncle Scrooge stories. Gladstone inspired life-long Barks fan, comics historian, and cartoonist Don Rosa to write and draw a new Uncle Scrooge novel, "Son of the Sun", which was published as *Uncle Scrooge* #219 (July 1987). It was an excellent story, and Rosa followed it up with a succession of laudable efforts.

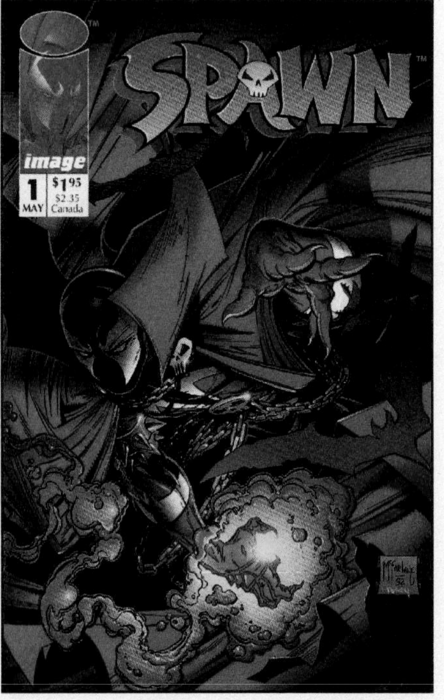

In 1988 DC got some media attention with Superman's 50th anniversary. This was more than matched by Batman's 50th anniversary in 1989— due to the release of the mega-hit Batman movie. DC also started the Vertigo series, designed for more mature readers, with *Sandman* #1 (Jan 1989), written by Neil Gaiman. More comic books were starting to appear in upscale formats, most often as graphic novels, perfect-bound on high-quality paper. An excellent example is 1988's *The Killing Joke* by Alan Moore and Brian Bolland, a Batman story that detailed the origin of the Joker.

In 1991 Marvel staged an ambitious marketing ploy by releasing the new *X-Men* #1 (by

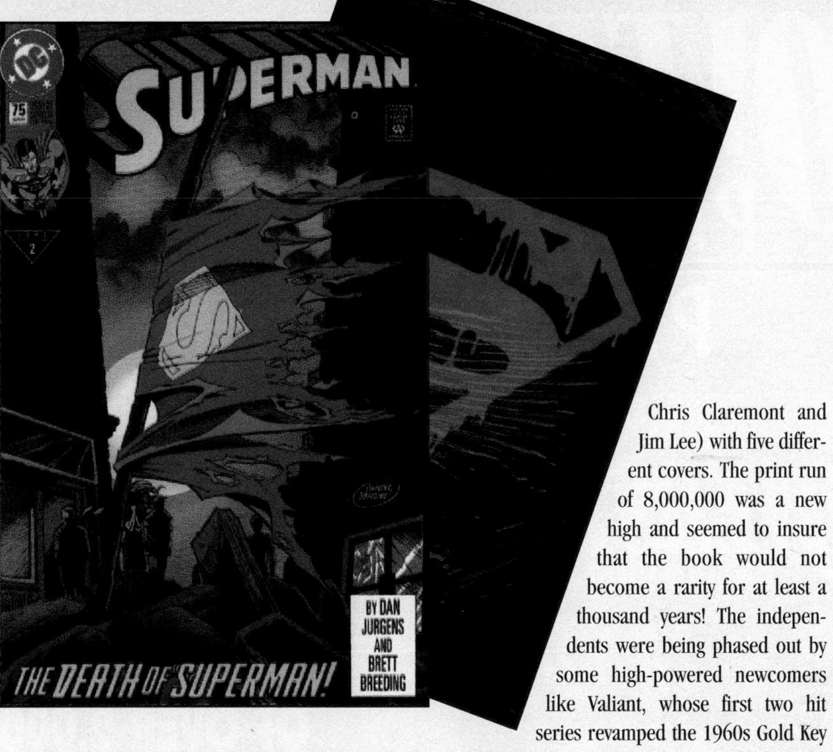

Chris Claremont and Jim Lee) with five different covers. The print run of 8,000,000 was a new high and seemed to insure that the book would not become a rarity for at least a thousand years! The independents were being phased out by some high-powered newcomers like Valiant, whose first two hit series revamped the 1960s Gold Key characters, Dr. Solar and Magnus- Robot Fighter. One indie that did make a splash— due to the old virtues of good story and art- was Jeff Smith's *Bone* (#1, July 1991).

In 1992 some of the hot young creators (Jim Lee, Todd McFarlane, Rob Liefeld, and Jim Valentino) grouped together to form their own company, Image Comics. McFarlane's *Spawn* (#1, May 1992) has been their most successful series. This year also saw a profusion of "cover enhancements" (hologram, prism, foil, gatefold, etc.) most often with enhanced prices to match. DC concocted the "death" of Superman, which received a lot of press outside the comics field and brought many newcomers into comics stores- most of them looking for the "black-bagged" *Superman* #75.

In 1993 the bubble-gum-card specialist Topps entered the comic book business with an adaptation of the blockbuster film Jurassic Park. Also Matt Groening, creator of the animated TV hit. The Simpsons, started Bongo Comics, featuring superhero spoofs like *Radioactive Man*. 1994 began auspiciously, with a comic from the writer and artist of the Batman animated TV series: *Mad Love* (Feb 1994) by Paul Dini and Bruce Timm shows that the 60—year old comic book medium is still going strong. And as for what 1995 will bring— wait and see. But with the 100-year history of comic strips and books that we have, there are always old wonders to explore while waiting for the new ones.

(Author's note: Space limitations have made it inevitable that a great many worthy strips, books, and creators did not get mentioned. Once comic books got going I veered away from newspaper strips, hence the omission of such classics as Charles Schulz's Peanuts. But I hope this overview adds to your appreciation of this super hobby. Thanks!- Pat S. Calhoun)

OVERSTREET PREMIUM RING PRICE GUIDE

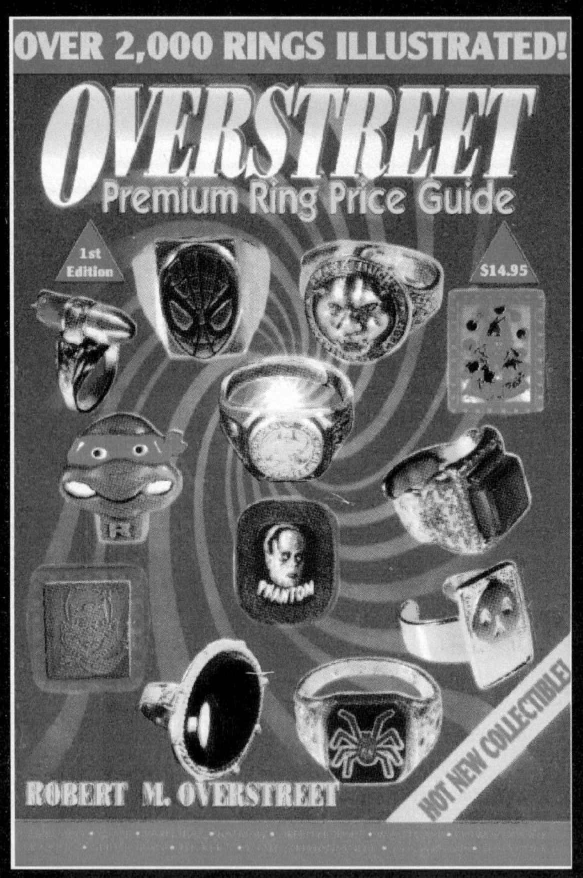

FEATURING PHOTOGRAPHS OF OVER 2,000 COLLECTIBLE PREMIUM RINGS!

AVAILABLE AT YOUR FAVORITE COMIC SHOP OR BOOKSTORE!

Your First Line of Defense

Comics worth collecting are worth protecting. Count on Comic Defense System® ProBags®, Backer Boards, and Storage Boxes for Maximum Collection Protection™ at a minimum cost per comic.

Bag 'em™

Secure the perimeters of all your comics with super-clear virgin polypropylene **ProBags**.

Board 'em™

Reinforce your defenses with all-white **Backer Boards**, safeguarding your comics from accidental bends and folds.

Box 'em™

Maintain your stronghold with double-wall corrugated cardboard **Storage Boxes** — easy to assemble and transport.

Command the full line of quality Comic Defense System products — your first, best line of defense for comics of any size, age and condition!

Look for the symbol of Maximum Collection Protection™ at a comic shop near you.

Superman soars to new heights at Sotheby's.

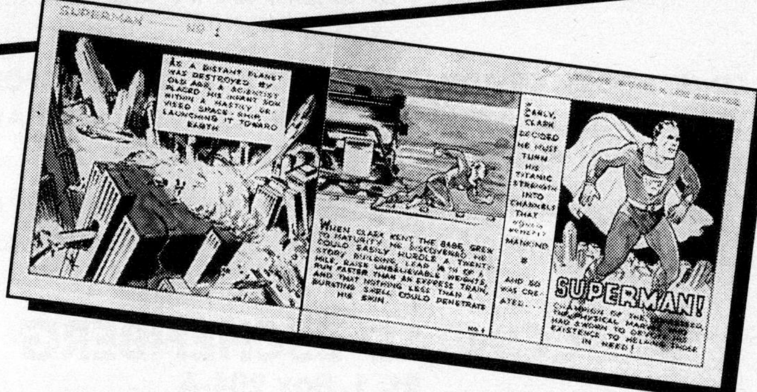

Each season Sotheby's offers a serious selection of Comic Books, Comic Art and Animation Art at auction. Joe Shuster's origin artwork to Superman Daily No. 1, shown here, sold privately for $77,000 at Sotheby's in 1994. So join us in 1995 as we celebrate 100 years of the comic art form.

Highlights from our spring 1995 sale include:

- **High grade copies of Action Comics No. 1, 3, 5**
- **Detective Comics No. 10, 14, 16, 27**
- **Adventure No. 61**
- **Marvel Comics No. 1**
- **Batman 1-20, Showcase No. 4**
- **All American 16 & 17**

- **The largest selection ever of newspaper comic strip artwork will be put on the auction block,** including Krazy Kat Sunday and E.C. Popeye Sunday Pages from the collection of Bud and Nadia Sagendorf, a special hand-colored Tarzan from Burne Hogard and **Little Nemo** Sundays.
- **The largest premium ring and button collection ever offered at auction will go up for sale** with over 135 precious and rare rings included.
- **Major examples from** the collections of Dick Ayers, Jack and Roz Kirby, Al Feldstein, Murphy Anderson, Johnny Craig, Harvey Kurtzman and other famed artists.

For more information, please call Jerry Weist or Dana Hawkes at (212) 606-7424, Sotheby's, 1334 York Avenue, New York, NY 10021.

THE WORLD'S LEADING FINE ART AUCTION HOUSE

SOTHEBY'S

FOUNDED 1744

The Origin Artwork by Bob Kane for Batman in the Newspaper Daily Format, Daily introduction original from B, or origin dailies 2. Auction estimate: $5,000-10,000

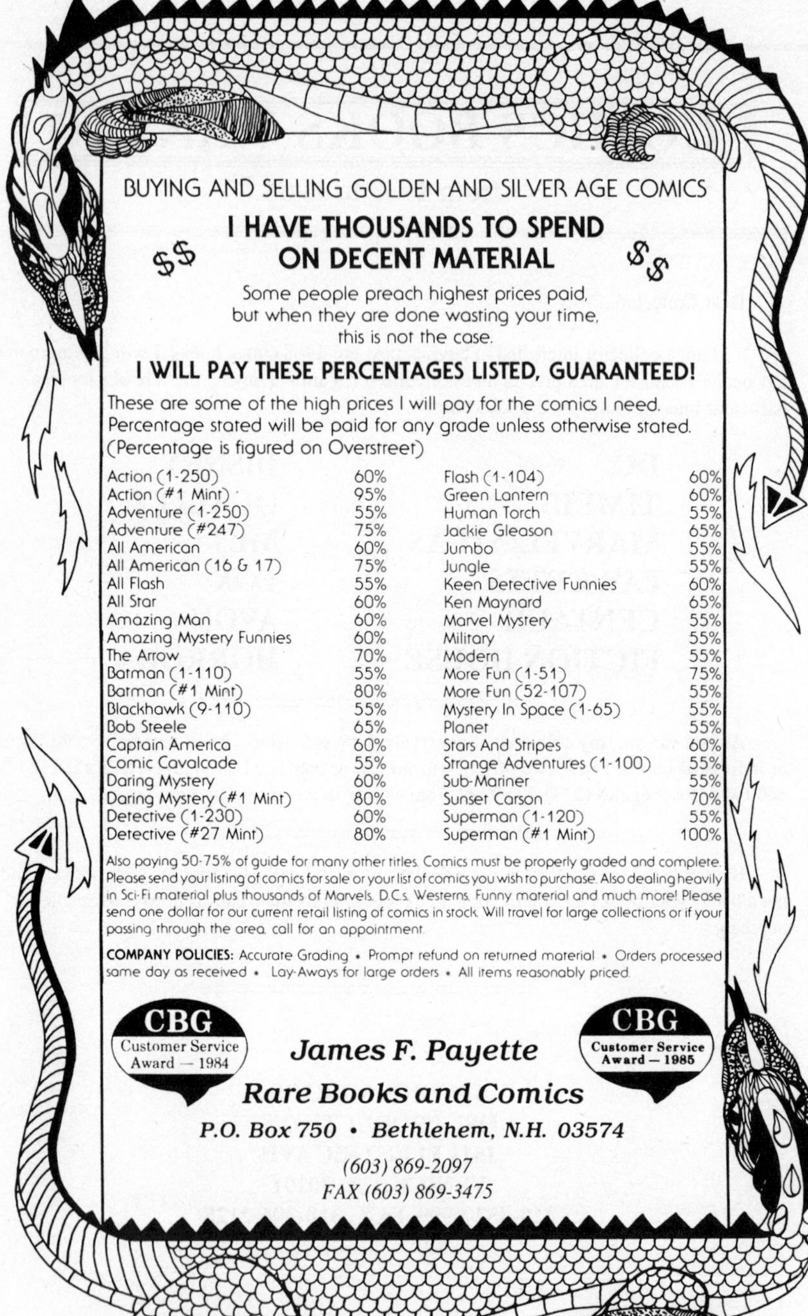

BUYING AND SELLING GOLDEN AND SILVER AGE COMICS
I HAVE THOUSANDS TO SPEND
$$ ON DECENT MATERIAL $$
Some people preach highest prices paid,
but when they are done wasting your time,
this is not the case.
I WILL PAY THESE PERCENTAGES LISTED, GUARANTEED!
These are some of the high prices I will pay for the comics I need.
Percentage stated will be paid for any grade unless otherwise stated.
(Percentage is figured on Overstreet)
Action (1-250) 60%
Action (#1 Mint) 95%
Adventure (1-250) 55%
Adventure (#247) 75%
All American 60%
All American (16 & 17) 75%
All Flash 55%
All Star 60%
Amazing Man 60%
Amazing Mystery Funnies 60%
The Arrow 70%
Batman (1-110) 55%
Batman (#1 Mint) 80%
Blackhawk (9-110) 55%
Bob Steele 65%
Captain America 60%
Comic Cavalcade 55%
Daring Mystery 60%
Daring Mystery (#1 Mint) 80%
Detective (1-230) 60%
Detective (#27 Mint) 80%
Flash (1-104) 60%
Green Lantern 60%
Human Torch 55%
Jackie Gleason 65%
Jumbo 55%
Jungle 55%
Keen Detective Funnies 60%
Ken Maynard 65%
Marvel Mystery 55%
Military 55%
Modern 55%
More Fun (1-51) 75%
More Fun (52-107) 55%
Mystery In Space (1-65) 55%
Planet 55%
Stars And Stripes 60%
Strange Adventures (1-100) 55%
Sub-Mariner 55%
Sunset Carson 70%
Superman (1-120) 55%
Superman (#1 Mint) 100%
Also paying 50-75% of guide for many other titles. Comics must be properly graded and complete. Please send your listing of comics for sale or your list of comics you wish to purchase. Also dealing heavily in Sci-Fi material plus thousands of Marvels. D.C.s. Westerns. Funny material and much more! Please send one dollar for our current retail listing of comics in stock. Will travel for large collections or if your passing through the area. call for an appointment.
COMPANY POLICIES: Accurate Grading • Prompt refund on returned material • Orders processed same day as received • Lay-Aways for large orders • All items reasonably priced.
CBG Customer Service Award — 1984
James F. Payette
CBG Customer Service Award — 1985
Rare Books and Comics
P.O. Box 750 • Bethlehem, N.H. 03574
(603) 869-2097
FAX (603) 869-3475

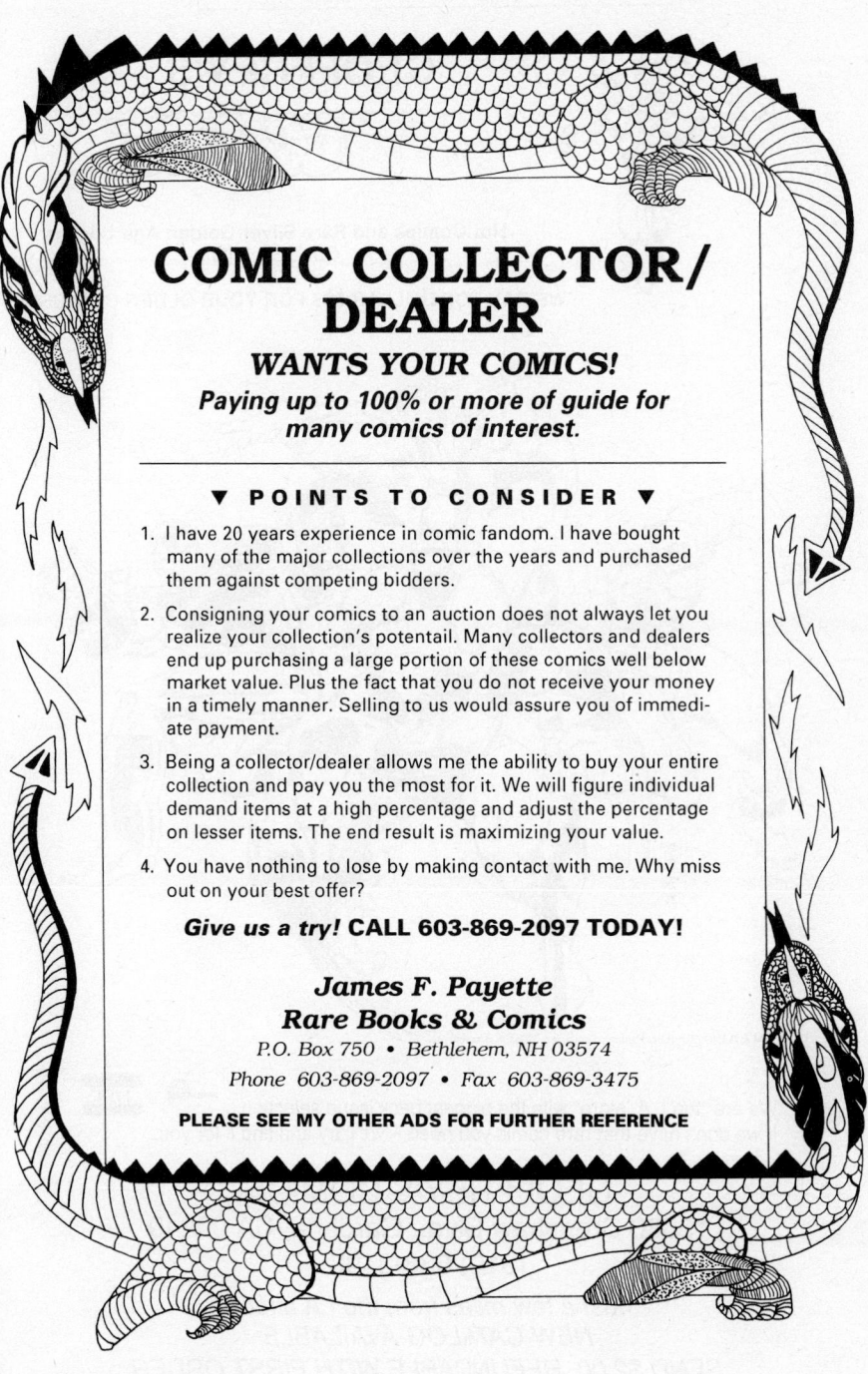

ART RESTORATION

Matthew Wilson, Conservator

P.O. BOX 881 / KELSO, WA 98626 / (360) 577-0351

FANTASY MASTERPIECES is a business dedicated to the art of paper conservation. It is our philosophy that art restoration should take the *whole* item into account. That means that not only should your item look as good as possible but that it should be made as structurally sound as possible. What good is a restored work of art if it disintegrates two years later? For that reason, I have developed various methods and techniques of paper art restoration unmatched anywhere else.

I am familiar with the construction of 19th & 20th century papers and have worked extensively on the most valuable of the Golden and Silver aged books from Action #1 to Amazing Fantasy #15.

When it comes to your paper art collection, whether it's a Superman #1 or a rare paper document that is priceless to you, why take a risk with anyone else? **FANTASY MASTERPIECES** is the answer.

Before

After

Our rate is $55.00 per hour.
Estimates are free & questions are always welcome.
Items to be restored should be worth at least $125.00 in their present condition.

We perform the following services with expert precision:

1) Cleaning
2) Whitening
3) Tape Removal
4) Piece Replacement
5) Repair Tears
6) Spine Roll Removal
7) Deacidification
8) Color Retouching
9)Staple Replacement
10) Page Lightening

Not Just
An Ordinary
Bookstore
NEW & USED:
COMICS
ADVENTURE GAMING
BOOKS
MAGAZINES
JAPANIMATION
ETC • ETC • ETC
O'Leary's Books
3828 100th SW, Tacoma, WA 98499 588-2503 1-800-542-1791

WANT LIST COMICS

Golden Age

Silver Age

WE FILL WANT LISTS

ATTENTION: INVESTORS AND COLLECTORS

Can't find those missing comic books **yet**? Are these books priced **TOO high** or are they just **IMPOSSIBLE** to find? Have local stores and conventions **not** produced what you want? **(Have you sent us a want list yet?)**

WHAT ARE YOU WAITING FOR?

"The **Batman #1** you sold me was in the **nicest, unrestored condition** I've seen!", **Bob Overstreet, author "The Official Overstreet Comic Book Price Guide".**

"I have been **very satisfied** in doing business with your company. Your fair price, great selection, accurate grading and professional service will keep me a **loyal customer** for years to come! I appreciate your **high standards** in this comic industry!" Drew Bloom, Huntington, VT

These are just two of the **many** satisfied customers that have bought books from us in the past. Over the years, we have developed a **very strong return customer base** because we **ACCURATELY** price, grade and describe books (in detail) over the phone and through the mail. For a small fee we will even videotape any comic book we have in stock. **Customer references are always available upon request.** If a book is restored, we will tell you **up front** so you won't be **UNpleasantly** surprised or deceived. As each year goes by, we complete more and more of our customers' comic want lists. For example, **in 1994 alone**, we acquired rare **Golden Age** treasures for our clients like **Detective 1, 27, 33, Silver Streak 6, More Fun 9, 14, World's Best 1, Wonder Comics 1, Jumbo 1, Human Torch 1, Submariner 1,** and the ultra-rare **New Fun 2** just to name a few. Yes, we can **definitely** find rare books - - we do all the time! We have in the past purchased **MULTIPLE** copies of all **Silver Age** "key" issues like Amazing Fantasy 15, Spiderman 1, FF1, Hulk 1, Showcase 4, 8, 22, JLA 1, Flash 105 and Brave and the Bold 28. **WE SPECIALIZE IN GOLDEN AGE AND SILVER AGE BOOKS (1933-1969)**, but we also have some later issues (up to 1985).

We don't claim that we can fill every list all the time, but if any company can accomplish this, it **would certainly** be us! We can say this with **much confidence** because we travel to the **majority** of the 50 states and Canada plus attend many of the major comic book conventions (San Diego, Chicago, Charlotte, etc.) to uncover books **you would not** have the opportunity to find. When we are not on the road, we spend **MANY** hours on the phone locating books from our **long** list of past and present comic sources we've developed over the **20 years** we have been dealing in comic books. When sending your want list, **please** include an SASE if possible, **your phone number,** and a good time to reach you. We **DON'T** send out catalogs, so **please** ask us for **specific** books and **conditions** desired. We will contact you **when** we find the items you've requested. **Phone calls are also welcomed. WE WILL GLADLY SUGGEST AND PERSONALLY PUT TOGETHER COMIC BOOK INVESTMENT PORTFOLIOS FOR BIG AND SMALL INVESTORS. OUR ADVICE IS ALWAYS FREE!**

SAVE YOURSELF ALL THE HASSLE AND LET US DO THE LOOKING FOR YOU CALL OR MAIL US YOUR WANT LIST!

YOU HAVE NOTHING TO LOSE AND EVERYTHING ON YOUR WANT LIST TO GAIN!!!

Competitive pricing always. Accurate grading. Friendly, courteous service. **Interest free time** payments/**layaways possible.** Visa, Mastercard and American Express accepted for total payment **OR** down payment on books. No collect calls. Books shipped within 48 hours of payment.

Our office/warehouse # is:

1-918-299-0440

Call us anytime between 1 pm and 8 pm CST

WANT LIST COMICS
BOX 701932
TULSA, OK 74170-1932

*** Advisor to the Overstreet Price Guide ***
References gladly provided!

Super Sales Catalog Only $2.00

Contains everything from Superheroes to Ducks! Includes Westerns, Independents, Combat, Space, Magazines, and much, much more.

MOST COMPLETE LISTING NEXT TO OVERSTREET'S!

Covers virtually every issue printed in the last 20 - 30 years and all available for sale in three different grades.

Order your catalog today!

Individual titles of interest sent FREE with a SASE.

Dealer Inquiries welcome!

Also available, complete inventory lists of pre -1964 books:

Super-hero, Adventure, etc. * Western
Classics Illustrated * Movie and T.V.
Funny Animal, Archie, Disney, etc.

EACH LIST ONLY $1.00 OR ALL FIVE FOR $2.00.

One list may be requested FREE when ordering Super Sales Catalog. Lists for **Independents, Non-sport Cards, Magazines, and Star Trek** will be sent free upon request with your catalog or list order.

WE SPECIALIZE IN BUYING ENTIRE COLLECTIONS.

We pay up to 100% of Overstreet for selected issues. Please write or call for our buying list and terms, or with any questions you may have.

Collectors Ink

932-A W. 8th Ave. ☆ Chico, CA ☆ 95926
(916) 345-0958 ☆ Mon.—Sat. 10-5

In association with

THE PENNY RANCH

SERVING THE COLLECTING COMMUNITY SINCE 1967

PACIFIC COMIC EXCHANGE, INC.

The Pacific Comic Exchange, Inc. (PCE) is the first computerized "on-line" comic book trading company specializing in Golden and Silver Age comics from 1933-1969. All comics listed on "The Exchange" have been graded and certified by the Comic Grading Service of America (CGSA), which has developed a new standardized numerical grading system that ensures an unprecedented degree of accuracy and consistency.

CGSA	M	NM/M	NM	VFN/NM	VFN	FN/VFN	FN	VG/FN	VG	G/VG	G	Fr	Pr
	100,99,98,97,96,95,94,93,92,91	90	88,85,80,75	70	65,60,55	50	45,40,35	30	25,20	15	10	6	3
PgQ	0 1 2 2.5	3	3.3 4	5	6	6.5	7	7.5	8	8.5	9	9.5	10

LIQUIDITY

- PCE is an international network of dealers, collectors, and retailers.
- Providing an excellent selection of Golden and Silver Age comics.
- Negotiable prices, prompt payment to sellers.
- Sellers enjoy the lowest brokerage commissions (8% to 13%) in the industry.

CONFIDENCE AND PROTECTION

- **CGSA** certified books are guaranteed to be in stated condition.
- Full disclosure of any restoration is certified by such respected experts as **Susan Ciccone** of **The Restoration Lab.**
- All books are uniquely identified and catalogued - Buyers and Sellers are protected from fraudulent substitution or damage.

ACCESS

- "The Exchange" is accessible via phone, computer, or mail.
- Detailed monthly reports (available through subscription) of sales data, updated listings, special market analyses, etc., help Buyers and Sellers make informed decisions.
- Buyers have access to a large selection of Golden and Silver age comics at negotiable prices.

COMPREHENSIVE ON-LINE SERVICE

- All statistics available "on-line": prices, market trends, grading, restoration information, etc.
- "Want Lists" link Sellers with interested Buyers.
- Buyers and Sellers can utilize extended "after hours" trading.

TRADE WITH CONFIDENCE, TRADE WITH PCE

Call or write (include your telephone number) for more information about opening a free trading account, viewing a demonstration of the PCE "on-line" service, or selling comics on "The Exchange."

Meeting and consultations are arranged by appointment only.

Copyright © 1995 by PACIFIC COMIC EXCHANGE, INC. All rights reserved

Item#	Publ	Title	Symbol	No	Year	P	R	CGSA	Grade	BidPrice	AskPrice	Status
8726	DC	ACTION COMICS	ACT	1	1938			VFN	60	$100000	$135000	BAK
9351	TIM	ALL WINNERS COMICS	AWC	2	1941			VF/NM	70	$2250	$3000	BAK
5467	DC	ALL-AMERICAN COMICS	AAC	17	1940			VFN	60	$4500	$5500	BAK
9430	DC	ALL-FLASH	ALLFL	1	1941			FN	35	$0	$2700	BAK
7213	MVL	AMAZING FANTASY	AMZ	15	1962			VFN	68	$0	$20000	BAK
8756	DC	BATMAN	B	3	1940			VFN	60	$2400	$4800	BAK
6490	DC	BOY COMMANDOS	BYC	1	1943	CC		VF/NM	70	$0	$2500	BAK
9206	DC	BRAVE AND THE BOLD	BB	34	1961			NM++	88	$2700	$4000	BAK
9444	FWC	CAPTAIN MARVEL ADVENTU	CMADV	1	1941		M	aFN	35	$0	$4000	BAK
9672	DC	DETECTIVE COMICS	DET	138	1948			VFN++	68	$650	$1109	BAK
9443	EAS	FAMOUS FUNNIES-CARNIVA	FFNCC	0	1933			VG+	25	$1300	$1300	ESC
9334	MVL	FANTASTIC FOUR	FF	1	1961			NM	80	$0	$30000	BAK
4904	NED	FIGHTING YANK	YANK	1	1942	MH		NM	80	$0	$2800	BAK
9692	DC	FLASH COMICS	FC	100	1948			VF/VF+	63	$1650	$2000	BAK
9243	DEL	FOUR COLOR	FRCLR	9	1942			VFN+	65	$2750	$3900	BAK
9588	TIM	HUMAN TORCH	HT	2	1940			VG	20	$1500	$2600	BAK
9347	MVL	INCREDIBLE HULK	IH	6	1963			NM	80	$1800	$2250	BAK
5482	EC	MAD	MAD	1	1952	GA		M	93	$7500	$15000	BAK
7002	DC	NEW FUN COMICS	NFC	2	1935			Fr	6	$0	$5000	BAK
8260	DC	NEW YORK WORLD'S FAIR	NYWF	39	1939			G	10	$1000	$1875	BAK
9247	DC	SHOWCASE	SHO	4	1956			NM	80	$0	$40000	BAK
9581	DC	SUPERMAN	S	1	1939		M	aVG/FN	30	$0	$18000	BAK
7112	EC	WEIRD FANTASY	WRDFY	10	1951	WM		NM	88	$0	$750	BAK
8262	DC	WORLD'S BEST COMICS	WF	1	1941			VFN	60	$0	$5000	BAK

<< hit any key to continue >>

Pacific Comic Exchange, Inc.
P.O. Box 34849 Los Angeles, CA 90034
Tel: (310) 836-7234(PCEI) Fax: (310) 836-7127 Modem: (310) 836-3076

DET27 25$29850 MFC52 15$3575 S1 20$7700 B1 15$5500 BB28 65$2750 SHO4 25$2300 AMZ15 40$2200

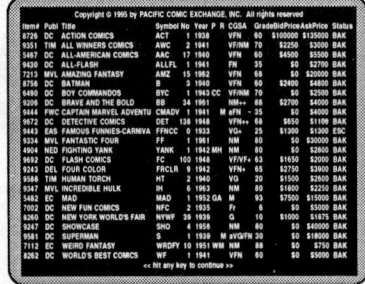

PACIFIC COMIC EXCHANGE, INC

P.O. BOX 34849, Los Angeles, CA 90034 ❖337 S. Robertson Blvd. Suite 203, Beverly Hills, CA 90211 ❖Tel:(310) 836-7234, Fax:(310) 836-7127

Instructions *(Please read before ordering)* :The following books are currently listed on the Exchange and are available for sale at the prices specified. All prices are "negotiable" and subject to change without notice. All orders are subject to a 10% buyers commission. The grade listed is the CGSA grade (see diagram below). Books may be returned (must be undamaged) if not satisfied and we are notified within 5 days of receipt by telephone .

a: Appears, d: Double Cover, t: Trimmed Book, R: Restored (C: Color Touch, S: Slight (e.g. tear sealed, cleaned, etc), L: Light, M: Moderate, E: Extensive),

PgQ: Page Quality (0.0, 1, 2, 2.5, 3: White; 3.3: Near White; 3.5: Off-White; 4: Beige or Cream Color). Page Quality follows the CGSA grade.

California residents please add 8 1/4% sales tax. *** Prices may be NEGOTIABLE ***

CGSA	M	NM/M	NM	VFN/NM	VFN	FN/VFN	FN	VG/FN	VG	G/VG	G	Fr	Pr
	100,99,98,97,96,95,94,93,92,91	90	88,85,80,75	70	65,60,55	50	45,40,35	30	25,20	15	10	6	3
PgQ	0 1 2 2.5	3	3.3 4	5	6	6.5	7	7.5	8	8.5	9	9.5	10

DC Action Comics 1
3rd Best Known Copy to Exist
VFN 60 (3.5) $135,000

DC Action Comics Ash Can 1
Very Rare
VFN+ 65 (5.0) $50,000

DC All Star Comics 10
Mile High / White Pages
M 93 (1.0) $7,500

MVL Amazing Fantasy 15
Origin/1st App Spider-Man
VFN++ 68 (3.5) $20,000

DC Batman 1
Cosmic Aeroplane/Tear Seals
S VFN 60 (3.5) $60,000

DC Boy Commandos 1
Carson City
VF/NM 70 (4.0) $2,500

DC Brave and the Bold 34
Origin/1st App SA Hawkman
NM++ 88 (3.5) $4,000

TIM Captain America 1
Origin/1st App Captain America
VG+ 25 (5.0) $10,000

FWCT Captain Marvel Adv. 1
Captain Marvel by Jack Kirby
M aFN 35 (7.0) $4,000

MVL Fantastic Four 1
Origin/1st App Fantastic Four
NM 80 (4.0) $30,000

NEDOR Fighting Yank 1
Mile High
NM 80 (2.5) $2,800

DC Green Lantern (GA) 1
Origin Retold
C VFN 55 (3.5) $6,500

DC Leading Comics 1
Origin Seven Soldiers Victory
FN/VFN 50 (5.0) $1,800

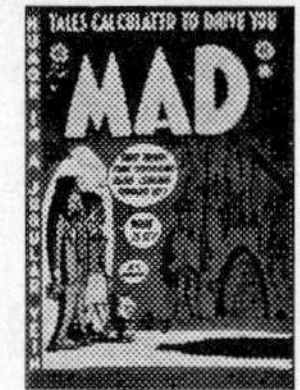

EC Mad 1
Gaines File Copy
M 93 (2.5) $15,000

DC More Fun Comics 9
Very Rare, 1st Comic-Sized
G/VG 15 (6.5) $2,000

DC New Fun Comics 2
Very Rare
Fr 6 (8.0) $5,000

DC NY World's Fair 1939
1st Published App Sandman
VG 20 (5.5) $3,600

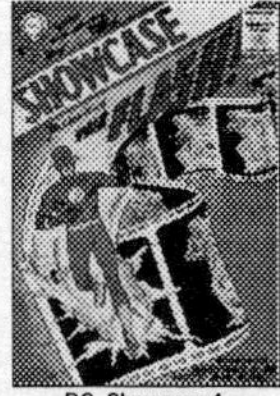

DC Showcase 4
Orig/1st App Silver Age Flash
NM 80 (4.0) $40,000

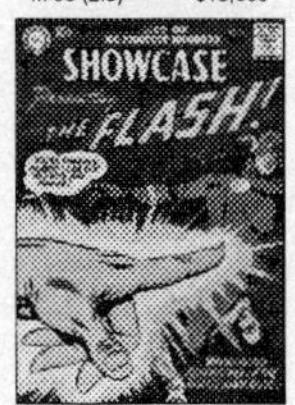

DC Showcase 8
2nd App SA Flash / Ohio Copy
FN/VFN 50 (3.5) $5,200

DC Star Spangled 84
Rare
VFN+ 65 (5.0) $1,350

DC Superman 1
Origin Superman
M aVG/FN 30 (6.5) $18,000

DC Superman 53
O. Superman Retold/10th Aniv.
VF/VF+ 63 (4.0) $2,000

EC Two-Fisted Tales 18
Gaines File Copy
NM/M 90 (3.3) $1,300

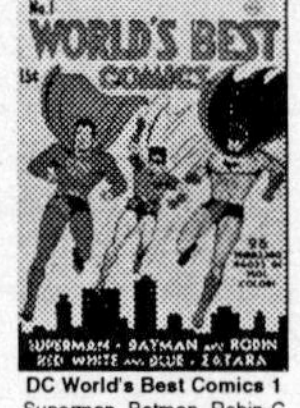

DC World's Best Comics 1
Superman, Batman, Robin-C
VFN 60 (4.5) $5,000

DC World's Finest Comics 2
Superman, Batman, Robin-C
VFN+ 65 (4.5) 2,500

TM

PACIFIC COMIC EXCHANGE, INC.

WANTED!

SELLERS: The following comics and others are wanted by collectors trading on the Pacific Comic Exchange. Please contact The Exchange if you would like to *consign* these or other books at full market value. All books should be graded according to CGSA standards.

CGSA	M	NM/M	NM	VFN/NM	VFN	FN/VFN	FN	VG/FN	VG	G/VG	G	Fr	Pr
	100.99.98.97.96.95.94.93.92.91	90	88.85.80.75	70	65.60.55	50	45.40.35	30	25.20	15	10	6	3
PgQ	0 1 2 2.5	3	3.3 4	5	6	6.5	7	7.5	8	8.5	9	9.5	10

Wanted immediately in all grades

© DC

Action Comics 1

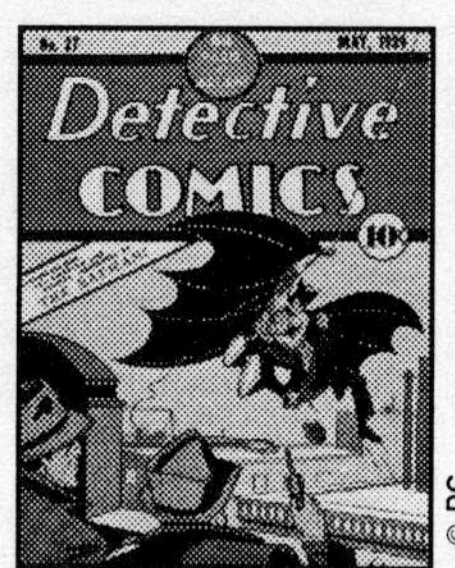

© DC

Detective Comics 27

	G 10	VG 20	FN 40	VFN 60	NM 80	NM/M 90
Action Comics 1	$18,000	$35,000	$60,000	$100,000	$200,000	$350,000
Detective Comics 27	$18,000	$35,000	$60,000	$90,000	$175,000	$300,000

Wanted Immediately in VFN 60 - NM/M 90

	VFN 60	NM 80	NM/M 90
Action Comics 1	$100,000	$200,000	$350,000
Adventure Comics 40	$20,000	$50,000	$75,000
Adventure Comics 210	$2,000	$5,000	$7,500
Adventure Comics 247	$2,500	$6,000	$10,000
All Star Comics 3	$25,000	$50,000	$100,000
All Star Comics 8	$15,000	$25,000	$50,000
All-American Comics 16	$40,000	$75,000	$125,000
Amazing Fantasy 15	---------	$25,000	$50,000
Amazing Spider-Man 1	---------	$15,000	$30,000
Batman 1	$35,000	$70,000	$120,000
Batman 100	$1,000	$2,000	$4,000
Captain America 1	$30,000	$60,000	$100,000
Detective Comics 1	$50,000	$100,000	$150,000
Detective Comics 27	$90,000	$175,000	$300,000
Detective Comics 33	$20,000	$40,000	$60,000
Detective Comics 38	$25,000	$40,000	$80,000
Fantastic Four 1	---------	$20,000	$40,000
Flash Comics 1	$40,000	$60,000	$120,000
Flash Comics 104	$4,500	$9,000	$15,000

	VFN 60	NM 80	NM/M 90
Green Lantern 1 (SA)	$1,400	$3,500	$7,000
Green Lantern 1 (GA)	$9,000	$20,000	$45,000
Incredible Hulk 1	$5,000	$12,000	$25,000
Jimmy Olsen 1	$2,500	$7,500	$15,000
Journey Into Mystery 83	$2,000	$5,000	$10,000
Justice League of America 1	$2,000	$4,000	$7,500
Lois Lane 1	$1,300	$4,000	$7,500
Marvel Comics 1	$50,000	$100,000	$175,000
More Fun Comics 52	$40,000	$75,000	$120,000
More Fun Comics 55	$10,000	$20,000	$40,000
Sensation Comics 1	$6,000	$12,000	$40,000
Showcase 4	$15,000	$30,000	$60,000
Showcase 22	$3,000	$6,000	$10,000
Sub-Mariner Comics 1	$6,000	$15,000	$30,000
Superman 1	$50,000	$100,000	$225,000
Superman 100	$1,000	$2,500	$4,500
Suspense Comics 3	$4,000	$6,000	$10,000
Wonder Woman 1	$6,000	$15,000	$30,000
X-Men 1	---------	$5,000	$9,000

Pacific Comic Exchange, Inc.

Corporate Office:
337 S. Robertson Blvd. Suite 203, Beverly Hills, CA 90211
Tel: (310) 836-7234 (PCEI)

Shipping Address:
P.O. Box 34849 Los Angeles, CA 90034
Fax: (310) 836-7127

Planning to sell an important Comic Book?

Call Us

We simply pay more than any other dealer for the items we want

Period!

Following are just a **few** examples of prices **we will pay**
Based on the NM+ condition grade.

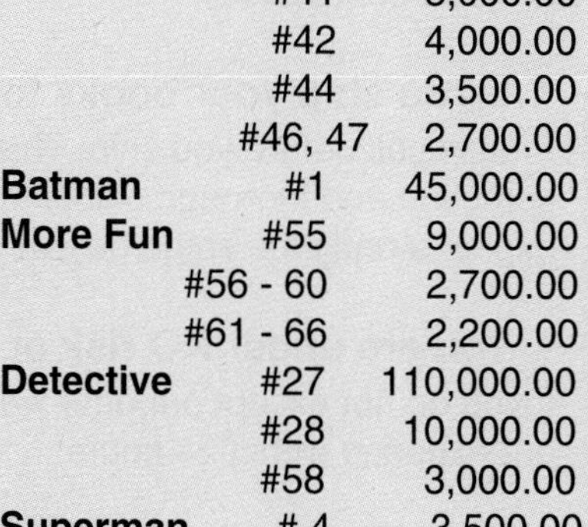

Action Comics	#1	$125,000.00
	#2	12,000.00
	#3	8,500.00
	#4	5,700.00
	#7	7,000.00
Adventure	#40	25,000.00
	#41	3,000.00
	#42	4,000.00
	#44	3,500.00
	#46, 47	2,700.00
Batman	#1	45,000.00
More Fun	#55	9,000.00
	#56 - 60	2,700.00
	#61 - 66	2,200.00
Detective	#27	110,000.00
	#28	10,000.00
	#58	3,000.00
Superman	# 4	3,500.00

World's Finest Comics & Collectibles

"The Right Choice"

Call - (360) 274-9163 **Fax** - (360) 274-2270

COMICS

Immediate Payment!

Price Guide Value!

Reputation

e have worked hard to build a reputation of complete stomer satisfaction, and welcome any inquiries you ght have. We invite you to contact the author of this ice Guide as a reference.

Expert in accurately grading and pricing

e use the standards written in this Price Guide, and will happy to go over the grading procedure with you.

We travel most ANYWHERE

purchase larger and more valuble collections.

Don't be afraid to ask questions.

e are aware that selling comic books might be something you have never done before. We are here to help d explain the process to you. That's good business.

We offer a TOLL FREE number to call

ll and leave a message at any time, day or night at **)0) 225-4189**. Or speak to us directly at **(360) 274-9163**.

Confidence

e are an advisor to the Overstreet Price Guide and the erstreet Grading Guide.

WORLD'S FINEST COMICS & COLLECTIBLES

"The Right Choice"

• Dedicated To Customer Service Since 1985 •

P.O. Box 340 Castle Rock, WA 98611

Theater Posters & Displays Wanted

I collect and deal in all types of theater posters and displays. My main focus is on **Animation**. Such as: early Disney characters, Superman, Popeye, Betty Boop, Tom & Jerry, Porky Pig, Bugs Bunny, Daffy Duck, and more; also **Classic movies**. Such as: Frankenstein, Dracula, The Mummy, King Kong, The Wolfman, Casablanca, early John Wayne, Gone With The Wind, Charlie Chaplin, The Wizard Of Oz, etc.

• 1890 - 1950 • Originals Only •

If you have a truly great theater piece

we want it!

World's Finest Comics & Collectibles

"The Right Choice"

Call - (360) 274-9163 **Fax** - (360) 274-2270

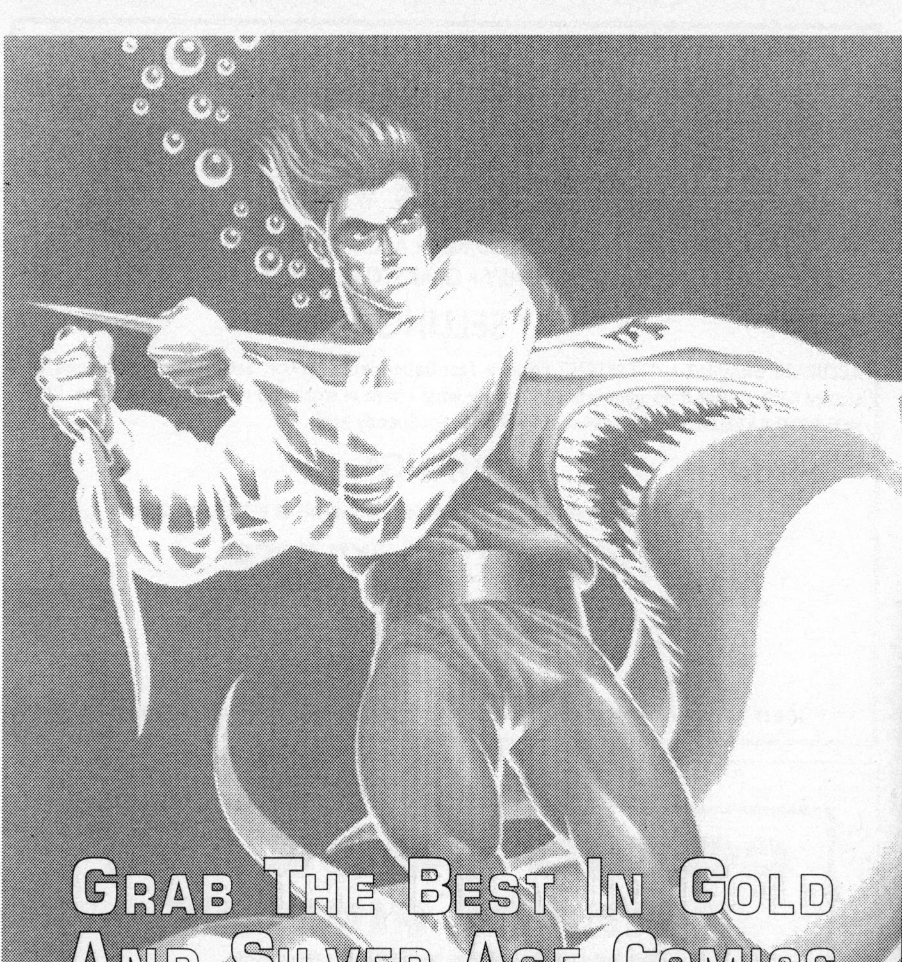

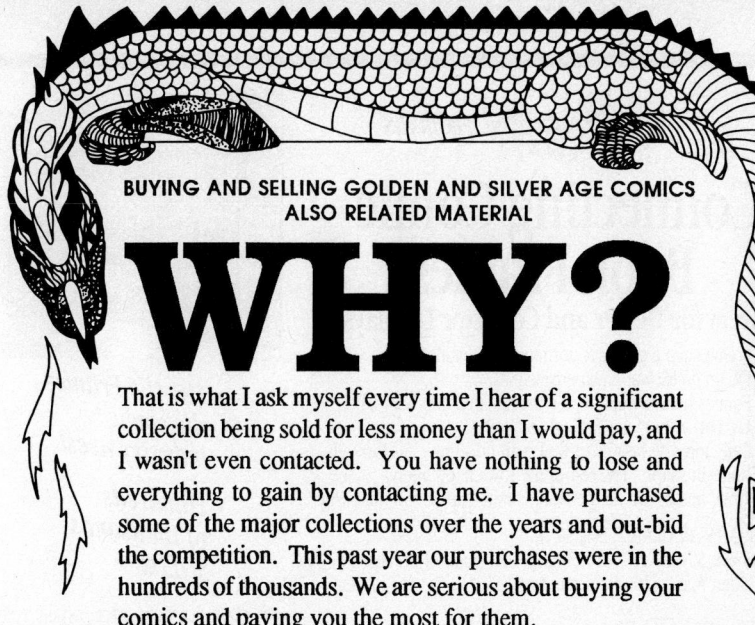

WE NOW SPECIALIZE IN
BUYING & SELLING
PRE-CODE COMICS
CRIME ★ HORROR ★ *GOOD GIRL*
UNDERGROUND'S & ALTERNATIVES TOO!

PHONE IN YER WANTS!
212-502-3991
OR MAIL EM' TO:
134 WEST 32 ST #602 NY NY 10001

BONZAI COMICS

A BRIEF HISTORICAL NOTE ABOUT "COMIC HEAVEN"

John Verzyl started collecting comic books in 1965, and within ten years, he had amassed thousands of Golden and Silver Age comic books. In 1979, with his wife Nanette, he opened "COMIC HEAVEN", a retail store devoted entirely to the buying and selling of comic books.

Over the years, John Verzyl has come to be recognized as an authority in the field of comic books,. He has served as an advisor to the "Overstreet Price Guide". Thousands of his "mint" comics were photographed for Ernst Gerbers newly-released "Photo-Journal Guide To Comic Books". His tables and displays at the annual San Diego Comic Convention draw customers from all over the country.

The first COMIC HEAVEN AUCTION was held in 1987, and today his Auction Catalogs are mailed out to more then ten thousand interested collectors (and dealers).

Comic Heaven
John and Nanette Verzyl
24 W. Main Street
Alhambra, CA 91801
1-818-289-3945

DIAMOND COMIC DISTRIBUTORS PRESENTS

The Photo-Journal Guide To Comic Books and Marvel Comics

Each of these four, full-color, coffee table-sized reference volumes chronicles and celebrates the history of comics with:
More than 8,000 color photos of classic comic covers!
Detailed chapters on every aspect of comic collecting!
Extensive cataloguing by:
Permanent ID Number • Scarcity Index
Relative Value Index • Issue Dates • Artist

Photo-Journal Guide To Comic Books Vol. 1 & 2
By Ernst Gerber.
Spotlighting thousands of Golden Age comics (from the late '30s to 1965).

Vol 1 (A-J)—HC, 11x14, 425pg, FC
Was $75.00—**Now $47.00 retail!**

Vol 2 (K-Z)—HC, 11x14, 425pg, FC
Was $75.00—**Now $47.00 retail!**

Photo-Journal Guide To Comic Books Vol. 3 & 4
By Ernst Gerber.
Showcasing all **Marvel Comics,** covers, and stories from 1961—the beginning of Marvel's heyday—through the late '70s and into the '80s!

Vol 3—HC, FC
Was $29.95—**Now $24.50 retail!**

Vol 4—HC, FC
Was $29.95—**Now $24.50 retail!**

"The best book ever in the history of comic book collecting!"
Steve Geppi, President,
Diamond Comic Distributors

Now available at a fine comic book specialty shop near you!

Retailers: Order your volumes of **The Photo-Journal Guide To Comic Books** today through the industry's leading source of backlist best-sellers, the **Diamond Star System!**

Abbie an' Slates #3 © UFS

Ace Comics #110 © DMP

Action Comics #15 © DC

The correct title listing for each comic book can be determined by consulting the indicia (publication data) on the beginning interior pages of the comic. The official title is determined by those words of the title in capital letters only, and not by what is on the cover.

Titles are listed in this book as if they were one word, ignoring spaces, hyphens, and apostrophes, to make finding titles easier. Comic books listed should be assumed to be in color unless noted "B&W".

Comic publishers are invited to send us sample copies for possible inclusion in future guides.

Near Mint is the highest value listed in this price guide. True mint books from the 1970s and 1990s do exist, so the Near Mint value listed should be interpreted as a Mint value for those books.

A-1 (See A-One)

ABBIE AN' SLATS (...With Becky No. 1-4) (See Comics On Parade, Fight for Love, Giant Comics Edition 2, Giant Comics Editions #1, Sparkler Comics, Tip Topper, Treasury of Comics, & United Comics)
1940; March, 1948 - No. 4, Aug, 1948 (Reprints)
United Features Syndicate

	GD25	FN65	NM94
Single Series 25 ('40)	27.00	81.00	190.00
Single Series 28	24.00	72.00	165.00
1 (1948)	12.00	36.00	85.00
2-4: 3-r/Sparkler #68-72	6.00	18.00	42.00

ABBOTT AND COSTELLO (...Comics)(See Giant Comics Editions #1 & Treasury of Comics)
Feb, 1948 - No. 40, Sept, 1956 (Mort Drucker art in most issues)
St. John Publishing Co.

	GD25	FN65	NM94
1	40.00	120.00	280.00
2	19.00	57.00	130.00
3-9 (#8, 8/49; #9, 2/50)	11.50	34.00	80.00
10-Son of Sinbad story by Kubert (new)	16.00	48.00	110.00
11,13-20 (#11, 10/50; #13, 8/51; #15, 12/52)	9.15	27.50	55.00
12-Movie issue	10.00	30.00	70.00
21-30: 28-r/#8. 30-Painted-c	6.70	20.00	40.00
31-40: 33,38-Reprints	5.85	17.50	35.00
3-D #1 (11/53, 25¢)-Infinity-c	27.00	81.00	190.00

ABBOTT AND COSTELLO (TV)
Feb, 1968 - No. 22, Aug, 1971 (Hanna-Barbera)
Charlton Comics

	GD25	FN65	NM94
1	6.50	19.00	45.00
2	3.25	9.50	22.00
3-10	2.60	7.50	18.00
11-22	1.70	5.00	12.00

ABC (See America's Best TV Comics)

ABRAHAM LINCOLN LIFE STORY (See Dell Giants)

ABSENT-MINDED PROFESSOR, THE (See 4-Color Comics No.1199)

ABYSS, THE (Dark Horse)(Value: cover or less)

ACE COMICS
April, 1937 - No. 151, Oct-Nov, 1949
David McKay Publications

	GD25	FN65	NM94
1-Jungle Jim by Alex Raymond, Blondie, Ripley's Believe It Or Not, Krazy Kat begin (1st app. of each)	250.00	750.00	1750.00
2	75.00	225.00	525.00
3-5	51.00	155.00	360.00
6-10	38.00	115.00	265.00
11-The Phantom begins (1st app., 2/38) (in brown costume)	48.00	145.00	335.00
12-20	29.00	86.00	200.00
21-25,27-30	25.00	75.00	175.00
26-Origin & 1st app. Prince Valiant (5/39); begins series?	68.00	205.00	475.00
31-40: 37-Krazy Kat ends	18.00	54.00	125.00
41-60	13.50	41.00	95.00
61-64,66-76-(7/43; last 68 pgs.)	12.00	36.00	85.00
65-(8/42)-Flag-c	13.00	40.00	90.00
77-84 (3/44; all 60 pgs.)	10.00	30.00	70.00
85-99 (52 pgs.)	9.15	27.50	55.00
100 (7/45; last 52 pgs.)	10.00	30.00	65.00
101-134: 128-(11/47)-Brick Bradford begins. 134-Last Prince Valiant (all 36 pgs.)	7.50	22.50	45.00
135-151: 135-(6/48)-Lone Ranger begins	6.35	19.00	38.00

ACE KELLY (See Tops Comics & Tops In Humor)

ACE KING (See Adventures of the Detective)

ACES (Eclipse)(Value: cover or less)

ACES HIGH
Mar-Apr, 1955 - No. 5, Nov-Dec, 1955
E.C. Comics

	GD25	FN65	NM94
1-Not approved by code	15.00	45.00	105.00
2	10.00	30.00	70.00
3-5	10.00	30.00	60.00

NOTE: *All have stories by* ***Davis, Evans, Krigstein****, and* ***Wood. Evans*** *c-1-5.*

ACTION ADVENTURE (War) (Formerly Real Adventure)
V1#2, June, 1955 - No. 4, Oct, 1955
Gillmor Magazines

	GD25	FN65	NM94
V1#2-4	3.60	9.00	18.00

ACTION COMICS (...Weekly #601-642; also see The Comics Magazine #1, More Fun #14-17 & Special Edition)
6/38 - No. 583, 9/86; No. 584, 1/87 - Present
National Periodical Publ./Detective Comics/DC Comics

	GD25	FN65	VF82	NM94
1-Origin & 1st app. Superman by Siegel & Shuster, Marco Polo, Tex Thompson, Pep Morgan, Chuck Dawson & Scoop Scanlon; 1st app. Zatara & Lois Lane; Superman story missing 4 pgs. which were included when reprinted in Superman #1; Clark Kent works for Daily Star; story continued in #2	12,500.00	37,500.00	81,250.00	125,000.00

(Estimated up to 75+ total copies exist, 4 in NM/Mint)
(Issues 1 through 10 are all scarce to rare)

1-Reprint, Oversize 13-1/2x10". **WARNING:** This comic is an exact reprint of the original except for its size. DC published it in 1974 with a second cover titling it as a Famous First Edition. There have been many reported cases of the outer cover being removed and the interior sold as the original edition. The reprint with the new outer cover removed is practically worthless. See Famous First Edition for value.

	GD25	FN65	NM94
1(1976,1983)-Giveaway; paper cover, 16pgs. in color; reprints complete Superman story from #1 ('38)	2.40	6.00	12.00
1(1987 Nestle Quik giveaway; 1988, 50¢)		.50	1.00
1(1993)-Came w/Reign of Superman packs	.30	.75	1.50
2	1145.00	3430.00	8000.00
3 (Scarce)-Superman apps. in costume in only one panel	1000.00	3000.00	7000.00
4-6: 6-1st Jimmy Olsen (called office boy)	571.00	1715.00	4000.00
7-2nd Superman cover	821.00	2465.00	5750.00
8,9	500.00	1500.00	3500.00
10-3rd Superman cover by Siegel & Shuster	745.00	2230.00	5200.00
11,14: 14-Clip Carson begins, ends #41	257.00	770.00	1800.00
12-Has 1 pg. Batman ad for Det. #27 (5/39); Zatara sci-fi cover (Zatara-c #14 also)	257.00	770.00	1800.00
13-Guardineer Superman-c; last Scoop Scanlon	400.00	1200.00	2800.00
15-Guardineer Superman-c	317.00	600.00	2400.00
16	200.00	500.00	1400.00
17-Superman cover; last Marco Polo	300.00	900.00	2100.00
18-Origin 3 Aces; 1st X-Ray Vision?	200.00	600.00	1400.00
19-Superman covers begin; has full pg. ad for New York World's Fair 1939	257.00	771.00	1800.00
20-The 'S' left off Superman's chest; Clark Kent works at 'Daily Star'	245.00	730.00	1700.00

Action Comics #36 © DC

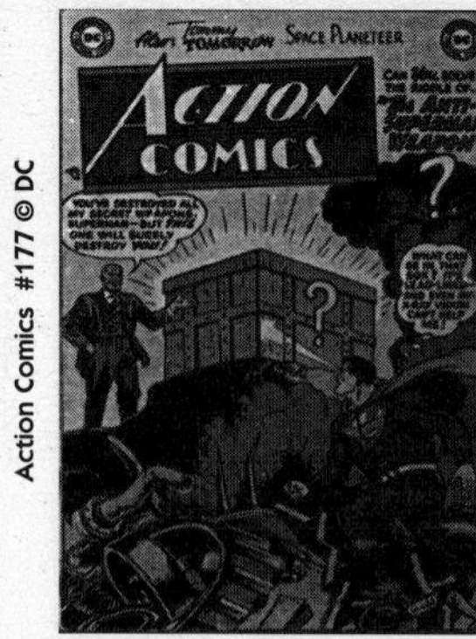

Action Comics #177 © DC

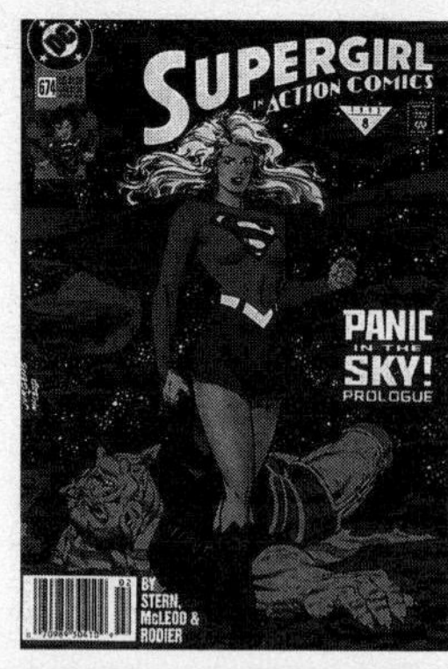

Action Comics #674 © DC

GD25 FN65 NM94

21,22,24,25: 24-Kent at Daily Planet. 25-Last app. Gargantua T. Potts, Tex Thompson's sidekick 143.00 430.00 1000.00
23-1st app. Luthor (w/red hair) & Black Pirate; Black Pirate by Moldoff; 1st mention of The Daily Planet (4/40) 500.00 1500.00 3500.00
26-30: 29-1st Lois Lane-c (10/40) 121.00 365.00 850.00
31,32: 32-Intro/1st app. Krypto Ray Gun in Superman story by Burnley 93.00 278.00 650.00
33-Origin Mr. America 107.00 321.00 750.00
34-40: 37-Origin Congo Bill. 40-(9/41)-Intro/1st app. Star Spangled Kid & Stripesy 93.00 278.00 650.00
41 86.00 257.00 600.00
42-1st app./origin Vigilante; Bob Daley becomes Fat Man; origin Mr. America's magic flying carpet; The Queen Bee & Luthor app; Black Pirate ends; not in #41 118.00 354.00 825.00
43-46,48-50: 44-Fat Man's i.d. revealed to Mr. America. 45-1st app. Stuff (Vigilante's oriental sidekick) 86.00 257.00 600.00
47-1st Luthor cover in comics (4/42) 107.00 321.00 750.00
51-1st app. The Prankster 86.00 257.00 600.00
52-Fat Man & Mr. America become the Ameri-commandos; origin Vigilante retold 93.00 278.00 650.00
53-60: 56-Last Fat Man. 57-2nd Lois Lane-c in Action (3rd anywhere, 2/43). 59-Kubert Vigilante begins?, ends #70. 60-First app. Lois Lane as Superwoman 57.00 171.00 400.00
61-63,65-70: 63-Last 3 Aces 50.00 150.00 350.00
64-Intro Toyman 61.00 182.00 425.00
71-79: 74-Last Mr. America 46.00 140.00 325.00
80-2nd app. & 1st Mr. Mxyztplk-c (1/45) 71.00 215.00 500.00
81-90: 83-Intro Hocus & Pocus 46.00 140.00 325.00
91-99: 93-X-Mas-c. 99-1st small logo (8/46) 43.00 130.00 300.00
100 100.00 300.00 700.00
101-Nuclear explosion-c 61.00 182.00 425.00
102-120: 105,117-X-Mas-c 43.00 130.00 300.00
121-126,128-140: 135,136,138-Zatara by Kubert 41.00 124.00 290.00
127-Vigilante by Kubert; Tommy Tomorrow begins (12/48, see Real Fact #6) 48.00 145.00 335.00
141-157,159-161: 151-Luthor/Mr. Mxyztplk/Prankster team-up. 156-Lois Lane as Super Woman. 160- Last 52 pgs. 39.00 118.00 275.00
158-Origin Superman retold 71.00 215.00 500.00
162-180: 168,176-Used in **POP**, pg. 90 30.00 90.00 210.00
181-201: 191-Intro. Janu in Congo Bill. 198-Last Vigilante. 201-Last pre-code issue 30.00 90.00 210.00
202-220 25.00 75.00 175.00
221-240: 224-1st Golden Gorilla story 20.00 60.00 140.00
241,243-251: 241-Batman x-over. 248-Congo Bill becomes Congorilla. 251-Last Tommy Tomorrow 15.00 45.00 105.00
242-Origin & 1st app. Brainiac (7/58); 1st mention of Shrunken City of Kandor 110.00 330.00 775.00
252-Origin & 1st app. Supergirl (5/59); intro new Metallo 130.00 375.00 875.00
253-2nd app. Supergirl 29.00 86.00 200.00
254-1st meeting of Bizarro & Superman-c/story 24.00 73.00 170.00
255-1st Bizarro Lois Lane-c/story & both Bizarros leave Earth to make Bizarro World 16.00 49.00 115.00
256-261: 259-Red Kryptonite used. 261-1st X-Kryptonite which gave Streaky his powers; last Congorilla in Action; origin & 1st app. Streaky The Super Cat 10.00 30.00 75.00
262,264-266,268-270 8.00 24.00 55.00
263-Origin Bizarro World 12.00 36.00 85.00
267(8/60)-3rd Legion app; 1st app. Chameleon Boy, Colossal Boy, & Invisible Kid 40.00 130.00 300.00
271-275,277-282: 282-Last 10¢ issue 7.50 22.00 52.00
276(5/61)-6th Legion app; 1st app. Brainiac 5, Phantom Girl, Triplicate Girl, Bouncing Boy, Sun Boy, & Shrinking Violet; Supergirl joins Legion 19.00 58.00 135.00
283(12/61)-Legion of Super-Villains app. 8.00 24.00 56.00
284(1/62)-Mon-el app. 8.00 24.00 56.00

GD25 FN65 NM94

285(2/62)-12th Legion app; Brainiac 5 cameo; Supergirl's existence revealed to world; JFK & Jackie cameos 8.00 24.00 56.00
286(3/62)-Legion of Super Villains app. 4.00 12.00 28.00
287(4/62)-14th Legion app.(cameo) 4.00 12.00 28.00
288-Mon-el app.; r-origin Supergirl 4.00 12.00 28.00
289(6/62)-16th Legion app.(Adult); Lightning Man & Saturn Woman's marriage 1st revealed 4.00 12.00 28.00
290(7/62)-17th Legion app. (cameo); Phantom Girl app. 290-1st Supergirl emergency squad 4.00 12.00 28.00
291,292,294-299: 291-1st meeting Supergirl & Mr. Mxyzptlk. 292-2nd app. Superhorse (see Adv. #293). 297-Mon-el app. 298-Legion cameo 3.30 10.00 23.00
293-Origin Comet(Superhorse) 9.00 26.00 60.00
300-(5/63) 4.00 12.00 28.00
301-303,305-308,310-320: 306-Brainiac 5, Mon-el app. 307-Saturn Girl app. 314-r-origin Supergirl; J.L.A. x-over. 317-Death of Nor-Kan of Kandor. 319-Shrinking Violet app. 2.00 5.00 14.00
304-Origin & 1st app. Black Flame (9/63) 2.70 8.00 19.00
309-(2/64)-Legion app.; Batman & Robin-c & cameo; JFK app. (he died 11/22/63; on stands same time as death?) 2.60 7.50 18.00
321-333,335-340: 336-Origin Akvar (Flamebird). 340-Origin, 1st app. Parasite 1.80 5.00 11.00
334-Giant G-20; origin Supergirl, Streaky, Superhorse & Legion (all-r) 3.00 9.00 21.00
341-346,348-359: 344-Batman x-over. 350-Batman, Green Arrow & Green Lantern app. in Supergirl back-up story 1.30 3.00 8.00
347,360-Giant Supergirl G-33,G-45; 347-Origin Comet-r plus 3 Bizarro stories. 360-Legion-r; r/origin Supergirl 2.00 6.00 14.00
361-372,374-380: 365-Legion app. 370-New facts about Superman's origin. 376-Last Supergirl in Action. 377-Legion begins 1.10 3.00 6.50
373-Giant Supergirl G-57; Legion-r 1.70 5.00 12.00
381-402: 392-Last Legion in Action. Saturn Girl gets new costume. 393-402-All Superman issues .90 2.30 5.50
403-413: All 52pg. issues. 411-Origin Eclipso-(r). 413-Metamorpho begins, ends #418 1.30 3.00 8.00
414-424: 419-Intro. Human Target. 421-Intro Capt. Strong; Green Arrow begins. 422,423-Origin Human Target .90 2.30 5.50
425-Neal Adams-a(p); The Atom begins 1.30 3.00 8.00
426-436,438,439: 432-1st S.A. app. The Toyman 1.00 2.00 5.00
437,443-(100 pg. giants) 1.30 3.00 7.50
440-1st Grell-a on Green Arrow 1.40 4.00 8.50
441-Grell-a on Green Arrow continues 1.10 2.70 6.50
442,444-499: 449-(68 pgs.). 454-Last Atom. 458-Last Green Arrow. 484-Earth II Superman & Lois Lane wed; 40th anniversary issue (6/78). 487,488-(44 pgs.). 487-Origin & 1st app. Microwave Man; origin Atom retold 1.40 3.50
500-($1.00, 68 pgs.)-Infinity-c; Superman life story; shows Legion statues in museum 1.40 3.50
501-551,554-582: 511-514-Airwave II solo stories. 513-The Atom begins. 517-Aquaman begins; ends #541. 521-1st app. The Vixen. 532,536-New Teen Titans cameo. 535,536-Omega Men app. 544-(Mando paper, 68 pgs.)-Origins new Luthor & Brainiac; Omega Men cameo. 544-Shuster-a (pin-up); article by Siegel. 546-J.L.A., New Teen Titans app. 551-Starfire becomes Red-Star .80 2.00
552,553-Animal Man-c & app. (2/84 & 3/84) 1.20 2.90 7.00
583-Alan Moore scripts 1.40 4.00 8.50
584-Byrne-a begins; New Teen Titans app. .80 2.00
585-599: 586-Legends x-over. 596-Millennium x-over. 598-1st app. Checkmate .60 1.50
600-($2.50, 84 pgs., 5/88) 1.90 4.75
601-642-Weekly issues ($1.50, 52 pgs.): 601-Re-intro The Secret Six. 611-614: Catwoman stories (new costume in #611). 613-618: Nightwing stories .70 1.75
643-Superman & monthly issues begin again; Perez-c/a/scripts begin; swipes cover to Superman #1 .70 1.75
644-649,651-661,663-666,668-679: 645-1st app. Maxima. 654-Part 3 of Batman

Adam-12 #9 © Gold Key

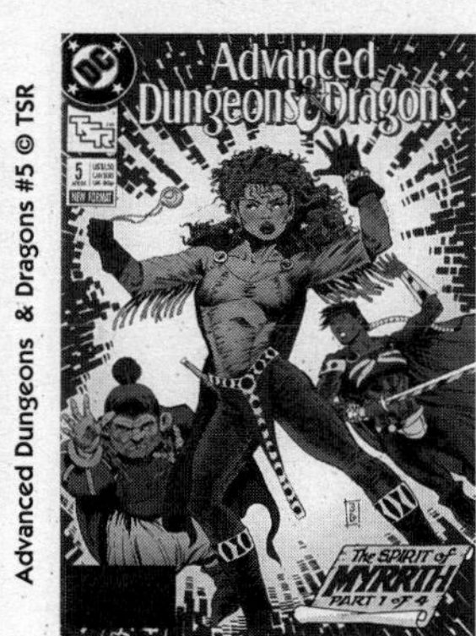

Advanced Dungeons & Dragons #5 © TSR

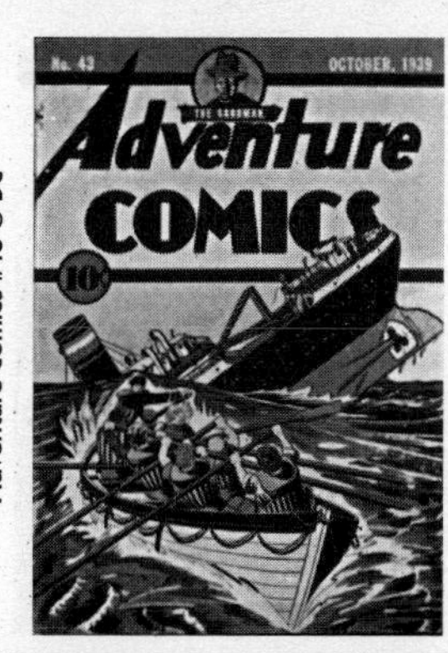

Adventure Comics #43 © DC

GD25 FN65 NM94

storyline. 655-Free extra 8 pgs. 660-Death of Lex Luthor. 661-Begin $1.00-c. 674-Supergirl logo & c/story (reintro). 675-Deathstroke cameo. 679-Last $1.00 issue 1.25
650-($1.50, 52 pgs.)-Lobo cameo (last panel) .70 1.75
662-Clark Kent reveals i.d. to Lois Lane; story continued in Superman #53 1.50 3.75
667-($1.75, 52 pgs.) .80 2.00
680-682 1.50
683-Doomsday cameo 1.30 3.00 8.00
683-2nd & 3rd printings 1.25
684-Doomsday battle issue 1.30 3.25 8.00
685,686-Funeral for a Friend issues; Supergirl app. .90 2.25
685-2nd & 3rd printings 1.25
687-($1.95)-Collector's Edition with die-cut-c .90 2.25
687-($1.50)-Newsstand Edition with mini-poster .70 1.70
688-699,701-709-($1.50): 688-Guy Gardner-c/story. 697-Bizarro-c/story. 703-(9/94)-Zero Hour 1.50
695-($2.50)-Collector's Edition w/embossed foil-c 1.00 2.50
700-($2.95, 68 pgs.)-Fall of Metropolis part 1; Pete Ross marries Lana Lang; Curt Swan & Murphy Anderson inks 1.20 3.00
0-(10/94) 1.50
Annual 1(1987)-Art Adams-c/a(p); Batman app. 1.10 2.70 6.50
Annual 2(1989, $1.75, 68 pgs.)-Perez-c/a(i) .80 2.00
Annual 3(1991, $2.00, 68 pgs.)-Armageddon 2001 .80 2.00
Annual 4(1992, $2.50, 68 pgs.)-Eclipso vs. Shazam 1.00 2.50
Annual 5(1993, $2.50, 68 pgs.) 1.00 2.50
Annual 6(1994, $2.95)-Elseworlds story 1.20 3.00
Theater Giveaway (1947, 32 pgs., 6-1/2 x 8-1/4", nn)-Vigilante story based on Columbia Vigilante serial; no Superman-c or story
64.00 192.00 450.00

NOTE:*Supergirl's origin in 262, 280, 285, 291, 305, 309.* ***N. Adams*** *c-356, 358, 359, 361-364, 366, 367, 370-374, 377-379i, 398-400, 402, 404-406, 419p, 466, 468, 473i, 485.* ***Austin*** *c/a-682i.* ***Baily*** *a-24, 25.* ***Burnley*** *a-28-33; c-48?, 53-55, 58, 59?, 60-63, 65, 66p, 67p, 70p, 71p, 79p, 82p, 84-86p, 90-92p, 93p?, 94p, 107p, 108p.* ***Byrne*** *a-584-598p, 599i, 600p; c-596-600.* ***Giffen*** *a-560, 563, 565, 577, 579; c-539, 560, 563, 565, 577, 579.* ***Grell*** *a-440-442, 444-446, 450-452, 456-458; c-456.* ***Guardineer*** *a-24, 25; c-8, 11, 12, 14-16, 18. 25.* ***Guice*** *a(p)-676-681, 683-698, 700; c-683, 685, 686, 687(direct), 688-693i, 694-696, 697i, 698-700.* ***Bob Kane's*** *Clip Carson-14-41.* ***Gil Kane*** *a-443r, 493r, 539-541, 544-546, 551-554, 601-605; c-535p, 540, 541, 544p, 545-549, 551-554.* ***Meskin*** *a-42-121(most).* ***Moldoff*** *a-23-25, 443r.* ***Mooney*** *a-667p.* ***Mortimer*** *c-153, 154, 159-172, 174, 178-181, 184, 186-189, 191-193, 196, 200, 206.* ***Perez*** *a-600i, 643-652p; c-529p, 643-651.* ***Quesada*** *c-Annual 4p.* ***Fred Ray*** *c-34, 36-46, 50-52.* ***Siegel & Shuster*** *a-1-27.* ***Starlin*** *a-509.* ***Leonard Starr*** *a-597i(part),* ***Staton*** *a-525p, 526p, 531p, 535p, 536p.* ***Swan/Moldoff*** *c-281, 286, 287, 293, 298, 334.* ***Thibert*** *c-676, 677p, 678-681, 684.* ***Toth*** *a-406, 407, 413, 431.* ***Tuska*** *a-486p, 550.* ***Williamson*** *a-568i.*

ACTION FORCE (Marvel)(Value: cover or less)

ACTUAL CONFESSIONS (Formerly Love Adventures)
No. 13, October, 1952 - No. 14, December, 1952
Atlas Comics (MPI)

13,14 3.20 8.00 16.00

ACTUAL ROMANCES (Becomes True Secrets #3 on?)
October, 1949 - No. 2, Jan, 1950 (52 pgs.)
Marvel Comics (IPS)

1 7.50 22.50 45.00
2-Photo-c 4.20 12.50 25.00

ADAM AND EVE (Spire Christian)(Value: cover or less)

ADAM STRANGE (DC)(Value: cover or less)(See Green Lantern #132, Mystery In Space #53 & Showcase #17)

ADAM-12 (TV)
Dec, 1973 - No. 10, Feb, 1976 (Photo covers)
Gold Key

1 3.25 9.50 22.00
2-10 1.80 4.60 11.00

ADDAMS FAMILY (TV cartoon)
Oct, 1974 - No. 3, Apr, 1975 (Hanna-Barbera)
Gold Key

GD25 FN65 NM94

1 5.50 17.00 40.00
2,3 3.25 9.50 22.00

ADLAI STEVENSON
December, 1966
Dell Publishing Co.

12-007-612-Life story; photo-c 4.00 11.00 22.00

ADOLESCENT RADIOACTIVE BLACK BELT HAMSTERS (Eclipse)(Value: cover or less)

ADULT TALES OF TERROR ILLUSTRATED (See Terror Illustrated)

ADVANCED DUNGEONS & DRAGONS (DC)(Value: cover or less)

ADVENTURE BOUND (See 4-Color Comics No. 239)

ADVENTURE COMICS (Formerly New Adventure)(...Presents Dial H For Hero #479-490)
No. 32, 11/38 - No. 490, 2/82; No. 491, 9/82 - No. 503, 9/83
National Periodical Publications/DC Comics

32-Anchors Aweigh (ends #52), Barry O'Neil (ends #60, not in #33), Captain Desmo (ends #47), Dale Daring (ends #47), Federal Men (ends #70), The Golden Dragon (ends #36), Rusty & His Pals (ends #52) by Bob Kane, Todd Hunter (ends #38) and Tom Brent (ends #39) begin
257.00 771.00 1800.00
33-38: 37-Cover used on Double Action #2 129.00 385.00 900.00
39(6/39):-Jack Wood begins, ends #42; 1st mention of Marijuana in comics
129.00 385.00 900.00

GD25 FN65 VF82 NM94

40-(Rare, 7/39, on stands 6/10/39)-The Sandman begins by Bert Christman (who died in WWII); believed to be 1st conceived story (see N.Y. World's Fair for 1st published app.); Socko Strong begins, ends #54
2445.00 7335.00 14,670.00 22,000.00

GD25 FN65 NM94

41 343.00 1030.00 2400.00
42,44-Sandman-c by Flessel. 44-Opium story 429.00 1285.00 3000.00
43,45 229.00 685.00 1600.00
46,47-Sandman covers by Flessel. 47-Steve Conrad Adventurer begins, ends #76 314.00 943.00 2200.00

GD25 FN65 VF82 NM94

48-Intro & 1st app. The Hourman by Bernard Bailey; Baily-c (Hourman c-48,50,52-59) 1333.00 4000.00 8000.00 12,000.00
(Estimated up to 80 total copies exist, 5 in NM/Mint)

GD25 FN65 NM94

49,50: 50-Cotton Carver by Jack Lehti begins, ends #64
171.00 515.00 1200.00
51,60-Sandman-c 200.00 600.00 1400.00
52-59: 53-1st app. Jimmy "Minuteman" Martin & the Minutemen of America in Hourman; ends #78. 58-Paul Kirk Manhunter begins (1st app.), ends #72
129.00 385.00 900.00

GD25 FN65 VF82 NM94

61-1st app. Starman by Jack Burnley (4/41); Starman c-61-72; Starman by Burnley in #61-80 800.00 2400.00 4800.00 7200.00
(Estimated up to 100+ total copies exist, 7 in NM/Mint)

GD25 FN65 NM94

62-65,67,68,70: 67-Origin & 1st app. The Mist. 70-Last Federal Men
121.00 365.00 850.00
66-Origin/1st app. Shining Knight (9/41) 150.00 450.00 1050.00
69-1st app. Sandy the Golden Boy (Sandman's sidekick) by Bob Kane; Sandman dons new costume 143.00 430.00 1000.00
71-Jimmy Martin becomes costume aide to the Hourman; 1st app.Hourman's Miracle Ray machine 107.00 321.00 750.00

GD25 FN65 VF82 NM94

72-1st Simon & Kirby Sandman (3/42, 1st DC work)
667.00 2000.00 4000.00 6000.00
(Estimated up to 100+ total copies exist, 8 in NM/Mint)
73-Origin Manhunter by Simon & Kirby; begin new series; Manhunter-c
700.00 2100.00 4200.00 6300.00
(Estimated up to 100+ total copies exist, 7 in NM/Mint)

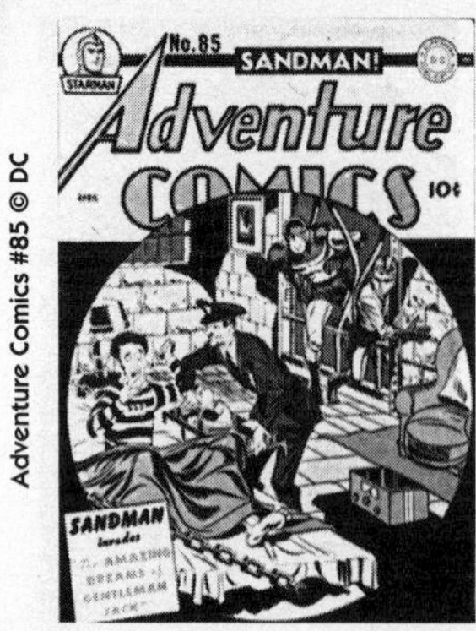

Adventure Comics #85 © DC

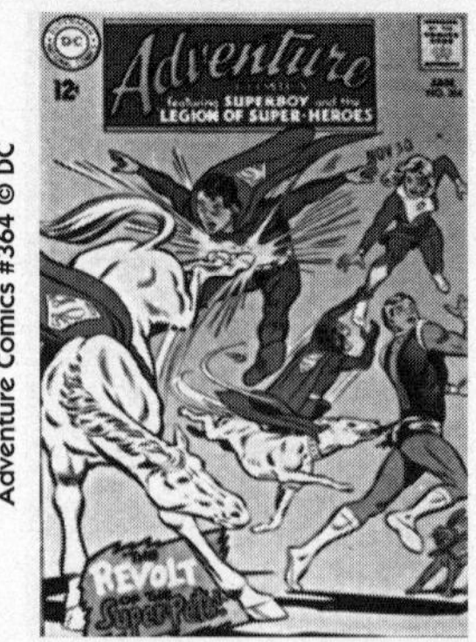

Adventure Comics #364 © DC

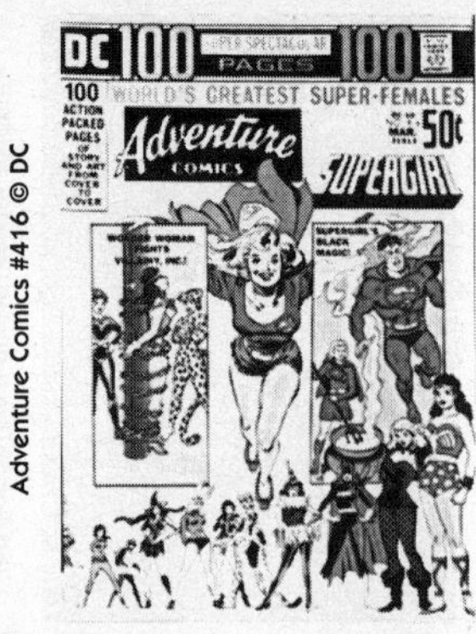

Adventure Comics #416 © DC

GD25 FN65 NM94 — GD25 FN65 NM94

	GD25	FN65	NM94
74-80: 74-Thorndyke replaces Jimmy, Hourman's assistant; new Sandman-c begin by S&K. 75-Thor app. by Kirby; 1st Kirby Thor (see Tales of the Unexpected #16). 77-Origin Genius Jones; Mist story. 79-Manhunter-c. 80-Last S&K Manhunter & Burnley Starman	143.00	430.00	1000.00
81-90: 83-Last Hourman. 84-Mike Gibbs begins, ends #102	93.00	280.00	650.00
91-Last Simon & Kirby Sandman	80.00	240.00	560.00
92-99,101,102: 92-Last Manhunter. 102-Last Starman, Sandman, & Genius Jones; most-S&K-c (Genius Jones cont'd in More Fun #108)	64.00	193.00	450.00
100-S&K cover	100.00	300.00	700.00
103-Aquaman, Green Arrow, Johnny Quick & Superboy all move over from More Fun Comics #107; 8th app. Superboy; Superboy-c begin; 1st small logo (4/46)	243.00	730.00	1700.00
104	86.00	257.00	600.00
105-110	57.00	170.00	400.00
111-120: 113-X-Mas-c	55.00	165.00	385.00
121-126,128-130: 128-1st meeting Superboy & Lois Lane	47.00	140.00	325.00
127-Brief origin Shining Knight retold	50.00	150.00	350.00
131-141,143-149: 132-Shining Knight 1st return to King Arthur time; origin aide Sir Butch	41.00	122.00	285.00
142-Origin Shining Knight & Johnny Quick retold	45.00	135.00	315.00
150,151,153,155,157,159,161,163-All have 6 pg. Shining Knight stories by Frank Frazetta. 159-Origin Johnny Quick	48.00	145.00	335.00
152,154,156,158,160,162,164-169: 166-Last Shining Knight. 168-Last 52 pg. issue	34.00	103.00	240.00
170-180	30.00	90.00	210.00
181-199: 189-B&W and color illo in **POP**	29.00	86.00	200.00
200 (5/54)	47.00	140.00	330.00
201-208: 207-Last Johnny Quick (not in 205)	31.00	94.00	220.00
209-Last pre-code issue; origin Speedy	32.00	96.00	225.00

	GD25	FN65	VF82	NM94
210-1st app. Krypto (Superdog)-c/story (3/55)	190.00	570.00	1422.00	2275.00

	GD25	FN65	NM94
211-213,215-220: 220-Krypto app.	25.00	75.00	175.00
214-2nd app. Krypto	39.00	116.00	270.00
221-246: 237-1st Intergalactic Vigilante Squadron (6/57)	21.00	62.00	145.00

	GD25	FN65	VF82	NM94
247(4/58)-1st Legion of Super Heroes app.; 1st app. Cosmic Boy, Lightning Boy (later Lightning Lad in #267), & Saturn Girl (origin)	285.00	855.00	1852.00	2850.00

	GD25	FN65	NM94
248-252,254,255-Green Arrow in all: 255-Intro. Red Kryptonite in Superboy (used in #252 but with no effect)	16.00	47.00	110.00
253-1st meeting of Superboy & Robin; Green Arrow by Kirby in #250-255 (also see World's Finest #96-99)	22.00	66.00	155.00
256-Origin Green Arrow by Kirby	64.00	190.00	445.00
257-259: 258-Green Arrow x-over in Superboy	14.00	43.00	100.00
260-1st Silver-Age origin Aquaman (5/59)	70.00	200.00	470.00
261-266,268,270: 262-Origin Speedy in Green Arrow. 266-(11/59)-Origin & 1st app. Aquagirl (tryout, not same as later character). 270-Congorilla begins, ends #281,283	10.00	31.00	72.00
267(12/59)-2nd Legion of Super Heroes; Lightning Boy now called Lightning Lad; new costumes for Legion	90.00	270.00	625.00
269-Intro. Aqualad (2/60); last Green Arrow (not in #206)	21.00	64.00	150.00
271-Origin Luthor retold	23.00	69.00	160.00
272-274,277-280: 279-Intro White Kryptonite in Superboy. 280-1st meeting Superboy-Lori Lemaris	8.00	24.00	55.00
275-Origin Superman-Batman team retold (see World's Finest #94)	19.00	58.00	135.00
276-(9/60) Re-intro Metallo (3rd app?); story similar to Superboy #49	8.00	24.00	55.00
281,284,287-289: 281-Last Congorilla. 284-Last Aquaman in Adv. 287,288-Intro Dev-Em, the Knave from Krypton. 287-1st Bizarro Perry White & J. Olsen. 288-Bizarro-c. 289-Legion cameo (statues)	8.00	24.00	55.00
282(3/61)-5th Legion app; intro/origin Star Boy	16.00	49.00	115.00
283-Intro. The Phantom Zone	18.00	54.00	125.00
285-1st Tales of the Bizarro World-c/story (ends #299) in Adv. (see Action #255)	13.00	40.00	90.00
286-1st Bizarro Mxyzptlk; Bizarro-c	11.00	34.00	80.00
290(11/61)-8th Legion app; origin Sunboy in Legion (last 10¢ issue)	16.00	49.00	115.00
291,292,295-298: 292-1st Bizarro Lana Lang & Lucy Lane. 295-Bizarro-c; 1st Bizarro Titano	5.00	15.00	36.00
293(2/62)-13th Legion app; Mon-el & Legion Super Pets (1st app./origin) app. (1st Superhorse). 1st Bizarro Luthor & Kandor	10.00	30.00	70.00
294-1st Bizarro M. Monroe, Pres. Kennedy	10.00	30.00	70.00
299-1st Gold Kryptonite (8/62)	6.50	20.00	46.00
300-Tales of the Legion of Super-Heroes series begins (9/62); Mon-el leaves Phantom Zone (temporarily), joins Legion	40.00	130.00	300.00
301-Origin Bouncing Boy	13.00	40.00	90.00
302-305: 303-1st app. Matter Eater Lad. 304-Death of Lightning Lad in Legion	9.00	26.00	60.00
306-310: 306-Intro. Legion of Substitute Heroes. 307-1st app. Element Lad in Legion. 308-1st app. Lightning Lass in Legion	6.00	19.00	44.00
311-320: 312-Lightning Lad back in Legion. 315-Last new Superboy story; Colossal Boy app. 316-Origins & powers of Legion given. 317-Intro. Dream Girl in Legion; Lightning Lass becomes Light Lass; Hall of Fame series begins. 320-Dev-Em 2nd app.	4.70	14.00	33.00
321-Intro Time Trapper	3.90	12.00	27.00
322-330: 327-Intro/1st app. Lone Wolf in Legion. 329-Intro The Bizarro Legionnaires	3.40	10.00	24.00
331-340: 337-Chlorophyll Kid & Night Girl app. 340-Intro Computo in Legion	3.00	7.50	18.00
341-Triplicate Girl becomes Duo Damsel	2.00	6.00	14.00
342-345,347,350,351: 345-Last Hall of Fame; returns in 356,371. 351-1st app. White Witch	1.65	4.40	10.50
346,348,349: 346-1st app. Karate Kid, Princess Projectra, Ferro Lad, & Nemesis Kid. 348-Origin Sunboy; intro Dr. Regulus in Legion. 349-Intro Universo & Rond Vidar	1.65	4.70	11.00
352,354-360: 355-Insect Queen joins Legion (4/67)	1.40	3.50	8.50
353-Death of Ferro Lad in Legion	2.15	6.50	15.00
361-364,366,368-370: 369-Intro Mordru in Legion	1.20	3.00	7.00
365,367,371,372: 365-Intro Shadow Lass; lists origins & powers of L.S.H. 367-New Legion headquarters. 371-Intro. Chemical King. 372-Timber Wolf & Chemical King join. 374-Article on comics fandom	1.30	3.25	8.00
373,374,376-380: Last Legion in Adventure	1.20	3.00	7.00
375-Intro Quantum Queen & The Wanderers	1.25	3.00	7.50
381-Supergirl begins; 1st full length supergirl story & her 1st solo book (6/69)		1.60	4.00
382-389,391-400: 399-Unpubbed G.A. Black Canary story. 400-New costume for Supergirl		1.00	2.50
390-Giant Supergirl G-69	1.50	3.75	9.00
401,402,404-410: 409-415,417-420-(52 pg. issues)		1.30	3.25
403-68pg. Giant G-81; Legion-r/#304,305,308,312	1.20	3.00	7.00
411,413: 413-Hawkman by Kubert r/B&B #44; G.A. Robotman-r/Det. #178; Zatanna by Morrow			1.40
412-Reprints origin/1st app. Animal Man/Strange Adventures #180	1.00	2.00	5.00
414-Reprints 2nd Animal Man/Strange Advs. #184		1.30	3.25
415,420-Animal Man reprints from Strange Adventures #190 (origin recap) & #195		.70	1.70
416-Giant DC-100 Page Super Spect. #10; GA-r; r/1st app. Black Canary from Flash #86; no Zatanna		1.00	2.50
417-Morrow Vigilante; Frazetta Shining Knight-r/Adv. #161; origin The Enchantress; no Zatanna			1.50

421-424-Last Supergirl in Adventure: 418-Previously unpublished Dr.

Adventure For Boys #1© Bailey Ent.

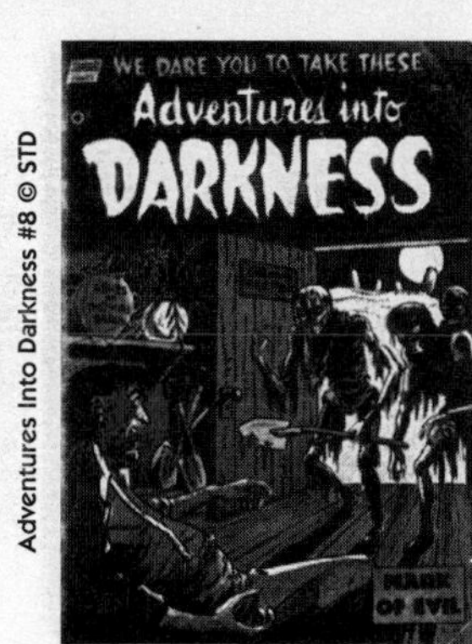

Adventures Into Darkness #8 © STD

Adventures Into Terror #43 © MEG

GD25 FN65 NM94 | GD25 FN65 NM94

Mid-Nite story from 1948; No Zatanna 1.20
425-New look, content change to adventure; Kaluta-c; Toth-a, origin Capt. Fear .70 1.80
426,427,431-458: 426-1st Adventurers Club. 427-Last Vigilante. 431-440-Spectre app. 433-437-Cover title is Weird Adv. Comics. 436-Last 20¢ issue. 440-New Spectre origin. 441-452-Aquaman app. 443-Re-intro Clay Face. 445-447-The Creeper app. 446-Flag-c. 449-451-Martian Manhunter app. 453-458-Super-boy app. 453-Intro Mighty Girl. 457,458-Eclipso app. 1.20
428-Origin/1st app. Black Orchid (c/story, 6-7/73) 1.30 3.25 8.00
429,430-Black Orchid-c/stories 1.60 4.00
459,460-New Gods/Darkseid storyline concludes from New Gods #19 (#459 is dated 9-10/78) without missing a month 1.40 3.50
461,462: 461-Justice Society begins; ends 466. 461,462-Death Earth II Batman (both $1.00, 68 pgs.) 1.00 2.00 5.00
463-466($1.00 size, 68 pgs.): 459-Flash (ends #466), Deadman (ends #466), Wonder Woman (ends #464), Green Lantern (ends #460), 460-Aquaman begins; ends #478 1.40
467-Starman by Ditko, Plastic Man begin .70 1.80
468-490: 469,470-Origin Starman. 478-Last Starman & Plastic Man. 479-Dial 'H' For Hero begins, ends #490 1.20
491-499: 488,489-Deathstroke-c/cameos. 491-100pg. Digest size begins; r/Legion of Super Heroes/Adv. #247,267; Spectre, Aquaman, Superboy, S&K Sandman, Bl. Canary-r & new Shazam by Newton begin. 493-Challengers of the Unknown begins by Tuska w/brief origin. 492,495,496,499-S&K Sand-man-r/Adventure in all; 494-499-Spectre-r/Spectre 1-3, 5-7. 493-495,497-499-G.A. Captain Marvel-r. 498-Plastic Man-r begin; origin Bouncing Boy-r/#301 1.40
500-All Legion-r (Digest size, 148 pgs.) .70 1.80
501-503-G.A.-r 1.35

NOTE: *Bizarro covers-285, 286, 288, 294, 295, 329. Vigilante app.-420, 426, 427.* ***N. Adams*** *a(r)-495i-498i; c-365-369, 371-373, 375-379, 381-383.* ***Austin*** *a-449i 451i.* ***Bernard Baily*** *c-48, 50, 52-59.* ***Bolland*** *c-475.* ***Burnley*** *c-61-72, 116-120p.* ***Chaykin*** *a-438.* ***Ditko*** *a-467-478p; c-467p.* ***Creig Flessel*** *c-32, 33, 40, 42, 44, 46, 47, 51, 60.* ***Giffen*** *c-491p-494p, 500p.* ***Grell*** *a-435-437, 440.* ***Guardineer*** *c-34, 35, 45.* ***Kaluta*** *c-425.* ***Bob Kane*** *a-38.* ***G. Kane*** *a-414r, 425; c-496-499, 537.* ***Kirby*** *a-250-256.* ***Kubert*** *a-413.* ***Meskin*** *a-81,127.* ***Moldoff*** *a-494i; c-49.* ***Morrow*** *a-413-415, 417, 422, 502r, 503r.* ***Newton*** *a-459-461, 464-466, 491p, 492p.* ***Orlando*** *a-457p, 458p.* ***Perez*** *c-484-486, 490p.* ***Simon/Kirby*** *c-73-97, 100-102.* ***Starlin*** *c-471.* ***Staton*** *a-445-447i, 456-458p, 459, 460, 461p-465p, 466,467p-478p, 502p(r); c-458, 461(back).* ***Toth*** *a-418, 419, 425, 431, 495p-497p.* ***Tuska*** *a-494p.*

ADVENTURE COMICS
No date (early 1940s) Paper cover, 32 pgs.
IGA
Two different issues; Super-Mystery reprints from 1941 17.00 51.00 120.00

ADVENTURE IN DISNEYLAND (Giveaway)
May, 1955 (16 pgs., soft-c) (Dist. by Richfield Oil)
Walt Disney Productions
nn 4.20 12.50 25.00

ADVENTURE INTO FEAR
1951
Superior Publ. Ltd.
1-Exist? 10.00 30.00 70.00

ADVENTURE INTO MYSTERY
May, 1956 - No. 8, July, 1957
Atlas Comics (BFP No. 1/OPI No. 2-8)
1-Powell s/f-a; Forte-a; Everett-c 22.00 65.00 150.00
2-Flying Saucer story 11.50 34.00 80.00
3,6-Everett-c 10.00 30.00 70.00
4-Williamson-a, 4 pgs; Powell-a 11.00 32.00 75.00
5-Everett-c/a, Orlando-a 11.00 32.00 75.00
7-Torres-a; Everett-c 11.00 32.00 75.00
8-Moriera, Sale, Torres, Woodbridge-a, Severin-c 10.00 30.00 70.00

ADVENTURE IS MY CAREER
1945 (44 pgs.)
U.S. Coast Guard Academy/Street & Smith
nn-Simon, Milt Gross-a 11.50 34.00 80.00

ADVENTURERS, THE (Aircel)(Value: cover or less)

ADVENTURES (No. 2 Spectacular... on cover)
Nov, 1949 - No. 2, Feb, 1950 (No. 1 ...in Romance on cover)
St. John Publishing Co. (Slightly large size)
1(Scarce); Bolle, Starr-a(2) 16.00 48.00 110.00
2(Scarce)-Slave Girl; China Bombshell app.; Bolle, L. Starr-a 26.00 78.00 180.00

ADVENTURES FOR BOYS
December, 1954
Bailey Enterprises
nn-Comics, text, & photos 4.00 11.00 22.00

ADVENTURES IN PARADISE (See 4-Color No. 1301)

ADVENTURES IN ROMANCE (See Adventures)

ADVENTURES IN SCIENCE (See Classics Illustrated Special Issue)

ADVENTURES IN 3-D
Nov, 1953 - No. 2, Jan, 1954 (25¢)
Harvey Publications
1-Nostrand, Powell-a, 2-Powell-a 14.00 43.00 100.00

ADVENTURES INTO DARKNESS (See Seduction of the Innocent 3-D)
No. 5, Aug, 1952 - No. 14, 1954
Better-Standard Publications/Visual Editions
5-Katz-c/a; Toth-a(p) 16.50 50.00 115.00
6-Tuska, Katz-a 10.00 30.00 65.00
7-Katz-c/a 11.00 32.00 75.00
8,9-Toth-a(p) 11.50 34.00 80.00
10,11-Jack Katz-a 10.00 30.00 60.00
12-Toth-a?; lingerie panels 10.00 30.00 60.00
13-Toth-a(p); Cannibalism story cited by T. E. Murphy articles 11.00 32.00 75.00
14 8.35 25.00 50.00

NOTE: ***Fawcette*** *a-13.* ***Moriera*** *a-5.* ***Sekowsky*** *a-10, 11, 13(2).*

ADVENTURES INTO TERROR (Formerly Joker Comics)
No. 43, Nov, 1950 - No. 31, May, 1954
Marvel/Atlas Comics (CDS)
43(#1) 30.00 90.00 210.00
44(#2, 2/51)-Sol Brodsky-c 21.00 63.00 145.00
3(4/51), 4 13.50 41.00 95.00
5-Wolverton-c panel/Mystic #6; Rico-c panel also; Atom Bomb story 16.50 50.00 115.00
6,8: 8-Wolverton text illo r-/Marvel Tales #104 12.00 36.00 85.00
7-Wolverton-a "Where Monsters Dwell", 6 pgs.; Tuska-c; Maneely-c panels 31.00 95.00 220.00
9,10,12-Krigstein-a. 9-Decapitation panels 11.50 34.00 80.00
11,13-20 10.00 30.00 60.00
21-24,26-31 9.15 27.50 55.00
25-Matt Fox-a 10.00 30.00 70.00

NOTE: ***Ayers*** *a-21.* ***Colan*** *a-3, 5, 14, 21, 24, 25, 28, 29; c-27.* ***Colletta*** *a-30.* ***Everett*** *c-13, 21, 25.* ***Fass*** *a-28, 29.* ***Forte*** *a-28.* ***Heath*** *a-43, 44, 4-6, 22, 24, 26; c-43, 9, 11.* ***Lazarus*** *a-7.* ***Maneely*** *a-7(3 pg.), 10, 11, 21., 22 c-15, 29.* ***Don Rico*** *a-4, 5(3 pg.).* ***Sekowsky*** *a-43, 3, 4.* ***Sinnott*** *a-8, 9, 11, 28.* ***Tuska*** *a-14; c-7.*

ADVENTURES INTO THE UNKNOWN
Fall, 1948 - No. 174, Aug, 1967 (No. 1-33: 52 pgs.)
American Comics Group
(1st continuous series horror comic; see Eerie #1)
1-Guardineer-a; adapt. of 'Castle of Otranto' by Horace Walpole 107.00 321.00 750.00
2 46.00 140.00 325.00
3-Feldstein-a (9 pgs) 50.00 150.00 350.00
4,5 26.00 78.00 180.00

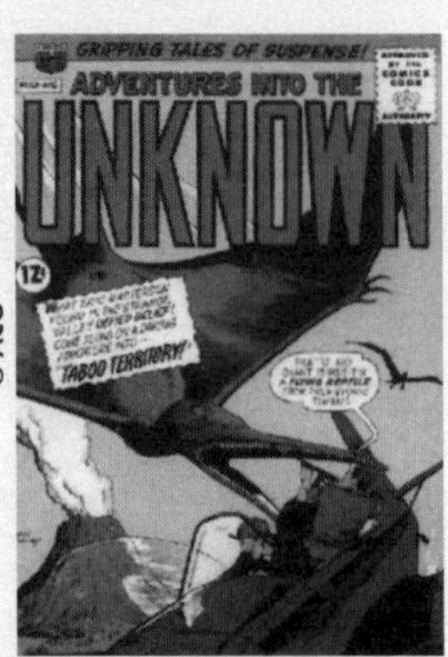

Adventures Into The Unknown #150 © ACG

Adventures Of Alan Ladd #8 © DC

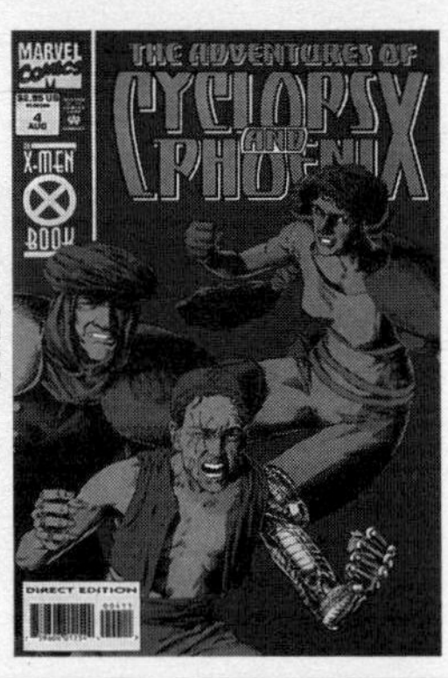

Adventures Of Cyclops And Phoenix #4 © MEG

	GD25	FN65	NM94
6-10	19.00	58.00	135.00
11-16,18-20: 13-Starr-a	14.00	43.00	100.00
17-Story similar to movie 'The Thing'	17.00	52.00	120.00
21-26,28-30	12.00	36.00	85.00
27-Williamson/Krenkel-a (8 pgs.)	17.00	52.00	120.00
31-50: 38-Atom bomb panels	10.00	30.00	65.00
51-(1/54)-(3-D effect-c/story)-Only white cover	21.00	63.00	145.00
52-58: (3-D effect-c/stories with black covers). 52-E.C. swipe/Haunt Of Fear #14	19.00	56.00	130.00
59-3-D effect story only; new logo	13.00	40.00	90.00
60-Woodesque-a by Landau	7.50	21.00	52.00
61-Last pre-code issue (1-2/55)	7.00	21.00	50.00
62-70	4.50	14.00	32.00
71-90	3.30	10.00	23.00
91,96(#95 on inside),107,116-All have Williamson-a	4.50	14.00	32.00
92-95,97-99,101-106,108-115,117-127: 109-113,118-Whitney painted-c	3.25	9.50	22.00
100	3.60	10.75	25.00
128-Williamson/Krenkel/Torres-a(r)/Forbidden Worlds #63; last 10¢ issue	3.25	9.50	22.00
129-152	2.40	7.25	17.00
153, 157-Magic Agent app.	2.15	6.50	15.00
154-Nemesis series begins (origin), ends #170	2.60	7.50	18.00
155,156,158-167,169-174	2.00	6.00	14.00
168-Ditko-a(p)	2.70	8.00	19.00

NOTE: *"Spirit of Frankenstein" series in 5, 6, 8-10, 12, 16.* ***Buscema*** *a-100, 106, 108-110, 158r, 165r.* ***Cameron*** *a-34.* ***Craig*** *a-152, 160.* ***Goode*** *a-45, 47, 60.* ***Landau*** *a-51, 59-63.* ***Lazarus*** *a-34, 48, 51, 52, 56, 58, 79, 87; c-31-56, 58.* ***Reinman*** *a-102, 111, 112, 115-118, 124, 130, 137, 141, 145, 164.* ***Whitney*** *c-12-30, 57, 59-on (most.)* ***Torres/Williamson*** *a-116.*

ADVENTURES INTO WEIRD WORLDS
Jan, 1952 - No. 30, June, 1954
Marvel/Atlas Comics (ACI)

	GD25	FN65	NM94
1-Atom bomb panels	30.00	90.00	210.00
2-Sci/fic stories (2); one by Maneely	18.00	54.00	125.00
3-10: 7-Tongue ripped out. 10-Krigstein, Everett-a	11.50	34.00	80.00
11-21: 21-Hitler in Hell story	10.00	30.00	70.00
22-26: 24-Man holds hypo & splits in two	9.15	27.50	55.00
27-Matt Fox end of world story-a; severed head-c	18.00	54.00	125.00
28-Atom bomb story; decapitation panels	10.00	30.00	70.00
29,30	6.70	20.00	40.00

NOTE: ***Ayers*** *a-8, 26.* ***Everett*** *a-4, 5; c-6, 8, 10-13, 18, 19, 22, 24, 25; a-4, 25.* ***Fass*** *a-7.* ***Forte*** *a-21, 24.* ***Al Hartley*** *a-2.* ***Heath*** *a-1, 4, 17, 22; c-7, 9, 20.* ***Maneely*** *a-2, 3, 11, 20, 22, 23, 25; c-1, 3, 22, 25-27, 29.* ***Reinman*** *a-24, 28.* ***Rico*** *a-13.* ***Robinson*** *a-13.* ***Sinnott*** *a-25, 30.* ***Tuska*** *a-1, 2, 12, 15.* ***Whitney*** *a-7.* ***Wildey*** *a-28. Bondage c-22.*

ADVENTURES IN WONDERLAND
April, 1955 - No. 5, Feb, 1956 (Jr. Readers Guild)
Lev Gleason Publications

	GD25	FN65	NM94
1-Maurer-a	5.85	17.50	35.00
2-4	4.00	11.00	22.00
5-Christmas issue	4.35	13.00	26.00

ADVENTURES OF ALAN LADD, THE
Oct-Nov, 1949 - No. 9, Feb-Mar, 1951 (All 52 pgs.)
National Periodical Publications

	GD25	FN65	NM94
1-Photo-c	71.00	215.00	500.00
2-Photo-c	43.00	130.00	300.00
3-6: Last photo-c	32.00	95.00	225.00
7-9	27.00	80.00	185.00

NOTE: ***Dan Barry*** *a-1.* ***Moreira*** *a-3-7.*

ADVENTURES OF ALICE
1945 (Also see Alice in Wonderland & ...at Monkey Island)
Civil Service Publ./Pentagon Publishing Co.

	GD25	FN65	NM94
1	9.15	27.50	55.00
2-Through the Magic Looking Glass	7.50	22.50	45.00

ADVENTURES OF BARON MUNCHAUSEN, THE (Now)(Value: cover or less)

ADVENTURES OF BAYOU BILLY, THE
Sept, 1989 - No. 5, June, 1990 ($1.00)
Archie Comics

	GD25	FN65	NM94
1-5: Esposito-c/a(i). 5-Kelley Jones-c			1.00

ADVENTURES OF BOB HOPE, THE (Also see True Comics #59)
Feb-Mar, 1950 - No. 109, Feb-Mar, 1968 (#1-10: 52pgs.)
National Periodical Publications

	GD25	FN65	NM94
1-Photo-c	114.00	343.00	800.00
2-Photo-c	57.00	170.00	400.00
3,4-Photo-c	36.00	107.00	250.00
5-10	29.00	86.00	200.00
11-20	16.50	50.00	115.00
21-31 (2-3/55; last precode)	11.50	34.00	80.00
32-40	10.00	30.00	60.00
41-50	8.35	25.00	50.00
51-70	5.00	15.00	35.00
71-93,95-105: 95-1st app. Super-Hip & 1st monster issue (11/65)	2.60	7.50	18.00
94-Aquaman cameo	2.85	8.00	20.00
106-109-All monster-c/stories by N. Adams-c/a	4.30	13.00	30.00

NOTE: *Buzzy in #34. Kitty Karr of Hollywood in #15, 17-20, 23, 28. Liz in #26, 109. Miss Beverly Hills of Hollywood in #7, 8, 10, 13, 14. Miss Melody Lane of Broadway in #15. Rusty in #23, 25. Tommy in #24. No 2nd feature in #2-4, 6, 8, 11, 12, 28-108.*

ADVENTURES OF CAPTAIN AMERICA
Sept, 1991 - No. 4, Jan, 1992 ($4.95, mini-series, 52 pgs.)
Marvel Comics

	GD25	FN65	NM94
1-4: 1-Embossed-c. 2-4-Austin-c/a(i)	1.00	2.00	5.00

ADVENTURES OF CHRISSIE CLAUS, THE (Hero)(Value: cover or less)

ADVENTURES OF CYCLOPS AND PHOENIX
May, 1994 - No. 4, Aug, 1994 ($2.95, mini-series)
Marvel Comics

	GD25	FN65	NM94
1-4-Characters from X-Men		1.20	3.00

ADVENTURES OF DEAN MARTIN AND JERRY LEWIS, THE
(The Adventures of Jerry Lewis #41 on; see Movie Love #12)
July-Aug, 1952 - No. 40, Oct, 1957
National Periodical Publications

	GD25	FN65	NM94
1	71.00	215.00	500.00
2	36.00	107.00	250.00
3-10: 3-3 pg origin on how they became a team; I Love Lucy text featurette	16.00	48.00	110.00
11-19: Last precode (2/55)	10.00	30.00	70.00
20-30	8.35	25.00	50.00
31-40	6.70	20.00	40.00

ADVENTURES OF FELIX THE CAT, THE
May, 1992 ($1.25)
Harvey Comics

	GD25	FN65	NM94
1-Messmer-r			1.25

ADVENTURES OF FORD FAIRLANE, THE
May, 1990 - No. 4, Aug, 1990 ($1.50, mini-series, mature readers)
DC Comics

	GD25	FN65	NM94
1-4: Movie tie-in; Don Heck inks			1.50

ADVENTURES OF G. I. JOE
1969 (3-1/4x7") (20 & 16 pgs.)
Giveaways

First Series: 1-Danger of the Depths. 2-Perilous Rescue. 3-Secret Mission to Spy Island. 4-Mysterious Explosion. 5-Fantastic Free Fall. 6-Eight Ropes of Danger. 7-Mouth of Doom. 8-Hidden Missile Discovery. 9-Space Walk Mystery. 10-Fight for Survival. 11-The Shark's Surprise. **Second Series:** 2-Flying Space Adventure. 4-White Tiger Hunt. 7-Capture of the Pygmy Gorilla. 12-Secret of the Mummy's Tomb. Third Series: Reprinted surviving titles of First Series. Fourth Series: 13-Adventure Team Headquarters. 14-Search For the Stolen Idol.

	GD25	FN65	NM94
each....			.80

ADVENTURES OF HAWKSHAW (See Hawkshaw The Detective)

Adventures of Jerry Lewis #86 © DC

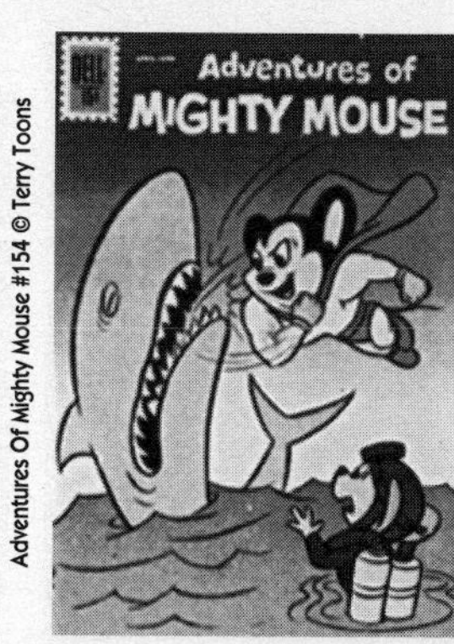

Adventures Of Mighty Mouse #154 © Terry Toons

Adventures O f Rex The Wonder Dog #44 © DC

GD25 FN65 NM94

1917 (9-3/4x13-1/2", 48 pgs., Color & two-tone)
The Saalfield Publishing Co.

nn-By Gus Mager (only 24 pgs. of strips, reverse of each pg. is blank) 25.00 75.00 225.00

ADVENTURES OF HOMER COBB, THE
September, 1947 (Oversized)
Say/Bart Prod. (Canadian)

1-(Scarce)-Feldstein-a 19.00 58.00 135.00

ADVENTURES OF HOMER GHOST (See Homer The Happy Ghost)
June, 1957 - No. 2, August, 1957
Atlas Comics

V1#1,2 4.20 12.50 25.00

ADVENTURES OF JERRY LEWIS, THE (Adventures of Dean Martin & Jerry Lewis No. 1-40)(See Super DC Giant)
No. 41, Nov, 1957 - No. 124, May-June, 1971
National Periodical Publications

41-60 5.35 16.00 32.00
61-80: 68,74-Photo-c 4.00 12.00 24.00
81-91,93-96,98-100: 89-Bob Hope app. 2.30 6.75 16.00
92-Superman cameo 2.85 8.00 20.00
97-Batman/Robin/Joker-c/story; Riddler & Penguin app. 4.00 12.00 28.00
101,103,104-Neal Adams-c/a 3.40 10.00 24.00
102-Beatles app.; Neal Adams c/a 4.00 12.00 28.00
105-Superman x-over 2.60 7.50 18.00
106-111,113-116 1.20 3.00 7.00
112-Flash x-over 2.60 7.50 18.00
117-Wonder Woman x-over 1.65 4.00 10.00
118-124 1.00 2.00 5.00

ADVENTURES OF JO-JOY, THE (See Jo-Joy)

ADVENTURES OF LUTHER ARKWRIGHT, THE (Dark Horse)(Value: cover or less)

ADVENTURES OF MARGARET O'BRIEN, THE
1947 (20 pgs. in color; slick cover; regular size) (Premium)
Bambury Fashions (Clothes)

In "The Big City" movie adaptation (scarce) 15.00 45.00 105.00

ADVENTURES OF MICKEY MOUSE
Book I, 1931 - Book II, 1932 (32pg, 5-1/2"x8-1/2")
David McKay Co., Inc.

Book I-First Disney book, by strict definition (1st printing-50,000 copies)(see Mickey Mouse Book by Bibo & Lang). Illustrated text refers to Clarabelle Cow as "Carolyn" and Horace Horsecollar as "Henry". The name "Donald Duck": appears with a non-costumed generic duck on back cover & inside, not in the context of the character that later debuted in the Wise Little Hen.
Version with Donald Duck on Back cover 14.00 43.00 100.00
Version without characters on back cover 10.00 30.00 60.00
Book II-Less common than Book I. Character development brought into conformity with the Mickey Mouse cartoon shorts and syndicated strips. Captain Church Mouse, Tanglefoot, Peg-Leg Pete and Pluto appear with Mickey & Minnie 13.00 43.00 100.00

ADVENTURES OF MIGHTY MOUSE (Mighty Mouse Adventures No. 1)
No. 2, Jan, 1952 - No. 18, May, 1955
St. John Publishing Co.

2 17.00 52.00 120.00
3-5 10.00 30.00 65.00
6-18 7.50 22.50 45.00

ADVENTURES OF MIGHTY MOUSE (2nd Series)
(Two No. 144's; formerly Paul Terry's Comics; No. 129-137 have nn's)
(Becomes Mighty Mouse No. 161 on)
No. 126, Aug, 1955 - No. 160, Oct, 1963
St. John/Pines/Dell/Gold Key

126(8/55), 127(10/55), 128(11/55)-St. John 5.35 16.00 32.00
nn(129, 4/56)-144(8/59)-Pines 4.70 14.00 28.00
144(10-12/59)-155(7-9/62) Dell 4.00 11.00 22.00
156(10/62)-160(10/63) Gold Key 4.00 11.00 22.00
NOTE: *Early issues titled "Paul Terry's Adventures of ...."*

ADVENTURES OF MIGHTY MOUSE (Formerly Mighty Mouse)
No. 166, Mar, 1979 - No. 172, Jan, 1980
Gold Key

166-172 1.10 2.70 6.50

ADVS. OF MR. FROG & MISS MOUSE (See Dell Junior Treasury No. 4)

ADVENTURES OF OZZIE AND HARRIET, THE (Radio)
Oct-Nov, 1949 - No. 5, June-July, 1950
National Periodical Publications

1-Photo-c 68.00 205.00 475.00
2 38.00 115.00 265.00
3-5 32.00 95.00 225.00

ADVENTURES OF PATORUZU
Aug, 1946 - Winter, 1946
Green Publishing Co.

nn's-Contains Animal Crackers reprints 4.00 11.00 22.00

ADVENTURES OF PINKY LEE, THE (TV)
July, 1955 - No. 5, Dec, 1955
Atlas Comics

1 20.00 60.00 140.00
2-5 11.50 34.00 80.00

ADVENTURES OF PIPSQUEAK, THE (Formerly Pat the Brat)
No. 34, Sept, 1959 - No. 39, July, 1960
Archie Publications (Radio Comics)

34 4.00 12.00 24.00
35-39 3.20 8.00 16.00

ADVENTURES OF QUAKE & QUISP, THE (See Quaker Oats "Plenty of Glutton")

ADVENTURES OF REX THE WONDER DOG, THE (Rex...No. 1)
Jan-Feb, 1952 - No. 45, May-June, 1959; No. 46, Nov-Dec, 1959
National Periodical Publications

1-(Scarce)-Toth-c/a 90.00 270.00 635.00
2-(Scarce)-Toth-c/a 45.00 135.00 315.00
3-(Scarce)-Toth-a 36.00 107.00 250.00
4,5 26.00 78.00 180.00
6-10 18.00 54.00 125.00
11-Atom bomb-c/story 19.00 58.00 135.00
12-19: 19-Last precode (1-2/55) 10.00 30.00 70.00
20-46 9.15 27.50 55.00
NOTE: ***Infantino, Gil Kane** art in 5-19 (most)*

ADVENTURES OF ROBIN HOOD, THE (Formerly Robin Hood)
No. 7, 9/57 - No. 8, 11/57 (Based on Richard Greene TV Show)
Magazine Enterprises (Sussex Publ. Co.)

7,8-Richard Greene photo-c. 7-Powell-a 10.00 30.00 70.00

ADVENTURES OF ROBIN HOOD, THE
March, 1974 - No. 7, Jan, 1975 (Disney cartoon) (36 pgs.)
Gold Key

1(90291-403)-Part-r of $1.50 editions 1.00 2.50 5.00
2-7: 1-7 are part-r .60 1.50 3.00

ADVENTURES OF SLIM AND SPUD, THE
1924 (3-3/4x 9-3/4")(104 pg. B&W strip reprints)
Prairie Farmer Publ. Co.

nn 14.00 43.00 100.00

ADVENTURES OF STUBBY, SANTA'S SMALLEST REINDEER, THE
nd (early 1940s) 12 pgs.
W. T. Grant Co. (Giveaway)

nn 4.00 10.00 20.00

Adventures of Superman #427 © DC

Adventures of Superman #516 © DC

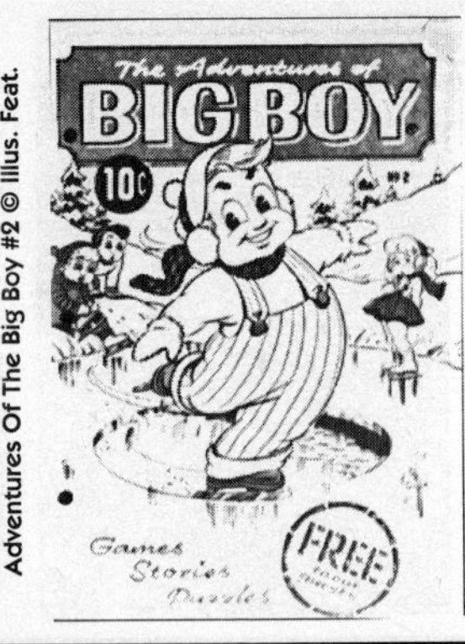

Adventures Of The Big Boy #2 © Illus. Feat.

ADVENTURES OF SUPERBOY, THE (See Superboy, 2nd series)

ADVENTURES OF SUPERMAN (Formerly Superman)
No. 424, Jan, 1987 - No. 499, Feb, 1993; No. 500, Early June, 1993 - Present
DC Comics

	GD25	FN65	NM94
424		.80	2.00
425-449: 426-Legends x-over. 432-1st app. Jose Delgado who becomes Gangbuster in #434. 436-Byrne scripts begin. 436,437-Millennium x-over. 438-New Brainiac app. 440-Batman app. 449-Invasion		.70	1.75
450-463: 457-Perez plots. 463-Superman/Flash race; cover swipe/Superman #199			1.50
464-Lobo-c & app. (pre-dates Lobo #1)		1.60	4.00
465-479,481-491: 467-Part 2 of Batman story. 473-Hal Jordan, Guy Gardner x-over. 477-Legion app. 491-Last $1.00-c			1.00
480-($1.75, 52 pgs.)		.70	1.75
492-495: 495-Forever People-c/story; Darkseid app.			1.25
496-Doomsday cameo	1.00	2.50	6.00
496,497-2nd printings			1.25
497-Doomsday battle issue	1.00	2.50	6.00
498,499-Funeral for a Friend; Supergirl app.		1.20	3.00
498-2nd & 3rd printings			1.25
500-($2.95, 68 pgs.)-Collector's edition w/card		1.20	3.00
500-($2.50, 68 pgs.)-Regular edition w/different-c		1.00	2.50
500-Platinum edition			90.00
501-($1.95)-Collector's edition with die-cut-c		.80	2.00
501-($1.50)-Regular edition w/mini-poster & diff.-c			1.50
502-518: 502-Supergirl-c/story. 508-Challengers of the Unknown app. 510-Bizarro-c/story. 518-(9/94)-Zero Hour			1.50
505-($2.50)-Holo-grafx foil-c edition		1.00	2.50
0,519-514: 0-(10/94)			1.50
Annual 1 (1987, $1.25, 52 pgs.)-Starlin-c & scripts			1.40
Annual 2,3 (1990, 1991, $2.00, 68 pgs.): 2-Byrne-c/a(i); Legion '90 (Lobo) app. 3-Armageddon 2001 x-over		.80	2.00
Annual 4,5 (1992, 1993, $2.50, 68 pgs.): 4-Guy Gardner/Lobo-c/story; Eclipso storyline; Quesada-c(p). 5-Bloodlines storyline		1.00	2.50
Annual 6 (1994, $2.95, 68 pgs.)-Elseworlds story		1.20	3.00

ADVENTURES OF THE BIG BOY (Giveaway)
1956 - Present (East & West editions of early issues)
Timely Comics/Webs Adv. Corp./Illus. Features

	GD25	FN65	NM94
1-Everett-a	45.00	135.00	320.00
2-Everett-a	23.00	70.00	160.00
3-5	8.65	26.00	52.00
6-10: 6-Sci/fic issue	5.35	16.00	32.00
11-20	3.20	8.00	16.00
21-30	1.80	4.50	9.00
31-50		1.80	4.50
51-100		1.00	2.50
101-150			1.20
151-240			.50
241-417: 266-Superman x-over. 417-(1992)			.20
1-50 ('76-'84,Paragon Prod.)			.20
Summer, 1959 issue, large size	3.60	9.00	18.00

ADVENTURES OF THE DETECTIVE
No date (1930's) (36 pgs.; 9-1/2x12"; B&W, paper cover)
Humor Publ. Co.

	GD25	FN65	NM94
nn-Not reprints; Ace King by Martin Nadle	11.00	32.00	75.00
2nd version (printed in red & blue)	11.00	32.00	75.00

ADVENTURES OF THE DOVER BOYS
September, 1950 - No. 2, 1950 (No month given)
Archie Comics (Close-up)

	GD25	FN65	NM94
1,2	6.70	20.00	40.00

ADVENTURES OF THE FLY (The Fly #1-6; Fly Man No. 32-39; See The Double Life of Private Strong, The Fly, Laugh Comics & Mighty Crusaders)
Aug, 1959 - No. 30, Oct, 1964; No. 31, May, 1965
Archie Publications/Radio Comics

	GD25	FN65	NM94
1-Shield app.; origin The Fly; S&K-c/a	60.00	170.00	385.00
2-Williamson, S&K-a	32.00	96.00	225.00
3-Origin retold; Davis, Powell-a	26.00	78.00	180.00
4-Neal Adams-a(p)(1 panel); S&K-c; Powell-a; 2 pg. Shield story	13.00	40.00	90.00
5-10: 7-1st S.A. app. Black Hood (7/60). 8-1st S.A. app. Shield (9/60). 9-Shield app. 9-1st app. Cat Girl. 10-Black Hood app.	9.00	26.00	60.00
11-13,15-20: 13-1st app. Fly Girl w/o costume. 16-Last 10¢ issue. 20-Origin Fly Girl retold	5.00	15.00	35.00
14-Origin & 1st app. Fly Girl in costume	7.00	21.00	50.00
21-30: 23-Jaguar cameo. 27-29-Black Hood 1 pg. strips. 30-Comet x-over (1st S.A. app.) in Fly Girl	3.40	10.00	24.00
31-Black Hood, Shield, Comet app.	4.00	12.00	28.00

NOTE: ***Simon*** c-2-4. ***Tuska*** a-1. *Cover title to #31 is Flyman; Advs. of the Fly inside.*

ADVENTURES OF THE JAGUAR, THE (See Blue Ribbon Comics, Laugh Comics & Mighty Crusaders)
Sept, 1961 - No. 15, Nov, 1963
Archie Publications (Radio Comics)

	GD25	FN65	NM94
1-Origin Jaguar (1st app?) by J. Rosenberger	18.00	54.00	125.00
2,3: 3-Last 10¢ issue	9.00	26.00	62.00
4-6-Catgirl app. (#4's-c is same as splash pg.)	6.00	19.00	44.00
7-10	4.30	13.00	30.00
11-15: 13,14-Catgirl, Black Hood app. in both	3.40	10.00	24.00

ADVENTURES OF THE OUTSIDERS, THE (Formerly Batman & The Outsiders; also see The Outsiders)
No. 33, May, 1986 - No. 46, June, 1987
DC Comics

	GD25	FN65	NM94
33-46: 39-45-r/Outsiders #1-7 by Aparo			1.00

ADVENTURES OF THE SUPER MARIO BROTHERS
1990 - No. 9?, 1990? ($1.50, color) (Also see Super Mario Brothers)
Valiant

	GD25	FN65	NM94
V2#1-9			1.50

ADVENTURES OF THE THING, THE (Also see The Thing)
Apr, 1992 - No. 4, July, 1992, ($1.25, mini-series)
Marvel Comics

	GD25	FN65	NM94
1-4: 1-r/Marvel Two-In-One #50 by Byrne; Kieth-c. 2-4-r/Marvel Two-In-One #80,51 & 77; 2-Ghost Rider-c/story. 3-Miller-r			1.25

ADVENTURES OF TINKER BELL (See 4-Color No. 982)

ADVENTURES OF TOM SAWYER (See Dell Junior Treasury No. 10)

ADVENTURES OF WILLIE GREEN, THE
1915 (8-1/2X16", 50¢, B&W, soft-c)
Frank M. Acton Co.

	GD25	FN65	NM94
Book 1-By Harris Brown; strip-r	15.00	45.00	105.00

ADVENTURES OF YOUNG DR. MASTERS, THE
Aug, 1964 - No. 2, Nov, 1964
Archie Comics (Radio Comics)

	GD25	FN65	NM94
1,2	1.00	2.50	6.00

ADVENTURES ON OTHER WORLDS (See Showcase #17 & 18)

ADVENTURES ON THE PLANET OF THE APES
Oct, 1975 - No. 11, Dec, 1976
Marvel Comics Group

	GD25	FN65	NM94
1-Planet of the Apes-r in color; Starlin-c		1.20	3.00
2-5		.90	2.20
6-11		.70	1.80

NOTE: ***Alcala*** a-6-11r. ***Buckler*** c-2p. ***Nasser*** c-7. ***Starlin*** c-6. ***Tuska*** a-1-5r.

ADVENTURES WITH SANTA CLAUS
No date (early 50's) (24 pgs.; 9-3/4x 6-3/4"; paper cover) (Giveaway)
Promotional Publ. Co. (Murphy's Store)

	GD25	FN65	NM94
nn-Contains 8 pgs. ads	4.00	10.00	21.00

Age Of Reptiles #1 © Dark Horse

Airboy #17 © Eclipse

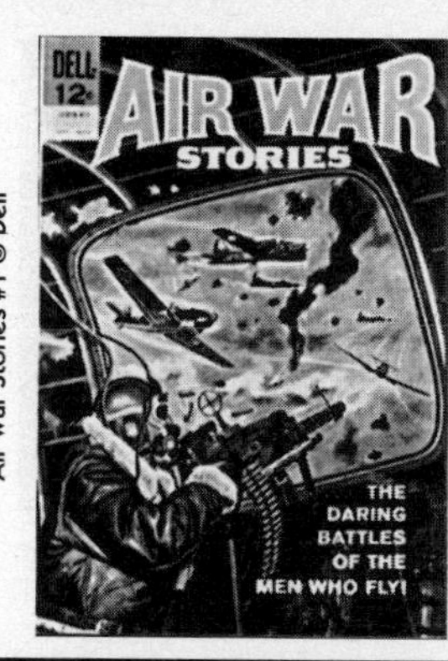

Air War Stories #1 © Dell

GD25 FN65 NM94

16 pg. version 4.00 10.00 21.00

AFRICA
1955
Magazine Enterprises
1(A-1#137)-Cave Girl,Thun'da;Powell-c/a(4) 16.00 48.00 110.00

AFRICAN LION (See 4-Color No. 665)

AFTER DARK
No. 6, May, 1955 - No. 8, Sept, 1955
Sterling Comics
6-8-Sekowsky-a in all 5.85 17.50 35.00

AGAINST BLACKSHARD 3-D (Sirius)(Value: cover or less)

AGENT LIBERTY SPECIAL
1992 ($2.00, 52 pgs.)
DC Comics
1-From Superman; 1st solo adv.; Guice-c/a(i) .80 2.00

AGENT THREE-ZERO
Sept, 1993 ($3.95, color, 52 pgs.)
Galaxinovels, Inc.
1-Polybagged with card & mini-poster; Platt-c/a(1st work) 1.60 4.00

AGE OF REPTILES
Nov, 1993 - No. 4, Feb, 1994 ($2.50, color, mini-series)
Dark Horse Comics
1-4: Delgado-c/a 1.00 2.50

AGGIE MACK
Jan, 1948 - No. 8, Aug, 1949
Four Star Comics Corp./Superior Comics Ltd.
1-Feldstein-a, "Johnny Prep" 16.00 48.00 110.00
2,3-Kamen-c 9.15 27.50 55.00
4-Feldstein "Johnny Prep"; Kamen-c 11.00 32.00 75.00
5-8-Kamen-c/a 10.00 30.00 60.00

AGGIE MACK (See 4-Color Comics No. 1335)

AIN'T IT A GRAND & GLORIOUS FEELING? (Also see Mr. & Mrs.)
1922 (52 pgs.; 9x9-3/4"; stiff cardboard cover)
Whitman Publishing Co.
nn-1921 daily strip-r; B&W, color-c; Briggs-a 15.00 45.00 135.00
nn-28 pgs.-(9x9-1/2")-Stiff cardboard-c; Sunday strip-r in color (inside front-c says "More of the Married Life of Mr. & Mrs".) 14.00 42.00 125.00

AIR ACE (Formerly Bill Barnes No. 1-12)
V2#1, Jan, 1944 - V3#8(No. 20), Feb-Mar, 1947
Street & Smith Publications
V2#1 13.50 41.00 95.00
V2#2-12: 7-Powell-a 8.35 25.00 50.00
V3#1-6 5.85 17.50 35.00
V3#7-Powell bondage-c/a; all atomic issue 11.00 32.00 75.00
V3#8 (V5#8 on-c)-Powell-c/a 6.70 20.00 40.00

AIRBOY (Eclipse)(Value: cover or less)

AIRBOY COMICS (Air Fighters Comics No. 1-22)
V2#11, Dec, 1945 - V10#4, May, 1953 (No V3#3)
Hillman Periodicals
V2#11 49.00 145.00 340.00
12-Valkyrie app. 32.00 96.00 225.00
V3#1,2(no #3) 27.00 80.00 185.00
4-The Heap app. in Skywolf 25.00 75.00 175.00
5-8,10,11: 6-Valkyrie app. 20.00 60.00 140.00
9-Origin The Heap 24.00 72.00 165.00
12-Skywolf & Airboy x-over; Valkyrie app. 25.00 75.00 175.00
V4#1-Iron Lady app. 24.00 72.00 165.00
2,3,12: 2-Rackman begins 14.00 43.00 100.00
4-Simon & Kirby-c 16.00 48.00 110.00
5-11-All S&K-a 22.00 65.00 150.00
V5#1-11: 4-Infantino Heap. 5-Skull-c. 10-Origin The Heap 11.00 32.00 75.00
12-Krigstein-a(p) 13.50 41.00 95.00
V6#1-3,5-12: 6,8-Origin The Heap 11.00 32.00 75.00
4-Origin retold 13.00 40.00 90.00
V7#1-12: 7,8,10-Origin The Heap 11.00 32.00 75.00
V8#1-3,5-12 10.00 30.00 65.00
4-Krigstein-a 11.00 32.00 75.00
V9#1-4,6-12: 2-Valkyrie app. 7-One pg. Frazetta ad 10.00 30.00 60.00
5(#100) 10.00 30.00 70.00
V10#1-4 10.00 30.00 60.00
NOTE: ***Barry*** *a-V2#3, 7.* ***Bolle*** *a-V4#12.* ***McWilliams*** *a-V3#7, 9.* ***Powell*** *a-V7#2, 3, V8#1, 6.* ***Starr*** *a-V5#1, 12.* ***Dick Wood*** *a-V4#12. Bondage-c V5#8.*

AIR FIGHTERS CLASSICS (Eclipse)(Value: cover or less)

AIR FIGHTERS COMICS (Airboy Comics #23 (V2#11) on)
Nov, 1941; No. 2, Nov, 1942 - V2#10, Fall, 1945
Hillman Periodicals
V1#1-(Produced by Funnies, Inc.); Black Commander only app. 143.00 430.00 1000.00
2(11/42)-(Produced by Quality artists & Biro for Hillman); Origin & 1st app. Airboy & Iron Ace; Black Angel (1st app.), Flying Dutchman & Skywolf (1st app.) begin; Fuje-a; Biro-c/a 236.00 707.00 1650.00
3-Origin/1st app. The Heap; origin Skywolf 118.00 354.00 825.00
4 82.00 245.00 575.00
5,6 64.00 193.00 450.00
7-12 49.00 145.00 340.00
V2#1,3-9: 5-Flag-c; Fuje-a. 7-Valkyrie app. 43.00 129.00 300.00
2-Skywolf by Giunta; Flying Dutchman by Fuje; 1st meeting Valkyrie & Airboy (she worked for the Nazis in beginning); 1st app. Valkyrie (11/43) 57.00 171.00 400.00
10-Origin The Heap & Skywolf 52.00 156.00 365.00
NOTE: ***Fuje*** *a-V1#2, 5, 7, V2#2, 3, 5, 7-9.* ***Giunta*** *a-V2#2, 3, 7, 9.*

AIRFIGHTERS MEET SGT. STRIKE SPECIAL, THE (Eclipse)(Value: cover or less)

AIR FORCES (See American Air Forces)

AIRMAIDENS SPECIAL (Eclipse)(Value: cover or less)

AIR POWER (CBS TV & the U.S. Air Force Presents)
1956 (32pgs, 5-1/4x7-1/4", soft-c)
Prudential Insurance Co. giveaway
nn-Toth-a? Based on 'You Are There' TV program by Walter Cronkite 8.35 25.00 50.00

AIR RAIDERS (Marvel)(Value: cover or less)

AIRTIGHT GARAGE, THE
July, 1993 - No. 4, Oct, 1993 ($2.50, mini-series)
Epic Comics (Marvel Comics)
1-4: By Moebius 1.00 2.50

AIR WAR STORIES
Sept-Nov, 1964 - No. 8, Aug, 1966
Dell Publishing Co.
1-Painted-c; Glanzman-c/a begins 4.00 12.00 24.00
2-8: 2-Painted-c (all painted?) 2.80 7.00 14.00

AKIRA
Sept, 1988 - No. 33, 1992 ($3.50/$3.95, deluxe, 68 pgs.)
Epic Comics (Marvel)
1 2.00 6.00 14.00
1,2-2nd printings ('89, $3.95) 1.40 3.50
2 1.30 3.30 8.00
3-5 1.10 2.70 6.50
6-15 1.80 4.50
16-33: 17-Begin $3.95-c 1.40 3.50

ALADDIN (Disney Comics)(Value: cover or less)(Also see Dell Junior Treasury No. 2)

Albedo: Anthropomorphics #1 ©S.A. Gallacci's

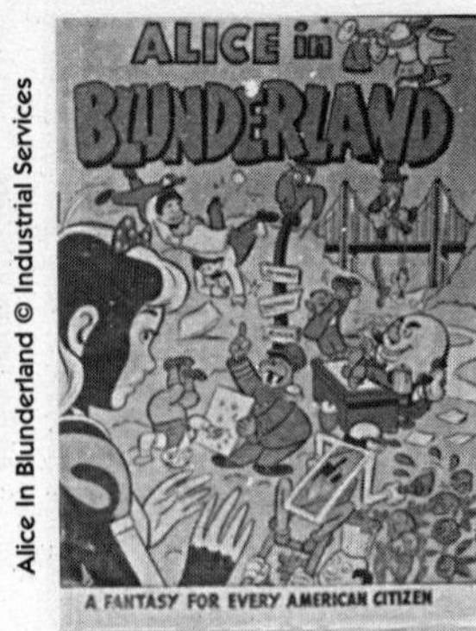

Alice In Blunderland © Industrial Services

Alien Legion #18 © MEG

ALAN LADD (See The Adventures of...)

ALARMING ADVENTURES
Oct, 1962 - No. 3, Feb, 1963
Harvey Publications

	GD25	FN65	NM94
1-Crandall/Williamson-a	6.00	18.00	42.00
2,3: 2-Williamson/Crandall-a	4.20	12.50	25.00

NOTE: ***Bailey** a-1, 3. **Crandall** a-1p, 2i. **Powell** a-2(2). **Severin** c-1-3. **Torres** a-2? **Tuska** a-1. **Williamson** a-1i, 2p.*

ALARMING TALES
Sept, 1957 - No. 6, Nov, 1958
Harvey Publications (Western Tales)

	GD25	FN65	NM94
1-Kirby-c/a(4); Kamandi prototype story by kirby	10.00	30.00	70.00
2-Kirby-a(4)	10.00	30.00	65.00
3,4-Kirby-a. 4-Powell, Wildey-a	7.50	22.50	45.00
5-Kirby/Williamson-a; Wildey-a; Severin-c	8.35	25.00	50.00
6-Williamson-a?; Severin-c	6.70	20.00	40.00

ALBEDO
April, 1985 - No. 14, Spring, 1989 (B&W)
Thoughts And Images

	GD25	FN65	NM94
0-Yellow cover; 50 copies	6.50	19.00	45.00
0-White cover, 450 copies	5.00	15.00	35.00
0-Blue, 1st printing, 500 copies	1.85	5.50	13.00
0-Blue, 2nd printing, 1000 copies	1.30	3.25	8.00
0-3rd printing		.80	2.00
0-4th printing			1.20
1-Dark red; 1st app. Usagi Yojimbo	1.60	3.80	9.75
1-Bright red	1.60	3.80	9.75
2	1.00	2.50	6.00
3-14		.80	2.00

ALBEDO ANTHROPOMORPHICS
Spring, 1994
Antartic Press

	GD25	FN65	NM94
V3#1-Steve Gallacci-c/a		1.20	3.00

ALBERTO (See The Crusaders)

ALBERT THE ALLIGATOR & POGO POSSUM (See 4-Color Comics #105, 148)

ALBUM OF CRIME (See Fox Giants)

ALBUM OF LOVE (See Fox Giants)

AL CAPP'S DOGPATCH (Also see Mammy Yokum)
No. 71, June, 1949 - No. 4, Dec, 1949
Toby Press

	GD25	FN65	NM94
71(#1)-Reprints from Tip Top #112-114	24.00	72.00	165.00
2-4: 4-Reprints from Li'l Abner #73	16.00	48.00	110.00

AL CAPP'S SHMOO (Also see Oxydol-Dreft & Washable Jones & Shmoo)
July, 1949 - No. 5, April, 1950 (None by Al Capp)
Toby Press

	GD25	FN65	NM94
1	30.00	90.00	210.00
2-5: 3-Sci-fi trip to moon. 4-X-Mas-c; origin/1st app. Super-Shmoo	22.00	65.00	150.00

AL CAPP'S WOLF GAL
1951 - No. 2, 1952
Toby Press

	GD25	FN65	NM94
1,2-Edited-r from Li'l Abner #63,64	30.00	90.00	210.00

ALEXANDER THE GREAT (See 4-Color No. 688)

ALF (TV) (See Star Comics Digest)
Mar, 1988 - No. 50, Feb, 1992 ($1.00)
Marvel Comics

	GD25	FN65	NM94
1-49: 22-X-Men parody			1.00
50-($1.75, 52 pgs.)-Final issue; photo-c		.70	1.75
Annual 1-3: 2-Sienkiewicz-c		.70	1.75
...Comics Digest 1 (1988)-Reprints Alf #1,2			1.50
Holiday Special 1 (1988, $1.75, 68 pgs.)		.70	1.75
Holiday Special 2 (Winter, 1989, $2.00, 68 pgs.)		.80	2.00
Spring Special 1 (Spr/89, $1.75, 68 pgs.)		.70	1.75

ALGIE
Dec, 1953 - No. 3, 1954
Timor Publ. Co.

	GD25	FN65	NM94
1-Teenage	4.00	10.00	20.00
1-Misprint exists w/Secret Mysteries #19 inside	4.00	11.00	22.00
2,3	3.20	8.00	16.00
Accepted Reprint #2(nd)	2.00	5.00	10.00
Super Reprint #15	1.60	4.00	8.00

ALIAS: (Now)(Value: cover or less)

ALICE (New Adventures in Wonderland)
No. 10, 7-8/51 - No. 2, 11-12/51
Ziff-Davis Publ. Co.

	GD25	FN65	NM94
10-Painted-c; Berg-a	16.00	48.00	110.00
11-Dave Berg-a	9.50	27.50	55.00
2-Dave Berg-a	7.50	22.50	45.00

ALICE AT MONKEY ISLAND (See The Adventures of Alice)
No. 3, 1946
Pentagon Publ. Co. (Civil Service)

	GD25	FN65	NM94
3	6.35	19.00	38.00

ALICE IN BLUNDERLAND
1952 (Paper cover, 16 pgs. in color)
Industrial Services

	GD25	FN65	NM94
nn-Facts about big government waste and inefficiency	12.00	36.00	84.00

ALICE IN WONDERLAND (See Advs. of Alice, 4-Color No. 331,341, Dell Jr. Treasury No. 1, The Dreamery, Movie Comics, Single Series No. 24, Walt Disney Showcase No. 22, and World's Greatest Stories)

ALICE IN WONDERLAND
1965; 1982
Western Printing Company/Whitman Publ. Co.

	GD25	FN65	NM94
Meets Santa Claus(1950s), nd, 16 pgs.	4.00	10.00	20.00
Rexall Giveaway(1965, 16 pgs., 5x7-1/4) Western Printing (TV, Hanna-Barbera)	3.60	9.00	18.00
Wonder Bakery Giveaway(16 pgs, color, nn, nd) (Continental Baking Company, 1969)	3.60	9.00	18.00
1-(Whitman; 1982)-r/4-Color #331			1.20

ALICE IN WONDERLAND MEETS SANTA
nd (16 pgs., 6-5/8x9-11/16", paper cover)
No publisher (Giveaway)

	GD25	FN65	NM94
nn	10.00	30.00	65.00

ALIEN ENCOUNTERS (Eclipse)(Value: cover or less)

ALIEN LEGION (See Epic & Marvel Graphic Novel #25)
April, 1984 - No. 20, Sept, 1987
Epic Comics (Marvel)

	GD25	FN65	NM94
1-$2.00 cover, high quality paper		.80	2.00
2-20			1.50

ALIEN LEGION (2nd series)
Aug, 1987 (indicia) (10/87 on-c) - No. 18, Aug, 1990 ($1.25)
Epic Comics (Marvel)

	GD25	FN65	NM94
V2#1-6			1.25
7-18: 7-Begin $1.50 cover			1.50

ALIEN LEGION: BINARY DEEP
1993 ($3.50, one-shot, 52 pgs.)
Epic Comics (Marvel)

	GD25	FN65	NM94
nn-With bound-in trading card		1.40	3.50

ALIEN LEGION: JUGGER GRIMROD

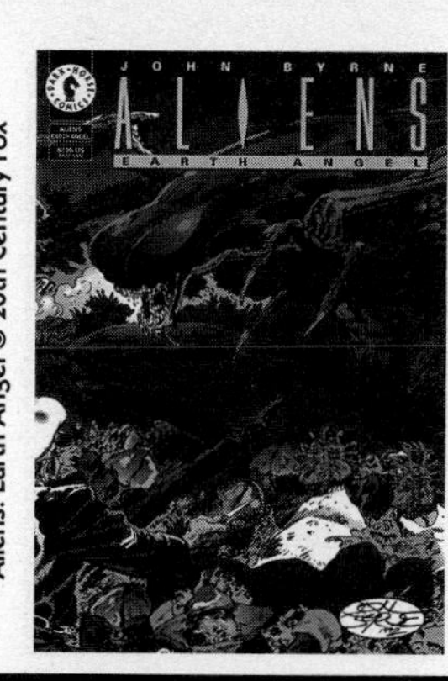

Aliens: Earth Angel © 20th Century Fox

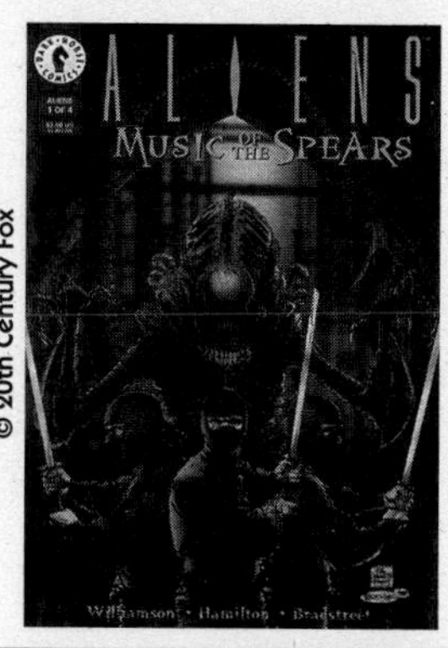

Aliens: Music of the Spears #1 © 20th Century Fox

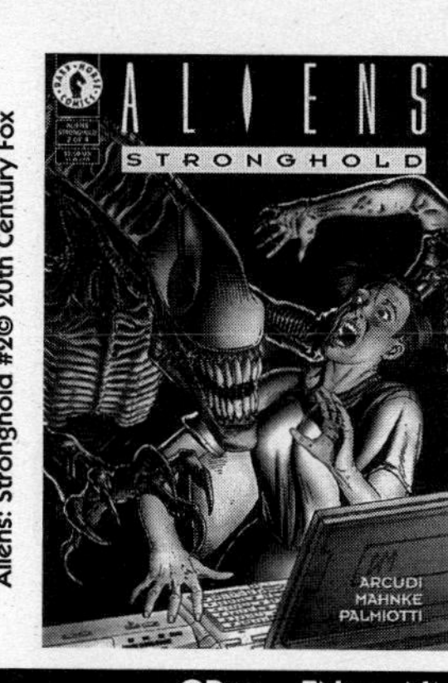

Aliens: Stronghold #2© 20th Century Fox

Aug, 1992 ($5.95, one-shot, 52 pgs.)
Epic Comics (Marvel)

	GD25	FN65	NM94
Book One	1.00	2.50	6.00

ALIEN LEGION: ONE PLANET AT A TIME
May, 1993 - No. 3, July, 1993 ($4.95, squarebound, 52 pgs.)
Epic Comics (Marvel)

	GD25	FN65	NM94
Book 1-3: Hoang Nguyen	1.00	2.00	5.00

ALIEN LEGION: ON THE EDGE (The... #2 & 3)
Nov, 1990 - No. 3, Jan, 1991 ($4.50, mini-series, 52 pgs.)
Epic Comics (Marvel)

	GD25	FN65	NM94
1-3		1.80	4.50

ALIEN LEGION: TENNANTS OF HELL
1991 - No. 2, 1991 ($4.50, color, squarebound, 52 pgs.)
Epic Comics (Marvel)

	GD25	FN65	NM94
Book 1,2-Stroman-c/a(p)		1.80	4.50

ALIEN NATION
Dec, 1988 ($2.50; 68 pgs.)
DC Comics

	GD25	FN65	NM94
1-Adapts movie; painted-c		1.00	2.50

ALIENS, THE (Captain Johner and...)(Also see Magnus Robot...)
Sept-Dec, 1967; No. 2, May, 1982
Gold Key

	GD25	FN65	NM94
1-Reprints from Magnus #1,3,4,6-10, all by Russ Manning	2.15	6.50	15.00
2-Same contents as #1		1.60	4.00

ALIENS (See Alien: The Illustrated..., Dark Horse Comics & Dark Horse Presents #24)
May, 1988 - No. 6, July, 1989 ($1.95, B&W, mini-series)
Dark Horse Comics

	GD25	FN65	NM94
1-Based on movie sequel;1st app. Aliens in comics	3.00	9.20	30.00
1-2nd printing	1.30	3.30	8.00
1-3rd - 6th printings; 4th w/new inside front-c		.80	2.00
2	2.90	8.70	20.00
2-2nd printing		1.40	3.50
2-3rd printing w/new inside f/c		.80	2.00
3	1.60	4.70	11.00
4	1.20	2.90	7.00
5,6	1.00	2.30	5.50
3-6-2nd printings		.80	2.00
...Mini Comic #1 (2/89, 4x6")-Was included with Aliens Portfolio	1.50	4.00	9.00
...Collection 1 ($10.95,)-r/#1-6 plus Dark Horse Presents #24 plus new-a	1.60	4.70	11.00
...Collection 1-2nd printing (1991, $11.95)-Printed on higher quality paper than 1st print; Dorman painted-c	1.70	5.00	12.00
Hardcover ('90, $24.95, B&W)-r/1-6, DHP #24	3.60	10.75	25.00

...Platinum Edition (See Dark Horse Presents: Aliens Platinum Edition)

ALIENS
V2#1, Aug, 1989 - No. 4, 1990 ($2.25, color, mini-series)
Dark Horse Comics

	GD25	FN65	NM94
V2#1-Adapts sequel	1.60	5.00	11.00
1-2nd printing (1990, $2.25)		.90	2.25
2-4	1.00	2.30	5.50

ALIENS: COLONIAL MARINES
Jan, 1993 - No. 10, July, 1994 ($2.50, color, limited series)
Dark Horse Comics

	GD25	FN65	NM94
1-10		1.00	2.50

ALIENS: EARTH ANGEL
Aug, 1994 ($2.95, color, one-shot)
Dark Horse Comics

	GD25	FN65	NM94
1-Byrne-a/story; wraparound-c		1.20	3.00

ALIENS: EARTH WAR
June, 1990 - No. 4, Oct, 1990 ($2.50, color, mini-series)
Dark Horse Comics

	GD25	FN65	NM94
1-All have Sam Kieth-a & Bolton painted-c	1.50	4.00	9.00
1-2nd printing		1.00	2.50
2	1.30	3.10	7.50
3,4	1.00	2.50	6.00

ALIENS: GENOCIDE
Nov, 1991 - No. 4, Feb, 1992 ($2.50, color, mini-series)
Dark Horse Comics

	GD25	FN65	NM94
1-4-Arthur Suydam painted-c. 4-Wraparound-c, poster		1.00	2.50

ALIENS: HIVE
Feb, 1992 - No. 4, May, 1992 ($2.50, color, mini-series)
Dark Horse Comics

	GD25	FN65	NM94
1-4: Kelley Jones-c/a in all		1.00	2.50

ALIENS: LABYRINTH
Sept, 1993 - No. 4, Jan, 1994 ($2.50, color, mini-series)
Dark Horse Comics

	GD25	FN65	NM94
1-4: 1-Painted-c		1.00	2.50

ALIENS: MUSIC OF THE SPEARS
Jan, 1994 - No. 4, Apr, 1994 ($2.50, color, mini-series)
Dark Horse Comics

	GD25	FN65	NM94
1-4		1.00	2.50

ALIENS: NEWT'S TALE (Dark Horse)(Value: cover or less)

ALIENS/PREDATOR: THE DEADLIEST OF SPECIES
July, 1993 - Present ($2.50, color, limited series:12, bi-monthly)
Dark Horse Comics

	GD25	FN65	NM94
1-10-Bolton painted-c: 1-3-Guice-a(p)		1.00	2.50
1-Embossed foil platinum edition			25.00

ALIENS: ROGUE
Apr, 1993 - No. 4, July, 1993 ($2.50, color, mini-series)
Dark Horse Comics

	GD25	FN65	NM94
1-4: Painted-c		1.00	2.50

ALIENS: SACRIFICE
May, 1993 ($4.95, color, one-shot, 52 pgs.)
Dark Horse Comics

	GD25	FN65	NM94
nn-Peter Milligan scripts; painted-c/a	1.00	2.00	5.00

ALIENS: SALVATION
Nov, 1993 ($4.95, color, one-shot, 52 pgs.)
Dark Horse Comics

	GD25	FN65	NM94
nn-Mike Mignola-c/a(p); D. Gibbons script	1.00	2.00	5.00

ALIENS: STRONGHOLD
May, 1994 - No. 4, Sept, 1994 ($2.50, color, mini-series)
Dark Horse Comics

	GD25	FN65	NM94
1-4		1.00	2.50

ALIENS VS. PREDATOR (See Dark Horse Presents #36)
June, 1990 - No. 4, Dec, 1990 ($2.50, color, mini-series)
Dark Horse Comics

	GD25	FN65	NM94
1-Painted-c	1.60	5.00	11.00
1-2nd printing		1.00	2.50
0-(7/90, $1.95, B&W)-r/Dark Horse Pres. #34-36	2.00	6.00	14.00
2,3	1.30	3.30	8.00
4-Dave Dorman painted-c	1.00	2.00	5.00

ALIEN TERROR (See 3-D Alien Terror)

ALIEN: THE ILLUSTRATED STORY (Also see Aliens)
1980 ($3.95, color, soft-c, 8X11")
Heavy Metal Books

All-American Comics #8 © DC

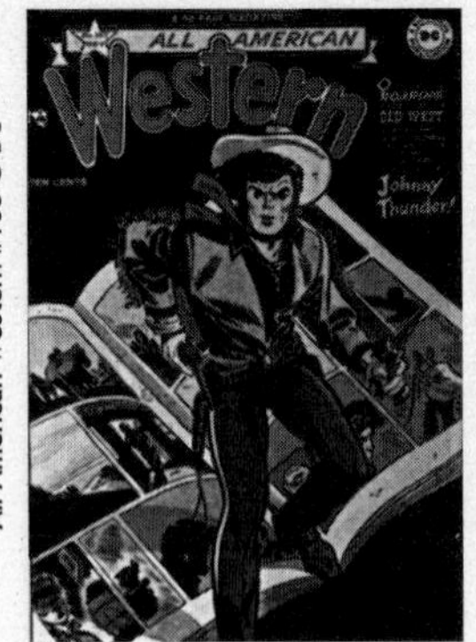

All-American Western #103 © DC

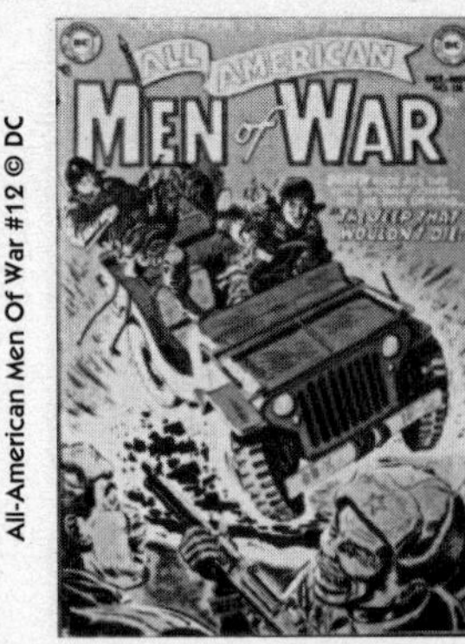

All-American Men Of War #12 © DC

GD25 FN65 NM94

nn-Movie adaptation; Simonson-a 1.60 4.00

ALIEN 3
June, 1992 - No. 3, July, 1992 ($2.50, color, mini-series)
Dark Horse Comics

1-3: Adapts 3rd movie; Suydam painted-c 1.00 2.50

ALIEN WORLDS (Also see Eclipse Graphic Album #22)
Dec, 1982 - No. 9, Jan, 1985
Pacific Comics/Eclipse

1 1.50
2-9: 2,4-Dave Stevens-c/a 1.00
3-D No. 1-Art Adams 1st published art 1.20 3.00

ALL-AMERICAN COMICS (...Western #103-126, ...Men of War #127 on; also see The Big All-American Comic Book)
April, 1939 - No. 102, Oct, 1948
All-American/National Periodical Publications

1-Hop Harrigan (1st app.), Scribbly by Mayer (1st app.), Toonerville Folks, Ben Webster, Spot Savage, Mutt & Jeff, Red White & Blue (1st app.), Adv. in the Unknown, Tippie, Reg'lar Fellers, Skippy, Bobby Thatcher, Mystery Men of Mars, Daiseybelle, Wiley of West Point begin 429.00 1285.00 3000.00
2-Ripley's Believe It or Not begins, ends #24 132.00 395.00 925.00
3-5: 5-The American Way begins, ends #10 96.00 290.00 675.00
6,7: 6-Last Spot Savage; Popsicle Pete begins, ends #26, 28. 7-Last Bobby Thatcher 82.00 245.00 575.00
8-The Ultra Man begins & 1st-c app. 121.00 365.00 850.00
9,10: 10-X-Mas-c 86.00 257.00 600.00
11-15: 11-Ultra Man-c. 12-Last Toonerville Folks. 15-Last Tippie & Reg'lar Fellars; Ultra Man-c 75.00 225.00 525.00

GD25 FN65 VF82 NM94

16-(Rare)-Origin/1st app. Green Lantern by Sheldon Moldoff (c/a)(7/40) & begin series; appears in costume on-c & only one panel inside; created by Martin Nodell. Inspired by Aladdin's Lamp; the suggested alter ego name Alan Ladd, was never capitalized on. It was changed to Alan Scott before Alan Ladd became a major film star; new logo begins
5,200.00 15,600.00 33,800.00 52,000.00
(Estimated up to 35+ total copies exist, 3 in NM/Mint)

GD25 FN65 NM94

17-(Scarce)-2nd Green Lantern 1215.00 3645.00 8500.00
18-N.Y. World's Fair-c/story 785.00 2360.00 5500.00

GD25 FN65 VF82 NM94

19-Origin/1st app. The Atom (10/40); last Ultra Man
1215.00 3645.00 6072.00 8500.00
(Estimated up to 80 total copies exist, 5 in NM/Mint)

GD25 FN65 NM94

20-Atom dons costume; Ma Hunkle becomes Red Tornado (1st app.)(1st DC costumed heroine, before Wonder Woman, 11/40); Rescue on Mars begins, ends #25; 1 pg. origin Green Lantern 321.00 965.00 2250.00
21-23: 21-Last Wiley of West Point & Skippy. 23-Last Daiseybelle; 3 Idiots begin, end #82 179.00 535.00 1250.00
24-Sisty & Dinky become the Cyclone Kids; Ben Webster ends; origin Dr. Mid-Nite & Sargon, The Sorcerer in text with app. 229.00 685.00 1600.00

GD25 FN65 VF82 NM94

25-Origin & 1st story app. Dr. Mid-Nite by Stan Asch; Hop Harrigan becomes Guardian Angel; last Adventure in the Unknown
785.00 2357.00 3928.00 5500.00
(Estimated up to 120 total copies exist, 6 in NM/Mint)

GD25 FN65 NM94

26-Origin/1st story app. Sargon, the Sorcerer 257.00 771.00 1800.00
27: #27-32 are misnumbered in indicia with correct No. appearing on-c. Intro. Doiby Dickles, Green Lantern's sidekick 314.00 945.00 2200.00
28-Hop Harrigan gives up costumed i.d. 114.00 345.00 800.00
29,30 114.00 345.00 800.00
31-40: 35-Doiby learns Green Lantern's i.d. 86.00 257.00 600.00
41-50: 50-Sargon ends 77.00 230.00 540.00
51-60: 59-Scribbly & the Red Tornado ends 64.00 193.00 450.00

GD25 FN65 NM94

61-Origin/1st app. Solomon Grundy (11/44) 300.00 900.00 2100.00
62-70: 70-Kubert Sargon; intro Sargon's helper, Maximillian O'Leary
55.00 165.00 385.00
71-88,90-99: 71-Last Red White & Blue. 72-Black Pirate begins (not in #74-82); last Atom. 73-Winky, Blinky & Noddy begins, ends #82. 79,83-Mutt & Jeff-c. 90-Origin/1st app. Icicle. 99-Last Hop Harrigan 50.00 150.00 350.00
89-Origin & 1st app. Harlequin 62.00 185.00 435.00
100-1st app. Johnny Thunder by Alex Toth (8/48); western theme begins
96.00 290.00 675.00
101-Last Mutt & Jeff 82.00 245.00 575.00
102-Last Green Lantern, Black Pirate & Dr. Mid-Nite
107.00 321.00 750.00

NOTE: *No Atom in 47, 62-69.* ***Kinstler*** *Black Pirate-89.* ***Stan Aschmeier*** *a (Dr. Mid-Nite) 25-84; c-7.* ***Mayer*** *c-1, 2(part), 6, 10.* ***Moldoff*** *c-16-23.* ***Nodell*** *c-31.* ***Paul Reinman*** *a (Green Lantern)-53-55p, 56-84, 87; (Black Pirate)-83-88, 90; c-52, 55-76, 78, 80, 81, 87.* ***Toth*** *a-88, 92, 96, 98-102; c(p)-92, 96-102. Scribbly by* ***Mayer*** *in #1-59. Ultra Man by* ***Mayer*** *in #8-19.*

ALL-AMERICAN MEN OF WAR (Previously All-American Western)
No. 127, Aug-Sept, 1952 - No. 117, Sept-Oct, 1966
National Periodical Publications

127 (#1, 1952) 70.00 214.00 500.00
128 (1952) 50.00 150.00 350.00
2(12-1/'52-53)-5 41.00 125.00 290.00
6-10 25.00 75.00 175.00
11-18: Last precode (2/55) 23.00 70.00 160.00
19-28 16.00 49.00 115.00
29,30,32-Wood-a 17.00 51.00 120.00
31,33-40 13.00 40.00 90.00
41-50 10.00 30.00 70.00
51-66 8.00 24.00 55.00
67-1st Gunner & Sarge by Andru & Esposito 17.00 51.00 120.00
68-70 8.00 24.00 55.00
71-80 5.00 15.00 35.00
81,83-88: 88-Last 10¢ issue 4.00 12.00 28.00
82-Johnny Cloud begins(1st app.), ends #111,114,115,117
7.00 21.00 50.00
89-100 3.00 10.00 23.00
101-117: 112-Balloon Buster series begins, ends #114,116. 117-Johnny Cloud-c & 3-part story 2.40 7.30 17.00

NOTE: ***Colan*** *a-112.* ***Drucker*** *a-47, 65, 71, 74, 77.* ***Grandenetti*** *c(p)-127, 128, 2-17(most).* ***Heath*** *a-27, 32, 47, 71, 95, 111, 112; c-85, 91, 94-96, 100, 101, 112, others?* ***Kirby*** *a-29.* ***Krigstein*** *a-128('52), 2, 3, 5.* ***Kubert*** *a-29, 36, 38, 41, 43, 47, 49, 50, 52, 53, 55, 56, 60, 63, 65, 69, 71-73, 102, 103, 105, 106, 108, 114; c-41, 77, 102, 103, 105, 106, 108, 114, others? Tank Killer in 69, 71, 76 by* ***Kubert. P. Reinman*** *c-55, 57, 61, 62, 71, 72, 74-76, 80.*

ALL-AMERICAN SPORTS
October, 1967
Charlton Comics

1 1.80 4.50 9.00

ALL-AMERICAN WESTERN (Formerly All-American Comics; Becomes All-American Men of War)
No. 103, Nov, 1948 - No. 126, June-July, 1952 (103-121: 52 pgs.)
National Periodical Publications

103-Johnny Thunder & his horse Black Lightning continues by Toth, ends #126; Foley of The Fighting 5th, Minstrel Maverick, & Overland Coach begin; Captain Tootsie by Beck; mentioned in Love and Death
39.00 118.00 275.00
104-Kubert-a 27.00 81.00 190.00
105,107-Kubert-a 23.00 70.00 160.00
106,108-110,112: 112-Kurtzman's "Pot-Shot Pete" (1 pg.)
17.00 52.00 120.00
111,114-116-Kubert-a 19.00 58.00 135.00
113-Intro. Swift Deer, J. Thunder's new sidekick (4-5/50); classic Toth-c; Kubert-a 22.00 65.00 150.00
117-126: 121-Kubert-a 14.00 43.00 100.00

NOTE: ***G. Kane*** *c(p)-119, 120, 123.* ***Kubert*** *a-103-105, 107, 111, 112(1 pg.), 113-116, 121.* ***Toth*** *a 103-126; c(p)-103-116, 121, 122, 124-126. Some copies of #125 have #12 on-c.*

ALL COMICS

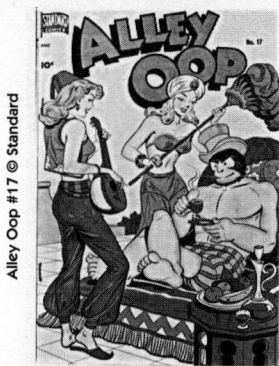

Alley Oop #17 © Standard

All Famous Police Cases #10 © STAR

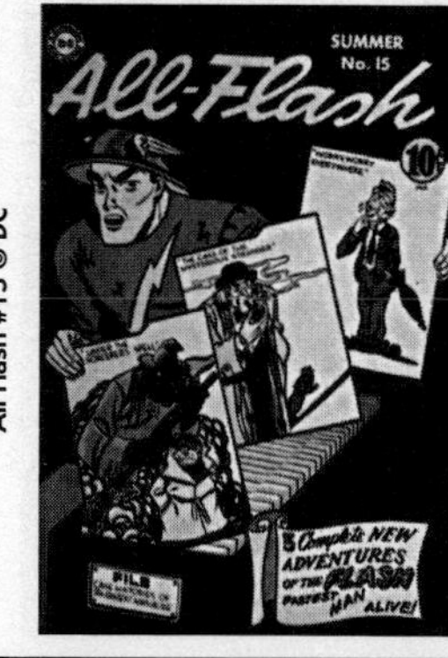

All Flash #15 © DC

GD25 FN65 NM94

1945
Chicago Nite Life News

	GD25	FN65	NM94
1	10.00	30.00	60.00

ALLEY OOP (See The Comics, 4-Color #3, The Funnies, Red Ryder and Super Book #9)

ALLEY OOP
No. 10, 1947 - No. 18, Oct, 1949
Standard Comics

	GD25	FN65	NM94
10	18.00	54.00	125.00
11-18: 17,18-Schomburg-c	13.50	41.00	95.00

ALLEY OOP
Nov, 1955 - No. 3, March, 1956 (Newspaper reprints)
Argo Publ.

	GD25	FN65	NM94
1	11.50	34.00	80.00
2,3	10.00	30.00	60.00

ALLEY OOP
12-2/62-63 - No. 2, 9-11/63
Dell Publishing Co.

	GD25	FN65	NM94
1,2	7.00	21.00	42.00

ALL-FAMOUS CRIME (Formerly Law Against Crime #1-3; becomes All-Famous Police Cases #6 on)
No. 4, 2/50 - No. 5, 5/50; No. 8, 5/51 - No. 10, 11/51
Star Publications

	GD25	FN65	NM94
4 (#1-1st series)-Formerly Law-Crime	10.00	30.00	65.00
5 (#2)	6.70	20.00	40.00
8 (#3-2nd series)	8.35	25.00	50.00
9 (#4)-Used in **SOTI**, illo- "The wish to hurt or kill couples in lovers' lanes is a not uncommon perversion;" L.B. Cole-c/a(r)/Law-Crime #3	13.50	41.00	95.00
10 (#5)-Becomes All-Famous Police Cases #6	6.70	20.00	40.00

NOTE: *All have* ***L.B. Cole*** *covers.*

ALL FAMOUS CRIME STORIES (See Fox Giants)

ALL-FAMOUS POLICE CASES (Formerly All Famous Crime #10 [#5])
No. 6, Feb, 1952 - No. 16, Sept, 1954
Star Publications

	GD25	FN65	NM94
6	7.50	22.50	45.00
7,8: 7-Kubert-a. 8-Marijuana story	5.85	17.50	35.00
9-16	5.00	15.00	30.00

NOTE: ***L. B. Cole*** *c-all; a-15, 1pg.* ***Hollingsworth*** *a-15.*

ALL-FLASH (...Quarterly No. 1-5)
Summer, 1941 - No. 32, Dec-Jan, 1947-48
National Periodical Publications/All-American

	GD25	FN65	VF82	NM94
1-Origin The Flash retold by E. E. Hibbard; Hibbard c-1-10,12-14,16,31p	1000.00	3000.00	5000.00	7000.00

(Estimated up to 200 total copies exist, 11 in NM/Mint)

	GD25	FN65	NM94
2-Origin recap	186.00	557.00	1300.00
3,4	118.00	355.00	825.00
5-Winky, Blinky & Noddy begins (1st app.), ends #32	86.00	257.00	600.00
6-10	71.00	215.00	500.00
11-13: 12-Origin/1st The Thinker. 13-The King app.	61.00	182.00	425.00
14-Green Lantern cameo	71.00	215.00	500.00
15-20: 18-Mutt & Jeff begins, ends #22	54.00	163.00	380.00
21-31	46.00	140.00	325.00
32-Origin/1st app. The Fiddler; 1st Star Sapphire	68.00	205.00	475.00

NOTE: *Book length stories in 2-13, 16. Bondage c-31, 32.* ***Martin Naydell*** *c-15, 17-28.*

ALL FOR LOVE (Young Love V3#5-on)
Apr-May, 1957 - V3#4, Dec-Jan, 1959-60
Prize Publications

	GD25	FN65	NM94
V1#1	5.85	17.50	35.00
2-6: 5-Orlando-c	4.00	10.00	20.00
V2#1-5(1/59), 5(3/59)	2.80	7.00	14.00
V3#1(5/59), 1(7/59)-4: 2-Powell-a	1.80	4.50	9.00

ALL FUNNY COMICS
Winter, 1943-44 - No. 23, May-June, 1948
Tilsam Publ./National Periodical Publications (Detective)

	GD25	FN65	NM94
1-Genius Jones (1st app.), Buzzy (1st app., ends #4), Dover & Clover (see More Fun #93) begin; Bailey-a	43.00	130.00	300.00
2	16.50	50.00	115.00
3-10	11.00	32.00	75.00
11-13,15,18,19-Genius Jones app.	9.15	27.50	55.00
14,17,20-23	7.50	22.50	45.00
16-DC Super Heroes app.	24.00	72.00	165.00

ALL GOOD
Oct, 1949 (260 pgs., 50¢)
St. John Publishing Co.

	GD25	FN65	NM94
nn-(8 St. John comics bound together)	54.00	160.00	375.00

NOTE: *Also see Li'l Audrey Yearbook & Treasury of Comics.*

ALL GOOD COMICS (See Fox Giants)
Spring, 1946 (36 pgs.)
Fox Features Syndicate

	GD25	FN65	NM94
1-Joy Family, Dick Transom, Rick Evans, One Round Hogan	13.00	40.00	90.00

ALL GREAT (See Fox Giants)
1946 (36 pgs.)
Fox Feature Syndicate

	GD25	FN65	NM94
1-Crazy House, Bertie Benson Boy Detective, Gussie the Gob	12.00	36.00	85.00

ALL GREAT
nd (1945?) (132 pgs.)
William H. Wise & Co.

	GD25	FN65	NM94
nn-Capt. Jack Terry, Joan Mason, Girl Reporter, Baron Doomsday; Torture scenes	27.00	81.00	190.00

ALL GREAT COMICS (Formerly Phantom Lady #13? Dagar, Desert Hawk No. 14 on)
No. 14, Oct, 1947 - No. 13, Dec, 1947 (Newspaper strip reprints)
Fox Features Syndicate

	GD25	FN65	NM94
14(#12)-Brenda Starr & Texas Slim-r (Scarce)	30.00	90.00	210.00
13-Origin Dagar, Desert Hawk; Brenda Starr (all-r); Kamen-c; Dagar covers begin	25.00	75.00	175.00

ALL-GREAT CONFESSIONS (See Fox Giants)

ALL GREAT CRIME STORIES (See Fox Giants)

ALL GREAT JUNGLE ADVENTURES (See Fox Giants)

ALL HALLOW'S EVE (Innovation)(Value: cover or less)

ALL HERO COMICS
March, 1943 (100 pgs.) (Cardboard cover)
Fawcett Publications

	GD25	FN65	NM94
1-Captain Marvel Jr., Capt. Midnight, Golden Arrow, Ibis the Invincible, Spy Smasher, Lance O'Casey; 1st Banshee O'Brien	114.00	343.00	800.00

ALL HUMOR COMICS
Spring, 1946 - No. 17, December, 1949
Quality Comics Group

	GD25	FN65	NM94
1	13.50	41.00	95.00
2-Atomic Tot story; Gustavson-a	7.50	22.50	45.00
3-9: 3-Intro Kelly Poole who is cover feature #3 on. 5-1st app. Hickory? 8-Gustavson-a	4.20	12.50	25.00
10-17	3.60	9.00	18.00

ALL LOVE (...Romances No. 26)(Formerly Ernie Comics)
No. 26, May, 1949 - No. 32, May, 1950

All New Comics #8 © Harvey

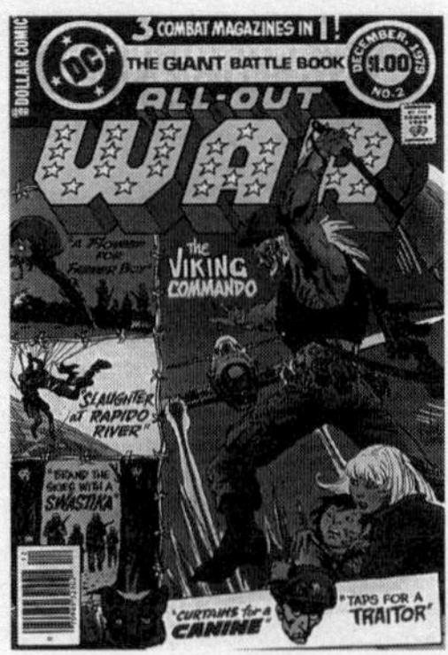

All Out War #2 © DC

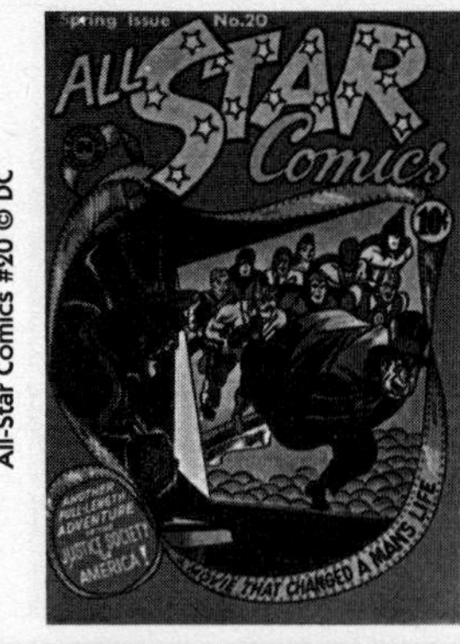

All-Star Comics #20 © DC

GD25 FN65 NM94

Ace Periodicals (Current Books)

26(No. 1)-Ernie, Lily Belle app. 5.85 17.50 35.00
27-L. B. Cole-a 6.35 19.00 38.00
28-32 4.00 10.00 20.00

ALL-NEGRO COMICS
June, 1947 (15¢)
All-Negro Comics

1 (Rare) 200.00 600.00 1400.00

NOTE: *Seldom found in fine or mint condition; many copies have brown pages.*

ALL-NEW COLLECTORS' EDITION (Formerly Limited ...)
Jan, 1978 - Vol. 8, No. C-62, 1979 (No. 54-58: 76 pgs.)
DC Comics, Inc.

C-53-Rudolph the Red-Nosed Reindeer 1.20 3.00
C-54-Superman Vs. Wonder Woman 1.20 3.00
C-55-Superboy & the Legion of Super-Heroes; marriage of Lightning Lad & Saturn Girl 1.00 2.50 6.00
C-56-Superman Vs. Muhammad Ali: story & wraparound N. Adams-c 1.60 4.00
C-58-Superman Vs. Shazam 1.20 3.00
C-60-Rudolph's Summer Fun(8/78) 1.20 3.00
C-61-See Famous First Edition
C-62-Superman the Movie (68 pgs.; 1979)-Photo-c from movie plus photos inside (also see DC Special Series #25) 1.20 3.00

ALL-NEW COMICS (...Short Story Comics No. 1-3)
Jan, 1943 - No. 14, Nov, 1946; No. 15, Mar-Apr, 1947 (10 x 13-1/2")
Family Comics (Harvey Publications)

1-Steve Case, Crime Rover, Johnny Rebel, Kayo Kane, The Echo, Night Hawk, Ray O'Light, Detective Shane begin (all 1st app.?); Red Blazer on cover only; Sultan-a 107.00 321.00 750.00
2-Origin Scarlet Phantom by Kubert 49.00 148.00 345.00
3 39.00 118.00 275.00
4,5 36.00 107.00 250.00
6-The Boy Heroes & Red Blazer (text story) begin, end #12; Black Cat app.; intro. Sparky in Red Blazer 39.00 118.00 275.00
7-Kubert, Powell-a; Black Cat & Zebra app. 39.00 118.00 275.00
8,9: 8-Shock Gibson app.; Kubert, Powell-a; Schomburg bondage-c. 9-Black Cat app.; Kubert-a 39.00 118.00 275.00
10-12: 10-The Zebra app. (from Green Hornet Comics); Kubert-a(3). 11-Girl Commandos, Man In Black app. 12-Kubert-a 32.00 96.00 225.00
13-Stuntman by Simon & Kirby; Green Hornet, Joe Palooka, Flying Fool app.; Green Hornet-c 39.00 118.00 275.00
14-The Green Hornet & The Man in Black Called Fate by Powell, Joe Palooka app.; J. Palooka-c by Ham Fisher 32.00 96.00 225.00
15-(Rare)-Small size (5-1/2x8-1/2"; B&W; 32 pgs.). Distributed to mail subscribers only. Black Cat and Joe Palooka app. Estimated value....$200-250

NOTE: *Also see Boy Explorers No. 2, Flash Gordon No. 5, and Stuntman No. 3.* **Powell** *a-11.* **Schomburg** *c-5, 7-11. Captain Red Blazer & Spark on c-5-11 (w/Boy Heroes #12).*

ALL NEW COMICS
Oct, 1993 (No cover price, 16 pgs.) (Hanna-Barbera)
Harvey Comics

1-Flintstones, Scooby Doo, Jetsons, Yogi Bear & Wacky Races previews for upcoming Harvey's new Hanna-Barbera line-up 1.00

ALL-OUT WAR
Sept-Oct, 1979 - No. 6, Aug, 1980 ($1.00, 68 pgs.)
DC Comics

1-6: 1-The Viking Commando(origin), Force Three(origin), & Black Eagle Squadron begin 1.50

NOTE: **Ayers** *a(p)-1-6.* **Elias** *r-2.* **Evans** *a-1-6.* **Kubert** *c-16.*

ALL PICTURE ADVENTURE MAGAZINE
Oct, 1952 - No. 2, Nov, 1952 (100 pg. Giants, 25¢, squarebound)
St. John Publishing Co.

1-War comics 18.00 54.00 125.00

GD25 FN65 NM94

2-Horror-crime comics 25.00 75.00 175.00

NOTE: *Above books contain three St. John comics rebound; variations possible.* **Baker** *art known in both.*

ALL PICTURE ALL TRUE LOVE STORY
October, 1952 (100 pgs., 25¢)
St. John Publishing Co.

1-Canteen Kate by Matt Baker 34.00 103.00 240.00

ALL-PICTURE COMEDY CARNIVAL
October, 1952 (100 pgs., 25¢)(Contains 4 rebound comics)
St. John Publishing Co.

1-Contents can vary; Baker-a 34.00 103.00 240.00

ALL REAL CONFESSION MAGAZINE (See Fox Giants)

ALL ROMANCES (Mr. Risk No. 7 on)
Aug, 1949 - No. 6, June, 1950
A. A. Wyn (Ace Periodicals)

1 6.35 19.00 38.00
2 3.20 8.00 16.00
3-6 2.80 7.00 14.00

ALL-SELECT COMICS (Blonde Phantom No. 12 on)
Fall, 1943 - No. 11, Fall, 1946
Timely Comics (Daring Comics)

1-Capt. America (by Rico #1), Human Torch, Sub-Mariner begin; Black Widow story (4 pgs.) 429.00 1285.00 3000.00
2-Red Skull app. 179.00 535.00 1250.00
3-The Whizzer begins 121.00 365.00 850.00
4,5-Last Sub-Mariner 86.00 257.00 600.00
6-9: 6-The Destroyer app. 8-No Whizzer 79.00 236.00 550.00
10-The Destroyer & Sub-Mariner app.; last Capt. America & Human Torch issue 79.00 236.00 550.00
11-1st app. Blonde Phantom; Miss America app.; all Blonde Phantom-c by Shores 136.00 407.00 950.00

NOTE: **Schomburg** *c-1-10.* **Sekowsky** *a-7. #7 & 8 show 1944 in indicia, but should be 1945.*

ALL SPORTS COMICS (Formerly Real Sports Comics; becomes All Time Sports Comics No. 4 on)
No. 2, Dec-Jan, 1948-49; No. 3, Feb-Mar, 1949
Hillman Periodicals

2-Krigstein-a(p), Powell, Starr-a 20.00 60.00 140.00
3-Mort Lawrence-a 16.00 48.00 110.00

ALL STAR COMICS (All Star Western No. 58 on)
Sum, '40 - No. 57, Feb-Mar, '51; No. 58, Jan-Feb, '76 -No. 74, Sept-Oct, '78
National Periodical Publ./All-American/DC Comics

GD25 FN65 VF82 NM94

1-The Flash(#1 by E.E. Hibbard), Hawkman(by Shelly), Hourman(by Bernard Baily), The Sandman(by Creig Flessel), The Spectre(by Baily), Biff Bronson, Red White & Blue(ends #2) begin; Ultra Man's only app. (#1-3 are quarterly; #4 begins bi-monthly issues) 1062.00 3190.00 5845.00 8500.00
(Estimated up to 200+ total copies exist, 6 in NM/Mint)

GD25 FN65 NM94

2-Green Lantern (by Martin Nodell), Johnny Thunder begin; Hibbard/Moldoff/Bailey-c 457.00 1371.00 3200.00

GD25 FN65 VF82 NM94

3-Origin & 1st app. The Justice Society of America (Win/40); Dr. Fate & The Atom begin, Red Tornado cameo 2500.00 7500.00 16,250.00 25,000.00
(Estimated up to 150+ total copies exist, 6 in NM/Mint)

3-Reprint, Oversize 13-1/2x10". **WARNING:** This comic is an exact reprint of the original except for its size. DC published it in 1974 with a second cover titling it as a Famous First Edition. There have been many reported cases of the outer cover being removed and the interior sold as the original edition. The reprint with the new outer cover removed is practically worthless. See Famous First Edition for value.

GD25 FN65 NM94

4-1st adventure for J.S.A. 429.00 1286.00 3000.00
5-1st app. Shiera Sanders as Hawkgirl (1st costumed super-heroine, 6-7/41) 414.00 1243.00 2900.00
6-Johnny Thunder joins JSA 271.00 815.00 1900.00

All-Star Squadron #47 © DC

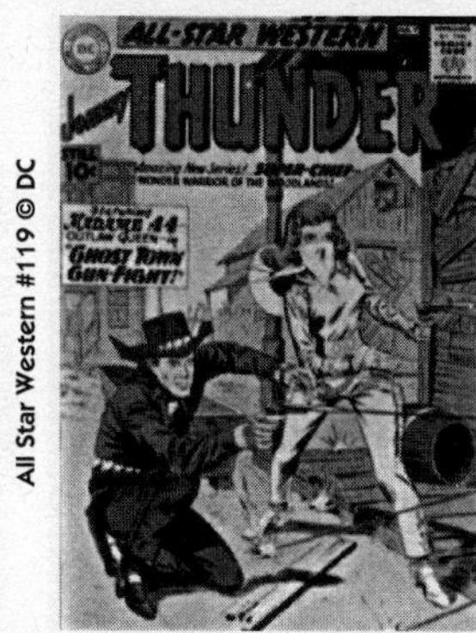

All Star Western #119 © DC

All Suprise #2 © MEG

GD25 FN65 NM94 GD25 FN65 NM94

7-Batman, Superman, Flash cameo; last Hourman; Doiby Dickles app. 314.00 943.00 2200.00

GD25 FN65 VF82 NM94

8-Origin & 1st app. Wonder Woman (12-1/41-42)(added as 9pgs. making book 76 pgs.; origin cont'd in Sensation #1; see W.W. #1 for more detailed origin); Dr. Fate dons new helmet; Hop Harrigan text stories & Starman begin; Shiera app.; Hop Harrigan JSA guest; Starman & Dr. Midnite become members 1190.00 3563.00 6531.00 9500.00

(Estimated up to 150 total copies exist, 6 in NM/Mint)

GD25 FN65 NM94

9,10: 9-JSA's girlfriends cameo; Shiera app.; J. Edgar Hoover of FBI made associate member of JSA. 10-Flash, Green Lantern cameo; Sandman new costume 264.00 793.00 1850.00
11,12: 11-Wonder Woman begins; Spectre cameo; Shiera app. 12- Wonder Woman becomes JSA Secretary 229.00 685.00 1600.00
13-15: Sandman w/Sandy in #14 & 15. 15-Origin & 1st app. Brain Wave; Shiera app. 214.00 643.00 1500.00
16-20: 19-Sandman w/Sandy. 20-Dr. Fate & Sandman cameo 164.00 493.00 1150.00
21-23: 21-Spectre & Atom cameo; Dr. Fate by Kubert; Dr. Fate, Sandman end. 22-Last Hop Harrigan; Flag-c. 23-Origin/1st app. Psycho Pirate; last Spectre & Starman 143.00 429.00 1000.00
24-Flash & Green Lantern cameo; Mr. Terrific only app.; Wildcat, JSA guest; Kubert Hawkman begins 143.00 429.00 1000.00
25-27: 25-Flash & Green Lantern start again. 26-Robot-c. 27-Wildcat, JSA guest (#24-26: only All-American imprint) 121.00 364.00 850.00
28-32 114.00 343.00 800.00
33-Solomon Grundy & Doiby Dickles app; classic Solomon Grundy cover 250.00 750.00 1750.00
34,35-Johnny Thunder cameo in both 104.00 310.00 725.00
36-Batman & Superman JSA guests 243.00 729.00 1700.00
37-Johnny Thunder cameo; origin & 1st app. Injustice Society; last Kubert Hawkman 132.00 396.00 925.00
38-Black Canary begins; JSA Death issue 157.00 471.00 1100.00
39,40: 39-Last Johnny Thunder 100.00 280.00 650.00
41-Black Canary joins JSA; Injustice Society app. (2nd app.?) 97.00 268.00 625.00
42-Atom & the Hawkman don new costumes 100.00 280.00 650.00
43-49,51-56: 43-New logo. 55-Sci/Fi story 100.00 280.00 650.00
50-Frazetta art, 3 pgs. 110.00 300.00 700.00
57-Kubert-a, 6 pgs. (Scarce); last app. G.A. Green Lantern, Flash & Dr. Mid-Nite 120.00 321.00 750.00
V12#58-74(1976-78)-Flash, Hawkman, Dr. Mid-Nite, Wildcat, Dr. Fate, Green Lantern, Star Spangled Kid, & Robin app.; intro Power Girl. 58-JSA app. 69-1st modern app. Huntress (see Sensation) .60 1.25

NOTE: *No Atom-27, 36; no Dr. Fate-13; no Flash-8, 9, 11-23; no Green Lantern-8, 9,11-23; Hawkman in 1-57 (only one to app. in all 57 issues); no Johnny Thunder-5, 36; no Wonder Woman-9, 10, 23. Book length stories in 4-9, 11-14, 18-22, 25, 26, 29, 30, 32-36, 42, 43. Johnny Peril in #42-46, 48, 49, 51, 52,54-57.* ***Baily*** *a-1-10, 12, 13, 14i, 15-20.* ***Burnley*** *Starman-8-13; c-12, 13.* ***Grell*** *c-58.* ***E.E. Hibbard*** *c-3, 4, 6-10.* ***Infantino*** *c-40.* ***Kubert*** *Hawkman-24-30, 33-37.* ***Lampert/Baily/Flessel*** *c-1, 2.* ***Moldoff*** *Hawkman-3-23; c-11.* ***Mart Naydell*** *c-25i, 26i, 27-32.* ***Purcell*** *c-5.* ***Simon & Kirby*** *Sandman 14-17, 19.* ***Staton*** *a-66-74p. c-74p.* ***Toth*** *a-37(2), 38(2), 40, 41; c-38, 41.* ***Wood*** *a-58i-63i, 64, 65; c-63i, 64, 65. Issues 1-7, 9-16 are 68 pgs.; #8 is 76 pgs.; #17-19 are 60 pgs.; #20-57 are 52 pgs.*

ALL STAR INDEX, THE (Eclipse)(Value: cover or less)

ALL-STAR SQUADRON (See Justice League of America #193)
Sept, 1981 - No. 67, March, 1987
DC Comics

1-Original Atom, Hawkman, Dr. Mid-Nite, Robotman (origin), Plastic Man, Johnny Quick, Liberty Belle, Shining Knight begin 1.00
2-24: 5-Danette Reilly becomes new Firebrand. 8-Re-intro Steel, the Indestructable Man. 12-Origin G.A. Hawkman retold. 23-Origin/1st app. The Amazing Man. 24-Batman app. 1.00
25-1st app. Infinity, Inc. (9/83) 1.00
26-Origin Infinity, Inc. (2nd app.); Robin app. 1.00
27-46,48,49: 33-Origin Freedom Fighters of Earth-X. 41-Origin Starman 1.00
47-Origin Dr. Fate; McFarlane-a (1st full story)/part-c (7/85) 1.60 4.00
50-Double size; Crisis x-over 1.00
51-67: 51-56-Crisis x-over. 61-Origin Liberty Belle. 62-Origin The Shining Knight. 63-Origin Robotman. 65-Origin Johnny Quick. 66-Origin Tarantula 1.00
Annual 1-3: 1(11/82)-Retells origin of G.A. Atom, Guardian & Wildcat. 2(11/83)-Infinity, Inc. app. 3(9/84) 1.00

NOTE: ***Kubert*** *c-2, 7-18. JLA app. in 14, 15. JSA app. in 4, 14, 15, 19, 27, 28.*

ALL-STAR STORY OF THE DODGERS, THE
April, 1979 (Full Color) ($1.00)
Stadium Communications

1 1.00

ALL STAR WESTERN (Formerly All Star Comics No. 1-57)
No. 58, Apr-May, 1951 - No. 119, June-July, 1961
National Periodical Publications

58-Trigger Twins (ends #116), Strong Bow, The Roving Ranger & Don Caballero begin 38.00 115.00 265.00
59,60: Last 52 pgs. 18.00 54.00 125.00
61-66: 61-64-Toth-a 15.00 45.00 105.00
67-Johnny Thunder begins; Gil Kane-a 18.00 54.00 125.00
68-81: Last precode (2-3/55) 9.15 27.50 55.00
82-98 8.35 25.00 50.00
99-Frazetta-r/Jimmy Wakely #4 9.15 27.50 55.00
100 9.15 27.50 55.00
101-107,109-116,118,119 5.85 17.50 35.00
108-Origin J. Thunder; J. Thunder logo begins 13.00 40.00 90.00
117-Origin Super Chie 10.00 30.00 60.00

NOTE: ***Gil Kane*** *c(p)-58, 59, 61, 63, 64, 68, 69, 70-95(most), 97-199(most).* ***Infantino*** *art in most issues. Madame .44 app.-#117-119.*

ALL-STAR WESTERN (Weird Western Tales No. 12 on)
Aug-Sept, 1970 - No. 11, Apr-May, 1972
National Periodical Publications

1-Pow-Wow Smith-r; Infantino-a 1.65 4.70 11.00
2-8: 2-Outlaw begins; El Diablo by Morrow begins; has cameos by Williamson, Torres, Gil Kane, Giordano & Phil Seuling. 3-Origin El Diablo. 5-Last Outlaw issue. 6-Billy the Kid begins, ends #8 1.60 4.00
9-Frazetta-a, 3pgs.(r) 1.00 2.50 5.50
10-Jonah Hex begins (1st app., 2-3/72) 9.00 28.00 65.00
11-2nd app. Jonah Hex 4.30 13.00 30.00

NOTE: ***Neal Adams*** *c-1-5;* ***Aparo*** *a-5.* ***G. Kane*** *a-3, 4, 6, 8.* ***Kubert*** *a-4r, 7-9r.* ***Morrow*** *a-2-4, 10, 11. No. 7-11 have 52 pgs..*

ALL SURPRISE (Becomes Jeanie #13 on) (Funny animal)
Fall, 1943 - No. 12, Winter, 1946-47
Timely/Marvel (CPC)

1-Super Rabbit, Gandy & Sourpuss begin 19.00 58.00 135.00
2 9.15 27.50 55.00
3-10,12 6.70 20.00 40.00
11-Kurtzman "Pigtales" art 9.15 27.50 55.00

ALL TEEN (Formerly All Winners; All Winners & Teen Comics No. 21 on)
No. 20, January, 1947
Marvel Comics (WFP)

20-Georgie, Mitzi, Patsy Walker, Willie app.; Syd Shores-c 6.70 20.00 40.00

ALL THE FUNNY FOLKS
1926 (hardcover, 112 pgs., 11-1/2x3-1/2") (Full color)
World Press Today, Inc.

nn-Barney Google, Spark Plug, Jiggs & Maggie, Tillie The Toiler, Happy Hooligan, Hans & Fritz, Toots & Casper, etc. 50.00 150.00 350.00

ALL-TIME SPORTS COMICS (Formerly All Sports Comics)
V2No. 4, Apr-May, 1949 - V2No. 7, Oct-Nov, 1949 (All 52 pgs.)
Hillman Periodicals

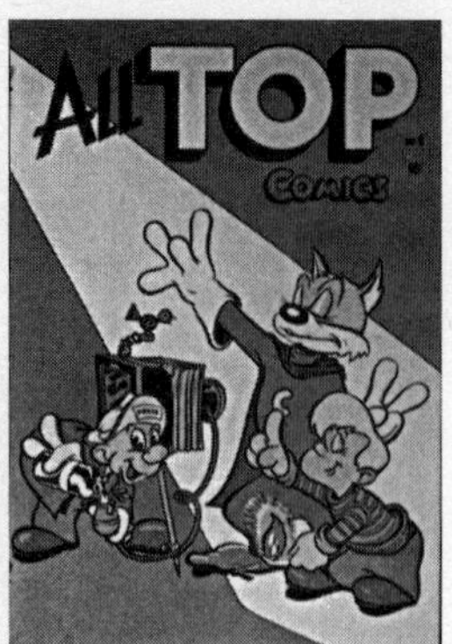

All Top Comics #6 © Fox

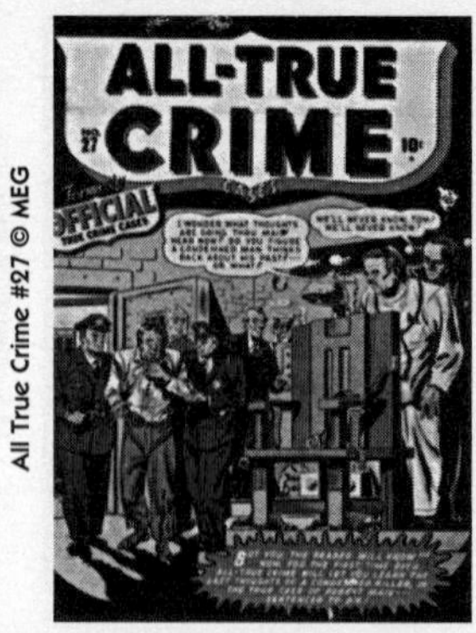

All True Crime #27 © MEG

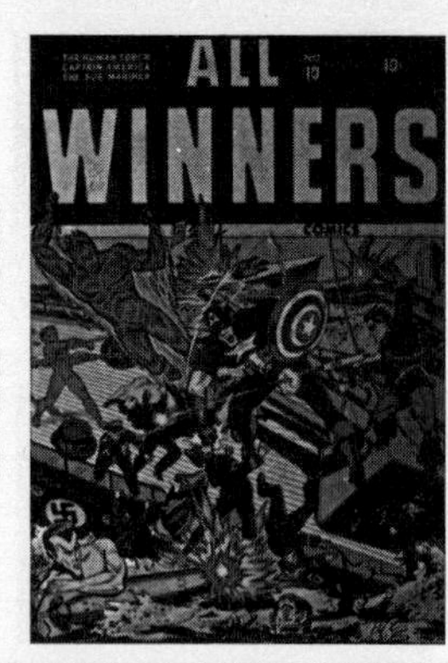

All Winners #10 © MEG

GD25 FN65 NM94

V2#4 14.00 43.00 100.00
5-7: 5-(V1#5 inside)-Powell-a. 7-Krigstein-p 11.00 32.00 75.00

ALL TOP
1944 (132 pgs.)
William H. Wise Co.

Capt. V, Merciless the Sorceress, Red Robbins, One Round Hogan, Mike the M.P., Snooky, Pussy Katnip app. 22.00 65.00 150.00

ALL TOP COMICS (My Experience No. 19 on)
1945; No. 2, Sum, 1946 - No. 18, Mar, 1949; 1957 - 1959
Fox Features Synd./Green Publ./Norlen Mag.

1-Cosmo Cat & Flash Rabbit begin (1st app.) 16.00 48.00 110.00
2 (#1-7 are funny animal) 8.65 26.00 52.00
3-7 6.35 19.00 38.00
8-Blue Beetle, Phantom Lady, & Rulah, Jungle Goddess begin (11/47); Kamen-c 100.00 300.00 700.00
9-Kamen-c 60.00 180.00 420.00
10-Kamen bondage-c 63.00 190.00 440.00
11-13,15-17: 15-No Blue Beetle 43.00 130.00 300.00
14-No Blue Beetle; used in **SOTI**, illo- "Corpses of colored people strung up by their wrists" 57.00 171.00 400.00
18-Dagar, Jo-Jo app; no Phantom Lady or Blue Beetle 36.00 107.00 250.00
6(1957-Green Publ.)-Patoruzu the Indian; Cosmo Cat on cover only 3.00 7.50 15.00
6(1958-Literary Ent.)-Muggy Doo; Cosmo Cat on cover only 3.00 7.50 15.00
6(1959-Norlen)-Atomic Mouse; Cosmo Cat on cover only 3.00 7.50 15.00
6(1959)-Little Eva 3.00 7.50 15.00
6(Cornell)-Supermouse on-c 3.00 7.50 15.00
NOTE: *Jo-Jo by **Kamen**-12,18.*

ALL TRUE ALL PICTURE POLICE CASES
Oct, 1952 - No. 2, Nov, 1952 (100 pgs.)
St. John Publishing Co.

1-Three rebound St. John crime comics 31.00 94.00 220.00
2-Three comics rebound 23.00 70.00 160.00
NOTE: *Contents may vary.*

ALL-TRUE CRIME (...Cases No. 26-35; formerly Official True Crime Cases)
No. 26, Feb, 1948 - No. 52, Sept, 1952
Marvel/Atlas Comics(OFI #26,27/CFI #28,29/LCC #30-46/LMC #47-52)

26(#1)-Syd Shores-c 15.00 45.00 105.00
27(4/48)-Electric chair-c 11.00 32.00 75.00
28-41,43-48,50-52: 35-37-Photo-c 5.00 15.00 30.00
42,49-Krigstein-a. 49-Used in **POP**, Pg 79 6.70 20.00 40.00
NOTE: ***Robinson** a-47, 50. **Shores** c-26. **Tuska** a-48(3).*

ALL-TRUE DETECTIVE CASES (Kit Carson No. 5 on)
Feb-Mar, 1954 - No. 4, Aug-Sept, 1954
Avon Periodicals

1 15.00 45.00 105.00
2-Wood-a 13.00 40.00 90.00
3-Kinstler-c 6.70 20.00 40.00
4-r/Gangsters And Gun Molls #2; Kamen-a 11.00 32.00 75.00
nn(100 pgs.)-7 pg. Kubert-a, Kinstler back-c 26.00 78.00 180.00

ALL TRUE ROMANCE (...Illustrated No. 3)
3/51 - No. 20, 12/54; No. 22, 3/55 - No. 30?, 7/57; No. 3(#31), 9/57; No. 4(#32), 11/57; No. 33, 2/58 - No. 34, 3/58
Artful Publ. #1-3/Harwell(Comic Media) #4-20?/Ajax-Farrell(Excellent Publ.) No. 22 on/Four Star Comic Corp.

1 (3/51) 10.00 30.00 65.00
2 (10/51; 11/51 on-c) 5.35 16.00 32.00
3(12/51) - #5(5/52) 4.35 13.00 26.00
6-Wood-a, 9 pgs. (exceptional) 12.00 36.00 85.00
7-10 4.00 10.00 20.00

GD25 FN65 NM94

11-13,16-19 (2/54) 3.20 8.00 16.00
14-Marijuana story 3.60 9.00 18.00
20,22: Last precode issue (Ajax, 3/55) 2.60 6.50 13.00
23-27,29,30 2.20 5.50 11.00
28 (9/56)-L. B. Cole, Disbrow-a 4.70 14.00 28.00
3,4,33,34 (Farrell, '57- '58) 1.40 3.50 7.00

ALL WESTERN WINNERS (Formerly All Winners; becomes Western Winners with No. 5; see Two-Gun Kid No. 5)
No. 2, Winter, 1948-49 - No. 4, April, 1949
Marvel Comics(CDS)

2-Black Rider (origin & 1st app.) & his horse Satan, Kid Colt & his horse Steel, & Two-Gun Kid & his horse Cyclone begin; Shores c-2-4 44.00 133.00 310.00
3-Anti-Wertham editorial 26.00 77.00 180.00
4-Black Rider i.d. revealed; Heath, Shores-a 26.00 77.00 180.00

ALL WINNERS COMICS (All Teen #20)
Summer, 1941 - No. 19, Fall, 1946; No. 21, Winter, 1946-47
(No #20) (No. 21 continued from Young Allies No. 20)
USA No. 1-7/WFP No. 10-19/YAI No. 21

GD25 FN65 VF82 NM94

1-The Angel & Black Marvel only app.; Capt. America by Simon & Kirby, Human Torch & Sub-Mariner begin (#1 was advertised as All Aces); 1st app. All-Winners Squad in text story by Stan Lee 1000.00 3000.00 5500.00 8000.00

GD25 FN65 NM94

2-The Destroyer & The Whizzer begin; Simon & Kirby Captain America &-c 300.00 900.00 2100.00
3 200.00 600.00 1400.00
4-Classic War-c by Al Avison 221.00 665.00 1550.00
5 121.00 365.00 850.00
6-The Black Avenger only app.; no Whizzer story; Hitler, Hirohito & Mussolini-c 129.00 385.00 900.00
7-10 100.00 300.00 700.00
11,13-18: 11-1st Atlas globe on-c (Winter, 1943-44; also see Human Torch #14). 14-16-No Human Torch 71.00 215.00 500.00
12-Red Skull story; last Destroyer; no Whizzer story 82.00 246.00 575.00
19-(Scarce)-1st story app. & origin All Winners Squad (Capt. America & Bucky, Human Torch & Toro, Sub-Mariner, Whizzer, & Miss America; r-in Fantasy Masterpieces #10 200.00 600.00 1400.00
21-(Scarce)-All Winners Squad; bondage-c 171.00 515.00 1200.00
NOTE: ***Everett** Sub-Mariner-1, 3, 4; **Burgos** Torch-1, 3, 4. **Schomburg** c-1, 7-18. **Shores** c-19p, 21.*

(2nd Series - August, 1948, Marvel Comics (CDS))
(Becomes All Western Winners with No. 2)

1-The Blonde Phantom, Capt. America, Human Torch, & Sub-Mariner app. 136.00 407.00 950.00

ALL YOUR COMICS (See Fox Giants)
Spring, 1946 (36 pgs.)
Fox Feature Syndicate (R. W. Voight)

1-Red Robbins, Merciless the Sorceress app. 11.50 34.00 80.00

ALMANAC OF CRIME (See Fox Giants)

AL OF FBI (See Little Al of the FBI)

ALONG THE FIRING LINE WITH ROGER BEAN
1916 (Hardcover, B&W) (6x17") (66 pgs.)
Chas. B. Jackson

3-By Chic Jackson (1915 daily strips) 14.00 43.00 100.00

ALPHA AND OMEGA (Spire Christian)(Value: cover or less)

ALPHA FLIGHT (See X-Men #120,121 & X-Men/Alpha Flight)
Aug, 1983 - No. 130, Mar, 1994 (#52-on are direct sale only)
Marvel Comics Group

1-Byrne-a begins (52pgs.)-Wolverine & Nightcrawler cameo 1.00 2.50

Alpha Flifgt #130 © MEG

Amazing Adult Fantasy #12 © MEG

Amazing Adventures #2 © MEG

GD25 FN65 NM94 — GD25 FN65 NM94

2-12: 2-Vindicator becomes Guardian; origin Marrina & Alpha Flight. 3-Concludes origin Alpha Flight. 6-Origin Shaman. 7-Origin Snowbird. 10,11-Origin Sasquatch. 12-(52 pgs.)-Death of Guardian .70 1.75
13-Wolverine app. 1.00 2.50 5.50
14-16,18-28: 16-Wolverine cameo. 20-New headquarters. 25-Return of Guardian. 28-Last Byrne issue 1.25
17-X-Men x-over (70% reprinted from X-Men #109); Wolverine cameo 1.20 3.00
29-32,35-49: 39-47,49-Portacio-a(i) 1.00
33,34: 33-X-Men (Wolverine) app. 34-Origin Wolverine 1.60 4.00
50-Double size; Portacio-a(i) 1.25
51-Jim Lee's 1st work at Marvel (10/87); Wolverine cameo; 1st Jim Lee Wolverine; Portacio-a(i) 1.00 2.00 5.00
52,53-Wolverine app.; Lee-a on Wolverine; Portacio-a(i); 53-Lee/Portacio-a 1.20 3.00
54,63,64-No Jim Lee-a; 54-Portacio-a(i) 1.00
55-62-Jim Lee-a(p) 1.00 2.50
65-74,76-86: 65-Begin $1.50-c. 71-Intro The Sorcerer (villain). 74-Wolverine, Spider-Man & The Avengers app. 89-Original Guardian returns 1.25
75-Double size ($1.95, 52 pgs.) 1.50
87-90-Wolverine 4 part story w/Jim Lee covers 1.40 3.50
91-99,101-104: 91-Dr. Doom app. 94-F.F. x-over. 99-Galactus, Avengers app. 102-Intro Weapon Omega. 104-Last $1.50-c 1.50
100-($2.00, 52 pgs.)-Avengers & Galactus app. .70 1.75
105,107-119,121-129: 107-X-Factor x-over. 110-112-Infinity War x-overs. 110, 111-Wolverine app. (brief). 111-Thanos cameo 1.50
106-Northstar revelation issue 1.10 2.75
106-2nd printing (direct sale only) 1.25
120-($2.25)-Polybagged w/Superpowers poster .70 1.75
130-($2.25, 52 pgs.) .90 2.25
Annual 1 (9/86, $1.25) 1.25
Annual 2(12/87, $1.25) 1.00
Special V2#1(6/92, $2.50, 52 pgs.)-Wolverine-c/story .90 2.25

NOTE: ***Austin*** *c-1i, 2i, 53i.* ***Byrne*** *c-81, 82.* ***Guice*** *c-85, 91-99.* ***Jim Lee*** *a(p)-51, 53, 55-62, 64; c-53, 87-90.* ***Whilce Portacio*** *a(i)-39-47, 49-54.*

ALPHA FLIGHT SPECIAL
July, 1991 - No. 4, Oct, 1991 ($1.50, limited series)
Marvel Comics

1-3: Reprints Flight #97-99 w/covers 1.50
4 ($2.00, 52 pgs.)-Reprints Alpha Flight #100 .80 2.00

ALPHA WAVE (Darkline)(Value: cover or less)

ALPHONSE & GASTON & LEON
1903 (15x10", Sunday strip reprints in color)
Hearst's New York American & Journal

nn-By Fred Opper 75.00 225.00 675.00

ALTER EGO (First)(Value: cover or less)

ALVIN (TV) (See 4-Color Comics No. 1042)
Oct-Dec, 1962 - No. 28, Oct, 1973
Dell Publishing Co.

12-021-212 (#1) 12.00 36.00 85.00
2 7.50 22.50 45.00
3-10 5.85 17.50 35.00
11-28 4.70 14.00 28.00
Alvin For President (10/64) 4.00 10.00 20.00
...& His Pals in Merry Christmas with Clyde Crashcup & Leonardo 1 (02-120-402)-(12-2/64), reprinted in 1966 (12-023-604) 6.65 20.00 40.00

ALVIN & THE CHIPMUNKS
July, 1992 - No. 5, May, 1994
Harvey Comics

1 1.25
2-5 1.50

AMAZING ADULT FANTASY (Formerly Amazing Adventures #1-6; becomes Amazing Fantasy #15)
No. 7, Dec, 1961 - No. 14, July, 1962
Marvel Comics Group (AMI)

7-Ditko-c/a begins, ends #14 35.00 106.00 425.00
8-Last 10¢ issue 29.00 90.00 350.00
9-13: 12-1st app. Mailbag. 13-Anti-communist story 26.00 80.00 310.00
14-Prototype ish. (Professor X) 28.00 84.00 335.00

AMAZING ADVENTURE FUNNIES (Fantoman No. 2 on)
June, 1940 - No. 2, Sept. 1940
Centaur Publications

1-The Fantom of the Fair by Gustavson (r/Amaz. Mystery Funnies V2#7,V2#8), The Arrow, Skyrocket Steele From the Year X by Everett (r/AMF #2); Burgos-a 136.00 407.00 950.00
2-Reprints; Published after Fantoman #2 93.00 280.00 650.00

NOTE: ***Burgos*** *a-1(2).* ***Everett*** *a-1(3).* ***Gustavson*** *a-1(5), 2(3).* ***Pinajian*** *a-2.*

AMAZING ADVENTURES (Also see Boy Cowboy & Science Comics)
1950; No. 1, Nov, 1950 - No. 6, Fall, 1952 (Painted covers)
Ziff-Davis Publ. Co.

1950 (no month given) (8-1/2x11) (8 pgs.) Has the front & back cover plus Schomburg story used in Amazing Advs. #1 (Sent to subscribers of Z-D s/f magazines & ordered through mail for 10¢. Used to test market) Estimated value... 220.00
1-Wood, Schomburg, Anderson, Whitney-a 43.00 129.00 300.00
2-5: 2-Schomburg-a. 2,4,5-Anderson-a. 3,5-Starr-a17.00 52.00 120.00
6-Krigstein-a 22.00 67.00 155.00

AMAZING ADVENTURES (Becomes Amazing Adult Fantasy #7 on)
June, 1961 - No. 6, Nov, 1961
Atlas Comics (AMI)/Marvel Comics No. 3 on

1-Origin Dr. Droom (1st Marvel-Age Superhero) by Kirby; Kirby/Ditko-a (5 pgs.) Ditko & Kirby-a in all; Kirby monster c-1-6 89.00 267.00 800.00
2 36.00 108.00 325.00
3-6: 6-Last Dr. Droom 31.00 92.00 275.00

AMAZING ADVENTURES
Aug, 1970 - No. 39, Nov, 1976
Marvel Comics Group

1-Inhumans by Kirby(p) & Black Widow (1st app. in Tales of Suspense #52) double feature begins 2.30 7.00 16.00
2-4: 2-F.F. brief app. 4-Last Kirby Inhumans 1.00 2.00 5.50
5-8-Neal Adams-a(p); 8-Last Black Widow 1.25 3.00 7.50
9,10: Magneto app. 10-Last Inhumans (origin-r by Kirby) 1.00 2.00 5.50
11-New Beast begins(1st app. in mutated form; origin in flashback); X-Men cameo in flashback (#11-17 are X-Men tie-ins) 1.65 4.70 11.00
12-17: 13-Brotherhood of Evil Mutants x-over from X-Men. 15-X-Men app. 17-Last Beast (origin); X-Men app. 1.25 3.00 7.50
18-War of the Worlds begins (5/73); 1st app. Killraven; Neal Adams-a(p) 1.85 5.50 13.00
19-39: 35-Giffen's first published story (art), along with Deadly Hands of Kung-Fu #22 (3/76) 1.60 4.00

NOTE: ***N. Adams*** *c-6-8.* ***Buscema*** *a-1p, 2p.* ***Colan*** *a-3-5p, 26p.* ***Ditko*** *a-24r.* ***Everett*** *a(i)3-5, 7-9.* ***Giffen*** *a-35i, 38p.* ***G. Kane*** *c-11, 25p, 29p.* ***Ploog*** *a-12i.* ***Russell*** *a-27-32, 34-37, 39; c-28, 30-32, 33i, 34, 35, 37, 39i.* ***Starliing*** *a-17.* ***Starlin*** *c-15p, 16, 17, 27.* ***Sutton*** *a-11-15p.*

AMAZING ADVENTURES
December, 1979 - No. 14, January, 1981
Marvel Comics Group

V2#1-Reprints story/X-Men #1 & 38 (origins) 1.70 4.25
2-14: 2-6-Early X-Men-r. 7,8-Origin Iceman 1.30 3.25

NOTE: ***Byrne*** *c-6p, 9p.* ***Kirby*** *a-1-14r; c-7, 9.* ***Steranko*** *a-12r.* ***Tuska*** *a-7-9.*

AMAZING ADVENTURES
July, 1988 ($4.95, One-shot, squarebound, 80 pgs.)
Marvel Comics

Amazing High Adventures #3 © MEG

Amazing-Man Comics #12 © CEN

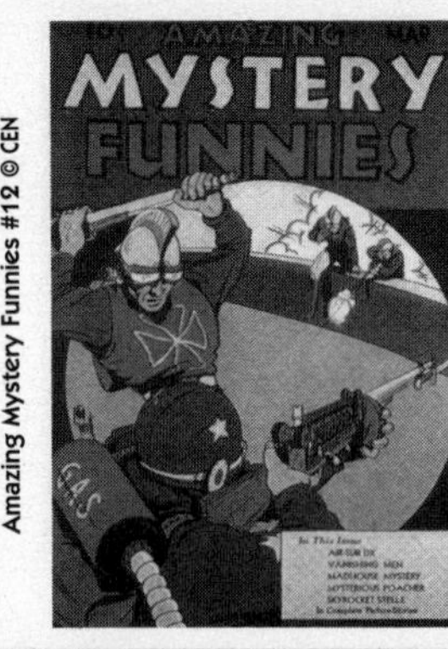

Amazing Mystery Funnies #12 © CEN

GD25 FN65 NM94

1-Anthology; Austin, Golden-a 1.00 2.00 5.00

AMAZING ADVENTURES OF CAPTAIN CARVEL AND HIS CARVEL CRUSADERS, THE (See Carvel Comics)

AMAZING CHAN & THE CHAN CLAN, THE (TV)
May, 1973 - No. 4, Feb, 1974 (Hanna-Barbera)
Gold Key

1-Warren Tufts-a in all 1.65 4.70 11.00
2-4 1.10 2.70 6.50

AMAZING COMICS (Complete Comics No. 2)
Fall, 1944
Timely Comics (EPC)

1-The Destroyer, The Whizzer, The Young Allies (by Sekowsky), Sergeant Dix; Schomburg-c 129.00 385.00 900.00

AMAZING DETECTIVE CASES (Formerly Suspense No. 2?)
No. 3, Nov, 1950 - No. 14, Sept, 1952
Marvel/Atlas Comics (CCC)

3 14.00 43.00 100.00
4-6 9.15 27.50 55.00
7-10 6.70 20.00 40.00
11,14: 11-(3/52)-Changes to horror 10.00 30.00 65.00
12-Krigstein-a 10.00 30.00 60.00
13-(Scarce)-Everett-a; electrocution-c/story 13.00 40.00 90.00
NOTE: ***Colan** a-9. **Maneely** c-13. **Sekowsky** a-12. **Sinnott** a-13. **Tuska** a-10.*

AMAZING FANTASY (Formerly Amazing Adult Fantasy #7-14)
No. 15, Aug, 1962 (Sept, 1962 shown in indicia)
Marvel Comics Group (AMI) **GD25 FN65 VF82 NM94**

15-Origin/1st app. of Spider-Man by Ditko (11 pgs.); 1st app. Aunt May & Uncle Ben; Kirby/Ditko-c 1470.00 4400.00 13,200.00 22,000.00

AMAZING GHOST STORIES (Formerly Nightmare)
No. 14, Oct, 1954 - No. 16, Feb, 1955
St. John Publishing Co. **GD25 FN65 NM94**

14-Pit & the Pendulum story by Kinstler; Baker-c 16.50 50.00 115.00
15-r/Weird Thrillers #5; Baker-c, Powell-a 11.50 34.00 80.00
16-Kubert reprints of Weird Thrillers #4; Baker-c; Roussos, Tuska-a; Kinstler-a (1 pg.) 12.00 36.00 85.00

AMAZING HIGH ADVENTURE
8/84; No. 2, 10/85; No. 3, 10/86 - No. 5, 1987 (Baxter No. 3,4)($2.00)
Marvel Comics

1-5 .80 2.00
NOTE: ***Bissette** a-4. **Bolton** c/a-4. **Severin** a-1, 3. **P. Smith** a-2. **Williamson** a-2i.*

AMAZING-MAN COMICS (Formerly Motion Picture Funnies Weekly?)
(Also see Stars And Stripes Comics)
No. 5, Sept, 1939 - No. 27, Feb, 1942
Centaur Publications **GD25 FN65 VF82 NM94**

5(#1)(Rare)-Origin/1st app. A-Man the Amazing Man by Bill Everett; The Cat-Man by Tarpe Mills (also #8), Mighty Man by Filchock, Minimidget & sidekick Ritty, & The Iron Skull by Burgos begins 1500.00 4500.00 8250.00 12,000.00
(Estimated up to 60 total copies exist, 3 in NM/Mint)

GD25 FN65 NM94

6-Origin The Amazing Man retold; The Shark begins; Ivy Menace by Tarpe Mills app. 285.00 857.00 2000.00
7-Magician From Mars begins; ends #11 171.00 515.00 1200.00
8-Cat-Man dresses as woman 121.00 365.00 850.00
9-Magician From Mars battles the 'Elemental Monster,' swiped into The Spectre in More Fun #54 & 55 1217.00 365.00 850.00
10,11: 11-Zardi, the Eternal Man begins; ends #16; Amazing Man dons costume; last Everett issue 107.00 321.00 750.00
12,13 96.00 289.00 675.00
14-Reef Kinkaid, Rocke Wayburn (ends #20), & Dr. Hypno (ends #21) begin; no Zardi or Chuck Hardy 82.00 246.00 575.00
15,17-20: 15-Zardi returns; no Rocke Wayburn. 17-Dr. Hypno returns; no Zardi 61.00 182.00 425.00
16-Mighty Man's powers of super strength & ability to shrink & grow explained; Rocke Wayburn returns; no Dr. Hypno; Al Avison (a character) begins, ends #18 (a tribute to the famed artist) 65.00 195.00 455.00
21-Origin Dash Dartwell (drug-use story); origin & only app. T.N.T. 61.00 182.00 425.00
22-Dash Dartwell, the Human Meteor & The Voice app; last Iron Skull & The Shark; Silver Streak app. 61.00 182.00 415.00
23-Two Amazing Man stories; intro/origin Tommy the Amazing Kid; The Marksman only app. 65.00 195.00 455.00
24,27: 24-King of Darkness, Nightshade, & Blue Lady begin; end #26; 1st app. Super-Ann 61.00 182.00 425.00
25,26 (Scarce)-Meteor Martin by Wolverton in both; 26-Electric Ray app. 93.00 280.00 650.00
NOTE: ***Everett** a-5-11; c-5-11. **Gilman** a-14-20. **Giunta/Mirando** a-7-10. **Sam Glanzman** a-14-16, 18-21, 23. **Louis Glanzman** a-6, 9-11, 14-21; c-13-19, 21. **Robert Golden** a-9. **Gustavson** a-6; c-22, 23. **Lubbers** a-14-21. **Simon** a-10. **Frank Thomas** a-6, 9-11, 14, 15, 17-21.*

AMAZING MYSTERIES (Formerly Sub-Mariner Comics No. 31)
No. 32, May, 1949 - No. 35, Jan, 1950
Marvel Comics (CCC)

32-The Witness app; 1st Marvel horror comic 54.00 160.00 375.00
33-Horror format 19.00 58.00 135.00
34,35-Change to Crime. 34,35-Photo-c 11.50 34.00 80.00

AMAZING MYSTERY FUNNIES
Aug, 1938 - No. 24, Sept, 1940 (All 52 pgs.)
Centaur Publications

V1#1-Everett-c(1st); Dick Kent Adv. story; Skyrocket Steele in the Year X on cover only 285.00 857.00 2000.00
2-Everett 1st-a (Skyrocket Steele) 135.00 407.00 950.00
3 71.00 215.00 500.00
3(#4, 12/38)-nn on cover, #3 on inside; bondage-c 64.00 193.00 450.00
V2#1-4,6: 2-Drug use story. 3-Air-Sub DX begins by Burgos. 4-Dan Hastings, Hastings, Sand Hog begins (ends #5). 6-Last Skyrocket Steele 60.00 180.00 420.00
5-Classic Everett-c 75.00 225.00 525.00
7 (Scarce)-Intro. The Fantom of the Fair & begins; Everett, Gustavson, Burgos-a 300.00 900.00 2100.00
8-Origin & 1st app. Speed Centaur 105.00 315.00 735.00
9-11: 11-Self portrait and biog. of Everett; Jon Linton begins; early Robot cover (11/39) 60.00 180.00 420.00
12 (Scarce)-1st Space Patrol; Wolverton-a (12/39); new costume Phantom of the Fair 150.00 450.00 1050.00
V3#1(#17, 1/40)-Intro. Bullet; Tippy Taylor serial begins, ends #24 (continued in The Arrow #2) 60.00 180.00 420.00
18,20: 18-Fantom of the Fair by Gustavson 57.00 171.00 400.00
19,21-24-Space Patrol by Wolverton in all 80.00 240.00 560.00
NOTE: ***Burgos** a-V2#3-9. **Eisner** a-V1#2, 3(2). **Everett** a-V1#2-4, V2#1, 3-6; c-V1#1-4,V2#3, 5, 18. **Filchock** a-V2#9. **Flessel** a-V2#6. **Guardineer** a-V1#4, V2#4-6; **Gustavson** a-V2#4, 5, 9-12, V3#1, 18, 19; c-V2#7, 9, 12, V3#1, 21, 22; **McWilliams** a-V2#9, 10. **TarpeMills** a-V2#2, 4-6, 9-12, V3#1. **Leo Morey**(Pulp artist) c-V2#10; text illo-V2#11. **FrankThomas** a-6-V2#11. **Webster** a-V2#4.*

AMAZING SAINTS (Logos)(Value: cover or less)

AMAZING SPIDER-MAN, THE (See All Detergent Comics, Amazing Fantasy, America's Best TV Comics, Aurora, Deadly Foes of Spider-Man, Giant-Size Spider-Man, Giant Size Super-Heroes Featuring..., Marvel Collectors Item Classics, Marvel Fanfare, Marvel Graphic Novel, Marvel Spec. Ed., Marvel Tales, Marvel Team-Up, Marvel Treasury Ed., Nothing Can Stop the Juggernaut, Official Marvel Index To..., Power Record Comics, Spectacular..., Spider-Man, Spider-Man Digest, Spider-Man Saga, Spider-Man 2099, Spider-Man Vs. Wolverine, Spidey Super Stories, Strange Tales Annual #2, Superman Vs. ..., Try-Out Winner Book, Web of Spider- Man & Within Our Reach)

AMAZING SPIDER-MAN, THE
March, 1963 - Present
Marvel Comics Group **GD25 FN65 VF82 NM94**

1-Retells origin by Steve Ditko; 1st Fantastic Four x-over (ties w/F.F. #12 as first Marvel x-over); intro. John Jameson & The Chameleon; Spider-Man's

The Amazing Spider-Man #9 © MEG

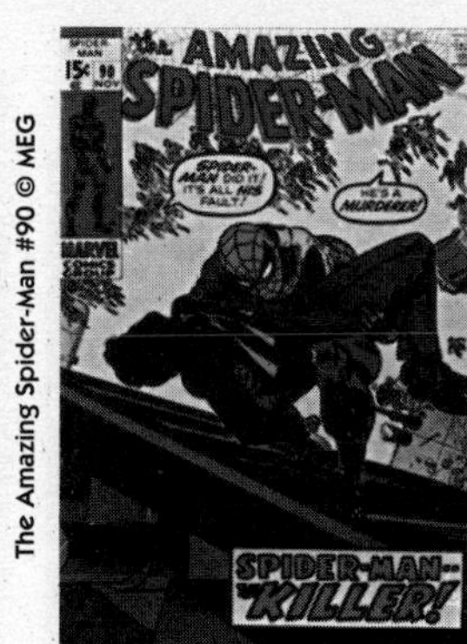

The Amazing Spider-Man #90 © MEG

The Amazing Spider-Man #196 © MEG

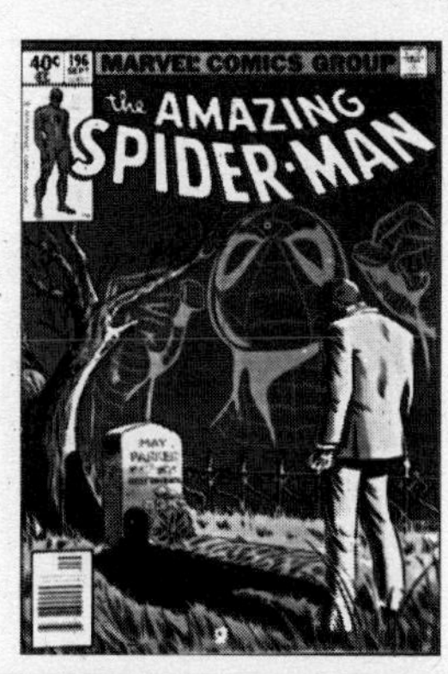

GD25 FN65 NM94 **GD25 FN65 NM94**

2nd app.; Kirby/Ditko-c; Ditko-c/a #1-38
970.00 2900.00 8700.00 14,500.00

	GD25	FN65	NM94
1-Reprint from the Golden Record Comic set	11.50	34.00	80.00
with record (1966)	27.00	81.00	190.00
2-1st app. the Vulture & the Terrible Tinkerer	220.00	660.00	2200.00
3-1st full-length story; Human Torch cameo; intro. & 1st app. Doc Octopus;	150.00	450.00	1350.00
4-Origin & 1st app. The Sandman (see Strange Tales #115 for 2nd app.); Intro. Betty Brant & Liz Allen	131.00	392.00	1175.00
5-Dr. Doom app.	120.00	360.00	960.00
6-1st app. Lizard	103.00	309.00	825.00
7,8,10: 7-Vs. The Vulture; 1st monthly issue. 8-Fantastic Four app. in back-up story by Kirby/Ditko. 10-1st app. Big Man & The Enforcers	79.00	236.00	550.00
9-Origin & 1st app. Electro (2/64)	86.00	257.00	600.00
11,12: 11-1st app. Bennett Brant. 12-Doc Octopus unmasks Spider-Man-c/story	42.00	126.00	295.00
13-1st app. Mysterio	61.00	184.00	430.00

	GD25	FN65	VF82	NM94
14-(7/64)-1st app. The Green Goblin (c/story)(Norman Osborn); Hulk x-over	110.00	330.00	715.00	1100.00

	GD25	FN65	NM94
15-1st app. Kraven the Hunter; 1st mention of Mary Jane Watson (not shown)	51.00	154.00	360.00
16-Spider-Man battles Daredevil (1st x-over 9/64); still in old yellow costume	37.00	111.00	260.00
17-2nd app. Green Goblin (c/story); Human Torch x-over (also in #18 & #21)	63.00	189.00	440.00
18-1st app. Ned Leeds who later becomes Hobgoblin; Fantastic Four back-up story; 3rd app. Sandman	40.00	120.00	280.00
19-Sandman app.	32.00	96.00	225.00
20-Origin & 1st app. The Scorpion	39.00	116.00	270.00
21-2nd app. The Beetle (see Strange Tales #123)	26.00	77.00	180.00
22-1st app. Princess Python	23.00	69.00	160.00
23-3rd app. The Green Goblin (c/story); Norman Osborn app.	39.00	116.00	270.00
24	21.00	64.00	150.00
25-(6/65)-1st app. Mary Jane Watson (cameo; face not shown); 1st app. Spencer Smythe; Norman Osborn app.	26.00	77.00	180.00
26-4th app. The Green Goblin (c/story); 1st app. Crime Master; dies in #27	29.00	86.00	200.00
27-5th app. The Green Goblin (c/story); Norman Osborn app.	26.00	79.00	185.00
28-Origin & 1st app. Molten Man (9/65, scarcer in high grade)	38.00	114.00	265.00
29,30	19.00	56.00	130.00
31-38: 31-1st app. Harry Osborn who later becomes 2nd Green Goblin, Gwen Stacy & Prof. Warren. 34-2nd app. Kraven the Hunter. 36-1st app. Looter. 37-Intro. Norman Osborn. 38-(7/66)-2nd app. Mary Jane Watson (cameo; face not shown); last Ditko issue	16.00	49.00	115.00
39-The Green Goblin-c/story; Green Goblin's i.d. revealed as Norman Osborn; Romita-a begins (8/66; see Daredevil #16 for 1st Romita-a on Spider-Man)	20.00	60.00	140.00
40-1st told origin The Green Goblin (c/story)	32.00	96.00	225.00
41-1st app. Rhino	15.00	50.00	105.00
42-(11/66)-3rd app. Mary Jane Watson (cameo in last 2 panels); 1st time face is shown	14.00	43.00	100.00
43-49: 44,45-2nd & 3rd app. The Lizard. 46-Intro. Shocker. 47-M. J. Watson & Peter Parker 1st date. 47-Green Goblin cameo; Harry & Norman Osborn app. 47,49-3rd & 4th app. Kraven the Hunter	9.00	28.00	65.00
50-1st app. Kingpin (7/67)	39.00	118.00	275.00
51-2nd app. Kingpin	16.00	47.00	110.00
52-60: 52-1st app. Joe Robertson & 3rd app. Kingpin. 56-1st app. Capt. George Stacy. 57,58-Ka-Zar app. 59-1st app. Brainwasher (alias Kingpin); 1st-c app. M. J. Watson	7.00	21.00	50.00
61-74: 67-1st app. Randy Robertson. 69-Kingpin-c. 69,70-Kingpin app. 73-1st app. Silvermane. 74-Last 12¢ issue	6.00	18.00	42.00
75-89,91-93,95,99: 78,79-1st app. The Prowler. 83-1st app. Schemer & Vanessa (Kingpin's wife). 84,85-Kingpin-c/story. 86-Re-intro & origin Black Widow in new costume. 93-1st app. Arthur Stacy	5.00	16.00	37.00
90-Death of Capt. Stacey	6.00	18.00	42.00
94-Origin retold	8.50	25.00	58.00
96-98-Green Goblin app. (97,98-Green Goblin-c); drug books not approved by CCA	11.00	32.00	75.00
100-Anniversary issue (9/71); Green Goblin cameo (2 pgs.)	22.00	66.00	155.00
101-1st app. Morbius the Living Vampire; Wizard cameo; last 15¢ issue (10/71)	23.00	69.00	160.00
101-Silver ink 2nd printing (9/92, $1.75)		1.00	2.50
102-Origin & 2nd app. Morbius (25¢, 52 pgs.)	16.00	47.00	110.00
103-118: 104,111-Kraven the Hunter-c/stories. 108-1st app. Sha-Shan. 109-Dr. Strange-c/story (6/72). 110-1st app. Gibbon. 113-1st app. Hammerhead	3.00	9.00	21.00
119,120-Spider-Man vs. Hulk (4 & 5/73)	4.85	15.00	34.00
121-Death of Gwen Stacy (6/73) (killed by Green Goblin) (reprinted in Marvel Tales #98 & 192)	13.00	40.00	90.00
122-Death of The Green Goblin (c/story, 7/73) (reprinted in Marvel Tales #99 & 192)	16.00	49.00	115.00
123-128: 123-Cage app. 124-1st app. Man-Wolf (9/73), origin in #125. 127-1st mention of Harry Osborn becoming Green Goblin	3.25	9.50	22.00
129-1st app. Jackal & The Punisher (2/74)	32.00	96.00	225.00
130-133,138-141,152-160: 131-Last 20¢ issue. 139-1st app. Grizzly. 140-1st app. Glory Grant. 159-Last 25¢ issue	1.85	5.50	13.00
134-Punisher cameo (7/74); 1st app. Tarantula	3.25	9.50	22.00
135-2nd full Punisher app. (8/74)	9.00	28.00	65.00
136-Reappearance of The Green Goblin (Harry Osborn; Norman Osborn's son)	4.70	14.00	33.00
137-Green Goblin-c/story (2nd Harry Osborn)	2.40	7.25	17.00
142,143-Gwen Stacy clone cameos: 143-1st app. Cyclone	1.70	5.00	12.00
144-Full app. of Gwen Stacy clone	1.70	5.00	12.00
145,146-Gwen Stacy clone storyline continues	1.70	5.00	12.00
147-Spider-Man learns Gwen Stacy is clone	1.70	5.00	12.00
148-Jackal revealed	1.70	5.00	12.00
149-Spider-Man clone story begins, clone dies (?); origin of Jackal	11.00	32.00	75.00
150-Spider-Man decides he is not the clone	5.00	15.00	35.00
151-Spider-Man disposes of clone body	2.40	7.20	17.00
161-Nightcrawler app. from X-Men; Punisher cameo	1.70	5.00	12.00
162-Punisher, Nightcrawler app.	3.25	9.50	22.00
163-173,181-190: 167-1st app. Will O' The Wisp. 169-Clone story recapped. 171-Nova app. 181-Origin retold; gives life history of Spidey; Punisher cameo in flashback (1 panel). 182-(7/78)-Peter proposes to Mary Jane for 1st time, but she refuses	1.40	3.50	8.50
174,175-Punisher app.	2.60	7.50	18.00
176-180-Green Goblin app	2.15	6.50	15.00
191-193,195-199,203-208,210-219: 193-Peter & Mary Jane break up. 196-Faked death of Aunt May. 203-2nd app. Dazzler. 209-1st app. Calypso (Kraven's girlfriend). 210-1st app. Madame Web. 212-1st app. Hydro Man; origin Sandman	1.25	3.00	7.50
194-1st app. Black Cat	2.15	6.50	15.00
200-Giant origin issue (1/80)	4.30	13.00	30.00
201,202-Punisher app.	3.25	9.50	22.00
209-Origin & 1st app. Calypso (10/80)	1.70	4.20	10.00
220-237: 225-(2/82)-Foolkiller-c/story. 226,227-Black Cat returns. 236-Tarantula dies. 234-Free 16 pg. insert "Marvel Guide to Collecting Comics". 235-Origin Will-'O-The-Wisp	1.30	3.25	8.00
238-(3/83)-1st app. Hobgoblin (Ned Leeds); came with skin "Tattooz" decal	11.00	33.00	78.00
238-Without tattooz decal	3.60	10.75	25.00
239-2nd app. Hobgoblin & 1st battle w/Spidey	6.00	18.00	42.00

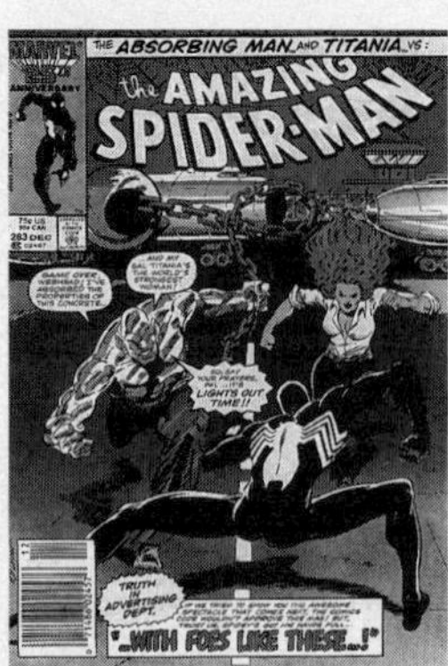

The Amazing Spider-Man #258 © MEG

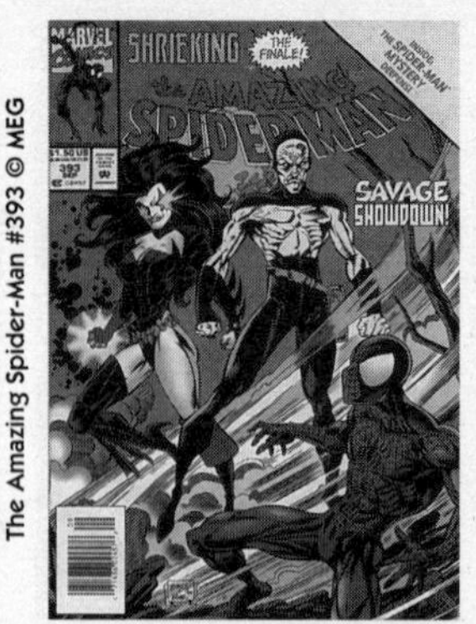

The Amazing Spider-Man #393 © MEG

The Amazing Spider-Man Annual #28 © MEG

GD25 FN65 NM94

240-243,246-248: 241-Origin The Vulture. 243-Reintro Mary Jane Watson after 4 year absence 1.30 3.25 8.00
244-3rd app. Hobgoblin (cameo only) 1.65 4.70 11.00
245-(10/83)-4th app. Hobgoblin (cameo only); Lefty Donovan gains powers of Hobgoblin & battles Spider-Man 2.30 6.75 16.00
249-251: 3 part Hobgoblin/Spider-Man battle. 249-Retells origin & death of 1st Green Goblin. 251-Last old costume 2.00 6.00 14.00
252-Spider-Man dons new black costume (5/84); ties with Marvel Team-Up #141 & Spectacular Spider-Man #90 for 1st new costume (See Marvel S-H Secret Wars #8) 4.50 14.00 32.00
253-1st app. The Rose 1.50 3.75 9.00
254 1.20 3.00 7.00
255,263,264,266-273,277-280,282,283: 277-Vess back-up art. 279-Jack O'Lantern-c/story. 282-X-Factor x-over 1.00 2.00 5.00
256-1st app. Puma 1.00 2.50 5.50
257-Hobgoblin cameo; 2nd app. Puma; M. J. Watson reveals she knows Spidey's i.d. 1.65 4.70 11.00
258-Hobgoblin app. (minor) 1.85 5.50 13.00
259-Full Hobgoblin app.; Spidey back to old costume; origin Mary Jane Watson 3.25 9.50 22.00
260-Hobgoblin app. 1.65 4.70 11.00
261-Hobgoblin-c/story; painted-c by Vess 1.85 5.50 13.00
262-Spider-Man unmasked; photo-c 1.50 3.75 9.00
265-1st app. Silver Sable (6/85) 2.15 6.50 15.00
265-Silver ink 2nd printing ($1.25) 1.40 3.50
274-Zarathos (The Spirit of Vengeance) app. (3/86) 1.80 4.50
275-($1.25, 52 pgs.)-Hobgoblin-c/story; origin-r by Ditko 2.00 6.00 14.00
276-Hobgoblin app. 1.65 4.70 11.00
281-Hobgoblin battles Jack O'Lantern 1.85 5.50 13.00
284-Punisher cameo; Gang War story begins; Hobgoblin-c/story 1.65 4.70 11.00
285-Punisher app.; minor Hobgoblin app. 2.70 8.00 19.00
286,287: 286-Hobgoblin-c & app. (minor). 287-Hobgoblin app. (minor) 1.10 2.70 6.50
288-Full Hobgoblin app.; last Gang War 1.65 4.00 10.00
289-(6/87, $1.25, 52 pgs.)-Hobgoblin's i.d. revealed as Ned Leeds; death of Ned Leeds; Macendale (Jack O'Lantern) becomes new Hobgoblin (1st app.) 3.85 11.50 27.00
290-292: 290-Peter proposes to Mary Jane. 292-She accepts; leads into Amazing Spider-Man Annual #21 .90 2.30 5.50
293,294-Part 2 & 5 of Kraven story from Web of Spider-Man. 294-Death of Kraven 1.70 4.20 10.00
295-297 1.10 2.70 6.50
298-Todd McFarlane-c/a begins (3/88); 1st app. Eddie Brock who becomes Venom; (cameo on last pg.) 6.40 19.00 45.00
299-1st app. Venom with costume (cameo) 4.00 12.00 28.00
300 ($1.50, 52 pgs.; 25th Anniversary)-1st full Venom app.; last black costume (5/88) 11.00 32.00 75.00
301-305: 301 ($1.00 issues begin). 304-1st bi-weekly issue 2.40 7.30 17.00
306-311,313,314: 306-Swipes-c from Action #1. 315-317-Venom app. 1.70 5.00 12.00
312-Hobgoblin battles Green Goblin 3.40 10.00 24.00
315-317-Venom app. 3.00 10.00 23.00
318-323,325: 319-Bi-weekly begins again 1.50 3.80 9.00
324-Sabretooth app.; McFarlane cover only 2.00 6.00 14.00
326,327,329: 327-Cosmic Spidey continues from Spectacular Spider-Man (no McFarlane-c/a) 1.80 4.50
328-Hulk x-over; last McFarlane issue 1.70 5.00 12.00
330,331-Punisher app. 331-Minor Venom app. 1.60 4.00
332,333-Venom-c/story 1.60 4.70 11.00
334-336,338-343: 341-Tarantula app. 1.60 4.00
337-Hobgoblin app. 1.00 2.00 5.00
344-1st app. Cletus Kasady (Carnage) 1.60 4.70 11.00
345-1st full app. Cletus Kasady; Venom cameo on last pg. 2.00 6.00 14.00
346,347-Venom app. 1.60 4.70 11.00
348,349,351-359: 348-Avengers x-over. 351,352-Nova of New Warriors app. 353-Darkhawk app.; brief Punisher app. 354-Punisher cameo & Nova, Night Thrasher (New Warriors), Darkhawk & Moon Knight app. 357,358-Punisher, Darkhawk, Moon Knight, Night Thrasher, Nova x-over. 358-3 part gatefold-c; last $1.00-c. 360-Carnage cameo 1.20 3.00
350-($1.50, 52pgs.)-Origin retold; Spidey vs. Dr. Doom; pin-ups; Uncle Ben app. 1.40 3.50
360-Carnage cameo 1.50 3.80 9.00
361-Intro Carnage (the Spawn of Venom); begin 3 part story; recap of how Spidey's alien costume became Venom 3.10 9.00 22.00
361-2nd printing ($1.25); silver-c 1.00 2.50
362,363-Carnage & Venom-c/story 2.00 5.00 12.00
362-2nd printing .70 1.75
364,366-374,376-387: 364-The Shocker app. (old villain). 366-Peter's parents-c/story. 369-Harry Osborn back-up (Gr. Goblin II). 373-Venom back-up. 374-Venom-c/story. 376-Cardiac app. 378-Maximum Carnage part 3. 381,382-Hulk app. 383-The Jury app. 384-Venom/carnage app. 387-New costume Vulture 1.50
365-($3.95, 84 pgs.)-30th anniversary issue w/silver hologram on-c; Spidey/Venom/Carnage pull-out poster; contains 5 pg. preview of Spider-Man 2099 (1st app.); Spidey's origin retold; Lizard app.; reintro Peter's parents in Stan Lee 3 pg. text w/illo (saga continues thru #370) 1.10 2.70 6.50
365-Second printing; gold hologram on-c 1.00 2.50 6.00
375-($3.95, 68 pgs.)-Holo-grafx foil-c; vs. Venom story; ties into Venom: Lethal Protector #1 1.00 2.50 6.00
388-(2.25, 68 pgs.)-Newsstand edition; Venom back-up & Cardiac & chance back-up 1.00 2.50
388-($2.95, 68 pgs.)-Collector's edition w/foil-c 1.30 3.25
389-401: 389-Begin $1.50-c; bound-in trading card sheet; Green Goblin app. 394-Power & Responsibility Pt. 2 .70 1.75
390-($2.95)-Collector's edition polybagged w/16 pg. insert of new animated Spidey TV show plus animation cel 1.30 3.25
394-($2.95, 48 pgs.)-Deluxe edition; flip book w/Birth of a Spider-Man Pt. 2; silver foil both-c 1.20 3.00
Annual 1 (1964, 72 pgs.)-Origin Spider-Man; 1st app. Sinister Six (Dr. Octopus, Electro, Kraven the Hunter, Mysterio, Sandman, Vulture) (41 pg. story); plus gallery of Spidey foes 44.00 133.00 400.00
Annual 2 (1965, 25¢, 72 pgs.)-Reprints from #1,2,5 plus new Doctor Strange story 18.00 53.00 175.00
Special 3 (11/66, 25¢, 72 pgs.)-Avengers & Hulk x-over; Doctor Octopus-r from #11,12; Romita-a 8.00 24.00 55.00
Special 4 (11/67, 25¢, 68 pgs.)-Spidey battles Human Torch (new 41 pg. story) 8.00 24.00 55.00
Special 5 (11/68, 25¢, 68 pgs.)-New 40 pg. Red Skull story; 1st app. Peter Parker's parents; last annual with new-a 9.00 26.00 60.00
Special 6 (11/69, 25¢, 68 pgs.)-Reprints 41 pg. Sinister Six story from annual #1 plus 2 Kirby/Ditko stories (r) 4.20 10.00 25.00
Special 7 (12/70, 25¢, 68 pgs.)-All-r(#1,2) 4.20 10.00 25.00
Special 8 (12/71)-All-r 4.20 10.00 25.00
King Size 9 ('73)-Reprints Spectacular Spider-Man (mag.) #2; 40 pg. Green Goblin-c/story (re-edited from 58 pgs.) 4.20 10.00 25.00
Annual 10 (1976)-Origin Human Fly (vs. Spidey); new-a begins 1.30 3.00 8.00
Annual 11,12: 11 (1977). 12 (1978)-Spider-Man vs. Hulk-r/#119,120 1.30 3.00 8.00
Annual 13 (1979)-Byrne/Austin-a (new) 1.50 3.80 9.00
Annual 14 (1980)-Miller-c/a(p), 40pgs. 1.50 3.80 9.00
Annual 15 (1981)-Miller-c/a(p); Punisher app. 3.30 9.90 23.00
Annual 16-20: 16 (1982)-Origin/1st app. new Capt. Marvel (female heroine). 17 (1983). 18 (1984). 19 (1985). 20 (1986)-Origin Iron Man of 2020 1.20 2.90 7.00
Annual 21 (1987)-Special wedding issue; newsstand & direct sale versions exist & are worth same 1.50 3.80 9.00
Annual 22 (1988, $1.75, 68 pgs.)-1st app. Speedball; Evolutionary War x-over;

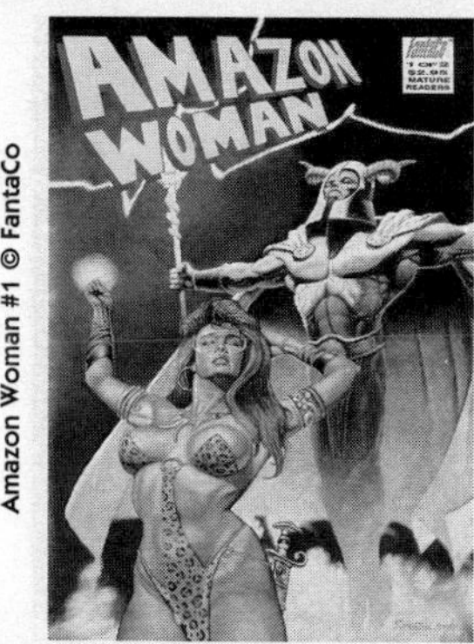

Amazon Woman #1 © FantaCo

Ambush Bug #3 © DC

American Air Forces #4 ©WHW

GD25 FN65 NM94

Daredevil app. 1.50 3.80 9.00
Annual 23 (1989, $2.00, 68 pgs.)-Atlantis Attacks; origin Spider-Man retold; She-Hulk app.; Byrne-c; Liefeld-a(p), 23 pgs. 1.20 2.90 7.00
Annual 24 (1990, $2.00, 68 pgs.)-Ant-Man app. 1.60 4.00
Annual 25 (1991, $2.00, 68 pgs.)-3 pg. origin recap; Iron Man app.; 1st Venom solo story; Ditko-a (6 pgs.) 2.00 5.00 12.00
Annual 26 (1992, $2.25, 68 pgs.)-New Warriors-c/story; Venom solo story cont'd in Spectacular Spider-Man Annual #12 1.20 2.90 7.00
Annual 27 (1993, $2.95, 68 pgs.)-Bagged w/card; 1st app. Annex 1.60 43.00
Annual 28 (1994, $2.95, 68 pgs.)-Carnage-c/story; Rhino & Cloak and Dagger back-ups 1.40 3.50
...: Skating on Thin Ice 1(1990, $1.25, Canadian)-McFarlane-c; anti-drug issue 1.00 2.00 5.00
...: Skating on Thin Ice 1 (2/93, $1.50, American) .80 2.00
...: Double Trouble 2 (1990, $1.25, Canadian) 1.20 3.00
...: Double Trouble 2 (2/93, $1.50, American) .80 2.00
...: Hit and Run 3 (1990, $1.25, Canadian)-Ghost Rider-c/story 1.20 3.00
...: Hit and Run 3 (2/93. $1.50, American) .80 2.00
...: Chaos in Calgary 4 (Canadian edition exist? part of 5 part series)
...: Chaos in Calgary 4 (2/93, $1.50, American) .80 2.00
...: Deadball 5 (1993, $1.60, Canadian)-Green Goblin-c/story; features Montreal Expos 1.50
...: Soul of the Hunter nn (8/92, $5.95, 52 pgs.)-Zeck-c/a(p) 1.00 2.50 6.00
Parallel Lives (1990, $8.95, 68pgs.)-Graphic novel 1.50 3.75 9.00
Aim Toothpaste giveaway(36 pgs., reg. size)-1 pg. origin recap; Green Goblin-c/story 1.00 2.50 6.00
Aim Toothpaste giveaway (16 pgs., reg. size)-Dr. Octopus app. 1.00 2.00 5.00
All Detergent Giveaway (1979, 36 pgs.), nn-Origin-r 1.65 4.00 10.00
Giveaway-Acme & Dingo Children's Boots (1980)-Spider-Woman app. 1.60 4.00
Amazing Spider-Man nn (1990, 6-1/8x9", 28 pgs.)-Shan-Lon giveaway; r/ Amazing Spider-Man #303 w/McFarlane-c/a 1.00
...& Power Pack (1984, nn)(Nat'l Committee for Prevention of Child Abuse (two versions, mail offer & store giveaway)-Mooney-a; Byrne-c 1.00
...& The Hulk (Special Edition)(6/8/80; 20 pgs.); Supplement to Chicago Tribune (giveaway) 1.30 3.25 8.00
...& The Incredible Hulk (1981, 1982; 36 pgs.), Sanger Harris supplement to Dallas Times, Dallas Herald, Denver Post, Kansas City Star, Tulsa World; Foley's supplement to Houston Chronicle (1982, 16 pgs.)-"Great Rodeo Robbery"; The Jones Store-giveaway (1983, 16 pgs.) 1.65 4.00 10.00
...And The New Mutants Featuring Skids nn (National Committee for Prevention of Child Abuse/K-Mart giveaway)-Williams-c(i) 1.00
..., Captain America, The Incredible Hulk, & Spider-Woman (1981) (7-11 Stores giveaway; 36 pgs.) 1.00 2.00 5.00
...: Christmas In Dallas (1983) (Supplement to Dallas Times Herald) giveaway 1.00 2.00 5.00
..., Fire-Star, and Iceman At the Dallas Ballet Nutcracker (1983; supplement to Dallas Times Herald)-Mooney-p 1.00 2.00 5.00
Giveaway-Esquire & Eye Magazines(2/69)-Miniature-Still attached 9.00 26.00 60.00
..., Storm & Powerman (1982; 20 pgs.)(American Cancer Society) giveaway 1.00 2.00 5.00
...Vs. The Hulk (Special Edition; 1979, 20 pgs.)(Supplement to Columbus Dispatch)-Giveaway 1.00 2.00 5.00
...Vs. the Prodigy Giveaway, 16 pgs. in color (1976, 5x6-1/2")-Sex education; (1 million printed; 35-50¢) 1.20 3.00

NOTE: ***Austin*** *a(i)-248, 335, 337, Annual 13; c(i)-188, 241, 242, 248, 331, 334, 343, Annual 25.* ***J. Buscema*** *a(p)-72, 73, 76-81, 84, 85.* ***Byrne*** *a-189p, 190p, 206p, Annual 3r, 6r, 7r, 13p; c-189p, 268, 296, Annual 12.* ***Ditko*** *a-1-38, Annual 1, Special 3(r), 2, 24(2); c-1i, 2-38.* ***Guice*** *c/a-Annual 18i.* ***Gil Kane*** *a(p)-89-105, 120-124, 150, Annual 10, 12i, 24p; c-90p, 96, 98, 99, 101-105p, 129p, 131p, 132p, 137-140p, 143p, 148p, 149p, 151p, 153p, 160p, 161p, Annual 10p, 24.* ***Kirby*** *a-8.* ***McFarlane*** *a-298p, 299p, 300-303, 304-323p, 325p, 328; c-298-325, 328.* ***Miller*** *c-218, 219.* ***Mooney*** *a-65i, 67-82i, 84-88i, 173i, 178i, 189i, 190i, 192i, 193i, 196-202i, 207i, 211-219i, 221i, 222i, 226i, 227i, 229-233i, Annual 11i, 17i.* ***Nasser*** *c-228p.* ***Nebres*** *a-Annual 24i.* ***Russell*** *c-357i.* ***Simonson*** *c-222, 337i.* ***Starlin*** *a-113i, 114i, 187p.*

AMAZING WILLIE MAYS, THE
No date (Sept, 1954)
Famous Funnies Publ.

nn 57.00 171.00 400.00

AMAZING WORLD OF SUPERMAN (See Superman)

AMAZON, THE (Comico)(Value: cover or less)

AMAZON ATTACK 3-D (3-D Zone)(Value: cover or less)

AMAZON WOMAN
Summer, 1994 - No. 2, Fall, 1994 ($2.95, B&W, mature)
FantaCo

1,2 1.20 3.00

AMBUSH (See 4-Color Comics No. 314)

AMBUSH BUG (Also see Son of...)
June, 1985 - No. 4, Sept, 1985 (75¢, mini-series)
DC Comics

1-4: Giffen-c/a in all 1.00
...Nothing Special 1 (9/92, $2.50, 68pg.)-Giffen-c/a 1.00 2.50
...Stocking Stuffer (2/86, $1.25)-Giffen-c/a 1.30

AMERICA IN ACTION
1942; Winter, 1945 (36 pgs.)
Dell(Imp. Publ. Co.)/Mayflower House Publ.

1942-Dell-(68 pgs.) 13.00 40.00 90.00
1(1945)-Has 3 adaptations from American history; Kiefer, Schrotter & Webb-a 10.00 30.00 65.00

AMERICA MENACED!
1950 (Paper cover)
Vital Publications

nn-Anti-communism estimated value... 175.00

AMERICAN, THE
July, 1987 - No. 8, 1989 ($1.50/$1.75, B&W)
Dark Horse Comics

1 ($1.50) 1.80 4.50
2-Begin $1.75-c? 1.30 3.25
3-5 .90 2.25
6-8 .70 1.75
...Collection ($5.95, B&W)-Reprints 1.00 2.50 6.00
...Special 1 (1990, $2.25, B&W) .90 2.25

AMERICAN AIR FORCES, THE (See A-1 Comics)
Sept-Oct, 1944 - No. 4, 1945; No. 5, 1951 - No. 12, 1954
William H. Wise(Flying Cadet Publ. Co./Hasan(No.1)/Life's Romances/ Magazine Ent. No. 5 on)

1-Article by Zack Mosley, creator of Smilin' Jack 10.00 30.00 65.00
2-4 6.35 19.00 38.00

NOTE: *All part comic, part magazine. Art by* ***Whitney, Chas. Quinlan, H. C. Kiefer,*** *and* ***Tony Dipreta.***

5(A-1 45)(Formerly Jet Powers), 6(A-1 54), 7(A-1 58), 8(A-1 65), 9(A-1 67), 10(A-1 74), 11(A-1 79), 12(A-1 91) 4.00 12.00 24.00

NOTE: ***Powell*** *c/a-5-12.*

AMERICAN COMICS
1940's
Theatre Giveaways (Liberty Theatre, Grand Rapids, Mich. known)

Many possible combinations. "Golden Age" superhero comics with new cover added and given away at theaters. Following known: Superman #59, Capt. Marvel #20, Capt. Marvel Jr. #5, Action #33, Classics Comics #8, Whiz #39. Value would vary with book and should be 70-80 percent of the original.

AMERICAN FLAGG! (First)(Value: cover or less)

AMERICAN FREAK: A TALE OF THE UN-MEN

American: Lost In America #4 ©DH

America's Best Comics #3 © STD

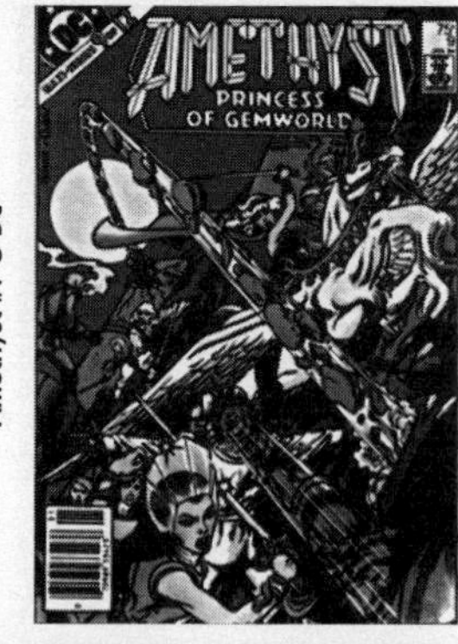

Amethyst #9 © DC

GD25 FN65 NM94

Feb, 1994 - No. 5, June, 1994 ($1.95, mini-series, mature readers)
DC Comics (Vertigo)

1-5 .80 2.00

AMERICAN GRAPHICS
No. 1, 1954; No. 2, 1957 (25¢)
Henry Stewart

1-The Maid of the Mist, The Last of the Eries (Indian Legends of Niagara) (sold at Niagara Falls) 7.50 22.50 45.00
2-Victory at Niagara & Laura Secord (Heroine of the War of 1812) 5.00 15.00 30.00

AMERICAN INDIAN, THE (See Picture Progress)

AMERICAN LIBRARY
1943 - No. 6, 1944 (68 pgs.) (15¢, B&W, text & pictures)
David McKay Publications

nn (#1)-Thirty Seconds Over Tokyo (movie) 29.00 86.00 200.00
nn (#2)-Guadalcanal Diary; painted-c (only 10¢) 22.00 65.00 150.00
3-6: 3-Look to the Mountain. 4-Case of the Crooked Candle (Perry Mason). 5-Duel in the Sun. 6-Wingate's Raiders 10.00 30.00 70.00

AMERICAN: LOST IN AMERICA, THE
July, 1992 - No. 4, Oct, 1992 ($2.50, color, mini-series)
Dark Horse Comics

1-4: 1-Dorman painted-c. 2-Joe Phillips painted-c. 3-Mignola-c. 4-Jim Lee-c. 1.00 2.50

AMERICAN SPLENDOR SPECIAL: A STEP OUT OF THE NEST
Aug, 1994 ($2.95, B&W, one-shot)
Dark Horse Comics

1-H. Pekar-story 1.20 3.00

AMERICAN TAIL: FIEVEL GOES WEST, AN
Early Jan, 1992 - No. 3, Early Feb, 1992 ($1.00, mini-series)
Marvel Comics

1-Adapts Universal animated movie; Wildman-a 1.00

AMERICA'S BEST COMICS
Feb, 1942; No. 2, Sept, 1942 - No. 31, July, 1949 (New logo with #9)
Nedor/Better/Standard Publications

1-The Woman in Red, Black Terror, Captain Future, Doc Strange, The Liberator, & Don Davis, Secret Ace begin 104.00 310.00 725.00
2-Origin The American Eagle; The Woman in Red ends 54.00 160.00 375.00
3-Pyroman begins (11/42, 1st app.; also see Startling Comics #18, 12/42) 39.00 118.00 275.00
4 34.00 100.00 235.00
5-Last Capt. Future (not in #4); Lone Eagle app. 30.00 90.00 210.00
6,7: 6-American Crusader app. 7-Hitler, Mussolini & Hirohito-c 26.00 80.00 185.00
8-Last Liberator 21.00 63.00 145.00
9-The Fighting Yank begins; The Ghost app. 24.00 72.00 165.00
10-14: 10-Flag-c. 14-American Eagle ends 19.00 58.00 135.00
15-20 16.50 50.00 115.00
21,22: 21-Infinity-c. 22-Capt. Future app. 15.00 45.00 105.00
23-Miss Masque begins; last Doc Strange 21.00 63.00 145.00
24-Miss Masque bondage-c 19.00 57.00 130.00
25-Last Fighting Yank; Sea Eagle app. 15.00 45.00 105.00
26-31: 26-The Phantom Detective & The Silver Knight app.; Frazetta text illo & some panels in Miss Masque. 27,28-Commando Cubs. 27-Doc Strange. 28-Tuska Black Terror. 29-Last Pyroman 19.00 57.00 130.00

NOTE: *American Eagle not in 3, 8, 9, 13. Fighting Yank not in 10, 12. Liberator not in 2, 6, 7. Pyroman not in 9, 11, 14-16, 23, 25-27.* ***Schomburg (Xela)*** *c-5, 7-31. Bondage c-18, 24.*

AMERICA'S BEST TV COMICS (TV)
1967 (Produced by Marvel Comics) (25¢, 68 pgs.)
American Broadcasting Company

1-Spider-Man, Fantastic Four (by Kirby/Ayers), Casper, King Kong, George of the Jungle, Journey to the Center of the Earth stories (promotes new TV cartoon show) 6.40 19.00 45.00

AMERICA'S BIGGEST COMICS BOOK
1944 (196 pgs.) (One Shot)
William H. Wise

1-The Grim Reaper, The Silver Knight, Zudo, the Jungle Boy, Commando Cubs, Thunderhoof app. 33.00 100.00 220.00

AMERICA'S FUNNIEST COMICS
1944 - No. 2, 1944 (15¢, 80 pgs.)
William H. Wise

nn(#1), 2 19.00 58.00 135.00

AMERICA'S GREATEST COMICS
May?, 1941 - No. 8, Summer, 1943 (15¢, 100 pgs.) (Soft cardboard covers)
Fawcett Publications

1-Bulletman, Spy Smasher, Capt. Marvel, Minute Man & Mr. Scarlet begin; Mac Raboy-c 200.00 600.00 1400.00
2 92.00 275.00 645.00
3 76.00 230.00 535.00
4,5: 4-Commando Yank begins; Golden Arrow, Ibis the Invincible & Spy Smasher cameo in Captain Marvel 57.00 171.00 400.00
6,7: 7-Balbo the Boy Magician app.; Captain Marvel, Bulletman cameo in Mr. Scarlet 46.00 140.00 325.00
8-Capt. Marvel Jr. & Golden Arrow app.; Spy Smasher x-over in Capt. Midnight; no Minute Man or Commando Yank 46.00 140.00 325.00

AMERICA'S SWEETHEART SUNNY (See Sunny, ...)

AMERICA VS. THE JUSTICE SOCIETY
Jan, 1985 - No. 4, Apr, 1985 ($1.00, mini-series)
DC Comics

1-Double size; Alcala-a(i) in all .30 .75 1.50
2-4 .50 1.00

AMERICOMICS (Americomics)(Value: cover or less)

AMETHYST
Jan, 1985 - No. 16, Aug, 1986 (75¢)
DC Comics

1-16: 8-Fire Jade's i.d. revealed 1.00
Special 1 (10/86, $1.25) 1.25

AMETHYST
Nov, 1987 - No. 4, Feb, 1988 ($1.25, mini-series)
DC Comics

1-4 1.25

AMETHYST, PRINCESS OF GEMWORLD
May, 1983 - No. 12, April, 1984 (12 issue maxi-series)
DC Comics

1-(60¢) 1.00
1,2 (35¢; tested in Austin & Kansas City) 2.15 6.50 15.00
2-12: Perez-c(p) #6-11 1.00
Annual 1(9/84) 1.25

ANARCHO DICTATOR OF DEATH (See Comics Novel)

ANCHORS ANDREWS (The Saltwater Daffy)
Jan, 1953 - No. 4, July, 1953 (Anchors the Saltwater... No. 4)
St. John Publishing Co.

1-Canteen Kate by Matt Baker (9 pgs.) 11.00 32.00 75.00
2-4 4.00 11.00 22.00

ANDREW VACHSS' UNDERGROUND (Dark Horse)(Value: cover or less)

ANDY & WOODY (See March of Comics No. 40, 55, 76)

ANDY BURNETT (See 4-Color Comics No. 865)

ANDY COMICS (Formerly Scream Comics; becomes Ernie Comics)
No. 20, June, 1948 - No. 21, Aug, 1948
Current Publications (Ace Magazines)

Angel Love #2 © DC

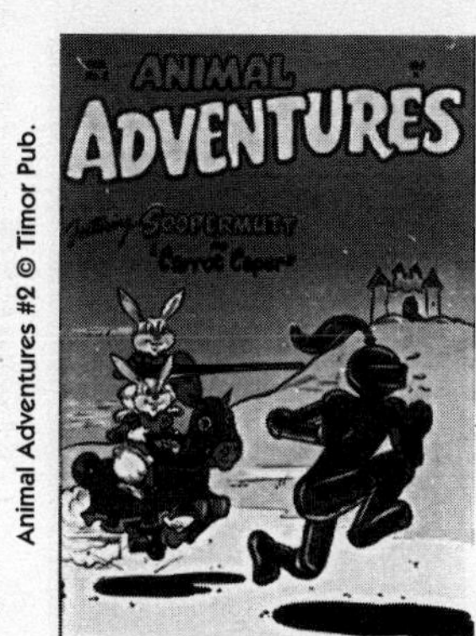

Animal Adventures #2 © Timor Pub.

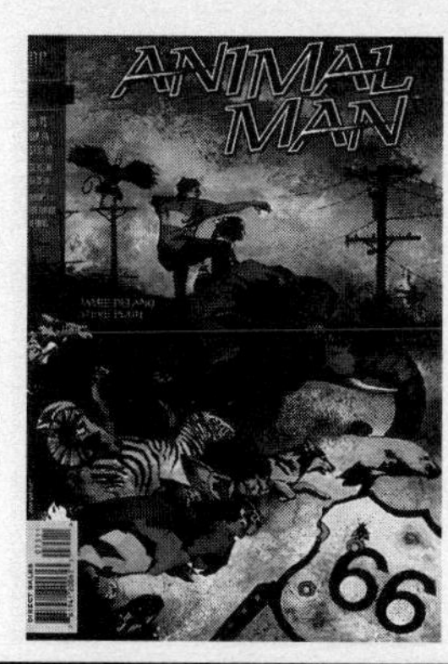

Animal Man # 75 © DC

	GD25	FN65	NM94
20,21-Archie-type comic	4.70	14.00	28.00

ANDY DEVINE WESTERN
Dec, 1950 - No. 2, 1951
Fawcett Publications

	GD25	FN65	NM94
1	43.00	129.00	300.00
2	32.00	96.00	225.00

ANDY GRIFFITH SHOW, THE (See 4-Color No. 1252, 1341)

ANDY HARDY COMICS (See Movie Comics No. 3 by Fiction House)
April, 1952 - No. 6, Sept-Nov, 1954
Dell Publishing Co.

	GD25	FN65	NM94
4-Color 389 (#1)	4.00	12.00	24.00
4-Color 447,480,515,5,6	3.20	8.00	16.00
...& the New Automatic Gas Clothes Dryer (1952, 16 pgs., 5x7-1/4") Bendix Giveaway (soft-c)	4.00	11.00	22.00

ANDY PANDA (Also see Crackajack Funnies #39, The Funnies, New Funnies & Walter Lantz...)
1943 - No. 56, Nov-Jan, 1961-62 (Walter Lantz)
Dell Publishing Co.

	GD25	FN65	NM94
4-Color 25(#1, 1943)	50.00	150.00	350.00
4-Color 54('44)	27.00	81.00	190.00
4-Color 85('45)	16.00	48.00	110.00
4-Color 130('46),154,198	10.00	30.00	65.00
4-Color 216,240,258,280,297	7.50	22.50	45.00
4-Color 326,345,358	4.00	11.00	22.00
4-Color 383,409	3.60	9.00	18.00
16(11-1/52-53) - 30	2.00	5.00	10.00
31-56	1.60	4.00	8.00

(See March of Comics #5, 22, 79, & Super Book #4, 15, 27.)

ANGEL
Aug, 1954 - No. 16, Nov-Jan, 1958-59
Dell Publishing Co.

	GD25	FN65	NM94
4-Color 576(#1, 8/54)	3.20	8.00	16.00
2(5-7/55) - 16	2.00	5.00	10.00

ANGEL AND THE APE (Meet Angel No. 7) (See Limited Collector's Edition C-34 & Showcase No. 77)
Nov-Dec, 1968 - No. 6, Sept-Oct, 1969
National Periodical Publications

	GD25	FN65	NM94
Showcase #77 (9/68)-1st app. Angel & the Ape	4.00	11.00	35.00
1-(11-12/68)-Not Wood-a	3.00	9.00	21.00
2-6-Wood inks in all	1.90	6.00	13.00

ANGEL AND THE APE (2nd series)
Mar, 1991 - No. 4, June, 1991 ($1.00, mini-series)
DC Comics

	GD25	FN65	NM94
1-4			1.00

ANGELIC ANGELINA
1909 (11-1/2x17"; 30 pgs.; 2 colors)
Cupples & Leon Company

	GD25	FN65	NM94
nn-By Munson Paddock	25.00	75.00	175.00

ANGEL LOVE
Aug, 1986 - No. 8, Mar, 1987 (75¢, mini-series)
DC Comics

	GD25	FN65	NM94
1-8			1.00
Special 1 (1987, $1.25, 52 pgs.)			1.25

ANGEL OF LIGHT, THE (See The Crusaders)

ANIMA
Mar, 1994 - Present ($1.75/$1.95)
DC Comics

	GD25	FN65	NM94
1-6		.70	1.75
7-(9/94)-Begin $1.95-c; Zero Hour		.80	2.00
0,8-13: 0-(10/94)		.80	2.00

ANIMAL ADVENTURES
Dec, 1953 - No. 3, May?, 1954
Timor Publications/Accepted Publications (reprints)

	GD25	FN65	NM94
1-Funny animal	4.00	11.00	22.00
2,3: 2-Featuring Soopermutt (2/54)	2.40	6.00	12.00
1-3 (reprints, nd)	1.60	4.00	8.00

ANIMAL ANTICS (Movie Town... No. 24 on)
Mar-Apr, 1946 - No. 23, Nov-Dec, 1949 (All 52 pgs.?)
National Periodical Publications

	GD25	FN65	NM94
1-Raccoon Kids begins by Otto Feur; some-c by Grossman; Seaman Sy Wheeler by Kelly in some issues	38.00	114.00	265.00
2	19.00	58.00	135.00
3-10: 10-Post-c/a	11.50	34.00	80.00
11-23: 14,15,18,19-Post-a	8.35	25.00	50.00

ANIMAL COMICS
Dec-Jan, 1941-42 - No. 30, Dec-Jan, 1947-48
Dell Publishing Co.

	GD25	FN65	NM94
1-1st Pogo app. by Walt Kelly (Dan Noonan art in most issues)	100.00	300.00	700.00
2-Uncle Wiggily begins	50.00	150.00	350.00
3,5	36.00	107.00	250.00
4,6,7-No Pogo	22.00	65.00	150.00
8-10	26.00	78.00	180.00
11-15	16.50	50.00	115.00
16-20	11.00	32.00	75.00
21-30: 25-30- "Jigger" by John Stanley	8.35	25.00	50.00

NOTE: ***Dan Noonan** a-18-30. **Gollub** art in most later issues; c-29, 30. **Kelly** c-7-26.*

ANIMAL CONFIDENTIAL (Dark Horse)(Value: cover or less)

ANIMAL CRACKERS (Also see Adventures of Patoruzu)
1946; No. 31, July, 1950; No. 9, 1959
Green Publ. Co./Norlen/Fox Feat.(Hero Books)

	GD25	FN65	NM94
1-Super Cat begins (1st app.)	10.00	30.00	70.00
2	6.70	20.00	40.00
3-10 (Exist?)	3.60	9.00	18.00
31(Fox)-Formerly My Love Secret	4.70	14.00	28.00
9(1959-Norlen)-Infinity-c	2.40	6.00	12.00
nn; nd ('50s), no publ.; infinity-c	2.40	6.00	12.00

ANIMAL FABLES
July-Aug, 1946 - No. 7, Nov-Dec, 1947
E. C. Comics(Fables Publ. Co.)

	GD25	FN65	NM94
1-Freddy Firefly (clone of Human Torch), Korky Kangaroo, Petey Pig, Danny Demon begin	31.00	94.00	220.00
2-Aesop Fables begin	21.00	63.00	145.00
3-6	17.00	52.00	120.00
7-Origin Moon Girl	50.00	150.00	350.00

ANIMAL FAIR (Fawcett's...)
March, 1946 - No. 11, Feb, 1947
Fawcett Publications

	GD25	FN65	NM94
1	19.00	58.00	135.00
2	10.00	30.00	65.00
3-6	7.50	22.50	45.00
7-11	5.00	15.00	30.00

ANIMAL FUN
1953 (25¢, came w/glasses)
Premier Magazines

	GD25	FN65	NM94
1-(3-D)-Ziggy Pig, Silly Seal, Billy & Buggy Bear	28.00	85.00	200.00

ANIMAL MAN (See Action Comics #552, 553, DC Comics presents #77, 78, Secret Origins #39, Strange Adventures #180 & Wonder Woman #267, 268)
Sept, 1988 - Present ($1.25/$1.50/$1.75/$1.95)
DC Comics (Vertigo imprint #57 on)

Annex #2 © MEG

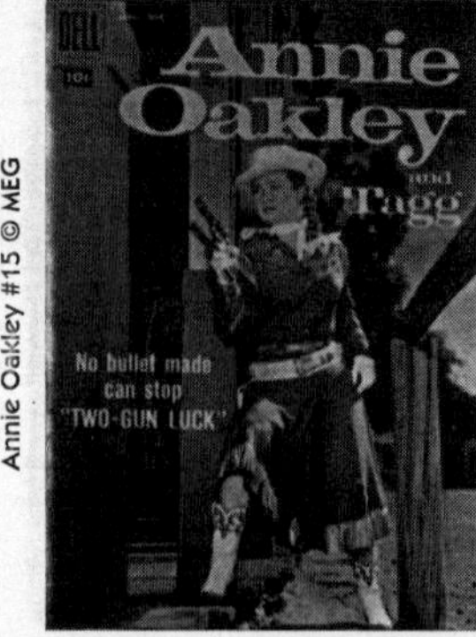

Annie Oakley #15 © MEG

A-1 Comics #1 © ME

GD25 FN65 NM94

1-Bolland c-1-63; Grant Morrison scripts begin 2.10 6.40 15.00
2-Superman cameo 1.70 4.20 10.00
3,4 1.00 2.50 6.00
5-10: 6-Invasion tie-in. 9-Manhunter-c/story 1.60 4.00
11-20: 11-Begin $1.50-c 1.10 2.75
21-26: 24-Arkham Asylum story; Bizarro Superman app. 25-Inferior Five app. 26-Last Morrison scripts; Morrison apps. in story; part photo-c (of Morrison?) 1.10 2.75
27-49,51-55,57-59: 41-Begin $1.75-c, end #59 .80 2.00
50-($2.95, 52 pgs.)-Last issue w/Veitch scripts 1.20 3.00
56-($3.50, 68 pgs.) 1.40 3.50
60-80: 60-Begin $1.95-c. 68-Photo-c. 71-Sutton-a(i) .80 2.00
Annual 1 (1993, $3.95, 68 pgs.)-Bolland-c; Children's Crusade Pt. 3 1.60 4.00

ANIMAL WORLD, THE (See 4-Color Comics No. 713)

ANIMATED COMICS
No date given (Summer, 1947?)
E. C. Comics

1 (Rare) 64.00 193.00 450.00

ANIMATED FUNNY COMIC TUNES (See Funny Tunes)

ANIMATED MOVIE-TUNES (Movie Tunes No. 3)
Fall, 1945 - No. 2, Sum, 1946
Margood Publishing Corp. (Timely)

1,2-Super Rabbit, Ziggy Pig & Silly Seal 14.00 43.00 100.00

ANIMAX
Dec, 1986 - No. 4, June, 1987
Star Comics (Marvel)

1-4: Based on toys 1.00

ANNE RICE'S THE MUMMY OR RAMSES THE DAMNED
Oct, 1990 - No. 12, 1991 ($2.50, color, high quality, mini-series)
Millennium Publications

1-12: Adapts novel; Mooney-p in all 1.00 2.50

ANNETTE (See 4-Color Comics No. 905)

ANNETTE'S LIFE STORY (See 4-Color No. 1100)

ANNEX
Aug, 1994 - Present ($1.75, color)
Marvel Comics
1-8: 1-Spider-Man app. .70 1.75

ANNIE
Oct, 1982 - No. 2, Nov, 1982 (60¢)
Marvel Comics Group

1,2-Movie adaptation 1.25
Treasury Edition ($2.00, tabloid size) .80 2.00

ANNIE OAKLEY (See Tessie The Typist #19, Two-Gun Kid & Wild Western)
Spring, 1948 - No. 4, 11/48; No. 5, 6/55 - No. 11, 6/56
Marvel/Atlas Comics(MPI No. 1-4/CDS No. 5 on)

1 (1st Series, 1948)-Hedy Devine app. 32.00 96.00 225.00
2 (7/48, 52 pgs.)-Kurtzman-a, "Hey Look", 1 pg; Intro. Lana; Hedy Devine app; Captain Tootsie by Beck 19.00 58.00 135.00
3,4 16.00 48.00 110.00
5 (2nd Series, 1955)-Reinman-a ; Maneely-c 10.00 30.00 75.00
6-9: 6,8-Woodbridge-a. 9-Williamson-a (4 pgs.) 10.00 30.00 60.00
10,11: 11-Severin-c 8.35 25.00 50.00

ANNIE OAKLEY AND TAGG (TV)
1953 - No. 18, Jan-Mar, 1959; July, 1965 (Gail Davis photo-c #3 on)
Dell Publishing Co./Gold Key

4-Color 438 (#1) 14.00 43.00 100.00
4-Color 481,575 (#2,3) 9.15 27.50 55.00
4(7-9/55)-10 8.35 25.00 50.00
11-18(1-3/59) 6.70 20.00 40.00
1(7/65-Gold Key)-Photo-c (c-r/#6) 5.85 17.50 35.00
NOTE: *Manning a-13. Photo back c-4, 9, 11.*

ANOTHER WORLD (See Strange Stories From...)

ANTHRO (See Showcase #74)
July-Aug, 1968 - No. 6, July-Aug, 1969
National Periodical Publications

Showcase #74 (5/68)-1st app. Anthro; Post-c/a 6.00 18.00 55.00
1-(7-8/68)-Howie Post-a in all 4.70 14.00 33.00
2-6: 6-Wood-c/a (inks) 2.60 7.70 18.00

ANTONY AND CLEOPATRA (See Ideal, a Classical Comic)

ANYTHING GOES
Oct, 1986 - No. 6, 1987 ($2.00, mini-series, mature readers)
Fantagraphics Books (#1-5: color & B&W; #6: B&W)

1-Flaming Carrot app. (1st in color?); G. Kane-c 1.20 3.00
2-4,6: 2-Miller-c(p); Alan Moore scripts; early Sam Kieth-a (2 pgs.). 3-Capt. Jack, Cerebus app.; Cerebus-c by N. Adams. 4-Perez-c .80 2.00
5-2nd color Teenage Mutant Ninja Turtles app. 1.20 3.00

A-1
1992 - No. 4, 1993 ($5.95, mini-series, mature readers)
Epic Comics (Marvel)

1-4: 3-Bisley-c 1.00 2.50 6.00

A-1 COMICS (A-1 appears on covers No. 1-17 only)(See individual title listings. First two issues not numbered.)
1944 - No. 139, Sept-Oct, 1955 (No #2)
Life's Romances Publ.-No. 1/Compix/Magazine Ent.

nn-Kerry Drake, Johnny Devildog, Rocky, Streamer Kelly (slightly large size) 19.00 57.00 130.00
1-Dotty Dripple (1 pg.), Mr. Ex, Bush Berry, Rocky, Lew Loyal (20 pgs.) 10.00 30.00 60.00
3-8,10-Texas Slim & Dirty Dalton, The Corsair, Teddy Rich, Dotty Dripple, Inca Dinca, Tommy Tinker, Little Mexico & Tugboat Tim, The Masquerader & others. 7-Corsair-c/s. 8-Intro. Rodeo Ryan 4.00 12.00 24.00
9-Texas Slim (all) 4.00 12.00 24.00
11-Teena; Ogden Whitney-c 6.35 19.00 38.00
12,15-Teena 5.35 16.00 32.00
13-Guns of Fact & Fiction (1948). Used in **SOTI**, pg. 19; Ingels & Johnny Craig-a 19.00 58.00 135.00
14-Tim Holt Western Adventures #1 (1948) 46.00 139.00 325.00
16-Vacation Comics; The Pixies, Tom Tom, Flying Fredd, & Koko & Kola 4.00 10.00 20.00
17-Tim Holt #2; photo-c; last issue to carry A-1 on cover (9-10/48) 27.00 80.00 185.00
18,20-Jimmy Durante; photo covers 30.00 90.00 210.00
19-Tim Holt #3; photo-c 19.00 58.00 135.00
21-Joan of Arc (1949)-Movie adaptation; Ingrid Bergman photo-covers & interior photos; Whitney-a 20.00 60.00 140.00
22-Dick Powell (1949)-Photo-c 20.00 60.00 140.00
23-Cowboys and Indians #6; Doc Holiday-c/story 6.35 19.00 38.00
24-Trail Colt #1-Frazetta, r-in Manhunt #13; Ingels-c; L. B. Cole-a 30.00 90.00 210.00
25-Fibber McGee & Molly (1949) (Radio) 8.35 25.00 50.00
26-Trail Colt #2-Ingels-c 24.00 73.00 170.00
27-Ghost Rider #1(1950)-Origin Ghost Rider 50.00 150.00 350.00
28-Christmas-(Koko & Kola #6) (1950) 4.00 11.00 22.00
29-Ghost Rider #2-Frazetta-c (1950) 45.00 135.00 315.00
30-Jet Powers #1-Powell-a 24.00 72.00 165.00
31-Ghost Rider #3-Frazetta-c & origin ('51) 45.00 135.00 315.00
32-Jet Powers #2 17.00 52.00 120.00
33-Muggsy Mouse #1('51) 5.00 15.00 30.00
34-Ghost Rider #4-Frazetta-c (1951) 45.00 135.00 315.00
35-Jet Powers #3-Williamson/Evans-a 28.00 84.00 195.00
36-Muggsy Mouse #2; Racist-c 5.85 17.50 35.00

A-1 Comics #59 © ME

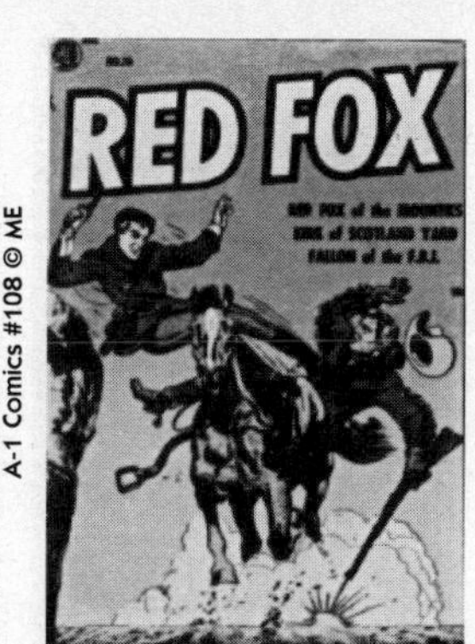

A-1 Comics #108 © ME

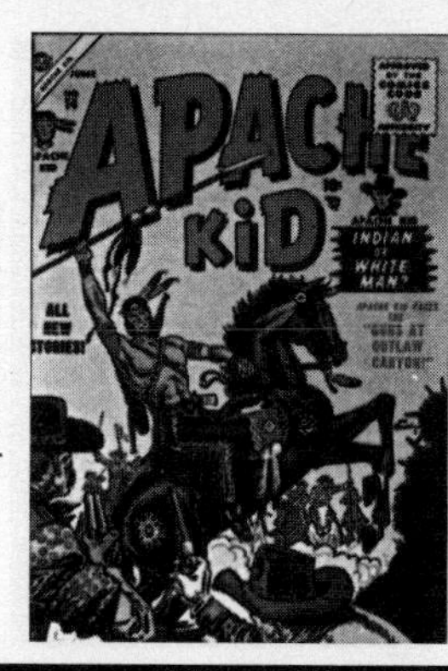

Apache Kid #14 © MEG

	GD25	FN65	NM94
37-Ghost Rider #5-Frazetta-c (1951)	45.00	135.00	315.00
38-Jet Powers #4-Williamson & Wood-a	28.00	84.00	195.00
39-Muggsy Mouse #3	3.20	8.00	16.00
40-Dogface Dooley #1('51)	4.70	14.00	28.00
41-Cowboys 'N' Indians #7	4.35	13.00	26.00
42-Best of the West #1-Powell-a	34.00	103.00	240.00
43-Dogface Dooley #2	4.00	10.00	20.00
44-Ghost Rider #6	18.00	54.00	125.00
45-American Air Forces #5-Powell-c/a	4.00	12.00	24.00
46-Best of the West #2	16.00	48.00	110.00
47-Thun'da, King of the Congo #1-Frazetta-c/a('52)	90.00	270.00	630.00
48-Cowboys 'N' Indians #8	4.35	13.00	26.00
49-Dogface Dooley #3	4.00	10.00	20.00
50-Danger Is Their Business #11 ('52)-Powell-a	10.00	30.00	60.00
51-Ghost Rider #7 ('52)	18.00	54.00	125.00
52-Best of the West #3	14.00	43.00	100.00
53-Dogface Dooley #4	4.00	10.00	20.00
54-American Air Forces #6(8/52)-Powell-a	4.00	12.00	24.00
55-U.S. Marines #5-Powell-a	4.00	12.00	24.00
56-Thun'da #2-Powell-c/a	14.00	43.00	100.00
57-Ghost Rider #8	16.00	48.00	110.00
58-American Air Forces #7-Powell-a	4.00	12.00	24.00
59-Best of the West #4	14.00	43.00	100.00
60-The U.S. Marines #6-Powell-a	4.00	12.00	24.00
61-Space Ace #5(1953)-Guardineer-a	34.00	103.00	240.00
62-Starr Flagg, Undercover Girl #5 (#1)	27.00	81.00	190.00
63-Manhunt #13-Frazetta reprinted from A-1 #24	20.00	60.00	140.00
64-Dogface Dooley #5	4.00	10.00	20.00
65-American Air Forces #8-Powell-a	4.00	12.00	24.00
66-Best of the West #5	14.00	43.00	100.00
67-American Air Forces #9-Powell-a	4.00	12.00	24.00
68-U.S. Marines #7-Powell-a	4.00	12.00	24.00
69-Ghost Rider #9(10/52)	16.00	48.00	110.00
70-Best of the West #6	10.00	30.00	70.00
71-Ghost Rider #10(12/52)-Vs. Frankenstein	16.00	48.00	110.00
72-U.S. Marines #8-Powell-a(3)	4.00	12.00	24.00
73-Thun'da #3-Powell-c/a	10.00	30.00	70.00
74-American Air Forces #10-Powell-a	4.00	12.00	24.00
75-Ghost Rider #11(3/52)	13.00	45.00	90.00
76-Best of the West #7	10.00	30.00	70.00
77-Manhunt #14	15.00	45.00	105.00
78-Thun'da #4-Powell-c/a	10.00	30.00	70.00
79-American Air Forces #11-Powell-a	4.00	12.00	24.00
80-Ghost Rider #12(6/52)-One-eyed Devil-c	13.00	40.00	90.00
81-Best of the West #8	10.00	30.00	70.00
82-Cave Girl #11(1953)-Powell-c/a; origin (#1)	30.00	90.00	210.00
83-Thun'da #5-Powell-c/a	10.00	30.00	65.00
84-Ghost Rider #13(7-8/53)	13.00	40.00	90.00
85-Best of the West #9	10.00	30.00	70.00
86-Thun'da #6-Powell-c/a	10.00	30.00	65.00
87-Best of the West #10(9-10/53)	10.00	30.00	70.00
88-Bobby Benson's B-Bar-B Riders #20	7.50	22.50	45.00
89-Home Run #3-Powell-a; Stan Musial photo-c	17.00	52.00	120.00
90-Red Hawk #11(1953)-Powell-c/a	10.00	30.00	60.00
91-American Air Forces #12-Powell-a	4.00	12.00	24.00
92-Dream Book of Romance #5-Photo-c; Guardineer-a	6.70	20.00	40.00
93-Great Western #8('54)-Origin The Ghost Rider; Powell-a	15.00	45.00	105.00
94-White Indian #11-Frazetta-a(r); Powell-c	17.00	52.00	120.00
95-Muggsy Mouse #4	3.20	8.00	16.00
96-Cave Girl #12, with Thun'da; Powell-c/a	22.00	67.00	155.00
97-Best of the West #11	10.00	30.00	70.00
98-Undercover Girl #6-Powell-c	25.00	75.00	175.00
99-Muggsy Mouse #5	3.20	8.00	16.00

	GD25	FN65	NM94
100-Badmen of the West #1-Meskin-a(?)	17.00	52.00	120.00
101-White Indian #12-Frazetta-a(r)	17.00	52.00	120.00
101-Dream Book of Romance #6 (4-6/54); Marlon Brando photo-c; Powell, Bolle, Guardineer-a	13.00	40.00	90.00
103-Best of the West #12-Powell-a	10.00	30.00	70.00
104-White Indian #13-Frazetta-a(r)('54)	17.00	52.00	120.00
105-Great Western #9-Ghost Rider app.; Powell-a, 6 pgs.; Bolle-c	9.15	27.50	55.00
106-Dream Book of Love #1 (6-7/54)-Powell, Bolle-a; Montgomery Clift, Donna Reed photo-c	8.35	25.00	50.00
107-Hot Dog #1	5.00	15.00	30.00
108-Red Fox #15 (1954)-L.B. Cole c/a; Powell-a	11.00	32.00	75.00
109-Dream Book of Romance #7 (7-8/54). Powell-a; movie photo-c	5.00	15.00	30.00
110-Dream Book of Romance #8 (10/54)-Movie photo-c	5.00	15.00	30.00
111-I'm a Cop #1 ('54); drug mention story; Powell-a	10.00	30.00	60.00
112-Ghost Rider #14 ('54)	13.00	40.00	90.00
113-Great Western #10; Powell-a	9.15	27.50	55.00
114-Dream Book of Love #2-Guardineer, Bolle-a; Piper Laurie, Victor Mature photo-c	6.70	20.00	40.00
115-Hot Dog #3	4.00	10.00	20.00
116-Cave Girl #13-Powell-c/a	22.00	67.00	155.00
117-White Indian #14	9.15	27.50	55.00
118-Undercover Girl #7-Powell-c	25.00	75.00	175.00
119-Straight Arrow's Fury #1 (origin); Fred Meagher-c/a	10.00	30.00	65.00
120-Badmen of the West #2	11.00	32.00	75.00
121-Mysteries of Scotland Yard #1; reprinted from Manhunt (5 stories)	11.00	32.00	75.00
122-Black Phantom #1 (11/54)	27.00	80.00	185.00
123-Dream Book of Love #3 (10-11/54)-Movie photo-c	5.00	15.00	30.00
124-Dream Book of Romance #8 (10-11/54)	5.00	15.00	30.00
125-Cave Girl #14-Powell-c/a	22.00	67.00	155.00
126-I'm a Cop #2-Powell-a	5.35	16.00	32.00
127-Great Western #11('54)-Powell-a	9.15	27.50	55.00
128-I'm a Cop #3-Powell-a	5.35	16.00	32.00
129-The Avenger #1('55)-Powell-c	26.00	77.00	180.00
130-Strongman #1-Powell-a	16.00	48.00	110.00
131-The Avenger #2('55)-Powell-c/a	17.00	52.00	120.00
132-Strongman #2	13.00	40.00	90.00
133-The Avenger #3-Powell-c/a	17.00	52.00	120.00
134-Strongman #3	13.00	40.00	90.00
135-White Indian #15	9.15	27.50	55.00
136-Hot Dog #4	4.00	10.00	20.00
137-Africa #1-Powell-c/a(4)	16.00	48.00	110.00
138-The Avenger #4-Powell-c/a	17.00	52.00	120.00
139-Strongman #4-Powell-a	13.00	40.00	90.00

NOTE: ***Bolle** a-110. Photo-c-17-22, 89, 92, 101, 106, 109, 110, 114, 123, 124.*

APACHE
1951
Fiction House Magazines

	GD25	FN65	NM94
1	14.00	43.00	100.00
I.W. Reprint No. 1-r/#1 above	2.40	6.00	12.00

APACHE HUNTER
1954 (18 pgs. in color) (promo copy) (saddle stitched)
Creative Pictorials

	GD25	FN65	NM94
nn-Severin, Heath stories	16.00	48.00	110.00

APACHE KID (Formerly Reno Browne; Western Gunfighters #20 on)
(Also see Two-Gun Western & Wild Western)
No. 53, 12/50 - No. 10, 1/52; No. 11, 12/54 - No. 19, 4/56
Marvel/Atlas Comics(MPC No. 53-10/CPS No. 11 on)

53(#1)-Apache Kid & his horse Nightwind (origin), Red Hawkins by Syd

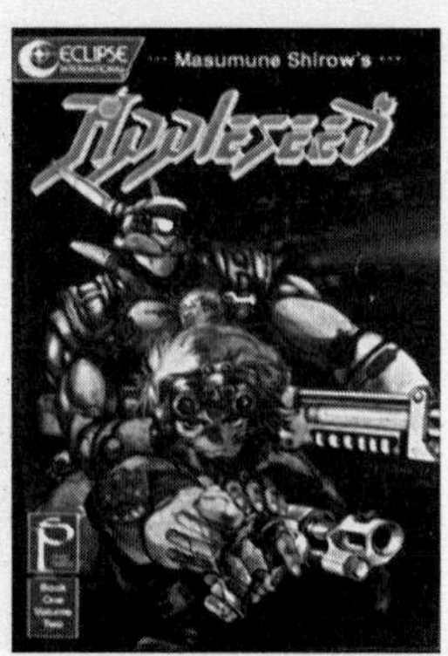

Appleseed (book 1) V2 © Eclipse

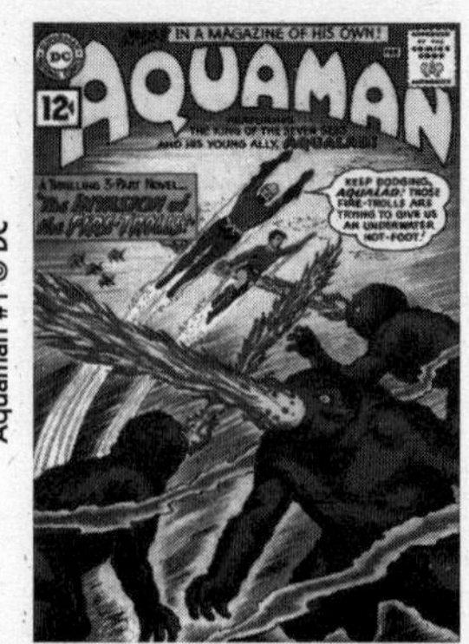

Aquaman #1 © DC

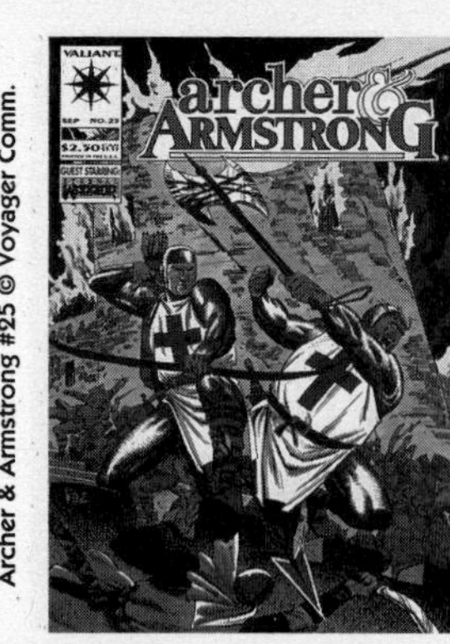

Archer & Armstrong #25 © Voyager Comm.

	GD25	FN65	NM94
Shores begins	22.00	65.00	150.00
2(2/51)	10.00	30.00	70.00
3-5	8.35	25.00	50.00
6-10 (1951-52)	5.85	17.50	35.00
11-19 (1954-56)	4.70	14.00	28.00

NOTE: **Heath** c-11, 13. **Maneely** a-53; c-53(#1), 12, 14-16. **Powell** a-14. **Severin** c-17.

APACHE MASSACRE (See Chief Victorio's...)

APACHE TRAIL
Sept, 1957 - No. 4, June, 1958
Steinway/America's Best

	GD25	FN65	NM94
1	6.70	20.00	40.00
2-4: 2-Tuska-a	4.00	11.00	22.00

APPLESEED
Sept, 1988 - Book 4, Vol. 4, Aug, 1991 (B&W, $2.50/$2.75, 52 pgs)
Eclipse Comics

	GD25	FN65	NM94
Book One, Volume 1 ($2.50)	1.65	4.00	10.00
Book One, Volume 2-5: 5-(1/89, $2.75 cover)		1.00	2.50
Book Two, Vol. 1(2/89) -5(7/89): Art Adams-c		1.00	2.50
Book Three, Volume 1(8/89) -4 ($2.75)		1.00	2.50
Book Three, Volume 5 ($3.50)		1.20	3.00
Book Four, Volume 1(1/91) -4 (3.50, 68 pgs.)		1.20	3.00

APPLESEED DATABOOK
Apr, 1994 - No. 2, May, 1994 ($3.50, B&W, limited series)
Dark Horse Comics

	GD25	FN65	NM94
1,2: 1-Flip book format		1.40	3.50

APPROVED COMICS
March, 1954 - No. 12, Aug, 1954 (All painted-c)
St. John Publishing Co. (Most have no c-price)

	GD25	FN65	NM94
1-The Hawk #5-r	6.70	20.00	40.00
2-Invisible Boy-r(3/54)-Origin; Saunders-c	11.50	34.00	80.00
3-Wild Boy of the Congo #11-r (4/54)	6.70	20.00	40.00
4,5: 4-Kid Cowboy-r. 5-Fly Boy-r	6.70	20.00	40.00
6-Daring Adv.-r (5/54); Krigstein-a(2); Baker-c	9.15	27.50	55.00
7-The Hawk #6-r	6.70	20.00	40.00
8-Crime on the Run (6/54); Powell-a; Saunders-c	6.70	20.00	40.00
9-Western Bandit Trails #3-r, with new-c; Baker-c/a	9.15	27.50	55.00
11-Fightin' Marines #3-r (8/54); Canteen Kate app; Baker-c/a	10.00	30.00	60.00
12-North West Mounties #4-r(8/54); new Baker-c	10.00	30.00	60.00

AQUAMAN (See Adventure #260, Brave & the Bold, DC Comics Presents #5, DC Special #28, DC Special Series #1, DC Super Stars #7, Detective, Justice League of America, More Fun #73, Showcase #30-33, Super DC Giant, Super Friends, and World's Finest Comics)

AQUAMAN (1st series)
Jan-Feb, 1962 - No. 56, Mar-Apr, 1971; No. 57, Aug-Sept, 1977 - No. 63, Aug-Sept, 1978
National Periodical Publications/DC Comics

	GD25	FN65	NM94
Showcase #30 (1-2/61)-Origin S.A. Aquaman	54.00	162.00	540.00
Showcase #31 (3-4/61)-Aquaman	30.00	90.00	300.00
Showcase #32 (5-6/61)-Aquaman	30.00	90.00	300.00
Showcase #33 (7-8/61)-Aquaman	36.00	108.00	360.00
1-(1-2/62)-Intro. Quisp	30.00	100.00	330.00
2	20.00	60.00	140.00
3-5	14.00	41.00	95.00
6-10: 9-Sea Devils app.	9.00	28.00	65.00
11-20: 11-1st app. Mera. 18-Aquaman weds Mera; JLA cameo	7.00	21.00	50.00
21-32,34-40: 23-Birth of Aquababy. 26-Huntress app.(3-4/66). 29-1st app. Ocean Master, Aquaman's step-brother. 30-Batman & Superman-c & cameo	5.00	15.00	35.00
33-1st app. Aqua-Girl (see Adventure #266)	7.00	21.00	50.00
41-47,49	2.10	6.50	15.00
48-Origin reprinted	2.60	7.70	18.00
50-52-Deadman by Neal Adams	3.60	11.00	25.00
53-56('71): 56-1st app. Crusader	1.40	4.00	8.50
57('77)-63: 58-Origin retold	1.00	2.00	5.00

NOTE: **Aparo** a-40-45, 46p, 47-59; c-58-63. **Nick Cardy** c-1-39. **Newton** a-60-63.

AQUAMAN (2nd series)
Feb, 1986 - No. 4, May, 1986 (Mini-series)
DC Comics

	GD25	FN65	NM94
1-New costume		1.60	4.00
2-4		1.00	2.50
...Special 1 ('88, $1.50, 52 pgs.)		.80	2.00

AQUAMAN (3rd series)
June, 1989 - No. 5, Oct, 1989 ($1.00, mini-series)
DC Comics

	GD25	FN65	NM94
1-5: Giffen plots/breakdowns; Swan-p			1.00
...Special 1 (Legend of..., $2.00, 1989, 52 pgs.)-Giffen plots/breakdowns; Swan-p		.80	2.00

AQUAMAN (4th series)
Dec, 1991 - No. 13, Dec, 1992 ($1.00/$1.25)
DC Comics

	GD25	FN65	NM94
1-5: 5-Last $1.00-c			1.00
6-13: 9-Sea Devils app.			1.25

AQUAMAN
Aug, 1994 - Present ($1.50)
DC Comics

	GD25	FN65	NM94
1,2-Peter David script: 2-(9/94)			1.50
0,3-7: 0-(10/94)			1.50

AQUAMAN: TIME & TIDE
Dec, 1993 - No. 4, March, 1994 ($1.50, mini-series)
DC Comics

	GD25	FN65	NM94
1-4: Peter David scripts; origin retold			1.50

AQUANAUTS (See 4-Color No. 1197)

ARABIAN NIGHTS (See Cinema Comics Herald)

ARACHNOPHOBIA
1990 ($5.95, color. 68 pg. graphic novel)
Hollywood Comics (Disney Comics)

	GD25	FN65	NM94
nn-Movie adaptation; Spiegle-a	1.00	2.50	6.00
Comic edition ($2.95, 68 pgs.)		1.20	3.00

ARAK/SON OF THUNDER (See Warlord #48)
Sept, 1981 - No. 50, Nov, 1985
DC Comics

	GD25	FN65	NM94
1-50: 1-Origin; 1st app. Angelica, Princess of White Cathay. 3-Intro Valda, The Iron Maiden. 12-Origin Valda. 20-Origin Angelica. 24,50-(52 pgs.)			1.00
Annual 1(10/84)			1.00

ARCANA ANNUAL
1994 ($3.95, 68 pgs.)
DC Comics (Vertigo)

	GD25	FN65	NM94
1-Bolton painted-c; Children's Crusade story		1.60	4.00

ARCHER & ARMSTRONG
July (June inside), 1992 - Present ($2.50, color)
Valiant

	GD25	FN65	NM94
0-(7/92)-B. Smith-c/a; Reese-i assists	1.50	4.00	9.00
0-(Gold Logo)			25.00
1-(8/92)-Origin & 1st app. Archer; Miller-c; B. Smith/Layton-a		1.60	4.00
2-2nd app. Turok(c/story); Smith/Layton-a; Simonson-c		1.50	3.75
3,4-Smith-c&a(p) & scripts		1.40	3.50
5-7		1.20	3.00
8-($4.50, 52 pgs.)-Combined with Eternal Warrior #8; B. Smith-c/a & scripts;			

Archie And Me #1 © AP

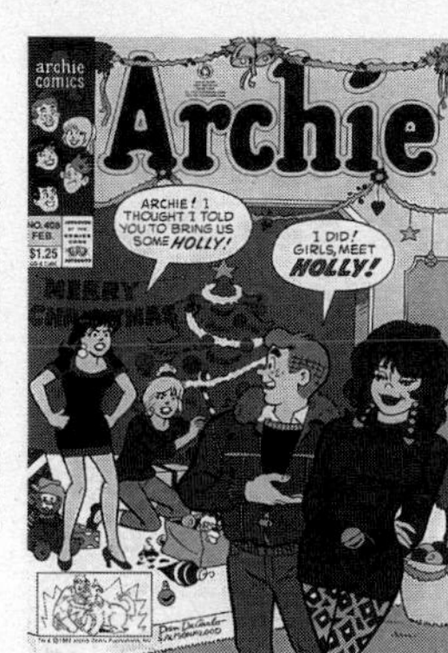

Archie Comics #408 © Archie

Archie Comics #422 © Archie

GD25 FN65 NM94

1st app. Ivar the Time Walker 1.50 3.75
9-25: 10-2nd app. Ivar. 10,11-B. Smith-c. 21,22-Shadowman app. 22-w/bound-in Upper Deck trading card. 25-Eternal Warrior app. 1.00 2.50

ARCHIE AND BIG ETHEL (Spire Christian)(Value: cover or less)

ARCHIE & FRIENDS
Dec, 1992 - Present ($1.25)
Archie Comics
1-14 1.25

ARCHIE AND ME (See Archie Giant Series Mag. #578, 591, 603, 616, 626)
Oct, 1964 - No. 161, Feb, 1987
Archie Publications

	GD25	FN65	NM94
1	16.00	48.00	110.00
2	9.15	27.50	55.00
3-5	4.70	14.00	28.00
6-10	3.20	8.00	16.00
11-20	1.60	4.00	8.00
21-30: 26-X-Mas-c	1.00	2.00	5.00
31-63: 43-63-(All Giants)		1.00	2.50
64-161-(Regular size)			1.00

ARCHIE AND MR. WEATHERBEE (Spire Christian)(Value: cover or less)

ARCHIE...ARCHIE ANDREWS, WHERE ARE YOU? (...Comics Digest #9, 10; ...Comics Digest Mag. No. 11 on)
Feb, 1977 - Present (Digest size, 160-128 pgs.)
Archie Publications

	GD25	FN65	NM94
1		1.60	4.00
2,3,5,7-9-N. Adams-a; 8-r-/origin The Fly by S&K. 9-Steel Sterling-r		1.20	3.00
4,6,10-50 ($1.00/$1.50): 17-Katy Keene story		.80	2.00
51-98		.70	1.75

ARCHIE AS PUREHEART THE POWERFUL (Also see Archie Giant Series #142, Jughead as Captain Hero, Life With Archie & Little Archie)
Sept, 1966 - No. 6, Nov, 1967
Archie Publications (Radio Comics)

	GD25	FN65	NM94
1-Super hero parody	7.40	22.00	52.00
2	5.00	14.00	32.00
3-6	3.00	9.00	22.00

NOTE: *Evilheart cameos in all. Title: Archie As Pureheart the Powerful #1-3; ...As Capt. Pureheart-#4-6.*

ARCHIE AT RIVERDALE HIGH (See Archie Giant Series Magazine #573, 586, 604 & Riverdale High)
Aug, 1972 - No. 113, Feb, 1987
Archie Publications

	GD25	FN65	NM94
1	4.50	14.00	32.00
2	2.00	6.00	14.00
3-5	1.20	3.00	7.00
6-10		1.60	4.00
11-30		.80	2.00
31-114: 96-Anti-smoking issue			1.00

ARCHIE COMICS (Also see Christmas & Archie, Everything's..., Explorers of the Unknown, Jackpot, Little..., Oxydol-Dreft, Pep, Riverdale High, Teenage Mutant Ninja Turtles Adventures & To Riverdale and Back Again)

ARCHIE COMICS (Archie #158 on)(First Teen-age comic)(Radio show 1st aired 6/2/45, by NBC)
Winter, 1942-43 - No. 19, 3-4/46; No. 20, 5-6/46 - Present
MLJ Magazines No. 1-19/Archie Publ.No. 20 on

	GD25	FN65	VF82	NM94
1 (Scarce)-Jughead, Veronica app.; 1st app. Mrs. Andrews	650.00	1950.00	4225.00	6500.00

(Estimated up to 50+ total copies exist, 5 in NM/Mint)

	GD25	FN65	NM94
2	214.00	643.00	1500.00
3 (60 pgs.)(scarce)	143.00	429.00	1000.00
4,5: 4-Article about Archie radio series	86.00	257.00	600.00
6-10: 6-X-Mas-c. 7-1st definitive love triangle story	64.00	193.00	450.00
11-20: 15,17,18-Dotty & Ditto by Woggon. 16-Woggon-a	43.00	129.00	300.00
21-30: 23-Betty & Veronica by Woggon. 25-Woggon-a. 30-Coach Piffle app., a Coach Kleets prototype. 34-Pre-Dilton try-out (named Dilbert)	29.00	86.00	200.00
31-40	16.50	50.00	115.00
41-50	11.00	32.00	75.00
51-70 (1954): 51,65-70,72-74-Katy Keene app.	7.50	22.50	45.00
71-99: 94-1st Coach Kleets	5.35	16.00	32.00
100	6.70	20.00	40.00
101-130 (1962)	3.20	8.00	16.00
131-160	1.60	4.00	8.00
161-200	1.00	2.50	5.00
201-240		1.00	2.00
241-282			1.50
283-Cover/story plugs "International Children's Appeal" which was a fraudulent charity, according to TV's 20/20 news program broadcast July 20, 1979		.80	2.10
284-435: 300-Anniversary issue. 393-Infinity-c; 1st comic book printed on recycled paper. 423-Dan DeCarlo-c			1.25
Annual 1('50)-116 pgs. (Scarce)	143.00	429.00	1000.00
Annual 2('51)	75.00	225.00	525.00
Annual 3('52)	50.00	150.00	350.00
Annual 4,5(1953-54)	34.00	100.00	235.00
Annual 6-10(1955-59)	17.00	52.00	120.00
Annual 11-15(1960-65)	8.35	25.00	50.00
Annual 16-20(1966-70)	2.60	7.70	18.00
Annual 21-26(1971-75)	1.00	2.50	6.00
Annual Digest 27('75)-65('83-'94, $1.50-1.75)(...Magazine #35 on)		1.00	2.50
...All-Star Specials(Winter '75, $1.25)-6 remaindered Archie comics rebound in each; titles: "The World of Giant Comics", "Giant Grab Bag of Comics", "Triple Giant Comics" & "Giant Spec. Comics	1.00	2.00	5.00
...And His Friends Help Raise Literacy Awareness In Mississippi nn (3/94)-Giveaway			1.00
...And the History of Electronics nn (5/90, 36 pgs.)-Radio Shack giveaway; Howard Bender-c/a			1.00
Mini-Comics (1970-Fairmont Potato Chips Giveaway-Miniature)(8 issues-nn's., 8 pgs. each)	1.65	4.00	10.00
Official Boy Scout Outfitter (1946, 9-1/2x6-1/2, 16 pgs.)-B. R. Baker Co. (Scarce)	39.00	120.00	275.00
Shoe Store giveaway (1948, Feb?)	13.00	40.00	90.00
...Vacation Special 1 (Summer 1994, $2.00, 52 pgs. plus poster)			2.00

NOTE: ***Al Fagly** c-17-35. **Bob Montana** c-38, 41-50, 58, Annual 1-4. **Bill Woggon** c-53, 54.*

ARCHIE COMICS DIGEST (...Magazine No. 37-95)
Aug, 1973 - Present (Small size, 160-128 pgs.)
Archie Publications

	GD25	FN65	NM94
1	4.30	13.00	30.00
2	2.30	6.75	16.00
3-5	1.30	3.25	8.00
6-10	1.00	2.00	5.00
11-33: 32,33-The Fly-r by S&K		1.00	2.50
34-133: 36-Katy Keene story		.70	1.75

NOTE: ***Neal Adams** a-1, 2, 4, 5, 19-21, 24, 25, 27, 29, 31, 33. X-mas c-88, 94, 100, 106.*

ARCHIE GETS A JOB (Spire Christian)(Value: cover or less)

ARCHIE GIANT SERIES MAGAZINE
1954 - No. 632, July, 1992 (No No. 36-135, no No. 252-451)(#1 not code approved)
Archie Publications

	GD25	FN65	NM94
1-Archie's Christmas Stocking	96.00	289.00	675.00
2-Archie's Christmas Stocking('55)	57.00	171.00	400.00
3-6-Archie's Christmas Stocking('56- '59)	39.00	118.00	275.00

Archie Giant Series #19 © AP

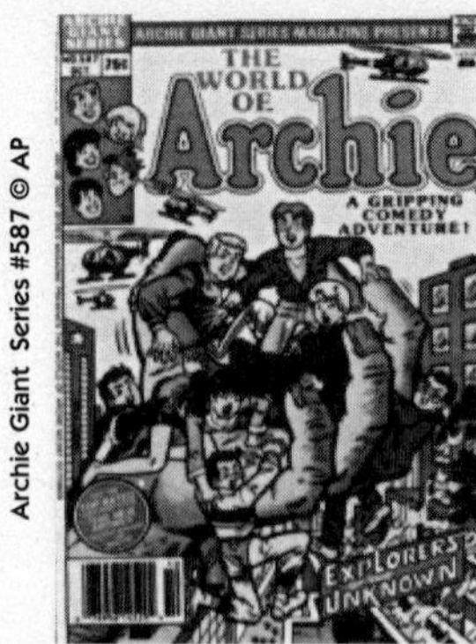

Archie Giant Series #587 © AP

Archie Giant Series #599 © AP

GD25 FN65 NM94

7-10: 7-Katy Keene Holiday Fun(9/60); Bill Woggon-c. 8-Betty & Veronica Summer Fun(10/60). 9-The World of Jughead (12/60). 10-Archie's Christmas Stocking(1/61) 25.00 75.00 175.00

11,13,16,18: 11-Betty & Veronica Spectacular (6/61). 13-Betty & Veronica Summer Fun (10/61). 16-Betty & Veronica Spectacular (6/62). 18-Betty & Veronica Summer Fun (10/62) 20.00 60.00 140.00

12,14,15,17,19,20: 12-Katy Keene Holiday Fun (9/61). 14-The World of Jughead (12/61). 15-Archie's Christmas Stocking (1/62). 17-Archie's Jokes (9/62); Katy Keene app. 19-The World of Jughead (12/62). 20-Archie's Christmas Stocking (1/63) 14.00 43.00 100.00

21,23,26,28: 21-Betty & Veronica Spectacular (6/63). 23-Betty & Veronica Summer Fun (10/63). 26-Betty & Veronica Spectacular (6/64). 28-Betty & Veronica Summer Fun (9/64) 11.00 32.00 75.00

22,24,25,27,29,30: 22-Archie's Jokes (9/63). 24-The World of Jughead (12/63). 25-Archie's Christmas Stocking (1/64). 27-Archie's Jokes (8/64). 29-Around the World with Archie (10/64). 30-The World of Jughead (12/64) 8.35 25.00 50.00

31-35,136-141: 31-Archie's Christmas Stocking (1/65). 32-Betty & Veronica Spectacular (6/65). 33-Archie's Jokes (8/65). 34-Betty & Veronica Summer Fun (9/65). 35-Around the World with Archie (10/65). 136-The World of Jughead (12/65). 137-Archie's Christmas Stocking (1/66). 138-Betty & Veronica Spectacular (6/66). 139-Archie's Jokes (6/66). 140-Betty & Veronica Summer Fun (8/66). 141-Around the World with Archie (9/66) 5.85 17.50 35.00

142-Archie's Super-Hero Special (10/66)-Origin Capt. Pureheart, Capt. Hero, and Evilheart 5.85 17.50 35.00

143-160: 143-The World of Jughead (12/66). 144-Archie's Christmas Stocking (1/67). 145-Betty & Veronica Spectacular (6/67). 146-Archie's Jokes (6/67). 147-Betty & Veronica Summer Fun (8/67) 148-World of Archie (9/67). 149-World of Jughead (10/67). 150-Archie's Christmas Stocking (1/68). 151-World of Archie (2/68). 152-World of Jughead (2/68). 153-Betty & Veronica Spectacular (6/68). 154-Archie Jokes (6/68). 155-Betty & VeronicaSummer Fun (8/68). 156-World of Archie (10/68). 157-World of Jughead (12/68). 158-Archie's Christmas Stocking (1/69). 159-Betty & Veronica Christmas Spectacular (1/69). 160-World of Archie (2/69) 3.20 8.00 16.00

161-200: 161-World of Jughead (2/69). 162-Betty & Veronica Spectacular (6/69). 163-Archie's Jokes(8/69). 164-Betty & Veronica Summer Fun (9/69). 165-World of Archie (9/69). 166-World of Jughead (9/69). 167-Archie's Christmas Stocking (1/70). 168-Betty & Veronica Christmas Spect. (1/70). 169-Archie's Christmas Love-In (1/70). 170-Jughead's Eat-Out Comic Book Mag. (12/69). 171-World of Archie (2/70). 172-World of Jughead (2/70). 173-Betty & Veronica Spectacular (6/70). 174-Archie's Jokes (8/70). 175-Betty & Veronica Summer Fun (9/70). 176-Li'l Jinx Giant Laugh-Out (8/70). 177-World of Archie (9/70). 178-World of Jughead (9/70). 179-Archie's Christmas Stocking (1/71). 180-Betty & Veronica Christmas Spect. (1/71). 181-Archie's Christmas Love-In (1/71). 182-World of Archie (2/71). 183-World of Jughead (2/71). 184-Betty & Veronica Spectacular (6/71). 185-Li'l Jinx Giant Laugh-Out (6/71). 186-Archie's Jokes (8/71). 187-Betty & Veronica Summer Fun (9/71). 188-World of Archie (9/71). 189-World of Jughead (9/71). 190-Archie's Christmas Stocking (12/71). 191-Betty & Veronica Christmas Spectacular (2/72). 192-Archie's Christmas Love-In (1/72). 193-World of Archie (3/72). 194-World of Jughead (4/72). 195-Li'l Jinx Christmas Bag (1/72). 196-Sabrina's Christmas Magic (1/72). 197-Betty & Veronica Spectacular (6/72). 198-Archie's Jokes (8/72). 199-Betty & Veronica Summer Fun (9/72). 200-World of Archie (10/72) 1.20 3.00 6.00

201-251: 201-Betty & Veronica Spectacular (10/72). 202-World of Jughead (11/72). 203-Archie's Christmas Stocking (12/72). 204-Betty & Veronica Christmas Spectacular (2/73). 205-Archie's Christmas Love-In (1/73). 206-Li'l Jinx Christmas Bag (12/72). 207-Sabrina's Christmas Magic (12/72). 208-World of Archie (3/73). 209-World of Jughead (4/73). 210-Betty & Veronica Spectacular (6/73). 211-Archie's Jokes (8/73). 212-Betty & Veronica Summer Fun (9/73). 213-World of Archie (10/73). 214-Betty & Veronica Spectacular (10/73). 215-World of Jughead (11/73). 216-Archie's Christmas Stocking (12/73). 217-Betty & Veronica Christmas Spectacular (2/74). 218-Archie's Christmas Love-In (1/74). 219-Li'l Jinx Christmas Bag (12/73). 220-Sabrina's Christmas Magic (12/73). 221-Betty & Veronica Spectacular (Advertised as World of Archie) (6/74). 222-Archie's Jokes (advertised as World of Jughead) (8/74). 223-Li'l Jinx (8/74). 224-Betty & Veronica Summer Fun (9/74). 225-World of Archie (9/74). 226-Betty & Veronica Spectacular (10/74). 227-World of Jughead (10/74). 228-Archie's Christmas Stocking (12/74). 229-Betty & Veronica Christmas Spectacular (12/74). 230-Archie's Christmas Love-In (1/75). 231-Sabrina's Christmas Magic (1/75). 232-World of Archie (3/75). 233-World of Jughead (4/75). 234-Betty & Veronica Spectacular (6/75). 235-Archie's Jokes (8/75). 236-Betty & Veronica Summer Fun (9/75). 237-World of Archie (9/75) 238-Betty & Veronica Spectacular (10/75). 239-World of Jughead (10/75). 240-Archie's Christmas Stocking (12/75). 241-Betty & Veronica Christmas Spectacular (12/75). 242-Archie's Christmas Love-In (1/76). 243-Sabrina's Christmas Magic (1/76). 244-World of Archie (3/76). 245-World of Jughead (4/76). 246-Betty & Veronica Spectacular (6/76). 247-Archie's Jokes (8/76). 248-Betty & Veronica Summer Fun (9/76). 249-World of Archie (9/76). 250-Betty & Veronica Spectacular (10/76). 251-World of Jughead each.... 1.20 3.00

GD25 FN65 NM94

452-500: 452-Archie's Christmas Stocking (12/76). 453-Betty & Veronica Christmas Spectacular (12/76). 454-Archie's Christmas Love-In (1/77). 455-Sabrina's Christmas Magic (1/77). 456-World of Archie (3/77). 457-World of Jughead (4/77). 458-Betty & Veronica Spectacular (6/77). 459-Archie's Jokes (8/77)-Shows 8/76 in error. 460-Betty & Veronica Summer Fun (9/77). 461-World of Archie (9/77). 462-Betty & Veronica Spectacular (10/77). 463-World of Jughead (10/77). 464-Archie's Christmas Stocking (12/77). 465-Betty & Veronica Christmas Spectacular (12/77). 466-Archie's Christmas Love-In (1/78). 467-Sabrina's Christmas Magic (1/78). 468-World of Archie (2/78). 469-World of Jughead (2/78). 470-Betty & Veronica Spectacular(6/78). 471-Archie's Jokes (8/78). 472-Betty & Veronica Summer Fun (9/78). 473-World of Archie (9/78). 474-Betty & Veronica Spectacular (10/78). 475-World of Jughead (10/78). 476-Archie's Christmas Stocking (12/78). 477-Betty & Veronica Christmas Spectacular (12/78). 478-Archie's Christmas Love-In (1/79). 479-Sabrina Christmas Magic (1/79). 480-The World of Archie (3/79). 481-World of Jughead (4/79). 482-Betty & Veronica Spectacular (6/79). 483-Archie's Jokes (8/79). 484-Betty & Veronica Summer Fun(9/79). 485-The World of Archie (9/79). 486-Betty & Veronica Spectacular(10/79). 487-The World of Jughead (10/79). 488-Archie's Christmas Stocking (12/79). 489-Betty & Veronica Christmas Spectacular (1/80). 490-Archie's Christmas Love-in (1/80). 491-Sabrina's Christmas Magic (1/80).492-The World of Archie (2/80). 493-The World of Jughead (4/80). 494-Betty & Veronica Spectacular (6/80). 495-Archie's Jokes (8/80). 496-Betty & Veronica Summer Fun (9/80). 497-The World of Archie (9/80). 498-Betty & Veronica Spectacular (10/80). 499-The World of Jughead (10/80). 500-Archie's Christmas Stocking (12/80) each... 1.50

501-550: 501-Betty & Veronica Christmas Spectacular (12/80). 502-Archie's Christmas Love-in (1/81). 503-Sabrina Christmas Magic (1/81). 504-The World of Archie (3/81). 505-The World of Jughead (4/81). 506-Betty & Veronica Spectacular (6/81). 507-Archie's Jokes (8/81). 508-Betty & Veronica Summer Fun (9/81). 509-The World of Archie (9/81). 510-Betty & Vernonica Spectacular (9/81). 511-The World of Jughead (10/81). 512-Archie's Christmas Stocking (12/81). 513-Betty & Veronica Christmas Spectacular (12/81). 514-Archie's Christmas Love-in (1/82). 515-Sabrina's Christmas Magic (1/82). 516-The World of Archie (3/82). 517-The World of Jughead (4/82). 518-Betty & Veronica Spectacular (6/82). 519-Archie's Jokes (8/82). 520-Betty & Veronica Summer Fun (9/82). 521-The World of Archie (9/82). 522-Betty & Veronica Spectacular (10/82). 523-The World of Jughead (10/82). 524-Archie's Christmas Stocking (1/83). 525-Betty and Veronica Christmas Spectacular (1/83). 526-Betty and Veronica Spectacular (5/83). 527-Little Archie (8/83). 528-Josie and the Pussycats (8/83). 529-Betty and Veronica Summer Fun (8/83). 530-Betty and Veronica Spectacular (9/83). 531-The World of Jughead (9/83). 532-The World of Archie (10/83). 533-Space Pirates by Frank Bolling (10/83). 534-Little Archie (1/84). 535-Archie's Christmas Stocking (1/84). 536-Betty and Veronica Christmas Spectacular (1/84). 537-Betty and Veronica Spectacular (6/84). 538-Little Archie (8/84). 539-Betty and Veronica Summer Fun (8/84). 540-Josie and the Pussycats (8/84). 541-Betty and Veronica Spec-

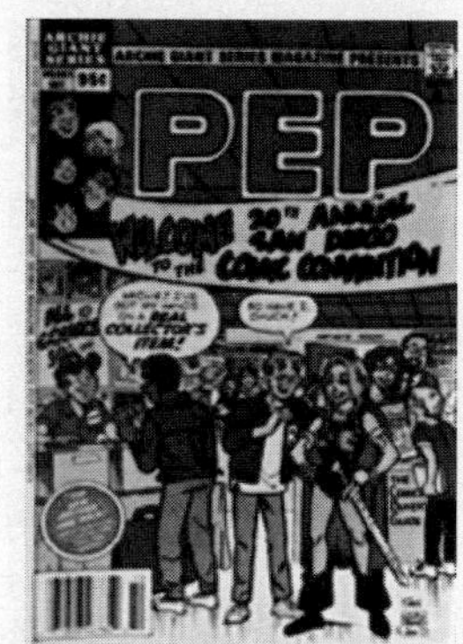

Archie Giant Series #601 © AP

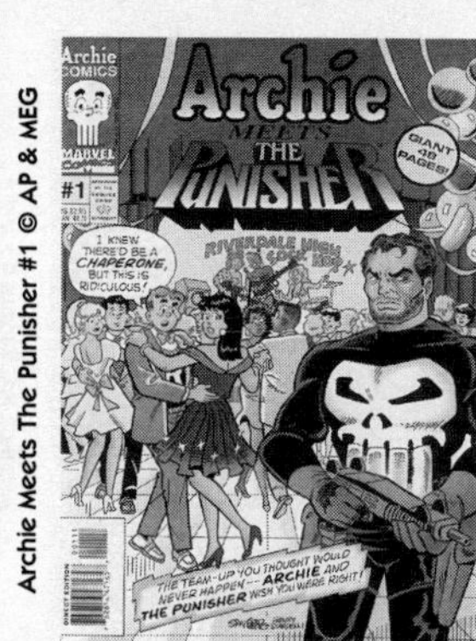

Archie Meets The Punisher #1 © AP & MEG

Archie's Girls Betty And Veronica #10 © AP

	GD25	FN65	NM94
tacular (9/84). 542-The World of Jughead (9/84). 543-The World of Archie (10/84). 544-Sabrina the Teen-Age Witch (10/84). 545-Little Archie (12/84). 546-Archie's Christmas Stocking (12/84). 547-Betty and Veronica Christmas Spectacular (12/84). 548-? 549-Little Archie. 550-Betty and Veronica Summer Fun each...			1.25
551-600: 551-Josie and the Pussycats. 552-Betty and Veronica Spectacular. 553-The World of Jughead. 554-The World of Archie. 555-Betty's Diary. 556-Little Archie (1/86). 557-Archie's Christmas Stocking (1/86). 558-Betty & Veronica Christmas Spectacular (1/86). 559-Betty & Veronica Spectacular. 560-Little Archie. 561-Betty & Veronica Summer Fun. 562-Josie and the Pussycats. 563-Betty & Veronica Spectacular. 564-World of Jughead. 565-World of Archie. 566-Little Archie. 567-Archie's Christmas Stocking. 568-Betty & Veronica Christmas Spectacular. 569-Betty & Veronica Spring Spectacular. 570-Little Archie. 571-Josie & the Pussycats. 572-Betty & Veronica Summer Fun. 573-Archie At Riverdale High. 574-World of Archie. 575-Betty & Veronica Spectacular. 576-Pep. 577-World of Jughead. 578-Archie And Me. 579-Archie's Christmas Stocking. 580-Betty and Veronica Christmas Spectacular. 581-Little Archie Christmas Special. 582-Betty & Veronica Spring Spectacular. 583-Little Archie. 584-Josie and the Pussycats. 585-Betty & Veronica Summer Fun. 586-Archie At Riverdale High. 587-The World of Archie (10/88); 1st app. Explorers of the Unknown. 588-Betty & Veronica Spectacular. 589-Pep (10/88). 590-The World of Jughead. 591-Archie & Me. 592-Archie's Christmas Stocking. 593-Betty & Veronica Christmas Spectacular. 594-Little Archie. 595-Betty & Veronica Spring Spectacular. 596-Little Archie. 597-Josie and the Pussycats. 598-Betty & Veronica Summer Fun. 599-The World of Archie (10/89); 2nd app. Explorers of the Unknown. 600-Betty and Veronica Spectacular each....			1.00
601-632: 601-Pep. 602-The World of Jughead. 603-Archie and Me. 604-Archie at Riverdale High. 605-Archie's Christmas Stocking. 606-Betty and Veronica Christmas Spectacular. 607-Little Archie. 608-Betty and Veronica Spectacular. 609-Little Archie. 610-Josie and the Pussycats. 611-Betty and Veronica Summer Fun. 612-The World of Archie. 613-Betty and Veronica Spectacular. 614-Pep (10/90). 615-Veronica's Summer Special. 616-Archie and Me. 617-Archie's Christmas Stocking. 618-Betty & Veronica Christmas Spectacular. 619-Little Archie. 620-Betty and Veronica Spectacular. 621-Betty and Veronica Summer Fun. 622-Josie & the Pussycats; not published. 623-Betty and Veronica Spectacular. 624-Pep Comics. 625-Veronica's Summer Special. 626-Archie and Me. 627-World of Archie. 628-Archie's Pals 'n' Gals Holiday Special. 629-Betty & Veronica Christmas Spectacular. 630-Archie's Christmas Stocking. 631-Archie's Pals 'n' Gals. 632-Betty & Veronica spectacular each....			1.00

ARCHIE MEETS THE PUNISHER (Same contents as The Punisher Meets Archie)
Aug, 1994 ($2.95, 52 pgs., one-shot)
Marvel Comics & Archie Comics Publications

	GD25	FN65	NM94
1-B. Lash-story, J. Buscema-a on Punisher, S. Goldberg-a on Archie		1.20	3.00

ARCHIE'S ACTIVITY COMICS DIGEST MAGAZINE
1985 - No. 4? (Annual, 128 pgs.; digest size)
Archie Enterprises

	GD25	FN65	NM94
1-4			1.50

ARCHIE'S CAR (Spire Christian)(Value: cover or less)

ARCHIE'S CHRISTMAS LOVE-IN (See Archie Giant Series Mag. No. 169, 181,192, 205, 218, 230, 242, 454, 466, 478, 490, 502, 514)

ARCHIE'S CHRISTMAS STOCKING (See Archie Giant Series Mag. No. 1-6,10, 15, 20, 25, 31, 137, 144, 150, 158, 167, 179, 190, 203, 216, 228, 240, 452, 464, 476, 488, 500, 512, 524, 535, 546, 557, 567, 579, 592, 605, 617, 630)

ARCHIE'S CHRISTMAS STOCKING
1993 ($2.00, 52 pgs.)
Archie Comics

	GD25	FN65	NM94
1-Calendar poster bound-in; Dan DeCarlo-c/a		.80	2.00

ARCHIE'S CLEAN SLATE (Spire Christian)(Value: cover or less)

ARCHIE'S DATE BOOK (Spire Christian)(Value: cover or less)

ARCHIE'S DOUBLE DIGEST QUARTERLY MAGAZINE
1981 - Present ($1.95/$2.75, 256pgs.) (A.D.D. Magazine No. 10 on)
Archie Comics

	GD25	FN65	NM94
1-30: 6-Katy Keene story. 29-Pureheart story		1.60	4.00
31-76		1.20	3.00

ARCHIE'S FAMILY ALBUM (Spire Christian)(Value: cover or less)

ARCHIE'S FESTIVAL (Spire Christian)(Value: cover or less)

ARCHIE'S GIRLS, BETTY AND VERONICA (Becomes Betty & Veronica)
1950 - No. 347, April, 1987 (Also see Veronica)
Archie Publications (Close-Up)

	GD25	FN65	NM94
1	114.00	343.00	800.00
2	57.00	171.00	400.00
3-5	34.00	103.00	240.00
6-10: 6-Dan DeCarlo's 1st Archie work; Betty's 1st ponytail. 10-Katy Keene app. (2 pgs.)	26.00	79.00	185.00
11-20: 11,13,14,17-19-Katy Keene app. 17-Last pre-code issue (3/55). 20-Debbie's Diary (2 pgs.)	19.00	57.00	130.00
21-30: 27,30-Katy Keene app.	13.00	40.00	90.00
31-50: 44-Elvis Presley 1 pg. photo & bio. 45-Fabian 1 pg. photo & bio. 46-Bobby Darin 1 pg. photo & bio	10.00	30.00	65.00
51-74: 73-Sci-fi-c	7.50	22.50	45.00
75-Betty & Veronica sell souls to Devil	11.50	34.00	80.00
76-99: Bobby Rydell 1 pg. illustrated bio	4.00	12.00	24.00
100	5.00	15.00	30.00
101-140: 118-Origin Superteen (see Betty & Me #3). 119-Last Superteen story	1.80	4.50	10.00
141-180		1.80	4.50
181-220		.70	2.00
221-347: 300-Anniversary issue			1.30
Annual 1 (1953)	71.00	215.00	500.00
Annual 2(1954)	33.00	100.00	230.00
Annual 3-5 ('55- '57)	25.00	75.00	175.00
Annual 6-8 ('58- '60)	16.00	48.00	110.00

ARCHIE SHOE-STORE GIVEAWAY
1944-49 (12-15 pgs. of games, puzzles, stories like Superman-Tim books, No nos. - came out monthly)
Archie Publications

	GD25	FN65	NM94
(1944-47)-issues	11.50	34.00	80.00
2/48-Peggy Lee photo-c	10.00	30.00	60.00
3/48-Marylee Robb photo-c	9.15	27.50	55.00
4/48-Gloria De Haven photo-c	9.15	27.50	55.00
5/48,6/48,7/48	9.15	27.50	55.00
8/48-Story on Shirley Temple	10.00	30.00	60.00
10/48-Archie as Wolf on cover	10.00	30.00	60.00
5/49-Kathleen Hughes photo-c	6.70	20.00	40.00
7/49	6.70	20.00	40.00
8/49-Archie photo-c from radio show	10.00	30.00	70.00
10/49-Gloria Mann photo-c from radio show	10.00	30.00	60.00
11/49,12/49	6.70	20.00	40.00

ARCHIE'S JOKEBOOK COMICS DIGEST ANNUAL (See Jokebook...)

ARCHIE'S JOKE BOOK MAGAZINE (See Joke Book ...)
1953 - No. 3, Sum, 1954; No. 15, Fall, 1954 - No. 288, 11/82
Archie Publications

	GD25	FN65	NM94
1953-One Shot (#1)	64.00	193.00	450.00
2	36.00	107.00	250.00
3 (no #4-14)	25.00	75.00	175.00
15-20: 15-Formerly Archie's Rival Reggie #14; last pre-code issue (Fall/54). 15-17-Katy Keene app.	17.00	52.00	120.00
21-30	11.00	32.00	75.00
31-40,42,43	7.50	22.50	45.00

Archie's Madhouse #1 © AP

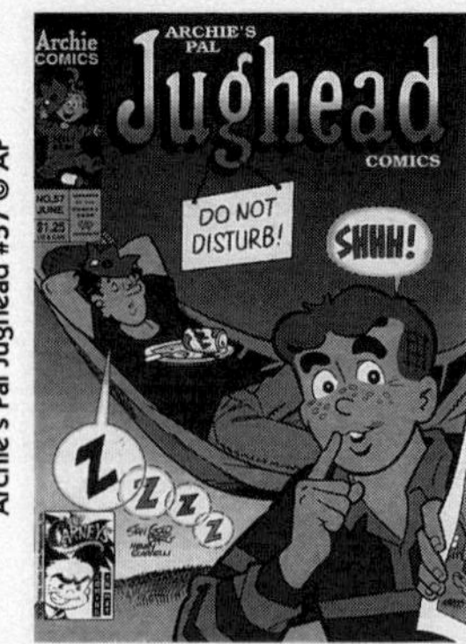

Archie's Pal Jughead #57 © AP

Archie's R/C Racers #3 © AP

	GD25	FN65	NM94
41-1st professional comic work by Neal Adams (9/59), 1 pg.	16.00	48.00	110.00
44-47-N. Adams-a in all, 1-3 pgs.	10.00	30.00	60.00
48-Four pgs. N. Adams-a	10.00	30.00	65.00
49-60 (1962)	3.60	9.00	18.00
61-80	2.00	5.00	10.00
81-100		1.80	4.50
101-140		.80	2.00
141-200			1.50
201-288			1.00
Drug Store Giveaway (No. 39 w/new-c)	3.60	9.00	18.00

ARCHIE'S JOKES (See Archie Giant Series Mag. No. 17, 22, 27, 33, 139, 146, 154, 163, 174, 186, 198, 211, 222, 235, 247, 459, 471, 483, 495, 519)

ARCHIE'S LOVE SCENE (Spire Christian)(Value: cover or less)

ARCHIE'S MADHOUSE (Madhouse Ma-ad No. 67 on)
Sept, 1959 - No. 66, Feb, 1969
Archie Publications

	GD25	FN65	NM94
1-Archie begins	25.00	75.00	175.00
2	12.00	36.00	85.00
3-5	9.15	27.50	55.00
6-10	6.35	19.00	38.00
11-17 (Last w/regular characters)	4.35	13.00	26.00
18-21,23-30 (New format): 25-1st app. Captain Sprocket (4/63)	2.00	5.00	10.00
22-1st app. Sabrina, the Teen-age Witch (10/62)	8.35	25.00	50.00
31-40: 34-Bordered-c begin. 35-Beatles cameo	1.00	2.50	5.00
41-66: 43-Mighty Crusaders cameo. 44-Swipes Mad #4 (Super-Duperman) in "Bird Monsters From Outer Space"			1.50
Annual 1 (1962-63)	8.35	25.00	50.00
Annual 2 (1964)	4.20	12.50	25.00
Annual 3 (1965)-Origin Sabrina the Teen-Age Witch	2.80	7.00	14.00
Annual 4-6('66-69)(Becomes Madhouse Ma-ad Annual #7 on)	1.80	4.50	9.00

NOTE: *Cover title to 61-65 is "Madhouse" and to 66 is "Madhouse Ma-ad Jokes".*

ARCHIE'S MECHANICS
Sept, 1954 - No. 3, 1955
Archie Publications

	GD25	FN65	NM94
1-(15¢; 52 pgs.)	75.00	225.00	525.00
2-(10¢)-Last pre-code issue	44.00	133.00	310.00
3-(10¢)	38.00	114.00	265.00

ARCHIE'S ONE WAY (Spire Christian)(Value: cover or less)

ARCHIE'S PAL, JUGHEAD (Jughead No. 122 on)
1949 - No. 126, Nov, 1965
Archie Publications

	GD25	FN65	NM94
1 (1949)-1st app. Moose (see Pep #33)	93.00	280.00	650.00
2 (1950)	46.00	139.00	325.00
3-5	30.00	90.00	210.00
6-10: 7-Suzie app.	19.00	57.00	130.00
11-20	13.00	40.00	90.00
21-30: 23-25,28-30-Katy Keene app. 28-Debbie's Diary app.	10.00	30.00	60.00
31-50	5.85	17.50	35.00
51-70	4.00	11.00	22.00
71-100	2.40	6.00	12.00
101-126	1.40	3.50	7.00
Annual 1 (1953, 25¢)	46.00	139.00	325.00
Annual 2 (1954, 25¢)-Last pre-code issue	29.00	86.00	200.00
Annual 3-5 (1955-57, 25¢)	20.00	60.00	140.00
Annual 6-8 (1958-60, 25¢)	13.00	40.00	90.00

ARCHIE'S PAL JUGHEAD COMICS (Formerly Jughead #1-45)
No. 46, June, 1993 - Present ($1.25)
Archie Comic Publications

	GD25	FN65	NM94
46-67		.65	1.25

ARCHIE'S PALS 'N' GALS (Also see Archie Giant Series Magazine #628)
1952-53 - No. 6, 1957-58; No. 7, 1958 - No. 224, Sept, 1991
Archie Publications

	GD25	FN65	NM94
1-(116 pgs., 25¢)	61.00	182.00	425.00
2(Annual)('54, 25¢)	32.00	96.00	225.00
3-5(Annual, '55-57, 25¢): 3-Last pre-code issue	23.00	69.00	160.00
6-10('58-'60)	12.00	36.00	85.00
11-20: 12-Harry Belafonte 2 pg. photo & bio	6.70	20.00	40.00
21-28,30-40	4.00	10.00	20.00
29-Beatles satire	5.35	16.00	32.00
41-60	1.60	4.00	8.00
61-80		1.60	4.00
81-110		.80	2.00
111-224: Later issues $1.00 cover. 197-G. Colan-a			1.00

ARCHIE'S PALS 'N' GALS DOUBLE DIGEST MAGAZINE
Nov, 1992 - Present ($2.50-2.75)
Archie Comic Publications

	GD25	FN65	NM94
1-3: 1-Capt. Hero story; Pureheart app. 2-Superduck story; Little Jinx in all		1.00	2.50
4-10-($2.75)		1.10	2.75

ARCHIE'S PARABLES
1973, 1975 (36 pgs., 39-49¢)
Spire Christian Comics (Fleming H. Revell Co.)

	GD25	FN65	NM94
nn-By Al Hartley			1.00

ARCHIE'S R/C RACERS
Sept, 1989 - No. 10, Mar, 1991 (#1,2: 95¢, #3-10: $1.00)
Archie Comics

	GD25	FN65	NM94
1-10: Radio control cars			1.00

ARCHIE'S RIVAL REGGIE (Reggie & Archie's Joke Book #15 on)
1950 - No. 14, Aug, 1954
Archie Publications

	GD25	FN65	NM94
1-Reggie 1st app. in Jackpot Comics #5	60.00	180.00	420.00
2	30.00	90.00	210.00
3-5	22.00	65.00	150.00
6-10	15.00	45.00	105.00
11-14: Katy Keene in No. 10-14, 1-2 pgs.	11.00	32.00	75.00

ARCHIE'S RIVERDALE HIGH (See Riverdale High)

ARCHIE'S ROLLER COASTER (Spire Christian)(Value: cover or less)

ARCHIE'S SOMETHING ELSE (Spire Christian)(Value: cover or less)

ARCHIE'S SONSHINE (Spire Christian)(Value: cover or less)

ARCHIE'S SPORTS SCENE (Spire Christian)(Value: cover or less)

ARCHIE'S STORY & GAME COMICS DIGEST MAGAZINE
Nov, 1986 - Present (Digest size, $1.25, $1.35, $1.50, 128 pgs.)
Archie Enterprises

	GD25	FN65	NM94
1-31		.80	2.00

ARCHIE'S SUPER HERO SPECIAL (See Archie Giant Series Mag. No. 142)

ARCHIE'S SUPER HERO SPECIAL (...Comics Digest Mag. 2)
Jan, 1979 - No. 2, Aug, 1979 (148 pgs., 95¢)
Archie Publications (Red Circle)

	GD25	FN65	NM94
1-Simon & Kirby r-/Double Life of Pvt. Strong #1,2; Black Hood, The Fly, Jaguar, The Web app.			1.00
2-Contains contents to the never published Black Hood #1; origin Black Hood; N. Adams, Wood, McWilliams, Morrow, S&K-a(r); N. Adams-c. The Shield, The Fly, Jaguar, Hangman, Steel Sterling, The Web, The Fox-r			1.00

ARCHIE'S SUPER TEENS
1994 - Present ($2.00, 52 pgs.)
Archie Comic Publications, Inc.

	GD25	FN65	NM94
1-Staton/Esposito-c/a; pull-out poster		.80	2.00

Archie 3000 #9 © AP

Armorines #9 © Voyager Comm.

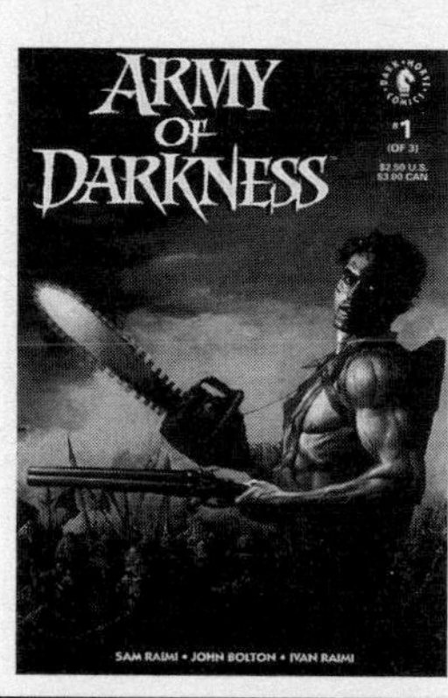

Army Of Darkness #1 © DH

ARCHIE'S TV LAUGH-OUT
Dec, 1969 - No. 106, April, 1986
Archie Publications

	GD25	FN65	NM94
1	4.00	12.00	28.00
2	1.65	4.00	10.00
3-5	1.00	2.00	5.00
6-10		.80	2.00
11-20			1.50
21-106			1.00

ARCHIE'S WORLD (Spire Christian)(Value: cover or less)

ARCHIE 3000
May, 1989 - No. 16, July, 1991 (75 & 95¢, #6-15: $1.00)
Archie Comics

	GD25	FN65	NM94
1-16: 6-X-Mas-c			1.00

ARCOMICS PREMIERE
July, 1993 ($2.95, color)
Arcomics

	GD25	FN65	NM94
1-1st linticular-c on a comic (flicker-c)		1.20	3.00

AREA 88 (Eclipse)(Value: cover or less)

ARENA (Alchemy)(Value: cover or less)

ARIANE AND BLUEBEARD (See Night Music #8)

ARIEL & SEBASTIAN (See Cartoon Tales & The Little Mermaid)

ARION, LORD OF ATLANTIS (Also see Warlord #55)
Nov, 1982 - No. 35, Sept, 1985
DC Comics

	GD25	FN65	NM94
1-35: 1-Story cont'd from Warlord #62			1.00
Special #1 (11/85)			1.00

ARION THE IMMORTAL
July, 1992 - No. 6, Dec, 1992 ($1.50, limited series)
DC Comics

	GD25	FN65	NM94
1-6: 4-Gustovich-a(i)			1.50

ARISTOCATS (See Movie Comics & Walt Disney Showcase No. 16)

ARISTOKITTENS, THE (...Meet Jiminy Cricket No. 1)(Disney)
Oct, 1971 - No. 9, Oct, 1975 (No. 6: 52 pgs.)
Gold Key

	GD25	FN65	NM94
1	3.70	11.00	26.00
2-9	2.10	6.50	15.00

ARIZONA KID, THE (Also see The Comics & Wild Western)
March, 1951 - No. 6, Jan, 1952
Marvel/Atlas Comics(CSI)

	GD25	FN65	NM94
1	14.00	43.00	100.00
2-4: 2-Heath-a(3)	8.35	25.00	50.00
5,6	7.50	22.50	45.00

NOTE: ***Heath** a-1-3; c-1-3. **Maneely** c-4-6. **Morisi** a-4-6. **Sinnott** a-6.*

ARK, THE (See The Crusaders)

ARKHAM ASYLUM (Also see Animal Man #24, Black Orchid #2 & The Saga of Swamp Thing #52, 53)
1989 ($24.95, hard-c, mature readers, 132 pgs.)
DC Comics

	GD25	FN65	NM94
nn-Joker-c/story; Grant Morrison scripts	4.30	13.00	30.00
nn-Soft cover reprint ($14.95)	2.15	6.50	15.00

ARMAGEDDON: ALIEN AGENDA
Nov, 1991 - No. 4, Feb, 1992 ($1.00, mini-series)
DC Comics

	GD25	FN65	NM94
1-4			1.00

ARMAGEDDON FACTOR, THE (AC)(Value: cover or less)

ARMAGEDDON: INFERNO
Apr, 1992 - No. 4, July, 1992 ($1.00, mini-series)
DC Comics

	GD25	FN65	NM94
1-4: Many DC heroes app. 3-A. Adams/Austin-a			1.00

ARMAGEDDON 2001
May, 1991 - No. 2, Oct, 1991 ($2.00, squarebound, 68 pgs.)
DC Comics

	GD25	FN65	NM94
1-Features many DC heroes; intro Waverider		1.10	2.75
1-2nd & 3rd printings; 3rd has silver ink-c		.70	1.75
2		1.00	2.50

ARMOR (Continuity Comics)(Value: cover or less)

ARMOR DEATHWATCH (Continuity Comics)(Value: cover or less)

ARMORINES (See X-O Manowar #25)
June, 1994 - Present ($2.25, color)
Valiant Comics

	GD25	FN65	NM94
1-9: 7-Wraparound-c		.90	2.25

ARMY AND NAVY COMICS (Supersnipe No. 6 on)
May, 1941 - No. 5, July, 1942
Street & Smith Publications

	GD25	FN65	NM94
1-Cap Fury & Nick Carter	36.00	107.00	250.00
2-Cap Fury & Nick Carter	19.00	58.00	135.00
3,4	13.50	41.00	95.00
5-Supersnipe app.; see Shadow V2#3 for 1st app.; Story of Douglas MacArthur; George Marcoux-c/a	35.00	105.00	245.00

ARMY ATTACK
July, 1964 - No. 4, Feb, 1965; V2#38, July, 1965 - No. 47, Feb, 1967
Charlton Comics

	GD25	FN65	NM94
V1#1	3.60	9.00	18.00
2-4(2/65)	2.00	5.00	10.00
V2#38(7/65)-47 (formerly U.S. Air Force #1-37)	2.00	5.00	10.00

NOTE: ***Glanzman** a-1-3. **Montes/Bache** a-44.*

ARMY AT WAR (Also see Our Army at War & Cancelled Comic Cavalcade)
Oct-Nov, 1978
DC Comics

	GD25	FN65	NM94
1-Kubert-c		.80	2.00

ARMY OF DARKNESS
Nov, 1992 - No. 2, Dec, 1992; No. 3, Oct, 1993 ($2.50, color, mini-series)
Dark Horse Comics

	GD25	FN65	NM94
1-3-Based on movie; Bolton painted-c/a		1.00	2.50

ARMY SURPLUS KOMIKZ FEATURING CUTEY BUNNY
1982 - No. 5, 1985 ($1.50, B&W)
Army Surplus Komikz/Eclipse Comics No. 5

	GD25	FN65	NM94
1-Cutey Bunny begins		.80	2.00
2-5: 5-JLA/X-Men/Batman parody			1.50

ARMY WAR HEROES (Also see Iron Corporal)
Dec, 1963 - No. 38, June, 1970
Charlton Comics

	GD25	FN65	NM94
1	3.60	9.00	18.00
2-38: 22-Origin & 1st app. Iron Corporal series by Glanzman. 24-Intro. Archer & Corp. Jack series	1.60	4.00	8.00
Modern Comics Reprint 36 ('78)		.80	2.00

NOTE: ***Montes/Bache** a-1, 16, 17, 21, 23-25, 27-30.*

AROUND THE BLOCK WITH DUNC & LOO (See Dunc and Loo)

AROUND THE WORLD IN 80 DAYS (See Four Color Comics #784 and A Golden Picture Classic)

AROUND THE WORLD UNDER THE SEA (See Movie Classics)

AROUND THE WORLD WITH ARCHIE (See Archie Giant Series Mag. #29, 35, 141)

AROUND THE WORLD WITH HUCKLEBERRY & HIS FRIENDS (See Dell Giant No. 44)

ARRGH! (Satire)
Dec, 1974 - No. 5, Sept, 1975 (25¢)

Art of Zen #1 © Entity

Astonishing #59 © MEG

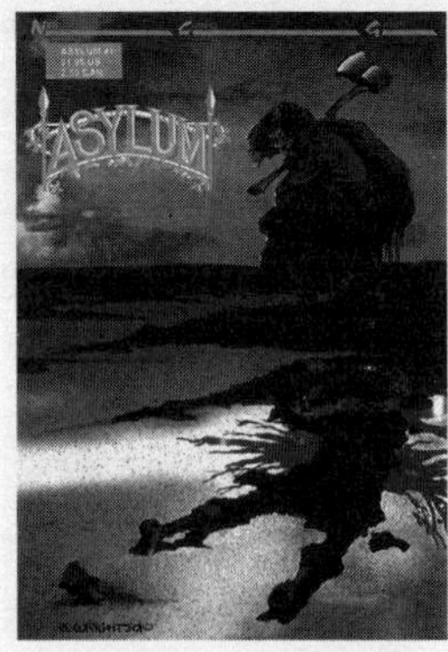

Asylum #1 © Millennium Pub.

GD25 FN65 NM94

Marvel Comics Group
1 1.30 3.25
2-5 .80 2.00
NOTE ***Alcala*** *a-2; c-3.* ***Everett*** *a-1r, 2r.* ***Maneely*** *a-4r.* ***Sekowsky*** *a-1p.* ***Sutton*** *a-1, 2.*

ARROW, THE (See Funny Pages)
Oct, 1940 - No. 2, Nov, 1940; No. 3, Oct, 1941
Centaur Publications
1-The Arrow begins(r/Funny Pages) 150.00 450.00 1050.00
2,3: 2-Tippy Taylor serial continues from Amazing Mystery Funnies #24. 3-Origin Dash Dartwell, the Human Meteor; origin The Rainbow-r; bondage-c 82.00 246.00 575.00
NOTE: ***Gustavson*** *a-1, 2; c-3.*

ARROWHEAD (See Black Rider and Wild Western)
April, 1954 - No. 4, Nov, 1954
Atlas Comics (CPS)
1-Arrowhead & his horse Eagle begin 10.00 30.00 70.00
2-4: 4-Forte-a 7.50 22.50 45.00
NOTE: ***Heath*** *c-3.* ***Jack Katz*** *a-3.* ***Maneely*** *c-2.* ***Pakula*** *a-2.* ***Sinnott*** *a-1-4; c-1.*

ART OF ZEN INTERGALACTIC NINJA, THE
1994 - No. 2, 1994 ($2.95, color)
Entity Comics
1,2 1.20 3.00

ASSASSINS, INC. (Silverline)(Value: cover or less)

ASTONISHING (Formerly Marvel Boy No. 1, 2)
No. 3, April, 1951 - No. 63, Aug, 1957
Marvel/Atlas Comics(20CC)
3-Marvel Boy continues; 3-5-Marvel Boy-c 61.00 182.00 425.00
4-6-Last Marvel Boy; 4-Stan Lee app. 41.00 122.00 285.00
7-10: 7-Maneely s/f story. 10-Sinnott s/f story 14.00 43.00 100.00
11,12,15,17,20 13.00 40.00 90.00
13,14,16,19-Krigstein-a 14.00 43.00 100.00
18-Jack The Ripper story 14.00 43.00 100.00
21,22,24 11.00 32.00 75.00
23-E.C. swipe "The Hole In The Wall" from Vault Of Horror #16 12.00 36.00 85.00
25-Crandall-a 11.00 32.00 75.00
26-28 10.00 30.00 65.00
29-Decapitation-c 11.00 32.00 75.00
30-Tentacled eyeball story 12.00 36.00 85.00
31-37-Last pre-code issue 9.15 27.50 55.00
38-43,46,48-52,56,58,59,61 7.50 22.50 45.00
44-Crandall swipe/Weird Fantasy #22 9.15 27.50 55.00
45,47-Krigstein-a 9.15 27.50 55.00
53,54: 53-Ditko-a. 54-Torres-a 8.35 25.00 50.00
55-Crandall, Torres-a 9.15 27.50 55.00
57-Williamson/Krenkel-a (4 pgs.) 9.15 27.50 55.00
60-Williamson/Mayo-a (4 pgs.) 9.15 27.50 55.00
62-Torres, Powell-a 6.70 20.00 40.00
63-Last issue; Woodbridge-a 6.70 20.00 40.00
NOTE: ***Ayers*** *a-16.* ***Berg*** *a-36, 53, 56.* ***Cameron*** *a-50.* ***Gene Colan*** *a-12, 20, 29, 56.* ***Ditko*** *a-53.* ***Drucker*** *a-41, 62.* ***Everett*** *a-3-6(3), 6, 10, 12, 37, 47, 48, 58; c-3-5, 13,15, 16, 18, 29, 47, 49, 51, 53-55, 57, 59-63.* ***Fass*** *a-11, 34.* ***Forte*** *a-53, 58, 60.* ***Fuje*** *a-11.* ***Heath*** *a-8, 29; c-8, 9, 19, 22, 25, 26.* ***Kirby*** *a-56.* ***Lawrence*** *a-28, 37, 38, 42.* ***Maneely*** *a-7(2); c-7, 31, 33, 34, 56.* ***Moldoff*** *a-33.* ***Morisi*** *a-10, 60.* ***Morrow*** *a-52, 61.* ***Orlando*** *a-47, 58, 61.* ***Pakula*** *a-10.* ***Powell*** *a-43, 44, 48.* ***Ravielli*** *a-28.* ***Reinman*** *a-32, 34, 38.* ***Robinson*** *a-20.* ***J. Romita*** *a-7, 18, 24, 43, 57,61.* ***Roussos*** *a-55.* ***Sale*** *a-28, 38, 59; c-32.* ***Sekowsky*** *a-13.* ***Severin*** *c-46.* ***Shores*** *a-16, 60.* ***Sinnott*** *a-11, 30.* ***Whitney*** *a-13.* ***Ed Win*** *a-20. Canadian reprints exist.*

ASTONISHING TALES (See Ka-Zar)
Aug, 1970 - No. 36, July, 1976 (#1-7: 15¢; #8: 25¢)
Marvel Comics Group
1-Ka-Zar (by Kirby(p) #1,2; by B. Smith #3-6) & Dr. Doom (by Wood #1-4; by Tuska #5,6; by Colan #7,8) double feature begins; Kraven the Hunter-c/story; Nixon cameo 3.40 10.00 24.00
2-Kraven the Hunter-c/story; Kirby, Wood-a 1.60 4.70 11.00

GD25 FN65 NM94

3-6: B. Smith-p; Wood-a-#3,4. 5,6-Red Skull 2-part story 2.30 6.90 16.00
7,8: 8-(25¢, 52 pgs.)-Last Dr. Doom 1.60 4.70 11.00
9-Lorna-r/Lorna #14 1.40 3.50
10-B. Smith/Sal Buscema-a 1.20 2.90 7.00
11-Origin Ka-Zar & Zabu 1.00 2.50 6.00
12-Man-Thing by Neal Adams (apps. #13 also) 1.00 2.50 6.00
13-24: 14-Jann of the Jungle-r (1950s). 19-Starlin-a(p). 20-Last Ka-Zar. 21-It! the Living Colossus begins, ends #24 .90 2.25
25-1st app. Deathlok the Demolisher; full length stories begin, end #36; Perez's 1st work, 2 pgs. (8/74) 5.70 17.00 40.00
26-28,30 1.70 4.20 10.00
29-r/origin/1st app. Guardians of the Galaxy from Marvel Super-Heroes #18 plus-c w/4 pgs. omitted; no Deathlok story 2.10 6.40 15.00
31-36: 31-Watcher-r/Silver Surfer #3 1.70 4.20 10.00
NOTE: ***Buckler*** *a-13i, 16p, 25, 26p, 27p, 28, 29p-36p; c-13, 25p, 26-30, 32-35p, 36.* ***John Buscema*** *a-9, 12p-14p, 16p; c-4-6p, 12p.* ***Colan*** *a-7p, 8p.* ***Ditko*** *a-21r.* ***Everett*** *a-6i.* ***G. Kane*** *a-11p, 15p; c-9, 10p, 11p, 14, 15p, 21p.* ***McWilliams*** *a-30i.* ***Starlin*** *a-19p; c-16p.* ***Sutton & Trimpe*** *a-8.* ***Tuska*** *a-5p, 6p, 8p.* ***Wood*** *a-1-4.* ***Wrightson*** *c-31i.*

ASTRO BOY (TV) (See March of Comics #285 & The Original...)
August, 1965 (12¢)
Gold Key
1(10151-508)-Scarce;1st app. Astro Boy in comics 38.00 1147.00 265.00

ASTRO COMICS
1969 - 1979 (Giveaway)
American Airlines (Harvey)
nn-Harvey's Casper, Spooky, Hot Stuff, Stumbo the Giant, Little Audrey, Little Lotta, & Richie Rich reprints 1.60 4.00

ASYLUM
1993 - Present ($2.50, color)
Millennium Publications
1-4: 1-Bolton-c/a; Russell 2-pg. illos 1.00 2.50

ATARI FORCE
1982 - No. 5, 1983; Jan, 1984 - No. 20, Aug, 1985 (Mando paper)
DC Comics
1-3 (1982, color, 52 pgs., 5X7")-Given away with Atari games 1.00
4,5 (1982, 1983, color, 52 pgs.)-Given away with Atari games (scarcer) 1.00
1-20: 1-(1/84)-1st app. Tempest, Packrat, Babe, Morphea, & Dart 1.00
Special 1 (4/86) 1.00
NOTE: ***Byrne*** *c-Special 1i.* ***Giffen*** *a-12p, 13i.* ***Rogers*** *a-18p, Special 1p.*

A-TEAM, THE (TV)
March, 1984 - No. 3, May, 1984
Marvel Comics Group
1-3 1.00

ATLANTIS CHRONICLES, THE
Mar, 1990 - No. 7, Sept, 1990 ($2.95, mini-series, 52 pgs.)
DC Comics
1-7: 7-True origin Aquaman; nudity panels 1.20 3.00

ATLANTIS, THE LOST CONTINENT (See 4-Color No. 1188)

ATLAS (See 1st Issue Special)

ATLAS
Feb, 1994 - No. 4, 1994 ($2.50, color, mini-series)
Dark Horse Comics
1-4 1.00 2.50

ATOM, THE (See Action #425, All-American #19, Brave & the Bold, D.C. Special Series #1, Detective, Flash Comics #80, Power Of The Atom, Showcase #34, Super Friends, Sword of The Atom & World's Finest)

ATOM, THE (...& the Hawkman No. 39 on)
June-July, 1962 - No. 38, Aug-Sept, 1968
National Periodical Publ. GD25 FN65 VF82 NM94

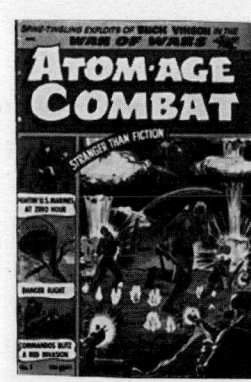

Atom-Age Combat #1 © Fago

Atoman #2 © Spark

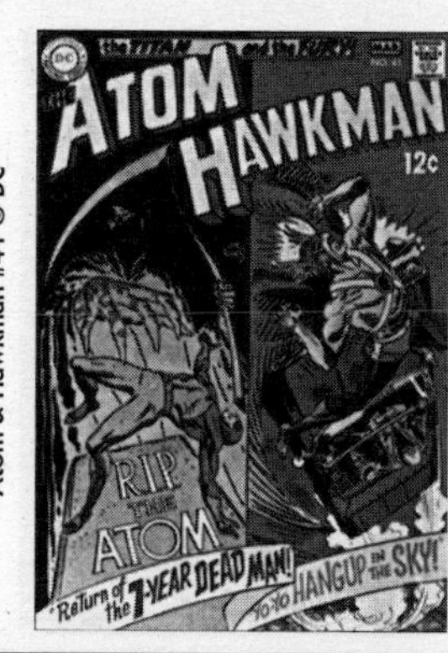

Atom & Hawkman #41 © DC

GD25 FN65 NM94

Showcase #34 (9-10/61)-Origin & 1st app. Silver Age Atom by Kane & Anderson 117.00 350.00 700.00 1050.00

	GD25	FN65	NM94
Showcase #35 (11-12/61)-2nd app. Atom by Gil Kane; last 10¢ issue	96.00	289.00	675.00
Showcase #36 (1-2/62)-3rd app. Atom by Kane	71.00	214.00	500.00
1-(6-7/62)-Intro Plant-Master; 1st app. Maya	96.00	289.00	675.00
2	37.00	111.00	260.00
3-1st Time Pool story; 1st app. Chronos (origin)	24.00	73.00	170.00
4,5: 4-Snapper Carr x-over	16.00	49.00	115.00
6,8-10: 8-Justice League, Dr. Light app.	13.00	39.00	90.00
7-Hawkman x-over (6-7/63; 1st Atom & Hawkman team-up); 1st app. Hawkman since Brave & the Bold tryouts	30.00	90.00	210.00
11-15: 13-Chronos-c/story	9.00	26.00	60.00
16-20: 19-Zatanna x-over	6.30	19.00	44.00
21-28,30: 28-Chronos-c/story	4.70	14.00	33.00
29-1st solo Golden Age Atom x-over in S.A.	14.00	43.00	100.00
31-35,37,38: 31-Hawkman x-over. 37-Intro. Major Mynah; Hawkman cameo	4.00	12.00	28.00
36-G.A. Atom x-over	5.70	17.00	40.00
Special 1 (1993, $2.50, 68 pgs.)		1.00	2.50

NOTE: ***Anderson** a-1-11i, 13i; c-inks-1-25, 31-35, 37. **Sid Greene** a-8i-38i. **Gil Kane** a-1p-38p; c-1p-28p, 29, 33p, 34. Time Pool stories also in 6, 9,12, 17, 21, 27, 35.*

ATOM AGE (See Classics Illustrated Special Issue)

ATOM-AGE COMBAT
June, 1952 - No. 5, April, 1953; Feb, 1958
St. John Publishing Co.

	GD25	FN65	NM94
1-Buck Vinson in all	31.00	94.00	220.00
2-Flying saucer story	17.00	52.00	120.00
3,5: 3-Mayo-a (6 pgs.). 5-Flying saucer-c/story	13.00	40.00	90.00
4 (Scarce)	16.50	50.00	115.00
1(2/58-St. John)	11.00	32.00	75.00

ATOM-AGE COMBAT
Nov, 1958 - No. 3, March, 1959
Fago Magazines

	GD25	FN65	NM94
1-All have Dick Ayers-c/a	15.00	45.00	105.00
2,3: 2-A-Bomb explosion-c	10.00	30.00	70.00

ATOMAN
Feb, 1946 - No. 2, April, 1946
Spark Publications

	GD25	FN65	NM94
1-Origin & 1st app. Atoman; Robinson/Meskin-a; Kidcrusaders, Wild Bill Hickok, Marvin the Great app.	36.00	107.00	250.00
2-Robinson/Meskin-a; Robinson c-1,2	27.00	81.00	190.00

ATOM & HAWKMAN, THE (Formerly The Atom)
No. 39, Oct-Nov, 1968 - No. 45, Oct-Nov, 1969
National Periodical Publications

	GD25	FN65	NM94
39-45: 43-Last 12¢ issue; 1st app. Gentleman Ghost, origin in #44	4.00	12.00	28.00

NOTE: ***M. Anderson** a-39, 40i, 41i, 43, 44. **Sid Greene** a-40i-45i. **Kubert** a-40p, 41p; c-39-45.*

ATOM ANT (TV) (See Golden Comics Digest #2)
January, 1966 (Hanna-Barbera, 12¢)
Gold Key

	GD25	FN65	NM94
1(10170-601)	17.00	51.00	170.00

ATOMIC AGE
Nov, 1990 - No. 4, Feb, 1991 ($4.50, mini-series, squarebound, 52 pgs.)
Epic Comics (Marvel)

	GD25	FN65	NM94
1-4: Williamson-a(i)		1.80	4.50

ATOMIC ATTACK (True War Stories; formerly Attack, first series)
No. 5, Jan, 1953 - No. 8, Oct, 1953
Youthful Magazines

	GD25	FN65	NM94
5-Atomic bomb-c	21.00	63.00	145.00
6-8	13.00	40.00	90.00

ATOMIC BOMB
1945 (36 pgs.)
Jay Burtis Publications

	GD25	FN65	NM94
1-Airmale & Stampy	32.00	96.00	225.00

ATOMIC BUNNY (Formerly Atomic Rabbit)
No. 12, Aug, 1958 - No. 19, Dec, 1959
Charlton Comics

	GD25	FN65	NM94
12	10.00	30.00	60.00
13-19	5.35	16.00	32.00

ATOMIC COMICS
Jan, 1946 - No. 4, 1946 (Reprints)
Daniels Publications (Canadian)

	GD25	FN65	NM94
1-Rocketman, Yankee Boy, Master Key; bondage-c	19.00	58.00	135.00
2-4 (Exist?)	10.00	30.00	70.00

ATOMIC COMICS
Jan, 1946 - No. 4, July-Aug, 1946 (#1-4 were printed without cover gloss)
Green Publishing Co.

	GD25	FN65	NM94
1-Radio Squad by Siegel & Shuster; Barry O'Neal app.; Fang Gow cover-r/ Detective Comics	86.00	257.00	600.00
2-Inspector Dayton; Kid Kane by Matt Baker; Lucky Wings, Congo King, Prop Powers (only app.) begin	40.00	120.00	280.00
3,4: 3-Zero Ghost Detective app.; Baker-a(2) each; 4-Baker-c	25.00	75.00	175.00

ATOMIC KNIGHTS (See Strange Adventures #117)

ATOMIC MOUSE (TV, Movies) (See Blue Bird, Funny Animals, Giant Comics Edition & Wotalife Comics)
3/53 - No. 54, 6/63; No. 1, 12/84; V2#10, 9/85 - No. 13, ?/86
Capitol Stories/Charlton Comics

	GD25	FN65	NM94
1-Origin & 1st app.; Al Fago-c/a in all?	16.50	50.00	115.00
2	9.15	27.50	55.00
3-10: 5-Timmy The Timid Ghost app.; see Zoo Funnies	6.70	20.00	40.00
11-13,16-25	4.00	11.00	22.00
14,15-Hoppy The Marvel Bunny app.	5.85	17.50	35.00
26-(68 pgs.)	7.50	22.50	45.00
27-40: 36,37-Atom The Cat app.	3.60	9.00	18.00
41-54	1.80	4.50	9.00
1 (1984)			1.00
V2#10 (10/85) -13-Fago-r. #12(1/86)			1.00

ATOMIC RABBIT (Atomic Bunny #12 on; see Giant Comics #3 & Wotalife)
August, 1955 - No. 11, March, 1958
Charlton Comics

	GD25	FN65	NM94
1-Origin & 1st app.; Al Fago-c/a in all?	16.00	48.00	110.00
2	8.35	25.00	50.00
3-10	5.85	17.50	35.00
11-(68 pgs.)	8.35	25.00	50.00

ATOMIC SPY CASES
Mar-Apr, 1950 (Painted-c)
Avon Periodicals

	GD25	FN65	NM94
1-No Wood-a; A-bomb blast panels; Fass-a	20.00	60.00	140.00

ATOMIC THUNDERBOLT, THE
Feb, 1946 (One shot)
Regor Company

	GD25	FN65	NM94
1-Intro. Atomic Thunderbolt & Mr. Murdo	34.00	103.00	240.00

ATOMIC WAR!
Nov, 1952 - No. 4, April, 1953
Ace Periodicals (Junior Books)

	GD25	FN65	NM94
1-Atomic bomb-c	50.00	150.00	350.00
2,3: 3-Atomic bomb-c	39.00	118.00	275.00
4-Used in **POP**, pg. 96 & illo.	39.00	118.00	275.00

Attack! #4 © CC

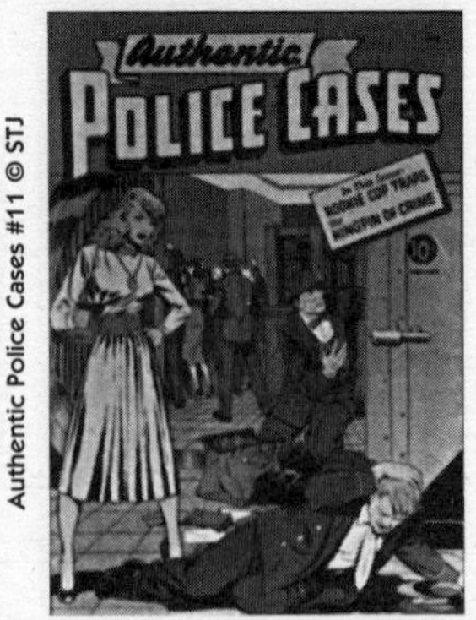

Authentic Police Cases #11 © STJ

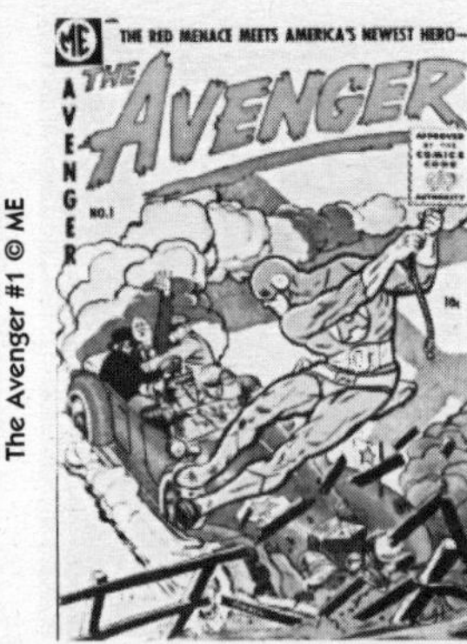

THE RED MENACE MEETS AMERICA'S NEWEST HERO—
THE AVENGER
AVENGER

The Avenger #1 © ME

GD25 FN65 NM94

ATOM SPECIAL
1993 ($2.50, 68 pgs.)
DC Comics

1 — 1.00 — 2.50

ATOM THE CAT (Formerly Tom Cat; see Giant Comics #3)
No. 9, Oct, 1957 - No. 17, Aug, 1959
Charlton Comics

9 — 5.85 — 17.50 — 35.00
10,13-17 — 4.00 — 10.00 — 20.00
11,12: 11(64pgs)-Atomic Mouse app. 12(100 pgs.) — 7.50 — 22.50 — 45.00

ATTACK
May, 1952 - No. 4, Nov, 1952; No. 5, Jan, 1953 - No. 5, Sept, 1953
Youthful Mag./Trojan No. 5 on

1-(1st series)-Extreme violence — 14.00 — 43.00 — 100.00
2,3: 3-Harrison-c/a; bondage, whipping — 8.35 — 25.00 — 50.00
4-Krenkel-a (7 pgs.); Harrison-a (becomes Atomic Attack #5 on) — 9.15 — 27.50 — 55.00
5-(#1, Trojan, 2nd series) — 7.50 — 22.50 — 45.00
6-8 (#2-4), 5 — 5.00 — 15.00 — 30.00

ATTACK
No. 54, 1958 - No. 60, Nov, 1959
Charlton Comics

54 (25¢, 100 pgs.) — 6.70 — 20.00 — 40.00
55-60 — 2.40 — 6.00 — 12.00

ATTACK!
1962 - No. 15, 3/75; No. 16, 8/79 - No. 48, 10/84
Charlton Comics

nn(#1)-('62) Special Edition — 4.00 — 11.00 — 22.00
2('63), 3(Fall, '64) — 2.40 — 6.00 — 12.00
V4#3(10/66), 4(10/67)-(Formerly Special War Series #2; becomes Attack At Sea V4#5) — 1.80 — 4.50 — 9.00
1(9/71) — 1.80 — 4.50
2-15(3/75): 4-American Eagle app. — .80 — 2.00
16(8/79) - 47 — 1.20
48(10/84)-Wood-r; S&K-c — 1.50
Modern Comics 13('78)-r — 1.00

ATTACK! (Spire Christian)(Value: cover or less)

ATTACK AT SEA (Formerly Attack!, 1967)
V4#5, October, 1968
Charlton Comics

V4#5 — 1.80 — 4.50 — 9.00

ATTACK ON PLANET MARS (See Strange Worlds #18)
1951
Avon Periodicals

nn-Infantino, Fawcette, Kubert & Wood-a; adaptation of Tarrano the Conqueror by Ray Cummings — 55.00 — 165.00 — 385.00

AUDREY & MELVIN (Formerly Little...)(See Little Audrey & Melvin)
No. 62, September, 1974
Harvey Publications

62 — .80 — 2.00

AUGIE DOGGIE (TV) (See Hanna-Barbera Band Wagon, Quick-Draw McGraw, Spotlight #2, Top Cat & Whitman Comic Books)
October, 1963 (Hanna-Barbera, 12¢)
Gold Key

1 — 11.00 — 32.00 — 75.00

AURORA COMIC SCENES INSTRUCTION BOOKLET
1974 (Slick paper, 8 pgs.)(6-1/4x9-3/4")(in full color)
(Included with superhero model kits)
Aurora Plastics Co.

181-140-Tarzan; Neal Adams-a — 1.60 — 4.00
182-140-Spider-Man. 183-140-Tonto(Gil Kane art). 184-140-Hulk. 185-140-Superman. 186-140-Superboy. 187-140-Batman. 188-140-The Lone Ranger(1974-by Gil Kane). 192-140-Captain America(1975). 193-140-Robin each.... — 1.20 — 3.00

GD25 FN65 NM94

AUTHENTIC POLICE CASES
2/48 - No. 6, 11/48; No. 7, 5/50 - No. 38, 3/55
St. John Publishing Co.

1-Hale the Magician by Tuska begins — 21.00 — 63.00 — 145.00
2-Lady Satan, Johnny Rebel app. — 13.50 — 41.00 — 95.00
3-Veiled Avenger app.; blood drainage story plus 2 Lucky Coyne stories; used in **SOTI**, illo. from Red Seal #16 — 27.00 — 80.00 — 185.00
4,5: 4-Masked Black Jack app. 5-Late 1930s Jack Cole-a(r); transvestism story — 13.50 — 41.00 — 95.00
6-Matt Baker-c; used in **SOTI**, illo- "An invitation to learning", r-in Fugitives From Justice #3; Jack Cole-a; also used by the N.Y. Legis. Comm. — 27.00 — 80.00 — 185.00
7,8,10-14: 7-Jack Cole-a; Matt Baker art begins #8, ends #?; Vic Flint in #10-14. 10-12-Baker-a(2 each) — 10.00 — 30.00 — 70.00
9-No Vic Flint — 10.00 — 30.00 — 60.00
15-Drug-c/story; Vic Flint app.; Baker-c — 10.00 — 30.00 — 70.00
16,18,20,21,23: Baker-a(i) — 6.70 — 20.00 — 40.00
17,19,22-Baker-c — 7.50 — 22.50 — 45.00
24-28 (All 100 pgs.): 26-Transvestism — 13.00 — 40.00 — 90.00
29,30 — 4.35 — 13.00 — 26.00
31,32,37-Baker-c: 37-r/#17 — 5.00 — 15.00 — 30.00
33-Transvestism; Baker-c — 5.85 — 17.50 — 35.00
34-Baker-c; r/#9 — 5.85 — 17.50 — 35.00
35-Baker-c/a(2); r/#10 — 5.35 — 16.00 — 32.00
36-r/#11; Vic Flint strip-r; Baker-c/a(2) unsigned — 5.85 — 17.50 — 35.00
38-Baker-c/a; r/#18 — 5.85 — 17.50 — 35.00

NOTE: ***Matt Baker** c-6-16, 17, 19, 22, 27, 29, 31-38; a-13, 16. Bondage c-1, 3.*

AUTUMN ADVENTURES (Walt Disney's...)
Autumn, 1990; No. 2, Aut, 1991 ($2.95, 68 pgs.)
Disney Comics

1-Donald Duck-r(2) by Barks, Pluto-r, & new-a — .60 — 1.50 — 3.00
2-D. Duck-r by Barks; new Super Goof story — .60 — 1.50 — 3.00

AVATAR
Feb, 1991 - No. 3, Apr, 1991 ($5.95, mini-series, 100 pgs.)
DC Comics

1-3: Based on TSR's Forgotten Realms — 1.20 — 3.00 — 6.00

AVENGER, THE (See A-1 Comics)
1955 - No. 4, Aug-Sept, 1955
Magazine Enterprises

1(A-1 #129)-Origin — 26.00 — 77.00 — 180.00
2(A-1 #131), 3(A-1 #133), 4(A-1 #138) — 17.00 — 52.00 — 120.00
IW Reprint #9('64)-Reprints #1 (new cover) — 3.20 — 8.00 — 16.00

NOTE: ***Powell** a-2-4; c-1-4.*

AVENGERS, THE (See Giant-Size..., Kree/Skrull War Starring..., Marvel Graphic Novel #27, Marvel Super Action, Marvel Super Heroes('66), Marvel Treasury Ed., Marvel Triple Action, Solo Avengers, Tales Of Suspense #49, West Coast Avengers & X-Men Vs....)

AVENGERS, THE (The Mighty Avengers on cover only #63-69)
Sept, 1963 - Present
Marvel Comics Group

	GD25	FN65	VF82	NM94
1-Origin & 1st app. The Avengers (Thor, Iron Man, Hulk, Ant-Man, Wasp); Loki app.	178.00	533.00	1154.00	1775.00

	GD25	FN65	NM94
2-Hulk leaves Avengers	68.00	204.00	475.00
3-1st Sub-Mariner x-over (outside the F.F.); Hulk & Sub-Mariner team-up & battle Avengers; Spider-Man cameo (1/64)	40.00	130.00	300.00
4-Revival of Captain America who joins the Avengers; 1st Silver Age app. of Captain America & Bucky (3/64)	103.00	308.00	1025.00
4-Reprint from the Golden Record Comic set	8.00	25.00	58.00
With Record (1966)	16.00	47.00	110.00

Avengers #16 © MEG

Avengers #223 © MEG

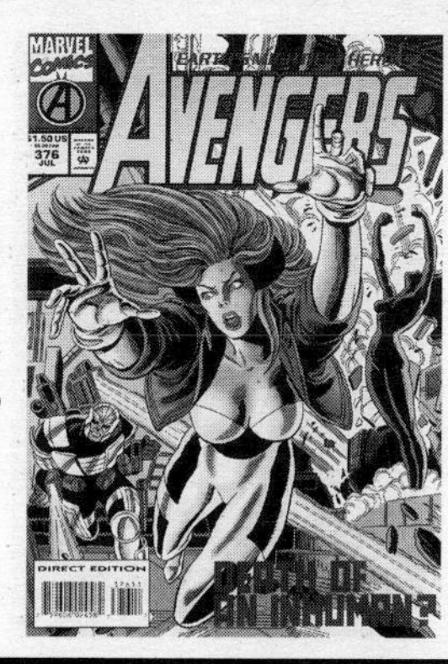

Avengers #376 © MEG

GD25 FN65 NM94

5-Hulk app. 27.00 81.00 190.00

6-8: 6-Intro/1st app. original Zemo & his Masters of Evil. 8-Intro Kang 21.00 62.00 145.00

9-Intro Wonder Man who dies in same story 22.00 66.00 155.00

10-Early Hercules app. 19.00 58.00 135.00

11-Spider-Man-c & x-over (12/64) 21.00 64.00 150.00

12-15: 15-Death of original Zemo 13.00 38.00 88.00

16-New Avengers line-up (Hawkeye, Quicksilver, Scarlet Witch join; Thor, Iron Man, Giant-Man, Wasp leave) 14.00 41.00 95.00

17-19: 19-Intro. Swordsman; origin Hawkeye 10.00 29.00 68.00

20-22: Wood inks 6.40 19.00 45.00

23-30: 25-Dr. Doom-c/story. 28-Giant-Man becomes Goliath (5/66) 4.60 14.00 32.00

31-40 3.20 8.00 23.00

41-52,54-56: 43,44-1st app. Red Guardian. 46-Ant-Man returns (re-intro, 11/67). 47-Magneto-c/story. 48-Origin/1st app. new Black Knight (1/68). 52-Black Panther joins; 1st app. The Grim Reaper. 54-1st app. new Masters of Evil 2.40 7.30 17.00

53-X-Men app. 3.00 9.00 22.00

57-1st app. S.A. Vision (10/68) 8.00 24.00 56.00

58-Origin The Vision 5.40 16.00 38.00

59-65: 59-Intro. Yellowjacket. 60-Wasp & Yellowjacket wed. 63-Goliath becomes Yellowjacket; Hawkeye becomes the new Goliath. 65-Last 12¢ issue 2.70 8.00 19.00

66,67: B. Smith-a 2.40 7.30 17.00

68-70: 70-Nighthawk on cover 2.00 5.00 12.00

71-1st app. The Invaders (12/69); 1st app. Nighthawk; Black Knight joins 2.70 8.00 19.00

72-82,84-86,88-91: 80-Intro. Red Wolf (9/70). 82-Daredevil app. 88-Written by Harlan Ellison 1.80 4.60 11.00

83-Intro. The Liberators (Wasp, Valkyrie, Scarlet Witch, Medusa & the Black Widow) 1.80 4.60 11.00

87-Origin The Black Panther 3.20 8.00 25.00

92-Last 15¢ issue; Neal Adams-c 1.90 6.00 13.00

93-(52 pgs.)-Neal Adams-c/a 6.30 19.00 44.00

94-96-Neal Adams-c/a 4.30 13.00 30.00

97-G.A. Capt. America, Sub-Mariner, Human Torch, Patriot, Vision, Blazing Skull, Fin, Angel, & new Capt. Marvel x-over 1.90 6.00 13.00

98-Goliath becomes Hawkeye; Smith c/a(i) 3.60 11.00 25.00

99-Smith-c, Smith/Sutton-a 3.60 11.00 25.00

100-(6/72)-Smith-c/a; featuring everyone who was an Avenger 10.00 29.00 68.00

101-106,108,109: 101-Harlan Ellison scripts 1.50 3.80 9.00

107-Starlin-a(p) 1.70 5.00 12.00

110,111-X-Men app. 2.40 7.30 17.00

112-1st app. Mantis 1.70 5.00 12.00

113-120: 116-118-Defenders/Silver Surfer app. 1.20 2.90 7.00

121-124,126-130: 123-Origin Mantis 1.20 2.90 7.00

125-Thanos-c & brief app. 2.30 6.90 16.00

131-140: 134,135-True origin Vision. 136-Ploog-r/Amazing Advs. #12 1.20 2.40 6.00

141-163: 144-Origin & 1st app. Hellcat. 146-25¢ & 30¢ variants exist. 150-Kirby-a(r); new line-up: Capt. America, Scarlet Witch, Iron Man, Wasp, Yellowjacket, Vision & The Beast. 151-Wonderman returns w/new costume 1.00 2.00 5.00

164-166: Byrne-a 1.20 2.40 6.00

167-180: 168-Guardians of the Galaxy app. 174-Thanos cameo. 176-Starhawk app. 1.30 3.25

181-191: Byrne-a. 181-New line-up: Capt. America, Scarlet Witch, Iron Man, Wasp, Vision, Beast & The Falcon. 183-Ms. Marvel joins. 185-Origin Quicksilver & Scarlet Witch 1.30 3.25

192-213,215-262: 195-1st Taskmaster. 200-(10/80, 52 pgs.)-Ms. Marvel leaves. 211-New line-up: Capt. America, Iron Man, Tigra, Thor, Wasp & Yellowjacket. 213-Yellowjacket leaves. 215,216-Silver Surfer app. 216-Tigra leaves. 217-Yellowjacket & Wasp return. 221-Hawkeye & She-Hulk join. 227-Capt. Marvel (female) joins; origins of Ant-Man, Wasp, Giant-Man, Goliath, Yellowjacket, & Avengers. 230-Yellowjacket quits. 231-Iron Man leaves. 232-Starfox (Eros) joins. 234-Origin Quicksilver, Scarlet Witch. 236-New logo. 238-Origin Blackout. 239-Avengers app. on Dave Letterman show. 240-Spider-Woman revived. 250-($1.00, 52 pgs.) .90 2.25

214-Ghost Rider-c/story 1.00 2.00 5.00

263-1st app. X-Factor (1/86)(story continues in Fantastic Four #286) 1.00 2.00 5.00

264-299: 272-Alpha Flight app. 291-$1.00 issues begin. 297-Black Knight, She-Hulk & Thor resign. 298-Inferno tie-in .80 2.00

300 (2/89, $1.75, 68 pgs.)-Thor joins; Simonson-a 1.20 3.00

301-304,306-325,327,329-343: 302-Re-intro Quasar. 314-318-Spider-Man x-over. 320-324-Alpha Flight app. (320-cameo). 327-2nd app. Rage. 341, 342-New Warriors app. 343-Last $1.00-c 1.00

305-Byrne scripts begin .80 2.00

326-1st app. Rage (11/90) 1.40 3.50 8.50

328-Origin Rage 1.20 3.00 7.00

344-346,348,349,351-359,361,362,364,365,367: 365-Contains coupon for Hunt for Magneto contest 1.50

347-($1.75, 56 pgs.) .80 2.00

350-($2.50, 68 pgs.)-Double gatefold-c showing-c to #1; r/#53 w/cover in flip book format; vs. The Starjammers 1.00 2.50

360-($2.95, 52 pgs.)-Embossed all-foil-c; 30th ann. 1.00 2.00 5.00

363-($2.95, 52 pgs.)-All silver foil-c 1.20 3.00

366-($3.95, 68 pgs.)-Embossed all gold foil-c 1.60 4.00

368-Bloodties part 1; Avengers/X-Men x-over 1.50

369-($2.95)-Foil embossed-c; Bloodties part 5 1.20 3.00

370-373 1.25

374-Begin $1.50-c; bound-in trading card sheet 1.50

375-($2.00, 52 pgs.)-Regular ed.; Thunderstrike returns .80 2.00

375-($2.50, 52 pgs.)-Collector's ed. w/bound-in poster 1.00 2.50

376-385 1.50

Special 1(9/67, 25¢, 68 pgs.)-New-a; original & new Avengers team-up 6.00 18.00 42.00

Special 2(9/68, 25¢, 68 pgs.)-New-a; original vs. new Avengers 2.30 7.00 16.00

Special 3(9/69, 25¢, 68 pgs.)-r/Avengers #4 plus 3 Capt. America stories by Kirby (art); origin Red Skull 2.85 8.00 20.00

Special 4(1/71, 25¢, 68 pgs.)-Kirby-r/Avengers #5,6 1.10 2.70 6.50

Special 5(1/72)-Spider-Man x-over 1.20 2.90 7.00

Annual 6(11/76) 1.10 2.20 5.50

Annual 7(11/77)-Starlin-c/a; Warlock dies; Thanos app. 4.60 14.00 32.00

Annual 8(1978)-Dr. Strange, Ms. Marvel app. 1.80 4.50

Annual 9(1979)-Newton-a(p) 1.40 3.50

Annual 10(1981)-Golden-p; X-Men cameo; 1st app. Rogue & Madelyne Pryor 1.30 3.25 8.00

Annual 11-16: 11(1982)-Vs. The Defenders. 12(1983). 13(1984). 14(1985). 15(1986). 16(1987) 1.50 3.75

Annual 17(1988)-Evolutionary War x-over 1.60 4.00

Annual 18(1989, $2.00, 68 pgs.)-Atlantis Attacks 1.20 3.00

Annual 19,20(1990, 1991)(both $2.00, 68 pgs.) 1.00 2.50

Annual 21(1992, $2.25, 68 pgs.) .90 2.25

Annual 22(1993, $2.95, 68 pgs.)-Bagged w/card 1.20 3.00

Annual 23(1994, $2.95, 68 pgs.) 1.20 3.00

Marvel Double Feature...Avengers/Giant-Man #379 ($2.50, 52 pgs.)-Same as Avengers #379 w/Giant-Man flip book 1.00 2.50

...: The Yesterday Quest ($6.95)-r/181,182,185-187 1.20 3.00 7.00

NOTE: **Austin** *c(i)-157, 167, 168, 170-177, 181, 183-188, 198-201, Annual 8.* **John Buscema** *a-41-44p, 46p, 47p, 49, 50, 51-62p, 74-77, 79-85, 87-91, 97, 105p, 121p, 124p,125p, 152, 153p, 255-279p, 281-302p; c-41-66, 68-71, 73-91, 97-99, 178, 256-259p, 261-279p, 281-302p.* **Byrne** *a-164-166p, 181-191p, 233p, Annual 13, 14p; c-186-190p, 233p, 260, 305p; scripts-305-312.* **Colan** *a(p)-63-65, 111, 206-208, 210, 211; c(p)-65, 206-208, 210, 211.* **Guice** *a-Annual 12p.* **Don Heck** *a-9-15, 17-40.* **Kane** *c-37p, 159p.* **Kane/Everett** *c-97.* **Kirby** *a-1-8p, Special 3r, 4r(p); c-1-30, 148, 151-158; layouts-14-16.* **Ron Lim** *c(p)-335-341.* **Miller** *c-193p.* **Mooney** *a-86i, 179p, 180p.* **Nebres** *a-178i; c-179i.* **Newton** *a-204p, Annual 9p.* **Perez** *a(p)-141, 143, 144, 148, 154, 155, 160, 161, 162, 167,168, 170, 171, 194-196, 198-202, Annual 6, 8; c(p)-160-162, 164-166, 170-174, 181,183-185, 191, 192, 194-201, Annual 8.* **Starlin** *c-121, 135.* **Staton** *a-127-134i.* **Tuska** *a-47i,48i, 51i, 53i, 54i, 106p, 107p, 135p, 137-140p, 163p. Guardians of the Galaxy app.*

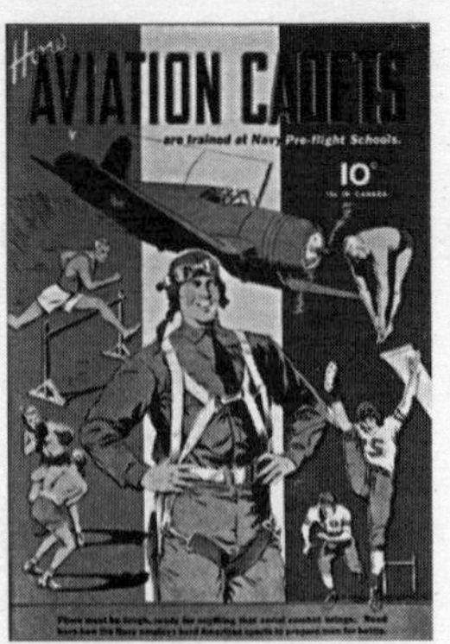

Aviation Cadets #1 © S & S

Axa #2 © ECL

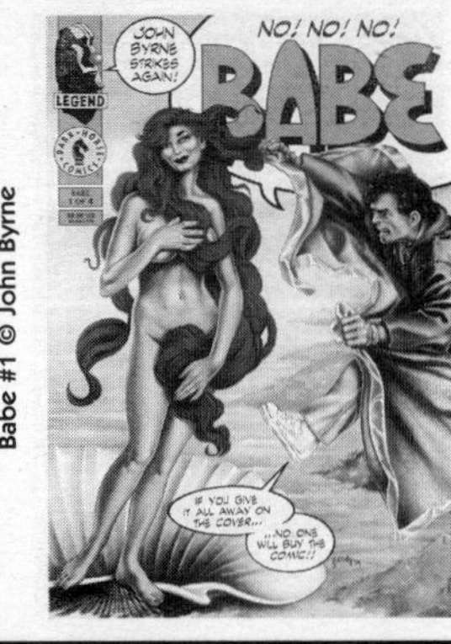

Babe #1 © John Byrne

	GD25	FN65	NM94

in #167, 168, 170, 173, 175, 181.

AVENGERS, THE (TV)(Also see Steed and Mrs. Peel)
Nov, 1968 ("John Steed & Emma Peel" cover title) (15¢)
Gold Key

	GD25	FN65	NM94
1-Photo-c	24.00	73.00	170.00

AVENGERS COLLECTOR'S EDITION, THE
1993 (Ordered through mail w/candy wrapper, 20 pgs.)
Marvel Comics

	GD25	FN65	NM94
1-Contains 4 bound-in trading cards		.80	2.00

AVENGERS LOG, THE
Feb, 1994 ($1.95)
Marvel Comics

	GD25	FN65	NM94
1-Gives history of all members; Perez-c		.80	2.00

AVENGERS SPOTLIGHT (Formerly Solo Avengers #1-20)
No. 21, Aug, 1989 - No. 40, Jan, 1991 (75¢/$1.00)
Marvel Comics

	GD25	FN65	NM94
21 (75¢)-Byrne-c/a			1.00
22-40 ($1.00): 26-Acts of Vengeance story. 31-34-U.S. Agent series. 36-Heck-i. 37-Mortimer-i. 40-The Black Knight app.			1.00

AVENGERS STRIKEFILE
Jan, 1994 ($1.75)
Marvel Comics

	GD25	FN65	NM94
1		.70	1.75

AVENGERS: THE TERMINATRIX OBJECTIVE
Sept, 1993 - No. 4, Dec, 1993 ($1.25)
Marvel Comics

	GD25	FN65	NM94
1-($2.50)-Holo-grafx foil-c		1.00	2.50
2-4-Old vs. new Avengers			1.25

AVENGERS WEST COAST (Formerly West Coast Avengers)
No. 48, Sept, 1989 - No. 102, Jan, 1994 ($1.00/$1.25)
Marvel Comics

	GD25	FN65	NM94
48,49: Byrne-c/a & scripts continue thru #57			1.10
50-Re-intro original Human Torch			1.50
51-74,76-99,101,102: 54-Cover swipe/F.F. #1. 70-Spider-Woman app. 78-Last $1.00-c. 79-Dr. Strange x-over. 84-Origin Spider-Woman retold; Spider-Man app. (also in #85,86). 87,88-Wolverine-c/story. 93-95-Darkhawk app. 101-X-Men x-over			1.25
75-($1.50, 52 pgs.)-Fantastic Four x-over			1.50
100-($3.95, 68 pgs.)-Embossed all red foil-c		1.60	4.00
Annual 8 (1993, $2.95, 68 pgs.)-Bagged w/card		1.20	3.00

AVIATION ADVENTURES AND MODEL BUILDING
No. 16, Dec, 1946 - No. 17, Feb, 1947 (True Aviation Advs. ...No. 15)
Parents' Magazine Institute

	GD25	FN65	NM94
16,17-Half comics and half pictures	5.00	15.00	30.00

AVIATION CADETS
1943
Street & Smith Publications

	GD25	FN65	NM94
nn	10.00	30.00	70.00

A-V IN 3-D
Dec, 1984 ($2.00, 28 pgs. w/glasses)
Aardvark-Vanaheim

	GD25	FN65	NM94
1-Cerebus, Flaming Carrot, Normalman & Ms. Tree		.80	2.00

AWFUL OSCAR (Formerly & becomes Oscar Comics with No. 13)
No. 11, June, 1949 - No. 12, Aug, 1949
Marvel Comics

	GD25	FN65	NM94
11,12	5.35	16.00	32.00

AXA (Eclipse)(Value: cover or less)

AXEL PRESSBUTTON (Eclipse)(Value: cover or less)

AZTEC ACE (Eclipse)(Value: cover or less)

BABE (...Darling of the Hills, later issues)(See Big Shot and Sparky Watts)
June-July, 1948 - No. 11, Apr-May, 1950
Prize/Headline/Feature

	GD25	FN65	NM94
1-Boody Rogers-a	13.00	40.00	90.00
2-Boody Rogers-a	10.00	30.00	60.00
3-11-All by Boody Rogers	7.00	21.00	48.00

BABE
July, 1994 - No. 4, Jan, 1994 ($2.50, color, limited series)
Dark Horse Comics

	GD25	FN65	NM94
1-4-John Byrne-stories/a		1.00	2.50

BABE AMAZON OF OZARKS
No. 5, 1948
Standard Comics

	GD25	FN65	NM94
5-Exist?	5.35	16.00	32.00

BABE RUTH SPORTS COMICS (Becomes Rags Rabbit #11 on?)
April, 1949 - No. 11, Feb, 1951
Harvey Publications

	GD25	FN65	NM94
1-Powell-a	27.00	80.00	185.00
2-Powell-a	20.00	60.00	140.00
3-11: Powell-a in most	16.50	50.00	115.00

NOTE: *Baseball c-2-4, 9. Basketball c-1, 6. Football c-5. Yogi Berra c/story-8. Joe DiMaggio c/story-3. Bob Feller c/story-4. Stan Musial c-9.*

BABES IN TOYLAND (See 4-Color No. 1282 & Golden Pix Story Book ST-3)

BABY HUEY
No. 100, Oct, 1990 - No. 101, Nov, 1990; No. 1, Oct, 1991 - No. 9, June, 1994 ($1.00/$1.25/$1.50, quarterly)
Harvey Comics

	GD25	FN65	NM94
100,101,1,2 ($1.00): 1-Cover says "Big Baby Huey"			1.00
3-7 ($1.25)			1.25
8,9 ($1.50)			1.50

BABY HUEY AND PAPA (See Paramount Animated...)
May, 1962 - No. 33, Jan, 1968 (Also see Casper The Friendly Ghost)
Harvey Publications

	GD25	FN65	NM94
1	14.00	43.00	100.00
2	6.35	19.00	38.00
3-5	4.00	10.00	20.00
6-10	2.40	6.00	14.00
11-20	1.40	3.50	7.00
21-33	1.20	3.00	6.00

BABY HUEY DUCKLAND
Nov, 1962 - No. 15, Nov, 1966 (25¢ Giants) (All 68 pgs.)
Harvey Publications

	GD25	FN65	NM94
1	10.00	30.00	60.00
2-5	4.00	11.00	22.00
6-15	2.40	6.00	12.00

BABY HUEY, THE BABY GIANT (Also see Big Baby Huey, Casper, Harvey Hits #22, Harvey Comics Hits #60, & Paramount Animated Comics)
9/56 - #97, 10/71; #98, 10/72; #99, 10/80; #100, 10/90 - #102?
Harvey Publications

	GD25	FN65	NM94
1-Infinity-c	32.00	96.00	225.00
2	16.00	48.00	110.00
3-Baby Huey takes anti-pep pills	10.00	30.00	65.00
4,5	8.35	25.00	50.00
6-10	4.20	12.50	25.00
11-20	3.20	8.00	16.00
21-40	2.60	6.50	13.00
41-60	1.60	4.00	9.00
61-79(12/67)	1.20	3.00	7.00
80(12/68) - 95-All 68 pg. Giants	1.60	4.00	9.00
96,97-Both 52 pg. Giants	1.20	3.00	7.00

Badger #51 © FC

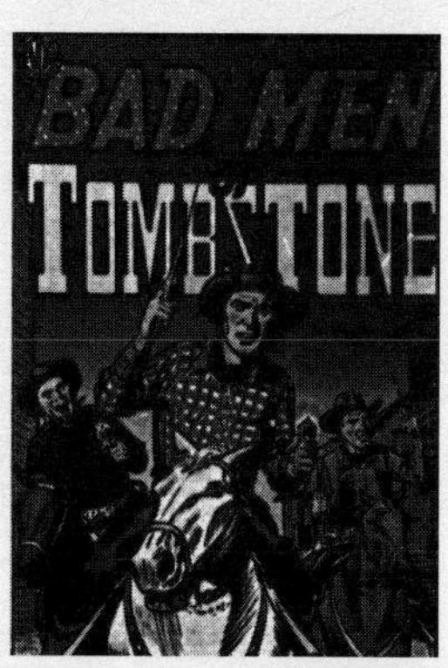

Badmen of Tombstone © AVON

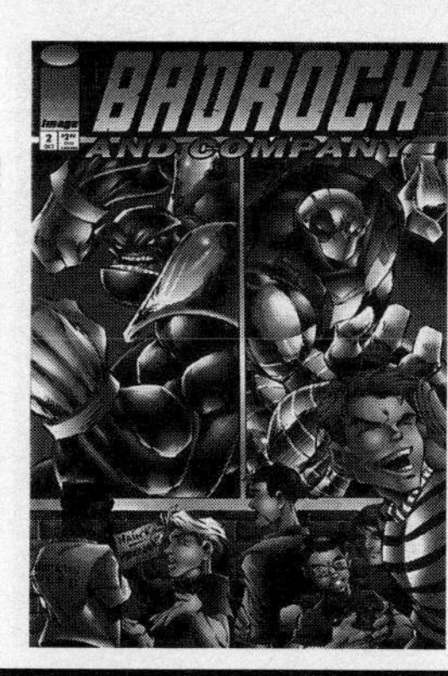

Badrock & Co. #2 © Rob Liefeld

	GD25	FN65	NM94
98-99: Regular size		1.20	3.00
100-102 ($1.00)			1.00

BABY SNOOTS (Also see March of Comics #359, 371, 396, 401, 419, 431, 443, 450, 462, 474, 485)
Aug, 1970 - No. 22, Nov, 1975
Gold Key

	GD25	FN65	NM94
1	1.50	3.75	9.00
2		1.60	4.00
3-22: 22-Titled Snoots, the Forgetful Elefink		.80	2.00

BACHELOR FATHER (TV)
No. 1332, 4-6/62 - No. 2, 1962
Dell Publishing Co.

	GD25	FN65	NM94
4-Color 1332 (#1)	9.15	27.50	55.00
2-Written by Stanley	9.15	27.50	55.00

BACHELOR'S DIARY
1949 (15¢)
Avon Periodicals

	GD25	FN65	NM94
1(Scarce)-King Features panel cartoons & text-r; pin-up, girl wrestling photos; similar to Sideshow	275.00	80.00	185.00

BACK DOWN THE LINE
1991 (Mature adults, 8-1/2 x 11", 52 pgs.)
Eclipse Books

	GD25	FN65	NM94
nn (Soft-c, $8.95)-Bolton-c/a	1.50	3.75	9.00
nn (Limited hard-c, $29.95)			30.00

BACKLASH
Nov,1994-Present(1.95,color)
Image Comics

	GD25	FN65	NM94
1-Double-c	0.40	0.80	2.00

BACK TO THE FUTURE (TV cartoon)
Nov, 1991 - No. 4, June, 1992 ($1.25)
Harvey Comics

	GD25	FN65	NM94
1-4: 1,2-Gil Kane-c; based on animated cartoon			1.25
Special nn (1991, 20 pgs.)-Brunner-c; given away at Universal Studios in Florida			1.00

BACK TO THE FUTURE: FORWARD TO THE FUTURE
Oct, 1992 - No. 3, Feb, 1993 ($1.50, mini-series)
Harvey Comics

	GD25	FN65	NM94
1-3			1.50

BAD COMPANY
Aug, 1988 - No. 19?, 1990 ($1.50/$1.75, color, high quality paper)
Quality Comics/Fleetway Quality #15 on

	GD25	FN65	NM94
1-15: 5,6-Guice-c			1.50
16-19: ($1.75-c)		.70	1.75

BADGE OF JUSTICE
No. 22, 1/55 - No. 23, 3/55; 4/55 - No. 4, 10/55
Charlton Comics

	GD25	FN65	NM94
22(1/55)	6.70	20.00	40.00
23(3/55), 1	4.70	14.00	28.00
2-4	3.60	9.00	18.00

BADGER, THE
Dec, 1983 - No. 70, Apr, 1991; V2#1, Spring, 1991
Capital Comics(#1-4)/First Comics

	GD25	FN65	NM94
1-4			1.50
5			1.50
6-49			1.00
50-($3.95, 52 pgs.)		1.40	3.50
51-70: 52-54-Tim Vigil-c/a		.80	2.00
V2#1 (Spring, 1991, $4.95)		1.60	4.00

BADGER GOES BERSERK (First)(Value: cover or less)

BADGER: SHATTERED MIRROR
July, 1994 - Present ($2.50, color, limited series)
Dark Horse Comics

	GD25	FN65	NM94
1,2		1.00	2.50

BADGER: ZEN POP FUNNY-ANIMAL VERSION
July, 1994 - No. 2, Aug, 1994 ($2.50, color, limited series)
Dark Horse Comics

	GD25	FN65	NM94
1,2		1.00	2.50

BADLANDS (Vortex)(Value: cover or less)

BADLANDS (Dark Horse)(Value: cover or less)

BADMEN OF THE WEST
1951 (Giant - 132 pgs.)(Painted-c)
Avon Periodicals

	GD25	FN65	NM94
1-Contains rebound copies of Jesse James, King of the Bad Men of Deadwood, Badmen of Tombstone; other combinations possible. Issues with Kubert-a...	25.00	75.00	175.00

BADMEN OF THE WEST! (See A-1 Comics)
1953 - No. 3, 1954
Magazine Enterprises

	GD25	FN65	NM94
1(A-1 100)-Meskin-a?	17.00	52.00	120.00
2(A-1 120), 3: 2-Larsen-a	11.00	32.00	75.00

BADMEN OF TOMBSTONE
1950
Avon Periodicals

	GD25	FN65	NM94
nn	10.00	30.00	70.00

BADROCK AND COMPANY
Sept, 1994-Present(2.50,color, limited series: 6)
Image

	GD25	FN65	NM94
1,2	0.50	1.00	2.50

BAFFLING MYSTERIES (Formerly Indian Braves No. 1-4; Heroes of the Wild Frontier No. 26-on)
No. 5, Nov, 1951 - No. 26, Oct, 1955
Periodical House (Ace Magazines)

	GD25	FN65	NM94
5	17.00	52.00	120.00
6-24: 8-Woodish-a by Cameron. 10-E.C. Crypt Keeper swipe on-c. 24-Last pre-code issue	11.00	32.00	75.00
25-Reprints; surrealistic-c	10.00	30.00	60.00
26-Reprints	8.35	25.00	50.00

NOTE: ***Cameron*** *a-8, 10, 16-18, 20-22.* ***Colan*** *a-5, 11, 25r/5.* ***Sekowsky*** *a-5, 6, 22. Bondage c-20, 23. Reprints in 18(1), 19(1), 24(3).*

BALBO (See Master Comics #33 & Mighty Midget Comics)

BALDER THE BRAVE
Nov, 1985 - No. 4, 1986 (Mini-series)
Marvel Comics Group

	GD25	FN65	NM94
1-4: Simonson-c/a; character from Thor			1.00

BALLAD OF HALO JONES, THE (Quality)(Value: cover or less)

BALLOONATIKS SUPER HEROES, THE (Best)(Value: cover or less)

BALOO & LITTLE BRITCHES
April, 1968 (Walt Disney)
Gold Key

	GD25	FN65	NM94
1-From the Jungle Book	3.40	10.00	24.00

BALTIMORE COLTS
1950 (Giveaway)
American Visuals Corp.

	GD25	FN65	NM94
nn-Eisner-c	45.00	135.00	315.00

BAMBI (See 4-Color No. 12, 30, 186, Movie Classics, Movie Comics, and Walt Disney Showcase No. 31)

BAMBI (Disney)

Barbie Fashion #45 © Mattel

Barb Wire #2 © DH

Barney Google & Snuffy Smith #1 © TOBY

1941, 1942, 1984
K. K. Publications (Giveaways)/Whitman Publ. Co.

	GD25	FN65	NM94
1941-Horlick's Malted Milk & various toy stores; text & pictures; most copies mailed out with store stickers on-c	22.00	65.00	150.00
1942-Same as 4-Color #12, but no price (Same as '41 issue?) (Scarce)	32.00	96.00	225.00
1-(Whitman, 1984; 60¢)-r/4-Color #186		1.60	4.00

BAMBI (Disney)
1942 (50 cents, 32pg, hard cover, 7"x8-1/2", w/dust jacket)
Grosset & Dunlap

nn-Given away w/a copy of Thumper for a $2.00, 2-yr. subscription to WDC&S in 1942 (Xmas offer)

	GD25	FN65	NM94
Book	15.00	45.00	100.00
Dust jacket only	7.00	21.00	50.00

BAMM BAMM & PEBBLES FLINTSTONE (TV)
Oct, 1964 (Hanna-Barbera)
Gold Key

	GD25	FN65	NM94
1	5.40	16.00	38.00

BANANA OIL
1924 (52 pgs.)(Black & White)
MS Publ. Co.

	GD25	FN65	NM94
nn-Milt Gross-a; not reprints	27.00	81.00	190.00

BANANA SPLITS, THE (TV) (See Golden Comics Digest & March of Comics No. 364)
June, 1969 - No. 8, Oct, 1971 (Hanna-Barbera)
Gold Key

	GD25	FN65	NM94
1-Photo-c	2.60	7.70	18.00
2-8	1.50	3.80	9.00

BAND WAGON (See Hanna-Barbera Band Wagon)

BANG-UP COMICS
Dec, 1941 - No. 3, June, 1942
Progressive Publishers

	GD25	FN65	NM94
1-Cosmo Mann & Lady Fairplay begin; Buzz Balmer by Rick Yager in all (origin #1)	61.00	182.00	425.00
2,3	36.00	107.00	250.00

BANNER COMICS (Becomes Captain Courageous No. 6)
No. 3, Sept, 1941 - No. 5, Jan, 1942
Ace Magazines

	GD25	FN65	NM94
3-Captain Courageous (1st app.) & Lone Warrior & Sidekick Dicky begin; Jim Mooney-c	75.00	225.00	525.00
4,5: 4-Flag-c	50.00	150.00	350.00

BARBARIANS, THE
June, 1975
Atlas Comics/Seaboard Periodicals

	GD25	FN65	NM94
1-Origin, only app. Andrax; Iron Jaw app.			1.00

BARBIE
Jan, 1991 - Present ($1.00/$1.25)
Marvel Comics

	GD25	FN65	NM94
1-Polybagged w/Barbie Pink Card; Romita-c		1.50	3.75
2-52: 13-Last $1.00-c			1.25

BARBIE & KEN
May-July, 1962 - No. 5, Nov-Jan, 1963-64
Dell Publishing Co.

	GD25	FN65	NM94
01-053-207(#1)-Based on Mattel toy dolls	35.00	105.00	245.00
2-4	25.00	75.00	175.00
5 (Rare)	29.00	86.00	200.00

BARBIE FASHION
Jan, 1991 - Present ($1.00/$1.25)
Marvel Comics

	GD25	FN65	NM94
1-Polybagged w/doorknob hanger		.80	2.00
2-52: 4-Contains preview to Sweet XVI. 13-Last $1.00-c			1.25

BARB WIRE (See Comics' Greatest World)
Apr, 1994 - Present ($2.00, color)
Dark Horse Comics

	GD25	FN65	NM94
1-6: 1-Foil logo		.80	2.00

BARKER, THE (Also see National Comics #42)
Autumn, 1946 - No. 15, Dec, 1949
Quality Comics Group/Comic Magazine

	GD25	FN65	NM94
1	13.00	40.00	90.00
2	6.70	20.00	40.00
3-10	5.00	15.00	30.00
11-14	4.00	11.00	22.00
15-Jack Cole-a(p)	5.00	15.00	30.00

NOTE: ***Jack Cole*** *art in some issues.*

BARNABY
1945 (25¢,102 pgs., digest size)
Civil Service Publications Inc.

	GD25	FN65	NM94
V1#1-r/Crocket Johnson strips from 1942	1.00	2.50	6.00

BARNEY AND BETTY RUBBLE (TV) (Flintstones' Neighbors)
Jan, 1973 - No. 23, Dec, 1976 (Hanna-Barbera)
Charlton Comics

	GD25	FN65	NM94
1	3.40	10.00	24.00
2-10	1.65	4.00	10.00
11-23: 11(2/75)-1st Mike Zeck-a (illos)	1.20	2.40	6.00

BARNEY BAXTER (Also see Magic Comics)
1938 - No. 2, 1956
David McKay/Dell Publishing Co./Argo

	GD25	FN65	NM94
Feature Books 15(McKay-1938)	20.00	60.00	200.00
4-Color 20(1942)	24.00	72.00	165.00
4,5	11.50	34.00	80.00
1,2(1956-Argo)	5.35	16.00	32.00

BARNEY BEAR ... (Spire Christian)(Value: cover or less)

BARNEY GOOGLE & SNUFFY SMITH
1942 - 1943; April, 1964
Dell Publishing Co./Gold Key

	GD25	FN65	NM94
4-Color 19(1942)	38.00	114.00	265.00
4-Color 40(1944)	22.00	65.00	150.00
Large Feature Comic 11(1943)	18.00	54.00	180.00
1(10113-404)-Gold Key (4/64)	4.00	11.00	22.00

BARNEY GOOGLE & SNUFFY SMITH
June, 1951 - No. 4, Feb, 1952 (Reprints)
Toby Press

	GD25	FN65	NM94
1	10.00	30.00	70.00
2,3	6.70	20.00	40.00
4-Kurtzman-a "Pot Shot Pete", 5 pgs.; reprints John Wayne #5	10.00	30.00	70.00

BARNEY GOOGLE AND SNUFFY SMITH
March, 1970 - No. 6, Jan, 1971
Charlton Comics

	GD25	FN65	NM94
1	2.30	6.90	16.00
2-6	1.70	4.20	10.00

BARNEY GOOGLE AND SPARK PLUG (See Comic Monthly & Giant Comic Album)
1923 - No. 6, 1928 (Daily strip reprints; B&W) (52 pgs.)
Cupples & Leon Co.

	GD25	FN65	NM94
1-By Billy DeBeck	30.00	90.00	270.00
2-6	20.00	60.00	180.00

NOTE: *Started in 1918 as newspaper strip; Spark Plug began 1922, 1923.*

BARNYARD COMICS (Dizzy Duck No. 32 on)

Bartman #2 © Matt Groeing

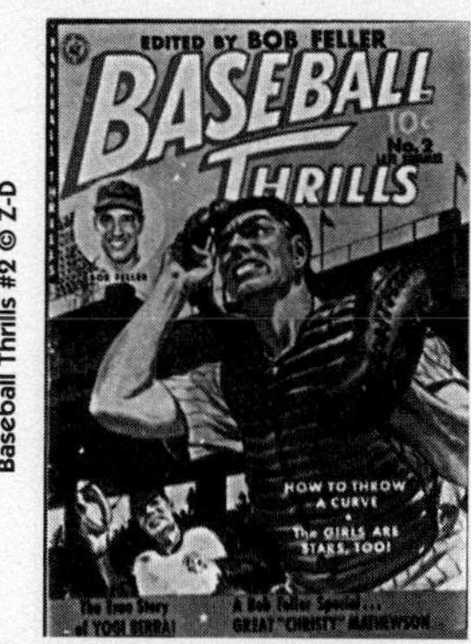

Baseball Thrills #2 © Z-D

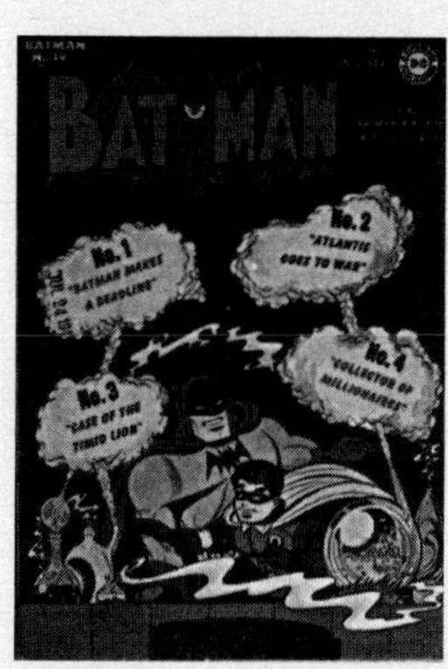

Batman #19 © DC

	GD25	FN65	NM94
June, 1944 - No. 31, Sept, 1950; No. 10, 1957			
Nedor/Polo Mag./Standard(Animated Cartoons)			
1(nn, 52 pgs.)-Funny animal	13.00	40.00	90.00
2 (52 pgs.)	7.50	22.50	45.00
3-5	5.00	15.00	30.00
6-12,16	4.00	12.00	24.00
13-15,17,21,23,26,27,29-All contain Frazetta text illos	5.00	15.00	30.00
18-20,22,24,25-All contain Frazetta-a & text illos	10.00	30.00	60.00
28,30,31	3.00	7.50	15.00
10(1957)(Exist?)	1.80	4.50	9.00

BARRY M. GOLDWATER
March, 1965 (Complete life story)
Dell Publishing Co.

	GD25	FN65	NM94
12-055-503-Photo-c	4.00	11.00	22.00

BARTMAN (Also see Simpson's Comics & Radioactive Man)
1993 - Present ($1.95, color)
Bongo Comics

	GD25	FN65	NM94
1-($2.95)-Foil-c; bound-in jumbo Bartman poster		1.40	3.50
2		.80	2.00
3-($2.25)-w/trading card		.90	2.25

BASEBALL COMICS
Spring, 1949 (Reprinted later as a Spirit section)
Will Eisner Productions

	GD25	FN65	NM94
1-Will Eisner-c/a	61.00	182.00	425.00

BASEBALL COMICS (Kitchen Sink)(Value: cover or less)

BASEBALL GREATS (Dark Horse)(Value: cover or less)

BASEBALL HEROES
1952 (One Shot)
Fawcett Publications

	GD25	FN65	NM94
nn (Scarce)-Babe Ruth photo-c; baseball's Hall of Fame biographies	64.00	193.00	450.00

BASEBALL'S GREATEST HEROES
Dec, 1991 - No. 2, May, 1992 ($1.75, color)
Magnum Comics

	GD25	FN65	NM94
1-Mickey Mantle #1; photo-c; Sinnott-a(p)		.70	1.75
2-Brooks Robinson #1; photo-c; Sinnott-a(i)		.70	1.75

BASEBALL THRILLS
No. 10, Sum, 1951 - No. 3, Sum, 1952 (Saunders painted-c No.1,2)
Ziff-Davis Publ. Co.

	GD25	FN65	NM94
10(#1)-Bob Feller story	30.00	90.00	210.00
2-Powell-a(2)(Late Sum, '51)-Babe Ruth story	22.00	65.00	150.00
3-Kinstler-c/a; Joe DiMaggio story	22.00	65.00	150.00

BASEBALL THRILLS 3-D (3-D Zone)(Value: cover or less)

BASICALLY STRANGE (Magazine)
December, 1982 (B&W, $1.95)
John C. Comics (Archie Comics Group)

	GD25	FN65	NM94
1-(21,000 printed; all but 1,000 destroyed; pgs. out of sequence)		.80	2.00
1-Wood, Toth-a; Corben-c; reprints & new art		.80	2.00

BASIC HISTORY OF AMERICA ILLUSTRATED
1976 (B&W) (Soft-c $1.50; Hard-c $4.50)
Pendulum Press

07-1999-America Becomes a World Power 1890-1920. 07-2251-The Industrial Era 1865-1915. 07-226x-Before the Civil War 1830-1860. 07-2278-Americans Move Westward 1800-1850. 07-2286-The Civil War 1850-1876; Redondo-a. 07-2294-The Fight for Freedom 1750-1783. 07-2308-The New World 1500-1750. 07-2316-Problems of the NewNation 1800-1830. 07-2324-Roaring Twenties and the Great Depression 1920-1940. 07-2332-The United States Emerges 1783-1800. 07-2340-America Today 1945-1976. 07-2359-World War II 1940-1945

BASIL (...the Royal Cat)
Jan, 1953 - No. 4, Sept, 1953
St. John Publishing Co.

	GD25	FN65	NM94
1-Funny animal	4.00	11.00	22.00
2-4	2.80	7.00	14.00
I.W. Reprint 1	1.20	3.00	6.00

BASIL WOLVERTON'S FANTASTIC FABLES
Oct, 1993 - No. 2, Dec, 1993 ($2.50, B&W, limited series)
Dark Horse Comics

	GD25	FN65	NM94
1,2-Wolverton-c/a(r)		1.00	2.50

BASIL WOLVERTON'S GATEWAY TO HORROR (Dark Horse)(Value: cover or less)

BASIL WOLVERTON'S PLANET OF TERROR (Dark Horse)(Value: cover or less)

BATGIRL SPECIAL (See Teen Titans #50)
1988 ($1.50, one-shot, 52 pgs)
DC Comics

	GD25	FN65	NM94
1		1.00	2.50

BAT LASH (See DC Special Series #16, Showcase #76, Weird Western Tales)
Oct-Nov, 1968 - No. 7, Oct-Nov, 1969 (All 12¢ issues)
National Periodical Publications

	GD25	FN65	NM94
Showcase #76 (8/68)-1st app. Bat Lash	4.00	11.00	35.00
1-(10-11/68)-2nd app. Bat Lash	2.00	6.00	14.00
2-7	1.40	3.50	8.50

BATMAN (See Arkham Asylum, Aurora, The Best of DC #2, Blind Justice, The Brave & the Bold, Cosmic Odyssey, DC 100-Page Super Spec. #14,20, DC Special, DC Special Series, Detective, Dynamic Classics, 80-Page Giants, Gotham By Gaslight, Gotham Nights, Greatest Batman Stories Ever Told, Greatest Joker Stories Ever Told, Heroes Against Hunger, The Joker, Justice League of America #250, Justice League Int., Legends of the Dark Knight, Limited Coll. Ed., Man-Bat, Power Record Comics, Real Fact #5, Saga of Ra's Al Ghul, Shadow of the..., Star Spangled, Super Friends, 3-D Batman, Untold Legend of..., Wanted... & World's Finest Comics)

BATMAN
Spring, 1940 - Present (#1-5 were quarterly)
National Periodical Publ./Detective Comics/DC Comics

	GD25	FN65	VF82	NM94
1-Origin The Batman reprinted (2 pgs.) from Det. #33 w/splash from #35 by Bob Kane; see Detective #33 for 1st origin; 1st app. Joker (2 stories intended for 2 separate issues of Det. Comics which would have been 1st & 2nd app.); splash pg. to 2nd Joker story is similar to cover of Det. #40 (story intended for #40); 1st app. The Cat (Catwoman)(1st villainess in comics); has Batman story (w/Hugo Strange) without Robin originally planned for Det. #38; mentions location (Manhattan) where Batman lives (see Det. #31). This book was created entirely from the inventory of Det. Comics; 1st Batman/Robin pin-up on back-c; has text piece & photo of Bob Kane	4,200.00	12,600.00	27,300.00	42,000.00

(Estimated up to 250+ total copies exist, 16 in NM/Mint)

1-Reprint, oversize 13-1/2x10". **WARNING**: This comic is an exact duplicate reprint of the original except for its size. DC published it in 1974 with a second cover titling it as a Famous First Edition. There have been many reported cases of the outer cover being removed and the interior sold as the original edition. The reprint with the new outer cover removed is practically worthless. See Famous First Edition for value.

	GD25	FN65	NM94
2-2nd app. The Joker; 2nd app. Catwoman (out of costume) in Joker story; 1st time called Catwoman	1000.00	3000.00	7000.00
3-3rd app Catwoman (1st in costume & 1st costumed villainess); 1st Puppet Master app.	714.00	2143.00	5000.00
4-4th app. The Joker (see Det. #45 for 4th); 1st mention of Gotham City in a Batman comic (on newspaper)(Win/40)	571.00	1715.00	4000.00
5-1st app. the Batmobile with its bat-head front	400.00	1200.00	2800.00
6-10: 8-Infinity-c. 9-1st Batman x-mas story; Burnley-c. 10-Cat-Woman story (gets new costume)	300.00	900.00	2100.00
11-Classic Joker-c by Ray/Robinson (3rd Joker-c, 6-7/42); Joker & Penguin app.	329.00	985.00	2300.00
12,13,15: 13-Jerry Siegel, creator of Superman appears in a Batman story. 15-New costume Catwoman	229.00	685.00	1600.00
14-2nd Penguin-c; Penguin app. (12-1/42-43)	250.00	750.00	1750.00
16-Intro/origin Alfred (4-5/43); cover is a reverse of #9 cover by Burnley; 1st small logo	471.00	1415.00	3300.00

Batman #52 © DC

Batman #64 © DC

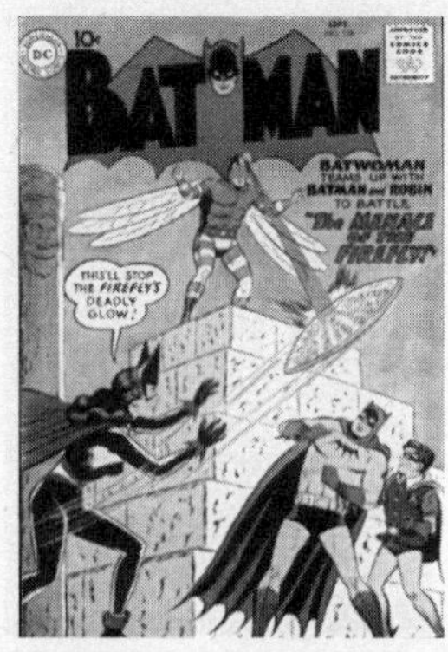

Batman #126 © DC

GD25 FN65 NM94

17-20: 17-Penguin app. 18-Hitler, Hirohito, Mussolini-c. 20-1st Batmobile-c (12-1/43-44) 143.00 430.00 1000.00
21,22,24,26,28-30: 21-1st skinny Alfred in Batman (2-3/44). 21,30-Penguin app. 22-1st Alfred solo-c/story (Alfred solo stories in 22-32,36); Catwoman app.; 2nd app. The Cavalier 118.00 354.00 825.00
23-Joker-c/story 171.00 514.00 1200.00
25-Only Joker/Penguin team-up; 1st team-up between two major villains 171.00 514.00 1200.00
27-Burnley Christmas-c; Penguin app. 143.00 430.00 1000.00
31,32,34-36,39: 32-Origin Robin retold. 35-Catwoman story (in new costume w/o cat head mask). 36-Penguin app. 86.00 257.00 600.00
33-Christmas-c 100.00 300.00 700.00
37,40,44-Joker-c/stories 111.00 332.00 775.00
38-Penguin-c/story 96.00 290.00 675.00
41,45,46: 41-Penguin app. 45-Christmas-c/story; Catwoman story; Vicki Vale app. (1st app?) 66.00 197.00 460.00
42-2nd Catwoman-c (1st in Batman)(8-9/47); Catwoman story also 82.00 246.00 575.00
43-Penguin-c/story 82.00 246.00 575.00
47-1st detailed origin The Batman (6-7/48); 1st Bat-signal-c this title (see Detective #108); Batman tracks down his parent's killer and reveals i.d. to him 229.00 686.00 1600.00
48-1000 Secrets of the Batcave; r-in #203; Penguin story 82.00 246.00 575.00
49-Joker-c/story; 1st app. Mad Hatter; Vicki Vale app. 111.00 332.00 775.00
50-Two-Face impostor app. 73.00 219.00 510.00
51,54,56,57,59: 57-Centerfold is a 1950 calendar. 59-1st app. Deadshot; Batman in the future-c/story 64.00 193.00 450.00
52,55-Joker-c/stories 79.00 236.00 550.00
53,60-Joker story 68.00 204.00 475.00
58-Penguin-c 68.00 204.00 475.00
61-Origin Batman Plane II 68.00 204.00 475.00
62-Origin Catwoman; Catwoman-c 86.00 257.00 600.00
63,80-Joker stories. 63-Flying saucer story(2-3/51) 55.00 165.00 385.00
64,67,70-72,74-77,79: 72-Last 52 pg. issue. 74-Used in **POP**, Pg. 90. 79-Vicki Vale in "The Bride of Batman" 51.00 154.00 360.00
65,69,84-Catwoman-c/stories. 84-Two-Face app. 55.00 165.00 385.00
66,73-Joker-c/stories. 66-Pre-2nd Batman & Robin team try-out. 73-Vicki Vale story 64.00 193.00 450.00
68,81-Two-Face-c/stories 51.00 154.00 360.00
78-(8-9/53)-Roh Kar, The Man Hunter from Mars story-the 1st lawman of Mars to come to Earth (green skinned) 64.00 193.00 450.00
82,83,85-89: 86-Intro Batmarine (Batman's submarine). 89-Last pre-code issue 48.00 144.00 335.00
90,91,93-99: 97-2nd app. Bat-Hound-c/story; Joker app. 38.00 114.00 265.00
92-1st app. Bat-Hound-c/story 48.00 144.00 335.00

	GD25	FN65	VF82	NM94
100 (6/56)	138.00	412.00	893.00	1375.00

GD25 FN65 NM94

101-104,106-109: 103-3rd Bat-Hound-c/story 39.00 118.00 275.00
105-1st Batwoman in Batman (2nd anywhere) 49.00 146.00 340.00
110-Joker story 39.00 118.00 275.00
111-120: 112-1st app. Signalman (super villain). 113-1st app. Fatman 28.00 84.00 195.00
121,122,124-126,128,130: 124-2nd app. Signal Man. 126-Batwoman-c/story. 128-Batwoman cameo. 130-Lex Luthor app. 20.00 60.00 140.00
123-Joker story; Bat-Hound app. 23.00 69.00 160.00
127-Batman vs. Thor the Thunder God-c/story (10/59); Joker story; Superman cameo 23.00 69.00 160.00
129-Origin Robin retold; bondage-c; Batwoman-c/story (reprinted in Batman Family #8) 24.00 73.00 170.00
131-135,137-139,141-143: 131-Intro 2nd Batman & Robin series (see #66; also in #135,145,154,159,164). 133-1st Bat-Mite in Batman (3rd app. anywhere). 134-Origin The Dummy. 139-Intro 1st Bat-Girl; only app. Signalman as the Blue Bowman. 141-2nd app. old Bat-Girl. 143-Last 10¢ issue 14.00 43.00 100.00
136-Joker-c/story 20.00 60.00 140.00
140,144-Joker stories. 140-Batwoman-c/story; Superman cameo. 144-3rd app. old Bat-Girl 14.00 41.00 95.00
145,148-Joker-c/stories 16.00 49.00 115.00
146,147,149,150 11.00 38.00 78.00
151,153,154,156-158,160-162,164-168,170: 153-4th app. old Bat-Girl. 156-Ant-Man/Robin team-up (6/63). 164-New Batmobile (6/64); new look & Mystery Analysts series begins 8.30 25.00 58.00
152-Joker story 8.30 25.00 58.00
155-1st S.A. app. The Penguin (4/63) 34.00 100.00 235.00
159,163-Joker-c/stories. 159-5th app. old Bat-Girl. 163-7th app. old Bat-Girl (last app. until Teen Titans #50); only app. old Bat-Girl as Batwoman II 10.00 29.00 68.00
169-2nd SA Penguin app. 13.00 39.00 90.00
171-1st Riddler app.(5/65) since Dec. 1948 50.00 144.00 335.00
172-175,177,178,180,181,183,184: 181-Batman & Robin poster insert; intro. Poison Ivy. 183-2nd app. Poison Ivy 5.00 16.00 37.00
176-(80-Pg. Giant G-17); Joker-c/story; Penguin app. in strip-r; Catwoman reprint 7.00 21.00 50.00
179-2nd app. Silver Age Riddler 12.00 36.00 85.00
182,187-(80 Pg. Giants G-24, G-30); Joker-c/stories 6.40 19.00 45.00
185-(80 Pg. Giant G-27) 6.00 17.00 40.00
186-Joker-c/story 3.60 10.70 25.00
188,189,191,192,194-196,199: 189-1st S.A. app. Scarecrow; retells origin of G.A. Scarecrow from World's Finest #3(1st app.) 2.40 7.30 17.00
190-Penguin app. 3.10 9.00 22.00
193-(80-Pg. Giant G-37) 5.00 13.70 32.00
197-4th S.A. Catwoman app. cont'd from Det. #369; 1st new Batgirl app. in Batman (4th anywhere) 7.00 21.00 48.00
198-(80-Pg. Giant G-43); Joker-c/story-r/World's Finest #61; Catwoman-r/ Det. #211; Penguin-r; origin-r/#47 9.00 27.00 64.00
200-(3/68)-Joker cameo; retells origin of Batman & Robin; 1st Neal Adams work this title (cover only) 19.00 58.00 135.00
201-Joker story 3.10 9.00 22.00
202,204-207,209,210 1.70 5.00 12.00
203-(80 Pg. Giant G-49); r/#48, 61, & Det. 185; Batcave Blueprints 3.10 9.00 22.00
208-(80 Pg. Giant G-55); New origin Batman by Gil Kane plus 3 G.A. Batman reprints w/Catwoman, Vicki Vale & Batwoman 3.10 9.00 22.00
211,212,214-217: 212-Last 12¢ issue. 214-Alfred given a new last name-"Pennyworth" (see Detective #96). 215-1st app. Batmen of all nations 1.90 6.00 13.00
213-(80-Pg. Giant G-61); 30th anniversary issue (7-8/69); origin Alfred (r/Batman #16), Joker(r/Det. #168), Clayface; new origin Robin with new facts 5.40 16.00 38.00
218-(80-Pg. Giant G-67) 3.10 9.00 22.00
219-Neal Adams-a 3.30 10.00 23.00
220,221,224-227,229-231 1.60 5.00 11.00
222-Beatles take-off; art lesson by Joe Kubert 3.60 11.00 25.00
223,228,233-(80-Pg. Giants G-73,G-79,G-85) 2.10 6.00 15.00
232,237-N. Adams-a. 232-Intro/1st app. Ras Al Ghul; origin Batman & Robin retold. 237-G.A. Batman-r/Det. #37; 1st app. The Reaper; Wrightson/Ellison plots 4.30 13.00 30.00
234-1st S.A. app. Two-Face; N. Adams-a; 52 pg. issues begin, end #242 9.00 28.00 65.00
235,236,239-242: 239-XMas-c. 241-Reprint/#5 1.70 4.20 10.00
238-DC-8 100 Page Super Spec.; G.A. Atom, Sargon (r/Sensation #57), Plastic Man (r/Police #14) stories; Doom Patrol origin-r; Batman, Legion, Aquaman-r; N. Adams wraparound-c 1.60 5.00 11.00
243-245-Neal Adams-a 2.60 7.70 18.00
246-250,252,253: 253-Shadow-c & app. 1.70 4.20 10.00
251-(9/73)-N. Adams-c/a; Joker-c/story 5.40 16.00 38.00
254,256-259,261-All 100 pg. editions; part-r: 254-(2/74)-Man-Bat-c & app. 258-Joker app.; The Cavalier-r. 259-Shadow-c & app.

Batman #251 © DC

Batman #429 © DC

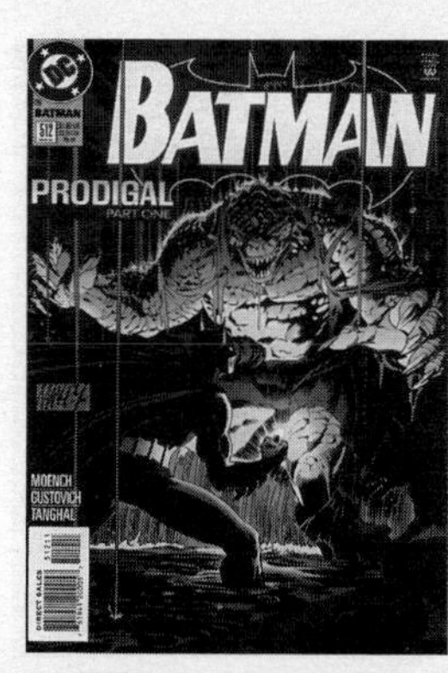

Batman #512 © DC

	GD25	FN65	NM94
	1.70	5.00	12.00
255-(100 pgs.)-N. Adams-c/a; tells of Bruce Wayne's father who wore bat costume & fought crime (r/Det. #235); r/story Batman #22	2.60	7.70	18.00
260-Joker-c/story (100 pgs.)	4.10	12.40	29.00
262-285,287-290,292,293,295-299: 262-(68pgs.). 266-Catwoman back to old costume	1.10	2.70	6.50
286,291,294-Joker-c/stories	1.40	3.50	8.50
300-Double-size	1.50	3.80	9.00
301-(7/78)-320,322-352: 304-(44 pgs.). 310-1st modern app. The Gentleman Ghost in Batman. 311-Bat-girl reteams w/Batman. 313-2nd app. Calendar Man. 313,314-Two-Face-c/stories. 316-Robin returns. 322-324-Catwoman (Selina Kyle) app. 322,323-Cat-Man cameos (1st in Batman, 1 panel each). 323-1st meeting Catwoman & Cat-Man. 324-1st full app. Cat-Man this title. 332-Catwoman's 1st solo. 325-Death of Comm. Gordon. 345-1st app. new Dr. Death. 357,358-1st app. Killer Croc. 361-1st app. Harvey Bullock	1.50	4.00	9.00
321,353,359-Joker-c/stories. 359-1st app. Killer Moth	1.70	4.20	10.00
354-356,358,360-365,369,370: 358-Killer Croc app.	1.10	2.70	6.50
357-1st app. Jason Todd (3/83); see Det. 524	1.50	3.75	9.00
366-Jason Todd 1st in Robin costume; Joker-c/story	2.90	9.00	20.00
368-1st new Robin in costume (Jason Todd)	2.10	6.40	15.00
371-399,401-403: 371-Cat-Man-c/story; brief origin Cat-Man (cont'd in Det. #538). 386,387-Intro Black Mask (villain). 401-2nd app. Magpie (see Man of Steel #3 for 1st). 403-Joker cameo		1.40	3.50

NOTE: *Most issues between 397 & 432 were reprinted in 1989 and sold in multi-packs. Some are not identified as reprints but have newer ads copyrighted after cover dates. 2nd and 3rd printings exist.*

	GD25	FN65	NM94
400 ($1.50, 68pgs.)-Dark Knight special; intro by Stephen King; Art Adams/Austin-a	2.40	7.30	17.00
404-Miller scripts begin (end 407); Year 1; 1st modern app. Catwoman (2/87)	2.30	7.00	16.00
405-407: 407-Year 1 ends (See Det. for Year 2)	1.20	2.90	7.00
408-410: New Origin Jason Todd (Robin)	1.00	2.50	6.00
411-416,421-425: 412-Origin/1st app. Mime. 414-Starlin scripts begin, end #429. 416-Nightwing-c/story. 423-McFarlane-c		1.20	3.00
417-420: "Ten Nights of the Beast" storyline	1.60	5.00	11.00
426-($1.50, 52 pgs.)- "A Death In The Family" storyline begins, ends #429	1.20	2.90	7.00
427- "A Death In The Family" part 2	1.00	2.50	6.00
428-Death of Robin (Jason Todd)	1.00	2.50	6.00
429-Joker-c/story; Superman app.	1.00	1.80	4.50
430-432		.80	2.00
433-435- "Many Deaths of the Batman" story by John Byrne-c/scripts		1.00	2.50
436-Year 3 begins (ends #439); origin original Robin retold by Nightwing (Dick Grayson); 1st app. Timothy Drake (8/89)	1.00	2.00	5.00
436-2nd printing			1.00
437-439: 437-Origin Robin continued		1.00	2.50
440,441: "A Lonely Place of Dying" Parts 1 & 3			1.00
442-1st app. Timothy Drake in Robin costume	1.00	2.00	5.00
443-456,458,459,462-464: 445-447-Batman goes to Russia. 448,449-"The Penguin Affair" parts 1 & 3. 450,451-Joker-c/stories. 452-454-"Dark Knight Dark City" storyline; Riddler app. 455-Alan Grant scripts begin, ends #466, 470. 464-Last solo Batman story; free 16 pg. preview of Impact Comics line			1.50
457-Timothy Drake officially becomes Robin & dons new costume	1.00	2.00	5.00
457-Direct sale edition (has #000 in indicia)	1.00	1.80	4.50
460,461-Two part Catwoman story		.80	2.00
465-Robin returns to action with Batman			1.25
466-487: 470-War of the Gods x-over. 475,476-The return of Scarface-c/story. 476-Last $1.00-c. 477,478-Photo-c			1.25
488-Cont'd from Batman: Sword of Azrael #4; Azrael-c & app.	1.70	4.20	10.00
489-Bane-c/story; 1st app. Azrael in Bat-costume	1.50	3.75	9.00
490-Riddler-c/story; Azrael & Bane app.	1.00	3.00	6.00
491-Knightfall lead-in; Joker-c/story; Azrael & Bane app.; Kelley Jones-c begin	1.00	1.60	4.00
492-Knightfall part 1; Bane app.	1.00	2.00	5.00
492-Platinum edition (promo copy)			20.00
493-Knightfall part 3		1.60	4.00
494-Knightfall part 5; Joker-c & app.		1.40	3.50
495-Knightfall part 7; brief Bane & Joker apps.		1.00	2.50
496-Knightfall part 9; Joker-c/story; Bane cameo			1.25
497-Knightfall part 11; has B&W outer-c; Bane vs. Batman-c/story	0.90	2.30	5.50
497-2nd printing			1.25
497-Newsstand edition w/o outer cover		.70	1.75
498-Knightfall part 15; Bane & Catwoman-c & app. (see Showcase 93 #7 & 8)		.70	1.75
499-Knightfall part 17; Bane app.		.70	1.75
500-($2.50, 68 pgs.)-Knightfall part 19; Azrael in new Bat-costume; Bane-c/story		1.00	2.50
500-($3.95, 68 pgs.)-Collector's Edition w/die-cut double-c w/foil by Joe Quesada & 2 bound-in post cards		1.60	4.00
501-508,510,511: 501-Begin $1.50-c. 501-508-Knightquest. 503,504-Catwoman app. 507-Ballistic app.; Jim Balent-a(p). 510-KnightsEnd Pt. 7. 511-(9/94)-Zero Hour			1.50
509-($2.50, 52 pgs.)-KnightsEnd Pt. 1		1.00	2.50
0,512-518: 0-(10/94)-Origin retold. 512-(11/94)-Dick Grayson assumes Batman role			1.50
Annual 1(8-10/61)-Swan-c	50.00	140.00	450.00
Annual 2	18.00	53.00	175.00
Annual 3(Summer, '62)-Joker-c/story	20.00	60.00	200.00
Annual 4,5	9.00	27.00	90.00
Annual 6,7(7/64, 25¢, 80 pgs.)	7.00	21.00	70.00
Annual V5#8(1982)-Painted-c		1.80	4.50
Annual 9,10,12: 9(7/85). 10(1986). 12(1988, $1.50)		1.20	3.00
Annual 11(1987, $1.25)-Penguin-c/story; Alan Moore scripts	1.00	2.00	5.00
Annual 13(1989, $1.75, 68 pgs.)-Gives history of Bruce Wayne, Dick Grayson, Jason Todd, Alfred, Comm. Gordon, Barbara Gordon (Batgirl) & Vicki Vale; Morrow-i		.90	2.25
Annual 14(1990, $2.00, 68 pgs.)-Origin Two-Face		.90	2.25
Annual 15(1991, $2.00, 68 pgs.)-Armageddon 2001 x-over; Joker app.;		.90	2.25
Annual 15(2nd printing)		.80	2.00
Annual 16(1992, $2.50, 68 pgs.)-Joker-c/s; Kieth-c		1.00	2.50
Annual 17(1993, $2.50, 68 pgs.)-Azrael in Bat-costume; intro Ballistic		1.00	2.50
Annual 18(1994, $2.95)		1.20	3.00
Special 1 (4/84)-Golden-c/a	1.00	2.00	5.00
Pizza Hut giveaway(12/77)-exact-r of #122,123; Joker-c/story		1.20	3.00
Prell Shampoo giveaway(1966, 16 pgs.)- "The Joker's Practical Jokes" (6-7/8x3-3/8")	3.60	9.00	18.00

NOTE: ***Art Adams** a-400p. **Neal Adams** c-200, 203, 210, 217, 219-222, 224-227, 229, 230, 232, 234, 236-241, 243-246, 251, 255, Annual 14. **Bolland** c-445-447. **Burnley** a-10, 12-18, 20, 22, 25, 27; c-9, 15, 16, 27, 28p, 40p, 42p. **Byrne** c-401, 433-435, 533-535, Annual 11. **Travis Charest** c-488-490p. **Colan** a-340p, 343-345p, 348-351p, 373p, 383p; c-343p, 345p, 350p. **J. Cole** a-238r. **Cowan** a-Annual 10p. **Golden** a-295p, 303p. **Alan Grant** scripts-455-466, 470, 474-476, 479, 480, Annual 16(part). **Grell** a-287, 288p, 289p, 290; c-287-290. **Infantino/Anderson** c-167, 173, 175, 181, 186, 191, 192, 194, 195, 198, 199. **Kelley Jones** c-491-499, 500(newsstand), 501-508. **Kaluta** c-242, 248, 253, Annual 12. **G. Kane/Anderson** c-178-180. **Bob Kane** a-1, 2, 5; c-1-5, 7, 17. **G. Kane** a-(r)-254, 255, 259, 261, 353i. **Kubert** a-238r, 400; c-310, 319p, 327, 328, 344. **McFarlane** c-423. **Moldoff** c-101-140. **Moldoff/Giella** a-164-175, 177-181, 183, 184, 186. **Moldoff/Greene** a-169, 172-174, 177-179, 181, 184. **Mooney** a-255r. **Newton** a-305, 306, 328p, 331p, 332p, 337p, 338p, 346p, 352-357p, 360-372p, 374-378p; c-374p, 378p. **Nino** a-Annual 9. **Irv Novick** c-201, 202. **Perez** a-400; c-436-442. **Fred Ray** c-8, 10; w/**Robinson**-11. **Robinson/Roussos** a-12-17, 20, 22, 24, 25, 27, 28, 31, 33, 37. **Robinson** a-12, 14, 18, 22-32,34, 36, 37, 255r, 260r, 261r; c-6, 8, 10, 12-15, 18, 21, 24, 26, 30, 37, 39. **Simonson** a-300p, 312p, 321p; c-300p, 312p, 366, 413i. **P. Smith** a-Annual 9. **Dick Sprang** c-19, 20, 22, 23, 25, 29, 31-36, 38, 51, 55, 66, 73, 76. **Starlin** c/a-402. **Staton** a-334. **Wrightson** a-265i, 400; c-320r. Bat-Hound app. in 92, 97, 103, 123, 125, 133, 156, 158. Bat-*

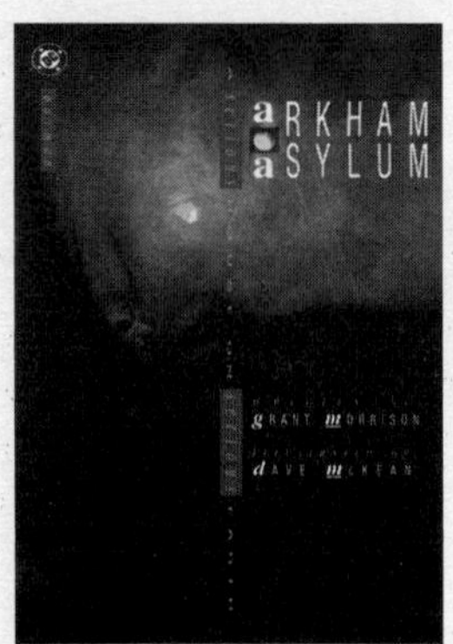

Batman: Arkham Asylum © DC

Batman/Spawn: War Devil © DC & Todd McFarlane

Batman and the Outsiders #11 © DC

GD25 FN65 NM94

Mite app. in 133, 136, 144, 146, 158, 161. Batwoman app. in 105, 116, 122, 125, 128, 129, 131, 133, 139, 140, 141, 144, 145, 150, 151, 153, 154, 157, 159, 162, 163. Catwoman back-ups in 332, 345, 346, 348-351. Joker app. in 1, 2, 4, 5, 7-9, 11-13, 19, 20, 23, 25, 28, 32 & many more. Robin solo back-up stories in 337-339, 341-343.

BATMAN (Books and trade paperbacks)

...: A Lonely Place of Dying (1990, $3.95, 132 pgs.)-r/Batman #440-442 & New Titans #60,61; Perez-c 1.60 4.00
...And Dracula: Red Rain nn(1991, $24.95)-Hard-c; Elseworlds storyline 5.70 17.00 40.00
...And Dracula: Red Rain nn(1992, $9.95)-Soft-c 1.70 4.00 10.00
Arkham Asylum Hard-c ('89, $24.95) 3.60 10.75 25.00
Arkham Asylum trade pb (#14.95) 2.15 6.50 15.00
Birth of the Demon Hard cover (1992, $24.95) 3.60 10.75 25.00
Birth of the Demon Soft cover (1993, $12.95) 1.85 5.50 13.00
Blind Justice nn (1992, $7.50)-r/Det. #598-600 1.25 3.00 7.50
Bride of the Demon Hard cover (1990, $19.95) 3.20 8.00 20.00
Bride of the Demon Soft cover ($12.95) 1.85 5.50 13.00
...: Collected Legends of the Dark Knight nn (1994, $12.95)-Reprints Legends of the Dark Knight #32-34,38,42,43 1.85 5.50 13.00
...: Dark Joker-The Wild(1993, $9.95)-Elseworlds sty 1.70 4.00 10.00
Death In The Family trade paperback (1988, $3.95)-r/Batman #426-429 by Aparo 1.00 2.00 5.00
Death In The Family: (2nd - 5th printings) 1.60 4.00
Digital Justice nn (1990, $24.95, hardcover)-Computer generated art 3.60 10.75 25.00
...Gothic nn (1992, $12.95)-r/Legends of the Dark Knight #6-10 1.85 5.50 13.00
Greatest Batman Stories Hard-c ($24.95) 6.00 19.00 45.00
Greatest Batman Stories Soft-c ($15.95) 2.30 6.90 16.00
Greatest Batman Stories Vol. 2 (1992, $16.95) 2.40 7.30 17.00
Greatest Joker Stories Hard-c ($19.95) 5.00 15.00 35.00
Greatest Joker Stories Soft-c ($14.95) 2.10 6.40 15.00
Greatest Joker Stories (Stacked Deck...Expanded Edition) (1992, $29.95)-Longmeadow Press Publ. 4.30 13.00 30.00
...: The Many Deaths of the Batman trade paperback (1992, $3.95, 84 pgs.)-r/Batman #433-435 w/new Byrne-c 1.60 4.00
...: Prey nn (1992, $12.95)-Gulacy/Austin-a 1.85 5.50 13.00
Shaman nn (1993, $12.95)-r/Legends/D.K. #1-5 1.85 5.50 13.00
...: Son of the Demon Hard cover (9/87, $14.95 6.00 19.00 45.00
...: Son of the Demon limited signed & numbered hard-c (1,700) 10.00 30.00 70.00
...: Son of the Demon softcover w/new-c ($8.95) 1.50 3.75 9.00
...: Son of the Demon softcover, 2nd printing (1989, $9.95) - 4th printing 1.65 4.00 10.00
...: Tales of the Demon nn (1991, $17.95, 212 pgs.)-Intro by Sam Hamm; reprints by N. Adams(3) & Golden; contains Saga of Ra's Al Ghul #1 2.60 7.50 18.00
...: Ten Nights of the Beast (1994, $5.95)-r/Batman #417-420 1.00 2.50 6.00
...: Venom trade paperback (1993, $9.95)-r/Legends of the Dark Knight #16-20; embossed-c 1.65 4.00 10.00
Year One Hardcover (1988, $12.95) 1.85 5.50 13.00
Year One trade paperback (1988, $9.95)-r/Batman #404-407 by Miller; introduction by Miller 1.65 4.00 10.00
Year One trade paperback: 2nd & 3rd prints 1.65 4.00 10.00
Year Two trade paperback (1990, $9.95)-r/Det. 575-578 by McFarlane; wraparound-c 1.65 4.00 10.00

BATMAN (One-Shots)

Batman and Other DC Classics 1 (1989, giveaway)-DC Comics/Diamond Comic Distributors; Batman origin-r/Batman #47, Camelot 3000-r by Bolland, Justice League-r('87), New Teen Titans-r by Perez 1.00
...: Catwoman Defiant nn (1992, $4.95, one-shot, prestige format)-Milligan scripts; c-interlocks w/Batman: Penguin Triumphant; special foil logo 1.00 2.00 5.00
Full Circle nn (1991, $5.95, stiff-c, 68 pgs.)-Sequel to Batman: Year Two 1.00 2.50 6.00
...Gallery, The 1 (1992, $2.95)-Reprints 1.20 3.00
...Gotham By Gaslight ('89, $3.95) 1.60 4.00
.../Green Arrow: The Poison Arrow nn (1992, $5.95, squarebound, 68 pgs.)-Netzer-c/a 1.00 2.50 6.00
Holy Terror nn (1991, $4.95, 52 pgs.)-Elseworlds 1.00 2.00 5.00
.../Houdini: The Devil's Workshop (1993, $5.95) 1.00 2.50 6.00
...: In Darkest Knight nn ('94, $4.95, 52 pgs.)-Elseworlds Batman with Green Lantern's ring 1.00 2.50 5.00
...Judge Dredd: Judgement on Gotham nn (1991, $5.95, 68 pgs.)-Grant/Wagner scripts; Simon Bisley-c/a 1.00 2.50 6.00
...Judge Dredd: Judgement on Gotham 2nd print 1.00 2.50 6.00
...Judge Dredd: Vendetta in Gotham (1993, $5.95) 1.00 2.50 6.00
...: Mask of the Phantasm ($2.95)-Movie adaptation 1.20 3.00
...: Mask of the Phantasm ($4.95)-Movie adaptation 1.00 2.50 5.00
...: Master of the Future nn (1991, $5.95, 68 pgs.)-Elseworlds storyline; sequel to Gotham By Gaslight; embossed-c 1.00 2.50 6.00
...Movie Special ('89, $2.50, regular) 1.00 2.50
...Movie Special ('89, $4.95, deluxe) 1.00 2.00 5.00
...: Penguin Triumphant nn (1992, $4.95, one-shot)-Staton-a(p); special foil logo 1.00 2.00 5.00
.../Punisher: Lake of Fire (1994, $4.95, DC/Marvel) 1.00 2.00 5.00
...Returns Movie Special ('92, $3.95) 1.60 4.00
...Returns Movie Prestige ('92, $5.95, squarebounded)-Dorman painted-c 1.00 2.50 6.00
...: Seduction of the Gun nn (1992, $2.50, 68 pgs.) 1.00 2.50
...-Spawn: War Devil nn (1994, $4.95, 52 pgs.) 1.00 2.00 5.00
...: The Blue, the Grey, & the Bat nn (1992, $5.95, 68 pgs.)-Weiss/Lopez-a 1.00 2.50 6.00
...: Vengeance of Bane Special 1 (1992, $2.50, 68 pgs.)-Origin & 1st app. Bane (see Batman #491) 3.20 8.00 20.00
...: Vengeance of Bane Special 1-2nd printing 1.00 2.50

BATMAN (Kellogg's Poptarts comics)
1966 (Set of 6) (16 pgs.)
National Periodical Publications

"The Man in the Iron Mask", "The Penguin's Fowl Play", "The Joker's Happy Victims", "The Catwoman's Catnapping Caper", "The Mad Hatter's Hat Crimes", "The Case of the Batman II"
each.... 4.00 10.00 20.00

NOTE: *All above were folded and placed in Poptarts boxes.* ***Infantino*** *art on Catwoman and Joker issues.*

BATMAN ADVENTURES, THE (TV cartoon)
Oct, 1992 - Present (1.25/1.50)
DC Comics

1-Based on Fox TV cartoon; Penguin-c/s 1.20 2.90 7.00
1-Silver Edition 2nd printing ($1.95) .90 2.25
2-6,8-19: 2,12-Catwoman-c/story. 3-Joker-c/story. 5-Scarecrow. 10-Riddler-c/s. 11-Man-Bat-c/s. 12-Batgirl-c/s 1.00 2.50
7-Spec. ed. polybagged with Man-Bat trading card 1.40 4.00 8.50
20-24,26-30: 16-Joker-c/s; begin $1.50-c. 18-Batgirl-c/s. 19-Scarecrow-c/s 1.50
25-($2.50, 52 pgs.)-Superman app. 1.00 2.50
...: Mad Love nn (2/94, $3.95, 68 pgs.)-Joker-c/story 1.40 2.80 7.00
...: The Collected Adventures Vol. 1 (1993, $5.95) 1.00 2.50 6.00
...: The Collected Adventures Vol. 2 (1994, $5.95) 1.00 2.50 6.00

BATMAN AND THE OUTSIDERS (The Adventures of the Outsiders#33 on)
(Also see Brave & The Bold #200 & The Outsiders)
Aug, 1983 - No. 32, Apr, 1986 (Mando paper #5 on)
DC Comics

1-32: 1-Batman, Halo, Geo-Force, Katana, Metamorpho & Black Lightning begin. 5-New Teen Titans x-over. 9-Halo begins. 11,12-Origin Katana. 18-More facts about Metamorpho's origin. 28-31-Lookers origin. 32-Team disbands 1.00
Annual 1(9/84)-Miller/Aparo-c; Aparo-i 1.00
Annual 2(9/85)-Metamorpho & Sapphire Stagg wed; Aparo-c 1.00

NOTE: ***Aparo*** *a-1-9, 11, 12p, 16-20; c-1-4, 5i, 6-21.* ***B. Kane*** *a-3r.* ***Layton*** *a-19i, 20i.* ***Lopez*** *a-*

Batman/Grendal #1© DC

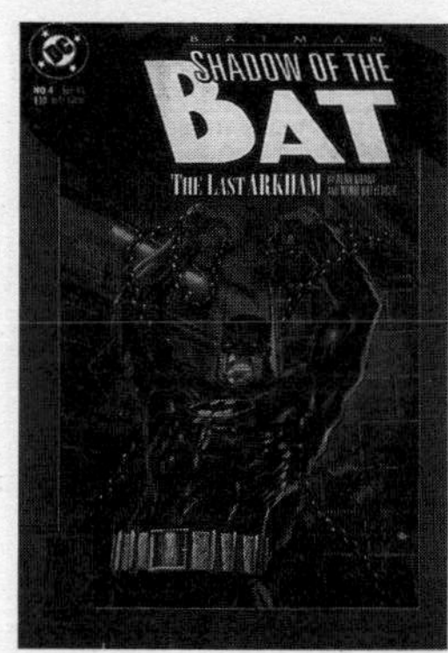

Batman: Shadow Of The Bat #4 © DC

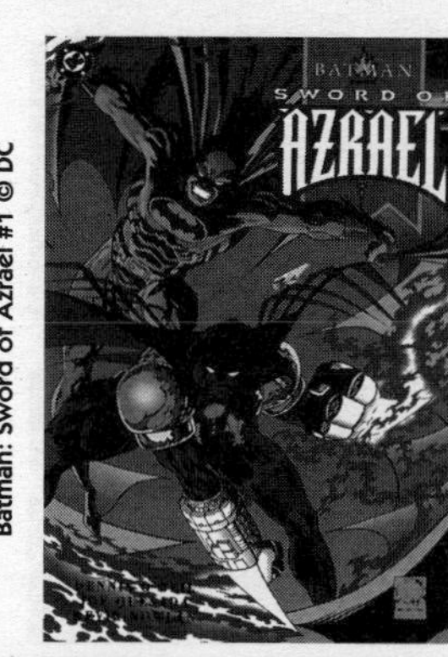

Batman: Sword of Azrael #1 © DC

GD25 FN65 NM94

*3p. **Perez** c-5p. **B. Willingham** a-14p.*

BATMAN FAMILY, THE
Sept-Oct, 1975 - No. 20, Oct-Nov, 1978 (#1-4, 17-on: 68 pgs.)
(Combined with Detective Comics with No. 481)
National Periodical Publications/DC Comics

1-Origin/2nd app. Batgirl-Robin team-up (The Dynamite Duo); reprints plus one new story begins; N. Adams-a(r); r/1st app. Man-Bat from Det. #400 — 1.60 4.00
2-5: 3-Batgirl & Robin learn each's i.d. — 1.10 2.75
6,9-Joker's daughter on cover (1st app?) — 1.20 3.00
7,8,10,14-16: 10-1st revival Batwoman; Cavalier app.; 2nd app. Killer Moth. 15-3rd app. Killer Moth. 16-Batgirl cameo; last app. in costume until New Teen Titans #47 — 1.10 2.75
11-13-Rogers-a(p): 11-New stories begin; Man-Bat begins — 1.60 4.00
17-($1.00 size)-Batman, Huntress begin; Batwoman & Catwoman 1st meet — 1.10 2.75
18-20: Huntress by Staton in all. 20-Origin Ragman retold — 1.50

NOTE: *Aparo* a-17; c-11-16. *Austin* a-12i. *Chaykin* a-14p. *Michael Golden* a-15-17,18-20p. *Grell* a-1; c-1. *Gil Kane* a-2r. *Kaluta* c-17, 19. *Newton* a-13. *Robinson* a-1r, 3i(r), 9r. *Russell* a-18i, 19i. *Starlin* a-17; c-18, 20.

BATMAN/GRENDEL
1993 - No. 2, 1993 ($4.95, mini-series, 52 pgs.)
DC Comics

1-Devil's Riddle; by Matt Wagner — 1.00 2.00 5.00
2-Devil's Masque; by Matt Wagner — 1.00 2.00 5.00

BATMAN: LEGENDS OF THE DARK KNIGHT (Legends of the Dark Knight #1-36)
Nov, 1989 - Present ($1.50/$1.75/$1.95)
DC Comics

1- "Shaman" begins, ends #5; outer cover has four different color variations, all worth same — 1.00 2.00 5.00
2 — 1.20 3.00
3-5 — .80 2.00
6-10- "Gothic" by Grant Morrison (scripts) — 1.20 3.00
11-15,17,18: 11-15-Gulacy/Austin-a. 14-Catwoman app. 18-Last $1.50-c — .80 2.00
16-Intro drug Bane uses; begin Venom story — 1.00 2.00 5.00
19-49,51-63: 38-Bat-Mite-c/story. 46-49-Catwoman app. w/Heath-c/a. 51-Ragman app.; Joe Kubert-c. 59,60-Knightquest x-over. 62,63-KnightsEnd Pt. 4 & 10 — .80 2.00
50-($3.95, 68 pgs.)-Bolland embossed gold foil-c; Joker-c/story; pin-ups by Chaykin, Simonson, Williamson, Kaluda, Russell, others — 1.60 4.00
64-(9/94)-Begin $1.95-c — .80 2.00
0,65-70: 0-(10/94)-Quesada/Palmiotti-c; various artists on sty — .80 2.00
Annual 1 (1991, $3.95, 68 pgs.)-Joker app. — 1.60 4.00
Annual 2 (1992, $3.50, 68 pgs.)-Netzer-c/a — 1.40 3.50
Annual 3 (1993, $3.50, 68 pgs.)-New Batman (Azrael) app. — 1.40 3.50
Annual 4 (1994, $3.50, 68 pgs.)-Elseworlds story — 1.40 3.50
Halloween Special 1 (12/93, $6.95, 84 pgs.)-Embossed & foil stamped-c — 1.20 3.00 7.00

NOTE: *Chaykin* scripts-24-26. *Alan Grant* scripts-38, 52, 53. *Gil Kane* c/a-24-26. *Russell* c/a-42, 43.

BATMAN MINIATURE (See Batman Kellogg's)

BATMAN RECORD COMIC
1966 (One Shot)
National Periodical Publications

1-With record (still sealed) — 16.00 48.00 110.00
Comic only — 2.80 7.00 14.00

BATMAN: RUN, RIDDLER, RUN
1992 - Book 3, 1992 ($4.95, mini-series)
DC Comics

Book 1-3: Mark Badger-a & plot — 1.00 2.00 5.00

BATMAN: SHADOW OF THE BAT
June, 1992 - Present ($1.50/$1.75/$1.95)
DC Comics

1-The Last Arkham-c/story begins; A. Grant scripts in all — 1.30 3.25
1-(2.50)-Deluxe edition polybagged w/poster, pop-up & book mark — 1.30 3.25
2-7: 4-The Last Arkham ends. 7-Last $1.50-c — 1.50
8-28: 14,15-Staton-a(p). 16-18-Knightfall tie-ins. 19-28-Knightquest tie-ins w/Azrael as Batman. 19,20-Painted-c. 25-Silver ink-c; anniversary issue — .70 1.75
29-($2.95, 52 pgs.)-KnightsEnd Pt. 2 — 1.20 3.00
30,31: 30-KnightsEnd Pt. 8. 31-(9.94)-Begin $1.95-c; Zero Hour — .80 2.00
0,32-36: 0-(10/94)-A. Grant-story — .80 2.00
Annual 1 (1993, $3.50, 68 pgs.) — 1.40 3.50
Annual 2 (1994, $3.95, 68 pgs.) — 1.60 4.00

BATMAN SPECTACULAR (See DC Special Series No. 15)

BATMAN: SWORD OF AZRAEL
Oct, 1992 - No. 4, Jan, 1993 ($1.75, mini-series)
DC Comics

1-Wraparound gatefold-c; Quesada-c/a(p) in all; 1st app. Azrael — 2.15 6.50 15.00
2-4: 4-Cont'd in Batman #488 — 1.65 4.00 10.00
Silver Edition 1-4 (1993, $1.95)-Reprints #1-4 — .80 2.00
Trade Paperback (1993, $9.95)-Reprints #1-4 — 1.65 4.00 10.00
Trade Paperback Gold Edition — 2.15 6.50 15.00

BATMAN: THE CULT
1988 - No. 4, Nov, 1988 ($3.50, deluxe mini-series)
DC Comics

1-Wrightson-a/painted-c in all — 1.00 2.00 5.00
2-4 — 1.60 4.00
Trade Paperback ('91, $14.95)-New Wrightson-c — 2.15 6.50 15.00

BATMAN: THE DARK KNIGHT
March, 1986 - No. 4, 1986 ($2.95, squarebound)
DC Comics

1-Miller story & c/a(p); set in the future — 2.15 6.50 15.00
1-2nd & 3rd printings — 1.20 3.00
2-Carrie Kelly becomes Robin (female) — 1.25 3.00 7.50
2-2nd & 3rd printings — 1.20 3.00
3-Death of Joker; Superman app. — 1.00 2.00 5.00
3-2nd printing — 1.20 3.00
4-Death of Alfred; Superman app. — 1.40 3.50
Hardcover, signed & numbered edition ($40.00)(4000 copies) — 150.00
Hardcover, trade edition — 4.30 13.00 30.00
Softcover, trade edition (1st printing only) — 1.65 4.00 10.00
Softcover, trade edition (2nd thru 8th printings) — 1.25 3.00 7.50

NOTE: *The #2 second printings can be identified by matching the grey background colors on the inside front cover and facing page. The inside front cover of the second printing has a dark grey background which does not match the lighter grey of the facing page. On the true 1st printings, the backgrounds are both light grey. All other issues areclearly marked.*

BATMAN: THE KILLING JOKE
1988 ($3.50, deluxe, 52 pgs., adults)
DC Comics

1-Bolland-c/a; Alan Moore scripts — 1.10 3.40 8.00
1-2nd thru 8th printings — 1.40 3.50

BATMAN: THE OFFICIAL COMIC ADAPTATION OF THE WARNER BROS. MOTION PICTURE
1989 ($2.50, $4.95, 68 pgs.) (Movie adaptation)
DC Comics

1-Regular format ($2.50)-Ordway-c/a — 1.60 4.00
1-Prestige format ($4.95)-Diff.-c, same insides — 1.00 2.50 6.00

BATMAN 3-D (Also see 3-D Batman)
1990 ($9.95, w/glasses, 8-1/8x10-3/4")

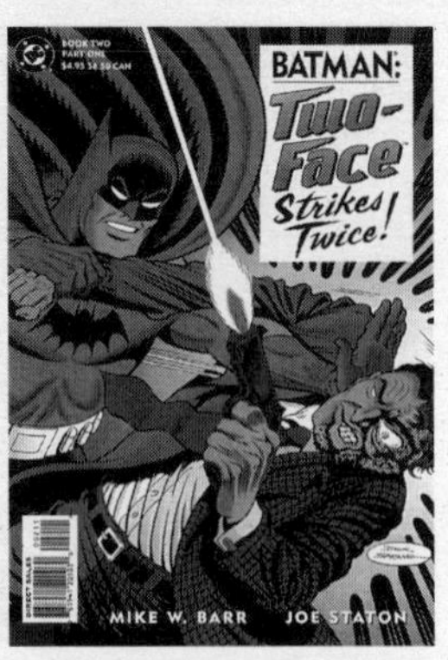

Batman: Two-Face Strikes Twice #2 © DC

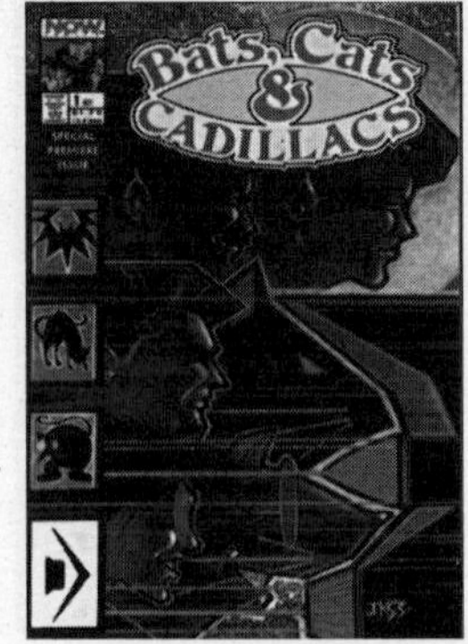

Bats, Cats & Cadillacs #1 © NOW

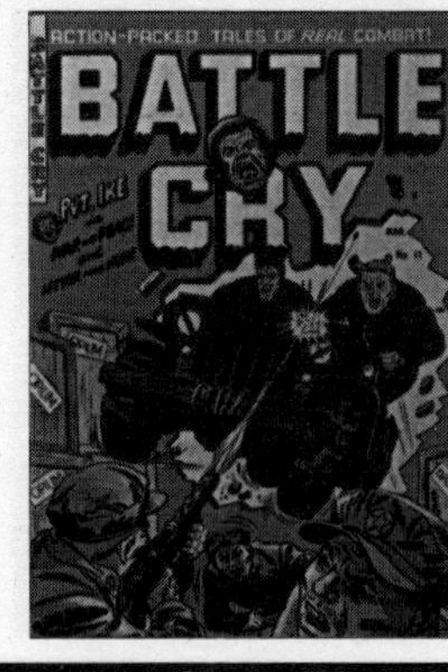

Battle Cry #11 © Stanmor Pub.

DC Comics
nn-Byrne-a/scripts; Riddler, Joker, Penguin & Two-Face app. plus r/1953 3-D Batman; pin-ups by many artists 1.65 4.00 10.00

BATMAN: TWO-FACE STRIKES TWICE
1993 - No. 2, 1993 ($4.95, 52 pgs.)
DC Comics
1,2-Flip book format w/Staton-a (G.A. side) 1.00 2.00 5.00

BATMAN VERSUS PREDATOR
1991 - No. 3, 1992 (Mini-series)
DC Comics/Dark Horse Comics
1 (Prestige format, $4.95)-1 & 3 contain 8 Batman/Predator trading cards; Andy & Adam Kubert-a; Suydam painted-c 1.00 2.50 5.00
1 (Regular format, $1.95)-No trading cards .80 2.00
2-(Prestige)-Extra pin-ups inside; Suydam-c 1.00 2.00 5.00
2-(Regular)-Without cards .80 2.00
3-(Prestige)-Suydam-c 1.00 2.00 5.00
3-(Regular)-Without cards .80 2.00
Trade paperback nn (1992, $5.95, 132pgs.)-r/#1-3 w/new introductions & forward plus new wraparound-c by Gibbons 1.00 2.50 6.00

BATMAN VS. THE INCREDIBLE HULK (See DC Special Series No. 27)

BAT MASTERSON (TV) (Also see Tim Holt #28)
Aug-Oct, 1959; Feb-Apr, 1960 - No. 9, Nov-Jan, 1961-62
Dell Publishing Co.
4-Color 1013 (#1) (8-10/59) 10.00 30.00 70.00
2-9: Gene Barry photo-c on all 6.70 20.00 40.00

BATS (See Tales Calculated to Drive You Bats)

BATS, CATS & CADILLACS (Now)(Value: cover or less)

BATTLE
March, 1951 - No. 70, June, 1960
Marvel/Atlas Comics(FPI No. 1-62/Male No. 63 on)
1 13.50 41.00 95.00
2 6.70 20.00 40.00
3-10: 4-1st Buck Pvt. O'Toole. 10-Pakula-a 4.70 14.00 28.00
11-20: 11-Check-a 4.00 11.00 22.00
21,23-Krigstein-a 5.35 16.00 32.00
22,24-36: 32-Tuska-a. 36-Everett-a 3.60 9.00 18.00
37-Kubert-a (Last precode, 2/55) 4.00 10.00 20.00
38-40,42-48 3.20 8.00 16.00
41-Kubert/Moskowitz-a 4.00 10.00 20.00
49-Davis-a 4.00 11.00 22.00
50-54,56-58 3.20 8.00 16.00
55-Williamson-a (5 pgs.) 5.00 15.00 30.00
59-Torres-a 3.60 9.00 18.00
60-62: 60,62-Combat Kelly app. 61-Combat Casey app. 3.20 8.00 16.00
63-66: 63-Ditko-a. 64-66-Kirby-a. 66-Davis-a; has story of Fidel Castro in pre-Communism days (an admiring profile) 5.85 17.50 35.00
67,68: 67-Williamson/Crandall-a (4 pgs.); Kirby, Davis-a. 68-Kirby/Williamson-a (4 pgs.); Kirby/Ditko-a 6.35 19.00 38.00
69,70: 69-Kirby-a. 70-Kirby/Ditko-a 5.35 16.00 32.00
NOTE: ***Andru*** *a-37.* ***Berg*** *a-38, 14, 60-62.* ***Colan*** *a-33, 55.* ***Everett*** *a-36, 50, 70; c-56, 57.* ***Heath*** *a-6, 9, 13, 31, 69; c-6, 9, 12, 26, 35, 37.* ***Kirby*** *c-64-69.* ***Maneely*** *a-4, 6, 31, 61; c-4, 33, 59, 61.* ***Orlando*** *a-47.* ***Powell*** *a-53, 55.* ***Reinman*** *a-8, 9, 26, 32.* ***Robinson*** *a-9, 39.* ***Romita*** *a-26.* ***Severin*** *a-28, 32-34, 66-69; c-36, 55.* ***Sinnott*** *a-33, 37.* ***Woodbridge*** *a-52, 55.*

BATTLE ACTION
Feb, 1952 - No. 12, 5/53; No. 13, 11/54 - No. 30, 8/57
Atlas Comics (NPI)
1-Pakula-a 12.00 36.00 85.00
2 6.35 19.00 38.00
3,4,6,7,9,10: 6-Robinson-c/a. 7-Partial nudity 4.20 12.50 25.00
5-Used in **POP**, pg. 93,94 4.70 14.00 28.00
8-Krigstein-a 5.00 15.00 30.00
11-15 (Last precode, 2/55) 4.00 11.00 22.00
16-26,28,29 3.20 8.00 16.00
27,30-Torres-a 4.00 10.00 20.00
NOTE: *Battle Brady app. 5-7, 10-12.* ***Berg*** *a-3.* ***Check*** *a-11.* ***Everett*** *a-7; c-13, 25.* ***Heath*** *a-3, 8, 18; c-3,15, 18, 21.* ***Maneely*** *a-1; c-5.* ***Reinman*** *a-1.* ***Robinson*** *a-6, 7; c-6.* ***Shores*** *a-7(2).* ***Sinnott*** *a-3.* ***Woodbridge*** *a-28, 30.*

BATTLE ATTACK
Oct, 1952 - No. 8, Dec, 1955
Stanmor Publications
1 6.35 19.00 38.00
2 4.00 10.00 20.00
3-8: 3-Hollingsworth-a 2.80 7.00 14.00

BATTLE BEASTS (Blackthorne)(Value: cover or less)

BATTLE BRADY (Formerly Men in Action No. 1-9; see 3-D Action)
No. 10, Jan, 1953 - No. 14, June, 1953
Atlas Comics (IPC)
10: 10-12-Syd Shores-c 9.15 27.50 55.00
11-Used in **POP**, pg. 95 plus B&W & color illos 5.00 15.00 30.00
12-14 4.00 12.00 24.00

BATTLE CLASSICS (See Cancelled Comic Cavalcade)
Sept-Oct, 1978 (44 pgs.)
DC Comics
1-Kubert-r; new Kubert-c 1.00

BATTLE CRY
1952(May) - No. 20, Sept, 1955
Stanmor Publications
1 7.50 22.50 45.00
2 4.00 11.00 22.00
3,5-10: 8-Pvt. Ike begins, ends #13,17 2.80 7.00 14.00
4-Classic E.C. swipe 4.00 11.00 22.00
11-20 2.00 5.00 10.00
NOTE: ***Hollingsworth*** *a-9; c-20.*

BATTLEFIELD (War Adventures on the...)
April, 1952 - No. 11, May, 1953
Atlas Comics (ACI)
1-Pakula, Reinman-a 10.00 30.00 70.00
2-5: 2-Heath, Maneely, Pakula, Reinman-a 5.85 17.50 35.00
6-11 3.60 9.00 18.00
NOTE: ***Colan*** *a-11.* ***Everett*** *a-8.* ***Heath*** *a-1, 2, 5p; c-2, 8, 9, 11.* ***Ravielli*** *a-11.*

BATTLEFIELD ACTION (Formerly Foreign Intrigues)
No. 16, Nov, 1957 - No. 62, 2-3/66; No. 63, 7/80 - No. 89, 11/84
Charlton Comics
V2#16 4.00 11.00 22.00
17,20-30 2.40 6.00 12.00
18,19-Check-a (2 stories in #18) 2.80 7.00 14.00
31-62(1966) 1.60 4.00 8.00
63-89(1983-84) 1.00
NOTE: ***Montes/Bache*** *a-43, 55, 62.* ***Glanzman*** *a-87r.*

BATTLE FIRE
April, 1955 - No. 7, 1955
Aragon Magazine/Stanmor Publications
1 5.00 15.00 30.00
2 3.20 8.00 16.00
3-7 2.00 5.00 10.00

BATTLE FOR A THREE DIMENSIONAL WORLD (3D Cosmic)(Value: cover or less)

BATTLEFORCE
Nov, 1987 - No. 2?, 1988 ($1.75) (#1: color; #2: B&W)
Blackthorne Publishing
1,2-Based on game .70 1.75

BATTLE FOR THE PLANET OF THE APES (See Power Record Comics)

BATTLEFRONT

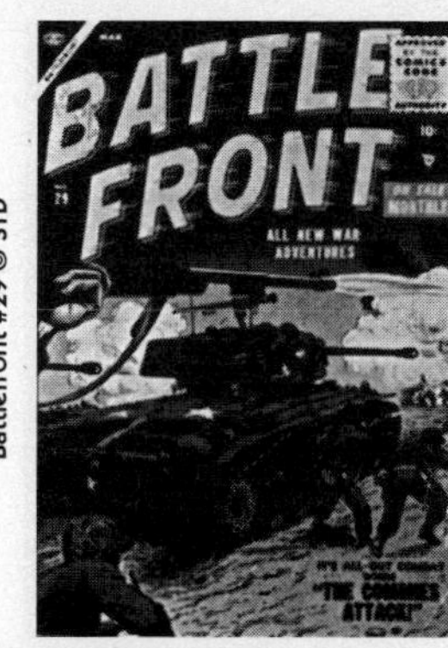

Battlefront #29 © STD

Battlestar Galactica #15 © MEG

Battle Tide II #2 © MEG

June, 1952 - No. 48, Aug, 1957
Atlas Comics (PPI)

	GD25	FN65	NM94
1-Heath-c	14.00	43.00	100.00
2-Robinson-a(4)	8.35	25.00	50.00
3-5-Robinson-a(4) in each	5.85	17.50	35.00
6-10: Combat Kelly in No. 6-10	5.35	16.00	32.00
11-22,24-28: 14,16-Battle Brady app. 22-Teddy Roosevelt & His Rough Riders story. 28-Last pre-code (2/55)	3.60	9.00	18.00
23,43-Check-a	4.00	12.00	24.00
29-39,41,44-47	3.20	8.00	16.00
40,42-Williamson-a	4.70	14.00	28.00
48-Crandall-a	4.00	11.00	22.00

NOTE: ***Ayers*** *a-19, 32.* ***Berg*** *a-44.* ***Colan*** *a-21, 22, 32, 33, 40.* ***Drucker*** *a-28, 29.* ***Everett*** *a-44.* ***Heath*** *c-23, 26, 27, 29, 32.* ***Maneely*** *a-22, 23; c-2, 13, 22, 35.* ***Morisi*** *a-42.* ***Morrow*** *a-41.* ***Orlando*** *a-47.* ***Powell*** *a-19, 21, 25, 29, 32, 40, 47.* ***Robinson*** *a-1-4, 5(4); c-4, 5.* ***Robert Sale*** *a-19.* ***Severin*** *a-32; c-40.* ***Woodbridge*** *a-45, 46.*

BATTLEFRONT
No. 5, June, 1952
Standard Comics

	GD25	FN65	NM94
5-Toth-a	10.00	30.00	65.00

BATTLE GROUND
Sept, 1954 - No. 20, Aug, 1957
Atlas Comics (OMC)

	GD25	FN65	NM94
1	11.00	32.00	75.00
2-Jack Katz-a	6.35	19.00	38.00
3,4-Last precode (3/55)	4.00	12.00	24.00
5-8,10	4.00	11.00	22.00
9-Krigstein-a	5.00	15.00	30.00
11,13,18-Williamson-a in each	5.00	15.00	30.00
12,15-17,19,20	3.60	9.00	18.00
14-Kirby-a	5.00	15.00	30.00

NOTE: ***Ayers*** *a-13.* ***Colan*** *a-11, 13.* ***Drucker*** *a-7, 12, 13, 20.* ***Heath*** *c-2, 5, 13.* ***Maneely*** *a-19; c-1, 19.* ***Orlando*** *a-17.* ***Pakula*** *a-11.* ***Severin*** *a-5, 12, 19. c-20.* ***Tuska*** *a-11.*

BATTLE HEROES
Sept, 1966 - No. 2, Nov, 1966 (25¢)
Stanley Publications

	GD25	FN65	NM94
1,2	1.20	3.00	6.00

BATTLE OF THE BULGE (See Movie Classics)

BATTLE OF THE PLANETS (TV)
6/79 - No. 10, 12/80 (Based on syndicated cartoon by Sandy Frank)
Gold Key/Whitman No. 6 on

	GD25	FN65	NM94
1			1.50
2-10: Mortimer a-1-4,7-10			1.00

BATTLE REPORT
Aug, 1952 - No. 6, June, 1953
Ajax/Farrell Publications

	GD25	FN65	NM94
1	5.00	15.00	30.00
2-6	4.00	10.00	20.00

BATTLE SQUADRON
April, 1955 - No. 5, Dec, 1955
Stanmor Publications

	GD25	FN65	NM94
1	4.00	12.00	24.00
2-5: 3-Iwo Jima & flag-c	2.80	7.00	14.00

BATTLESTAR GALACTICA (TV)(Also see Marvel Comics Super Special #8)
March, 1979 - No. 23, January, 1981
Marvel Comics Group

	GD25	FN65	NM94
1: 1-5 adapt TV episodes		.70	1.75
2-23: 1-3-Partial-r			1.50

NOTE: ***Austin*** *c-9i, 10i.* ***Golden*** *c-18.* ***Simonson*** *a(p)-4, 5, 11-13, 15-20, 22, 23; c(p)-4, 5,11-17, 19, 20, 22, 23.*

BATTLE STORIES (See XMas Comics)
Jan, 1952 - No. 11, Sept, 1953
Fawcett Publications

	GD25	FN65	NM94
1-Evans-a	10.00	30.00	60.00
2	5.00	15.00	30.00
3-11	4.00	11.00	22.00

BATTLE STORIES
1963 - 1964
Super Comics

	GD25	FN65	NM94
Reprints #10-12,15-18: 10-r/U.S Tank Commandos #? 11-r/? 12,17-r/Monty Hall #?; 15-r/American Air Forces #7 by Powell; Bolle-r	.60	1.75	3.00

BATTLETECH (Blackthorne)(Value: cover or less)

BATTLETIDE (Death's Head II & Killpower...)
Dec, 1992 - No. 4, Mar, 1993 ($1.75, color, mini-series)
Marvel Comics UK, Ltd.

	GD25	FN65	NM94
1-4: Wolverine, Psylocke, Dark Angel app.		.70	1.75

BATTLETIDE II (Death's Head II & Killpower...)
Aug, 1993 - No. 4, Nov, 1993 ($1.75, color, mini-series)
Marvel Comics UK, Ltd.

	GD25	FN65	NM94
1-($2.95)-Foil embossed logo		.70	1.75
2-4: 2-Hulk-c/story		.70	1.75

BEACH BLANKET BINGO (See Movie Classics)

BEAGLE BOYS, THE (Walt Disney)(See The Phantom Blot)
11/64; No. 2, 11/65; No. 3, 8/66 - No. 47, 2/79 (See WDC&S #134)
Gold Key

	GD25	FN65	NM94
1	4.20	12.50	25.00
2-5	2.40	6.00	12.00
6-10	1.60	4.00	8.00
11-20: 11,14,19-r	1.00	2.00	5.00
21-47: 27-r		1.00	2.50

BEAGLE BOYS VERSUS UNCLE SCROOGE
March, 1979 - No. 12, Feb, 1980
Gold Key

	GD25	FN65	NM94
1	1.30	3.25	8.00
2-12: 9-r		1.60	4.00

BEANBAGS
Winter, 1951 - No. 2, Spring, 1952
Ziff-Davis Publ. Co. (Approved Comics)

	GD25	FN65	NM94
1,2	7.00	21.00	42.00

BEANIE THE MEANIE
1958 - No. 3, May, 1959
Fago Publications

	GD25	FN65	NM94
1-3	3.60	9.00	18.00

BEANY AND CECIL (TV) (Bob Clampett's...)
Jan, 1952 - 1955; July-Sept, 1962 - No. 5, July-Sept, 1963
Dell Publishing Co.

	GD25	FN65	NM94
4-Color 368	24.00	73.00	170.00
4-Color 414,448,477,530,570,635(1/55)	19.00	58.00	135.00
01-057-209 (#1)	17.00	52.00	120.00
2-5	11.50	34.00	80.00

BEAR COUNTRY (Disney) (See 4-Color No. 758)

B.E.A.S.T.I.E.S.
Apr, 1994 ($1.95, color)
Axis Comics

	GD25	FN65	NM94
1-By Javier Saltares		.80	2.00

BEATLES, THE (See Girls' Romances #109, Go-Go, Heart Throbs #101, Herbie #5, Howard the Duck Mag. #4, Laugh #166, Marvel Comics Super Special #4, My LittleMargie #54, Not Brand Echh, Strange Tales #130, Summer Love, Superman's Pal Jimmy Olsen #79, Teen Confessions #37, Tippy's Friends & Tippy Teen)

BEATLES, THE (Life Story)

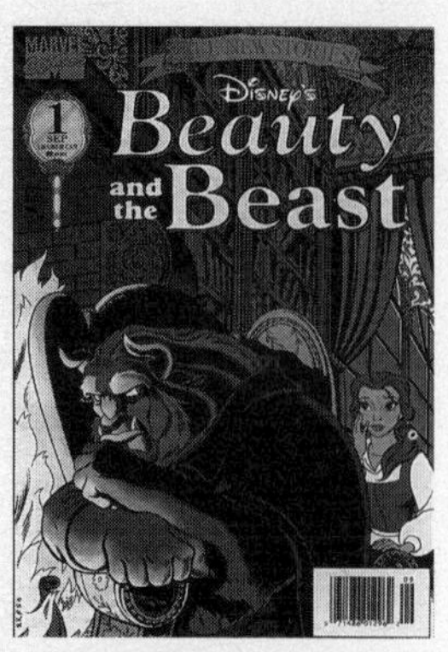

Beauty and the Beast #1 © WDC

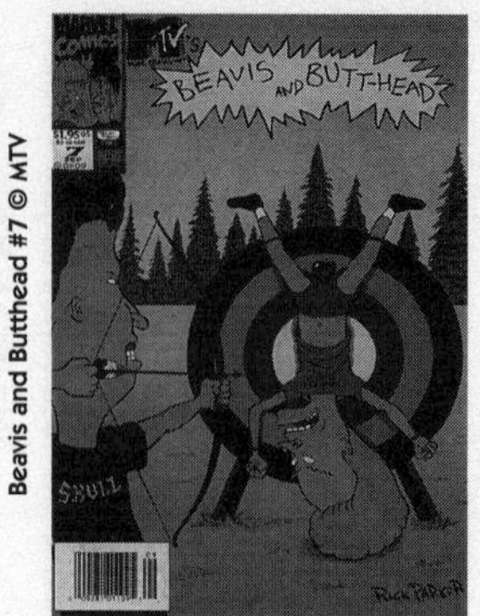

Beavis and Butthead #7 © MTV

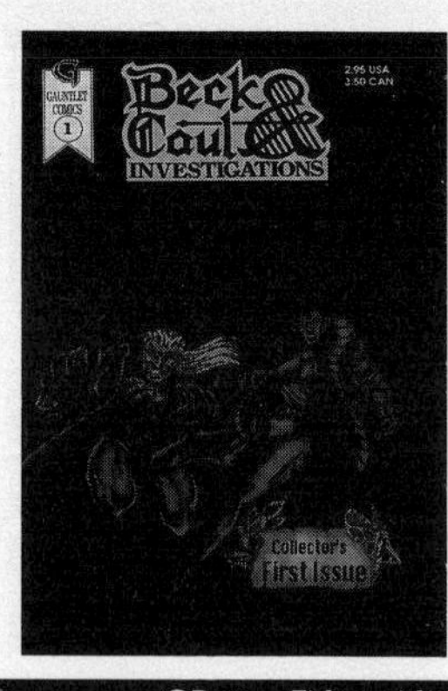

Beck & Caul Investigations #1 © Calibur

GD25 FN65 NM94

Sept-Nov, 1964 (35¢)
Dell Publishing Co.

1-(Scarce)-Stories with color photo pin-ups 45.00 135.00 450.00

BEATLES EXPERIENCE, THE
Mar, 1991 - No. 8, 1991 ($2.50, B&W, limited series)
Revolutionary Comics

1-8: 1-Gold logo 1.00 2.50

BEATLES YELLOW SUBMARINE (See Movie Comics under Yellow...)

BEAUTIFUL STORIES FOR UGLY CHILDREN
1989 - Present ($2.00/$2.50, B&W, mature readers)
Piranha Press (DC Comics)

Vol. 1-11 ($2.00) .80 2.00
12-30 ($2.50) 1.00 2.50

BEAUTY AND THE BEAST, THE
Jan, 1985 - No. 4, Apr, 1985 (Mini-series)
Marvel Comics Group

1-4: Dazzler & the Beast from X-Men 1.50

BEAUTY AND THE BEAST (Graphic novel)(Also see Cartoon Tales & Disney's New Adventures of...)
1992
Disney Comics

nn-($4.95, prestige edition)-Adapts animated film 1.00 2.00 5.00
nn-($2.50, newsstand edition) 1.00 2.50

BEAUTY AND THE BEAST: PORTRAIT OF LOVE (TV)
May, 1989 - No. 2, Mar, 1990 ($5.95, 60 pgs., color, squarebound)
First Comics

1-Based on TV show, Wendy Pini-a/scripts 1.00 2.50 6.00
2-...: Night of Beauty; by Wendy Pini 1.00 2.50 6.00

BEAUTY AND THE BEAST
Sept., 1992 - No. 2, 1992 ($1.50, mini-series)
Disney Comics

1 .80 2.00
2 1.50

BEAVER VALLEY (See 4-Color No. 625)

BEAVIS AND BUTTHEAD (TV)
Mar, 1994 - Present ($1.95)
Marvel Comics

1-Silver ink-c. 1, 2-Punisher & Devil Dinosaur app. 1.00 2.50 6.00
1-2nd printing .80 2.00
2,3: 2-Wolverine app. 3-Man-Thing, Spider-Man, Venom, Carnage, Mary Jane & Stan Lee cameos; John Romita, Sr. art (2 pgs.) 1.40 3.50
4-13: 5-War Machine, Thor, Loki, Hulk, Captain America & Rhino cameos. 6-Psylocke, Polaris, Daredevil & Bullseye app. 7-Ghost Rider & Sub-Mariner app. 8-Quasar & Eon app. .80 2.00

BECK & CAUL INVESTIGATIONS
Jan, 1994 - Present ($2.95, B&W)
Gauntlet Comics (Caliber)

1-4 1.20 3.00
... Special 1 ($4.95) 1.00 2.00 5.00

BEDKNOBS AND BROOMSTICKS (See Walt Disney Showcase No. 6 & 50)

BEDLAM! (Eclipse)(Value: cover or less)

BEDTIME STORY (See Cinema Comics Herald)

BEEP BEEP, THE ROAD RUNNER (TV)(See Daffy & Kite Fun Book)
July, 1958 - No. 14, Aug-Oct, 1962; Oct, 1966 - No. 105, 1983
Dell Publishing Co./Gold Key No. 1-88/Whitman No. 89 on

4-Color 918 (#1, 7/58) 10.00 30.00 60.00
4-Color 1008,1046 (11-1/59-60) 5.35 16.00 32.00
4(2-4/60)-14(Dell) 4.00 12.00 24.00
1(10/66, Gold Key) 4.70 14.00 28.00
2-5 3.20 8.00 16.00
6-14 (1962) 2.40 6.00 12.00
15-18,20-40 1.60 4.00 8.00
19-With pull-out poster 3.20 8.00 16.00
41-50 1.00 2.00 5.00
51-70 .70 1.75 3.50
71-105 1.50

NOTE: *See March of Comics #351, 353, 375, 387, 397, 416, 430, 442, 455. #5, 8-10, 35, 53, 59-62, 68-r; 96-102, 104 are 1/3-r.*

BEETLE BAILEY (See Comics Reading Library, Giant Comic Album & Sarge Snorkel)
#459, 5/53 - #38, 5-7/62; #39, 11/62 - #53, 5/66; #54, 8/66 - #65, 12/67; #67, 2/69 - #119, 11/76; #120, 4/78 - #132, 4/80
Dell Publishing Co./Gold Key #39-53/King #54-66/Charlton #67-119/ Gold Key #120-131/Whitman #132

4-Color 469 (#1)-By Mort Walker 10.00 30.00 60.00
4-Color 521,552,622 5.00 15.00 30.00
5(2-4/56)-10(5-7/57) 4.00 11.00 22.00
11-20(4-5/59) 3.20 8.00 16.00
21-38(5-7/62) 2.00 5.00 10.00
39-53(5/66) 1.20 3.00 6.00
54-119 (No. 66 publ. overseas only?) .60 1.50 3.00
120-132 .80 2.00
Bold Detergent Giveaway('69)-same as regular issue (#67) minus price .60 1.50 3.00
Cerebral Palsy Assn. Giveaway V2#71('69)-V2#73; (#1), 1/70 (Charlton) .60 1.50 3.00
Red Cross Giveaway, 16pp, 5x7", 1969, paper-c .60 1.50 3.00

BEETLE BAILEY
Sept, 1992 - No. 9, Aug, 1994 ($1.25/$1.50)
Harvey Comics

V2#1-4 1.25
5-9-($1.50) 1.50
...Big Book 1(11/92),2(5/93)(Both $1.95, 52 pgs.) .80 2.00
...Giant Size V2#1(10/92),2(3/93)(Both $2.25,68 pgs.) .90 2.25

BEETLEJUICE (TV)
Oct, 1991 ($1.25)
Harvey Comics

1 1.25

BEETLEJUICE CRIMEBUSTERS ON THE HAUNT
Sept, 1992 - No. 3, Jan, 1993 ($1.50, mini-series)
Harvey Comics

1-3 1.50

BEE 29, THE BOMBARDIER
Feb, 1945
Neal Publications

1-(Funny animal) 13.00 40.00 90.00

BEHIND PRISON BARS
1952
Realistic Comics (Avon)

1-Kinstler-c 19.00 58.00 135.00

BEHOLD THE HANDMAID
1954 (Religious) (25¢ with a 20¢ sticker price)
George Pflaum

nn 3.20 8.00 16.00

BELIEVE IT OR NOT (See Ripley's...)

BEN AND ME (See 4-Color No. 539)

BEN BOWIE AND HIS MOUNTAIN MEN
1952 - No. 17, Nov-Jan, 1958-59
Dell Publishing Co.

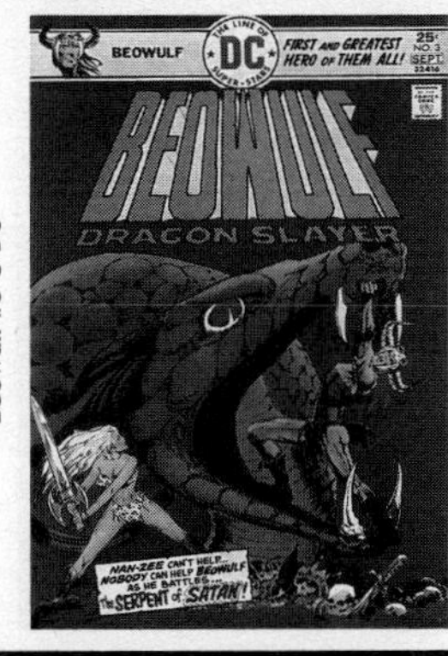

Beowulf #3 © DC

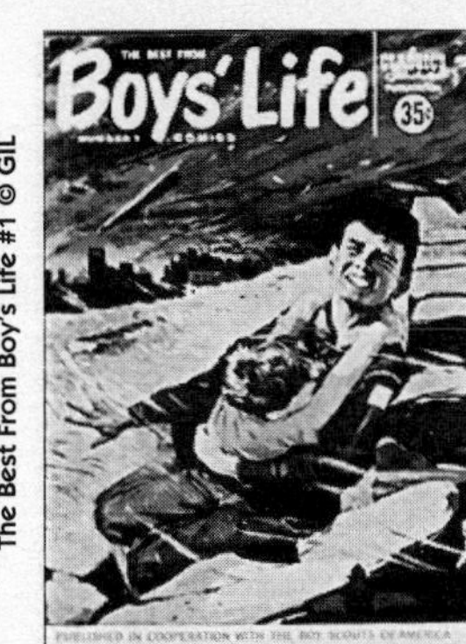

The Best From Boy's Life #1 © GIL

Best of The Brave And The Bold #2 © DC

GD25 FN65 NM94

4-Color 443 (#1) 8.35 25.00 50.00
4-Color 513,557,599,626,657 4.35 13.00 26.00
7(5-7/56)-11: 11-Intro/origin Yellow Hair 4.00 10.00 20.00
12-17 3.20 8.00 16.00

BEN CASEY (TV)
June-July, 1962 - No. 10, June-Aug, 1965 (Photo-c)
Dell Publishing Co.

12-063-207 (#1) 5.35 16.00 32.00
2(10/62)-10: 4-Marijuana & heroin use story 4.00 10.00 20.00

BEN CASEY FILM STORY (TV)
November, 1962 (25¢) (Photo-c)
Gold Key

30009-211-All photos 9.15 27.50 55.00

BENEATH THE PLANET OF THE APES (See Movie Comics & Power Record Comics)

BEN FRANKLIN (See Kite Fun Book)

BEN HUR (See 4-Color No. 1052)

BEN ISRAEL (Logos Int.)(Value: cover or less)

BEOWULF (See First Comics Graphic Novel #1)
April-May, 1975 - No. 6, Feb-Mar, 1976
National Periodical Publications

1 1.50
2-6: 5-Flying saucer-c/story 1.00

BERNI WRIGHTSON, MASTER OF THE MACABRE
July, 1983 - No. 5, Nov, 1984 ($1.50; Baxter paper)
Pacific Comics/Eclipse Comics No. 5

1-5: Wrightson-c/a(r). 4-Jeff Jones-r (11 pgs.) 1.50

BERRYS, THE (Also see Funny World)
May, 1956
Argo Publ.

1-Reprints daily & Sunday strips & daily Animal Antics by Ed Nofziger 4.20 12.50 25.00

BEST COMICS
Nov, 1939 - No. 4, Feb, 1940 (Large size, reads sideways)
Better Publications

1-(Scarce)-Red Mask begins(1st app.) & c/s-all 54.00 160.00 375.00
2-4: 4-Cannibalism story 35.00 105.00 245.00

BEST FROM BOY'S LIFE, THE
Oct, 1957 - No. 5, Oct, 1958 (35¢)
Gilberton Company

1-Space Conquerors & Kam of the Ancient Ones begin, end #5 7.50 22.50 45.00
2,3,5 4.20 12.50 25.00
4-L.B. Cole-a 5.00 15.00 30.00

BEST LOVE (Formerly Sub-Mariner Comics No. 32)
No. 33, Aug, 1949 - No. 36, April, 1950 (Photo-c 33-36)
Marvel Comics (MPI)

33-Kubert-a 8.35 25.00 50.00
34 4.00 11.00 22.00
35,36-Everett-a 5.85 17.50 35.00

BEST OF BUGS BUNNY, THE
Oct, 1966 - No. 2, Oct, 1968
Gold Key

1,2-Giants 3.75 11.25 30.00

BEST OF DC, THE (Blue Ribbon Digest) (See Limited Coll. Ed. C-52)
Sept-Oct, 1979 - No. 71, Apr, 1986 (100-148 pgs; all reprints)
DC Comics

1-17,19-34,36-71: 28,29,41,47,58,65,68-Sugar & Spike. 28,29,39,45,70-Binky. 34-Has #497 on-c from Adv. Comics. 37,43,49,55-Funny Stuff. 60-Plop!; Wood-c(r) & Aragones-r (5/85). 63-Plop! 1.00
18-The New Teen Titans .65 1.60
35-The Year's Best Comics Stories(148 pgs.) 1.20

NOTE: ***N. Adams*** *a-26, 51.* ***Aparo*** *a-9, 14, 26, 30; c-9, 14, 26.* ***Austin*** *a-51i.* ***Buckler*** *a-40p; c-22.* ***Giffen*** *a-50, 52; c-33p.* ***Grell*** *a-33p.* ***Grossman*** *a-37.* ***Heath*** *a-26.* ***Kaluta*** *a-40.* ***G. Kane*** *c-40, 44.* ***Kubert*** *a-21, 26.* ***Layton*** *a-21.* ***S. Mayer*** *c-29, 37, 41, 43, 47; a-28, 29, 37, 41, 43, 47, 58, 65, 68.* ***Moldoff*** *c-64p.* ***Morrow*** *a-40; c-40.* ***W. Mortimer*** *a-39p.* ***Newton*** *a-5, 51.* ***Perez*** *a-24, 50p; c-18, 21, 23.* ***Rogers*** *a-14, 51p.* ***Spiegle*** *a-52.* ***Starlin*** *a-51.* ***Staton*** *a-5, 21.* ***Tuska*** *a-24.* ***Wolverton*** *a-60.* ***Wood*** *a-60, 63; c-60, 63.* ***Wrightson*** *a-60. New art in #14, 18, 24.*

BEST OF DENNIS THE MENACE, THE
Summer, 1959 - No. 5, Spring, 1961 (100 pgs.)
Hallden/Fawcett Publications

1-All reprints; Wiseman-a 6.70 20.00 40.00
2-5 4.70 14.00 28.00

BEST OF DONALD DUCK, THE
Nov, 1965 (12¢, 36 pgs.)(Says 2nd printing in indicia)
Gold Key

1-Reprints 4-Color #223 by Barks 10.00 30.00 60.00

BEST OF DONALD DUCK & UNCLE SCROOGE, THE
Nov, 1964 - No. 2, Sept, 1967 (25¢ giants)
Gold Key

1(30022-411)('64)-Reprints 4-Color #189 & 408 by Carl Barks; cover of F.C. #189 redrawn by Barks 10.00 30.00 60.00
2(30022-709)('67)-Reprints 4-Color #256 & "Seven Cities of Cibola" & U.S. #8 by Barks 10.00 30.00 60.00

BEST OF HORROR AND SCIENCE FICTION COMICS (Webster)(Value: cover or less)

BEST OF MARMADUKE, THE
1960 (A dog)
Charlton Comics

1-Brad Anderson's strip reprints 3.60 9.00 18.00

BEST OF MS. TREE, THE (Pyramid)(Value: cover or less)

BEST OF THE BRAVE AND THE BOLD, THE (See Super DC Giant)
Oct, 1988 - No. 6, Jan, 1989 ($2.50, mini-series)
DC Comics

1-6: Neal Adams-r in all 1.00 2.50

BEST OF THE WEST (See A-1 Comics)
1951 - No. 12, April-June, 1954
Magazine Enterprises

1(A-1 42)-Ghost Rider, Durango Kid, Straight Arrow, Bobby Benson begin 34.00 103.00 240.00
2(A-1 46) 16.00 48.00 110.00
3(A-1 52), 4(A-1 59), 5(A-1 66) 14.00 43.00 100.00
6(A-1 70), 7(A-1 76), 8(A-1 81), 9(A-1 85), 10(A-1 87), 11(A-1 97), 12(A-1 103) 10.00 30.00 70.00

NOTE: ***Bolle*** *a-9.* ***Borth*** *a-12.* ***Guardineer*** *a-5, 12.* ***Powell*** *a-1, 12.*

BEST OF UNCLE SCROOGE & DONALD DUCK, THE
November, 1966 (25¢)
Gold Key

1(30030-611)-Reprints part 4-Color #159 & 456 & Uncle Scrooge #6,7 by Carl Barks 10.00 30.00 60.00

BEST OF WALT DISNEY COMICS, THE
1974 (In color; $1.50; 52 pgs.) (Walt Disney)
(8-1/2x11" cardboard covers; 32,000 printed of each)
Western Publishing Co.

96170-Reprints 1st two stories less 1 pg. each from 4-Color #62 2.85 8.00 20.00
96171-Reprints Mickey Mouse and the Bat Bandit of Inferno Gulch from 1934 (strips) by Gottfredson 2.85 8.00 20.00
96172-r/Uncle Scrooge #386 & two other stories 2.85 8.00 20.00
96173-Reprints "Ghost of the Grotto" (from 4-Color #159) & "Christmas on Bear Mountain" (from 4-Color #178) 2.85 8.00 20.00

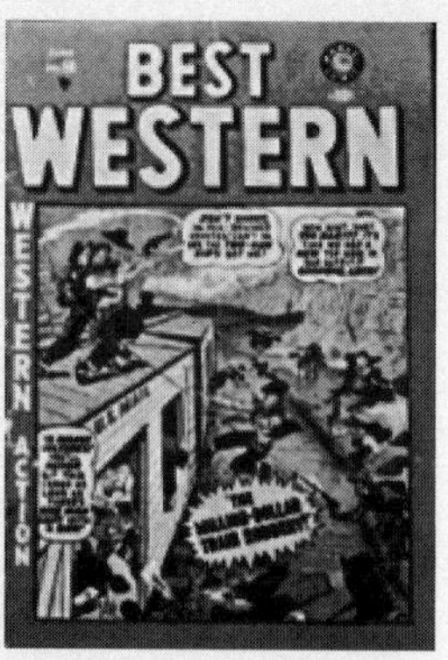

Best Western #58 © MEG

Betty's Diary #1 © AP

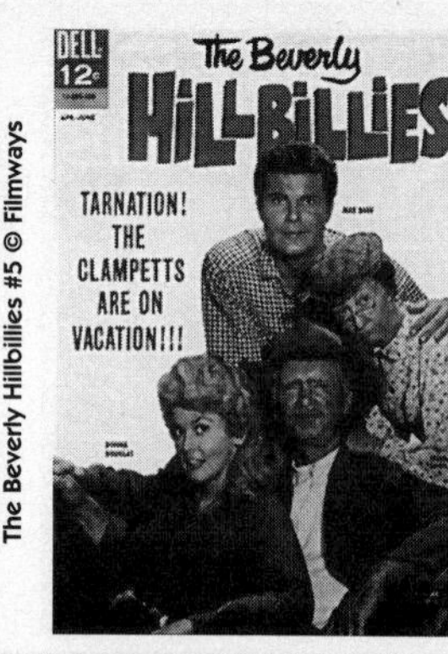

The Beverly Hillbillies #5 © Filmways

GD25 FN65 NM94

BEST ROMANCE
No. 5, Feb-Mar, 1952 - No. 7, Aug, 1952
Standard Comics (Visual Editions)

5-Toth-a; photo-c 9.15 27.50 55.00
6,7-Photo-c 4.00 10.00 20.00

BEST SELLER COMICS (See Tailspin Tommy)

BEST WESTERN (Formerly Terry Toons? or Miss America Magazine V7#24(#57)?; Western Outlaws & Sheriffs No. 60 on)
No. 58, June, 1949 - No. 59, Aug, 1949
Marvel Comics (IPC)

58,59-Black Rider, Kid Colt, Two-Gun Kid app.; both have Syd Shores-c
13.00 40.00 90.00

BETTY (See Pep Comics #22 for 1st app.)
Sept, 1992 - Present ($1.25)
Archie Comics

1-24 1.25

BETTY AND HER STEADY (Going Steady with Betty No. 1)
No. 2, Mar-Apr, 1950
Avon Periodicals

2 8.00 24.00 48.00

BETTY AND ME
Aug, 1965 - No. 200, Aug, 1992
Archie Publications

1 11.00 32.00 75.00
2 6.35 19.00 38.00
3-5: 3-Origin Superteen. Superteen in new costume #4-7; dons new helmet in #5, ends #8 (see Archie's Girls #118) 4.00 11.00 22.00
6-10 2.40 6.00 12.00
11-30 1.20 3.00 6.00
31-55 (52 pgs. #36-55) 1.50 3.00
56-100 1.50
101-199: Later issues $1.00 cover 1.00
200-($1.50)-Last issue 1.50

BETTY AND VERONICA (Also see Archie's Girls...)
June, 1987 - Present (75¢ - $1.25)
Archie Enterprises

1-87 .60 1.25
...Summer Fun 1 (1994, $2.00, 52 pgs. plus poster .80 2.00

BETTY & VERONICA ANNUAL DIGEST (...Digest Magazine #1-4, 44 on; ...Comics Digest Mag. #5-43)
November, 1980 - Present ($1.00/$1.50, digest size)
Archie Publications

1,2(11/81-Katy Keene story), 3(8/82)-70 1.50

BETTY & VERONICA ANNUAL DIGEST MAGAZINE
Sept, 1989 - Present ($1.50/$1.75, 128 pgs.)
Archie Comics

1-11: 9-Neon ink logo .70 1.75

BETTY & VERONICA CHRISTMAS SPECTACULAR (See Archie Giant Series Magazine #159, 168, 180, 191, 204, 217, 229, 241, 453, 465, 477, 489, 501, 513, 525, 536, 547, 558, 568, 580, 593, 606, 618)

BETTY & VERONICA DOUBLE DIGEST MAGAZINE
1987 - Present (Digest size, 256 pgs., $2.25/$2.75)(...Digest #12 on)
Archie Enterprises

1-47: 5,17-Xmas-c. 16-Capt. Hero story 1.10 2.75

BETTY & VERONICA SPECTACULAR (See Archie Giant Series Mag. #11, 16, 21, 26, 32, 138, 145, 153, 162, 173, 184, 197, 201, 210, 214, 221, 226, 234, 238, 246, 250, 458, 462, 470, 482, 486, 494, 498, 506, 510, 518, 522, 526, 530, 537, 552, 559, 563, 569, 575, 582, 588, 600, 608, 613, 620, 623, and Betty & Veronica)

BETTY AND VERONICA SPECTACULAR
Oct, 1992 - Present ($1.25)
Archie Comics

1-13: 1-Dan DeCarlo-c/a 1.25

BETTY & VERONICA SPRING SPECTACULAR (See Archie Giant Series Magazine #569, 582, 595)

BETTY & VERONICA SUMMER FUN (See Archie Giant Series Mag. #8, 13, 18, 23, 28, 34, 140, 147, 155, 164, 175, 187, 199, 212, 224, 236, 248, 460, 484, 496, 508, 520, 529, 539, 550, 561, 572, 585, 598, 611, 621)

BETTY BOOP'S BIG BREAK (First)(Value: cover or less)

BETTY PAGE 3-D COMICS (3-D Zone)(Value: cover or less)

BETTY'S DIARY (See Archie Giant Series Magazine No. 555)
April, 1986 - No. 40, Apr, 1991 (#1:65¢; 75¢/95¢)
Archie Enterprises

1-40 1.00

BEVERLY HILLBILLIES (TV)
4-6/63 - No. 18, 8/67; No. 19, 10/69; No. 20, 10/70; No. 21, Oct, 1971
Dell Publishing Co.

1-Photo-c 15.00 45.00 105.00
2-Photo-c 8.35 25.00 50.00
3-9: All have photo covers 5.85 17.50 35.00
10: No photo cover 3.60 9.00 18.00
11-21: All have photo covers. 18-Last 12¢ issue 4.35 13.00 26.00
NOTE: *#1-9, 11-21 are photo covers. #19 reprints cover to #1, but not insides.*

BEWARE (Formerly Fantastic; Chilling Tales No. 13 on)
No. 10, June, 1952 - No. 12, Oct, 1952
Youthful Magazines

10-E.A. Poe's Pit & the Pendulum adaptation by Wildey; Harrison/Bache-a; atom bomb and shrunken head-c 22.00 65.00 150.00
11-Harrison-a; Ambrose Bierce adapt. 16.00 48.00 110.00
12-Used in **SOTI**, pg. 388; Harrison-a 16.00 48.00 110.00

BEWARE
No. 13, 1/53 - No. 16, 7/53; No. 5, 9/53 - No. 15, 5/55
Trojan Magazines/Merit Publ. No. ?

13(#1)-Harrison-a 23.00 70.00 160.00
14(#2, 3/53)-Krenkel/Harrison-c; dismemberment, severed head panels
16.00 48.00 110.00
15,16(#3, 5/53; #4, 7/53)-Harrison-a 11.50 34.00 80.00
5,9,12,13 11.50 34.00 80.00
6-Ill. in **SOTI**- "Children are first shocked and then desensitized by all this brutality." Corpse on cover swipe/V.O.H. #26; girl on cover swipe/Advs. Into Darkness #10 24.00 73.00 170.00
7,8-Check-a 13.00 40.00 90.00
10-Frazetta/Check-c; Disbrow, Check-a 36.00 107.00 250.00
11-Disbrow-a; heart torn out, blood drainage 14.00 43.00 100.00
14,15: 14-Myron Fass-c. 15-Harrison-a 10.00 30.00 70.00
NOTE: ***Fass** a-5, 6, 8; c-6, 11, 14. **Forte** a-8. **Hollingsworth** a-15(#3), 16(#4), 9; c-16(#4), 8, 9. **Kiefer** a-16(#4), 5, 6, 10.*

BEWARE (Becomes Tomb of Darkness No. 9 on)
March, 1973 - No. 8, May, 1974 (All reprints)
Marvel Comics Group

1-Everett-c; Sinnott-r ('54) 1.30 3.25
2-8: 2-Forte, Colan-r. 6-Tuska-a. 7-Torres-r/Mystical Tales #7
1.60

BEWARE TERROR TALES
May, 1952 - No. 8, July, 1953
Fawcett Publications

1-E.C. art swipe/Haunt of Fear #5 & Vault of Horror #26
24.00 72.00 165.00
2 13.00 40.00 90.00
3-8: 8-Tothish-a 11.50 34.00 80.00
NOTE: ***Andru** a-2. **Bernard Bailey** a-1; c-1-5. **Powell** a-1, 2, 8. **Sekowsky** a-2.*

BEWARE THE CREEPER (See Adventure, Best of the Brave & the Bold, Brave

Beyond #11 © ACE

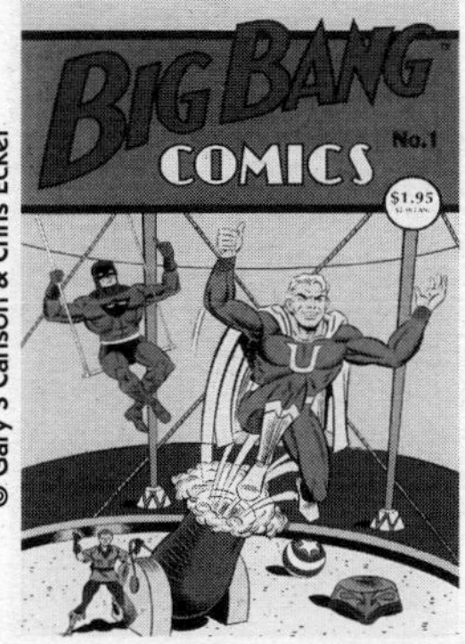

Big Bang Comics #1 © Gary S Carlson & Chris Ecker

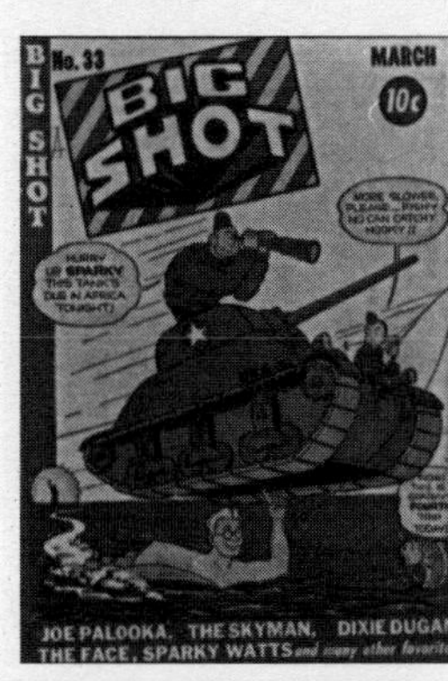

Big Shot Comics #33 © CCG

GD25 FN65 NM94

& the Bold, 1st Issue Special, Flash #318-323, Showcase, World's Finest #249)
May-June, 1968 - No. 6, March-April, 1969 (All 12¢ issues)
National Periodical Publications

Showcase #73 (3-4/68)-Origin & 1st app. The Creeper; Ditko-c/a 10.00 30.00 90.00
1-(5-6/68)-Ditko-a in all; c-1-5 7.00 21.00 50.00
2-6: 6-Gil Kane-c 5.00 14.00 32.00

BEWITCHED (TV)
4-6/65 - No. 11, 10/67; No. 12, 10/68 - No. 13, 1/69; No. 14, 10/69
Dell Publishing Co.

1-Photo-c 13.00 40.00 90.00
2-No photo-c 7.50 22.50 45.00
3-13-All have photo-c 5.00 15.00 35.00
14-No photo-c 3.10 9.00 22.00

BEYOND, THE
Nov, 1950 - No. 30, Jan, 1955
Ace Magazines

1-Bakerish-a(p) 23.00 70.00 160.00
2-Bakerish-a(p) 13.00 40.00 90.00
3-10: 10-Woodish-a by Cameron 9.15 27.50 55.00
11-20: 18-Used in **POP**, pgs. 81,82 7.50 22.50 45.00
21-26,28-30 6.70 20.00 40.00
27-Used in **SOTI**, pg. 111 8.35 25.00 50.00

NOTE: ***Cameron** a-10, 11p, 12p, 15, 16, 21-27, 30; c-20. **Colan** a-6, 13, 17. **Sekowsky** a-2, 3, 5, 7, 11, 14, 27r. No. 1 was to appear as Challenge of the Unknown No. 7.*

BEYOND THE GRAVE
July, 1975 - No. 6, June, 1976; No. 7, Jan, 1983 - No. 17, Oct, 1984
Charlton Comics

1-Ditko-a (6 pgs.); Sutton painted-c 1.60 4.00
2-6: 2-5-Ditko-a; Ditko c-2,3,6 .80 2.00
7-17: ('83-'84) Reprints. 13-Aparo-c(r). 15-Sutton-c 1.25
Modern Comics Reprint 2('78) 1.00

BIBLE TALES FOR YOUNG FOLK (...Young People No. 3-5)
Aug, 1953 - No. 5, Mar, 1954
Atlas Comics (OMC)

1 14.00 43.00 100.00
2-Everett, Krigstein-a 11.50 34.00 80.00
3-5: 4-Robinson-c 9.15 27.50 55.00

BIG (Hit)(Value: cover or less)

BIG ALL-AMERICAN COMIC BOOK, THE (See All-American Comics)
1944 (One Shot) (132 pgs.) (Early DC Annual)
All-American/National Per.l Publ. GD25 FN65 VF82 NM94

1-Wonder Woman, Green Lantern, Flash, The Atom, Wildcat, Scribbly, The Whip, Ghost Patrol, Hawkman by Kubert (1st on Hawkman), Hop Harrigan, Johnny Thunder, Little Boy Blue, Mr. Terrific, Mutt & Jeff app.; Sargon on cover only; cover by Kubert/Hibbard/Mayer/others 800.00 2400.00 5200.00 8000.00
(Estimated up to 80+ total copies exist, 6 in NM/Mint)

BIG BABY HUEY (Also see Baby Huey)
Oct, 1991 - Present ($1.00, quarterly)
Harvey Comics GD25 FN65 NM94

1-4 1.00

BIG BANG COMICS
Spring, 1994 - Present ($1.95, color)
Big Bang Comics

1,2 .80 2.00

BIG BOOK OF FUN COMICS (See New Book of Comics)
Spring, 1936 (52 pgs., large size)(1st comic book annual & DC annual)
National Periodical Publications GD25 FN65 VF82

1 (Very rare)-r/New Fun #1-5 1600.00 4800.00 8000.00
(Estimated up to 15 total copies exist, none in NM/Mint)

GD25 FN65 NM94

BIG BOOK ROMANCES
February, 1950(no date given) (148 pgs.)
Fawcett Publications GD25 FN65 NM94

1-Contains remaindered Fawcett romance comics - several combinations possible 25.00 75.00 175.00

BIG BOY (See Adventures of the Big Boy)

BIG CHIEF WAHOO
July, 1942 - No. 23, 1945? (Quarterly)
Eastern Color Printing/George Dougherty (distr. by Fawcett)

1-Newspaper-r (on sale 6/15/42) 31.00 94.00 220.00
2-Steve Roper app. 16.00 48.00 110.00
3-5: 4-Chief is holding a Katy Keene comic 11.50 34.00 80.00
6-10: 8-23-Exist? 9.15 27.50 55.00
11-23 6.35 19.00 38.00

NOTE: *Kerry Drake in some issues.*

BIG CIRCUS, THE (See 4-Color No. 1036)

BIG COUNTRY, THE (See 4-Color No. 946)

BIG DADDY ROTH
Oct-Nov, 1964 - No. 4, Apr-May, 1965 (35¢, magazine)
Millar Publications

1-Toth-a 16.50 50.00 115.00
2-4-Toth-a 12.00 36.00 85.00

BIG HERO ADVENTURES (See Jigsaw)

BIG JIM'S P.A.C.K.
No date (1975) (16 pgs.)
Mattel, Inc. (Marvel Comics)

nn-Giveaway with Big Jim doll; Buscema/Sinnott-c/a .50

BIG JON & SPARKIE (Radio)(Formerly Sparkie, Radio Pixie)
No. 4, Sept-Oct, 1952 (Painted-c)
Ziff-Davis Publ. Co.

4-Based on children's radio program 13.00 40.00 90.00

BIG LAND, THE (See 4-Color No. 812)

BIG RED (See Movie Comics)

BIG SHOT COMICS
May, 1940 - No. 104, Aug, 1949
Columbia Comics Group

1-Intro. Skyman; The Face (1st app.; Tony Trent), The Cloak (Spy Master), Marvelo, Monarch of Magicians, Joe Palooka, Charlie Chan, Tom Kerry, Dixie Dugan, Rocky Ryan begin; Charlie Chan moves over from Feature Comics #31 (4/40) 129.00 385.00 900.00
2 51.00 154.00 360.00
3-The Cloak called Spy Chief; Skyman-c 44.00 133.00 310.00
4,5 37.00 111.00 260.00
6-10: 8-Christmas-c 30.00 90.00 210.00
11-14: 14-Origin & 1st app. Sparky Watts (6/41) 27.00 81.00 190.00
15-Origin The Cloak 30.00 90.00 210.00
16-20 21.00 63.00 145.00
21-27,29,30: 24-Tojo-c. 29-Intro. Capt. Yank; Bo (a dog) newspaper strip-r by by Frank Beck begin, ends #104. 30-X-Mas-c 16.50 50.00 115.00
28-Hitler, Tojo & Mussolini-c 19.00 57.00 130.00
31,33-40 12.00 36.00 85.00
32-Vic Jordan newspaper strip reprints begin, ends #52; Hitler, Tojo & Mussolini-c 13.50 41.00 95.00
41-50: 42-No Skyman. 43,46-Hitler-c. 50-Origin The Face retold 10.00 30.00 70.00
51-60 9.15 27.50 55.00
61-70: 63 on-Tony Trent, the Face 6.70 20.00 40.00
71-80: 73-The Face cameo. 74-(2/47)-Mickey Finn begins. 74,80-The Face app. in Tony Trent. 78-Last Charlie Chan strip-r 5.85 17.50 35.00
81-90: 85-Tony Trent marries Babs Walsh. 86-Valentines-c 5.00 15.00 30.00

Big Shot Comics #98 © CCG

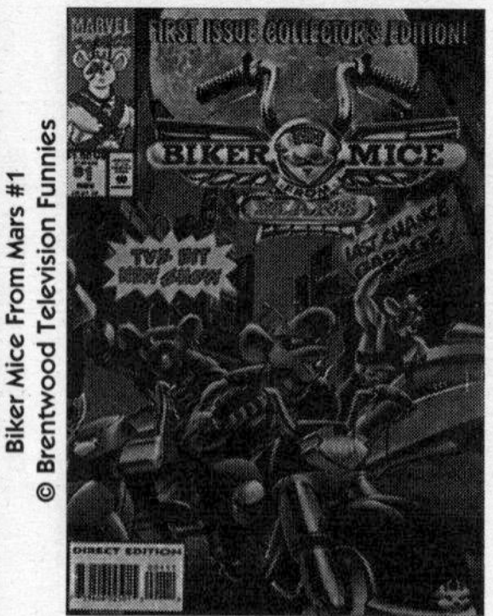

Biker Mice From Mars #1 © Brentwood Television Funnies

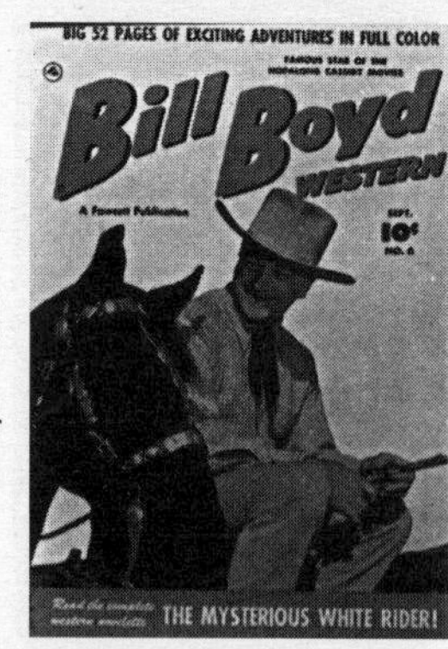

Bill Boyd Western #6 © FAW

	GD25	FN65	NM94
91-99,101-104: 69-94-Skyman in Outer Space. 96-Xmas-c	4.35	13.00	26.00
100	5.85	17.50	35.00

NOTE: ***Mart Bailey*** *art on "The Face" No. 1-104.* ***Guardineer*** *a-5. Sparky Watts by* ***Boody Rogers****-No. 14-42, 77-104, (by others No. 43-76). Others than Tony Trent wear "The Face" mask in No. 46-63, 93. Skyman by* ***Ogden Whitney****-No. 1, 2, 4, 12-37, 49, 70-101. Skyman covers-No. 1, 3, 7-12, 14, 16, 20, 27, 89, 95, 100.*

BIG TEX
June, 1953
Toby Press

	GD25	FN65	NM94
1-Contains (3) John Wayne stories-r with name changed to Big Tex	6.70	20.00	40.00

BIG-3
Fall, 1940 - No. 7, Jan, 1942
Fox Features Syndicate

	GD25	FN65	NM94
1-Blue Beetle, The Flame, & Samson begin	121.00	365.00	850.00
2	57.00	171.00	400.00
3-5	43.00	129.00	300.00
6-Last Samson; bondage-c	36.00	107.00	250.00
7-V-Man app.	36.00	107.00	250.00

BIG TOP COMICS, THE (TV's Great Circus Show)
1951 - No. 2, 1951 (No month)
Toby Press

	GD25	FN65	NM94
1,2	5.85	17.50	35.00

BIG TOWN (Radio/TV) (Also see Movie Comics, 1946)
Jan, 1951 - No. 50, Mar-Apr, 1958 (No. 1-9: 52pgs.)
National Periodical Publications

	GD25	FN65	NM94
1-Dan Barry-a begins	46.00	140.00	325.00
2	22.00	65.00	150.00
3-10	13.50	41.00	95.00
11-20	10.00	30.00	65.00
21-31: Last pre-code (1-2/55)	7.50	22.50	45.00
32-50	5.35	16.00	32.00

BIG VALLEY, THE (TV)
June, 1966 - No. 5, Oct, 1967; No. 6, Oct, 1969
Dell Publishing Co.

	GD25	FN65	NM94
1: Photo-c #1-5	5.85	17.50	35.00
2-6: 6-Reprints #1	3.60	9.00	18.00

BIKER MICE FROM MARS
Nov, 1993 - No. 3, Jan, 1994 ($1.50, based on TV cartoon)
Marvel Comics

	GD25	FN65	NM94
1-3: 1-Intro Vinnie, Modo & Throttle. 2-Origin			1.50

BILL & TED'S BOGUS JOURNEY
Sept, 1991 ($2.95, squarebound, 84 pgs.)
Marvel Comics

	GD25	FN65	NM94
1-Adapts movie sequel		1.20	3.00

"BILL AND TED'S EXCELLENT ADVENTURE" MOVIE ADAPTATION
1989 (No cover price)
DC Comics

	GD25	FN65	NM94
nn-Torres-a			1.00

BILL & TED'S EXCELLENT COMIC BOOK
Dec, 1991 - No. 12, 1992 ($1.00/$1.25)
Marvel Comics

	GD25	FN65	NM94
1,2: 2-Last $1.00-c			1.00
3-12			1.25

BILL BARNES COMICS (...America's Air Ace Comics No. 2 on)
(Becomes Air Ace V2#1 on; also see Shadow Comics)
Oct, 1940(No. month given) - No. 12, Oct, 1943
Street & Smith Publications

	GD25	FN65	NM94
1-23 pgs.-comics; Rocket Rooney begins	57.00	171.00	400.00
2-Barnes as The Phantom Flyer app.; Tuska-a	34.00	100.00	235.00
3-5	25.00	75.00	175.00
6-12	22.00	65.00	150.00

BILL BATTLE, THE ONE MAN ARMY (Also see Master Comics No. 133)
Oct, 1952 - No. 4, Apr, 1953 (All photo-c)
Fawcett Publications

	GD25	FN65	NM94
1	5.85	17.50	35.00
2	4.00	11.00	22.00
3,4	3.20	8.00	16.00

BILL BLACK'S FUN COMICS (Americomics)(Value: cover or less)

BILL BOYD WESTERN (Movie star; see Hopalong Cassidy & Western Hero)
Feb, 1950 - No. 23, June, 1952 (1-3,7,11,14-on: 36 pgs.)
Fawcett Publications

	GD25	FN65	NM94
1-Bill Boyd & his horse Midnite begin; photo front/back-c	38.00	114.00	265.00
2-Painted-c	19.00	58.00	135.00
3-Photo-c begin, end #23; last photo back-c	16.00	48.00	110.00
4-6(52 pgs.)	13.00	40.00	90.00
7,11(36 pgs.)	10.00	30.00	70.00
8-10,12,13(52 pgs.)	11.00	32.00	75.00
14-22	10.00	30.00	65.00
23-Last issue	11.00	32.00	75.00

BILL BUMLIN (See Treasury of Comics No. 3)

BILL ELLIOTT (See Wild Bill Elliott)

BILLI 99 (Dark Horse)(Value: cover or less)

BILL STERN'S SPORTS BOOK
Spring-Summer, 1951 - V2#2, Winter, 1952
Ziff-Davis Publ. Co.(Approved Comics)

	GD25	FN65	NM94
V1#10-(1951)	13.00	40.00	90.00
2-(Sum/52; reg. size)	10.00	30.00	70.00
V2#2-(1952, 96 pgs.)-Krigstein, Kinstler-a	13.00	40.00	90.00

BILLY AND BUGGY BEAR (See Animal Fun)
1958; 1964
I.W. Enterprises/Super

	GD25	FN65	NM94
I.W. Reprint #1(early Timely funny animal-r), #7('58)	.80	2.00	4.00
Super Reprint #10(1964)	.80	2.00	4.00

BILLY BUCKSKIN WESTERN (2-Gun Western No. 4)
Nov, 1955 - No. 3, March, 1956
Atlas Comics (IMC No. 1/MgPC No. 2,3)

	GD25	FN65	NM94
1-Mort Drucker-a; Maneely-c/a	10.00	30.00	70.00
2-Mort Drucker-a	7.50	22.50	45.00
3-Williamson, Drucker-a	8.35	25.00	50.00

BILLY BUNNY (Black Cobra No. 6 on)
Feb-Mar, 1954 - No. 5, Oct-Nov, 1954
Excellent Publications

	GD25	FN65	NM94
1	5.00	15.00	30.00
2	3.60	9.00	18.00
3-5	2.80	7.00	14.00

BILLY BUNNY'S CHRISTMAS FROLICS
1952 (100 pgs., 25¢ giant)
Farrell Publications

	GD25	FN65	NM94
1	11.50	34.00	80.00

BILLY COLE
May, 1994 - No. 4, Aug, 1994 ($2.75, B&W, mini-series)
Cult Press

	GD25	FN65	NM94
1-4		1.10	2.75

BILLY MAKE BELIEVE (See Single Series No. 14)

BILLY NGUYEN, PRIVATE EYE (Caliber Press)(Value: cover or less)

BILLY THE KID (Formerly The Masked Raider; also see Doc Savage Comics

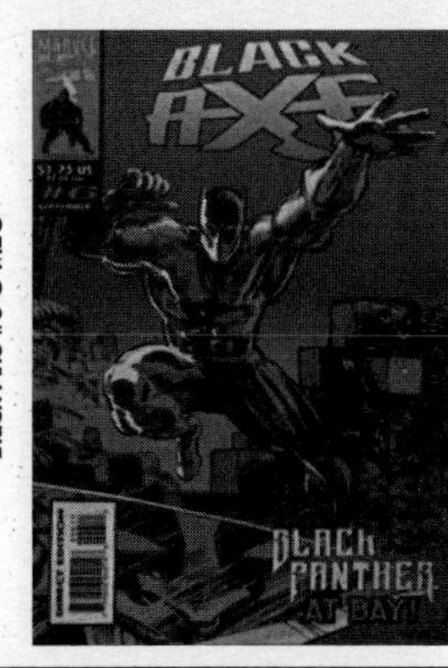

Black Axe #6 © MEG

Black & White #1 © Rob Liefeld

Black Canary #10 © DC

& Return of the Outlaw)
No. 9, Nov, 1957 - No. 121, Dec, 1976; No. 122, Sept, 1977 - No. 123, Oct, 1977; No. 124, Feb, 1978 - No. 153, Mar, 1983
Charlton Publ. Co.

9 7.50 22.50 45.00
10,12,14,17-19 4.70 14.00 28.00
11-(68 pgs.)-Origin & 1st app. The Ghost Train 5.35 16.00 32.00
13-Williamson/Torres-a 5.85 17.50 35.00
15-Origin; 2 pgs. Williamson-a 5.85 17.50 35.00
16 5.85 17.50 35.00
20-26-Severin-a(3-4 each) 5.85 17.50 35.00
27-30 4.00 10.00 20.00
31-40 2.80 7.00 14.00
41-60 1.80 4.50 9.00
61-80: 66-Bounty Hunter series begins. Not in #79,82,84-863 .90 2.25 4.50
81-99,101-123: 87-Last Bounty Hunter. 111-Origin The Ghost Train. 117-Gunsmith & Co., The Cheyenne Kid app. 1.20 3.00
100 .80 2.00
124(2/78)-153 1.50
Modern Comics 109 (1977 reprint) 1.20

NOTE: ***Severin** a(r)-121-129, 134; c-23, 25. **Sutton** a-111.*

BILLY THE KID ADVENTURE MAGAZINE
Oct, 1950 - No. 30, 1955
Toby Press

1-Williamson/Frazetta-a (2 pgs) r/from John Wayne Adventure Comics #2; photo-c 22.00 65.00 150.00
2-Photo-c 7.50 22.50 45.00
3-Williamson/Frazetta "The Claws of Death", 4 pgs. plus Williamson art 24.00 72.00 165.00
4,5,7,8,10: 4,7-Photo-c 5.00 15.00 30.00
6-Frazetta assist on "Nightmare"; photo-c 10.00 30.00 65.00
9-Kurtzman Pot-Shot Pete; photo-c 10.005 30.00 60.00
11,12,15-20: 11-Photo-c 4.30 13.00 26.00
13-Kurtzman-r/John Wayne #12 (Genius) 5.00 15.00 30.00
14-Williamson/Frazetta; r-of #1 (2 pgs.) 7.50 22.50 45.00
21,23-30 4.00 10.00 20.00
22-Williamson/Frazetta-r(1pg.)/#1; photo-c 4.70 14.00 28.00

BILLY THE KID AND OSCAR (Also see Fawcett's Funny Animals)
Winter, 1945 - No. 3, Summer, 1946 (Funny animal)
Fawcett Publications

1 10.00 30.00 70.00
2,3 6.70 20.00 40.00

BILLY WEST (Bill West No. 9,10)
1949 - No. 9, Feb, 1951; No. 10, Feb, 1952
Standard Comics (Visual Editions)

1 6.70 20.00 40.00
2 4.00 10.00 20.00
3-10: 7,8-Schomburg-c 3.20 8.00 16.00

NOTE: ***Celardo** a-1-6, 9; c-1-3. **Moreira** a-3. **Roussos** a-2.*

BING CROSBY (See Feature Films)

BINGO (...Comics) (H. C. Blackerby)
1945 (Reprints National material)
Howard Publ.

1-L. B. Cole opium-c 16.00 48.00 110.00

BINGO, THE MONKEY DOODLE BOY
Aug, 1951; Oct, 1953
St. John Publishing Co.

1(8/51)-By Eric Peters 4.70 14.00 28.00
1(10/53) 4.00 11.00 22.00

BINKY (Formerly Leave It to...)
No. 72, 4-5/70 - No. 81, 10-11/71; No. 82, Summer/77
National Periodical Publ./DC Comics

72-81: 78-1 pg. story on Barry Williams of Brady Bunch 1.60 4.00
82('77)-(One Shot) .80 2.00

BINKY'S BUDDIES
Jan-Feb, 1969 - No. 12, Nov-Dec, 1970
National Periodical Publications

1 1.20 3.00 7.00
2-12 1.60 4.00

BIONEERS
Aug, 1994 - Present ($2.75, color)
Mirage Publishing

1-w/bound-in trading card 1.10 2.75

BIONIC WOMAN, THE (TV)
October, 1977 - No. 5, June, 1978
Charlton Publications

1-5 1.25

BIZARRE ADVENTURES (Formerly Marvel Preview)
No. 25, 3/81 - No. 34, 2/83 (#25-33: Magazine-$1.50)
Marvel Comics Group

25-Lethal Ladies. 26-King Kull 1.25
27-Phoenix, Iceman & Nightcrawler app. 28-The Unlikely Heroes; Elektra by Miller; Neal Adams-a 1.50
29-Horror. 30-Tomorrow. 31-After The Violence Stops; new Hangman story; Miller-a. 32-Gods. 33-Horror; photo-c 1.25
34 ($2.00, Baxter paper, comic size)-Son of Santa; Christmas special; Howard the Duck by Paul Smith 1.50

NOTE: ***Alcala** a-27i. **Austin** a-25i, 28i. **J. Buscema** a-27p, 29, 30p; c-26. **Byrne** a-31 (2 pg.). **Golden** a-25p, 28p. **Perez** a-27p. **Rogers** a-25p. **Simonson** a-29; c-29. **Paul Smith** a-34.*

BLACK AND WHITE (See Large Feature Comic, Series I)

BLACK & WHITE
Oct,1994-Present(1.95, color)
Image Comics, Inc.

1-Thibert-c/story 0.60 1.20 3.00

BLACK & WHITE MAGIC (Innovation)(Value: cover or less)

BLACK AXE (Marvel Comics UK)(Value: cover or less)

BLACKBALL COMICS
Mar, 1994 - Present ($3.00)
Blackball Comics

1-Trencher by Giffen (c/a); John Pain by O'Neill 1.20 3.00

BLACKBEARD'S GHOST (See Movie Comics)

BLACK BEAUTY (See 4-Color No. 440)

BLACK CANARY (See All Star Comics #38, Flash Comics #86, Justice League of America #75 & World's Finest #244)
Nov, 1991 - No. 4, Feb, 1992 ($1.75, mini-series)
DC Comics

1-4 .70 1.75

BLACK CANARY
Jan, 1993 - No. 12, Dec, 1993 ($1.75)
DC Comics

1-12: 8-The Ray-c/story. 9,10-Huntress-c/story .70 1.75

BLACK CAT COMICS (...Western #16-19; ...Mystery #30 on)
(See All-New #7,9, The Original Black Cat, Pocket & Speed Comics)
June-July, 1946 - No. 29, June, 1951
Harvey Publications (Home Comics)

1-Kubert-a; Joe Simon c-1-3 41.00 120.00 285.00
2-Kubert-a 21.00 62.00 145.00
3,4: 4-The Red Demons begin (The Demon #4 & 5) 16.00 49.00 115.00

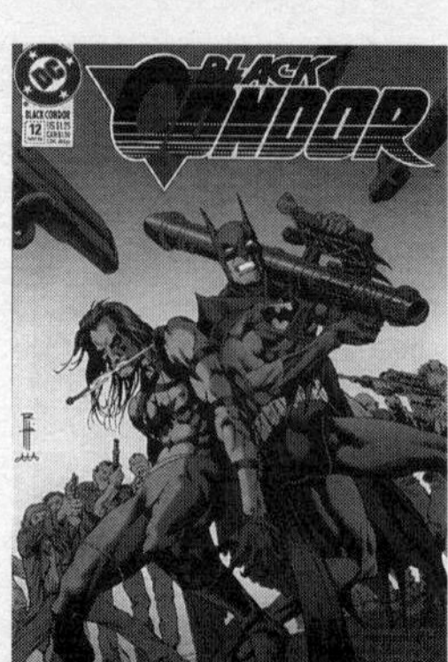

Black Condor #12 © DC

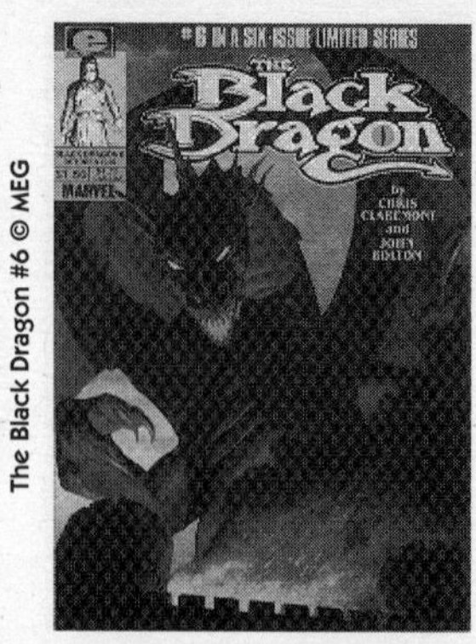

The Black Dragon #6 © MEG

Black Flag #1 © Rob Liefeld

	GD25	FN65	NM94
5,6-The Scarlet Arrow app. in ea. by Powell; S&K-a in both. 6-Origin Red Demon	22.00	65.00	150.00
7-Vagabond Prince by S&K plus 1 more story	22.00	65.00	150.00
8-S&K-a; Kerry Drake begins, ends #13	19.00	57.00	130.00
9-Origin Stuntman (r/Stuntman #1)	24.00	72.00	165.00
10-20: 14,15,17-Mary Worth app. plus Invisible Scarlet O'Neil-#15,20,24	14.00	43.00	100.00
21-26	11.50	34.00	80.00
27-Used in **SOTI**, pg. 193; X-Mas-c; 2 pg. John Wayne story	14.00	43.00	100.00
28-Intro. Kit, Black Cat's new sidekick	14.00	43.00	100.00
29-Black Cat bondage-c; Black Cat stories	13.00	40.00	90.00

BLACK CAT MYSTERY (Formerly Black Cat; ...Western Mystery #54; ...Western #55,56; ...Mystery #57; ...Mystic #58-62; Black Cat #63-65)
No. 30, Aug, 1951 - No. 65, April, 1963
Harvey Publications

	GD25	FN65	NM94
30-Black Cat on cover only	13.00	40.00	90.00
31,32,34,37,38,40	10.00	30.00	65.00
33-Used in **POP**, pg. 89; electrocution-c	10.00	30.00	70.00
35-Atomic disaster cover/story	11.50	34.00	80.00
36,39-Used in **SOTI**: #36-Pgs. 270,271; #39-Pgs. 386-388	13.50	41.00	95.00
41-43	10.00	30.00	65.00
44-Eyes, ears, tongue cut out; Nostrand-a	10.00	30.00	70.00
45-Classic "Colorama" by Powell; Nostrand-a	15.00	45.00	105.00
46-49,51-Nostrand-a in all	10.00	30.00	70.00
50-Check-a; Warren Kremer?-c showing a man's face burning away	14.00	43.00	100.00
52,53 (r/#34 & 35)	8.35	25.00	50.00
54-Two Black Cat stories (2/55, last pre-code)	10.00	30.00	70.00
55,56-Black Cat app.	8.35	25.00	50.00
57(7/56)-Kirby-c	6.70	20.00	40.00
58-60-Kirby-a(4). 58,59-Kirby-c. 60,61-Simon-c	10.00	30.00	60.00
61-Nostrand-a; "Colorama" r/#45	8.35	25.00	50.00
62(3/58)-E.C. story swipe	6.70	20.00	40.00
63-Giant(10/62); Reprints; Black Cat app.; origin Black Kitten	10.00	30.00	65.00
64-Giant(1/63); Reprints; Black Cat app.	10.00	30.00	65.00
65-Giant(4/63); Reprints; Black Cat app.; 1 pg. Powell-a	10.00	30.00	65.00

NOTE: ***Kremer*** *a-37, 39, 43; c-36, 37, 47.* ***Meskin*** *a-51.* ***Palais*** *a-30, 31(2), 32(2), 33-35, 37-40.* ***Powell*** *a-32-35, 36(2), 40, 41, 43-53, 57.* ***Simon*** *c-63-65.* ***Sparling*** *a-44. Bondage c-32, 34, 43.*

BLACK COBRA (Bride's Diary No. 4 on) (See Captain Flight #8)
No. 1, 10-11/54; No. 6(No. 2), 12-1/54-55; No. 3, 2-3/55
Ajax/Farrell Publications(Excellent Publ.)

	GD25	FN65	NM94
1-Re-intro Black Cobra & The Cobra Kid (costumed heroes)	17.00	52.00	120.00
6(#2)-Formerly Billy Bunny	11.00	32.00	75.00
3-(Pre-code)-Torpedoman app.	11.00	32.00	75.00

BLACK CONDOR (Also see Crack Comics & Freedom Fighters)
June, 1992 - No. 12, May, 1993 ($1.25)
DC Comics

	GD25	FN65	NM94
1-12: 1-10,12-Heath-c. 9,10-The Ray app. 12-Batman-c/s			1.25

BLACK CROSS SPECIAL (Dark Horse)(Value: cover or less)(See Dark Horse Presents)

BLACK DIAMOND (Americomics)(Value: cover or less)

BLACK DIAMOND WESTERN (Formerly Desperado No. 1-8)
No. 9, Mar, 1949 - No. 60, Feb, 1956 (No. 9-28: 52 pgs.)
Lev Gleason Publications

	GD25	FN65	NM94
9-Black Diamond & his horse Reliapon begin; origin Black Diamond	13.00	40.00	90.00
10	7.50	22.50	45.00
11-15	5.85	17.50	35.00
16-28(11/49-11/51)-Wolverton's Bing Bang Buster	7.50	22.50	45.00
29-40: 31-One pg. Frazetta anti-drug ad	4.00	11.00	22.00
41-50,53-59	3.60	9.00	18.00
51-3-D effect-c/story	10.00	30.00	60.00
52-3-D effect story	9.15	27.50	55.00
60-Last issue	4.00	12.00	24.00

NOTE: ***Biro*** *c-9-35?.* ***Fass*** *a-58, c-54-56, 58.* ***Guardineer*** *a-9, 15, 18.* ***Kida*** *a-9.* ***Maurer*** *a-10.* ***Ed Moore*** *a-16.* ***Morisi*** *a-55.* ***Tuska*** *a-10, 48.*

BLACK DRAGON, THE
May, 1985 - No. 6, Oct, 1985 (Baxter paper; mini-series; adults only)
Epic Comics (Marvel)

	GD25	FN65	NM94
1-Bolton-c/a in all		.80	2.00
2-6			1.00

BLACK FLAG, PREVIEW EDITION
June, 1994 - Present ($1.95, B&W)
Image Comics

	GD25	FN65	NM94
1-Fraga/McFarlane-c		.80	2.00

BLACK FURY (Becomes Wild West No. 58) (See Blue Bird)
May, 1955 - No. 57, Mar-Apr, 1966 (Horse stories)
Charlton Comics Group

	GD25	FN65	NM94
1	5.00	15.00	30.00
2	2.80	7.00	14.00
3-10	1.80	4.50	9.00
11-15,19,20	1.40	3.50	7.00
16-18-Ditko-a	4.70	14.00	28.00
21-30	1.00	2.50	5.00
31-57	.70	1.75	3.50

BLACK GOLD
1945? (8 pgs. in color)
Esso Service Station (Giveaway)

	GD25	FN65	NM94
nn-Reprints from True Comics	4.00	11.00	22.00

BLACK GOLIATH
Feb, 1976 - No. 5, Nov, 1976
Marvel Comics Group

	GD25	FN65	NM94
1: 1-3-Tuska-a(p)		1.70	4.25
2-5		.90	2.25

BLACKHAWK (Formerly Uncle Sam #1-8; see Military & Modern Comics)
No. 9, Winter, 1944 - No. 243, 10-11/68; No. 244, 1-2/76 - No. 250, 1-2/77; No. 251, 10/82 - No. 273, 11/84
Comic Magazines(Quality)No. 9-107(12/56); National Periodical Publications No. 108(1/57)-250; DC Comics No. 251 on

	GD25	FN65	NM94
9 (1944)	257.00	771.00	1800.00
10 (1946)	79.00	235.00	650.00
11-15: 14-Ward-a; 13,14-Fear app.	54.00	160.00	400.00
16-20: 20-Ward Blackhawk	46.00	140.00	350.00
21-30	33.00	100.00	265.00
31-40: 31-Chop Chop by Jack Cole	24.00	72.00	185.00
41-49,51-60	19.00	55.00	145.00
50-1st Killer Shark; origin in text	22.00	65.00	160.00
61-Used in **POP**, pg. 91	17.00	50.00	130.00
62-Used in **POP**, pg. 92 & color illo	17.00	50.00	130.00
63-70,72-80: 65-H-Bomb explosion panel. 66-B&W & color illos **POP**. 70-Return of Killer Shark; atomic explosion panel. 75-Intro. Blackie the Hawk	15.00	45.00	120.00
71-Origin retold; flying saucer-c; A-Bomb panels	18.00	55.00	140.00
81-86: Last precode (3/55)	14.00	42.50	115.00
87-92,94-99,101-107	12.00	35.00	90.00
93-Origin in text	12.50	37.50	95.00
100	15.00	45.00	115.00
108-1st DC issue (1/57); re-intro. Blackie, the Hawk, their mascot; not in #115	46.00	139.00	325.00
109-117	14.00	43.00	100.00
118-Frazetta-r/Jimmy Wakely #4 (3 pgs.)	15.00	45.00	105.00
119-130	10.00	30.00	70.00

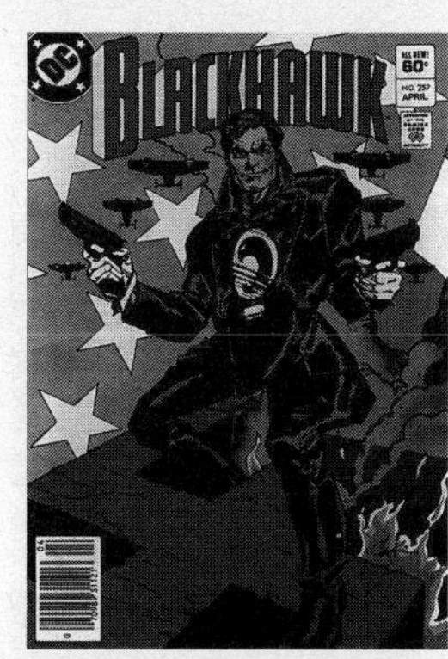

Blackhawk #257 © DC

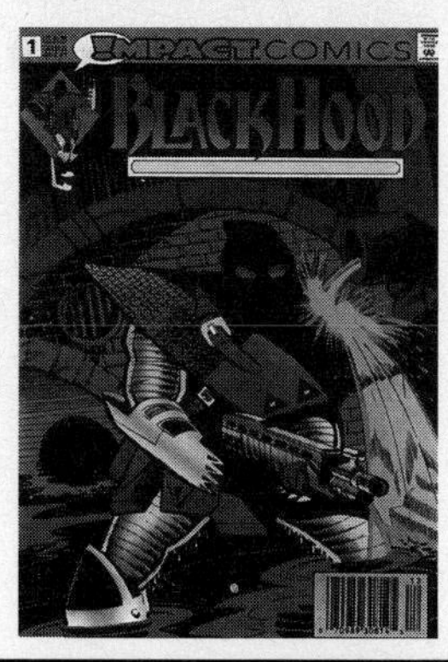

Black Hood #1 © Impact

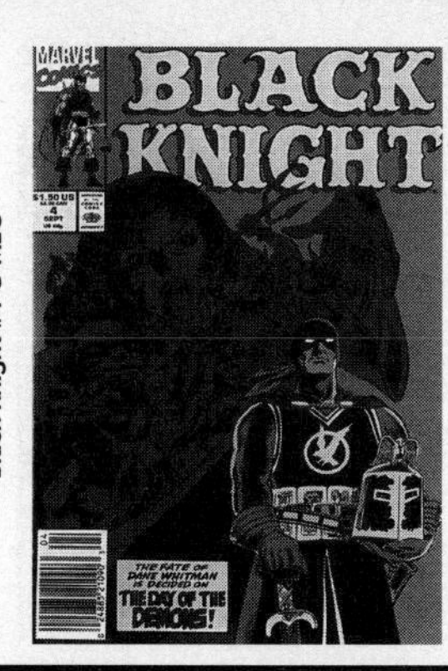

Black Knight #4 © MEG

GD25 FN65 NM94

131-140: 133-Intro. Lady Blackhawk 7.00 21.00 50.00
141-163,165,166: 143-Kurtzman-r/Jimmy Wakely #4. 166-Last 10¢ issue 5.30 16.00 37.00
164-Origin retold 5.00 15.00 35.00
167-180 2.00 6.00 14.00
181-190 1.70 4.20 10.00
191-197,199-202,204-210: 196-Combat Diary series begins. 197-New look for Blackhawks 1.30 3.00 8.00
198-Origin retold 1.70 4.20 10.00
203-Origin Chop Chop (12/64) 1.40 3.50 8.50
211-243(1968): 228-Batman, Green Lantern, Superman, The Flash cameos. 230-Blackhawks become superheroes. 242-Return to old costumes .90 2.00 5.50
244 ('76) -250: 250-Chuck dies .80 2.00
251-273: 251-Origin retold; Black Knights return. 252-Intro Domino. 253-Part origin Hendrickson. 258-Blackhawk's Island destroyed. 259-Part origin Chop-Chop. 265-273 (75¢ cover price) 1.50

NOTE: ***Chaykin** a-260; c-257-260, 262. **Crandall** a-10, 11, 13, 16?, 18-20, 22-26, 30-33, 35p, 36(2), 37, 38?, 39-44, 46-50, 52-58, 60, 63, 64, 66, 67; c-14-20, 22-63(most except #28-33, 36, 37, 39). **Evans** a-244, 245,246i, 248-250i. **G. Kane** c-263, 264. **Kubert** c-244, 245. **Newton** a-266p. **Severin** a-257.**Spiegle** a-261-267, 269-273; c-265-272. **Toth** a-260p. **Ward** a-16-27(Chop Chop, 8pgs. ea.); pencilled stories-No. 17-63(approx.). **Wildey** a-268. Chop Chop solo stories in #10-95?*

BLACKHAWK
Mar, 1988 - No. 3, May, 1988 ($2.95, mini-series)
DC Comics

1-3: Chaykin painted-c/a 1.20 3.00

BLACKHAWK
March, 1989 - No. 16, Aug, 1990 ($1.50, mature readers)
DC Comics

1-6,8-16: 16-Crandall-c swipe 1.50
7-($2.50, 52 pgs.)-Story-r/Military #1 1.00 2.50
Annual 1 (1989, $2.95, 68 pgs.)-Recaps origin of Blackhawk, Lady Blackhawk, and others 1.20 3.00
Special 1 (1992, $3.50, 68 pgs.)-Mature readers 1.40 3.50

BLACKHAWK INDIAN TOMAHAWK WAR, THE
1951 (Also see Fighting Indians of the Wild West)
Avon Periodicals

nn-Kinstler-c; Kit West story 11.00 32.00 75.00

BLACK HEART ASSASSIN
Jan, 1994 ($2.95, color)
Iguana Comics

1 1.20 3.00

BLACK HOLE (See Walt Disney Showcase #54)
March, 1980 - No. 4, September, 1980 (Disney movie)
Whitman Publishing Co.

11295(#1)-4: 1-Photo-c; Spiegle-a. 1,2-Movie adaptation. 2-4-Spiegle-a. 3-McWilliams-a; photo-c. 3,4-New stories 1.00

BLACK HOOD, THE (See Blue Ribbon, Flyman & Mighty Comics)
June, 1983 - No. 3, Oct, 1983 (Printed on Mandell paper)
Red Circle Comics (Archie)

1-Morrow, McWilliams, Wildey-a; Toth-c 1.50
2,3: MLJ's The Fox by Toth, c/a. 3-Morrow-a 1.00
(Also see Archie's Super-Hero Special Digest #2)

BLACK HOOD
Dec, 1991 - No. 12, Dec, 1992 ($1.00)
DC/Impact Comics

1-12: 11-Intro The Fox. 12-Origin Black Hood 1.00
Annual 1 (1992, $2.50, 68 pgs.)-W/Trading card 1.00 2.50

BLACK HOOD COMICS (Formerly Hangman #2-8; Laugh Comics #20 on; also see Black Swan, Jackpot, Roly Poly & Top-Notch #9)
No. 9, Winter, 1943-44 - No. 19, Summer, 1946 (on radio in 1943)
MLJ Magazines

9-The Hangman & The Boy Buddies cont'd 61.00 182.00 425.00
10-Hangman & Dusty, the Boy Detective app. 36.00 107.00 250.00
11-Dusty app.; no Hangman 25.00 75.00 175.00
12-18: 14-Kinstler blood-c. 17-Hal Foster swipe from Prince Valiant; 1st issue with "An Archie Magazine" on-c 25.00 75.00 175.00
19-I.D. exposed 31.00 95.00 220.00

NOTE: *Hangman by **Fuje** in 9, 10. **Kinstler** a-15, c-14-16.*

BLACK JACK (Rocky Lane's...; formerly Jim Bowie)
No. 20, Nov, 1957 - No. 30, Nov, 1959
Charlton Comics

20 5.85 17.50 35.00
21,27,29,30 3.60 9.00 18.00
22-(68 pgs.) 4.70 14.00 28.00
23-Williamson/Torres-a 5.35 16.00 32.00
24-26,28-Ditko-a 6.35 19.00 38.00

BLACK KNIGHT, THE
May, 1953; 1963
Toby Press

1-Bondage-c 14.00 430.00 100.00
Super Reprint No. 11 (1963)-Reprints 1953 issue 3.20 8.00 16.00

BLACK KNIGHT, THE (Also see The Avengers #48, Marvel Super Heroes & Tales To Astonish #52)
May, 1955 - No. 5, April, 1956
Atlas Comics (MgPC)

1-Origin Crusader; Maneely-c/a 68.00 205.00 475.00
2-Maneely-c/a(4) 49.00 145.00 340.00
3-5: 4-Maneely-c/a. 5-Maneely-c, Shores-a 40.00 120.00 280.00

BLACK KNIGHT
June, 1990 - No. 4, Sept, 1990 ($1.50, mini-series)
Marvel Comics

1-4: 1-Original Black Knight returns 1.50

BLACK LIGHTNING (See Brave & The Bold, Cancelled Comic Cavalcade, DC Comics Presents #16, Detective #490 and World's Finest #257)
April, 1977 - No. 11, Sept-Oct, 1978
National Periodical Publications/DC Comics

1 .80 2.00
2-11: 4-Intro Cyclotronic Man. 11-The Ray app. 1.00

NOTE: ***Buckler** c-1-3p, 6-11p. #11 is 44 pgs.*

BLACK MAGIC (...Magazine) (Becomes Cool Cat V8#6 on)
10-11/50 - V4#1, 6-7/53: V4#2, 9-10/53 - V5#3, 11-12/54; V6#1, 9-10/57 - V7#2, 11-12/58: V7#3, 7-8/60 - V8#5, 11-12/61
(V1#1-5, 52pgs.; V1#6-V3#3, 44pgs.)
Crestwood Publ. V1#1-4,V6#1-V7#5/Headline V1#5-V5#3,V7#6-V8#5

V1#1-S&K-a, 10 pgs.; Meskin-a(2) 64.00 193.00 450.00
2-S&K-a, 17 pgs.; Meskin-a 31.00 92.00 215.00
3-6(8-9/51)-S&K, Roussos, Meskin-a 24.00 72.00 165.00
V2#1(10-11/51),4,5,7(#13),9(#15),12(#18)-S&K-a 17.00 52.00 120.00
2,3,6,8,10,11(#17) 12.00 36.00 85.00
V3#1(#19, 12/52) - 6(#24, 5/53)-S&K-a 13.50 41.00 95.00
V4#1(#25, 6-7/53), 2(#26, 9-10/53)-S&K-a(3-4) 14.00 43.00 100.00
3(#27, 11-12/53)-S&K-a; Ditko-a (1st published-a); also see Captain 3-D & Fantastic Fears #5 (Fantastic Fears #5 was 1st drawn, but not 1st published Ditko-a) 31.00 92.00 215.00
4(#28)-Eyes ripped out/story-S&K, Ditko-a 20.00 60.00 140.00
5(#29, 3-4/54)-S&K, Ditko-a 16.00 48.00 110.00
6(#30, 5-6/54)-S&K, Powell?-a 10.00 30.00 70.00
V5#1(#31, 7-8/54 - 3(#33, 11-12/54)-S&K-a 10.00 30.00 60.00
V6#1(#34, 9-10/57), 2(#35, 11-12/57) 5.35 16.00 32.00
3(1-2/58) - 6(7-8/58) 5.35 16.00 32.00
V7#1(9-10/58) - 3(7-8/60) 4.35 13.00 26.00
4(9-10/60), 5(11-12/60)-Torres-a 5.35 16.00 32.00

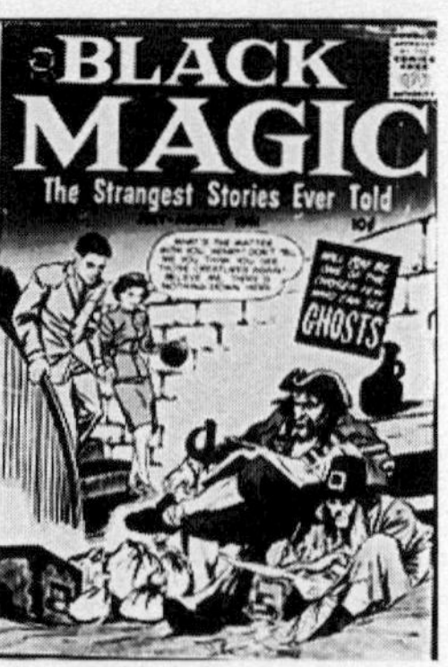

Black Magic V8 #3 © PRIZE

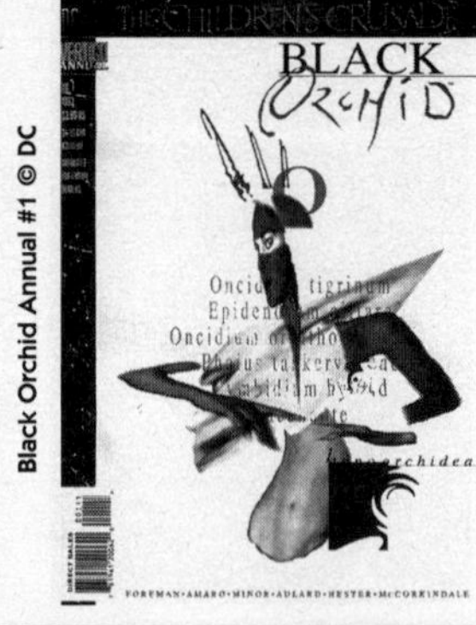

Black Orchid Annual #1 © DC

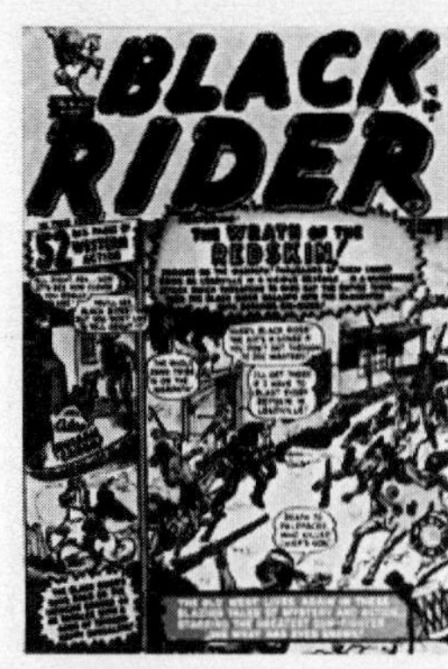

Black Rider #9 © MEG

	GD25	FN65	NM94
6(1-2/61)-Powell-a(2)	4.35	13.00	26.00
V8#1(3-4/61)-Powell-c/a	4.35	13.00	26.00
2(5-6/61)-E.C. story swipe/W.F. #22; Ditko, Powell-a	5.35	16.00	32.00
3(7-8/61)-E.C. story swipe/W.F. #22; Powell-a(2)	5.35	16.00	32.00
4(9-10/61)-Powell-a(5)	4.35	13.00	26.00
5-E.C. story swipe/W.S.F. #28; Powell-a(3)	5.35	16.00	32.00

NOTE: ***Bernard Baily** a-V4#6?, V5#3(2). **Grandenetti** a-V2#3, 11. **Kirby** c-V1#1-6, V2#1-12, V3#1-6, V4#1, 2, 4-6, V5#1-3. **McWilliams** a-V3#2i. **Meskin** a-V1#1(2), 2, 3, 4(2), 5(2), 6, V2/1, 2, 3(2), 4(3), 5, 6(2), 7-9, 11, 12i, V3#1(2), 5, 6, V5#1(2), 2. **Orlando** a-V6#1, 4, V7#2; c-V6/1-6. **Powell** a-V5#1?. **Roussos** a-V1#3-5, 6(2), V2#3(2), 4, 5(2), 6, 8, 9, 10(2), 11, 12p, V3#1(2), 2i, 5, V5#2. **Simon** a-V2#12, V3#2, V7#5? c-V4#3?, V7#3?, 4, 5?, 6?, V8#1-5. **Simon & Kirby** a-V1#1, 2(2), 3-6, V2#1, 4, 5, 7, 9, 12, V3#1-6, V4#1(3), 2(4), 3(2), 4(2), 5, 6, V5#1-3; c-V2#1. **Leonard Starr** a-V1#1. **Tuska** a-V6#3, 4. **Woodbridge** a-V7#4.*

BLACK MAGIC
Oct-Nov, 1973 - No. 9, Apr-May, 1975
National Periodical Publications

	GD25	FN65	NM94
1-S&K reprints			1.50
2-9-S&K reprints			1.00

BLACK MAGIC (Eclipse)(Value: cover or less)

BLACKMAIL TERROR (See Harvey Comics Library)

BLACK MASK
1993 - No. 3, 1994 ($4.95, mini-series, 52 pgs.)
DC Comics

	GD25	FN65	NM94
1-3	1.00	2.00	5.00

BLACK ORCHID (See Adventure Comics #428 & Phantom Stranger)
Holiday, 1988-89 - No. 3, 1989 ($3.50, mini-series, prestige format)
DC Comics

	GD25	FN65	NM94
Book 1,3: Neil Gaiman scripts & McKean-a in all	1.00	2.50	6.00
Book 2-Arkham Asylum story; Batman app.	1.30	3.00	7.50

BLACK ORCHID
Sept, 1993 - Present ($1.95)
DC Comics

	GD25	FN65	NM94
1-10: Dave McKean c-1-9		.90	2.25
1-Platinum Edition	2.00	6.40	15.00
11-20		.80	2.00
Annual 1 (1993, $3.95, 68 pgs.)-Children's Crusade		1.60	4.00

BLACKOUTS (See Broadway Hollywood...)

BLACK PANTHER, THE (Also see Avengers #52, Fantastic Four #52, Jungle Action & Marvel Premiere #51-53)
Jan, 1977 - No. 15, May, 1979
Marvel Comics Group

	GD25	FN65	NM94
1	1.00	2.50	6.00
2		1.40	3.50
3-10		1.00	2.50
11-15: 14,15-Avengers x-over		.80	2.00

NOTE: ***J. Buscema** c-15p. **Kirby** c/a & scripts-1-12. **Layton** c-13i.*

BLACK PANTHER
July, 1988 - No. 4, Oct, 1988 ($1.25)
Marvel Comics Group

	GD25	FN65	NM94
1-4			1.25

BLACK PANTHER: PANTHER'S PREY
1991 - No. 4, 1991 ($4.95, squarebound, mini-series, 52 pgs.)
Marvel Comics

	GD25	FN65	NM94
1-4	1.00	2.00	5.00

BLACK PHANTOM (See Tim Holt #25, 38)
Nov, 1954 (One shot) (Female outlaw)
Magazine Enterprises

	GD25	FN65	NM94
1 (A-1 #122)-The Ghost Rider story plus 3 Black Phantom stories; Headlight-c/a	27.00	80.00	185.00

BLACK PHANTOM
1989 - No. 3, 1990 ($2.50, B&W; #2 color)(Reprints & new-a)
AC Comics

	GD25	FN65	NM94
1,2: 1-Ayers-r, Bolle-r/B.P. #1. 2-Redmask-r		1.00	2.50
3 ($2.75, B&W)-B.P., Redmask-r & new-a		1.10	2.75

BLACK PHANTOM, RETURN OF THE (See Wisco)

BLACK RIDER (Formerly Western Winners; Western Tales of Black Rider #28-31; Gunsmoke Western #32 on)(Also see All Western Winners, Best Western, Kid Colt, Outlaw Kid, Rex Hart, Two-Gun Kid, Two-Gun Western, Western Gunfighters, Western Winners, & Wild Western)
No. 8, 3/50 - No. 18, 1/52; No. 19, 11/53 - No. 27, 3/55
Marvel/Atlas Comics(CDS No. 8-17/CPS No. 19 on)

	GD25	FN65	NM94
8 (#1)-Black Rider & his horse Satan begin; 36 pgs; Stan Lee photo-c as Black Rider)	31.00	95.00	220.00
9-52 pgs. begin, end #14	16.00	48.00	110.00
10-Origin Black Rider	19.00	57.00	130.00
11-14: 14-Last 52pgs.	11.50	34.00	80.00
15-19: 19-Two-Gun Kid app.	10.00	30.00	65.00
20-Classic-c; Two-Gun Kid app.	11.00	32.00	75.00
21-26: 21-23-Two-Gun Kid app. 24,25-Arrowhead app. 26-Kid Colt app.	10.00	30.00	60.00
27-Last issue; last precode. Kid Colt app. The Spider (a villain) burns to death	10.00	30.00	60.00

NOTE: ***Ayers** c-22. **Jack Keller** a-15, 26, 27. **Maneely** a-14; c-16, 17, 25, 27. **Syd Shores** a-19, 21, 22, 23(3), 24(3), 25-27; c-19, 21, 23. **Sinnott** a-24, 25. **Tuska** a-12, 19-21.*

BLACK RIDER RIDES AGAIN!, THE
September, 1957
Atlas Comics (CPS)

	GD25	FN65	NM94
1-Kirby-a(3); Powell-a; Severin-c	16.00	48.00	110.00

BLACKSTONE (See Super Magician Comics & Wisco Giveaways)

BLACKSTONE, MASTER MAGICIAN COMICS
Mar-Apr, 1946 - No. 3, July-Aug, 1946
Vital Publications/Street & Smith Publ.

	GD25	FN65	NM94
1	17.00	52.00	120.00
2,3	13.50	41.00	95.00

BLACKSTONE, THE MAGICIAN (...Detective on cover only #3 & 4)
No. 2, May, 1948 - No. 4, Sept, 1948 (No #1)(Cont'd from E.C. #1?)
Marvel Comics (CnPC)

	GD25	FN65	NM94
2-The Blonde Phantom begins, ends #4	43.00	129.00	300.00
3,4: 3-Blonde Phantom by Sekowsky	29.00	86.00	200.00

BLACKSTONE, THE MAGICIAN DETECTIVE FIGHTS CRIME
Fall, 1947
E. C. Comics

	GD25	FN65	NM94
1-1st app. Happy Houlihans	37.00	110.00	260.00

BLACK SWAN COMICS
1945
MLJ Magazines (Pershing Square Publ. Co.)

	GD25	FN65	NM94
1-The Black Hood reprints from Black Hood No. 14; Bill Woggon-a; Suzie app.	15.00	45.00	105.00

BLACK TARANTULA (See Feature Presentations No. 5)

BLACK TERROR (See America's Best Comics & Exciting Comics)
Wint, 1942-43 - No. 27, June, 1949
Better Publications/Standard

	GD25	FN65	NM94
1-Black Terror, Crime Crusader begin	121.00	365.00	850.00
2	52.00	156.00	365.00
3	41.00	125.00	290.00
4,5	34.00	100.00	235.00
6-10: 7-The Ghost app.	25.00	75.00	175.00
11-20: 20-The Scarab app.	22.00	65.00	150.00
21-Miss Masque app.	24.00	72.00	165.00
22-Part Frazetta-a on one Black Terror story	24.00	72.00	165.00
23,25-27	21.00	63.00	145.00

Blackwulf #3 © MEG

Blade: The Vampire Hunter #3 © MEG

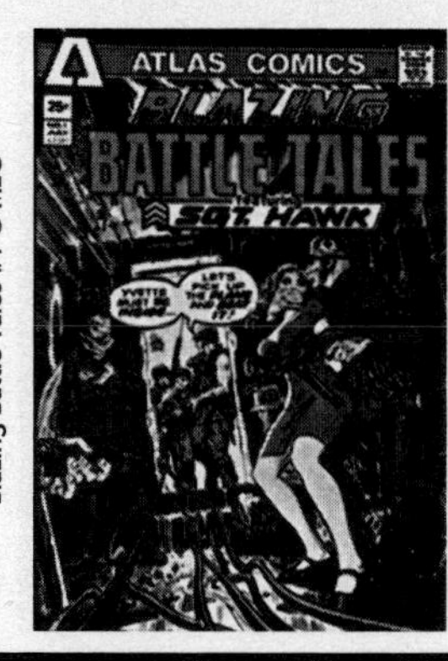

Blazing Battle Tales #1 © MEG

	GD25	FN65	NM94
24-Frazetta-a (1/4 pg.)	22.00	65.00	150.00

NOTE: ***Schomburg (Xela)*** *c-2-27; bondage c-2, 17, 24.* ***Meskin*** *a-27.* ***Moreira*** *a-27.* ***Robinson/Meskin*** *a-23, 24(3), 25, 26.* ***Roussos/Mayo*** *a-24.* ***Tuska*** *a-26, 27.*

BLACK TERROR, THE (Eclipse)(Value: cover or less) (Also see Total Eclipse)

BLACKTHORNE 3-D SERIES (Blackthorne)(Value: cover or less)

BLACKWULF
June, 1994 - Present ($1.50)
Marvel Comics

	GD25	FN65	NM94
1-($2.50)-Embossed-c; Angel Medina-a		1.00	2.50
2-11			1.50

BLACK ZEPPELIN (See Gene Day's...)

BLADE RUNNER
Oct, 1982 - No. 2, Nov, 1982 (Movie adaptation)
Marvel Comics Group

	GD25	FN65	NM94
1,2-r/Marvel Super Special #22; 1-Williamson-c/a. 2-Williamson-a			.75

BLADESMEN UNDERSEA
1994 ($3.50, B&W)
Blue Comet Press

	GD25	FN65	NM94
1-Polybagged w/trading card		1.40	3.50

BLADE: THE VAMPIRE-HUNTER
July, 1994 - Present ($1.95)
Marvel Comics

	GD25	FN65	NM94
1-($2.95)-Foil-c		1.20	3.00
2-9		.80	2.00

BLAKE HARPER (See City Surgeon...)

BLAST (Satire Magazine)
Feb, 1971 - No. 2, May, 1971
G & D Publications

	GD25	FN65	NM94
1-Wrightson & Kaluta-a	3.60	9.00	18.00
2-Kaluta-a	2.80	7.00	14.00

BLASTERS SPECIAL
1989 ($2.00, one-shot)
DC Comics

	GD25	FN65	NM94
1-Invasion spin-off		.80	2.00

BLAST-OFF (Three Rocketeers)
October, 1965 (12¢)
Harvey Publications (Fun Day Funnies)

	GD25	FN65	NM94
1-Kirby/Williamson-a(2); Williamson/Crandall-a; Williamson/Torres/Krenkel-a; Kirby/Simon-c	3.30	10.00	23.00

BLAZE
Aug, 1994 - Present ($1.95)
Marvel Comics

	GD25	FN65	NM94
1-($2.95)-Foil embossed-c		1.20	3.00
2-6: 2-Man-Thing-c/story		.80	2.00

BLAZE CARSON (Becomes Rex Hart No. 6 on)(See Kid Colt, Tex Taylor, Wild Western, Wisco)
Sept, 1948 - No. 5, June, 1949
Marvel Comics (USA)

	GD25	FN65	NM94
1: 1,2-Shores-c	17.00	52.00	120.00
2,4,5: 4-Two-Gun Kid app. 5-Tex Taylor app.	12.00	36.00	85.00
3-Used by N.Y. State Legis. Comm. (injury to eye splash); Tex Morgan app.	14.00	43.00	100.00

BLAZE: LEGACY OF BLOOD (See Ghost Rider & Ghost Rider/Blaze)
Dec, 1993 - No. 4, Mar, 1994 ($1.75, mini-series)
Marvel Comics (Midnight Sons imprint)

	GD25	FN65	NM94
1-4		.70	1.75

BLAZE THE WONDER COLLIE (Formerly Molly Manton's Romances #1?)
No. 2, Oct, 1949 - No. 3, Feb, 1950 (Both have photo covers)
Marvel Comics(SePI)

	GD25	FN65	NM94
2(#1), 3-(Scarce)	16.00	48.00	110.00

BLAZING BATTLE TALES
July, 1975
Seaboard Periodicals (Atlas)

	GD25	FN65	NM94
1-Intro. Sgt. Hawk & the Sky Demon; Severin, McWilliams, Sparling-a; Thorne-c			1.00

BLAZING COMBAT (Magazine)
Oct, 1965 - No. 4, July, 1966 (Black & White, 35¢)
Warren Publishing Co.

	GD25	FN65	NM94
1-Frazetta painted-c on all	10.00	30.00	70.00
2	4.00	10.00	20.00
3,4: 4-Frazetta half pg. ad	3.00	8.00	15.00
...Anthology (reprints from No. 1-4)	.80	2.00	4.00

NOTE: *Above has art by* ***Colan, Crandall, Evans, Morrow, Orlando, Severin, Torres, Toth, Williamson,*** *and* ***Wood.***

BLAZING COMBAT: WORLD WAR I AND WORLD WAR II
Mar, 1994 ($3.75, B&W)
Apple Press

	GD25	FN65	NM94
1,2: 1-r/Colan, Toth, Goodwin, Severin, Wood-a. 2-r/Crandall, Evans, Severin, Torres, Williamson-a		1.50	3.75

BLAZING COMICS
6/44 - #3, 9/44; #4, 2/45; #5, 3/45; #5(V2#2), 3/55 - #6(V2#3), 1955?
Enwil Associates/Rural Home

	GD25	FN65	NM94
1-The Green Turtle, Red Hawk, Black Buccaneer begin; origin Jun-Gal	32.00	96.00	225.00
2-5: 3-Briefer-a. 5-(V2#2 inside)	19.00	58.00	135.00
5(3/55, V2#2-inside)-Black Buccaneer-c, 6(V2#3-inside, 1955)-Indian/Japanese-c	8.35	25.00	50.00

NOTE: *No. 5 & 6 contain remaindered comics rebound and the contents can vary. Cloak & Daggar, Will Rogers, Superman 64, Star Spangled 130, Kaanga known. Value would be half of contents.*

BLAZING SIXGUNS
December, 1952
Avon Periodicals

	GD25	FN65	NM94
1-Kinstler-c/a; Larsen/Alascia-a(2), Tuska?-a; Jesse James, Kit Carson, Wild Bill Hickok app.	10.00	30.00	70.00

BLAZING SIXGUNS
1964
I.W./Super Comics

	GD25	FN65	NM94
I.W. Reprint #1,8,9: 1-r/Wild Bill Hickok #26 & Blazing Sixguns #1 by Avon; Kinstler-c. 8-r/Blazing Western #?; Kinstler-c. 9-r/Blazing Western #1; Ditko-r	1.80	4.50	9.00
Super Reprint #10,11,15,16: 10,11-r/The Rider #2,1. 15-r/Silver Kid Western #?. 16-r/Buffalo Bill #?; Wildey-r; Severin-c. 17(1964)-r/Western True Crime #?	1.60	4.00	8.00
12-Reprints Bullseye #3; S&K-a	4.00	10.00	20.00
18-r/Straight Arrow #? by Powell; Severin-c	2.00	5.00	10.00

BLAZING SIX-GUNS (Also see Sundance Kid)
Feb, 1971 - No. 2, April, 1971 (52 pgs.)
Skywald Comics

	GD25	FN65	NM94
1-The Red Mask, Sundance Kid begin, Avon's Geronimo reprint by Kinstler; Wyatt Earp app.		1.60	4.00
2-Wild Bill Hickok, Jesse James, Kit Carson-r plus M.E. Red Mask-r		.80	2.00

BLAZING WEST (Also see The Hooded Horseman)
Fall, 1948 - No. 22, Mar-Apr, 1952
American Comics Group(B&I Publ./Michel Publ.)

	GD25	FN65	NM94
1-Origin & 1st app. Injun Jones, Tenderfoot & Buffalo Belle; Texas Tim & Ranger begins, ends #13	14.00	43.00	100.00
2,3	8.35	25.00	50.00

Blazing West #7 © ACG

Blonde Phantom #18 © MEG

Blood of Dracula #1 © Apple Comics

	GD25	FN65	NM94
4-Origin & 1st app. Little Lobo; Starr-a	5.85	17.50	35.00
5-10: 5-Starr-a	5.00	15.00	30.00
11-13	4.00	11.00	22.00
14-Origin & 1st app. The Hooded Horseman	8.35	25.00	50.00
15-22: 15,16,18,19-Starr-a	5.85	17.50	35.00

BLAZING WESTERN
Jan, 1954 - No. 5, Sept, 1954
Timor Publications

	GD25	FN65	NM94
1-Ditko-a; Text story by Bruce Hamilton	10.00	30.00	70.00
2-4	4.20	12.50	25.00
5-Disbrow-a	5.00	15.00	30.00

BLESSED PIUS X
No date (32 pgs.; text, comics) (Paper cover)
Catechetical Guild (Giveaway)

	GD25	FN65	NM94
nn	3.20	8.00	16.00

BLIND JUSTICE (Also see Batman: Blind Justice)
1989 (Giveaway, squarebound)
DC Comics/Diamond Comic Distributors

	GD25	FN65	NM94
nn-Contains Detective #598-600 by Batman movie writer Sam Hamm, w/covers; published same time as originals?		.80	2.00

BLITZKRIEG
Jan-Feb, 1976 - No. 5, Sept-Oct, 1976
National Periodical Publications

	GD25	FN65	NM94
1-Kubert-c on all			1.25
2-5			.75

BLONDE PHANTOM (Formerly All-Select #1-11; Lovers #23 on)(Also see Blackstone, Marvel Mystery, Millie The Model #2, Sub-Mariner Comics #25 & Sun Girl)
No. 12, Winter, 1946-47 - No. 22, March, 1949
Marvel Comics (MPC)

	GD25	FN65	NM94
12-Miss America begins, ends #14	82.00	246.00	575.00
13-Sub-Mariner begins (not in #16)	54.00	160.00	375.00
14,15: 15-Kurtzman's "Hey Look"	44.00	133.00	310.00
16-Captain America with Bucky story by Rico(p), 6 pgs.; Kurtzman's "Hey Look" (1 pg.)	64.00	193.00	450.00
17-22: 22-Anti Wertham editorial	41.00	122.00	285.00

NOTE: ***Shores** c-12-18.*

BLONDIE (See Ace Comics, Comics Reading Libraries, Dagwood, Daisy & Her Pups, Eat Right to Work..., King & Magic Comics)
1942 - 1946
David McKay Publications

	GD25	FN65	NM94
Feature Books 12 (Rare)	45.00	135.00	450.00
Feature Books 27-29,31,34(1940)	13.00	40.00	90.00
Feature Books 36,38,40,42,43,45,47	11.50	34.00	80.00
...1944 (Hard-c, 1938, B&W, 128 pgs.)-1944 daily strip-r	11.50	34.00	80.00

BLONDIE & DAGWOOD FAMILY
Oct, 1963 - No. 4, Dec, 1965 (68 pgs.)
Harvey Publications (King Features Synd.)

	GD25	FN65	NM94
1	3.20	8.00	16.00
2-4	1.00	5.00	10.00

BLONDIE COMICS (...Monthly No. 16-141)
Spring, 1947 - No. 163, Nov, 1965; No. 164, Aug, 1966 - No. 175, Dec, 1967; No. 177, Feb, 1969 - No. 222, Nov, 1976
David McKay #1-15/Harvey #16-163/King #164-175/Charlton #177 on

	GD25	FN65	NM94
1	16.00	48.00	110.00
2	9.15	27.50	55.00
3-5	6.35	19.00	38.00
6-10	4.70	14.00	28.00
11-15	4.00	10.00	20.00
16-(3/50; 1st Harvey issue)	4.35	13.00	26.00
17-20: 20-(3/51)-Becomes Daisy & Her Pups #21 & Chamber of Chills #21	3.60	9.00	18.00
21-30	2.80	7.00	14.00
31-50	2.00	5.00	10.00
51-80	1.80	4.50	9.00
81-124,126-130	1.60	4.00	8.00
125 (80 pgs.)	2.00	5.00	10.00
131-136,138,139	1.40	3.50	7.00
137,140-(80 pgs.)	1.80	4.50	9.00
141-167(#148,155,157-159,161-163 are 68 pgs.)	1.80	4.50	9.00
168-175,177-222 (no #176)	.90	2.25	4.50
Blondie, Dagwood & Daisy 1(100 pgs., 1953)	13.00	40.00	90.00
1950 Giveaway	3.20	8.00	16.00
1962,1964 Giveaway	1.20	3.00	6.00
N. Y. State Dept. of Mental Hygiene Giveaway-('50, '56, '61) Regular size (Diff. issues) 16 pgs.; no #	1.80	4.50	9.00

BLOOD
Feb, 1988 - No. 4, Apr, 1988 ($3.25, adults)
Epic Comics (Marvel)

	GD25	FN65	NM94
1-4		1.30	3.25

BLOOD AND GLORY (Punisher & Captain America)
Oct, 1992 - No. 3, Dec, 1992 ($5.95, mini-series)
Marvel Comics

	GD25	FN65	NM94
1-3: 1-Embossed wraparound-c	1.00	2.50	6.00

BLOOD & ROSES: FUTURE PAST TENSE (Bob Hickey's...)
Dec, 1993 ($2.25, color)
Sky Comics

	GD25	FN65	NM94
1-Silver ink logo		.90	2.25

BLOOD & ROSES: SEARCH FOR THE TIME-STONE (Bob Hickey's...)
Apr, 1994 - Present ($2.50, color)
Sky Comics

	GD25	FN65	NM94
1		1.00	2.50

BLOODBATH
Early Dec, 1993 - No. 2, Late Dec, 1993 ($3.50, limited series, 68 pgs.)
DC Comics

	GD25	FN65	NM94
1,2-Neon ink-c; Superman app.: 1-New Batman-c & app.		1.40	3.50

BLOODFIRE
June, 1993 - Present ($2.95, color)
Lightning Comics

	GD25	FN65	NM94
1-($3.50)-Foil-c; 1st app. Bloodfire		1.60	4.00
2-12: 2-Origin; contracts HIV virus via transfusion. 5-Polybagged w/card & collectors warning on bag. 12-(5/94)		1.20	3.00
0-(MAY on-c, June 1994 inside, $3.50)		1.40	3.50

BLOOD IS THE HARVEST
1950 (32 pgs.) (paper cover)
Catechetical Guild

	GD25	FN65	NM94
(Scarce)-Anti-communism(13 known copies)	80.00	2405.00	560.00
Black & white version (5 known copies), saddle stitched	30.00	90.00	200.00

Untrimmed version (only one known copy); estimated value-$600
NOTE: *In 1979 nine copies of the color version surfaced from the old Guild's files plus the five black & white copies.*

BLOOD IS THE HARVEST (Eclipse)(Value: cover or less)

BLOODLINES: A TALE FROM THE HEART OF AFRICA
1992 ($5.95, 52 pgs.)(See Tales From the Heart of Africa)
Epic Comics (Marvel)

	GD25	FN65	NM94
1-Story cont'd from Tales From...	1.00	2.50	6.00

BLOOD OF DRACULA
Nov, 1987 - No. 20?, 1990 ($1.75/$1.95, B&W)($2.25 #14,16 on)
Apple Comics

Bloodstrike #12 © Rob Liefeld

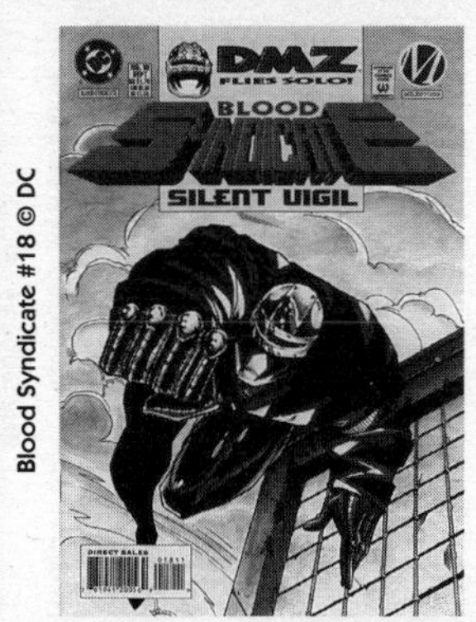

Blood Syndicate #18 © DC

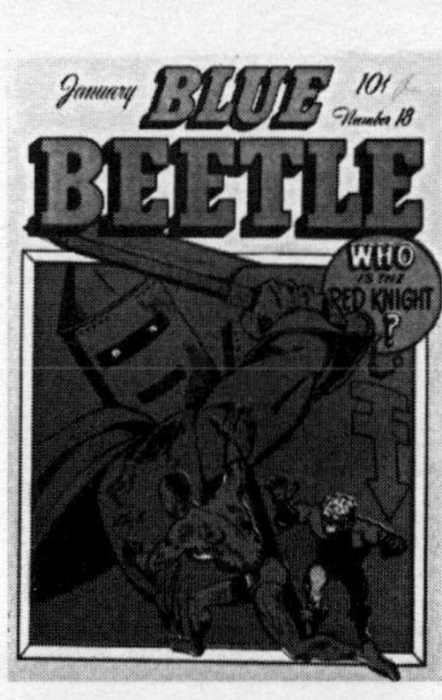

Blue Beetle #18 © CC

GD25 FN65 NM94

1-13: 6-Begin $1.95-c. 10-Chadwick-c .80 2.00
14,16-20 ($2.25): 14,16-19-Lost Frankenstein pgs. by Wrightson
.90 2.25
15-Contains stereo flexidisc ($3.75) 1.50 3.75

BLOOD OF THE INNOCENT (WaRP)(Value: cover or less)

BLOODSCENT (Comico)(Value: cover or less)

BLOODSEED
Oct, 1993 - No. 2, Nov, 1993 ($1.95, mini-series, adult)
Marvel Frontier Comics
1,2: Sharp/Cam Smith-a .80 2.00

BLOODSHOT (See Eternal Warrior #4 & Rai #0)
Nov, 1992 - Present ($2.25, color)
Valiant
1-($3.50)-Chromium embossed-c by B. Smith w/poster 1.70 4.25
2-($2.50) 1.00 2.50
3-5,8-14: 3-Begin $2.25-c; cont'd in Hard Corps #5. 4-Eternal Warrior-c/story. 5-Rai & Eternal Warrior app. 14-(3/94)-Reese-c(i) .90 2.25
6-1st app. Ninjak (out of costume) 1.40 3.50
7-1st app. Ninjak in costume 2.00 4.75
0-(3/94, $3.50)-Wraparound chromium-c by Quesada(p); origin
1.40 3.50
0-Gold variant 1.40 3.50
15-22: 15-(4/94). 16-w/bound-in trading card .90 2.25
...Yearbook 1 (1994, $3.95) 1.60 4.00

BLOODSTRIKE (See Supreme V2#3)
1993 - Present ($1.95, color)
Image Comics
1-10: 1-Blood Brothers prelude. 2-1st app. Lethal. 5-1st app. Noble. 6-1st app. Chaple as team leader. 9-Black and White part 6 by Art Thibert; Liefeld pin-up. 9,10-Have coupon #3 & 7 for Extreme Prejudice #0. 10-(4/94)
.80 2.00
25-(5/94)-Liefeld/Fraga-c .80 2.00
11,12: 11-(7/94) .80 2.00
NOTE: ***Giffen** story/layouts-4-6. **Jae Lee** c-7, 8. **Rob Liefeld** layouts-1-3. **Art Thibert** c-6i.*

BLOOD SWORD, THE (Jademan)(Value: cover or less)

BLOOD SWORD DYNASTY (Jademan)(Value: cover or less)

BLOOD SYNDICATE
Apr, 1993 - Present ($1.50/$1.75)
DC Comics (Milestone)
1-($2.95)-Collector's Edition; polybagged with poster, trading card, & acid-free backing board (direct sale only) 1.20 3.00
1-9,11-17: 8-Intro Kwai. 15-Byrne-c. 16-Worlds Collide Pt. 6; Superman-c & app. 17-Worlds Collide Pt. 13 1.50
10-($2.50, 52 pgs.)-Simonson-c 1.00 2.50
18-24: 18-Begin $1.75-c 1.75

BLUE BEETLE, THE (Also see All Top, Big-3, Mystery Men & Weekly Comic Magazine)
Winter, 1939-40 - No. 57, 7/48; No. 58, 4/50 - No. 60, 8/50
Fox Publ. No. 1-11, 31-60; Holyoke No. 12-30
1-Reprints from Mystery Men 1-5; Blue Beetle origin; Yarko the Great-r/from Wonder/Wonderworld 2-5 all by Eisner; Master Magician app.; (Blue Beetle in 4 different costumes) 243.00 730.00 1700.00
2-K-51-r by Powell/Wonderworld 8,9 93.00 280.00 650.00
3-Simon-c 71.00 215.00 500.00
4-Marijuana drug mention story 46.00 139.00 325.00
5-Zanzibar The Magician by Tuska 39.00 118.00 275.00
6-Dynamite Thor begins (1st); origin Blue Beetle 37.00 110.00 260.00
7,8-Dynamo app. in both. 8-Last Thor 34.00 103.00 240.00
9,10-The Blackbird & The Gorilla app. in both. 10-Bondage/hypo-c
32.00 96.00 225.00
11(2/42)-The Gladiator app. 32.00 96.00 225.00
12(6/42)-The Black Fury app. 32.00 96.00 225.00
13-V-Man begins (1st app.), ends #18; Kubert-a 37.00 110.00 260.00
14,15-Kubert-a in both. 14-Intro. side-kick (c/text only), Sparky (called Spunky #17-19) 36.00 107.00 250.00
16-18: 17-Brodsky-c 28.00 84.00 195.00
19-Kubert-a 30.00 90.00 210.00
20-Origin/1st app. Tiger Squadron; Arabian Nights begin
32.00 96.00 225.00
21-26: 24-Intro. & only app. The Halo. 26-General Patton story & photo
20.00 60.00 140.00
27-Tamaa, Jungle Prince app. 19.00 57.00 130.00
28-30(2/44) 17.00 52.00 120.00
31(6/44), 33-40: 34-38-"The Threat from Saturn" serial. 35-Extreme violence
13.00 40.00 90.00
32-Hitler-c 16.00 48.00 110.00
41-45 11.00 32.00 75.00
46-The Puppeteer app. 12.00 36.00 85.00
47-Kamen & Baker-a begin 59.00 175.00 410.00
48-50 45.00 135.00 315.00
51,53 41.00 122.00 285.00
52-Kamen bondage-c; true crime stories begin 59.00 178.00 415.00
54-Used in **SOTI**. Illo, "Children call these 'headlights' comics"
79.00 235.00 550.00
55,57(7/48)-Last Kamen issue; becomes Western Killers?
38.00 114.00 265.00
56-Used in **SOTI**, pg. 145 38.00 114.00 265.00
58(4/50)-60-No Kamen-a 10.00 30.00 70.00
NOTE: ***Kamen** a-47-51, 53, 55-57; c-47, 49-52. **Powell** a-4(2). Bondage-c 9-12, 46, 52.*

BLUE BEETLE (Formerly The Thing; becomes Mr. Muscles No. 22 on) (See Charlton Bullseye & Space Adventures)
No. 18, Feb, 1955 - No. 21, Aug, 1955
Charlton Comics
18,19-(Pre-1944-r). 18-Last pre-code ossue. 19-Bouncer, Rocket Kelly-r
11.50 34.00 80.00
20-Joan Mason by Kamen 13.50 41.00 95.00
21-New material 10.00 30.00 65.00

BLUE BEETLE (Unusual Tales #1-49; Ghostly Tales #55 on)(Also see Captain Atom & Charlton Bullseye)
V2#1, June, 1964 - V2#5, Mar-Apr, 1965; V3#50, July, 1965 - V3#54, Feb-Mar, 1966; #1, June, 1967 - #5, Nov, 1968
Charlton Comics
V2#1-Origin/1st S.A. app. Dan Garrett-Blue Beetle 6.00 18.00 42.00
2-5: 5-Weiss illo; 1st published-a? 4.40 13.00 31.00
V3#50-54-Formerly Unusual Tales 4.40 13.00 31.00
1(1967)-Question series begins by Ditko 9.70 29.00 68.00
2-Origin Ted Kord-Blue Beetle (see Capt. Atom #83 for 1st Ted Kord Blue Beetle); Dan Garrett x-over 4.00 11.00 26.00
3-5 (All Ditko-c/a in #1-5) 3.00 9.00 21.00
1,3(Modern Comics-1977)-Reprints 1.00
NOTE: *#6 only appeared in the fanzine 'The Charlton Portfolio.'*

BLUE BEETLE (Also see Americomics & Crisis On Infinite Earths)
June, 1986 - No. 24, May, 1988
DC Comics
1-Origin retold; intro. Firefist 1.00
2-24: 2-Origin Firefist. 5-7-The Question app. 11-14-New Teen Titans x-over. 20-Justice League app. 20,21-Millennium tie-ins 1.00

BLUEBERRY (See Lt. Blueberry & Marshal Blueberry)
1989 - No. 5, 1990 ($12.95/$14.95, graphic novel)
Epic Comics (Marvel)
1,3,4,5-($12.95)-Moebius-a in all 1.85 5.50 13.00
2-($14.95) 2.15 6.50 15.00

BLUE BIRD COMICS
Late 1940's - 1964 (Giveaway)
Various Shoe Stores/Charlton Comics

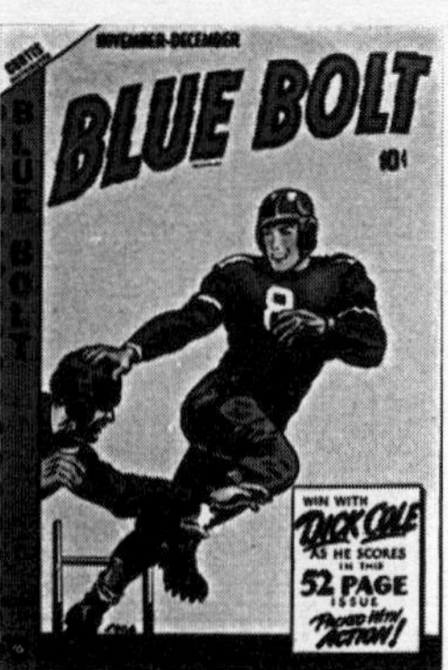

Blue Bolt #6/V9 © NOVP

Blue Devil #18 © DC

Blue Ribbon #7 © STJ

GD25 FN65 NM94

nn(1947-50)(36 pgs.)-Several issues; Human Torch, Sub-Mariner app. in some 10.00 30.00 60.00
1959-Li'l Genius, Timmy the Timid Ghost, Wild Bill Hickok (All #1) 1.40 3.50 7.00
1959-(6 titles; all #2) Black Fury #1,4,5, Freddy #4, Li'l Genius, Timmy the Timid Ghost #4, Masked Raider #4, Wild Bill Hickok (Charlton) 1.40 3.50 7.00
1959-(#5) Masked Raider #21 1.40 3.50 7.00
1960-(6 titles)(All #4) Black Fury #8,9, Masked Raider, Freddy #8,9, Timmy the Timid Ghost #9, Li'l Genius #7,9 (Charlt.) 1.40 3.50 7.00
1961,1962-(All #10's) Atomic Mouse #12,13,16, Black Fury #11,12, Freddy, Li'l Genius, Masked Raider, Six Gun Heroes, Texas Rangers in Action, Timmy the Ghost, Wild Bill Hickok, Wyatt Earp #3,11-13,16-18 (Charlton) 1.20 3.00 6.00
1963-Texas Rangers #17 (Charlton) .60 1.75 3.00
1964-Mysteries of Unexplored Worlds #18, Teenage Hotrodders #18, War Heroes #18 (Charlton) 1.00 2.50 5.00
1965-War Heroes #18 .40 1.00 2.00
NOTE: *More than one issue of each character could have been published each year. Numbering is sporadic.*

BLUE BIRD CHILDREN'S MAGAZINE, THE
V1#2, 1957 - No. 10 1958 (16 pgs.; soft cover; regular size)
Graphic Information Service
V1#2-10: Pat, Pete & Blue Bird app. .80 2.00 4.00

BLUE BOLT
June, 1940 - No. 101 (V10No.2), Sept-Oct, 1949
Funnies, Inc. No. 1/Novelty Press/Premium Group of Comics
V1#1-Origin Blue Bolt by Joe Simon, Sub-Zero Man, White Rider & Super Horse, Dick Cole, Wonder Boy & Sgt. Spook (1st app. of each) 200.00 600.00 1400.00
2-Simon & Kirby's 1st art & 1st super-hero (Blue Bolt) 93.00 280.00 650.00
3-1 pg. Space Hawk by Wolverton; 2nd S&K-a on Blue Bolt (same cover date as Red Raven #1); 1st time S&K names app. in a comic; Simon-c 79.00 235.00 550.00
4,5-S&K-a in each; 5-Everett-a begins on Sub-Zero 71.00 215.00 500.00
6,8-10-S&K-a 64.00 193.00 450.00
7-S&K-c/a 71.00 215.00 500.00
11,12: 11-Robot-c 71.00 215.00 500.00
V2#1-Origin Dick Cole & The Twister; Twister x-over in Dick Cole, Sub-Zero, & Blue Bolt; origin Simba Karno who battles Dick Cole thru V2#5 & becomes main supporting character V2#6 on; battle-c 21.00 63.00 145.00
2-Origin The Twister retold in text 16.00 48.00 110.00
3-5: 5-Intro. Freezum 13.50 41.00 95.00
6-Origin Sgt. Spook retold 10.00 30.00 85.00
7-12: 7-Lois Blake becomes Blue Bolt's costume aide; last Twister 10.00 30.00 65.00
V3#1-3 8.35 25.00 50.00
4-12: 4-Blue Bolt abandons costume 6.35 19.00 38.00
V4#1-Hitler, Tojo, Mussolini-c 8.65 26.00 52.00
V4#2-12: 3-Shows V4#3 on-c, V4#4 inside (9-10/43). 5-Infinity-c. 8-Last Sub-Zero 5.35 16.00 32.00
V5#1-8, V6#1-3,5-10, V7#1-12 4.00 12.00 24.00
V6#4-Racist cover 5.85 17.50 35.00
V8#1-6,8-12, V9#1-5,7,8 4.00 11.00 22.00
V8#7,V9#6,9-L. B. Cole-c 4.70 14.00 28.00
V10#1(#100) 4.00 12.00 24.00
V10#2(#101)-Last Dick Cole, Blue Bolt 4.00 12.00 24.00
NOTE: ***Everett** c-V1#4, 11, V2#1, 2. **Gustavson** a-V1#1-12, V2#1-7. **Kiefer** c-V3#1. **Rico** a-V6#10, V7#4. Blue Bolt not in V9#8.*

BLUE BOLT (Becomes Ghostly Weird Stories #120 on; continuation of Novelty Blue Bolt) (...Weird Tales #112-119)
No. 102, Nov-Dec, 1949 - No. 119, May-June, 1953
Star Publications
102-The Chameleon, & Target app. 17.00 52.00 120.00
103,104-The Chameleon app. 104-Last Target 16.00 48.00 110.00
105-Origin Blue Bolt (from #1) retold by Simon; Chameleon & Target app.; opium den story 30.00 90.00 210.00
106-Blue Bolt by S&K begins; Spacehawk reprints from Target by Wolverton begin, ends #110; Sub-Zero begins; ends #109 27.00 80.00 185.00
107-110: 108-Last S&K Blue Bolt reprint. 109-Wolverton-c(r)/inside Spacehawk splash. 110-Target app. 25.00 75.00 175.00
111-Red Rocket & The Mask-r; last Blue Bolt; 1pg. L. B. Cole-a 24.00 72.00 165.00
112-Last Torpedo Man app. 24.00 72.00 165.00
113-Wolverton's Spacehawk-r/Target V3#7 25.00 75.00 175.00
114,116: 116-Jungle Jo-r 24.00 72.00 165.00
115-Sgt. Spook app. 26.00 78.00 180.00
117-Jo-Jo & Blue Bolt-r 24.00 72.00 165.00
118-"White Spirit" by Wood 26.00 78.00 180.00
119-Disbrow/Cole-c; Jungle Jo-r 24.00 72.00 165.00
Accepted Reprint #103(1957?, nd) 6.70 20.00 40.00
NOTE: ***L. B. Cole** c-102-108, 110 on. **Disbrow** a-112(2), 113(3), 114(2), 115(2), 116-118. **Hollingsworth** a-117. **Palais** a-112r. Sci/Fi c-105-110. Horror c-111.*

BLUE BULLETEER, THE (AC)(Value: cover or less)

BLUE CIRCLE COMICS (Also see Roly Poly Comic Book)
June, 1944 - No. 5, Mar, 1945; No. 6, 1950s
Enwil Associates/Rural Home
1-The Blue Circle begins (1st app.); origin & 1st app. Steel Fist 15.00 45.00 105.00
2,3: 3-Hitler parody-c 10.00 30.00 65.00
4,5: 5-Last Steel Fist 6.70 20.00 40.00
6-(1950s)-Colossal Features-r 6.70 20.00 40.00

BLUE DEVIL (See Fury of Firestorm #24)
June, 1984 - No. 31, Dec, 1986 (75¢)
DC Comics
1-30: 4-Origin Nebiros. 7-Gil Kane-a. 8-Giffen-a. 17-19-Crisis x-over 1.00
31-($1.25, 52 pgs.) 1.25
Annual 1 (11/85)-Team-ups w/Black Orchid, Creeper, Demon, Madame Xanadu, Man-Bat & Phantom Stranger 1.25

BLUE PHANTOM, THE
June-Aug, 1962
Dell Publishing Co.
1(01-066-208)-by Fred Fredericks 4.00 10.00 20.00

BLUE RIBBON COMICS (...Mystery Comics No. 9-18)
Nov, 1939 - No. 22, March, 1942 (1st MLJ series)
MLJ Magazines
1-Dan Hastings, Richy the Amazing Boy, Rang-A-Tang the Wonder Dog begin (1st app. of each); Little Nemo app. (not by W. McCay); Jack Cole-a(3) 229.00 685.00 1600.00
2-Bob Phantom, Silver Fox (both in #3), Rang-A-Tang Club & Cpl. Collins begin (1st app. of each); Jack Cole-a 86.00 257.00 600.00
3-J. Cole-a 57.00 171.00 400.00
4-Doc Strong, The Green Falcon, & Hercules begin (1st app. each); origin & 1st app. The Fox & Ty-Gor, Son of the Tiger 62.00 186.00 435.00
5-8: 8-Last Hercules; 6,7-Biro, Meskin-a. 7-Fox app. on-c 43.00 130.00 300.00
9-(Scarce)-Origin & 1st app. Mr. Justice (2/41) 164.00 493.00 1150.00
10-13: 12-Last Doc Strong. 13-Inferno, the Flame Breather begins, ends #19; Devil-c 71.00 215.00 500.00
14,15,17,18: 15-Last Green Falcon 61.00 182.00 425.00
16-Origin & 1st app. Captain Flag (9/41) 116.00 350.00 815.00
19-22: 20-Last Ty-Gor. 22-Origin Mr. Justice retold 57.00 171.00 400.00
NOTE: ***Biro** c-3-5; a-2 (Cpl. Collins & Scoop Cody). **S. Cooper** c-9-17. 20-22 contain "Tales From the Witch's Cauldron" (same strip as "Stories of the Black Witch" in Zip Comics). Mr. Justice c-9-18. Captain Flag c-16(w/Mr. Justice), 19-22.*

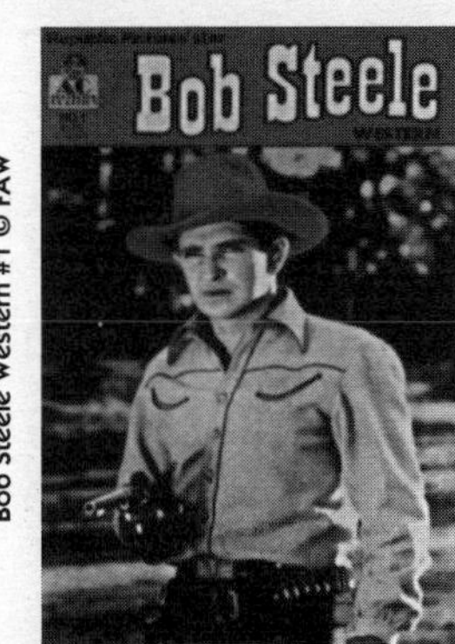

Bob Steele Western #1 © FAW

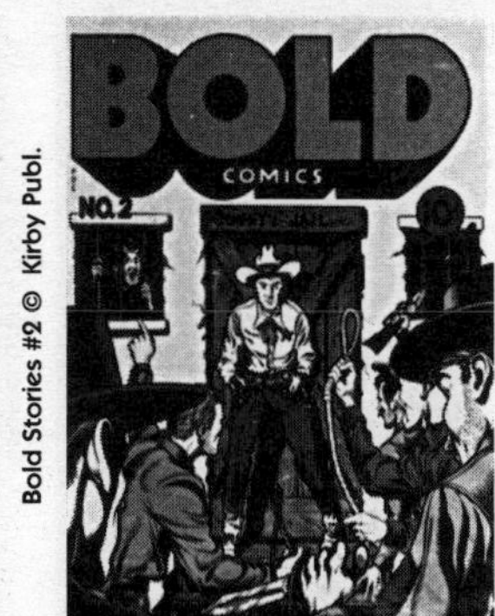

Bold Stories #2 © Kirby Publ.

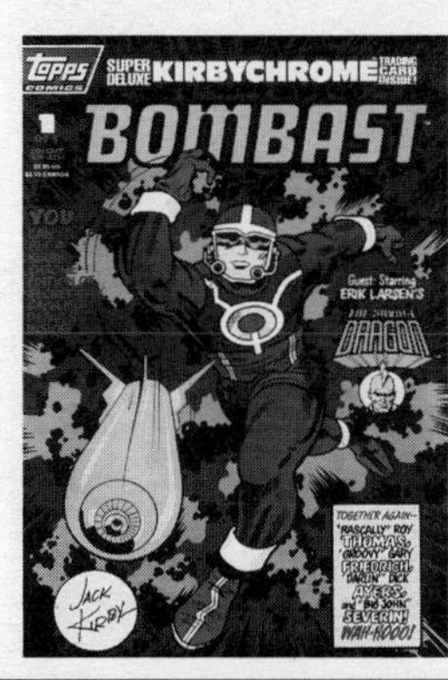

Bombast #1 © Jack Kirby

GD25 FN65 NM94

BLUE RIBBON COMICS (Becomes Teen-Age Diary Secrets #4)
Feb, 1949 - No. 6, Aug, 1949 (See Heckle & Jeckle)
Blue Ribbon (St. John)

1,3-Heckle & Jeckle 6.70 20.00 40.00
2(4/49)-Diary Secrets; Baker-c 10.00 30.00 65.00
4(6/49)-Teen-Age Diary Secrets; Baker c/a(2) 10.00 30.00 70.00
5(8/49)-Teen-Age Diary Secrets; Oversize; photo-c; Baker-a(2)- Continues as Teen-Age Diary Secrets 14.00 43.00 100.00
6-Dinky Duck(8/49) 3.00 7.50 15.00

BLUE-RIBBON COMICS
Nov, 1983 - No. 14, Dec, 1984
Red Circle Prod./Archie Ent. No. 5 on

1-S&K-r/Advs. of the Fly #1,2; Williamson/Torres-r/Fly #2; Ditko-c 1.00
2-14: 3-Origin Steel Sterling. 5-S&K Shield-r. 6,7-The Fox app. 8-Toth centerspread. 8,11-Black Hood. 12-Thunder Agents. 13-Thunder Bunny. 14-Web & Jaguar 1.00

NOTE: ***N. Adams*** *a(r)-8.* ***Buckler*** *a-4i.* ***Nino*** *a-2i.* ***McWilliams*** *a-8.* ***Morrow*** *a-8.*

BLUE STREAK (See Holyoke One-Shot No. 8)

BLYTHE (See 4-Color No. 1072)

B-MAN (See Double-Dare Adventures)

BO (Tom Cat #4 on; also see Big Shot #29 & Dixie Dugan)
June, 1955 - No. 3, Oct, 1955 (a dog)
Charlton Comics Group

1-3-Newspaper reprints by Frank Beck 5.70 17.00 34.00

BOATNIKS, THE (See Walt Disney Showcase No. 1)

BOB & BETTY & SANTA'S WISHING WELL
1941 (12 pgs.) (Christmas giveaway)
Sears Roebuck & Co.

nn 9.15 27.50 55.00

BOBBY BENSON'S B-BAR-B RIDERS (Radio) (See Best of The West, The Lemonade Kid & Model Fun)
May-June, 1950 - No. 20, May-June, 1953
Magazine Enterprises

1-The Lemonade Kid begins; Powell-a 25.00 75.00 175.00
2 11.00 32.00 75.00
3-5: 4,5-Lemonade Kid-c (#4-Spider-c) 10.00 30.00 60.00
6-8,10 8.35 25.00 50.00
9,11,13-Frazetta-c; Ghost Rider in #13-15 by Ayers-a. 13-Ghost Rider-c 21.00 63.00 145.00
12,17-20: 20-(A-1 #88) 7.50 22.50 45.00
14-Decapitation/Bondage-c & story; horror-c 10.00 30.00 70.00
15-Ghost Rider-c 10.00 30.00 70.00
16-Photo-c 10.00 30.00 60.00
...in the Tunnel of Gold-(1936, 5-1/4x8"; 100 pgs.) Radio giveaway by Hecker-H.O. Company(H.O. Oats); contains 22 color pgs. of comics, rest in novel form 9.15 27.50 55.00
...And The Lost Herd-same as above 9.15 27.50 55.00

NOTE: ***Ayers*** *a-13-15, 20.* ***Powell*** *a-1-12(4 ea.), 13(3), 14-16(Red Hawk only); c-1-8,1 0, 12. Lemonade Kid in most 1-13.*

BOBBY COMICS
May, 1946
Universal Phoenix Features

1-By S. M. Iger 6.35 19.00 38.00

BOBBY SHELBY COMICS
1949
Shelby Cycle Co./Harvey Publications

nn 4.00 10.00 20.00

BOBBY SHERMAN (TV)
Feb, 1972 - No. 7, Oct, 1972
Charlton Comics

1-Based on TV show "Getting Together" 4.00 10.00 20.00
2-7: 4-Photo-c 2.40 6.00 12.00

BOBBY THATCHER & TREASURE CAVE
1932 (86 pgs.; B&W; hardcover; 7x9")
Altemus Co.

nn-Reprints; Storm-a 9.15 27.50 55.00

BOBBY THATCHER'S ROMANCE
1931 (7x8-3/4")
The Bell Syndicate/Henry Altemus Co.

nn-By Storm 9.15 27.50 55.00

BOB COLT (Movie star)(See XMas Comics)
Nov, 1950 - No. 10, May, 1952
Fawcett Publications

1-Bob Colt, his horse Buckskin & sidekick Pablo begin; photo front/back-c begin 34.00 103.00 240.00
2 22.00 65.00 150.00
3-5 18.00 54.00 125.00
6-Flying Saucer story 15.00 45.00 105.00
7-10: 9-Last photo back-c 13.50 41.00 95.00

BOB HOPE (See Adventures of... & Calling All Boys #12)

BOB POWELL'S TIMELESS TALES (Eclipse)(Value: cover or less)

BOB SCULLY, TWO-FISTED HICK DETECTIVE
No date (1930's) (36 pgs.; 9-1/2x12"; B&W; paper cover)
Humor Publ. Co.

nn-By Howard Dell; not reprints 10.00 30.00 60.00

BOB SON OF BATTLE (See 4-Color No. 729)

BOB STEELE WESTERN (Movie star)
Dec, 1950 - No. 10, June, 1952; 1990
Fawcett Publications/AC Comics

1-Bob Steele & his horse Bullet begin; photo front/back-c begin 43.00 130.00 300.00
2 22.00 67.00 155.00
3-5: 4-Last photo back-c 18.00 54.00 125.00
6-10: 10-Last photo-c 13.50 41.00 95.00
1 (1990, $2.75, B&W)-Bob Steele & Rocky Lane reprints; photo-c & inside covers .55 1.60 2.75

BOB SWIFT (Boy Sportsman)
May, 1951 - No. 5, Jan, 1952
Fawcett Publications

1 6.70 20.00 40.00
2-5: Saunders painted-c #1-5 4.00 11.00 22.00

BOLD ADVENTURES (Pacific)(Value: cover or less)

BOLD STORIES (Also see Candid Tales & It Rhymes With Lust)
Mar, 1950 - July, 1950 (Digest size; 144 pgs.; full color)
Kirby Publishing Co.

March issue (Very Rare) - Contains "The Ogre of Paris" by Wood 54.00 160.00 375.00
May issue (Very Rare) - Contains "The Cobra's Kiss" by Graham Ingels (21 pgs.) 43.00 129.00 300.00
July issue (Very Rare) - Contains "The Ogre of Paris" by Wood 47.00 141.00 330.00

BOLT AND STAR FORCE SIX (Americomics)(Value: cover or less)

BOMBARDIER (See Bee 29, the Bombardier & Cinema Comics Herald)

BOMBAST
1993 ($2.95, one-shot)
Topps Comics

1-Polybagged w/Kirbychrome trading card; Savage Dragon app.; Kirby-c; has coupon for Amberchrome Secret City Saga #0 1.20 3.00

BOMBA THE JUNGLE BOY (TV)

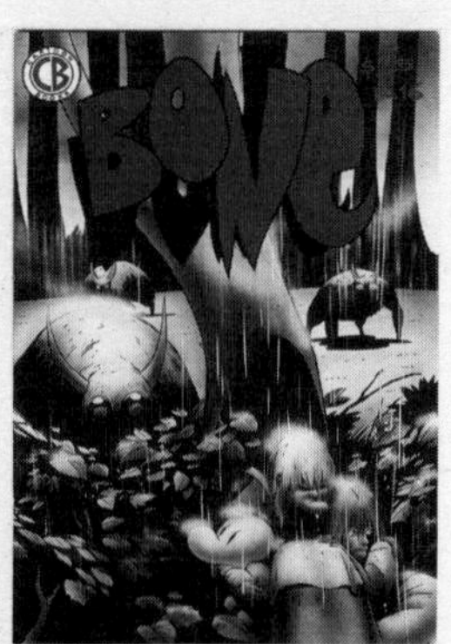

Bone #16 © Jeff Smith

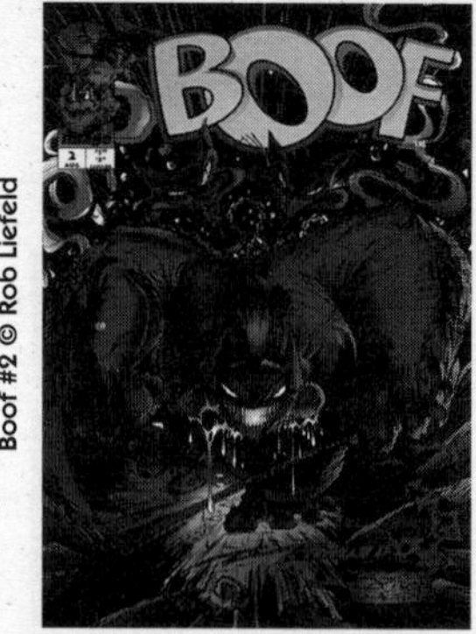

Boof #2 © Rob Liefeld

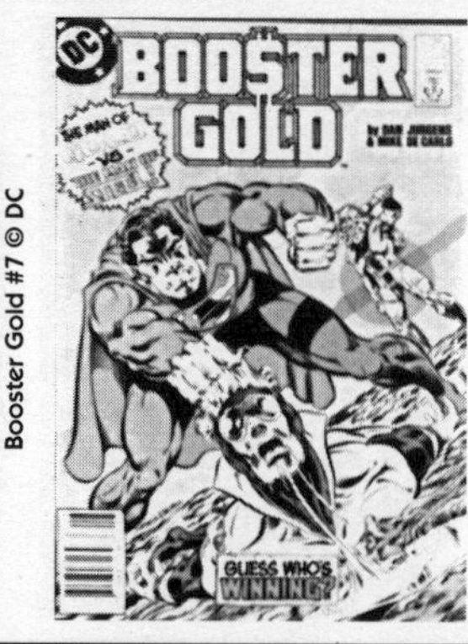

Booster Gold #7 © DC

GD25 FN65 NM94

Sept-Oct, 1967 - No. 7, Sept-Oct, 1968 (12¢)
National Periodical Publications

1-Intro. Bomba; Infantino/Anderson-c 2.15 6.50 15.00
2-7 1.25 3.00 7.50

BOMBER COMICS
March, 1944 - No. 4, Winter, 1944-45
Elliot Publ. Co./Melverne Herald/Farrell/Sunrise Times

1-Wonder Boy, & Kismet, Man of Fate begin 29.00 86.00 200.00
2-4: 2-4-Have Classics Comics ad to HRN 20 21.00 63.00 145.00

BONANZA (TV)
June-Aug, 1960 - No. 37, Aug, 1970 (All Photo-c)
Dell/Gold Key

4-Color 1110 (6-8/60) 34.00 103.00 240.00
4-Color 1221,1283, & #01070-207, 01070-210 17.00 52.00 120.00
1(12/62-Gold Key) 17.00 52.00 120.00
2 9.15 27.50 55.00
3-10 5.00 15.00 30.00
11-20 4.00 11.00 22.00
21-37: 29-Reprints 3.20 8.00 16.00

BONE
July, 1991 - Present ($2.95, B&W)
Cartoon Books

1-Jeff Smith-c/a in all 18.00 54.00 125.00
1-2nd printing 2.10 6.40 15.00
1-3rd thru 5th printings 1.00 2.00 5.00
2-1st printing 7.00 21.00 50.00
2-2nd & 3rd printings 1.00 2.00 5.00
3-1st printing 4.30 13.00 30.00
3-2nd thru 4th printings 1.00 2.00 5.00
4-10 1.60 4.00
11-15 1.20 3.00
Holiday Special (1993, giveaway) 1.00
Complete Bone Adventures Vol 1 (1993, r/#1-6), Vol 2 (1994, r/#7-12): Both $12.95-c 2.00 5.50 13.00
NOTE: *Printings not listed sell for cover price.*

BONGO (See Story Hour Series)

BONGO & LUMPJAW (See 4-Color #706,886, & Walt Disney Showcase #3)

BON VOYAGE (See Movie Classics)

BOOF
July, 1994 - Present ($1.95, color)
Image Comics

1-3 .80 2.00

BOOF AND THE BRUISE CREW
July, 1994 - Present ($1.95, color)
Image Comics

1-3 .80 2.00

BOOK AND RECORD SET (See Power Record Comics)

BOOK OF ALL COMICS
1945 (196 pgs.)(Inside f/c has Green Publ. blacked out)
William H. Wise

nn-Green Mask, Puppeteer & The Bouncer 29.00 86.00 200.00

BOOK OF COMICS, THE
No date (1944) (25¢, 132 pgs.)
William H. Wise

nn-Captain V app. 29.00 86.00 200.00

BOOK OF LOVE (See Fox Giants)

BOOK OF NIGHT, THE (Dark Horse)(Value: cover or less)

BOOK OF THE DEAD
Dec, 1993 - No. 4, Mar, 1994 ($1.75, mini-series, 52 pgs.)
Marvel Comics

1-4: 1-Ploog Frankenstein & Morrow Man-Thing-r begin; Wrightson-r/Chamber of Darkness #7. 2-Morrow new painted-c; Chaykin/Morrow Man-Thing; Krigstein-r/Uncanny Tales #54; r/Fear #10. 3-r/Astonishing Tales #10 & Starlin Man-Thing. 3,4-Painted-c .70 1.75

BOOKS OF MAGIC
1990 - No. 4, 1991 ($3.95, mini-series, mature readers, 52 pgs.)
DC Comics

1-Bolton painted-c/a; Phantom Stranger app.; Gaiman scripts in all 1.70 5.00 12.00
2,3: 2-John Constantine, Dr. Fate, Spectre, Deadman app. 3-Dr. Occult app.; minor Sandman app. 1.30 3.00 7.50
4-Early-c & app. of Death (early 1991) 1.40 3.50 8.50

BOOKS OF MAGIC
May, 1994 - Present ($1.95, mature readers)
DC Comics (Vertigo)

1-10: Vess-c .80 2.00

BOOSTER GOLD (See Justice League #4)
Feb, 1986 - No. 25, Feb, 1988 (75¢)
DC Comics

1-25: 4-Rose & Thorn app. 6-Origin. 6,7,23-Superman app. 8,9-LSH app. 22-JLI app. 24,25-Millennium tie-ins 1.00
NOTE: ***Austin** c-22i. **Byrne** c-23i.*

BOOTS AND HER BUDDIES
No. 5, 9/48 - No. 9, 9/49; 12/55 - No. 3, 1956
Standard Comics/Visual Editions/Argo (NEA Service)

5-Strip-r 11.00 32.00 75.00
6,8 8.35 25.00 50.00
7-(Scarce)-Spanking panels(3) 10.00 30.00 60.00
9-(Scarce)-Frazetta-a (2 pgs.) 19.00 57.00 130.00
1-3(Argo-1955-56)-Reprints 4.00 11.00 22.00

BOOTS & SADDLES (See 4-Color No. 919, 1029, 1116)

BORDER PATROL
May-June, 1951 - No. 3, Sept-Oct, 1951
P. L. Publishing Co.

1 8.35 25.00 50.00
2,3 5.85 17.50 35.00

BORDER WORLDS (Kitchen Sink)(Value: cover or less)

BORIS KARLOFF TALES OF MYSTERY (TV) (...Thriller No. 1,2)
No. 3, April, 1963 - No. 97, Feb, 1980
Gold Key

3-8,10-(Two #5's, 10/63,11/63): 5-(10/63)-11 pgs. Toth-a. 10-Orlando-a 4.00 10.00 20.00
9-Wood-a 4.00 12.00 24.00
11-Williamson-a, 8 pgs.; Orlando-a, 5 pgs. 4.00 12.00 24.00
12-Torres, McWilliams-a; Orlando-a(2) 3.60 9.00 18.00
13,14,16-20 2.80 7.00 14.00
15-Crandall 3.20 8.00 16.00
21-Jeff Jones-a(3 pgs.) "The Screaming Skull" 3.20 8.00 16.00
22-30: 23-Reprint; photo-c 2.00 5.00 10.00
31-50: 36-Weiss-a 1.20 3.00 6.00
51-74: 74-Origin & 1st app. Taurus 1.60 4.00
75-97: 80-86-(52 pgs.). 90-r/Torres, McWilliams-a/#12; Morrow-c .80 2.00

Story Digest 1(7/70-Gold Key)-All text 1.30 3.25 8.00
(See Mystery Comics Digest No. 2, 5, 8, 11, 14, 17, 20, 23, 26)
NOTE: ***Bolle** a-51-54, 56, 58, 59. **McWilliams** a-12, 14, 18, 19, 72, 80, 81, 93. **Orlando** a-11-15, 21. Reprints: 78, 81-86, 88, 90, 92, 95, 97.*

BORIS KARLOFF THRILLER (TV) (Becomes Boris Karloff Tales...)
Oct, 1962 - No. 2, Jan, 1963 (80 pgs.)

BORIS THE BEAR
Slaughters the Teenage Radioactive Black Belt Mutant Ninja Critters

Boris The Bear #1 © DH

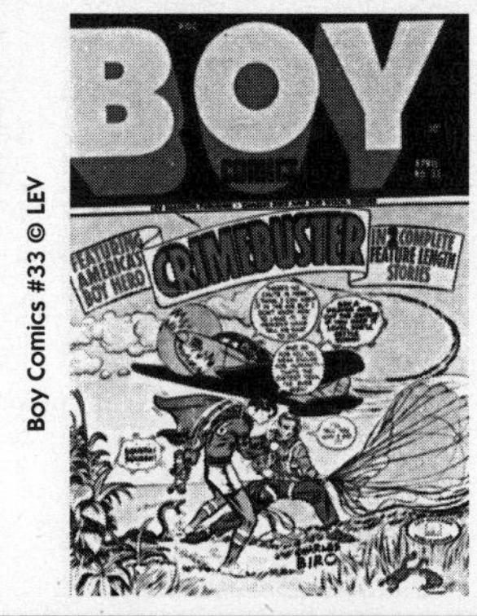

Boy Comics #33 © LEV

Boy Commandos #35, © DC

GD25 FN65 NM94

Gold Key
1-Photo-c 8.35 25.00 50.00
2 5.85 17.50 35.00

BORIS THE BEAR INSTANT COLOR CLASSICS (Dark Horse)(Value: cover or less)

BORN AGAIN (Spire Christian)(Value: cover or less)

BOUNCER, THE (Formerly Green Mask #9)
1944 - No. 14, Jan, 1945
Fox Features Syndicate
nn(1944, #10?) 17.00 52.00 120.00
11(#1)(9/44)-Origin; Rocket Kelly, One Round Hogan app. 14.00 43.00 100.00
12-14: 14-Reprints no # issue 11.00 32.00 75.00

BOUNTY GUNS (See 4-Color No. 739)

BOY AND HIS 'BOT, A (Now)(Value: cover or less)

BOY AND THE PIRATES, THE (See 4-Color No. 1117)

BOY COMICS (Captain Battle No. 1 & 2; Boy Illustories No. 43-108)
(Stories by Charles Biro)
No. 3, April, 1942 - No. 119, March, 1956
Lev Gleason Publications (Comic House)
3(No.1)-Origin Crimebuster, Bombshell & Young Robin Hood; Yankee Longago, Case 1001-1008, Swoop Storm, & Boy Movies begin; 1st app. Iron Jaw 200.00 600.00 1400.00
4-Hitler, Tojo, Mussolini-c 75.00 225.00 525.00
5 57.00 171.00 400.00
6-Origin Iron Jaw; origin & death of Iron Jaw's son; Little Dynamite begins, ends #39 135.00 407.00 950.00
7,9: 7-Flag & Hitler, Tojo, Mussolini-c 50.00 150.00 350.00
8-Death of Iron Jaw 57.00 171.00 400.00
10-Return of Iron Jaw; classic Biro-c 79.00 235.00 550.00
11-14: 11-Classic Iron Jaw-c. 14-Iron Jaw-c 36.00 107.00 250.00
15-Death of Iron Jaw 43.00 129.00 300.00
16,18-20 24.00 73.00 170.00
17-Flag-c 26.00 78.00 180.00
21-26 16.50 50.00 115.00
27-29,31,32-(All 68 pgs.). 28-Yankee Longago ends. 32-Swoop Storm & Young Robin Hood end 16.50 50.00 115.00
30-(68 pgs.)-Origin Crimebuster retold 24.00 72.00 165.00
33-40: 34-Crimebuster story(2); suicide-c/story 11.50 34.00 80.00
41-50 10.00 30.00 70.00
51-59: 57-Dilly Duncan begins, ends #71 10.00 30.00 60.00
60-Iron Jaw returns 10.00 30.00 70.00
61-Origin Crimebuster & Iron Jaw retold 11.50 34.00 80.00
62-Death of Iron Jaw explained 11.00 32.00 75.00
63-73: 73-Frazetta 1-pg. ad 9.15 27.50 55.00
74-88: 80-1st app. Rocky X of the Rocketeers; becomes "Rocky X" #101; Iron Jaw, Sniffer & the Deadly Dozen in 80-118 7.50 22.50 45.00
89-92-The Claw serial app. in all 8.35 25.00 50.00
93-Claw cameo; Rocky X by Sid Check 7.50 22.50 45.00
94-97,99 6.70 20.00 40.00
98-Rocky X by Sid Check 7.50 22.50 45.00
100 7.50 22.50 45.00
101-107,109,111,119: 111-Crimebuster becomes Chuck Chandler. 119-Last Crimebuster 5.85 17.50 35.00
108,110,112-118-Kubert-a 7.50 22.50 45.00
(See Giant Boy Book of Comics)
NOTE: *Boy Movies in 3-5,40,41. Iron Jaw app.-3, 4, 6, 8, 10, 11, 13-15; returns-60-62, 68, 69, 72-79, 81-118.* ***Biro*** *c-all.* ***Briefer*** *a-5, 13, 14, 16-20 among others.* ***Fuje*** *a-55, 18 pgs.* ***Palais*** *a-14, 16, 17, 19, 20 among others.*

BOY COMMANDOS (See Detective #64 & World's Finest Comics #8)
Winter, 1942-43 - No. 36, Nov-Dec, 1949
National Periodical Publications
1-Origin Liberty Belle; The Sandman & The Newsboy Legion x-over in Boy Commandos; S&K-a, 48 pgs.; S&K cameo? 270.00 800.00 2600.00
2-Last Liberty Belle; Hitler-c; S&K-a, 46 pgs. 110.00 332.00 775.00
3-S&K-a, 45 pgs. 79.00 235.00 550.00
4-6: 6-S&K-a 53.00 160.00 370.00
7-10 36.00 107.00 250.00
11-Infinity-c 22.00 67.00 155.00
12-16,18-19 17.00 52.00 120.00
17,20-Sci/fi-c/stories 20.00 60.00 140.00
21,22,24,25: 22-Judy Canova x-over 14.00 43.00 100.00
23-S&K-c/a(all) 16.50 50.00 115.00
26-Flying Saucer story (3-4/48)-4th of this theme 16.00 48.00 110.00
27,28,30: 30-Cleveland Indians story 14.00 43.00 100.00
29-S&K story (1) 16.50 50.00 115.00
31-35: 32-Dale Evans app. on-c & in story. 34-Intro. Wolf, their mascot 14.00 43.00 100.00
36-Intro The Atomobile c/sci-fi story 16.50 50.00 115.00
NOTE: *Most issues signed by* ***Simon & Kirby*** *are not by them.* ***S&K*** *c-1-9, 13, 14, 17, 21, 23, 30-32.* ***Feller*** *c-30.*

BOY COMMANDOS
Sept-Oct, 1973 - No. 2, Nov-Dec, 1973 (G.A. S&K reprints)
National Periodical Publications
1,2: 1-Reprints story from Boy Commandos #1 plus-c & Detective #66 by S&K. 2-Infantino/Orlando-c .40 1.00 2.00

BOY COWBOY (Also see Amazing Adventures & Science Comics)
1950 (8 pgs. in color)
Ziff-Davis Publ. Co.
nn-Sent to subscribers of Ziff-Davis mags. & ordered through mail for 10¢; used to test market for Kid Cowboy
Estimated value 140.00

BOY DETECTIVE
May-June, 1951 - No. 4, May, 1952
Avon Periodicals
1 13.00 40.00 90.00
2,3: 3-Kinstler-c 8.35 25.00 50.00
4-Kinstler-c 11.50 34.00 80.00

BOY EXPLORERS COMICS (Terry and The Pirates No. 3 on)
May-June, 1946 - No. 2, Sept-Oct, 1946
Family Comics (Harvey Publications)
1-Intro The Explorers, Duke of Broadway, Calamity Jane & Danny Dixon... Cadet; S&K-c/a, 24 pgs. 52.00 156.00 365.00
2-(Scarce)-Small size (5-1/2x8-1/2"; B&W; 32 pgs.) Distributed to mail subscribers only; S&K-a Estimated value $250.00-$400.00
(Also see All New No. 15, Flash Gordon No. 5, and Stuntman No. 3)

BOY ILLUSTORIES (See Boy Comics)

BOY LOVES GIRL (Boy Meets Girl No. 1-24)
No. 25, July, 1952 - No. 57, June, 1956
Lev Gleason Publications
25(#1) 4.35 13.00 26.00
26,27,29-42: 30-33-Serial, 'Loves of My Life.' 39-Lingerie panels 2.80 7.00 14.00
28-Drug propaganda story 3.60 9.00 18.00
43-Toth-a 4.35 13.00 26.00
44-50: 50-Last pre-code (2/55) 2.00 5.00 10.00
51-57: 57-Ann Brewster-a 1.60 4.00 8.00

BOY MEETS GIRL (Boy Loves Girl No. 25 on)
Feb, 1950 - No. 24, June, 1952 (No. 1-17: 52 pgs.)
Lev Gleason Publications
1-Guardineer-a 5.00 15.00 30.00
2 3.00 7.50 15.00
3-10 2.40 6.00 12.00
11-24 2.00 5.00 10.00
NOTE: ***Briefer*** *a-24.* ***Fuje*** *c-3,7. Painted-c 1-17. Photo-c 19-21, 23.*

BOYS' AND GIRLS' MARCH OF COMICS (See March of Comics)

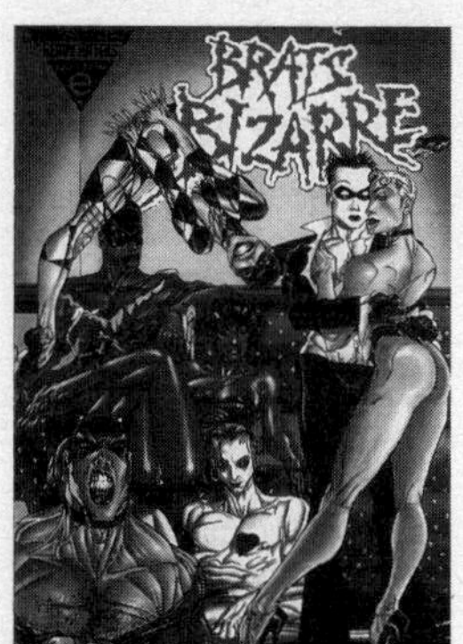

Brats Bizzare #1 © MEG

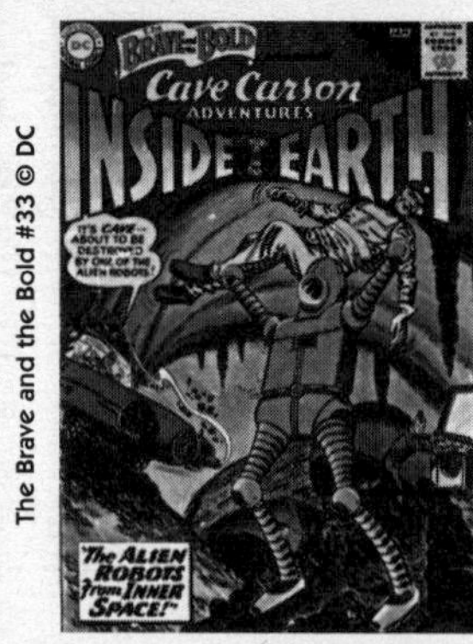

The Brave and the Bold #33 © DC

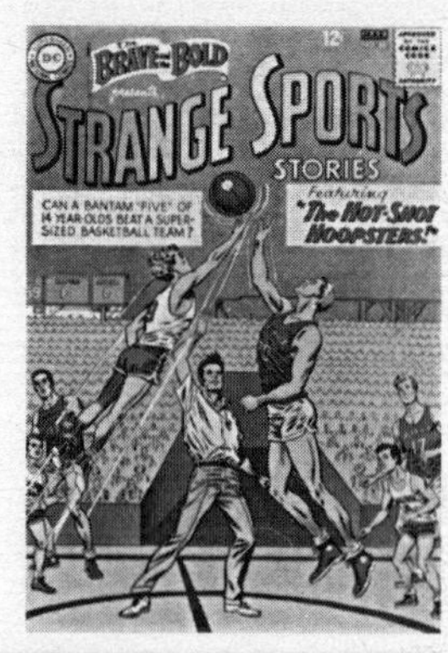

The Brave and the Bold #46 © DC

GD25 FN65 NM94

BOYS' RANCH (Also see Western Tales & Witches' Western Tales)
Oct, 1950 - No. 6, Aug, 1951 (No.1-3, 52 pgs.; No. 4-6, 36 pgs.)
Harvey Publications

	GD25	FN65	NM94
1-S&K-c/a(3)	48.00	144.00	335.00
2-S&K-c/a(3)	37.00	110.00	260.00
3-S&K-c/a(2); Meskin-a	34.00	100.00	235.00
4-S&K-c/a, 5 pgs.	29.00	86.00	200.00
5,6-S&K-c, splashes & centerspread only; Meskin-a	16.00	48.00	110.00
Shoe Store Giveaway #5,6 (Identical to regular issues except S&K centerfold replaced with ad)	13.00	40.00	90.00

BOZO (Larry Harmon's Bozo, the World's Most Famous Clown)
1992 ($6.95, color, 68 pgs.)
Innovation Publishing

1-Reprints Four Color #285(#1)	1.20	3.00	7.00

BOZO THE CLOWN (TV) (Bozo No. 7 on)
July, 1950 - No. 4, Oct-Dec, 1963
Dell Publishing Co.

4-Color 285(#1)	16.50	50.00	115.00
2(7-9/51)-7(10-12/52)	11.00	32.00	75.00
4-Color 464,508,551,594(10/54)	11.00	32.00	75.00
1(nn, 5-7/62) - 4(1963)	7.50	22.50	45.00
Giveaway-1961, 16 pgs., 3-1/2x7-1/4", Apsco Products	4.70	14.00	28.00

BOZZ CHRONICLES, THE
Dec, 1985 - No. 6, 1986 (Adults only)(Mini-series)
Epic Comics (Marvel)

1-6			1.50

BRADY BUNCH, THE (TV)(See Kite Fun Book and Binky #78)
Feb, 1970 - No. 2, May, 1970
Dell Publishing Co.

1,2	6.35	19.00	38.00

BRAIN, THE
Sept, 1956 - No. 7, 1958
Sussex Publ. Co./Magazine Enterprises

1-Dan DeCarlo-a in all including reprints	5.00	15.00	30.00
2,3	3.20	8.00	16.00
4-7	2.00	5.00	10.00
I.W. Reprints #1-4,8-10('63),14: 2-Reprints Sussex #2 with new cover added	1.40	3.50	7.00
Super Reprint #17,18(nd)	1.40	3.50	7.00

BRAIN BOY
April-June, 1962 - No. 6, Sept-Nov, 1963 (Painted c-5,6)
Dell Publishing Co.

4-Color 1330(#1)-Gil Kane-a; origin	13.00	40.00	90.00
2(7-9/62),3-6: 4-Origin retold	7.00	21.00	50.00

BRAM STOKER'S DRACULA (Also see Dracula: Vlad the Impaler)
10/92 - No. 4, 1/93 ($2.95, mini-series, polybagged, adapts movie)
Topps Comics

1-4 trading cards & poster; photo scenes of movie		1.20	3.00
1-2nd printing		1.20	3.00
1-Crimson foil edition (limited to 500)	3.50	11.00	25.00
2-Bound-in poster & cards; Mignola-c/a in all		1.20	3.00
3,4-4 trading cards: 3-Contains coupon to win 1 of 500 crimson foil-c edition of #1. 4-Contains coupon to win 1 of 500 uncut sheets of all 16 trading cards		1.30	3.25
3,4-With coupon missing		1.20	3.00

BRAND ECHH (See Not Brand Echh)

BRAND OF EMPIRE (See 4-Color No. 771)

BRATS BIZZARE
1994 - No. 4, 1994 ($2.50, mini-series)
Epic Comics (Marvel)

	GD25	FN65	NM94
1-4: All w/bound-in trading cards		1.00	2.50

BRAVADOS, THE (See Wild Western Action)
August, 1971 (52 pgs.) (One-Shot)
Skywald Publ. Corp.

1-Red Mask, The Durango Kid, Billy Nevada-r	.30	.75	1.50

BRAVE AND THE BOLD, THE (See Best Of... & Super DC Giant)
Aug-Sept, 1955 - No. 200, July, 1983
National Periodical Publications/DC Comics

1-Viking Prince by Kubert, Silent Knight, Golden Gladiator begin; part Kubert-c	160.00	480.00	1600.00
2	80.00	240.00	800.00
3,4	47.50	142.00	475.00
5-Robin Hood begins (4-5/56, 1st DC app.), ends #15; see Robin Hood Tales #7	49.00	147.00	490.00
6-10: 6-Robin Hood by Kubert; last Golden Gladiator app.; Silent Knight; no Viking Prince	39.00	116.00	310.00
11-22,24: 12,14-Robin Hood-c. 18,21-23-Grey tone-c. 22-Last Silent Knight. 24-Last Viking Prince by Kubert (2nd solo book)	28.00	84.00	225.00
23-Viking Prince origin by Kubert; 1st B&B single theme issue & 1st Viking Prince solo book	38.00	113.00	300.00
25-1st app. Suicide Squad (8-9/59)	36.00	107.00	250.00
26,27-Suicide Squad	31.00	94.00	220.00

	GD25	FN65	VF82	NM94
28-(2-3/60)-Justice League intro./1st app.; origin/1st app. Snapper Carr	275.00	825.00	2062.00	3300.00
29-Justice League (4-5/60)-2nd app.	190.00	570.00	1235.00	1900.00
30-Justice League (6-7/60)-3rd app.	155.00	465.00	1007.00	1550.00

	GD25	FN65	NM94
31-1st app. Cave Carson (8-9/60); scarce in high grade; 1st try-out series	30.00	90.00	210.00
32,33-Cave Carson	21.00	64.00	150.00

	GD25	FN65	VF82	NM94
34-Origin/1st app. Silver-Age Hawkman, Hawkgirl & Byth by Kubert (2-3/61); 1st S.A. Hawkman tryout series; all predate Hawkman #1	121.00	363.00	906.00	1450.00

	GD25	FN65	NM94
35-Hawkman by Kubert (4-5/61)-2nd app.	40.00	110.00	450.00
36-Hawkman by Kubert; origin & 1st app. Shadow Thief (6-7/61)-3rd app.	38.00	113.00	375.00
37-Suicide Squad (2nd tryout series)	22.00	67.00	200.00
38,39-Suicide Squad. 38-Last 10¢ issue	25.00	75.00	175.00
40,41-Cave Carson Inside Earth (2nd try-out series). 40-Kubert-a. 41-Meskin-a	16.00	47.00	110.00
42-Hawkman by Kubert (2nd tryout series)	25.00	75.00	250.00
43-Hawkman by Kubert; more detailed origin	30.00	90.00	300.00
44-Hawkman by Kubert; grey-tone-c	20.00	60.00	200.00
45-49-Strange Sports Stories by Infantino	6.40	19.00	45.00
50-The Green Arrow & Manhunter From Mars (10-11/63); 1st Manhunter x-over outside of Detective (pre-dates House of Mystery #143); team-ups begin	16.00	49.00	115.00
51-Aquaman & Hawkman (12-1/63-64); pre-dates Hawkman #1	17.50	52.00	175.00
52-(2-3/64)-3 Battle Stars; Sgt. Rock, Haunted Tank, Johnny Cloud, & Mlle. Marie team-up for 1st time by Kubert (c/a)	12.00	36.00	85.00
53-Atom & The Flash by Toth	6.40	19.00	45.00
54-Kid Flash, Robin & Aqualad; 1st app./origin Teen Titans (6-7/64)	29.00	86.00	200.00
55-Metal Men & The Atom	4.00	12.00	28.00
56-The Flash & Manhunter From Mars	4.00	12.00	28.00
57-Origin & 1st app. Metamorpho (12-1/64-65)	15.00	45.00	105.00
58-2nd app. Metamorpho by Fradon	7.00	21.00	48.00
59-Batman & Green Lantern; 1st Batman team-up in Brave and the Bold	10.00	31.00	72.00

60-Teen Titans (2nd app.)-1st app. new Wonder Girl (Donna Troy), who joins

The Brave and the Bold #154, © DC

The Brave and the Bold #198, © DC

Breed #6 © Jim Starlin

GD25 FN65 NM94

Titans (6-7/65) 9.70 29.00 68.00
61,62-Origin Starman & Black Canary by Anderson. 62-1st S.A. app. Wildcat (10-11/65); 1st S.A. app. of G.A. Huntress 11.00 32.00 75.00
63-Supergirl & Wonder Woman 2.40 7.30 17.00
64-Batman Versus Eclipso (see H.O.S. #61) 7.00 21.00 48.00
65-Flash & Doom Patrol (4-5/66) 1.70 5.00 12.00
66-Metamorpho & Metal Men (6-7/66) 1.70 5.00 12.00
67-Batman & The Flash by Infantino; Batman team-ups begin, end #200 (8-9/66) 4.60 14.00 32.00
68-Batman/Metamorpho/Joker/Riddler/Penguin-c/story; Batman as Bat-Hulk (Hulk parody) 7.40 221.00 52.00
69-Batman & Green Lantern 3.00 9.00 21.00
70-Batman & Hawkman; Craig-a(p) 3.00 9.00 21.00
71-Batman & Green Arrow 3.00 9.00 21.00
72-Spectre & Flash (6-7/67); 4th app. The Spectre; predates Spectre #1 3.10 9.40 22.00
73-Aquaman & The Atom 2.60 7.70 18.00
74-Batman & Metal Men 2.60 7.70 18.00
75-Batman & The Spectre (12-1/67-68); 6th app. Spectre; came out between Spectre #1 & #2 2.90 8.60 20.00
76-Batman & Plastic Man (2-3/68); came out between Plastic Man #8 & #9 2.60 7.70 18.00
77-Batman & The Atom 2.60 7.70 18.00
78-Batman, Wonder Woman & Batgirl 2.60 7.70 18.00
79-Batman & Deadman by Neal Adams (8-9/68); early Deadman app. 4.60 14.00 32.00
80-Batman & Creeper (10-11/68); N. Adams-a; early app. The Creeper; came out between Creeper #3 & #4 4.30 13.00 30.00
81-Batman & Flash; N. Adams-a 4.30 13.00 30.00
82-Batman & Aquaman; N. Adams-a; origin Ocean Master retold (2-3/69) 4.30 13.00 30.00
83-Batman & Teen Titans; N. Adams-a (4-5/69); last 12¢ issue 5.40 16.00 38.00
84-Batman (G.A., 1st S.A. app.) & Sgt. Rock; N. Adams-a 4.00 12.00 28.00
85-Batman & Green Arrow; 1st new costume for Green Arrow by Neal Adams (8-9/69) 4.00 12.00 28.00
86-Batman & Deadman (10-11/69); N. Adams-a; story concludes from Strange Adventures #216 (1-2/69) 4.00 12.00 28.00
87-Batman & Wonder Woman 2.70 8.10 19.00
88-Batman & Wildcat 2.70 8.10 19.00
89-Batman & Phantom Stranger (4-5/70); early Phantom Stranger app. (came out between Phantom Stranger #6 & 7 2.70 8.10 19.00
90-Batman & Adam Strange 2.70 8.10 19.00
91-Batman & Black Canary (8-9/70) 2.70 8.10 19.00
92-Batman; intro the Bat Squad 2.70 8.10 19.00
93-Batman-House of Mystery; N. Adams-a 3.70 11.00 26.00
94-Batman-Teen Titans 1.60 4.70 11.00
95-Batman & Plastic Man 1.70 4.20 10.00
96-Batman & Sgt. Rock 1.70 4.20 10.00
97-Batman & Wildcat; 52 pg. issues begin, end #102; reprints origin & 1st app. Deadman from Strange Advs. #205 1.70 4.20 10.00
98-Batman & Phantom Stranger 1.70 4.20 10.00
99-Batman & Flash 1.70 4.20 10.00
100-(2-3/72, 25¢, 52 pgs.)-Batman-Gr. Lantern-Gr. Arrow-Black Canary-Robin; Deadman-r by Adams/Str. Advs. #210 3.60 10.70 25.00
101-Batman & Metamorpho; Kubert Viking Prince .90 2.30 5.50
102-Batman-Teen Titans; N. Adams-a(p) 1.40 3.50 8.50
103-110: Batman team-ups: 103-Metal Men. 104-Deadman. 105-Wonder Woman. 106-Green Arrow. 107-Black Canary. 108-Sgt. Rock. 109-Demon. 110-Wildcat .90 2.30 5.50
111-Batman/Joker-c/story 1.60 4.70 11.00
112-117: All 100 pgs.; Batman team-ups: 112-Mr. Miracle. 113-Metal Men; reprints origin/1st Hawkman from Brave and the Bold #34; r/origin Multi-Man/ Challengers #14. 114-Aquaman. 115-Atom; r/origin Viking Prince from #23; r/Dr. Fate/Hourman/Solomon Grundy/Green Lantern from Showcase #55.

GD25 FN65 NM94

116-Spectre. 117-Sgt. Rock; last 100 pg. issue 1.10 2.70 6.50
118-Batman/Wildcat/Joker-c/story 1.60 4.70 11.00
119-128,132-140: Batman team-ups: 119-Man-Bat. 120-Kamandi(68 pgs.). 121-Metal Men. 122-Swamp Thing. 123-Plastic Man/Metamorpho. 124-Sgt. Rock. 125-Flash. 126-Aquaman. 127-Wildcat. 128-Mr. Miracle. 132-Kung-Fu Fighter. 133-Deadman. 134-Green Lantern. 135-Metal Men. 136-Metal Men/Green Arrow. 137-Demon. 138-Mr. Miracle. 139-Hawkman. 140-Wonder Woman 1.40 3.50
129,130-Batman/Green Arrow/Atom parts 1 & 2; Joker & Two Face-c/stories 1.80 4.60 11.00
131-Batman & Wonder Woman vs. Catwoman-c/sty 1.10 2.70 6.50
141-Batman/Black Canary vs. Joker-c/story 1.60 4.70 11.00
142-190,192-199: Batman team-ups: 142-Aquaman. 143-Creeper; origin Human Target (44 pgs.). 144-Green Arrow; origin Human Target part 2 (44 pgs.). 145-Phantom Stranger. 146-G.A. Batman/Unknown Soldier. 147-Supergirl. 148-Plastic Man; X-Mas-c. 149-Teen Titans. 150-Anniversary issue; Superman. 151-Flash. 152-Atom. 153-Red Tornado. 154-Metamorpho. 155-Green Lantern. 156-Dr. Fate. 157-Batman vs. Kamandi (ties into Kamandi #59). 158-Wonder Woman. 159-Ra's Al Ghul. 160-Supergirl. 161-Adam Strange. 162-G.A. Batman/Sgt. Rock. 163-Black Lightning. 164-Hawkman. 165-Man-Bat. 166-Black Canary; Nemesis (intro) back-up story begins, ends #192; Penguin-c/story. 167-G.A. Batman/Blackhawk; origin Nemesis. 168-Green Arrow. 169-Zatanna. 170-Nemesis. 171-Scalphunter. 172-Firestorm. 173-Guardians of the Universe. 174-Green Lantern. 175-Lois Lane. 176-Swamp Thing. 177-Elongated Man. 178-Creeper. 179-Legion. 180-Spectre. 181-Hawk & Dove. 182-G.A. Robin; G.A. Starman app.; 1st modern app. G.A. Batwoman. 183-Riddler. 184-Huntress. 185-Green Arrow. 186-Hawkman. 187-Metal Men. ,188,189-Rose & the Thorn. 190-Adam Strange. 192-Superboy vs. Mr. I.Q. 193-Nemesis. 194-Flash. 195-I... Vampire. 196-Ragman; origin Ragman retold. 197-Catwoman; Earth II Batman & Catwoman marry; 2nd modern app. of G.A. Batwoman. 198-Karate Kid. 199-Batman vs. The Spectre 1.30 3.25
191-Batman/Joker-c/story; Nemesis app. 1.30 3.00 7.50
200-Double-sized (64 pgs.); printed on Mando paper; Earth One & Earth Two Batman app. in separate stories; intro/1st app. Batman & The Outsiders 1.40 3.50 8.50

NOTE: ***Neal Adams*** *a-79-86, 93, 100r, 102; c-75, 76, 79-86, 88-90, 93, 95, 99, 100r.* ***M. Anderson*** *a-115r; c-72i, 96i.* ***Andru/Esposito*** *c-25-27.* ***Aparo*** *a-98, 100-102, 104-125, 126i, 127-136, 138-145, 147, 148i, 149-152, 154, 155, 157-162, 168-170, 173-178, 180-182, 184, 186i-189i, 191i-193i, 195, 196, 200; c-105-109, 111-136, 137i, 138-175, 177, 180-184, 186-200.* ***Austin*** *a-166i.* ***Bernard Baily*** *c-32, 33.* ***Buckler*** *a-185, 186p; c-137, 178p, 185p, 186p.* ***Giordano*** *a-143, 144.* ***Infantino*** *a-67p, 72p, 97r, 98r, 172p, 183p, 190p, 194p; c-45-49, 67p, 69p, 70p, 72p, 96p, 98r.* ***Kaluta*** *c-176.* ***Kane*** *a-115r.* ***Kubert*** *&/or* ***Heath*** *a-1-24; reprints-101, 113, 115, 117.* ***Kubert*** *c-22-24, 34-36, 40, 42-44, 52.* ***Mooney*** *a-114r.* ***Newton*** *a-153p, 156p, 165p.* ***Irv Novick*** *c-1(part), 2-21.* ***Roussos*** *a-114r.* ***Staton*** *148p. 52 pgs.-97, 100; 68 pgs.-120; 100 pgs.-112-117.*

BRAVE AND THE BOLD, THE
Dec, 1991 - No. 6, June, 1992 ($1.75, mini-series)
DC Comics

1-6: Green Arrow, The Butcher, The Question in all; Grell scripts in all; Grell c-3,4,6 .70 1.75

BRAVE AND THE BOLD SPECIAL, THE (See DC Special Series No. 8)

BRAVE EAGLE (See 4-Color No. 705, 770, 816, 879, 929)

BRAVE ONE, THE (See 4-Color No. 773)

BREAK-THRU
Dec, 1993 - No. 2, Jan, 1994 ($2.50, color, 44 pgs.)
Malibu Comics (Ultraverse)

1,2-Perez-c/a(p); has x-overs in Ultraverse titles 1.00 2.50

BREATHTAKER
1990 - No. 4, 1990 ($4.95, prestige format, mature readers, 52 pgs.)
DC Comics

Book 1-4: By Hempel & Wheatley painted-c/a 1.00 2.00 5.00

'BREED
Jan, 1994 - No. 6, 1994 ($2.50, color, limited series)
Malibu Comics (Bravura)

Brigade #3 © Rob Liefeld

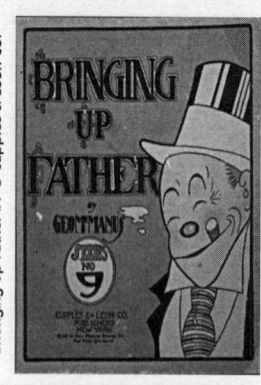

Bribnging Up Father #9 © Cupples & Leon Co.

Binke of Eternity #1 © Brinke Stevens

GD25 FN65 NM94

1-(48 pgs.)-Origin & 1st app. of 'Breed by Starlin; contains Bavura stamps; spot varnish-c 1.40 3.50
2-6-Jim Starlin-c/a/scripts; Bravura stamps in all. 6-Death of Rachel 1.00 2.50

BREEZE LAWSON, SKY SHERIFF (See Sky Sheriff)

BRENDA LEE STORY, THE
September, 1962
Dell Publishing Co.

01-078-209 10.00 30.00 70.00

BRENDA STARR (Also see All Great)
No. 13, 9/47; No. 14, 3/48; V2#3, 6/48 - V2#12, 12/49
Four Star Comics Corp./Superior Comics Ltd.

V1#13-By Dale Messick 54.00 160.00 375.00
14-Kamen bondage-c 54.00 160.00 375.00
V2#3-Baker-a? 44.00 133.00 310.00
4-Used in **SOTI**, pg. 21; Kamen bondage-c 46.00 139.00 325.00
5-10 39.00 118.00 275.00
11,12 (Scarce) 43.00 129.00 300.00

NOTE: *Newspaper reprints plus original material through #6. All original #7 on.*

BRENDA STARR (...Reporter)(Young Lovers No. 16 on?)
No. 13, June, 1955 - No. 15, Oct, 1955
Charlton Comics

13-15-Newspaper-r 26.00 78.00 180.00

BRENDA STARR REPORTER
October, 1963
Dell Publishing Co.

1 19.00 58.00 135.00

BRER RABBIT (See 4-Color No. 129, 208, 693, Kite Fun Book, Walt Disney Showcase #28 and Wheaties)

BRER RABBIT IN "ICE CREAM FOR THE PARTY"
1955 (16 pgs., 5x7-1/4", soft-c) (Walt Disney) (Premium)
American Dairy Association

nn-(Rare) 20.00 60.00 225.00

BRIAN BOLLAND'S BLACK BOOK (Eclipse)(Value: cover or less)

BRICK BRADFORD (Also see Ace Comics & King Comics)
No. 5, July, 1948 - No. 8, July, 1949 (Ritt & Grey reprints)
King Features Syndicate/Standard

5 11.50 34.00 80.00
6-8: 6-Robot-c (by Schomburg?). 7-Schomburg-c. 8-Says #7 inside, #8 on-c 10.00 30.00 65.00

BRIDE'S DIARY (Formerly Black Cobra No. 3)
No. 4, May, 1955 - No. 10, Aug, 1956
Ajax/Farrell Publ.

4 (#1) 4.70 14.00 28.00
5-8 3.20 8.00 16.00
9,10-Disbrow-a 4.70 14.00 28.00

BRIDES IN LOVE (Hollywood Romances & Summer Love No. 46 on)
Aug, 1956 - No. 45, Feb, 1965
Charlton Comics

1 4.70 14.00 28.00
2 3.00 7.50 15.00
3-10 2.00 5.00 10.00
11-20 1.40 3.50 7.00
21-45 .70 1.75 3.50

BRIDES ROMANCES
Nov, 1953 - No. 23, Dec, 1956
Quality Comics Group

1 9.25 27.50 55.00
2 4.35 13.00 26.00
3-10: Last precode (3/55) 3.60 9.00 18.00

GD25 FN65 NM94

11-14,16,17,19-22 2.40 6.00 12.00
15-Baker-a(p)?; Colan-a 2.80 7.00 14.00
18-Baker-a 3.60 9.00 18.00
23-Baker-c/a 4.35 13.00 26.00

BRIDE'S SECRETS
Apr-May, 1954 - No. 19, May, 1958
Ajax/Farrell(Excellent Publ.)/Four-Star Comic

1 7.50 22.50 45.00
2 4.00 12.00 24.00
3-6: Last precode (3/55) 3.20 8.00 16.00
7-19: 12-Disbrow-a. 18-Hollingsworth-a 2.80 7.00 14.00

BRIDE-TO-BE ROMANCES (See True...)

BRIGADE
Aug, 1992 - No. 4, 1992 ($1.95, color, mini-series)
V2#1, May, 1993 - Present ($1.95, color, on-going series)
Image Comics

1-Liefeld part plots/scripts in all, Liefeld-c(p); contains 2 Brigade trading cards; 1st app. Genocide 1.20 3.00
1-Gold foil stamped logo edition 2.90 9.00 20.00
2-Contains coupon for Image Comics #0 & 2 trading cards 1.60 4.00
2-With coupon missing .80 2.00
3-Contains 2 bound-in trading cards; 1st Birds of Prey .80 2.00
4-Flip book format featuring Youngblood #5 .80 2.00
V2#1-Gatefold-c; Liefeld co-plots; Blood Brothers part 1; Bloodstrike app.; 1st app. Boone & Hacker .80 2.00
2-9: 2-(6/93, V2#1 on inside)-Foil merricote-c. 3-1st app. Roman; Perez-c(i); Liefeld scripts. 6-1st app. Coral & Worlok. 6-8-Thibert-c(i). 8-Liefeld scripts; Black and White part 5 by Art Thibert. 8,9-Coupons #2 & 6 for Extreme Prejudice #0 bound-in. 9-(4/94) .80 2.00
V2#2-($1.95)-Newsstand edition w/o foil-c .80 2.00
0-(9/93)-Liefeld scripts; 1st app. Warcry; Youngblood & Wildcats app.; Thibert-c(i) 1.20 3.00
25-(5/94) .80 2.00
10-(6/94) .80 2.00
11-(8/94, $2.50)-WildC.A.T.S app. 1.00 2.50

BRIGAND, THE (See Fawcett Movie Comics No. 18)

BRINGING UP FATHER (See 4-Color #37 & Large Feature Comic #9)

BRINGING UP FATHER
1917 (16-1/2x5-1/2"; cardboard cover; 100 pgs.; B&W)
Star Co. (King Features)

nn-(Rare) Daily strip reprints by George McManus (no price on-c) 50.00 150.00 450.00

BRINGING UP FATHER
1919 - 1934 (by George McManus)(No. 22 is 9-1/4x9-1/2")
(10x10"; stiff cardboard covers; B&W; daily strip reprints; 52 pgs.)
Cupples & Leon Co.

1 36.00 108.00 325.00
2-10 18.00 54.00 160.00
11-26 (Scarcer) 30.00 90.00 225.00
The Big Book 1(1926)-Thick book (hardcover); 10-1/4x10-1/4", 142 pgs. 45.00 135.00 400.00
The Big Book 2(1929) 40.00 120.00 360.00

NOTE: *The Big Books contain 3 regular issues rebound and probably w/dust jackets.*

BRINGING UP FATHER, THE TROUBLE OF
1921 (9x15") (Sunday reprints in color)
Embee Publ. Co.

nn-(Rare) 50.00 150.00 450.00

BRINKE OF ETERNITY
Apr, 1994 ($2.75, color, one-shot)
Chaos! Comics

Bruce Lee #2 © Bruce Lee Estate

Brute & Babe #2 © Bart Sears

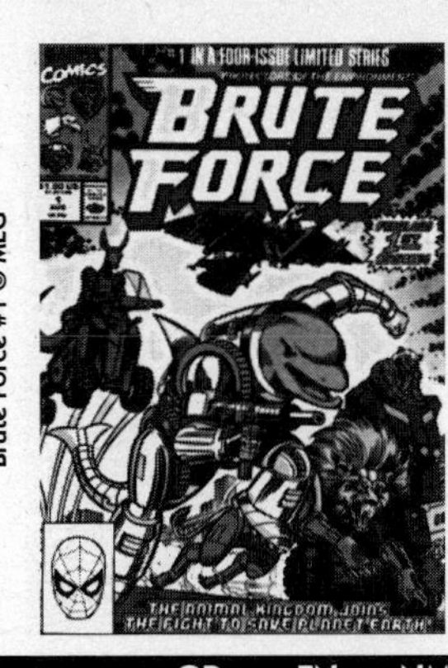

Brute Force #1 © MEG

GD25 FN65 NM94

1 1.10 2.75

BROADWAY HOLLYWOOD BLACKOUTS
Mar-Apr, 1954 - No. 3, July-Aug, 1954
Stanhall

1 9.15 27.50 55.00
2,3 5.85 17.50 35.00

BROADWAY ROMANCES
January, 1950 - No. 5, Sept, 1950
Quality Comics Group

1-Ward-c/a (9 pgs.); Gustavson-a 19.00 58.00 135.00
2-Ward-a (9 pgs.); photo-c 12.00 36.00 85.00
3-5: 4,5-Photo-c 7.00 21.00 42.00

BROKEN ARROW (See 4-Color No. 855,947)

BROKEN CROSS, THE (See The Crusaders)

BRONCHO BILL (See Comics On Parade, Sparkler & Tip Top Comics)
1939 - 1940; No. 5, 1?/48 - No. 16, 8?/50
United Features Syndicate/Standard(Visual Editions) No. 5-on

Single Series 2 ('39) 38.00 114.00 265.00
Single Series 19 ('40)(#2 on cvr) 31.00 94.00 220.00
5 8.15 27.50 55.00
6(4/48)-10(4/49) 5.00 15.00 30.00
11(6/49)-16 4.00 11.00 22.00
NOTE: ***Schomburg*** *c-6, 7, 9-13, 16.*

BROOKS ROBINSON (See Baseball's Greatest Heroes #2)

BROTHER POWER, THE GEEK (See Saga of Swamp Thing Annual)
Sept-Oct, 1968 - No. 2, Nov-Dec, 1968 (Also see Vertigo Visions)
National Periodical Publications

1-Origin; Simon-c(i?) 3.00 9.00 20.00
2 2.00 6.00 15.00

BROTHERS, HANG IN THERE, THE (Spire Christian)(Value: cover or less)

BROTHERS OF THE SPEAR (Also see Tarzan)
June, 1972 - No. 17, Feb, 1976; No. 18, May, 1982
Gold Key/Whitman No. 18

1 2.10 6.00 15.00
2-Painted-c begin, end #17 1.30 3.25 8.00
3-10 1.80 4.50
11-17: 12-Line drawn-c. 13-17-Spiegle-a .80 2.00
18-r/#2; Leopard Girl-r 1.00

BROTHERS, THE CULT ESCAPE, THE (Spire Christian)(Value: cover or less)

BROWNIES (See 4-Color No. 192, 244, 293, 337, 365, 398, 436, 482, 522, 605 & New Funnies)

BROWN'S BLUE RIBBON BOOK OF JOKES AND JINGLES (See Buster Brown's...)

BRUCE GENTRY
Jan, 1948 - No. 2, Nov, 1948; No. 3, Jan, 1949 - No. 8, July, 1949
Better/Standard/Four Star Publ./Superior No. 3

1-Ray Bailey strip reprints begin, end #3; E. C. emblem appears as a monogram on stationery in story; negligee panels 29.00 86.00 200.00
2,3 22.00 65.00 150.00
4-8 14.00 43.00 100.00
NOTE: ***Kamenish*** *a-2-7; c-1-8.*

BRUCE LEE
July, 1994 - Present ($2.95, color)
Malibu Comics Entertainment, Inc.

1-(44 pgs.)-Mortal Kombat preview, 1st app. in comics 1.20 3.00
2,3-(36 pgs.) 1.20 3.00

BRU-HEAD: AMERICA'S FAVORITE BLOCKHEAD
Mar, 1994 - No. 4, 1994 ($2.50, B&W, mini-series)
Schism Comics

GD25 FN65 NM94

1 1.00 2.50

BRUISER
Feb, 1994 - Present ($2.45, color)
Anthem Publications

1 1.00 2.45

BRUTE, THE
Feb, 1975 - No. 3, July, 1975
Seaboard Publ. (Atlas)

1-Origin & 1st app; Sekowsky-a(p) 1.50
2,3: 2-Sekowsky-a(p). 3-Weiss-a(p) 1.00

BRUTE & BABE
July, 1994 - Present (Color)
Ominous Press

1-($3.95, 8 tablets plus-c)-"...It Begins..."; tablet format 1.60 4.00
2-($2.50, 36 pgs.)-"Mael's Rage" 1.00 2.50
2-(40 pgs.)-Stiff additional variant-c 1.00 2.50

BRUTE FORCE
Aug, 1990 - No. 4, Nov, 1990 ($1.00, limited series)
Marvel Comics

1-4: Animal super-heroes 1.00

BUBBLEGUM CRISIS: GRAND MAL
Mar, 1994 - No. 4, June, 1994 ($2.50, color, mini-series)
Dark Horse Comics

1-4-Japanese manga 1.00 2.50

BUCCANEER
No date (1963)
I. W. Enterprises

I.W. Reprint #1(r-/Quality #20), #8(r-/#23): Crandall-a in each 3.60 9.00 18.00

BUCCANEERS (Formerly Kid Eternity)
No. 19, Jan, 1950 - No. 27, May, 1951 (No. 24-27: 52 pgs.)
Quality Comics Group

19-Captain Daring, Black Roger, Eric Falcon & Spanish Main begin; Crandall-a 38.00 114.00 265.00
20,23-Crandall-a 25.00 75.00 175.00
21-Crandall-c/a 31.00 94.00 220.00
22-Bondage-c 20.00 60.00 140.00
24-26: 24-Adam Peril, U.S.N. begins. 25-Origin & 1st app. Corsair Queen. 26-last Spanish Main 16.50 50.00 115.00
27-Crandall-c/a 26.00 78.00 180.00
Super Reprint #12 (1964)-Crandall-r/#21 3.60 9.00 18.00

BUCCANEERS, THE (See 4-Color No. 800)

BUCKAROO BANZAI
Dec, 1984 - No. 2, Feb, 1985 (Movie adaptation)
Marvel Comics Group

1,2-r/Marvel Super Special #33 1.00

BUCK DUCK
June, 1953 - No. 4, Dec, 1953
Atlas Comics (ANC)

1-Funny animal stories in all 7.50 22.50 45.00
2-4: 2-Ed Win-a(5) 4.20 12.50 25.00

BUCK JONES (Also see Crackajack Funnies, Famous Feature Stories, Master Comics #7 & Wow Comics #1, 1936)
No. 299, Oct, 1950 - No. 850, Oct, 1957 (All Painted-c)
Dell Publishing Co.

4-Color 299(#1)-Buck Jones & his horse Silver-B begin; painted back-c begins, ends #5 14.00 43.00 100.00
2(4-6/51) 8.35 25.00 50.00
3-8(10-12/52) 6.70 20.00 40.00

Buck Rogers #3 (TSR), © Dille Family Trust

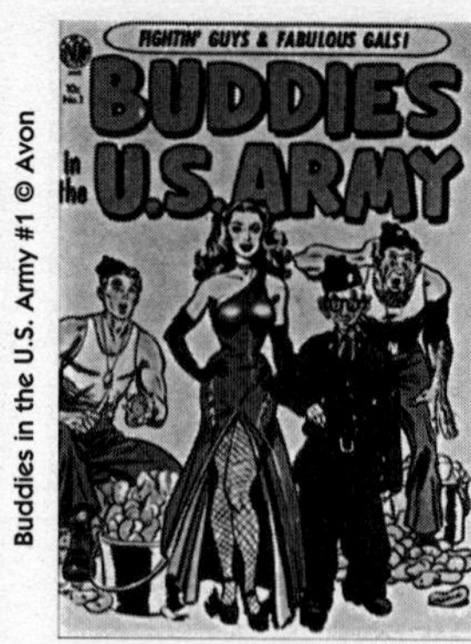

Buddies in the U.S. Army #1 © Avon

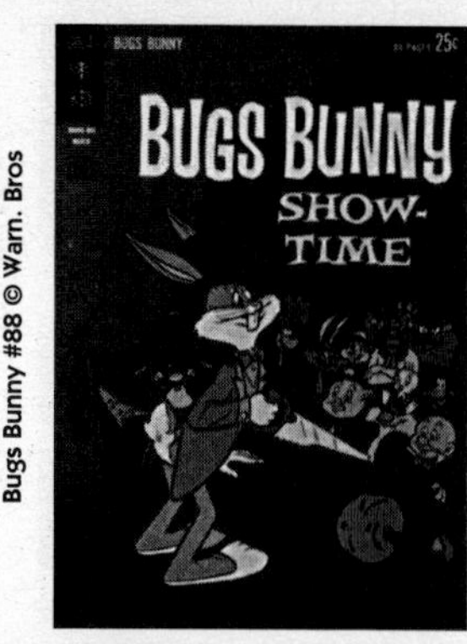

Bugs Bunny #88 © Warn. Bros

	GD25	FN65	NM94
4-Color 460,500,546,589	5.85	17.50	35.00
4-Color 652,733,850	4.00	11.00	22.00

BUCK ROGERS (In the 25th Century)
1933 (36 pgs. in color) (6x8")
Kelloggs Corn Flakes Giveaway

	GD25	FN65	NM94
370A-By Phil Nowlan & Dick Calkins; 1st Buck Rogers radio premium & 1st app. in comics (tells origin)	46.00	140.00	325.00

BUCK ROGERS (Also see Famous Funnies, Pure Oil Comics, Salerno Carnival of Comics, 24 Pages of Comics, & Vicks Comics)
Winter, 1940-41 - No. 6, Sept, 1943
Famous Funnies

	GD25	FN65	NM94
1-Sunday strip reprints by Rick Yager; begins with strip #190; Calkins-c	214.00	643.00	1500.00
2 (7/41)-Calkins-c	107.00	321.00	750.00
3 (12/41), 4 (7/42)	86.00	257.00	600.00
5-Story continues with Famous Funnies No. 80; Buck Rogers, Sky Roads	76.00	229.00	535.00
6-Reprints of 1939 dailies; contains B.R. story "Crater of Doom" (2 pgs.) by Calkins not-r from Famous Funnies	76.00	229.00	535.00

BUCK ROGERS
No. 100, Jan, 1951 - No. 9, May-June, 1951
Toby Press

	GD25	FN65	NM94
100(#7)-All strip-r begin	20.00	60.00	140.00
101(#8), 9-All Anderson-a(1947-49-r/dailies)	17.00	52.00	120.00

BUCK ROGERS (...in the 25th Century No. 5 on) (TV)
Oct, 1964; No. 2, July, 1979 - No. 16, May, 1982 (No #10)
Gold Key/Whitman No. 7 on

	GD25	FN65	NM94
1(10128-410, 12¢)-1st S.A. app. Buck Rogers & 1st new B. R. in comics since 1933 giveaway; painted-c; back-c pin-up	5.80	18.00	35.00
2(7/79)-Movie adaptation; painted-c		1.20	3.00
3-9,11-16: 3,4-Movie adaptation. 5-New stories			1.50
Giant Movie Edition 11296(64pp, Whitman, $1.50), reprints GK #2-4 minus cover; tabloid size		.80	2.00
Giant Movie Edition 02489(Western/Marvel, $1.50), reprints GK #2-4 minus cover		.80	2.00

NOTE: ***Bolle** a-2p,3p, Movie Ed.(p). **McWilliams** a-2i,3i, 5-11, Movie Ed.(i). Painted c-1-9,11-13.*

BUCK ROGERS (Comics Module)
1990 - No. 10, 1991 ($2.95, color, 44 pgs.)
TSR, Inc.

	GD25	FN65	NM94
1-5 (1990): 1-Begin origin in 3 parts. 2-Indicia says #1. 2,3-Black Barney back-up story. 4-All Black Barney issue; B. B.-c. 5-Indicia says #6; Black Barney-c & lead story; Buck Rogers back-up story.		1.20	3.00
6-10 (1991): 10-Flip book (72 pgs.)		1.20	3.00

BUCKSKIN (Movie) (See 4-Color No. 1011,1107)

BUCKY O'HARE (Continuity)(Value: cover or less)

BUDDIES IN THE U.S. ARMY
Nov, 1952 - No. 2, 1953
Avon Periodicals

	GD25	FN65	NM94
1-Lawrence-c	9.15	27.50	55.00
2-Mort Lawrence-c/a	6.35	19.00	38.00

BUDDY TUCKER & HIS FRIENDS (Also see Buster Brown)
1906 (11x17") (In color)
Cupples & Leon Co.

	GD25	FN65	NM94
1905 Sunday strip reprints by R. F. Outcault	46.00	139.00	325.00

BUFFALO BEE (See 4-Color No. 957, 1002, 1061)

BUFFALO BILL (Also see Frontier Fighters, Super Western Comics & Western Action Thrillers)
No. 2, Oct, 1950 - No. 9, Dec, 1951
Youthful Magazines

	GD25	FN65	NM94
2-Annie Oakley story	8.35	25.00	50.00
3-9: 2-4-Walter Johnson-c/a. 9-Wildey-a	5.00	15.00	30.00

BUFFALO BILL CODY (See Cody of the Pony Express)

BUFFALO BILL, JR. (TV) (See Western Roundup under Dell Giants)
Jan, 1956 - No. 13, Aug-Oct, 1959; 1965 (All photo-c)
Dell Publishing Co./Gold Key

	GD25	FN65	NM94
4-Color 673 (#1)	7.50	22.50	45.00
4-Color 742,766,798,828,856(11/57)	5.00	15.00	30.00
7(2-4/58)-13	4.00	11.00	22.00
1(6/65, Gold Key)-Photo-c(r/F.C. #798); photo-b/c	3.20	8.00	16.00

BUFFALO BILL PICTURE STORIES
June-July, 1949 - No. 2, Aug-Sept, 1949
Street & Smith Publications

	GD25	FN65	NM94
1,2-Wildey, Powell-a in each	9.15	27.50	55.00

BUFFALO BILL'S PICTURE STORIES
1909 (Soft cardboard cover)
Street & Smith Publications

	GD25	FN65	NM94
nn	18.00	54.00	180.00

BUGALOOS (TV)
Sept, 1971 - No. 4, Feb, 1972
Charlton Comics

	GD25	FN65	NM94
1-4	1.20	3.00	6.00

NOTE: *No. 3(1/72) went on sale late in 1972 (after No. 4) with the 1/73 issues.*

BUGHOUSE (Satire)
Mar-Apr, 1954 - No. 4, Sept-Oct, 1954
Ajax/Farrell (Excellent Publ.)

	GD25	FN65	NM94
V1#1	11.50	34.00	80.00
2-4	8.35	25.00	50.00

BUGHOUSE FABLES
1921 (48 pgs.) (4x4-1/2") (10¢)
Embee Distributing Co. (King Features)

	GD25	FN65	NM94
1-Barney Google	20.00	60.00	140.00

BUG MOVIES
1931 (52 pgs.) (B&W)
Dell Publishing Co.

	GD25	FN65	NM94
nn-Not reprints; Stookie Allen-a	16.00	48.00	110.00

BUGS BUNNY (See The Best of..., Camp Comics, Comic Album #2, 6, 10, 14, Dell Giant #28, 32, 46, Dynabrite, Golden Comics Digest #1, 3, 5, 6, 8, 10, 14, 15, 17, 21, 26, 30, 34, 39, 42, 47, Kite Fun Book, Large Feature Comic #8, Looney Tunes and Merry Melodies, March of Comics #44, 59, 75, 83, 97, 115, 132, 149, 160, 179, 188, 201, 220, 231, 245, 259, 273, 287, 301, 315, 329, 343, 363, 367, 380, 392, 403, 415, 428, 440, 452, 464, 476, 487, Porky Pig, Puffed Wheat, Story Hour Series #802, Super Book #14, 26 and Whitman Comic Books)

BUGS BUNNY (See Dell Giants for annuals)
1942 - No. 245, 1983
Dell Publishing Co./Gold Key No. 86-218/Whitman No. 219 on

	GD25	FN65	NM94
Large Feature Comic 8(1942)-(Rarely found in fine-mint condition)	70.00	210.00	700.00
4-Color 33 ('43)	57.00	171.00	400.00
4-Color 51	34.00	100.00	235.00
4-Color 88	20.00	60.00	140.00
4-Color 123('46),142,164	14.00	43.00	100.00
4-Color 187,200,217,233	11.50	34.00	80.00
4-Color 250-Used in **SOTI**, pg. 309	11.50	34.00	80.00
4-Color 266,274,281,289,298('50)	10.00	30.00	65.00
4-Color 307,317(#1),327(#2),338,347,355,366,376,393	8.35	25.00	50.00
4-Color 407,420,432	5.85	17.50	35.00
28(12-1/52-53)-30	4.00	11.00	22.00
31-50	3.00	7.50	15.00
51-85(7-9/62)	2.00	5.00	10.00
86(10/62)-88-Bugs Bunny's Showtime-(25¢, 80pgs.)	5.25	15.75	42.00
89-100	1.30	3.25	8.00

Bulletman #6 © FAW

Bulls-Eye #5 © CHES

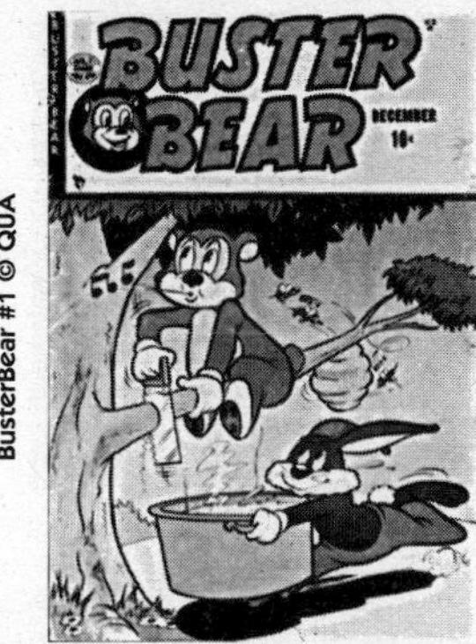

BusterBear #1 © QUA

GD25 FN65 NM94

101-120 1.00 2.00 5.00
121-140 1.60 4.00
141-170 1.20 3.00
171-245: 229-Swipe of Barks story/WDC&S #223 .80 2.00
NOTE: *Reprints-100, 102, 104, 123, 143, 144, 147, 167, 173, 175-177, 179-185, 187, 190.*
...Comic-Go-Round 11196-(224 pgs.)($1.95)(Golden Press, 1979) 1.20 3.00
...Winter Fun 1(12/67-Gold Key)-Giant 3.50 10.50 28.00

BUGS BUNNY (Puffed Rice Giveaway)
1949 (32 pgs. each, 3-1/8x6-7/8")
Quaker Cereals

A1-Traps the Counterfeiters, A2-Aboard Mystery Submarine, A3- Rocket to the Moon, A4-Lion Tamer, A5-Rescues the Beautiful Princess, B1-Buried Treasure, B2-Outwits the Smugglers, B3-Joins the Marines, B4-Meets the Dwarf Ghost, B5-Finds Aladdin's Lamp, C1-Lost in the Frozen North, C2-Secret Agent, C3-Captured by Cannibals, C4-Fights the Man from Mars, C5-And the Haunted Cave
each.... 5.00 15.00 30.00

BUGS BUNNY (3-D)
1953 (Pocket size) (15 titles)
Cheerios Giveaway
each.... 6.70 20.00 40.00

BUGS BUNNY
June, 1990 - No. 3, Aug, 1990 ($1.00, mini-series)
DC Comics
1-3: Daffy Duck, Elmer Fudd, others app. 1.00

BUGS BUNNY (...Monthly on-c)
1993 - Present ($1.95)
DC Comics
1-3-Bugs, Porky Pig, Daffy, Road Runner .80 2.00

BUGS BUNNY & PORKY PIG
Sept, 1965 (100 pgs.; paper cover; giant)
Gold Key
1(30025-509) 10.00 30.00 60.00

BUGS BUNNY'S ALBUM (See 4-Color No. 498,585,647,724)

BUGS BUNNY LIFE STORY ALBUM (See 4-Color No. 838)

BUGS BUNNY MERRY CHRISTMAS (See 4-Color No. 1064)

BULLET CROW, FOWL OF FORTUNE (Eclipse)(Value: cover or less)

BULLETMAN (See Fawcett Miniatures, Master Comics, Mighty Midget Comics, Nickel Comics & XMas Comics)
Sum, 1941 - #12, 2/12/43; #14, Spr, 1946 - #16, Fall, 1946 (No #13)
Fawcett Publications
1 229.00 685.00 1600.00
2 107.00 321.00 750.00
3 75.00 225.00 525.00
4,5 66.00 197.00 460.00
6-10: 7-Ghost Stories told by night watchman of cemetery begins; Eisnerish-a; hidden message "Chic Stone is a jerk" 57.00 171.00 400.00
11,12,14-16 (nn 13) 48.00 145.00 335.00
Well Known Comics (1942)-Paper-c, glued binding; printed in red (Bestmaid/Samuel Lowe giveaway) 12.50 37.50 85.00
NOTE: ***Mac Raboy** c-1-3, 5, 6, 10. "Bulletman the Flying Detective" on cover #8 on.*

BULLS-EYE (Cody of The Pony Express No. 8 on)
7-8/54 - No. 5, 3-4/55; No. 6, 6/55; No. 7, 8/55
Mainline No. 1-5/Charlton No. 6,7
1-S&K-c, 2 pgs.-a 41.00 122.00 285.00
2-S&K-c/a 36.00 107.00 250.00
3-5-S&K-c/a(2 each). 4-Last pre-code issue (1-2/55). 5-Censored issue with tomahawks removed in battle scene 27.00 81.00 190.00
6-S&K-c/a 20.00 60.00 140.00
7-S&K-c/a(3) 27.00 80.00 185.00
Great Scott Shoe Store giveaway-Reprints #2 with new cover 14.00 43.00 100.00

BULLS-EYE COMICS (Formerly Komik Pages #10; becomes Kayo #12)
No. 11, 1944
Harry 'A' Chesler
11-Origin K-9, Green Knight's sidekick, Lance; The Green Knight, Lady Satan, Yankee Doodle Jones app. 24.00 72.00 165.00

BULLWHIP GRIFFIN (See Movie Comics)

BULLWINKLE (TV) (...and Rocky No. 20 on; See March of Comics #233 and Rocky & Bullwinkle) (Jay Ward)
3-5/62 - #11, 4/74; #12, 6/76 - #19, 3/78; #20, 4/79 - #25, 2/80
Dell Publishing/Gold Key
4-Color 1270 (3-5/62) 17.00 51.00 120.00
01-090-209 (Dell, 7-9/62) 16.00 47.00 110.00
1(11/62, Gold Key) 12.00 36.00 85.00
2(2/63) 9.00 28.00 65.00
3(4/72)-11(4/74-Gold Key) 4.00 15.00 35.00
12(6/76)-Reprints 1.70 4.00 10.00
13(9/76), 14-New stories 1.90 6.00 13.00
15-25 1.30 3.30 8.00
Mother Moose Nursery Pomes 01-530-207 (5-7/62, Dell) 11.00 34.00 80.00
NOTE: *Reprints: 6, 7, 20-24.*

BULLWINKLE (...& Rocky No. 2 on)(TV)
July, 1970 - No. 7, July, 1971
Charlton Comics
1 3.70 11.00 26.00
2-7 2.30 6.90 16.00

BULLWINKLE AND ROCKY
Nov, 1987 - No. 9, Mar, 1989
Star Comics/Marvel Comics No. 3 on
1-9 1.00

BUNNY (Also see Rock Happening)
Dec, 1966 - No. 20, Dec, 1971; No. 21, Nov, 1976
Harvey Publications
1: 68 pg. Giant 3.00 7.50 15.00
2-18: 68 pg. Giants 2.40 6.00 12.00
19-21-52 pg. Giants: 21-Fruitman app. 1.65 4.00 10.00

BURKE'S LAW (TV)
1-3/64; No. 2, 5-7/64; No. 3, 3-5/65 (All have Gene Barry photo-c)
Dell Publishing Co.
1-Photo-c 5.00 15.00 30.00
2,3-Photo-c 4.00 10.00 20.00

BURNING ROMANCES (See Fox Giants)

BUSTER BEAR
Dec, 1953 - No. 10, June, 1955
Quality Comics Group (Arnold Publ.)
1-Funny animal 5.85 17.50 35.00
2 3.60 9.00 18.00
3-10 2.80 7.00 14.00
I.W. Reprint #9,10 (Super on inside) 1.40 3.50 7.00

BUSTER BROWN (Also see Brown's Blue Ribbon Book of Jokes and Jingles & Buddy Tucker & His Friends)
1903 - 1916 (11x17" strip reprints in color) (All rare or scarce)
Frederick A. Stokes Co.
GD25 FN65 VF82
...& His Resolutions (1903) by R. F. Outcault 133.00 400.00 1200.00
...Abroad (1904)-86 pgs.; hardback; 8x10-1/4"; B&W; by R. F. Outcault 121.00 365.00 850.00
...His Dog Tige & Their Troubles (1904) 121.00 365.00 850.00
...Pranks (1905) 121.00 365.00 850.00
...Antics (1906)-11x17", 66 pgs. 121.00 365.00 850.00

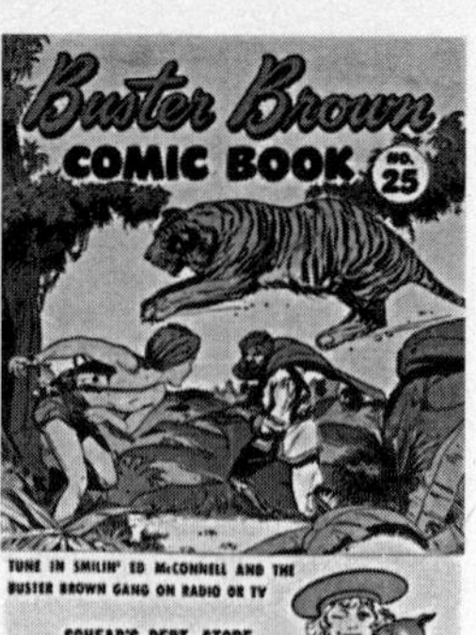

Buster Brown Comics #25, © Buster Brown

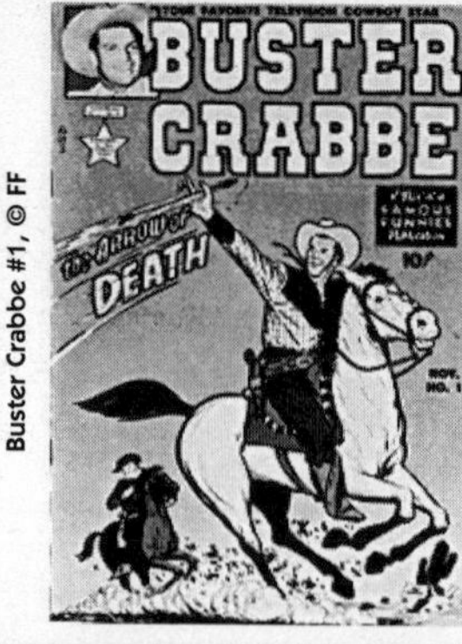

Buster Crabbe #1, © FF

The Butcher #1, © DC

	GD25	FN65	NM94
...And Company (1906)-11x17" in color	121.00	365.00	850.00
...Mary Jane & Tige (1906)	121.00	365.00	850.00
...My Resolutions (1906)-68 pgs.; B&W; hardcover; Sunday panel reprints	121.00	365.00	850.00
Collection of Buster Brown Comics (1908)	121.00	365.00	850.00
Buster Brown Up to Date (1910)	121.00	365.00	850.00
...The Fun Maker (1912)	121.00	365.00	850.00
...The Little Rogue (1916)(10x15-3/4", 62 pgs., in color)	100.00	300.00	700.00

NOTE: *Rarely found in fine or mint condition.*

BUSTER BROWN
1904 - 1912 (3x5" to 5x7"; sizes vary)(Advertising premium booklets)
Various Publishers

The Brown Shoe Company, St. Louis, USA
(Color, 5x7", 16 pgs.set of five books)

	GD25	FN65	VF82
Brown's Blue Ribbon Book of Jokes and Jingles Book 1 (nn, 1904)-By R. F. Outcault; Buster Brown & Tige, Little Tommy Tucker, Jack & Jill, Little Boy Blue, Dainty Jane; The Yellow Kid app. on back-c (1st comic book premium)	360.00	720.00	2500.00
Buster Brown's Blue Ribbon Book of Jokes and Jingles Book 2 (1905)-Original color art by Outcault	185.00	560.00	1300.00
Buster's Book of Jokes & Jingles Book 3 (1909)-r/Blue Ribbon post cards not signed by R.F. Outcault	185.00	560.00	1300.00
Buster's Book of Instructive Jokes and Jingles Book 4 (1910)-Original color art not signed by R.F. Outcault	185.00	560.00	1300.00
...Book of Travels nn (1912, 3x5")-Original color art not signed by Outcault	79.00	235.00	550.00

NOTE: *Estimated 5 to 6 known copies exist of books #1-4.*

The Buster Brown Bread Company

"Buster Brown" Bread Book of Rhymes, The nn (1904, 4x6", 12 pgs.)-Original color art not signed by R.F. Outcault	107.00	320.00	750.00

The Buster Brown Stocking Company

Buster Brown Drawing Book, The nn (nd, 5x6", 20 pgs.)-B&W reproductions of 1903 R.F. Outcault art to trace	54.00	160.00	375.00

Collins Baking Company

Buster Brown Drawing Book nn (1904, 3x5", 12 pgs.)-Original B&W art to trace not signed by R.F. Outcault	54.00	160.00	375.00

C. H. Morton, St. Albans, VT

Merry Antics of Buster Brown, Buddy Tucker & Tige nn (nd, 3-1/2x5-1/2", 16 pgs.)-Original B&W art by R.F. Outcault	54.00	160.00	375.00

Ivan Frank & Company

Buster Brown nn (1904, 3x5", 12 pgs.)-B&W repros of R. F. Outcault Sunday pages (First premium to actually reproduce Sunday comic pages – may be first premium comic book?)	54.00	160.00	375.00

Pond's Extract

Buster Brown's Experiences With Pond's Extract nn (1904, 4-1/2x6-3/4", 28 pgs.)-Original color art by R.F. Outcault	107.00	321.00	750.00

Ringen Stove Company

Quick Meal Steel Ranges nn (nd, 3x5", 16 pgs.)-Original B&W art not signed by R.F. Outcault	50.00	150.00	350.00

No Publisher Listed

The Drawiing Book nn (1906, 3-9/16x5", 8 pgs.)-Original B&W art to trace not signed by R.F. Outcault	50.00	150.00	350.00

BUSTER BROWN
1906 - 1917 (11x17" strip reprints in color)
Cupples & Leon Co./N. Y. Herald Co.
(By R. F. Outcault)

	GD25	FN65	VF82
...His Dog Tige & Their Jolly Times (1906, 58 pgs.)	55.00	165.00	550.00
...Latest Frolics (1906, 58 pgs.)	55.00	165.00	550.00
...Amusing Capers (1908, 46 pgs.)	55.00	165.00	550.00
...And His Pets (1909)	55.00	165.00	550.00
...On His Travels (1910)	55.00	165.00	550.00
...Happy Days (1911)	55.00	165.00	550.00
...In Foreign Lands (1912)	50.00	150.00	500.00
...And the Cat (1917)	50.00	150.00	500.00

NOTE: *Rarely found in fine or mint condition.*

BUSTER BROWN COMICS (Radio)(Also see My Dog Tige)
1945 - No. 43, 1959 (No. 5: paper cover)
Brown Shoe Co

	GD25	FN65	NM94
nn, nd (#1,scarce)-Covers mention diff. shoe stores	43.00	129.00	300.00
2	16.00	48.00	110.00
3-10: 4-(Rare)-Low print run due to paper shortage	10.00	30.00	60.00
11-20	6.35	19.00	38.00
21-24,26-28	4.70	14.00	28.00
25,33-37,40,41-Crandall-a in all	10.00	30.00	60.00
29-32-"Interplanetary Police Vs. the Space Siren" by Crandall (pencils only #29)	10.00	30.00	60.00
38,39,42,43	5.00	15.00	30.00
...Goes to Mars (2/58-Western Printing), slick-c, 20 pgs., reg. size	9.15	27.50	55.00
...In "Buster Makes the Team!" (1959-Custom Comics)	5.85	17.50	35.00
...In The Jet Age ('50s), slick-c, 20 pgs., 5x7-1/4"	9.15	27.50	55.00
...Of the Safety Patrol ('60-Custom Comics)	4.00	11.00	22.00
...Out of This World ('59-Custom Comics)	5.85	17.50	35.00
...Safety Coloring Book ('58, 16 pgs.)-Slick paper	5.85	17.50	35.00

BUSTER BUNNY
Nov, 1949 - No. 16, Oct, 1953
Standard Comics(Animated Cartoons)/Pines

1-Frazetta 1 pg. text illo.	5.85	17.50	35.00
2	3.60	9.00	18.00
3-16: 15-Racist-c	2.40	6.00	12.00

BUSTER CRABBE (TV)
Nov, 1951 - No. 12, 1953
Famous Funnies Publ.

1-1st app.(?) Frazetta anti-drug ad; text story about Buster Crabbe & Billy the Kid	25.00	75.00	175.00
2-Williamson/Evans-c; text story about Wild Bill Hickok & Pecos Bill	27.00	80.00	185.00
3-Williamson/Evans-c/a	30.00	90.00	210.00
4-Frazetta-c/a, 1pg.; bondage-c	35.00	105.00	245.00
5-Frazetta-c; Williamson/Krenkel/Orlando-a, 11pgs. (per Mr. Williamson)	93.00	280.00	650.00
6,8	11.50	34.00	80.00
7-Frazetta one pg. ad	14.00	43.00	100.00
9-One pg. Frazetta Boy Scouts ad (1st?)	11.50	34.00	80.00
10-12	8.35	25.00	50.00

NOTE: Eastern Color sold 3 dozen each NM file copies of #s 9-12 a few years ago.

BUSTER CRABBE (The Amazing Adventures of...)
Dec, 1953 - No. 4, June, 1954
Lev Gleason Publications

1,4: 1-Photo-c. 4-Flash Gordon-c	13.00	40.00	90.00
2,3-Toth-a	15.00	45.00	105.00

BUTCH CASSIDY
June, 1971 - No. 3, Oct, 1971 (52 pgs.)
Skywald Comics

1-Red Mask reprint, retitled Maverick; Bolle-a		.80	2.00
2,3: 2-Whip Wilson-r. 3-Dead Canyon Days reprint/Crack Western No. 63; Sundance Kid app.; Crandall-a			1.50

BUTCH CASSIDY (...& the Wild Bunch)
1951
Avon Periodicals

Buzzy #17 © DC

Cable #16 © MEG

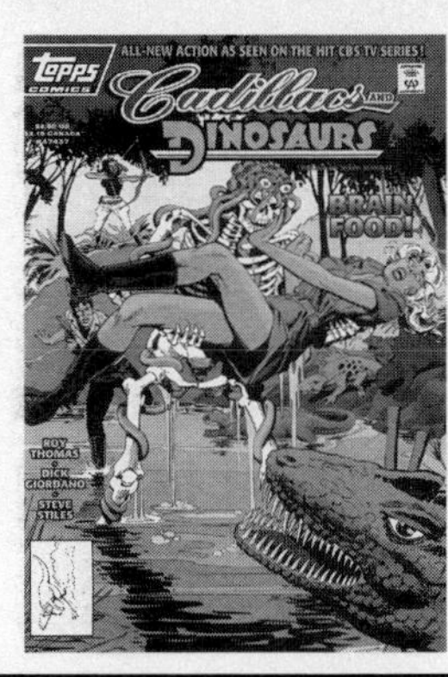

Cadillacs & Dinosaurs #2 © TOPS

GD25 FN65 NM94

1-Kinstler-c/a 13.00 40.00 90.00
NOTE: ***Reinman*** *story; Issue number on inside spine.*

BUTCH CASSIDY (See Fun-In No. 11 & Western Adventure Comics)

BUTCHER, THE (Also see Brave and the Bold, 2nd series)
May, 1990 - No. 5, Sept, 1990 ($1.50, mature readers)
DC Comics
1-5: 1-No indicia inside 1.50

BUTTONS & FATTY IN THE FUNNIES
nd (1927)(10-1/4"x15-1/2")(28pg. in color)
Whitman Publishing Co.
W936-Signed "M.E.B.", probably Merrill Blosser; strips in color copyright The Brooklyn Daily Eagle; thought to be one of the first two western Publ. Co. books (very rare) 45.00 120.00 270.00

BUZ SAWYER (Sweeney No. 4 on)
June, 1948 - No. 3, 1949
Standard Comics
1-Roy Crane-a 16.00 48.00 110.00
2-Intro his pal Sweeney 10.00 30.00 65.00
3 9.15 27.50 55.00

BUZ SAWYER'S PAL, ROSCOE SWEENEY (See Sweeney)

BUZZY (See All Funny Comics)
Winter, 1944-45 - No. 75, 1-2/57; No. 76, 10/57; No. 77, 10/58
National Periodical Publications/Detective Comics
1 (52 pgs. begin) 23.00 70.00 160.00
2 11.00 32.00 75.00
3-5 7.50 22.50 45.00
6-10 5.35 16.00 32.00
11-20 4.70 14.00 28.00
21-30 4.00 10.00 20.00
31,35-38 3.20 8.00 16.00
32-34,39-Last 52 pgs. Scribbly story by Mayer in each (these four stories were done for Scribbly #14 which was delayed for a year) 4.00 10.00 20.00
40-77: 62-Last precode (2/55) 3.00 7.50 15.00

BUZZY THE CROW (See Harvey Comics Hits #60 & 62, Harvey Hits #18 & Paramount Animated Comics #1)

BY BIZARRE HANDS
Apr, 1994 - No. 3, June, 1994 ($2.50, B&W, limited series, mature readers)
Dark Horse Comics
1-3 1.00 2.50

CABLE (See Ghost Rider &..., & New Mutants #87)
May, 1993 - Present ($2.00)
Marvel Comics
1-($3.50, 52 pgs.)-Gold foil & embossed-c; Thibert a-1-4p; c-1-3; Liefeld-a assist #4 1.40 3.50
2-15: 3-Extra 16 pg. X-Men/Avengers ann. preview. 4-Liefeld-a assist; last Thibert-a(p). 6-8-Reveals that Baby Nathan is Cable; gives background on Stryfe. 9-Omega Red-c/story. 11-Bound-in trading card sheet .80 2.00
16-Newsstand edition 1.00 2.50
16-Enhanced edition 1.40 3.50
17-($1.95)-Deluxe edition .80 2.00

CABLE - BLOOD AND METAL
Oct, 1992 - No. 2, Nov, 1992 ($2.50, mini-series, 52 pgs.)
Marvel Comics
1-Wraparound-c; Cable vs. Stryfe; Romita, Jr.-c/a in both 1.40 3.50
2-Prelude to X-Cutioner's Song x-overs 1.00 2.50

CADET GRAY OF WEST POINT (See Dell Giants)

CADILLACS & DINOSAURS (TV)
Nov, 1990 - No. 6, Apr, 1991 ($2.50, limited series, coated paper)
Epic Comics (Marvel)
1-6: r/Xenozoic Tales in color w/new-c 1.00 2.50
...In 3-D #1 (7/92, $3.95, Kitchen Sink)-With glasses 1.60 4.00

CADILLACS AND DINOSAURS (TV)
Feb, 1994 - No. 6, July, 1994 ($2.50, limited series)
Topps Comics
V2#1-($2.95)-Collector's edition w/Stout-c & bound-in poster; Buckler-a; foil stamped logo; Giordano-a in all 1.40 3.00
V2#1-Newsstand edition w/Giordano-c 1.00 2.50
V2#2,3-Collector's editions w/Stout-c & posters 1.00 2.50
V2#2,3-Newsstand ed. w/Giordano-c; w/o posters 1.00 2.50
V2#4-6-Collectors edition; Kieth-c 1.00 2.50
V2#4-6-Newsstand edition 1.00 2.50

CAGE (Also see Hero for Hire, Power Man & Punisher)
Apr, 1992 - No. 20, Nov, 1993 ($1.25)
Marvel Comics
1-($1.50)-Has extra color on-c .80 2.00
2-11,13-20: 3-Punisher-c & minor app. 9-Rhino-c/story; Hulk cameo. 10-Rhino & Hulk-c/story 1.25
12-($1.75, 52 pgs.)-Iron Fist app. .70 1.75

CAGES
1991 - No. 10, 1992? ($3.50/$3.95, color, limited series)
Tundra Publ.
1-Dave McKean-c/a in all 1.70 5.00 12.00
2-Misprint exists 1.20 3.00 7.00
3-10: 5-Begin $3.95-c 1.60 4.00

CAIN'S HUNDRED (TV)
May-July, 1962 - No. 2, Sept-Nov, 1962
Dell Publishing Co.
nn(01-094-207) 2.80 7.00 14.00
2 1.80 4.50 9.00

CALIBER PRESENTS
Jan, 1989 - No. 24, 1991 ($1.95/$2.50, B&W, 52 pgs.)
Caliber Press
1-Anthology; 1st app. The Crow; Tim Vigil-c/a 10.00 30.00 70.00
2-Deadworld story; Tim Vigil-a 1.00 2.00 5.00
3-14: 9-Begin $2.50-c 1.20 3.00
15-24 ($3.50, 68 pgs.) 1.40 3.50

CALIPER PRESENTS: CINDERELLA ON FIRE
1994 ($2.95, B&W, mature readers)
Caliper Press
1 1.20 3.00

CALIFORNIA GIRLS
June, 1987 - No. 8, May, 1988 ($2.00, B&W, 40 pgs)
Eclipse Comics
1-8: All contain color paper dolls .80 2.00

CALL FROM CHRIST
1952 (36 pgs.) (Giveaway)
Catechetical Educational Society
nn 2.00 5.00 10.00

CALLING ALL BOYS (Tex Granger No. 18 on)
Jan, 1946 - No. 17, May, 1948 (Photo c-1-5,7,8)
Parents' Magazine Institute
1 8.35 25.00 50.00
2 4.00 11.00 22.00
3-7,9,11,14-17: 6-Painted-c. 11-Rin Tin Tin photo on-c; Tex Granger begins. 14-J. Edgar Hoover photo on-c. 15-Tex Granger-c begin 2.80 7.00 14.00
8-Milton Caniff story 4.70 14.00 28.00
10-Gary Cooper photo on-c 4.35 13.00 26.00

Camelot 3000 #12 © DC

Candid Tales © Kirby Pub.

Candy #46 © QUA

	GD25	FN65	NM94
12-Bob Hope photo on-c	6.35	19.00	38.00
13-Bing Crosby photo on-c	5.00	15.00	30.00

CALLING ALL GIRLS
Sept, 1941 - No. 89, Sept, 1949 (Part magazine, part comic)
Parents' Magazine Institute

	GD25	FN65	NM94
1	10.00	30.00	65.00
2-Photo-c	5.00	15.00	30.00
3-Shirley Temple photo-c	6.35	19.50	38.00
4-10: 4,5,7,9-Photo-c. 9-Flag-c	3.60	9.00	18.00
11-20: 11-Tina Thayer photo-c; Mickey Rooney photo-b/c; B&W photo inside of Gary Cooper as Lou Gehrig in "Pride of Yankees"	2.80	7.00	14.00
21-39,41-43(10-11/45)-Last issue with comics	2.00	5.00	10.00
40-Liz Taylor photo-c	6.35	19.50	38.00
44-51(7/46)-Last comic book size issue	1.60	4.00	8.00
52-89	1.40	3.50	7.00

NOTE: ***Jack Sparling** art in many issues; becomes a girls' magazine "Senior Prom" with #90.*

CALLING ALL KIDS (Also see True Comics)
Dec-Jan, 1945-46 - No. 26, Aug, 1949
Parents' Magazine Institute

	GD25	FN65	NM94
1-Funny animal	7.00	21.00	42.00
2	4.00	10.00	20.00
3-10	2.00	5.00	10.00
11-26	1.60	4.00	8.00

CALVIN (See Li'l Kids)

CALVIN & THE COLONEL (TV)
No. 1354, Apr-June, 1962 - No. 2, July-Sept, 1962
Dell Publishing Co.

	GD25	FN65	NM94
4-Color 1354(#1)	9.15	27.50	55.00
2	5.85	17.50	35.00

CAMELOT 3000
12/82 - No. 11, 7/84; No. 12, 4/85 (Direct Sale; Mando paper)
DC Comics (Maxi-series)

	GD25	FN65	NM94
1-12: 5-Intro Knights of New Camelot		1.00	2.50

NOTE: ***Austin** a-7i-12i. **Bolland** a-1-12p; c-1-12.*

CAMERA COMICS
July, 1944 - No. 9, Summer, 1946
U.S. Camera Publishing Corp./ME

	GD25	FN65	NM94
nn (7/44)	16.00	48.00	110.00
nn (9/44)	13.00	40.00	90.00
1(10/44)-The Grey Comet	13.00	40.00	90.00
2	10.00	30.00	65.00
3-Nazi WW II-c; photos	9.15	27.50	55.00
4-9: All half photos	8.35	25.00	50.00

CAMP CANDY (TV)
May, 1990 - No. 6, Oct, 1990 ($1.00)
Marvel Comics

	GD25	FN65	NM94
1-6: Post-c/a(p); featuring John Candy		.50	1.00

CAMP COMICS
Feb, 1942 - No. 3, April, 1942 (All have photo-c)
Dell Publishing Co.

	GD25	FN65	NM94
1- "Seaman Sy Wheeler" by Kelly, 7 pgs.; Bugs Bunny app.; Mark Twain adaptation	49.00	145.00	340.00
2-Kelly-a, 12 pgs.; Bugs Bunny app.	36.00	107.00	250.00
3-(Scarce)-Dave Berg & Walt Kelly-a	49.00	145.00	340.00

CAMP RUNAMUCK (TV)
April, 1966
Dell Publishing Co.

	GD25	FN65	NM94
1-Photo-c	3.60	9.00	18.00

CAMPUS LOVES
Dec, 1949 - No. 5, Aug, 1950
Quality Comics Group (Comic Magazines)

	GD25	FN65	NM94
1-Ward-c/a (9 pgs.)	19.00	57.00	130.00
2-Ward-c/a	13.50	41.00	95.00
3-5: 5-Spanking panels (2)	7.50	22.50	45.00

NOTE: ***Gustavson** a-1-5. Photo c-3-5.*

CAMPUS ROMANCE (...Romances on cover)
Sept-Oct, 1949 - No. 3, Feb-Mar, 1950
Avon Periodicals/Realistic

	GD25	FN65	NM94
1-Walter Johnson-a; c-/Avon paperback #348	14.00	43.00	100.00
2-Grandenetti-a; c-/Avon paperback #151	11.00	32.00	75.00
3-c-/Avon paperback #201	11.00	32.00	75.00
Realistic reprint	5.00	15.00	30.00

CANADA DRY PREMIUMS (See Swamp Fox, The & Terry & The Pirates)

CANCELLED COMIC CAVALCADE
Summer, 1978 - No. 2, Fall, 1978 (8-1/2x11"; B&W)
(Xeroxed pgs. on one side only w/blue cover and taped spine)
DC Comics, Inc.

1-(412 pgs.) Contains xeroxed copies of art for: Black Lightning #12, cover to #13; Claw #13, 14; The Deserter #1; Doorway to Nightmare #6; Firestorm #6; The Green Team #2,3.

2-(532 pgs.) Contains xeroxed copies of art for: Kamandi #60 (including Omac), #61; Prez #5; Shade #9 (including The Odd Man); Showcase #105 (Deadman), 106 (The Creeper); The Vixen #1; and covers to Army at War #2, Battle Classics #3, Demand Classics #1 & 2, Dynamic Classics #3, Mr. Miracle #26, Ragman #6, Weird Mystery #25 & 26, & Western Classics #1 & 2. (Rare) (One set sold in 1989 for $1,200.00)

NOTE: *In June, 1978, DC cancelled several of their titles. For copyright purposes, the unpublished original art for these titles was xeroxed, bound in the above books, published and distributed. Only 35 copies were made.*

CANDID TALES (Also see Bold Stories & It Rhymes With Lust)
April, 1950; June, 1950 (Digest size) (144 pgs.) (Full color)
Kirby Publishing Co.

	GD25	FN65	NM94
nn-(Scarce) Contains Wood female pirate story, 15 pgs., and 14 pgs. in June issue; Powell-a	54.00	160.00	375.00

NOTE: *Another version exists with Dr. Kilmore by Wood; no female pirate story.*

CANDY
Fall, 1944 - No. 3, Spring, 1945
William H. Wise & Co.

	GD25	FN65	NM94
1-Two Scoop Scuttle stories by Wolverton	22.00	65.00	150.00
2,3-Scoop Scuttle by Wolverton, 2-4 pgs.	17.00	52.00	120.00

CANDY (Teen-age)(Also see Police Comics #37)
Autumn, 1947 - No. 64, July, 1956
Quality Comics Group (Comic Magazines)

	GD25	FN65	NM94
1-Gustavson-a	12.00	36.00	85.00
2-Gustavson-a	7.50	22.50	45.00
3-10	4.70	14.00	28.00
11-30	3.60	9.00	18.00
31-63	3.20	8.00	16.00
64-Ward-c(p)?	3.60	9.00	18.00
Super Reprint No. 2,10,12,16,17,18('63-'64)	1.60	4.00	8.00

NOTE: ***Jack Cole** 1-2 pg. art in many issues.*

CANNONBALL COMICS
Feb, 1945 - No. 2, Mar, 1945
Rural Home Publishing Co.

	GD25	FN65	NM94
1-The Crash Kid, Thunderbrand, The Captive Prince & Crime Crusader begin; skull-c	39.00	118.00	275.00
2-Devil-c	34.00	100.00	235.00

CANTEEN KATE (See All Picture All True Love Story & Fightin' Marines)
June, 1952 - No. 3, Nov, 1952
St. John Publishing Co.

	GD25	FN65	NM94
1-Matt Baker-c/a	30.00	90.00	210.00
2-Matt Baker-c/a	25.00	75.00	175.00
3-(Rare)-Used in **POP**, pg. 75; Baker-c/a	30.00	90.00	210.00

CAP'N CRUNCH COMICS (See Quaker Oats)
1963; 1965 (16 pgs.; miniature giveaways; 2-1/2x6-1/2")

Captain Aero #3 © HOKE

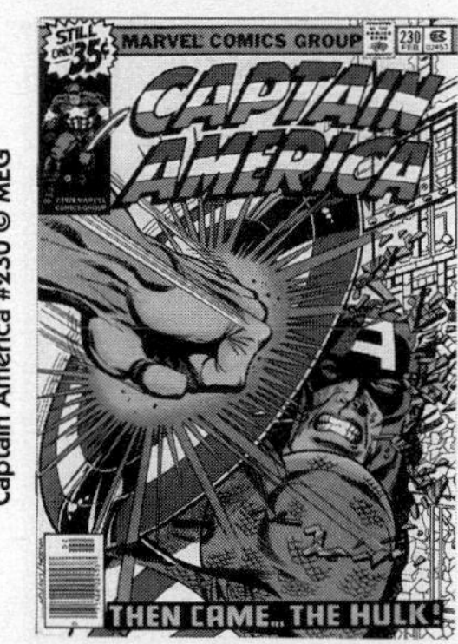

Captain America #230 © MEG

Captain America #431 © MEG

GD25 FN65 NM94 — GD25 FN65 NM94

Quaker Oats Co.
(1963 titles)- "The Picture Pirates", "The Fountain of Youth", "I'm Dreaming of a Wide Isthmus". (1965 titles)- "Bewitched, Betwitched, & Betweaked", "Seadog Meets the Witch Doctor" (another 1965 title suspected) 5.00 15.00 30.00

CAP'N QUICK & A FOOZLE (Eclipse)(Value: cover or less)

CAPTAIN ACTION
Oct-Nov, 1968 - No. 5, June-July, 1969 (Based on Ideal toy)
National Periodical Publications
1-Origin; Wood-a; Superman-c app. 7.00 21.00 48.00
2,3,5-Kane/Wood-a 4.00 12.00 28.00
4 3.00 9.40 22.00
...& Action Boy('67)-Ideal Toy Co. giveaway (1st app. Captain Action) 7.00 21.00 50.00

CAPTAIN AERO COMICS (Samson No. 1-6; also see Veri Best Sure Fire & Veri Best Sure Shot Comics)
V1#7(#1), Dec, 1941 - V2#4(#10), Jan, 1943; V3#9(#11), Sept, 1943 - V4#3(#17), Oct, 1944; #21, Dec, 1944 - #26, Aug, 1946 (No #18-20)
Holyoke Publishing Co.
V1#7(#1)-Flag-Man & Solar, Master of Magic, Captain Aero, Cap Stone, Adventurer begin 85.00 257.00 600.00
8(#2)-Pals of Freedom app. 46.00 139.00 325.00
9(#3)-Alias X begins; Pals of Freedom app. 46.00 139.00 325.00
10(#4)-Origin The Gargoyle; Kubert-a 46.00 139.00 325.00
11,12(#5,6)-Kubert-a; Miss Victory in #6 38.00 114.00 265.00
V2#1,2(#7,8): 8-Origin The Red Cross; Miss Victory app.; Brodsky-c(i) 23.00 70.00 160.00
3(#9)-Miss Victory app. 17.00 52.00 120.00
4(#10)-Miss Victory app. 13.00 40.00 90.00
V3#9 - V3#13(#11-15): 11,15-Miss Victory app. 10.00 30.00 70.00
V4#2, V4#3(#16,17) 10.00 30.00 60.00
21-24,26-L. B. Cole covers. 22-Intro/origin Mighty Mite. 26-Palais-a(2) 13.00 40.00 90.00
25-L. B. Cole S/F-c 15.00 45.00 105.00
NOTE: *L.B. Cole* c-17. ***Hollingsworth*** a-23. ***Infantino*** a-23, 26. ***Schomburg*** c-15, 16.

CAPTAIN AMERICA (See Adventures of..., All-Select, All Winners, Aurora, Avengers #4, Blood and Glory, Captain Britain 16-20, Giant-Size..., The Invaders, Marvel Double Feature, Marvel Fanfare, Marvel Mystery, Marvel Super-Action, Marvel Super Heroes V2#3, Marvel Team-Up, Marvel Treasury Special, Power Record Comics, USA Comics, Young Allies & Young Men)

CAPTAIN AMERICA (Formerly Tales of Suspense #1-99; Captain America and the Falcon #134-223 on cover only)
No. 100, April, 1968 - Present
Marvel Comics Group
100-Flashback on Cap's revival with Avengers & Sub-Mariner; story continued from Tales of Suspense #99; Kirby-c/a begins 34.00 103.00 275.00
101-The Sleeper-c/story; Red Skull app. 9.00 26.00 70.00
102-108: 102-Sleeper-c/s. 103,104-Red Skull-c/sty 4.40 13.00 35.00
109-Origin Capt. America retold 8.00 23.00 62.00
110,111,113-Classic Steranko-c/a: 110-Rick becomes Cap's partner; Hulk x-over; 1st app. Viper. 111-Death of Steve Rogers. 113-Cap's funeral 6.90 21.00 55.00
112-Origin retold; last Kirby-c/a 3.40 10.00 27.00
114-116,118-120: 115-Last 12¢ issue 2.30 7.00 18.00
117-1st app. The Falcon (9/69) 3.40 10.00 27.00
121-140: 121-Retells origin. 133-The Falcon becomes Cap's partner; origin Modok. 137,138-Spider-Man x-over. 140-Origin Grey Gargoyle retold 1.40 3.50 8.50
141-153,155-171,176-179: 142-Last 15¢ issue. 143-(52 pgs). 144-New costume Falcon. 153-1st app. (cameo) Jack Monroe. 155-Origin; redrawn w/Falcon added; origin J. Monroe. 158-Cap's strength increased. 160-1st app. Solarr. 164-1st app. Nightshade. 176-End of Capt. Am. 1.00 3.00 6.00
154-1st full app. Jack Monroe (Nomad)(10/72) 1.20 2.90 7.00
172-175-X-Men x-over 1.40 4.10 9.50
180-Intro/origin of Nomad (Steve Rogers) 1.10 3.00 6.50
181-Intro/origin new Cap. .90 2.30 5.50
182,184-200(8/76): 186-True origin The Falcon 1.40 3.50
183-Death of new Cap; Nomad becomes Cap .90 2.30 5.50
201-240,242-246: 215-Retells Cap's origin. 216-r/story from Strange Tales #114. 217-1st app. Marvel Man (later Quasar). 229-Marvel Man app. 230-Battles Hulk-c/story cont'd in Hulk #232. 233-Death of Sharon Carter. 234,235-Daredevil x-over; 235(7/79)-Miller pencils. 244,245-Miller-c 1.00 2.50
241-Punisher app.; Miller-c 5.70 17.00 40.00
247-255-Byrne-a. 255-Origin; Miller-c 1.20 3.00
256-281,284,285,289-322,324-326,329-331: 264-Old X-Men cameo in flash-back. 265,266-Nick Fury & Spider-Man app. 267-1st app. Everyman. 269-1st Team America. 279-(3/83)-Contains Tattooz skin decals. 281-1950s Bucky returns. 284-Patriot (Jack Mace) app. 285-Death of Patriot. 298-Origin Red Skull .80 2.00
282-Bucky becomes new Nomad (Jack Monroe) 1.40 4.10 9.50
282-Silver ink 2nd print ($1.75) w/original date (6/83) .70 1.75
283-2nd app. Nomad 1.80 4.50
286-288-Deathlok app. 1.00 2.50
323-1st app. new Super Patriot (see Nick Fury) 1.40 3.50
327-Captain America battles Super Patriot 1.00 2.50
328-Origin & 1st app. D-Man 1.00 2.50
332-Old Cap resigns 1.40 4.00 10.00
333-Intro & origin new Captain (Super Patriot) 1.30 3.90 9.00
334 1.80 4.50
335-340: 339-Fall of the Mutants tie-in 1.70 4.25
341-343,345-349 .60 1.50
344-($1.50, 52 pgs.)-Ronald Reagan cameo .80 1.90
350-($1.75, 68 pgs.)-Return of Steve Rogers (original Cap) to original costume 1.60 4.00
351-354: 351-Nick Fury app. 354-1st app. U.S. Agent (6/89, see Avengers West Coast) 1.50
355-382,384-396: 373-Bullseye app. 375-Daredevil app. 386-U.S. Agent app. 387-389-Red Skull back-up stories. 396-Last $1.00-c. 396,397-1st app. all new Jack O'Lantern 1.40
383-($2.00, 68 pgs.)-50th anniversary issue; Red Skull story; Jim Lee-c(i) 1.80 4.50
397-399,401-424,426: 402-Begin 6 part Man-Wolf story w/Wolverine in #403-407. 405-410-New Jack O'Lantern app. in back-up story. 406-Cable & Shatterstar cameo. 407-Capwolf vs. Cable-c/story. 408-Infinity War x-over; Falcon solo back-up. 423-Vs. Namor-c/story 1.10
400-($2.25, 84 pgs.)-Flip book format w/double gatefold-c; r/Avengers #4 plus-c; contains cover pin-ups 1.20 3.00
425-($2.95, 52 pgs.)-Embossed Foil-c edition; Fighting Chance Pt. 1 1.20 3.00
425-($1.75, 52 pgs.)-Regular edition .70 1.80
427-438: 427-Begin $1.50-c; bound-in trading card sheet 1.50
Special 1(1/71)-Origin retold 2.00 6.00 14.00
Special 2(1/72)-Colan-r/Not Brand Echh; all-r 1.60 5.00 11.00
Annual 3,5-7: 3(1976), 5('81, 52 pgs.). 6('82, 52 pgs.). 7('83, 52 pgs.) 1.00 2.50
Annual 4(1977, 52 pgs.)-Kirby0c/a(new); Magneto0c/story (34 pgs.) 1.20 3.00
Annual 8(9/86)-Wolverine-c/story 5.70 17.00 40.00
Annual 9(1990, $2.00, 68 pgs.)-Nomad back-up 1.80 4.50
Annual 10(1991, $2.00, 68 pgs.)-Origin retold (2 pgs.) .80 2.00
Annual 11(1992, $2.25, 68 pgs.)-Falcon solo story .90 2.25
Annual 12(1993, $2.95, 68 pgs.)-Bagged w/card 1.20 3.00
Annual 13(1994, $2.95, 68 pgs.)-Red Skull-c/story 1.20 3.00
...: Deathlok Lives! nn(10/93, $4.95)-r/#286-288 1.00 2.00 5.00
...Drug War 1-(1994, $2.00, 52 pgs.)-New Warriors app. .80 2.00
...Medusa Effect 1 (1994, $2.95, 68 pgs.)-Origin Baron Zemo 1.20 3.00
...Streets of Poison ($15.95)-r/#372-378 2.30 6.90 16.00
...: The Movie Special nn (5/92, $3.50, 52 pgs.)-Adapts movie; printed on coated stock; The Red Skull app. 1.20 3.00

Captain America Comics #21 © MEG

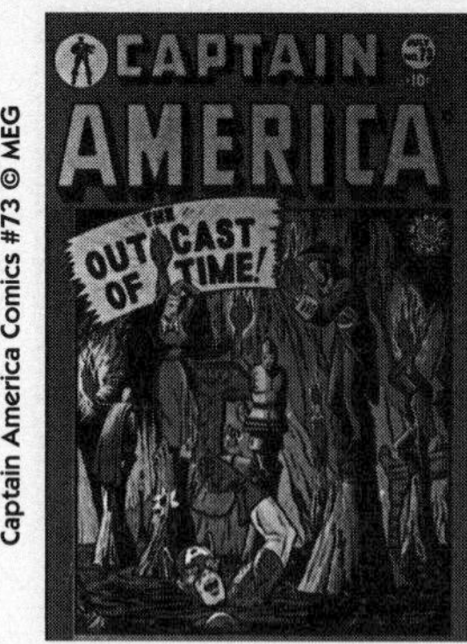

Captain America Comics #73 © MEG

Captain Atom #2 (modern) © DC

GD25 FN65 NM94

...& The Campbell Kids (1980, 36pg. giveaway, Campbell's Soup/U.S. Dept. of Energy) .80 2.00
...Goes to War Against Drugs (1990, no #, giveaway)-Distributed to direct sales shops; 2nd printing exists 1.00
...Meets the Asthma Monster (1987, no #, giveaway, Your Physician and Glaxo, Inc.) 1.00
...Vs. Asthma Monster (1990, no #, giveaway, Your Physician & Allen & Hanbury's) 1.00

NOTE: ***Austin*** *c-225i, 239i, 246i.* ***Buscema*** *a-115p, 217p; c-136p, 217.* ***Byrne*** *c-223(part), 238, 239, 247p-254p, 290, 291, 313p; a-247-254p, 255, 313p, 350.* ***Colan*** *a(p)-116-137, 256, Annual 5; c(p)-116-123, 126, 129.* ***Everett*** *a-136i, 137i; c-126i.* ***Gil Kane*** *a-145p; c-147p, 149p, 150p, 170p, 172-174, 180, 181p, 183-190p, 215, 216, 220, 221.* ***Kirby*** *a(p)-100-109, 112, 193-214, 216, Special 1, 2(layouts), Annual 3, 4; c-100-109, 112, 126p, 193-214.* ***Ron Lim*** *a(p)-366, 368-378, 380-386; c-366p, 368-378p, 379, 380-393p.* ***Miller*** *c-241p, 244p, 245p, 255p, Annual 5.* ***Mooney*** *a-149i.* ***Morrow*** *a-144.* ***Perez*** *c-243p, 246p.* ***Robbins*** *c(p)-183-187, 189-192, 225.* ***Roussos*** *a-140i, 168i.* ***Starlin/Sinnott*** *c-162.* ***Sutton*** *a-244i.* ***Tuska*** *a-112i, 215p, Special 2.* ***Williamson*** *a-313i.* ***Wood*** *a-127i.*

CAPTAIN AMERICA COMICS
Mar, 1941 - No. 75, Jan, 1950; No. 76, 5/54 - No. 78, 9/54
(No. 74 & 75 titled Capt. America's Weird Tales)
Timely/Marvel Comics (TCI 1-20/CmPS 21-68/MjMC 69-75/Atlas Comics (PrPI 76-78)

	GD25	FN65	VF82	NM94
1-Origin & 1st app. Captain America & Bucky by S&K; Hurricane, Tuk the Caveboy begin by S&K; 1st app. Red Skull; Hitler-c (by Simon?); indicia reads Vol. 2, Number 1	4,500.00	13,500.00	29,250.00	45,000.00

(Estimated up to 180 total copies exist, 8 in NM/Mint)

	GD25	FN65	NM94
2-S&K Hurricane; Tuk by Avison (Kirby splash); classic Hitler-c	923.00	2785.00	6500.00
3-Red Skull-c & app; Stan Lee's 1st text (1st work for Marvel)	714.00	2143.00	5000.00
4-1st full pg. panel in comics	464.00	1393.00	3250.00
5	414.00	1243.00	2900.00
6-Origin Father Time; Tuk the Caveboy ends	357.00	1071.00	2500.00
7-Red Skull app.; classic-c	385.00	1157.00	2700.00
8-10-Last S&K issue, (S&K centerfold #6-10)	286.00	857.00	2000.00
11-Last Hurricane, Headline Hunter; Al Avison Captain America begins, ends #20; Avison-c(p)	243.00	730.00	1700.00
12-The Imp begins, ends #16; last Father Time	229.00	685.00	1600.00
13-Origin The Secret Stamp; classic-c	250.00	750.00	1750.00
14,15	229.00	685.00	1600.00
16-Red Skull unmasks Cap	257.00	771.00	1800.00
17-The Fighting Fool only app.	193.00	580.00	1350.00
18,19-Human Torch begins #19	157.00	471.00	1100.00
20-Sub-Mariner app.; no H. Torch	157.00	471.00	1100.00
21-25: 25-Cap drinks liquid opium	143.00	430.00	1000.00
26-30: 27-Last Secret Stamp; last 68 pg. issue. 28-60 pg. issues begin.	136.00	407.00	950.00
31-35,38-40: 34-Centerfold poster of Cap	114.00	343.00	800.00
36-Classic Hitler-c	171.00	515.00	1200.00
37-Red Skull app.	121.00	365.00	850.00
41-47: 41-Last Jap War-c. 46-German Holocaust-c. 47-Last German War-c	100.00	300.00	700.00
48-58,60	96.00	290.00	675.00
59-Origin retold	186.00	557.00	1300.00
61-Red Skull-c/story	143.00	430.00	1000.00
62,64,65: 65-Kurtzman's "Hey Look"	100.00	300.00	700.00
63-Intro/origin Asbestos Lady	107.00	321.00	750.00
66-Bucky is shot; Golden Girl teams up with Captain America & learns his i.d; origin Golden Girl	111.00	332.00	775.00
67-Captain America/Golden Girl team-up; Mxyztplk swipe; last Toro in Human Torch	100.00	300.00	700.00
68,70-Sub-Mariner/Namora, and Captain America/Golden Girl team-up in each. 70-Science fiction-c/story	100.00	300.00	700.00
69,71-73: 69-Human Torch/Sun Girl team-up. 71-Anti Wertham editorial; The Witness, Bucky app.	100.00	300.00	700.00
74-(Scarce)(1949)-Titled "Captain America's Weird Tales"; Red Skull app.	186.00	557.00	1300.00
75(2/50)-Titled "C.A.'s Weird Tales"; no C.A. app.; horror cover/stories	100.00	300.00	700.00
76-78(1954): Human Torch/Toro stories; all have communist-c/stories	64.00	193.00	450.00
132-Pg. Issue (B&W-1942)(Canadian)-Has blank inside-c and back-c; contains Marvel Mystery #33 & Capt. America #18 w/cover from Capt. America #22; same contents as Marvel Mystery annual	1100.00	3200.00	7500.00
Shoestore Giveaway #77	38.00	114.00	265.00

NOTE: ***Crandall*** *a-2i, 3i, 9i, 10i.* ***Kirby*** *c-8p.* ***Rico*** *c-69-71.* ***Romita*** *c-77, 78.* ***Schomburg*** *c-3, 4, 26-29, 31, 33, 37-39, 41, 42, 45-54, 58.* ***Sekowsky*** *c-55, 56.* ***Shores*** *c-1, 2, 5-7, 11i, 20-25, 30, 32, 34, 35, 40, 57, 59-67.* ***S&K*** *c-1, 2, 5-7, 9, 10. Bondage c-3, 7, 15, 16, 34, 38.*

CAPTAIN AMERICA SPECIAL EDITION
Feb, 1984 - No. 2, Mar, 1984 ($2.00, Baxter paper)
Marvel Comics Group

1,2-Steranko-c/a(r) .80 2.00

CAPTAIN AND THE KIDS, THE (See Famous Comics Cartoon Books)

CAPTAIN AND THE KIDS, THE (See Comics on Parade, Katzenjammer Kids, Okay Comics & Sparkler Comics)
1938 -12/39; Sum, 1947 - No. 32, 1955; 4-Color No. 881, Feb, 1958
United Features Syndicate/Dell Publ. Co.

	GD25	FN65	NM94
Single Series 1(1938)	71.00	215.00	500.00
Single Series 1(Reprint)(12/39- "Reprint" on-c)	39.00	118.00	275.00
1(Summer, 1947-UFS)-Katzenjammer Kids	10.00	30.00	65.00
2	5.85	17.50	35.00
3-10	4.35	13.00	26.00
11-20	4.00	10.00	20.00
21-32(1955)	3.20	8.00	16.00
50th Anniversary issue-(1948)-Contains a 2 pg. history of the strip, including an account of the famous Supreme Court decision allowing both Pulitzer & Hearst to run the same strip under different names	6.35	19.00	38.00
Special Summer issue, Fall issue (1948)	4.70	14.00	28.00
4-Color 881 (Dell)	4.00	10.00	20.00

CAPTAIN ATOM
1950 - No. 7, 1951 (5x7-1/4") (5¢, 52 pgs.)
Nationwide Publishers

	GD25	FN65	NM94
1-Sci/fic	24.00	72.00	165.00
2-7	12.00	36.00	85.00
...- Secret of the Columbian Jungle (16 pgs. in color, paper-c, 3-3/4x5-1/8")-Fireside Marshmallow giveaway	4.00	10.00	20.00

CAPTAIN ATOM (Formerly Strange Suspense Stories No. 77)
V2#78, Dec, 1965 - V2#89, Dec, 1967 (Also see Space Adventures)
Charlton Comics

	GD25	FN65	NM94
78-Origin retold; Bache-a (3 pgs.)	8.00	25.00	58.00
79-82: 79-1st app. Dr. Spectro; 3 pg. Ditko cut & paste /Space Adventures #24. 82-Intro. Nightshade (9/66)	5.40	16.00	38.00
83-86: Ted Kord Blue Beetle in all. 83-(11/66)-1st app. Ted Kord. 84-1st app. new Captain Atom	4.70	14.00	33.00
87-89-Nightshade by Aparo in all	4.70	14.00	33.00
83-85(Modern Comics-1977)-reprints			1.00

NOTE: ***Aparo*** *a-87-89.* ***Ditko*** *c/a(p) 78-89. #90 only published in fanzine 'The Charlton Bullseye' #1, 2.*

CAPTAIN ATOM (Also see Americomics & Crisis On Infinite Earths)
March, 1987 - No. 57, Sept, 1991 (Direct sale only #35 on)
DC Comics

	GD25	FN65	NM94
1-(44 pgs.)-Origin/1st app. with new costume		.80	2.00
2-49: 5-Firestorm x-over. 6-Intro. new Dr. Spectro. 11-Millennium tie-in. 14-Nightshade app. 16-Justice League app. 17-$1.00-c begins; Swamp Thing app. 20-Blue Beetle x-over. 24,25-Invasion tie-in			1.20
50-($2.00, 52 pgs.)		.80	2.00
51-57: 57-War of the Gods x-over			1.00
Annual 1 (1988, $1.25)-Intro Major Force			1.50

Captain Canuck #4 © Comely

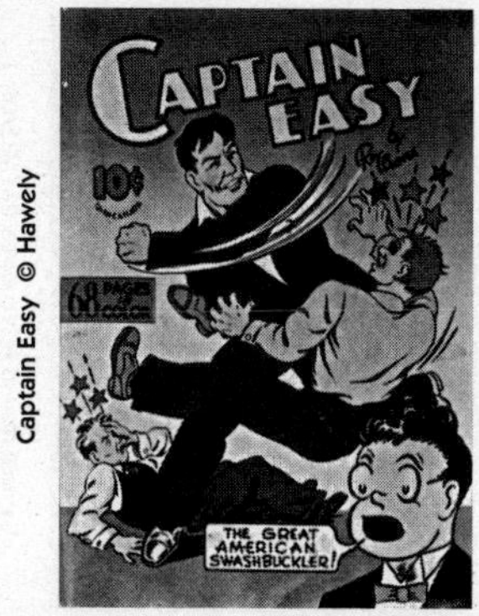

Captain Easy © Hawely

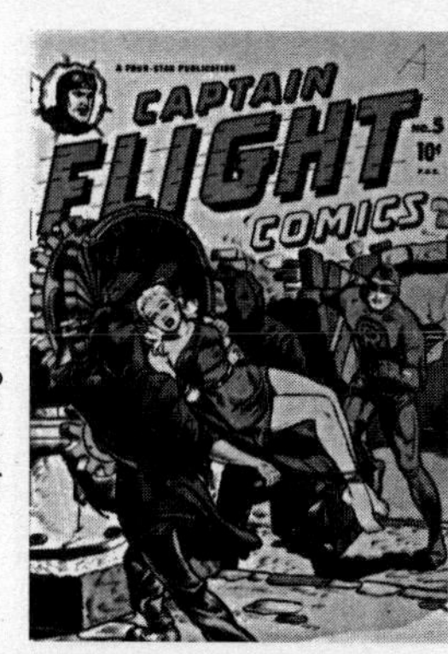

Captain Flight #5 © Four Star

GD25 FN65 NM94

Annual 2 (1988, $1.50) 1.50

CAPTAIN BATTLE (Boy Comics #3 on) (See Silver Streak Comics)
Summer, 1941 - No. 2, Fall, 1941
New Friday Publ./Comic House

1-Origin Blackout by Rico; Captain Battle begins (1st appeared in Silver Streak #10, 5/41) 86.00 257.00 600.00
2 57.00 171.00 400.00

CAPTAIN BATTLE (2nd Series)
No. 3, Wint, 1942-43 - No. 5, Sum, 1943 (#3: 52pgs., nd)(#5: 68pgs.)
Magazine Press/Picture Scoop No. 5

3-Origin Silver Streak-r/SS#3; origin Lance Hale-r/Silver Streak; Simon-a(r) 50.00 150.00 350.00
4,5: 5-Origin Blackout retold 37.00 111.00 260.00

CAPTAIN BATTLE, JR.
Fall, 1943 - No. 2, Winter, 1943-44
Comic House (Lev Gleason)

1-The Claw vs. The Ghost 71.00 215.00 500.00
2-Wolverton's Scoop Scuttle; Don Rico-c/a; The Green Claw story is reprinted from Silver Streak #6 57.00 171.00 400.00

CAPTAIN BRITAIN (Also see Marvel Team-Up No. 65, 66)
Oct. 13, 1976 - No. 39, July 6, 1977 (Weekly)
Marvel Comics International

1-Origin; with Capt. Britain's face mask inside 1.70 4.20 10.00
2-Origin, part II; Capt. Britain's Boomerang inside 1.00 2.50 6.00
3-8: 3,8-Vs. Bank Robbers. 4-7-Vs. Hurricane 1.60 4.00
9-15: 9-13-Vs. Dr. Synne. 14,15-Vs. Mastermind .80 2.00
16-20-With Capt. America; 17 misprinted & color section reprinted in #18 .70 1.80
21-23,25,26-With Capt. America .70 1.80
24-With C.B.'s Jet Plane inside 1.45 3.60
27,33-35: 27-Origin retold. 33-35-More on origin .70 1.80
28-32,36-39: 28-32-Vs. Lord Hawk. 36-Star Sceptre. 37-39-Vs. Highwayman & Munipulator 1.50
Annual (1978, Hardback, 64 pgs.)-Reprints #1-7 with pin-ups of Marvel characters 1.30 3.25 8.00
Summer Special (1980, 52 pgs.)-Reprints .80 2.00

NOTE: *No. 1, 2, & 24 are rarer in mint due to inserts. Distributed in Great Britain only. Nick Fury-r by* **Steranko** *in 1-20, 24-31, 35-37. Fantastic Four-r by* **J. Buscema** *in all. New* **Buscema**-*a in 24-30. Story from No. 39 continues in Super Spider-Man (British weekly) No. 231-247. Following cancellation of his series, new Captain Britain stories appeared in "Super Spider-Man" (British weekly) No. 231-247. Captain Britain stories which appear in Super-Spider-Man No 248-253 are reprints of Marvel Team-Up No. 65&66. Capt. Britain strips also appeared in Hulk Comic (weekly) 1, 3-30, 42-55, 57-60, in Marvel Superheroes (monthly) 377-388, in Daredevils (monthly) 1-11, Mighty World of Marvel (monthly) 7-16 & Captain Britain (monthly) 1-14. Issues 1-23 have B&W & color, paper-c, & are 32 pgs. Issues 24 on are all B&W w/glossy-c & are 36 pgs.*

CAPTAIN CANUCK
7/75 - No. 4, 7/77; No. 4, 7-8/79 - No. 14, 3-4/81
Comely Comix (Canada) (All distr. in U. S.)

1-1st app. Bluefox 1.00 2.50
2-1st app. Dr. Walker, Redcoat & Kebec .70 1.80
3(5-7/76)-1st app. Heather .70 1.80
4(1st printing-2/77)-10x14-1/2"; (5.00); B&W; 300 copies serially numbered and signed with one certificate of authenticity 2.15 6.50 15.00
4(2nd printing-7/77)-11x17", B&W; only 15 copies printed; signed by creator Richard Comely, serially #'d and two certificates of authenticity inserted; orange cardboard covers (Very Rare) 4.30 13.00 30.00
4-14: 4(7-8/79)-1st app. Tom Evans & Mr. Gold; origin The Catman. 5-Origin Capt. Canuck's powers; 1st app. Earth Patrol & Chaos Corps. 8-Jonn 'The Final Chapter'. 9-1st World Beyond. 11-1st 'Chariots of Fire' story 1.00
Summer Special 1(7-9/80, 95¢, 64 pgs.) 1.00

NOTE: *30,000 copies of No. 2 were destroyed in Winnipeg.*

CAPTAIN CANUCK (Semple Comics)(Value: cover or less)

CAPTAIN CARROT AND HIS AMAZING ZOO CREW (Also see New Teen Titans & Oz-Wonderland War)
March, 1982 - No. 20, Nov, 1983
DC Comics

1-20: 1-Superman app. 3-Re-intro Dodo & The Frog. 9-Re-intro Three Mouseketeers, the Terrific Whatzit. 10,11- Pig Iron reverts back to Peter Porkchops. 20-The Changeling app. 1.00

CAPTAIN CARVEL AND HIS CARVEL CRUSADERS (See Carvel Comics)

CAPTAIN CONFEDERACY
Nov, 1991 - No. 4, Feb, 1992 ($1.95)
Epic Comics (Marvel)

1-4: All new stories .80 2.00

CAPTAIN COURAGEOUS COMICS (Banner No. 3-5; see Four Favorites #5)
No. 6, March, 1942
Periodical House (Ace Magazines)

6-Origin & 1st app. The Sword; Lone Warrior, Capt. Courageous app.; Capt. moves to Four Favorites #5 in May 55.00 165.00 385.00

CAPT'N CRUNCH COMICS (See Cap'n...)

CAPTAIN DAVY JONES (See 4-Color No. 598)

CAPTAIN EASY (See The Funnies & Red Ryder #3-32)
1939 - No. 17, Sept, 1949; April, 1956
Hawley/Dell Publ./Standard(Visual Editions)/Argo

nn-Hawley(1939)-Contains reprints from The Funnies & 1938 Sunday strips by Roy Crane 79.00 235.00 550.00
4-Color 24 (1943) 43.00 129.00 300.00
4-Color 111(6/46) 14.00 43.00 100.00
10(Standard-10/47) 10.00 30.00 60.00
11-17: All contain 1930s & '40s strip-r 6.70 20.00 40.00
Argo 1(4/56)-Reprints 5.35 16.00 32.00

NOTE: ***Schomburg*** *c-13, 16.*

CAPTAIN EASY & WASH TUBBS (See Famous Comics Cartoon Books)

CAPTAIN ELECTRON (Brick Computer)(Value: cover or less)

CAPTAIN EO 3-D (Eclipse)(Value: cover or less) (Disney)

CAPTAIN FEARLESS COMICS (Also see Holyoke One-Shot #6, Old Glory Comics & Silver Streak #1)
August, 1941 - No. 2, Sept, 1941
Helnit Publishing Co. (Holyoke Publishing Co.)

1-Origin Mr. Miracle, Alias X, Captain Fearless, Citizen Smith Son of the Unknown Soldier; Miss Victory (1st app.) begins (1st patriotic heroine? before Wonder Woman) 55.00 165.00 385.00
2-Grit Grady, Captain Stone app. 34.00 103.00 240.00

CAPTAIN FLAG (See Blue Ribbon Comics #16)

CAPTAIN FLASH
Nov, 1954 - No. 4, July, 1955
Sterling Comics

1-Origin; Sekowsky-a; Tomboy (female super hero) begins; only pre-code issue; atomic rocket-c 22.00 65.00 150.00
2-4: 4-Flying saucer invasion-c 13.00 40.00 90.00

CAPTAIN FLEET (Action Packed Tales of the Sea)
Fall, 1952
Ziff-Davis Publishing Co.

1-Painted-c 10.00 30.00 70.00

CAPTAIN FLIGHT COMICS
Mar, 1944 - No. 10, Dec, 1945; No. 11, Feb-Mar, 1947
Four Star Publications

nn 20.00 60.00 140.00
2 11.00 32.00 75.00
3,4: 4-Rock Raymond begins, ends #7 10.00 30.00 70.00
5-Bondage, torture-c; Red Rocket begins; the Grenade app. 15.00 45.00 105.00

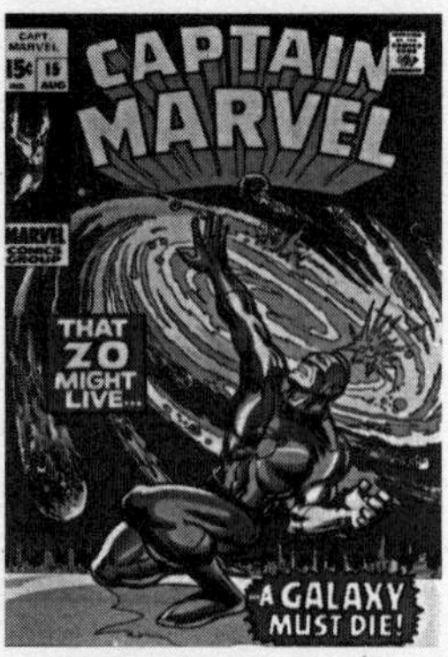

Captain Marvel #15 © MEG

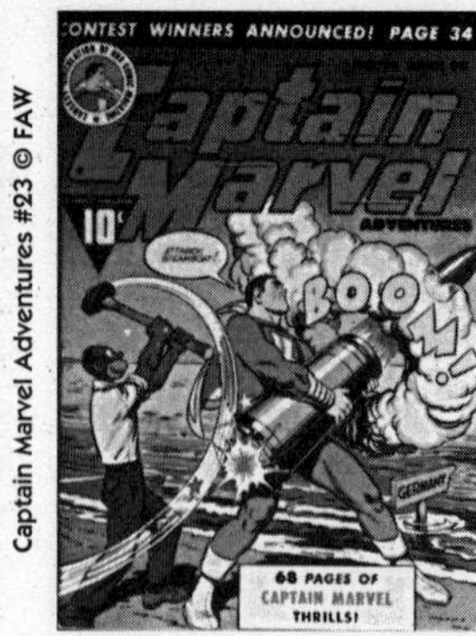

Captain Marvel Adventures #23 © FAW

Captain Marvel Adventures #67 © FAW

GD25 FN65 NM94

6,7: 7-L. B. Cole covers begin, end #11 10.00 30.00 70.00
8,9: 8-Yankee Girl begins; intro. Black Cobra & Cobra Kid & begins. 9-Torpedoman app.; last Yankee Girl; Kinstler-a 15.00 45.00 105.00
10-Deep Sea Dawson, Zoom of the Jungle, Rock Raymond, Red Rocket, & Black Cobra app; bondage-c 15.00 45.00 105.00
11-Torpedoman, Blue Flame (Human Torch clone) app.; last Black Cobra, Red Rocket; L. B. Cole-c 15.00 45.00 105.00

CAPTAIN FORTUNE PRESENTS
1955 - 1959 (16 pgs.; 3-1/4x6-7/8") (Giveaway)
Vital Publications

"Davy Crockett in Episodes of the Creek War", "Davy Crockett at the Alamo", "In Sherwood Forest Tells Strange Tales of Robin Hood" ('57), "Meets Bolivar the Liberator" ('59), "Tells How Buffalo Bill Fights the Dog Soldiers" ('57), "Young Davy Crockett" 1.80 4.50 9.00

CAPTAIN GALLANT (...of the Foreign Legion) (TV) (Texas Rangers in Action No. 5 on?)
1955; No. 2, Jan, 1956 - No. 4, Sept, 1956
Charlton Comics

Heinz Foods Premium (#1?)(1955; regular size)-U.S. Pictorial; contains Buster Crabbe photos; Don Heck-a 1.80 4.50 9.00
Non-Heinz version (same as above except pictures of show replaces ads) (#1)-Buster Crabbe photo on-c; full page Buster Crabbe photo inside front-c 9.15 27.50 55.00
2-4: Buster Crabbe in all 7.50 22.50 45.00

CAPTAIN GLORY
April, 1993 ($2.95) (Created by Jack Kirby)
Topps Comics

1-Polybagged w/Kirbychrome trading card; Ditko-a & Kirby-c; has coupon for Amberchrome Secret City Saga #0 1.20 3.00

CAPTAIN HERO (See Jughead as...)

CAPTAIN HERO COMICS DIGEST MAGAZINE
Sept, 1981
Archie Publications

1-Reprints of Jughead as Super-Guy 1.00

CAPTAIN HOBBY COMICS
Feb, 1948 (Canadian)
Export Publication Ent. Ltd. (Dist. in U.S. by Kable News Co.)

1 5.00 15.00 30.00

CAPT. HOLO IN 3-D (See Blackthorne 3-D Series #65)

CAPTAIN HOOK & PETER PAN (See 4-Color No. 446 and Peter Pan)

CAPTAIN JET (Fantastic Fears No. 7 on)
May, 1952 - No. 5, Jan, 1953
Four Star Publ./Farrell/Comic Media

1-Bakerish-a 11.00 32.00 75.00
2 8.35 25.00 50.00
3-5,6(?) 5.85 17.50 35.00

CAPTAIN JUSTICE
March, 1988 - No. 2, April, 1988
Marvel Comics

1,2-Based on TV series, True Colors 1.25

CAPTAIN KANGAROO (See 4-Color No. 721, 780, 872)

CAPTAIN KIDD (Formerly Dagar; My Secret Story #26 on)(Also see Comic Comics & Fantastic Comics)
No. 24, June, 1949 - No. 25, Aug, 1949
Fox Feature Syndicate

24,25: 24-Features Blackbeard the Pirate 10.00 30.00 70.00

CAPTAIN MARVEL (See All Hero, All-New Collectors' Ed., America's Greatest, Fawcett Miniature, Gift, Legends, Limited Collectors' Ed., Marvel Family, Master No. 21, Mighty Midget Comics, Shazam, Special Edition Comics, Whiz, Wisco, World's Finest #253 and XMas Comics)

GD25 FN65 NM94

CAPTAIN MARVEL (Becomes ...Presents the Terrible 5 No. 5)
April, 1966 - No. 4, Nov, 1966 (25¢ Giants)
M. F. Enterprises

nn-(#1 on pg. 5)-Origin; created by Carl Burgos 2.40 7.30 17.00
2-4: 3-(#3 on pg. 4)-Fights the Bat 1.50 3.80 9.00

CAPTAIN MARVEL (Marvel's Space-Born Super-Hero! Captain Marvel #1-6; see Giant-Size..., Life Of..., Marvel Graphic Novel #1, Marvel Spotlight V2#1 & Marvel Super-Heroes #12)
May, 1968 - No. 19, Dec, 1969; No. 20, June, 1970 - No. 21, Aug, 1970; No. 22, Sept, 1972 - No. 62, May, 1979
Marvel Comics Group

1 12.00 36.00 95.00
2-Super Skrull-c/story 4.60 11.00 32.00
3-5: 4-Captain Marvel battles Sub-Mariner 2.40 7.00 22.00
6-11: 11-Capt. Marvel given great power by Zo the Ruler; Smith/Trimpe-c; Death of Una 2.00 6.00 14.00
12-24: 14-Capt. Marvel vs. Iron Man; last 12¢ issue. 16,17-New costume. 21-Capt. Marvel battles Hulk; last 15¢ issue 1.00 3.00 9.00
25-Starlin-c/a begins; Starlin's 1st Thanos saga begins (3/73), ends #34; Thanos cameo (5 panels) 4.10 11.00 29.00
26-Minor Thanos app. (see Iron Man #55); 1st Thanos-c 4.00 13.00 31.00
27,28-1st & 2nd full app. Thanos. 28-Thanos-c/s 3.00 9.00 26.00
29,30-Thanos cameos. 29-C.M. gains more powers 1.00 4.00 10.00
31,32: Thanos app. 31-Last 20¢ issue. 32-Thanos-c 2.00 7.00 16.00
33-Thanos-c & app.; Capt. Marvel battles Thanos; 1st origin Thanos 4.00 11.00 31.00
34-1st app. Nitro; C.M. contracts cancer which eventually kills him; last Starlin-c/a 1.00 3.00 7.50
35,37-56,58-62: 39-Origin Watcher. 41,43-Wrightson part inks; #43-c(i). 49-Starlin & Weiss-p assists. 58-Thanos cameo .70 1.75
36-Reprints origin/1st app. Capt. Marvel from Marvel Super-Heroes #12; Starlin-a (3 pgs.) 1.00 2.00 5.00
57-Thanos appears in flashback 1.00 3.00 7.00

NOTE: ***Alcala*** *a-35.* ***Austin*** *a-46i, 49-53i; c-52i.* ***Buscema*** *a-18p-21p.* ***Colan*** *a(p)-1-4; c(p)-1-4, 8, 9.* ***Heck*** *a-5-10p, 16p.* ***Gil Kane*** *a-17-21p; c-17-24p, 37p, 53.* ***McWilliams*** *a-40i. #25-34 were reprinted in The Life of Captain Marvel.*

CAPTAIN MARVEL
Nov, 1989 ($1.50, one-shot, 52 pgs.)
Marvel Comics

1-Super-hero from Avengers; new powers 1.50

CAPTAIN MARVEL
Feb, 1994 ($1.75, 52 pgs.)
Marvel Comics

1-(Indicia says Vol 2 #2)-Minor Captain America app. .70 1.75

CAPTAIN MARVEL ADVENTURES (See Special Edition Comics for pre #1)
1941 (March) - No. 150, Nov, 1953 (#1 on stands 1/16/41)
Fawcett Publications

GD25 FN65 VF82 NM94

nn(#1)-Captain Marvel & Sivana by Jack Kirby. The cover was printed on unstable paper stock and is rarely found in Fine or Mint condition; blank back inside-c 1900.00 5700.00 12,300.00 19,000.00
(Estimated up to 140 total copies exist, 3 in NM/Mint)

GD25 FN65 NM94

2-(Advertised as #3, which was counting Special Edition Comics as the real #1); Tuska-a 314.00 943.00 2200.00
3-Metallic silver-c 200.00 600.00 1400.00
4-Three Lt. Marvels app. 121.00 365.00 850.00
5 93.00 279.00 650.00
6-10: 9-1st Otto Binder scripts on Capt. Marvel 71.00 215.00 500.00
11-15: 12-Capt. Marvel joins the Army. 13-Two pg. Capt. Marvel pin-up. 15-Comic cards on back-c begin, end #26 57.00 171.00 400.00
16,17: 17-Painted-c 52.00 156.00 365.00
18-Origin & 1st app. Mary Marvel & Marvel Family (12/11/42); painted-c; Mary Marvel by Marcus Swayze 93.00 280.00 650.00

Captain Marvel #42 © FAW

Captain Marvel Jr. #22 © FAW

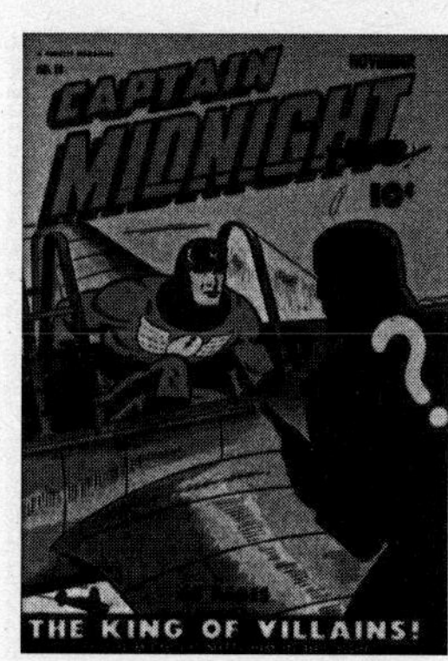

Captain Midnight #14 © The Wander Co.

GD25 FN65 NM94

19-Mary Marvel x-over; Christmas-c 49.00 138.00 340.00
20,21-Attached to the cover, each has a miniature comic just like the Mighty Midget Comics #11, except that each has a full color promo ad on the back cover. Most copies were circulated without the miniature comic. These issues with miniatures attached are very rare, and should not be mistaken for copies with the similar Mighty Midget glued in its place. The Mighty Midgets had blank back covers except for a small victory stamp seal. Only the Capt. Marvel and Captain Marvel Jr. No. 11 miniatures have been positively documented as having been affixed tothese covers. Each miniature was only partially glued by its back cover to the Captain Marvel comic making it easy to see if it's the genuine miniature rather than a Mighty Midget.
with comic attached.... 307.00 921.00 2150.00
20,21-Without miniature 45.00 135.00 315.00
22-Mr. Mind serial begins; 1st app. Mr. Mind 64.00 193.00 450.00
23-25 45.00 135.00 315.00
26-30: 26-Flag-c. 29-1st Mr. Mind-c & 1st app. (his voice was heard over the radio before now)(11/43) 36.00 107.00 250.00
31-35: 35-Origin Radar (5/44, see Master #50) 34.00 101.00 235.00
36-40: 37-Mary Marvel x-over 27.00 81.00 190.00
41-46: 42-Christmas-c. 43-Capt. Marvel 1st meets Uncle Marvel (1st app.); Mary Batson cameo. 46-Mr. Mind serial ends 24.00 72.00 165.00
47-50 21.00 63.00 145.00
51-53,55-60: 51-63-Bi-weekly issues. 52-Origin & 1st app. Sivana Jr.; Capt. Marvel Jr. x-over 17.00 52.00 120.00
54-Special oversize 68 pg. issue 19.00 57.00 130.00
61-The Cult of the Curse serial begins 22.00 67.00 155.00
62-66-Serial ends; Mary Marvel x-over in #65. 66-Atomic War-c 17.00 52.00 120.00
67-77,79: 69-Billy Batson's Christmas; Uncle Marvel, Mary Marvel, Capt. Marvel Jr. x-over. 71-Three Lt. Marvels app. 79-Origin Mr. Tawny 16.50 50.00 115.00
78-Origin Mr. Atom 19.00 57.00 130.00
80-Origin Capt. Marvel retold 33.00 100.00 230.00
81-84,86-90: 81,90-Mr. Atom app. 82-Infinity-c. 86-Mr. Tawny app. 15.00 45.00 105.00
85-Freedom Train issue 19.00 57.00 130.00
91-99: 96-Mr. Tawny app. 14.00 43.00 100.00
100-Origin retold 29.00 86.00 200.00
101-115,117-120 13.50 41.00 95.00
116-Flying Saucer issue (1/51) 15.00 45.00 105.00
121-Origin retold 19.00 57.00 130.00
122-137,139-149: 141-Pre-code horror story "The Hideous Head-Hunter". 142-used in **POP**, pgs. 92,96 13.50 41.00 95.00
138-Flying Saucer issue (11/52) 14.00 43.00 100.00
150-(Low distribution) 19.00 57.00 130.00
Bond Bread Giveaways-(24 pgs.; pocket size-7-1/4x3-1/2"; paper cover): "...& the Stolen City" ('48), "The Boy Who Never Heard of Capt. Marvel", "Meets the Weatherman" -(1950)(reprint) each.... 23.00 68.00 150.00
...Well Known Comics (1944; 12 pgs.; 8-1/2x10-1/2")-printed in red & in blue; soft-c; glued binding)-Bestmaid/Samuel Lowe Co. giveaway 16.00 48.00 100.00

NOTE: ***Swayze*** *a-12, 14, 15, 18, 19, 40; c-12, 15, 19.*

CAPTAIN MARVEL ADVENTURES
1945 (6x8") (Full color, paper cover)
Fawcett Publications (Wheaties Giveaway)

nn- "Captain Marvel & the Threads of Life" plus 2 other stories (32 pgs.) 50.00 150.00 350.00

NOTE: *All copies were taped at each corner to a box of Wheaties and are never found in Fine or Mint condition. Prices listed for each grade include tape.*

CAPTAIN MARVEL AND THE GOOD HUMOR MAN (Movie)
1950

Fawcett Publicationsnn-Partial photo-c w/Jack Carson & the Captain Marvel Club Boys 32.00 96.00 225.00

CAPTAIN MARVEL AND THE LTS. OF SAFETY
1950 - 1951 (3 issues - no No.'s)
Ebasco Services/Fawcett Publications

GD25 FN65 VF82

"Danger Flies a Kite" ('50, scarce), "Danger Takes to Climbing" ('50), "Danger Smashes Street Lights" ('51) 100.00 300.00 500.00

CAPTAIN MARVEL COMIC STORY PAINT BOOK (See Comic Story...)

CAPTAIN MARVEL, JR. (See Fawcett Miniatures, Marvel Family, Master Comics, Mighty Midget Comics, Shazam & Whiz Comics)

CAPTAIN MARVEL, JR.
Nov, 1942 - No. 119, June, 1953 (No #34)
Fawcett Publications

1-Origin Capt. Marvel Jr. retold (Whiz No. 25); Capt. Nazi app. 257.00 771.00 1800.00
2-Vs. Capt. Nazi; origin Capt. Nippon 114.00 343.00 800.00
3,4 71.00 214.00 500.00
5-Vs. Capt. Nazi 64.00 193.00 450.00
6-10: 8-Vs. Capt. Nazi. 9-Flag-c. 10-Hitler-c 52.00 156.00 365.00
11,12,15-Capt. Nazi app. 43.00 129.00 300.00
13,14,16-20: 13-Hitler-c. 14-X-Mas-c. 16-Capt. Marvel & Sivana x-over. 19-Capt. Nazi & Capt. Nippon app. 36.00 107.00 250.00
21-30: 25-Flag-c 26.00 80.00 185.00
31-33,36-40: 37-Infinity-c 17.00 52.00 120.00
35-#34 on inside; cover shows origin of Sivana Jr. which is not on inside. Evidently the cover to #35 was printed out of sequence and bound with contents to #34 17.00 52.00 120.00
41-70: 53-Atomic Bomb-c/story 13.00 40.00 90.00
71-99,101-104: 104-Used in **POP**, pg. 89 11.00 32.00 70.00
100 11.00 32.00 75.00
105-114,116-119: 116-Vampira, Queen of Terror app. 119-Electric chair-c 10.00 30.00 70.00
115-Injury to eye-c; Eyeball story w/injury-to-eye panels 12.00 36.00 85.00
...Well Known Comics (1944; 12 pgs.; 8-1/2x10-1/2")(Printed in blue; paper-c, glued binding)-Bestmaid/Samuel Lowe Co. giveaway 13.00 40.00 80.00

NOTE: ***Mac Raboy*** *c-1-10, 12-14, 16, 19, 21, 22, 25, 27, 28, 30-33, 57 among others.*

CAPTAIN MARVEL PRESENTS THE TERRIBLE FIVE
Aug, 1966; V2#5, Sept, 1967 (No #2-4) (25¢)
M. F. Enterprises

1 2.10 6.00 15.00
V2#5-(Formerly Captain Marvel) 1.40 3.50 8.50

CAPTAIN MARVEL'S FUN BOOK
1944 (1/2" thick) (cardboard covers)
Samuel Lowe Co.

nn-Puzzles, games, magic, etc.; infinity-c 25.00 75.00 175.00

CAPTAIN MARVEL SPECIAL EDITION (See Special Edition)

CAPTAIN MARVEL STORY BOOK
Summer, 1946 - No. 4, Summer?, 1948
Fawcett Publications

1-Half text 45.00 135.00 315.00
2-4 30.00 90.00 210.00

CAPTAIN MARVEL THRILL BOOK (Large-Size)
1941 (Black & White; color cover)
Fawcett Publications

GD25 FN65 VF82

1-Reprints from Whiz #8,10, & Special Edition #1 (Rare) 200.00 600.00 2000.00

NOTE: *Rarely found in Fine or Mint condition.*

CAPTAIN MIDNIGHT (Radio, films, TV) (See The Funnies & Popular Comics)
(Becomes Sweethearts No. 68 on)
Sept, 1942 - No. 67, Fall, 1948 (#1-14: 68 pgs.)
Fawcett Publications

GD25 FN65 NM94

1-Origin Captain Midnight; Captain Marvel cameo on cover 200.00 600.00 1400.00
2 93.00 280.00 650.00
3-5 64.00 193.00 450.00
6-10: 9-Raboy-c. 10-Raboy Flag-c 46.00 139.00 325.00

Captain Savage and His Leatherneck Raiders #4 © MEG

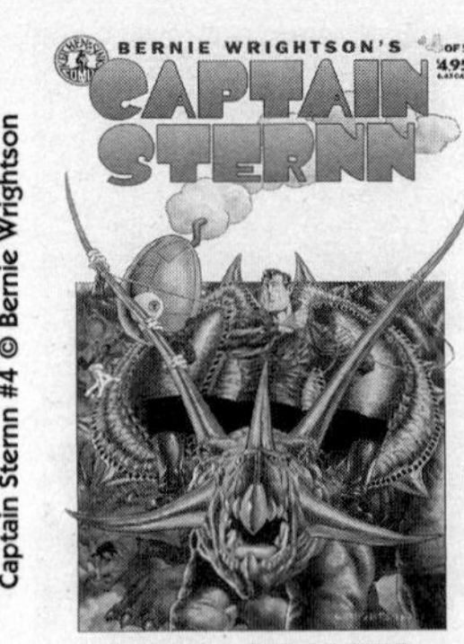

Captain Sternn #4 © Bernie Wrightson

Caravan Kidd #5 © DH

GD25 FN65 NM94

11-20: 11,17,18-Raboy-c 34.00 103.00 240.00
21-30 25.00 75.00 175.00
31-40 19.00 57.00 130.00
41-59,61-67: 50-Sci/fi theme begins? 15.00 45.00 105.00
60-Flying Saucer issue (2/48)-3rd of this theme; see Shadow Comics V7#10 & Boy Commandos #26 20.00 60.00 140.00

CAPTAIN NICE (TV)
Nov, 1967 (One Shot)
Gold Key
1(10211-711)-Photo-c 5.00 15.00 35.00

CAPTAIN N: THE GAME MASTER (TV)
1990 - No. 6? ($1.95, color, thick stock, coated-c)
Valiant Comics
1-6: 4-6-Layton-c .80 2.00

CAPTAIN PARAGON (Americomics)(Value: cover or less)

CAPTAIN PARAGON AND THE SENTINELS OF JUSTICE (AC)(Value: cover or less)

CAPTAIN PLANET AND THE PLANETEERS (TV)
Oct, 1991 - No. 12, Oct, 1992 ($1.00/$1.25, based on cartoon series)
Marvel Comics
1-12: 1-N. Adams painted-c. 3-Romita-c 1.25

CAPTAIN POWER AND THE SOLDIERS OF THE FUTURE (TV)(Continuity)(Value: cover or less)

CAPTAIN PUREHEART (See Archie as...)

CAPTAIN ROCKET
November, 1951
P. L. Publ. (Canada)
1 27.00 80.00 185.00

CAPT. SAVAGE AND HIS LEATHERNECK RAIDERS (...And His Battlefield Raiders #9 on)
Jan, 1968 - No. 19, Mar, 1970 (See Sgt. Fury No. 10)
Marvel Comics Group (Animated Timely Features)
1-Sgt. Fury & Howlers cameo 1.60 5.00 11.00
2-10: 2-Origin Hydra. 1-5,7-Ayers/Shores-a. 7-Pre-"Thing" Ben Grimm story 1.10 2.70 6.50
11-19 .90 2.30 5.50

CAPTAIN SCIENCE (Fantastic No. 8 on)
Nov, 1950 - No. 7, Dec, 1951
Youthful Magazines
1-Wood-a; origin 57.00 171.00 400.00
2 29.00 86.00 200.00
3,6,7; 3,6-Bondage c-swipes/Wings #94,91 26.00 77.00 180.00
4,5-Wood/Orlando-c/a(2) each 57.00 171.00 400.00
NOTE: *Fass a-4. Bondage c-3, 6, 7.*

CAPTAIN SILVER'S LOG OF SEA HOUND (See Sea Hound)

CAPTAIN SINDBAD (Movie Adaptation) (See Fantastic Voyages of... & Movie Comics)

CAPTAIN STERNN: RUNNING OUT OF TIME
Sept, 1993 - No. 5, 1994 ($4.95, color, mini-series, coated stock, 52 pgs.)
Kitchen Sink Press
1-5-Bernie Wrightson-c/a/scripts 1.00 2.00 5.00
1-Gold ink variant 2.10 6.00 15.00

CAPTAIN STEVE SAVAGE (...& His Jet Fighters, No. 2-13)
1950 - No. 8, 1/53; No. 5, 9-10/54 - No. 13, 5-6/56
Avon Periodicals
nn(1st series)-Wood art, 22 pgs. (titled "...Over Korea") 30.00 90.00 210.00
1(4/51)-Reprints nn issue (Canadian) 13.00 40.00 90.00
2-Kamen-a 8.65 26.00 52.00
3-11 (#6, 9-10/54, last precode) 5.00 15.00 30.00

GD25 FN65 NM94

12-Wood-a (6 pgs.) 9.65 29.00 58.00
13-Check, Lawrence-a 6.35 19.00 38.00
NOTE: ***Kinstler** c-2-5, 7-9, 11. **Lawrence** a-8. **Ravielli** a-5, 9.*
5(9-10/54-2nd series)(Formerly Sensational Police Cases) 5.35 16.00 32.00
6-Reprints nn issue; Wood-a 8.00 24.00 48.00
7-13: 9,10-Kinstler-c. 10-r/cover #2 (1st series). 13-r/cover #8 (1st series) 4.00 10.00 20.00

CAPTAIN STONE (See Holyoke One-Shot No. 10)

CAPT. STORM (Also see G. I. Combat #138)
May-June, 1964 - No. 18, Mar-Apr, 1967 (Grey tone c-8)
National Periodical Publications
1-Origin 2.90 8.60 20.00
2-18: 3,6,13-Kubert-a. 4-Colan-a. 12-Kubert-c 1.60 5.00 11.00

CAPTAIN 3-D (Super hero)
December, 1953 (25¢, came with 2 pair of glasses)
Harvey Publications
1-Kirby/Ditko-a (Ditko's 2nd work, see Black Magic & Fantastic Fears); shows cover in 3-D on inside; Kirby/Meskin-c 8.35 25.00 50.00

CAPTAIN THUNDER AND BLUE BOLT (Hero)(Value: cover or less)

CAPTAIN TOOTSIE & THE SECRET LEGION (Advs. of...)(Also see Monte Hale #30, 39 & Real Western Hero)
Oct, 1950 - No. 2, Dec, 1950
Toby Press
1-Not Beck-a; both have sci/fi covers 19.00 57.00 130.00
2-The Rocketeer Patrol app.; not Beck-a 12.00 36.00 85.00

CAPTAIN TRIUMPH (See Crack Comics #27)

CAPTAIN VENTURE & THE LAND BENEATH THE SEA
Oct, 1968 - No. 2, Oct, 1969 (See Space Family Robinson)
Gold Key
1,2: 1-r/Space Family Robinson serial; Spiegle-a in both 4.70 14.00 28.00

CAPTAIN VICTORY AND THE GALACTIC RANGERS (Pacific)(Value: cover or less)

CAPTAIN VIDEO (TV) (See XMas Comics)
Feb, 1951 - No. 6, Dec, 1951 (No. 1,5,6-36pgs.; 2-4, 52pgs.)
Fawcett Publications
1-George Evans-a(2) 61.00 182.00 425.00
2-Used in **SOTI**, pg. 382 46.00 139.00 325.00
3-6-All Evans-a except #5 mostly Evans 39.00 118.00 275.00
NOTE: *Minor **Williamson** assists on most issues. Photo c-1, 5, 6; painted c-2-4.*

CAPTAIN WILLIE SCHULTZ (Also see Fightin' Army)
No. 76, Oct, 1985 - No. 77, Jan, 1986
Charlton Comics
76,77 1.00

CAPTAIN WIZARD COMICS (See Meteor, Red Band & Three Ring Comics)
1946
Rural Home
1-Capt. Wizard dons new costume; Impossible Man, Race Wilkins app. 17.00 52.00 120.00

CARAVAN KIDD (Dark Horse)(Value: cover or less)

CARDINAL MINDSZENTY (The Truth Behind the Trial of...)
1949 (24 pgs.; paper cover, in color)
Catechetical Guild Education Society
nn-Anti-communism 5.85 17.50 35.00
Press Proof-(Very Rare)-(Full color, 7-1/2x11-3/4", untrimmed) Only two known copies 150.00
Preview Copy (B&W, stapled), 18 pgs.; contains first 13 pgs. of Cardinal Mindszenty and was sent out as an advance promotion. Only one known copy 150.00 - 200.00

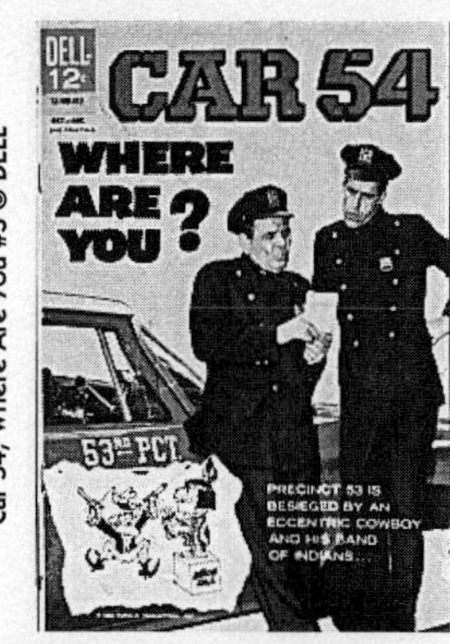

Car 54, Where Are You #3 © DELL

The Carneys #1 © AP

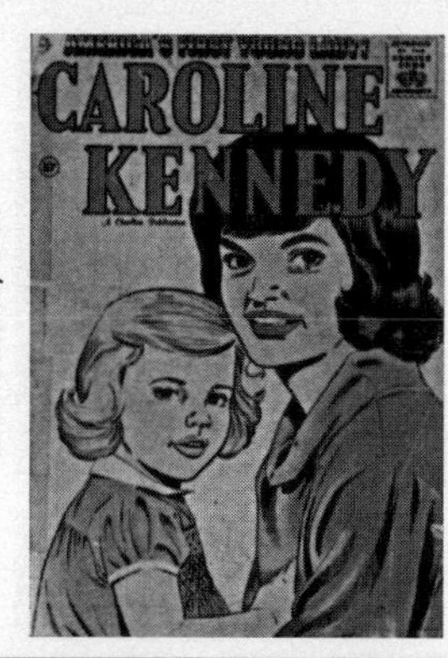

Caroline Kenndy © CC

GD25 FN65 NM94 | GD25 FN65 NM94

NOTE: *Regular edition also printed in French. There was also a movie released in 1949 called "Guilty of Treason" which is a fact-based account of the trial and imprisonment of Cardinal Mindszenty by the Communist regime in Hungary.*

CARE BEARS (TV, Movie)(See Star Comics Magazine)
Nov, 1985 - No. 20, Jan, 1989 ($1.00 #11 on)
Star Comics/Marvel Comics No. 15 on

1-20: Post-a begins 1.00

CAREER GIRL ROMANCES (Formerly Three Nurses)
June, 1964 - No. 78, Dec, 1973
Charlton Comics

V4#24-31,33-50 .80 2.00 4.00
32-Elvis Presley, Hermans Hermits, Johnny Rivers line drawn-c 8.35 25.00 50.00
51-78 .40 1.00 2.00

CAR 54, WHERE ARE YOU? (TV)
Mar-May, 1962 - No. 7, Sept-Nov, 1963; 1964 - 1965 (All photo-c)
Dell Publishing Co.

4-Color 1257(#1, 3-5/62) 8.35 25.00 50.00
2(6-8/62)-7 4.70 14.00 28.00
2,3(10-12/64), 4(1-3/65)-Reprints #2,3,&4 of 1st series 4.00 10.00 20.00

CARL BARKS LIBRARY OF WALT DISNEY'S GYRO GEARLOOSE COMICS AND FILLERS IN COLOR, THE
1993 ($7.95, 52 pgs., 8-1/2x11")(mini-series)
Gladstone

1-6-Carl Barks reprints 1.30 3.25 8.00

CARL BARKS LIBRARY OF WALT DISNEY'S COMICS AND STORIES IN COLOR, THE
Jan, 1992 - Present ($8.95, 60 pgs., 8-1/2x11")(51 ish. series)
Gladstone

1-36: 1-Barks Donald Duck-r/WDC&S #31-35; 2-r/#36,38-41; 3-r/#47-51; 4-r/#47-51; 5-r/#52-56; 6-r/#57-61; 7-r/#62-66; 8-r/#67-71; 9-r/#72-76; 10-r/#77-81; 11-r/#82-86; 12-r/#87-91; 13-r/#92-96; 14-r/#97-101; 15-r/#102-106; 16-r/#107-111; 17-r/#112,114,117,124,125; 18-r/#126-130; 19-r/#131,132(2),133,134; 20-r/#135-139; 21-r/#140-144; 22-r/#145-149; 23-r/#150-154; 24-r/#155-159; 25-r/#160-164; 26-r/#165-169; 27-r/#170-174; 28-r/#175-179; 29-r/#180-184; 30-r/#185-189; 31-r/#190-194; 32-r/#195-199; 33-r/#200-204; 34-r/#205-209; 35-r/#210-214; 36-r/#215-219
All contain one Heroes & Villains tradingcard ea. 1.50 3.75 9.00

CARL BARKS LIBRARY OF WALT DISNEY'S DONALD DUCK ADVENTURES IN COLOR, THE
1994 - Present ($7.95/$9.95, 44-68pgs., 8-1/2"x11")(29 issue series)
(all contain one Donald Duck trading card each)
Gladstone

1-15-Carl Barks-r: 1-r/FC #9; 2-r/FC #29; 3-r/FC #62; 4-r/FC #108; 5-r/FC #147 & #79(Mickey Mouse); 6-r/MOC #4, Cheerios "Atom Bomb," D.D. Tells About Kites; 7-r/FC #159. 8-r/FC #178 & 189. 9-r/FC #199 & 203; 10-r/FC 223 & 238; 11-r/Christmas Parade #1 & 2; 12-r/FC #296; 13-r/FC #263; 14-r/MOC #20 & 41; 15-r/FC 275 & 282 1.70 4.20 10.00

CARL BARKS LIBRARY OF WALT DISNEY'S DONALD DUCK CHRISTMAS STORIES IN COLOR, THE
1992 ($7.95, 44pgs.)(one shot)
Gladstone

nn-Reprints Firestone giveaways 1945-1949 1.30 3.25 8.00

CARL BARKS LIBRARY OF WALT DISNEY'S UNCLE SCROOGE COMICS ONE PAGERS IN COLOR, THE
1992 - No. 2, 1993 ($8.95, 60 pgs., 8-1/2x11")(2-part mini-series)
Gladstone

1,2-Carl Barks one pg. reprints 1.50 3.75 9.00

CARNATION MALTED MILK GIVEAWAYS (See Wisco)

CARNEYS, THE
Summer, 1994-Present ($2.00, 52 pgs.)(Published annually)
Archie Comics

1-Bound-in pull-out poster .80 2.00

CARNIVAL COMICS (Formerly Kayo #12; becomes Red Seal Comics #14)
1945
Harry 'A' Chesler/Pershing Square Publ. Co.

nn (#13)-Guardineer-a 10.00 30.00 70.00

CARNIVAL OF COMICS
1954 (Giveaway)
Fleet-Air Shoes

nn-Contains a comic bound with new cover; several combinations possible; Charlton's Eh! known 2.00 5.00 10.00

CAROLINE KENNEDY
1961 (One Shot)
Charlton Comics

nn 10.00 30.00 60.00

CAROUSEL COMICS
V1#8, April, 1948
F. E. Howard, Toronto

V1#8 4.70 14.00 28.00

CARTOON KIDS
1957 (no month)
Atlas Comics (CPS)

1-Maneely-c/a; Dexter The Demon, Willie The Wise-Guy, Little Zelda app. 5.85 17.50 35.00

CARTOON TALES (Disney's...)
No date (1992) ($2.95, 6-5/8x9-1/2", 52 pgs.)
W.D. Publications (Disney)

nn-Ariel & Sebastian - Serpent Teen 1.20 3.00
nn-Beauty and the Beast - A Tale of Enchantment 1.20 3.00
nn-Darkwing Duck - Just Us Justice Ducks 1.20 3.00
nn-101 Dalmations - Canine Classics 1.20 3.00
nn-Tale Spin - Surprise in the Skies 1.20 3.00
nn-Uncle Scrooge - Blast to the Past 1.20 3.00

CARVEL COMICS (Amazing Advs. of Capt. Carvel)
1975 - No. 5, 1976 (25¢; #3-5: 35¢) (#4,5: 3-1/4x5")
Carvel Corp. (Ice Cream)

1-3 1.00
4,5(1976)-Baseball theme 1.00 2.50 6.00

CAR WARRIORS
June, 1991 - No. 4, Sept, 1991 ($2.25, mini-series)
Epic Comics (Marvel)

1-4: 1-Says April in indicia .90 2.25

CASE OF THE SHOPLIFTER'S SHOE (Perry Mason) (See Feature Book No.50)

CASE OF THE WASTED WATER, THE
1972? (Giveaway)
Rheem Water Heating

nn-Neal Adams-a 4.20 12.50 25.00

CASE OF THE WINKING BUDDHA, THE
1950 (132 pgs.; 25¢; B&W; 5-1/2x7-5-1/2x8")
St. John Publ. Co.

nn-Charles Raab-a; reprinted in Authentic Police Cases No. 25 17.00 52.00 120.00

CASEY-CRIME PHOTOGRAPHER (Two-Gun Western No. 5 on)
Aug, 1949 - No. 4, Feb, 1950 (Radio)
Marvel Comics (BFP)

1-Photo-c; 52 pgs. 11.50 34.00 80.00
2-4: Photo-c 9.15 27.50 55.00

Casper And Friends #1

Casper Cat #1 © I.W.

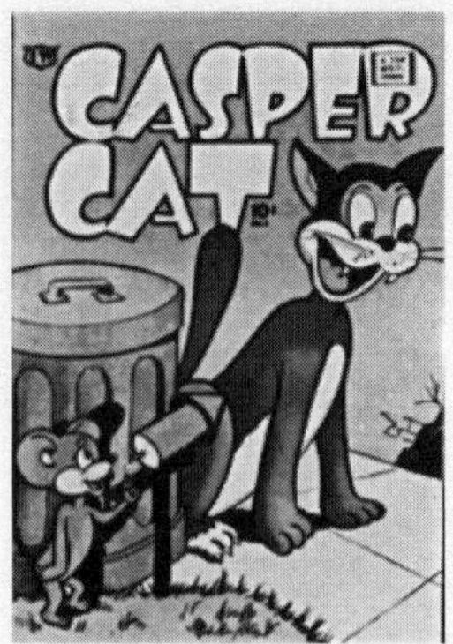

Casper The Friendly Ghost #3 © Paramount

GD25 FN65 NM94

CASEY JONES (See 4-Color No. 915)

CASPER ADVENTURE DIGEST
Oct, 1992 - Present ($1.75, digest-size)
Harvey Comics

V2#1,2-Casper, Richie Rich, Spooky, Wendy .70 1.75

CASPER AND...
Nov, 1987 - No. 12, June, 1990 (.75/$1.00, all reprints)
Harvey Comics

1-12: 1-Ghostly Trio. 2-Spooky; begin $1.00-c. 3-Wendy. 4-Nightmare. 5-Ghostly Trio. 6-Spooky. 7-Wendy. 8-Hot Stuff. 9-Baby Huey. 10-Wendy. 11-Ghostly Trio. 12-Spooky 1.00

CASPER AND FRIENDS
Oct, 1991 - No. 5, July, 1992 (#1,2: $1.00/#3-5: $1.25)
Harvey Comics

1-5: Nightmare, Ghostly Trio, Wendy, Spooky 1.25

CASPER AND NIGHTMARE (See Harvey Hits# 37, 45, 52, 56, 59, 62, 65, 68,71, 75)

CASPER AND NIGHTMARE (Nightmare & Casper No. 1-5)
No. 6, 11/64 - No. 44, 10/73; No. 45, 6/74 - No. 46, 8/74 (25¢)
Harvey Publications

	GD25	FN65	NM94
6: 68 pg. Giants begin, ends #32	4.00	10.00	20.00
7-10	2.00	5.00	10.00
11-20	1.00	2.50	6.00
21-46: 33-37-(52 pg. Giants)		1.60	4.00

NOTE: *Many issues contain reprints.*

CASPER AND SPOOKY (See Harvey Hits No. 20)
Oct, 1972 - No. 7, Oct, 1973
Harvey Publications

	GD25	FN65	NM94
1	1.20	3.00	7.00
2-7		1.40	3.50

CASPER AND THE GHOSTLY TRIO
Nov, 1972 - No. 7, Nov, 1973; No. 8, Aug, 1990 - No. 10, Dec, 1990
Harvey Publications

	GD25	FN65	NM94
1	1.20	3.00	7.00
2-7		1.40	3.50
8-10			1.00

CASPER AND WENDY
Sept, 1972 - No. 8, Nov, 1973
Harvey Publications

	GD25	FN65	NM94
1: 52 pg. Giant	1.20	3.00	7.00
2-8		1.40	3.50

CASPER CAT (See Dopey Duck)
1958; 1963
I. W. Enterprises/Super

1,7-Reprint, Super No. 14('63) 1.00 2.50 5.00

CASPER DIGEST (...Magazine #?; ...Halloween Digest #8, 10)
Oct, 1986 - No. 20? ($1.25/$1.75, digest-size)
Harvey Publications

1-20: 11-Valentine-c. 18-Halloween-c 1.50

CASPER DIGEST (...Magazine #? on)
Sept, 1991 - No. 14, Nov, 1994 ($1.75, digest-size)
Harvey Comics

1-14 .70 1.75

CASPER DIGEST STORIES
Feb, 1980 - No. 4, Nov, 1980 (95¢; 132 pgs.; digest size)
Harvey Publications

	GD25	FN65	NM94
1		1.20	3.00
2-4		.80	2.00

CASPER DIGEST WINNERS
April, 1980 - No. 3, Sept, 1980 (95¢; 132 pgs.; digest size)
Harvey Publications

	GD25	FN65	NM94
1		.80	2.00
2,3			1.50

CASPER ENCHANTED TALES DIGEST
May, 1992 - No. 10, Oct, 1994 ($1.75, digest-size, 98 pgs.)
Harvey Comics

1-10-Casper, Spooky, Wendy stories .70 1.75

CASPER GHOSTLAND
May, 1992 ($1.25)
Harvey Comics

1 1.25

CASPER GIANT SIZE
Oct, 1992 - No. 4, Nov, 1993 ($2.25, 68 pgs.)
Harvey Comics

V2#1-4-Casper, Wendy, Spooky stories .90 2.25

CASPER HALLOWEEN TRICK OR TREAT
January, 1976 (52 pgs.)
Harvey Publications

1 1.20 3.00

CASPER IN SPACE (Formerly Casper Spaceship)
No. 6, June, 1973 - No. 8, Oct, 1973
Harvey Publications

6-8 1.40 3.50

CASPER'S GHOSTLAND
Winter, 1958-59 - No. 97, 12/77; No. 98, 12/79 (25¢)
Harvey Publications

	GD25	FN65	NM94
1: 68 pgs. begin, ends #61	14.00	43.00	100.00
2	8.35	25.00	50.00
3-10	5.00	15.00	30.00
11-20: 13-X-Mas-c	4.00	10.00	20.00
21-40	3.20	8.00	16.00
41-61: 61-Last 68 pg. issue	1.70	4.20	10.00
62-77: All 52 pgs.	1.00	2.50	5.50
78-98: 94-X-Mas-c		1.60	4.00

NOTE: *Most issues contain reprints.*

CASPER SPACESHIP (Casper in Space No. 6 on)
Aug, 1972 - No. 5, April, 1973
Harvey Publications

	GD25	FN65	NM94
1: 52 pg. Giant	1.30	3.25	8.00
2-5		1.40	3.50

CASPER SPECIAL
nd (Dec, 1990) (Giveaway with $1.00 cover)
Target Stores (Harvey)

Three issues-Given away with Casper video 1.00

CASPER STRANGE GHOST STORIES
October, 1974 - No. 14, Jan, 1977 (All 52 pgs.)
Harvey Publications

	GD25	FN65	NM94
1	1.00	2.50	6.00
2-14		1.00	2.50

CASPER, THE FRIENDLY GHOST (See America's Best TV Comics, Famous TV Funday Funnies, The Friendly Ghost..., Nightmare &..., Richie Rich and..., Tastee-Freez, Treasury of Comics, Wendy the Good Little Witch & Wendy Witch World)

CASPER, THE FRIENDLY GHOST (Becomes Harvey Comics Hits No. 61 (No. 6), and then continued with Harvey issue No. 7)
Sept, 1949 - No. 5, Aug, 1951
St. John Publishing Co.

1(1949)-Origin & 1st app. Baby Huey & Herman the Mouse (1st time the name Casper app. in any media, even films) 79.00 236.00 550.00

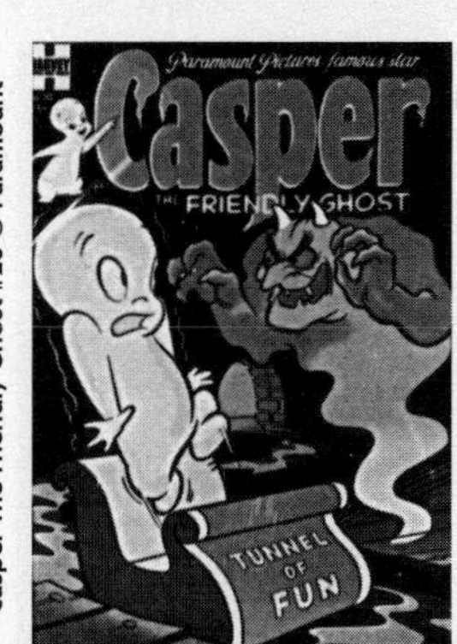

Casper The Friendly Ghost #20 © Paramount

The Cat #1 © MEG

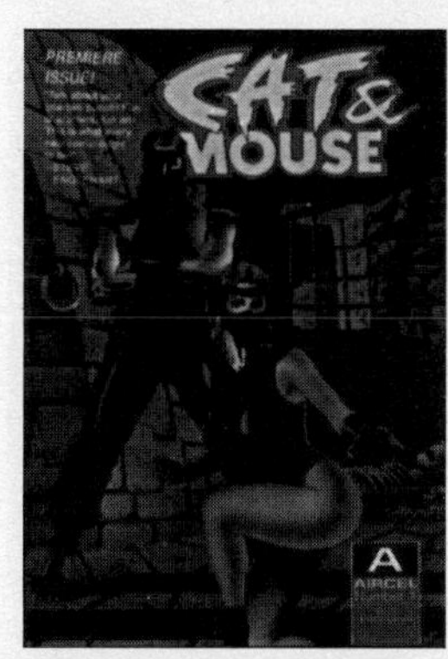

Cat & Mouse #1 © EF Graphics

GD25 FN65 NM94

2,3 (2/50 & 8/50) 46.00 137.00 320.00
4,5 (3/51 & 8/51) 36.00 107.00 250.00

CASPER, THE FRIENDLY GHOST (Paramount Picture Star...)
No. 7, Dec, 1952 - No. 70, July, 1958
Harvey Publications (Family Comics)
Note: No. 6 is Harvey Comics Hits No. 61 (10/52)

7-Baby Huey begins, ends #9 27.00 81.00 190.00
8,9 13.50 41.00 95.00
10-Spooky begins (1st app., 6/53), ends #70? 16.50 50.00 115.00
11-18: Alfred Harvey app. in story 9.15 27.50 55.00
19-1st app. Nightmare (4/54) 11.00 32.00 75.00
20-Wendy the Witch begins (1st app., 5/54) 14.00 43.00 100.00
21-30: 24-Infinity-c 7.50 22.50 45.00
31-40 5.35 16.00 32.00
41-50 4.35 13.00 26.00
51-70 (Continues as Friendly Ghost... 8/58) 4.00 10.00 20.00
American Dental Association (Giveaways):
...'s Dental Health Activity Book-1977 1.20 3.00
...Presents Space Age Dentistry-1972 1.40 3.50
..., His Den, & Their Dentist Fight the Tooth Demons-1974 1.40 3.50

CASPER THE FRIENDLY GHOST (Formerly The Friendly Ghost...)
No. 254, July, 1990 - No. 260, Jan, 1991 ($1.00)
Harvey Comics

254-260 1.00

CASPER THE FRIENDLY GHOST
Mar, 1991 - No. 28, Nov, 1994 ($1.00/$1.25/$1.50)
Harvey Comics

1-14: 1-Casper becomes Mighty Ghost; Spooky & Wendy app. 7,8-Post-a. 7-14-($1.25) 1.25
15-28-($1.50) 1.50

CASPER BIG BOOK
V2#1, Aug, 1992 - No. 3, May, 1993 ($1.95, 52 pgs.)
Harvey Comics

V2#1-3: 1-Spooky app. .80 2.00

CASPER T.V. SHOWTIME
Jan, 1980 - No. 5, Oct, 1980
Harvey Comics

1 .80 2.00
2-5 1.00

CASSETTE BOOKS
(Classics Illustrated)
1984 (48 pgs, b&w comic with cassette tape)
Cassette Book Co./I.P.S. Publ.

NOTE: *This series was illegal. The artwork was illegally obtained, and the Classics Illustrated copyright owner, Twin Circle Publ. sued to get an injunction to prevent the continued sale of this series. Many C.I. collectors obtained copies before the 1987 injunction, but now they are already scarce. Here again the market is just developing, but sealed mint copies of com ic and tape should be worth at least $25.*

1001 (CI#1-A2)New-PC 1002(CI#3-A2)CI-PC 1003(CI#13-A2)CI-PC 1004(CI#25)CI-LDC 1005(CI#10-A2)New-PC 1006(CI#64)CI-LDC

CASTILIAN (See Movie Classics)

CAT, T.H.E. (TV) (See T.H.E. Cat)

CAT, THE (See Movie Classics)

CAT, THE
Nov, 1972 - No. 4, June, 1973
Marvel Comics Group

1-Origin & 1st app. The Cat (who later becomes Tigra); Mooney-a(i); Wood-c(i)/a(i) 1.90 6.00 13.00
2,3: 2-Marie Severin/Mooney-a. 3-Everett inks 1.40 3.50 8.50
4-Starlin/Weiss-a(p) 1.40 3.50 8.50

GD25 FN65 NM94

CATALYST: AGENTS OF CHANGE (Also see Comics' Greatest World)
Feb, 1994 - Present ($2.00)
Dark Horse Comics

1-9: 1-Foil stamped logo .80 2.00

CAT & MOUSE
Dec, 1988 ($1.75, color w/part B&W)
EF Graphics (Silverline)

1-1st printing (12/88, 32 pgs.) .70 1.75
1-2nd printing (5/89, 36 pgs.) .70 1.75

CAT FROM OUTER SPACE (See Walt Disney Showcase #46)

CATHOLIC COMICS (See Heroes All Catholic...)
June, 1946 - V3#10, July, 1949
Catholic Publications

1 17.00 52.00 120.00
2 10.00 30.00 60.00
3-13(7/47) 7.50 22.50 45.00
V2#1-10 4.20 12.50 25.00
V3#1-10: Reprints 10-part Treasure Island serial from Target V2#2-11 (see Key Comics #5) 5.00 15.00 30.00

CATHOLIC PICTORIAL
1947
Catholic Guild

1-Toth-a(2) (Rare) 25.00 75.00 175.00

CATMAN COMICS (Formerly Crash Comics No. 1-5)
5/41 - No. 17, 1/43; No. 18, 7/43 - No. 22, 12/43; No. 23, 3/44 - No. 26, 11/44; No. 27, 4/45 - No. 30, 12/45; No. 31, 6/46 - No. 32, 8/46
Holyoke Publishing Co./Continental Magazines V2#12, 7/44 on

1(V1#6)-Origin The Deacon & Sidekick Mickey, Dr. Diamond & Rag-Man; The Black Widow app.; The Catman by Chas. Quinlan & Blaze Baylor begin 143.00 430.00 1000.00
2(V1#7) 57.00 171.00 400.00
3(V1#8), 4(V1#9): 3-The Pied Piper begins 41.00 122.00 285.00
5(V2#10)-Origin Kitten; The Hood begins (c-redated), 6,7(V2#11,12) 34.00 100.00 235.00
8(V2#13,3/42)-Origin Little Leaders; Volton by Kubert begins (his 1st comic book work) 45.00 135.00 315.00
9,10(V2#14,15): 10-Origin Blackout retold; Phantom Falcon begins 30.00 90.00 210.00
11(V3#1)-Kubert-a 30.00 90.00 210.00
12(V3#2) - 15, 17, 18(V3#8, 7/43) 23.00 70.00 160.00
16 (V3#5)-Hitler, Tojo, Mussolini, Stalin-c 27.00 81.00 190.00
19 (V2#6)-Hitler, Tojo, Mussolini-c 27.00 81.00 190.00
20(V2#7) - 23(V2#10, 3/44): 20-Hitler-c 23.00 70.00 160.00
nn(V3#13, 5/44)-Rico-a; Schomburg bondage-c 20.00 60.00 140.00
nn(V2#12, 7/44) 20.00 60.00 140.00
nn(V3#1, 9/44)-Origin The Golden Archer; Leatherface app. 20.00 60.00 140.00
nn(V3#2, 11/44)-L. B. Cole-c 27.00 81.00 190.00
27-Origin Kitten retold; L. B. Cole Flag-c 30.00 90.00 210.00
28-Catman learns Kitten's I.D.; Dr. Macabre, Deacon app.; L. B. Cole c/a 31.00 92.00 215.00
29-32-L. B. Cole-c; bondage-#30 27.00 810.00 190.00

NOTE: ***Fuje** a-11, 29(3), 30. **Palais** a-11, 29(2), 30(2), 32; c-25(7/44). **Rico** a-11(2).*

CAT TALES (3-D)
April, 1989 ($2.95)
Eternity Comics

1-Felix the Cat-r in 3-D 1.20 3.00

CATWOMAN (Also see Action Comics Weekly #611, Batman #1, Detective Comics, Showcase 93 & Superman's Girlfriend Lois Lane #70, 71)
Feb, 1989 - No. 4, May, 1989 ($1.50, mini-series, mature readers)
DC Comics

1 1.00 2.50 6.00

Catwoman #13 © DC

Cave Girl #1 © AC

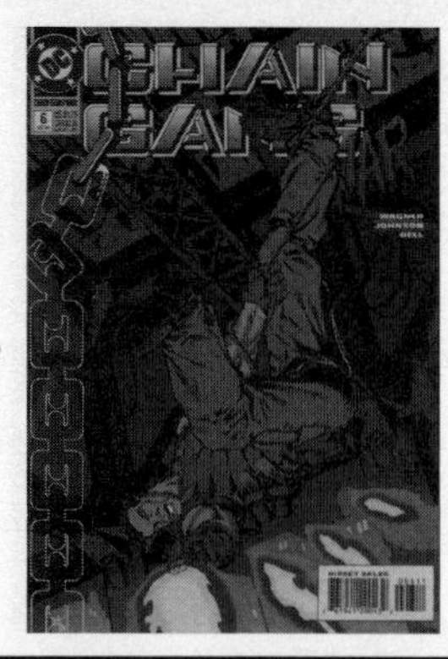
Chain Gang War #6 © DC

GD25 FN65 NM94

2 — 1.40 3.50
3,4: 3-Batman cameo. 4-Batman app. — 1.00 2.50
...: Her Sister's Keeper (1991, $9.95)-r/#1-4 — 1.65 4.00 10.00

CATWOMAN
Aug, 1993 - Present ($1.50)
DC Comics

1-($1.95)-Embossed-c; Bane app.; Balent c-1-10; a-1-10p — 1.30 3.25
2-14: 3-Bane flashback cameo. 4-Brief Bane app. 6,7-Knightquest tie-ins; new Batman (Azrael) app. 8-1st app. Zephyr. 12-KnightsEnd Pt. 6. 13-KnightsEnd Aftermath. 14-(9/94)-Zero Hour — 1.50
0,15-20: 0-(10/94)-Origin retold — 1.50
Annual 1 (1994, $2.95, 68 pgs.)-Elseworlds story; Batman app.; no Balent-a — 1.20 3.00

CAUGHT
Aug, 1956 - No. 5, April, 1957
Atlas Comics (VPI)

1 — 11.50 34.00 80.00
2,4: 4-Maneely-a (4 pgs.) — 6.70 20.00 40.00
3-Maneely, Pakula, Torres-a — 6.70 20.00 40.00
5-Crandall, Krigstein-a — 8.35 25.00 50.00
NOTE: ***Drucker** a-2. **Heck** a-4. **Severin** c-1, 2, 4, 5. **Shores** a-4.*

CAVALIER COMICS
1945; 1952 (Early DC reprints)
A. W. Nugent Publ. Co.

2(1945)-Speed Saunders, Fang Gow — 12.00 36.00 85.00
2(1952) — 6.70 20.00 40.00

CAVE GIRL (Also see Africa)
No. 11, 1953 - No. 14, 1954
Magazine Enterprises

11(A-1 82)-Origin; all Cave Girl stories — 30.00 90.00 210.00
12(A-1 96), 13(A-1 116), 14(A-1 125)-Thunda by Powell in each — 22.00 67.00 155.00
NOTE: ***Powell** c/a in all.*

CAVE GIRL
1988 ($2.95, 44 pgs., 16 pgs. of color, rest B&W)
AC Comics

1-Powell-r/Cave Girl #11; Nyoka photo back-c from movie; Powell/Bill Black-c; Special Limited Edition on-c — 1.20 3.00

CAVE KIDS (TV)
Feb, 1963 - No. 16, Mar, 1967 (Hanna-Barbera)
Gold Key

1 — 4.00 10.70 25.00
2-5 — 1.70 5.00 12.00
6-16: 7,12-Pebbles & Bamm Bamm app. — 1.50 3.75 9.00

CENTURION OF ANCIENT ROME, THE
1958 (no month listed) (36 pgs.) (B&W)
Zondervan Publishing House

(Rare) All by Jay Disbrow
Estimated Value.... — 200.00

CENTURIONS (TV)
June, 1987 - No. 4, Sept, 1987 (75¢, mini-series)
DC Comics

1-4 — 1.00

CENTURY OF COMICS
1933 (100 pgs.) (Probably the 3rd comic book)
Eastern Color Printing Co.

Bought by Wheatena, Milk-O-Malt, John Wanamaker, Kinney Shoe Stores, & others to be used as premiums and radio giveaways. No publisher listed.

GD25 FN65 VF82
nn-Mutt & Jeff, Joe Palooka, etc. reprints — 2000.00 6000.00 10,000.00
(Estimated up to 20 total copies exist, none in NM-Mint)

GD25 FN65 NM94

CEREBUS BI-WEEKLY
Dec. 2, 1988 - No. 26, Nov. 11, 1989 ($1.25, B&W)
Aardvark-Vanaheim

GD25 FN65 NM94
1-26: Reprints Cerebus #1-26 — 1.25

CEREBUS: CHURCH & STATE
Feb, 1991 - No. 30, Apr, 1992 ($2.00, B&W, bi-weekly)
Aardvark-Vanaheim

1-30: r/Cerebus #51-80 — .80 2.00

CEREBUS: HIGH SOCIETY
Feb, 1990 - No. 25, 1991 ($1.70, B&W)
Aardvark-Vanaheim

1-25: r/Cerebus #26-50 — .70 1.70

CEREBUS JAM
Apr, 1985
Aardvark-Vanaheim

1-Eisner, Austin, Dave Sim-a (Cerebus vs. Spirit) — 1.20 3.00

CEREBUS THE AARDVARK (See A-V in 3-D, Nucleus, Power Comics)
Dec, 1977 - Present ($1.70/$2.00, B&W)
Aardvark-Vanaheim

1-1st app. Cerebus; 2000 print run; most copies poorly printed — 26.00 77.00 180.00
Note: *There is a counterfeit version known to exist. It can be distinguished from the original in the following ways: inside cover is glossy instead of flat, black background on the front cover is blotted or spotty. Reports show that a counterfeit #2 also exists.*
2-Dave Sim art in all — 7.00 22.00 52.00
3-Origin Red Sophia — 6.00 18.00 42.00
4-Origin Elrod the Albino — 3.70 11.00 26.00
5,6 — 3.00 9.00 21.00
7-10 — 2.30 6.90 16.00
11,12: 11-Origin Capt. Coachroach — 2.60 7.70 18.00
13-15: 14-Origin Lord Julius — 1.50 3.80 9.00
16-20 — .90 2.30 5.50
21-Scarcer; B. Smith letter in letter column — 4.60 14.00 32.00
22-Low distribution; no cover price — 1.70 5.00 12.00
23-30: 26-High Society storyline begins — .90 2.30 5.50
31-Origin Moonroach — 1.30 3.00 7.50
32-40 — 1.80 4.50
41-50,52: 52-Cutey Bunny app. — 1.40 3.50
51-Not reprinted; Cutey Bunny app. — 1.90 6.00 13.00
53-Intro. Wolveroach (cameo) — .90 2.30 5.50
54-1st full Wolveroach story — 1.30 3.00 7.50
55,56-Wolveroach app.; Normalman back-ups by Valentino — .90 2.30 5.50
57-79: 61,62: Flaming Carrot app. — 1.00 2.50
80-180: 104-Flaming Carrot app. 112/113-Double issue. 137-Begin $2.25-c. 175-(44 pgs., same price) — .90 2.25
151-153-2nd printings — .90 2.25
Free Cerebus (Giveaway, 1991-92?, 36 pgs.)-All-r — 1.00

CHAIN GANG WAR
July, 1993 - Present ($1.75)
DC Comics

1-($2.50)-Embossed silver foil-c — 1.00 2.50
2-4,6-15: 3-Deathstroke app. 4-Brief Deathstroke app. 6-New Batman cameo. 11-New Batman-c/story — .70 1.75
5-($2.50)-Foil embossed-c; Deathstroke app.; new Batman cameo (Azrael, 1 panel) — 1.00 2.50

CHALLENGE OF THE UNKNOWN (Formerly Love Experiences)
No. 6, Sept, 1950 (See Web Of Mystery No. 19)
Ace Magazines

6- "Villa of the Vampire" used in N.Y. Joint Legislative Comm. Publ; Sekowsky-a — 15.00 45.00 105.00

CHALLENGER, THE

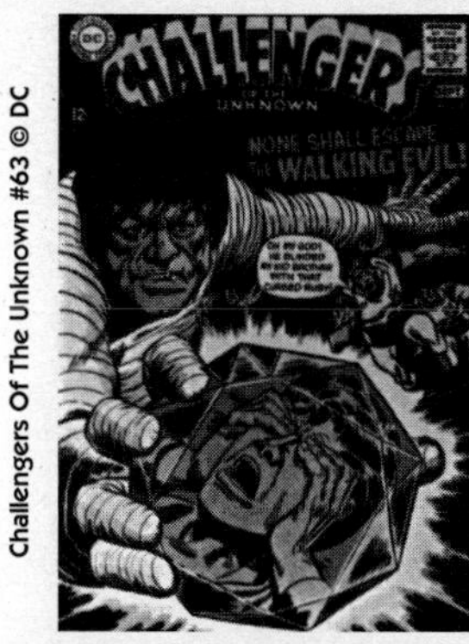

Challengers Of The Unknown #63 © DC

Chamber Of Darkness #2 © MEG

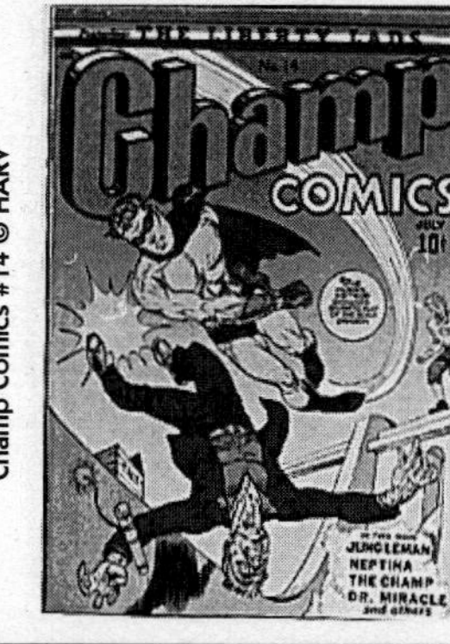

Champ Comics #14 © HARV

GD25 FN65 NM94

1945 - No. 4, Oct-Dec, 1946
Interfaith Publications/T.C. Comics

nn; nd; 32 pgs.; Origin the Challenger Club; Anti-Fascist with funny animal filler 22.00 65.00 150.00
2-4-Kubert-a; 4-Fuje-a 18.00 54.00 125.00

CHALLENGERS OF THE UNKNOWN (See Showcase #6, 7, 11, 12, Super DC Giant, and Super Team Family)
4-5/58 - No. 77, 12-1/70-71; No. 78, 2/73 - No. 80, 6-7/73; No. 81, 6-7/77 - No. 87, 6-7/78
National Per. Publ./DC Comics

GD25 FN65 VF82 NM94

Showcase #6 (1-2/57)-Origin & 1st app. Challengers of the Unknown by Kirby (1st Silver Age super-hero team) (1st original concept S.A. series) 160.00 480.00 1440.00 2400.00

GD25 FN65 NM94

Showcase #7 (3-4/57)-2nd app. by Kirby 108.00 325.00 1300.00
Showcase #11 (11-12/57)-3rd app. by Kirby; 2nd tryout series 115.00 345.00 1150.00
Showcase #12 (1-2/58)-4th app. by Kirby 100.00 300.00 1200.00

GD25 FN65 VF82 NM94

1-(4-5/58)-Kirby/Stein-a(2); Kirby-c 152.00 457.00 991.00 1525.00

GD25 FN65 NM94

2-Kirby/Stein-a(2) 64.00 193.00 580.00
3-Kirby/Stein-a(2) 53.00 158.00 475.00
4-8-Kirby/Wood-a plus cover to #8 45.00 135.00 405.00
9,10 22.00 65.00 195.00
11-15: 11-Grey tone-c. 14-Origin/1st app. Multi-Man (villain) 15.00 45.00 135.00
16-22: 18-Intro. Cosmo, the Challengers Spacepet. 22-Last 10¢ issue 13.00 38.00 115.00
23-30 8.00 24.00 55.00
31-Retells origin of the Challengers 9.00 26.00 60.00
32-40 4.00 12.00 28.00
41-60: 43-New look begins. 48-Doom Patrol app. 49-Intro. Challenger Corps. 51-Sea Devils app. 55-Death of Red Ryan. 60-Red Ryan returns 1.70 5.10 12.00
61-73,75-77: 64,65-Kirby origin-r, parts 1 & 2. 66-New logo. 68-Last 12¢ issue. 69-1st app. Corinna 1.00 2.50 6.00
74-Deadman by Tuska/N. Adams; 1 pg. Wrightson-a 2.00 6.00 14.00
78-87: 82-Swamp Thing begins; Wrightson partial-i 1.50 3.75

NOTE: ***N. Adams*** *c-67, 68, 70, 72, 74i, 81i.* ***Buckler*** *c-83-86p.* ***Giffen*** *a-83-87p.* ***Kirby*** *a-75-80r; c-75, 77, 78.* ***Kubert*** *c-64, 66, 69, 76, 79.* ***Nasser*** *c/a-81p, 82p.* ***Tuska*** *a-73.* ***Wood*** *r-76.*

CHALLENGERS OF THE UNKNOWN
Mar, 1991 - No. 8, Oct, 1991 ($1.75, limited series)
DC Comics

1-Bolland-c .80 2.00
2-8: 6-G. Kane-c(p). 7-Steranko-c swipe by Arthur Adams .70 1.75

CHALLENGE TO THE WORLD
1951 (10¢, 36 pgs.)
Catechetical Guild

nn 3.20 8.00 16.00

CHAMBER OF CHILLS (Formerly Blondie Comics #20; ...of Clues No. 27 on)
No. 21, June, 1951 - No. 26, Dec, 1954
Harvey Publications/Witches Tales

21 (#1) 21.00 63.00 145.00
22,24 (#2,3) 11.00 32.00 75.00
23 (#4)-Excessive violence; eyes torn out 13.00 40.00 90.00
5(2/52)-Decapitation, acid in face scene 13.00 40.00 90.00
6-Woman melted alive 12.00 36.00 85.00
7-Used in **SOTI**, pg. 389; decapitation/severed head panels 11.00 32.00 75.00
8-10: 8-Decapitation panels 10.00 30.00 65.00
11,12,14 8.35 25.00 50.00
13,15-24-Nostrand-a in all. 13,21-Decapitation panels. 18-Atom bomb panels.
20-Nostrand-c 11.00 32.00 75.00
25,26 6.70 20.00 40.00

NOTE: *About half the issues contain bondage, torture, sadism, perversion, gore, cannabalism, eyes ripped out, acid in face, etc.* ***Elias*** *c-4-11, 14-19, 21-26.* ***Kremer*** *a-12, 17.* ***Palais*** *a-21(1), 23.* ***Nostrand/Powell*** *a-13, 15, 16.* ***Powell*** *a-21, 23, 24('51), 5-8, 11, 13, 18-21, 23-25. Bondage-c-21, 24('51), 7. 25-r/#5; 26-r/#9.*

CHAMBER OF CHILLS
Nov, 1972 - No. 25, Nov, 1976
Marvel Comics Group

1-Harlan Ellison adaptation 1.30 3.25
2-25 .70 1.75

NOTE: ***Adkins*** *a-1i, 2i.* ***Brunner*** *a-2-4; c-4.* ***Ditko*** *r-14, 16, 19, 23, 24.* ***Everett*** *a-3i, 11r,21r.* ***Heath*** *a-1r.* ***Gil Kane*** *c-2p.* ***Powell*** *a-13r.* ***Russell*** *a-1p, 2p.* ***Williamson/Mayo*** *a-13r.* ***Robert E. Howard*** *horror story adaptation-2, 3.*

CHAMBER OF CLUES (Formerly Chamber of Chills)
No. 27, Feb, 1955 - No. 28, April, 1955
Harvey Publications

27-Kerry Drake-r/#19; Powell-a; last pre-code 8.35 25.00 50.00
28-Kerry Drake 5.00 15.00 30.00

CHAMBER OF DARKNESS (Monsters on the Prowl #9 on)
Oct, 1969 - No. 8, Dec, 1970
Marvel Comics Group

1-Buscema-a(p) 4.60 14.00 32.00
2-Neal Adams scripts 1.90 6.00 13.00
3-Smith, Buscema-a 1.90 6.00 13.00
4-A Conanesque tryout by Smith (4/70); reprinted in Conan #16; Marie Severin/Everett-c 5.30 16.00 37.00
5,6,8: 5-H.P. Lovecraft adaptation .90 2.30 5.50
7-Wrightson-c/a, 7pgs. (his 1st work at Marvel); Wrightson draws himself in 1st & last panels; Kirby/Ditko-r 1.70 5.00 12.00
1-(1/72; 25¢ Special) 1.10 2.70 6.50

NOTE: ***Adkins/Everett*** *a-8.* ***Craig*** *a-5.* ***Ditko*** *a-6-8r.* ***Kirby*** *a(p)-4, 5, 7r.* ***Kirby/Everett*** *c-5.* ***Severin/Everett*** *c-6.* ***Wrightson*** *c-7, 8.*

CHAMP COMICS (Formerly Champion No. 1-10)
No. 11, Oct, 1940 - No. 29, March, 1944
Worth Publ. Co./Champ Publ./Family Comics(Harvey Publ.)

11-Human Meteor cont'd. from Champion 54.00 160.00 375.00
12-20: 14,15-Crandall-c. 18,19-Kirbyish-c. 19-The Wasp app. 20-The Green Ghost app. 43.00 130.00 300.00
21-29: 22-The White Mask app. 23-Flag-c 34.00 103.00 240.00

CHAMPION (See Gene Autry's...)

CHAMPION COMICS (Formerly Speed Comics #1?; Champ Comics No. 11 on)
No. 2, Dec, 1939 - No. 10, Aug, 1940 (no No.1)
Worth Publ. Co.(Harvey Publications)

2-The Champ, The Blazing Scarab, Neptina, Liberty Lads, Jungleman, Bill Handy, Swingtime Sweetie begin 86.00 257.00 600.00
3-7: 7-The Human Meteor begins? 43.00 130.00 300.00
8-10: 8-Simon-c. 9-1st S&K-c (1st collaboration together). 10-Bondage-c by Kirby 48.00 145.00 335.00

CHAMPIONS, THE
October, 1975 - No. 17, Jan, 1978
Marvel Comics Group

1-Origin & 1st app. The Champions (The Angel, Black Widow, Ghost Rider, Hercules, Ice Man); Venus x-over 2.30 6.90 16.00
2-10,16: 2,3-Venus x-over 1.60 4.70 11.00
11-15,17-Byrne-a 1.70 5.00 12.00

NOTE: ***Buckler/Adkins*** *c-3.* ***Kane/Adkins*** *c-1.* ***Kane/Layton*** *c-11.* ***Tuska*** *a-3p, 4p, 6p. Ghost Rider c-1-4, 7, 8, 10, 14, 16, 17 (4, 10, 14 are more prominent).*

CHAMPIONS (Eclipse)(Value: cover or less)

CHAMPIONS (Hero)(Value: cover or less)

CHAMPION SPORTS
Oct-Nov, 1973 - No. 3, Feb-Mar, 1974
National Periodical Publications

The Chaos Effect: Omega © Voyager

Charlemagne #2 © EEP

Checkmate #3 © DC

GD25 FN65 NM94

1-3 1.50

CHAOS (See The Crusaders)

CHAOS EFFECT, THE
1994
Valiant

Alpha-w/trading card checklist 1.00
Omega-(11/94, $2.25) .90 2.25

CHARLEMAGNE
Mar, 1994 - Present ($2.50, color)
Defiant Comics

1-($3.50, 52 pgs.) 1.40 3.50
2,3,5: 2-War Dancer app. 1.00 2.50
4-($3.25, 52 pgs.) 1.30 3.25

CHARLIE CHAN (See Big Shot Comics, Columbia Comics, Feature Comics & The New Advs. of...)

CHARLIE CHAN (The Adventures of...) (Zaza The Mystic No. 10 on) (TV)
6-7/48 - No. 5, 2-3/49; No.6, 6/55 - No. 9, 3/56
Crestwood(Prize) No. 1-5; Charlton No. 6(6/55) on

1-S&K-c, 2 pgs.; Infantino-a 50.00 150.00 350.00
2-S&K-c 31.00 92.00 215.00
3-S&K-c/a 31.00 92.00 215.00
4,5 S&K-c 31.00 94.00 220.00
6(6/55-Charlton)-S&K-c 22.00 65.00 150.00
7-9 11.00 32.00 75.00

CHARLIE CHAN
Oct-Dec, 1965 - No. 2, Mar, 1966
Dell Publishing Co.

1-Springer-a 5.00 15.00 30.00
2 3.60 9.00 18.00

CHARLIE CHAPLIN
1917 (9x16"; large size; softcover; B&W)
Essanay/M. A. Donohue & Co.

Series 1, #315-Comic Capers (9-3/4x15-3/4")-18pp by Segar, Series 1, #316-In the Movies 100.00 300.00 900.00
Series 1, #317-Up in the Air. 318-In the Army 100.00 300.00 900.00
Funny Stunts-(12-1/2x16-3/8") in color 55.00 170.00 500.00
NOTE: *All contain* ***Segar*** *-a; pre-Thimble Theatre.*

CHARLIE McCARTHY (See Edgar Bergen Presents...)
No. 171, Nov, 1947 - No. 571, July, 1954 (See True Comics #14)
Dell Publishing Co.

4-Color 171 18.00 54.00 125.00
4-Color 196-Part photo-c; photo back-c 16.00 48.00 110.00
1(3-5/49)-Part photo-c; photo back-c 16.00 48.00 110.00
2-9(7/52; #5,6-52 pgs.) 7.50 22.50 45.00
4-Color 445,478,527,571 5.85 17.50 35.00

CHARLTON BULLSEYE
1975 - No. 5, 1976 ($1.50, B&W, bi-monthly, magazine format)
CPL/Gang Publications

1: 1 & 2 are last Capt. Atom by Ditko/Byrne intended for the never published Capt. Atom #90; Nightshade app.; Jeff Jones-a 1.60 4.70 11.00
2-Part 2 Capt. Atom story by Ditko/Byrne 1.70 4.20 10.00
3-Wrong Country by Sanho Kim 1.20 2.90 7.00
4-Doomsday + 1 by John Byrne 1.60 4.00 9.50
5-Doomsday + 1 by Byrne, The Question by Toth; Neal Adams back-c; Toth-c 1.60 4.70 11.00

CHARLTON BULLSEYE
June, 1981 - No. 10, Dec, 1982; Nov, 1986 (Color)
Charlton Publications

1-Blue Beetle, The Question app.; 1st app. Rocket Rabbit .80 2.00
2-10: 2-1st app. Neil The Horse; Rocket Rabbit app. 6-Origin & 1st app. Thunderbunny 1.50
Special 1(11/86)(Half in B&W) 1.20 3.00
Special 2-Atomic Mouse app. ('87) .80 2.00

CHARLTON CLASSICS
April, 1980 - No. 9, Aug, 1981
Charlton Comics

1 .80 2.00
2-9 1.00

CHARLTON CLASSICS LIBRARY (1776)
V10 No.1, March, 1973 (One Shot)
Charlton Comics

1776 (title) - Adaptation of the film musical "1776"; given away at movie theatres 1.60 4.00

CHARLTON PREMIERE (Formerly Marine War Heroes)
V1#19, July, 1967; V2#1, Sept, 1967 - No. 4, May, 1968
Charlton Comics

V1#19-Marine War Heroes. V2#1-Trio; intro. Shape. Tyro Team. & Spookman. 2-Children of Doom. 3-Sinistro Boy Fiend; Blue Beetle & Peacemaker x-over. 4-Unlikely Tales; Aparo, Ditko-a 1.00 2.00 5.00

CHARLTON SPORT LIBRARY - PROFESSIONAL FOOTBALL
Winter, 1969-70 (Jan. on cover) (68 pgs.)
Charlton Comics

1 1.70 5.00 12.00

CHASING THE BLUES
1912 (52 pgs.) (7-1/2x10"; B&W; hardcover)
Doubleday Page

nn-by Rube Goldberg 64.00 193.00 450.00

CHECKMATE (TV)
Oct, 1962 - No. 2, Dec, 1962
Gold Key

1,2-Photo-c 4.70 14.00 28.00

CHECKMATE (See Action Comics #598)
April, 1988 - No. 33, Jan, 1991 ($1.25)
DC Comics

1-12 1.25
13-33: $1.50/$2.00, new format 1.50
NOTE: ***Gil Kane*** *c-2, 4, 7, 8, 10, 11, 15-19.*

CHEERIOS PREMIUMS (Disney)
1947 (32 pgs.) (Pocket size; 16 titles)
Walt Disney Productions

Set "W"
W1-Donald Duck & the Pirates 5.35 16.00 32.00
W2-Bucky Bug & the Cannibal King 4.00 10.00 20.00
W3-Pluto Joins the F.B.I. 4.00 10.00 20.00
W4-Mickey Mouse & the Haunted House 4.70 14.00 28.00

Set "X"
X1-Donald Duck, Counter Spy 4.35 13.00 26.00
X2-Goofy Lost in the Desert 3.60 9.00 18.00
X3-Br'er Rabbit Outwits Br'er Fox 3.60 9.00 18.00
X4-Mickey Mouse at the Rodeo 4.35 13.00 28.00

Set "Y"
Y1-Donald Duck's Atom Bomb by Carl Barks. Disney has banned reprinting this book 85.00 257.00 600.00
Y2-Br'er Rabbit's Secret 3.60 9.00 18.00
Y3-Dumbo & the Circus Mystery 4.35 13.00 26.00
Y4-Mickey Mouse Meets the Wizard 4.70 14.00 28.00

Set "Z"
Z1-Donald Duck Pilots a Jet Plane (not by Barks) 4.35 13.00 26.00
Z2-Pluto Turns Sleuth Hound 3.60 9.00 18.00
Z3-The Seven Dwarfs & the Enchanted Mtn. 4.35 13.00 26.00
Z4-Mickey Mouse's Secret Room 4.70 14.00 28.00

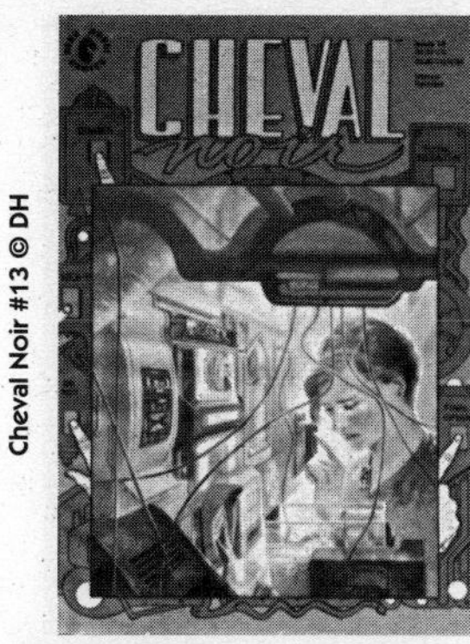

Cheval Noir #13 © DH

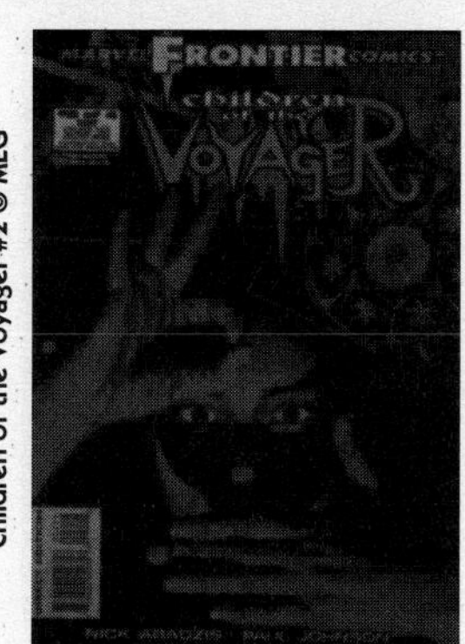

Children of the Voyager #2 © MEG

Chiller #2 © MEG

CHEERIOS 3-D GIVEAWAYS (Disney)
1954 (Pocket size) (24 titles) (Glasses were cut-outs on boxes)
Walt Disney Productions

	GD25	FN65	NM94
Glasses only...	6.70	20.00	40.00
(Set 1) 1-Donald Duck & Uncle Scrooge, the Firefighters			
2-Mickey Mouse & Goofy, Pirate Plunder			
3-Donald Duck's Nephews, the Fabulous Inventors			
4-Mickey Mouse, Secret of the Ming Vase			
5-Donald Duck with Huey, Dewey, & Louie; ...the Seafarers (title on 2nd page)			
6-Mickey Mouse, Moaning Mountain			
7-Donald Duck, Apache Gold			
8-Mickey Mouse, Flight to Nowhere (per book)	8.35	25.00	50.00
(Set 2) 1-Donald Duck, Treasure of Timbuktu			
2-Mickey Mouse & Pluto, Operation China			
3-Donald Duck in the Magic Cows			
4-Mickey Mouse & Goofy, Kid Kokonut			
5-Donald Duck, Mystery Ship			
6-Mickey Mouse, Phantom Sheriff			
7-Donald Duck, Circus Adventures			
8-Mickey Mouse, Arctic Explorers (per book)	8.35	25.00	50.00
(Set 3) 1-Donald Duck & Witch Hazel			
2-Mickey Mouse in Darkest Africa			
3-Donald Duck & Uncle Scrooge, Timber Trouble			
4-Mickey Mouse, Rajah's Rescue			
5-Donald Duck in Robot Reporter			
6-Mickey Mouse, Slumbering Sleuth			
7-Donald Duck in the Foreign Legion			
8-Mickey Mouse, Airwalking Wonder (per book)....	8.35	25.00	50.00

CHESTY AND COPTIE
1946 (4 pgs.) (Giveaway) (Disney)
Los Angeles Community Chest

	GD25	FN65	NM94
nn-(One known copy) by Floyd Gottfredson	93.00	280.00	650.00

CHESTY AND HIS HELPERS
1943 (12 pgs., Disney giveaway, 5-1/2x7-1/4")
Los Angeles War Chest

	GD25	FN65	NM94
nn-Chesty & Coptie	64.00	193.00	450.00

CHEVAL NOIR
1989 - No. 48, Nov, 1993 ($3.50, B&W, 68 pgs.)
Dark Horse Comics

	GD25	FN65	NM94
1-8,10 ($3.50): 6-Moebius poster insert		1.40	3.50
9,11,13,15,17,20,22 ($4.50, 84 pgs.)		1.80	4.50
12,18,19,21,23,25,26 ($3.95): 12-Geary-a; Mignola-c. 26-Moebius-a begins		1.60	4.00
14 ($4.95, 76 pgs.)(7 pgs. color)	1.00	2.00	5.00
16,24 ($3.75): 16-19-Contain trading cards		1.50	3.75
27-48 ($2.95)		1.20	3.00

NOTE: ***Bolland** a-2, 6, 7, 13, 14. **Bolton** a-2, 4, 45; c-4, 20. **Chadwick** c-13. **Dorman** painted c-16. **Geary** a-13, 14. **Kelley Jones** c-27. **Kaluta** a-6; c-6, 18. **Moebius** c-5, 9, 26. **Dave Stevens** c-1, 7. **Sutton** painted c-36.*

CHEYENNE (TV)
No. 734, Oct, 1956 - No. 25, Dec-Jan, 1961-62
Dell Publishing Co.

	GD25	FN65	NM94
4-Color 734(#1)-Clint Walker photo-c	13.50	41.00	95.00
4-Color 772,803: Clint Walker photo-c	8.35	25.00	50.00
4(8-10/57) - 12: 4-9-Clint Walker photo-c. 10-12-Ty Hardin photo-c	5.85	17.50	35.00
13-25 (All Clint Walker photo-c)	5.00	15.00	30.00

CHEYENNE AUTUMN (See Movie Classics)

CHEYENNE KID (Formerly Wild Frontier No. 1-7)
No. 8, July, 1957 - No. 99, Nov, 1973
Charlton Comics

	GD25	FN65	NM94
8 (#1)	5.35	16.00	32.00
9,15-19	3.60	9.00	18.00
10-Williamson/Torres-a(3); Ditko-c	7.50	22.50	45.00
11,12-Williamson/Torres-a(2) ea.; 11-(68 pgs.)-Cheyenne Kid meets Geronimo	8.00	24.00	48.00
13-Williamson/Torres-a (5 pgs.)	5.00	15.00	30.00
14-Williamson-a (5 pgs.?)	5.00	15.00	30.00
20-22,24,25-Severin c/a(3) each	4.00	10.00	20.00
23,27-29	1.80	4.50	9.00
26,30-Severin-a	2.80	7.00	14.00
31-59	1.00	2.30	5.50
60-99: 66-Wander by Aparo begins, ends #87. Apache Red begins #88, origin in #89		1.40	3.50
Modern Comics Reprint 87,89(1978)			1.00

CHICAGO MAIL ORDER (See C-M-O Comics)

CHIEF, THE (Indian Chief No. 3 on)
No. 290, Aug, 1950 - No. 2, Apr-June, 1951
Dell Publishing Co.

	GD25	FN65	NM94
4-Color 290(#1), 2	5.35	16.00	32.00

CHIEF CRAZY HORSE (See Wild Bill Hickok #21)
1950 (Also see Fighting Indians of the Wild West!)
Avon Periodicals

	GD25	FN65	NM94
nn-Fawcette-c	14.00	431.00	100.00

CHIEF VICTORIO'S APACHE MASSACRE
1951 (Also see Fighting Indians of the Wild West!)
Avon Periodicals

	GD25	FN65	NM94
nn-Williamson/Frazetta-a (7 pgs.); Larsen-a; Kinstler-c	30.00	90.00	210.00

CHILDREN OF FIRE (Fantagor)(Value: cover or less)

CHILDREN OF THE VOYAGER (See Marvel Frontier Comics Unlimited)
Sept, 1993 - No. 4, Dec, 1993 ($1.95, mini-series)
Marvel Frontier Comics

	GD25	FN65	NM94
1-($2.95)-Embossed glow-in-the-dark-c		1.00	2.50
2-4			1.50

CHILDREN'S BIG BOOK
1945 (25¢, 68 pgs.; stiff covers)
Dorene Publ. Co.

	GD25	FN65	NM94
nn-Comics & fairy tales; David Icove-a	9.15	27.50	55.00

CHILDREN'S CRUSADE, THE
Dec, 1993 - No. 2, Jan, 1994 ($3.95, limited series, mature readers)
DC Comics

	GD25	FN65	NM94
1,2-By Gaiman/Bachalo		1.60	4.00

CHILD'S PLAY: THE SERIES (Innovation)(Value: cover or less)

CHILD'S PLAY 2 THE OFFICIAL MOVIE ADAPTATION (Innovation)(Value: cover or less)

CHILI (Millie's Rival)
5/69 - No. 17, 9/70; No. 18, 8/72 - No. 26, 12/73
Marvel Comics Group

	GD25	FN65	NM94
1	3.20	8.00	20.00
2-5	1.65	4.00	10.00
6-17	1.20	3.00	7.00
18-26	1.00	2.00	5.00
Special 1(12/71)	1.70	4.20	10.00

CHILLER
Nov, 1993 - No. 2, Dec, 1993 ($7.95, limited series, 68 pgs.)
Epic Comics (Marvel)

	GD25	FN65	NM94
1,2	1.30	3.25	8.00

CHILLING ADVENTURES IN SORCERY (...as Told by Sabrina #1, 2)

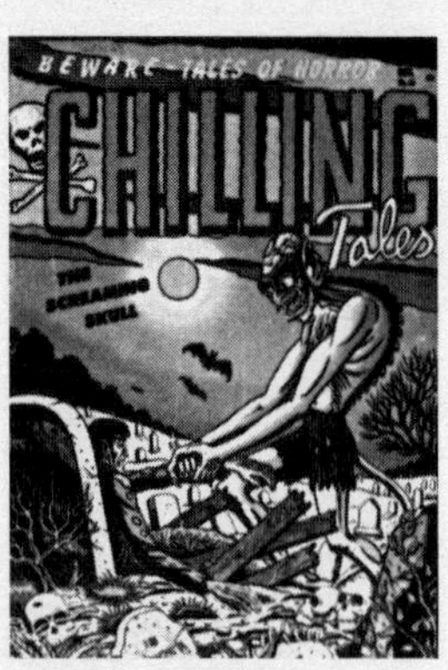

Chilling Tales #13 © YM

Christmas Carnival © Z-D

Christmas Coloring Fun © H. Burnside

(Red Circle Sorcery No. 6 on)
9/72 - No. 2, 10/72; No. 3, 10/73 - No. 5, 2/74
Archie Publications (Red Circle Prod.)

	GD25	FN65	NM94
1,2-Sabrina cameo in both	1.00	2.50	6.00
3-Morrow-c/a, all		1.40	3.50
4,5-Morrow-c/a (5 & 6 pgs.)		1.40	3.50

CHILLING TALES (Formerly Beware)
No. 13, Dec, 1952 - No. 17, Oct, 1953
Youthful Magazines

	GD25	FN65	NM94
13(No.1)-Harrison-a; Matt Fox-c/a	27.00	80.00	185.00
14-Harrison-a	16.00	48.00	110.00
15-Has #14 on-c; Matt Fox-c; Harrison-a	19.00	57.00	130.00
16-Poe adapt.-'Metzengerstein'; Rudyard Kipling adapt.- 'Mark of the Beast,' by Kiefer; bondage-c	14.00	43.00	100.00
17-Matt Fox-c; Sir Walter Scott & Poe adapt.	19.00	57.00	130.00

CHILLING TALES OF HORROR (Magazine)
V1#1, 6/69 - V1#7, 12/70; V2#2, 2/71 - V2#5, 10/71 (50¢, B&W, 52 pgs.)
Stanley Publications

	GD25	FN65	NM94
V1#1	3.20	8.00	20.00
2-7: 7-Cameron-a	1.70	5.00	12.00
V2#2,3,5: 2-Spirit of Frankenstein-r/Adventures into the Unknown #16	1.70	4.20	10.00
V2#4-r/9 pg. Feldstein-a from Adventures into the Unknown #3	1.70	5.00	12.00

NOTE: *Two issues of V2#2 exist, Feb, 1971 and April, 1971.*

CHILLY WILLY (See 4-Color #740, 852, 967, 1017, 1074, 1122, 1177, 1212, 1281)

CHINA BOY (See Wisco)

CHIP 'N' DALE (Walt Disney)(See Walt Disney's C&S #204)
Nov, 1953 - No. 30, June-Aug, 1962; Sept, 1967 - No. 83, 1982
Dell Publishing Co./Gold Key/Whitman No. 65 on

	GD25	FN65	NM94
4-Color 517(#1)	8.35	25.00	50.00
4-Color 581,636	5.00	15.00	30.00
4(12/55-2/56)-10	4.00	10.00	20.00
11-30	3.00	7.50	15.00
1(Gold Key, 1967)-Reprints	2.80	7.00	14.00
2-10	1.00	2.50	6.00
11-20		1.20	3.00
21-83			1.50

NOTE: *All Gold Key/Whitman issues have reprints except No. 32-35, 38-41, 45-47. No. 23-28, 30-42, 45-47, 49 have new covers.*

CHIP 'N DALE RESCUE RANGERS
June, 1990 - No. 19, Dec, 1991 ($1.50)
Disney Comics

	GD25	FN65	NM94
1-19: New stories; 1,2-Origin			1.50

CHITTY CHITTY BANG BANG (See Movie Comics)

CHOICE COMICS
Dec, 1941 - No. 3, Feb, 1942
Great Publications

	GD25	FN65	NM94
1-Origin Secret Circle; Atlas the Mighty app.; Zomba, Jungle Fight, Kangaroo Man, & Fire Eater begin	75.00	225.00	525.00
2	48.00	144.00	335.00
3-Double feature; Features movie "The Lost City" (classic cover); continued from Great Comics #3	66.00	200.00	465.00

CHOO CHOO CHARLIE
Dec, 1969
Gold Key

	GD25	FN65	NM94
1-John Stanley-a (scarce)	11.00	32.00	75.00

CHRISTIAN HEROES OF TODAY
1964 (36 pgs.)
David C. Cook

	GD25	FN65	NM94
nn	.80	2.00	4.00

CHRISTMAS (See A-1 No. 28)

CHRISTMAS ADVENTURE, A (See Classics Comics Giveaways, 12/69)

CHRISTMAS ADVENTURE, THE
1963 (16 pgs.)
S. Rose (H. L. Green Giveaway)

	GD25	FN65	NM94
nn	1.20	3.00	6.00

CHRISTMAS ALBUM (See March of Comics No. 312)

CHRISTMAS & ARCHIE
Jan, 1975 ($1.00, 68 pgs.) (10-1/4x13-1/4")
Archie Comics

	GD25	FN65	NM94
1	1.70	5.00	12.00

CHRISTMAS AT THE ROTUNDA (Titled Ford Rotunda Christmas Book 1957 on) (Regular size)
1954 - 1961 (Given away every Christmas at one location)
Ford Motor Co. (Western Printing)

	GD25	FN65	NM94
1954-56 issues (nn's)	4.20	12.50	25.00
1957-61 issues (nn's)	4.00	10.00	20.00

CHRISTMAS BELLS (See March of Comics No. 297)

CHRISTMAS CARNIVAL
1952 (25¢, 100 pgs.) (One Shot)
Ziff-Davis Publ. Co./St. John Publ. Co. No. 2

	GD25	FN65	NM94
nn	20.00	60.00	140.00
2-Reprints Ziff-Davis issue plus-c	11.50	34.00	80.00

CHRISTMAS CAROL, A (See March of Comics No. 33)

CHRISTMAS CAROL, A
No date (1942-43) (32 pgs.; 8-1/4x10-3/4"; paper cover)
Sears Roebuck & Co. (Giveaway)

	GD25	FN65	NM94
nn-Comics & coloring book	10.00	30.00	60.00

CHRISTMAS CAROL, A
1940s ? (20 pgs.)
Sears Roebuck & Co. (Christmas giveaway)

	GD25	FN65	NM94
nn-Comic book & animated coloring book	8.35	25.00	50.00

CHRISTMAS CAROLS
1959 ? (16 pgs.)
Hot Shoppes Giveaway

	GD25	FN65	NM94
nn	2.40	6.00	12.00

CHRISTMAS COLORING FUN
1964 (20 pgs.; slick cover; B&W inside)
H. Burnside

	GD25	FN65	NM94
nn	1.60	4.00	8.00

CHRISTMAS DREAM, A
1950 (16 pgs.) (Kinney Shoe Store Giveaway)
Promotional Publishing Co.

	GD25	FN65	NM94
nn	2.40	6.00	12.00

CHRISTMAS DREAM, A
1952? (16 pgs.; paper cover)
J. J. Newberry Co. (Giveaway)

	GD25	FN65	NM94
nn	2.40	6.00	12.00

CHRISTMAS DREAM, A
1952 (16 pgs.; paper cover)
Promotional Publ. Co. (Giveaway)

	GD25	FN65	NM94
nn	2.40	6.00	12.00

CHRISTMAS EVE, A (See March of Comics No. 212)

CHRISTMAS FUN AROUND THE WORLD
No date (early 50's) (16 pgs.; paper cover)
No publisher

	GD25	FN65	NM94
nn	3.20	8.00	16.00

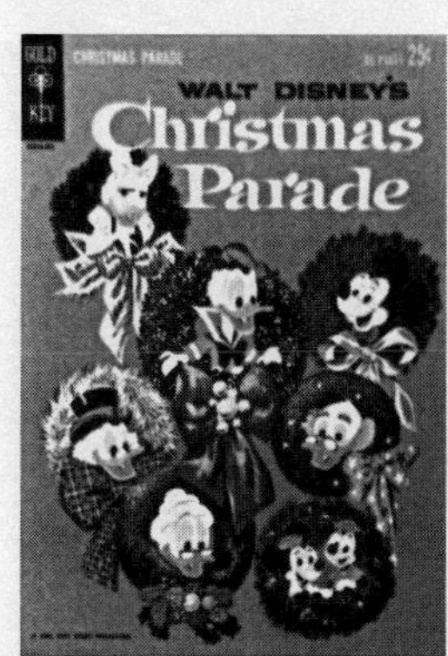

Christmas Parade #1 © WDC

Christmas With The Super-Heroes #1 © DC

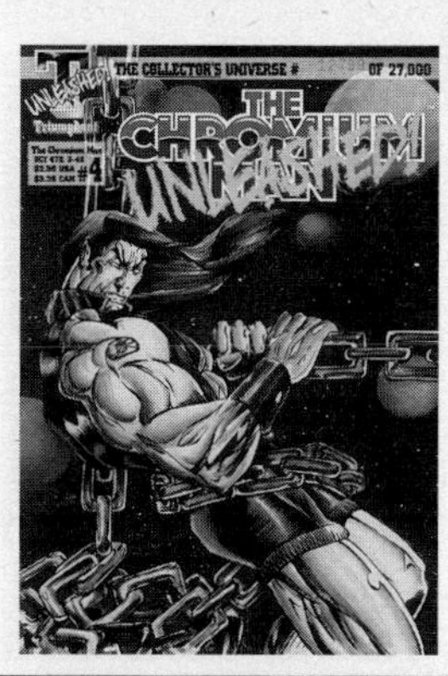

The Chromium Man #4 © Triumphant

GD25 FN65 NM94

CHRISTMAS IN DISNEYLAND (See Dell Giants)

CHRISTMAS JOURNEY THROUGH SPACE
1960
Promotional Publishing Co.

nn-Reprints 1954 issue Jolly Christmas Book with new slick cover 4.00 10.00 20.00

CHRISTMAS ON THE MOON
1958 (20 pgs.; slick cover)
W. T. Grant Co. (Giveaway)

nn 4.20 12.50 25.00

CHRISTMAS PARADE (See Dell Giant No. 26, Dell Giants, March of Comics No. 284, Walt Disney Christmas Parade & Walt Disney's...)

CHRISTMAS PARADE (Walt Disney's)
Jan, 1963 (no month) - No. 9, Jan, 1972 (#1,5: 80 pgs.; #2-4,7-9: 36 pgs.)
Gold Key

1 (30018-301)-Giant 10.00 30.00 60.00
2-6: 2-r/F.C. #367 by Barks. 3-r/F.C. #178 by Barks. 4-r/F.C. #203 by Barks. 5-r/Christ. Parade #1 (Dell) by Barks; giant. 6-r/Christmas Parade #2 (Dell) by Barks (64 pgs.); giant 7.50 22.50 45.00
7,9: 7-Pull-out poster 4.00 10.00 20.00
8-r/F.C. #367 by Barks; pull-out poster 7.50 22.50 45.00

CHRISTMAS PARTY (See March of Comics No. 256)

CHRISTMAS PLAY BOOK
1946 (16 pgs.; paper cover)
Gould-Stoner Co. (Giveaway)

nn 4.20 12.50 25.00

CHRISTMAS ROUNDUP
1960
Promotional Publishing Co.

nn-Marv Levy-c/a 1.80 4.50 9.00

CHRISTMAS STORIES (See 4-Color No. 959, 1062)

CHRISTMAS STORY (See March of Comics No. 326)

CHRISTMAS STORY BOOK (See Woolworth's Christmas Story Book)

CHRISTMAS STORY CUT-OUT BOOK, THE
No. 393, 1951 (36 pgs.) (15¢)
Catechetical Guild

393-Half text & half comics 4.20 12.50 25.00

CHRISTMAS TREASURY, A (See Dell Giants & March of Comics No. 227)

CHRISTMAS USA (Through 300 Years) (Also see Uncle Sam's...)
1956
Promotional Publ. Co. (Giveaway)

nn-Marv Levy-c/a 1.80 4.50 9.00

CHRISTMAS WITH ARCHIE
1973, 1974 (52 pgs.) (49¢)
Spire Christian Comics (Fleming H. Revell Co.)

nn .80 2.00

CHRISTMAS WITH MOTHER GOOSE (See 4-Color No. 90, 126, 172, 201, 253)

CHRISTMAS WITH SANTA (See March of Comics No. 92)

CHRISTMAS WITH SNOW WHITE AND THE SEVEN DWARFS
1953 (16 pgs., paper cover)
Kobackers Giftstore of Buffalo, N.Y.

nn 4.70 14.00 28.00

CHRISTMAS WITH THE SUPER-HEROES (See Limited Collectors' Edition)
1988; No. 2, 1989 ($2.95)
DC Comics

1-(100 pgs.)-All reprints; N. Adams-r, Byrne-c; Batman, Superman, JLA, LSH Christmas stories; r-Miller's 1st Batman/DC Special Series #21 1.20 3.00
2-(68 pgs.)-Superman by Chadwick; Batman, Wonder Woman, Deadman, Gr. Lantern, Flash app.; Morrow-a; Enemy Ace by Byrne; all new-a 1.20 3.00

GD25 FN65 NM94

CHRISTOPHERS, THE
1951 (36 pgs.) (Some copies have 15¢ sticker)
Catechetical Guild (Giveaway)

nn-Stalin as Satan in Hell 20.00 60.00 140.00

CHROMA-TICK, THE (...Special Edition, #1,2) (Also see The Tick)
Feb, 1992 - No. 8, Nov, 1993 ($3.95/$3.50, color, 44 pgs.)
New England Comics Press

1,2-Includes serially numbered trading card set 1.60 4.00
3-8 ($3.50, 36 pgs.): 6-Bound-in card 1.40 3.50

CHROME (Hot)(Value: cover or less)

CHROMIUM MAN, THE
Aug, 1993 - Present ($2.50, color)
Triumphant Comics

1-1st app. Mr. Death; all serially numbered 1.00 2.50
2-9: 2-1st app. Prince Vandal. 3-1st app. Candi, Breaker & Coil. 4,5-Triumphant Unleashed x-over. 8,9-(3/94) 1.00 2.50
0-(4/94)-Four color-c 1.00 2.50
0-All pink-c & all blue-c; no cover price 1.00 2.50
10-(5/94) 1.00 2.50

CHROMIUM MAN: VIOLENT PAST, THE
Jan, 1994 - No. 2, Jan, 1994 ($2.50, color, limited series)
Triumphant Comics

1,2-Serially numbered to 22,000 each 1.00 2.50

CHRONICLES OF CORUM, THE (First)(Value: cover or less)

CHUCKLE, THE GIGGLY BOOK OF COMIC ANIMALS
1945 (132 pgs.) (One Shot)
R. B. Leffingwell Co.

1-Funny animal 17.00 52.00 120.00

CHUCK NORRIS (TV)
Jan, 1987 - No. 3, May, 1987
Star Comics (Marvel)

1-3: Ditko-a 1.00

CHUCK WAGON (See Sheriff Bob Dixon's...)

CICERO'S CAT
July-Aug, 1959 - No. 2, Sept-Oct, 1959
Dell Publishing Co.

1,2-Cat from Mutt & Jeff 4.20 12.50 25.00

CIMARRON STRIP (TV)
January, 1968
Dell Publishing Co.

1-Stuart Whitman photo-c 4.00 11.00 22.00

CINDER AND ASHE
May, 1988 - No. 4, Aug, 1988 ($1.75, mini-series)
DC Comics

1-4: Mature readers .70 1.75

CINDERELLA (See 4-Color No. 272, 786, & Movie Comics)

CINDERELLA
April, 1982
Whitman Publishing Co.

nn-Reprints 4-Color #272 1.00

CINDERELLA IN "FAIREST OF THE FAIR"
1955 (16 pgs., 5x7-1/4", soft-c) (Walt Disney)
American Dairy Association (Premium)

nn 10.00 30.00 60.00

Cinderella Love #7 © Z-D

The Clandestine Preview © MEG

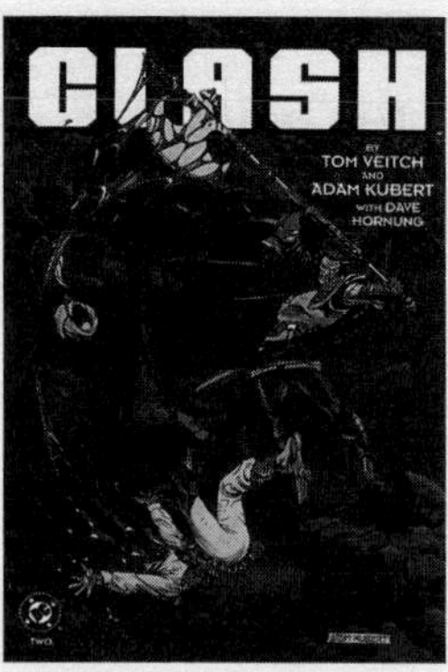

Clash #2 © DC

GD25 FN65 NM94

CINDERELLA LOVE
No. 10, 1950; No. 11, 4-5/51; No. 12, 9/51; No. 4, 10-11/51 - No. 11, Fall, 1952; No. 12, 10/53 - No. 15, 8/54; No. 25, 12/54 - No. 29, 10/55 (No #16-24)
Ziff-Davis/St. John Publ. Co. No. 12 on

	GD25	FN65	NM94
10(#1)(1st Series, 1950)	9.15	27.50	55.00
11(#2, 4-5/51)-Crandall-a; Saunders painted-c	5.85	17.50	35.00
12(#3, 9/51)	4.35	13.00	26.00
4-8: 4,7-Photo-c	4.00	11.00	22.00
9-Kinstler-a; photo-c	5.00	15.00	30.00
10,11(Fall/'52): 10-Whitney painted-c. 11-Photo-c	4.35	13.00	26.00
12(St. John-10/53)-#14:13-Painted-c.14-Baker-a?	4.00	10.00	20.00
15 (8/54)-Matt Baker-c	4.35	13.00	26.00
25(2nd Series)(Formerly Romantic Marriage)	3.60	9.00	18.00
26-Baker-c; last precode (2/55)	4.35	13.00	26.00
27,29-Matt Baker-c	4.35	13.00	26.00
28	3.00	7.50	15.00

CINDY COMICS (...Smith No. 39, 40; Crime Can't Win No. 41 on)
(Formerly Krazy Komics)(See Junior Miss & Teen Comics)
No. 27, Fall, 1947 - No. 40, July, 1950
Timely Comics

	GD25	FN65	NM94
27-Kurtzman-a, 3 pgs: Margie, Oscar begin	11.50	34.00	80.00
28-31-Kurtzman-a	8.35	25.00	50.00
32-40: 33-Georgie story; anti-Wertham editorial	5.35	16.00	32.00

NOTE: *Kurtzman's "Hey Look"-#27(3), 29(2), 30(2), 31; "Giggles 'n' Grins"-28.*

CINEMA COMICS HERALD
1941 - 1943 (4-pg. movie "trailers", paper-c, 7-1/2x10-1/2")(Giveaway)
Paramount Pictures/Universal/RKO/20th Century Fox/Republic

	GD25	FN65	NM94
"Mr. Bug Goes to Town" (1941)	4.20	12.50	25.00
"Bedtime Story"	4.00	11.00	22.00
"Lady For A Night", John Wayne, Joan Blondell (1942)	6.70	20.00	40.00
"Reap The Wild Wind" (1942)	4.00	11.00	22.00
"Thunder Birds" (1942)	4.00	11.00	22.00
"They All Kissed the Bride"	4.00	11.00	22.00
"Arabian Nights" (nd)	4.70	14.00	28.00
"Bombardie" (1943)	4.00	11.00	22.00
"Crash Dive" (1943)-Tyrone Power	4.70	14.00	28.00

NOTE: *The 1941-42 issues contain line art with color photos. 1943 issues are line art.*

CIRCUS (...the Comic Riot)
June, 1938 - No. 3, Aug, 1938
Globe Syndicate

	GD25	FN65	NM94
1-(Scarce)-Spacehawks (2 pgs.), & Disk Eyes by Wolverton (2 pgs.), Pewee Throttle by Cole (2nd comic book work; see Star Comics V1#11), Beau Gus, Ken Craig & The Lords of Crillon, Jack Hinton by Eisner, Van Bragger by Kane	357.00	1071.00	2500.00
2,3-(Scarce)-Eisner, Cole, Wolverton, Bob Kane-a in each	200.00	600.00	1400.00

CIRCUS BOY (See 4-Color No. 759, 785, 813 & Movie Classics)

CIRCUS COMICS
1945 - No. 2, June, 1945; Winter, 1948-49
Farm Women's Publishing Co./D. S. Publ.

	GD25	FN65	NM94
1-Funny animal	8.35	25.00	50.00
2	5.85	17.50	35.00
1(1948)-D.S. Publ.; 2 pgs. Frazetta	17.00	52.00	120.00

CIRCUS OF FUN COMICS
1945 - No. 3, Dec, 1947 (A book of games & puzzles)
A. W. Nugent Publishing Co.

	GD25	FN65	NM94
1	10.00	30.00	60.00
2,3	6.70	20.00	40.00

CISCO KID, THE (TV)
July, 1950 - No. 41, Oct-Dec, 1958
Dell Publishing Co.

	GD25	FN65	NM94
4-Color 292(#1)-Cisco Kid, his horse Diablo, & sidekick Pancho & his horse Loco begin; painted-c begin	20.00	60.00	140.00
2(1/51)-5	10.00	30.00	70.00
6-10	9.15	27.50	55.00
11-20	7.50	22.50	45.00
21-36-Last painted-c	5.85	17.50	35.00
37-41: All photo-c	10.00	30.00	70.00

NOTE: ***Buscema** a-40. **Ernest Nordli** painted c-5-16, 20, 35.*

CISCO KID COMICS
Winter, 1944 - No. 3?, 1945
Bernard Bailey/Swappers Quarterly

	GD25	FN65	NM94
1-Illustrated Stories of the Operas: Faust; Funnyman by Giunta; Cisco Kid (1st app.) & Superbaby begin; Giunta-c	36.00	107.00	250.00
2,3 (Exist?)	29.00	86.00	200.00

CITIZEN SMITH (See Holyoke One-Shot No. 9)

CITY OF THE LIVING DEAD (See Fantastic Tales No. 1)
1952
Avon Periodicals

	GD25	FN65	NM94
nn-Hollingsworth-c/a	25.00	75.00	175.00

CITY SURGEON (Blake Harper...)
August, 1963
Gold Key

	GD25	FN65	NM94
1(10075-308)-Painted-c	2.40	6.00	12.00

CIVIL WAR MUSKET, THE (Kadets of America Handbook)
1960 (36 pgs.) (Half-size; 25¢)
Custom Comics, Inc.

	GD25	FN65	NM94
nn	2.80	7.00	14.00

CLAIRE VOYANT (Also see Keen Teens)
1946 - No. 4, 1947 (Sparling strip reprints)
Leader Publ./Standard/Pentagon Publ.

	GD25	FN65	NM94
nn	38.00	115.00	265.00
2,4: 2-Kamen-c. 4-Kamen bondage-c	31.00	92.00	215.00
3-Kamen bridal-c; contents mentioned in Love and Death, a book by Gershom Legman(1949) referenced by Dr. Wertham	34.00	103.00	240.00

CLANCY THE COP
1930 - No. 2, 1931 (52 pgs.; B&W) (not reprints) (10x10")
Dell Publishing Co. (Soft cover)

	GD25	FN65	NM94
1,2-Vep-a	15.00	45.00	105.00

CLANDESTINE PREVIEW, THE
Oct, 1994 ($1.50)
Marvel Comics

	GD25	FN65	NM94
1			1.50

CLASH
1991 - No. 3, 1991 ($4.95, mini-series, 52 pgs.)
DC Comics

	GD25	FN65	NM94
Book One - Three: Adam Kubert-c/a	1.00	2.50	5.00

CLASSIC COMICS/ILLUSTRATED - INTRODUCTION
by Dan Malan

Further revisions have been made to help in understanding the **Classics** section. **Classics** reprint editions prior to 1963 had either incorrect dates or no dates listed. Those reprint editions should be identified only by the highest number on the reorder list (HRN). Past price guides listed what were calculated to be approximately correct dates, but many people found it confusing for the price guide to list a date not listed in the comic itself.

We have also attempted to clear up confusion about edition variations, such as color, printer, etc. Such variations will be identified by letters. Editions will now be determined by three categories. Original edition variations will be Edition 1A, 1B, etc. All reprint editions prior to 1963 will be identified by HRN only. All reprint editions from 9/63 on will be identified by the correct date listed in the comic.

We have also included new information on four recent reprintings of **Classics** not previously listed. From 1968-1976 Twin Circle, the Catholic newspaper, serialized over 100 **Classics** titles. That list can be found under non-series items at the end of this section. In 1972 twelve **Classics** were reissued as **Now Age Books Illustrated**. They are listed under **Pendulum Illustrated Classics**. In 1982, 20 **Classics** were reissued, adapted for teaching English as a second language. They are listed under **Regents Illustrated Classics**. Then in 1984, six **Classics** were reissued with cassette tapes. See the listing under **Cassette Books**.

UNDERSTANDING CLASSICS ILLUSTRATED
by Dan Malan

Since **Classics Illustrated** is the most complicated comic book series, with all its reprint editions and variations, with changes in covers and artwork, with a variety of means of identifying editions, and with the most extensive worldwide distribution of any comic-book series; therefore this introductory section is provided to assist you in gaining expertise about this series.

THE HISTORY OF CLASSICS

The **Classics** series was the brain child of Albert L. Kanter, who saw in the new comic-book medium a means of introducing children to the great classics of literature. In October of 1941 his Gilberton Co. began the **Classic Comics** series with **The Three Musketeers**, with 64 pages of storyline. In those early years, the struggling series saw irregular schedules and numerous printers, not to mention variable art quality and liberal story adaptations. With No.13 the page total was reduced to 56 (except for No. 33, originally scheduled to be No. 9), and with No. 15 the coming-next ad on the outside back cover moved inside. In 1945 the Jerry Iger Shop began producing all new CC titles, beginning with No. 23. In 1947 the search for a classier logo resulted in **Classics Illustrated**, beginning with No. 35, **Last Days of Pompeii**. With No. 45 the page total dropped again to 48, which was to become the standard.

Two new developments in 1951 had a profound effect upon the success of the series. One was the introduction of painted covers, instead of the old line drawn covers, beginning with No. 81, **The Odyssey**. The second was the switch to the major national distributor Curtis. They raised the cover price from 10 to 15 cents, making it the highest priced comic-book, but it did not slow the growth of the series, because they were marketed as books, not comics. Because of this higher quality image, **Classics** flourished during the fifties while other comic series were reeling from outside attacks. They diversified with their new **Juniors**, **Specials**, and **World Around Us** series.

Classics artwork can be divided into three distinct periods. The pre-Iger era (1941-44) was mentioned above for its variable art quality. The Iger era (1945-53) was a major improvement in art quality and adaptations. It came to be dominated by artists Henry Kiefer and Alex Blum, together accounting for some 50 titles. Their styles gave the first real personality to the series. The EC era (1954-62) resulted from the demise of the EC horror series, when many of their artists made the major switch to classical art.

But several factors brought the production of new CI titles to a complete halt in 1962. Gilberton lost its 2nd class mailing permit. External factors like television, cheap paperback books, and Cliff Notes were all eating away at their market. Production halted with No.167, **Faust**, even though many more titles were already in the works. Many of those found their way into foreign series, and are very desirable to collectors. In 1967, **Classics Illustrated** was sold to Patrick Frawley and his Catholic publication, Twin Circle. They issued two new titles in 1969 as part of an attempted revival, but succumbed to major distribution problems in 1971. In 1988, the trio: First Publishing, Berkley Press, and Classics Media Group acquired the use rights for the old CI series art, logo, and name from the Frawley Group. So far they have used only the name in the new series, but do have plans to reprint the old CI.

One of the unique aspects of the **Classics Illustrated** (CI) series was the proliferation of reprint variations. Some titles had as many as 25 editions. Reprinting began in 1943. Some **Classic Comics** (CC) reprints (r) had the logo format revised to a banner logo, and added a motto under the banner. In 1947 CC titles changed to the CI logo, but kept their line drawn covers (LDC). In 1948, Nos. 13, 18, 29 and 41 received second covers (LDC2), replacing covers considered too violent, and reprints of Nos. 13-44 had pages reduced to 48, except for No. 26, which had 48 pages to begin with.

Starting in the mid-1950s, 70 of the 80 LDC titles were reissued with new painted covers (PC). Thirty of them also received new interior artwork (A2). The new artwork was generally higher quality with larger art panels and more faithful but abbreviated storylines. Later on, there were 29 second painted covers (PC2), mostly by Twin Circle. Altogether there were 199 interior art variations (169 (O)s and 30 A2 editions) and 272 different covers (169 (O)s, four LDC2s, 70 new PCs of LDC (O)s, and 29 PC2s). It is mildly astounding to realize that there are nearly 1400 different editions in the U.S. CI series.

FOREIGN CLASSICS ILLUSTRATED

If U.S. Classics variations are mildly astounding, the veritable plethora of foreign CI variations will boggle your imagination. While we still anticipate additional discoveries, we presently know about series in 25 languages and 27 countries. There were 250 new CI titles in foreign series, and nearly 400 new foreign covers of U.S. titles. The 1400 U.S. CI editions pale in comparison to the 4000 plus foreign editions. The very nature of CI lent itself to flourishing as an international series. Worldwide, they published over one billion copies! The first foreign CI series consisted of six Canadian Classic Comic reprints in 1946.

Here is a chart showing when CI series first began in each country:

1946: Canada. 1947: Australia. 1948: Brazil/The Netherlands. 1950: Italy. 1951: Greece/Japan/Hong Kong(?)/England/Argentina/Mexico. 1952: West Germany. 1954: Norway. 1955: New Zealand/South Africa. 1956: Denmark/Sweden/Iceland. 1957: Finland/France. 1962: Singapore(?). 1964: India (8 languages). 1971: Ireland (Gaelic). 1973: Belgium(?) /Philippines(?) & Malaysia(?).

Significant among the early series were Brazil and Greece. In 1950, Brazil was the first country to begin doing its own new titles. They issued nearly 80 new CI titles by Brazilian authors. In Greece in 1951 they actually had debates in parliament about the effects of Classics Illustrated on Greek culture, leading to the inclusion of 88 new Greek History & Mythology titles in the CI series.

But by far the most important foreign CI development was the joint European series which began in 1956 in 10 countries simultaneously. By 1960, CI had the largest European distribution of any American publication, not just comics! So when all the problems came up with U.S. distribution, they literally moved the CI operation to Europe in 1962, and continued producing new titles in all four CI series. Many of them were adapted and drawn in the U.S., the most famous of which was the British CI #158A. Dr. No, drawn by Norman Nodel. Unfortunately, the British CI series ended in late 1963, which limited the European CI titles available in English to 15. Altogether there were 82 new CI art titles in the joint European series, which ran until 1976.

IDENTIFYING CLASSICS EDITIONS

HRN: This is the highest number on the reorder list. It should be listed in ( ) after the title number. It is crucial to understanding various CI editions.

ORIGINALS (O): This is the all-important First Edition. To determine (O)s,there is one primary rule and two secondary rules (with exceptions):

Rule No. 1: All (O)s and only (O)s have coming-next ads for the next number. **Exceptions**: No. 14(15) (reprint) has an ad on the last inside text page only. No. 14(0) also has a full-page outside back cover ad (also rule 2). Nos.55(75) and 57(75) have coming-next ads. (Rules 2 and 3 apply here). Nos. 168(0) and 169(0) do not have coming-next ads. No.168 was never reprinted; No. 169(0) has HRN (166). No. 169(169) is the only reprint.

Rule No. 2: On nos.1-80, all (O)s and only (O)s list 10c on the front cover. **Exceptions**: Reprint variations of Nos. 37(62), 39(71), and 46(62) list 10c on the front cover. (Rules 1 and 3 apply here.)

Rule No. 3: All (O)s have HRN close to that title No. **Exceptions**: Some reprints also have HRNs close to that title number: a few CC(r)s, 58(62), 60(62), 149(149), 152(149) 153(149), and title nos. in the 160's. (Rules 1 and 2 apply here.)

DATES: Many reprint editions list either an incorrect date or no date. Since Gilberton apparently kept track of CI editions by HRN, they often left the (O) date on reprints. Often, someone with a CI collection for sale will swear that all their copies are originals. That is why we are so detailed in pointing out how to identify original editions. Except for original editions, which should have a coming-next ad, etc., all CI dates prior to 1963 are incorrect! So you want to go by HRN only if it is (165) or below, and go by listed date if it is 1963 or later. There are a few (167) editions with incorrect dates. They could be listed either as (167) or (62/3), which is meant to indicate that they were issued sometime between late 1962 and early 1963.

COVERS: A change from CC to LDC indicates a logo change, not a cover change; while a change from LDC to LDC2, LDC to PC, or from PC to PC2 does indicate a new cover. New PCs can be identified by HRN, and PC2s can be identified by HRN and date. Several covers had color changes, particularly from purple to blue.

Notes: If you see 15 cents in Canada on a front cover, it does not necessarily indicate a Canadian edition. Editions with an HRN between 44 and 75, with 15 cents on the cover are Canadian. Check the publisher's address. An HRN listing two numbers with a / between them indicates that there are two different reorder lists in the front and back covers. Official Twin Circle editions have a full-page back cover ad for their TC magazine, with no CI reorder list. Any CI with just a Twin Circle sticker on the front is not an official TC edition.

TIPS ON LISTING CLASSICS FOR SALE

It may be easy to just list Edition 17, but Classics collectors keep track of CI editions in terms of HRN and/or date, (O) or (r), CC or LDC, PC or PC2, A1 or A2, soft or stiff cover, etc. Try to help them out. For originals, just list (0), unless there are variations such as color (Nos. 10 and 61), printer (Nos. 18-22), HRN (Nos. 95, 108, 160), etc. For reprints, just list HRN if its (165) or below. Above that, list HRN and date. Also, please list type of logo/cover/art for the convenience of buyers. They will appreciate it.

CLASSIC COMICS (Also see Best from Boys Life, Cassette Books, Famous Stories, Fast Fiction, Golden Picture Classics, King Classics, Marvel Classics Comics, Pendulum Illustrated Classics, Picture Parade, Picture Progress, Regents Ill. Classics, Spitfire, Stories by Famous Authors, Superior Stories, and World Around Us.)

CLASSIC COMICS (Classics Illustrated No. 35 on)
10/41 - No. 34, 2/47; No. 35, 3/47 - No. 169, Spring 1969
(Reprint Editions of almost all titles 5/43 - Spring 1971)
(Painted Covers (0)s No. 81 on, and (r)s of most Nos. 1-80)
Elliot Publishing #1-3 (1941-1942)/Gilberton Publications #4-167 (1942-1967)/
Twin Circle Pub. (Frawley) #168-169 (1968-1971)

Abbreviations:
A–Art; C or c–Cover; CC–Classic Comics; CI–Classics Ill.;
Ed–Edition; LDC–Line Drawn Cover; PC–Painted Cover; r–Reprint

1. The Three Musketeers

Ed	HRN	Date	Details	A	C	GD25	FN65	NM94
1	–	10/41	Date listed-1941; Elliot Pub; 68 pgs.	1	1	457.00	1370.00	3200.00

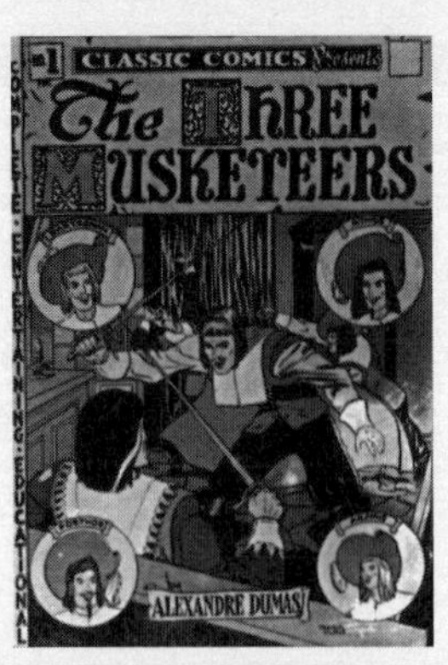

Classic Comics #1 © GIL

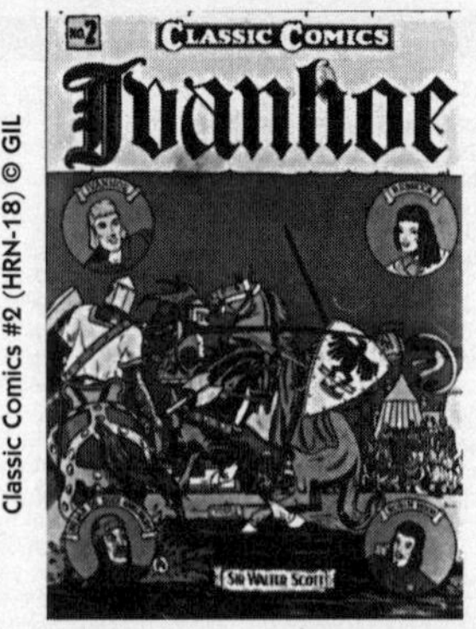

Classic Comics #2 (HRN-18) © GIL

Classic Comics #3 (HRN-20) © GIL

Ed	HRN	Date	Details	A	C	GD25	FN65	NM94
2	10	–	10¢ price removed on all (r)s; Elliot Pub; CC-r	1	1	26.00	809.00	185.00
3	15	–	Long Isl. Ind. Ed.; CC-r	1	1	19.00	57.00	130.00
4	18/20		Sunrise Times Ed.; CC-r	1	1	15.00	45.00	105.00
5	21	–	Richmond Courier Ed.; CC-r	1	1	13.50	41.00	95.00
6	28	1946	CC-r	1	1	10.00	30.00	70.00
7	36	–	LDC-r	1	1	5.85	17.50	35.00
8	60	–	LDC-r	1	1	4.00	11.00	22.00
9	64	–	LDC-r	1	1	3.60	9.00	18.00
10	78	–	C-price 15¢;LDC-r	1	1	3.20	8.00	16.00
11	93	–	LDC-r	1	1	3.20	8.00	16.00
12	114	–	Last LDC-r	1	1	2.40	6.00	12.00
13	134	–	New-c; old-a; 64 pg. PC-r	1	2	2.40	6.00	12.00
14	143	–	Old-a; PC-r; 64 pg.	1	2	2.00	5.00	10.00
15	150	–	New-a; PC-r; Evans/Crandall-a	2	2	2.40	6.00	12.00
16	149	–	PC-r	2	2	1.25	2.50	5.00
17	167	–	PC-r	2	2	1.25	2.50	5.00
18	167	4/64	PC-r	2	2	1.25	2.50	5.00
19	167	1/65	PC-r	2	2	1.25	2.50	5.00
20	167	3/66	PC-r	2	2	1.25	2.50	5.00
21	166	11/67	PC-r	2	2	1.25	2.50	5.00
22	166	Spr/69	C-price 25¢ ; stiff-c; PC-r	2	2	1.25	2.50	5.00
23	169	Spr/71	PC-r; stiff-c	2	2	1.25	2.50	5.00

2. Ivanhoe

Ed	HRN	Date	Details	A	C	GD25	FN65	NM94
1	(O)	12/41?	Date listed-1941; Elliot Pub; 68 pgs.	1	1	170.00	515.00	1200.00
2	10	–	Price & 'Presents' removed; Elliot Pub; CC-r	1	1	23.00	70.00	160.00
3	15	–	Long Isl. Ind. ed.; CC-r	1	1	17.00	52.00	120.00
4	18/20		Sunrise Times ed.; CC-r	1	1	15.00	45.00	105.00
5	21	–	Richmond Courier ed.; CC-r	1	1	13.50	41.00	95.00
6	28	1946	Last 'Comics'-r	1	1	10.00	30.00	70.00
7	36	–	1st LDC-r	1	1	5.85	17.50	35.00
8	60	–	LDC-r	1	1	4.00	11.00	22.00
9	64	–	LDC-r	1	1	4.00	10.00	20.00
10	78	–	C-price 15¢; LDC-r	1	1	3.20	8.00	16.00
11	89	–	LDC-r	1	1	2.80	7.00	14.00
12	106	–	LDC-r	1	1	2.40	6.00	12.00
13	121	–	Last LDC-r	1	1	2.40	6.00	12.00
14	136	–	New-c&a; PC-r	2	2	2.80	7.00	14.00
15	142	–	PC-r	2	2	1.25	2.50	5.00
16	153	–	PC-r	2	2	1.25	2.50	5.00
17	149	–	PC-r	2	2	1.25	2.50	5.00
18	167	–	PC-r	2	2	1.25	2.50	5.00
19	167	5/64	PC-r	2	2	1.25	2.50	5.00
20	167	1/65	PC-r	2	2	1.25	2.50	5.00
21	167	3/66	PC-r	2	2	1.25	2.50	5.00
22A	166	9/67	PC-r	2	2	1.25	2.50	5.00
22B	166	–	Center ad for Children's Digest & Young Miss; rare; PC-r	2	2	8.35	25.00	50.00
23	166	R/68	C-Price 25¢; PC-r	2	2	1.25	2.50	5.00
24	169	Win/69	Stiff-c	2	2	1.25	2.50	5.00
25	169	Win/71	PC-r; stiff-c	2	2	1.25	2.50	5.00

3. The Count of Monte Cristo

Ed	HRN	Date	Details	A	C	GD25	FN65	NM94
1	(O)	3/42	Elliot Pub; 68 pgs.	1	1	121.00	365.00	850.00
2	10	–	Conray Prods; CC-r	1	1	123.00	70.00	160.00
3	15	–	Long Isl. Ind. ed.; CC-r	1	1	17.00	52.00	120.00
4	18/20	–	Sunrise Times ed.; CC-r	1	1	15.00	45.00	105.00
5	20	–	Sunrise Times ed.; CC-r	1	1	13.50	41.00	95.00
6	21	–	Richmond Courier ed.; CC-r	1	1	13.00	40.00	90.00
7	28	1946	CC-r; new Banner logo	1	1	10.00	30.00	70.00
8	36	–	1st LDC-r	1	1	5.85	17.50	35.00
9	60	–	LDC-r	1	1	4.00	11.00	22.00
10	62	–	LDC-r	1	1	4.35	13.00	26.00
11	71	–	LDC-r	1	1	3.60	9.00	18.00
12	87	–	C-price 15¢; LDC-r	1	1	3.20	8.00	16.00
13	113	–	LDC-r	1	1	2.40	6.00	12.00
14	135	–	New-c&a; PC-r; Cameron-a	2	2	2.40	6.00	12.00
15	143	–	PC-r	2	2	1.25	2.50	5.00
16	153	–	PC-r	2	2	1.25	2.50	5.00
17	161	–	PC-r	2	2	1.25	2.50	5.00
18	167	–	PC-r	2	2	1.25	2.50	5.00
19	167	7/64	PC-r	2	2	1.25	2.50	5.00
20	167	7/65	PC-r	2	2	1.25	2.50	5.00
21	167	7/66	PC-r	2	2	1.25	2.50	5.00
22	166	R/68	C-price 25¢; PC-r	2	2	1.25	2.50	5.00
23	169	–	Win/69 Stiff-c; PC-r	2	2	1.25	2.50	5.00

4. The Last of the Mohicans

Ed	HRN	Date	Details	A	C	GD25	FN65	NM94
1	(O)	8/42?	Date listed-1942; Gilberton #4(0) on; 68 pgs.	1	1	107.00	320.00	750.00
2	12	–	Elliot Pub; CC-r	1	1	22.00	65.00	150.00
3	15	–	Long Isl. Ind. ed.; CC-r	1	1	17.00	52.00	120.00
4	20	–	Long Isl. Ind. ed.; CC-r; banner logo	1	1	15.00	45.00	105.00
5	21	–	Queens Home News ed.; CC-r	1	1	13.50	41.00	95.00
6	28	1946	Last CC-r; new	1	1	10.00	30.00	70.00
7	36	–	1st LDC-r	1	1	5.85	17.50	35.00
8	60	–	LDC-r	1	1	4.00	11.00	22.00
9	64	–	LDC-r	1	1	3.60	9.00	18.00
10	78	–	C-price 15¢; LDC-r	1	1	3.20	8.00	16.00
11	89	–	LDC-r	1	1	2.80	7.00	14.00
12	117	–	Last LDC-r	1	1	2.40	6.00	12.00
13	135	–	New-c; PC-r	1	2	2.40	6.00	12.00
14	141	–	PC-r	1	2	2.00	5.00	10.00
15	150	–	New-a; PC-r; Severin, L.B. Cole-a	2	2	2.40	6.00	12.00
16	161	–	PC-r	2	2	1.25	2.50	5.00
17	167	–	PC-r	2	2	1.25	2.50	5.00
18	167	6/64	PC-r	2	2	1.25	2.50	5.00
19	167	8/65	PC-r	2	2	1.25	2.50	5.00
20	167	8/66	PC-r	2	2	1.25	2.50	5.00
21	166	R/67	C-price 25¢; PC-r	2	2	1.25	2.50	5.00
22	169	Spr/69	Stiff-c; PC-r	2	2	1.25	2.50	5.00

5. Moby Dick

Ed	HRN	Date	Details	A	C

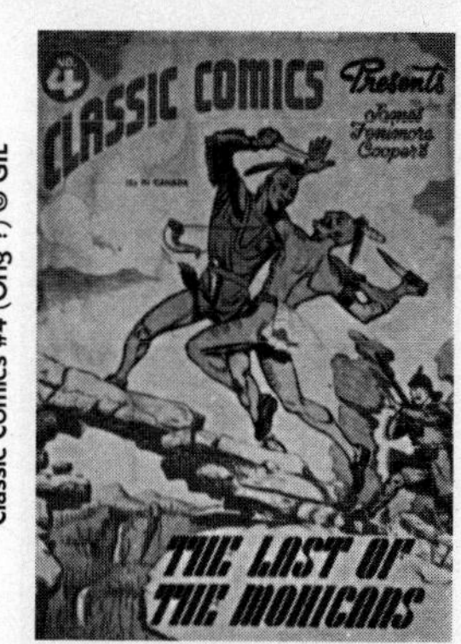

Classic Comics #4 (Orig ?) © GIL

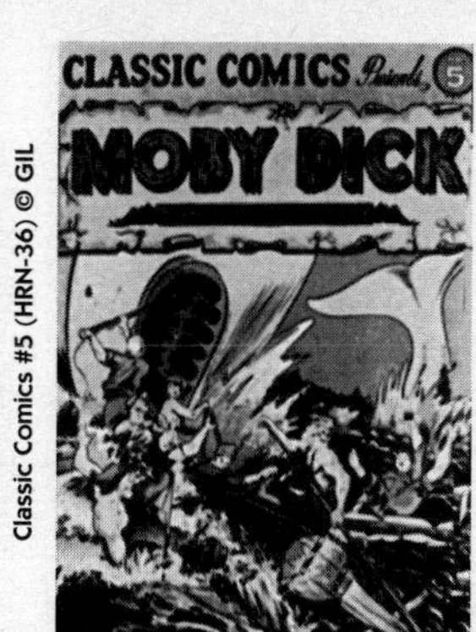

Classic Comics #5 (HRN-36) © GIL

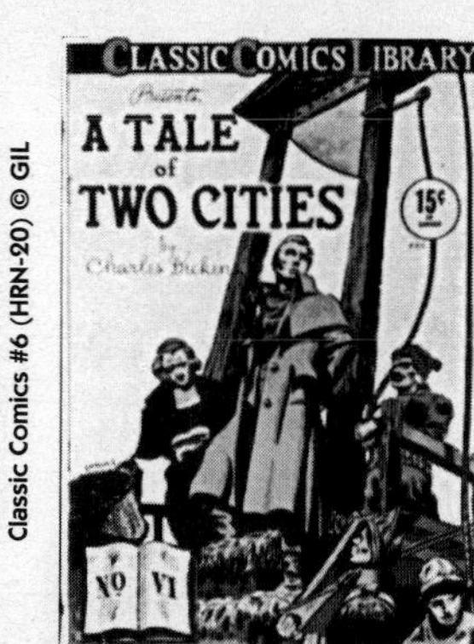

Classic Comics #6 (HRN-20) © GIL

Ed	HRN	Date	Details	A	C	GD25	FN65	NM94
1	(O)	9/42?	Date listed-1942; Gilberton; 68 pgs.	1	1	129.00	385.00	900.00
2	10	–	Conray Prods; Pg. 64 changed from 105 title list to letter from Editor; CC-r	1	1	23.00	70.00	160.00
3	15	–	Long Isl. Ind. ed.; Pg. 64 changed from Letter to the Editor to Ill. poem-Concord Hymn; CC-r	1	1	17.00	52.00	120.00
4	18/20	–	Sunrise Times ed.; CC-r	1	1	16.00	48.00	110.00
5	20	–	Sunrise Times ed.; CC-r	1	1	15.00	45.00	105.00
6	21	–	Sunrise Times ed.; CC-r	1	1	13.50	41.00	95.00
7	28	1946	CC-r; new banner logo	1	1	10.00	30.00	70.00
8	36	–	1st LDC-r	1	1	5.85	17.50	35.00
9	60	–	LDC-r	1	1	4.00	11.00	22.00
10	62	–	LDC-r	1	1	4.35	13.00	26.00
11	71	–	LDC-r	1	1	3.60	9.00	18.00
12	87	–	C-price 15¢; LDC-r	1	1	3.20	8.00	16.00
13	118	–	LDC-r	1	1	2.40	6.00	12.00
14	131	–	New c&a; PC-r	2	2	2.40	6.00	12.00
15	138	–	PC-r	2	2	1.25	2.50	5.00
16	148	–	PC-r	2	2	1.25	2.50	5.00
17	158	–	PC-r	2	2	1.25	2.50	5.00
18	167	–	PC-r	2	2	1.25	2.50	5.00
19	167	6/64	PC-r	2	2	1.25	2.50	5.00
20	167	7/65	PC-r	2	2	1.25	2.50	5.00
21	167	3/66	PC-r	2	2	1.25	2.50	5.00
22	166	9/67	PC-r	2	2	1.25	2.50	5.00
23	166	Win/69	New-c & c-price 25¢; Stiff-c; PC-r	2	3	2.00	5.00	10.00
24	169	Win/71	PC-r	2	3	2.00	5.00	10.00

6. A Tale of Two Cities

Ed	HRN	Date	Details	A	C	GD25	FN65	NM94
1	(O)	10/42	Date listed-1942; 68 pgs. Zeckerberg c/a	1	1	110.00	330.00	775.00
2	14	–	Elliot Pub; CC-r	1	1	20.00	60.00	140.00
3	18	–	Long Isl. Ind. ed.; CC-r	1	1	17.00	50.00	115.00
4	20	–	Sunrise Times ed.; CC-r	1	1	15.00	45.00	105.00
5	28	1946	Last CC-r; new banner logo	1	1	10.00	30.00	70.00
6	51	–	1st LDC-r	1	1	5.35	16.00	32.00
7	64	–	LDC-r	1	1	4.00	10.50	21.00
8	78	–	C-price 15¢; LDC-r	1	1	3.20	8.00	16.00
9	89	–	LDC-r	1	1	2.40	6.00	12.00
10	117	–	LDC-r	1	1	2.40	6.00	12.00
11	132	–	New-c&a; PC-r; Joe Orlando-a	2	2	2.40	6.00	12.00
12	140	–	PC-r	2	2	1.25	2.50	5.00
13	147	–	PC-r	2	2	1.25	2.50	5.00
14	152	–	PC-r; very rare	2	2	11.50	34.00	80.00
15	153	–	PC-r	2	2	1.25	2.50	5.00
16	149	–	PC-r	2	2	1.25	2.50	5.00
17	167	–	PC-r	2	2	1.25	2.50	5.00
18	167	6/64	PC-r	2	2	1.25	2.50	5.00
19	167	8/65	PC-r	2	2	1.25	2.50	5.00
20	166	5/67	PC-r	2	2	1.25	2.50	5.00
21	166	Fall/68	New-c & 25¢; PC-r	2	3	2.00	5.00	10.00
22	169	Sum/70	Stiff-c; PC-r	2	3	2.00	5.00	10.00

7. Robin Hood

Ed	HRN	Date	Details	A	C	GD25	FN65	NM94
1	(O)	12/42	Date listed-1942; first Gift Box ad-bc; 68 pgs.	1	1	85.00	257.00	600.00
2	12	–	Elliot Pub; CC-r	1	1	20.00	60.00	140.00
3	18	–	Long Isl. Ind. ed.; CC-r	1	1	16.00	48.00	110.00
4	20	–	Nassau Bulletin ed.; CC-r	1	1	15.00	45.00	105.00
5	22	–	Queens Cty. Times ed.; CC-r	1	1	13.50	41.00	95.00
6	28	–	CC-r	1	1	10.00	30.00	70.00
7	51	–	LDC-r	1	1	5.35	16.00	32.00
8	64	–	LDC-r	1	1	4.00	10.50	21.00
9	78	–	LDC-r	1	1	3.20	8.00	16.00
10	97	–	LDC-r	1	1	2.80	7.00	14.00
11	106	–	LDC-r	1	1	2.40	6.00	12.00
12	121	–	LDC-r	1	1	2.40	6.00	12.00
13	129	–	New-c; PC-r	1	2	2.40	6.00	12.00
14	136	–	New-a; PC-r	2	2	2.40	6.00	12.00
15	143	–	PC-r	2	2	1.25	2.50	5.00
16	153	–	PC-r	2	2	1.25	2.50	5.00
17	164	–	PC-r	2	2	1.25	2.50	5.00
18	167	–	PC-r	2	2	1.25	2.50	5.00
19	167	6/64	PC-r	2	2	1.50	3.00	6.00
20	167	5/65	PC-r	2	2	1.25	2.50	5.00
21	167	7/66	PC-r	2	2	1.25	2.50	5.00
22	166	12/67	PC-r	2	2	1.50	3.00	6.00
23	169	Sum/69	Stiff-c; c-price 25¢; PC-r	2	2	1.25	2.50	5.00

8. Arabian Nights

Ed	HRN	Date	Details	A	C	GD25	FN65	NM94
1	(O)	2/43	Original; 68 pgs. Lilian Chestney-c/a	1	1	229.00	685.00	1600.00
2	17	–	Long Isl. ed.; pg. 64 changed from Gift Box ad to Letter from British Medical Worker; CC-r	1	1	64.00	193.00	450.00
3	20	–	Nassau Bulletin; Pg. 64 changed from letter to article-Three Men Named Smith; CC-r	1	1	50.00	150.00	350.00
4A	28	1946	CC-r; new banner logo, slick-c	1	1	32.00	96.00	225.00
4B	28	1946	Same, but w/stiff-c	1	1	32.00	96.00	225.00
5	51	–	LDC-r	1	1	23.00	70.00	160.00
6	64	–	LDC-r	1	1	19.00	57.00	130.00
7	78	–	LDC-r	1	1	17.00	51.00	120.00
8	164	–	New-c&a; PC-r	2	2	14.00	43.00	100.00

9. Les Miserables

Ed	HRN	Date	Details	A	C	GD25	FN65	NM94
1A	(O)	3/43	Original; slick paper cover; 68 pgs.	1	1	75.00	225.00	525.00
1B	(O)	3/43	Original; rough, pulp type-c; 68 pgs.	1	1	79.00	235.00	550.00
2	14	–	Elliot Pub; CC-r	1	1	22.00	65.00	150.00
3	18	3/44	Nassau Bul. Pg. 64 changed from Gift Box ad to Bill of Rights article; CC-r	1	1	17.00	52.00	120.00
4	20	–	Richmond Courier	1	1	14.00	43.00	100.00

Classic Comics #7 © GIL

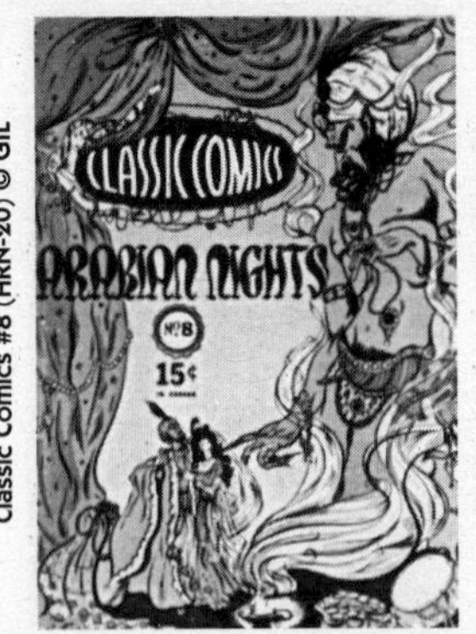

Classic Comics #8 (HRN-20) © GIL

CLASSIC COMICS
ROBINSON CRUSOE

Classic Comics #10 (HRN-14) © GIL

Ed	HRN	Date	Details	A	C	GD25	FN65	NM94
			ed.; CC-r					
5	28	1946	Gilberton; pgs. 60-64 rearranged/ illos added; CC-r	1	1	11.00	32.00	75.00
6	51	–	LDC-r	1	1	5.85	17.50	35.00
7	71	–	LDC-r	1	1	4.35	13.00	26.00
8	87	–	C-price 15¢; LDC-r	1	1	4.00	10.50	21.00
9	161	–	New-c&a; PC-r	2	2	4.00	12.00	24.00
10	167	9/63	PC-r	2	2	3.20	8.00	16.00
11	167	12/65	PC-r	2	2	3.20	8.00	16.00
12	166	R/1968	New-c & price 25¢; PC-r	2	3	3.60	9.00	18.00

10. Robinson Crusoe (Used in **SOTI**, pg. 142)

Ed	HRN	Date	Details	A	C	GD25	FN65	NM94
1A	(O)	4/43	Original; Violet-c; 68 pgs; Zuckerberg c/a	1	1	75.00	225.00	525.00
1B	(O)	4/43	Original; blue-grey-c, 68 pgs.	1	1	79.00	235.00	550.00
2A	14	–	Elliot Pub; violet-c; 68 pgs; CC-r	1	1	20.00	60.00	140.00
2B	14	–	Elliot Pub; blue-grey-c; CC-r	1	1	22.00	65.00	150.00
3	18	–	Nassau Bul. Pg. 64 changed from Gift Box ad to Bill of Rights article; CC-r	1	1	16.00	48.00	110.00
4	20	–	Queens Home News ed.; CC-r	1	1	13.50	41.00	95.00
5	28	1946	Gilberton; pg. 64 changes from Bill of Rights to WWII article-One Leg Shot Away; last CC-r	1	1	10.00	30.00	70.00
6	51	–	LDC-r	1	1	5.35	16.00	32.00
7	64	–	LDC-r	1	1	4.00	10.50	21.00
8	78	–	C-price 15¢; LDC-r	1	1	3.20	8.00	16.00
9	97	–	LDC-r	1	1	2.80	7.00	14.00
10	114	–	LDC-r	1	1	2.40	6.00	12.00
11	130	–	New-c; PC-r	1	2	2.40	6.00	12.00
12	140	–	New-a; PC-r	2	2	2.40	6.00	12.00
13	153	–	PC-r	2	2	1.25	2.50	5.00
14	164	–	PC-r	2	2	1.25	2.50	5.00
15	167	–	PC-r	2	2	1.25	2.50	5.00
16	167	7/64	PC-r	2	2	1.25	2.50	5.00
17	167	5/65	PC-r	2	2	1.80	4.50	9.00
18	167	6/66	PC-r	2	2	1.25	2.50	5.00
19	166	Fall/68	C-price 25¢; PC-r	2	2	1.25	2.50	5.00
20	166	R/68	(No Twin Circle ad)	2	2	1.50	3.00	6.00
21	169	Sm/70	Stiff-c; PC-r	2	2	1.50	3.00	6.00

11. Don Quixote

Ed	HRN	Date	Details	A	C	GD25	FN65	NM94
1	10	5/43	First (O) with HRN list; 68 pgs.	1	1	79.00	235.00	550.00
2	18	–	Nassau Bulletin ed.; CC-r	1	1	20.00	60.00	140.00
3	21	–	Queens Home News ed.; CC-r	1	1	16.00	48.00	110.00
4	28	–	CC-r	1	1	10.00	30.00	70.00
5	110	–	New-PC; PC-r	1	2	4.00	10.00	20.00
6	156	–	Pgs. reduced 68 to 52; PC-r	1	2	2.40	6.00	12.00
7	165	–	PC-r	1	2	1.75	3.50	7.00
8	167	1/64	PC-r	1	2	1.75	3.50	7.00
9	167	11/65	PC-r	1	2	1.75	3.50	7.00
10	166	R/1968	New-c & price 25¢; PC-r	1	3	2.80	7.00	14.00

12. Rip Van Winkle and the Headless Horseman

Ed	HRN	Date	Details	A	C	GD25	FN65	NM94
1	11	6/43	Original; 68 pgs.	1	1	79.00	235.00	550.00
2	15	–	Long Isl. Ind. ed.; CC-r	1	1	21.00	62.00	145.00
3	20	–	Long Isl. Ind. ed.;	1	1	16.00	48.00	110.00
4	22	–	Queens Cty. Times ed.; CC-r	1	1	13.50	41.00	95.00
5	28	–	CC-r	1	1	10.00	30.00	70.00
6	60	–	1st LDC-r	1	1	4.70	14.00	28.00
7	62	–	LDC-r	1	1	4.00	11.00	22.00
8	71	–	LDC-r	1	1	3.20	8.00	16.00
9	89	–	C-price 15¢; LDC-r	1	1	2.80	7.00	14.00
10	118	–	LDC-r	1	1	2.40	6.00	12.00
11	132	–	New-c; PC-r	1	2	2.40	6.00	12.00
12	150	–	New-a; PC-r	2	2	2.40	6.00	12.00
13	158	–	PC-r	2	2	1.25	2.50	5.00
14	167	–	PC-r	2	2	1.25	2.50	5.00
15	167	12/63	PC-r	2	2	1.25	2.50	5.00
16	167	4/65	PC-r	2	2	1.50	3.00	6.00
17	167	4/66	PC-r	2	2	1.25	2.50	5.00
18	166	R/1968	New-c&price 25¢; PC-r; stiff-c	2	3	2.00	5.00	10.00
19	169	Sm/70	PC-r; stiff-c	2	3	2.00	5.00	10.00

13. Dr. Jekyll and Mr. Hyde (Used in **SOTI**, pg. 143)

Ed	HRN	Date	Details	A	C	GD25	FN65	NM94
1	12	8/43	Original 60 pgs.	1	1	100.00	300.00	700.00
2	15	–	Long Isl. Ind. ed.; CC-r	1	1	24.00	73.00	170.00
3	20	–	Long Isl. Ind. ed.; CC-r	1	1	17.00	52.00	120.00
4	28	–	No c-price; CC-r	1	1	14.00	43.00	100.00
5	60	–	New-c; Pgs. reduced from 60 to 52; H.C. Kiefer-c; LDC-r	1	2	4.70	14.00	28.00
6	62	–	LDC-r	1	2	4.00	12.00	24.00
7	71	–	LDC-r	1	2	3.60	9.00	18.00
8	87	–	Date returns (erroneous); LDC-r	1	2	3.20	8.00	16.00
9	112	–	New-c&a; PC-r; Cameron-a	2	3	3.20	8.00	16.00
10	153	–	PC-r	2	3	1.25	2.50	5.00
11	161	–	PC-r	2	3	1.25	2.50	5.00
12	167	–	PC-r	2	3	1.25	2.50	5.00
13	167	8/64	PC-r	2	3	1.25	2.50	5.00
14	167	11/65	PC-r	2	3	1.25	2.50	5.00
15	166	R/68	C-price 25¢; PC-r	2	3	1.50	3.00	6.00
16	169	Wn/69	PC-r; stiff-c	2	3	1.25	2.50	5.00

14. Westward Ho!

Ed	HRN	Date	Details	A	C	GD25	FN65	NM94
1	13	9/43	Original; last outside bc coming-next ad; 60 pgs.	1	1	171.00	515.00	1200.00
2	15	–	Long Isl. Ind. ed.; CC-r	1	1	50.00	150.00	350.00
3	21	–	Queens Home News; Pg. 56 changed from coming-next ad to Three Men Named Smith; CC-r	1	1	36.00	107.00	250.00
4	28	1946	Gilberton; Pg. 56 changed again to WWII article-Speaking for America; last CC-r	1	1	29.00	86.00	200.00
5	53	–	Pgs. reduced from	1	1	26.00	78.00	180.00

Classics Illustrated #12 (HRN-167) © GIL

Classic Comics #14 (HRN-21) © GIL

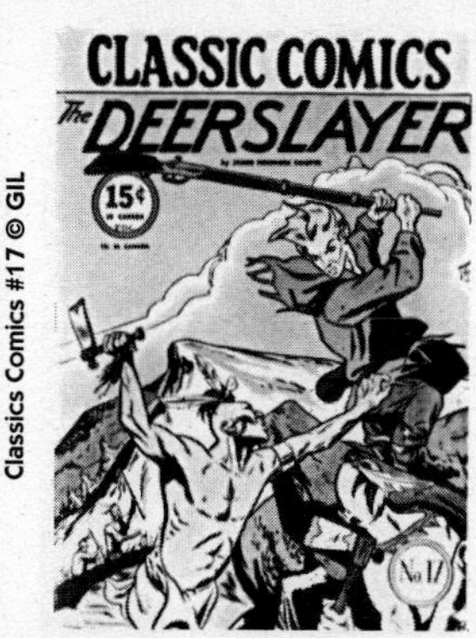

Classics Comics #17 © GIL

60 to 52; LDC-r

15. Uncle Tom's Cabin (Used in **SOTI**, pgs. 102, 103)

Ed	HRN	Date	Details	A	C	GD25	FN65	NM94
1	14	11/43	Original; Outside-bc ad: 2 Gift Boxes; 60 pgs.	1	1	64.00	193.00	450.00
2	15	–	Long Isl. Ind. listed- bottom inside-fc; also Gilberton listed bottom-pg. 1; CC-r	1	1	22.00	65.00	150.00
3	21	–	Nassau Bulletin ed.; CC-r	1	1	18.00	54.00	125.00
4	28	–	No c-price; CC-r	1	1	11.00	32.00	75.00
5	53	–	Pgs. reduced 60 to 52; LDC-r	1	1	5.35	16.00	32.00
6	71	–	LDC-r	1	1	4.00	11.00	22.00
7	89	–	C-price 15¢; LDC-r	1	1	4.00	10.00	20.00
8	117	–	New-c/lettering changes; PC-r	1	2	2.40	6.00	12.00
9	128	–	'Picture Progress' promo; PC-r	1	2	1.60	4.00	8.00
10	137	–	PC-r	1	2	1.25	2.50	5.00
11	146	–	PC-r	1	2	1.25	2.50	5.00
12	154	–	PC-r	1	2	1.25	2.50	5.00
13	161	–	PC-r	1	2	1.25	2.50	5.00
14	167	–	PC-r	1	2	1.25	2.50	5.00
15	167	6/64	PC-r	1	2	1.25	2.50	5.00
16	167	5/65	PC-r	1	2	1.25	2.50	5.00
17	166	5/67	PC-r	1	2	1.25	2.50	5.00
18	166	Wn/69	New-stiff-c; PC-r	1	3	2.00	5.00	10.00
19	169	Sm/70	PC-r; stiff-c	1	3	2.00	5.00	10.00

16. Gullivers Travels

Ed	HRN	Date	Details	A	C	GD25	FN65	NM94
1	15	12/43	Original-Lilian Chestney c/a; 60 pgs.	1	1	60.00	182.00	425.00
2	18/20	–	Price deleted; Queens Home News ed; CC-r	1	1	19.00	57.00	130.00
3	22	–	Queens Cty. Times ed.; CC-r	1	1	15.00	45.00	105.00
4	28	–	CC-r	1	1	10.00	30.00	70.00
5	60	–	Pgs. reduced to 48; LDC-r	1	1	4.35	13.00	26.00
6	62	–	LDC-r	1	1	4.00	10.00	20.00
7	78	–	C-price 15¢; LDC-r	1	1	3.20	8.00	16.00
8	89	–	LDC-r	1	1	2.40	6.00	12.00
9	155	–	New-c; PC-r	1	2	2.40	6.00	12.00
10	165	–	PC-r	1	2	1.25	2.50	5.00
11	167	5/64	PC-r	1	2	1.25	2.50	5.00
12	167	11/65	PC-r	1	2	1.25	2.50	5.00
13	166	R/1968	C-price 25¢; PC-r	1	2	1.25	2.50	5.00
14	169	Wn/69	PC-r; stiff-c	1	2	1.25	2.50	5.00

17. The Deerslayer

Ed	HRN	Date	Details	A	C	GD25	FN65	NM94
1	16	1/44	Original; Outside-bc ad: 3 Gift Boxes; 60 pgs.	1	1	57.00	170.00	400.00
2A	18	–	Queens Cty Times (inside-fc); CC-r	1	1	19.00	57.00	130.00
2B	18	–	Gilberton (bottom-pg. 1); CC-r; Scarce	1	1	26.00	78.00	180.00
3	22	–	Queens Cty. Times ed.; CC-r	1	1	15.00	45.00	105.00
4	28	–	CC-r	1	1	10.00	30.00	70.00
5	60	–	Pgs.reduced to 52; LDC-r	1	1	4.35	13.00	26.00
6	64	–	LDC-r	1	1	3.60	9.00	18.00
7	85	–	C-price 15¢; LDC-r	1	1	2.80	7.00	14.00
8	118	–	LDC-r	1	1	2.40	6.00	12.00
9	132	–	LDC-r	1	1	2.40	6.00	12.00
10	167	11/66	Last LDC-r	1	1	2.00	5.00	10.00
11	166	R/1968	New-c & price 25¢; PC-r	1	2	2.40	6.00	12.00
12	169	Spr/71	Stiff-c; letters from parents & educators; PC-r	1	2	2.00	5.00	10.00

18. The Hunchback of Notre Dame

Ed	HRN	Date	Details	A	C	GD25	FN65	NM94
1A	17	3/44	Orig.; Gilberton ed; 60 pgs.	1	1	71.00	215.00	500.00
1B	17	3/44	Orig.; Island Pub. Ed.; 60 pgs.	1	1	64.00	193.00	450.00
2	18/20	–	Queens Home News ed.; CC-r	1	1	20.00	60.00	140.00
3	22	–	Queens Cty. Times ed.; CC-r	1	1	16.00	48.00	110.00
4	28	–	CC-r	1	1	11.50	34.00	80.00
5	60	–	New-c; 8pgs. deleted; Kiefer-c; LDC-r	1	2	4.70	14.00	28.00
6	62	–	LDC-r	1	2	3.60	9.00	18.00
7	78	–	C-price 15¢; LDC-r	1	2	3.20	8.00	16.00
8A	89	–	H.C.Kiefer on bottom right-fc; LDC-r	1	2	2.80	7.00	14.00
8B	89	–	Name omitted; LDC-r	1	2	3.60	9.00	18.00
9	118	–	LDC-r	1	2	2.80	7.00	14.00
10	140	–	New-c; PC-r	1	3	4.00	10.00	20.00
11	146	–	PC-r	1	3	3.20	8.00	16.00
12	158	–	New-c&a; PC-r; Evans/Crandall-a	2	4	2.80	7.00	14.00
13	165	–	PC-r	2	4	1.50	3.00	6.00
14	167	9/63	PC-r	2	4	1.50	3.00	6.00
15	167	10/64	PC-r	2	4	1.50	3.00	6.00
16	167	4/66	PC-r	2	4	1.25	2.50	5.00
17	166	R/1968	New price 25¢; PC-r	2	4	1.25	2.50	5.00
18	169	Sp/70	Stiff-c; PC-r	2	4	1.25	2.50	5.00

19. Huckleberry Finn

Ed	HRN	Date	Details	A	C	GD25	FN65	NM94
1A	18	4/44	Orig.; Gilberton ed.; 60 pgs.	1	1	50.00	150.00	350.00
1B	18	4/44	Orig.; Island Pub.; 60 pgs.	1	1	54.00	160.00	375.00
2	18	–	Nassau Bulletin ed.; fc-price 15¢-Canada; no coming-next ad; CC-r	1	1	20.00	60.00	140.00
3	22	–	Queens City Times ed.; CC-r	1	1	15.00	45.00	105.00
4	28	–	CC-r	1	1	10.00	30.00	70.00
5	60	–	Pgs. reduced to 48; LDC-r	1	1	4.35	13.00	26.00
6	62	–	LDC-r	1	1	4.00	10.00	20.00
7	78	–	LDC-r	1	1	3.20	8.00	16.00
8	89	–	LDC-r	1	1	2.80	7.00	14.00
9	117	–	LDC-r	1	1	2.40	6.00	12.00
10	131	–	New-c&a; PC-r	2	2	2.40	6.00	12.00
11	140	–	PC-r	2	2	1.25	2.50	5.00
12	150	–	PC-r	2	2	1.25	2.50	5.00
13	158	–	PC-r	2	2	1.25	2.50	5.00
14	165	–	PC-r	2	2	1.25	2.50	5.00

Classics Comics #18 © GIL

Classic Comics #20 © GIL

Classic Comics #22 © GIL

Ed	HRN	Date	Details	A	C	GD25	FN65	NM94
15	167	–	PC-r	2	2	1.25	2.50	5.00
16	167	6/64	PC-r	2	2	1.25	2.50	5.00
17	167	6/65	PC-r	2	2	1.25	2.50	5.00
18	167	10/65	PC-r	2	2	1.25	2.50	5.00
19	166	9/67	PC-r	2	2	1.25	2.50	5.00
20	166	Win/69	C-price 25¢; PC-r; stiff-c	2	2	1.25	2.50	5.00
21	169	Sm/70	PC-r; stiff-c	2	2	1.25	2.50	5.00

20. The Corsican Brothers

Ed	HRN	Date	Details	A	C	GD25	FN65	NM94
1A	20	6/44	Orig.; Gilberton ed.; bc-ad: 4 Gift Boxes; 60 pgs.	1	1	57.00	170.00	400.00
1B	20	6/44	Orig.; Courier ed.; 60 pgs.	1	1	54.00	160.00	375.00
1C	20	6/44	Orig.; Long Island Ind. ed.; 60 pgs.	1	1	54.00	160.00	375.00
2	22	–	Queens Cty. Times ed.; white logo banner; CC-r	1	1	23.00	70.00	160.00
3	28	–	CC-r	1	1	20.00	60.00	140.00
4	60	–	CI logo; no price; 48 pgs.; LDC-r	1	1	16.00	48.00	110.00
5A	62	–	LDC-r; Classics Ill. logo at top of pgs.	1	1	14.00	43.00	100.00
5B	62	–	w/o logo at top of pg. (scarcer)	1	1	14.00	43.00	100.00
6	78	–	C-price 15¢; LDC-r	1	1	13.00	40.00	90.00
7	97	–	LDC-r	1	1	11.50	34.00	80.00

21. 3 Famous Mysteries ("The Sign of the 4", "The Murders in the Rue Morgue", "The Flayed Hand")

Ed	HRN	Date	Details	A	C	GD25	FN65	NM94
1A	21	7/44	Orig.; Gilberton ed.; 60 pgs.	1	1	85.00	257.00	600.00
1B	21	7/44	Orig. Island Pub. Co.; 60 pgs.	1	1	89.00	268.00	625.00
1C	21	7/44	Original; Courier Ed.; 60 pgs.	1	1	79.00	235.00	550.00
2	22	–	Nassau Bulletin ed.; CC-r	1	1	31.00	93.00	215.00
3	30	–	CC-r	1	1	24.50	73.00	170.00
4	62	–	LDC-r; 8 pgs. deleted; LDC-r	1	1	19.00	57.00	130.00
5	70	–	LDC-r	1	1	17.00	52.00	120.00
6	85	–	C-price 15¢; LDC-r	1	1	15.00	45.00	105.00
7	114	–	New-c; PC-r	1	2	15.00	45.00	105.00

22. The Pathfinder

Ed	HRN	Date	Details	A	C	GD25	FN65	NM94
1A	22	10/44	Orig.; No printer listed; ownership statement inside fc lists Gilberton & date; 60 pgs.	1	1	43.00	129.00	300.00
1B	22	10/44	Orig.; Island Pub. ed.; 60 pgs.	1	1	36.00	107.00	250.00
1C	22	10/44	Orig.; Queens Cty Times ed. 60 pgs.	1	1	36.00	107.00	250.00
2	30	–	C-price removed; CC-r	1	1	10.00	30.00	70.00
3	60	–	Pgs. reduced to 52; LDC-r	1	1	4.00	12.00	24.00
4	70	–	LDC-r	1	1	4.00	10.00	20.00
5	85	–	C-price 15¢; LDC-r	1	1	3.20	8.00	16.00
6	118	–	LDC-r	1	1	2.80	7.00	14.00
7	132	–	LDC-r	1	1	2.40	6.00	12.00
8	146	–	LDC-r	1	1	2.40	6.00	12.00
9	167	11/63	New-c; PC-r	1	2	4.00	10.00	20.00
10	167	12/65	PC-r	1	2	2.80	7.00	14.00
11	166	8/67	PC-r	1	2	2.80	7.00	14.00

23. Oliver Twist (1st Classic produced by the Iger Shop)

Ed	HRN	Date	Details	A	C	GD25	FN65	NM94
1	23	7/45	Original; 60 pgs.	1	1	36.00	107.00	250.00
2A	30	–	Printers Union logo on bottom left-fc same as 23(Orig.) (very rare); CC-r	1	1	22.00	65.00	150.00
2B	30	–	Union logo omitted; CC-r	1	1	10.00	30.00	70.00
3	60	–	Pgs. reduced to 48; LDC-r	1	1	4.00	12.00	24.00
4	62	–	LDC-r	1	1	4.00	10.00	20.00
5	71	–	LDC-r	1	1	3.20	8.00	16.00
6	85	–	C-price 15¢; LDC-r	1	1	2.80	7.00	14.00
7	94	–	LDC-r	1	1	2.40	6.00	12.00
8	118	–	LDC-r	1	1	2.40	6.00	12.00
9	136	–	New-PC, old-a; PC-r	1	2	2.40	6.00	12.00
10	150	–	Old-a; PC-r	1	2	1.80	4.50	9.00
11	164	–	Old-a; PC-r	1	2	1.80	4.50	9.00
12	164	–	New-a; PC-r; Evans/Crandall-a	2	2	2.80	7.00	14.00
13	167	–	PC-r	2	2	1.80	4.50	9.00
14	167	8/64	PC-r	2	2	1.25	2.50	5.00
15	167	12/65	PC-r	2	2	1.25	2.50	5.00
16	166	R/1968	New 25¢; PC-r	2	2	1.00	2.00	5.00
17	169	Win/69	Stiff-c; PC-r	2	2	1.25	2.50	5.00

24. A Connecticut Yankee in King Arthur's Court

Ed	HRN	Date	Details	A	C	GD25	FN65	NM94
1	9/45	–	Original	1	1	36.00	107.00	250.00
2	30	–	No price circle; CC-r	1	1	10.00	30.00	70.00
3	60	–	8 pgs. deleted; LDC-r	1	1	4.00	12.00	24.00
4	62	–	LDC-r	1	1	4.00	10.00	20.00
5	71	–	LDC-r	1	1	3.20	8.00	16.00
6	87	–	C-price 15¢; LDC-r	1	1	2.80	7.00	14.00
7	121	–	LDC-r	1	1	2.40	6.00	12.00
8	140	–	New-c&a; PC-r	2	2	2.40	6.00	12.00
9	153	–	PC-r	2	2	1.25	2.50	5.00
10	164	–	PC-r	2	2	1.25	2.50	5.00
11	167	–	PC-r	2	2	1.25	2.50	5.00
12	167	7/64	PC-r	2	2	1.25	2.50	5.00
13	167	6/66	PC-r	2	2	1.25	2.50	5.00
14	166	R/1968	C-price 25¢; PC-r	2	2	1.25	2.50	5.00
15	169	Spr/71	PC-r; stiff-c	2	2	1.25	2.50	5.00

25. Two Years Before the Mast

Ed	HRN	Date	Details	A	C	GD25	FN65	NM94
1	10/45	–	Original; Webb/Heames-a&c	1	1	36.00	107.00	250.00
2	30	–	Price circle blank; CC-r	1	1	11.00	32.00	75.00
3	60	–	8 pgs. deleted; LDC-r	1	1	4.00	12.00	24.00
4	62	–	LDC-r	1	1	4.00	10.50	21.00
5	71	–	LDC-r	1	1	3.20	8.00	16.00
6	85	–	C-price 15¢; LDC-r	1	1	2.80	7.00	14.00
7	114	–	LDC-r	1	1	2.40	6.00	12.00
8	156	–	3 pgs. replaced by fillers; new-c; PC-r	1	2	2.40	6.00	12.00
9	167	12/63	PC-r	1	2	1.25	2.50	5.00

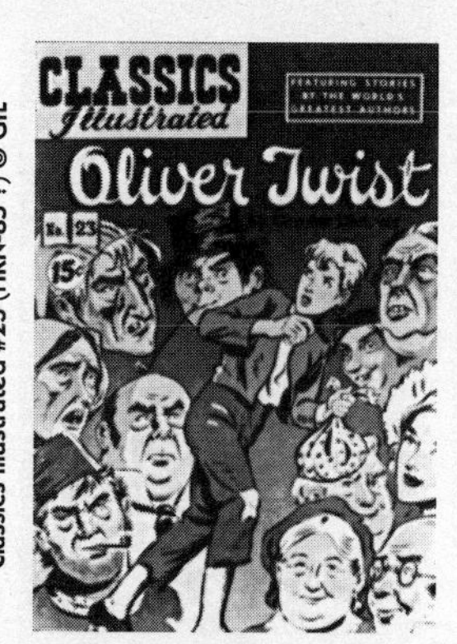

Classics Illustrated #23 (HRN-85 ?) © GIL

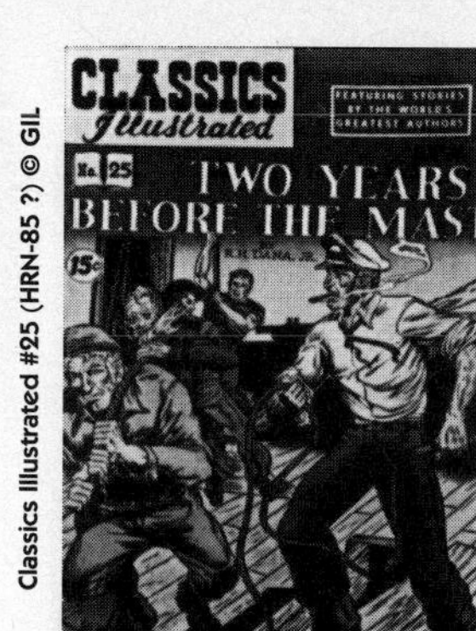

Classics Illustrated #25 (HRN-85 ?) © GIL

Classics Illustrated #26 © GIL

Ed	HRN	Date	Details	A	C	GD25	FN65	NM94
10	167	12/65	PC-r	1	2	1.25	2.50	5.00
11	166	9/67	PC-r	1	2	1.25	2.50	5.00
12	169	Win/69	C-price 25¢; stiff-c PC-r	1	2	1.25	2.50	5.00

26. Frankenstein

Ed	HRN	Date	Details	A	C	GD25	FN65	NM94
1	26	12/45	Orig.; Webb/Brewster a&c; 52 pgs.	1	1	86.00	257.00	600.00
2A	30	–	Price circle blank; no indicia; CC-r	1	1	23.00	70.00	160.00
2B	30	–	With indicia; scarce; CC-r	1	1	27.00	80.00	190.00
3	60	–	LDC-r	1	1	6.70	20.00	40.00
4	62	–	LDC-r	1	1	10.00	30.00	60.00
5	71	–	LDC-r	1	1	4.20	12.50	25.00
6A	82	–	C-price 15¢; soft-c LDC-r	1	1	4.00	11.00	22.00
6B	82	–	Stiff-c; LDC-r	1	1	4.70	14.00	28.00
7	117	–	LDC-r	1	1	2.80	7.00	14.00
8	146	–	New Saunders-c; PC-r	1	2	2.80	7.00	14.00
9	152	–	Scarce; PC-r	1	2	4.00	12.00	24.00
10	153	–	PC-r	1	2	1.25	2.50	5.00
11	160	–	PC-r	1	2	1.25	2.50	5.00
12	165	–	PC-r	1	2	1.25	2.50	5.00
13	167	–	PC-r	1	2	1.25	2.50	5.00
14	167	6/64	PC-r	1	2	1.25	2.50	5.00
15	167	6/65	PC-r	1	2	1.25	2.50	5.00
16	167	10/65	PC-r	1	2	1.25	2.50	5.00
17	166	9/67	PC-r	1	2	1.25	2.50	5.00
18	169	Fall/69	C-price 25¢; stiff-c PC-r	1	2	1.25	2.50	5.00
19	169	Spr/71	PC-r; stiff-c	1	2	1.25	2.50	5.00

27. The Adventures of Marco Polo

Ed	HRN	Date	Details	A	C	GD25	FN65	NM94
1	4/46	–	Original	1	1	36.00	107.00	250.00
2	30	–	Last 'Comics' reprint; CC-r	1	1	10.00	30.00	70.00
3	70	–	8 pgs. deleted; no c-price; LDC-r	1	1	4.00	10.50	21.00
4	87	–	C-price 15¢; LDC-r	1	1	3.20	8.00	16.00
5	117	–	LDC-r	1	1	2.40	6.00	12.00
6	154	–	New-c; PC-r	1	2	2.40	6.00	12.00
7	165	–	PC-r	1	2	1.25	2.50	5.00
8	167	4/64	PC-r	1	2	1.25	2.50	5.00
9	167	6/66	PC-r	1	2	1.25	2.50	5.00
10	169	Spr/69	New price 25¢; stiff-c; PC-r	1	2	1.25	2.50	5.00

28. Michael Strogoff

Ed	HRN	Date	Details	A	C	GD25	FN65	NM94
1	6/46	–	Original	1	1	36.00	107.00	250.00
2	51	–	8 pgs. cut; LDC-r	1	1	10.00	30.00	70.00
3	115	–	New-c; PC-r	1	2	3.20	8.00	16.00
4	155	–	PC-r	1	2	1.60	4.00	8.00
5	167	11/63	PC-r	1	2	1.60	4.00	8.00
6	167	7/66	PC-r	1	2	1.60	4.00	8.00
7	169	Sm/69	C-price 25¢; stiff-c PC-r	1	3	2.00	5.00	10.00

29. The Prince and the Pauper

Ed	HRN	Date	Details	A	C	GD25	FN65	NM94
1	7/46	–	Orig.; "Horror"-c	1	1	64.00	193.00	450.00
2	60	–	8 pgs. cut; new-c by Kiefer; LDC-r	1	2	4.35	13.00	26.00
3	62	–	LDC-r	1	2	4.00	11.00	22.00
4	71	–	LDC-r	1	2	3.20	8.00	16.00
5	93	–	LDC-r	1	2	2.80	7.00	14.00
6	114	–	LDC-r	1	2	2.40	6.00	12.00
7	128	–	New-c; PC-r	1	3	2.40	6.00	12.00
8	138	–	PC-r	1	3	1.25	2.50	5.00
9	150	–	PC-r	1	3	1.25	2.50	5.00
10	164	–	PC-r	1	3	1.25	2.50	5.00
11	167	–	PC-r	1	3	1.25	2.50	5.00
12	167	7/64	PC-r	1	3	1.25	2.50	5.00
13	167	11/65	PC-r	1	3	1.25	2.50	5.00
14	166	R/68	C-price 25¢; PC-r	1	3	1.25	2.50	5.00
15	169	Sm/70	PC-r; stiff-c	1	3	1.25	2.50	5.00

30. The Moonstone

Ed	HRN	Date	Details	A	C	GD25	FN65	NM94
1	9/46	–	Original; Rico-c/a	1	1	36.00	107.00	250.00
2	60	–	LDC-r; 8pgs. cut	1	1	5.00	15.00	30.00
3	70	–	LDC-r	1	1	4.00	12.00	24.00
4	155	–	New L.B. Cole-c; PC-r	1	2	5.85	17.50	35.00
5	165	–	PC-r; L.B. Cole-c	1	2	2.80	7.00	14.00
6	167	1/64	PC-r; L.B. Cole-c	1	2	1.60	4.00	8.00
7	167	9/65	PC-r; L.B. Cole-c	1	2	1.50	3.00	6.00
8	166	R/1968	C-price 25¢; PC-r	1	2	1.25	2.50	5.00

31. The Black Arrow

Ed	HRN	Date	Details	A	C	GD25	FN65	NM94
1	10/46	–	Original	1	1	29.00	86.00	200.00
2	51	–	CI logo; LDC-r 8pgs. deleted	1	1	4.70	14.00	28.00
3	64	–	LDC-r	1	1	3.60	9.00	18.00
4	87	–	C-price 15¢; LDC-r	1	1	3.20	8.00	16.00
5	108	–	LDC-r	1	1	2.80	7.00	14.00
6	125	–	LDC-r	1	1	2.40	6.00	12.00
7	131	–	New-c; PC-r	1	2	2.40	6.00	12.00
8	140	–	PC-r	1	2	1.25	2.50	5.00
9	148	–	PC-r	1	2	1.25	2.50	5.00
10	161	–	PC-r	1	2	1.25	2.50	5.00
11	167	–	PC-r	1	2	1.25	2.50	5.00
12	167	7/64	PC-r	1	2	1.25	2.50	5.00
13	167	11/65	PC-r	1	2	1.25	2.50	5.00
14	166	R/1968	C-price 25¢; PC-r	1	2	1.25	2.50	5.00

32. Lorna Doone

Ed	HRN	Date	Details	A	C	GD25	FN65	NM94
1	12/46	–	Original; Matt Baker c&a	1	1	36.00	107.00	250.00
2	53/64	–	8 pgs. deleted; LDC-r	1	1	5.35	16.00	32.00
3	85	–	C-price 15¢; LDC-r; Baker c&a	1	1	4.00	12.00	24.00
4	118	–	LDC-r	1	1	3.20	8.00	16.00
5	138	–	New-c; old-c becomes new title pg.; PC-r	1	2	2.80	7.00	14.00
6	150	–	PC-r	1	2	1.25	2.50	5.00
7	165	–	PC-r	1	2	1.25	2.50	5.00
8	167	1/64	PC-r	1	2	1.25	2.50	5.00
9	167	11/65	PC-r	1	2	1.25	2.50	5.00
10	166	R/1968	New-c; PC-r	1	3	2.40	6.00	12.00

33. The Adventures of Sherlock Holmes

Ed	HRN	Date	Details	A	C	GD25	FN65	NM94
1	33	1/47	Original; Kiefer-c; contains Study in Scarlet & Hound of the Baskervilles; 68 pgs.	1	1	107.00	320.00	750.00
2	53	–	"A Study in Scarlet" (17 pgs.)	1	1	38.00	115.00	265.00

Classics Illustrated #30 © GIL

Classics Illustrated #34 (HRN-167) © GIL

Classics Illustrated #40 (Orig.) © GIL

Ed	HRN	Date	Details	A	C	GD25	FN65	NM94
			deleted; LDC-r					
3	71	–	LDC-r	1	1	28.00	86.00	200.00
4A	89	–	C-price 15¢; LDC-r	1	1	23.00	70.00	160.00
4B	89	–	Kiefer's name omitted from-c	1	1	23.00	70.00	160.00

34. Mysterious Island (Last "Classic Comic")

Ed	HRN	Date	Details	A	C	GD25	FN65	NM94
1	2/47	–	Original; Webb/ Heames-c/a	1	1	36.00	107.00	250.00
2	60	–	8 pgs. deleted; LDC-r	1	1	4.00	12.00	24.00
3	62	–	LDC-r	1	1	4.00	10.00	20.00
4	71	–	LDC-r	1	1	4.35	13.00	26.00
5	78	–	C-price 15¢ in circle; LDC-r	1	1	3.20	8.00	16.00
6	92	–	LDC-r	1	1	2.80	7.00	14.00
7	117	–	LDC-r	1	1	2.40	6.00	12.00
8	140	–	New-c; PC-r	1	2	2.40	6.00	12.00
9	156	–	PC-r	1	2	1.25	2.50	5.00
10	167	10/63	PC-r	1	2	1.25	2.50	5.00
11	167	5/64	PC-r	1	2	1.25	2.50	5.00
12	167	6/66	PC-r	1	2	1.25	2.50	5.00
13	166	R/1968	C-price 25¢; PC-r	1	2	1.25	2.50	5.00

35. Last Days of Pompeii (First "Classics Illustrated")

Ed	HRN	Date	Details	A	C	GD25	FN65	NM94
1	–	3/47	Original; LDC; Kiefer-c/a	1	1	36.00	107.00	250.00
2	161	–	New c&a; 15¢; PC-r; Kirby/Ayers-a	2	2	3.60	9.00	18.00
3	167	1/64	PC-r	2	2	1.60	4.00	8.00
4	167	7/66	PC-r	2	2	1.60	4.00	8.00
5	169	Spr/70	New price 25¢; stiff-c; PC-r	2	2	1.60	4.00	8.00

36. Typee

Ed	HRN	Date	Details	A	C	GD25	FN65	NM94
1	4/47	–	Original	1	1	17.00	52.00	120.00
2	64	–	No c-price; 8 pg. ed.; LDC-r	1	1	4.70	14.00	28.00
3	155	–	New-c; PC-r	1	2	2.40	6.00	12.00
4	167	9/63	PC-r	1	2	1.40	3.50	7.00
5	167	7/65	PC-r	1	2	1.40	3.50	7.00
6	169	Sm/69	C-price 25¢; stiff-c PC-r	1	2	1.50	3.50	7.00

37. The Pioneers

Ed	HRN	Date	Details	A	C	GD25	FN65	NM94
1	37	5/47	Original; Palais-c/a	1	1	16.00	48.00	110.00
2A	62	–	8 pgs. cut; LDC-r; price circle blank	1	1	4.00	11.00	22.00
2B	62	–	10¢; LDC-r;	1	1	10.00	30.00	70.00
3	70	–	LDC-r	1	1	3.20	8.00	16.00
4	92	–	15¢; LDC-r	1	1	2.80	7.00	14.00
5	118	–	LDC-r	1	1	2.40	6.00	12.00
6	131	–	LDC-r	1	1	2.40	6.00	12.00
7	132	–	LDC-r	1	1	2.40	6.00	12.00
8	153	–	LDC-r	1	1	2.00	5.00	10.00
9	167	5/64	LDC-r	1	1	1.60	4.00	8.00
10	167	6/66	LDC-r	1	1	1.60	4.00	8.00
11	166	R/1968	New-c; 25¢; PC-r	1	2	3.20	8.00	16.00

38. Adventures of Cellini

Ed	HRN	Date	Details	A	C	GD25	FN65	NM94
1	6/47	–	Original; Froehlich c/a	1	1	30.00	90.00	210.00
2	164	–	New-c&a; PC-r	2	2	2.80	7.00	14.00
3	167	12/63	PC-r	2	2	1.60	4.00	8.00
4	167	7/66	PC-r	2	2	1.60	4.00	8.00
5	169	Spr/70	Stiff-c; new price 25¢; PC-r	2	2	1.60	4.00	8.00

39. Jane Eyre

Ed	HRN	Date	Details	A	C	GD25	FN65	NM94
1	7/47	–	Original	1	1	23.00	70.00	160.00
2	60	–	No c-price; 8 pgs. cut; LDC-r	1	1	4.35	13.00	26.00
3	62	–	LDC-r	1	1	4.00	10.50	21.00
4	71	–	LDC-r; c-price 10¢	1	1	3.00	9.00	18.00
5	92	–	C-price 15¢; LDC-r	1	1	2.80	7.00	14.00
6	118	–	LDC-r	1	1	2.40	6.00	12.00
7	142	–	New-c; old-a; PC-r	1	2	2.80	7.00	14.00
8	154	–	Old-a; PC-r	1	2	2.40	6.00	12.00
9	165	–	New-a; PC-r	2	2	2.80	7.00	14.00
10	167	12/63	PC-r	2	2	2.80	7.00	14.00
11	167	4/65	PC-r	2	2	2.40	6.00	12.00
12	167	8/66	PC-r	2	2	2.40	6.00	12.00
13	166	R/1968	New-c; PC-r	2	3	4.70	14.00	28.00

40. Mysteries ("The Pit and the Pendulum", "The Advs. of Hans Pfall" & "The Fall of the House of Usher")

Ed	HRN	Date	Details	A	C	GD25	FN65	NM94
1	8/47	–	Original; Kiefer-c/a, Froehlich, Griffiths-a	1	1	64.00	193.00	450.00
2	62	–	LDC-r; 8pgs. cut	1	1	23.00	70.00	160.00
3	75	–	LDC-r	1	1	20.00	60.00	140.00
4	92	–	C-price 15¢; LDC-r	1	1	16.00	48.00	110.00

41. Twenty Years After

Ed	HRN	Date	Details	A	C	GD25	FN65	NM94
1	9/47	–	Original; 'horror'-c	1	1	50.00	150.00	350.00
2	62	–	New-c; no c-price 8 pgs. cut; LDC-r; Kiefer-c	1	2	4.35	13.00	26.00
3	78	–	C-price 15¢; LDC-r	1	2	3.60	9.00	18.00
4	156	–	New-c; PC-r	1	3	2.40	6.00	12.00
5	167	12/63	PC-r	1	3	1.20	3.00	6.00
6	167	11/66	PC-r	1	3	1.20	3.00	6.00
7	169	Spr/70	New price 25¢; stiff-c; PC-r	1	3	1.20	2.50	5.00

42. Swiss Family Robinson

Ed	HRN	Date	Details	A	C	GD25	FN65	NM94
1	42	10/47	Orig.; Kiefer-c&a;	1	1	17.00	52.00	120.00
2A	62	–	8 pgs. cut; outside bc: Gift Box ad; LDC-r	1	1	4.00	12.00	24.00
2B	62	–	8 pgs. cut; outside-bc: Reorder list; scarce; LDC-r	1	1	7.50	22.50	45.00
3	75	–	LDC-r	1	1	3.20	8.00	16.00
4	93	–	LDC-r	1	1	2.80	7.00	14.00
5	117	–	LDC-r	1	1	2.40	6.00	12.00
6	131	–	New-c; old-a; PC-r	1	2	2.40	6.00	12.00
7	137	–	Old-a; PC-r	1	2	2.00	5.00	10.00
8	141	–	Old-a; PC-r	1	2	2.00	5.00	10.00
9	152	–	New-a; PC-r	2	2	2.40	6.00	12.00
10	158	–	PC-r	2	2	1.25	2.50	5.00
11	165	–	PC-r	2	2	1.80	4.50	9.00
12	167	12/63	PC-r	2	2	1.50	3.00	6.00
13	167	4/65	PC-r	2	2	1.50	3.00	6.00
14	167	5/66	PC-r	2	2	1.50	3.00	6.00
15	166	11/67	PC-r	2	2	1.25	2.50	5.00
16	169	Spr/69	PC-r; stiff-c	2	2	1.25	2.50	5.00

43. Great Expectations (Used in **SOTI**, pg. 311)

Ed	HRN	Date	Details	A	C	GD25	FN65	NM94
1	11/47	–	Original; Kiefer-a/c	1	1	79.00	235.00	550.00

CLASSICS
Illustrated
No. 42
10¢
Swiss Family
Robinson

Classics Illustrated #42 (Orig.?) © GIL

Classics Illustrated #46 © GIL

Classics Illustrated #51 (Orig.) © GIL

Ed	HRN	Date	Details	A	C	GD25	FN65	NM94
2	62	–	No c-price; 8 pgs. cut; LDC-r	1	1	43.00	130.00	300.00

44. Mysteries of Paris (Used in **SOTI**, pg. 323)

Ed	HRN	Date	Details	A	C	GD25	FN65	NM94
1A	44	12/47	Original; 56 pgs.; Kiefer-c/a	1	1	61.00	182.00	425.00
1B	44	12/47	Orig.; printed on white/heavier paper; (rare)	1	1	64.00	193.00	450.00
2A	62	–	8 pgs. cut; outside-bc: Gift Box ad; LDC-r	1	1	23.00	70.00	160.00
2B	62	–	8 pgs. cut; outside-bc: reorder list; LDC-r	1	1	23.00	70.00	160.00
3	78	–	C-price 15¢; LDC-r	1	1	20.00	60.00	140.00

45. Tom Brown's School Days

Ed	HRN	Date	Details	A	C	GD25	FN65	NM94
1	44	1/48	Original; 1st 48pg. issue	1	1	11.50	34.00	80.00
2A	64	–	No c-price; LDC-r	1	1	4.70	14.00	28.00
2B	64	–	15¢ price below box w/15¢ in Canada	1	1	4.70	14.00	28.00
3	161	–	New-c&a; PC-r	2	2	2.40	6.00	12.00
4	167	2/64	PC-r	2	2	1.60	4.00	8.00
5	167	8/66	PC-r	2	2	1.60	4.00	8.00
6	166	R/1968	C-price 25¢; PC-r	2	2	1.60	4.00	8.00

46. Kidnapped

Ed	HRN	Date	Details	A	C	GD25	FN65	NM94
1	47	4/48	Original; Webb-c/a	1	1	11.00	32.00	75.00
2A	62	–	Price circle blank; LDC-r	1	1	4.00	11.00	22.00
2B	62	–	C-price 10¢; rare; LDC-r	1	1	11.00	32.00	75.00
3	78	–	C-price 15¢; LDC-r	1	1	3.20	8.00	16.00
4	87	–	LDC-r	1	1	2.80	7.00	14.00
5	118	–	LDC-r	1	1	2.40	6.00	12.00
6	131	–	New-c; PC-r	1	2	2.40	6.00	12.00
7	140	–	PC-r	1	2	1.25	2.50	5.00
8	150	–	PC-r	1	2	1.25	2.50	5.00
9	164	–	Reduced pg.width; PC-r	1	2	1.25	2.50	5.00
10	167	–	PC-r	1	2	1.25	2.50	5.00
11	167	3/64	PC-r	1	2	1.25	2.50	5.00
12	167	6/65	PC-r	1	2	1.25	2.50	5.00
13	167	12/65	PC-r	1	2	1.25	2.50	5.00
14	166	9/67	PC-r	1	2	1.25	2.50	5.00
15	166	Win/69	New price 25¢; PC-r; stiff-c	1	2	1.25	2.50	5.00
16	169	Sm/70	PC-r; stiff-c	1	2	1.25	2.50	5.00

47. Twenty Thousand Leagues Under the Sea

Ed	HRN	Date	Details	A	C	GD25	FN65	NM94
1	47	5/48	Orig.; Kiefer-a&c;	1	1	11.00	32.00	75.00
2A	64	–	No c-price; LDC-r	1	1	4.00	11.00	22.00
2B	64	–	With 15¢ sticker	1	1	4.00	11.00	22.00
3	78	–	C-price 15¢; LDC-r	1	1	3.20	8.00	16.00
4	94	–	LDC-r	1	1	2.80	7.00	14.00
5	118	–	LDC-r	1	1	2.40	6.00	12.00
6	128	–	New-c; PC-r	1	2	2.40	6.00	10.00
7	133	–	PC-r	1	2	1.80	4.50	9.00
8	140	–	PC-r	1	2	1.25	2.50	5.00
9	148	–	PC-r	1	2	1.25	2.50	5.00
10	156	–	PC-r	1	2	1.25	2.50	5.00
11	165	–	PC-r	1	2	1.25	2.50	5.00
12	167	–	PC-r	1	2	1.25	2.50	5.00
13	167	3/64	PC-r	1	2	1.25	2.50	5.00
14	167	8/65	PC-r	1	2	1.25	2.50	5.00
15	167	10/66	PC-r	1	2	1.25	2.50	5.00
16	166	R/1968	C-price 25¢; new-c PC-r	1	3	2.00	5.00	10.00
17	169	Spr/70	Stiff-c; PC-r	1	3	2.00	5.00	10.00

48. David Copperfield

Ed	HRN	Date	Details	A	C	GD25	FN65	NM94
1	47	6/48	Original; Kiefer-c/a	1	1	11.00	32.00	75.00
2	64	–	Price circle replaced by motif of boy reading; LDC-r	1	1	4.00	11.00	22.00
3	87	–	C-price 15¢; LDC-r	1	1	3.20	8.00	16.00
4	121	–	New-c; PC-r	1	2	2.40	6.00	12.00
5	130	–	PC-r	1	2	1.50	3.00	6.00
6	140	–	PC-r	1	2	1.50	3.00	6.00
7	148	–	PC-r	1	2	1.50	3.00	6.00
8	156	–	PC-r	1	2	1.50	3.00	6.00
9	167	–	PC-r	1	2	1.25	2.50	5.00
10	167	4/64	PC-r	1	2	1.25	2.50	5.00
11	167	6/65	PC-r	1	2	1.25	2.50	5.00
12	166	5/67	PC-r	1	2	1.25	2.50	5.00
13	166	R/67	PC-r; C-price 25¢	1	2	1.80	4.50	9.00
14	166	Spr/69	C-price 25¢; stiff-c PC-r	1	2	1.25	2.50	5.00
15	169	Win/69	Stiff-c; PC-r	1	2	1.25	2.50	5.00

49. Alice in Wonderland

Ed	HRN	Date	Details	A	C	GD25	FN65	NM94
1	47	7/48	Original; 1st Blum a & c	1	1	14.00	43.00	100.00
2	64	–	No c-price; LDC-r	1	1	4.70	14.00	28.00
3A	85	–	C-price 15¢; soft-c LDC-r	1	1	4.00	10.50	21.00
3B	85	–	Stiff-c; LDC-r	1	1	4.00	12.00	24.00
4	155	–	New PC, similar to orig.; PC-r	1	2	4.00	10.50	21.00
5	165	–	PC-r	1	2	3.20	8.00	16.00
6	167	3/64	PC-r	1	2	2.80	7.00	14.00
7	167	6/66	PC-r	1	2	2.80	7.00	14.00
8A	166	Fall/68	New-c; soft-c; 25¢ c-price; PC-r	1	3	4.00	10.00	20.00
8B	166	Fall/68	New-c; stiff-c; 25¢ c-price; PC-r	1	3	5.85	17.50	35.00

50. Adventures of Tom Sawyer (Used in **SOTI**, pg. 37)

Ed	HRN	Date	Details	A	C	GD25	FN65	NM94
1A	51	8/48	Orig.; Aldo Rubano a&c	1	1	11.50	34.00	80.00
1B	51	9/48	Orig.; Rubano c&a	1	1	11.50	34.00	80.00
1C	51	9/48	Orig.; outside-bc: blue & yellow only; rare	1	1	16.00	48.00	110.00
2	64	–	No c-price; LDC-r	1	1	4.00	10.00	20.00
3	78	–	C-price 15¢; LDC-r	1	1	2.80	7.00	14.00
4	94	–	LDC-r	1	1	2.40	6.00	12.00
5	117	–	LDC-r	1	1	2.00	5.00	10.00
6	132	–	LDC-r	1	1	2.00	5.00	10.00
7	140	–	New-c; PC-r	1	2	2.00	5.00	10.00
8	150	–	PC-r	1	2	1.60	4.00	8.00
9	164	–	New-a; PC-r	2	2	2.00	5.00	10.00
10	167	–	PC-r	2	2	1.25	2.50	5.00
11	167	1/65	PC-r	2	2	1.25	2.50	5.00
12	167	5/66	PC-r	2	2	1.25	2.50	5.00
13	166	12/67	PC-r	2	2	1.25	2.50	5.00
14	169	Fall/69	C-price 25¢; stiff-c; PC-r	2	2	1.25	2.50	5.00

Classics Illustrated #52 © GIL

Classics Illustrated #53 (Orig.) © GIL

Classics Illustrated #56 (Orig.) © GIL

Ed	HRN	Date	Details	A	C	GD25	FN65	NM94
15	169	Win/71	PC-r	2	2	1.25	2.50	5.00

51. The Spy

Ed	HRN	Date	Details	A	C	GD25	FN65	NM94
1A	51	9/48	Original; inside-bc illo: Christmas Carol	1	1	11.00	32.00	75.00
1B	51	9/48	Original; inside-bc illo: Man in Iron Mask	1	1	11.00	32.00	75.00
1C	51	8/48	Original; outside-bc: full color	1	1	11.00	32.00	75.00
1D	51	8/48	Original; outside-bc: blue & yellow only; scarce	1	1	14.00	43.00	100.00
2	89	–	C-price 15¢; LDC-r	1	1	3.60	9.00	18.00
3	121	–	LDC-r	1	1	2.80	7.00	14.00
4	139	–	New-c; PC-r	1	2	2.40	6.00	12.00
5	156	–	PC-r	1	2	1.25	2.50	5.00
6	167	11/63	PC-r	1	2	1.25	2.50	5.00
7	167	7/66	PC-r	1	2	1.25	2.50	5.00
8A	166	Win/69	C-price 25¢; soft-c; scarce; PC-r	1	2	2.40	6.00	12.00
8B	166	Win/69	C-price 25¢; stiff-c; PC-r	1	2	1.25	2.50	5.00

52. The House of the Seven Gables

Ed	HRN	Date	Details	A	C	GD25	FN65	NM94
1	53	10/48	Orig.; Griffiths a&c	1	1	10.00	30.00	70.00
2	89	–	C-price 15¢; LDC-r	1	1	3.60	9.00	18.00
3	121	–	LDC-r	1	1	2.80	7.00	14.00
4	142	–	New-c&a; PC-r; Woodbridge-a	2	2	2.40	6.00	12.00
5	156	–	PC-r	2	2	1.25	2.50	5.00
6	165	–	PC-r	2	2	1.25	2.50	5.00
7	167	5/64	PC-r	2	2	1.25	2.50	5.00
8	167	3/66	PC-r	2	2	1.25	2.50	5.00
9	166	R/1968	C-price 25¢; PC-r	2	2	1.25	2.50	5.00
10	169	Spr/70	Stiff-c; PC-r	2	2	1.25	2.50	5.00

53. A Christmas Carol

Ed	HRN	Date	Details	A	C	GD25	FN65	NM94
1	53	11/48	Original & only ed; Kiefer-c/a	1	1	11.50	34.00	80.00

54. Man in the Iron Mask

Ed	HRN	Date	Details	A	C	GD25	FN65	NM94
1	55	12/48	Original; Froehlich-a, Kiefer-c	1	1	10.00	30.00	70.00
2	93	–	C-price 15¢; LDC-r	1	1	3.60	9.00	18.00
3A	111	–	(O) logo lettering; scarce; LDC-r	1	1	4.00	12.00	24.00
3B	111	–	New logo as PC; LDC-r	1	1	3.20	8.00	16.00
4	142	–	New-c&a; PC-r	2	2	2.40	6.00	12.00
5	154	–	PC-r	2	2	1.25	2.50	5.00
6	165	–	PC-r	2	2	1.25	2.50	5.00
7	167	5/64	PC-r	2	2	1.25	2.50	5.00
8	167	4/66	PC-r	2	2	1.25	2.50	5.00
9A	166	Win/69	C-price 25¢; soft-c PC-r	2	2	2.80	7.00	14.00
9B	166	Win/69	Stiff-c	2	2	1.25	2.50	5.00

55. Silas Marner (Used in **SOTI**, pgs. 311, 312)

Ed	HRN	Date	Details	A	C	GD25	FN65	NM94
1	55	1/49	Original-Kiefer-c	1	1	10.00	30.00	70.00
2	75	–	Price circle blank; 'Coming Next' ad; LDC-r	1	1	4.00	11.00	22.00
3	97	–	LDC-r	1	1	2.80	7.00	14.00
4	121	–	New-c; PC-r	1	2	2.40	6.00	12.00
5	130	–	PC-r	1	2	1.25	2.50	5.00
6	140	–	PC-r	1	2	1.25	2.50	5.00
7	154	–	PC-r	1	2	1.25	2.50	5.00
8	165	–	PC-r	1	2	1.25	2.50	5.00
9	167	2/64	PC-r	1	2	1.25	2.50	5.00
10	167	6/65	PC-r	1	2	1.25	2.50	5.00
11	166	5/67	PC-r	1	2	1.25	2.50	5.00
12A	166	Win/69	C-price 25¢; soft-c PC-r	1	2	2.80	7.00	14.00
12B	166	Win/69	C-price 25¢; stiff-c PC-r	1	2	1.25	2.50	5.00

56. The Toilers of the Sea

Ed	HRN	Date	Details	A	C	GD25	FN65	NM94
1	55	2/49	Original; A.M. Froehlich-c/a	1	1	16.00	48.00	110.00
2	165	–	New-c&a; PC-r; Angelo Torres-a	2	2	4.00	10.50	21.00
3	167	3/64	PC-r	2	2	2.80	7.00	14.00
4	167	10/66	PC-r	2	2	2.80	7.00	14.00

57. The Song of Hiawatha

Ed	HRN	Date	Details	A	C	GD25	FN65	NM94
1	55	3/49	Original; Alex Blum-c/a	1	1	10.00	30.00	70.00
2A	75	–	No c-price w/15¢ sticker; 'Coming Next' ad; LDC-r	1	1	4.00	11.00	22.00
2B	75	–	15¢ in circle	1	1	4.00	11.00	22.00
3	94	–	C-price 15¢; LDC-r	1	1	3.20	8.00	16.00
4	118	–	LDC-r	1	1	2.80	7.00	14.00
5	134	–	New-c; PC-r	1	2	2.40	6.00	12.00
6	139	–	PC-r	1	2	1.25	2.50	5.00
7	154	–	PC-r	1	2	1.25	2.50	5.00
8	167	–	Has orig.date; PC-r	1	2	1.25	2.50	5.00
9	167	9/64	PC-r	1	2	1.25	2.50	5.00
10	167	10/65	PC-r	1	2	1.25	2.50	5.00
11	166	F/1968	C-price 25¢; PC-r	1	2	1.25	2.50	5.00

58. The Prairie

Ed	HRN	Date	Details	A	C	GD25	FN65	NM94
1	60	4/49	Original; Palais c/a	1	1	10.00	30.00	70.00
2	62	–	No c-price; no coming-next ad; LDC-r	1	1	5.85	17.50	35.00
3	78	–	C-price 15¢ in dbl. circle; LDC-r	1	1	3.60	9.00	18.00
4	114	–	LDC-r	1	1	2.80	7.00	14.00
5	131	–	LDC-r	1	1	2.40	6.00	12.00
6	132	–	LDC-r	1	1	2.40	6.00	12.00
7	146	–	New-c; PC-r	1	2	2.40	6.00	12.00
8	155	–	PC-r	1	2	1.25	2.50	5.00
9	167	5/64	PC-r	1	2	1.25	2.50	5.00
10	167	4/66	PC-r	1	2	1.25	2.50	5.00
11	169	Sm/69	New price 25¢; stiff-c; PC-r	1	2	1.25	2.50	5.00

59. Wuthering Heights

Ed	HRN	Date	Details	A	C	GD25	FN65	NM94
1	60	5/49	Original; Kiefer-c/a	1	1	10.00	30.00	70.00
2	85	–	C-price 15¢; LDC-r	1	1	4.00	12.00	24.00
3	156	–	New-c; PC-r	1	2	2.40	6.00	12.00
4	167	1/64	PC-r	1	2	1.50	3.00	6.00
5	167	10/66	PC-r	1	2	1.50	3.00	6.00
6	169	Sm/69	C-price 25¢; stiff-c; PC-r	1	2	1.25	2.50	5.00

60. Black Beauty

Ed	HRN	Date	Details	A	C	GD25	FN65	NM94
1	62	6/49	Original;	1	1	10.00	30.00	70.00

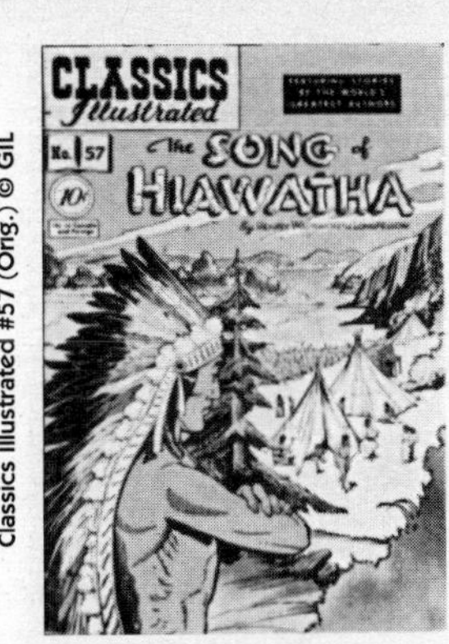

Classics Illustrated #57 (Orig.) © GIL

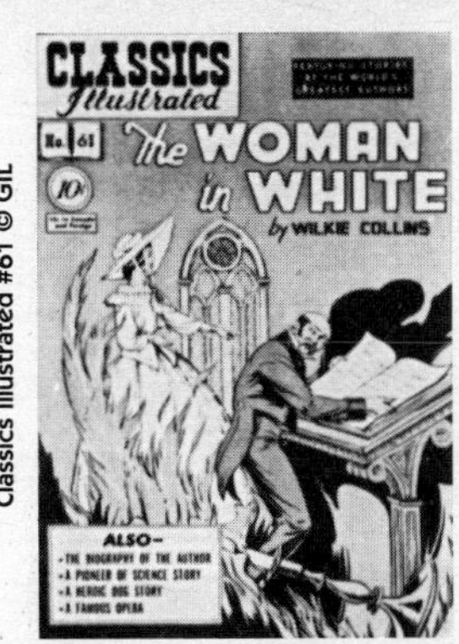

Classics Illustrated #61 © GIL

Classics Illustrated #66 (Orig.) © GIL

Ed	HRN	Date	Details	A	C	GD25	FN65	NM94
			Froehlich-c/a					
2	62	–	No c-price; no coming-next ad; LDC-r (rare)	1	1	10.00	30.00	70.00
3	85	–	C-price 15¢; LDC-r	1	1	4.00	10.00	20.00
4	158	–	New L.B. Cole-c/a; PC-r	2	2	3.60	9.00	18.00
5	167	2/64	PC-r	2	2	2.40	6.00	12.00
6	167	3/66	PC-r	2	2	2.40	6.00	12.00
7	166	R/1968	New-c&price, 25¢; PC-r	2	3	5.85	17.50	35.00

61. The Woman in White

Ed	HRN	Date	Details	A	C	GD25	FN65	NM94
1A	62	7/49	Original; Blum-c/a fc-purple; bc: top illos light blue	1	1	10.00	30.00	70.00
1B	62	7/49	Original; Blum-c/a fc-pink; bc: top illos light violet	1	1	10.00	30.00	70.00
2	156	–	New-c; PC-r	1	2	3.20	8.00	16.00
3	167	1/64	PC-r	1	2	2.40	6.00	12.00
4	166	R/1968	C-price 25¢; PC-r	1	2	2.40	6.00	12.00

62. Western Stories ("The Luck of Roaring Camp" and "The Outcasts of Poker Flat")

Ed	HRN	Date	Details	A	C	GD25	FN65	NM94
1	62	8/49	Original; Kiefer-c/a	1	1	10.00	30.00	65.00
2	89	–	C-price 15¢; LDC-r	1	1	4.00	10.00	20.00
3	121	–	LDC-r	1	1	3.20	8.00	16.00
4	137	–	New-c; PC-r	1	2	2.40	6.00	12.00
5	152	–	PC-r	1	2	1.50	3.00	6.00
6	167	10/63	PC-r	1	2	1.50	3.00	6.00
7	167	6/64	PC-r	1	2	1.25	2.50	5.00
8	167	11/66	PC-r	1	2	1.25	2.50	5.00
9	166	R/1968	New-c&price 25¢; PC-r	1	3	2.80	7.00	14.00

63. The Man Without a Country

Ed	HRN	Date	Details	A	C	GD25	FN65	NM94
1	62	9/49	Original; Kiefer-c/a	1	1	10.00	30.00	70.00
2	78	–	C-price 15¢ in double circle; LDC-r	1	1	4.00	11.00	22.00
3	156	–	New-c, old-a; PC-r	1	2	3.20	8.00	16.00
4	165	–	New-a & text pgs.; PC-r; A. Torres-a	2	2	2.40	6.00	12.00
5	167	3/64	PC-r	2	2	1.25	2.50	5.00
6	167	8/66	PC-r	2	2	1.25	2.50	5.00
7	169	Sm/69	New price 25¢; stiff-c; PC-r	2	2	1.25	2.50	5.00

64. Treasure Island

Ed	HRN	Date	Details	A	C	GD25	FN65	NM94
1	62	10/49	Original; Blum-c/a	1	1	10.00	30.00	70.00
2A	82	–	C-price 15¢; soft-c LDC-r	1	1	4.00	10.00	20.00
2B	82	–	Stiff-c; LDC-r	1	1	4.00	11.00	22.00
3	117	–	LDC-r	1	1	3.20	8.00	16.00
4	131	–	New-c; PC-r	1	2	2.40	6.00	12.00
5	138	–	PC-r	1	2	1.25	2.50	5.00
6	146	–	PC-r	1	2	1.25	2.50	5.00
7	158	–	PC-r	1	2	1.25	2.50	5.00
8	165	–	PC-r	1	2	1.25	2.50	5.00
9	167	–	PC-r	1	2	1.25	2.50	5.00
10	167	6/64	PC-r	1	2	1.25	2.50	5.00
11	167	12/65	PC-r	1	2	1.25	2.50	5.00
12A	166	10/67	PC-r	1	2	1.80	4.50	9.00
12B	166	10/67	w/Grit ad stapled in book	1	2	10.00	30.00	60.00
13	169	Spr/69	New price 25¢; stiff-c; PC-r	1	2	1.25	2.50	5.00
14	–	1989	Long John Silver's Seafood Shoppes; $1.95, First/Berkley Publ.; Blum-r	1	2	.40	1.00	2.00

65. Benjamin Franklin

Ed	HRN	Date	Details	A	C	GD25	FN65	NM94
1	64	11/49	Original; Kiefer-c; Iger Shop-a	1	1	10.00	30.00	70.00
2	131	–	New-c; PC-r	1	2	2.80	7.00	14.00
3	154	–	PC-r	1	2	1.25	2.50	5.00
4	167	2/64	PC-r	1	2	1.25	2.50	5.00
5	167	4/66	PC-r	1	2	1.25	2.50	5.00
6	169	Fall/69	New price 25¢; stiff-c; PC-r	1	2	1.25	2.50	5.00

66. The Cloister and the Hearth

Ed	HRN	Date	Details	A	C	GD25	FN65	NM94
1	67	12/49	Original & only ed; Kiefer-a & c	1	1	23.00	70.00	160.00

67. The Scottish Chiefs

Ed	HRN	Date	Details	A	C	GD25	FN65	NM94
1	67	1/50	Original; Blum-a&c	1	1	10.00	30.00	60.00
2	85	–	C-price 15¢; LDC-r	1	1	4.00	10.00	20.00
3	118	–	LDC-r	1	1	3.20	8.00	16.00
4	136	–	New-c; PC-r	1	2	2.40	6.00	12.00
5	154	–	PC-r	1	2	1.60	4.00	8.00
6	167	11/63	PC-r	1	2	1.60	4.00	8.00
7	167	8/65	PC-r	1	2	1.60	4.00	8.00

68. Julius Caesar (Used in **SOTI**, pgs. 36, 37)

Ed	HRN	Date	Details	A	C	GD25	FN65	NM94
1	70	2/50	Original; Kiefer-c/a	1	1	10.00	30.00	65.00
2	85	–	C-price 15¢; LDC-r	1	1	4.00	10.00	20.00
3	108	–	LDC-r	1	1	3.20	8.00	16.00
4	156	–	New L.B. Cole-c; PC-r	1	2	3.20	8.00	16.00
5	165	–	New-a by Evans, Crandall; PC-r	2	2	3.20	8.00	16.00
6	167	2/64	PC-r	2	2	1.25	2.50	5.00
7	167	10/65	Tarzan books inside cover; PC-r	2	2	1.25	2.50	5.00
8	166	R/1967	PC-r	2	2	1.25	2.50	5.00
9	169	Win/69	PC-r; stiff-c	2	2	1.25	2.50	5.00

69. Around the World in 80 Days

Ed	HRN	Date	Details	A	C	GD25	FN65	NM94
1	70	3/50	Original; Kiefer-c/a	1	1	10.00	30.00	65.00
2	87	–	C-price 15¢; LDC-r	1	1	4.00	10.00	20.00
3	125	–	LDC-r	1	1	3.20	8.00	16.00
4	136	–	New-c; PC-r	1	2	2.40	6.00	12.00
5	146	–	PC-r	1	2	1.25	2.50	5.00
6	152	–	PC-r	1	2	1.25	2.50	5.00
7	164	–	PC-r	1	2	1.25	2.50	5.00
8	167	–	PC-r	1	2	1.25	2.50	5.00
9	167	7/64	PC-r	1	2	1.25	2.50	5.00
10	167	11/65	PC-r	1	2	1.25	2.50	5.00
11	166	7/67	PC-r	1	2	1.25	2.50	5.00
12	169	Spr/69	C-price 25¢; stiff-c; PC-r	1	2	1.25	2.50	5.00

70. The Pilot

Ed	HRN	Date	Details	A	C	GD25	FN65	NM94
1	71	4/50	Original; Blum-c/a	1	1	8.35	25.00	50.00
2	92	–	C-price 15¢; LDC-r	1	1	4.00	10.00	20.00
3	125	–	LDC-r	1	1	3.20	8.00	16.00

Classics Illustrated #71 © GIL

Classics Illustrated #72 (Orig.) © GIL

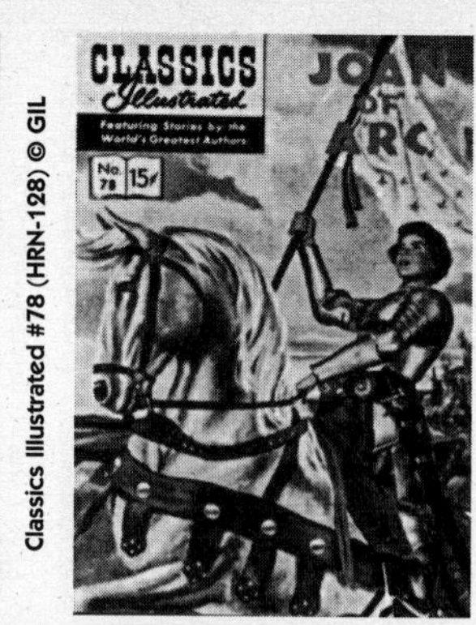

Classics Illustrated #78 (HRN-128) © GIL

Ed	HRN	Date	Details	A	C	GD25	FN65	NM94
4	156	–	New-c; PC-r	1	2	2.40	6.00	12.00
5	167	2/64	PC-r	1	2	1.60	4.00	8.00
6	167	5/66	PC-r	1	2	1.60	4.00	8.00

71. The Man Who Laughs

Ed	HRN	Date	Details	A	C	GD25	FN65	NM94
1	71	5/50	Original; Blum-c/a	1	1	13.00	40.00	90.00
2	165	–	New-c&a; PC-r	2	2	8.35	25.00	50.00
3	167	4/64	PC-r	2	2	6.70	20.00	40.00

72. The Oregon Trail

Ed	HRN	Date	Details	A	C	GD25	FN65	NM94
1	73	6/50	Original; Kiefer-c/a	1	1	8.35	25.00	50.00
2	89	–	C-price 15¢; LDC-r	1	1	4.00	10.00	20.00
3	121	–	LDC-r	1	1	3.20	8.00	16.00
4	131	–	New-c; PC-r	1	2	2.40	6.00	12.00
5	140	–	PC-r	1	2	1.50	3.00	6.00
6	150	–	PC-r	1	2	1.25	2.50	5.00
7	164	–	PC-r	1	2	1.25	2.50	5.00
8	167	–	PC-r	1	2	1.25	2.50	5.00
9	167	8/64	PC-r	1	2	1.25	2.50	5.00
10	167	10/65	PC-r	1	2	1.25	2.50	5.00
11	166	R/1968	C-price 25¢; PC-r	1	2	1.25	2.50	5.00

73. The Black Tulip

Ed	HRN	Date	Details	A	C	GD25	FN65	NM94
1	75	7/50	1st & only ed.; Alex Blum-c/a	1	1	26.00	77.00	180.00

74. Mr. Midshipman Easy

Ed	HRN	Date	Details	A	C	GD25	FN65	NM94
1	75	8/50	1st & only edition	1	1	26.00	77.00	180.00

75. The Lady of the Lake

Ed	HRN	Date	Details	A	C	GD25	FN65	NM94
1	75	9/50	Original; Kiefer-c/a	1	1	7.50	22.50	45.00
2	85	–	C-price 15¢; LDC-r	1	1	4.00	10.00	20.00
3	118	–	LDC-r	1	1	3.20	8.00	16.00
4	139	–	New-c; PC-r	1	2	2.40	6.00	12.00
5	154	–	PC-r	1	2	1.25	2.50	5.00
6	165	–	PC-r	1	2	1.25	2.50	5.00
7	167	4/64	PC-r	1	2	1.25	2.50	5.00
8	167	5/66	PC-r	1	2	1.25	2.50	5.00
9	169	Spr/69	New price 25¢; stiff-c; PC-r	1	2	1.25	2.50	5.00

76. The Prisoner of Zenda

Ed	HRN	Date	Details	A	C	GD25	FN65	NM94
1	75	10/50	Original; Kiefer-c/a	1	1	7.50	22.50	45.00
2	85	–	C-price 15¢; LDC-r	1	1	4.00	10.00	20.00
3	111	–	LDC-r	1	1	3.20	8.00	16.00
4	128	–	New-c; PC-r	1	2	2.40	6.00	12.00
5	152	–	PC-r	1	2	1.25	2.50	5.00
6	165	–	PC-r	1	2	1.25	2.50	5.00
7	167	4/64	PC-r	1	2	1.25	2.50	5.00
8	167	9/66	PC-r	1	2	1.25	2.50	5.00
9	169	Fall/69	New price 25¢; stiff-c; PC-r	1	2	1.25	2.50	5.00

77. The Iliad

Ed	HRN	Date	Details	A	C	GD25	FN65	NM94
1	78	11/50	Original; Blum-c/a	1	1	7.50	22.50	45.00
2	87	–	C-price 15¢; LDC-r	1	1	4.00	10.00	20.00
3	121	–	LDC-r	1	1	3.20	8.00	16.00
4	139	–	New-c; PC-r	1	2	2.40	6.00	12.00
5	150	–	PC-r	1	2	1.25	2.50	5.00
6	165	–	PC-r	1	2	1.25	2.50	5.00
7	167	10/63	PC-r	1	2	1.25	2.50	5.00
8	167	7/64	PC-r	1	2	1.25	2.50	5.00
9	167	5/66	PC-r	1	2	1.25	2.50	5.00
10	166	R/1968	C-price 25¢; PC-r	1	2	1.25	2.50	5.00

78. Joan of Arc

Ed	HRN	Date	Details	A	C	GD25	FN65	NM94
1	78	12/50	Original; Kiefer-c/a	1	1	7.50	22.50	45.00
2	87	–	C-price 15¢; LDC-r	1	1	4.00	10.00	20.00
3	113	–	LDC-r	1	1	3.20	8.00	16.00
4	128	–	New-c; PC-r	1	2	2.40	6.00	12.00
5	140	–	PC-r	1	2	1.25	2.50	5.00
6	150	–	PC-r	1	2	1.25	2.50	5.00
7	159	–	PC-r	1	2	1.25	2.50	5.00
8	167	–	PC-r	1	2	1.25	2.50	5.00
9	167	12/63	PC-r	1	2	1.25	2.50	5.00
10	167	6/65	PC-r	1	2	1.25	2.50	5.00
11	166	6/67	PC-r	1	2	1.25	2.50	5.00
12	166	Win/69	New-c&price, 25¢; PC-r; stiff-c	1	3	2.40	6.00	12.00

79. Cyrano de Bergerac

Ed	HRN	Date	Details	A	C	GD25	FN65	NM94
1	78	1/51	Orig.; movie promo inside front-c; Blum-c/a	1	1	7.50	22.50	45.00
2	85	–	C-price 15¢; LDC-r	1	1	4.00	10.00	20.00
3	118	–	LDC-r	1	1	3.20	8.00	16.00
4	133	–	New-c; PC-r	1	2	2.80	7.00	14.00
5	156	–	PC-r	1	2	2.00	5.00	10.00
6	167	8/64	PC-r	1	2	2.00	5.00	10.00

80. White Fang (Last line drawn cover)

Ed	HRN	Date	Details	A	C	GD25	FN65	NM94
1	79	2/51	Orig.; Blum-c/a	1	1	7.50	22.50	45.00
2	87	–	C-price 15¢; LDC-r	1	1	4.00	10.00	20.00
3	125	–	LDC-r	1	1	3.20	8.00	16.00
4	132	–	New-c; PC-r	1	2	2.40	6.00	12.00
5	140	–	PC-r	1	2	1.25	2.50	5.00
6	153	–	PC-r	1	2	1.25	2.50	5.00
7	167	–	PC-r	1	2	1.25	2.50	5.00
8	167	9/64	PC-r	1	2	1.25	2.50	5.00
9	167	7/65	PC-r	1	2	1.25	2.50	5.00
10	166	6/67	PC-r	1	2	1.25	2.50	5.00
11	169	Fall/69	New price 25¢; PC-r; stiff-c	1	2	1.25	2.50	5.00

81. The Odyssey (1st painted cover)

Ed	HRN	Date	Details	A	C	GD25	FN65	NM94
1	82	3/51	First 15¢ Original; Blum-c	1	1	5.35	16.00	32.00
2	167	8/64	PC-r	1	1	2.00	5.00	10.00
3	167	10/66	PC-r	1	1	2.00	5.00	10.00
4	169	Spr/69	New, stiff-c; PC-r	1	2	2.40	6.00	12.00

82. The Master of Ballantrae

Ed	HRN	Date	Details	A	C	GD25	FN65	NM94
1	82	4/51	Original; Blum-c	1	1	5.00	15.00	30.00
2	167	8/64	PC-r	1	1	2.40	6.00	12.00
3	166	Fall/68	New, stiff-c; PC-r	1	2	2.40	6.00	12.00

83. The Jungle Book

Ed	HRN	Date	Details	A	C	GD25	FN65	NM94
1	85	5/51	Original; Blum-c Bossert/Blum-a	1	1	5.00	15.00	30.00
2	110	–	PC-r	1	1	1.40	3.50	7.00
3	125	–	PC-r	1	1	1.25	2.50	5.00
4	134	–	PC-r	1	1	1.25	2.50	5.00
5	142	–	PC-r	1	1	1.25	2.50	5.00
6	150	–	PC-r	1	1	1.25	2.50	5.00
7	159	–	PC-r	1	1	1.25	2.50	5.00
8	167	–	PC-r	1	1	1.25	2.50	5.00
9	167	3/65	PC-r	1	1	1.25	2.50	5.00
10	167	11/65	PC-r	1	1	1.25	2.50	5.00
11	167	5/66	PC-r	1	1	1.25	2.50	5.00

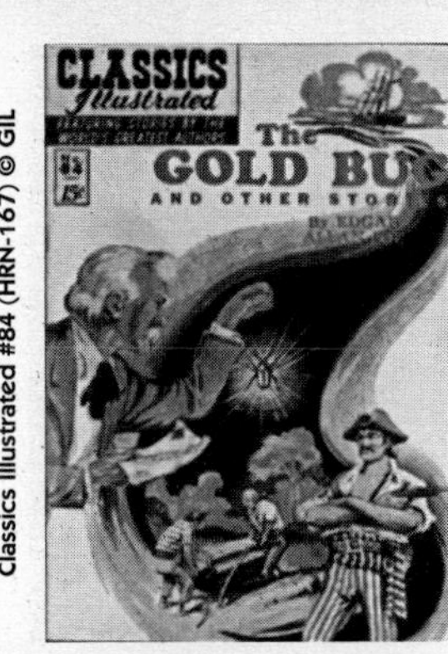

Classics Illustrated #84 (HRN-167) © GIL

Classics Illustrated #90 © GIL

Classics Illustrated #91 (HRN-112) © GIL

Ed	HRN	Date	Details	A	C	GD25	FN65	NM94
12	166	R/1968	New c&a; stiff-c; PC-r	2	2	2.40	6.00	12.00

84. The Gold Bug and Other Stories ("The Gold Bug", "The Tell-Tale Heart", "The Cask of Amontillado")

Ed	HRN	Date	Details	A	C	GD25	FN65	NM94
1	85	6/51	Original; Blum-c/a; Palais, Laverly-a	1	1	11.00	32.00	75.00
2	167	7/64	PC-r	1	1	6.70	20.00	40.00

85. The Sea Wolf

Ed	HRN	Date	Details	A	C	GD25	FN65	NM94
1	85	7/51	Original; Blum-c/a	1	1	4.00	11.00	22.00
2	121	–	PC-r	1	1	1.00	2.00	4.00
3	132	–	PC-r	1	1	1.00	2.00	4.00
4	141	–	PC-r	1	1	1.00	2.00	4.00
5	161	–	PC-r	1	1	1.00	2.00	4.00
6	167	2/64	PC-r	1	1	1.00	2.00	4.00
7	167	11/65	PC-r	1	1	1.00	2.00	4.00
8	169	Fall/69	New price 25¢; stiff-c; PC-r	1	1	1.00	2.00	4.00

86. Under Two Flags

Ed	HRN	Date	Details	A	C	GD25	FN65	NM94
1	87	8/51	Original; first delBourgo-a	1	1	4.00	11.00	22.00
2	117	–	PC-r	1	1	1.00	2.00	4.00
3	139	–	PC-r	1	1	1.00	2.00	4.00
4	158	–	PC-r	1	1	1.00	2.00	4.00
5	167	2/64	PC-r	1	1	1.00	2.00	4.00
6	167	8/66	PC-r	1	1	1.00	2.00	4.00
7	169	Sm/69	New price 25¢; stiff-c; PC-r	1	1	1.00	2.00	4.00

87. A Midsummer Nights Dream

Ed	HRN	Date	Details	A	C	GD25	FN65	NM94
1	87	9/51	Original; Blum c/a	1	1	4.00	11.00	22.00
2	161	–	PC-r	1	1	1.25	2.50	5.00
3	167	4/64	PC-r	1	1	1.00	2.00	4.00
4	167	5/66	PC-r	1	1	1.00	2.00	4.00
5	169	Sm/69	New price 25¢; stiff-c; PC-r	1	1	1.00	2.00	4.00

88. Men of Iron

Ed	HRN	Date	Details	A	C	GD25	FN65	NM94
1	89	10/51	Original	1	1	4.00	12.00	24.00
2	154	–	PC-r	1	1	1.25	2.50	5.00
3	167	1/64	PC-r	1	1	1.25	2.50	5.00
4	166	R/1968	C-price 25¢; PC-r	1	1	1.25	2.50	5.00

89. Crime and Punishment (Cover illo. in **POP**)

Ed	HRN	Date	Details	A	C	GD25	FN65	NM94
1	89	11/51	Original; Palais-a	1	1	4.00	12.00	24.00
2	152	–	PC-r	1	1	1.00	2.00	4.00
3	167	4/64	PC-r	1	1	1.00	2.00	4.00
4	167	5/66	PC-r	1	1	1.00	2.00	4.00
5	169	Fall/69	New price 25¢ stiff-c; PC-r	1	1	1.00	2.00	4.00

90. Green Mansions

Ed	HRN	Date	Details	A	C	GD25	FN65	NM94
1	89	12/51	Original; Blum-c/a	1	1	4.35	13.00	26.00
2	148	–	New L.B. Cole-c; PC-r	1	2	2.00	5.00	10.00
3	165	–	PC-r	1	2	1.00	2.00	4.00
4	167	4/64	PC-r	1	2	1.00	2.00	4.00
5	167	9/66	PC-r	1	2	1.00	2.00	4.00
6	169	Sm/69	New price 25¢; stiff-c; PC-r	1	2	1.00	2.00	4.00

91. The Call of the Wild

Ed	HRN	Date	Details	A	C	GD25	FN65	NM94
1	92	1/52	Orig.; delBourgo-a	1	1	4.00	11.00	22.00
2	112	–	PC-r	1	1	1.25	2.50	5.00
3	125	–	'Picture Progress' on back-c; PC-r	1	1	1.00	2.00	4.00
4	134	–	PC-r	1	1	1.00	2.00	4.00
5	143	–	PC-r	1	1	1.00	2.00	4.00
6	165	–	PC-r	1	1	1.00	2.00	4.00
7	167	–	PC-r	1	1	1.00	2.00	4.00
8	167	4/65	PC-r	1	1	1.00	2.00	4.00
9	167	3/66	PC-r	1	1	1.00	2.00	4.00
10	166	11/67	PC-r	1	1	1.00	2.00	4.00
11	169	Spr/70	New price 25¢; stiff-c; PC-r	1	1	1.00	2.00	4.00

92. The Courtship of Miles Standish

Ed	HRN	Date	Details	A	C	GD25	FN65	NM94
1	92	2/52	Original; Blum-c/a	1	1	4.00	11.00	22.00
2	165	–	PC-r	1	1	1.00	2.00	4.00
3	167	3/64	PC-r	1	1	1.00	2.00	4.00
4	166	5/67	PC-r	1	1	1.00	2.00	4.00
5	169	Win/69	New price 25¢ stiff-c; PC-r	1	1	1.00	2.00	4.00

93. Pudd'nhead Wilson

Ed	HRN	Date	Details	A	C	GD25	FN65	NM94
1	94	3/52	Orig.; Kiefer-c/a;	1	1	4.35	13.00	26.00
2	165	–	New-c; PC-r	1	2	1.80	4.50	9.00
3	167	3/64	PC-r	1	2	1.40	3.50	7.00
4	166	R/1968	New price 25¢; soft-c; PC-r	1	2	1.40	3.50	7.00

94. David Balfour

Ed	HRN	Date	Details	A	C	GD25	FN65	NM94
1	94	4/52	Original; Palais-a	1	1	4.35	13.00	26.00
2	167	5/64	PC-r	1	1	2.00	5.00	10.00
3	166	R/1968	C-price 25¢; PC-r	1	1	2.00	5.00	10.00

95. All Quiet on the Western Front

Ed	HRN	Date	Details	A	C	GD25	FN65	NM94
1A	96	5/52	Orig.; del Bourgo-a	1	1	9.15	27.50	55.00
1B	99	5/52	Orig.; del Bourgo-a	1	1	8.35	25.00	50.00
2	167	10/64	PC-r	1	1	2.80	7.00	14.00
3	167	11/66	PC-r	1	1	2.80	7.00	14.00

96. Daniel Boone

Ed	HRN	Date	Details	A	C	GD25	FN65	NM94
1	97	6/52	Original; Blum-a	1	1	4.00	11.00	22.00
2	117	–	PC-r	1	1	1.00	2.00	4.00
3	128	–	PC-r	1	1	1.00	2.00	4.00
4	132	–	PC-r	1	1	1.00	2.00	4.00
5	134	–	"Story of Jesus" on back-c; PC-r	1	1	1.00	2.00	4.00
6	158	–	PC-r	1	1	1.00	2.00	4.00
7	167	1/64	PC-r	1	1	1.00	2.00	4.00
8	167	5/65	PC-r	1	1	1.00	2.00	4.00
9	167	11/66	PC-r	1	1	1.00	2.00	4.00
10	166	Win/69	New-c; price 25¢; PC-r; stiff-c	1	2	2.00	5.00	10.00

97. King Solomon's Mines

Ed	HRN	Date	Details	A	C	GD25	FN65	NM94
1	96	7/52	Orig.; Kiefer-a	1	1	4.00	11.00	22.00
2	118	–	PC-r	1	1	1.50	3.50	7.00
3	131	–	PC-r	1	1	1.00	2.00	4.00
4	141	–	PC-r	1	1	1.00	2.00	4.00
5	158	–	PC-r	1	1	1.00	2.00	4.00
6	167	2/64	PC-r	1	1	1.00	2.00	4.00
7	167	9/65	PC-r	1	1	1.00	2.00	4.00
8	169	Sm/69	New price 25¢; stiff-c; PC-r	1	1	1.25	2.50	5.00

Classics Illustrated #97 (HRN-131) © GIL

Classics Illustrated #101 (Orig.) © GIL

Classics Illustrated #105 (HRN-167) © GIL

98. The Red Badge of Courage

Ed	HRN	Date	Details	A	C	GD25	FN65	NM94
1	98	8/52	Original	1	1	4.00	11.00	22.00
2	118	–	PC-r	1	1	1.00	2.00	4.00
3	132	–	PC-r	1	1	1.00	2.00	4.00
4	142	–	PC-r	1	1	1.00	2.00	4.00
5	152	–	PC-r	1	1	1.00	2.00	4.00
6	161	–	PC-r	1	1	1.00	2.00	4.00
7	167	–	Has orig.date; PC-r	1	1	1.00	2.00	4.00
8	167	9/64	PC-r	1	1	1.00	2.00	4.00
9	167	10/65	PC-r	1	1	1.00	2.00	4.00
10	166	R/1968	New-c&price 25¢; PC-r; stiff-c	1	2	2.40	6.00	12.00

99. Hamlet (Used in POP, pg. 102)

Ed	HRN	Date	Details	A	C	GD25	FN65	NM94
1	98	9/52	Original; Blum-a	1	1	4.00	12.00	24.00
2	121	–	PC-r	1	1	1.00	2.00	4.00
3	141	–	PC-r	1	1	1.00	2.00	4.00
4	158	–	PC-r	1	1	1.00	2.00	4.00
5	167	–	Has orig.date; PC-r	1	1	1.00	2.00	4.00
6	167	7/65	PC-r	1	1	1.00	2.00	4.00
7	166	4/67	PC-r	1	1	1.00	2.00	4.00
8	169	Spr/69	New-c&price 25¢; PC-r; stiff-c	1	2	2.00	5.00	10.00

100. Mutiny on the Bounty

Ed	HRN	Date	Details	A	C	GD25	FN65	NM94
1	100	10/52	Original	1	1	4.00	11.00	22.00
2	117	–	PC-r	1	1	1.00	2.00	4.00
3	132	–	PC-r	1	1	1.00	2.00	4.00
4	142	–	PC-r	1	1	1.00	2.00	4.00
5	155	–	PC-r	1	1	1.00	2.00	4.00
6	167	–	Has orig. date;PC-r	1	1	1.00	2.00	4.00
7	167	5/64	PC-r	1	1	1.00	2.00	4.00
8	167	3/66	PC-r	1	1	1.00	2.00	4.00
9	169	Spr/70	PC-r; stiff-c	1	1	1.00	2.00	4.00

101. William Tell

Ed	HRN	Date	Details	A	C	GD25	FN65	NM94
1	101	11/52	Original; Kiefer-c delBourgo-a	1	1	4.00	11.00	22.00
2	118	–	PC-r	1	1	1.00	2.00	4.00
3	141	–	PC-r	1	1	1.00	2.00	4.00
4	158	–	PC-r	1	1	1.00	2.00	4.00
5	167	–	Has orig.date; PC-r	1	1	1.00	2.00	4.00
6	167	11/64	PC-r	1	1	1.00	2.00	4.00
7	166	4/67	PC-r	1	1	1.00	2.00	4.00
8	169	Win/69	New price 25¢; stiff-c; PC-r	1	1	1.00	2.00	4.00

102. The White Company

Ed	HRN	Date	Details	A	C	GD25	FN65	NM94
1	101	12/52	Original; Blum-a	1	1	6.70	20.00	40.00
2	165	–	PC-r	1	1	3.60	9.00	18.00
3	167	4/64	PC-r	1	1	3.60	9.00	18.00

103. Men Against the Sea

Ed	HRN	Date	Details	A	C	GD25	FN65	NM94
1	104	1/53	Original; Kiefer-c; Palais-a	1	1	4.35	13.00	26.00
2	114	–	PC-r	1	1	2.80	7.00	14.00
3	131	–	New-c; PC-r	1	2	2.00	5.00	10.00
4	158	–	PC-r	1	2	2.00	5.00	10.00
5	149	–	White reorder list; came after HRN-158; PC-r	1	2	3.60	9.00	18.00
6	167	3/64	PC-r	1	2	1.40	3.50	7.00

104. Bring 'Em Back Alive

Ed	HRN	Date	Details	A	C	GD25	FN65	NM94
1	105	2/53	Original; Kiefer-c/a	1	1	4.00	10.50	21.00
2	118	–	PC-r	1	1	1.00	2.00	4.00
3	133	–	PC-r	1	1	1.00	2.00	4.00
4	150	–	PC-r	1	1	1.00	2.00	4.00
5	158	–	PC-r	1	1	1.00	2.00	4.00
6	167	10/63	PC-r	1	1	1.00	2.00	4.00
7	167	9/65	PC-r	1	1	1.00	2.00	4.00
8	169	Win/69	New price 25¢; stiff-c; PC-r	1	1	1.00	2.00	4.00

105. From the Earth to the Moon

Ed	HRN	Date	Details	A	C	GD25	FN65	NM94
1	106	3/53	Original; Blum-a	1	1	4.00	10.50	21.00
2	118	–	PC-r	1	1	1.00	2.00	4.00
3	132	–	PC-r	1	1	1.00	2.00	4.00
4	141	–	PC-r	1	1	1.00	2.00	4.00
5	146	–	PC-r	1	1	1.00	2.00	4.00
6	156	–	PC-r	1	1	1.00	2.00	4.00
7	167	–	Has orig. date; PC-r	1	1	1.00	2.00	4.00
8	167	5/64	PC-r	1	1	1.00	2.00	4.00
9	167	5/65	PC-r	1	1	1.00	2.00	4.00
10A	166	10/67	PC-r	1	1	1.00	2.00	4.00
10B	166	10/67	w/Grit ad stapled in book	1	1	9.35	28.00	56.00
11	169	Sm/69	New price 25¢; stiff-c; PC-r	1	1	1.00	2.00	4.00
12	169	Spr/71	PC-r	1	1	1.00	2.00	4.00

106. Buffalo Bill

Ed	HRN	Date	Details	A	C	GD25	FN65	NM94
1	107	4/53	Orig.; delBourgo-a	1	1	4.00	10.50	21.00
2	118	–	PC-r	1	1	1.00	2.00	4.00
3	132	–	PC-r	1	1	1.00	2.00	4.00
4	142	–	PC-r	1	1	1.00	2.00	4.00
5	161	–	PC-r	1	1	1.00	2.00	4.00
6	167	3/64	PC-r	1	1	1.00	2.00	4.00
7	166	7/67	PC-r	1	1	1.00	2.00	4.00
8	169	Fall/69	PC-r; stiff-c	1	1	1.00	2.00	4.00

107. King of the Khyber Rifles

Ed	HRN	Date	Details	A	C	GD25	FN65	NM94
1	108	5/53	Original	1	1	4.00	11.00	22.00
2	118	–	PC-r	1	1	1.00	2.00	4.00
3	146	–	PC-r	1	1	1.00	2.00	4.00
4	158	–	PC-r	1	1	1.00	2.00	4.00
5	167	–	Has orig.date; PC-r	1	1	1.00	2.00	4.00
6	167	–	PC-r	1	1	1.00	2.00	4.00
7	167	10/66	PC-r	1	1	1.00	2.00	4.00

108. Knights of the Round Table

Ed	HRN	Date	Details	A	C	GD25	FN65	NM94
1A	108	6/53	Original; Blum-a	1	1	4.00	11.00	22.00
1B	109	6/53	Original; scarce	1	1	5.35	16.00	32.00
2	117	–	PC-r	1	1	1.00	2.00	4.00
3	165	–	PC-r	1	1	1.00	2.00	4.00
4	167	4/64	PC-r	1	1	1.00	2.00	4.00
5	166	4/67	PC-r	1	1	1.00	2.00	4.00
6	169	Sm/69	New price 25¢; stiff-c; PC-r	1	1	1.00	2.00	4.00

109. Pitcairn's Island

Ed	HRN	Date	Details	A	C	GD25	FN65	NM94
1	110	7/53	Original; Palais-a	1	1	4.00	12.00	24.00
2	165	–	PC-r	1	1	1.50	3.50	7.00
3	167	3/64	PC-r	1	1	1.50	3.50	7.00
4	166	6/67	PC-r	1	1	1.50	3.50	7.00

Classics Illustrated #111 (HRN-167) © GIL

Classics Illustrated #115 (Orig.) © GIL

Classics Illustrated #124 (HRN-167) © GIL

110. A Study in Scarlet

Ed	HRN	Date	Details	A	C	GD25	FN65	NM94
1	111	8/53	Original	1	1	11.00	32.00	75.00
2	165	–	PC-r	1	1	7.00	21.00	42.00

111. The Talisman

Ed	HRN	Date	Details	A	C	GD25	FN65	NM94
1	112	9/53	Original; last H.C. Kiefer-a	1	1	5.35	16.00	32.00
2	165	–	PC-r	1	1	1.25	2.50	5.00
3	167	5/64	PC-r	1	1	1.25	2.50	5.00
4	166	Fall/68	C-price 25¢; PC-r	1	1	1.25	2.50	5.00

112. Adventures of Kit Carson

Ed	HRN	Date	Details	A	C	GD25	FN65	NM94
1	113	10/53	Original; Palais-a	1	1	5.35	16.00	32.00
2	129	–	PC-r	1	1	1.00	2.00	4.00
3	141	–	PC-r	1	1	1.00	2.00	4.00
4	152	–	PC-r	1	1	1.00	2.00	4.00
5	161	–	PC-r	1	1	1.00	2.00	4.00
6	167	–	PC-r	1	1	1.00	2.00	4.00
7	167	2/65	PC-r	1	1	1.00	2.00	4.00
8	167	5/66	PC-r	1	1	1.00	2.00	4.00
9	166	Win/69	New-c&price 25¢; PC-r; stiff-c	1	2	2.00	5.00	10.00

113. The Forty-Five Guardsmen

Ed	HRN	Date	Details	A	C	GD25	FN65	NM94
1	114	11/53	Orig.; delBourgo-a	1	1	7.50	22.50	45.00
2	166	7/67	PC-r	1	1	4.00	10.50	21.00

114. The Red Rover

Ed	HRN	Date	Details	A	C	GD25	FN65	NM94
1	115	12/53	Original	1	1	7.50	22.50	45.00
2	166	7/67	PC-r	1	1	4.00	10.50	21.00

115. How I Found Livingstone

Ed	HRN	Date	Details	A	C	GD25	FN65	NM94
1	116	1/54	Original	1	1	7.50	22.50	45.00
2	167	1/67	PC-r	1	1	4.00	10.50	21.00

116. The Bottle Imp

Ed	HRN	Date	Details	A	C	GD25	FN65	NM94
1	117	2/54	Orig.; Cameron-a	1	1	7.50	22.50	45.00
2	167	1/67	PC-r	1	1	4.00	10.50	21.00

117. Captains Courageous

Ed	HRN	Date	Details	A	C	GD25	FN65	NM94
1	118	3/54	Orig.; Costanza-a	1	1	6.35	19.00	38.00
2	167	2/67	PC-r	1	1	2.40	6.00	12.00
3	169	Fall/69	New price 25¢; stiff-c; PC-r	1	1	2.00	5.00	10.00

118. Rob Roy

Ed	HRN	Date	Details	A	C	GD25	FN65	NM94
1	119	4/54	Original; Rudy & Walter Palais-a	1	1	7.50	22.50	45.00
2	167	2/67	PC-r	1	1	4.00	10.50	21.00

119. Soldiers of Fortune

Ed	HRN	Date	Details	A	C	GD25	FN65	NM94
1	120	5/54	Original Shaffenberger-a	1	1	7.00	21.00	42.00
2	166	3/67	PC-r	1	1	2.80	7.00	14.00
3	169	Spr/70	New price 25¢; stiff-c; PC-r	1	1	2.00	5.00	10.00

120. The Hurricane

Ed	HRN	Date	Details	A	C	GD25	FN65	NM94
1	121	6/54	Orig.; Cameron-a	1	1	7.50	22.50	45.00
2	166	3/67	PC-r	1	1	4.00	12.00	24.00

121. Wild Bill Hickok

Ed	HRN	Date	Details	A	C	GD25	FN65	NM94
1	122	7/54	Original	1	1	4.00	11.00	22.00
2	132	–	PC-r	1	1	1.00	2.00	4.00
3	141	–	PC-r	1	1	1.00	2.00	4.00
4	154	–	PC-r	1	1	1.00	2.00	4.00
5	167	–	PC-r	1	1	1.00	2.00	4.00
6	167	8/64	PC-r	1	1	1.00	2.00	4.00
7	166	4/67	PC-r	1	1	1.00	2.00	4.00
8	169	Win/69	PC-r; stiff-c	1	1	1.00	2.00	4.00

122. The Mutineers

Ed	HRN	Date	Details	A	C	GD25	FN65	NM94
1	123	9/54	Original	1	1	4.00	11.00	22.00
2	136	–	PC-r	1	1	1.00	2.00	4.00
3	146	–	PC-r	1	1	1.00	2.00	4.00
4	158	–	PC-r	1	1	1.00	2.00	4.00
5	167	11/63	PC-r	1	1	1.00	2.00	4.00
6	167	3/65	PC-r	1	1	1.00	2.00	4.00
7	166	8/67	PC-r	1	1	1.00	2.00	4.00

123. Fang and Claw

Ed	HRN	Date	Details	A	C	GD25	FN65	NM94
1	124	11/54	Original	1	1	4.00	11.00	22.00
2	133	–	PC-r	1	1	1.00	2.00	4.00
3	143	–	PC-r	1	1	1.00	2.00	4.00
4	154	–	PC-r	1	1	1.00	2.00	4.00
5	167	–	Has orig.date; PC-r	1	1	1.00	2.00	4.00
6	167	9/65	PC-r	1	1	1.00	2.00	4.00

124. The War of the Worlds

Ed	HRN	Date	Details	A	C	GD25	FN65	NM94
1	125	1/55	Original; Cameron-c/a	1	1	5.00	15.00	30.00
2	131	–	PC-r	1	1	1.40	3.50	7.00
3	141	–	PC-r	1	1	1.40	3.50	7.00
4	148	–	PC-r	1	1	1.40	3.50	7.00
5	156	–	PC-r	1	1	1.40	3.50	7.00
6	165	–	PC-r	1	1	1.40	3.50	7.00
7	167	–	PC-r	1	1	1.40	3.50	7.00
8	167	11/64	PC-r	1	1	1.40	3.50	7.00
9	167	11/65	PC-r	1	1	1.40	3.50	7.00
10	166	R/1968	C-price 25¢; PC-r	1	1	1.40	3.50	7.00
11	169	Sm/70	PC-r; stiff-c	1	1	1.40	3.50	7.00

125. The Ox Bow Incident

Ed	HRN	Date	Details	A	C	GD25	FN65	NM94
1	3/55	–	Original; Picture Progress replaces reorder list	1	1	4.00	11.00	22.00
2	143	–	PC-r	1	1	1.00	2.00	4.00
3	152	–	PC-r	1	1	1.00	2.00	4.00
4	149	–	PC-r	1	1	1.00	2.00	4.00
5	167	–	PC-r	1	1	1.00	2.00	4.00
6	167	11/64	PC-r	1	1	1.00	2.00	4.00
7	166	4/67	PC-r	1	1	1.00	2.00	4.00
8	169	Win/69	New price 25¢; stiff-c; PC-r	1	1	1.00	2.00	4.00

126. The Downfall

Ed	HRN	Date	Details	A	C	GD25	FN65	NM94
1	5/55	–	Orig.; 'Picture Progress' replaces reorder list; Cameron-c/a	1	1	4.00	11.00	22.00
2	167	8/64	PC-r	1	1	1.60	4.00	8.00
3	166	R/1968	C-price 25¢; PC-r	1	1	1.60	4.00	8.00

127. The King of the Mountains

Ed	HRN	Date	Details	A	C	GD25	FN65	NM94
1	128	7/55	Original	1	1	4.00	11.00	22.00
2	167	6/64	PC-r	1	1	1.60	4.00	8.00

Classics Illustrated #127 (Orig.) © GIL

Classics Illustrated #130 (Orig) © GIL

Classics Illustrated #138 © GIL

Ed	HRN	Date	Details	A	C	GD25	FN65	NM94
3	166	F/1968	C-price 25¢; PC-r	1	1	1.60	4.00	8.00

128. Macbeth (Used in **POP**, pg. 102)

Ed	HRN	Date	Details	A	C	GD25	FN65	NM94
1	128	9/55	Orig.; last Blum-a	1	1	4.00	11.00	22.00
2	143	–	PC-r	1	1	1.00	2.00	4.00
3	158	–	PC-r	1	1	1.00	2.00	4.00
4	167	–	PC-r	1	1	1.00	2.00	4.00
5	167	6/64	PC-r	1	1	1.00	2.00	4.00
6	166	4/67	PC-r	1	1	1.00	2.00	4.00
7	166	R/1968	C-Price 25¢; PC-r	1	1	1.00	2.00	4.00
8	169	Spr/70	Stiff-c; PC-r	1	1	1.00	2.00	4.00

129. Davy Crockett

Ed	HRN	Date	Details	A	C	GD25	FN65	NM94
1	129	11/55	Orig.; Cameron-a	1	1	10.00	30.00	60.00
2	167	9/66	PC-r	1	1	5.35	16.00	32.00

130. Caesar's Conquests

Ed	HRN	Date	Details	A	C	GD25	FN65	NM94
1	130	1/56	Original; Orlando-a	1	1	4.00	11.00	22.00
2	142	–	PC-r	1	1	1.00	2.00	4.00
3	152	–	PC-r	1	1	1.00	2.00	4.00
4	149	–	PC-r	1	1	1.00	2.00	4.00
5	167	–	PC-r	1	1	1.00	2.00	4.00
6	167	10/64	PC-r	1	1	1.00	2.00	4.00
7	167	4/66	PC-r	1	1	1.00	2.00	4.00

131. The Covered Wagon

Ed	HRN	Date	Details	A	C	GD25	FN65	NM94
1	131	3/56	Original	1	1	4.00	11.00	22.00
2	143	–	PC-r	1	1	1.00	2.00	4.00
3	152	–	PC-r	1	1	1.00	2.00	4.00
4	158	–	PC-r	1	1	1.00	2.00	4.00
5	167	–	PC-r	1	1	1.00	2.00	4.00
6	167	11/64	PC-r	1	1	1.00	2.00	4.00
7	167	4/66	PC-r	1	1	1.00	2.00	4.00
8	169	Win/69	New price 25¢; stiff-c; PC-r	1	1	1.00	2.00	4.00

132. The Dark Frigate

Ed	HRN	Date	Details	A	C	GD25	FN65	NM94
1	132	5/56	Original	1	1	4.00	11.00	22.00
2	150	–	PC-r	1	1	1.40	3.50	7.00
3	167	1/64	PC-r	1	1	1.40	3.50	7.00
4	166	5/67	PC-r	1	1	1.40	3.50	7.00

133. The Time Machine

Ed	HRN	Date	Details	A	C	GD25	FN65	NM94
1	132	7/56	Orig.; Cameron-a	1	1	5.00	15.00	30.00
2	142	–	PC-r	1	1	1.40	3.50	7.00
3	152	–	PC-r	1	1	1.40	3.50	7.00
4	158	–	PC-r	1	1	1.40	3.50	7.00
5	167	–	PC-r	1	1	1.40	3.50	7.00
6	167	6/64	PC-r	1	1	1.40	3.50	7.00
7	167	3/66	PC-r	1	1	1.40	3.50	7.00
8	166	12/67	PC-r	1	1	1.40	3.50	7.00
9	169	Win/71	New price 25¢; stiff-c; PC-r	1	1	1.40	3.50	7.00

134. Romeo and Juliet

Ed	HRN	Date	Details	A	C	GD25	FN65	NM94
1	134	9/56	Original; Evans-a	1	1	4.00	11.00	22.00
2	161	–	PC-r	1	1	1.00	2.00	4.00
3	167	9/63	PC-r	1	1	1.00	2.00	4.00
4	167	5/65	PC-r	1	1	1.00	2.00	4.00
5	166	6/67	PC-r	1	1	1.00	2.00	4.00
6	166	Win/69	New c&price 25¢; stiff-c; PC-r	1	2	3.60	9.00	18.00

135. Waterloo

Ed	HRN	Date	Details	A	C	GD25	FN65	NM94
1	135	11/56	Orig.; G. Ingels-a	1	1	4.00	11.00	22.00
2	153	–	PC-r	1	1	1.00	2.00	4.00
3	167	–	PC-r	1	1	1.00	2.00	4.00
4	167	9/64	PC-r	1	1	1.00	2.00	4.00
5	166	R/1968	C-price 25¢; PC-r	1	1	1.00	2.00	4.00

136. Lord Jim

Ed	HRN	Date	Details	A	C	GD25	FN65	NM94
1	136	1/57	Original; Evans-a	1	1	4.00	11.00	22.00
2	165	–	PC-r	1	1	1.00	2.00	4.00
3	167	3/64	PC-r	1	1	1.00	2.00	4.00
4	167	9/66	PC-r	1	1	1.00	2.00	4.00
5	169	Sm/69	New price 25 ¢; stiff-c; PC-r	1	1	1.00	2.00	4.00

137. The Little Savage

Ed	HRN	Date	Details	A	C	GD25	FN65	NM94
1	136	3/57	Original; Evans-a	1	1	4.00	11.00	22.00
2	148	–	PC-r	1	1	1.00	2.00	4.00
3	156	–	PC-r	1	1	1.00	2.00	4.00
4	167	–	PC-r	1	1	1.00	2.00	4.00
5	167	10/64	PC-r	1	1	1.00	2.00	4.00
6	166	8/67	PC-r	1	1	1.00	2.00	4.00
7	169	Spr/70	New price 25¢; stiff-c; PC-r	1	1	1.00	2.00	4.00

138. A Journey to the Center of the Earth

Ed	HRN	Date	Details	A	C	GD25	FN65	NM94
1	136	5/57	Original	1	1	4.70	14.00	28.00
2	146	–	PC-r	1	1	1.25	2.50	5.00
3	156	–	PC-r	1	1	1.25	2.50	5.00
4	158	–	PC-r	1	1	1.25	2.50	5.00
5	167	–	PC-r	1	1	1.25	2.50	5.00
6	167	6/64	PC-r	1	1	1.25	2.50	5.00
7	167	4/66	PC-r	1	1	1.25	2.50	5.00
8	166	R/68	C-price 25¢; PC-r	1	1	1.25	2.50	5.00

139. In the Reign of Terror

Ed	HRN	Date	Details	A	C	GD25	FN65	NM94
1	139	7/57	Original; Evans-a	1	1	4.00	11.00	22.00
2	154	–	PC-r	1	1	1.00	2.00	4.00
3	167	–	Has orig.date; PC-r	1	1	1.00	2.00	4.00
4	167	7/64	PC-r	1	1	1.00	2.00	4.00
5	166	R/1968	C-price 25¢; PC-r	1	1	1.00	2.00	4.00

140. On Jungle Trails

Ed	HRN	Date	Details	A	C	GD25	FN65	NM94
1	140	9/57	Original	1	1	4.00	11.00	22.00
2	150	–	PC-r	1	1	1.00	2.00	4.00
3	160	–	PC-r	1	1	1.00	2.00	4.00
4	167	9/63	PC-r	1	1	1.00	2.00	4.00
5	167	9/65	PC-r	1	1	1.00	2.00	4.00

141. Castle Dangerous

Ed	HRN	Date	Details	A	C	GD25	FN65	NM94
1	141	11/57	Original	1	1	4.00	11.00	22.00
2	152	–	PC-r	1	1	1.25	2.50	5.00
3	167	–	PC-r	1	1	1.25	2.50	5.00
4	166	7/67	PC-r	1	1	1.25	2.50	5.00

142. Abraham Lincoln

Ed	HRN	Date	Details	A	C	GD25	FN65	NM94
1	142	1/58	Original	1	1	4.00	11.00	22.00
2	154	–	PC-r	1	1	1.00	2.00	4.00
3	158	–	PC-r	1	1	1.00	2.00	4.00
4	167	10/63	PC-r	1	1	1.00	2.00	4.00
5	167	7/65	PC-r	1	1	1.00	2.00	4.00
6	166	11/67	PC-r	1	1	1.00	2.00	4.00
7	169	Fall/69	New price 25¢; stiff-c; PC-r	1	1	1.00	2.00	4.00

143. Kim

Classics Illustrated #140 (HRN-160) © GIL

Classics Illustrated #148 © GIL

Classics Illustrated #149 © GIL

Ed	HRN	Date	Details	A	C	GD25	FN65	NM94
1	143	3/58	Original; Orlando-a	1	1	4.00	11.00	22.00
2	165	–	PC-r	1	1	1.00	2.00	4.00
3	167	11/63	PC-r	1	1	1.00	2.00	4.00
4	167	8/65	PC-r	1	1	1.00	2.00	4.00
5	169	Win/69	New price 25¢; stiff-c; PC-r	1	1	1.00	2.00	4.00

144. The First Men in the Moon

Ed	HRN	Date	Details	A	C	GD25	FN65	NM94
1	143	5/58	Original; Woodbridge/Williamson/Torres-a	1	1	4.70	14.00	28.00
2	152	–	(Rare)-PC-r	1	1	5.85	17.50	35.00
3	153	–	PC-r	1	1	1.25	2.50	5.00
4	161	–	PC-r	1	1	1.25	2.50	5.00
5	167	–	PC-r	1	1	1.25	2.50	5.00
6	167	12/65	PC-r	1	1	1.25	2.50	5.00
7	166	Fall/68	New-c&price 25¢; PC-r; stiff-c	1	2	1.80	4.50	9.00
8	169	Win/69	Stiff-c; PC-r	1	2	1.80	4.50	9.00

145. The Crisis

Ed	HRN	Date	Details	A	C	GD25	FN65	NM94
1	143	7/58	Original; Evans-a	1	1	4.00	11.00	22.00
2	156	–	PC-r	1	1	1.00	2.00	4.00
3	167	10/63	PC-r	1	1	1.00	2.00	4.00
4	167	3/65	PC-r	1	1	1.00	2.00	4.00
5	166	R/68	C-price 25¢; PC-r	1	1	1.00	2.00	4.00

146. With Fire and Sword

Ed	HRN	Date	Details	A	C	GD25	FN65	NM94
1	143	9/58	Original; Woodbridge-a	1	1	4.00	11.00	22.00
2	156	–	PC-r	1	1	1.40	3.50	7.00
3	167	11/63	PC-r	1	1	1.40	3.50	7.00
4	167	3/65	PC-r	1	1	1.40	3.50	7.00

147. Ben-Hur

Ed	HRN	Date	Details	A	C	GD25	FN65	NM94
1	147	11/58	Original; Orlando-a	1	1	4.00	11.00	22.00
2	152	–	Scarce; PC-r	1	1	4.00	12.00	24.00
3	153	–	PC-r	1	1	1.00	2.00	4.00
4	158	–	PC-r	1	1	1.00	2.00	4.00
5	167	–	Orig.date; but PC-r	1	1	1.00	2.00	4.00
6	167	2/65	PC-r	1	1	1.00	2.00	4.00
7	167	9/66	PC-r	1	1	1.00	2.00	4.00
8A	166	Fall/68	New-c&price 25¢; PC-r; soft-c	1	2	2.40	6.00	12.00
8B	166	Fall/68	New-c&price 25¢; PC-r; stiff-c; scarce	1	2	4.00	12.00	24.00

148. The Buccaneer

Ed	HRN	Date	Details	A	C	GD25	FN65	NM94
1	148	1/59	Orig.; Evans/Jenny-a; Saunders-c	1	1	4.00	11.00	22.00
2	568	–	Juniors list only PC-r	1	1	1.40	3.50	7.00
3	167	–	PC-r	1	1	1.00	2.00	4.00
4	167	9/65	PC-r	1	1	1.00	2.00	4.00
5	169	Sm/69	New price 25¢; PC-r; stiff-c	1	1	1.00	2.00	4.00

149. Off on a Comet

Ed	HRN	Date	Details	A	C	GD25	FN65	NM94
1	149	3/59	Orig.;G.McCann-a; blue reorder list	1	1	4.00	11.00	22.00
2	155	–	PC-r	1	1	1.00	2.00	4.00
3	149	–	PC-r; white reorder list; no coming-next ad	1	1	1.00	2.00	4.00
4	167	12/63	PC-r	1	1	1.00	2.00	4.00
5	167	2/65	PC-r	1	1	1.00	2.00	4.00
6	167	10/66	PC-r	1	1	1.00	2.00	4.00
7	166	Fall/68	New-c&price 25¢; PC-r	1	2	2.40	6.00	12.00

150. The Virginian

Ed	HRN	Date	Details	A	C	GD25	FN65	NM94
1	150	5/59	Original	1	1	5.00	15.00	30.00
2	164	–	PC-r	1	1	2.40	6.00	12.00
3	167	10/63	PC-r	1	1	2.00	5.00	10.00
4	167	12/65	PC-r	1	1	2.00	5.00	10.00

151. Won By the Sword

Ed	HRN	Date	Details	A	C	GD25	FN65	NM94
1	150	7/59	Original	1	1	5.00	15.00	30.00
2	164	–	PC-r	1	1	2.00	5.00	10.00
3	167	10/63	PC-r	1	1	1.80	4.50	9.00
4	166	7/67	PC-r	1	1	1.80	4.50	9.00

152. Wild Animals I Have Known

Ed	HRN	Date	Details	A	C	GD25	FN65	NM94
1	152	9/59	Orig.; L.B. Cole c/a	1	1	5.00	15.00	30.00
2A	149	–	PC-r; white reorder list; no coming-next ad; IBC: Jr. list #572	1	1	1.25	2.50	5.00
2B	149	–	PC-r; inside-bc: Jr. list to #555	1	1	1.40	3.50	7.00
2C	149	–	PC-r; inside-bc: has World Around Us ad; scarce	1	1	2.80	7.00	14.00
3	167	9/63	PC-r	1	1	1.00	2.00	4.00
4	167	8/65	PC-r	1	1	1.00	2.00	4.00
5	169	Fall/69	New price 25¢; stiff-c; PC-r	1	1	1.00	2.00	4.00

153. The Invisible Man

Ed	HRN	Date	Details	A	C	GD25	FN65	NM94
1	153	11/59	Original	1	1	5.00	15.00	30.00
2A	149	–	PC-r; white reorder list; no coming-next ad; inside-bc: Jr. list to #572	1	1	1.25	2.50	5.00
2B	149	–	PC-r; inside-bc: Jr. list to #555	1	1	1.40	3.50	7.00
3	167	–	PC-r	1	1	1.00	2.00	4.00
4	167	2/65	PC-r	1	1	1.00	2.00	4.00
5	167	9/66	PC-r	1	1	1.00	2.00	4.00
6	166	Win/69	New price 25¢; PC-r; stiff-c	1	1	1.00	2.00	4.00
7	169	Spr/71	Stiff-c; letters spelling 'Invisible Man' are 'solid' not 'invisible;' PC-r	1	1	1.00	2.00	4.00

154. The Conspiracy of Pontiac

Ed	HRN	Date	Details	A	C	GD25	FN65	NM94
1	154	1/60	Original	1	1	5.00	15.00	30.00
2	167	11/63	PC-r	1	1	2.40	6.00	12.00
3	167	7/64	PC-r	1	1	2.40	6.00	12.00
4	166	12/67	PC-r	1	1	2.40	6.00	12.00

155. The Lion of the North

Ed	HRN	Date	Details	A	C	GD25	FN65	NM94
1	154	3/60	Original	1	1	4.70	14.00	28.00
2	167	1/64	PC-r	1	1	2.00	5.00	10.00
3	166	R/1967	C-price 25¢; PC-r	1	1	1.80	4.50	9.00

156. The Conquest of Mexico

Ed	HRN	Date	Details	A	C

Classics Illustrated #160 (HRN-160) © GIL

Classics Illustrated #161 (HRN-167) © GIL

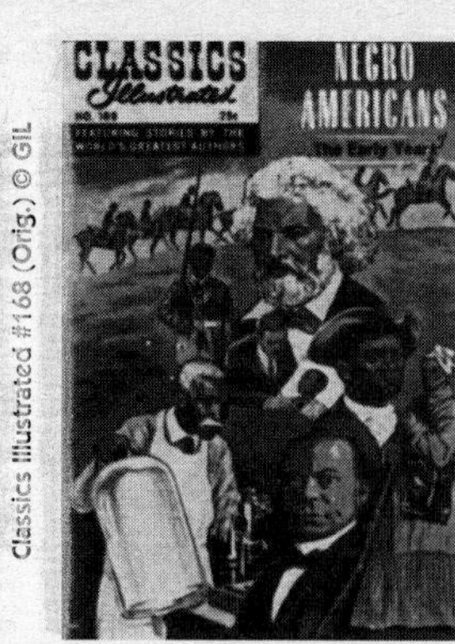

Classics Illustrated #168 (Orig.) © GIL

Ed	HRN	Date	Details	A	C	GD25	FN65	NM94
1	156	5/60	Orig.; Bruno Premiani-c/a	1	1	4.70	14.00	28.00
2	167	1/64	PC-r	1	1	1.40	3.50	7.00
3	166	8/67	PC-r	1	1	1.40	3.50	7.00
4	169	Spr/70	New price 25¢; stiff-c; PC-r	1	1	1.25	2.50	5.00

157. Lives of the Hunted

Ed	HRN	Date	Details	A	C	GD25	FN65	NM94
1	156	7/60	Orig.; L.B. Cole-c	1	1	5.00	15.00	30.00
2	167	2/64	PC-r	1	1	2.40	6.00	12.00
3	166	10/67	PC-r	1	1	2.40	6.00	12.00

158. The Conspirators

Ed	HRN	Date	Details	A	C	GD25	FN65	NM94
1	156	9/60	Original	1	1	5.00	15.00	30.00
2	167	7/64	PC-r	1	1	2.40	6.00	12.00
3	166	10/67	PC-r	1	1	2.40	6.00	12.00

159. The Octopus

Ed	HRN	Date	Details	A	C	GD25	FN65	NM94
1	159	11/60	Orig.; Gray Morrow-a; L.B. Cole-c	1	1	5.00	15.00	30.00
2	167	2/64	PC-r	1	1	2.00	5.00	10.00
3	166	R/1967	C-price 25¢; PC-r	1	1	2.00	5.00	10.00

160. The Food of the Gods

Ed	HRN	Date	Details	A	C	GD25	FN65	NM94
1A	159	1/61	Original	1	1	5.00	15.00	30.00
1B	160	1/61	Original; same, except for HRN	1	1	5.00	15.00	30.00
2	167	1/64	PC-r	1	1	2.00	5.00	10.00
3	166	6/67	PC-r	1	1	2.00	5.00	10.00

161. Cleopatra

Ed	HRN	Date	Details	A	C	GD25	FN65	NM94
1	161	3/61	Original	1	1	5.85	17.50	35.00
2	167	1/64	PC-r	1	1	2.80	7.00	14.00
3	166	8/67	PC-r	1	1	2.80	7.00	14.00

162. Robur the Conqueror

Ed	HRN	Date	Details	A	C	GD25	FN65	NM94
1	162	5/61	Original	1	1	5.00	15.00	30.00
2	167	7/64	PC-r	1	1	2.00	5.00	10.00
3	166	8/67	PC-r	1	1	2.00	5.00	10.00

163. Master of the World

Ed	HRN	Date	Details	A	C	GD25	FN65	NM94
1	163	7/61	Original; Gray Morrow-a	1	1	5.00	15.00	30.00
2	167	1/65	PC-r	1	1	2.00	5.00	10.00
3	166	R/1968	C-price 25¢; PC-r	1	1	2.00	5.00	10.00

164. The Cossack Chief

Ed	HRN	Date	Details	A	C	GD25	FN65	NM94
1	164	(1961)	Orig.; nd(10/61?)	1	1	5.00	15.00	30.00
2	167	4/65	PC-r	1	1	2.00	5.00	10.00
3	166	Fall/68	C-price 25¢; PC-r	1	1	2.00	5.00	10.00

165. The Queen's Necklace

Ed	HRN	Date	Details	A	C	GD25	FN65	NM94
1	164	1/62	Original; Morrow-a	1	1	5.00	15.00	30.00
2	167	4/65	PC-r	1	1	2.00	5.00	10.00
3	166	Fall/68	C-price 25¢; PC-r	1	1	2.00	5.00	10.00

166. Tigers and Traitors

Ed	HRN	Date	Details	A	C	GD25	FN65	NM94
1	165	5/62	Original	1	1	8.00	24.00	48.00
2	167	2/64	PC-r	1	1	3.60	9.00	18.00
3	167	11/66	PC-r	1	1	3.60	9.00	18.00

167. Faust

Ed	HRN	Date	Details	A	C	GD25	FN65	NM94
1	165	8/62	Original	1	1	11.00	32.00	75.00
2	167	2/64	PC-r	1	1	5.35	16.00	32.00
3	166	6/67	PC-r	1	1	5.35	16.00	32.00

168. In Freedom's Cause

Ed	HRN	Date	Details	A	C	GD25	FN65	NM94
1	169	Win/69	Original; Evans/Crandall-a; stiff-c; 25¢; no coming-next ad;	1	1	10.00	30.00	70.00

169. Negro AmericansThe Early Years

Ed	HRN	Date	Details	A	C	GD25	FN65	NM94
1	166	Spr/69	Orig. & last issue; 25¢; Stiff-c; no coming-next ad; other sources indicate publication date of 5/69	1	1	10.00	30.00	70.00
2	169	Spr/69	Stiff-c	1	1	6.70	20.00	40.00

NOTE: *Many other titles were prepared or planned but were only issued in British/European series.*

CLASSICS GIVEAWAYS (Arranged in chronological order)

	GD25	FN65	NM94
12/41–Walter Theatre Enterprises (Huntington, WV) giveaway containing #2 (orig.) w/new generic-c (only 1 known copy)	93.00	280.00	650.00
1942–Double Comics containing CC#1 (orig.) (diff. cover) (not actually a giveaway) (very rare) (also see Double Comics) (only one known copy)	200.00	600.00	1400.00
12/42–Saks 34th St. Giveaway containing CC#7 (orig.) (diff. cover) (very rare; only 6 known copies)	600.00	1800.00	4200.00
2/43–American Comics containing CC#8 (orig.) (Liberty Theatre giveaway) (different cover) (only one known copy) (see American Comics)	129.00	385.00	900.00
12/44–Robin Hood Flour Co. Giveaway - #7-CC(R) (diff. cover) (rare) (edition probably 5 [22])	257.00	771.00	1800.00

NOTE: How are above editions determined without CC covers? 1942 is dated 1942, and CC#1-first reprint did not come out until 5/43. 12/42 and 2/43 are determined by blue note at bottom of first text page only in original edition. 12/44 is estimated from page width each reprint edition had progressively slightly smaller page width.

	GD25	FN65	NM94
1951–Shelter Thru the Ages (C.I. Educational Series) (actually Giveaway by the Ruberoid Co.) (16 pgs.) (contains original artwork by H. C. Kiefer) (there are 5 diff. back cover ad variations: "Ranch" house ad, "Igloo" ad, "Doll House" ad, "Tree House" ad & blank)(scarce)	71.00	215.00	500.00
1952–George Daynor Biography Giveaway (CC logo) (partly comic book/pictures/newspaper articles) (story of man who built Palace Depression out of junkyard swamp in NJ) (64 pgs.)(very rare; only 3 known copies, one missing-bc)	785.00	2360.00	5500.00
1953–Westinghouse/Dreams of a Man (C.I. Educational Series) (Westinghouse bio./Westinghouse Co. giveaway) (contains original artwork by H. C. Kiefer) (16 pgs.) (also French/Spanish/Italian versions) (scarce)	79.00	235.00	550.00

NOTE: Reproductions of 1951, 1952, and 1953 exist with color photocopy covers and black & white photocopy interior ("W.C.N. Reprint")

	GD25	FN65	NM94
	2.00	5.00	10.00
1951-53–Coward Shoe Giveaways (all editions very rare); 2 variations of back-c ad exist:			
With back-c photo ad: 5 (87), 12 (89), 22 (85), 49 (85), 69 (87), 72 (no HRN), 80 (0), 91 (0), 92 (0), 96 (0), 98 (0), 100 (0), 101 (0), 103-105 (all Os)	36.00	107.00	250.00
With back-c cartoon ad: 106-109 (all 0s), 110 (111), 112 (0)	43.00	130.00	300.00
1956–Ben Franklin 5-10 Store Giveaway (#65-PC with back cover ad) (scarce)	30.00	90.00	210.00
1956–Ben Franklin Insurance Co. Giveaway (#65-PC with diff. back cover ad) (very rare)	71.00	215.00	500.00
11/56–Sealtest Co. Edition - #4 (135) (identical to regular edition except for Sealtest logo printed, not stamped, on front cover) (only two copies known to exist)	36.00	107.00	250.00

1958–Get-Well Giveaway containing #15-CI (new cartoon-type cover)(Pressman

Classics Illustrated Christmas Giveaway
Stacy's Dept. Store © GIL

Classics Illustrated Jr. #522 © GIL

Classics Illustrated Jr. #558 © GIL

	GD25	FN65	NM94
Pharmacy) (only one copy known to exist)	36.00	107.00	250.00
1967-68–Twin Circle Giveaway Editions - all HRN 166, with back cover ad for National Catholic Press.			
2(R68), 4(R67), 10(R68), 13(R68)	4.00	12.00	24.00
48(R67), 128(R68), 535(576-R68)	5.00	15.00	30.00
16(R68), 68(R67)	6.70	20.00	40.00
12/69–Christmas Giveaway ("A Christmas Adventure") (reprints Picture Parade #4-1953, new cover) (4 ad variations)			
Stacy's Dept. Store	4.00	10.00	20.00
Anne & Hope Store	7.50	22.50	45.00
Gibson's Dept. Store (rare)	7.50	22.50	45.00
"Merry Christmas" & blank ad space	4.00	10.00	20.00

CLASSICS ILLUSTRATED GIANTS
October, 1949 (One-Shots - "OS")
Gilberton Publications

These Giant Editions, all with new Kiefer front and back covers, were advertised from 10/49 to 2/52. They were 50¢ on the newsstand and 60¢ by mail. They are actually fourclassics in one volume. All the stories are reprints of the Classics Illustrated Series. NOTE: There were also British hardback Adventure & Indian Giants in 1952, with the same covers but different contents: Adventure - 2, 7, 10; Indian - 17, 22, 37, 58. They are also rare.

	GD25	FN65	NM94
"An Illustrated Library of Great Adventure Stories" - reprints of No. 6,7,8,10 (Rare); Kiefer-c	107.00	320.00	750.00
"An Illustrated Library of Exciting Mystery Stories" - reprints of No. 30,21,40, 13 (Rare)	115.00	343.00	800.00
"An Illustrated Library of Great Indian Stories" - reprints of No. 4,17,22,37 (Rare)	100.00	300.00	700.00

INTRODUCTION TO CLASSICS ILLUSTRATED JUNIOR

Collectors of Juniors can be put into one of two categories those who want any copy of each title, and those who want all the originals. Those seeking every original and reprint edition are a limited group, primarily because Juniors have no changes in art or covers to spark interest, and because reprints are so low in value it is difficult to get dealers to look for specific reprint editions.

In recent years it has become apparent that most serious Classics collectors seek Junior originals. Those seeking reprints seek them for low cost. This has made the previous note about the comparative market value of reprints inadequate. Most dealers report difficulty in moving reprints for more than $2-$4 for mint copies. Some may be worth $5-$7, just because of the popularity of the title, such as Snow White, Sleeping Beauty, and Wizard of Oz. Others may be worth $5-$7, because of the scarcity of particular title nos., such as 514, 560, 562, 575 & 576. Three particular reprint editions are worth even more. For the 535-Twin Circle edition, see Giveaways. There are also reprint editions of 501 and 503 which have a full-page bc ad for the very rare Junior record. Those may sell as high as $10-$15 in mint. Original editions of 557 and 558 also have that ad.

There are no reprint editions of 577. The only edition, from 1969, is a 25 cent stiff-cover edition with no ad for the next issue. All other original editions have coming-next ad. But 577, like C.I. #168, was prepared in 1962 but not issued. Copies of 577 can be found in 1963 British/European series, which then continued with dozens of additional new Junior titles.

PRICES LISTED BELOW ARE FOR ORIGINAL EDITIONS, WHICH HAVE AN AD FOR THE NEXT ISSUE.

CLASSICS ILLUSTRATED JUNIOR
Oct, 1953 - Spring, 1971
Famous Authors Ltd. (Gilberton Publications)

	GD25	FN65	NM94
501-Snow White & the Seven Dwarfs; Alex Blum-a	9.35	28.00	56.00
502-The Ugly Duckling	5.85	17.50	35.00
503-Cinderella	4.00	10.50	21.00
504-512: 504-The Pied Piper. 505-The Sleeping Beauty. 506-The Three Little Pigs. 507-Jack & the Beanstalk. 508-Goldilocks & the Three Bears. 509-Beauty and the Beast. 510-Little Red Riding Hood. 511-Puss-N Boots. 512-Rumpelstiltskin	2.80	7.00	14.00
513-Pinocchio	4.00	10.50	21.00
514-The Steadfast Tin Soldier	4.70	14.00	28.00
515-Johnny Appleseed	2.80	7.00	14.00
516-Aladdin and His Lamp	4.00	10.50	21.00
517-519: 517-The Emperor's New Clothes. 518-The Golden Goose. 519-Paul Bunyan	2.80	7.00	14.00
520-Thumbelina	4.00	10.50	21.00
521-King of the Golden River	2.80	7.00	14.00
522-530: 522-The Nightingale. 523-The Gallant Tailor. 524-The Wild Swans. 525-The Little Mermaid. 526-The Frog Prince. 527-The Golden-Haired Giant. 528-The Penny Prince. 529-The Magic Servants. 530-The Golden Bird	2.00	5.00	10.00
531-Rapunzel	2.80	7.00	14.00
532-534: 532-The Dancing Princesses. 533-The Magic Fountain. 534-The Golden Touch	2.00	5.00	10.00
535-The Wizard of Oz	4.70	14.00	28.00
536-538: 536-The Chimney Sweep. 537-The Three Fairies. 538-Silly Hans	2.00	5.00	10.00
539-The Enchanted Fish	4.00	10.50	21.00
540-The Tinder-Box	4.00	10.50	21.00
541-Snow White & Rose Red	2.80	7.00	14.00
542-The Donkey's Tale	2.80	7.00	14.00
543-The House in the Woods	2.00	5.00	10.00
544-The Golden Fleece	4.70	14.00	28.00
545-The Glass Mountain	2.80	7.00	14.00
546-The Elves & the Shoemaker	2.80	7.00	14.00
547-551: 547-The Wishing Table. 548-The Magic Pitcher. 549-Simple Kate. 550-The Singing Donkey. 551-The Queen Bee	2.00	5.00	10.00
552-The Three Little Dwarfs	2.80	7.00	14.00
553-556: 553-King Thrushbeard. 554-The Enchanted Deer. 555-The Three Golden Apples. 556-The Elf Mound	2.00	5.00	10.00
557-Silly Willy	4.00	10.50	21.00
558-The Magic Dish; L.B. Cole-c; soft and stiff-c exist on original	4.00	10.50	21.00
559-The Japanese Lantern; 1 pg. Ingels-a; L.B. Cole-c	4.00	10.50	21.00
560-The Doll Princess; L.B. Cole-c	4.00	10.50	21.00
561-Hans Humdrum; L.B. Cole-c	2.00	5.00	10.00
562-The Enchanted Pony; L.B. Cole-c	4.00	10.50	21.00
563-570: 563-The Wishing Well; L.B. Cole-c. 564-The Salt Mountain; L.B.Cole-c. 565-The Silly Princess; L.B. Cole-c. 566-Clumsy Hans; L.B. Cole-c. 567-The Bearskin Soldier; L.B. Cole-c. 568-The Happy Hedgehog; L.B. Cole-c. 569-The Three Giants. 570-The Pearl Princess	2.00	5.00	10.00
571-574: 571-How Fire Came to the Indians. 572-The Drummer Boy. 573-The Crystal Ball. 574-Brightboots	2.40	6.00	12.00
575-The Fearless Prince	2.80	7.00	14.00
576-The Princess Who Saw Everything	4.00	10.50	21.00
577-The Runaway Dumpling	4.70	14.00	28.00

NOTE: *Prices are for original editions. Last reprint - Spring, 1971.* ***Costanza*** *&* ***Shaffenberger*** *art in many issues.*

CLASSICS ILLUSTRATED SPECIAL ISSUE
Dec, 1955 - July, 1962 (35¢, 100 pgs.)
Gilberton Co. (Came out semi-annually)

	GD25	FN65	NM94
129-The Story of Jesus (titled ...Special Edition) "Jesus on Mountain" cover	5.85	17.50	35.00
"Three Camels" cover (12/58)	8.35	25.00	50.00
"Mountain" cover (no date)-Has checklist on inside b/c to HRN #161 & different testimonial on back-c	4.20	12.50	25.00
"Mountain" cover (1968 re-issue; has white 50¢ circle)	4.00	10.00	20.00
132A-The Story of America (6/56); Cameron-a	4.70	14.00	28.00
135A-The Ten Commandments(12/56)	5.35	16.00	32.00
138A-Adventures in Science(6/57); HRN to 137	4.70	14.00	28.00
138A-(6/57)-2nd version w/HRN to 149	4.00	11.00	22.00
138A-(12/61)-3rd version w/HRN to 149	4.00	10.00	20.00
141A-The Rough Rider (Teddy Roosevelt)(12/57); Evans-a			

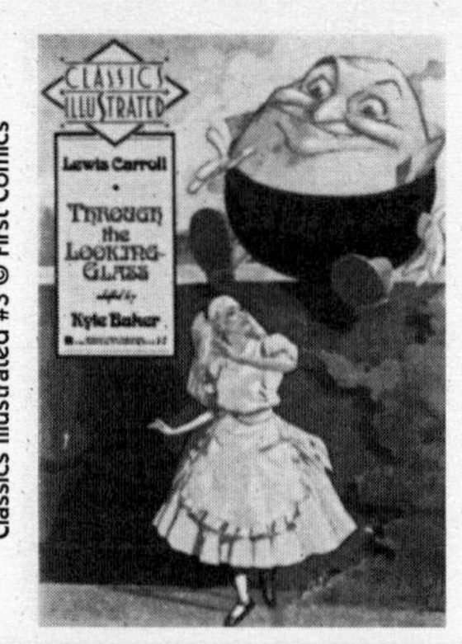

Classics Illustrated #3 © First Comics

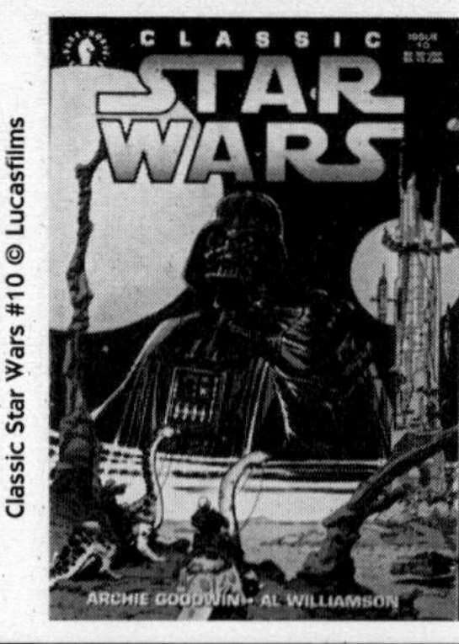

Classic Star Wars #10 © Lucasfilms

Claw #2 © DC

4.70 14.00 28.00
144A-Blazing the Trails West(6/58)- 73 pgs. of Crandall/Evans plus Severin-a 4.70 14.00 28.00
147A-Crossing the Rockies(12/58)-Crandall/Evans-a 5.35 16.00 32.00
150A-Royal Canadian Police(6/59)-Ingels, Sid Check-a 5.35 16.00 32.00
153A-Men, Guns & Cattle(12/59)-Evans-a (26 pgs.); Kinstler-a 5.85 17.50 35.00
156A-The Atomic Age(6/60)-Crandall/Evans, Torres-a 4.70 14.00 28.00
159A-Rockets, Jets and Missiles(12/60)-Evans, Morrow-a 4.70 14.00 28.00
162A-War Between the States(6/61)-Kirby & Crandall/Evans-a; Ingels-a 10.00 30.00 70.00
165A-To the Stars(12/61)-Torres, Crandall/Evans, Kirby-a 4.70 14.00 28.00
166A-World War II('62)-Torres, Crandall/Evans, Kirby-a 5.85 17.50 35.00
167A-Prehistoric World(7/62)-Torres & Crandall/Evans-a; two versions exist (HRN to 165 & HRN to 167) 5.85 17.50 35.00
nn Special Issue-The United Nations (1964; 50¢; scarce); this is actually part of the European Special Series, which cont'd on after the U.S. series stopped issuing new titles in 1962. This English edition was prepared specifically for sale at the U.N. It was printed in Norway 29.00 85.00 200.00

*NOTE: There was another U.S. Special Issue prepared in 1962 with artwork by **Torres** entitled World War I. Unfortunately, it was never issued in any English-language edition. It was issued in 1964 in West Germany, The Netherlands, and some Scandanavian countries, with another edition in 1974 with a new cover.*

CLASSIC PUNISHER (Also see Punisher)
Dec, 1989 ($4.95, B&W, deluxe format, 68 pgs.)
Marvel Comics
1-Reprints Marvel Super Action #1 & Marvel Preview #2 plus new story 1.00 2.00 5.00

CLASSICS ILLUSTRATED
Feb, 1990 - No. 27, July?, 1991 ($3.75/$3.95, 52 pgs.)
First Publishing/Berkley Publishing
1-17: 1-Gahan Wilson-c/a. 4-Sienkiewicz painted-c/a. 6-Russell scripts/layouts. 7-Spiegle-a. 9-Ploog-c/a. 16-Staton-a 1.50 3.75
18-27: 18-Gahan Wilson-c/a; begin $3.95-c. 20-Geary-a. 26-Aesop's Fables (6/91). 26,27-Direct sale only 1.60 4.00

CLASSICS LIBRARY (See King Classics)

CLASSIC STAR WARS (Also see Star Wars)
Aug, 1992 - No. 20, June, 1994 ($2.50)
Dark Horse Comics
1-19-Star Wars strip-r by Williamson; Williamson redrew portions of the panels to fit comic book format; Williamson c-1-5,7,9,10,14,15,20: 8-Polybagged w/ Star Wars Galaxy trading card. 8,17-M. Schultz-c. 13-Yeates-c. 19-Evans-c 1.00 2.50
20-($3.50, 52 pgs.)-Polybagged w/trading card 1.40 3.50

CLASSIC STAR WARS: A NEW HOPE
June, 1994 - No. 2, July, 1994 ($3.95)
Dark Horse Comics
1-r/Star Wars 1-3, 7-9/1977 series 1.60 4.00
2-r/Star Wars 4-6, 10-12/1977 series 1.60 4.00

CLASSIC STAR WARS: THE EARLY ADVENTURES
Aug, 1994 - Present ($2.50)
Dark Horse Comics
1-4 1.00 2.50

CLASSIC STAR WARS: THE EMPIRE STRIKES BACK
Aug, 1994 ($3.95, one-shot)
Dark Horse Comics
1-r/Star Wars #39-44 1.60 4.00

CLASSIC X-MEN (Becomes X-Men Classic #46 on)
Sept, 1986 - No. 45, Mar, 1990 (#27 on: $1.25)
Marvel Comics Group
1-Begins-r of New X-Men 1.00 2.00 5.00
2-4 1.60 4.00
5-9 1.20 3.00
10-Sabretooth app. 1.60 4.00
11-15: 11-1st origin of Magneto in back-up story 1.00 2.50
16,18-20 .80 2.00
17-Wolverine-c 1.60 4.00
21-25,27-30: 27-r/X-Men #121; begin $1.25-c .70 1.75
26-r/X-Men #120; Wolverine-c/app. 1.60 4.00
31-38,40-42,44,45: 35-r/X-Men #129 1.50
39-New Jim Lee back-up story (2nd-a on X-Men) 1.00 2.00 5.00
43-Byrne-c/a(r); $1.75, double-size .80 2.00

*NOTE: **Art Adams** c(p)-1-10, 12-16, 18, 19, 25. **Austin** c-19i. **Bolton** back up stories in 1-28 at least. **Williamson** c-12-14i.*

CLAW (See Capt. Battle, Jr. Daredevil Comics & Silver Streak Comics)

CLAW THE UNCONQUERED (See Cancelled Comic Cavalcade)
5-6/75 - No. 9, 9-10/76; No. 10, 4-5/78 - No. 12, 8-9/78
National Periodical Publications/DC Comics
1-1st app. Claw .80 2.00
2,3: 3-Nudity panel 1.50
4-12: 9-Origin 1.20

*NOTE: **Giffen** a-8-12p. **Kubert** c-10-12. **Layton** a-9i, 12i.*

CLAY CODY, GUNSLINGER
Fall, 1957
Pines Comics
1-Painted-c 4.00 11.00 22.00

CLEAN FUN, STARRING "SHOOGAFOOTS JONES"
1944 (24 pgs.; B&W; oversized covers) (10¢)
Specialty Book Co.
nn-Humorous situations involving Negroes in the Deep South
White cover issue... 4.00 10.00 20.00
Dark grey cover issue... 4.00 11.00 22.00

CLEMENTINA THE FLYING PIG (See Dell Jr. Treasury)

CLEOPATRA (See Ideal, a Classical Comic No. 1)

CLIFF MERRITT SETS THE RECORD STRAIGHT
Giveaway (2 different issues)
Brotherhood of Railroad Trainsmen
...and the Very Candid Candidate by Al Williamson .60 1.50 3.00
...Sets the Record Straight by Al Williamson (2 different-c: one by Williamson, the other by McWilliams) .60 1.50 3.00

CLIFFORD McBRIDE'S IMMORTAL NAPOLEON & UNCLE ELBY
1932 (12x17"; softcover cartoon book)
The Castle Press
nn-Intro. by Don Herod 15.00 45.00 135.00

CLIMAX!
July, 1955 - No. 2, Sept, 1955
Gillmor Magazines
1,2 (Mystery) 10.00 30.00 60.00

CLINT (Elcipse)(Value: cover or less)

CLINT & MAC (See 4-Color No. 889)

CLIVE BARKER'S BOOK OF THE DAMNED: A HELLRAISER COMPANION
Oct, 1991 - No. 3, Nov, 1992 ($4.95, semi-annual, 52 pgs.)
Epic Comics (Marvel)
Volume 1-3: 1-Simon Bisley-c. 2-(4/92). 3-(11/92)-McKean-a (1 pg.) 1.00 2.00 5.00

CLIVE BARKER'S HELLRAISER (Also see Epic, Hellraiser Nightbreed – Jihad, Revelations, Son of Celluloid, Tapping the Vein & Weaveworld)

Clive Barker's Hellraiser #6 © Clive Barker

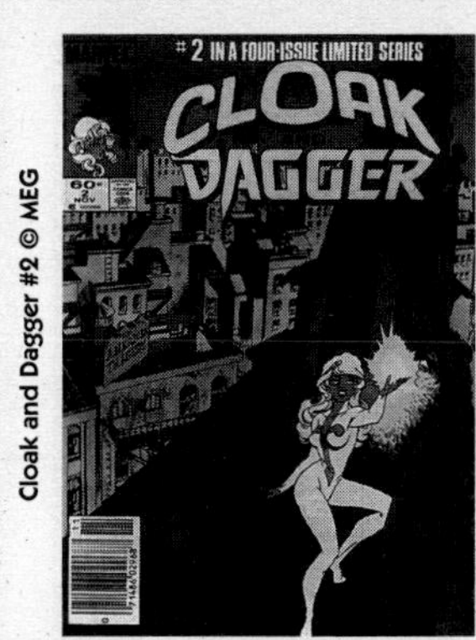

Cloak and Dagger #2 © MEG

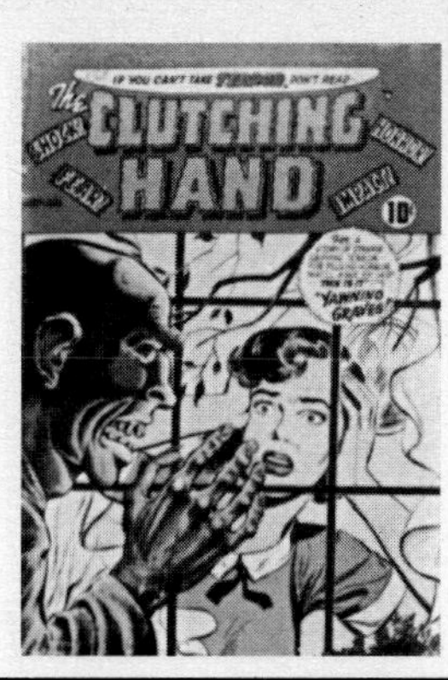

The Clutching Hand #1 © ACG

	GD25	FN65	NM94

1989 - No. 20, 1993 ($4.95, mature readers, quarterly, 68 pgs.)
Epic Comics (Marvel)

	GD25	FN65	NM94
Book 1-Based on Hellraiser & Hellbound movies; Bolton-c/a; Spiegle & Wrightson-a (graphic album)	1.00	2.00	5.00
Book 2-4,14-20: 20-By Gaiman/McKean	1.00	2.00	5.00
Book 5-9 ($5.95): 7-Bolton-a. 8-Morrow-a	1.00	2.50	6.00
Book 10,11,13($4.50, 52 pgs.): 10-Foil-c. 11-Guice-p		1.80	4.50
Book 12-Sam Kieth-a		1.80	4.50
...Dark Holiday Special ('92, $4.95)-Conrad-a	1.00	2.00	5.00
...Spring Slaughter 1 ('94, $6.95, 52 pgs.)-Painted-c	1.20	2.90	7.00
...Summer Special 1 ('92, $5.95, 68 pgs.)	1.00	2.50	6.00

CLIVE BARKER'S NIGHTBREED (Also see Epic)
Apr, 1990 - No. 24, Feb, 1993 ($1.95/$2.25/$2.50, adults)
Epic Comics (Marvel)

	GD25	FN65	NM94
1: 1-4-Adapt horror movie		1.20	3.00
2-19: 5-New stories & $2.25-c begin; Guice-a(p)		.90	2.25
20-24: 20-Begin $2.50-c		1.00	2.50

CLIVE BARKER'S THE HARROWERS
Dec, 1993 - Present ($2.50)
Epic Comics (Marvel)

	GD25	FN65	NM94
1-($2.95)-Glow-in-the-dark-c; Colan-c/a in all		1.20	3.00
2-9		1.00	2.50

NOTE: ***Colan*** *a(p)-1-6; c-1-3, 4p, 5p.* ***Williamson*** *a(i)-2, 4, 5(part).*

CLOAK AND DAGGER
Fall, 1952
Ziff-Davis Publishing Co.

	GD25	FN65	NM94
1-Saunders painted-c	16.00	48.00	110.00

CLOAK AND DAGGER (Also see Marvel Fanfare)
Oct, 1983 - No. 4, Jan, 1984 (Mini-series)(See Spectacular Spider-Man #64)
Marvel Comics Group

	GD25	FN65	NM94
1-4-Austin-c/a(i) in all. 4-Origin			1.50

CLOAK AND DAGGER (Also see Marvel Graphic Novel #34, Mutant Misadventures Of... & Strange Tales, 2nd series)
July, 1985 - No. 11, Jan, 1987
Marvel Comics Group

	GD25	FN65	NM94
1			1.50
2-8,10,11			1.00
9-Art Adams-p		.80	2.00
...And Power Pack (1990, $7.95, 68 pgs.)	1.30	3.25	8.00

CLONEZONE SPECIAL
1989 ($2.00, B&W)
Dark Horse Comics/First Comics

	GD25	FN65	NM94
1-Back-up series from Badger & Nexus		.80	2.00

CLOSE ENCOUNTERS (See Marvel Comics Super Special & Marvel Special Edition)

CLOSE SHAVES OF PAULINE PERIL, THE (TV?)
June, 1970 - No. 4, March, 1971 (Jay Ward?)
Gold Key

	GD25	FN65	NM94
1	1.65	4.00	10.00
2-4	1.00	2.50	6.00

CLOWN COMICS (No. 1 titled Clown Comic Book)
1945 - No. 3, Wint, 1946
Clown Comics/Home Comics/Harvey Publ.

	GD25	FN65	NM94
nn (#1)	6.70	20.00	40.00
2,3	4.20	12.50	25.00

CLUBHOUSE RASCALS (#1 titled ...Presents?)
June, 1956 - No. 2, Oct, 1956 (Also see Three Rascals)
Sussex Publ. Co. (Magazine Enterprises)

	GD25	FN65	NM94
1,2: The Brain app.	4.00	11.00	22.00

CLUB "16"
June, 1948 - No. 4, Dec, 1948
Famous Funnies

	GD25	FN65	NM94
1-Teen-age humor	8.35	25.00	50.00
2-4	4.70	14.00	28.00

CLUE COMICS (Real Clue Crime V2#4 on)
Jan, 1943 - No. 15(V2#3), May, 1947
Hillman Periodicals

	GD25	FN65	NM94
1-Origin The Boy King, Nightmare, Micro-Face, Twilight, & Zippo	70.00	210.00	490.00
2	34.00	100.00	235.00
3-5	24.00	72.00	165.00
6,8,9: 8-Palais-c/a(2)	16.50	50.00	115.00
7-Classic torture-c	23.00	70.00	160.00
10-Origin/1st app. The Gun Master & begin series; content changes to crime	17.00	52.00	120.00
11	12.00	36.00	85.00
12-Origin Rackman; McWilliams-a, Guardineer-a(2)	15.00	45.00	105.00
V2#1-Nightmare new origin; Iron Lady app.; Simon & Kirby-a	25.00	75.00	175.00
V2#2-S&K-a(2)-Bondage/torture-c; man attacks & kills people with electric iron. Infantino-a	25.00	75.00	175.00
V2#3-S&K-a(3)	25.00	75.00	175.00

CLUTCHING HAND, THE
July-Aug, 1954
American Comics Group

	GD25	FN65	NM94
1	19.00	58.00	135.00

CLYDE BEATTY COMICS (Also see Crackajack Funnies)
October, 1953 (84 pgs.)
Commodore Productions & Artists, Inc.

	GD25	FN65	NM94
1-Photo front/back-c; movie scenes and comics	20.00	60.00	140.00
...African Jungle Book('56)-Richfield Oil Co. 16 pg. giveaway, soft-c	10.00	30.00	60.00

CLYDE CRASHCUP (TV)
Aug-Oct, 1963 - No. 5, Sept-Nov, 1964
Dell Publishing Co.

	GD25	FN65	NM94
1-All written by John Stanley	11.50	34.00	80.00
2-5	10.00	30.00	60.00

C-M-O COMICS
1942 - No. 2, 1942 (68 pgs., full color)
Chicago Mail Order Co.(Centaur)

	GD25	FN65	NM94
1-Invisible Terror, Super Ann, & Plymo the Rubber Man app. (all Centaur costume heroes)	66.00	200.00	465.00
2-Invisible Terror, Super Ann app.	41.00	122.00	285.00

COBALT BLUE (Innovation)(Value: cover or less)

COCOMALT BIG BOOK OF COMICS
1938 (Regular size; full color; 52 pgs.)
Harry 'A' Chesler (Cocomalt Premium)

	GD25	FN65	NM94
1-(Scarce)-Biro-c/a; Little Nemo by Winsor McCay Jr., Dan Hastings; Jack Cole, Guardineer, Gustavson, Bob Wood-a	143.00	430.00	1000.00

CODE NAME: ASSASSIN (See 1st Issue Special)

CODENAME: DANGER (Lodestone)(Value: cover or less)

CODENAME: GENETIX
Jan, 1993 - No. 4, May, 1993 ($1.75, mini-series)
Marvel Comics UK

	GD25	FN65	NM94
1-4: Wolverine in all		.70	1.75

CODENAME SPITFIRE (Formerly Spitfire And The Troubleshooters)
No. 10, July, 1987 - No. 13, Oct, 1987
Marvel Comics Group

	GD25	FN65	NM94
10-13: 10-Rogers-c/a			1.00

Codename: Stryke Force #4 © Rob Liefeld

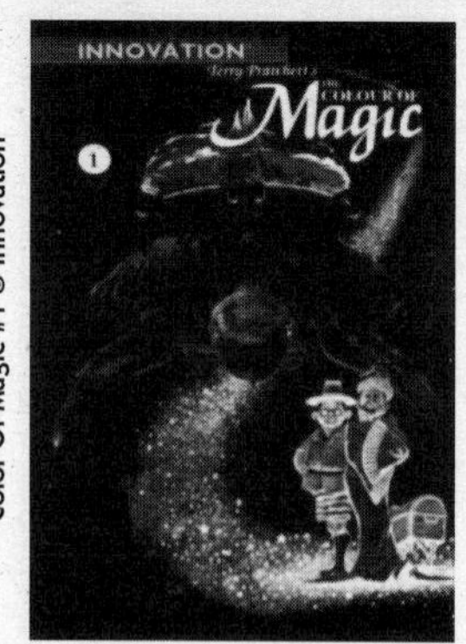

Color Of Magic #1 © Innovation

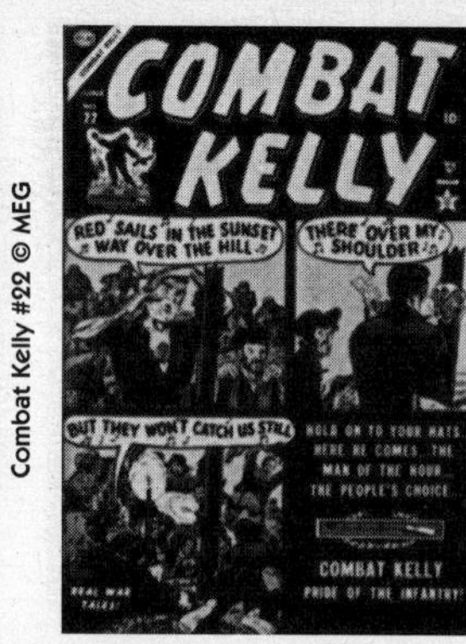

Combat Kelly #22 © MEG

GD25 FN65 NM94 GD25 FN65 NM94

CODENAME: STRYKE FORCE
Jan, 1994 - Present ($1.95)
Image Comics

1-8-Silvestri stories, Peterson-a. 1-Wraparound-c. 4-Stormwatch app. .80 2.00

CODE NAME: TOMAHAWK
Sept, 1986 ($1.75, high quality paper)
Fantasy General Comics

1-Sci/fi .70 1.75

CODY OF THE PONY EXPRESS (See Colossal Features Magazine)
Sept, 1950 - No. 3, Jan, 1951 (See Women Outlaws)
Fox Features Syndicate

1-3 (Actually #3-5). 1-Painted-c 10.00 30.00 60.00

CODY OF THE PONY EXPRESS (Buffalo Bill...) (Outlaws of the West #11 on; Formerly Bullseye)
No. 8, Oct, 1955; No. 9, Jan, 1956; No. 10, June, 1956
Charlton Comics

8-Bullseye on splash pg; not S&K-a 5.35 16.00 32.00
9,10: Buffalo Bill app. in all 4.00 11.00 22.00

CODY STARBUCK (1st app. in Star Reach #1)
July, 1978 (2nd printing exists)
Star Reach Productions

nn-Howard Chaykin-c/a .80 2.00
NOTE: *Both printings say First Printing. True first printing is on lower-grade paper, somewhat off-register, and snow in snow sequence has green tint.*

CO-ED ROMANCES
November, 1951
P. L. Publishing Co.

1 4.70 14.00 28.00

COLLECTORS DRACULA, THE
1994 - No. 2, 1994 ($3.95, color/B&W, 52 pgs., limited series)
Millennium Publications

1-Bolton-a (7 pgs.) 1.60 4.00

COLLECTORS ITEM CLASSICS (See Marvel Collectors Item Classics)

COLOSSAL FEATURES MAGAZINE (Formerly I Loved) (See Cody of the Pony Express)
No. 33, May, 1950 - No. 34, July, 1950; No. 3, Sept, 1950
Fox Features Syndicate

33,34-Cody of the Pony Express begins (based on Columbia serial).
33-Painted-c. 34-Photo-c 7.50 22.50 45.00
3-Authentic criminal cases 7.50 22.50 45.00

COLOSSAL SHOW, THE (TV)
October, 1969
Gold Key

1 4.70 14.00 28.00

COLOSSUS COMICS (See Green Giant & Motion Picture Funnies Weekly)
March, 1940
Sun Publications (Funnies, Inc.?)

1-(Scarce)-Tulpa of Tsang(hero); Colossus app. 221.00 665.00 1550.00
NOTE: *Cover by artist that drew Colossus in Green Giant Comics.*

COLOUR OF MAGIC, THE (Terry Pratchett's...)
1991 - No. 4, 1991 ($2.50, mini-series)
Innovation Publishing

1-4: Adapts 1st novel of the Discworld series 1.00 2.50

COLT .45 (TV)
No. 924, 8/58 - No. 1058, 11-1/59-60; No. 4, 2-4/60 - No. 9, 5-7/61
Dell Publishing Co.

4-Color 924(#1)-Wayde Preston photo-c on all 10.00 30.00 70.00
4-Color 1004,1058, #4,5,7-9: 1004-Photo-b/c 8.35 25.00 50.00
6-Toth-a 9.15 27.50 55.00

COLUMBIA COMICS
1943
William H. Wise Co.

1-Joe Palooka, Charlie Chan, Capt. Yank, Sparky Watts, Dixie Dugan app. 19.00 58.00 135.00

COLUMBUS
Sept, 1992 ($2.50, B&W, one-shot)
Dark Horse Comics

1-Yeates painted-c 1.00 2.50

COMANCHE (See 4-Color No. 1350)

COMANCHEROS, THE (See 4-Color No. 1300)

COMBAT
June, 1952 - No. 11, April, 1953
Atlas Comics (ANC)

1 11.00 32.00 75.00
2-Heath-c/a 5.85 17.50 35.00
3,5-9,11: 9-Robert Q. Sale-a 4.00 12.00 24.00
4-Krigstein-a 5.35 16.00 32.00
10-B&W and color illos. in **POP** 4.70 14.00 28.00
NOTE: *Combat Casey in 7-11.* ***Heath*** *c-1, 2, 9.* ***Maneely*** *a-1; c-3.* ***Pakula*** *a-1.* ***Reinman*** *a-1.*

COMBAT
Oct-Nov, 1961 - No. 40, Oct, 1973 (No #9)
Dell Publishing Co.

1 5.35 16.00 32.00
2-5: 4-John F. Kennedy c/story (P.T. 109) 3.20 8.00 16.00
6,7,8(4-6/63), 8(7-9/63) 2.60 6.50 13.00
10-26 2.00 5.00 10.00
27-40(reprints #1-14). 30-r/#4 1.40 3.50 7.00
NOTE: ***Glanzman*** *c/a-1-27, 28-40r.*

COMBAT CASEY (Formerly War Combat)
No. 6, Jan, 1953 - No. 34, July, 1957
Atlas Comics (SAI)

6 (Indicia shows 1/52 in error) 8.35 25.00 50.00
7-Spanking panel 6.70 20.00 40.00
8-Used in **POP**, pg. 94 4.20 12.50 25.00
9 4.00 10.00 20.00
10,13-19-Violent art by R. Q. Sale; Battle Brady x-over #10 5.85 17.50 35.00
11,12,20-Last Precode (2/55) 4.00 10.00 20.00
21-34 3.60 9.00 18.00
NOTE: ***Everett*** *a-6.* ***Heath*** *c-10, 17, 19, 30.* ***Maneely*** *c-6, 8.* ***Powell*** *a-29(5), 30(5), 34.* ***Severin*** *c-26, 33.*

COMBAT KELLY
Nov, 1951 - No. 44, Aug, 1957
Atlas Comics (SPI)

1-1st app. Combat Kelly; Heath-a 14.00 43.00 100.00
2 7.50 22.50 45.00
3-10 5.00 15.00 30.00
11-Used in **POP**, pgs. 94,95 plus color illo. 4.20 12.50 25.00
12-Color illo. in **POP** 4.20 12.50 25.00
13-16 3.60 9.00 18.00
17-Violent art by R. Q. Sale; Combat Casey app. 5.85 17.50 35.00
18-20,22-44: 18-Battle Brady app. 28-Last precode (1/55). 38-Green Berets story (8/56) 3.60 9.00 18.00
21-Transvestism-c 4.20 12.50 25.00
NOTE: ***Berg*** *a-8, 12-14, 16, 17, 19-23, 25, 26, 28, 31-36, 42-44; c-2.* ***Colan*** *a-42.* ***Heath*** *a-4; c-31.* ***Lawrence*** *a-23.* ***Maneely*** *a-4(2), 6, 7(3), 8; c-4, 5, 7, 8, 10, 25.* ***R.Q. Sale*** *a-17, 25.* ***Severin*** *c-41, 42.* ***Whitney*** *a-5.*

COMBAT KELLY (...and the Deadly Dozen)
June, 1972 - No. 9, Oct, 1973
Marvel Comics Group

Comic Album #12 © M.G.M.

Comic Books #1 Tallulah © Metropolitan

Comic Cavalcade #16 © DC

GD25 FN65 NM94

1-Intro & origin new Combat Kelly; Ayers/Mooney-a; Severin-c (20¢) 1.10 2.75
2-9 1.50

COMBINED OPERATIONS (See The Story of the Commandos)

COMEDY CARNIVAL
no date (1950's) (100 pgs.)
St. John Publishing Co.

nn-Contains rebound St. John comics 25.00 75.00 175.00

COMEDY COMICS (1st Series) (Formerly Daring Mystery No. 1-8)
(Becomes Margie Comics No. 35 on)
No. 9, April, 1942 - No. 34, Fall, 1946
Timely Comics (TCI 9,10)

9-(Scarce)-The Fin by Everett, Capt. Dash, Citizen V, & The Silver Scorn app.; Wolverton-a; 1st app. Comedy Kid; satire on Hitler & Stalin; The Fin, Citizen V & Silver Scorn cont. from Daring Mystery 143.00 430.00 1000.00
10-(Scarce)-Origin The Fourth Musketeer, Victory Boys; Monstro, the Mighty app. 100.00 300.00 700.00
11-Vagabond, Stuporman app. 34.00 103.00 240.00
12,13 10.00 30.00 70.00
14-Origin/1st app. Super Rabbit (3/43) plus-c 35.00 105.00 245.00
15-20 10.00 30.00 60.00
21-32 6.70 20.00 40.00
33-Kurtzman-a (5 pgs.) 9.15 27.50 55.00
34-Intro Margie; Wolverton-a (5 pgs.) 12.00 36.00 85.00

COMEDY COMICS (2nd Series)
May, 1948 - No. 10, Jan, 1950
Marvel Comics (ACI)

1-Hedy, Tessie, Millie begin; Kurtzman's "Hey Look" (he draws himself) 22.00 67.00 155.00
2 9.15 27.50 55.00
3,4-Kurtzman's "Hey Look" (?&3) 10.00 30.00 70.00
5-10 5.00 15.00 30.00

COMET, THE (See The Mighty Crusaders & Pep Comics #1)
Oct, 1983 - No. 2, Dec, 1983
Red Circle Comics (Archie)

1,2: 1-Re-intro & origin The Comet; The American Shield begins. 2-Origin continues 1.00

COMET, THE
July, 1991 - No. 18, Dec, 1992 ($1.00/$1.25)
Impact Comics (DC)

1-13: 4-Black Hood app. 6-Re-intro Hangman. 8-Web x-over. 10-Contains Crusaders trading card. 13-Last $1.00-c 1.00
14-18: 14-Origin. Netzer(Nasser) c(p)-11,14-17 1.25
Annual 1 (1992, $2.50, 68 pgs.)-Contains Impact trading card; Shield back-up story 1.00 2.50

COMET MAN, THE
Feb, 1987 - No. 6, July, 1987 (Mini-series)
Marvel Comics Group

1-6 1.00

COMIC ALBUM (Also see Disney Comic Album)
Mar-May, 1958 - No. 18, June-Aug, 1962
Dell Publishing Co.

1-Donald Duck 8.35 25.00 50.00
2-Bugs Bunny 4.00 11.00 22.00
3-Donald Duck 6.70 20.00 40.00
4-6,8-10: 4-Tom & Jerry. 5-Woody Woodpecker. 6,10-Bugs Bunny. 8-Tom & Jerry. 9-Woody Woodpecker 3.60 9.00 18.00
7,11: 7-Popeye (9-11/59). 11-Popeye (9-11/60) 4.20 12.50 25.00
12-14: 12-Tom & Jerry. 13-Woody Woodpecker. 14-Bugs Bunny 3.20 8.00 16.00
15-Popeye 4.20 12.50 25.00
16-Flintstones (12-2/61-62)-3rd app. 7.00 21.00 42.00
17-Space Mouse (3rd app.) 4.20 12.50 25.00
18-Three Stooges; photo-c 7.50 22.50 45.00

COMIC BOOK (Also see Comics From Weatherbird)
1954 (Giveaway)
American Juniors Shoe

Contains a comic rebound with new cover. Several combinations possible. Contents determines price.

COMIC BOOK MAGAZINE
1940 - 1943 (Similar to Spirit Sections)(7-3/4x10-3/4"; full color; 16-24 pgs. ea.)
Chicago Tribune & other newspapers

1940 issues 5.85 17.50 35.00
1941, 1942 issues 4.70 14.00 28.00
1943 issues 4.00 12.00 24.00

NOTE: *Published weekly. Texas Slim, Kit Carson, Spooky, Josie, Nuts & Jolts, Lew Loyal, Brenda Starr, Daniel Boone, Captain Storm, Rocky, Smokey Stover, Tiny Tim, Little Joe, Fu Manchu appear among others. Early issues had photo stories with pictures from the movies; later issues had comic art.*

COMIC BOOKS (Series 1)
1950 (16 pgs.; 5-1/4x8-1/2"; full color; bound at top; paper cover)
Metropolitan Printing Co. (Giveaway)

1-Boots and Saddles; intro The Masked Marshal 4.70 14.00 28.00
1-The Green Jet; Green Lama by Raboy 25.00 75.00 175.00
1-My Pal Dizzy (Teen-age) 2.40 6.00 12.00
1-New World; origin Atomaster (costumed hero) 8.35 25.00 50.00
1-Talullah (Teen-age) 2.40 6.00 12.00

COMIC CAPERS
Fall, 1944 - No. 6, Summer, 1946
Red Circle Mag./Marvel Comics

1-Super Rabbit, The Creeper, Silly Seal, Ziggy Pig, Sharpy Fox begin 16.00 48.00 110.00
2 9.15 27.50 55.00
3-6 6.70 20.00 40.00

COMIC CAVALCADE
Winter, 1942-43 - No. 63, June-July, 1954
(Contents change with No. 30, Dec-Jan, 1948-49 on)
All-American/National Periodical Publications

GD25 FN65 VF82 NM94

1-The Flash, Green Lantern, Wonder Woman, Wildcat, The Black Pirate by Moldoff (also #2), Ghost Patrol, and Red White & Blue begin; Scribbly app.; Minute Movie 625.00 1875.00 3437.00 5000.00
(Estimated up to 175 total copies exist, 6 in NM/Mint)

GD25 FN65 NM94

2-Mutt & Jeff begin; last Ghost Patrol & Black Pirate; Minute Movies 171.00 515.00 1200.00
3-Hop Harrigan & Sargon, the Sorcerer begin; The King app. 129.00 385.00 900.00
4,5: 4-The Gay Ghost, The King, Scribbly, & Red Tornado app. 5-Christmas-c 107.00 321.00 750.00
6-10: 7-Red Tornado & Black Pirate app.; last Scribbly. 9-Fat & Slat app.; X-Mas-c 86.00 257.00 600.00
11,12,14-20: 12-Last Red White & Blue. 15-Johnny Peril begins (1st app., 6-7/46), ends #29. 19-Christmas-c 71.00 215.00 500.00
13-Solomon Grundy app.; X-Mas-c 121.00 365.00 850.00
21-23: 23-Harry Lampert-c (Toth swipes) 71.00 215.00 500.00
24-Solomon Grundy x-over in Green Lantern 86.00 257.00 600.00
25-28: 25-Black Canary app.; X-Mas-c. 26-28-Johnny Peril app. 28-Last Mutt & Jeff 54.00 160.00 375.00
29-(10-11/48)-Last Flash, Wonder Woman, Green Lantern & Johnny Peril; Wonder Woman invents "Thinking Machine"; 1st computer in comics?; Leave It to Binky story (early app.) 61.00 182.00 425.00
30-(12-1/48-49)-The Fox & the Crow, Dodo & the Frog & Nutsy Squirrel begin 36.00 110.00 255.00
31-35 17.00 52.00 120.00

Comico Christmas Special #1 © Comico

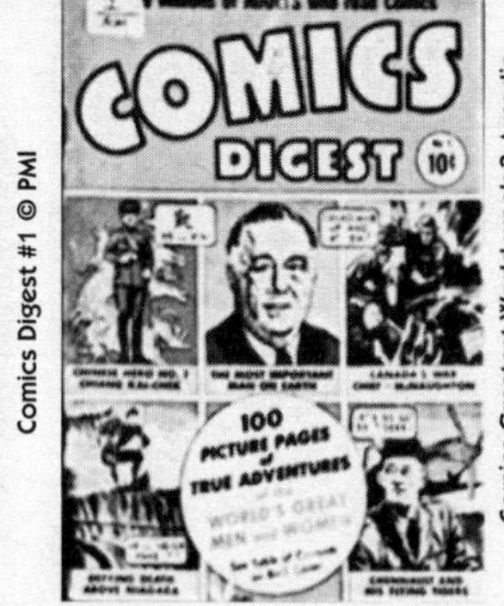

Comics Digest #1 © PMI

Comics Greatest World week 3 Arcadia © DH

GD25 FN65 NM94

36-49 12.00 36.00 85.00
50-62(Scarce) 16.00 48.00 110.00
63(Rare) 27.00 80.00 185.00
Giveaway (1944, 8 pgs., paper-c, in color)-One Hundred Years of Co-operation-r/Comic Cavalcade #9 57.00 171.00 400.00
Giveaway (1945, 16 pgs., paper-c, in color)-Movie "Tomorrow The World" (Nazi theme); r/Comic Cavalcade #10 86.00 257.00 600.00
Giveaway (c. 1944-45; 8 pgs, paper-c, in color)-The Twain Shall Meet-r/Comic Cavalcade #8 71.00 214.00 500.00

NOTE: ***Grossman*** *a-30-63.* ***E.E. Hibbard*** *c-(Flash only)-1-4, 7-14, 16-19, 21.* ***Sheldon Mayer*** *a(2-3)-40-63.* ***Moulson*** *c(G.L.)-7, 15.* ***Nodell*** *c(G.L.)-9.* ***H.G. Peter*** *c(W. Woman only)-1, 3-21, 24.* ***Post*** *a-31, 36.* ***Purcell*** *c(G.L.)-2-5, 10.* ***Reinman*** *a(Green Lantern)-4-6, 8, 9, 13, 15-21; c(Gr. Lantern)-6, 8, 19.* ***Toth*** *a(Green Lantern)-26-28; c-27. Atom app.-22, 23.*

COMIC COMICS
April, 1946 - No. 10, Feb, 1947
Fawcett Publications

1-Captain Kidd; Nutty Comics #1 in indicia 9.15 27.50 55.00
2-10-Wolverton-a, 4 pgs. each. 5-Captain Kidd app. Mystic Moot by Wolverton in #2-10? 10.00 30.00 65.00

COMIC CUTS (Also see The Funnies)
5/19/34 - 7/28/34 (5¢, 24 pgs.) (Tabloid size in full color)
(Not reprints; published weekly; created for newsstand sale)
H. L. Baker Co., Inc.

V1#1 - V1#7(6/30/34), V1#8(7/14/34), V1#9(7/28/34)-Idle Jack strips 8.70 26.00 52.00

COMIC LAND
March, 1946
Fact and Fiction Publ.

1-Sandusky & the Senator, Sam Stupor, Sleuth, Marvin the Great, Sir Passer, Phineas Gruff app.; Irv Tirman & Perry Williams art 10.00 30.00 60.00

COMIC MONTHLY
Jan, 1922 - No. 12, Dec, 1922 (10¢, 28 pgs.)(8-1/2"x9")(2-color covers)
(1st monthly newsstand comic publication) (Reprints 1921 B&W dailies)
Embee Dist. Co.

1-Polly & Her Pals 60.00 180.00 600.00
2-Mike & Ike by Rube Goldberg 20.00 60.00 200.00
3-S'Matter, Pop? 11.00 32.00 100.00
4-Barney Google 25.00 75.00 250.00
5-Tillie the Toiler 15.00 45.00 135.00
6-12: 6-Indoor Sports. 7-Little Jimmy. 8-Toots and Casper. 9,10-Foolish Questions. 11-Barney Google & Spark Plug in the Abadaba Handicap. 12-Polly & Her Pals 11.00 32.00 100.00

COMICO CHRISTMAS SPECIAL (Comico)(Value: cover or less)

COMICO PRIMER (See Primer)

COMIC PAGES (Formerly Funny Picture Stories)
V3#4, July, 1939 - V3#6, Dec, 1939
Centaur Publications

V3#4-Bob Wood-a 49.00 145.00 340.00
5,6: 6-Schwab-c 33.00 100.00 230.00

COMIC PAINTING AND CRAYONING BOOK
1917 (32 pgs.)(10x13-1/2")(No price on cover)
Saalfield Publ. Co.

nn-Tidy Teddy by F. M. Follett, Clarence the Cop, Mr. & Mrs. Butt-In. Regular comic stories to read or color 15.00 45.00 105.00

COMICS (See All Good)

COMICS, THE
March, 1937 - No. 11, Nov, 1938 (Newspaper strip-r; bi-monthly)
Dell Publishing Co.

1-1st app. Tom Mix in comics; Wash Tubbs, Tom Beatty, Myra North, Arizona Kid, Erik Noble & International Spy w/Doctor Doom begin 121.00 365.00 850.00
2 57.00 170.00 400.00
3-11: 3-Alley Oop begins 50.00 150.00 350.00

COMICS AND STORIES (See Walt Disney's.Comics and Stories)

COMICS CALENDAR, THE (The 1946...)
1946 (25¢, 116 pgs.)(Stapled at top)
True Comics Press (ordered through the mail)

nn-(Rare) Has a "strip" story for every day of the year in color 32.00 95.00 225.00

COMICS DIGEST (Pocket size)
Winter, 1942-43 (100 pgs.) (Black & White)
Parents' Magazine Institute

1-Reprints from True Comics (non-fiction World War II stories) 8.00 24.00 48.00

COMIC SELECTIONS (Shoe store giveaway)
1944-46 (Reprints from Calling All Girls, True Comics, True Aviation, & Real Heroes)
Parents' Magazine Press

1 3.60 9.00 18.00
2-5 3.00 7.50 15.00

COMICS EXPRESS (Eclipse)(Value: cover or less)

COMICS FOR KIDS
1945 (no month); No. 2, Sum, 1945 (Funny animal)
London Publishing Co./Timely

1,2-Puffy Pig, Sharpy Fox 10.00 30.00 60.00

COMICS FROM WEATHER BIRD (Also see Comic Book, Edward's Shoes, Free Comics to You & Weather Bird)
1954 - 1957 (Giveaway)
Weather Bird Shoes

Contains a comic bound with new cover. Many combinations possible. Contents would determine price. Some issues do not contain complete comics, but only parts of comics.Value equals 40 to 60 percent of contents.

COMICS' GREATEST WORLD
June, 1993 - V4#4, Sept, 1993 ($1.00)
Dark Horse Comics

Arcadia 1-4: 1-X: Frank Miller-c. 2-Pit Bulls. 3-Ghost; Dorman-c; Hughes-a. 4-Monster 1.00
1-B&W Press Proof Edition (1500 copies) 2.15 6.50 15.00
1-Silver-c; distr. retailer bonus w/print & cards 1.40 4.00 10.00
Retailer's Premium Embossed Silver Foil Logo (r/1-4)2.90 9.00 20.00
Golden City 1-4: 1-Rebel; Ordway-c. 2-Mecha; Dave Johnson-c. 3-Titan; Walt Simonson-c. 4-Catalyst; Perez-c 1.00
1-Gold-c; distr. retailer bonus w/print & cards 1.40 4.00 10.00
Retailer's Premium Embossed Gold Foil Logo (r/1-4) 2.90 9.00 20.00
Steel Harbor 1-4: 1-Barb Wire; Dorman-c; Gulacy-a(p). 2-The Machine; Mignola-c. 3-Wolfgang; Warner-c. 4-Motorhead 1.00
1-Silver-c; distr. retailer bonus w/print & cards 1.40 4.00 10.00
Retailer's Premium Embossed Red Foil Logo (r/1-4) 2.90 9.00 20.00
Vortex 1-4: 1-Division 13; Dorman-c. 2-Hero Zero; Art Adams-c. 3-King Tiger; Chadwick-a(p); Darrow-c. 4-Vortex; Miller-c 1.00
1-Gold-c; distr. retailer bonus w/print & cards 1.40 4.00 10.00
Retailer's Premium Embossed Blue Foil Logo (r/1-4) 2.90 9.00 205.00

COMICS' GREATEST WORLD: OUT OF THE VORTEX(See out of The Vortex)

COMICS HITS (See Harvey Comics Hits)

COMICS MAGAZINE, THE (...Funny Pages #3)(Funny Pages #6 on)
May, 1936 - No. 5, Sept, 1936 (Paper covers)
Comics Magazine Co.

GD25 FN65 VF82

1-Dr. Mystic, The Occult Detective (1st Superman prototype & 1st super hero) by Siegel & Shuster (1st episode of "The Koth and the Seven"; continues in More Fun #14; originally scheduled for publication at DC). 1 pg. Kelly-a; Sheldon Mayer-a 1167.00 3500.00 7000.00

Comics On Parade #54 © UFS

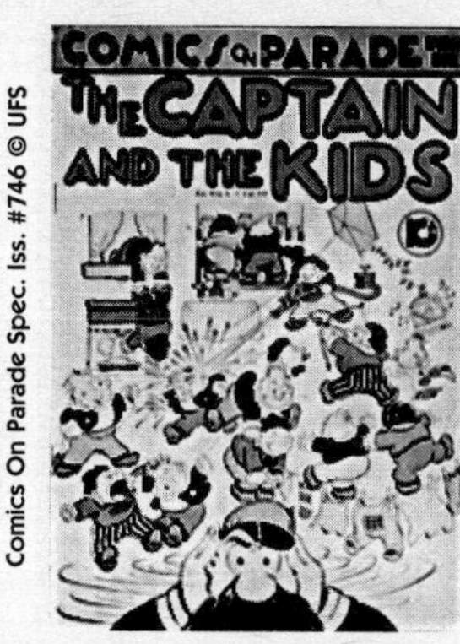

Comics On Parade Spec. Iss. #746 © UFS

Commander Battle #1 © ACG

(Estimated up to 10 total copies exist)

	GD25	FN65	NM94
2-Federal Agent (a.k.a. Federal Men) by Siegel & Shuster; 1 pg. Kelly-a	150.00	450.00	1050.00
3-5	121.00	365.00	850.00

COMICS NOVEL (Anarcho, Dictator of Death)
1947
Fawcett Publications

	GD25	FN65	NM94
1-All Radar	22.00	65.00	150.00

COMICS ON PARADE (No. 30 on are a continuation of Single Series)
April, 1938 - No. 104, Feb, 1955
United Features Syndicate

	GD25	FN65	NM94
1-Tarzan by Foster; Captain & the Kids, Little Mary Mixup, Abbie & Slats, Ella Cinders, Broncho Bill, Li'l Abner begin	221.00	665.00	1550.00
2 (Tarzan & others app. on-c of #1-3,17)	93.00	280.00	650.00
3	75.00	225.00	525.00
4,5	57.00	171.00	400.00
6-10	39.00	118.00	275.00
11-20	34.00	100.00	235.00
21-29: 22-Son of Tarzan begins. 22,24,28-Tailspin Tommy-c. 29-Last Tarzan issue	28.00	85.00	195.00
30-Li'l Abner	18.00	54.00	125.00
31-The Captain & the Kids	13.00	40.00	90.00
32-Nancy & Fritzi Ritz	10.00	30.00	70.00
33-Li'l Abner	16.00	48.00	110.00
34-The Captain & the Kids (10/41)	12.00	36.00	85.00
35-Nancy & Fritzi Ritz	10.00	30.00	70.00
36-Li'l Abner	16.00	48.00	110.00
37-The Captain & the Kids (6/42)	12.00	36.00	85.00
38-Nancy & Fritzi Ritz; infinity-c	10.00	30.00	70.00
39-Li'l Abner	16.00	48.00	110.00
40-The Captain & the Kids (3/43)	12.00	36.00	85.00
41-Nancy & Fritzi Ritz	8.65	26.00	52.00
42-Li'l Abner	16.50	50.00	115.00
43-The Captain & the Kids	12.00	36.00	85.00
44-Nancy & Fritzi Ritz (3/44)	8.65	26.00	52.00
45-Li'l Abner	13.00	40.00	90.00
46-The Captain & the Kids	10.00	30.00	70.00
47-Nancy & Fritzi Ritz	8.65	26.00	52.00
48-Li'l Abner (3/45)	13.00	40.00	90.00
49-The Captain & the Kids	10.00	30.00	70.00
50-Nancy & Fritzi Ritz	9.15	27.50	52.00
51-Li'l Abner	11.00	32.00	75.00
52-The Captain & the Kids (3/46)	8.00	24.00	48.00
53-Nancy & Fritzi Ritz	8.00	24.00	48.00
54-Li'l Abner	11.00	32.00	75.00
55-Nancy & Fritzi Ritz	8.00	24.00	48.00
56-The Captain & the Kids (r/Sparkler)	8.00	24.00	48.00
57-Nancy & Fritzi Ritz	8.00	24.00	48.00
58-Li'l Abner; continues as Li'l Abner #61?	11.00	32.00	75.00
59-The Captain & the Kids	7.00	21.00	42.00
60-70-Nancy & Fritzi Ritz	7.00	21.00	42.00
71-76-Nancy only	5.00	15.00	30.00
77-99,101-104-Nancy & Sluggo	5.00	15.00	30.00
100-Nancy & Sluggo	6.35	19.00	38.00
Special Issue, 7/46; Summer, 1948 - The Captain & the Kids app.	5.00	15.00	30.00
NOTE: Bound Volume (Very Rare) includes No. 1-12; bound by publisher in pictorial comic boards & distributed at the 1939 World's Fair and through mail order from ads in comic books (also see Tip Top)	221.00	665.00	1550.00

NOTE: *Li'l Abner reprinted from Tip Top.*

COMICS READING LIBRARIES (Educational Series)
1973, 1977, 1979 (36 pgs. in color) (Giveaways)
King Features (Charlton Publ.)

	GD25	FN65	NM94
R-01-Tiger, Quincy		.80	2.00
R-02-Beetle Bailey, Blondie & Popeye		.80	2.00
R-03-Blondie, Beetle Bailey		.80	2.00
R-04-Tim Tyler's Luck, Felix the Cat	1.65	4.00	10.00
R-05-Quincy, Henry		.80	2.00
R-06-The Phantom, Mandrake	2.30	6.75	16.00
1977 reprint(R-04)	1.00	2.00	5.00
R-07-Popeye, Little King	1.00	2.00	5.00
R-08-Prince Valiant(Foster), Flash Gordon	3.40	10.00	24.00
1977 reprint	1.30	3.25	8.00
R-09-Hagar the Horrible, Boner's Ark		.80	2.00
R-10-Redeye, Tiger		.80	2.00
R-11-Blondie, Hi & Lois		.80	2.00
R-12-Popeye-Swee'pea, Brutus	1.00	2.50	6.00
R-13-Beetle Bailey, Little King		.80	2.00
R-14-Quincy-Hamlet		.80	2.00
R-15-The Phantom, The Genius	2.30	6.75	16.00
R-16-Flash Gordon, Mandrake	3.40	10.00	24.00
1977 reprint	1.30	3.25	8.00
Other 1977 editions....		.50	1.00
1979 editions(68pgs.)		.50	1.00

NOTE: *Above giveaways available with purchase of $45.00 in merchandise. Used as a reading skills aid for small children.*

COMICS REVUE
June, 1947 - No. 5, Jan, 1948
St. John Publ. Co. (United Features Synd.)

	GD25	FN65	NM94
1-Ella Cinders & Blackie	8.35	25.00	50.00
2-Hap Hopper (7/47)	5.35	16.00	32.00
3-Iron Vic (8/47)	4.70	14.00	28.00
4-Ella Cinders (9/47)	5.35	16.00	32.00
5-Gordo No. 1 (1/48)	4.70	14.00	28.00

COMIC STORY PAINT BOOK
1943 (68 pgs.) (Large size)
Samuel Lowe Co.

	GD25	FN65	NM94
1055-Captain Marvel & a Captain Marvel Jr. story to read & color; 3 panels in color per pg. (reprints)	45.00	135.00	450.00

COMIX BOOK (B&W Magazine - $1.00)
1974 - No. 5, 1976
Marvel Comics Group/Krupp Comics Works No. 4,5

	GD25	FN65	NM94
1-Underground comic artists; 2 pgs. Wolverton-a	1.20	2.90	7.00
2-Wolverton-a (1 pg.)		1.40	3.50
3-Low distribution (3/75)	1.00	2.00	5.00
4(2/76), 4(5/76), 5		1.20	3.00

NOTE: *Print run No. 1-3: 200-250M; No. 4&5: 10M each.*

COMIX INTERNATIONAL
July, 1974 - No. 5, Spring, 1977 (Full color)
Warren Magazines

	GD25	FN65	NM94
1-Low distribution; all Corben story remainders from Warren	3.40	10.00	24.00
2-Wood, Wrightson-r	1.65	4.00	10.00
3-5: 4-Crandall-a. 5-Spirit story	1.00	2.50	6.00

NOTE: *No. 4 had two printings with extra **Corben** story in one. No. 3 may also have a variation. No. 3 has two Jeff Jones reprints from Vampirella.*

COMMANDER BATTLE AND THE ATOMIC SUB
July-Aug, 1954 - No. 7, Aug-Sept, 1955
American Comics Group (Titan Publ. Co.)

	GD25	FN65	NM94
1 (3-D effect)-Moldoff flying saucer-c	34.00	100.00	235.00
2,4-7: 2-Moldoff-c. 4-(1-2/55)-Last pre-code; Landau-a. 5-3-D effect story (2 pgs.). 6,7-Landau-a. 7-Flying saucer-c	16.50	50.00	115.00
3-H-Bomb-c; Atomic Sub becomes Atomic Spaceship	18.00	54.00	125.00

COMMANDMENTS OF GOD
1954, 1958
Catechetical Guild

Commando Adventures #1 © MEG

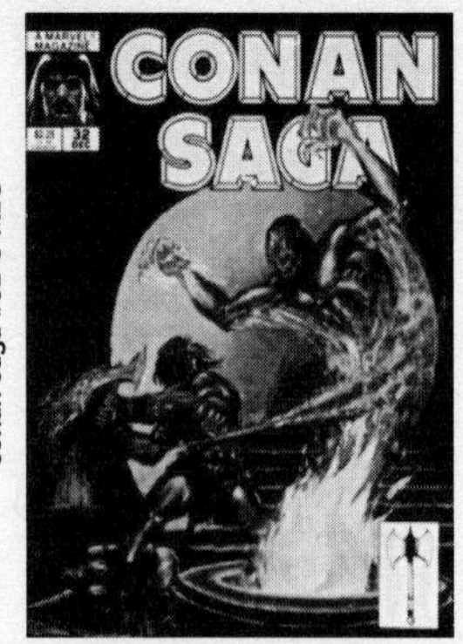

Conan Saga #32 © MEG

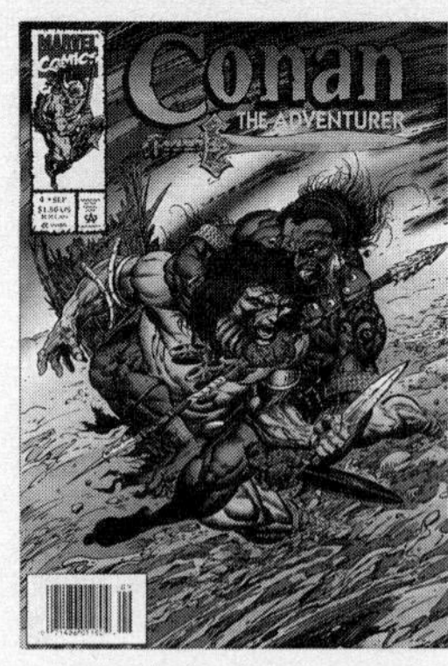

Conan The Adventurer #4 © MEG

GD25 FN65 NM94

300-Same contents in both editions; diff-c 2.00 5.00 10.00

COMMANDO ADVENTURES
June, 1957 - No. 2, Aug, 1957
Atlas Comics (MMC)

1,2-Severin-c. 2-Drucker-a? 5.35 16.00 32.00

COMMANDO YANK (See The Mighty Midget Comics & Wow Comics)

COMPLETE BOOK OF COMICS AND FUNNIES
1944 (196 pgs.) (One Shot) (25¢)
William H. Wise & Co.

1-Origin Brad Spencer, Wonderman; The Magnet, The Silver Knight by Kinstler, & Zudo the Jungle Boy app. 30.00 90.00 210.00

COMPLETE BOOK OF TRUE CRIME COMICS
No date (Mid 1940's) (132 pgs.) (25¢)
William H. Wise & Co.

nn-Contains Crime Does Not Pay rebound (includes #22) 71.00 215.00 500.00

COMPLETE COMICS (Formerly Amazing Comics No. 1)
No. 2, Winter, 1944-45
Timely Comics (EPC)

2-The Destroyer, The Whizzer, The Young Allies & Sergeant Dix; Schomburg-c 100.00 300.00 700.00

COMPLETE LOVE MAGAZINE (Formerly a pulp with same title)
V26#2, May-June, 1951 - V32#4(#191), Sept, 1956
Ace Periodicals (Periodical House)

V26#2-Painted-c (52 pgs.) 4.00 11.00 22.00
V26#3-6(2/52), V27#1(4/52)-6(1/53) 3.00 7.50 15.00
V28#1(3/53), V28#2(5/53), V29#3(7/53)-6(12/53) 2.40 6.00 12.00
V30#1(2/54), V30#1(#176, 4/54),2,4-6(#181, 1/55) 2.40 6.00 12.00
V30#3(#178)-Rock Hudson photo-c 4.00 10.00 20.00
V31#1(#182, 3/55)-Last precode 2.40 6.00 12.00
V31#2(5/55)-6(#187, 1/56) 1.60 4.00 8.00
V32#1(#188, 3/56)-4(#191, 9/56) 1.60 4.00 8.00
NOTE: *(34 total issues). Photo-c V27#5-on. Painted-c V26#3.*

COMPLETE MYSTERY (True Complete Mystery No. 5 on)
Aug, 1948 - No. 4, Feb, 1949 (Full length stories)
Marvel Comics (PrPl)

1-Seven Dead Men 25.00 75.00 175.00
2-Jigsaw of Doom! 19.00 58.00 135.00
3-Fear in the Night; Burgos-c/a (28 pgs.) 19.00 58.00 135.00
4-A Squealer Dies Fast 19.00 58.00 135.00

COMPLETE ROMANCE
1949
Avon Periodicals

1-(Scarce)-Reprinted as Women to Love 27.00 81.00 190.00

COMPLIMENTARY COMICS
No date (1950's)
Sales Promotion Publ. (Giveaway)

1-Strongman by Powell, 3 stories 5.35 16.00 32.00

CONAN (See Chamber of Darkness #4, Giant-Size..., Handbook of..., King Conan, Marvel Graphic Novel #19, 28, Marvel Treasury Ed., Power Record Comics, Robert E. Howard's.., Savage Sword of Conan, and Savage Tales)

CONAN CLASSIC
June, 1994 - Present ($1.50)
Marvel Comics

1-11-r/Conan 1-6 by B. Smith, r/covers w/changes 1.50

CONAN SAGA, THE
June, 1987 - Present ($2.00/$2.25, B&W magazine)
Marvel Comics

1-Barry Smith-r 1-9,11; new Barry Smith-c 1-9 .80 2.00
2-27: 13,15-Boris-c. 17-Adams-r. 18,25-Chaykin-r. 22-r/Giant-Size Conan 1,2 .80 2.00
28-91 ($2.25): 31-Red Sonja-r by N. Adams/SSOC #1; 1 pg. Jeff Jones-r. 32-Newspaper strip-r begin by Buscema. 33-Smith/Conrad-a. 39-r/Kull #1('71) by Andru/Wood. 44-Swipes-c/Savage Tales #1. 57-Brunner-r/SSOC #30. 66-r/Conan Annual #2 by Buscema. 79-r/Conan #43-45 w/Red Sonja. 85-Based on Conan #57-63 .90 2.25
NOTE: ***J. Buscema*** *r-32-on; c-86.* ***Chaykin*** *r-34.* ***Chiodo*** *painted c-63, 65, 66, 82.* ***G. Colan*** *a-47p.* ***Jusko*** *painted c-64, 83.* ***Kaluta*** *c-84.* ***Nino*** *a-37.* ***Ploog*** *a-50.* ***N. Redondo*** *painted c-48, 50, 51, 53, 57, 62.* ***Simonson*** *r-50-54, 56.* ***B. Smith*** *r-51.* ***Starlin*** *c-34.* ***Williamson*** *r-50i.*

CONAN THE ADVENTURER
June, 1994 - Present ($1.50)
Marvel Comics

1-($2.50)-Embossed foil-c; Kayaran-a 1.00 2.50
2-11 1.50

CONAN THE BARBARIAN
Oct, 1970 - No. 275, Dec, 1993
Marvel Comics Group

1-Origin/1st app. Conan (in comics) by Barry Smith; Kull app.; #1-9 are 15¢ issues 23.00 70.00 210.00
2 9.00 28.00 85.00
3-(Low distribution in some areas) 18.00 53.00 160.00
4,5 8.00 25.00 58.00
6-9: 8-Hidden panel message, pg. 14 5.40 16.00 38.00
10,11 (25¢ giants): 10-Black Knight-r; Kull story by Severin 6.90 21.00 48.00
12,13: 12-Wrightson-c(i) 3.90 11.60 27.00
14,15-Elric app. 6.00 18.00 42.00
16,19,20: 16-Conan-r/Savage Tales #1 3.40 10.00 24.00
17,18-No Barry Smith-a 1.60 5.00 11.00
21,22: 22-Has reprint from #1 3.30 10.00 23.00
23-1st app. Red Sonja (2/73) 4.70 14.00 33.00
24-1st full Red Sonja story; last Smith-a 3.90 12.00 27.00
25-John Buscema-c/a begins 1.70 4.20 10.00
26-30 .90 2.30 5.50
31-36,38-40 1.40 3.50
37-Neal Adams-c/a; last 20¢ issue; contains pull-out subscription form 1.00 2.70 6.50
41-57,59,60: 44,45-N. Adams-i(Crusty Bunkers). 45-Adams-c. 48-Origin retold. 59-Origin Belit .80 2.00
58-2nd Belit app. (see Giant-Size Conan #1) 1.40 3.50
61-99: 68-Red Sonja story cont'd from Marvel Feature #7. 84-Intro. Zula. 85-Origin Zula. 87-r/Savage Sword of Conan #3 in color 1.25
100-(52 pg. Giant)-Death of Belit 1.40 3.50
101-114,116-199: 116-r/Power Record Comic PR31 1.25
115-Double size 1.50
200,250 ($1.50): 200-(52 pgs.). 250-(60 pgs.) 1.70
201-249,251,252: 232-Young Conan storyline begins; Conan is born. 244-Return of Zula. 252-Last $1.00-c 1.25
253-274: 262-Adapted from R.E. Howard story 1.35
275-($2.50, 68 pgs.)-Final issue; painted-c 1.00 2.50
King Size 1(1973, 35¢)-Smith-r/#2,4; Smith-c 1.50 3.80 9.00
Annual 2(1976, 50¢)-New full length story 1.50 3.75
Annual 3(1978)-Chaykin/N. Adams-r/SSOC #2 .90 2.25
Annual 4-6: 4(1978)-New full length story. 5(1979)-New full length Buscema story & part-c, 6(1981)-Kane-c/a 1.75
Annual 7-12: 7(1982)-Based on novel "Conan of the Isles" (new-a). 8(1984). 9(1984), 10(1986). 11(1986). 12(1987) 1.35
Special Edition 1 (Red Nails) 1.50 3.75
NOTE: ***Arthur Adams*** *c-248, 249.* ***Neal Adams*** *a-116r(i); c-49i.* ***Austin*** *a-125, 126; c-125i, 126i.* ***Brunner*** *c-17i. c-40.* ***Buscema*** *a-25-36p, 38, 39, 41-56p, 58-63p, 65-67p, 68, 70-78p, 84-86p, 88-91p, 93-126p, 136p, 140, 141-144p, 146-158p, 159, 161, 162, 163p, 165-185p. 187-190p, Annual 2(3pgs.). 3-5p, 7p; c(p)-26, 36, 44, 46, 52, 56, 58, 59, 64, 65, 72, 78-80, 83-91, 93-103, 105-126, 136-151, 155-159, 161, 162, 168, 169, 171, 172, 174, 175, 178-185, 188, 189, Annual 4, 5, 7.* ***Chaykin*** *a-79-83.* ***Golden*** *c-152.* ***Kaluta*** *c-167.* ***Gil Kane*** *a-12p, 17p, 18p, 127-130, 131-134p; c-12p, 17p, 18p, 23, 25, 27-32, 34, 35, 38, 39, 41-43, 45-51, 53-55, 57, 60-63, 65-71, 73p, 76p, 127-134.* ***Jim Lee*** *c-242.* ***McFarlane*** *c-241p.* ***Ploog*** *a-57.* ***Russell*** *a-21; c-251i.* ***Simonson***

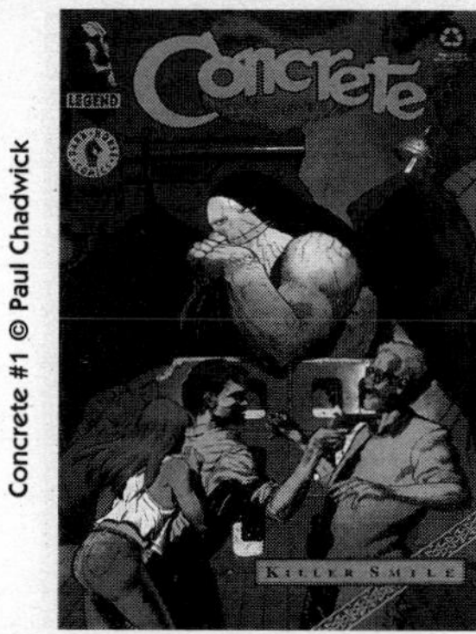

Concrete #1 © Paul Chadwick

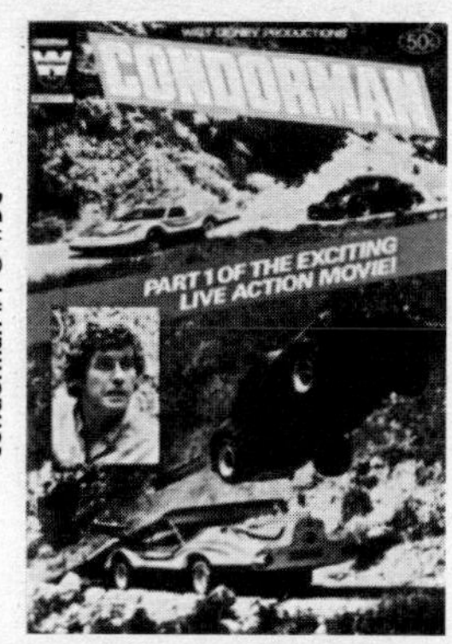

Condorman #1 © WDC

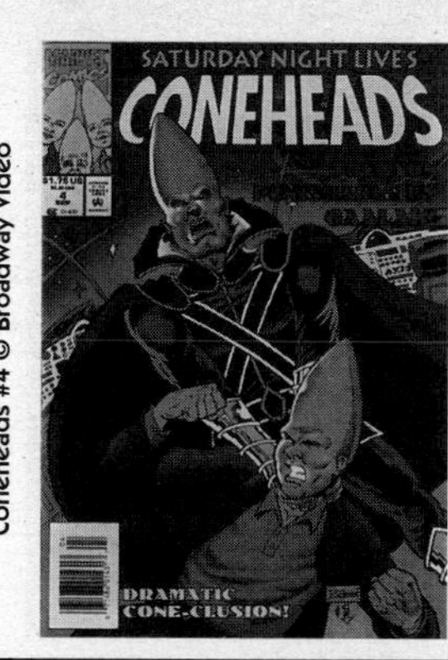

Coneheads #4 © Broadway Video

c-135. ***B. Smith*** *a-1-11p, 12, 13-15p, 16, 19-21, 23, 24; c-1-11, 13-16, 19-24p.* ***Starlin*** *a-64.* ***Wood*** *a-47r. Issue Nos. 3-5, 7-9, 11, 16-18, 21, 23, 25, 27-30, 35, 37, 38, 42, 45, 52, 57, 58, 65, 69-71, 73, 79-83, 99, 100, 104, 114, Annual 2 have original Robert E. Howard stories adapted. Issues #32-34 adapted from Norvell Page's novel* ***Flame Winds.***

CONAN THE BARBARIAN MOVIE SPECIAL
Oct, 1982 - No. 2, Nov, 1982
Marvel Comics Group

	GD25	FN65	NM94
1,2-Movie adaptation; Buscema-a			1.00

CONAN THE DESTROYER
Jan, 1985 - No. 2, Mar, 1985 (Movie adaptation)
Marvel Comics Group

	GD25	FN65	NM94
1,2-r/Marvel Super Special			1.00

CONAN THE KING (Formerly King Conan)
No. 20, Jan, 1984 - No. 55, Nov, 1989
Marvel Comics Group

	GD25	FN65	NM94
20-55: 48-55 ($1.50)			1.50

NOTE: ***Kaluta*** *c-20-23, 24i, 26, 27, 30, 50, 52.* ***Williamson*** *a-37i; c-37i, 38i.*

CONCRETE (Also see Dark Horse Presents & Within Our Reach)
March, 1987 - No. 10, Nov, 1988 ($1.50, B&W)
Dark Horse Comics

	GD25	FN65	NM94
1-Paul Chadwick-c/a in all	1.50	3.80	9.00
1-2nd print		.90	2.25
2	.90	2.30	5.50
3-Origin		1.30	3.25
4-10		.90	2.25
...: A New Life 1 (1989, $2.95, B&W)-r/#3,4 plus new-a (11 pgs.)		1.30	3.25
...Celebrates Earth Day 1990 ($3.50, 52 pgs.)		1.40	3.50
...Color Special 1 (2/89, $2.95, 44 pgs.)-r/1st two Conrete apps. from Dark Horse Presents #1,2 plus new-a		1.40	3.50
...: Eclectica 1,2 (4/93-5/93, $2.95)		1.20	3.00
...: Fragile Creature 1-4 ($2.50, 6/91-2/92, mini-series)		1.00	2.50
...: Killer Smile 1-4 ($2.95, 7/94-10/94, mini-series)		1.20	3.00
...: Land And Sea 1 (2/89, $2.95, B&W)-r/#1,2		1.20	3.00
...: Odd Jobs 1 (7/90, $3.50)-r/5,6 plus new-a		1.40	3.50

CONCRETE: KILLER SMILE
July, 1994 ($2.95, color, limited series)
Dark Horse Comics

	GD25	FN65	NM94
1		1.20	3.00

CONDORMAN (Walt Disney)
Oct, 1981 - No. 3, Jan, 1982
Whitman Publishing

	GD25	FN65	NM94
1-3: 1,2-Movie adaptation; photo-c			1.00

CONEHEADS
June, 1994 - No. 4, 1994 ($1.75, mini-series)
Marvel Comics

	GD25	FN65	NM94
1-4		.70	1.75

CONFESSIONS ILLUSTRATED (Magazine)
Jan-Feb, 1956 - No. 2, Spring, 1956
E. C. Comics

	GD25	FN65	NM94
1-Craig, Kamen, Wood, Orlando-a	11.00	32.00	75.00
2-Craig, Crandall, Kamen, Orlando-a	10.00	30.00	65.00

CONFESSIONS OF LOVE
Apr, 1950 - No. 2, July, 1950 (25¢; 132 pgs. in color)(7-1/4x5-1/4")
Artful Publ.

	GD25	FN65	NM94
1-Bakerish-a	19.00	58.00	135.00
2-Art & text; Bakerish-a	11.00	32.00	75.00

CONFESSIONS OF LOVE (Formerly Startling Terror Tales #10; becomes Confessions of Romance No. 7 on)
No. 11, 7/52 - No. 14, 1/53; No. 4, 3/53- No. 6, 8/53
Star Publications

	GD25	FN65	NM94
11-13: 12,13-Disbrow-a	8.35	25.00	50.00
14,5,6	4.70	14.00	28.00
4-Disbrow-a	5.85	17.50	35.00

NOTE: *All have* ***L. B. Cole*** *covers.*

CONFESSIONS OF ROMANCE (Formerly Confessions of Love)
No. 7, Nov, 1953 - No. 11, Nov, 1954
Star Publications

	GD25	FN65	NM94
7	7.00	21.00	42.00
8	4.70	14.00	28.00
9-Wood-a	9.15	27.50	55.00
10,11-Disbrow-a	5.85	17.50	35.00

NOTE: *All have* ***L. B. Cole*** *covers.*

CONFESSIONS OF THE LOVELORN (Formerly Lovelorn)
No. 52, Aug, 1954 - No. 114, June-July, 1960
American Comics Group (Regis Publ./Best Synd. Features)

	GD25	FN65	NM94
52 (3-D effect)	16.00	48.00	110.00
53,55	4.20	12.50	25.00
54 (3-D effect)	15.00	45.00	105.00
56-Anti-communist propaganda story, 10 pgs; last pre-code (2/55)	5.35	16.00	32.00
57-90	3.20	8.00	16.00
91-Williamson-a	5.35	16.00	32.00
92-99,101-114	2.40	6.00	12.00
100	3.20	8.00	16.00

NOTE: ***Whitney*** *a-most issues; c-52, 53. Painted c-106, 107.*

CONFIDENTIAL DIARY (Formerly High School Confidential Diary; Three Nurses No. 18 on)
No. 12, May, 1962 - No. 17, March, 1963
Charlton Comics

	GD25	FN65	NM94
12-17	1.20	3.00	6.00

CONGO BILL (See Action Comics & More Fun Comics #56)
Aug-Sept, 1954 - No. 7, Aug-Sept, 1955
National Periodical Publication

	GD25	FN65	VF82
1 (Scarce)	68.00	205.00	475.00
2,7 (Scarce)	57.00	170.00	400.00
3-6 (Scarce). 4-Last pre-code issue	50.00	150.00	350.00

NOTE: *(Rarely found in fine to mint condition.)* ***Nick Cardy*** *c-1-7.*

CONGORILLA (Also see Actions Comics #224)
Nov, 1992 - No. 4, Feb, 1993 ($1.75, mini-series)
DC Comics

	GD25	FN65	NM94
1-4: 1,2-Brian Bolland-c		.70	1.75

CONNECTICUT YANKEE, A (See King Classics)

CONQUEROR, THE (See 4-Color No. 690)

CONQUEROR COMICS
Winter, 1945
Albrecht Publishing Co.

	GD25	FN65	NM94
nn	11.50	34.00	80.00

CONQUEROR OF THE BARREN EARTH
Feb, 1985 - No. 4, May, 1985 (Mini-series)
DC Comics

	GD25	FN65	NM94
1-4: Back-up series from Warlord			1.00

CONQUEST
1953 (6¢)
Store Comics

	GD25	FN65	NM94
1-Richard the Lion Hearted, Beowulf, Swamp Fox	4.00	11.00	22.00

CONQUEST
Spring, 1955
Famous Funnies

1-Crandall-a, 1 pg.; contains contents of 1953 issue

Contact Comics #3 © Aviation Press

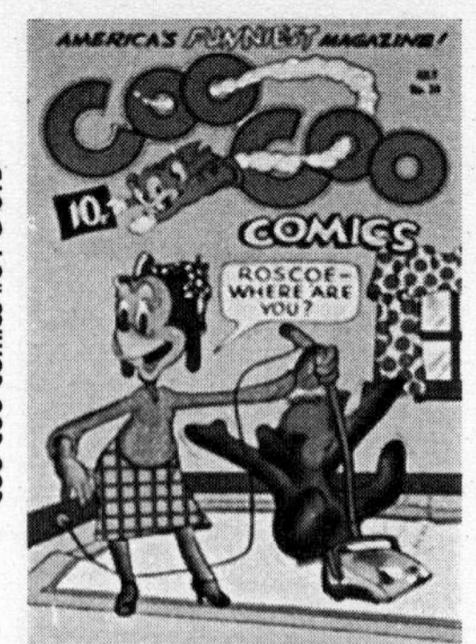

Coo Coo Comics #34 © STD

Cosmic Powers #1 © MEG

GD25 FN65 NM94

3.60 9.00 18.00

CONTACT COMICS
July, 1944 - No. 12, May, 1946
Aviation Press

nn-Black Venus, Flamingo, Golden Eagle, Tommy Tomahawk begin 25.00 75.00 175.00
2-5: 3-Last Flamingo. 3,4-Black Venus by L. B. Cole. 5-The Phantom Flyer app. 18.00 54.00 125.00
6,11-Kurtzman's Black Venus; 11-Last Golden Eagle, last Tommy Tomahawk; Feldstein-a 22.00 65.00 150.00
7-10,12: 12-Sky Rangers, Air Kids, Ace Diamond app. 16.00 48.00 110.00
NOTE: ***L. B. Cole** a-9; c-1-12. **Giunta** a-3. **Hollingsworth** a-5, 7, 10. **Palais** a-11, 12.*

CONTEMPORARY MOTIVATORS
1977 - 1978 (5-3/8x8")(31 pgs., B&W, $1.45)
Pendelum Press

14-3002 The Caine Mutiny; 14-3010 Banner in the Sky; 14-3029 God Is My Co-Pilot;14-3037 Guadalcanal Diary; 14-3045 Hiroshima; 14-3053 Hot Rod; 14-3061 Just Dial a Number; 14-307x Star Wars; 14-3088 The Diary of Anne Frank; 14-3096 Lost Horizon 1.50

NOTE: *Also see Now Age Illustrated. Above may have been distributed the same.*

CONTEST OF CHAMPIONS (See Marvel Super-Hero...)

CONTRACTORS (Eclipse)(Value: cover or less)

COO COO COMICS (...the Bird Brain No. 57 on)
Oct, 1942 - No. 62, April, 1952
Nedor Publ. Co./Standard (Animated Cartoons)

1-Origin/1st app. Super Mouse & begin series (cloned from Superman); the first funny animal super hero series (see Looney Tunes #5 for 1st funny animal super hero) 18.00 54.00 125.00
2 10.00 30.00 60.00
3-10: 10-(3/44) 5.35 16.00 32.00
11-33: 33-1 pg. Ingels-a 4.00 12.00 24.00
34-40,43-46,48-Text illos by Frazetta in all. 36-Super Mouse covers begin 5.85 17.50 35.00
41-Frazetta-a (6-pg. story & 3 text illos) 11.00 32.00 75.00
42,47-Frazetta-a & text illos. 8.35 25.00 50.00
49-(1/50)-3-D effect story; Frazetta text illo 7.00 21.00 42.00
50,51-3-D effect-c only. 50-Frazetta text illo 6.35 19.00 38.00
52-62: 56-Last Supermouse? 3.60 9.00 18.00

"COOKIE" (Also see Topsy-Turvy)
April, 1946 - No. 55, Aug-Sept, 1955
Michel Publ./American Comics Group(Regis Publ.)

1-Teen-age humor 13.50 41.00 95.00
2 7.50 22.50 45.00
3-10 5.35 16.00 32.00
11-20 4.35 13.00 26.00
21-23,26,28-30 4.00 10.00 20.00
24,25,27-Starlet O'Hara stories 4.00 11.00 22.00
31-34,37-55 3.60 9.00 18.00
35,36-Starlett O'Hara stories 4.00 10.00 20.00

COOL CAT (Formerly Black Magic)
V8#6, Mar-Apr, 1962 - V9#2, July-Aug, 1962
Prize Publications

V8#6, nn(V9#1, 5-6/62), V9#2 4.00 10.00 20.00

COOL WORLD
Apr, 1992 - No. 4, Sept, 1992 ($1.75, mini-series)
DC Comics

1-4: Prequel to animated/live action movie by Ralph Bakshi. 1-Bakshi-c. Bill Wray inks in all .70 1.75
...Movie Adaptation nn ('92, $3.50, 68pg.)-Bakshi-c 1.40 3.50

COPPER CANYON (See Fawcett Movie Comics)

COPS (TV)
Aug, 1988 - No. 15, Aug, 1989 ($1.00)
DC Comics

1 ($1.50, 52 pgs.)-Based on Hasbro Toys 1.50
2-15: 14-Orlando-c(p) 1.00

COPS: THE JOB
June, 1992 - No. 4, Sept, 1992 ($1.25, mini-series)
Marvel Comics

1-4: All have Jusko scripts & Golden-c 1.25

CORBEN SPECIAL, A (Pacific)(Value: cover or less)

CORKY & WHITE SHADOW (See 4-Color No. 707)

CORLISS ARCHER (See Meet Corliss Archer)

CORMAC MAC ART (Dark Horse)(Value: cover or less)

CORPORAL RUSTY DUGAN (See Holyoke One-Shot #2)

CORPSES OF DR. SACOTTI, THE (See Ideal a Classical Comic)

CORSAIR, THE (See A-1 Comics No. 5, 7, 10)

CORTEZ AND THE FALL OF THE AZTECS
1993 ($2.95, B&W, limited series)
Tome Press

1,2 1.20 3.00

CORUM: THE BULL AND THE SPEAR (First)(Value: cover or less)

COSMIC BOOK, THE (Ace)(Value: cover or less)

COSMIC BOY (See The Legion of Super-Heroes)
Dec, 1986 - No. 4, Mar, 1987 (Mini-series)
DC Comics

1-4: Legends tie-ins all issues 1.00

COSMIC ODYSSEY
1988 - No. 4, 1988 ($3.50, squarebound)
DC Comics

1-4: Superman, Batman, Green Lantern; Starlin scripts 1.40 3.50

COSMIC POWERS
Mar, 1994 - No. 6, Aug, 1994 ($2.50, limited series)
Marvel Comics

1-6: 1-Ron Lim-c/a(p). 1,2-Thanos app. 2-Terrax. 3-Ganymede & Jack of Hearts app. 1.00 2.50

COSMO CAT (Becomes Sunny #11 on; also see All Top & Wotalife Comics)
July-Aug, 1946 - No. 10, Oct, 1947; 1957; 1959
Fox Publications/Green Publ. Co./Norlen Mag.

1 14.00 43.00 100.00
2 7.50 22.50 45.00
3-Origin (11-12/46) 8.35 25.00 50.00
4-10 5.35 16.00 32.00
2-4(1957-Green Publ. Co.) 3.20 8.00 16.00
2-4(1959-Norlen Mag.) 2.00 5.00 10.00
I.W. Reprint #1 1.40 3.50 7.00

COSMO THE MERRY MARTIAN
Sept, 1958 - No. 6, Oct, 1959
Archie Publications (Radio Comics)

1-Bob White-a in all 11.00 32.00 75.00
2-6 8.35 25.00 50.00

COTTON WOODS (See 4-Color No. 837)

COUGAR, THE (Cougar No. 2)
April, 1975 - No. 2, July, 1975
Seaboard Periodicals (Atlas)

1,2: 1-Adkins-a(p). 2-Origin; Buckler-c(p) 1.00

COUNTDOWN (See Movie Classics)

COUNT DUCKULA (TV)

Count Duckula #9 © MEG

Cowboy Western #27 © CC

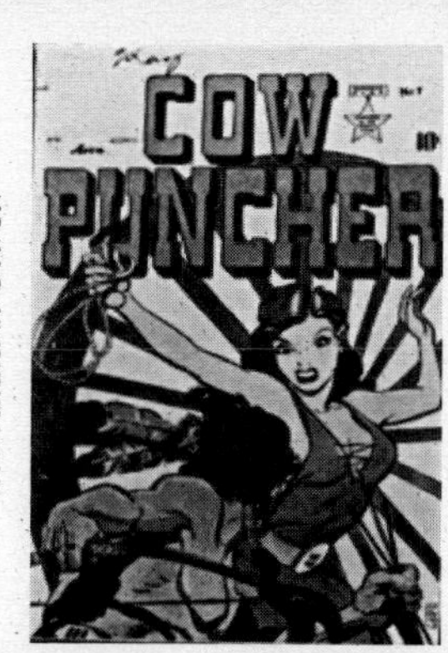

Cow Puncher #7 © AVON

GD25 FN65 NM94

Nov, 1988 - No. 15, Jan, 1991 ($1.00)
Marvel Comics

1-15: Dangermouse back-ups. 8-Geraldo Rivera photo-c; Sienkiewicz-a(i) 1.00

COUNT OF MONTE CRISTO, THE (See 4-Color No. 794)

COURAGE COMICS
1945
J. Edward Slavin

1,2,77 7.50 22.50 45.00

COURTSHIP OF EDDIE'S FATHER (TV)
Jan, 1970 - No. 2, May, 1970
Dell Publishing Co.

1,2-Bill Bixby photo-c 3.10 9.00 22.00

COVERED WAGONS, HO (See 4-Color No. 814)

COWBOY ACTION (Formerly Western Thrillers No. 1-4; Becomes Quick-Trigger Western No. 12 on)
No. 5, March, 1955 - No. 11, March, 1956
Atlas Comics (ACI)

5 8.35 25.00 50.00
6-10: 6-8-Heath-c 5.35 16.00 32.00
11-Williamson-a (4 pgs.); Baker-a 6.35 19.00 38.00
NOTE: ***Ayers** a-8. **Drucker** a-6. **Maneely** c/a-5, 6. **Severin** c-10. **Shores** a-7.*

COWBOY COMICS (...Stories No. 14; formerly Star Ranger)(Star Ranger Funnies No. 15 on)
No. 13, July, 1938 - No. 14, Aug, 1938
Centaur Publishing Co.

13-(Rare)-Ace and Deuce, Lyin Lou, Air Patrol, Aces High, Lee Trent, Trouble Hunters begin 86.00 257.00 600.00
14-Filchock-c 57.00 171.00 400.00
NOTE: ***Guardineer** a-13, 14. **Gustavson** a-13, 14.*

COWBOY IN AFRICA (TV)
March, 1968
Gold Key

1(10219-803)-Chuck Connors photo-c 4.00 12.00 28.00

COWBOY LOVE (Becomes Range Busters?)
7/49 - V2#10, 6/50; No. 11, 1951; No. 28, 2/55 - No. 31, 8/55
Fawcett Publications/Charlton Comics No. 28 on

V1#1-Rocky Lane photo back-c 11.50 34.00 80.00
2 4.00 12.00 24.00
V1#3,4,6 (12/49) 4.00 10.00 20.00
5-Bill Boyd photo back-c (11/49) 5.85 17.50 35.00
V2#7-Williamson/Evans-a 7.00 21.00 42.00
V2#8-11 3.60 9.00 18.00
V1#28 (Charlton)-Last precode (2/55) (Formerly Romantic Story?) 3.60 9.00 18.00
V1#29-31 (Charlton; becomes Sweetheart Diary #32 on) 3.20 8.00 16.00
NOTE: ***Powell** a-10. **Marcus Swayze** a-2, 3. Photo c-1-11. No. 1-3, 5-7, 9, 10 are 52 pgs.*

COWBOY ROMANCES (Young Men No. 4 on)
Oct, 1949 - No. 3, Mar, 1950 (All photo-c & 52 pgs.)
Marvel Comics (IPC)

1-Photo-c 14.00 43.00 100.00
2-William Holden, Mona Freeman "Streets of Laredo" photo-c 10.00 30.00 70.00
3-Photo-c 9.15 27.50 55.00

COWBOYS 'N' INJUNS (...and Indians No. 6 on)
1946 - No. 5, 1947; No. 6, 1949 - No. 8, 1952
Com No. 1-5/Magazine Enterprises No. 6 on

1 6.70 20.00 40.00
2-5-All funny animal western 4.35 13.00 26.00

GD25 FN65 NM94

6(A-1 23)-Half violent, half funny; Ayers-a 6.35 19.00 38.00
7(A-1 41, 1950), 8(A-1 48)-All funny 4.35 13.00 26.00
I.W. Reprint No. 1,7 (Reprinted in Canada by Superior, No. 7) 1.20 3.00 6.00
Super Reprint #10 (1963) 1.20 3.00 6.00

COWBOY WESTERN COMICS (TV)(Formerly Jack In The Box; Becomes Space Western No. 40-45 & Wild Bill Hickok & Jingles No. 68 on; title: Cowboy Western Heroes No. 47 & 48; Cowboy Western No. 49 on)
No. 17, 7/48 - No. 39, 8/52; No. 46, 10/53; No. 47, 12/53; No. 48, Spr, '54; No. 49, 5-6/54 - No. 67, 3/58 (nn 40-45)
Charlton (Capitol Stories)

17-Jesse James, Annie Oakley, Wild Bill Hickok begin; Texas Rangers app. 11.50 34.00 80.00
18,19-Orlando-c/a. 18-Paul Bunyan begins. 19-Wyatt Earp story 8.35 25.00 50.00
20-25: 21-Buffalo Bill story. 22-Texas Rangers-c/story. 24-Joel McCrea photo-c & adaptation from movie "Three Faces West". 25-James Craig photo-c & adaptation from movie "Northwest Stampede" 6.70 20.00 40.00
26-George Montgomery photo-c and adaptation from movie "Indian Scout"; 1 pg. bio on Will Rogers 9.15 27.50 55.00
27-Sunset Carson photo-c & adapts movie "Sunset Carson Rides Again" plus 1 other Sunset Carson story 54.00 160.00 375.00
28-Sunset Carson line drawn-c; adapts movies "Battling Marshal" & "Fighting Mustangs" starring Sunset Carson 25.00 75.00 175.00
29-Sunset Carson line drawn-c; adapts movies "Rio Grande" with Sunset Carson & "Winchester '73" w/James Stewart plus 5 pg. life history of Sunset Carson featuring Tom Mix 25.00 75.00 175.00
30-Sunset Carson photo-c; adapts movie "Deadline" starring Sunset Carson plus 1 other Sunset Carson story 54.00 160.00 375.00
31-34,38,39,47-50 (no #40-45): 50-Golden Arrow, Rocky Lane & Blackjack (r?) stories 5.35 16.00 32.00
35,36-Sunset Carson-c/stories (2 in each). 35-Inside front-c photo of Sunset Carson plus photo on-c 25.00 75.00 175.00
37-Sunset Carson stories (2) 14.00 43.00 100.00
46-(Formerly Space Western)-Space western story 12.00 36.00 85.00
51-57,59-66: 51-Golden Arrow(r?) & Monte Hale-r renamed Rusty Hall. 53,54-Tom Mix-r. 55-Monte Hale story(r?). 66-Young Eagle story. 67-Wild Bill Hickok and Jingles-c/story 4.00 11.00 22.00
58-(1/56, 15¢, 68 pgs.)-Wild Bill Hickok, Annie Oakley & Jesse James stories; Forgione-a 4.35 13.00 26.00
67-(15¢, 68 pgs.)-Williamson/Torres-a, 5 pgs. 7.50 22.50 45.00
NOTE: *Many issues trimmed 1" shorter. **Maneely** a-67(5). Inside front/back photo c-29.*

COWGIRL ROMANCES (Formerly Jeanie Comics)
No. 28, Jan, 1950 (52 pgs.)
Marvel Comics (CCC)

28(#1)-Photo-c 14.00 43.00 100.00

COWGIRL ROMANCES
1950 - No. 12, Winter, 1952-53 (No. 1-3: 52 pgs.)
Fiction House Magazines

1-Kamen-a 22.00 65.00 150.00
2 11.50 34.00 80.00
3-5: 5-12-Whitman-c (most) 10.00 30.00 70.00
6-9,11,12 10.00 30.00 60.00
10-Frazetta?/Williamson?-a; Kamen?/Baker-a; r/Mitzi story from Movie Comics #4 w/all new dialogue 22.00 65.00 150.00

COW PUNCHER (...Comics)
Jan, 1947; No. 2, Sept, 1947 - No. 7, 1949
Avon Periodicals

1-Clint Cortland, Texas Ranger, Kit West, Pioneer Queen begin; Kubert-a; Alabam stories begin 25.00 75.00 175.00
2-Kubert, Kamen/Feldstein-a; Kamen-c 22.00 65.00 150.00
3-5,7: 3-Kiefer story 14.00 43.00 100.00
6-Opium drug mention story; bondage, headlight-c; Reinman-a 17.00 52.00 120.00

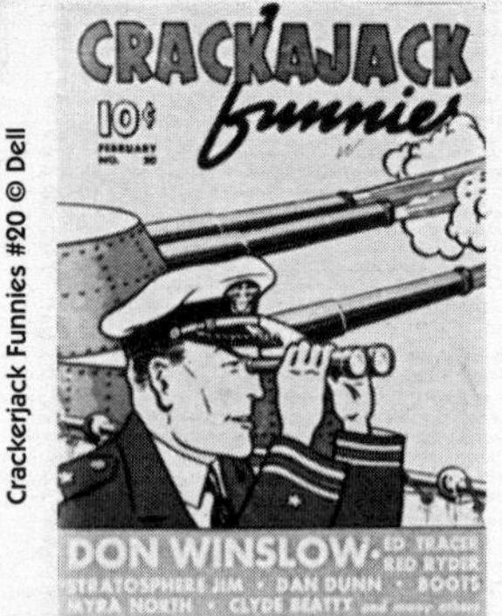

Crackerjack Funnies #20 © Dell

Crack Comics #42 © QUA

Crack Comics #52 © QUA

GD25 FN65 NM94

COWPUNCHER
1953 (nn) (Reprints Avon's No. 2)
Realistic Publications

nn-Kubert-a 8.35 25.00 50.00

COWSILLS, THE (See Harvey Pop Comics)

COYOTE
June, 1983 - No. 16, Mar, 1986
Epic Comics (Marvel)

1-16: 11-1st McFarlane-a. 12-14-McFarlane-a 1.25

CRACKAJACK FUNNIES (Giveaway)
1937 (32 pgs.; full size; soft cover; full color)(Before No. 1?)
Malto-Meal

nn-Features Dan Dunn, G-Man, Speed Bolton, Freckles, Buck Jones, Clyde Beatty, The Nebbs, Major Hoople, Wash Tubbs 71.00 215.00 500.00

CRACKAJACK FUNNIES
June, 1938 - No. 43, Jan, 1942
Dell Publishing Co.

1-Dan Dunn, Freckles, Myra North, Wash Tubbs, Apple Mary, The Nebbs, Don Winslow, Tom Mix, Buck Jones, Major Hoople, Clyde Beatty, Boots begin 143.00 430.00 1000.00
2 71.00 215.00 500.00
3 54.00 160.00 375.00
4,5: 5-Nude woman on cover 39.00 118.00 275.00
6-8,10: 8-Speed Bolton begins (1st app.) 32.00 96.00 225.00
9-(3/39)-Red Ryder strip-r begin by Harman; 1st app. in comics & 1st cover app. 44.00 133.00 310.00
11-14 30.00 90.00 210.00
15-Tarzan text feature begins by Burroughs (9/39); not in #26,35 32.00 96.00 225.00
16-24: 18-Stratosphere Jim begins (1st app., 12/39). 23-Ellery Queen begins plus-c (1st comic book app., 5/40) 22.00 65.00 150.00
25-The Owl begins (1st app., 7/40); in new costume #26 by Frank Thomas (also see Popular Comics #72) 51.00 154.00 360.00
26-30: 28-Part Owl-c 41.00 122.00 285.00
31-Owl covers begin, end #42 34.00 103.00 240.00
32-Origin Owl Girl 44.00 133.00 310.00
33-38: 36-Last Tarzan issue. 37-Cyclone & Midge begin (1st app.) 26.00 78.00 180.00
39-Andy Panda begins (intro/1st app., 9/41) 34.00 103.00 240.00
40-43: 42-Last Owl-c. 43-Terry & the Pirates-r 24.00 72.00 165.00
NOTE: ***McWilliams*** *art in most issues.*

CRACK COMICS (Crack Western No. 63 on)
May, 1940 - No. 62, Sept, 1949
Quality Comics Group

1-Origin & 1st app. The Black Condor by Lou Fine, Madame Fatal, Red Torpedo, Rock Bradden & The Space Legion; The Clock, Alias the Spider (by Gustavson), Wizard Wells, & Ned Brant begin; Powell-a; Note: Madame Fatal is a man dressed as a woman 315.00 945.00 2200.00
2 136.00 407.00 950.00
3 96.00 290.00 675.00
4 86.00 257.00 600.00
5-10: 5-Molly The Model begins. 10-Tor, the Magic Master begins 69.00 208.00 485.00
11-20: 13-1 pg. J. Cole-a. 18-1st app. Spitfire? 60.00 182.00 425.00
21-24: 23-Pen Miller begins; continued from National Comics #22. 24-Last Fine Black Condor 46.00 140.00 325.00
25,26: 26-Flag-c 32.00 96.00 225.00
27-(1/43)-Intro & origin Captain Triumph by Alfred Andriola (Kerry Drake artist) & begin series 69.00 210.00 485.00
28-30 29.00 86.00 200.00
31-39: 31-Last Black Condor 16.50 50.00 115.00
40-46 11.00 32.00 75.00
47-57,59,60-Capt. Triumph by Crandall 12.00 36.00 85.00

GD25 FN65 NM94

58,61,62-Last Captain Triumph 10.00 30.00 65.00
NOTE: *Black Condor by* ***Fine****: No. 1, 2, 4-6, 8, 10-24; by* ***Sultan****: No. 3, 7; by* ***Fugitani****: No. 9.* ***Cole*** *a-34.* ***Crandall*** *a-61(unsigned); c-48, 49, 51-61.* ***Guardineer*** *a-17.* ***Gustavson*** *a-1, 13, 17.* ***McWilliams*** *a-15-27. Black Condor c-2, 4, 6, 8, 10, 12, 14, 16, 18, 20-26. Capt. Triumph c-27-62. The Clock c-1, 3, 5, 7, 9, 11, 13, 15, 17, 19.*

CRACKED (Magazine) (Satire) (Also see The 3-D Zone #19)
Feb-Mar, 1958 - Present
Major Magazines(#1-212)/Globe Communications(#213 on)

1-One pg. Williamson-a 13.00 40.00 90.00
2-1st Shut-Ups & Bonus Cut-Outs 5.85 17.50 35.00
3-6 4.00 11.00 22.00
7-10: 7-Reprints 1st 6 covers on-c 3.60 9.00 18.00
11-12, 13(nn,3/60), 14-17, 18(nn,2/61), 19,20 3.20 8.00 16.00
21-27(11/62), 27(No.28, 2/63; mis-#d), 29(5/63) 2.80 7.00 14.00
31-60 1.80 4.50 9.00
61-98,100 1.40 3.50 7.00
99-Alfred E. Neuman on-c 4.00 10.00 20.00
101-200: 234-Don Martin-a begins ($1.75 #? on) 1.50 3.50
201-298 1.00 2.00
Biggest... (Winter, 1977) 1.40 3.50 7.00
Biggest, Greatest... nn('65) 4.00 10.00 20.00
Biggest, Greatest... 2('66) - #12('76) 2.00 5.00 10.00
...Blockbuster 1,2 ('88) .55 1.60 2.75
...Digest 1(Fall, '86, 148 pgs.) - #5 .40 1.00 2.00
...Collectors' Edition 4 ('73; formerly ...Special) 1.40 3.50 7.00
5-70: 23-Ward-a .60 1.50 3.00
71-84: 83-Elvis, Batman parodies .70 1.75 3.50
...Party Pack 1,2('88) .70 1.75 3.50
...Shut-Ups (2/72-'72; Cracked Spec. #3) 1;2 1.20 3.00 6.00
...Special 3('73; formerly Cracked Shut-Ups; ...Collectors' Edition#4 on) 1.20 3.00 6.00
Extra Special... 1('76), 2('76) .60 1.50 3.00
Giant... nn('65) 4.20 12.50 25.00
Giant... 2('66)-12('76), nn(9/77)-48('87) 3.00 7.50 15.00
King Sized... 1('67) 5.00 15.00 30.00
King Sized... 2('68)-11('77) 4.00 10.00 20.00
King Sized... 12-22 (Sum/'86) .40 1.00 2.00
Super... 1('68) 4.20 12.50 25.00
Super... 2('69)-24('88) 3.60 9.00 18.00
Super... 1('87, 100 pgs.)-Severin & Elder-a .55 1.40 2.75
NOTE: ***Burgos*** *a-1-10.* ***Colan*** *a-257.* ***Davis*** *a-5, 11-17, 24, 40, 80; c-12-14, 16.* ***Elder*** *a-5, 6, 10-13; c-10.* ***Everett*** *a-1-10, 23-25, 61; c-1.* ***Heath*** *a-1-3, 6, 13, 14, 17, 110; c-6.* ***Jaffee*** *a-5, 6.* ***Don Martin*** *c-235, 244, 247, 259, 261, 264.* ***Morrow*** *a-8-10.* ***Reinman*** *a-1-4.* ***Severin*** *c/a-in most all issues.* ***Shores*** *a-3-7.* ***Torres*** *a-7-10.* ***Ward*** *a-22-24, 27, 35, 40, 143, 144, 149, 150, 152, 153, 156.* ***Williamson*** *a-1 (1 pg.).* ***Wolverton*** *a-10 (2 pgs.), Giant nn('65).* ***Wood*** *a-27, 35, 40. Alfred E. Neuman c-177, 200, 202. Batman c-234, 248, 249, 256. Captain America c-256. Christmas c-234, 243. Spider-Man c-260. Star Trek c-127, 169, 207, 228. Star Wars c-145, 146, 148, 149, 152, 155, 173, 174, 199. Superman c-183, 233. #144, 146 have free full-color pre-glued stickers. #145, 147, 155, 163 have free full-color postcards. #123, 137, 154, 157 have free iron-ons.*

CRACKED MONSTER PARTY
July, 1988 - Present
Globe Communications

1-26 .80 2.00

CRACKED'S FOR MONSTERS ONLY
Sept, 1969 - No. 9, Sept, 1969
Major Magazines

1-9 1.00

CRACKED SPACED OUT
Fall, 1993 - Present
Globe Communications

1-4 .80 2.00

CRACK WESTERN (Formerly Crack Comics; Jonesy No. 85 on)
No. 63, Nov, 1949 - No. 84, May, 1953 (36 pgs., 63-68,74-on)
Quality Comics Group

63(#1)-Two-Gun Lil (origin & 1st app.)(ends #84), Arizona Ames, his horse

Crack Western #71 © QUA

Crazy #2 © MEG

Creatures On The Loose #23 © MEG

GD25 FN65 NM94

Thunder (with sidekick Spurs & his horse Calico), Frontier Marshal (ends #70), & Dead Canyon Days (ends #69) begin; Crandall-a 16.00 48.00 110.00
64,65-Crandall-a 12.00 36.00 85.00
66,68-Photo-c. 66-Arizona Ames becomes A. Raines (ends #84) 11.00 32.00 75.00
67-Randolph Scott photo-c; Crandall-a 12.00 36.00 85.00
69(52pgs.)-Crandall-a 11.00 32.00 75.00
70(52pgs.)-The Whip (origin & 1st app.) & his horse Diablo begin (ends #84); Crandall-a 11.00 32.00 75.00
71(52pgs.)-Frontier Marshal becomes Bob Allen F. Marshal (ends #84); Crandall-c/a 12.00 36.00 85.00
72(52pgs.)-Tim Holt photo-c 10.00 30.00 70.00
73(52pgs.)-Photo-c 7.50 22.50 45.00
74-76,78,79,81,83-Crandall-c. 83-Crandall-a(p) 10.00 30.00 60.00
77,80,82 5.85 17.50 35.00
84-Crandall-c/a 10.00 30.00 70.00

NOTE: ***Crandall** c-71p, 74-81, 83p(w/**Cuidera**-i).*

CRASH COMICS (Catman Comics No. 6 on)
May, 1940 - No. 5, Nov, 1940
Tem Publishing Co.

1-The Blue Streak, Strongman (origin), The Perfect Human, Shangra begin (1st app. of each); Kirby-a 171.00 515.00 1200.00
2-Simon & Kirby-a 86.00 257.00 600.00
3,5-Simon & Kirby-a 68.00 205.00 475.00
4-Origin & 1st app. The Catman; S&K-a 114.00 343.00 800.00

NOTE: *Solar Legion by **Kirby** No. 1-5 (5 pgs. each). Strongman c-1-4. Catman c-5.*

CRASH DIVE (See Cinema Comics Herald)

CRASH RYAN (Also see Dark Horse Presents #44)
Oct, 1984 - No. 4, Jan, 1985 (Baxter paper, limited series)
Epic Comics (Marvel)

1-4 1.50

CRAZY (Also see This Magazine is Crazy)
Dec, 1953 - No. 7, July, 1954
Atlas Comics (CSI)

1-Everett-c/a 16.50 50.00 115.00
2 13.00 40.00 90.00
3-7: 4-I Love Lucy satire. 5-Satire on censorship 11.00 32.00 75.00

NOTE: ***Ayers** a-5. **Berg** a-1, 2. **Burgos** c-5, 6. **Drucker** a-6. **Everett** a-1-4. **Al Hartley** a-4. **Heath** a-3, 7; c-7. **Maneely** a-1-7, c-3, 4. **Post** a-3-6. Funny monster c-1-4.*

CRAZY (Satire)
Feb, 1973 - No. 3, June, 1973
Marvel Comics Group

1-3-Not Brand Echh-r. 1-Beatles cameo (r) 1.00

CRAZY MAGAZINE (Satire)
Oct, 1973 - No. 94, Apr, 1983 (40-90¢, B&W magazine)
(#1, 44 pgs; #2-90, reg. issues, 52 pgs; #92-95, 68 pgs)'
Marvel Comics Group

1-Wolverton(1 pg.), Bode-a; 3 pg. photo story of Neal Adams & Dick Giordano .80 2.00
2-Kurtzman's "Hey Look" 2 pg. reprint 1.20
3-16: 8-Casper parody. 9-Has 1st 8 covers on-c 1.00
17-29,31-36,38-41,43,48,50,51,53,54,56,57,59,60: 20-Superheroes song sheet. 41-Kiss-c. 43-E.C. swipe from Mad #131. 60,92-Star Trek parodies 1.00
30,37,42,49,52,55,61,64,67,70,73,76,85,88: Super Specials ($1.00, all 84 pgs.). 85-Flintstones. 88-X-Men 1.20
58-Super Special ($1.25); contains free Crazy #1 (2/73) comic reprint 1.25
62,63,65,66,68,69,71,72,74,75,77,78,80,81,83,84,86,87,89,90: 62-Kiss-c & 2 pg. story. 63-Obnoxio app. 69-Richie Rich. 80-X-Men. 81-Wolverine/Hulk. 87-Obnoxio origin 1.00
79-Super Special ($1.25)-Full color looney labels 1.25
82-Super Special ($1.25); X-Men on-c 1.25
91-94: ($1.25) 91-Super Special; Black Knight by Maneely. 93-E.T.-c, & parody. 94-Avengers parody 1.25
Super Special 1(Summer, 1975, 100 pgs.)-Ploog, Neal Adams-r .65 1.60

NOTE: ***N. Adams** a-2, 61r, 94p. **Austin** a-82i. **Buscema** a-2, 82. **Byrne** c-82p. **Nick Cardy** c-7, 8, 10, 12-16, Super Special 1. **Crandall** a-76r. **Ditko** a-68r, 79r, 82r. **Drucker** a-3. **Eisner** a-9-16. **Kelly Freas** c-1-6, 9, 11; a-7. **Ploog** a-1, 4, 7, 67r, 73r. **Rogers** a-82. **Sparling** a-92. **Wood** a-65r. Howard the Duck in 36, 50, 51, 53, 54, 59, 63, 65, 66, 68, 69, 71, 72, 74, 75, 77. Hulk in 46, c-42, 46, 57, 73. Star Wars in 32, 66; c-37.*

CRAZYMAN
Apr, 1992 - No. 5, 1992 ($2.50, high quality paper)
Continuity Comics

1-($3.95, 52 pgs.)-Embossed-c; N. Adams part-i 1.60 4.00
2-5 ($2.50): 2-N. Adams/Bolland-c 1.00 2.50

CRAZYMAN
V2#1, May, 1993 - No. 4, Jan, 1994 ($2.50, high quality paper)
Continuity Comics

V2#1-($2.50)-Entire book is die-cut 1.00 2.50
2-4: 2-(12/93)-Adams-c(p) & part scripts. 3-(12/93). 4-Indicia says #3, Jan. 1993 1.00 2.50

CRAZY, MAN, CRAZY (Magazine) (Becomes This Magazine is...?)
V2#2, June, 1956 (Formerly From Here to Insanity
Humor Magazines (Charlton)

V2#2-Satire; Wolverton-a, 3 pgs. 9.15 27.50 55.00

CREATURE, THE (See Movie Classics)

CREATURES ON THE LOOSE (Formerly Tower of Shadows No. 1-9)(See Kull)
No. 10, March, 1971 - No. 37, Sept, 1975 (New-a & reprints)
Marvel Comics Group

10-First King Kull story; see Monsters on the Prowl (next app.?); Wrightson-a; 15¢ 3.90 11.60 27.00
11-37: 16-Origin Warrior of Mars (begins? ends #21). 21,22-Steranko-c. 22-29-Thongor-c/stories. 30-Manwolf begins 1.10 2.75

NOTE: ***Crandall** a-13. **Ditko** r-15, 17, 18, 20, 22, 24, 27, 28. **Everett** a-16i(new). **Matt Fox** r-21i. **Howard** a-26i. **Gil Kane** a-16p, 17p; c-16, 20, 25, 29, 33p, 35p, 36p. **Kirby** r-16(2). **Morrow** a-20, 21. **Perez** a-33-37; c-34p. **Sinnott** r-21. **Tuska** a-31p, 32p.*

CREEPER, THE (See Beware... & 1st Issue Special)

CREEPY (Magazine)(See Warren Presents)
1964 - No. 145, Feb, 1983; No. 146, 1985 (B&W)
Warren Publishing Co./Harris Publ. #146

1-Frazetta-a (his last story in comics?); Jack Davis-c; 1st Warren all comics magazine 10.00 30.00 70.00
2: 2-Frazetta-c & 1 pg. strip 5.00 16.00 37.00
3-13: 3-7,9-11-Frazetta-c. 7-Frazetta 1 pg. strip. 9-Creepy fan club sketch by Wrightson (1st published-a); has 1/2 pg. anti-smoking strip by Frazetta. 10-Brunner fan club sketch (1st published work) 2.30 6.90 16.00
14-Neal Adams 1st Warren work 3.00 9.00 21.00
15-25: 15-17-Frazetta-c 1.70 4.20 10.00
26-40: 27,32-Frazetta-c. 32-Harlan Ellison story 1.50 4.00 9.00
41-47,49-54,56-61: 61-Wertham parody 1.30 3.30 8.00
48,55,65-(1973, 1974, 1975 Annuals) 1.50 4.00 9.00
62-64,66-112,114-145: 93-Sports issue. 96-Aliens issue. 102-All monster issue. 121-All Severin-r issue. 125-All N. Adams-r issue. 137-All Williamson-r issue. 139-All Toth-r issue. 144-Giant, $2.25; Frazetta-c 1.20 2.90 7.00
113-All Wrightson-r issue 1.40 4.00 8.50
146 ($2.95) 1.50 3.80 9.00
Year Book 1968, 1969 1.50 3.80 9.00
Year Book 1970-Neal Adams, Ditko-a(r) 1.50 3.80 9.00
Annual 1971,1972 1.50 3.80 9.00
1993 Fearbook (1993, $3.95)-Harris Publications 1.00 2.00 5.00

NOTE: *All issues contain many good artists works: **Neal Adams, Brunner, Corben, Craig (Taycee), Crandall, Ditko, Evans, Frazetta, Heath, Jeff Jones, Krenkel, McWilliams, Morrow, Nino, Orlando, Ploog, Severin, Torres, Toth, Williamson, Wood, & Wrightson**; covers by **Crandall, Davis, Frazetta, Morrow, San Julian, Todd/Bode**; Otto Binder's "Adam Link"*

Crime And Punishment #37 © LEV

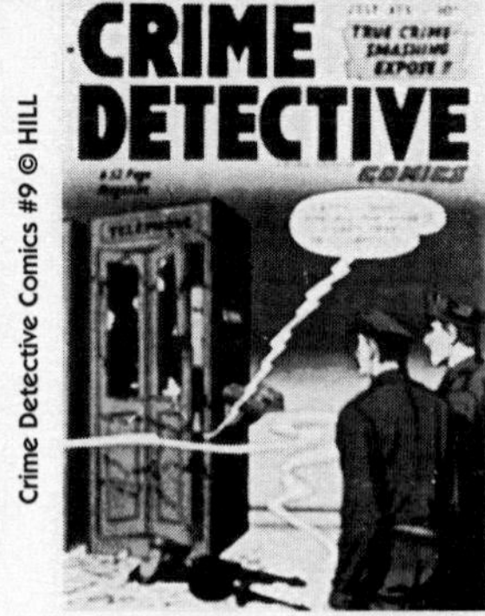

Crime Detective Comics #9 © HILL

Crime Does Not Pay #40 © LEV

	GD25	FN65	NM94

*stories in No. 2, 4, 6, 8, 9, 12, 13, 15 with **Orlando** art. **Frazetta** c-2-7, 9-11, 15-17, 27, 32, 83r, 89r, 91r. **E.A. Poe** adaptations in 66, 69, 70.*

CREEPY THINGS
July, 1975 - No. 6, June, 1976
Charlton Comics

	GD25	FN65	NM94
1			1.50
2-6: Ditko-a in 3,5. Sutton c-3,4			1.00
Modern Comics Reprint 2-6(1977)			1.00

CRIME AND JUSTICE (Rookie Cop? No. 27 on)
March, 1951 - No. 26, Sept, 1955
Capitol Stories/Charlton Comics

	GD25	FN65	NM94
1	19.00	57.00	130.00
2	5.85	17.50	35.00
3-8,10-13: 6-Negligee panels	5.00	15.00	30.00
9-Classic story "Comics Vs. Crime"	11.50	34.00	80.00
14-Color illos in **POP**; gory story of man who beheads women	9.15	27.50	55.00
15-17,19-26	4.00	10.00	20.00
18-Ditko-a	13.00	40.00	90.00

*NOTE: **Alascia** c-20. **Ayers** a-17. **Shuster** a-19-21; c-19. Bondage c-11, 12.*

CRIME AND PUNISHMENT (Title inspired by 1935 film)
April, 1948 - No. 74, Aug, 1955
Lev Gleason Publications

	GD25	FN65	NM94
1-Mr. Crime app. on-c	17.00	52.00	120.00
2	10.00	30.00	65.00
3-Used in **SOTI**, pg. 112; injury-to-eye panel; Fuje-a	10.00	30.00	70.00
4,5	7.50	22.50	45.00
6-10	6.35	19.00	38.00
11-20	5.00	15.00	30.00
21-30	4.20	12.50	25.00
31-38,40-44,46: 46-One pg. Frazetta-a	4.00	10.00	20.00
39-Drug mention story "The 5 Dopes"	5.85	17.50	35.00
45- "Hophead Killer" drug story	5.85	17.50	35.00
47-58,60-65,70-74: 58-Used in **POP**, pg. 79	3.60	9.00	18.00
59-Used in **SOTI**, illo "What comic-book America stands for"	16.00	48.00	110.00
66-Toth-c/a(4); 3-D effect issue (3/54); 1st "Deep Dimension" process	24.00	72.00	165.00
67- "Monkey on His Back" heroin story; 3-D effect issue	17.00	528.00	120.00
68-3-D effect issue; Toth-c (7/54)	16.00	48.00	110.00
69- "The Hot Rod Gang" dope crazy kids	5.85	17.50	35.00

*NOTE: **Biro** c-most. **Everett** a-31. **Fuje** a-3, 4, 12, 13, 17, 18, 20, 26, 27. **Guardineer** a-2-4, 10, 14, 17, 18, 20, 26-28, 32, 38-44. **Kinstler** c-69. **McWilliams** a-41, 48, 49. **Tuska** a-28, 30, 51, 64, 70.*

CRIME AND PUNISHMENT: MARSHALL LAW TAKES MANHATTAN
1989 ($4.95, 52 pgs., direct sale only, mature readers)
Epic Comics (Marvel)

	GD25	FN65	NM94
nn-Graphic album featuring Marshall Law	1.00	2.00	5.00

CRIME CAN'T WIN (Formerly Cindy Smith)
No. 41, 9/50 - No. 43, 2/51; No. 4, 4/51 - No. 12, 9/53
Marvel/Atlas Comics (TCI 41/CCC 42,43,4-12)

	GD25	FN65	NM94
41(#1)	13.50	41.00	95.00
42(#2)	8.35	25.00	50.00
43(#3)-Horror story	10.00	30.00	60.00
4(4/51),5-12: 10-Possible use in **SOTI**, pg. 161	6.35	19.00	38.00

*NOTE: **Robinson** a-9-11. **Tuska** a-43.*

CRIME CASES COMICS (Formerly Willie Comics)
No. 24, 8/50 - No. 27, 3/51; No. 5, 5/51 - No. 12, 7/52
Marvel/Atlas Comics(CnPC No.24-8/MJMC No.9-12)

	GD25	FN65	NM94
24 (#1, 52 pgs.)-True police cases	10.00	30.00	60.00
25-27(#2-4): 27-Morisi-a	6.70	20.00	40.00
5-12: 11-Robinson-a. 12-Tuska-a	5.35	16.00	32.00

CRIME CLINIC
No. 10, July-Aug, 1951 - No. 5, Summer, 1952
Ziff-Davis Publishing Co.

	GD25	FN65	NM94
10(#1)-Painted-c; origin Dr. Tom Rogers	14.00	43.00	100.00
11,3-5: 3-Used in **SOTI**, pg. 18. 4,5-Painted-c	10.00	30.00	70.00

*NOTE: All have painted covers by **Saunders**. **Starr** a-10.*

CRIME DETECTIVE COMICS
Mar-Apr, 1948 - V3#8, May-June, 1953
Hillman Periodicals

	GD25	FN65	NM94
V1#1-The Invisible 6, costumed villains app; Fuje-c/a, 15 pgs.	15.00	45.00	105.00
2,5: 5-Krigstein-a	6.70	20.00	40.00
3,4,6,7,10-12: 6-McWilliams-a	5.35	16.00	32.00
8-Kirbyish-a by McCann	5.00	15.00	30.00
9-Used in **SOTI**, pg. 16 & "Caricature of the author in a position comic book publishers wish he were in permanently" illo.	20.00	60.00	140.00
V2#1,4,7-Krigstein-a: 1-Tuska-a	5.85	17.50	35.00
2,3,5,6,8-12 (1-2/52)	4.00	12.00	24.00
V3#1-Drug use-c	4.00	12.00	24.00
2-8	4.00	10.00	20.00

*NOTE: **Briefer** a-11, V3#1. **Kinstlerish**-a by **McCann**-V2#7, V3#2. **Powell** a-10, 11. **Starr** a-10.*

CRIME DETECTOR
Jan, 1954 - No. 5, Sept, 1954
Timor Publications

	GD25	FN65	NM94
1	10.00	30.00	70.00
2	5.35	16.00	32.00
3,4	4.70	14.00	28.00
5-Disbrow-a (classic)	10.00	30.00	75.00

CRIME DOES NOT PAY (Formerly Silver Streak Comics No. 1-21)
No. 22, June, 1942 - No. 147, July, 1955 (1st crime comic)
Comic House/Lev Gleason/Golfing (Title inspired by film)

	GD25	FN65	NM94
22(23 on cover, 22 on indicia)-Origin The War Eagle & only app.; Chip Gardner begins; #22 was rebound in Complete Book of True Crime (Scarce)	143.00	430.00	1000.00
23 (Scarce)	75.00	225.00	525.00
24-Intro. & 1st app. Mr. Crime (Scarce)	68.00	205.00	475.00
25-30	39.00	116.00	270.00
31-40	22.00	65.00	150.00
41-Origin & 1st app. Officer Common Sense	16.00	48.00	110.00
42-Electrocution-c	19.00	57.00	130.00
43-46,48-50: 44,45,50 are 68 pg. issues	11.00	32.00	75.00
47-Electric chair-c	18.00	54.00	125.00
51-70: 63,64-Possible use in **SOTI**, pg. 306. 63-Contains Biro & Gleason's self censorship code of 12 listed restrictions (5/48)	10.00	30.00	60.00
71-99: 87-Chip Gardner begins, ends #99	7.50	22.50	45.00
100	8.35	25.00	50.00
101-105,107-110: 102-Chip Gardner app. 105-Used in **POP**, pg. 84	5.35	16.00	32.00
106,114-Frazetta-a, 1 pg.	5.35	16.00	32.00
111-Used in **POP**, pgs. 80 & 81; injury-to-eye story illo	5.35	16.00	32.00
112,113,115-130	4.20	12.50	25.00
131-140	4.00	10.00	20.00
141,142-Last pre-code issue; Kubert-a(1)	5.85	17.50	35.00
143,147-Kubert-a, one story each	5.85	17.50	35.00
144-146	3.60	9.00	18.00
1(Golfing-1945)	4.20	12.50	25.00
The Best of...(1944, 128 pgs.)-Series contains 4 rebound issues	68.00	205.00	475.00
...1945 issue	50.00	150.00	350.00
...1946-48 issues	35.00	105.00	245.00
...1949-50 issues	30.00	90.00	210.00
...1951-53 issues	27.00	80.00	185.00

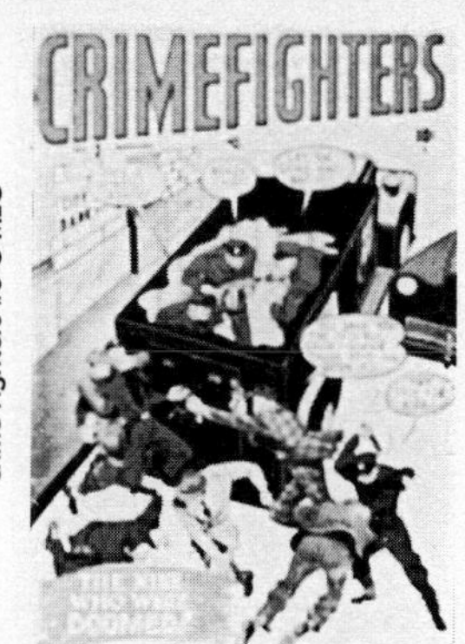

Crime Fighters #3 © MEG

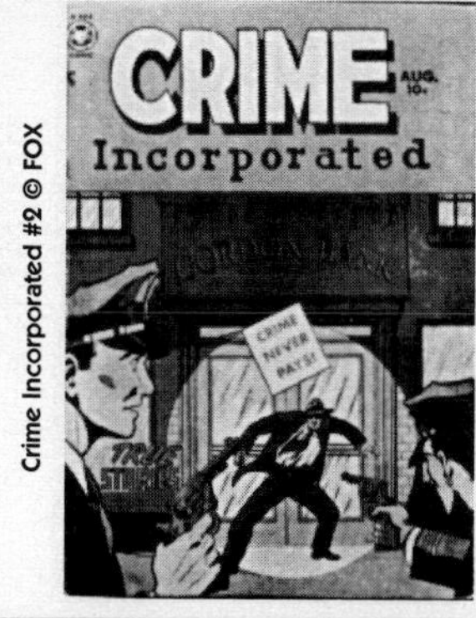

Crime Incorporated #2 © FOX

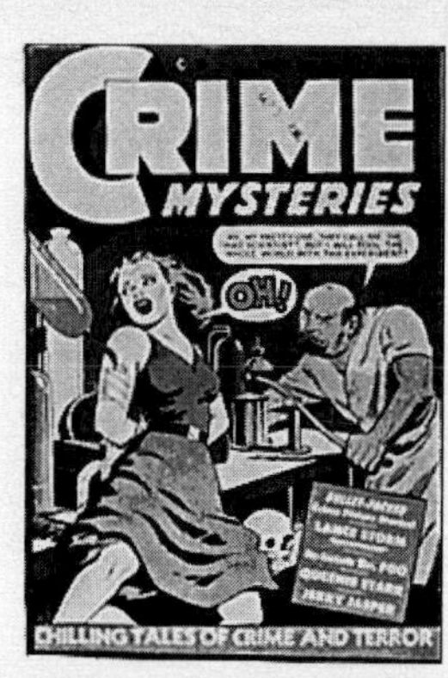

Crime Mysteries #4 © TM

NOTE: *Many issues contain violent covers and stories. Who Dunnit by* ***Guardineer****-39-42, 44-105, 108-110; Chip Gardner by* ***Bob Fujitani (Fuje)****-88-103.* ***Alderman*** *a-29, 41-44, 49.* ***Dan Barry*** *a-75.* ***Biro*** *c-1-76, 122, 142.* ***Briefer*** *a-29(2), 30, 31, 33, 37, 39.* ***G. Colan*** *a-105.* ***Fuje*** *c-88, 89, 91-94, 96, 98, 99, 102, 103.* ***Guardineer*** *a-57, 71.* ***Kubert*** *c-143.* ***Landau*** *a-118.* ***Maurer*** *a-29, 39, 41, 42.* ***McWilliams*** *a-91, 93, 95, 100-103.* ***Palais*** *a-30, 33, 37, 39, 41-43, 44(2), 46, 49.* ***Powell*** *a-146, 147.* ***Tuska*** *a-48, 50(2), 51, 52, 56, 57(2), 60-64, 66, 67, 71. Painted c-87-102. Bondage c-43, 62, 98.*

CRIME EXPOSED
June, 1948; Dec, 1950 - No. 14, June, 1952
Marvel Comics (PPI)/Marvel Atlas Comics (PrPI)

	GD25	FN65	NM94
1(6/48)	18.00	54.00	125.00
1(12/50)	11.00	32.00	75.00
2	8.35	25.00	50.00
3-11,14: 10-Used in **POP**, pg. 81	5.85	17.50	35.00
12-Krigstein & Robinson-a	6.70	20.00	40.00
13-Used in **POP**, pg. 81; Krigstein-a	7.50	22.50	45.00

NOTE: ***Maneely*** *c-8.* ***Robinson*** *a-11, 12.* ***Tuska*** *a-3, 4.*

CRIMEFIGHTERS
April, 1948 - No. 10, Nov, 1949
Marvel Comics (CmPS 1-3/CCC 4-10)

	GD25	FN65	NM94
1-Some copies are undated & could be reprints	14.00	43.00	100.00
2,3: 3-Morphine addict story	7.50	22.50	45.00
4-10: 6-Anti-Wertham editorial. 9,10-Photo-c	6.70	20.00	40.00

CRIME FIGHTERS (...Always Win)
No. 11, Sept, 1954 - No. 13, Jan, 1955
Atlas Comics (CnPC)

	GD25	FN65	NM94
11-13: 11-Maneely-a,13-Pakula, Reinman, Severin-a	7.50	22.50	45.00

CRIME FIGHTING DETECTIVE (Shock Detective Cases No. 20 on; formerly Criminals on the Run)
No. 11, Apr-May, 1950 - No. 19, June, 1952 (Based on true crime cases)
Star Publications

	GD25	FN65	NM94
11-L. B. Cole-c/a (2 pgs.); L. B. Cole-c on all	8.35	25.00	50.00
12,13,15-19: 17-Young King Cole & Dr. Doom app.	5.85	17.50	35.00
14-L. B. Cole-c/a, r/Law-Crime #2	7.50	22.50	45.00

CRIME FILES
No. 5, Sept, 1952 - No. 6, Nov, 1952
Standard Comics

	GD25	FN65	NM94
5-Alex Toth-a; used in **SOTI**, pg. 4 (text)	16.00	48.00	110.00
6-Sekowsky-a	8.35	25.00	50.00

CRIME ILLUSTRATED (Magazine, 25¢)
Nov-Dec, 1955 - No. 2, Spring, 1956 (Adult Suspense Stories on-c)
E. C. Comics

	GD25	FN65	NM94
1-Ingels & Crandall-a	10.00	30.00	65.00
2-Ingels & Crandall-a	9.15	27.50	55.00

NOTE: ***Craig*** *a-2.* ***Crandall*** *a-1, 2; c-2.* ***Evans*** *a-1.* ***Davis*** *a-2.* ***Ingels*** *a-1, 2.* ***Krigstein/Crandall*** *a-1.* ***Orlando*** *a-1, 2; c-1.*

CRIME INCORPORATED (Formerly Crimes Incorporated)
No. 2, Aug, 1950; No. 3, Aug, 1951
Fox Features Syndicate

	GD25	FN65	NM94
2	13.00	40.00	90.00
3(1951)-Hollingsworth-a	10.00	30.00	70.00

CRIME MACHINE (Magazine)
Feb, 1971 - No. 2, May, 1971 (B&W)
Skywald Publications

	GD25	FN65	NM94
1-Kubert-a(2)(r)(Avon)	2.60	7.50	18.00
2-Torres, Wildey-a; violent-c/a	2.00	6.00	14.00

CRIME MUST LOSE! (Formerly Sports Action?)
No. 4, Oct, 1950 - No. 12, April, 1952
Sports Action (Atlas Comics)

	GD25	FN65	NM94
4-Ann Brewster-a in all; c-used in N.Y. Legis. Comm. documents	10.00	30.00	70.00
5-12: 9-Robinson-a. 11-Used in **POP**, pg. 89	6.70	20.00	40.00

CRIME MUST PAY THE PENALTY (Formerly Four Favorites; Penalty #47, 48)
No. 33, Feb, 1948; No. 2, June, 1948 - No. 48, Jan, 1956
Ace Magazines (Current Books)

	GD25	FN65	NM94
33(#1, 2/48)-Becomes Four Teeners #34?	17.00	52.00	120.00
2(6/48)-Extreme violence; Palais-a?	11.50	34.00	80.00
3- "Frisco Mary" story used in Senate Investigation report, pg. 7	7.50	22.50	45.00
4,8-Transvestism stories	9.15	27.50	55.00
5-7,9,10	5.35	16.00	32.00
11-20	4.35	13.00	26.00
21-32,34-40,42-48	4.00	11.00	22.00
33(7/53)- "Dell Fabry-Junk King" drug story; mentioned in Love and Death	5.35	16.00	32.00
41-Drug story "Dealers in White Death"	5.35	16.00	32.00

NOTE: ***Cameron*** *a-29-31, 34, 35, 39-41.* ***Colan*** *a-20, 31.* ***Kremer*** *a-3, 37r.* ***Larsen*** *a-32.* ***Palais*** *a-5?,37.*

CRIME MUST STOP
October, 1952 (52 pgs.)
Hillman Periodicals

	GD25	FN65	NM94
V1#1(Scarce)-Similar to Monster Crime; Mort Lawrence, Krigstein-a	40.00	120.00	280.00

CRIME MYSTERIES (Secret Mysteries No. 16 on; combined with Crime Smashers No. 7 on)
May, 1952 - No. 15, Sept, 1954
Ribage Publishing Corp. (Trojan Magazines)

	GD25	FN65	NM94
1-Transvestism story; crime & terror stories begin	29.00	86.00	200.00
2-Marijuana story (7/52)	19.00	57.00	130.00
3-One pg. Frazetta-a	16.00	48.00	110.00
4-Cover shows girl in bondage having her blood drained; 1 pg. Frazetta-a	27.00	80.00	185.00
5-10	13.00	40.00	90.00
11,12,14	11.50	34.00	80.00
13-(5/54)-Angelo Torres 1st comic work (inks over Check's pencils); Check-a	16.00	48.00	110.00
15-Acid in face-c	19.00	57.00	130.00

NOTE: ***Fass*** *a-13; c-4, 10.* ***Hollingsworth*** *a-10-13, 15; c-2, 12, 13, 15.* ***Kiefer*** *a-4.* ***Woodbridge*** *a-13? Bondage-c-1, 8, 12.*

CRIME ON THE RUN (See Approved Comics #8)

CRIME ON THE WATERFRONT (Formerly Famous Gangsters)
No. 4, May, 1952 (Painted cover)
Realistic Publications

	GD25	FN65	NM94
4	18.00	54.00	125.00

CRIME PATROL (Formerly International #1-5; International Crime Patrol #6; becomes Crypt of Terror #17 on)
No. 7, Summer, 1948 - No. 16, Feb-Mar, 1950
E. C. Comics

	GD25	FN65	NM94
7-Intro. Captain Crime	47.00	141.00	330.00
8-14: 12-Ingels-a	43.00	130.00	300.00
15-Intro. of Crypt Keeper (inspired by Witches Tales radio show) & Crypt of Terror (see Tales From the Crypt #33 for origin); used by N.Y. Legis. Comm.; last pg. Feldstein-a	200.00	600.00	1400.00
16-2nd Crypt Keeper app.; Roussos-a	129.00	385.00	900.00

NOTE: ***Craig*** *c/a in most issues.* ***Feldstein*** *a-9-16.* ***Kiefer*** *a-8, 10, 11.* ***Moldoff*** *a-7.*

CRIME PHOTOGRAPHER (See Casey...)

CRIME REPORTER
Aug, 1948 - No. 3, Dec, 1948 (Shows Oct.)
St. John Publ. Co.

	GD25	FN65	NM94
1-Drug club story	27.00	81.00	190.00
2-Used in **SOTI**: illo- "Children told me what the man was going to do with the red-hot poker;" r/Dynamic #17 with editing; Baker-c; Tuska-a	46.00	140.00	325.00
3-Baker-c; Tuska-a	22.00	65.00	150.00

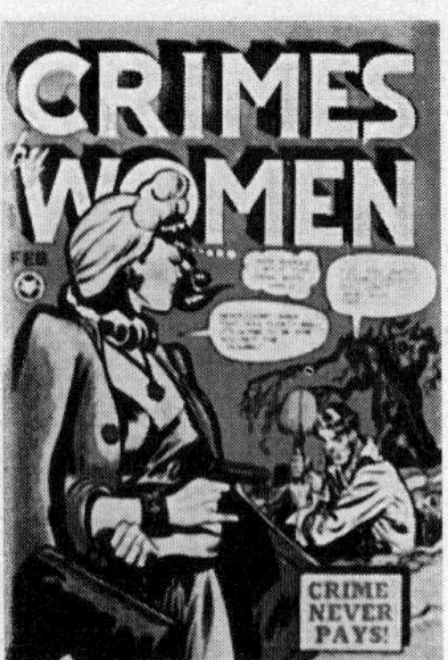

Crimes By Women #5 © FOX

Crime Suspenstories #13 © E.C. Comics

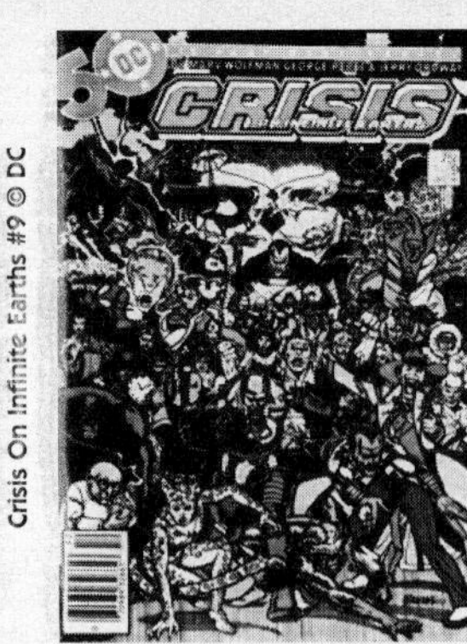

Crisis On Infinite Earths #9 © DC

CRIMES BY WOMEN
June, 1948 - No. 15, Aug, 1951; 1954 (True crime cases)
Fox Features Syndicate

	GD25	FN65	NM94
1-True story of Bonnie Parker	71.00	215.00	500.00
2,3: 3-Used in **SOTI**, pg. 234	39.00	118.00	275.00
4,5,7-9,11-15: 8-Used in **POP**.	33.00	100.00	230.00
6-Classic girl fight-c; acid-in-face panel	39.00	118.00	275.00
10-Used in **SOTI**, pg. 72	33.00	100.00	230.00
54(M.S. Publ.-'54)-Reprint; (formerly My Love Secret)	14.00	43.00	100.00

CRIMES INCORPORATED (Formerly My Past)
No. 12, June, 1950 (Crime Incorporated No. 2 on)
Fox Features Syndicate

	GD25	FN65	NM94
12	9.15	27.50	55.00

CRIMES INCORPORATED (See Fox Giants)

CRIME SMASHER
Summer, 1948 (One Shot)
Fawcett Publications

	GD25	FN65	NM94
1-Formerly Spy Smasher; see Whiz #76	27.00	81.00	190.00

CRIME SMASHERS (Becomes Secret Mysteries No. 16 on)
Oct, 1950 - No. 15, Mar, 1953
Ribage Publishing Corp.(Trojan Magazines)

	GD25	FN65	NM94
1-Used in **SOTI**, pg. 19,20, & illo "A girl raped and murdered;" Sally the Sleuth begins	46.00	140.00	325.00
2-Kubert-c	24.00	72.00	165.00
3,4	17.00	52.00	120.00
5-Wood-a	23.00	70.00	160.00
6,8-11	13.50	41.00	95.00
7-Female heroin junkie story	14.00	43.00	100.00
12-Injury to eye panel; 1 pg. Frazetta-a	15.00	45.00	105.00
13-Used in **POP**, pgs. 79,80; 1 pg. Frazetta-a	14.00	43.00	100.00
14,15	13.00	40.00	90.00

NOTE: ***Hollingsworth*** *a-14.* ***Kiefer*** *a-15. Bondage c-7, 9.*

CRIME SUSPENSTORIES (Formerly Vault of Horror No. 12-14)
No. 15, Oct-Nov, 1950 - No. 27, Feb-Mar, 1955
E. C. Comics

	GD25	FN65	NM94
15-Identical to #1 in content; #1 printed on outside front cover. #15 (formerly "The Vault of Horror") printed and blackened out on inside front cover with Vol. 1, No. 1 printed over it. Evidently, several of No. 15 were printed before a decision was made not to drop the Vault of Horror and Haunt of Fear series. The print run was stopped on No. 15 and continued on No. 1. All of No. 15 were changed as described above.	115.00	343.00	800.00
1	81.00	242.00	565.00
2	48.00	145.00	335.00
3-5: 3-Poe adaptation. 4,5-Old Witch stories	33.00	100.00	230.00
6-10	27.00	80.00	185.00
11,12,14,15: 15-The Old Witch guest stars	20.00	60.00	140.00
13,16-Williamson-a	23.00	70.00	160.00
17-Williamson/Frazetta-a (6 pgs.)	25.00	75.00	175.00
18,19: 19-Used in **SOTI**, pg. 235	17.00	52.00	120.00
20-Cover used in **SOTI**, illo "Cover of a children's comic book"	23.00	70.00	160.00
21,24-27: 24- "Food For Thought" similar to "Cave In" in Amazing Detective Cases #13 (1952)	12.00	36.00	85.00
22,23-Used in Senate investigation on juvenile delinquency. 22-Ax decapitation-c	17.00	52.00	120.00

NOTE: ***Craig*** *a-1-21; c-1-18, 20-22.* ***Crandall*** *a-18-26.* ***Davis*** *a-4, 5, 7, 9-12, 20.* ***Elder*** *a-17,18.* ***Evans*** *a-15, 19, 21, 23, 25, 27; c-23, 24.* ***Feldstein*** *c-19.* ***Ingels*** *a-1-12, 14, 15, 27.* ***Kamen*** *a-2, 4-18, 20-27; c-25-27.* ***Krigstein*** *a-22, 24, 25, 27.* ***Kurtzman*** *a-1, 3.* ***Orlando*** *a-16, 22, 24, 26.* ***Wood*** *a-1, 3. Issues No. 11-15 have E. C. "quickie" stories. No. 25 contains the famous "Are You a Red Dupe?" editorial. Ray Bradbury adaptations-15, 17.*

CRIME SUSPENSTORIES
Nov, 1992 - Present ($1.50/$2.00)
Russ Cochran

	GD25	FN65	NM94
1-3: 1,2-r/Crime SuspenStories #1,2			1.50
4-8 ($2.00)		.80	2.00

CRIMINALS ON THE RUN (Formerly Young King Cole)
(Crime Fighting Detective No. 11 on)
V4#1, Aug-Sept, 1948 - #10, Dec-Jan, 1949-50
Premium Group (Novelty Press)

	GD25	FN65	NM94
V4#1-Young King Cole continues	13.00	40.00	90.00
2-6: 6-Dr. Doom app.	10.00	30.00	70.00
7-Classic "Fish in the Face" c by L. B. Cole	25.00	75.00	175.00
V5#1,2 (#8,9): 9-L. B. Cole-c	10.00	30.00	65.00
10-L. B. Cole-c	10.00	30.00	65.00

NOTE: *Most issues have* ***L. B. Cole*** *covers.* ***McWilliams*** *a-V4#6, 7, V5#2; c-V4#5.*

CRIMSON AVENGER, THE (See Detective Comics #20 for 1st app.)
(Also see Leading Comics #1 & World's Best/Finest Comics)
June, 1988 - No. 4, Sept, 1988 ($1.00, limited series)
DC Comics

	GD25	FN65	NM94
1-4		.50	1.00

CRISIS ON INFINITE EARTHS (Also see Official... Index)
Apr, 1985 - No. 12, Mar, 1986 (12 issue maxi-series)
DC Comics

	GD25	FN65	NM94
1-1st DC app. Blue Beetle & Detective Karp from Charlton; Perez-c on all		1.70	4.25
2-6: 6-Intro Charlton's Capt. Atom, Nightshade, Question, Judomaster, Peacemaker & Thunderbolt		.90	2.25
7-Double size; death of Supergirl		1.70	4.25
8-Death of Flash	.90	2.30	5.50
9-11: 9-Intro. Charlton's Ghost. 10-Intro. Charlton's Banshee, Dr. Spectro, Image, Punch & Jewellee		.90	2.25
12-(52 pgs.)-Deaths of Dove, Kole, Lori Lemaris, Sunburst, G.A. Robin & Huntress; Kid Flash becomes new Flash; 3rd & final DC app. 3 Lt. Marvels		1.70	4.25

CRITICAL ERROR (Dark Horse)(Value: cover or less)

CRITICAL MASS (See A Shadowline Saga: Critical Mass)

CRITTERS (Also see Usagi Yojimbo Summer Special)
1986 - No. 50, 1990 ($1.70/$2.00, B&W)
Fantagraphics Books

	GD25	FN65	NM94
1-Cutey Bunny, Usagi Yojimbo app.		1.10	2.75
2-11: 3,10,11-Usagi Yojimbo app. 11-Christmas Special (68 pgs.); Usagi Yojimbo		.90	2.25
12-22,24-49: 14,38-Usagi Yojimbo app. 22-Watchmen parody; two diff. covers exist		.70	1.80
23-With Alan Moore Flexi-disc ($3.95)		1.70	4.25
50 ($4.95, 84 pgs.)-Neil the Horse, Capt. Jack, Sam & Max & Usagi Yojimbo app.; Quagmire, Shaw-a	1.00	2.00	5.00
Special 1 (1/88, $2.00)		.80	2.00

CROMWELL STONE (Dark Horse)(Value: cover or less)

CROSLEY'S HOUSE OF FUN (Also see Tee and Vee Crosley...)
1950 (32 pgs.; full color; paper cover)
Crosley Div. AVCO Mfg. Corp. (Giveaway)

	GD25	FN65	NM94
nn-Strips revolve around Crosley appliances	4.00	12.00	24.00

CROSS AND THE SWITCHBLADE, THE (Spire Christian)(Value: cover or less)

CROSSFIRE (Spire Christian)(Value: cover or less)

CROSSFIRE (Eclipse)(Value: cover or less)

CROSSFIRE AND RAINBOW (Eclipse)(Value: cover or less)

CROSSING THE ROCKIES (See Classics Illustrated Special Issue)

CROSSROADS (First)(Value: cover or less)

CROW, THE (Also see Caliber Presents)
Feb, 1989 - No. 4, 1989 ($1.95, B&W, mini-series)
Caliber Press

	GD25	FN65	NM94
1-By Jim O'Barr	7.00	21.00	50.00

Crown Comics #5

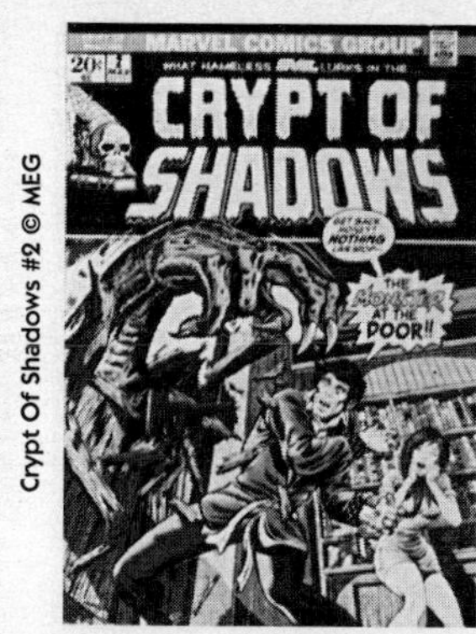

Crypt Of Shadows #2 © MEG

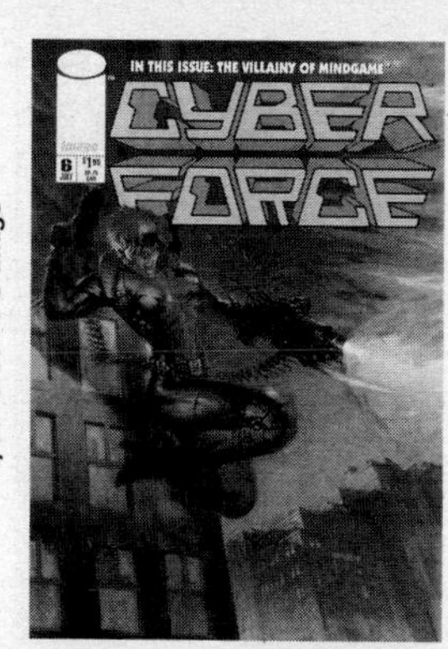

IN THIS ISSUE: THE VILLAINY OF MINDGAME
CYBER
FORCE

Cyberforce #6 © Image

	GD25	FN65	NM94
1-3-2nd printings		1.80	4.50
2,4	2.50	6.00	15.00
2-3rd printing		1.80	4.50
3-(Scarcer)	2.90	8.60	20.00

CROW, THE
Jan, 1992 - No. 3, 1992 ($4.95, B&W, 68 pgs.)
Tundra Publishing, Ltd.

1-3-Reprints	1.30	3.00	7.50

CROWN COMICS
Winter, 1944-45; No. 2, Sum, 1945 - No. 19, July, 1949
Golfing/McCombs Publ.

1- "The Oblong Box" E.A. Poe adaptation	24.00	73.00	170.00
2,3-Baker-a	13.00	40.00	90.00
4-6-Baker-c/a; Voodah app. #4,5	13.50	41.00	95.00
7-Feldstein, Baker, Kamen-a; Baker-c	13.00	40.00	90.00
8-Baker-a; Voodah app.	12.00	36.00	85.00
9-11,13-19: Voodah in #10-19. 13-New logo	7.50	22.50	45.00
12-Feldstein?, Starr-a	8.35	25.00	50.00

NOTE: ***Bolle** a-11, 13-16, 18, 19; c-11p, 15. **Powell** a-19. **Starr** a-11-13; c-11i.*

CRUCIBLE
Feb, 1993 - No. 6, July, 1993 ($1.25, mini-series)
DC Comics

1-(99¢)-Quesada-c(p) & layouts begin; neon ink-c			1.00
2-6: 2-Last Quesada-c. 4-Last Quesada layouts			1.25

CRUSADER FROM MARS (See Tops in Adventure)
Jan-Mar, 1952 - No. 2, Fall, 1952 (Painted-c)
Ziff-Davis Publ. Co.

1-Cover is dated Spring	50.00	150.00	350.00
2-Bondage-c	41.00	122.00	285.00

CRUSADER RABBIT (See 4-Color No. 735,805)

CRUSADERS, THE (Chick)(Value: cover or less)

CRUSADERS (Southern Knights No. 2 on)
1982 (Magazine size, B&W)
Guild Publications

1-1st app. Southern Knights	1.00	2.00	5.00

CRUSADERS, THE (Also see Black Hood, The Jaguar, The Comet, The Fly, Legend of the Shield, The Mighty... & The Webb)
May, 1992 - No. 8, Dec, 1992 ($1.00/$1.25)
Impact Comics (DC Comics)

1-Contains 3 Impact trading cards			1.25
2-8			1.00

CRY FOR DAWN
1989 - No. 9 ($2.25, B&W, adult readers)
Cry For Dawn Pub.

1	3.70	11.00	26.00
1-2nd, 3rd printing		1.20	3.00
2	1.60	4.70	11.00
2-2nd printing		.80	2.00
3	1.20	2.90	7.00
4-9		1.20	3.00

CRYING FREEMAN (Viz)(Value: cover or less)

CRYIN' LION COMICS
Fall, 1944 - No. 3, Spring, 1945
William H. Wise Co.

1-Funny animal	11.00	32.00	75.00
2,3: 2-Hitler app.	7.50	22.50	45.00

CRYPT OF SHADOWS
Jan, 1973 - No. 21, Nov, 1975 (#1 & 2 are 20¢)
Marvel Comics Group

	GD25	FN65	NM94
1-Wolverton-r/Advs. Into Terror #7		1.80	4.50
2-21: 2-Starlin/Everett-c		.90	2.25

NOTE: ***Briefer** a-2r. **Ditko** a-13r, 18-20r. **Everett** a-6, 14r; c-2i. **Heath** a-1r. **Mort Lawrence** a-1r, 8r. **Maneely** a-2r. **Moldoff** a-8. **Powell** a-12r, 14r.*

CRYPT OF TERROR (Formerly Crime Patrol; Tales From the Crypt No. 20 on)
No. 17, Apr-May, 1950 - No. 19, Aug-Sept, 1950
E. C. Comics

17-1st New Trend to hit stands	200.00	600.00	1400.00
18,19	129.00	385.00	900.00

NOTE: ***Craig** c/a-17-19. **Feldstein** a-17-19. **Ingels** a-19. **Kurtzman** a-18. **Wood** a-18. Canadian reprints known; see Table of Contents.*

CUPID
Dec, 1949 - No. 2, Mar, 1950
Marvel Comics (U.S.A.)

1-Photo-c	10.00	30.00	60.00
2-Betty Page ('50s pin-up queen) photo-c; Powell-a (see My Love #4)	17.00	52.00	120.00

CURIO
1930's(?) (Tabloid size, 16-20 pgs.)
Harry 'A' Chesler

nn	13.50	41.00	95.00

CURLY KAYOE COMICS (Boxing)
1946 - No. 8, 1950; Jan, 1958
United Features Syndicate/Dell Publ. Co.

1 (1946)-Strip-r (Fritzi Ritz); biography of Sam Leff, Kayoe's artist	11.00	32.00	75.00
2	6.35	19.00	38.00
3-8	4.35	13.00	26.00
United Presents...(Fall, 1948)	4.35	13.00	26.00
4-Color 871 (Dell, 1/58)	4.00	11.00	22.00

CURSE OF THE WEIRD
Dec, 1993 - No. 4, Mar, 1994 ($1.25, mini-series)(Pre-code horror-r)
Marvel Comics

1-4: 1,3,4-Wolverton-r(1-Eye of Doom; 3-Where Monsters Dwell; 4-The End of the World). 2-Orlando-r. 4-Zombie-r by Everett; painted-c			1.25

NOTE: ***Briefer** r-2. **Ditko** r-1, 2; c(r)-1. **Everett** r-1. **Heath** r-1-3. **Kubert** r-3. **Wolverton** r-1, 3.*

CUSTER'S LAST FIGHT
1950
Avon Periodicals

nn-Partial reprint of Cowpuncher #1	12.00	36.00	85.00

CUTEY BUNNY (See Army Surplus Komikz Featuring...)

CUTIE PIE
May, 1955 - No. 3, Dec, 1955; No. 4, Feb, 1956; No. 5, Aug, 1956
Junior Reader's Guild (Lev Gleason)

1	4.20	12.50	25.00
2-5: 4-Misdated 2/55	3.00	7.50	15.00

CYBER CRUSH (Fleetway/Quality)(Value: cover or less)

CYBERFORCE
Oct, 1992 - No. 4, 1993; No. 0, Sept, 1993 ($1.95, mini-series)
Image Comics

1-Coupon for Image Comics #0; Silvestri-c/a in all	1.00	2.00	5.00
1-With coupon missing		.80	2.00
2 (3/93), 3,4: 3-Pitt-c/story. 4-Foil-c; Stryke Force back-up (1st app. in comics)		.80	2.00
0 (9/93)-By Walt Simonson (c/a/script)		.80	2.00

CYBERFORCE
Nov, 1993 - Present ($1.95)
Image Comics

1-9-Marc Silvestri/Keith Williams-a (covers #1-5)		.80	2.00

CYBERFORCE UNIVERSE SOURCEBOOK

Cyber 7 #3 © Shuho Itahashi's

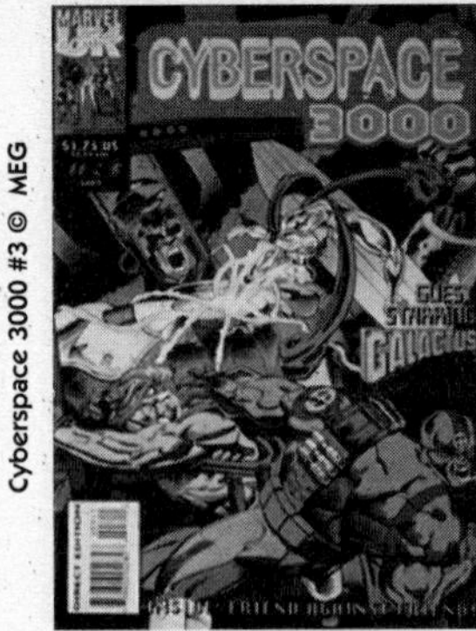

Cyberspace 3000 #3 © MEG

Daffy Duck #22 © Warner Bros.

GD25 FN65 NM94

Aug, 1994 ($2.50)
Image Comics
1-Silvestri-c 1.00 2.50

CYBERPUNK (Innovation)(Value: cover or less)

CYBERPUNK: THE SERAPHIM FILES (Innovation)(Value: cover or less)

CYBERRAD
1991 - No. 7, 1992 ($2.00)(Direct sale & newsstand-c variations)
V2#1, - Present ($2.00)
Continuity Comics
1-7: 5-Glow-in-the-dark-c by N. Adams (direct sale only). 6-Contains 4 pg. fold-out poster; N. Adams layouts .80 2.00
V2#1-($2.95, direct sale ed.)-Die-cut-c w/B&W hologram on-c; Neal Adams sketches 1.20 3.00
V2#1-($2.50, newsstand ed.)-Without sketches 1.00 2.50
V2#2-5: 2-N. Adams-c .80 2.00

CYBERRAD DEATHWATCH 2000 (Becomes CyberRad w/#2, 7/93)
Apr, 1993 - Present ($2.50)
Continuity Comics
1,2: 1-Bagged w/2 cards; Adams-c & layouts & plots. 2-Bagged w/card; Adams scripts 1.00 2.50

CYBER 7 (Eclipse)(Value: cover or less)

CYBERSPACE 3000 (Marvel Comics UK)(Value: cover or less)

CYCLONE COMICS (Also see Whirlwind Comics)
June, 1940 - No. 5, Nov, 1940
Bilbara Publishing Co.
1-Origin Tornado Tom; Volton (the human generator), Tornado Tom, Kingdom of the Moon, Mister Q begin (1st app. of each) 71.00 215.00 500.00
2 39.00 118.00 275.00
3-5 34.00 100.00 235.00

CYNTHIA DOYLE, NURSE IN LOVE (Formerly Sweetheart Diary)
No. 66, Oct, 1962 - No. 74, Feb, 1964
Charlton Publications
66-74 .80 2.00 4.00

DAFFY (Daffy Duck No. 18 on)(See Looney Tunes)
#457, 3/53 - #30, 7-9/62; #31, 10-12/62 - #145, 1983 (No #132,133)
Dell Publishing Co./Gold Key No. 31-127/Whitman No. 128 on
4-Color 457(#1)-Elmer Fudd x-overs begin 10.00 30.00 60.00
4-Color 536,615('55) 5.00 15.00 30.00
4(1-3/56)-11('57) 3.60 9.00 18.00
12-19(1958-59) 2.80 7.00 14.00
20-40(1960-64) 1.40 3.50 7.00
41-60(1964-68) 1.00 2.50 5.00
61-90(1969-74)-Road Runner in most 1.40 3.50
91-131,134-145(1974-83) 1.75
Mini-Comic 1 (1976; 3-1/4x6-1/2") 1.00
NOTE: *Reprint issues-No.41-46, 48, 50, 53-55; 58, 59, 65, 67, 69, 73, 81, 96, 103-108; 136-142, 144, 145(1/3-2/3-r). (See March of Comics No. 277, 288, 303, 313, 331, 347, 357,375, 387, 397, 402, 413, 425, 437, 460).*

DAFFYDILS
1911 (52 pgs.; 6x8"; B&W; hardcover)
Cupples & Leon Co.
nn-By Tad 20.00 60.00 140.00

DAFFY TUNES COMICS
June, 1947; No. 12, Aug, 1947
Four-Star Publications
nn 6.35 19.00 38.00
12-Al Fago-c/a; funny animal 5.35 16.00 32.00

DAGAR, DESERT HAWK (Captain Kidd No. 24 on; formerly All Great)
No. 14, Feb, 1948 - No. 23, Apr, 1949 (No #17,18)
Fox Features Syndicate
14-Tangi & Safari Cary begin; Edmond Good bondage-c/a 44.00 133.00 310.00
15,16-E. Good-a; 15-Bondage-c 27.00 81.00 190.00
19,20,22: 19-Used in **SOTI**, pg. 180 (Tangi) 24.00 72.00 165.00
21- "Bombs & Bums Away" panel in "Flood of Death" story used in **SOTI** 27.00 80.00 185.00
23-Bondage-c 25.00 75.00 175.00
NOTE: *Tangi by* ***Kamen****-14-16, 19, 20; c-20, 21.*

GD25 FN65 NM94

DAGAR THE INVINCIBLE (Tales of Sword & Sorcery...) (Also see Dan Curtis Giveaways & Gold Key Spotlight)
Oct, 1972 - No. 18, Dec, 1976; No. 19, Apr, 1982
Gold Key
1-Origin; intro. Villains Olstellon & Scor 1.70 5.00 12.00
2-5: 3-Intro. Graylin, Dagar's woman; Jarn x-over 1.00 2.50 6.00
6-1st Dark Gods story 1.00 2.00 5.00
7-10: 9-Intro. Torgus. 10-1st Three Witches story 1.60 4.00
11-18: 13-Durak & Torgus x-over; story continues in Dr. Spektor #15. 14-Dagar's origin retold. 18-Origin retold 1.00 2.50
19-Origin-r/#18 1.20
NOTE: *Durak app. in 7, 12, 13. Tragg app. in 5, 11.*

DAGWOOD (Chic Young's) (Also see Blondie Comics)
Sept, 1950 - No. 140, Nov, 1965
Harvey Publications
1 10.00 30.00 65.00
2 5.35 16.00 32.00
3-10 4.35 13.00 26.00
11-30 3.20 8.00 16.00
31-70 1.80 4.50 9.00
71-100 1.40 3.50 7.00
101-128,130,135 1.00 2.50 5.00
129,131-134,136-140-All are 68-pg. issues 1.50 3.75 7.50
NOTE: *Popeye and other one page strips appeared in early issues.*

DAGWOOD SPLITS THE ATOM (Also see Topix V8#4)
1949 (Science comic with King Features characters) (Giveaway)
King Features Syndicate
nn-Half comic, half text; Popeye, Olive Oyl, Henry, Mandrake, Little King, Katzenjammer Kids app. 4.00 12.00 24.00

DAI KAMIKAZE! (Now)(Value: cover or less)

DAISY AND DONALD (See Walt Disney Showcase No. 8)
May, 1973 - No. 59, 1984 (no No. 48)
Gold Key/Whitman No. 42 on
1-Barks-r/WDC&S #280,308 1.70 5.00 12.00
2-5: 4-Barks-r/WDC&S #224 1.00 2.50 6.00
6-10 1.00 2.00 5.00
11-20 1.60 4.00
21-47,49,50: 32-r/WDC&S #308. 50-r/#3 1.20 3.00
51-Barks-r/4-Color #1150 .80 2.00
52-59: 52-r/#2. 55-r/#5 1.50

DAISY & HER PUPS (Blondie's Dogs)(Formerly Blondie Comics #20)
No. 21, 7/51 - No. 27, 7/52; No. 8, 9/52 - No. 25, 7/55
Harvey Publications
21-27 (#1-7): 26,27 have No. 6 & 7 on cover but No. 26 & 27 on inside 1.80 4.50 9.00
8-25: 19-25-Exist? 1.40 3.50 7.00

DAISY COMICS
Dec, 1936 (Small size: 5-1/4x7-1/2")
Eastern Color Printing Co.
nn-Joe Palooka, Buck Rogers (2 pgs. from Famous Funnies No. 18), Napoleon Flying to Fame, Butty & Fally 27.00 80.00 185.00

DAISY DUCK & UNCLE SCROOGE PICNIC TIME (See Dell Giant #33)

DAISY DUCK & UNCLE SCROOGE SHOW BOAT (See Dell Giant #55)

Dale Evans Comics #20 © DC

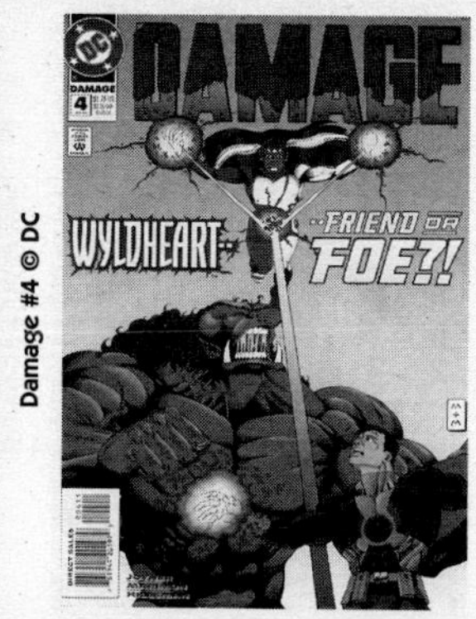

Damage #4 © DC

Dances With Demons #2 © MEG

GD25 FN65 NM94

DAISY DUCK'S DIARY (See Dynabrite Comics, Four Color No. 600, 659, 743, 858, 948, 1055, 1150, 1247 & Walt Disney's Comics & Stories #298)

DAISY HANDBOOK
1946; No. 2, 1948 (10¢, 132 pgs.)(Pocket-size)
Daisy Manufacturing Co.

1-Buck Rogers, Red Ryder; Wolverton-a(2 pgs.) 30.00 90.00 210.00
2-Captain Marvel & Ibis the Invincible, Red Ryder, Boy Commandos & Robotman; Wolverton-a (2 pgs.); contains 8 pg. color catalog
30.00 90.00 210.00

DAISY LOW OF THE GIRL SCOUTS
1954, 1965 (16 pgs.; paper cover)
Girl Scouts of America

1954-Story of Juliette Gordon Low 4.00 10.00 20.00
1965 1.60 4.00 8.00

DAISY MAE (See Oxydol-Dreft)

DAISY'S RED RYDER GUN BOOK
1955 (25¢, 132 pgs.)(Pocket-size)
Daisy Manufacturing Co.

nn-Boy Commandos, Red Ryder; 1 pg. Wolverton-a 19.00 58.00 135.00

DAKOTA LIL (See Fawcett Movie Comics)

DAKOTA NORTH
June, 1986 - No. 5, Feb, 1987
Marvel Comics Group

1-5 1.00

DAKTARI (Ivan Tors) (TV)
July, 1967 - No. 3, Oct, 1968; No. 4, Sept, 1969 (All have photo-c)
Dell Publishing Co.

1 4.00 11.00 22.00
2-4 3.00 7.50 15.00

DALE EVANS COMICS (Also see Queen of the West...)
Sept-Oct, 1948 - No. 24, July-Aug, 1952 (No. 1-19: 52 pgs.)
National Periodical Publications

1-Dale Evans & her horse Buttermilk begin; Sierra Smith begins by Alex Toth
57.00 171.00 400.00
2-Alex Toth-a 29.00 86.00 200.00
3-11-Alex Toth-a 24.00 72.00 165.00
12-24: 12-Target-c 11.50 34.00 80.00
NOTE: *Photo-c-1, 2, 4-14.*

DALGODA (Fantagraphics)(Value: cover or less)

DALTON BOYS, THE
1951
Avon Periodicals

1-(Number on spine)-Kinstler-c 11.00 32.00 75.00

DAMAGE
Apr, 1994 - Present ($1.75/$1.95)
DC Comics

1-4 .70 1.75
5,6: 5-Begin $1.95-c. 6-(9/94)-Zero Hour .80 2.00
0,7-11: 0-(10/94) .80 2.00

DAMAGE CONTROL (See Marvel Comics Presents #19)
5/89 - No. 4, 8/89; V2#1, 12/89 - No. 4, 2/90 ($1.00)
V3#1, 6/91 - No. 4, 9/91 ($1.25, all are mini-series)
Marvel Comics

V1#1-4,V2#1,3: V1#4-Wolverine app. 1.00
V2#2,4-Punisher app. 1.00
V3#1-4: 1-Spider-Man app. 2-New Warriors app. 3,4-Silver Surfer app. 4-Infinity Guantlet parody 1.00

DANCE OF LIFEY DEATH, THE (Dark Horse)(Value: cover or less)

DANCES WITH DEMONS (See Marvel Frontier Comics Unlimited)
Sept, 1993 - No. 4, Dec, 1993 ($1.95, mini-series)
Marvel Frontier Comics

1-($2.95)-Foil embossed-c 1.20 3.00
2-4 .80 2.00

DAN CURTIS GIVEAWAYS
1974 (24 pgs.) (3x6") (In color, all reprints)
Western Publishing Co.

1-Dark Shadows, 2-Star Trek, 3-The Twilight Zone, 4-Ripley's Believe It or Not!, 5-Turok, Son of Stone (partial-r/Turok #78), 6-Star Trek, 7-The Occult Files of Dr. Spektor, 8-Dagar the Invincible, 9-Grimm's Ghost Stories
Set... 3.00 9.00 30.00

DANDEE
1947
Four Star Publications

nn 4.70 14.00 28.00

DAN DUNN (See Crackajack Funnies, Detective Dan, Famous Feature Stories & Red Ryder)

DANDY COMICS (Also see Happy Jack Howard)
Spring, 1947 - No. 7, Spring, 1948
E. C. Comics

1-Funny animal; Vince Fago-a in all; Dandy in all 25.00 75.00 175.00
2 18.00 54.00 125.00
3-7: 3-Intro Handy Andy who is c-feature #3 on 13.50 41.00 95.00

DANGER
January, 1953 - No. 11, Aug, 1954
Comic Media/Allen Hardy Assoc.

1-Heck-c/a 10.00 30.00 65.00
2,3,5-7,9-11: 6- "Narcotics" story; begin spy theme 5.00 15.00 30.00
4-Marijuana cover/story 7.00 21.00 42.00
8-Bondage/torture/headlights panels 8.00 24.00 48.00
NOTE: ***Morisi** a-2, 5, 6(3), 10; c-2. Contains some reprints from Danger & Dynamite.*

DANGER (Jim Bowie No. 15 on; formerly Comic Media title)
No. 12, June, 1955 - No. 14, Oct, 1955
Charlton Comics Group

12(#1) 5.85 17.50 35.00
13,14: 14-r/#12 4.70 14.00 28.00

DANGER
1964
Super Comics

Super Reprint #10-12 (Black Dwarf; #10-r/Great Comics #1 by Novack. #11-r/Johnny Danger #1. #12-r/Red Seal #?), #15-r/Spy Cases #26. #16-Unpublished Chesler material (Yankee Girl), #17-r/Scoop #8 (Capt. Courage & Enchanted Dagger), #18(nd)-r/Guns Against Gangsters #5 (Gun-Master, Annie Oakley, The Chameleon; L.B. Cole-r)
1.60 4.00 8.00

DANGER AND ADVENTURE (Formerly This Magazine Is Haunted; Robin Hood and His Merry Men No. 28 on)
No. 22, Feb, 1955 - No. 27, Feb, 1956
Charlton Comics

22-Ibis the Invincible-c/story; Nyoka app.; last pre-code issue; Ditko-a in all
8.35 25.00 50.00
23-Lance O'Casey-c/story; Nyoka app. 8.35 25.00 50.00
24-27: 24-Mike Danger & Johnny Adventure begin 5.00 15.00 30.00

DANGER IS OUR BUSINESS!
1953(Dec.) - No. 10, June, 1955
Toby Press

1-Captain Comet by Williamson/Frazetta-a, 6 pgs. (science fiction)
36.00 107.00 250.00
2 8.35 25.00 50.00
3-10 6.70 20.00 40.00
I.W. Reprint #9('64)-Williamson/Frazetta-r/#1; Kinstler-c
8.35 25.00 50.00

DANGER IS THEIR BUSINESS (See A-1 Comics No. 50)

Daredevil #11 © MEG

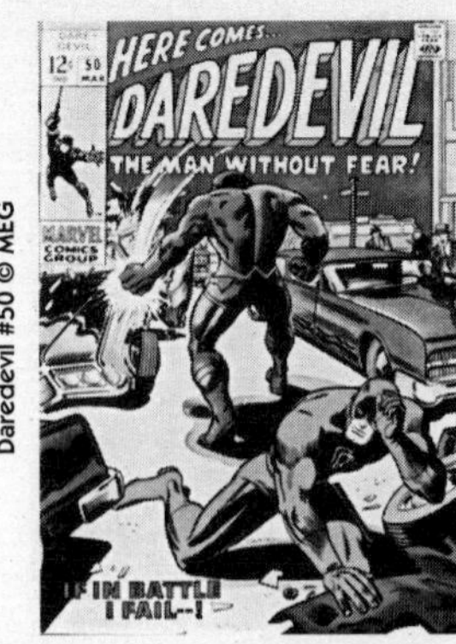

Daredevil #50 © MEG

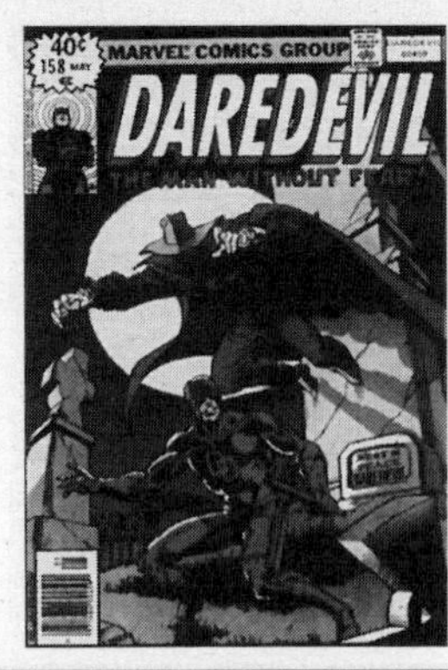

Daredevil #158 © MEG

GD25 FN65 NM94

DANGER MAN (See 4-Color No. 1231)

DANGER TRAIL (Also see Showcase #50, 51)
July-Aug, 1950 - No. 5, Mar-Apr, 1951 (52 pgs.)
National Periodical Publications

1-King Faraday begins, ends #4; Toth-a in all 82.00 246.00 575.00
2 60.00 182.00 425.00
3-(Rare; considered the rarest early '50s DC comic)
91.00 272.00 635.00
4,5: 5-Johnny Peril-c/story (moves to Sensation Comics #107); new logo
54.00 160.00 375.00

DANGER TRAIL
Apr, 1993 - No. 4, July, 1993 ($1.50, mini-series)
National Periodical Publications

1-4: Gulacy-c on all 1.50

DANGER UNLIMITED
Feb, 1994 - No. 4, May, 1994 ($2.00, mini-series)
Dark Horse Comics (Legend)

1-4: 1-1st app. Thermal; Byrne-a & scripts; intro Torch of Liberty & Golgotha (cameo) by Byrne (scripts) in back-up story. 2-Byrne-a. 3,4-Byrne-a/stories
.80 2.00

DANIEL BOONE (See The Exploits of..., Fighting..., 4-Color No. 1163, Frontier Scout..., The Legends of... & March of Comics No. 306)

DAN'L BOONE
Sept, 1955 - No. 8, Sept, 1957
Magazine Enterprises/Sussex Publ. Co. No. 2 on

1 10.00 30.00 70.00
2 7.00 21.00 42.00
3-8 5.35 16.00 32.00

DANIEL BOONE (TV) (See March of Comics No. 306)
Jan, 1965 - No. 15, Apr, 1969 (All have Fess Parker photo-c)
Gold Key

1 10.00 30.00 65.00
2 5.35 16.00 32.00
3-5 4.00 10.00 20.00
6-15 2.40 6.00 12.00

DANNY BLAZE (...Firefighter) (Nature Boy No. 3 on)
Aug, 1955 - No. 2, Oct, 1955
Charlton Comics

1,2 5.35 16.00 32.00

DANNY DINGLE (See Single Series #17 & Sparkler Comics)

DANNY KAYE'S BAND FUN BOOK
1959
H & A Selmer (Giveaway)

nn 4.70 14.00 28.00

DANNY THOMAS SHOW, THE (See 4-Color No. 1180,1249)

DARBY O'GILL & THE LITTLE PEOPLE (See 4-Color No. 1024 & Movie Comics)

DARE (Fantagraphics)(Value: cover or less)

DAREDEVIL (...& the Black Widow #92-107 on-c only; see Giant-Size..., Marvel Advs., Marvel Graphic Novel #24, Marvel Super Heroes, '66 & Spider-Man and...)
April, 1964 - Present
Marvel Comics Group GD25 FN65 VF82 NM94

1-Origin & 1st app. Daredevil; reprinted in Marvel Super Heroes #1 (1966); death of Battling Murdock; intro Foggy Nelson & Karen Page; Everett-c/a
144.00 430.00 865.00 1300.00
GD25 FN65 NM94
2-Fantastic Four cameo; 2nd app. Electro (Spidey villain); Thing guest star;
39.00 117.00 390.00
3-Origin & 1st app. The Owl (villain) 27.00 81.00 270.00

GD25 FN65 NM94

4 26.00 78.00 260.00
5-Minor costume change; Wood-a begins 17.00 50.00 165.00
6,8-10: 8-Origin/1st app. Stilt-Man 10.00 35.00 115.00
7-Daredevil battles Sub-Mariner & dons new red costume (4/65)
17.00 50.00 165.00
11-15: 12-Romita's 1st work at Marvel; 1st app. Plunderer; Ka-Zar app. 13-Facts about Ka-Zar's origin; Kirby-a 7.00 20.00 60.00
16,17-Spider-Man x-over. 16-1st Romita-a on Spider-Man (5/66)
8.00 23.00 75.00
18-20: 18-Origin & 1st app. Gladiator 4.40 13.00 44.00
21-26,28-30: 24-Ka-Zar app. 4.00 8.00 30.00
27-Spider-Man x-over 3.30 10.00 33.00
31-40: 38-Fantastic Four x-over; cont'd in F.F. #73. 39-1st Exterminator (later becomes Death-Stalker) 2.20 7.00 22.00
41-49: 41-Death Mike Murdock. 42-1st app. Jester. 43-Daredevil battles Captain America; origin partially retold. 45-Statue of Liberty photo-c
2.00 6.00 17.00
50-52-B. Smith-a 2.00 6.00 20.00
53-Origin retold; last 12¢ issue 3.70 9.00 22.00
54-56,58-60: 54-Spider-Man cameo. 56-1st app. Death's Head (9/69); story cont'd in #57 (not same as new Death's Head) 1.70 4.20 10.00
57-Reveals i.d. to Karen Page; Death's Head app. 2.00 6.00 11.00
61-99: 79-Stan Lee cameo. 81-Oversize issue; Black Widow begins (11/71). 83-B. Smith layouts/Weiss-p. 87-Electro-c/story 1.50 3.80 9.00
100-Origin retold 3.70 9.00 22.00
101-104,106,108-113,115-120: 113-1st app. Deathstalker (cameo)
1.10 2.70 6.50
105-Origin Moondragon by Starlin (12/73); Thanos cameo in flashback (early app.) 1.90 6.00 13.00
107-Starlin-c; Thanos cameo 1.30 3.00 7.50
114-1st full app. Deathstalker 1.40 3.50 8.50
121-130,133-137: 124-1st app. Copperhead; Black Widow leaves. 126-1st new Torpedo 1.60 4.00
131-Origin/1st app. new Bullseye (see Nick Fury #15)
3.70 9.00 22.00
132-Bullseye app. .90 2.00 5.50
138-Ghost Rider-c/story; Death's Head is reincarnated; Byrne-a
1.70 5.00 12.00
139-157: 142-Nova cameo. 146-Bullseye app. 148-(30 & 35¢ issues exist). 150-1st app. Paladin. 151-Reveals i.d. to Heather Glenn. 155-Black Widow returns. 156-The 1960s Daredevil app. 1.50 3.75
158-Frank Miller art begins (5/79); origin/death of Deathstalker (see Captain America #235 & Spectacular Spider-Man #27 5.40 16.00 38.00
159 2.40 7.30 17.00
160,161 1.30 3.00 8.00
162-Ditko-a; no Miller-a 1.10 2.75
163,164: 163-Hulk cameo. 164-Origin retold 1.20 2.90 7.00
165-167,170 .90 2.00 5.50
168-Origin/1st app. Elektra 3.10 9.40 22.00
169-Elektra app. 1.30 3.00 7.50
171-175: 174,175-Elektra app. 1.80 4.50
176-180-Elektra app. 178-Cage app. 179-Anti-smoking issue mentioned in the Congressional Record 1.40 3.50
181-(52 pgs.)-death of Elektra; Punisher cameo out of costume
1.30 3.00 7.50
182-184-Punisher app. by Miller (drug issues) 2.00 6.00 11.00
185-191: 187-New Black Widow. 189-Death of Stick. 190-($1.00, 52 pgs.)-Elektra returns, part origin. 191-Last Miller Daredevil 1.00 2.50
192-195,197-210: 197,200-Bullseye app. 208-Harlan Ellison scripts borrowed from Avengers TV episode "House that Jack Built" 1.75
196-Wolverine app. 1.90 6.00 13.00
211-225: 219-Miller scripts 1.25
226-Frank Miller plots begin .90 2.25
227-Miller scripts begin 1.60 4.00
228-233-Last Miller scripts 1.20 3.00
234-237,239,240,242-247 1.25

Daredevil #319 © MEG

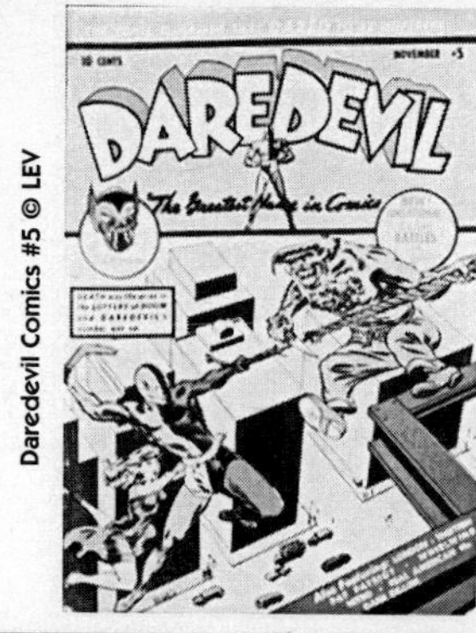

Daredevil Comics #5 © LEV

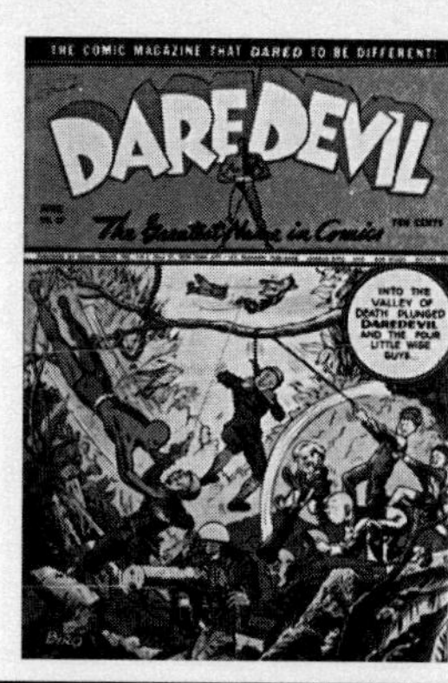

Daredevil Comics #17 © LEV

GD25 FN65 NM94

238-Mutant Massacre; Sabretooth app. 1.10 2.70 6.50
241-Todd McFarlane-a(p) 1.40 3.50
248,249-Wolverine app. 1.10 2.70 6.50
250,251,253,258: 250-1st app. Bullet. 258-Intro The Bengal (a villain) 1.25
252-(52 pgs.); Fall of the Mutants 1.40 3.50
254-Origin & 1st app. Typhoid Mary (5/88) 2.10 6.00 15.00
255-2nd app. Typhoid Mary 1.10 2.70 6.50
256-3rd app. Typhoid Mary .90 2.00 5.50
257-Punisher app. (x-over w/Punisher #10) 2.70 8.00 19.00
259,260-Typhoid Mary app. 260-(52 pgs.) 1.40 3.50
261-291,294,296-299: 272-Intro Shotgun (villain). 282-Silver Surfer app. (cameo in #281). 283-Capt. America app. 297-Typhoid Mary app.; Kingpin storyline begins. 299-Last $1.00-c 1.25
292,293-Punisher app. 292-Chichester scripts begin .90 2.25
295-Ghost Rider app. 1.10 2.75
300-($2.00, 52 pgs.)-Kingpin story ends 1.30 3.25
301-318: 301-303-Re-intro the Owl. 305,306-Spider-Man-c/story. 309-Punisher c/story; Terror app. 310-Calypso-c/story 1.35
319-Prologue to "Fall From Grace"; Elektra returns 1.40 4.30 10.00
319-2nd printing w/black-c 1.25
320- "Fall From Grace", chapter 1 1.10 2.70 6.50
321- "Fall From Grace" regular ed.; chapter 2; new costume; Venom app. 1.30 3.00
321-($2.00)-Wraparound Glow-in-the-dark-c ed. .80 2.00 5.50
322- "Fall From Grace" part 3; Eddie Brock app. 1.40 3.50
323,324- "Fall From Grace" Pt. 4 & 5: 323-Vs. Venon-c/story. 324-Morbius-c/story .70 1.75
325-($2.50, 52 pgs.)- "Fall From Grace" ends; contains bound-in poster 1.00 2.50
326,327: 326-New logo 1.25
328-339: 328-Begin $1.50-c; bound-in trading card sheet. 330-Gambit app. 1.50
Special 1(9/67, 25¢, 68 pgs.)-New art/story 4.00 12.00 28.00
Special 2,3: 2(2/71, 25¢, 52 pgs.)-Entire book has Powell/Wood-r; Wood-c. 3(1/72)-Reprints 1.60 4.70 11.00
Annual 4(10/76) .90 2.00 5.50
Annual 4(#5)(1989, $2.00, 68 pgs.)-Atlantis Attacks 1.00 2.50
Annual 6(1990, $2.00, 68 pgs.)-Sutton-a .80 2.00
Annual 7(1991, $2.00, 68 pgs.)-Guice-a (7 pgs.) .80 2.00
Annual 8(1992, $2.25, 68 pgs.)-Deathlok-c/story .90 2.25
Annual 9(1993, $2.95, 68 pgs.)-Polybagged w/card 1.20 3.00
Annual 10(1994, $2.95, 68 pgs.) 1.20 3.00
.../Punisher TPB (1988, $4.95)-r/D.D. #182-184 1.10 2.70 6.50
.../Punisher TPB, 2nd & 3rd printings 1.00 2.00 5.00

NOTE: **Art Adams** *c-238p, 239.* **Austin** *a-191i; c-151i, 200i.* **John Buscema** *a-136, 137p, 234p, 235p; c-86p, 136i, 137p, 142, 219.* **Byrne** *c-200p, 201, 203, 223.* **Capullo** *a-286p.* **Colan** *a(p)-20-49, 53-82, 84-98, 100, 110, 112, 124, 153, 154, 156, 157, Spec. 1p; c(p)-20-42, 44-49, 53-60, 71, 92, 98, 138, 153, 154, 156, 157, Annual 1.* **Craig** *a-50i, 52i.* **Ditko** *a-162, 234p, 235p, 264p; c-162.* **Everett** *c/a-1; inks-21, 83.* **Gil Kane** *a-141p, 146-148p, 151p; c(p)-85, 90, 91, 93, 94, 115, 116, 119, 120, 125-128, 133, 139, 147, 152.* **Kirby** *c-2-4, 5p, 12p, 13p, 43, 136p.* **Layton** *c-202.* **Miller** *scripts-168-182, 183(part), 184-191, 219, 227-233; a-158-161p, 163-184p, 191p; c-158-161p, 163-184p, 185-189, 190p, 191.* **Orlando** *a-2-4p.* **Powell** *a-9p, 11p, Special 1r, 2r.* **Simonson** *c-199, 236p.* **B. Smith** *a-236p; c-51p, 52p.* **Starlin** *a-105p.* **Steranko** *c-44i.* **Tuska** *a-39i, 145p.* **Williamson** *a(i)-237, 239, 240, 243, 248-257, 259-282, 283(part), 284, 285, 287, 288(part), 289(part), 293-300; c(i)-237, 243, 244, 248-257, 259-263, 265-278, 280-289, Annual 8.* **Wood** *a-5-8, 9i, 10, 11i, Spec. 2i; c-5i, 6-11, 164i.*

DAREDEVIL COMICS (See Silver Streak Comics)
July, 1941 - No. 134, Sept, 1956 (Charles Biro stories)
Lev Gleason Publications (Funnies, Inc. No. 1)

GD25 FN65 VF82 NM94

1-No. 1 titled "Daredevil Battles Hitler"; The Silver Streak, Lance Hale, Cloud Curtis, Dickey Dean, Pirate Prince team up w/Daredevil and battle Hitler; Daredevil battles the Claw; Origin of Hitler feature story. Hitler photo app. on-c 688.00 2062.00 3781.00 5500.00
(Estimated up to 215 total copies exist, 12 in NM/Mint)

GD25 FN65 NM94

2-London, Pat Patriot (by Reed Crandall), Nightro, Real American No. 1 (by Briefer #2-11), Dickie Dean, Pirate Prince, & Times Square begin; intro. & only app. The Pioneer, Champion of America 243.00 730.00 1700.00
3-Origin of 13 135.00 407.00 950.00
4 121.00 365.00 850.00
5-Intro. Sniffer & Jinx; Ghost vs. Claw begins by Bob Wood, ends #20 103.00 310.00 720.00
6-(#7 in indicia) 86.00 257.00 600.00
7-10: 8-Nightro ends 71.00 215.00 500.00
11-London, Pat Patriot end; bondage/torture-c 68.00 205.00 475.00
12-Origin of The Claw; Scoop Scuttle by Wolverton begins (2-4 pgs.), ends #22, not in #21 104.00 310.00 725.00
13-Intro. of Little Wise Guys (10/42) 100.00 300.00 700.00
14 50.00 150.00 350.00
15-Death of Meatball 75.00 225.00 525.00
16,17 46.00 140.00 325.00
18-New origin of Daredevil (not same as Silver Streak #6) 100.00 300.00 700.00
19,20 41.00 122.00 285.00
21-Reprints cover of Silver Streak #6 (on inside) plus intro. of The Claw from Silver Streak #1 62.00 186.00 435.00
22-30: 27-Bondage/torture-c 25.00 75.00 175.00
31-Death of The Claw 57.00 171.00 400.00
32-37,39,41: 35-Two Daredevil stories begin, end #68 (35-41 are 64 pgs.) 20.00 60.00 140.00
38-Origin Daredevil retold from #18 34.00 103.00 240.00
42-50: 42-Intro. Kilroy in Daredevil; 1 panel Steranko-a 16.00 48.00 110.00
51-69-Last Daredevil issue (12/50) 11.50 34.00 80.00
70-Little Wise Guys take over book; McWilliams-a; Hot Rock Flanagan begins, ends #80 10.00 30.00 65.00
71-79,81: 79-Daredevil returns 8.35 25.00 50.00
80-Daredevil x-over 9.15 27.50 55.00
82,90-One pg. Frazetta ad in both 8.35 25.00 50.00
83-89,91-99,101-134 6.70 20.00 40.00
100 8.35 25.00 50.00

NOTE: ***Wolverton's*** *Scoop Scuttle-12-20, 22.* **Biro** *c/a-all?* **Bolle** *a-125.* **Maurer** *a-75.* **McWilliams** *a-73, 75, 79, 80.*

DAREDEVIL THE MAN WITHOUT FEAR
Oct, 1993 - No. 5, Feb, 1994 ($2.95, limited series)
Marvel Comics

1-5: Foil embossed etched-c; Miller scripts; Romita, Jr./Williamson-c/a 1.60 4.00

DARE THE IMPOSSIBLE (Fleetway/Quality)(Value: cover or less)

DARING ADVENTURES (Also see Approved Comics)
Nov, 1953 (3-D, 25¢, came w/glasses)
St. John Publishing Co.

1 (3-D)-Reprints lead story from Son of Sinbad #1 by Kubert 30.00 90.00 210.00

DARING ADVENTURES
1963 - 1964
I.W. Enterprises/Super Comics

I.W. Reprint #9-r/Blue Bolt #115; Disbrow-a(3) 4.70 14.00 28.00
Super Reprint #10,11('63)-r/Dynamic #24,16; 11-Marijuana story; Yankee Boy app. 2.80 7.00 14.00
Super Reprint #12('64)-Phantom Lady from Fox (r/#14 only? w/splash pg. omitted) 11.50 34.00 80.00
Super Reprint #15('64)-r/Hooded Menace #1 7.50 22.50 45.00
Super Reprint #16('64)-r/Dynamic #12 2.80 7.00 14.00
Super Reprint #17('64)-r/Green Lama #3 by Raboy 4.20 12.50 25.00
Super Reprint #18-Origin Atlas from unpublished Atlas Comics #1 3.60 9.00 18.00

DARING COMICS (Formerly Daring Mystery) (Jeanie Comics No. 13 on)
No. 9, Fall, 1944 - No. 12, Fall, 1945

Dark Angel #14 © MEG

Darker Image #1 © Image

Darkhawk #43 © MEG

GD25 FN65 NM94

Timely Comics (HPC)

9-Human Torch, Toro & Sub-Mariner begin 71.00 215.00 500.00
10-The Angel only app. 64.00 193.00 450.00
11,12-The Destroyer app. 64.00 193.00 450.00

NOTE: ***Schomburg*** *c-9-11.* ***Sekowsky*** *c-12? Human Torch, Toro & Sub-Mariner c-9-12.*

DARING CONFESSIONS (Formerly Youthful Hearts)
No. 4, 11/52 - No. 7, 5/53; No. 8, 10/53
Youthful Magazines

4-Doug Wildey-a; Tony Curtis story 8.35 25.00 50.00
5-8: 5-Ray Anthony photo on-c. 6,8-Wildey-a 5.85 17.50 35.00

DARING LOVE (Radiant Love No. 2 on)
Sept-Oct, 1953
Gilmor Magazines

1 6.35 19.00 38.00

DARING LOVE (Formerly Youthful Romances)
No. 15, 12/52; No. 16, 2/53-c, 4/53-Indicia; No. 17-4/53-c & indicia
Ribage/Pix

15 6.70 20.00 40.00
16,17: 17-Photo-c 5.35 16.00 32.00

NOTE: ***Colletta*** *a-15.* ***Wildey*** *a-17.*

DARING LOVE STORIES (See Fox Giants)

DARING MYSTERY COMICS (Comedy Comics No. 9 on; title changed to Daring Comics with No. 9)
1/40 - No. 5, 6/40; No. 6, 9/40; No. 7, 4/41 - No. 8, 1/42
Timely Comics (TPI 1-6/TCI 7,8) GD25 FN65 VF82 NM94

1-Origin The Fiery Mask (1st app.) by Joe Simon; Monako, Prince of Magic (1st app.), John Steele, Soldier of Fortune (1st app.), Doc Doyle (1st app.) begin; Flash Foster & Barney Mullen, Sea Rover only app; bondage-c 1375.00 4125.00 7562.00 11,000.00
(Estimated up to 60 total copies exist, 5 in NM/Mint)

GD25 FN65 NM94

2-(Rare)-Origin The Phantom Bullet (1st & only app.); The Laughing Mask & Mr. E only app.; Trojak the Tiger Man begins, ends #6; Zephyr Jones & K-4 & His Sky Devils app., also #4 514.00 1543.00 3600.00
3-The Phantom Reporter, Dale of FBI, Breeze Barton, Captain Strong & Marvex the Super-Robot only app.; The Purple Mask begins 329.00 985.00 2300.00
4-Last Purple Mask; Whirlwind Carter begins; Dan Gorman, G-Man app. 207.00 621.00 1450.00
5-The Falcon begins (1st app.); The Fiery Mask, Little Hercules app. by Sagendorf in the Segar style; bondage-c 207.00 621.00 1450.00
6-Origin & only app. Marvel Boy by S&K; Flying Flame, Dynaman, & Stuporman only app.; The Fiery Mask by S&K; S&K-c 271.00 815.00 1900.00
7-Origin The Blue Diamond, Captain Daring by S&K, The Fin by Everett, The Challenger, The Silver Scorn & The Thunderer by Burgos; Mr. Millions app 250.00 750.00 1750.00
8-Origin Citizen V; Last Fin, Silver Scorn, Capt. Daring by Borth, Blue Diamond & The Thunderer; Kirby & part solo Simon-c; Rudy the Robot only app.; Citizen V, Fin & Silver Scorn continue in Comedy #9 186.00 557.00 1300.00

NOTE: ***Schomburg*** *c-1-4, 7.* ***Simon*** *a-2, 3, 5. Cover features: 1-Fiery Mask; 2-Phantom Bullet; 3-Purple Mask; 4-G-Man; 5-The Falcon; 6-Marvel Boy; 7, 8-Multiple characters.*

DARING NEW ADVENTURES OF SUPERGIRL, THE
Nov, 1982 - No. 13, Nov, 1983 (Supergirl No. 14-on)
DC Comics

1-Origin retold; Lois Lane back-ups in #2-12 1.50
2-13: 8,9-Doom Patrol app. 13-New costume; flag-c 1.00

NOTE: ***Buckler*** *c-1p, 2p.* ***Giffen*** *c-3p, 4p.* ***Gil Kane*** *c-6, ,8, 9, 11-13.*

DARK, THE
Nov, 1990 - No. 4, Feb, 1993; V2#1, May, 1993 - V2#7, Apr?, 1994 ($1.95)
Continum Comics

1-($2.00)-Bright-p; Panosian, Hanna-i; Stroman-c .80 2.00
2-(1/92, $2.25)-Stroman-c/a(p) .90 2.25
3,4-($2.50): 4-Perez-c & part-i 1.00 2.50
V2#1-Red foil Bart Sears-c .80 2.00
V2#1-Red non-foil variant-c .80 2.00
V2#1-2nd printing w/blue foil Bart Sears-c .80 2.00
V2#2-6: 2-Stroman/Bryant-a. 3-6-Foil-c. 3-Perez-c(i). 4-Perez-c & part-i; bound-in trading cards. 5,6-(2,3/94)-Perez-c(i) .80 2.00
V2#7-(B&W)-Perez-c(i) .80 2.00
...Convention Book 1 (Fall/94, $2.00)-Perez-c .80 2.00
...Convention Book 2 (10/94, &2.00)-Perez-c(i) .80 2.00

DARK ANGEL (Formerly Hell's Angel)
No. 6, Dec, 1992 - No. 16, Dec, 1993 ($1.75)
Marvel Comics UK, Ltd.

6-16: 6-Excalibur-c/story. 8-Psylocke app. .70 1.75

DARK CRYSTAL, THE
April, 1983 - No. 2, May, 1983
Marvel Comics Group

1,2-Movie adaptation, part 1&2 .50 1.00

DARK DOMINION
Oct, 1993 - Present ($2.50)
Defiant Comics

1-9-Len Wein scripts. 4-Free extra 16 pgs. 1.00 2.50
10-Shooter/Wein script 1.00 2.50

DARKER IMAGE
Mar, 1993 ($1.95)
Image Comics

1-Polybagged w/1 of 3 cards by Kieth, Lee or Liefeld; The Maxx by Sam Kieth begins; 1st app. Bloodwulf by Rob Liefeld & Deathblow by Jim Lee & begins 1.00 2.50
1-B&W interior pgs. w/silver foil logo 7.50

DARKEWOOD (Aircel)(Value: cover or less)

DARK GUARD
Oct, 1993 - Present? ($1.75)
Marvel Comics UK

1-($2.95)-Foil stamped-c 1.20 3.00
2-4 .70 1.75

DARKHAWK
Mar, 1991 - Present ($1.00,/$1.25)
Marvel Comics

1-Origin/1st app. Darkhawk; Hobgoblin cameo 1.60 4.70 11.00
2-Spider-Man & Hobgoblin app. 1.10 3.00 7.50
3-Spider-Man & Hobgoblin app. 1.10 2.70 6.50
4 1.00 2.00 5.00
5 1.00 2.00 5.00
6-Capt. America & Daredevil x-over 1.60 4.00
7,8 1.20 3.00
9-Punisher app. 1.00 2.00 5.00
10-12: 11-Last $1.00-c. 11,12-Tombstone app. .80 2.00
13,14-Venom-c/story 1.60 4.00
15-24,26-38: 19-Spider-Man & Brotherhood of Evil Mutants-c/story. 20-Spider-Man app. 22-Ghost Rider-c/story. 23-Origin begins, ends #25. 27-New Warriors-c/story. 35-Begin 3 part Venom story 1.25
25-($2.95, 52 pgs.)-Red holo-grafx foil-c w/double gatefold poster; origin of Darkhawk armor revealed 1.20 3.00
39-49: 39-Begin $1.50-c; bound-in trading card sheet 1.50
Annual 1 (1992, $2.25, 68 pgs.)-Vs. Iron Man 1.20 3.00
Annual 2 (1993, $2.95, 68 pgs.)-Polybagged w/card 1.20 3.00
Annual 3 (1994, $2.95) 1.20 3.00

DARKHOLD: PAGES FROM THE BOOK OF SINS
Oct, 1992 - No. 16, Jan, 1994 ($1.75) (See Midnight Sons Unlimited)
Marvel Comics (Midnight Sons imprint #15 on)

Dark Horse Comics #22 © DH

Darkman #3 © MEG

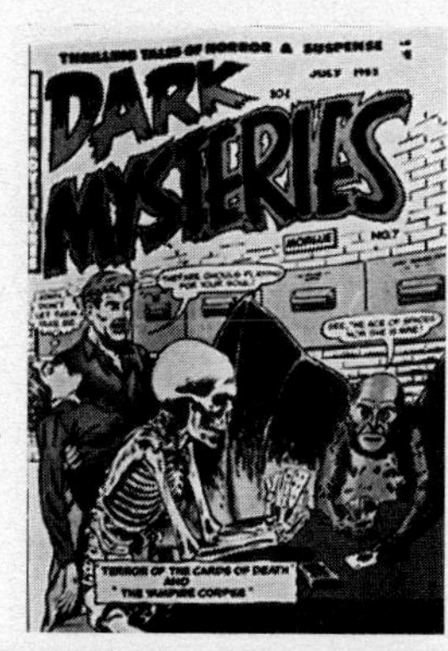

Dark Mysteries #7 © Master Pub.

GD25 FN65 NM94

1-($2.75, 52 pgs.)-Polybagged w/poster by Andy & Adam Kubert; part 4 of Rise of the Midnight Sons storyline 1.10 2.75
2-10,12-16: 3-Reintro Modred the Mystic (see Marvel Chillers #1). 5-Punisher & Ghost Rider app. 15-Spot varnish-c. 15,16-Siege of Darkness part 4&12 .70 1.75
11-($2.25)-Outer-c is a Darkhold envelope made of black parchment w/gold ink .90 2.25

DARK HORSE CLASSICS
1992 ($3.95, B&W, 52 pgs.)
Dark Horse Comics

nn's: The Last of the Mohicans. 20,000 Leagues Under the Sea 1.60 4.00

DARK HORSE COMICS
Aug, 1992 - Present ($2.50)
Dark Horse Comics

1-Dorman double gategold painted-c; Predator, Robocop, Timecop (3-part) & Renegade stories begin; 1st app. of Timecop 1.10 2.75
2-6,11-26: 2-Mignola-c. 3-Begin 3-part Aliens story; Aliens-c. 4-Predator-c. 6-Begin 4 part Robocop story. 12-Begin 2-part Aliens & 3-part Predator stories. 13-Thing From Another World begins w/Nino-a(i). 15-Begin 2-part Aliens: Cargo story. 16-Begin 3-part Predator story. 17-Begin 3-part Star Wars: Droids story & 3-part Aliens: Alien story; Droids-c. 19-Begin 2-part X story; X cover .50 1.25 2.50
7-Begin Star Wars: Tales of the Jedi 3-part story 1.20 3.00
8-1st app. X and begins; begin 4-part James Bond 1.60 4.00
9,10: 9-Star Wars ends. 10-X ends; Begin 3-part Predator & Godzilla stories 1.10 2.75

DARK HORSE DOWN UNDER
June, 1994 - No. 3, Oct, 1994 ($2.50, B&W, limited series)
Dark Horse Comics

1-3 1.00 2.50

DARK HORSE PRESENTS
July, 1986 - Present ($1.50/$1.75/$1.95/$2.25/$2.50, B&W)
Dark Horse Comics

1-1st app. Concrete by Paul Chadwick 1.65 4.00 10.00
1-2nd printing (1988, $1.50) 1.00 2.50
1-Silver ink 3rd printing (1992, $2.25)-Says 2nd printing inside .90 2.25
2-Concrete app. 1.20 3.00 7.00
3-Concrete app. 1.00 2.00 5.00
4,5-Concrete app. 1.60 4.00
6-10: 6,8,10-Concrete app. 10-1st app. The Mask 1.20 3.00
11-14,16-19,21-23: 11-19,21-Mask stories. 12,14,16,18,22-Concrete app. 17-All Roachmill issue .80 2.00
15(2/88) .80 2.00 5.00
20-($2.95, 68 pgs.)-Concrete, Flaming Carrot, Mask 1.20 3.00
24-Origin Aliens-c/story (11/88); Mr. Monster app. 2.90 8.60 20.00
25-31,33: 28-($2.95, 52 pgs.)-Concrete app.; Mr. Monster story (homage to Graham Ingels). 33-($2.25, 44 pgs.) 1.20 3.00
32-($3.50, 68 pgs.)-Annual; Concrete, American 1.60 4.00
34-Aliens-c/story 1.00 3.00 6.00
35-Predator-c/story; begin $1.95-c 1.00 3.00 6.00
36-1st Aliens Vs. Predator story; painted-c 1.50 4.00 9.00
36-Same as above, but line drawn-c 1.20 2.90 7.00
37-39,41,44,45,47-50: 38-Concrete. 44-Crash Ryan. 48-50-Contain 2 trading cards. 50-S/F story by Perez .80 2.00
40-($2.95, 52 pgs.)-1st Argosy story 1.20 3.00
42,43-Aliens-c/stories 1.00 2.00 5.00
46-Prequel to new Predator II mini-series 1.40 3.50
51-53-Sin City by Frank Miller, parts 2-4; 51,53-Miller-c 1.00 2.50
54-The Next Men begins(1st app.) by Byrne(9/91); Miller-a 1.30 3.10 7.50
55-2nd app. The Next Men; parts 5 & 6 of Sin City by Miller; Homocide by Morrow in both. 54-Morrow-c; begin $2.25-c. 55-Miller-c 1.50 3.75
56-($3.95, 68 pg. annual)-2-part prologue to Aliens: Genocide; part 7 of Sin City by Miller; Next Men by Byrne 1.60 4.00
57-($3.50, 52 pgs.)-Part 8 of Sin City by Miller; Next Men by Byrne; Byrne & Miller-c; Alien Fire story; swipes cover to Daredevil #1 1.40 3.50
58-66,68-84-($2.25): 58,59-Part 9,10 Sin City by Miller; Alien Fire stories. 60,61-Part 11,12 Sin City by Miller. 62-Last Sin City (entire book by Miller, c/a; 52 pgs.). 64-Dr. Giggles begins (1st app.), ends #66; Boris the Bear story. 66-New Concrete-c/story by Chadwick. 71-Begin 3 part Dominque story by Jim Balent; Balent-c. 72-(3/93)-Begin 3-part Eudaemon (1st app.) story by Nelson. 80-Art Adams-c/a (Monkeyman & O'Brien) .90 2.25
67-($3.95, 68 pgs.)-Begin 3-part prelude to Predator: Race War mini-series; Oscar Wilde adapt. by Russell 1.60 4.00
85-94: 85-Begin $2.50-c 1.00 2.50
...Fifth Anniversary Special nn (4/91, $9.95)-Part 1 of Sin City by Frank Miller (c/a); Aliens, Aliens vs. Predator, Concrete, Roachmill, Give Me Liberty & The American stories 1.65 4.00 10.00
...Aliens Platinum Edition (1992)-r/DHP #24,43,43,56 & Special 2.90 8.60 20.00

NOTE: ***Geary*** *a-59, 60.* ***Miller*** *a-Special, 51-53, 55-62; c-59-62.* ***Moebius*** *a-63; c-63, 70.* ***Vess*** *a-78; c-75, 78.*

DARK KNIGHT (See Batman: The Dark Knight Returns & Legends of the...)

DARKLON THE MYSTIC (Pacific)(Value: cover or less)

DARKMAN
Sept, 1990; Oct, 1990 - No. 3, Dec, 1990 ($1.50, movie adapt.)
Marvel Comics

1 (9/90, $2.25, B&W mag., 68 pgs.) .90 2.25
1-3: Reprints B&W magazine 1.50

DARKMAN
V2#1, Apr, 1993 -No. 6, Sept, 1993 ($2.95, limited series)
Marvel Comics

V2#1 ($3.95, 52 pgs.) 1.60 4.00
2-6 1.20 3.00

DARK MANSION OF FORBIDDEN LOVE, THE (Becomes Forbidden Tales of Dark Mansion No. 5 on)
Sept-Oct, 1971 - No. 4, Mar-Apr, 1972 (52 pgs.)
National Periodical Publications

1 2.00 5.00 12.00
2-4: 2-Adams-c. 3-Jeff Jones-c 1.10 2.70 6.50

DARK MYSTERIES (Thrilling Tales of Horror & Suspense)
June-July, 1951 - No. 25?, 1955
"Master" - "Merit" Publications

1-Wood-c/a (8 pgs.) 46.00 140.00 325.00
2-Wood/Harrison-c/a (8 pgs.) 36.00 107.00 250.00
3-9: 7-Dismemberment, hypo blood drainage stories 16.00 48.00 110.00
10-Cannibalism story; witch burning-c 16.50 50.00 115.00
11-13,15-18: 11-Severed head panels. 13-Dismemberment-c/story. 17-The Old Gravedigger host 11.50 34.00 80.00
14-Several E.C. Craig swipes 12.00 36.00 85.00
19-Injury-to-eye panel; E.C. swipe; torture-c 16.00 48.00 110.00
20-Female bondage, blood drainage story 13.50 41.00 95.00
21,22-Last pre-code issue, mis-dated 3/54 instead of 3/55 10.00 30.00 60.00
23-25 (#25-Exist?) 8.35 25.00 50.00

NOTE: ***Cameron*** *a-1, 2.* ***Myron Fass*** *c/a-21.* ***Harrison*** *a-3, 7; c-3.* ***Hollingsworth*** *a-7-17, 20, 21, 23.* ***Wildey*** *a-5. Woodish art by* ***Fleishman****-9; c-10, 14-17. Bondage c-10, 18, 19.*

DARK SHADOWS
October, 1957 - No. 3, May, 1958
Steinway Comic Publications (Ajax)(America's Best)

1 10.00 30.00 70.00
2,3 8.35 25.00 50.00

DARK SHADOWS (TV) (See Dan Curtis Giveaways)

Darkstars #12 © DC

Date With Danger #6 © STD

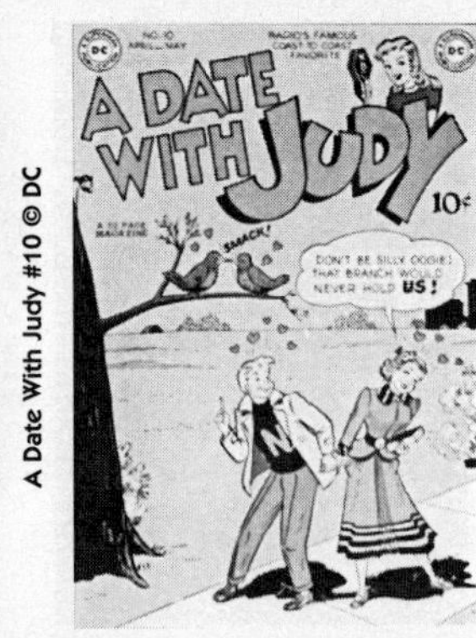

A Date With Judy #10 © DC

March, 1969 - No. 35, Feb, 1976 (Photo-c: 1-7)
Gold Key

	GD25	FN65	NM94
1(30039-903)-With pull-out poster (25¢)	25.00	75.00	175.00
1-With poster missing	9.00	27.00	62.00
2	8.00	25.00	58.00
3-With pull-out poster	13.00	406.00	90.00
3-With poster missing	6.60	20.00	46.00
4-7: 7-Last photo-c	8.00	24.00	56.00
8-10	6.00	18.00	42.00
11-20	4.60	14.00	32.00
21-35: 30-Last painted-c	3.00	9.40	22.00
Story Digest 1 (6/70)-Photo-c	6.00	18.00	42.00

DARK SHADOWS (TV) (See Nightmare on Elm Street)
June, 1992 - No. 4, Spring, 1993 ($2.50, mini-series, coated stock)
Innovation Publishing

	GD25	FN65	NM94
1-Based on 1991 NBC TV mini-series; painted-c		1.10	2.75
2-4		1.00	2.50

DARK SHADOWS: BOOK TWO
1993 - No. 4, July, 1993 ($2.50, mini-series)
Innovation Publishing

	GD25	FN65	NM94
1-4-Painted-c. 4-Maggie Thompson scripts		1.00	2.50

DARK SHADOWS: BOOK THREE
Nov, 1993 ($2.50)
Innovation Publishing

	GD25	FN65	NM94
1-(Whole #9)		1.00	2.50

DARKSTARS, THE
Oct, 1992 - Present ($1.75/$1.95)
DC Comics

	GD25	FN65	NM94
1-1st app. The Darkstars		.80	2.00
2-21: 5-Hawkman & Hawkwoman app. 18-20-Flash app.		.70	1.75
22-24: 22-Begin $1.95-c. 24-(9/94)-Zero Hour		.80	2.00
0,25-29: 0-(10/94)		.80	2.00

NOTE: ***Travis Charest*** *a(p)-4-7; c(p)-2-5; c-6-11.* ***Stroman*** *a-1-3; c-1.*

DARKWING DUCK (TV cartoon) (Also see Cartoon Tales)
Nov, 1991 - No. 4, Feb, 1992 ($1.50, limited series)
Disney Comics

	GD25	FN65	NM94
1-4: Adapts hour-long premiere TV episode			1.50

DARLING LOVE
Oct-Nov, 1949 - No. 11, 1952 (no month) (52 pgs.)(All photo-c?)
Close Up/Archie Publ. (A Darling Magazine)

	GD25	FN65	NM94
1-Photo-c	9.15	27.50	55.00
2-Photo-c	5.85	17.50	35.00
3-8,10,11: 3,5,6-photo-c	4.70	14.00	28.00
9-Krigstein-a	5.85	17.50	35.00

DARLING ROMANCE
Sept-Oct, 1949 - No. 7, 1951 (All photo-c)
Close Up (MLJ Publications)

	GD25	FN65	NM94
1-(52 pgs.)-Betty Page photo-c?	10.00	30.00	65.00
2	5.85	17.50	35.00
3-7	5.00	15.00	30.00

DASTARDLY & MUTTLEY (See Fun-In No. 1-4, 6 and Kite Fun Book)

DATE WITH DANGER
No. 5, Dec, 1952 - No. 6, Feb, 1953
Standard Comics

	GD25	FN65	NM94
5,6-Secret agent stories	5.00	15.00	30.00

DATE WITH DEBBI (Also see Debbi's Dates)
Jan-Feb, 1969 - No. 17, Sept-Oct, 1971; No. 18, Oct-Nov, 1972
National Periodical Publications

	GD25	FN65	NM94
1-Teenage	2.40	6.00	12.00
2-5	1.40	3.50	7.00
6-18	1.00	2.50	5.00

DATE WITH JUDY, A (Radio/TV, and 1948 movie)
Oct-Nov, 1947 - No. 79, Oct-Nov, 1960 (No. 1-25: 52 pgs.)
National Periodical Publications

	GD25	FN65	NM94
1-Teenage	22.00	65.00	150.00
2	10.00	30.00	70.00
3-10	8.35	25.00	50.00
11-20	5.00	15.00	30.00
21-40	4.00	12.00	24.00
41-45: 45-Last pre-code (2-3/55)	4.00	10.00	20.00
46-79: 79-Drucker-c/a	3.20	8.00	16.00

DATE WITH MILLIE, A (Life With Millie No. 8 on)(Teenage)
Oct, 1956 - No. 7, Aug, 1957; Oct, 1959 - No. 7, Oct, 1960
Atlas/Marvel Comics (MPC)

	GD25	FN65	NM94
1(10/56)-(1st Series)-Dan DeCarlo-a in #1-7	16.00	48.00	110.00
2	9.15	27.50	55.00
3-7	6.35	19.00	38.00
1(10/59)-(2nd Series)	10.00	30.00	60.00
2-7	5.85	17.50	35.00

DATE WITH PATSY, A (Also see Patsy Walker)
September, 1957 (One-shot)
Atlas Comics

	GD25	FN65	NM94
1-Starring Patsy Walker	7.50	22.50	45.00

DAVID AND GOLIATH (See 4-Color No. 1205)

DAVID CASSIDY (TV)(See Partridge Family, Swing With Scooter #33 & Time For Love #30)
Feb, 1972 - No. 14, Sept, 1973
Charlton Comics

	GD25	FN65	NM94
1	2.10	6.50	15.00
2-14: 5,7,9,14-Photo-c	1.70	4.20	10.00

DAVID LADD'S LIFE STORY (See Movie Classics)

DAVY CROCKETT (See Dell Giants, Fightin..., Frontier Fighters, It's Game Time, Power Record Comics, Western Tales & Wild Frontier)

DAVY CROCKETT (Frontier Fighter...)
1951
Avon Periodicals

	GD25	FN65	NM94
nn-Tuska?, Reinman-a; Fawcette-c	12.00	36.00	85.00

DAVY CROCKETT (...King of the Wild Frontier No. 1,2)(TV)
5/55 - No. 671, 12/55; No. 1, 12/63; No. 2, 11/69 (Walt Disney)
Dell Publishing Co./Gold Key

	GD25	FN65	NM94
4-Color 631(#1)-Fess Parker photo-c	14.00	43.00	100.00
4-Color 639-Photo-c	14.00	43.00	100.00
4-Color 664,671(Marsh-a)-Photo-c	13.00	40.00	90.00
1(12/63-Gold Key)-Fess Parker photo-c; reprints	13.00	40.00	90.00
2(11/69)-Fess Parker photo-c; reprints	4.00	10.00	20.00
...Christmas Book (no date, 16 pgs., paper-c)-Sears giveaway	4.70	14.00	28.00
...In the Raid at Piney Creek (1955, 16 pgs., 5x7-1/4")-American Motors giveaway; slick, photo-c	6.35	19.00	38.00
...Safety Trails (1955, 16pgs, 3-1/4x7")-Cities Service giveaway	6.35	19.00	38.00

DAVY CROCKETT (...Frontier Fighter #1,2; Kid Montana #9 on)
Aug, 1955 - No. 8, Jan, 1957
Charlton Comics

	GD25	FN65	NM94
1	6.70	20.00	40.00
2	4.00	12.00	24.00
3-8	3.60	9.00	18.00
Hunting With... nn ('55, 16 pgs.)-Ben Franklin Store giveaway (Publ.-S. Rose)	4.00	11.00	22.00

DC Challenge #4 © DC

DC Comics Presents #19 © DC

DC 100 Page Super Spectacular #18 © DC

GD25 FN65 NM94

DAYS OF THE MOB (See In the Days of the Mob)

DAYTONA SPECIAL (Vortex)(Value: cover or less)

DAZEY'S DIARY
June-Aug, 1962
Dell Publishing Co.

01-174-208: Bill Woggon-c/a 4.35 13.00 26.00

DAZZLER, THE (Also see Marvel Graphic Novel & X-Men #130)
March, 1981 - No. 42, Mar, 1986
Marvel Comics Group

1,2-X-Men app. .80 2.00
3-37,39-42: 10,11-Galactus app. 21-Double size; photo-c. 42-The Beast app. 1.00
38-Wolverine-c/app.; X-Men app. .90 2.30 5.50

NOTE: *No. 1 distributed only through comic shops.* ***Alcala*** *a-1i, 2i.* ***Chadwick*** *a-38-42p; c(p)-39, 41, 42.* ***Guice*** *a-38i, 42i; c-38, 40.*

DC CHALLENGE
Nov, 1985 - No. 12, Oct, 1986 ($1.25, 12 issue maxi-series)
DC Comics

1-11: 1-Colan-a. 4-Gil Kane-c/a 1.25
12-($2.00)-Perez/Austin-c .80 2.00

NOTE: *Batman app. in 1-4, 6-12. Joker app. in 7.* ***Giffen*** *c/a-11.* ***Swan/Austin*** *c-10.*

DC COMICS PRESENTS
July-Aug, 1978 - No. 97, Sept, 1986 (Superman team-ups in all)
DC Comics

1,2-4th & final Superman/Flash race .50 1.00
3-12,14-25: 4-Metal Men. 9-Wonder Woman. 19-Batgirl .50 1.00
13-Legion of Super Heroes (also in #43 & 80) .80 2.00
26-(10/80)-Green Lantern; intro Cyborg, Starfire, Raven (1st app. New Teen Titans in 16 pg. preview); Starlin-c/a; Sargon the Sorcerer back-up 1.30 3.00 7.50
27-40,42-71,73-76,79-84,86-97: 31,58-Robin. 35-Man-Bat. 42,47-Sandman. 52-Doom Patrol. 82-Adam Strange. 83-Batman & Outsiders. 86-88-Crisis x-over. 88-Creeper .50 1.00
41-Superman/Joker-c/story 1.10 2.75
72-Joker/Phantom Stranger-c/story 1.10 2.75
77,78-Animal Man app. (77-cover app. also) 1.30 3.25
85-Swamp Thing; Alan Moore scripts 1.30 3.25
Annual 1-4: 1(9/82)-G.A. Superman. 2(7/83)-Intro/origin Superwoman. 3(9/84)-Shazam. 4(10/85)-Superwoman 1.35

NOTE: ***Adkins*** *a-2, 54; c-2.* ***Gil Kane*** *a-28, 35, Annual 3; c-48p, 56, 58, 60, 62, 64, 68, Annual 2, 3.* ***Kirby*** *c/a-84.* ***Kubert*** *c/a-66.* ***Morrow*** *c/a-65.* ***Newton*** *c/a-54p.* ***Orlando*** *c-53i.* ***Perez*** *a-26p, 61p; c-38, 61, 94.* ***Starlin*** *a-26-29p, 36p, 37p; c-26-29, 36, 37, 93.* ***Toth*** *a-84.* ***Williamson*** *i-79, 85, 87.*

DC GRAPHIC NOVEL (Also see DC Science Fiction...)
Nov, 1983 - No. 7, 1986 ($5.95, 68 pgs.)
DC Comics

1-5,7: 1-Star Raiders. 2-Warlords; not from regular Warlord series. 3-The Medusa Chain; Ernie Colon story/a. 4-The Hunger Dogs; Kirby-c/a(p). 5-Me and Joe Priest; Chaykin-c. 7-Space Clusters; Nino-c/a 1.00 2.50 6.00
6-Metalzoic; Sienkiewicz-c ($6.95) 1.20 3.00 7.00

DC 100 PAGE SUPER SPECTACULAR
(Title is 100 Page... No. 14 on)(Square bound) (Reprints, 50¢)
No. 4, Summer, 1971 - No. 13, 6/72; No. 14, 2/73 - No. 22, 11/73 (No #1-3)
National Periodical Publications

4-Weird Mystery Tales; Johnny Peril & Phantom Stranger; cover & splashes by Wrightson; origin Jungle Boy of Jupiter 1.80 4.50
5-Love Stories; Wood inks (7 pgs.)(scarcer) 1.30 2.60 6.50
6- "World's Greatest Super-Heroes"; JLA, JSA, Spectre, Johnny Quick, Vigilante & Hawkman; contains unpublished Wildcat story; N. Adams wrap-around-c; r/JLA #21,22 1.80 4.50
7-13: 7-(See Superman #245). 8-(See Batman #238). 9-(See Our Army at War #242). 10-(See Adventure #416). 11-(See Flash #214).12-(See Superboy #185). 13-(See Superman #252)
14-Batman-r/Detective #31,32,156; Atom-r/Showcase #34 1.10 2.70 6.50
15-22: 15-r/2nd Boy Commandos/Det. #65. 17-JSA-r/All Star #37(38 pgs.); Sandman-r/Adv. #66. 20-Batman-r/Det. #66,68, others; origin Two-Face. 21-r/Brave & the Bold #54. 22-r/All-Flash #13 .90 2.25

NOTE: ***Anderson*** *r-11, 14, 18i, 22.* ***B. Baily*** *r-18, 20.* ***Burnley*** *r-18, 20.* ***Crandall*** *r-14p, 20.* ***Drucker*** *r-4.* ***Infantino*** *r-17, 20, 22.* ***G. Kane*** *r-18.* ***Kubert*** *r-6, 7, 16, 17; c-16, 19.* ***Meskin*** *r-4, 22.* ***Mooney*** *r-15, 21.* ***Toth*** *r-17, 20.*

DC SCIENCE FICTION GRAPHIC NOVEL
1985 - No. 7, 1987 ($5.95)
DC Comics

SF1-SF7: SF1-Hell on Earth by Robert Bloch; Giffen-p. SF2-Nightwings by Robert Silverberg; G. Colan-p. SF3-Frost & Fire by Bradbury. SF4-Merchants of Venus. SF5-Demon With A Glass Hand by Ellison; M. Rogers-a. SF6-The Magic Goes Away by Niven. SF7-Sandkings by George R.R. Martin 1.00 2.50 6.00

DC SILVER AGE CLASSICS
1992 ($1.00, all reprints)
DC Comics

...Action Comics #252; r/1st Supergirl; Adventure Comics #247; r/1st Legion of S.H....The Brave and the Bold #28; r/1st JLA; Detective Comics #225; r/1st Martian Manhunter; Detective Comics #327; r/1st new look Batman; Green Lantern #76; r/Green Lantern/Gr. Arrow; House of Secrets #92; r/1st Swamp Thing; Showcase #4; r/1st S.A. Flash; Showcase #22; r/1st S.A. Green Lantern; Sugar and Spike #99; 2 unpublished stories 1.00

DC SPECIAL (Also see Super DC...)
10-12/68 - No. 15, 11-12/71; No. 16, Spr/75 - No. 29, 8-9/77
National Periodical Publications

1-All Infantino issue; Flash, Batman, Adam Strange-r; begin 68 pg. issues, end #21 1.40 3.50 8.50
2-15: 2-Teen humor. 5-All Kubert issue; Viking Prince, Sgt. Rock-r. 12-Viking Prince; Kubert-c/a(r/B&B almost entirely). 15-G.A. Plastic Man origin-r/Police #1; origin Woozy by Cole; 14,15-(52 pgs.) 1.10 2.70 6.50
16-29: 16-Super Heroes Battle Super Gorillas; r/Capt. Storm #1, 1st Johnny Cloud/All-Amer. Men of War #82. 17-Early S.A. Green Lantern-r. 22-Origin Robin Hood. 26-Enemy Ace on-c only. 27-Untold Origin of the Justice Society. 28-Earth Shattering Disaster Stories; Legion of Super-Heroes story. 29-Secret Origin of the Justice Society 1.40 3.50

NOTE: ***N. Adams*** *c-3, 4, 6, 11, 29.* ***Grell*** *a-20; c-17, 20.* ***Heath*** *a-12r.* ***G. Kane*** *a-6p, 13r, 17r, 19-21r.* ***Kubert*** *a-6r, 12r, 22.* ***Meskin*** *a-10.* ***Moreira*** *a-10.* ***Staton*** *a-29p.* ***Toth*** *a-13, 20r. #1-15: 25¢; 16-27: 50¢; 28, 29: 60¢. #1-13, 16-21: 68 pgs.; 14, 15: 52 pgs.; 25-27: oversized.*

DC SPECIAL BLUE-RIBBON DIGEST
Mar-Apr, 1980 - No. 24, Aug, 1982
DC Comics

1-24: All reprints? 1.00

NOTE: ***N. Adams*** *a-16(6)r, 17r, 23r; c-16.* ***Aparo*** *a-6r, 24r; c-23.* ***Grell*** *a-8, 10; c-10.* ***Heath*** *a-14.* ***Kaluta*** *a-17r.* ***Gil Kane*** *a-22r.* ***Kirby*** *a-23r.* ***Kubert*** *a-3, 18r, 21r; c-7, 12, 14, 17, 18, 21, 24.* ***Morrow*** *a-24r.* ***Orlando*** *a-17r, 22r; c-1, 20.* ***Perez*** *c-19p.* ***Toth*** *a-21r, 24r.* ***Wood*** *a-3, 17r, 24r.* ***Wrightson*** *a-16r, 17r, 24r.*

DC SPECIAL SERIES
9/77 - No. 16, Fall, 1978; No. 17, 8/79 - No. 27, Fall, 1981
(No. 19, 23, 24 - digest size, 100 pgs.; No. 25-27 - over-sized)
National Periodical Publications/DC Comics

1-Five-Star Super-Hero Spectacular; Atom, Flash, Green Lantern, Aquaman, Batman, Kobra app.; N. Adams-c 1.30 3.25
2(#1)-The Original Swamp Thing Saga (1977)-r/Swamp Thing #1&2 by Wrightson; Wrightson wraparound-c 1.30 3.25
3-20,22-24: 6-Jones-a. 7-Ghosts Special. 10-Origin Dr. Fate, Lightray & Black Canary. 14,17,20-Original Swamp Thing Saga; r/Swamp Thing #3-10 by Wrightson (52-68 pgs.). 15-Batman Spectacular. 16-Jonah Hex Spectacular; death of Jonah Hex; Bat Lash story. 19-Secret Origins of Super-Heroes; origins Wonder Woman (new-a), Robin, & Batman-Superman team. 22-G.I. Combat .90 2.25
21-Miller-a (1st on Batman, Spring, 1980) 1.90 6.00 13.00

DC Trinity #1 © DC

Deadly Foes Of Spider-Man #2 © MEG

Deadman #3 © DC

GD25 FN65 NM94

V5#25-($2.95, Sum/81)-Superman II the Adventure Continues; photos from movie & photo-c (see All-New Coll. Ed. C-62) 1.30 3.25
26-($2.95, Sum/81)-Superman and His Incredible Fortress of Solitude 1.30 3.25
27-($2.50)-Batman vs. The Incredible Hulk .90 2.30 5.50

NOTE: ***Golden** a-15. **Heath** a-12i, 16. **Kubert** c-13. **Nasser** a-1. **Rogers** c/a-15. **Starlin** c-12. **Staton** a-1. #25 & 26 were advertised as All-New Collectors' Edition C-63, C-64. #26 was originally planned as All-New Collectors' Ed. C-30?; has C-630 & A.N.C.E. on cover.*

DC SPOTLIGHT
1985 (50th anniversary special)
DC Comics (giveaway)

1 1.20

DC SUPER-STARS
March, 1976 - No. 18, Winter, 1978 (No.3-18: 52 pgs.)
National Periodical Publications/DC Comics

1-(68 pgs.)-Re-intro Teen Titans (predates T. T. #44 (11/76); tryout iss.) plus r/Teen Titans; W.W. as girl was original Wonder Girl 1.80 4.50
2-7,9,11-14,16,18: 2,4-6,8-Adam Strange; 2-(68 pgs.)-r/1st Adam Strange/Hawkman team-up from Mystery in Space #90 plus Atomic Knights origin-r. 3-Legion issue. 4-r/Tales/Unexpected #45. 13-Sergio Aragones Special 1.25
8-r/1st Space Ranger from Showcase #15, Adam Strange-r/Mystery in Space #89 & Star Rovers-r/M.I.S. #80 1.50 3.75
10-Strange Sports Stories; Batman/Joker-c/story 1.70 4.25
15-Batman Spectacular; Golden & Rogers-a 1.10 2.75
17-Secret Origins of Super-Heroes (origin of The Huntress); origin Green Arrow by Grell; Legion app.; Earth II Batman & Catwoman marry (1st revealed; also see B&B #197 & Superman Family #211) .90 2.25

NOTE: ***M. Anderson** r-2, 4, 6. **Aparo** c-7, 14, 18. **Austin** a-11i. **Buckler** a-14p; c-10. **Grell** a-17. **G. Kane** a-1r, 10r. **Kubert** c-15. **Layton** c/a-16i, 17i. **Mooney** a-4r, 6r. **Morrow** c/a-11r. **Nasser** a-11. **Newton** c/a-16p. **Staton** a-17; c-17. No. 10, 12-18 contain all new material; the rest are reprints. #1 contains new and reprint material.*

DC UNIVERSE: TRINITY
Aug, 1993 - No. 2, Sept, 1993 ($2.95, 52 pgs.)
DC Comics

1,2-Foil-c; Green Lantern, Darkstars, Legion app. 1.20 3.00

D-DAY (Also see Special War Series)
Sum/63; No. 2, Fall/64; No. 4, 9/66; No. 5, 10/67; No. 6, 11/68
Charlton Comics (no No. 3)

1(1963)-Montes/Bache-c 3.00 7.50 15.00
2(Fall,'64)-Wood-a(4) 3.60 9.00 18.00
4-6('66-'68)-Montes/Bache-a #5 2.00 5.00 10.00

DEAD CLOWN (Malibu)(Value: cover or less)

DEAD END CRIME STORIES
April, 1949 (52 pgs.)
Kirby Publishing Co.

nn-(Scarce)-Powell, Roussos-a; painted-c 36.00 107.00 250.00

DEAD-EYE WESTERN COMICS
Nov-Dec, 1948 - V3#1, Apr-May, 1953
Hillman Periodicals

V1#1-(52 pgs.)-Krigstein, Roussos-a 11.50 34.00 80.00
V1#2,3-(52 pgs.) 6.70 20.00 40.00
V1#4-12-(52 pgs.) 4.20 12.50 25.00
V2#1,2,5-8,10-12: 1-7-(52 pgs.) 4.00 10.00 20.00
3,4-Krigstein-a 5.85 17.50 35.00
9-One pg. Frazetta ad 4.00 10.00 20.00
V3#1 3.60 9.00 18.00

NOTE: ***Briefer** a-V1#8. Kinstleresque stories by **McCann**-12, V2#1, 2, V3#1. **McWilliams** a-V1#5. **Ed Moore** a-V1#4.*

DEADFACE: DOING THE ISLANDS WITH BACCHUS
July, 1991 - No. 3, Sept, 1991 ($2.95, B&W, mini-series, 52 pgs.)
Dark Horse Comics

1-3: By Eddie Campbell 1.20 3.00

DEADFACE: EARTH, WATER, AIR, AND FIRE
July, 1992 - No. 4, Oct, 1992 ($2.50, B&W, mini-series; British-r)
Dark Horse Comics

1-4: By Eddie Campbell 1.00 2.50

DEAD IN THE WEST
Oct, 1993 - No. 2, Mar, 1994 ($3.95, B&W, adults, 52 pgs.)
Dark Horse Comics

1,2-Timothy Truman-c 1.60 4.00

DEADLIEST HEROES OF KUNG FU
Summer, 1975 (Magazine)
Marvel Comics Group

1 .70 1.80

DEADLINE USA
Apr, 1992 - No. 8, Nov, 1992 ($3.95, B&W, 52 pgs.)
Dark Horse Comics

1-8: Johnny Nemo w/Milligan scripts in all 1.60 4.00

DEADLY FOES OF SPIDER-MAN (Marvel)(Value: cover or less)

DEADLY FOES OF SPIDER-MAN (See Lethal Foes of...)
May, 1991 - No. 4, Aug, 1991 ($1.00, mini-series)
Marvel Comics

1-4: 1-Punisher, Kingpin, Rhino app. 1.00

DEADLY HANDS OF KUNG FU, THE (See Master of Kung Fu)
April, 1974 - No. 33, Feb, 1977 (75¢) (B&W, magazine)
Marvel Comics Group

1(V1#4 listed in error)-Origin Sons of the Tiger; Shang-Chi, Master of Kung Fu begins (ties w/Master of Kung Fu #17 as 3rd app. Shang-Chi); Bruce Lee photo pin-up 1.40 3.50
2,3,5 .90 2.25
4-Bruce Lee painted-c by Neal Adams; 8 pg. biog of Bruce Lee 1.30 3.25
6-14 .90 2.25
15-(Annual 1, Summer '75)-Origin Iron Fist retold (predates Iron Fist #1) .90 2.25
16-19,21-27,29-33: 17-1st Giffen-a (1 pg.; 11/75). 19-1st White Tiger. 22-1st app. Jack of Hearts; 1st Giffen story-a (along with Amazing Adventures #35, 3/76) 1.60
20-Origin The White Tiger; Perez-a .80 2.00
28-Origin Jack of Hearts; Bruce Lee life story 1.20 3.00
Special Album Edition 1(Summer, '74)-Iron Fist-c/story (very early app., 3rd?); Adams-i .90 2.25

NOTE: ***N. Adams** a-1i(part), 27i; c-1, 2-4, 11, 12, 14, 17. **Giffen** a-22p, 24p. **G. Kane** a-23p. **Kirby** a-5r. **Nasser** a-27p, 28. **Perez** a(p)-6-14, 16, 17, 19, 21. **Rogers** a-26, 32, 33. **Starlin** a-1, 2r, 15r. **Staton** a-28p, 31, 32. Iron Fist in #10, 15, 18-24. Shang Chi, Master of Kung Fu in #1-9, 11-18, 33. Sons of the Tiger in #1, 3, 4, 6-14, 16-19 (White Tiger #20-24, 26, 27, 29-31).*

DEADMAN (See The Brave and the Bold & Phantom Stranger #39)
May, 1985 - No. 7, Nov, 1985 ($1.75, Baxter paper)
DC Comics

1-Deadman-r by Infantino, N. Adams in all .70 1.75
2-7: 5-Batman-c/story-r/Str. Advs. 7-Batman-r .70 1.75

DEADMAN
Mar, 1986 - No. 4, June, 1986 (75¢, mini-series)
DC Comics

1-4: Lopez-c/a. 4-Byrne-c(p) 1.00

DEADMAN: EXORCISM
1992 - No. 2, 1992 ($4.95, mini-series, 52 pgs.)
DC Comics

1,2-Kelley Jones-c/a 1.00 2.00 5.00

DEADMAN: LOVE AFTER DEATH
1989 - No. 2, 1990 ($3.95, 2 issue series, mature readers, 52 pgs.)
DC Comics

Deadpool #2 © MEG

Deathblow #7 © Image

Deathlok #6 © MEG

GD25 FN65 NM94

Book One, Two: 1-Contains nudity 1.60 4.00

DEAD MEAT (Fleetway/Quality)(Value: cover or less)

DEAD OF NIGHT
Dec, 1973 - No. 11, Aug, 1975
Marvel Comics Group

1-Horror reprints .80 1.90
2-11: 11-Intro Scarecrow; Kane/Wrightson-c 1.10
NOTE: ***Ditko** r-7, 10. **Everett** c-2. **Sinnott** r-1.*

DEADPOOL
Aug, 1994 - No. 4, Nov, 1994 ($2.50, limited series)
Marvel Comics

1-4 1.00 2.50

DEADPOOL: THE CIRCLE CHASE (See New Mutants #98)
Aug, 1993 - No. 4, Nov, 1993 ($2.00, mini-series)
Marvel Comics

1-($2.50)-Embossed-c 1.00 2.50
2-4 .80 2.00

DEADSHOT (See Batman #59 & Detective Comics #474)
Nov, 1988 - No. 4, Feb, 1989 ($1.00, mini-series)
DC Comics

1-4: Deadshot is a Batman villain 1.00

DEAD WHO WALK, THE (See Strange Mysteries, Super Reprint #15, 16)
1952 (One Shot)
Realistic Comics

nn 35.00 105.00 245.00

DEADWOOD GULCH
1931 (52 pgs.) (B&W)
Dell Publishing Co.

nn-By Charles "Boody" Rogers 16.00 48.00 110.00

DEADWORLD (Also see The Realm)
Dec, 1986 - No. 28? ($1.50/$1.95/#15-28: $2.50, B&W, adults)
Arrow Comics/Caliber Comics

1 1.50 3.75
2 1.10 2.75
3,4 .70 1.70
5-11: Graphic covers .60 1.60
5-11: Tame covers .80 1.90
12-28: Graphic covers, 12-28: Tame covers .80 1.90
...Archives 1 (1992, $2.50) .80 1.90

DEAN MARTIN & JERRY LEWIS (See Adventures of...)

DEAR BEATRICE FAIRFAX
No. 5, Nov, 1950 - No. 9, Sept, 1951 (Vern Greene art)
Best/Standard Comics(King Features)

5-All have Schomburg air brush-c 5.35 16.00 32.00
6-9 4.00 10.00 20.00

DEAR HEART (Formerly Lonely Heart)
No. 15, July, 1956 - No. 16, Sept, 1956
Ajax

15,16 3.60 9.00 18.00

DEAR LONELY HEART (...Illustrated No. 1-6)
Mar, 1951; No. 2, Oct, 1951 - No. 8, Oct, 1952
Artful Publications

1 11.00 32.00 75.00
2 5.35 16.00 32.00
3-Matt Baker Jungle Girl story 10.00 30.00 70.00
4-8 4.70 14.00 28.00

DEAR LONELY HEARTS (Lonely Heart #9 on)
Aug, 1953 - No. 8, Oct, 1954
Harwell Publ./Mystery Publ. Co. (Comic Media)

GD25 FN65 NM94

1 5.35 16.00 32.00
2-8 3.60 9.00 18.00

DEARLY BELOVED
Fall, 1952
Ziff-Davis Publishing Co.

1-Photo-c 10.00 30.00 70.00

DEAR NANCY PARKER
June, 1963 - No. 2, Sept, 1963
Gold Key

1,2-Painted-c 3.00 7.50 15.00

DEATHBLOW (Also see Darker Image)
May (April inside), 1993 - Present ($1.75/$1.95)
Image Comics

1-($2.50)-Red foil stamped logo on black varnish-c; Jim Lee-c/a; flip-book side has Cybernary -c/story (#2 also) 1.10 2.75
1-($1.95)-Newsstand version w/o foil-c & varnish .80 2.00
2-4: 2-(8/93)-Lee/Choi-a; with bound-in poster. 4-Jim Lee-c .70 1.75
2-($1.75)-Newsstand version w/o poster .70 1.75
5-8-Jim Lee-c: 5-Begin $1.95-c .80 2.00
5-Alternate Portacio-c, forms larger picture when combined with alternate-c for Gen 13 #5, Kindred #3, Stormwatch #10, Team 7 #1, Union #0, Wetworks #2 & WildC.A.T.s # 11 .70 2.00 5.00

DEATHLOK (Also see Astonishing Tales #25)
July, 1990 - No. 4, Oct, 1990 ($3.95, limited series, 52 pgs.)
Marvel Comics

1-Guice-a(p) 1.00 3.00 7.00
2-4: 2-Guice-a(p). 3,4-Denys Cowan-a, c-4 .80 2.10 5.00

DEATHLOK
July, 1991 - Present ($1.75)
Marvel Comics

1-Silver ink cover; Denys Cowan-c/a(p) begins 1.10 2.75
2-5: 2-Forge (X-Men) app. 3-Vs. Dr. Doom. 5-X-Men & F.F. x-over 1.00 2.50
6-10: 6,7-Punisher x-over. 9,10-Ghost Rider-c/story .70 1.75
11-18,20-24,26-39: 16-Infinity War x-over. 17-Jae Lee-c. 22-Black Panther app. 27-Siege app. .70 1.75
19-($2.25)-Foil-c .90 2.25
25-($2.95, 52 pgs.)-Holo-grafx foil-c 1.20 3.00
Annual 1 (1992, $2.25, 68 pgs.)-Guice-p; Quesada-c(p) 1.00 2.50
Annual 2 (1993, $2.95, 68 pgs.)-Bagged w/card; intro Tracer 1.20 3.00
NOTE: ***Denys Cowan** a(p)-9-13, 15, Annual 1; c-9-12, 13p, 14. **Guice/Cowan** c-8.*

DEATHLOK SPECIAL
May, 1991 - No. 4, Late-June, 1991 ($2.00, bi-weekly mini-series)
Marvel Comics

1-4: r/1-4(1990) w/new Guice-c #1,2; Cowan c-3,4 1.00 2.50
1-2nd printing w/white-c .90 2.25

DEATHMATE
Sept, 1993 - Feb, 1994 ($2.95/$4.95, limited series)
Valiant (Prologue/Yellow/Blue)/Image Comics (Black/Epilogue)

Preview-(7/93, 8 pgs.) 1.00
Prologue (#1)–Silver foil; Jim Lee/Layton-c; B. Smith/Lee-a; Liefeld-a(p) 1.20 3.00
Prologue–Special gold foil ed. of silver ed. 1.40 4.00 10.00
Black (#2)-(9/93, $4.95, 52 pgs.)-Silvestri/Jim Lee-c; pencils by Peterson/Silvestri/Capullo/Jim Lee/Portacio; 1st app. Gen 13 1.60 4.00
Black-Special gold foil edition 1.40 4.00 10.00
Yellow (#3)-(10/93, $4.95, 52 pgs)-Yellow foil-c; Indicia says Prologue Sept 1993 by mistake; 3rd app. Ninjak; Thibert-c(i) 1.60 4.00
Yellow-Special gold foil edition 1.40 4.00 10.00
Blue (#4)-(10/93, $4.95, 52 pgs.)-Thibert blue foil-c(i); Reese-a(i) 1.60 4.00

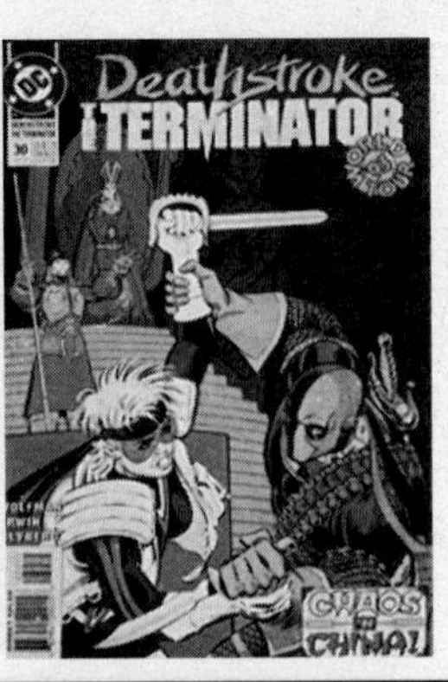

Deathstroke: The Terminator #30 © DC

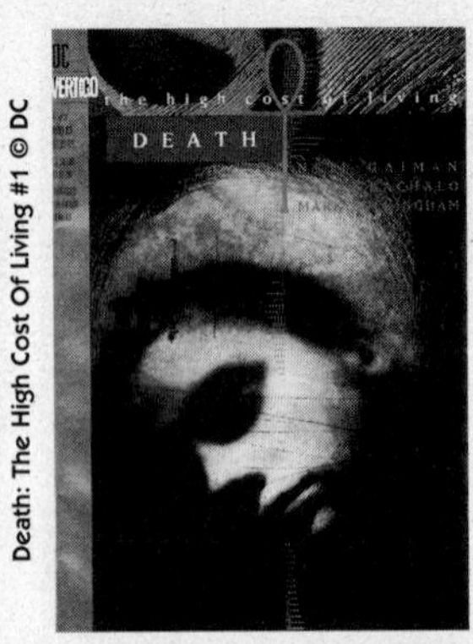

Death: The High Cost Of Living #1 © DC

Death Valley #1 © Comic Media

GD25 FN65 NM94

Blue-Special gold foil edition 1.40 4.00 10.00
Red (#5) 1.60 4.00
Epilogue (#6)-(2/94, $2.95)-Silver foil Quesada/Silvestri-c; Silvestri-a(p) 1.20 3.00

DEATH METAL
Jan, 1994 - No. 4, Apr, 1994 ($1.95, mini-series)
Marvel Comics UK
1-4: 1-Silver ink-c. Alpha Flight app. .80 2.00

DEATH METAL VS. GENETIX
Dec, 1993 - No. 2, Jan, 1994 (Limited series)
Marvel Comics UK
1-($2.95)-Polybagged w/2 trading cards 1.20 3.00
2-($2.50)-Polybagged w/2 trading cards 1.00 2.50

DEATH OF CAPTAIN MARVEL (See Marvel Graphic Novel #1)

DEATH OF MR. MONSTER, THE (See Mr. Monster #8)

DEATH OF SUPERMAN (See Superman, 2nd series)

DEATH RATTLE (Kitchen Sink)(Value: cover or less)

DEATH RATTLE
1986-?
Kitchen Sink
1-7 .80 2.00
8-(12/86)-1st app. Mark Schultz's Xenozoic Tales/Cadillacs & Dinosaurs 1.00 2.00 5.00
8-(1994)-r plus interview w/Mark Schultz 1.20 3.00

DEATH'S HEAD (See Daredevil #56, Dragon's Claws #5 & Incomplete...)
Dec, 1988 - No. 10, Sept, 1989 ($1.75)(Dragon's Claws spin-off)
Marvel Comics
1-Dragon's Claws spin-off .90 3.00 6.50
2-Fantastic Four app.; Dragon's Claws x-over 1.60 4.00
3,4 .80 2.00
5-10: 8-Dr. Who app. 9-F. F. x-over; Simonson-c(p) .80 2.00
...Gold 1 (1/94, $3.95, 68 pgs.)-Gold foil-c 1.60 4.00

DEATH'S HEAD II (Also see Battletide)
Mar, 1992 - No. 4, June (May inside), 1992 ($1.75, mini-series)
Marvel Comics UK, Ltd.
1 1.10 3.00 6.50
1,2-Silver ink 2nd printiings .70 1.75
2-Fantastic Four app. 1.60 4.00
3,4: 4-Punisher, Spider-Man , Daredevil, Dr. Strange, Capt. America & Wolverine in the year 2020 .80 2.00

DEATH'S HEAD II (Also see Battletide)
Dec, 1992 - Present ($1.75/$1.95)
Marvel Comics UK, Ltd.
V2#1-5: 1-Gatefold-c. 1-4-X-Men app. .70 1.75
6-13,15,16 ($1.95): 15-Capt. America & Wolverine app. .80 2.00
14-($2.95)-Foil flip-c w/Death's Head II Gold #0 1.20 3.00

DEATH'S HEAD II & THE ORIGIN OF DIE CUT
Aug, 1993 - No. 2, Sept, 1993 (Limited series)
Marvel Comics UK, Ltd.
1-($2.95)-Embossed-c 1.20 3.00
2 ($1.75) .70 1.75

DEATHSTROKE: THE TERMINATOR (Also see Marvel & DC Present, New Teen Titans #2, New Titans & Tales of the Teen Titans #42-44)
Aug, 1991 - Present ($1.75/$1.95)
DC Comics
1-New Titans spin-off; Mike Zeck c-1-28 1.60 4.00
1-Gold ink 2nd printing ($1.75) .70 1.80
2 1.20 3.00
3-5 .80 2.00
6-37: 6,8-Batman cameo. 7,9-Batman-c/story. 9-1st new Vigilante (female) in cameo. 10-1st full app. new Vigilante; Perez-i. 13-Vs. Justice League; Team Titans cameo on last pg. 14-Total Chaos, part 1; Team Titans-c/story cont'd in New Titans #90. 15-Total Chaos, part 4 .70 1.75
38-40: 38-Begin $1.95-c. 40-(9/94) .80 2.00
0-(10/94)-Begin Deathstroke, The Hunted .80 2.00
41-(11/94)-46 .80 2.00
Annual 1,2 ('92, '93, $3.50, 68 pgs.): 1-Nightwing & Vigilante app.; minor Eclipso app. 2-Bloodlines Deathstorm; 1st app. Gunfire 1.40 3.50
Annual 3 (1994, $3.95, 68 pgs.)-Elseworlds story 1.60 4.00

DEATH: THE HIGH COST OF LIVING (See Books of Magic & Sandman #8)
Mar, 1993 - No. 3, May, 1993 ($1.95, mini-series)
DC Comics (Vertigo)
1-Neil Gaiman scripts in all 1.20 2.90 7.00
1-Platinum edition 5.30 16.00 37.00
2 1.80 4.50
3-Pgs. 19 & 20 had wrong placement 1.40 3.50
3-Corrected version w/pgs. 19 & 20 facing each other; has no-c price plus has ads for Sebastion O & The Geek added 1.40 3.50
...Trade paperback (6/94, $12.95, Titan Books)-r/#1-3 & Death Talks About Life; prism-c 1.85 5.50 13.00

DEATH 3
Sept, 1993 - No. 4, Dec, 1993 ($1.75, mini-series)
Marvel Comics UK
1-($2.95)-Embossed-c 1.20 3.00
2-4 .70 1.75

DEATH VALLEY (Cowboys and Indians)
Oct, 1953 - No. 6, Aug, 1954?
Comic Media
1-Billy the Kid; Morisi-a; Andru/Esposito-c/a 7.00 21.00 42.00
2-Don Heck-c 4.35 13.00 26.00
3-6: 3,5-Morisi-a. 5-Discount-a 4.00 11.00 22.00

DEATH VALLEY (Becomes Frontier Scout, Daniel Boone No.10-13)
No. 7, 6/55 - No. 9, 10/55 (Continued from Comic Media series)
Charlton Comics
7-9: 8-Wolverton-a (half pg.) 4.00 10.00 20.00

DEATH WRECK
Jan, 1994 - No. 4, Apr, 1994 ($1.95, mini-series
Marvel Comics UK
1-4: 1-Metallic ink logo; Death's Head II app. .80 2.00

DEBBIE DEAN, CAREER GIRL
April, 1945 - No. 2, July, 1945
Civil Service Publ.
1,2-Newspaper reprints by Bert Whitman 11.00 32.00 75.00

DEBBI'S DATES (Also see Date With Debbi)
Apr-May, 1969 - No. 11, Dec-Jan, 1970-71
National Periodical Publications
1 2.40 6.00 12.00
2,3,5,7-11 1.20 3.00 6.00
4,6: 4-Neal Adams text illo, 6-Superman cameo 1.30 3.25 8.00

DEEP, THE (Movie)
November, 1977
Marvel Comics Group
1-Infantino-c/a 1.50

DEFENDERS, THE (TV)
Sept-Nov, 1962 - No. 2, Feb-Apr, 1963
Dell Publishing Co.
12-176-211(#1), 12-176-304(#2) 4.00 10.00 20.00

DEFENDERS, THE (Also see Giant-Size..., Marvel Feature, Marvel Treasury Edition, Secret Defenders & Sub-Mariner #34, 35; The New...#140-on)

Defenders #25 © MEG

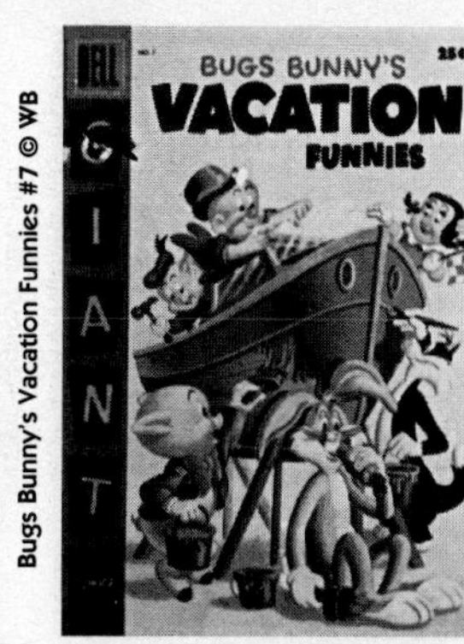

Bugs Bunny's Vacation Funnies #7 © WB

Walt Disney's Christmas Parade #3 © WDC

GD25 FN65 NM94 GD25 FN65 NM94

Aug, 1972 - No. 152, Feb, 1986
Marvel Comics Group
1-The Hulk, Doctor Strange, Sub-Mariner begin 9.00 27.00 64.00
2-Silver Surfer x-over 4.60 14.00 32.00
3-5: 3-Silver Surfer x-over. 4-Valkyrie joins 3.00 9.00 21.00
6-9: 6,8-Silver Surfer x-over. 9-Avengers app. 2.30 6.90 16.00
10-Hulk vs. Thor battle; Avengers app. 3.00 9.00 21.00
11-14: 11-Silver Surfer x-over. 12-Last 20¢ issue 1.70 4.20 10.00
15,16-Magneto & Brotherhood of Evil Mutants app. from X-Men
1.90 6.00 13.00
17-20: 17-Power Man x-over (11/74) 1.30 3.00 7.50
21-25: 24,25-Son of Satan app. 1.10 2.70 6.50
26-29-Guardians of the Galaxy app. (#26 is 8/75; pre-dates Marvel Presents #3): 28-1st full app. Starhawk (cameo #27). 29-Starhawk joins Guardians
1.70 5.00 12.00
30-50: 31,32-Origin Nighthawk. 35-Intro New Red Guardian. 44-Hellcat joins. 45-Dr. Strange leaves. 47-49-Early Moon Knight app. (5/77)
1.00 2.00 5.00
51-60: 53-1st app. Lunatik (cameo, Lobo lookalike). 55-Origin Red Guardian; Lunatik cameo. 56-1st full Lunatik story 1.70 4.25
61-72: 61-Lunatik & Spider-Man app. 70-73-Lunatik (origin #71)
1.50 3.75
73-75-Foolkiller II app. (Greg Salinger). 74-Nighthawk resigns
1.50 3.75
76-95,97-124,126-149,151: 77-Origin Omega. 78-Original Defenders return thru #101. 94-1st Gargoyle. 100-(52 pgs.)-Hellcat (Patsy Walker) revealed as Satan's daughter. 101-Silver Surfer-c & app. 104-The Beast joins. 105-Son of Satan joins. 106-Death of Nighthawk. 120,121-Son of Satan-c/stories. 122-Final app. Son of Satan (2 pgs.). 129-New Mutants cameo (3/84, early x-over) .90 2.25
96-Ghost Rider app. 1.90 4.75
125-(52 pgs.)-Intro new Defenders 1.30 3.25
150-(52 pgs.)-Origin Cloud 1.30 3.25
152-(52 pgs.)-Ties in with X-Factor & Secret Wars II 1.30 3.25
Annual 1 (1976, 52 pgs.)-New book-length story 1.70 4.25
NOTE: ***Art Adams*** *c-142p.* ***Austin*** *a-53i; c-65i, 119i, 145i.* ***Frank Bolle*** *a-7i, 10i, 11i.* ***Buckler*** *c(p)-34, 38, 76, 77, 79-86, 90, 91.* ***J. Buscema*** *c-66.* ***Giffen*** *a-42-49p, 50, 51-54p.* ***Golden*** *a-53p, 54p; c-94, 96.* ***Guice*** *c-129.* ***G. Kane*** *c(p)-13, 16, 18, 19, 21-26, 31-33, 35-37, 40, 41, 52, 55.* ***Kirby*** *c-42-45.* ***Mooney*** *a-3i, 31-34i, 62i, 63i, 85i.* ***Nasser*** *c-88p.* ***Perez*** *c(p)-51, 53, 54.* ***Rogers*** *c-98.* ***Starlin*** *c-110.* ***Tuska*** *a-57p. Silver Surfer in No. 2, 3, 6, 8-11, 92, 98-101, 107, 112-115, 122-125.*

DEFENDERS OF DYNATRON CITY
Feb, 1992 - No. 6, July, 1992 ($1.25, limited series)
Marvel Comics
1-6-Lucasarts characters. 2-Origin 1.25

DEFENDERS OF THE EARTH (TV)
Jan, 1987 - No. 5, Sept, 1987
Star Comics (Marvel)
1-5: The Phantom, Mandrake The Magician, Flash Gordon begin
1.00

DEFINITIVE DIRECTORY OF THE DC UNIVERSE, THE (See Who's Who...)

DELECTA OF THE PLANETS (See Don Fortune & Fawcett Miniatures)

DELLA VISION (...The Television Queen) (Patty Powers #4 on)
April, 1955 - No. 3, Aug, 1955
Atlas Comics
1-Al Hartley-c 10.00 30.00 70.00
2,3 8.35 25.00 50.00

DELL GIANT COMICS

Dell Publishing began to release square bound comics in 1949 with a 132-page issue called Christmas Parade #1. The covers were of a heavier stock to accommodate the increased number of pages. The books proved profitable at 25 cents, but the average number of pages was quickly reduced to 100. Ten years later they were converted to a numbering system similar to the Four Color Comics, for greater ease in distribution and the page counts cut back to mostly 84 pages. The label "Dell Giant" began to appear on the covers in 1954. Because of the size of the books and the heavier, less pliant cover stock, they are rarely found in high grade condition, and with the exception of a small quantity of copies released from Western Publishing's warehouse–are almost never found in near mint.

Abraham Lincoln Life Story 1(3/58) 6.00 18.00 42.00 90.00
Bugs Bunny Christmas Funnies 1(11/50, 116pp)
16.00 48.00 112.00 240.00
...Christmas Funnies 2(11/51, 116pp) 10.50 32.00 75.00 160.00
...Christmas Funnies 3-5(11/52-11/54,)-Becomes Christmas Party #6
9.50 29.00 68.00 145.00
...Christmas Funnies 7-9(12/56-12/58) 8.50 26.00 61.00 130.00
...Christmas Party 6(11/55)-Formerly Bugs Bunny Christmas Funnies
7.00 21.00 49.00 105.00
...County Fair 1(9/57) 10.50 32.00 75.00 160.00
...Halloween Parade 1(10/53) 9.50 29.00 68.00 145.00
...Halloween Parade 2(10/54)-Trick 'N' Treat Halloween Fun #3 on
8.50 26.00 61.00 130.00
...Trick 'N' Treat Halloween Fun 3,4(10/55-10/56)-Formerly Halloween Parade #2 9.50 28.00 65.00 140.00
...Vacation Funnies 1(7/51, 112pp) 16.00 48.00 112.00 240.00
...Vacation Funnies 2('52) 13.00 39.00 91.00 195.00
...Vacation Funnies 3-5('53-'55) 9.50 29.00 68.00 145.00
...Vacation Funnies 6-9('54-6/59) 8.50 26.00 61.00 130.00
Cadet Gray of West Point 1(4/58)-Williamson-a, 10pgs.; Buscema-a; photo-c
5.00 15.00 35.00 75.00
Christmas In Disneyland 1(12/57)-Barks-a, 18 pgs.
24.00 72.00 168.00 360.00
Christmas Parade 1(11/49)(132 pgs.)(1st Dell Giant)-Donald Duck (25pgs. by Barks, r-in G.K. Christmas Parade #5); Mickey Mouse & other film oriented stories; Cinderella (prior to movie), 7 Dwarfs, Bambi & Thumper, So Dear To My Heart, Flying Mouse, Dumbo, Cookieland & others
54.00 162.00 378.00 800.00
Christmas Parade 2('50)-Donald Duck (132 pgs.)(25 pgs. by Barks, r-in G.K. Christmas Parade #6). Mickey, Pluto, Chip & Dale, etc. Contents shift to a holiday expansion of W.D. C&S type format
40.00 120.00 280.00 600.00
Christmas Parade 3-7('51-'55, #3-116pgs; #4-7, 100 pgs.)
11.50 35.00 82.00 175.00
Christmas Parade 8(12/56)-Barks-a, 8 pgs.
20.00 60.00 140.00 300.00
Christmas Parade 9(12/58)-Barks-a, 20 pgs.
24.00 72.00 168.00 360.00
Christmas Treasury, A 1(11/54) 7.50 23.00 54.00 115.00
Davy Crockett, King Of The Wild Frontier 1(9/55)-Fess Parker photo-c; Marsh-a 15.00 45.00 105.00 225.00
Disneyland Birthday Party 1(10/58)-Barks-a, 16 pgs. r-by Gladstone
24.00 72.00 168.00 360.00
Donald and Mickey In Disneyland 1(5/58)10.50 32.00 75.00 160.00
Donald Duck Beach Party 1(7/54)-Has an Uncle Scrooge story (not by Barks) that prefigures the later rivalry with Flintheart Glomgold and tells of Scrooge's wild rivalry with another millionaire 13.50 40.00 93.00 200.00
...Beach Party 2(1955)-Lady & Tramp sty10.00 30.00 70.00 150.00
...Beach Party 3-5(1956-58) 10.00 30.00 70.00 150.00
...Beach Party 6(8/59, 84pp)-Stapled 6.50 20.00 47.00 100.00
Donald Duck Fun Book 1,2(1953 & 10/54)-Games, puzzles, comics & cut-outs (very rare in unused condition)(most copies commonly have defaced interior pgs.) 33.50 100.00 233.00 500.00
Donald Duck In Disneyland 1(9/55)-1st Disneyland Dell Giant
12.00 36.00 84.00 180.00
Golden West Rodeo Treasury 1(10/57) 7.00 20.00 50.00 105.00
Huey, Dewey and Louie Back To School 1(9/58)
8.00 24.00 56.00 120.00
Lady and The Tramp 1(6/55) 16.50 50.00 117.00 250.00
Life Stories of American Presidents 1(11/57)-Buscema-a

Walt Disney's Silly Symphonies #9 © WDC

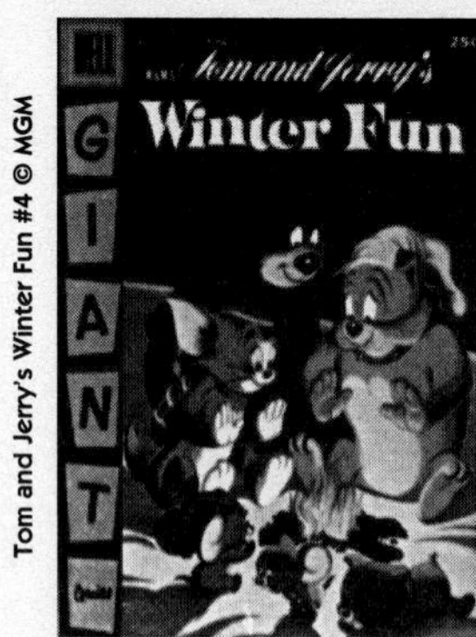

Tom and Jerry's Winter Fun #4 © MGM

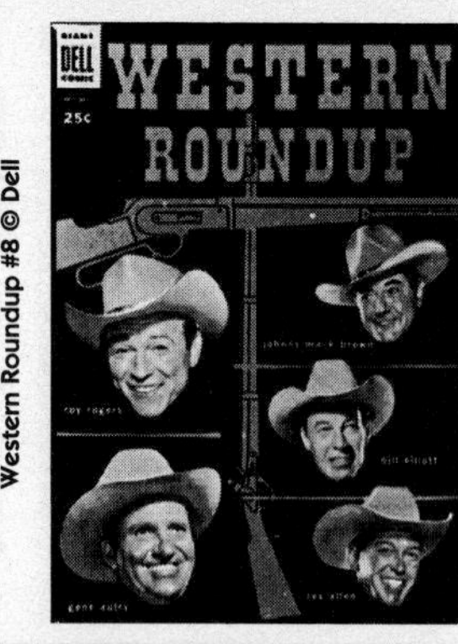

Western Roundup #8 © Dell

GD25 FN65 NM94

4.50 13.00 30.00 65.00
Lone Ranger Golden West 3(8/55)-Formerly Lone Ranger Western Treasury
15.00 45.00 105.00 225.00
Lone Ranger Movie Story nn(3/56)-Origin Lone Ranger in text; Clayton Moore photo-c 29.00 87.00 203.00 435.00
...Western Treasury 1(9/53)-Origin Lone Ranger, Silver, & Tonto; painted cover
17.00 51.00 119.00 255.00
...Western Treasury 2(8/54)-Becomes Lone Ranger Golden West #3
9.50 29.00 68.00 145.00
Marge's Little Lulu & Alvin Story Telling Time 1(3/59)-r/#2,5,3,11,30,10,21,17,8, 14,16; Stanley-a 11.50 35.00 82.00 175.00
...& Her Friends 4(3/56)-Tripp-a 10.00 30.00 70.00 150.00
...& Her Special Friends 3(3/55)-Tripp-a 12.00 36.00 84.00 180.00
...& Tubby At Summer Camp 5(10/57)-Tripp-a
10.00 30.00 70.00 150.00
...& Tubby At Summer Camp 2(10/58)-Tripp-a
10.00 30.00 70.00 150.00
...& Tubby Halloween Fun 6(10/57)-Tripp-a
10.00 30.00 70.00 150.00
...& Tubby Halloween Fun 2(10/58)-Tripp-a
10.00 30.00 70.00 150.00
...& Tubby In Alaska 1(7/59)-Tripp-a 10.00 30.00 70.00 150.00
...On Vacation 1(7/54)-r/4C-110,14,4C-146,5,4C-97,4,4C-158,3,1;Stanley-a
22.00 66.00 154.00 330.00
...& Tubby Annual 1(3/53)-r/4C-165,4C-74,4C-146,4C-97,4C-158, 4C-139, 4C -131; Stanley-a (1st Lulu Dell Gnt) 27.00 81.00 189.00 405.00
...& Tubby Annual 2('54)-r/4C-139,6,4C-115,4C-74,5,4C-97,3,4C-146,18; Stanley-a 24.00 72.00 168.00 360.00
Marge's Tubby & His Clubhouse Pals 1(10/56)-1st app. Gran'pa Feeb;1st app. Janie; written by Stanley; Tripp-a 11.50 35.00 82.00 175.00
Mickey Mouse Almanac 1(12/57)-Barks-a, 8pgs.
25.00 75.00 175.00 370.00
...Birthday Party 1(9/53)-r/entire 48pgs. of Gottfredson's "Mickey Mouse in Love Trouble" from WDC&S 36-39. Quality equal to original. Also reprints one story each from 4-Color 27, 29, & 181 plus 6 panels of highlights in the career of Mickey Mouse 30.00 90.00 210.00 450.00
...Club Parade 1(12/55)-r/4-Color 16 with some death trap scenes redrawn by Paul Murry & recolored with night turned into day; quality less than original
24.00 72.00 168.00 360.00
...In Fantasy Land 1(5/57) 12.00 36.00 84.00 180.00
...In Frontier Land 1(5/56)-Mickey Mouse Club issue
12.00 36.00 84.00 180.00
...Summer Fun 1(8/58)-Mobile cut-outs on back-c; becomes Summer Fun with #2 12.00 36.00 84.00 180.00
Moses & The Ten Commandments 1(8/57)-Not based on movie; Dell's adaptation; Sekowsky-a 5.00 15.00 35.00 75.00
Nancy & Sluggo Travel Time 1(9/58) 6.25 19.00 44.00 95.00
Peter Pan Treasure Chest 1(1/53, 212pp)-Disney; contains 54-page movie adaptation & other P. Pan stories; plus Donald & Mickey stories w/P. Pan; a 32-page retelling of "D. Duck Finds Pirate Gold" with yellow beak, called "Capt. Hook & the Buried Treasure" 100.00 300.00 700.00 1500.00
Picnic Party 6,7(7/55-6/56)(Formerly Vacation Parade)-UncleScrooge, Mickey & Donald 10.00 30.00 70.00 150.00
Picnic Party 8(7/57)-Barks-a, 6pgs 20.00 60.00 140.00 300.00
Pogo Parade 1(9/53)-Kelly-a(r-/Pogo from Animal Comics in this order: #11,13,21,14,27,16,23,9,18,15,17) 27.00 81.00 189.00 405.00
Raggedy Ann & Andy 1(2/55) 15.00 45.00 105.00 225.00
Santa Claus Funnies 1(11/52)-Dan Noonan -A Christmas Carol adaptation
7.50 23.00 54.00 115.00
Silly Symphonies 1(9/52)-Redrawing of Gotfredson's Mickey Mouse strip of "The Brave Little Tailor;" 2 Good Housekeeping pages (from 1943); Lady and the Two Siamese Cats, three years before "Lady & the Tramp;" a retelling of Donald Duck's first app. in "The Wise Little Hen" & other stories based on 1930's Silly Symphony cartoons 27.00 81.00 189.00 405.00
Silly Symphonies 2(9/53)-M. Mouse in "The Sorcerer's Apprentice", 2 Good Housekeeping pages (from 1944); The Pelican & the Snipe, Elmer Elephant, Peculiar Penguins, Little Hiawatha, & others
24.00 72.00 168.00 360.00
Silly Symphonies 3(2/54)-r/Mickey & The Beanstalk (4-Color #157, 39pgs.), Little Minnehaha, Pablo, The Flying Gauchito, Pluto, & Bongo, & 2 Good Housekeeping pages (1944) 20.00 60.00 140.00 300.00
Silly Symphonies 4(8/54)-r/Dumbo (4-Color 234), Morris The Midget Moose, The Country Cousin, Bongo, & Clara Cluck
20.00 60.00 140.00 300.00
Silly Symphonies 5(2/55)-r/Cinderella (4-Color 272), Bucky Bug, Pluto, Little Hiawatha, The 7 Dwarfs & Dumbo, Pinocchio
17.00 51.00 119.00 250.00
Silly Symphonies 6(8/55)-r/Pinocchio(WDC&S 63), The 7 Dwarfs & Thumper (WDC&S 45), M. Mouse "Adventures With Robin Hood" (40 pgs.), Johnny Appleseed, Pluto & Peter Pan, & Bucky Bug; Cut-out on back-c
17.00 51.00 119.00 250.00
Silly Symphonies 7(2/57)-r/Reluctant Dragon, Ugly Duckling, M. Mouse & Peter Pan, Jiminy Cricket, Peter & The Wolf, Brer Rabbit, Bucky Bug; Cut-out on back-c 17.00 51.00 119.00 250.00
Silly Symphonies 8(2/58)-r/Thumper Meets The 7 Dwarfs (4-Color #19), Jiminy Cricket, Niok, Brer Rabbit; Cut-out on back-c
17.00 51.00 119.00 250.00
Silly Symphonies 9(2/59)-r/Paul Bunyan, Humphrey Bear, Jiminy Cricket, The Social Lion, Goliath II; cut-out on back-c
15.00 45.00 105.00 225.00
Sleeping Beauty 1(4/59) 27.00 81.00 189.00 405.00
Summer Fun 2(8/59, 84pp, stapled binding)(Formerly Mickey Mouse...)-Barks-a(2), 24 pgs. 24.00 72.00 168.00 360.00
Tarzan's Jungle Annual 1(8/52)-Lex Barker photo on-c of #1,2
12.00 36.00 84.00 180.00
...Annual 2(8/53) 9.00 27.00 63.00 135.00
...Annual 3-7('54-9/58)(two No. 5s)-Manning-a-No. 3,5-7; Marsh-a in No. 1-7 plus painted-c 1-7 7.50 22.00 51.00 110.00
Tom And Jerry Back To School 1(9/56) 12.50 38.00 89.00 190.00
...Picnic Time 1(7/58) 9.50 29.00 68.00 145.00
...Summer Fun 1(7/54)-Droopy written by Barks
14.00 42.00 98.00 210.00
...Summer Fun 2-4(7/55-7/57) 6.50 19.00 44.00 95.00
...Toy Fair 1(6/58) 9.50 29.00 68.00 145.00
...Winter Carnival 1(12/52)-Droopy written by Barks
20.00 60.00 140.00 300.00
...Winter Carnival 2(12/53)-Droopy written by Barks
17.00 51.00 119.00 255.00
...Winter Fun 3(12/54) 6.50 19.00 44.00 95.00
...Winter Fun 4-7(12/55-11/58) 5.50 16.00 37.00 80.00
Treasury of Dogs, A 1(10/56) 5.00 15.00 35.00 75.00
Treasury of Horses, A (9/55) 5.00 15.00 35.00 75.00
Uncle Scrooge Goes To Disneyland 1(8/57p)-Barks-a, 20pgs.r-by Gladstone
24.00 72.00 168.00 360.00
Vacation In Disneyland 1(8/58) 10.50 32.00 75.00 160.00
Vacation Parade 1(7/50, 132pp)-Donald Duck & Mickey Mouse; Barks-a, 55 pgs. 80.00 240.00 560.00 1200.00
Vacation Parade 2(7/51,116pp) 27.00 81.00 189.00 405.00
Vacation Parade 3-5(7/52-7/54)-Becomes Picnic Party No. 6 on. #4-Robin Hood Advs. 13.50 40.00 93.00 200.00
Western Roundup 1(6/52)-Photo-c; Gene Autry, Roy Rogers, Johnny Mack Brown, Rex Allen, & Bill Elliott begin; photo back-c begin, end No. 14,16,18
19.00 58.00 135.00 290.00
Western Roundup 2(2/53)-Photo-c 11.50 35.00 82.00 175.00
Western Roundup 3-5(7-9/53 - 1-3/54)-Photo-c
9.00 27.00 63.00 135.00
Western Roundup 6-10(4-6/54 - 4-6/55)-Photo-c
8.50 26.00 61.00 130.00
Western Roundup 11-13,16,17-Photo-c; Manning-a. 11-Flying A's Range Rider, Dale Evans begin 7.50 23.00 54.00 115.00
Western Roundup 14,15,25(1-3/59)-Photo-c
7.50 23.00 54.00 115.00

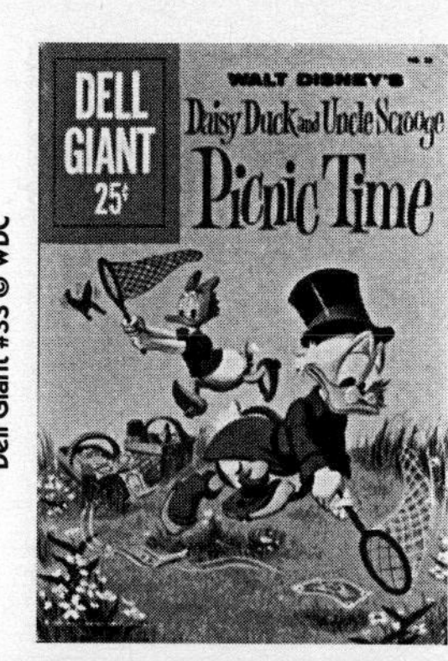

Dell Giant #33 © WDC

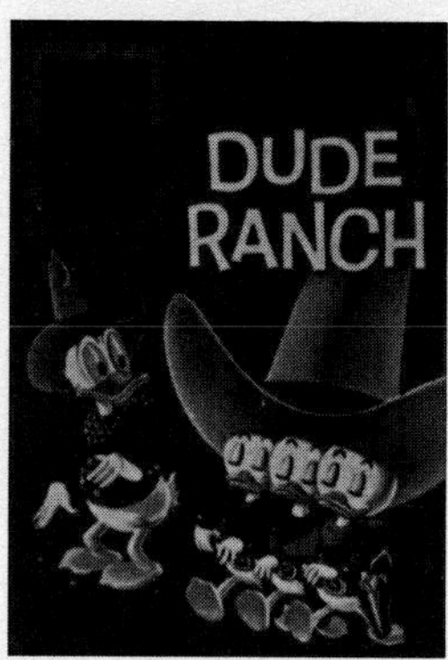

Dell Giant #52 © WDC

Demon #1 © DC

GD25 FN65 NM94

Western Roundup 18-Toth-a; last photo-c; Gene Autry ends
8.00 24.00 56.00 120.00
Western Roundup 19-24-Manning-a. 19-Buffalo Bill Jr. begins (7-9/57; early app.). 19,20,22-Toth-a. 21-Rex Allen, Johnny Mack Brown end. 22-Jace Pearson's Texas Rangers, Rin Tin Tin, Tales of Wells Fargo (2nd app., 4-6/58) & Wagon Train (2nd app.) begin 7.00 21.00 49.00 105.00
Woody Woodpecker Back To School 1(10/52)
9.50 28.00 65.00 140.00
...Back To School 2-4,6('53-10/57)-County Fair No. 5
6.50 19.00 44.00 95.00
...County Fair 5(9/56)-Formerly Back To School
6.50 19.00 44.00 95.00
...County Fair 2(11/58) 5.50 16.00 37.00 80.00

DELL GIANTS (Consecutive numbering)
No. 21, Sept, 1959 - No. 55, Sept, 1961 (Most 84 pgs., 25¢)
Dell Publishing Co.

GD25 FN65 VF82 NM94

21-(#1)-M.G.M.'s Tom & Jerry Picnic Time (84pp, stapled binding)-Painted-c
10.50 32.00 75.00 160.00
22-Huey, Dewey & Louie Back to School (Disney; 10/59, 84pp, square binding begins) 8.00 24.00 56.00 120.00
23-Marge's Little Lulu & Tubby Halloween Fun (10/59)-Tripp-a
10.00 30.00 70.00 150.00
24-Woody Woodpecker's Family Fun (11/59)(Walter Lantz)
7.50 23.00 54.00 115.00
25-Tarzan's Jungle World(11/59)-Marsh-a; painted-c
10.00 30.00 70.00 150.00
26-Christmas Parade(Disney; 12/59)-Barks-a, 16pgs.; Barks draws himself on wanted poster pg. 13 20.00 60.00 140.00 300.00
27-Man in Space r-/4-Color 716,866, & 954 (100 pgs., 35¢)(Disney)(TV)
9.50 29.00 68.00 145.00
28-Bugs Bunny's Winter Fun (2/60) 9.50 29.00 68.00 145.00
29-Marge's Little Lulu & Tubby in Hawaii (4/60)-Tripp-a
10.00 30.00 70.00 150.00
30-Disneyland USA(Disney; 6/60) 8.50 26.00 61.00 130.00
31-Huckleberry Hound Summer Fun (7/60)(TV)(HannaBarbera)-Yogi Bear & Pixie & Dixie app. 13.00 39.00 91.00 195.00
32-Bugs Bunny Beach Party 5.50 17.00 40.00 85.00
33-Daisy Duck & Uncle Scrooge Picnic Time (Disney; 9/60)
8.50 26.00 61.00 130.00
34-Nancy & Sluggo Summer Camp (8/60)
6.50 20.00 47.00 100.00
35-Huey, Dewey & Louie Back to School (Disney; 10/60)-1st app. Daisy Duck's Nieces, April, May & June 10.00 30.00 70.00 150.00
36-Marge's Little Lulu & Witch Hazel Halloween Fun (10/60)-Tripp-a
10.00 30.00 70.00 150.00
37-Tarzan, King of the Jungle (11/60)-Marsh-a; painted-c
9.00 27.00 63.00 135.00
38-Uncle Donald & His Nephews Family Fun (Disney; 11/60)-Cover painting based on a pencil sketch by Barks 13.00 39.00 91.00 195.00
39-Walt Disney's Merry Christmas (Disney; 12/60)-Cover painting based on a pencil sketch by Barks 13.00 39.00 91.00 195.00
40-Woody Woodpecker Christmas Parade (12/60)(Walter Lantz)
5.50 17.00 40.00 85.00
41-Yogi Bear's Winter Sports (12/60)(TV)(Hanna-Barbera)-Huckleberry Hound & Top Cat app. 12.50 38.00 89.00 190.00
42-Marge's Little Lulu & Tubby in Australia (4/61)
10.00 30.00 70.00 150.00
43-Mighty Mouse in Outer Space (5/61) 19.00 57.00 133.00 285.00
44-Around the World with Huckleberry and His Friends (7/61)(TV)(Hanna-Barbera)-Yogi Bear app. 12.50 38.00 89.00 190.00
45-Nancy & Sluggo Summer Camp (8/61)
5.50 17.00 40.00 85.00
46-Bugs Bunny Beach Party (8/61) 5.50 17.00 40.00 85.00
47-Mickey & Donald in Vacationland (Disney; 8/61)
8.00 24.00 56.00 120.00
48-The Flintstones (No. 1)(Bedrock Bedlam)(7/61)(TV)(Hanna-Barbera)
17.00 50.00 119.00 250.00
49-Huey, Dewey & Louie Back to School (Disney; 9/61)
8.00 24.00 56.00 120.00
50-Marge's Little Lulu & Witch Hazel Trick 'N' Treat (10/61)
10.00 30.00 70.00 150.00
51-Tarzan, King of the Jungle by Jesse Marsh (11/61)-Painted-c
7.00 21.00 49.00 105.00
52-Uncle Donald & His Nephews Dude Ranch (Disney; 11/61)
6.50 20.00 47.00 100.00
53-Donald Duck Merry Christmas (Disney; 12/61)
6.50 20.00 47.00 100.00
54-Woody Woodpecker's Christmas Party (12/61)-Issued after No. 55
6.50 20.00 47.00 100.00
55-Daisy Duck & Uncle Scrooge Showboat (Disney; 9/61)
8.00 24.00 56.00 120.00
NOTE: All issues printed with & without ad on back cover.

DELL JUNIOR TREASURY
June, 1955 - No. 10, Oct, 1957 (15¢) (All painted-c)
Dell Publishing Co.

GD25 FN65 NM94

1-Alice in Wonderland; r/4-Color #331 (52 pgs.) 11.50 34.00 80.00
2-Aladdin & the Wonderful Lamp 9.15 27.50 55.00
3-Gulliver's Travels (1/56) 7.50 22.50 45.00
4-Adventures of Mr. Frog & Miss Mouse 8.35 25.00 50.00
5-The Wizard of Oz (7/56) 9.15 27.50 55.00
6-Heidi (10/56) 7.50 22.50 45.00
7-Santa and the Angel 7.50 22.50 45.00
8-Raggedy Ann and the Camel with the Wrinkled Knees
7.50 22.50 45.00
9-Clementina the Flying Pig 7.50 22.50 45.00
10-Adventures of Tom Sawyer 7.50 22.50 45.00

DEMOLITION MAN
Nov, 1993 - No. 4, Feb, 1994 ($1.75, mini-series)
DC Comics
1-4-Movie adaptation .70 1.75

DEMON, THE (See Detective Comics No. 482-485)
Aug-Sept, 1972 - V3#16, Jan, 1974
National Periodical Publications
1-Origin; Kirby-c/a in all 3.90 11.60 27.00
2-5 2.20 5.40 13.00
6-16 1.50 3.80 9.00

DEMON, THE (2nd series)
Jan, 1987 - No. 4, Apr, 1987 (75¢, mini-series)(#2 has #4 of 4 on-c)
DC Comics
1-4: Matt Wagner-a(p) & scripts 1.00

DEMON, THE (3rd series)
July, 1990 - Present ($1.50/$1.75/$1.95)
DC Comics
1-Grant scripts begin: 1-4-Painted-c .70 1.80
2-18,20-27: 3,8-Batman app. (cameo #4). 12-Bisley painted-c. 12-15,21-Lobo app. (1 pg. cameo #11). 23-Robin app. .65 1.60
19-($2.50, 44 pgs.)-Lobo poster stapled inside 1.20 3.00
28-47: 28-Superman-c/story; begin $1.75-c. 29-Superman app. 31,33-39-Lobo app. 46-Return of The Haunted Tank-c/s (also in #47,48) .70 1.75
48,49,51: 48-Begin $1.95-c. 51-(9/94) .80 2.00
50 ($2.95, 52 pgs.) 1.20 3.00
0,52-56: 0-(10/94) .80 2.00
Annual 1 (1992, $3.00, 68 pgs.)-Eclipso-c/story 1.20 3.00
Annual 2 (1993, $3.50, 68 pgs.) 1.40 3.50
NOTE: ***Alan Grant*** *scripts in #1-16, 20, 21, 23-25, 30-39, Annual 1.* ***Wagner*** *a/scripts-22.*

DEMON DREAMS (Pacific)(Value: cover or less)

DEMON-HUNTER

Demon Hunter #1 © Aircel

Dennis the Menace Giant #40 © KFS

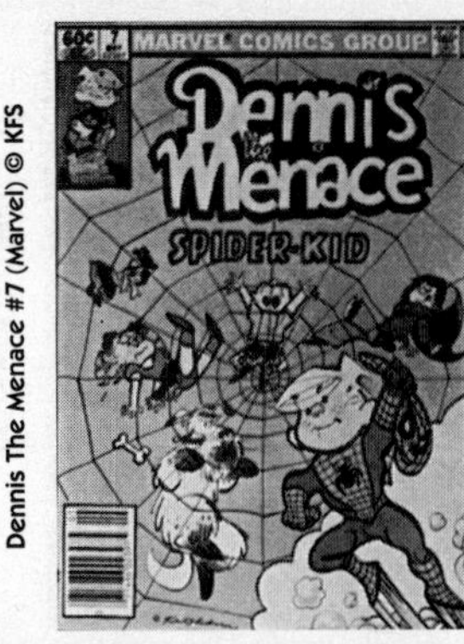

Dennis The Menace #7 (Marvel) © KFS

GD25 FN65 NM94 GD25 FN65 NM94

September, 1975
Seaboard Periodicals (Atlas)

1-Origin; Buckler-c/a 1.00

DEMONIC TOYS (Eternity)(Value: cover or less)

DEMON KNIGHT: A GRIMJACK GRAPHIC NOVEL (First)(Value: cover or less)

DENNIS THE MENACE (TV with 1959 issues) (Becomes ...Fun Fest Series; See The Best of... & The Very Best of...)(...Fun Fest on-c only to #156-166)
8/53 - #14, 1/56; #15, 3/56 - #31, 11/58; #32, 1/59 - #166, 11/79
Standard Comics/Pines No.15-31/Hallden (Fawcett) No.32 on

1-1st app. Dennis, Mr. & Mrs. Wilson, Ruff & Dennis' mom & dad; Wiseman-a, written by Fred Toole-most issues 46.00 140.00 325.00
2 20.00 60.00 140.00
3-10: 8-Last pre-code issue 11.50 342.00 80.00
11-20 10.00 30.00 60.00
21-30: 22-1st app. Margaret w/blonde hair 6.70 20.00 40.00
31-40: 31-1st app. Joey. 37-A-Bomb blast panel. 39-1st app. Gina (11/59) 4.00 12.00 24.00
41-60 3.20 8.00 16.00
61-90 2.20 5.50 11.00
91-166 1.00 2.50 6.00
...& Dirt('59,'68)-Soil Conservation giveaway; r-# 36; Wiseman-c/a 1.20 3.00 6.00
...Away We Go('70)-Caladayl giveaway 1.20 3.00 6.00
...Coping with Family Stress-giveaway .80 2.00 4.00
...Takes a Poke at Poison('61)-Food & Drug Assn. giveaway; Wiseman-c/a 1.20 3.00 6.00
...Takes a Poke at Poison-Revised 1/66, 11/70, 1972, 1974, 1977, 1981 1.60 4.00

NOTE: ***Wiseman** c/a-1-46, 53, 68, 69.*

DENNIS THE MENACE (Giants) (No. 1 titled Giant Vacation Special; becomes Dennis the Menace Bonus Magazine No. 76 on)
(#1-8,18,23,25,30,38: 100 pgs.; rest to #41: 84 pgs.; #42-75: 68 pgs.)
Summer, 1955 - No. 75, Dec, 1969
Standard/Pines/Hallden(Fawcett)

nn-Giant Vacation Special(Summ/55-Standard) 14.00 43.00 100.00
nn-Christmas issue (Winter '55) 12.00 36.00 85.00
2-Giant Vacation Special (Summer '56-Pines)
3-Giant Christmas issue (Winter '56-Pines)
4-Giant Vacation Special (Summer '57-Pines)
5-Giant Christmas issue (Winter '57-Pines)
6-In Hawaii (Giant Vacation Special)(Summer '58-Pines)
6-In Hawaii (Summer '59-Hallden)-2nd printing; says 3rd large printing on-c
6-In Hawaii (Summer '60)-3rd printing; says 4th large printing on-c
6-In Hawaii (Summer '62)-4th printing; says 5th large printing on-c
6-Giant Christmas issue (Winter '58)
each.... 10.00 30.00 60.00
7-In Hollywood (Winter '59-Hallden)
7-In Hollywood (Summer '61)-2nd printing
8-In Mexico (Winter '60, 100 pgs.-Hallden/Fawcett)
8-In Mexico (Summer '62, 2nd printing)
9-Goes to Camp (Summer '61, 84 pgs.)-1st CCA approved issue
9-Goes to Camp (Summer '62)-2nd printing
10-X-Mas issue (Winter '61)
11-Giant Christmas issue (Winter '62)
12-Triple Feature (Winter '62)
each.... 8.35 25.00 50.00
13-Best of Dennis the Menace (Spring '63)-Reprints
14-And His Dog Ruff (Summer '63)
15-In Washington, D.C. (Summer '63)
16-Goes to Camp (Summer '63)-Reprints No. 9
17-& His Pal Joey (Winter '63)
18-In Hawaii (Reprints No. 6)
19-Giant Christmas issue (Winter '63)
20-Spring Special (Spring '64)
each.... 4.20 12.50 25.00
21-40: 30-r/#6 2.40 6.00 12.00
41-75: 68-Partial-r/#6 1.60 4.00 8.00

NOTE: ***Wiseman** c/a-1-8, 12, 14, 15, 17, 20, 22, 27, 28, 31, 35, 36, 41, 49.*

DENNIS THE MENACE
Nov, 1981 - No. 13, Nov, 1982
Marvel Comics Group

1-13: 1,2-New art. 3-Part-r. 4,5-r. 5-X-Mas-c & issue 1.00

NOTE: ***Hank Ketcham** c-most; a-3, 12. **Wiseman** a-4, 5.*

DENNIS THE MENACE AND HIS DOG RUFF
Summer, 1961
Hallden/Fawcett

1-Wiseman-c/a 5.85 17.50 35.00

DENNIS THE MENACE AND HIS FRIENDS
1969; No. 5, Jan, 1970 - No. 46, April, 1980 (All reprints)
Fawcett Publications

Dennis the Menace & Joey No. 2 (7/69) 2.40 6.00 12.00
Dennis the Menace & Ruff No. 2 (9/69) 2.00 5.00 10.00
Dennis the Menace & Mr. Wilson No. 1 (10/69) 2.40 6.00 12.00
Dennis & Margaret No. 1 (Winter '69) 1.20 3.00 6.00
5-20: 5-Dennis the Menace & Margaret. 6-...& Joey. 7-...& Ruff. 8-...& Mr. Wilson 1.60 4.00
21-37 1.20 3.00
38-46 (Digest size, 148 pgs., 4/78, 95¢) 1.60 4.00

NOTE: *Titles rotate every four issues, beginning with No. 5.*

DENNIS THE MENACE AND HIS PAL JOEY
Summer, 1961 (10¢) (See Dennis the Menace Giants No. 45)
Fawcett Publications

1-Wiseman-c/a 5.85 17.50 35.00

DENNIS THE MENACE AND THE BIBLE KIDS
1977 (36 pgs.)
Word Books

1-10: 1-Jesus. 2-Joseph. 3-David. 4-The Bible Girls. 5-Moses. 6-More About Jesus. 7-The Lord's Prayer. 8-Stories Jesus told. 9-Paul, God's Traveller. 10-In the Beginning 1.00

NOTE: ***Ketcham** c/a in all.*

DENNIS THE MENACE BIG BONUS SERIES
No. 10, Feb, 1980 - No. 11, Apr, 1980
Fawcett Publications

10,11 1.50

DENNIS THE MENACE BONUS MAGAZINE (Formerly Dennis the Menace Giants Nos. 1-75)
No. 76, 1/70 - No. 194, 10/79; (No. 76-124: 68 pgs.; No. 125-163: 52 pgs.; No. 164 on: 36 pgs.)
Fawcett Publications

76-90 1.60 4.00
91-110 1.20 3.00
111-194: 166-Indicia printed backwards 1.20

DENNIS THE MENACE COMICS DIGEST
April, 1982 - No. 3, Aug, 1982 (Digest Size, $1.25)
Marvel Comics Group

1-3-Reprints .80 2.00

NOTE: ***Ketcham** c-all. **Wiseman** a-all. A few thousand #1's were published with a DC emblem on cover.*

DENNIS THE MENACE FUN BOOK
1960 (100 pgs.)
Fawcett Publications/Standard Comics

1-Part Wiseman-a 7.50 22.50 45.00

DENNIS THE MENACE FUN FEST SERIES (Formerly Dennis the Menace #166)
No. 16, Jan, 1980 - No. 17, Mar, 1980 (40¢)

The Destroyer V2 #1 © MEG

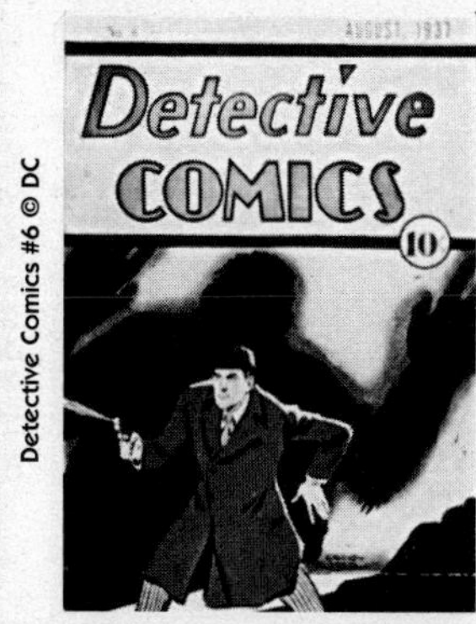

Detective Comics #6 © DC

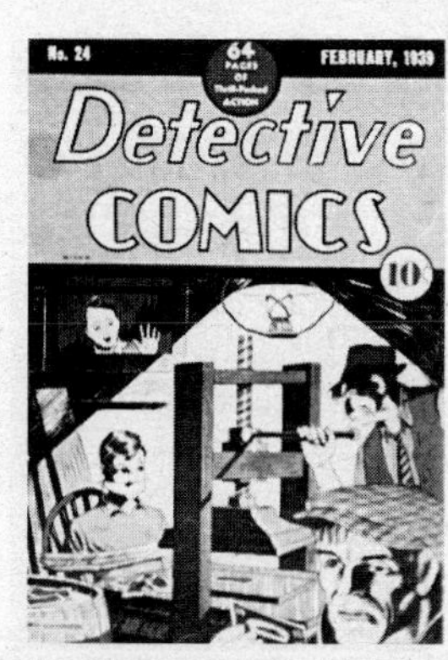

Detective Comics #24 © DC

GD25 FN65 NM94 GD25 FN65 NM94

Hallden (Fawcett)

16,17-By Hank Ketcham 1.00

DENNIS THE MENACE POCKET FULL OF FUN!
Spring, 1969 - No. 50, March, 1980 (196 pgs.) (Digest size)
Fawcett Publications (Hallden)

1-Reprints in all issues 2.40 6.00 12.00
2-10 1.20 3.00 6.00
11-28 .80 2.00 4.00
29-50: 35,40,46-Sunday strip-r .80 2.00
NOTE: *No. 1-28 are 196 pgs.; No. 29-36: 164 pgs.; No. 37: 148 pgs.; No. 38 on: 132 pgs. No. 8, 11, 15, 21, 25, 29 all contain strip reprints.*

DENNIS THE MENACE TELEVISION SPECIAL
Summer, 1961 - No. 2, Spring, 1962 (Giant)
Fawcett Publications (Hallden Div.)

1 6.70 20.00 40.00
2 4.00 11.00 22.00

DENNIS THE MENACE TRIPLE FEATURE
Winter, 1961 (Giant)
Fawcett Publications

1-Wiseman-c/a 6.70 20.00 40.00

DEPUTY, THE (See 4-Color No. 1077, 1130, 1225)

DEPUTY DAWG (TV) (Also see New Terrytoons)
Oct-Dec, 1961 - No. 1299, 1962; No. 1, Aug, 1965
Dell Publishing Co./Gold Key

4-Color 1238,1299 11.50 34.00 80.00
1(10164-508)(8/65)-Gold Key 10.00 30.00 70.00

DEPUTY DAWG PRESENTS DINKY DUCK AND HASHIMOTO-SAN
August, 1965 (TV)
Gold Key

1(10159-508) 10.00 30.00 65.00

DESIGN FOR SURVIVAL (Gen. Thomas S. Power's...)
1968 (36 pgs. in color) (25¢)
American Security Council Press

nn-Propaganda against the Threat of Communism-Aircraft cover
4.00 10.00 20.00
Twin Circle Edition-Cover shows panels from inside 2.40 6.00 12.00

DESPERADO (Becomes Black Diamond Western No. 9 on)
June, 1948 - No. 8, Feb, 1949 (All 52 pgs.)
Lev Gleason Publications

1-Biro-c on all; contains inside photo-c of Charles Biro, Lev Gleason & Bob Wood 10.00 30.00 65.00
2 5.35 16.00 32.00
3-Story with over 20 killings 5.35 16.00 32.00
4-8 4.00 12.00 24.00
NOTE: ***Barry** a-2. **Fuje** a-4, 8. **Guardineer** a-5-7. **Kida** a-3-7. **Ed Moore** a-4, 6.*

DESTINATION MOON (See Fawcett Movie Comics, Space Adventures #20, 23, & Strange Adventures #1)

DESTROY!! (Eclipse)(Value: cover or less)

DESTROYER, THE
Nov, 1989 - No. 9, June, 1990 ($2.25, B&W, magazine, 52 pgs.)
Marvel Comics

1-Based on Remo Williams movie, paperbacks .90 2.25
2-9: 2-Williamson part inks. 4-Ditko-a .90 2.25

DESTROYER, THE
V2#1, March, 1991 ($1.95, 52 pgs.)
V3#1, Dec, 1991 - No. 4, Mar, 1992 ($1.95, mini-series)
Marvel Comics

V2#1-Based on Remo Williams paperbacks .80 2.00
V3#1-4: 1-4-Simonson-c. 3-Morrow-a .80 2.00

DESTROYER DUCK
Feb, 1982 - No. 7, May, 1984 (#2-7: Baxter paper) ($1.50)
Eclipse Comics

1-Origin Destroyer Duck; 1st app. Groo 1.30 3.25
2-7: 2-Starling back-up begins 1.25
NOTE: ***Neal Adams** c-1i. **Kirby** c/a-1-5p. **Miller** c-7.*

DESTRUCTOR, THE
February, 1975 - No. 4, Aug, 1975
Atlas/Seaboard

1-Origin; Ditko/Wood-a; Wood-c(i) 1.50
2-4: 2-Ditko/Wood-a. 3,4-Ditko-a(p) 1.00

DETECTIVE COMICS (Also see Batman and Special Edition)
March, 1937 - Present
National Periodical Publications/DC Comics

GD25 FN65 VF82

1-(Scarce)-Slam Bradley & Spy by Siegel & Shuster, Speed Saunders by Guardineer, Flat Foot Flannigan by Gustavson, Cosmo, the Phantom of Disguise, Buck Marshall, Bruce Nelson begin; Chin Lung in 'Claws of the Red Dragon' serial begins; Fu Manchu-c by Vincent Sullivan
7,200.00 21,600.00 36,000.00
(Estimated up to 30 total copies exist, 1 in NM/Mint)
2 (Rare)-Creig Flessel-c begin; new logo 1285.00 3857.00 9000.00
3 (Rare) 929.00 2785.00 6500.00

GD25 FN65 NM94

4,5: 5-Larry Steele begins 571.00 1715.00 4000.00
6,7,9,10 400.00 1200.00 2800.00
8-Mister Chang-c 457.00 1371.00 3200.00
11-17,19: 14-Superman ad for Action #1 (4/38). 17-1st app. Fu Manchu in Det.
300.00 900.00 2100.00
18-Fu Manchu-c; last Flessel-c 400.00 1200.00 2800.00
20-The Crimson Avenger begins (1st app.) 471.00 1415.00 3300.00
21,23-25 243.00 730.00 1700.00
22-1st & only Crimson Avenger-c (12/38) 300.00 900.00 2100.00
26 243.00 730.00 1700.00

GD25 FN65 VF82 NM94

27-The Batman & Commissioner Gordon begin (1st app.) by Bob Kane (5/39); Batman-c (1st) 11,500.00 34,500.00 74,750.00 115,000.00
(Estimated up to 50+ total copies exist, 3 in NM/Mint)
27-Reprint, Oversize 13-1/2x10". WARNING: This comic is an exact duplicate reprint of the original except for its size. DC published it in 1974 with a second cover titling it as Famous First Edition. There have been many reported cases of the outer cover being removed and the interior sold as the original edition. The reprint with the new outer cover removed is practically worthless; see Famous First Edition for value.

GD25 FN65 NM94

27(1984)-Oreo Cookies giveaway (32 pgs., paper-c, r-/Det. 27, 38 & Batman No. 1 (1st Joker) 4.35 13.00 26.00
28-2nd app. The Batman (6 pg. story) 1214.00 3643.00 8500.00

GD25 FN65 VF82 NM94

29-Batman-c; Doctor Death-c/story; Batman story now 10 pgs.
1650.00 4950.00 10,725.00 16,500.00
(Estimated up to 75+ total copies exist, 6 in NM/Mint)

GD25 FN65 NM94

30,32: 30-Dr. Death app. cont'd from #29. 32-Batman uses gun
500.00 1500.00 3500.00

GD25 FN65 VF82 NM94

31-Classic Batman-c; 1st Julie Madison (Bruce Wayne's fiancee), Bat Plane (Bat-Gyro) & Batarang; 1st mention of Locale (New York City) of where Batman lives. 31,32-1st 2 part Batman story
1600.00 4800.00 10,400.00 16,000.00
(Estimated up to 75+ total copies exist, 6 in NM/Mint)
33-Origin The Batman (1st told origin); Batman gunholster-c; Batman story now 12 pgs. 2200.00 6600.00 14,300.00 22,000.00
(Estimated up to 75+ total copies exist, 7 in NM/Mint)

GD25 FN65 NM94

34-Steve Malone begins 400.00 1200.00 2800.00
35-Batman-c begin; hypo-c; cover of #35 goes with story to #34
671.00 2015.00 4700.00

Detective Comics #45 © DC

Detective Comics #107 © DC

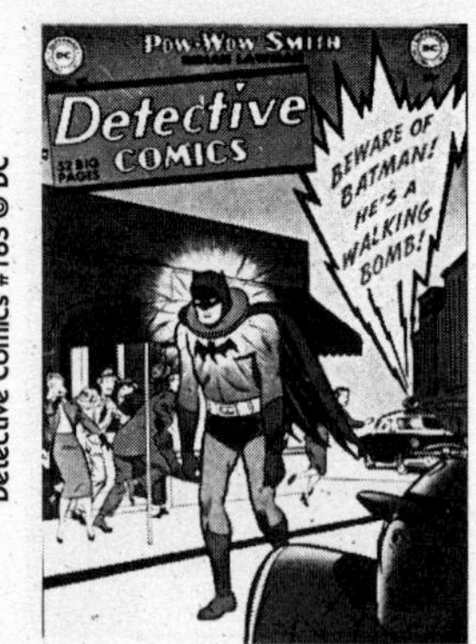

Detective Comics #163 © DC

GD25 FN65 NM94

36,37: 36-Origin & 1st app. Hugo Strange (1st major Batman villain, 2/40). 37-Cliff Crosby begins; last solo Batman story 471.00 1415.00 3300.00

GD25 FN65 VF82 NM94

38-Origin/1st app. Robin the Boy Wonder (4/40); Batman and Robin-c begin; cover by Kane & Robinson taken from splash pg. 2100.00 6300.00 13,650.00 21,000.00

(Estimated up to 85+ total copies exist, 9 in NM/Mint)

GD25 FN65 NM94

39-Opium story 400.00 1200.00 2800.00
40-Origin & 1st app. Clay Face (Basil Karlo); 1st Joker cover app. (6/40); Joker story intended for this issue was used in Batman #1 instead; cover is similar to splash pg. in 2nd Joker story in Batman #1 500.00 1500.00 3500.00
41-Robin's 1st solo 257.00 771.00 1800.00
42-44: 44-Crimson Avenger-new costume 171.00 515.00 1200.00
45-1st Joker story in Det. (3rd book app. & 4th story app. over all, 11/40) 257.00 771.00 1800.00
46-50: 46-Death of Hugo Strange. 48-1st time car called Batmobile (2/41); Gotham City 1st mention in Det. (1st mentioned in Wow #1; also see Batman #4). 49-Last Clay Face 150.00 450.00 1050.00
51-57 114.00 343.00 800.00
58-1st Penguin app. (12/41); last Speed Saunders; Fred Ray-c 300.00 900.00 2100.00
59-Last Steve Malone; 2nd Penguin; Wing becomes Crimson Avenger's aide 129.00 386.00 900.00
60-Intro. Air Wave; Joker app. (2nd in Det.) 129.00 386.00 900.00
61,63: 63-Last Cliff Crosby; 1st app. Mr. Baffle 114.00 343.00 800.00
62-Joker-c/story (2nd Joker-c, 4/42) 164.00 493.00 1150.00
64-Origin & 1st app. Boy Commandos by Simon & Kirby (6/42); Joker app. 286.00 857.00 2000.00
65-1st Boy Commandos-c (S&K-a on Boy Commandos & Ray/Robinson-a on Batman & Robin on-c; 4 artists on one-c) 243.00 729.00 1700.00
66-Origin & 1st app. Two-Face 243.00 729.00 1700.00
67-1st Penguin-c (9/42) 150.00 450.00 1050.00
68-Two-Face-c/story; 1st Two-Face-c 121.00 365.00 850.00
69-Joker-c/story 125.00 375.00 875.00
70 93.00 279.00 650.00
71-Joker-c/story 105.00 315.00 735.00
72-75: 73-Scarecrow-c/story (1st Scarecrow-c). 74-1st Tweedledum & Tweedledee plus-c; S&K-a 82.00 246.00 575.00
76-Newsboy Legion & The Sandman x-over in Boy Commandos; S&K-a; Joker-c/story 136.00 407.00 950.00
77-79: All S&K-a 93.00 279.00 650.00
80-Two-Face app.; S&K-a 100.00 300.00 700.00
81,82,84,86-90: 81-1st Cavalier-c & app. 89-Last Crimson Avenger; 2nd Cavalier-c & app. 73.00 219.00 510.00
83-1st "skinny" Alfred (2/44)(see Batman #21; last S&K Boy Commandos. (also #92,128); most issues #84 on signed S&K are not by them 83.00 249.00 580.00
85-Joker-c/story; last Spy; Kirby/Klech Boy Commandos 96.00 289.00 675.00
91,102-Joker-c/story 87.00 260.00 610.00
92-98: 96-Alfred's last name 'Beagle' revealed, later changed to 'Pennyworth' in #214 64.00 192.00 450.00
99-Penguin-c 96.00 289.00 675.00
100 (6/45) 100.00 300.00 700.00
101,103-108,110-113,115-117,119: 108-1st Bat-signal-c (2/46). 114-1st small logo (8/46) 61.00 182.00 425.00
109,114,118-Joker-c/stories 82.00 246.00 575.00
120-Penguin-c (white-c, rare above fine) 96.00 289.00 675.00
121,123,125,127,129,130 61.00 182.00 425.00
122-1st Catwoman-c (4/47) 100.00 300.00 700.00
124,128-Joker-c/stories 75.00 225.00 525.00
126-Penguin-c 81.00 242.00 565.00
131-136,139: 135-Frankenstein-c/story 49.00 146.00 340.00
137-Joker-c/story; last Air Wave 64.00 192.00 445.00
138-Origin Robotman (see Star Spangled #7 for 1st app.); series ends #202 95.00 285.00 665.00
140-The Riddler-c/story (1st app., 10/48) 314.00 943.00 2200.00
141,143-148,150: 150-Last Boy Commandos 52.00 156.00 365.00
142-2nd Riddler-c/story 93.00 279.00 650.00
149-Joker-c/story 67.00 201.00 470.00
151-Origin & 1st app. Pow Wow Smith, Indian lawman (9/49) & begins series 59.00 176.00 410.00
152,154,155,157-160: 152-Last Slam Bradley 52.00 156.00 365.00
153-1st app. Roy Raymond TV Detective (11/49) ; origin The Human Fly 56.00 167.00 390.00
156(2/50)-The new classic Batmobile 69.00 206.00 480.00
161-167,169,170,172-176: Last 52 pg. issue 55.00 165.00 385.00
168-Origin the Joker 271.00 815.00 1900.00
171-Penguin-c 75.00 225.00 525.00
177-179,181-186,188,189,191,192,194-199,201,202,204,206-210,212,214-216: 184-1st app. Fire Fly. 185-Secret of Batman's utility belt. 187-Two-Face app. 202-Last Robotman & Pow Wow Smith. 216-Last precode (2/55) 42.00 126.00 295.00
180,193-Joker-c/story 44.00 131.00 305.00
187-Two-Face-c/story 44.00 131.00 305.00
190-Origin Batman retold 59.00 176.00 410.00
200 (10/53) 55.00 165.00 385.00
203,211-Catwoman-c/stories 44.00 131.00 305.00
205-Origin Batcave 55.00 165.00 385.00
213-Origin & 1st app. Mirror Man 49.00 146.00 340.00
217-224: 218-Batman Jr. & Robin Sr. app. 33.00 99.00 230.00

GD25 FN65 VF82 NM94

225-(11/55)-1st app. Martian Manhunter, John Jones; later changed to J'onn J'onzz; origin begins; also see Batman #78 260.00 770.00 2310.00 3850.00

GD25 FN65 NM94

226-Origin Martian Manhunter cont'd (2nd app.) 129.00 386.00 900.00
227-229: Martian Manhunter stories in all 50.00 150.00 350.00
230-1st app. Mad Hatter; brief recap origin of Martian Manhunter 51.00 154.00 360.00
231-Brief origin recap Martian Manhunter 32.00 96.00 225.00
232,234,237-240: 239-Early DC grey tone-c 30.00 90.00 210.00
233-Origin & 1st app. Batwoman (7/56) 123.00 369.00 860.00
235-Origin Batman & his costume; tells how Bruce Wayne's father (Thomas Wayne) wore Bat costume & fought crime (reprinted in Batman #255) 60.00 170.00 385.00
236-J'onn J'onzz talks to parents and Mars-1st since being stranded on earth; 1st app. Bat-Tank? 36.00 107.00 250.00
241-260: 246-Intro. Diane Meade, John Jones' girl. 249-4th app. Batwoman. 253-1st app. The Terrible Trio. 254-Bat-Hound-c/story. 257-Intro. & 1st app. Whirly Bats. 259-1st app. The Calendar Man 24.00 73.00 170.00
261-J. Jones tie-in to sci/fi movie "Incredible Shrinking Man" 19.00 56.00 130.00
262-264,266,269,270: 261-1st app. Dr. Double X. 262-Origin Jackal 19.00 56.00 130.00
265-Batman's origin retold with new facts 29.00 86.00 200.00
267-Origin & 1st app. Bat-Mite (5/59) 26.00 79.00 185.00
268,271-Manhunter origin recap 19.00 56.00 130.00
272,274-280: 276-2nd app. Bat-Mite 13.60 41.00 95.00
273-J'onn J'onzz i.d. revealed for 1st time 15.00 45.00 105.00
281-292, 294-297: 287-Origin J'onn J'onzz retold. 289-Bat-Mite-c/story. 292-Last Roy Raymond. 297-Last 10¢ issue (11/61) 11.00 32.00 75.00
293-(7/61)-Aquaman begins (pre #1); ends #300 11.00 34.00 80.00
298-(12/61)-1st modern Clayface (Matt Hagen) 20.00 60.00 140.00
299,300: 300-(2/62)-Aquaman ends 8.00 24.00 55.00
301-(3/62)-J'onn J'onzz returns to Mars (1st since stranded on earth 6 years before) 7.40 22.00 52.00
302-326,329,330: 311-Intro. Zook in John Jones; 1st app. Cat-Man. 318,325-Cat-Man-c/story (2nd & 3rd app.); also 1st & 2nd app. Batwoman as the Cat-Woman. 321-2nd Terrible Trio. 322-Bat-Girl's 1st/only app. in Det. (6th in all); Batman cameo in J'onn J'onzz (only hero to app. in series). 326-Last

Detective Comics #400 © DC

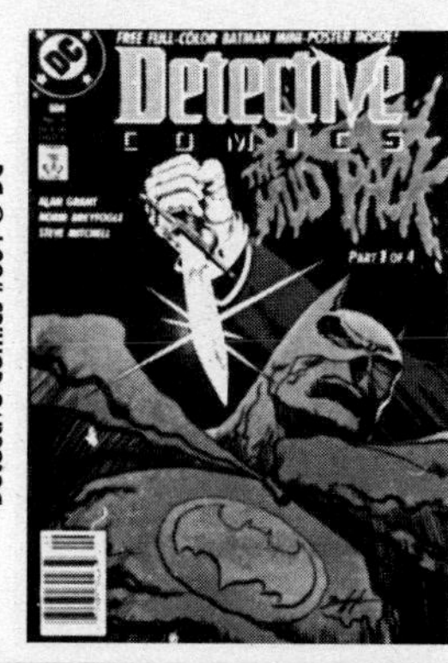

Detective Comics #604 © DC

Detective Comics #677 © DC

GD25 FN65 NM94   GD25 FN65 NM94

J'onn J'onzz, story cont'd in H.O.M. #143; intro. Idol-Head of Diabolu 5.40 16.00 38.00

327-(5/64)-Elongated Man begins, ends #383; 1st new look Batman with new costume; Infantino/Giella new look-a begins; Batman with gun 10.00 29.00 68.00

328-Death of Alfred; Bob Kane biog, 2 pgs. 9.00 28.00 65.00

331,333-340,342-358,360-364,366-368,370: 334-1st app. The Outsider. 345-Intro Block Buster. 347-"What If" theme story (1/66). 351-Elongated Man new costume. 355-Zatanna x-over in Elongated Man. 356-Alfred brought back in Batman, 1st SA app.? 362,364-S.A. Riddler app. (early). 363-2nd app. new Batgirl. 370-1st Neal Adams-a on Batman (cover only, 12/67) 3.60 10.70 25.00

332,341,365-Joker-c/stories 4.60 14.00 32.00

359-Intro/origin new Batgirl-c/story (1/67) 5.00 15.00 35.00

369(11/67)-N. Adams-a (Elongated Man); 3rd app. S.A. Catwoman (cameo; leads into Batman #197); 4th app. new Batgirl 6.00 17.00 40.00

371-1st new Batmobile from TV show (1/68) 3.60 10.70 25.00

372-386,389,390: 375-New Batmobile-c. 377-S.A. Riddler app. 2.10 6.00 15.00

387-r/1st Batman story from #27 (30th anniversary, 5/69); Joker-c 5.10 15.00 36.00

388-Joker-c/story; last 12¢ issue 3.00 9.40 22.00

391-394,396,398,399,401,403,405,406,409: 392-1st app. Jason Bard. 401-2nd Batgirl/Robin team-up 1.70 5.00 12.00

395,397,402,404,407,408,410-Neal Adams-a. 404-Tribute to Enemy Ace 2.40 7.30 17.00

400-(6/70)-Origin & 1st app. Man-Bat; 1st Batgirl/Robin team-up (cont'd in #401); Neal Adams-a 4.30 13.00 30.00

411-420: 413-Last 15¢ issue. 414-25¢, 52 pgs. begin, end #424. 418-Creeper x-over 1.70 4.20 10.00

421-436: 424-Last Batgirl. 426,430,436-Elongated Man app. 428,434-Hawkman begins, ends #467 1.50 3.80 9.00

437-New Manhunter begins (10-11/73, 1st app.) by Simonson, ends #443 1.90 6.00 13.00

438-445 (All 100 Page Super Spectaculars): 438-Kubert Hawkman-r. 439-Origin Manhunter. 440-G.A. Manhunter(Adv. #79) by S&K, Hawkman, Dollman, Gr. Lantern; Toth-a. 441-G.A. Plastic Man, Batman, Ibis-r. 442-G.A. Newsboy Legion, Bl. Canary, Elongated Man, Dr. Fate-r. 443-Origin The Creeper-r; death of Manhunter; G.A. Green Lantern, Spectre-r; Batman-r/Batman #18. 444-G.A. Kid Eternity-r. 445-G.A. Dr. Midnite-r 2.20 5.00 13.00

446-460: 457-Origin retold & updated 1.30 3.00 7.50

461-465,469,470,480: 480-(44 pgs.). 463,464-1st app. Black Spider 1.20 2.40 6.00

466-468,471-474,478,479-Rogers-a in all: 466-1st app. Signalman since Batman #139. 469-Intro/origin Dr. Phosphorous. 470,471-1st modern app. Hugo Strange. 474-1st app. new Deadshot. 478-1st app. 3rd Clayface (Preston Payne). 479-(44 pgs.) 1.90 6.00 13.00

475,476-Joker-c/stories; Rogers-a 3.00 9.40 22.00

477-Neal Adams-a(r); Rogers-a (3 pgs.) 2.30 6.90 16.00

481-(Combined with Batman Family, 12-1/78-79, begin $1.00, 68 pg. issues, ends #495); 481-495-Batgirl, Robin solo stories 1.60 5.00 11.00

482-Starlin/Russell, Golden-a; The Demon begins (origin-r), ends #485 (by Ditko #483-485) 1.30 3.00 7.50

483-40th Anniversary issue; origin retold; Newton Batman begins 1.50 3.80 9.00

484-499: 484-Origin Robin. 485-Death of Batwoman. 487-The Odd Man by Ditko. 489-Robin/Batgirl team-up. 490-Black Lightning begins. 491-(#492 on inside) 1.80 4.50

500-($1.50, 52 pgs.)-Batman/Deadman team-up; new Hawkman story by Joe Kubert; incorrectly says 500th anniv. of Det. 1.60 5.00 11.00

501-503,505-523: 512-2nd app. new Dr. Death. 519-Last Batgirl. 521-Green Arrow series begins. 523-Solomon Grundy app. 1.50 3.75

504-Joker-c/story 1.20 2.90 7.00

524-2nd app. Jason Todd (cameo)(3/83) 1.00 2.00 5.00

525-3rd app. Jason Todd (See Batman #357) 1.60 4.00

526-Batman's 500th app. in Detective Comics ($1.50, 68 pgs.); Joker-c/story (55 pgs.); Bob Kane pin-up 1.60 4.70 11.00

527-531,533,534,536-568,571,573: 538-Cat-Man-c/story cont'd from Batman #371. 542-Jason Todd quits as Robin (becomes Robin again #547). 549, 550-Alan Moore scripts (Gr. Arrow). 554-1st new Black Canary (9/85). 566-Batman villains profiled. 567-Harlan Ellison scripts 1.10 2.75

532,569,570-Joker-c/stories 1.20 2.40 6.00

535-Intro new Robin (Jason Todd)-1st appeared in Batman 1.20 2.40 6.00

572-(3/87, $1.25, 60 pgs.)-50th Anniv. of Det. Comics 1.60 4.00

574-Origin Batman & Jason Todd retold .90 2.30 5.50

575-Year 2 begins, ends #578 2.00 6.00 14.00

576-578: McFarlane-c/a. 578-Clay Face app. 1.70 5.00 12.00

579-597,601-610: 579-New bat wing logo. 583-1st app. villains Scarface & Vintriloquist. 589-595-(52 pgs.)-Each contain free 16 pg. Batman stories. 604-607-Mudpack storyline; 604,607-Contain Batman mini-posters. 610-Faked death of Penguin; artists names app. on tombstone on-c 1.50

598-($2.95, 84 pgs.)- "Blind Justice" storyline begins by Batman movie writer Sam Hamm, ends #600 1.60 4.00

599 1.20 3.00

600-(5/89, $2.95, 84 pgs.)-50th Anniv. of Batman in Det.; 1 pg. Neal Adams pin-up, among other artists 1.40 3.50

611-626,628-658: 612-1st new look Cat-Man; Catwoman app. 615- "The Penquin Affair" part 2 (See Batman #448,449). 617-Joker-c/story. 624-1st new Catwoman (w/death) & 1st new Batwoman. 626-Batman's 600th app. in Det. 642-Return of Scarface, part 2. 644-Last $1.00-c. 652,653-Huntress-c/story w/new costume plus Travis Charest-c on both 1.25

627-($2.95, 84 pgs.)-Batman's 601st app. in Det.; reprints 1st story/#27 plus 3 versions (2 new) of same story 1.20 3.00

659-Knightfall part 2; Kelley Jones-c 1.20 3.00

660-Knightfall part 4; Bane-c by Sam Keith 1.80 4.50

661-Knightfall part 6; brief Joker & Riddler app. 1.30 3.25

662-Knightfall part 8; Riddler app.; Sam Kieth-c 1.30 3.25

663-Knightfall part 10; Kelley Jones-c 1.30 3.25

664-Knightfall part 12; Bane-c/story; Joker app.; continued in Showcase 93 #7 & 8; Jones-c 1.30 3.25

665,666-Knightfall parts 16 & 18; 666-Bane-c/story .80 2.00

667,668: 667-Knightquest: The Crusade & new Batman begins (1st app. in Batman #500) 1.50

669-675: 669-Begin $1.50-c; Knightquest, cont'd in Robin #1. 671,673-Joker app. .70 1.75

675-($2.95)-Collectors edition w/foil-c 1.20 3.00

676-($2.50, 52 pgs.)-KnightsEnd Pt. 3 1.00 2.50

677,678: 677-KnightsEnd Pt. 9. 678-(9/94)-Zero Hour 1.50

0,679-683: 0-(10/94) 1.50

Annual 1 (1988, $1.50) 1.00 2.00 5.00

Annual 2 (1989, $2.00, 68 pgs.) 1.60 4.00

Annual 3 (1990, $2.00, 68 pgs.) .80 2.00

Annual 4 (1991, $2.00, 68 pgs.)-Painted-c .80 2.00

Annual 5 (1992, $2.50, 68 pgs.)-Joker-c/story (54 pgs.) continued in Robin Annual #1; Sam Kieth-c; Eclipso app. 1.00 2.50

Annual 6 (1993, $2.50, 68 pgs.)-Azrael as Batman in new costume; intro Geist the Twilight Man; Bloodlines storyline 1.00 2.50

Annual 7 (1994, $2.95, 68 pgs.)-Elseworlds story 1.20 3.00

NOTE: **Neal Adams** *c-370, 372, 383, 385, 389, 391, 392, 394-422, 439.* **Aparo** *a-437, 438, 444-446, 500, 625-632p, 638-641p; c-430, 437, 440-446, 448, 468-470, 480, 484(back), 492-502,508, 509, 515, 518-522, 641.* **Austin** *a(i)-450, 451, 463-468, 471-476; c(i)-474-476, 478.* **Baily** *a-443r.* **Buckler** *a-434, 446p, 479p; c(p)-467, 482, 505, 506, 511, 513-516, 518.* **Burnley** *a(Batman)-65, 75, 78, 83, 100, 103, 125; c-62i, 63i, 64, 73i, 78, 83p, 96p, 103p, 105p, 106, 108, 121p, 123p, 125p.* **Chaykin** *a-441.* **Colan** *a(p)-510, 512, 517, 523, 528-538, 540-546, 555-567; c(p)-510, 512, 528, 530-535, 537, 538, 540, 541, 543-545, 556-558, 560-564.* **J. Craig** *a-488.* **Ditko** *a-443r, 483-485, 487.* **Golden** *a-482p.* **Alan Grant** *scripts-584-597, 601-621, 641, 642, Annual 5.* **Grell** *a-445, 455, 463p, 464p; c-455.* **Guardineer** *c-23, 24, 26, 28, 30, 32.* **Gustavson** *a-441r.* **Infantino/Anderson** *c-333, 337-340, 343, 344, 347, 351, 352, 359, 361-368, 371.* **Kelley Jones** *c-651, 657i, 658i, 659, 661, 663-675.* **Kaluta** *c-423, 424, 426-428, 431, 434, 438, 484, 486, 572.* **Bob Kane** *a-Most early issues #27 on, 297r, 356r, 438-440r, 442r, 443r.* **Kane/Robinson** *c-33.* **Gil Kane** *a(p)-368, 370-374, 384, 385, 388-407, 438r, 439r, 520.* **Kane/Anderson** *c-369.* **Sam Kieth** *c-654-656 (657, 658 w/***Kelley Jones***), 660, 662, Annual #5.* **Kubert** *a-438r, 439r, 500; c-348, 350.* **McFarlane** *c/a(p)-576-578.* **Meskin** *a-420r.* **Moldoff** *c-*

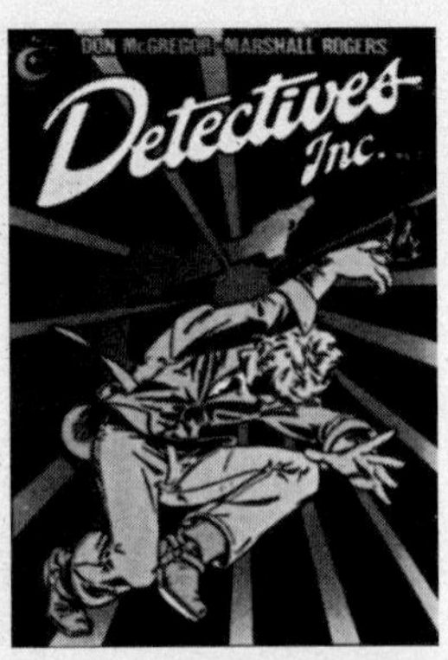

Detectives Inc. #2 © Eclipse

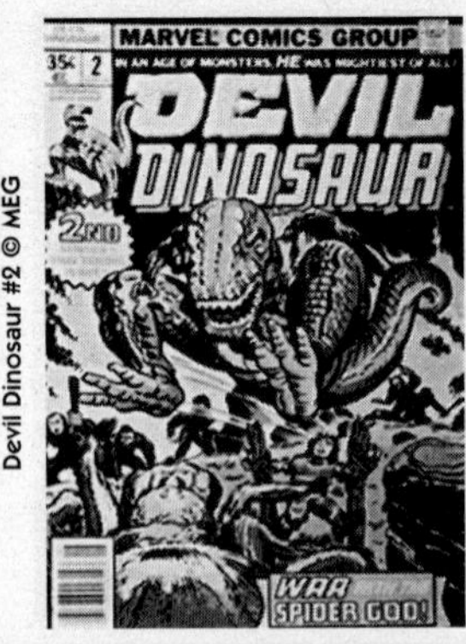

Devil Dinosaur #2 © MEG

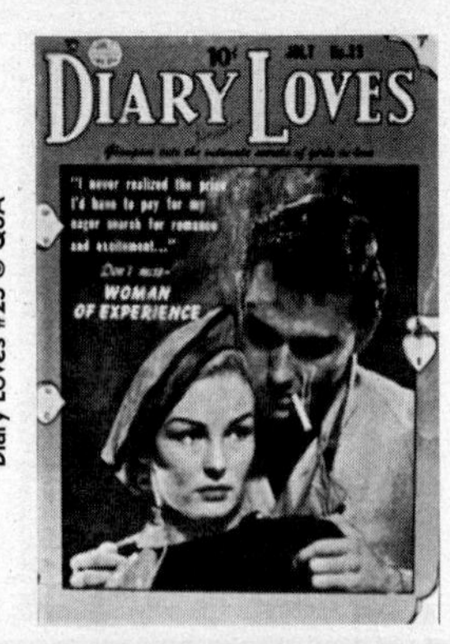

Diary Loves #23 © QUA

GD25 FN65 NM94

233-354, 259, 266, 267, 275, 287, 289, 290, 297, 300. ***Moldoff/Giella*** *a-328, 330, 332, 334, 336, 338, 340, 342, 344, 346, 348, 350, 352, 354, 356.* ***Mooney*** *a-444r.* ***Moreira*** *a-153-300, 419r, 444r, 445r.* ***Newton*** *a(p)-480, 481, 483-499, 501-509, 511, 513-516, 518-520, 524, 526, 539; c-526p.* ***Irv Novick*** *c-375-377.* ***Robbins*** *a-426p, 429p.* ***Robinson*** *a-part: 66, 68, 71-73; all: 74-76, 79, 80; c-62, 64, 66, 68-74, 76, 79, 82, 86, 88, 442r, 443r.* ***Rogers*** *a-466-468, 471-479p, 481p; c-471p, 472p, 473, 474-479p.* ***Roussos*** *Airwave-76-105(most); c(i)-71, 72, 74-76, 79, 107.* ***Russell*** *a-481i, 482i.* ***Simon/Kirby*** *a-440r, 442r.* ***Simonson*** *a-437-443, 450, 469, 470, 500.* ***Dick Sprang*** *c-77, 82, 84, 85, 87, 89-93, 95-100, 102, 103i, 104i, 106, 108, 114, 117, 118, 122, 123, 128, 129, 131, 133, 135, 141, 148, 149, 168, 622-624.* ***Starlin*** *a-481p, 482p; c-503, 504, 567p.* ***Starr*** *a-444r.* ***Toth*** *r-414, 416, 418, 424, 440-444.* ***Tuska*** *a-486p, 490p.* ***Wrightson*** *c-425.*

DETECTIVE DAN, SECRET OP. 48
1933 (36 pgs.; 9-1/2x12") (B&W; Softcover)
Humor Publ. Co.

nn-By Norman Marsh; forerunner of Dan Dunn 14.00 43.00 100.00

DETECTIVE EYE (See Keen Detective Funnies)
Nov, 1940 - No. 2, Dec, 1940
Centaur Publications

1-Air Man (see Keen Detective) & The Eye Sees begins; The Masked Marvel & Dean Denton app. 136.00 407.00 950.00
2-Origin Don Rance and the Mysticape; Binder-a; Frank Thomas-c 96.00 289.00 675.00

DETECTIVE PICTURE STORIES (Keen Detective Funnies No. 8 on?)
Dec, 1936 - No. 7, June?, 1937 (1st comic of a single theme)
Comics Magazine Company

1 229.00 685.00 1600.00
2-The Clock app. (1/37, early app.) 93.00 279.00 650.00
3,4: 4-Eisner-a 86.00 257.00 600.00
5-7: 5-The Clock-c/s (4/37); Kane-a; 6,7 (Exist)? 77.00 231.00 540.00

DETECTIVES, THE (See 4-Color No. 1168, 1219, 1240)

DETECTIVES, INC. (Eclipse)(Value: cover or less)

DEVIL DINOSAUR
April, 1978 - No. 9, Dec, 1978
Marvel Comics Group

1-9: Kirby/Royer-a in all; all have Kirby-c .90 2.25

DEVIL-DOG DUGAN (Tales of the Marines No. 4 on)
July, 1956 - No. 3, Nov, 1956
Atlas Comics (OPI)

1-Severin-c 6.70 20.00 40.00
2-Iron Mike McGraw x-over; Severin-c 5.00 15.00 30.00
3 4.00 109.00 20.00

DEVIL DOGS
1942
Street & Smith Publishers

1-Boy Rangers, U.S. Marines 19.00 57.00 130.00

DEVILINA
Feb, 1975 - No. 2, May, 1975 (Magazine) (B&W)
Atlas/Seaboard

1,2: 1-Reese-a 1.20 3.00

DEVIL KIDS STARRING HOT STUFF
July, 1962 - No. 107, Oct, 1981 (Giant-Size #41-55)
Harvey Publications (Illustrated Humor)

1 (12¢ cover price #1-?) 12.00 36.00 85.00
2 6.70 20.00 40.00
3-10 (1/64) 4.00 11.00 22.00
11-20 2.80 7.00 14.00
21-30 2.00 5.00 10.00
31-40 ('71) 1.30 3.25 8.00
41-50: All 68 pg. Giants 1.70 4.20 10.00
51-55: All 52 pg. Giants 1.50 3.80 9.00
56-70 1.00 2.00 5.00
71-90 1.20 3.00
91-107 1.50

DEXTER COMICS
Summer, 1948 - No. 5, July, 1949
Dearfield Publ.

1-Teen-age humor 5.85 17.50 35.00
2-Junie Prom app. 4.35 13.00 26.00
3-5 3.60 9.00 18.00

DEXTER THE DEMON (Formerly Melvin The Monster)
No. 7, Sept, 1957 (Also see Cartoon Kids & Peter the Little Pest)
Atlas Comics (HPC)

7 4.00 10.00 20.00

DIARY CONFESSIONS (Formerly Ideal Romance)
No. 9, May, 1955 - No. 14, April, 1955
Stanmor/Key Publ.(Medal Comics)

9 4.00 12.00 24.00
10-14 3.00 7.50 15.00

DIARY LOVES (Formerly Love Diary #1; G. I. Sweethearts #32 on)
No. 2, Nov, 1949 - No. 31, April, 1953
Quality Comics Group

2-Ward-c/a, 9 pgs. 10.00 30.00 65.00
3 (1/50)-Photo-c begin, end #27? 4.00 11.00 22.00
4-Crandall-a 6.00 18.00 36.00
5-7,10 3.20 8.00 16.00
8,9-Ward-a 6,8 pgs. 8-Gustavson-a 7.00 21.00 42.00
11,13,14,17-20 2.80 7.00 14.00
12,15,16-Ward-a 9,7,8 pgs. 6.00 18.00 36.00
21-Ward-a, 7 pgs. 5.00 15.00 30.00
22-31: 31-Whitney-a 2.00 5.00 10.00
NOTE: *Photo c-3-10, 12-27.*

DIARY OF HORROR
December, 1952
Avon Periodicals

1-Hollingsworth-c/a; bondage-c 24.00 72.00 165.00

DIARY SECRETS (Formerly Teen-Age Diary Secrets)
No. 10, Feb, 1952 - No. 30, Sept, 1955
St. John Publishing Co.

10-Baker-c/a most issues 9.15 27.50 55.00
11-16,18,19 7.00 21.00 42.00
17,20-Kubert-a 7.50 22.50 45.00
21-30: 28-Last precode (3/55) 4.70 14.00 28.00
(See Giant Comics Edition for Annual)

DICK COLE (Sport Thrills No. 11 on)(See Blue Bolt & Four Most #1)
Dec-Jan, 1948-49 - No. 10, June-July, 1950
Curtis Publ./Star Publications

1-Sgt. Spook; L. B. Cole-c; McWilliams-a; Curt Swan's 1st work 12.00 36.00 85.00
2 8.35 25.00 50.00
3-10: 10-Joe Louis story 6.70 20.00 40.00
Accepted Reprint #7(V1#6 on-c)(1950's)-Reprints #7; L.B. Cole-c 4.35 13.00 26.00
Accepted Reprint #9(nd)-(Reprints #9 & #8-c) 4.35 13.00 26.00
NOTE: ***L. B. Cole*** *c-1, 3, 4, 6-10.* ***Al McWilliams*** *a-6. Dick Cole in 1-9. Baseball c-10. Basketball c-9. Football c-8.*

DICKIE DARE
1941 - No. 4, 1942 (#3 on sale 6/15/42)
Eastern Color Printing Co.

1-Caniff-a, Everett-c 29.00 86.00 200.00
2 18.00 54.00 125.00
3,4-Half Scorchy Smith by Noel Sickles who was very influential in Milton Caniff's development 19.00 58.00 135.00

DICK POWELL (See A-1 Comics No. 22)

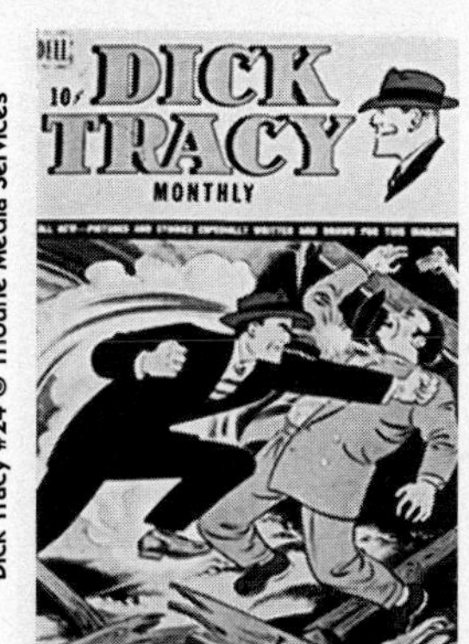

Dick Tracy #24 © Tribune Media Services

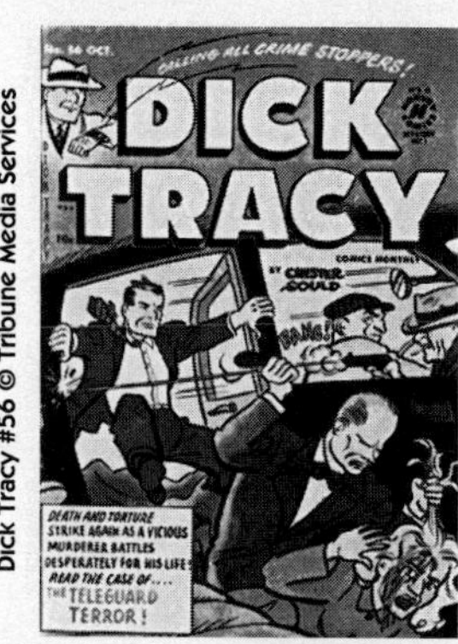

Dick Tracy #56 © Tribune Media Services

Dick Tracy #105 © Tribune Media Services

GD25 FN65 NM94

DICK QUICK, ACE REPORTER (See Picture News #10)

DICK'S ADVENTURES IN DREAMLAND (See 4-Color No. 245)

DICK TRACY (See Famous Feature Stories, Harvey Comics Library, Limited Collectors' Ed., Mammoth Comics, Merry Christmas, The Original..., Popular Comics, Super Book No. 1, 7, 13, 25, Super Comics & Tastee-Freez)

DICK TRACY
May, 1937 - Jan, 1938
David McKay Publications

Feature Books nn - 100 pgs., partially reprinted as 4-Color No. 1 (appeared before Large Feature Comics, 1st Dick Tracy comic book) (Very Rare-three known copies)
Estimated Value.... 500.00 1500.00 5000.00
Feature Books 4 - Reprints nn issue but with new cover added 80.00 240.00 800.00
Feature Books 6,9 65.00 195.00 650.00

DICK TRACY (...Monthly #1-24)
1939 - No. 24, Dec, 1949
Dell Publishing Co.

	GD25	FN65	NM94
Large Feature Comic 1(1939)	100.00	300.00	1000.00
Large Feature Comic 4,8	50.00	150.00	500.00
Large Feature Comic 11,13,15	60.00	180.00	600.00

	GD25	FN65	VF82	NM94
4-Color 1(1939)('35-r)	470.00	1410.00	3055.00	4700.00

(Estimated up to 75+ total copies exist, 5 in NM/Mint)

	GD25	FN65	NM94
4-Color 6(1940)('37-r)-(Scarce)	129.00	385.00	900.00
4-Color 8(1940)('38-'39-r)	75.00	225.00	525.00
Large Feature Comic 3(1941, Series II)	50.00	150.00	500.00
4-Color 21('41)('38-r)	64.00	195.00	450.00
4-Color 34('43)('39-'40-r)	43.00	130.00	300.00
4-Color 56('44)('40-r)	34.00	105.00	240.00
4-Color 96('46)('40-r)	26.00	78.00	180.00
4-Color 133('47)('40-'41-r)	22.00	65.00	150.00
4-Color 163('47)('41-r)	17.00	52.00	120.00
4-Color 215('48)-Titled "Sparkle Plenty", Tracy-r	10.00	30.00	70.00
1(1/48)('34-r)	43.00	130.00	300.00
2,3	24.00	73.00	150.00
4-10	22.00	65.00	150.00
11-18: 13-Bondage-c	14.00	43.00	100.00
19-1st app. Sparkle Plenty, B.O. Plenty & Gravel Gertie in a 3-pg. strip not by Gould	16.00	48.00	110.00
20-1st app. Sam Catchem; c/a not by Gould	12.00	36.00	85.00
21-24-Only 2 pg. Gould-a in each	12.00	36.00	85.00

NOTE: *No. 19-24 have a 2 pg. biography of a famous villain illustrated by* ***Gould****: 19-Little Face; 20-Flattop; 21-Breathless Mahoney; 22-Measles; 23-Itchy; 24-The Brow.*

DICK TRACY (Continued from Dell series)(...Comics Monthly #25-140)
No. 25, Mar, 1950 - No. 145, April, 1961
Harvey Publications

	GD25	FN65	NM94
25-Flat Top-c/story (also #26,27)	17.00	52.00	120.00
26-28,30: 28-Bondage-c. 28,29-The Brow-c/stories	12.00	36.00	85.00
29-1st app. Gravel Gertie in a Gould-r	16.00	48.00	110.00
31,32,34,35,37-40: 40-Intro/origin 2-way wrist radio (6/51)	11.00	32.00	75.00
33- "Measles the Teen-Age Dope Pusher"	12.00	36.00	85.00
36-1st app. B.O. Plenty in a Gould-r	12.00	36.00	85.00
41-50	9.30	28.00	65.00
51-56,58-80: 51-2pgs Powell-a	8.50	25.50	60.00
57-1st app. Sam Catchem in a Gould-r	11.00	32.00	75.00
81-99,101-140	7.50	22.50	45.00
100	8.35	25.00	50.00
141-145 (25¢)(titled "Dick Tracy")	7.00	21.00	42.00

NOTE: ***Powell*** *a(1-2pgs.)-43, 44, 104, 108, 109, 145. No. 110-120, 141-145 are all reprints from earlier issues.*

DICK TRACY (Blackthorne)(Value: cover or less)

DICK TRACY (Disney)(Value: cover or less)

DICK TRACY ADVENTURES (Gladstone)(Value: cover or less)

DICK TRACY & DICK TRACY JR. CAUGHT THE RACKETEERS, HOW
1933 (88 pgs.) (7x8-1/2") (Hardcover)
Cupples & Leon Co.

	GD25	FN65	NM94
2-(Numbered on pg. 84)-Continuation of Stooge Viller book (daily strip reprints from 8/3/33 thru 11/8/33) (Rarer than No. 1)	43.00	130.00	300.00
With dust jacket...	60.00	180.00	420.00
Book 2 (32 pgs.; soft-c; has strips 9/18/33-11/8/33)	19.00	57.00	132.00

DICK TRACY & DICK TRACY JR. AND HOW THEY CAPTURED "STOOGE" VILLER (See Treasure Box of Famous Comics)
1933 (7x8-1/2") (Hard cover; One Shot; 100 pgs.)
Reprints 1932 & 1933 Dick Tracy daily strips
Cupples & Leon Co.

	GD25	FN65	NM94
nn(No.1)-1st app. of "Stooge" Viller	34.00	105.00	240.00
with dust jacket...	46.00	140.00	325.00

DICK TRACY, EXPLOITS OF
1946 (Strip reprints) (Hardcover) ($1.00)
Rosdon Books, Inc.

	GD25	FN65	NM94
1-Reprints the near complete case of "The Brow" from 6/12/44 to 9/24/44 (story starts a few weeks late)	22.00	65.00	150.00
with dust jacket...	36.00	107.00	250.00

DICK TRACY GIVEAWAYS
1939 - 1958; 1990

	GD25	FN65	NM94
Buster Brown Shoes Giveaway (1940s?, 36 pgs. in color); 1938-39-r by Gould	25.00	75.00	175.00
Gillmore Giveaway (See Superbook)			
...Hatful of Fun (No date, 1950-52, 32pgs.; 8-1/2x10")-Dick Tracy hat promotion; Dick Tracy games, magic tricks. Miller Bros. premium	11.00	32.00	75.00
Motorola Giveaway (1953)-Reprints Harvey Comics Library #2; "The Case of the Sparkle Plenty TV Mystery"	4.00	12.00	24.00
Original Dick Tracy by Chester Gould, The (Aug, 1990, 16 pgs., 5-1/2x8-1/2")-Gladstone Publ.; Bread Giveaway	4.00	10.00	20.00
Popped Wheat Giveaway (1947, 16 pgs. in color)-1940-r; Sig Feuchtwanger Publ.; Gould-a	2.00	5.00	10.00
...Presents the Family Fun Book; Tip Top Bread Giveaway, no date or number (1940, Fawcett Publ., 16 pgs. in color)-Spy Smasher, Ibis, Lance O'Casey app.	54.00	160.00	375.00
Same as above but without app. of heroes & Dick Tracy on cover only	10.00	30.00	60.00
Service Station Giveaway (1958, 16 pgs. in color)(regular size, slick cover)-Harvey Info. Press	3.20	8.00	16.00
Shoe Store Giveaway (Weatherbird)(1939, 16 pgs.)-Gould-a	11.00	32.00	75.00

DICK TRACY MONTHLY/WEEKLY
May, 1986 - No. 99, 1989 ($2.00, B&W) (Becomes Weekly #26 on)
Blackthorne Publishing

	GD25	FN65	NM94
1-99: Gould-r. 30,31-Mr. Crime app.	.40	1.00	2.00

NOTE: *#1-10 reprint strips 3/10/40-7/13/41; #10(pg.8)-51 reprint strips 4/6/49-12/31/55; #52-99 reprint strips 12/26/56-4/26/64.*

DICK TRACY SHEDS LIGHT ON THE MOLE
1949 (16 pgs.) (Ray-O-Vac Flashlights giveaway)
Western Printing Co.

	GD25	FN65	NM94
nn-Not by Gould	5.85	17.50	35.00

DICK TRACY SPECIAL (Blackthorne)(Value: cover or less)

DICK TRACY: THE EARLY YEARS (Blackthorne)(Value: cover or less)

DICK TRACY UNPRINTED STORIES (Blackthorne)(Value: cover or less)

DICK TURPIN (See Legend of Young...)

DICK WINGATE OF THE U.S. NAVY

Die Cut #4 © MEG

Dilton's Strange Science #3 © AP

Ding Dong #3 © CME

GD25 FN65 NM94

1951; 1953 (no month)
Superior Publ./Toby Press

nn-U.S. Navy giveaway 2.00 5.00 10.00
1(1953, Toby)-Reprints nn issue? (same-c) 3.60 9.00 18.00

DIE-CUT
Nov, 1993 - No. 4, Feb, 1994 ($1.75, mini-series)
Marvel Comics UK, Ltd

1-($2.50)-Die-cut-c; The Beast app. 1.00 2.50
2-4 .70 1.75

DIE-CUT VS. G-FORCE
Nov, 1993 - No. 2, Dec, 1993 ($2.75, mini-series)
Marvel Comics UK, Ltd

1,2-($2.75)-Gold foil-c on both 1.10 2.75

DIE, MONSTER, DIE (See Movie Classics)

DIG 'EM
1973 (16 pgs.) (2-3/8x6")
Kellogg's Sugar Smacks Giveaway

nn-4 different issues 1.00 2.00 5.00

DIGITEK
Dec, 1992 - No. 4, Mar, 1993 ($1.95/$2.25, mini-series)
Marvel Comics UK, Ltd

1-4: 1,2 ($1.95). 3,4 ($2.25): 3-Deathlock-c/story .80 2.00

DILLY (Dilly Duncan from Daredevil Comics; see Boy Comics #57)
May, 1953 - No. 3, Sept, 1953
Lev Gleason Publications

1-Teenage; Biro-c 4.20 12.50 25.00
2,3-Biro-c 3.00 7.50 15.00

DILTON'S STRANGE SCIENCE (See Pep Comics #78)
May, 1989 - No. 5, May, 1990 (.75/$1.00)
Archie Comics

1-5 1.00

DIME COMICS
1945; 1951
Newsbook Publ. Corp.

1-Silver Streak-c/story; L. B. Cole-c 20.00 603.00 140.00
1(1951), 5 3.20 8.00 16.00

DINGBATS (See 1st Issue Special)

DING DONG
Summer?, 1946 - No. 5, 1947 (52 pgs.)
Compix/Magazine Enterprises

1-Funny animal 11.50 34.00 80.00
2 (9/46) 6.35 19.00 38.00
3 (Wint '46-'47) - 5 5.00 15.00 30.00

DINKY DUCK (Paul Terry's...) (See Blue Ribbon, Giant Comics Edition #5A & New Terrytoons)
Nov, 1951 - No. 16, Sept, 1955; No. 16, Fall, 1956; No. 17, May, 1957 - No. 19, Summer, 1958
St. John Publishing Co./Pines No. 16 on

1-Funny animal 7.50 22.50 45.00
2 4.00 11.00 22.00
3-10 2.80 7.00 14.00
11-16(9/55) 2.00 5.00 10.00
16(Fall,'56) - 19 1.60 4.00 8.00

DINKY DUCK & HASHIMOTO-SAN (See Deputy Dawg Presents...)

DINO (TV)(The Flintstones)
Aug, 1973 - No. 20, Jan, 1977 (Hanna-Barbera)
Charlton Publications

1 1.10 2.70 6.50
2-20 1.40 3.50

DINO ISLAND
Feb, 1994 - No. 2, Mar, 1994 ($2.75, limited series)
Mirage Studios

1,2-By Jim Lawson 1.10 2.75

DINO RIDERS
Feb, 1989 - No. 3, 1989 ($1.00)
Marvel Comics

1-3: Based on toys 1.00

DINOSAUR REX (Fantagraphics)(Value: cover or less)

DINOSAURS, A CELEBRATION
Oct, 1992 - No. 4, Oct, 1992 ($4.95, mini-series, 52 pgs.)
Epic Comics (Marvel)

1-4: 2-Bolton painted-c 1.00 2.00 5.00

DINOSAURS ATTACK! THE GRAPHIC NOVEL
1991 - Book 3, 1992 ($3.95, mini-series, coated stock, stiff-c)
Eclipse Comics

Book One - Three: Based on Topps trading cards 1.60 4.00

DINOSAURS FOR HIRE (Malibu)(Value: cover or less)

DINOSAURS FOR HIRE
Feb, 1993 - No. 12, Feb, 1994 ($1.95/$2.50)
Malibu Comics

1-Flip book .80 2.00
2-12: 8-($2.50)-Bagged w/Skycap; Staton-c. 10-Flip book 1.00 2.50

DINOSAURS GRAPHIC NOVEL (TV)
1992 - No. 2, 1993 ($2.95, 52 pgs.)
Disney Comics

1,2-Staton-a; based on Dinosaurs TV show 1.20 3.00

DINOSAURUS (See 4-Color No. 1120)

DIPPY DUCK
October, 1957
Atlas Comics (OPI)

1-Maneely-a; code approved 5.00 15.00 30.00

DIRECTORY TO A NONEXISTENT UNIVERSE (Eclipse)(Value: cover or less)

DIRTY DOZEN (See Movie Classics)

DIRTY PAIR
Dec, 1988 - No. 4, April, 1989 ($2.00, B&W, mini-series)
Eclipse Comics

1-4: Japanese manga with original stories .80 2.00

DIRTY PAIR: SIM HELL (Dark Horse)(Value: cover or less)

DIRTY PAIR II
June, 1989 - No. 5, Mar, 1990 ($2.00, B&W, mini-series)
Eclipse Comics

1-5: 3-Cover is misnumbered as #1 .80 2.00

DIRTY PAIR III, THE (A Plague of Angels)
Aug, 1990 - No. 5, Aug, 1991 ($2.00, B&W, mini-series)
Eclipse Comics

1,2 .40 1.00 2.00
3-5: ($2.25) .45 1.15 2.25

DISHMAN (Eclipse)(Value: cover or less)

DISNEY COMIC ALBUM
1990(no month, year) - No. 8, 1991 ($6.95/$7.95)
Disney Comics

1,2 ($6.95): 1-Donald Duck and Gyro Gearloose by Barks(r). 2-Uncle Scrooge by Barks(r); Jr. Woodchucks app. 1.20 3.00 7.00
3-8: 3-Donald Duck-r/F.C. 308 by Barks; begin $7.95-c. 4-Mickey Mouse Meets the Phantom Blot; strip-r. 5-Chip 'n' Dale Rescue Rangers; new-a.

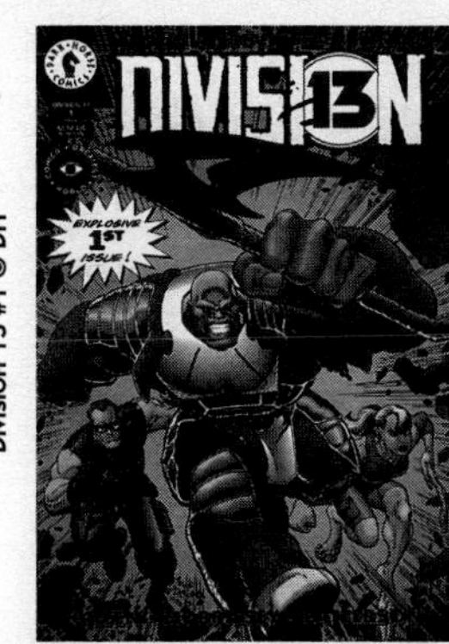

Division 13 #1 © DH

Dixie Dugan #1 © McNaught

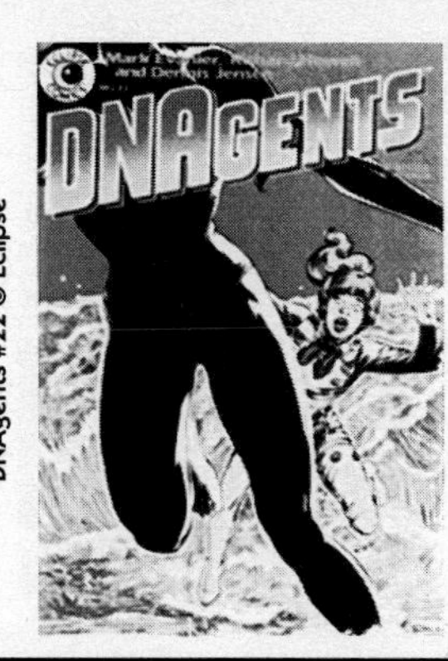

DNAgents #22 © Eclipse

6-Uncle Scrooge. 7-Donald Duck in Too Many Pets; Barks-r(4). 8-Super Goof; r/S.G. #1, D.D. #102 1.30 3.25 8.00

DISNEY COMICS
June, 1990
Disney Comics

Boxed set of #1 issues includes Donald Duck Advs., Ducktales, Chip 'n Dale Rescue Rangers, Roger Rabbit, Mickey Mouse Advs. & Goofy Advs.; limited to 10,000 sets 0.00 00.00 00.00

DISNEYLAND BIRTHDAY PARTY (Also see Dell Giants)
Aug, 1985 ($2.50)
Gladstone Publishing Co.

1-Reprints Dell Giant with new-photo-c 1.00 2.00 5.00
...Comics Digest #1-(Digest) 1.00 2.50

DISNEYLAND MAGAZINE
Feb. 15, 1972 - ? (10-1/4"x12-5/8", 20 pgs, weekly)
Fawcett Publications

1-One or two page painted art features on Dumbo, Snow White, Lady & the Tramp, the Aristocats, Brer Rabbit, Peter Pan, Cinderella, Jungle Book, Alice & Pinocchio. Most standard characters app. 3.00 9.00 20.00

DISNEYLAND, USA (See Dell Giant No. 30)

DISNEY MOVIE BOOK
1990 (8-1/2"x11")($7.95, 52 pgs.)(w/pull-out poster)
Walt Disney Productions/(produced by Gladstone)

1-Roger Rabbit in Tummy Trouble; from the cartoon film strips adapted to the comic format. Ron Dias-c 1.70 5.00 12.00

DISNEY'S ALADDIN
Oct, 1994 - Present ($1.50)
Marvel Comics

1-9 1.50

DISNEY'S BEAUTY AND THE BEAST
Sept, 1994 - Present ($1.50)
Marvel Comics

1-9 1.50

DISNEY'S COLOSSAL COMICS COLLECTION
1991 - No. 10, 1993 ($1.95, digest-size, 96-132 pgs.)
Disney Comics

1-10: Ducktales, Talespin, Chip 'n Dale's Rescue Rangers. 4-r/Darkwing Duck #1-4. 6-Goofy begins. 8-Little Mermaid .80 2.00

DISNEY'S COMICS IN 3-D
1992 ($2.95, w/glasses, polybagged)
Disney Comics

1-Infinity-c; Barks, Rosa, Gottfredson-r 1.20 3.00

DISNEY'S NEW ADVENTURES OF BEAUTY AND THE BEAST (Also see Beauty and the Beast & Disney's Beauty and the Beast)
1992 - No. 2, 1992 ($1.50, mini-series)
Disney Comics

1,2-New stories based on movie 1.50

DISNEY'S TALESPIN LIMITED SERIES: "TAKE OFF" (See Talespin)
Jan, 1991 - No. 4, Apr, 1991 ($1.50, mini-series, 52 pgs.)
W. D. Publications (Disney Comics)

1-4: Based on animated series; 4 part origin 1.50

DISNEY'S THE LION KING
July, 1994 - No. 2, July, 1994 ($1.50)
Marvel Comics

1,2: 2-part movie adaptation 1.50
1-($2.50, 52 pgs.)-Complete story 1.00 2.50

DISNEY'S THE LITTLE MERMAID
Sept, 1994 - Present ($1.50)
Marvel Comics

1-9 1.50

DISNEY'S THE LITTLE MERMAID LIMITED SERIES
Feb, 1992 - No. 4, May, 1992 ($1.50, limited series)
Disney Comics

1-4-All new adventures 1.50

DISNEY'S THE THREE MUSKETEERS
Jan, 1994 - No. 2, Feb, 1994 ($1.50, limited series)
Marvel Comics

1,2-Morrow-c; Spiegle-a; Movie adaptation 1.50

DIVER DAN (TV)
Feb-Apr, 1962 - No. 2, June-Aug, 1962
Dell Publishing Co.

4-Color 1254(#1), 2 7.00 21.00 42.00

DIVISION 13
Sept, 1994 - Present ($2.50)
Dark Horse Comics

1-4: 1-Art Adams-c 1.00 2.50

DIXIE DUGAN (See Big Shot, Columbia Comics & Feature Funnies)
July, 1942 - No. 13, 1949 (Strip reprints in all)
McNaught Syndicate/Columbia/Publication Ent.

1-Joe Palooka x-over by Ham Fisher 22.00 65.00 150.00
2 11.00 32.00 75.00
3 10.00 30.00 60.00
4,5(1945-46)-Bo strip-r 6.35 19.00 38.00
6-13(1/47-49): 6-Paperdoll cut-outs 5.00 15.00 30.00

DIXIE DUGAN
V3#1, Nov, 1951 - V4#4, Feb, 1954
Prize Publications (Headline)

V3#1 5.85 17.50 35.00
2-4 4.00 12.00 24.00
V4#1-4(#5-8) 3.60 9.00 18.00

DIZZY DAMES
Sept-Oct, 1952 - No. 6, July-Aug, 1953
American Comics Group (B&M Distr. Co.)

1-Whitney-c 7.50 22.50 45.00
2 4.70 14.00 28.00
3-6 4.00 10.00 20.00

DIZZY DON COMICS
1942 - No. 22, Oct, 1946; No. 3, Apr, 1947 (B&W)
F. E. Howard Publications/Dizzy Don Ent. Ltd (Canada)

1 6.70 20.00 40.00
2 4.00 10.00 20.00
4-21 3.60 9.00 18.00
22-Full color, 52 pgs. 6.70 20.00 40.00
3 (4/47)-Full color, 52 pgs. 5.00 15.00 30.00

DIZZY DUCK (Formerly Barnyard Comics)
No. 32, Nov, 1950 - No. 39, Mar, 1952
Standard Comics

32-Funny animal 6.35 19.00 38.00
33-39 4.00 10.00 20.00

DNAGENTS (Eclipse)(Value: cover or less)

DOBERMAN (See Sgt. Bilko's Private...)

DOBIE GILLIS (See The Many Loves of...)

DOC CARTER VD COMICS
1949 (16 pgs. in color) (Paper cover)
Health Publications Institute, Raleigh, N. C. (Giveaway)

nn 17.00 52.00 120.00

Doc Savage Comics #4 © S&S

Dr. Fate #10 © DC

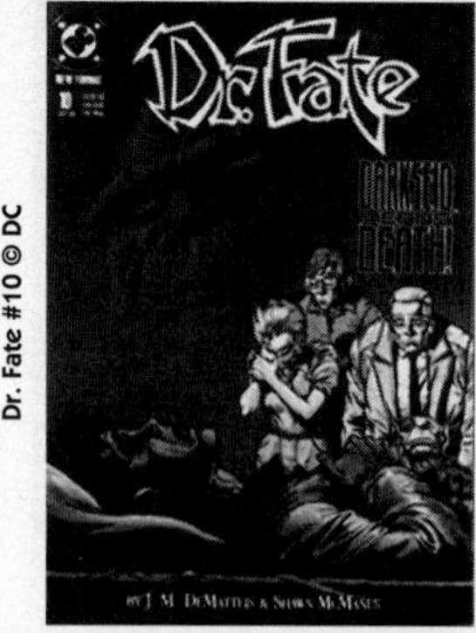

Doctor Solor, Man Of The Atom #1 © WEST

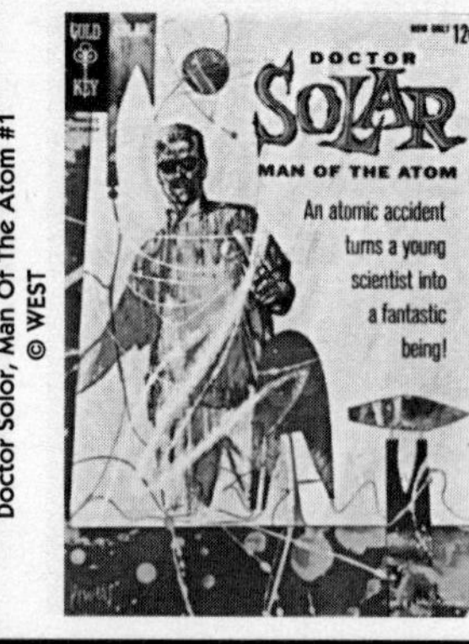

GD25 FN65 NM94

DOC CHAOS: THE STRANGE ATTRACTOR (Vortex)(Value: cover or less)

DOC SAVAGE
November, 1966
Gold Key

1-Adaptation of the Thousand-Headed Man; James Bama c-r/1964 Doc Savage paperback 8.00 24.00 56.00

DOC SAVAGE (Also see Giant-Size...)
Oct, 1972 - No. 8, Jan, 1974
Marvel Comics Group

1 1.30 3.00 7.50
2-8: 2,3-Steranko-c 1.80 4.50

NOTE: *Gil Kane c-5, 6. Mooney a-1i. No. 1, 2 adapts pulp story "The Man of Bronze"; No. 3, 4 adapts "Death in Silver"; No. 5, 6 adapts "The Monsters"; No. 7, 8 adapts "The Brand of The Werewolf".*

DOC SAVAGE (Magazine)
Aug, 1975 - No. 8, Spring, 1977 ($1.00, B&W)
Marvel Comics Group

1-Cover from movie poster; Ron Ely photo-c 1.70 4.25
2-8: 1,3-Buscema-a. 5-Adams-a(1 pg.), Rogers-a(1 pg) 1.10 2.75

DOC SAVAGE
Nov, 1987 - No. 4, Feb, 1988 ($1.75, mini-series)
DC Comics

1-4 .70 1.75

DOC SAVAGE
Nov, 1988 - No. 24, Oct, 1990 ($1.75/$2.00: #13-24)
DC Comics

1-24 .80 2.00
Annual 1 (1989, $3.50, 68 pgs.) 1.40 3.50

DOC SAVAGE COMICS (Also see Shadow Comics)
May, 1940 - No. 20, Oct, 1943 (1st app. in Doc Savage pulp, 3/33)
Street & Smith Publications

1-Doc Savage, Cap Fury, Danny Garrett, Mark Mallory, The Whisperer, Captain Death, Billy the Kid, Sheriff Pete & Treasure Island begin; Norgil, the Magician app. 285.00 857.00 2000.00
2-Origin & 1st app. Ajax, the Sun Man; Danny Garrett, The Whisperer end 100.00 300.00 700.00
3 86.00 257.00 600.00
4-Treasure Island ends; Tuska-a 68.00 205.00 475.00
5-Origin & 1st app. Astron, the Crocodile Queen, not in #9 & 11; Norgi the Magician app. 51.00 154.00 360.00
6-10: 6-Cap Fury ends; origin & only app. Red Falcon in Astron story. 8-Mark Mallory ends; Charlie McCarthy app. on-c plus true life story. 9-Supersnipe app. 10-Origin & only app. The Thunderbolt 44.00 133.00 310.00
11,12 36.00 107.00 250.00
V2#1-8(#13-20): 16-The Pulp Hero, The Avenger app.; Fanny Brice story. 17-Sun Man ends; Nick Carter begins; Duffy's Tavern part photo-c & story. 18-Huckleberry Finn part-c/story. 19-Henny Youngman part photo-c & life story. 20-Only all funny-c w/Huckleberry Finn 36.00 107.00 250.00

DOC SAVAGE: THE MAN OF BRONZE
1991 - No. 4, 1991 ($2.50, mini-series)
Millennium Publications

1-4: 1-Bronze logo 1.00 2.50
...: The Manual of Bronze 1 ($2.50, B&W, color, one-shot)-Unpublished proposed Doc Savage strip in color, B&W strip-r 1.00 2.50

DOC SAVAGE: THE MAN OF BRONZE, DOOM DYNASTY
1992 (Says 1991) - No. 2, 1992 ($2.50, mini-series)
Millennium Publications

1,2 1.00 2.50

DOC SAVAGE: THE MAN OF BRONZE - REPEL
1992 ($2.50)
Innovation Publishing

1-Dave Dorman painted-c 1.00 2.50

DOC SAVAGE: THE MAN OF BRONZE THE DEVIL'S THOUGHTS
1992 (Says 1991) - No. 2, 1992 ($2.50, mini-series)
Millennium Publications

1,2 1.00 2.50

DOC STEARN...MR. MONSTER (See Mr. Monster)

DR. ANTHONY KING, HOLLYWOOD LOVE DOCTOR
1952(Jan) - No. 3, May, 1953; No. 4, May, 1954
Minoan Publishing Corp./Harvey Publications No. 4

1 8.35 25.00 50.00
2-4: 4-Powell-a 5.35 16.00 32.00

DR. ANTHONY'S LOVE CLINIC (See Mr. Anthony's...)

DR. BOBBS (See 4-Color No. 212)

DOCTOR BOOGIE (Media)(Value: cover or less)

DOCTOR CHAOS
Nov, 1993 - Present ($2.50)
Triumphant Comics

1-6: 1,2-Triumphant Unleashed x-over. 2-1st app. War Dancer in pin-up. 3-Intro The Cry 1.00 2.50

DR. DOOM'S REVENGE
1989 (Came w/computer game from Paragon Software)
Marvel Comics

V1#1-Spider-Man & Captain America fight Dr. Doom 1.00

DR. FATE (See 1st Issue Special, The Immortal..., Justice League, More Fun #55, & Showcase)

DOCTOR FATE
July, 1987 - No. 4, Oct, 1987 ($1.50, mini-series, Baxter)
DC Comics

1-4: Giffen-c/a in all 1.50

DOCTOR FATE
Winter, 1988-'89 - No. 41, June, 1992 ($1.25/$1.50 #5 on)
DC Comics

1-31: 15-Justice League app. 25-1st new Dr. Fate .75 1.50
32-41: 32-Begin $1.75-c. 36-Original Dr. returns .70 1.75
Annual 1(1989, $2.95, 68 pgs.)-Sutton-a 1.20 3.00

DR. FU MANCHU (See The Mask of...)
1964
I.W. Enterprises

1-r/Avon's "Mask of Dr. Fu Manchu"; Wood-a 8.35 25.00 50.00

DR. GIGGLES (See Dark Horse Presents #64-66)
Oct, 1992 - No. 2, Oct, 1992 ($2.50, mini-series)
Dark Horse Comics

1,2-Based on movie 1.00 2.50

DOCTOR GRAVES (Formerly The Many Ghosts of...)
No. 73, Sept, 1985 - No. 75, Jan, 1986
Charlton Comics

73-75 1.00

DR. JEKYLL AND MR. HYDE (See A Star Presentation & Supernatural Thrillers #4)

DR. KILDARE (TV)
No. 1337, 4-6/62 - No. 9, 4-6/65 (All Richard Chamberlain photo-c)
Dell Publishing Co.

4-Color 1337(#1, 1962) 7.50 22.50 45.00
2-9 5.85 17.50 35.00

DR. MASTERS (See The Adventures of Young...)

DOCTOR SOLAR, MAN OF THE ATOM (Also see The Occult Files of Dr. Spektor #14 & Solar)
10/62 - No. 27, 4/69; No. 28, 4/81 - No. 31, 3/82 (1-27 have painted-c)

Doctor Strange #169 © MEG

Doctor Strange, Sorcerer Supreme #69 © MEG

Dods Of War #1 © EEP

GD25 FN65 NM94

Gold Key/Whitman No. 28 on
1-(#10000-210)-Origin/1st app. Dr. Solar (1st original Gold Key character)
40.00 120.00 280.00
2-Prof. Harbinger begins 13.00 40.00 90.00
3-5: 5-Intro. Man of the Atom in costume 9.00 26.00 60.00
6-10 5.70 17.00 40.00
11-14,16-20 4.70 14.00 33.00
15-Origin retold 6.30 19.00 44.00
21-27 3.00 9.40 22.00
28-31: 29-Magnus Robot Fighter begins. 31-The Sentinel app.
1.70 4.20 10.00

NOTE: ***Frank Bolle*** *a-6-19, 29-31; c-29i, 30i.* ***Bob Fugitani*** *a-1-5.* ***Spiegle*** *a-29-31.* ***Al McWilliams*** *a-20-23.*

DOCTOR SOLAR, MAN OF THE ATOM
1990 - No. 2, 1991 ($7.95, card stock-c, high quality, 96 pgs.)
Valiant Comics
1,2: Reprints Gold Key series 1.30 3.25 8.00

DOCTOR SPEKTOR (See The Occult Files of..., & Spine-Tingling Tales)

DOCTOR STRANGE (Formerly Strange Tales #1-168) (Also see The Defenders, Giant-Size..., Marvel Fanfare, Marvel Graphic Novel, Marvel Premiere, Marvel Treasury Edition & Strange Tales, 2nd Series)
No. 169, 6/68 - No. 183, 11/69; 6/74 - No. 81, 2/87
Marvel Comics Group
169(#1)-Origin retold; panel swipe/M.D. #1-c 18.00 54.00 125.00
170-176 6.00 18.00 42.00
177-New costume 5.30 16.00 37.00
178-183: 178-Black Knight app. 179-Spider-Man story-r. 180-Photo montage-c. 181-Brunner-c(part-i) 4.90 15.00 34.00
1(6/74, 2nd series)-Brunner-c/a 4.60 14.00 32.00
2 2.40 7.30 17.00
3-5 1.30 3.00 8.00
6-10 1.00 2.50 6.00
11-20: 14-Dracula app. 1.80 4.50
21-26: 21-Origin-r/Doctor Strange #169 1.40 3.50
27-77,79-81: 31-Sub-Mariner-c/story. 56-Origin retold. 58-Re-intro Hannibal King (cameo). 59-Hannibal King full app. 59-62-Dracula app. (Darkhold storyline). 61,62-Doctor Strange, Blade, Hannibal King & Frank Drake team-up to battle Dracula. 62-Death of Dracula & Lilith .70 1.70
78-New costume 1.10 2.75
Annual 1(1976, 52 pgs.)-New Russell-a (35 pgs.) 1.70 4.25
.../Silver Dagger Special Edition 1 (3/83, $2.50)-r/#1,2,4,5; Wrightson-c
1.10 2.75

NOTE: ***Adkins*** *a-169, 170, 171i; c-169-171, 172i, 173.* ***Adams*** *a-4i.* ***Austin*** *a(i)-48-60, 66, 68, 70, 73; c(i)-38, 47-53, 55, 58-60, 70.* ***Brunner*** *a-1-5p; c-1-6, 22, 28-30, 33.* ***Colan*** *a(p)-172-178, 180-183, 6-18, 36-45, 47; c(p)-172, 174-183, 11-21, 23, 27, 35, 36, 47.* ***Ditko*** *a-179r, 3r.* ***Everett*** *c-183i.* ***Golden*** *a-46p, 55p; c-42-44, 46, 55p.* ***G. Kane*** *c(p)-8-10.* ***Miller*** *c-46p.* ***Nebres*** *a-20, 22, 23, 24i, 26i, 32i; c-32i, 34.* ***Rogers*** *a-48-53p; c-47p-53p.* ***Russell*** *a-34i, 46i, Annual 1.* ***B. Smith*** *c-179.* ***Paul Smith*** *a-54p, 56p, 65, 66p, 68p, 69, 71-73; c-56, 65, 66, 68, 71.* ***Starlin*** *a-23p, 26; c-25, 26.* ***Sutton*** *a-27-29p, 34p. Painted c-62, 63.*

DOCTOR STRANGE CLASSICS
Mar, 1984 - No. 4, June, 1984 ($1.50 cover price; Baxter paper)
Marvel Comics Group
1-4: Ditko-r; Byrne-c. 4-New Golden pin-up .80 2.00

DOCTOR STRANGE, SORCERER SUPREME
Nov, 1988 - Present (Mando paper, $1.25/$1.50/$1.75/$1.95, direct sales only)
Marvel Comics (Midnight Sons imprint #60 on)
1 ($1.25) 1.60 4.00
2-9,12-14,16-27,29,30 ($1.50): 3-New Defenders app. 5-Guice-c/a begins. 14-18-Morbius story line. 26-Werewolf by Night app. 1.50
10-Re-intro Morbius w/new costume (11/89) .80 2.00
11-Hobgoblin app. 1.00 2.00 5.00
15-Unauthorized Amy Grant photo-c 1.00 2.50 5.50
28-Ghost Rider story cont'd from G.R. #12; same book published at same time as Doctor Strange/Ghost Rider Special #1 (4/91) 1.60 4.00
31-36-Infinity Gauntlet x-overs: 31-Silver Surfer app. 33-Thanos-c & cameo. 36-Warlock app. 1.20 3.00
37-49,51-64: 37-Silver Surfer app. 38-Begin $1.75-c. 40-Daredevil x-over. 41-Wolverine-c/story. 42-47-Infinity War x-overs. 47-Gamora app. 52,53-Morbius-c/stories. 60,61-Siege of Darkness pt. 7 & 15. 60-Spot varnish-c. 61-New Doctor Strange begins (cameo, 1st app.). 62-Dr. Doom & Morbius app. .70 1.75
50-($2.95, 52 pgs.)-Holo-grafx foil-c; Hulk, Ghost Rider & Silver Surfer app.; leads into new Secret Defenders series 1.20 3.00
65-76: 65-Begin $1.95-c; bound-in card sheet; Namor-c/s .80 2.00
Annual 2 ('92, $2.25, 68 pgs.)-Return of Defenders .90 2.25
Annual 3 ('93, $2.95, 68 pgs.)-Polybagged w/card 1.20 3.00
Annual 4 ('94, $2.95) 1.20 3.00
.../Ghost Rider Special 1 (4/91, $1.50)-Same book as D.S.S.S. #28
1.50 3.75
...Vs. Dracula 1 (3/94, $1.75, 52 pgs.)-r/Tomb of Dracula #44 & Dr. Strange #14
.70 1.75

NOTE: ***Colan*** *c/a-19.* ***Guice*** *a-5-16, 18, 20-24; c-5-12, 20-24. See 1st series for Annual #1.*

DR. TOM BRENT, YOUNG INTERN
Feb, 1963 - No. 5, Oct, 1963
Charlton Publications
1 1.80 4.50 9.00
2-5 1.00 2.50 5.00

DR. VOLTZ (See Mighty Midget Comics)

DR. WEIRD SPECIAL
Feb, 1994 ($3.95, B&W, 68 pgs.)
Big Bang Comics
1-Origin-r by Starlin; Starlin-c 1.60 4.00

DOCTOR WHO (Also see Marvel Premiere #57-60)
Oct, 1984 - No. 23, Aug, 1986 ($1.50, Direct sales, Baxter paper)
Marvel Comics Group
1-23-British-r 1.00

DR. WHO & THE DALEKS (See Movie Classics)

DOCTOR ZERO
April, 1988 - No. 8, Aug, 1989 ($1.25/$1.50)
Epic Comics (Marvel)
1-8: 1-Sienkiewicz-c (a-3i,4i). 6,7-Spiegle-a 1.50

DO-DO (Funny Animal Circus Stories)
1950 - No. 7, 1951 (5x7-1/4" Miniature) (5¢)
Nation Wide Publishers
1 (52 pgs.) 13.00 40.00 90.00
2-7 7.50 22.50 45.00

DODO & THE FROG, THE (Formerly Funny Stuff; also see It's Game Time #2)
No. 80, 9-10/54 - No. 88, 1-2/56; No. 89, 8-9/56; No. 90, 10-11/56; No. 91, 9/57; No. 92, 11/57 (See Comic Cavalcade)
National Periodical Publications
80-1st app. Doodles Duck by Sheldon Mayer 16.00 48.00 110.00
81-91: Doodles Duck by Mayer in #81,83-90 10.00 30.00 70.00
92-(Scarce)-Doodles Duck by S. Mayer 13.50 41.00 95.00

DOGFACE DOOLEY
1951 - No. 5, 1953
Magazine Enterprises
1(A-1 40) 4.70 14.00 28.00
2(A-1 43), 3(A-1 49), 4(A-1 53), 5(A-1 64) 4.00 10.00 20.00
I.W. Reprint #1('64), Super Reprint #17 1.60 4.00 8.00

DOG OF FLANDERS, A (See 4-Color No. 1088)

DOGPATCH (See Al Capp's... & Mammy Yokum)

DOGS OF WAR
Apr, 1994 - Present ($2.50)
Defiant Comics

Doll Man #30 © QUA

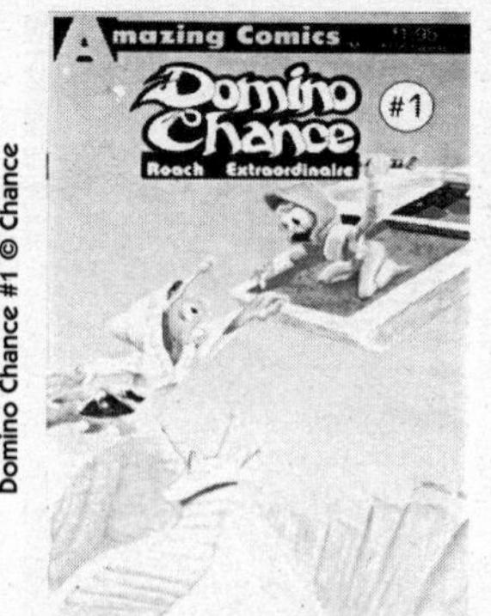

Domino Chance #1 © Chance

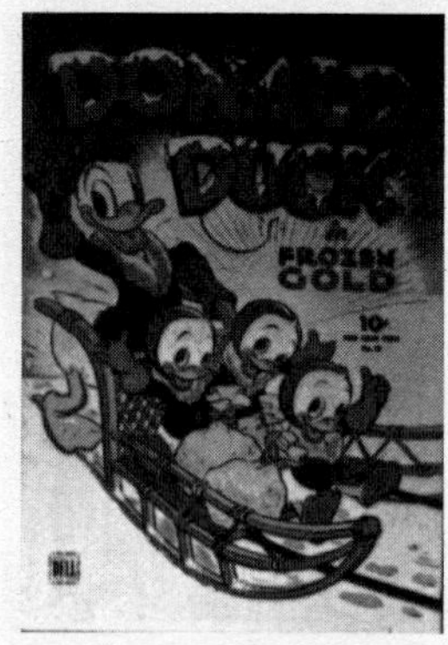

4-Color #62 Donald Duck © WDC

GD25 FN65 NM94 — GD25 FN65 NM94

1-5 — 1.00 — 2.50

DOINGS OF THE DOO DADS, THE
1922 (34 pgs.; 7-3/4x7-3/4"; B&W) (50¢)(red & white-c, square binding)
Detroit News (Universal Feat. & Specialty Co.)

nn-Reprints 1921 newspaper strip "Text & Pictures" given away as prize in the Detroit News Doo Dads contest; by Arch Dale — 14.00 — 43.00 — 100.00

DOLLFACE & HER GANG (See 4-Color No. 309)

DOLLMAN
Sept, 1991 - No. 4, Dec, 1991 ($2.50, mini-series)
Eternity Comics

1-4: Based on new movie — 1.00 — 2.50

DOLL MAN QUARTERLY, THE (Doll Man #17 on; also see Feature Comics #27 & Freedom Fighters)
Fall, 1941 - No. 7, Fall, '43; No. 8, Spring, '46 - No. 47, Oct, 1953
Quality Comics Group

1-Dollman (by Cassone), Justin Wright begin — 193.00 — 580.00 — 1350.00
2-The Dragon begins; Crandall-a(5) — 82.00 — 246.00 — 575.00
3,4 — 61.00 — 182.00 — 425.00
5-Crandall-a — 46.00 — 139.00 — 325.00
6,7(1943) — 36.00 — 107.00 — 250.00
8(1946)-1st app. Torchy by Bill Ward — 41.00 — 122.00 — 285.00
9 — 31.00 — 92.00 — 215.00
10-20 — 25.00 — 75.00 — 175.00
21-30: 28-Vs. The Flame — 22.00 — 65.00 — 150.00
31-36,38,40: 31-(12/50)-Intro Elmo, the wonder dog (Dollman's faithful dog). 32-34-Jeb Rivers app.; 34 by Crandall(p) — 17.00 — 52.00 — 120.00
37-Origin & 1st app. Dollgirl; Dollgirl bondage-c — 25.00 — 75.00 — 175.00
39- "Narcotics...the Death Drug" c-/story — 17.00 — 52.00 — 120.00
41-47 — 13.00 — 40.00 — 90.00
Super Reprint #11('64, r/#20),15(r/#23),17(r/#28): 15,17-Torchy app.; Andru/Esposito-c — 3.60 — 9.00 — 18.00
NOTE: *Ward Torchy in 8, 9, 11, 12, 14-24, 26, 27; by Fox-#30, 35-47. **Crandall** a-2, 5, 10, 13 & Super #11, 17, 18. **Crandall/Cuidera** c-40-42. **Guardineer** a-3. Bondage c-27, 37, 38, 39.*

DOLLY
No. 10, July-Aug, 1951 (Funny animal)
Ziff-Davis Publ. Co.

10-Painted-c — 4.00 — 11.00 — 22.00

DOLLY DILL
1945
Marvel Comics/Newsstand Publ.

1 — 11.00 — 32.00 — 75.00

DOLLY DIMPLES & BOBBY BOONCE'
1933
Cupples & Leon Co.

nn — 12.00 — 36.00 — 85.00

DOMINION (Eclipse)(Value: cover or less)

DOMINO CHANCE (Chance)(Value: cover or less)

DONALD AND MICKEY IN DISNEYLAND (See Dell Giants)

DONALD AND MICKEY MERRY CHRISTMAS (Formerly Famous Gang Book Of Comics)
1943 - 1949 (20 pgs.)(Giveaway) Put out each Christmas; 1943 issue titled "Firestone Presents Comics" (Disney)
K. K. Publ./Firestone Tire & Rubber Co.

1943-Donald Duck-r/WDC&S #32 by Carl Barks — 50.00 — 150.00 — 450.00
1944-Donald Duck-r/WDC&S #35 by Barks — 50.00 — 150.00 — 450.00
1945- "Donald Duck's Best Christmas", 8 pgs. Carl Barks; intro. & 1st app. Grandma Duck in comic books — 67.00 — 200.00 — 600.00
1946-Donald Duck in "Santa's Stormy Visit", 8 pgs. Carl Barks — 56.00 — 167.00 — 500.00
1947-Donald Duck in "Three Good Little Ducks", 8 pgs. Carl Barks — 44.00 — 133.00 — 400.00
1948-Donald Duck in "Toyland", 8 pgs. Carl Barks — 44.00 — 133.00 — 400.00
1949-Donald Duck in "New Toys", 8 pgs. Barks — 44.00 — 133.00 — 400.00

DONALD AND SCROOGE
1992 ($8.95, squarebound, 100 pgs.)
Disney Comics

nn-Don Rosa reprint special; r/U.S., D.D. Advs. — 1.50 — 3.75 — 9.00
1-3 (1992, $1.50)-r/D.D. Advs. (Disney) #1,22,24 & U.S. #261-263,269 — 1.50

DONALD AND THE WHEEL (See 4-Color No. 1190)

DONALD DUCK (See Cheerios, Donald & Mickey, Ducktales, Dynabrite Comics, Gladstone Comic Album, Mickey & Donald, Mickey Mouse Mag., Story Hour Series, Uncle Scrooge, Walt Disney's Comics & Stories, W. D.'s Donald Duck, Wheaties & Whitman Comic Books)

DONALD DUCK
1935, 1936 (All pages on heavy linen-like finish cover stock in color;1st book ever devoted to Donald Duck; see The Wise Little Hen for earlier app.) (9-1/2x13")
Whitman Publishing Co./Grosset & Dunlap/K.K.

978(1935)-16 pgs.; Illustrated text story book — 300.00 — 900.00 — 2000.00
nn(1936)-36 pgs.plus hard cover & dust jacket. Story completely rewritten with B&W illos added. Mickey appears and his nephews are named Morty & Monty
Book only — 300.00 — 900.00 — 2000.00
Dust jacket only.... — 70.00 — 210.00 — 500.00

DONALD DUCK (Walt Disney's) (10¢)
1938 (B&W) (8-1/2x11-1/2") (Cardboard-c)(Has D. Duck with bubble pipe on-c)
Whitman/K.K. Publications

GD25 — FN65 — VF82 — NM94

nn-The first Donald Duck & Walt Disney comic book; 1936 & 1937 Sunday strip-r(in B&W); same format as the Feature Books; 1st strips with Huey, Dewey & Louie from 10/17/37 — 180.00 — 540.00 — 1170.00 — 1800.00

DONALD DUCK (Walt Disney's...#262 on; see 4-Color listings for titles & 4-Color No. 1109 for origin story)
1940 - No. 84, Sept-Nov, 1962; No. 85, Dec, 1962 - No. 245, 1984; No. 246, Oct, 1986 - No. 279, May, 1990; No. 280, Sept, 1993 - Present
Dell Publishing Co./Gold Key #85-216/Whitman #217-245/ Gladstone #246 on

GD25 — FN65 — VF82 — NM94

4-Color 4(1940)-Daily 1939 strip-r by Al Taliaferro — 700.00 — 2100.00 — 4550.00 — 7000.00
(Estimated up to 175 total copies exist, 9 in NM/Mint)
Large Feature Comic 16(1/41?)-1940 Sunday strips-r in B&W — 250.00 — 750.00 — 1625.00 — 2500.00
Large Feature Comic 20('41)-Comic Paint Book, r-single panels from Large Feature #16 at top of each pg. to color; daily strip-r across bottom of each pg. — 350.00 — 1050.00 — 2275.00 — 3500.00
4-Color 9('42)- "Finds Pirate Gold"; 64 pgs. by Carl Barks & Jack Hannah (pgs. 1,2,5,12-40 are by Barks, his 1st comic book art work; © 8/17/42) — 600.00 — 1800.00 — 3900.00 — 6000.00
(Estimated up to 270 total copies exist, 18 in NM/Mint)
4-Color 29(9/43)- "Mummy's Ring" by Barks; reprinted in Uncle Scrooge & Donald Duck #1('65), W. D. Comics Digest #44('73) & Donald Duck Advs. #14 — 500.00 — 1500.00 — 3250.00 — 5000.00
(Estimated up to 300 total copies exist, 14 in NM/Mint)

GD25 — FN65 — NM94

4-Color 62(1/45)- "Frozen Gold"; 52 pgs. by Barks, reprinted in The Best of W.D. Comics & Donald Duck Advs. #4 — 144.00 — 433.00 — 1300.00
4-Color 108(1946)- "Terror of the River"; 52 pgs. by Carl Barks; reprinted in Gladstone Comic Album #2 — 111.00 — 333.00 — 1000.00
4-Color 147(5/47)-in "Volcano Valley" by Barks — 72.00 — 217.00 — 650.00
4-Color 159(8/47)-in "The Ghost of the Grotto";52 pgs. by Carl Barks; reprinted in Best of Uncle Scrooge & Donald Duck #1 ('66) & The Best of W.D. Comics & D.D. Advs. #9; two Barks stories — 64.00 — 192.00 — 575.00
4-Color 178(12/47)-1st app. Uncle Scrooge by Carl Barks; reprinted in Gold Key Christmas Parade #3 & The Best of Walt Disney Comics — 72.00 — 217.00 — 650.00
4-Color 189(6/48)-by Carl Barks; reprinted in Best of Donald Duck & Uncle

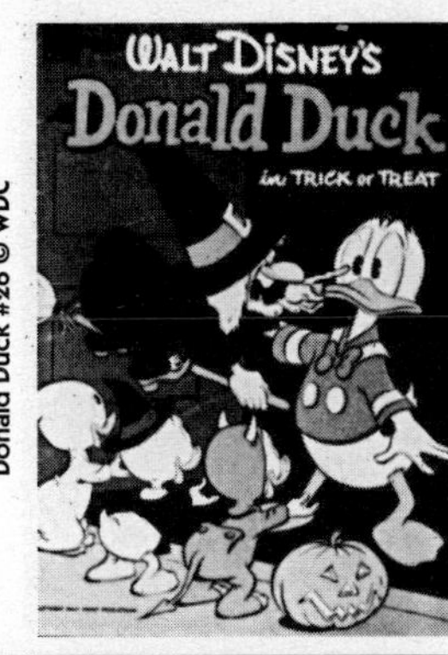

Donald Duck #26 © WDC

Donald Duck #246 © WDC

Donald Duck Album #1 © WDC

	GD25	FN65	NM94
Scrooge #1('64) & D.D. Advs. #19	59.00	178.00	535.00
4-Color 199(10/48)-by Carl Barks; mentioned in Love and Death; r/in Gladstone Comic Album #5	59.00	178.00	535.00
4-Color 203(12/48)-by Barks; reprinted as Gold Key Christmas Parade #4	44.00	133.00	400.00
4-Color 223(4/49)-by Barks; reprinted as Best of Donald Duck #1 & Donald Duck Advs. #3	56.00	167.00	500.00
4-Color 238(8/49)-in "Voodoo Hoodoo" by Barks	44.00	133.00	400.00
4-Color 256(12/49)-by Barks; reprinted in Best of Donald Duck & Uncle Scrooge #2('67), Gladstone Comic Album #16 & W.D. Comics Digest #44('73)	32.00	95.00	285.00
4-Color 263(2/50)-Two Barks stories; r-in D.D. #278	32.00	95.00	285.00
4-Color 275(5/50), 282(7/50), 291(9/50), 300(11/50)-All by Carl Barks; 275, 282 reprinted in W.D. Comics Digest #44('73). #275 r/in Gladstone Comic Album #10. #291 r/in D. Duck Advs. #16	29.00	88.00	265.00
4-Color 308(1/51), 318(3/51)-by Barks; #318-reprinted in W.D. Comics Digest #34 & D.D. Advs. #2,19	25.00	75.00	225.00
4-Color 328(5/51)-by Carl Barks	27.00	80.00	240.00
4-Color 339(7-8/51), 379-not by Barks	8.35	25.00	50.00
4-Color 348(9-10/51), 356,394-Barks-c only	14.00	43.00	100.00
4-Color 367(1-2/52)-by Barks; reprinted as Gold Key Christmas Parade #2 & #8	23.00	70.00	210.00
4-Color 408(7-8/52), 422(9-10/52)-All by Carl Barks. #408-r-in Best of Donald Duck & Uncle Scrooge #1('64) & Gladstone Comic Album #13	23.00	70.00	210.00
26(11-12/52)-In "Trick or Treat" (Barks-a, 36pgs.) 1st story r-in Walt Disney Digest #16 & Gladstone C.A. #23	24.00	73.00	220.00
27-30-Barks-c only	11.00	32.00	75.00
31-44,47-50	5.85	17.50	35.00
45-Barks-a (6 pgs.)	14.00	43.00	100.00
46- "Secret of Hondorica" by Barks, 24 pgs.; reprinted in Donald Duck #98 & 154	22.00	65.00	150.00
51-Barks-a,1/2 pg.	5.85	17.50	35.00
52- "Lost Peg-Leg Mine" by Barks, 10 pgs.	14.00	43.00	100.00
53,55-59	4.20	12.50	25.00
54- "Forbidden Valley" by Barks, 26 pgs. (10¢ & 15¢ versions exist)	14.00	43.00	100.00
60- "Donald Duck & the Titanic Ants" by Barks, 20 pgs. plus 6 more pgs.	14.00	43.00	100.00
61-67,69,70	4.20	12.50	25.00
68-Barks-a, 5 pgs.	11.00	32.00	75.00
71-Barks-r, 1/2 pg.	4.00	10.00	20.00
72-78,80,82-97,99,100: 96-Donald Duck Album	4.00	10.00	20.00
79,81-Barks-a, 1pg.	4.00	10.00	20.00
98-Reprints #46 (Barks)	4.20	12.50	25.00
101-133: 102-Super Goof. 112-1st Moby Duck	2.10	6.50	15.00
134-Barks-r/#52 & WDC&S 194	2.10	6.50	15.00
135-Barks-r/WDC&S 198, 19 pgs.	2.10	6.50	15.00
136-153,155,156,158	1.70	4.20	10.00
154-Barks-r(#46)	1.70	5.00	12.00
157,159,160,164: 157-Barks-r(#45). 159-Reprints/WDC&S #192 (10 pgs.). 160-Barks-r(#26). 164-Barks-r(#79)	1.70	4.20	10.00
161-163,165-173,175-187,189-191	1.00	2.50	6.00
174,188: 174-r/4-Color #394. 188-Barks-r/#68	1.30	3.25	8.00
192-Barks-r(40 pgs.) from Donald Duck #60 & WDC&S #226,234 (52 pgs.)	1.30	3.25	8.00
193-200,202-207,209-211,213-218: 217 has 216 on-c		1.60	4.00
201,208,212: 201-Barks-r/Christmas Parade #26, 16pgs. 208-Barks-r/#60 (6 pgs.). 212-Barks-r/WDC&S #130		1.60	4.00
219-Barks-r/WDC&S #106,107, 10 pgs. ea.		1.60	4.00
220-227,231-245		1.20	3.00
228-230: 228-Barks-r/F.C. #275. 229-Barks-r/F.C. #282. 230-Barks-r/ #52 & WDC&S #194		1.60	4.00
246-(1st Gladstone issue)-Barks-r/FC #422	1.65	4.00	10.00
247-249: 248,249-Barks-r/DD #54 & 26		1.60	4.00
250-($1.50, 68 pgs.)-Barks-r/4-Color #9	1.70	5.10	12.00
251-256: 251-Barks-r/1945 Firestone. 254-Barks-r/FC #328. 256-Barks-r/FC #147		1.50	3.75
257-($1.50, 52 pgs.)-Barks-r/Vacaction Parade #1		1.60	4.00
258-260		1.20	3.00
261-277: 261-Barks-r/FC #300. 275-Kelly-r/FC #92		.75	1.90
278-($1.95, 68 pgs.)-Rosa-a; Barks-r/FC #263		1.00	2.50
279-($1.95, 68 pgs.)-Rosa-c; Barks-r/MOC #4		1.00	2.50
280-285,287-291: 283-Don Rosa-a, part-c & scripts		.70	1.80
286 ($2.95, 68 pgs.)-Happy Birthday, Donald		1.20	3.00
Mini-Comic #1(1976)-(3-1/4x6-1/2"); r/D.D. #150			.10

NOTE: ***Carl Barks*** *wrote all issues he illustrated, but #117, 126, 138 contain his script only. Issues 4-Color #189, 199, 203, 223, 238, 256, 263, 275, 282, 308, 348, 356, 367, 394, 408, 422, 26-30, 35, 44, 46, 52, 55, 57, 60, 65, 70-73, 77-80, 83, 101, 103, 105, 106, 111, 126, 246r, 266r, 268r, 271r, 275r, 278r(F.C. 263) all have* ***Barks*** *covers.* ***Barks*** *r-263-267, 269-278-282, 284, 285. #96 titled "Comic Album", #99-"Christmas Album". New art issues (not reprints)-106-46, 148-63, 167, 169, 170, 172, 173, 175, 178, 179, 196, 209, 223, 225, 236.* ***Tallaferro*** *daily newspaper strips #284, 285; Sunday strips #280-283.*

DONALD DUCK
1944 (16 pg. Christmas giveaway)(paper cover)(2 versions)
K. K. Publications

	GD25	FN65	NM94
nn-Kelly cover reprint	50.00	150.00	450.00

DONALD DUCK ALBUM (See Comic Album No. 1,3 & Duck Album)
5-7/59 - F.C. No. 1239, 10-12/61; 1962; 8/63 - No. 2, Oct, 1963
Dell Publishing Co./Gold Key

	GD25	FN65	NM94
4-Color 995 (#1)	5.00	15.00	35.00
1182, 01204-207 (1962-Dell)	4.70	14.00	28.00
4-Color 1099,1140,1239-Barks-c	6.70	20.00	40.00
1(8/63-Gold Key)-Barks-c	5.85	17.50	35.00
2(10/63)	4.00	10.00	20.00

DONALD DUCK AND THE BOYS (Also see Story Hour Series)
1948 (Hardcover book; 5-1/4x5-1/2") (100pgs., art, text)
Whitman Publishing Co.

	GD25	FN65	NM94
845-(49) new illos by Barks based on his Donald Duck 10-pager in WDC&S #74, Expanded text not written by Barks; Cover not by Barks	50.00	150.00	350.00

(Prices vary widely on this book)

DONALD DUCK AND THE CHRISTMAS CAROL
1960 (A Little Golden Book, 28pgs, color, 6-3/8"x7-5/8")
Whitman Publishing Co.

	GD25	FN65	NM94
nn-Story book pencilled by Carl Barks with the intended title "Uncle Scrooge's Christmas Carol." Finished art adapted by Norman McGary. (Rare)-Reprinted in Uncle Scrooge in Color.	90.00	270.00	600.00

DONALD DUCK AND THE RED FEATHER
1948 (4 pgs.) (8-1/2x11") (Black & White)
Red Feather Giveaway

	GD25	FN65	NM94
nn	11.50	34.00	80.00

DONALD DUCK BEACH PARTY (Also see Dell Giants)
Sept, 1965 (12¢)
Gold Key

	GD25	FN65	NM94
1(#10158-509)-Barks-r/WDC&S #45; painted-c	8.35	25.00	50.00

DONALD DUCK BOOK (See Story Hour Series)

DONALD DUCK COMIC PAINT BOOK (See Large Feature Comic No. 20)

DONALD DUCK COMICS DIGEST
Nov, 1986 - No. 5, July, 1987 ($1.25/$1.50, 96 pgs.)
Gladstone Publishing

	GD25	FN65	NM94
1-5: 1-Barks-c/a-r. 4,5-$1.50-c		.80	2.00

DONALD DUCK FUN BOOK (See Dell Giants)

DONALD DUCK IN DISNEYLAND (See Dell Giants)

DONALD DUCK IN "THE LITTERBUG"
1963 (16 pgs., 5x7-1/4", soft-c) (Disney giveaway)

Don Simpson's Bizarre Heroes #1 © Don Simpson

Don Winslow of the Navy #17 © FAW

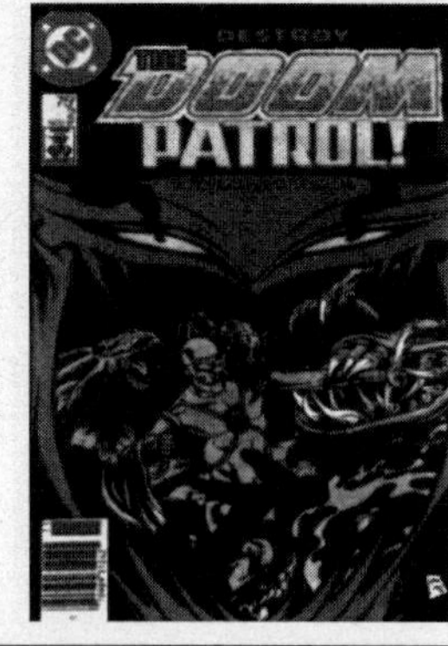

Doom Patrol #2 © DC

GD25 FN65 NM94 GD25 FN65 NM94

Keep America Beautiful
nn 5.00 15.00 30.00

DONALD DUCK MARCH OF COMICS
No. 4, 1947 - No. 69, 1951; No. 263, 1964 (Giveaway) (Disney)
K. K. Publications
nn(No.4)- "Maharajah Donald"; 30 pgs. by Carl Barks-(1947) 857.00 2571.00 6000.00
20- "Darkest Africa" by Barks-(1948); 22 pgs. 500.00 1500.00 3500.00
41- "Race to South Seas" by Carl Barks-(1949); 22 pgs. 500.00 1500.00 3500.00
56-(1950)-Barks-a on back-c 34.00 103.00 240.00
69-(1951)-Not by Barks; Barks-a on back-c 29.00 86.00 200.00
263-Not by Barks 10.00 30.00 60.00

DONALD DUCK MERRY CHRISTMAS (See Dell Giant No. 53)

DONALD DUCK PICNIC PARTY (See Picnic Party listed under Dell Giants)

DONALD DUCK "PLOTTING PICNICKERS" (Also see Ludwig Von Drake & Mickey Mouse)
1962 (16 pgs., 3-1/4x7", soft-c) (Disney)
Fritos Giveaway
nn 5.35 16.00 32.00

DONALD DUCK'S SURPRISE PARTY
1948 (16 pgs.) (Giveaway for Icy Frost Twins Ice Cream Bars)
Walt Disney Productions
nn-(Rare)-Kelly-c/a 285.00 857.00 2000.00

DONALD DUCK TELLS ABOUT KITES (See Kite Fun Book)

DONALD DUCK, THIS IS YOUR LIFE (See 4-Color No. 1109)

DONALD DUCK XMAS ALBUM (See regular Donald Duck No. 99)

DONALD IN MATHMAGIC LAND (See 4-Color No. 1051, 1198)

DONATELLO, TEENAGE MUTANT NINJA TURTLE
Aug, 1986 ($1.50, one-shot, B&W, 44 pgs.)
Mirage Studios
1 1.50 4.00 9.00

DONDI (See 4-Color No. 1176,1276)

DON FORTUNE MAGAZINE
Aug, 1946 - No. 6, Feb, 1947
Don Fortune Publishing Co.
1-Delecta of the Planets by C. C. Beck in all 13.00 40.00 90.00
2 10.00 30.00 60.00
3-6: 3-Bondage-c 6.70 20.00 40.00

DONNA MATRIX
Aug, 1993 ($2.95, 52 pgs.)
Reactor, Inc.
1-Computer generated-c/a by Mike Saenz; 3-D effects 1.20 3.00

DON NEWCOMBE
1950 (Baseball)
Fawcett Publications
nn-Photo-c 30.00 901.00 210.00

DON SIMPSON'S BIZARRE HEROES
May, 1994 - Present ($2.95, B&W, adult)
Fiasco Comics
1-9: 1,2-Megaton Man-c/story 1.20 3.00

DON'T GIVE UP THE SHIP (See 4-Color #1049)

DON WINSLOW OF THE NAVY (See Crackajack Funnies, Famous Feature Stories, Four Color #2, 22, Popular Comics & Super Book #5,6)

DON WINSLOW OF THE NAVY (See TV Teens; Movie, Radio, TV)
(Fightin' Navy No. 74 on)
2/43 - #64, 12/48; #65, 1/51 - #69, 9/51; #70, 3/55 - #73, 9/55
Fawcett Publications/Charlton No. 70 on
1-(68 pgs.)-Captain Marvel on cover 71.00 215.00 500.00
2 36.00 107.00 250.00
3 26.00 78.00 180.00
4-6: 6-Flag-c 20.00 60.00 140.00
7-10: 8-Last 68 pg. issue? 14.00 43.00 100.00
11-20 11.00 32.00 75.00
21-40 8.35 25.00 50.00
41-64: 51,60-Singapore Sal (villain) app. 64-(12/48) 6.70 20.00 40.00
65(1/51)-Flying Saucer attack; photo-c 8.35 25.00 50.00
66 - 69(9/51): All photo-c 8.35 25.00 50.00
70(3/55)-73: 70-73 r-/#26,58 & 59 5.85 17.50 35.00

DOOM FORCE SPECIAL
July, 1992 ($2.95, mature readers, 68 pgs.)
DC Comics
1-X-Force parody; Morrison scripts; Simonson, Steacy, others-a; Giffen/Mignola-c 1.20 3.00

DOOM PATROL, THE (Formerly My Greatest Adventure No. 1-85; see Brave and the Bold, DC Special Blue Ribbon Digest 19, Official... Index & Showcase No. 94-96)
No. 86, 3/64 - No. 121, 9-10/68; No. 122, 2/73 - No. 124, 6-7/73
National Periodical Publications
86-1 pg. origin (#86-121 are 12¢ issues) 12.00 36.00 85.00
87-99: 88-Origin The Chief. 91-Intro. Mento. 99-Intro. Beast Boy (later became the Changeling in New Teen Titans 7.00 22.00 52.00
100-Origin Beast Boy; Robot-Maniac series begins (12/65) 9.00 27.00 62.00
101-110: 102-Challengers of the Unknown app. 105-Robot-Maniac series ends. 106-Negative Man begins (origin) 4.30 13.00 30.00
111-120 3.40 10.00 24.00
121-Death of Doom Patrol; Orlando-c 10.00 29.00 68.00
122-124: All reprints 1.20 3.00

DOOM PATROL
Oct, 1987 - Present (New format, direct sale, 75¢/$1.00/$1.50/$1.75/$1.95)
DC Comics (Vertigo imprint #64 on)
1-Begin 75¢-c .90 2.25
2-18: 3-1st app. Lodestone. 4-1st app. Karma. 8,15,16-Art Adams-c(i). 10-Begin $1.00-c. 18-Invasion 1.10
19-New format & Grant Morrison scripts begin; begin $1.50-c 2.30 6.90 16.00
20-25 1.50 3.75 9.00
26-30: 29-Superman app. 30-Night Breed fold-out 1.60 4.00
31-40: 39-Preview of World Without End .80 2.00
41-49,51-56,58-60: 60-Last $1.50-c .70 1.80
50,57-($2.50, 52 pgs.) 1.00 2.50
61-65-($1.75): 61-Photo-c. 63-Last Morrison scripts .70 1.80
66-88 ($1.95): 70-Photo-c. 73-Death cameo(2 panels) .80 2.00
...And Suicide Squad 1 (3/88, $1.50, 52 pgs.)-Wraparound-c .65 1.60
Annual 1('88, $1.50, 52 pgs.) .65 1.60
Annual 2 ('94, $3.95, 68 pgs.)-Children's Crusade 1.60 4.00
NOTE: ***Simon Bisley*** *painted c-26-48, 55-58.* ***Bolland*** *c-64, 75.* ***Steacy*** *a-53.*

DOOMSDAY + 1 (Also see Charlton Bullseye)
July, 1975 - No. 6, June, 1976; No. 7, June, 1978 - No. 12, May, 1979
Charlton Comics
1: #1-5 are 25¢ issues 1.00 2.00 5.00
2 1.30 3.25
3-6: 4-Intro Lor. 5-Ditko-a(1 pg.) 6-Begin 30¢ issues 1.20 3.00
V3#7-12 (reprints #1-6) .65 1.60
5 (Modern Comics reprint, 1977) 1.00
NOTE: ***Byrne*** *c/a-1-12; Painted covers-2-7.*

DOOMSDAY SQUAD, THE (Fantagraphics)(Value: cover or less)

DOOM'S IV
July, 1994 - Present ($2.50)

Doom 2099 #20 © MEG

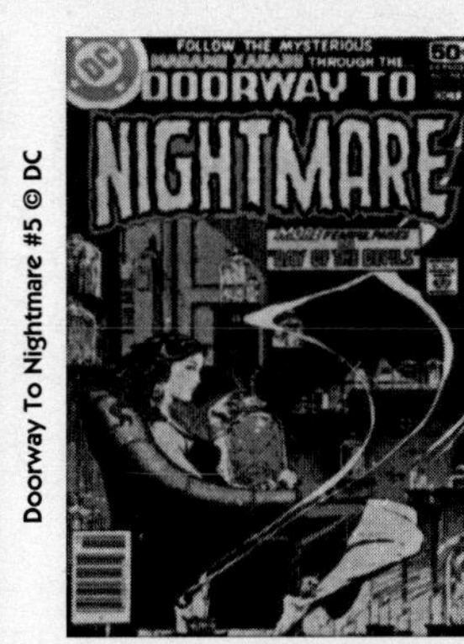

Doorway To Nightmare #5 © DC

Double Dragon #3 © Technos Japan Corp.

	GD25	FN65	NM94

Image Comics

	GD25	FN65	NM94
1,2-Liefeld story		1.00	2.50
1,2-Two alternate Liefeld-c each, 4 covers form 1 picture		1.60	4.00

DOOM 2099 (See Marvel Comics Presents #118)
Jan, 1993 - Present ($1.25)
Marvel Comics

	GD25	FN65	NM94
1-($1.75)-Metallic foil stamped-c		.80	1.90
1-2nd printing		.70	1.75
2-16: 14-Ron Lim-c(p)			1.25
17-28: 17-Begin $1.50-c; bound-in trading card sheet			1.50

DOORWAY TO NIGHTMARE (See Cancelled Comic Cavalcade)
Jan-Feb, 1978 - No. 5, Sept-Oct, 1978
DC Comics

	GD25	FN65	NM94
1-5-Madame Xanadu in all. 4-Craig-a			1.00

NOTE: ***Kaluta** covers on all. Merged into The Unexpected with No. 190.*

DOPEY DUCK COMICS (Wacky Duck No. 3) (See Super Funnies)
Fall, 1945 - No. 2, April, 1946
Timely Comics (NPP)

	GD25	FN65	NM94
1,2-Casper Cat, Krazy Krow	12.00	36.00	85.00

DOROTHY LAMOUR (Formerly Jungle Lil)(Stage, screen, radio)
No. 2, June, 1950 - No. 3, Aug, 1950
Fox Features Syndicate

	GD25	FN65	NM94
2,3-Wood-a(3) each, photo-c	14.00	43.00	100.00

DOT AND DASH AND THE LUCKY JINGLE PIGGIE
1942 (12 pgs.)
Sears Roebuck Christmas giveaway

	GD25	FN65	NM94
nn-Contains a war stamp album and a punch out Jingle Piggie bank	6.70	20.00	40.00

DOT DOTLAND (Formerly Little Dot Dotland)
No. 62, Sept, 1974 - No. 63, November, 1974
Harvey Publications

	GD25	FN65	NM94
62,63		.80	2.00

DOTTY (...& Her Boy Friends)(Formerly Four Teeners; Glamorous Romances No. 41 on)
No. 35, June, 1948 - No. 40, May, 1949
Ace Magazines (A. A. Wyn)

	GD25	FN65	NM94
35-Teen-age	5.00	15.00	30.00
36,38-40	3.20	8.00	16.00
37-Transvestism story	3.60	9.00	18.00

DOTTY DRIPPLE (Horace & Dotty Dripple No. 25 on)
1946 - No. 24, June, 1952 (See A-1 No. 1-8, 10)
Magazine Ent.(Life's Romances)/Harvey No. 3 on

	GD25	FN65	NM94
1 (nd) (10¢)	4.00	11.00	22.00
2	2.00	5.00	10.00
3-10: 3,4-Powell-a	1.40	3.50	7.00
11-24	1.00	2.50	5.00

DOTTY DRIPPLE AND TAFFY
No. 646, Sept, 1955 - No. 903, May, 1958
Dell Publishing Co.

	GD25	FN65	NM94
4-Color 646 (#1)	4.00	11.00	22.00
4-Color 691,718,746,801,903	3.60	9.00	18.00

DOUBLE ACTION COMICS
No. 2, Jan, 1940 (Regular size; 68 pgs.; B&W, color cover)
National Periodical Publications

	GD25	FN65	NM94
2-Contains original stories(?); pre-hero DC contents; same cover as Adventure No. 37. (six known copies) (not an ashcan) Estimated value....			8500.00

NOTE: *The cover to this book was probably reprinted from Adventure #37. #1 exists as an ash can copy with B&W cover; contains a coverless comic on inside with 1st & last page missing.*

DOUBLE COMICS
1940 - 1944 (132 pgs.)
Elliot Publications

	GD25	FN65	NM94
1940 issues; Masked Marvel-c & The Mad Mong vs. The White Flash covers known	171.00	515.00	1200.00
1941 issues; Tornado Tim-c, Nordac-c, & Green Light covers known	119.00	358.00	835.00
1942 issues	93.00	278.00	650.00
1943,1944 issues	67.00	200.00	470.00

NOTE: *Double Comics consisted of an almost endless combination of pairs of remaindered, unsold issues of comics representing most publishers and usually mixed publishers in the same book; e.g., a Captain America with a Silver Streak, or a Feature with a Detective, etc., could appear inside the same cover. The actual contents would have to determine its price. Prices listed are for average contents. Any containing rare origin or first issues are worth much more. Covers also vary in same year. Value would be approximately 50 percent of contents.*

DOUBLE-CROSS (See The Crusaders)

DOUBLE-DARE ADVENTURES
Dec, 1966 - No. 2, March, 1967 (35-25¢, 68 pgs.)
Harvey Publications

	GD25	FN65	NM94
1-Origin Bee-Man, Glowing Gladiator, & Magic-Master; Simon/Kirby-a (last S&K art as a team?)	5.10	15.00	36.00
2-Williamson/Crandall-a; r/Alarming Adv. #3('63)	3.70	11.00	26.00

NOTE: ***Powell** a-1. **Simon/Sparling** c-1, 2.*

DOUBLE DRAGON
July, 1991 - No. 6, Dec, 1991 (1.00, mini-series)
Marvel Comics

	GD25	FN65	NM94
1-6: Based on video game. 2-Arthur Adams-c			1.00

DOUBLE LIFE OF PRIVATE STRONG, THE
June, 1959 - No. 2, Aug, 1959
Archie Publications/Radio Comics

	GD25	FN65	NM94
1-Origin & re-intro The Shield; Simon & Kirby-c/a, their re-entry into the super-hero genre; intro./1st app. The Fly; 1st S.A. super-hero for Archie Publ.	59.00	176.00	410.00
2-S&K-c/a; Tuska-a; The Fly app. (2nd or 3rd?)	37.00	111.00	260.00

DOUBLE TALK (Also see Two-Faces)
No date (1962?) (32 pgs.; full color; slick cover)
Christian Anti-Communism Crusade (Giveaway)
Feature Publications

	GD25	FN65	NM94
nn-Sickle with blood-c	10.00	30.00	65.00

DOUBLE TROUBLE
Nov, 1957 - No. 2, Jan-Feb, 1958
St. John Publishing Co.

	GD25	FN65	NM94
1,2	4.00	11.00	22.00

DOUBLE TROUBLE WITH GOOBER
No. 417, Aug, 1952 - No. 556, May, 1954
Dell Publishing Co.

	GD25	FN65	NM94
4-Color 417	3.60	9.00	18.00
4-Color 471,516,556	2.80	7.00	14.00

DOUBLE UP
1941 (200 pgs.) (Pocket size)
Elliott Publications

	GD25	FN65	NM94
1-Contains rebound copies of digest sized issues of Pocket Comics, Speed Comics, & Spitfire Comics	62.00	188.00	435.00

DOVER & CLOVER (See All Funny & More Fun Comics #93)

DOVER BOYS (See Adventures of the...)

DOVER THE BIRD
Spring, 1955
Famous Funnies Publishing Co.

	GD25	FN65	NM94
1-Funny animal; code approved	4.00	11.00	22.00

DOWN WITH CRIME

Dracula #1 © Steve Jones

Dragonflight © Anne McCaffrey

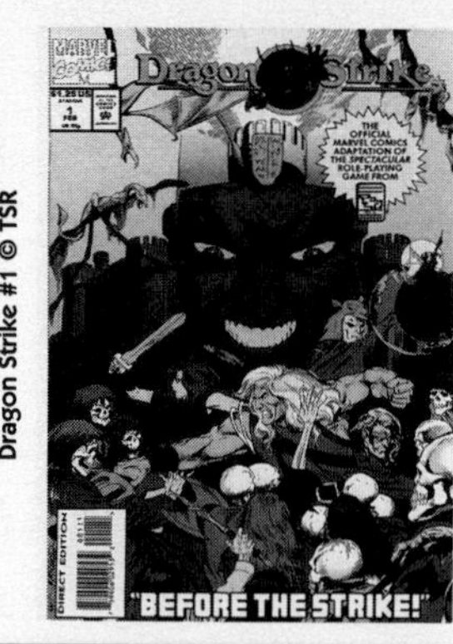

Dragon Strike #1 © TSR

Nov, 1952 - No. 7, Nov, 1953
Fawcett Publications

	GD25	FN65	NM94
1	13.00	40.00	100.00
2-5: 2,4-Powell-a in each. 3-Used in **POP**, pg. 106; "H is for Heroin" drug story. 5-Bondage-c	9.15	27.50	55.00
6,7: 6-Used in **POP**, pg. 80	6.70	20.00	40.00

DO YOU BELIEVE IN NIGHTMARES?
Nov, 1957 - No. 2, Jan, 1958
St. John Publishing Co.

	GD25	FN65	NM94
1-Mostly Ditko-c/a	25.00	75.00	175.00
2-Ayers-a	13.50	41.00	95.00

D.P. 7
Nov, 1986 - No. 32, June, 1989 (26 on: $1.50)
Marvel Comics Group

	GD25	FN65	NM94
1-32			1.25
Annual #1 (11/87)-Intro. The Witness			1.25

NOTE: ***Williamson*** *a-9i, 11i; c-9i.*

DRACULA (See Bram Stoker's Dracula, Giant-Size..., Little Dracula, Marvel Graphic Novel, Requiem for Dracula, Spider-Man Vs...., Tomb of... & Wedding of...; also see Movie Classics under Universal Presents as well as Dracula)

DRACULA (See Movie Classics for #1)(Also see Frankenstein & Werewolf)
No. 2, 11/66 - No. 4, 3/67; No. 6, 7/72 - No. 8, 7/73 (No #5)
Dell Publishing Co.

	GD25	FN65	NM94
2-Origin & 1st app. Dracula (11/66) (super hero)	2.40	6.50	13.00
3,4: 4-Intro. Fleeta ('67)	1.30	4.00	8.00
6-('72)-r/#2 w/origin	.90	2.30	5.50
7,8-r/#3, #4		1.70	4.25

DRACULA (Magazine)
1979 (120 pgs., full color)
Warren Publishing Co.

	GD25	FN65	NM94
Book 1-Maroto art; Spanish material translated into English	1.30	3.25	8.00

DRACULA LIVES! (Magazine)(Also see Tomb of Dracula)
1973(no month) - No. 13, July, 1975 (75¢, B&W)
Marvel Comics Group

	GD25	FN65	NM94
1	1.00	2.50	6.00
2,3: 2-Origin; Starlin-a		1.70	4.25
4-Ploog-a		1.10	2.75
5(V2#1)-13: 5-Dracula series begins		.90	2.25
Annual 1(Summer, 1975, $1.25)-Morrow painted-c		1.00	2.50

NOTE: ***N. Adams*** *a-2, 3i, 10i, Annual 1r(2, 3i).* ***Alcala*** *a-9.* ***Buscema*** *a-3p, 6p, Annual 1p.* ***Colan*** *a(p)-1, 2, 5, 6, 8.* ***Evans*** *a-7.* ***Heath*** *a-1r, 13.* ***Pakula*** *a-6r.* ***Weiss*** *r-Annual 1p.*

DRACULA 3-D (3-D Zone)(Value: cover or less)

DRACULA VERSUS ZORRO
Oct, 1993 - No. 2, Nov, 1993 ($2.95, limited series)
Topps Comics

	GD25	FN65	NM94
1,2: 1-Spot varnish & red foil-c. 2-Polybagged w/16 pg. Zorro #0		1.20	3.00

DRACULA: VLAD THE IMPALER (Also see Bram Stoker's Dracula)
Feb, 1993 - No. 3, Apr, 1993 ($2.95, mini-series)
Topps Comics

	GD25	FN65	NM94
1-3-Polybagged with 3 trading cards each; Maroto-c/a		1.20	3.00

DRAFT, THE
1988 (One shot, $3.50, squarebound)
Marvel Comics

	GD25	FN65	NM94
1-Sequel to "The Pitt"		1.40	3.50

DRAG 'N' WHEELS (Formerly Top Eliminator)
No. 30, Sept, 1968 - No. 59, May, 1973
Charlton Comics

	GD25	FN65	NM94
30-40-Scot Jackson begins	2.00	6.00	14.00
41-50	1.50	3.80	9.00
51-59: Scot Jackson	1.00	2.50	6.00
Modern Comics Reprint 58('78)		1.20	3.00

DRAGON CHIANG (Eclipse)(Value: cover or less)

DRAGONFLIGHT (Eclipse)(Value: cover or less)

DRAGONFLY (Americomics)(Value: cover or less)(See Americomics #4)

DRAGONFORCE
1988 - No. 13, 1989 ($2.00)
Aircel Publishing

	GD25	FN65	NM94
1-Dale Keown-c/a/scripts in #1-12		1.50	3.75
2,3		1.30	3.25
4-6		.90	2.25
7-12		.80	2.00
13-No Keown-a		.80	2.00
...Chronicles Book 1-5 ($2.95, B&W, 60 pgs.): Dale Keown-r/Dragonring & Dragonforce		1.20	3.00

DRAGONLANCE (DC)(Value: cover or less)(Also see TSR Worlds)

DRAGON LINES
May, 1993 - No. 4, Aug, 1993 ($1.95, mini-series)
Epic Comics (Marvel)

	GD25	FN65	NM94
1-($2.50)-Embossed-c; Ron Lim-c/a in all		1.00	2.50
2-4		.80	2.00

DRAGON LINES: WAY OF THE WARRIOR
Nov, 1993 - No. 2, Jan, 1994 ($2.25, limited series)
Epic Comics (Marvel)

	GD25	FN65	NM94
1,2-Ron Lim-c/a(p)		.90	2.25

DRAGONQUEST
Dec, 1986 - No. 3, 1987 ($1.50, B&W, 28 pgs.)
Silverwolf Comics

	GD25	FN65	NM94
1-Tim Vigil-c/a in all	1.30	3.30	8.00
2,3	1.00	2.00	5.00

DRAGONRING (Aircel)(Value: cover or less)

DRAGON'S CLAWS
July, 1988 - No. 10, Apr, 1989 ($1.25/$1.50/$1.75, British)
Marvel Comics UK, Ltd.

	GD25	FN65	NM94
1-4: 2-Begin $1.50-c. 3-Death's Head 1 pg. strip on back-c (1st app.). 4-Silhouette of Death's Head on last pg.			1.50
5-1st full app. new Death's Head; begin $1.75-c	1.30	3.10	7.50
6-10		.70	1.75

DRAGONSLAYER
October, 1981 - No. 2, Nov, 1981
Marvel Comics Group

	GD25	FN65	NM94
1,2-Paramount Disney movie adaptation			1.00

DRAGON'S STAR 2
1994 - Present ($2.95, B&W)
Caliber Press

	GD25	FN65	NM94
1		1.20	3.00

DRAGON STRIKE
Feb, 1994 ($1.25)
Marvel Comics

	GD25	FN65	NM94
1-Based on TSR role playing game			1.25

DRAGOON WELLS MASSACRE (See 4-Color No. 815)

DRAGSTRIP HOTRODDERS (World of Wheels No. 17 on)
Sum, 1963; No. 2, Jan, 1965 - No. 16, Aug, 1967
Charlton Comics

	GD25	FN65	NM94
1	4.00	12.00	24.00
2-5	3.20	8.00	16.00
6-16	2.40	6.00	12.00

Drama #1 © JML

Dreadstar #46 © First

Duck Tales #6 © WDC

GD25 FN65 NM94

DRAMA
June, 1994 ($2.95, mature)
Sirius
1-1st full color Dawn app. 1.20 3.00
1-Limited edition (1400 copies); signed & numbered; fingerprint authenticity 1.70 4.00 10.00

DRAMA OF AMERICA, THE
1973 (224 pgs.) ($1.95)
Action Text
1- "Students' Supplement to History" 1.20 3.00

DREAD (Eclipse)(Value: cover or less)(Clive Barker) (Graphic album)

DREADLANDS (Also see Epic)
1992 - No. 4, 1992 ($3.95, mini-series, coated stock, 52 pgs.)
Epic Comics (Marvel)
1-4: Stiff-c 1.60 4.00

DREAD OF NIGHT (Hamilton)(Value: cover or less)

DREADSTAR (Epic/First)(Value: Cover or less)

DREADSTAR
Nov, 1982 - No. 64, Mar, 1991
Epic Comics/First Comics (No. 27 on)
1-64: 1-Starlin-a begins 1.25
Annual 1 (12/83)-r/The Price .70 1.75

DREADSTAR
Apr, 1994 - Present ($2.50, limited series:6)
Malibu Comics (Bravura imprint)
1-3-Peter David scripts: 1,2-Starlin-c 1.00 2.50
NOTE: *Issues 1-6 will contain Bravura stamps.*

DREADSTAR AND COMPANY (Epic)(Value: cover or less)

DREAM BOOK OF LOVE (See A-1 Comics No. 106, 114, 123)

DREAM BOOK OF ROMANCE (See A-1 No. 92, 101, 109, 110, 124)

DREAMERY, THE (Eclipse)(Value: cover or less)

DREAM OF LOVE
1958 (Reprints)
I. W. Enterprises
1,2,8: 1-Powell-a. 8-Kinstler-c 1.40 3.50 7.00
9-Kinstler-c; 1pg. John Wayne interview & Frazetta illo from John Wayne Adv. Comics #2 1.20 3.00 6.00

DREAMS OF THE RAREBIT FIEND
1905
Doffield & Co.?
nn-By Winsor McCay (Very Rare) (Three copies known to exist)
Estimated value.... $1200.00–$2200.00

DREDD RULES (Fleetway/Quality)(Value: cover or less)

DRIFT MARLO
May-July, 1962 - No. 2, Oct-Dec, 1962
Dell Publishing Co.
01-232-207(#1), 2(12-232-212) 3.60 9.00 18.00

DRISCOLL'S BOOK OF PIRATES
1934 (124 pgs.) (B&W; hardcover; 7x9")
David McKay Publ. (Not reprints)
nn-By Montford Amory 14.00 43.00 100.00

DROIDS (Also see Dark Horse Comics)
April, 1986 - No. 8, June, 1987 (Based on Saturday morning cartoon)
Star Comics (Marvel)
1-8: R2D2, C-3PO from Star Wars app. 1.00
NOTE: ***Romita** a-3p. **Williamson** a-2i, 5i, 7i, 8i. **Sinnott** a-3i.*

DROWNED GIRL, THE
1990 ($5.95, mature readers, 52 pgs.)
Piranha Press (DC)
nn 1.00 2.50 6.00

GD25 FN65 NM94

DRUG WARS (Pioneer)(Value: cover or less)

DRUM BEAT (See 4-Color No. 610)

DRUNKEN FIST (Jademan)(Value: cover or less)

DUCK ALBUM (See Donald Duck Album)
No. 353, Oct, 1951 - No. 840, Sept, 1957
Dell Publishing Co.
4-Color 353 (#1)-Barks-c 8.35 25.00 50.00
4-Color 450-Barks-c 6.70 20.00 40.00
4-Color 492,531,560,586,611,649,686 5.85 17.50 35.00
4-Color 726,782,840 5.85 17.50 35.00

DUCKTALES
Oct, 1988 - No. 13, May, 1990 (1,2,9-11: $1.50; 3-8: 95¢)
Gladstone Publishing
1-Barks-r 1.90 4.75
2-11: 2,4-6,9-11-Barks-r. 7-Barks-r(1 pg.) .80 2.00
12,13 ($1.95, 68 pgs.)-Barks-r; 12-r/F.C. #495 .90 2.25

DUCKTALES
June, 1990 - No. 18, Nov, 1991 ($1.50)
Disney Comics
1-All new stories 1.10 2.75
2-18 .65 1.60
...: The Movie nn (1990, 7.95, 68 pgs.)-Graphic novel adapting animated movie 1.30 3.25 8.00

DUDLEY (Teen-age)
Nov-Dec, 1949 - No. 3, Mar-Apr, 1950
Feature/Prize Publications
1-By Boody Rogers 11.00 32.00 75.00
2,3 7.50 22.50 45.00

DUDLEY DO-RIGHT (TV)
Aug, 1970 - No. 7, Aug, 1971 (Jay Ward)
Charlton Comics
1 6.00 18.00 42.00
2-7 4.00 12.00 28.00

DUKE OF THE K-9 PATROL
April, 1963
Gold Key
1 (10052-304) 3.60 9.00 18.00

DUMBO (See 4-Color #17,234,668, Movie Comics, & Walt Disney Showcase #12)

DUMBO (Walt Disney's...)
1941 (K.K. Publ. Giveaway)
Weatherbird Shoes/Ernest Kern Co.(Detroit)
nn-16 pgs., 9x10" (Rare) 30.00 90.00 210.00
nn-52 pgs., 5-1/2x8-1/2", slick cover in color; B&W interior; half text, half reprints 4-Color No. 17 19.00 58.00 135.00

DUMBO COMIC PAINT BOOK (See Large Feature Comic No. 19)

DUMBO WEEKLY
1942 (Premium supplied by Diamond D-X Gas Stations)
Walt Disney Productions
1 25.00 75.00 175.00
2-16 12.00 36.00 85.00
NOTE: *A cover and binder came separate at gas stations. Came with membership card.*

DUNC AND LOO (1-3 titled "Around the Block with Dunc and Loo")
Oct-Dec, 1961 - No. 8, Oct-Dec, 1963
Dell Publishing Co.
1 11.50 34.00 80.00

Durango Kid #28 © ME

Dynamic Comics #1 © CHES

Dynamo #3 © TC

	GD25	FN65	NM94
2	7.50	22.50	45.00
3-8	5.85	17.50	35.00

NOTE: *Written by* ***John Stanley; Bill Williams*** *art.*

DUNE
April, 1985 - No. 3, June, 1985
Marvel Comics

1-3-r/Marvel Super Special; movie adaptation 1.00

DURANGO KID, THE (Also see Best of the West, Great Western & White Indian) (Charles Starrett starred in Columbia's Durango Kid movies)
Oct-Nov, 1949 - No. 41, Oct-Nov, 1955 (All 36 pgs.)
Magazine Enterprises

	GD25	FN65	NM94
1-Charles Starrett photo-c; Durango Kid & his horse Raider begin; Dan Brand & Tipi (origin) begin by Frazetta & continue through #16	54.00	160.00	375.00
2(Starrett photo-c)	27.00	81.00	190.00
3-5(All have Starrett photo-c)	24.00	72.00	165.00
6-10: 7-Atomic weapon-c/story	12.00	36.00	85.00
11-16-Last Frazetta issue	10.00	30.00	60.00
17-Origin Durango Kid	12.00	36.00	85.00
18-Fred Meagher-a on Dan Brand begins	8.35	25.00	50.00
19-30: 19-Guardineer-c/a(3) begin, end #41. 23-Intro. The Red Scorpion	8.35	25.00	50.00
31-Red Scorpion returns	7.50	22.50	45.00
32-41-Bolle/Frazettaish-a (Dan Brand; true in later issues?)	7.50	22.50	45.00

NOTE: *#6, 8, 14, 15 contain* ***Frazetta*** *art not reprinted in White Indian.* ***Ayers*** *c-18.* ***Guardineer*** *a(3)-19-41; c-19-41.* ***Fred Meagher*** *a-18-29 at least.*

DURANGO KID, THE (AC)(Value: cover or less)

DWIGHT D. EISENHOWER
December, 1969
Dell Publishing Co.

	GD25	FN65	NM94
01-237-912 - Life story	3.20	8.00	16.00

DYNABRITE COMICS
1978 - 1979 (69¢; 48 pgs.)(10x7-1/8"; cardboard covers)
(Blank inside covers)
Whitman Publishing Co.

11350 - Walt Disney's Mickey Mouse & the Beanstalk (4-C 157). 11350-1 - Mickey Mouse Album (4-C 1057,1151,1246). 11351 - Mickey Mouse & His Sky Adventure (4-C 214, 343). 11352 - Donald Duck (4-C 408, Donald Duck 45,52)-Barks-a. 11352-1 - Donald Duck (4-C 318, 10 pg. Barks/WDC&S 125,128)-Barks-c(r). 11353 - Daisy Duck's Diary (4-C 1055,1150) Barks-a. 11354 - Goofy: A Gaggle of Giggles. 11354-1 - Super Goof Meets Super Thief. 11355 - Uncle Scrooge (Barks-a/U.S. 12,33). 11355-1 - Uncle Scrooge (Barks-a/U.S. 13,16) - Barks-c(r). 11356 - (?). 11357 - Star Trek (r/-Star Trek 33,41). 11358 - Star Trek (r/-Star Trek 34,36). 11359 - Bugs Bunny-r. 11360 - Winnie the Pooh Fun and Fantasy (Disney-r). 11361 - Gyro Gearloose & the Disney Ducks (r/4-C 1047,1184)-Barks-c(r)

each.... 1.00

DYNAMIC ADVENTURES
No. 8, 1964 - No. 9, 1964
I. W. Enterprises

	GD25	FN65	NM94
8-Kayo Kirby-r by Baker?/Fight Comics #?	2.40	6.00	12.00
9-Reprints Avon's "Escape From Devil's Island"; Kinstler-c	2.80	7.00	14.00
nn(no date)-Reprints Risks Unlimited with Rip Carson, Senorita Rio	2.40	6.00	12.00

DYNAMIC CLASSICS (See Cancelled Comic Cavalcade)
Sept-Oct, 1978 (44 pgs.)
DC Comics

	GD25	FN65	NM94
1-Neal Adams Batman, Simonson Manhunter-r		1.00	2.50

DYNAMIC COMICS (No #4-7)
Oct, 1941 - No. 3, Feb, 1942; No. 8, 1944 - No. 25, May, 1948
Harry 'A' Chesler

	GD25	FN65	NM94
1-Origin Major Victory by Charles Sultan (reprinted in Major Victory #1), Dynamic Man & Hale the Magician; The Black Cobra only app.; Major Victory & Dynamic Man begin	89.00	268.00	625.00
2-Origin Dynamic Boy & Lady Satan; intro. The Green Knight & sidekick Lance Cooper	50.00	150.00	350.00
3	39.00	118.00	275.00
8-Dan Hastings, The Echo, The Master Key, Yankee Boy begin; Yankee Doodle Jones app.; hypo story	39.00	118.00	275.00
9-Mr. E begins; Mac Raboy-c	41.00	122.00	285.00
10	31.00	94.00	220.00
11-15: 15-The Sky Chief app.	27.00	80.00	185.00
16-Marijuana story	27.00	81.00	190.00
17(1/46)-Illustrated in **SOTI**, "The children told me what the man was going to do with the hot poker," but Wertham saw this in Crime Reporter #2	36.00	109.00	255.00
18,19,21,22,24,25	17.00	52.00	120.00
20-Bare-breasted woman-c	24.00	73.00	170.00
23-Yankee Girl app.	16.50	50.00	115.00
I.W. Reprint #1,8('64): 1-r/#23. 8-Exist?	2.80	7.00	14.00

NOTE: ***Kinstler*** *c-IW #1.* ***Tuska*** *art in many issues, #3, 9, 11, 12, 16, 19. Bondage c-16.*

DYNAMITE (Becomes Johnny Dynamite No. 10 on)
May, 1953 - No. 9, Sept, 1954
Comic Media/Allen Hardy Publ.

	GD25	FN65	NM94
1-Pete Morisi-a; Don Heck-c; r-as Danger #6	11.50	34.00	80.00
2	7.50	22.50	45.00
3-Marijuana story; Johnny Dynamite (1st app.) begins by Pete Morisi(c/a); Heck text-a; man shot in face at close range	9.15	27.50	55.00
4-Injury-to-eye, prostitution; Morisi-c/a	11.00	32.00	65.00
5-9-Morisi-c/a in all. 7-Prostitute story plus reprints	6.70	20.00	40.00

DYNAMO (Also see Tales of Thunder & T.H.U.N.D.E.R. Agents)
Aug, 1966 - No. 4, June, 1967 (25¢)
Tower Comics

	GD25	FN65	NM94
1-Crandall/Wood, Ditko/Wood-a; Weed series begins; NoMan & Lightning cameos; Wood-c/a	4.90	15.00	34.00
2-4: Wood-c/a in all	3.30	9.90	23.00

NOTE: ***Adkins/Wood*** *a-2.* ***Ditko*** *a-4?.* ***Tuska*** *a-2, 3.*

DYNAMO JOE (Also see First Adventures & Mars)
May, 1986 - No. 15, Jan, 1988 (#12-15: $1.75)
First Comics

	GD25	FN65	NM94
1-15: 4-Cargonauts begin			1.50
Special 1(1/87)-Mostly-r/Mars			1.50

DYNOMUTT (TV)(See Scooby-Doo, 3rd series)
Nov, 1977 - No. 6, Sept, 1978 (Hanna-Barbera)
Marvel Comics Group

	GD25	FN65	NM94
1-The Blue Falcon, Scooby Doo in all		1.10	2.75
2-6:			1.60

EAGLE, THE (1st Series) (See Science Comics & Weird Comics #8)
July, 1941 - No. 4, Jan, 1942
Fox Features Syndicate

	GD25	FN65	NM94
1-The Eagle begins; Rex Dexter of Mars app. by Briefer; all issues feature German war covers	114.00	343.00	800.00
2-The Spider Queen begins (origin)	60.00	180.00	420.00
3,4: 3-Joe Spook begins (origin)	50.00	150.00	350.00

EAGLE (2nd Series)
Feb-Mar, 1945 - No. 2, Apr-May, 1945
Rural Home Publ.

	GD25	FN65	NM94
1-Aviation stories	14.00	43.00	100.00
2-Lucky Aces	11.50	34.00	80.00

NOTE: ***L. B. Cole*** *c/a in each.*

EAGLE
Sept, 1986 - No. 26?, 1989 ($1.50/1.75/1.95, B&W)
Crystal Comics/Apple Comics #17 on

	GD25	FN65	NM94
1		.80	2.00
1-Signed and limited		1.10	2.75

Earth Man on Venus © AVON

Eclipso #1 © DC

The Eden Matrix #1 © Adhesive Media

GD25 FN65 NM94

2-26: 12-Double size origin issue ($2.50) 1.50

EAGLES DARE
Aug, 1994 - Present ($1.95, B&W, limited series:5)
Aager comics, Inc.

1,2 .80 2.00

EARTH 4/EARTH 4 DEATHWATCH 2000 (Continuity)(Value: cover or less)

EARTH MAN ON VENUS (An...) (Also see Strange Planets)
1951
Avon Periodicals

nn-Wood-a (26 pgs.); Fawcette-c 86.00 257.00 600.00

EASTER BONNET SHOP (See March of Comics No. 29)

EASTER WITH MOTHER GOOSE (See 4-Color No. 103, 140, 185, 220)

EAST MEETS WEST (Innovation)(Value: cover or less)

EAT RIGHT TO WORK AND WIN
1942 (16 pgs.) (Giveaway)
Swift & Company

Blondie, Henry, Flash Gordon by Alex Raymond, Toots & Casper, Thimble Theatre(Popeye), Tillie the Toiler, The Phantom, The Little King, & Bringing up Father - original strips just for this book -(in daily strip form which shows what foods we should eat and why)
20.00 60.00 140.00

E. C. CLASSIC REPRINTS
May, 1973 - No. 12, 1976 (E. C. Comics reprinted in color minus ads)
East Coast Comix Co.

1-The Crypt of Terror #1 (Tales from the Crypt #46) 1.00 2.50 6.00
2-Weird Science #15('52) 1.60 4.00
3-12: 3-Shock SuspenStories #12. 4-Haunt of Fear #12. 5-Weird Fantasy #13 ('52). 6-Crime SuspenStories #25. 7-Vault of Horror #26. 8-Shock SuspenStories #6. 9-Two-Fisted Tales #34. 10-Haunt of Fear #23. 11-Weird Science #12(#1). 12-Shock SuspenStories #2 1.20 3.00

EC CLASSICS
Aug, 1985 - No. 12, 1986? (High quality paper; each-r 8 stories in color)
Russ Cochran (#2-12 were resolicited in 1990)($4.95, 56 pgs., 8x11")

1-12: 1-Tales From the Crypt. 2-Weird Science. 3-Two-Fisted Tales. 4-Shock SuspenStories. 5-Weird Fantasy. 6-Vault of Horror. 7-Weird Science-Fantasy (r/23,24). 8-Crime SuspensStories. 9-Haunt of Fear. 10-Panic (r/1,2). 11-Tales From the Crypt (r/23,24). 12-Weird Science (r/20,22)
1.00 2.00 5.00

ECHO OF FUTUREPAST (Pacific)(Value: cover or less)

ECLIPSE GRAPHIC ALBUM SERIES
Oct, 1978 - Present (8-1/2x11") (B&W #1-5)
Eclipse Comics

1-Sabre (10/78, B&W, 1st print.); Gulacy-a; 1st direct sale graphic novel
1.30 3.25 8.00
1-Sabre (2nd printing, 1/79) 1.30 3.25 8.00
1-Sabre (3rd printing, $5.95) 1.00 2.50 6.00
2-Night Music (11/79, B&W)-Russell-a 1.00 2.00 5.00
3-Detectives, Inc. (5/80, B&W)-Rogers-a 1.20 3.00 7.00
4-Stewart The Rat ('80, B&W)-G. Colan-a 1.20 3.00 7.00
5-The Price (10/81, B&W)-Starlin-a 1.70 5.00 12.00
6-I Am Coyote (11/84, color)-Rogers-c/a 1.30 3.25 8.00
7-The Rocketeer (9/85, color)-Dave Stevens-a (r/chapters 1-5)(see Pacific Presents & Starslayer); has 7 pgs. new-a 1.30 3.25 8.00
7-The Rocketeer (2nd print, $7.95) 1.30 3.25 8.00
7-The Rocketeer (3rd print, 1991, $8.95) 1.50 3.75 9.00
7-The Rocketeer, signed & limited hardcover 9.00 26.00 60.00
7-The Rocketeer, hard-c (1986, $19.95) 4.00 10.00 20.00
7-The Rocketeer, unsigned hard-c (3rd, $32.95) 4.70 14.00 33.00
8-Zorro In Old California ('86, color) 1.30 3.25 8.00
8-Hard cover 1.70 5.00 12.00
9-Sacred And The Profane ('86)-Steacy-a 2.30 6.75 16.00
9-Hard cover ($24.95) 3.60 10.75 25.00
10-Somerset Holmes ('86, $15.95)-Adults, soft-c 2.30 6.75 16.00
10-Hard cover ($24.95) 3.60 10.75 25.00
11-Floyd Farland, Citizen of the Future ('87, $3.95, B&W) 1.60 4.00
12-Silverheels ('87, $8.95, color) 1.50 3.75 9.00
12-Hard cover ($14.95) 2.15 6.50 15.00
12-Hard cover, signed & #'d ($24.95) 3.60 10.75 25.00
13-The Sisterhood of Steel ('87, $9.95, color) 1.65 4.00 10.00
14-Samurai, Son of Death ('87, $4.95, B&W) 1.00 2.00 5.00
14-Samurai, Son of Death ($3.95, 2nd printing) 1.60 4.00
15-Twisted Tales (11/87, color)-Dave Stevens-c 1.60 4.00
16-See Airfighters Classics #1
17-Valkyrie, Prisoner of the Past ('88, $3.95, color) 1.60 4.00
18-See Airfighters Classics #2
19-Scout: The Four Monsters ('88, $14.95, color)-r/Scout #1-7; soft-c
2.15 6.50 15.00
20-See Airfighters Classics #3
21-XYR-Multiple ending comic ('88, $3.95, B&W) 1.60 4.00
22-Alien Worlds #1 (5/88, $3.95, 52 pgs.)-Nudity 1.60 4.00
23-See Airfighters Classics #4
24-Heartbreak ($4.95, B&W) 1.00 2.00 5.00
25-Alex Toth's Zorro Vol. 1 ($10.95, B&W) 1.65 4.70 11.00
26-Alex Toth's Zorro Vol. 2 ($10.95, B&W) 1.65 4.70 11.00
27-Fast Fiction (She) ($5.95, B&W) 1.00 2.50 6.00
28-Miracleman Book I ($5.95) 1.00 2.50 6.00
29-Real Love: The Best of the Simon and Kirby Romance Comics (10/88, $12.95) 1.85 5.50 13.00
30-Brought To Light; Alan Moore scripts (1989) 1.65 4.70 11.00
30-Limited hardcover ed. ($29.95) 4.30 13.00 30.00
31-Pigeons From Hell by R. E. Howard (11/88) 1.30 3.25 8.00
31-Signed & Limited Edition ($29.95) 4.30 13.00 30.00

ECLIPSE MAGAZINE (Eclipse)(Value: cover or less)

ECLIPSE MONTHLY (Eclipse)(Value: cover or less)

ECLIPSO (See Brave and the Bold #64, House of Secrets #61 & Phantom Stranger, 1987)
Nov, 1992 - No. 18, Apr, 1994 ($1.25)
DC Comics

1-14: 1-Giffen plots/breakdowns begin. 10-Darkseid app. 1.25
15-18: 15-Begin $1.50-c; Creeper in #3-6,9,11-13. 18-Spectre-c/s 1.50
Annual 1 (1993, $2.50, 68 pgs.)-Intro Prism 1.00 2.50

ECLIPSO: THE DARKNESS WITHIN
July, 1992 - No. 2, Oct, 1992 ($2.50, 68 pgs.)
DC Comics

1-With purple gem attached to-c 1.50 3.75
1-Without gem; Superman, Creeper app. 1.00 2.50
2-Concludes Eclipso storyline from annuals 1.00 2.50

E. C. 3-D CLASSICS (See Three Dimensional...)

ECTOKID (See Razorline)
Sept, 1993 - No. 9, May, 1994 ($1.75/$1.95)
Marvel Comics

1-($2.50)-Foil embossed-c; created by C. Barker 1.00 2.50
2-8: 2-Origin. 5-Saint Sinner x-over .70 1.75
9-Begin $1.95-c .80 2.00
...: Unleased! 1 (10/94, $2.95, 52 pgs.) 1.20 3.00

EDDIE STANKY (Baseball Hero)
1951 (New York Giants)
Fawcett Publications

nn-Photo-c 22.00 65.00 150.00

EDEN MATRIX, THE
1994 ($2.95)
Adhesive Comics

1,2-Two variant-c; alternate-c on inside back-c 1.20 3.00

EDGAR BERGEN PRESENTS CHARLIE McCARTHY

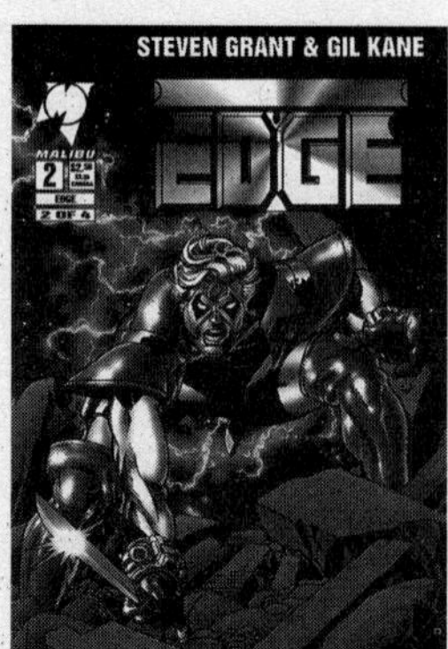

Edge #2 © Steven Grant & Gil Kane

Eerie #14 © AVON

Eerie #1 © WP

GD25 FN65 NM94

No. 764, 1938 (36 pgs.; 15x10-1/2"; in color)
Whitman Publishing Co. (Charlie McCarthy Co.)

764 (Scarce) 71.00 215.00 500.00

EDGE
July, 1994 - Present ($2.50, limited series:4)
Malibu Comics

1-S. Grant-story, Gil Kane-c/a; w/Bravura stamp 1.00 2.50

EDGE OF CHAOS (Pacific)(Value: cover or less)

EDWARD'S SHOES GIVEAWAY
1954 (Has clown on cover)
Edward's Shoe Store

Contains comic with new cover. Many combinations possible. Contents determines price, 50-60 percent of original. (Similar to Comics From Weatherbird & Free Comics to You)

ED WHEELAN'S JOKE BOOK STARRING FAT & SLAT (See Fat & Slat)

EERIE (Strange Worlds No. 18 on)
No. 1, Jan, 1947; No. 1, May-June, 1951 - No. 17, Aug-Sept, 1954
Avon Periodicals

1(1947)-1st horror comic; Kubert, Fugitani-a; bondage-c
107.00 321.00 750.00
1(1951)-Reprints story from 1947 #1 37.00 111.00 260.00
2-Wood-c/a; bondage-c 41.00 122.00 285.00
3-Wood-c; Kubert, Wood/Orlando-a 41.00 122.00 285.00
4,5-Wood-c 34.00 100.00 235.00
6,8,13,14: 8-Kinstler-a; bondage-c; Phantom Witch Doctor story
14.00 43.00 100.00
7-Wood/Orlando-c; Kubert-a 25.00 75.00 175.00
9-Kubert-a; Check-c 16.00 48.00 110.00
10,11: 10-Kinstler-a. 11-Kinstlerish-a by McCann 13.00 40.00 90.00
12-Dracula story from novel, 25 pgs. 16.50 50.00 115.00
15-Reprints No. 1('51)minus-c(bondage) 10.00 30.00 65.00
16-Wood-a r-/No. 2 11.00 32.00 75.00
17-Wood/Orlando & Kubert-a; reprints #3 minus inside & outside Wood-c
13.50 41.00 95.00

NOTE: ***Hollingsworth** a-9-11; c-10, 11.*

EERIE
1964
I. W. Enterprises

I.W. Reprint #1('64)-Wood-c(r); r-story/Spook #1 3.60 9.00 18.00
I.W. Reprint #2,6,8: 8-Dr. Drew by Grandenetti from Ghost #9
2.80 7.00 14.00
I.W. Reprint #9-r/Tales of Terror #1(Toby); Wood-c 3.60 9.00 18.00

EERIE (Magazine)(See Warren Presents)
No. 1, Sept, 1965; No. 2, Mar, 1966 - No. 139, Feb, 1983
Warren Publishing Co.

1-24 pgs., black & white, small size (5-1/4x7-1/4"), low distribution; cover from inside back cover of Creepy No. 2; stories reprinted from Creepy No. 7, 8. At least three different versions exist.

First Printing - B&W, 5-1/4" wide x 7-1/4" high, evenly trimmed. On page 18, panel 5, in the upper left-hand corner, the large rear view of a bald headed man blends into solid black and is unrecognizable. Overall printing quality is poor. 31.00 94.00 220.00

Second Printing - B&W, 5-1/4x7-1/4", with uneven, untrimmed edges (if one of these were trimmed evenly, the size would be less than as indicated). The figure of the bald headed man on page 18, panel 5 is clear and discernible. The staples have a 1/4" blue stripe.
13.00 39.00 90.00

Other unauthorized reproductions for comparison's sake would be practically worthless. One known version was probably shot off a first printing copy with some loss of detail; the finer lines tend to disappear in this version which can be determined by looking at the lower right-hand corner of page one, first story. The roof of the house is shaded with straight lines. These lines are sharp and distinct on original, but broken on this version.

NOTE: ***The Overstreet Comic Book Price Guide** recommends that, before buying a 1st issue, you consult an expert.*

2-Frazetta-c (also #3,5,7,8) 5.70 17.00 40.00
3-Frazetta-c & half pg. ad (rerun in #4) 4.00 12.00 28.00
4-10: 4-Frazetta-a (1/2 pg. ad). 5,7,8-Frazetta-c. 9-Headlight-c
2.30 6.90 16.00
11-22,24,25: 25-Steranko-c 1.80 4.60 11.00
23-Frazetta-c 2.00 5.00 12.00
26-41,43-45 1.10 2.70 6.50
42,51-(1973 & 1974 Annuals) 1.40 3.50 8.50
46-50,52,53,56-59,61-78: 46-Dracula series by Sutton begins. 78-The Mummy-r
1.20 2.40 6.00
54,55-Color Spirit story by Eisner, reprints sections 12/21/47 & 6/16/46
1.10 2.70 6.50
60-Summer Giant (9/74, $1.25) 1.30 3.00 7.50
79,80-Origin Darklon the Mystic by Starlin (1st app.) 1.20 2.40 6.00
81-139: 82-1st app. The Rook. 84-All sports issue 1.60 4.00
Year Book 1970, 1971-Reprints in both 2.00 5.00 12.00
Year Book 1972-Reprints 1.50 3.80 9.00

NOTE: *The above books contain art by many good artists: **N. Adams, Brunner, Corben, Craig (Taycee), Crandall, Ditko, Eisner, Evans, Jeff Jones, Krenkel, McWilliams, Morrow, Orlando, Ploog, Severin, Starlin, Torres, Toth, Williamson, Wood,** and **Wrightson**; covers by **Bode', Corben, Davis, Frazetta, Morrow,** and **Orlando. Frazetta** c-2, 3, 7, 8, 23. Annuals from 1973-on are included in regular numbering. 1970-74 Annuals are complete reprints. Annuals from 1975-on are in the format of the regular issues.*

EERIE ADVENTURES (Also see Weird Adventures)
Winter, 1951 (Painted-c)
Ziff-Davis Publ. Co.

1-Powell-a(2), McCann-a; used in **SOTI;** bondage-c; Krigstein back-c
19.00 58.00 135.00

NOTE: *Title dropped due to similarity to Avon's Eerie & legal action.*

EERIE TALES (Magazine)
1959 (Black & White)
Hastings Associates

1-Williamson, Torres, Tuska-a, Powell(2), & Morrow(2)-a
7.50 22.50 45.00

EERIE TALES
1963-1964
Super Comics

Super Reprint No. 10,11,12,18: 10('63)-r/Spook #27. Purple Claw in #11,12 ('63); #12-r/Avon's Eerie #1('51)-Kida-r 2.00 5.00 10.00
15-Wolverton-a, Spacehawk-r/Blue Bolt Weird Tales #113; Disbrow-a
4.35 13.00 26.00

EGBERT
Spring, 1946 - No. 20, 1950
Arnold Publications/Quality Comics Group

1-Funny animal; intro Egbert & The Count 14.00 43.00 100.00
2 9.15 27.50 55.00
3-10 5.00 15.00 30.00
11-20 4.00 10.00 20.00

EH! (...Dig This Crazy Comic) (From Here to Insanity No. 8 on)
Dec, 1953 - No. 7, Nov-Dec, 1954 (Satire)
Charlton Comics

1-Davisish-c/a by Ayers, Woodish-a by Giordano; Atomic Mouse app.
18.00 54.00 125.00
2-Ayers-c/a 12.00 36.00 85.00
3-7: 4,6-Sexual innuendo-c. 6-Ayers-a 11.50 34.00 80.00

EIGHT IS ENOUGH KITE FUN BOOK (See Kite Fun Book)

80 PAGE GIANT (...Magazine No. 2-15)
8/64 - No. 15, 10/65; No. 16, 11/65 - No. 89, 7/71 (25¢)(All reprints)
National Periodical Publications (#1-56: 84 pgs.; #57-89: 68 pgs.)

1-Superman Annual; originally planned as Superman Annual #9 (8/64)
25.00 75.00 300.00
2-Jimmy Olsen 13.00 38.00 150.00
3,4: 3-Lois Lane. 4-Flash-G.A.-r; Infantino-a 10.00 30.00 120.00
5-Batman; has Sunday newspaper strip; Catwoman-r; Batman's Life Story-r (25th anniversary special) 8.00 25.00 100.00

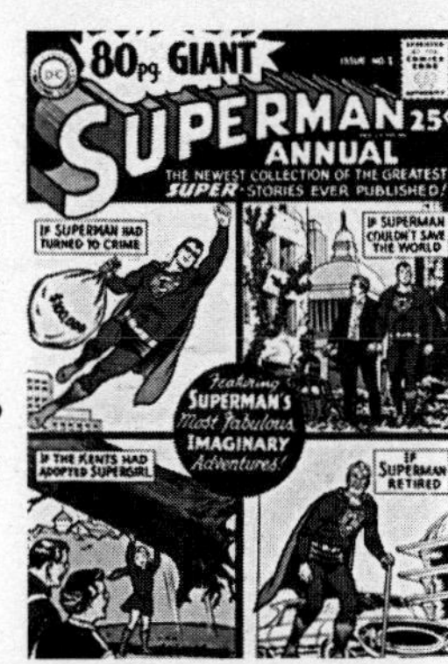

80 Page Giant #1 © DC

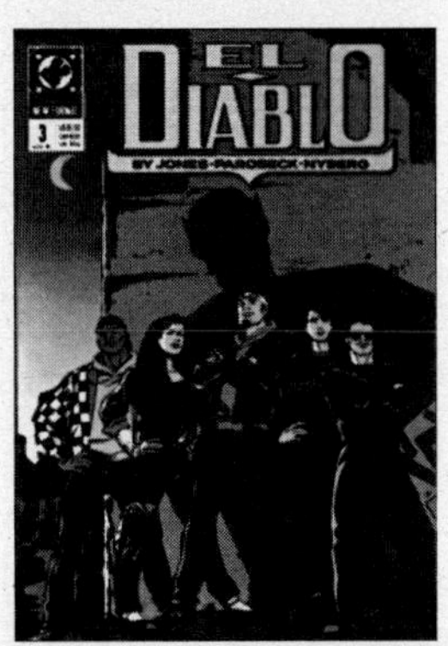

El Diablo #3 © DC

Elf Quest #1 © Warp

GD25 FN65 NM94

6-Superman 8.00 24.00 95.00
7-Sgt. Rock's Prize Battle Tales; Kubert-c/a 8.00 24.00 95.00
8-More Secret Origins-origins of JLA, Aquaman, Robin, Atom, & Superman; Infantino-a 21.00 64.00 255.00
9-11: 9-Flash (r/Flash #106,117,123 & Showcase #14); Infantino-a. 10-Superboy. 11-Superman; all Luthor issue 8.00 23.00 90.00
12-Batman; has Sunday newspaper strip 8.00 23.00 90.00
13,14: 13-Jimmy Olsen. 14-Lois Lane 8.00 23.00 90.00
15-Superman and Batman; Joker-c/story 8.00 24.00 95.00

Continued as part of regular series under each title in which that particular book came out, a Giant being published instead of the regular size. Issues No. 16 to No. 89 are listed for your information. See individual titles for prices.

16-JLA #39 (11/65), 17-Batman #176, 18-Superman #183, 19-Our Army at War #164, 20-Action #334, 21-Flash #160, 22-Superboy #129, 23-Superman #187, 24-Batman #182, 25-Jimmy Olsen #95, 26-Lois Lane #68, 27-Batman #185, 28-World's Finest #161, 29-JLA #48, 30-Batman #187, 31-Superman #193, 32-Our Army at War #177, 33-Action #347, 34-Flash #169, 35-Superboy #138, 36-Superman #197, 37-Batman #193, 38-Jimmy Olsen #104, 39-Lois Lane #77, 40-World's Finest #170, 41-JLA #58, 42-Superman #202, 43-Batman #198, 44-Our Army at War #190, 45-Action #360, 46-Flash #178, 47-Superboy #147, 48-Superman #207, 49-Batman #203, 50-Jimmy Olsen #113, 51-Lois Lane #86, 52-World's Finest #179, 53-JLA #67, 54-Superman #212, 55-Batman #208, 56-Our Army at War #203, 57-Action #373, 58-Flash #187, 59-Superboy #156, 60-Superman #217, 61-Batman #213, 62-Jimmy Olsen #122, 63-Lois Lane #95, 64-World's Finest #188, 65-JLA #76, 66-Superman #222, 67-Batman #218, 68-Our Army at War #216, 69-Adventure #390, 70-Flash #196, 71-Superboy #165, 72-Superman #227, 73-Batman #223, 74-Jimmy Olsen #131, 75-Lois Lane #104, 76-World's Finest #197, 77-JLA #85, 78-Superman #232, 79-Batman #228, 80-Our Army at War #229, 81-Adventure #403, 82-Flash #205, 83-Superboy #174, 84-Superman #239, 85-Batman #233, 86-Jimmy Olsen #140, 87-Lois Lane #113, 88-World's Finest #206, 89-JLA #93.

87TH PRECINCT (TV)
Apr-June, 1962 - No. 2, July-Sept, 1962
Dell Publishing Co.

4-Color 1309(#1); Krigstein-a 10.00 30.00 65.00
2 8.35 25.00 50.00

EL BOMBO COMICS
1946
Standard Comics/Frances M. McQueeny

nn(1946) 9.15 27.50 55.00
1(no date) 9.15 27.50 55.00

EL CID (See 4-Color No. 1259)

EL DIABLO (DC)(Value: cover or less)

EL DORADO (See Movie Classics)

ELECTRIC UNDERTOW (See Strikeforce Morituri: Electric Undertow)

ELECTRIC WARRIOR (DC)(Value: cover or less)

ELEKTRA: ASSASSIN
Aug, 1986 - No. 8, June, 1987 (Limited series, adults)
Epic Comics (Marvel)

1-Miller scripts in all 1.60 4.00
2 1.20 3.00
3-7 .80 2.00
8 1.90 4.75
Signed & numbered hardcover (Graphitti Designs, $39.95, 2000 print run)-reprints 1-8 40.00

ELEKTRA SAGA, THE
Feb, 1984 - No. 4, June, 1984 ($2.00, Baxter paper)
Marvel Comics Group

1-4-r/Daredevil 168-190; Miller-c/a 1.60 4.00

ELEMENTALS, THE (See The Justice Machine & Morningstar Spec.)
June, 1984 - No. 29, Sept, 1988; V2#1, Mar, 1989 - No. 28, 1994?
Comico The Comic Co. ($1.50/$2.50, Baxter paper)

1-Willingham-c/a, 1-8 1.50 3.75
2 .90 2.25
3-10: 9-Bissette-a(p). 10-Photo-c .80 2.00
11-29 1.50

GD25 FN65 NM94

V2#1-28: 1-3-$1.95-c. 4-Begin $2.50-c. 16-1st app. Strike Force America. 18-Prelude to Avalon mini-series. 37-Prequel to Strike Force America series .80 2.00
Special 1 (3/86)-Willingham-a(p) .70 1.75
Special 2 (1/89, $1.95) .75 1.90

ELFLORD (Aircel)(Value: cover or less)

ELFLORD: DRAGON'S EYE
1993 ($2.50, B&W)
Night Wynd Enterprises

1 1.00 2.50

ELFQUEST (Also see Fantasy Quarterly & Warp Graphics Annual)
No. 2, Aug, 1978 - No. 21, Feb, 1985 (All magazine size)
No. 1, April, 1979
WaRP Graphics, Inc.

NOTE: ***Elfquest*** was originally published as one of the stories in **Fantasy Quarterly** #1. When the publisher went out of business, the creative team, Wendy and Richard Pini, formed WaRP Graphics and continued the series, beginning with **Elfquest** #2. **Elfquest** #1, which reprinted the story from **Fantasy Quarterly**, was published about the same time **Elfquest** #4 was released. Thereafter, most issues were reprinted as demand warranted, until Marvel announced it would reprint the entire series under its Epic imprint (Aug., 1985).

1(4/79)-Reprints Elfquest story from Fantasy Quarterly No. 1
1st printing ($1.00-c) 4.30 13.00 30.00
2nd printing ($1.25-c) 1.50 3.80 9.00
3rd printings ($1.50-c) 1.60 4.00
4th printing; different-c ($1.50-c) 1.25
2(8/78)-5: 1st printings ($1.00-c) 2.90 8.60 20.00
2nd printings ($1.25-c) 1.40 3.50
3rd & 4th printings ($1.50-c)(all 4th prints 1989) .80 2.00
6-9: 1st printings ($1.25-c) 1.20 2.90 7.00
2nd printings ($1.50-c) 1.00 2.50
3rd printings ($1.50-c) .70 1.75
10-14: ($1.50-c); 16-8pg. preview of A Distant Soil 1.80 4.50
10-14: 2nd printings ($1.50) 1.50
15-21 (only one printing) 1.90 4.50

ELFQUEST
Aug, 1985 - No. 32, Mar, 1988
Epic Comics (Marvel)

1-Reprints in color the Elfquest epic by WaRP Graphics 1.50 3.75
2-5 .80 2.00
6-10 .70 1.75
11-20 .60 1.60
21-32 1.25

ELFQUEST
1989 - No. 4, 1989 ($1.50, B&W)
WaRP Graphics

1-4: Reprints original Elfquest series 1.50

ELFQUEST: BLOOD OF TEN CHIEFS
July, 1993 - Present ($2.00, color)
WaRP Graphics

1-12-By Richard & Wendy Pini .80 2.00

ELFQUEST: HIDDEN YEARS (WaRP Graphics)(Value: cover or less)

ELFQUEST: KINGS OF THE BROKEN WHEEL
June, 1990 - No. 9, Feb, 1992 ($2.00, B&W) (3rd Elfquest saga)
WaRP Graphics

1-9: By Richard & Wendy Pini; 1-Color insert .80 2.00
1-2nd printing .80 2.00

ELFQUEST: NEW BLOOD (...Summer Special on-c #1 only)
Aug, 1992 - Present ($2.00/$2.25, color, bi-monthly)
WaRP Graphics

1-($3.95, 68 pgs.)-Byrne-a/scripts (16 pgs.) 1.60 4.00
2-17: Barry Blair-a in all .90 2.25

Ellery Queen #1 © SUPR

Elvira #2 © ECL

E-Man #2 © CC

GD25 FN65 NM94

18-23: 18-Begin $2.25-c .90 2.25

ELFQUEST: SHARDS
Aug, 1994 - Present ($2.25)
Warp Graphics

1-3 .90
2.25

ELFQUEST: SIEGE AT BLUE MOUNTAIN
Mar, 1987 - No. 8, Dec, 1988 ($1.75/$1.95, B&W, mini-series)
WaRP Graphics/Apple Comics

	GD25	FN65	NM94
1-Staton-a(i) in all; 2nd Elfquest saga		1.50	3.75
1-2nd printing		.70	1.75
2		.80	2.00
2,3-2nd printings		.70	1.75
3-8		.70	1.75

ELFQUEST: WAVE DANCERS
Dec, 1993 - Present ($2.00/$2.25, color)
WaRP Graphics

	GD25	FN65	NM94
1,2: 1-Foil-c & poster		1.00	2.50
3-8: 3-Begin $2.25-c		.90	2.25

ELF-THING (Eclipse)(Value: cover or less)

ELIMINATOR FULL COLOR SPECIAL (Eternity)(Value: cover or less)

ELLA CINDERS (See Comics On Parade, Comics Revue #1,4, Famous Comics Cartoon Book, Giant Comics Editions, Sparkler Comics, Tip Top & Treasury of Comics)

ELLA CINDERS
1938 - 1940
United Features Syndicate

	GD25	FN65	NM94
Single Series 3(1938)	32.00	96.00	225.00
Single Series 21(#2 on-c, #21 on inside), 28('40)	28.00	84.00	195.00

ELLA CINDERS
March, 1948 - No. 5, March, 1949
United Features Syndicate

	GD25	FN65	NM94
1-(#2 on cover)	11.00	32.00	75.00
2	7.00	21.00	42.00
3-5	5.00	15.00	30.00

ELLERY QUEEN
May, 1949 - No. 4, Nov, 1949
Superior Comics Ltd.

	GD25	FN65	NM94
1-Kamen-c; L.B. Cole-a; r-in Haunted Thrills	31.00	95.00	220.00
2-4: 3-Drug use stories(2)	22.00	65.00	150.00

NOTE: *Iger shop art in all issues.*

ELLERY QUEEN (TV)
1-3/52 (Spring on-c) - No. 2, Summer/52 (Saunders painted covers)
Ziff-Davis Publishing Co.

	GD25	FN65	NM94
1-Saunders-c	31.00	95.00	220.00
2-Saunders bondage, torture-c	27.00	80.00	185.00

ELLERY QUEEN (See Crackajack Funnies #23 & 4-Color No. 1165, 1243, 1289)

ELMER FUDD (Also see Camp Comics, Daffy, Looney Tunes #1 & Super Book #10, 22)
No. 470, May, 1953 - No. 1293, Mar-May, 1962
Dell Publishing Co.

	GD25	FN65	NM94
4-Color 470,558,628,689('56)	3.20	8.00	16.00
4-Color 725,783,841,888,938,977,1032,1081,1131,1171,1222,1293('62)	2.80	7.00	14.00

ELMO COMICS
January, 1948 (Daily strip-r)
St. John Publishing Co.

	GD25	FN65	NM94
1-By Cecil Jensen	8.35	25.00	50.00

ELONGATED MAN (See Flash #112 & Justice League of America #105)
Jan, 1992 - No. 4, Apr, 1992 ($1.00, mini-series)
DC Comics

	GD25	FN65	NM94
1-4: 3-The Flash app.			1.00

ELRIC (Pacific/First, all titles)(Value; cover or less)

EL SALVADOR - A HOUSE DIVIDED (Eclipse)(Value: cover or less)

ELSEWHERE PRINCE, THE (Moebius' Airtight Garage)
May, 1990 - No. 6, Oct, 1990 ($1.95, color, limited series)
Epic Comics (Marvel)

	GD25	FN65	NM94
1-6: Moebius scripts & back-up-a in all		.80	2.00

ELSIE THE COW
Oct-Nov, 1949 - No. 3, July-Aug, 1950
D. S. Publishing Co.

	GD25	FN65	NM94
1-(36 pgs.)	18.00	54.00	125.00
2,3	14.00	43.00	100.00
Borden Milk Giveaway-(16 pgs., nn) (3 issues, 1957)	7.50	22.50	45.00
Elsie's Fun Book(1950; Borden Milk)	8.35	25.00	50.00
Everyday Birthday Fun With... (1957; 20 pgs.)(100th Anniversary); Kubert-a	7.50	22.50	45.00

ELSON'S PRESENTS
1981 (100 pgs., no cover price)
DC Comics

	GD25	FN65	NM94
Series 1-6: Repackaged 1981 DC comics; Superman, Action, Flash, DC Comics Presents & Batman known. Series I has a Batman/Joker-c. Series 3-New Teen Titans #3('81)	1.00	2.00	5.00

ELVIRA MISTRESS OF THE DARK
May, 1993 - Present ($2.50, B&W)
Claypool Comics (Eclipse)

	GD25	FN65	NM94
1-14-Photo-c: 1-Austin-a(i). 1-6-Spiegle-a		1.00	2.50

ELVIRA'S HOUSE OF MYSTERY
Jan, 1986 - No. 11, Jan, 1987
DC Comics

	GD25	FN65	NM94
1-($1.50)			1.50
2-11: 9-Photo-c. 11-Dave Stevens-c			1.25
Special 1 (3/87, $1.25)			1.25

ELVIRA'S MISTRESS OF THE DARK (Marvel)(Value: cover or less)

ELVIS MANDIBLE, THE
1990 ($3.50, B&W, mature readers, 52 pgs.)
Piranha Press (DC)

	GD25	FN65	NM94
nn		1.40	3.50

ELVIS PRESLEY (See Career Girl Romances #32, Go-Go, Howard Chaykin's American Flagg #10, Humbug #8, I Love You #60 & Young Lovers #18)

E-MAN
Oct, 1973 - No. 10, Sept, 1975 (Painted-c No. 7-10)
Charlton Comics

	GD25	FN65	NM94
1-Origin & 1st app. E-Man; Staton c/a in all	2.30	6.90	16.00
2-4: 2,4-Ditko-a. 3-Howard-a	1.40	3.50	8.50
5-Miss Liberty Belle app. by Ditko	1.10	2.70	6.50
6,7,9,10-Early Byrne-a in all (#6 is 1/75)	1.30	3.00	8.00
8-Full-length story; Nova begins as E-Man's partner	1.50	3.80	9.00
1-4,9,10(Modern Comics reprints, '77)			1.00

NOTE: *Killjoy app.-No. 2, 4. Liberty Belle app.-No. 5. Rog 2000 app.-No. 6, 7, 9, 10. Travis app.-No. 3.* ***Tom Sutton*** *a-1.*

E-MAN
Oct, 1993 ($2.75)
Alpha Productions

	GD25	FN65	NM94
V5#1-Staton-c/a; 20th anniversary issue		1.00	2.50

E-MAN RETURNS
1994 ($2.75, B&W)
Alpha Productions

Enchanting Love #2 © Kirby

Enemy Ace #1 © DC

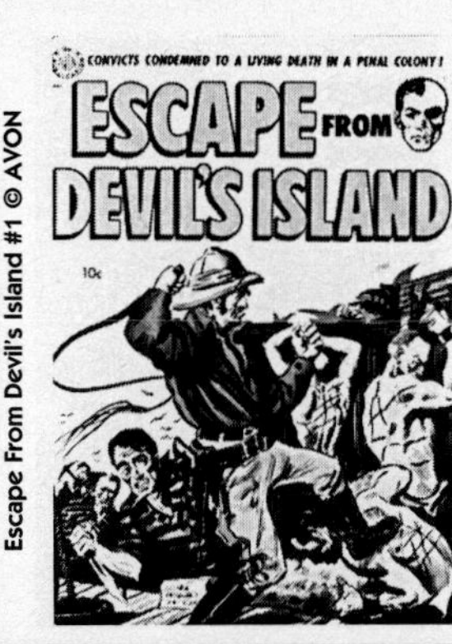

Escape From Devil's Island #1 © AVON

GD25 FN65 NM94

1-Joe Staton-c/a(p) 1.10 2.75

E-MAN (First & Comico)(Value: cover or less)

EMERALD DAWN
1991 ($4.95, squarebound)
DC Comics

nn-Reprints Green Lantern: Emerald Dawn #1-6 1.00 2.00 5.00

EMERALD DAWN II (See Green Lantern...)

EMERGENCY (Magazine)
June, 1976 - No. 4, Jan, 1977 (B&W)
Charlton Comics

1-Neal Adams-c/a; Heath, Austin-a 1.00 2.50
2,4: 2-N. Adams-c. 4-Alcala-a .65 1.60
3-N. Adams-a .70 1.80

EMERGENCY (TV)
June, 1976 - No. 4, Dec, 1976
Charlton Comics

1-Staton-c; Byrne-a 1.00 2.50
2-4: 2-Staton-c 1.50

EMERGENCY DOCTOR
Summer, 1963 (One Shot)
Charlton Comics

1 1.20 3.00 6.00

EMIL & THE DETECTIVES (See Movie Comics)

EMMA PEEL & JOHN STEED (See The Avengers)

EMPEROR'S NEW CLOTHES, THE
1950 (10¢, 68 pgs., 1/2 size, oblong)
Dell

nn - (Surprise Books series) 2.80 7.00 14.00

EMPIRE STRIKES BACK, THE (See Marvel Comics Super Special #16 & Marvel Special Edition)

ENCHANTED APPLES OF OZ, THE (See First Comics Graphic Novel #5)

ENCHANTER (Eclipse)(Value: cover or less)

ENCHANTING LOVE
Oct, 1949 - No. 6, July, 1950 (All 52 pgs.)
Kirby Publishing Co.

1-Photo-c 8.35 25.00 50.00
2-Photo-c; Powell-a 5.00 15.00 30.00
3,4,6: 3-Jimmy Stewart photo-c 4.00 11.00 22.00
5-Ingels-a, 9 pgs.; photo-c 10.00 30.00 70.00

ENCHANTMENT VISUALETTES (Magazine)
Dec, 1949 - No. 5, April, 1950 (Painted c-1)
World Editions

1-Contains two romance comic strips each 11.00 32.00 75.00
2 10.00 30.00 60.00
3-5 8.35 25.00 50.00

ENEMY
May, 1994 - No. 5, Jan, 1995 ($2.50, limited series)
Dark Horse Comics

1-5 1.00 2.50

ENEMY ACE SPECIAL (Also see Our Army at War #151, Showcase #57, 58 & Star Spangled War Stories #138)
1990 ($1.00, one-shot)
DC Comics

1-Kubert-r/Our Army #151,153; c-r/Showcase 57 1.50

ENFORCE (Reoccurring Images)(Value: cover or less)

ENIGMA
March, 1993 - No. 8, Oct, 1993 ($2.50, limited series)
DC Comics (Vertigo)

1-8: Milligan scripts 1.00 2.50

ENSIGN O'TOOLE (TV)
Aug-Oct, 1963 - No. 2, 1964
Dell Publishing Co.

1,2 3.20 8.00 16.00

ENSIGN PULVER (See Movie Classics)

EPIC
1992 - Book 4, 1992 ($4.95, mini-series, 52 pgs.)
Epic Comics (Marvel)

Book One-Four: 2-Dorman painted-c 1.00 2.00 5.00

NOTE: *Alien Legion in #3. Cholly & Flytrap by* ***Burden****(scripts) &* ***Suydam****(art) in 3, 4. Dinosaurs in #4. Dreadlands in #1. Hellraiser in #1. Nightbreed in #2. Sleeze Brothers in #2. Stalkers in #1-4. Wild Cards in #1-4.*

EPIC ILLUSTRATED (Magazine)
Spring, 1980 - No. 36, Feb, 1986 ($2.00/$2.50, B&W/Color, adults)
Marvel Comics Group

1-Frazetta-c .80 2.00
2-26: 12-Wolverton Spacehawk-r edited & recolored w/article on him. 13-Bladerunner preview by Williamson. 14-Elric of Melnibone by Russell; Revenge of the Jedi preview. 15-Vallejo-c & interview; 1st Dreadstar story (cont'd in Dreadstar #1). 16-B. Smith-c/a(2). 20-The Sacred & the Profane begins by Ken Steacy. 26-Galactus series begins, ends #34; Cerebus the Aardvark story by Dave Sim 1.50
27-36: ($2.50): 27-Groo. 28-Cerebus app. 1.00 2.50

NOTE: ***N. Adams*** *a-7; c-6.* ***Austin*** *a-15-20i.* ***Bode*** *a-19, 23, 27r.* ***Bolton*** *a-7, 10-12, 15, 18, 22-25; c-10, 18, 22, 23.* ***Boris*** *c/a-15.* ***Brunner*** *c-12.* ***Buscema*** *a-1p, 9p, 11-13p.* ***Byrne/Austin*** *a-26-34.* ***Chaykin*** *a-2; c-8.* ***Conrad*** *a-2-5, 7-9, 25-34; c-17.* ***Corben*** *a-15; c-2.* ***Frazetta*** *c-1.* ***Golden*** *a-3r.* ***Gulacy*** *c/a-3.* ***Jeff Jones*** *c-25.* ***Kaluta*** *a-17r, 21, 24r, 26; c-4, 28.* ***Nebres*** *a-1.* ***Reese*** *a-12.* ***Russell*** *a-2-4, 9, 14, 33; c-14.* ***Simonson*** *a-17.* ***B. Smith*** *c/a-7, 16.* ***Starlin*** *a-1-9, 14, 15, 34.* ***Steranko*** *c-19.* ***Williamson*** *a-13, 27, 34.* ***Wrightson*** *a-13p, 22, 25, 27, 34; c-30.*

EPIC LITE
Sept, 1991 ($3.95, one-shot, 52 pgs.)
Epic Comics (Marvel)

1-Bob the Alien, Normalman by Valentino 1.60 4.00

EPICURUS THE SAGE
1991 - Vol. 2, 1991 ($9.95, 8-1/8x10-7/8")
Piranha Press (DC Comics)

Volume 1,2-Sam Kieth-c/a 1.65 4.00 10.00

EPSILON WAVE (Independent/Elite)(Value: cover or less)

ERNIE COMICS (Formerly Andy Comics #21; All Love Romances #26 on)
No. 22, Sept, 1948 - No. 25, Mar, 1949
Current Books/Ace Periodicals

nn(9/48,11/48; #22,23)-Teenage humor 5.00 15.00 30.00
24,25 4.00 10.00 20.00

ESCAPADE IN FLORENCE (See Movie Comics)

ESCAPE FROM DEVIL'S ISLAND
1952
Avon Periodicals

1-Kinstler-c; r/as Dynamic Adventures #9 24.00 73.00 170.00

ESCAPE FROM FEAR
1956, 1962, 1969 (8 pgs. full color) (On birth control)
Planned Parenthood of America (Giveaway)

1956 edition 10.00 30.00 60.00
1962 edition 6.70 20.00 40.00
1969 edition 4.00 10.00 20.00

ESCAPE FROM THE PLANET OF THE APES (See Power Record Comics)

ESCAPE TO WITCH MOUNTAIN (See Walt Disney Showcase No. 29)

ESPERS (Eclipse)(Value: cover or less)

ESPIONAGE (TV)

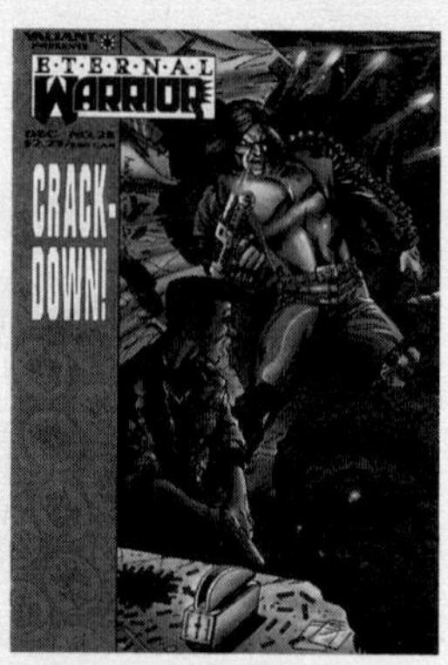

Eternal Warrior #28 © Voyager

The Everyman #1 © MEG

Excaliber Special © MEG

	GD25	FN65	NM94

May-July, 1964 - No. 2, Aug-Oct, 1964
Dell Publishing Co.

1,2	3.60	9.00	18.00

ETC
1989 - No. 5, 1990 ($4.50, color, mini-series, adults, 60 pgs.)
Piranha Press (DC Comics)

Book 1-5: Conrad scripts/layouts in all		1.80	4.50

ETERNAL BIBLE, THE
1946 (Large size) (16 pgs. in color)
Authentic Publications

1	10.00	30.00	70.00

ETERNALS, THE
July, 1976 - No. 19, Jan, 1978
Marvel Comics Group

1-Origin & 1st app. Eternals		1.70	4.25
2-19: 2-1st app. Ajak & The Celestials; 25¢ & 30¢ issues exist. 14,15-Cosmic powered Hulk-c/story		1.10	2.75
Annual 1(10/77)		1.10	2.75

NOTE: ***Kirby** c/a(p) in all. Price changed from 25¢ to 30¢ during run of #1.*

ETERNALS, THE
Oct, 1985 - No. 12, Sept, 1986 (Maxi-series, mando paper)
Marvel Comics Group

1,12 ($1.25, 52 pgs.): 12-Williamson-a(i)			1.25
2-11-(75¢)			1.00

ETERNALS: THE HEROD FACTOR
Nov, 1991 ($2.50, 68 pgs.)
Marvel Comics

1		1.00	2.50

ETERNAL WARRIOR (See Solar #10 & 11)
Aug, 1992 - Present ($2.25)
Valiant

1-Miller-c; B. Smith/Layton-a (Unity x-over); origin Eternal Warrior & Armstrong	1.70	4.00	10.00
1-Gold logo	3.00	9.00	20.00
1-Gold foil logo	4.00	11.00	25.00
2-Unity x-over; Simonson-c	.90	2.30	5.50
3-Archer & Armstrong x-over		2.00	4.75
4-1st app. Bloodshot (last pg. cameo); see Rai #0 for 1st full app.; Cowan-c	1.10	3.20	7.50
5-2nd full app. Bloodshot (12/92; see Rai #0)	.80	2.00	4.75
6,7: 6-2nd app. Master Darque		1.00	2.50
8-See Archer & Armstrong #8 for value; combined with Eternal Warrior #8		1.50	3.50
9-25,27,28: 9-1st Book of Geomancer. 14-16-Bloodshot app. 18-Doctor Mirage cameo. 19-Doctor Mirage app. 22-W/bound-in trading card. 25-Archer & Armstrong app. cont'd from A&A #25		.90	2.25
26-($2.75, 44 pgs.)-Flip book w/Archer & Armstrong		1.10	2.75
Year Book 1 (1993, $3.95)		1.60	4.00

ETERNITY SMITH (Renegade & Hero)(Value: cover or less)

ETTA KETT
No. 11, Dec, 1948 - No. 14, Sept, 1949
King Features Syndicate/Standard

11-Teenage	7.50	22.50	45.00
12-14	5.00	15.00	30.00

EUDAEMON, THE (See Dark Horse Presents #72-74)
Aug, 1993 - No. 3, Nov, 1993 ($2.50, mini-series)
Dark Horse Comics

1-3: Nelson-a, painted-c & scripts		1.00	2.50

EVANGELINE (Comico/First)(Value: cover or less)

EVA THE IMP
1957 - No. 2, Nov, 1957
Red Top Comic/Decker

1,2	2.80	7.00	14.00

EVEL KNIEVEL
1974 (20 pgs.) (Giveaway)
Marvel Comics Group (Ideal Toy Corp.)

nn-Contains photo on inside back-c			1.00

EVERYBODY'S COMICS (See Fox Giants)

EVERYMAN, THE
Nov, 1991 ($4.50, one-shot, 52 pgs.)
Epic Comics (Marvel)

1		1.80	4.50

EVERYTHING HAPPENS TO HARVEY
Sept-Oct, 1953 - No. 7, Sept-Oct, 1954
National Periodical Publications

1	19.00	57.00	130.00
2	11.00	32.00	75.00
3-7	10.00	30.00	60.00

EVERYTHING'S ARCHIE
May, 1969 - No. 157, Sept, 1991 (Giant issues No. 1-20)
Archie Publications

1	8.35	25.00	50.00
2	4.00	12.00	24.00
3-5	2.00	6.00	14.00
6-10	1.30	3.25	8.00
11-20	1.00	2.00	5.00
21-50		.80	2.00
51-157: 142,148-Gene Colan-a			1.25

EVERYTHING'S DUCKY (See 4-Color No. 1251)

EVIL ERNIE
Dec, 1991 - No. 5, 1992 ($2.50, B&W, mini-series)
Eternity Comics

1-1st app. Lady Death by Steven Hughes (12,000 print run); Lady Death app. in all issues	3.00	8.60	20.00
2-1st Lady Death-c. 2,3-(7,000 print run)	2.00	5.00	12.00
3-5: 3,4-(8,000 print run)	1.30	3.10	7.50

EWOKS (TV) (See Star Comics Magazine)
June, 1985 - No. 15, Sept, 1987 (#15 exists?) (75¢; $1.00 #14 on)
Star Comics (Marvel)

1-15 (From Star Wars): 10-Williamson-a			1.00

EXCALIBUR (Also see Marvel Comics Presents #31)
Apr, 1988; Oct, 1988 - Present ($1.50, Baxter)($1.75 #24 on)
Marvel Comics

Special Edition nn (The Sword is Drawn)(4/88, $3.25)-This is the 1st Excalibur comic	1.20	2.90	7.00
Special Edition nn (2nd print, 10/88, $3.50)		1.50	3.75
Special Edition nn (3rd print, 12/89, 4.50)		1.60	4.00
...The Sword is Drawn (Apr, '92, 4.95)		1.80	4.50
1($1.50, 10/88)-X-Men spin-off; Nightcrawler, Shadowcat(Kitty Pryde), Capt. Britain, Phoenix & Meggan begin	.90	2.30	5.50
2		1.20	3.00
3-10		.80	2.00
11-15: 10,11-Rogers/Austin-a		.60	1.60
16-23: 19-Austin-i. 21-Intro Crusader X. 22-Iron Man x-over			1.50
24-40,42-49,51-70,72-74,76: 32-($1.50). 24-John Byrne app. in story; begin $1.75-c. 26-Ron Lim-c/a. 27-B. Smith-a(p). 37-Dr. Doom & Iron Man app. 49-Neal Adams c-swipe. 52,57-X-Men (Cyclops, Wolverine) app. 53-Spider-Man-c/story. 58-X-Men(Wolverine, Gambit, Cyclops, etc.)-c/story. 61-Phoenix returns. 68-Starjammers-c/story			1.50
41-X-Men (Wolverine) app.; Cable cameo		.70	1.75
50-($2.75, 56 pgs.)-New logo		1.00	2.50

Exciting Comics #13 © STD

Ex-Mutants #9 © Malibu

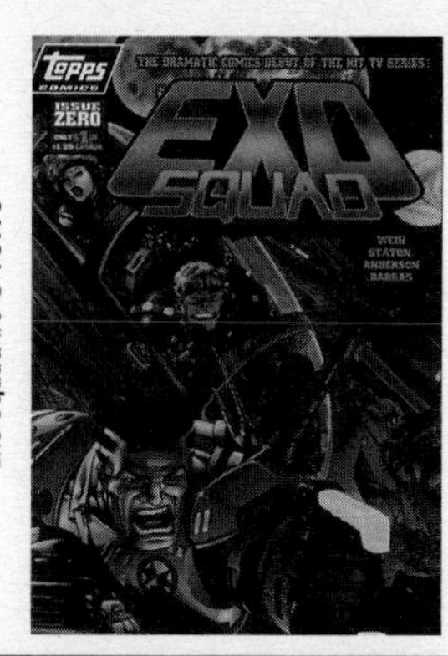

Exo Squad #0 © TOPPS

GD25 FN65 NM94

71-($3.95, 52 pgs.)-Hologram on-c; 30th anniversary 1.40 3.50
75-($3.50, 52 pgs.)-Holo-grafx foil cover edition 1.20 3.00
75-($2.25, 52 pgs.)-Regular edition .80 2.00
77-81,83-86: 77-Begin $1.95-c; bound-in trading card sheet .70 1.75
82-($2.50)-Newsstand edition 1.00 2.50
82-($3.50)-Enhanced edition 1.40 3.50
Annual 1 ('93, $2.95)-1st app. Khaos 1.00 2.50
Annual 2 ('94, $2.95, 68 pgs.)-X-men & Psylocke app. 1.20 3.00
...Air Apparent nn (12/91, $4.95)-Simonson-c 1.60 4.00
...Mojo Mayhem nn (12/89, $4.50)-Art Adams/Austin-c/a 1.60 4.00
...: The Possession nn (7/91, $2.95, 52 pgs.) 1.00 2.50
...: XX Crossing (7/92, 5/92-inside, $2.50)-Vs. The X-Men .80 2.00

EXCITING COMICS
April, 1940 - No. 69, Sept, 1949
Nedor/Better Publications/Standard Comics

1-Origin & 1st app. The Mask, Jim Hatfield, Sgt. Bill King, Dan Williams begin; early Robot-c (see Smash #1) 100.00 300.00 700.00
2-The Sphinx begins; The Masked Rider app.; Son of the Gods begins, ends #8 46.00 139.00 325.00
3-5: 3,6-Robot-c 39.00 118.00 275.00
6-8 27.00 80.00 185.00
9-Origin/1st app. of The Black Terror & sidekick Tim, begin series (5/41) (Black Terror c-9-52,54,55) 157.00 471.00 1100.00
10-2nd app. Black Terror 57.00 171.00 400.00
11-13 45.00 135.00 315.00
14-Last Sphinx, Dan Williams 32.00 96.00 225.00
15-The Liberator begins (origin) 36.00 107.00 250.00
16-20: 20-The Mask ends 22.00 65.00 150.00
21,23-27 19.00 58.00 135.00
22-Origin The Eaglet; The American Eagle begins 28.00 84.00 195.00
28-30: 28-Schomburg-c begin. 28-Crime Crusader begins, ends #58 27.00 80.00 185.00
31-38: 35-Liberator ends, not in 31-33 22.00 67.00 155.00
39-Origin Kara, Jungle Princess 29.00 86.00 200.00
40-50: 42-The Scarab begins. 49-Last Kara, Jungle Princess. 50-Last American Eagle 27.00 80.00 185.00
51-Miss Masque begins (1st app.) 30.00 90.00 210.00
52-54: Miss Masque ends. 53-Miss Masque-c 24.00 73.00 170.00
55-58: 55-Judy of the Jungle begins (origin), ends #69; 1 pg. Ingels-a; Judy of the Jungle c-56-66. 56-58: All airbrush-c 30.00 90.00 210.00
59-Frazetta art in Caniff style; signed Frank Frazeta (one t), 9 pgs. 30.00 90.00 210.00
60-66: 60-Rick Howard, the Mystery Rider begins. 66-Robinson/Meskin-a 22.00 65.00 150.00
67-69-All western covers 13.00 40.00 90.00

NOTE: ***Schomburg (Xela)** c-28-68; airbrush c-57-66. Black Terror by **R. Moreira**-#65. **Roussos** a-62. Bondage-c 9, 12, 13, 20, 23, 25, 30, 59.*

EXCITING ROMANCES
1949 (nd); No. 2, Spring, 1950 - No. 5, 10/50; No. 6 (1951, nd); No. 7, 9/51 - No. 14, 1/53
Fawcett Publications

1(1949) 9.15 27.50 55.00
2-5-(1950) 5.35 16.00 32.00
6-14 4.00 12.00 24.00

NOTE: ***Powell** a-8-10. **Marcus Swayze** a-5, 6, 9. Photo c-1-7, 10-12.*

EXCITING ROMANCE STORIES (See Fox Giants)

EXCITING WAR (Korean war)
No. 5, Sept, 1952 - No. 8, May, 1953; No. 9, Nov, 1953
Standard Comics (Better Publ.)

5 5.35 16.00 32.00
6,7,9 3.60 9.00 18.00
8-Toth-a 5.85 17.50 35.00

EXILE EARTH (River City Comics)(Value: cover or less)

EXILES
Aug, 1993 - No. 4, Nov, 1993 ($1.95)
Malibu Comics (Ultraverse)

1,2,4: 1,2-Bagged copies of each exist. 2-Gustovich-c .80 2.00
3-($2.50, 40 pgs.)-Rune flip-c/story by B. Smith (3 pgs.) 1.00 2.50

EX-MUTANTS
Nov, 1992 - Present ($1.95)
Malibu Comics

1-10 .80 2.00
11-14 ($2.25): 11-Polybagged w/Skycap .90 2.25
15-21 ($2.50) 1.00 2.50

EXORCISTS (See The Crusaders)

EXOSQUAD (TV)
Jan, 1994 ($1.25)
Topps Comics

0($1.00, 20 pgs.)-1st app.; Staton-a(p); wraparound-c 1.00

EXOTIC ROMANCES (Formerly True War Romances)
No. 22, Oct, 1955 - No. 31, Nov, 1956
Quality Comics Group (Comic Magazines)

22 5.85 17.50 35.00
23-26,29 4.00 10.00 20.00
27,31-Baker-c/a 6.35 19.00 38.00
28,30-Baker-a 5.85 17.50 35.00

EXPLOITS OF DANIEL BOONE
Nov, 1955 - No. 6, Oct, 1956
Quality Comics Group

1-All have Cuidera-c(i) 17.00 52.00 120.00
2 10.00 30.00 70.00
3-6 10.00 30.00 60.00

EXPLOITS OF DICK TRACY (See Dick Tracy)

EXPLORER JOE
Winter, 1951 - No. 2, Oct-Nov, 1952
Ziff-Davis Comic Group (Approved Comics)

1-Saunders painted-c 9.15 27.50 55.00
2-Saunders painted-c; Krigstein-a 9.15 27.50 55.00

EXPLORERS OF THE UNKNOWN (See Archie Giant Series #587, 599)
June, 1990 - No. 6, Apr, 1991 ($1.00)
Archie Comics

1-6: Featuring Archie and the gang 1.00

EXPOSED (...True Crime Cases; ...Cases in the Crusade Against Crime #5-9)
Mar-Apr, 1948 - No. 9, July-Aug, 1949
D. S. Publishing Co.

1 11.50 34.00 80.00
2-Giggling killer story with excessive blood; two injury-to-eye panels; electrocution panel 13.00 40.00 90.00
3,8,9 6.70 20.00 40.00
4-Orlando-a 7.50 22.50 45.00
5-Breeze Lawson, Sky Sheriff by E. Good 7.50 22.50 45.00
6-Ingels-a; used in **SOTI**, illo. "How to prepare an alibi" 23.00 70.00 160.00
7-Illo. in **SOTI**, "Diagram for housebreakers;" used by N.Y. Legis. Committee 23.00 70.00 160.00

EXTRA!
Mar-Apr, 1955 - No. 5, Nov-Dec, 1955
E. C. Comics

1-Not code approved 13.00 40.00 90.00
2-5 10.00 30.00 60.00

NOTE: ***Craig, Crandall, Severin** art in all.*

EXTRA COMICS
1948 (25¢, 3 comics in one)
Magazine Enterprises

Fairy Tale Parade #2 © DELL

The Falcon #1 © MEG

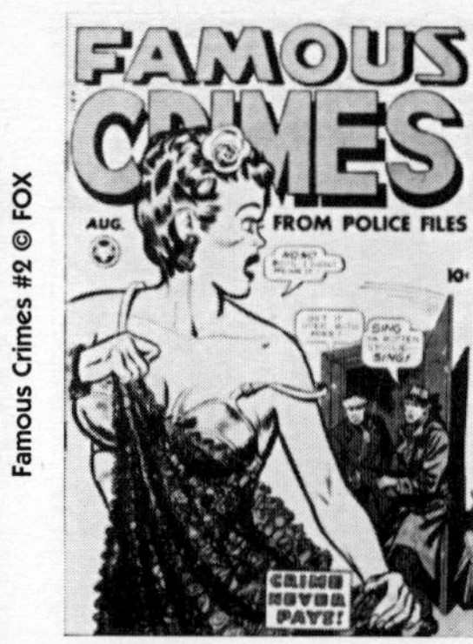

Famous Crimes #2 © FOX

GD25 FN65 NM94

1-Giant; consisting of rebound ME comics. Two versions known; (1)-Funnyman by Siegel & Shuster, Space Ace, Undercover Girl, Red Fox by L.B. Cole, Trail Colt & (2)-All Funnyman 39.00 116.00 270.00

EXTREMIST, THE
Sept, 1993 - No. 4, Dec, 1993 ($1.95, mini-series)
DC Comics (Vertigo)

1-4-Peter Milligan scripts; McKeever-c/a .80 2.00
1-Platinum Edition 8.00

EYEBALL KID, THE (Dark Horse)(Value; cover or less)

FACE, THE (Tony Trent, the Face No. 3 on) (See Big Shot Comics)
1941 - No. 2, 1941?
Columbia Comics Group

1-The Face; Mart Bailey-c 57.00 171.00 400.00
2-Bailey-c 36.00 107.00 250.00

FACULTY FUNNIES
June, 1989 - No. 5, May, 1990 (75¢; 95¢ #2 on)
Archie Comics

1-5: 1,2-The Awesome Four app. 1.00

FAFHRD AND THE GREY MOUSER (Also see Sword of Sorcery & Wonder Woman #202)
Oct, 1990 - No. 4, 1991 ($4.50, 52 pgs.)
Marvel Comics

1-4: Mignola/Williamson-a; Chaykin scripts 1.80 4.50

FAIRY TALE PARADE (See Famous Fairy Tales)
June-July, 1942 - No. 121, Oct, 1946 (Most all by Walt Kelly)
Dell Publishing Co.

1-Kelly-a begins 107.00 321.00 750.00
2(8-9/42) 57.00 171.00 400.00
3-5 (10-11/42 - 2-4/43) 39.00 118.00 275.00
6-9 (5-7/43 - 11-1/43-44) 30.00 90.00 210.00
4-Color 50('44) 26.00 78.00 180.00
4-Color 69('45), 87('45) 26.00 78.00 180.00
4-Color 104,114('46)-Last Kelly issue 20.00 60.00 140.00
4-Color 121('46)-Not by Kelly 11.50 34.00 80.00
NOTE: *#1-9, 4-Color #50, 69 have **Kelly** c/a; 4-Color #87, 104, 114-**Kelly** art only. #9 has a redrawn version of The Reluctant Dragon. This series contains all the classic fairy tales from Jack In The Beanstalk to Cinderella.*

FAIRY TALES
No. 10, Apr-May, 1951 - No. 11, June-July, 1951
Ziff-Davis Publ. Co. (Approved Comics)

10,11-Painted-c 11.50 34.00 80.00

FAITHFUL
November, 1949 - No. 2, Feb, 1950 (52 pgs.)
Marvel Comics/Lovers' Magazine

1,2-Photo-c 5.85 17.50 35.00

FALCON (Also see Avengers #181 & Captain America #117 & 133)
Nov, 1983 - No. 4, Feb, 1984 (Mini-series)(See Marvel Premiere #49)
Marvel Comics Group

1-4: 1-Paul Smith-c/a(p). 2-P. Smith-c 1.00

FALLEN ANGELS
April, 1987 - No. 8, Nov, 1987 (Mini-series)
Marvel Comics Group

1 .80 2.00
2-8 1.40

FALLING IN LOVE
Sept-Oct, 1955 - No. 143, Oct-Nov, 1973
Arleigh Publ. Co./National Periodical Publications

1 26.00 78.00 180.00
2 13.00 40.00 90.00
3-10 7.50 22.50 45.00

GD25 FN65 NM94

11-20 5.85 17.50 35.00
21-40 4.20 12.50 25.00
41-47: 47-Last 10¢ issue? 3.60 9.00 18.00
48-100,108: 108-Wood-a (4 pgs., 7/69) 1.80 4.50 9.00
101-107,109-143 1.00 2.00 5.00
NOTE: ***Colan** c/a-75, 81. 52 pgs.-#125-133.*

FALL OF THE HOUSE OF USHER, THE (See A Corben Special & Spirit section 8/22/48)

FALL OF THE ROMAN EMPIRE (See Movie Comics)

FAMILY AFFAIR (TV)
Feb, 1970 - No. 4, Oct, 1970 (25¢)
Gold Key

1-With pull-out poster; photo-c 3.60 10.75 25.00
1-With poster missing 1.70 5.00 12.00
2-4: 3,4-Photo-c 2.15 6.50 15.00

FAMILY FUNNIES
No. 9, Aug-Sept, 1946
Parents' Magazine Institute

9 3.60 9.00 18.00

FAMILY FUNNIES (Tiny Tot Funnies No. 9)
Sept, 1950 - No. 8, April, 1951
Harvey Publications

1-Mandrake (has over 30 King Feature strips) 5.00 15.00 30.00
2-Flash Gordon, 1 pg. 4.00 10.00 20.00
3-8: 4,5,7-Flash Gordon, 1 pg. 3.60 9.00 18.00
1(Black & white) 2.00 5.00 10.00

FAMOUS AUTHORS ILLUSTRATED (See Stories by...)

FAMOUS COMICS (Also see Favorite Comics)
No date; Mid 1930's (24 pgs.) (paper cover)
Zain-Eppy/United Features Syndicate

nn-Reprinted from 1933 & 1934 newspaper strips in color; Joe Palooka, Hairbreadth Harry, Napoleon, The Nebbs, etc. (Many different versions known) 38.00 114.00 265.00

FAMOUS COMICS
1934 (100 pgs., daily newspaper reprints)
(3-1/2x8-1/2"; paper cover) (came in a box)
King Features Syndicate (Whitman Publ. Co.)

684(#1)-Little Jimmy, Katzenjammer Kids, & Barney Google 23.00 70.00 160.00
684(#2)-Polly, Little Jimmy, Katzenjammer Kids 23.00 70.00 160.00
684(#3)-Little Annie Rooney, Polly and her Pals, Katzenjammer Kids 23.00 70.00 160.00
....Box price.... 18.00 54.00 125.00

FAMOUS COMICS CARTOON BOOKS
1934 (72 pgs.; 8x7-1/4"; daily strip reprints)
Whitman Publishing Co. (B&W; hardbacks)

1200-The Captain & the Kids (1st app?); Dirks reprints credited to Bernard Dibble 20.00 60.00 140.00
1202-Captain Easy (1st app?) & Wash Tubbs by Roy Crane 25.00 75.00 175.00
1203-Ella Cinders (1st app?) 20.00 60.00 140.00
1204-Freckles & His Friends (1st app?) 17.00 52.00 120.00
NOTE: *Called Famous Funnies Cartoon Books inside.*

FAMOUS CRIMES
June, 1948 - No. 19, Sept, 1950; No. 20, Aug, 1951; No. 51, 52, 1953
Fox Features Syndicate/M.S. Dist. No. 51,52

1-Blue Beetle app. & crime story-r/Phantom Lady #16 26.00 78.00 180.00
2-Has woman dissolved in acid; lingerie-c/panels 20.00 60.00 140.00
3-Injury-to-eye story used in **SOTI**, pg. 112; has two electrocution stories 25.00 75.00 175.00

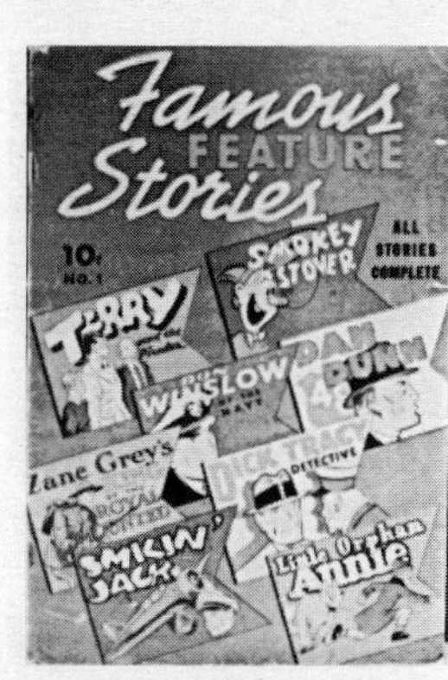

Famous Feature Stories #1 © DELL

Famous Funnies #43 © EAS

Famous Funnies #151 © EAS

GD25 FN65 NM94

4-6 10.00 30.00 70.00
7- "Tarzan, the Wyoming Killer" used in **SOTI**, pg. 44; drug trial/possession story 22.00 65.00 150.00
8-20: 17-Morisi-a 8.35 25.00 50.00
51(nd, 1953) 8.35 25.00 50.00
52 4.35 13.00 26.00

FAMOUS FAIRY TALES
1942; 1943 (32 pgs.); 1944 (16 pgs.) (Soft covers)
K. K. Publ. Co. (Giveaway)

1942-Kelly-a 37.00 111.00 260.00
1943-r-/Fairy Tale Parade No. 2,3; Kelly-a 29.00 86.00 200.00
1944-Kelly-a 26.00 77.00 180.00

FAMOUS FEATURE STORIES
1938 (68 pgs., 7-1/2x11")
Dell Publishing Co.

1-Tarzan, Terry & the Pirates, King of the Royal Mtd., Buck Jones, Dick Tracy, Smilin' Jack, Dan Dunn, Don Winslow, G-Man, Tailspin Tommy, Mutt & Jeff, Little Orphan Annie reprints - all illustrated text 62.00 188.00 425.00

FAMOUS FIRST EDITION (See Limited Collectors' Edition)
($1.00; 10x13-1/2"-Giant Size)(72 pgs.; No.6-8, 68 pgs.)
1974 - No. 8, Aug-Sept, 1975; C-61, 1979
National Periodical Publications/DC Comics

C-26-Action Comics #1; gold ink outer cover 1.20 4.00 12.00
C-28-Detective #27; silver ink outer cover 3.50 11.00 35.00
C-28-Hardbound edition 6.80 20.00 68.00
C-30-Sensation #1(1974); bronze ink outer cover 1.20 4.00 12.00
F-4-Whiz Comics #2(#1)(10-11/74)-Cover not identical to original (dropped "Gangway for Captain Marvel" from cover); gold ink on outer cover 1.20 4.00 12.00
F-5-Batman #1(F-6 inside); silver ink on outer-c 2.40 7.00 24.00
V2#F-6-Wonder Woman #1 1.20 4.00 12.00
F-7-All-Star Comics #3 1.20 4.00 12.00
F-8-Flash Comics #1(8-9/75) 1.20 4.00 12.00
V8#C-61-Superman #1(1979, $2.00) 1.20 4.00 12.00
Hardbound editions (w/dust jackets $5.00 extra) (Lyle Stuart, Inc.)
C-26,C-30,F-4,F-6 known 2.00 6.00 17.00

Warning: The above books are almost **exact** reprints of the originals that they represent except for the Giant-Size format. None of the originals are Giant-Size. The first five issues and C-61 were printed with two covers. Reprint information can be found on the outside cover, but not on the inside cover which was reprinted exactly like the original (inside and out).

FAMOUS FUNNIES
1933 - No. 218, July, 1955
Eastern Color

GD25 FN65 VF82 NM94

A Carnival of Comics (probably the second comic book), 36 pgs., no date given, no publisher, no number; contains strip reprints of The Bungle Family, Dixie Dugan, Hairbreadth Harry, Joe Palooka, Keeping Up With the Jones, Mutt & Jeff, Reg'lar Fellers, S'Matter Pop, Strange As It Seems, and others. This book was sold by M. C. Gaines to Wheatena, Milk-O-Malt, John Wanamaker, Kinney Shoe Stores, & others to be given away as premiums and radio give-aways (1933). 650.00 1950.00 4225.00 6500.00
(Estimated up to 50 total copies exist, 2 in NM/Mint)

Series 1-(Very rare)(nd-early 1934)(68 pgs.) No publisher given (Eastern Color PrintingCo.); sold in chain stores for 10¢. 35,000 print run. Contains Sunday strip reprints of Mutt & Jeff, Reg'lar Fellers, Nipper, Hairbreadth Harry, Strange As It Seems, Joe Palooka, Dixie Dugan, The Nebbs, Keeping Up With the Jones, and others. Inside front and back covers and pages 1-16 of Famous Funnies Series 1, #s 49-64 reprinted from **Famous Funnies**, **A Carnival of Comics**, and most of pages 17-48 reprinted from **Funnies on Parade**. This was the first comic book sold. 2285.00 6857.00 11,428.00 16,000.00
(Estimated up to 12 copies exist, 1 in NM/Mint)

No. 1 (Rare)(7/34-on stands 5/34) - Eastern Color Printing Co. First monthly newsstand comic book. Contains Sunday strip reprints of Toonerville Folks, Mutt & Jeff, Hairbreadth Harry, S'Matter Pop, Nipper, Dixie Dugan, The Bungle Family, Connie, Ben Webster, Tailspin Tommy, The Nebbs, Joe Palooka, & others. 1643.00 4930.00 8215.00 11,500.00
(Estimated up to 30 total copies exist, 2 in NM/Mint)

GD25 FN65 VF82

GD25 FN65 NM94

2 (Rare, 9/34) 314.00 943.00 2200.00
3-Buck Rogers Sunday strip reprints by Rick Yager begins, ends #218; not in #191-208; the number of the 1st strip reprinted is pg. 190, Series No. 1 386.00 1157.00 2700.00
4 114.00 343.00 800.00
5-1st Christmas-c on a newsstand comic 93.00 279.00 650.00
6-10 79.00 236.00 550.00

GD25 FN65 NM94

11,12,18-Four pgs. of Buck Rogers in each issue, completes stories in Buck Rogers #1 which lacks these pages. 18-Two pgs. of Buck Rogers reprinted in Daisy Comics #1 68.00 205.00 475.00
13-17,19,20: 14-Has two Buck Rogers panels missing. 17-2nd Christmas-c on a newsstand comic (12/35) 50.00 150.00 350.00
21,23-30: 27-(10/36)-War on Crime begins (4 pgs.); 1st true crime in comics (reprints); part photo-c. 29-X-Mas-c (12/36) 38.00 114.00 265.00
22-Four pgs. of Buck Rogers needed to complete stories in Buck Rogers #1 41.00 124.00 290.00
31-34,36,37,39,40: 33-Careers of Baby Face Nelson & John Dillinger traced 29.00 86.00 200.00
35-Two pgs. Buck Rogers omitted in Buck Rogers #2 31.00 94.00 220.00
38-Full color portrait of Buck Rogers 29.00 86.00 200.00
41-60: 41,53-X-Mas-c. 55-Last bottom panel, pg. 4 in Buck Rogers redrawn in Buck Rogers #3 20.00 60.00 140.00
61,63,64,66,67,69,70 16.00 48.00 110.00
62,65,68-Two pgs. Kirby-a "Lightnin' & the Lone Rider". 65-X-Mas-c 17.00 52.00 120.00
71,73,77-80: 77-X-Mas-c. 80-(3/41)-Buck Rogers story continues from Buck Rogers #5 12.00 36.00 85.00
72-Speed Spaulding begins by Marvin Bradley (artist), ends #88. This series was written by Edwin Balmer & Philip Wylie (later appeared as film & book "When Worlds Collide") 13.00 40.00 90.00
74-76-Two pgs. Kirby-a in all 11.50 34.00 80.00
81-Origin & 1st app. Invisible Scarlet O'Neil (4/41); strip begins #82, ends #167; 1st non-funny-c (Scarlet O'Neil) 10.00 30.00 65.00
82-Buck Rogers-c 11.50 34.00 80.00
83-87,90: 86-Connie vs. Monsters on the Moon-c (sci/fi). 87 has last Buck Rogers full page-r. 90-Bondage-c 10.00 30.00 65.00
88-Buck Rogers in "Moon's End" by Calkins, 2 pgs.(not reprints). Beginning with #88, all Buck Rogers pgs. have rearranged panels 10.00 30.00 70.00
89-Origin & 1st app. Fearless Flint, the Flint Man 10.00 30.00 70.00
91-93,95,96,98-99,101-110: 102-Chief Wahoo vs. Hitler, Tojo & Mussolini-c (1/43). 105-Series 2 begins (Strip Page #1) 9.15 27.50 55.00
94-Buck Rogers in "Solar Holocaust" by Calkins, 3 pgs.(not reprints) 10.00 30.00 60.00
97-War Bond promotion, Buck Rogers by Calkins, 2 pgs.(not reprints) 10.00 30.00 60.00
100 10.00 30.00 60.00
111-130: 113-X-Mas-c 6.70 20.00 40.00
131-150: 137-Strip page No. 110 omitted 5.00 15.00 30.00
151-162,164-168 4.35 13.00 26.00
163-St. Valentine's Day-c 5.35 16.00 32.00
169,170-Two text illos. by Williamson, his 1st comic book work 9.15 27.50 55.00
171-180: 171-Strip pgs. 227,229,230, Series 2 omitted. 172-Strip Pg. 232 omitted 4.00 12.00 24.00
181-190: Buck Rogers ends with start of strip pg. 302, Series 2. 190-Oaky Doaks-c/story 4.00 12.00 24.00
191-197,199,201,203,206-208: No Buck Rogers 4.00 11.00 22.00
198,202,205-One pg. Frazetta ads; no B. Rogers 4.00 12.00 24.00
200-Frazetta 1 pg. ad 4.00 12.00 24.00
204-Used in **POP**, pg. 79,99; war-c begin, end #208 4.00 12.00 24.00
209-Buck Rogers begins (12/53) with strip pg. 480, Series 2; Frazetta-c 41.00 122.00 285.00
210-216: Frazetta-c. 211-Buck Rogers ads by Anderson begins, ends #217.

Famous Stars #1 © Z-D

Fantastic Comics #22 © FOX

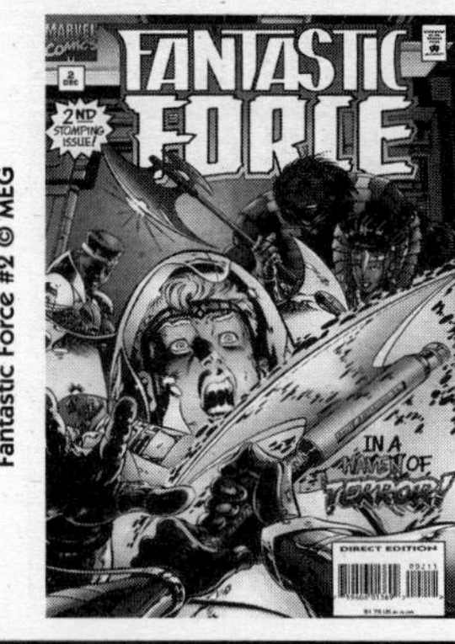

Fantastic Force #2 © MEG

GD25 FN65 NM94 | GD25 FN65 NM94

#215-Contains B. Rogers strip pg. 515-518, series 2 followed by pgs. 179-181, Series 3 — 41.00 122.00 285.00
217,218-B. Rogers ends with pg. 199, Series 3. 218-Wee Three-c/story — 4.00 12.00 24.00

NOTE: ***Rick Yager*** *did the Buck Rogers Sunday strips reprinted in Famous Funnies. The Sundays were formerly done by Russ Keaton and Lt. Dick Calkins did the dailies, but would sometimes assist Yager on a panel or two from time to time. Strip No. 169 is Yager's first full Buck Rogers page. Yager did the strip until 1958 when* ***Murphy Anderson*** *took over.* ***Tuska*** *art from 4/26/59 - 1965. Virtually every panel was rewritten for Famous Funnies. Not iden#tical to the original Sunday page. The Buck Rogers reprints run continuously through Famous Funnies issue No. 190 (Strip No. 302) with no break in story line. The story line has no continuity after No. 190. The Buck Rogers newspaper strips came out in four series: Series 1, 3/30/30 - 9/21/41 (No. 1 - 600); Series 2, 9/28/41 -10/21/51 (No. 1 -525)(Strip No. 110-1/2 (1/2 pg.) published in only a few newspapers); Series 3, 10/28/51 -2/9/58 (No. 100-428)(No No.1-99); Series 4, 2/16/58 - 6/13/65 (No numbers, dates only).* ***Everett*** *c-85, 86.* ***Moulton*** *a-100. Chief Wahoo c-93, 97, 102, 116, 136, 139, 151. Dickie Dare c-83, 88. Fearless Flint c-89. Invisible Scarlet O'Neil c-81, 87, 95, 121(part), 132. Scorchy Smith c-84, 90.*

FAMOUS FUNNIES
1964
Super Comics

Super Reprint Nos. 15-18 — 1.80 4.50 9.00

FAMOUS GANG BOOK OF COMICS (Becomes Donald & Mickey Merry Christmas 1943 on)
Dec, 1942 (32 pgs.; paper cover) (Christmas giveaway)
Firestone Tire & Rubber Co.

nn-(Rare)-Porky Pig, Bugs Bunny, Mary Jane & Sniffles, Elmer Fudd; r/Looney Tunes — 60.00 180.00 600.00

FAMOUS GANGSTERS (Crime on the Waterfront No. 4)
April, 1951 - No. 3, Feb, 1952
Avon Periodicals/Realistic No. 3

1-Capone, Dillinger; c-/Avon paperback #329 — 22.00 65.00 150.00
2-Dillinger Machine Gun Killer; Wood-c/a (1 pg.); r/Saint #7 & retitled "Mike Strong" — 23.00 70.00 160.00
3-Lucky Luciano & Murder, Inc; c-/Avon paperback #66 — 23.00 70.00 160.00

FAMOUS INDIAN TRIBES
July-Sept, 1962; No. 2, July, 1972
Dell Publishing Co.

12-264-209(#1) (The Sioux) — 2.00 5.00 10.00
2(7/72)-Reprints above — .40 1.00 2.00

FAMOUS STARS
Nov-Dec, 1950 - No. 6, Spring, 1952 (All have photo covers)
Ziff-Davis Publ. Co.

1-Shelley Winters, Susan Peters, Ava Gardner, Shirley Temple;Jimmy Stewart & Shelley Winters photo-c; Whitney-a — 22.00 65.00 150.00
2-Betty Hutton, Bing Crosby, Colleen Townsend, Gloria Swanson; Betty Hutton photo-c; Everett-a(2) — 15.00 45.00 105.00
3-Farley Granger, Judy Garland's ordeal, Alan Ladd; Farley Granger & Judy Garland photo-c; Whitney-a — 13.50 41.00 95.00
4-Al Jolson, Bob Mitchum, Ella Raines, Richard Conte, Vic Damone; Bob Mitchum photo-c; Crandall-a, 6pgs. — 13.00 40.00 90.00
5-Liz Taylor, Betty Grable, Esther Williams, George Brent, Mario Lanza; Liz Taylor photo-c; Krigstein-a — 16.00 48.00 110.00
6-Gene Kelly, Hedy Lamarr, June Allyson, William Boyd, Janet Leigh, Gary Cooper; Gene Kelly photo-c — 11.50 34.00 80.00

FAMOUS STORIES (...Book No. 2)
1942 - No. 2, 1942
Dell Publishing Co.

1,2: 1-Treasure Island. 2-Tom Sawyer — 23.00 70.00 160.00

FAMOUS TV FUNDAY FUNNIES
Sept, 1961
Harvey Publications

1-Casper the Ghost — 4.70 14.00 28.00

FAMOUS WESTERN BADMEN (Formerly Redskin)
No. 13, Dec, 1952 - No. 15, Apr, 1953
Youthful Magazines

13-Redskin story — 8.35 25.00 50.00
14,15: 15-The Dalton Boys story — 6.35 19.00 38.00

FANTASTIC (Formerly Captain Science; Beware No. 10 on)
No. 8, Feb, 1952 - No. 9, April, 1952
Youthful Magazines

8-Capt. Science by Harrison; decapitation, shrunken head panels — 20.00 60.00 140.00
9-Harrison-a — 13.00 40.00 90.00

FANTASTIC ADVENTURES
1963 - 1964 (Reprints)
Super Comics

9,10,12,15,16,18: 9-r/? 10-r/He-Man #2(Toby). 12-Unpublished Chesler material? 15-r/Spook #23. 16-r/Dark Shadows #2(Steinway); Briefer-a. 18-r/Superior Stories #1 — 2.40 6.00 12.00
11-Wood-a; r/Blue Bolt #118 — 4.00 10.00 20.00
17-Baker-a(2) r/Seven Seas #6 — 3.60 9.00 18.00

FANTASTIC COMICS
Dec, 1939 - No. 23, Nov, 1941
Fox Features Syndicate

1-Intro/origin Samson; Stardust, The Super Wizard, Sub Saunders (by Kiefer), Space Smith, Capt. Kidd begin — 243.00 730.00 1700.00
2-Powell text illos — 107.00 321.00 750.00
3-5: 3-Early Robot-c; Powell text illos — 82.00 246.00 575.00
6-9: 6,7-Simon-c — 63.00 190.00 440.00
10-Intro/origin David, Samson's aide — 54.00 161.00 375.00
11-17,19,20,22: 16-Stardust ends — 46.00 137.00 320.00
18-1st app. Black Fury & sidekick Chuck; ends #23 — 50.00 150.00 350.00
21,23: 21-The Banshee begins(origin); ends #23; Hitler-c. 22-Likeness of Hitler as furnace on cover. 23-Origin The Gladiator — 50.00 150.00 350.00

NOTE: ***Lou Fine*** *c-1-5.* ***Tuska*** *a-3-5, 8. Bondage c-6, 8, 9. Issue #11 has indicia to Mystery Men Comics #15. All issues feature Samson covers.*

FANTASTIC COMICS (Fantastic Fears #1-9; Becomes Samson #12)
No. 10, Nov-Dec, 1954 - No. 11, Jan-Feb, 1955
Ajax/Farrell Publ.

10,11: 11-Robot-c — 10.00 30.00 65.00

FANTASTIC FABLES
Feb, 1987 ($1.50, B&W, 28 pgs.)
Silverwolf Comics

1-Tim Vigil-a (6 pgs.) — 1.10 2.75

FANTASTIC FEARS (Formerly Captain Jet) (Fantastic Comics #10 on)
No. 7, May, 1953 - No. 9, Sept-Oct, 1954
Ajax/Farrell Publ.

7(#1, 5/53)-Tales of Stalking Terror — 19.00 57.00 130.00
8(#2, 7/53) — 12.00 36.00 85.00
3,4 — 10.00 30.00 65.00
5-(1-2/54)-Ditko story (1st in book) is written by Bruce Hamilton; r-in Weird V2#8 (Ditko's 3rd published-a) (1st pro work for Ditko but Black Magic #27 was published 1st) — 57.00 171.00 400.00
6-Decapitation of girl's head with paper cutter (classic) — 25.00 75.00 175.00
7(5-6/54), 9(9-10/54) — 10.00 30.00 60.00
8(7-8/54)-Contains story intended for Jo-Jo; name changed to Kaza; decapitation story — 11.50 34.00 80.00

FANTASTIC FORCE
Nov, 1994-Present(1.75, color Marvel Comics)
1-(2.50)-Foil wraparound-c; intro Fantastic Force w/Huntara, Delvor, Psi-Lord & Vibraxas — 0.50 1.00 2.50
2,3 — 0.40 0.70 1.75

Fantastic Four #15 © MEG

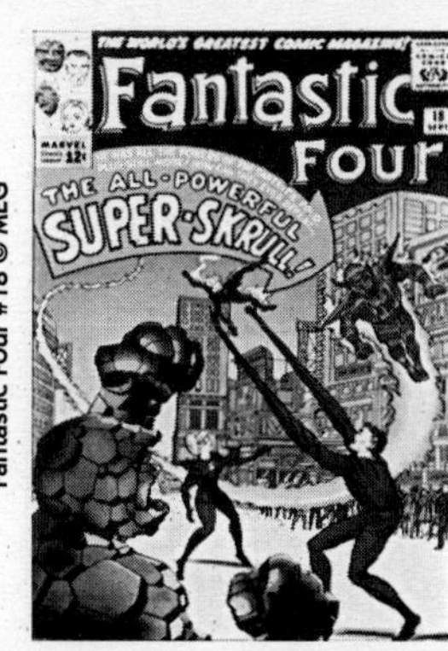

Fantastic Four #18 © MEG

Fantastic Four Annual #113 © MEG

GD25 FN65 NM94 GD25 FN65 NM94

FANTASTIC FOUR (See America's Best TV..., Giant- Size..., Giant Size Super- Stars, Marvel Collectors Item Classics, Marvel Milestone Edition, Marvel's Greatest,Marvel Treasury Edition, Marvel Triple Action, Official Marvel Index to... & Power Record Comics)

FANTASTIC FOUR
Nov, 1961 - Present
Marvel Comics Group

	GD25	FN65	VF82	NM94
1-Origin & 1st app. The Fantastic Four (Reed Richards: Mr. Fantastic, Johnny Storm: The Human Torch, Sue Storm: The Invisible Girl, & Ben Grimm: The Thing–Marvel's 1st super-hero group since the G.A.; 1st app. S.A. Human Torch); origin/1st app. The Mole Man	1080.00	3250.00	8,125.00	13,000.00

	GD25	FN65	NM94
1-Golden Record Comic Set Reprint (1966)-cover not identical to original	16.00	47.00	110.00
with Golden Record	26.00	79.00	185.00
2-Vs. The Skrulls (last 10¢ issue)	220.00	650.00	2175.00
3-Fantastic Four don costumes & establish Headquarters; brief 1pg. origin; intro The Fantasti-Car; Human Torch drawn w/two left hands on-c	150.00	450.00	1500.00

	GD25	FN65	VF82	NM94
4-1st Silver Age Sub-Mariner app. (5/62)	185.00	555.00	1202.00	1850.00
5-Origin & 1st app. Doctor Doom	200.00	600.00	1300.00	2000.00

	GD25	FN65	NM94
6-Sub-Mariner, Dr. Doom team up; 1st Marvel villain team-up (2nd S.A. Sub-Mariner app.	111.00	332.00	775.00
7-10: 7-1st app. Kurrgo. 8-1st app. Puppet-Master & Alicia Masters. 9-3rd Sub-Mariner app. 10-Stan Lee (1st app. in comics?) & Jack Kirby app. in story	79.00	236.00	550.00
11-Origin/1st app. The Impossible Man (2/63)	64.00	193.00	450.00
12-Fantantic Four Vs. The Hulk (1st meeting); 1st Hulk x-over & ties w/Amazing Spider-Man #1 as 1st Marvel x-over; (3/63)	79.00	236.00	550.00
13-Intro. The Watcher; 1st app. The Red Ghost	48.00	144.00	335.00
14-19: 14-Sub-Mariner x-over. 15-1st app. Mad Thinker. 16-1st Ant-Man x-over (7/63); Wasp cameo. 18-Origin/1st app. The Super Skrull. 19-Intro. Rama-Tut; Stan Lee & Jack Kirby cameo	32.00	96.00	225.00
20-Origin/1st app. The Molecule Man	37.00	111.00	260.00
21-Intro. The Hate Monger; 1st Sgt. Fury x-over (12/63)	24.00	71.00	165.00
22-24: 22-Sue Storm gains more powers	14.00	43.00	100.00
25,26-The Hulk vs. The Thing (their 1st battle). 25-3rd Avengers x-over (1st time w/Capt. America)(cameo, 4/64); 2nd S.A. app. Cap (takes place between Avengers #4 & 5. 26-4th Avengers x-over	44.00	133.00	310.00
27-1st Doctor Strange x-over (6/64)	17.00	51.00	120.00
28-Early X-Men x-over (7/64); same date as X-Men #6	21.00	64.00	150.00
29,30: 30-Intro. Diablo	12.00	35.00	82.00
31-40: 31-Early Avengers x-over (10/64). 33-1st app. Attuma; part photo-c. 35-Intro/1st app. Dragon Man. 36-Intro/1st app. Madam Medusa & the Frightful Four (Sandman, Wizard, Paste Pot Pete). 39-Wood inks on Daredevil (early x-over)	10.00	29.00	68.00
41-47: 41-43-Frightful Four app. 44-Intro. Gorgon. 45-Intro/1st app. The Inhumans (c/story, 12/65); also see Incredible Hulk Special #1 & Thor #146, & 147; 1st Black Bolt-c (Kirby) & 1st full app.	6.60	20.00	46.00
48-Partial origin/1st app. The Silver Surfer & Galactus (3/66); Galactus cameo in last panel; 1st of 3 part story	65.00	195.00	650.00
49-2nd app. Silver Surfer & Galactus	14.00	41.00	135.00
50-Silver Surfer battles Galactus	16.00	48.00	160.00
51,54: 54-Inhumans cameo	43.00	11.00	36.00
52-1st app. The Black Panther (7/66)	6.00	19.00	62.00
53-Origin & 2nd app. The Black Panther	5.00	16.00	52.00
55-Thing battles Silver Surfer; 4th app. Silver Surfer	5.00	16.00	52.00
56-60: Silver Surfer x-over. 59,60-Inhumans cameos	5.00	14.00	46.00
61-65,68-70: 61-Silver Surfer cameo; Sandman-c/s	3.00	10.00	32.00
66-Begin 2 part origin of Him (Warlock); does not app. (9/67)	8.00	24.00	80.00
67-Origin/1st app. Him (Warlock); 1 pg. cameo; see Thor #165,166 for 1st full app.	9.00	27.00	90.00
71,73,78-80: 73-Spider-Man, D.D., Thor x-over; cont'd from Daredevil #38	3.00	8.00	25.00
72-Silver Surfer-c/story (pre-dates Silver Surfer #1)	3.00	8.00	27.00
74-77: Silver Surfer app.(#77 is same date/S.S. #1)	3.00	8.00	27.00
81-88: 81-Crystal joins & dons costume. 82,83-Inhumans app. 84-87-Dr. Doom app. 88-Last 12¢ issue	2.00	6.00	19.00
89-99,101,102: 94-Intro. Agatha Harkness. 102,103-Fantastic Four vs. Sub-Mariner	1.00	4.00	13.00
100 (7/70)	6.00	18.00	60.00
103-111: 104-Magneto-c/story. 108-Last Kirby issue (not in #103-107). 110-Variant in cover color	1.70	5.00	12.00
112-Hulk Vs. Thing (7/71)	5.70	17.00	40.00
113-115: 115-Last 15¢ issue	1.60	5.00	11.00
116-120: 116-(52 pgs.)	1.40	3.50	8.50
121-123-Silver Surfer-c/stories. 122,123-Galactus	1.70	5.00	12.00
124,125,127,129-149: 129-Intro. Thundra. 130-Sue leaves F.F. 131-Quicksilver app. 132-Medusa joins. 133-Thundra Vs. Thing. 142-Kirbyish-a by Buckler begins. 143-Dr. Doom-c/story. 147-Sub-Mariner	1.30	3.00	7.50
126-Origin F.F. retold; cover swipe of F.F. #1	1.40	3.50	8.50
128-Four pg. insert of F.F. Friends & Foes	1.40	3.50	8.50
150-Crystal & Quicksilver's wedding	1.40	3.50	8.50
151-154,158-160: 151-Origin Thundra. 159-Medusa leaves; Sue rejoins	1.10	2.70	6.50
155-157: Silver Surfer in all	1.30	3.00	7.50
161-180: 164-The Crusader (old Marvel Boy) revived (origin #165). 168-170-Cage app. 176-Re-intro Impossible Man; Marvel artists app. 180-r/#101 by Kirby		1.40	3.50
181-199: 189-G.A. Human Torch app. & origin retold. 190,191-Fantastic Four break up		.90	2.25
200-(11/78, 52 pgs.)-F.F. re-united vs. Dr. Doom		1.80	4.50
201-208,219,222-231: 207-Human Torch vs. Spider-Man-c/story. 211-1st app. Terrax		.70	1.75
209-216,218,220,221-Byrne-a. 209-1st Herbie the Robot. 220-Brief origin		.90	2.25
217-Dazzler app. by Byrne		1.30	3.25
232-Byrne-a begins		1.50	3.75
233-235,237-249,251-260: All Byrne-a. 238-Origin Frankie Raye. 244-Frankie Raye becomes Nova, Herald of Galactus. 252-Reads sideways; Annihilus app.; contains skin "Tattooz" decals		1.10	2.75
236-20th Anniversary issue(11/81, 68 pgs., $1.00)-Brief origin F.F.; Byrne-c/a(p); new Kirby-a(p)		1.50	3.75
250-(52 pgs)-Spider-Man x-over; Byrne-a; Skrulls impersonate New X-Men		1.50	3.75
261-285: 261-Silver Surfer. 262-Origin Galactus; Byrne writes & draws himself into story. 264-Swipes-c of F.F. #1. 274-Spider-Man's alien costume app. (4th app., 1/85, 2 pgs.)		1.10	2.75
286-2nd app. X-Factor continued from Avengers #263; story continues in X-Factor #1		1.90	4.75
287-295: 292-Nick Fury app. 293-Last Byrne-a		.70	1.75
296-($1.50)-Barry Smith-c/a; Thing rejoins		.90	2.25
297-305,307-318,320-330: 300-Johnny Storm & Alicia Masters wed. 311-Re-intro The Black Panther. 312-X-Factor x-over. 327-Mr. Fantastic & Invisible Girl return		.70	1.80
306-New team begins (9/87)		.70	1.80
319-Double size		1.10	2.75
331-346,351-357,359,360: 334-Simonson-c/scripts begin. 337-Simonson-a begins. 342-Spider-Man cameo. 356-F.F. vs. The New Warriors; Paul Ryan-c/a begins. 360-Last $1.00-c		.60	1.60
347-Ghost Rider, Wolverine, Spider-Man, Hulk-c/stories thru #349; Arthur Adams-c/a(p) in each	1.00	2.50	6.00
347-Gold 2nd printing		1.00	2.50
348,349		1.50	3.75

Fantastuic Four #391 © MEG

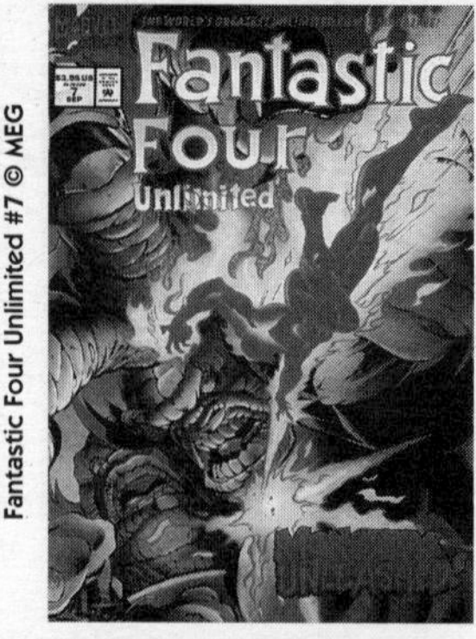

Fantastic Four Unlimited #7 © MEG

Fantoman #2 © CEN

GD25 FN65 NM94

348-Gold 2nd printing .60 1.60
350-($1.50, 52 pgs.)-Dr. Doom app. 1.30 3.25
358-(11/91, $2.25, 88 pgs.)-30th anniversary issue; gives history of F.F.; die cut-c; Art Adams back-up story-a 1.30 3.25
361-368,370,372-374,376-380,382-386: 362-Spider-Man app. 367-Wolverine app. (brief). 370-Infinity War x-over; Thanos & Magus app. 374-Secret Defenders (Ghost Rider, Hulk, Wolverine) x-over .60 1.60
369-Infinity War x-over; Thanos app. 1.10 2.75
371-All white embossed-c ($2.00) 1.60 4.00
371-All red 2nd printing ($2.00) .90 2.25
375-($2.95, 52 pgs.)-Holo-grafx foil-c; ann. issue 1.20 3.00
381-Death of Reed Richards & Dr. Doom 1.50 3.75
387-Newsstand ed. ($1.25) 1.25
387-($2.95)-Collector's Ed. w/Die-cut foil-c 1.20 3.00
388-399: 388-Begin $1.50-c; bound-in trading card sheet 1.50
Annual 1('63)-Origin F.F.; Ditko-i 45.00 135.00 450.00
Annual 2('64)-Dr. Doom origin & c/story 28.00 84.00 280.00
Annual 3('65)-Reed & Sue wed; r/#6,11 12.00 35.00 115.00
Special 4(11/66)-G.A. Torch x-over (1st S.A. app.) & origin retold; r/#25,26 (Hulk vs. Thing); Torch vs. Torch battle 6.00 19.00 62.00
Special 5(11/67)-New art; Intro. Psycho-Man; early Black Panther, Inhumans & Silver Surfer (1st solo story) app. 7.00 20.00 68.00
Special 6(11/68)-Intro. Annihilus; birth of Franklin Richards; new 48 pg. movie length epic; last non-reprint annual 4.00 11.00 36.00
Special 7(11/69)-r/F.F. #1-5; Marvel staff photos 2.70 8.10 19.00
Special 8-10: All reprints. 8(12/70)-F.F. vs. Sub-Mariner plus gallery of F.F. foes. 9(12/71). 10('73) 1.70 4.20 10.00
Annual 11-14: 11(1976)-New art begins again. 12(1978). 13(1978). 14(1979) 1.00 2.50 6.00
Annual 15-20: 15(1980). 16(1981). 17(1983)-Byrne-c/a. 18(1984). 19(1985). 20(1987) 1.50 3.75
Annual 21(1988)-Evolutionary War x-over 1.60 4.00
Annual 22-24 (1989-91, $2.00, 68 pgs.): 22-Atlantis Attacks x-over; Sub-Mariner & The Avengers app.; Buckler-a. 23-Byrne-c; Guice-p. 24-2 pg. origin recap of Fantastic Four; Guardians of the Galaxy x-over .90 2.25
Annual 25(1992, $2.25, 68 pgs.)-Moondragon story .90 2.25
Annual 26,27('93,'94, $2.95, 68 pgs.). 26-Bagged w/card 1.20 3.00
Special Edition 1(5/84)-r/Annual #1; Byrne-c/a 1.00 2.50
...: Monsters Unleashed nn(1992, $5.95)-r/F.F. #347-349 w/new Arthur Adams-c 1.00 2.50 6.00
Giveaway (nn, 1981, 32pgs., Young Model Builders Club) .65 1.60

NOTE: ***Arthur Adams*** *c/a-347-349p.* ***Austin*** *c(i)-232-236, 238, 240-242, 250i, 286i.* ***John Buscema*** *a(p)-107, 108(w/**Kirby** & **Romita**),109-130, 132, 134-141, 160, 173-175, 202, 296-309p, Annual 11, 13; c(p)-107-122, 124-129, 133-139, 202, Annual 12p, Special 10.* ***Byrne*** *a-209-218p, 220p, 221p, 232-265, 266i, 267-273, 274-293p, Annual 17, 19; c-211-214p, 220p, 232-236p, 237, 238p, 239, 240-242p, 243-249, 250p, 251-267, 269-277, 278-281p, 283p, 284, 285, 286p, 288-293, Annual 17.* ***Ditko*** *a-13i, 14i(w/**Kirby**-p), Annual 16.* ***G. Kane*** *c-150p, 160p.* ***Kirby*** *a-1-102p, 108, 180r, 189r, 236p, Special 1-10; c-1-101, 164, 167, 171-177, 180, 181, 190, 200, Annual 11, Special 1-7, 9.* ***Marcos*** *a-Annual 14i.* ***Mooney*** *a-118i, 152i.* ***Perez*** *a(p)-164-167, 170-172, 176-178, 184-188, 191p, 192p. Annual 14p, 15p; c(p)-183-188, 191, 192, 194-197.* ***Simonson*** *a-337-341, 343, 344p, 345p, 346, 350p, 353, 354; c-212, 334-341, 342p, 343-346, 350, 353, 354.* ***Steranko*** *c-130-132p.* ***Williamson*** *c-357i.*

FANTASTIC FOUR INDEX (See Official...)

FANTASTIC FOUR ROAST
May, 1982 (75¢, one shot, direct sale only)
Marvel Comics Group

1-Celebrates 20th anniversary of F.F.#1; X-Men, Ghost Rider & many others cameo; Golden, Miller, Buscema, Rogers, Byrne, Anderson art; Hembeck/Austin-c 1.60 4.00

FANTASTIC FOUR UNLIMITED
Mar, 1993 - Present ($3.95, 68 pgs.)
Marvel Comics

1-11: 1-Black Panther app. 4-Thing vs. Hulk. 5-Vs. The Frightful Four. 6-Vs. Namor. 7-Wraparound-c 1.60 4.00

FANTASTIC FOUR VS. X-MEN
Feb, 1987 - No. 4, June, 1987 (Mini-series)
Marvel Comics

1 1.20 3.00
2-4: 4-Austin-a(i) .80 2.00

FANTASTIC GIANTS (Formerly Konga #1-23)
V2#24, September, 1966 (25¢, 68 pgs.)
Charlton Comics

V2#24-Special Ditko issue; origin Konga & Gorgo reprinted plus two new Ditko stories 6.70 20.00 40.00

FANTASTIC TALES
1958 (no date) (Reprint)
I. W. Enterprises

1-Reprints Avon's "City of the Living Dead" 3.20 8.00 16.00

FANTASTIC VOYAGE (See Movie Comics)
Aug, 1969 - No. 2, Dec, 1969
Gold Key

1,2 (TV) 2.60 7.70 18.00

FANTASTIC VOYAGES OF SINDBAD, THE
Oct, 1965 - No. 2, June, 1967
Gold Key

1,2-Painted-c 4.20 12.50 25.00

FANTASTIC WORLDS
No. 5, Sept, 1952 - No. 7, Jan, 1953
Standard Comics

5-Toth, Anderson-a 19.00 58.00 135.00
6-Toth-c/a 17.00 52.00 120.00
7 10.00 30.00 70.00

FANTASY FEATURES (Americomics)(Value: cover or less)

FANTASY MASTERPIECES (Marvel Super Heroes No. 12 on)
Feb, 1966 - No. 11, Oct, 1967; V2#1, Dec, 1979 - No. 14, Jan, 1981
Marvel Comics Group

1-Photo of Stan Lee (12¢-c #1,2) 4.60 143.00 32.00
2-r/1st Fin Fang Foom from Strange Tales #89 1.70 4.30 12.00
3-8: 3-G.A. Capt. America-r begin, end #11; 1st 25¢ Giant; Colan-r. 3-6-Kirby-c (p). 4-Kirby-c(p)(i). 7-Begin G.A. Sub-Mariner, Torch-r/M. Mystery. 8-Torch battles the Sub-Mariner-r/Marvel Mystery #9 1.90 6.00 13.00
9-Origin Human Torch-r/Marvel Comics #1 2.30 6.90 16.00
10,11: 10-r/origin & 1st app. All Winners Squad from All Winners #19. 11-r/origin of Toro (H.T. #1) & Black Knight #1 1.70 5.00 12.00
V2#1(12/79, 75¢, 52 pgs.)-r/origin Silver Surfer from Silver Surfer #1 with editing plus reprints cover; J. Buscema-a 1.90 4.75
2-14-Reprints Silver Surfer #2-14 w/covers 1.50 3.75

NOTE: ***Buscema*** *c-V2#7-9(in part).* ***Ditko*** *r-1-3, 7, 9.* ***Everett*** *r-1,7-9.* ***Matt Fox*** *r-9i.* ***Kirby*** *r-1-11; c(p)-3, 4i, 5, 6.* ***Starlin*** *r-8-13. Some direct sale V2#14's had a 50¢ cover price. #3-11 contain Capt. America-r/Capt. America #3-10. #7-11 contain G.A.Human Torch & Sub-Mariner-r.*

FANTASY QUARTERLY (Also see Elfquest)
Spring, 1978 (B&W) (2nd printing exist?)
Independent Publishers Syndicate

1-1st app. Elfquest; Dave Sim-a (6 pgs.) 5.00 15.00 35.00

FANTOMAN (Formerly Amazing Adventure Funnies)
No. 2, Aug, 1940 - No. 4, Dec, 1940
Centaur Publications

2-The Fantom of the Fair, The Arrow, Little Dynamite-r begin; origin The Ermine by Filchock; Fantoman app. in 2-4; Burgos, J. Cole, Ernst, Gustavson-a 100.00 300.00 700.00
3,4: Gustavson-r. 4-Red Blaze story 81.00 242.00 565.00

FARGO KID (Formerly Justice Traps the Guilty)(See Feature Comics #47
V11#3(#1), June-July, 1958 - V11#5, Oct-Nov, 1958
Prize Publications

V11#3(#1)-Origin Fargo Kid, Severin-c/a; Williamson-a(2); Heath-a

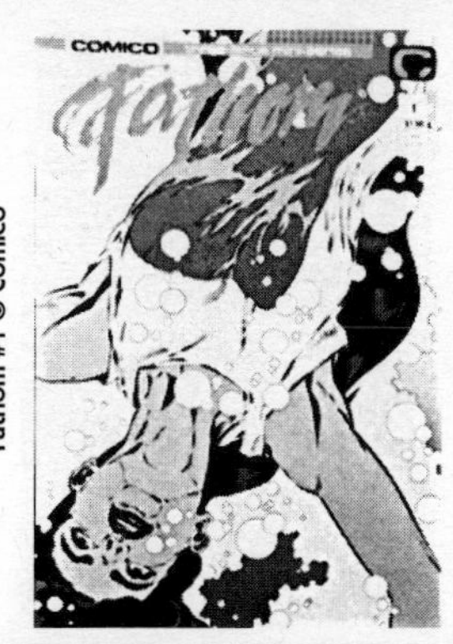

Fathom #1 © Comico

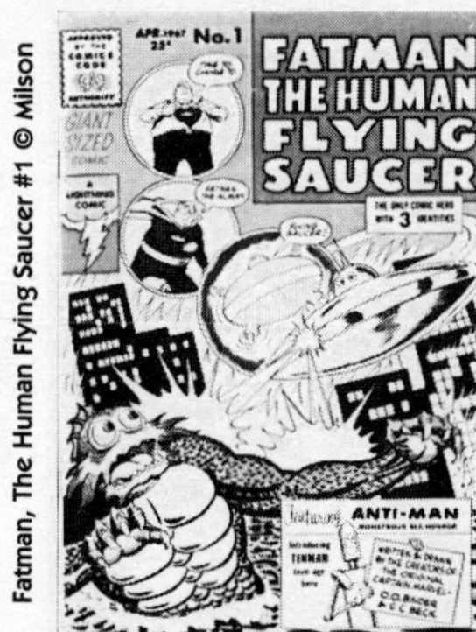

Fatman, The Human Flying Saucer #1 © Milson

Faust #10 © Tim Vigil

	GD25	FN65	NM94
	12.00	36.00	85.00
V11#4,5-Severin-c/a	10.00	30.00	60.00

FARMER'S DAUGHTER, THE
Feb-Mar, 1954 - No. 3, June-July, 1954; No. 4, Oct, 1954
Stanhall Publ./Trojan Magazines

	GD25	FN65	NM94
1-Lingerie, nudity panel	12.00	36.00	85.00
2-4(Stanhall)	10.00	30.00	60.00

FASHION IN ACTION (Eclipse)(Value: cover or less)

FASTEST GUN ALIVE, THE (See 4-Color No. 741)

FAST FICTION (...Action) (Stories by Famous Authors Illustrated #6 on)
Oct, 1949 - No. 5, Mar, 1950 (All have Kiefer-c)(48 pgs.)
Seaboard Publ./Famous Authors Ill.

	GD25	FN65	NM94
1-Scarlet Pimpernel; Jim Lavery-c/a	29.00	86.00	200.00
2-Captain Blood; H. C. Kiefer-c/a	26.00	78.00	180.00
3-She, by Rider Haggard; Vincent Napoli-a	34.00	100.00	235.00
4-(1/50, 52 pgs.)-The 39 Steps; Lavery-c/a	21.00	63.00	145.00
5-Beau Geste; Kiefer-c/a	21.00	63.00	145.00

NOTE: ***Kiefer** a-2, 5; c-2, 3,5. **Lavery** c/a-1, 4. **Napoli** a-3.*

FAST FORWARD
1992 - No. 3, 1993 ($4.95, 68 pgs.)
Piranha Press (DC)

	GD25	FN65	NM94
1-3: 1-Morrison script/McKean-c/a. 3-Sam Kieth-a	1.00	2.00	5.00

FAST WILLIE JACKSON
October, 1976 - No. 7, 1977
Fitzgerald Periodicals, Inc.

	GD25	FN65	NM94
1-7			1.00

FAT ALBERT (...& the Cosby Kids) (TV)
March, 1974 - No. 29, Feb, 1979
Gold Key

	GD25	FN65	NM94
1		1.20	3.00
2-29			1.00

FAT AND SLAT (Ed Wheelan) (Becomes Gunfighter No. 5 on)
Summer, 1947 - No. 4, Spring, 1948
E. C. Comics

	GD25	FN65	NM94
1-Intro/origin Voltage, Man of Lightning; "Comics" McCormick, the World's No. 1 Comic Book Fan begins, ends #4	24.00	72.00	165.00
2-4: 4-Comics McCormick-c feature	17.00	52.00	120.00

FAT AND SLAT JOKE BOOK
Summer, 1944 (One Shot, 52 pgs.)
All-American Comics (William H. Wise)

	GD25	FN65	NM94
nn-by Ed Wheelan	19.00	57.00	130.00

FATE (See Hand of Fate & Thrill-O-Rama)

FATHER OF CHARITY
No date (32 pgs.; paper cover)
Catechetical Guild Giveaway

	GD25	FN65	NM94
nn	2.50	5.00	10.00

FATHOM (Comico)(Value: cover or less)

FATIMA...CHALLENGE TO THE WORLD
1951, 36 pgs. (15¢ cover)
Catechetical Guild

	GD25	FN65	NM94
nn (not same as 'Challenge to the World')	2.40	6.00	12.00

FATMAN, THE HUMAN FLYING SAUCER
April, 1967 - No. 3, Aug-Sept, 1967 (68 pgs.)
Lightning Comics(Milson Publ. Co.) (Written by Otto Binder)

	GD25	FN65	NM94
1-Origin/1st app. Fatman & Tinman by Beck	5.30	16.00	37.00
2-C. C. Beck-a	3.60	11.00	25.00
3-(Scarce)-Beck-a	6.00	18.00	42.00

FAUNTLEROY COMICS (Super Duck Presents...)
1950 - No. 3, 1952
Close-Up/Archie Publications

	GD25	FN65	NM94
1-Super Duck-c/stories by Al Fagaly in all	6.70	20.00	40.00
2,3	4.20	12.50	25.00

FAUST
1989?(nd) - No. 12 (B&W; 1,2: $2.00, 3-on: $2.25; adults, violent)
Northstar Publishing/Rebel Studios #7 on

	GD25	FN65	NM94
1-Decapitation-c; Tim Vigil-c/a in all	5.00	15.00	35.00
1-2nd printing	1.60	5.00	11.00
1-3rd printing		1.00	2.50
2	3.60	10.50	25.00
2-2nd & 3rd printings		1.00	2.50
3-Begin $2.25-c	2.10	6.40	15.00
3-2nd printing		1.00	2.50
4	1.10	3.00	6.50
5-10		1.10	2.75

FAVORITE COMICS (Also see Famous Comics)
1934 (36 pgs.)
Grocery Store Giveaway (Diff. Corp.) (detergent)

	GD25	FN65	NM94
Book 1-The Nebbs, Strange As It Seems, Napoleon, Joe Palooka, Dixie Dugan, S'Matter Pop, Hairbreadth Harry, etc. reprints	54.00	160.00	375.00
Book 2,3	41.00	122.00	285.00

FAWCETT MINIATURES (See Mighty Midget)
1946 (12-24 pgs.; 3-3/4x5") (Wheaties giveaways)
Fawcett Publications

	GD25	FN65	NM94
Captain Marvel "And the Horn of Plenty"; Bulletman story	9.15	27.50	55.00
Captain Marvel "& the Raiders From Space"; Golden Arrow story	9.15	27.50	55.00
Captain Marvel Jr. "The Case of the Poison Press!" Bulletman story	9.15	27.50	55.00
Delecta of the Planets; C. C. Beck art; B&W inside; 12 pgs.; 3 printing variations (coloring) exist	17.00	52.00	120.00

FAWCETT MOTION PICTURE COMICS (See Motion Picture Comics)

FAWCETT MOVIE COMIC
1949 - No. 20, Dec, 1952 (All photo-c)
Fawcett Publications

	GD25	FN65	NM94
nn- "Dakota Lil"; George Montgomery & Rod Cameron (1949)	27.00	80.00	185.00
nn- "Copper Canyon"; Ray Milland & Hedy Lamarr (1950)	20.00	60.00	140.00
nn- "Destination Moon" (1950)	57.00	171.00	400.00
nn- "Montana"; Errol Flynn & Alexis Smith (1950)	20.00	60.00	140.00
nn- "Pioneer Marshal"; Monte Hale (1950)	20.00	60.00	140.00
nn- "Powder River Rustlers"; Rocky Lane (1950)	23.00	70.00	160.00
nn- "Singing Guns"; Vaughn Monroe, Ella Raines & Walter Brennan (1950)	18.00	54.00	125.00
7- "Gunmen of Abilene"; Rocky Lane; Bob Powell-a (1950)	23.00	70.00	160.00
8- "King of the Bullwhip"; Lash LaRue; Bob Powell-a (1950)	35.00	105.00	245.00
9- "The Old Frontier"; Monte Hale; Bob Powell-a(2/51; mis-dated 2/50)	22.00	65.00	150.00
10- "The Missourians"; Monte Hale (4/51)	22.00	65.00	150.00
11- "The Thundering Trail"; Lash LaRue (6/51)	29.00	86.00	200.00
12- "Rustlers on Horseback"; Rocky Lane (8/51)	23.00	70.00	160.00
13- "Warpath"; Edmond O'Brien & Forrest Tucker (10/51)	15.00	45.00	105.00
14- "Last Outpost"; Ronald Reagan (12/51)	36.00	109.00	255.00
15-(Scarce)- "The Man From Planet X"; Robert Clark; Shaffenberger-a (2/52)	157.00	471.00	1100.00
16- "10 Tall Men"; Burt Lancaster	11.50	34.00	80.00
17- "Rose of Cimarron"; Jack Buetel & Mala Powers	10.00	30.00	60.00

F.B.I. #1 © DELL

Feature Books #125 © DMP

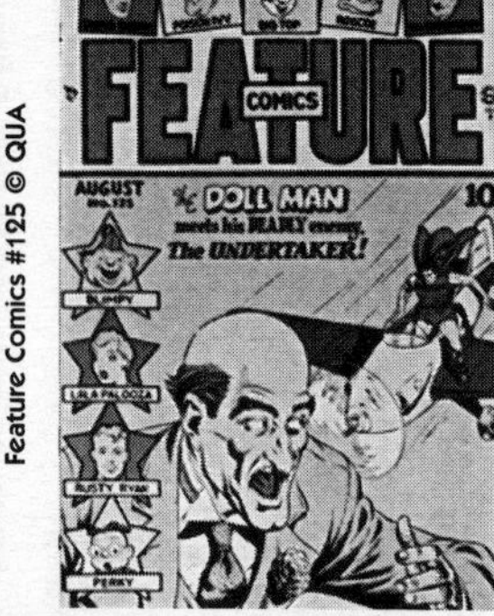

Feature Comics #125 © QUA

GD25 FN65 NM94

18- "The Brigand"; Anthony Dexter & Anthony Quinn; Shaffenberger-a
10.00 30.00 60.00
19- "Carbine Williams"; James Stewart; Costanza-a; James Stewart photo-c
10.00 30.00 70.00
20- "Ivanhoe"; Robert Taylor & Liz Taylor photo-c 15.00 45.00 105.00

FAWCETT'S FUNNY ANIMALS (No. 1-26, 80-on titled "Funny Animals"; becomes Li'l Tomboy No. 92 on?)
12/42 - #79, 4/53; #80, 6/53 - #83, 12?/53; #84, 4/54 - #91, 2/56
Fawcett Publications/Charlton Comics No. 84 on

1-Capt. Marvel on cover; intro. Hoppy The Captain Marvel Bunny, cloned from Capt. Marvel; Billy the Kid & Willie the Worm begin
46.00 139.00 325.00
2-Xmas-c 24.00 72.00 165.00
3-5: 3-Spirit of '43-c 14.00 43.00 100.00
6,7,9,10 10.00 30.00 65.00
8-Flag-c 10.00 30.00 70.00
11-20: 14-Cover is a 1944 calendar 7.50 22.50 45.00
21-40: 25-Xmas-c. 26-St. Valentines Day-c 5.00 15.00 30.00
41-87,90,91 4.00 11.00 22.00
87-89(10-54-2/55)-Merry Mailman ish (TV/Radio)-part photo-c
5.00 15.00 30.00

NOTE: *Marvel Bunny in all issues to at least No. 68 (not in 49-54).*

FAZE ONE FAZERS (Americomics)(Value: cover or less)

F.B.I., THE
April-June, 1965
Dell Publishing Co.

1-Sinnott-a 2.80 7.00 14.00

F.B.I. STORY, THE (See 4-Color No. 1069)

FEAR (Adventure into...)
Nov, 1970 - No. 31, Dec, 1975 (No.1-6: Giant Size)
Marvel Comics Group

1-Fantasy & Sci-Fi reprints in early issues 1.50 3.80 9.00
2-6 .90 2.00 5.50
7-9 1.30 3.25
10-Man-Thing begins (10/72, early app.), ends #19; see Savage Tales #1 for 1st app.; Chaykin/Morrow-c/a 1.50 3.80 9.00
11,12: 11-N. Adams-c. 12-Starlin/Buckler-a 1.70 4.25
13,14,16-18: 17-Origin/1st app. Wundarr 1.30 3.25
15-1st full-length Man-Thing story (8/73) 1.70 4.25
19-Intro. Howard the Duck; Val Mayerik-a (12/73) 2.40 7.25 17.00
20-Morbius, the Living Vampire begins, ends #31; has history recap of Morbius with X-Men & Spider-Man 3.10 9.00 22.00
21-25 2.00 5.00 12.00
26-31 1.50 3.80 9.00

NOTE: ***Bolle** a-13i. **Brunner** c-15-17. **Buckler** a-11p, 12i. **Chaykin** a-10i. **Colan** a-23r. **Craig** a-10p. **Ditko** a-6-8r. **Evans** a-30. **Everett** a-9, 10i, 21r. **Gulacy** a-20p. **Gil Kane** a-21p; c(p)-20, 21, 23-28, 31. **Kirby** a-8r, 9r. **Maneely** a-24r. **Mooney** a-11i, 26r. **Morrow** a-11i. **Paul Reinman** a-14r. **Robbins** a(p)-25-27, 31. **Russell** a-23p, 24p. **Severin** c-8. **Starlin** c-12p.*

FEARBOOK (Eclipse)(Value: cover or less)

FEAR IN THE NIGHT (See Complete Mystery No. 3)

FEARLESS FAGAN (See 4-Color No. 441)

FEATURE BOOK (Dell) (See Large Feature Comic)

FEATURE BOOKS (Newspaper-r, early issues)
May, 1937 - No. 57, 1948 (B&W; Full color, 68 pgs. begin #26 on)
David McKay Publications

GD25 FN65 VF82

nn-Popeye & the Jeep (#1, 100 pgs.); reprinted as Feature Books #3 (Very Rare; only 3 known copies, 1-VF, 2-in low grade)
Estimated value.... 500.00 1500.00 5000.00
nn-Dick Tracy (#1)-Reprinted as Feature Book #4 (100 pgs.) & in part as 4-Color #1 (Rare, less than 10 known copies)
Estimated value.... 500.00 1500.00 5000.00

NOTE: *Above books were advertised together with different covers from Feat. Books #3 & 4.*

GD25 FN65 NM94

1-King of the Royal Mtd. (#1) 55.00 165.00 550.00
2-Popeye (6/37) by Segar 55.00 165.00 550.00
3-Popeye (7/37) by Segar; same as nn issue but a new cover added
50.00 150.00 500.00
4-Dick Tracy (8/37)-Same as nn issue but a new cover added
80.00 240.00 800.00
5-Popeye (9/37) by Segar 45.00 135.00 450.00
6-Dick Tracy (10/37) 65.00 195.00 650.00
7-Little Orphan Annie (#1, 11/37) (Rare)-Reprints strips from 12/31/34 to 7/17/35 75.00 225.00 750.00
8-Secret Agent X-9 (12/37)-Not by Raymond 30.00 90.00 300.00
9-Dick Tracy (1/38) 65.00 195.00 650.00
10-Popeye (2/38) 45.00 135.00 450.00
11-Little Annie Rooney (#1, 3/38) 20.00 60.00 200.00
12-Blondie (#1) (4/38) (Rare) 45.00 135.00 450.00
13-Inspector Wade (5/38) 15.00 45.00 150.00
14-Popeye (6/38) by Segar (Scarce) 55.00 165.00 550.00
15-Barney Baxter (#1) (7/38) 20.00 60.00 200.00
16-Red Eagle (8/38) 15.00 45.00 150.00
17-Gangbusters (#1, 9/38) (1st app.) 40.00 120.00 400.00
18,19-Mandrake 30.00 90.00 300.00
20-Phantom (#1, 12/38) 55.00 165.00 550.00
21-Lone Ranger 50.00 150.00 500.00
22-Phantom 45.00 135.00 450.00
23-Mandrake 30.00 90.00 300.00
24-Lone Ranger (1941) 50.00 150.00 500.00
25-Flash Gordon (#1)-Reprints not by Raymond 55.00 165.00 550.00
26-Prince Valiant (1941)-Harold Foster-c/a; newspaper strips reprinted, pgs. 1-28,30-63; color & 68 pg. issues begin; Foster cover is only original comic book artwork by him 86.00 257.00 600.00
27-29,31,34-Blondie 13.00 40.00 90.00
30-Katzenjammer Kids (#1, 1942) 13.00 40.00 90.00
32,35,41,44-Katzenjammer Kids 11.50 34.00 80.00
33(nn)-Romance of Flying; World War II photos 11.00 32.00 75.00
36('43),38,40('44),42,43,45,47-Blondie 11.50 34.00 80.00
37-Katzenjammer Kids; has photo & biog. of Harold H. Knerr(1883-1949) who took over strip from Rudolph Dirks in 1914 13.00 40.00 90.00
39-Phantom 43.00 130.00 300.00
46-Mandrake in the Fire World-(58 pgs.) 29.00 86.00 200.00
48-Maltese Falcon by Dashiell Hammett('46) 57.00 171.00 400.00
49,50-Perry Mason; based on Gardner novels 19.00 57.00 130.00
51,54-Rip Kirby; Raymond-c/s; origin-#51 27.00 81.00 190.00
52,55-Mandrake 25.00 75.00 175.00
53,56,57-Phantom 31.00 94.00 220.00

NOTE: *All Feature Books through #25 are over-sized 8-1/2x11-3/8" comics with color covers and black and white interiors. The covers are rough, heavy stock. The page counts, including covers, are as follows: nn, #3, 4-100 pgs.; #1, 2-52 pgs.; #5-25 are all 76 pgs. #33 was found in bound set from publisher.*

FEATURE COMICS (Formerly Feature Funnies)
No. 21, June, 1939 - No. 144, May, 1950
Quality Comics Group

21-The Clock, Jane Arden & Mickey Finn continue from Feature Funnies
43.00 130.00 300.00
22-26: 23-Charlie Chan begins (8/39, 1st app.) 30.00 90.00 210.00
26-(nn, nd)-Cover in one color, (10¢, 36 pgs.; issue No. blanked out. Two variations exist, each contain half of the regular #26) 9.15 27.50 55.00
27-(Rare)-Origin/1st app. Doll Man by Eisner (scripts) & Lou Fine (art); Doll Man begins, ends #139 243.00 730.00 1700.00
28-2nd app. Doll Man by Lou Fine 100.00 300.00 700.00
29,30: 30-1st Doll Man-c 61.00 182.00 425.00
31-Last Clock & Charlie Chan issue (4/40); Charlie Chan moves to Big Shot #1 following month (5/40) 52.00 156.00 365.00
32-37: 32-Rusty Ryan & Samar begin. 34-Captain Fortune app. 37-Last Fine Doll Man 38.00 114.00 265.00
38-41: 38-Origin the Ace of Space. 39-Origin The Destroying Demon, ends #40; X-Mas-c. 40-Bruce Blackburn in costume 31.00 92.00 215.00

Feature Films #1 © DC

Felicia Hardy: The Black Cat #2 © MEG

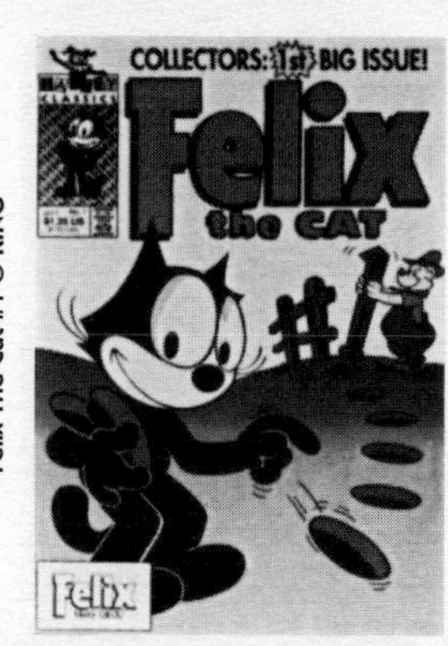

Felix The Cat #1 © KING

GD25 FN65 NM94

42,43,45-50: 42-USA, the Spirit of Old Glory begins. 46-Intro. Boyville Brigadiers in Rusty Ryan. 47-Fargo Kid begins. 48-USA ends 21.00 63.00 145.00
44-Doll Man by Crandall begins, ends #63; Crandall-a(2) 31.00 92.00 215.00
51-60: 56-Marijuana story in Swing Sisson strip. 57-Spider Widow begins. 60-Raven begins, ends #71 16.00 48.00 110.00
61-68 (5/43) 15.00 45.00 105.00
69,70-Phantom Lady x-over in Spider Widow 16.50 50.00 115.00
71-80,100: 71-Phantom Lady x-over. 72-Spider Widow ends 10.00 30.00 75.00
81-99 10.00 30.00 65.00
101-144: 139-Last Doll Man & last Doll Man-c. 140-Intro. Stuntman Stetson (Stuntman Stetson c-140-144) 8.35 25.00 50.00

NOTE: ***Celardo** a-37-43. **Crandall** a-44-60, 62, 63-on(most). **Gustavson** a-(Rusty Ryan)- 32-134. **Powell** a-34, 64-73. The Clock c-25, 28, 29. Doll Man c-30, 32, 34, 36, 38, 40, 42, 44, 46, 48, 50, 52, 54, 56, 58, 60, 62, 64, 66, 68, 70, 72, 74, 77-139. Joe Palooka c-21, 24, 27.*

FEATURE FILMS
Mar-Apr, 1950 - No. 4, Sept-Oct, 1950 (All photo-c)
National Periodical Publications

1- "Captain China" with John Payne, Gail Russell, Lon Chaney & Edgar Bergen 50.00 150.00 350.00
2- "Riding High" with Bing Crosby 57.00 171.00 400.00
3- "The Eagle & the Hawk" with John Payne, Rhonda Fleming & D. O'Keefe 50.00 150.00 350.00
4- "Fancy Pants"; Bob Hope & Lucille Ball 57.00 171.00 400.00

FEATURE FUNNIES (Feature Comics No. 21 on)
Oct, 1937 - No. 20, May, 1939
Harry 'A' Chesler

1(V9#1-indicia)-Joe Palooka, Mickey Finn (1st app.), The Bungles, Jane Arden, Dixie Dugan (1st app.), Big Top, Ned Brant, Strange As It Seems, & Off the Record strip reprints begin 200.00 600.00 1400.00
2-The Hawk app. (11/37); Goldberg-c 93.00 280.00 650.00
3-Hawks of Seas begins by Eisner, ends #12; The Clock begins; Christmas-c 68.00 205.00 475.00
4,5 50.00 150.00 350.00
6-12: 11-Archie O'Toole by Bud Thomas begins, ends #22 41.00 122.00 285.00
13-Espionage, Starring Black X begins by Eisner, ends #20 45.00 135.00 315.00
14-20 35.00 105.00 245.00

NOTE: *Joe Palooka covers 1, 6, 9, 12, 15, 18.*

FEATURE PRESENTATION, A (Feature Presentations Magazine #6) (Formerly Women in Love) (Also see Startling Terror Tales #11)
No. 5, April, 1950
Fox Features Syndicate

5(#1)-Black Tarantula 26.00 78.00 180.00

FEATURE PRESENTATIONS MAGAZINE (Formerly A Feature Presentation #5; becomes Feature Stories Magazine #3 on)
No. 6, July, 1950
Fox Features Syndicate

6(#2)-Moby Dick; Wood-c 20.00 60.00 140.00

FEATURE STORIES MAGAZINE (Formerly Feature Presentations Mag. #6)
No. 3, Aug, 1950 - No. 4, Oct, 1950
Fox Features Syndicate

3-Jungle Lil, Zegra stories; bondage-c 18.00 54.00 125.00
4 13.50 41.00 95.00

FEDERAL MEN COMICS (See Adventure Comics #32, The Comics Magazine, New Adventure Comics, New Book of Comics, New Comics & Star Spangled Comics #91)
No. 2, 1945 (DC reprints from 1930's)
Gerard Publ. Co.

2-Siegel & Shuster-a; cover redrawn from Detective #9; spanking panel 21.00 63.00 145.00

FELICIA HARDY: THE BLACK CAT
July, 1994 - No. 4, Oct, 1994 ($1.50, mini-series)
Marvel Comics

1-4: 1,4-Spider-Man app. 1.50

FELIX
1931 (52 pgs., hardcover, full color, 6-1/2"x8-1/4", with dust jacket)
Henry Altemus Company

1-3-Sunday strip reprints of Felix the Cat by Otto Messmer. Book No. 2 r/1931 Sunday panels mostly two to a page in a continuity format oddly arranged so each tier of panels reads across two pages, then drops to the next tier. (Books 1 & 3 have not been documented.)(Rare)
Each 50.00 150.00 350.00
Dust jacket only 20.00 60.00 135.00

FELIX'S NEPHEWS INKY & DINKY
Sept, 1957 - No. 7, Oct, 1958
Harvey Publications

1-Cover shows Inky's left eye with 2 pupils 8.35 25.00 50.00
2-7 4.00 11.00 22.00

NOTE: ***Messmer** art in 1-6. **Oriolo** a-1-7.*

FELIX THE CAT (See Cat Tales 3-D, The Funnies, March of Comics #24,36, 51, New Funnies & Popular Comics)
1943 - No. 118, Nov, 1961; Sept-Nov, 1962 - No. 12, July-Sept, 1965
Dell Publ. No. 1-19/Toby No. 20-61/Harvey No. 62-118/Dell No. 1-12

4-Color 15 71.00 215.00 500.00
4-Color 46('44) 43.00 130.00 300.00
4-Color 77('45) 40.00 120.00 280.00
4-Color 119('46)-All new stories begin 34.00 100.00 235.00
4-Color 135('46) 25.00 75.00 175.00
4-Color 162(9/47) 19.00 57.00 130.00
1(2-3/48)(Dell) 25.00 75.00 175.00
2 13.00 40.00 90.00
3-5 11.00 32.00 70.00
6-19(2-3/51-Dell) 8.35 25.00 50.00
20-31,32,33,36-61(6/55)-All Messmer issues.(Toby): 28-(2/52)-Some copies have #29 on cover, #28 on inside (Rare in high grade) 15.00 45.00 150.00
31,34,35-No Messmer-a; Messmer-c only 5.00 15.00 45.00
62(8/55)-100 (Harvey) 3.20 8.00 16.00
101-118(11/61): 101-117-Reprints. 118-All new-a 2.80 7.00 14.00
12-269-211(#1, 9-11/62)(Dell) 4.00 12.00 24.00
2-12(7-9/65)(Dell, TV) 3.20 8.00 16.00
3-D Comic Book 1(1953-One Shot, 25¢)-w/glasses 32.00 96.00 225.00
Special nn ('52, 25¢, 100 pgs., Toby)-All new stories; X-Mas-c 33.00 100.00 300.00
Summer Annual nn ('53, 25¢, 100 pgs., Toby)-All new stories 33.00 100.00 300.00
Winter Annual 2 ('54, 25¢, 100 pgs., Toby)-1930s daily & Sunday-r 33.00 100.00 300.00

(Special note: Despite the covers on two above proclaiming "all new stories," they were merely reformatted newspaper reprints)

NOTE: ***Otto Messmer** went to work for Universal Film as an animater in 1915 and then worked for the Pat Sullivan animation studio in 1916. He created a black cat in the cartoon short, Feline Follies in 1919 that became known as Felix in the early 1920s. The Felix Sunday strip began Aug. 14, 1923 and continued until Sept. 19, 1943 whjen **Messmer** took the character to Dell (Western Publishing) and began doing Felix comic books, first adapting strips to the comic format. The first all new Felix comic was Four Color #119 in 1946 (#4 in the Dell run). The daily Felix was begun on May 9, 1927 by another artist, but by the following year, **Messmer** did it too. King Features took the daily away from **Messmer** in 1954 and he began to do some of his most dynamic art for Toby Press. The daily was continued by **Joe Oriolo** who drew it until it was discontinued Jan. 9, 1967. **Oriolo** was **Messmer's** assistant for many years and inked some of **Messmer's** pencils through the Toby run, as well as doing some of the stories by himself. Though **Messmer** continued to work for Harvey, his contirubitons were limited, and no all **Messmer** stories appeared after the Toby run until some early Toby reprints were published in the 1990s Harvey revival of the title. 4-Color No. 15, 46, 77 and the Toby Annuals are all daily or Sunday newspaper reprints from the 1930's drawn by **Otto Messmer**. #101-r/#64; 102-r/#65; 103-r/#67; 104-117-r/#68-81. **Messmer**-a in all Dell/Toby/Harvey issues except #31, 34, 35, 97,*

Femforce #32 © Aircel

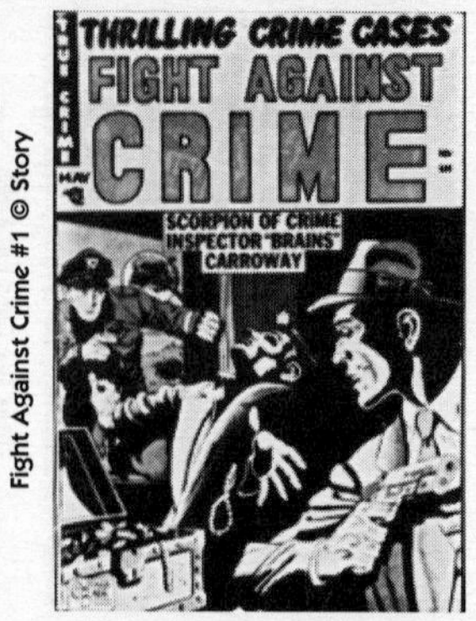

Fight Against Crime #1 © Story

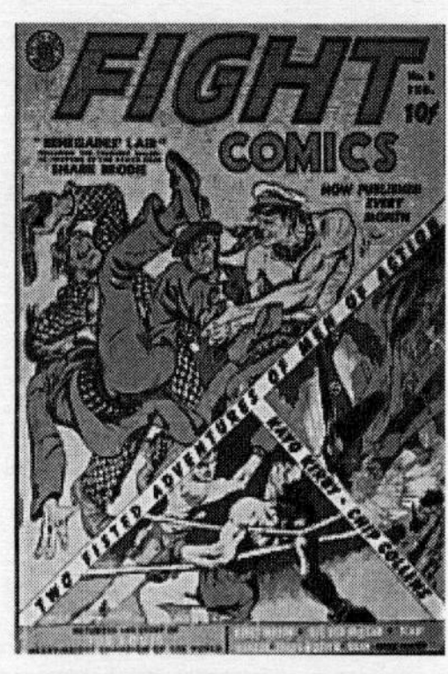

Fight Comics #2 © FH

*98, 100, 118. **Oriolo** a-20, 31-on.*

FELIX THE CAT (Also see The Nine Lives of...)
Sept, 1991 - No. 7, Jan, 1993 ($1.25/$1.50, bi-monthly)
Harvey Comics/Gladstone

1-5: Reprints 1950s Toby issues by Messmer. 1-Inky and Dinky back-up story (produced by Gladstone) 1.25
6,7-($1.50-c) 1.50
Big Book V2#1 (9/92, $1.95, 52 pgs.) .80 2.00

FELIX THE CAT AND FRIENDS
1992 - Present? ($1.95)
Felix Comics

1-4: 1-Contains Felix trading cards .80 2.00

FELIX THE CAT & HIS FRIENDS (Pat Sullivan's...)
Dec, 1953 - No. 3, 1954 (Indicia title for #2&3 as listed)
Toby Press

1 (Indicia title, "Felix and His Friends," #1 only) 15.00 45.00 150.00
2-3 10.00 30.00 100.00

FELIX THE CAT BOOK
1927 (52pgs., 8"x15-3/4", 1/2 in color, 1/2 in B&W)
McLoughlin Bros. **GD FN VF NM**

nn-Reprints 23 Sunday strips by Otto Messmer from 1926 & 1927, every other one in color, two pages per strip. (Rare)
80.00 240.00 520.00 800.00
260-Reissued (1931), reformatted to 9-1/2"x10-1/4" (same color plates, but one strip per every three pages), retitled ("Book" dropped from title) and abridged (only eight strips repeated from first issue, 28 pgs.).(Rare)
40.00 120.00 260.00 400.00

FELIX THE CAT DIGEST MAGAZINE
July, 1992 ($1.75, digest-size, 98 pgs.)
Harvey Comics **GD FN NM**

1-Felix, Richie Rich stories .70 1.75

FELIX THE CAT KEEPS ON WALKIN'
1991, ($15.95, color, 8-1/2"x11", 132 pgs.)
Hamilton Comics

nn-Reprints 15 Toby Press Felix the Cat and Felix and His Friends stories in new computer color 2.30 6.90 16.00

FEM FANTASTIQUE (AC)(Value: cover or less)

FEMFORCE (Also see Untold Origin of the Femforce)
Apr, 1985 - Present? ($1.75/1.95/2.25; in color; B&W #16-56)
Americomics

1-Black-a in most; Nightveil, Ms. Victory begin 1.00 2.00 5.00
2 1.30 3.25
3-30: 12-15-$1.95-c. 16-19-$2.25-c. 20-Begin $2.50-c, 44 pgs. 25-Origin/1st app. new Ms. Victory. 28-Colt leaves. 29,30-Camilla-r by Mayo from Jungle Comics 1.10 2.75
31-35,37-49,51-62: 31-Begin $2.75-c. 44-Contains mini-comic insert, Catman & Kitten #0. 51-Photo-c from movie. 57-Begin color issues
1.00 2.50
36-($2.95, 52 pgs.) 1.00 2.50
50-($2.95, 52 pgs.)-Contains flexi-disc; origin retold; most AC characters app. 1.00 2.50
63-68 ($2.95-c): 64-Re-intro Black Phantom 1.00 2.50
Special 1 (Fall, '84)(B&W, 52pgs.)-1st app. Ms. Victory, She-Cat, Blue Bulleteer, Rio Rita & Lady Luger .80 2.00
Frightbook 1 ('92, $2.95, B&W)-Halloween special 1.20 3.00
In the House of Horror 1 ('89, $2.50, B&W) 1.00 2.50
Night of the Demon 1 ('90, $2.75, B&W) 1.10 2.75
Out of the Asylum Special 1 ('87, B&W, $1.95) .80 2.00
Pin-Up Portfolio .80 2.00

FEMFORCE UP CLOSE
Apr, 1992 - Present ($2.75, color, quarterly)
AC Comics

1-4: 1-Stars Nightveil; inside f/c photo from Femforce movie. 2-Stars Stardust. 3-Stars Dragonfly. 4-Stars She-Cat 1.10 2.75

FERDINAND THE BULL (See Mickey Mouse Magazine V4#3)
1938 (10¢)(Large size; some color, rest B&W)
Dell Publishing Co.

nn 14.00 43.00 100.00

FERRET
Sept, 1992; May, 1993 - No. 10, Feb, 1994 ($1.95)
Malibu Comics

1-(1992, one-shot) .80 2.00
1-($2.50)-Completely die-cut cover 1.00 2.50
2-4-($2.50)-Collector's Edition w/poster 1.00 2.50
2-4-($1.95)-Newsstand Edition w/different-c .80 2.00
5-8-($2.25): 5-Polybagged w/Skycap .90 2.25
9,10: 9-Begin $2.50-c 1.00 2.50

FEUD
July, 1993 - No. 4, Oct, 1993 ($1.95, mini-series)
Epic Comics (Marvel)

1-($2.50)-Embossed-c 1.00 2.50
2-4 .80 2.00

FIBBER McGEE & MOLLY (See A-1 Comics No. 25)

55 DAYS AT PEKING (See Movie Comics)

FIGHT AGAINST CRIME (Fight Against the Guilty #22, 23)
May, 1951 - No. 21, Sept, 1954
Story Comics

1-True crime stories #1-4 18.00 54.00 125.00
2 9.15 27.50 55.00
3,5: 5-Frazetta-a, 1 pg.; content change to horror & suspense
7.50 22.50 45.00
4-Drug story "Hopped Up Killers" 9.15 27.50 55.00
6,7: 6-Used in **POP**, pgs. 83,84 6.70 20.00 40.00
8-Last crime format issue 6.70 20.00 40.00

NOTE: *No. 9-21 contain violent, gruesome stories with blood, dismemberment, decapitation, E.C. style plot twists and several E.C. swipes. Bondage c-4, 6, 18, 19.*

9-11,13 13.50 41.00 95.00
12-Morphine drug story "The Big Dope" 15.00 45.00 105.00
14-Tothish art by Ross Andru; electrocution-c 13.50 41.00 95.00
15-B&W & color illos in **POP** 13.00 40.00 90.00
16-E.C. story swipe/Haunt of Fear #19; Tothish-a by Ross Andru; bondage-c 15.00 45.00 105.00
17-Wildey E.C. swipe/Shock SuspenStories #9; knife through neck-c (1/54)
15.00 45.00 105.00
18,19: 19-Bondage/torture-c 13.00 40.00 90.00
20-Decapitation cover; contains hanging, ax murder, blood & violence
24.00 72.00 165.00
21-E.C. swipe 11.50 34.00 80.00

NOTE: ***Cameron** a-4, 5, 8. **Hollingsworth** a-3-7, 9, 10, 13. **Wildey** a-6, 15, 16.*

FIGHT AGAINST THE GUILTY (Formerly Fight Against Crime)
No. 22, Dec, 1954 - No. 23, Mar, 1955
Story Comics

22-Tothish-a by Ross Andru; Ditko-a; E.C. story swipe; electrocution-c (Last pre-code) 11.50 34.00 80.00
23-Hollingsworth-a 10.00 30.00 60.00

FIGHT COMICS
Jan, 1940 - No. 83, 11/52; No. 84, Wint, 1952-53; No. 85, Spring, 1953; No. 86, Summer, 1954
Fiction House Magazines

1-Origin Spy Fighter, Starring Saber; Jack Dempsey life story; Shark Brodie & Chip Collins begin; Fine/Eisner-c; Eisner-a 164.00 493.00 1150.00
2-Joe Louis life story 71.00 215.00 500.00
3-Rip Regan, the Power Man begins (3/40) 54.00 160.00 375.00

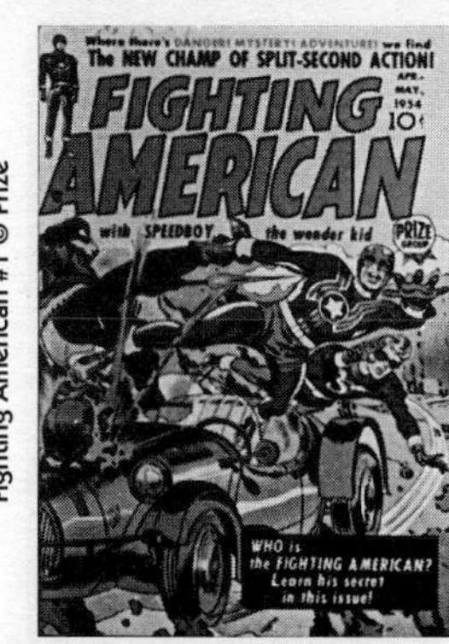

Fighting American #1 © Prize

Fighting American #6 © DC

Fighting Army #17 © CC

	GD25	FN65	NM94
4,5: 4-Fine-c	45.00	135.00	315.00
6-10: 6,7-Powell-c	36.00	107.00	250.00
11-14: Rip Regan ends	32.00	96.00	225.00
15-1st app. Super American plus-c (10/41)	45.00	135.00	315.00
16-Captain Fight begins (12/41); Spy Fighter ends	45.00	135.00	315.00
17,18: Super American ends	36.00	107.00	250.00
19-Captain Fight ends; Senorita Rio begins (6/42, origin & 1st app.); Rip Carson, Chute Trooper begins	36.00	107.00	250.00
20	29.00	86.00	200.00
21-30	18.00	54.00	125.00
31,33-50: 31-Decapitation-c. 44-Capt. Fight returns. 48-Used in Love and Death by Legman. 49-Jungle-c begin, end #81	16.00	48.00	110.00
32-Tiger Girl begins (6/44, 1st app.?)	17.00	52.00	120.00
51-Origin Tiger Girl; Patsy Pin-Up app.	25.00	75.00	175.00
52-60,62-64-Last Baker issue	12.00	36.00	85.00
61-Origin Tiger Girl retold	16.00	48.00	110.00
65-78: 78-Used in **POP**, pg. 99	11.50	34.00	80.00
79-The Space Rangers app.	11.50	34.00	80.00
80-85: 81-Last jungle-c. 82-85-War-c/stories	10.00	30.00	70.00
86-Two Tigerman stories by Evans-r/Rangers Comics #40,41; Moreira-r/Rangers Comics #45	10.00	30.00	70.00

NOTE: *Bondage covers, Lingerie, headlights panels are common. Captain Fight by* ***Kamen****-51-66. Kayo Kirby by* ***Baker****-#43-64, 67(not by Baker). Senorita Rio by* ***Kamen****-#57-64; by* ***Grandenetti****-#65, 66. Tiger Girl by* ***Baker****-#36-60, 62-64;* ***Eisner*** *c-1-3, 5, 10, 11.* ***Kamen*** *a-54?, 57?* ***Tuska*** *a-1, 5, 8, 10, 21, 29, 34.* ***Whitman*** *c-73-84.* ***Zolnerwich*** *c-16, 17, 22. Power Man c-5, 6, 9. Super American c-15-17. Tiger Girl c-49-81.*

FIGHT FOR FREEDOM
1949, 1951 (16 pgs.) (Giveaway)
National Association of Mfgrs./General Comics

	GD25	FN65	NM94
nn-Dan Barry-c/a; used in **POP**, pg. 102	5.00	15.00	30.00

FIGHT FOR LOVE
1952 (no month)
United Features Syndicate

	GD25	FN65	NM94
nn-Abbie & Slats newspaper-r	9.15	27.50	55.00

FIGHTING AIR FORCE (See United States Fighting Air Force)

FIGHTIN' AIR FORCE (Formerly Sherlock Holmes?; Never Again? War and Attack #54 on)
No. 3, Feb, 1956 - No. 53, Feb-Mar, 1966
Charlton Comics

	GD25	FN65	NM94
V1#3	4.20	12.50	25.00
4-10	2.80	7.00	14.00
11(3/58, 68 pgs.)	3.60	9.00	18.00
12 (100 pgs.)	4.00	11.00	22.00
13-30: 13,24-Glanzman-a. 24-Glanzman-c	2.40	6.00	12.00
31-50: 50-American Eagle begins	1.60	4.00	8.00
51-53	1.00	2.50	5.00

FIGHTING AMERICAN
Apr-May, 1954 - No. 7, Apr-May, 1955
Headline Publications/Prize (Crestwood)

	GD25	FN65	NM94
1-Origin & 1st app. Fighting American & Speedboy (Capt. America & Bucky clones); S&K-c/a(3); 1st super hero satire series	121.00	365.00	850.00
2-S&K-a(3)	61.00	182.00	425.00
3,4-S&K-a(3)	51.00	154.00	360.00
5-S&K-a(2); Kirby/?-a	51.00	154.00	360.00
6-Origin-r (4 pgs.) plus 2 pgs. by S&K	46.00	140.00	325.00
7-Kirby-a	43.00	130.00	300.00

NOTE: ***Simon*** *&* ***Kirby*** *covers on all. 6 is last pre-code issue.*

FIGHTING AMERICAN
October, 1966 (25¢)
Harvey Publications

	GD25	FN65	NM94
1-Origin Fighting American & Speedboy by S&K-r; S&K-c/a(3); 1 pg. Neal Adams ad	2.40	7.30	17.00

FIGHTING AMERICAN
Feb, 1994 - No. 6, 1994 ($1.50, limited series)
DC Comics

	GD25	FN65	NM94
1-6			1.50

FIGHTIN' ARMY (Formerly Soldier and Marine Comics; see Captain Willy Schultz)
No. 16, 1/56 - No. 127, 12/76; No. 128, 9/77 - No. 172, 11/84
Charlton Comics

	GD25	FN65	NM94
16	4.20	12.50	25.00
17-19,21-23,25-30	2.80	7.00	14.00
20-Ditko-a	4.00	11.00	22.00
24 (3/58, 68 pgs.)	3.20	8.00	16.00
31-45	2.40	6.00	12.00
46-60	1.60	4.00	8.00
61-80: 75-92-The Lonely War of Willy Schultz	1.00	2.00	5.00
81-172: 89,90,92-Ditko-a; Devil Brigade in #79,82,83		1.00	2.50
108(Modern Comics-1977)-Reprint			1.50

NOTE: ***Aparo*** *c-154.* ***Montes/Bache*** *a-48, 49, 51, 69, 75, 76, 170r.*

FIGHTING DANIEL BOONE
1953
Avon Periodicals

	GD25	FN65	NM94
nn-Kinstler-c/a, 22 pgs.	13.00	40.00	90.00
I.W. Reprint #1-Reprints #1 above; Kinstler-c/a; Lawrence/Alascia-a	2.00	5.00	10.00

FIGHTING DAVY CROCKETT (Formerly Kit Carson)
No. 9, Oct-Nov, 1955
Avon Periodicals

	GD25	FN65	NM94
9-Kinstler-c	6.70	20.00	40.00

FIGHTIN' FIVE, THE (Fightin' 5 #40 on?; formerly Space War; also see The Peacemaker)
July, 1964 - No. 41, Jan, 1967; No. 42, Oct, 1981 - No. 49, Dec, 1982
Charlton Comics

	GD25	FN65	NM94
V2#28-Origin & 1st app. Fightin' Five	3.00	9.00	21.00
29-39,41	2.00	5.00	12.00
40-Peacemaker begins (1st app.)	3.00	9.00	21.00
42-49: Reprints		.70	1.70

FIGHTING FRONTS!
Aug, 1952 - No. 5, Jan, 1953
Harvey Publications

	GD25	FN65	NM94
1	5.00	15.00	30.00
2-Extreme violence; Nostrand/Powell-a	5.85	17.50	35.00
3-5: 3-Powell-a	3.60	9.00	18.00

FIGHTING INDIAN STORIES (See Midget Comics)

FIGHTING INDIANS OF THE WILD WEST!
Mar, 1952 - No. 2, Nov, 1952
Avon Periodicals

	GD25	FN65	NM94
1-Geronimo, Chief Crazy Horse, Chief Victorio, Black Hawk begin; Larsen-a; McCann-a(2)	10.00	30.00	70.00
2-Kinstler-c & inside-c only; Larsen, McCann-a	7.50	22.50	45.00
100 Pg. Annual (1952, 25¢)-Contains three comics rebound; Geronimo, Chief Crazy Horse, Chief Victorio; Kinstler-c	20.00	60.00	140.00

FIGHTING LEATHERNECKS
Feb, 1952 - No. 6, Dec, 1952
Toby Press

	GD25	FN65	NM94
1- "Duke's Diary"; full pg. pin-ups by Sparling	10.00	30.00	65.00
2- "Duke's Diary"	7.50	22.50	45.00
3-5- "Gil's Gals"; full pg. pin-ups	7.50	22.50	45.00
6-(Same as No. 3-5?)	5.35	16.00	32.00

FIGHTING MAN, THE (War)
May, 1952 - No. 8, July, 1953
Ajax/Farrell Publications(Excellent Publ.)

Fighting Man #6 © Ajax

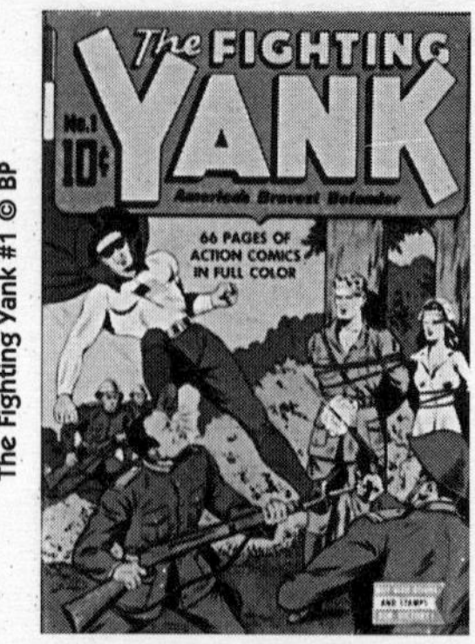

The Fighting Yank #1 © BP

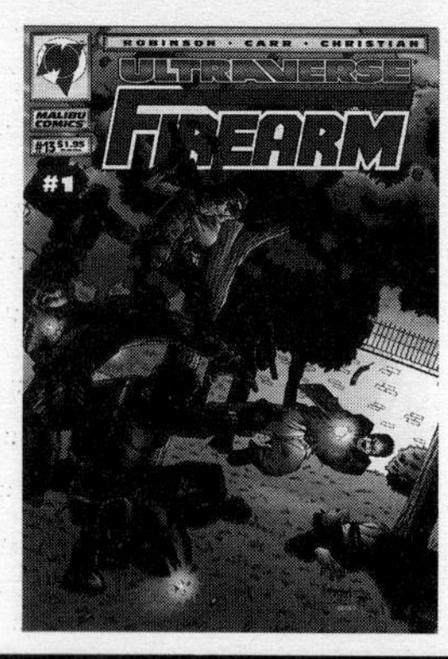

Firearm #13 © Malibu

	GD25	FN65	NM94
1	7.50	22.50	45.00
2	4.00	11.00	22.00
3-8	3.60	9.00	18.00
Annual 1 (1952, 25¢, 100 pgs.)	16.00	48.00	110.00

FIGHTIN' MARINES (Formerly The Texan; also see Approved Comics)
No. 15, 8/51 - No. 12, 3/53; No. 14, 5/55 - No. 132, 11/76;
No. 133, 10/77 - No. 176, 9/84 (No #13?) (Korean war #1-3)
St. John(Approved Comics)/Charlton Comics No. 14 on

	GD25	FN65	NM94
15(#1)-Matt Baker c/a "Leatherneck Jack"; slightly large size; Fightin' Texan No. 16 & 17?	19.00	57.00	130.00
2-1st Canteen Kate by Baker; slightly large size	21.00	63.00	145.00
3-9,11-Canteen Kate by Baker; Baker c-#2,3,5-11	11.00	32.00	75.00
10-Matt Baker-c	4.20	12.50	25.00
12-No Baker-a; Last St. John issue?	3.00	7.50	15.00
14 (5/55; 1st Charlton issue; formerly?)-Canteen Kate by Baker; all stories reprinted from #2	10.00	30.00	65.00
15-Baker-c	4.00	12.00	24.00
16,18-20-Not Baker-c	2.60	6.50	13.00
17-Canteen Kate by Baker	7.50	22.50	45.00
21-24	2.60	6.50	13.00
25-(68 pgs.)(3/58)-Check-a?	4.00	11.00	22.00
26-(100 pgs.)(8/58)-Check-a(5)	5.35	16.00	32.00
27-50	2.00	5.00	10.00
51-81,83-100: 78-Shotgun Harker & the Chicken series begin	1.00	2.00	5.00
82-(100 pgs.)	1.30	3.25	8.00
101-122: 122-Pilot issue for "War" title (Fightin' Marines Presents War)		1.20	3.00
123-176			1.50
120(Modern Comics reprint, 1977)			1.50

NOTE: *No. 14 & 16 (CC) reprint St. John issues; No. 16 reprints St. John insignia on cover.* ***Colan*** *a-3, 7.* ***Glanzman*** *c/a-92, 94.* ***Montes/Bache*** *a-48, 53, 55, 64, 65, 72-74, 77-83, 176r.*

FIGHTING MARSHAL OF THE WILD WEST (See The Hawk)

FIGHTIN' NAVY (Formerly Don Winslow)
No. 74, 1/56 - No. 125, 4-5/66; No. 126, 8/83 - No. 133, 10/84
Charlton Comics

	GD25	FN65	NM94
74	4.20	12.50	25.00
75-81	2.60	6.50	13.00
82-Sam Glanzman-a	1.80	4.50	9.00
83-99,101-105,106-125('66)	1.20	3.00	6.00
100	1.40	3.50	7.00
126-133 (1984)			1.50

NOTE: ***Montes/Bache*** *a-109.* ***Glanzman*** *a-82, 131r.*

FIGHTING PRINCE OF DONEGAL, THE (See Movie Comics)

FIGHTIN' TEXAN (Formerly The Texan & Fightin' Marines?)
No. 16, Oct, 1952 - No. 17, Dec, 1952
St. John Publishing Co.

	GD25	FN65	NM94
16,17-Tuska-a each. 17-Cameron-c/a	5.00	15.00	30.00

FIGHTING UNDERSEA COMMANDOS (See Undersea Fighting...)
May, 1952 - No. 5, April, 1953 (U.S. Navy frogmen)
Avon Periodicals

	GD25	FN65	NM94
1-Cover title is Undersea Fighting... #1 only	8.35	25.00	50.00
2	5.85	17.50	35.00
3-5: 1,3-Ravielli-c. 4-Kinstler-c	5.00	15.00	30.00

FIGHTING WAR STORIES
Aug, 1952 - No. 5, 1953
Men's Publications/Story Comics

	GD25	FN65	NM94
1	6.35	19.00	38.00
2-5	4.00	11.00	22.00

FIGHTING YANK (See America's Best Comics & Startling Comics)
Sept, 1942 - No. 29, Aug, 1949
Nedor/Better Publ./Standard

	GD25	FN65	NM94
1-The Fighting Yank begins; Mystico, the Wonder Man app; bondage-c	121.00	365.00	850.00
2	54.00	160.00	375.00
3	37.00	111.00	260.00
4	31.00	92.00	215.00
5-10: 7-Grim Reaper app. 8,10-Bondage/torture-c	25.00	75.00	175.00
11-20: 11-The Oracle app. 12-Hirohito bondage-c. 15-Bondage/torture-c. 18-The American Eagle app.	22.00	65.00	150.00
21,23,24: 21-Kara, Jungle Princess app. 24-Miss Masque app.	24.00	73.00	170.00
22-Miss Masque-c/story	31.00	92.00	215.00
25-Robinson/Meskin-a; strangulation, lingerie panel; The Cavalier app.	31.00	92.00	215.00
26-29: All-Robinson/Meskin-a. 28-One pg. Williamson-a	24.00	72.00	165.00

NOTE: ***Schomburg (Xela)*** *c-4-29; airbrush-c 28, 29. Bondage c-1, 4, 8, 10, 11, 12, 15, 17.*

FIGHTMAN
June, 1993 ($2.00, one-shot, 52 pgs.)
Marvel Comics

	GD25	FN65	NM94
1		.80	2.00

FIGHT THE ENEMY
Aug, 1966 - No. 3, Mar, 1967 (25¢, 68 pgs.)
Tower Comics

	GD25	FN65	NM94
1-Lucky 7 & Mike Manly begin	3.20	9.00	21.00
2-Boris Vallejo, McWilliams-a	2.40	7.25	17.00
3-Wood-a (1/2 pg.); McWilliams, Bolle-a	2.40	7.25	17.00

FILM FUNNIES
Nov, 1949 - No. 2, Feb, 1950 (52 pgs.)
Marvel Comics (CPC)

	GD25	FN65	NM94
1-Krazy Krow, Wacky Duck	13.00	40.00	90.00
2-Wacky Duck	10.00	30.00	70.00

FILM STARS ROMANCES (True life stories of movie stars)
Jan-Feb, 1950 - No. 3, May-June, 1950
Star Publications

	GD25	FN65	NM94
1-Rudy Valentino & Gregory Peck stories; L. B. Cole-c; lingerie panels	22.00	65.00	150.00
2-Liz Taylor/Robert Taylor photo-c & true life story	24.00	72.00	165.00
3-Douglas Fairbanks story; photo-c	17.00	52.00	120.00

FINAL CYCLE, THE (Dragon's Teeth)(Value: cover or less)

FIRE
1993 - No. 2, 1993 ($2.95, B&W, mini-series, 52 pgs.)
Caliber Press

	GD25	FN65	NM94
1,2-Photo-c		1.20	3.00

FIRE AND BLAST
1952 (16 pgs.; paper cover) (Giveaway)
National Fire Protection Assoc.

	GD25	FN65	NM94
nn-Mart Baily A-Bomb-c; about fire prevention	15.00	45.00	105.00

FIREARM (See Night Man #4)
Sept, 1993 - Present ($1.95)
Malibu Comics (Ultraverse)

	GD25	FN65	NM94
1,3-6: 1-4-Chaykin-c; Hamner-a. 4-Break-Thru x-over. 5-2 pg. origin Prime; 6-Prime app.; Brereton-c		.80	2.00
1-($2.50)-Newsstand edition polybagged w/card		1.00	2.50
1-Ultra Limited silver foil-c	1.70	4.20	10.00
2-($2.50, 44 pgs.)-Rune flip-c/story by B. Smith (3 pgs.)		1.00	2.50
3-10,12-17: 1-4-Chaykin-c; Hamner/Lowe-a. 5-Origin Prime. 6-Brereton-c; Prime app.		.80	2.00
11-($3.50, 68 pgs.)-Flip book w/Ultraverse Premiere #5		1.40	3.50

FIRE BALL XL5 (See Steve Zodiac & The ...)

FIRE CHIEF AND THE SAFE OL' FIREFLY, THE
1952 (16 pgs.) (Safety brochure given away at schools)

The Fury Of Firestorm #24 © DC

Firestorm #92 © DC

First Love Illustrated #21 © Harv

GD25 FN65 NM94 — GD25 FN65 NM94

National Board of Fire Underwriters (produced by American Visuals Corp.) (Eisner)
nn-(Rare) Eisner-c/a 50.00 150.00 350.00

FIREHAIR COMICS (Formerly Pioneer West Romances #3-6; also see Rangers Comics)
Winter/48-49; No. 2, Wint/49-50; No. 7, Spr/51 - No. 11, Spr/52
Fiction House Magazines (Flying Stories)
1-Origin Firehair 31.00 94.00 220.00
2 16.00 48.00 110.00
7-11 13.00 40.00 90.00
I.W. Reprint 8-(nd)-Kinstler-c; reprints Rangers #57; Dr. Drew story by Grandenetti 2.80 7.00 14.00

FIRESTAR
March, 1986 - No. 4, June, 1986 (75¢)(From Spider-Man TV series)
Marvel Comics Group
1-X-Men & New Mutants app. 1.20 3.00
2-Wolverine-c(not real Wolverine?); Art Adams-a(p) .90 2.30 5.50
3,4: 3-Art Adams/Sienkiewicz-c. 4-B. Smith-c .80 2.00

FIRESTONE (See Donald And Mickey Merry Christmas)

FIRESTORM (See Cancelled Comic Cavalcade, DC Comics Presents, Flash #289, The Fury of... & Justice League of America #179)
March, 1978 - No. 5, Oct-Nov, 1978
DC Comics
1-Origin & 1st app. 1.10 2.75
2-5: 2-Origin Multiplex. 3-Origin & 1st app. Killer Frost. 4-1st app. Hyena .70 1.75

FIRESTORM, THE NUCLEAR MAN (Formerly Fury of Firestorm)
No. 65, Nov, 1987 - No. 100, Aug, 1990
DC Comics
65-99: 66-1st app. Zuggernaut; Firestorm vs. Green Lantern. 71-Death of Capt. X. 67,68-Millennium tie-ins. 83-1st new look 1.00
100-($2.95, 68 pgs.) 1.20 3.00
Annual 5 (10/87)-1st app. new Firestorm 1.25

FIRST ADVENTURES (First)(Value: cover or less)

FIRST AMERICANS, THE (See 4-Color No. 843)

FIRST CHRISTMAS, THE (3-D)
1953 (25¢) (Oversized - 8-1/4x10-1/4")(Came w/glasses)
Fiction House Magazines (Real Adv. Publ. Co.)
nn-(Scarce)-Kelly Freas painted-c; Biblical theme, birth of Christ; Nativity-c 34.00 102.00 240.00

FIRST COMICS GRAPHIC NOVEL
Jan, 1984 - No. 20? (52-176 pgs., high quality paper)
First Comics
1-Beowulf ($5.95) 1.00 2.50 6.00
1-2nd printing ($6.95) 1.20 3.00 7.00
2-Time Beavers ($5.95) 1.00 2.50 6.00
3($11.95, 100 pgs.)-American Flagg! Hard Times (2nd printing exists) 1.70 5.00 12.00
4-Nexus ($6.95)-r/B&W 1-3 1.30 3.25 8.00
5-The Enchanted Apples of Oz ($7.95, 52 pgs.)-Intro by Harlan Ellison (1986) 1.30 3.25 8.00
6-Elric of Melnibone ($14.95, 176 pgs.)-Reprints with new color 2.15 6.50 15.00
7-The Secret Island Of Oz ($7.95) 1.30 3.25 8.00
8-Teenage Mutant Ninja Turtles Book I ($9.95, 132 pgs.)-r/TMNT #1-3 in color w/12 pgs. new-a; origin 1.65 4.00 10.00
9-Time 2: The Epiphany by Chaykin (11/86, $7.95, 52pgs. - indicia says #8) 1.30 3.25 8.00
10-Teenage Mutant Ninja Turtles Book II ($9.95)-r/TMNT #4-6 in color 1.65 4.00 10.00
11-Sailor On The Sea of Fate ($14.95) 2.15 6.50 15.00
nn-Time 2: The Satisfaction of Black Mariah (9/87) 1.30 3.25 8.00
12-American Flagg! Southern Comfort (10/87, $11.95) 1.70 5.00 12.00
13-The Ice King Of Oz ($7.95) 1.30 3.25 8.00
14-Teenage Mutant Ninja Turtles Book III ($9.95)-r/TMNT #7,8 in color plus new 12 pg. story 1.65 4.00 10.00
15-Hex Breaker: Badger ($7.95, 68 pgs.) 1.30 3.25 8.00
16-The Forgotten Forest of Oz ($8.95) 1.50 3.75 9.00
17-Mazinger (68 pgs., $8.95) 1.50 3.75 9.00
18-Teenage Mutant Ninja Turtles Book IV ($9.95)-r/TMNT #10,11 plus 3 pg. fold-out 1.65 4.00 10.00
19-The Original Nexus Graphic Novel ($7.95, 104 pgs.)-Reprints First Comics Graphic Novel #4 ($7.95) 1.30 3.25 8.00
20-American Flagg!: State of the Union; r/A.F. 7-9 ($11.95, 96 pgs.) 1.70 5.00 12.00
NOTE: *Most or all issues have been reprinted.*

1ST FOLIO (The Joe Kubert School Presents...)
March, 1984 ($1.50)
Pacific Comics
1-Kubert-c/a(2 pgs.); Adam & Andy Kubert-a 1.50

1ST ISSUE SPECIAL
April, 1975 - No. 13, April, 1976 (Try out series)
National Periodical Publications
1-7,9-12: 1-Intro. Atlas; Kirby-c/a/script. 2-Green Team (see Cancelled Comic Cavalcade). 3-Metamorpho by Ramona Fraden. 4-Lady Cop. 5-Manhunter; Kirby-c/a/script. 6-Dingbats; Kirby-c/a/script. 7-The Creeper by Ditko(c/a). 9-Dr. Fate; Kubert-c; Simonson-a. 10-The Outsiders. 11-Code Name: Assassin; Grell-c. 12-Origin/1st app. new Starman; Kubert-c 1.10 2.75
8-Origin/1st app. The Warlord; Grell-c/a (11/75) 2.10 6.40 15.00
13-Return of the New Gods; Darkseid app.; 1st new costume Orion; predates New Gods #12 by more than a year 1.70 4.25

FIRST KISS
Dec, 1957 - No. 40, Jan, 1965
Charlton Comics
V1#1 3.60 9.00 18.00
V1#2-10 2.00 4.00 10.00
11-40 1.00 2.50 5.00

FIRST LOVE ILLUSTRATED
2/49 - No. 9, 6/50; No. 10, 1/51 - No. 86, 3/58; No. 87, 9/58 - No. 88, 11/58; No. 89, 11/62, No. 90, 2/63
Harvey Publications(Home Comics)(True Love)
1-Powell-a(2) 10.00 30.00 60.00
2-Powell-a 5.00 15.00 30.00
3-"Was I Too Fat To Be Loved" story 5.00 15.00 30.00
4-10 4.00 10.00 20.00
11-30: 13-"I Joined a Teen-age Sex Club" story. 30-Lingerie panel 2.80 7.00 14.00
31-34,37,39-49: 49-Last pre-code (2/55) 2.40 6.00 12.00
35-Used in **SOTI**, illo "The title of this comic book is First Love" 10.00 30.00 70.00
36-Communism story, "Love Slaves" 3.60 9.00 18.00
38-Nostrand-a 4.00 12.00 24.00
50-90 1.80 4.50 9.00
NOTE: ***Disbrow** a-13. **Orlando** c-87. **Powell** a-1, 3-5, 7, 10, 11, 13-17, 19-24, 26-29, 33,35-41, 43, 45, 46, 50, 54, 55, 57, 58, 61-63, 65, 71-73, 76, 79r, 82, 84, 88.*

FIRST MEN IN THE MOON (See Movie Comics)

FIRST ROMANCE MAGAZINE
8/49 - #6, 6/50; #7, 6/51 - #50, 2/58; #51, 9/58 - #52, 11/58
Home Comics(Harvey Publ.)/True Love
1 10.00 30.00 60.00
2 5.00 15.00 30.00
3-5 4.00 12.00 24.00

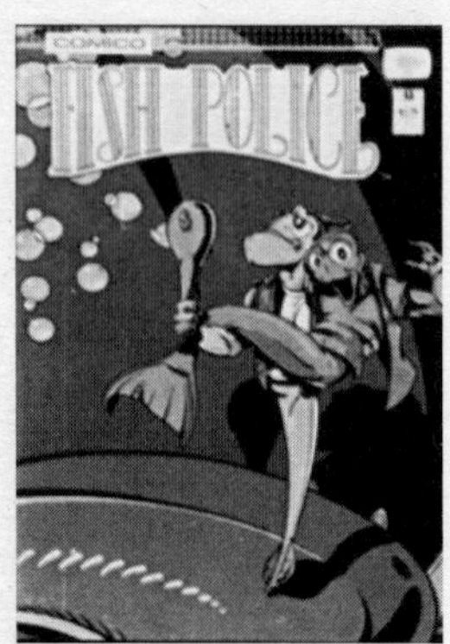

Fish Police #13 © Comico

Flare #5 © Hero Comics

The Flash #105 © DC

	GD25	FN65	NM94
6-10	4.00	10.00	20.00
11-20	2.80	7.00	14.00
21-27,29-32: 32-Last pre-code issue (2/55)	2.40	6.00	12.00
28-Nostrand-a(Powell swipe)	4.00	11.00	22.00
33-52	1.80	4.50	9.00

NOTE: ***Powell** a-1-5, 8-10, 14, 18, 20-22, 24, 25, 28, 36, 46, 48, 51.*

FIRST TRIP TO THE MOON (See Space Adventures No. 20)

FISH POLICE (Fishwrap/Apple)(Value: cover or less)

FISH POLICE
V2#1, Oct, 1992 - No. 6, Mar, 1993 ($1.25)
Marvel Comics

	GD25	FN65	NM94
V2#1-6: 1-Hairballs Saga begins; r/#1 (1985)			1.25

5-STAR SUPER-HERO SPECTACULAR (See DC Special Series No. 1)

FLAME, THE (See Big 3 & Wonderworld Comics)
Summer, 1940 - No. 8, Jan, 1942 (#1,2: 68 pgs; #3-8: 44 pgs.)
Fox Features Syndicate

	GD25	FN65	NM94
1-Flame stories reprinted from Wonderworld #5-9; origin The Flame; Lou Fine-a (36 pgs.), r/Wonderworld #3,10	186.00	557.00	1300.00
2-Fine-a(2); Wing Turner by Tuska	93.00	280.00	650.00
3-8: 3-Powell-a	61.00	182.00	425.00

FLAME, THE (Formerly Lone Eagle)
No. 5, Dec-Jan, 1954-55 - No. 3, April-May, 1955
Ajax/Farrell Publications (Excellent Publ.)

	GD25	FN65	NM94
5(#1)-1st app. new Flame	24.00	72.00	165.00
2,3	16.50	50.00	115.00

FLAMING CARROT (...Comics #6? on; see Anything Goes, Cerebus, Teenage Mutant Ninja Turtles/Flaming Carrot Crossover & Visions)
5/84 - No. 5, 1/85; No. 6, 3/85 - Present ($1.70/$2.00, B&W)
Aardvark-Vanaheim/Renegade Press #6-17/Dark Horse #18 on

	GD25	FN65	NM94
1-Bob Burden story/art	4.30	13.00	30.00
2	2.00	6.40	15.00
3	1.40	4.30	10.00
4-6	.90	2.80	6.50
7-9		1.70	4.00
10-12		1.20	3.00
13-15		.90	2.25
15-Variant without cover price		1.70	4.00
16-20: 18-1st Dark Horse issue		1.10	2.75
21-23,25: 25-Contains trading cards; TMNT app.		.80	2.00
24-($2.50, 52 pgs.)-10th anniversary issue		1.00	2.50
26-28: 26-Begin $2.25-c. 26,27-Teenage Mutant Ninja Turtles x-over. 27-Todd McFarlane-c		.90	2.25
29,30-($2.50-c)		1.00	2.50

FLAMING CARROT COMICS (Also see Junior Carrot Patrol)
Summer-Fall, 1981 ($1.95, one shot) (Large size, 8-1/2x11")
Killian Barracks Press

	GD25	FN65	NM94
1-By Bob Burden; serially numbered to 6500	8.00	24.00	55.00

FLAMING LOVE
Dec, 1949 - No. 6, Oct, 1950 (Photo covers #2-6) (52 pgs.)
Quality Comics Group (Comic Magazines)

	GD25	FN65	NM94
1-Ward-c/a (9 pgs.)	23.00	70.00	160.00
2	10.00	30.00	70.00
3-Ward-a (9 pgs.); Crandall-a	15.00	45.00	105.00
4-6: 4-Gustavson-a	10.00	30.00	65.00

FLAMING WESTERN ROMANCES (Formerly Target Western Romances)
No. 3, Mar-Apr, 1950
Star Publications

	GD25	FN65	NM94
3-Robert Taylor, Arlene Dahl photo on-c with biographies inside; L. B. Cole-c	24.00	72.00	165.00

FLARE (Also see Champions for 1st app. & League of Champions)
Nov, 1988 - No. 3, Jan, 1989 ($2.75, color, 52 pgs)
V2#1, Nov, 1990 - No. 7, Nov, 1991 ($2.95/$3.50, color, mature, 52 pgs.)
V2#8, Oct, 1992 - No. 16, Feb, 1994 ($3.50/$3.95, B&W, mature, 36 pgs.)
Hero Comics/Hero Graphics Vol. 2 on

	GD25	FN65	NM94
1-3		1.10	2.75
V2#1-3,16 ($2.95)		1.20	3.00
V2#4-6,8-10: 4-Begin $3.50-c. 5-Eternity Smith returns. 6-Intro The Tigress		1.40	3.50
V2#7,11-15 ($3.95)		1.60	4.00
Annual 1(1992, $4.50, B&W, 52 pgs.)-Champions-r		1.80	4.50

FLARE ADVENTURES
Feb, 1992 - No. 12, 1993? ($3.50/$3.95)
Hero Graphics

	GD25	FN65	NM94
1 (90¢, color, 20 pgs.)			1.00
2-7 ($3.50)-Flip books w/Champions Classics		1.40	3.50
8-12 ($3.95)-Flip books w/Champions Classics		1.60	4.00

FLASH, THE (See Adventure, The Brave and the Bold, Crisis On Infinite Earths, DC Comics Presents, DC Special, DC Special Series, DC Super-Stars, Green Lantern, Justice League of America, Showcase, Super Team Family, & World's Finest)

FLASH, THE (Formerly Flash Comics)
No. 105, Feb-Mar, 1959 - No. 350, Oct, 1985
National Periodical Publ./DC

	GD25	FN65	VF82	NM94
Showcase #4 (9-10/56)-Origin/1st app. The Flash (1st DC S.A. superhero) Turtle; Kubert-a	1400.00	4200.00	12,600.00	21,000.00
Showcase #8 (5-6/57)-2nd app. The Flash; origin & 1st app. Capt. Cold	975.00	2925.00	5800.00	–

	GD25	FN65	NM94
Showcase #13 (3-4/58)-Origin/1st Mr. Element	270.00	810.00	2700.00
Showcase #14 (5-6/58)-Origin & 1st app. Dr. Alchemy, formerly Mr. Element	292.00	875.00	3500.00

	GD25	FN65	VF82	NM94
105-(2-3/59)-Origin Flash(retold), & Mirror Master (1st app.)	310.00	930.00	2065.00	3100.00

	GD25	FN65	NM94
106-Origin Grodd & Pied Piper; Flash's 1st visit to Gorilla City; begin Grodd the Super Gorilla trilogy (Scarce)	86.00	258.00	775.00
107-Grodd trilogy, part 2	51.00	153.00	460.00
108-Grodd trilogy ends	44.00	133.00	400.00
109-2nd app. Mirror Master	39.00	117.00	350.00
110-Intro/origin The Weather Wizard & Kid Flash who later becomes Flash in Crisis On Infinite Earths #12; begin Kid Flash trilogy, ends #112 (also in #114,116,118)	94.00	283.00	660.00
111-2nd Kid Flash tryout; Cloud Creatures	32.00	96.00	225.00
112-Origin & 1st app. Elongated Man (4-5/60); also apps. in #115,119,130	35.00	105.00	245.00
113-Origin & 1st app. Trickster	34.00	101.00	235.00
114-Captain Cold app. (see Showcase #8)	26.00	79.00	185.00
115,116,118-120: 119-Elongated Man marries Sue Dearborn. 120-Flash & Kid Flash team-up for 1st time	19.00	58.00	135.00
117-Origin & 1st app. Capt. Boomerang; 1st & only S.A. app. Winky Blinky & Noddy	27.00	81.00	190.00
121,122: 122-Origin & 1st app. The Top	14.00	43.00	100.00
123-(9/61)-Re-intro. Golden Age Flash; origins of both Flashes; 1st mention of an Earth II where DC G. A. heroes live	73.00	218.00	725.00
124-Last 10¢ issue	13.00	40.00	90.00
125-128,130: 127-Return of Grodd-c/story. 128-Origin & 1st app. Abra Kadabra	12.00	36.00	85.00
129-2nd G.A. Flash x-over; J.S.A. cameo in flashback (1st S.A. app. G.A. Green Lantern, Hawkman, Atom, Black Canary & Dr. Mid-Nite)	31.00	92.00	215.00
131-136,138,140: 130-(7/62)-1st Gauntlet of Super-Villains (Mirror Master, Capt. Cold, The Top, Capt. Boomerang & Trickster). 131-Early Green Lantern x-over (9/62). 136-1st Dexter Miles. 140-Origin & 1st app. Heat Wave	12.00	36.00	85.00

137-G.A. Flash x-over; J.S.A. cameo (1st S.A. app.)(1st real app. since 2-3/51);

The Flash #129 © DC

The Flash #202 © DC

Flash #5(new series) © DC

GD25 FN65 NM94 GD25 FN65 NM94

1st S.A. app. Vandall Savage & Johnny Thunder; JSA team decides to re-form 45.00 135.00 315.00
139-Origin & 1st app. Prof. Zoom 14.00 41.00 95.00
141-150: 142-Trickster app. 8.00 24.00 55.00
151-G.A. Flash vs. The Shade 9.00 28.00 68.00
152-159 5.00 15.00 36.00
160-(80-Pg. Giant G-21); G.A. Flash & Johnny Quick-r 8.00 24.00 55.00
161-168,170: 165-Silver Age Flash weds Iris West. 167-New facts about Flash's origin. 168-Green Lantern-c/story. 170-Dr. Mid-Nite, Dr. Fate, G.A. Flash x-over 4.60 14.00 32.00
169-(80-Pg. Giant G-34)-New facts about origin 8.00 24.00 55.00
171-174,176,177,179,180: 171-JLA, Green Lantern, Atom flashbacks. 173-G.A. Flash x-over. 174-Barry Allen reveals I.D. to wife 3.70 11.00 26.00
175-2nd Superman/Flash race (12/67; see Superman #199 & World's Finest #198,199); JLA cameo; gold kryptonite used (on J'onn J'onzz impersonating Superman) 16.00 36.00 90.00
178-(80-Pg. Giant G-46) 5.40 16.00 38.00
181-186,188-195,197-200: 186-Re-intro. Sargon 1.70 5.10 12.00
187,196: (68-Pg. Giants G-58, G-70) 4.00 11.60 27.00
201-204,206-210: 201-New G.A. Flash story. 208-52 pg. begin, end #213, 215,216. 206-Elongated Man begins 1.10 2.70 6.50
205-(68-Pg. Giant G-82) 2.10 6.40 15.00
211-213,216,220: 211-G.A. Flash origin-r/#104. 213-Reprints #137. 220-1st app. Turtle since Showcase 4 1.10 2.70 6.50
214-DC 100 Page Super Spectacular DC-11; origin Metal Men-r/Showcase #37; never before pubbed G.A. Flash story 1.70 4.20 10.00
215 (52 pgs.)-Flash-r/Showcase #4; G.A. Flash x-over, reprinted in #216 1.90 6.00 13.00
217-219: Neal Adams-a in all. 217-Green Lantern/Green Arrow series begins (9/72); 2nd G.L. & G.A. team-up series (see Green Lantern #76). 219-Last Green Arrow 1.70 5.00 12.00
221-225,227,228,230,231,233: 222-G. Lantern x-over1.10 2.70 6.50
226-Neal Adams-a 1.60 4.00 9.50
229,232-(100 pg. issues)-G.A. Flash-r & new-a 1.40 4.00 8.50
234-288,290: 235-Green Lantern x-over. 243-Death of The Top. 245-Origin The Floronic Man in Green Lantern back-up, ends #246. 246-Last Green Lantern 256-Death of The Top retold. 250-Intro Golden Glider. 265-267-(44 pgs.). 267-Origin of Flash's uniform. 270-Intro The Clown. 275,276-Iris West Allen dies. 286-Intro/origin Rainbow Raider 1.30 3.25
289-1st Perez DC art (Firestorm); new Firestorm back-up series begins (9/80), ends #304 1.20 2.40 6.00
291-299,301-305: 291-1st app. Saber-Tooth (villain). 295-Gorilla Grodd-c/story. 298-Intro/origin new Shade. 301-Atomic bomb-c. 303-The Top returns. 304-Intro/origin Colonel Computron; 305-G.A. Flash x-over 1.10 2.75
300-(52 pgs.)-Origin Flash retold; 25th ann. issue 1.70 4.25
306-Dr. Fate by Giffen begins, ends #313 1.10 2.75
307-313-Giffen-a. 309-Origin Flash retold .90 2.25
314-349: 318-323-Creeper back-ups. 323,324-Two part Flash vs. Flash story. 324-Death of Reverse Flash (Prof. Zoom). 328-Iris West Allen's death retold. 344-Origin Kid Flash .80 2.00
350-Double size ($1.25) .90 2.30 5.50
Annual 1(10-12/63, 84 pgs.)-Origin Elongated Man & Kid Flash-r; origin Grodd; G.A. Flash-r 30.00 90.00 300.00

NOTE: ***N. Adams*** *c-194, 195, 203, 204, 206-208, 211, 213, 215, 246.* ***M. Anderson*** *a-202i.* ***Austin*** *a-233i, 234i, 246i.* ***Buckler*** *a-271p, 272p; c(p)-247-250, 252, 253p, 255, 256p, 258, 262, 265-267, 269-271.* ***Giffen*** *a-306-313p; c-310p, 315.* ***Sid Greene*** *a-167-174i, 229i(r).* ***Grell*** *a-237p, 238p, 240-243p; c-236.* ***Infantino/Anderson*** *c-201.* ***Infantino/Giella*** *c-105-112.* ***G. Kane*** *a-195p, 197-199p, 229r, 232r; c-197-199, 312p.* ***Kubert*** *a-108p, 215i(r); c-189-191.* ***Lopez*** *c-272.* ***Meskin*** *a-229r, 232r.* ***Perez*** *a-289-293p; c-293.* ***Starlin*** *a-294-296p.* ***Staton*** *c-263p, 264p. Green Lantern x-over-131, 143, 168, 171, 191.*

FLASH
June, 1987 - Present (75¢, $1.00 #17 on)
DC Comics

1-Guice-c/a begins; New Teen Titans app. 1.80 4.50
2,3: 3-Intro. Kilgore 1.10 2.75
4-10: 5-Intro. Speed McGee. 7-1st app. Blue Trinity. 8,9-Millennium tie-ins. 9-1st app. The Chunk .90 2.25
11-20: 12-Free extra 16 pg. Dr. Light story. 19-Free extra 16 pg. Flash story .80 1.90
21-30: 28-Capt. Cold app. 29-New Phantom Lady app. 1.40
31-49,51-65: 40-Dr. Alchemy app. 62-Flash: Year One begins, ends #65. 65-Last $1.00-c 1.00
50-($1.75, 52 pgs.) .70 1.75
66-78,80-84: 66-Aquaman app. 69,70-Green Lantern app. 70-Gorilla Grodd story ends. 73-Re-intro Barry Allen & begin saga (Barry Allen revealed as Reverse Flash in #78). 80-Regular ed. 81,82-Nightwing & Starfire app. 84-Razer app. 1.25
79-($2.50, 68 pgs.)-Barry Allen saga ends 1.00 2.50
80-($2.50)-Foil cover edition 1.00 2.50
85-94: 85-Begin $1.50-c; 94-Zero Hour 1.50
0,95-101 1.50
Annual 1 (1987, $1.25) .70 1.75
Annual 2, 3: 2-(1988, $1.50) 3-(1989, $1.75, 68 pgs.)-Gives history of G.A., Silver Age, & new Flash in text .70 1.75
Annual 4 (1991, $2.00, 68 pgs.)-Armaggedon 2001 .80 2.00
Annual 5 (1992, $2.50, 68 pgs.)-Eclipso-c/story 1.00 2.50
Annual 6 (1993, $2.50, 68 pgs.) 1.00 2.50
Annual 7 (1994, $2.95)-Elseworlds story 1.20 3.00
Special 1 (1990, $2.95, 84 pgs.)-50th anniversary issue; Kubert-c 1.20 3.00
...TV Special 1 (1991, $3.95, 76 pgs.)-Photo-c plus behind the scenes photos of TV show; Saltares-a, Byrne scripts 1.60 4.00

NOTE: ***Guice*** *a-1-9p, 11p, Annual 1p; c-1-9p, Annual 1p.* ***Perez*** *c-15-17, Annual 2i.* ***Travest Charest*** *c/a-Annual 5p.*

FLASH COMICS (Whiz Comics No. 2 on)
Jan, 1940 (12 pgs., B&W, regular size)
(Not distributed to newsstands; printed for in-house use)
Fawcett Publications

NOTE*:* ***Whiz Comics*** *#2 was preceded by two books,* ***Flash Comics*** *and* ***Thrill Comics****, both dated Jan, 1940, (12 pgs, B&W, regular size) and were not distributed. These two books are identical except for the title, and were sent out to major distributors as ad copies to promote sales. It is believed that the complete 68 page issue of Fawcett's* ***Flash*** *and* ***Thrill Comics #1*** *was finished and ready for publication with the January date. Since DC Comics was also about to publish a book with the same date and title, Fawcett hurriedly printed up the black and white version of* ***Flash Comics*** *to secure copyright before DC The inside covers are blank, with the covers and inside pages printed on a high quality uncoated paper stock.The eight page origin story of Captain Thunder is composed of pages 1-7 and 13 of the Captain Marvel story essentially as they appeared in the first issue of* ***Whiz Comics****. The balloon dialogue on page thirteen was relettered to tie the story into the end of page seven in* ***Flash*** *and* ***Thrill Comics*** *to produce a shorter version of the origin story for copyright purposes. Obviously, DC acquired the copyright and Fawcett dropped* ***Flash*** *as well as* ***Thrill*** *and came out with* ***Whiz Comics*** *a month later. Fawcett never used the cover to* ***Flash*** *and* ***Thrill #1****, designing a new cover for* ***Whiz Comics****. Fawcett also must have discovered that Captain Thunder had already been used by another publisher (Captain Terry Thunder by Fiction House). All references to Captain Thunder were relettered to Captain Marvel before appearing in* ***Whiz****.*

1 (nn on-c, #1 on inside)-Origin & 1st app. Captain Thunder. Eight copies of Flash and three copies of Thrill exist. All 3 copies of Thrill sold in 1986 for between $4,000-$10,000 each. A NM copy of Thrill sold in 1987 for $12,000. A vg copy of Thrill sold in 1987 for $9000 cash; another copy sold in 1987 for $2000 cash, $10,000 trade; cover by Leo O'Mealia

FLASH COMICS (The Flash No. 105 on) (Also see All-Flash)
Jan, 1940 - No. 104, Feb, 1949
National Periodical Publications/All-American

GD25 FN65 VF82 NM94

1-The Flash (origin/1st app.) by Harry Lampert, Hawkman (origin/1st app.) by Gardner Fox, The Whip, & Johnny Thunder (origin/1st app.) by Stan Asch; Cliff Cornwall by Moldoff, Flash Picture Novelets (later Minute Movies w/#12) begin; Moldoff (Shelly) cover; 1st app. Shiera Sanders who later becomes Hawkgirl, #24; reprinted in Famous First Edition (on sale 11/10/39); The Flash-c 3200.00 9600.00 20,800.00 32,000.00
(Estimated up to 75+ total copies exist, 7 in NM/Mint)
1-Reprint, Oversize 13-1/2x10". **WARNING:** This comic is an exact reprint of the original except for its size. DC published it in 1974 with a second cover titling it as a Famous First Edition. There have been many reported cases of the outer cover being removed and the interior

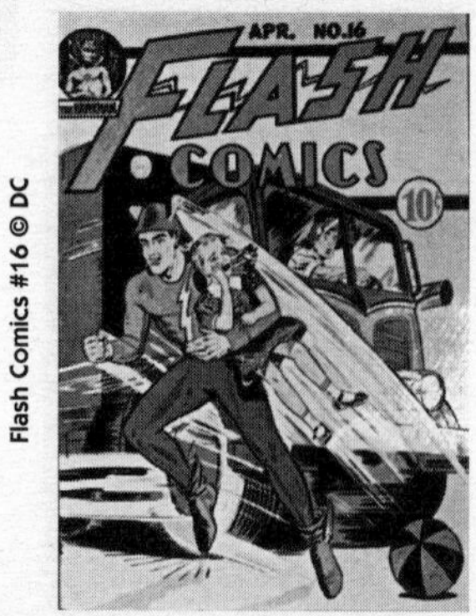

Flash Comics #16 © DC

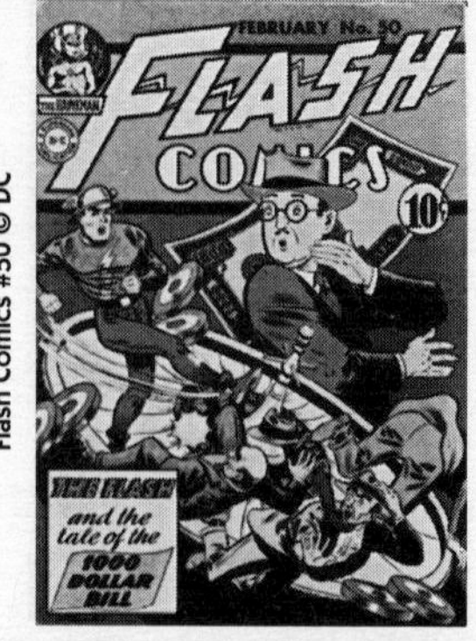

Flash Comics #50 © DC

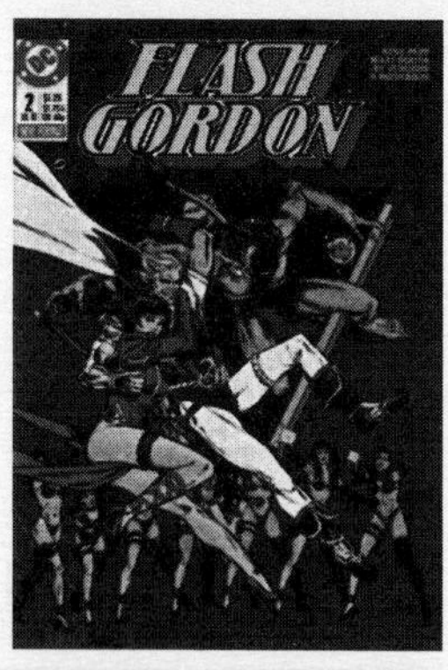

Flash Gordon #2 © DC

GD25 FN65 NM94

GD25 FN65 NM94

sold as the original edition. The reprint with the new outer cover removed is practically worthless. See Famous First Edition for value.

	GD25	FN65	NM94
2-Rod Rian begins, ends #11; Hawkman-c	500.00	1500.00	3500.00
3-King Standish begins (1st app.), ends #41 (called The King #16-37,39-41); E.E. Hibbard-a begins on Flash	400.00	1200.00	2800.00
4-Moldoff (Shelly) Hawkman begins; The Whip-c	343.00	1030.00	2400.00
5-The King-c	314.00	943.00	2200.00
6-2nd Flash-c (alternates w/Hawkman #6 on)	357.00	1071.00	2500.00
7-10: 7-2nd Hawkman-c. 8-New logo	200.00	600.00	1400.00
11-20: 12-Les Watts begins; "Sparks" #16 on. 17-Last Cliff Cornwall	132.00	396.00	925.00
21-23	107.00	321.00	750.00
24-Shiera becomes Hawkgirl (12/41); see All-Star Comics #5 for 1st app.	143.00	429.00	1000.00
25-28,30: 28-Last Les Sparks.	86.00	257.00	600.00
29-Ghost Patrol begins(origin, 1st app.), ends #104	100.00	300.00	700.00
31-40: 33-Origin Shade	79.00	236.00	550.00
41-50	71.00	215.00	500.00
51-61: 59-Last Minute Movies. 61-Last Moldoff Hawkman	61.00	182.00	425.00
62-Hawkman by Kubert begins	79.00	236.00	550.00
63-70: 66-68-Hop Harrigan in all. 70-Mutt & Jeff app.	61.00	182.00	425.00
71-85: 80-Atom begins, ends #104	61.00	182.00	425.00
86-Intro. The Black Canary in Johnny Thunder (8/47); see All-Star #38; rare in Mint due to black ink smearing on white-c	171.00	515.00	1200.00
87-90: 88-Origin Ghost. 89-Intro villain The Thorn	82.00	246.00	575.00
91,93-99: 98-Atom & Hawkman don new costumes	93.00	279.00	650.00
92-1st solo Black Canary plus-c	229.00	685.00	1600.00
100 (10/48),103(Scarce)-52 pgs. each	229.00	685.00	1600.00
101,102(Scarce)	186.00	557.00	1300.00
104-Origin The Flash retold (Scarce)	457.00	1371.00	3200.00
Wheaties Giveaway (1946, 32 pgs., 6-1/2x8-1/4")-Johnny Thunder, Ghost Patrol, The Flash & Kubert Hawkman app. NOTE: All known copies were taped to Wheaties boxes and are never found in mint condition. Copies with light tape residue bring the listed prices in all grades	250.00	750.00	–

NOTE: ***E.E. Hibbard*** *c-6, 12, 20, 24, 26, 28, 30, 44, 46, 48, 50, 62, 66, 68, 69, 72, 74, 76, 78, 80, 82.* ***Infantino*** *a-86p, 90, 93-95, 99-104; c-90, 92, 93, 97, 99, 101, 103.* ***Kinstler*** *a-87, 89(Hawkman); c-87.* ***Chet Kozlak*** *c-77, 79, 81.* ***Krigstein*** *a-94.* ***Kubert*** *a-62-76, 83, 85, 86, 88-104; c-63, 65, 67, 70, 71, 73, 75, 83, 85, 86, 88, 89, 91, 94, 96, 98, 100, 104.* ***Moldoff*** *a-3; c-3, 7-11, 13-17, plus odd #'s 19-61.* ***Martin Naydell*** *c-52, 54, 56, 58, 60, 64, 84.*

FLASH DIGEST, THE (See DC Special Series #24)

FLASH GORDON (See Defenders Of The Earth, Eat Right to Work..., Feature Book #25, Giant Comic Album, King Classics, King Comics, March of Comics #118, 133, 142, The Phantom #18, Street Comix & Wow Comics, 1st series)

FLASH GORDON
No. 10, 1943 - No. 512, Nov, 1953
Dell Publishing Co.

	GD25	FN65	NM94
4-Color 10(1943)-by Alex Raymond; reprints "The Ice Kingdom"	57.00	171.00	400.00
4-Color 84(1945)-by Alex Raymond; reprints "The Fiery Desert"	39.00	118.00	275.00
4-Color 173,190: 190-Bondage-c	13.50	41.00	95.00
4-Color 204,247	11.00	32.00	75.00
4-Color 424-Painted-c	9.15	27.50	55.00
2(5-7/53-Dell)-Painted-c; Evans-a?	5.00	15.00	30.00
4-Color 512-Painted-c	5.00	15.00	30.00
Macy's Giveaway(1943)-(Rare)-20 pgs.; not by Raymond	60.00	160.00	360.00

FLASH GORDON (See Tiny Tot Funnies)
Oct, 1950 - No. 4, April, 1951
Harvey Publications

	GD25	FN65	NM94
1-Alex Raymond-a; bondage-c; reprints strips from 7/14/40 to 12/8/40	19.00	58.00	135.00
2-Alex Raymond-a; r/strips 12/15/40-4/27/41	14.00	43.00	100.00
3,4-Alex Raymond-a; 3-bondage-c; r/strips 5/4/41-9/21/41. 4-r/strips 10/24/37-3/27/38	13.00	40.00	90.00
5-(Rare)-Small size-5-1/2x8-1/2"; B&W; 32 pgs.; Distributed to some mail subscribers only. Estimated value		$200.00–$300.00	

(Also see All-New No. 15, Boy Explorers No. 2, and Stuntman No. 3)

FLASH GORDON
1951 (Paper cover; 16 pgs. in color; regular size)
Harvey Comics (Gordon Bread giveaway)

	GD25	FN65	NM94
1,2: 1-r/strips 10/24/37 - 2/6/38. 2-r/strips 7/14/40 - 10/6/40; Reprints by Raymond each....	1.50	4.50	10.00

NOTE: *Most copies have brittle edges.*

FLASH GORDON
June, 1965
Gold Key

	GD25	FN65	NM94
1 (1947 reprint)-Painted-c	2.70	8.00	19.00

FLASH GORDON (Also see Comics Reading Libraries)
9/66 - #11, 12/67; #12, 2/69 - #18, 1/70; #19, 10-11/78 - #37, 3/82
(Painted covers No. 19-30, 34)
King #1-11/Charlton #12-18/Gold Key #19-23/Whitman #28 on

	GD25	FN65	NM94
1-Williamson c/a(2); E.C. swipe/Incredible S.F. #32. Mandrake story	3.00	9.00	21.00
1-Army giveaway(1968)("Complimentary" on cover)(Same as regular #1 minus Mandrake story & back-c)	1.90	6.00	13.00
2-Bolle, Gil Kane-c; Mandrake story	1.90	6.00	13.00
3-Williamson-c	2.10	6.50	15.00
4-Secret Agent X-9 begins, Williamson-c/a(3)	2.10	6.50	15.00
5-Williamson-c/a(2)	2.10	6.50	15.00
6,8-Crandall-a. 8-Secret Agent X-9-r	2.90	9.00	20.00
7-Raboy-a (last in comics?)	2.10	6.50	15.00
9,10-Raymond-r. 10-Buckler's 1st pro work (11/67)	2.60	7.70	18.00
11-Crandall-a	1.90	6.00	13.00
12-Crandall-c/a	2.10	6.50	15.00
13-Jeff Jones-a (15 pgs.)	2.10	6.50	15.00
14-17: 17-Brick Bradford story	1.30	3.00	7.50
18-Kaluta-a (3rd pro work?)(see Teen Confessions)	1.40	3.50	8.50
19(9/78, G.K.), 20-30(10/80)		1.40	3.50
30 (7/81; re-issue)		.60	1.60
31-33: Movie adaptation; Williamson-a		.70	1.70
34-37: Movie adaptation			1.50

NOTE: ***Aparo*** *a-8.* ***Bolle*** *a-21, 22.* ***Boyette*** *a-14-18.* ***Briggs*** *c-10.* ***Buckler*** *a-10.* ***Crandall*** *c-6.* ***Estrada*** *a-3.* ***Gene Fawcette*** *a-29, 30, 34, 37.* ***McWilliams*** *a-31-33, 36.*

FLASH GORDON
June, 1988 - No. 9, Holiday, 1988-'89 ($1.25, mini-series)
DC Comics

	GD25	FN65	NM94
1-9: 1,5-Painted-c			1.25

FLASH GORDON THE MOVIE
1980 ($1.95. color, 68 pgs., 8-1/4 x 11")
Western Publishing Co.

	GD25	FN65	NM94
11294-Williamson-c/a; adapts movie		.80	2.00
13743-Hardback edition	1.00	2.00	5.00

FLASH SPECTACULAR, THE (See DC Special Series No. 11)

FLAT-TOP
11/53 - No. 3, 5/54; No. 4, 3/55 - No. 7, 9/55
Mazie Comics/Harvey Publ.(Magazine Publ.) No. 4 on

	GD25	FN65	NM94
1-Teenage; Flat-Top, Mazie, Mortie & Stevie begin	4.00	12.00	24.00
2,3	2.80	7.00	14.00
4-7	2.00	5.00	10.00

FLAXEN (Dark Horse)(Value: cover or less)

FLESH AND BONES (Fantagraphics)(Value: cover or less)

FLESH: THE LEGEND OF SHAMANA (Fleetway)(Value: cover or less)

Flintstones #14 © H-B

The Fly #5 (new series) © AP

The Flying A's Range Rider #18 © DELL

FLINTSTONE KIDS, THE (TV; See Star Comics Digest)
Aug, 1987 - No. 11, April, 1989
Star Comics/Marvel Comics #5 on

	GD25	FN65	NM94
1-11			1.00

FLINTSTONES, THE (TV)(See Dell Giant #48 for No. 1)
No. 2, Nov-Dec, 1961 - No. 60, Sept, 1970 (Hanna-Barbera)
Dell Publ. Co./Gold Key No. 7 (10/62) on

	GD25	FN65	NM94
2-2nd app. (TV show debuted on 9/30/60)	9.00	28.00	65.00
3-6(7-8/62): 2-5: 15¢. 6-Begin 12¢ issues	6.90	21.00	48.00
7 (10/62; 1st GK)	6.30	19.00	44.00
8-10: Mr. & Mrs. J. Evil Scientist begin?	5.40	16.00	38.00
11-1st app. Pebbles (6/63)	8.00	24.00	55.00
12-15,17-20	4.70	14.00	33.00
16-1st app. Bamm-Bamm (1/64)	6.40	19.00	45.00
21-30: 24-1st app. The Grusomes	3.90	12.00	27.00
31-33,35-40: 31-Xmas-c. 33-Meet Frankenstein & Dracula. 39-Reprints	3.60	10.70	25.00
34-1st app. The Great Gazoo	4.60	14.00	32.00
41-60: 45-Last 12¢ issue	3.10	9.00	22.00
At N. Y. World's Fair('64)-J.W. Books(25¢)-1st printing; no date on-c (29¢ version exists, 2nd print?)	5.00	15.00	35.00
At N. Y. World's Fair (1965 on-c; re-issue). NOTE: Warehouse find in 1984	1.10	2.70	6.50
Bigger & Boulder 1(#30013-211) (Gold Key Giant, 11/62, 25¢, 84 pgs.)	9.00	28.00	66.00
Bigger & Boulder 2-(1966, 25¢)-Reprints B&B No. 1	8.00	24.00	55.00
...With Pebbles & Bamm Bamm (100 pgs., G.K.)-30028-511 (paper-c, 25¢) (11/65)	8.00	24.00	55.00

NOTE: *(See Comic Album #16, Bamm-Bamm & Pebbles Flintstone, Dell Giant 48, Golden Comics Digest, March of Comics #229, 243, 271, 289, 299, 317, 327, 341, Pebbles Flintstone, Top Comics #2-4, and Whitman Comic Books.)*

FLINTSTONES, THE (TV)(...& Pebbles)
Nov, 1970 - No. 50, Feb, 1977 (Hanna-Barbera)
Charlton Comics

	GD25	FN65	NM94
1	5.00	15.00	35.00
2	2.60	7.50	18.00
3-7,9,10	1.70	5.00	12.00
8- "Flintstones Summer Vacation" (Summer, 1971, 52 pgs.)	2.15	6.50	15.00
11-20	1.65	4.70	11.00
21-50: 36-Mike Zeck illos (early work). 37-Byrne text illos (early work; see Nightmare #20). 42-Byrne-a (2 pgs.)	1.65	4.70	11.00

(Also see Barney & Betty Rubble, Dino, The Great Gazoo, & Pebbles & Bamm-Bamm)

FLINTSTONES, THE (TV)(See Yogi Bear, 3rd series)
October, 1977 - No. 9, Feb, 1979 (Hanna-Barbera)
Marvel Comics Group

	GD25	FN65	NM94
1-9: Yogi Bear app. 4-The Jetsons app.		.80	2.00

FLINTSTONES, THE
Sept, 1992 - No. 13, June, 1994 ($1.25/$1.50) (Hanna-Barbera)
Harvey Comics

	GD25	FN65	NM94
V2#1-4			1.25
5-13: 5-Begin $1.50-c			1.50
...Big Book 1,2 (11/92, 3/93; both $1.95, 52 pgs.)		.80	2.00
...Giant Size 1-3 (10/92, 4/93, 11/93; $2.25, 68 pgs.)		.90	2.25

FLINTSTONES CHRISTMAS PARTY, THE (See The Funtastic World of Hanna-Barbera No. 1)

FLIP
April, 1954 - No. 2, June, 1954 (Satire)
Harvey Publications

	GD25	FN65	NM94
1,2-Nostrand-a each. 2-Powell-a	16.00	48.00	110.00

FLIPPER (TV)
April, 1966 - No. 3, Nov, 1967 (All have photo-c)
Gold Key

	GD25	FN65	NM94
1	6.70	20.00	40.00
2,3	4.20	12.50	25.00

FLIPPITY & FLOP
12-1/51-52 - No. 46, 8-10/59; No. 47, 9-11/60
National Periodical Publ. (Signal Publ. Co.)

	GD25	FN65	NM94
1-Twiddle and Twaddle begin	20.00	60.00	140.00
2	11.50	34.00	80.00
3-5	10.00	30.00	60.00
6-10	8.35	25.00	50.00
11-20: 20-Last precode (3/55)	6.70	20.00	40.00
21-47	5.00	15.00	30.00

FLOATERS
Sept, 1993 - No. 5, Jan, 1994 ($2.50, B&W, limited series)
Dark Horse Comics

	GD25	FN65	NM94
1-5		1.00	2.50

FLOOD RELIEF
Jan, 1994 (36 pgs.)(ordered thru mail w/$5.00 to Red Cross)
Malibu Comics (Ultraverse)

	GD25	FN65	NM94
1-Hardcase, Prime & Prototype app.	1.00	2.00	5.00

FLOYD FARLAND (See Eclipse Graphic Album Series #11)

FLY, THE (Also see Adventures of..., Blue Ribbon Comics & Flyman)
May, 1983 - No. 9, Oct, 1984
Archie Enterprises, Inc.

	GD25	FN65	NM94
1-9: 1-Mr. Justice app; origin Shield. 2-Flygirl app.			1.00

NOTE: ***Buckler** a-1, 2. **Ditko** a-2-9; c-4-8p. **Nebres** c-3, 4, 5i, 6, 7i. **Steranko** c-1, 2.*

FLY, THE
Aug, 1991 - No. 17, Dec, 1992 ($1.00)
Impact Comics (DC)

	GD25	FN65	NM94
1-17: 4-Vs. The Black Hood. 9-Trading card inside			1.00
Annual 1 ('92, $2.50, 68 pgs.)-Impact trading card		1.00	2.50

FLY BOY (Flying Cadets)(Also see Approved Comics)
Spring, 1952 - No. 4, 1953
Ziff-Davis Publ. Co. (Approved)

	GD25	FN65	NM94
1-Saunders painted-c	11.50	34.00	80.00
2-(10-11/52)-Saunders painted-c	10.00	30.00	60.00
3,4-Saunders painted-c	6.70	20.00	40.00

FLYING ACES (Aviation stories)
July, 1955 - No. 5, March, 1956
Key Publications

	GD25	FN65	NM94
1	4.00	11.00	22.00
2-5: 2-Trapani-a	2.80	7.00	14.00

FLYING A'S RANGE RIDER, THE (TV) (See Western Roundup under Dell Giants)
#404, 6-7/52; #2, June-Aug, 1953 - #24, Aug, 1959 (All photo-c)
Dell Publishing Co.

	GD25	FN65	NM94
4-Color 404(#1)-Titled "The Range Rider"	11.50	34.00	80.00
2	7.00	21.00	42.00
3-10	5.85	17.50	35.00
11-16,18-24	5.35	16.00	32.00
17-Toth-a	6.70	20.00	40.00

FLYING CADET (WW II Plane Photos)
Jan, 1943 - V2#8, 1947 (Half photos, half comics)
Flying Cadet Publishing Co.

	GD25	FN65	NM94
V1#1-Painted-c	10.00	30.00	70.00
2	5.35	16.00	32.00
3-9 (Two #6's, Sept. & Oct.): 5,6a,6b-Photo-c	4.70	14.00	28.00
V2#1-7(#10-16)	4.00	11.00	22.00
8(#17)-Bare-breasted woman-c	10.00	30.00	70.00

FLYIN' JENNY

Foodang #1 © Continuity

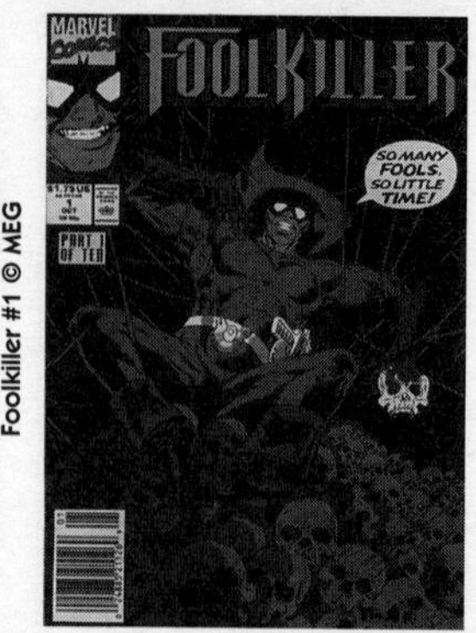

Foolkiller #1 © MEG

Forbidden Worlds #86 © ACG

GD25 FN65 NM94

1946 - No. 2, 1947 (1945 strip reprints)
Pentagon Publ. Co./Leader Enterprises #2

nn-Marcus Swayze strip-r (entire insides) 9.15 27.50 55.00
2-Baker-c; Swayze strip reprints 10.00 30.00 65.00

FLYING MODELS
V61#3, May, 1954 (5¢, 16 pgs.)
H-K Publ. (Health-Knowledge Publs.)

V61#3 (Rare) 5.85 17.50 35.00

FLYING NUN (TV)
Feb, 1968 - No. 4, Nov, 1968
Dell Publishing Co.

1-Sally Field photo-c 5.00 15.00 30.00
2-4: 2-Sally Field photo-c 3.60 9.00 18.00

FLYING NURSES (See Sue & Sally Smith...)

FLYING SAUCERS
1950; 1952; 1953
Avon Periodicals/Realistic

1(1950)-Wood-a, 21 pgs.; Fawcette-c 50.00 150.00 350.00
nn(1952)-Cover altered plus 2 pgs. of Wood-a not in original 46.00 140.00 325.00
nn(1953)-Reprints above 27.00 81.00 190.00

FLYING SAUCERS (Comics)
April, 1967 - No. 4, Nov, 1967; No. 5, Oct, 1969
Dell Publishing Co.

1 1.65 4.70 11.00
2-5 1.00 2.50 6.00

FLY IN MY EYE: EXPOSED (Eclipse)(Value: cover or less) (Graphic Album)

FLY MAN (Formerly Adventures of The Fly; Mighty Comics #40 on)
No. 32, July, 1965 - No. 39, Sept, 1966 (Also see Mighty Crusaders)
Mighty Comics Group (Radio Comics) (Archie)

32,33-Comet, Shield, Black Hood, The Fly & Flygirl x-over. 33-Re-intro Wizard, Hangman (1st S.A. appearances) 3.70 11.00 26.00
34-36: 34-Shield begins. 35-Origin Black Hood. 36-Hangman x-over in Shield; re-intro. & origin of Web (1st S.A. app.) 2.40 7.30 17.00
37-39: 37-Hangman, Wizard x-over in Flyman; last Shield issue. 38-Web story. 39-Steel Sterling story (1st S.A. app.) 2.40 7.30 17.00

FOES (Ram)(Value: cover or less)

FOLLOW THE SUN (TV)
May-July, 1962 - No. 2, Sept-Nov, 1962 (Photo-c)
Dell Publishing Co.

01-280-207(No.1), 12-280-211(No.2) 4.35 13.00 26.00

FOODANG
July, 1994 ($1.95, B&W, bi-monthly)
Continum Comics

1 .80 2.00

FOODINI (TV)(The Great...; see Jingle Dingle & Pinhead &...)
March, 1950 - No. 5, 1950 (All have 52 pgs.)
Continental Publications (Holyoke)

1-Based on TV puppet show (very early TV comic) 11.00 32.00 75.00
2-Jingle Dingle begins 7.00 21.00 42.00
3-5: 4-(8/50) 5.35 16.00 32.00

FOOEY (Magazine) (Satire)
Feb, 1961 - No. 4, May, 1961
Scoff Publishing Co.

1 5.35 16.00 32.00
2-4 4.00 10.00 20.00

FOOFUR (TV)
Aug, 1987 - No. 6, June, 1988
Star Comics/Marvel Comics No. 5 on

GD25 FN65 NM94

1-6 1.00

FOOLKILLER (Also see The Amazing Spider-Man #225, The Defenders #73 Man-Thing #3 & Omega the Unknown #8)
Oct, 1990 - No. 10, Oct, 1991 ($1.75, limited series)
Marvel Comics

1-Origin 3rd Foolkiller; Greg Salinger app. .70 1.75
2-7,9,10: DeZuniga-a(i) in 1-4 .70 1.75
8-Spider-Man x-over .90 2.25

FOOTBALL THRILLS (See Tops In Adventure)
Fall-Winter, 1951-52 - No. 2, Fall, 1952 (Edited by "Red" Grange)
Ziff-Davis Publ. Co.

1-Powell a(2); Saunders painted-c; Red Grange, Jim Thorpe stories 20.00 60.00 140.00
2-Saunders painted-c 13.50 41.00 95.00

FOR A NIGHT OF LOVE
1951
Avon Periodicals

nn-Two stories adapted from the works of Emile Zola; Astarita, Ravielli-a; Kinstler-c 19.00 58.00 135.00

FORBIDDEN LOVE
Mar, 1950 - No. 4, Sept, 1950 (52 pgs.)
Quality Comics Group

1-(Scarce)-Classic photo-c; Crandall-a 54.00 160.00 375.00
2,3-(Scarce)-Photo-c 24.00 72.00 165.00
4-(Scarce)-Ward/Cuidera-a; photo-c 27.00 80.00 185.00

FORBIDDEN LOVE (See Dark Mansion of...)

FORBIDDEN PLANET
May, 1992 - No. 4, 1992 ($2.50, mini-series)
Innovation Publishing

1-4: Adapts movie; painted covers 1.00 2.50

FORBIDDEN TALES OF DARK MANSION (Formerly Dark Mansion of Forbidden Love #1-4)
No. 5, May-June, 1972 - No. 15, Feb-Mar, 1974
National Periodical Publications

5-15: 5-(52 pgs.). 13-Kane/Howard-a 1.00 2.00 5.00
NOTE: ***N. Adams*** *c-9.* ***Alcala*** *a-9-11, 13.* ***Chaykin*** *a-7,15.* ***Evans*** *a-14.* ***Kaluta*** *a-7i, 8-13; c-7, 8, 13.* ***G. Kane*** *a-13.* ***Kirby*** *a-6.* ***Nino*** *a-8, 12, 15.* ***Redondo*** *a-14.*

FORBIDDEN WORLDS
7-8/51 - No. 34, 10-11/54; No. 35, 8/55 - No. 145, 8/67
(No. 1-5: 52 pgs.; No. 6-8: 44 pgs.)
American Comics Group

1-Williamson/Frazetta-a (10 pgs.) 86.00 257.00 700.00
2 43.00 130.00 350.00
3-Williamson/Orlando-a (7 pgs.); Wood (2 panels); Frazetta (1 panel) 45.00 135.00 365.00
4 22.00 65.00 170.00
5-Krenkel/Williamson-a (8 pgs.) 36.00 110.00 285.00
6-Harrison/Williamson-a (8 pgs.) 30.00 90.00 240.00
7,8,10: 7-1st monthly issue 15.00 45.00 125.00
9-A-Bomb explosion story 17.00 52.00 140.00
11-20 11.00 32.00 85.00
21-33: 24-E.C. swipe by Landau 8.00 24.00 65.00
34(10-11/54)(Scarce)(becomes Young Heroes #35 on)-Last pre-code issue; A-Bomb explosion story 8.00 24.00 65.00
35(8/55)-Scarce 7.40 22.00 52.00
36-62 4.70 14.00 33.00
63,69,76,78-Williamson-a in all; w/Krenkel #69 6.00 17.00 40.00
64,66-68,70-72,74,75,77,79-85,87-90 4.30 12.90 30.00
65- "There's a New Moon Tonight" listed in #114 as holding 1st record fan mail response 5.00 15.00 35.00
73-1st app. Herbie by Ogden Whitney 26.00 79.00 185.00
86-Flying saucer-c by Schaffenberger 5.00 15.00 35.00

Force Works #3 © MEG

Forever People #7 © DC

Fuor Color #3 © DELL

GD25 FN65 NM94

91-93,95-100 3.00 9.40 22.00
94-Herbie app. 7.00 20.00 46.00
101-109,111-113,115,117-120 2.60 7.70 18.00
110,114,116-Herbie app. 114-1st Herbie-c; contains list of editor's top 20 ACG stories. 116-Herbie goes to Hell 4.10 12.40 29.00
121-124: 124-Magic Agent app. 2.60 7.70 18.00
125-Magic Agent app.; intro. & origin Magicman series, ends #141 2.90 9.00 20.00
126-130 2.40 7.30 17.00
131-139: 133-Origin/1st app. Dragonia in Magicman (1-2/66); returns in #138. 136-Nemesis x-over in Magicman 2.10 6.00 15.00
140-Mark Midnight app. by Ditko 2.40 7.30 17.00
141-145 1.70 5.00 12.00

NOTE: ***Buscema** a-75, 79, 81, 82, 140r. **Cameron** a-5. **Disbrow** a-10. **Ditko** a-137p, 138, 140. **Landau** a-24, 27-29, 31-34, 48, 86r, 96, 143-45. **Lazarus** a-18, 23, 24, 57. **Moldoff** a-27, 31, 139r. **Reinman** a-93. **Whitney** a-115, 116, 137; c-40, 46, 57, 60, 68, 78, 79, 90, 93, 94, 100, 102, 103, 106-108, 114, 129.*

FORCE, THE (See The Crusaders)

FORCE OF BUDDHA'S PALM THE (Jademan)(Value: cover or less)

FORCE WORKS
July, 1994 - Present ($1.50)
Marvel Comics
1-($3.95)-Fold-out pop-up-c; Iron Man, Wonder Man, Spider-Woman,U.S. Agent & Scarlet Witch (new costume) 1.60 4.00
2-9: 5-Blue logo version & pink logo version 1.50

FORD ROTUNDA CHRISTMAS BOOK (See Christmas at the Rotunda)

FOREIGN INTRIGUES (Formerly Johnny Dynamite; becomes Battlefield Action #16 on)
No. 13, 1956 - No. 15, Aug, 1956
Charlton Comics
13-15-Johnny Dynamite continues 4.35 13.00 26.00

FOREMOST BOYS (See 4Most)

FOREST FIRE (Also see Smokey The Bear)
1949 (dated-1950) (16 pgs., paper-c)
American Forestry Assn.(Commerical Comics)
nn-Intro/1st app. Smokey The Forest Fire Preventing Bear; created by Rudy Wendelein; Wendelein/Sparling-a; 'Carter Oil Co.' on back-c of original 16.00 48.00 110.00

FOREVER, DARLING (See 4-Color No. 681)

FOREVER PEOPLE, THE
Feb-Mar, 1971 - No. 11, Oct-Nov, 1972
National Periodical Publications
1-1st app. Forever People; Superman x-over; Kirby-c/a begins; 1st full app. Darkseid (3rd anywhere, 3 weeks before New Gods #1); Darkseid storyline begins, ends #8(app. in 1-4,6,8; cameos in 5,11) 5.10 15.00 36.00
2-5: 4-G.A. reprints begin, end #9 3.00 9.40 22.00
6-11: 9,10-Deadman app. 1.70 4.20 10.00
NOTE: ***Kirby** c/a(p)-1-11; #4-9 contain Sandman reprints from Adventure #85, 84, 75, 80, 77, 74 in that order. #1-3, 10-11 are 36pgs; #4-9 are 52pgs.*

FOREVER PEOPLE
Feb, 1988 - No. 6, July, 1988 ($1.25, mini-series)
DC Comics
1-6 1.25

FOR GIRLS ONLY
Nov, 1953 (Digest size, 100 pgs.)
Bernard Bailey Enterprises
1-Half comic book, half magazine 10.00 30.00 70.00

FORGOTTEN FOREST OF OZ, THE (See First Comics Graphic Novel #16)

FORGOTTEN REALMS (DC)(Value: cover or less)

FORGOTTEN STORY BEHIND NORTH BEACH, THE
No date (8 pgs.; paper cover)
Catechetical Guild
nn 2.40 6.00 12.00

GD25 FN65 NM94

FOR LOVERS ONLY (Formerly Hollywood Romances)
No. 60, Aug, 1971 - No. 87, Nov, 1976
Charlton Comics
60-87: 73-Spanking scene-c/story 1.20

40 BIG PAGES OF MICKEY MOUSE
No. 945, Jan, 1936 (44 pgs.; 10-1/4x12-1/2"; cardboard cover)
Whitman Publishing Co.
945-Reprints Mickey Mouse Magazine #1, but with a different cover; ads were eliminated and some illustrated stories had expanded text. The book is 3/4" shorter than Mickey Mouse Mag. #1, but the reprints are the same size (Rare) 150.00 450.00 1000.00

48 FAMOUS AMERICANS
1947 (Giveaway) (Half-size in color)
J. C. Penney Co. (Cpr. Edwin H. Stroh)
nn-Simon & Kirby-a 9.15 27.50 55.00

FOR YOUR EYES ONLY (See James Bond...)

FOUR COLOR
Sept?, 1939 - No. 1354, Apr-June, 1962 (Series I are all 68 pgs.)
Dell Publishing Co.

NOTE: *Four Color only appears on issues #19-25, 1-99,101. Dell Publishing Co. filed these as Series I, #1-25, and Series II, #1-1354. Issues beginning with #710? were printed with and without ads on back cover. Issues without ads are worth more.*

SERIES I: GD25 FN65 VF82 NM94
1(nn)-Dick Tracy 470.00 1410.00 3055.00 4700.00
(Estimated up to 115 total copies exist, 5 in NM/Mint)
GD25 FN65 NM94
2(nn)-Don Winslow of the Navy (#1) (Rare) (11/39?) 126.00 377.00 880.00
3(nn)-Myra North (1/40?) 79.00 235.00 550.00
GD25 FN65 VF82 NM94
4-Donald Duck by Al Taliaferro (1940)(Disney)(3/40?) 700.00 2100.00 4550.00 7000.00
(Prices vary widely on this book)
GD25 FN65 NM94
5-Smilin' Jack (#1) (5/40?) 63.00 190.00 440.00
6-Dick Tracy (Scarce) 129.00 385.00 900.00
7-Gang Busters 37.00 111.00 260.00
8-Dick Tracy 75.00 225.00 525.00
9-Terry and the Pirates-r/Super #9-29 63.00 190.00 440.00
10-Smilin' Jack 57.00 170.00 400.00
11-Smitty (#1) 38.00 115.00 265.00
12-Little Orphan Annie; reprints strips from 12/19/37 to 6/4/38 51.00 154.00 360.00
13-Walt Disney's Reluctant Dragon('41)-Contains 2 pgs. of photos from film; 2 pg. foreword to Fantasia by Leopold Stokowski; Donald Duck, Goofy, Baby Weems & Mickey Mouse (as the Sorcerer's Apprentice) app. (Disney) 150.00 450.00 1000.00
14-Moon Mullins (#1) 36.00 107.00 250.00
15-Tillie the Toiler (#1) 36.00 107.00 250.00
GD25 FN65 VF82
16-Mickey Mouse (#1) (Disney) by Gottfredson 600.00 1800.00 6000.00
GD25 FN65 NM94
17-Walt Disney's Dumbo, the Flying Elephant (#1)(1941)-Mickey Mouse, Donald Duck, & Pluto app. (Disney) 180.00 535.00 1250.00
18-Jiggs and Maggie (#1)(1936-38-r) 39.00 118.00 275.00
19-Barney Google and Snuffy Smith (#1)-(1st issue with Four Color on the cover) 38.00 114.00 265.00
20-Tiny Tim 31.00 94.00 220.00
21-Dick Tracy 64.00 195.00 450.00
22-Don Winslow 31.00 94.00 220.00
23-Gang Busters 28.00 84.00 195.00
24-Captain Easy 43.00 129.00 300.00
25-Popeye (1942) 71.00 215.00 500.00

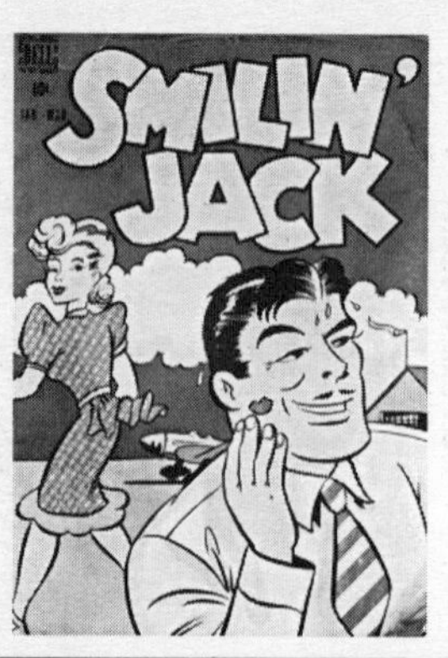

Four Color #4© N.Y. News Syndicate

Four Color #42 © DELL

Four Color #94 © DELL

SERIES II:

	GD25	FN65	VF82	NM94
1-Little Joe (1942)	47.00	141.00		330.00
2-Harold Teen	26.00	78.00		180.00
3-Alley Oop (#1)	50.00	150.00		350.00
4-Smilin' Jack	47.00	141.00		330.00
5-Raggedy Ann and Andy (#1)	50.00	150.00		350.00
6-Smitty	22.00	65.00		150.00
7-Smokey Stover (#1)	34.00	103.00		240.00
8-Tillie the Toiler	22.00	65.00		150.00
9-Donald Duck Finds Pirate Gold, by Carl Barks & Jack Hannah (Disney) (© 8/17/42)	6000.00	1800.00	3900.00	6000.00
10-Flash Gordon by Alex Raymond; reprinted from "The Ice Kingdom"	57.00	171.00		400.00
11-Wash Tubbs	31.00	94.00		220.00
12-Walt Disney's Bambi (#1)	57.00	171.00		400.00
13-Mr. District Attorney (#1)-See The Funnies #35 for 1st app.	29.00	86.00		200.00
14-Smilin' Jack	37.00	111.00		260.00
15-Felix the Cat (#1)	71.00	215.00		500.00
16-Porky Pig (#1)(1942)- "Secret of the Haunted House"	71.00	215.00		500.00
17-Popeye	57.00	171.00		400.00
18-Little Orphan Annie's Junior Commandos; Flag-c; reprints strips from 6/14/42 to 11/21/42	41.00	125.00		290.00
19-Walt Disney's Thumper Meets the Seven Dwarfs (Disney); reprinted in Silly Symphonies	57.00	171.00		400.00
20-Barney Baxter	24.00	72.00		165.00
21-Oswald the Rabbit (#1)(1943)	50.00	150.00		350.00
22-Tillie the Toiler	17.00	52.00		120.00
23-Raggedy Ann and Andy	37.00	111.00		260.00
24-Gang Busters	28.00	84.00		195.00
25-Andy Panda (#1) (Walter Lantz)	50.00	150.00		350.00
26-Popeye	57.00	171.00		400.00
27-Walt Disney's Mickey Mouse and the Seven Colored Terror	86.00	257.00		600.00
28-Wash Tubbs	23.00	70.00		160.00
29-Donald Duck and the Mummy's Ring, by Carl Barks (Disney) (9/43)	500.00	1500.00	3250.00	5000.00
30-Bambi's Children (1943)-Disney	57.00	171.00		400.00
31-Moon Mullins	19.00	57.00		130.00
32-Smitty	17.00	52.00		120.00
33-Bugs Bunny "Public Nuisance #1"	57.00	171.00		400.00
34-Dick Tracy	43.00	130.00		300.00
35-Smokey Stover	17.00	52.00		120.00
36-Smilin' Jack	24.00	72.00		165.00
37-Bringing Up Father	19.00	57.00		130.00
38-Roy Rogers (#1, © 4/44)-1st western comic with photo-c	100.00	300.00		700.00
39-Oswald the Rabbit (1944)	35.00	105.00		245.00
40-Barney Google and Snuffy Smith	22.00	65.00		150.00
41-Mother Goose and Nursery Rhyme Comics (#1)-All by Walt Kelly	22.00	65.00		150.00
42-Tiny Tim (1934-r)	17.00	52.00		120.00
43-Popeye (1938-'42-r)	33.00	100.00		230.00
44-Terry and the Pirates (1938-r)	43.00	130.00		300.00
45-Raggedy Ann	30.00	90.00		210.00
46-Felix the Cat and the Haunted Castle	43.00	130.00		300.00
47-Gene Autry (copyright 6/16/44)	43.00	130.00		300.00
48-Porky Pig of the Mounties by Carl Barks (7/44)	100.00	300.00		700.00
49-Snow White and the Seven Dwarfs (Disney)	57.00	171.00		400.00
50-Fairy Tale Parade-Walt Kelly art (1944)	26.00	78.00		180.00
51-Bugs Bunny Finds the Lost Treasure	34.00	100.00		235.00
52-Little Orphan Annie; reprints strips from 6/18/38 to 11/19/38	31.00	94.00		220.00
53-Wash Tubbs	17.00	52.00		120.00
54-Andy Panda	27.00	81.00		190.00
55-Tillie the Toiler	13.00	40.00		90.00
56-Dick Tracy	34.00	105.00		240.00
57-Gene Autry	38.00	115.00		265.00
58-Smilin' Jack	24.00	72.00		165.00
59-Mother Goose and Nursery Rhyme Comics-Kelly-c/a	19.00	57.00		130.00
60-Tiny Folks Funnies	14.00	43.00		100.00
61-Santa Claus Funnies(11/44)-Kelly art	24.00	72.00		165.00
62-Donald Duck in Frozen Gold, by Carl Barks (Disney) (1/45)	144.00	433.00		1300.00
63-Roy Rogers; color photo-all 4 covers	47.00	141.00		330.00
64-Smokey Stover	13.00	40.00		90.00
65-Smitty	13.00	40.00		90.00
66-Gene Autry	38.00	115.00		265.00
67-Oswald the Rabbit	17.00	52.00		120.00
68-Mother Goose and Nursery Rhyme Comics, by Walt Kelly	19.00	57.00		130.00
69-Fairy Tale Parade, by Walt Kelly	26.00	78.00		180.00
70-Popeye and Wimpy	27.00	81.00		190.00
71-Walt Disney's Three Caballeros, by Walt Kelly (© 4/45)-(Disney)	86.00	257.00		600.00
72-Raggedy Ann	25.00	75.00		175.00
73-The Gumps (#1)	11.00	32.00		75.00
74-Marge's Little Lulu (#1)	107.00	321.00		750.00
75-Gene Autry and the Wildcat	31.00	94.00		220.00
76-Little Orphan Annie; reprints strips from 2/28/40 to 6/24/40	26.00	78.00		180.00
77-Felix the Cat	40.00	120.00		280.00
78-Porky Pig and the Bandit Twins	24.00	72.00		165.00
79-Walt Disney's Mickey Mouse in The Riddle of the Red Hat by Carl Barks (8/45)	114.00	343.00		800.00
80-Smilin' Jack	17.00	52.00		120.00
81-Moon Mullins	10.00	30.00		70.00
82-Lone Ranger	39.00	118.00		275.00
83-Gene Autry in Outlaw Trail	31.00	94.00		220.00
84-Flash Gordon by Alex Raymond-Reprints from "The Fiery Desert"	39.00	118.00		275.00
85-Andy Panda and the Mad Dog Mystery	16.00	48.00		110.00
86-Roy Rogers; photo-c	34.00	100.00		235.00
87-Fairy Tale Parade by Walt Kelly; Dan Noonan-c	26.00	78.00		180.00
88-Bugs Bunny's Great Adventure (Sci/fi)	20.00	60.00		140.00
89-Tillie the Toiler	13.00	40.00		90.00
90-Christmas with Mother Goose by Walt Kelly (11/45)	18.00	54.00		125.00
91-Santa Claus Funnies by Walt Kelly (11/45)	19.00	57.00		130.00
92-Walt Disney's The Wonderful Adventures Of Pinocchio (1945); Donald Duck by Kelly, 16 pgs. (Disney)	57.00	171.00		400.00
93-Gene Autry in The Bandit of Black Rock	26.00	78.00		180.00
94-Winnie Winkle (1945)	13.00	40.00		90.00
95-Roy Rogers Comics; photo-c	34.00	100.00		235.00
96-Dick Tracy	26.00	78.00		180.00
97-Marge's Little Lulu (1946)	50.00	150.00		350.00
98-Lone Ranger, The	30.00	90.00		210.00
99-Smitty	11.50	34.00		80.00
100-Gene Autry Comics; photo-c	26.00	78.00		180.00
101-Terry and the Pirates	29.00	86.00		200.00

NOTE: *No. 101 is last issue to carry "Four Color" logo on cover; all issues beginning with No. 100 are marked "...O. S." (One Shot) which can be found in the bottom left-hand panel on the first page; the numbers following "O. S." relate to the year/month issued.*

	GD25	FN65	NM94
102-Oswald the Rabbit-Walt Kelly art, 1 pg.	15.00	45.00	105.00
103-Easter with Mother Goose by Walt Kelly	20.00	60.00	140.00
104-Fairy Tale Parade by Walt Kelly	20.00	60.00	140.00

Four Color #144 © Roy Rogers

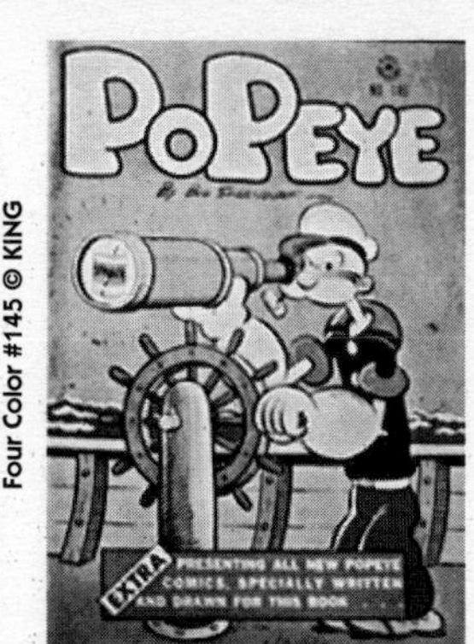

Four Color #145 © KING

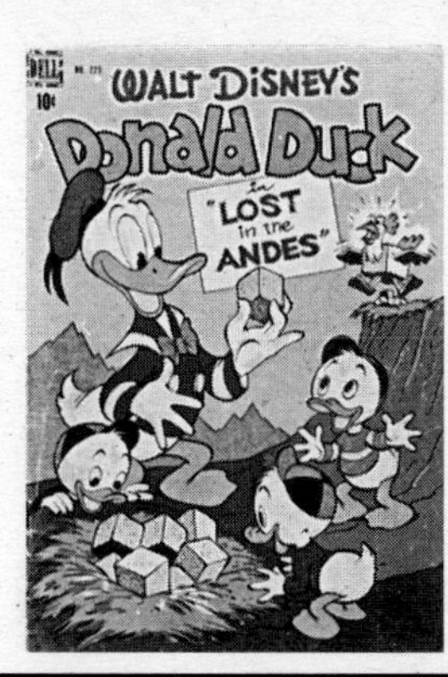

Four Color #223 © WDC

	GD25	FN65	NM94
105-Albert the Alligator and Pogo Possum (#1) by Kelly (4/46)	75.00	220.00	515.00
106-Tillie the Toiler	10.00	30.00	65.00
107-Little Orphan Annie; reprints strips from 11/16/42 to 3/24/43	22.00	67.00	155.00
108-Donald Duck in The Terror of the River, by Carl Barks (Disney) (© 4/16/46)	111.00	333.00	1000.00
109-Roy Rogers Comics; photo-c	27.00	80.00	185.00
110-Marge's Little Lulu	36.00	107.00	250.00
111-Captain Easy	14.00	43.00	100.00
112-Porky Pig's Adventure in Gopher Gulch	14.00	43.00	100.00
113-Popeye; all new Popeye stories begin	14.00	43.00	100.00
114-Fairy Tale Parade by Walt Kelly	20.00	60.00	140.00
115-Marge's Little Lulu	36.00	107.00	250.00
116-Mickey Mouse and the House of Many Mysteries (Disney)	24.00	72.00	165.00
117-Roy Rogers Comics; photo-c	19.00	57.00	130.00
118-Lone Ranger, The	30.00	90.00	210.00
119-Felix the Cat; all new Felix stories begin	34.00	100.00	235.00
120-Marge's Little Lulu	31.00	94.00	220.00
121-Fairy Tale Parade-(not Kelly)	11.50	34.00	80.00
122-Henry (#1) (10/46)	11.50	34.00	80.00
123-Bugs Bunny's Dangerous Venture	14.00	43.00	100.00
124-Roy Rogers Comics; photo-c	19.00	57.00	130.00
125-Lone Ranger, The	22.00	67.00	155.00
126-Christmas with Mother Goose by Walt Kelly (1946)	14.00	43.00	100.00
127-Popeye	14.00	43.00	100.00
128-Santa Claus Funnies- "Santa & the Angel" by Gollub; "A Mouse in the House" by Kelly	14.00	43.00	100.00
129-Walt Disney's Uncle Remus and His Tales of Brer Rabbit (#1) (1946)- Adapted from Disney movie "Song of the South"	29.00	86.00	200.00
130-Andy Panda (Walter Lantz)	10.00	30.00	65.00
131-Marge's Little Lulu	31.00	94.00	220.00
132-Tillie the Toiler (1947)	10.00	30.00	65.00
133-Dick Tracy	22.00	65.00	150.00
134-Tarzan and the Devil Ogre; Marsh-c/a	64.00	193.00	450.00
135-Felix the Cat	25.00	75.00	175.00
136-Lone Ranger, The	22.00	67.00	155.00
137-Roy Rogers Comics; photo-c	19.00	57.00	130.00
138-Smitty	10.00	30.00	65.00
139-Marge's Little Lulu (1947)	29.00	86.00	200.00
140-Easter with Mother Goose by Walt Kelly	16.00	48.00	110.00
141-Mickey Mouse and the Submarine Pirates (Disney)	21.00	63.00	145.00
142-Bugs Bunny and the Haunted Mountain	14.00	43.00	100.00
143-Oswald the Rabbit & the Prehistoric Egg	9.15	27.50	55.00
144-Roy Rogers Comics (1947)-Photo-c	19.00	57.00	130.00
145-Popeye	14.00	43.00	100.00
146-Marge's Little Lulu	29.00	86.00	200.00
147-Donald Duck in Volcano Valley, by Carl Barks (Disney) (5/47)	72.00	217.00	650.00
148-Albert the Alligator and Pogo Possum by Walt Kelly (5/47)	68.00	205.00	475.00
149-Smilin' Jack	11.50	34.00	80.00
150-Tillie the Toiler (6/47)	9.15	27.50	55.00
151-Lone Ranger, The	19.00	57.00	130.00
152-Little Orphan Annie; reprints strips from 1/2/44 to 5/6/44	14.00	43.00	100.00
153-Roy Rogers Comics; photo-c	16.00	48.00	110.00
154-Walter Lantz Andy Panda	10.00	30.00	65.00
155-Henry (7/47)	9.15	27.50	55.00
156-Porky Pig and the Phantom	10.00	30.00	70.00
157-Mickey Mouse & the Beanstalk (Disney)	21.00	63.00	145.00
158-Marge's Little Lulu	29.00	86.00	200.00
159-Donald Duck in the Ghost of the Grotto, by Carl Barks (Disney) (8/47)	64.00	192.00	575.00
160-Roy Rogers Comics; photo-c	16.00	48.00	110.00
161-Tarzan and the Fires Of Tohr; Marsh-c/a	55.00	165.00	385.00
162-Felix the Cat (9/47)	19.00	57.00	130.00
163-Dick Tracy	17.00	52.00	120.00
164-Bugs Bunny Finds the Frozen Kingdom	14.00	43.00	100.00
165-Marge's Little Lulu	29.00	86.00	200.00
166-Roy Rogers Comics (52 pgs.)-Photo-c	16.00	48.00	110.00
167-Lone Ranger, The	19.00	57.00	130.00
168-Popeye (10/47)	14.00	43.00	100.00
169-Woody Woodpecker (#1)- "Manhunter in the North"; drug use story	16.00	48.00	110.00
170-Mickey Mouse on Spook's Island (11/47)(Disney)-reprinted in Mickey Mouse #103	17.00	52.00	120.00
171-Charlie McCarthy (#1) and the Twenty Thieves	18.00	54.00	125.00
172-Christmas with Mother Goose by Walt Kelly (11/47)	14.00	43.00	100.00
173-Flash Gordon	13.50	41.00	95.00
174-Winnie Winkle	8.35	25.00	50.00
175-Santa Claus Funnies by Walt Kelly (1947)	14.00	43.00	100.00
176-Tillie the Toiler (12/47)	9.15	27.50	55.00
177-Roy Rogers Comics-(36 pgs.); Photo-c	16.00	48.00	110.00
178-Donald Duck "Christmas on Bear Mountain" by Carl Barks; 1st app. Uncle Scrooge (Disney)(12/47)	72.00	217.00	650.00
179-Uncle Wiggily (#1)-Walt Kelly-c	16.00	48.00	110.00
180-Ozark Ike (#1)	10.00	30.00	60.00
181-Walt Disney's Mickey Mouse in Jungle Magic	17.00	52.00	120.00
182-Porky Pig in Never-Never Land (2/48)	10.00	30.00	70.00
183-Oswald the Rabbit (Lantz)	9.15	27.50	55.00
184-Tillie the Toiler	9.15	27.50	55.00
185-Easter with Mother Goose by Walt Kelly (1948)	14.00	43.00	100.00
186-Walt Disney's Bambi (4/48)-Reprinted as Movie Classic Bambi #3 (1956)	17.00	52.00	120.00
187-Bugs Bunny and the Dreadful Dragon	11.50	34.00	80.00
188-Woody Woodpecker (Lantz, 5/48)	11.50	34.00	80.00
189-Donald Duck in The Old Castle's Secret, by Carl Barks (Disney) (6/48)	59.00	178.00	535.00
190-Flash Gordon ('48)	13.50	41.00	95.00
191-Porky Pig to the Rescue	10.00	30.00	70.00
192-The Brownies (#1)-by Walt Kelly (7/48)	13.00	40.00	90.00
193-M.G.M. Presents Tom and Jerry (#1)(1948)	14.00	43.00	100.00
194-Mickey Mouse in The World Under the Sea (Disney)-Reprinted in Mickey Mouse #101	17.00	52.00	120.00
195-Tillie the Toiler	6.35	19.00	38.00
196-Charlie McCarthy in The Haunted Hide-Out; part photo-c	16.00	48.00	110.00
197-Spirit of the Border (#1) (Zane Grey) (1948)	13.00	40.00	90.00
198-Andy Panda	10.00	30.00	65.00
199-Donald Duck in Sheriff of Bullet Valley, by Carl Barks; Barks draws himself on wanted poster, last page; used in Love & Death (Disney) (10/48)	59.00	178.00	535.00
200-Bugs Bunny, Super Sleuth (10/48)	11.50	34.00	80.00
201-Christmas with Mother Goose by W. Kelly	12.00	36.00	85.00
202-Woody Woodpecker	7.50	22.50	45.00
203-Donald Duck in the Golden Christmas Tree, by Carl Barks (Disney) (12/48)	44.00	133.00	400.00
204-Flash Gordon (12/48)	11.00	32.00	75.00
205-Santa Claus Funnies by Walt Kelly	13.00	40.00	90.00
206-Little Orphan Annie; reprints strips from 11/10/40 to 1/11/41	8.35	25.00	50.00
207-King of the Royal Mounted (#1) (12/48)	17.00	52.00	120.00
208-Brer Rabbit Does It Again (Disney) (1/49)	11.50	34.00	80.00
209-Harold Teen	4.35	13.00	26.00
210-Tippie and Cap Stubbs	4.35	13.00	26.00
211-Little Beaver (#1)	8.35	25.00	50.00
212-Dr. Bobbs	4.70	14.00	28.00

Four Color #226 © Warner Bros.

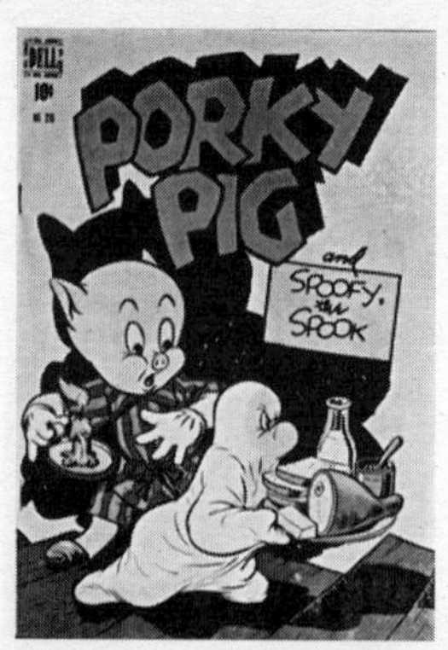

Four Color #228 © Johnston McCulley

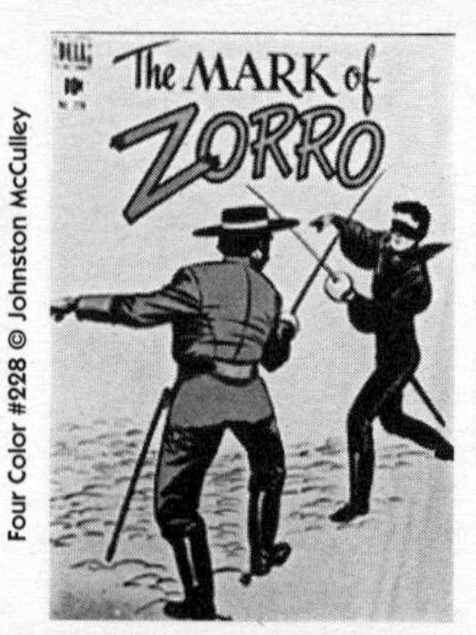

Four Color #305 © Walter Lantz Prod.

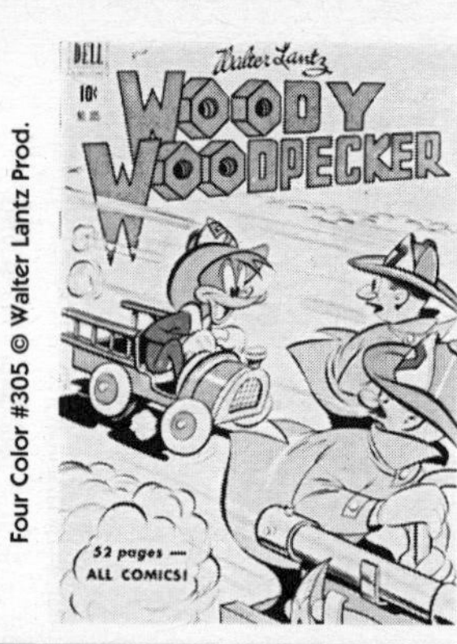

	GD25	FN65	NM94
213-Tillie the Toiler	6.35	19.00	38.00
214-Mickey Mouse and His Sky Adventure (2/49)(Disney)-Reprinted in Mickey Mouse #105	14.00	43.00	100.00
215-Sparkle Plenty (Dick Tracy-r by Gould)	10.00	30.00	70.00
216-Andy Panda and the Police Pup (Lantz)	7.50	22.50	45.00
217-Bugs Bunny in Court Jester	11.50	34.00	80.00
218-3 Little Pigs and the Wonderful Magic Lamp (Disney) (3/49)(#1)	13.00	40.00	90.00
219-Swee'pe	10.00	30.00	65.00
220-Easter with Mother Goose by Walt Kelly	13.00	40.00	90.00
221-Uncle Wiggily-Walt Kelly cover in part	10.00	30.00	70.00
222-West of the Pecos (Zane Grey)	8.35	25.00	50.00
223-Donald Duck "Lost in the Andes" by Carl Barks (Disney-4/49) (square egg story)	56.00	167.00	500.00
224-Little Iodine (#1), by Hatlo (4/49)	10.00	30.00	70.00
225-Oswald the Rabbit (Lantz)	5.85	17.50	35.00
226-Porky Pig and Spoofy, the Spook	8.35	25.00	50.00
227-Seven Dwarfs (Disney)	11.00	32.00	75.00
228-Mark of Zorro, The (#1) (1949)	24.00	72.00	165.00
229-Smokey Stover	5.35	16.00	32.00
230-Sunset Pass (Zane Grey)	8.35	25.00	50.00
231-Mickey Mouse and the Rajah's Treasure (Disney)	14.00	43.00	100.00
232-Woody Woodpecker (Lantz, 6/49)	7.50	22.50	45.00
233-Bugs Bunny, Sleepwalking Sleuth	11.50	34.00	80.00
234-Dumbo in Sky Voyage (Disney)	10.00	30.00	70.00
235-Tiny Tim	5.85	17.50	35.00
236-Heritage of the Desert (Zane Grey) (1949)	8.35	25.00	50.00
237-Tillie the Toiler	6.35	19.00	38.00
238-Donald Duck in Voodoo Hoodoo, by Carl Barks (Disney) (8/49)	44.00	133.00	400.00
239-Adventure Bound (8/49)	5.35	16.00	32.00
240-Andy Panda (Lantz)	7.50	22.50	45.00
241-Porky Pig, Mighty Hunter	8.35	25.00	50.00
242-Tippie and Cap Stubbs	4.35	13.00	26.00
243-Thumper Follows His Nose (Disney)	10.00	30.00	70.00
244-The Brownies by Walt Kelly	11.50	34.00	80.00
245-Dick's Adventures in Dreamland (9/49)	5.35	16.00	32.00
246-Thunder Mountain (Zane Grey)	5.35	16.00	32.00
247-Flash Gordon	11.00	32.00	75.00
248-Mickey Mouse and the Black Sorcerer (Disney)	14.00	43.00	100.00
249-Woody Woodpecker in the "Globetrotter" (10/49)	7.50	22.50	45.00
250-Bugs Bunny in Diamond Daze; used in **SOTI**, pg. 309	11.50	34.00	80.00
251-Hubert at Camp Moonbeam	5.35	16.00	32.00
252-Pinocchio (Disney)-not by Kelly; origin	10.00	30.00	70.00
253-Christmas with Mother Goose by W. Kelly	11.00	32.00	75.00
254-Santa Claus Funnies by Walt Kelly; Pogo & Albert story by Kelly (11/49)	13.00	40.00	90.00
255-The Ranger (Zane Grey) (1949)	5.35	16.00	32.00
256-Donald Duck in "Luck of the North" by Carl Barks (Disney) (12/49)-Shows #257 on inside	32.00	95.00	285.00
257-Little Iodine	8.35	25.00	50.00
258-Andy Panda and the Balloon Race (Lantz)	7.50	22.50	45.00
259-Santa and the Angel (Gollub art-condensed from #128) & Santa at the Zoo (12/49)-two books in one	5.85	17.50	35.00
260-Porky Pig, Hero of the Wild West (12/49)	8.35	25.00	50.00
261-Mickey Mouse and the Missing Key (Disney)	14.00	43.00	100.00
262-Raggedy Ann and Andy	7.00	21.00	42.00
263-Donald Duck in "Land of the Totem Poles" by Carl Barks (Disney) (2/50)-Has two Barks stories	32.00	95.00	285.00
264-Woody Woodpecker in the Magic Lantern (Lantz)	7.50	22.50	45.00
265-King of the Royal Mounted (Zane Grey)	10.00	30.00	65.00
266-Bugs Bunny on the "Isle of Hercules" (2/50)-Reprinted in Best of Bugs Bunny #1	10.00	30.00	65.00
267-Little Beaver; Harmon-c/a	4.35	13.00	26.00
268-Mickey Mouse's Surprise Visitor (1950) (Disney)	14.00	43.00	100.00
269-Johnny Mack Brown (#1)-Photo-c	22.00	65.00	150.00
270-Drift Fence (Zane Grey) (3/50)	5.35	16.00	32.00
271-Porky Pig in Phantom of the Plains	8.35	25.00	50.00
272-Cinderella (Disney) (4/50)	10.00	30.00	70.00
273-Oswald the Rabbit (Lantz)	5.85	17.50	35.00
274-Bugs Bunny, Hare-brained Reporter	10.00	30.00	65.00
275-Donald Duck in "Ancient Persia" by Carl Barks (Disney) (5/50)	29.00	88.00	265.00
276-Uncle Wiggily	8.35	25.00	50.00
277-Porky Pig in Desert Adventure (5/50)	8.35	25.00	50.00
278-Bill Elliott Comics (#1)-Photo-c	13.00	40.00	90.00
279-Mickey Mouse and Pluto Battle the Giant Ants (Disney); reprinted in Mickey Mouse #102 & 245	11.50	34.00	80.00
280-Andy Panda in The Isle Of Mechanical Men (Lantz)	7.50	22.50	45.00
281-Bugs Bunny in The Great Circus Mystery	10.00	30.00	65.00
282-Donald Duck and the Pixilated Parrot by Carl Barks (Disney) (© 5/23/50)	29.00	88.00	265.00
283-King of the Royal Mounted (7/50)	10.00	30.00	65.00
284-Porky Pig in The Kingdom of Nowhere	8.35	25.00	50.00
285-Bozo the Clown & His Minikin Circus (#1) (TV)	16.50	50.00	115.00
286-Mickey Mouse in The Uninvited Guest (Disney	11.50	34.00	80.00
287-Gene Autry's Champion in The Ghost Of Black Mountain; photo-c	10.00	30.00	70.00
288-Woody Woodpecker in Klondike Gold (Lantz)	7.50	22.50	45.00
289-Bugs Bunny in "Indian Trouble"	10.00	30.00	65.00
290-The Chief (#1) (8/50)	5.35	16.00	32.00
291-Donald Duck in "The Magic Hourglass" by Carl Barks (Disney) (9/50)	29.00	88.00	265.00
292-The Cisco Kid Comics (#1)	20.00	60.00	140.00
293-The Brownies-Kelly-c/a	11.00	32.00	75.00
294-Little Beaver	4.35	13.00	26.00
295-Porky Pig in President Porky (9/50)	8.35	25.00	50.00
296-Mickey Mouse in Private Eye for Hire (Disney)	11.50	34.00	80.00
297-Andy Panda in The Haunted Inn (Lantz, 10/50)	7.50	22.50	45.00
298-Bugs Bunny in Sheik for a Day	10.00	30.00	65.00
299-Buck Jones & the Iron Horse Trail (#1)	14.00	43.00	100.00
300-Donald Duck in "Big-Top Bedlam" by Carl Barks (Disney) (11/50)	29.00	88.00	265.00
301-The Mysterious Rider (Zane Grey)	5.35	16.00	32.00
302-Santa Claus Funnies (11/50)	4.00	12.00	24.00
303-Porky Pig in The Land of the Monstrous Flies	5.85	17.50	35.00
304-Mickey Mouse in Tom-Tom Island (Disney) (12/50)	9.15	27.50	55.00
305-Woody Woodpecker (Lantz)	4.70	14.00	28.00
306-Raggedy Ann	5.35	16.00	32.00
307-Bugs Bunny in Lumber Jack Rabbit	8.35	25.00	50.00
308-Donald Duck in "Dangerous Disguise" by Carl Barks (Disney) (1/51)	25.00	75.00	225.00
309-Betty Betz' Dollface and Her Gang (1951)	5.35	16.00	32.00
310-King of the Royal Mounted (1/51)	7.50	22.50	45.00
311-Porky Pig in Midget Horses of Hidden Valley	5.85	17.50	35.00
312-Tonto (#1)	13.00	40.00	90.00
313-Mickey Mouse in The Mystery of the Double-Cross Ranch (#1) (Disney) (2/51)	9.15	27.50	55.00

Note: Beginning with the above comic in 1951 Dell/Western began adding #1 in small print on the covers of several long running titles with the evident intention of switching these titles to their own monthly numbers, but when the conversions were made, there was no connection. It is thought that the post office may have stepped in and decreed the sequences should commence as though the first four colors printed had each begun with number one, or the first issues sold by subscription. Since the regular series' numbers don't correctly match to the num-

Four Color #335 © UFS

Four Color #337 © DELL

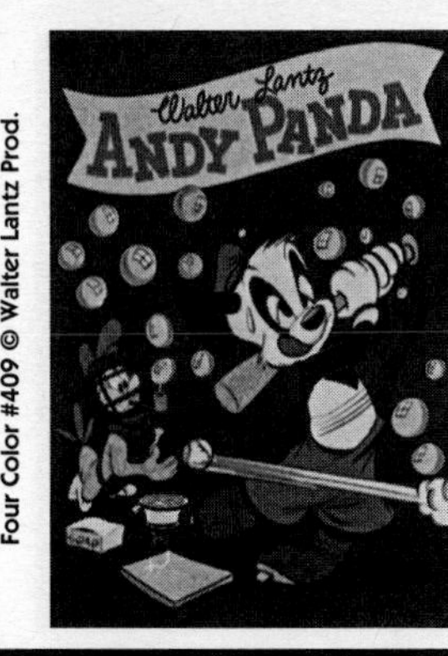

Four Color #409 © Walter Lantz Prod.

	GD25	FN65	NM94
bers of earlier issues published, it's not known whether or not the numbering was in error.			
314-Ambush (Zane Grey)	5.35	16.00	32.00
315-Oswald the Rabbit (Lantz)	4.00	11.00	22.00
316-Rex Allen (#1)-Photo-c; Marsh-a	17.00	52.00	120.00
317-Bugs Bunny in Hair Today Gone Tomorrow (#1)	8.35	25.00	50.00
318-Donald Duck in "No Such Varmint" by Carl Barks (#1)-Indicia shows #317 (Disney, © 1/23/51)	25.00	75.00	225.00
319-Gene Autry's Champion; painted-c	4.70	14.00	28.00
320-Uncle Wiggily (#1)	7.50	22.50	45.00
321-Little Scouts (#1) (3/51)	4.00	10.00	20.00
322-Porky Pig in Roaring Rockets (#1 on-c)	5.85	17.50	35.00
323-Susie Q. Smith (#1) (3/51)	4.70	14.00	28.00
324-I Met a Handsome Cowboy (3/51)	9.15	27.50	55.00
325-Mickey Mouse in The Haunted Castle (#2) (Disney) (4/51)	9.15	27.50	55.00
326-Andy Panda (#1) (Lantz)	4.00	11.00	22.00
327-Bugs Bunny and the Rajah's Treasure (#2)	8.35	25.00	50.00
328-Donald Duck in Old California (#2) by Carl Barks-Peyote drug use issue (Disney) (5/51)	27.00	80.00	240.00
329-Roy Roger's Trigger (#1)(5/51)-Photo-c	11.00	32.00	75.00
330-Porky Pig Meets the Bristled Bruiser (#2)	5.85	17.50	35.00
331-Alice in Wonderland (Disney) (1951)	16.00	48.00	110.00
332-Little Beaver	4.35	13.00	26.00
333-Wilderness Trek (Zane Grey) (5/51)	5.35	16.00	32.00
334-Mickey Mouse and Yukon Gold (Disney) (6/51)	9.15	27.50	55.00
335-Francis the Famous Talking Mule (#1, 6/51)-1st Dell non animated movie comic (all issues based on movie)	10.00	30.00	60.00
336-Woody Woodpecker (Lantz)	4.70	14.00	28.00
337-The Brownies-not by Walt Kelly	4.00	12.00	24.00
338-Bugs Bunny and the Rocking Horse Thieves	8.35	25.00	50.00
339-Donald Duck and the Magic Fountain-not by Carl Barks (Disney) (7-8/51)	8.35	25.00	50.00
340-King of the Royal Mounted (7/51)	7.50	22.50	45.00
341-Unbirthday Party with Alice in Wonderland (Disney) (7/51)	16.00	48.00	110.00
342-Porky Pig the Lucky Peppermint Mine	4.00	12.00	24.00
343-Mickey Mouse in The Ruby Eye of Homar-Guy-Am (Disney)-Reprinted in Mickey Mouse #104	7.50	22.50	45.00
344-Sergeant Preston from Challenge of The Yukon (#1) (TV)	12.00	36.00	85.00
345-Andy Panda in Scotland Yard (8-10/51) (Lantz)	4.00	11.00	22.00
346-Hideout (Zane Grey)	5.35	16.00	32.00
347-Bugs Bunny the Frigid Hare (8-9/51)	8.35	25.00	50.00
348-Donald Duck "The Crocodile Collector"; Barks-c only (Disney) (9-10/51)	14.00	43.00	100.00
349-Uncle Wiggily	7.50	22.50	45.00
350-Woody Woodpecker (Lantz)	4.70	14.00	28.00
351-Porky Pig & the Grand Canyon Giant (9-10/51)	4.00	12.00	24.00
352-Mickey Mouse in The Mystery of Painted Valley (Disney)	7.50	22.50	45.00
353-Duck Album (#1)-Barks-c (Disney)	8.35	25.00	50.00
354-Raggedy Ann & Andy	5.35	16.00	32.00
355-Bugs Bunny Hot-Rod Hare	8.35	25.00	50.00
356-Donald Duck in "Rags to Riches"; Barks-c only	14.00	43.00	100.00
357-Comeback (Zane Grey)	4.70	14.00	28.00
358-Andy Panda (Lantz) (11-1/52)	4.00	11.00	22.00
359-Frosty the Snowman (#1)	8.35	25.00	50.00
360-Porky Pig in Tree of Fortune (11-12/51)	4.00	12.00	24.00
361-Santa Claus Funnies	4.00	12.00	24.00
362-Mickey Mouse and the Smuggled Diamonds (Disney)	7.50	22.50	45.00
363-King of the Royal Mounted	6.70	20.00	40.00
364-Woody Woodpecker (Lantz)	4.00	11.00	22.00
365-The Brownies-not by Kelly	4.00	12.00	24.00
366-Bugs Bunny Uncle Buckskin Comes to Town (12-1/52)	8.35	25.00	50.00
367-Donald Duck in "A Christmas for Shacktown" by Carl Barks (Disney) (1-2/52)	23.00	70.00	210.00
368-Bob Clampett's Beany and Cecil (#1)	24.00	73.00	170.00
369-The Lone Ranger's Famous Horse Hi-Yo Silver (#1); Silver's origin	10.00	30.00	60.00
370-Porky Pig in Trouble in the Big Trees	4.00	12.00	24.00
371-Mickey Mouse in The Inca Idol Case (1952) (Disney)	7.50	22.50	45.00
372-Riders of the Purple Sage (Zane Grey)	4.70	14.00	28.00
373-Sergeant Preston (TV)	7.50	22.50	45.00
374-Woody Woodpecker (Lantz)	4.00	11.00	22.00
375-John Carter of Mars (E. R. Burroughs)-Jesse Marsh-a; origin	25.00	75.00	175.00
376-Bugs Bunny, "The Magic Sneeze"	8.35	25.00	50.00
377-Susie Q. Smith	4.00	11.00	22.00
378-Tom Corbett, Space Cadet (#1) (TV)-McWilliams-a	17.00	52.00	120.00
379-Donald Duck in "Southern Hospitality"; Not by Barks (Disney)	5.85	17.50	35.00
380-Raggedy Ann & Andy	5.35	16.00	32.00
381-Marge's Tubby (#1)	16.00	48.00	110.00
382-Snow White and the Seven Dwarfs (Disney)-origin; partial reprint of 4-Color #49 (Movie)	13.00	40.00	90.00
383-Andy Panda (Lantz)	3.60	9.00	18.00
384-King of the Royal Mounted (3/52)(Zane Grey)	6.70	20.00	40.00
385-Porky Pig in The Isle of Missing Ships (3-4/52)	4.00	12.00	24.00
386-Uncle Scrooge (#1)-by Carl Barks (Disney) in "Only a Poor Old Man" (3/52)	100.00	300.00	700.00
387-Mickey Mouse in High Tibet (Disney) (4-5/52)	7.50	22.50	45.00
388-Oswald the Rabbit (Lantz)	4.00	11.00	22.00
389-Andy Hardy Comics (#1)	4.00	12.00	24.00
390-Woody Woodpecker (Lantz)	4.00	11.00	22.00
391-Uncle Wiggily	5.85	17.50	35.00
392-Hi-Yo Silver	5.00	15.00	30.00
393-Bugs Bunny	8.35	25.00	50.00
394-Donald Duck in Malayalaya-Barks-c only (Disney)	14.00	43.00	100.00
395-Forlorn River(Zane Grey)-First Nevada (5/52)	4.70	14.00	28.00
396-Tales of the Texas Rangers(#1)(TV)-Photo-c	11.50	34.00	80.00
397-Sergeant Preston of the Yukon (TV) (5/52)	7.50	22.50	45.00
398-The Brownies-not by Kelly	4.00	12.00	24.00
399-Porky Pig in The Lost Gold Mine	4.00	12.00	24.00
400-Tom Corbett, Space Cadet (TV)-McWilliams-c/a	10.00	30.00	70.00
401-Mickey Mouse and Goofy's Mechanical Wizard (Disney) (6-7/52)	5.35	16.00	32.00
402-Mary Jane and Sniffles	10.00	30.00	65.00
403-Li'l Bad Wolf (Disney) (6/52)(#1)	8.35	25.00	50.00
404-The Range Rider (#1) (TV)-Photo-c	11.50	34.00	80.00
405-Woody Woodpecker (Lantz) (6-7/52)	4.00	11.00	22.00
406-Tweety and Sylvester (#1)	7.50	22.50	45.00
407-Bugs Bunny, Foreign-Legion Hare	5.85	17.50	35.00
408-Donald Duck and the Golden Helmet by Carl Barks (Disney) (7-8/52)	23.00	70.00	210.00
409-Andy Panda (7-9/52)	3.60	9.00	18.00
410-Porky Pig in The Water Wizard (7/52)	4.00	12.00	24.00
411-Mickey Mouse and the Old Sea Dog (Disney) (8-9/52)	5.35	16.00	32.00
412-Nevada (Zane Grey)	4.70	14.00	28.00
413-Robin Hood (Disney-Movie) (8/52)-Photo-c (1st Disney movie four color book)	11.00	32.00	75.00
414-Bob Clampett's Beany and Cecil (TV)	19.00	58.00	135.00
415-Rootie Kazootie (#1) (TV)	11.00	32.00	75.00
416-Woody Woodpecker (Lantz)	4.00	11.00	22.00
417-Double Trouble with Goober (#1) (8/52)	3.60	9.00	18.00

Four Color #471 © DELL

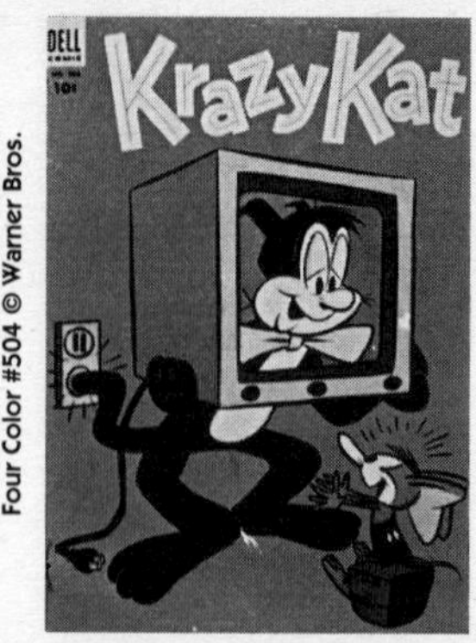

Four Color #504 © Warner Bros.

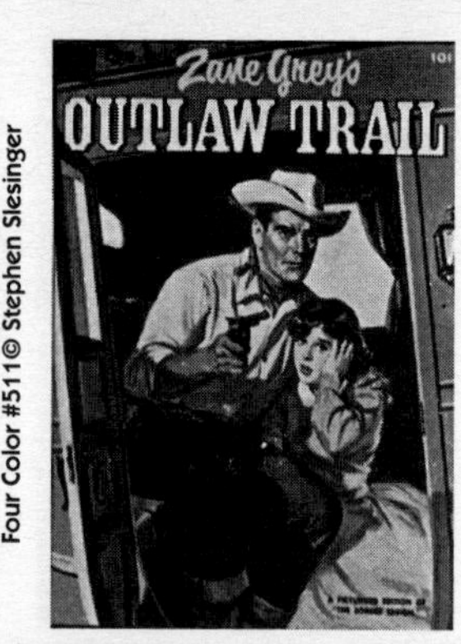

Four Color #511© Stephen Slesinger

	GD25	FN65	NM94
418-Rusty Riley, a Boy, a Horse, and a Dog (#1)-Frank Godwin-a (strip reprints) (8/52)	5.00	15.00	30.00
419-Sergeant Preston (TV)	7.50	22.50	45.00
420-Bugs Bunny in The Mysterious Buckaroo (8-9/52)	5.85	17.50	35.00
421-Tom Corbett, Space Cadet(TV)-McWilliams-a	10.00	30.00	70.00
422-Donald Duck and the Gilded Man, by Carl Barks (Disney) (9-10/52) (#423 on inside)	23.00	70.00	210.00
423-Rhubarb, Owner of the Brooklyn Ball Club (The Millionaire Cat) (#1)-Painted cover	5.00	15.00	30.00
424-Flash Gordon-Test Flight in Space (9/52)	9.15	27.50	55.00
425-Zorro, the Return of	14.00	43.00	100.00
426-Porky Pig in The Scalawag Leprechaun	4.00	12.00	24.00
427-Mickey Mouse and the Wonderful Whizzix (Disney) (10-11/52)-Reprinted in Mickey Mouse #100	5.35	16.00	32.00
428-Uncle Wiggily	5.35	16.00	32.00
429-Pluto in "Why Dogs Leave Home" (Disney) (10/52)(#1)	10.00	30.00	60.00
430-Marge's Tubby, the Shadow of a Man-Eater	10.00	30.00	60.00
431-Woody Woodpecker (10/52) (Lantz)	4.00	11.00	22.00
432-Bugs Bunny and the Rabbit Olympics	5.85	17.50	35.00
433-Wildfire (Zane Grey) (11-1/52-53)	4.70	14.00	28.00
434-Rin Tin Tin "In Dark Danger" (#1) (TV) (11/52)-Photo-c	19.00	58.00	135.00
435-Frosty the Snowman (11/52)	4.35	13.00	26.00
436-The Brownies-not by Kelly (11/52)	4.00	10.00	20.00
437-John Carter of Mars (E. R. Burroughs)-Marsh-a	17.00	52.00	120.00
438-Annie Oakley (#1) (TV)	14.00	43.00	100.00
439-Little Hiawatha (Disney) (12/52)j(#1)	6.70	20.00	40.00
440-Black Beauty (12/52)	4.00	10.00	20.00
441-Fearless Fagan	4.00	10.00	20.00
442-Peter Pan (Disney) (Movie)	10.00	30.00	70.00
443-Ben Bowie and His Mountain Men (#1)	8.35	25.00	50.00
444-Marge's Tubby	10.00	30.00	60.00
445-Charlie McCarthy	5.85	17.50	35.00
446-Captain Hook and Peter Pan (Disney) (Movie) (1/53)	10.00	30.00	70.00
447-Andy Hardy Comics	3.20	8.00	16.00
448-Bob Clampett's Beany and Cecil (TV)	19.00	58.00	135.00
449-Tappan's Burro (Zane Grey) (2-4/53)	4.70	14.00	28.00
450-Duck Album; Barks-c (Disney)	6.70	20.00	40.00
451-Rusty Riley-Frank Godwin-a (strip-r) (2/53)	4.00	11.00	22.00
452-Raggedy Ann & Andy (1953)	5.35	16.00	32.00
453-Susie Q. Smith (2/53)	4.00	10.00	20.00
454-Krazy Kat Comics; not by Herriman	4.35	13.00	26.00
455-Johnny Mack Brown Comics(3/53)-Photo-c	6.70	20.00	40.00
456-Uncle Scrooge Back to the Klondike (#2) by Barks (3/53) (Disney)	57.00	171.00	400.00
457-Daffy (#1)	10.00	30.00	60.00
458-Oswald the Rabbit (Lantz)	3.60	9.00	18.00
459-Rootie Kazootie (TV)	8.35	25.00	50.00
460-Buck Jones (4/53)	5.85	17.50	35.00
461-Marge's Tubby	9.15	27.50	55.00
462-Little Scouts	2.40	6.00	12.00
463-Petunia (4/53)	4.00	11.00	22.00
464-Bozo (4/53)	11.00	32.00	75.00
465-Francis the Famous Talking Mule	5.35	16.00	32.00
466-Rhubarb, the Millionaire Cat; painted-c	4.00	10.00	20.00
467-Desert Gold (Zane Grey) (5-7/53)	4.70	14.00	28.00
468-Goofy (#1) (Disney)	14.00	43.00	100.00
469-Beetle Bailey (#1) (5/53	10.00	30.00	60.00
470-Elmer Fudd	3.20	8.00	16.00
471-Double Trouble with Goober	2.80	7.00	14.00
472-Wild Bill Elliott (6/53)-Photo-c	5.85	17.50	35.00
473-Li'l Bad Wolf (Disney) (6/53)(#2)	5.85	17.50	35.00
474-Mary Jane and Sniffles	10.00	30.00	60.00
475-M.G.M.'s The Two Mouseketeers (#1)	7.50	22.50	45.00
476-Rin Tin Tin (TV)-Photo-c	10.00	30.00	65.00
477-Bob Clampett's Beany and Cecil (TV)	19.00	58.00	135.00
478-Charlie McCarthy	5.85	17.50	35.00
479-Queen of the West Dale Evans (#1)-Photo-c	14.00	43.00	100.00
480-Andy Hardy Comics	3.20	8.00	16.00
481-Annie Oakley And Tagg (TV)	9.15	27.50	55.00
482-Brownies-not by Kelly	4.00	10.00	20.00
483-Little Beaver (7/53)	4.00	11.00	22.00
484-River Feud (Zane Grey) (8-10/53)	4.70	14.00	28.00
485-The Little People-Walt Scott (#1)	7.50	22.50	45.00
486-Rusty Riley-Frank Godwin strip-r	4.00	11.00	22.00
487-Mowgli, the Jungle Book (Rudyard Kipling's)	5.35	16.00	32.00
488-John Carter of Mars (Burroughs)-Marsh-a; painted-c	17.00	52.00	120.00
489-Tweety and Sylvester	4.00	11.00	22.00
490-Jungle Jim (#1)	7.50	22.50	45.00
491-Silvertip (#1) (Max Brand)-Kinstler-a (8/53)	10.00	30.00	60.00
492-Duck Album (Disney)	5.85	17.50	35.00
493-Johnny Mack Brown; photo-c	6.70	20.00	40.00
494-The Little King (#1)	10.00	30.00	65.00
495-Uncle Scrooge (#3) (Disney)-by Carl Barks (9/53)	43.00	130.00	300.00
496-The Green Hornet; painted-c	27.00	81.00	190.00
497-Zorro (Sword of...)-Kinstler-a	15.00	45.00	105.00
498-Bugs Bunny's Album (9/53)	5.35	16.00	32.00
499-M.G.M.'s Spike and Tyke (#1) (9/53)	3.60	9.00	18.00
500-Buck Jones	5.85	17.50	35.00
501-Francis the Famous Talking Mule	5.35	16.00	32.00
502-Rootie Kazootie (TV)	8.35	25.00	50.00
503-Uncle Wiggily (10/53)	5.35	16.00	32.00
504-Krazy Kat; not by Herriman	4.35	13.00	26.00
505-The Sword and the Rose (Disney) (10/53)(Movie)-Photo-c	10.00	30.00	60.00
506-The Little Scouts	2.40	6.00	12.00
507-Oswald the Rabbit (Lantz)	3.60	9.00	18.00
508-Bozo (10/53)	11.00	32.00	75.00
509-Pluto (Disney) (10/53)	6.70	20.00	40.00
510-Son of Black Beauty	4.00	10.00	20.00
511-Outlaw Trail (Zane Grey)-Kinstler-a	5.00	15.00	30.00
512-Flash Gordon (11/53)	5.00	15.00	30.00
513-Ben Bowie and His Mountain Men	4.35	13.00	26.00
514-Frosty the Snowman (11/53)	4.00	11.00	22.00
515-Andy Hardy	3.20	8.00	16.00
516-Double Trouble With Goober	2.80	7.00	14.00
517-Chip 'N' Dale (#1) (Disney)	8.35	25.00	50.00
518-Rivets (11/53)	3.20	8.00	16.00
519-Steve Canyon (#1)-Not by Milton Caniff	9.15	27.50	55.00
520-Wild Bill Elliott-Photo-c	5.85	17.50	35.00
521-Beetle Bailey (12/53)	5.00	15.00	30.00
522-The Brownies	4.00	10.00	20.00
523-Rin Tin Tin (TV)-Photo-c (12/53)	10.00	30.00	65.00
524-Tweety and Sylvester	4.00	11.00	22.00
525-Santa Claus Funnies	4.00	11.00	22.00
526-Napoleon	2.80	7.00	14.00
527-Charlie McCarthy	5.85	17.50	35.00
528-Queen of the West Dale Evans; photo-c	10.00	30.00	60.00
529-Little Beaver	4.00	11.00	22.00
530-Bob Clampett's Beany and Cecil (TV) (1/54)	19.00	58.00	135.00
531-Duck Album (Disney)	5.85	17.50	35.00
532-The Rustlers (Zane Grey) (2-4/54)	4.70	14.00	28.00
533-Raggedy Ann and Andy	5.35	16.00	32.00
534-Western Marshal(Ernest Haycox's)-Kinstler-a	6.35	19.00	38.00
535-I Love Lucy (#1) (TV) (2/54)-Photo-c	37.00	110.00	260.00
536-Daffy (3/54)	5.00	15.00	30.00
537-Stormy, the Thoroughbred... (Disney-Movie) on top 2/3 of each page;			

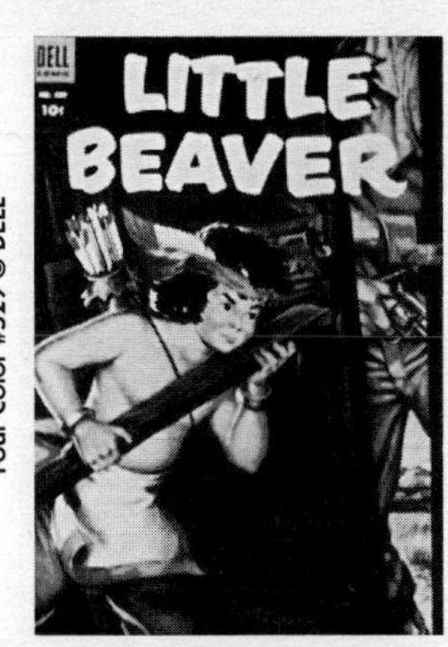

Four Color #529 © DELL

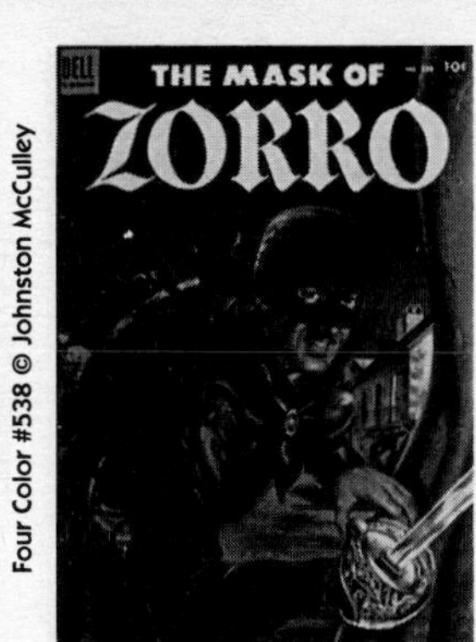

Four Color #538 © Johnston McCulley

Four Color #646 © DELL

	GD25	FN65	NM94
Pluto story on bottom 1/3 of each page (2/54)	4.70	14.00	28.00
538-The Mask of Zorro; Kinstler-a	15.00	45.00	105.00
539-Ben and Me (Disney) (3/54)	4.00	10.00	20.00
540-Knights of the Round Table (3/54) (Movie)-Photo-c	7.50	22.50	45.00
541-Johnny Mack Brown; photo-c	6.70	20.00	40.00
542-Super Circus Featuring Mary Hartline (TV) (3/54)	5.85	17.50	35.00
543-Uncle Wiggily (3/54)	5.35	16.00	32.00
544-Rob Roy (Disney-Movie)-Manning-a; photo-c	10.00	30.00	65.00
545-The Wonderful Adventures of Pinocchio-Partial reprint of 4-Color #92 (Disney-Movie)	8.35	25.00	50.00
546-Buck Jones	5.85	17.50	35.00
547-Francis the Famous Talking Mule	5.35	16.00	32.00
548-Krazy Kat; not by Herriman (4/54)	4.00	11.00	22.00
549-Oswald the Rabbit (Lantz)	3.60	9.00	18.00
550-The Little Scouts	2.40	6.00	12.00
551-Bozo (4/54)	11.00	32.00	75.00
552-Beetle Bailey	5.00	15.00	30.00
553-Susie Q. Smith	4.00	10.00	20.00
554-Rusty Riley (Frank Godwin strip-r)	4.00	11.00	22.00
555-Range War (Zane Grey)	4.70	14.00	28.00
556-Double Trouble With Goober (5/54)	2.80	7.00	14.00
557-Ben Bowie and His Mountain Men	4.35	13.00	26.00
558-Elmer Fudd (5/54)	3.20	8.00	16.00
559-I Love Lucy (#2) (TV)-Photo-c	25.00	75.00	175.00
560-Duck Album (Disney) (5/54)	5.85	17.50	35.00
561-Mr. Magoo (5/54)	10.00	30.00	65.00
562-Goofy (Disney)(#2)	8.35	25.00	50.00
563-Rhubarb, the Millionaire Cat (6/54)	4.00	10.00	20.00
564-Li'l Bad Wolf (Disney)(#3)	5.85	17.50	35.00
565-Jungle Jim	4.00	11.00	22.00
566-Son of Black Beauty	4.00	10.00	20.00
567-Prince Valiant (#1)-By Bob Fuje (Movie)-Photo-c	10.00	30.00	65.00
568-Gypsy Colt (Movie) (6/54)	5.35	16.00	32.00
569-Priscilla's Pop	4.00	10.00	20.00
570-Bob Clampett's Beany and Cecil (TV)	19.00	58.00	135.00
571-Charlie McCarthy	5.85	17.50	35.00
572-Silvertip (Max Brand) (7/54); Kinstler-a	5.35	16.00	32.00
573-The Little People by Walt Scott	4.00	11.00	22.00
574-The Hand of Zorro; Kinstler-a	15.00	45.00	105.00
575-Annie Oakley and Tagg (TV)-Photo-c	9.15	27.50	55.00
576-Angel (#1) (8/54)	3.20	8.00	16.00
577-M.G.M.'s Spike and Tyke	2.80	7.00	14.00
578-Steve Canyon (8/54)	5.35	16.00	32.00
579-Francis the Famous Talking Mule	5.35	16.00	32.00
580-Six Gun Ranch (Luke Short-8/54)	4.20	12.50	25.00
581-Chip 'N' Dale (#2) (Disney)	5.00	15.00	30.00
582-Mowgli Jungle Book (Kipling) (8/54)	4.00	12.00	24.00
583-The Lost Wagon Train (Zane Grey)	4.70	14.00	28.00
584-Johnny Mack Brown-Photo-c	6.70	20.00	40.00
585-Bugs Bunny's Album	5.00	15.00	30.00
586-Duck Album (Disney)	5.85	17.50	35.00
587-The Little Scouts	2.40	6.00	12.00
588-King Richard and the Crusaders (Movie) (10/54) Matt Baker-a; photo-c	10.00	30.00	70.00
589-Buck Jones	5.85	17.50	35.00
590-Hansel and Gretel; partial photo-c	6.35	19.00	38.00
591-Western Marshal(Ernest Haycox's)-Kinstler-a	6.35	19.00	38.00
592-Super Circus (TV)	5.85	17.50	35.00
593-Oswald the Rabbit (Lantz)	3.60	9.00	18.00
594-Bozo (10/54)	11.00	32.00	75.00
595-Pluto (Disney)	5.00	15.00	30.00
596-Turok, Son of Stone (#1)	75.00	225.00	525.00
597-The Little King	7.50	22.50	45.00

	GD25	FN65	NM94
598-Captain Davy Jones	4.00	10.00	20.00
599-Ben Bowie and His Mountain Men	4.35	13.00	26.00
600-Daisy Duck's Diary (#1) (Disney) (11/54)	6.70	20.00	40.00
601-Frosty the Snowman	4.00	11.00	22.00
602-Mr. Magoo and Gerald McBoing-Boing	10.00	30.00	65.00
603-M.G.M.'s The Two Mouseketeers	4.00	11.00	22.00
604-Shadow on the Trail (Zane Grey)	4.70	14.00	28.00
605-The Brownies-not by Kelly (12/54)	4.00	10.00	20.00
606-Sir Lancelot (not TV)	9.15	27.50	55.00
607-Santa Claus Funnies	4.00	11.00	22.00
608-Silvertip- "Valley of Vanishing Men" (Max Brand)-Kinstler-a	5.35	16.00	32.00
609-The Littlest Outlaw (Disney-Movie) (1/55)-Photo-c	8.35	25.00	50.00
610-Drum Beat (Movie); Alan Ladd photo-c	11.00	32.00	75.00
611-Duck Album (Disney)	5.85	17.50	35.00
612-Little Beaver (1/55)	4.00	10.00	20.00
613-Western Marshal (Ernest Haycox's) (2/55)-Kinstler-a	6.35	19.00	38.00
614-20,000 Leagues Under the Sea (Disney) (Movie) (2/55)-Painted-c	10.00	30.00	60.00
615-Daffy	5.00	15.00	30.00
616-To the Last Man (Zane Grey)	4.70	14.00	28.00
617-The Quest of Zorro	14.00	43.00	100.00
618-Johnny Mack Brown; photo-c	6.70	20.00	40.00
619-Krazy Kat; not by Herriman	4.00	11.00	22.00
620-Mowgli Jungle Book (Kipling)	4.00	12.00	24.00
621-Francis the Famous Talking Mule (4/55)	4.70	14.00	28.00
622-Beetle Bailey	5.00	15.00	30.00
623-Oswald the Rabbit (Lantz)	2.80	7.00	14.00
624-Treasure Island(Disney-Movie)(4/55)-Photo-c	10.00	30.00	60.00
625-Beaver Valley (Disney-Movie)	8.35	25.00	50.00
626-Ben Bowie and His Mountain Men	4.35	13.00	26.00
627-Goofy (Disney) (5/55)	8.35	25.00	50.00
628-Elmer Fudd	3.20	8.00	16.00
629-Lady and the Tramp with Jock (Disney)	6.70	20.00	40.00
630-Priscilla's Pop	4.00	10.00	20.00
631-Davy Crockett, Indian Fighter (#1) (Disney) (5/55) (TV)-Fess Parker photo-c	14.00	43.00	100.00
632-Fighting Caravans (Zane Grey)	4.70	14.00	28.00
633-The Little People by Walt Scott (6/55)	4.00	11.00	22.00
634-Lady and the Tramp Album (Disney) (6/55)	5.85	17.50	35.00
635-Bob Clampett's Beany and Cecil (TV)	19.00	58.00	135.00
636-Chip 'N' Dale (Disney)	3.60	9.00	18.00
637-Silvertip (Max Brand)-Kinstler-a	5.35	16.00	32.00
638-M.G.M.'s Spike and Tyke (8/55)	2.80	7.00	14.00
639-Davy Crockett at the Alamo (Disney) (7/55) (TV)-Fess Parker photo-c	14.00	43.00	100.00
640-Western Marshal(Ernest Haycox's)-Kinstler-a	6.35	19.00	38.00
641-Steve Canyon (1955)-by Caniff	5.35	16.00	32.00
642-M.G.M.'s The Two Mouseketeers	4.00	11.00	22.00
643-Wild Bill Elliott; photo-c	4.70	14.00	28.00
644-Sir Walter Raleigh (5/55)-Based on movie "The Virgin Queen"; photo-c	8.35	25.00	50.00
645-Johnny Mack Brown; photo-c	6.70	20.00	40.00
646-Dotty Dripple and Taffy (#1)	4.00	11.00	22.00
647-Bugs Bunny's Album (9/55)	5.00	15.00	30.00
648-Jace Pearson of the Texas Rangers (TV)-Photo-c	6.70	20.00	40.00
649-Duck Album (Disney)	5.35	17.50	35.00
650-Prince Valiant; by Bob Fuje	6.35	19.00	38.00
651-King Colt (Luke Short) (9/55)-Kinstler-a	4.70	14.00	28.00
652-Buck Jones	4.00	11.00	22.00
653-Smokey the Bear (#1) (10/55)	10.00	30.00	60.00
654-Pluto (Disney)	5.00	15.00	30.00
655-Francis the Famous Talking Mule	4.70	14.00	28.00

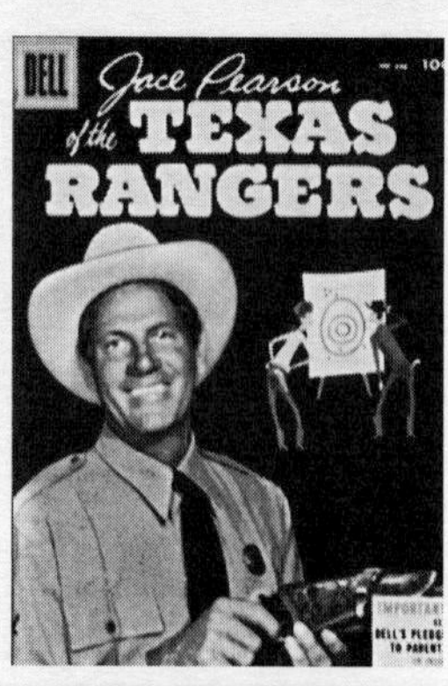

Four Color #648 © DELL

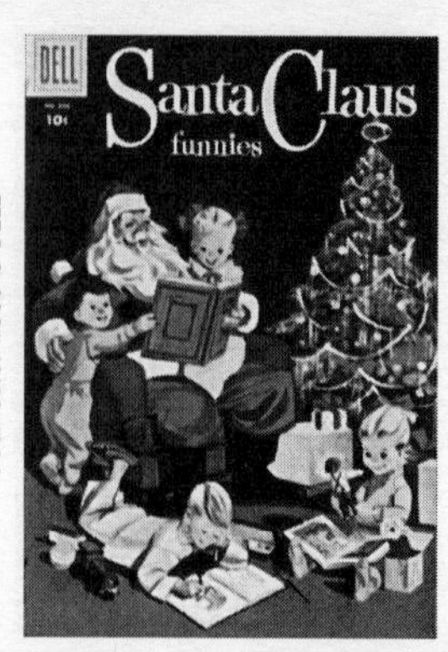

Four Color #666 © DELL

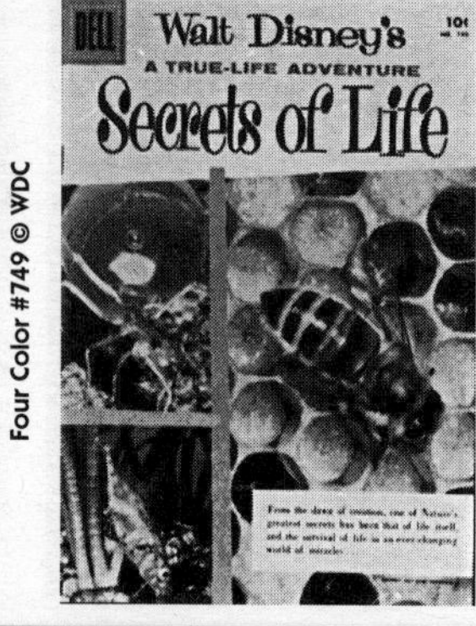

Four Color #749 © WDC

	GD25	FN65	NM94
656-Turok, Son of Stone (#2) (10/55)	45.00	135.00	315.00
657-Ben Bowie and His Mountain Men	4.35	13.00	26.00
658-Goofy (Disney)	8.35	25.00	50.00
659-Daisy Duck's Diary (Disney)(#2)	5.85	17.50	35.00
660-Little Beaver	4.00	10.00	20.00
661-Frosty the Snowman	4.00	11.00	22.00
662-Zoo Parade (TV)-Marlin Perkins (11/55)	5.85	17.50	35.00
663-Winky Dink (TV)	8.35	25.00	50.00
664-Davy Crockett in the Great Keelboat Race (TV) (Disney) (11/55)-Fess Parker photo-c	13.00	40.00	90.00
665-The African Lion (Disney-Movie) (11/55)	6.70	20.00	40.00
666-Santa Claus Funnies	4.00	11.00	22.00
667-Silvertip and the Stolen Stallion (Max Brand) (12/55)-Kinstler-a	5.35	16.00	32.00
668-Dumbo (Disney) (12/55)-First of two printings. Dumbo on cover with starry sky. Reprints 4-Color #234?; same-c as #234	8.35	25.00	50.00
668-Dumbo (Disney) (1/58)-Second printing. Same cover altered, with Timothy Mouse added. Same contents as above	6.70	20.00	40.00
669-Robin Hood (Disney-Movie) (12/55)-Reprints #413 plus-c; photo-c	5.85	17.50	35.00
670-M.G.M's Mouse Musketeers (#1) (1/56)-Formerly the Two Mouseketeers	3.60	9.00	18.00
671-Davy Crockett and the River Pirates (TV) (Disney) (12/55)-Jesse Marsh-a; Fess Parker photo-c	13.00	40.00	90.00
672-Quentin Durward (1/56) (Movie)-Photo-c	7.50	22.50	45.00
673-Buffalo Bill, Jr. (#1) (TV)-James Arness photo-c	7.50	22.50	45.00
674-The Little Rascals (#1) (TV)	7.50	22.50	45.00
675-Steve Donovan, Western Marshal (#1) (TV)-Kinstler-a; photo-c	8.35	25.00	50.00
676-Will-Yum!	3.60	9.00	18.00
677-Little King	7.50	22.50	45.00
678-The Last Hunt (Movie)-Photo-c	7.50	22.50	45.00
679-Gunsmoke (#1) (TV)-Photo-c	13.00	40.00	90.00
680-Out Our Way with the Worry Wart (2/56)	3.60	9.00	18.00
681-Forever, Darling (Movie) with Lucille Ball & Desi Arnaz (2/56)-; photo-c	11.00	32.00	75.00
682-When Knighthood Was in Flower (Disney-Movie)-Reprint of #505; Renamed the Sword & the Rose for the novel; photo-c	8.35	25.00	50.00
683-Hi and Lois (3/56)	3.20	8.00	16.00
684-Helen of Troy (Movie)-Buscema-a; photo-c	11.50	34.00	80.00
685-Johnny Mack Brown; photo-c	6.70	20.00	40.00
686-Duck Album (Disney)	5.85	17.50	35.00
687-The Indian Fighter (Movie)-Kirk Douglas photo-c	6.70	20.00	40.00
688-Alexander the Great (Movie) (5/56)-Buscema-a; photo-c	7.50	22.50	45.00
689-Elmer Fudd (3/56)	3.20	8.00	16.00
690-The Conqueror (Movie) - John Wayne photo-c	16.00	48.00	110.00
691-Dotty Dripple and Taffy	3.60	9.00	18.00
692-The Little People-Walt Scott	4.00	10.00	20.00
693-Song of the South (Disney) (1956)-Partial reprint of #129	10.00	30.00	60.00
694-Super Circus (TV)-Photo-c	5.85	17.50	35.00
695-Little Beaver	4.00	10.00	20.00
696-Krazy Kat; not by Herriman (4/56)	4.00	11.00	22.00
697-Oswald the Rabbit (Lantz)	2.80	7.00	14.00
698-Francis the Famous Talking Mule (4/56)	4.70	14.00	28.00
699-Prince Valiant-by Bob Fuje	6.35	19.00	38.00
700-Water Birds and the Olympic Elk (Disney-Movie) (4/56)	6.70	20.00	40.00
701-Jiminy Cricket (#1) (Disney) (5/56)	9.15	27.50	55.00
702-The Goofy Success Story (Disney)	8.35	25.00	50.00
703-Scamp (#1) (Disney)	10.00	30.00	60.00
704-Priscilla's Pop (5/56)	4.00	10.00	20.00
705-Brave Eagle (#1) (TV)-Photo-c	5.85	17.50	35.00
706-Bongo and Lumpjaw (Disney) (6/56)	4.35	13.00	26.00
707-Corky and White Shadow (Disney) (5/56)-Mickey Mouse Club (TV); photo-c	8.35	25.00	50.00
708-Smokey the Bear	5.00	15.00	30.00
709-The Searchers (Movie) - John Wayne photo-c	29.00	85.00	200.00
710-Francis the Famous Talking Mule	4.70	14.00	28.00
711-M.G.M's Mouse Musketeers	2.80	7.00	14.00
712-The Great Locomotive Chase (Disney-Movie) (9/56)-Photo-c	8.35	25.00	50.00
713-The Animal World (Movie) (8/56)	5.85	17.50	35.00
714-Spin and Marty (#1) (TV) (Disney)-Mickey Mouse Club (6/56); photo-c	11.50	34.00	80.00
715-Timmy (8/56)	4.00	10.00	20.00
716-Man in Space (Disney)(A science feature from Tomorrowland)	10.00	30.00	60.00
717-Moby Dick (Movie)-Gregory Peck photo-c	9.15	27.50	55.00
718-Dotty Dripple and Taffy	3.60	9.00	18.00
719-Prince Valiant; by Bob Fuje (8/56)	6.35	19.00	38.00
720-Gunsmoke (TV)-James Arness photo-c	7.00	21.00	42.00
721-Captain Kangaroo (TV)-Photo-c	16.00	48.00	110.00
722-Johnny Mack Brown-Photo-c	6.70	20.00	40.00
723-Santiago (Movie)-Kinstler-a (9/56); Alan Ladd photo-c	11.50	34.00	80.00
724-Bugs Bunny's Album	5.00	15.00	30.00
725-Elmer Fudd (9/56)	2.80	7.00	14.00
726-Duck Album (Disney) (9/56)	5.85	17.50	35.00
727-The Nature of Things (TV) (Disney)-Jesse Marsh-a	8.35	25.00	50.00
728-M.G.M's Mouse Musketeers	2.80	7.00	14.00
729-Bob Son of Battle (11/56)	4.00	10.00	20.00
730-Smokey Stover	4.00	10.00	20.00
731-Silvertip and The Fighting Four (Max Brand)-Kinstler-a	5.35	16.00	32.00
732-Zorro, the Challenge of (10/56)	14.00	43.00	100.00
733-Buck Jones	4.00	11.00	22.00
734-Cheyenne (#1) (TV) (10/56)-Clint Walker photo-c	13.50	41.00	95.00
735-Crusader Rabbit (#1) (TV)	25.00	75.00	175.00
736-Pluto (Disney)	5.00	15.00	30.00
737-Steve Canyon-Caniff-a	5.35	16.00	32.00
738-Westward Ho, the Wagons (Disney-Movie)-Fess Parker photo-c	10.00	30.00	70.00
739-Bounty Guns (Luke Short)-Drucker-a	4.20	12.50	25.00
740-Chilly Willy (#1) (Walter Lantz)	4.70	14.00	28.00
741-The Fastest Gun Alive (Movie)(9/56)-Photo-c	8.35	25.00	50.00
742-Buffalo Bill, Jr. (TV)-Photo-c	5.00	15.00	30.00
743-Daisy Duck's Diary (Disney) (11/56)	5.85	17.50	35.00
744-Little Beaver	4.00	10.00	20.00
745-Francis the Famous Talking Mule	4.70	14.00	28.00
746-Dotty Dripple and Taffy	3.60	9.00	18.00
747-Goofy (Disney)	8.35	25.00	50.00
748-Frosty the Snowman (11/56)	4.00	10.00	20.00
749-Secrets of Life (Disney-Movie)-Photo-c	6.70	20.00	40.00
750-The Great Cat Family (Disney-TV/Movie)-Pinocchio & Alice app.	6.70	20.00	40.00
751-Our Miss Brooks (TV)-Photo-c	8.35	25.00	50.00
752-Mandrake, the Magician	10.00	30.00	60.00
753-Walt Scott's Little People (11/56)	4.00	10.00	20.00
754-Smokey the Bear	5.00	15.00	30.00
755-The Littlest Snowman (12/56)	4.00	12.00	24.00
756-Santa Claus Funnies	4.00	11.00	22.00
757-The True Story of Jesse James (Movie)-Photo-c	10.00	30.00	65.00
758-Bear Country (Disney-Movie)	6.70	20.00	40.00
759-Circus Boy (TV)-The Monkees' Mickey Dolenz photo-c (12/56)	11.00	32.00	75.00
760-The Hardy Boys (#1) (TV) (Disney)-Mickey Mouse Club; photo-c	11.50	34.00	80.00

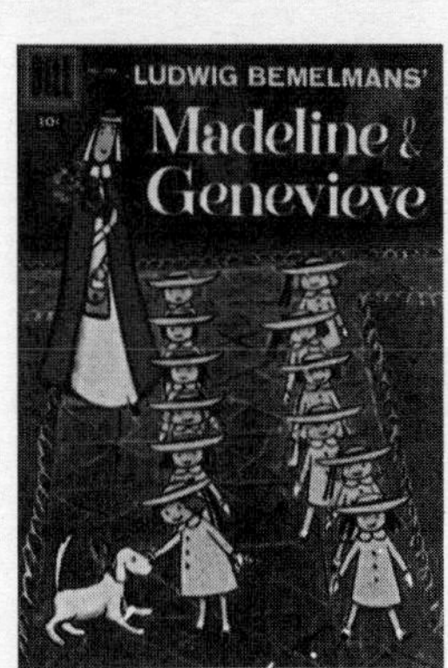

Four Color #796 © Ludwig Bemelmans'

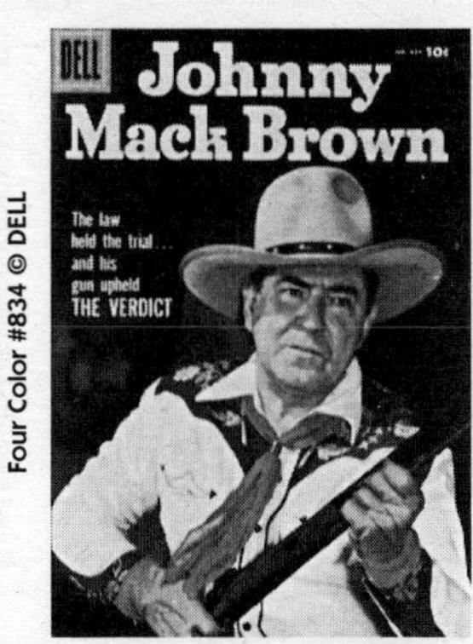

DELL
10¢
Johnny Mack Brown
The law held the trial... and his gun upheld THE VERDICT

Four Color #834 © DELL

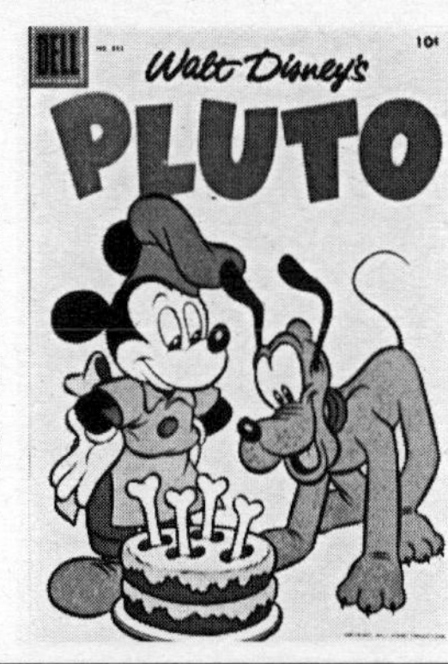

Four Color #853 © WDC

	GD25	FN65	NM94
761-Howdy Doody (TV) (1/57)	10.00	30.00	65.00
762-The Sharkfighters (Movie) (1/57); Buscema-a; photo-c	11.50	34.00	80.00
763-Grandma Duck's Farm Friends (#1) (Disney)	8.35	25.00	50.00
764-M.G.M's Mouse Musketeers	2.80	7.00	14.00
765-Will-Yum!	3.60	9.00	18.00
766-Buffalo Bill, Jr. (TV)-Photo-c	5.00	15.00	30.00
767-Spin and Marty (TV) (Disney)-Mickey Mouse Club (2/57)	10.00	30.00	60.00
768-Steve Donovan, Western Marshal (TV)-Kinstler-a; photo-c	6.70	20.00	40.00
769-Gunsmoke (TV)-James Arness photo-c	7.00	21.00	42.00
770-Brave Eagle (TV)-Photo-c	4.00	10.00	20.00
771-Brand of Empire (Luke Short)(3/57)-Drucker-a	4.20	12.50	25.00
772-Cheyenne (TV)-Clint Walker photo-c	8.35	25.00	50.00
773-The Brave One (Movie)-Photo-c	5.35	16.00	32.00
774-Hi and Lois (3/57)	3.20	8.00	16.00
775-Sir Lancelot and Brian (TV)-Buscema-a; photo-c	10.00	30.00	65.00
776-Johnny Mack Brown; photo-c	6.70	20.00	40.00
777-Scamp (Disney) (3/57)	7.50	22.50	45.00
778-The Little Rascals (TV)	4.00	11.00	22.00
779-Lee Hunter, Indian Fighter (3/57)	5.85	17.50	35.00
780-Captain Kangaroo (TV)-Photo-c	14.00	43.00	100.00
781-Fury (#1) (TV) (3/57)-Photo-c	10.00	30.00	65.00
782-Duck Album (Disney)	5.85	17.50	35.00
783-Elmer Fudd	2.80	7.00	14.00
784-Around the World in 80 Days (Movie) (2/57)-Photo-c	7.50	22.50	45.00
785-Circus Boy (TV) (4/57)-The Monkees' Mickey Dolenz photo-c	11.00	32.00	75.00
786-Cinderella (Disney) (3/57)-Partial-r of #272	6.70	20.00	40.00
787-Little Hiawatha (Disney) (4/57)(#2)	5.85	17.50	35.00
788-Prince Valiant; by Bob Fuje	6.35	19.00	38.00
789-Silvertip-Valley Thieves (Max Brand) (4/57)-Kinstler-a	5.35	16.00	32.00
790-The Wings of Eagles (Movie) (John Wayne)-Toth-a; John Wayne photo-c; 10 & 15¢ editions exist	16.50	50.00	115.00
791-The 77th Bengal Lancers (TV)-Photo-c	7.50	22.50	45.00
792-Oswald the Rabbit (Lantz)	2.80	7.00	14.00
793-Morty Meekle	3.60	9.00	18.00
794-The Count of Monte Cristo (5/57) (Movie)-Buscema-a	10.00	30.00	65.00
795-Jiminy Cricket (Disney)(#2)	6.70	20.00	40.00
796-Ludwig Bemelman's Madeleine and Genevieve	4.00	12.00	24.00
797-Gunsmoke (TV)-Photo-c	7.00	21.00	42.00
798-Buffalo Bill, Jr. (TV)-Photo-c	5.00	15.00	30.00
799-Priscilla's Pop	4.00	10.00	20.00
800-The Buccaneers (TV)-Photo-c	7.00	21.00	42.00
801-Dotty Dripple and Taffy	3.60	9.00	18.00
802-Goofy (Disney) (5/57)	8.35	25.00	50.00
803-Cheyenne (TV)-Clint Walker photo-c	8.35	25.00	50.00
804-Steve Canyon-Caniff-a (1957)	5.35	16.00	32.00
805-Crusader Rabbit (TV)	22.00	65.00	150.00
806-Scamp (Disney) (6/57)	7.50	22.50	45.00
807-Savage Range (Luke Short)-Drucker-a	4.20	12.50	25.00
808-Spin and Marty (TV)(Disney)-Mickey Mouse Club; photo-c	10.00	30.00	60.00
809-The Little People (Walt Scott)	4.00	10.00	20.00
810-Francis the Famous Talking Mule	4.00	11.00	22.00
811-Howdy Doody (TV) (7/57)	10.00	30.00	65.00
812-The Big Land (Movie); Alan Ladd photo-c	10.00	30.00	70.00
813-Circus Boy (TV)-The Monkees' Mickey Dolenz photo-c	11.00	32.00	75.00
814-Covered Wagons, Ho! (Disney)-Donald Duck (TV) (6/57); Mickey Mouse app.	6.70	20.00	40.00

	GD25	FN65	NM94
815-Dragoon Wells Massacre (Movie)-photo-c	9.15	27.50	55.00
816-Brave Eagle (TV)-photo-c	4.00	10.00	20.00
817-Little Beaver	4.00	10.00	20.00
818-Smokey the Bear (6/57)	5.00	15.00	30.00
819-Mickey Mouse in Magicland (Disney) (7/57)	4.00	12.00	24.00
820-The Oklahoman (Movie)-Photo-c	10.00	30.00	60.00
821-Wringle Wrangle (Disney)-Based on movie "Westward Ho, the Wagons"; Marsh-a; Fess Parker photo-c	10.00	30.00	60.00
822-Paul Revere's Ride with Johnny Tremain (TV) (Disney)-Toth-a	14.00	43.00	100.00
823-Timmy	3.20	8.00	16.00
824-The Pride and the Passion (Movie) (8/57)-Frank Sinatra & Cary Grant photo-c	10.00	30.00	60.00
825-The Little Rascals (TV)	4.00	11.00	22.00
826-Spin and Marty and Annette (TV) (Disney)-Mickey Mouse Club; Annette Funicello photo-c	26.00	78.00	180.00
827-Smokey Stover (8/57)	4.00	10.00	20.00
828-Buffalo Bill, Jr. (TV)-Photo-c	5.00	15.00	30.00
829-Tales of the Pony Express (TV) (8/57)-Painted-c	5.00	15.00	30.00
830-The Hardy Boys (TV) (Disney)-Mickey Mouse Club (8/57); photo-c	10.00	30.00	70.00
831-No Sleep 'Til Dawn (Movie)-Karl Malden photo-c	7.50	22.50	45.00
832-Lolly and Pepper (#1)	4.00	10.00	20.00
833-Scamp (Disney) (9/57)	7.50	22.50	45.00
834-Johnny Mack Brown; photo-c	6.70	20.00	40.00
835-Silvertip-The False Rider (Max Brand)	4.70	14.00	28.00
836-Man in Flight (Disney) (TV) (9/57)	8.35	25.00	50.00
837-All-American Athlete Cotton Woods	5.85	17.50	35.00
838-Bugs Bunny's Life Story Album (9/57)	5.35	16.00	32.00
839-The Vigilantes (Movie)	8.35	25.00	50.00
840-Duck Album (Disney) (9/57)	5.85	17.50	35.00
841-Elmer Fudd	2.80	7.00	14.00
842-The Nature of Things (Disney-Movie) ('57)-Jesse Marsh-a (TV series)	8.35	25.00	50.00
843-The First Americans (Disney) (TV)-Marsh-a	10.00	30.00	60.00
844-Gunsmoke (TV)-Photo-c	7.00	21.00	42.00
845-The Land Unknown (Movie)-Alex Toth-a	16.00	48.00	110.00
846-Gun Glory (Movie)-by Alex Toth; photo-c	13.00	40.00	90.00
847-Perri (squirrels) (Disney-Movie)-Two different covers published	8.35	25.00	50.00
848-Marauder's Moon (Luke Short)	5.85	17.50	35.00
849-Prince Valiant; by Bob Fuje	6.35	19.00	38.00
850-Buck Jones	4.00	11.00	22.00
851-The Story of Mankind (Movie) (1/58)-Hedy Lamarr & Vincent Price photo-c	7.50	22.50	45.00
852-Chilly Willy (2/58) (Lantz)	3.60	9.00	18.00
853-Pluto (Disney) (10/57)	5.00	15.00	30.00
854-The Hunchback of Notre Dame (Movie)-Photo-c	13.00	40.00	90.00
855-Broken Arrow (TV)-Photo-c	5.85	17.50	35.00
856-Buffalo Bill, Jr. (TV)-Photo-c	5.00	15.00	30.00
857-The Goofy Adventure Story (Disney) (11/57)	8.35	25.00	50.00
858-Daisy Duck's Diary (Disney) (11/57)	4.35	13.00	26.00
859-Topper and Neil (TV) (11/57)	4.00	10.00	20.00
860-Wyatt Earp (#1) (TV)-Manning-a; photo-c	12.00	36.00	85.00
861-Frosty the Snowman	4.00	10.00	20.00
862-The Truth About Mother Goose (Disney-Movie) (11/57)	8.35	25.00	50.00
863-Francis the Famous Talking Mule	4.00	11.00	22.00
864-The Littlest Snowman	4.00	12.00	24.00
865-Andy Burnett (TV) (Disney) (12/57)-Photo-c	11.50	34.00	80.00
866-Mars and Beyond (Disney-TV)(A science feature from Tomorrowland)	10.00	30.00	60.00
867-Santa Claus Funnies	4.00	11.00	22.00
868-The Little People (12/57)	4.00	10.00	20.00
869-Old Yeller (Disney-Movie)-Photo-c	8.35	25.00	50.00
870-Little Beaver (1/58)	4.00	10.00	20.00

Four Color #894 © Walter Lantz Prod.

Four Color #918 © Warner Bros.

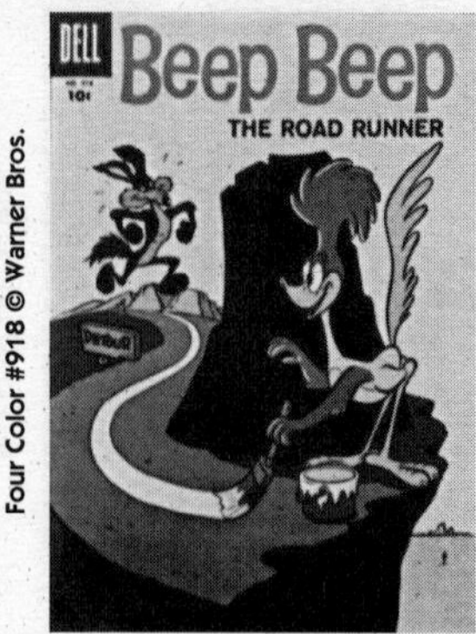

Four Color #957 © National Biscuit Co.

	GD25	FN65	NM94
871-Curly Kayoe	4.00	11.00	22.00
872-Captain Kangaroo (TV)-Photo-c	14.00	43.00	100.00
873-Grandma Duck's Farm Friends (Disney)	6.70	20.00	40.00
874-Old Ironsides (Disney-Movie with Johnny Tremain) (1/58)	8.35	25.00	50.00
875-Trumpets West (Luke Short) (2/58)	4.20	12.50	25.00
876-Tales of Wells Fargo (#1)(TV)(2/58)-Photo-c	10.00	30.00	70.00
877-Frontier Doctor with Rex Allen (TV)-Alex Toth-a; Rex Allen photo-c	11.50	34.00	80.00
878-Peanuts (#1)-Schulz-c only (2/58)	14.00	43.00	100.00
879-Brave Eagle (TV) (2/58)-Photo-c	4.00	10.00	20.00
880-Steve Donovan, Western Marshal-Drucker-a (TV)-Photo-c	4.70	14.00	28.00
881-The Captain and the Kids (2/58)	4.00	10.00	20.00
882-Zorro (Disney)-1st Disney issue; by Alex Toth (TV) (2/58); photo-c	22.00	65.00	150.00
883-The Little Rascals (TV)	4.00	10.00	20.00
884-Hawkeye and the Last of the Mohicans (TV) (3/58); photo-c	7.50	22.50	45.00
885-Fury (TV) (3/58)-Photo-c	7.50	22.50	45.00
886-Bongo and Lumpjaw (Disney) (3/58)	4.00	10.00	20.00
887-The Hardy Boys (Disney) (TV)-Mickey Mouse Club (1/58)-Photo-c	10.00	30.00	70.00
888-Elmer Fudd (3/58)	2.80	7.00	14.00
889-Clint and Mac (Disney) (TV) (3/58)-Alex Toth-a; photo-c	14.00	43.00	100.00
890-Wyatt Earp (TV)-by Russ Manning; photo-c	8.35	25.00	50.00
891-Light in the Forest (Disney-Movie) (3/58)-Fess Parker photo-c	10.00	30.00	60.00
892-Maverick (#1) (TV) (4/58)-James Garner photo-c	16.00	48.00	110.00
893-Jim Bowie (TV)-Photo-c	6.35	19.00	38.00
894-Oswald the Rabbit (Lantz)	2.80	7.00	14.00
895-Wagon Train (#1) (TV) (3/58)-Photo-c	10.00	30.00	70.00
896-The Adventures of Tinker Bell (Disney)	8.35	25.00	50.00
897-Jiminy Cricket (Disney)	6.70	20.00	40.00
898-Silvertip (Max Brand)-Kinstler-a (5/58)	5.35	16.00	32.00
899-Goofy (Disney) (5/58)	5.85	17.50	35.00
900-Prince Valiant; by Bob Fuje	6.35	19.00	38.00
901-Little Hiawatha (Disney)	5.85	17.50	35.00
902-Will-Yum!	3.60	9.00	18.00
903-Dotty Dripple and Taffy	3.60	9.00	18.00
904-Lee Hunter, Indian Fighter	4.70	14.00	28.00
905-Annette (Disney) (TV) (5/58)-Mickey Mouse Club; Annette Funicello photo-c	29.00	86.00	200.00
906-Francis the Famous Talking Mule	4.00	11.00	22.00
907-Sugarfoot (#1) (TV)Toth-a; photo-c	13.00	40.00	90.00
908-The Little People and the Giant-Walt Scott (5/58)	4.00	10.00	20.00
909-Smitty	3.60	9.00	18.00
910-The Vikings (Movie)-Buscema-a; Kirk Douglas photo-c	10.00	30.00	70.00
911-The Gray Ghost (TV)-Photo-c	9.15	27.50	55.00
912-Leave It to Beaver (#1) (TV)-Photo-c	20.00	60.00	140.00
913-The Left-Handed Gun (Movie) (7/58); Paul Newman photo-c	11.00	32.00	75.00
914-No Time for Sergeants (Movie)-Andy Griffith photo-c; Toth-a	10.00	30.00	65.00
915-Casey Jones (TV)-Alan Hale photo-c	7.50	22.50	45.00
916-Red Ryder Ranch Comics (7/58)	4.00	10.00	20.00
917-The Life of Riley (TV)-Photo-c	13.00	40.00	90.00
918-Beep Beep, the Roadrunner (#1) (7/58)-Published with two different back covers	10.00	30.00	60.00
919-Boots and Saddles (#1) (TV)-Photo-c	9.15	27.50	55.00
920-Zorro (Disney) (TV) (6/58)Toth-a; photo-c	14.00	43.00	100.00
921-Wyatt Earp (TV)-Manning-a; photo-c	8.35	25.00	50.00

	GD25	FN65	NM94
922-Johnny Mack Brown by Russ Manning; photo-c	7.50	22.50	45.00
923-Timmy	3.20	8.00	16.00
924-Colt .45 (#1) (TV) (8/58)-W. Preston photo-c	10.00	30.00	70.00
925-Last of the Fast Guns (Movie) (8/58)-Photo-c	7.50	22.50	45.00
926-Peter Pan (Disney)-Reprint of #442	5.85	17.50	35.00
927-Top Gun (Luke Short) Buscema-a	4.20	12.50	25.00
928-Sea Hunt (#1) (9/58) (TV)-Lloyd Bridges photo-c	13.00	40.00	90.00
929-Brave Eagle (TV)-Photo-c	4.00	10.00	20.00
930-Maverick (TV) (7/58)-James Garner photo-c	10.00	30.00	60.00
931-Have Gun, Will Travel (#1) (TV)-Photo-c	11.50	34.00	80.00
932-Smokey the Bear (His Life Story)	5.00	15.00	30.00
933-Zorro (Disney, 9/58) (TV)-Alex Toth-a; photo-c	14.00	43.00	100.00
934-Restless Gun (#1) (TV)-Photo-c	11.50	34.00	80.00
935-King of the Royal Mounted	4.70	14.00	28.00
936-The Little Rascals (TV)	4.00	10.00	20.00
937-Ruff and Reddy (#1) (9/58) (TV) (1st Hanna-Barbera comic book)	12.00	36.00	85.00
938-Elmer Fudd (9/58)	2.80	7.00	14.00
939-Steve Canyon - not by Caniff	5.00	15.00	30.00
940-Lolly and Pepper (10/58)	3.20	8.00	16.00
941-Pluto (Disney) (10/58)	4.00	10.00	20.00
942-Pony Express (TV)	5.00	15.00	30.00
943-White Wilderness (Disney-Movie) (10/58)	8.35	25.00	50.00
944-The 7th Voyage of Sinbad (Movie) (9/58)-Buscema-a; photo-c	14.00	43.00	100.00
945-Maverick (TV)-James Garner/Jack Kelly photo-c	10.00	30.00	60.00
946-The Big Country (Movie)-Photo-c	7.50	22.50	45.00
947-Broken Arrow (TV)-Photo-c (11/58)	5.85	17.50	35.00
948-Daisy Duck's Diary (Disney) (11/58)	4.35	13.00	26.00
949-High Adventure(Lowell Thomas')(TV)-Photo-c	5.85	17.50	35.00
950-Frosty the Snowman	4.00	10.00	20.00
951-The Lennon Sisters Life Story (TV)-Toth-a, 32 pgs.; photo-c	16.00	48.00	110.00
952-Goofy (Disney) (11/58)	5.85	17.50	35.00
953-Francis the Famous Talking Mule	4.00	11.00	22.00
954-Man in Space-Satellites (TV)	8.35	25.00	50.00
955-Hi and Lois (11/58)	3.20	8.00	16.00
956-Ricky Nelson (#1) (TV)-Photo-c	23.00	70.00	160.00
957-Buffalo Bee (#1) (TV)	10.00	30.00	60.00
958-Santa Claus Funnies	4.00	10.00	20.00
959-Christmas Stories-(Walt Scott's Little People) (1951-56 strip reprints)	4.00	10.00	20.00
960-Zorro (Disney) (TV) (12/58)-Toth art; photo-c	14.00	43.00	100.00
961-Jace Pearson's Tales of the Texas Rangers (TV)-Spiegle-a; photo-c	5.35	16.00	32.00
962-Maverick (TV) (1/59)-James Garner/Jack Kelly photo-c	10.00	30.00	60.00
963-Johnny Mack Brown; photo-c	6.70	20.00	40.00
964-The Hardy Boys (TV) (Disney) (1/59)-Mickey Mouse Club; photo-c	10.00	30.00	70.00
965-Grandma Duck's Farm Friends (Disney)(1/59)	5.85	17.50	35.00
966-Tonka (starring Sal Mineo; Disney-Movie)-Photo-c	10.00	30.00	70.00
967-Chilly Willy (2/59) (Lantz)	3.60	9.00	18.00
968-Tales of Wells Fargo (TV)-Photo-c	9.15	27.50	55.00
969-Peanuts (2/59)	10.00	30.00	70.00
970-Lawman (#1) (TV)-Photo-c	10.00	30.00	70.00
971-Wagon Train (TV)-Photo-c	6.35	19.00	38.00
972-Tom Thumb (Movie)-George Pal (1/59)	11.50	34.00	80.00
973-Sleeping Beauty and the Prince(Disney)(5/59)	14.00	43.00	100.00
974-The Little Rascals (TV) (3/59)	4.00	10.00	20.00
975-Fury (TV)-Photo-c	7.50	22.50	45.00
976-Zorro (Disney) (TV)-Toth-a; photo-c	14.00	43.00	100.00
977-Elmer Fudd (3/59)	2.80	7.00	14.00
978-Lolly and Pepper	3.20	8.00	16.00

Four Color #964 © WDC

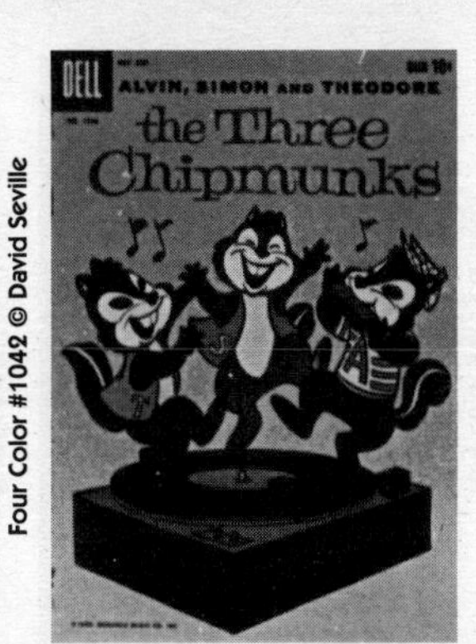

Four Color #1042 © David Seville

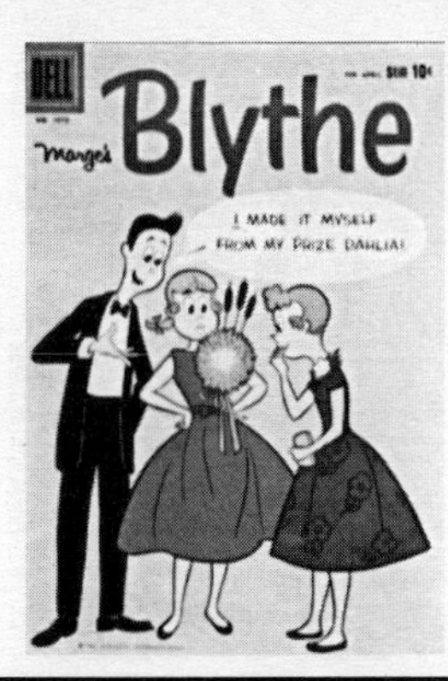

Four Color #1072 © WEST

	GD25	FN65	NM94
979-Oswald the Rabbit (Lantz)	2.80	7.00	14.00
980-Maverick (TV) (4-6/59)-James Garner/Jack Kelly photo-c	10.00	30.00	60.00
981-Ruff and Reddy (TV) (Hanna-Barbera)	9.15	27.50	55.00
982-The New Adventures of Tinker Bell (TV) (Disney)	8.35	25.00	50.00
983-Have Gun, Will Travel (TV) (4-6/59)-Photo-c	8.35	25.00	50.00
984-Sleeping Beauty's Fairy Godmothers (Disney)	11.50	34.00	80.00
985-Shaggy Dog (Disney-Movie)-Photo-all four covers; Annette on back-c(5/59)	5.85	17.50	35.00
986-Restless Gun (TV)-Photo-c	8.35	25.00	50.00
987-Goofy (Disney) (7/59)	5.85	17.50	35.00
988-Little Hiawatha (Disney)	5.85	17.50	35.00
989-Jiminy Cricket (Disney) (5-7/59)	5.85	17.50	35.00
990-Huckleberry Hound (#1)(TV)(Hanna-Barbera); 1st app. Huck, Yogi Bear, & Pixie & Dixie & Mr. Jinx	10.00	30.00	65.00
991-Francis the Famous Talking Mule	4.00	11.00	22.00
992-Sugarfoot (TV)-Toth-a; photo-c	13.00	40.00	90.00
993-Jim Bowie (TV)-Photo-c	6.35	19.00	38.00
994-Sea Hunt (TV)-Lloyd Bridges photo-c	9.15	27.50	55.00
995-Donald Duck Album (Disney) (5-7/59)(#1)	5.85	17.50	35.00
996-Nevada (Zane Grey)	4.00	11.00	22.00
997-Walt Disney Presents-Tales of Texas John Slaughter (#1) (TV) (Disney)-Photo-c; photo of W. Disney inside-c	8.35	25.00	50.00
998-Ricky Nelson (TV)-Photo-c	23.00	70.00	160.00
999-Leave It to Beaver (TV)-Photo-c	18.00	54.00	125.00
1000-The Gray Ghost (TV) (6-8/59)-Photo-c	9.15	27.50	55.00
1001-Lowell Thomas' High Adventure (TV) (8-10/59)-Photo-c	5.85	17.50	35.00
1002-Buffalo Bee (TV)	7.50	22.50	45.00
1003-Zorro (TV) (Disney)-Toth-a; photo-c	14.00	43.00	100.00
1004-Colt .45 (TV) (6-8/59)-Photo-c	8.35	25.00	50.00
1005-Maverick (TV)-James Garner/Jack Kelly photo-c	10.00	30.00	60.00
1006-Hercules (Movie)-Buscema-a; photo-c	11.00	32.00	75.00
1007-John Paul Jones (Movie)-Robert Stack photo-c	5.85	17.50	35.00
1008-Beep Beep, the Road Runner (7-9/59)	5.35	16.00	32.00
1009-The Rifleman (#1) (TV)-Photo-c	17.00	52.00	120.00
1010-Grandma Duck's Farm Friends (Disney)-by Carl Barks	14.00	43.00	100.00
1011-Buckskin (#1) (TV)-Photo-c	10.00	30.00	65.00
1012-Last Train from Gun Hill (Movie) (7/59)-Photo-c	9.15	27.50	55.00
1013-Bat Masterson (#1) (TV) (8/59)-Gene Barry photo-c	10.00	30.00	70.00
1014-The Lennon Sisters (TV)-Toth-a; photo-c	16.00	48.00	110.00
1015-Peanuts-Schulz-c	10.00	30.00	70.00
1016-Smokey the Bear Nature Stories	4.00	11.00	22.00
1017-Chilly Willy (Lantz)	3.60	9.00	18.00
1018-Rio Bravo (Movie)(6/59)-John Wayne; Toth-a; John Wayne, Dean Martin & Ricky Nelson photo-c	22.00	65.00	150.00
1019-Wagon Train (TV)-Photo-c	6.35	19.00	38.00
1020-Jungle Jim-McWilliams-a	3.60	9.00	18.00
1021-Jace Pearson's Tales of the Texas Rangers (TV)-Photo-c	5.00	15.00	30.00
1022-Timmy	3.20	8.00	16.00
1023-Tales of Wells Fargo (TV)-Photo-c	9.15	27.50	55.00
1024-Darby O'Gill and the Little People (Disney-Movie)-Toth-a; photo-c	14.00	43.00	100.00
1025-Vacation in Disneyland (8-10/59)-Carl Barks-a(24pgs.) (Disney)	22.00	65.00	150.00
1026-Spin and Marty (TV) (Disney) (9-11/59)-Mickey Mouse Club; photo-c	8.35	25.00	50.00
1027-The Texan (#1)(TV)-Photo-c	8.35	25.00	50.00
1028-Rawhide (#1) (TV) (9-11/59)-Clint Eastwood photo-c; Tufts-a	24.00	70.00	165.00
1029-Boots and Saddles (TV) (9/59)-Photo-c	6.35	19.00	38.00

	GD25	FN65	NM94
1030-Spanky and Alfalfa, the Little Rascals (TV)	4.00	10.00	20.00
1031-Fury (TV)-Photo-c	7.50	22.50	45.00
1032-Elmer Fudd	2.80	7.00	14.00
1033-Steve Canyon-not by Caniff; photo-c	5.00	15.00	30.00
1034-Nancy and Sluggo Summer Camp (9-11/59)	3.60	9.00	18.00
1035-Lawman (TV)-Photo-c	6.70	20.00	40.00
1036-The Big Circus (Movie)-Photo-c	5.85	17.50	35.00
1037-Zorro (Disney) (TV)-Tufts-a; Annette Funicello photo-c	18.00	54.00	125.00
1038-Ruff and Reddy (TV)(Hanna-Barbera)(1959)	9.15	27.50	55.00
1039-Pluto (Disney) (11-1/60)	4.00	10.00	20.00
1040-Quick Draw McGraw (#1) (TV) (Hanna-Barbera) (12-2/60)	11.50	34.00	68.00
1041-Sea Hunt (TV) (10-12/59)-Toth-a; Lloyd Bridges photo-c	10.00	30.00	65.00
1042-The Three Chipmunks (Alvin, Simon & Theodore) (#1) (TV) (10-12/59)	4.00	11.00	22.00
1043-The Three Stooges (#1)-Photo-c	19.00	58.00	135.00
1044-Have Gun, Will Travel (TV)-Photo-c	8.35	25.00	50.00
1045-Restless Gun (TV)-Photo-c	8.35	25.00	50.00
1046-Beep Beep, the Road Runner (11-1/60)	5.35	16.00	32.00
1047-Gyro Gearloose (#1) (Disney)-All Barks-c/a	11.00	32.00	125.00
1048-The Horse Soldiers (Movie) (John Wayne)-Sekowsky-a; painted cover featuring John Wayne	17.00	52.00	120.00
1049-Don't Give Up the Ship (Movie) (8/59)-Jerry Lewis photo-c	7.50	22.50	45.00
1050-Huckleberry Hound (TV) (Hanna-Barbera) (10-12/59)	7.50	22.50	45.00
1051-Donald in Mathmagic Land (Disney-Movie)	10.00	30.00	70.00
1052-Ben-Hur (Movie) (11/59)-Manning-a	10.00	30.00	65.00
1053-Goofy (Disney) (11-1/60)	5.85	17.50	35.00
1054-Huckleberry Hound Winter Fun (TV) (Hanna-Barbera) (12/59)	7.50	22.50	45.00
1055-Daisy Duck's Diary (Disney)-by Carl Barks (11-1/60)	10.00	30.00	70.00
1056-Yellowstone Kelly (Movie)-Clint Walker photo-c	5.85	17.50	35.00
1057-Mickey Mouse Album (Disney)	4.00	10.00	20.00
1058-Colt .45 (TV)-Photo-c	8.35	25.00	50.00
1059-Sugarfoot (TV)-Photo-c	9.15	27.50	55.00
1060-Journey to the Center of the Earth (Movie)-Pat Boone & James Mason photo-c	13.00	40.00	90.00
1061-Buffalo Bee (TV)	7.50	22.50	45.00
1062-Christmas Stories (Walt Scott's Little People strip-r)	4.00	10.00	20.00
1063-Santa Claus Funnies	4.00	10.00	20.00
1064-Bugs Bunny's Merry Christmas (12/59)	5.00	15.00	30.00
1065-Frosty the Snowman	4.00	10.00	20.00
1066-77 Sunset Strip (#1) (TV)-Toth-a (1-3/60)-Efrem Zimbalist, Jr. & Edd "Kookie" Byrnes photo-c	12.00	36.00	85.00
1067-Yogi Bear (#1) (TV) (Hanna-Barbera)	11.50	34.00	80.00
1068-Francis the Famous Talking Mule	4.00	11.00	22.00
1069-The FBI Story (Movie)-Toth-a; James Stewart photo on-c	11.00	32.00	75.00
1070-Solomon and Sheba (Movie)-Sekowsky-a; photo-c	10.00	30.00	65.00
1071-The Real McCoys (#1) (TV) (1-3/60)-Toth-a; Walter Brennan photo-c	11.50	34.00	80.00
1072-Blythe (Marge's)	5.00	15.00	30.00
1073-Grandma Duck's Farm Friends-Barks-c/a (Disney)	14.00	43.00	100.00
1074-Chilly Willy (Lantz)	3.60	9.00	18.00
1075-Tales of Wells Fargo (TV)-Photo-c	9.15	27.50	55.00
1076-The Rebel (#1) (TV)-Sekowsky-a; photo-c	11.00	32.00	75.00
1077-The Deputy (#1) (TV)-Buscema-a; Henry Fonda photo-c	13.00	40.00	90.00
1078-The Three Stooges (2-4/60)-Photo-c	10.00	30.00	70.00

Four Color #1078 © Norman Maurer Prod.

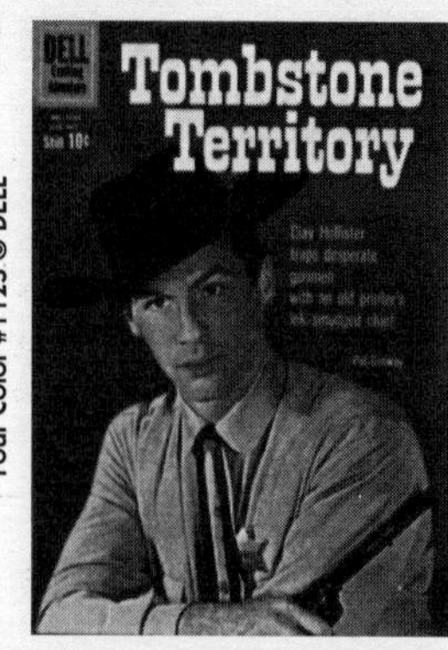

Four Color #1123 © DELL

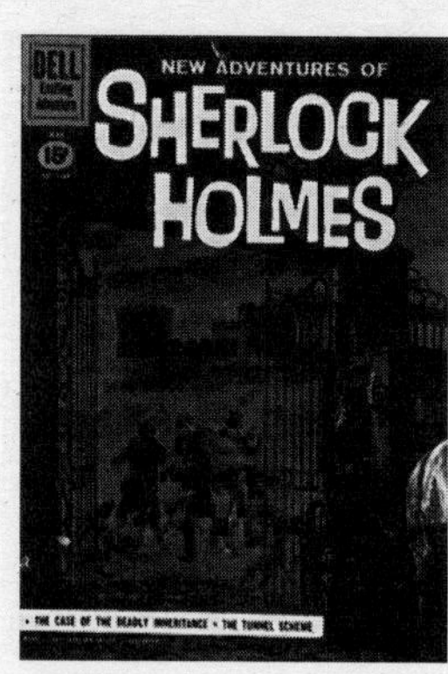

Four Color #1169 © DELL

	GD25	FN65	NM94
1079-The Little Rascals (TV) (Spanky & Alfalfa)	4.00	10.00	20.00
1080-Fury (TV) (2-4/60)-Photo-c	7.50	22.50	45.00
1081-Elmer Fudd	2.80	7.00	14.00
1082-Spin and Marty (Disney) (TV)-Photo-c	8.35	25.00	50.00
1083-Men into Space (TV)-Anderson-a; photo-c	6.70	20.00	40.00
1084-Speedy Gonzales	3.60	9.00	18.00
1085-The Time Machine (H.G. Wells) (Movie) (3/60)-Alex Toth-a; Rod Taylor photo-c	16.00	48.00	110.00
1086-Lolly and Pepper	3.20	8.00	16.00
1087-Peter Gunn (TV)-Photo-c	10.00	30.00	65.00
1088-A Dog of Flanders (Movie)-Photo-c	5.35	16.00	32.00
1089-Restless Gun (TV)-Photo-c	8.35	25.00	50.00
1090-Francis the Famous Talking Mule	4.00	11.00	22.00
1091-Jacky's Diary (4-6/60)	5.85	17.50	35.00
1092-Toby Tyler (Disney-Movie)-Photo-c	8.35	25.00	50.00
1093-MacKenzie's Raiders (Movie/TV)-Richard Carlson photo-c from TV show	7.50	22.50	45.00
1094-Goofy (Disney)	5.85	17.50	35.00
1095-Gyro Gearloose (Disney)-All Barks-c/a	11.50	34.00	80.00
1096-The Texan (TV)-Rory Calhoun photo-c	8.35	25.00	50.00
1097-Rawhide (TV)-Manning-a; Clint Eastwood photo-c	16.00	48.00	110.00
1098-Sugarfoot (TV)-Photo-c	9.15	27.50	55.00
1099-Donald Duck Album (Disney) (5-7/60)-Barks-c	6.70	20.00	40.00
1100-Annette's Life Story (Disney-Movie) (5/60)-Annette Funicello photo-c	22.00	65.00	150.00
1101-Robert Louis Stevenson's Kidnapped (Disney-Movie) (5/60); photo-c	6.70	20.00	40.00
1102-Wanted: Dead or Alive (#1) (TV) (5-7/60); Steve McQueen photo-c	14.00	43.00	100.00
1103-Leave It to Beaver (TV)-Photo-c	18.00	54.00	125.00
1104-Yogi Bear Goes to College (TV) (Hanna-Barbera) (6-8/60)	8.35	25.00	50.00
1105-Gale Storm (Oh! Susanna) (TV)-Toth-a; photo-c	14.00	43.00	100.00
1106-77 Sunset Strip(TV)(6-8/60)-Toth-a; photo-c	10.00	30.00	65.00
1107-Buckskin (TV)-Photo-c	8.35	25.00	50.00
1108-The Troubleshooters (TV)-Keenan Wynn photo-c	6.70	20.00	40.00
1109-This Is Your Life, Donald Duck (Disney) (TV) (8-10/60)-Gyro flashback to WDC&S #141; origin Donald Duck (1st told)	19.00	57.00	130.00
1110-Bonanza (#1) (TV) (6-8/60)-Photo-c	34.00	103.00	240.00
1111-Shotgun Slade (TV)-Photo-c	6.70	20.00	40.00
1112-Pixie and Dixie and Mr. Jinks (#1) (TV) (Hanna-Barbera) (7-9/60)	7.50	22.50	45.00
1113-Tales of Wells Fargo (TV)-Photo-c	9.15	27.50	55.00
1114-Huckleberry Finn (Movie) (7/60)-Photo-c	5.85	17.50	35.00
1115-Ricky Nelson (TV)-Manning-a; photo-c	18.00	54.00	125.00
1116-Boots and Saddles (TV) (8/60)-Photo-c	6.35	19.00	38.00
1117-Boy and the Pirates (Movie)-Photo-c	7.50	22.50	45.00
1118-The Sword and the Dragon (Movie) (6/60)-Photo-c	9.15	27.50	55.00
1119-Smokey the Bear Nature Stories	4.00	11.00	22.00
1120-Dinosaurus (Movie)-Painted-c	8.35	25.00	50.00
1121-Hercules Unchained (Movie) (8/60)-Crandall/Evans-a	10.00	30.00	65.00
1122-Chilly Willy (Lantz)	3.60	9.00	18.00
1123-Tombstone Territory (TV)-Photo-c	10.00	30.00	65.00
1124-Whirlybirds (#1) (TV)-Photo-c	10.00	30.00	65.00
1125-Laramie (#1) (TV)-Photo-c; G. Kane/Heath-a	10.00	30.00	60.00
1126-Sundance (TV) (8-10/60)-Earl Holliman photo-c	10.00	30.00	65.00
1127-The Three Stooges-Photo-c (8-10/60)	10.00	30.00	70.00
1128-Rocky and His Friends (#1) (TV) (Jay Ward) (8-10/60)	29.00	86.00	200.00
1129-Pollyanna (Disney-Movie)-Hayley Mills photo-c	11.00	32.00	75.00
1130-The Deputy (TV)-Buscema-a; Henry Fonda photo-c	10.00	30.00	65.00
1131-Elmer Fudd (9-11/60)	2.80	7.00	14.00
1132-Space Mouse (Lantz) (8-10/60)	4.70	14.00	28.00
1133-Fury (TV)-Photo-c	7.50	22.50	45.00
1134-Real McCoys (TV)-Toth-a; photo-c	11.50	34.00	80.00
1135-M.G.M.'s Mouse Musketeers (9-11/60)	2.80	7.00	14.00
1136-Jungle Cat (Disney-Movie)-Photo-c	8.35	25.00	50.00
1137-The Little Rascals (TV)	4.00	10.00	20.00
1138-The Rebel (TV)-Photo-c	10.00	30.00	65.00
1139-Spartacus (Movie) (11/60)-Buscema-a; Kirk Douglas photo-c	13.00	40.00	90.00
1140-Donald Duck Album (Disney)-Barks-c	6.70	20.00	40.00
1141-Huckleberry Hound for President (TV) (Hanna-Barbera) (10/60)	7.50	22.50	45.00
1142-Johnny Ringo (TV)-Photo-c	9.15	27.50	55.00
1143-Pluto (Disney) (11-1/61)	4.00	10.00	20.00
1144-The Story of Ruth (Movie)-Photo-c	11.50	34.00	80.00
1145-The Lost World (Movie)-Gil Kane-a; photo-c; 1 pg. Conan Doyle biography by Torres	12.00	36.00	85.00
1146-Restless Gun (TV)-Photo-c; Wildey-a	8.35	25.00	50.00
1147-Sugarfoot (TV)-Photo-c	9.15	27.50	55.00
1148-I Aim at the Stars-the Wernher Von Braun Story (Movie) (11-1/61)-Photo-c	7.50	22.50	45.00
1149-Goofy (Disney) (11-1/61)	5.85	17.50	35.00
1150-Daisy Duck's Diary (Disney) (12-1/61) by Carl Barks	10.00	30.00	70.00
1151-Mickey Mouse Album (Disney) (11-1/61)	4.00	10.00	20.00
1152-Rocky and His Friends (TV) (Jay Ward) (12-2/61)	24.00	72.00	165.00
1153-Frosty the Snowman	4.00	10.00	20.00
1154-Santa Claus Funnies	4.00	10.00	20.00
1155-North to Alaska (Movie)-John Wayne photo-c	16.00	48.00	110.00
1156-Walt Disney Swiss Family Robinson (Movie) (12/60)-Photo-c	8.35	25.00	50.00
1157-Master of the World (Movie) (7/61)	6.35	19.00	38.00
1158-Three Worlds of Gulliver (2 issues exist with different covers) (Movie)-Photo-c	5.85	17.50	35.00
1159-77 Sunset Strip (TV)-Toth-a; photo-c	10.00	30.00	65.00
1160-Rawhide (TV)-Clint Eastwood photo-c	16.00	48.00	110.00
1161-Grandma Duck's Farm Friends (Disney) by Carl Barks (2-4/61)	14.00	43.00	100.00
1162-Yogi Bear Joins the Marines (TV) (Hanna-Barbera) (5-7/61)	8.35	25.00	50.00
1163-Daniel Boone (3-5/61); Marsh-a	6.70	20.00	40.00
1164-Wanted: Dead or Alive (TV)-Steve McQueen photo-c	11.50	34.00	80.00
1165-Ellery Queen (#1) (3-5/61)	11.50	34.00	80.00
1166-Rocky and His Friends (TV) (Jay Ward)	24.00	72.00	165.00
1167-Tales of Wells Fargo (TV)-Photo-c	8.35	25.00	50.00
1168-The Detectives (TV)-Robert Taylor photo-c	10.00	30.00	60.00
1169-New Adventures of Sherlock Holmes	17.00	52.00	120.00
1170-The Three Stooges (3-5/61)-Photo-c	10.00	30.00	70.00
1171-Elmer Fudd	2.80	7.00	14.00
1172-Fury (TV)-Photo-c	7.50	22.50	45.00
1173-The Twilight Zone (#1) (TV) (5/61)-Crandall/Evans-c/a; Crandall tribute to Ingles	19.00	58.00	135.00
1174-The Little Rascals (TV)	3.60	9.00	18.00
1175-M.G.M.'s Mouse Musketeers (3-5/61)	2.80	7.00	14.00
1176-Dondi (Movie)-Origin; photo-c	5.85	17.50	35.00
1177-Chilly Willy (Lantz) (4-6/61)	3.20	8.00	16.00
1178-Ten Who Dared (Disney-Movie) (12/60)-Painted-c; cast member photo on back-c	8.35	25.00	50.00
1179-The Swamp Fox (TV) (Disney)-Leslie Nielson photo-c	10.00	30.00	60.00

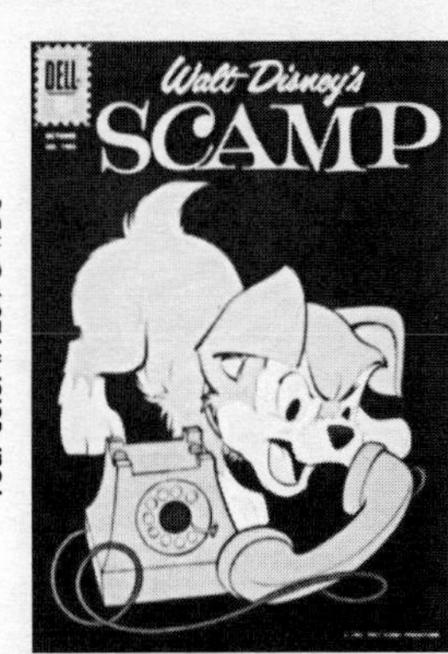

Four Color #1204 © WDC

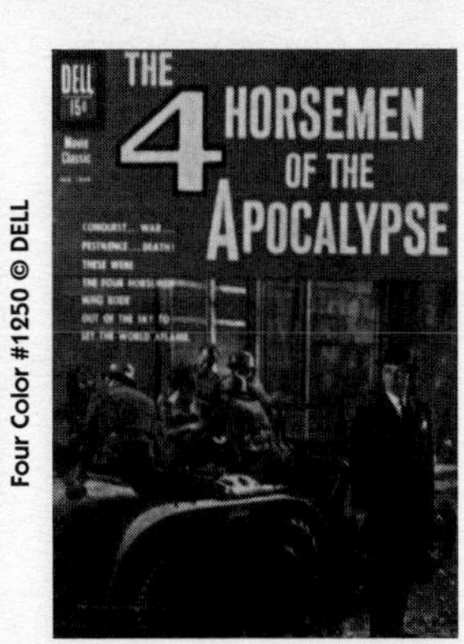

Four Color #1250 © DELL

Four Color #1279 © WDC

	GD25	FN65	NM94
1180-The Danny Thomas Show (TV)-Toth-a; photo-c	17.00	52.00	120.00
1181-Texas John Slaughter (TV) (Disney) (4-6/61)-Photo-c	8.35	25.00	50.00
1182-Donald Duck Album (Disney) (5-7/61)	4.70	14.00	28.00
1183-101 Dalmatians (Disney-Movie) (3/61)	10.00	30.00	60.00
1184-Gyro Gearloose; All Barks-c/a (Disney) (5-7/61) Two variations exist	11.50	34.00	80.00
1185-Sweetie Pie	4.00	11.00	22.00
1186-Yak Yak (#1) by Jack Davis (2 versions - one minus 3-pg. Davis-c/a)	10.00	30.00	60.00
1187-The Three Stooges (6-8/61)-Photo-c	10.00	30.00	70.00
1188-Atlantis, the Lost Continent (Movie) (5/61)-Photo-c	11.00	32.00	75.00
1189-Greyfriars Bobby (Disney-Movie) (11/61)-Photo-c (scarce)	8.35	25.00	50.00
1190-Donald and the Wheel (Disney-Movie) (11/61); Barks-c	7.50	22.50	45.00
1191-Leave It to Beaver (TV)-Photo-c	18.00	54.00	125.00
1192-Ricky Nelson (TV)-Manning-a; photo-c	18.00	54.00	125.00
1193-The Real McCoys (TV) (6-8/61)-Photo-c	10.00	30.00	60.00
1194-Pepe (Movie) (4/61)-Photo-c	4.70	14.00	28.00
1195-National Velvet (#1) (TV)-Photo-c	7.50	22.50	45.00
1196-Pixie and Dixie and Mr. Jinks (TV) (Hanna-Barbera) (7-9/61)	5.85	17.50	35.00
1197-The Aquanauts (TV) (5-7/61)-Photo-c	7.50	22.50	45.00
1198-Donald in Mathmagic Land (Disney-Movie)-Reprint of #1051	7.50	22.50	45.00
1199-The Absent-Minded Professor (Disney-Movie) (4/61)-Photo-c	8.35	25.00	50.00
1200-Hennessey (TV) (8-10/61)-Gil Kane-a; photo-c	7.50	22.50	45.00
1201-Goofy (Disney) (8-10/61)	5.85	17.50	35.00
1202-Rawhide (TV)-Clint Eastwood photo-c	16.00	48.00	110.00
1203-Pinocchio (Disney) (3/62)	5.85	17.50	35.00
1204-Scamp (Disney)	4.00	10.00	20.00
1205-David and Goliath (Movie) (7/61)-Photo-c	6.70	20.00	40.00
1206-Lolly and Pepper (9-11/61)	3.20	8.00	16.00
1207-The Rebel (TV)-Sekowsky-a; photo-c	10.00	30.00	65.00
1208-Rocky and His Friends (Jay Ward) (TV)	24.00	72.00	165.00
1209-Sugarfoot (TV)-Photo-c (10-12/61)	9.15	27.50	55.00
1210-The Parent Trap (Disney-Movie) (8/61)-Hayley Mills photo-c	11.00	32.00	75.00
1211-77 Sunset Strip (TV)-Manning-a; photo-c	10.00	30.00	60.00
1212-Chilly Willy (Lantz) (7-9/61)	3.20	8.00	16.00
1213-Mysterious Island (Movie)-Photo-c	9.15	27.50	55.00
1214-Smokey the Bear	4.00	11.00	22.00
1215-Tales of Wells Fargo (TV) (10-12/61)-Photo-c	8.35	25.00	50.00
1216-Whirlybirds (TV)-Photo-c	9.15	27.50	55.00
1218-Fury (TV)-Photo-c	7.50	22.50	45.00
1219-The Detectives (TV)-Robert Taylor & Adam West photo-c	8.35	25.00	50.00
1220-Gunslinger (TV)-Photo-c	9.15	27.50	55.00
1221-Bonanza (TV) (9-11/61)-Photo-c	17.00	52.00	120.00
1222-Elmer Fudd (9-11/61)	2.80	7.00	14.00
1223-Laramie (TV)-Gil Kane-a; photo-c	6.70	20.00	40.00
1224-The Little Rascals (TV) (10-12/61)	3.60	9.00	18.00
1225-The Deputy (TV)-Henry Fonda photo-c	10.00	30.00	65.00
1226-Nikki, Wild Dog of the North (Disney-Movie) (9/61)-Photo-c	6.70	20.00	40.00
1227-Morgan the Pirate (Movie)-Photo-c	10.00	30.00	65.00
1229-Thief of Baghdad (Movie)-Crandall/Evans-a; photo-c	11.00	32.00	75.00
1230-Voyage to the Bottom of the Sea (#1) (Movie)-Photo insert on-c	10.00	30.00	60.00
1231-Danger Man (TV) (9-11/61)-Patrick McGoohan photo-c	10.00	30.00	60.00

	GD25	FN65	NM94
1232-On the Double (Movie)	5.35	16.00	32.00
1233-Tammy Tell Me True (Movie) (1961)	7.50	22.50	45.00
1234-The Phantom Planet (Movie) (1961)	6.70	20.00	40.00
1235-Mister Magoo (#1) (12-2/62)	9.15	27.50	55.00
1235-Mister Magoo (3-5/65) 2nd printing; reprint of 12-2/62 issue	5.00	15.00	30.00
1236-King of Kings (Movie)-Photo-c	9.15	27.50	55.00
1237-The Untouchables (#1) (TV)-Not by Toth; photo-c	16.00	48.00	110.00
1238-Deputy Dawg (TV)	11.50	34.00	80.00
1239-Donald Duck Album (Disney) (10-12/61)-Barks-c	6.70	20.00	40.00
1240-The Detectives (TV)-Tufts-a; Robert Taylor photo-c	8.35	25.00	50.00
1241-Sweetie Pie	4.00	11.00	22.00
1242-King Leonardo and His Short Subjects (#1) (TV) (11-1/62)	14.00	43.00	100.00
1243-Ellery Queen	9.15	27.50	55.00
1244-Space Mouse (Lantz) (11-1/62)	4.70	14.00	28.00
1245-New Adventures of Sherlock Holmes	17.00	52.00	120.00
1246-Mickey Mouse Album (Disney)	4.00	10.00	20.00
1247-Daisy Duck's Diary (Disney) (12-2/62)	4.35	13.00	26.00
1248-Pluto (Disney)	4.00	10.00	20.00
1249-The Danny Thomas Show (TV)-Manning-a; photo-c	17.00	52.00	120.00
1250-The Four Horsemen of the Apocalypse (Movie)-Photo-c	7.50	22.50	45.00
1251-Everything's Ducky (Movie) (1961)	5.85	17.50	35.00
1252-The Andy Griffith Show (TV)-Photo-c; 1st show aired 10/3/60	27.00	81.00	190.00
1253-Space Man (#1) (1-3/62)	8.35	25.00	50.00
1254- "Diver Dan" (#1) (TV) (2-4/62)-Photo-c	7.00	21.00	42.00
1255-The Wonders of Aladdin (Movie) (1961)	7.50	22.50	45.00
1256-Kona, Monarch of Monster Isle (#1) (2-4/62)-Glanzman-a	6.70	20.00	45.00
1257-Car 54, Where Are You? (#1) (TV) (3-5/62)-Photo-c	8.35	25.00	50.00
1258-The Frogmen (#1)-Evans-a	8.35	25.00	50.00
1259-El Cid (Movie) (1961)-Photo-c	7.50	22.50	45.00
1260-The Horsemasters (TV, Movie) (Disney) (12-2/62)-Annette Funicello photo-c	11.50	34.00	80.00
1261-Rawhide (TV)-Clint Eastwood photo-c	16.00	48.00	110.00
1262-The Rebel (TV)-Photo-c	10.00	30.00	65.00
1263-77 Sunset Strip (TV) (12-2/62)-Manning-a; photo-c	10.00	30.00	60.00
1264-Pixie and Dixie and Mr. Jinks (TV) (Hanna-Barbera)	5.85	17.50	35.00
1265-The Real McCoys (TV)-Photo-c	10.00	30.00	60.00
1266-M.G.M.'s Spike and Tyke (12-2/62)	2.40	6.00	12.00
1267-Gyro Gearloose; Barks-c/a, 4 pgs. (Disney) (12-2/62)	8.35	25.00	50.00
1268-Oswald the Rabbit (Lantz)	2.80	7.00	14.00
1269-Rawhide (TV)-Clint Eastwood photo-c	16.00	48.00	110.00
1270-Bullwinkle and Rocky (#1) (TV) (Jay Ward) (3-5/62)	17.00	51.00	120.00
1271-Yogi Bear Birthday Party (TV) (Hanna-Barbera) (11/61)	5.85	17.50	35.00
1272-Frosty the Snowman	4.00	10.00	20.00
1273-Hans Brinker (Disney-Movie)-Photo-c (2/62)	8.35	25.00	50.00
1274-Santa Claus Funnies (12/61)	4.00	10.00	20.00
1275-Rocky and His Friends (TV) (Jay Ward)	24.00	72.00	165.00
1276-Dondi	4.00	11.00	22.00
1278-King Leonardo and His Short Subjects (TV)	14.00	43.00	100.00
1279-Grandma Duck's Farm Friends (Disney)	5.85	17.50	35.00
1280-Hennessey (TV)-Photo-c	7.50	22.50	45.00
1281-Chilly Willy (Lantz) (4-6/62)	3.20	8.00	16.00

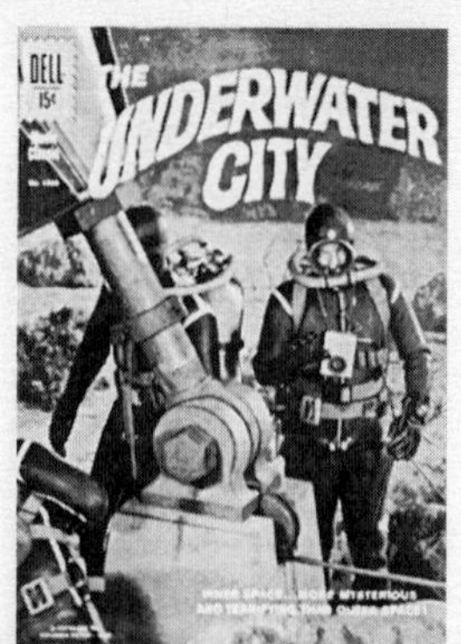

Four Color #1328 © DELL

4-Most V8#1 © STAR

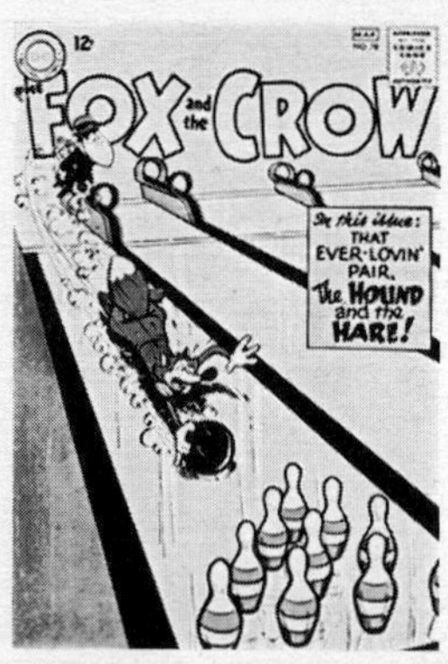

Fox and the Crow #78 © DC

1282-Babes in Toyland (Disney-Movie) (1/62); Annette Funicello photo-c 13.00 40.00 90.00
1283-Bonanza (TV) (2-4/62)-Photo-c 17.00 52.00 120.00
1284-Laramie (TV)-Heath-a; photo-c 6.70 20.00 40.00
1285-Leave It to Beaver (TV)-Photo-c 18.00 54.00 125.00
1286-The Untouchables (TV)-Photo-c 16.00 48.00 110.00
1287-Man from Wells Fargo (TV)-Photo-c 5.00 15.00 30.00
1288-The Twilight Zone (TV) (4/62)-Crandall/Evans-c/a 11.50 34.00 80.00
1289-Ellery Queen 9.15 27.50 55.00
1290-M.G.M.'s Mouse Musketeers 2.80 7.00 14.00
1291-77 Sunset Strip (TV)-Manning-a; photo-c 10.00 30.00 60.00
1293-Elmer Fudd (3-5/62) 2.80 7.00 14.00
1294-Ripcord (TV) 7.50 22.50 45.00
1295-Mister Ed, the Talking Horse (#1) (TV) (3-5/62)-Photo-c 13.00 40.00 90.00
1296-Fury (TV) (3-5/62)-Photo-c 7.50 22.50 45.00
1297-Spanky, Alfalfa and the Little Rascals (TV) 3.60 9.00 18.00
1298-The Hathaways (TV)-Photo-c 5.85 17.50 35.00
1299-Deputy Dawg (TV) 11.50 34.00 80.00
1300-The Comancheros (Movie) (1961)-John Wayne photo-c 16.50 50.00 115.00
1301-Adventures in Paradise (TV) (2-4/62) 5.00 15.00 30.00
1302-Johnny Jason, Teen Reporter (2-4/62) 3.20 8.00 16.00
1303-Lad: A Dog (Movie)-Photo-c 4.35 13.00 26.00
1304-Nellie the Nurse (3-5/62)-Stanley-a 10.00 30.00 65.00
1305-Mister Magoo (3-5/62) 9.15 27.50 55.00
1306-Target: The Corruptors (#1) (TV) (3-5/62)-Photo-c 5.00 15.00 30.00
1307-Margie (TV) (3-5/62) 4.35 13.00 26.00
1308-Tales of the Wizard of Oz (TV) (3-5/62) 11.50 34.00 80.00
1309-87th Precinct (#1) (TV) (4-6/62)-Krigstein-a; photo-c 10.00 30.00 65.00
1310-Huck and Yogi Winter Sports (TV) (Hanna-Barbera) (3/62) 7.50 22.50 45.00
1311-Rocky and His Friends (TV) (Jay Ward) 24.00 72.00 165.00
1312-National Velvet (TV)-Photo-c 4.00 12.00 24.00
1313-Moon Pilot (Disney-Movie)-Photo-c 8.35 25.00 50.00
1328-The Underwater City (Movie) (1961)-Evans-a; photo-c 8.35 25.00 50.00
1329-See Gyro Gearloose #01329-207
1330-Brain Boy (#1)-Gil Kane-a 13.00 40.00 90.00
1332-Bachelor Father (TV) 9.15 27.50 55.00
1333-Short Ribs (4-6/62) 5.85 17.50 35.00
1335-Aggie Mack (4-6/62) 4.00 12.00 24.00
1336-On Stage; not by Leonard Starr 5.35 16.00 32.00
1337-Dr. Kildare (#1) (TV) (4-6/62)-Photo-c 7.50 22.50 45.00
1341-The Andy Griffith Show (TV) (4-6/62)-Photo-c 27.00 81.00 190.00
1348-Yak Yak (#2)-Jack Davis-c/a 9.15 27.50 55.00
1349-Yogi Bear Visits the U.N. (TV) (Hanna-Barbera) (1/62)-Photo-c 10.00 30.00 70.00
1350-Comanche (Disney-Movie)(1962)-Reprints 4-Color #966 (title change from "Tonka" to "Comanche") (4-6/62)-Sal Mineo photo-c 6.70 20.00 40.00
1354-Calvin & the Colonel (#1) (TV) (4-6/62) 9.15 27.50 55.00
NOTE: *Missing numbers probably do not exist.*

4-D MONKEY, THE (Leung's)(Value: cover or less)

FOUR FAVORITES (Crime Must Pay the Penalty No. 33 on)
Sept, 1941 - No. 32, Dec, 1947
Ace Magazines

1-Vulcan, Lash Lightning (formerly Flash Lightning in Sure-Fire), Magno the Magnetic Man & The Raven begin; flag-c 86.00 257.00 600.00
2-The Black Ace only app. 38.00 115.00 265.00
3-Last Vulcan 31.00 92.00 215.00
4,5: 4-The Raven & Vulcan end; Unknown Soldier begins (see Our Flag), ends #28. 5-Captain Courageous begins (5/42), ends #28 (moves over from Captain Courageous #6); not in #6 29.00 88.00 205.00
6-8: 6-The Flag app.; Mr. Risk begins (7/42) 25.00 75.00 175.00
9,11-Kurtzman-a (Lash Lightning); 11-Hitler, Mussolini, Hirohito-c; L.B. Cole-a; Unknown Soldier by Kurtzman 31.00 92.00 215.00
10-Classic Kurtzman-c/a (Magno & Davey) 38.00 115.00 265.00
12-L.B. Cole-a 19.00 57.00 130.00
13-20: 18,20-Palais-c/a 16.50 50.00 115.00
21-No Unknown Soldier; The Unknown app. 11.50 34.00 80.00
22-26: 22-Captain Courageous drops costume. 23-Unknown Soldier drops costume. 25-29-Hap Hazard app. 26-Last Magno 11.50 34.00 80.00
27-32: 30-Funny-c begin (teen humor), end #32 10.00 30.00 65.00
NOTE: ***Dave Berg** c-5. **Jim Mooney** a-6; c-1-3. **Palais** a-18-20; c-18-25. Torture chamber c-5.*

FOUR HORSEMEN, THE (See The Crusaders)

FOUR HORSEMEN OF THE APOCALYPSE, THE (See 4-Color No. 1250)

4MOST (Foremost Boys No. 32-40; becomes Thrilling Crime Cases #41 on)
Winter, 1941-42 - V8#5(#36), 9-10/49; #37, 11-12/49 - #40, 4-5/50
Novelty Publications/Star Publications No. 37-on

V1#1-The Target by Sid Greene, The Cadet & Dick Cole begin with origins retold; produced by Funnies Inc.; quarterly issues begin, end V6#3 79.00 235.00 550.00
2-Last Target (Spr/42) 36.00 107.00 250.00
3-Dan'l Flannel begins; flag-c 30.00 90.00 210.00
4-1pg. Dr. Seuss (signed) (Aut/42) 24.00 73.00 170.00
V2#1-4: 4-Hitler, Tojo & Mussolini app. as pumpkins on-c 7.50 22.50 45.00
V3#1-4 7.50 22.50 45.00
V4#1-4: 2-Walter Johnson-c 5.85 17.50 35.00
V5#1-4: 1-The Target & Targeteers app. 4.70 14.00 28.00
V6#1-4: 1-White Rider & Super Horse begin 4.70 14.00 28.00
5-L. B. Cole-c 6.70 20.00 40.00
V7#1,3,5, V8#1 4.70 14.00 28.00
2,4,6-L. B. Cole-c. 6-Last Dick Cole 7.00 21.00 42.00
V8#2,3,5-L. B. Cole-c/a 9.15 27.50 55.00
4-L. B. Cole-a 5.85 17.50 35.00
37-40: 38-Johnny Weismuller (Tarzan) life story & Jim Braddock (boxer) life story. 38-40-L.B. Cole-c. 40-Last White Rider 5.85 17.50 35.00
Accepted Reprint 38-40 (nd): 40-r/Johnny Weismuller life story; all have L.B. Cole-c 4.70 14.00 28.00

FOUR-STAR BATTLE TALES
Feb-Mar, 1973 - No. 5, Nov-Dec, 1973
National Periodical Publications

1-5: All reprints 1.00
NOTE: ***Drucker** r-1, 3-5. **Heath** r-2, 5; c-1. **Krigstein** r-5. **Kubert** r-4; c-2.*

FOUR STAR SPECTACULAR
Mar-Apr, 1976 - No. 6, Jan-Feb, 1977
National Periodical Publications

1-6: Reprints in all. 2-Infinity cover 1.00
NOTE: *All contain DC Superhero reprints. #1 has 68 pgs.; #2-6, 52 pgs.. #1, 4-Hawkman app.; #2-Kid Flash app.; #3-Green Lantern app; #2, 4, 5-Wonder Woman, Superboy app; #5-Green Arrow, Vigilante app; #6-Blackhawk G.A.-r.*

FOUR TEENERS (Formerly Crime Must Pay The Penalty; Dotty No. 35 on)
No. 34, April, 1948 (52 pgs.)
A. A. Wyn

34-Teen-age comic; Dotty app.; Curly & Jerry continue from Four Favorites 4.00 11.00 22.00

FOX AND THE CROW (Stanley & His Monster No. 109 on) (See Comic Cavalcade & Real Screen Comics)
Dec-Jan, 1951-52 - No. 108, Feb-Mar, 1968
National Periodical Publications

1 82.00 246.00 575.00
2(Scarce) 41.00 122.00 285.00

Fox Giant (1950) © FOX

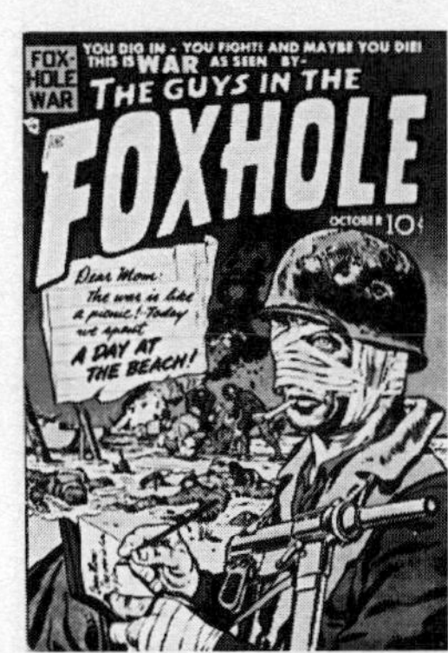

Foxhole #1 © CC

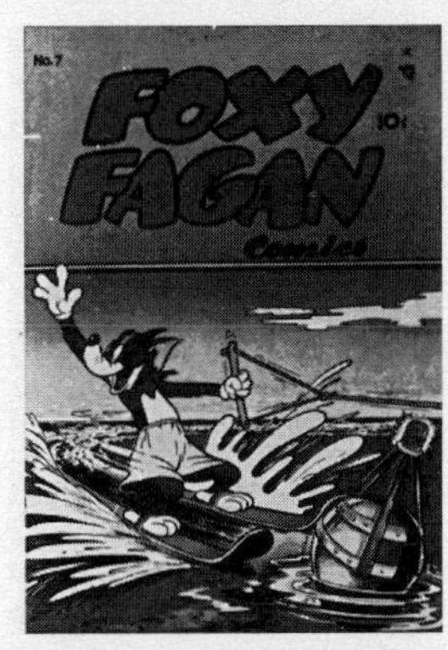

Foxy Fagan #7 © Dearfield Publ.

	GD25	FN65	NM94
3-5	25.00	75.00	175.00
6-10	18.00	54.00	125.00
11-20	13.00	40.00	90.00
21-40: 22-Last precode issue (2/55)	9.15	27.50	55.00
41-60	6.35	19.00	38.00
61-80	4.35	13.00	26.00
81-94	3.60	9.00	18.00
95-Stanley & His Monster begins(origin)(1st app?)	4.00	10.00	20.00
96-99,101-108	1.80	4.50	9.00
100 (10-11/66)	2.40	6.00	12.00

NOTE: *Many covers by* ***Mort Drucker.***

FOX AND THE HOUND, THE (Disney)
Aug, 1981 - No. 3, Oct, 1981
Whitman Publishing Co.

	GD25	FN65	NM94
11292(#1),2,3-Based on animated movie			1.00

FOX GIANTS
1944 - 1950 (25¢, 132 - 196 pgs.)
Fox Features Syndicate

	GD25	FN65	NM94
Album of Crime nn(1949, 132p)	34.00	103.00	240.00
Album of Love nn(1949, 132p)	29.00	88.00	205.00
All Famous Crime Stories nn('49, 132p)	34.00	103.00	240.00
All Good Comics 1(1944, 132p)(R.W. Voigt)-The Bouncer, Purple Tigress,Rick Evans, Puppeteer, Green Mask; Infinity-c	29.00	86.00	200.00
All Great nn(1944, 132p)-Capt. Jack Terry, Rick Evans, Jaguar Man	29.00	86.00	200.00
All Great nn(Chicago Nite Life News)(1945, 132p)-Green Mask, Bouncer, Puppeteer, Rick Evans, Rocket Kelly	31.00	92.00	215.00
All-Great Confessions nn(1949, 132p)	27.00	81.00	190.00
All Great Crime Stories nn('49, 132p)	33.00	100.00	230.00
All Great Jungle Adventures nn('49, 132p)	39.00	118.00	275.00
All Real Confession Magazine 3 (3/49, 132p)	27.00	81.00	190.00
All Real Confession Magazine 4 (4/49, 132p)	27.00	81.00	190.00
All Your Comics 1(1944, 132p)-The Puppeteer, Red Robbins, & Merciless the Sorcerer	30.00	90.00	210.00
Almanac Of Crime nn(1948, 148p)	34.00	103.00	240.00
Almanac Of Crime 1(1950, 132p)	33.00	100.00	230.00
Book Of Love nn(1950, 132p)	27.00	80.00	185.00
Burning Romances 1(1949, 132p)	31.00	94.00	220.00
Crimes Incorporated nn(1950, 132p)	31.00	92.00	215.00
Daring Love Stories nn(1950, 132p)	27.00	80.00	185.00
Everybody's Comics 1(1944, 50¢, 196p)-The Green Mask, The Puppeteer, The Bouncer, Rocket Kelly, Rick Evans	32.00	96.00	225.00
Everybody's Comics 1(1946, 196p)-Green Lama, The Puppeteer	26.00	78.00	180.00
Everybody's Comics 1(1946, 196p)-Same as 1945 Ribtickler	20.00	60.00	140.00
Everybody's Comics nn(1947, 132p)-Jo-Jo, Purple Tigress, Cosmo Cat, Bronze Man	25.00	75.00	175.00
Exciting Romance Stories nn(1949, 132p)	27.00	80.00	185.00
Famous Love nn(1950, 132p)	27.00	80.00	185.00
Intimate Confessions nn(1950, 132p)	27.00	80.00	185.00
Journal Of Crime nn(1949, 132p)	33.00	100.00	230.00
Love Problems nn(1949, 132p)	28.00	84.00	195.00
Love Thrills nn(1950, 132p)	28.00	84.00	195.00
March of Crime nn('48, 132p)-Female w/rifle-c	31.00	92.00	215.00
March of Crime nn('49, 132p)-Cop w/pistol-c	31.00	92.00	215.00
March of Crime nn(1949, 132p)-Coffin & man w/machine-gun-c	31.00	92.00	215.00
Revealing Love Stories nn(1950, 132p)	27.00	80.00	185.00
Ribtickler nn(1945, 50¢, 196p)-Chicago Nite Life News; Marvel Mutt, Cosmo Cat, Flash Rabbit, The Nebbs app.	24.00	72.00	165.00
Romantic Thrills nn(1950, 132p)	27.00	80.00	185.00
Secret Love nn(1949, 132p)	27.00	80.00	185.00
Secret Love Stories nn(1949, 132p)	27.00	80.00	185.00
Strange Love nn(1950, 132p)-Photo-c	31.00	94.00	220.00
Sweetheart Scandals nn(1950, 132p)	27.00	80.00	185.00
Teen-Age Love nn(1950, 132p)	27.00	80.00	185.00
Throbbing Love nn(1950, 132p)-Photo-c; used in **POP**, pg. 107	31.00	94.00	220.00
Truth About Crime nn(1949, 132p)	33.00	100.00	230.00
Variety Comics 1(1946, 132p)-Blue Beetle, Jungle Jo	27.00	80.00	185.00
Variety Comics nn(1950, 132p)-Jungle Jo, My Secret Affair(w/Harrison/Wood-a), Crimes by Women & My Story	25.00	75.00	175.00
Western Roundup nn('50, 132p)-Hoot Gibson; Cody of the Pony Express app.	29.00	86.00	200.00

NOTE: *Each of the above usually contain four remaindered Fox books minus covers. Since these missing covers often had the first page of the first story, most Giants therefore are incomplete. Approximate values are listed. Books with appearances of Phantom Lady, Rulah, Jo-Jo, etc. could bring more.*

FOXHOLE (Becomes Never Again #8?)
9-10/54 - No. 4, 3-4/55; No. 5, 7/55 - No. 7, 3/56
Mainline/Charlton Comics No. 5 on

	GD25	FN65	NM94
1-Classic Kirby-c	16.50	50.00	115.00
2-Kirby-c/a(2); Kirby scripts based on his war time experiences	13.00	40.00	90.00
3-5-Kirby-c only	8.35	25.00	50.00
6-Kirby-c/a(2)	11.00	32.00	75.00
7	4.00	10.00	20.00
Super Reprints #10-12,15-18: 10-r/? 11,12,18-r/Foxhole #1,2,3. 15,16-r/United States Marines #5,8. 17-r/Monty Hall #?	1.20	3.00	6.00

NOTE: ***Kirby*** *a(r)-Super #11, 12.* ***Powell*** *a(r)-Super #15, 16. Stories by actual veterans.*

FOXY FAGAN COMICS
Dec, 1946 - No. 7, Summer, 1948
Dearfield Publishing Co.

	GD25	FN65	NM94
1-Foxy Fagan & Little Buck begin	10.00	30.00	65.00
2	5.35	16.00	32.00
3-7: 6-Rocket ship-c	4.35	13.00	26.00

FOXY GRANDPA (Also see The Funnies, 1st series)
1901 - 1916 (Hardcover; strip reprints)
N. Y. Herald/Frederick A. Stokes Co./M. A. Donahue & Co./Bunny Publ.
(L. R. Hammersly Co.)

	GD25	FN65	VF82
1901-9x15" in color-N. Y. Herald	60.00	180.00	600.00
1902- "Latest Larks of...", 32 pgs. in color, 9-1/2x15-1/2"	50.00	150.00	500.00
1902- "The Many Advs. of...", 9x12", 148 pgs. in color (Hammersly)	55.00	165.00	550.00
1903- "Latest Advs.", 9x15", 24 pgs. in color, Hammersly Co.	50.00	150.00	500.00
1903- "...'s New Advs.", 10x15", 32 pgs. in color, Stokes	50.00	150.00	500.00
1904- "Up to Date", 10x15", 28 pgs. in color, Stokes	50.00	150.00	500.00
1905- "& Flip Flaps", 9-1/2x15-1/2", 52 pgs., in color	50.00	150.00	500.00
1905- "The Latest Advs. of", 9x15", 28, 52, & 66 pgs, in color, M.A. Donohue Co.; re-issue of 1902 issue	35.00	105.00	350.00
1905- "Merry Pranks of", 9-1/2x15-1/2", 52 pgs. in color, Donahue	35.00	105.00	350.00
1905- "Latest Larks of", 9-1/2x15-1/2", 52 pgs. in color, Donahue; re-issue of 1902 issue	35.00	105.00	350.00
1905- "Latest Larks of", 9-1/2x15-1/2", 24 pg. edition in color, Donahue; re-issue of 1902 issue	35.00	105.00	350.00
1906- "Frolics", 10x15", 30 pgs. in color, Stokes	35.00	105.00	350.00
1907	35.00	105.00	350.00
1908?- "Triumphs", 10x15"	35.00	105.00	350.00
1908?- "...& Little Brother", 10x15"	35.00	105.00	350.00
1911- "Latest Tricks", r-1910,1911 Sundays in color-Stokes Co.	35.00	105.00	350.00
1914-(9-1/2x15-1/2", 24 pgs.)-6 color cartoons/page, Bunny Publ.	30.00	90.00	300.00

Frank #1 © Nemesis Comics

Franenstein #25 © PRIZE

Freak Force #7 © Rob Liefeld

GD25 FN65 NM94

1916- "Merry Book", 10x15", 30 pgs. in color, Stokes
30.00 90.00 300.00

FOXY GRANDPA SPARKLETS SERIES
1908 (6-1/2x7-3/4"; 24 pgs. in color)
M. A. Donahue & Co.

"... Rides the Goat", "...& His Boys", "...Playing Ball", "...Fun on the Farm", "...Fancy Shooting", "...Show the Boys Up Sports",... "Plays Santa Claus" each.... 40.00 120.00 400.00
900- "Playing Ball"; Bunny illos; 8 pgs., linen like pgs., no date
30.00 90.00 300.00

FRACTURED FAIRY TALES (TV)
October, 1962 (Jay Ward)
Gold Key

	GD25	FN65	NM94
1 (10022-210)-From Bullwinkle TV show	12.00	36.00	85.00

FRAGGLE ROCK (TV)
Apr, 1985 - No. 8, Sept, 1986; V2#1, Apr, 1988 - No. 6, Sept, 1988
Star Comics (Marvel)/Marvel V2#1 on

1-8 (75¢) 1.00
V2#1-6($1.00): Reprints 1st series 1.00

FRANCIS, BROTHER OF THE UNIVERSE
1980 (75¢) (52 pgs.) (One Shot)
Marvel Comics Group

nn-Buscema/Marie Severin-a; story of Francis Bernadone celebrating his 800th birthday in 1982 1.00

FRANCIS THE FAMOUS TALKING MULE (All based on movie) (See 4-Color #335, 465, 501, 547, 579, 621, 655, 698, 710, 745, 810, 863, 906, 953, 991, 1068, 1090)

FRANK
Apr (March inside), 1994 - No. 4, 1994 ($1.75/$2.50, mini-series)
Nemesis Comics (Harvey)

1-4-($2.50, direct sale): 1-Foil-c Edition 1.00 2.50
1-4-($1.75)-Newsstand Editions; Cowan-a in all .70 1.75

FRANK BUCK (Formerly My True Love)
No. 70, May, 1950 - No. 3, Sept, 1950
Fox Features Syndicate

70-Wood a(p)(3 stories)-Photo-c 14.00 43.00 100.00
71,3: 71-Wood a? (9 pgs.). 71,3-Photo/painted-c 10.00 30.00 65.00
NOTE: *Based on "Bring 'Em Back Alive" TV show.*

FRANKENSTEIN (See Dracula, Movie Classics & Werewolf)
Aug-Oct, 1964; No. 2, Sept, 1966 - No. 4, Mar, 1967
Dell Publishing Co.

1(12-283-410)(1964) 2.30 6.90 16.00
2-Intro. & origin super-hero character (9/66) 1.70 4.20 10.00
3,4 1.30 3.00 8.00

FRANKENSTEIN (The Monster of...; also see Monsters Unleashed #2, Power Record Comics, Psycho & Silver Surfer #7)
Jan, 1973 - No. 18, Sept, 1975
Marvel Comics Group

1-Ploog-c/a begins, ends #6 2.40 7.30 17.00
2-5,8,9: 8,9-Dracula app. 9-Death of Dracula 1.40 4.30 10.00
6,7,10 1.00 3.00 6.00
11-18 1.30 3.25
NOTE: ***Adkins** c-17i. **Buscema** a-7-10p. **Ditko** a-12r. **G. Kane** c-15p. **Orlando** a-8r. **Ploog** a-1-3, 4p, 5p, 6; c-1-6. **Wrightson** c-18i.*

FRANKENSTEIN COMICS (Also See Prize Comics)
Sum, 1945 - V5#5(#33), Oct-Nov, 1954
Prize Publications (Crestwood/Feature)

1-Frankenstein begins by Dick Briefer (origin); Frank Sinatra parody
71.00 215.00 500.00
2 36.00 107.00 250.00
3-5 27.00 80.00 185.00
6-10: 7-S&K a(r)/Headline Comics. 8(7-8/47)-Superman satire
22.00 65.00 150.00
11-17(1-2/49)-11-Boris Karloff parody-c/story. 17-Last humor issue
19.00 57.00 130.00
18(3/52)-New origin, horror series begins 24.00 72.00 165.00
19,20(V3#4, 8-9/52) 15.00 45.00 105.00
21(V3#5), 22(V3#6) 13.50 41.00 95.00
23(V4#1) - #28(V4#6) 13.50 41.00 95.00
29(V5#1) - #33(V5#5) 13.50 41.00 95.00
NOTE: ***Briefer** c/a-all. **Meskin** a-21, 29.*

FRANKENSTEIN, JR. (...& the Impossibles) (TV)
January, 1967 (Hanna-Barbera)
Gold Key

1-Super hero 2.30 6.90 16.00

FRANK FRAZETTA'S THUN'DA TALES (Fantagrahics)(Value: cover or less)

FRANK FRAZETTA'S UNTAMED LOVE (Fantagraphics)(Value: cover or less)

FRANKIE COMICS (...& Lana No. 13-15) (Formerly Movie Tunes; becomes Frankie Fuddle No. 16 on)
No. 4, Wint, 1946-47 - No. 15, June, 1949
Marvel Comics (MgPC)

4-Mitzi, Margie, Daisy app. 10.00 30.00 60.00
5-9 5.35 16.00 32.00
10-15: 13-Anti-Wertham editorial 4.35 13.00 26.00

FRANKIE DOODLE (See Single Series #7 and Sparkler, both series)

FRANKIE FUDDLE (Formerly Frankie & Lana)
No. 16, Aug, 1949 - No. 17, Nov, 1949
Marvel Comics

16,17 4.70 14.00 28.00

FRANK LUTHER'S SILLY PILLY COMICS (See Jingle Dingle...)
1950 (10¢)
Children's Comics (Maltex Cereal)

1-Characters from radio, records, & TV 4.00 12.00 24.00

FRANK MERRIWELL AT YALE (Speed Demons No. 5 on?)
June, 1955 - No. 4, Jan, 1956 (Also see Shadow Comics)
Charlton Comics

1 4.00 11.00 22.00
2-4 3.20 8.00 16.00

FRANTIC (Magazine) (See Ratfink & Zany)
Oct, 1958 - V2#2, April, 1959 (Satire)
Pierce Publishing Co.

V1#1,2 4.70 14.00 28.00
V2#1,2: 1-Burgos-a, Severin-c/a; Powell-a? 3.60 9.00 18.00

FREAK FORCE
Dec, 1993 - Present ($1.95)
Image Comics

1-10-Superpatriot & Mighty Man in all; Erik Larsen scripts in all. 4-Vanguard app. .80 2.00

FREAKS' ARMOUR (Dark Horse)(Value: cover or less)

FRECKLES AND HIS FRIENDS (See Crackajack Funnies, Famous Comics Cartoon Book, Honeybee Birdwhistle... & Red Ryder)

FRECKLES AND HIS FRIENDS
No. 5, 11/47 - No. 12, 8/49; 11/55 - No. 4, 6/56
Standard Comics/Argo

5-Reprints 5.35 16.00 32.00
6-12-Reprints. 7-9-Airbrush-c (by Schomburg?). 11-Lingerie panels
4.00 10.00 20.00
NOTE: *Some copies of No. 8 & 9 contain a printing oddity. The negatives were elongated in the engraving process, probably to conform to page dimensions on the filler pages. Those pages only look normal when viewed at a 45 degree angle.*
1(Argo,'55)-Reprints (NEA Service) 4.00 11.00 22.00
2-4 3.00 7.50 15.00

Freex #5 © Malibu

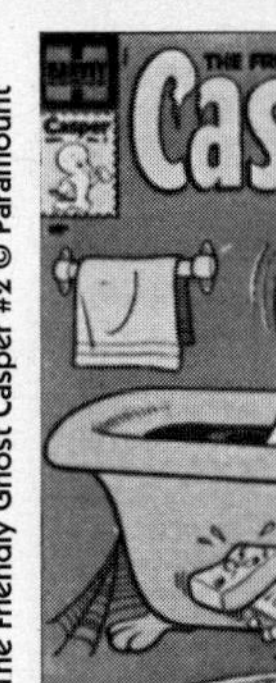

The Friendly Ghost Casper #2 © Paramount

Fritzi Ritz #3 © UFS

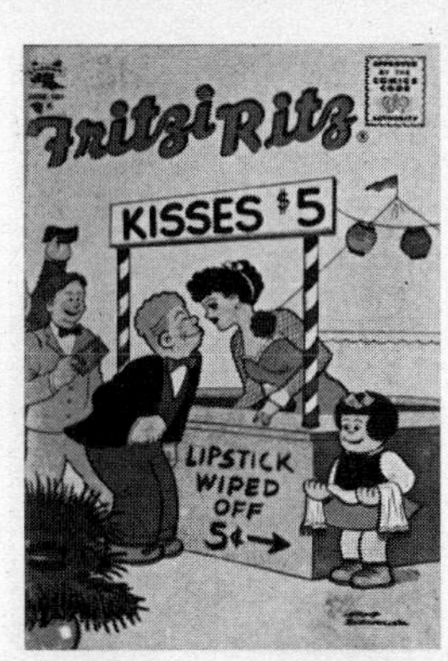

FREDDY (Formerly My Little Margie's Boy Friends) (Also see Blue Bird)
V2#12, June, 1958 - No. 47, Feb, 1965
Charlton Comics

	GD25	FN65	NM94
V2#12	2.80	7.00	14.00
13-15	1.40	3.50	7.00
16-47	.80	2.00	4.00
Schiff's Shoes Presents... #1 (1959)-Giveaway	.80	2.00	4.00

FREDDY
May-July, 1963 - No. 3, Oct-Dec, 1964
Dell Publishing Co.

	GD25	FN65	NM94
1-3	1.40	3.50	7.00

FREDDY KRUEGER'S A NIGHTMARE ON ELM STREET (Marvel)(Value: cover or less)

FREDDY'S DEAD: THE FINAL NIGHTMARE (Innovation)(Value: cover or less)

FRED HEMBECK DESTROYS THE MARVEL UNIVERSE
July, 1989 ($1.50, one-shot)
Marvel Comics

	GD25	FN65	NM94
1-Punisher app.; Staton-i (5 pgs.)			1.50

FRED HEMBECK SELLS THE MARVEL UNIVERSE
Oct, 1990 ($1.25, one-shot)
Marvel Comics

	GD25	FN65	NM94
1-Punisher, Wolverine parodies; Hembeck/Austin-c			1.25

FREE COMICS TO YOU FROM... (name of shoe store) (Has clown on cover & another with a rabbit) (Like comics from Weather Bird & Edward's Shoes)
Circa 1956, 1960-61
Shoe Store Giveaway

Contains a comic bound with new cover - several combinations possible; some Harvey titles known. Contents determines price.

FREEDOM AGENT (Also see John Steele)
April, 1963 (12¢)
Gold Key

	GD25	FN65	NM94
1 (10054-304)-Painted-c	1.60	4.70	11.00

FREEDOM FIGHTERS (See Justice League of America #107,108)
Mar-Apr, 1976 - No. 15, July-Aug, 1978
National Periodical Publications/DC Comics

	GD25	FN65	NM94
1-Uncle Sam, The Ray, Black Condor, Doll Man, Human Bomb, & Phantom Lady begin (all former Quality characters)	.40	1.00	2.00
2-15: 4,5-Wonder Woman x-over. 7-1st app. Crusaders. 10-Origin Doll Man; Cat-Man-c/story (4th app; 1st revival since Det. #325). 11-Origin The Ray. 12-Origin Firebrand. 13-Origin Black Condor. 14,15-Batgirl & Batwoman app. 15-Origin Phantom Lady			1.00

NOTE: *Buckler c-5-11p, 13p, 14p.*

FREEDOM TRAIN
1948 (Giveaway)
Street & Smith Publications

	GD25	FN65	NM94
nn-Powell-c	4.00	11.00	22.00

FREEJACK (Now)(Value: cover or less)

FREEX
July, 1993 - Present ($1.95)
Malibu Comics (Ultraverse)

	GD25	FN65	NM94
1-3,5-16: 1-Polybagged w/trading card. 2-Some were polybagged w/card. 4-Night Man 3 pg. preview. 6-Nightman-c/story. 7-2 pg. origin Hardcase by Zeck		.80	2.00
1-Holographic cover edition			25.00
1-Ultra 5,000 limited silver ink-c			10.00
4-($2.50, 48 pgs.)-Rune flip-c/story by B. Smith (3 pgs.)		1.00	2.50
Giant Size 1 ('94, $2.50)-Prime app.		1.00	2.50

FRENZY (Magazine) (Satire)
April, 1958 - No. 6, March, 1959
Picture Magazine

	GD25	FN65	NM94
1	5.00	15.00	30.00
2-6	3.60	9.00	18.00

FRIDAY FOSTER
October, 1972
Dell Publishing Co.

	GD25	FN65	NM94
1	3.20	8.00	16.00

FRIENDLY GHOST, CASPER, THE (Becomes Casper... #254 on)
Aug, 1958 - No. 224, Oct, 1982; No. 225, Oct, 1986 - No. 253, June, 1990
Harvey Publications

	GD25	FN65	NM94
1-Infinity-c	22.00	67.00	155.00
2	10.00	30.00	70.00
3-10: 6-X-Mas-c	5.85	17.50	35.00
11-20: 18-X-Mas-c	4.00	12.00	24.00
21-30	2.60	6.50	13.00
31-50	1.80	4.50	9.00
51-100: 54-X-Mas-c	1.20	3.00	6.00
101-159	.80	2.00	4.00
160-163: All 52 pg. Giants	.90	2.25	4.50
164-237: 173,179,185-Cub Scout Specials. 230-X-mas-c. 232-Valentine's-c		.80	2.00
238-253: 238-Begin $1.00-c. 238,244-Halloween-c. 243-Last new material			1.00
American Dental Assoc. giveaway-Small size (1967, 16 pgs.)	.80	2.00	4.00

FRIGHT
June, 1975 (August on inside)
Atlas/Seaboard Periodicals

	GD25	FN65	NM94
1-Origin The Son of Dracula; Frank Thorne-c/a		.50	1.00

FRIGHT NIGHT (Now)(Value: cover or less)

FRIGHT NIGHT II (Now)(Value: cover or less)

FRISKY ANIMALS (Formerly Frisky Fables; Super Cat #56 on)
No. 44, Jan, 1951 - No. 55, Sept, 1953
Star Publications

	GD25	FN65	NM94
44-Super Cat	11.00	32.00	75.00
45-Classic L. B. Cole-c	15.00	45.00	105.00
46-51,53-55: Super Cat. 54-Super Cat-c begin	10.00	30.00	65.00
52-L. B. Cole-c/a, 3 1/2 pgs.; X-Mas-c	11.00	32.00	75.00

NOTE: *All have* **L. B. Cole**-*c. No. 47-No Super Cat.* **Disbrow** *a-49, 52.* **Fago** *a-51.*

FRISKY ANIMALS ON PARADE (Formerly Parade Comics; becomes Superspook)
Sept, 1957 - No. 3, Dec-Jan, 1957-1958
Ajax-Farrell Publ. (Four Star Comic Corp.)

	GD25	FN65	NM94
1-L. B. Cole-c	10.00	30.00	60.00
2-No L. B. Cole-c	5.00	15.00	30.00
3-L. B. Cole-c	7.50	22.50	45.00

FRISKY FABLES (Frisky Animals No. 44 on)
Spring, 1945 - No. 43, Oct, 1950
Premium Group/Novelty Publ./Star Publ. V5#4 on

	GD25	FN65	NM94
V1#1-Funny animal; Al Fago-c/a #1-38	10.00	30.00	70.00
2,3(Fall & Winter, 1945)	6.35	19.00	38.00
V2#1(#4, 4/46) - 9,11,12(#15, 3/47): 4-Flag-c	4.00	10.00	20.00
10-Christmas-c	4.00	11.00	22.00
V3#1(#16, 4/47) - 12(#27, 3/48): 4-Flag-c. 7,9-Infinity-c. 10-X-Mas-c	3.60	9.00	18.00
V4#1(#28, 4/48) - 7(#34, 2-3/49)	3.60	9.00	18.00
V5#1(#35, 4-5/49) - 4(#38, 10-11/49)	3.60	9.00	18.00
39-43-L. B. Cole-c; 40-X-mas-c	10.00	30.00	60.00
Accepted Reprint No. 43 (nd); L.B. Cole-c	4.35	13.00	26.00

FRITZI RITZ (See Comics On Parade, Single Series #5, 1(reprint), Tip Top & United Comics)

FRITZI RITZ (United Comics No. 8-26)
Fall, 1948 - No. 7, 1949; No. 27, 3-4/53 - No. 36, 9-10/54; No. 42, 1/55;

Frogman #7 © HILL

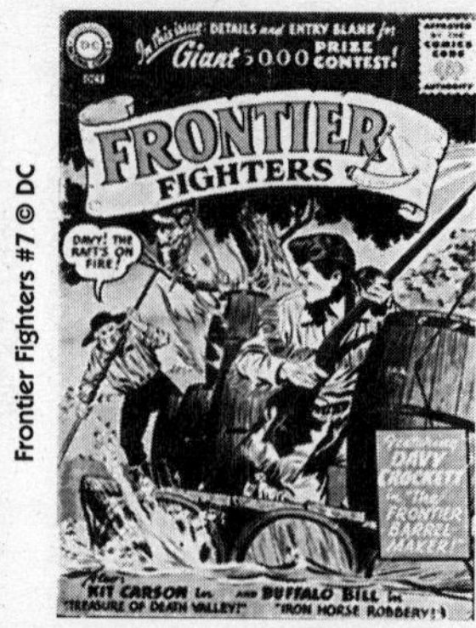

Frontier Fighters #7 © DC

Frontline Combat #1 © E.C.

	GD25	FN65	NM94

No. 43, 6/56 - No. 55, 9-11/57; No. 56, 12-2/57-58 - No. 59, 9-11/58
United Features Synd./St. John No. 37?-55/Dell No. 56 on

	GD25	FN65	NM94
nn(1948)-Special Fall issue; by Ernie Bushmiller	10.00	30.00	65.00
2	5.35	16.00	32.00
3-7(1949): 6-Abbie & Slats app.	4.35	13.00	26.00
27-29(1953): 29-Five pg. Abbie & Slats; 1 pg. Mamie by Russell Patterson	3.60	9.00	18.00
30-59: 31-Peanuts by Schulz (1st app.?, 11-12/53). 36-1 pg. Mamie by Patterson	3.20	8.00	16.00

NOTE: *Abbie & Slats in #6,7, 27-31. Li'l Abner in #33, 35, 36. Peanuts in #31, 43, 58, 59.*

FROGMAN COMICS
Jan-Feb, 1952 - No. 11, May, 1953
Hillman Periodicals

	GD25	FN65	NM94
1	9.15	27.50	55.00
2	4.70	14.00	28.00
3,4,6-11: 4-Meskin-a	4.00	11.00	22.00
5-Krigstein-a	5.85	17.50	35.00

FROGMEN, THE
No. 1258, Feb-Apr, 1962 - No. 11, Nov-Jan, 1964-65 (Painted-c)
Dell Publishing Co.

	GD25	FN65	NM94
4-Color 1258(#1)-Evans-a	8.35	25.00	50.00
2,3-Evans-a; part Frazetta inks in #2,3	6.70	20.00	40.00
4,6-11	3.60	9.00	18.00
5-Toth-a	4.35	13.00	26.00

FROM BEYOND THE UNKNOWN
10-11/69 - No. 25, 11-12/73 (No. 7-11: 64 pgs.; No. 12-17: 52 pgs.)
National Periodical Publications

	GD25	FN65	NM94
1	1.20	2.90	7.00
2-10: 7-Intro. Col. Glenn Merrit. 13-Wood-a(i)(r)		1.80	4.50
11-25: Star Rovers-r begin #18,19. Space Museum in #23-25		1.10	2.75

NOTE: ***N. Adams** c-3, 6, 8, 9. **Anderson** c-2, 4, 5, 10, 11i, 15-17, 22; reprints-3, 4, 6-8, 10, 11, 13-16, 24, 25. **Infantino** r-1-5, 7-19, 23-25; c-11p. **Kaluta** c-18, 19. **Kubert** c-1, 7, 12-14. **Toth** a-2r. **Wood** a-13i. Photo c-22.*

FROM HERE TO INSANITY (Satire) (Formerly Eh! #1-7)
(See Frantic & Frenzy)
No. 8, Feb, 1955 - V3#1, 1956
Charlton Comics

	GD25	FN65	NM94
8	10.00	30.00	65.00
9	8.35	25.00	50.00
10-Ditko-c/a (3 pgs.)	11.50	34.00	80.00
11,12-All Kirby except 4 pgs.	14.00	43.00	100.00
V3#1(1956)-Ward-c/a(2) (signed McCartney); 5 pgs. Wolverton-a; 3 pgs. Ditko-a; magazine format (cover says "Crazy, Man, Crazy" and becomes Crazy, Man, Crazy with V2#2)	25.00	75.00	175.00

FROM THE PIT
1994 ($4.95, quarterly, mature readers)
Fantagor Press

	GD25	FN65	NM94
1-R. Corben/a; HP Lovecraft b/u story	1.00	2.00	5.00

FRONTIER DAYS
1956 (Giveaway)
Robin Hood Shoe Store (Brown Shoe)

	GD25	FN65	NM94
1	2.40	6.00	12.00

FRONTIER DOCTOR (See 4-Color No. 877)

FRONTIER FIGHTERS
Sept-Oct, 1955 - No. 8, Nov-Dec, 1956
National Periodical Publications

	GD25	FN65	NM94
1-Davy Crockett, Buffalo Bill (by Kubert), Kit Carson begin (Scarce)	46.00	139.00	325.00
2	34.00	100.00	235.00
3-8	29.00	86.00	200.00

NOTE: *Buffalo Bill by **Kubert** in all.*

FRONTIER ROMANCES
Nov-Dec, 1949 - No. 2, Feb-Mar, 1950 (Painted-c)
Avon Periodicals/I. W.

	GD25	FN65	NM94
1-Used in **SOTI**, pg. 180(General reference) & illo. "Erotic spanking in a western comic book"	36.00	107.00	250.00
2 (Scarce)-Woodish-a by Stallman	24.00	72.00	165.00
I.W. Reprint #1-Reprints Avon's #1	4.00	12.00	24.00
I.W. Reprint #9-Reprints ?	2.80	7.00	14.00

FRONTIER SCOUT: DAN'L BOONE (Formerly Death Valley; The Masked Raider No. 14 on)
No. 10, Jan, 1956 - No. 13, Aug, 1956; V2#14, March, 1965
Charlton Comics

	GD25	FN65	NM94
10	7.50	22.50	45.00
11-13(1956)	4.20	12.50	25.00
V2#14(3/65)	3.00	7.50	15.00

FRONTIER TRAIL (The Rider No. 1-5)
No. 6, May, 1958
Ajax/Farrell Publ.

	GD25	FN65	NM94
6	4.00	10.00	20.00

FRONTIER WESTERN
Feb, 1956 - No. 10, Aug, 1957
Atlas Comics (PrPI)

	GD25	FN65	NM94
1	12.00	36.00	85.00
2,3,6-Williamson-a, 4 pgs. each	10.00	30.00	60.00
4,7,9,10: 10-Check-a	5.35	16.00	32.00
5-Crandall, Baker, Davis-a; Williamson text illos	7.50	22.50	45.00
8-Crandall, Morrow, & Wildey-a	5.35	16.00	32.00

NOTE: ***Baker** a-9. **Colan** a-2, 6. **Drucker** a-3, 4. **Heath** c-5. **Maneely** c/a-2, 7, 9. **Maurera** a-2. **Romita** a-7. **Severin** c-6, 8, 10. **Tuska** a-2. **Wildey** a-5, 8. Ringo Kid in No. 4.*

FRONTLINE COMBAT
July-Aug, 1951 - No. 15, Jan, 1954
E. C. Comics

	GD25	FN65	NM94
1-Severin/Kurtzman-a	56.00	167.00	390.00
2	33.00	100.00	230.00
3	24.00	72.00	165.00
4-Used in **SOTI**, pg. 257; contains "Airburst" by Kurtzman which is his personal all-time favorite story	20.00	60.00	140.00
5	18.00	54.00	125.00
6-10	15.00	45.00	105.00
11-15	11.00	32.00	75.00

NOTE: ***Davis** a-in all; c-11, 12. **Evans** a-10-15. **Heath** a-1. **Kubert** a-14. **Kurtzman** a-1-5; c-1-9. **Severin** a-5-7, 9, 13, 15. **Severin/Elder** a-2-11; c-10. **Toth** a-8, 12. **Wood** a-1-4, 6-10, 12-15; c-13-15. Special issues: No. 7 (Iwo Jima), No. 9 (Civil War), No. 12 (Air Force). (Canadian reprints known; see Table of Contents.)*

FRONT PAGE COMIC BOOK
1945
Front Page Comics (Harvey)

	GD25	FN65	NM94
1-Kubert-a; intro. & 1st app. Man in Black by Powell; Fuje-c	27.00	80.00	185.00

FROST AND FIRE (See DC Science Fiction Graphic Novel)

FROSTY THE SNOWMAN
No. 359, Nov, 1951 - No. 1272, Dec-Feb?/1961-62
Dell Publishing Co.

	GD25	FN65	NM94
4-Color 359 (#1)	8.35	25.00	50.00
4-Color 435	4.35	13.00	26.00
4-Color 514,601,661	4.00	11.00	22.00
4-Color 748,861,950,1065,1153,1272	4.00	10.00	20.00

FRUITMAN SPECIAL
Dec, 1969 (68 pgs.)
Harvey Publications

	GD25	FN65	NM94
1-Funny super hero	3.20	8.00	16.00

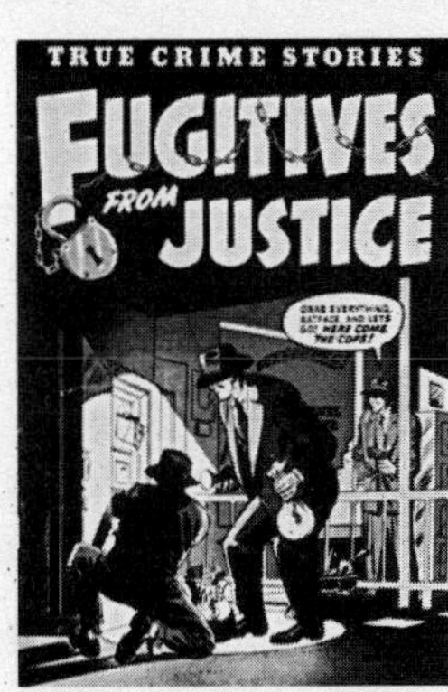

Fugitives From Justice #1 © STJ

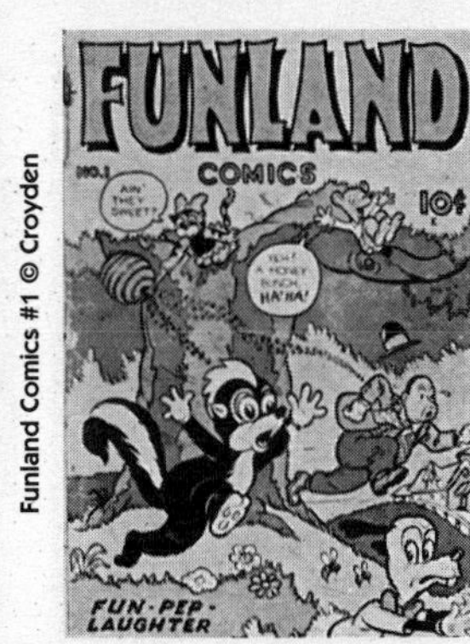

Funland Comics #1 © Croyden

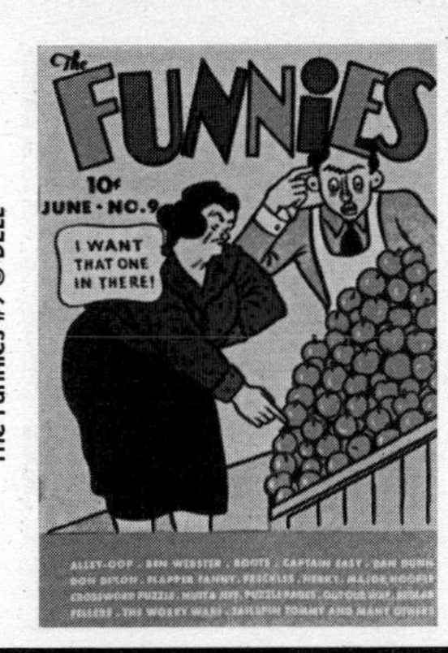

The Funnies #9 © DELL

GD25 FN65 NM94

F-TROOP (TV)
Aug, 1966 - No. 7, Aug, 1967 (All have photo-c)
Dell Publishing Co.

1 7.50 22.50 45.00
2-7 4.20 12.50 25.00

FUGITIVES FROM JUSTICE
Feb, 1952 - No. 5, Oct, 1952
St. John Publishing Co.

1 11.50 34.00 80.00
2-Matt Baker-r/Northwest Mounties #2; Vic Flint strip reprints begin 11.50 34.00 80.00
3-Reprints panel from Authentic Police Cases that was used in **SOTI** with changes; Tuska-a 11.50 34.00 80.00
4 5.85 17.50 35.00
5-Last Vic Flint-r; bondage-c 7.50 22.50 45.00

FUGITOID
1985 (One shot, B&W, magazine size)
Mirage Studios

1-Ties into Teenage Mutant Ninja Turtles #5 1.50 4.00 9.00

FULL COLOR COMICS
1946
Fox Features Syndicate

nn 10.00 30.00 60.00

FULL OF FUN
Aug, 1957 - No. 2, Nov, 1957; 1964
Red Top (Decker Publ.)(Farrell)/I. W. Enterprises

1(1957)-Funny animal; Dave Berg-a 4.35 13.00 26.00
2-Reprints Bingo, the Monkey Doodle Boy 3.60 9.00 18.00
8-I.W. Reprint('64) 1.00 3.00 6.00

FUN AT CHRISTMAS (See March of Comics No. 138)

FUN CLUB COMICS (See Interstate Theatres...)

FUN COMICS (Formerly Holiday Comics #1-8; Mighty Bear #13 on)
No. 9, Jan, 1953 - No. 12, Oct, 1953
Star Publications

9-(25¢ Giant)-L. B. Cole X-Mas-c; X-Mas issue 11.00 32.00 75.00
10-12-L. B. Cole-c. 12-Mighty Bear-c/story 8.35 25.00 50.00

FUNDAY FUNNIES (See Famous TV..., and Harvey Hits No. 35,40)

FUN-IN (TV)(Hanna-Barbera)
Feb, 1970 - No. 10, Jan, 1972; No. 11, 4/74 - No. 15, 12/74
Gold Key

1-Dastardly & Muttley in Their Flying Machines; Perils of Penelope Pitstop in #1-4; It's the Wolf in all 2.40 7.30 17.00
2-4,6-Cattanooga Cats in 2-4 1.30 3.00 8.00
5,7-Motormouse & Autocat, Dastardly & Muttley in both; It's the Wolf in #7 1.70 4.20 10.00
8,10-The Harlem Globetrotters, Dastardly & Muttley in #10 1.30 3.00 7.50
9-Where's Huddles?, Dastardly & Muttley, Motormouse & Autocat app. 1.70 4.20 10.00
11-15: 11-Butch Cassidy. 12,15-Speed Buggy. 13-Hair Bear Bunch. 14-Inch High Private Eye 1.00 2.50 6.00

FUNKY PHANTOM, THE (TV)
Mar, 1972 - No. 13, Mar, 1975 (Hanna-Barbera)
Gold Key

1 1.90 6.00 13.00
2-5 1.10 2.70 6.50
6-13 1.50 3.75

FUNLAND
No date (1940s) (25¢)
Ziff-Davis (Approved Comics)

nn-Contains games, puzzles, cut-outs, etc. 11.00 32.00 75.00

FUNLAND COMICS
1945
Croyden Publishers

1-Funny animal 11.00 32.00 75.00

FUNNIES, THE (Also see Comic Cuts)
1929 - No. 36, 10/18/30 (10¢; 5¢ No. 22 on) (16 pgs.)
Full tabloid size in color; not reprints; published every Saturday
Dell Publishing Co.

1-My Big Brudder, Johnathan, Jazzbo & Jim, Foxy Grandpa, Sniffy, Jimmy Jams & other strips begin; first four-color comic newsstand publication; also contains magic, puzzles & stories 43.00 130.00 300.00
2-21 (1930, 30¢) 17.00 52.00 120.00
22(nn-7/12/30-5¢) 13.00 40.00 90.00
23(nn-7/19/30-5¢), 24(nn-7/26/30-5¢), 25(nn-8/2/30), 26(nn-8/9/30), 27(nn-8/16/30), 28(nn-8/23/30), 29(nn-8/30/30), 30(nn-9/6/30), 31(nn-9/13/30), 32(nn-9/20/30), 33(nn-9/27/30), 34(nn-10/4/30), 35(nn-10/11/30), 36(nn, no date-10/18/30) each.... 13.00 40.00 90.00

FUNNIES, THE (New Funnies No. 65 on)
Oct, 1936 - No. 64, May, 1942
Dell Publishing Co.

1-Tailspin Tommy, Mutt & Jeff, Alley Oop (1st app?), Capt. Easy (1st app.), Don Dixon begin 193.00 580.00 1350.00
2-Scribbly by Mayer begins (1st app.) 86.00 257.00 600.00
3 69.00 208.00 485.00
4,5: 4-Christmas-c 51.00 154.00 360.00
6-10 43.00 129.00 300.00
11-20: 16-Christmas-c 38.00 115.00 265.00
21-29: 25-Crime Busters by McWilliams(4pgs.) 30.00 90.00 210.00
30-John Carter of Mars (origin/1st app.) begins by Edgar Rice Burroughs; Warner Bros.' Bosko-c (4/39) 82.00 246.00 575.00
31-44: 33-John Coleman Burroughs art begins on John Carter. 34-Last funny-c. 35-(9/39)-Mr. District Attorney begins; based on radio show 51.00 152.00 355.00
45-Origin/1st app. Phantasmo, the Master of the World (Dell's 1st super-hero, 7/40) & his sidekick Whizzer McGee 41.00 122.00 285.00
46-50: 46-The Black Knight begins, ends #62 30.00 90.00 210.00
51-56-Last ERB John Carter of Mars 30.00 90.00 210.00
57-Intro. & origin Captain Midnight (7/41) 89.00 268.00 625.00
58-60: 58-Captain Midnight-c begin, end #63 33.00 100.00 230.00
61-Andy Panda begins by Walter Lantz 36.00 107.00 250.00
62,63: 63-Last Captain Midnight-c; bondage-c 29.00 88.00 205.00
64-Format change; Oswald the Rabbit, Felix the Cat, Li'l Eight Ball app.; origin & 1st app. Woody Woodpecker in Oswald; last Capt. Midnight; Oswald, Andy Panda, Li'l Eight Ball-c 68.00 205.00 475.00

NOTE: ***Mayer** c-26, 48. **McWilliams** art in many issues on "Rex King of the Deep". Alley Oop c-17, 20. Captain Midnight c-57(i/2), 58-63. John Carter c-35-37, 40. Phantasmo c-45-56, 57(1/2), 58-61(part). Rex King c-38, 39, 42. Tailspin Tommy c-41.*

FUNNIES ANNUAL, THE
1959 ($1.00)(B&W; tabloid-size, approx. 7x10")
Avon Periodicals

1-(Rare)-Features the best newspaper comic strips of the year: Archie, Snuffy Smith, Beetle Bailey, Henry, Blondie, Steve Canyon, Buz Sawyer, The Little King, Hi & Lois, Popeye, & others. Also has a chronological history of the comics from 2000 B.C. to 1959. 38.00 115.00 265.00

FUNNIES ON PARADE (Premium)
1933 (Probably the 1st comic book) (36 pgs.; slick cover)
No date or publisher listed
Eastern Color Printing Co.

GD25 FN65 VF82 NM94

nn-Contains Sunday page reprints of Mutt & Jeff, Joe Palooka, Hairbreadth Harry, Reg'lar Fellers, Skippy, & others (10,000 print run). This book was printed for Proctor & Gamble to be given away & came out before Famous Funnies or Century of Comics. 820.00 2460.00 5330.00 8200.00
(Estimated up to 50 total copies exist, 3 in NM/Mint)

Funny Book #6 © PMI

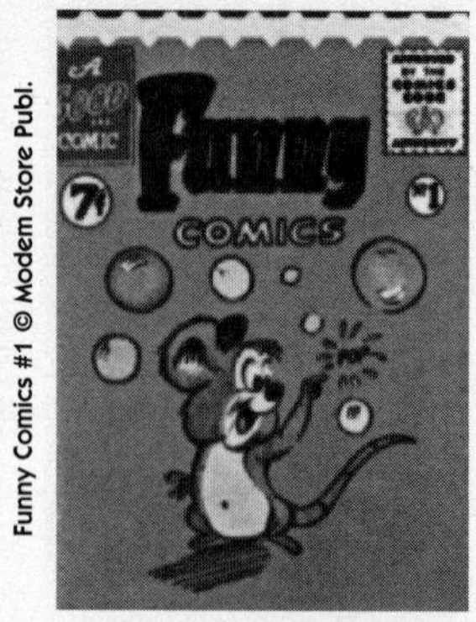

Funny Comics #1 © Modern Store Publ.

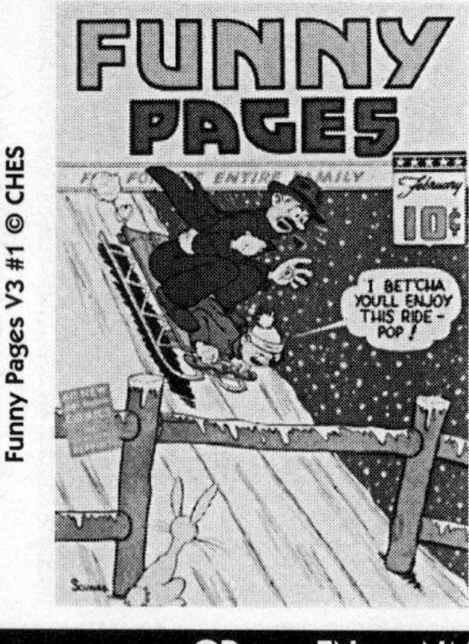

Funny Pages V3 #1 © CHES

	GD25	FN65	NM94

FUNNY ANIMALS (See Fawcett's Funny Animals)
Sept, 1984 - No. 2, Nov, 1984
Charlton Comics

	GD25	FN65	NM94
1,2-Atomic Mouse-r			1.00

FUNNYBONE (... The Laugh-Book of Comical Comics)
1944 (25¢, 132 pgs.)
La Salle Publishing Co.

nn	22.00	65.00	150.00

FUNNY BOOK (...Magazine for Young Folks) (Hocus Pocus No. 9)
Dec, 1942 - No. 9, Aug-Sept, 1946 (Comics, stories, puzzles, games)
Parents' Magazine Press (Funny Book Publishing Corp.)

1-Funny animal; Alice In Wonderland app.	11.00	32.00	75.00
2-Gulliver in Giant-Land	6.35	19.00	38.00
3-9: 4-Advs. of Robin Hood. 9-Hocus-Pocus strip	4.35	13.00	26.00

FUNNY COMICS (7¢)
1955 (36 pgs.; 5x7"; in color)
Modern Store Publ.

1-Funny animal	1.20	3.00	6.00

FUNNY COMIC TUNES (See Funny Tunes)

FUNNY FABLES
Aug, 1957 - V2#2, Nov, 1957
Decker Publications (Red Top Comics)

V1#1	3.60	9.00	18.00
V2#1,2	2.40	6.00	12.00

FUNNY FILMS (Features funny animal characters from films)
Sept-Oct, 1949 - No. 29, May-June, 1954 (No. 1-4: 52 pgs.)
American Comics Group(Michel Publ./Titan Publ.)

1-Puss An' Boots, Blunderbunny begin	14.00	43.00	100.00
2	8.35	25.00	50.00
3-10: 3-X-Mas-c	5.00	15.00	30.00
11-20	4.00	11.00	22.00
21-29	3.60	9.00	18.00

FUNNY FOLKS (Hollywood... on cover only No. 16-26; becomes Hollywood Funny Folks No. 27 on)
April-May, 1946 - No. 26, June-July, 1950 (52 pgs., #16 on)
National Periodical Publications

1-Nutsy Squirrel begins (1st app.) by Rube Grossman	36.00	107.00	250.00
2	16.00	48.00	110.00
3-5: 4-1st Nutsy Squirrel-c	11.50	34.00	80.00
6-10: 6,9-Nutsy Squirrel-c begin	9.15	27.50	55.00
11-26: 16-Begin 52 pg. issues (10-11/48)	7.50	22.50	45.00

NOTE: ***Sheldon Mayer*** *a-in some issues.* ***Post*** *a-18. Christmas c-12.*

FUNNY FROLICS
Summer, 1945 - No. 5, Dec, 1946
Timely/Marvel Comics (SPI)

1-Sharpy Fox, Puffy Pig, Krazy Krow	14.00	43.00	100.00
2	8.35	25.00	50.00
3,4	6.70	20.00	40.00
5-Kurtzman-a	8.35	25.00	50.00

FUNNY FUNNIES
April, 1943 (68 pgs.)
Nedor Publishing Co.

1-Funny animals; Peter Porker app.	14.00	43.00	100.00

FUNNYMAN (Also see Cisco Kid Comics & Extra Comics)
Dec, 1947; No. 1, Jan, 1948 - No. 6, Aug, 1948
Magazine Enterprises

nn(12/47)-Prepublication B&W undistributed copy by Siegel & Shuster-(5-3/4x8"), 16 pgs.; Sold in San Francisco in 1976 for $300.00

1-Siegel & Shuster-a in all; Dick Ayers 1st pro work (as assistant) on 1st few issues	24.00	73.00	170.00
2	17.00	52.00	120.00
3-6	14.00	43.00	100.00

FUNNY MOVIES (See 3-D Funny Movies)

FUNNY PAGES (Formerly The Comics Magazine)
No. 6, Nov, 1936 - No. 42, Oct, 1940
Comics Magazine Co./Ultem Publ.(Chesler)/Centaur Publications

V1#6 (nn, nd)-The Clock begins (2 pgs., 1st app.), ends #11; The Clock is the 1st masked comic book hero	86.00	257.00	600.00
7-11	48.00	145.00	335.00
V2#1 (9/37)(V2#2 on-c; V2#1 in indicia)	36.00	110.00	255.00
V2#2 (10/37)(V2#3 on-c; V2#2 in indicia)	36.00	110.00	255.00
3(11/37)-5	36.00	110.00	255.00
6(1st Centaur, 3/38)	63.00	190.00	440.00
7-9	44.00	133.00	310.00
10(Scarce, 9/38)-1st app. of The Arrow by Gustavson (Blue costume)	164.00	493.00	1150.00
11,12	76.00	229.00	535.00
V3#1-6: 6,8-Last funny covers	76.00	229.00	535.00
7-1st Arrow-c (9/39)	93.00	280.00	650.00
8,9: 9-Tarpe Mills jungle-c	71.00	214.00	500.00
10-2nd Arrow-c	86.00	257.00	600.00
V4#1(1/40, Arrow-c)-(Rare)-The Owl & The Phantom Rider app.; origin Mantoka, Maker of Magic by Jack Cole. Mad Ming begins, ends #42; Tarpe Mills-a	91.00	272.00	635.00
35-Classic Arrow-c	82.00	246.00	575.00
36-38-Mad Ming-c	69.00	208.00	485.00
39-42-Arrow-c. 42-Last Arrow	75.00	225.00	525.00

NOTE: ***Biro*** *c-V2#9.* ***Burgos*** *c-V3#10.* ***Jack Cole*** *a-V2#3, 7, 8, 10, 11, V3#2, 6, 9, 10, V4#1, 37; c-V3#2, 4.* ***Eisner*** *a-V1#7, 8?, 10.* ***Ken Ernst*** *a-V1#7, 8.* ***Everett*** *a-V2#11 (illos).* ***Filchock*** *c-V2#10, V3#6.* ***Gill Fox*** *a-V2#11.* ***Sid Greene*** *a-39.* ***Guardineer*** *a-V2#2, 3, 5.* ***Gustavson*** *a-V2#5, 11, 12, V3#1-10, 35, 38-42; c-V3#7, 35, 39-42.* ***Bob Kane*** *a-V3#1.* ***McWilliams*** *a-V2#12, V3#1, 3-6.* ***Tarpe Mills*** *a-V3#8-10, V4#1; c-V3#9.* ***Ed Moore Jr.*** *a-V2#12.* ***Schwab*** *c-V3#1.* ***Bob Wood*** *a-V2#2, 3, 8, 11, V3#6, 9, 10; c-V2#6, 7. Arrow c-V3#7, 10, V4#1, 35, 40-42.*

FUNNY PICTURE STORIES (Comic Pages V3#4 on)
Nov, 1936 - V3#3, May, 1939
Comics Magazine Co./Centaur Publications

V1#1-The Clock begins (c-feature)(see Funny Pages for 1st app.)	157.00	471.00	1100.00
2	71.00	215.00	500.00
3-9: 4-Eisner-a; X-Mas-c. 7-Racial humor-c	51.00	152.00	355.00
V2#1 (9/37; V1#10 on-c; V2#1 in indicia)-Jack Strand begins	38.00	115.00	265.00
2 (10/37; V1#11 on-c; V2#2 in indicia)	38.00	115.00	265.00
3-5: 4-Xmas-c	34.00	100.00	235.00
6-(1st Centaur, 3/38)	59.00	178.00	415.00
7-11	34.00	100.00	235.00
V3#1-3	30.00	90.00	210.00
Laundry giveaway (16-20 pgs., 1930s)-slick-c	20.00	60.00	140.00

NOTE: ***Biro*** *c-V2#1, 8, 9, 11.* ***Guardineer*** *a-V1#11; c-V2#6, V3#5.* ***Bob Wood*** *c/a-V1#11, V2#2; c-V2#3, 5.*

FUNNY STUFF (Becomes The Dodo & the Frog No. 80)
Summer, 1944 - No. 79, July-Aug, 1954 (#1-7 are quarterly)
All-American/National Periodical Publications No. 7 on

1-The Three Mouseketeers (ends #28) & The "Terrific Whatzit" begin; Sheldon Mayer-a	82.00	246.00	575.00
2-Sheldon Mayer-a	41.00	124.00	290.00
3-5: 3-Flash parody. 5-All Mayer-a/scripts issue	27.00	80.00	185.00
6-10 10-(6/46)	17.00	52.00	120.00
11-17,19,20: 20-1st Dodo & the Frog-c (4/47)	13.00	40.00	90.00
18-The Dodo & the Frog (2/47, 1st app?) begin?; X-Mas-c	22.00	67.00	155.00
21,23-30: 24-Infinity-c	9.15	27.50	55.00
22-Superman cameo	31.00	94.00	220.00
31-79: 70-1st Bo Bunny by Mayer & begins	7.00	21.00	42.00

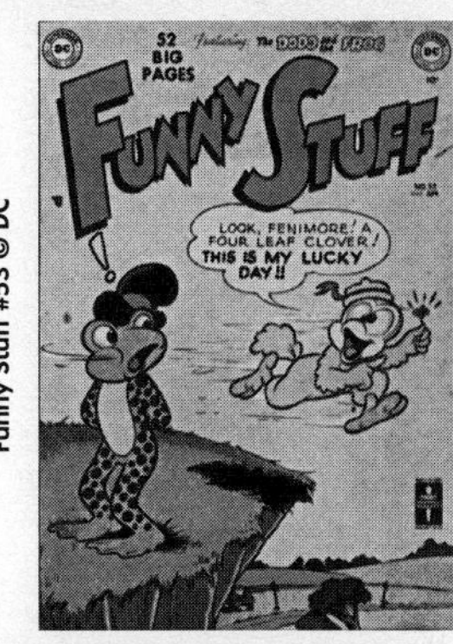

Funny Stuff #53 © DC

Fury #1 © MEG

The Fury Of Firestorm #24 © DC

	GD25	FN65	NM94

Wheaties Giveaway(1946, 6-1/2x8-1/4") (Scarce)-Dodo & the Frog, Three Mouseketeers, etc.; came taped to Wheaties box; never found in better than fine 50.00 150.00

NOTE: ***Mayer** a-1-8, 55, ,57, 58, 61, 62, 64, 65, 68, 70, 72, 74-79; c-2, 5, 6, 8.*

FUNNY STUFF STOCKING STUFFER
March, 1985 ($1.25, 52 pgs.)
DC Comics

	GD25	FN65	NM94
1-Almost every DC funny animal featured			1.25

FUNNY 3-D
December, 1953 (25¢, came with 2 pair of glasses)
Harvey Publications

	GD25	FN65	NM94
1-Shows cover in 3-D on inside	10.00	30.00	65.00

FUNNY TUNES (Animated Funny Comic Tunes No. 16-22; Funny Comic Tunes No. 23, on covers only; formerly Krazy Komics #15; Oscar No. 24 on)
No. 16, Summer, 1944 - No. 23, Fall, 1946
U.S.A. Comics Magazine Corp. (Timely)

	GD25	FN65	NM94
16-Silly Seal, Ziggy Pig, Krazy Krow begin	10.00	30.00	60.00
17 (Fall/44)-Becomes Gay Comics #18 on?	7.00	21.00	42.00
18-22: 21-Super Rabbit app.	5.85	17.50	35.00
23-Kurtzman-a	7.50	22.50	45.00

FUNNY TUNES (Becomes Space Comics #4 on)
July, 1953 - No. 3, Dec-Jan, 1953-54
Avon Periodicals

	GD25	FN65	NM94
1-Space Mouse, Peter Rabbit, Merry Mouse, Spotty the Pup, Cicero the Cat begin; all continue in Space Comics	6.70	20.00	40.00
2,3	4.35	13.00	26.00

FUNNY WORLD
1947 - No. 3, 1948
Marbak Press

	GD25	FN65	NM94
1-The Berrys, The Toodles & other strip-r begin	6.35	19.00	38.00
2,3	4.70	14.00	28.00

FUNTASTIC WORLD OF HANNA-BARBERA, THE (TV)
Dec, 1977 - No. 3, June, 1978 ($1.25) (Oversized)
Marvel Comics Group

	GD25	FN65	NM94
1-3: 1-The Flintstones Christmas Party(12/77). 2-Yogi Bear's Easter Parade(3/78). 3-Laff-a-lympics(6/78)	.90	2.30	5.50

FUN TIME
Spring, 1953; No. 2, Sum, 1953; No. 3(nn), Fall, 1953; No. 4, Wint, 1953-54
Ace Periodicals

	GD25	FN65	NM94
1-(25¢, 100 pgs.)-Funny animal	4.20	12.50	25.00
2-4 (All 25¢, 100 pgs.)	10.00	30.00	60.00

FUN WITH SANTA CLAUS (See March of Comics No. 11, 108, 325)

FURTHER ADVENTURES OF INDIANA JONES, THE (Also see Indiana Jones and the Last Crusade & Indiana Jones and the Temple of Doom)
Jan, 1983 - No. 34, Mar, 1986
Marvel Comics Group

	GD25	FN65	NM94
1-34: 1,2-Byrne/Austin-c/a			1.10

NOTE: ***Austin** a-6i, 9i; c-1i, 2i, 6i, 9i. **Chaykin** a-6p; c-6p, 8p-10p. **Ditko** a-21p, 25-28, 34. **Golden** c-24, 25. **Simonson** c-9. Painted c-14.*

FURTHER ADVENTURES OF NYOKA, THE JUNGLE GIRL, THE (AC)(Value: cover or less)

FURY (Straight Arrow's Horse...) (See A-1 No. 119)

FURY (TV) (See March Of Comics #200)
No. 781, Mar, 1957 - Nov, 1962 (All photo-c)
Dell Publishing Co./Gold Key

	GD25	FN65	NM94
4-Color 781	10.00	30.00	65.00
4-Color 885,975,1031,1080,1133,1172,1218,1296, 01292-208(#1-'62)	7.50	22.50	45.00
10020-211(11/62-G.K.)	7.50	22.50	45.00

FURY
May, 1994 ($2.95, One-shot)
Marvel Comics

	GD25	FN65	NM94
1-Ironman, Red Skull, FF, Hatemonger, Logan, Scorpio app.; Origin Nick Fury		1.20	3.00

FURY OF FIRESTORM, THE (Becomes Firestorm The Nuclear Man #65 on; also see Firestorm)
June, 1982 - No. 64, Oct, 1987 (#19-on: 75¢)
DC Comics

	GD25	FN65	NM94
1-Intro The Black Bison; brief origin		.80	2.00
2-64: 4-JLA x-over. 17-1st app. Firehawk. 21-Death of Killer Frost. 22-Origin. 23-Intro. Byte. 24-(6/84)-1st app. Blue Devil & Bug (origin); origin Byte. 34-1st app./origin Killer Frost II. 39-Weasel's i.d. revealed 41,42-Crisis x-over. 48-Intro. Moonbow. 53-Origin/1st app. Silver Shade. 55,56-Legends x-over. 58-1st app./origin Parasite			1.00
61-Test cover variant; Superman logo	3.60	11.00	25.00
Annual 1(1983)			1.25
Annual 2-4: 2(1984), 3(1985), 4(1986)			1.25

NOTE: ***Colan** a-19p, Annual 4p. **Giffen** a-Annual 4p. **Gil Kane** c-30. **Nino** a-37. **Tuska** a-(p)-17, 18, 32, 45.*

FUSION (Eclipse)(Value: cover or less)

FUTURE COMICS
June, 1940 - No. 4, Sept, 1940
David McKay Publications

	GD25	FN65	NM94
1-Origin The Phantom; The Lone Ranger, & Saturn Against the Earth begin	157.00	471.00	1100.00
2	86.00	257.00	600.00
3,4	71.00	214.00	500.00

FUTURE COURSE (Reoccurring Images)(Value: cover or less)

FUTURE WORLD COMICS
Summer, 1946 - No. 2, Fall, 1946
George W. Dougherty

	GD25	FN65	NM94
1,2-H. C. Kiefer covers	16.50	50.00	115.00

FUTURE WORLD COMIX (Warren Presents... on cover)
September, 1978
Warren Publications

	GD25	FN65	NM94
1-Corben-a; Todd-c			1.50

FUTURIANS, THE (Lodestone)(Value: cover or less)

G-8 (See G-Eight)

GABBY (Formerly Ken Shannon) (Teen humor)
No. 11, July, 1953; No. 2, Sept, 1953 - No. 9, Sept, 1954
Quality Comics Group

	GD25	FN65	NM94
11(#1)(7/53)	5.85	17.50	35.00
2	4.00	10.00	20.00
3-9	2.80	7.00	14.00

GABBY GOB (See Harvey Hits No. 85, 90, 94, 97, 100, 103, 106, 109)

GABBY HAYES ADVENTURE COMICS
Dec, 1953
Toby Press

	GD25	FN65	NM94
1-Photo-c	11.50	34.00	80.00

GABBY HAYES WESTERN (Movie star) (See Monte Hale, Real Western Hero & Western Hero)
Nov, 1948 - No. 50, Jan, 1953; No. 51, Dec, 1954 - No. 59, Jan, 1957
Fawcett Publications/Charlton Comics No. 51 on

	GD25	FN65	NM94
1-Gabby & his horse Corker begin; photo front/back-c begin	37.00	111.00	260.00
2	18.00	54.00	125.00
3-5	11.50	34.00	80.00
6-10: 9-Young Falcon begins	10.00	30.00	70.00
11-20: 19-Last photo back-c	8.65	26.00	52.00
21-49: 20,22,24,26,28,29-(52 pgs.)	5.85	17.50	35.00

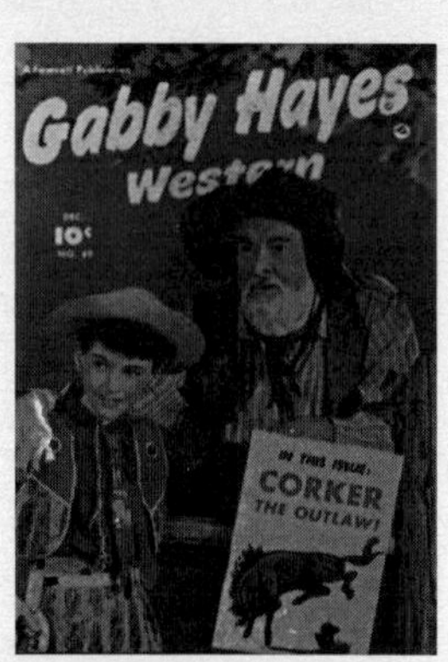

Gabby Hayes Western #49 © FAW

Gameboy #1 © Nintendo

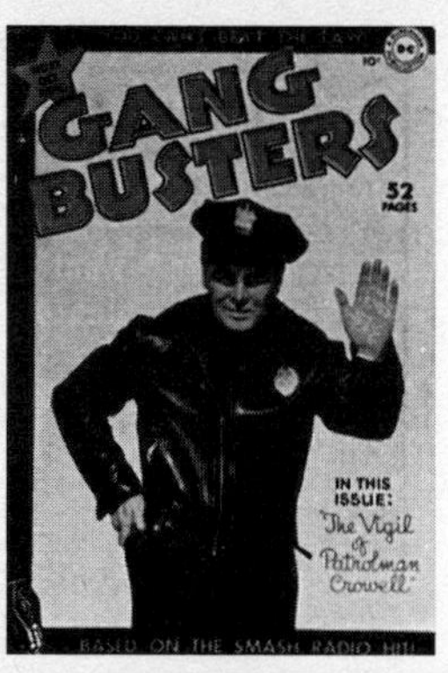

Gangbusters #12 © DC

	GD25	FN65	NM94
50-(1/53)-Last Fawcett issue; last photo-c?	7.00	21.00	42.00
51-(12/54)-1st Charlton issue; photo-c	7.00	21.00	42.00
52-59(1955-57): 53,55-Photo-c. 58-Swayze-a	4.00	11.00	22.00
Quaker Oats Giveaway nn's(#1-5, 1951, 2-1/2x7") (Kagran Corp.)-...In Tracks of Guilt, ...In the Fence Post Mystery, ...In the Accidental Sherlock, ... In the Frame-Up known	9.15	27.50	55.00

GAGS
July, 1937 - V3#10, Oct, 1944 (13-3/4x10-3/4")
United Features Synd./Triangle Publ. No. 9 on

	GD25	FN65	NM94
1(7/37)-52 pgs.; 20 pgs. Grin & Bear It, Fellow Citizen	5.00	15.00	30.00
V1#9 (36 pgs.) (7/42)	3.60	9.00	18.00
V3#10	2.40	7.00	14.00

GALACTIC GUARDIANS
July, 1994 - No. 4, Oct, 1994 ($1.50, limited series)
Marvel Comics

	GD25	FN65	NM94
1-4			1.50

GALACTIC WAR COMIX (Warren Presents... on cover)
December, 1978
Warren Publications

	GD25	FN65	NM94
nn-Wood, Williamson-r			1.50

GALLANT MEN, THE (TV)
October, 1963 (Photo-c)
Gold Key

	GD25	FN65	NM94
1(1008-310)-Manning-a	2.80	7.00	14.00

GALLEGHER, BOY REPORTER (TV)
May, 1965 (Disney)
Gold Key

	GD25	FN65	NM94
1(10149-505)-Photo-c	2.00	5.00	10.00

GAMBIT (See X-Men #266 & X-Men Annual #14)
Dec, 1993 - No. 4, Mar, 1994 ($2.00, mini-series)
Marvel Comics

	GD25	FN65	NM94
1-($2.50)-Gold foil stamped-c		1.00	2.50
2-4		.80	2.00

GAMEBOY
1990 - No. 6? ($1.95, coated-c)
Valiant Comics

	GD25	FN65	NM94
1-6: 3,4,6-Layton-c. 4-Morrow-a. 5-Layton-c(i)		.80	2.00

GAMMARAUDERS (DC)(Value: cover or less)

GANDY GOOSE (Movies/TV)(See All Surprise, Giant Comics Edition #5A &10, Paul Terry's Comics & Terry-Toons)
Mar, 1953 - No. 5, Nov, 1953; No. 5, Fall, 1956 - No. 6, Sum/58
St. John Publ. Co./Pines No. 5,6

	GD25	FN65	NM94
1-All St. John issues are pre-code	7.50	22.50	45.00
2	4.00	11.00	22.00
3-5(1953)(St. John)	3.60	9.00	18.00
5,6(1956-58)(Pines)-CBS Televison Presents...	2.80	7.00	14.00

GANG BUSTERS (See Popular Comics #38)
1938 - 1943
David McKay/Dell Publishing Co.

	GD25	FN65	NM94
Feature Books 17(McKay)('38)-1st app.	40.00	120.00	400.00
Large Feature Comic 10('39)-(Scarce)	40.00	120.00	400.00
Large Feature Comic 17('41)	25.00	75.00	250.00
4-Color 7(1940)	37.00	111.00	260.00
4-Color 23,24('42-43)	28.00	84.00	195.00

GANG BUSTERS (Radio/TV)(Gangbusters #14 on)
Dec-Jan, 1947-48 - No. 67, Dec-Jan, 1958-59 (No. 1-23: 52 pgs.)
National Periodical Publications

	GD25	FN65	NM94
1	62.00	186.00	435.00
2	28.00	84.00	195.00
3-5	19.00	58.00	135.00
6-10: 9,10-Photo-c	16.50	50.00	115.00
11-13-Photo-c	14.00	43.00	100.00
14,17-Frazetta-a, 8 pgs. each. 14-Photo-c	25.00	75.00	175.00
15,16,18-20	10.00	30.00	70.00
21-30: 26-Kirby-a	10.00	30.00	60.00
31-44: 44-Last Pre-code (2-3/55)	8.35	25.00	50.00
45-67	6.70	20.00	40.00

NOTE: ***Barry** a-6, 8, 10. **Drucker** a-51. **Moreira** a-48, 50, 59. **Roussos** a-8.*

GANGSTERS AND GUN MOLLS
Sept, 1951 - No. 4, June, 1952 (Painted c-1-3)
Avon Periodical/Realistic Comics

	GD25	FN65	NM94
1-Wood-a, 1 pg; c-/Avon paperback #292	30.00	90.00	210.00
2-Check-a, 8 pgs.; Kamen-a; Bonnie Parker story	22.00	67.00	155.00
3-Marijuana mention story; used in **POP**, pg. 84,85	21.00	63.00	145.00
4-Syd Shores-c	16.00	48.00	110.00

GANGSTERS CAN'T WIN
Feb-Mar, 1948 - No. 9, June-July, 1949 (All 52 pgs?)
D. S. Publishing Co.

	GD25	FN65	NM94
1-True crime stories	18.00	54.00	125.00
2	10.00	30.00	60.00
3-6: 4-Acid in face story	8.00	24.00	48.00
7-9	6.35	19.00	38.00

NOTE: ***Ingles** a-5, 6. **McWilliams** a-5, 7. **Reinman** c-6.*

GANG WORLD
No. 5, Nov, 1952 - No. 6, Jan, 1953
Standard Comics

	GD25	FN65	NM94
5-Bondage-c	10.00	30.00	70.00
6	8.35	25.00	50.00

GARGOYLE (See The Defenders #94)
June, 1985 - No. 4, Sept, 1985 (75¢, limited series)
Marvel Comics Group

	GD25	FN65	NM94
1-4: 1-Wrightson-c; character from Defenders			1.00

GARRISON'S GORILLAS (TV)
Jan, 1968 - No. 4, Oct, 1968; No. 5, Oct, 1969 (Photo-c)
Dell Publishing Co.

	GD25	FN65	NM94
1	3.60	11.00	25.00
2-5: 5-Reprints #1	2.40	7.30	17.00

GASOLINE ALLEY (Also see Popular Comics & Super Comics)
1929 (B&W daily strip reprints)(7x8-3/4"; hardcover)
Reilly & Lee Publishers

	GD25	FN65	NM94
nn-By King (96 pgs.)	19.00	58.00	135.00

GASOLINE ALLEY (Top Love Stories No. 3 on?)
Sept-Oct, 1950 - No. 2, Dec, 1950 (Newspaper reprints)
Star Publications

	GD25	FN65	NM94
1-Contains 1 pg. intro. history of the strip (The Life of Skeezix); reprints 15 scenes of highlights from 1921-1935, plus an adventure from 1935 and 1936 strips; a 2-pg. filler is included on the life of the creator Frank King, with photo of the cartoonist.	16.00	48.00	110.00
2-(1936-37 reprints)-L. B. Cole-c	15.00	45.00	105.00

(See Super Book No. 21)

GASP!
March, 1967 - No. 4, Aug, 1967 (12¢)
American Comics Group

	GD25	FN65	NM94
1	3.30	9.90	23.00
2-4	2.00	6.00	14.00

GAY COMICS (Honeymoon No. 41)
Mar, 1944 (no month); No. 18, Fall, 1944 - No. 40, Oct, 1949
Timely Comics/USA Comic Mag. Co. No. 18-24

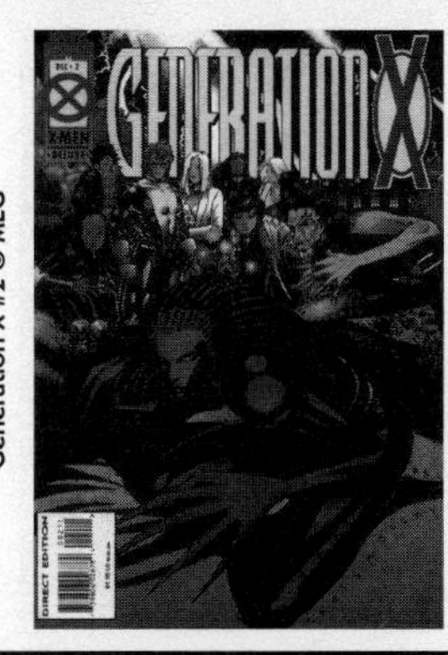

Generation X #2 © MEG

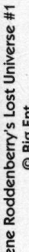

Gene Roddenberry's Lost Universe #1 © Big Ent.

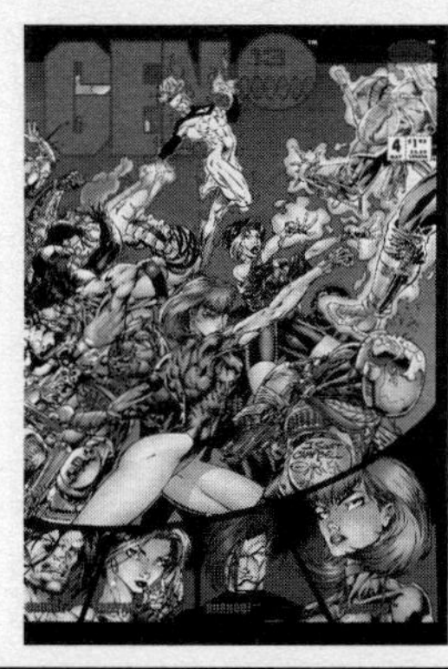

GEN 13 #4 © Jim Lee

GD25 FN65 NM94

1-Wolverton's Powerhouse Pepper; Tessie the Typist begins; 1st app. Millie the Model & Willie (one shot) 33.00 100.00 230.00
18-(Formerly Funny Tunes #17?)-Wolverton-a 16.50 50.00 115.00
19-29-Wolverton-a in all(21,24-6 pg., 7 pg. Powerhouse Pepper; additional 2 pg. sty in 24). 24,29-Kurtzman-a (24-"Hey Look"(2)) 13.50 41.00 95.00
30,33,36,37-Kurtzman's "Hey Look" 6.35 19.00 38.00
31-Kurtzman's "Hey Look" (1), Giggles 'N' Grins (1-1/2) 6.35 19.00 38.00
32,35,38-40: 35-Nellie The Nurse begins? 4.70 14.00 28.00
34-Three Kurtzman's "Hey Look" 7.00 21.00 42.00

GAY COMICS (Also see Smile, Tickle, & Whee Comics)
1955 (52 pgs.; 5x7-1/4"; 7¢)
Modern Store Publ.

1 .80 2.00 4.00

GAY PURR-EE (See Movie Comics)

GEEK, THE (See Brother Power... & Vertigo Visions)

G-8 AND HIS BATTLE ACES
October, 1966
Gold Key

1 (10184-610)-Painted-c 4.00 11.00 22.00

G-8 AND HIS BATTLE ACES
1991 ($1.50, one-shot)
Blazing Comics

1-Glanzman-a; Truman-c 1.50
NOTE: *Flip book format with "The Spider's Web" #1 on other side w/**Glanzman**-a, **Truman**-c.*

GEM COMICS
April, 1945 (52 pgs.) (Bondage-c)
Spotlight Publishers

1-Little Mohee, Steve Strong app. 17.00 52.00 120.00

GENE AUTRY (See March of Comics No. 25, 28, 39, 54, 78, 90, 104, 120, 135, 150 & Western Roundup under Dell Giants)

GENE AUTRY COMICS (Movie, Radio star; singing cowboy)
(Dell takes over with No. 11)
1941 (On sale 12/31/41) - No. 10, 1943 (68 pgs.)
Fawcett Publications

1 (Rare)-Gene Autry & his horse Champion begin 320.00 960.00 3200.00
2-(1942) 75.00 210.00 750.00
3-5: 3-(11/1/42) 52.00 156.00 520.00
6-10 45.00 135.00 450.00

GENE AUTRY COMICS (...& Champion No. 102 on)
No. 11, 1943 - No. 121, Jan-Mar, 1959 (TV - later issues)
Dell Publishing Co.

11 (1943, 60 pgs.)-Continuation of Fawcett series; photo back-c 57.00 171.00 400.00
12 (2/44, 60 pgs.) 51.00 154.00 360.00
4-Color 47(1944, 60 pgs.) 43.00 130.00 300.00
4-Color 57(11/44),66('45)(52 pgs. each) 38.00 115.00 265.00
4-Color 75,83('45, 36 pgs. each) 31.00 94.00 220.00
4-Color 93,100('45-46, 36 pgs. each): 100-Photo-c 26.00 78.00 180.00
1(5-6/46, 52 pgs.) 43.00 130.00 300.00
2(7-8/46)-Photo-c begin, end #111 22.00 67.00 155.00
3-5: 4-Intro Flapjack Hobbs 17.00 52.00 120.00
6-10 13.00 40.00 90.00
11-20: 20-Panhandle Pete begins 10.00 30.00 70.00
21-29(36pgs.) 8.35 25.00 50.00
30-40(52pgs.) 8.35 25.00 50.00
41-56(52pgs.) 6.70 20.00 40.00
57-66(36pgs.): 58-X-mas-c 4.20 12.50 25.00
67-80(52pgs.) 4.70 14.00 28.00
81-90(52pgs.): 82-X-mas-c. 87-Blank inside-c 4.00 11.00 22.00

GD25 FN65 NM94

91-99(36pgs. No. 91-on). 94-X-mas-c 3.20 8.00 16.00
100 4.00 11.00 22.00
101-111-Last Gene Autry photo-c 3.20 8.00 16.00
112-121-All Champion painted-c, most by Sam Savitt 2.40 6.00 12.00
...Adventure Comics And Play-Fun Book ('47)-32 pgs., 8x6-1/2"; games, comics, magic (Pillsbury premium) 24.00 73.00 170.00
Quaker Oats Giveaway(1950)-2-1/2x6-3/4"; 5 different versions; "Death Card Gang", "Phantoms of the Cave", "Riddle of Laughing Mtn.", "Secret of Lost Valley", "Bond of the Broken Arrow" (came in wrapper) each... 10.30 31.00 72.00
3-D Giveaway(1953)-Pocket-size; 5 different 12.00 36.00 85.00
NOTE: *Photo back covers 4-18, 20-45, 48-65. **Manning** a-118. **Jesse Marsh** art: 4-Color No. 66, 75, 93, 100, No. 1-25, 27-37, 39, 40.*

GENE AUTRY'S CHAMPION (TV)
No. 287, 8/50; No. 319, 2/51; No. 3, 8-10/51 - No. 19, 8-10/55
Dell Publishing Co.

4-Color 287(#1)('50, 52pgs.)-Photo-c 10.00 30.00 70.00
4-Color 319(#2, '51), 3: 2-Painted-c begin, most by Sam Savitt 4.70 14.00 28.00
4-19: 19-Last painted-c 3.00 7.50 15.00

GENE AUTRY TIM (Formerly Tim) (Becomes Tim in Space)
1950 (Half-size) (Black & White Giveaway)
Tim Stores

nn-Several issues (All Scarce) 10.00 30.00 60.00

GENE DOGS
Oct, 1993 - No. 4, Jan, 1994 ($1.75, mini-series)
Marvel Comics UK

1-($2.75)-Polybagged w/4 trading cards 1.10 2.75
2-4: 2-Vs. Genetix .70 1.75

GENERAL DOUGLAS MACARTHUR
1951
Fox Features Syndicate

nn-True life story 14.00 43.00 100.00

GENERIC COMIC, THE
April, 1984 (One-shot)
Marvel Comics Group

1 1.00

GENERATION X
Oct, 1994-Present (1.50, color)
Marvel Comics

...Collectors Preview(1.75) 0.40 0.70 1.75
..."Ashcan" Edition 0.20 0.30 0.75
1-(3.95)-Wraparound chromium-c 0.80 1.60 4.00
2,3-(1.95)-Deluxe edition 0.40 0.80 2.00
2-(1.50)-Standard edition 0.30 0.60 1.50

GENE RODDENBERRY'S LOST UNIVERSE
Apr, 1995-Present (1.95, color)
Tekno Comix

1; bound in game piece and trading card 0.40 0.80 2.00

GENETIX
Oct, 1993 - No. 6, Mar, 1994 ($1.75, limited series)
Marvel Comics UK

1-($2.75)-Polybagged w/4 cards; Dark Guard app. 1.10 2.75
2-6: 2-Intro Tektos. 4-Vs. Gene Dogs .70 1.75

GEN^{13}
Feb, 1994 - No. 4, 1994 ($1.95)
Image Comics

1-($2.50)-Created by Jim Lee 2.90 5.70 20.00
2-($2.50) 1.70 4.20 10.00

Georgie Comics #12 © MEG

Geronimo #2 © AVON

Ghostly Haunts #44 © CC

	GD25	FN65	NM94
3-5: 3,4-Pitt-c & story. 4-Wraparound-c		1.60	4.00
5-Alternate Portacio-c; see Deathblow #5	1.20	2.40	6.00

NOTE: *Issues 1-4 contain coupons redeemable for ashcan edition of Gen 13 #0. Price listed is for complete books.*

GENTLE BEN (TV)
Feb, 1968 - No. 5, Oct, 1969 (All photo-c)
Dell Publishing Co.

	GD25	FN65	NM94
1	4.00	11.00	22.00
2-5: 5-Reprints #1	2.40	6.00	12.00

GEOMANCER
Nov, 1994 - Present ($2.25, color)
Valiant

	GD25	FN65	NM94
1-($3.75)-Chromium wraparound-c; Eternal Warrior app.		1.50	3.75
2-5		.90	2.25

GEORGE OF THE JUNGLE (TV)(See America's Best TV Comics)
Feb, 1969 - No. 2, Oct, 1969 (Jay Ward)
Gold Key

	GD25	FN65	NM94
1,2	7.00	21.00	50.00

GEORGE PAL'S PUPPETOONS
Dec, 1945 - No. 18, Dec, 1947; No. 19, 1950
Fawcett Publications

	GD25	FN65	NM94
1-Captain Marvel app. on cover	35.00	105.00	245.00
2	17.00	52.00	120.00
3-10	11.00	32.00	75.00
11-19	10.00	30.00	60.00

GEORGIE COMICS (...& Judy Comics #20-35?; see All Teen & Teen Comics)
Spring, 1945 - No. 39, Oct, 1952 (#1-3 are quarterly)
Timely Comics/GPI No. 1-34

	GD25	FN65	NM94
1-Dave Berg-a	14.00	43.00	100.00
2	8.35	25.00	50.00
3-5,7,8	5.85	17.50	35.00
6-Georgie visits Timely Comics	8.35	25.00	50.00
9,10-Kurtzman's "Hey Look" (1 & ?); Margie app.	7.50	22.50	45.00
11,12: 11-Margie, Millie app.	4.35	13.00	26.00
13-Kurtzman's "Hey Look", 3 pgs.	6.70	20.00	40.00
14-Wolverton-a(1 pg.); Kurtzman's "Hey Look"	8.00	24.00	48.00
15,16,18-20	4.00	11.00	22.00
17,29-Kurtzman's "Hey Look", 1 pg.	5.85	17.50	35.00
21-24,27,28,30-39: 21-Anti-Wertham editorial	3.60	9.00	18.00
25-Painted-c by classic pin-up artist Peter Driben	6.70	20.00	40.00
26-Logo design swipe from Archie Comics	4.00	11.00	22.00

GERALD McBOING-BOING AND THE NEARSIGHTED MR. MAGOO (TV)
(Mr. Magoo No. 6 on)
Aug-Oct, 1952 - No. 5, Aug-Oct, 1953
Dell Publishing Co.

	GD25	FN65	NM94
1	9.15	27.50	55.00
2-5	7.50	22.50	45.00

GERONIMO (See Fighting Indians of the Wild West!)
1950 - No. 4, Feb, 1952
Avon Periodicals

	GD25	FN65	NM94
1-Indian Fighter; Maneely-a; Texas Rangers-r/Cowpuncher #1; Fawcette-c	11.50	34.00	80.00
2-On the Warpath; Kit West app.; Kinstler-c/a	7.50	22.50	45.00
3-And His Apache Murderers; Kinstler-c/a(2); Kit West-r/Cowpuncher #6	7.50	22.50	45.00
4-Savage Raids of; Kinstler-c & inside front-c; Kinstlerish-a by McCann(3)	6.35	19.00	38.00

GERONIMO JONES
Sept, 1971 - No. 9, Jan, 1973
Charlton Comics

	GD25	FN65	NM94
1	1.00	2.00	5.00
2-9		1.00	2.50
Modern Comics Reprint #7('78)			1.50

GETALONG GANG, THE (TV)
May, 1985 - No. 6, March, 1986
Star Comics (Marvel)

	GD25	FN65	NM94
1-6: Saturday morning TV stars			1.00

GET LOST
Feb-Mar, 1954 - No. 3, June-July, 1954 (Satire)
Mikeross Publications/New Comics

	GD25	FN65	NM94
1-Andru/Esposito-a in all?	17.00	52.00	120.00
2-Andru/Esposito-c; has 4 pg. E.C. parody featuring "The Sewer Keeper"	12.00	36.00	85.00
3-John Wayne 'Hondo' parody	10.00	30.00	70.00
1,2 (10,12/87-New Comics)-B&W r-original			1.00

GET SMART (TV)
June, 1966 - No. 8, Sept, 1967 (All have Don Adams photo-c)
Dell Publishing Co.

	GD25	FN65	NM94
1	9.00	29.00	64.00
2-Ditko-a	6.40	19.00	45.00
3-8: 3-Ditko-a(p)	5.70	17.00	40.00

GHOST (...Comics #9)
1951(Winter) - No. 11, Summer, 1954
Fiction House Magazines

	GD25	FN65	NM94
1-Most covers by Whitman	46.00	137.00	320.00
2-Ghost Gallery & Werewolf Hunter stories	22.00	65.00	150.00
3-9: 3,6,7,9-Bondage-c. 9-Abel, Discount-a	18.00	54.00	125.00
10,11-Dr. Drew by Grandenetti in each, reprinted from Rangers; 11-Evans-r/Rangers #39; Grandenetti-r/Rangers #49	22.00	65.00	150.00

GHOST BREAKERS (Also see Racket Squad in Action, Red Dragon & (CC) Sherlock Holmes Comics)
Sept, 1948 - No. 2, Dec, 1948 (52 pgs.)
Street & Smith Publications

	GD25	FN65	NM94
1-Powell-c/a(3); Dr. Neff (magician) app.	26.00	78.00	180.00
2-Powell-c/a(2); Maneely-a	20.00	60.00	140.00

GHOSTBUSTERS (TV)(First)(Value: cover or less)

GHOSTBUSTERS II (Now)(Value: cover or less)

GHOST CASTLE (See Tales of...)

GHOSTLY HAUNTS (Formerly Ghost Manor)
#20, 9/71 - #53, 12/76; #54, 9/77 - #55, 10/77; #56, 1/78 - #58, 4/78
Charlton Comics

	GD25	FN65	NM94
20-58: 27-Dr. Graves x-over. 32-New logo. 33-Back to old logo. 39-Origin & 1st app. Destiny Fox		1.20	3.00
40,41(Modern Comics-r, 1977, 1978)			1.50

NOTE: ***Ditko*** *a-22-25, 27, 28, 31-34, 36-41, 43-48, 50, 52, 54, 56r; c-22-27, 30, 33-37, 47, 54, 56.* ***Glanzman*** *a-20.* ***Howard*** *a-27, 30, 35, 42.* ***Newton*** *c/a-42.* ***Staton*** *a-35; c-28, 46.* ***Sutton*** *c-33, 37, 39, 41.*

GHOSTLY TALES (Formerly Blue Beetle No. 50-54)
No. 55, 4-5/66 - No. 124, 12/76; No. 125, 9/77 - No. 169, 10/84
Charlton Comics

	GD25	FN65	NM94
55-Intro. & origin Dr. Graves	1.60	4.00	8.00
56-70-Dr. Graves ends	.80	2.00	4.00
71-169: 107-Sutton, Wood-a. 114-Newton-a		1.20	3.00

NOTE: ***Aparo*** *a-65, 66, 68, 72, 141r, 142r; c-71, 72, 74-76, 81, 146r.* ***Ditko*** *a-55-58, 60, 61, 67, 69-73, 75-90, 92-95, 97, 99-118, 120-122, 125r, 126r, 131-133r, 136-141r, 143r, 144r, 152, 155, 161, 163; c-67, 69, 73, 77, 78, 83, 84, 86-90, 92-97, 99, 102, 109, 111, 118, 120-122, 125, 131-133, 163.* ***Glanzman*** *a-167.* ***Howard*** *a-95, 98, 99, 117; c-98, 107, 120, 121, 161.* ***Morisi*** *a-83, 84, 86.* ***Newton*** *a-114; c-115(painted).* ***Palais*** *a-61.* ***Staton*** *a-161; c-117.* ***Sutton*** *a-107, 112-114; c-100, 106, 110, 113(painted).* ***Wood*** *a-107.*

GHOSTLY WEIRD STORIES (Formerly Blue Bolt Weird)
No. 120, Sept, 1953 - No. 124, Sept, 1954
Star Publications

Ghost Manor #19 © CC

Ghostr Rider #7 © MEG

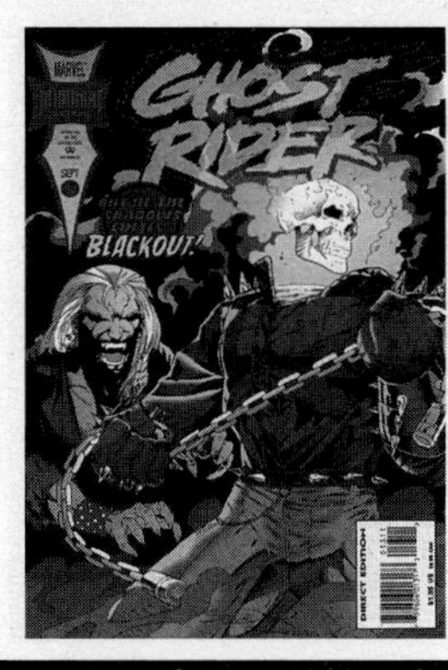

Ghost Rider V2 #52 © MEG

GD25 FN65 NM94 | GD25 FN65 NM94

120-Jo-Jo-r 19.00 57.00 130.00
121-Jo-Jo-r 13.50 41.00 95.00
122-The Mask-r/Capt. Flight #5; Rulah-r; has 1pg. story 'Death and the Devil Pills'-r/Western Outlaws #17 13.50 41.00 95.00
123-Jo-Jo; Disbrow-a(2) 13.50 41.00 95.00
124-Torpedo Man 13.50 41.00 95.00
NOTE: ***Disbrow** a-120-124. **L. B. Cole** covers-all issues (#122 is a sci-fi cover).*

GHOST MANOR (Ghostly Haunts No. 20 on)
July, 1968 - No. 19, July, 1971
Charlton Comics

1 1.30 3.25 8.00
2-5 1.60 4.00
6-12,17: 17-Morisi-a 1.20 3.00
13-16,18,19-Ditko-a; c-15,18,19 1.60 4.00

GHOST MANOR (2nd Series)
Oct, 1971 - No. 32, Dec, 1976; No. 33, Sept, 1977 - No. 77, 11/84
Charlton Comics

1 1.30 3.25 8.00
2-7,9,10 1.60 4.00
8-Wood-a 1.00 2.00 5.00
11-56,58-77: 18-Newton's 1st pro art. 19-20-Newton-a. 22-Newton-c/a. 21-E-Man, Blue Beetle, Capt. Atom cameos. 28-Nudity panels. 40-Torture & drug use. 77-Aparo-r/Space Adventures V3#60 (Paul Mann) 1.20 3.00
57-Wood, Ditko, Howard-a 1.60 4.00
19(Modern Comics reprint, 1977) 1.00
NOTE: ***Ditko** a-4, 8, 10, 11(2), 13, 14, 18, 20-22, 24-26, 28, 29, 31, 37r, 38r, 40r, 42-44r, 46r, 47, 51r, 52r, 54r, 57, 60, 62(4), 64r, 71; c-2-7, 9-11, 14-16, 28, 31, 37, 38, 42, 43, 46, 47, 51, 52, 60, 62, 64. **Howard** a-4, 8, 19-21, 57. **Newton** a-18-20, 22, 64. **Sutton** a-19;c-8, 18.*

GHOST RIDER (See A-1 Comics, Best of the West, Black Phantom, Bobby Benson, Great Western, Red Mask & Tim Holt)
1950 - No. 14, 1954
Magazine Enterprises
NOTE: *The character was inspired by Vaughn Monroe's "Ghost Riders in the Sky", and Disney's movie "The Headless Horseman".*

1(A-1 #27)-Origin Ghost Rider 50.00 150.00 350.00
2-5: 2(A-1 #29), 3(A-1 #31), 4(A-1 #34), 5(A-1 #37)-All Frazetta-c only 45.00 135.00 315.00
6,7: 6(A-1 #44)-Loco weed story, 7(A-1 #51) 18.00 54.00 125.00
8,9: 8(A-1 #57)-Drug use story, 9(A-1 #69) 16.00 48.00 110.00
10(A-1 #71)-Vs. Frankenstein 16.00 48.00 110.00
11-14: 11(A-1 #75). 12(A-1 #80)-Bondage-c; one-eyed Devil-c. 13(A-1 #84). 14(A-1 #112) 13.00 40.00 90.00
NOTE: ***Dick Ayers** art in all; c-1, 6-14.*

GHOST RIDER, THE (See Night Rider & Western Gunfighters)
Feb, 1967 - No. 7, Nov, 1967 (Western hero)(All 12¢)
Marvel Comics Group

1-Origin & 1st app. Ghost Rider; Kid Colt-r begin 3.60 10.75 25.00
2-7: 6-Last Kid Colt-r; All Ayers-c/a(p) 1.65 4.70 11.00

GHOST RIDER (See The Champions, Marvel Spotlight #5, Marvel Team-Up #15, 58, Marvel Treasury Edition #18, Marvel Two-In-One #8, The Original Ghost Rider & The Original Ghost Rider Rides Again)
Sept, 1973 - No. 81, June, 1983 (Super-hero)
Marvel Comics Group

1-Johnny Blaze, the Ghost Rider begins; 1st app. Daimon Hellstrom (Son of Satan) in cameo 10.00 30.00 70.00
2-1st full app. Daimon Hellstrom; gives glimpse of costume (1 panel); story continues in Marvel Spotlight #12 4.30 13.00 30.00
3-5: 3-Ghost Rider gets new cycle; Son of Satan app. 3.10 9.40 22.00
6-10: 10-Reprints origin/1st app. from Marvel Spotlight #5; Ploog-a 2.00 6.00 14.00
11-19: 18-Spider-Man-c & app. 1.60 4.70 11.00
20-Daredevil x-over; ties into D.D. #138; Byrne-a 2.00 6.00 14.00
21-30: 22-1st app. Enforcer. 29,30-Vs. Dr. Strange 1.00 2.50 6.00
31-49 .80 2.10 5.00
50-Double size 1.00 3.00 6.00
51-67,69-76,78-80: 80-Brief origin recap 1.60 4.00
68,77-Origin retold .80 2.10 5.00
81-Death of Ghost Rider (Demon leaves Blaze) 1.30 3.30 8.00
NOTE: ***Anderson** c-64p. **Infantino** a(p)-43, 44, 51. **G. Kane** a-21p; c(p)-1, 2, 4, 5, 8, 9, 11-13, 19, 20, 24, 25. **Kirby** c-21-23. **Mooney** a-2-9p, 30i. **Nebres** c-26i. **Newton** a-23i. **Perez** c-26p. **Shores** a-2i. J. **Sparling** a-62p, 64p, 65p. **Starlin** a(p)-35. **Sutton** a-1p, 44i, 64i, 65i, 66, 67i. **Tuska** a-13p, 14p, 16p.*

GHOST RIDER (Also see Doctor Strange/Ghost Rider Special, Marvel Comics Presents & Midnight Sons Unlimited)
V2#1, May, 1990 - Present ($1.50/$1.75)
Marvel Comics (Midnight Sons imprint #44 on)

V2#1-($1.95, 52 pgs.)-Origin/1st app. new Ghost Rider; Kingpin app. 2.10 6.00 15.00
1-2nd printing (not gold) 1.60 3.75
2 1.60 5.00 11.00
3-Kingpin app. 1.50 3.80 9.00
4-Scarcer 1.90 5.60 13.00
5-Punisher app.; Jim Lee-c 1.90 5.60 13.00
5-Gold background 2nd printing 1.10 2.70 6.50
6-Punisher app. 1.10 2.70 6.50
7-10: 9-X-Factor app. 10-Reintro Johnny Blaze on last pg. 1.20 3.00
11-14: 11-Stroman-c/a(p). 12,13-Dr. Strange x-over cont'd in D.S. #28. 13-Painted-c. 14-Johnny Blaze vs. Ghost Rider; origin recap 1st Ghost Rider (Blaze) .90 2.25
15-Glow in the dark-c; begin $1.75-c .80 2.10 5.00
15-Gold background 2nd printing .80 2.00
16,17-Spider-Man/Hobgoblin-c/story 1.10 2.75
18-24,29,30,32-39: 18-Painted-c by Nelson. 29-Wolverine-c/story. 32-Dr. Strange x-over; Johnny Blaze app. 34-Williamson-a(i). 36-Daredevil app. 37-Archangel app. 1.50
25-($2.75)-Contains pop-up scene insert .90 2.25
26,27-X-Men x-over; Lee/Williams-c on both .90 2.25
28-($2.50, 52 pgs.)-Polybagged w/poster; part 1 of Rise of the Midnight Sons storyline (see Ghost Rider/Blaze #1) 1.30 3.25
31-($2.50, 52 pgs.)-Polybagged w/poster; part 6 of Rise of the Midnight Sons .80 2.00
40-($2.25)-Outer-c is Darkhold envelope made of black parchment w/gold ink; Midnight Massacre; Demogoblin app. .75 1.90
41-48: 41-Lilith & Centurious app.; begin $1.75-c. 41-43-Neon ink-c. 43-Has free extra 16 pg. insert on Siege of Darkness. 44,45-Siege of Darkness parts 2 & 10. 44-Spot varnish-c. 46-Intro new Ghost Rider. 48-Spider-Man app. .70 1.75
49,51-61: 49-Begin $1.95-c; bound-in trading card sheet; Hulk app. 55-Werewolf by Night app. .80 2.00
50-($2.50, 52 pgs.)-Regular edition 1.00 2.50
50-($2.95, 52 pgs.)-Collectors ed. die cut foil-c 1.20 3.00
Annual 1 ('93, $2.95, 68 pgs.)-Bagged w/card 1.00 2.50
Annual 2 ('94, $2.95, 68 pgs.) 1.00 2.50
...And Cable 1 (9/92, $3.95, stiff-c, 68 pgs.)-Reprints Marvel Comics Presents #90-98 w/new Kieth-c 1.40 3.50
NOTE: ***Andy & Joe Kubert** c/a-28-31. **Williamson** a(i)-33-35; c-33i.*

GHOST RIDER/BLAZE: SPIRITS OF VENGEANCE (Also see Blaze)
Aug, 1992 - No. 23, June, 1994 ($1.75)
Marvel Comics (Midnight Sons imprint #17 on)

1-($2.75, 52 pgs.)-Polybagged w/poster; part 2 of Rise of the Midnight Sons storyline; Adam Kubert-c/a begins 1.10 2.75
2-11,14-21: 4-Art Adams & Joe Kubert-p. 5,6-Spirits of Venom parts 2 & 4 cont'd from Web of Spider-Man #95,96 w/Demogoblin. 14-17-Neon ink-c. 15-Intro Blaze's new costume & power. 17,18-Siege of Darkness parts 8 & 13. 17-Spot varnish-c .70 1.75
12-($2.95)-Glow-in-the-dark-c 1.20 3.00
13-($2.25)-Outer-c is Darkhold envelope made of black parchment w/gold

Ghost Rider 2099 #5 © MEG

Ghosts #80 © DC

Ghost Special Edition #1 © DH

	GD25	FN65	NM94
ink; Midnight Massacre x-over		.90	2.25
22,23: 22-Begin $1.95-c; bound-in trading card sheet		.80	2.00

NOTE: ***Adam & Joe Kubert** c-7, 8. **Adam Kubert/Steacy** c-6. **J. Kubert** a-13p(6 pgs.)*

GHOST RIDER/CAPTAIN AMERICA: FEAR
Oct, 1992 ($5.95, 52 pgs.)
Marvel Comics

	GD25	FN65	NM94
nn-Wraparound gatefold-c; Williamson inks	1.00	2.50	6.00

GHOST RIDER 2099
May, 1994 - Present ($1.50)
Marvel Comics

	GD25	FN65	NM94
1-($2.25)-Collector's Edition w/prismatic foil-c		.90	2.25
1-($1.50)-Regular Edition; bound-in trading card sheet			1.50
2-12: 7-Spider-Man 2099 app.			1.50

GHOST RIDER; WOLVERINE; PUNISHER: HEARTS OF DARKNESS
Dec, 1991 ($4.95, one-shot, 52 pgs.)
Marvel Comics

	GD25	FN65	NM94
1-Double gatefold-c; John Romita, Jr.-c/a(p)	1.00	2.00	5.00

GHOSTS (Ghost No. 1)
Sept-Oct, 1971 - No. 112, May, 1982 (No. 1-5: 52 pgs.)
National Periodical Publications/DC Comics

	GD25	FN65	NM94
1-Aparo-a	1.65	4.00	10.00
2-Wood-a(i)		1.60	4.00
3-5		1.20	3.00
6-20		.80	2.00
21-96: 40-(68 pgs.)			1.50
97-99-The Spectre app. 97,98-Spectre-c by Aparo		.80	2.00
100-112: 100-Infinity-c			1.00

NOTE: ***B. Baily** a-77. **J. Craig** a-108. **Ditko** a-77, 111. **Giffen** a-104p, 106p, 111p. **Golden** a-88. **Kaluta** c-7, 93, 101. **Kubert** c-89, 105-108, 111. **Mayer** a-111. **McWilliams** a-99. **Win Mortimer** a-89, 91, 94. **Newton** a-92p, 94p. **Nino** a-35, 37, 57. **Orlando** a-74i; c-80. **Redondo** a-8, 13, 45. **Sparling** a(p)-90, 93, 94. **Spiegle** a-103, 105. Dr. 13, the Ghostbreaker back-ups in 95-99, 101.*

GHOSTS SPECIAL (See DC Special Series No. 7)

GHOST SPECIAL
July, 1994 ($3.95, 48 pgs, one-shot)
Dark Horse Comics

	GD25	FN65	NM94
1		1.60	4.00

GHOST STORIES (See Amazing Ghost Stories)

GHOST STORIES
Sept-Nov, 1962; No. 2, Apr-June, 1963 - No. 37, Oct, 1973
Dell Publishing Co.

	GD25	FN65	NM94
12-295-211(#1)-Written by John Stanley	5.35	16.00	32.00
2	3.20	8.00	16.00
3-10: Two No. 6's exist with different c/a(12-295-406 & 12-295-503) #12-295-503 is actually #9 with indicia to #6	2.40	6.00	12.00
11-20	1.40	3.50	7.00
21-37	1.00	2.00	5.00

NOTE: *#21-34, 36, 37 all reprint earlier issues.*

GHOUL TALES (Magazine)
Nov, 1970 - No. 5, July, 1971 (52 pgs.) (B&W)
Stanley Publications

	GD25	FN65	NM94
1-Aragon pre-code reprints; Mr. Mystery as host; bondage-c	3.25	9.50	22.00
2,3: 2-(1/71)Reprint/Climax #1. 3-(3/71)	1.65	4.00	10.00
4-(5/71)Reprints story "The Way to a Man's Heart" used in **SOTI**	3.25	9.50	22.00
5-ACG reprints	1.65	4.00	10.00

NOTE: *No. 1-4 contain pre-code Aragon reprints.*

GIANT BOY BOOK OF COMICS (Also see Boy Comics)
1945 (Hardcover) (240 pgs.)
Newsbook Publications (Gleason)

	GD25	FN65	NM94
1-Crimebuster & Young Robin Hood; Biro-c	75.00	225.00	525.00

GIANT COMIC ALBUM
1972 (52 pgs., 11x14", B&W, 59¢, cardboard-c)
King Features Syndicate

Newspaper reprints: Little Iodine, Katzenjammer Kids, Henry, Mandrake the Magician ('59 Falk), Popeye, Beetle Bailey, Barney Google, Blondie, Flash Gordon ('68-69 Dan Barry), & Snuffy Smith

	GD25	FN65	NM94
each...	1.65	4.00	10.00

GIANT COMICS
Summer, 1957 - No. 3, Winter, 1957 (25¢, 100 pgs.)
Charlton Comics

	GD25	FN65	NM94
1-Atomic Mouse, Hoppy app.	14.00	43.00	100.00
2,3: 2-Romance. 3-Christmas Book; Atomic Mouse, Atomic Rabbit, Li'l Genius, Li'l Tomboy & Atom the Cat stories	11.00	32.00	75.00

NOTE: *The above may be rebound comics; contents could vary.*

GIANT COMICS (See Wham-O Giant Comics)

GIANT COMICS EDITION (See Terry-Toons)
1947 - No. 17, 1950 (All 100-164 pgs.) (25¢)
St. John Publishing Co.

	GD25	FN65	NM94
1-Mighty Mouse	35.00	105.00	350.00
2-Abbie & Slats	16.00	48.00	160.00
3-Terry-Toons Album; 100 pgs.	26.00	80.00	260.00
4-Crime comics; contains Red Seal No. 16, used & illo. in **SOTI**	38.00	115.00	380.00
5-Police Case Book (4/49, 132 pgs.)-Contents varies; contains remaindered St. John books - some volumes contain 5 copies rather than 4, with 160 pages; Matt Baker-c	36.00	110.00	360.00
5A-Terry-Toons Album (132 pgs.)-Mighty Mouse, Heckle & Jeckle, Gandy Goose & Dinky stories	25.00	75.00	250.00
6-Western Picture Stories; Baker-c/a(3); Tuska-a; The Sky Chief, Blue Monk, Ventrilo app., 132 pgs.	34.00	100.00	340.00
7-Contains a teen-age romance plus 3 Mopsy comics	22.00	65.00	220.00
8-The Adventures of Mighty Mouse (10/49)	25.00	75.00	250.00
9-Romance and Confession Stories; Kubert-a(4); Baker-a; photo-c (132 pgs.)	34.00	100.00	340.00
10-Terry-Toons Album (132 pgs.)-Mighty Mouse, Heckle & Jeckle, Gandy Goose stories	25.00	75.00	250.00
11-Western Picture Stories-Baker-c/a(4); The Sky Chief, Desperado, & Blue Monk app.; another version with Son of Sinbad by Kubert (132 pgs.)	32.00	95.00	320.00
12-Diary Secrets; Baker prostitute-c; 4 St. John romance comics; Baker-a	54.00	160.00	540.00
13-Romances; Baker, Kubert-a	28.00	85.00	280.00
14-Mighty Mouse Album (132 pgs.)	25.00	75.00	250.00
15-Romances (4 love comics)-Baker-c	30.00	90.00	300.00
16-Little Audrey; Abbott & Costello, Casper	25.00	75.00	250.00
17(nn)-Mighty Mouse Album (nn, no date, but did follow No. 16); 100 pgs. on cover but has 148 pgs.	25.00	75.00	250.00

NOTE: *The above books contain remaindered comics and contents could vary with each issue. No. 11, 12 have part photo magazine insides.*

GIANT COMICS EDITIONS
1940's (132 pgs.)
United Features Syndicate

	GD25	FN65	NM94
1-Abbie & Slats, Abbott & Costello, Jim Hardy, Ella Cinders, Iron Vic, Gordo, & Bill Bumlin	29.00	86.00	200.00
2-Jim Hardy, Ella Cinders, Elmo & Gordo	22.00	65.00	150.00

NOTE: *Above books contain rebound copies; contents can vary.*

GIANT GRAB BAG OF COMICS (See Archie All-Star Specials under Archie Comics)

GIANTS (See Thrilling True Story of the Baseball...)

GIANT-SIZE...
May, 1974 - Dec, 1975 (35-50¢, 52-68 pgs.)(Some titles quarterly)
Marvel Comics Group

Avengers 1(8/74)-New-a plus G.A. H. Torch-r; 1st modern app. The Whizzer;

Giant-Size Captain America #1 © MEG

Giant-Size Spider-Man #1 © MEG

G.I. Combat #5 © QUA

GD25 FN65 NM94

1st & only modern app. Miss America 1.10 2.80 6.75
Avengers 2,3: 2(11/74)-Death of the Swordsman. 3(2/75) 1.90 4.75
Avengers 4,5: 4(6/75)-Vision marries Scarlet Witch. 5(12/75)-Reprints Avengers Special #1 1.50 3.75
Captain America 1(12/75)-r/stories T.O.S. 59-63 by Kirby (#63 reprints origin) 1.50 3.80 9.00
Captain Marvel 1(12/75)-r/Capt. Marvel #17, 20 by Gil Kane (p) 1.30 3.00 8.00
Chillers 1(6/74, 52 pgs)-Curse of Dracula; origin/1st app. Lilith, Dracula's daughter; Heath-r, Colan-c/a(p); becomes Giant-Size Dracula #2 on 1.50 3.75
Chillers 1(2/75, 50¢, 68 pgs.)-Alacala-a 1.30 3.25
Chillers 2(5/75)-All-r; Everett-r from Advs. into Weird Worlds 1.10 2.75
Chillers 3(8/75)-Wrightson-c(new)/a(r); Colan, Kirby, Smith-r 1.50 3.75
Conan 1(9/74)-B. Smith-r/#3; start adaptation of Howard's "Hour of the Dragon" (ends #4); 1st app. Belit; new-a begins 1.20 2.90 7.00
Conan 2(12/74)-B. Smith-r/#5; Sutton-a(i)(#1 also); Buscema-c 1.00 2.50 6.00
Conan 3-5: 3(4/75)-B. Smith-r/#6; Sutton-a(i). 4(6/75)-B. Smith-r/#7. 5(1975)-B. Smith-r/#14,15; Kirby-c 1.50 3.75
Creatures 1(5/74, 52 pgs.)-Werewolf app; 1st app. Tigra (formerly Cat); Crandall-r; becomes Giant-Size Werewolf w/#2 1.50 3.75
Daredevil 1(1975) 1.20 2.90 7.00
Defenders 1(7/74)-Silver Surfer app.; Starlin-a; Ditko, Everett & Kirby reprints 1.70 4.20 10.00
Defenders 2(10/74, 68 pgs.)-New G. Kane-c/a(p); Son of Satan app.; Sub-Mariner-r by Everett; Ditko-r/Strange Tales #119 (Dr. Strange) 1.00 2.50 6.00
Defenders 3-5: 3(1/75)-Newton, Starlin-a; Ditko, Everett-r. 4(4/75)-Ditko, Everett-r; G. Kane-c. 5-(7/75)-Guardians app. 1.00 2.00 5.00
Doc Savage 1(1975, 68 pgs.)-r/#1,2; Mooney-r 1.50 3.75
Doctor Strange 1(11/75)-Reprints stories from Strange Tales #164-168; Lawrence, Tuska-r 1.00 2.50 6.00
Dracula 2(9/74, 50¢)-Formerly Giant-Size Chillers 1.00 2.00 5.00
Dracula 3(12/74)-Fox-r/Uncanny Tales #6 1.50 3.75
Dracula 4(3/75)-Ditko-r(2) 1.10 2.75
Dracula 5(6/75)-1st Byrne art at Marvel 1.00 2.50 6.00
Fantastic Four 2-4: 2(8/74)-Formerly Giant-Size Super-Stars; Ditko-r. 3(11/74). 4(2/75)-1st Madrox; 2-4-All have Buscema-a 1.50 3.80 9.00
Fantastic Four 5,6: 5(5/75)-All-r; Kirby, G. Kane-r. 6(10/75)-All-r; Kirby-r 1.20 2.90 7.00
Hulk 1(1975) 1.70 5.00 12.00
Invaders 1(6/75, 50¢, 68 pgs.)-Origin; G.A. Sub-Mariner-r/Sub-Mariner #1; intro Master Man 1.00 2.50 6.00
Iron Man 1(1975)-Ditko reprint 1.50 3.80 9.00
Kid Colt 1-3: 1(1/75). 2(4/75). 3(7/75) 1.50 3.75
Man-Thing 1(8/74)-New Ploog-c/a (25 pgs.); Ditko-r/Amazing Adv. #11; Kirby-r/ Strange Tales Ann. #2 & T.O.S. #15; (#1-5 all have new Man-Thing stories, pre-hero-r & are 68 pgs.) 1.00 2.50 6.00
Man-Thing 2,3: 2(11/74)-Buscema-c/a(p); Kirby, Powell-r. 3(2/75)-Alcala-a; Ditko, Kirby, Sutton-r; Gil Kane-c 1.50 3.75
Man-Thing 4,5: 4(5/75)-Howard the Duck by Brunner-c/a; Ditko-r. 5(8/75)-Howard the Duck by Brunner (p); Dracaula cameo in Howard the Duck; Buscema-a(p); Sutton-a(i); G. Kane-c 1.00 2.50 6.00
Marvel Triple Action 1,2: 1(5/75). 2(7/75) 1.10 2.75
Master of Kung Fu 1(9/74)-Russell-a; Yellow Claw-r in #1-4; Gulacy-a in #1,2 1.20 2.90 7.00
Master of Kung Fu 2(12/74)-r/Yellow Claw #1 1.70 4.25
Master of Kung Fu 3(3/75)-Gulacy-a 1.50 3.75
Master of Kung Fu 4(6/75) 1.50 3.75
Power Man 1(1975) 1.00 2.50 6.00
Spider-Man 1(7/74)-Kirby/Ditko, Byrne-r plus new-a (Dracula-c/story) 3.30 10.00 23.00
Spider-Man 2,3: 2(10/74). 3(1/75)-Byrne-r 1.50 3.80 9.00
Spider-Man 4(4/75)-3rd Punisher app.; Byrne, Ditko-r 9.00 27.00 64.00
Spider-Man 5,6: 5(7/75)-Byrne-r. 6(9/75) 1.30 3.00 8.00
Super-Heroes Featuring Spider-Man 1(6/74, 35¢, 52 pgs.)-Spider-Man vs. Man-Wolf; Morbius, the Living Vampire app.; Ditko-r; G. Kane-a(p); Spidey villains app. 6.00 18.00 42.00
Super-Stars 1(5/74, 35¢, 52 pgs.)-Fantastic Four; Thing vs. Hulk; Kirbyish-c/a by Buckler/Sinnott; F.F. villains profiled; becomes Giant-Size Fantastic Four #2 on 2.00 6.00 14.00
Super-Villain Team-Up 1(3/75, 68 pgs.)-Craig-r(i) (Also see Fantastic Four #6 for 1st super-villain team-up) 1.20 2.90 7.00
Super-Villain Team-Up 2(6/75, 68 pgs.)-Dr. Doom, Sub-Mariner app.; Spider-Man-r/Amazing Spider-Man #8 by Ditko; Sekowsky-a(p) 1.00 2.00 5.00
Thor 1(7/75) 1.00 2.50 6.00
Werewolf 2(10/74, 68 pgs.)-Formerly Giant-Size Creatures; Ditko-r; Frankenstein app. 1.50 3.75
Werewolf 3,5: 3(1/75, 68 pgs.). 5(7/75, 68 pgs.) 1.50 3.75
Werewolf 4(4/75, 68 pgs.)-Morbius the Living Vampire app. 1.90 4.75
X-Men 1(Summer, 1975, 50¢, 68 pgs.)-1st app. new X-Men; intro Nightcrawler, Storm, Colossus & Thunderbird; 2nd full app. Wolverine after Incredible Hulk #181 36.00 110.00 250.00
X-Men 2(11/75)-N. Adams-r (51 pgs) 4.30 12.90 30.00

GIANT SPECTACULAR COMICS (See Archie All-Star Special under Archie Comics)

GIANT SUMMER FUN BOOK (See Terry-Toons...)

G. I. COMBAT
Oct, 1952 - No. 43, Dec, 1956
Quality Comics Group

	GD25	FN65	NM94
1-Crandall-c; Cuidera a-1-43i	41.00	122.00	285.00
2	16.50	50.00	115.00
3-5,10-Crandall-c/a	16.00	48.00	110.00
6-Crandall-a	14.00	43.00	100.00
7-9	12.00	36.00	85.00
11-20	10.00	30.00	65.00
21-31,33,35-43	8.35	25.00	50.00
32-Nuclear attack-c/story "Atomic Rocket Assault"	10.00	30.00	65.00
34-Crandall-a	9.15	27.50	55.00

G. I. COMBAT (See DC Special Series #22)
No. 44, Jan, 1957 - No. 288, Mar, 1987
National Periodical Publications/DC Comics

	GD25	FN65	NM94
44-Grey tone-c	29.00	87.00	250.00
45	20.00	60.00	140.00
46-50	14.00	43.00	100.00
51-60: 51-Grey tone-c	11.00	34.00	80.00
61-66,68-80: 75-109-Grey tone-c	7.90	24.00	55.00
67-1st Tank Killer	10.00	30.00	70.00
81,82,84-86,88-90: 90-Last 10¢ issue	6.00	18.00	42.00
83-1st Big Al, Little Al, & Charlie Cigar	6.60	20.00	46.00
87-1st Haunted Tank	21.00	64.00	150.00
91-100: 91-1st Haunted Tank-c	4.60	14.00	32.00
101-110: 108-1st Sgt. Rock x-over. 109-Grey tone-c	3.90	11.60	27.00
111-113,115-120: 113-Grey tone-c	3.10	9.40	22.00
114-Origin Haunted Tank	7.40	22.00	52.00
121-137,139,140: 121-1st app. Sgt. Rock's father. 136-Last 12¢ issue	2.90	8.60	20.00
138-Intro. The Losers (Capt. Storm, Gunner/Sarge, Johnny Cloud) in Haunted Tank (10-11/69)	2.90	9.00	20.00
141-200: 146-148-(25¢, 68 pgs.). 149-154-(52 pgs.). 150-Ice Cream Soldier story (tells how he got his name). 151-Capt. Storm story. 151,153-Medal of Honor series by Maurer	1.00	2.00	5.00

201-281: 201-245,247-259 are $1.00 size. 232-Origin Kana the Ninja. 244-Death of Slim Stryker; 1st app. The Mercenaries. 246-(76 pgs., $1.50)-30th Anniversary issue. 257-Intro. Stuart's Raiders. 260-Begin $1.25, 52 pg.

G.I. Joe V2#6 © Hasbro

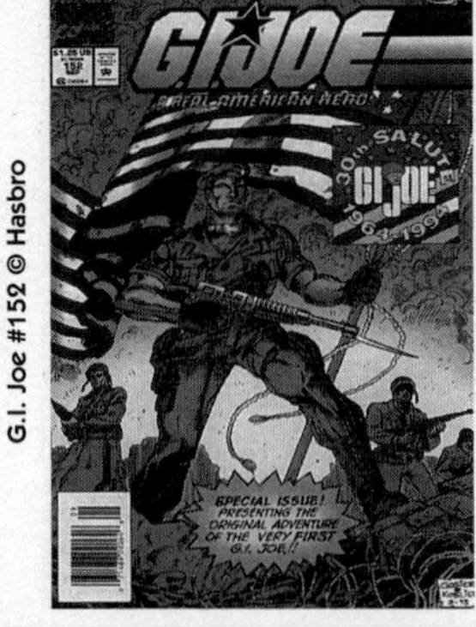

G.I. Joe #152 © Hasbro

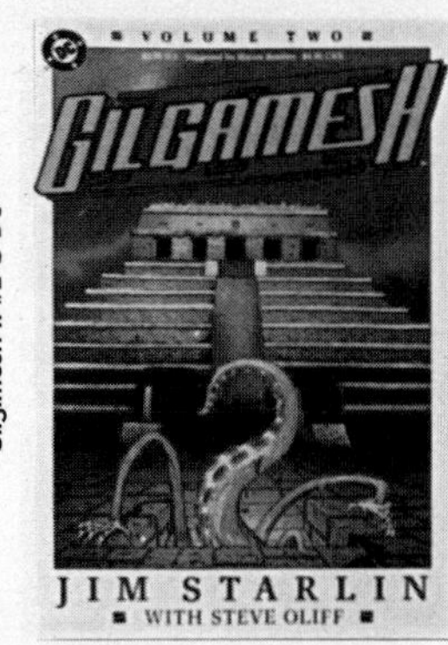

Gilgimesh II #2 © DC

GD25 FN65 NM94

issues, end #281. 264-Intro Sgt. Bullet; origin Kana. 269-Intro. The Bravos of Vietnam 1.20 3.00
282-288 (75¢): 282-New advs. begin 1.20 3.00

NOTE: ***N. Adams** c-168, 201, 202. **Check** a-168, 173. **Drucker** a-48, 61, 63, 66, 71, 72, 76, 134, 140, 141, 144, 147, 148, 153. **Evans** a-135, 138, 158, 164, 166, 201, 202, 204, 205, 215, 256. Giffen a-267. **Glanzman** a-most issues. **Kubert/Heath** a-most issues; **Kubert** covers most issues. **Morrow** a-159-161(2 pgs.). **Redondo** a-189, 240i, 243i. **Sekowsky** a-162p. **Severin** a-147, 152, 154. **Simonson** c-169. **Thorne** a-152, 156. **Wildey** a-153. Johnny Cloud app.-112, 115, 120. Mlle. Marie app.-123, 132, 200. Sgt. Rock app.-111-113, 115, 120, 125, 141, 146, 147, 149, 200. USS Stevens by **Glanzman**-145, 150-153, 157. **Grandenetti** c-44-48.*

G. I. COMICS (Also see Jeep & Overseas Comics)
1945 - No. 73?, 1946 (Distributed to U. S. armed forces)
Giveaways

1-73-Contains Prince Valiant by Foster, Blondie, Smilin' Jack, Mickey Finn, Terry & the Pirates, Donald Duck, Alley Oop, Moon Mullins & Capt. Easy strip reprints (at least 73 issues known to exist) 4.00 12.00 28.00

GIDGET (TV)
April, 1966 - No. 2, Dec, 1966
Dell Publishing Co.

1,2: 1-Sally Field photo-c 7.50 22.50 45.00

GIFT (See The Crusaders)

GIFT COMICS (50¢)
1942 - No. 4, 1949 (No. 1-3: 50¢, 324 pgs.; No. 4: 25¢, 152 pgs.)
Fawcett Publications

1-Captain Marvel, Bulletman, Golden Arrow, Ibis the Invincible, Mr. Scarlet, & Spy Smasher begin. Not rebound, remaindered comics, printed at same time as originals 175.00 525.00 1750.00
2-Commando Yank, Phantom Eagle, others app. 120.00 360.00 1200.00
3 75.00 225.00 750.00
4-The Marvel Family, Captain Marvel, etc.; each issue can vary in contents 50.00 150.00 500.00

GIFTS FROM SANTA (See March of Comics No. 137)

GIGGLE COMICS (Spencer Spook No. 100) (Also see Ha Ha Comics)
Oct, 1943 - No. 99, Jan-Feb, 1955
Creston No.1-63/American Comics Group No. 64 on

1-Funny animal 23.00 70.00 160.00
2 11.00 32.00 75.00
3-5: Ken Hultgren-a begins? 8.35 25.00 50.00
6-10: 9-1st Superkatt (6/44) 6.70 20.00 40.00
11-20 5.00 15.00 30.00
21-40: 32-Patriotic-c. 37,61-X-Mas-c. 39-St. Valentine's Day-c 4.00 12.00 24.00
41-54,56-59,61-99: 95-Spencer Spook begins? 4.00 10.00 20.00
55,60-Milt Gross-a 4.70 14.00 28.00

G-I IN BATTLE (G-I No. 1 only)
Aug, 1952 - No. 9, July, 1953; Mar, 1957 - No. 6, May, 1958
Ajax-Farrell Publ./Four Star

1 6.35 19.00 38.00
2 4.00 10.00 20.00
3-9 3.20 8.00 16.00
Annual 1(1952, 25¢, 100 pgs.) 17.00 52.00 120.00
1(1957-Ajax) 4.00 12.00 24.00
2-6 2.80 7.00 14.00

G. I. JANE
May, 1953 - No. 11, Mar, 1955 (Misdated 3/54)
Stanhall/Merit No. 11

1-PX Pete begins; Bill Williams-c/a 8.35 25.00 50.00
2-7(5/54) 4.20 12.50 25.00
8-10(12/54, Stanhall) 4.00 10.00 20.00
11 (3/55, Merit) 3.20 8.00 16.00

G. I. JOE (Also see Advs. of..., Showcase #53, 54 & The Yardbirds)
No. 10, 1950; No. 11, 4-5/51 - No. 51, 6/57 (52pgs.: 10-14,6-17?)
Ziff-Davis Publ. Co. (Korean War)

10(#1, 1950)-Saunders painted-c begin 9.15 27.50 55.00
11-14(#2-5, 10/51): 11-New logo. 12-New logo 5.85 17.50 35.00
V2#6(12/51)-17-(11/52; Last 52 pgs.?) 5.00 15.00 30.00
18-(25¢, 100 pg. Giant, 12-1/52-53) 12.00 36.00 85.00
19-30: 20-22,24,28-31-The Yardbirds app. 4.00 12.00 24.00
31-47,49-51 4.00 11.00 22.00
48-Atom bomb story 4.00 12.00 24.00

NOTE: ***Powell** a-V2#7, 8, 11. **Norman Saunders** painted c-10-14, V2#6-14, 26, 30, 31, 35, 38, 39. **Tuska** a-7. Bondage c-29, 35, 38.*

G. I. JOE (America's Movable Fighting Man)
1967 (36 pgs.) (5-1/8x8-3/8")
Custom Comics

nn-Schaffenberger-a; based on Hasbro toy 1.00

G. I. JOE AND THE TRANSFORMERS
Jan, 1987 - No. 4, Apr, 1987 (Mini-series)
Marvel Comics Group

1-4 1.00

G. I. JOE, A REAL AMERICAN HERO (...Starring Snake-Eyes on-c #135 on)
June, 1982 - No. 155, Dec, 1994
Marvel Comics Group

1-Printed on Baxter paper; based on Hasbro toy 1.90 4.75
2-Printed on reg. paper 1.80 4.50
3-10 1.10 2.75
11-20: 11-Intro Airborne 1.50
21,22,26,27: 26,27-Origin Snake-Eyes parts 1 & 2 .70 1.80
23-25,28-30 .70 1.70
31-134,139-143: 33-New headquarters. 60-Todd McFarlane-a. 139-142-New Transformers app. 1.50
135-138-($1.75)-Polybagged w/trading card .60 1.60
144-149,151-155-($1.25): 144-Origin Snake-Eyes 1.25
All 2nd printings 1.00
150-($2.00, 52 pgs.) .80 2.00
Special Treasury Edition (1982)-r/#1 1.20 3.00
...Yearbook 1 (3/85)-r/#1; Golden-c .80 2.00
...Yearbook 2 (3/86)-Golden-c/a , 3(3/87, 68 pgs.) .70 1.80
...Yearbook 4 (2/88) 1.50

NOTE: ***Golden** c-23, 29, 34, 36. **Heath** a-24. **Rogers** a(p)-75, 77-82, 84, 86; c-77.*

G. I. JOE COMICS MAGAZINE
Dec, 1986 - No. 13, 1988 ($1.50, digest-size)
Marvel Comics Group

1-13: G.I. Joe-r 1.50

G.I. JOE EUROPEAN MISSIONS (Action Force in indicia)
June, 1988 - No. 15, Dec, 1989 ($1.50/$1.75 #12 on)
Marvel Comics Ltd. (British)

1-15: Reprints Action Force 1.50

G. I. JOE ORDER OF BATTLE, THE
Dec, 1986 - No. 4, Mar, 1987 (Mini-series)
Marvel Comics Group

1-4 1.00

G. I. JOE SPECIAL MISSIONS (Indicia title: Special Missions)
Oct, 1986 - No. 28, Dec, 1989 ($1.00)
Marvel Comics Group

1-28 1.00

G. I. JUNIORS (See Harvey Hits No. 86, 91, 95, 98, 101, 104, 107, 110, 112, 114, 116, 118, 120, 122)

GILGAMESH II
1989 - No. 4, 1989 ($3.95, mini-series, prestige format)
DC Comics

1-4: Starlin-c/a, scripts; mature readers 1.60 4.00

GIL THORP

Ginger #5 © AP

Give Me Liberty #3 © Frank Miller

Gizmo #1 © Mirage Studios

	GD25	FN65	NM94

May-July, 1963
Dell Publishing Co.

	GD25	FN65	NM94
1-Caniffish-a	3.20	8.00	16.00

GINGER (Li'l Jinx No. 11 on?)
1951 - No. 10, Summer, 1954
Archie Publications

	GD25	FN65	NM94
1-Teenage humor	11.00	32.00	75.00
2-(1952)	6.70	20.00	40.00
3-6: 6-(Sum/53)	4.70	14.00	28.00
7-10-Katy Keene app.	7.00	21.00	42.00

GINGER FOX (Also see The World of Ginger Fox)
Sept, 1988 - No. 4, Dec, 1988 ($1.75, color, mini-series)
Comico

	GD25	FN65	NM94
1-4: 1-4-part photo-c		.70	1.75

G.I. R.A.M.B.O.T.
April, 1987 - No. 2? ($1.95, color)
Wonder Color Comics/Pied Piper #2

	GD25	FN65	NM94
1,2: 2-Exist?		.80	2.00

GIRL COMICS (Becomes Girl Confessions No. 13 on)
Oct, 1949 - No. 12, Jan, 1952 (Photo-c 1-4) (#1-4: 52 pgs.)
Marvel/Atlas Comics(CnPC)

	GD25	FN65	NM94
1	13.00	40.00	90.00
2-Kubert-a	8.35	25.00	50.00
3-Everett-a; Liz Taylor photo-c	10.00	30.00	65.00
4-11: 10-12-Sol Brodsky-c	5.85	17.50	35.00
12-Krigstein-a; Al Hartley-c	7.50	22.50	45.00

GIRL CONFESSIONS (Formerly Girl Comics)
No. 13, Mar, 1952 - No. 35, Aug, 1954
Atlas Comics (CnPC/ZPC)

	GD25	FN65	NM94
13-Everett-a	8.00	24.00	48.00
14,15,19,20	5.00	15.00	30.00
16-18-Everett-a	5.85	17.50	35.00
21-35: Robinson-a	3.60	9.00	18.00

GIRL FROM U.N.C.L.E., THE (TV) (Also see The Man From...)
Jan, 1967 - No. 5, Oct, 1967
Gold Key

	GD25	FN65	NM94
1-McWilliams-a; Stephanie Powers photo front/back-c & pin-ups (no ads, 12¢)	7.50	22.50	45.00
2-5-Leonard Swift-Courier No. 5	5.00	15.00	30.00

GIRLS' FUN & FASHION MAGAZINE (Formerly Polly Pigtails)
V5#44, Jan, 1950 - V5#47, July, 1950
Parents' Magazine Institute

	GD25	FN65	NM94
V5#44	4.00	10.00	20.00
45-47	2.40	6.00	12.00

GIRLS IN LOVE
May, 1950 - No. 2, July, 1950
Fawcett Publications

	GD25	FN65	NM94
1,2-Photo-c	6.70	20.00	40.00

GIRLS IN LOVE (Formerly G. I. Sweethearts No. 45)
No. 46, Sept, 1955 - No. 57, Dec, 1956
Quality Comics Group

	GD25	FN65	NM94
46	4.70	14.00	28.00
47-56: 54- 'Commie' story	3.60	9.00	18.00
57-Matt Baker-c/a	5.00	15.00	30.00

GIRLS IN WHITE (See Harvey Comics Hits No. 58)

GIRLS' LIFE (Patsy Walker's Own Magazine For Girls!)
Jan, 1954 - No. 6, Nov, 1954
Atlas Comics (BFP)

	GD25	FN65	NM94
1	7.50	22.50	45.00
2-Al Hartley-c	4.00	11.00	22.00
3-6	3.60	9.00	18.00

GIRLS' LOVE STORIES
Aug-Sept, 1949 - No. 180, Nov-Dec, 1973 (No. 1-13: 52 pgs.)
National Comics(Signal Publ. No. 9-65/Arleigh No. 83-117)

	GD25	FN65	NM94
1-Toth, Kinstler-a, 8 pgs. each; photo-c	39.00	118.00	275.00
2-Kinstler-a?	22.00	65.00	150.00
3-10: 1-9-Photo-c. 7-Infantino-c(p)	13.00	40.00	90.00
11-20	10.00	30.00	70.00
21-33: 21-Kinstler-a. 33-Last pre-code (1-2/55)	7.50	22.50	45.00
34-50	6.35	19.00	38.00
51-99: 83-Last 10¢ issue	4.20	12.50	25.00
100	4.70	14.00	28.00
101-146: 113-117-April O'Day app.	2.40	6.00	12.00
147-151- "Confessions" serial	1.30	3.25	8.00
152-180: 161-170, 52 pgs.	1.00	2.00	5.00

GIRLS' ROMANCES
Feb-Mar, 1950 - No. 160, Oct, 1971 (No. 1-11: 52 pgs.)
National Periodical Publ.(Signal Publ. No. 7-79/Arleigh No. 84)

	GD25	FN65	NM94
1-Photo-c	39.00	118.00	275.00
2-Photo-c; Toth-a	20.00	60.00	140.00
3-10: 3-6-Photo-c	13.00	40.00	90.00
11,12,14-20	10.00	30.00	65.00
13-Toth-c	11.00	32.00	75.00
21-31: 31-Last pre-code (2-3/55)	6.35	19.00	38.00
32-50	5.35	16.00	32.00
51-99: 80-Last 10¢ issue	4.00	11.00	22.00
100	4.35	13.00	26.00
101-108,110-120	2.10	6.50	15.00
109-Beatles-c/story	6.40	19.00	45.00
121-133,135-140	1.30	3.25	8.00
134-Neal Adams-c (splash pg. is same as-c)	1.70	4.20	10.00
141-160: 159,160-52 pgs.	1.00	2.00	5.00

G. I. SWEETHEARTS (Formerly Diary Loves; Girls In Love #46 on)
No. 32, June, 1953 - No. 45, May, 1955
Quality Comics Group

	GD25	FN65	NM94
32	4.70	14.00	28.00
33-45: 44-Last pre-code (3/55)	3.60	9.00	18.00

G.I. TALES (Formerly Sgt. Barney Barker No. 1-3)
No. 4, Feb, 1957 - No. 6, July, 1957
Atlas Comics (MCI)

	GD25	FN65	NM94
4-Severin-a(4)	5.00	15.00	30.00
5	4.00	10.00	20.00
6-Orlando, Powell, & Woodbridge-a	4.00	11.00	22.00

GIVE ME LIBERTY (Dark Horse)(Value: cover or less)

G. I. WAR BRIDES
April, 1954 - No. 8, June, 1955
Superior Publishers Ltd.

	GD25	FN65	NM94
1	4.70	14.00	28.00
2	2.80	7.00	14.00
3-8: 4-Kamenesque-a; lingerie panels	2.00	5.00	10.00

G. I. WAR TALES
Mar-Apr, 1973 - No. 4, Oct-Nov, 1973
National Periodical Publications

	GD25	FN65	NM94
1-4: Reprints. 2-N. Adams-a(r), 4-Krigstein-a(r)			1.00

NOTE: ***Drucker*** *a-3r, 4r.* ***Heath*** *a-4r.* ***Kubert*** *a-2, 3; c-4r.*

GIZMO (Also see Domino Chance)
May-June, 1985 (B&W, one shot)
Chance Ent.

	GD25	FN65	NM94
1	1.00	2.00	5.00

GIZMO

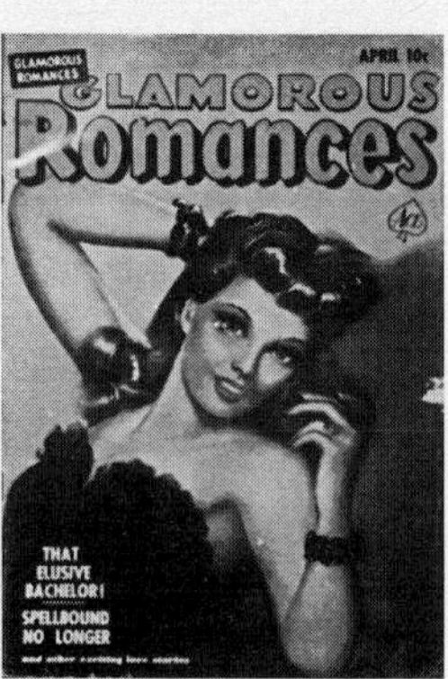

Glamorous Romances #60 © ACE

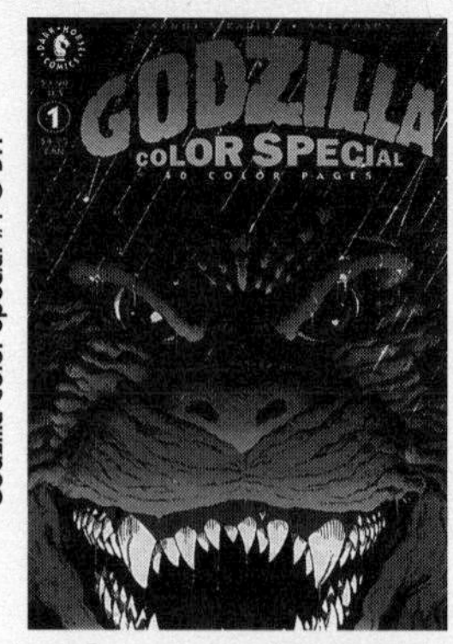

Godzilla Color Special #1 © DH

Golden Age #1 © DC

GD25 FN65 NM94

1986 - No. 6, July, 1987 ($1.50, B&W)
Mirage Studios

1 1.60 4.00
2-6 1.00 2.50

GLADSTONE COMIC ALBUM (Also see The Original Dick Tracy Comic...)
1987 - No. 28, 1990 (8-1/2x11")($5.95)(#26-28: $9.95)
Gladstone

1-10: 1-Uncle Scrooge; Barks-r; Beck-c. 2-Donald Duck; r/F.C. #108 by Barks. 3-Mickey Mouse-r by Gottfredson. 4-Uncle Scrooge; r/F.C. #456 by Barks w/ unedited story. 5-Donald Duck Advs.; r/F.C. #199. 6-Uncle Scrooge-r by Barks. 7-Donald Duck-r by Barks. 8-Mickey Mouse-r. 9-Bambi; r/F.C. #186? 10-Donald Duck Advs.; r/F.C. #275 1.00 2.50 6.00
11-20: 11-Uncle Scrooge; r/U.S. #4. 12-Donald And Daisy; r/F.C. #1055, WDC&S. 13-Donald Duck Advs.; r/F.C. #408. 14-Uncle Scrooge; Barks-r/ U.S #21. 15-Donald And Gladstone; Barks-r. 16-Donald Duck Advs.; r/F.C. #238. 17-Mickey Mouse strip-r (The World of Tomorrow, The Pirate Ghost Ship). 18-Donald Duck and the Junior Woodchucks; Barks-r. 19-Uncle Scrooge; r/U.S. #12; Rosa-c. 20-Uncle Scrooge; r/F.C. #386; Barks-c/a(r) 1.00 2.50 6.00
21-25: 21-Donald Duck Family; Barks-c/a(r). 22-Mickey Mouse strip-r. 23-Donald Duck; Barks-r/D.D. #26 w/unedited story. 24-Uncle Scrooge; Barks-r; Rosa-c. 25-D. Duck; Barks-c/a-r/F.C. #367 1.00 2.50 6.00
26-28: 26-Mickey and Donald; Gottfredson-c/a(r). 27-Donald Duck; r/WDC&S by Barks; Barks painted-c. 28-Uncle Scrooge & Donald Duck; Rosa-c/a (4 stories) 1.65 4.00 10.00
Special 1 (1989, $9.95)-Donald Duck Finds Pirate Gold; r/F.C. #9 1.65 4.00 10.00
Special 2 (1989, $8.95)-Uncle Scrooge and Donald Duck; Barks-r/Uncle Scrooge #5; Rosa-c 1.50 3.75 9.00
Special 3 (1989, $8.95)-Mickey Mouse strip-r 1.50 3.75 9.00
Special 4 (1989, $11.95)-Uncle Scrooge; Rosa-c/a-r/Son of the Sun from U.S. #219 plus Barks-r/U.S. 1.70 5.00 12.00
Special 5 (1990, $11.95)-Donald Duck Advs.; Barks-r/F.C. #282 & 422 plus Barks painted-c 1.70 5.00 12.00
Special 6 (1990, $12.95)-Uncle Scrooge; Barks-c/a-r/Uncle Scrooge 1.85 5.50 13.00
Special 7 (1990, $13.95)-Mickey Mouse; Gottfredson strip-r 2.00 6.00 14.00

GLAMOROUS ROMANCES (Formerly Dotty)
No. 41, July, 1949 - No. 90, Oct, 1956 (Photo-c 68-90)
Ace Magazines (A. A. Wyn)

41-Dotty app. 5.85 17.50 35.00
42-72,74-80: 44-Begin 52 pg. issues. 45,50-61-Painted-c. 80-Last pre-code (2/55) 3.60 9.00 18.00
73-L.B. Cole-r/All Love #27 4.00 10.00 20.00
81-90 3.00 7.50 15.00

GLOBAL FORCE (Silverline)(Value: cover or less)

GNOME MOBILE, THE (See Movie Comics)

GOBBLEDYGOOK
1984 - No. 2, 1984 (B&W)(1st Mirage comic, published at same time)
Mirage Studios

1,2-(24 pgs.)-1st Teenage Mutant Ninja Turtles 29.00 86.00 200.00

GOBBLEDYGOOK
Dec, 1986 (One shot, $3.50, B&W, 100 pgs.)
Mirage Studios

1-New 8 pg. TMNT story plus a Donatello/Michaelangelo 7 pg. story & a Gizmo story; Corben-i(r)/TMNT #7 1.60 4.00

GOBLIN, THE
June, 1982 - No. 4, Dec, 1982 (Magazine, $2.25)
Warren Publishing Co.

1-The Gremlin app; Golden-a(p) .90 2.25
2-4: 2-1st Hobgoblin .90 2.25

GD25 FN65 NM94

GODFATHERS, THE (See The Crusaders)

GOD IS (Spire Christian)(Value: cover or less)

GODS FOR HIRE (Hot Comics)(Value; cover or less)

GOD'S HEROES IN AMERICA
1956 (nn) (68 pgs.) (25-35¢)
Catechetical Guild Educational Society

307 1.60 4.00 8.00

GOD'S SMUGGLER (Spire Christian)(Value: cover or less)

GODZILLA
August, 1977 - No. 24, July, 1979 (Based on movie series)
Marvel Comics Group

1-Mooney-i 1.00 2.50 6.00
2-10: 2-Tuska-i. 3-Champions app.(w/o Ghost Rider). 4,5-Sutton-a 1.60 4.00
11-24: 14-Shield app. 20-F.F. app. 21,22-Devil Dinosaur app. 1.10 2.75

GODZILLA
May, 1988 - No. 6, 1988 ($1.95, B&W, mini-series)
Dark Horse Comics

1 .90 2.30 5.50
2-6 1.10 2.75
...Collection (1990, $10.95)-r/1-6 with new-c 1.65 4.70 11.00
...Color Special 1 (Sum, 1992, $3.50, color, 44 pgs.)-Arthur Adams wrap-around-c/a & part scripts 1.40 3.50
...King Of The Monsters Special (8/87, $1.50)-Origin; Bissette-c/a 1.10 2.75
...Vs. Barkley nn (12/93, $2.95, color)-Dorman painted-c 1.20 3.00

GO-GO
June, 1966 - No. 9, Oct, 1967
Charlton Comics

1-Miss Bikini Luv begins; Rolling Stones, Beatles, Elvis, Sonny & Cher, Bob Dylan, Sinatra, parody; Herman's Hermits pin-ups; D'Agostino-c/a in #1-8 3.70 11.00 26.00
2-Ringo Starr, David McCallum & Beatles photos on cover; Beatles story and photos 3.70 11.00 26.00
3,4: 3-Blooperman begins, ends #6; 1 pg. Batman & Robin satire; full pg. photo pin-ups Lovin' Spoonful & The Byrds 2.30 6.90 16.00
5-9: 5-Super Hero & TV satire by Jim Aparo & Grass Green begins. 6-8-Aparo-a. 6-Petula Clark photo-c. 7-Photo of Brian Wilson of Beach Boys on-c & Beach Boys photo inside f/b-c. 8-Monkees photo on-c & photo inside f/b-c; 9-Aparo-c/a 2.30 6.90 16.00

GO-GO AND ANIMAL (See Tippy's Friends...)

GOING STEADY (Formerly Teen-Age Temptations)
No. 10, Dec, 1954 - No. 13, June, 1955; No. 14, Oct, 1955
St. John Publishing Co.

10(1954)-Matt Baker-c/a 10.00 30.00 70.00
11(2/55, last precode), 12(4/55)-Baker-c 6.70 20.00 40.00
13(6/55)-Baker-c/a 7.50 22.50 45.00
14(10/55)-Matt Baker-c/a, 25 pgs. 8.35 25.00 50.00

GOING STEADY (Formerly Personal Love)
V3#3, Feb, 1960 - V3#6, Aug, 1960; V4#1, Sept-Oct, 1960
Prize Publications/Headline

V3#3-6, V4#1 2.00 5.00 10.00

GOING STEADY WITH BETTY (Becomes Betty & Her Steady No. 2)
Nov-Dec, 1949
Avon Periodicals

1 10.00 30.00 65.00

GOLDEN AGE, THE
1993 - No. 4, 1994 ($4.95, mini-series)
DC Comics

Golden Arrow #1 © FAW

Golden Lad #1 © Spark

Golden Picture Story Book #3 © WDC

GD25 FN65 NM94

1-4-Gold foil embossed-c: Elseworlds storyline 1.10 2.10 5.25

GOLDEN ARROW (See Fawcett Miniatures, Mighty Midget & Whiz Comics)

GOLDEN ARROW (...Western No. 6)
Spring, 1942 - No. 6, Spring, 1947 (68 pgs.)
Fawcett Publications

1-Golden Arrow begins 46.00 137.00 320.00
2-(1943) 16.00 48.00 110.00
3-5: 3-(Win/45-46). 4-(Spr/46). 5-(Fall/46) 10.00 30.00 65.00
6-Krigstein-a 10.00 30.00 70.00
...Well Known Comics (1944; 12 pgs.; 8-1/2x10-1/2"; paper-c; glued binding)-Bestmaid/Samuel Lowe giveaway; printed in green 7.50 22.50 45.00

GOLDEN COMICS DIGEST
May, 1969 - No. 48, Jan, 1976
Gold Key
NOTE: *Whitman editions exist of many titles and are generally valued less.*

1-Tom & Jerry, Woody Woodpecker, Bugs Bunny 2.40 6.00 12.00
2-Hanna-Barbera TV Fun Favorites; Space Ghost, Flintstones, Atom Ant, Jetsons, Yogi Bear, Banana Splits, others app. 2.30 6.90 16.00
3-Tom & Jerry, Woody Woodpecker 1.00 2.50 6.00
4-Tarzan; Manning & Marsh-a 2.30 6.90 16.00
5,8-Tom & Jerry, W. Woodpecker, Bugs Bunny 1.00 2.00 5.00
6-Bugs Bunny 1.00 2.00 5.00
7-Hanna-Barbera TV Fun Favorites 1.70 4.20 10.00
9-Tarzan 2.00 6.00 14.00
10-17: 10-Bugs Bunny. 11-Hanna-Barbera TV Fun Favorites. 12-Tom & Jerry, Bugs Bunny, W. Woodpecker Journey to the Sun. 13-Tom & Jerry. 14-Bugs Bunny Fun Packed Funnies. 15-Tom & Jerry, Woody Woodpecker, Bugs Bunny. 16-Woody Woodpecker Cartoon Special. 17-Bugs Bunny 1.00 2.00 5.00
18-Tom & Jerry; Barney Bear-r by Barks 1.00 2.50 6.00
19-Little Lulu 2.00 6.00 14.00
20-22: 20-Woody Woodpecker Falltime Funtime. 21-Bugs Bunny Showtime. 22-Tom & Jerry Winter Wingding 1.00 2.00 5.00
23-Little Lulu & Tubby Fun Fling 2.00 6.00 14.00
24-26,28: 24-Woody Woodpecker Fun Festival. 25-Tom & Jerry. 26-Bugs Bunny Halloween Hulla-Boo-Loo; Dr. Spektor article, also #25. 28-Tom & Jerry 1.00 2.00 5.00
27-Little Lulu & Tubby in Hawaii 1.65 4.70 11.00
29-Little Lulu & Tubby 1.65 4.70 11.00
30-Bugs Bunny Vacation Funnies 1.00 2.00 5.00
31-Turok, Son of Stone; r/4-Color #596,656; c-r/#9 2.00 6.00 14.00
32-Woody Woodpecker Summer Fun 1.00 2.00 5.00
33,36: 33-Little Lulu & Tubby Halloween Fun; Dr. Spektor app. 36-Little Lulu & Her Friends 2.00 6.00 14.00
34,35,37-39: 34-Bugs Bunny Winter Funnies. 35-Tom & Jerry Snowtime Funtime. 37-Woody Woodpecker County Fair. 38-The Pink Panther. 39-Bugs Bunny Summer Fun 1.00 2.00 5.00
40,43: 40-Little Lulu & Tubby Trick or Treat; all by Stanley. 43-Little Lulu in Paris 2.00 6.00 14.00
41,42,44,45,47: 41-Tom & Jerry Winter Carnival. 42-Bugs Bunny. 44-Woody Woodpecker Family Fun Festival. 45-The Pink Panther. 47-Bugs Bunny 1.60 4.00
46-Little Lulu & Tubby 1.65 4.70 11.00
48-The Lone Ranger 1.00 2.50 6.00
NOTE: *#1-30, 164 pgs.; #31 on, 132 pgs..*

GOLDEN LAD
July, 1945 - No. 5, June, 1946 (#4, 5: 52 pgs.)
Spark Publications

1-Origin & 1st app. Golden Lad & Swift Arrow; Sandusky and the Senator begins 49.00 146.00 340.00
2-Mort Meskin-c/a 24.00 73.00 170.00
3,4-Mort Meskin-c/a 20.00 60.00 140.00
5-Origin/1st Golden Girl; Shaman & Flame app. 24.00 73.00 170.00
NOTE: *All have* ***Robinson,*** *and* ***Roussos*** *art plus* ***Meskin*** *covers and art.*

GD25 FN65 NM94

GOLDEN LEGACY
1966 - 1972 (Black History) (25¢)
Fitzgerald Publishing Co.

1-Toussaint L'Ouverture (1966), 2-Harriet Tubman (1967), 3-Crispus Attucks & the Minutemen (1967), 4-Benjamin Banneker (1968), 5-Matthew Henson (1969), 6-Alexander Dumas & Family (1969), 7-Frederick Douglass, Part 1 (1969), 8-Frederick Douglass, Part 2 (1970), 9-Robert Smalls (1970), 10-J. Cinque & the Amistad Mutiny (1970), 11-Men in Action: White, Marshall J. Wilkins (1970), 12-Black Cowboys (1972), 13-The Life of Martin Luther King, Jr. (1972), 14-The Life of Alexander Pushkin (1971), 15-Ancient African Kingdoms (1972), 16-Black Inventors (1972)
each.... 1.50
1-10,12,13,15,16(1976)-Reprints 1.00

GOLDEN LOVE STORIES (Formerly Golden West Love)
No. 4, April, 1950
Kirby Publishing Co.

4-Powell-a; Glenn Ford/Janet Leigh photo-c 10.00 30.00 70.00

GOLDEN PICTURE CLASSIC, A
1956-1957 (Text stories w/illustrations in color; 100 pgs. each)
Western Printing Co. (Simon & Shuster)

CL-401: Treasure Island 8.35 25.00 50.00
CL-402: Tom Sawyer 7.00 21.00 42.00
CL-403: Black Beauty 7.00 21.00 42.00
CL-404: Little Women 7.00 21.00 42.00
CL-405: Heidi 7.00 21.00 42.00
CL-406: Ben Hur 4.70 14.00 28.00
CL-407: Around the World in 80 Days 4.70 14.00 28.00
CL-408: Sherlock Holmes 5.85 17.50 35.00
CL-409: The Three Musketeers 4.70 14.00 28.00
CL-410: The Merry Advs. of Robin Hood 4.70 14.00 28.00
CL-411: Hans Brinker 5.85 17.50 35.00
CL-412: The Count of Monte Cristo 5.85 17.50 35.00
(Both soft & hardcover editions are valued the same)
NOTE: *Recent research has uncovered new information. Apparently #s 1-6 were issued in 1956 and #7-12 in 1957. But they can be found in five different series listings: CL-1 to CL-12 (softbound); CL-401 to CL-412 (also softbound); CL-101 to CL-112 (hardbound); plus two new series discoveries: A Golden Reading Adventure, publ. by Golden Press; edited down to 60 pages and reduced in size to 6x9"; only #s discovered so far are #381 (CL-4), #382 (CL-6) & #387 (CL-3). They have no reorder list and some have covers different from GPC. There have also been found British hardbound editions of GPC with dust jackets. Copies of all five listed series vary from scarce to very rare. Some editions of some series have not yet been found at all.*

GOLDEN PICTURE STORY BOOK
Dec, 1961 (52 pgs.; 50¢; large size)(All are scarce)
Racine Press (Western)

ST-1-Huckleberry Hound (TV) 16.00 48.00 110.00
ST-2-Yogi Bear (TV) 16.00 48.00 110.00
ST-3-Babes in Toyland (Walt Disney's...)-Annette Funicello photo-c 22.00 65.00 150.00
ST-4-(...of Disney Ducks)-Walt Disney's Wonderful World of Ducks (Donald Duck, Uncle Scrooge, Donald's Nephews, Grandma Duck, Ludwig Von Drake, & Gyro Gearloose stories) 22.00 65.00 150.00

GOLDEN RECORD COMIC (See Amazing Spider-Man #1, Avengers #4, Fantastic Four #1, Journey Into Mystery #83)

GOLDEN STORY BOOKS
1949 (128pgs, heavy covers; digest size (Illustrated text in color)
Western Printing Co. (Simon & Shuster)

7-Walt Disney's Mystery in Disneyville, a book-length adventure starring Donald and Nephews, Mickey and Nephews, and with Minnie, Daisy and Goofy. Art by Dick Moores & Marvel Gonzales (scarce) 22.00 65.00 150.00
10-Bugs Bunny's Treasure Hunt, a book-length adventure starring Bugs & Porky Pig, with Petunia Pig & Nephew, Cicero. Art by Tom McKimson (scarce) 14.00 43.00 100.00

GOLDEN WEST LOVE (Golden Love Stories No. 4)
Sept-Oct, 1949 - No. 3, Feb, 1950 (All 52 pgs.)
Kirby Publishing Co.

Good Girl Art Quarterly (winter '91) © AC

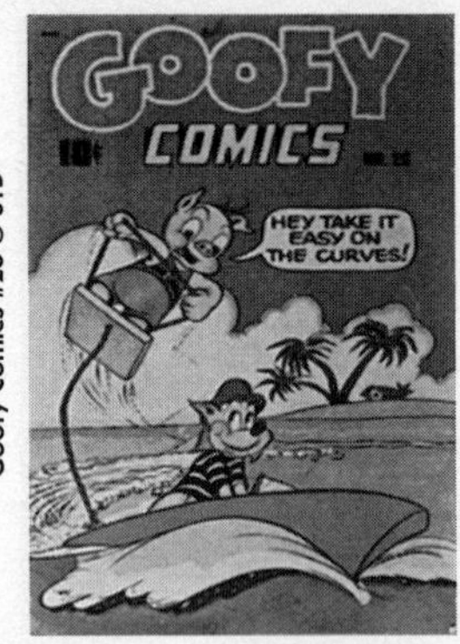

Goofy Comics #26 © STD

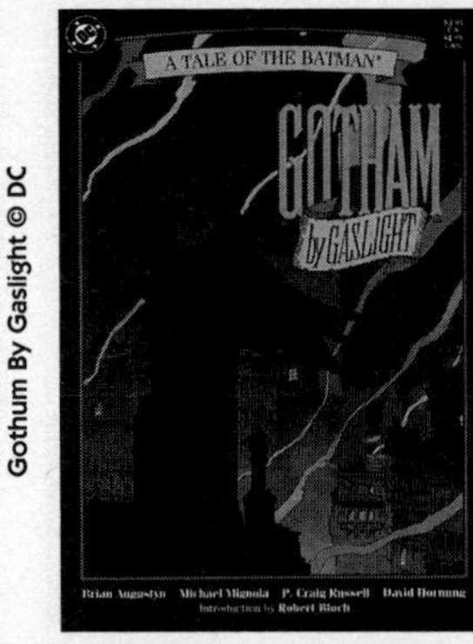

Gothum By Gaslight © DC

	GD25	FN65	NM94
1-Powell-a in all; Roussos-a; painted-c	13.00	40.00	90.00
2,3: Photo-c	10.00	30.00	60.00

GOLDEN WEST RODEO TREASURY (See Dell Giants)

GOLDILOCKS (See March of Comics No. 1)

GOLDILOCKS & THE THREE BEARS
1943 (Giveaway)
K. K. Publications

nn	9.15	27.50	55.00

GOLD KEY CHAMPION
Mar, 1978 - No. 2, May, 1978 (52 pgs.) (50¢)
Gold Key

1-Space Family Robinson; half-r		.80	2.00
2-Mighty Samson; half-r		.80	2.00

GOLD KEY SPOTLIGHT
May, 1976 - No. 11, Feb, 1978
Gold Key

1-Tom, Dick & Harriet		1.60	4.00
2-5,710,11: 2-Wacky Advs. of Cracky. 3-Wacky Witch. 4-Tom, Dick & Harriet. 5-Wacky Advs. of Cracky. 7-Wacky Witch & Greta Ghost 10-O. G. Whiz. 11-Tom, Dick & Harriet		1.20	3.00
6,8,9: 6-Dagar the Invincible; Santos-a; origin Demonomicon. 8-The Occult Files of Dr. Spektor, Simbar, Lu-sai; Santos-a. 9-Tragg		1.60	4.00

GOLD MEDAL COMICS
1945 (25¢, 132 pgs.) (One shot)
Cambridge House

nn-Captain Truth by Fugitani, Crime Detector, The Witch of Salem, Luckyman, others app.	19.00	57.00	130.00

GOMER PYLE (TV)
July, 1966 - No. 3, Jan, 1967
Gold Key

1-Photo front/back-c	5.50	17.00	40.00
2,3	5.00	15.00	35.00

GOODBYE, MR. CHIPS (See Movie Comics)

GOOD GIRL ART QUARTERLY (AC)(Value: cover or less)

GOOD GIRL ART QUARTERLY
Summer, 1990 - Present (Color & B&W, 52 pgs.)
AC Comics

1 ($3.50)-All have one new story (often FemForce) & rest reprints by Baker, Ward & other "good girl" artists		1.40	3.50
2 ($3.95)		1.60	4.00
3-16		1.40	3.50

GOOD GUYS, THE
Nov, 1993 - Present ($2.50, color)
Defiant

1-($3.50, 52 pgs.)-Glory x-over from Plasm		1.40	3.50
2,3,5-11		1.00	2.50
4-($3.25, 52 pgs.)		1.30	3.25

GOOFY (Disney)(See Dynabrite Comics, Mickey Mouse Magazine V4#7, Walt Disney Showcase #35 & Wheaties)
No. 468, May, 1953 - Sept-Nov, 1962
Dell Publishing Co.

4-Color 468 (#1)	14.00	43.00	100.00
4-Color 562,627,658,702,747,802,857	8.35	25.00	50.00
4-Color 899,952,987,1053,1094,1149,1201	5.85	17.50	35.00
12-308-211(Dell, 9-11/62)	5.85	17.50	35.00

GOOFY ADVENTURES
June, 1990 - No. 17, 1991 ($1.50)
Disney Comics

1-17: Most new stories. 2-Joshua Quagmire-a w/free poster. 7-WDC&S-r plus new-a. 9-Gottfredson-r. 14-Super Goof story. 15-All Super Goof issue. 17-Gene Colan-a(p)			1.50

GOOFY ADVENTURE STORY (See 4-Color No. 857)

GOOFY COMICS (Companion to Happy Comics)(Not Disney)
June, 1943 - No. 48, 1953
Nedor Publ. Co. No. 1-14/Standard No. 14-48 (Animated Cartoons)

	GD25	FN65	NM94
1-Funny animal; Oriolo-c	19.00	57.00	130.00
2	10.00	30.00	65.00
3-10	7.50	22.50	45.00
11-19	5.35	16.00	32.00
20-35-Frazetta text illos in all	7.00	21.00	42.00
36-48	4.00	12.00	24.00

GOOFY SUCCESS STORY (See 4-Color No. 702)

GOOSE (Humor magazine)
Sept, 1976 - No. 3, 1976 (52 pgs.) (75¢)
Cousins Publ. (Fawcett)

1-3			1.00

GORDO (See Comics Revue No. 5 & Giant Comics Edition)

GORGO (Based on M.G.M. movie) (See Return of...)
May, 1961 - No. 23, Sept, 1965
Charlton Comics

1-Ditko-a, 22 pgs.	24.00	70.00	170.00
2,3-Ditko-c/a	12.00	36.00	85.00
4-10: 4-Ditko-c	7.00	21.00	50.00
11,13-16-Ditko-a	5.70	17.00	40.00
12,17-23: 12-Reptisaurus x-over; Montes/Bache-a-No. 17-23. 20-Giordano-c	2.90	9.00	20.00
Gorgo's Revenge('62)-Becomes Return of...	5.00	15.00	35.00

GOSPEL BLIMP, THE (Spire Christian)(Value: cover or less)

GOTHAM BY GASLIGHT (A Tale of the Batman)(See Batman: Master of...)
1989 ($3.95, one-shot, squarebound, 52 pgs.)
DC Comics

nn-Mignola/Russell-a; intro by Robert Bloch		1.60	4.00

GOTHAM NIGHTS
Mar, 1992 - No. 4, June, 1992 ($1.25, mini-series)
DC Comics

1-4: Featuring Batman			1.25

GOTHIC ROMANCES
December, 1974 (B&W Magazine) (75¢)
Atlas/Seaboard Publ.

1-Text w/ illos by N. Adams, Chaykin, Heath (2 pgs. ea.)		.70	1.80

GOVERNOR & J. J., THE (TV)
Feb, 1970 - No. 3, Aug, 1970 (Photo-c)
Gold Key

1	3.60	10.75	25.00
2,3	2.60	7.50	18.00

GRAFIK MUZIK (Caliber)(Value: cover or less)

GRANDMA DUCK'S FARM FRIENDS (See 4-Color #763, 873, 965, 1010, 1073, 1161, 1279, Walt Disney's Comics & Stories #293 & Wheaties)

GRAND PRIX (Formerly Hot Rod Racers)
No. 16, Sept, 1967 - No. 31, May, 1970
Charlton Comics

16-Features Rick Roberts	2.10	6.50	15.00
17-20	1.70	4.20	10.00
21-31	1.20	2.90	7.00

GRAVESTONE
July, 1993 - No. 7, Feb, 1994 ($2.25)
Malibu Comics

1-6: 3-Polybagged w/Skycap		.90	2.25
7-($2.50)		1.00	2.50

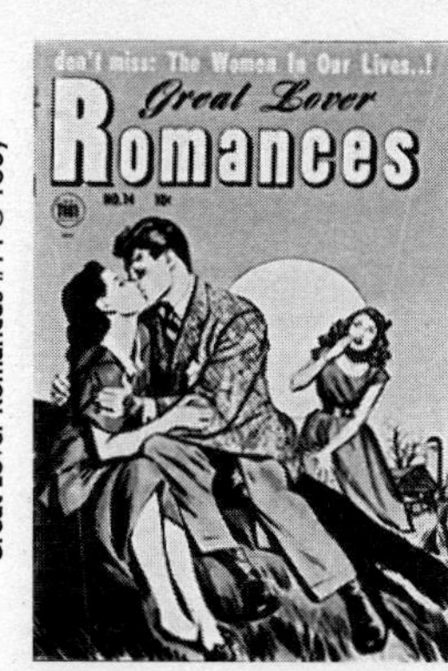

Great Lover Romances #14 © Toby

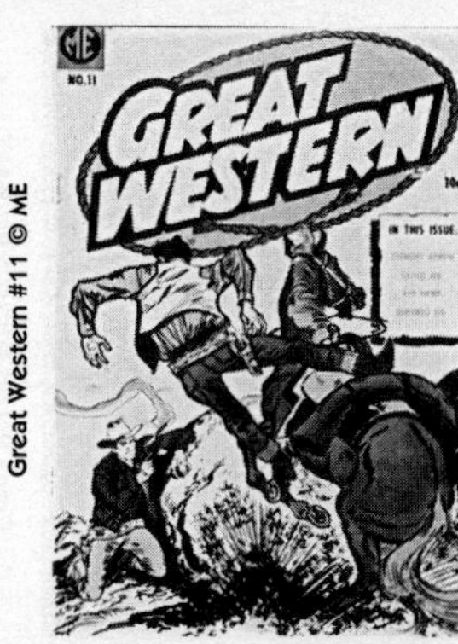

Great Western #11 © ME

Green Arrow #4 © DC

GD25 FN65 NM94

GRAVE TALES (Also see Maggots)
Oct, 1991 - No. 3, Feb, 1992 ($3.95, B&W, magazine, 52 pgs.)
Hamilton Comics

1-3: 1-Staton-c/a. 2-Staton-a; Morrow-c 1.60 4.00

GRAY GHOST, THE (See 4-Color No. 911, 1000)

GREAT ACTION COMICS
1958 (Reprints with new covers)
I. W. Enterprises

1-Captain Truth reprinted from Gold Medal #1 2.40 6.00 12.00
8,9-Reprints Phantom Lady #15 & 23 10.00 30.00 60.00

GREAT AMERICAN COMICS PRESENTS - THE SECRET VOICE
1945 (10¢)
Peter George 4-Star Publ./American Features Syndicate

1-Anti-Nazi; "What Really Happened to Hitler" 13.00 40.00 90.00

GREAT AMERICAN WESTERN, THE (AC)(Value: cover or less)

GREAT CAT FAMILY, THE (See 4-Color No. 750)

GREAT COMICS
Nov, 1941 - No. 3, Jan, 1942
Great Comics Publications

1-Origin/1st app. The Great Zarro; Madame Strange & Guy Gorham, Wizard of Science & The Great Zarro begin 81.00 242.00 565.00
2-Buck Johnson, Jungle Explorer app.; X-Mas-c 46.00 140.00 325.00
3-Futuro Takes Hitler to Hell-c/s; "The Lost City" movie story (starring William Boyd); continues in Choice Comics #3 82.00 246.00 575.00

GREAT COMICS
1945
Novack Publishing Co./Jubilee Comics/Barrel O' Fun

1-(Novack)-The Defenders, Capt. Power app.; L. B. Cole-c 17.00 52.00 120.00
1-(Jubilee)-Same cover; Boogey Man, Satanas, & The Sorcerer & His Apprentice 11.00 32.00 75.00
1-(Barrel O' Fun)-L. B. Cole-c; Barrel O' Fun overprinted in indicia; Li'l Cactus, Cuckoo Sheriff (humorous) 5.85 17.50 35.00

GREAT DOGPATCH MYSTERY (See Mammy Yokum & the...)

GREATEST BATMAN STORIES EVER TOLD, THE
1988 (Color reprints) (Greatest Stories Vol. 2)
DC Comics

Hardcover ($24.95) with dust jacket 4.60 13.70 32.00
Softcover ($15.95)-Simonson-c 2.30 6.90 16.00
Softcover (1992, $16.95, Vol. 2)-Catwoman & Penguin stories 2.40 7.25 17.00

GREATEST JOKER STORIES EVER TOLD, THE
1988 (Color reprints) (Greatest Stories Vol. 3)
DC Comics

Hardcover ($19.95) with dust jacket 3.60 11.00 25.00
Softcover ($14.95)-Brian Bolland Joker-c 2.10 6.50 15.00
Stacked Deck ...Expanded Edition (1990, $29.95)-Longmeadow Press Publ. 4.30 13.00 30.00

GREAT EXPLOITS
October, 1957
Decker Publ./Red Top

1-Krigstein-a(2) (re-issue on cover); reprints Daring Advs. #6 by Approved Comics 5.85 17.50 35.00

GREAT FOODINI, THE (See Foodini)

GREAT GAZOO, THE (The Flintstones)(TV)
Aug, 1973 - No. 20, Jan, 1977 (Hanna-Barbera)
Charlton Comics

1 1.20 2.90 7.00
2-20 1.60 4.00

GD25 FN65 NM94

GREAT GRAPE APE, THE (TV)(See TV Stars #1)
Sept, 1976 - No. 2, Nov, 1976 (Hanna-Barbera)
Charlton Comics

1,2 1.10 2.70 6.50

GREAT LOCOMOTIVE CHASE, THE (See 4-Color No. 712)

GREAT LOVER ROMANCES (Young Lover Romances #4,5)
3/51; #2, 1951(nd); #3, 1952 (nd); #6, Oct?, 1952 - No. 22, May, 1955
Toby Press (Photo-c #1-5, 10 ,13, 15, 17) (no #4, 5)

1-Jon Juan story-r/Jon Juan #1 by Schomburg; Dr. Anthony King app. 10.00 30.00 65.00
2-Jon Juan, Dr. Anthony King app. 5.85 17.50 35.00
3,7,9-14,16-22: 10-Rita Hayworth photo-c. 17-Rita Hayworth & Aldo Ray photo-c 3.60 9.00 18.00
6-Kurtzman-a (10/52) 6.35 19.00 38.00
8-Five pgs. of "Pin-Up Pete" by Sparling 6.35 19.00 38.00
15-Liz Taylor photo-c 7.50 22.50 45.00

GREAT PEOPLE OF GENESIS, THE
No date (64 pgs.) (Religious giveaway)
David C. Cook Publ. Co.

nn-Reprint/Sunday Pix Weekly 2.00 6.00 12.00

GREAT RACE, THE (See Movie Classics)

GREAT SACRAMENT, THE
1953 (36 pgs., giveaway)
Catechetical Guild

nn 200 5.00 10.00

GREAT SCOTT SHOE STORE (See Bulls-Eye)

GREAT WEST (Magazine)
1969 (52 pgs.) (Black & White)
M. F. Enterprises

V1#1 .80 2.00

GREAT WESTERN
No. 8, Jan-Mar, 1954 - No. 11, Oct-Dec, 1954
Magazine Enterprises

8(A-1 93)-Trail Colt by Guardineer; Powell Red Hawk-r/Straight Arrow begins, ends #11; Durango Kid story 15.00 45.00 105.00
9(A-1 105), 11(A-1 127)-Ghost Rider, Durango Kid app. in each. 9-Red Mask-c, but no app. 9.15 27.50 55.00
10(A-1 113)-The Calico Kid by Guardineer-r/Tim Holt #8; Straight Arrow, Durango Kid app. 9.15 27.50 55.00
I.W. Reprint #1,2 9: 1,2-r/Straight Arrow #36,42. 9-r/Straight Arrow #? 2.40 6.00 12.00
I.W. Reprint #8-Origin Ghost Rider(r/Tim Holt #11); Tim Holt app.; Bolle-a 3.20 8.00 16.00

NOTE: ***Guardineer** c-8. **Powell** a(r)-8-11 (from Straight Arrow).*

GREEN ARROW (See Action #440, Adventure, Brave & the Bold, DC Super Stars #17, Detective #521, Flash #217, Green Lantern #76, Justice League of America #4, Leading, More Fun #73 (1st app.) and World's Finest Comics)

GREEN ARROW
May, 1983 - No. 4, Aug, 1983 (Mini-series)
DC Comics

1-Origin; Speedy cameo 1.50 3.75
2-4 1.10 2.75

GREEN ARROW
Feb, 1988 - Present ($1.00, mature readers)(Painted-c #1-3)
DC Comics

1-Mike Grell scripts in #1-80 1.00 2.00 5.00
2 .90 2.25
3-49,51-74,76-86: 27,28-Warlord app. 35-38-Co-stars Black Canary; Bill Wray-i. 40-Grell-a. 47-Begin $1.50-c. 63-No longer has mature readers on-c. 63-66-Shado app. 68-Last $1.50-c. 83-Huntress-c/story. 85-Deathstroke-c/s.

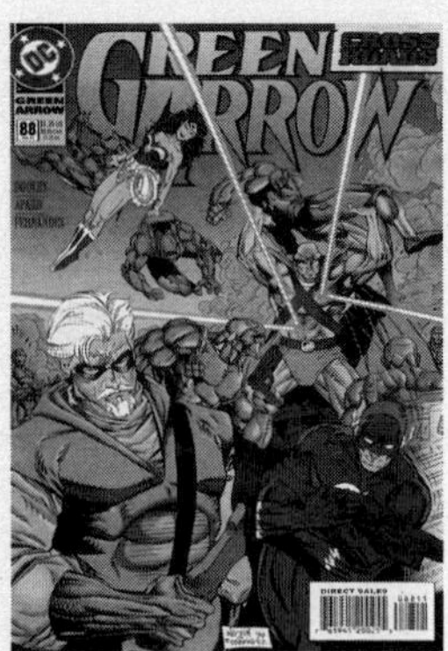

Green Arrow #88 © DC

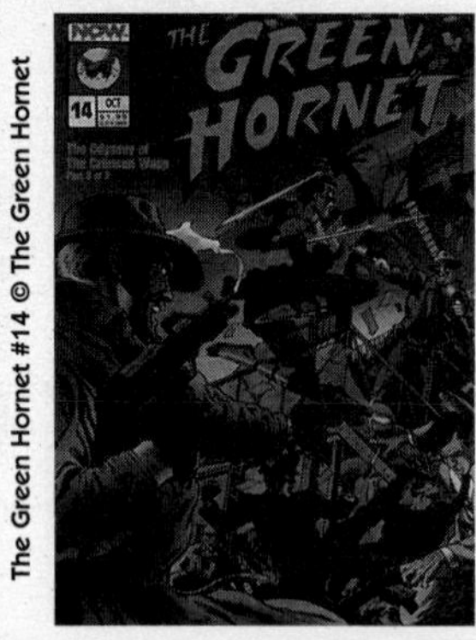

The Green Hornet #14 © The Green Hornet

Green Hornet Comics #7 © HARV

86-Catwoman-c/s w/Jim Balent layouts .60 1.50
50,75-($2.50, 52 pgs.)-Anniversary issues 1.00 2.50
87-90: 87-Begin $1.95-c. 88-Wonder Woman-c. 90-(9/94)-Zero Hour .80 2.00
0,91-93: 0-(10/94)-Aparo-a(p) .80 2.00
Annual 1(1988, $2.00)-No Grell scripts .80 2.00
Annual 2(1989, $2.50, 68pgs.)-No Grell scripts; recaps origin Green Arrow, Speedy, Black Canary & others 1.00 2.50
Annual 3(1990, $2.50, 68pgs.)-Bill Wray-a 1.20 3.00
Annual 4(1991, $2.95, 68pgs.)-50th anniversary issue .80 2.00
Annual 5(1992, $3.00, 68pgs.)-Batman, Eclipso app. 1.20 3.00
Annual 6(1993, $3.50, 68pgs.)-Bloodlines; Hook app. 1.40 3.50

NOTE: ***Denys Cowan** a(p)-39, 41-43, 47, 48; c(p)-41-43. **Mike Grell** c-1-4, 10p, 39, 40, 44, 45, 47-73, 75-80, Annual 4, 5. **Springer** a-67, 68.*

GREEN ARROW: THE LONG BOW HUNTERS
Aug, 1987 - No. 3, Oct, 1987 ($2.95, mature readers)
DC Comics

1-Grell-c/a in all 1.20 3.00 7.00
1,2-2nd printings .80 2.00
2 1.50 3.75
3 1.20 3.00
Trade paperback (1989, $12.95)-Reprints #1-3 1.85 5.50 13.00

GREEN ARROW: THE WONDER YEAR
Feb, 1993 - No. 4, May, 1993 ($1.75, mini-series)
DC Comics

1-4: By Grell (scripts & pencils) & Morrow (inks) .70 1.75

GREEN BERET, THE (See Tales of...)

GREEN GIANT COMICS (Also see Colossus Comics)
1940 (No price on cover; distributed in New York City only)
Pelican Publ. (Funnies, Inc.)

	GD25	FN65	VF82	NM94
1-Dr. Nerod, Green Giant, Black Arrow, Mundoo & Master Mystic app.; origin Colossus (Rare)	750.00	2250.00	4125.00	6000.00

(Estimated up to 17 copies exist, 3 in NM/Mint)

NOTE: *The idea for this book came from George Kapitan. Printed by Moreau Publ. of Orange, N.J. as an experiment to see if they could profitably use the idle time of their 40-page Hoe color press. The experiment failed due to the difficulty of obtaining good quality color registration and Mr. Moreau believes the book never reached the stands. The book has no price or date which lends credence to this. Contains five pages reprinted from Motion Picture Funnies Weekly.*

GREEN-GREY SPONGE-SUIT SUSHI TURTLES (Mirage)(Value: cover or less)

GREENHAVEN (Aircel)(Value: cover or less)

GREEN HORNET, THE (TV)(See Four Color #496)
Feb, 1967 - No. 3, Aug, 1967
Gold Key

1-All have Bruce Lee photo-c 18.00 54.00 125.00
2,3 14.00 40.00 95.00

GREEN HORNET, THE (Also see Kato of the... & Tales of the...)
Nov, 1989 - No. 14, Feb, 1991 ($1.75, color)
V2#1, Sept, 1991 - Present ($1.95, color)
Now Comics

1 ($2.95, double-size)-Steranko painted-c; G.A. Green Hornet 2.10 6.00 15.00
1-2nd printing ('90, $3.95)-New Butler-c 1.60 4.00
2 1.50 4.00 9.00
3-5: 5-Death of original (1930s) Green Hornet .90 2.30 5.50
6-8: 6-Dave Dorman painted-c 1.10 2.75
9-14 .70 1.80
V2#1-11,13-21,24-26,28-38: 1-Butler painted-c. 9-Mayerik-c .80 2.00
12-(2.50)-Color Green Hornet button polybagged inside 1.00 2.50
22,23-($2.95)-Bagged w/color hologravure card 1.20 3.00
27-($2.95)-Newsstand ed. polybagged w/multi-dimensional card (1993 Anniversary Special on cover) 1.20 3.00
27-($2.95)-Direct Sale ed. polybagged w/multi-dimensional card; cover variations 1.20 3.00
31-($2.50)-Polybagged w/trading card 1.00 2.50
1-($2.50)-Polybagged w/button (same as #12) 1.00 2.50
2,3-($1.95)-Same as #13 & 14 .80 2.00
Annual 1 (12/92, 2.50) 1.00 2.50

GREEN HORNET: SOLITARY SENTINEL, THE
Dec, 1992 - No. 3, 1993 ($2.50, color, mini-series)
Now Comics

1-3 1.00 2.50

GREEN HORNET COMICS (...Racket Buster #44) (Radio, movies)
Dec, 1940 - No. 47, Sept, 1949 (See All New #13,14)(Early issues: 68 pgs.)
Helnit Publ. Co.(Holyoke) No. 1-6/Family Comics(Harvey) No. 7-on

1-Green Hornet begins(1st app.); painted-c 250.00 750.00 1750.00
2-Early issues based on radio adventures 100.00 300.00 700.00
3 86.00 257.00 600.00
4-6: 6-(8/41) 68.00 205.00 475.00
7 (6/42)-Origin The Zebra & begins; Robin Hood, Spirit of '76, Blonde Bomber & Mighty Midgets begin; new logo 60.00 180.00 420.00
8-10: 9-Kirby-c 55.00 165.00 385.00
11,12-Mr. Q in both 50.00 150.00 350.00
13-20: 13-1st Nazi-c; shows Hitler poster on-c 40.00 120.00 280.00
21-30: 24-Sci-Fi-c 30.00 90.00 210.00
31-The Man in Black Called Fate begins (11-12/45, early app.) 33.00 100.00 230.00
32-36 29.00 86.00 200.00
37-Shock Gibson app. by Powell; S&K Kid Adonis reprinted from Stuntman #3 29.00 88.00 205.00
38-Shock Gibson, Kid Adonis app. 29.00 86.00 200.00
39-Stuntman story by S&K 34.00 103.00 240.00
40,41 21.00 63.00 145.00
42-47-Kerry Drake in all. 45-Boy Explorers on-c only. 46- "Case of the Marijuana Racket" cover/story; Kerry Drake app. 21.00 63.00 145.00

NOTE: ***Fuje** a-23, 24, 26. **Henkle** c-7-9. **Kubert** a-20, 30. **Powell** a-7-10, 12, 14, 16-21, 30, 31(2), 32(3), 33, 34(3), 35, 36, 37(2), 38. **Robinson** a-27. **Schomburg** c-15, 17-23. Kirbyish c-7, 15. Bondage c-8, 14, 18, 26, 36.*

GREEN JET COMICS, THE (See Comic Books, Series 1)

GREEN LAMA (Also see Comic Books, Series 1, Daring Adventures #17 & Prize Comics #7)
Dec, 1944 - No. 8, March, 1946
Spark Publications/Prize No. 7 on

1-Intro. Lt. Hercules & The Boy Champions; Mac Raboy-c/a #1-8 100.00 300.00 700.00
2-Lt. Hercules borrows the Human Torch's powers for one panel 60.00 180.00 420.00
3,6,8: 7-X-mas-c; Raboy craft tint-c/a 50.00 150.00 350.00
4-Dick Tracy take-off in Lt. Hercules story by H. L. Gold (sci-fiction writer) 50.00 150.00 350.00
5-Lt. Hercules story; Little Orphan Annie, Smilin' Jack & Snuffy Smith take-off (5/45) 50.00 150.00 350.00
7-X-mas-c; Raboy craft tint c/a (note: a small quantity of NM copies surfaced) 36.00 107.00 250.00

NOTE: ***Robinson** a-3-5, 8. Roussos a-8. Formerly a pulp hero who began in 1940.*

GREEN LANTERN (1st Series) (See All-American, All Flash Quarterly, All Star Comics, The Big All-American & Comic Cavalcade)
Fall, 1941 - No. 38, May-June, 1949 (#1-18 are quarterly)
National Periodical Publications/All-American

	GD25	FN65	VF82	NM94
1-Origin retold	1,750.00	5,250.00	11,375.00	17,500.00

(Estimated up to 200 total copies exist, 8 in NM/Mint)

	GD25	FN65	NM94
2-1st book-length story	500.00	1500.00	3500.00
3-Classic German war-c by Mart Nodell	371.00	1115.00	2600.00
4-Green Lantern & Doiby Dickles join the Army	293.00	880.00	2050.00
5	186.00	557.00	1300.00

Green Lantern #19 © DC

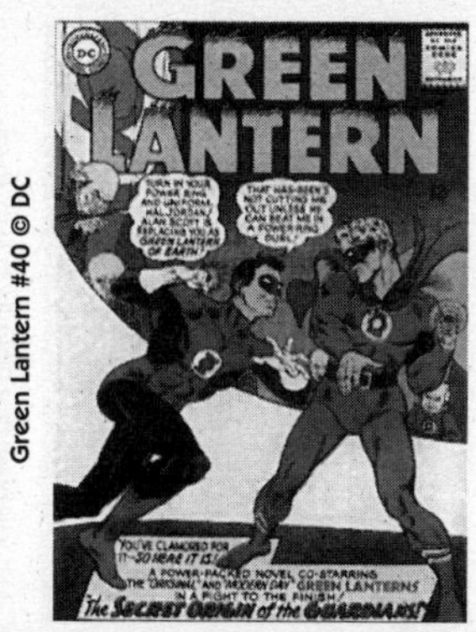

Green Lantern #40 © DC

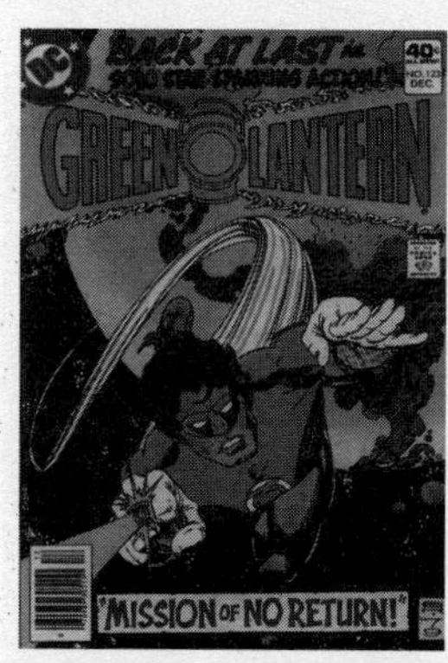

Green Lantern #123 © DC

GD25 FN65 NM94

6-8: 7-Robot-c. 8-Hop Harrigan begins 143.00 430.00 1000.00
9 129.00 385.00 900.00
10-Origin/1st app. Vandal Savage 136.00 407.00 950.00
11-17,19,20: 12-Origin/1st app. Gambler 107.00 321.00 750.00
18-Christmas-c 121.00 365.00 850.00
21-26,28-30: 30-Origin/1st app. Streak the Wonder Dog by Toth (2-3/48)
100.00 300.00 700.00
27-Origin/1st app. Sky Pirate 107.00 321.00 750.00
31-35: 35-Kubert-c. 35-38-New logo 79.00 235.00 550.00
36-38: 37-Sargon the Sorcerer app. 104.00 311.00 725.00
NOTE: *Book-length stories #2-7.* ***Mayer/Moldoff*** *c-9.* ***Mayer/Purcell*** *c-8.* ***Purcell*** *c-1.* ***Mart Nodell*** *c-2, 3, 7.* ***Paul Reinman*** *c-11, 12, 15-22.* ***Toth*** *a-28, 30, 31, 34-38; c-28, 30, 34p, 36-38p. Cover to #8 says Fall while the indicia says Summer Issue. Streak the Wonder Dog c-30(w/Green Lantern), 34, 36, 38.*

GREEN LANTERN (See Action Comics Weekly, Adventure Comics, Brave & the Bold, DC Special, DC Special Series, Flash, Guy Gardner, Guy Gardner Reborn, Justice League of America, Showcase & Tales of The...Corps)

GREEN LANTERN (2nd series)(Green Lantern Corps #206 on)
7-8/60 - No. 89, 4-5/72; No. 90, 8-9/76 - No. 205, 10/86
National Periodical Publ./DC Comics GD25 FN65 VF82 NM94
Showcase #22 (9-10/59)-Origin & 1st app. Silver Age Green Lantern by Gil Kane
1st Ferris (becomes Star Sapphire) 325.00 975.00 2060.00 3900.00
Showcase #23 (11-12/59) 144.00 433.00 867.00 1300.00
Showcase #24 (1-2/60) 147.00 442.00 883.00 1325.00
1-(7-8/60)-Origin retold; Gil Kane-c/a continues; 1st app. Guardians of the Universe 194.00 583.00 1166.00 1750.00
GD25 FN65 NM94
2-1st Pieface 73.00 219.00 585.00
3-Contains readers poll 40.00 130.00 350.00
4,5: 5-Origin & 1st app. Hector Hammond 34.00 101.00 270.00
6-10: 6-Intro Tomar-re the alien G.L. 7-Origin/1st app. Sinestro (7-8/61). 8-1st 5700 A.D. story; grey tone-c. 9-1st Jordan Brothers; last 10¢ issue
23.00 69.00 185.00
11,12 18.00 50.00 125.00
13-Flash x-over 22.00 66.00 155.00
14-20: 14-Origin/1st app. Sonar. 16-Origin & 1st app. Star Sapphire. 20-Flash x-over 16.00 49.00 115.00
21-30: 21-Origin & 1st app. Dr. Polaris. 23-1st Tattooed Man. 24-Origin & 1st app. Shark. 29-JLA cameo; 1st Blackhand 13.00 39.00 92.00
31-39: 37-1st app. Evil Star (villain) 10.00 31.00 72.00
40-1st app. Crisis (10/65); 2nd solo G.A. Green Lantern in Silver Age (see Showcase #55); origin The Guardians; Doiby Dickles app.
49.00 148.00 395.00
41-44,46-50: 42-Zatanna x-over. 43-Flash x-over 7.00 20.00 46.00
45-2nd S.A. app. G.A. Green Lantern in title (6/66) 10.00 31.00 72.00
51,53-58 4.60 14.00 32.00
52-G.A. Green Lantern x-over 5.40 16.00 38.00
59-1st app. Guy Gardner (3/68) 24.00 70.00 170.00
60,62-69: 69-Wood inks; last 12 cent issue 3.00 9.00 21.00
61-G.A. Green Lantern x-over 4.30 12.90 30.00
70-75 2.40 7.30 17.00
76-(4/70)-Begin Green Lantern/Green Arrow series (by Neal Adams #76-89) ends #122 (see Flash #217 for 2nd series) 16.00 49.00 115.00
77 6.00 18.00 42.00
78-80 4.60 14.00 32.00
81-84: 82-Wrightson-i(1 pg.). 83-G.L. reveals i.d. to Carol Ferris. 84-N. Adams/Wrightson-a(22 pgs.); last 15¢-c; partial photo-c 3.70 11.00 26.00
85,86-(52 pgs.)-Anti-drug issues. 86-G.A. Green Lantern-r; Toth-a
5.10 15.00 36.00
87-(52 pgs.): 2nd app. Guy Gardner (cameo); 1st app. John Stewart (12-1/71-72) (becomes 3rd Green Lantern in #182) 3.40 10.30 24.00
88-(2-3/72, 52 pgs.)-Unpubbed G.A. Green Lantern story; Green Lantern-r/Showcase #23. N. Adams-c/a (1 pg.) 1.00 2.50 6.00
89-(4-5/72, 52 pgs.)-G.A. Green Lantern-r; Green Lantern & Green Arrow move to Flash #217 (2nd team-up series) 1.60 4.70 11.00
90-99: 90-(8-9/76)-Begin 3rd Green Lantern/Green Arrow team-up series; Mike Grell-c/a begins, ends #111 1.40 3.50
100-(1/78, Giant)-1st app. Air Wave II 1.00 2.70 6.50
101-111,113-115,117-119: 107-1st Tales of the G.L. Corps story. 108-110-(44 pgs)-G.A. Green Lantern back-ups in each. 111-Origin retold; G.A. Green Lantern app. 1.10 2.75
112-G.A. Green Lantern origin retold 1.10 2.70 6.50
116-1st app. Guy Gardner as a Gr. Lantern (5/79) 3.70 11.00 26.00
120,121,124-135,138-140,142-149: 130-132-Tales of the G.L. Corps. 132-Adam Strange series begins, ends 147. 142,143-Omega Men app.; Perez-c. 144-Omega Men cameo. 148-Tales of the G.L. Corps begins, ends #173
.70 1.80
122-Last Green Lantern/Green Arrow team-up .90 2.25
123-Green Lantern back to solo action; 2nd app. Guy Gardner as Green Lantern 1.00 2.50 6.00
136,137-1st app. Citadel; Space Ranger app. 1.10 2.75
141-1st app. Omega Men (6/81) 1.00 2.50
150-Anniversary issue, 52 pgs.; no G.L. Corps 1.10 2.75
151-170: 159-Origin Evil Star. 160,161-Omega Men app. 181-Hal Jordan resigns as G.L. 182-John Stewart becomes new G.L.; origin recap of Hal Jordan as G.L. .70 1.80
171-193,196-199,201-205: (75¢ cover). 185-Origin new G.L. (John Stewart). 188-I.D. revealed; Alan Moore back-up scripts. 191-Re-intro Star Sapphire (cameo). 192-Re-intro Star Sapphire (1st full app.). 194,198-Crisis x-over. 199-Hal Jordan returns as a member of G.L. Corps (3 G.L.s now). 201-Green Lantern Corps begins (is cover title, says premiere issue)
.70 1.80
194-Hal Jordan/Guy Gardner battle; Guardians choose Guy Gardner to become new Green Lantern 1.00 2.50 6.00
195-Guy Gardner becomes Green Lantern; Crisis x-over
2.40 7.30 17.00
200-Double-size 1.10 2.75
Annual 1 (See Tales Of The...)
Annual 3 (See Green Lantern Corps Annual #3)
Special 1 (1988), 2 (1989)-(Both $1.50, 52 pgs.) 1.00 2.50
NOTE: ***N. Adams*** *a-76, 77-87p, 89; c-63, 76-89.* ***M. Anderson*** *a-137i.* ***Austin*** *a-93i, 94i, 171i.* ***Greene*** *a-39-49i, 58-63i; c-54-58i.* ***Grell*** *a-90-106, 108-111; c-90-106, 108-112.* ***Gil Kane*** *a-1-49p, 50-57, 58-61p, 68-75p, 85p(r), 87p(r), 88p(r), 156, 177, 184p; c-1-52, 54-61p, 67-75, 123, 154, 156, 165-171, 177, 184.* ***Newton*** *a-148p, 149p, 181.* ***Perez*** *c-132p, 141-144.* ***Sekowsky*** *a-65p, 170p.* ***Sparling*** *a-63p.* ***Starlin*** *c-129, 133.* ***Staton*** *a-117p, 123-127p, 128, 129-131p, 132-139, 140p, 141-146, 147p, 148-150, 151-155p; c-107p, 117p, 135(i), 136p, 145p, 146, 147, 148-152p, 155p.* ***Toth*** *a-86r, 171p.* ***Tuska*** *a-166-168p, 170p.*

GREEN LANTERN (3rd series)
June, 1990 - Present ($1.00/$1.25)
DC Comics
1-Hal Jordan, John Stewart & Guy Gardner return; Batman app.
1.10 2.75
2,3 .80 1.90
4-8 1.20
9-12-Guy Gardner solo story .90 2.25
13-($1.75, 52 pgs.) .80 1.90
14-18,20-24,26: 18-Guy Gardner solo story. 26-Last $1.00-c 1.00
19-($1.75, 52 pgs.)-50th anniversary issue; Mart Nodell (original G.A. artist) part-p on G.A. Gr. Lantern; G. Kane-c .70 1.75
25-($1.75, 52 pgs.)-Hal Jordan/Guy Gardner battle .80 1.90
27-45,47: 30,31-Gorilla Grodd-c/story(see Flash #69). 38,39-Adam Strange-c/story. 42-Deathstroke-c/s. 47-Green Arrow x-over 1.25
46-Superman app. cont'd in Superman #82 1.80 4.50
48,49: 48-Emerald Twilight part 1; begin $1.50-c 1.10 2.75
50-($2.95, 52 pgs.)-Glow-in-the-dark-c 1.20 3.00
51-55: 51-1st app. New Green Lantern with new costume. 53-Superman-c/sty. 55-(9/94)-Zero Hour 1.50
0,56-59: 0-(10/94) 1.50
Annual 1 (1992, $2.50, 68 pgs.)-Eclipso app. 1.00 2.50
Annual 2 (1993, $2.50, 68 pgs.)-Intro Nightblade 1.00 2.50
Annual 3 (1994, $2.95)-Elseworlds story 1.20 3.00
...: Emerald Twilight nn (1994, $5.95)-r/#48-50 1.00 2.50 6.00
...: Ganthet's Tale nn (1992, $5.95, 68 pgs.)-Silver foil stamped logo; Byrne-c/a

Green Lantern: Emerald Dawn #5 © DC

Green Lantern: Mosaic #15 © DC

Grendel: War Child #1 © Matt Wagner

GD25 FN65 NM94 | GD25 FN65 NM94

1.00 2.50 6.00
.../Green Arrow Collection, Vol. 2-r/Gl #84-87,89 & Flash #217-219 & GL/GA #5-7 by O'Neil/Adams/Wrightson 1.90 5.60 13.00
...The Road Back nn (1992, $8.95)-r/1-8 w/covers 1.50 3.75 9.00
NOTE: *Staton a(p)-9-12; c-9-12.*

GREEN LANTERN CORPS, THE (Formerly Green Lantern; see Tales of...)
No. 206, Nov, 1986 - No. 224, May, 1988
DC Comics
206-223: 220,221-Millennium tie-ins 1.00
224-Double size last issue 1.50
...Corps Annual 2 (12/86)-Formerly Tales of ...Annual #1; Alan Moore scripts 1.50
...Corps Annual 3 (8/87)-Indicia says Green Lantern Annual #3; Moore scripts; Byrne-a 1.50
NOTE: ***Austin** a-Annual 3i. **Gil Kane** a-223, 224p; c-223, 224. **Russell** a-Annual 3i. **Staton** a-207-213p, 217p, 221p, 222p, Annual 3; c-207-213p, 217p, 221p, 222p. **Willingham** a-213p, 219p, 220p, 218p, 219p, Annual 2, 3p; c-218p, 219p.*

GREEN LANTERN CORPS QUARTERLY
Summer, 1992 - No. 8, Spring, 1994 ($2.50/$2.95, 68 pgs.)
DC Comics
1-5: 1-G.A. Green Lantern story; Staton-a(p). 2-G.A. G.L.-c/story; Austin-c(i); Gulacy-a(p). 3-G.A. G.L. story. 4-Austin-i 1.00 2.50
6-8: 6-Begin $2.95-c. 7-Painted-c; Tim Vigil-a. 8-Lobo-c/s 1.20 3.00

GREEN LANTERN: EMERALD DAWN (Also see Emerald Dawn)
Dec, 1989 - No. 6, May, 1990 ($1.00, mini-series)
DC Comics
1-Origin retold; Giffen plots in all 1.50 3.75
2 1.10 2.75
3,4 .80 1.90
5,6 1.40

GREEN LANTERN: EMERALD DAWN II (Emerald Dawn II #1 & 2)
Apr, 1991 - No. 6, Sept, 1991 ($1.00, mini-series)
DC Comics
1 1.25
2-6 1.00

GREEN LANTERN/GREEN ARROW (Also see The Flash #217)
Oct, 1983 - No. 7, April, 1984 (52-60 pgs.)
DC Comics
1-7: Reprints Green Lantern #76-89 1.10 2.75
NOTE: ***Neal Adams** r-1-7; c-1-4. **Wrightson** r-4, 5.*

GREEN LANTERN: MOSAIC
June, 1992 - No. 18, Nov, 1993 ($1.25)
DC Comics
1-18: Featuring John Stewart. 1-Painted-c 1.25

GREEN MASK, THE (See Mystery Men)
Summer, 1940 - No. 9, 2/42; No. 10, 8/44 - No. 11, 11/44; V2#1, Spring, 1945 - No. 6, 10-11/46
Fox Features Syndicate
V1#1-Origin The Green Mask & Domino; reprints/Mystery Men #1-3,5-7; Lou Fine-c 157.00 471.00 1100.00
2-Zanzibar The Magician by Tuska 79.00 235.00 550.00
3-Powell-a; Marijuana story 46.00 140.00 325.00
4-Navy Jones begins, ends #6 39.00 118.00 275.00
5 34.00 100.00 235.00
6-The Nightbird begins, ends #9; bondage/torture-c 27.00 80.00 185.00
7-9: 9(2/42)-Becomes The Bouncer #10(nn) on? & Green Mask #10 on 22.00 65.00 150.00
10,11: 10-Origin One Round Hogan & Rocket Kelly 19.00 57.00 130.00
V2#1 15.00 45.00 105.00
2-6 13.00 40.00 90.00

GREEN PLANET, THE
1962 (One Shot) (12¢)
Charlton Comics
nn-Giordano-c 6.70 20.00 40.00

GREEN TEAM (See Cancelled Comic Cavalcade & 1st Issue Special)

GREETINGS FROM SANTA (See March of Comics No. 48)

GREGORY (Piranha Press/DC)(Value: cover or less)

GRENDEL (Also see Primer No. 2 and Mage)
Mar, 1983 - No. 3, Feb, 1984 ($1.50, B&W)(#1 has indicia to Skrog #1)
Comico
1-Origin Hunter Rose 7.10 21.00 50.00
2,3: 2-Origin Argent 5.50 17.00 40.00

GRENDEL
Oct, 1986 - No. 40, Feb, 1991 ($1.50/$1.95/$2.50, color) (Mature readers)
Comico
1 1.50 3.25
1,2-2nd printings .60 1.60
2 .90 2.25
3-10: 4-Dave Stevens-c(i) .80 1.90
11-15: 13-15-Ken Steacy-c .70 1.75
16-Re-intro Mage (series begins, ends #19) 1.20 3.00
17-32: 18-26-$1.75-c; 27-32-$1.95-c .80 2.00
33-($2.75, 44 pgs.) 1.10 2.75
34-40: 34-Begin $2.50 cover price 1.00 2.50
Devil by the Deed (Graphic Novel, 10/86, $5.95, 52 pgs.)-r/Grendel back-ups/ Mage 6-14; Alan Moore intro. 1.20 3.00 7.00
Devil's Legacy ($14.95, 1988, Graphic Novel) 2.15 6.50 15.00
Devil's Vagary (10/87, B&W & red)-No price; included in Comico Collection 1.70 5.00 12.00

GRENDEL: DEVIL BY THE DEED
July, 1993 ($3.95, color, one-shot, spot varnish-c)
Dark Horse Comics
nn-r/Grendel back-ups from Mage #6-14 1.60 4.00

GRENDEL TALES: FOUR DEVILS, ONE HELL
Aug, 1993 - No. 6, Jan, 1994 ($2.95, color, limited series, mature readers)
Dark Horse Comics
1-6: Wagner painted-c 1.20 3.00

GRENDEL TALES: THE DEVIL IN OUR MIDST
May, 1994 - No. 5, Sept, 1994 ($2.95, limited series, adult)
Dark Horse Comics
1-5-Wagner painted-c 1.20 3.00

GRENDEL TALES: THE DEVIL'S HAMMER
Feb, 1994 - No. 3, Apr, 1994 ($2.95, color, mini-series, mature readers)
Dark Horse Comics
1-3 1.20 3.00

GRENDEL: WAR CHILD
Aug, 1992 - No. 10, 1993 ($2.50, color, limited series, mature readers)
Dark Horse Comics
1-9: Bisley painted-c; Wagner-i & scripts 1.00 2.50
10-($3.50, 52 pgs.) 1.40 3.50

GREYFRIARS BOBBY (See 4-Color No. 1189)

GREYLORE (Sirius)(Value: cover or less)

GRIFFIN, THE (DC)(Value: cover or less)

GRIM GHOST, THE
Jan, 1975 - No. 3, July, 1975
Atlas/Seaboard Publ.
1-3: 1-Origin. 3-Heath-c 1.00

GRIMJACK (Also see Demon Knight & Starslayer)

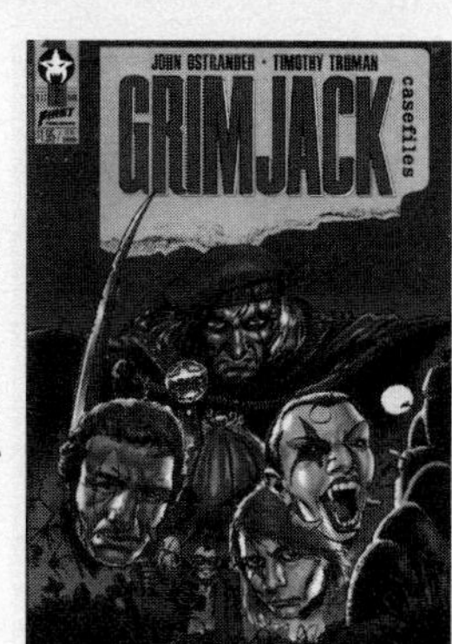

Grimjack #2 © First Comics

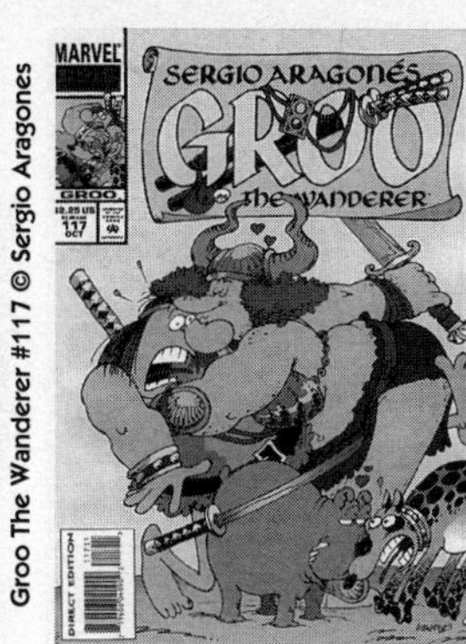

Groo The Wanderer #117 © Sergio Aragones

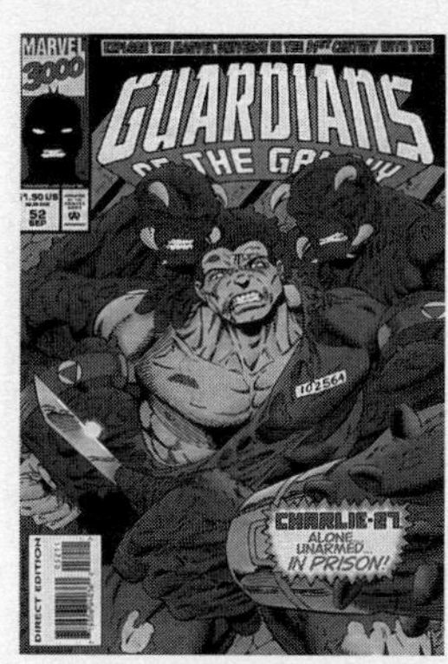

Guardians of the Galaxy #52 © MEG

GD25 FN65 NM94

Aug, 1984 - No. 81, Apr, 1991 (Later issues $1.95, $2.25)
First Comics

1 .80 2.00
2-25: 20-Sutton-c/a begins. 22-Bolland-a 1.50
26-2nd color Teenage Mutant Ninja Turtles 1.50 3.75
27-74,76-81 (Later issues $1.95, $2.25): 30-Dynamo Joe x-over; 31-Mandrake-c/a begins. 73,74-Kelley Jones-a 1.25
75-($5.95, 52 pgs.)-Fold-out map; coated stock 1.00 2.50 6.00

GRIMJACK CASEFILES (First)(Value: cover or less)

GRIMM'S GHOST STORIES (See Dan Curtis)
Jan, 1972 - No. 60, June, 1982 (Painted-c #1-42,44,46-56)
Gold Key/Whitman No. 55 on

1 1.00 2.50 6.00
2-4,6,7,9,10 1.20 3.00
5,8-Williamson-a 1.60 4.00
11-35: 32,34-Reprints .80 2.00
36-58,60: 43,44-(52 pgs.). 43,45-Photo-c 1.50
59-Williamson-a(r/#8) .80
2.00
Mini-Comic No. 1 (3-1/4x6-1/2", 1976) 1.00

NOTE: Reprints-#32?, 34?, 39, 43, 44, 47?, 53; 56-60(1/3). ***Bolle*** *a-8, 17, 22-25, 27, 29(2), 33, 35, 41, 43r, 45(2), 48(2), 50, 52.* ***Celardo*** *a-17, 26, 28p, 30, 31, 43(2), 45.* ***Lopez*** *a-24, 25.* ***McWilliams*** *a-33, 44r, 48, 54(2), 57, 58.* ***Win Mortimer*** *a-31, 33, 49, 51, 55, 56, 58(2), 59, 60.* ***Roussos*** *a-25, 30.* ***Sparling*** *a-23, 24, 28, 30, 31, 33, 43r, 44, 45, 51(2), 52, 56, 58, 59(2), 60.* ***Spiegle*** *a-44.*

GRIN (The American Funny Book) (Magazine)
Nov, 1972 - No. 3, April, 1973 (52 pgs.) (Satire)
APAG House Pubs

1 .80 2.00
2,3 1.00

GRIN & BEAR IT (See Gags & Large Feature Comic No. 28)

GRIPS (Extreme violence)
Sept, 1986 - No. 4, Dec, 1986 ($1.50, B&W, adults)
Silverwolf Comics

1-Tim Vigil-c/a in all 2.30 6.90 16.00
2 1.60 4.70 11.00
3 1.70 4.00 10.00
4 1.50 4.00 9.00

GRIT GRADY (See Holyoke One-Shot No. 1)

GROO CARNIVAL, THE
Dec, 1991 ($8.95, trade paperback)
Epic Comics (Marvel)

nn-Reprints Groo #9-12 by Aragones 1.50 3.75 9.00

GROO CHRONICLES, THE (Sergio Aragones)
June, 1989 - No. 6, Feb, 1990 ($3.50)
Epic Comics (Marvel)

Book 1-6: Reprints early Pacific issues 1.40 3.50

GROO SPECIAL
Oct, 1984 ($2.00, 52 pgs., Baxter paper)
Eclipse Comics

1-Aragones-c/a 5.10 15.00 36.00

GROO THE WANDERER (See Destroyer Duck #1, Marvel Graphic Novel #32 & & Starslayer #5)
Dec, 1982 - No. 8, Apr, 1984
Pacific Comics

1-Aragones-c/a(p) in all; Aragones biog., photo 4.00 12.00 28.00
2 2.60 7.70 18.00
3-7: 5-Deluxe paper (1.00-c) 2.10 6.50 15.00
8 1.70 5.10 12.00

GROO THE WANDERER (Sergio Aragones'...)
March, 1985 - Present
Epic Comics (Marvel)

1-Aragones-c/a in all 2.00 4.70 11.00
2 1.30 2.60 6.50
3-10 1.70 4.25
11-20 1.10 2.75
21-30 .90 2.25
31-86: 50-($1.50, double size) 1.40
87-99,101-122: 87-Begin $2.25, direct sale only, high quality paper issues .90 2.25
100-($2.95, 52 pgs.) 1.20 3.00
Marvel Graphic Novel 32: Death of Groo 1.20 2.90 7.00
Death of Groo 2nd printing ($5.95) 1.00 2.50 6.00
Groo Garden, The (4/94, $10.95)-r/25-28 1.60 4.70 11.00

GROOVY (Cartoon Comics - not CCA approved)
March, 1968 - No. 3, July, 1968
Marvel Comics Group

1-Monkees, Ringo Starr, Sonny & Cher, Mamas & Papas photos 3.40 10.00 24.00
2,3 2.60 7.70 18.00

GROUP LARUE, THE (Innovation)(Value: cover or less)

GUADALCANAL DIARY (See American Library)

GUARDIANS OF JUSTICE & THE O-FORCE (Shadow)(Value: cover or less)

GUARDIANS OF THE GALAXY (Also see The Defenders #26, Marvel Presents #3, Marvel Super-Heroes #18, Marvel Two-In-One #5)
June, 1990 - Present ($1.00)
Marvel Comics

1-Valentino-c/a(p) begin 1.00 3.00 6.00
2,3: 2-Zeck-c(i) 1.50 3.75
4-6: 5-McFarlane-c(i) 1.30 3.25
7-10: 7-Intro Malevolence (Mephisto's daughter); Perez-c(i). 8-Intro Rancor (descendant of Wolverine) in cameo. 9-1st full app. Rancor; Rob Liefeld-c(i). 10-Jim Lee-c(i) 1.10 2.75
11,12,15: 15-Starlin-c(i) .80 1.90
13,14-1st app. Spirit of Vengeance (futuristic Ghost Rider). 14-Spirit of Vengeance vs. The Guardians 1.80 4.25
16-($1.50, 52 pgs.)-Starlin-c(i) .80 1.90
17-23,26-38,40-47: 17-20-31st century Punishers storyline. 20-Last $1.00-c. 21-Rancor app. 22-Reintro Starhawk. 26-Origin retold. 27-28-Infinity War x-over; 27-Inhumans app. 43-Intro Wooden (son of Thor) 1.25
24-Silver Surfer-c/story; Ron Lim-c 1.10 2.75
25-($2.50)-Prism foil-c; Silver Surfer/Galactus-c/s 1.30 3.25
25-($2.50)-Without foil-c; newsstand edition .80 2.00
39-($2.95, 52 pgs.)-Embossed & holo-grafx foil-c; Dr. Doom vs. Rancor 1.20 3.00
48,49,51-59: 48-Begin $1.50-c; bound-in trading card sheet 1.50
50-($2.00, 52 pgs.)-Newsstand edition .80 2.00
50-($2.95, 52 pgs.)-Collectors ed. w/foil embossed-c 1.20 3.00
Annual 1 (1991, $2.00, 68 pgs.)-2 pg. origin 1.00 2.50
Annual 2 (1992, $2.25, 68 pgs.)-Spirit of Vengeance-c/story .90 2.25
Annual 3 (1993, $2.95, 68 pgs.)-Bagged w/card 1.20 3.00
Annual 4 (1994, $2.95) 1.20 3.00

GUERRILLA WAR (Formerly Jungle War Stories)
No. 12, July-Sept, 1965 - No. 14, Mar, 1966
Dell Publishing Co.

12-14 2.00 5.00 10.00

GUILTY (See Justice Traps the Guilty)

GULF FUNNY WEEKLY (Gulf Comic Weekly No. 1-4)
1933 - No. 422, 5/23/41 (in full color; 4 pgs.; tabloid size to 2/3/39; 2/10/39 on, regular comic book size)(early issues undated)
Gulf Oil Company (Giveaway)

The Gumps #1 © C & L

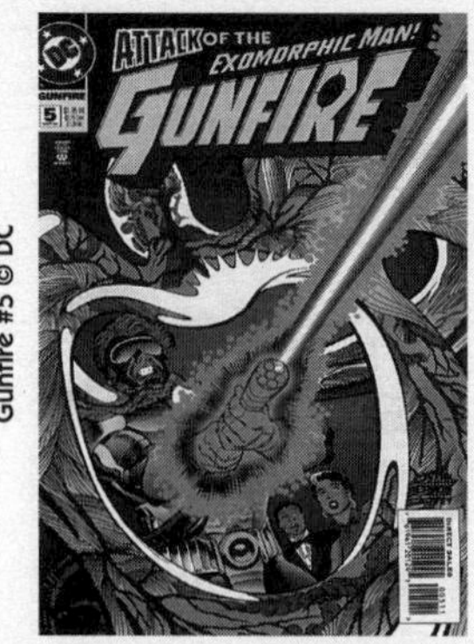

Gunfire #5 © DC

Gun Runner #1 © MEG

	GD25	FN65	NM94
1	43.00	130.00	300.00
2-5	14.00	43.00	100.00
6-30	4.20	25.00	50.00
31-100	5.85	17.50	35.00
101-196	4.20	12.50	25.00
197-Wings Winfair begins(1/29/37); by Fred Meagher beginning in 1938	22.00	65.00	150.00
198-300 (Last tabloid size)	10.00	30.00	70.00
301-350 (Regular size)	5.85	17.50	35.00
351-422	4.20	12.50	25.00

GULLIVER'S TRAVELS (See Dell Jr. Treasury No. 3)
Sept-Nov, 1965 - No. 3, May, 1966
Dell Publishing Co.

	GD25	FN65	NM94
1	4.35	13.00	26.00
2,3	3.60	9.00	18.00

GUMBY'S SUMMER FUN SPECIAL
July, 1987 ($2.50, color)
Comico

	GD25	FN65	NM94
1-Art Adams-c/a, B. Burden story		1.00	2.50

GUMBY'S WINTER FUN SPECIAL
Dec, 1988 ($2.50, color, 44 pgs.)
Comico

	GD25	FN65	NM94
1-Art Adams-c/a		1.00	2.50

GUMPS, THE
No. 2, 1918; 1924 - No. 8, 1931 (10x10")(52 pgs.; black & white)
Landfield-Kupfer/Cupples & Leon No. 2

	GD25	FN65	NM94
Book No.2(1918)-(Rare); 5-1/4x13-1/3"; paper cover; 36 pgs. daily strip reprints by Sidney Smith	36.00	108.00	360.00
nn(1924)-By Sidney Smith	25.00	75.00	250.00
2,3	16.00	48.00	160.00
4-7	13.00	40.00	130.00
8-(10x14"); 36 pgs.; B&W; National Arts Co.	13.00	40.00	130.00

GUMPS, THE (See Merry Christmas..., Popular & Super Comics)
No. 73, 1945; Mar-Apr, 1947 - No. 5, Nov-Dec, 1947
Dell Publ. Co./Bridgeport Herald Corp.

	GD25	FN65	NM94
4-Color 73 (Dell)(1945)	11.00	32.00	75.00
1 (3-4/47)	11.00	32.00	75.00
2-5	7.50	22.50	45.00

GUNFIGHTER (Fat & Slat #1-4) (Becomes Haunt of Fear #15 on)
No. 5, Summer, 1948 - No. 14, Mar-Apr, 1950
E. C. Comics (Fables Publ. Co.)

	GD25	FN65	NM94
5,6-Moon Girl in each	41.00	122.00	285.00
7-14: 14-Bondage-c	28.00	84.00	195.00

NOTE: ***Craig & H. C. Kiefer*** *art in most issues.* ***Craig*** *c-5, 6, 13, 14.* ***Feldstein/Craig*** *a-10.* ***Feldstein*** *a-7-11.* ***Harrison/Wood*** *a-13, 14.* ***Ingels*** *a-5-14; c-7-12.*

GUNFIGHTERS, THE
1963 - 1964
Super Comics (Reprints)

	GD25	FN65	NM94
10-12,15,16,18: 10,11-r/Billy the Kid #s? 12-r/The Rider #5(Swift Arrow). 15-r/Straight Arrow #42; Powell-r. 16-r/Billy the Kid #?(Toby). 18-r/ The Rider #3; Severin-c	1.40	3.50	7.00

GUNFIGHTERS, THE (Formerly Kid Montana)
No. 51, 10/66 - No. 52, 10/67; No. 53, 6/79 - No. 85, 7/84
Charlton Comics

	GD25	FN65	NM94
51,52	1.20	3.00	6.00
53-85: 53,54-Williamson/Torres-r/Six Gun Heroes #47,49. 56-Williamson/ Severin-c; Severin-r/Sheriff of Tombstone #1. 85-S&K-r/1955 Bullseye		1.20	3.00

GUNFIRE (See Deathstroke Annual #2 & Showcase 94)
May, 1994 - Present ($1.75)
DC Comics

	GD25	FN65	NM94
1-5: 2-Ricochet-c/story. 5-(9/94)		.70	1.75
0,6-8: 0-(10/94)		.80	2.00

GUN GLORY (See 4-Color No. 846)

GUNHAWK, THE (Formerly Whip Wilson)(See Wild Western)
No. 12, Nov, 1950 - No. 18, Dec, 1951 (Also see Two-Gun Western #5)
Marvel Comics/Atlas (MCI)

	GD25	FN65	NM94
12	11.50	34.00	80.00
13-18: 13-Tuska-a. 16-Colan-a. 18-Maneely-c	10.00	30.00	60.00

GUNHAWKS (Gunhawk No. 7)
October, 1972 - No. 7, October, 1973
Marvel Comics Group

	GD25	FN65	NM94
1-Reno Jones, Kid Cassidy; Shores-c/a(p)		1.60	4.00
2-7: 6-Kid Cassidy dies. 7-Reno Jones solo		1.20	3.00

GUNHED (Viz)(Value: cover or less)

GUNMASTER (Becomes Judo Master #89 on)
9/64 - No. 4, 1965; No. 84, 7/65 - No. 88, 3-4/66; No. 89, 10/67
Charlton Comics

	GD25	FN65	NM94
V1#1	3.20	8.00	16.00
2-4	1.80	4.50	9.00
V5#84-86: 84-Formerly Six-Gun Heroes	1.80	4.50	9.00
V5#87-89	1.20	3.00	6.00

NOTE: *Vol. 5 was originally cancelled with #88 (3-4/66). #89 on, became Judo Master, then later in 1967, Charlton issued #89 as a Gunmaster one-shot.*

GUN RUNNER
Oct, 1993 - No. 6, Mar, 1994 ($1.75, limited series)
Marvel Comics UK

	GD25	FN65	NM94
1-($2.75)-Polybagged w/4 trading cards; Spirits of Vengeance app.		1.10	2.75
2-6: 2-Ghost Rider & Blaze app.		.70	1.75

GUNS AGAINST GANGSTERS (True-To-Life Romances #8 on)
Sept-Oct, 1948 - No. 6, July-Aug, 1949; V2#1, Sept-Oct, 1949 - No. 2, 11-12/49
Curtis Publications/Novelty Press

	GD25	FN65	NM94
1-Toni & Greg Gayle begins by Schomburg	16.50	50.00	115.00
2	11.50	34.00	80.00
3-6, V2#1,2: 6-Toni Gayle-c	10.00	30.00	70.00

NOTE: ***L. B. Cole*** *c-1-6, V2#1, 2; a-1, 2, 3(2), 4-6.*

GUNSLINGER (See 4-Color No. 1220)

GUNSLINGER (Formerly Tex Dawson...)
No. 2, April, 1973 - No. 3, June, 1973
Marvel Comics Group

	GD25	FN65	NM94
2,3			1.00

GUNSMOKE (Blazing Stories of the West)
Apr-May, 1949 - No. 16, Jan, 1952
Western Comics (Youthful Magazines)

	GD25	FN65	NM94
1-Gunsmoke & Masked Marvel begin by Ingels; Ingels bondage-c	27.00	81.00	190.00
2-Ingels-c/a(2)	16.50	50.00	115.00
3-Ingels bondage-c/a	13.00	40.00	90.00
4-6: Ingels-c	11.00	32.00	75.00
7-10	7.50	22.50	45.00
11-16: 15,16-Western/horror stories	5.35	16.00	32.00

NOTE: ***Stallman*** *a-11, 14.* ***Wildey*** *a-15, 16.*

GUNSMOKE (TV)
No. 679, Feb, 1956 - No. 27, June-July, 1961; Feb, 1969 - No. 6, Feb, 1970
Dell Publishing Co./Gold Key (All have James Arness photo-c)

	GD25	FN65	NM94
4-Color 679(#1)	13.00	40.00	90.00
4-Color 720,769,797,844 (#2-5)	7.00	21.00	42.00
6(11-1/57-58), 7	7.00	21.00	42.00
8,9,11,12-Williamson-a in all, 4 pgs. each	8.35	25.00	50.00

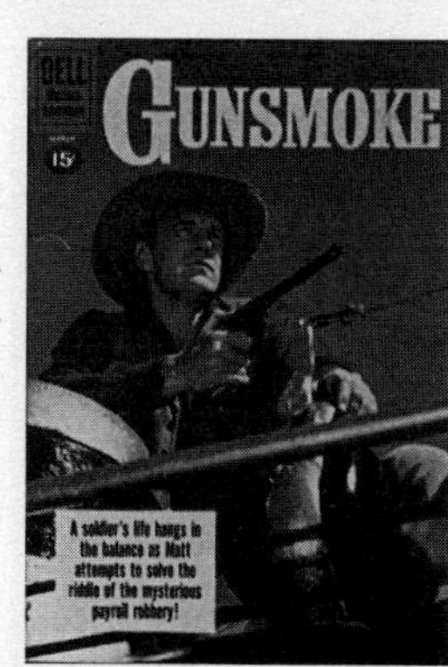

Gunsmoke #25 (Dell) © CBS

Guy Gardner #8 © DC

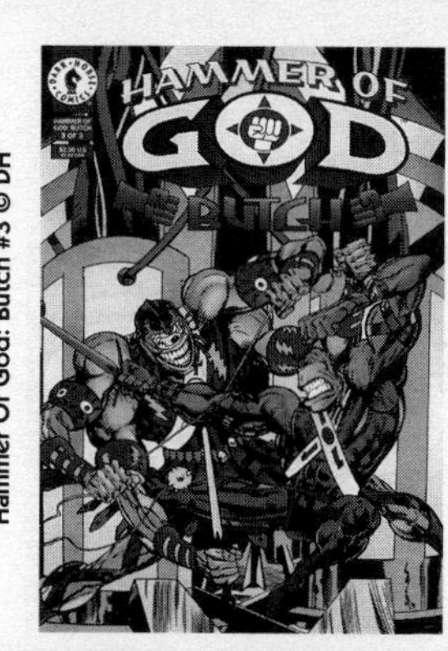

Hammer Of God: Butch #3 © DH

	GD25	FN65	NM94
10-Williamson/Crandall-a, 4 pgs.	8.35	25.00	50.00
13-27	6.35	19.00	38.00
Gunsmoke Film Story (11/62-G.K. Giant) No. 30008-211	9.15	27.50	55.00
1 (Gold Key)	4.35	13.00	26.00
2-6('69-70)	2.30	6.90	16.00

GUNSMOKE TRAIL
June, 1957 - No. 4, Dec, 1957
Ajax-Farrell Publ./Four Star Comic Corp.

	GD25	FN65	NM94
1	7.50	22.50	45.00
2-4	4.35	13.00	26.00

GUNSMOKE WESTERN (Formerly Western Tales of Black Rider)
No. 32, Dec, 1955 - No. 77, July, 1963
Atlas Comics No. 32-35(CPS/NPI); Marvel No. 36 on

	GD25	FN65	NM94
32-Baker & Drucker-a	10.00	30.00	70.00
33,35,36-Williamson-a in each: 5,6 & 4 pgs. plus Drucker-a #33. 33-Kinstler-a?	10.00	30.00	60.00
34-Baker-a, 4 pgs.	5.85	17.50	35.00
37-Davis-a(2); Williamson text illo	6.70	20.00	40.00
38,39: 39-Williamson text illo (unsigned)	4.70	14.00	28.00
40-Williamson/Mayo-a (4 pgs.)	6.70	20.00	40.00
41,42,45-49,51-54,57-60: 49,52-Kid from Texas story. 57-1st Two Gun Kid by Severin. 60-Sam Hawk app. in Kid Colt	4.00	10.00	20.00
43,44-Torres-a	4.00	12.00	24.00
50,61-Crandall-a	4.70	14.00	28.00
55,56-Matt Baker-a	4.00	12.00	24.00
62-71,73-77	3.20	8.00	16.00
72-Origin Kid Colt	4.00	11.00	22.00

NOTE: ***Colan** a-35-37, 39, 72, 76. **Davis** a-37, 52, 54, 55; c-50, 54. **Ditko** a-66; c-56p. **Drucker** a-32-34. **Heath** c-33. **Jack Keller** a-35, 40, 60, 72; c-72. **Kirby** a-47, 50, 51, 59, 62(3), 63-67, 69, 71, 73, 77; c-56(w/**Ditko**),57, 58, 60, 61(w/**Ayers**), 62, 63, 66, 68, 69, 71-77. **Robinson** a-35. **Severin** a-35, 59-61; c-34, 35, 39, 42, 43. **Tuska** a-34. **Wildey** a-10, 37, 42, 56, 57. Kid Colt in all. Two-Gun Kid in No. 57, 59, 60-63. Wyatt Earp in No. 45, 48, 49, 52, 54, 55, 58.*

GUNS OF FACT & FICTION (See A-1 Comics No. 13)

GUN THAT WON THE WEST, THE
1956 (24 pgs.; regular size) (Giveaway)
Winchester-Western Division & Olin Mathieson Chemical Corp.

	GD25	FN65	NM94
nn-Painted-c	4.20	12.50	25.00

GUY GARDNER (Guy Gardner: Warrior #17 on)(Also see Green Lantern #59)
Oct, 1992 - Present ($1.25/$1.50)
DC Comics

	GD25	FN65	NM94
1-15: 1-Staton-c/a(p) begins. 6-Guy vs. Hal Jordan. 8-Vs. Lobo-c/story. 15-JLA x-over			1.25
16-24: 16-Begin $1.50-c. 18-Begin 4-part Emerald Fallout story; splash page x-over GL #50. 18-21-Vs. Hal Jordan. 24-(9/94)-Zero Hour			1.50
0,25-29: 0-(10/94)			1.50

GUY GARDNER REBORN
1992 - Book 3, 1992 ($4.95, mini-series)
DC Comics

	GD25	FN65	NM94
1-3: Staton-c/a(p). 1-Lobo-c/cameo. 2,3-Lobo-c/s	1.00	2.00	5.00

GYPSY COLT (See 4-Color No. 568)

GYRO GEARLOOSE (See Dynabrite Comics, Walt Disney's C&S #140 & Walt Disney Showcase #18)
No. 1047, Nov-Jan/1959-60 - May-July, 1962 (Disney)
Dell Publishing Co.

	GD25	FN65	NM94
4-Color 1047 (No. 1)-All Barks-c/a	18.00	54.00	125.00
4-Color 1095,1184-All by Carl Barks	11.50	34.00	80.00
4-Color 1267-Barks c/a, 4 pgs.	8.35	25.00	50.00
01329-207 (#1, 5-7/62)-Barks-c only (intended as 4-Color 1329?)	5.85	17.50	35.00

HACKER FILES, THE
Aug, 1992 - No. 12, July, 1993 ($1.95)
DC Comics

	GD25	FN65	NM94
1-12: 1-Sutton-a(p) begins; computer generated-c		.80	2.00

HAGAR THE HORRIBLE (See Comics Reading Libraries)

HA HA COMICS (Teepee Tim No. 100 on; also see Giggle Comics)
Oct, 1943 - No. 99, Jan, 1955
Scope Mag.(Creston Publ.) No. 1-80/American Comics Group

	GD25	FN65	NM94
1-Funny animal	23.00	70.00	160.00
2	11.00	32.00	75.00
3-5: Ken Hultgren-a begins?	8.35	25.00	50.00
6-10	6.70	20.00	40.00
11-20: 14-Infinity-c	5.00	15.00	30.00
21-40	4.00	12.00	24.00
41-94,96-99: 49-X-Mas-c	4.00	10.00	20.00
95-3-D effect-c	10.00	30.00	70.00

HAIR BEAR BUNCH, THE (TV) (See Fun-In No. 13)
Feb, 1972 - No. 9, Feb, 1974 (Hanna-Barbera)
Gold Key

	GD25	FN65	NM94
1	1.40	3.50	8.50
2-9	1.00	2.00	5.00

HALLELUJAH TRAIL, THE (See Movie Classics)

HALL OF FAME FEATURING THE T.H.U.N.D.E.R. AGENTS
May, 1983 - No. 3, Dec, 1983
JC Productions(Archie Comics Group)

	GD25	FN65	NM94
1-3: Thunder Agents-r(Crandall, Tuska, Wood-a)		.50	1.00

HALLOWEEN HORROR (Eclipse)(Value: cover or less)

HALO JONES (See The Ballad of...)

HAMMERLOCKE
Sept, 1992 - No. 9, May, 1993 ($1.75, mini-series)
DC Comics

	GD25	FN65	NM94
1-($2.50, 52 pgs.)		1.00	2.50
2-9		.70	1.75

HAMMER OF GOD (First)(Value: cover or less)

HAMMER OF GOD: BUTCH
May, 1994 - No. 3, Aug, 1994 ($2.50, limited series)
Dark Horse Comics

	GD25	FN65	NM94
1-3		1.00	2.50

HAMMER OF GOD: PENTATHLON
Jan, 1994 ($2.50)
Dark Horse Comics

	GD25	FN65	NM94
1-Character from Nexus		1.00	2.50

HAMMER OF GOD: SWORD OF JUSTICE (First)(Value: cover or less)

HANDBOOK OF THE CONAN UNIVERSE, THE
June, 1985 ($1.25, one-shot)
Marvel Comics

	GD25	FN65	NM94
1			1.25

HAND OF FATE (Formerly Men Against Crime)
No. 8, Dec, 1951 - No. 26, March, 1955 (Weird/horror stories)(Two #25's)
Ace Magazines

	GD25	FN65	NM94
8-Surrealistic text story	21.00	63.00	145.00
9,10	11.00	32.00	75.00
11-18,20,22,23	10.00	30.00	60.00
19-Bondage, hypo needle scenes	11.00	32.00	70.00
21-Necronomicon story; drug belladonna used	11.00	32.00	75.00
24-Electric chair-c	14.00	43.00	100.00
25a(11/54), 25b(12/54)-Both have Cameron-a	8.00	24.00	48.00
26-Nostrand-a; exist?	10.00	30.00	65.00

NOTE: ***Cameron** a-9, 10, 19-25a, 25b; c-13. **Sekowsky** a-8, 9, 13, 14.*

The Hand of Fate #18 © ACE

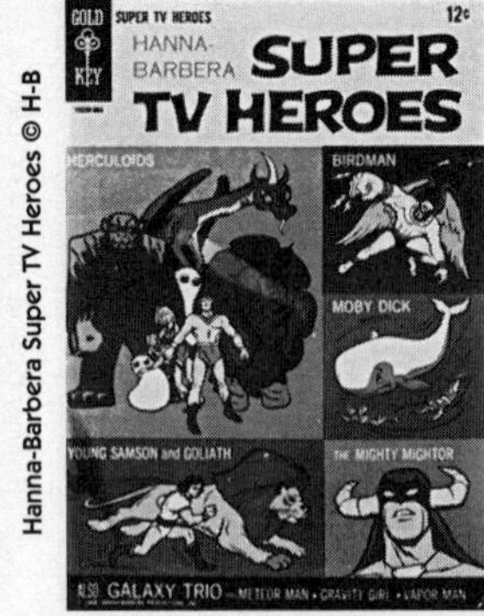

Hanna-Barbera Super TV Heroes © H-B

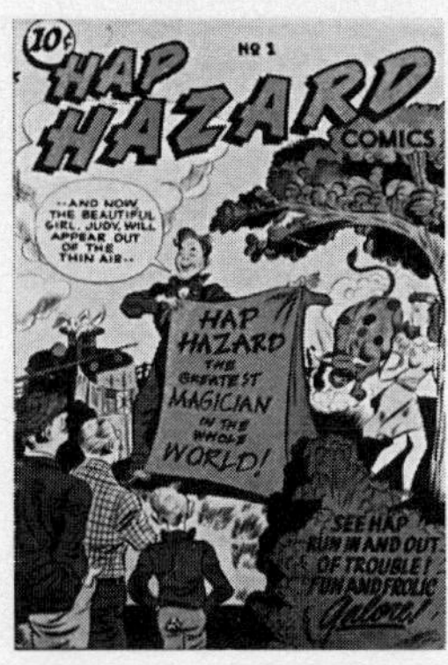

Hap Hazard Comics #1 © ACE

HAND OF FATE (Eclipse)(Value: cover or less)

HANDS OF THE DRAGON
June, 1975
Seaboard Periodicals (Atlas)

	GD25	FN65	NM94
1-Origin; Mooney inks			1.00

HANGMAN COMICS (Special Comics No. 1; Black Hood No. 9 on)
(Also see Flyman, Mighty Comics, Mighty Crusaders & Pep Comics)
No. 2, Spring, 1942 - No. 8, Fall, 1943
MLJ Magazines

	GD25	FN65	NM94
2-The Hangman, Boy Buddies begin	118.00	354.00	825,00
3-8: 3-Beheading splash pg.; 1st Nazi war-c. 5-1st Jap war-c. 8-2nd app. Super Duck (ties w/Jolly Jingles #11)	62.00	186.00	435.00

NOTE: ***Fuje** a-7(3), 8(3); c-3. **Reinman** c/a-3. Bondage c-3. **Sahle** c-6.*

HANK
1946
Pentagon Publishing Co.

	GD25	FN65	NM94
nn-Coulton Waugh's newspaper reprint	6.35	19.00	38.00

HANNA-BARBERA (See Golden Comics Digest No. 2, 7, 11)

HANNA-BARBERA BAND WAGON (TV)
Oct, 1962 - No. 3, April, 1963
Gold Key

	GD25	FN65	NM94
1,2-Giants, 84 pgs. 1-Augie Doggie & Lippy the Lion app. (pre-#1's)	9.15	27.50	55.00
3-Regular size; Mr. & Mrs. J. Evil Scientist app. (pre-#1) & Snagglepuss app.	5.85	17.50	35.00

HANNA-BARBERA GIANT SIZE
Oct, 1992 ($2.25, 68 pgs.)
Harvey Comics

	GD25	FN65	NM94
V2#1-Flintstones, Yogi Bear, Magilla Gorilla, Huckleberry Hound, Quick Draw McGraw, Yakky Doodle & Chopper, Jetsons & others		.90	2.25

HANNA-BARBERA HI-ADVENTURE HEROES (See Hi-Adventure...)

HANNA-BARBERA PARADE (TV)
Sept, 1971 - No. 10, Dec, 1972
Charlton Comics

	GD25	FN65	NM94
1	4.60	14.00	32.00
2-10: 7-(52 pgs.)- "Summer Picnic"	2.60	7.70	18.00

NOTE: *No. 4 (1/72) went on sale late in 1972 with the January 1973 issues.*

HANNA-BARBERA SPOTLIGHT (See Spotlight)

HANNA-BARBERA SUPER TV HEROES (TV)
April, 1968 - No. 7, Oct, 1969 (Hanna-Barbera)
Gold Key

	GD25	FN65	NM94
1-The Birdman, The Herculoids(ends #6; not in #2), Moby Dick, Young Samson & Goliath(ends #2,4), and The Mighty Mightor begin; Spiegle-a in all	12.00	36.00	85.00
2-The Galaxy Trio app.; Shazzan begins; 12 & 15 cent versions exist	10.00	29.00	78.00
3-7: 3,6,7-The Space Ghost app.	10.00	31.00	72.00

HANNA-BARBERA TV FUN FAVORITES (See Golden Comics Digest #2,7,11)

HANNA-BARBERA (TV STARS) (See TV Stars)

HANS BRINKER (See 4-Color No. 1273)

HANS CHRISTIAN ANDERSEN
1953 (100 pgs. - Special Issue)
Ziff-Davis Publ. Co.

	GD25	FN65	NM94
nn-Danny Kaye (movie)-Photo-c; fairy tales	13.00	40.00	90.00

HANSEL & GRETEL (See 4-Color No. 590)

HANSI, THE GIRL WHO LOVED THE SWASTIKA (Spire Christian)(Value: cover or less)

HANS UND FRITZ
1929 (28 pgs., B&W, 10x13-1/2")
The Saalfield Publishing Co.

	GD25	FN65	NM94
193-(Rare)-By R. Dirks; contains 1916 Sunday strip reprints of Katzenjammer Kids & Hawkshaw the Detective	45.00	135.00	450.00
...The Funny Larks Of 2(1929)	40.00	120.00	400.00

HAP HAZARD COMICS (Real Love No. 25 on)
Summer, 1944 - No. 24, Feb, 1949 (#1-6 are quarterly issues)
Ace Magazines (Readers' Research)

	GD25	FN65	NM94
1	10.00	30.00	60.00
2	5.00	15.00	30.00
3-10	4.00	10.00	20.00
11-13,15-24	3.20	8.00	16.00
14-Feldstein-c (4/47)	6.35	19.00	38.00

HAP HOPPER (See Comics Revue No. 2)

HAPPIEST MILLIONAIRE, THE (See Movie Comics)

HAPPINESS AND HEALING FOR YOU (Also see Oral Roberts'...)
1955 (36 pgs.; slick cover) (Oral Roberts Giveaway)
Commercial Comics

	GD25	FN65	NM94
nn	8.35	25.00	50.00

NOTE: *The success of this book prompted Oral Roberts to go into the publishing business himself to produce his own material.*

HAPPI TIM (See March of Comics No. 182)

HAPPY COMICS (Happy Rabbit No. 41 on)
Aug, 1943 - No. 40, Dec, 1950 (Companion to Goofy Comics)
Nedor Publ./Standard Comics (Animated Cartoons)

	GD25	FN65	NM94
1-Funny animal	19.00	57.00	130.00
2	10.00	30.00	65.00
3-10	7.00	21.00	42.00
11-19	4.70	14.00	28.00
20-31,34-37-Frazetta text illos in all (2 in #34&35, 3 in #27,28,30). 27-Al Fago-a	5.35	16.00	32.00
32-Frazetta-a, 7 pgs. plus 2 text illos; Roussos-a	11.00	32.00	75.00
33-Frazetta-a(2), 6 pgs. each (Scarce)	17.00	52.00	120.00
38-40	4.00	10.00	20.00

HAPPY DAYS (TV)(See Kite Fun Book)
March, 1979 - No. 6, Feb, 1980
Gold Key

	GD25	FN65	NM94
1-Photo-c of TV cast	1.00	2.00	5.00
2-6		1.20	3.00

HAPPY HOLIDAY (See March of Comics No. 181)

HAPPY HOOLIGAN (See Alphonse...)
1903 (18 pgs.) (Sunday strip reprints in color)
Hearst's New York American-Journal

	GD25	FN65	NM94
Book 1-By Fred Opper	50.00	150.00	500.00
50 Pg. Edition(1903)-10x15" in color	60.00	180.00	600.00

HAPPY HOOLIGAN (Handy...) (See The Travels of...)
1908 (32 pgs. in color) (10x15"; cardboard covers)
Frederick A. Stokes Co.

	GD25	FN65	NM94
nn	40.00	120.00	400.00

HAPPY HOOLIGAN (Story of...)
No. 281, 1932 (16 pgs.; 9-1/2x12"; softcover)
McLoughlin Bros.

	GD25	FN65	NM94
281-Three-color text, pictures on heavy paper	15.00	45.00	150.00

HAPPY HOULIHANS (Saddle Justice No. 3 on; see Blackstone, The Magician Detective)
Fall, 1947 - No. 2, Winter, 1947-48
E. C. Comics

	GD25	FN65	NM94
1-Origin Moon Girl (same date as Moon Girl #1)	36.00	107.00	250.00
2	19.00	57.00	130.00

Harbinger #9 © Voyager Comm.

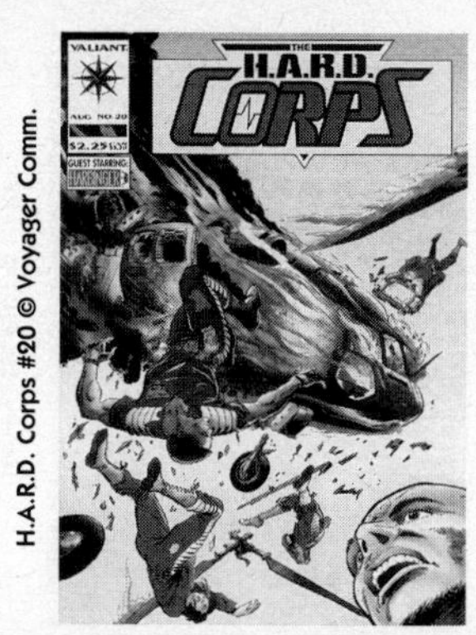

H.A.R.D. Corps #20 © Voyager Comm.

Harvey Comics Hits #56 © HARV

GD25 FN65 NM94

HAPPY JACK
August, 1957 - No. 2, Nov, 1957
Red Top (Decker)

V1#1,2 3.20 8.00 16.00

HAPPY JACK HOWARD
1957
Red Top (Farrell)/Decker

nn-Reprints Handy Andy story from E. C. Dandy Comics #5, renamed "Happy Jack" 4.00 10.00 20.00

HAPPY RABBIT (Formerly Happy Comics)
No. 41, Feb, 1951 - No. 48, April, 1952
Standard Comics (Animated Cartoons)

41-Funny animal 4.00 12.00 24.00
42-48 2.80 7.00 14.00

HARBINGER
Jan, 1992 - Present ($1.95/$2.50, color)
Valiant

0-(Advance) 7.15 21.50 50.00
1-1st app. 5.70 17.10 40.00
2 2.90 9.00 20.00
3 1.45 4.35 10.00
4-Low print run 2.15 6.45 15.00
5,6 1.40 4.30 10.00
7-9: 8,9-Unity x-overs. 8-Miller-c. 9-Simonson-c 1.00 3.00 7.00
10-1st app. H.A.R.D Corps (10/92) 1.00 2.00 5.00
11-16: 14-1st app. Stronghold 1.00 2.50
17-24,26-36: 18-Intro Screen. 19-1st app. Stunner. 22-Archer & Armstrong app. 24-Cover similar to #1. 26-Intro New Harbingers. 29-Bound-in trading card. 30-H.A.R.D. Corps app. 32-Eternal Warrior app. 33-Dr. Eclipse app. 1.00 2.50
25-($3.50, 52 pgs.)-Harada vs. Sting 1.40 3.50
...Files 1 (8/94, $2.50) 1.00 2.50
Trade paperback nn (11/92, $9.95)-Reprints #1-4 & comes polybagged with a copy of Harbinger #0 w/new-c 2.90 9.00 20.00
NOTE: *Issues 1-6 have coupons with origin of Harada and are redeemable for Harbinger #0.*

HARD BOILED (Dark Horse)(Value: cover or less)

HARDCASE (See Flood Relief)
June, 1993 - Present ($1.95, color)
Malibu Comics (Ultraverse)

1-Intro Hardcase; Dave Gibbons-c; has coupon for Ultraverse Premiere #0; Jim Callahan-a(p) begin, end #3 1.20 3.00
1-With coupon missing 1.50
1-Platinum Edition 10.00
1-Holographic Cover Edition; 1st full-c holograph tied w/Prime 1 & Strangers 1 25.00
1-Ultra Limited silver foil-c 10.00
2,3-Callahan-a .90 2.25
2-($2.50)-Newsstand edition bagged w/trading card 1.00 2.50
4,6-14: 4-Strangers app. 7-Break-Thru x-over. 8-Solution app. 9-Vs. Turf. 12-Silver foil logo, wraparound-c .80 2.00
5-($2.50, 48 pgs.)-Rune flip-c/story by B. Smith (3 pgs.) 1.00 2.50

H.A.R.D. CORPS, THE (See Harbinger #10)
Dec, 1992 - Present ($2.25, color) (Harbinger spin-off)
Valiant

1-(Advance) 30.00
1-($2.50)-Gatefold-c by Jim Lee & Bob Layton 1.10 2.75
1-Gold variant 10.00
2-6: 5-Bloodshot-c/story cont'd from Bloodshot #3 .90 2.25
5-Variant edition; came w/Comic Defense System 1.40 3.50
7-25: 10-Turok app. 17-Vs. Armorines. 18-Bound-in trading card. 20-Harbinger app. .90 2.25

HARD LOOKS (Dark Horse)(Value: cover or less)

GD25 FN65 NM94

HARDWARE
Apr, 1993 - Present ($1.50/$1.75)
DC Comics (Milestone)

1-($2.95)-Collector's Edition polybagged w/poster & trading card (direct sale only) 1.20 3.00
1-Platinum Edition 10.00
1-15,17-19: 11-Shadow War x-over. 11,14-Simonson-c. 12-Buckler-a(p). 17-Worlds Collide Pt. 2. 18-Simonson-c; Worlds Collide Pt. 9 1.50
16-($3.95, 52 pgs.)-Collector's Edition w/gatefold 2nd cover by Byrne; new armor; Icon app. 1.60 4.00
16-($2.50, 52 pgs.)-Newsstand Edition 1.00 2.50
20-24: 20-Begin $1.75-c .70 1.75

HARDY BOYS, THE (Disney)(See 4-Color No. 760, 830, 887, 964)

HARDY BOYS, THE (TV)
April, 1970 - No. 4, Jan, 1971
Gold Key

1 1.70 5.00 12.00
2-4 1.30 3.25 8.00

HARLEM GLOBETROTTERS (TV) (See Fun-In No. 8, 10)
April, 1972 - No. 12, Jan, 1975 (Hanna-Barbera)
Gold Key

1 1.30 3.25 8.00
2-12 1.60 4.00
NOTE: *#4, 8, and 12 contain 16 extra pages of advertising.*

HAROLD TEEN (See 4-Color #2, 209, Popular Comics, Super Comics & Treasure Box of Famous Comics)

HAROLD TEEN (Adventures of...)
1929-31 (36-52 pgs.) (Paper covers)
Cupples & Leon Co.

nn-B&W daily strip reprints by Carl Ed 16.00 48.00 110.00

HARROWERS, THE (See Clive Barker's...)

HARSH REALM
1994 - Present ($2.95)
Harris Comics

1-4-Painted-c 1.20 3.00

HARVEY
Oct, 1970; No. 2, 12/70; No. 3, 6/72 - No. 6, 12/72
Marvel Comics Group

1 1.20 2.90 7.00
2-6 1.60 4.00

HARVEY COLLECTORS COMICS (Richie Rich Collectors Comics #10 on, cover title only)
Sept, 1975 - No. 15, Jan, 1978; No. 16, Oct, 1979 (52 pgs.)
Harvey Publications

1-Reprints Richie Rich #1,2 1.00 2.00 5.00
2-10: 7-Splash pg. shows-c to Friendly Ghost Casper #1 1.20 3.00
11-16: 16-Sad Sack-r 1.25
NOTE: *All reprints: Casper-#2, 7, Richie Rich-#1, 3, 5, 6, 8-15, Sad Sack-#16. Wendy-#4. #6 titled 'Richie Rich...'on inside.*

HARVEY COMICS HITS (Formerly Joe Palooka #50)
No. 51, Oct, 1951 - No. 62, Apr, 1953
Harvey Publications

51-The Phantom 19.00 57.00 130.00
52-Steve Canyon's Air Power(Air Force sponsored) 10.00 30.00 65.00
53-Mandrake the Magician 13.50 41.00 95.00
54-Tim Tyler's Tales of Jungle Terror 9.15 27.50 55.00
55-Love Stories of Mary Worth 4.35 13.00 26.00
56-The Phantom; bondage-c 15.00 45.00 105.00
57-Rip Kirby Exposes the Kidnap Racket; entire book by Alex Raymond 10.00 30.00 70.00

Harvey Comics Library #1 © HARV

Harvey Hits #48 © HARV

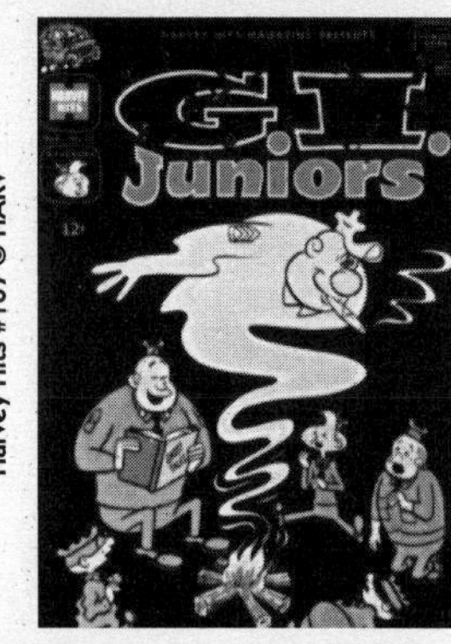

Harvey Hits #107 © HARV

	GD25	FN65	NM94
58-Girls in White (nurses stories)	4.00	12.00	24.00
59-Tales of the Invisible featuring Scarlet O'Neil	8.00	24.00	48.00
60-Paramount Animated Comics #1 (2nd app. Baby Huey); 1st Harvey app. Baby Huey & Casper the Friendly Ghost; 1st app. Herman & Catnip (c/story) & Buzzy the Crow (9/52)	30.00	90.00	210.00
61-Casper the Friendly Ghost #6 (2nd Harvey Casper, 10/52)-Casper-c	28.00	84.00	195.00
62-Paramount Animated Comics #2; Herman & Catnip, Baby Huey & Buzzy the Crow	10.00	30.00	60.00

HARVEY COMICS LIBRARY
April, 1952 - No. 2, 1952
Harvey Publications

	GD25	FN65	NM94
1-Teen-Age Dope Slaves as exposed by Rex Morgan, M.D.; drug propaganda story; used in **SOTI,** pg. 27	55.00	165.00	385.00
2-Dick Tracy Presents Sparkle Plenty in "Blackmail Terror"	13.00	40.00	90.00

HARVEY COMICS SPOTLIGHT
Sept, 1987 - No. 4, Mar, 1988 (#1-3: 75 cents, #4: $1.00)
Harvey Comics

	GD25	FN65	NM94
1-4: 1,2-new material. 1-Sad Sack, 2-Baby Huey, 3-Little Dot. 4-Little Audrey. #5 was advertised but not published			1.00

HARVEY HITS
Sept, 1957 - No. 122, Nov, 1967
Harvey Publications

	GD25	FN65	NM94
1-The Phantom	21.00	63.00	145.00
2-Rags Rabbit (10/57)	3.00	7.50	15.00
3-Richie Rich (11/57)-r/Little Dot; 1st book devoted to Richie Rich; see Little Dot for 1st app.	68.00	205.00	475.00
4-Little Dot's Uncles (12/57)	12.00	36.00	85.00
5-Stevie Mazie's Boy Friend (1/58)	2.00	5.00	10.00
6-The Phantom (2/58); Kirby-c; 2pg. Powell-a	13.00	40.00	90.00
7-Wendy the Good Little Witch (3/58, pre-dates Wendy #1; 1st book devoted to Wendy)	12.00	36.00	85.00
8-Sad Sack's Army Life; George Baker-c	5.00	15.00	30.00
9-Richie Rich's Golden Deeds; reprints (2nd book devoted to Richie Rich)	39.00	118.00	275.00
10-Little Lotta's Lunch Box	10.00	30.00	65.00
11-Little Audrey Summer Fun (7/58)	6.70	20.00	40.00
12-The Phantom; Kirby-c; 2pg. Powell-a (8/58)	11.00	32.00	75.00
13-Little Dot's Uncles (9/58); Richie Rich 1pg.	8.35	25.00	50.00
14-Herman & Katnip (10/58, TV/movies)	3.00	7.50	15.00
15-The Phantom (12/58)-1 pg. origin	11.00	32.00	75.00
16-Wendy the Good Little Witch (1/59); Casper app.	8.35	25.00	50.00
17-Sad Sack's Army Life (2/59)	4.20	12.50	25.00
18-Buzzy & the Crow	3.60	9.00	18.00
19-Little Audrey (4/59)	4.20	12.50	25.00
20-Casper & Spooky	5.85	17.50	35.00
21-Wendy the Witch	5.00	15.00	30.00
22-Sad Sack's Army Life	4.00	10.00	20.00
23-Wendy the Witch (8/59)	4.70	14.00	28.00
24-Little Dot's Uncles (9/59); Richie Rich 1pg.	6.70	20.00	40.00
25-Herman & Katnip (10/59)	2.40	6.00	12.00
26-The Phantom (11/59)	10.00	30.00	65.00
27-Wendy the Good Little Witch (12/59)	4.70	14.00	28.00
28-Sad Sack's Army Life (1/60)	2.40	6.00	12.00
29-Harvey-Toon (No.1)('60); Casper, Buzzy	4.00	11.00	22.00
30-Wendy the Witch (3/60)	4.70	14.00	28.00
31-Herman & Katnip (4/60)	1.40	3.50	7.00
32-Sad Sack's Army Life (5/60)	2.00	5.00	10.00
33-Wendy the Witch (6/60)	4.70	14.00	28.00
34-Harvey-Toon (7/60)	2.80	7.00	14.00
35-Funday Funnies (8/60)	1.40	3.50	7.00
36-The Phantom (1960)	8.35	25.00	50.00
37-Casper & Nightmare	4.00	11.00	22.00
38-Harvey-Toon	2.80	7.00	14.00
39-Sad Sack's Army Life (12/60)	2.00	5.00	10.00
40-Funday Funnies (1/61)	1.00	2.50	5.00
41-Herman & Katnip	1.20	3.00	6.00
42-Harvey-Toon (3/61)	2.00	5.00	10.00
43-Sad Sack's Army Life (4/61)	1.60	4.00	8.00
44-The Phantom (5/61)	7.50	22.50	45.00
45-Casper & Nightmare	3.20	8.00	16.00
46-Harvey-Toon (7/61)	1.60	4.00	8.00
47-Sad Sack's Army Life (8/61)	1.60	4.00	8.00
48-The Phantom (9/61)	7.50	22.50	45.00
49-Stumbo the Giant (1st app. in Hot Stuff)	8.35	25.00	50.00
50-Harvey-Toon (11/61)	1.60	4.00	8.00
51-Sad Sack's Army Life (12/61)	1.60	4.00	8.00
52-Casper & Nightmare	3.20	8.00	16.00
53-Harvey-Toons (2/62)	1.20	3.00	6.00
54-Stumbo the Giant	4.35	13.00	26.00
55-Sad Sack's Army Life (4/62)	1.60	4.00	8.00
56-Casper & Nightmare	3.20	8.00	16.00
57-Stumbo the Giant	4.35	13.00	26.00
58-Sad Sack's Army Life	1.60	4.00	8.00
59-Casper & Nightmare (7/62)	3.20	8.00	16.00
60-Stumbo the Giant (9/62)	4.35	13.00	26.00
61-Sad Sack's Army Life	1.60	4.00	8.00
62-Casper & Nightmare	2.80	7.00	14.00
63-Stumbo the Giant	4.35	13.00	26.00
64-Sad Sack's Army Life (1/63)	1.60	4.00	8.00
65-Casper & Nightmare	2.80	7.00	14.00
66-Stumbo The Giant (3/63)	4.35	13.00	26.00
67-Sad Sack's Army Life (4/63)	1.60	4.00	8.00
68-Casper & Nightmare	2.80	7.00	14.00
69-Stumbo the Giant (6/63)	4.35	123.00	26.00
70-Sad Sack's Army Life (7/63)	1.60	4.00	8.00
71-Casper & Nightmare (8/63)	2.00	5.00	10.00
72-Stumbo the Giant	4.35	13.00	26.00
73-Little Sad Sack (10/63)	1.60	4.00	8.00
74-Sad Sack's Muttsy... (11/63)	1.60	4.00	8.00
75-Casper & Nightmare	1.80	4.50	9.00
76-Little Sad Sack	1.60	4.00	8.00
77-Sad Sack's Muttsy...	1.60	4.00	8.00
78-Stumbo the Giant (3/64); JFK caricature	4.35	13.00	26.00
79-87: 79-Little Sad Sack (4/64). 80-Sad Sack's Muttsy... (5/64). 81-Little Sad Sack. 82-Sad Sack's Muttsy... 83-Little Sad Sack(8/64). 84-Sad Sack's Muttsy... 85-Gabby Gob (#1)(10/64). 86-G. I. Juniors (#1)(11/64). 87-Sad Sack's Muttsy... (12/64)	1.60	4.00	8.00
88-Stumbo the Giant (1/65)	4.35	13.00	26.00
89-122: 89-Sad Sack's Muttsy... 90-Gabby Gob. 91-G. I. Juniors. 92-Sad Sack's Muttsy... (5/65). 93-Sadie Sack (6/65). 94-Gabby Gob. 95-G. I. Juniors (8/65). 96-Sad Sack's Muttsy... (9/65). 97-Gabby Gob (10/65). 98-G. I. Juniors (11/65). 99-Sad Sack's Muttsy... (12/65). 100-Gabby Gob(1/66). 101-G. I. Juniors (2/66). 102-Sad Sack's Muttsy... (3/66). 103-Gabby Gob. 104- G. I. Juniors. 105-Sad Sack's Muttsy... 106-Gabby Gob (7/66). 107-G. I. Juniors (8/66). 108-Sad Sack's Muttsy... 109-Gabby Gob. 110-G. I. Juniors (11/66). 111-Sad Sack's Muttsy... (12/66). 112-G. I. Juniors. 113-Sad Sack's Muttsy... 114-G. I. Juniors. 115-Sad Sack's Muttsy... 116-G. I. Juniors (5/67). 117-Sad Sack's Muttsy... 118-G. I. Juniors. 119-Sad Sack's Muttsy... (8/67). 120-G. I. Juniors (9/67). 121-Sad Sack's Muttsy... (10/67). 122-G. I. Juniors (11/67)	1.00	2.50	6.00

HARVEY HITS COMICS
Nov, 1986 - No. 6, Oct, 1987
Harvey Publications

	GD25	FN65	NM94
1-6-Little Lotta, Little Dot, Wendy & Baby Huey: 3-Xmas-c			1.00

HARVEY POP COMICS (Teen Humor)
Oct, 1968 - No. 2, Nov, 1969 (Both are 68 pg. Giants)
Harvey Publications

Haunted #17 © CC

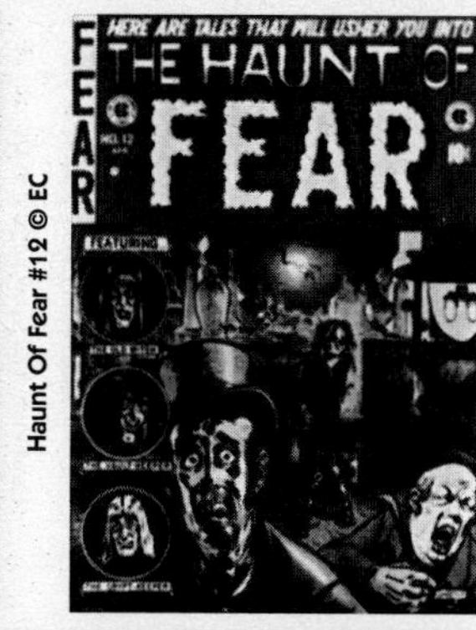

Haunt Of Fear #12 © EC

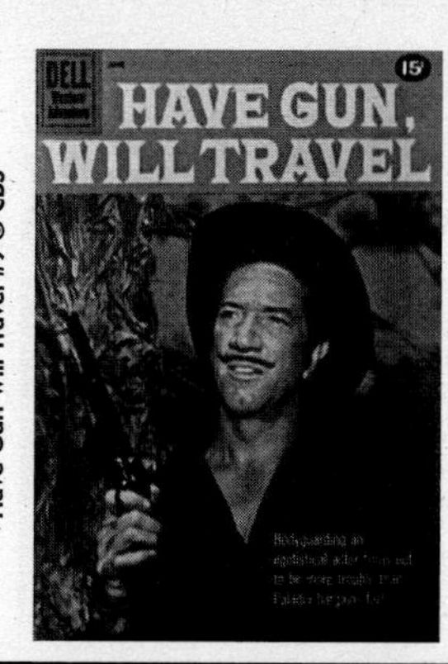

Have Gun Will Travel #9 © CBS

	GD25	FN65	NM94
1,2-The Cowsills	2.00	6.00	14.00

HARVEY 3-D HITS (See Sad Sack)

HARVEY-TOON (...S) (See Harvey Hits No. 29, 34, 38, 42, 46, 50, 53)

HARVEY WISEGUYS (...Digest #? on)
Nov, 1987; #2, Nov, 1988; #3, Apr, 1989 - No. 4, Nov, 1989 (98 pgs., digest-size, $1.25/$1.75)
Harvey Comics

	GD25	FN65	NM94
1,2: 1-Hot Stuff, Spooky, etc. 2 (68 pgs.)			1.25
3,4		.70	1.75

HATARI (See Movie Classics)

HATHAWAYS, THE (See 4-Color No. 1298)

HAUNTED (See This Magazine Is Haunted)

HAUNTED (Baron Weirwulf's Haunted Library #21 on)
9/71 - No. 30, 11/76; No. 31, 9/77 - No. 75, 9/84
Charlton Comics

	GD25	FN65	NM94
1	1.30	3.25	8.00
2-5		1.60	4.00
6-21		1.20	3.00
22-75: 51-Reprints #1. 64,75-Reprints			1.50

NOTE: ***Aparo** c-45. **Ditko** a-1-8, 11-16, 18, 23, 24, 28, 30, 34r, 36r, 39-42r, 47r, 49-51r, 57, 60, 74. c-1-7, 11, 13, 14, 16, 30, 41, 47, 49-51, 74. **Howard** a-18, 22, 32. **Morisi** a-13. **Newton** a-17, 21, 59r; c-21, 22(painted). **Staton** a-18, 21, 22, 30, 33; c-18, 33. **Sutton** a-21, 22, 38; c-15, 17, 18, 23(painted), 24(painted), 64r. #49 reprints Tales of the Mysterious Traveler #4.*

HAUNTED LOVE
April, 1973 - No. 11, Sept, 1975
Charlton Comics

	GD25	FN65	NM94
1-Tom Sutton-a (16 pgs.)	1.00	2.00	5.00
2,3,6-11		.80	2.00
4,5-Ditko-a		1.00	2.50
Modern Comics #1(1978)			1.00

NOTE: ***Howard** a-8i. **Newton** c-8, 9. **Staton** a-5.*

HAUNTED THRILLS (Tales of Horror and Terror)
June, 1952 - No. 18, Nov-Dec, 1954
Ajax/Farrell Publications

	GD25	FN65	NM94
1-r/Ellery Queen #1	21.00	63.00	145.00
2-L. B. Cole-a r-/Ellery Queen #1	12.00	36.00	85.00
3-5: 3-Drug use story	10.00	30.00	70.00
6-10,12: 7-Hitler story.	10.00	30.00	60.00
11-Nazi death camp story	10.00	30.00	70.00
13,16-18: 18-Lingerie panels	8.35	25.00	50.00
14-Jesus Christ apps. in story by Webb	8.35	25.00	50.00
15-Jo-Jo-r	8.35	25.00	50.00

NOTE: ***Kamenish** art in most issues. **Webb** a-12.*

HAUNT OF FEAR (Formerly Gunfighter)
No. 15, May-June, 1950 - No. 28, Nov-Dec, 1954
E. C. Comics

	GD25	FN65	NM94
15(#1, 1950)(Scarce)-1st app. Old Witch	200.00	600.00	1400.00
16	86.00	257.00	600.00
17-Origin of Crypt of Terror, Vault of Horror, & Haunt of Fear; used in **SOTI**, pg. 43; last pg. Ingels-a used by N.Y. Legis. Comm.; story "Monster Maker" based on Frankenstein	86.00	257.00	600.00
4	64.00	193.00	450.00
5-Injury-to-eye panel, pg. 4 of Wood story	49.00	145.00	340.00
6-10: 8-Shrunken head cover. 10-Ingels biog.	34.00	100.00	235.00
11-13,15-18: 11-Kamen biog. 12-Feldstein biog. 16,18-Ray Bradbury adaptations. 18-Ray Bradbury biography	24.00	73.00	170.00
14-Origin Old Witch by Ingels	37.00	111.00	260.00
19-Used in **SOTI**, ill. "A comic book baseball game" & Senate investigation on juvenile delinq. bondage/decapitation-c	34.00	100.00	235.00
20-Feldstein-r/Vault of Horror #12	22.00	67.00	155.00
21,22,25,27: 27-Cannibalism story; Wertham cameo	15.00	45.00	105.00
23-Used in **SOTI**, pg. 241	16.00	48.00	110.00
24-Used in Senate Investigative Report, pg.8	14.00	43.00	100.00
26-Contains anti-censorship editorial, 'Are you a Red Dupe?'	14.00	43.00	100.00
28-Low distribution	16.00	48.00	110.00

NOTE: *(Canadian reprints known; see Table of Contents). **Craig** a-15-17, 5, 7, 10, 12, 13; c-15-17, 5-7. **Crandall** a-20, 21, 26, 27. **Davis** a-4-26, 28. **Evans** a-15-19, 22-25, 27. **Feldstein** a-15-17, 20; c-4, 8-10. **Ingels** a-16, 17, 4-28; c-11-28. **Kamen** a-16, 4, 6, 7, 9-11, 13-19, 21-28. **Krigstein** a-28. **Kurtzman** a-15(#1), 17(#3). **Orlando** a-9, 12. **Wood** a-15, 16, 4-6.*

HAUNT OF FEAR, THE
May, 1991 - No. 2, July, 1991 ($2.00, 68 pgs.)
Gladstone Publishing

	GD25	FN65	NM94
1,2: 1-Ghastly Ingels-c(r); 2-Craig-c(r)		1.00	2.50

HAUNT OF FEAR
Sept, 1991 - No. 5, 1992 ($2.00, color, 68 pgs.)
Nov, 1992 - Present ($1.50, color)
Russ Cochran

	GD25	FN65	NM94
1-Ingels-c(r)		1.00	2.50
2-5		.80	2.00
1-3: 1-3-r/HOF #15-17 with original-c			1.50
4,5-r/HOF #4,5 with original-c		.80	2.00

HAUNT OF HORROR, THE (Magazine)
May, 1974 - No. 5, Jan, 1975 (75 cents) (B&W)
Cadence Comics Publ. (Marvel)

	GD25	FN65	NM94
1	1.00	2.50	6.00
2,4: 2-Origin & 1st app. Gabriel the Devil Hunter; Satana begins. 4-Neal Adams-a	1.00	2.00	5.00
3,5: 5-Evans-a(2)		1.60	4.00

NOTE: ***Alcala** a-2. **Colan** a-2p. **Heath** r-1. **Krigstein** r-3. **Reese** a-1. **Simonson** a-1.*

HAVE GUN, WILL TRAVEL (TV)
No. 931, 8/58 - No. 14, 7-9/62 (All Richard Boone photo-c)
Dell Publishing Co.

	GD25	FN65	NM94
4-Color 931 (#1)	11.50	34.00	80.00
4-Color 983,1044 (#2,3)	8.35	25.00	50.00
4 (1-3/60) - 14	6.35	19.00	38.00

HAVOK & WOLVERINE - MELTDOWN (See Marvel Comics Presents #24)
Mar, 1989 - No. 4, Oct, 1989 ($3.50, mini-series, squarebound)
Epic Comics (Marvel)

	GD25	FN65	NM94
1-4: Mature readers, violent		1.40	3.50

HAWAIIAN EYE (TV)
July, 1963 (Troy Donahue, Connie Stevens photo-c)
Gold Key

	GD25	FN65	NM94
1 (10073-307)	5.00	15.00	30.00

HAWAIIAN ILLUSTRATED LEGENDS SERIES
1975 (B&W)(Cover printed w/blue, yellow, and green)
Hogarth Press

	GD25	FN65	NM94
1-Kalelealuaka, the Mysterious Warrior			1.20
2,3(Exist?)			1.00

HAWK, THE (Also see Approved Comics #1, 7 & Tops In Adventure)
Wint/51 - No. 3, 11-12/52; No. 4, 1953 - No. 12, 5/55 (Painted c-1-4)
Ziff-Davis/St. John Publ. Co. No. 4 on

	GD25	FN65	NM94
1-Anderson-a	14.00	43.00	100.00
2 (Sum, '52)-Kubert, Infantino-a	9.15	27.50	55.00
3-8,11: 8-Reprints #3 w/different-c by Baker. 11-Buckskin Belle & The Texan app.	6.70	20.00	40.00
9-Baker-c/a; Kubert-a(r)/#2	7.50	22.50	45.00
10-Baker-c/a; r/one story from #2	7.50	22.50	45.00
12-Baker-c/a; Buckskin Belle app.	7.50	22.50	45.00
3-D 1(11/53, 25¢)-Came w/glasses; Baker-c	26.00	78.00	180.00

NOTE: ***Baker** c-8-12. **Larsen** a-10. **Tuska** a-1, 9, 12. Painted c-1, 7.*

HAWK AND DOVE (2nd series)

Hawk & Dove #6 ('89) © DC

Hawkman #4 © DC

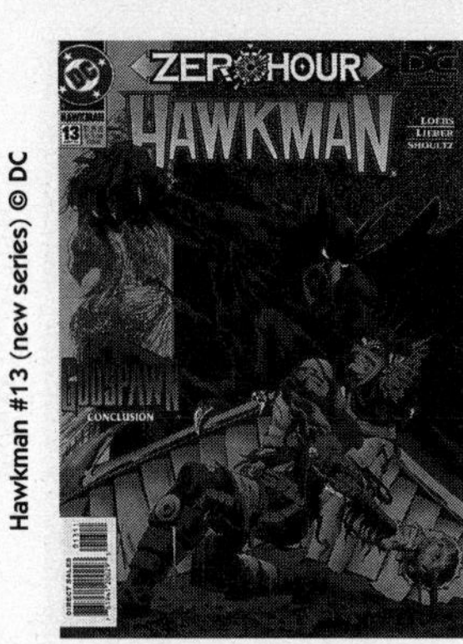

Hawkman #13 (new series) © DC

GD25 FN65 NM94

Oct, 1988 - No. 5, Feb, 1989 ($1.00, mini-series)
DC Comics

1-Rob Liefeld-c/a(p) in all 1.40 3.50
2-5 .80 2.00
Trade paperback ('93, $9.95)-Reprints #1-5 1.65 4.00 10.00

HAWK AND DOVE
June, 1989 - No. 28, Oct, 1991 ($1.00)
DC Comics

1-28 1.00
Annual 1 (1990, $2.00)-Liefeld pin-up .80 2.00
Annual 2 (1991)-Armageddon 2001 x-over .80 2.00

HAWK AND THE DOVE, THE (See Showcase #75 & Teen Titans)
Aug-Sept, 1968 - No. 6, June-July, 1969 (1st series)
National Periodical Publications

Showcase #75 (7-8/67)-Origin & 1st app. The Hawk and the Dove; Ditko-c/a 8.00 23.00 75.00
1-Ditko-c/a 5.70 17.00 40.00
2-6: 5-Teen Titans cameo 4.30 13.00 30.00
NOTE: ***Ditko** c/a-1, 2. **Gil Kane** a-3p, 4p, 5, 6p; c-3-6.*

HAWKEYE (See The Avengers #16 & Tales Of Suspense #57)
Sept, 1983 - No. 4, Dec, 1983 (Mini-series)
Marvel Comics Group

1-4: 1-Origin Hawkeye. 3-Origin Mockingbird 1.00

HAWKEYE
Jan, 1994 - No. 4, Apr, 1994 ($1.75, mini-series)
Marvel Comics

1-4 .70 1.75

HAWKEYE & THE LAST OF THE MOHICANS (See 4-Color No. 884)

HAWKMAN (See Atom & Hawkman, The Brave & the Bold, DC Comics Presents, Detective, Flash Comics, Hawkworld, Justice League of America #31, Mystery in Space, Shadow War Of..., Showcase, & World's Finest #256)

HAWKMAN (1st series) (Also see The Atom #7)
Apr-May, 1964 - No. 27, Aug-Sept, 1968
National Periodical Publications

	GD25	FN65	VF82	NM94
Brave and the Bold #34 (2-3/61)-Origin & 1st app. S.A. Hawkman & Byth by Kubert; 1st S.A. Hawkman tryout	121.00	363.00	906.00	1450.00

	GD25	FN65	NM94
Brave and the Bold #35 (4-5/61)-2nd app. Hawkman by Kubert. 36-Origin & 1st app. Shadow Thief	40.00	110.00	450.00
Brave and the Bold #36 (6-7/61)-3rd app. Hawkman by Kubert; origin Shadow Thief	38.00	113.00	375.00
Brave and the Bold #42 (6-7/62)-Hawkman by Kubert; #42-44 is 2nd Hawkman tryout series	25.00	75.00	250.00
Brave and the Bold #43 (8-9/62)-Gives more detailed origin Hawkman by Kubert	30.00	90.00	300.00
Brave and the Bold #44 (10-11/62)-Hawkman by Kubert	20.00	60.00	200.00
Brave and the Bold #51 (12-1/63-64)-Aquaman & Hawkman team-up	17.50	52.50	175.00
1-(4-5/64)-Anderson-c/a begins, ends #21	33.00	100.00	400.00
2	16.00	47.00	155.00
3,5	10.00	29.00	88.00
4-Origin & 1st app. Zatanna (10-11/64)	10.00	30.00	100.00
6-10: 9-Atom cameo; Hawkman & Atom learn each other's I.D.; 2nd app. Shadow Thief	8.30	25.00	58.00
11-15	6.00	18.00	42.00
16-27: 18-Adam Strange x-over (cameo #19). 25-G.A. Hawkman-r by Moldoff. 27-Kubert-c	4.30	12.90	30.00

HAWKMAN (2nd series)
Aug, 1986 - No. 17, Dec, 1987
DC Comics

1-17: 10-Byrne-c 1.00

Special #1 (1986, $1.25) 1.50
Trade paperback (1989, $19.95)-r/Brave and the Bold #34-36,42-44 by Kubert; Kubert-c 3.20 8.00 20.00

HAWKMAN (3rd series)
Sept, 1993 - Present ($1.75)
DC Comics

1-($2.50)-Gold foil embossed-c; new costume & powers 1.00 2.50
2-11: 2-Green Lantern x-over. 3-Airstryke app. 4,6-Wonder Woman app. .70 1.75
12,13: 12 -Begin $1.95-c. 13-(9/94)-Zero Hour .80 2.00
0,14-16: 0-(10/94) .80 2.00
Annual 1 ('93, $2.50, 68 pgs.)-Bloodlines Eathplague 1.00 2.50

HAWKMOON: (First Comics, all titles)(Value: cover or less)

HAWKSHAW THE DETECTIVE (See Advs. of..., Hans Und Fritz & Okay)
1917 (24 pgs.; B&W; 10-1/2x13-1/2") (Sunday strip reprints)
The Saalfield Publishing Co.

nn-By Gus Mager 16.00 48.00 110.00

HAWKWORLD
1989 - No. 3, 1989 ($3.95, prestige format, mini-series)
DC Comics

Book 1-Hawkman dons new costume 1.60 4.00
Book 2,3-Truman-c/a/scripts in #1-3 1.60 4.00

HAWKWORLD
June, 1990 - No. 32, Mar, 1993 ($1.50/$1.75)
DC Comics

1-Hawkman spin-off 1.00 2.50
2-32: 15,16-War of the Gods x-over. 22-J'onn J'onzz app. .70 1.75
Annual 1-3 ('90-'92, $2.95, 68 pgs.) 1.20 3.00
Annual 2-2nd printing with silver ink-c 1.20 3.00

HAWTHORN-MELODY FARMS DAIRY COMICS
No date (1950's) (Giveaway)
Everybody's Publishing Co.

nn-Cheerie Chick, Tuffy Turtle, Robin Koo Koo, Donald & Longhorn Legends 1.60 4.00 8.00

HAYWIRE (DC)(Value: cover or less)

HEADLINE COMICS (...For the American Boy) (...Crime No. 32-39)
Feb, 1943 - No. 22, Nov-Dec, 1946; No. 23, 1947 - No. 77, Oct, 1956
Prize Publications

	GD25	FN65	NM94
1-Junior Rangers-c/stories begin; Yank & Doodle x-over in Junior Rangers (Junior Rangers are Uncle Sam's nephews)	30.00	90.00	210.00
2	13.00	40.00	90.00
3-Used in **POP**, pg. 84	10.00	30.00	70.00
4-7,9,10: 4,9,10-Hitler stories in each	10.00	30.00	70.00
8-Classic Hitler-c	20.00	60.00	140.00
11,12	7.50	22.50	45.00
13-15-Blue Streak in all	8.35	25.00	50.00
16-Origin & 1st app. Atomic Man (11-12/45)	15.00	45.00	105.00
17,18,20,21: 21-Atomic Man ends (9-10/46)	8.35	25.00	50.00
19-S&K-a	17.00	52.00	120.00
22-Last Junior Rangers; Kiefer-c	5.00	15.00	30.00
23,24: (All S&K-a). 23-Valentine's Day Massacre story; content changes to true crime. 24-Dope-crazy killer story	15.00	45.00	105.00
25-35-S&K-c/a. 25-Powell-a	13.00	40.00	90.00
36-S&K-a; photo-c begin	10.00	30.00	70.00
37-One pg. S&K, Severin-a; Jack Kirby photo-c	6.70	20.00	40.00
38,40-Meskin-a	4.00	11.00	22.00
39,41,42,46-48,50-55: 41-J. Edgar Hoover 26th Anniversary Issue with photo on-c. 51-Kirby-c	3.00	7.50	15.00
43,49-Meskin-a	3.20	8.00	16.00
44-S&K-c; Severin/Elder, Meskin-a	6.70	20.00	40.00
45-Kirby-a	5.00	15.00	30.00

Headline Comics #8 © Prize

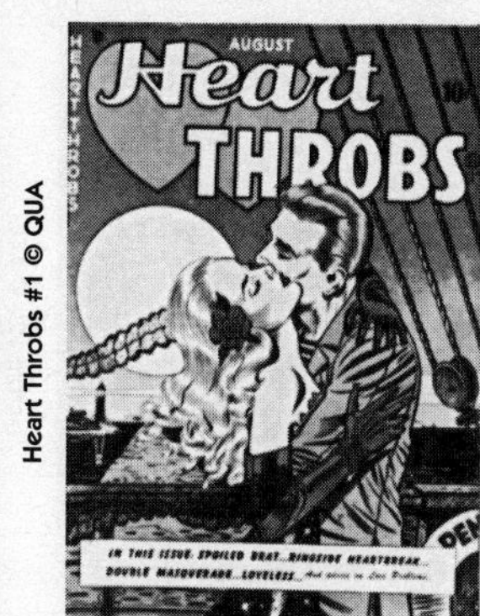

Heart Throbs #1 © QUA

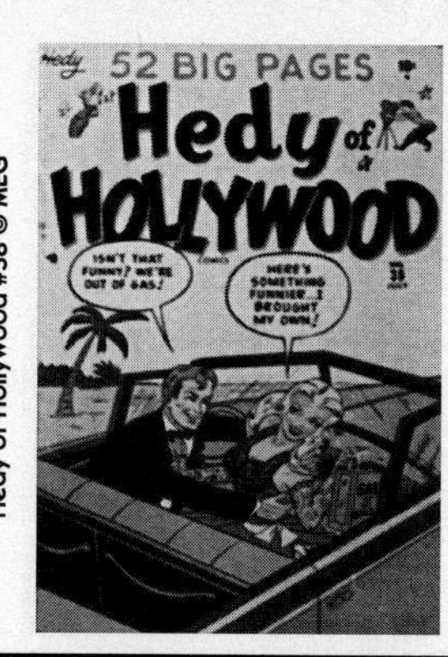

Hedy of Hollywood #38 © MEG

GD25 FN65 NM94

56-S&K-a 6.70 20.00 40.00
57-77: 72-Meskin-c/a(i) 2.80 7.00 14.00
NOTE: **Hollingsworth** a-30. Photo c-36-43. **H. C. Kiefer** c-12-16, 22. Atomic Man c-17-19.

HEADMAN (Innovation)(Value: cover or less)

HEAP, THE
Sept, 1971 (52 pgs.)
Skywald Publications
1-Kinstler-r/Strange Worlds #8 1.20 3.00

HEART AND SOUL
April-May, 1954 - No. 2, June-July, 1954
Mikeross Publications
1,2 5.00 15.00 30.00

HEART OF DARKNESS
1994 - Present ($2.95, bimonthly)
Hardline Studios
1-Brereton-c 1.20 3.00

HEART OF THE BEAST, THE
1994 ($19.95, adult)
DC Comics
1-Hardcover 3.00 8.60 20.00

HEARTS OF DARKNESS (See Ghost Rider; Wolverine; Punisher: Hearts of...)
Dec, 1992 ($4.95, double gatefold-c)
Marvel Comics
1-Ghost Rider, Punisher, Wolverine app. 1.00 2.00 5.00

HEART THROBS (Love Stories No. 147 on)
8/49 - No. 8, 10/50; No. 9, 3/52 - No. 146, Oct, 1972
Quality Comics/National Periodical #47(4-5/57) on (Arleigh #48-101)
1-Classic Ward-c, Gustavson-a, 9 pgs. 27.00 81.00 190.00
2-Ward-c/a (9 pgs); Gustavson-a 13.50 41.00 95.00
3-Gustavson-a 5.85 17.50 35.00
4,6,8-Ward-a, 8-9 pgs. 9.15 27.50 55.00
5,7 4.00 11.00 22.00
9-Robert Mitchum, Jane Russell photo-c 7.00 21.00 42.00
10,15-Ward-a 7.00 21.00 42.00
11-14,16-20: 12 (7/52) 3.60 9.00 18.00
21-Ward-c 5.35 16.00 32.00
22,23-Ward-a(p) 4.00 12.00 24.00
24-33: 33-Last pre-code (3/55) 3.20 8.00 16.00
34-39,41-46 (12/56; last Quality issue) 2.80 7.00 14.00
40-Ward-a; r-7 pgs./#21 4.00 11.00 22.00
47-(4-5/57; 1st DC issue) 20.00 60.00 140.00
48-60 9.15 27.50 55.00
61-70 6.35 19.00 38.00
71-100: 74-Last 10 cent issue 4.70 14.00 28.00
101-The Beatles app. on-c 10.00 30.00 60.00
102-120: 102-123-(Serial)-Three Girls, Their Lives, Their Loves. 120-Neal Adams-c 2.40 6.00 12.00
121-146: #133-142, 52 pgs. 1.00 2.50 6.00
NOTE: **Gustavson** a-8. **Tuska** a-128. Photo c-4, 5, 8-10, 15, 17.

HEATHCLIFF (See Star Comics Magazine)
Apr, 1985 - No. 56, Feb, 1991 (#16-on, $1.00)
Star Comics/Marvel Comics No. 23 on
1-49,51-56: Post-a most issues. 43-X-Mas issue. 47-Batman parody (Catman vs. the Soaker) 1.00
50-($1.50, 52 pgs.) 1.50
Annual 1 ('87) 1.20

HEATHCLIFF'S FUNHOUSE
May, 1987 - No. 10, 1988
Star Comics/Marvel Comics No. 6 on
1-10 1.00

HEAVY HITTERS
1993 ($3.75, 68 pgs.)
Epic Comics (Marvel)
1-Bound w/trading card; Lawdog, Feud, Alien Legion, Trouble With Girls, & Spyke 1.50 3.75

HECKLE AND JECKLE (See Blue Ribbon, Giant Comics Edition #5A & 10, Paul Terry's, Terry-Toons Comics)
10/51 - No. 24, 10/55; No. 25, Fall/56 - No. 34, 6/59
St. John Publ. Co. No. 1-24/Pines No. 25 on
1-Funny animal 23.00 70.00 160.00
2 11.50 34.00 80.00
3-5 10.00 30.00 60.00
6-10 6.70 20.00 40.00
11-20 5.00 15.00 30.00
21-34: 25-Begin CBS Television Presents on-c 4.00 11.00 22.00

HECKLE AND JECKLE (TV) (See New Terrytoons)
11/62 - No. 4, 8/63; 5/66; No. 2, 10/66; No. 3, 8/67
Gold Key/Dell Publishing Co.
1 (11/62; Gold Key) 4.70 14.00 33.00
2-4 2.40 7.30 17.00
1 (5/66; Dell) 3.00 9.40 22.00
2,3 2.40 7.30 17.00
(See March of Comics No. 379, 472, 484)

HECKLE AND JECKLE 3-D (Spotlight)(Value: cover or less)

HECKLER, THE (DC Comics)(Value: cover or less)

HECTOR COMICS (The Keenest Teen in Town)
Nov, 1953 - No. 3, 1954
Key Publications
1-Teen humor 3.60 9.00 18.00
2,3 2.40 6.00 12.00

HECTOR HEATHCOTE (TV)
March, 1964
Gold Key
1 (10111-403) 5.00 15.00 30.00

HECTOR THE INSPECTOR (See Top Flight Comics)

HEDY DEVINE COMICS (Formerly All Winners #21? or Teen #22?(6/47); Hedy of Hollywood #36 on; also see Annie Oakley, Comedy & Venus)
No. 22, Aug, 1947 - No. 50, Sept, 1952
Marvel Comics (RCM)/Atlas #50
22-1st app. Hedy Devine (also see Joker #32) 10.00 30.00 65.00
23,24,27-30: 23-Wolverton-a, 1 pg; Kurtzman's "Hey Look", 2 pgs. 24,27-30-"Hey Look" by Kurtzman, 1-3 pgs. 11.00 32.00 70.00
25-Classic "Hey Look" by Kurtzman, "Optical Illusion" 11.00 32.00 75.00
26- "Giggles 'n' Grins" by Kurtzman 8.35 25.00 50.00
31-34,36-50: 32-Anti-Wertham editorial 5.00 15.00 30.00
35-Four pgs. "Rusty" by Kurtzman 10.00 30.00 60.00

HEDY-MILLIE-TESSIE COMEDY (See Comedy Comics)

HEDY WOLFE (Also see Patsy & Hedy & Miss America Magazine V1#2)
August, 1957
Atlas Publishing Co. (Emgee)
1-Patsy Walker's rival; Al Hartley-c 7.50 22.50 45.00

HEE HAW (TV)
July, 1970 - No. 7, Aug, 1971
Charlton Press
1 2.00 6.00 14.00
2-7 1.60 3.80 9.00

HEIDI (See Dell Jr. Treasury No. 6)

HELEN OF TROY (See 4-Color No. 684)

HELLBLAZER (John Constantine) (See Saga of Swamp Thing #37)

Hellblazer #70 © DC

Hellstrom #18 © MEG

Herbie #21 © ACG

GD25 FN65 NM94

Jan, 1988 - Present ($1.25/1.50, adults)
DC Comics (Vertigo imprint #63 on)

1-(44 pgs.)-John Constantine 1.70 5.00 12.00
2-5 1.10 2.70 6.50
6-10: 9-X-over w/Swamp Thing #76. 9,10-Swamp Thing cameo 1.40 3.50
11-20: 19-Dave McKean-c 1.40 3.50
21-30: 24-Contains bound-in Shocker movie poster. 25,26-Grant Morrison scripts. 27-Neil Gaiman scripts; Dave McKean-a; fold-out guide to Nightbreed 1.20 3.00
31-39,41-49: 36-Preview of World Without End. 44-Begin $1.75-c. 44,45-Sutton-a(i) 1.00 2.50
40-($2.25, 52 pgs.)-Dave McKean-a & colors; preview of Kid Eternity 1.20 3.00
50-($3.00, 52 pgs.) 1.20 3.00
51-65: 52-Glenn Fabry painted-c begin. 62-Special Death insert by McKean. 63-Silver metallic ink on-c .70 1.75
66-74,76-87: 66-Begin $1.95-c. 77-Totleben-c .80 2.00
75-($2.95, 52 pgs.) 1.20 3.00
Annual 1 (1989, $2.95, 68 pgs.) 1.80 4.50
Special 1 (1993, $3.95, 68 pgs.)-With pin-ups 1.60 4.00

HELLBOY: SEED OF DESTRUCTION
Mar, 1994 - No. 4, 1994 ($2.50, color, limited series)
Dark Horse Comics

1,2-Mignola & Byrne-a; Monkeyman & O'Brien back-up story (origin parts 1 & 2) 1.00 2.50

HELLHOUNDS (...: Panzer Cops #3-6)
1994 - No. 6, July, 1994 ($2.50, B&W, limited series)
Dark Horse Comics

1,3-5: 1-Hamner-c. 3-(4/94) 1.00 2.50
2,6-($2.95, 52 pgs.): 2-Joe Phillips-c 1.20 3.00

HELLHOUND, THE REDEMPTION QUEST
Dec, 1993 - No. 4, Mar, 1994 ($2.25, mini-series, coated stock)
Epic Comics (Marvel)

1-4 .90 2.25

HELLO, I'M JOHNNY CASH (Spire Christian)(Value: cover or less)

HELL ON EARTH (See DC Science Fiction Graphic Novel)

HELLO PAL COMICS (Short Story Comics)
Jan, 1943 - No. 3, May, 1943 (Photo-c)
Harvey Publications

1-Rocketman & Rocketgirl begin; Yankee Doodle Jones app.; Mickey Rooney photo-c 50.00 150.00 350.00
2-Charlie McCarthy photo-c 35.00 105.00 245.00
3-Bob Hope photo-c 41.00 122.00 285.00

HELLRAISER NIGHTBREED – JIHAD (Epic)(Value: cover or less)

HELLRAISER III: HELL ON EARTH (Epic)(Value: cover or less)(Movie Special)

HELL-RIDER (Magazine)
Aug, 1971 - No. 2, Oct, 1971 (B&W)
Skywald Publications

1,2: 1-Origin & 1st app.; Butterfly & Wildbunch begins 1.00 2.00 5.00

NOTE: *#3 advertised in Psycho #5 but did not come out.* ***Buckler*** *a-1, 2.* ***Morrow*** *c-3.*

HELL'S ANGEL (Becomes Dark Angel #6 on)
July, 1992 - No. 5, Nov, 1993 ($1.75)
Marvel Comics UK

1-5: X-Men (Wolverine, Cyclops)-c/stories. 1-Origin. 3-Jim Lee cover swipe .70 1.75

HELLSHOCK
July, 1994 - Present ($1.95, limited series:4)
Image Comics

GD25 FN65 NM94

1-Jae Lee-story/a .80 2.00

HELLSTORM: PRINCE OF LIES (See Ghost Rider #1 & Marvel Spotlight #12)
Apr, 1993 - Present ($2.00)
Marvel Comics

1-($2.95)-Parchment-c w/red thermographic ink 1.20 3.00
2-22: 14-Bound-in trading card sheet. P. Craig Russell-c .80 2.00

HE-MAN (See Masters Of The Universe)

HE-MAN (Also see Tops In Adventure)
Fall, 1952
Ziff-Davis Publ. Co. (Approved Comics)

1-Kinstler painted-c; Powell-a 10.00 30.00 70.00

HE-MAN
May, 1954 - No. 2, July, 1954 (Painted-c by B. Safran)
Toby Press

1 10.00 30.00 60.00
2 8.35 25.00 50.00

HENNESSEY (See 4-Color No. 1200, 1280)

HENRY
1935 (52 pgs.) (Daily B&W strip reprints)
David McKay Publications

1-By Carl Anderson 11.50 34.00 80.00

HENRY (See King Comics & Magic Comics)
No. 122, Oct, 1946 - No. 65, Apr-June, 1961
Dell Publishing Co.

4-Color 122-All new stories begin 11.50 34.00 80.00
4-Color 155 (7/47) 9.15 27.50 55.00
1 (1-3/48)-All new stories 10.00 30.00 60.00
2 4.20 12.50 25.00
3-10 4.00 10.00 20.00
11-20: 20-Infinity-c 2.80 7.00 14.00
21-30 2.00 5.00 10.00
31-40 1.60 4.00 8.00
41-65 1.20 3.00 6.00

HENRY (See Giant Comic Album and March of Comics No. 43, 58, 84, 101, 112, 129, 147, 162, 178, 189)

HENRY ALDRICH COMICS (TV)
Aug-Sept, 1950 - No. 22, Sept-Nov, 1954
Dell Publishing Co.

1-Part series written by John Stanley; Bill Williams-a 10.00 30.00 60.00
2 5.00 15.00 30.00
3-5 4.35 13.00 26.00
6-10 4.00 11.00 22.00
11-22 3.200 8.00 16.00
Giveaway (16 pgs., soft-c, 1951)-Capehart radio 4.00 11.00 22.00

HENRY BREWSTER
Feb, 1966 - V2#7, Sept, 1967 (All 25¢ Giants)
Country Wide (M.F. Ent.)

1 1.20 3.00 6.00
2-6(12/66)-Powell-a in most .80 2.00 4.00
V2#7 .60 1.50 3.00

HERBIE (See Forbidden Worlds & Unknown Worlds)
April-May, 1964 - No. 23, Feb, 1967 (All 12 cents)
American Comics Group

1-Whitney-c/a in most issues 16.00 49.00 115.00
2-4 8.00 25.00 58.00
5-Beatles, Dean Martin, F. Sinatra app. 11.00 33.00 78.00
6,7,9,10 7.00 20.00 46.00
8-Origin & 1st app. The Fat Fury 8.00 25.00 58.00
11-23: 14-Nemesis & Magicman app. 17-r/2nd Herbie from Forbidden Worlds

Hercules #11 © CC

Hero #2 © MEG

Heroic Comics #18 © EAS

GD25 FN65 NM94

#94. 23-r/1st Herbie from F.W. #73 4.60 14.00 32.00

HERBIE
Oct, 1992 - No. 12, 1993 ($2.50, color, limited series)
Dark Horse Comics

1-6: Whitney-r plus new-c/a. 1-Byrne-c/a/scripts. 3-Bob Burden-c/a. 4-Art Adams-c 1.00 2.50

HERBIE GOES TO MONTE CARLO, HERBIE RIDES AGAIN (See Walt Disney Showcase No. 24, 41)

HERCULES (See Hit Comics #1-21, Journey Into Mystery Annual, Marvel Graphic Novel #37, Marvel Premiere #26 & The Mighty...)

HERCULES
Oct, 1967 - No. 13, Sept, 1969; Dec, 1968
Charlton Comics

1-Thane of Bagarth series begins; Glanzman 1.40 3.50 8.50
2-13: 1-5,7,9,10-Aparo-a .90 2.30 5.50
8-(Low distribution)(12/68, 35¢, B&W); magazine format; new Hercules story plus-r story/#1; Thane-r/#1-3 2.40 7.00 17.00
Modern Comics reprint 10('77), 11('78) 1.00

HERCULES (Prince of Power) (Also see The Champions)
Sept, 1982 - No. 4, Dec, 1982; Mar, 1984 - No. 4, June, 1984
Marvel Comics Group

1-4 .65 1.60
V2#1-4 (Mini-series) 1.00
NOTE: ***Layton** a-1, 2, 3p, 4p, V2#1-4; c-1-4, V2#1-4.*

HERCULES UNBOUND
Oct-Nov, 1975 - No. 12, Aug-Sept, 1977
National Periodical Publications

1-Wood inks begin 1.40
2-12: 10-Atomic Knights x-over 1.20
NOTE: ***Buckler** c-7p. **Layton** inks-No. 9, 10. **Simonson** a-7-10p, 11, 12; c- 8p, 9-12. **Wood** a-1-8i; c-7i, 8i.*

HERCULES UNCHAINED (See 4-Color No. 1006, 1121)

HERE COMES SANTA (See March of Comics No. 30, 213, 340)

HERE IS SANTA CLAUS
1930s (16 pgs., 8 in color) (stiff paper covers)
Goldsmith Publishing Co. (Kann's in Washington, D.C.)

nn 7.50 22.50 45.00

HERE'S HOW AMERICA'S CARTOONISTS HELP TO SELL U.S. SAVINGS BONDS
1950? (16 pgs.; paper cover)
Harvey Comics giveaway

Contains: Joe Palooka, Donald Duck, Archie, Kerry Drake, Red Ryder, Blondie & Steve Canyon 12.00 36.00 85.00

HERE'S HOWIE COMICS
Jan-Feb, 1952 - No. 18, Nov-Dec, 1954
National Periodical Publications

1 18.00 54.00 125.00
2 10.00 30.00 60.00
3-5: 5-Howie in the Army issues begin (9-10/52) 7.50 22.50 45.00
6-10 5.85 17.50 35.00
11-18 4.35 13.00 26.00

HERMAN & KATNIP (See Harvey Comics Hits #60 & 62, Harvey Hits #14,25,31,41 & Paramount Animated Comics #1)

HERO (Marvel)(Value: cover or less)

HERO ALLIANCE, THE (Sirius)(Value: cover or less)

HERO ALLIANCE (Wonder)(Value: cover or less)

HERO ALLIANCE (Innovation, all titles)(Value: cover or less)

HEROES AGAINST HUNGER
1986 ($1.50, one shot) (For famine relief)
DC Comics

1-Superman, Batman app.; Neal Adams-c(p); includes many artists work; Jeff Jones assist (2 pg.) on B. Smith-a 1.50

HEROES ALL CATHOLIC ACTION ILLUSTRATED
1943 - V6#5, March 10, 1948 (paper covers)
Heroes All Co.

V1#1,2-(16 pgs., 8x11") 10.00 30.00 70.00
V2#1(1/44)-3(3/44)-(16 pgs., 8x11") 8.35 25.00 50.00
V3#1(1/45)-10(12/45)-(16 pgs., 8x11") 6.70 20.00 40.00
V4#1-35 (12/20/46)-(16 pgs.) 5.00 15.00 30.00
V5#1(1/10/47)-8(2/28/47)-(16 pgs.) 4.00 11.00 22.00
V5#9(3/7/47)-20(11/25/47)-(32 pgs.) 4.00 11.00 22.00
V6#1(1/10/48)-5(3/10/48)-(32 pgs.) 4.00 11.00 22.00

HEROES FOR HOPE STARRING THE X-MEN
Dec, 1985 ($1.50, one-shot, 52pgs., proceeds donated to famine relief)
Marvel Comics Group

1-Stephen King scripts; Byrne, Miller, Corben-a; Wrightson/J. Jones-a (3 pgs.); Art Adams-c; Starlin back-c 1.50

HEROES, INC. PRESENTS CANNON
1969 - No. 2, 1976 (Sold at Army PX's)
Wally Wood/CPL/Gang Publ. No. 2

nn-Ditko, Wood-a; Wood-c; Reese-a(p) 1.60 4.00 8.00
2-Wood-c; Ditko, Byrne, Wood-a; 8-1/2x10-1/2"; B&W; $2.00 1.60 4.00
NOTE: *First issue not distributed by publisher; 1,800 copies were stored and 900 copies were stolen from warehouse. Many copies have surfaced in recent years.*

HEROES OF THE WILD FRONTIER (Formerly Baffling Mysteries)
No. 27, Jan, 1956 - No. 2, Apr, 1956
Ace Periodicals

27(#1),2-Davy Crockett, Daniel Boone, Buffalo Bill 4.00 10.00 20.00

HERO FOR HIRE (Power Man No. 17 on; also see Cage)
June, 1972 - No. 16, Dec, 1973
Marvel Comics Group

1-Origin & 1st app. Luke Cage; Tuska-a(p) 4.30 13.00 30.00
2-5: 2,3-Tuska-a(p). 3-1st app. Mace. 4-1st app. Phil Fox of the Bugle 1.70 5.00 12.00
6-10: 8,9-Dr. Doom app. 9-F.F. app. 1.00 2.50 6.00
11-16: 14-Origin retold. 15-Everett Subby-r('53). 16-Origin Stilletto; death of Rackham 1.00 2.50 5.50

HERO-GRAPHICS SUPER-SAMPLER (Hero)(Value: cover or less)

HERO HOTLINE (DC)(Value: cover or less)

HEROIC ADVENTURES (See Adventures)

HEROIC COMICS (Reg'lar Fellers...#1-15; New Heroic #41 on)
Aug, 1940 - No. 97, June, 1955
Eastern Color Printing Co./Famous Funnies(Funnies, Inc. No. 1)

1-Hydroman (origin) by Bill Everett, The Purple Zombie (origin) & Mann of India by Tarpe Mills begins (all 1st apps.) 93.00 280.00 650.00
2 46.00 140.00 325.00
3,4 36.00 109.00 255.00
5,6 27.00 81.00 190.00
7-Origin & 1st app. Man O'Metal (1 pg.) 31.00 94.00 220.00
8-10: 10-Lingerie panels 18.00 54.00 125.00
11,13: 13-Crandall/Fine-a 17.00 52.00 120.00
12-Music Master (origin/1st app.) begins by Everett, ends No. 31; last Purple Zombie & Mann of India 19.00 58.00 135.00
14,15-Hydroman x-over in Rainbow Boy. 14-Origin & 1st app. Rainbow Boy (super hero). 15-1st app. Downbeat 19.00 58.00 135.00
16-20: 16-New logo. 17-Rainbow Boy x-over in Hydroman. 19-Rainbow Boy x-over in Hydroman & vice versa 14.00 43.00 100.00
21-30:25-Rainbow Boy x-over in Hydroman. 28-Last Man O'Metal. 29-Last Hydroman 10.00 30.00 65.00

Hickory #2 © QUA

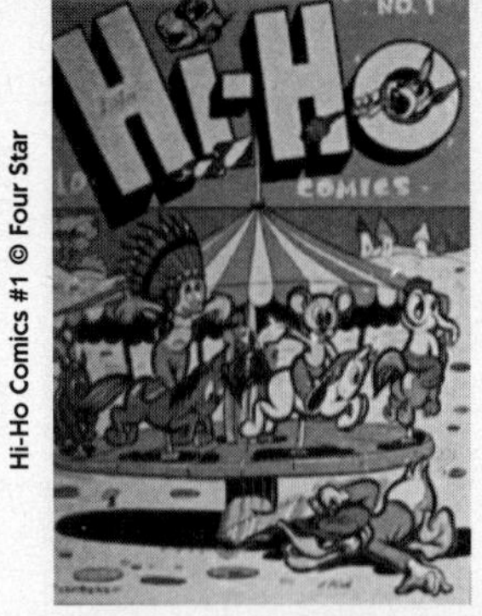

Hi-Ho Comics #1 © Four Star

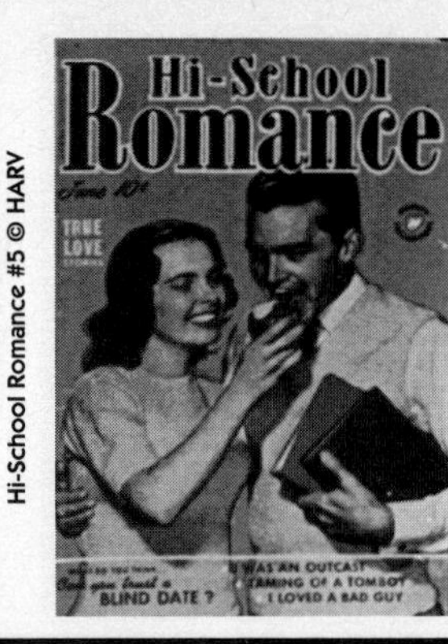

Hi-School Romance #5 © HARV

	GD25	FN65	NM94
31,34,38	3.60	9.00	18.00
32,36,37-Toth-a (3-4 pgs. each)	5.00	15.00	30.00
33,35-Toth-a (8 & 9 pgs.)	5.35	16.00	32.00
39-42-Toth, Ingels-a	5.35	16.00	32.00
43,46,47,49-Toth-a (2-4 pgs.). 47-Ingels-a	4.00	12.00	24.00
44,45,50-Toth-a (6-9 pgs.)	4.70	14.00	28.00
48,53,54	3.20	8.00	16.00
51-Williamson-a	5.00	15.00	30.00
52-Williamson-a (3 pg. story)	4.00	11.00	22.00
55-Toth-c/a	4.35	13.00	26.00
56-60-Toth-c. 60-Everett-a	4.00	11.00	22.00
61-Everett-a	3.20	8.00	16.00
62,64-Everett-c/a	3.60	9.00	18.00
63-Everett-c	2.80	7.00	14.00
65-Williamson/Frazetta-a; Evans-a (2 pgs.)	6.35	19.00	38.00
66,75,94-Frazetta-a (2 pgs. each)	4.00	10.00	20.00
67,73-Frazetta-a (4 pgs. each)	4.00	12.00	24.00
68,74,76-80,84,85,88-93,95-97: 95-Last pre-code	2.80	7.00	14.00
69,72-Frazetta-a (6 & 8 pgs. each); 1st (?) app. Frazetta Red Cross ad	6.35	19.00	38.00
70,71,86,87-Frazetta, 3-4 pgs. each; 1 pg. ad by Frazetta in #70	4.00	10.00	20.00
81,82-Frazetta art (1 pg. each): 81-1st (?) app. Frazetta Boy Scout ad (tied w/ Buster Crabbe #9	2.80	7.00	14.00
83-Frazetta-a (1/2 pg.)	2.80	7.00	14.00

NOTE: ***Evans*** *a-64, 65.* ***Everett*** *a-(Hydroman-c/a-No. 1-9), 44, 60-64; c-1-9, 62-64.* ***Harvey Fuller*** *c-28-35.* ***Sid Greene*** *a-38-43, 46.* ***Guardineer*** *a-42(3), 43, 44, 45(2), 49(3), 50, 60, 61(2), 65, 67(2) 70-72.* ***Ingels*** *c-41.* ***Kiefer*** *a-46, 48; c-19-22, 24, 44, 46, 48, 51-53, 65, 67-69, 71-74, 76, 77, 79, 80, 82, 85, 86, 88, 89, 94, 95.* ***Mort Lawrence*** *a-45.* ***Tarpe Mills*** *a-2(2), 3(2), 10.* ***Ed Moore*** *a-49, 52-54, 56-63, 65-69, 72-74, 76, 77.* ***H.G. Peter*** *a-58-74, 76, 77, 87.* ***Paul Reinman*** *a-49.* ***Rico*** *a-31. Captain Tootsie by* ***Beck****-31, 32. Painted-c #16 on. Hydroman c-1-11. Music Master c-12, 13, 15. Rainbow Boy c-14.*

HEX (Replaces Jonah Hex)
Sept, 1985 - No. 18, Feb, 1987 (Story continues from Jonah Hex 92)
DC Comics

	GD25	FN65	NM94
1-10,14-18: 1-Hex in post-atomic war world; origin. 6-Origin Stiletta			1.00
11-13: All contain future Batman storyline. 13-Intro The Dogs of War (origin #15)		.80	2.00

NOTE: ***Giffen*** *a(p)-15-18; c(p)-15,17,18.* ***Texeira*** *a-1, 2p, 3p, 5-7p, 9p, 11-14p; c(p)-1, 2, 4-7, 12.*

HEXBREAKER (See First Comics Graphic Novel #15)

HEY THERE, IT'S YOGI BEAR (See Movie Comics)

HI-ADVENTURE HEROES (TV)
May, 1969 - No. 2, Aug, 1969 (Hanna-Barbera)
Gold Key

	GD25	FN65	NM94
1-Three Musketeers, Gulliver, Arabian Knights	2.90	9.00	20.00
2-Three Musketeers, Micro-Venture, Arabian Knights	2.40	7.30	17.00

HI AND LOIS (See 4-Color No. 683, 774, 955)

HI AND LOIS
Nov, 1969 - No. 11, July, 1971
Charlton Comics

	GD25	FN65	NM94
1	2.00	6.00	14.00
2-11	1.20	2.90	7.00

HICKORY (See All Humor Comics)
Oct, 1949 - No. 6, Aug, 1950
Quality Comics Group

	GD25	FN65	NM94
1-Sahl-c/a in all; Feldstein?-a	10.00	30.00	70.00
2	5.35	16.00	32.00
3-6	4.35	13.00	26.00

HIDDEN CREW, THE (See The United States Air Force Presents:...)

HIDE-OUT (See 4-Color No. 346)

HIDING PLACE, THE (Spire Christian)(Value: cover or less)

HIGH ADVENTURE
October, 1957
Red Top(Decker) Comics (Farrell)

	GD25	FN65	NM94
1-Krigstein-r from Explorer Joe (re-issue on-c)	3.60	9.00	18.00

HIGH ADVENTURE (See 4-Color No. 949, 1001)

HIGH CHAPPARAL (TV)
August, 1968 (Photo-c)
Gold Key

	GD25	FN65	NM94
1 (10226-808)-Tufts-a	5.35	17.50	35.00

HIGH SCHOOL CONFIDENTIAL DIARY (Confidential Diary #12 on)
June, 1960 - No. 11, March, 1962
Charlton Comics

	GD25	FN65	NM94
1	3.20	8.00	16.00
2-11	1.60	4.00	8.00

HI-HO COMICS
nd (2/46?) - No. 3, 1946
Four Star Publications

	GD25	FN65	NM94
1-Funny Animal; L. B. Cole-c	14.00	43.00	100.00
2,3: 2-L. B. Cole-c	10.00	30.00	60.00

HI-JINX (Teen-age Animal Funnies)
1945; July-Aug, 1947 - No. 7, July-Aug, 1948
La Salle Publ. Co./B&I Publ. Co.(American Comics Group)/Creston

	GD25	FN65	NM94
nn-(© 1945, 25 cents, 132 Pgs.)(La Salle)	13.00	40.00	90.00
1-Teen-age, funny animal	11.00	32.00	75.00
2,3	7.50	22.50	45.00
4-7-Milt Gross. 4-X-Mas-c	9.15	27.50	55.00

HI-LITE COMICS
Fall, 1945
E. R. Ross Publishing Co.

	GD25	FN65	NM94
1-Miss Shady	10.00	30.00	70.00

HILLBILLY COMICS
Aug, 1955 - No. 4, July, 1956 (Satire)
Charlton Comics

	GD25	FN65	NM94
1	5.85	17.50	35.00
2-4	4.00	10.00	20.00

HIP-IT-TY HOP (See March of Comics No. 15)

HI-SCHOOL ROMANCE (...Romances No. 41 on)
Oct, 1949 - No. 5, June, 1950; No. 6, Dec, 1950 - No. 73, Mar, 1958; No. 74, Sept, 1958 - No. 75, Nov, 1958
Harvey Publications/True Love(Home Comics)

	GD25	FN65	NM94
1-Photo-c	9.15	27.50	55.00
2-Photo-c	4.35	13.00	26.00
3-9: 3,5-Photo-c	3.60	9.00	18.00
10-Rape story	4.20	12.50	25.00
11-20	2.40	6.00	12.00
21-31	2.00	5.00	10.00
32- "Unholy passion" story	4.00	10.00	20.00
33-36: 36-Last pre-code (2/55)	1.60	4.00	8.00
37-75	1.40	3.50	7.00

NOTE: ***Powell*** *a-1-3, 5, 8, 12-16, 18, 21-23, 25-27, 30-34, 36, 37, 39, 45-48, 50-52, 57, 58, 60, 64, 65, 67, 69.*

HI-SCHOOL ROMANCE DATE BOOK
Nov, 1962 - No. 3, Mar, 1963 (25¢ Giants)
Harvey Publications

	GD25	FN65	NM94
1-Powell, Baker-a	3.20	8.00	16.00
2,3	1.40	3.50	7.00

HIS NAME IS SAVAGE (Magazine format)
June, 1968 (35¢, 52 pgs.)
Adventure House Press

Hit Comics #52 © QUA

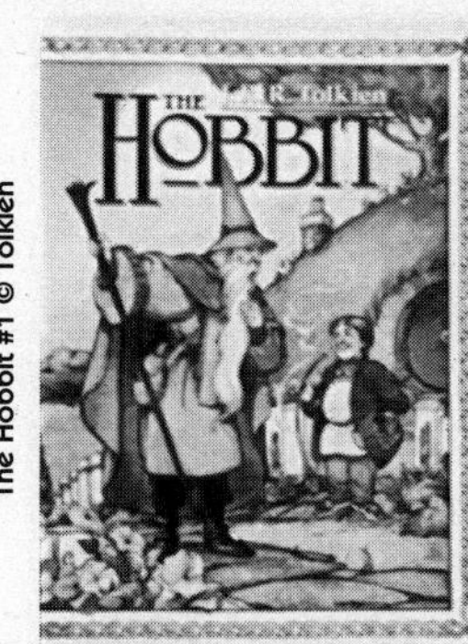

The Hobbit #1 © Tolkien

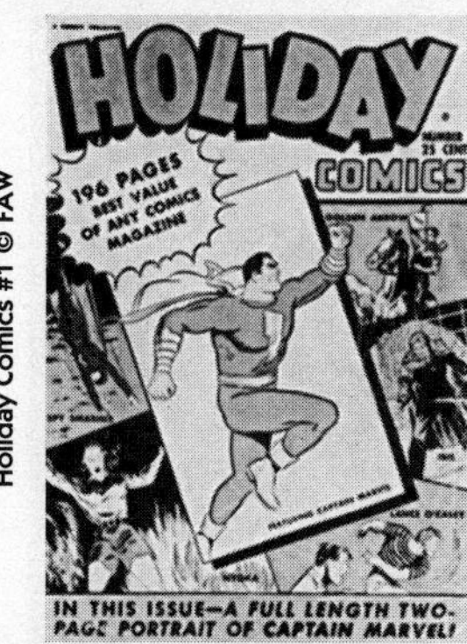

Holiday Comics #1 © FAW

GD25 FN65 NM94

1-Gil Kane-a 3.20 8.00 20.00

HI-SPOT COMICS (Red Ryder No. 1 & No. 3 on)
No. 2, Nov, 1940
Hawley Publications

2-David Innes of Pellucidar; art by J. C. Burroughs; written by Edgar Rice Burroughs 86.00 257.00 600.00

HISTORY OF THE DC UNIVERSE
Sept, 1986 - No. 2, Nov, 1986 ($2.95)
DC Comics

1,2: 1-Perez-c/a 1.20 3.00
Limited Edition hardcover 45.00

HITCHHIKERS GUIDE TO THE GALAXY
1993 - No. 3, 1993 ($4.95, color, limited series)
DC Comics

1-3-Adaptation of D. Adams book 1.00 2.00 5.00

HIT COMICS
July, 1940 - No. 65, July, 1950
Quality Comics Group

1-Origin/1st app. Neon, the Unknown & Hercules; intro. The Red Bee; Bob & Swab, Blaze Barton, the Strange Twins, X-5 Super Agent, Casey Jones & Jack & Jill (ends #7) begin 357.00 1071.00 2500.00
2-The Old Witch begins, ends #14 136.00 407.00 950.00
3-Casey Jones ends; transvestism story "Jack & Jill" 114.00 343.00 800.00
4-Super Agent (ends #17), & Betty Bates (ends #65) begin; X-5 ends 100.00 300.00 700.00
5-Classic cover 200.00 600.00 1400.00
6-10: 10-Old Witch by Crandall (4 pgs.); 1st work in comics (4/41) 81.00 242.00 565.00
11-17: 13-Blaze Barton ends. 17-Last Neon; Crandall Hercules in all 71.00 214.00 500.00
18-Origin & 1st app. Stormy Foster, the Great Defender (12/41); The Ghost of Flanders begins; Crandall-c 84.00 250.00 585.00
19,20 70.00 210.00 490.00
21-24: 21-Last Hercules. 24-Last Red Bee & Strange Twins 63.00 190.00 440.00
25-Origin & 1st app. Kid Eternity and begins by Moldoff (12/42); 1st app. The Keeper (Kid Eternity's aide) 104.00 310.00 725.00
26-Blackhawk x-over in Kid Eternity 66.00 200.00 465.00
27-29 37.00 111.00 260.00
30,31- "Bill the Magnificent" by Kurtzman, 11 pgs. in each 33.00 100.00 230.00
32-40: 32-Plastic Man x-over. 34-Last Stormy Foster 16.50 50.00 115.00
41-50 11.50 34.00 80.00
51-60-Last Kid Eternity 10.00 30.00 70.00
61-63-Crandall-c/a; 61-Jeb Rivers begins 11.00 32.00 75.00
64,65-Crandall-a 10.00 30.00 70.00

NOTE: ***Crandall** a-11-17(Hercules), 23, 24(Stormy Foster); c-18-20, 23, 24. **Fine** c-1-14, 16, 17(most). **Ward** c-33. Bondage c-7, 64. Hercules c-3, 10-17. Jeb Rivers c-61-65. Kid Eternity c-25-60 (w/Keeper-28-34, 36, 39-43, 45-55). Neon the Unknown c-2, 4, 8, 9. Red Bee c-1, 5-7. Stormy Foster c-18-24.*

HI-YO SILVER (See Lone Ranger's Famous Horse... and also see The Lone Ranger and March of Comics No. 215)

HOBBIT, THE (Eclipse)(Value: cover or less)

HOCUS POCUS (Formerly Funny Book)
No. 9, Aug-Sept, 1946
Parents' Magazine Press

9 4.00 11.00 22.00

HOGAN'S HEROES (TV)
June, 1966 - No. 8, Sept, 1967; No. 9, Oct, 1969
Dell Publishing Co.

GD25 FN65 NM94

1: #1-7 photo-c 6.00 17.00 39.00
2,3-Ditko-a(p) 3.60 11.00 25.00
4-9: 9-Reprints #1 2.60 7.70 18.00

HOKUM & HEX (See Razorline)
Sept, 1993 - No. 9, May, 1994 ($1.75/$1.95)
Marvel Comics

1-($2.50)-Foil embossed-c; by Clive Barker 1.00 2.50
2-8: 5-Hyperkind x-over .70 1.75
9-($1.95) .80 2.00

HOLIDAY COMICS
1942 (25¢, 196 pgs.)
Fawcett Publications

1-Contains three Fawcett comics plus two page portrait of Captain Marvel; Capt. Marvel, Nyoka #1, & Whiz. Not rebound, remaindered comics; printed at the same time as originals 110.00 330.00 1100.00

HOLIDAY COMICS (Becomes Fun Comics #9-12)
January, 1951 - No. 8, Oct, 1952
Star Publications

1-Funny animal contents (Frisky Fables) in all; L. B. Cole X-Mas-c 18.00 54.00 125.00
2-Classic L. B. Cole-c 20.00 60.00 140.00
3-8: 5,8-X-Mas-c; all L.B. Cole-c 11.50 34.00 80.00
Accepted Reprint 4 (nd)-L.B. Cole-c 6.70 20.00 40.00

HOLIDAY DIGEST
1988 ($1.25, digest-size)
Harvey Comics

1 1.25

HOLIDAY PARADE (Walt Disney's...)
Winter, 1990-91(no yr. given) - No. 2, Winter, 1990-91 ($2.95, 68 pgs.)
W. D. Publications (Disney)

1-Reprints 1947 Firestone by Barks plus new-a 1.20 3.00
2-Barks-r plus other stories 1.20 3.00

HOLI-DAY SURPRISE (Formerly Summer Fun)
V2#55, Mar, 1967 (25¢ Giant)
Charlton Comics

V2#55 1.00 2.00 5.00

HOLLYWOOD COMICS
Winter, 1944 (52 pgs.)
New Age Publishers

1-Funny animal 12.00 36.00 85.00

HOLLYWOOD CONFESSIONS
Oct, 1949 - No. 2, Dec, 1949
St. John Publishing Co.

1-Kubert-c/a (entire book) 15.00 45.00 105.00
2-Kubert-c/a (entire book) (Scarce) 23.00 70.00 160.00

HOLLYWOOD DIARY
Dec, 1949 - No. 5, July-Aug, 1950
Quality Comics Group

1-No photo-c 11.50 34.00 80.00
2-Photo-c 8.35 25.00 50.00
3-5-Photo-c. 5-June Allyson/Peter Lawford photo-c 6.70 20.00 40.00

HOLLYWOOD FILM STORIES
April, 1950 - No. 4, Oct, 1950 (All photo-c; "Fumetti" type movie comic)
Feature Publications/Prize

1-June Allyson photo-c 11.50 34.00 80.00
2-4: 2-Lizabeth Scott photo-c. 3-Barbara Stanwick photo-c. 4-Betty Hutton photo-c 10.00 30.00 60.00

HOLLYWOOD FUNNY FOLKS (Formerly Funny Folks; Becomes Nutsy Squirrel #61 on)

Homer The Haspy Ghost #16 © MEG

Homicide #1 © DH

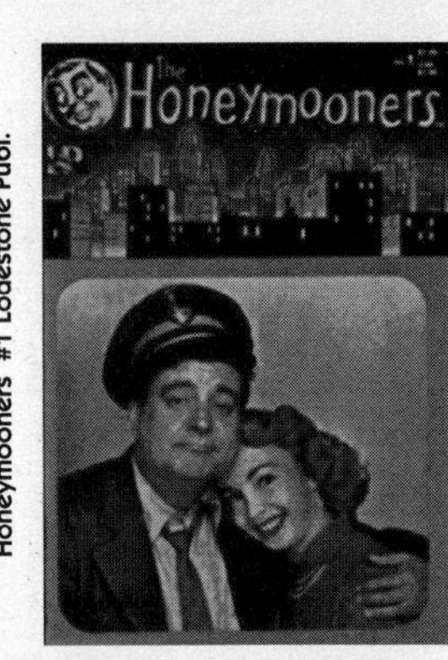

Honeymooners #1 Lodestone Publ.

GD25 FN65 NM94

No. 27, Aug-Sept, 1950 - No. 60, July-Aug, 1954
National Periodical Publications

	GD25	FN65	NM94
27	10.00	30.00	70.00
28-40	7.50	22.50	45.00
41-60	5.85	17.50	35.00

NOTE: ***Sheldon Mayer** a-27-35, 37-40, 43-46, 48-51, 53, 56, 57, 60.*

HOLLYWOOD LOVE DOCTOR (See Doctor Anthony King...)

HOLLYWOOD PICTORIAL (...Romances on cover)
No. 3, January, 1950
St. John Publishing Co.

	GD25	FN65	NM94
3-Matt Baker-a; photo-c	12.00	36.00	85.00

(Becomes a movie magazine - Hollywood Pictorial Western with No. 4.)

HOLLYWOOD ROMANCES (Formerly Brides In Love; becomes For Lovers Only #60 on)
V2#46, 11/66; #47, 10/67; #48, 11/68; V3#49, 11/69 - V3#59, 6/71
Charlton Comics

	GD25	FN65	NM94
V2#46-Rolling Stones-c/story	6.35	19.00	38.00
V2#47-V3#59: 56- "Born to Heart Break" begins	1.00	2.50	5.00

HOLLYWOOD SECRETS
Nov, 1949 - No. 6, Sept, 1950
Quality Comics Group

	GD25	FN65	NM94
1-Ward-c/a (9 pgs.)	21.00	63.00	145.00
2-Crandall-a, Ward-c/a (9 pgs.)	12.00	36.00	85.00
3-6: All photo-c. 5-Lex Barker (Tarzan)-c	7.50	22.50	45.00
...of Romance, I.W. Reprint #9; r/#2 above w/Kinstler-c	1.40	3.50	7.00

HOLLYWOOD SUPERSTARS (Epic)(Value: cover or less)

HOLO-MAN (See Power Record Comics)

HOLYOKE ONE-SHOT
1944 - No. 10, 1945 (All reprints)
Holyoke Publishing Co. (Tem Publ.)

	GD25	FN65	NM94
1-Grit Grady (on cover only), Miss Victory, Alias X (origin)-All reprints from Captain Fearless	8.35	25.00	50.00
2-Rusty Dugan (Corporal); Capt. Fearless (origin), Mr. Miracle (origin) app.	8.35	25.00	50.00
3-Miss Victory; r/Crash #4; Cat Man (origin), Solar Legion by Kirby app.; Miss Victory on cover only (1945)	15.00	45.00	105.00
4-Mr. Miracle; The Blue Streak app.	7.50	22.50	45.00
5-U.S. Border Patrol Comics (Sgt. Dick Carter of the...), Miss Victory (story matches cover to #3), Citizen Smith, & Mr. Miracle app.	8.35	25.00	50.00
6-Capt. Fearless, Alias X, Capt. Stone (splash used as-c to #10); Diamond Jim & Rusty Dugan (splash from cover of #2)	7.50	22.50	45.00
7-Secret Agent Z-2, Strong Man, Blue Streak (story matches cover to #8); Reprints from Crash #2	8.65	26.00	52.00
8-Blue Streak, Strong Man (story matches cover to #7)-Crash reprints	7.50	22.50	45.00
9-Citizen Smith, The Blue Streak, Solar Legion by Kirby & Strongman, the Perfect Human app.; reprints from Crash #4 & 5; Citizen Smith on cover only-from story in #5 (1944-before #3)	10.00	30.00	70.00
10-Captain Stone; r/Crash; Solar Legion by S&K	10.00	30.00	70.00

HOMER COBB (See Adventures of...)

HOMER HOOPER
July, 1953 - No. 4, Dec, 1953
Atlas Comics

	GD25	FN65	NM94
1-Teenage humor	7.50	22.50	45.00
2-4	4.70	14.00	28.00

HOMER, THE HAPPY GHOST (See Adventures of...)
3/55 - No. 22, 11/58; V2#1, 11/69 - V2#5, 7/70
Atlas(ACI/PPI/WPI)/Marvel Comics

	GD25	FN65	NM94
V1#1-Dan DeCarlo-c/a begins, ends #22	10.00	30.00	70.00
2-1st code approved issue	5.85	17.50	35.00
3-10	4.20	12.50	25.00
11-22	4.00	10.00	20.00
V2#1 - V2#5 (1969-70)	1.80	4.50	9.00

HOME RUN (See A-1 Comics No. 89)

HOME, SWEET HOME
1925 (10-1/4x10")
M.S. Publishing Co.

	GD25	FN65	NM94
nn-By Tuthill	19.00	57.00	130.00

HOMICIDE (Dark Horse)(Value: cover or less)

HONEYBEE BIRDWHISTLE AND HER PET PEPI (Introducing...)
1969 (24 pgs.; B&W; slick cover)
Newspaper Enterprise Association (Giveaway)

	GD25	FN65	NM94
nn-Contains Freckles newspaper strips with a short biography of Henry Fornhals (artist) & Fred Fox (writer) of the strip	5.35	16.00	32.00

HONEYMOON (Formerly Gay Comics)
No. 41, January, 1950
A Lover's Magazine(USA) (Marvel)

	GD25	FN65	NM94
41-Photo-c; article by Betty Grable	6.35	19.00	38.00

HONEYMOONERS, THE (TV)
Oct, 1986 ($1.50)
Lodestone

	GD25	FN65	NM94
1-Photo-c			1.50

HONEYMOONERS, THE (TV)
Sept, 1987 - No. 13? ($2.00)
Triad Publications

	GD25	FN65	NM94
1-13		.80	2.00

HONEYMOON ROMANCE
April, 1950 - No. 2, July, 1950 (25¢, digest size)
Artful Publications(Canadian)

	GD25	FN65	NM94
1,2-(Rare)	22.00	65.00	150.00

HONEY WEST (TV)
September, 1966 (Photo-c)
Gold Key

	GD25	FN65	NM94
1 (10186-609)	11.00	32.00	75.00

HONG KONG PHOOEY (TV)
June, 1975 - No. 9, Nov, 1976 (Hanna-Barbera)
Charlton Comics

	GD25	FN65	NM94
1	1.65	4.00	10.00
2	1.00	2.00	5.00
3-9		1.20	3.00

HOODED HORSEMAN, THE (Also see Blazing West)
No. 21, 1-2/52 - No. 27, 1-2/53; No. 18, 12-1/54-55 - No. 27, 6-7/56
American Comics Group (Michel Publ.)

	GD25	FN65	NM94
21(1-2/52)-Hooded Horseman, Injun Jones continue	11.00	32.00	75.00
22	7.50	22.50	45.00
23-25,27(1-2/53)	5.85	17.50	35.00
26-Origin/1st app. Cowboy Sahib by L. Starr	8.65	26.00	52.00
18(11-12/54)(Formerly Out of the Night)	7.50	22.50	45.00
19-Last precode (1-2/55)	5.00	15.00	30.00
20-Origin Johnny Injun	6.70	20.00	40.00
21-24,26,27(6-7/56)	5.00	15.00	30.00
25-Cowboy Sahib on cover only; Hooded Horseman i.d. revealed	5.85	17.50	35.00

NOTE: ***Whitney** c/a-21('52), 20-22.*

HOODED MENACE, THE (Also see Daring Adventures)
1951 (One Shot)
Realistic/Avon Periodicals

Hook #1 © Amblin Ent.

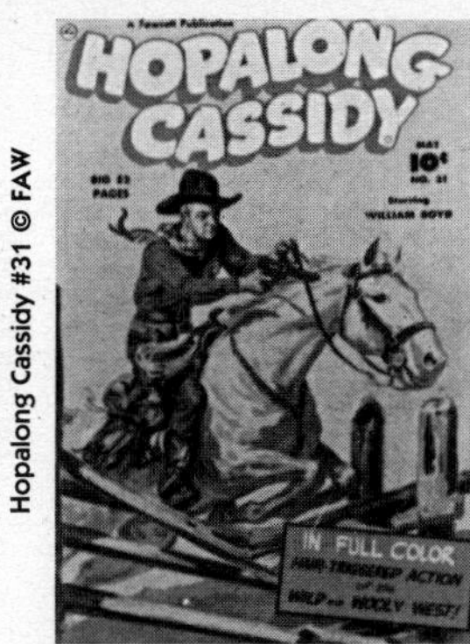

Hopalong Cassidy #31 © FAW

Horace and Dotty Dripple #25 © HARV

GD25 FN65 NM94

nn-Based on a band of hooded outlaws in the Pacific Northwest, 1900-1906; reprinted in Daring Advs. #15 36.00 107.00 250.00

HOODS UP
1953 (16 pgs.; 15¢) (Eisner-c/a in all)
Fram Corp. (Dist. to service station owners)

1-(Very Rare; only 2 known) 50.00 150.00 350.00
2-6-(Very Rare; only 1 known of #3, 4, 2 known of #2) 50.00 150.00 350.00
NOTE: *Convertible Connie gives tips for service stations, selling Fram oil filters.*

HOOK
Early Feb, 1992 - No. 4, Late Mar, 1992 ($1.00, mini-series)
Marvel Comics

1-4: Adapts movie; Vess-c; 1-Morrow-a(p) 1.00
nn (1991, $5.95, 84 pgs.)-Contains #1-4; Vess-c 1.00 2.50 6.00
1 (1991, $2.95, magazine, 84 pgs.)-Contains #1-4; Vess-c (same cover as nn issue) 1.20 3.00

HOOT GIBSON'S WESTERN ROUNDUP (See Western Roundup under Fox Giants)

HOOT GIBSON WESTERN (Formerly My Love Story)
No. 5, May, 1950 - No. 3, Sept, 1950
Fox Features Syndicate

5,6(#1,2): 5-Photo-c. 6-Photo/painted-c 19.00 57.00 130.00
3-Wood-a; painted-c 21.00 63.00 145.00

HOPALONG CASSIDY (Also see Bill Boyd Western, Master Comics, Real Western Hero, Six Gun Heroes & Western Hero; Bill Boyd starred as H. Cassidy in the movies; H. Cassidy in movies, radio & TV)
Feb, 1943; No. 2, Summer, 1946 - No. 85, Jan, 1954
Fawcett Publications

1 (1943, 68 pgs.)-H. Cassidy & his horse Topper begin (on sale 1/8/43)-Captain Marvel app. on-c 421.00 1265.00 2950.00
2-(Sum, '46) 57.00 171.00 400.00
3,4: 3-(Fall, '46, 52 pgs. begin) 27.00 80.00 185.00
5- "Mad Barber" story mentioned in **SOTI**, pgs. 308,309; photo-c 24.00 73.00 170.00
6-10: 8-Photo-c 19.00 57.00 130.00
11-19: 11,13-19-Photo-c 13.50 41.00 95.00
20-29 (52 pgs.)-Painted/photo-c 10.00 30.00 70.00
30,31,33,34,37-39,41 (52 pgs.)-Painted-c 7.50 22.50 45.00
32,40 (36pgs.)-Painted-c 6.35 19.00 38.00
35,42,43,45 (52 pgs.)-Photo-c 7.50 22.50 45.00
36,44,48 (36 pgs.)-Photo-c 6.35 19.00 38.00
46,47,49-51,53,54,56 (52 pgs.)-Photo-c 7.00 21.00 42.00
52,55,57-70 (36 pgs.)-Photo-c 5.00 15.00 30.00
71-84-Photo-c 4.35 13.00 26.00
85-Last Fawcett issue; photo-c 5.35 16.00 32.00
NOTE: *Line-drawn c-1-4, 6, 7, 9, 10, 12.*
Grape Nuts Flakes giveaway (1950,9x6") 11.00 32.00 75.00
...& the Mad Barber (1951 Bond Bread giveaway)-7x5"; used in **SOTI**, pgs. 308,309 19.00 57.00 130.00
...Meets the Brend Brothers Bandits (1951 Bond Bread giveaway, color, paper-c, 16pgs. 3-1/2x7")-Fawcett Publ. 9.15 27.50 55.00
...Strange Legacy (1951 Bond Bread giveaway) 9.15 27.50 55.00
White Tower Giveaway (1946, 16pgs., paper-c) 9.15 27.50 55.00

HOPALONG CASSIDY (TV)
No. 86, Feb, 1954 - No. 135, May-June, 1959 (All-36pgs.)
National Periodical Publications

86-Photo covers continue 25.00 75.00 175.00
87 15.00 45.00 105.00
88-90 11.00 32.00 75.00
91-99 (98 has #93 on-c; last precode issue, 2/55) 10.00 30.00 60.00
100 10.00 30.00 70.00
101-108-Last photo-c 8.35 25.00 50.00
109-135: 124-Painted-c 6.70 20.00 40.00
NOTE: ***Gil Kane** art-1956 up. **Kubert** a-123.*

GD25 FN65 NM94

HOPE SHIP
June-Aug, 1963
Dell Publishing Co.

1 1.80 4.50 9.00

HOPPY THE MARVEL BUNNY (See Fawcett's Funny Animals)
Dec, 1945 - No. 15, Sept, 1947
Fawcett Publications

1 22.00 65.00 150.00
2 11.00 32.00 75.00
3-15: 7-Xmas-c 10.00 30.00 60.00
...Well Known Comics (1944,8-1/2x10-1/2", paper-c) Bestmaid/Samuel Lowe (printed in red or blue) 7.50 22.50 45.00

HORACE & DOTTY DRIPPLE (Dotty Dripple No. 1-24)
No. 25, Aug, 1952 - No. 43, Oct, 1955
Harvey Publications

25-43 1.20 3.00 6.00

HORIZONTAL LIEUTENANT, THE (See Movie Classics)

HOROBI (Viz)(Value: cover or less)

HORRIFIC (Terrific No. 14 on)
Sept, 1952 - No. 13, Sept, 1954
Artful/Comic Media/Harwell/Mystery

1 19.00 57.00 130.00
2 10.00 30.00 65.00
3-Bullet in head-c 16.00 48.00 110.00
4,5,7,9,10: 4-Shrunken head-c. 7-Guillotine-c 8.35 25.00 50.00
6-Jack The Ripper story 9.15 27.50 55.00
8-Origin & 1st app. The Teller (E.C. parody) 10.00 30.00 65.00
11-13: 11-Swipe/Witches Tales #6,27; Devil-c 5.85 17.50 35.00
NOTE: ***Don Heck** a-8; c-3-13. **Hollingsworth** a-4. **Morisi** a-8. **Palais** a-5, 7-12.*

HORROR FROM THE TOMB (Mysterious Stories No. 2 on)
Sept, 1954
Premier Magazine Co.

1-Woodbridge/Torres, Check-a; The Keeper of the Graveyard is host 19.00 57.00 130.00

HORRORS, THE (Formerly Startling Terror Tales #10)
No. 11, Jan, 1953 - No. 15, Apr, 1954
Star Publications

11-Horrors of War; Disbrow-a(2) 12.00 36.00 85.00
12-Horrors of War; color illo in **POP** 11.50 34.00 80.00
13-Horrors of Mystery; crime stories 11.00 32.00 75.00
14,15-Horrors of the Underworld; crime stories 11.50 34.00 80.00
NOTE: *All have **L. B. Cole** covers; a-12. **Hollingsworth** a-13. **Palais** a-13r.*

HORROR TALES (Magazine)
V1#7, 6/69 - V6#6, 12/74; V7#1, 2/75; V7#2, 5/76 - V8#5, 1977; V9#3, 8/78; (V1-V6: 52 pgs.; V7, V8#2: 112 pgs.; V8#4 on: 68 pgs.) (No V5#3, V8#1,3)
Eerie Publications

V1#7 2.10 6.50 15.00
V1#8,9 1.70 4.20 10.00
V2#1-6('70), V3#1-6('71) 1.30 3.25 8.00
V4#1-3,5-7('72) 1.30 3.25 8.00
V4#4-LSD story reprint/Weird V3#5 2.10 6.50 15.00
V5#1,2,4,5(6/73),5(10/73),6(12/73),V6#1-6('74),V7#1,2,4('76),V7#3('76)-Giant issue,V8#2,4,5('77),V9#3(8/78, $1.50) 1.30 3.25 8.00
NOTE: *Bondage-c-V6#1, 3, V7#2.*

HORSE FEATHERS COMICS
Nov, 1945 - No. 4, July(Summer on-c), 1948 (52 pgs.)
Lev Gleason Publications

1-Wolverton's Scoop Scuttle, 2 pgs. 14.00 43.00 100.00
2 7.00 21.00 42.00
3,4: 3-(5/48) 5.35 16.00 32.00

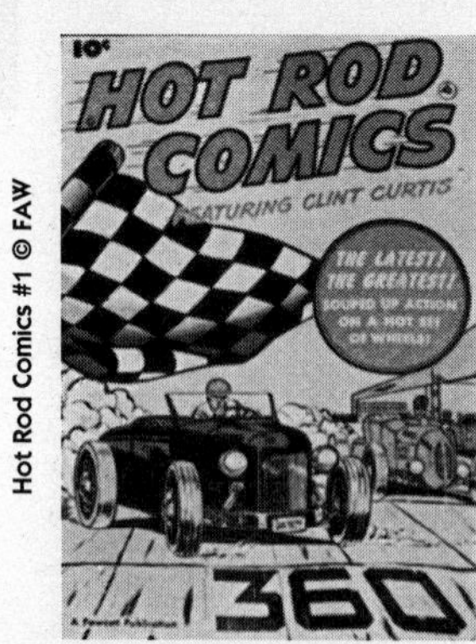

Hot Rod Comics #1 © FAW

Hotspur #2 © ECL

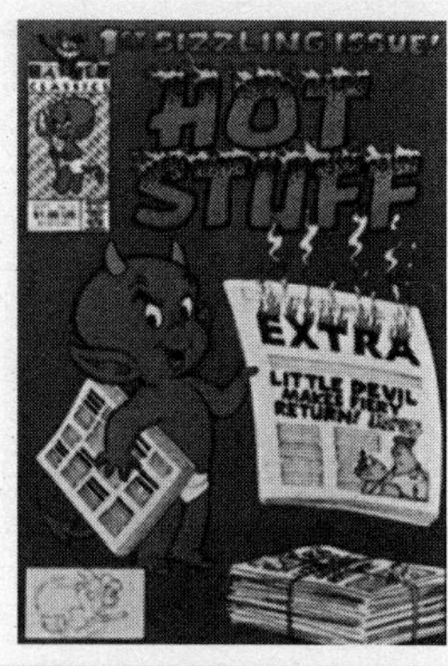

Hot Stuff #1 © HARV

HORSEMASTERS, THE (See 4-Color No. 1260)

HORSE SOLDIERS, THE (See 4-Color No. 1048)

HORSE WITHOUT A HEAD, THE (See Movie Comics)

HOT DOG
June-July, 1954 - No. 4, Dec-Jan, 1954-55
Magazine Enterprises

	GD25	FN65	NM94
1(A-1 #107)	5.00	15.00	30.00
2,3(A-1 #115),4(A-1 #136)	4.00	10.00	20.00

HOT DOG (See Jughead's Pal, Hotdog)

HOTEL DEPAREE - SUNDANCE (See 4-Color No. 1126)

HOT ROD AND SPEEDWAY COMICS
Feb-Mar, 1952 - No. 5, Apr-May, 1953
Hillman Periodicals

	GD25	FN65	NM94
1	14.00	43.00	100.00
2-Krigstein-a	11.00	32.00	75.00
3-5	5.85	17.50	35.00

HOT ROD COMICS (...Featuring Clint Curtis) (See XMas Comics)
Nov, 1951 (no month given) - V2#7, Feb, 1953
Fawcett Publications

	GD25	FN65	NM94
nn (V1#1)-Powell-c/a in all	18.00	54.00	125.00
2 (4/52)	11.00	32.00	75.00
3-6, V2#7	8.35	25.00	50.00

HOT ROD KING (Also see Speed Smith the Hot Rod King)
Fall, 1952
Ziff-Davis Publ. Co.

	GD25	FN65	NM94
1-Giacoia-a; Saunders painted-c	16.00	48.00	110.00

HOT ROD RACERS (Grand Prix No. 16 on)
Dec, 1964 - No. 15, July, 1967
Charlton Comics

	GD25	FN65	NM94
1	6.70	20.00	40.00
2-5	4.00	10.00	20.00
6-15	3.00	7.50	15.00

HOT RODS AND RACING CARS
Nov, 1951 - No. 120, June, 1973
Charlton Comics (Motor Mag. No. 1)

	GD25	FN65	NM94
1-Speed Davis begins; Indianapolis 500 story	16.00	48.00	110.00
2	9.15	27.50	55.00
3-10	6.35	19.00	38.00
11-20	5.00	15.00	30.00
21-34,36-40	4.00	10.00	20.00
35 (6/58, 68 pgs.)	4.70	14.00	28.00
41-60	3.00	7.50	15.00
61-80	2.00	5.00	10.00
81-100	1.30	3.25	8.00
101-120	1.00	2.00	5.00

HOT SHOT CHARLIE
1947 (Lee Elias)
Hillman Periodicals

	GD25	FN65	NM94
1	5.85	17.50	35.00

HOTSPUR (Eclipse)(Value: cover or less)

HOT STUFF (See Stumbo Tinytown)
V2#1, Sept, 1991 - No. 12, June, 1994 ($1.00)
Harvey Comics

	GD25	FN65	NM94
V2#1,2: 1-Stumbo back-up story			1.00
3-8 ($1.25)			1.25
9-12 ($1.50)			1.50
...Big Book 1 (11/92), 2 (6/93) (Both $1.95, 52 pgs.)		.80	2.00

HOT STUFF CREEPY CAVES
Nov, 1974 - No. 7, Nov, 1975
Harvey Publications

	GD25	FN65	NM94
1	1.00	2.00	5.00
2-5		1.20	3.00
6,7			1.50

HOT STUFF DIGEST
July, 1992 - No. 5, 1993 ($1.75, digest size)
Harvey Comics

	GD25	FN65	NM94
V2#1-5: Hot Stuff, Stumbo, Richie Rich stories		.70	1.75

HOT STUFF GIANT SIZE
Oct, 1992 - No. 3, Oct, 1993 ($2.25, 68 pgs.)
Harvey Comics

	GD25	FN65	NM94
V2#1-3: Hot Stuff & Stumbo stories		.90	2.25

HOT STUFF SIZZLERS
July, 1960 - No. 59, Mar, 1974; V2#1, Aug, 1992
Harvey Publications

	GD25	FN65	NM94
1: 68 pgs. begin; Hot Stuff, Stumbo begin	10.00	30.00	70.00
2-5	5.00	15.00	30.00
6-10	3.60	9.00	18.00
11-20	2.40	6.00	12.00
21-45: Last 68 pgs.	1.40	3.50	7.00
46-52: All 52 pgs.	1.00	2.00	5.00
53-59		1.60	4.00
V2#1-(8/92, $1.25)-Stumbo back-up			1.25

HOT STUFF, THE LITTLE DEVIL (Also see Devil Kids & Harvey Hits)
10/57 - No. 141, 7/77; No. 142, 2/78 - No. 164, 8/82; No. 165, 10/86 - No. 171, 11/87; No. 172, 11/88; No. 173, Sept, 1990 - No. 177, 1/91
Harvey Publications (Illustrated Humor)

	GD25	FN65	NM94
1	29.00	86.00	200.00
2-1st app. Stumbo the Giant (12/57)	14.00	43.00	100.00
3-5	11.50	34.00	80.00
6-10	7.50	22.50	45.00
11-20	5.00	15.00	30.00
21-40	3.60	9.00	18.00
41-60	2.00	5.00	10.00
61-105	1.00	2.50	6.00
106-112: All 52 pg. Giants	1.60	4.00	8.00
113-125		1.20	3.00
126-177: 172-177-($1.00)			1.00
Shoestore Giveaway('63)	1.60	4.00	8.00

HOT WHEELS (TV)
Mar-Apr, 1970 - No. 6, Jan-Feb, 1971
National Periodical Publications

	GD25	FN65	NM94
1	5.40	16.00	38.00
2,4,5	2.60	7.70	18.00
3-Neal Adams-c	3.70	11.00	26.00
6-Neal Adams-c/a	4.30	12.90	30.00

NOTE: ***Toth** a-1p, 2-5; c-1p, 5.*

HOURMAN (See Adventure Comics #48)

HOUSE OF MYSTERY (See Brave and the Bold #93, Elvira's House of Mystery, Limited Collectors' Edition & Super DC Giant)

HOUSE OF MYSTERY, THE
Dec-Jan, 1951-52 - No. 321, Oct, 1983 (No. 199-203: 52 pgs.)
National Periodical Publications/DC Comics

	GD25	FN65	NM94
1	157.00	471.00	1100.00
2	64.00	193.00	450.00
3	52.00	156.00	365.00
4,5	41.00	124.00	290.00
6-10	31.00	94.00	220.00
11-15	25.00	75.00	175.00
16(7/53)-25	19.00	57.00	130.00
26-35(2/55)-Last pre-code issue; 30-Woodish-a	13.00	40.00	90.00
36-49	11.00	32.00	75.00

House Of Mystery #77 © DC

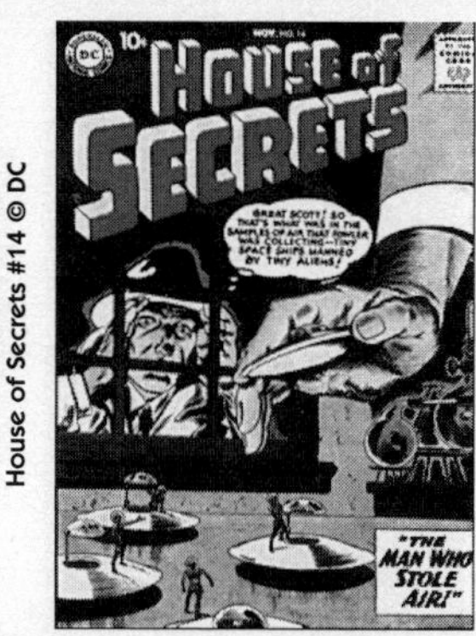

House of Secrets #14 © DC

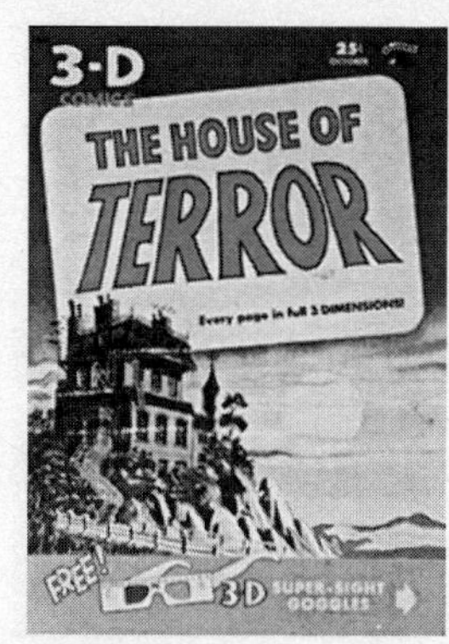

House of Terroe #10 © STJ

GD25 FN65 NM94

50-Text story of Orson Welles' War of the Worlds broadcast 11.00 32.00 75.00
51-60 9.00 27.00 62.00
61,63,65,66,70,72,76,84,85-Kirby-a 9.00 26.00 60.00
62,64,67-69,71,73-75,77-83,86-99 5.30 16.00 37.00
100 (7/60) 8.00 25.00 50.00
101-116: 109-Toth, Kubert-a. 116-Last 10¢ issue 4.00 11.00 36.00
117-130: 117-Swipes-c to HOS #20. 120-Toth-a 3.00 8.00 26.00
131-142 2.00 6.00 21.00
143-J'onn J'onzz, Manhunter begins (6/64), ends #173; story continues from Detective #326 20.00 70.00 205.00
144 12.00 35.00 105.00
145-155,157-159: 149-Toth-a. 155-The Human Hurrican app. (12/65), Red Tornado prototype. 158-Origin/1st app. Diabolu Idol-Head in J'onn J'onzz 8.00 23.00 68.00
156-Robby Reed begins (origin/1st app.), ends #173 9.00 26.00 78.00
160-(7/66)-Robby Reed becomes Plastic Man in this issue only; 1st S.A. app. Plastic Man; intro Marco Xavier (Martian Manhunter) & Vulture Crime Organization; ends #173 10.00 31.00 92.00
161-173: 169-Origin/1st app. Gem Girl 5.00 14.00 42.00
174-177,182: 174-Mystery format begins. 176-1st app. Cain (HOM host). 182-Toth-a 2.00 5.00 12.00
178-Neal Adams-a (2/68) 2.00 6.00 16.00
179-N. Adams/Orlando, Wrightson-a (1st pro work, 3 pgs.) 6.00 17.00 44.00
180,181,183: Wrightson-a (3,10, & 3 pgs.). 180-Last 12¢ issue; Kane/Wood-a(2). 183-Wood-a 2.00 5.00 13.00
184-Kane/Wood, Toth-a 1.00 4.00 11.00
185-Williamson/Kaluta-a; Howard-a (3 pgs.) 1.00 4.00 11.00
186-N. Adams-a; Wrightson-a (10 pgs.) 1.00 4.00 11.00
187,190: 187-Toth-a. 190-Toth-a(r) 1.00 3.00 7.00
188,191,195-Wrightson-a (8, 3 & 10 pgs.). 195-Swamp creature story by Wrightson similar to Swamp Thing (10/71) 2.00 5.00 12.00
189,192-194,196-198: 189-Wood-a(i). 194-Toth, Kirby-a; 52 pg. issues begin, end #203 1.00 3.00 7.00
199-Wood-a (8pg.); Kirby-a 1.00 3.00 8.00
200-203-(25¢, 52 pgs.)-One third-r. 200-(3/72) 1.00 2.00 6.00
204-Wrightson-c/a, 9 pgs. 1.00 2.00 6.00
205-223,225,227: 207-Wrightson, Starlin, Redondo art. 221-Wrightson/Kaluta-a (8 pgs.) 1.00 2.00 5.00
224-N. Adams/Wrightson-a(r); begin 100 pg. issues; Phantom Stranger-r 1.60 3.20 8.00
226-Wrightson/Redondo-a Phantom Stranger-r 1.10 2.20 5.50
228-N. Adams inks; Wrightson-r 1.10 2.20 5.50
229-235,237-321: 229-Wrightson-a(r); Toth-r; last 100 pg. issue. 230-(68 pgs.) 251-259-(84 pgs.). 251-Wood-a. 282-(68 pgs.)-Has extra story "The Computers That Saved Metropolis" Radio Shack giveaway by Jim Starlin 1.10 2.20 5.50
236-Ditko-a(p); N. Adams-i; Wrightson-c 1.10 2.20 5.50

NOTE: **Neal Adams** a-236i; c-175-192, 197, 199, 251-254. **M. Anderson** c/a-37. **Aragones** a-185, 186, 194, 196, 200, 202, 229, 251. **Baily** a-279p. **Cameron** a-76, 79. **Colan** a-202r. **Craig** a-263, 275, 295, 300. **Ditko** a-236p, 247, 254, 258, 276; c-277. **Drucker** a-37. **Evans** c-218. **Fraden** a-251. **Giunta** a-199. **Golden** a-257, 259. **Heath** a-194r; c-203. **Howard** a-182, 185, 187, 196, 229r, 247i, 254, 279i. **Kaluta** a-195, 200, 250r; c-200-202, 210, 212, 233, 260, 261, 263, 265, 267, 268, 273, 276, 284, 287, 288, 293-295, 300, 302, 304, 305, 309-319, 321. **Bob Kane** a-84. **Gil Kane** a-196p, 253p, 300p. **Kirby** a-194r, 199r; c-65, 76, 78, 79, 85. **Kubert** c-282, 283, 285, 286, 289-292, 297-299, 301, 303, 306-308. **Maneely** a-68. **Mayer** a-317p. **Meskin** a-52-144 (most), 224r, 229r; c-63, 66, 124, 127. **Mooney** a-24, 159, 160. **Moreira** a-3, 4, 20-50, 58, 59, 62, 68, 77, 79, 90, 108, 113, 123, 201r, 228; c-4-28, 44, 47, 50, 54, 59, 62, 64, 68, 70, 73. **Morrow** a-192, 196, 255, 320i. **Mortimer** a-204(3 pgs.). **Nasser** a-276. **Newton** a-259, 272. **Nino** a-204, 212, 213, 220, 224, 225, 245, 250, 252-256, 283. **Orlando** a-175(2 pgs.), 178, 240i; c-240, 258p, 262, 264p, 270p, 271, 272, 274, 275, 278, 296i. **Redondo** a-194, 195, 197, 202, 203, 207, 211, 214, 217, 219, 226, 227, 229, 235, 241, 287(layout), 302p, 303i, 308; c-229. **Reese** a-195, 200, 205i. **Rogers** a-254, 274, 277. **Roussos** a-65, 84, 224i. **Sekowsky** a-282p. **Sparling** a-203. **Starlin** a-207(2 pgs.), 282p; c-281. **Leonard Starr** a-9. **Staton** a-300p. **Sutton** a-271, 290, 291, 293, 295, 297-299, 302, 303, 306-309, 310-313i, 314. **Tuska** a-293p, 294p, 316p. **Wrightson** c-193-195, 204, 207, 209, 211, 213, 214, 217, 221, 231, 236, 255, 256.

HOUSE OF SECRETS (Combined with The Unexpected after #154)
11-12/56 - No. 80, 9-10/66; No. 81, 8-9/69 - No. 140, 2-3/76; No. 141, 8-9/76 - No. 154, 10-11/78
National Periodical Publications/DC Comics

1-Drucker-a; Moreira-c 60.00 180.00 600.00
2-Moreira-a 34.00 103.00 310.00
3-Kirby-c/a 25.00 75.00 225.00
4,8-Kirby-a 16.00 47.00 140.00
5-7,9-11: 11,12-Lou Cameron-a(#11 is unsigned) 11.00 33.00 100.00
12-Kirby-c/a 12.00 37.00 110.00
13-15: 14-Flying saucer-c 8.00 24.00 72.00
16-20 7.00 21.00 62.00
21,22,24-30 6.00 19.00 56.00
23-1st app. Mark Merlin & begin series (8/59) 8.00 23.00 70.00
31-50: 48-Toth-a. 50-Last 10¢ issue 4.00 13.00 40.00
51-60: 58-Origin Mark Merlin 4.00 13.00 34.00
61-First Eclipso (7-8/63) and begin series 16.00 49.00 130.00
62 8.00 24.00 64.00
63-65,67-Toth-a on Eclipso (see Brave and the Bold #64) 6.00 19.00 50.00
66-1st Eclipso-c (also #67,70,78,79); Toth-a 9.00 28.00 75.00
68-80: 73-Mark Merlin becomes Prince Ra-Man (1st app.). 76-Prince Ra-Man vs. Eclipso. 80-Eclipso, Prince Ra-Man end 5.00 14.00 37.00
81-91: 81-Mystery format begins; 1st app. Abel (HOS host). 82-Neal Adams-c(i). 85-N. Adams-a(i). 87-Wrightson & Kaluta-a. 90-Buckler (early work)/N. Adams-a(i) 1.00 3.00 9.00
92-1st app. Swamp Thing-c/story (8 pgs.)(6-7/71) by Berni Wrightson(p) w/JeffJones/Kaluta/Weiss ink assists 38.00 113.00 415.00
93-100: 94-Wrightson inks. 96-Wood-a 1.10 2.20 5.50
101-154: 140-Origin The Patchworkman 1.10 2.75

NOTE: **Neal Adams** c-81, 82, 84-88, 90, 91. **Cameron** a-13, 15. **Colan** a-63. **Ditko** a-139p, 148. **Elias** a-58. **Evans** a-118. **Finlay** a-7r(Real Fact?). **Glanzman** a-91. **Golden** a-151. **Heath** a-31. **Kaluta** a-87, 98, 99; c-98, 99, 101, 102, 149, 151, 154. **Bob Kane** a-18, 21. **G. Kane** a-85p. **Kirby** c-3, 11, 12. **Kubert** a-39. **Meskin** a-2-68 (most); c-55-60. **Moreira** a-7, 8, 51, 54, 102-104, 106, 108, 113, 116, 118, 121, 123, 127; c-1, 2, 4-10, 13-20. **Morrow** a-86, 89, 90; c-89, 146-148. **Nino** a-101, 103, 106, 109, 115, 117, 126, 128, 131, 147, 153. **Redondo** a-95, 99, 102, 104p, 113, 116, 134, 136, 139, 140. **Reese** a-85. **Starlin** c-150. **Sutton** a-154. **Toth** a-63-67, 83, 93r, 94r, 96r, 98r, 123. **Tuska** a-90, 104. **Wrightson** a-134; c-92-94, 96, 100, 103, 106, 107, 135, 136, 139.

HOUSE OF TERROR (3-D)
October, 1953 (25¢, came w/glasses)
St. John Publishing Co.

1-Kubert, Baker-a 25.00 75.00 175.00

HOUSE OF YANG, THE (See Yang)
July, 1975 - No. 6, June, 1976; 1978
Charlton Comics

1 1.50
2-6, Modern Comics #1,2(1978) 1.00

HOUSE II: THE SECOND STORY
Oct, 1987 (One-shot)
Marvel Comics

1-Adapts movie .80 2.00

HOWARD CHAYKIN'S AMERICAN FLAGG! (First)(Value: cover or less)

HOWARD THE DUCK (See Bizarre Adventures #34, Crazy Magazine, Fear, Man-Thing, Marvel Treasury Edition & Sensational She-Hulk #14-17)
Jan, 1976 - No. 31, May, 1979; No. 32, Jan, 1986; No. 33, Sept, 1986
Marvel Comics Group

1-Brunner-c/a; Spider-Man x-over (low distr.) 1.50 4.00 9.00
2-11: 2-Brunner-c/a (low distr.). 3-Buscema-a(p) .80 1.90
12-1st app. Kiss (cameo, 3/77) 1.50 3.75
13-Kiss app. (1st full story, 6/77); Daimon Hellstrom app. plus cameo of Howard as Son of Satan 1.70 4.25
14-33: 14-Howard as Son of Satan-c/story; Son of Satan app. 16-Album issue; 3 pgs. comics. 22,23-Man-Thing-c/stories 1.00
Annual 1(1977, 52 pgs.)-Mayerik-a 1.00

NOTE: **Austin** c-29i. **Bolland** c-33. **Brunner** a-1p, 2p; c-1, 2. **Buckler** c-3p. **Buscema** a-3p. **Colan** a(p)-4-15, 17-20, 24-27, 30, 31; c(p)-4-31, Annual 1p. **Leialoha** a-1-13i; c(i)-3-5, 8-11.

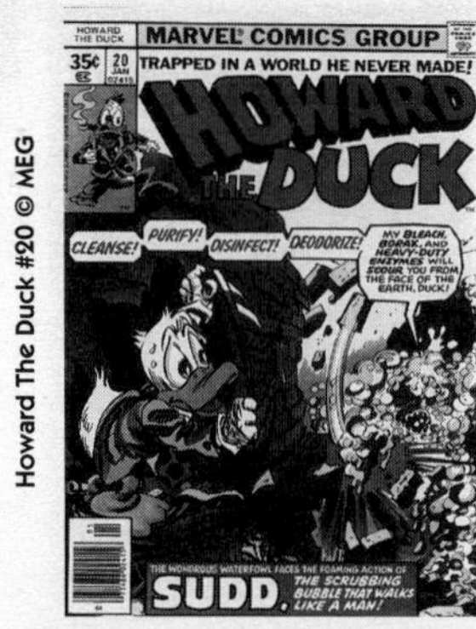

Howard The Duck #20 © MEG

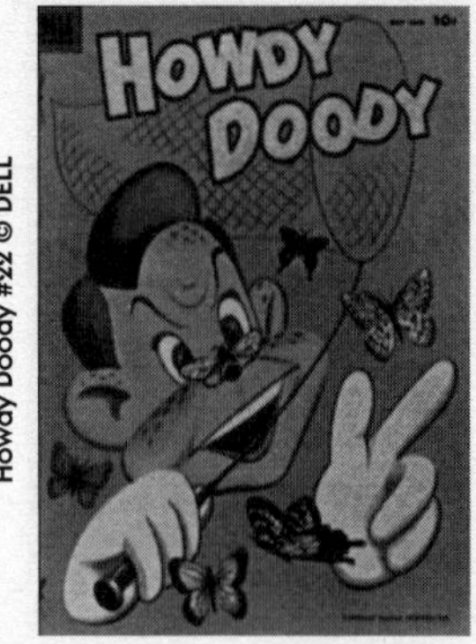

Howdy Doody #22 © DELL

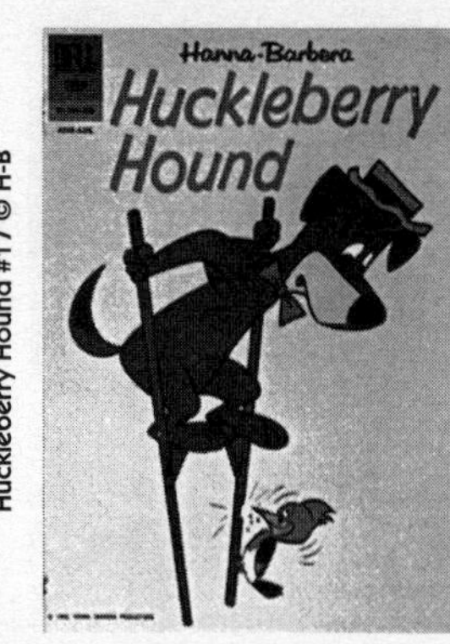

Huckleberry Hound #17 © H-B

Mayerik a-22, 23, 33. ***P. Smith*** *a-30p. Man-Thing app. in #22, 23.*

HOWARD THE DUCK (Magazine)
October, 1979 - No. 9, March, 1981 (B&W, 68 pgs.)
Marvel Comics Group

	GD25	FN65	NM94
1			1.50
2,3,5-9: 3-Xmas issue. 7-Has poster by Byrne			1.00
4-Beatles, John Lennon, Elvis, Kiss & Devo cameos; Hitler app.			1.20

NOTE: ***Buscema*** *a-4p.* ***Colan*** *a-1-5p, 7-9p.* ***Jack Davis*** *c-3.* ***Golden*** *a(p)-1, 5, 6(51pgs.).* ***Rogers*** *a-7, 8.* ***Simonson*** *a-7.*

HOWARD THE DUCK: THE MOVIE
Dec, 1986 - No. 3, Feb, 1987 (Mini-series)
Marvel Comics Group

	GD25	FN65	NM94
1-3: Movie adaptation; r/Marvel Super Special			1.00

HOW BOYS AND GIRLS CAN HELP WIN THE WAR
1942 (One Shot) (10¢)
The Parents' Magazine Institute

	GD25	FN65	NM94
1-All proceeds used to buy war bonds	19.00	57.00	130.00

HOWDY DOODY (TV)(See Poll Parrot)
1/50 - No. 38, 7-9/56; No. 761, 1/57; No. 811, 7/57
Dell Publishing Co.

	GD25	FN65	NM94
1-(Scarce)-Photo-c; 1st TV comic	71.00	215.00	500.00
2-Photo-c	22.00	67.00	155.00
3-5: All photo-c	15.00	45.00	105.00
6-Used in **SOTI**, pg. 309; painted-c begin	14.00	43.00	100.00
7-10	11.50	34.00	80.00
11-20: 13-X-Mas-c	10.00	30.00	60.00
21-38	9.15	27.50	55.00
4-Color 761,811	10.00	30.00	65.00

HOW IT BEGAN (See Single Series No. 15)

HOW SANTA GOT HIS RED SUIT (See March of Comics No. 2)

HOW STALIN HOPES WE WILL DESTROY AMERICA
1951 (16 pgs.) (Giveaway)
Joe Lowe Co. (Pictorial News)

	GD25	FN65	NM94
nn	43.00	130.00	300.00

(Prices vary widely on this book)

HOW THE WEST WAS WON (See Movie Comics)

HOW TO DRAW FOR THE COMICS
No date (1942?) (64 pgs.; B&W & color) (10¢) (No ads)
Street and Smith

	GD25	FN65	NM94
nn-Art by Winsor McCay, George Marcoux(Supersnipe artist), Vernon Greene (The Shadow artist), Jack Binder(with biog.), Thorton Fisher, Jon Small, & Jack Farr; has biographies of each artist	19.00	57.00	130.00

H. P. LOVECRAFT'S CTHULHU
Dec, 1991 - No. 3, Feb?, 1992 ($2.50, color, mini-series)
Millennium Publications

	GD25	FN65	NM94
1-3: 1-Contains trading cards on thin stock		1.00	2.50

H. R. PUFNSTUF (TV) (See March of Comics #360)
Oct, 1970 - No. 8, July, 1972
Gold Key

	GD25	FN65	NM94
1-Photo-c (all have photo-c?)	11.00	32.00	75.00
2-8	5.00	15.00	30.00

HUBERT (See 4-Color No. 251)

HUCK & YOGI JAMBOREE (TV)
March, 1961 (116 pgs.; $1.00) (B&W original material)
(6-1/4x9"; cardboard cover; high quality paper)
Dell Publishing Co.

	GD25	FN65	NM94
nn	9.15	27.50	50.00

HUCK & YOGI WINTER SPORTS (See 4-Color No. 1310)

HUCK FINN (See The New Adventures of... & Power Record Comics)

HUCKLEBERRY FINN (See 4-Color No. 1114)

HUCKLEBERRY HOUND (See Dell Giant #31,44, Golden Picture Story Book, Kite Fun Book, March of Comics #199, 214, 235, Spotlight #1 & Whitman Comic Books)

HUCKLEBERRY HOUND (TV)
No. 990, 5-7/59 - No. 43, 10/70 (Hanna-Barbera)
Dell/Gold Key No. 18 (10/62) on

	GD25	FN65	NM94
4-Color 990(#1)-1st app. Huckleberry Hound, Yogi Bear, & Pixie & Dixie & Mr. Jinx	10.00	30.00	65.00
4-Color 1050,1054 (12/59)	7.50	22.50	45.00
3(1-2/60) - 7 (9-10/60)	7.50	22.50	45.00
4-Color 1141 (10/60)	7.50	22.50	45.00
8-10	5.50	17.00	33.00
11-17 (6-8/62)	4.70	14.00	28.00
18,19 (84pgs.; 18-20 titled ...Chuckleberry Tales)	6.90	21.00	55.00
20-30: 20-Titled Chuckleberry Tales	3.30	10.00	20.00
31-43: 37-Reprints	2.70	8.00	16.00

HUCKLEBERRY HOUND (TV)
Nov, 1970 - No. 8, Jan, 1972 (Hanna-Barbera)
Charlton Comics

	GD25	FN65	NM94
1	2.30	6.75	16.00
2-8	1.65	4.70	11.00

HUEY, DEWEY, & LOUIE (See Donald Duck, 1938 for 1st app. Also see Mickey Mouse Magazine V4#2, V5#7 & Walt Disney's Junior Woodchucks Limited Series)

HUEY, DEWEY, & LOUIE BACK TO SCHOOL (See Dell Giant #22, 35, 49 & Dell Giants)

HUEY, DEWEY AND LOUIE JUNIOR WOODCHUCKS (Disney)
Aug, 1966 - No. 81, 1984 (See Walt Disney's Comics & Stories #125)
Gold Key No. 1-61/Whitman No. 62 on

	GD25	FN65	NM94
1	5.00	15.00	35.00
2,3(12/68)	2.85	8.00	20.00
4,5(4/70)-r/two WDC&S Donald Duck stories	3.70	11.00	26.00
6-17,19-23,25-New storyboarded scripts by Barks, 13-25 pgs. per issue	5.00	15.00	35.00
18,24,27-34,36-40,42-57,59-61	1.70	4.20	10.00
26,58-r/Barks Donald Duck WDC&S stories	2.85	8.00	20.00
35,41-r/Barks J.W. scripts	1.90	6.00	13.00
62-81	1.00	2.50	6.00

HUGGA BUNCH (TV) (Marvel)(Value: cover or less)

HULK (Formerly The Rampaging Hulk; also see The Incredible Hulk)
No. 11, Oct, 1978 - No. 27, June, 1981 (Magazine)($1.50)
Marvel Comics Group

	GD25	FN65	NM94
11-Moon Knight begins, ends 20		1.90	4.75
12-15: Moon Knight stories		1.30	3.25
16,19,21,22,24-27: 24-Part color. 25-27 are B&W		.80	2.00
17,18,20: Moon Knight stories		1.20	3.00
23-Last full color issue; Banner is attacked		1.10	2.75

NOTE: ***Alcala*** *a(i)-15, 17-20, 22, 24-27.* ***Buscema*** *a-23; c-26.* ***Chaykin*** *a-21-25.* ***Colan*** *a(p)-11, 19, 24-27.* ***Jusko*** *painted c-12.* ***Nebres*** *a-16. Moon Knight by* ***Sienkiewicz*** *in 13-15, 17, 18, 20.* ***Simonson*** *a-27; c-23. Dominic Fortune appears in #21-24.*

HULK: FUTURE IMPERFECT
Jan, 1993 - No. 2, Dec, 1992 (In error) ($5.95, 52 pgs.)
Marvel Comics

	GD25	FN65	NM94
1,2-Embossed-c; Perez-c/a	1.00	2.50	6.00

HUMAN FLY
1963 - 1964 (Reprints)
I.W. Enterprises/Super

	GD25	FN65	NM94
I.W. Reprint #1-Reprints Blue Beetle #44('46)	1.60	4.00	8.00
Super Reprint #10-R/Blue Beetle #46('47)	1.60	4.00	8.00

HUMAN FLY, THE
Sept, 1977 - No. 19, Mar, 1979

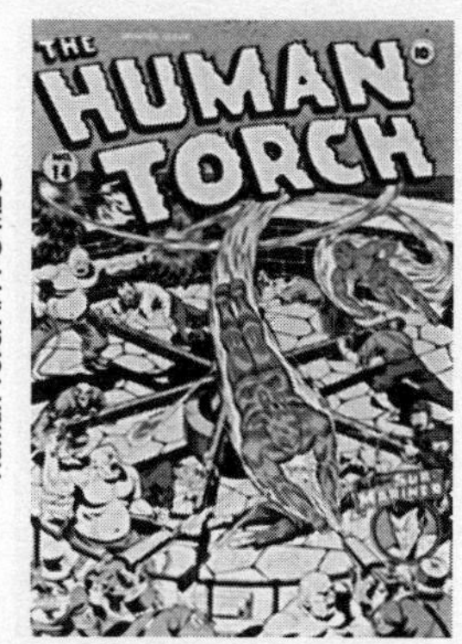
Human Torch #14 © MEG

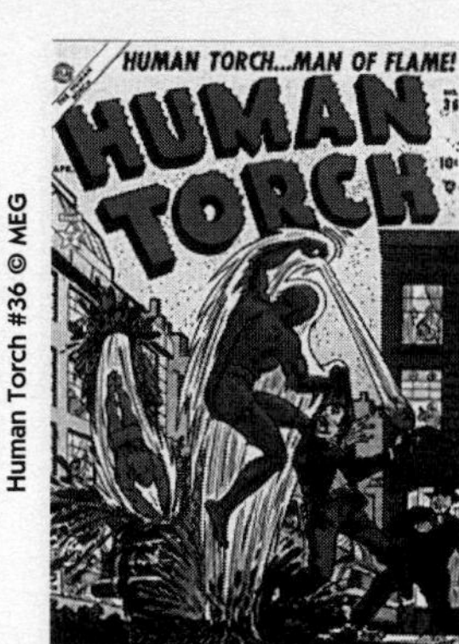
Human Torch #36 © MEG

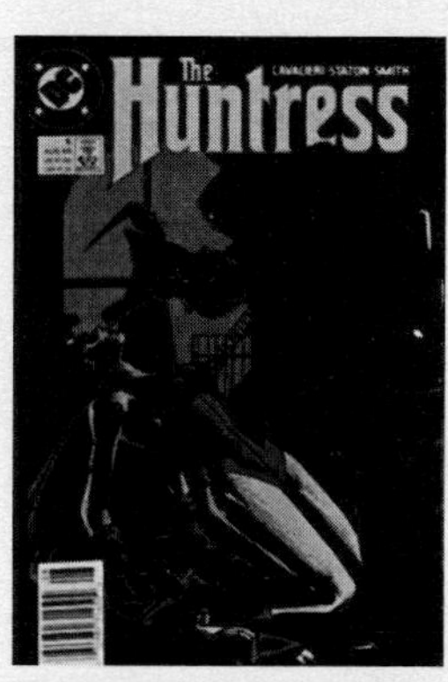
The Huntress #5 © DC

GD25 FN65 NM94

Marvel Comics Group
1-Origin; Spider-Man x-over 1.60 4.00
2-Ghost Rider app. 1.90 4.75
3-19: 9-Daredevil x-over; Byrne-c(p) .70 1.80
NOTE: **Austin** c-4i, 9i. **Elias** a-1, 3p, 4p, 7p, 10-12p, 15p, 18p, 19p. **Layton** c-19.

HUMAN TARGET SPECIAL (TV)
Nov, 1991 ($2.00, 52 pgs.)
DC Comics
1 .80 2.00

HUMAN TORCH, THE (Red Raven #1)(See All-Select, All Winners, Marvel Mystery, Men's Adventures, Mystic Comics (2nd series), Sub-Mariner, USA & Young Men)
No. 2, Fall, 1940 - No. 15, Spring, 1944;
No. 16, Fall, 1944 - No. 35, Mar, 1949 (Becomes Love Tales #36 on);
No. 36, April, 1954 - No. 38, Aug, 1954
Timely/Marvel Comics (TP 2,3/TCI 4-9/SePI 10/SnPC 11-25/CnPC 26-35/Atlas Comics (CPC 36-38)) GD25 FN65 VF82 NM94
2(#1)-Intro & Origin Toro; The Falcon, The Fiery Mask, Mantor the Magician, & Microman only app.; Human Torch by Burgos, Sub-Mariner by Everett begin (origin of each in text) 1500.00 4500.00 9750.00 15,000.00
(Estimated up to 190 total copies exist, 10 in NM/Mint)
GD25 FN65 NM94
3(#2)-40pg. H.T. story; H.T. & S.M. battle over who is best artist in text-Everett or Burgos 400.00 1200.00 2800.00
4(#3)-Origin The Patriot in text; last Everett Sub-Mariner; 1st Nazi war-c this title (see Marvel Mystery #4); Sid Greene-a 300.00 900.00 2100.00
5(#4)-The Patriot app; Angel x-over in Sub-Mariner (Summer, 1941) 214.00 643.00 1500.00
5-Human Torch battles Sub-Mariner (Fall, '41) 357.00 1071.00 2500.00
6,7,9: 7-1st Japanese war-c 136.00 407.00 950.00
8-Human Torch battles Sub-Mariner; Wolverton-a, 1 pg. 229.00 685.00 1600.00
10-Human Torch battles Sub-Mariner; Wolverton-a, 1 pg. 157.00 471.00 1100.00
11-15: 14-1st Atlas Globe logo (Winter, 1943-44; see All Winners #11 also) 104.00 311.00 725.00
16-20: 20-Last War issue 79.00 236.00 550.00
21-30: 23(Sum/46)-Becomes Junior Miss 24? 68.00 205.00 475.00
31-Namora x-over in Sub-Mariner (also #30); last Toro 61.00 182.00 425.00
32-Sungirl, Namora app.; Sungirl-c 61.00 182.00 425.00
33-Capt. America x-over 63.00 190.00 440.00
34-Sungirl solo 59.00 175.00 410.00
35-Captain America & Sungirl app. (1949) 63.00 190.00 440.00
36-38(1954)-Sub-Mariner in all 50.00 150.00 350.00
NOTE: **Ayers** Human Torch in 36(3). **Brodsky** c-25, 31-33?, 37, 38. **Burgos** c-36. **Everett** a-1-3, 27, 28, 30, 37, 38. **Powell** a-36(Sub-Mariner). **Schomburg** c-1-3, 5-8, 10-23. **Sekowsky** c-28, 34?, 35? **Shores** c-24, 26, 27, 29, 30. **Mickey Spillane** text 4-6. Bondage c-2, 12, 19.

HUMAN TORCH, THE (Also see Avengers West Coast, Fantastic Four, The Invaders, Saga of the Original... & Strange Tales #101)
Sept, 1974 - No. 8, Nov, 1975
Marvel Comics Group
1: 1-8-r/stories from Strange Tales #101-108 1.80 4.50
2-8: 1st H.T. title since G.A. 7-vs. Sub-Mariner 1.20 3.00
NOTE: Golden Age & Silver Age Human Torch-r #1-8. **Ayers** r-6, 7. **Kirby/Ayers** r-1-5, 8.

HUMBUG (Satire by Harvey Kurtzman)
Aug, 1957 - No. 9, May, 1958; No. 10, June, 1958; No. 11, Oct, 1958
Humbug Publications
1-Wood-a (intro pgs. only) 17.00 52.00 120.00
2 9.15 27.50 55.00
3-9: 8-Elvis in Jailbreak Rock 6.70 20.00 40.00
10,11-Magazine format. 10-Photo-c 10.00 30.00 60.00
Bound Volume(#1-6)-Sold by publisher 29.00 86.00 200.00
Bound Volume(#1-9) 34.00 103.00 240.00

GD25 FN65 NM94

NOTE: **Davis** a-1-11. **Elder** a-2-4, 6-9, 11. **Heath** a-2, 4-8, 10. **Jaffee** a-2, 4-9. **Kurtzman** a-11.

HUMDINGER (Becomes White Rider and Super Horse #3 on?)
May-June, 1946 - V2#2, July-Aug, 1947
Novelty Press/Premium Group
1-Jerkwater Line, Mickey Starlight by Don Rico, Dink begin 17.00 52.00 120.00
2 8.35 25.00 50.00
3-6, V2#1,2 5.00 15.00 30.00

HUMOR (See All Humor Comics)

HUMPHREY COMICS (Joe Palooka Presents...; also see Joe Palooka)
October, 1948 - No. 22, April, 1952
Harvey Publications
1-Joe Palooka's pal (r); (52 pgs.)-Powell-a 10.00 30.00 65.00
2,3: Powell-a 5.00 15.00 30.00
4-Boy Heroes app.; Powell-a 5.85 17.50 35.00
5-8,10: 5,6-Powell-a. 7-Little Dot app. 4.00 11.00 22.00
9-Origin Humphrey 5.00 15.00 30.00
11-22 3.20 8.00 16.00

HUNCHBACK OF NOTRE DAME, THE (See 4-Color No. 854)

HUNK
August, 1961 - No. 11, 1963
Charlton Comics
1 3.00 7.50 15.00
2-11 1.60 4.00 8.00

HUNTED (Formerly My Love Memoirs)
No. 13, July, 1950 - No. 2, Sept, 1950
Fox Features Syndicate
13(#1)-Used in **SOTI**, pg. 42 & illo. "Treating police contemptuously" (lower left); Hollingsworth bondage-c 19.00 58.00 135.00
2 9.15 27.50 55.00

HUNTRESS, THE (See All-Star Comics #69, Batman Family, Brave & the Bold #62, DC Super Stars #17, Detective #652, Infinity, Inc. #1, Sensation Comics #68 & Wonder Woman #271)
April, 1989 - No. 19, Oct, 1990 ($1.00, mature readers)
DC Comics
1-19: Staton-c/a(p) in all. 17-19-Batman-c/stories 1.00

HUNTRESS, THE
June, 1994 - No. 4, Sept, 1994 ($1.50, mini-series)
DC Comics
1-4-Netzer-c/a: 2-Batman app. 1.50

HURRICANE COMICS
1945 (52 pgs.)
Cambridge House
1-(Humor, funny animal) 14.00 43.00 100.00

HYBRIDS
Jan, 1994 - Present ($2.50)
Continuity Comics
1-Neal Adams-c(p) & part-i; embossed-c 1.00 2.50

HYBRIDS DEATHWATCH 2000
Apr, 1993 - No. 3, Aug, 1993 ($2.50, color)
Continuity Comics
0-(Giveaway)-Foil-c; Neal Adams-c(i) & plots (also #1,2) 1.00 2.50
1-5: 1-Polybagged w/card; die-cut-c. 2-Thermal-c. 3-Polybagged w/card; indestructible-c; Adams plot. 4,5-Valeria She-Bat; origin Hybrids; Adams-c(p) 1.00 2.50

HYBRIDS ORIGIN
1993 - Present ($2.50)
Continuity Comics
1-5: 2,3-Neal Adams-c. 4,5-Valeria the She-Bat app. Adams-c(i)

Hyperkind Unleashed #1 © MEG

Iceman #4 © MEG

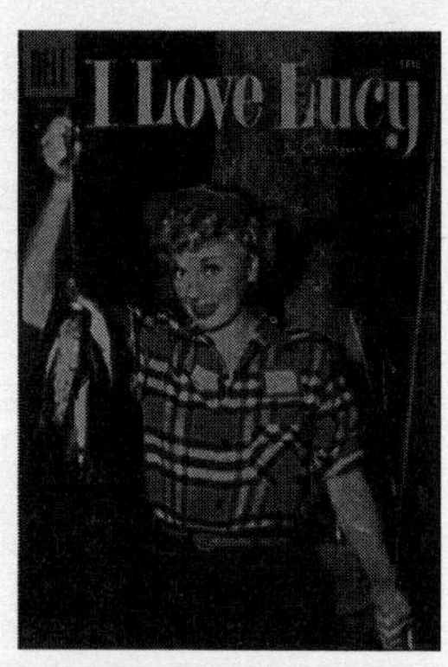

I Love Lucy #7 © Desilu

	GD25	FN65	NM94
		1.00	2.50

HYDROMAN (See Heroic Comics)

HYPERKIND (See Razorline)
Sept, 1993 - No. 9, May, 1994 ($1.75/$1.95)
Marvel Comics

	GD25	FN65	NM94
1-($2.50)-Foil embossed-c; by Clive Barker		.80	2.00
2-8		.70	1.75
9-($1.95)		.80	2.00

HYPERKIND UNLEASED
Aug, 1994 ($2.95, 52 pgs.)
Marvel Comics

	GD25	FN65	NM94
1		1.20	3.00

HYPER MYSTERY COMICS
May, 1940 - No. 2, June, 1940 (68 pgs.)
Hyper Publications

	GD25	FN65	NM94
1-Hyper, the Phenomenal begins	121.00	365.00	850.00
2	79.00	236.00	550.00

I AIM AT THE STARS (See 4-Color No. 1148)

I AM COYOTE (See Eclipse Graphic Album Series & Eclipse Magazine #2)

I AM LEGEND (Eclipse)(Value: cover or less)

IBIS, THE INVINCIBLE (See Fawcett Miniatures, Mighty Midget & Whiz)
1943 (Feb) - #2, 1943; #3, Wint, 1945 - #5, Fall, 1946; #6, Spring, 1948
Fawcett Publications

	GD25	FN65	NM94
1-Origin Ibis; Raboy-c; on sale 1/2/43	121.00	365.00	850.00
2-Bondage-c	64.00	193.00	450.00
3-Wolverton-a #3-6 (4 pgs. each)	51.00	154.00	360.00
4-6: 5-Bondage-c	39.00	118.00	275.00

NOTE: ***Mac Raboy** c(p)-3-5. **Shaffenberger** c-6.*

ICE KING OF OZ, THE (See First Comics Graphic Novel #13)

ICEMAN (Also see The Champions & X-Men #94)
Dec, 1984 - No. 4, June, 1985 (Limited series)
Marvel Comics Group

	GD25	FN65	NM94
1		.80	2.00
2,4		.70	1.70
3-The Defenders, Champions (Ghost Rider) & the original X-Men x-over		1.10	2.75

ICICLE (Hero)(Value: cover or less)

I COME IN PEACE (Greater Mercury)(Value: cover or less)

ICON
May, 1993 - Present ($1.50/$1.75)
DC Comics (Milestone)

	GD25	FN65	NM94
1-($2.95)-Collector's Edition polybagged w/poster & trading card (direct sale only)		1.20	3.00
1-14: 9-Simonson-c			1.50
15-21: 15-Begin $1.75-c. 15,16-Worlds Collide Pt. 4 & 11. 15-Superboy app. 16-Superman-c/sty.		.70	1.75

IDAHO
June-Aug, 1963 - No. 8, July-Sept, 1965
Dell Publishing Co.

	GD25	FN65	NM94
1	2.40	6.00	12.00
2-8: 5-7-Painted-c	1.40	3.50	7.00

IDEAL (... a Classical Comic) (2nd Series) (Love Romances No. 6 on)
July, 1948 - No. 5, March, 1949 (Feature length stories)
Timely Comics

	GD25	FN65	NM94
1-Antony & Cleopatra	23.00	70.00	160.00
2-The Corpses of Dr. Sacotti	20.00	60.00	140.00
3-Joan of Arc; used in **SOTI**, pg. 308 'Boer War'	17.00	52.00	120.00
4-Richard the Lion-hearted; titled "...the World's Greatest Comics"; The Witness app.	27.00	80.00	185.00
5-Ideal Love & Romance; change to love; photo-c	11.00	32.00	75.00

IDEAL COMICS (1st Series) (Willie Comics No. 5 on)
Fall, 1944 - No. 4, Spring, 1946
Timely Comics (MgPC)

	GD25	FN65	NM94
1-Funny animal; Super Rabbit in all	13.00	40.00	90.00
2	10.00	30.00	60.00
3,4	9.15	27.50	55.00

IDEAL LOVE & ROMANCE (See Ideal, A Classical Comic)

IDEAL ROMANCE (Formerly Tender Romance)
No. 3, April, 1954 - No. 8, Feb, 1955 (Diary Confessions No. 9 on)
Key Publications

	GD25	FN65	NM94
3-Bernard Baily-c	5.00	15.00	30.00
4-8: 4,5-B. Baily-c	3.20	8.00	16.00

IDOL
1992 - No. 3, 1992 ($2.95, mini-series, 52 pgs.)
Epic Comics (Marvel)

	GD25	FN65	NM94
Book 1-3		1.20	3.00

I DREAM OF JEANNIE (TV)
April, 1965 - No. 2, Dec, 1966 (Photo-c)
Dell Publishing Co.

	GD25	FN65	NM94
1,2-Barbara Eden photo-c	10.00	30.00	60.00

IF THE DEVIL WOULD TALK
1950; 1958 (32 pgs.; paper cover; in full color)
Roman Catholic Catechetical Guild/Impact Publ.

	GD25	FN65	NM94
nn-(Scarce)-About secularism (20-30 copies known to exist); very low distribution	57.00	171.00	400.00
1958 Edition-(Impact Publ.); art & script changed to meet church criticism of earlier edition; 80 plus copies known to exist	36.00	107.00	250.00
Black & White version of nn edition; small size; only 4 known copies exist	30.00	90.00	200.00

NOTE: *The original edition of this book was printed and killed by the Guild's board of directors. It is believed that a very limited number of copies were distributed. The 1958 version was a complete bomb with very limited, if any, circulation. In 1979, 11 original, 4 1958 reprints, and 4 B&W's surfaced from the Guild's old files in St. Paul, Minnesota.*

ILLUMINATOR
1993 - No. 4, 1993 ($2.95, 52 pgs.)
Marvel Comics/Nelson Publ.

	GD25	FN65	NM94
1,2-($4.99)	1.00	2.00	5.00
3,4		1.20	3.00

ILLUSTRATED GAGS (See Single Series No. 16)

ILLUSTRATED LIBRARY OF..., AN (See Classics Illustrated Giants)

ILLUSTRATED STORIES OF THE OPERAS
1943 (16 pgs.; B&W) (25 cents) (cover-B&W & red)
Baily (Bernard) Publ. Co.

	GD25	FN65	NM94
nn-(Rare)-Faust (part-r in Cisco Kid #1)	43.00	130.00	300.00
nn-(Rare)-Aida	43.00	130.00	300.00
nn-(Rare)-Carmen; Baily-a	43.00	130.00	300.00
nn-(Rare)-Rigoleito	43.00	130.00	300.00

ILLUSTRATED STORY OF ROBIN HOOD & HIS MERRY MEN, THE
(See Classics Giveaways, 12/44)

ILLUSTRATED TARZAN BOOK, THE (See Tarzan Book)

I LOVED (Formerly Rulah; Colossal Features Magazine No. 33 on)
No. 28, July, 1949 - No. 32, Mar, 1950
Fox Features Syndicate

	GD25	FN65	NM94
28	5.85	17.50	35.00
29-32	4.00	11.00	22.00

I LOVE LUCY (Eternity)(Value: cover or less)

I LOVE LUCY COMICS (TV) (Also see The Lucy Show)
No. 535, Feb, 1954 - No. 35, Apr-June, 1962 (All have Lucille Ball photo-c)

I Love You #8 © CC

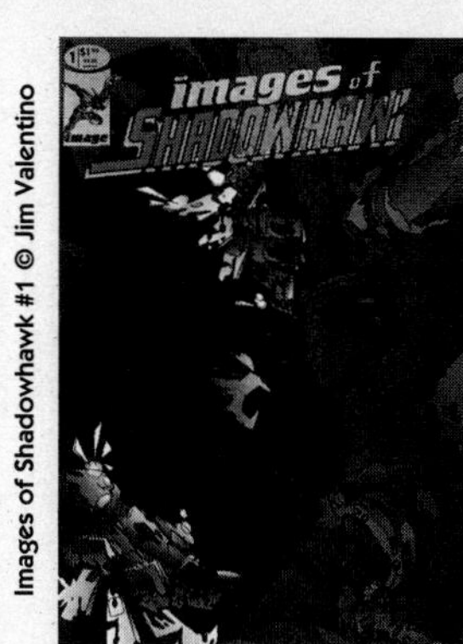

Images of Shadowhawk #1 © Jim Valentino

Impossible Man #1 © MEG

	GD25	FN65	NM94
Dell Publishing Co.			
4-Color 535(#1)	37.00	110.00	260.00
4-Color 559(#2, 5/54)	25.00	75.00	175.00
3 (8-10/54) - 5	16.00	48.00	110.00
6-10	11.50	34.00	80.00
11-20	10.00	30.00	70.00
21-35	10.00	30.00	60.00

I LOVE YOU
June, 1950 (One shot)
Fawcett Publications

1-Photo-c 10.00 30.00 65.00

I LOVE YOU (Formerly In Love)
No. 7, 9/55 - No. 121, 12/76; No. 122, 3/79 - No. 130, 5/80
Charlton Comics

	GD25	FN65	NM94
7-Kirby-c; Powell-a	8.35	25.00	50.00
8-10	3.60	9.00	18.00
11-16,18-20	2.00	5.00	10.00
17-(68 pg. Giant)	2.80	7.00	14.00
21-25,27-50	1.20	3.00	6.00
26-Torres-a	1.40	3.50	7.00
51-59		1.60	4.00
60(1/66)-Elvis Presley line drawn c/story	10.00	30.00	70.00
61-85		1.20	3.00
86-130			1.00

I'M A COP
1954 - No. 3, 1954?
Magazine Enterprises

1(A-1 #111)-Powell-c/a in all 10.00 30.00 60.00
2(A-1 #126), 3(A-1 #128) 5.35 16.00 32.00

IMAGE GRAPHIC NOVEL (Image International)(Value: cover or less)

IMAGES OF SHADOWHAWK (Also see Shadowhawk)
Sept, 1993 - No. 3, 1994 ($1.95, color, limited series)
Image Comics

1-3-Keith Giffen-c/a .80 2.00

IMAGE ZERO
1993 (Received through mail w/coupons from Image books)
Image Comics

0-Savage Dragon, Stormwatch, Shadowhawk, Strykeforce; 1st app. Troll; 1st app. McFarlane's Freak, Blotch, Sweat and Bludd 2.10 6.40 15.00

I'M DICKENS - HE'S FENSTER (TV)
May-July, 1963 - No. 2, Aug-Oct, 1963 (Photo-c)
Dell Publishing Co.

1,2 4.20 12.50 25.00

I MET A HANDSOME COWBOY (See 4-Color No. 324)

IMMORTALIS (See Mortigan Goth: Immortalis)

IMMORTAL DOCTOR FATE, THE (DC)(Value: cover or less)

IMPACT
Mar-Apr, 1955 - No. 5, Nov-Dec, 1955
E. C. Comics

	GD25	FN65	NM94
1-Not code approved	13.00	40.00	90.00
2	10.00	30.00	60.00
3-5: 4-Crandall-a	7.50	22.50	45.00

NOTE: ***Crandall*** *a-1-4.* ***Davis*** *a-2-4; c-1-5.* ***Evans*** *a-1, 4, 5.* ***Ingels*** *a-in all.* ***Kamen*** *a-3.* ***Krigstein*** *a-1, 5.* ***Orlando*** *a-2, 5.*

IMPACT CHRISTMAS SPECIAL
1991 ($2.50, color, 68 pgs.)
Impact Comics (DC Comics)

1-Gift of the Magi by Infantino/Rogers; The Black Hood, The Fly, The Jaguar, & The Shield stories 1.00 2.50

IMPOSSIBLE MAN SUMMER VACATION SPECTACULAR, THE (Marvel)
(Value: cover or less)

INCAL, THE
Nov, 1988 - No. 3, Jan, 1989 ($10.95/$12.95, adults)
Epic Comics (Marvel)

1,3: Moebius-c/a in all; sexual content 1.65 4.70 11.00
2-($12.95) 1.85 5.50 13.00

INCOMPLETE DEATH'S HEAD (Also see Death's Head)
Jan, 1993 - No. 12, Dec, 1993 ($1.75, limited series)
Marvel Comics UK

1-($2.95, 56 pgs.)-Die-cut cover 1.20 3.00
2-11: 2-Re-intro original Death's Head. 3-Original Death's Head vs. Dragon's Claws .70 1.75
12-($2.50, 52 pgs.)-She Hulk app. 1.00 2.50

INCREDIBLE HULK, THE (See Aurora, The Avengers #1, The Defenders #1, Giant-Size..., Hulk, Marvel Collectors Item Classics, Marvel Comics Presents #26, Marvel Fanfare, Marvel Treasury Edition, Power Record Comics, Rampaging Hulk, She-Hulk & 2099 Unlimited)

INCREDIBLE HULK, THE
May, 1962 - No. 6, Mar, 1963; No. 102, Apr, 1968 - Present
Marvel Comics Group

	GD25	FN65	VF82	NM94
1-Origin & 1st app. (skin is grey colored); Kirby pencils begin, end #5	708.00	2125.00	5312.00	8500.00
2-1st green skinned Hulk; Kirby/Ditko-a	180.00	540.00	1170.00	1800.00

	GD25	FN65	NM94
3-Origin retold; 1st app. Ringmaster & Hercules (9/62)	114.00	342.00	1025.00
4,5: 4-Brief origin retold	92.00	275.00	825.00
6-Intro. Teen Brigade; all Ditko-a	158.00	475.00	1425.00
102-(Formerly Tales to Astonish)-Origin retold; story continued from Tales to Astonish #101	24.00	73.00	170.00
103	9.00	27.00	64.00
104-Rhino app.	8.00	25.00	58.00
105-108: 105-1st Missing Link	7.00	21.00	48.00
109,110: 109-Ka-Zar app.	4.60	14.00	32.00
111-117: 117-Last 12 cent issue	3.40	10.30	24.00
118-Hulk vs. Sub-Mariner	2.70	8.10	19.00
119-121,123-125	1.90	5.60	13.00
122-Hulk battles Thing (12/69)	2.90	9.00	20.00
126-140: 126-1st Barbara Norriss (Valkyrie). 131-Hulk vs. Iron Man; 1st Jim Wilson, Hulk's new sidekick. 136-1st Xeron, The Star-Slayer. 140-Written by Harlan Ellison; 1st Jarella, Hulk's love	1.40	3.50	8.50
141-1st app. Doc Samson (7/71)	1.50	3.80	9.00
142-144,146-157,159-161: 149-1st app. The Inheritor. 155-1st app. Shaper. 161-The Mimic dies; Beast app.	1.00	2.50	6.00
145-(52 pgs.)-Origin retold	1.30	3.30	8.00
158-Warlock cameo(12/72)	1.10	2.70	6.50
162-1st app. The Wendigo (4/73); Beast app.	1.30	3.00	8.00
163-171,173-175: 163-1st app. The Gremlin. 164-1st Capt. Omen & Colonel John D. Armbruster. 166-1st Zzzax. 168-1st The Harpy; nudity panels of Betty Brant. 169-1st app. Bi-Beast	1.00	2.50	6.00
165-Variant w/4 extra pgs. of ads on slick paper (7/73)	1.10	2.70	6.50
172-X-Men cameo; origin Juggernaut retold	1.20	2.90	7.00
176-Warlock cameo (2 panels only); same date as Strange Tales #178 (6/74)	1.10	2.70	6.50
177-1st actual death of Warlock (last panel only)	1.30	3.90	9.00
178-Rebirth of Warlock	2.30	6.90	16.00
179-No Warlock	1.00	2.00	5.00
180-(10/74)-1st app. Wolverine (cameo last pg.)	8.00	24.00	55.00
181-(11/74)-1st full Wolverine story	40.00	120.00	270.00
182-Wolverine cameo; see Giant-Size X-Men #1 for next app.; 1st Crackajack Jackson	6.30	19.00	44.00
183-199: 185-Death of Col. Armbruster		1.50	3.75

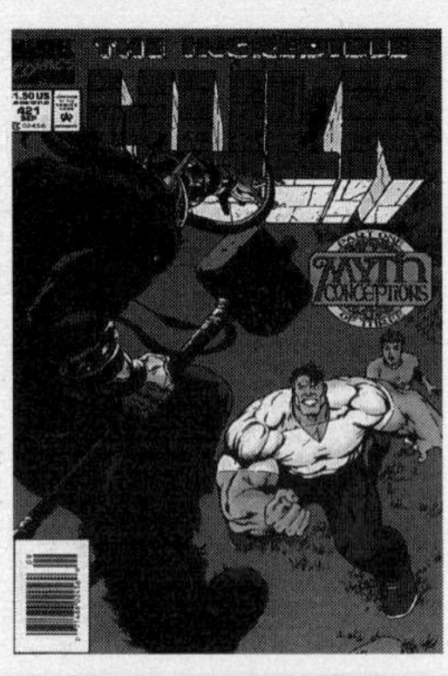

The Incredible Hulk #421 © MEG

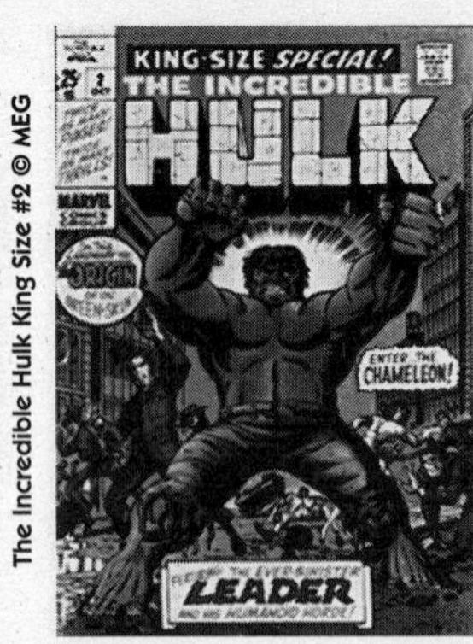

The Incredible Hulk King Size #2 © MEG

Indiana Jones and the Golden Fleece #1 © Lucasfilms

GD25 FN65 NM94

200-Silver Surfer app.; anniversary issue 3.00 9.40 22.00
201-240: 212-1st app. The Constrictor. 227-Original Avengers app. 232-Capt. America x-over from C.A. #230. 233-Marvel Man app. 234-(4/79)-1st app. Quasar (formerly Marvel Man & changes name to Quasar) 1.30 3.25
241-249,251-299: 243-Cage app. 271-Rocket Raccoon app. 272-Sasquatch & Wendigo app.; Wolverine & Alpha Flight cameo in flashback. 278,279-Most Marvel characters app. (Wolverine in both). 279-X-Men & Alpha Flight cameos. 282-284-She-Hulk app. 293-F.F. app. .90 2.25
250-Giant size; Silver Surfer app. 1.50 3.80 9.00
300-(11/84, 52 pgs.)-Spider-Man app in new black costume on-c & 2 pg. cameo 1.70 4.25
301-313: 312-Origin Hulk retold 1.10 2.75
314-Byrne-c/a begins, ends #319 2.00 5.00
315-319: 319-Bruce Banner & Betty Talbot wed 1.10 2.75
320-323,325,327-329 .90 2.25
324-1st app. Grey Hulk since #1 (c-swipe of #1) 1.70 5.00 12.00
326-Grey vs. Green Hulk 1.00 2.00 5.00
330-1st McFarlane issue (4/87) 3.00 9.40 22.00
331-Grey Hulk series begins 2.30 6.90 16.00
332-334,336-339: 336,337-X-Factor app. 1.70 5.00 12.00
335-No McFarlane-a 1.30 3.25
340-Hulk battles Wolverine by McFarlane 6.30 19.00 44.00
341-344 1.30 3.00 7.50
345-($1.50, 52 pgs.) 1.40 3.50 8.50
346-Last McFarlane issue 1.10 2.70 6.50
347-349,351-358,360-366 1.30 3.25
350-Hulk/Thing battle 1.80 4.50
359-Wolverine app. (illusion only) 1.90 4.75
367-1st Dale Keown-a on Hulk (3/90) 3.30 9.90 23.00
368-Sam Kieth-c/a 2.40 7.30 17.00
369,370-Dale Keown-c/a. 370,371-Original Defenders app. 2.00 5.00 12.00
371,373-376: Keown-c/a. 376-Green vs. Grey Hulk 1.20 2.90 7.00
372-Green Hulk app.; Keown-c/a 2.90 9.00 20.00
377-1st all new Hulk; fluorescent-c; Keown-c/a 3.10 9.00 22.00
377-Fluorescent green logo 2nd printing 1.00 2.30 5.50
378,380,389: No Keown-a. 380-Doc Samson app. 1.30 3.25
379-Keown-a 1.30 3.00 8.00
381-388,390-392-Keown-a. 385-Infinity Gauntlet x-over. 389-Last $1.00-c. 392-X-Factor app. 1.70 4.25
393-($2.50, 72 pgs.)-30th anniversary issue; green foil stamped-c; swipes-c to #1; has pin-ups of classic battles; Keown-c/a 1.30 3.00 8.00
393-2nd printing 1.30 3.25
394-No Keown-c/a; intro Trauma .70 1.80
395,396-Punisher-c/stories; Keown-c/a .90 2.25
397-Begin "Ghost of the Past" 4-part sty; Keown c/a .90 2.25
398,399: 398-Last Keown-c/a .70 1.80
400-($2.50, 68 pgs.)-Holo-grafx foil-c & r/TTA #63 1.10 2.75
401-416: 402-Return of Doc Samson .70 1.80
417-427: 417-Begin $1.50-c; bound-in trding card sheet. 418-Regular edition; Death app. 420-Death of Jim Wilson. 421-Peter David story 1.50
418-($2.50)-Collector's Edition w/Gatefold die-cut-c 1.00 2.50
Special 1 (10/68, 25¢, 68 pg.)-New 51 pg. story, Hulk battles The Inhumans (early app.; Steranko-c 9.00 26.00 60.00
Special 2 (10/69, 25¢, 68 pg.)-Origin retold 5.00 15.00 35.00
Special 3 (1/71, 25¢, 68 pg.) 1.30 3.00 8.00
Special 4 (1/72) 1.00 2.50 6.00
Annual 5 (1976) 1.70 4.25
Annual 6 (1977) .90 2.25
Annual 7 (1978)-Byrne/Layton-c/a; Iceman & Angel app. in book-length story 1.30 3.25
Annual 8-17: 8('79)-Book-length Sasquatch-c/story. 9('80). 10('81). 11('82)-Doc Samson back-up by Miller(p)(5 pgs.); Spider-Man & Avengers app. Buckler-a(p). 12('83). 13('84). 14('85). 15('86). 16('90, $2.00, 68 pgs.)-She-Hulk app. 17(1991, $2.00)-Origin retold .80 2.00
Annual 18 (1992, $2.25, 68 pgs.)-Return of the Defenders, Pt. I; no Keown-c/a .90 2.25
Annual 19 (1993, $2.95, 68 pgs.)-Bagged w/card 1.20 3.00
Annual 20 (1994, $2.95, 68 pgs.) 1.20 3.00
...Versus Quasimodo 1 (3/83, one-shot)-Based on Saturday morning cartoon .65 1.60
...Versus Venom 1 (4/94, $2.50, one-shot)-Embossed-c; red foil logo 1.00 2.50

NOTE: **Adkins** *a-111-116i.* **Austin** *a(i)-350, 351, 353, 354; c-302i, 350i.* **Ayers** *a-3-5i.* **John Buscema** *c-202p.* **Byrne** *a-314-319p; c-314-316, 318, 319, 359.* **Colan** *c-363.* **Ditko** *a-2i, 6, 249, Annual 2r(5), 3r, 9p; c-2i, 6, 235, 249.* **Everett** *c-133i.* **Golden** *c-248, 251.* **Kane** *c(p)-193, 194, 196, 198.* **Dale Keown** *a(p)-367, 369-377, 379, 381-388, 390-393, 395-398; c-369-377p, 381, 382p, 384, 385, 386, 387p, 388, 390p, 391-393, 395p, 396, 397p, 398.* **Kirby** *a-1-5p, Special 2, 3p, Annual 5p; c-1-5, Annual 5.* **McFarlane** *a-330-334p, 336-339p, 340-343, 344-346p; c-330p, 340p, 341-343, 344p, 345, 346p.* **Miller** *c-258p, 261, 264, 268.* **Mooney** *a-230p, 287i, 288i.* **Powell** *a-Special 3r(2).* **Romita** *a-Annual 17p.* **Severin** *a(i)-108-110, 131-133, 141-151, 153-155; c(i)-109, 110, 132, 142, 144-155.* **Simonson** *c-283, 364-367.* **Starlin** *a-222p; c-217.* **Staton** *a(i)-187-189, 191-209.* **Tuska** *a-102i, 105i, 106i, 218p.* **Williamson** *a-310i; c-310i, 311i.* **Wrightson** *c-197.*

INCREDIBLE HULK AND WOLVERINE, THE
Oct, 1986 ($2.50)
Marvel Comics Group

1-r-/1st app. Wolverine from Incred. Hulk #180,181; Wolverine back-up by Austin(i); Byrne-c 1.60 5.00 11.00

INCREDIBLE MR. LIMPET, THE (See Movie Classics)

INCREDIBLE SCIENCE FICTION (Formerly Weird Science-Fantasy)
No. 30, July-Aug, 1955 - No. 33, Jan-Feb, 1956
E. C. Comics

30,33: 33-Story-r/Weird Fantasy #18 30.00 90.00 210.00
31-Williamson/Krenkel-a, Wood-a(2) 32.00 96.00 225.00
32-Williamson/Krenkel-a 32.00 96.00 225.00

NOTE: **Davis** *a-30, 32, 33; c-30-32.* **Krigstein** *a-in all.* **Orlando** *a-30, 32, 33("Judgement Day" reprint).* **Wood** *a-30, 31, 33; c-33.*

INDIANA JONES (See Dark Horse Comics & Further Adventures of...)

INDIANA JONES AND THE ARMS OF GOLD
Feb, 1994 - No. 4, May, 1994 ($2.50, mini-series)
Dark Horse Comics

1-4 1.00 2.50

INDIANA JONES AND THE FATE OF ATLANTIS
March, 1991 - No. 4, Sept, 1991 ($2.50, mini-series)
Dark Horse Comics

1-4: Dorman painted-c on all; 1,2-Contain trading cards (#1 has a 2nd printing, 10/91) 1.00 2.50

INDIANA JONES AND THE GOLDEN FLEECE
June, 1994 - July, 1994 ($2.50, limited series)
Dark Horse Comics

1,2 1.00 2.50

INDIANA JONES AND THE LAST CRUSADE
1989 - No. 4, 1989 ($1.00, limited series, movie adaptation)
Marvel Comics

1-4: Williamson-i assist 1.00
1 (1989, $2.95, B&W mag., 80 pgs.) 1.20 3.00

INDIANA JONES AND THE TEMPLE OF DOOM
Sept, 1984 - No. 3, Nov, 1984 (Movie adaptation)
Marvel Comics Group

1-3-r/Marvel Super Special; Guice-a 1.00

INDIANA JONES: THUNDER IN THE ORIENT
Sept, 1993 - No. 6, 1994 ($2.50, limited series)
Dark Horse Comics

1-6: Dan Barry story & art in all; 1-Dorman painted-c 1.00 2.50

INDIAN BRAVES (Baffling Mysteries No. 5 on)
March, 1951 - No. 4, Sept, 1951

Indian Chief #23 © DELL

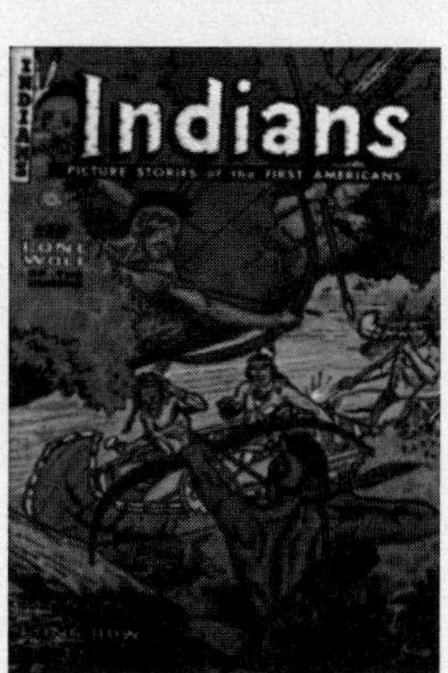

Indians #12 © FH

Infinity Gauntlet #3 © MEG

GD25 FN65 NM94 GD25 FN65 NM94

Ace Magazines
1-Green Arrowhead begins, ends #3 7.50 22.50 45.00
2 4.00 11.00 22.00
3,4 3.60 9.00 18.00
I.W. Reprint #1 (nd)-r/Indian Braves #4 1.40 3.50 7.00

INDIAN CHIEF (White Eagle...) (Formerly The Chief)
No. 3, July-Sept, 1951 - No. 33, Jan-Mar, 1959 (All painted-c)
Dell Publishing Co.
3 4.20 12.50 25.00
4-11: 6-White Eagle app. 3.20 8.00 16.00
12-1st White Eagle(10-12/53)-Not same as earlier character
4.00 11.00 22.00
13-29 2.40 6.00 12.00
30-33-Buscema-a 2.80 7.00 14.00

INDIAN CHIEF (See March of Comics No. 94, 110, 127, 140, 159, 170, 187)

INDIAN FIGHTER, THE (See 4-Color No. 687)

INDIAN FIGHTER
May, 1950 - No. 11, Jan, 1952
Youthful Magazines
1 8.35 25.00 50.00
2-Wildey-a/c(bondage) 4.70 14.00 28.00
3-11: 3,4-Wildey-a 3.60 9.00 18.00
NOTE: ***Walter Johnson*** *c-1, 3, 4, 6.* ***Palais*** *a-10.* ***Stallman*** *a-7.* ***Wildey*** *a-2-4; c-2, 5.*

INDIAN LEGENDS OF THE NIAGARA (See American Graphics)

INDIANS
Spring, 1950 - No. 17, Spring, 1953 (1-8: 52 pgs.)
Fiction House Magazines (Wings Publ. Co.)
1-Manzar The White Indian, Long Bow & Orphan of the Storm begin
17.00 52.00 120.00
2-Starlight begins 10.00 30.00 60.00
3-5: 5-17-Most-c by Whitman 8.35 25.00 50.00
6-10 6.70 20.00 40.00
11-17 5.00 15.00 30.00

INDIANS OF THE WILD WEST
Circa 1958? (no date) (Reprints)
I. W. Enterprises
9-Kinstler-c; Whitman-a; r/Indians #? 1.80 4.50 9.00

INDIANS ON THE WARPATH
No date (Late 40s, early 50s) (132 pgs.)
St. John Publishing Co.
nn-Matt Baker-c; contains St. John comics rebound. Many combinations possible 20.00 60.00 140.00

INDIAN TRIBES (See Famous Indian Tribes)

INDIAN WARRIORS (Formerly White Rider and Super Horse; becomes Western Crime Cases #9)
No. 7, June, 1951 - No. 8, Sept, 1951
Star Publications
7-White Rider & Superhorse continue; "Last of the Mohicans" serial begins;
L.B. Cole-c 8.35 25.00 50.00
8-L. B. Cole-c 6.70 20.00 40.00
3-D 1(12/53, 25¢)-Came w/glasses; L. B. Cole-c 27.00 81.00 190.00
Accepted Reprint(nn)(inside cover shows White Rider & Superhorse #11)-r/cover to #7; origin White Rider &...;. L. B. Cole-c 4.00 10.00 20.00
Accepted Reprint #8 (nd); L.B. Cole-c (r-cover to #8) 4.00 10.00 20.00

INDOORS-OUTDOORS (See Wisco)

INDOOR SPORTS
nd (64 pgs.; 6x9"; B&W reprints; hardcover)
National Specials Co.
nn-By Tad 4.35 13.00 26.00

INFERIOR FIVE, THE (Inferior 5 #11, 12) (See Showcase #62, 63, 65)
3-4/67 - No. 10, 9-10/68; No. 11, 8-9/72 - No. 12, 10-11/72
National Periodical Publications (#1-10: 12 cents)
Showcase #62 (5-6/66)-Origin & 1st app. 6.00 18.00 55.00
Showcase #63,65 (7-8/66, 11-12/66)-2nd & 3rd app. 4.00 10.50 28.00
1-(3-4/67)-Sekowsky-a(p); 4th app. 4.70 14.00 33.00
2-Plastic Man, F.F. app.; Sekowsky-a(p) 2.40 7.30 17.00
3-10: 4-Thor app. 6-Stars DC staff. 10-Superman x-over; F.F., Spider-Man & Sub-Mariner app. 1.70 5.00 12.00
11,12-Orlando-c/a; both r/Showcase #62,63 1.70 5.00 12.00

INFINITY CRUSADE
June, 1993 - No. 6, Nov, 1993 ($2.50, limited series, 52 pgs.)
Marvel Comics
1-6: By Jim Starlin & Ron Lim 1.00 2.50

INFINITY GAUNTLET (The... #2 on; see Infinity Crusade, The Infinity War & Warlock & the Infinity Watch)
July, 1991 - No. 6, Dec, 1991 ($2.50, limited series)
Marvel Comics
1-Thanos-c/stories in all; Starlin scripts in all 1.90 4.50
2 1.10 2.75
3-6: 5,6-Ron Lim-c/a 1.00 2.50
NOTE: ***Lim*** *a-3p(part), 5p, 6p; c-5i, 6i.* ***Perez*** *a-1-3p, 4p(part); c-1(painted), 2-4, 5i, 6i.*

INFINITY, INC. (See All-Star Squadron #25)
Mar, 1984 - No. 53, Aug, 1988 ($1.25, Baxter paper, 36 pgs.)
DC Comics
1-Brainwave, Jr., Fury, The Huntress, Jade, Northwind, Nuklon, Obsidian, Power Girl, Silver Scarab & Star Spangled Kid begin 1.50
2-5: 2-Dr. Midnite, G.A. Flash, W. Woman, Dr. Fate, Hourman, Green Lantern, Wildcat app. 5-Nudity panels 1.20
6-13,38-49,51-53: 46,47-Millennium tie-ins 1.20
14-Todd McFarlane-a (5/85, 2nd full story) 1.20 3.00
15-37-McFarlane-a (20,23,24: 5 pgs. only; 33: 2 pgs.); 18-24-Crisis x-over. 21-Intro new Hourman & Dr. Midnight. 26-New Wildcat app. 31-Star Spangled Kid becomes Skyman. 32-Green Fury becomes Green Flame. 33-Origin Obsidian. 35-1st modern app. G.A. Fury .70 1.80
50 ($2.50, 52 pgs.) 1.00 2.50
Annual 1,2: 1(12/85)-Crisis x-over. 2('88, $2.00) .80 2.00
Special 1 (1987, $1.50) 1.50
NOTE: ***Kubert*** *r-4.* ***McFarlane*** *a-14-37p, Annual 1p; c(p)-14-19, 22, 25, 26, 31-33, 37, Annual 1.* ***Newton*** *a-12p, 13p(last work 4/85).* ***Tuska*** *a-11p. JSA app. 3-10.*

INFINITY WAR, THE (Also see Infinity Gauntlet & Warlock and the Infinity...)
June, 1992 - No. 6, Nov, 1992 ($2.50, mini-series)
Marvel Comics
1-Starlin scripts, Lim-c/a(p), Thanos app. in all 1.60 4.00
2-6: All have wraparound gatefold covers 1.00 2.50

INFORMER, THE
April, 1954 - No. 5, Dec, 1954
Feature Television Productions
1-Sekowsky-a begins 7.50 22.50 45.00
2 5.00 15.00 30.00
3-5 4.20 12.50 25.00

IN HIS STEPS (Spire Christiain)(Value: cover or less)

INHUMANOIDS, THE (TV) (Marvel)(Value: cover or less)

INHUMANS, THE (See Amazing Adventures, Fantastic Four #54 & Special #5, Incredible Hulk Special #1, Marvel Graphic Novel & Thor #146)
Oct, 1975 - No. 12, Aug, 1977
Marvel Comics Group
1: #1-4 are 25¢ issues 1.30 3.25
2-12: 9-Reprints Amazing Adventures #1,2('70) .70 1.80
Special 1(4/90, $1.50, 52 pgs.)-F.F. cameo .70 1.70
NOTE: ***Buckler*** *c-2-4p, 5.* ***Gil Kane*** *a-5-7p; c-1p, 7p, 8p.* ***Kirby*** *a-9r.* ***Mooney*** *a-11i.* ***Perez*** *a-1-4p, 8p.*

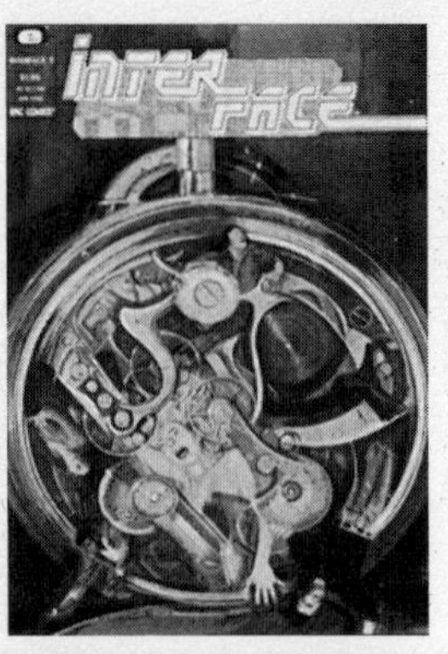

Interface #2 © MEG

International Crime Patrol #6 © EC

The Invaders #7 © MEG

INKY & DINKY (See Felix's Nephews...)

IN LOVE (...Magazine on-c; I Love You No. 7 on)
Aug-Sept, 1954 - No. 6, July, 1955 ('Adult Reading' on-c)
Mainline/Charlton No. 5 (5/55)-on

	GD25	FN65	NM94
1-Simon & Kirby-a; book-length novel in all issues	17.00	52.00	120.00
2-S&K-a	10.00	30.00	70.00
3,4-S&K-a. 3-Last pre-code (12-1/54-55)	9.15	27.50	55.00
5-S&K-c only	5.85	17.50	35.00
6-No S&K-a	3.20	8.00	16.00

IN LOVE WITH JESUS
1952 (36 pgs.) (Giveaway)
Catechetical Educational Society

	GD25	FN65	NM94
nn	3.00	7.50	15.00

INNOVATION SPECTACULAR (Innovation)(Value: cover or less)

INNOVATION SUMMER FUN SPECIAL (Innovation)(Value: cover or less)

INSANE (Dark Horse)(Value: cover or less)

IN SEARCH OF THE CASTAWAYS (See Movie Comics)

INSIDE CRIME (Formerly My Intimate Affair)
No. 3, July, 1950 - No. 2, Sept, 1950
Fox Features Syndicate (Hero Books)

	GD25	FN65	NM94
3-Wood-a (10 pgs.); L. B. Cole-c	14.00	43.00	100.00
2-Used in **SOTI**, pg. 182,183; r/Spook #24	11.00	32.00	75.00
nn(no publ. listed, nd)	5.85	17.50	35.00

INSPECTOR, THE (TV) (Also see The Pink Panther)
July, 1974 - No. 19, Feb, 1978
Gold Key

	GD25	FN65	NM94
1	1.30	3.25	8.00
2-5		1.60	4.00
6-19: 11-Reprints		.80	2.00

INSPECTOR GILL OF THE FISH POLICE (See Fish Police)

INSPECTOR WADE (See Feature Books #13)

INSTANT PIANO
Aug, 1994 - Present ($3.95, B&W, bimonthly)
Dark Horse Comics

	GD25	FN65	NM94
1-4		1.60	4.00

INTERFACE (Epic)(Value: cover or less)

INTERNATIONAL COMICS (...Crime Patrol No. 6)
Spring, 1947 - No. 5, Nov-Dec, 1947
E. C. Comics

	GD25	FN65	NM94
1-Schaffenberger-a begins, ends #4	53.00	160.00	370.00
2	38.00	115.00	265.00
3-5	31.00	94.00	220.00

INTERNATIONAL CRIME PATROL (Formerly International Comics #1-5; becomes Crime Patrol No. 7 on)
No. 6, Spring, 1948
E. C. Comics

	GD25	FN65	NM94
6-Moon Girl app.	53.00	160.00	370.00

INTERSTATE THEATRES' FUN CLUB COMICS
Mid 1940's (10¢ on cover) (B&W cover) (Premium)
Interstate Theatres

	GD25	FN65	NM94
Cover features MLJ characters looking at a copy of Top-Notch Comics, but contains an early Detective Comic on inside; many combinations possible2	5.35	16.00	32.00

IN THE DAYS OF THE MOB (Magazine)
Fall, 1971 (Black & White)
Hampshire Dist. Ltd. (National)

	GD25	FN65	NM94
1-Kirby-a; John Dillinger wanted poster inside	1.70	4.20	10.00

IN THE PRESENCE OF MINE ENEMIES (Spire Christian)(Value: cover or less)

INTIMATE (Teen-Age Love No. 4 on)
December, 1957 - No. 3, May, 1958
Charlton Comics

	GD25	FN65	NM94
1-3	1.80	4.50	9.00

INTIMATE CONFESSIONS (See Fox Giants)

INTIMATE CONFESSIONS
July-Aug, 1951 - No. 7, Aug, 1952; No. 8, Mar, 1953 (All painted-c)
Realistic Comics

	GD25	FN65	NM94
1-Kinstler-c/a; c/Avon paperback #222	55.00	165.00	385.00
2	10.00	30.00	70.00
3-c/Avon paperback #250; Kinstler-c/a	13.00	40.00	90.00
4-6,8: 4-c/Avon paperback #304; Kinstler-c. 6-c/Avon paperback #120. 8-c/Avon paperback #375; Kinstler-a	10.00	30.00	70.00
7-Spanking panel	11.00	32.00	75.00

INTIMATE CONFESSIONS
1964
I. W. Enterprises/Super Comics

	GD25	FN65	NM94
I.W. Reprint #9,10	1.20	3.00	6.00
Super Reprint #12,18	1.20	3.00	6.00

INTIMATE LOVE
No. 5, 1950 - No. 28, Aug, 1954
Standard Comics

	GD25	FN65	NM94
5	4.35	13.00	26.00
6-8-Severin/Elder-a	5.00	15.00	30.00
9	2.80	7.00	14.00
10-Jane Russell, Robert Mitchum photo-c	5.00	15.00	30.00
11-18,20,23,25,27,28	2.00	5.00	10.00
19,21,22,24,26-Toth-a	5.00	15.00	30.00

NOTE: ***Celardo** a-8, 10. **Colletta** a-23. **Moreira** a-13(2). Photo-c-6, 7, 10, 12, 14, 15, 18-20, 24, 26, 27.*

INTIMATE SECRETS OF ROMANCE
Sept, 1953 - No. 2, April, 1954
Star Publications

	GD25	FN65	NM94
1,2-L. B. Cole-c	8.35	25.00	50.00

INTRIGUE
January, 1955
Quality Comics Group

	GD25	FN65	NM94
1-Horror; Jack Cole reprint/Web of Evil	17.00	52.00	120.00

INTRUDER (TSR)(Value; cover or less)

INVADERS, THE (TV)
Oct, 1967 - No. 4, Oct, 1968 (All have photo-c)
Gold Key

	GD25	FN65	NM94
1-Spiegle-a in all	6.70	20.00	40.00
2-4	4.00	12.00	28.00

INVADERS, THE (Also see The Avengers #71 & Giant-Size Invaders)
August, 1975 - No. 40, May, 1979; No. 41, Sept, 1979
Marvel Comics Group

	GD25	FN65	NM94
1-Captain America & Bucky, Human Torch & Toro, & Sub-Mariner begin; #1-7 are 25¢ issues	1.30	3.25	8.00
2-10: 2-1st app. Mailbag & Brain-Drain. 3-Battle issue; Cap vs. Namor vs. Torch; intro U-Man. 6-Liberty Legion app; two cover prices, 25¢ & 30¢. 7-Intro Baron Blood & intro/1st app. Union Jack; Human Torch origin retold. 8-Union Jack-c/story. 9-Origin Baron Blood. 10-G.A. Capt. America-r/C.A #22	1.00	2.50	5.50
11-19: 11-Origin Spitfire; intro The Blue Bullet. 14-1st app. The Crusaders. 16-Re-intro The Destroyer. 17-Intro Warrior Woman. 18-Re-intro The Destroyer w/new origin. 19-Hitler-c/story		1.60	4.00
20-Reprints origin/1st app. Sub-Mariner from Motion Picture Funnies Weekly with color added & brief write-up about MPFW; 1st app. new Union Jack II	1.00	2.50	5.50
21-Reprints Marvel Mystery #10 (battle issue)		1.40	3.50

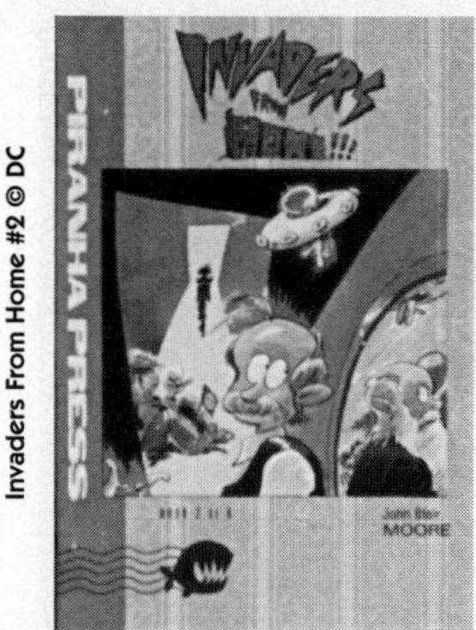

Invaders From Home #2 © DC

Iron Man #61 © MEG

Iron Man #306 © MEG

GD25 FN65 NM94

22,23,25-40: 22-New origin Toro. 25-All new-a begins. 28-Intro new Human Top & Golden Girl. 29-Intro Teutonic Knight. 31-Frankenstein-c/story. 32,33-Thor app. 34-Mighty Destroyer joins. 35-The Whizzer app. 1.00 2.50
24-r/Marvel Mystery #17 (team-up issue; all-r) 1.20 3.00
41-Double size last issue 1.20 3.00
Annual 1 (9/77)-Schomburg, Rico stories (new); Schomburg-c/a (1st for Marvel in 30 years); Avengers app.; re-intro The Shark & The Hyena 1.20 3.00

NOTE: ***Buckler*** *a-5.* ***Everett*** *r-20('39), 21(1940), 24, Annual 1.* ***Gil Kane*** *c(p)-13, 17, 18, 20-27.* ***Kirby*** *c(p)-3-12, 14-16, 32, 33.* ***Mooney*** *a-5i, 16, 22.* ***Robbins*** *a-1-4, 6-9, 10(3 pg.), 11-15, 17-21, 23, 25-28; c-28.*

INVADERS (See Namor, the Sub-Mariner #12)
May, 1993 - No. 4, Aug, 1993 ($1.75, mini-series)
Marvel Comics Group

1-4 .70 1.75

INVADERS FROM HOME (DC)(Value: cover or less)

INVASION
Holiday, 1988-'89 - No. 3, Jan, 1989 ($2.95, mini-series, 84 pgs.)
DC Comics

1-McFarlane/Russell-a 1.20 3.00
2,3: 2-McFarlane/Russell-a 1.20 3.00

INVINCIBLE FOUR OF KUNGFU & NINJA (Leung)(Value: cover or less)

INVISIBLE BOY (See Approved Comics)

INVISIBLE MAN, THE (See Superior Stories #1 & Supernatural Thrillers #2)

INVISIBLES, THE
Sept, 1994 - Present ($1.95, mature)
DC Comics

1-($2.95, 52 pgs.)-G. Morrison story 1.20 3.00
2-5 .80 2.00

INVISIBLE SCARLET O'NEIL (Also see Famous Funnies #81 & Harvey Comics Hits #59)
Dec, 1950 - No. 3, April, 1951
Famous Funnies (Harvey)

1 10.00 30.00 70.00
2,3 8.35 25.00 50.00

IRON CORPORAL, THE (See Army War Heroes #22)
No. 23, Oct, 1985 - No. 25, Feb, 1986
Charlton Comics

23-25: Glanzman-a(r) 1.00

IRON FIST (See Deadly Hands of Kung Fu, Marvel Premiere & Power Man)
Nov, 1975 - No. 15, Sept, 1977
Marvel Comics Group

1-Iron Fist battles Iron Man (#1-6: 25¢) 3.90 12.00 27.00
2 2.40 7.30 17.00
3-5 1.70 5.00 12.00
6-10: 8-Origin retold 1.40 3.50 8.50
11-13: 12-Capt. America app. 1.30 3.00 7.50
14-1st app. Sabretooth (8/77)(see Power Man) 15.00 45.00 105.00
15-X-Men app., Byrne-a (30¢ & 35¢ variants) 3.90 12.00 27.00

NOTE: ***Adkins*** *a-8p, 10i, 13i; c-8i.* ***Byrne*** *a-1-15p; c-8p, 15p.* ***G. Kane*** *c-4-6p.* ***McWilliams*** *a-1i.*

IRONHAND OF ALMURIC (Dark Horse)(Value: cover or less)

IRON HORSE (TV)
March, 1967 - No. 2, June, 1967
Dell Publishing Co.

1,2-Dale Robertson photo covers 2.40 6.00 12.00

IRONJAW (Also see The Barbarians)
Jan, 1975 - No. 4, July, 1975
Atlas/Seaboard Publ.

1-1st app. Iron Jaw; Neal Adams-c; Sekowsky-a(p) 1.50
2-4: 2-Neal Adams-c. 4-Origin 1.00

GD25 FN65 NM94

IRON MAN (Also see The Avengers #1, Giant-Size..., Marvel Collectors Item Classics, Marvel Double Feature, Marvel Fanfare & Tales of Suspense #39)
May, 1968 - Present
Marvel Comics Group

1-Origin; Colan-c/a(p); story continued from Iron Man & Sub-Mariner #1 46.00 139.00 325.00
2 14.00 40.00 100.00
3 10.00 30.00 70.00
4,5 6.30 19.00 50.00
6-10: 9-Iron Man battles green Hulk-like android 5.00 14.00 38.00
11-15: 15-Last 12¢ issue 3.00 9.00 25.00
16-20 2.00 7.00 19.00
21-24,26-42: 22-Death of Janice Cord. 27-Intro Fire Brand. 33-1st app. Spymaster. 35-Nick Fury & Daredevil x-over. 42-Last 15¢ issue 1.80 5.00 14.00
25-Iron Man battles Sub-Mariner 2.00 7.00 19.00
43-Intro The Guardsman; 25¢ giant 1.80 5.00 14.00
44-46,48-50: 43-Giant-Man back-up by Ayers. 44-Ant-Man by Tuska. 46-The Guardsman dies. 50-Princess Python app. 1.30 4.00 10.00
47-Origin retold; Barry Smith-a(p) 2.00 6.00 15.00
51-53: 53-Starlin part pencils 1.20 2.90 7.00
54-Iron Man battles Sub-Mariner; 1st app. Moondragon (1/73) as Madame MacEvil; Everett part-c 1.70 4.00 12.00
55-1st app. Thanos (cameo), Drax the Destroyer, Mentor, Starfox & Kronos (2/73); Starlin-c/a 11.00 34.00 90.00
56-Starlin-a 3.00 7.20 18.00
57-67,69,70: 59-Firebrand returns. 65-Origin Dr. Spectrum. 66-Iron Man vs. Thor. 67-Last 20¢ issue 1.20 2.90 7.00
68-Sunfire & Unicorn app.; origin retold; Starlin-c 1.00 3.60 9.00
71-99: 72-Cameo portraits of N. Adams, Brunner. 76-r/#9. 86-1st app. Blizzard. 87-Origin Blizzard. 88-Thanos app. 89-Daredevil app.; last 25¢ issue. 96-1st app. new Guardsman .80 2.10 5.00
100-(7/77)-Starlin-c 1.00 3.60 9.00
101-117: 101-Intro DreadKnight. 109-1st app. new Crimson Dynamo; 1st app. Vanguard. 110-Origin Jack of Hearts retold .80 2.10 5.00
118-Byrne-a(p) 1.00 2.50 6.00
119,120,123-128-Tony Stark recovers from alcohol problem. 120,121-Sub-Mariner x-over. 125-Ant-Man app. 1.70 4.25
121,122,129-149: 122-Origin. 131,132-Hulk x-over 1.00 2.50
150-Double size 1.40 3.50
151-168: 152-New armor. 161-Moon Knight app. 167-Tony Stark alcohol problem starts again .90 2.25
169-New Iron Man (Jim Rhodes replaces Tony Stark) 1.30 3.30 8.00
170 1.60 4.00
171 1.20 3.00
172-199: 172-Captain America x-over. 186-Intro Vibro. 190-Scarlet Witch app. 191-198-Tony Stark returns as original Iron Man. 192-Both Iron Men battle .80 2.00
200-(11/85, $1.25, 52 pgs.)-Tony Stark returns as new Iron Man (red & white armor) thru #230 1.70 4.25
201-224: 213-Intro new Dominic Fortune. 214-Spider-Woman apps. in new black costume (1/87) .60 1.60
225-Double size ($1.25) 1.70 4.25
226-243,245-249: 228-Vs. Capt. America. 231-Intro new Iron Man. 233-Ant-Man app. 234-Spider-Man x-over. 243-Tony Stark looses use of legs. 247-Hulk x-over .60 1.60
244-($1.50, 52 pgs.)-New Armor makes him walk 1.60 4.00
250-($1.50, 52 pgs.)-Dr. Doom-c/story .60 1.60
251-274,276-283,285-287,289,291-299: 258-277-Byrne scripts. 271-Fin Fang Foom app. 276-Black Widow-c/story; last $1.00-c. 281-1st app. ;War Machine (cameo). 282-1st full app. War Machine (7/92). 283-2nd full app. War Machine 1.00
275-($1.50, 52 pgs.) .60 1.60
284-Death of Iron Man (Tony Stark) 1.90 4.50
288-($2.50, 52pg.)-Silver foil stamped-c; Iron Man's 350th app. in comics 1.00 2.50

Iron Man Annual #15 © MEG

Isis #3 © DC

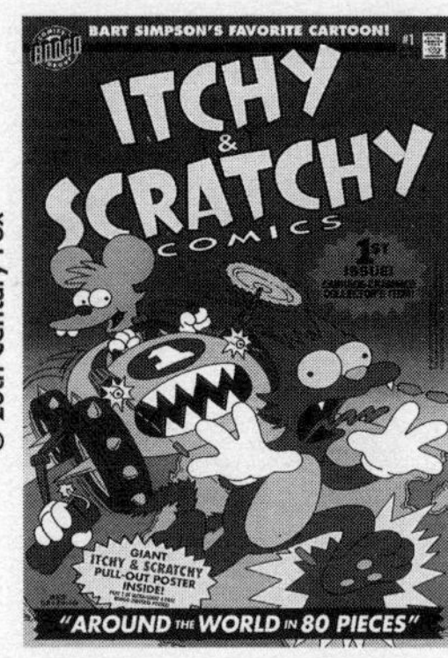

Itchy & Scratchy Comics #1 © 20th Century Fox

GD25 FN65 NM94

290-($2.95, 52pg.)-Gold foil stamped-c; 30th ann. 1.30 3.25
300-($3.95, 68 pgs.)-Collector's Edition w/embossed foil-c; anniversary issue; War Machine-c/story 1.60 4.00
300-($2.50, 68 pgs.)-Newsstand Edition 1.10 2.75
301-303: 302-Venom-c/story (cameo #301) 1.25
304-314: 304-Begin $1.50-c; bound-in trading card sheet; Thunderstrike -c/story .60 1.60
Special 1(8/70)-Sub-Mariner x-over; Everett-c 2.30 6.90 16.00
Special 2(11/71)-r/TOS #81,82,91 (all-r) 1.20 2.90 7.00
Annual 3(1976)-Man-Thing app. 1.40 3.50
King Size 4(8/77)-The Champions (w/Ghost Rider) app.; Newton-a(i) 1.00 2.50
Annual 5-9: 5(1982)-New-a. 6(1983)-New Iron Man(J. Rhodes) app. 7(1984). 8(1986)-X-Factor app. 9(1987) .80 2.00
Annual 10(1989, $2.00, 68 pgs.)-Atlantis Attacks x-over; P. Smith-a; Layton/Guice-a; Sub-Mariner app. 1.00 2.50
Annual 11,12 ($2.00, 68 pgs.): 11-(1990)-Origin of Mrs. Arbogast by Ditko (p&i). 12-(1991)-1 pg. origin recap; Ant-Man back-up story .80 2.00
Annual 13 (1992, $2.25, 68 pgs.)-Darkhawk & Avengers West Coast app.; Colan/Williamson-a .90 2.25
Annual 14 (1993, $2.95, 68 pgs.)-Bagged w/card 1.20 3.00
Annual 15 (1994, $2.95, 68 pgs.) 1.20 3.00
Manual 1 (1993, $1.75)-Operations handbook .70 1.75
Graphic Novel: Crash (1988, $12.95, Adults, 72 pgs?)-Computer generated art & color; violence & nudity 1.85 5.50 13.00
...2020 (6/94, $5.95) 1.00 2.50 6.00

NOTE: ***Austin*** *c-105i, 109-111i, 151i.* ***Byrne*** *a-118p; c-109p, 253.* ***Colan*** *a-1p, 253, Special 1p(3); c-1p.* ***Craig*** *a-1i, 2-4, 5-13i, 14, 15-19i, 24p, 25p, 26-28i; c-2-4.* ***Ditko*** *a-160p.* ***Everett*** *c-29.* ***Guice*** *a-233-241p.* ***G. Kane*** *c(p)-52-54, 63, 67, 72-75, 77, 78, 88, 98.* ***Kirby*** *a-Special 1p; c-13, 80p, 90, 92-95.* ***Mooney*** *a-40i, 43i, 47i.* ***Perez*** *c-103p.* ***Simonson*** *c-Annual 8.* ***B. Smith*** *a-232p, 243i; c-232.* ***P. Smith*** *a-159p, 245p, Annual 10p; c-159.* ***Starlin*** *a-53p(part), 55p, 56p; c-55p, 160, 163.* ***Tuska*** *a-5-13p, 15-23p, 24i, 32p, 38-46p, 48-54p, 57-61p, 63-69p, 70-72p, 78p, 86-92p, 95-106p, Annual 4p.* ***Wood*** *a-Special 1i.*

IRON MAN & SUB-MARINER
April, 1968 (One Shot, 12¢) (Pre-dates Iron Man #1 & Sub-Mariner #1)
Marvel Comics Group

1-Iron Man story by Colan/Craig continued from Tales of Suspense #99 & continued in Iron Man #1; Sub-Mariner story by Colan continued from Tales to Astonish #101 & continued in Sub-Mariner #1; Colan/Everett-c 20.00 60.00 140.00

IRON MARSHALL (Jademan)(Value: cover or less)

IRON VIC (See Comics Revue No. 3 & Giant Comics Editions)
1940; Aug, 1947 - No. 3, 1947
United Features Syndicate/St. John Publ. Co.

Single Series 22 23.00 70.00 160.00
2,3(St. John) 5.00 15.00 30.00

IRONWOLF (DC)(Value: cover or less)

ISIS (TV) (Also see Shazam)
Oct-Nov, 1976 - No. 8, Dec-Jan, 1977-78
National Periodical Publications/DC Comics

1-Wood inks 1.50
2-8: 5-Isis new look. 7-Origin 1.00

ISLAND AT THE TOP OF THE WORLD (See Walt Disney Showcase #27)

ISLAND OF DR. MOREAU, THE (Movie)
October, 1977 (52 pgs.)
Marvel Comics Group

1-Gil Kane-c 1.00

I SPY (TV)
Aug, 1966 - No. 6, Sept, 1968 (All have photo-c)
Gold Key

1-Bill Cosby, Robert Culp photo covers 17.00 50.00 120.00
2-6: 3,4-McWilliams-a 10.00 31.00 72.00

IS THIS TOMORROW?
1947 (One Shot) (3 editions) (52 pgs.)
Catechetical Guild

1-Theme of communists taking over the USA; (no price on cover) Used in **POP**, pg. 102 10.00 30.00 70.00
1-(10¢ on cover) 14.00 42.00 100.00
1-Has blank circle with no price on cover 14.00 42.00 100.00
Black & White advance copy titled "Confidential" (52 pgs.)-Contains script and art edited out of the color edition, including one page of extreme violence showing mob nailing a Cardinal to a door; (only two known copies) 43.00 130.00 300.00

NOTE: *The original color version first sold for 10 cents. Since sales were good, it was later printed as a giveaway. Approximately four million in total were printed. The two black and white copies listed plus two other versions as well as a full color untrimmed version surfaced in 1979 from the Guild's old files in St. Paul, Minnesota.*

IT! (See Astonishing Tales No. 21-24 & Supernatural Thrillers No. 1)

ITCHY & SCRATCHY COMICS (Simpson's TV show)
1993 - Present ($1.95, three times yearly)
Bongo Comics

1-($2.25)-Bound-in jumbo poster 1.10 2.75
2 .80 2.00
3-($2.25)-w/decoder screen trading card .90 2.25

IT HAPPENS IN THE BEST FAMILIES
1920 (52 pgs.) (B&W Sundays)
Powers Photo Engraving Co.

nn-By Briggs 14.00 43.00 100.00
Special Railroad Edition (30¢)-r/strips from 1914-1920 12.00 36.00 85.00

IT REALLY HAPPENED
1944 - No. 11, Oct, 1947
William H. Wise No. 1,2/Standard (Visual Editions)

1-Kit Carson & Ben Franklin stories 13.00 40.00 90.00
2 7.50 22.50 45.00
3,4,6,9,11: 6-Joan of Arc story. 9-Captain Kidd & Frank Buck stories 5.00 15.00 30.00
5-Lou Gehrig & Lewis Carroll stories 10.00 30.00 65.00
7-Teddy Roosevelt story 5.35 16.00 32.00
8-Story of Roy Rogers 11.50 34.00 80.00
10-Honus Wagner & Mark Twain stories 9.15 27.50 55.00

NOTE: ***Guardineer*** *a-7(2), 8(2), 11.* ***Schomburg*** *c-1-7, 9-11.*

IT RHYMES WITH LUST (Also see Bold Stories & Candid Tales)
1950 (Digest size) (128 pgs.)
St. John Publishing Co.

nn (Rare)-Matt Baker & Ray Osrin-a 28.00 85.00 200.00

IT'S ABOUT TIME (TV)
January, 1967
Gold Key

1 (10195-701)-Photo-c 4.20 12.50 25.00

IT'S A DUCK'S LIFE
Feb, 1950 - No. 11, Feb, 1952
Marvel Comics/Atlas(MMC)

1-Buck Duck, Super Rabbit begin 10.00 30.00 65.00
2 5.35 16.00 32.00
3-11 4.00 11.00 22.00

IT'S FUN TO STAY ALIVE (Giveaway)
1948 (16 pgs.) (Heavy stock paper)
National Automobile Dealers Association

Featuring: Bugs Bunny, The Berrys, Dixie Dugan, Elmer, Henry, Tim Tyler, Bruce Gentry, Abbie & Slats, Joe Jinks, The Toodles, & Cokey; all art copyright 1946-48 drawn especially for this book. 14.00 43.00 100.00

IT'S GAMETIME
Sept-Oct, 1955 - No. 4, Mar-Apr, 1956
National Periodical Publications

Jace Pearson of the Texas Rangers #4 © DELL

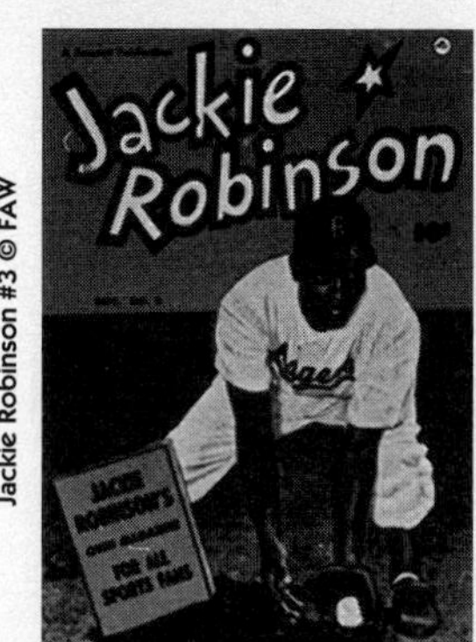

Jackie Robinson #3 © FAW

Jack Kirby's Secret City Saga #4 © Jack Kirby

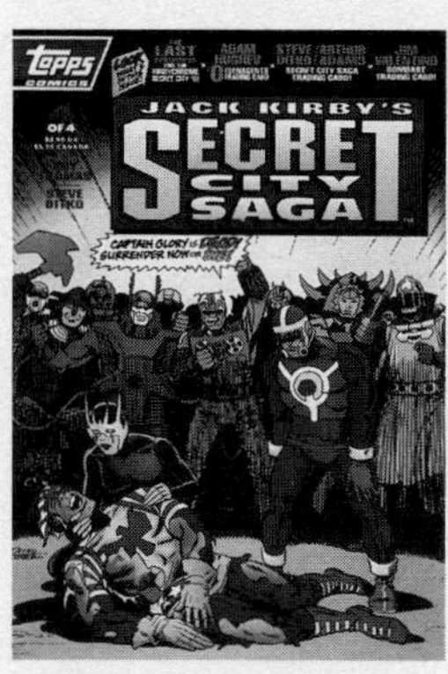

	GD25	FN65	NM94
1-(Scarce)-Infinity-c; Davy Crockett app. in puzzle	56.00	170.00	395.00
2-4(Scarce): 2-Dodo & The Frog	48.00	145.00	335.00

IT'S LOVE, LOVE, LOVE
November, 1957 - No. 2, Jan, 1958 (10 cents)
St. John Publishing Co.

	GD25	FN65	NM94
1,2	3.20	8.00	16.00

IVANHOE (See Fawcett Movie Comics No. 20)

IVANHOE
July-Sept, 1963
Dell Publishing Co.

	GD25	FN65	NM94
1 (12-373-309)	4.00	11.00	22.00

IWO JIMA (See Spectacular Features Magazine)

JACE PEARSON OF THE TEXAS RANGERS (4-Color #396 is titled Tales of the Texas Rangers; ...'s Tales of ... #11-on)(See Western Roundup under Dell Giants)(Radio/TV)
No. 396, 5/52 - No. 1021, 8-10/59 (No #10) (All-Photo-c)
Dell Publishing Co.

	GD25	FN65	NM94
4-Color 396 (#1)	11.50	34.00	80.00
2(5-7/53) - 9(2-4/55)	6.70	20.00	40.00
4-Color 648(#10, 9/55)	6.70	20.00	40.00
11(11-2/55-56) - 14,17-20(6-8/58)	5.00	15.00	30.00
15,16-Toth-a	6.35	19.00	38.00
4-Color 961-Spiegle-a	5.35	16.00	32.00
4-Color 1021	5.00	15.00	30.00

NOTE: *Joel McCrea photo c-1-9, F.C. 648 (starred on radio show only); Willard Parker photo c-11-on (starred on TV series).*

JACK & JILL VISIT TOYTOWN WITH ELMER THE ELF
1949 (16 pgs.) (paper cover)
Butler Brothers (Toytown Stores Giveaway)

	GD25	FN65	NM94
nn	2.80	7.00	14.00

JACK ARMSTRONG (Radio)(See True Comics)
Nov, 1947 - No. 9, Sept, 1948; No. 10, Mar, 1949 - No. 13, Sept, 1949
Parents' Institute

	GD25	FN65	NM94
1	17.00	52.00	120.00
2	10.00	30.00	70.00
3-5	10.00	30.00	60.00
6-13: 7-Vic Hardy's Crime Lab begins?	8.35	25.00	50.00
12-Premium version(distr. in Chicago only); Free printed on upper right-c; no price (Rare)	12.00	36.00	85.00

JACK HUNTER (Blackthorne)(Value: cover or less)

JACKIE GLEASON (TV) (Also see The Honeymooners)
1948 - No. 2, 1948; Sept, 1955 - No. 4, Dec, 1955?
St. John Publishing Co.

	GD25	FN65	NM94
1(1948)	63.00	190.00	440.00
2(1948)	50.00	150.00	350.00
1(1955)(TV)-Photo-c	51.00	154.00	360.00
2-4	36.00	107.00	250.00

JACKIE GLEASON AND THE HONEYMOONERS (TV)
June-July, 1956 - No. 12, Apr-May, 1958
National Periodical Publications

	GD25	FN65	NM94
1-1st app. Ralph Kramden	69.00	206.00	480.00
2	50.00	160.00	370.00
3-11	39.00	116.00	270.00
12 (Scarce)	56.00	172.00	400.00

JACKIE JOKERS (Became Richie Rich &...)
March, 1973 - No. 4, Sept, 1973 (#5 was advertised, but not published)
Harvey Publications

	GD25	FN65	NM94
1-4: 1-1st app. 2-President Nixon app.			1.00

JACKIE ROBINSON (Famous Plays of...) (Also see Negro Heroes #2 & Picture News #4)
May, 1950 - No. 6, 1952 (Baseball hero) (All photo-c)
Fawcett Publications

	GD25	FN65	NM94
nn	64.00	193.00	450.00
2	41.00	124.00	290.00
3-6	34.00	103.00	240.00

JACK IN THE BOX (Formerly Yellowjacket Comics #1-10; becomes Cowboy Western Comics #17 on)
Feb, 1946; No. 11, Oct, 1946 - No. 16, Nov-Dec, 1947
Frank Comunale/Charlton Comics No. 11 on

	GD25	FN65	NM94
1-Stitches, Marty Mouse & Nutsy McKrow	10.00	30.00	60.00
11-Yellowjacket (early Charlton comic)	10.00	30.00	65.00
12,14,15	4.35	13.00	26.00
13-Wolverton-a	13.50	41.00	95.00
16-12 pg. adapt. of Silas Marner; Kiefer-a	7.50	22.50	45.00

JACK KIRBY'S SECRET CITY SAGA
No. 0, Apr, 1993; No. 1, 5/93 - No. 4, 8/93 ($2.95, mini-series)
Topps Comics

	GD25	FN65	NM94
0-(No cover price, 20 pgs.)-Simonson-c/a		1.80	2.00
1-4-Bagged w/3 trading cards; Ditko-c/a: 1-Ditko/Art Adams-c. 2-Ditko/Byrne-c; has coupon for Pres. Clinton holo-foil trading card. 3-Dorman poster; has coupon for Gore holo-foil trading card. 4-Ditko/Perez-c		1.20	3.00

NOTE: *Issues #1-4 contain coupons redeemable for Kirbychrome version of #1*

JACK KIRBY'S SILVER STAR (Also see Silver Star)
Oct, 1993 ($2.95, intended as 4-issue mini-series)
Topps Comics

	GD25	FN65	NM94
1-Silver ink-c; Austin-c/a(i); polybagged w/3 cards		1.20	3.00

JACK KIRBY'S TEENAGENTS (See Satan's Six)
Aug, 1993 - No. 3, Oct, 1993 ($2.95, intended as 4-issue mini-series)
Topps Comics

	GD25	FN65	NM94
1-3-Polybagged with/3 trading cards; 1-3-Austin-c(i): 3-Liberty Project app.		1.20	3.00

JACK OF HEARTS (Also see The Deadly Hands of Kung Fu #22 & Marvel Premiere #44)
Jan, 1984 - No. 4, April, 1984 (60¢, mini-series)
Marvel Comics Group

	GD25	FN65	NM94
1-4			1.00

JACKPOT COMICS (Jolly Jingles #10 on)
Spring, 1941 - No. 9, Spring, 1943
MLJ Magazines

	GD25	FN65	NM94
1-The Black Hood, Mr. Justice, Steel Sterling & Sgt. Boyle begin; Biro-c	186.00	557.00	1300.00
2-S. Cooper-c	86.00	257.00	600.00
3-Hubbell-c	68.00	205.00	475.00
4-Archie begins (Win/41; on sale 12/41)-(also see Pep Comics #22); 1st app. Mrs. Grundy, the principal; Novick-c	171.00	515.00	1200.00
5-Hitler-c by Montana; 1st definitive Mr. Weatherbee; 1st app. Reggie in 1 panel cameo	86.00	257.00	600.00
6-9: 6,7-Bondage-c by Novick. 8,9-Sahle-c	71.00	215.00	500.00

JACK Q FROST (See Unearthly Spectaculars)

JACK THE GIANT KILLER (See Movie Classics)

JACK THE GIANT KILLER (New Adventures of...)
Aug-Sept, 1953
Bimfort & Co.

	GD25	FN65	NM94
V1#1-H. C. Kiefer-c/a	14.00	43.00	100.00

JACKY'S DIARY (See 4-Color No. 1091)

JADEMAN COLLECTION (Jademan)(Value: cover or less)

JADEMAN KUNG FU SPECIAL (Jademan)(Value: cover or less)

JAGUAR, THE (Also see The Adventures of...)
Aug, 1991 - No. 14, Oct, 1992 ($1.00, color)

Jaguar #1 © DC

James Bond : Permission To Die #1 © Ian Fleming

Jerry Drummer V3 #11 © CC

GD25 FN65 NM94

Impact Comics (DC)
1-14: 4-The Black Hood x-over. 7-Sienkiewicz-c. 9-Contains Crusaders trading card 1.00
Annual 1 (1992, $2.50, 68 pgs.)-With trading card 1.00 2.50

JAKE THRASH (Aircel)(Value: cover or less)

JAMBOREE
Feb, 1946(no mo. given) - No. 3, April, 1946
Round Publishing Co.
1-Funny animal 14.00 43.00 100.00
2,3 10.00 30.00 60.00

JAMES BOND 007: A SILENT ARMAGEDDON
Mar, 1993 - No. 2, May, 1993
Dark Horse Comics/Acme Comics
1,2 1.25 3.00

JAMES BOND 007: SERPENT'S TOOTH
July, 1992 - No. 3, Sept, 1992 ($4.95, mini-series)
Acme Comics/Dark Horse Comics
1-3: Paul Gulacy-c/a 1.00 2.00 5.00

JAMES BOND 007: SHATTERED HELIX
1994 - No. 2, July, 1994 ($2.50, limited series)
Dark Horse Comics
1,2 1.20 3.00

JAMES BOND FOR YOUR EYES ONLY
Oct, 1981 - No. 2, Nov, 1981
Marvel Comics Group
1,2-Movie adapt.; r/Marvel Super Special #19 1.00

JAMES BOND JR. (TV)
Jan, 1992 - No. 12, Dec, 1992 (#1: $1.00, #2-on: $1.25)
Marvel Comics
1-12: Based on animated TV show 1.25

JAMES BOND: LICENCE TO KILL (See Licence To Kill)

JAMES BOND: PERMISSION TO DIE
1989 - No. 3, 1991 ($3.95, color, mini-series, squarebound, 52 pgs.)
Eclipse Comics/ACME Press
1-3: Mike Grell-c/a/scripts in all. 3-($4.95) 1.00 2.00 5.00

JAM: SUPER COOL COLOR INJECTED TURBO ADVENTURE #1 FROM HELL!, THE (Comico)(Value: cover or less)

JANE ARDEN (See Feature Funnies & Pageant of Comics)
March, 1948 - No. 2, June, 1948
St. John (United Features Syndicate)
1-Newspaper reprints 13.00 40.00 90.00
2 10.00 30.00 60.00

JANN OF THE JUNGLE (Jungle Tales No. 1-7)
No. 8, Nov, 1955 - No. 17, June, 1957
Atlas Comics (CSI)
8(#1) 17.00 52.00 120.00
9,11-15 10.00 30.00 60.00
10-Williamson/Colletta-c 10.00 30.00 65.00
16,17-Williamson/Mayo-a(3), 5 pgs. each 11.50 34.00 80.00
NOTE: *Everett c-15-17. Heck a-8, 15, 17. Maneely c-11. Shores a-8.*

JASON & THE ARGONAUTS (See Movie Classics)

JASON GOES TO HELL: THE FINAL FRIDAY
July, 1993 - No. 3, Sept, 1993 ($2.95, mini-series)
Topps Comics
1-3: Adapts movie. 1-Glow-in-the-dark-c 1.20 3.00

JASON'S QUEST (See Showcase #88-90)

JAWS 2 (See Marvel Comics Super Special, A)

GD25 FN65 NM94

JCP FEATURES
Feb, 1982-c; Dec, 1981-indicia ($2.00, one-shot, B&W)
J.C. Productions (Archie)
1-T.H.U.N.D.E.R. Agents; Black Hood by Morrow & Neal Adams .80 2.00

JEANIE COMICS (Formerly All Surprise; Cowgirl Romances #28)
No. 13, April, 1947 - No. 27, Oct, 1949
Marvel Comics/Atlas(CPC)
13-Mitzi, Willie begin 10.00 30.00 70.00
14,15 8.35 25.00 50.00
16-Used in Love and Death by Legman; Kurtzman's "Hey Look" 10.00 30.00 70.00
17-19,22-Kurtzman's "Hey Look", (1-3 pgs. each) 8.00 24.00 48.00
20,21,23-27 5.35 16.00 32.00

JEEP COMICS (Also see G.I. Comics and Overseas Comics)
Winter, 1944 - No. 3, Mar-Apr, 1948
R. B. Leffingwell & Co.
1-Capt. Power, Criss Cross & Jeep & Peep (costumed) begin 19.00 58.00 135.00
2 11.50 34.00 80.00
3-L. B. Cole dinosaur-c 13.00 40.00 90.00
1-46(Giveaways)-Strip reprints in all; Tarzan, Flash Gordon, Blondie, The Nebbs, Little Iodine, Red Ryder, Don Winslow, The Phantom, Johnny Hazard, Katzenjammer Kids; distr. to U.S. Armed Forces from 1945-1946 4.00 10.00 20.00

JEFF JORDAN, U.S. AGENT
Dec, 1947 - Jan, 1948
D. S. Publishing Co.
1 9.15 27.50 55.00

JEMM, SON OF SATURN
Sept, 1984 - No. 12, Aug, 1985 (12 part maxi-series; mando paper)
DC Comics
1-12: Colan p-all; c-1-5p, 7-12p. 3-Origin 1.00

JERRY DRUMMER (Formerly Soldier & Marine V2#9)
V2#10, Apr, 1957 - V3#12, Oct, 1957
Charlton Comics
V2#10, V3#11,12: 11-Whitman-c/a 4.00 10.00 20.00

JERRY IGER'S... (All titles, Blackthorne/First)(Value: cover or less)

JERRY LEWIS (See The Adventures of...)

JESSE JAMES (See 4-Color No. 757 & The Legend of...)

JESSE JAMES (See Badmen of the West & Blazing Sixguns)
8/50 - No. 9, 11/52; No. 15, 10/53 - No. 29, 8-9/56
Avon Periodicals
1-Kubert Alabam-r/Cowpuncher #1 13.50 41.00 95.00
2-Kubert-a(3) 11.00 32.00 75.00
3-Kubert Alabam-r/Cowpuncher #2 10.00 30.00 65.00
4,9-No Kubert 4.35 13.00 26.00
5,6-Kubert Jesse James-a(3); 5-Wood-a(1pg.) 10.00 30.00 65.00
7-Kubert Jesse James-a(2) 8.65 26.00 52.00
8-Kinstler-a(3) 5.85 17.50 35.00
15-Kinstler-r/#3 4.00 11.00 22.00
16-Kinstler-r/#3 & story-r/Butch Cassidy #1 4.00 12.00 24.00
17-19,21: 17-Jesse James-r/#4; Kinstler-c idea from Kubert splash in #6. 18-Kubert Jesse James-r/#5. 19-Kubert Jesse James-r/#6. 21-Two Jesse James-r/#4, Kinstler-r/#4 3.60 9.00 18.00
20-Williamson/Frazetta-a; r/Chief Vic. Apache Massacre; Kubert Jesse James-r/#6; Kit West story by Larsen 10.00 30.00 70.00
22,23-No Kubert 3.60 9.00 18.00
24-New McCarty strip by Kinstler; Kinstler-r 3.60 9.00 18.00
25-New McCarty Jesse James strip by Kinstler; Jesse James-r/#7,9 3.60 9.00 18.00

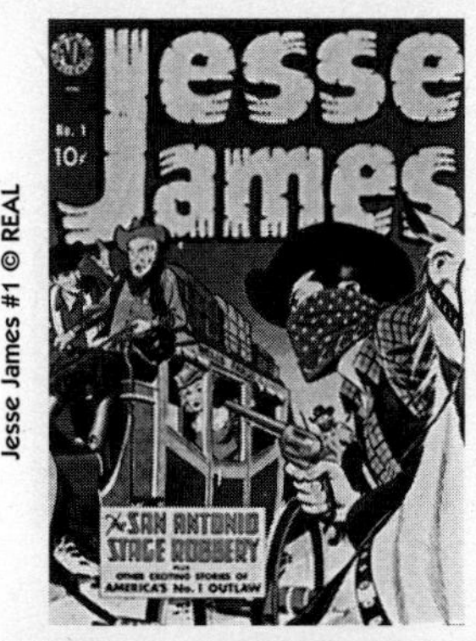

Jesse James #1 © REAL

Jet Power #1 © I.W.

Jetsons #1 © H-B

	GD25	FN65	NM94
26,27-New McCarty Jesse James strip plus a Kinstler/McCann Jesse James-r	3.60	9.00	18.00
28,29: 28-Reprints most of Red Mountain, Featuring Quantrells Raiders	3.60	9.00	18.00
Annual nn (1952; 25¢, 100 pgs.)- "...Brings Six-Gun Justice to the West"- 3 earlier issues rebound; Kubert, Kinstler-a(3)	22.00	65.00	150.00

*NOTE: Mostly reprints #10 on. **Fawcette** c-1, 2. **Kida** a-5. **Kinstler** a-3, 4, 7-9, 15r, 16r(2), 21-27; c-3, 4, 9, 17-27. Painted c-5-8. 22 has 2 stories r/Sheriff Bob Dixon's Chuck Wagon #1 with name changed to Sheriff Bob Trent.*

JESSE JAMES
July, 1953
Realistic Publications

nn-Reprints Avon's #1; same-c, colors different	7.50	22.50	45.00

JEST (Formerly Snap; becomes Kayo #12)
No. 10, 1944; No. 11, 1944
Harry 'A' Chesler

10-Johnny Rebel & Yankee Boy app. in text	10.00	30.00	65.00
11-Little Nemo in Adventure Land	10.00	30.00	70.00

JESTER
No. 10, 1945
Harry 'A' Chesler

10	9.15	27.50	55.00

JESUS (Spire Christian)(Value: cover or less)

JET (See Jet Powers)

JET ACES
1952 - No. 4, 1953
Fiction House Magazines

1	10.00	30.00	60.00
2-4	5.85	17.50	35.00

JET DREAM (...and Her Stunt-Girl Counterspies)(See The Man from Uncle #7)
June, 1968 (12¢)
Gold Key

1-Painted-c	2.40	7.25	17.00

JET FIGHTERS (Korean War)
No. 5, Nov, 1952 - No. 7, Mar, 1953
Standard Magazines

5,7-Toth-a. 5-Toth-c	9.15	27.50	55.00
6-Celardo-a	4.00	11.00	22.00

JET POWER
1963
I.W. Enterprises

I.W. Reprint 1,2-r/Jet Powers #1,2	3.60	9.00	18.00

JET POWERS (American Air Forces No. 5 on)
1950 - No. 4, 1951
Magazine Enterprises

1(A-1 #30)-Powell-c/a begins	24.00	72.00	165.00
2(A-1 #32)	17.00	52.00	120.00
3(A-1 #35)-Williamson/Evans-a	28.00	84.00	195.00
4(A-1 #38)-Williamson/Wood-a; "The Rain of Sleep" drug story	28.00	84.00	195.00

JET PUP (See 3-D Features)

JETSONS, THE (TV) (See March of Comics #276, 330, 348 & Spotlight #3)
Jan, 1963 - No. 36, Oct, 1970 (Hanna-Barbera)
Gold Key

1	19.00	58.00	175.00
2	10.00	30.00	90.00
3-10	8.00	23.00	70.00
11-20	5.00	16.00	48.00
21-36	4.00	12.00	36.00

JETSONS, THE (TV) (Also see Golden Comics Digest)
Nov, 1970 - No. 20, Dec, 1973 (Hanna-Barbera)
Charlton Comics

1	7.70	23.00	54.00
2	3.90	12.00	27.00
3-10	3.10	9.00	22.00
11-20	2.00	6.00	14.00

JETSONS, THE (TV)
V2#1, Sept, 1992 - No. 5, Nov, 1993 ($1.25/$1.50) (Hanna-Barbera)
Harvey Comics

V2#1-4			1.25
5 ($1.50)			1.50
...Big Book V2#1,2,3 ($1.95, 52 pgs.): 1-(11/92). 2-(4/93). 3-(7/93)		.80	2.00
...Giant Size 1,2,3 ($2.25, 68 pgs): 1-(10/92). 2-(4/93). 3-(10/93)		.90	2.25

JETTA OF THE 21ST CENTURY
No. 5, Dec, 1952 - No. 7, Apr, 1953 (Teen-age Archie type)
Standard Comics

5	14.00	43.00	100.00
6,7	10.00	30.00	60.00

JEZEBEL JADE (Comico)(Hanna-Barbera)(Value: cover or less)

JIGGS & MAGGIE (See 4-Color No. 18)

JIGGS & MAGGIE
No. 11, 1949(June) - No. 21, 2/53; No. 22, 4/53 - No. 27, 2-3/54
Standard Comics/Harvey Publications No. 22 on

11	8.35	25.00	50.00
12-15,17-21	4.35	13.00	26.00
16-Wood text illos.	5.85	17.50	35.00
22-25,27: 22-24-Little Dot app.	4.00	10.00	20.00
26-Four pgs. partially in 3-D	11.00	32.00	75.00

NOTE: Sunday page reprints by McManus loosely blended into story continuity. Based on Bringing Up Father strip. Advertised on covers as "All New."

JIGSAW (Big Hero Adventures)
Sept, 1966 - No. 2, Dec, 1966 (36 pgs.)
Harvey Publications (Funday Funnies)

1-Origin & 1st app.; Crandall-a (5 pgs.)	1.30	3.00	8.00
2-Man From S.R.A.M.	1.00	2.50	6.00

JIGSAW OF DOOM (See Complete Mystery No. 2)

JIM BOWIE (Formerly Danger; Black Jack No. 20 on)
No. 15, 1955? - No. 19, April, 1957
Charlton Comics

15	5.35	16.00	32.00
16-19	4.00	10.00	20.00

JIM BOWIE (See 4-Color No. 893, 993, & Western Tales)

JIM DANDY
May, 1956 - No. 3, Sept, 1956 (Charles Biro)
Dandy Magazine (Lev Gleason)

1-Biro-c	5.00	15.00	30.00
2,3	3.60	9.00	18.00

JIM HARDY (See Giant Comics Eds., Sparkler & Treasury of Comics #2 & 5)
1939; 1942; 1947 - No. 2, 1947
United Features Syndicate/Spotlight Publ.

Single Series 6 ('39)	31.00	94.00	220.00
Single Series 27('42)	24.00	73.00	170.00
1('47)-Spotlight Publ.	10.00	30.00	60.00
2	5.35	16.00	32.00

JIM HARDY
1944 (25¢, 132 pgs.) (Tip Top, Sparkler-r)
Spotlight/United Features Syndicate

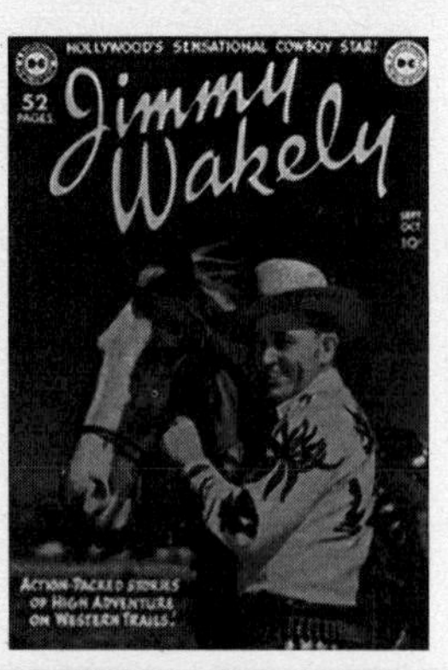

Jimmy Wakely #1 © DC

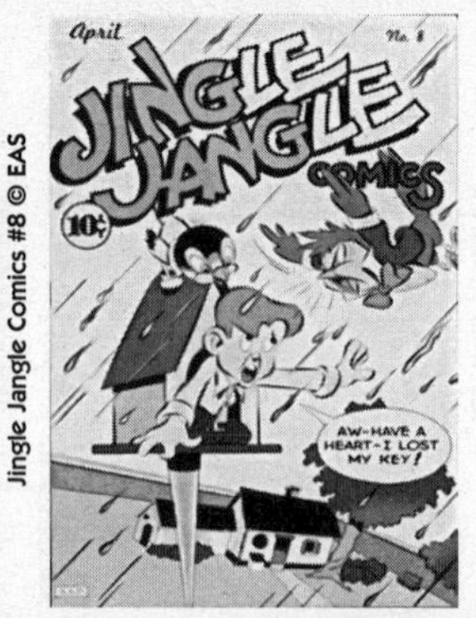

Jingle Jangle Comics #8 © EAS

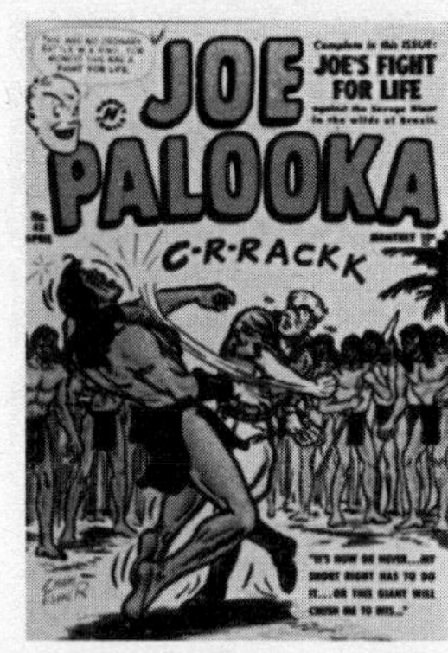

Joe Palooka #43 © CCG

GD25 FN65 NM94

nn-Origin Mirror Man; Triple Terror app. 33.00 100.00 230.00

JIMINY CRICKET (See 4-Color No. 701, 795, 897, 989, Mickey Mouse Mag. V5#3 & Walt Disney Showcase #37)

JIMMY (James Swinnerton)
1905 (10x15") (40 pgs. in color)
N. Y. American & Journal

nn 39.00 116.00 270.00

JIMMY DURANTE (See A-1 Comics No. 18, 20)

JIMMY OLSEN (See Superman's Pal...)

JIMMY WAKELY (Cowboy movie star)
Sept-Oct, 1949 - No. 18, July-Aug, 1952 (1-13: 52pgs.)
National Periodical Publications

1-Photo-c, 52 pgs. begin; Alex Toth-a; Kit Colby Girl Sheriff begins
71.00 215.00 500.00
2-Toth-a 39.00 116.00 270.00
3,6,7-Frazetta-a in all, 3 pgs. each; Toth-a in all. 7-Last photo-c
43.00 130.00 300.00
4-Frazetta-a (3 pgs.); Kurtzman "Pot-Shot Pete", 1 pg; Toth-a
43.00 130.00 300.00
5,8-15,18-Toth-a; 12,14-Kubert-a (3 & 2 pgs.) 31.00 95.00 220.00
16,17 25.00 75.00 175.00

NOTE: ***Gil Kane** c-10-19p.*

JIM RAY'S AVIATION SKETCH BOOK
Mar-Apr, 1946 - No. 2, May-June, 1946
Vital Publishers

1,2-Picture stories about planes and pilots 18.00 55.00 125.00

JIM SOLAR (See Wisco/Klarer)

JINGLE BELLS (See March of Comics No. 65)

JINGLE BELLS CHRISTMAS BOOK
1971 (20 pgs.; B&W inside; slick cover)
Montgomery Ward (Giveaway)

nn .80 2.00

JINGLE DINGLE CHRISTMAS STOCKING COMICS (See Foodini #2)
V2#1, 1951 (no date listed) (25¢, 100 pgs.; giant-size)
Stanhall Publications (Publ. annually)

V2#1-Foodini & Pinhead, Silly Pilly plus games & puzzles
11.50 34.00 80.00

JINGLE JANGLE COMICS (Also see Puzzle Fun Comics)
Feb, 1942 - No. 42, Dec, 1949
Eastern Color Printing Co.

1-Pie-Face Prince of Old Pretzleburg, Jingle Jangle Tales by George Carlson, Hortense, & Benny Bear begin 34.00 103.00 240.00
2,3-No Pie-Face Prince 16.00 48.00 110.00
4-Pie-Face Prince cover 16.00 48.00 110.00
5 13.50 41.00 95.00
6-10: 8-No Pie-Face Prince 12.00 36.00 85.00
11-15 10.00 30.00 60.00
16-30: 17,18-No Pie-Face Prince. 30-XMas-c 7.50 22.50 45.00
31-42: 36,42-Xmas-c 5.00 15.00 30.00

NOTE: ***George Carlson** a-(2) in all except No. 2, 3, 8; c-1-6. **Carlson** 1 pg. puzzles in 9, 10, 12-15, 18, 20. **Carlson** illustrated a series of Uncle Wiggily books in 1930's.*

JING PALS
Feb, 1946 - No. 4, Aug?, 1946 (Funny animal)
Victory Publishing Corporation

1-Wishing Willie, Puggy Panda & Johnny Rabbit begin
10.00 30.00 60.00
2-4 5.35 16.00 32.00

JINKS, PIXIE, AND DIXIE (See Kite Fun Book & Whitman Comic Books)

JOAN OF ARC (See A-1 Comics No. 21 & Ideal a Classical Comic)

GD25 FN65 NM94

JOAN OF ARC
No date (28 pgs.)
Catechetical Guild (Topix) (Giveaway)

nn 9.15 27.50 55.00

NOTE: *Unpublished version exists which came from the Guild's files.*

JOE COLLEGE
Fall, 1949 - No. 2, Winter, 1950 (Teen-age humor, 52 pgs.)
Hillman Periodicals

1,2-Powell-a; 1-Briefer-a 7.00 21.00 42.00

JOE JINKS (See Single Series No. 12)

JOE LOUIS (See Fight Comics #2, Picture News #6 & True Comics #5)
Sept, 1950 - No. 2, Nov, 1950 (Photo-c) (Boxing champ)(See Dick Cole #10)
Fawcett Publications

1-Photo-c; life story 46.00 139.00 325.00
2-Photo-c 31.00 95.00 220.00

JOE PALOOKA
1933 (B&W daily strip reprints) (52 pgs.)
Cupples & Leon Co.

nn-(Scarce)-by Fisher 79.00 236.00 550.00

JOE PALOOKA (1st Series)(Also see Big Shot Comics, Columbia Comics & Feature Funnies)
1942 - No. 4, 1944
Columbia Comic Corp. (Publication Enterprises)

1-1st to portray American president; gov't permission required
57.00 171.00 400.00
2 (1943)-Hitler-c 34.00 103.00 240.00
3,4: 3-Nazi Sub-c 24.00 73.00 170.00

JOE PALOOKA (2nd Series) (Battle Adv. #68-74; ...Advs. #75, 77-81, 83-85, 87; Champ of the Comics #76, 82, 86, 89-93) (See All-New)
Nov, 1945 - No. 118, Mar, 1961
Harvey Publications

1 41.00 125.00 290.00
2 19.00 57.00 130.00
3,4,6,7-1st Flyin' Fool, ends #25 11.50 34.00 80.00
5-Boy Explorers by S&K (7-8/46) 16.50 50.00 115.00
8-10 10.00 30.00 60.00
11-14,16-20: 19-Freedom Train-c 7.50 22.50 45.00
15-Origin & 1st app. Humphrey (12/47); Super heroine Atoma app. by Powell 11.50 34.00 80.00
21-30: 27-1st app. Little Max? (12/48). 30-Nude female painting
5.85 17.50 35.00
31-61: 35-Little Max-c/story. 36-Humphrey story. 39-Humphrey & Little Max begin (12/49). 41-Bing Crosby photo on-c. 44-Palooka marries Ann Howe. 50-(11/51)-Becomes Harvey Comics Hits #51 4.35 13.00 26.00
62-S&K Boy Explorers-r 5.35 16.00 32.00
63-80: 66,67-'Commie' torture story 4.00 11.00 22.00
81-99,101-115 3.60 9.00 18.00
100 4.00 11.00 22.00
116-S&K Boy Explorers-r (Giant, '60) 5.35 16.00 32.00
117,118-Giants 4.70 14.00 28.00
...Body Building Instruction Book (1958 B&M Sports Toy giveaway, 16pgs., 5-1/4x7")-Origin 9.15 27.50 55.00
...Fights His Way Back (1945 Giveaway, 24 pgs.) Family Comics
16.00 48.00 110.00
...in Hi There! (1949 Red Cross giveaway, 12 pgs., 4-3/4x6")
8.35 25.00 50.00
...in It's All in the Family (1945 Red Cross giveaway, 16 pgs., regular size)
10.00 30.00 60.00
...**Visits the Lost City** nn (1945)(One Shot)(50¢)-164 page continuous story strip reprint. Has biography & photo of Ham Fisher; possibly the single longest comic book story published (159 pgs.?) 100.00 300.00 1000.00

NOTE: ***Nostrand/Powell** a-73. **Powell** a-7, 8, 10, 12, 14, 17, 19, 26-45, 47-53, 70, 73 at least. Black Cat text stories #8, 12, 13, 19.*

John Byrne's Next Men #18 © John Byrne

John Carter Warlord of Mars #4 © MEG

Johnny Thunder #3 © DC

JOE YANK (Korean War)
No. 5, March, 1952 - No. 16, 1954
Standard Comics (Visual Editions)

	GD25	FN65	NM94
5-Toth, Celardo, Tuska-a	4.35	13.00	26.00
6-Toth, Severin/Elder-a	6.35	19.00	38.00
7	3.60	9.00	18.00
8-Toth-c	4.35	13.00	26.00
9-16: 9-Andru-c. 12-Andru-a	3.20	8.00	16.00

JOHN BOLTON'S HALLS OF HORROR (Eclipse)(Value: cover or less)

JOHN BYRNE'S NEXT MEN (See Dark Horse Presents #54)
Jan, 1992 - Present ($2.50, mature)
Dark Horse Comics (Legend imprint #19 on)

	GD25	FN65	NM94
1-Silver foil embossed-c; Byrne-c/a/scripts in all	1.10	3.00	6.50
1-2nd printing with gold ink logo		1.30	3.25
0-(2/92)-r/chapters 1-4 from DHP w/new Byrne-c		1.90	4.75
2		1.30	3.25
3,4		1.10	2.75
5-32: 7-10-MA #1-4 mini-series on flip side. 16-Origin of Mark IV. 17-Miller-c. 19-22-Faith storyline. 23-26-Power storyline. 27,28-Lies storyline Pt. 1,2		1.00	2.50
...Parallel, Book 2 ($16.95)-TPB; r/#7-12	2.40	7.30	17.00

NOTE: *Issues 1 through 6 contain certificates redeemable for an exclusive Next Men trading card set by Byrne. Prices are for complete books.* ***Cody*** *painted c-23-26.* ***Mignola*** *a-21(part); c-21.*

JOHN CARTER OF MARS (See 4-Color #375, 437, 488, The Funnies & Tarzan #207)

JOHN CARTER OF MARS
April, 1964 - No. 3, Oct, 1964
Gold Key

	GD25	FN65	NM94
1(10104-404)-r/4-Color #375; Jesse Marsh-a	4.00	12.00	28.00
2(407), 3(410)-r/4-Color #437 & 488; Marsh-a	2.90	9.00	20.00

JOHN CARTER OF MARS
1970 (72 pgs.; paper cover; 10-1/2x16-1/2"; B&W)
House of Greystroke

	GD25	FN65	NM94
1941-42 Sunday strip reprints; John Coleman Burroughs-a	3.20	8.00	20.00

JOHN CARTER, WARLORD OF MARS (Also see Weird Worlds)
June, 1977 - No. 28, Oct, 1979
Marvel Comics Group

	GD25	FN65	NM94
1-17,19-28: 1-Origin. 11-Origin Dejah Thoris			1.00
18-Miller-a(p)			1.50
Annuals 1-3: 1(1977). 2(1978). 3(1979)-All 52 pgs. with new book-length stories			1.00

NOTE: ***Austin*** *c-24i.* ***Gil Kane*** *a-1-10p; c-1p, 2p, 3, 4-9p, 10, 15p, Annual 1p.* ***Layton*** *a-17i.* ***Miller*** *c-25, 26p.* ***Nebres*** *a-2-4i, 8-16i; c(i)-6-9, 11-22, 25, Annual 1.* ***Perez*** *c-24p.* ***Simonson*** *a-15p.* ***Sutton*** *a-7i.*

JOHN F. KENNEDY, CHAMPION OF FREEDOM
1964 (no month) (25 cents)
Worden & Childs

	GD25	FN65	NM94
nn-Photo-c	7.50	22.50	45.00

JOHN F. KENNEDY LIFE STORY
Aug-Oct, 1964; Nov, 1965; June, 1966 (12 cents)
Dell Publishing Co.

	GD25	FN65	NM94
12-378-410-Photo-c	5.35	16.00	32.00
12-378-511 (reprint, 11/65)	4.00	11.00	22.00
12-378-606 (reprint, 6/66)	4.00	10.00	20.00

JOHN FORCE (See Magic Agent)

JOHN HIX SCRAP BOOK, THE
Late 1930's (no date) (10¢, 68 pgs.; regular size)
Eastern Color Printing Co. (McNaught Synd.)

	GD25	FN65	NM94
1-Strange As It Seems (resembles Single Series books)	25.00	75.00	175.00
2-Strange As It Seems	20.00	60.00	140.00

JOHN LAW DETECTIVE (Eclipse)(Value: cover or less)(See Smash Comics #3)

JOHNNY APPLESEED (See Story Hour Series)

JOHNNY CASH (See Hello, I'm...)

JOHNNY DANGER (See Movie Comics, 1946)
1950 (Based on movie serial)
Toby Press

	GD25	FN65	NM94
1-Photo-c; Sparling-a	11.00	32.00	75.00

JOHNNY DANGER PRIVATE DETECTIVE
1954 (Reprinted in Danger #11 by Super)
Toby Press

	GD25	FN65	NM94
1-Opium den story	10.00	30.00	60.00

JOHNNY DYNAMITE (Formerly Dynamite #1-9; Foreign Intrigues #13 on)
No. 10, June, 1955 - No. 12, Oct, 1955
Charlton Comics

	GD25	FN65	NM94
10-12	5.00	15.00	30.00

JOHNNY HAZARD
No. 5, Aug, 1948 - No. 8, May, 1949; No. 35, date?
Best Books (Standard Comics) (King Features)

	GD25	FN65	NM94
5-Strip reprints by Frank Robbins (c/a)	10.00	30.00	70.00
6,8-Strip reprints by Frank Robbins	8.35	25.00	50.00
7-New art, not Robbins	6.70	20.00	40.00
35	6.70	20.00	40.00

JOHNNY JASON (...Teen Reporter)
Feb-Apr, 1962 - No. 2, June-Aug, 1962
Dell Publishing Co.

	GD25	FN65	NM94
4-Color 1302, 2(01380-208)	3.20	8.00	16.00

JOHNNY JINGLE'S LUCKY DAY
1956 (16 pgs.; 7-1/4x5-1/8") (Giveaway) (Disney)
American Dairy Association

	GD25	FN65	NM94
nn	4.00	10.00	20.00

JOHNNY LAW, SKY RANGER
Apr, 1955 - No. 3, Aug, 1955; No. 4, Nov, 1955
Good Comics (Lev Gleason)

	GD25	FN65	NM94
1-Edmond Good-c/a	5.35	16.00	32.00
2-4	4.00	10.00	20.00

JOHNNY MACK BROWN (TV western star; see Western Roundup under Dell Giants)
No. 269, Mar, 1950 - No. 963, Feb, 1959 (All Photo-c)
Dell Publishing Co.

	GD25	FN65	NM94
4-Color 269(#1)(3/50, 52pgs.)-Johnny Mack Brown & his horse Rebel begin; photo front/back-c begin; Marsh-a in #1-9	22.00	65.00	150.00
2(10-12/50, 52pgs.)	11.00	32.00	75.00
3(1-3/51, 52pgs.)	10.00	30.00	60.00
4-10 (9-11/52)(36pgs.)	6.70	20.00	40.00
4-Color 455,493,541,584,618	6.70	20.00	40.00
4-Color 645,685,722,776,834,963	6.70	20.00	40.00
4-Color 922-Manning-a	7.50	22.50	45.00

JOHNNY NEMO
Sept, 1985 - No. 3, Feb, 1986 (Mini-series)
Eclipse Comics

	GD25	FN65	NM94
1,2 ($1.75 cover)		.70	1.80
3 ($2.00 cover)		.80	2.00

JOHNNY PERIL (See Comic Cavalcade #15, Danger Trail #5, Sensation Comics #107 & SensationMystery)

JOHNNY RINGO (See 4-Color No. 1142)

JOHNNY STARBOARD (See Wisco)

JOHNNY THUNDER

John Wayne Adventure Comics # 6 © TOBY

Jo-Jo Comics #28 © FOX

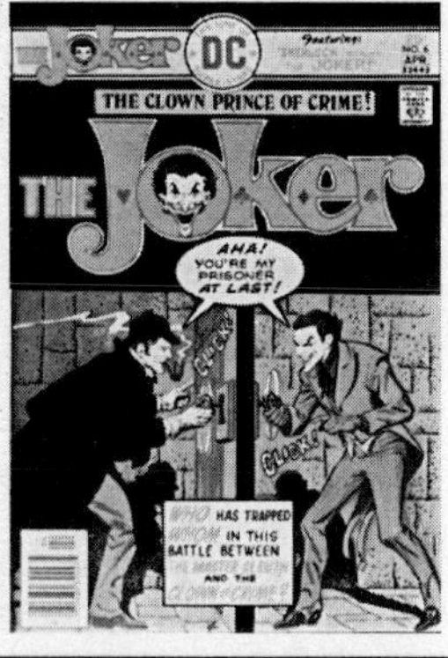

The Joker #6 © DC

GD25 FN65 NM94

Feb-Mar, 1973 - No. 3, July-Aug, 1973
National Periodical Publications

1-3: Johnny Thunder & Nighthawk-r. 2-Trigger Twins app. 1.00

NOTE: *All contain 1950s DC reprints from All-American Western.* ***Drucker*** *r-2, 3.* ***G. Kane*** *r-2, 3.* ***Moriera*** *r-1.* ***Toth*** *r-1, 3; c-1r, 3r. Also see All-American, All-Star Western, Flash Comics, Western Comics, World's Best & World's Finest.*

JOHN PAUL JONES (See Four Color No. 1007)

JOHN STEED & EMMA PEEL (See The Avengers, Gold Key series)

JOHN STEELE SECRET AGENT (Also see Freedom Agent)
December, 1964
Gold Key

1-Freedom Agent 9.00 27.00 64.00

JOHN WAYNE ADVENTURE COMICS (Movie star; See Big Tex, Oxydol-Dreft, Tim McCoy, & With The Marines...#1)
Winter, 1949-50 - No. 31, May, 1955 (Photo-c: 1-12,17,25-on)
Toby Press

1 (36pgs.)-Photo-c begin (1st time in comics on-c) 68.00 205.00 475.00
2 (4/50, 36pgs.)-Williamson/Frazetta-a(2) 6 & 2 pgs. (one story-r/Billy the Kid #1); photo back-c 49.00 148.00 345.00
3 (36pgs.)-Williamson/Frazetta-a(2), 16 pgs. total; photo back-c 49.00 148.00 345.00
4 (52pgs.)-Williamson/Frazetta-a(2), 16 pgs. total 49.00 148.00 345.00
5 (52pgs.)-Kurtzman-a-(Alfred "L" Newman in Potshot Pete) 39.00 115.00 270.00
6 (52pgs.)-Williamson/Frazetta-a (10 pgs.); Kurtzman-a "Pot-Shot Pete", (5 pgs.); & "Genius Jones", (1 pg.) 48.00 144.00 335.00
7 (52pgs.)-Williamson/Frazetta-a (10 pgs.) 39.00 116.00 270.00
8 (36pgs.)-Williamson/Frazetta-a(2) (12 & 9 pgs.) 48.00 145.00 335.00
9-11: Photo western-c 27.00 80.00 185.00
12,14-Photo war-c. 12-Kurtzman-a(2 pg.) "Genius" 27.00 80.00 185.00
13,15: 13,15-Line-drawn-c begin, end #24 24.00 72.00 165.00
16-Williamson/Frazetta-r/Billy the Kid #1 25.00 75.00 175.00
17-Photo-c 27.00 80.00 185.00
18-Williamson/Frazetta-a (r/#4 & 8, 19 pgs.) 29.00 86.00 200.00
19-24: 23-Evans-a? 21.00 63.00 145.00
25-Photo-c resume; end #31; Williamson/Frazetta-r/Billy the Kid #3 29.00 86.00 200.00
26-28,30-Photo-c 24.00 73.00 170.00
29,31-Williamson/Frazetta-a in each (r/#4, 2) 26.00 78.00 180.00

NOTE: *Williamsonish art in later issues by* ***Gerald McCann.***

JO-JO COMICS (...Congo King #7-29; My Desire #30 on)
(Also see Fantastic Fears and Jungle Jo)
1945 - No. 29, July, 1949 (Two No.7's; no #13)
Fox Feature Syndicate

nn(1945)-Funny animal, humor 10.00 30.00 65.00
2(Sum,'46)-6(4-5/47): Funny animal. 2-Ten pg. Electro story (Fall/46) 5.35 16.00 32.00
7(7/47)-Jo-Jo, Congo King begins (1st app.); Bronze Man & Purlpe Tigress app. 46.00 140.00 325.00
7(#8) (9/47) 34.00 103.00 240.00
8-10(#9-11): 8-Tanee begins 28.00 84.00 195.00
11,12(#12,13),14,16: 11,16-Kamen bondage-c 24.00 72.00 165.00
15-Cited by Dr. Wertham in 5/47 Saturday Review of Literature 25.00 75.00 175.00
17-Kamen bondage-c 25.00 75.00 175.00
18-20 24.00 72.00 165.00
21-29: 21-Hollingsworth-a(4 pgs.; 23-1 pg.) 22.00 65.00 150.00

NOTE: *Many bondage-c/a by* ***Baker/Kamen/Feldstein/Good.*** *No. 7's have Princesses Gwenna, Geesa, Yolda, & Safra before settling down on Tanee.*

JO-JOY (The Adventures of...)
1945 - 1953 (Christmas gift comic, 16 pgs., 7-1/16x10-1/4")
W. T. Grant Dept. Stores

1945-53 issues 4.00 11.00 22.00

GD25 FN65 NM94

JOKEBOOK COMICS DIGEST ANNUAL (...Magazine No. 5 on)
Oct, 1977 - No. 13, Oct, 1983 (Digest Size)
Archie Publications

1(10/77)-Reprints; Neal Adams-a 1.20 3.00
2(4/78)-13 1.20 3.00

JOKER, THE (See Batman #1, Batman: The Killing Joke, Brave & the Bold, Detective, Greatest Joker Stories & Justice League Annual #2)
May, 1975 - No. 9, Sept-Oct, 1976
National Periodical Publications

1-Two-Face app. 1.40 4.30 10.00
2,3: 3-The Creeper app. 1.20 3.00 7.00
4-6: 4-Green Arrow-c/sty. 6-Sherlock Holmes-c/sty 0.90 2.50 5.50
7-9: 7-Lex Luthor-c/story. 8-Scarecrow-c/story. 9-Catwoman-c/story 1.00 2.00 5.00

JOKER COMICS (Adventures Into Terror No. 43 on)
April, 1942 - No. 42, August, 1950
Timely/Marvel Comics No. 36 on (TCI/CDS)

1-(Rare)-Powerhouse Pepper (1st app.) begins by Wolverton; Stuporman app. from Daring Comics 150.00 450.00 1050.00
2-Wolverton-a; 1st app. Tessie the Typist & begin series 57.00 171.00 400.00
3-5-Wolverton-a 38.00 115.00 265.00
6-10-Wolverton-a. 6-Tessie-c begin 26.00 80.00 185.00
11-20-Wolverton-a 22.00 65.00 150.00
21,22,24-27,29,30-Wolverton cont'd. & Kurtzman's "Hey Look" in #23-27 17.00 52.00 120.00
23-1st "Hey Look" by Kurtzman; Wolverton-a 19.00 57.00 130.00
28,32,34,37-41: 28-Millie the Model begins. 32-Hedy begins. 41-Nellie the Nurse app. 5.00 15.00 30.00
31-Last Powerhouse Pepper; not in #28 12.00 36.00 85.00
33,35,36-Kurtzman's "Hey Look" 7.50 22.50 45.00
42-Only app. 'Patty Pinup,' clone of Millie the Model 6.70 20.00 40.00

JOLLY CHRISTMAS, A (See March of Comics No. 269)

JOLLY CHRISTMAS BOOK (See Christmas Journey Through Space)
1951; 1954; 1955 (36 pgs.; 24 pgs.)
Promotional Publ. Co.

1951-(Woolworth giveaway)-slightly oversized; no slick cover; Marv Levy-c/a 5.35 16.00 32.00
1954-(Hot Shoppes giveaway)-regular size-reprints 1951 issue; slick cover added; 24 pgs.; no ads 5.35 16.00 32.00
1955-(J. M. McDonald Co. giveaway)-reg. size 4.00 11.00 22.00

JOLLY COMICS
1947
Four Star Publishing Co.

1 5.85 17.50 35.00

JOLLY JINGLES (Formerly Jackpot Comics)
No. 10, Sum, 1943 - No. 16, Wint, 1944/45
MLJ Magazines

10-Super Duck begins (origin & 1st app.); Woody The Woodpecker begins (not same as Lantz character) 29.00 86.00 200.00
11 (Fall, '43)-2nd Super Duck(see Hangman #8) 14.00 43.00 100.00
12-Hitler-c 11.00 32.00 75.00
13-16: 13-Sahle-c. 15-Vigoda-c 9.15 27.50 55.00

JONAH HEX (See All-Star Western, Hex and Weird Western Tales)
Mar-Apr, 1977 - No. 92, Aug, 1985
National Periodical Publications/DC Comics

1 4.60 14.00 32.00
2-6,9,10: 9-Wrightson-c 1.50 3.80 9.00
7,8-Explains Hex's face disfigurement (origin) 1.50 3.80 9.00
11-20: 12-Starlin-c 1.00 2.00 5.00
21-50: 31,32-Origin retold 1.60 4.00
51-92: 92-Story continued in Hex #1 1.20 3.00

Jonah Hex: Two Gun Mojo #4 © DC

Journey Into Fear #11 © SUPR

Journey Into Mystery #7 © MEG

NOTE: **Ayers** *a(p)-35-37, 40, 41, 44-53, 56, 58-82.* **Kubert** *c-43-46.* **Morrow** *a-90-92; c-10.* **Spiegle(Tothish)** *a-34, 38, 40, 49, 52.* **Texeira** *a-89p. Batlash back-ups in 49, 52. El Diablo back-ups in 48, 56-60, 73-75. Scalphunter back-ups in 40, 41, 45-47.*

JONAH HEX AND OTHER WESTERN TALES (Blue Ribbon Digest)
Sept-Oct, 1979 - No. 3, Jan-Feb, 1980 (100 pgs.)
DC Comics

	GD25	FN65	NM94
1-3: 1-Origin Scalphunter-r; painted-c. 2-Weird Western Tales-r; Neal Adams, Toth, Aragones, Gil Kane-a			1.00

JONAH HEX SPECTACULAR (See DC Special Series No. 16)

JONAH HEX: TWO-GUN MOJO
Aug, 1993 - No. 5, Dec, 1993 ($2.95, mini-series)
DC Comics (Vertigo)

	GD25	FN65	NM94
1-Truman/Glanzman-a in all w/Truman-c	1.20	2.90	7.00
1-Silver ink edition with no price on cover	2.10	6.40	15.00
2-5		1.70	4.25

JONESY (Formerly Crack Western)
No. 85, Aug, 1953; No. 2, Oct, 1953 - No. 8, Oct, 1954
Comic Favorite/Quality Comics Group

	GD25	FN65	NM94
85(#1)-Teen-age humor	4.70	14.00	28.00
2	3.60	9.00	18.00
3-8	2.40	6.00	12.00

JON JUAN (Also see Great Lover Romances)
Spring, 1950
Toby Press

	GD25	FN65	NM94
1-All Schomburg-a (signed Al Reid on-c); written by Siegel; used in **SOTI**, pg. 38	17.00	52.00	120.00

JONNI THUNDER (...A.K.A. Thunderbolt)
Feb, 1985 - No. 4, Aug, 1985 (75¢, mini-series)
DC Comics

	GD25	FN65	NM94
1-4: 1-Origin & 1st app.			1.00

JONNY DEMON
May, 1994 - No. 3, July, 1994 ($2.50, limited series)
Dark Horse Comics

	GD25	FN65	NM94
1-3		1.00	2.50

JONNY QUEST (TV)
December, 1964 (Hanna-Barbera)
Gold Key

	GD25	FN65	NM94
1 (10139-412)	24.00	728.00	240.00

JONNY QUEST (TV) (Comico)(Value: cover or less)

JONNY QUEST CLASSICS (TV) (First)(Value: cover or less)

JON SABLE, FREELANCE (First)(Value: cover or less)

JOSEPH & HIS BRETHREN (See The Living Bible)

JOSIE (She's... #1-16) (...& the Pussycats #45 on) (See Archie Giant Series Magazine #528, 540, 551, 562, 571, 584, 597, 610, 622)
Feb, 1963; No. 2, Aug, 1963 - No. 106, Oct, 1982
Archie Publications/Radio Comics

	GD25	FN65	NM94
1	14.00	43.00	100.00
2	8.35	25.00	50.00
3-5	4.70	14.00	28.00
6-10	4.00	10.00	20.00
11-20	3.20	8.00	16.00
21-30: 22-Mighty Man & Mighty (Josie Girl) app.	2.00	5.00	10.00
31-54	1.00	2.50	6.00
55-74(52pg. issues)		1.00	2.50
75-106			1.50

JOSIE & THE PUSSYCATS (TV)
1993 - Present ($2.00, 52 pgs.)(Published annually)
Archie Comics

	GD25	FN65	NM94
1,2-Bound-in pull-out poster in each. 2-(Spr/94)		.80	2.00

JOURNAL OF CRIME (See Fox Giants)

JOURNEY (Also see Journey: Wardrums)
1983 - No. 14, 9/84; No. 15, 4/85 - No. 27, 7/86 (B&W)
Aardvark-Vanaheim #1-14/Fantagraphics Books #15-on

	GD25	FN65	NM94
1	1.00	2.00	5.00
2		1.20	3.00
3-27: 20-Sam Kieth-a			1.25

JOURNEY INTO FEAR
May, 1951 - No. 21, Sept, 1954
Superior-Dynamic Publications

	GD25	FN65	NM94
1-Baker-r(2)	30.00	90.00	210.00
2	18.00	54.00	125.00
3,4	14.00	43.00	100.00
5-10,15: 15-Used in **SOTI**, pg. 389	11.00	32.00	75.00
11-14,16-21	10.00	30.00	65.00

NOTE: *Kamenish 'headlight'-a most issues.* **Robinson** *a-10.*

JOURNEY INTO MYSTERY (1st Series) (Thor No. 126 on)
6/52 - No. 48, 8/57; No. 49, 11/58 - No. 125, 2/66
Atlas(CPS No. 1-48/AMI No. 49-68/Marvel No. 69 (6/61) on)

	GD25	FN65	NM94
1-Weird/horror stories begin	130.00	390.00	1575.00
2	66.00	197.00	525.00
3,4	50.00	150.00	400.00
5-11	31.00	94.00	250.00
12-20,22: 15-Atomic explosion panel. 22-Davisesque-a; last pre-code issue (2/55)	29.00	88.00	205.00
21-Kubert-a; Tothish-a by Andru	27.00	81.00	215.00
23-32,35-38,40: 24-Torres?-a. 38-Ditko-a	16.00	47.00	125.00
33-Williamson-a; Ditko-a (his 1st for Atlas?)	18.00	53.00	140.00
34,39: 34-Krigstein-a. 39-Wood-a	16.00	49.00	130.00
41-Crandall-a; Frazettaesque-a by Morrow	13.00	39.00	105.00
42,48-Torres-a	13.00	39.00	105.00
43,44-Williamson/Mayo-a in both	14.00	43.00	115.00
45,47,52,53	11.00	34.00	90.00
46-Torres & Krigstein-a	13.00	39.00	105.00
49-Matt Fox, Check-a	14.00	41.00	110.00
50,54: 50-Davis-a. 54-Williamson-a	9.00	26.00	88.00
51-Kirby/Wood-a	10.50	32.00	105.00
55-61,63-65,67-69,71,72,74,75: 58-Ad for Fantastic Four #1-c. 74-Contents change to Fantasy. 75-Last 10¢ issue	9.50	29.00	95.00
62-Prototype ish. (The Hulk); 1st app. Xemnu (Titan) called "The Hulk"	14.00	40.00	140.00
66-Prototype ish. (The Hulk)-Return of Xemnu "The Hulk"	12.00	36.00	120.00
70-Prototype ish. (The Sandman)(7/61); similar to Spidey villain	11.00	33.00	110.00
73-Prototype ish. (Spider-Man)	15.00	40.00	145.00
76,77,80-82: 80-Anti-communist propaganda story	8.20	25.00	82.00
78-The Sorceror (Dr. Strange prototype) app. (3/62)	13.00	39.00	130.00
79-Prototype ish. (Mr. Hyde)	11.00	33.00	110.00

	GD25	FN65	VF82	NM94
83-Origin & 1st app. The Mighty Thor by Kirby (8/62) and begin series; Thor-c also begin	295.00	890.00	1920.00	2950.00

	GD25	FN65	NM94
83-Reprint from the Golden Record Comic Set	9.00	26.00	70.00
with the record (1966)	17.00	51.00	135.00
84-2nd app. Thor	88.00	263.00	700.00
85-1st app. Loki & Heimdall; Odin cameo (1 panel)	45.00	135.00	360.00
86-1st full app. Odin	30.00	90.00	255.00
87-89: 89-Origin Thor retold	20.00	60.00	170.00
90-No Kirby-a	13.00	38.00	105.00
91,92,94-96-Sinnott-a	12.00	36.00	95.00
93,97-Kirby-a; Tales of Asgard series begins #97 (origin which concludes in #99)	16.00	47.00	125.00

Journey Into Mystery (2nd series) #2 © MEG

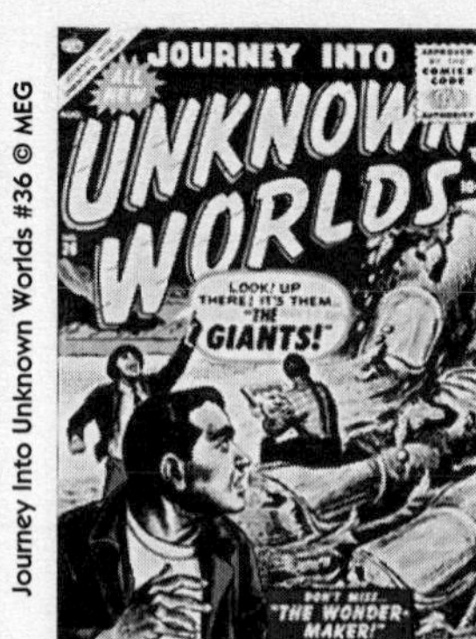

Journey Into Unknown Worlds #36 © MEG

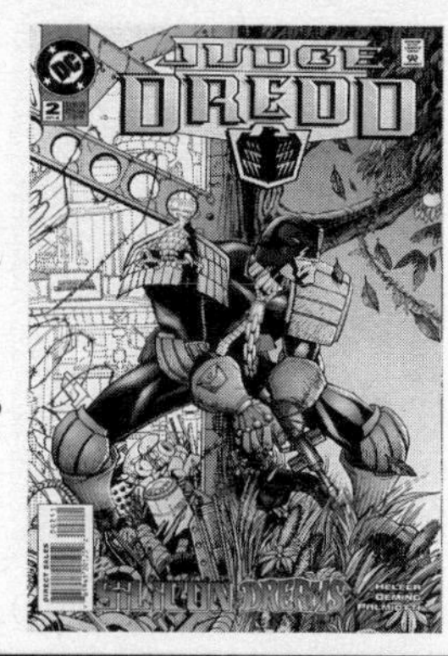

Judge Dredd #2 © DC

GD25 FN65 NM94

98-100-Kirby/Heck-a. 98-Origin/1st app. The Human Cobra. 99-1st app. Surtur & Mr. Hyde 11.00 32.00 85.00
101-108,110: 101-(2/64)-2nd Avengers x-over (w/o Capt. America); see Tales Of Suspense #49 for 1st x-over. 102-Intro Sif. 103-1st app. Enchantress. 105-109-Ten extra pgs. Kirby-a in each. 107-1st app. Grey Gargoyle. 108-(9/64)-Early Dr. Strange & Avengers x-over 7.00 21.00 56.00
109-Magneto-c & app. (1st x-over, 10/64) 10.00 30.00 80.00
111,113,114,116-125: 114-Origin/1st app. Absorbing Man. 118-1st app. Destroyer. 119-Intro Hogun, Fandrall, Volstagg. 124-Hercules-c/story 7.00 21.00 55.00
112-Thor Vs. Hulk (1/65). 112,113-Origin Loki 15.00 45.00 120.00
115-Origin Loki 8.00 23.00 60.00
Annual 1(1965, 25 cents, 72 pgs.)-New Thor vs. Hercules(1st app.)-c/story (see Incredible Hulk #3); Kirby-c/a; r/#85,93,95,97 14.00 41.00 110.00

NOTE: ***Ayers** a-14, 39, 64i, 71i, 74i, 80i. **Bailey** a-43. **Briefer** a-5, 12. **Cameron** a-35. **Check** a-17. **Colan** a-23, 81; c-14. **Ditko** a-33, 38, 50-96; c-58, 67, 71, 88i. **Kirby/Ditko** a-50-83. **Everett** a-20, 48; c-4-7, 9, 36, 37, 39-42, 44, 45, 47. **Forte** a-19, 35, 40, 53. **Heath** a-4-6, 11, 14; c-1, 8, 11, 15, 51. **Heck** a-53, 73. **Kirby** a(p)-51, 52, 56, 57, 60, 62, 64, 66, 69, 71-74, 76, 79, 80-89, 93, 97, 98, 100(w/**Heck**), 101-125; c-50-57, 59-66, 68-70, 72-82, 88(w/**Ditko**), 83 & 84(w/**Sinnott**), 85-96(w/**Ayers**), 97-152p. **Leiber/Fox** a-93, 98-102. **Maneely** c-20-22. **Morisi** a-42. **Morrow** a-41, 42. **Orlando** a-30, 45, 57. **Mac Pakula** (Tothish) a-9, 35, 41. **Powell** a-20, 27, 34. **Reinman** a-39, 87, 92, 96i. **Robinson** a-9. **Roussos** a-39. **Robert Sale** a-14. **Severin** a-27; c-30. **Sinnott** a-41; c-50. **Tuska** a-11. **Wildey** a-16.*

JOURNEY INTO MYSTERY (2nd Series)
Oct, 1972 - No. 19, Oct, 1975
Marvel Comics Group

1-Robert Howard adaptation; Starlin/Ploog-a 1.10 2.70 6.50
2,3,5-Bloch adaptation; 5-Last new story 1.30 3.25
4,6-19: 4-H. P. Lovecraft adaptation .90 2.25

NOTE: ***N. Adams** a-2i. **Ditko** r-7, 10, 12, 14, 15, 19; c-10. **Everett** r-9, 14. **G. Kane** a-1p, 2p; c-1-3p. **Kirby** r-7, 13, 18, 19; c-7. **Mort Lawrence** r-2. **Maneely** r-3. **Orlando** r-16. **Reese** a-1, 2i. **Starlin** a-1p, 3p. **Torres** r-16. **Wildey** r-9, 14.*

JOURNEY INTO UNKNOWN WORLDS (Formerly Teen)
No. 36, 9/50 - No. 38, 2/51; No. 4, 4/51 - No. 59, 8/57
Atlas Comics (WFP)

36(#1)-Science fiction/weird; "End Of The Earth" c/story 129.00 385.00 900.00
37(#2)-Science fiction; "When Worlds Collide" c/story; Everett-c/a; Hitler story 62.00 186.00 435.00
38(#3)-Science fiction 54.00 160.00 375.00
4-6,8,10-Science fiction/weird 33.00 100.00 230.00
7-Wolverton-a "Planet of Terror", 6 pgs; electric chair c-inset/story 55.00 165.00 385.00
9-Giant eyeball story 39.00 118.00 275.00
11,12-Krigstein-a 25.00 75.00 175.00
13,16,17,20 18.00 54.00 125.00
14-Wolverton-a "One of Our Graveyards Is Missing", 4 pgs; Tuska-a 43.00 130.00 300.00
15-Wolverton-a "They Crawl by Night", 5 pgs.; 2 pg. Maneely s/f story 43.00 130.00 300.00
18,19-Matt Fox-a 22.00 65.00 150.00
21-33: 21-Decapitation-c. 24-Sci/fic story. 26-Atom bomb panel. 27-Sid Check-a. 33-Last pre-code (2/55) 13.00 40.00 90.00
34-Kubert, Torres-a 10.00 30.00 70.00
35-Torres-a 10.00 30.00 65.00
36-42 10.00 30.00 60.00
43,44: 43-Krigstein-a. 44-Davis-a 10.00 30.00 65.00
45,55,59-Williamson-a in all; with Mayo #55,59. 55-Crandall-a 10.00 30.00 65.00
46,47,49,52,56-58 9.15 27.50 55.00
48,53-Crandall-a (4 pgs. #48). 48-Check-a 10.00 30.00 65.00
50-Davis, Crandall-a 10.00 30.00 65.00
51-Ditko, Wood-a 10.00 30.00 70.00
54-Torres-a 9.15 27.50 55.00

NOTE: ***Ayers** a-24, 43, **Berg** a-38(#3), 43. **Lou Cameron** a-33. **Colan** a-37(#2), 6, 17, 19, 20, 23, 39. **Ditko** a-45, 51. **Drucker** a-35, 58. **Everett** a-37(#2), 11, 14, 41, 55, 56; c-37(#2), 11, 13, 14, 17, 22, 47, 48, 50, 53-55, 59. **Forte** a-49. **Fox** a-21i. **Heath** a-36(#1), 4, 6-8, 17, 20, 22, 36i; c-18. **Keller** a-15. **Mort Lawrence** a-38, 39. **Maneely** a-7, 8, 15, 16, 22, 49, 58; c-19, 25, 52. **Morrow** a-48. **Orlando** a-44, 57. **Pakula** a-36. **Powell** a-42, 53, 54. **Reinman** a-8. **Rico** a-21. **Robert Sale** a-24, 49. **Sekowsky** a-4, 5, 9. **Severin** a-38, 51; c-38, 48i, 56. **Sinnott** a-9, 21, 24. **Tuska** a-38(#3), 14. **Wildey** a-25, 43, 44.*

GD25 FN65 NM94

JOURNEY OF DISCOVERY WITH MARK STEEL (See Mark Steel)

JOURNEY TO THE CENTER OF THE EARTH (See 4-Color No. 1060)

JUDE, THE FORGOTTEN SAINT
1954 (16 pgs.; 8x11"; full color; paper cover)
Catechetical Guild Education Society

nn 2.00 5.00 10.00

JUDGE COLT
Oct, 1969 - No. 4, Sept, 1970
Gold Key

1 1.30 3.25 8.00
2-4 1.00 2.00 5.00

JUDGE DREDD (...Classics #62 on; also see Batman - Judge Dredd, Dredd Rules, The Law of Dredd & 2000 A.D. Monthly)
Nov, 1983 - No. 35, 1986; V2#1, Oct, 1986 - No. 77, 1993
Eagle Comics/IPC Magazines Ltd./Quality Comics #34-35, V2#1-37/ Fleetway #38 on

1-Bolland-c/a in #1-10,15 1.50 3.75 9.00
2-35 1.20 3.00
V2#1-('86)-New look begins .80 2.00
V2#2-6 1.50
V2#7-21/22: 14-Bolland-a. 20-Begin $1.50-c 1.30
V2#23/24-Two issue numbers in one 1.50
25-38: 28-1st app. Megaman (super-hero) 1.50
39-50: 39-Begin $1.75-c .70 1.75
51-77: 51-Begin $1.95-c. 53-Bolland-a. 57-Reprints 1st published Judge Dredd story .80 2.00
Special 1 1.40

NOTE: ***Guice** c-V2#23/24, 26, 27.*

JUDGE DREDD (3rd series)
Aug, 1994 - Present ($1.95)
DC Comics

1-5 .80 2.00

JUDGE DREDD (Definitive Editions) (Fleetway/Quality)(Value: cover or less)

JUDGE DREDD'S CRIME FILE (Eagle & Quality)(Value: cover or less)

JUDGE DREDD'S HARDCASE PAPERS (Fleetway/Quality)(Value: cover or less)

JUDGE DREDD: THE EARLY CASES (Eagle)(Value: cover or less)

JUDGE DREDD: THE JUDGE CHILD QUEST (Eagle)(Value: cover or less)

JUDGE DREDD: THE MEGAZINE (Fleetway/Quality)(Value: cover or less)

JUDGEMENT DAY
Sept, 1993 - No. 8, Apr, 1994 ($2.95, color)
Lightning Comics

1-($3.50)-Red foil-c 1.40 3.50
1-Gold Prism Edition 9.00
1-Purple-c Edition 1.90 4.50
2-8: 2-Polybagged with trading card. 7-Origin 1.20 3.00

JUDGE PARKER
Feb, 1956 - No. 2, 1956
Argo

1-Newspaper strip reprints 4.70 14.00 28.00
2 3.60 9.00 18.00

JUDO JOE
Aug, 1953 - No. 3, Dec, 1953 (Judo lessons in each issue)
Jay-Jay Corp.

1-Drug ring story 5.85 17.50 35.00
2,3: 3-Hypo needle story 4.00 12.00 24.00

JUDOMASTER (Gun Master #84-89) (Also see Crisis on Infinite Earths, Sarge

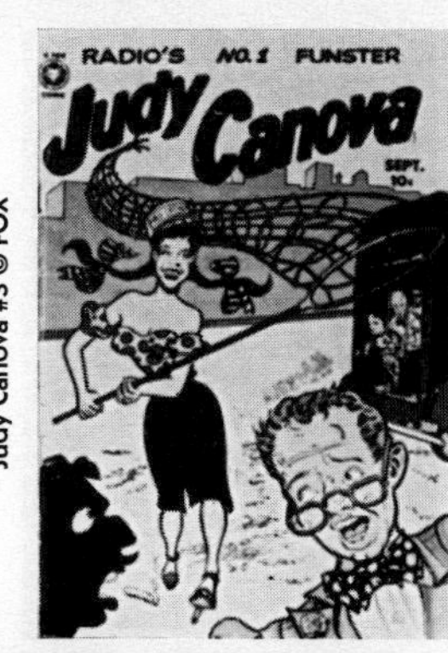

Judy Canova #3 © FOX

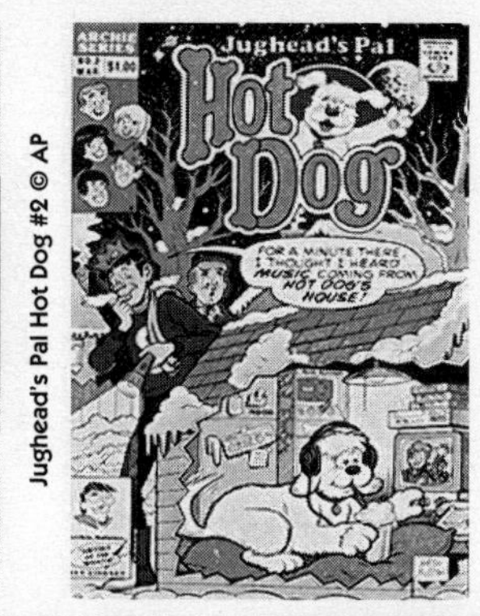

Jughead's Pal Hot Dog #2 © AP

Juke Box Comics #1 © FF

	GD25	FN65	NM94

Steel #6 & Special War Series)
No. 89, May-June, 1966 - No. 98, Dec, 1967 (Two No. 89's)
Charlton Comics

89-3rd app. Judomaster	2.40	7.30	17.00
90-98: 91-Sarge Steel begins. 93-Intro. Tiger	1.90	6.00	13.00
93,94,96,98(Modern Comics reprint, 1977)			1.25

NOTE: ***Morisi*** *Thunderbolt #90. #91 has 1 pg. biography on writer/artist Frank McLoughlin.*

JUDY CANOVA (Formerly My Experience) (Stage, screen, radio)
No. 23, May, 1950 - No. 3, Sept, 1950
Fox Features Syndicate

23(#1)-Wood-c,a(p)?	12.00	36.00	85.00
24-Wood-a(p)	12.00	36.00	85.00
3-Wood-c; Wood/Orlando-a	14.00	43.00	100.00

JUDY GARLAND (See Famous Stars)

JUDY JOINS THE WAVES
1951 (For U.S. Navy)
Toby Press

nn	4.35	13.00	26.00

JUGHEAD (Formerly Archie's Pal...)
No. 127, Dec, 1965 - No. 352, June, 1987
Archie Publications

127-130	1.90	6.00	13.00
131,133,135-160	1.70	4.20	10.00
132,134: 132-Shield-c; The Fly & Black Hood app.; Shield cameo. 134-Shield-c	1.60	4.70	11.00
161-200	1.00	2.00	5.00
201-240		.80	2.00
241-352: 300-Anniversary issue; infinity-c			1.50

JUGHEAD (2nd series)(Becomes Archie's Pal Jughead Comics #46 on)
Aug, 1987 - No. 45, May, 1993 (.75/$1.00/$1.25)
Archie Enterprises

1-45: 4-X-Mas issue. 17-Colan-c/a			1.25

JUGHEAD AS CAPTAIN HERO (See Archie as Purehear the Powerful, Archie Giant Series Magazine #142 & Life With Archie)
Oct, 1966 - No. 7, Nov, 1967
Archie Publications

1-Super hero parody	3.85	11.50	28.00
2	2.60	7.70	18.00
3-7	1.70	5.10	12.00

JUGHEAD JONES COMICS DIGEST, THE (...Magazine No. 10-64; Jughead Jones Digest Magazine #65)
June, 1977 - Present ($1.35/$1.50, digest-size, 128 pgs.)
Archie Publications

1-Neal Adams-a; Capt. Hero-r	1.00	2.50	6.00
2(9/77)-Neal Adams-a		1.60	4.00
3-50: 7-Origin Jaguar-r; N. Adams-a. 13-r/1957 Jughead's Folly		.80	2.00
51-96			1.50

JUGHEAD'S BABY TALES
Spring, 1994 ($2.00, 52 pgs.)
Archie Comics

1-Bound-in pull-out poster		.80	2.00

JUGHEAD'S DINER
Apr, 1990 - No. 7, Apr, 1991 ($1.00)
Archie Comics

1-7			1.00

JUGHEAD'S DOUBLE DIGEST (...Magazine #5)
Oct, 1989 - Present ($2.25/$2.50, quarterly, 256 pgs.)
Archie Comics

1-28: 2,5-Capt. Hero stories		1.00	2.50

JUGHEAD'S EAT-OUT COMIC BOOK MAGAZINE (See Archie Giant Series Magazine No. 170)

JUGHEAD'S FANTASY
Aug, 1960 - No. 3, Dec, 1960
Archie Publications

1	17.00	52.00	120.00
2	11.50	34.00	80.00
3	10.00	30.00	70.00

JUGHEAD'S FOLLY
1957 (36 pgs.)(One Shot)
Archie Publications (Close-Up)

1-Jughead a la Elvis (Rare) (1st reference to Elvis in comics?)	39.00	118.00	275.00

JUGHEAD'S JOKES
Aug, 1967 - No. 78, Sept, 1982
(No. 1-8, 38 on: reg. size; No. 9-23: 68 pgs.; No. 24-37: 52 pgs.)
Archie Publications

1	6.00	18.00	42.00
2	3.10	9.00	22.00
3-5	1.70	5.00	12.00
6-10	1.00	2.50	6.00
11-30		1.60	4.00
31-50		.80	2.00
51-78			1.50

JUGHEAD'S PAL HOT DOG (See Laugh #14 for 1st app.)
Jan, 1990 - No. 5, Oct, 1990 ($1.00)
Archie Comics

1-5			1.00

JUGHEAD'S SOUL FOOD (Spire Christian)(Value: cover or less)

JUGHEAD'S TIME POLICE
July, 1990 - No. 6, May, 1991 ($1.00, bi-monthly)
Archie Comics

1-6: Colan a-3-6p; c-3-6			1.00

JUGHEAD WITH ARCHIE DIGEST (...Plus Betty & Veronica & Reggie Too No. 1,2; ...Magazine #33-?, 101-on; ...Comics Digest Mag.)
March, 1974 - Present (Digest Size; $1.00/$1.25/$1.35/$1.50)
Archie Publications

1	2.15	6.50	15.00
2	1.20	3.00	7.00
3-10		1.60	4.00
11-20: Capt. Hero-r in #14-16; Pureheart the Powerful #18,21,22; Capt. Pureheart #17,19		1.20	3.00
21-50: 29-The Shield-r. 30-The Fly-r		.80	2.00
51-124			1.50

JUKE BOX COMICS
March, 1948 - No. 6, Jan, 1949
Famous Funnies

1-Toth-c/a; Hollingsworth-a	32.00	95.00	225.00
2-Transvestism story	18.00	54.00	125.00
3-6: 3-Peggy Lee story. 4-Jimmy Durante line drawn-c. 6-Features Desi Arnaz plus Arnaz line drawn-c	13.00	40.00	90.00

JUMBO COMICS (Created by S.M. Iger)
Sept, 1938 - No. 167, Mar, 1953 (No. 1-3: 68 pgs.; No. 4-8: 52 pgs.)
(No. 1-8 oversized-10-1/2x14-1/2"; black & white)
Fiction House Magazines (Real Adv. Publ. Co.)

	GD25	FN65	VF82

1-(Rare)-Sheena Queen of the Jungle(1st app.) by Meskin, Hawks of the Seas (The Hawk #10 on; see Feature Funnies #3) by Eisner, The Hunchback by Dick Briefer (ends #8), Wilton of the West (ends #24), Inspector Dayton (ends #67) & ZX-5 (ends #140) begin; 1st comic art by Jack Kirby (Count of Monte Cristo & Wilton of the West); Mickey Mouse appears (1 panel) with brief biography of Walt Disney; 1st app. Peter Pupp by Bob Kane. Note:

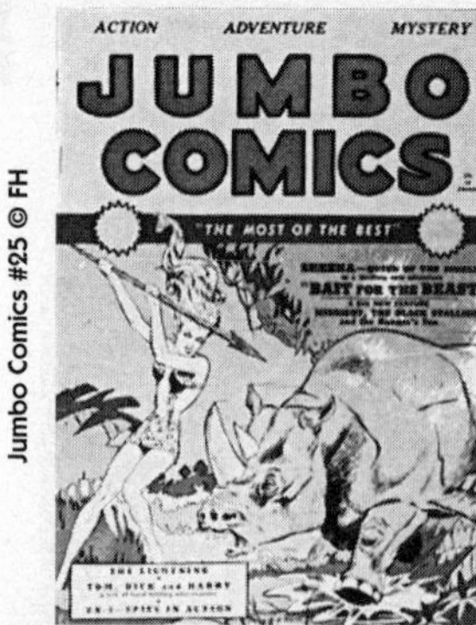

Jumbo Comics #25 © FH

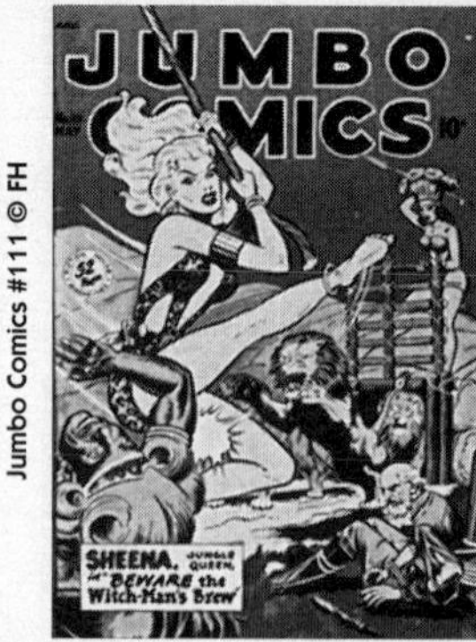

Jumbo Comics #111 © FH

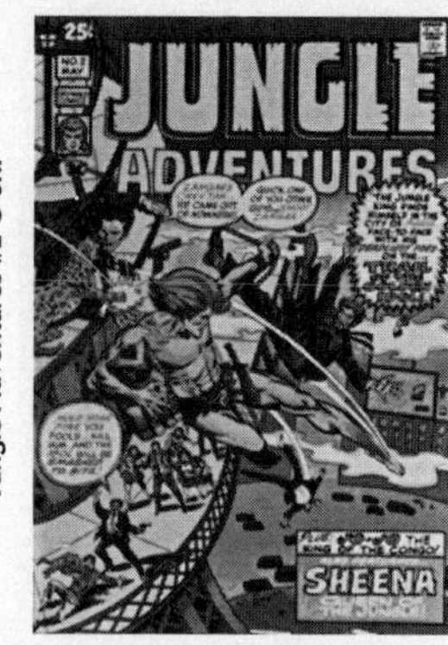

Jungle Adventures #2 © SKY

GD25 FN65 NM94

Sheena was created by Iger for publication in England as a newspaper strip. The early issues of Jumbo contain Sheena strip-r; mutiple panel-c 1,2,7 1000.00 3000.00 10,000.00
(Estimated up to 45 total copies exist, 1 in NM/Mint)
2-(Rare)-Origin Sheena. Diary of Dr. Hayward by Kirby (also #3) plus 2 other stories; contains strip from Universal Film featuring Edgar Bergen & Charlie McCarthy plus-c (preview of film) 471.00 1415.00 3300.00
3-Last Kirby issue 343.00 1030.00 2400.00
4-(Scarce)-Origin The Hawk by Eisner; Wilton of the West by Fine (ends #14)(1st comic work); Count of Monte Cristo by Fine (ends #15); The Diary of Dr. Hayward by Fine (cont'd #8,9) 329.00 985.00 2300.00
5-Christmas-c 257.00 771.00 1800.00
6-8-Last B&W issue. #8 was a 1939 N. Y. World's Fair Special Edition; Frank Buck's Jungleland story 185.00 557.00 1300.00
9-Stuart Taylor begins by Fine (ends #140); Fine-c; 1st color issue (8-9/39)-1st Sheena (jungle) cover; 8-1/4x10-1/4" (oversized in width only) 207.00 621.00 1450.00

GD25 FN65 NM94

10-13: 10-Regular size 68 pg. issues begin; Sheena dons new costume w/ origin costume; Stuart Taylor sci/fi-c. 12-The Hawk-c 90.00 270.00 635.00
14-Intro. Lightning (super-hero) on-c only 102.00 306.00 715.00
15,17-20: 15-1st Lightning story and begins, ends #41. 17-Lightning part-c 59.00 178.00 415.00
16-Lightning-c 74.00 220.00 515.00
21-30: 22-1st Tom, Dick & Harry; origin The Hawk retold. 25-Midnight the Black Stallion begins, ends #65 44.00 133.00 310.00
31-40: 31-(9/41)-1st app. Mars God of War in Stuart Taylor story (see Planet Comics #15. 35-Shows V2#11 (correct number does not appear) 39.00 118.00 275.00
41-50: 42-Ghost Gallery begins, ends #167 31.00 92.00 215.00
51-60: 52-Last Tom, Dick & Harry 27.00 80.00 185.00
61-70: 68-Sky Girl begins, ends #130; not in #79 19.00 58.00 135.00
71-99: 89-ZX5 becomes a private eye. 94-Used in Love and Death by Legman 16.00 48.00 110.00
100 19.00 57.00 130.00
101-110 14.00 43.00 100.00
111-140,150-158: 155-Used in **POP**, pg. 98 13.00 40.00 90.00
141-149-Two Sheena stories. 141-Long Bow, Indian Boy begins, ends #160 14.00 43.00 100.00
159-163: Space Scouts serial in all. 160-Last jungle-c (6/52). 161-Ghost Gallery covers begin, end #167. 163-Suicide Smith app. 11.50 34.00 80.00
164-The Star Pirate begins, ends #165 11.50 34.00 80.00
165-167: 165,167-Space Rangers app. 11.50 34.00 80.00

NOTE: *Bondage covers, negligee panels, torture, etc. are common in this series. Hawks of the Seas, Inspector Dayton, Spies in Action, Sports Shorts, & Uncle Otto by Eisner, #1-7. Hawk by* ***Eisner****-#10-15.* ***Eisner*** *c-1-7, 11-13, 15. 1pg. Patsy pin-ups in 92-97, 99-101. Sheena by* ***Meskin****-#1, 4; by* ***Powell****-#2, 3, 5-28;* ***Powell*** *c-14, 16, 17, 19. Sky Girl by* ***Matt Baker****-#69-78, 80-130. ZX-5 & Ghost Gallery by* ***Kamen****-#90-130.* ***Bailey*** *a-3-8.* ***Briefer*** *a-1-8, 10.* ***Fine*** *a-14; c-8-10.* ***Kamen*** *a-101, 105, 123, 132; c-105, 121-145.* ***Bob Kane*** *a-1-8.* ***Whitman*** *c-146-167(most). Jungle c-9, 13, 15, 17 on.*

JUMPING JACKS PRESENTS THE WHIZ KIDS
1978 (In 3-D) with glasses (4 pgs.)
Jumping Jacks Stores giveaway

nn 1.00

JUNGLE ACTION
Oct, 1954 - No. 6, Aug, 1955
Atlas Comics (IPC)

1-Leopard Girl begins by Al Hartley (#1,3); Jungle Boy by Forte; Maneely-a in all 20.00 60.00 140.00
2-(3-D effect cover) 25.00 75.00 175.00
3-6: 3-Last precode (2/55) 13.00 40.00 90.00

NOTE: ***Maneely*** *c-1, 2, 5, 6.* ***Romita*** *a-3, 6.* ***Shores*** *a-3, 6; c-3, 4?.*

JUNGLE ACTION (...& Black Panther #18-21?)
Oct, 1972 - No. 24, Nov, 1976
Marvel Comics Group

GD25 FN65 NM94

1-Lorna, Jann-r (All reprints in 1-4) 1.10 2.70 6.50
2-4 1.30 3.25
5-Black Panther begins; new stories begin 1.10 2.70 6.50
6-18: 8-Origin Black Panther. 9-Contains pull-out centerfold ad by Mark Jewelers 1.30 3.25
19-24: 19-23-KKK x-over. 23-r/#22. 24-1st Wind Eagle .90 2.25

NOTE: ***Buckler*** *a-6-9p, 22; c-8p, 12p.* ***Buscema*** *a-5p; c-22.* ***Byrne*** *c-23.* ***Gil Kane*** *a-8p; c-2, 4, 10p, 11p, 13-17, 19, 24.* ***Kirby*** *c-18.* ***Maneely*** *r-1.* ***Russell*** *a-13i.* ***Starlin*** *c-3p.*

JUNGLE ADVENTURES
1963 - 1964 (Reprints)
Super Comics

10,12,15: 10-r/Terrors of the Jungle #10(Rulah). 12-r/Zoot #14(Rulah).15-r/ Kaanga from Jungle #152 & Tiger Girl 4.00 10.00 20.00
17-All Jo-Jo reprints 4.00 10.00 20.00
18-Reprints/White Princess of the Jungle #1; no Kinstler-a; origin of both White Princess & Cap'n Courage 4.20 12.50 25.00

JUNGLE ADVENTURES
March, 1971 - No. 3, June, 1971 (25 cents, 52 pgs.)
Skywald Comics

1-Zangar origin; reprints of Jo-Jo, Blue Gorilla(origin)/White Princess #3, Kinstler-r/White Princess #2 1.30 3.25 8.00
2-Zangar, Sheena-r/Sheena #17 & Jumbo #162, Jo-Jo, origin Slave Girl Princess-r 1.30 3.25 8.00
3-Zangar, Jo-Jo, White Princess-r 1.30 3.25 8.00

JUNGLE BOOK (See King Louie and Mowgli, Movie Comics, Walt Disney Showcase #45 & Walt Disney's The Jungle Book)

JUNGLE CAT (See 4-Color No. 1136)

JUNGLE COMICS
1/40 - No. 157, 3/53; No. 158, Spr, 1953 - No. 163, Summer, 1954
Fiction House Magazines

1-Origin The White Panther, Kaanga, Lord of the Jungle, Tabu, Wizard of the Jungle; Wambi, the Jungle Boy, Camilla & Capt. Terry Thunder begin (all 1st app.) 243.00 730.00 1700.00
2-Fantomah, Mystery Woman of the Jungle begins, ends #51; The Red Panther begins, ends #26 96.00 290.00 675.00
3,4 86.00 257.00 600.00
5 68.00 205.00 475.00
6-10: 7,8-Powell-c 51.00 152.00 355.00
11-20: 13-Tuska-c 40.00 120.00 280.00
21-30: 25-Shows V2#1 (correct number does not appear). #27-New origin Fantomah, Daughter of the Pharoahs; Camilla dons new costume 32.00 96.00 225.00
31-40 26.00 78.00 180.00
41,43-50 22.00 65.00 150.00
42-Kaanga by Crandall, 12 pgs. 24.00 72.00 165.00
51-60 20.00 60.00 140.00
61-70: 67-Cover swipes Crandall splash pg. in #42 17.00 52.00 120.00
71-80: 79-New origin Tabu 15.00 45.00 105.00
81-97,99,101-110 14.00 43.00 100.00
98-Used in **SOTI**, pg. 185 & illo "In ordinary comic books, there are pictures within pictures for children who know how to look;" used by N.Y. Legis. Comm. 22.00 65.00 150.00
100 16.00 48.00 110.00
111-163: 104-In Camilla story villain is Dr. Wertham. 118-Clyde Beatty app. 135-Desert Panther begins in Terry Thunder (origin), not in #137; ends (dies) #138. 139-Last 52 pg. issue. 141-Last Tabu. 143,145-Used in **POP**, pg. 99. 151-Last Camilla & Terry Thunder. 152-Tiger Girl begins. 158-Last Wambi; Sheena app. 13.00 40.00 90.00
I.W. Reprint #1,9: 1-r/? 9-r/#151 3.20 8.00 16.00

NOTE: *Bondage covers, negligee panels, torture, etc. are common to this series. Camilla by* ***Fran Hopper****-#70-92; by* ***Baker****-#69, 100-113, 115, 116; by* ***Lubbers****-#97-99 by* ***Tuska****-#63, 65. Kaanga by* ***John Celardo****-#80-113; by* ***Larsen****-#71, 75-79; by* ***Moreira****-#58, 60, 61, 63-70, 72-74; by* ***Tuska****-#37, 62; by* ***Whitman****-#114-163. Tabu by* ***Larsen****-#59-75, 82-92; by* ***Whitman****-#93-115. Terry Thunder by* ***Hopper****-#71, 72; by* ***Celardo****-#78, 79; by* ***Lubbers****-#80-85. Tiger Girl-r by* ***Baker****-#152, 153, 155-157, 159. Wambi by* ***Baker****-#62-67, 74.* ***Astarita*** *c-46.* ***Celardo*** *a-78;*

Jungle Comics #82 © FH

Jungle Tales #5 © MEG

Jungle War Stories #8 © DELL

	GD25	FN65	NM94

c-98-113. ***Eisner*** *c-2, 5, 6.* ***Fine*** *c-1.* ***Larsen*** *a-65, 66, 71, 72, 74, 75, 79, 83, 84, 87-90.* ***Moriera*** *c-43, 44.* ***Morisi*** *a-51.* ***Powell*** *c-7, 8.* ***Sultan*** *c-3, 4.* ***Tuska*** *c-13.* ***Whitman*** *c-132-163(most).* ***Zolnerwich*** *c-11, 12, 18-41.*

JUNGLE COMICS (Blackthorne)(Value: cover or less)

JUNGLE GIRL (See Lorna, the...)

JUNGLE GIRL (Nyoka, Jungle Girl No. 2 on)
Fall, 1942 (One shot)(No month listed)
Fawcett Publications

	GD25	FN65	NM94
1-Bondage-c; photo of Kay Aldridge who played Nyoka in movie serial app. on-c. Adaptation of the classic Republic movie serial Perils of Nyoka. 1st comic to devote entire contents to a movie serial adaptation	71.00	215.00	500.00

JUNGLE GIRLS
1989 - No. 16, 1993 (B&W)
AC Comics

	GD25	FN65	NM94
1-($1.95)-New story & "good girl" reprints		.80	2.00
2-($2.25)-New story & "good girl" reprints		.90	2.25
3-16: 3,4,10,13-16-New story & g.g. reprints. 5-9,11,12-All g.g. reprints (Baker, Powell, Lubbers, others)		1.00	2.50

JUNGLE JIM (Also see Ace Comics)
No. 11, Jan, 1949 - No. 20, Apr, 1951
Standard Comics (Best Books)

	GD25	FN65	NM94
11	5.85	17.50	35.00
12-20	4.00	10.00	20.00

JUNGLE JIM
No. 490, 8/53 - No. 1020, 8-10/59 (Painted-c)
Dell Publishing Co.

	GD25	FN65	NM94
4-Color 490(#1)	7.50	22.50	45.00
4-Color 565(#2, 6/54)	4.00	11.00	22.00
3(10-12/54)-5	4.00	10.00	20.00
6-19(1-3/59)	3.60	9.00	18.00
4-Color 1020(#20)	3.60	9.00	18.00

JUNGLE JIM
No. 5, December, 1967
King Features Syndicate

	GD25	FN65	NM94
5-Reprints Dell #5; Wood-c	2.80	7.00	14.00

JUNGLE JIM (Continued from Dell series)
No. 22, Feb, 1969 - No. 28, Feb, 1970 (#21 was an overseas edition only)
Charlton Comics

	GD25	FN65	NM94
22-Dan Flagg begins; Ditko/Wood-a	3.60	11.00	25.00
23-26: 23-Last Dan Flagg; Howard-c. 24-Jungle People begin	2.30	6.90	16.00
27,28: 27-Ditko/Howard-a. 28-Ditko-a	2.85	8.00	20.00

JUNGLE JO
Mar, 1950 - No. 6, Mar, 1951
Fox Feature Syndicate (Hero Books)

	GD25	FN65	NM94
nn-Jo-Jo blanked out, leaving Congo King; came out after Jo-Jo #29 (intended as Jo-Jo #30?)	22.00	65.00	150.00
1-Tangi begins; part Wood-a	24.00	73.00	170.00
2	19.00	57.00	130.00
3-6	17.00	52.00	120.00

JUNGLE LIL (Dorothy Lamour #2 on; also see Feature Stories Magazine)
April, 1950
Fox Feature Syndicate (Hero Books)

	GD25	FN65	NM94
1	20.00	60.00	140.00

JUNGLE TALES (Jann of the Jungle No. 8 on)
Sept, 1954 - No. 7, Sept, 1955
Atlas Comics (CSI)

	GD25	FN65	NM94
1-Jann of the Jungle	20.00	60.00	140.00
2-7: 3-Last precode (1/55)	14.00	43.00	100.00

NOTE: ***Heath*** *c-5.* ***Heck*** *a-6, 7.* ***Maneely*** *a-2; c-1, 3.* ***Shores*** *a-5-7; c-4, 6.* ***Tuska*** *a-2.*

JUNGLE TALES OF TARZAN
Dec, 1964 - No. 4, July, 1965
Charlton Comics

	GD25	FN65	NM94
1	4.00	11.00	22.00
2-4	3.60	9.00	18.00

NOTE: ***Giordano*** *c-3p.* ***Glanzman*** *a-1-3.* ***Montes/Bache*** *a-4.*

JUNGLE TERROR (See Harvey Comics Hits No. 54)

JUNGLE THRILLS (Formerly Sports Thrills; Terrors of the Jungle #17 on)
No. 16, Feb, 1952; Dec, 1953; No. 7, 1954
Star Publications

	GD25	FN65	NM94
16-Phantom Lady & Rulah story-reprint/All Top No. 15; used in **POP**, pg. 98,99; L. B. Cole-c	25.00	75.00	175.00
3-D 1(12/53, 25¢)-Came w/glasses; Jungle Lil & Jungle Jo appear; L. B. Cole-c	30.00	90.00	210.00
7-Titled 'Picture Scope Jungle Adventures;' (1954, 36 pgs, 15¢)-3-D effect c/stories; story & coloring book; Disbrow-a/script; L.B. Cole-c	27.00	81.00	190.00

JUNGLE TWINS, THE (Tono & Kono)
Apr, 1972 - No. 17, Nov, 1975; No. 18, May, 1982
Gold Key/Whitman No. 18

	GD25	FN65	NM94
1	1.00	2.50	6.00
2-5		1.40	3.50
6-18: 18-Reprints		.80	2.00

NOTE: *UFO c/story No. 13. Painted-c No. 1-17.* ***Spiegle*** *c-18.*

JUNGLE WAR STORIES (Guerrilla War No. 12 on)
July-Sept, 1962 - No. 11, Apr-June, 1965 (Painted-c)
Dell Publishing Co.

	GD25	FN65	NM94
01-384-209 (#1)	3.20	8.00	16.00
2-11	2.00	5.00	10.00

JUNIE PROM (Also see Dexter Comics)
Winter, 1947-48 - No. 7, Aug, 1949
Dearfield Publishing Co.

	GD25	FN65	NM94
1-Teen-age	9.15	27.50	55.00
2	5.00	15.00	30.00
3-7	4.00	10.00	20.00

JUNIOR CARROT PATROL (Dark Horse)(Value: cover or less)

JUNIOR COMICS (Formerly Li'l Pan; becomes Western Outlaws with #17)
No. 9, Sept, 1947 - No. 16, July, 1948
Fox Feature Syndicate

	GD25	FN65	NM94
9-Feldstein-c/a; headlights-c	44.00	133.00	310.00
10-16-Feldstein-c/a; headlights-c on all	41.00	122.00	285.00

JUNIOR FUNNIES (Formerly Tiny Tot Funnies No. 9)
No. 10, Aug, 1951 - No. 13, Feb, 1952
Harvey Publications (King Features Synd.)

	GD25	FN65	NM94
10-Partial reprints in all; Blondie, Dagwood, Daisy, Henry, Popeye, Felix, Katzenjammer Kids	2.80	7.00	14.00
11-13	2.40	6.00	12.00

JUNIOR HOPP COMICS
Feb, 1952 - No. 3, July, 1952
Stanmor Publ.

	GD25	FN65	NM94
1-Teenage humor	7.00	21.00	42.00
2,3: 3-Dave Berg-a	4.00	11.00	22.00

JUNIOR MEDICS OF AMERICA, THE
No. 1359, 1957 (15 cents)
E. R. Squire & Sons

	GD25	FN65	NM94
1359	2.40	6.00	12.00

JUNIOR MISS
Winter, 1944; No. 24, April, 1947 - No. 39, Aug, 1950

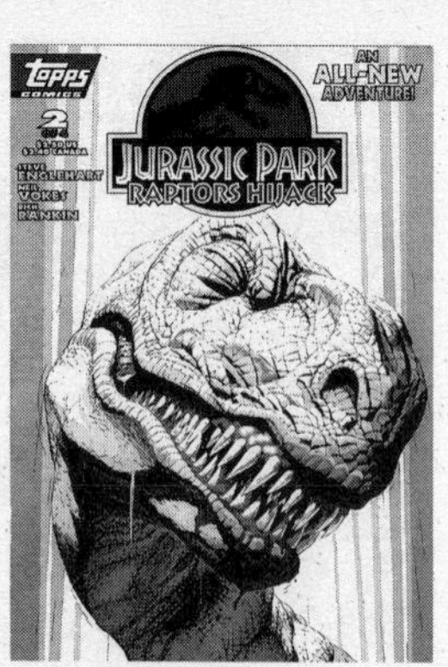

Jurassic Park: Raptors Attack #2
© Universal City Studios & Amblin Entertainment

Justice #1 © MEG

Justice Comics #8 © MEG

Timely/Marvel Comics (CnPC)

	GD25	FN65	NM94
1-Frank Sinatra & June Allyson life story	17.00	52.00	120.00
24-Formerly The Human Torch #23?	7.50	22.50	45.00
25-38: 29,31,34-Cindy-c/stories (others?)	4.35	13.00	26.00
39-Kurtzman-a	5.85	17.50	35.00

NOTE: *Painted-c 35-37. 35, 37-all romance. 36, 38-mostly teen humor.*

JUNIOR PARTNERS (Formerly Oral Roberts' True Stories)
No. 120, Aug, 1959 - V3#12, Dec, 1961
Oral Roberts Evangelistic Assn.

	GD25	FN65	NM94
120(#1)	4.20	12.50	25.00
2(9/59)	3.20	8.00	16.00
3-12(7/60)	2.00	5.00	10.00
V2#1(8/60)-5(12/60)	1.40	3.50	7.00
V3#1(1/61)-12	1.20	3.00	6.00

JUNIOR TREASURY (See Dell Junior...)

JUNIOR WOODCHUCKS LIMITED SERIES (Walt Disney's...)
July, 1991 - No. 4, Oct, 1991 ($1.50, limited series; new & reprint-a)
W. D. Publications (Disney)

	GD25	FN65	NM94
1-4: 1-The Beagle Boys app.; Barks-r			1.50

JUNIOR WOODCHUCKS (See Huey, Dewey & Louie...)

JUNKER (Fleetway)(Value: cover or less)

JURASSIC PARK
June, 1993 - No. 4, Aug, 1993 (Color, mini-series, movie adaptation)
Topps Comics

	GD25	FN65	NM94
1-($2.50)-Newsstand Edition; Kane/Perez-a in all		1.50	3.75
1-($2.95)-Collector's Ed.; polybagged w/3 cards	.90	2.30	5.50
1-Amberchrome Edition w/no price or ads			15.00
2-4-($2.50)-Newsstand Edition		1.00	2.50
2,3-($2.95)-Collector's Ed.; polybagged w/3 cards		1.20	3.00
4-($2.95)-Collector's Ed.; polybagged w/1 of 4 different action hologram trading card; Gil Kane/Perez-a		1.20	3.00
Trade paperback (1993, $9.95)-r/#1-4; bagged w/#0	1.65	4.00	10.00

JURASSIC PARK: RAPTOR
Nov, 1993 - No. 2, Dec, 1993 ($2.95, limited series)
Topps Comics

	GD25	FN65	NM94
1,2: 1-Bagged w/3 trading cards & Zorro #0; Golden c-1,2		1.20	3.00

JURASSIC PARK: RAPTORS ATTACK
Mar, 1994 - No. 4, June, 1994 ($2.50, limited series)
Topps Comics

	GD25	FN65	NM94
1-4-Michael Golden-c/frontispiece		1.00	2.50

JURASSIC PARK: RAPTORS HIJACK
July, 1994 - No. 4, Oct, 1994 ($2.50, limited series)
Topps Comics

	GD25	FN65	NM94
1-4-Michael Golden-c/frontispiece		1.00	2.50

JUSTICE
Nov, 1986 - No. 32, June, 1989
Marvel Comics Group

	GD25	FN65	NM94
1-32: 26-32-$1.50-c			1.00

JUSTICE COMICS (Formerly Wacky Duck; Tales of Justice #53 on)
No. 7, Fall/47 - No. 9, 6/48; No. 4, 8/48 - No. 52, 3/55
Marvel/Atlas Comics (NPP 7-9,4-19/CnPC 20-23/MjMC 24-38/Male 39-52

	GD25	FN65	NM94
7(#1, 1947)	16.00	48.00	110.00
8(#2)-Kurtzman-a "Giggles 'n' Grins" (3)	10.00	30.00	70.00
9(#3, 6/48)	10.00	30.00	65.00
4	10.00	30.00	60.00
5-9: 8-Anti-Wertham editorial	7.50	22.50	45.00
10-15-Photo-c	6.70	20.00	40.00
16-30	5.35	16.00	32.00
31-40,42-47,49-52-Last precode	4.70	14.00	28.00
41-Electrocution-c	10.00	30.00	65.00
48-Pakula & Tuska-a	4.70	14.00	28.00

NOTE: **Heath** *a-24.* **Maneely** *c-44, 52.* **Pakula** *a-43, 45, 48.* **Louis Ravielli** *a-39.* **Robinson** *a-22, 25, 41.* **Shores** *c-7(#1), 8(#2)?* **Tuska** *a-48.* **Wildey** *a-52.*

JUSTICE: FOUR BALANCE
Sept, 1994 - No. 4, Dec, 1994 ($1.75, limited series)
Marvel Comics

	GD25	FN65	NM94
1-4: 1-Thing & Firestar app.		.70	1.75

JUSTICE, INC. (The Avenger)
May-June, 1975 - No. 4, Nov-Dec, 1975
National Periodical Publications

	GD25	FN65	NM94
1-McWilliams-a, Kubert-c; origin			1.25
2-4: 2-4-Kirby-a(p), c-2,3p. 4-Kubert-c			1.00

NOTE: *Adapted from Kenneth Robeson novel, creator of Doc Savage.*

JUSTICE, INC. (DC)(Value: cover or less)

JUSTICE LEAGUE (...International #7-25; ...America #26 on)
May, 1987 - Present (Also see Legends #6)
DC Comics

	GD25	FN65	NM94
1-Batman, Green Lantern(Guy Gardner), Blue Beetle, Mr. Miracle, Capt. Marvel & Martian Manhunter begin	1.20	3.00	7.00
2		1.60	4.00
3-Regular cover (white background)		1.20	3.00
3-Limited cover (yellow background, Superman logo)	13.00	39.00	90.00
4-6: 4-Booster Gold joins. 5-Origin Gray Man; Batman vs. Guy Gardner; Creeper app.		.90	2.25
7-($1.25, 52 pgs.)-Capt. Marvel & Dr. Fate resign; Capt. Atom, Rocket Red join		1.10	2.75
8-10: 9,10-Millennium x-over			1.50
11-23: 16-Bruce Wayne-c/story. 18-21-Lobo app.			1.20
24-($1.50)-1st app. Justice League Europe			1.50
25-49,51-62: 31,32-Justice League Europe x-over. 58-Lobo app. 61-New team begins; swipes-c to JLA #1(10-11/60). 62-Last $1.00-c			1.00
50-($1.75, 52 pgs.)		.70	1.75
63-68,72-82: 80-Intro new Booster Gold. 82,83-Guy Gardner-c/stories			1.25
69-Doomsday tie-in; takes place between Superman: The Man of Steel #18 & Superman #74	2.10	6.40	15.00
69,70-2nd printings			1.25
70-Funeral for a Friend part 1; red 3/4 outer-c	1.50	4.00	9.00
70-Newsstand version w/o outer-c		1.60	4.00
71-Direct sale version w/black outer-c		.80	2.00
71-Newsstand version w/o outer-c			1.25
83-95: 83-Begin $1.50-c. 92-(9/94)-Zero Hour			1.50
0-(10/94)-New membership - Hawkman, Wonder Woman, Metamorpho, Flash, Nuklon, Crimson Fox, Obsidian & Fire			1.50
Annual 1 (1987)		.80	2.00
Annual 2 (1988)-Joker-c/story; Batman cameo		.80	2.00
Annual 3 (1989, $1.75, 68 pgs.)		.80	2.00
Annual 4 (1990, $2.00, 68 pgs.)		.80	2.00
Annual 5 (1991, $2.00, 68 pgs.)-Armageddon 2001 x-over		.80	2.00
Annual 5-Silver ink 2nd printing		.80	2.00
Annual 6 (1992, $2.50, 68 pgs.)		1.00	2.50
Annual 7 (1993, $2.50, 68 pgs.)-Bloodlines x-over		1.00	2.50
Annual 8 (1994, $2.95, 68 pgs.)-Elseworlds story		1.20	3.00
Special 1 (1990, $1.50, 52 pgs.)-Giffen plots			1.50
Special 2 (1991, $2.95, 52 pgs.)-Staton-a(p)		1.20	3.00
Spectacular 1 (1992, $1.50, 52 pgs.)-Intro new JLI & JLE teams; ties into JLI #61 & JLE #37			1.50
A New Beginning Trade Paperback (1989, $12.95)-r/1-7	1.85	5.50	13.00

NOTE: **Austin** *a-1i, 60i; c-1i.* **Giffen** *a-8-10; c-21p.* **Guice** *a-62i.* **Russell** *c-54i.* **Willingham** *a-30p, Annual 2.*

JUSTICE LEAGUE EUROPE (Justice League International #51 on)
April, 1989 - No. 68, 1994 (75¢/ $1.00/$1.25/$1.50)

Justice League International #19 © DC

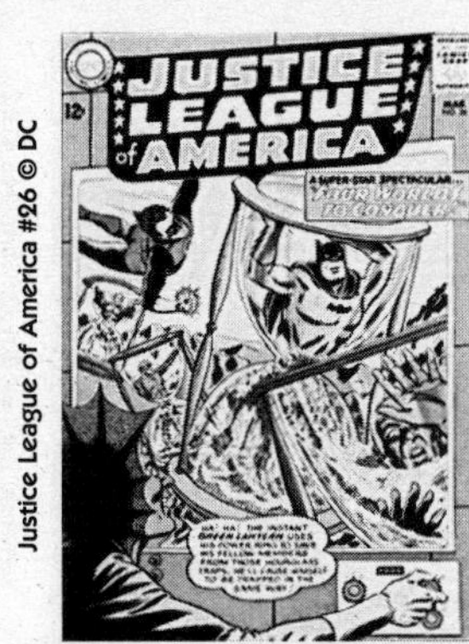

Justice League of America #26 © DC

Justice League of America #178 © DC

GD25 FN65 NM94

DC Comics
1-Giffen plots in all; breakdowns in 1-8,13-30 .80 2.00
2-49,51-57: 5-Begin $1.00-c. 7-9-Batman app. 7,8-JLA x-over. 8,9-Superman app. 12-Metal Men app. 20,21-Rogers-c/a(p). 33,34-Lobo vs. Despero. 37-New team begins; swipes-c to JLA #9; see JLA Spectacular. 38-Last $1.00-c 1.25
50-($2.50, 68 pgs.)-Battles Sonar 1.00 2.50
58-68: 58-Begin $1.50-c. 68-Zero Hour 1.50
Annual 1 (1990, $2.00, 68 pgs.)-Return of the Global Guardians; Giffen plots/breakdowns .80 2.00
Annual 2 (1991, $2.00, 68pgs.)-Armageddon 2001; Giffen-p; Golden-i; Rogers-p .80 2.00
Annual 3 (1992, $2.50, 68 pgs.)-Eclipso app. 1.00 2.50
Annual 4 (1993, $2.50, 68 pgs.)-Intro Lionheart 1.00 2.50
Annual 5 (1994, $2.95)-Elseworlds story 1.20 3.00

JUSTICE LEAGUE INTERNATIONAL (See Justice League Europe)

JUSTICE LEAGUE OF AMERICA (See Brave & the Bold #28-30, Mystery In Space #75 & Official... Index)
Oct-Nov, 1960 - No. 261, Apr, 1987 (91-99,139-157: 52 pgs.)
National Periodical Publ./DC Comics GD25 FN65 VF82 NM94
Brave and the Bold #28 (2-3/60)-Intro/1st app. Justice League of America; origin & 1st app. Snapper Carr 275.00 825.00 2062.00 3300.00
Brave and the Bold #29 (4-5/60) 190.00 570.00 1235.00 1900.00
Brave and the Bold #30 (6-7/60) 155.00 465.00 1007.00 1550.00
1-(10-11/60)-Origin & 1st app. Despero; Aquaman, Batman, Flash, Green Lantern, J'onn J'onzz, Superman & Wonder Woman continue from Brave and the Bold 250.00 750.00 1625.00 2500.00
GD25 FN65 NM94
2 80.00 240.00 640.00
3-Origin/1st app. Kanjar Ro (see Mystery in Space #75) 56.00 167.00 500.00
4-Green Arrow joins JLA 36.00 108.00 325.00
5-Origin & 1st app. Dr. Destiny 33.00 98.00 260.00
6-8,10: 6-Origin/1st app. Prof. Amos Fortune. 7-Last 10¢ issue. 10-Origin & 1st app. Felix Faust; 1st app. Time Lord 26.00 79.00 210.00
9-Origin J.L.A. (1st origin) 39.00 117.00 350.00
11-15: 12-Origin & 1st app. Dr. Light. 13-Speedy app. 14-Atom joins JLA 20.00 60.00 140.00
16-20: 17-Adam Strange flashback 16.00 49.00 115.00
21- "Crisis on Earth-One"; re-intro. of JSA in this title (8/63)(see Flash #129)(1st S.A. app. Hourman & Dr. Fate) 36.00 109.00 255.00
22- "Crisis on Earth-Two"; JSA x-over (story continued from #21) 34.00 101.00 235.00
23-28: 24-Adam Strange app. 28-Robin app. 8.00 24.00 55.00
29,30-JSA x-over. 29-1st Silver Age app. Starman; "Crisis on Earth-Three" 10.00 30.00 70.00
31-Hawkman joins JLA, Hawkgirl cameo (11/64) 7.10 21.00 50.00
32-Intro & Origin Brain Storm 4.00 12.00 33.00
33,35,36,40,41: 40-3rd S.A. Penguin app. 41-Intro & origin The Key 3.00 10.00 27.00
34-Joker-c/story 4.00 13.00 34.00
37,38-JSA x-over (1st S.A. app. Mr. Terrific #37). 37-1st S.A. app. Mr. Terrific; Batman cameo. 38-"Crisis on Earth-A" 7.00 17.00 48.00
39-Giant G-16; r/B&B #28,30 & JLA #5 8.00 20.00 70.00
42-45: 42-Metamorpho app. 43-Intro. Royal Flush Gang 2.00 7.00 17.00
46-JSA x-over; 1st S.A. app. Sandman; 3rd S.A. app. of G.A. Spectre (8/66) 7.00 21.00 55.00
47-JSA x-over 3.60 11.00 25.00
48-Giant G-29; r/JLA #2,3 & B&B #29 3.60 11.00 25.00
49-54,57,59,60 2.10 6.50 15.00
55-Intro. Earth 2 Robin (1st G.A. Robin in S.A.) 4.60 13.70 32.00
56-JLA vs. JSA (1st G.A. Wonder Woman in S.A.) 2.00 6.00 17.00
58-Giant G-41; r/JLA #6,8,1 2.00 6.00 15.00
61-63,66,68-72: 69-Wonder Woman quits. 71-Manhunter leaves. 72-Last 12¢ issue 1.60 4.00 10.00
64,65-JSA story. 64-Origin/1st app. S.A. Red Tornado (8/68) 1.00 4.00 11.00
67-Giant G-53; r/JLA #4,14,31 1.00 4.00 12.00
73-1st S.A. app. of G.A. Superman; 1st S.A. app. of Black Canary 1.00 4.00 11.00
74,77-80: 74-Black Canary joins; 1st meeting of G.A. & S.A. Superman. 78-Re-intro Vigilante (1st S.A. app?) 1.00 3.00 6.50
75-2nd app. Green Arrow in new costume (see Brave & the Bold #85) 1.00 2.00 7.50
76-Giant G-65 1.00 2.00 7.50
81-84,86-92: 82-1st S.A. app. of G.A. Batman (cameo). 83-Death of Spectre. 91,92-Begin 25¢, 52 pgs. issues, ends #99 1.00 2.00 5.50
85,93-(Giant G-77,G-89; 68 pgs.) 1.00 2.00 8.00
94-Reprints 1st Sandman story (Adv. #40) & origin/1st app. Starman (Adv. #61); Deadman x-over; N. Adams-a(4 pgs.) 2.00 7.00 20.00
95-Origin Dr. Fate & Dr. Midnight reprint (from More Fun #67, All-American #25) 1.00 3.00 7.50
96-Origin Hourman (Adv. #48); Wildcat-r 1.00 3.00 7.50
97-Origin JLA retold; Sargon, Starman-r 1.00 2.00 5.50
98,99: 98-G.A. Sargon, Starman-r. 99-G.A. Sandman, Starman, Atom-r; last 52 pg. issue 1.00 2.00 5.50
100-(8/72)-1st meeting of G.A. & S.A. W. Woman 1.00 2.00 6.50
101,102: JSA x-overs. 102-Red Tornado dies 1.00 2.00 6.00
103-106,109: 103-Phantom Stranger joins. 105-Elongated Man joins. 106-New Red Tornado joins. 109-Hawkman resigns 1.40 3.50
107,108-G.A. Uncle Sam, Black Condor, The Ray, Dollman, Phantom Lady & The Human Bomb (JSA) x-over, 1st S.A. app. 1.10 2.70 6.50
110-116: All 100 pgs. 111-Shining Knight, Green Arrow-r. 112-Crimson Avenger, Vigilante-r; origin Starman-r/Adv. #81. 115-Martian Manhunter app. 1.00 2.00 5.00
117-190: 117-Hawkman rejoins. 120,121,138-Adam Strange app. 128-Wonder Woman rejoins. 129-Death of Red Tornado. 135-137-G.A. Bulletman, Bulletgirl, Spy Smasher, Mr. Scarlet, Pinky & Ibis x-over, 1st S.A. app. 137-Superman battles G.A. Capt. Marvel. 138-Adam Strange-c by Neal Adams. 139-Adam Strange app. 139-157-(52 pgs.). 144-Origin retold; origin J'onn J'onnz. 145-Red Tornado resurrected. 147,148-Legion x-over. 158-160-(44 pgs.). 161-Zatanna joins & new costume. 171-Mr. Terrific murdered. 178-Cover similar to #1; J'onn J'onzz app. 179-Firestorm joins. 181-Green Arrow leaves 1.00 2.50
191-199: 192,193-Real origin Red Tornado. 193-1st app. All-Star Squadron as free 16 pg. insert .80 2.00
200-Anniversary issue (76pgs., $1.50); origin retold; Green Arrow rejoins 1.30 3.25
201-250: 203-Intro/origin new Royal Flush Gang. 207,208-JSA, JLA, & All-Star Squadron team-up. 219,220-True origin Black Canary. 228-Re-intro Martian Manhunter. 233-New JLA begins. 243-Aquaman leaves. 244,245-Crisis x-over. 250-Batman rejoins .80 2.00
251-260: 253-Origin Despero. 258-Death of Vibe. 258-261-Legends x-over. 260-Death of Steel 1.25
261-Last issue 1.20 3.00
Annual 1(1983) 1.10 2.75
Annual 2(1984)-Intro new J.L.A. .80 2.00
Annual 3(1985)-Crisis x-over .80 2.00

NOTE: ***Neal Adams*** *c-63, 66, 67, 70, 74, 79, 81, 82, 86-89, 91, 92, 94, 96-98, 138, 139.* ***M. Anderson*** *c-1-4, 6, 7, 10, 12-14.* ***Aparo*** *a-200.* ***Austin*** *a-200i.* ***Baily*** *a-96r.* ***Burnley*** *r-94, 98, 99.* ***Greene*** *a-46-61i, 64-73i, 110i(r).* ***Grell*** *c-117, 122.* ***Kaluta*** *c-154p.* ***Gil Kane*** *a-200.* ***Krigstein*** *a-96(r/Sensation #84).* ***Kubert*** *a-200; c-72, 73.* ***Nino*** *a-228i, 230i.* ***Orlando*** *c-151i.* ***Perez*** *a-184-186p, 192-197p, 200p; c-184p, 186, 192-195, 196p, 197p, 199, 200, 201p, 202, 203-205p, 207-209, 212-215, 217, 219, 220.* ***Reinman*** *r-97.* ***Roussos*** *a-62i.* ***Sekowsky*** *a-37, 38, 44-63p, 110-112p(r); c-46-48p, 51p.* ***Sekowsky/Anderson*** *c-5, 8, 9, 11, 15.* ***B. Smith*** *c-185i.* ***Starlin*** *c-178-180, 183, 185p.* ***Staton*** *a-244p; c-157p, 244p.* ***Toth*** *r-110.* ***Tuska*** *a-153, 228p, 241-243p. JSA x-overs-21, 22, 29, 30, 37, 38, 46, 47, 55, 56, 64, 65, 73, 74, 82, 83, 91, 92, 100, 101, 102, 107, 108, 110, 113, 115, 123, 124, 135-137, 147, 148, 159, 160, 171, 172, 183-185, 195-197, 207-209, 219, 220, 231, 232, 244.*

JUSTICE LEAGUE QUARTERLY (DC)(Value: cover or less)

JUSTICE LEAGUE TASK FORCE

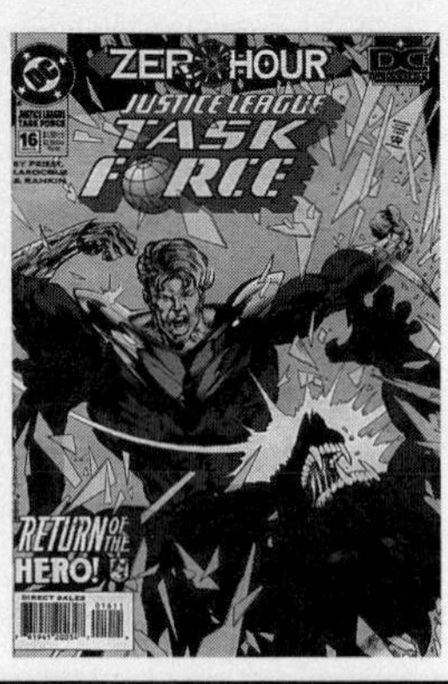

Justice League Task Force #16 © DC

Justice Traps The Guilty V11 #1 © PRIZE

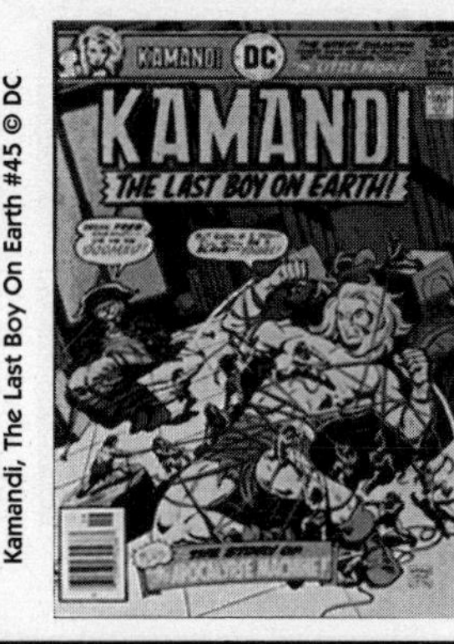

Kamandi, The Last Boy On Earth #45 © DC

GD25 FN65 NM94 GD25 FN65 NM94

June, 1993 - Present ($1.25)
DC Comics

1-7: Aquaman, Nightwing, Flash, J'onn J'onzz, & Gypsy begin. 5,6-Knight-quest tie-ins (new Batman cameo #5, 1 pg.) 1.25
8-16: 8-Begin $1.50-c. 16-(9/94)-Zero Hour 1.50
0,17-21: 0-(10/94) 1.50

JUSTICE MACHINE, THE
June, 1981 - No. 5, Nov, 1983 ($2.00, No. 1-3, Magazine size)
Noble Comics

	GD25	FN65	NM94
1-Byrne-c(p)	1.10	2.70	6.50
2-Austin-c(i)		1.80	4.50
3		1.20	3.00
4,5		1.00	2.50
Annual 1 (1/84, 68 pgs.)(published by Texas Comics); 1st app. The Elementals; Golden-c(p)		1.60	4.00

JUSTICE MACHINE (Comico)(Value: cover or less)

JUSTICE MACHINE, THE (Innovation & Millennium)(Value: cover or less)

JUSTICE MACHINE FEATURING THE ELEMENTALS (Comico)(Value: cover or less)

JUSTICE SOCIETY OF AMERICA (See Adventure #461 & All-Star #3)
April, 1991 - No. 8, Nov, 1991 ($1.00, limited series)
DC Comics

1-8: 1-Flash. 2-Black Canary. 3-Green Lantern. 4-Hawkman. 5-Flash/Hawkman. 6-Gr. Lantern/Black Canary. 7-JSA 1.00

JUSTICE SOCIETY OF AMERICA (Also see Last Days of the... Special)
Aug, 1992 - No. 10, May, 1993 ($1.25)
DC Comics

1-10 1.25

JUSTICE TRAPS THE GUILTY (Fargo Kid V11#3 on)
Oct-Nov, 1947 - V11#2(#92), Apr-May, 1958 (True FBI Cases)
Prize/Headline Publications

	GD25	FN65	NM94
V2#1-S&K-c/a; electrocution-c	34.00	103.00	240.00
2-S&K-c/a	17.00	52.00	120.00
3-5-S&K-c/a	16.00	48.00	110.00
6-S&K-c/a; Feldstein-a	17.00	52.00	120.00
7,9-S&K-c/a. 7-9-V2#1-3 in indicia; #7-9 on-c	13.50	41.00	95.00
8,10-Krigstein-a; S&K-c. 10-S&K-a	16.00	48.00	110.00
11,19-S&K-c	9.15	27.50	55.00
12,14-17,20-No S&K. 14-Severin/Elder-a (8pg.)	4.20	12.50	25.00
13-Used in **SOTI**, pg. 110-111	5.85	17.50	35.00
18-S&K-c, Elder-a	5.35	16.00	32.00
21,30-S&K-c/a	6.70	20.00	40.00
22,23,27-S&K-c	4.70	14.00	28.00
24-26,28,29,31-50	3.20	8.00	16.00
51-57,59-70: 56-Ben Oda, Joe Simon, Joe Genola, Mort Meskin, & Jack Kirby app. in police line-up on-c	2.80	7.00	14.00
58-Illo. in **SOTI**, "Treating police contemptuously" (top left); text on heroin	16.00	48.00	110.00
71-92: 76-Orlando-a	2.80	7.00	14.00

NOTE: ***Bailey*** *a-12, 13.* ***Elder*** *a-8.* ***Kirby*** *a-19p.* ***Meskin*** *a-22, 27, 63, 64; c-45, 46.* ***Robinson/Meskin*** *a-5, 19.* ***Severin*** *a-8, 11p. Photo c-12, 15-17.*

JUST KIDS
No. 283, 1932 (16 pgs.; 9-1/2x12"; paper cover)
McLoughlin Bros.

	GD25	FN65	NM94
283-Three-color text, pictures on heavy paper	11.00	32.00	75.00

JUST MARRIED
January, 1958 - No. 114, Dec, 1976
Charlton Comics

	GD25	FN65	NM94
1	4.20	12.50	25.00
2	2.80	7.00	14.00
3-10	1.60	4.00	9.00
11-30	.90	2.25	4.50
31-50	.40	1.00	2.00
51-114		.50	1.00

JUSTY (Viz)(Value: cover or less)

KA'A'NGA COMICS (...Jungle King)(See Jungle Comics)
Spring, 1949 - No. 20, Summer, 1954
Fiction House Magazines (Glen-Kel Publ. Co.)

	GD25	FN65	NM94
1-Ka'a'nga, Lord of the Jungle begins	41.00	124.00	290.00
2 (Winter, '49-'50)	20.00	60.00	140.00
3,4	15.00	45.00	105.00
5-Camilla app.	11.00	32.00	75.00
6-10: 7-Tuska-a. 9-Tabu, Wizard of the Jungle app. 10-Used in **POP**, pg. 99	10.00	30.00	60.00
11-15: 15-Camilla-r by Baker/Jungle #106	8.35	25.00	50.00
16-Sheena app.	9.15	27.50	55.00
17-20	7.50	22.50	45.00
I.W. Reprint #1,8: 1-r/#18; Kinstler-c. 8-r/#10	2.00	5.00	10.00

NOTE: ***Celardo*** *c-1.* ***Whitman*** *c-8-20(most).*

KAMANDI: AT EARTH'S END
June, 1993 - No. 6, Nov, 1993 ($1.75, limited series)
DC Comics

1-6: Elseworlds storyline .70 1.75

KAMANDI, THE LAST BOY ON EARTH (Also see Alarming Tales #1, Brave and the Bold #120 & 157 & Cancelled Comic Cavalcade)
Oct-Nov, 1972 - V7#59, Sept-Oct, 1978
National Periodical Publications/DC Comics

	GD25	FN65	NM94
1-Origin & 1st app. Kamandi	4.60	14.00	32.00
2	2.60	7.70	18.00
3-5: 4-Intro. Prince Tuftan of the Tigers	1.70	5.00	12.00
6-10	1.30	3.00	8.00
11-20	.90	2.30	5.50
21-40: 24-Last 20¢ issue. 29-Superman x-over. 31-Intro Pyra. 32-(68 pgs.)-r/origin from #1 plus one new story; 4 pg. biog. of Jack Kirby with B&W photos		1.60	4.00
41-59: 58-Karate Kid x-over from LSH. 59-(44 pgs.)-Cont'd in B&B #157; The Return of Omac back-up by Starlin-c/a(p)		1.10	2.75

NOTE: ***Ayers*** *a(p)-48-59 (most).* ***Giffen*** *a-44p, 45p.* ***Kirby*** *a-1-40p; c-1-33.* ***Kubert*** *c-34-41.* ***Nasser*** *a-45p, 46p.* ***Starlin*** *a-59p; c-57, 59p.*

KAMUI (Eclipse)(Value: cover or less)

KARATE KID (See Action, Adventure, Legion of Super-Heroes, & Superboy)
Mar-Apr, 1976 - No. 15, July-Aug, 1978 (Legion spin-off)
National Periodical Publications/DC Comics

1-Meets Iris Jacobs; Estrada/Staton-a .80 2.00
2-15: 2-Major Disaster app. 15-Continued into Kamandi #58 .70 1.80

NOTE: ***Grell*** *c-1-4, 5p, 6p, 7, 8.* ***Staton*** *a-1-9i. Legion x-over-No. 1, 2, 4, 6, 10, 12, 13. Princess Projectra x-over-#8, 9.*

KASCO KOMICS
1945; No. 2, 1949 (regular size; paper cover)
Kasko Grainfeed (Giveaway)

	GD25	FN65	NM94
1(1945)-Similar to Katy Keene; Bill Woggon-a; 28 pgs.; 6-7/8x9-7/8"	11.50	34.00	80.00
2(1949)-Woggon-c/a	10.00	30.00	70.00

KATHY
September, 1949 - No. 17, Sept, 1955
Standard Comics

	GD25	FN65	NM94
1-Teen-age	7.50	22.50	45.00
2-Schomburg-c	4.00	11.00	22.00
3-5	3.20	8.00	16.00
6-17: 17-Code approved	2.40	6.00	12.00

KATHY (The Teenage Tornado)
Oct, 1959 - No. 27, Feb, 1964

Katy Keene #57 © AP

Katzenjammer Kids #16 © STD

Ka-Zar #1 © MEG

GD25 FN65 NM94

Atlas Comics/Marvel (ZPC)

	GD25	FN65	NM94
1-Teen-age	5.85	17.50	35.00
2	3.60	9.00	18.00
3-15	2.00	5.00	10.00
16-27	1.40	3.50	7.00

KAT KARSON
No date (Reprint)
I. W. Enterprises

	GD25	FN65	NM94
1-Funny animals	1.40	3.50	7.00

KATO OF THE GREEN HORNET (Now)(Value: cover or less)

KATY AND KEN VISIT SANTA WITH MISTER WISH
1948 (16 pgs.; paper cover)
S. S. Kresge Co. (Giveaway)

	GD25	FN65	NM94
nn	4.00	10.00	20.00

KATY KEENE (Also see Kasco Komics, Laugh, Pep, Suzie, & Wilbur)
1949 - No. 4, 1951; No. 5, 3/52 - No. 62, Oct, 1961 (50-53-Adventures of...on-c)
Archie Publ./Close-Up/Radio Comics

	GD25	FN65	NM94
1-Bill Woggon-c/a begins; swipes-c to Mopsy #1	86.00	257.00	600.00
2-(1950)	43.00	129.00	300.00
3-5: 3-(1951). 4-(1951)	36.00	107.00	250.00
6-10	30.00	90.00	210.00
11,13-21: 21-Last pre-code issue (3/55)	25.00	75.00	175.00
12-(Scarce)	29.00	86.00	200.00
22-40	19.00	57.00	130.00
41-62: 54-Wedding Album plus wedding pin-up	14.00	43.00	100.00
Annual 1('54, 25¢)-All new stories; last pre-code	46.00	139.00	325.00
Annual 2-6('55-59, 25¢)-All new stories	25.00	75.00	175.00
3-D 1(1953, 25¢, large size)-Came w/glasses	38.00	115.00	265.00
Charm 1(9/58)-Woggon-c/a; new stories, cut-outs	24.00	72.00	165.00
Glamour 1(1957)-Puzzles, games, cut-outs	24.00	72.00	165.00
Spectacular 1('56)	24.00	72.00	165.00

NOTE: *Debby's Diary in #45, 47-49, 52, 57.*

KATY KEENE COMICS DIGEST MAGAZINE
1987 - No. 10, July, 1990 ($1.25/$1.35/$1.50, digest size)
Close-Up, Inc. (Archie Ent.)

	GD25	FN65	NM94
1-10			1.50

KATY KEENE FASHION BOOK MAGAZINE
1955 - No. 13, Sum, '56 - N. 23, Wint, '58-59 (nn 3-10)
Radio Comics/Archie Publications

	GD25	FN65	NM94
1-Bill Woggon-c/a	41.00	124.00	290.00
2	25.00	75.00	175.00
11-18: 18-Photo Bill Woggon	19.00	57.00	130.00
19-23	14.00	43.00	100.00

KATY KEENE HOLIDAY FUN (See Archie Giant Series Magazine No. 7, 12)

KATY KEENE PINUP PARADE
1955 - No. 15, Summer, 1961 (25¢)
Radio Comics/Archie Publications

	GD25	FN65	NM94
1-Cut-outs in all?; last pre-code issue	41.00	124.00	290.00
2-(1956)	25.00	75.00	175.00
3-5: 3-(1957)	21.00	63.00	145.00
6-10,12-14: 8-Mad parody. 10-Photo of Bill Woggon	19.00	52.00	120.00
11-Story of how comics get CCA approved, narrated by Katy	22.00	65.00	150.00
15(Rare)-Photo artist & family	41.00	124.00	290.00

KATY KEENE SPECIAL (Katy Keene #7 on; see Laugh Comics Digest)
Sept, 1983 - No. 33, 1990 (Later issues published quarterly)
Archie Enterprises

	GD25	FN65	NM94
1-33: 1-Woggon-r; new Woggon-c. 3-Woggon-r			1.00

KATZENJAMMER KIDS, THE (Also see Hans Und Fritz)
1903 (50 pgs.; 10x15-1/4"; in color)
New York American & Journal
(By Rudolph Dirks; strip 1st appeared in 1898)

	GD25	FN65	NM94
1903 (Rare)	60.00	180.00	600.00
1905-Tricks of...(10x15)	40.00	120.00	400.00
1906-Stokes-10x16", 32 pgs. in color	40.00	120.00	400.00
1910-The Komical...(10x15)	35.00	105.00	350.00
1921-Embee Dist. Co., 10x16", 20 pgs. in color	30.00	90.00	300.00

KATZENJAMMER KIDS, THE (See Captain & the Kids & Giant Comic Album)
1945-1946; Summer, 1947 - No. 27, Feb-Mar, 1954
David McKay Publ./Standard No. 12-21(Spring/'50 - 53)/Harvey No. 22, 4/53 on

	GD25	FN65	NM94
Feature Books 30	13.00	40.00	90.00
Feature Books 32,35('45),41,44('46)	11.50	34.00	80.00
Feature Book 37-Has photos & biography of Harold Knerr	13.00	40.00	90.00
1(1947)-All new stories begin	13.00	40.00	90.00
2	7.50	22.50	45.00
3-11	5.00	15.00	30.00
12-14(Standard)	4.00	12.00	24.00
15-21(Standard)	4.00	10.00	20.00
22-25,27(Harvey): 22-24-Henry app.	3.20	8.00	16.00
26-Half in 3-D	17.00	52.00	120.00

KAYO (Formerly Bullseye & Jest; becomes Carnival Comics)
No. 12, March, 1945
Harry 'A' Chesler

	GD25	FN65	NM94
12-Green Knight, Capt. Glory, Little Nemo (not by McCay)	10.00	30.00	65.00

KA-ZAR (Also see Marvel Comics #1, Savage Tales #6 & X-Men #10)
Aug, 1970 - No. 3, Mar, 1971 (Giant-Size, 68 pgs.)
Marvel Comics Group

	GD25	FN65	NM94
1-Reprints earlier Ka-Zar stories; Avengers x-over in Hercules; Daredevil, X-Men app.; hidden profanity-c	1.90	6.00	13.00
2,3-Daredevil-r. 2-r/Daredevil #12 w/Kirby layouts; Ka-Zar origin, Angel-r from X-Men by Tuska. 3-Romita & Heck-a (no Kirby)	1.50	3.80	9.00

NOTE: ***Buscema** r-2. **Colan** a-1p(r). **Kirby** c/a-1, 2. #1-Reprints X-Men #10? & Daredevil #13?*

KA-ZAR
Jan, 1974 - No. 20, Feb, 1977 (Regular Size)
Marvel Comics Group

	GD25	FN65	NM94
1		1.10	2.75
2-20		.80	2.00

NOTE: ***Alcala** a-6i, 8i. **Brunner** c-4. **J. Buscema** a-6-10p; c-1, 5, 7. **Heath** a-12. **G. Kane** c(p)-3, 5, 8-11, 15, 20. **Kirby** c-12p. **Reinman** a-1p.*

KA-ZAR THE SAVAGE (See Marvel Fanfare)
Apr, 1981 - No. 34, Oct, 1984 (Regular size) (Mando paper #10 on)
Marvel Comics Group

	GD25	FN65	NM94
1-34: 11-Origin Zabu. 12-Two versions: With & without panel missing (1600 printed with panel). 20-Kraven the Hunter-c/story (also apps. in #21). 21-23,25,26-Spider-Man app. 26-Photo-c. 29-Double size; Ka-Zar & Shanna wed			1.00

NOTE: ***B. Anderson** a-1-15p, 18, 19; c-1-17, 18p, 20(back). **G. Kane** a(back-up)-11, 12, 14.*

KEEN DETECTIVE FUNNIES (Formerly Detective Picture Stories?)
No. 8, July, 1938 - No. 24, Sept, 1940
Centaur Publications

	GD25	FN65	NM94
V1#8-The Clock continues-r/Funny Picture Stories #1; Roy Crane-a (1st?)	129.00	386.00	900.00
9-Tex Martin by Eisner; The Gang Buster app.	61.00	182.00	425.00
10,11: 11-Dean Denton story (begins?)	55.00	165.00	385.00
V2#1,2-The Eye Sees by Frank Thomas begins; ends #23(Not in V2#3&5). 2-Jack Cole-a	49.00	146.00	340.00
3-6,9-11: 3-TNT Todd begins. 4-Gabby Flynn begins. 5,6-Dean Denton story	49.00	146.00	340.00
7-The Masked Marvel by Ben Thompson begins (7/39, 1st app.)	87.00	261.00	610.00

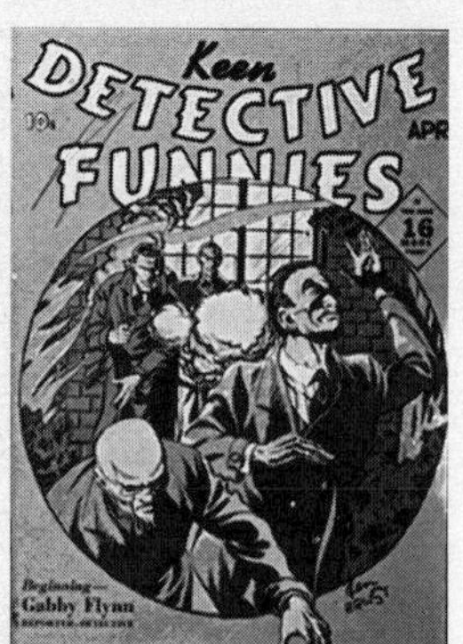

Keen Detective Funnies V2 #4 © CEN

Kerry Drake #2 © ARGO

Key Ring Comics #1 © DELL

GD25 FN65 NM94

8-Nudist ranch panel w/four girls 52.00 156.00 365.00
12(12/39)-Origin The Eye Sees by Frank Thomas; death of Masked Marvel's sidekick ZL 61.00 182.00 425.00
V3#1,2 52.00 156.00 365.00
18,19,21,22: 18-Bondage/torture-c 52.00 156.00 365.00
20-Classic Eye Sees-c by Thomas 66.00 200.00 465.00
23,24: 23-Air Man begins (intro). 23,24-Air Man-c 61.00 182.00 425.00

NOTE: ***Burgos*** *a-V2#2.* ***Jack Cole*** *a-V2#2.* ***Eisner*** *a-10, V2#6r.* ***Ken Ernst*** *a-V2#4-7, 9, 10, 19, 21; c-V2#4.* ***Everett*** *a-V2#6, 7, 9, 11, 12, 20.* ***Guardineer*** *a-V2#5, 66.* ***Gustavson*** *a-V2#4-6.* ***Simon*** *c-V3#1.* ***Thompson*** *c-V2#7, 9, 10, 22.*

KEEN KOMICS
V2#1, May, 1939 - V2#3, Nov, 1939
Centaur Publications

V2#1(Large size)-Dan Hastings (s/f), The Big Top, Bob Phantom the Magician, The Mad Goddess app. 71.00 215.00 500.00
V2#2(Reg. size)-The Forbidden Idol of Machu Picchu; Cut Carson by Burgos begins 44.00 133.00 310.00
V2#3-Saddle Sniffl by Jack Cole, Circus Pays, Kings Revenge app. 44.00 133.00 310.00

NOTE: ***Binder*** *a-V2#2.* ***Burgos*** *a-V2#2, 3.* ***Ken Ernst*** *a-V2#3.* ***Gustavson*** *a-V2#2.* ***Jack Cole*** *a-V2#3.*

KEEN TEENS (Girls magazine)
1945 - No. 6, Aug-Sept, 1947
Life's Romances Publ./Leader/Magazine Enterprises

nn (#1)-14 pgs. Claire Voyant (cont'd. in other nn issue) movie photos, Dotty Dripple, Gertie O'Grady & Sissy; Van Johnson, Frank Sinatra photo-c 17.00 52.00 120.00
nn (#2, 1946)-16 pgs. Claire Voyant & 16 pgs. movie photos 17.00 52.00 120.00
3-6: 4-Glenn Ford photo-c. 5-Perry Como-c 5.85 17.50 35.00

KEEPING UP WITH THE JONESES
1920 - No. 2, 1921 (52 pgs.; 9-1/4x9-1/4"; B&W daily strip reprints)
Cupples & Leon Co.

1,2-By Pop Momand 19.00 57.00 130.00

KELLYS, THE (Formerly Rusty Comics; Spy Cases No. 26 on)
No. 23, Jan, 1950 - No. 25, June, 1950 (52 pgs.)
Marvel Comics (HPC)

23-Teenage 10.00 30.00 60.00
24,25: 24-Margie app. 5.85 17.50 35.00

KELVIN MACE (Vortex)(Value: cover or less)

KEN MAYNARD WESTERN (Movie star)(See Wow Comics, 1936)
Sept, 1950 - No. 8, Feb, 1952 (All 36 pgs; photo front/back-c)
Fawcett Publications

1-Ken Maynard & his horse Tarzan begin 46.00 137.00 320.00
2 29.00 88.00 205.00
3-8: 6-Atomic bomb explosion panel 23.00 70.00 160.00

KEN SHANNON (Becomes Gabby #11 on) (Also see Police Comics #103)
Oct, 1951 - No. 10, Apr, 1953 (A private eye)
Quality Comics Group

1-Crandall-a 22.00 65.00 150.00
2-Crandall c/a(2) 17.00 52.00 120.00
3-5-Crandall-a. 3-Horror-c 12.00 36.00 85.00
6-Crandall-c/a; "The Weird Vampire Mob"-c/s 13.00 40.00 90.00
7-Crandall-a 10.00 30.00 70.00
8,9: 8-Opium den drug use story 10.00 30.00 60.00
10-Crandall-c 10.00 30.00 70.00

NOTE: ***Crandall/Cuidera*** *c-1-10.* ***Jack Cole*** *a-1-9. #1-15 published after title change to Gabby.*

KEN STUART
Jan, 1949 (Sea Adventures)
Publication Enterprises

1-Frank Borth-c/a 6.70 20.00 40.00

KENT BLAKE OF THE SECRET SERVICE (Spy)
May, 1951 - No. 14, July, 1953
Marvel/Atlas Comics(20CC)

1-Injury to eye, bondage, torture; Brodsky-c 11.50 34.00 80.00
2-Drug use w/hypo scenes; Brodsky-c 8.35 25.00 50.00
3-14: 8-R.Q. Sale-a (2 pgs.) 5.35 16.00 32.00

NOTE: ***Heath*** *c-5, 7, 8.* ***Infantino*** *c-12.* ***Maneely*** *c-3.* ***Sinnott*** *a-2(3).* ***Tuska*** *a-8(3pg.).*

KERRY DRAKE
Jan, 1956 - No. 2, March, 1956
Argo

1,2-Newspaper-r 5.00 15.00 30.00

KERRY DRAKE DETECTIVE CASES (...Racket Buster No. 32,33)
(Also see Chamber of Clues & Green Hornet Comics #42-47)
1944 - No. 5, 1944; No. 6, Jan, 1948 - No. 33, Aug, 1952
Life's Romances/Com/Magazine Ent. No.1-5/Harvey No.6 on

nn(1944)(A-1 Comics)(slightly over-size) 19.00 57.00 130.00
2 11.50 34.00 80.00
3-5(1944) 10.00 30.00 60.00
6,8(1948): Lady Crime by Powell. 8-Bondage-c 5.85 17.50 35.00
7-Kubert-a; biog of Andriola (artist) 7.00 21.00 42.00
9,10-Two-part marijuana story; Kerry smokes marijuana in #10 10.00 30.00 60.00
11-15 5.00 15.00 30.00
16-33 4.00 12.00 24.00
...in the Case of the Sleeping City-(1951-Publishers Synd.)-16 pg. giveaway for armed forces; paper cover 4.00 11.00 22.00

NOTE: ***Andiola*** *c-6-9.* ***Berg*** *a-5.* ***Powell*** *a-10-23, 28, 29.*

KEWPIES
Spring, 1949
Will Eisner Publications

1-Feiffer-a; Kewpie Doll ad on back cover 35.00 105.00 245.00

KEY COMICS
Jan, 1944 - No. 5, Aug, 1946
Consolidated Magazines

1-The Key, Will-O-The-Wisp begin 23.00 70.00 160.00
2 (3/44) 11.50 34.00 80.00
3,4: 4-(5/46)-Origin John Quincy The Atom (begins); Walter Johnson c-3-5 10.00 30.00 65.00
5-4pg. Faust Opera adaptation; Kiefer-a; back-c advertises "Masterpieces Illustrated" by Lloyd Jacquet after he left Classic Comics (no copies of Masterpieces Illustrated known) 12.00 36.00 85.00

KEY COMICS
1951 - 1956 (32 pgs.) (Giveaway)
Key Clothing Co./Peterson Clothing
Contains a comic from different publishers bound with new cover. Cover changed each year. Many combinations possible. Distributed in Nebraska, Iowa, & Kansas. Contents would determine price, 40-60 percent of original.

KEY RING COMICS
1941 (16 pgs.; two colors) (sold 5 for 10¢)
Dell Publishing Co.

1-Sky Hawk 3.00 7.50 15.00
1-Viking Carter 3.00 7.50 15.00
1-Features Sleepy Samson 3.20 8.00 16.00
1-Origin Greg Gilday-r/War Comics #2 3.20 8.00 16.00
1-Radior(Super hero) 2.80 7.00 14.00

NOTE: *Each book has two holes in spine to put in binder.*

KICKERS, INC. (Marvel)(Value: cover or less)

KID CARROTS
September, 1953
St. John Publishing Co.

1-Funny animal 4.20 12.50 25.00

KID COLT OUTLAW (Kid Colt #1-4; ...Outlaw #5-on)(Also see All Western

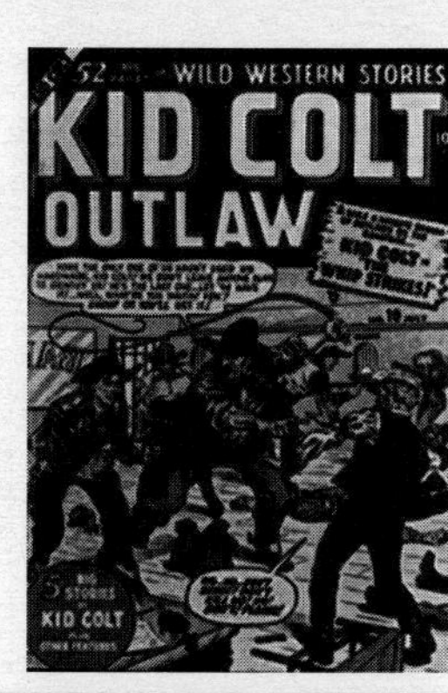

Kid Colt Outlaw #10 © MEG

Kid Eternity #16 © DC

Kid Montana V2 #21 © CC

GD25 FN65 NM94

Winners, Best Western, Black Rider, Giant-Size..., Two-Gun Kid, Two-Gun Western, Western Winners, Wild Western, Wisco)
8/48 - No. 139, 3/68; No. 140, 11/69 - No. 229, 4/79
Marvel Comics(LCC) 1-16; Atlas(LMC) 17-102; Marvel 103-on

1-Kid Colt & his horse Steel begin; Two-Gun Kid app. 68.00 205.00 475.00
2 31.00 95.00 220.00
3-5: 4-Anti-Wertham editorial; Tex Taylor app. 5-Blaze Carson app. 24.00 72.00 165.00
6-8: 6-Tex Taylor app; 7-Nimo the Lion begins, ends #10 16.00 48.00 110.00
9,10 (52 pgs.) 16.50 50.00 115.00
11-Origin 19.00 58.00 135.00
12-20 11.50 34.00 80.00
21-32 10.00 30.00 60.00
33-45: Black Rider in all 8.35 25.00 50.00
46,47,49,50 7.50 22.50 45.00
48-Kubert-a 8.35 25.00 50.00
51-53,55,56 5.85 17.50 35.00
54-Williamson/Maneely-c 6.70 20.00 40.00
57-60,66: 4-pg. Williamson-a in all. 59-Reprints Rawhide Kid #79; Colan text illo 7.50 22.50 45.00
61-63,67-78,80-86: 86-Kirby-a(r) 4.20 12.50 25.00
64,65-Crandall-a 5.35 16.00 32.00
79,87: 79-Origin retold. 87-Davis-a(r) 5.00 15.00 30.00
88,89-Williamson-a in both (4 pgs.). 89-Redrawn Matt Slade #2 5.85 17.50 35.00
90-99,101: 101-Last 10¢ issue 3.20 8.00 16.00
100 4.00 10.00 22.00
101-120 2.40 6.00 12.00
121-140: 121-Rawhide Kid x-over. 125-Two-Gun Kid x-over. 130-132-68 pg. issues with one new story each. 130-Origin. 140-Reprints begin 1.30 3.25 8.00
141-160: 156-Giant; reprints (later issues all-r) 1.60 4.00
161-229: 170-Origin retold. 229-Rawhide Kid-r .80 2.00
...Album (no date; 1950's; Atlas Comics)-132 pgs.; random binding, cardboard cover, B&W stories; contents can vary (Rare) 68.00 205.00 475.00

NOTE: ***Ayers*** *a-many.* ***Colan*** *a-52, 53; c(p)-223, 228, 229.* ***Crandall*** *a-140r, 167r.* ***Everett*** *a-90, 137i, 225i(r).* ***Heath*** *a-8(2); c-34, 35, 39, 44, 46, 48, 49, 57, 64.* ***Jack Keller*** *a-25(2), 26-68(3-4), 78, 94p, 98, 99, 108, 110, 132.* ***Kirby*** *a-86r, 93, 96, 119, 176(part); c-87, 92-95, 97, 99-112, 114-117, 121-123, 197r; w/****Ditko*** *c-89.* ***Maneely*** *a-12, 68, 81; c-17, 19, 40-43, 47, 52, 53, 62, 65, 68, 78, 81.* ***Morrow*** *a-173r, 216r.* ***Rico*** *a-13, 18.* ***Severin*** *c-58, 59.* ***Shores*** *a-39, 41-43; c-1-10(most), 24.* ***Sutton*** *a-137p, 225p(r).* ***Wildey*** *a-47, 54, 82.* ***Williamson*** *r-147, 170, 172, 216.* ***Woodbridge*** *a-64, 81. Black Rider in #33-45, 74, 86. Iron Mask in #110, 114, 121, 127. Sam Hawk in #84, 101, 111, 121, 146, 174, 181, 188.*

KID COWBOY (Also see Approved Comics #4 & Boy Cowboy)
1950 - No. 14, 1954 (Painted covers #1-10, 14)
Ziff-Davis Publ./St. John (Approved Comics)

1-Lucy Belle & Red Feather begin 10.00 30.00 60.00
2-Maneely-c 5.85 17.50 35.00
3-14: 5-Berg-a. 14-Code approved 4.70 14.00 28.00

KIDDIE KAPERS
1945?(nd); Oct, 1957; 1963 - 1964
Kiddie Kapers Co., 1945/Decker Publ. (Red Top-Farrell)

1(nd, 1945-46?, 36 pgs.)-Infinity-c; funny animal 5.70 17.00 34.00
1(10/57)(Decker)-Little Bit reprints from Kiddie Karnival 3.20 8.00 16.00
Super Reprint #7, 10('63), 12, 14('63), 15,17('64), 18('64) 1.00 2.50 5.00

KIDDIE KARNIVAL
1952 (25¢, 100 pgs.) (One Shot)
Ziff-Davis Publ. Co. (Approved Comics)

nn-Rebound Little Bit #1,2; painted-c 27.00 80.00 185.00

KID ETERNITY (Becomes Buccaneers) (See Hit Comics)
Spring, 1946 - No. 18, Nov, 1949
Quality Comics Group

1 50.00 150.00 350.00
2 25.00 75.00 175.00
3-Mac Raboy-a 27.00 81.00 190.00
4-10 14.00 43.00 100.00
11-18 10.00 30.00 70.00

KID ETERNITY
1991 - No. 3, Nov, 1991 ($4.95, mini-series)
DC Comics

1-3: Grant Morrison scripts 1.00 2.00 5.00

KID ETERNITY
May, 1993 - Present ($1.95, mature readers)
DC Comics (Vertigo)

1-21: 1-Gold ink-c. 6-Photo-c .80 2.00

KID FROM DODGE CITY, THE
July, 1957 - No. 2, Sept, 1957
Atlas Comics (MMC)

1-Don Heck-c 6.70 20.00 40.00
2-Everett-c 4.00 12.00 24.00

KID FROM TEXAS, THE (A Texas Ranger)
June, 1957 - No. 2, Aug, 1957
Atlas Comics (CSI)

1-Powell-a; Severin-c 7.50 22.50 45.00
2 4.20 12.50 25.00

KID KOKO
1958
I. W. Enterprises

Reprint #1,2-(r/M.E.'s Koko & Kola #4, 1947) 1.20 3.00 6.00

KID KOMICS (Kid Movie Komics No. 11)
Feb, 1943 - No. 10, Spring, 1946
Timely Comics (USA 1,2/FCI 3-10)

1-Origin Captain Wonder & sidekick Tim Mullrooney, & Subbie; intro the Sea-Going Lad, Pinto Pete, & Trixie Trouble; Knuckles & Whitewash Jones (from Young Allies) app.; Wolverton-a (7 pgs.) 257.00 771.00 1800.00
2-The Young Allies, Red Hawk, & Tommy Tyme begin; last Captain Wonder & Subbie 107.00 321.00 750.00
3-The Vision, Daredevils & Red Hawk app. 75.00 225.00 525.00
4-The Destroyer begins; Sub-Mariner app.; Red Hawk & Tommy Tyme end 68.00 205.00 475.00
5,6: 5-Tommy Tyme begins, ends #10 55.00 165.00 385.00
7-10: 7,10-The Whizzer app. Destroyer not in #7,8. 10-Last Destroyer, Young Allies & Whizzer 52.00 156.00 365.00

NOTE: ***Brodsky*** *c-5.* ***Schomburg*** *c-2-4, 6-10.* ***Shores*** *c-1. Captain Wonder c-1, 2. The Young Allies c-3-10.*

KID MONTANA (Formerly Davy Crockett Frontier Fighter; The Gunfighters No. 51 on)
V2#9, Nov, 1957 - No. 50, Mar, 1965
Charlton Comics

V2#9 6.00 18.00 36.00
10 3.60 9.00 18.00
11,12,14-20 2.40 6.00 14.00
13-Williamson-a 4.00 10.00 20.00
21-35 1.40 3.50 7.00
36-50 .80 2.00 4.00

NOTE: *Title change to Montana Kid on cover only #44 & 45; remained Kid Montana on inside.*

KID MOVIE KOMICS (Formerly Kid Komics; Rusty Comics #12 on)
No. 11, Summer, 1946
Timely Comics

11-Silly Seal & Ziggy Pig; 2 pgs. Kurtzman "Hey Look" plus 6 pg. "Pigtales" story 18.00 54.00 125.00

KIDNAPPED (See 4-Color No. 1101 & Movie Comics)

Kid 'n Play #1 ©

The Kindred #4 © Jim Lee

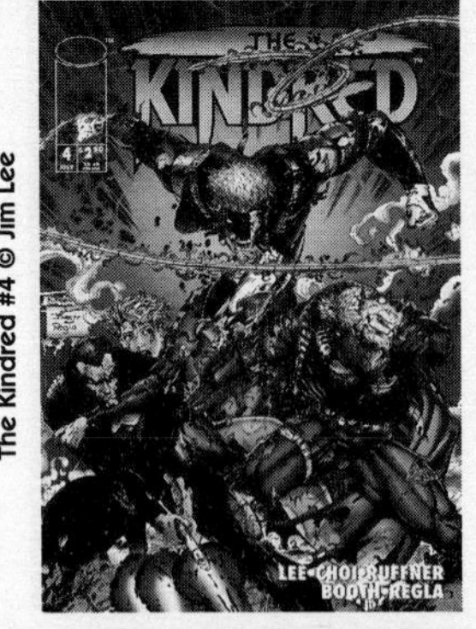

King Comics #17 © DMP

	GD25	FN65	NM94

KIDNAP RACKET (See Harvey Comics Hits No. 57)

KID 'N PLAY (Marvel)(Value: cover or less)

KID SLADE GUNFIGHTER (Formerly Matt Slade...)
No. 5, Jan, 1957 - No. 8, July, 1957
Atlas Comics (SPI)

	GD25	FN65	NM94
5-Maneely, Roth, Severin-a in all; Maneely-c	8.35	25.00	50.00
6,8-Severin-c	4.00	12.00	24.00
7-Williamson/Mayo-a, 4 pgs.	7.00	21.00	42.00

KID ZOO COMICS
July, 1948 (52 pgs.)
Street & Smith Publications

	GD25	FN65	NM94
1-Funny Animal	19.00	57.00	130.00

KILLER (...Tales By Timothy Truman)
March, 1985 ($1.75, one-shot, color, Baxter paper)
Eclipse Comics

	GD25	FN65	NM94
1-Timothy Truman-c/a		.70	1.75

KILLERS, THE
1947 - No. 2, 1948 (No month)
Magazine Enterprises

	GD25	FN65	NM94
1-Mr. Zin, the Hatchet Killer; mentioned in **SOTI**, pgs. 179,180; used by N.Y. Legis. Comm.; L. B. Cole-c	55.00	165.00	385.00
2-(Scarce)-Hashish smoking story; "Dying, Dying, Dead" drug story; Whitney, Ingels-a; Whitney hanging-c	50.00	150.00	350.00

KILLING JOKE, THE (See Batman: The Killing Joke)

KILLPOWER: THE EARLY YEARS
Sept, 1993 - No. 4, Dec, 1993 ($1.75, mini-series)
Marvel Comics UK

	GD25	FN65	NM94
1-($2.95)-Foil embossed-c		1.20	3.00
2-4: 2-Genetix app. 3-Punisher app.		.70	1.75

KILROYS, THE
June-July, 1947 - No. 54, June-July, 1955
B&I Publ. Co. No. 1-19/American Comics Group

	GD25	FN65	NM94
1	17.00	52.00	120.00
2	10.00	30.00	60.00
3-5: 5-Gross-a	7.50	22.50	45.00
6-10: 8-Milt Gross's Moronica	5.35	16.00	32.00
11-20: 14-Gross-a	4.70	14.00	28.00
21-30	4.00	10.00	20.00
31-47,50-54	3.60	9.00	18.00
48,49-(3-D effect-c/stories)	14.00	43.00	100.00

KINDRED, THE
Mar, 1994 - Present ($1.95)
Image Comics

	GD25	FN65	NM94
1-($2.50)-Bound-in trading card; Booth-c/a		1.00	2.50
2,3-($1.95)		.80	2.00
2-Variant-c	2.10	6.40	15.00
3-Alternate-c by Portacio, see Deathblow #5	1.00	2.00	5.00
4-($2.50)		1.00	2.50

NOTE: *The first four issues contain coupons redeemable for a Jim Lee Grifter/Backlash print.*

KING ARTHUR AND THE KNIGHTS OF JUSTICE
Dec, 1993 - No. 3, Feb, 1994 ($1.25, mini-series)
Marvel Comics UK

	GD25	FN65	NM94
1-3: TV adaptation			1.25

KING CLASSICS
1977 (85¢ each) (36 pgs., cardboard covers)
King Features (Printed in Spain for U.S. distr.)

	GD25	FN65	NM94
1-Connecticut Yankee, 2-Last of the Mohicans, 3-Moby Dick, 4-Robin Hood, 5-Swiss Family Robinson, 6-Robinson Crusoe, 7-Treasure Island, 8-20,000 Leagues, 9-Christmas Carol, 10-Huck Finn, 11-Around the World in 80 Days, 12-Davy Crockett, 13-Don Quixote, 14-Gold Bug, 15-Ivanhoe, 16-Three Musketeers, 17-Baron Munchausen, 18-Alice in Wonderland, 19-Black Arrow, 20-Five Weeks in a Balloon, 21-Great Expectations, 22-Gulliver's Travels, 23-Prince & Pauper, 24-Lawrence of Arabia (Originals, 1977-78) each....	1.30	3.25	8.00
Reprints, 1979; HRN-24)	1.00	2.50	6.00

NOTE: *The first eight issues were not numbered. Issues No. 25-32 were advertised but not published. The 1977 originals have HRN 32a; the 1978 originals have HRN 32b.*

KING COLT (See 4-Color No. 651)

KING COMICS (Strip reprints)
4/36 - No. 155, 11-12/49; No. 156, Spr/50 - No. 159, 2/52 (Winter on-c)
David McKay Publications/Standard #156-on

	GD25	FN65	VF82
1-1st app. Flash Gordon by Alex Raymond; Brick Bradford (1st app.), Popeye, Henry (1st app.) & Mandrake the Magician (1st app.) begin; Popeye-c begin	800.00	2400.00	4800.00

(Estimated up to 25 total copies exist, none in NM/Mint)

	GD25	FN65	NM94
2	214.00	643.00	1500.00
3	143.00	430.00	1000.00
4	114.00	343.00	800.00
5	86.00	257.00	600.00
6-10: 9-X-Mas-c	57.00	171.00	400.00
11-20	44.00	133.00	310.00
21-30: 21-X-Mas-c	34.00	103.00	240.00
31-40: 33-Last Segar Popeye	29.00	86.00	200.00
41-50: 46-Little Lulu, Alvin & Tubby app. as text illos by Marge Buell. 50-The Lone Ranger begins	27.00	80.00	185.00
51-60: 52-Barney Baxter begins?	19.00	57.00	130.00
61-The Phantom begins	16.50	50.00	115.00
62-80: 76-Flag-c. 79-Blondie begins	13.50	41.00	95.00
81-99	11.50	34.00	80.00
100	14.00	43.00	100.00
101-114: 114-Last Raymond issue (1 pg.); Flash Gordon by Austin Briggs begins, ends #155	10.00	30.00	70.00
115-145: 117-Phantom origin retold	9.15	27.50	55.00
146,147-Prince Valiant in both	6.70	20.00	40.00
148-155: 155-Flash Gordon ends (11-12/49)	6.70	20.00	40.00
156-159: 156-New logo begins (Standard)	5.85	17.50	35.00

NOTE: *Marge Buell text illos in No. 24-46 at least.*

KING CONAN (Conan The King No. 20 on)
March, 1980 - No. 19, Nov, 1983 (52 pgs.)
Marvel Comics Group

	GD25	FN65	NM94
1		1.00	2.50
2-19: 4-Death of Thoth Amon. 7-1st Paul Smith-a, 1 pg. pin-up (9/81)		.70	1.75

NOTE: ***J. Buscema** a-1-9p, 17p; c(p)-1-5, 7-9, 14, 17. **Kaluta** c-19. **Nebres** a-17i, 18, 19i. **Severin** c-18. **Simonson** c-6.*

KING KONG (See Movie Comics)

KING LEONARDO & HIS SHORT SUBJECTS (TV)
Nov-Jan, 1961-62 - No. 4, Sept, 1963
Dell Publishing Co./Gold Key

	GD25	FN65	NM94
4-Color 1242,1278	14.00	43.00	100.00
01390-207(5-7/62)(Dell)	11.00	32.00	75.00
1 (10/62)	11.00	32.00	75.00
2-4	9.15	27.50	55.00

KING LOUIE & MOWGLI (See Jungle Book under Movie Comics)
May, 1968 (Disney)
Gold Key

	GD25	FN65	NM94
1 (#10223-805)-Characters from Jungle Book	2.15	6.50	15.00

KING OF DIAMONDS (TV)
July-Sept, 1962
Dell Publishing Co.

	GD25	FN65	NM94
01-391-209-Photo-c	4.20	12.50	25.00

KING OF KINGS (See 4-Color No. 1236)

KING OF THE BAD MEN OF DEADWOOD
1950 (See Wild Bill Hickok #16)

King Of THe Royal Mounted #21 © DELL

Kit Carson #7 © AVON

Kitty Pride & Wolverine #1 © MEG

	GD25	FN65	NM94

Avon Periodicals
nn-Kinstler-c; Kamen/Feldstein-r/Cowpuncher #2 11.50 34.00 80.00

KING OF THE ROYAL MOUNTED (See Famous Feature Stories, Feature Books #1, Large Feature Comic #9, King Comics, Red Ryder #3 & Super Book #2, 6)

KING OF THE ROYAL MOUNTED (Zane Grey's...)
No. 207, Dec, 1948 - No. 935, Sept-Nov, 1958
Dell Publishing Co.

	GD25	FN65	NM94
4-Color 207(#1, 12/48)	17.00	52.00	120.00
4-Color 265,283	10.00	30.00	65.00
4-Color 310,340	7.50	22.50	45.00
4-Color 363,384	6.70	20.00	40.00
8(6-8/52)-10	6.70	20.00	40.00
11-20	5.35	16.00	32.00
21-28(3-5/58)	4.70	14.00	28.00
4-Color 935(9-11/58)	4.70	14.00	28.00

NOTE: *4-Color No. 207, 265, 283, 310, 340, 363, 384 are all newspaper reprints with **Jim Gary** art. No. 8 on are all Dell originals. Painted c-No. 9-on.*

KING RICHARD & THE CRUSADERS (See 4-Color No. 588)

KINGS OF THE NIGHT (Dark Horse)(Value: cover or less)

KING SOLOMON'S MINES
1951 (Movie)
Avon Periodicals

	GD25	FN65	NM94
nn(#1 on 1st page)	25.00	75.00	175.00

KISS (See Crazy Magazine, Howard the Duck #12, 13, Marvel Comics Super Special #1, 5, Rock Fantasy Comics #10 & Rock N' Roll Comics #9)

KISSYFUR (TV) (DC)(Value: cover or less)

KIT CARSON (Formerly All True Detective Cases No. 4; Fighting Davy Crockett No. 9; see Blazing Sixguns & Frontier Fighters)
1950; No. 2, 8/51 - No. 3, 12/51; No. 5, 11-12/54 - No. 8, 9/55 (No #4)
Avon Periodicals

	GD25	FN65	NM94
nn(#1) (1950)- "...Indian Scout"	10.00	30.00	65.00
2(8/51)	6.70	20.00	40.00
3(12/51)- "...Fights the Comanche Raiders"	5.35	16.00	32.00
5-6,8(11-12/54-9/55): 5-Formerly All True Detective Cases (last pre-code); titled "...and the Trail of Doom"	5.00	15.00	30.00
7-McCann-a?	5.35	16.00	32.00
I.W. Reprint #10('63)-r/Kit Carson #1; Severin-c	1.80	4.50	9.00

NOTE: ***Kinstler** c-1-3, 5-8.*

KIT CARSON & THE BLACKFEET WARRIORS
1953
Realistic

	GD25	FN65	NM94
nn-Reprint; Kinstler-c	7.50	22.50	45.00

KITE FUN BOOK
1954 - 1981 (16pgs, 5x7-1/4", soft-c)
Pacific, Gas & Electric/Sou. California Edison/Florida Power & Light

	GD25	FN65	NM94
1954-Donald Duck Tells About Kites-Fla. Power, S.C.E. & version with label issues-Barks pencils-8 pgs.; inks-7 pgs. (Rare)	400.00	1200.00	2800.00
1954-Donald Duck Tells About Kites-P.G.&E. issue -7th page redrawn changing middle 3 panels to show P.G.&E. in story line; (All barks; last page Barks pencils only) Scarce	300.00	900.00	2100.00
1954-Pinocchio Learns About Kites (Disney)	39.00	116.00	270.00
1955-Brer Rabbit in "A Kite Tail" (Disney)	29.00	86.00	200.00
1956-Woody Woodpecker (Lantz)	11.00	32.00	75.00
1957-?			
1958-Tom And Jerry (M.G.M.)	6.70	20.00	45.00
1960-Porky Pig (Warner Bros.)	5.35	16.00	32.00
1960-Bugs Bunny (Warner Bros.)	5.35	16.00	32.00
1961-Huckleberry Hound (Hanna-Barbera)	6.70	20.00	40.00
1962-Yogi Bear (Hanna-Barbera)	4.70	14.00	28.00
1963-Rocky and Bullwinkle (TV)(Jay Ward)	11.00	32.00	75.00
1963-Top Cat (TV)(Hanna-Barbera)	5.00	15.00	30.00
1964-Magilla Gorilla (TV)(Hanna-Barbera)	4.20	12.50	25.00
1965-Jinks, Pixie and Dixie (TV)(Hanna-Barbera)	3.60	9.00	18.00
1965-Tweety and Sylvester (Warner); S.C.E. version with Reddy Kilowatt app.	1.80	4.50	9.00
1966-Secret Squirrel (Hanna-Barbera); S.C.E. version with Reddy Kilowatt app.	8.00	24.00	55.00
1967-Beep! Beep! The Road Runner (TV)(Warner)	2.60	7.70	18.00
1968-Bugs Bunny (Warner Bros.)	2.30	6.90	16.00
1969-Dastardly and Muttley (TV)(Hanna-Barbera)	3.60	11.00	25.00
1970-Rocky and Bullwinkle (TV)(Jay Ward)	8.00	24.00	55.00
1971-Beep! Beep! The Road Runner (TV)(Warner)	1.70	5.00	12.00
1972-The Pink Panther (TV)	1.30	3.25	8.00
1973-Lassie (TV)	3.10	9.00	22.00
1974-Underdog (TV)	2.00	6.00	14.00
1975-Ben Franklin		1.60	4.00
1976-The Brady Bunch (TV)	1.70	5.00	12.00
1977-Ben Franklin		1.60	4.00
1977-Popeye	1.70	5.00	12.00
1978-Happy Days (TV)	1.20	2.90	7.00
1979-Eight is Enough (TV)	1.50	3.80	9.00
1980-The Waltons (TV, released in 1981)	1.70	4.20	10.00

KIT KARTER
May-July, 1962
Dell Publishing Co.

	GD25	FN65	NM94
1	3.20	8.00	16.00

KITTY
October, 1948
St. John Publishing Co.

	GD25	FN65	NM94
1-Teenage; Lily Renee-c/a	5.35	16.00	32.00

KITTY PRYDE AND WOLVERINE
Nov, 1984 - No. 6, April, 1985 (Mini-series)
Marvel Comics Group

	GD25	FN65	NM94
1 (From X-Men)		1.30	3.25
2-6		.80	2.00

KLARER GIVEAWAYS (See Wisco)

KNIGHTS OF PENDRAGON, THE (Also see Pendragon)
July, 1990 - No. 18, Dec, 1991 ($1.95)
Marvel Comics Ltd.

	GD25	FN65	NM94
1-18: 1-Capt. Britain app. 2,8-Free poster inside. 9,10-Bolton-c. 11,18-Iron Man app.		.80	2.00

KNIGHTS OF THE ROUND TABLE (See 4-Color No. 540)

KNIGHTS OF THE ROUND TABLE
No. 10, April, 1957
Pines Comics

	GD25	FN65	NM94
10	3.60	9.00	18.00

KNIGHTS OF THE ROUND TABLE
Nov-Jan, 1963-64
Dell Publishing Co.

	GD25	FN65	NM94
1 (12-397-401)-Painted-c	4.00	11.00	22.00

KNOCK KNOCK (...Who's There?)
No. 801, 1936 (52 pgs.) (8x9", B&W)
Whitman Publ./Gerona Publications

	GD25	FN65	NM94
801-Joke book; Bob Dunn-a	5.35	16.00	32.00

KNOCKOUT ADVENTURES
Winter, 1953-54
Fiction House Magazines

	GD25	FN65	NM94
1-Reprints Fight Comics #53 w/Rip Carson-c/s	10.00	30.00	70.00

KNOW YOUR MASS
No. 303, 1958 (35¢, 100 Pg. Giant) (Square binding)
Catechetical Guild

	GD25	FN65	NM94
303-In color	3.20	8.00	16.00

Kobra #5 © DC

Kong The Untamed #1 © DC

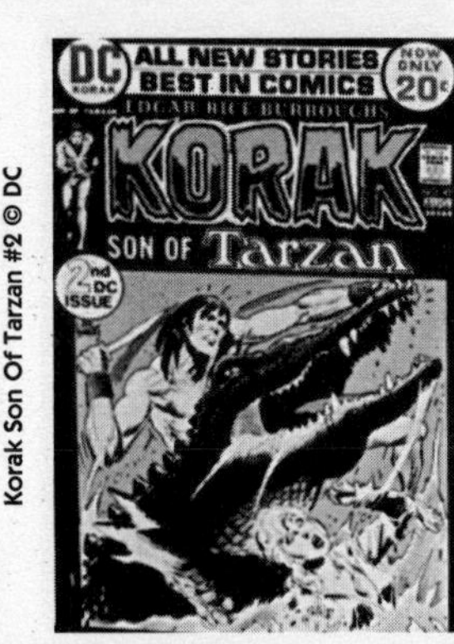

Korak Son Of Tarzan #2 © DC

KOBALT
June, 1994 - Present ($1.75)
DC Comics (Milestone)

	GD25	FN65	NM94
1-9: 1-Byrne-c. 4-Intro Page		.70	1.75

KOBRA (See DC Special Series No. 1)
Feb-Mar, 1976 - No. 7, Mar-Apr, 1977
National Periodical Publications

	GD25	FN65	NM94
1-1st app.; Kirby-a redrawn by Marcos; only 25¢ issue		.80	2.00
2-7: (All 30¢ issues) 3-Giffen-a		.65	1.60

NOTE: ***Austin** a-3i. **Buckler** a-5p; c-5p. **Kubert** c-4. **Nasser** a-6p, 7; c-7.*

KOKEY KOALA (...and the Magic Button)
May, 1952
Toby Press

	GD25	FN65	NM94
1	7.50	22.50	45.00

KOKO AND KOLA (Also see A-1 Comics #16 & Tick Tock Tales)
Fall, 1946 - No. 5, May, 1947; No. 6, 1950
Com/Magazine Enterprises

	GD25	FN65	NM94
1-Funny animal	8.35	25.00	50.00
2-X-Mas-c	4.20	12.50	25.00
3-6: 6(A-1 28)	4.00	11.00	22.00

KO KOMICS
October, 1945
Gerona Publications

	GD25	FN65	NM94
1-The Duke of Darkness & The Menace (hero)	40.00	120.00	280.00

KOMIC KARTOONS
Fall, 1945 - No. 2, Winter, 1945
Timely Comics (EPC)

	GD25	FN65	NM94
1,2-Andy Wolf, Bertie Mouse	14.00	43.00	100.00

KOMIK PAGES (Formerly Snap; becomes Bullseye #11)
April, 1945 (All reprints)
Harry 'A' Chesler, Jr. (Our Army, Inc.)

	GD25	FN65	NM94
10(#1 on inside)-Land O' Nod by Rick Yager (2 pgs.), Animal Crackers, Foxy GrandPa, Tom, Dick & Mary, Cheerio Minstrels, Red Starr plus other 1-2 pg. strips; Cole-a	16.00	48.00	110.00

KONA (...Monarch of Monster Isle)
Feb-Apr, 1962 - No. 21, Jan-Mar, 1967 (Painted-c)
Dell Publishing Co.

	GD25	FN65	NM94
4-Color 1256 (#1)	7.50	22.50	45.00
2-10: 4-Anak begins	4.00	10.00	20.00
11-21	3.00	7.50	15.00

NOTE: ***Glanzman** a-all issues.*

KONGA (Fantastic Giants No. 24) (See Return of...)
1960; No. 2, Aug, 1961 - No. 23, Nov, 1965
Charlton Comics

	GD25	FN65	NM94
1(1960)-Based on movie; Giordano-c	27.00	81.00	190.00
2-Giordano-c	13.00	39.00	90.00
3-5	11.00	32.00	75.00
6-15	7.00	21.00	48.00
16-23	5.00	15.00	35.00

NOTE: ***Ditko** a-1, 3-15; c-4, 6-9. **Glanzman** a-12. **Montes & Bache** a-16-23.*

KONGA'S REVENGE (Formerly Return of...)
No. 2, Summer, 1963 - No. 3, Fall, 1964; Dec, 1968
Charlton Comics

	GD25	FN65	NM94
2,3: 2-Ditko-c/a	5.00	15.00	35.00
1(12/68)-Reprints Konga's Revenge #3	2.60	7.70	18.00

KONG THE UNTAMED
June-July, 1975 - V2#5, Feb-Mar, 1976
National Periodical Publications

	GD25	FN65	NM94
1-1st app. Kong; Wrightson-c; Alcala-a			1.50
2-5: 2-Wrightson-c. 2,3-Alcala-a			1.00

KOOKIE
Feb-Apr, 1962 - No. 2, May-July, 1962 (15 cents)
Dell Publishing Co.

	GD25	FN65	NM94
1,2-Written by John Stanley; Bill Williams-a	9.15	27.50	55.00

KOOSH KINS
Oct, 1991 - No. 3, Feb, 1992 ($1.00, bi-monthly, mini-series)
Archie Comics

	GD25	FN65	NM94
1-3 (#4 planned but cancelled)			1.00

K. O. PUNCH, THE (Also see Lucky Fights It Through)
1948 (Educational giveaway)
E. C. Comics

	GD25	FN65	NM94
nn-Feldstein-splash; Kamen-a	125.00	375.00	750.00

KORAK, SON OF TARZAN (Edgar Rice Burroughs)(See Tarzan #139)
Jan, 1964 - No. 45, Jan, 1972 (Painted-c No. 1-?)
Gold Key

	GD25	FN65	NM94
1-Russ Manning-a	5.70	17.00	40.00
2-11-Russ Manning-a	3.00	9.40	22.00
12-21: 12,13-Warren Tufts-a. 14-Jon of the Kalahari ends. 15-Mabu, Jungle Boy begins. 21-Manning-a	2.30	6.90	16.00
22-30	1.70	4.20	10.00
31-45	1.30	3.00	8.00

KORAK, SON OF TARZAN (Tarzan Family #60 on; see Tarzan #230)
V9#46, May-June, 1972 - V12#56, Feb-Mar, 1974; No. 57, May-June, 1975 - No. 59, Sept-Oct, 1975 (Edgar Rice Burroughs)
National Periodical Publications

	GD25	FN65	NM94
46-(52 pgs.)-Carson of Venus begins (origin), ends #56; Pellucidar feature; Weiss-a		1.50	3.75
47-59: 49-Origin Korak retold		.80	2.00

NOTE: ***Kaluta** a-46-56. All have covers by **Joe Kubert**. **Manning** strip reprints-No. 57-59. **Frank Thorn** a-46-51.*

KOREA MY HOME (Also see Yalta to Korea)
nd (1950s)
Johnstone and Cushing

	GD25	FN65	NM94
nn-Anti-communist; Korean War	22.00	65.00	150.00

KORG: 70,000 B. C. (TV)
May, 1975 - No. 9, Nov, 1976 (Hanna-Barbera)
Charlton Publications

	GD25	FN65	NM94
1		1.90	4.75
2-9: 2-Painted-c; Byrne text illos		1.00	2.50

KORNER KID COMICS
1947
Four Star Publications

	GD25	FN65	NM94
1	5.35	16.00	32.00

KRAZY KAT
1946 (Hardcover)
Holt

	GD25	FN65	NM94
Reprints daily & Sunday strips by Herriman	64.00	193.00	450.00
dust jacket only	50.00	150.00	350.00

KRAZY KAT (See Ace Comics & March of Comics No. 72, 87)

KRAZY KAT COMICS (...& Ignatz the Mouse early issues)
May-June, 1951 - F.C. #696, Apr, 1956; Jan, 1964 (None by Herriman)
Dell Publishing Co./Gold Key

	GD25	FN65	NM94
1(1951)	8.35	25.00	50.00
2-5 (#5, 8-10/52)	5.85	17.50	35.00
4-Color 454,504	4.35	13.00	26.00
4-Color 548,619,696 (4/56)	4.00	11.00	22.00
1(10098-401)(1/64-Gold Key)(TV)	4.00	11.00	22.00

KRAZY KOMICS (1st Series) (Cindy Comics No. 27 on)

Krazy Komics #1 ('42) © MEG

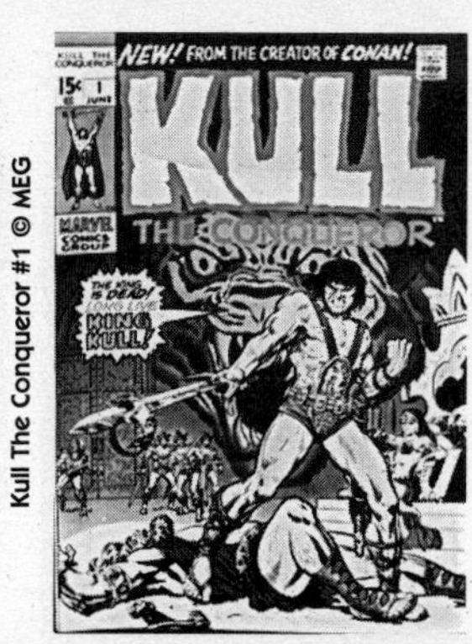

Kull The Conqueror #1 © MEG

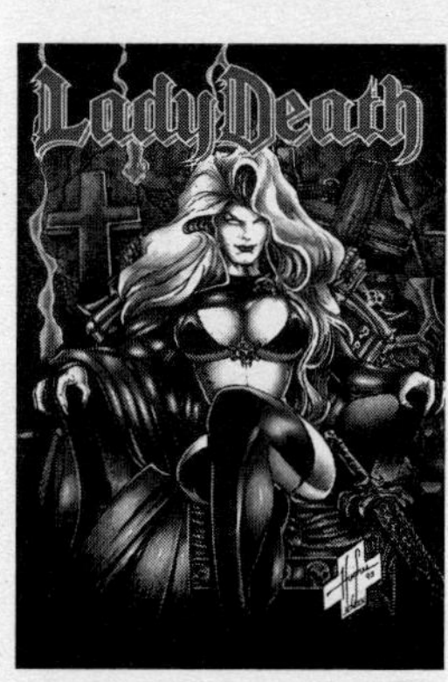

Lady Death #2 © Brian Paludo

GD25 FN65 NM94

July, 1942 - No. 26, Spr, 1947 (Also see Ziggy Pig)
Timely Comics (USA No. 1-21/JPC No. 22-26)

1-Toughy Tomcat, Ziggy Pig (by Jaffee) & Silly Seal begin 33.00 100.00 230.00
2 16.00 48.00 110.00
3-10: 9-Hitler parody 11.50 34.00 80.00
11,13,14 9.15 27.50 55.00
12-Timely's entire art staff drew themselves into a Creeper story 14.00 43.00 100.00
15-(8-9/44)-Becomes Funny Tunes #16; has "Super Soldier" by Pfc. Stan Lee 9.15 27.50 55.00
16-24,26: 16-(10-11/44). 26-Super Rabbit-c/story 6.70 20.00 40.00
25-Wacky Duck-c/story & begin; Kurtzman-a (6pgs.) 9.15 27.50 55.00

KRAZY KOMICS (2nd Series)
Aug, 1948 - No. 2, Nov, 1948
Timely/Marvel Comics

1-Wolverton (10 pgs.) & Kurtzman (8 pgs.)-a; Eustice Hayseed begins (Li'l Abner swipe) 30.00 90.00 210.00
2-Wolverton-a (10 pgs.); Powerhouse Pepper cameo 20.00 60.00 140.00

KRAZY KROW (Also see Dopey Duck, Film Funnies, Funny Frolics & Movie Tunes)
Summer, 1945 - No. 3, Wint, 1945/46
Marvel Comics (ZPC)

1 12.00 36.00 85.00
2,3 9.15 27.50 55.00
I.W. Reprint #1('57), 2('58), 7 1.80 4.50 9.00

KRAZYLIFE (Becomes Nutty Life #2)
1945 (no month)
Fox Feature Syndicate

1-Funny animal 10.00 30.00 65.00

KREE/SKRULL WAR STARRING THE AVENGERS, THE
Sept, 1983 - No. 2, Oct, 1983 ($2.50, 68 pgs.; Baxter paper)
Marvel Comics Group

1,2 1.00 2.50
NOTE: ***Neal Adams*** *p-1r, 2.* ***Buscema*** *a-1r, 2r.* ***Simonson*** *a-1p; c-1p.*

KRIM-KO KOMICS
5/18/35 - No. 6, 6/22/35; 1936 - 1939 (Giveaway) (weekly)
Krim-ko Chocolate Drink

1-(16 pgs., soft-c, Dairy giveaways)-Tom, Mary & Sparky Advs. by Russell Keaton, Jim Hawkins by Dick Moores, Mystery Island! by Rick Yager begin 10.00 30.00 70.00
2-6 (6/22/35) 8.35 25.00 50.00
Lola, Secret Agent; 184 issues, 4 pg. giveaways - all original stories each.... 5.85 17.50 35.00

KROFFT SUPERSHOW (TV)
April, 1978 - No. 6, Jan, 1979
Gold Key

1-Photo-c 1.20 3.00
2-6: 6-Photo-c 1.50

KRULL
Nov, 1983 - No. 2, Dec, 1983 (Movie adaptation)
Marvel Comics Group

1,2-r/Marvel Super Special. 1-Photo-c from movie 1.00

KRYPTON CHRONICLES
Sept, 1981 - No. 3, Nov, 1981
DC Comics

1-Buckler-c(p) 1.50
2,3 1.00

KULL AND THE BARBARIANS (Magazine)
May, 1975 - No. 3, Sept, 1975 ($1.00, B&W, 84 pgs.)
Marvel Comics Group

1-3: 1-Andru/Wood-r/Kull #1; 2 pgs. Neal Adams; Gil Kane(p), Marie & John Severin-a(r); Krenkel text illo. 2-Red Sonja by Chaykin begins; Soloman Kane by Weiss/N. Adams; Gil Kane-a. 3-Origin Red Sonja by Chaykin; N. Adams-a; Solomon Kane app. 1.00

KULL THE CONQUEROR (...the Destroyer #11 on; see Creatures on the Loose #10 and Marvel Preview)
June, 1971 - No. 2, Sept, 1971; No. 3, July, 1972 - No. 15, Aug, 1974; No. 16, Aug, 1976 - No. 29, Oct, 1978
Marvel Comics Group

1-Andru/Wood-a; origin Kull; 15¢ issue 1.50 3.75 9.00
2-5: 2-Last 15¢ issue. 3-13: 20¢ issues 1.70 4.25
6-10 1.30 3.25
11-29: 11-15-Ploog-a. 14-16: 25¢ issues .90 2.25
NOTE: *No. 1, 2, 7-9, 11 are based on Robert E. Howard stories.* ***Alcala*** *a-17p, 18-20i; c-24.* ***Ditko*** *a-12r, 15r.* ***Gil Kane*** *c-15p, 21.* ***Nebres*** *a-22i-27i; c-25i, 27i.* ***Ploog*** *c-11, 12p, 13.* ***Severin*** *a-2-9i; c-2-10i, 19.* ***Starlin*** *c-14.*

KULL THE CONQUEROR (Marvel, 1982)(Value: cover or less)

KULL THE CONQUEROR (Marvel, 1983)(Value: cover or less)

KUNG FU (See Deadly Hands of..., & Master of...)

KUNG FU FIGHTER (See Richard Dragon...)

LABOR IS A PARTNER
1949 (32 pgs. in color; paper cover)
Catechetical Guild Educational Society

nn-Anti-communism 17.00 51.00 120.00
Confidential Preview-(B&W, 8-1/2x11", saddle stitched)-only one known copy; text varies from color version, advertises next book on secularism (If the Devil Would Talk) 35.00 100.00 200.00

LABYRINTH (Marvel)(Value: cover or less)

LAD: A DOG
1961 - No. 2, July-Sept, 1962
Dell Publishing Co.

4-Color 1303 (movie), 2 4.35 13.00 26.00

LADY AND THE TRAMP (See Dell Giants, 4-Color No. 629, 634, & Movie Comics)

LADY AND THE TRAMP IN "BUTTER LATE THAN NEVER"
1955 (16 pgs., 5x7-1/4", soft-c) (Walt Disney)
American Dairy Association (Premium)

nn 10.00 30.00 60.00

LADY ARCANE (Hero)(Value: cover or less)

LADY BOUNTIFUL
1917 (10-1/4x13-1/2"; 24 pgs.; B&W; cardboard cover)
Saalfield Publ. Co./Press Publ. Co.

nn-By Gene Carr; 2 panels per page 14.00 43.00 140.00

LADY COP (See 1st Issue Special)

LADY DEATH (See Evil Ernie)
Jan, 1994 - No. 3, Mar, 1994 ($2.75, limited series)
Chaos! Comics

1-($3.50)-Chromium-c; S. Hughes-c/a in all 3.60 11.00 25.00
2 1.70 5.00 12.00
3 .90 2.00 5.50
...Swimsuit Special #1-($2.50)-Wraparound-c 1.00 2.50
...Swimsuit Special #1-Red velvet-c 5.00 15.00 35.00
...: The Reckoning (7/94, $6.95)-r/#1-3 1.20 3.00 7.00

LADY FOR A NIGHT (See Cinema Comics Herald)

LADY LUCK (Formerly Smash #1-85) (Also see Spirit Sections #1)
No. 86, Dec, 1949 - No. 90, Aug, 1950
Quality Comics Group

86(#1) 54.00 160.00 375.00

Lamce O'Casey #2 © FAW

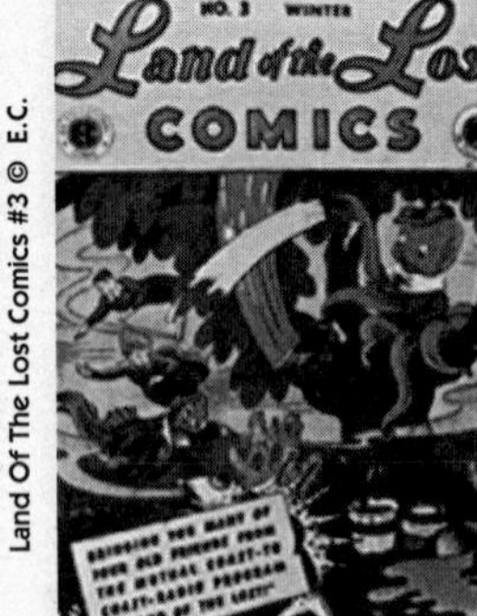

Land Of The Lost Comics #3 © E.C.

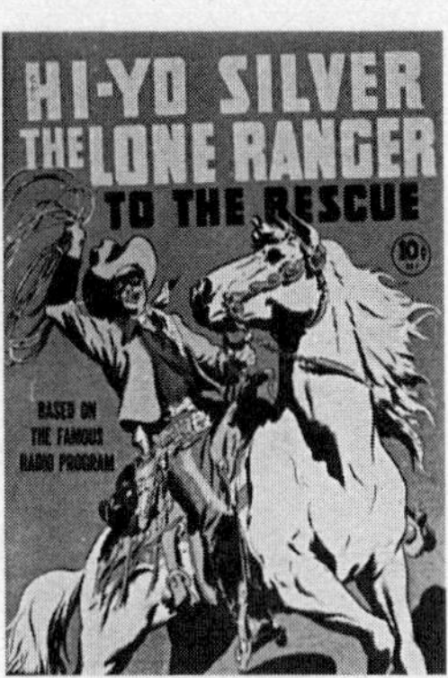

Large Feature Comics #7 © DELL

	GD25	FN65	NM94
87-90	45.00	135.00	315.00

LAFF-A-LYMPICS (TV)(See The Funtastic World of Hanna-Barbera)
Mar, 1978 - No. 13, Mar, 1979 (Hanna-Barbera)
Marvel Comics Group

1-13: Yogi Bear, Scooby Doo, Pixie & Dixie, etc. 11-Jetsons x-over; 1 pg. illustrated bio of Mighty Mightor, Herculoids, Shazzan, Galaxy Trio & Space Ghost — 1.00

LAFFY-DAFFY COMICS
Feb, 1945 - No. 2, March, 1945
Rural Home Publ. Co.

	GD25	FN65	NM94
1,2-Funny animal	5.85	17.50	35.00

LANA (Little Lana No. 8 on)
Aug, 1948 - No. 7, Aug, 1949 (Also see Annie Oakley)
Marvel Comics (MjMC)

	GD25	FN65	NM94
1-Rusty, Millie begin	11.50	34.00	80.00
2-Kurtzman's "Hey Look" (1); last Rusty	8.35	25.00	50.00
3-7: 3-Nellie begins	5.35	16.00	32.00

LANCELOT & GUINEVERE (See Movie Classics)

LANCELOT LINK, SECRET CHIMP (TV)
April, 1971 - No. 8, Feb, 1973
Gold Key

	GD25	FN65	NM94
1-Photo-c	2.00	6.00	14.00
2-8: 2-Photo-c	1.30	3.25	8.00

LANCELOT STRONG (See The Shield)

LANCE O'CASEY (See Mighty Midget & Whiz Comics)
Spring, 1946 - No. 3, Fall, 1946; No. 4, Summer, 1948
Fawcett Publications

	GD25	FN65	NM94
1-Captain Marvel app. on-c	19.00	58.00	135.00
2	11.00	32.00	75.00
3,4	9.15	27.50	55.00

NOTE: *The cover for the 1st issue was done in 1942 but was not published until 1946. The cover shows 68 pages but actually has only 36 pages.*

LANCER (TV)(Western)
Feb, 1969 - No. 3, Sept, 1969 (All photo-c)
Gold Key

	GD25	FN65	NM94
1	3.10	9.00	22.00
2,3	2.30	6.90	16.00

LAND OF THE GIANTS (TV)
Nov, 1968 - No. 5, Sept, 1969 (All have photo-c)
Gold Key

	GD25	FN65	NM94
1	5.50	17.00	40.00
2-5	3.10	9.00	22.00

LAND OF THE LOST COMICS (Radio)
July-Aug, 1946 - No. 9, Spring, 1948
E. C. Comics

	GD25	FN65	NM94
1	25.00	75.00	175.00
2	16.50	50.00	115.00
3-9	13.50	41.00	95.00

LAND UNKNOWN, THE (See 4-Color No. 845)

LARAMIE (TV)
Aug, 1960 - July, 1962 (All photo-c)
Dell Publishing Co.

	GD25	FN65	NM94
4-Color 1125-Gil Kane/Heath-a	10.00	30.00	60.00
4-Color 1223,1284	6.70	20.00	40.00
01-418-207 (7/62)	6.70	20.00	40.00

LAREDO (TV)
June, 1966
Gold Key

	GD25	FN65	NM94
1 (10179-606)-Photo-c	3.60	9.00	18.00

LARGE FEATURE COMIC (Formerly called Black & White in previous guides)
1939 - No. 13, 1943
Dell Publishing Co.

	GD	FN	VF	NM
1 (Series I)-Dick Tracy Meets the Blank	100.00	300.00	650.00	1000.00
2-Terry and the Pirates (#1)	50.00	150.00	325.00	500.00
3-Heigh-Yo Silver! The Lone Ranger (text & ill.)(76 pgs.); also exists as a Whitman #710; based on radio program	50.00	150.00	325.00	500.00
4-Dick Tracy Gets His Man	50.00	150.00	325.00	500.00
5-Tarzan of the Apes (#1) by Harold Foster (origin); reprints 1st Tarzan dailies from 1929	90.00	270.00	585.00	900.00
6-Terry & the Pirates & The Dragon Lady; reprints dailies from 1936	50.00	150.00	325.00	500.00
7-(Scarce, 52 pgs.)-Hi-Yo Silver the Lone Ranger to the Rescue; also exists as a Whitman #715; based on radio program	65.00	195.00	422.00	650.00
8-Dick Tracy the Racket Buster	50.00	150.00	325.00	500.00
9-King of the Royal Mounted (Zane Grey's...)	30.00	90.00	195.00	300.00
10-(Scarce)-Gang Busters (No. appears on inside front cover); first slick cover (based on radio program)	40.00	120.00	260.00	400.00
11-Dick Tracy Foils the Mad Doc Hump	60.00	180.00	390.00	600.00
12-Smilin' Jack; no number on-c	40.00	120.00	260.00	400.00
13-Dick Tracy and Scottie of Scotland Yard	60.00	180.00	390.00	600.00
14-Smilin' Jack Helps G-Men Solve a Case!	40.00	120.00	260.00	400.00
15-Dick Tracy and the Kidnapped Princes	60.00	180.00	390.00	600.00
16-Donald Duck; 1st app. Daisy Duck on back cover (6/41-Disney)	250.00	750.00	1625.00	2500.00
17-Gang Busters (1941)	25.00	75.00	162.00	250.00
18-Phantasmo (see The Funnies #45)	20.00	60.00	130.00	200.00
19-Dumbo Comic Paint Book (Disney); partial-r from 4-Color #17	200.00	600.00	1300.00	2000.00
20-Donald Duck Comic Paint Book (rarer than #16) (Disney)	350.00	1050.00	2275.00	3500.00

(Prices vary widely on this book)

	GD	FN	VF	NM
21,22: 21-Private Buck. 22-Nuts & Jolts	8.00	24.00	52.00	80.00
23-The Nebbs	12.00	36.00	78.00	120.00
24-Popeye in "Thimble Theatre" by Segar	40.00	120.00	260.00	400.00
25-Smilin' Jack-1st issue to show title on-c	40.00	120.00	260.00	400.00
26-Smitty	20.00	60.00	130.00	200.00
27-Terry and the Pirates; Caniff-c/a	40.00	120.00	260.00	400.00
28-Grin and Bear It	8.00	24.00	52.00	80.00
29-Moon Mullins	20.00	60.00	130.00	200.00
30-Tillie the Toiler	18.00	54.00	117.00	180.00
1 (Series II)-Peter Rabbit by Harrison Cady; arrival date-3/27/42	30.00	90.00	195.00	300.00
2-Winnie Winkle (#1)	14.00	42.00	91.00	140.00
3-Dick Tracy	50.00	150.00	325.00	500.00
4-Tiny Tim (#1)	26.00	78.00	169.00	260.00
5-Toots and Casper	9.00	27.00	58.00	90.00
6-Terry and the Pirates; Caniff-a	40.00	120.00	260.00	400.00
7-Pluto Saves the Ship (#1)(Disney)-Written by Carl Barks, Jack Hannah, & Nick George (Barks' 1st comic book work)	90.00	270.00	585.00	900.00
8-Bugs Bunny (#1)('42)	70.00	210.00	455.00	700.00
9-Bringing Up Father	14.00	42.00	91.00	140.00
10-Popeye (Thimble Theatre)	35.00	105.00	228.00	350.00
11-Barney Google and Snuffy Smith	18.00	54.00	117.00	180.00
12-Private Buck	8.00	24.00	52.00	80.00

13-(nn)-1001 Hours Of Fun; puzzles & games; by A. W. Nugent. This book was bound as #13 with Large Feature Comics in publisher's files

Lars Of Mars #11 © Z-D

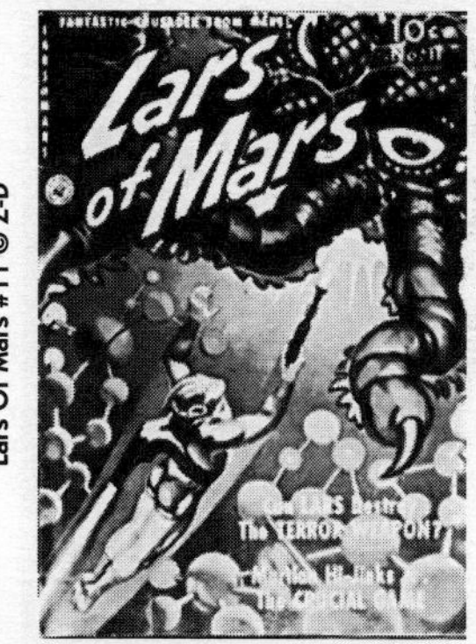

Lash Laure Western #1 © FAW

Lassie #1 © DELL

GD25 FN65 NM94

15.00 45.00 98.00 150.00

NOTE: *The Black & White Feature Books are oversized 8-1/2x11-3/8" comics with color covers and black and white interiors. The first nine issues all have rough, heavy stock covers and, except for #7, all have 76 pages, including covers. #7 and #10-on all have 52 pages. Beginning with #10 the covers are slick and thin and, because of their size, are difficult to handle without damaging. For this reason, they are seldom found in fine to mint condition. The paper stock, unlike Wow #1 and Capt. Marvel #1, is itself not unstable ...just thin.*

LARRY DOBY, BASEBALL HERO
1950 (Cleveland Indians)
Fawcett Publications

nn-Bill Ward-a; photo-c 57.00 171.00 400.00

LARRY HARMON'S LAUREL AND HARDY (...Comics)
July-Aug, 1972 (Regular size)
National Periodical Publications

1 1.60 4.00

LARS OF MARS
No. 10, Apr-May, 1951 - No. 11, July-Aug, 1951 (Painted-c)
Ziff-Davis Publishing Co.

10-Origin; Anderson-a(3) in each 46.00 140.00 325.00
11-Gene Colan-a 39.00 118.00 275.00

LARS OF MARS 3-D (Eclipse)(Value: cover or less)

LASER ERASER & PRESSBUTTON (Eclipse)(Value: cover or less)

LASH LARUE WESTERN (Movie star; king of the bullwhip)(See Fawcett Movie Comic, Motion Picture Comics & Six-Gun Heroes)
Sum, 1949 - No. 46, Jan, 1954 (36pgs., 1-7,9,13,16-on)
Fawcett Publications

1-Lash & his horse Black Diamond begin; photo front/back-c begin
89.00 268.00 625.00
2(11/49) 39.00 118.00 275.00
3-5 33.00 100.00 230.00
6,7,9: 6-Last photo back-c; intro. Frontier Phantom (Lash's twin brother)
25.00 75.00 175.00
8,10 (52pgs.) 27.00 80.00 185.00
11,12,14,15 (52pgs.) 16.50 50.00 115.00
13,16-20 (36pgs.) 15.00 45.00 105.00
21-30: 21-The Frontier Phantom app. 13.00 40.00 90.00
31-45 11.00 32.00 75.00
46-Last Fawcett issue & photo-c 11.50 34.00 80.00

LASH LARUE WESTERN (Continues from Fawcett series)
No. 47, Mar-Apr, 1954 - No. 84, June, 1961
Charlton Comics

47-Photo-c 14.00 43.00 100.00
48 10.00 30.00 70.00
49-60 8.35 25.00 50.00
61-66,69,70: 52-r/#8; 53-r/#22 7.50 22.50 45.00
67,68-(68 pgs.). 68-Check-a 7.50 22.50 45.00
71-83 4.70 14.00 28.00
84-Last issue 5.85 17.50 35.00

LASH LARUE WESTERN (AC)(Value: cover or less)

LASSIE (TV)(M-G-M's... #1-36; see Kite Fun Book)
June, 1950 - No. 70, July, 1969
Dell Publishing Co./Gold Key No. 59 (10/62) on

1 (52 pgs.)-Photo-c; inside lists One Shot #282 in error
14.00 43.00 100.00
2-Painted-c begin 7.50 22.50 45.00
3-10 4.70 14.00 28.00
11-19: 12-Rocky Langford (Lassie's master) marries Gerry Lawrence. 15-1st app. Timbu 4.00 10.00 20.00
20-22-Matt Baker-a 4.20 12.50 25.00
23-40: 33-Robinson-a. 39-1st app. Timmy as Lassie picks up her TV family
3.20 8.00 16.00
41-70: 63-Last Timmy (10/63). 64-r/#19. 65-Forest Ranger Corey Stuart begins, ends #69. 70-Forest Rangers Bob Ericson & Scott Turner app. (Lassie's new masters) 2.00 5.00 10.00
11193(1978, $1.95, 224 pgs., Golden Press)-Baker-r (92 pgs.)
1.00 2.50 5.00
The Adventures of... nn-(Red Heart Dog Food giveaway, 1949)-16 pgs, soft-c; 1st app. Lassie in comics 14.00 43.00 100.00

NOTE: *Photo c-57, 63. (See March of Comics #210, 217, 230, 254, 266, 278, 296, 308, 324, 334, 346, 358, 370, 381, 394, 411, 432)*

LAST AMERICAN, THE
Dec, 1990 - No. 4, March, 1991 ($2.25, mini-series)
Epic Comics (Marvel)

1-4: Alan Grant scripts .90 2.25

LAST DAYS OF THE JUSTICE SOCIETY SPECIAL
1986 ($2.50, one shot, 68 pgs.)
DC Comics

1-62 pg. JSA story plus unpubbed G.A. pg. 1.00 2.50

LAST GENERATION, THE (Black Tie)(Value: cover or less)

LAST HUNT, THE (See 4-Color No. 678)

LAST KISS (Acme)(Value: cover or less)

LAST OF THE COMANCHES (See Wild Bill Hickok #28)
1953 (Movie)
Avon Periodicals

nn-Kinstler-c/a, 21pgs.; Ravielli-a 11.50 34.00 80.00

LAST OF THE ERIES, THE (See American Graphics)

LAST OF THE FAST GUNS, THE (See 4-Color No. 925)

LAST OF THE MOHICANS (See King Classics & White Rider and...)

LAST OF THE VIKING HEROES, THE (Also see Silver Star #1)
Mar, 1987 - No. 12 ($1.50/$1.95)
Genesis West Comics

1-4: 4-Intro The Phantom Force 1.00 2.50
1-Signed edition ($1.50) 1.50
5A-Kirby/Stevens-c 1.30 3.25
5B,6 ($1.95) .80 2.00
7-Art Adams-c 1.30 3.25
8-12: 8-Kirby back-c. 9,10,12-($2.50) 1.00 2.50
Summer Special 1-3: 1-(1988)-Frazetta-c & illos. 2(1990, $2.50)-A TMNT app. 3 (1991, $2.50)-Teenage Mutant Ninja Turtles 1.20 3.00
Summer Special 1-Signed edition (sold for $1.95) .80 2.00

NOTE: ***Art Adams** c-7. **Byrne** c-3. **Kirby** c-1p, 5p. **Perez** c-2i. **Stevens** c-5Ai.*

LAST ONE, THE
July, 1993 - No. 6, Dec, 1993 ($2.50, limited series, mature readers)
DC Comics (Vertigo)

1-6 1.00 2.50

LAST STARFIGHTER, THE
Oct, 1984 - No. 3, Dec, 1984 (75¢, movie adaptation)
Marvel Comics Group

1-3: r/Marvel Super Special; Guice-c 1.00

LAST TEMPTATION, THE
May, 1994 - Present ($4.95, limited series)
Marvel Comics

1,2-Gaiman story 1.00 2.00 5.00

LAST TRAIN FROM GUN HILL (See 4-Color No. 1012)

LATEST ADVENTURES OF FOXY GRANDPA (See Foxy Grandpa)

LATEST COMICS (Super Duper No. 3?)
March, 1945 - No. 2, 1945?
Spotlight Publ./Palace Promotions (Jubilee)

1-Super Duper 10.00 30.00 70.00
2-Bee-29 (nd); Jubilee in indicia blacked out 8.35 25.00 50.00

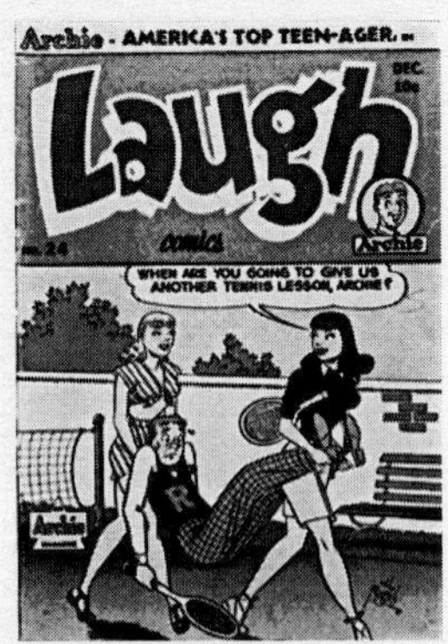

Laugh Comics #24 © AP

Larry Harmon's Laurel and Hardy #3 © DELL

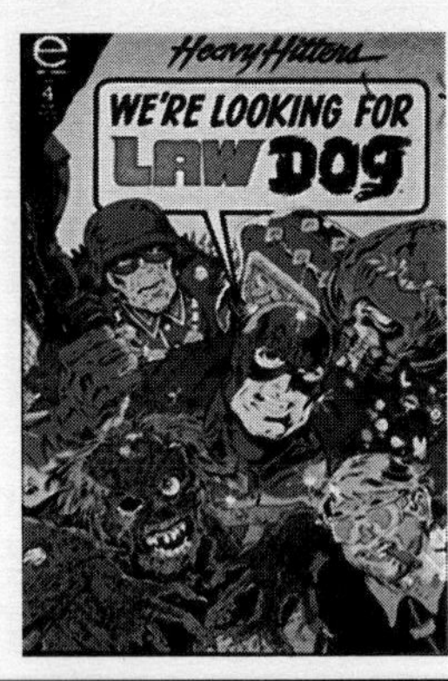

Lawdog #4 © MEG

LAUGH
June, 1987 - No. 29, Aug, 1991 (.75/$1.00)
Archie Enterprises

	GD25	FN65	NM94
V2#1-29: 5,19-X-Mas issues. 14-1st app. Hot Dog. 24-Re-intro Super Duck			1.00

LAUGH COMICS (Teenage) (Formerly Black Hood #9-19) (Laugh #226 on)
No. 20, Fall, 1946 - No. 400, Apr, 1987
Archie Publications (Close-Up)

	GD25	FN65	NM94
20-Archie begins; Katy Keene & Taffy begin by Woggon; Suzie & Wilbur also begin; Archie covers begin	53.00	160.00	370.00
21-23,25	25.00	75.00	175.00
24- "Pipsy" by Kirby (6 pgs.)	27.00	80.00	185.00
26-30	13.50	41.00	95.00
31-40	11.00	32.00	70.00
41-60: 41,54-Debbi by Woggon	7.00	21.00	42.00
61-80: 67-Debbi by Woggon	4.70	14.00	28.00
81-99	4.00	11.00	22.00
100	5.00	15.00	30.00
101-126: 125-Debbi app.	3.20	8.00	16.00
127-144: Super-hero app. in all (see note)	3.60	9.00	18.00
145-160: 157-Josie app.	1.30	3.25	8.00
161-165,167-200	1.00	2.00	5.00
166-Beatles-c	2.30	6.75	16.00
201-240		1.20	3.00
241-280			1.50
281-400: 381-384-Katy Keene app.; by Woggon-381,382			1.00

NOTE: *The Fly app. in 128, 129, 132, 134, 138, 139. Flygirl app. in 136, 137, 143. Flyman app. in 137. The Jaguar app. in 127, 130, 131, 133, 135, 140-142, 144. Josie app. in 145, 160, 164. Katy Keene app. in 20-125, 129, 130, 133. Many issues contain paper dolls.* ***Al Fagaly*** *c-20-29.* ***Montana*** *c-33, 36, 37, 42.* ***BillVigoda*** *c-30, 50.*

LAUGH COMICS DIGEST (...Magazine #23-89; Laugh Digest Mag. #90 on)
8/74; No. 2, 9/75; No. 3, 3/76 - Present (Digest-size)
Archie Publications (Close-Up No. 1, 3 on)

	GD25	FN65	NM94
1-Neal Adams-a	1.30	3.25	8.00
2,7,8,19-Neal Adams-a		1.60	4.00
3-6,9-18,20-50		1.00	2.50
51-119: Later issues $1.35,$1.50-c			1.50

NOTE: *Katy Keene in 23, 25, 27, 32-38, 40, 45-48, 50. The Fly-r in 19, 20. The Jaguar-r in 25, 27. Mr. Justice-r in 21. The Web-r in 23.*

LAUGH COMIX (Formerly Top Notch Laugh; Suzie Comics No. 49 on)
No. 46, Summer, 1944 - No. 48, Winter, 1944-45
MLJ Magazines

	GD25	FN65	NM94
46-Wilbur & Suzie in all; Harry Sahle-c	14.00	43.00	100.00
47,48: 47-Sahle-c. 48-Bill Vigoda-c	11.00	32.00	75.00

LAUGH-IN MAGAZINE (TV)(Magazine)
Oct, 1968 - No. 12, Oct, 1969 (50¢) (Satire)
Laufer Publ. Co.

	GD25	FN65	NM94
V1#1	2.60	7.70	18.00
2-12	1.30	3.25	8.00

LAUREL & HARDY (See Larry Harmon's... & March of Comics No. 302, 314)

LAUREL AND HARDY (...Comics)
3/49 - No. 3, 9/49; No. 26, 11/55 - No. 28, 3/56 (No #4-25)
St. John Publishing Co.

	GD25	FN65	NM94
1	50.00	150.00	350.00
2	30.00	90.00	210.00
3	22.00	65.00	150.00
26-28 (Reprints)	12.00	36.00	85.00

LAUREL AND HARDY (TV)
Oct, 1962 - No. 4, Sept-Nov, 1963
Dell Publishing Co.

	GD25	FN65	NM94
12-423-210 (8-10/62)	6.35	19.00	38.00
2-4 (Dell)	4.70	14.00	28.00

LAUREL AND HARDY (Larry Harmon's...)
Jan, 1967 - No. 2, Oct, 1967
Gold Key

	GD25	FN65	NM94
1,2: 1-Photo back-c	4.00	12.00	24.00

LAW AGAINST CRIME (Law-Crime on cover)
April, 1948 - No. 3, Aug, 1948 (Real Stories from Police Files)
Essenkay Publishing Co.

	GD25	FN65	NM94
1-(#1-3 are half funny animal, half crime stories)-L. B. Cole-c/a in all; electrocution-c	40.00	120.00	280.00
2-L. B. Cole-c/a	29.00	86.00	200.00
3-Used in **SOTI**, pg. 180,181 & illo "The wish to hurt or kill couples in lovers' lanes;" reprinted in All-Famous Crime #9	38.00	115.00	265.00

LAWBREAKERS (...Suspense Stories No. 10 on)
Mar, 1951 - No. 9, Oct-Nov, 1952
Law and Order Magazines (Charlton Comics)

	GD25	FN65	NM94
1	18.00	54.00	125.00
2	10.00	30.00	60.00
3,5,6,8,9	7.50	22.50	45.00
4- "White Death" junkie story	10.00	30.00	60.00
7- "The Deadly Dopesters" drug story	10.00	30.00	60.00

LAWBREAKERS ALWAYS LOSE!
Spring, 1948 - No. 10, Oct, 1949
Marvel Comics (CBS)

	GD25	FN65	NM94
1-2pg. Kurtzman-a, "Giggles 'n' Grins"	17.00	52.00	120.00
2	10.00	30.00	60.00
3-5: 4-Vampire story	8.35	25.00	50.00
6(2/49)-Has editorial defense against charges of Dr. Wertham	9.15	27.50	55.00
7-Used in **SOTI**, illo "Comic-book philosophy"	17.00	52.00	120.00
8-10: 9,10-Photo-c	6.70	20.00	40.00

NOTE: ***Brodsky*** *c-4, 5.* ***Shores*** *c-1-3, 6-8.*

LAWBREAKERS SUSPENSE STORIES (Formerly Lawbreakers; Strange Suspense Stories No. 16 on)
No. 10, Jan, 1953 - No. 15, Nov, 1953
Capitol Stories/Charlton Comics

	GD25	FN65	NM94
10	12.00	36.00	85.00
11 (3/53)-Severed tongues-c/story & woman negligee scene	37.00	111.00	260.00
12-14: 13-Giordana-c begin, end #15	7.50	22.50	45.00
15-Acid-in-face-c/story; hands dissolved in acid sty	19.00	58.00	135.00

LAW-CRIME (See Law Against Crime)

LAWDOG (Epic Comics)(Value: cover or less)

LAWDOG/GRIMROD: TERROR AT THE CROSSROADS
Sept, 1993 ($3.50)
Epic Comics (Marvel)

	GD25	FN65	NM94
1		1.40	3.50

LAWMAN (TV)
No. 970, Feb, 1959 - No. 11, Apr-June, 1962 (All photo-c)
Dell Publishing Co.

	GD25	FN65	NM94
4-Color 970(#1)	10.00	30.00	70.00
4-Color 1035('60)	6.70	20.00	40.00
3(2-4/60)-Toth-a	7.00	21.00	42.00
4-11	5.00	15.00	30.00

LAW OF DREDD, THE (Quality)(Value: cover or less)

LAWRENCE (See Movie Classics)

LAZARUS CHURCHYARD
June, 1992 - No. 3, 1992 ($3.95, color, coated stock, 44 pgs.)
Tundra Publishing

	GD25	FN65	NM94
1-3		1.60	4.00

LEADING COMICS (...Screen Comics No. 42 on)

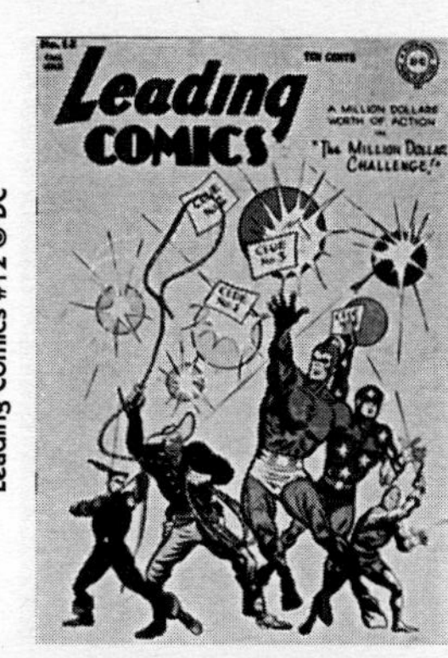

Leading Comics #12 © DC

The Legend of the Shield #3 © DC

The Legends of Daniel Boone #2 © DC

Winter, 1941-42 - No. 41, Feb-Mar, 1950
National Periodical Publications

	GD25	FN65	NM94
1-Origin The Seven Soldiers of Victory; Crimson Avenger, Green Arrow & Speedy, Shining Knight, The Vigilante, Star Spangled Kid & Stripesy begin; The Dummy (Vigilante villain) app.	300.00	900.00	2100.00
2-Meskin-a;Fred Ray-c	100.00	300.00	700.00
3	86.00	256.00	600.00
4,5	68.00	205.00	475.00
6-10	57.00	171.00	400.00
11-14(Spring, 1945)	43.00	129.00	300.00
15-(Sum,'45)-Contents change to funny animal	19.00	58.00	135.00
16-22,24-30: 16-Nero Fox-c begin, end #22	10.00	30.00	60.00
23-1st app. Peter Porkchops by Otto Feur & begins	20.00	60.00	140.00
31,32,34-41: 34-41-Leading Screen... on-c only	8.35	25.00	50.00
33-(Scarce)	16.00	48.00	110.00

NOTE: ***Rube Grossman**-a(Peter Porkchops)-most #15-on; c-15-41. **Post** a-23-37, 39, 41.*

LEADING SCREEN COMICS (Formerly Leading Comics)
No. 42, Apr-May, 1950 - No. 77, Aug-Sept, 1955
National Periodical Publications

	GD25	FN65	NM94
42-Peter Porkchops-c/stories continue	9.15	27.50	55.00
43-77	7.50	22.50	45.00

NOTE: ***Grossman** a-most. **Mayer** a-45-48, 50, 54-57, 60, 62-74, 75(3), 76, 77.*

LEAGUE OF CHAMPIONS, THE (Hero)(Value: cover or less)

LEATHERFACE (Arpad)(Value: cover or less)

LEATHERNECK THE MARINE (See Mighty Midget Comics)

LEAVE IT TO BEAVER (TV)
No. 912, June, 1958 - May-July, 1962 (All photo-c)
Dell Publishing Co.

	GD25	FN65	NM94
4-Color 912	20.00	60.00	140.00
4-Color 999,1103,1191,1285, 01-428-207	18.00	54.00	125.00

LEAVE IT TO BINKY (Binky No. 72 on) (Super DCGiant) (No. 1-22: 52 pgs.)
2-3/48 - #60, 10/58; #61, 6-7/68 - #71, 2-3/70 (Teen-age humor)
National Periodical Publications

	GD25	FN65	NM94
1-Lucy wears Superman costume	25.00	75.00	175.00
2	13.00	40.00	90.00
3,4	7.50	22.50	45.00
5-Superman cameo	12.00	36.00	85.00
6-10	7.00	21.00	42.00
11-14,16-20	5.35	16.00	32.00
15-Scribbly story by Mayer	9.15	27.50	55.00
21-28,30-45: 45-Last pre-code (2/55)	4.00	11.00	22.00
29-Used in **POP**, pg. 78	4.00	11.00	22.00
46-60: 60-(10/58)	3.20	8.00	16.00
Showcase #70 (9-10/67)-Tryout issue	2.80	7.00	14.00
61-71: 61-(6-7/68)	1.80	4.50	9.00

NOTE: ***Drucker** a-28. **Mayer** a-1, 2, 15. Created by **Mayer**.*

LEE HUNTER, INDIAN FIGHTER (See 4-Color No. 779, 904)

LEFT-HANDED GUN, THE (See 4-Color No. 913)

LEGACY
Oct, 1993 - Present ($2.25)
Majestic Entertainment

	GD25	FN65	NM94
1-2: 1-Glow-in-the-dark-c		.90	2.25
0-Platinum	1.10	3.00	6.50

LEGEND OF CUSTER, THE (TV)
January, 1968
Dell Publishing Co.

	GD25	FN65	NM94
1-Wayne Maunder photo-c	1.70	5.00	12.00

LEGEND OF JESSE JAMES, THE (TV)
February, 1966
Gold Key

	GD25	FN65	NM94
10172-602-Photo-c	3.20	8.00	16.00

LEGEND OF KAMUI, THE (See Kamui)

LEGEND OF LOBO, THE (See Movie Comics)

LEGEND OF THE SHIELD, THE
July, 1991 - No. 16, Oct, 1992 ($1.00, color)
Impact Comics (DC)

	GD25	FN65	NM94
1-16: 6,7-The Fly x-over. 12-Contains trading card			1.00
Annual 1 (1992, $2.50, 68 pgs.)-With trading card		1.00	2.50

LEGEND OF WONDER WOMAN, THE (DC)(Value: cover or less)

LEGEND OF YOUNG DICK TURPIN, THE (TV)
May, 1966 (Disney TV episode)
Gold Key

	GD25	FN65	NM94
1 (10176-605)-Photo/painted-c	2.00	5.00	10.00

LEGEND OF ZELDA, THE (Link: The Legend... in indicia)
1990 - No. 4, 1990 ($1.95, color, coated stiff-c)
V2#1, 1991 - No. 5, 1991 ($1.50, color)
Valiant Comics

	GD25	FN65	NM94
1-4: 4-Layton-c(i)		.80	2.00
V2#1-5			1.50

LEGENDS
Nov, 1986 - No. 6, Apr, 1987 (75¢, mini-series)
DC Comics

	GD25	FN65	NM94
1-Byrne-c/a(p) in all; 1st app. new Capt. Marvel		.80	2.00
2-5: 3-1st app. new Suicide Squad; death of Blockbuster		.60	1.60
6-1st app. new Justice League		1.60	4.00

LEGENDS OF DANIEL BOONE, THE (...Frontier Scout)
Oct-Nov, 1955 - No. 8, Dec-Jan, 1956-57
National Periodical Publications

	GD25	FN65	NM94
1 (Scarce)-Nick Cardy c-1-8	50.00	150.00	350.00
2 (Scarce)	38.00	115.00	265.00
3-8 (Scarce)	34.00	100.00	235.00

LEGENDS OF NASCAR, THE
Nov, 1990 - No. 14? (Color)(#1 3rd printing (1/91) says 2nd printing inside)
Vortex Comics

	GD25	FN65	NM94
1-Bill Elliott biog.; Trimpe-a ($1.50)	1.50	4.00	9.00
1-2nd printing (11/90, $2.00)		1.40	3.50
1-3rd print; contains Maxx racecards ($3.00)		1.70	4.25
2-Richard Petty ($2.00)		1.10	2.75
3-14: 3-Ken Schrader (7/91). 4-Bobby Allison; Spiegle-a(p); Adkins part-i. 5-Sterling Marlin. 6-Bill Elliott. 7-Junior Johnson; Spiegle-c/a. 8-Benny Parsons; Heck-a		.70	1.80
1-13-Hologram cover versions. 2-Hologram shows Bill Elliott's car by mistake (all are numbered & limited)		1.80	4.50
2-Hologram corrected version		1.80	4.50
...Christmas Special($5.95)	1.00	2.50	6.00

LEGENDS OF THE DARK KNIGHT (See Batman: ...)

LEGENDS OF THE STARGRAZERS (Innovation)(Value: cover or less)

LEGENDS OF THE WORLD'S FINEST (See World's Finest)
1994 - No. 3, 1994 ($4.95, limited series)
DC Comics

	GD25	FN65	NM94
1-3-By Simonson/Brereton; embossed foil logos	1.00	2.00	5.00

L.E.G.I.O.N. (The # to right of title represents year of print; also see Lobo)
Feb, 1989 - No. 70, Sept, 1994 ($1.50/$1.75)
DC Comics

	GD25	FN65	NM94
1-Giffen plots/breakdowns in #1-12		.70	1.80
2-22,24-47: 3-Lobo app. #3 on. 4-1st Lobo-c this title. 5-Lobo joins Legion. 28-Giffen-c(p). 31-Capt. Marvel app. 35-L.E.G.I.O.N. '92 begins			1.50
23-($2.50, 52 pgs.)-L.E.G.I.O.N. '91 begins		1.00	2.50
48,49,51-69: 48-Begin $1.75-c. 63-L.E.G.I.O.N. '94 begins; Superman x-over			

L.E.G.I.O.N. #70 © DC

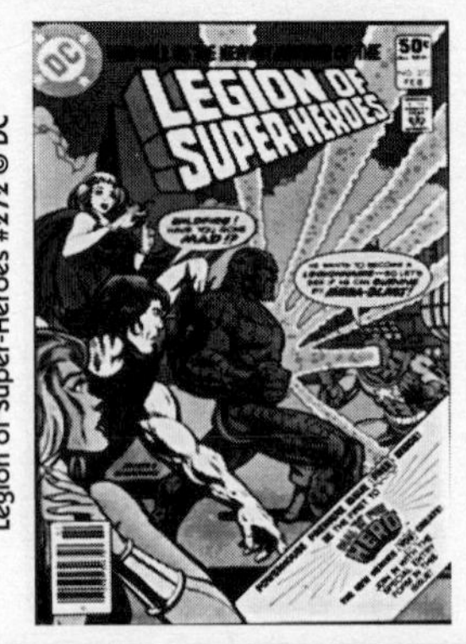

Legion of Super-Heroes #272 © DC

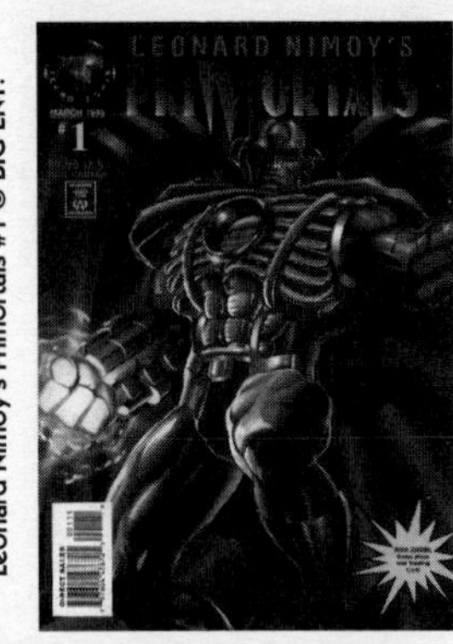

Leonard Nimoy's Primortals #1 © BIG ENT.

GD25 FN65 NM94

.70 1.75
50-($3.50, 68 pgs.) 1.40 3.50
70-($2.50, 52 pgs.)-Zero Hour 1.00 2.50
Annual 1-3 (1990-1992, $2.95, 68 pgs.): 1-Lobo, Superman app. 2-Alan Grant scripts 1.20 3.00
Annual 4 (1993, $3.50, 68 pgs.) 1.40 3.50
Annual 5 (1994, $3.50, 68 pgs.)-Elseworlds story; Lobo app. 1.40 3.50
NOTE: ***Alan Grant*** *scripts in #1-39, 51, Annual 1, 2.*

LEGIONNAIRES (See Legion of Super-Heroes #40, 41)
Apr, 1992 - Present ($1.25/$1.50)
DC comics

1-8: 1-Polybagged w/SkyBox trading card 1.25
9-18: 9-Begin $1.50-c. 11-Kid Quantum joins. 18-(9/94)-Zero Hour 1.50
0,19-23: 0-(10/94) 1.50
Annual 1 (1994, $2.95)-Elseworlds story 1.20 3.00

LEGIONNAIRES THREE
Jan, 1986 - No. 4, May, 1986 (75¢, mini-series)
DC comics

1-4 1.00

LEGION OF MONSTERS (Also see Marvel Premiere #28 & Marvel Preview #8)
September, 1975 ($1.00, B&W, 76 pgs.)(Magazine)
Marvel Comics Group

1-Origin & 1st app. Legion of Monsters; Neal Adams-c; Morrow-a; origin & only app. The Manphibian; Frankenstein by Mayerik; Bram Stoker's Dracula adaptation; Reese-a; painted-c (#2 was advertised with Morbius & Satana, but was never published) 1.30 3.25

LEGION OF NIGHT, THE
Oct, 1991 - No. 2, Oct, 1991 ($4.95, 52 pgs.)
Marvel Comics

1,2-Whilce Portacio-c/a(p) 1.00 2.00 5.00

LEGION OF SUBSTITUTE HEROES SPECIAL (DC)(Value: cover or less)

LEGION OF SUPER-HEROES (See Action, Adventure, All New Collectors Edition, Limited Collectors Edition, Secrets of the..., Superboy & Superman)
Feb, 1973 - No. 4, July-Aug, 1973
National Periodical Publications

1-Legion & Tommy Tomorrow reprints begin 1.10 2.70 6.50
2-4: 2-Forte-r. 3-r/Adv. #340. Action #240. 4-r/Adv. #341, Action #233; Mooney-r 1.00 1.90 4.75

LEGION OF SUPER-HEROES, THE (Formerly Superboy and...; Tales of The Legion No. 314 on)
No. 259, Jan, 1980 - No. 313, July, 1984
DC Comics

259(#1)-Superboy leaves Legion 1.20 3.00
260-270: 265-Contains 28 pg. insert "Superman & the TRS-80 Computer"; origin Tyroc; Tyroc leaves Legion .80 2.00
271-284: 272-Blok joins; origin; 20pg. insert-Dial 'H' For Hero. 277-Intro Reflecto. 280-Superboy re-joins legion. 282-Origin Reflecto. 283-Origin Wildfire .65 1.60
285,286-Giffen back up story .80 2.00
287-Giffen-a on Legion begins 1.10 2.80
288-290: 290-294-Great Darkness saga .80 2.00
291-293 .65 1.60
294-Double size (52 pgs.); Giffen-a(p) .70 1.80
295-299,301-305: 297-Origin retold. 298-Free 16pg. Amethyst preview .65 1.60
300-(68 pgs., Mando paper)-Anniversary issue; has c/a by almost everyone at DC .80 2.00
306-313 (75¢): 306-Brief origin Star Boy 1.00
Annual 1(1982, 52 pgs.)-Giffen-c/a; 1st app./origin new Invisible Kid who joins Legion .80 2.00
Annual 2,3: 2(1983, 52 pgs.)-Giffen-c; Karate Kid & Princess Projectra wed & resign. 3(1984, 52 pgs.) .65 1.60
...The Great Darkness Saga (1989, $17.95, 196 pgs.)-r/LSH #287,290-294 & Annual #3; Giffen-c/a 2.60 7.50 18.00
NOTE: ***Aparo*** *c-282, 283, 300(part).* ***Austin*** *c-268i.* ***Buckler*** *c-273p, 274p, 276p.* ***Colan*** *a-311p.* ***Ditko*** *a(p)-267, 268, 272, 274, 276, 281.* ***Giffen*** *a-285-313p, Annual 1p; c-287p, 288p, 289, 290p, 291p, 292, 293, 294-299p, 300, 301-313p, Annual 1p, 2p.* ***Perez*** *c-268p, 277-280, 281p.* ***Starlin*** *a-265.* ***Staton*** *a-259p, 260p, 280.* ***Tuska*** *a-308p.*

LEGION OF SUPER-HEROES (Reprinted in Tales of the Legion)
Aug, 1984 - No. 63, Aug, 1989 ($1.25/$1.75, deluxe format)
DC Comics

1-Silver ink logo .70 1.80
2-10: 4-Death of Karate Kid. 5-Death of Nemesis Kid 1.50
11-14: 12-Cosmic Boy, Lightning Lad, & Saturn Girl resign. 14-Intro new members: Tellus, Sensor Girl, Quislet 1.20
15-18: 15-17-Crisis tie-ins. 18-Crisis x-over 1.50
19-25: 25-Sensor Girl i.d. revealed as Princess Projectra 1.20
26-36,39-44: 35-Saturn Girl rejoins. 40-$1.75 cover price begins. 42,43-Millennium tie-ins. 44-Origin Quislet 1.10
37,38-Death of Superboy 1.70 4.20 10.00
45 ($2.95, 68 pgs.)-Anniversary issue 1.20 3.00
46-49,51-62 1.00
50-Double size, $2.50 1.00 2.50
63-Final issue 1.40
Annual 1 (10/85, 52 pgs.)-Crisis tie-in .70 1.80
Annual 2,3: 2 (1986, 52 pgs.). 3 (1987, $2.25, 52 pgs.) .65 1.60
Annual 4 (1988, $2.50, 52 pgs.) .80 2.00
NOTE: ***Byrne*** *c-36p.* ***Giffen*** *a(p)-1, 2, 50-55, 57-63, Annual 1p, 2; c-1-5p, 54p, Annual 1.* ***Orlando*** *a-6p.* ***Steacy*** *c-45-50, Annual 3.*

LEGION OF SUPER-HEROES
Nov, 1989 - Present ($1.75/$1/.95)
DC Comics

1-Giffen-c/a(p) & scripts begin (4 pg.-a only #18) .70 1.75
2-49,51-53,55-58: 8-Origin. 13-Free poster by Giffen showing new costumes. 21-24-Lobo & Darkseid storyline. 26-New map of headquarters. 34-Six pg. preview of Timber Wolf mini-series. 40-Minor Legionnaires app. 41-Intro Legionnaires (3/93) .70 1.75
50-($3.50, 68 pgs.) 1.40 3.50
54-($2.95)-Die-cut & foil stamped-c 1.20 3.00
59-61: 59-Begin $1.95-c. 61-(9/94)-Zero Hour .80 2.00
0-(10/94) .80 2.00
62-(11/94)-67 .80 2.00
Annual 1-5 (1990-4, $3.50, 68 pgs.): 4-Bloodlines. 5-Elseworlds story 1.40 3.50
NOTE: ***Giffen*** *a-1-24; breakdowns-26-32, 34-36; c-1-7, 8(part), 9-24.* ***Brandon Peterson*** *a(p)-15(1st for DC), 16, 18, Annual 2(54 pgs.); c-Annual 2p.* ***Swan/Anderson*** *c-8(part).*

LEMONADE KID, THE (See Bobby Benson's B-Bar-B Riders)
1990 ($2.50, color, 28 pgs.)
AC Comics

1-Powell-c(r); Red Hawk-r by Powell; Lemonade Kid-r/Bobby Benson by Powell (2 stories) 1.00 2.50

LENNON SISTERS LIFE STORY, THE (See 4-Color No. 951, 1014)

LEONARD NIMOY'S PRIMORTALS
Mar, 1995-Present (1.95, color)
Tekno Comix

1-Concept by Leonard Nimoy & Isaac Asimov; w/bound-in game piece & trading card 0.40 0.80 2.00

LEONARDO (Also see Teenage Mutant Ninja Turtles)
Dec, 1986 ($1.50, B&W, One shot)
Mirage Studios

1 1.30 3.10 7.50

LEO THE LION
No date(1960s) (10¢)
I. W. Enterprises

Leroy #1 © STD

Lex Luthor #1 © DC

Liberty Scouts #3 © CEN

	GD25	FN65	NM94
1-Reprint	1.20	3.00	6.00

LEROY (Teen-age)
Nov, 1949 - No. 6, Nov, 1950
Standard Comics

	GD25	FN65	NM94
1	5.35	16.00	32.00
2-Frazetta text illo.	4.00	12.00	24.00
3-6: 3-Lubbers-a	4.00	10.00	20.00

LETHAL FOES OF SPIDER-MAN (Sequel to Deadly Foes of Spider-Man)
Sept, 1993 - No. 4, Dec, 1993 ($1.75, mini-series)
Marvel Comics

	GD25	FN65	NM94
1-4			1.00

LET'S PRETEND (CBS radio)
May-June, 1950 - No. 3, Sept-Oct, 1950
D. S. Publishing Co.

	GD25	FN65	NM94
1	10.00	30.00	70.00
2,3	9.15	27.50	55.00

LET'S READ THE NEWSPAPER
1974
Charlton Press

	GD25	FN65	NM94
nn-Features Quincy by Ted Sheares			1.00

LET'S TAKE A TRIP (TV) (CBS Television Presents)
Spring, 1958
Pines Comics

	GD25	FN65	NM94
1-Marv Levy-c/a	3.20	8.00	16.00

LETTERS TO SANTA (See March of Comics No. 228)

LEX LUTHOR: THE UNAUTHORIZED BIOGRAPHY (DC)(Value: cover or less)

LIBERTY COMICS (Miss Liberty No. 1)
No. 4, 1945 - No. 15, July, 1946 (MLJ & other reprints)
Green Publishing Co.

	GD25	FN65	NM94
4	11.50	34.00	80.00
5 (5/46)-The Prankster app; Starr-a	10.00	30.00	65.00
10-Hangman & Boy Buddies app.; Suzie & Wilbur begin; reprints Hangman story from Hangman #8	13.00	40.00	90.00
11(V2#2, 1/46)-Wilbur in women's clothes	11.00	32.00	75.00
12-Black Hood & Suzie app.	11.00	32.00	75.00
14,15-Patty of Airliner; Starr-a in both	7.50	22.50	45.00

LIBERTY GUARDS
No date (1946?)
Chicago Mail Order

	GD25	FN65	NM94
nn-Reprints Man of War #1 with cover of Liberty Scouts #1; Gustavson-c	25.00	75.00	175.00

LIBERTY PROJECT, THE (Eclipse)(Value: cover or less)

LIBERTY SCOUTS (See Liberty Guards & Man of War)
No. 2, June, 1941 - No. 3, Aug, 1941
Centaur Publications

	GD25	FN65	NM94
2(#1)-Origin The Fire-Man, Man of War; Vapo-Man & Liberty Scouts begin; intro Liberty Scouts; Gustavson-c/a in both	104.00	310.00	725.00
3(#2)-Origin & 1st app. The Sentinel	82.00	246.00	575.00

LICENCE TO KILL (Eclipse)(Value: cover or less)

LIDSVILLE (TV)
Oct, 1972 - No. 5, Oct, 1973
Gold Key

	GD25	FN65	NM94
1	1.70	5.00	12.00
2-5	1.00	2.50	6.00

LIEUTENANT, THE (TV)
April-June, 1964
Dell Publishing Co.

	GD25	FN65	NM94
1-Photo-c	2.40	6.00	12.00

LIEUTENANT BLUEBERRY (Also see Blueberry)
1991 - No. 3, 1991 (Color, graphic novel)
Epic Comics (Marvel)

	GD25	FN65	NM94
1,2 ($8.95)-Moebius-a in all	1.50	3.75	9.00
3 ($14.95)	2.15	6.50	15.00

LT. ROBIN CRUSOE, U.S.N. (See Movie Comics & Walt Disney Showcase #26)

LIFE OF CAPTAIN MARVEL, THE
Aug, 1985 - No. 5, Dec, 1985 ($2.00 cover; Baxter paper)
Marvel Comics Group

	GD25	FN65	NM94
1-All reprint Starlin issues of Iron Man #55, Capt. Marvel #25-34 plus Marvel Feature #12 (all with Thanos)		.80	2.00
2-5: 4-New Thanos back-c by Starlin		.80	2.00

LIFE OF CHRIST, THE
No. 301, 1949 (35¢, 100 pgs.)
Catechetical Guild Educational Society

	GD25	FN65	NM94
301-Reprints from Topix(1949)-V5#11,12	3.60	9.00	18.00

LIFE OF CHRIST: THE EASTER STORY, THE
1993 ($2.99, slick stock)
Marvel Comics/Nelson

	GD25	FN65	NM94
nn		1.20	3.00

LIFE OF CHRIST VISUALIZED
1942 - No. 3, 1943
Standard Publishers

	GD25	FN65	NM94
1-3: All came in cardboard case	3.60	9.00	18.00
With case.....	6.70	20.00	40.00

LIFE OF CHRIST VISUALIZED
1946? (48 pgs. in color)
The Standard Publ. Co.

	GD25	FN65	NM94
nn	1.60	4.00	8.00

LIFE OF ESTHER VISUALIZED
No. 2062, 1947 (48 pgs. in color)
The Standard Publ. Co.

	GD25	FN65	NM94
2062	1.60	4.00	8.00

LIFE OF JOSEPH VISUALIZED
No. 1054, 1946 (48 pgs. in color)
The Standard Publ. Co.

	GD25	FN65	NM94
1054	1.60	4.00	8.00

LIFE OF PAUL (See The Living Bible)

LIFE OF POPE JOHN PAUL II, THE
Jan, 1983
Marvel Comics Group

	GD25	FN65	NM94
1			1.50

LIFE OF RILEY, THE (See 4-Color No. 917)

LIFE OF THE BLESSED VIRGIN
1950 (68pgs.) (square binding)
Catechetical Guild (Giveaway)

	GD25	FN65	NM94
nn-Contains "The Woman of the Promise" & "Mother of Us All" rebound	3.60	9.00	18.00

LIFE'S LIKE THAT
1945 (25¢, B&W, 68 pgs.)
Croyden Publ. Co.

	GD25	FN65	NM94
nn-Newspaper Sunday strip-r by Neher	4.70	14.00	28.00

LIFE'S LITTLE JOKES
No date (1924) (B&W, 52 pgs.)
M.S. Publ. Co.

	GD25	FN65	NM94
nn-By Rube Goldberg	32.00	95.00	225.00

LIFE STORIES OF AMERICAN PRESIDENTS (See Dell Giants)

Life Story #45 © FAW

Life With Archie #50 © AP

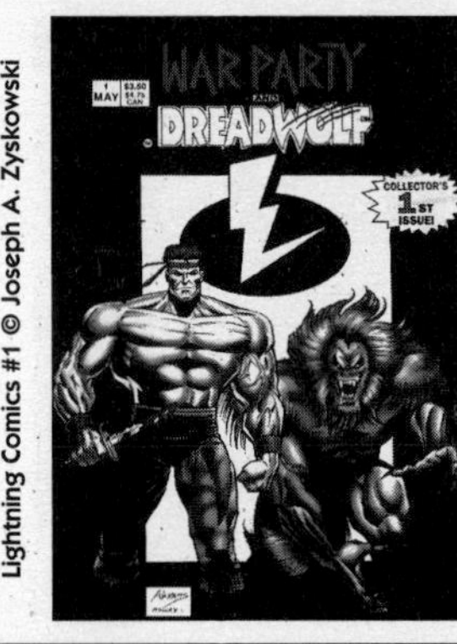

Lightning Comics #1 © Joseph A. Zyskowski

LIFE STORY
Apr, 1949 - V8#46, Jan, 1953; V8#47, Apr, 1953 (All have photo-c?)
Fawcett Publications

	GD25	FN65	NM94
V1#1	9.15	27.50	55.00
2	4.20	12.50	25.00
3-6	4.00	10.00	20.00
V2#7-12	4.00	10.00	20.00
V3#13-Wood-a	10.00	30.00	65.00
V3#14-18, V4#19-21,23,24	3.60	9.00	18.00
V4#22-Drug use story	4.00	10.00	20.00
V5#25-30, V6#31-35	3.60	9.00	18.00
V6#36- "I sold drugs" on-c	4.00	10.00	20.00
V7#37,40-42, V8#44,45	2.40	6.00	12.00
V7#38, V8#43-Evans-a	4.00	11.00	22.00
V7#39-Drug Smuggling & Junkie story	3.60	9.00	18.00
V8#46,47 (Scarce)	3.60	9.00	18.00

NOTE: ***Powell*** *a-13, 23, 24, 26, 28, 30, 32, 39.* ***Marcus Swayze*** *a-1-3, 10-12, 15, 16, 20, 21, 23-25, 31, 35, 37, 40, 44, 46.*

LIFE WITH ARCHIE
Sept, 1958 - No. 285, 1991
Archie Publications

	GD25	FN65	NM94
1	22.00	65.00	215.00
2-(9/59)	14.00	40.00	100.00
3-5: 3-(7/60)	10.00	30.00	70.00
6-10	5.00	15.00	35.00
11-20	3.00	9.40	22.00
21-30	2.40	7.30	17.00
31-41	1.70	4.20	10.00
42-45: 42-Pureheart begins (1st app., 1965?)	1.30	3.00	8.00
46-Origin Pureheart	1.70	5.00	12.00
47-59: 50-United Three begin: Pureheart (Archie), Superteen (Betty), Captain Hero (Jughead). 59-Pureheart ends	1.00	2.50	6.00
60-100: 60-Archie band begins		1.40	3.50
101-285: 208-Reintro Veronica. 238-(9/83)-25th anniversary issue; Ol' Betsy (jalopy) replaced. 279-Intro Mustang Sally ($1.00)			1.50

NOTE: ***Gene Colan*** *a-272-279, 285, 286.*

LIFE WITH MILLIE (Formerly A Date With Millie) (Modeling With Millie #21 on)
No. 8, Dec, 1960 - No. 20, Dec, 1962
Atlas/Marvel Comics Group

	GD25	FN65	NM94
8-Teenage	6.70	20.00	40.00
9-11	4.70	14.00	28.00
12-20	4.00	10.00	20.00

LIFE WITH SNARKY PARKER (TV)
August, 1950
Fox Feature Syndicate

	GD25	FN65	NM94
1-Early TV comic; photo-c from TV puppet show	19.00	57.00	130.00

LIGHT AND DARKNESS WAR, THE
Oct, 1988 - No. 6, Dec, 1989 ($1.95, limited series)
Epic Comics (Marvel)

	GD25	FN65	NM94
1-6		.80	2.00

LIGHT FANTASTIC, THE (Terry Pratchett's)
June, 1992 - No. 4, Sept, 1992 ($2.50, color, mini-series)
Innovation Publishing

	GD25	FN65	NM94
1-4: Adapts 2nd novel in Discworld series		1.00	2.50

LIGHT IN THE FOREST (See 4-Color No. 891)

LIGHTNING COMICS (Formerly Sure-Fire No. 1-3)
No. 4, Dec, 1940 - No. 13(V3#1), June, 1942
Ace Magazines

	GD25	FN65	NM94
4-Characters continue from Sure-Fire	61.00	182.00	425.00
5,6: 6-Dr. Nemesis begins	45.00	135.00	315.00
V2#1-6: 2- "Flash Lightning" becomes "Lash..."	36.00	107.00	250.00
V3#1-Intro. Lightning Girl & The Sword	36.00	107.00	250.00

NOTE: ***Anderson*** *a-V2#6.* ***Mooney*** *c-V1#5, 6, V2#1-6, V3#1. Bondage c-V2#6. Lightning-c on all.*

LIGHTNING COMICS PRESENTS
May, 1994 ($3.50)
Lightning Comics

	GD25	FN65	NM94
1-Red foil-c distributed by Diamond Distributors		1.20	3.00
1-Black/yellow/blue-c distrib. by Capital Distributors		1.20	3.00
1-Red/yellow-c distributed by H. World		1.20	3.00
1-Platinum		1.20	3.00

LI'L (See Little)

LILY OF THE ALLEY IN THE FUNNIES
No date (1927) (10-1/4x15-1/2"; 28 pgs. in color)
Whitman Publishing Co.(one of their first two books)

	GD25	FN65	NM94
W936 - By T. Burke (very rare)	40.00	120.00	270.00

LIMITED COLLECTORS' EDITION (See Famous First Edition & Rudolph the Red Nosed Reindeer; becomes All-New Collectors' Edition)
(#21-34,51-59: 84 pgs.; #35-41: 68 pgs.; #42-50: 60 pgs.)
C-21, Summer, 1973 - No. C-59, 1978 ($1.00) (10x13-1/2")
National Periodical Publications/DC Comics

	GD25	FN65	NM94
nn(C-20)-Rudolph (date?)	1.30	3.25	8.00
C-21: Shazam (TV); r/Captain Marvel Jr. #11 by Raboy; C.C. Beck-c, biog. & photo	1.00	2.50	6.00
C-22: Tarzan; complete origin reprinted from #207-210; all Kubert-c/a; Joe Kubert biography & photo inside	1.00	2.50	6.00
C-23: House of Mystery; Wrightson, N. Adams/Orlando, G. Kane/Wood, Toth, Aragones, Sparling reprints		1.60	4.00
C-24: Rudolph The Red-nosed Reindeer		1.60	4.00
C-25: Batman; Neal Adams-c/a(r); G.A. Joker-r; Batman/Enemy Ace-r; has photos from TV show	1.30	3.25	8.00
C-26: See Famous First Edition C-26 (same contents)			
C-27: Shazam (TV); G.A. Capt. Marvel & Mary Marvel-r; Beck-r		1.60	4.00
C-29: Tarzan; reprints "Return of Tarzan" from #219-223 by Kubert; Kubert-c	1.00	2.50	6.00
C-31: Superman; origin-r; N. Adams-a; photos of George Reeves from 1950s TV show on inside b/c; Burnley, Boring-r	1.00	2.50	6.00
C-32: Ghosts (new-a)		1.60	4.00
C-33: Rudolph The Red-nosed Reindeer(new-a)		1.60	4.00
C-34: Christmas with the Super-Heroes; unpublished Angel & Ape story by Oksner & Wood; Batman & Teen Titans-r	1.00	2.50	6.00
C-35: Shazam (TV); photo cover features TV's Captain Marvel, Jackson Bostwick; Beck-r; TV photos inside b/c		1.60	4.00
C-36: The Bible; all new adaptation beginning with Genesis by Kubert, Redondo & Mayer; Kubert-c	1.00	2.50	6.00
C-37: Batman; r-1946 Sundays; inside b/c photos of Batman TV show villains (all villain issue; r/G.A. Joker, Catwoman, Penguin, Two-Face, & Scarecrow stories plus 1946 Sundays-r)	1.30	3.25	8.00
C-38: Superman; 1 pg. N. Adams; part photo-c; photos from TV show on inside back-c		1.60	4.00
C-39: Secret Origins of Super-Villains; N. Adams-i(r); G.A. Batman-r; Beck-r		1.60	4.00
C-40: Dick Tracy by Gould featuring Flattop; newspaper-r from 12/21/43 - 5/17/44; biog. of Chester Gould	1.00	2.50	6.00
C-41: Super Friends (TV); JLA-r(1965); Toth-c/a		1.60	4.00
C-42: Rudolph		1.60	4.00
C-43: Christmas with the Super-Heroes; Wrightson, S&K, Neal Adams-a	1.00	2.50	6.00
C-44: Batman; N. Adams-p(r) & G.A.-r; painted-c	1.30	3.25	8.00
C-45: More Secret Origins of Super-Villains; Flash-r/#105; G.A. Wonder Woman & Batman/Catwoman-r		1.60	4.00
C-46: Justice League of America(1963-r); 3 pgs. Toth-a	1.00	2.50	6.00
C-47: Superman Salutes the Bicentennial (Tomahawk interior); 2 pgs. new-a		1.20	3.00

Limited Collectors' Edition #16 © DC

Lippy the Lion and Hardy Har Har #1 © H-B

Li'l Abner #70 © UFS

	GD25	FN65	NM94
C-48: Superman Vs. The Flash (Superman/Flash race); swipes-c to Superman #199; r/Superman #199 & Flash #175; 6 pgs. Neal Adams-a	1.00	2.50	6.00
C-49: Superboy & the Legion of Super-Heroes		1.60	4.00
C-50: Rudolph The Red-nosed Reindeer		1.20	3.00
C-51: Batman; Neal Adams-c/a	1.30	3.25	8.00
C-52: The Best of DC; Neal Adams-c/a; Toth, Kubert-a	1.00	2.50	6.00
C-57: Welcome Back, Kotter-r(TV)(5/78)		1.20	3.00
C-59: Batman's Strangest Cases; N. Adams-r; Wrightson-r/Swamp Thing #7; N. Adams/Wrightson-c	1.30	3.25	8.00

NOTE: *All-r with exception of some special features and covers.* ***Aparo*** *a-52r; c-37.* ***Grell*** *c-49.* ***Infantino*** *a-25, 39, 44, 45, 52.* ***Bob Kane*** *r-25.* ***Robinson*** *r-25, 44.* ***Sprang*** *r-44. Issues #21-31, 35-39, 45, 48 have back cover cut-outs.*

LINDA (Everybody Loves...) (Phantom Lady No. 5 on)
Apr-May, 1954 - No. 4, Oct-Nov, 1954
Ajax-Farrell Publ. Co.

	GD25	FN65	NM94
1-Kamenish-a	10.00	30.00	70.00
2-Lingerie panel	8.35	25.00	50.00
3,4	6.70	20.00	40.00

LINDA CARTER, STUDENT NURSE
Sept, 1961 - No. 9, Jan, 1963
Atlas Comics (AMI)

	GD25	FN65	NM94
1-Al Hartley-c	4.70	14.00	28.00
2-9	4.00	10.00	20.00

LINDA LARK
Oct-Dec, 1961 - No. 8, Aug-Oct, 1963
Dell Publishing Co.

	GD25	FN65	NM94
1	3.20	8.00	16.00
2-8	1.60	4.00	8.00

LINUS, THE LIONHEARTED (TV)
September, 1965
Gold Key

	GD25	FN65	NM94
1 (10155-509)	8.35	25.00	50.00

LION, THE (See Movie Comics)

LION OF SPARTA (See Movie Classics)

LIPPY THE LION AND HARDY HAR HAR (TV)
March, 1963 (Hanna-Barbera) (12¢) (See Hanna-Barbera Band Wagon #1)
Gold Key

	GD25	FN65	NM94
1 (10049-303)	8.35	25.00	50.00

LI'L ABNER (See Comics on Parade, Sparkle, Sparkler Comics, Tip Top Comics & Tip Topper)
1939 - 1940
United Features Syndicate

	GD25	FN65	NM94
Single Series 4 ('39)	57.00	170.00	400.00
Single Series 18 ('40) (#18 on inside, #2 on-c)	50.00	150.00	350.00

LI'L ABNER (Al Capp's; continued from Comics on Parade #58)
No. 61, Dec, 1947 - No. 97, Jan, 1955 (See Oxydol-Dreft)
Harvey Publ. No. 61-69 (2/49)/Toby Press No. 70 on

	GD25	FN65	NM94
61(#1)-Wolverton & Powell-a	25.00	75.00	175.00
62-65: 63-The Wolf Girl app. 65-Powell-a	16.00	48.00	110.00
66,67,69,70	13.00	40.00	90.00
68-Full length Fearless Fosdick-c/story	14.00	43.00	100.00
71-74,76,80	10.00	30.00	70.00
75,77-79,86,91-All with Kurtzman art; 91-r/#77	13.00	40.00	90.00
81-85,87-90,92-94,96,97: 93-reprints #71	10.00	30.00	60.00
95-Full length Fearless Fosdick story	11.50	34.00	80.00
...& the Creatures from Drop-Outer Space-nn (Job Corps giveaway; 36 pgs., in color)(entire book by Frank Frazetta)	22.00	65.00	150.00
...Joins the Navy (1950) (Toby Press Premium)	10.00	30.00	60.00
...by Al Capp Giveaway (Circa 1955, nd)	10.00	30.00	60.00

LI'L ABNER
1951
Toby Press

	GD25	FN65	NM94
1	14.00	43.00	100.00

LI'L ABNER'S DOGPATCH (See Al Capp's...)

LITTLE AL OF THE F.B.I.
No. 10, 1950 (no month) - No. 11, Apr-May, 1951 (Saunders painted-c)
Ziff-Davis Publications

	GD25	FN65	NM94
10(1950)	10.00	30.00	70.00
11(1951)	8.35	25.00	50.00

LITTLE AL OF THE SECRET SERVICE
No. 10, 7-8/51; No. 2, 9-10/51; No. 3, Winter, 1951 (Saunders painted-c)
Ziff-Davis Publications

	GD25	FN65	NM94
10(#1)-Spanking panels (2)	11.00	32.00	75.00
2,3	8.35	25.00	50.00

LITTLE ALONZO
1938 (B&W, 5-1/2x8-1/2")(Christmas giveaway)
Macy's Dept. Store

	GD25	FN65	NM94
nn-By Ferdinand the Bull's Munro Leaf	6.70	20.00	40.00

LITTLE AMBROSE
September, 1958
Archie Publications

	GD25	FN65	NM94
1-Bob Bolling-c	10.00	30.00	70.00

LITTLE ANGEL
No. 5, Sept, 1954; No. 6, Sept, 1955 - No. 16, Sept, 1959
Standard (Visual Editions)/Pines

	GD25	FN65	NM94
5-Last pre-code issue	4.70	14.00	28.00
6-16	3.20	8.00	16.00

LITTLE ANNIE ROONEY
1935 (25¢, B&W dailies, 48 pgs.)
David McKay Publications

	GD25	FN65	NM94
Book 1-Daily strip-r by Darrell McClure	13.50	41.00	95.00

LITTLE ANNIE ROONEY (See King Comics & Treasury of Comics)
1938; Aug, 1948 - No. 3, Oct, 1948
David McKay/St. John/Standard

	GD25	FN65	NM94
Feature Books 11 (McKay, 1938)	20.00	60.00	200.00
1 (St. John)	10.00	30.00	70.00
2,3	6.70	20.00	40.00

LITTLE ARCHIE (The Adventures of... #13-on) (See Archie Giant Series Mag. #527, 534, 538, 545, 549, 556, 560, 566, 570, 583, 594, 596, 607, 609, 619)
1956 - No. 180, Feb, 1983 (Giants No. 3-84)
Archie Publications

	GD25	FN65	NM94
1-(Scarce)	49.00	145.00	340.00
2 (1957)	22.00	65.00	150.00
3-5: 3-(1958)-Bob Bolling-c & giant issues begin	14.00	43.00	100.00
6-10	10.00	30.00	70.00
11-20	6.70	20.00	40.00
21-30	4.20	12.50	25.00
31-40: Little Pureheart apps. #40-42,44	2.80	7.00	14.00
41-60: 42-Intro The Little Archies. 59-Little Sabrina begins	1.60	4.00	8.00
61-84: 84-Last Giant-Size	1.00	2.50	6.00
85-100		1.20	3.00
101-180			1.50
...In Animal Land 1(1957)	11.50	34.00	80.00
...In Animal Land 17(Winter, 1957-58)-19(Summer,1958)-Formerly Li'l Jinx	6.70	20.00	40.00

LITTLE ARCHIE CHRISTMAS SPECIAL (See Archie Giant Series #581)

LITTLE ARCHIE COMICS DIGEST ANNUAL (...Magazine #5 on)
10/77 - No. 48, 5/91 (Digest-size, 128 pgs., later issues $1.35-$1.50)

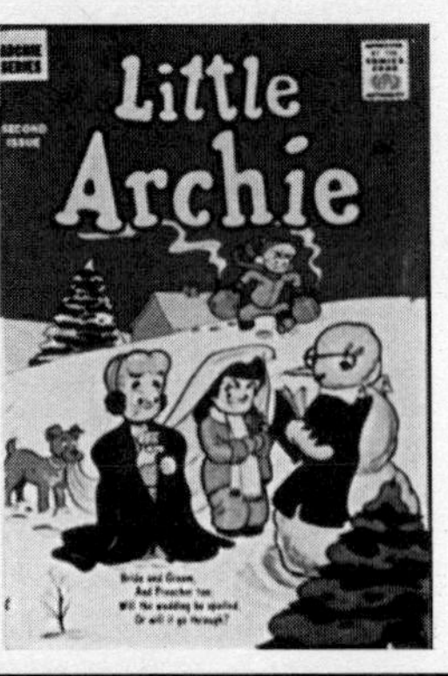

Little Archie #2 © AP

Little Audry and Melvin #1 © HARV

Little Dot #11 © HARV

Archie Publications

	GD25	FN65	NM94
1(10/77)-Reprints		.80	2.00
2(4/78)-Neal Adams-a			1.40
3(11/78)-The Fly-r by S&K; Neal Adams-a			1.40
4(4/79) - 48: 28,40,46-Christmas-c			1.40

NOTE: *Little Archie, Little Jinx, Little Jughead & Little Sabrina in most issues.*

LITTLE ARCHIE DIGEST MAGAZINE
July, 1991 - Present ($1.50, digest size)
Archie Comics

	GD25	FN65	NM94
V2#1-16			1.50

LITTLE ARCHIE MYSTERY
Aug, 1963 - No. 2, Oct, 1963 (12¢ issues)
Archie Publications

	GD25	FN65	NM94
1	11.00	32.00	75.00
2	6.35	19.00	38.00

LITTLE ASPIRIN (See Little Lenny & Wisco)
July, 1949 - No. 3, Dec, 1949 (52 pgs.)
Marvel Comics (CnPC)

	GD25	FN65	NM94
1-Oscar app.; Kurtzman-a (4 pgs.)	11.00	32.00	75.00
2-Kurtzman-a (4 pgs.)	7.00	21.00	42.00
3-No Kurtzman-a	4.00	11.00	22.00

LITTLE AUDREY (Also see Playful...)
April, 1948 - No. 24, May, 1952
St. John Publ.

	GD25	FN65	NM94
1-1st app. Little Audrey	27.00	81.00	190.00
2	13.00	40.00	90.00
3-5	10.00	30.00	60.00
6-10	5.85	17.50	35.00
11-20: 16-X-Mas-c	4.00	11.00	22.00
21-24	3.20	8.00	16.00

LITTLE AUDREY (See Harvey Hits #11, 19)
No. 25, Aug, 1952 - No. 53, April, 1957
Harvey Publications

	GD25	FN65	NM94
25-(Paramount Pictures Famous Star... on-c)	8.35	25.00	50.00
26-30: 26-28-Casper app.	4.35	13.00	26.00
31-40: 32-35-Casper app.	4.00	10.00	20.00
41-53	2.80	7.00	14.00
...Clubhouse 1 (9/61, 68 pg. Giant) w/reprints	6.35	19.00	38.00

LITTLE AUDREY
Aug, 1992 - No. 8, July, 1993 ($1.25/$1.50)
Harvey Comics

	GD25	FN65	NM94
V2#1-5			1.25
6-8 ($1.50)			1.50

LITTLE AUDREY (...Yearbook)
1950 (50¢, 260 pgs.)
St. John Publishing Co.

	GD25	FN65	NM94
Contains 8 complete 1949 comics rebound; Casper, Alice in Wonderland, Little Audrey, Abbott & Costello, Pinocchio, Moon Mullins, Three Stooges (from Jubilee), Little Annie Rooney app. (Rare)	57.00	171.00	400.00

(Also see All Good & Treasury of Comics)

NOTE: *This book contains remaindered St. John comics; many variations possible.*

LITTLE AUDREY & MELVIN (Audrey & Melvin No. 62)
May, 1962 - No. 61, Dec, 1973
Harvey Publications

	GD25	FN65	NM94
1	8.35	25.00	50.00
2-5	4.20	12.50	25.00
6-10	3.20	8.00	16.00
11-20	2.00	5.00	10.00
21-40: 22-Richie Rich app.	1.20	2.90	7.00
41-50,54-61	1.00	2.00	5.00
51-53: All 52 pg. Giants	1.00	2.50	6.00

LITTLE AUDREY TV FUNTIME
Sept, 1962 - No. 33, Oct, 1971 (#1-31: 68 pgs.; #32,33: 52 pgs.)
Harvey Publications

	GD25	FN65	NM94
1-Richie Rich app.	5.85	17.50	35.00
2,3: Richie Rich app.	4.00	10.00	20.00
4,5: 5-25¢ & 35¢ issues exist	3.20	8.00	16.00
6-10	1.60	4.00	8.00
11-20	1.20	2.90	7.00
21-33	1.00	2.00	5.00

LITTLE BAD WOLF (See 4-Color #403, 473, 564, Walt Disney's C&S #52, Walt Disney Showcase #21 & Wheaties)

LITTLE BEAVER
No. 211, Jan, 1949 - No. 870, Jan, 1958 (All painted-c)
Dell Publishing Co.

	GD25	FN65	NM94
4-Color 211('49)-All Harman-a	8.35	25.00	50.00
4-Color 267,294,332(5/51)	4.35	13.00	26.00
3(10-12/51)-8(1-3/53)	4.00	11.00	22.00
4-Color 483(8-10/53),529	4.00	11.00	22.00
4-Color 612,660,695,744,817,870	4.00	10.00	20.00

LITTLE BIT
March, 1949 - No. 2, June, 1949
Jubilee/St. John Publishing Co.

	GD25	FN65	NM94
1,2	4.00	11.00	22.00

LITTLE DOT (See Humphrey, Li'l Max, Sad Sack, and Tastee-Freez Comics)
Sept, 1953 - No. 164, April, 1976
Harvey Publications

	GD25	FN65	NM94
1-Intro./1st app. Richie Rich & Little Lotta	66.00	197.00	460.00
2-1st app. Freckles & Pee Wee (Richie Rich's poor friends)	33.00	100.00	230.00
3	20.00	60.00	140.00
4	16.00	48.00	110.00
5-Origin dots on Little Dot's dress	23.00	70.00	160.00
6-Richie Rich, Little Lotta, & Little Dot all on cover; 1st Richie Rich cover featured	19.00	57.00	130.00
7-10: 8-Last pre-code issue? (11/54)	10.00	30.00	65.00
11-20	8.35	25.00	50.00
21-40	4.20	12.50	25.00
41-60	2.80	7.00	14.00
61-80	1.80	4.50	9.00
81-100	1.00	2.00	5.00
101-141		1.40	3.50
142-145: All 52 pg. Giants	1.00	2.00	5.00
146-164			1.50
Shoe store giveaway 2	5.00	15.00	30.00

NOTE: *Richie Rich & Little Lotta in all.*

LITTLE DOT
Sept, 1992 - No. 7, June, 1994 ($1.25/$1.50)
Harvey Comics

	GD25	FN65	NM94
V2#1-3: Little Dot, Little Lotta, Richie Rich in all			1.25
4-7 ($1.50)			1.50

LITTLE DOT DOTLAND (Dot Dotland No. 62, 63)
July, 1962 - No. 61, Dec, 1973
Harvey Publications

	GD25	FN65	NM94
1-Richie Rich begins	8.35	25.00	50.00
2,3	4.00	12.00	24.00
4,5	3.60	9.00	18.00
6-10	2.40	6.00	12.00
11-20	1.80	4.50	9.00
21-30	1.00	2.00	5.00
31-50,55-61		1.40	3.50
51-54: All 52 pg. Giants	1.00	2.50	6.00

LITTLE DOT'S UNCLES & AUNTS (See Harvey Hits No. 4, 13, 24)

Little Eva #1 © STJ

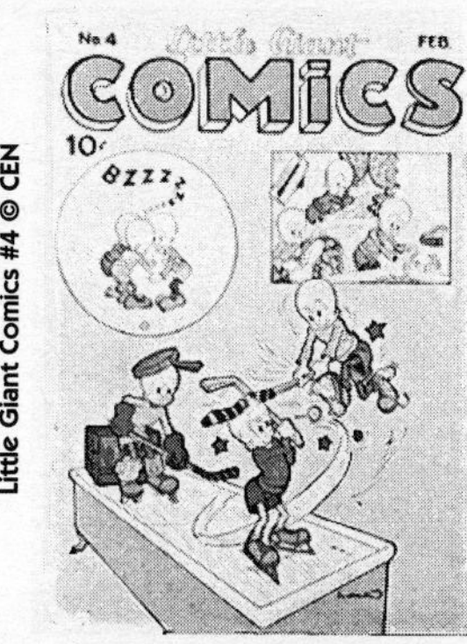

Little Giant Comics #4 © CEN

Little Jack Frost #1 © AVON

Oct, 1961; No. 2, Aug, 1962 - No. 52, April, 1974
Harvey Enterprises

	GD25	FN65	NM94
1-Richie Rich begins; 68 pgs. begin	9.15	27.50	55.00
2,3	4.70	14.00	28.00
4,5	3.20	8.00	16.00
6-10	2.40	6.00	12.00
11-20	1.80	4.50	9.00
21-37: Last 68 pg. issue	1.00	2.50	6.00
38-52: All 52 pg. Giants	1.00	2.00	5.00

LITTLE DRACULA
Jan, 1992 - No. 3, May, 1992 ($1.25, quarterly, mini-series)
Harvey Comics

	GD25	FN65	NM94
1-3			1.25

LITTLE EVA
May, 1952 - No. 31, Nov, 1956
St. John Publishing Co.

	GD25	FN65	NM94
1	10.00	30.00	60.00
2	5.00	15.00	30.00
3-5	4.00	10.00	20.00
6-10	2.80	7.00	14.00
11-31	2.40	6.00	12.00
3-D 1,2(10/53, 11/53, 25¢)-Both came w/glasses. 1-Infinity-c	14.00	43.00	100.00
I.W. Reprint #1-3,6-8	.80	2.00	4.00
Super Reprint #10,12('63),14,16,18('64)	.80	2.00	4.00

LITTLE FIR TREE, THE
nd (1942) (8-1/2x11") (12 pgs. with cover, color & B&W, heavy paper)
W. T. Grant Co. (Christmas giveaway)

nn-Story by Hans Christian Anderson; 8 pg. Kelly-r/Santa Claus Funnies (not signed); X-Mas-c
(One copy in Mint sold for $1750.00 in 1986 & another copy in VF sold for $1000.00 in 1991)

LI'L GENIUS (Summer Fun No. 54) (See Blue Bird & Giant Comics #3)
1954 - No. 52, 1/65; No. 53, 10/65; No. 54, 10/85 - No. 55, 1/86
Charlton Comics

	GD25	FN65	NM94
1	8.35	25.00	50.00
2	4.20	12.50	25.00
3-15,19,20	3.20	8.00	16.00
16,17-(68 pgs.)	4.00	11.00	22.00
18-(100 pgs., 10/58)	5.35	16.00	32.00
21-35	2.80	7.00	14.00
36-53	1.40	3.50	7.00
54,55			1.50

LI'L GHOST
Feb, 1958; Nov?, 1958 - No. 3, Mar, 1959
St. John Publishing Co./Fago No. 1 on

	GD25	FN65	NM94
1(St. John)	6.35	19.00	38.00
1(Fago)-Al Fago-c/a begins	4.00	12.00	24.00
2,3: 2-(1/59)	3.60	9.00	18.00

LITTLE GIANT COMICS
7/38 - No. 3, 10/38; No. 4, 2/39 (132 pgs.) (6-3/4x4-1/2")
Centaur Publications

	GD25	FN65	NM94
1-B&W with color-c; stories, puzzles, magic	39.00	118.00	275.00
2,3-B&W with color-c	33.00	100.00	230.00
4 (6-5/8x9-3/8")(68 pgs., B&W inside)	34.00	103.00	240.00

NOTE: ***Filchock** c-2, 4. **Gustavson** a-1. **Pinajian** a-4. **Bob Wood** a-1.*

LITTLE GIANT DETECTIVE FUNNIES
Oct, 1938 - No. 4, Jan, 1939 (132 pgs., B&W) (6-3/4x4-1/2")
Centaur Publications

	GD25	FN65	NM94
1-B&W with color-c	39.00	118.00	275.00
2,3	33.00	100.00	230.00
4(1/39, B&W; color-c; 68 pgs., 6-1/2x9-1/2")-Eisner-r	34.00	103.00	240.00

LITTLE GIANT MOVIE FUNNIES
Aug, 1938 - No. 2, Oct, 1938 (132 pgs., B&W) (6-3/4x4-1/2")
Centaur Publications

	GD25	FN65	NM94
1-Ed Wheelan's "Minute Movies" reprints	39.00	118.00	275.00
2-Ed Wheelan's "Minute Movies" reprints	30.00	90.00	210.00

LITTLE GROUCHO (...the Red-Headed Tornado; ...Grouchy No. 2)
No. 16; Feb-Mar, 1955 - No. 2, June-July, 1955 (See Tippy Terry)
Reston Publ. Co.

	GD25	FN65	NM94
16, 1 (2-3/55)	5.85	17.50	35.00
2(6-7/55)	4.00	11.00	22.00

LITTLE HIAWATHA (See 4-Color #439, 787, 901, 988 & Walt Disney's C&S #143)

LITTLE IKE
April, 1953 - No. 4, Oct, 1953
St. John Publishing Co.

	GD25	FN65	NM94
1	7.50	22.50	45.00
2	4.00	11.00	22.00
3,4	3.60	9.00	18.00

LITTLE IODINE (See Giant Comic Album)
No. 224, 4/49 - No. 257, 1949: 3-5/50 - No. 56, 4-6/62 (1-4: 52pgs.)
Dell Publishing Co.

	GD25	FN65	NM94
4-Color 224-By Jimmy Hatlo	10.00	30.00	70.00
4-Color 257	8.35	25.00	50.00
1(3-5/50)	10.00	30.00	60.00
2-5	4.00	12.00	24.00
6-10	3.20	8.00	16.00
11-20	2.80	7.00	14.00
21-30: 27-Xmas-c	2.40	6.00	12.00
31-40	1.80	4.50	9.00
41-56	1.40	3.50	7.00

LITTLE JACK FROST
1951
Avon Periodicals

	GD25	FN65	NM94
1	5.35	16.00	32.00

LI'L JINX (Formerly Ginger?) (Little Archie in Animal Land #17)
(Also see Pep Comics #62)
No. 11, Nov, 1956 - No. 16, Sept, 1957
Archie Publications

	GD25	FN65	NM94
11 (#1)-By Joe Edwards	8.35	25.00	50.00
12-16	5.35	16.00	32.00

LI'L JINX (See Archie Giant Series Magazine No. 223)

LI'L JINX CHRISTMAS BAG (See Archie Giant Series Mag. No. 195, 206, 219)

LI'L JINX GIANT LAUGH-OUT (See Archie Giant Series Mag. No. 176, 185)
No. 33, Sept, 1971 - No. 43, Nov, 1973 (52 pgs.)
Archie Publications

	GD25	FN65	NM94
33-43		1.20	3.00

LITTLE JOE (See 4-Color #1, Popular Comics & Super Comics)

LITTLE JOE
April, 1953
St. John Publishing Co.

	GD25	FN65	NM94
1	3.20	8.00	16.00

LITTLE JOHNNY & THE TEDDY BEARS
1907 (10x14") (32 pgs. in color)
Reilly & Britton Co.

	GD25	FN65	NM94
nn-By J. R. Bray	25.00	75.00	175.00

LI'L KIDS (Also see Li'l Pals)
8/70 - No. 2, 10/70; No. 3, 11/71 - No. 12, 6/73
Marvel Comics Group

Little Lizzie #2 © MEG

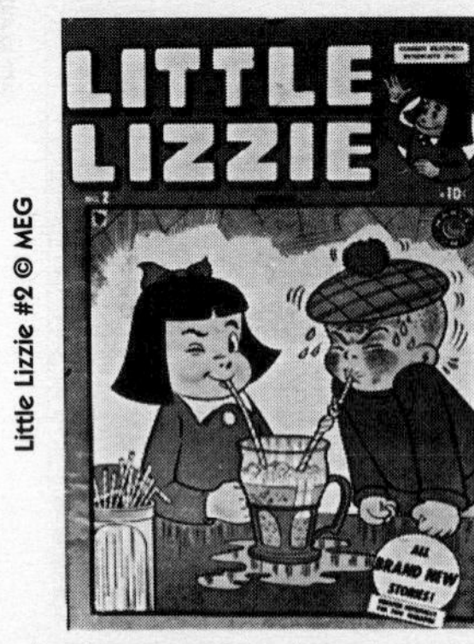

Li'l Menace #1 © FAGO

Little Mermaid #1© WDC

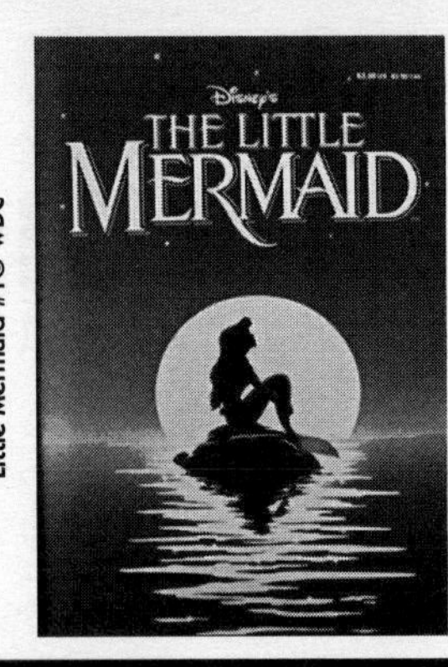

	GD25	FN65	NM94
1	1.50	3.75	9.00
2-12: 10-12-Calvin app.		1.80	4.50

LITTLE KING (See 4-Color No. 494, 597, 677)

LITTLE KLINKER
Nov, 1960 (20 pgs.) (slick cover)
Little Klinker Ventures (Montgomery Ward Giveaway)

	GD25	FN65	NM94
nn	2.00	5.00	10.00

LITTLE LANA (Formerly Lana)
No. 8, Nov, 1949; No. 9, Mar, 1950
Marvel Comics (MjMC)

	GD25	FN65	NM94
8,9	4.70	14.00	28.00

LITTLE LENNY
June, 1949 - No. 3, Nov, 1949
Marvel Comics (CDS)

	GD25	FN65	NM94
1-Little Aspirin app.	7.50	22.50	45.00
2,3	4.00	11.00	22.00

LITTLE LIZZIE
6/49 - No. 5, 4/50; 9/53 - No. 3, Jan, 1954
Marvel Comics (PrPI)/Atlas (OMC)

	GD25	FN65	NM94
1	9.15	27.50	55.00
2-5	4.00	14.00	28.00
1 (9/53, 2nd series by Atlas)-Howie Post-c	5.35	16.00	32.00
2,3	4.00	11.00	22.00

LITTLE LOTTA (See Harvey Hits No. 10)
11/55 - No. 110, 11/73; No. 111, 9/74 - No. 121, 5/76
V2#1, Oct, 1992 - No. 4, July, 1993 ($1.25)
Harvey Publications

	GD25	FN65	NM94
1-Richie Rich (r) & Little Dot begin	32.00	96.00	225.00
2,3	14.00	43.00	100.00
4,5	9.15	27.50	55.00
6-10	7.50	22.50	45.00
11-20	4.70	14.00	28.00
21-40	3.00	7.50	15.00
41-60	2.40	6.00	12.00
61-80	1.30	3.25	8.00
81-99	1.00	2.00	5.00
100-103: All 52 pg. Giants	1.00	2.50	6.00
104-121: 121-Exist?		1.00	2.50
V2#1-4 (1992-93)			1.25

LITTLE LOTTA FOODLAND
9/63 - No. 14, 10/67; No. 15, 10/68 - No. 29, Oct, 1972
Harvey Publications

	GD25	FN65	NM94
1-Little Lotta, Little Dot, Richie Rich, 68 pgs. begin	10.00	30.00	70.00
2,3	6.35	19.00	38.00
4,5	4.00	12.00	24.00
6-10	3.20	8.00	16.00
11-20	2.00	6.00	12.00
21-26: 26-Last 68 pg. issue	1.80	4.50	9.00
27,28: Both 52 pgs.	1.00	2.50	6.00
29-(36 pgs.)		1.80	4.50

LITTLE LULU (Formerly Marge's...)
No. 207, Sept, 1972 - No. 268, April, 1984
Gold Key 207-257/Whitman 258 on

	GD25	FN65	NM94
207,209,220-Stanley-r. 207-1st app. Henrietta	1.00	2.50	6.00
208,210-219: 208-1st app. Snobbly, Wilbur's brother	1.00	2.00	5.00
221-240,242-249, 250(r/#166), 251-254(r/#206)		1.60	4.00
241,263,268-Stanley-r		1.60	4.00
255-262,264-267: 256-r/#212		.80	2.00

LITTLE MARY MIXUP (See Comics On Parade & Single Series #10, 26)

LITTLE MAX COMICS (Joe Palooka's Pal; see Joe Palooka)
Oct, 1949 - No. 73, Nov, 1961
Harvey Publications

	GD25	FN65	NM94
1-Infinity-c; Little Dot begins; Joe Palooka on-c	12.00	36.00	85.00
2-Little Dot app.; Joe Palooka on-c	7.00	21.00	42.00
3-Little Dot app.; Joe Palooka on-c	5.00	15.00	30.00
4-10: 5-Little Dot app., 1pg.	3.60	9.00	18.00
11-20	2.80	7.00	14.00
21-73: 23-Little Dot app. 38-r/#20. 70-73-Little Lotta, Richie Rich app.	1.80	4.50	9.00

LI'L MENACE
Dec, 1958 - No. 3, May, 1959
Fago Magazine Co.

	GD25	FN65	NM94
1-Peter Rabbit app.	5.00	15.00	30.00
2-Peter Rabbit (Vincent Fago's)	4.00	11.00	22.00
3	3.60	9.00	18.00

LITTLE MERMAID, THE (Walt Disney's...; also see Disney's...)
1990 (no date given)($5.95, no ads, 52 pgs.)
W. D. Publications (Disney)

	GD25	FN65	NM94
nn-Adapts animated movie	1.00	2.50	6.00
nn-Comic version ($2.50)		1.00	2.50

LITTLE MERMAID, THE
1992 - No. 4, 1992 ($1.50, mini-series)
Disney Comics

	GD25	FN65	NM94
1-4: Based on movie			1.50
1-4: 2nd printings sold at Wal-Mart w/different-c			1.50

LITTLE MISS MUFFET
No. 11, Dec, 1948 - No. 13, March, 1949
Best Books (Standard Comics)/King Features Synd.

	GD25	FN65	NM94
11-Strip reprints; Fanny Cory-c/a	6.70	20.00	40.00
12,13-Strip reprints; Fanny Cory-c/a	4.35	13.00	26.00

LITTLE MISS SUNBEAM COMICS
June-July, 1950 - No. 4, Dec-Jan, 1950-51
Magazine Enterprises/Quality Bakers of America

	GD25	FN65	NM94
1	10.00	30.00	65.00
2-4	5.35	16.00	32.00
...Advs. In Space ('55)	4.00	11.00	22.00
Bread Giveaway 1-4(Quality Bakers, 1949-50)-14 pgs. each	4.00	10.00	20.00
Bread Giveaway (1957,61; 16pgs, reg. size)	3.60	9.00	18.00

LITTLE MONSTERS, THE (See March of Comics #423, Three Stooges #17)
Nov, 1964 - No. 44, Feb, 1978
Gold Key

	GD25	FN65	NM94
1	3.60	9.00	18.00
2	1.80	4.50	9.00
3-10	1.40	3.50	7.00
11-20		1.40	3.50
21-44: 20,34-39,43-Reprints			1.50

LITTLE MONSTERS (Now)(Value: cover or less)

LITTLE NEMO (See Cocomalt, Future Comics, Help, Jest, Kayo, Punch, Red Seal, & Superworld; most by Winsor McCay Jr., son of famous artist) (Other McCay books: see Little Sammy Sneeze & Dreams of the Rarebit Fiend)

LITTLE NEMO (...in Slumberland)
1906, 1909 (Sunday strip reprints in color) (cardboard covers)
Doffield & Co.(1906)/Cupples & Leon Co.(1909)

	GD25	FN65	NM94
1906-11x16-1/2" in color by Winsor McCay; 30 pgs. (Very Rare)	250.00	750.00	2500.00
1909-10x14" in color by Winsor McCay (Very Rare)	200.00	600.00	2000.00

LITTLE NEMO (...in Slumberland)
1945 (28 pgs.; 11x7-1/4"; B&W)
McCay Features/Nostalgia Press('69)

Little Orphan Annie Sparkies Giveaway © Newsv Synd.

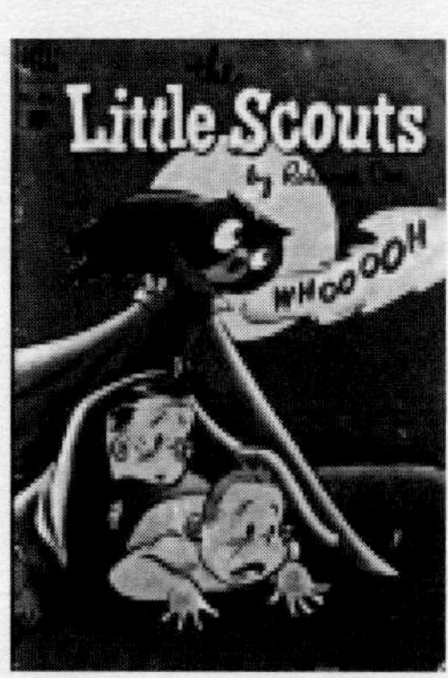

Little Scouts #2 © Roland Coe

Li'l Willie #21 © MEG

GD25 FN65 NM94

1905 & 1911 reprints by Winsor McCay 8.35 25.00 50.00
1969-70 (Exact reprint) 1.30 4.00 8.00

LITTLE ORPHAN ANNIE (See Annie, Famous Feature Stories, Feature Books #7, Marvel Super Special, Merry Christmas..., Popular Comics, Super Book #7, 11, 23 & Super Comics)

LITTLE ORPHAN ANNIE (See Treasure Box of Famous Comics)
1926 - 1934 (Daily strip reprints) (7x8-3/4") (B&W)
Cupples & Leon Co.
(Hardcover Editions, 100 pgs.)

1(1926)-Little Orphan Annie 25.00 75.00 175.00
1(1926)Hardcover 39.00 118.00 275.00
2('27)-In the Circus 17.00 52.00 120.00
2(/27)Hardcover 27.00 81.00 190.00
3('28)-The Haunted House 17.00 52.00 120.00
3('28)Hardcover 27.00 81.00 190.00
4('29)-Bucking the World 17.00 52.00 120.00
4('29)Hardcover 26.00 78.00 180.00
5('30)-Never Say Die 17.00 52.00 120.00
5(-30)Hardcover 26.00 78.00 180.00
6('31)-Shipwrecked 17.00 52.00 120.00
6('31)Hardcover 7('32) 23.00 70.00 160.00
7('32)-A Willing Helper 13.00 40.00 90.00
7('32)Hardcover 17.00 52.00 120.00
8('33)-In Cosmic City 13.00 40.00 90.00
8('33)Hardcover 17.00 52.00 120.00
9('34)-Uncle Dan 17.00 52.00 120.00
9('34)Hardcover 22.00 65.00 150.00
NOTE: *Each book reprints dailies from the previous year.*

LITTLE ORPHAN ANNIE
No. 7, 1937 - No. 3, Sept-Nov, 1948; No. 206, Dec, 1948
David McKay Publ./Dell Publishing Co.

Feature Books(McKay) 7-(1937) (Rare) 75.00 225.00 750.00
4-Color 12(1941) 51.00 154.00 360.00
4-Color 18(1943)-Flag-c 41.00 125.00 290.00
4-Color 52(1944) 31.00 94.00 220.00
4-Color 76(1945) 26.00 78.00 180.00
4-Color 107(1946) 22.00 67.00 155.00
4-Color 152(1947) 14.00 43.00 100.00
1(3-5/48)-r/strips from 5/7/44 to 7/30/44 15.50 45.00 105.00
2-r/strips from 7/21/40 to 9/9/40 10.00 30.00 60.00
3-r/strips from 9/10/40 to 11/9/40 10.00 30.00 60.00
4-Color 206(12/48) 8.35 25.00 50.00
Junior Commandos Giveaway (same-c as 4-Color #18, K.K. Publ.)(Big Shoe Store); same back cover as '47 Popped Wheat giveaway; 16 pgs; flag-c; r/strips 9/7/42-10/10/42 24.00 72.00 165.00
Popped Wheat Giveaway ('47)-16 pgs. full color; reprints strips from 5/3/40 to 6/20/40 1.60 4.00 8.00
Quaker Sparkies Giveaway (1940) 13.00 40.00 90.00
Quaker Sparkies Giveaway (1941, Full color, 20 pgs.); "LOA and the Rescue"; r/strips 4/13/39-6/21/39 & 7/6/39-7/17/39. "LOA and the Kidnappers"; r/strips 11/28/38-1/28/39 11.00 32.00 75.00
Quaker Sparkies Giveaway (1942, Full color, 20 pgs.); "LOA and Mr. Gudge"; r/strips 2/13/38-3/21/38 & 4/18/37-5/30/37. "LOA and the Great Am" 10.00 30.00 65.00

LI'L PALS (Also see Li'l Kids)
Sept, 1972 - No. 5, May, 1973
Marvel Comics Group

1-5 1.40 3.50

LI'L PAN (Formerly Rocket Kelly; becomes Junior Comics with #9)
No. 6, Dec-Jan, 1946-47 - No. 8, Apr-May, 1947 (Also see Wotalife Comics)
Fox Features Syndicate

6 6.35 19.00 38.00
7,8: 7-Atomic bomb story 4.00 12.00 24.00

LITTLE PEOPLE (See 4-Color #485, 573, 633, 692, 753, 809, 868, 908, 959, 1024, 1062)

LITTLE RASCALS (See 4-Color #674, 778, 825, 883, 936, 974, 1030, 1079, 1137, 1174, 1224, 1297)

LI'L RASCAL TWINS (Formerly Nature Boy)
No. 6, 1957 - No. 18, Jan, 1960
Charlton Comics

6-Li'l Genius & Tomboy in all 4.70 14.00 28.00
7-18 2.80 7.00 14.00

LITTLE ROQUEFORT COMICS (See Paul Terry's Comics #105)
June, 1952 - No. 9, Oct, 1953; No. 10, Summer, 1958
St. John Publishing Co.(all pre-code)/Pines No. 10

1-By Paul Terry 7.50 22.50 45.00
2 4.00 11.00 22.00
3-10: 10-CBS Television Presents on-c 3.20 8.00 16.00

LITTLE SAD SACK (See Harvey Hits No. 73, 76, 79, 81, 83)
Oct, 1964 - No. 19, Nov, 1967
Harvey Publications

1-Richie Rich app. on cover only 3.20 8.00 16.00
2-19 1.20 3.00 6.00

LITTLE SAMMY SNEEZE
1905 (28 pgs. in color; 11x16-1/2")
New York Herald Co.

nn-By Winsor McCay (Rare) 314.00 943.00 2200.00
NOTE: *Rarely found in fine to mint condition.*

LITTLE SCOUTS
No. 321, Mar, 1951 - No. 587, Oct, 1954
Dell Publishing Co.

4-Color #321 (#1, 3/51) 4.00 10.00 20.00
2(10-12/51) - 6(10-12/52) 2.40 6.00 12.00
4-Color #462,506,550,587 2.40 6.00 12.00

LITTLE SHOP OF HORRORS SPECIAL (DC)(Value: cover or less)

LITTLE SPUNKY
No date (1963?) (10¢)
I. W. Enterprises

1-Reprint 1.00 2.50 5.00

LITTLE STOOGES, THE (The Three Stooges' Sons)
Sept, 1972 - No. 7, Mar, 1974
Gold Key

1-Norman Maurer cover/stories in all 1.30 3.25 8.00
2-7 1.60 4.00

LITTLEST OUTLAW (See 4-Color #609)

LITTLEST SNOWMAN, THE
No. 755, 12/56; No. 864, 12/57; 12-2/1963-64
Dell Publishing Co.

4-Color #755,864, 1(1964) 4.00 12.00 24.00

LI'L TOMBOY (Formerly Fawcett's Funny Animals; see Giant Comics #3)
V14#92, Oct, 1956; No. 93, Mar, 1957 - No. 107, Feb, 1960
Charlton Comics

V14#92 4.00 11.00 22.00
93-107: 97-Atomic Bunny app. 3.20 8.00 16.00

LITTLE TREE THAT WASN'T WANTED, THE
1960, (Color, 28 pgs.)
W. T. Grant Co. (Giveaway)

nn-Christmas giveaway 1.60 4.00 8.00

LI'L WILLIE COMICS (Formerly & becomes Willie Comics #22 on)
No. 20, July, 1949 - No. 21, Sept, 1949
Marvel Comics (MgPC)

20,21: 20-Little Aspirin app. 5.00 15.00 30.00

LITTLE WOMEN (See Power Record Comics)

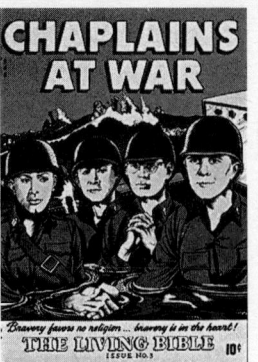

The Living Bible #3 © LBC

Lobo #7 © DC

Logan's Run #7 © MEG

GD25 FN65 NM94

LIVE IT UP (Spire Christian)(Value: cover or less)

LIVING BIBLE, THE
Fall, 1945 - No. 3, Spring, 1946
Living Bible Corp.

	GD25	FN65	NM94
1-The Life of Paul; all have L. B. Cole-c	17.00	52.00	120.00
2-Joseph & His Brethren; Jonah & the Whale	11.50	34.00	80.00
3-Chaplains At War (classic-c)	19.00	58.00	135.00

LOBO
Dec, 1965; No. 2, Oct, 1966
Dell Publishing Co.

	GD25	FN65	NM94
1,2	1.80	4.50	9.00

LOBO (Also see Action #650, Adventures of Superman, Justice League, L.E.G.I.O.N., Mister Miracle, Omega Men #3 & Superman #41)
Nov, 1990 - No. 4, Feb, 1991 ($1.50, mini-series)
DC Comics

	GD25	FN65	NM94
1-(99¢)-Giffen plots/Breakdowns in all		1.50	3.75
2-Legion '89 spin-off		.90	2.25
3,4: 1-4 have Bisley painted covers & art		.70	1.75
Annual 1 (1993, $3.50, 68 pgs.)-Bloodlines x-over		1.40	3.50
...: Blazing Chain of Love 1 (9/92, $1.50)-Denys Cowan-c/a; Alan Grant scripts			1.00
...Convention Special 1 (1993, $1.75)			1.50
...Paramilitary Christmas Special 1 (1991, $2.39, 52 pgs.)-Bisley-c/a		.80	2.00
...: Portrait of a Victim 1 (1993, $1.75)			1.50

LOBO
Dec, 1993 - Present ($1.75, mature readers)
DC Comics

	GD25	FN65	NM94
1-($2.95)-Foil enhanced-c; Alan Grant scripts begin		.80	2.00
2-7-Alan Grant scripts			1.50
8,9: 8-Begin $1.95-c. 9-(9/94)		.70	1.75
0,10-14: 0-(10/94)-Origin retold		.80	2.00
Annual 2 (1994, $3.50)-21 artists (20 listed on-c); Alan Grant script; Elseworlds story		1.40	3.50
Lobocop 1 (2/94, $1.95)-Alan Grant scripts; painted-c		.80	2.00
...In the Chair 1 (8/94, $1.95, 36 pgs.)		.80	2.00

LOBO: A CONTRACT ON GAWD
Apr, 1994 - No. 4, July, 1994 ($1.75, mini-series, mature readers)
DC Comics

	GD25	FN65	NM94
1-4: Alan Grant scripts. 3-Groo cameo		.70	1.75

LOBO: INFANTICIDE
Oct, 1992 - No. 4, Jan, 1993 ($1.50, mini-series, mature readers)
DC Comics

	GD25	FN65	NM94
1-4: Giffen-c/a; Alan Grant scripts			1.50

LOBO'S BACK
May, 1992 - No. 4, Nov, 1992 ($1.50, mini-series, mature readers)
DC Comics

	GD25	FN65	NM94
1-4: 1-Has 3 outer covers. Bisley painted-c 1,2; a-1-3. 3-Sam Kieth-c; all have Giffen plots/breakdown & Grant scripts			1.50
Trade paperback (1993, $9.95)-r/1-4	1.70	4.20	10.00

LOBO: UNAMERICAN GLADIATORS
June, 1993 - No. 4, Sept, 1993 ($1.75, mini-series, mature readers)
DC Comics

	GD25	FN65	NM94
1-4: Mignola-c; Grant/Wagner scripts		.70	1.75

LOCKE! (Blackthorne)(Value: cover or less)

LOCO (Magazine) (Satire)
Aug, 1958 - V1#3, Jan, 1959
Satire Publications

	GD25	FN65	NM94
V1#1-Chic Stone-a	4.00	12.00	24.00
V1#2,3-Severin-a, 2 pgs. Davis; 3-Heath-a	3.60	9.00	18.00

GD25 FN65 NM94

LOGAN'S RUN
Jan, 1977 - No. 7, July, 1977
Marvel Comics Group

	GD25	FN65	NM94
1: 1-5-Based on novel & movie		1.20	3.00
2-5,7: 6,7-New stories adapted from novel			1.50
6-1st Thanos solo story (back-up) by Zeck (6/77)	1.70	5.10	12.00

NOTE: ***Austin** a-6i. **Gulacy** c-6. **Kane** c-7p. **Perez** a-1-5p; c-1-5p. **Sutton** a-6p, 7p.*

LOIS & CLARK, THE NEW ADVENTURES OF SUPERMAN
1994 ($9.95)
DC Comics

	GD25	FN65	NM94
1-r/Man of Steel #2, Superman Annual 1, Superman #9 & 11, Action #600 & 655, Adventures of Superman #445, 462 & 466	1.70	4.20	10.00

LOIS LANE (DC)(Value: cover or less)(Also see Daring, Man of Steel #2, New Adventures of Supergirl, Showcase & Superman's Girlfriend Lois Lane)

LOLLY AND PEPPER
No. 832, Sept, 1957 - July, 1962
Dell Publishing Co.

	GD25	FN65	NM94
4-Color 832(#1)	4.00	10.00	20.00
4-Color 940,978,1086,1206	3.20	8.00	16.00
01-459-207 (7/62)	3.20	8.00	16.00

LOMAX (See Police Action)

LONE EAGLE (The Flame No. 5 on)
Apr-May, 1954 - No. 4, Oct-Nov, 1954
Ajax/Farrell Publications

	GD25	FN65	NM94
1	9.15	27.50	55.00
2-4: 3-Bondage-c	5.35	16.00	32.00

LONELY HEART (Formerly Dear Lonely Hearts; Dear Heart #15 on)
No. 9, March, 1955 - No. 14, Feb, 1956
Ajax/Farrell Publ. (Excellent Publ.)

	GD25	FN65	NM94
9-Kamenesque-a; (Last precode)	5.85	17.50	35.00
10-14	4.00	10.00	20.00

LONE RANGER, THE (See Ace Comics, Aurora, Dell Giants, Feature Books #21, 24, Future Comics, Golden Comics Digest #48, King Comics, Magic Comics & March of Comics #165, 174, 193, 208, 225, 238, 310, 322, 338, 350)

LONE RANGER, THE
No. 3, 1939 - No. 167, Feb, 1947
Dell Publishing Co.

	GD25	FN65	NM94
Large Feature Comic 3(1939)-Heigh-Yo Silver; text with illus. by Robert Weisman; also exists as a Whitman #710	50.00	150.00	500.00
Large Feature Comic 7(1939)-Illustr. by Henry Vallely; Hi-Yo Silver the Lone Ranger to the Rescue; also exists as a Whitman #715	65.00	195.00	650.00
Feature Book 21(1940), 24(1941)	50.00	150.00	500.00
4-Color 82(1945)	39.00	118.00	275.00
4-Color 98(1945),118(1946)	30.00	90.00	210.00
4-Color 125(1946),136(1947)	22.00	67.00	155.00
4-Color 151,167(1947)	19.00	57.00	130.00

LONE RANGER, THE (Movie, radio & TV; Clayton Moore starred as Lone Ranger in the movies; No. 1-37: strip reprints)(See Dell Giants)
Jan-Feb, 1948 - No. 145, May-July, 1962
Dell Publishing Co.

	GD25	FN65	NM94
1 (36 pgs.)-The Lone Ranger, his horse Silver, companion Tonto & his horse Scout begin	64.00	193.00	450.00
2 (52 pgs. begin, end #41)	30.00	90.00	210.00
3-5	23.00	70.00	160.00
6,7,9,10	19.00	57.00	130.00
8-Origin retold; Indian back-c begin, end #35	24.00	72.00	165.00
11-20: 11- "Young Hawk" Indian boy serial begins, ends #145	12.00	36.00	85.00
21,22,24-31: 51-Reprint. 31-1st Mask logo	10.00	30.00	70.00
23-Origin retold	13.50	41.00	95.00

32-37: 32-Painted-c begin. 36-Animal photo back-c begin, end #49. 37-Last

The Lone Ranger # 7 © Lone Ranger

The Lone Rangers' Famous Horse Hi-Yo Silver #4 © Lone Ranger

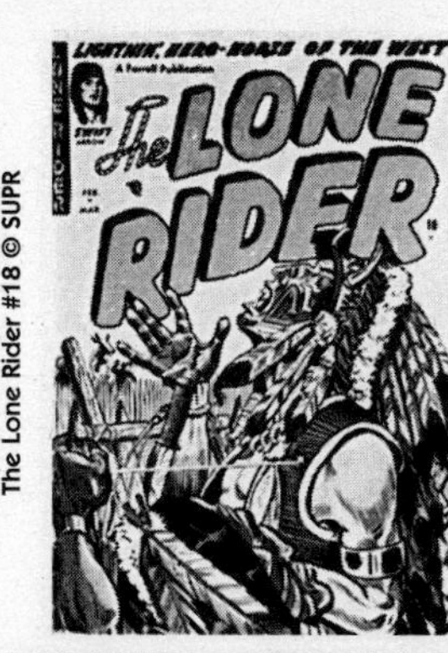

The Lone Rider #18 © SUPR

	GD25	FN65	NM94
newspaper-r issue; new outfit	9.15	27.50	55.00
38-41 (All 52 pgs.)	7.50	22.50	45.00
42-50 (36 pgs.)	6.35	19.00	38.00
51-74 (52 pgs.): 56-One pg. origin story of Lone Ranger & Tonto. 71-Blank inside-c	6.35	19.00	38.00
75-99: 76-Flag-c. 79-X-mas-c	5.00	15.00	30.00
100	7.50	22.50	45.00
101-111: Last painted-c	5.35	16.00	32.00
112-Clayton Moore photo-c begin, end #145	17.00	52.00	120.00
113-117	10.00	30.00	60.00
118-Origin Lone Ranger, Tonto, & Silver retold; Special anniversary issue	16.00	48.00	110.00
119-145: 139-Last issue by Fran Striker	9.15	27.50	55.00
Cheerios Giveaways (1954, 16 pgs., 2-1/2x7", soft-c) #1- "The Lone Ranger, His Mask & How He Met Tonto". #2- "The Lone Ranger & the Story of Silver" each....	13.00	40.00	95.00
Doll Giveaways (Gabriel Ind.)(1973, 3-1/4x5")- "The Story of The Lone Ranger" & "The Carson City Bank Robbery"	1.60	4.00	8.00
How the Lone Ranger Captured Silver Book(1936)-Silvercup Bread giveaway	50.00	150.00	350.00
...In Milk for Big Mike (1955, Dairy Association giveaway), soft-c; 5x7-1/4", 16 pgs.	11.50	34.00	80.00
Merita Bread giveaway (1954, 16 pgs., 5x7-1/4")- "How to Be a Lone Ranger Health & Safety Scout"	11.50	34.00	80.00

NOTE: ***Hank Hartman*** *painted c(signed)-65, 66, 70, 75, 82; unsigned-64?, 67-69?, 71, 72, 73?, 74?, 76-78, 80, 81, 83-91, 92?, 93-111.* ***Ernest Nordli*** *painted c(signed)-42, 50, 52, 53, 56, 59, 60; unsigned-39-41, 44-49, 51, 54, 55, 57, 58, 61-63?*

LONE RANGER, THE
9/64 - No. 16, 12/69; No. 17, 11/72; No. 18, 9/74 - No. 28, 3/77
Gold Key (Reprints in #13-20)

	GD25	FN65	NM94
1-Retells origin	4.00	11.00	22.00
2	2.40	6.00	12.00
3-10: Small Bear-r in #6-12	1.60	4.00	8.00
11-17	1.20	3.00	6.00
18-28	1.00	2.50	5.00
Golden West 1(30029-610, 10/66)-Giant; r/most Golden West #3 including Clayton Moore photo front/back-c	8.35	25.00	50.00

LONE RANGER AND TONTO, THE
Aug, 1994 - No. 4, Nov, 1994 ($2.50, limited series)
Topps Comics

	GD25	FN65	NM94
1-4		1.00	2.50

LONE RANGER COMICS, THE
1939(inside) (shows 1938 on-c) (52 pgs. in color; regular size)
Lone Ranger, Inc. (Ice cream mail order)

	GD25	FN65	VF82
nn-(Scarce)-The first western comic devoted to a single character; not by Vallely	383.00	1150.00	2300.00

(Estimated up to 20 total copies exist, none in NM/Mint)

LONE RANGER'S COMPANION TONTO, THE (TV)
No. 312, Jan, 1951 - No. 33, Nov-Jan/58-59 (All painted-c)
Dell Publishing Co.

	GD25	FN65	NM94
4-Color 312(#1, 1/51)	13.00	40.00	90.00
2(8-10/51),3: (#2 titled "Tonto")	7.50	22.50	45.00
4-10	5.00	15.00	30.00
11-20	4.00	12.00	24.00
21-33	3.60	9.00	18.00

NOTE: ***Ernest Nordli*** *painted c(signed)-2, 7; unsigned-3-6, 8-11, 12?, 13, 14, 18?, 22-24? See Aurora Comic Booklets.*

LONE RANGER'S FAMOUS HORSE HI-YO SILVER, THE (TV)
No. 369, Jan, 1952 - No. 36, Oct-Dec, 1960 (All painted-c, most by Sam Sevitt)
Dell Publishing Co.

	GD25	FN65	NM94
4-Color 369(#1)-Silver's origin as told by The Lone Ranger	10.00	30.00	60.00
4-Color 392(#2, 4/52)	5.00	15.00	30.00
3(7-9/52)-10(4-6/52)	4.00	10.00	20.00
11-36	3.00	7.50	15.00

LONE RIDER (Also see The Rider)
April, 1951 - No. 26, July, 1955 (#3-on: 36 pgs.)
Superior Comics(Farrell Publications)

	GD25	FN65	NM94
1 (52 pgs.)-The Lone Rider & his horse Lightnin' begin; Kamenish-a begins	12.00	36.00	85.00
2 (52 pgs.)-The Golden Arrow begins (origin)	7.50	22.50	45.00
3-6: 6-Last Golden Arrow	5.85	17.50	35.00
7-Golden Arrow becomes Swift Arrow; origin of his shield	7.50	22.50	45.00
8-Origin Swift Arrow	9.15	27.50	55.00
9,10	5.00	15.00	30.00
11-14	4.00	12.00	24.00
15-Golden Arrow origin-r from #2, changing name to Swift Arrow	5.00	15.00	30.00
16-20,22-26: 23-Apache Kid app.	4.00	11.00	22.00
21-3-D effect-c	10.00	30.00	65.00

LONE WOLF AND CUB (First)(Value: cover or less)

LONG BOW (...Indian Boy)(See Indians & Jumbo Comics #141)
1951 - No. 9, Wint, 1952/53
Fiction House Magazines (Real Adventures Publ.)

	GD25	FN65	NM94
1-Most covers by Maurice Whitman	10.00	30.00	70.00
2	7.50	22.50	45.00
3-9	6.00	18.00	36.00

LONG JOHN SILVER & THE PIRATES (Formerly Terry & the Pirates)
No. 30, Aug, 1956 - No. 32, March, 1957 (TV)
Charlton Comics

	GD25	FN65	NM94
30-32: Whitman-c	6.70	20.00	40.00

LONGSHOT (Also see X-Men #10, 1992)
Sept, 1985 - No. 6, Feb, 1986 (Limited series)
Marvel Comics Group

	GD25	FN65	NM94
1-Arthur Adams/Whilce Portacio-c/a in all	1.30	4.00	9.00
2	1.30	3.00	8.00
3-5: 4-Spider-Man app.	1.00	2.50	6.00
6-Double size	1.20	2.90	7.00
Trade Paperback (1989, $16.95)-r/#1-6	2.40	7.25	17.00

LOONEY TUNES (2nd Series)
April, 1975 - No. 47, July, 1984
Gold Key/Whitman

	GD25	FN65	NM94
1		.80	2.00
2-47: Reprints: #1-4,16; 38-46(1/3-r)			1.00

LOONEY TUNES (3th Series)
Apr, 1994 - Present ($1.50)
DC Comics

	GD25	FN65	NM94
1-12: 1-Marvin Martian-c/sty; Bugs Bunny, Roadrunner, Daffy, Tweety begin			1.50

LOONEY TUNES AND MERRIE MELODIES COMICS ("Looney Tunes" #166 (8/55) on)
1941 - No. 246, July-Sept, 1962
Dell Publishing Co.

	GD25	FN65	VF82	NM94
1-Porky Pig, Bugs Bunny, Daffy Duck, Elmer Fudd, Mary Jane & Sniffles, Pat Patsy and Pete begin (1st comic book app. of each). Bugs Bunny story by Win Smith (early Mickey Mouse artist)	500.00	1500.00	3250.00	5000.00

(Estimated up to 171 total copies exist, 8 in NM/Mint)

	GD25	FN65	NM94
2 (11/41)	111.00	334.00	780.00
3-Kandi the Cave Kid begins by Walt Kelly; also in #4-6,8,11,15	93.00	280.00	650.00
4-Kelly-a	83.00	250.00	580.00
5-Bugs Bunny The Super-Duper Rabbit story (1st funny animal super hero, 3/42; also see Coo Coo); Kelly-a	69.00	205.00	480.00

Loony Tunes #46 © Warner Bros.

Lost In Space #1 © CBS

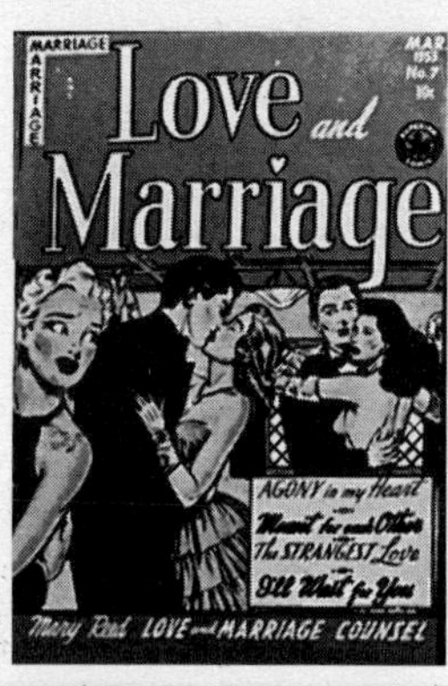

Love and Marriage #7 © SUPR

	GD25	FN65	NM94
6,8-Kelly-a	51.00	154.00	360.00
7,9,10: 9-Painted-c. 10-Flag-c	41.00	122.00	285.00
11,15-Kelly-a; 15-X-Mas-c	41.00	122.00	285.00
12-14,16-19	36.00	109.00	255.00
20-25: Pat, Patsy & Pete by Walt Kelly in all	36.00	109.00	255.00
26-30	26.00	78.00	180.00
31-40: 33-War bond-c. 39-X-Mas-c	19.00	57.00	130.00
41-50	15.00	45.00	105.00
51-60	10.00	30.00	60.00
61-80	7.50	22.50	45.00
81-99: 87-X-Mas-c	5.00	15.00	30.00
100	5.85	17.50	35.00
101-120	4.00	12.00	24.00
121-150	3.60	9.00	18.00
151-200: 159-X-Mas-c	2.40	6.00	12.00
201-246	1.80	4.50	9.00

LOONY SPORTS (Magazine)
Spring, 1975 (68 pgs.)
3-Strikes Publishing Co.

	GD25	FN65	NM94
1-Sports satire		.80	2.00

LOOY DOT DOPE (See Single Series No. 13)

LORD JIM (See Movie Comics)

LORDS OF THE ULTRA-REALM (DC)(Value: cover or less)

LORNA THE JUNGLE GIRL (...Jungle Queen #1-5)
July, 1953 - No. 26, Aug, 1957
Atlas Comics (NPI 1/OMC 2-11/NPI 12-26)

	GD25	FN65	NM94
1-Origin & 1st app.	20.00	60.00	140.00
2-Intro. & 1st app. Greg Knight	10.00	30.00	70.00
3-5	9.15	27.50	55.00
6-11: 11-Last pre-code (1/55)	7.50	22.50	45.00
12-17,19-26: 14-Colletta & Maneely-c	5.85	17.50	35.00
18-Williamson/Colleta-c	6.70	20.00	40.00

NOTE: ***Brodsky*** *c-1-3, 5, 9.* ***Everett*** *c-21, 23-26.* ***Heath*** *c-6, 7.* ***Maneely*** *c-12, 15.* ***Romita*** *a-20, 22, 24, 26.* ***Shores*** *a-14-16, 24, 26; c-11, 13, 16.* ***Tuska*** *a-6.*

LOSERS SPECIAL (DC)(Value: cover or less)(See G.I. Combat & Our Fighting Forces)

LOST CONTINENT (Eclipse)(Value: cover or less)

LOST IN SPACE (TV)(Also see Space Family Robinson)
Aug, 1991 - No. 12, Jan, 1993 ($2.50, color, limited series)
Innovation Publishing

	GD25	FN65	NM94
1-12: Bill Mumy (Will Robinson) scripts in #1-9. 9-Perez-c		1.00	2.50
1,2-Special Ed.; r/#1,2 plus new art & new-c		1.00	2.50
Annual 1,2 (1991, 1992, $2.95, 52 pgs.)		1.20	3.00

LOST IN SPACE: PROJECT ROBINSON (TV)
Nov, 1993 ($2.50, limited series intended)
Innovation Publishing

	GD25	FN65	NM94
1-Takes place after #12		1.00	2.50

LOST IN SPACE: VOYAGE TO THE BOTTOM OF THE SOUL
No. 13, Aug, 1993 - No. 18, 1994 ($2.50, limited series: 12 issues intended)
Innovation Publishing

	GD25	FN65	NM94
13(V1#1, $2.95)-Embossed silver logo edition; Bill Mumy scripts begin; painted-c		1.00	2.50
13(V1#1, $4.95)-Embossed gold logo edition bagged w/poster	1.00	2.00	5.00
14-18: Painted-c		1.00	2.50

LOST PLANET (Eclipse)(Value: cover or less)

LOST WORLD, THE (See 4-Color #1145)

LOST WORLDS (Weird Tales of the Past and Future)
No. 5, Oct, 1952 - No. 6, Dec, 1952
Standard Comics

	GD25	FN65	NM94
5- "Alice in Terrorland" by Alex Toth; J. Katz-a	23.00	70.00	160.00
6-Toth-a	19.00	58.00	135.00

LOTS 'O' FUN COMICS
1940's? (5¢) (Heavy stock; blue covers)
Robert Allen Co.

nn-Contents can vary; Felix, Planet Comics known; contents would determine value. Similar to Up-To-Date Comics. Remainders - re-packaged.

LOU GEHRIG (See The Pride of the Yankees)

LOVE ADVENTURES (Actual Confessions #13)
Oct, 1949; No. 2, Jan, 1950; No. 3, Feb, 1951 - No. 12, Aug, 1952
Marvel (IPS)/Atlas Comics (MPI)

	GD25	FN65	NM94
1-Photo-c	10.00	30.00	60.00
2-Powell-a; Tyrone Power, Gene Tierney photo-c	10.00	30.00	60.00
3-8,10-12: 8-Robinson-a	4.00	14.00	28.00
9-Everett-a	5.85	17.50	35.00

LOVE AND MARRIAGE
March, 1952 - No. 16, Sept, 1954
Superior Comics Ltd.

	GD25	FN65	NM94
1	8.35	25.00	50.00
2	4.20	12.50	25.00
3-10	3.20	9.00	18.00
11-16	2.80	7.00	14.00
I.W. Reprint #1,2,8,11,14	1.00	2.50	5.00
Super Reprint #10('63),15,17('64)	1.00	2.50	5.00

NOTE: *All issues have* ***Kamenish*** *art.*

LOVE AND ROCKETS
July, 1982 - Present? (B&W, adults only)
Fantagraphics Books

	GD25	FN65	NM94
1-B&W-c ($2.95; small size, publ. by Hernandez Bros.)(800 printed)	6.90	21.00	48.00
1 (Fall, '82; color-c)	3.30	9.90	23.00
1-2nd & 3rd printing		1.10	2.75
2	1.70	5.00	12.00
2-11,29-31: 2nd printings ($2.50)		1.00	2.50
3-5	1.20	3.00	7.00
6-10		1.60	4.00
11-40: 30($2.95, 52 pgs.). 31-on: $2.50-c		1.00	2.50

LOVE AND ROMANCE
Sept, 1971 - No. 24, Sept, 1975
Charlton Comics

	GD25	FN65	NM94
1		1.20	3.00
2-24			1.00

LOVE AT FIRST SIGHT
Oct, 1949 - No. 42, Aug, 1956 (Photo-c: 21-42)
Ace Magazines (RAR Publ. Co./Periodical House)

	GD25	FN65	NM94
1-Painted-c	9.15	27.50	55.00
2-Painted-c	4.20	12.50	25.00
3-10: 4-Painted-c	3.60	9.00	18.00
11-20	2.80	7.00	14.00
21-33: 33-Last pre-code	2.00	5.00	10.00
34-42	1.60	4.00	8.00

LOVE BUG, THE (See Movie Comics)

LOVE CLASSICS
Nov, 1949 - No. 2, Feb, 1950 (Photo-c, 52 pgs.)
A Lover's Magazine/Marvel Comics

	GD25	FN65	NM94
1,2: 2-Virginia Mayo photo-c; 30 pg. story "I Was a Small Town Flirt"	9.15	27.50	55.00

LOVE CONFESSIONS
Oct, 1949 - No. 54, Dec, 1956 (Photo-c: 3,4,6,7,9,11-18,21)
Quality Comics Group

	GD25	FN65	NM94
1-Ward-c/a, 9 pgs; Gustavson-a	17.00	52.00	120.00
2-Gustavson-a; Ward-c	7.00	21.00	42.00

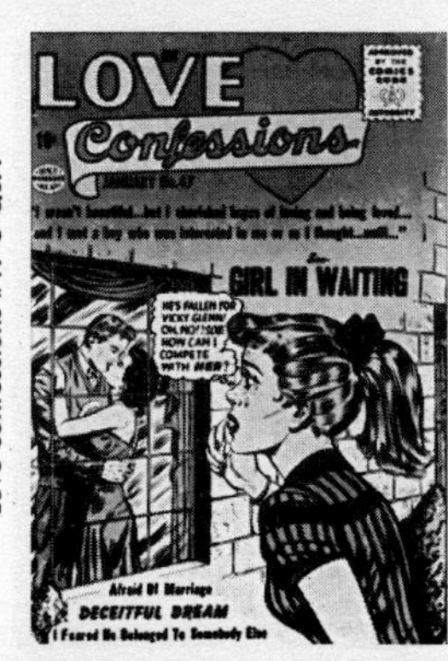

Love Confessions #47 © QUA

Love Diary #34 © Our Publ.

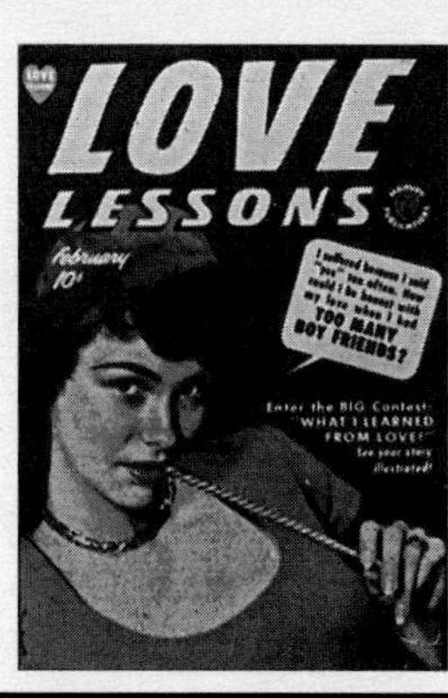

Love Lessons #3 © HARV

	GD25	FN65	NM94
3	4.70	14.00	28.00
4-Crandall-a	6.35	19.00	38.00
5-Ward-a, 7 pgs.	7.00	21.00	42.00
6,7,9,11-13,15,16,18: 7-Van Johnson photo-c. 8-Robert Mitchum & Jane Russell photo-c	3.20	8.00	16.00
8,10-Ward-a(2 stories in #10)	6.35	19.00	38.00
14,17,19,22-Ward-a; 17-Faith Domerque photo-c	5.35	16.00	32.00
20-Ward-a(2)	6.35	19.00	38.00
21,23-28,30-38,40-42: Last precode, 4/55	2.00	5.00	10.00
29-Ward-a	5.00	15.00	30.00
39-Matt Baker-a	3.60	9.00	18.00
43,44,46-48,50-54: 47-Ward-c?	1.80	4.50	9.00
45-Ward-a	3.60	9.00	18.00
49-Baker-c/a	4.00	11.00	22.00

LOVE DIARY
July, 1949 - No. 48, Oct, 1955 (Photo-c: 1-24,27-29) (52 pgs. #1-11?)
Our Publishing Co./Toytown/Patches

	GD25	FN65	NM94
1-Krigstein-a	11.00	32.00	75.00
2,3-Krigstein & Mort Leav-a in each	7.50	22.50	45.00
4-8	4.00	10.00	20.00
9,10-Everett-a	4.00	12.00	24.00
11-20: 16,20-Mort Leav-a	3.20	8.00	16.00
21-30,32-48: 45-Leav-a. 47-Last precode(12/54)	2.40	6.00	12.00
31-John Buscema headlights-c	3.20	8.00	16.00

LOVE DIARY (Diary Loves #2 on; title changed due to previously published title above?)
September, 1949
Quality Comics Group

	GD25	FN65	NM94
1-Ward-c/a, 9 pgs.	14.00	43.00	100.00

LOVE DIARY
July, 1958 - No. 102, Dec, 1976
Charlton Comics

	GD25	FN65	NM94
1	5.85	17.50	35.00
2	3.60	9.00	18.00
3-5,7-10: 10-Photo-c	2.40	6.00	12.00
6-Torres-a	3.20	8.00	16.00
11-20: 20-Photo-c	1.80	4.50	9.00
21-40	1.20	3.00	6.00
41-60		1.40	3.50
61-102			1.00

LOVE DOCTOR (See Dr. Anthony King...)

LOVE DRAMAS (True Secrets No. 3 on?)
Oct, 1949 - No. 2, Jan, 1950
Marvel Comics (IPS)

	GD25	FN65	NM94
1-Jack Kamen-a; photo-c	11.00	32.00	75.00
2	8.35	25.00	50.00

LOVE EXPERIENCES (Challenge of the Unknown No. 6)
Oct, 1949 - No. 5, June, 1950; No. 6, Apr, 1951 - No. 38, June, 1956
Ace Periodicals (A.A. Wyn/Periodical House)

	GD25	FN65	NM94
1-Painted-c	7.50	22.50	45.00
2	4.00	11.00	22.00
3-5: 5-Painted-c	3.20	8.00	16.00
6-10	2.80	7.00	14.00
11-30: 30-Last pre-code (2/55)	2.00	5.00	10.00
31-38: 38-Indicia date-6/56; c-date-8/56	1.80	4.50	9.00

NOTE: ***Anne Brewster** a-15. Photo c-4, 15-35, 38.*

LOVE JOURNAL
No. 10, Oct, 1951 - No. 25, July, 1954
Our Publishing Co.

	GD25	FN65	NM94
10	6.35	19.00	38.00
11-25: 19-Mort Leav-a	4.00	10.00	20.00

LOVELAND
Nov, 1949 - No. 2, Feb, 1950 (52 pgs.)
Mutual Mag./Eye Publ. (Marvel)

	GD25	FN65	NM94
1,2-Photo-c	6.35	19.00	38.00

LOVE LESSONS
Oct, 1949 - No. 5, June, 1950
Harvey Comics/Key Publ. No. 5

	GD25	FN65	NM94
1-Metallic silver-c printed over the cancelled covers of Love Letters #1; indicia title is "Love Letters"	8.35	25.00	50.00
2-Powell-a; photo-c	4.00	11.00	22.00
3-5: 3-Photo-c	3.60	9.00	18.00

LOVE LETTERS (10/49, Harvey; advertised but never published; covers were printed before cancellation and were used as the cover to Love Lessons #1)

LOVE LETTERS (Love Secrets No. 32 on)
11/49 - #6, 9/50; #7, 3/51 - #31, 6/53; #32, 2/54 - #51, 12/56
Quality Comics Group

	GD25	FN65	NM94
1-Ward-c, Gustavson-a	12.00	36.00	85.00
2-Ward-c, Gustavson-a	10.00	30.00	70.00
3-Gustavson-a	8.35	25.00	50.00
4-Ward-a, 9 pgs.	10.00	30.00	70.00
5-8,10	3.60	9.00	18.00
9-One pg. Ward "Be Popular with the Opposite Sex"; Robert Mitchum photo-c	4.70	14.00	28.00
11-Ward-r/Broadway Romances #2 & retitled	4.70	14.00	28.00
12-15,18-20	2.80	7.00	14.00
16,17-Ward-a; 16-Anthony Quinn photo-c. 17-Jane Russell photo-c	6.70	20.00	40.00
21-29	2.40	6.00	12.00
30,31(6/53)-Ward-a	4.00	12.00	24.00
32(2/54)-39: 38-Crandall-a. 39-Last precode (4/55)	2.00	5.00	10.00
40-48	1.60	4.00	8.00
49,50-Baker-a	4.00	11.00	22.00
51-Baker-c	3.60	9.00	18.00

NOTE: *Photo-c on most 3-28.*

LOVE LIFE
Nov, 1951
P. L. Publishing Co.

	GD25	FN65	NM94
1	5.35	16.00	32.00

LOVELORN (Confessions of the Lovelorn #52 on)
Aug-Sept, 1949 - No. 51, July, 1954 (No. 1-26: 52 pgs.)
American Comics Group (Michel Publ./Regis Publ.)

	GD25	FN65	NM94
1	10.00	30.00	60.00
2	5.00	15.00	30.00
3-10	4.00	11.00	22.00
11-20,22-48: 18-Drucker-a(2 pgs.). 46-Lazarus-a	3.20	8.00	16.00
21-Prostitution story	4.35	13.00	26.00
49-51-Has 3-D effect-c/stories	11.00	32.00	75.00

LOVE MEMORIES
1949 (no month) - No. 4, July, 1950 (All photo-c)
Fawcett Publications

	GD25	FN65	NM94
1	7.50	22.50	45.00
2-4: 2-(Win/49-50)	4.35	13.00	26.00

LOVE MYSTERY
June, 1950 - No. 3, Oct, 1950 (All photo-c)
Fawcett Publications

	GD25	FN65	NM94
1-George Evans-a	14.00	43.00	100.00
2,3-Evans-a. 3-Powell-a	11.00	32.00	75.00

LOVE PROBLEMS (See Fox Giants)

LOVE PROBLEMS AND ADVICE ILLUSTRATED (Becomes Romance Stories of True Love No. 45 on)
June, 1949 - No. 6, Apr, 1950; No. 7, Jan, 1951 - No. 44, Mar, 1957
McCombs/Harvey Publ./Home Comics

Lovers #52 © MEG

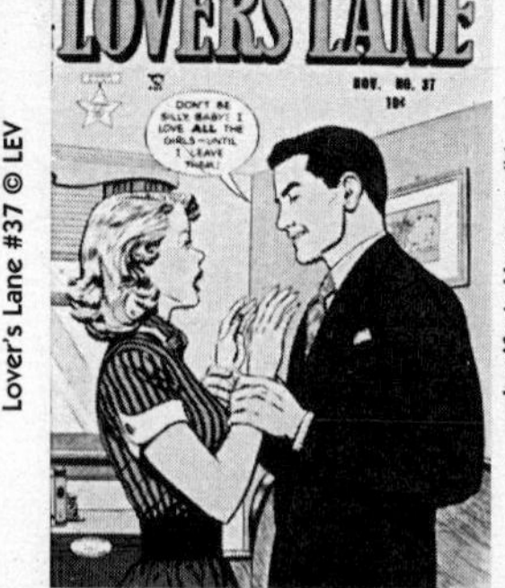

Lover's Lane #37 © LEV

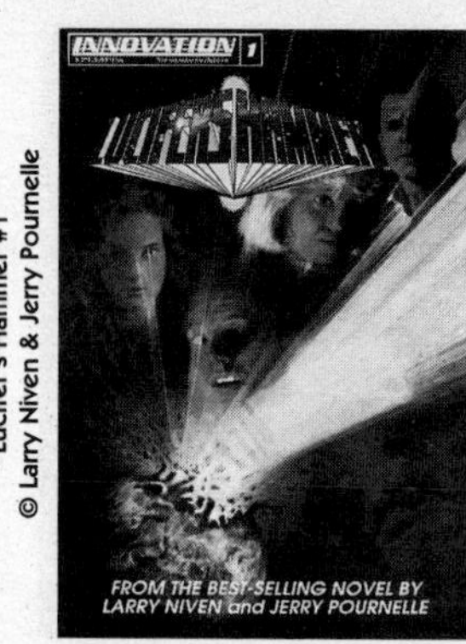

INNOVATION 1
FROM THE BEST-SELLING NOVEL BY LARRY NIVEN and JERRY POURNELLE

Lucifer's Hammer #1 © Larry Niven & Jerry Pournelle

	GD25	FN65	NM94
V1#1	9.15	27.50	55.00
2	4.70	14.00	28.00
3-10: 7-9-Elias-c	4.00	10.00	20.00
11-13,15-23,25-31: 31-Last pre-code (1/55)	2.80	7.00	14.00
14,24-Rape scene	3.20	8.00	16.00
32-37,39-44	2.00	5.00	10.00
38-S&K-c	4.00	12.00	24.00

NOTE: **Powell** a-1, 2, 7-14, 17-25, 28, 29, 33, 40, 41. #3 has True Love... on inside.

LOVE ROMANCES (Formerly Ideal #5)
No. 6, May, 1949 - No. 106, July, 1963
Timely/Marvel/Atlas(TCI No. 7-71/Male No. 72-106)

	GD25	FN65	NM94
6-Photo-c	8.35	25.00	50.00
7-Photo-c; Kamen-a	5.35	16.00	32.00
8-Kubert-a; photo-c	5.85	17.50	35.00
9-20: 9-12-Photo-c	4.00	11.00	22.00
21,24-Krigstein-a	5.85	17.50	35.00
22,23,25-35,37,39,40	3.60	9.00	18.00
36,38-Krigstein-a	5.00	15.00	30.00
41-44,46,47: Last precode (2/55)	3.60	9.00	18.00
45,57-Matt Baker-a	4.00	11.00	22.00
48,50-52,54-56,58-74	2.80	7.00	14.00
49,53-Toth-a, 6 & ? pgs.	5.35	16.00	32.00
75,77,82-Matt Baker-a	4.00	10.00	20.00
76,78-81,84,86-95: Last 10¢ issue?	2.80	7.00	14.00
83-Kirby-c, Severin-a	4.20	12.50	25.00
85,96-Kirby-c/a	4.70	14.00	28.00
97,100-104	2.40	6.00	12.00
98-Kirby-a(4)	6.70	20.00	40.00
99,105,106-Kirby-a	4.20	12.50	25.00

NOTE: **Anne Brewster** a-67, 72. **Colletta** a-37, 40, 42, 44, 67(2); c-42, 44, 49, 80. **Everett** c-70. **Heath** a-87. **Kirby** c-80, 85, 88. **Robinson** a-29.

LOVERS (Formerly Blonde Phantom)
No. 23, May, 1949 - No. 86, Aug?, 1957
Marvel Comics No. 23,24/Atlas No. 25 on (ANC)

	GD25	FN65	NM94
23-Photo-c begin, end #28	8.35	25.00	50.00
24-Tothish plus Robinson-a	4.20	12.50	25.00
25,30-Kubert-a; 7, 10 pgs.	5.00	15.00	30.00
26-29,31-36,39,40	3.60	9.00	18.00
37,38-Krigstein-a	5.85	17.50	35.00
41-Everett-a(2)	4.20	12.50	25.00
42,44-65: 65-Last pre-code (1/55)	3.20	8.00	16.00
43-Frazetta 1 pg. ad	3.20	8.00	16.00
66,68-86	2.80	7.00	14.00
67-Toth-a	5.00	15.00	30.00

NOTE: **Anne Brewster** a-86. **Colletta** a-54, 59, 62, 64, 65, 69, 85; c-61, 64, 65, 75. **Heath** a-61. **Maneely** a-57. **Powell** a-27, 30. **Robinson** a-54, 56.

LOVERS' LANE
Oct, 1949 - No. 41, June, 1954 (No. 1-18: 52 pgs.)
Lev Gleason Publications

	GD25	FN65	NM94
1-Biro-c	7.50	22.50	45.00
2-Biro-c	4.00	11.00	22.00
3-20: 3,4-Painted-c. 20-Frazetta 1 pg. ad	3.20	8.00	16.00
21-38,40,41	2.00	5.00	10.00
39-Story narrated by Frank Sinatra	4.00	11.00	22.00

NOTE: **Briefer** a-6, 21. **Fuje** a-4, 16; c-many. **Guardineer** a-1. **Kinstler** c-41. **Tuska** a-6. Painted c-3-18. Photo c-19-22, 26-28.

LOVE SCANDALS
Feb, 1950 - No. 5, Oct, 1950 (Photo-c #2-5) (All 52 pgs.)
Quality Comics Group

	GD25	FN65	NM94
1-Ward-c/a, 9 pgs.	14.00	43.00	100.00
2,3: 2-Gustavson-a	5.85	17.50	35.00
4-Ward-a, 18 pgs; Gil Fox-a	11.50	34.00	80.00
5-C. Cuidera-a; tomboy story "I Hated Being a Woman"	5.85	17.50	35.00

LOVE SECRETS
Oct, 1949 - No. 2, Jan, 1950 (52 pgs., photo-c)
Marvel Comics(IPC)

	GD25	FN65	NM94
1	8.35	25.00	50.00
2	5.85	17.50	35.00

LOVE SECRETS (Formerly Love Letters #31)
No. 32, Aug, 1953 - No. 56, Dec, 1956
Quality Comics Group

	GD25	FN65	NM94
32	5.85	17.50	35.00
33,35-39	3.20	8.00	16.00
34-Ward-a	5.35	16.00	32.00
40-Matt Baker-c	4.00	12.00	24.00
41-43: 43-Last precode (3/55)	2.80	7.00	14.00
44,47-50,53,54	2.00	5.00	10.00
45,46-Ward-a. 46-Baker-a	4.35	13.00	26.00
51,52-Ward(r). 52-r/Love Confessions #17	3.60	9.00	18.00
55,56-Baker-a. 56-Baker-c	3.60	9.00	18.00

LOVE STORIES (Formerly My Love Affair #5)
No. 6, 1950 - No. 12, 1951
Fox Feature Syndicate

	GD25	FN65	NM94
6,8-Wood-a	11.50	34.00	80.00
7,9-12	5.35	16.00	32.00

LOVE STORIES (Formerly Heart Throbs)
No. 147, Nov, 1972 - No. 152, Oct-Nov, 1973
National Periodical Publications

	GD25	FN65	NM94
147-152		1.60	4.00

LOVE STORIES OF MARY WORTH (See Harvey Comics Hits #55 & Mary Worth)
Sept, 1949 - No. 5, May, 1950
Harvey Publications

	GD25	FN65	NM94
1-1940's newspaper reprints-#1-4	4.70	14.00	28.00
2	4.00	11.00	22.00
3-5: 3-Kamen/Baker-a?	4.00	10.00	20.00

LOVE TALES (Formerly The Human Torch #35)
No. 36, 5/49 - No. 58, 8/52; No. 59, date? - No. 75, Sept, 1957
Marvel/Atlas Comics (ZPC No. 36-50/MMC No. 67-75)

	GD25	FN65	NM94
36-Photo-c	8.35	25.00	50.00
37	5.00	15.00	30.00
38-44,46-50: 39-41-Photo-c	4.00	10.00	20.00
45-Powell-a	4.00	11.00	22.00
51,69-Everett-a	4.00	12.00	24.00
52-Krigstein-a	4.35	13.00	26.00
53-60: 60-Last pre-code (2/55)	2.40	6.00	12.00
61-68,70-75: 75-Brewster, Cameron, Colletta-a	2.00	5.00	10.00

LOVE THRILLS (See Fox Giants)

LOVE TRAILS (Western romance)
Dec, 1949 - No. 2, Mar, 1950 (52 pgs.)
A Lover's Magazine (CDS)(Marvel)

	GD25	FN65	NM94
1,2: 1-Photo-c	7.50	22.50	45.00

LOWELL THOMAS' HIGH ADVENTURE (See 4-Color #949, 1001)

LT. (See Lieutenant)

LUCIFER'S HAMMER (Larry Niven & Jerry Pournelle's...)
Nov, 1993 - No. 6, 1994 ($2.50, color, limited series)
Innovation Publishing

	GD25	FN65	NM94
1-6-Painted-c & art; adapts novel		1.00	2.50

LUCKY COMICS
Jan, 1944; No. 2, Summer, 1945 - No. 5, Summer, 1946
Consolidated Magazines

	GD25	FN65	NM94
1-Lucky Starr & Bobbie begin	11.50	34.00	80.00
2-5: 5-Devil-c by Walter Johnson	7.50	22.50	45.00

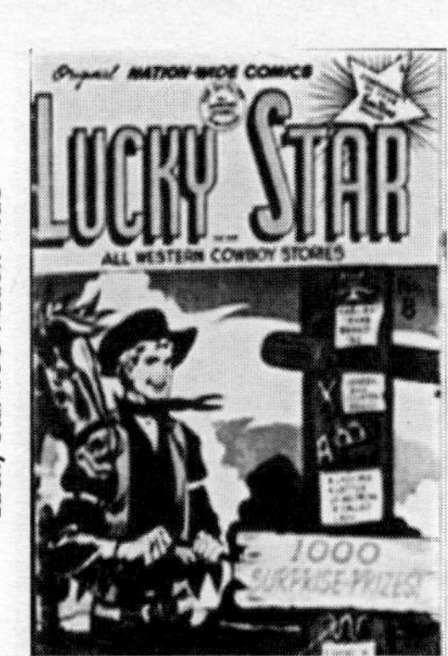

Lucky Star #8© Nation Wide

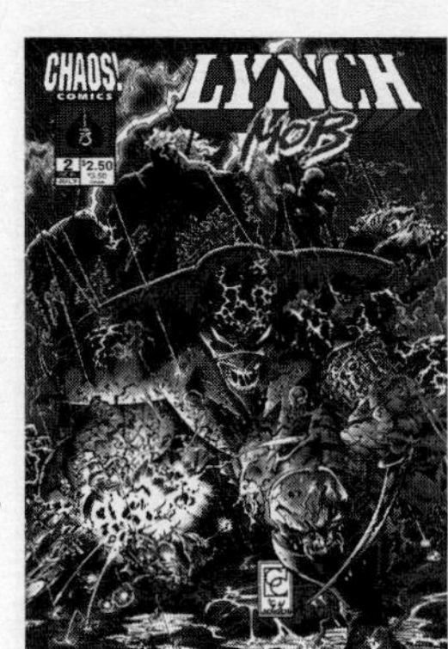

Lynch Mob #2 © Brian Paludo

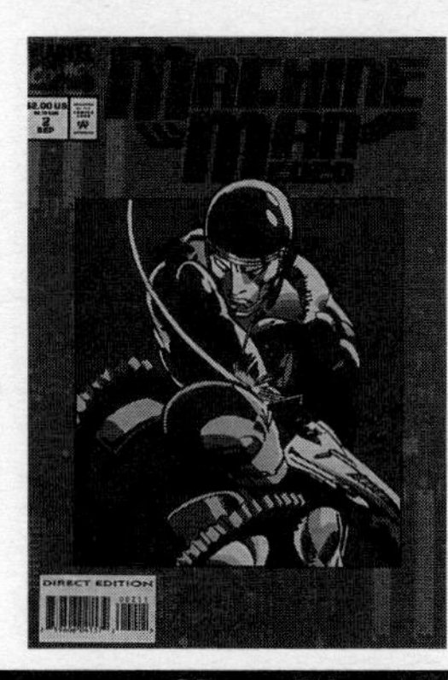

Machine Man 2020 #2 © MEG

LUCKY DUCK
No. 5, Jan, 1953 - No. 8, Sept, 1953
Standard Comics (Literary Ent.)

	GD25	FN65	NM94
5-Funny animal; Irving Spector-a	10.00	30.00	60.00
6-8-Irving Spector-a	8.35	25.00	50.00

NOTE: Harvey Kurtzman tried to hire Spector for Mad #1.

LUCKY FIGHTS IT THROUGH (Also see The K. O. Punch)
1949 (16 pgs. in color; paper cover) (Giveaway)
Educational Comics

	GD25	FN65	NM94
nn-(Very Rare)-1st Kurtzman work for E. C.; V.D. prevention	171.00	515.00	1200.00
nn-Reprint in color (1977)		.80	2.00

NOTE: *Subtitled "The Story of That Ignorant, Ignorant Cowboy". Prepared for Communications Materials Center, Columbia University.*

LUCKY "7" COMICS
1944 (No date listed)
Howard Publishers Ltd.

	GD25	FN65	NM94
1-Pioneer, Sir Gallagher, Dick Royce, Congo Raider, Punch Powers; bondage-c	19.00	58.00	135.00

LUCKY STAR (Western)
1950 - No. 7, 1951; No. 8, 1953 - No. 14, 1955 (5x7-1/4"; full color, 5¢)
Nation Wide Publ. Co.

	GD25	FN65	NM94
nn (#1)-(10¢, 52 pgs.)-Davis-a	8.35	25.00	50.00
2,3-(5¢, 52 pgs.)-Davis-a	5.35	16.00	32.00
4-7-(5¢, 52 pgs.)-Davis-a	4.70	14.00	28.00
8-14-(36 pgs.)	3.60	9.00	18.00
Given away with Lucky Star Western Wear by the Juvenile Mfg. Co.	3.60	9.00	18.00

LUCY SHOW, THE (TV) (Also see I Love Lucy)
June, 1963 - No. 5, June, 1964 (Photo-c: 1,2)
Gold Key

	GD25	FN65	NM94
1	10.00	30.00	72.00
2	7.00	21.00	50.00
3-5: Photo back c-1,2,4,5	6.30	19.00	44.00

LUCY, THE REAL GONE GAL (Meet Miss Pepper #5 on)
June, 1953 - No. 4, Dec, 1953
St. John Publishing Co.

	GD25	FN65	NM94
1-Negligee panels	9.15	27.50	55.00
2	5.00	15.00	30.00
3,4: 3-Drucker-a	4.00	12.00	24.00

LUDWIG BEMELMAN'S MADELEINE & GENEVIEVE (See 4-Color #796)

LUDWIG VON DRAKE (TV)(Disney)(See Walt Disney's C&S #256)
Nov-Dec, 1961 - No. 4, June-Aug, 1962
Dell Publishing Co.

	GD25	FN65	NM94
1	6.70	20.00	40.00
2-4	4.35	13.00	26.00
...Fish Stampede (1962, Fritos giveaway)-16 pgs., 3-1/4x7", soft-c; also see Donald Duck & Mickey Mouse	4.00	12.00	24.00

LUGER (Eclipse)(Value: cover or less)

LUKE CAGE (See Cage & Hero for Hire)

LUKE SHORT'S WESTERN STORIES
No. 580, Aug, 1954 - No. 927, Aug, 1958
Dell Publishing Co.

	GD25	FN65	NM94
4-Color 580(8/54)	4.20	12.50	25.00
4-Color 651(9/55)-Kinstler-a	4.70	14.00	28.00
4-Color 739,771,807,875,927	4.20	12.50	25.00
4-Color 848	5.85	17.50	35.00

LUNATIC FRINGE, THE (Innovation)(Value: cover or less)

LUNATICKLE (Magazine) (Satire)
Feb, 1956 - No. 2, Apr, 1956
Whitstone Publ.

	GD25	FN65	NM94
1,2-Kubert-a	2.40	6.00	12.00

LYCANTHROPE LEO
1994 ($2.95, B&W, limited series intended, 44 pgs.)
Viz Communications

	GD25	FN65	NM94
1		1.20	3.00

LYNCH MOB
June, 1994 - No. 4, Sept, 1994 ($2.50, limited series)
Chaos! Comics

	GD25	FN65	NM94
1-4		1.00	2.50
1-Special edition full foil-c	2.90	8.60	20.00

LYNDON B. JOHNSON
March, 1965
Dell Publishing Co.

	GD25	FN65	NM94
12-445-503-Photo-c	2.80	7.00	14.00

M (Eclipse)(Value: cover or less)

MACHINE MAN (Also see 2001, A Space Odyssey)
Apr, 1978 - No. 9, Dec, 1978; No. 10, Aug, 1979 - No. 19, Feb, 1981
Marvel Comics Group

	GD25	FN65	NM94
1		1.30	3.25
2-17		.70	1.80
18-Wendigo, Alpha Flight-ties into X-Men #140	.90	2.30	5.50
19-Intro/1st app. Jack O'Lantern (Macendale), later becomes 2nd Hobgoblin	2.30	6.90	16.00

NOTE: ***Austin** c-7i, 19i. **Buckler** c-17p, 18p. **Byrne** c-14p. **Ditko** a-10-19; c-10-13, 14i, 15, 16. **Kirby** a-1-9p; c-1-5, 7-9p. **Layton** c-7i. **Miller** c-19p. **Simonson** c-6.*

MACHINE MAN
Oct, 1984 - No. 4, Jan, 1985 (Limited-series)
Marvel Comics Group

	GD25	FN65	NM94
1-Barry Smith-c/a(p) & colors in all		.60	1.60
2-4			1.20

MACHINE MAN 2020
Aug, 1994 - Nov, 1994 ($2.00, 52 pgs., limited series)
Marvel Comics

	GD25	FN65	NM94
1-4-Barry Windsor-Smith-c/a(r)		.80	2.00

MACK BOLAN: THE EXECUTIONER (Don Pendleton's...)
July, 1993 ($2.50)
Innovation Publishing

	GD25	FN65	NM94
1-($3.95)-Indestructible Cover Edition		1.60	4.00
1-($2.95)-Collector's Gold Edition; foil stamped		1.20	3.00
1-($3.50)-Double Cover Edition; red foil outer-c		1.40	3.50

MACKENZIE'S RAIDERS (See 4-Color #1093)

MACO TOYS COMIC
1959 (36 pgs.; full color) (Giveaway)
Maco Toys/Charlton Comics

	GD25	FN65	NM94
1-All military stories featuring Maco Toys	1.20	3.00	6.00

MACROSS (Becomes Robotech: The Macross Saga #2 on)
Dec, 1984 ($1.50)
Comico

	GD25	FN65	NM94
1	1.25	3.00	7.50

MACROSS II
1992 - No. 10, 1993 ($2.75, B&W, limited series)
Viz Select Comics

	GD25	FN65	NM94
1-10: Based on video series		1.10	2.75

MAD (Tales Calculated to Drive You...)
Oct-Nov, 1952 - Present (No. 24 on are magazine format)
(Kurtzman editor No. 1-28, Feldstein No. 29 - No. ?)
E. C. Comics (Educational Comics)

	GD25	FN65	NM94
1-Wood, Davis, Elder start as regulars	457.00	1371.00	3200.00

MAD #41 © EC

Mad-Dog #4 © MEG

The Mad Hatter #1 © OW Comics

GD25 FN65 NM94

2-Dick Tracy cameo 107.00 321.00 750.00

3,4: 3-Stan Lee mentioned. 4-Reefer mention story "Flob Was a Slob" by Davis; Superman parody 68.00 205.00 475.00

5-Low distr.; W.M. Gaines biog. 111.00 332.00 775.00

6-11: 6-Popeye cameo. 7,8- "Hey Look" reprints by Kurtzman. 11-Wolverton-a; Davis story was-r/Crime Suspenstories #12 w/new Kurtzman dialogue 50.00 150.00 350.00

12-15: 15,18-Pot Shot Pete-r by Kurtzman 40.00 120.00 280.00

16-23(5/55): 18-Alice in Wonderland by Jack Davis. 21-1st app. Alfred E. Neuman on-c in fake ad. 22-All by Elder plus photo-montages by Kurtzman. 23-Special cancel announcement 31.00 92.00 215.00

24(7/55)-1st magazine issue (25¢); Kurtzman logo & border on-c; 1st "What? Me Worry?" on-c; 2nd printing exists 89.00 268.00 625.00

25-Jaffee starts as regular writer 36.00 107.00 250.00

26,27: 27-Jaffee starts as story artist; new logo 29.00 86.00 200.00

28-Last issue edited by Kurtzman; (three cover variations exist with different wording on contents banner on lower right of cover; value of each the same) 25.00 75.00 175.00

29-Kamen-a; Don Martin starts as regular; Feldstein editing begins 25.00 75.00 175.00

30-1st A. E. Neuman cover by Mingo; last Elder-a; Bob Clarke starts as regular; Disneyland & Elvis Presley spoof 37.00 111.00 260.00

31-Freas starts as regular; last Davis-a until #99 20.00 60.00 140.00

32,33: 32-Orlando, Drucker, Woodbridge start as regulars; Wood back-c. 33-Orlando back-c 18.00 54.00 125.00

34-Berg starts as regular 16.00 48.00 110.00

35-Mingo wraparound-c; Crandall-a 16.00 48.00 110.00

36-40 10.00 30.00 70.00

41-50 9.15 27.50 55.00

51-60: 60-Two Clarke-c; Prohias starts as regular 8.00 24.00 48.00

61-70: 64-Rickard starts as regular. 68-Martin-c 5.85 17.50 35.00

71-80: 76-Aragones starts as regular 5.00 15.00 30.00

81-90: 86-1st Fold-in. 89-One strip by Walt Kelly. 90-Frazetta back-c; Beatles app. 4.20 12.50 25.00

91-100: 91-Jaffee starts as story artist. 99-Davis-a resumes 4.00 11.00 22.00

101-104,106-120: 101-Infinity-c. 106-Frazetta back-c 3.60 9.00 18.00

105-Batman TV show take-off 4.20 12.50 25.00

121-140: 121-Beatles app. 122-Ronald Reagan photo inside; Drucker & Mingo-c. 128-Last Orlando. 130-Torres begins as reg. 131-Reagan photo back-c. 135,139-Davis-c 1.70 5.00 12.00

141-170: 165-Martin-c. 169-Drucker-c 1.70 4.20 10.00

171-200: 182-Bob Jones starts as regular. 186-Star Trek take-off. 187-Harry North starts as regular. 196-Star Wars take-off 1.30 3.25 8.00

201-250: 203-Star Wars take-off. 204-Hulk TV show take-off. 208-Superman movie take-off. 245- Last Rikard-a. 1.60 4.00

251-300: 256-Last issue edited by Feldstein. 274-Last Martin-a. 284-Roger Rabbit-c/story. 289-Batman movie parody. 291-TMNT-c only. 299-Simpson's-c/story 1.20 3.00

301-350: 306-TMNT III movie parody. 308-Terminator parody. 311-Addams Family-c/story. 314-Batman Returns-c/story. 315-Tribute to William Gaines. 316-Photo-c. 322-Batman animated series parody .80 2.00

300-303 (1/91-6/91)-Special Hussein Asylum Editions; only distributed to the troops in the Middle East(see Mad Super Spec.) 1.00 2.00 5.00

NOTE: **Aragones** *c-210, 293.* **Davis** *c-2, 27, 135, 139, 173, 178, 212, 213, 219, 246, 260, 296, 308.* **Drucker** *c-122, 169, 176, 225, 234, 264, 266, 274, 280, 285, 297, 299, 303, 314, 315, 321.* **Elder** *c-5, 259, 261, 268.* **Elder/Kurtzman** *a-258-274.* **Jules Feiffer** *a(r)-42.* **Freas** *c-39-59, 62-67, 69-70, 72, 74.* **Heath** *a-14, 27.* **Jaffee** *c-199, 217, 224, 258.* **Kamen** *a-29.* **Krigstein** *a-12, 17, 24, 26.* **Kurtzman** *c-1, 3, 4, 6-10, 13, 16, 18.* **Martin** *c-68, 165, 229.* **Mingo** *c-30-37, 61, 71, 75-80, 82-114, 117-124, 126, 129, 131, 133, 134, 136, 140, 143-148, 150-162, 164, 166-168, 171, 172, 174, 175, 177, 179, 181, 183, 185, 198, 206, 209, 211, 214, 218, 221, 222, 300.* **John Severin** *a-1-6, 9, 10.* **Wolverton** *c-11; a-11, 17, 29, 31, 36, 40, 82, 137.* **Wood** *a-24-45, 59; c-26, 28, 29.* **Woodbridge** *a-43. Issues 1-23 are 36 pgs.; 24-28 are 58 pgs.; 29 on are 52 pgs.*

MAD (See Mad Follies, ...Special, More Trash from..., and The Worst from...)

MAD ABOUT MILLIE (Also see Millie the Model)
April, 1969 - No. 17, Dec, 1970
Marvel Comics Group

1-Giant issue 4.60 13.70 32.00

2-17: 16,17-r 2.30 6.90 16.00

Annual 1(11/71) 1.65 4.00 10.00

MADAME XANADU (DC)(Value: cover or less)

MADBALLS
Sept, 1986 - No. 3, Nov, 1986; No. 4, June, 1987 - No. 10, June, 1988
Star Comics/Marvel Comics #9 on

1-10: Based on toys. 9-Post-a 1.00

MAD DISCO
1980 (One shot)(36 pgs.)
E.C. Comics

1-Includes 30 minute flexi-disc of Mad disco music .80 2.00

MAD-DOG (Marvel)(Value: cover or less)

MAD DOGS
Feb, 1992 - No. 3, July, 1992 ($2.50, B&W, mini-series)
Eclipse Comics

1-3 1.00 2.50

MAD 84 (Mad Extra)
1984 (84 pgs.)
E.C. Comics

1 .80 2.00

MAD FOLLIES (Special)
1963 - No. 7, 1969
E. C. Comics

nn(1963)-Paperback book covers 22.00 65.00 150.00

2(1964)-Calendar 15.00 45.00 105.00

3(1965)-Mischief Stickers 11.50 34.00 80.00

4(1966)-Mobile; Frazetta-r/back-c Mad #90 13.00 40.00 90.00

5(1967)-Stencils 10.00 30.00 60.00

6(1968)-Mischief Stickers 7.50 22.50 45.00

7(1969)-Nasty Cards 7.50 22.50 45.00

NOTE: **Clarke** *c-4.* **Frazetta** *r-4, 6 (1 pg. ea.).* **Mingo** *c-1-3.* **Orlando** *a-5.*

MAD HATTER, THE (Costumed Hero)
Jan-Feb, 1946; No. 2, Sept-Oct, 1946
O. W. Comics Corp.

1-Freddy the Firefly begins; Giunta-c/a 50.00 150.00 350.00

2-Has ad for E.C.'s Animal Fables #1 27.00 81.00 190.00

MADHOUSE
3-4/54 - No. 4, 9-10/54; 6/57 - No. 4, Dec?, 1957
Ajax/Farrell Publ. (Excellent Publ./4-Star)

1(1954) 18.00 54.00 125.00

2,3 10.00 30.00 65.00

4-Surrealistic-c 16.00 48.00 110.00

1(1957, 2nd series) 7.50 22.50 45.00

2-4 5.85 17.50 35.00

MAD HOUSE (Formerly Madhouse Glads; ...Comics #104? on)
No. 95, 9/74 - No. 97, 1/75; No. 98, 8/75 - No. 130, 10/82
Red Circle Productions/Archie Publications

95,96-Horror stories through #97 1.20 3.00

97-Intro. Henry Hobson; Morrow, Thorne-a 1.50

98-130-Satire/humor stories 1.50

Annual 8(1970-71)- 12(1974-75)-Formerly Madhouse Ma-ad Annual. 11-Wood-a(r) .80 2.00

...Comics Digest 1('75-76)- 8(8/82)(...Mag. #5 on) 1.00 2.50

NOTE: **B. Jones** *a-96.* **McWilliams** *a-97.* **Morrow** *a-96, 97; c-95-97.* **Wildey** *a-95, 96. See Archie Comics Digest #1, 13.*

MADHOUSE GLADS (Formerly ...Ma-ad; Madhouse #95 on)
No. 73, May, 1970 - No. 94, Aug, 1974 (No. 78-92: 52 pgs.)

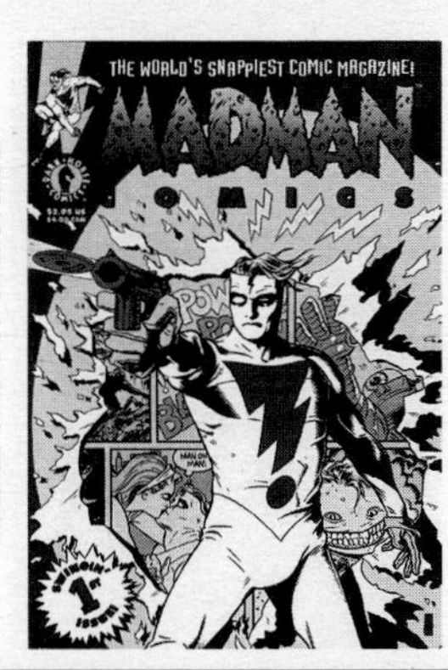

Madman Comics #1 © Mike Allred

Mage #1 © Comico

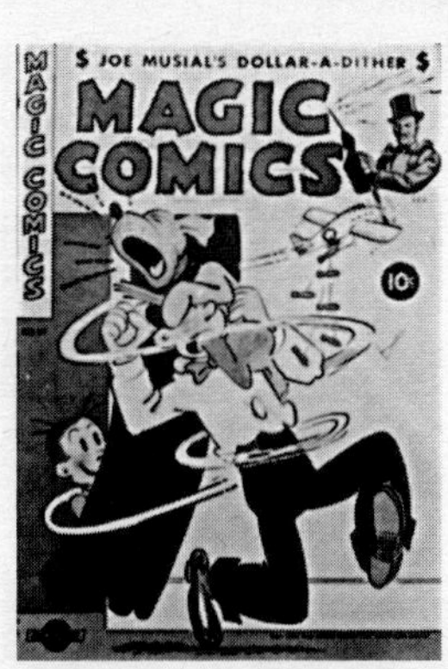

Magic Comics #51 © DMP

GD25 FN65 NM94

Archie Publications

73 1.00 2.00 5.00
74-94 1.60 4.00

MADHOUSE MA-AD (...Jokes #67-70; ...Freak-Out #71-74)
(Formerly Archie's Madhouse) (Becomes Madhouse Glads #75 on)
No. 67, April, 1969 - No. 72, Jan, 1970
Archie Publications

67-72 1.00 2.00 5.00
...Annual 7(1969-70)-Formerly Archie's Madhouse Annual; becomes Madhouse Annual 1.00 2.00 5.00

MADMAN
Mar, 1992 - No. 3, 1992 ($3.95, duotone, high quality, 52 pgs.)
Tundra Publishing

1-Mike Allred-c/a in all 1.30 3.00 8.00
1-2nd printing 1.60 4.00
2,3 .90 2.00 5.50

MADMAN ADVENTURES
1992 - No. 3, 1993 ($2.95, color, mini-series)
Tundra Publishing

1-3-Mike Allred-c/a in all 1.20 3.00

MADMAN COMICS
Apr, 1994 - Present ($2.95)
Dark Horse Comics
1-6-Alfred-c/a: 1-F. Miller back-c. 3-Alex Toth back-c 1.20 3.00

MAD MONSTER PARTY (See Movie Classics)

MADNESS IN MURDERWORLD
1989 (Came with computer game from Paragon Software)
Marvel Comics

V1#1-Starring The X-men 1.00

MAD SPECIAL (...Super Special)
Fall, 1970 - Present (84 - 116 pgs.)
E. C. Publications, Inc.

Fall 1970(#1)-Bonus-Voodoo Doll; contains 17 pgs. new material 9.00 26.00 60.00
Spring 1971(#2)-Wall Nuts; 17 pgs. new material 5.00 15.00 35.00
3-Protest Stickers 5.00 15.00 35.00
4-8: 4-Mini Posters. 5-Mad Flag. 6-Mad Mischief Stickers. 7-Presidential candidate posters, Wild Shocking Message posters. 8-TV Guise 4.30 13.00 30.00
9(1972)-Contains Nostalgic Mad #1 (28 pgs.) 3.10 9.00 22.00
10,11,13: 10-Nonsense Stickers (Don Martin). 11-33-1/3 RPM record. 13-Sickie Stickers; 3 pgs. Wolverton-r/Mad #137 3.10 9.00 22.00
12-Contains Nostalgic Mad #2 (36 pgs.); Davis, Wolverton-a 3.10 9.00 22.00
14-Vital Message posters & Art Depreciation paintings 1.70 5.00 12.00
15-Contains Nostalgic Mad #3 (28 pgs.) 2.15 6.50 15.00
16,17,19,20: 16-Mad-hesive Stickers. 17-Don Martin posters. 20-Martin Stickers 1.70 5.00 12.00
18-Contains Nostalgic Mad #4 (36 pgs.) 1.70 5.00 12.00
21,24-Contains Nostalgic Mad #5 (28 pgs.) & #6 (28 pgs.) 1.70 5.00 12.00
22,23,25,27,29,30: 22-Diplomas. 23-Martin Stickers. 25-Martin Posters.27-Mad Shock-Sticks. 29-Mad Collectable-Correctables Posters. 30-The Movies 1.00 2.50 6.00
26-Has 33-1/3 RPM record 1.70 4.20 10.00
28-Contains Nostalgic Mad #7 (36 pgs.) 1.20 3.00 7.00
31,33-60: 36-Has 96 pgs. of comic book & comic strip spoofs: titles "The Comics" on-c 1.00 2.50 6.00
32-Contains Nostalgic Mad #8 1.30 3.25 8.00
61-88,90-96: 71-Batman parodies-r by Wood, Drucker. 72-Wolverton-c r-from 1st panel in Mad #11; Wolverton-s r/new dialogue. 83-All Star Trek spoof issue 1.40 3.50
76-(Fall, 1991)-Special Hussein Asylum Edition; distributed only to the troops in the Middle East (see Mad #300-303) 1.00 2.00 5.00
89-($3.95)-Polybaged w/1st of 3 Spy vs. Spy hologram trading cards (direct sale only issue)(other cards came w/card set) 1.60 4.00
NOTE: *#28-30 have no number on cover.* ***Freas*** *c-76.* ***Mingo*** *c-9, 11, 15, 19, 23.*

MAGE (The Hero Discovered...; also see Grendel #16)
Feb, 1984 (no month) - #15, Dec, 1986 ($1.50, Mando paper)
Comico

1-Violence; Comico's 1st color comic .90 2.00 5.00
2 1.80 4.50
3-5: 3-Intro Edsel 1.00 2.50
6-Grendel begins (1st in color) 1.90 5.60 13.00
7-1st new Grendel story 1.20 2.90 7.00
8-14: 13-Grendel dies. 14-Grendel story ends .90 2.25
15-$2.95, Double size w/pullout poster 1.10 2.75

MAGGOTS (Hamilton)(Value: cover or less)

MAGIC AGENT (See Forbidden Worlds & Unknown Worlds)
Jan-Feb, 1962 - No. 3, May-June, 1962
American Comics Group

1-Origin & 1st app. John Force 2.60 7.70 18.00
2,3 2.00 5.00 12.00

MAGIC COMICS
Aug, 1939 - No. 123, Nov-Dec, 1949
David McKay Publications

1-Mandrake the Magician, Henry, Popeye , Blondie, Barney Baxter, Secret Agent X-9 (not by Raymond), Bunky by Billy DeBeck & Thornton Burgess text stories illustrated by Harrison Cady begin; Henry covers begin 171.00 515.00 1200.00
2 68.00 205.00 475.00
3 51.00 154.00 360.00
4 44.00 133.00 310.00
5 35.00 105.00 245.00
6-10: 8-11,21-Mandrake/Henry-c 29.00 86.00 200.00
11-16,18-20: 12-Mandrake-c begin. 19-Robot-c 24.00 73.00 170.00
17-The Lone Ranger begins 26.00 78.00 180.00
21-30: 25-Only Blondie-c. 26-Dagwood-c begin 16.50 50.00 115.00
31-40: 36-Flag-c 12.00 36.00 85.00
41-50 10.00 30.00 65.00
51-60 9.15 27.50 55.00
61-70 6.35 19.00 38.00
71-99 5.00 15.00 30.00
100 6.35 19.00 38.00
101-106,109-123: 123-Last Dagwood-c 4.35 13.00 26.00
107,108-Flash Gordon app; not by Raymond 5.00 15.00 30.00

MAGICA DE SPELL (See Walt Disney Showcase #30)

MAGIC FLUTE, THE (See Night Music #9-11)

MAGIC OF CHRISTMAS AT NEWBERRYS, THE
1967 (20 pgs.; slick cover; B&W inside)
E. S. London (Giveaway)

nn 1.20 3.00

MAGIC SWORD, THE (See Movie Classics)

MAGIK (Illyana and Storm Limited Series)
Dec, 1983 - No. 4, Mar, 1984 (60¢, mini-series)
Marvel Comics Group

1-Characters from X-Men; Inferno begins; X-Men cameo (Buscema pencils in #1,2; c-1p 1.20 3.00
2-4: 2-Nightcrawler app. & X-Men cameo 1.20 3.00

MAGILLA GORILLA (TV) (See Kite Fun Book)
May, 1964 - No. 10, Dec, 1968 (Hanna-Barbera)
Gold Key

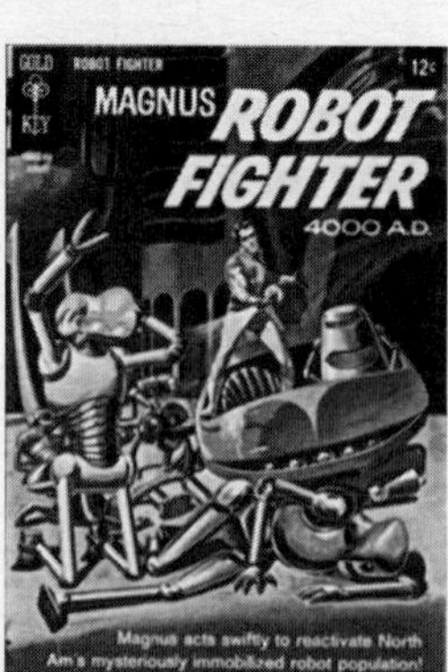

Magnus Robot Fighter #23 (old series) © WEST

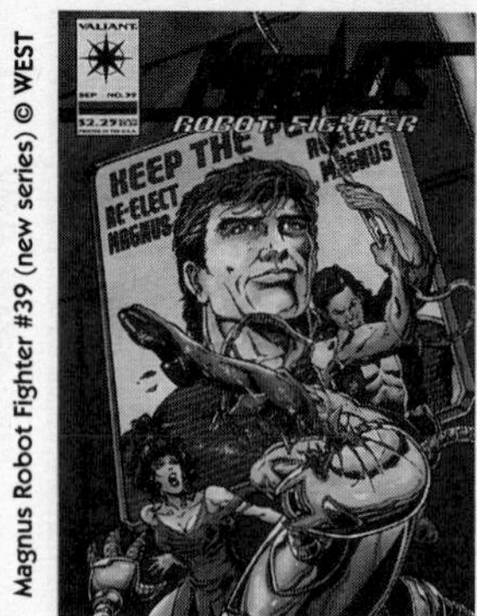

Magnus Robot Fighter #39 (new series) © WEST

Man Comics #4 © MEG

GD25 FN65 NM94

1 6.00 18.00 42.00
2-10: 3-Vs. Yogi Bear for President 3.30 9.90 23.00

MAGILLA GORILLA (TV)(See Spotlight #4)
Nov, 1970 - No. 5, July, 1971 (Hanna-Barbera)
Charlton Comics

1 2.90 9.00 20.00
2-5 2.00 6.00 14.00

MAGNETO (See X-Men #1)
Sept, 1993 (no date given) (Giveaway, one-shot)
Marvel Comics

0-Embossed foil-c by Sienkiewicz; r/Classic X-Men #19 & 12 by John Bolton 1.00 1.90 4.75

MAGNUS, ROBOT FIGHTER (...4000 A.D.)(See Doctor Solar)
Feb, 1963 - No. 46, Jan, 1977 (Painted covers)
Gold Key

1-Origin & 1st app. Magnus; Aliens (1st app.) series begins 33.00 99.00 230.00
2,3 17.00 51.00 120.00
4-10: 10-Simonson fan club illo (5/65, 1st-a?) 10.00 29.00 68.00
11-20 6.40 19.00 45.00
21,24-28: 28-Aliens ends 4.30 12.90 30.00
22,23-12¢ and 15¢ editions exist: 22-Origin-r/#1 3.90 12.00 27.00
29-46-Reprints 1.70 5.00 12.00

NOTE: ***Manning** a-1-22, 28-43(r). **Spiegle** a-23, 44r.*

MAGNUS ROBOT FIGHTER (Also see Vintage Magnus)
May, 1991 - Present ($1.75/$1.95/$2.25, color, high quality paper)
Valiant Comics

1-Nichols/Layton-c/a; 1-8 have trading cards 3.00 7.70 18.00
2 1.40 4.00 10.00
3,4: 4-Rai cameo 1.70 5.00 12.00
5-Origin & 1st full app. Rai (10/91); 5-8 are in flip book format and back-c & half of book are Rai #1-4 mini-series 2.10 6.40 15.00
6-8: 6-1st Solar x-over. 7-Magnus vs. Rai-c/story; 1st X-O Armor. 8-Begin $1.95-c 1.20 2.90 7.00
0-Origin issue; Layton-a; ordered through mail w/coupons from 1st 8 issues plus 50¢; B. Smith trading card 7.00 21.00 50.00
0-Sold thru comic shops without trading card 3.10 9.00 22.00
9-11: 11-Last $1.95-c .90 2.30 5.50
12-($3.25, 44 pgs.)-Turok-c/story (1st app. in Valiant universe, 5/92); has 8 pg. Magnus story insert 5.40 16.00 38.00
13-20,22-24,26-43: 14-1st app. Isak. 15,16-Unity x-overs. 15-Miller-c. 16-Birth of Magnus. 24-Story cont'd in Rai & the Future Force #9. 33-Timewalker app. 36-Bound-in trading cards. 37-Rai & Starwatchers app. .90 2.25
21-New direction & new logo; Reese inks 1.10 2.75
21-Gold ink variant 10.00
25-($2.95)-Embossed silver foil-c; new costume 1.20 3.00
...Yearbook (1994, $3.95, 52 pgs.) 1.60 4.00

NOTE: ***Ditko/Reese** a-18. **Layton** a(i)-5; c-6-9i, 25; back(i)-5-8. **Reese** a(i)-22, 25, 28; c(i)-22, 24, 28. **Simonson** c-16. Prices for issues 1-8 are for trading cards and coupons intact.*

MAGNUS ROBOT FIGHTER 4000 A.D.
1990 - No. 2?, 1991 ($7.95, color, high quality paper, card stock-c, 96 pgs.)
Valiant Comics

1,2-Russ Manning-r. 1-Origin 1.30 3.25 8.00

MAGNUS ROBOT FIGHTER/NEXUS
Dec, 1993 - No. 2, Apr, 1994 ($2.95, color, limited series)
Valiant/Dark Horse Comics

1,2-Steve Rude painted-c & pencils 1.20 3.00

MAID OF THE MIST (See American Graphics)

MAI, THE PSYCHIC GIRL (Eclipse)(Value: cover or less)

MAJOR HOOPLE COMICS (See Crackajack Funnies)
nd (Jan, 1943)
Nedor Publications

1-Mary Worth, Phantom Soldier app. by Moldoff 27.00 80.00 185.00

MAJOR INAPAK THE SPACE ACE
1951 (20 pgs.) (Giveaway)
Magazine Enterprises (Inapac Foods)

1-Bob Powell-c/a 1.00

NOTE: *Many warehouse copies surfaced in 1973.*

MAJOR VICTORY COMICS (Also see Dynamic Comics)
1944 - No. 3, Summer, 1945
H. Clay Glover/Service Publ./Harry 'A' Chesler

1-Origin Major Victory (patriotic hero) by C. Sultan (reprint from Dynamic #1); 1st app. Spider Woman 41.00 124.00 290.00
2-Dynamic Boy app. 27.00 80.00 185.00
3-Rocket Boy app. 21.00 63.00 145.00

MALTESE FALCON (See Feature Books No. 48)

MALU IN THE LAND OF ADVENTURE
1964 (See White Princess of Jungle #2)
I. W. Enterprises

1-r/Avon's Slave Girl Comics #1; Severin-c 5.00 15.00 30.00

MAMMOTH COMICS
1938 (84 pgs.) (Black & White, 8-1/2x11-1/2")
Whitman Publishing Co.(K. K. Publications)

1-Alley Oop, Terry & the Pirates, Dick Tracy, Little Orphan Annie, Wash Tubbs, Moon Mullins, Smilin' Jack, Tailspin Tommy, Don Winslow, Dan Dunn, Smokey Stover & other reprints 96.00 288.00 675.00

MAMMY YOKUM & THE GREAT DOGPATCH MYSTERY
1951 (Giveaway)
Toby Press

nn-Li'l Abner 17.00 52.00 120.00
nn-Reprint (1956) 4.00 12.00 24.00

MAN-BAT (See Batman Family, Brave & the Bold, & Detective #400)
Dec-Jan, 1975-76 - No. 2, Feb-Mar, 1976; Dec, 1984
National Periodical Publications/DC Comics

1-Ditko-a(p); Aparo-c; Batman app.; 1st app. She-Bat? 1.00 2.00 5.00
2-Aparo-c 1.30 3.25
1 (12/84)-N. Adams-r(3)/Det.(Vs. Batman on-c) 1.60 4.00

MAN COMICS
Dec, 1949 - No. 28, Sept, 1953 (#1-6: 52 pgs.)
Marvel/Atlas Comics (NPI)

1-Tuska-a 12.00 36.00 85.00
2-Tuska-a 7.00 21.00 42.00
3-6 5.85 17.50 35.00
7,8 4.70 14.00 28.00
9-13,15: 9-Format changes to war 4.00 12.00 24.00
14-Henkel (3 pgs.); Pakula-a 5.35 16.00 32.00
16-21,23-28: 28-Crime issue (Bob Brant) 4.00 10.00 20.00
22-Krigstein-a, 5 pgs. 6.70 20.00 40.00

NOTE: ***Berg** a-14, 15, 19. **Colan** a-9, 21. **Everett** a-8, 22; c-22, 25. **Heath** a-11, 17, 21. Kubertish a-by **Bob Brown**-3. **Maneely** a-11; c-10, 11. **Reinman** a-11. **Robinson** a-7, 10, 14. **Robert Sale** a-9, 11. **Sinnott** a-22, 23. **Tuska** a-14, 23.*

MANDRAKE THE MAGICIAN (See Defenders Of The Earth, Feature Books #18, 19, 123, 46, 52, 55, Giant Comic Album, King Comics, Magic Comics, The Phantom #21, Tiny Tot Funnies & Wow Comics, '36)

MANDRAKE THE MAGICIAN (See Harvey Comics Hits #53)
Sept, 1966 - No. 10, Nov, 1967 (Also see Four Color #752)
King Comics (All 12¢)

1-Begin S.O.S. Phantom, ends #3 3.70 11.00 26.00
2-7,9: 4-Girl Phantom app. 5-Flying Saucer-c/story. 5,6-Brick Bradford app. 7-Origin Lothar. 9-Brick Bradford app. 2.00 6.00 14.00
8-Jeff Jones-a (4 pgs.) 2.90 9.00 20.00
10-Rip Kirby app.; Raymond-a (14 pgs.) 3.60 11.00 25.00

Man From Atlantis #2 © MEG

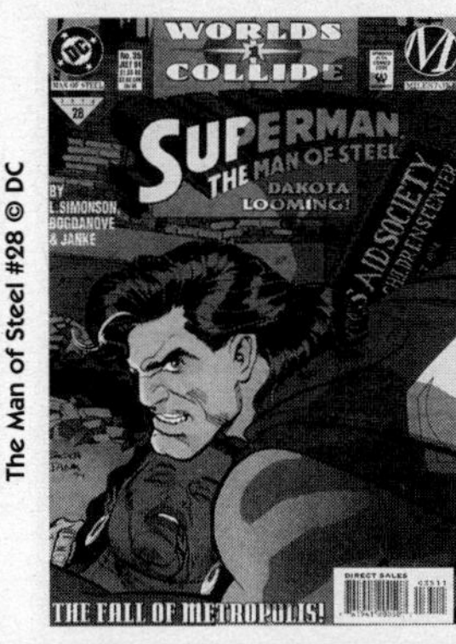

The Man of Steel #28 © DC

Mantra #13 © Malibu

GD25 FN65 NM94

MAN FROM ATLANTIS (TV)
Feb, 1978 - No. 7, Aug, 1978
Marvel Comics Group

1-($1.00, 84 pgs.)-Sutton-a(p), Buscema-c; origin 1.20
2-7 (#1: cast photos & origin Mark Harris inside) 1.00

MAN FROM PLANET X, THE (Planet X Productions)(Value: cover or less)

MAN FROM U.N.C.L.E., THE (TV) (Also see The Girl From Uncle)
Feb, 1965 - No. 22, April, 1969 (All photo covers)
Gold Key

1 13.00 39.00 90.00
2-Photo back c-2-8 8.60 26.00 60.00
3-10: 7-Jet Dream begins (1st app., also see Jet Dream) (all new stories) 5.70 17.00 40.00
11-22: 21,22-Reprint #10 & 7 4.30 13.00 30.00

MAN FROM U.N.C.L.E., THE (Entertainment)(Value: cover or less)

MAN FROM WELLS FARGO (TV)
No. 1287, Feb-Apr, 1962 - May-July, 1962 (Photo-c)
Dell Publishing Co.

4-Color 1287, #01-495-207 5.00 15.00 30.00

MANGLE TANGLE TALES (Innovation)(Value: cover or less)

MANHUNT! (Becomes Red Fox #15 on)
Oct, 1947 - No. 14, 1953
Magazine Enterprises

1-Red Fox by L. B. Cole, Undercover Girl by Whitney, Space Ace begin (1st app.); negligee panels 27.00 81.00 190.00
2-Electrocution-c 22.00 65.00 150.00
3-6 18.00 54.00 125.00
7-10: 7-Space Ace ends. 8-Trail Colt begins (intro/1st app., 5/48) by Guardineer; Trail Colt-c. 10-G. Ingels-a 15.00 45.00 105.00
11(8/48)-Frazetta-a, 7 pgs.; The Duke, Scotland Yard begin 22.00 67.00 155.00
12 11.50 34.00 80.00
13(A-1 #63)-Frazetta, r-/Trail Colt #1, 7 pgs. 20.00 60.00 140.00
14(A-1 #77)-Bondage/hypo-c; last L. B. Cole Red Fox; Ingels-a 15.00 45.00 105.00

NOTE: ***Guardineer** a-1-5; c-8. **Whitney** a-2-14; c-1-6, 10. Red Fox by **L. B. Cole**-#1-14. #15 was advertised but came out as Red Fox #15. Bondage c-6.*

MANHUNTER (See Adventure #58, 73, Brave & the Bold, Detective Comics, 1st Issue Special, House of Mystery #143 and Justice League of America)
1984 ($2.50, 76 pgs; high quality paper)
DC Comics

1-Simonson-c/a(r)/Detective; Batman app. 1.00 2.50

MANHUNTER (DC Comics, 1988-90)(Value: cover or less)

MANHUNTER
No. 0, Oct, 1994 - Present ($1.95)
DC Comics

0-3 .80 2.00

MAN IN BLACK (See Thrill-O-Rama) (Also see All New Comics, Front Page, Green Hornet #31, Strange Story & Tally-Ho Comics)
Sept, 1957 - No. 4, Mar, 1958
Harvey Publications

1-Bob Powell-c/a 10.00 30.00 65.00
2-4: Powell-c/a 7.50 22.50 45.00

MAN IN BLACK
1990 - No. 2, July, 1991 (B&W)
Lorne-Harvey Publications (Recollections)

1,2 .80 2.00

MAN IN FLIGHT (See 4-Color #836)

MAN IN SPACE (See Dell Giant #27 & 4-Color #716, 954)

GD25 FN65 NM94

MAN OF PEACE, POPE PIUS XII
1950 (See Pope Pius XII... & To V2#8)
Catechetical Guild

nn-All Powell-a 4.00 10.50 21.00

MAN OF STEEL, THE (Also see Superman: The Man of Steel)
1986 (June release) - No. 6, 1986 (75¢, mini-series)
DC Comics

1-Silver logo; Byrne-c/a/scripts in all; origin 1.00
1-Alternate-c for newsstand sales 1.00
1-Distr. to toy stores by So Much Fun 1.00
2-6: 2-Intro. Lois Lane, Jimmy Olsen. 3-Intro/origin Magpie; Batman-c/story. 4-Intro. new Lex Luthor 1.00
1-6-Silver Editions (1993, $1.95)-r/1-6 .80 2.00
...The Complete Saga nn-Contains #1-6, given away in contest .80 2.00
Limited Edition, softcover 3.60 11.00 25.00

NOTE: *Issues 1-6 were released between Action #583 (9/86) & Action #584 (1/87) plus Superman #423 (9/86) & Advs. of Superman #424 (1/87).*

MAN OF WAR (See Liberty Guards & Liberty Scouts)
Nov, 1941 - No. 2, Jan, 1942
Centaur Publications

1-The Fire-Man, Man of War, The Sentinel, Liberty Guards, & Vapo-Man begin; Gustavson-c/a; Flag-c 114.00 343.00 800.00
2-Intro The Ferret; Gustavson-c/a 100.00 300.00 700.00

MAN OF WAR (Eclipse Comics)(Value: cover or less)

MAN OF WAR (See The Protectors)
1993 - Present ($1.95/$2.50/$2.25)
Malibu Comics

1-5 ($1.95)-Newsstand Editions w/different-c .80 2.00
1-5 ($2.50)-Collector's Editions w/poster 1.00 2.50
6-11 ($2.25): 6-Polybagged w/Skycap. 8-Vs. Rocket Rangers .90 2.25

MAN O' MARS
1953; 1964
Fiction House Magazines

1-Space Rangers; Whitman-c 27.00 81.00 190.00
I.W. Reprint #1-r/Man O'Mars #1 & Star Pirate; Murphy Anderson-a 5.35 16.00 32.00

MANTECH ROBOT WARRIORS (Archie)(Value: cover or less)

MAN-THING (See Fear, Giant-Size..., Marvel Comics Presents, Marvel Fanfare, Monsters Unleashed, Power Record Comics & Savage Tales)
Jan, 1974 - No. 22, Oct, 1975; V2#1, Nov, 1979 - V2#11, July, 1981
Marvel Comics Group

1-Howard the Duck(2nd app.) cont'd/Fear #19 2.40 7.25 17.00
2 1.30 3.25 8.00
3-1st app. original Foolkiller 1.20 3.00 7.00
4-Origin Foolkiller; last app. 1st Foolkiller 1.60 4.00
5-11-Ploog-a. 11-Foolkiller cameo (flashback) 1.20 3.00
12-22: 19-1st app. Scavenger. 20-Spidey cameo. 21-Origin Scavenger, Man-Thing. 22-Howard the Duck cameo .90 2.25
V2#1(1979) - 11 1.30

NOTE: ***Alcala** a-14. **Brunner** c-1. J. **Buscema** a-12p, 13p, 16p. **Gil Kane** c-4p, 10p, 12-20p, 21. **Mooney** a-17, 18, 19p, 20-22, V2#1-3p. **Ploog** Man-Thing-5p, 6p, 7, 8, 9-11p; c-5, 6, 8, 9, 11. **Sutton** a-13i. No. 19 says #10 in indicia.*

MANTRA
July, 1993 - Present ($1.95)
Malibu Comics (Ultraverse)

1-Polybagged w/trading card & coupon 1.60 4.00
1-Newsstand edition w/o trading card or coupon 1.20 3.00
1-Full cover holographic edition 25.00
1-Ultra-limited silver foil-c 1.40 4.20 10.00
2,3,5,6: 3-Intro Warstrike & Kismet. 6-Break-Thru x-over .90 2.25
2-($2.50- Newsstand edition bagged w/card 1.00 2.50

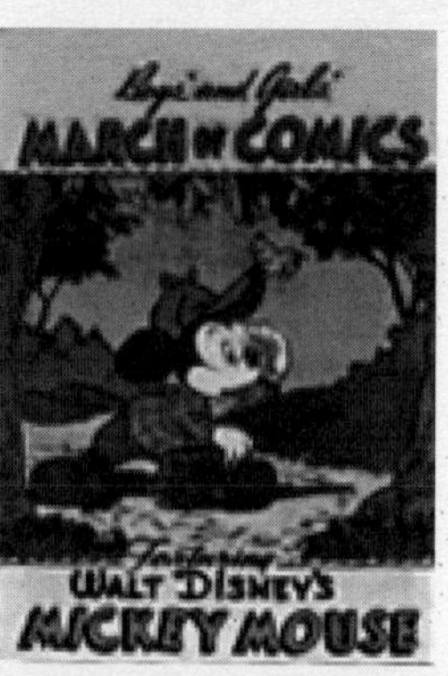

March of Comics #27 © WDC

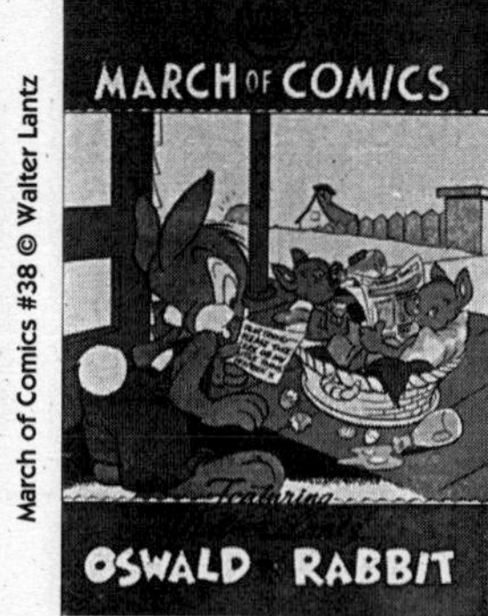

March of Comics #38 © Walter Lantz

March of Comics #41 © WDC

GD25 FN65 NM94

4-($2.50, 48 pgs.)-Rune flip-c/story by B. Smith (3 pgs.) 1.00 2.50
7-9,11-16: 7-Prime app.; origin Prototype by Jurgens/Austin (2 pgs.). 11-New costume .80 2.00
10-($3.50, 68 pgs.)-Flip-c w/Ultraverse Premiere #2 1.40 3.50
Giant Size 1 (7/94, $2.50, 44 pgs.) 1.00 2.50

MAN WITH THE X-RAY EYES, THE (See X,... under Movie Comics)

MANY GHOSTS OF DR. GRAVES, THE (Doctor Graves #73 on)
5/67 - No. 60, 12/76; No. 61, 9/77 - No. 62, 10/77; No. 63, 2/78 - No. 65, 4/78; No. 66, 6/81 - No. 72, 5/82
Charlton Comics

1-Palais-a; early issues 12¢-c 1.70 4.20 10.00
2-10 1.00 2.00 5.00
11-20 1.40 3.50
21-44,46-72: 47,49-Newton-a .80 2.00
45-1st Newton comic work (8 pgs.); new logo 1.20 3.00
Modern Comics Reprint 12,25 (1978) 1.00

NOTE: **Aparo** *a-4, 5, 7, 8, 66r, 69r; c-8, 14, 19, 66r, 67r.* **Byrne** *c-54.* **Ditko** *a-1, 7, 9, 11-13, 15-18, 20-22, 24, 26, 27, 35, 37, 38, 40-44, 47, 48, 51-54, 58, 60r-65r, 70, 72; c-11-13, 16-18, 22, 24, 26-35, 38, 40, 55, 58, 62-65.* **Howard** *a-45i; c-48.* **Morisi** *a-13, 14, 23, 26.* **Newton** *a-45, 47p, 49p; c-49, 52.* **Sutton** *a-42, 49; c-42, 44, 45; painted c-53.*

MANY LOVES OF DOBIE GILLIS (TV)
May-June, 1960 - No. 26, Oct, 1964
National Periodical Publications

1-Most covers by Bob Oskner 20.00 60.00 160.00
2-5 10.00 30.00 80.00
6-10 8.00 24.00 65.00
11-26: 20-Drucker-a 7.00 21.00 55.00

MARAUDER'S MOON (See 4-Color #848)

MARCH OF COMICS (Boys' and Girls'...#3-353)
1946 - No. 488, April, 1982 (#1-4 are not numbered)
(K.K. Giveaway) (Founded by Sig Feuchtwanger)
K. K. Publications/Western Publishing Co.

Early issues were full size, 32 pages, and were printed with and without an extra cover of slick stock, just for the advertiser. The binding was stapled if the slick cover was added; otherwise, the pages were glued together at the spine. Most 1948 - 1951 issues were full size,24 pages, pulp covers. Starting in 1952 they were half-size and 32 pages with slick covers.1959 and later issues had only 16 pages plus covers. 1952 -1959 issues read oblong; 1960 and later issues read upright. All have new stories except where noted.

nn (#1, 1946)-Goldilocks; Kelly back-c (16 pgs., stapled) 33.00 100.00 230.00
nn (#2, 1946)-How Santa Got His Red Suit; Kelly-a (11 pgs., r/4-Color #61 from 1944) (16pgs., stapled) 33.00 100.00 230.00
nn (#3, 1947)-Our Gang (Walt Kelly) 46.00 137.00 320.00
nn (#4)-Donald Duck by Carl Barks, "Maharajah Donald", 28 pgs.; Kelly-c? (Disney) 857.00 2571.00 6000.00
5-Andy Panda (Walter Lantz) 19.00 57.00 130.00
6-Popular Fairy Tales; Kelly-c; Noonan-a(2) 22.00 67.00 155.00
7-Oswald the Rabbit 22.00 67.00 155.00
8-Mickey Mouse, 32 pgs. (Disney) 71.00 215.00 500.00
9(nn)-The Story of the Gloomy Bunny 10.00 30.00 70.00
10-Out of Santa's Bag 10.00 30.00 60.00
11-Fun With Santa Claus 7.50 22.50 45.00
12-Santa's Toys 7.50 22.50 45.00
13-Santa's Surprise 7.50 22.50 45.00
14-Santa's Candy Kitchen 7.50 22.50 45.00
15-Hip-It-Ty Hop & the Big Bass Viol 7.50 22.50 45.00
16-Woody Woodpecker (1947)(Walter Lantz) 13.50 41.00 95.00
17-Roy Rogers (1948) 24.00 72.00 165.00
18-Popular Fairy Tales 12.00 36.00 85.00
19-Uncle Wiggily 10.00 30.00 70.00
20-Donald Duck by Carl Barks, "Darkest Africa", 22 pgs.; Kelly-c (Disney) 5007.00 1500.00 3500.00
21-Tom and Jerry 11.50 34.00 80.00
22-Andy Panda (Lantz) 10.00 30.00 70.00
23-Raggedy Ann & Andy; Kerr-a 16.00 48.00 110.00

GD25 FN65 NM94

24-Felix the Cat, 1932 daily strip reprints by Otto Messmer 25.00 75.00 175.00
25-Gene Autry 23.00 70.00 160.00
26-Our Gang; Walt Kelly 25.00 75.00 175.00
27-Mickey Mouse; r/in M. M. #240 (Disney) 50.00 150.00 350.00
28-Gene Autry 23.00 70.00 160.00
29-Easter Bonnet Shop 5.35 16.00 32.00
30-Here Comes Santa 4.35 13.00 26.00
31-Santa's Busy Corner 4.35 13.00 26.00
32-No book produced
33-A Christmas Carol (12/48) 4.35 13.00 26.00
34-Woody Woodpecker 10.00 30.00 70.00
35-Roy Rogers (1948) 23.00 70.00 160.00
36-Felix the Cat(1949); by Messmer; 1934 daily strip-r 21.00 63.00 145.00
37-Popeye 17.00 52.00 120.00
38-Oswald the Rabbit 9.15 27.50 55.00
39-Gene Autry 23.00 70.00 160.00
40-Andy and Woody 9.15 27.50 55.00
41-Donald Duck by Carl Barks, "Race to the South Seas", 22 pgs.; Kelly-c 500.00 1500.00 3500.00
42-Porky Pig 9.15 27.50 55.00
43-Henry 7.50 22.50 45.00
44-Bugs Bunny 10.00 30.00 70.00
45-Mickey Mouse (Disney) 39.00 116.00 270.00
46-Tom and Jerry 10.00 30.00 70.00
47-Roy Rogers 20.00 60.00 140.00
48-Greetings from Santa 4.00 11.00 22.00
49-Santa Is Here 4.00 11.00 22.00
50-Santa Claus' Workshop (1949) 4.00 11.00 22.00
51-Felix the Cat (1950) by Messmer 17.00 52.00 120.00
52-Popeye 14.00 43.00 100.00
53-Oswald the Rabbit 9.15 27.50 55.00
54-Gene Autry 19.00 57.00 130.00
55-Andy and Woody 8.35 25.00 50.00
56-Donald Duck; not by Barks; Barks art on back-c (Disney) 34.00 103.00 240.00
57-Porky Pig 8.35 25.00 50.00
58-Henry 5.85 17.50 35.00
59-Bugs Bunny 10.00 30.00 60.00
60-Mickey Mouse (Disney) 35.00 105.00 245.00
61-Tom and Jerry 8.35 25.00 50.00
62-Roy Rogers 19.00 57.00 130.00
63-Welcome Santa (1/2-size, oblong) 4.00 11.00 22.00
64(nn)-Santa's Helpers (1/2-size, oblong) 4.00 11.00 22.00
65(nn)-Jingle Bells (1950) (1/2-size, oblong) 4.00 11.00 22.00
66-Popeye (1951) 12.00 36.00 85.00
67-Oswald the Rabbit 7.50 22.50 45.00
68-Roy Rogers 17.00 52.00 120.00
69-Donald Duck; Barks-a on back-c (Disney) 29.00 86.00 200.00
70-Tom and Jerry 7.50 22.50 45.00
71-Porky Pig 7.50 22.50 45.00
72-Krazy Kat 10.00 30.00 60.00
73-Roy Rogers 14.00 43.00 100.00
74-Mickey Mouse (1951)(Disney) 29.00 86.00 200.00
75-Bugs Bunny 8.35 25.00 50.00
76-Andy and Woody 7.50 22.50 45.00
77-Roy Rogers 14.00 42.00 95.00
78-Gene Autry (1951); last regular size issue 14.00 42.00 95.00
79-Andy Panda (1952, 5x7" size) 4.35 13.00 26.00
80-Popeye 11.00 32.00 75.00
81-Oswald the Rabbit 4.70 14.00 28.00
82-Tarzan; Lex Barker photo-c 19.00 52.00 120.00
83-Bugs Bunny 6.35 19.00 38.00
84-Henry 4.00 11.00 22.00
85-Woody Woodpecker 4.00 11.00 22.00

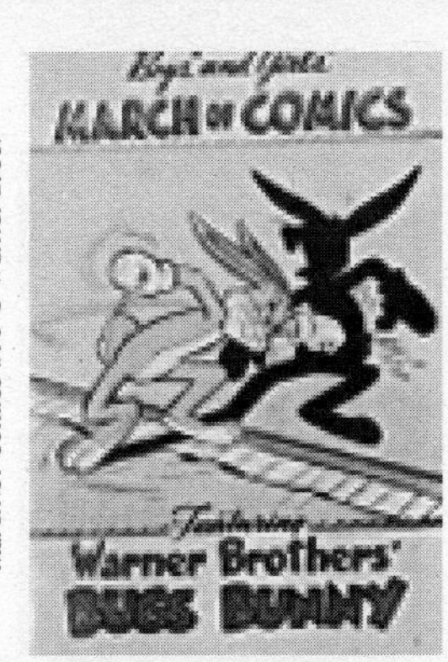

March of Comics #75 © Warner Bros.

March of Comics #208 © Broadway Video

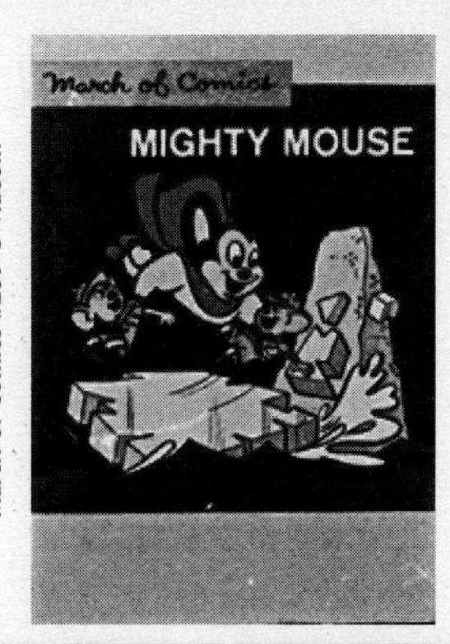

March of Comics #257 © Viacom

	GD25	FN65	NM94
86-Roy Rogers	11.50	34.00	80.00
87-Krazy Kat	8.35	25.00	50.00
88-Tom and Jerry	5.35	16.00	32.00
89-Porky Pig	4.00	11.00	22.00
90-Gene Autry	11.50	34.00	80.00
91-Roy Rogers & Santa	11.50	34.00	80.00
92-Christmas with Santa	3.60	9.00	18.00
93-Woody Woodpecker (1953)	4.00	11.00	22.00
94-Indian Chief	10.00	30.00	60.00
95-Oswald the Rabbit	4.00	11.00	22.00
96-Popeye	10.00	30.00	65.00
97-Bugs Bunny	5.35	16.00	32.00
98-Tarzan; Lex Barker photo-c	19.00	57.00	130.00
99-Porky Pig	4.00	11.00	22.00
100-Roy Rogers	10.00	30.00	65.00
101-Henry	4.00	10.00	20.00
102-Tom Corbett (TV)('53, early app).; painted-c	16.00	48.00	110.00
103-Tom and Jerry	4.00	11.00	22.00
104-Gene Autry	10.00	30.00	65.00
105-Roy Rogers	10.00	30.00	65.00
106-Santa's Helpers	3.60	9.00	18.00
107-Santa's Christmas Book - not published			
108-Fun with Santa (1953)	3.60	9.00	18.00
109-Woody Woodpecker (1954)	4.00	10.00	20.00
110-Indian Chief	5.35	16.00	32.00
111-Oswald the Rabbit	4.00	10.00	20.00
112-Henry	3.60	9.00	18.00
113-Porky Pig	4.00	10.00	20.00
114-Tarzan; Russ Manning-a	19.00	57.00	130.00
115-Bugs Bunny	4.35	13.00	26.00
116-Roy Rogers	10.00	30.00	65.00
117-Popeye	10.00	30.00	65.00
118-Flash Gordon; painted-c	13.00	40.00	90.00
119-Tom and Jerry	4.00	10.00	20.00
120-Gene Autry	10.00	30.00	65.00
121-Roy Rogers	10.00	30.00	65.00
122-Santa's Surprise (1954)	2.80	7.00	14.00
123-Santa's Christmas Book	2.80	7.00	14.00
124-Woody Woodpecker (1955)	3.60	9.00	18.00
125-Tarzan; Lex Barker photo-c	17.00	52.00	120.00
126-Oswald the Rabbit	3.60	9.00	18.00
127-Indian Chief	4.70	14.00	28.00
128-Tom and Jerry	3.60	9.00	18.00
129-Henry	3.20	8.00	16.00
130-Porky Pig	3.60	9.00	18.00
131-Roy Rogers	10.00	30.00	65.00
132-Bugs Bunny	4.00	11.00	22.00
133-Flash Gordon; painted-c	11.50	34.00	80.00
134-Popeye	7.50	22.50	45.00
135-Gene Autry	10.00	30.00	60.00
136-Roy Rogers	10.00	30.00	60.00
137-Gifts from Santa	2.40	6.00	12.00
138-Fun at Christmas (1955)	2.40	6.00	12.00
139-Woody Woodpecker (1956)	3.60	9.00	18.00
140-Indian Chief	4.70	14.00	28.00
141-Oswald the Rabbit	3.60	9.00	18.00
142-Flash Gordon	11.50	34.00	80.00
143-Porky Pig	3.60	9.00	18.00
144-Tarzan; Russ Manning-a; painted-c	16.00	48.00	110.00
145-Tom and Jerry	3.60	9.00	18.00
146-Roy Rogers; photo-c	10.00	30.00	65.00
147-Henry	2.80	7.00	14.00
148-Popeye	7.50	22.50	45.00
149-Bugs Bunny	4.00	10.00	20.00
150-Gene Autry	10.00	30.00	60.00
151-Roy Rogers	10.00	30.00	60.00
152-The Night Before Christmas	2.40	6.00	12.00
153-Merry Christmas (1956)	2.40	6.00	12.00
154-Tom and Jerry (1957)	3.60	9.00	18.00
155-Tarzan; photo-c	16.00	48.00	110.00
156-Oswald the Rabbit	3.60	9.00	18.00
157-Popeye	6.35	19.00	38.00
158-Woody Woodpecker	3.60	9.00	18.00
159-Indian Chief	4.70	14.00	28.00
160-Bugs Bunny	4.00	10.00	20.00
161-Roy Rogers	8.35	25.00	50.00
162-Henry	2.80	7.00	14.00
163-Rin Tin Tin (TV)	6.35	19.00	38.00
164-Porky Pig	3.60	9.00	18.00
165-The Lone Ranger	9.15	27.50	55.00
166-Santa and His Reindeer	2.40	6.00	12.00
167-Roy Rogers and Santa	8.35	25.00	50.00
168-Santa Claus' Workshop (1957)	2.40	6.00	12.00
169-Popeye (1958)	6.35	19.00	38.00
170-Indian Chief	4.70	14.00	28.00
171-Oswald the Rabbit	3.20	8.00	16.00
172-Tarzan	12.00	36.00	85.00
173-Tom and Jerry	3.20	8.00	16.00
174-The Lone Ranger	9.15	27.50	55.00
175-Porky Pig	3.20	8.00	16.00
176-Roy Rogers	7.50	22.50	45.00
177-Woody Woodpecker	3.20	8.00	16.00
178-Henry	2.80	7.00	14.00
179-Bugs Bunny	3.20	8.00	16.00
180-Rin Tin Tin (TV)	5.35	16.00	32.00
181-Happy Holiday	2.00	5.00	10.00
182-Happi Tim	3.20	8.00	16.00
183-Welcome Santa (1958)	2.00	5.00	10.00
184-Woody Woodpecker (1959)	3.20	8.00	16.00
185-Tarzan; photo-c	12.00	36.00	85.00
186-Oswald the Rabbit	3.20	8.00	16.00
187-Indian Chief	4.70	14.00	28.00
188-Bugs Bunny	3.20	8.00	16.00
189-Henry	2.80	7.00	14.00
190-Tom and Jerry	3.20	8.00	16.00
191-Roy Rogers	7.50	22.50	45.00
192-Porky Pig	3.20	8.00	16.00
193-The Lone Ranger	9.15	27.50	55.00
194-Popeye	5.85	17.50	35.00
195-Rin Tin Tin (TV)	5.35	16.00	32.00
196-Sears Special - not published			
197-Santa Is Coming	2.00	5.00	10.00
198-Santa's Helpers (1959)	2.00	5.00	10.00
199-Huckleberry Hound (TV)(1960, early app.)	6.70	20.00	40.00
200-Fury (TV)	5.35	16.00	32.00
201-Bugs Bunny	3.20	8.00	16.00
202-Space Explorer	8.35	25.00	50.00
203-Woody Woodpecker	2.80	7.00	14.00
204-Tarzan	10.00	30.00	65.00
205-Mighty Mouse	6.35	19.00	38.00
206-Roy Rogers; photo-c	7.50	22.50	45.00
207-Tom and Jerry	2.80	7.00	14.00
208-The Lone Ranger; Clayton Moore photo-c	11.50	34.00	80.00
209-Porky Pig	2.80	7.00	14.00
210-Lassie (TV)	5.35	16.00	32.00
211-Sears Special - not published			
212-Christmas Eve	2.00	5.00	10.00
213-Here Comes Santa (1960)	2.00	5.00	10.00
214-Huckleberry Hound (TV)(1961)	5.85	17.50	35.00
215-Hi Yo Silver	5.35	16.00	32.00
216-Rocky & His Friends (TV)(1961); predates Rocky and His Fiendish Friends #1 (see Four Color #1128)	10.00	30.00	70.00

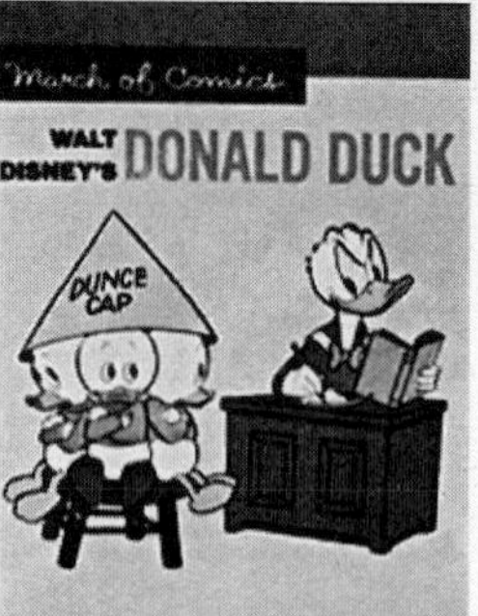

March of Comics #263 © WDC

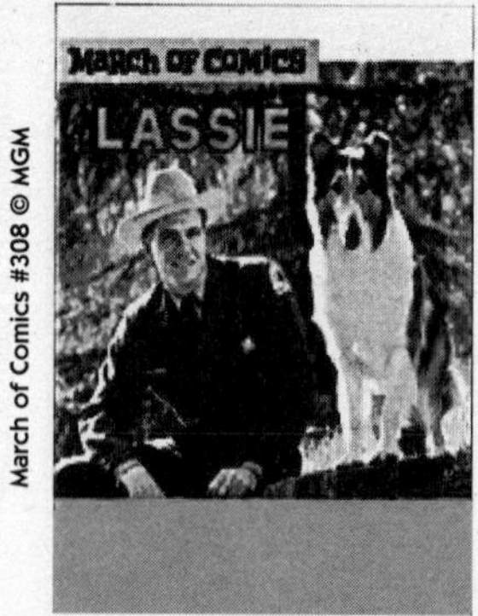

March of Comics #308 © MGM

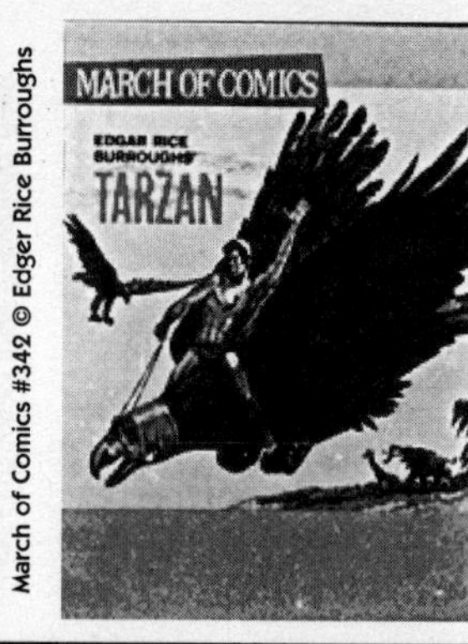

March of Comics #342 © Edger Rice Burroughs

	GD25	FN65	NM94
217-Lassie (TV)	4.35	13.00	26.00
218-Porky Pig	2.80	7.00	14.00
219-Journey to the Sun	5.35	16.00	32.00
220-Bugs Bunny	3.20	8.00	16.00
221-Roy and Dale; photo-c	6.70	20.00	40.00
222-Woody Woodpecker	2.80	7.00	14.00
223-Tarzan	10.00	30.00	65.00
224-Tom and Jerry	2.80	7.00	14.00
225-The Lone Ranger	6.70	20.00	40.00
226-Christmas Treasury (1961)	2.00	5.00	10.00
227-Sears Special - not published?			
228-Letters to Santa (1961)	2.00	5.00	10.00
229-The Flintstones (TV)(1962); early app.; predates 1st Flintstones Gold Key issue (#7)	10.00	30.00	60.00
230-Lassie (TV)	4.35	13.00	26.00
231-Bugs Bunny	3.20	8.00	16.00
232-The Three Stooges	10.00	30.00	60.00
233-Bullwinkle (TV) (1962, very early app.)	11.00	32.00	75.00
234-Smokey the Bear	4.00	10.00	20.00
235-Huckleberry Hound (TV)	5.85	17.50	35.00
236-Roy and Dale	5.35	16.00	32.00
237-Mighty Mouse	4.70	14.00	28.00
238-The Lone Ranger	6.70	20.00	40.00
239-Woody Woodpecker	2.80	7.00	14.00
240-Tarzan	8.35	25.00	50.00
241-Santa Claus Around the World	2.00	5.00	10.00
242-Santa's Toyland (1962)	2.00	5.00	10.00
243-The Flintstones (TV)(1963)	9.15	27.50	55.00
244-Mister Ed (TV); early app.; photo-c	5.85	17.50	35.00
245-Bugs Bunny	3.20	8.00	16.00
246-Popeye	4.35	13.00	26.00
247-Mighty Mouse	4.70	14.00	28.00
248-The Three Stooges	10.00	30.00	60.00
249-Woody Woodpecker	2.80	7.00	14.00
250-Roy and Dale	5.35	16.00	32.00
251-Little Lulu & Witch Hazel	14.00	43.00	100.00
252-Tarzan; painted-c	8.35	25.00	50.00
253-Yogi Bear (TV)	6.35	19.00	38.00
254-Lassie (TV)	4.35	13.00	26.00
255-Santa's Christmas List	2.00	5.00	10.00
256-Christmas Party (1963)	2.00	5.00	10.00
257-Mighty Mouse	4.70	14.00	28.00
258-The Sword in the Stone (Disney)	9.15	27.50	55.00
259-Bugs Bunny	3.20	8.00	16.00
260-Mister Ed (TV)	4.70	14.00	28.00
261-Woody Woodpecker	2.80	7.00	14.00
262-Tarzan	8.35	25.00	50.00
263-Donald Duck; not by Barks (Disney)	10.00	30.00	60.00
264-Popeye	4.35	13.00	26.00
265-Yogi Bear (TV)	4.70	14.00	28.00
266-Lassie (TV)	4.00	11.00	22.00
267-Little Lulu; Irving Tripp-a	11.50	34.00	80.00
268-The Three Stooges	9.15	27.50	55.00
269-A Jolly Christmas	2.00	5.00	10.00
270-Santa's Little Helpers	2.00	5.00	10.00
271-The Flintstones (TV)(1965)	9.15	27.50	55.00
272-Tarzan	8.35	25.00	50.00
273-Bugs Bunny	3.20	8.00	16.00
274-Popeye	4.35	13.00	26.00
275-Little Lulu; Irving Tripp-a	10.00	30.00	65.00
276-The Jetsons (TV)	14.00	43.00	100.00
277-Daffy Duck	3.20	8.00	16.00
278-Lassie (TV)	4.00	11.00	22.00
279-Yogi Bear (TV)	4.70	14.00	28.00
280-The Three Stooges; photo-c	9.15	27.50	55.00
281-Tom and Jerry	2.40	6.00	12.00

	GD25	FN65	NM94
282-Mister Ed (TV)	4.70	14.00	28.00
283-Santa's Visit	2.00	5.00	10.00
284-Christmas Parade (1965)	2.00	5.00	10.00
285-Astro Boy (TV); 2nd app. Astro Boy	33.00	100.00	230.00
286-Tarzan	7.50	22.50	45.00
287-Bugs Bunny	3.20	8.00	16.00
288-Daffy Duck	2.80	7.00	14.00
289-The Flintstones (TV)	8.35	25.00	50.00
290-Mister Ed (TV); photo-c	4.00	12.00	24.00
291-Yogi Bear (TV)	4.00	12.00	24.00
292-The Three Stooges; photo-c	9.15	27.50	55.00
293-Little Lulu; Irving Tripp-a	9.15	27.50	55.00
294-Popeye	4.35	13.00	26.00
295-Tom and Jerry	2.40	6.00	12.00
296-Lassie (TV); photo-c	4.00	10.00	20.00
297-Christmas Bells	2.00	5.00	10.00
298-Santa's Sleigh (1966)	2.00	5.00	10.00
299-The Flintstones (TV)(1967)	8.35	25.00	50.00
300-Tarzan	7.50	22.50	45.00
301-Bugs Bunny	2.80	7.00	14.00
302-Laurel and Hardy (TV); photo-c	5.00	15.00	30.00
303-Daffy Duck	2.00	5.00	10.00
304-The Three Stooges; photo-c	8.35	25.00	50.00
305-Tom and Jerry	2.00	5.00	10.00
306-Daniel Boone (TV); Fess Parker photo-c	5.00	15.00	30.00
307-Little Lulu; Irving Tripp-a	7.50	22.50	45.00
308-Lassie (TV); photo-c	3.60	9.00	18.00
309-Yogi Bear (TV)	4.00	11.00	22.00
310-The Lone Ranger; Clayton Moore photo-c	11.50	34.00	80.00
311-Santa's Show	2.00	5.00	10.00
312-Christmas Album (1967)	2.00	5.00	10.00
313-Daffy Duck (1968)	2.00	5.00	10.00
314-Laurel and Hardy (TV)	4.70	14.00	28.00
315-Bugs Bunny	2.80	7.00	14.00
316-The Three Stooges	6.70	20.00	40.00
317-The Flintstones (TV)	6.70	20.00	40.00
318-Tarzan	6.70	20.00	40.00
319-Yogi Bear (TV)	4.00	11.00	22.00
320-Space Family Robinson (TV); Spiegle-a	13.00	40.00	90.00
321-Tom and Jerry	2.00	5.00	10.00
322-The Lone Ranger	5.85	17.50	35.00
323-Little Lulu; not by Stanley	4.35	13.00	26.00
324-Lassie (TV); photo-c	3.60	9.00	18.00
325-Fun with Santa	2.00	5.00	10.00
326-Christmas Story (1968)	2.00	5.00	10.00
327-The Flintstones (TV)(1969)	6.70	20.00	40.00
328-Space Family Robinson (TV); Spiegle-a	13.00	40.00	90.00
329-Bugs Bunny	2.80	7.00	14.00
330-The Jetsons (TV)	10.00	30.00	70.00
331-Daffy Duck	2.00	5.00	10.00
332-Tarzan	5.35	16.00	32.00
333-Tom and Jerry	2.00	5.00	10.00
334-Lassie (TV)	3.20	8.00	16.00
335-Little Lulu	4.35	13.00	26.00
336-The Three Stooges	6.70	20.00	40.00
337-Yogi Bear (TV)	4.00	11.00	22.00
338-The Lone Ranger	5.85	17.50	35.00
339-(Was not published)			
340-Here Comes Santa (1969)	2.00	5.00	10.00
341-The Flintstones (TV)	6.70	20.00	40.00
342-Tarzan	5.35	16.00	32.00
343-Bugs Bunny	2.40	6.00	12.00
344-Yogi Bear (TV)	4.00	10.00	20.00
345-Tom and Jerry	2.00	5.00	10.00
346-Lassie (TV)	3.20	8.00	16.00
347-Daffy Duck	2.00	5.00	10.00

March of Comics #378 © WEST

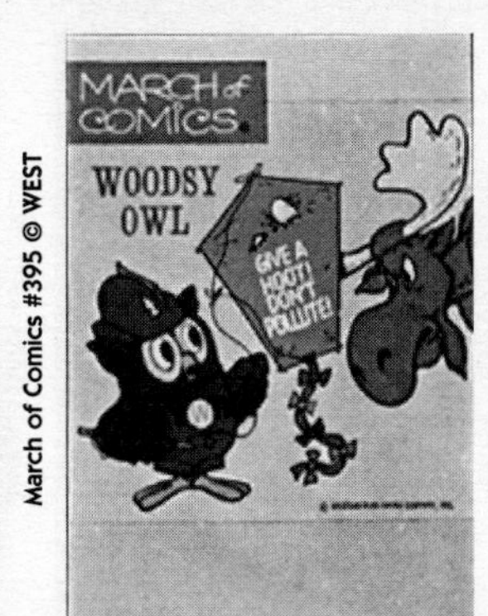

March of Comics #395 © WEST

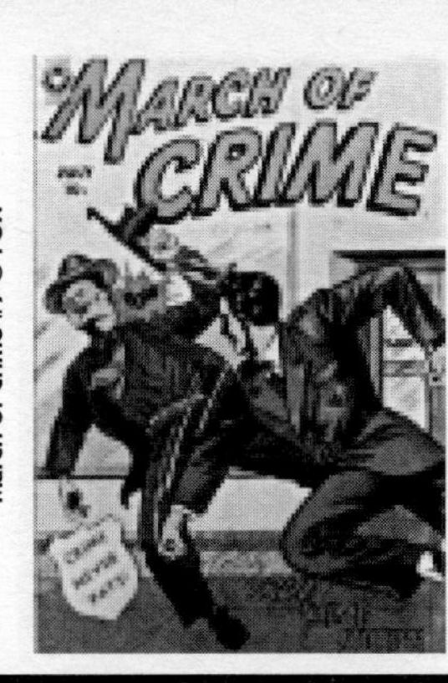

March of Crime #7 © FOX

	GD25	FN65	NM94
348-The Jetsons (TV)	10.00	30.00	60.00
349-Little Lulu; not by Stanley	4.00	11.00	22.00
350-The Lone Ranger	5.00	15.00	30.00
351-Beep-Beep, the Road Runner (TV)	2.80	7.00	14.00
352-Space Family Robinson (TV); Spiegle-a	13.00	40.00	90.00
353-Beep-Beep, the Road Runner (1971) (TV)	2.80	7.00	14.00
354-Tarzan (1971)	4.70	14.00	28.00
355-Little Lulu; not by Stanley	4.00	11.00	22.00
356-Scooby Doo, Where Are You? (TV)	4.00	11.00	22.00
357-Daffy Duck & Porky Pig	2.00	5.00	10.00
358-Lassie (TV)	3.20	8.00	16.00
359-Baby Snoots	2.80	7.00	14.00
360-H. R. Pufnstuf (TV); photo-c	2.80	7.00	14.00
361-Tom and Jerry	2.00	5.00	10.00
362-Smokey the Bear (TV)	2.00	5.00	10.00
363-Bugs Bunny & Yosemite Sam	2.40	6.00	12.00
364-The Banana Splits (TV); photo-c	2.40	6.00	12.00
365-Tom and Jerry (1972)	2.00	5.00	10.00
366-Tarzan	4.35	13.00	26.00
367-Bugs Bunny & Porky Pig	2.40	6.00	12.00
368-Scooby Doo (TV)(4/72)	4.00	10.00	20.00
369-Little Lulu; not by Stanley	3.60	9.00	18.00
370-Lassie (TV); photo-c	3.20	8.00	16.00
371-Baby Snoots	2.40	6.00	12.00
372-Smokey the Bear (TV)	2.00	5.00	10.00
373-The Three Stooges	5.85	17.50	35.00
374-Wacky Witch	2.00	5.00	10.00
375-Beep-Beep & Daffy Duck (TV)	2.00	5.00	10.00
376-The Pink Panther (1972) (TV)	2.80	7.00	14.00
377-Baby Snoots (1973)	2.40	6.00	12.00
378-Turok, Son of Stone; new-a	14.00	43.00	100.00
379-Heckle & Jeckle New Terrytoons (TV)	2.00	5.00	10.00
380-Bugs Bunny & Yosemite Sam	2.00	5.00	10.00
381-Lassie (TV)	2.80	7.00	14.00
382-Scooby Doo, Where Are You? (TV)	3.60	9.00	18.00
383-Smokey the Bear (TV)	1.60	4.00	8.00
384-Pink Panther (TV)	2.00	5.00	10.00
385-Little Lulu	3.00	7.50	15.00
386-Wacky Witch	1.60	4.00	8.00
387-Beep-Beep & Daffy Duck (TV)	1.60	4.00	8.00
388-Tom and Jerry (1973)	1.60	4.00	8.00
389-Little Lulu; not by Stanley	3.00	7.50	15.00
390-Pink Panther (TV)	1.60	4.00	8.00
391-Scooby Doo (TV)	3.20	8.00	16.00
392-Bugs Bunny & Yosemite Sam	1.20	3.00	6.00
393-New Terrytoons (Heckle & Jeckle) (TV)	1.20	3.00	6.00
394-Lassie (TV)	2.00	5.00	10.00
395-Woodsy Owl	1.20	3.00	6.00
396-Baby Snoots	1.60	4.00	8.00
397-Beep-Beep & Daffy Duck (TV)	1.20	3.00	6.00
398-Wacky Witch	1.20	3.00	6.00
399-Turok, Son of Stone; new-a	11.00	32.00	75.00
400-Tom and Jerry	1.20	3.00	6.00
401-Baby Snoots (1975) (r/#371)	1.60	4.00	8.00
402-Daffy Duck (r/#313)	1.00	2.50	5.00
403-Bugs Bunny (r/#343)	1.20	3.00	6.00
404-Space Family Robinson (TV)(r/#328)	10.00	30.00	65.00
405-Cracky	1.00	2.50	5.00
406-Little Lulu (r/#355)	2.40	6.00	12.00
407-Smokey the Bear (TV)(r/#362)	1.20	3.00	6.00
408-Turok, Son of Stone; c-r/Turok #20 w/changes; new-a	8.35	25.00	55.00
409-Pink Panther (TV)	1.00	2.50	5.00
410-Wacky Witch	.80	2.00	4.00
411-Lassie (TV)(r/#324)	1.80	4.50	9.00
412-New Terrytoons (1975) (TV)	.80	2.00	4.00
413-Daffy Duck (1976)(r/#331)	.80	2.00	4.00
414-Space Family Robinson (r/#328)	8.35	25.00	55.00
415-Bugs Bunny (r/#329)	.80	2.00	4.00
416-Beep-Beep, the Road Runner (r/#353)(TV)	.80	2.00	4.00
417-Little Lulu (r/#323)	2.40	6.00	12.00
418-Pink Panther (r/#384) (TV)	.80	2.00	4.00
419-Baby Snoots (r/#377)	1.00	2.50	5.00
420-Woody Woodpecker	.80	2.00	4.00
421-Tweety & Sylvester	.80	2.00	4.00
422-Wacky Witch (r/#386)	.80	2.00	4.00
423-Little Monsters	1.00	2.50	5.00
424-Cracky (12/76)	.80	2.00	4.00
425-Daffy Duck	.80	2.00	4.00
426-Underdog (TV)	3.00	7.50	15.00
427-Little Lulu (r/#335)	1.60	4.00	8.00
428-Bugs Bunny	.60	1.50	3.00
429-The Pink Panther (TV)	.60	1.50	3.00
430-Beep-Beep, the Road Runner (TV)	.60	1.50	3.00
431-Baby Snoots	.80	2.00	4.00
432-Lassie (TV)	1.00	2.50	5.00
433-437: 433-Tweety & Sylvester. 434-Wacky Witch. 435-New Terrytoons (TV). 436-Wacky Advs. of Cracky. 437-Daffy Duck	.60	1.50	3.00
438-Underdog (TV)	3.00	7.50	15.00
439-Little Lulu (r/#349)	1.60	4.00	8.00
440-442,444-446: 440-Bugs Bunny. 441-The Pink Panther (TV). 442-Beep-Beep, the Road Runner (TV). 444-Tom and Jerry. 445-Tweety and Sylvester. 446-Wacky Witch	.60	1.50	3.00
443-Baby Snoots	.80	2.00	4.00
447-Mighty Mouse	1.20	3.00	6.00
448-455,457,458: 448-Cracky. 449-Pink Panther (TV). 450-Baby Snoots 451-Tom and Jerry. 452-Bugs Bunny. 453-Popeye. 454-Woody Woodpecker. 455-Beep-Beep, the Road Runner (TV). 457-Tweety & Sylvester. 458-Wacky Witch	.60	1.50	3.00
456-Little Lulu (r/#369)	1.20	3.00	6.00
459-Mighty Mouse	1.20	3.00	6.00
460-466: 460-Daffy Duck. 461-The Pink Panther (TV). 462-Baby Snoots. 463-Tom and Jerry. 464-Bugs Bunny. 465-Popeye. 466-Woody Woodpecker	.60	1.50	3.00
467-Underdog (TV)	2.40	6.00	12.00
468-Little Lulu (r/#385)	.80	2.00	4.00
469-Tweety & Sylvester	.60	1.50	3.00
470-Wacky Witch	.60	1.50	3.00
471-Mighty Mouse	.80	2.50	5.00
472-474,476-478: 472-Heckle & Jeckle(12/80). 473-Pink Panther(1/81)(TV). 474-Baby Snoots. 476-Bugs Bunny. 477-Popeye. 478-Woody Woodpecker	.60	1.50	3.00
475-Little Lulu (r/#323)	.80	2.00	4.00
479-Underdog (TV)	2.00	5.00	10.00
480-482: 480-Tom and Jerry. 481-Tweety and Sylvester. 482-Wacky Witch	.60	1.50	3.00
483-Mighty Mouse	.80	2.00	5.00
484-487: 484-Heckle & Jeckle. 485-Baby Snoots. 486-The Pink Panther (TV). 487-Bugs Bunny	.60	1.50	3.00
488-Little Lulu (4/82) (r/#335)	.80	2.00	4.00

MARCH OF CRIME (Formerly My Love Affair #1-6) (See Fox Giants)
No. 7, July, 1950 - No. 2, Sept, 1950; No. 3, Sept, 1951
Fox Features Syndicate

	GD25	FN65	NM94
7(#1)(7/50)-True crime stories; Wood-a	22.00	65.00	150.00
2(9/50)-Wood-a (exceptional)	22.00	65.00	150.00
3(9/51)	10.00	30.00	65.00

MARCO POLO
1962 (Movie classic)
Charlton Comics Group

	GD25	FN65	NM94
nn (Scarce)-Glanzman-c/a (25 pgs.)	11.50	34.00	80.00

MARC SPECTOR: MOON KNIGHT (Also see Moon Knight)

Marc Spector: Moon Knight #15 © MEG

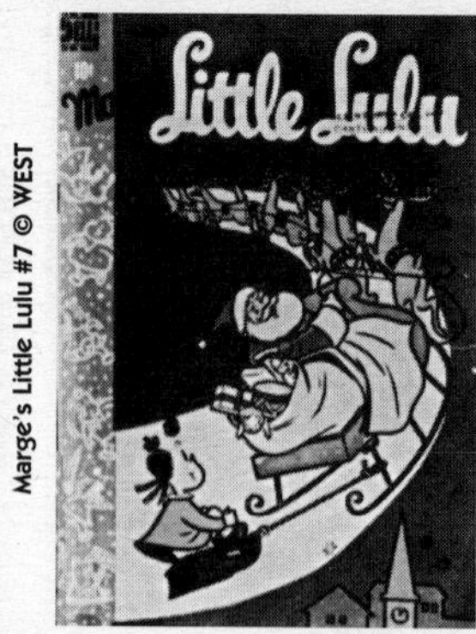

Marge's Little Lulu #7 © WEST

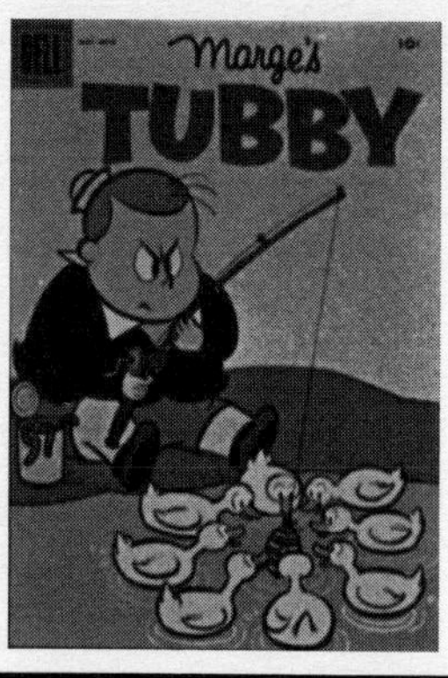

Marge's Tubby #22 © WEST

June, 1989 - No. 60, Mar, 1994 ($1.50/$1.75, direct sale only)
Marvel Comics

	GD25	FN65	NM94
1		1.30	3.25
2-7: 4-Intro new Midnight		.90	2.25
8,9-Punisher app.	1.20	3.00	7.00
10-18: 15-Silver Sable app. 20-Guice-c. 21-23-Cowan-c(p)		.90	2.25
19-21-Spider-Man & Punisher app.	1.10	2.70	6.50
22-24,26-31,34: 34-Last $1.50-c		.70	1.80
25-($2.50, 52 pgs.)-Ghost Rider app.		1.30	3.25
32,33-Hobgoblin II (Macendale) & Spider-Man (in black costume) app.		1.30	3.25
35-38-Punisher story		.90	2.25
39-49,51-54: 42-44-Infinity War x-over. 46-Demogoblin app. 51,53-Gambit app.		.70	1.75
50-($2.95, 56 pgs.)-Special die-cut cover		1.30	3.25
55-New look & Stephen Platt-c/a begin	1.40	4.00	10.00
56,57-Platt-c/a. 57-Spider-Man-c/story		1.60	4.00
58,59-S. Platt-c only		1.00	2.50
60-S.Platt-c/a; death of Moon Knight		.70	1.75
...: Divided We Fall ($4.95, 52 pgs.)	1.00	2.00	5.00
Special 1 (1992, $2.50)		1.00	2.50

MARGARET O'BRIEN (See The Adventures of...)

MARGE'S LITTLE LULU (Little Lulu #207 on)
No. 74, 6/45 - No. 164, 7-9/62; No. 165, 10/62 - No. 206, 8/72
Dell Publishing Co./Gold Key #165-206

Marjorie Henderson Buell, born in Philadelphia, Pa., in 1904, created Little Lulu, a cartoon character that appeared weekly in the Saturday Evening Post from Feb. 23, 1935 through Dec. 30, 1944. She was not responsible for any of the comic books. **John Stanley** did pencils only on all Little Lulu comics through at least #135 (1959). He did pencils and inks on Four Color #74 & 97. **Irving Tripp** began inking stories from #1 on, and remained the comic's illustrator throughout its entire run. **Stanley** did storyboards (layouts), pencils, and scripts in all cases and inking only on covers. His word balloons were written in cursive. **Tripp** and occasionally other artists at Western Publ. in Poughkeepsie, N.Y. blew up the pencilled pages, inked the blowups, and lettered them. **Arnold Drake** did storyboards, pencils and scripts starting with #197 (1970) on, amidst reprinted issues. **Buell** sold her rights exclusively to Western Publ. in Dec., 1971. The earlier issues had to be approved by **Buell** prior to publication.

	GD25	FN65	NM94
4-Color 74('45)-Intro Lulu, Tubby & Alvin	107.00	321.00	750.00
4-Color 97(2/46)	50.00	150.00	350.00
(Above two books are all John Stanley - cover, pencils, and inks.)			
4-Color 110('46)-1st Alvin Story Telling Time; 1st app. Willy	36.00	107.00	250.00
4-Color 115-1st app. Boys' Clubhouse	36.00	107.00	250.00
4-Color 120, 131: 120-1st app. Eddie	31.00	94.00	220.00
4-Color 139('47),146,158	29.00	86.00	200.00
4-Color 165 (10/47)-Smokes doll hair & has wild hallucinations. 1st Tubby detective story	29.00	86.00	200.00
1(1-2/48)-Lulu's Diary feature begins	59.00	175.00	410.00
2-1st app. Gloria; 1st Tubby story in a L.L. comic; 1st app. Miss Feeny	30.00	90.00	210.00
3-5	27.00	80.00	185.00
6-10: 7-1st app. Annie; Xmas-c	19.00	58.00	135.00
11-20: 18-X-Mas-c. 19-1st app. Wilbur. 20-1st app. Mr. McNabbem	17.00	52.00	120.00
21-30: 26-r/F.C. 110. 30-Xmas-c	13.00	40.00	90.00
31-38,40: 35-1st Mumday story	10.00	30.00	70.00
39-Intro. Witch Hazel in "That Awful Witch Hazel"	12.00	36.00	85.00
41-60: 42-Xmas-c. 45-2nd Witch Hazel app. 49-Gives Stanley & others credit	10.00	30.00	65.00
61-80: 63-1st app. Chubby (Tubby's cousin). 68-1st app. Prof. Cleff. 78-Xmas-c. 80-Intro. Little Itch (2/55)	8.35	25.00	50.00
81-99: 90-Xmas-c	5.85	17.50	35.00
100	6.70	20.00	40.00
101-130: 123-1st app. Fifi	5.00	15.00	30.00
131-164: 135-Last Stanley-p	4.35	13.00	26.00
165-Giant; ...n Paris ('62)	12.00	36.00	120.00
166-Giant; ...Christmas Diary (1962 - '63)	12.00	36.00	120.00
167-169	4.00	10.00	20.00
170,172,175,176,178-196,198-200-Stanley-r. 182-1st app. Little Scarecrow Boy	2.80	7.00	14.00
171,173,174,177,197	1.60	4.00	8.00
201,203,206-Last issue to carry Marge's name	1.20	3.00	6.00
202,204,205-Stanley-r	1.80	4.50	9.00
...& Tubby in Japan (12¢)(5-7/62) 01476-207	10.00	30.00	60.00
...Summer Camp 1(8/67-G.K.-Giant) '57-58-r	7.00	21.00	42.00
...Trick 'N' Treat 1(12¢)(12/62-Gold Key)	8.35	25.00	50.00

NOTE: *See Dell Giant Comics #23, 29, 36, 42, 50, & Dell Giants for annuals. All Giants not by Stanley from L.L. on Vacation (7/54) on. Irving Tripp a-#1-on. Christmas c-7, 18, 30, 42, 78, 90, 126, 166, 250. Summer Camp issues #173, 177, 181, 189, 197, 201, 206.*

MARGE'S LITTLE LULU (See Golden Comics Digest #19, 23, 27, 29, 33, 36, 40, 43, 46, & March of Comics #251, 267, 275, 293, 307, 323, 335, 349, 355, 369, 385, 406, 417, 427, 439, 456, 468, 475, 488)

MARGE'S TUBBY (Little Lulu)(See Dell Giants)
No. 381, Aug, 1952 - No. 49, Dec-Feb, 1961-62
Dell Publishing Co./Gold Key

	GD25	FN65	NM94
4-Color 381(#1)-Stanley script; Irving Tripp-a	16.00	48.00	110.00
4-Color 430,444-Stanley-a	10.00	30.00	60.00
4-Color 461 (4/53)-1st Tubby & Men From Mars story; Stanley-a	9.15	27.50	55.00
5 (7-9/53)-Stanley-a	7.50	22.50	45.00
6-10	5.00	15.00	30.00
11-20	4.20	12.50	25.00
21-30	4.00	11.00	22.00
31-49	4.00	10.00	20.00
...& the Little Men From Mars No. 30020-410(10/64-G.K.)-25¢, 68 pgs.	9.15	27.50	55.00

NOTE: ***John Stanley** did all storyboards & scripts through at least #35 (1959). **Lloyd White** did all art except F.C. 381, 430, 444, 461 & #5.*

MARGIE (See My Little...)

MARGIE (TV)
No. 1307, Mar-May, 1962 - No. 2, July-Sept, 1962 (Photo-c)
Dell Publishing Co.

	GD25	FN65	NM94
4-Color 1307(#1), 2	4.35	13.00	26.00

MARGIE COMICS (Formerly Comedy Comics; Reno Browne #50 on)
(Also see Cindy Comics & Teen Comics)
No. 35, Winter, 1946-47 - No. 49, Dec, 1949
Marvel Comics (ACI)

	GD25	FN65	NM94
35	9.15	27.50	55.00
36-38,42,45,47-49	5.00	15.00	30.00
39,41,43(2),44,46-Kurtzman's "Hey Look"	7.00	21.00	42.00
40-Three "Hey Looks", three "Giggles 'n' Grins" by Kurtzman	8.35	25.00	50.00

MARINES (See Tell It to the...)

MARINES ATTACK
Aug, 1964 - No. 9, Feb-Mar, 1966
Charlton Comics

	GD25	FN65	NM94
1	2.40	6.00	12.00
2-9	1.20	3.00	6.00

MARINES AT WAR (Formerly Tales of the Marines #4)
No. 5, April, 1957 - No. 7, Aug, 1957
Atlas Comics (OPI)

	GD25	FN65	NM94
5-7	4.00	10.00	20.00

NOTE: ***Colan** a-5. **Drucker** a-5. **Everett** a-5. **Maneely** a-5. **Orlando** a-7. **Severin** c-5.*

MARINES IN ACTION
June, 1955 - No. 14, Sept, 1957
Atlas News Co.

	GD25	FN65	NM94
1-Rock Murdock, Boot Camp Brady begin	5.85	17.50	35.00
2-14	4.00	10.00	20.00

NOTE: ***Berg** a-2, 8, 9, 11, 14. **Heath** c-2, 9. **Maneely** c-1. **Severin** a-4; c-7-11, 14.*

MARINES IN BATTLE

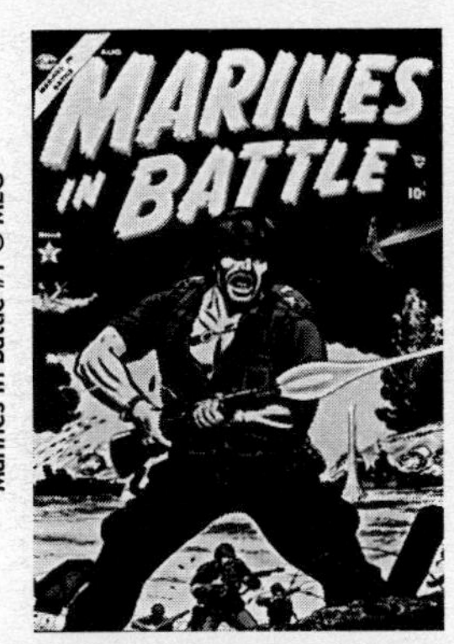

Marines In Battle #1 © MEG

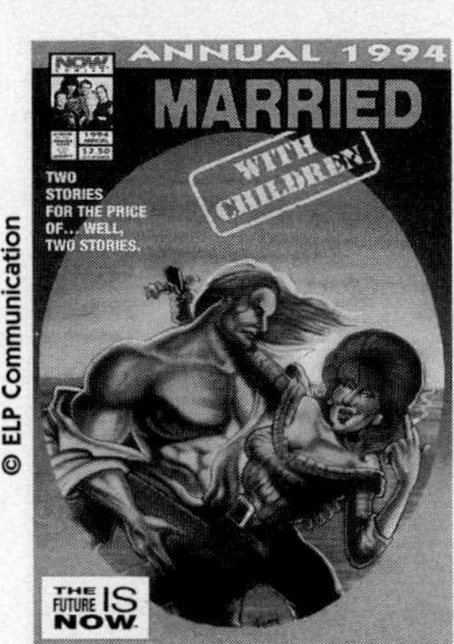

Married... With Children Annual 1994 © ELP Communication

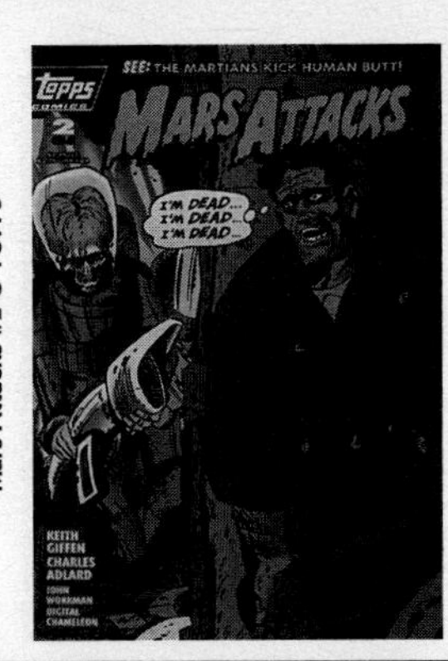

Mars Attacks #2 © TOPPS

GD25 FN65 NM94

Aug, 1954 - No. 25, Sept, 1958
Atlas Comics (ACI No. 1-12/WPI No. 13-25)

1-Heath-c; Iron Mike McGraw by Heath; history of U.S. Marine Corps. begins 10.00 30.00 65.00
2-Heath-c 5.35 16.00 32.00
3-6,8-10: 4-Last precode (2/55) 4.20 12.50 25.00
7-Kubert/Moskowitz-a (6 pgs.) 5.35 16.00 32.00
11-16,18-21,24 4.00 10.00 20.00
17-Williamson-a (3 pgs.) 6.35 19.00 38.00
22,25-Torres-a 4.20 12.50 25.00
23-Crandall-a; Mark Murdock app. 5.00 15.00 30.00

NOTE: ***Berg*** *a-22.* ***G. Colan*** *a-22, 23.* ***Drucker*** *a-6.* ***Everett*** *a-4, 15; c-21.* ***Heath*** *c-1, 2, 4.* ***Maneely*** *c-23, 24.* ***Orlando*** *a-14.* ***Pakula*** *a-6, 23.* ***Powell*** *a-16.* ***Severin*** *a-22; c-12.* ***Sinnott*** *a-23.* ***Tuska*** *a-15.*

MARINE WAR HEROES (Charlton Premiere #19 on)
Jan, 1964 - No. 18, Mar, 1967
Charlton Comics

1-Montes/Bache-c/a 2.40 6.00 12.00
2-18: 14,18-Montes/Bache-a 1.20 3.00 6.00

MARK, THE (Also see Mayhem)
Dec, 1993 - No. 4, Mar, 1994 ($2.50, limited series)
Dark Horse Comics

1-4 1.00 2.50

MARK HAZZARD: MERC (Marvel)(Value: cover or less)

MARK OF ZORRO (See 4-Color #228)

MARKSMAN, THE (Hero Comics)(Value: cover or less)(Also see Champions)

MARK STEEL
1967, 1968, 1972 (24 pgs.) (Color)
American Iron & Steel Institute (Giveaway)

1967,1968- "Journey of Discovery with..."; Neal Adams art 3.60 9.00 18.00
1972- "...Fights Pollution"; N. Adams-a 1.50 3.75 9.00

MARK TRAIL
Oct, 1955; No. 5, Summer, 1959
Standard Magazines (Hall Syndicate)/Fawcett Publ. No. 5

1(1955)-Sunday strip-r 5.00 15.00 30.00
5(1959) 3.60 9.00 18.00
...Adventure Book of Nature 1 (Summer, 1958, 25¢, Pines)-100 pg. Giant; Special Camp Issue; contains 78 Sunday strip-r 7.50 22.50 45.00

MARMADUKE MONK
No date; 1963 (10¢)
I. W. Enterprises/Super Comics

1-I.W. Reprint(nd), 14-(Super Reprint)(1963) 1.00 2.50 5.00

MARMADUKE MOUSE
Spring, 1946 - No. 65, Dec, 1956 (Early issues: 52 pgs.)
Quality Comics Group (Arnold Publ.)

1-Funny animal 11.50 34.00 80.00
2 6.70 20.00 40.00
3-10 5.00 15.00 30.00
11-30 4.00 11.00 22.00
31-65: Later issues are 36 pgs. 3.20 8.00 16.00
Super Reprint #14(1963) 1.60 4.00 8.00

MARRIED ... WITH CHILDREN (TV)
June, 1990 - No. 7, Feb, 1991(12/90 inside) ($1.75, color)
V2#1, Sept, 1991 - No. 12, 1992 ($1.95, color)
Now Comics

1-Based on Fox TV show 1.90 4.50
1-2nd printing ($1.75) .70 1.75
2-Photo-c 1.60 4.00
2-2nd printing ($1.75) .60 1.60
3 .70 1.80
4-7 .65 1.60
V2#1-12: 1,4,5,9-Photo-c .80 2.00
...Buck's Tale (6/94, $1.95) .80 2.00
...1994 Annual nn (2/94, $2.50, 52 pgs.)-Flip book format 1.00 2.50
Special 1 (7/92, $1.95)-Kelly Bundy photo-c/poster .80 2.00

MARRIED ... WITH CHILDREN: KELLY BUNDY
Aug, 1992 - No. 3, Oct, 1992 ($1.95, color, mini-series)
Now Comics

1-3: Kelly Bundy photo-c & poster in each .80 2.00

MARRIED ... WITH CHILDREN: QUANTUM QUARTET
Oct, 1993 - No. 4, 1994, ($1.95, color, mini-series)
Now Comics

1-4-Fantastic Four parody .80 2.00

MARRIED ... WITH CHILDREN: 2099
June, 1993 - No. 3, Aug, 1993 ($1.95, color, mini-series)
Now Comics

1-3 .80 2.00

MARS (First Comics)(Value: cover or less)

MARS & BEYOND (See 4-Color #866)

MARS ATTACKS
May, 1994 - No. 5, Sept, 1994 ($2.95, mini-series)
Topps Comics

1-5-Flip books 1.20 3.00

MARSHAL BLUEBERRY (See Blueberry)
1991 ($14.95, graphic novel)
Epic Comics (Marvel)

1-Moebius-a 2.15 6.50 15.00

MARSHAL LAW (Also see Crime And Punishment: Marshall Law...)
Oct, 1987 - No. 6, May, 1989 ($1.95, adults) (See Pinhead Vs....)
Epic Comics (Marvel)

1-6 .80 2.00

MARSHALL LAW - KINGDOM OF THE BLIND (Apocalypse Publishing)(Value: cover or less)

MARSHALL LAW: SECRET TRIBUNAL (Dark Horse)(Value: cover or less)

MARSHALL LAW: SUPER BABYLON (Dark Horse)(Value: cover or less)

M.A.R.S. PATROL TOTAL WAR (Formerly Total War #1,2)
No. 3, Sept, 1966 - No. 10, Aug, 1969 (All-Painted-c)
Gold Key

3-Wood-a 4.60 14.00 32.00
4-10 2.30 6.90 16.00

MARTHA WASHINGTON GOES TO WAR
May, 1994 - No. 5, Sept, 1994 ($2.95, limited series)
Dark Horse Comics

1-5-Miller story; Gibbons-c/a 1.20 3.00

MARTHA WAYNE (See The Story of...)

MARTIAN MANHUNTER (DC, 1988)(Value: cover or less)(See Detective Comics)

MARTIAN MANHUNTER: AMERICAN SECRETS (DC Comics)(Value: cover or less)

MARTIN KANE (William Gargan as... Private Eye)(Stage/Screen/Radio/TV)
No. 4, June, 1950 - No. 2, Aug, 1950 (Formerly My Secret Affair)
Fox Features Syndicate (Hero Books)

4(#1)-True crime stories; Wood-c/a(2); used in **SOTI**, pg. 160; photo back-c 20.00 60.00 140.00
2-Orlando-a, 5 pgs; Wood-a(2) 15.00 45.00 105.00

MARTY MOUSE
No date (1958?) (10¢)
I. W. Enterprises

1-Reprint 1.00 2.50 5.00

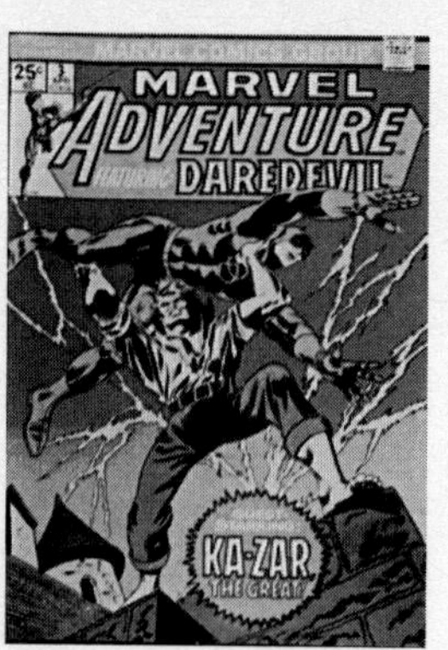

Marvel Adventures Starring Daredevil #3 © MEG

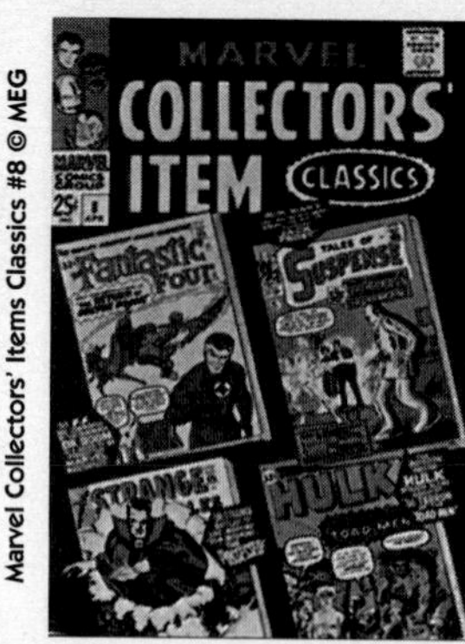

Marvel Collectors' Items Classics #8 © MEG

Marvel Comics Presents #163 © MEG

MARVEL ACTION UNIVERSE (TV)
Jan, 1989 ($1.00, one-shot)
Marvel Comics

1-r/Spider-Man And His Amazing Friends 1.00

MARVEL ADVENTURES STARRING DAREDEVIL (...Adventure #4 on)
Dec, 1975 - No. 6, Oct, 1976
Marvel Comics Group

1-6-r/Daredevil #22-27 by Colan 1.00

MARVEL AND DC PRESENT FEATURING THE UNCANNY X-MEN AND THE NEW TEEN TITANS
1982 ($2.00, one shot, 68 pgs., printed on Baxter paper)
Marvel Comics Group/DC Comics

1-3rd app. Deathstroke the Terminator; Darkseid app.; Simonson/Austin-c/a 1.10 3.00 7.50

MARVEL BOY (Astonishing #3 on; see Marvel Super Action #4)
Dec, 1950 - No. 2, Feb, 1951
Marvel Comics (MPC)

1-Origin Marvel Boy by Russ Heath 57.00 171.00 400.00
2-Everett-a 50.00 150.00 350.00

MARVEL CHILLERS (Also see Giant-Size Chillers)
Oct, 1975 - No. 7, Oct, 1976 (All 25¢ issues)
Marvel Comics Group

1,2-Intro. Modred the Mystic, ends #2; Kane-c(p) 1.30 3.25
3-7: 3-Tigra, the Were-Woman begins (origin), ends #7 (see Giant-Size Creatures #1). Chaykin/Wrightson-c. 4-Kraven app. 5,6-Red Wolf app. 6-Byrne-a(p); Buckler-c(p). 7-Kirby-c; Tuska-p .90 2.25

MARVEL CLASSICS COMICS SERIES FEATURING... (Also see Pendulum Illustrated Classics)
1976 - No. 36, Dec, 1978 (52 pgs., no ads)
Marvel Comics Group

1-Dr. Jekyll and Mr. Hyde 1.60 4.00
2-27,29-36 1.10 2.75
28-1st Golden-c/a; The Pit and the Pendulum 1.10 2.70 6.50

NOTE: ***Adkins** c-1i, 4i, 12i. **Alcala** a-34i; c-34. **Bolle** a-35. **Buscema** c-17p, 19p, 26p. **Golden** c/a-28. **Gil Kane** c-1-16p, 21p, 22p, 24p, 32p. **Nebres** a-5; c-24i. **Nino** a-2, 8, 12. **Redondo** a-1, 9. No. 1-12 were reprinted from Pendulum Illustrated Classics.*

MARVEL COLLECTOR'S EDITION
1992 (Ordered thru mail with Charleston Chew candy wrapper)
Marvel Comics

1-Flip-book format; Spider-Man, Silver Surfer, Wolverine (by Sam Keith), & Ghost Rider stories; Wolverine back-c by Kieth .90 2.25

MARVEL COLLECTOR'S EDITION: X-MEN
1993 (Color, 3-3/4x6-1/2")
Marvel Comics

1-4-Pizza Hut giveaways .80 2.00

MARVEL COLLECTORS' ITEM CLASSICS (Marvel's Greatest #23 on)
Feb, 1965 - No. 22, Aug, 1969 (25¢, 68 pgs.)
Marvel Comics Group(ATF)

1-Fantastic Four, Spider-Man, Thor, Hulk, Iron Man-r begin 6.90 21.00 48.00
2 (4/66) - 4 3.70 11.00 26.00
5-22: 22-r/The Man in the Ant Hill/TTA #27 1.60 5.00 11.00

NOTE: *All reprints; **Ditko, Kirby** art in all.*

MARVEL COMICS (Marvel Mystery Comics #2 on)
October, November, 1939
Timely Comics (Funnies, Inc.)

NOTE: The first issue was originally dated October 1939. Most copies have a black circle stamped over the date (on cover and inside) with "November" printed over it. However, some copies do not have the November overprint and could have a higher value. Most No. 1's have printing defects, i.e., tilted pages which caused trimming into the panels usually on right side and bottom. Covers exist with and without gloss finish.

GD25 FN65 VF82 NM94

1-Origin Sub-Mariner by Bill Everett(1st newsstand app.); 1st 8 pgs. were produced for Motion Picture Funnies Weekly #1 which was probably not distributed outside of advance copies; intro Human Torch by Carl Burgos, Kazar the Great (1st Tarzan clone), & Jungle Terror(only app.); intro. The Angel by Gustavson, The Masked Raider & his horse Lightning (ends #12); cover by sci/fi pulp illustrator Frank R. Paul 9,445.00 28,335.00 56,667.00 85,000.00
(Estimated up to 50 total copies exist, 4 in NM/Mint)

MARVEL COMICS PRESENTS
Early Sept, 1988 - Present ($1.25/$1.50/$1.75, bi-weekly)
Marvel Comics (Midnight Sons imprint #143 on)

GD25 FN65 NM94

1-Wolverine by Buscema in #1-10 1.70 5.00 12.00
2-5 .90 2.30 5.50
6-10: 6-Sub-Mariner app. 10-Colossus begins 1.60 4.00
11-32,34-37: 17-Cyclops begins. 19-1st app. Damage Control. 24-Havok begins. 25-Origin/1st app. Nth Man. 26-Hulk begins by Rogers. 29-Quasar app. 31-Excalibur begins by Austin (i). 32-McFarlane-a(p). 37-Devil-Slayer app. .80 2.00
33-Capt. America; Jim Lee-a 1.10 2.75
38-Wolverine begins by Buscema; Hulk app. 1.00 2.00 5.00
39-47,51-53: 39-Spider-Man app. 46-Liefeld Wolverine-c. 51-53-Wolverine by Rob Liefeld 1.10 2.75
48-50-Wolverine & Spider-Man team-up by Erik Larsen-c/a. 48-Wasp app. 49, 50-Savage Dragon prototype app. by Larsen. 50-Silver Surfer. 50-53-Comet Man; Bill Mumy scripts 1.00 2.50 5.50
54-61-Wolverine/Hulk story: 54-Werewolf by Night begins; The Shroud by Ditko. 58-Iron Man by Ditko. 59-Punisher 1.00 2.50 6.00
62-Deathlok & Wolverine stories 1.25 3.00 7.50
63-Wolverine 1.50 3.75
64-71-Wolverine/Ghost Rider 8-part story. 70-Liefeld Ghost Rider/Wolverine-c 1.60 4.00
72-Begin 13-part Weapon-X story (Wolverine origin) by B. Windsor-Smith (prologue) 1.25 3.00 7.50
73-Weapon-X part 1; Black Knight, Sub-Mariner 1.00 2.00 5.00
74-Weapon-X part 2; Black Knight, Sub-Mariner 1.50 3.75
75-80: 76-Death's Head story. 77-Mr. Fantastic story. 78-Iron Man by Steacy. 80,81-Capt. America by Ditko/Austin 1.10 2.75
81-84: 81-Daredevil by Rogers/Williamson. 82-Power Man. 83-Human Torch by Ditko(a&scripts); $1.00-c direct, $1.25 newsstand. 84-Last Weapon-X (24 pg. conclusion) .90 2.25
85-Begin 8-part Wolverine story by Sam Kieth (c/a); 1st Kieth-a on Wolverine; begin 8-part Beast story by Jae Lee(p) with Liefeld part pencils #85,86; 1st Jae Lee-a (assisted w/Liefeld, 1991) 1.25 3.00 7.50
86-89-Wolverine, Beast stories continue 1.50 3.75
90-Begin 8-part Ghost Rider & Cable story, ends #97; begin flip book format with two covers 1.90 4.75
91-94: 93-Begin 6-part Wolverine story, ends #98 1.10 2.75
95-98: 95-Begin $1.50-c. 98-Begin 2-part Ghost Rider story .70 1.80
99,101-107,112-116: 99-Spider-Man story. 101-Begin 6-part Ghost Rider/Dr. Strange story & begin 8-part Wolverine/Nightcrawler story by Colan/Williamson; Punisher story. 107-Begin 6-part Ghost Rider/Werewolf by Night story. 112-Demogoblin story by Colan/Williamson; Pip the Troll story w/Starlin scripts & Gamora cameo. 113-Begin 6-part Giant-Man & begin 6-part Ghost Rider/Iron Fist stories .65 1.60
100-Full-length Ghost Rider/Wolverine story by Sam Kieth w/Tim Vigil assists; anniversary issue, non flip-book 1.00 2.50
108-111: 108-Begin 4 part Thanos story; Starlin scripts. 109-Begin 8 part Wolverine/Typhoid Mary story. 111-Iron Fist .80 2.00
117-Preview of Ravage 2099 (1st app.); begin 6 part Wolverine/Venom story w/Kieth-a 1.00 2.50
118-Preview of Doom 2099 (1st app.) 1.00 2.50
119-142,147-152: 119-Begin Ghost Rider/Cloak & Dagger story by Colan. 120,136,138-Spider-Man. 123-Begin 8-part Ghost Rider/Typhoid Mary story; begin 4-part She Hulk story; begin 8-partWolverine/Lynx story. 125-Begin 6-part Iron Fist story. 129-Jae Lee back-c. 130-Begin 6-part Ghost Rider/Cage story. 131-Begin 6-part Ghost Rider/Cage story. 132-Begin 5-part

Marvel Super Special #24 © MEG

Marvel Double Feature #4 © MEG

Marvel Fanfare #55 © MEG

Wolverine story. 133-136-Iron Fist vs. Sabretooth. 136-Daredevil. 137-Begin 6-part Wolverine story & 6-part Ghost Rider story. 147-Begin 2-part Vengeance-c/s w/new Ghost Rider. 149-Vengeance-c/s w/new Ghost Rider. 150-Silver ink-c; begin 2-part Bloody Mary story w/Typhoid Mary, Wolverine, Daredevil, new Ghost Rider; intro Steel Raven. 152-Begin 4-part Wolverine, 4-part War Machine, 4-part Vengeance, 3-part Moon Knight stories; same date as War Machine #1 .70 1.80

143-146-($1.75)-Siege of Darkness parts 3,6,11,14; all have spot-varnished covers. 143-Ghost Rider/Scarlet Witch; intro new Werewolf. 144-Begin 2-part Morbius story. 145-Begin 2-part Nightstalkers story. .70 1.75

153-164: 153-Begin $1.75-c. 153-155-Bound-in Spider-Man trading card sheet .70 1.75

NOTE: ***Austin*** *a-31-37i; c(i)-48, 50, 99, 122.* ***Buscema*** *a-1-10, 38-47; c-6.* ***Byrne*** *a-79; c-71.* ***Colan*** *a(p)-36, 37.* ***Colan/Williamson*** *a-101-108.* ***Ditko*** *a-7p, 10, 56p, 58, 80, 81, 83.* ***Guice*** *a-62.* ***Sam Kieth*** *a-85-92, 117-122; c-85-98, 99p, 100-108, 117, 118, 120-122; back c-109-113, 117.* ***Jae Lee*** *c-129(back).* ***Liefeld*** *a-51, 52, 53p(2), 85p; c-46, 70.* ***McFarlane*** *c-32.* ***Mooney*** *a-73.* ***Rogers*** *a-26, 38, 46i, 81p.* ***Russell*** *a-10i; c-4i.* ***Saltares*** *a-8p(early), 38-45p.* ***Simonson*** *c-1.* ***B. Smith*** *a-72-84; c-72-84.* ***P. Smith*** *c-34.* ***Sparling*** *a-33.* ***Starlin*** *a-89i.* ***Staton*** *a-74.* ***Steacy*** *a-78.* ***Sutton*** *a-101-105.* ***Williamson*** *c-62i. Two Gun Kid by* ***Gil Kane*** *in #116, 122.*

MARVEL COMICS SUPER SPECIAL, A (Marvel Super Special #5 on)
Sept, 1977 - No. 41(?), Nov, 1986 (nn 7) (Magazine; $1.50)
Marvel Comics Group

1-Kiss, 40 pgs. comics plus photos & features; Simonson-a(p); also see Howard the Duck #12 8.00 24.00 55.00
2-Conan (1978) 1.50
3-Close Encounters of the Third Kind (1978); Simonson-a 1.50
4-The Beatles Story (1978)-Perez/Janson-a; has photos & articles 1.40 4.00 10.00
5-Kiss (1978)-Includes poster 4.30 13.00 30.00
6-Jaws II (1978) 1.50
7-Sgt. Pepper; Beatles movie adaptation; withdrawn from U.S. distribution
8-Battlestar Galactica; tabloid size ($1.50, 1978); adapts TV show 1.50
8-Battlestar Galactica; publ. in regular magazine format; low distribution ($1.50, 8-1/2x11") 1.50
9,10: 9-Conan. 10-Star-Lord 1.50
11-13-Weirdworld begins #11; 25 copy special press run of each with gold seal and signed by artists (Proof quality), Spring-June, 1979 8.00 24.00 55.00
11-13-Weirdworld (regular issues): 11-Fold-out centerfold 1.50
14-Miller-c(p); adapts movie "Meteor" 1.20
15-Star Trek with photos & pin-ups($1.50) 1.20
15-With $2.00 price (scarce); the price was changed at tail end of a 200,000 press run .80 2.00
16-20 (Movie adaptations): 16-Empire Strikes Back; Williamson-a. 17-Xanadu. 18-Raiders of the Lost Ark. 19-For Your Eyes Only (James Bond). 20-Dragonslayer .70 1.75
21-41 (Movie adaptations): 21-Conan. 22-Bladerunner; Williamson-a; Steranko-c. 23-Annie. 24-The Dark Crystal. 25-Rock and Rule-w/photos; artwork is from movie. 26-Octopussy (James Bond). 27-Return of the Jedi. 28-Krull; photo-c. 29-Tarzan of the Apes (Greystoke movie). 30-Indiana Jones and the Temple of Doom. 31-The Last Star Fighter. 32-The Muppets Take Manhattan. 33-Buckaroo Bonzai. 34-Sheena. 35-Conan The Destroyer. 36-Dune. 37-2010. 38-Red Sonja. 39-Santa Claus: The Movie. 40-Labyrinth. 41-Howard The Duck .70 1.75

NOTE: ***J. Buscema*** *a-1, 2, 9, 11-13, 18p, 21, 35, 40; c-11(part), 12.* ***Chaykin*** *a-9, 19p; c-18, 19.* ***Colan*** *a(p)-6, 10, 14.* ***Morrow*** *a-34; c-1i, 34.* ***Nebres*** *a-11.* ***Spiegle*** *a-29.* ***Stevens*** *a-27.* ***Williamson*** *a-27. #22-28 contain photos from movies.*

MARVEL DOUBLE FEATURE
Dec, 1973 - No. 21, Mar, 1977
Marvel Comics Group

1-Capt. America, Iron Man-r/T.O.S. begin 1.60 4.00
2-16,20,21: 3-Last 20¢ issue. 17-Last 25¢ issue .80 2.00
17-Reprints story/Iron Man & Sub-Mariner #1 1.20 3.00
18,19-Colan/Craig-r from Iron Man #1 in both 1.60 4.00

NOTE: ***Colan*** *r-1-19p.* ***Craig*** *r-17-19i.* ***G. Kane*** *r-15p; c-15p.* ***Kirby*** *r-1-16p, 20, 21; c-17-20.*

MARVEL FAMILY (Also see Captain Marvel Adventures No. 18)
Dec, 1945 - No. 89, Jan, 1954
Fawcett Publications

1-Origin Captain Marvel, Captain Marvel Jr., Mary Marvel, & Uncle Marvel retold; origin/1st app. Black Adam 121.00 365.00 850.00
2-The 3 Lt. Marvels & Uncle Marvel app. 57.00 171.00 400.00
3 39.00 118.00 275.00
4,5 34.00 100.00 235.00
6-10: 7-Shazam app. 27.00 80.00 185.00
11-20 19.00 58.00 135.00
21-30 15.00 45.00 105.00
31-40 12.00 36.00 85.00
41-46,48-50 11.00 32.00 75.00
47-Flying Saucer-c/story (5/50) 14.00 43.00 100.00
51-76,78-89: 78,81-Used in **POP**, pg. 92,93. 79-Horror satire-c 10.00 30.00 70.00
77-Communist Threat-c 14.00 43.00 100.00

MARVEL FANFARE
March, 1982 - No. 60, Jan, 1992 ($1.25/$2.25, slick paper, direct sale)
Marvel Comics Group

1-Spider-Man/Angel team-up; 1st Paul Smith-a (1st full story; see King Conan #7); Daredevil app. 1.80 5.00 11.00
2-Spider-Man, Ka-Zar, The Angel. F.F. origin retold .90 2.30 5.50
3,4-X-Men & Ka-Zar. 4-Deathlok, Spidey app. 1.90 4.75
5-Dr. Strange, Capt. America 1.20 3.00
6-15: 6-Spider-Man, Scarlet Witch. 7-Incredible Hulk; D.D. back-up(also 15). 8-Dr. Strange; Wolf Boy begins. 9-Man-Thing. 10-13-Black Widow. 14-The Vision. 15-The Thing by Barry Smith, c/a 1.00 2.50
16-32,34-50: 16,17-Skywolf. 16-Sub-Mariner back-up. 17-Hulk back-up. 18-Capt. America by Miller. 19-Cloak and Dagger. 20-Thing/Dr. Strange. 21-Thing/Dr. Strange/Hulk. 22,23-Iron Man vs. Dr. Octopus. 24-26-Weirdworld. 24-Wolverine back-up. 27-Daredevil/Spider-Man. 28-Alpha Flight. 29-Hulk. 30-Moon Knight. 31,32-Captain America. 34-37-Warriors Three. 38-Moon Knight/Dazzler. 39-Moon Knight/Hawkeye. 40-Angel/Rogue & Storm. 41-Dr. Strange. 42-Spider-Man. 43-Sub-Mariner/Human Torch. 44-Iron Man vs. Dr. Doom by Ken Steacy. 45-All pin-up issue by Steacy, Art Adams & others. 46-Fantastic Four. 47-Hulk. 48-She-Hulk/Vision. 49-Dr. Strange/Nick Fury. 50-X-Factor; begin $2.25-c 1.00 2.50
33-X-Men, Wolverine app.; Punisher pin-up 1.00 2.50 5.50
51-($2.95, 52 pgs.)-Silver Surfer; Fantastic Four & Capt. Marvel app.; 51,52-Colan/Williamson back-up (Dr. Strange) 1.20 3.00
52,53: 52-54-Black Knight; 53-Iron Man back up 1.00 2.50
54,55-Wolverine back-ups. 55-Power Pack 1.20 3.00
56-60: 56-59-Shanna the She-Devil. 58-Vision & Scarlet Witch back-up. 60-Black Panther/Rogue/Daredevil stories 1.00 2.50

NOTE: ***Art Adams*** *c-13.* ***Austin*** *a-1i, 4i, 33i, 38i; c-8i, 33i.* ***Buscema*** *a-51p.* ***Byrne*** *a-1p, 29, 48; c-29.* ***Chiodo*** *painted c-56-59.* ***Colan*** *a-51p.* ***Cowan/Simonson*** *c/a-60.* ***Golden*** *a-1, 2, 4p, 47; c-1, 2, 47.* ***Infantino*** *c/a(p)-8.* ***Gil Kane*** *a-8-11p.* ***Miller*** *a-18; c-1(Back-c), 18.* ***Perez*** *a-10, 11p, 12, 13p; c-10-13p.* ***Rogers*** *a-5p; c-5p.* ***Russell*** *a-5i, 6i, 8-11i, 43i; c-5i, 6.* ***Paul Smith*** *a-1p, 4p, 32, 60; c-4p. Staton c/a-50(p).* ***Williamson*** *a-30i, 51i.*

MARVEL FEATURE (See Marvel Two-In-One)
Dec, 1971 - No. 12, Nov, 1973 (1,2: 25¢ giants)(1-3: quarterly)
Marvel Comics Group

1-Origin/1st app. The Defenders (Sub-Mariner, Hulk & Dr. Strange); see Sub-Mariner #34,35 for prequel; Dr. Strange solo story (predates D.S. #1) plus 1950s Sub-Mariner-r; Neal Adams-c 10.00 30.00 72.00
2-2nd app. Defenders; 1950s Sub-Mariner-r 4.60 14.00 32.00
3-Defenders ends 4.60 14.00 32.00
4-Re-intro Antman (1st app. since 1960s), begin series; brief origin; Spider-Man app. 1.85 5.50 13.00
5-10: 6-Wasp app. & begins team-ups. 8-Origin Antman & Wasp-r/TTA #44. 9-Iron Man app. 10-Last Antman 1.00 2.50 5.50
10-(7/73)-Variant w/4 extra pgs. ads on slick paper 1.00 2.50 6.00
11-Thing vs. Hulk; 1st Thing solo book (9/73); origin Fantastic Four retold 1.25 3.00 7.50
12-Thing/Iron Man; early Thanos app.; occurs after Capt. Marvel #33;

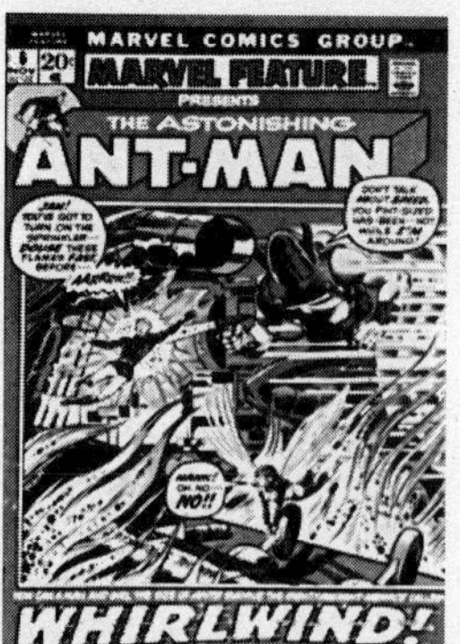

Marvel Feature #6 © MEG

Marvel Masterpieces 2 Collection #2 © MEG

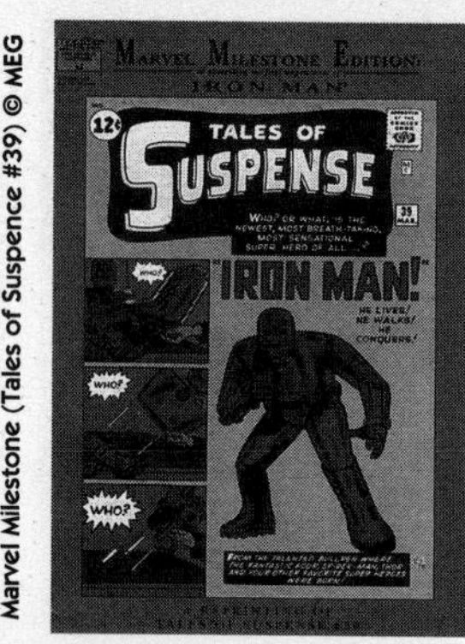

Marvel Milestone (Tales of Suspence #39) © MEG

GD25 FN65 NM94

Starlin-a(p) 1.65 4.00 10.00

NOTE: ***Bolle** a-9i. **Everett** a-1i, 3i. **Hartley** r-10. **Kane** c-3p, 7p. **Russell** a-7-10p. **Starlin** a-8, 11, 12; c-8.*

MARVEL FEATURE (Also see Red Sonja)
Nov, 1975 - No. 7, Nov, 1976 (Story continues in Conan #68)
Marvel Comics Group

1-Red Sonja begins (pre-dates Red Sonja #1); adapts Howard short story; Adams-r/Savage Sword of Conan #1 1.70 4.25
2-7: Thorne-c/a in #2-7. 7-Battles Conan .90 2.25

MARVEL FRONTIER COMICS UNLIMITED
Jan, 1994 - Present ($2.95, quarterly, 68 pgs.)
Marvel Frontier Comics

1-Dances with Demons, Immortalis, Children of the Voyager, Evil Eye, The Fallen stories 1.20 3.00

MARVEL FUMETTI BOOK
April, 1984 (One shot) ($1.00 cover price)
Marvel Comics Group

1-All photos; Stan Lee photo-c; Art Adams touch-ups 1.00

MARVEL GRAPHIC NOVEL
1982 - No. 38, 1990? ($5.95/$6.95)
Marvel Comics Group (Epic Comics)

1-Death of Captain Marvel (1st Marvel graphic novel); Capt. Marvel battles Thanos by Jim Starlin (c/a/scripts) 4.50 13.50 27.00
1 (2nd & 3rd printings) 1.20 3.00 5.50
2-Elric: The Dreaming City 1.60 4.00 8.50
3-Dreadstar; Starlin-c/a, 52 pgs. 1.40 3.50 7.50
4-Origin/1st app. The New Mutants (1982) 3.00 6.50 16.00
4,5-2nd printings 1.20 3.00 5.50
5-X-Men; book-length story (1982) 2.40 6.00 13.00
6-18: 6-The Star Slammers. 7-Killraven. 8-Super Boxers; Byrne scripts. 9-The Futurians. 10-Heartburst. 11-Void Indigo. 12-The Dazzler. 13-Starstruck. 14-The Swords Of The Swashbucklers. 15-The Raven Banner (Asgard). 16-The Aladdin Effect. 17-Revenge Of The Living Monolith. 18-She Hulk 1.20 3.00 5.50
19-32: 19-The Witch Queen of Acheron (Conan). 20-Greenberg the Vampire. 21-Marada the She-Wolf. 22-Amaz. Spider-Man in Hooky by Wrightson. 23-Dr. Strange. 24-Love and War (Daredevil); Miller scripts. 25-Alien Legion. 26-Dracula. 27-Avengers (Emperor Doom). 28-Conan the Reaver. 29-The Big Chance (Thing vs. Hulk). 30-A Sailor's Story. 31-Wolfpack. 32-Death of Groo 1.40 3.50 7.50
32-2nd printing ($5.95) 1.20 3.00 6.00
33,34,36,37: 33-Thor. 34-Predator & Prey (Cloak & Dagger). 36-Willow (movie adapt.). 37-Hercules 1.40 3.50 7.50
35-Hitler's Astrologer (Shadow, $12.95, hard-c) 1.85 5.50 13.00
35-Soft cover reprint (1990, $10.95) 1.65 4.70 11.00
38-Silver Surfer (Judgement Day)($14.95) 2.15 6.50 15.00
nn-Inhumans (1988, $7.95)-Williamson-i 1.30 3.25 8.00
nn-Last of the Dragons (1988, $6.95) 1.20 3.00 7.00
nn-Who Framed Roger Rabbit (1989, $6.95) 1.20 3.00 7.00
nn-Roger Rabbit In The Resurrection Of Doom (1989, $8.95) 1.50 3.75 9.00
nn-Arena by Bruce Jones ($5.95) 1.00 2.50 6.00

NOTE: ***Aragones** a-27, 32. **Byrne** c/a-18. **Kaluta** a-13, 35p; c-13. **Miller** a-24p. **Simonson** a-6; c-6. **Starlin** c/a-1,3. **Williamson** a-34. **Wrightson** c-29i.*

MARVEL HOLIDAY SPECIAL
1991 ($2.25, 84 pgs.); Jan, 1993 ($2.95, 68 pgs.)
Marvel Comics

1-X-Men, Fantastic Four, Punisher, Thor, Capt. America, Ghost Rider, Capt. Ultra, Spidey stories; Art Adams-c/a .90 2.25
nn-Wolverine, Thanos (by Starlin/Lim/Austin) 1.20 3.00

MARVEL ILLUSTRATED: SWIMSUIT ISSUE (See Marvel Swimsuit Spec.)
1991 ($3.95, magazine, 52 pgs.)
Marvel Comics

GD25 FN65 NM94

V1#1-Parody of Sports Illustrated swimsuit issue; Mary Jane Parker centerfold pin-up by Jusko; 2nd print exists 1.60 4.00

MARVEL MASTERPIECES COLLECTION, THE
May, 1993 - No. 4, Aug, 1993 ($2.95, coated paper, mini-series)
Marvel Comics

1-4-Reprints Marvel Masterpieces trading cards w/ new Jusko paintings in each; Jusko painted-c/a 1.20 3.00

MARVEL MASTERPIECES 2 COLLECTION, THE
July, 1994 - Present ($2.95)
Marvel Comics

1-3: 1-Kaluta-c; r/trading cards; new Steranko centerfold 1.20 3.00

MARVEL MILESTONE EDITION
1991 - Present ($2.95, coated stock)(r/originals with original ads w/silver ink-c)
Marvel Comics

...: X-Men #1-Reprints X-Men #1 (1991) 1.20 3.00
...: Giant Size X-Men #1-(1991, $3.95, 68 pgs.) 1.60 4.00
...: Fantastic Four #1 (11/91) 1.20 3.00
...: Incredible Hulk #1 (3/92, says 3/91 by error) 1.20 3.00
...: Amazing Fantasy #15 (3/92) 1.20 3.00
...: Fantastic Four #5 (11/92) 1.20 3.00
...: Amazing Spider-Man #129 (11/92) 1.20 3.00
...: Iron Man #55 (11/92) 1.20 3.00
...: Iron Fist #14 (11/92) 1.20 3.00
...: Amazing Spider-Man #1 (1/93) 1.20 3.00
...: Tales of Suspense #39 (3/93) 1.20 3.00
...: Avengers #1 (9/93) 1.20 3.00
...: X-Men #9 (10/93) 1.20 3.00
...: Avengers #16 (10/93) 1.20 3.00

MARVEL MINI-BOOKS
1966 (50 pgs., B&W; 5/8x7/8") (6 different issues)
Marvel Comics Group (Smallest comics ever published)

Captain America, Spider-Man, Sgt. Fury, Hulk, Thor 3.20 8.00 16.00
Millie the Model 3.20 8.00 16.00

NOTE: *Each came in six different color covers, usually one color: Pink, yellow, green, etc.*

MARVEL MOVIE PREMIERE (Magazine)
Sept, 1975 (One Shot) (Black & White)
Marvel Comics Group

1-Burroughs' "The Land That Time Forgot" adaptation .80 2.00

MARVEL MOVIE SHOWCASE FEATURING STAR WARS
Nov, 1982 - No. 2, Dec, 1982 ($1.25, 68 pgs.)
Marvel Comics Group

1,2-Star Wars movie adaptation; reprints Star Wars #1-6 by Chaykin; 1-Reprints-c to Star Wars #1. 2-Stevens-r 1.25

MARVEL MOVIE SPOTLIGHT FEATURING RAIDERS OF THE LOST ARK
Nov, 1982 ($1.25, 68 pgs.)
Marvel Comics Group

1-Edited-r/Raiders of the Lost Ark #1-3; Buscema-c/a(p); movie adaptation 1.25

MARVEL MYSTERY COMICS (Formerly Marvel Comics) (Becomes Marvel Tales No. 93 on)
No. 2, Dec, 1939 - No. 92, June, 1949
Timely /Marvel Comics (TP #2-17/TCI #18-54/MCI #55-92)

GD25 FN65 VF82 NM94

2-American Ace begins, ends #3; Human Torch (blue costume) by Burgos, Sub-Mariner by Everett continue; 2 pg. origin recap of Human Torch 1714.00 5143.00 8571.00 12,000.00
(Estimated up to 50 total copies exist, 5 in NM/Mint)

GD25 FN65 NM94

3-New logo from Marvel pulp begins 714.00 2143.00 5000.00
4-Intro. Electro, the Marvel of the Age (ends #19), The Ferret, Mystery Detective (ends #9); 1st Nazi war-c on a comic book & 1st German flag

Marvel Mystery Comics #28 © MEG

Marvel Mystery Comics #37 © MEG

Marvel Premiere #48 © MEG

GD25 FN65 NM94

(Swastika) on-c of a comic (2/40) 571.00 1714.00 4000.00

GD25 FN65 VF82 NM94

5 (Scarce) 1286.00 3857.00 6428.00 9000.00
(Estimated up to 75 total copies exist, 3 in NM/Mint)

GD25 FN65 NM94

6,7: 6-Gustavson Angel story 357.00 1071.00 2500.00
8-1st Human Torch & Sub-Mariner battle(6/40) 429.00 1286.00 3000.00

GD25 FN65 VF82 NM94

9-(Scarce)-Human Torch & Sub-Mariner battle (cover/story); 1st Television in comics? 1357.00 4071.00 6785.00 9500.00
(Estimated up to 75 total copies exist, 6 in NM/Mint)

GD25 FN65 NM94

10-Human Torch & Sub-Mariner battle, conclusion; Terry Vance, the Schoolboy Sleuth begins, ends #57 329.00 985.00 2300.00
11 257.00 771.00 1800.00
12-Classic Kirby-c 239.00 718.00 1675.00
13-Intro. & 1st app. The Vision by S&K (11/40); Sub-Mariner dons new costume, ends #15 279.00 835.00 1950.00
14-16: 14-Shows-c to Human Torch #1 on-c (12/40). 15-S&K Vision, Gustavson Angel story 157.00 471.00 1100.00
17-Human Torch/Sub-Mariner team-up by Burgos/Everett; pin-up on back-c; shows-c to Human Torch #2 on-c 171.00 515.00 1200.00
18 143.00 430.00 1000.00
19-Origin Toro in text; shows-c to Sub-Mariner #1 on-c 150.00 450.00 1050.00
20-Origin The Angel in text 150.00 450.00 1050.00
21-Intro. & 1st app. The Patriot (7/41); not in #46-48; pin-up on back-c 136.00 407.00 950.00
22-25: 23-Last Gustavson Angel; origin The Vision in text. 24-Injury-to-eye story 107.00 321.00 750.00
26-30: 27-Ka-Zar ends; last S&K Vision who battles Satan. 28-Jimmy Jupiter in the Land of Nowhere begins, ends #48; Sub-Mariner vs. The Flying Dutchman. 30-1st Japanese war-c 104.00 311.00 725.00
31-Sub-Mariner by Everett ends, begins again #84 100.00 300.00 700.00
32-1st app. The Boboes 100.00 300.00 700.00
33,35-40: 40-Zeppelin-c 100.00 300.00 700.00
34-Everett, Burgos, Martin Goodman, Funnies, Inc. office appear in story & battles Hitler; last Burgos Human Torch 114.00 343.00 800.00
41-43,45-48: 46-Hitler-c. 48-Last Vision; flag-c 93.00 280.00 650.00
44-Classic Super Plane-c 93.00 280.00 650.00
49-Origin Miss America 121.00 365.00 850.00
50-Mary becomes Miss Patriot (origin) 93.00 280.00 650.00
51-60: 53-Bondage-c. 60-Last Japanese war-c 79.00 235.00 550.00
61,62,64-Last German war-c 75.00 225.00 525.00
63-Classic Hitler War-c; The Villainess Cat-Woman only app. 79.00 235.00 550.00
65,66-Last Japanese War-c 75.00 225.00 525.00
67-75: 74-Last Patriot. 75-Young Allies begin 71.00 215.00 500.00
76-78: 76-Ten Chapter Miss America serial begins, ends #85 71.00 215.00 500.00
79-New cover format; Super Villains begin on cover; last Angel 71.00 215.00 500.00
80-1st app. Capt. America in Marvel Comics 86.00 257.00 600.00
81-Captain America app. 74.00 220.00 515.00
82-Origin & 1st app. Namora (5/47); 1st Sub-Mariner/Namora team-up; Captain America app. 132.00 395.00 925.00
83,85: 83-Last Young Allies. 85-Last Miss America; Blonde Phantom app. 68.00 205.00 475.00
84-Blonde Phantom begins (on-c of #84,88,89); Sub-Mariner by Everett begins; Captain America app. 93.00 280.00 650.00
86-Blonde Phantom i.d. revealed; Captain America app.; last Bucky app. 75.00 225.00 525.00
87-1st Capt. America/Golden Girl team-up 79.00 235.00 550.00
88-Golden Girl, Namora, & Sun Girl (1st in Marvel Comics) x-over; Captain America, Blonde Phantom app.; last Toro 74.00 220.00 515.00
89-1st Human Torch/Sun Girl team-up; 1st Captain America solo; Blonde Phantom app. 75.00 225.00 525.00
90-Blonde Phantom un-masked; Captain America app. 79.00 235.00 550.00
91-Capt. America app.; Blonde Phantom & Sub-Mariner end; early Venus app. (4/49) 79.00 235.00 550.00
92-Feature story on the birth of the Human Torch and the death of Professor Horton (his creator); 1st app. The Witness in Marvel Comics; Captain America app. 132.00 396.00 925.00
132 Pg. issue, B&W, 25¢ (1943-44)-printed in N. Y.; square binding, blank inside covers; has Marvel No. 33-c in color; contains Capt. America #18 & Marvel Mystery Comics #33; same contents as Captain America Annual (only three copies known to exist) 1300.00 4000.00 9100.00

NOTE: ***Brodsky*** *c-49, 72, 86, 88-92.* ***Crandall*** *a-26i.* ***Everett*** *c-7-9, 27, 84.* ***Gabrielle*** *c-30-32.* ***Schomburg*** *c-3-11, 13-29, 33-36, 39-48, 50-59, 63-69, 74, 76, 132 pg. issue.* ***Shores*** *c-37, 38, 75p, 77, 78p, 79p, 80, 81p, 82-84, 85p, 87p.* ***Sekowsky*** *c-73. Bondage covers-3, 4, 7, 12, 28, 29, 49, 50, 52, 56, 57, 58, 59, 65. Angel c-2, 3, 8, 12. Remember Pearl Harbor issues-#30-32.*

MARVEL NO-PRIZE BOOK, THE (The Official... on-c)
Jan, 1983 (One Shot, Direct Sale only)
Marvel Comics Group

1-Golden-c 1.00

MARVEL PREMIERE
April, 1972 - No. 61, Aug, 1981 (A tryout book for new characters)
Marvel Comics Group

1-Origin Warlock (pre-#1) by Gil Kane/Adkins; origin Counter-Earth; Hulk & Thor cameo (#1-14 are 20¢-c) 6.90 21.00 48.00
2-Warlock ends; Kirby Yellow Claw-r 3.70 11.00 26.00
3-Dr. Strange series begins (pre #1, 7/72), B. Smith-a(p); Smith-c? 4.10 12.40 29.00
4-Smith/Brunner-a 1.65 4.70 11.00
5-9: 8-Starlin-c/a(p) 1.10 2.70 6.50
10-Death of the Ancient One 1.50 3.75 9.00
11-14: 11-Dr. Strange origin-r by Ditko. 14-Last Dr. Strange (3/74), gets own title 3 months later 1.80 4.50
15-Origin/1st app. Iron Fist (5/74), ends #25 6.50 19.00 45.00
16-2nd app. Iron Fist; origin cont'd from #15; Hama's 1st Marvel-a 2.10 6.40 15.00
17-24: Iron Fist in all 1.85 5.50 13.00
25-1st Byrne Iron Fist (moves to own title next) 2.30 6.75 16.00
26,27: 26-Hercules. 27-Satana 1.80 4.50
28-Legion of Monsters (Ghost Rider, Man-Thing, Morbius, Werewolf) 1.70 5.00 12.00
29-49,51-56,61: 29,30-The Liberty Legion. 29-1st modern app. Patriot. 31-1st app. Woodgod; last 25¢ issue. 32-1st app. Monark Starstalker. 33,34-1st color app. Solomon Kane (Robert E. Howard adaptation "Red Shadows". 35-Origin/1st app. 3-D Man. 36,37-3-D Man. 38-1st Weirdworld. 39,40-Torpedo. 41-1st Seeker 3001! 42-Tigra. 43-Paladin. 44-Jack of Hearts (1st solo book, 10/78). 45,46-Man-Wolf. 47-Origin/1st app. new Ant-Man. 48-Ant-Man. 49-The Falcon (1st solo book, 8/79). 51-53-Black Panther. 54-1st Caleb Hammer. 55-Wonder Man. 56-1st color app. Dominic Fortune. 61-Star Lord .65 1.60
50-1st app. Alice Cooper; co-plotted by Alice 1.00 2.50 5.50
57-Dr. Who (2nd U.S. app.-see Movie Classics) 1.40 3.50
58-60-Dr. Who .90 2.25

NOTE: ***N. Adams*** *(Crusty Bunkers) part inks-10, 12, 13.* ***Austin*** *a-50i, 56i; c-46i, 50i, 56i, 58.* ***Brunner*** *a-4i, 6p, 9-14p; c-9-14.* ***Byrne*** *a-47p, 48p.* ***Chaykin*** *a-32-34; c-32, 33, 56.* ***Giffen*** *a-31p, 44p; c-44.* ***Gil Kane*** *a(p)-1, 2, 15; c(p)-1, 2, 15, 16, 22-24, 27, 36, 37.* ***Kirby*** *c-26, 29-31, 35.* ***Layton*** *a-47i, 48i; c-47.* ***McWilliams*** *a-25i.* ***Miller*** *c-49p, 53p, 58p.* ***Nebres*** *a-44i; c-38i.* ***Nino*** *a-38i.* ***Perez*** *c/a-38p, 45p, 46p.* ***Ploog*** *a-38; c-5-7.* ***Russell*** *a-7p.* ***Simonson*** *a-60(2pgs.); c-57.* ***Starlin*** *a-8p; c-8.* ***Sutton*** *a-41, 43, 50p, 61; c-50p, 61. #57-60 published w/two different prices on-c.*

MARVEL PRESENTS
October, 1975 - No. 12, Aug, 1977 (#1-5 are 25¢ issues)
Marvel Comics Group

1-Origin & 1st app. Bloodstone 1.00 2.00 5.00
2-Origin Bloodstone continued; Kirby-c 1.60 4.00
3-Guardians of the Galaxy (1st solo book, 2/76) begins, ends #12

Marvel Preview #20 © MEG

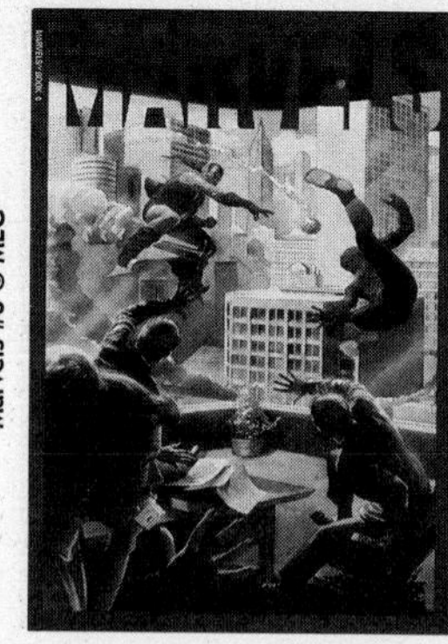
Marvels #0 © MEG

Marvel Spotlight #9 © MEG

GD25 FN65 NM94

3.00 7.70 18.00
4-7,9-12: 9,10-Origin Starhawk 1.70 5.00 12.00
8-r/story from Silver Surfer #2 plus 4 pgs. new-a 1.90 5.60 13.00
NOTE: ***Austin*** *a-6i.* ***Buscema*** *r-8p.* ***Chaykin*** *a-5p.* ***Kane*** *c-1p.* ***Starlin*** *layouts-10.*

MARVEL PREVIEW (Magazine) (Bizarre Adventures #25 on)
Feb (no month), 1975 - No. 24, Winter, 1980 (B&W) ($1.00)
Marvel Comics Group

1-Man-Gods From Beyond the Stars; Crusty Bunkers (Neal Adams)-a(i) & cover; Nino-a .80 2.00
2-1st origin The Punisher (see Amaz. Spider-Man #129 & Classic Punisher); 1st app. Dominic Fortune; Morrow-c 20.00 60.00 140.00
3-7,9,10: 3-Blade the Vampire Slayer. 4-Star-Lord & Sword in the Star (origins & 1st app.). 5,6-Sherlock Holmes. 6-N. Adams frontispiece. 7-Satana, Sword in the Star app. 9-Man-God; origin Star Hawk, ends #20. 10-Thor the Mighty. 10,11-Starlin frontispiece in each .80 2.00
8-Legion of Monsters; Morbius app. 1.30 3.30 8.00
11-20,22-24: 11-Star-Lord; Byrne-a. 12-Haunt of Horror. 14,15-Star-Lord. 14-Starlin painted-c. 16-Masters of Terror. 17-Blackmark by G. Kane (see SSOC #1-3). 18-Star-Lord. 19-Kull. 20-Bizarre Advs. 22-King Arthur. 23-Bizarre Advs.; Miller-a. 24-Debut Paradox .80 2.00
21-Moon Knight (Spr/80)-Predates Moon Knight #1; The Shroud by Ditko 1.00 2.00 5.00

NOTE: ***N. Adams*** *(C. Bunkers) r-20i.* ***Buscema*** *a-22, 23.* ***Byrne*** *a-11.* ***Chaykin*** *a-20r; c-20 (new).* ***Colan*** *a-8, 16p(3), 18p, 23p; c-16p.* ***Elias*** *a-18.* ***Giffen*** *a-7.* ***Infantino*** *a-14p.* ***Kaluta*** *a-12; c-15.* ***Miller*** *a-23.* ***Morrow*** *a-8i; c-2-4.* ***Perez*** *a-20p.* ***Ploog*** *a-8.* ***Starlin*** *c-13, 14. Nudity in some issues*

MARVELS
Jan, 1994 - No. 4, Apr, 1994 ($5.95, mini-series, 52 pgs.)
Marvel Comics

1-4: Painted-c/a; double-c w/acetate overlay 1.00 2.50 6.00
...Marvel Classic Collectors Pack ($11.90)-Issues #1 & 2 boxed-1st printings 1.70 5.00 12.00
0-(8.94, $2.95) 1.20 3.00

MARVEL SAGA, THE
Dec, 1985 - No. 25, Dec, 1987
Marvel Comics Group

1 1.50
2-25 1.00
NOTE: ***Williamson*** *a(i)-9, 10; c(i)-7, 10-12, 14, 16.*

MARVEL'S GREATEST COMICS (Marvel Collectors' Item Classics #1-22)
No. 23, Oct, 1969 - No. 96, Jan, 1981
Marvel Comics Group

23-30: Begin Fantastic Four-r/#30s?-116 1.20 3.00
31-34,38-96: 42-Silver Surfer-r/F.F.(others?) .80 2.00
35-37-Silver Surfer-r/Fantastic Four #48-50 .80 2.00
NOTE: *Dr. Strange, Fantastic Four, Iron Man, Watcher-#23, 24. Capt. America, Dr. Strange, Iron Man, Fantastic Four-#25-28. Fantastic Four-#38-96.* ***Buscema*** *r-85-92; c-87-92r.* ***Ditko*** *r-23-28.* ***Kirby*** *r-23-82; c-75, 77p, 80p. #81 reprints Fantastic Four #100.*

MARVELS OF SCIENCE
March, 1946 - No. 4, June, 1946
Charlton Comics

1-A-Bomb story 14.00 43.00 100.00
2-4 10.00 30.00 65.00

MARVEL SPECIAL EDITION FEATURING... (Also see Special Collectors' Ed.)
1975 - 1978 (84 pgs.) (Oversized)
Marvel Comics Group

1-The Spectacular Spider-Man ($1.50); r/Amazing Spider-Man #6,35, Annual 1; Ditko-a(r) .80 2.00
1-Star Wars (1977, $1.00); r/Star Wars #1-3 .80 2.00
2-Star Wars (1978, $1.00); r/Star Wars #4-6 1.50
3-Star Wars ('78, $2.50, 116pgs.); r/S. Wars #1-6 1.00 2.50
3-Close Encounters of the Third Kind (1978, $1.50, 56 pgs.)-Movie adaptation; Simonson-a(p) 1.50
V2#2(Spring, 1980, $2.00, oversized)- "Star Wars: The Empire Strikes Back"; r/Marvel Comics Super Special #16 1.50
NOTE: ***Chaykin*** *c/a(r)-1(1977), 2, 3.* ***Stevens*** *a(r)-2i, 3i.* ***Williamson*** *a(r)-V2#2.*

GD25 FN65 NM94

MARVEL SPECTACULAR
Aug, 1973 - No. 19, Nov, 1975
Marvel Comics Group

1-Thor-r from mid-sixties begin by Kirby .80 2.00
2-19 1.50

MARVEL SPOTLIGHT (...& Son of Satan #19, 20, 23, 24)
Nov, 1971 - No. 33, Apr, 1977; V2#1, July, 1979 - V2#11, Mar, 1981
Marvel Comics Group (A try-out book for new characters)

1-Origin Red Wolf (western hero)(1st solo book, pre-#1); Wood inks, Neal Adams-c; only 15¢ issue 3.00 9.90 23.00
2-(25¢, 52 pgs.)-Venus-r by Everett; origin/1st app. Werewolf By Night (begins) by Ploog; N. Adams-c 5.70 17.00 40.00
3,4: 4-Werewolf By Night ends (6/72); gets own title 9/72 1.70 5.00 12.00
5-Origin/1st app. Ghost Rider (8/72) & begins 16.00 50.00 110.00
6-8: 6-Origin G.R. retold. 8-Last Ploog issue 7.00 21.00 50.00
9-11-Last Ghost Rider (gets own title next mo.) 5.50 17.00 40.00
12-Origin & 2nd full app. The Son of Satan (10/73); story cont'd from Ghost Rider #2 & into #3; series begins, ends #24 1.50 3.75 9.00
12-Variant w/4 extra pgs. of ads on slick paper plus a Mark Jeweler pull-out centerfold ad 1.65 4.00 10.00
13-21,23,24: 13-Partial origin Son of Satan. 14-Last 20¢ issue. 24-Last Son of Satan (10/75); gets own title 12/75 1.60 4.00
22-Ghost Rider-c & cameo (5 panels) 1.50 3.75 9.00
25-27,30,31: 25-Sinbad; contains pull-out Mark Jewelers ad. 26-Scarecrow. 27-Sub-Mariner. 30-The Warriors Three. 31-Nick Fury 1.20 3.00
28,29: Moon Knight. 28-1st solo Moon Knight app., (6/76). 29-Last 25¢ issue 1.80 5.00 11.00
32-1st app./partial origin Spider-Woman (2/77); Nick Fury app. 1.30 3.00 8.00
33-Deathlok; 1st app. Devil-Slayer 1.30 3.00 8.00
V2#1-11: 1-4,8-Capt. Marvel. 5-Dragon Lord. 6,7-StarLord; origin #6. 9-11-Capt. Universe (see Micronauts #8) 1.00
NOTE: ***Austin*** *c-V2#2i, 8.* ***J. Buscema*** *c/a-30p.* ***Chaykin*** *a-31; c-26, 31.* ***Colan*** *a-18p, 19p.* ***Ditko*** *a-V2#4, 5, 9-11; c-V2#4, 9-11.* ***Kane*** *c-21p, 32p.* ***Kirby*** *c-29p.* ***McWilliams*** *a-20i.* ***Miller*** *a-V2#8p; c(p)-V2#2, 5, 7, 8.* ***Mooney*** *a-8i, 10i, 14p, 15, 16p, 17p, 24p, 27, 32i.* ***Nasser*** *a-33p.* ***Ploog*** *a-2-5, 6-8p; c-3-9.* ***Romita*** *c-13.* ***Sutton*** *a-9-11p, V2#6, 7. #29-25¢ & 30¢ issues exist.*

MARVEL SUPER ACTION (Magazine)
January, 1976 (B&W, 76 pgs.)
Marvel Comics Group

1-Origin/2nd app. Dominic Fortune(see Marv. Preview); early Punisher app.; Weird World & The Huntress; Evans, Ploog-a 11.00 32.00 75.00

MARVEL SUPER ACTION
May, 1977 - No. 37, Nov, 1981
Marvel Comics Group

1-Reprints Capt. America #100 by Kirby 1.00 2.50
2,3,5-13: r/Capt. America #101,102,103-111. 11-Origin-r. 12,13-Classic Steranko-c/a(r) 1.50
4-Marvel Boy-r(origin)/M. Boy #1 1.50
14-37: r/Avengers #55,56, Annual 2, others. 30-r/Hulk #6 from U.K. 1.00
NOTE: ***Buscema*** *a(r)-14p, 15p; c-18-20, 22, 35r-37.* ***Everett*** *a-4.* ***Heath*** *a-4r.* ***Kirby*** *r-1-3, 5-11.* ***B. Smith*** *a-27r, 28r.* ***Steranko*** *a(r)-12p, 13p; c-12r, 13r.*

MARVEL SUPER HERO CONTEST OF CHAMPIONS
June, 1982 - No. 3, Aug, 1982 (Mini-Series)
Marvel Comics Group

1-3: Features nearly all Marvel characters currently appearing in their comics; 1st Marvel limited series 1.60 4.00

MARVEL SUPER HEROES
October, 1966 (25¢, 68 pgs.) (1st Marvel one-shot)
Marvel Comics Group

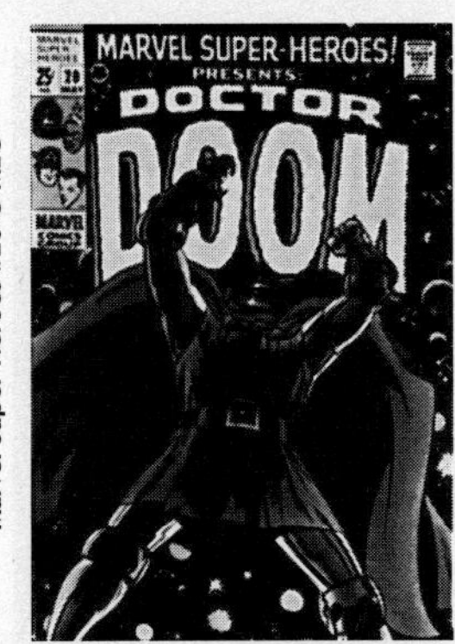

Marvel Super-Heroes #20 © MEG

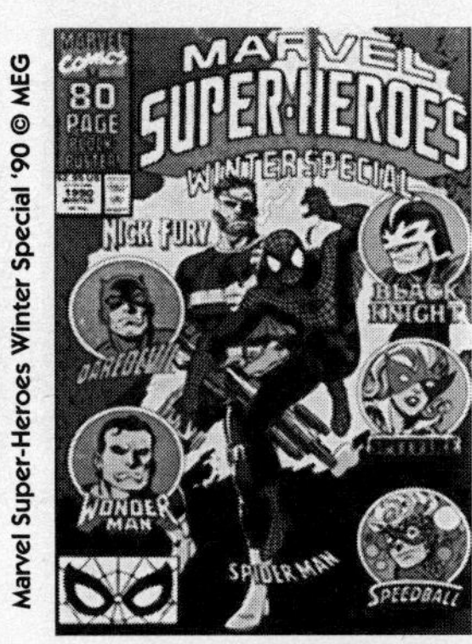

Marvel Super-Heroes Winter Special '90 © MEG

Marvel Tales #130 © MEG

GD25 FN65 NM94

1-r/origin Daredevil from D.D. #1; r/Avengers #2; G.A. Sub-Mariner-r/Marvel Mystery #8 (Human Torch app.) 10.00 30.00 70.00

MARVEL SUPER-HEROES (Formerly Fantasy Masterpieces #1-11)
(Also see Giant-Size Super Heroes) (#12-20: 25¢, 68 pgs.)
No. 12, 12/67 - No. 31, 11/71; No. 32, 9/72 - No. 105, 1/82
Marvel Comics Group

12-Origin & 1st app. Capt. Marvel of the Kree; G.A. Human Torch, Destroyer, Capt. America, Black Knight, Sub-Mariner-r (#12-20 all contain new stories and reprints) 16.00 47.00 110.00
13-2nd app. Capt. Marvel; G.A. Black Knight, Torch, Vision, Capt. America, Sub-Mariner-r 8.00 24.00 55.00
14-Amazing Spider-Man (5/68, new-a by Andru/Everett); G.A. Sub-Mariner, Torch, Mercury (1st Kirby-a at Marvel), Black Knight, Capt. America reprints 14.00 43.00 100.00
15-Black Bolt cameo in Medusa (new-a); Black Knight, Sub-Mariner, Black Marvel, Capt. America-r 2.30 6.90 16.00
16-Origin & 1st app. S. A. Phantom Eagle; G.A. Torch, Capt. America, Black Knight, Patriot, Sub-Mariner-r 2.30 6.90 16.00
17-Origin Black Knight (new-a); G.A. Torch, Sub-Mariner-r; reprint from All-Winners Squad #21 (cover & story) 2.30 6.90 16.00
18-Origin/1st app. Guardians of the Galaxy (1/69); G.A. Sub-Mariner, All-Winners Squad-r 9.00 27.00 62.00
19-Ka-Zar (new-a); G.A. Torch, Marvel Boy, Black Knight, Sub-Mariner reprints; Smith-c(p); Tuska-a(r) 1.70 5.00 12.00
20-Doctor Doom (5/69); r/Young Men #24 w/-c 1.90 6.00 13.00
21-31: All-r issues. 21-X-Men, Daredevil, Iron Man-r begin, end #31. 31-Last Giant issue 1.00 2.50 6.00
32-105: 32-Hulk/Sub-Mariner-r begin from TTA. 56-r/origin Hulk/Inc. Hulk #102; Hulk-r begin 1.00

NOTE: ***Austin** a-104. **Colan** a(p)-12, 13, 15, 18; c-12, 13, 15, 18. **Everett** a-14i(new); r-14, 15i, 18, 19, 33; c-85(r). New **Kirby** c-22, 27, 54. **Maneely** r-14, 15, 19. **Severin** r-83-85i, 100-102; c-100-102r. **Starlin** c-47. **Tuska** a-19p. Black Knight-r by **Maneely** in 12-16, 19. Sub-Mariner-r by **Everett** in 12-20.*

MARVEL SUPER-HEROES
May, 1990 - Present ($2.95/$2.25/$2.50, quarterly, 68-84 pgs.)
Marvel Comics

1-Moon Knight, Hercules, Black Panther, Magik, Brother Voodoo, Speedball (by Ditko) & Hellcat; Hembeck-a 1.20 3.00
2,4,5: 2-Summer Special(7/90); Rogue, Speedball (by Ditko), Iron Man, Falcon, Tigra & Daredevil. 4-Spider-Man/Nick Fury, Daredevil, Speedball, Wonder Man, Spitfire & Black Knight; Byrne-c. 5-Thor, Dr. Strange, Thing & She-Hulk; Speedball by Ditko(p) 1.20 3.00
V2#3-Retells origin Capt. America w/new facts; Blue Shield, Capt. Marvel, Speedball, Wasp; Hulk by Ditko/Rogers 1.20 3.00
V2#6-9: 6-8-$2.25-c. 6,7-X-Men, Cloak & Dagger, The Shroud (by Ditko) & Marvel Boy in each. 8-X-Men, Namor & Iron Man (by Ditko); Larsen-c. 9-W.C Avengers, Iron Man app.; Kieth-c(p); begin $2.50-c 1.00 2.50
V2#10-Ms. Marvel/Sabretooth-c/story (intended for Ms. Marvel #24; shows-c to #24); Namor, Vision, Scarlet Witch stories 1.00 2.50
V2#11,12 ($2.50): 11-Original Ghost Rider-c/story; Giant-Man, Ms. Marvel stories. 12-Dr. Strange, Falcon, Iron Man 1.00 2.50
V2#13-16 ($2.75, 84 pgs.): 13-All Iron Man issue; 30th anniversary. 15-Iron Man/Thor/Volstagg/Dr. Druid 1.10 2.75

MARVEL SUPER-HEROES MEGAZINE
Oct, 1994 - Present ($2.95, 100 pgs.)
Marvel Comics

1-5: 1-r/FF #232, DD #159, Iron Man #115, Incred. Hulk #314 1.20 3.00

MARVEL SUPER-HEROES SECRET WARS (See Secret Wars II)
May, 1984 - No. 12, Apr, 1985 (Limited series)
Marvel Comics Group

1 1.20 3.00
1-3-2nd printings (sold in multi-packs) 1.00
2-7,9-12: 6-The Wasp dies. 7-Intro. new Spider-Woman. 12-($1.00, 52 pgs.) .80 2.00
8-Spider-Man's new black costume explained as alien costume (1st app. Venom as alien costume) 2.90 8.60 20.00

MARVEL SUPER SPECIAL A (See Marvel Comics Super...)

MARVEL SWIMSUIT SPECIAL (Also see Marvel Illustrated...)
1992 ($3.95/$4.50, magazine, 52 pgs.)
Marvel Comics

1-Silvestri-c; pin-ups by many good artists 1.60 4.00
2-Jusko painted-c; all pin-ups 1.80 4.50

MARVEL TAILS STARRING PETER PORKER THE SPECTACULAR SPIDER-HAM (Also see Peter Porker...)
Nov, 1983 (One Shot)
Marvel Comics Group

1-Peter Porker, the Spectacular Spider-Ham, Captain Americat, Goose Rider, Hulk Bunny app. 1.50

MARVEL TALES (Formerly Marvel Mystery Comics #1-92)
No. 93, Aug, 1949 - No. 159, Aug, 1957
Marvel/Atlas Comics (MCI)

93-Horror/weird stories begin 79.00 236.00 550.00
94-Everett-a 57.00 171.00 400.00
95,96,99,101,103,105: 95-New logo 33.00 100.00 285.00
97-Sun Girl, 2 pgs; Kirbyish-a; one story used in N.Y. State Legislative document 46.00 139.00 325.00
98-Krigstein-a 39.00 118.00 275.00
100 39.00 118.00 275.00
102-Wolverton-a "The End of the World", (6 pgs.) 54.00 160.00 375.00
104-Wolverton-a "Gateway to Horror", (6 pgs.) 49.00 148.00 345.00
106,107-Krigstein-a. 106-Decapitation story 33.00 100.00 230.00
108-120: 118-Hypo-c/panels in End of World story. 120-Jack Katz-a 22.00 65.00 150.00
121,123-131: 128-Flying Saucer-c. 131-Last precode (2/55) 16.50 50.00 115.00
122-Kubert-a 17.00 52.00 120.00
132,133,135-141,143,145 10.00 30.00 70.00
134-Krigstein, Kubert-a; flying saucer-c 12.00 36.00 85.00
142-Krigstein-a 11.00 32.00 70.00
144-Williamson/Krenkel-a, 3 pgs. 11.00 32.00 70.00
146,148-151,154-156,158: 156-Torres-a 9.15 27.50 55.00
147-Ditko-a 11.00 32.00 70.00
152-Wood, Morrow-a 11.00 32.00 70.00
153-Everett End of World c/story 11.00 32.00 75.00
157,159-Krigstein-a 10.00 30.00 65.00

NOTE: ***Andru** a-103. **Briefer** a-118. **Check** a-147. **Colan** a-105, 107, 118, 120, 121, 127, 131. **Drucker** a-127, 135, 141, 146, 150. **Everett** a-98, 104, 106(2), 108(2), 131, 148, 151, 153, 155; c-107, 109, 111, 112, 114, 117, 127, 143, 147-151, 153, 155, 156. **Forte** a-119, 125, 130. **Heath** a-110, 113, 118, 119; c-104-106, 110, 130. **Gil Kane** a-117. **Lawrence** a-130. **Maneely** a-111, 126, 129; c-108, 116, 120, 129, 152. **Mooney** a-114. **Morisi** a-153. **Morrow** a-150, 152, 156. **Orlando** a-149, 151, 157. **Pakula** a-119, 121, 135, 144, 150, 152, 156. **Powell** a-136, 137, 150, 154. **Ravielli** a-117. **Rico** a-97, 99. **Romita** a-108. **Sekowsky** a-96-98. **Shores** a-110; c-96. **Sinnott** a-105, 116. **Tuska** a-114. **Whitney** a-107. **Wildey** a-126, 138.*

MARVEL TALES (...Annual #1,2; ...Starring Spider-Man #123 on)
1964 - Present (No. 1-32: 72 pgs.)
Marvel Comics Group (NPP earlier issues)

1-Reprints origins of Spider-Man/Amazing Fantasy #15, Hulk/Inc. Hulk#1, Ant-Man/T.T.A. #35, Giant Man/T.T.A. #49, Iron Man/T.O.S. #39,48, Thor/J.I.M. #83 & r/Sgt. Fury #1 31.00 94.00 250.00
2 ('65)-r/X-Men #1(origin), Avengers #1(origin), origin Dr. Strange-r/Strange Tales #115 & origin Hulk(Hulk #3) 11.00 32.00 75.00
3 (7/66)-Spider-Man, Strange Tales (H. Torch), Journey into Mystery (Thor), Tales to Astonish (Ant-Man)-r begin (r/Strange Tales #101) 5.00 15.00 35.00
4,5 2.40 7.00 17.00
6-8,10: 10-Reprints 1st Kraven/Amaz. S-M #15 1.70 4.20 10.00
9-r/Amazing Spider-Man #14 w/cover 1.70 5.00 12.00
11-32: 11-Spider-Man battles Daredevil-r/Amaz. Spider-Man #16. 13-Origin Marvel Boy-r/M. Boy #1. 22-Green Goblin-c/story-r/Amaz. Spider-Man #27.

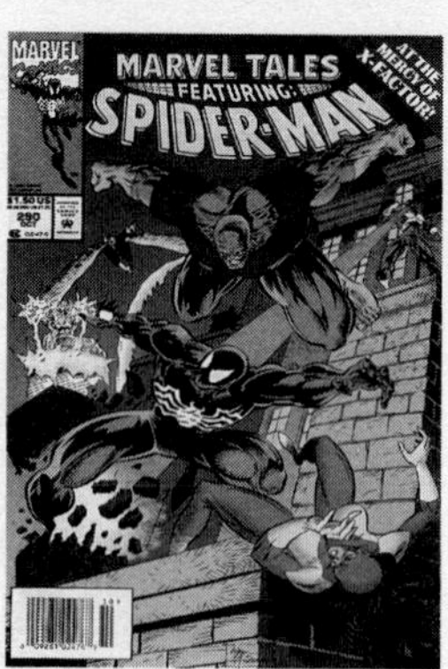

Marvel Tales #290 © MEG

Marvel Team-up #23 © MEG

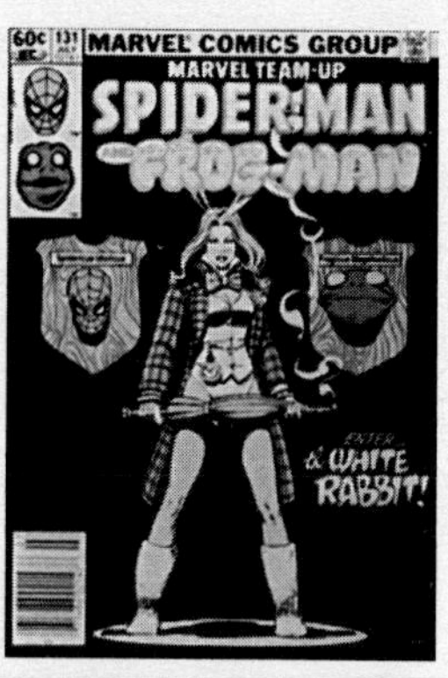

Marvel Team-up #131 © MEG

GD25 FN65 NM94

30-New Angel story. 32-Last 72 pg. issue 1.10 2.70 6.50
33-105: 33-(52 pgs.,)-Kraven-r. 34-Begin regular size issues. 75-Origin Spider-Man-r. 77-79-Drug issues-r/A. Spider-Man #96-98. 98-Death of Gwen Stacy-r/A. Spider-Man #121 (Green Goblin). 99-Death Green Goblin-r/A. Spider-Man #122. 100-(52 pgs.)-New Hawkeye/Two Gun Kid story. 101-105-All Spider-Man-r 1.50
106-1st Punisher-r/Amazing Spider-Man #129 1.50 3.75 9.00
107-133-All Spider-Man-r. 111,112-r/Spider-Man #134,135 (Punisher). 113, 114-r/Spider-Man #136,137(Green Goblin). 126-128-r/clone story from Amazing Spider-Man #149-151 1.00
134-136-Dr. Strange-r begin; SpM stories continue. 134-Dr. Strange-r/ Strange Tales #110 1.00
137-Origin-r Dr. Strange; shows original unprinted-c & origin Spider-Man/ Amazing Fantasy #15 1.80 4.50
137-Nabisco giveaway 1.00
138-Reprints all Amazing Spider-Man #1; begin reprints of Spider-Man with covers similar to originals 1.80 4.50
139-144: r/Amazing Spider-Man #2-7 .80 2.00
145-191,193-199: Spider-Man-r continue w/#8 on. 149-Contains skin "Tattooz" decals. 150-($1.00, 52pgs.)-r/Spider-Man Annual 1(Kraven app.). 153-r/1st Kraven/Spider-Man #15. 155-r/2nd Green Goblin/Spider-Man #17. 161,164,165-Gr. Goblin-c/stories-r/Spider-Man #23,26,27. 178,179-Green Goblin-c/story-r/Spider-Man #39,40. 187,189-Kraven-r. 191-($1.50, 68 pgs.)-r/Spider-Man #96-98. 193-Byrne-r/Marvel Team-Up begin w/scripts 1.20
192-($1.25, 52 pgs.)-r/Spider-Man #121,122 .80 2.00
200-Double size ($1.25)-Miller-c & r/Annual #14 1.50
201-208,210-222: 208-Last Byrne-r. 210,211-r/Spidey #134,135. 212,213-r/ Giant-Size Spidey #4. 213-r/1st solo Silver Surfer story/F.F. Annual #5. 214, 215-r/Spidey #161,162. 222-Reprints origin Punisher/Spectacular Spider-Man #83; last Punisher reprint 1.00
209-Reprints 1st app. The Punisher/Amazing Spider-Man #129; Punisher reprints begin, end #222 1.00 2.50
223-McFarlane-c begin, end #239 1.50
224-249,251,252,254-257: 233-Spider-Man/X-Men team-ups begin; r/X-Men #35. 234-r/Marvel Team-Up #4. 235,236-r/M. Team-Up Annual #1. 237, 238-r/M. Team-Up #150. 239,240-r/M. Team-Up #38,90(Beast). 242-r/M. Team-Up #89. 243-r/M. Team-Up #117(Wolverine). 251-r/Spider-Man #100 (Green Goblin-c/story). 252-r/1st app. Morbius/Amaz. Spider-Man #101. 254-r/M. Team-Up #15(Ghost Rider); new painted-c. 255,256-Spider-Man & Ghost Rider-r/Marvel Team-Up #58,91. 257-Hobgoblin-r begin(r/Amazing Spider-Man #238); last $1.00-c 1.00
250-($1.50, 52pgs.)-r/1st Karma/M. Team-Up #100 1.50
253-($1.50, 52 pgs.)-r/Amaz. S-M #102 1.50
258-289: 258-261-r/A. Spider-Man #239,249-251(Hobgoblin). 262,263-r/Marv. Team-Up #53,54. 262-New X-Men vs. Sunstroke story. 263-New Woodgod origin story. 264,265-r/A. Spider-Man Annual 5. 266-273-Reprints alien costume stories/A. S-M 252-259. 277-r/1st Silver Sable/A. S-M 265. 283-r/ A. S-M 275 (Hobgoblin). 284-r/A. S-M 276 (Hobgoblin) 1.25
285-variant w/Wonder-Con logo on c-no price-giveaway 1.00
286-($2.95)-p/bagged w/16 page insert & animation print 1.20 3.00
290-295: 290-Begin $1.50-c 1.50

NOTE: *All contain reprints; some have new art. #89-97-r/Amazing Spider-Man #110-118; #98-136-r/#121-159; #137-150-r/Amazing Fantasy #15, #1-12 & Annual 1; #151-167-r/#13-28 & Annual 2; #168-186-r/#29-46.* **Austin** *a-100i; c-272i, 273i.* **Byrne** *a(r)-193-198p, 201-208p.* **Ditko** *a-1-30, 83, 100, 137-155.* **G. Kane** *a-71, 81, 98-101p, 249r; c-125-127p, 130p, 137-155.* **Sam Kieth** *c-255, 262, 263.* **Ron Lim** *c-266p-281p, 283p-285p.* **McFarlane** *c-223-239.* **Mooney** *a-63, 95-97i, 103(i).* **Nasser** *a-100p.* **Nebres** *a-242i.* **Perez** *c-259-261.* **Rogers** *c-240, 241, 243-251.*

MARVEL TEAM-UP (See Marvel Treasury Edition #18 & Official Marvel Index To...)
March, 1972 - No. 150, Feb, 1985
Marvel Comics Group
NOTE: *Spider-Man team-ups in all but Nos. 18, 23, 26, 29, 32, 35, 97, 104, 105, 137.*

1-Human Torch 11.00 32.00 75.00
2-Human Torch 3.90 11.60 27.00
3-Spider-Man/Human Torch vs. Morbius (part 1); 3rd app. of Morbius (7/72) 5.70 17.00 40.00

GD25 FN65 NM94

4-Spider-Man/X-Men vs. Morbius (part 2 of story); 4th app. of Morbius 7.00 21.00 50.00
5-10: 5-Vision. 6-Thing. 7-Thor. 8-The Cat (4/73, came out between The Cat #3 & 4). 9-Iron Man. 10-H-T 2.50 6.30 15.00
11-14,16-20: 11-Inhumans. 12-Werewolf (8/73, 1 month before Werewolf #1). 13-Capt. America. 14-Sub-Mariner. 16-Capt. Marvel. 17-Mr. Fantastic. 18-H-T/Hulk. 19-Ka-Zar. 20-Black Panther; last 20¢ issue 1.70 4.20 10.00
15-1st Spider-Man/Ghost Rider team-up (11/73) 2.10 6.40 15.00
21-30: 21-Dr. Strange. 22-Hawkeye. 23-H-T/Iceman (X-Men cameo). 24-Brother Voodoo. 25-Daredevil. 26-H-T/Thor. 27-Hulk. 28-Hercules. 29-H-T/Iron Man. 30-Falcon 1.00 2.50 6.00
31-45,47-50: 31-Iron Fist. 32-H-T/Son of Satan. 33-Nighthawk. 34-Valkyrie. 35-H-T/Dr. Strange. 36-Frankenstein. 37-Man-Wolf. 38-Beast. 39-H-T. 40-Sons of the Tiger/H-T. 41-Scarlet Witch. 42-The Vision. 43-Dr. Doom; retells origin. 44-Moondragon. 45-Killraven. 47-Thing. 48-Iron Man; last 25¢ issue. 49-Dr. Strange; Iron Man app. 50-Iron Man; Dr. Strange app. 1.00 2.00 5.00
46-Spider-Man/Deathlok team-up 1.90 6.00 13.00
51,52,56,57: 51-Iron Man; Dr. Strange app. 52-Capt. America. 56-Daredevil. 57-Black Widow 1.60 4.00
53-Hulk; Woodgod & X-Men app., 1st Byrne-a on X-Men (1/77) 2.10 6.40 15.00
54,59,60: 54-Hulk; Woodgod app. 59-Yellowjacket/The Wasp. 60-The Wasp (Byrne-a in all) 1.00 2.50 6.00
55-Warlock-c/story; Byrne-a 1.30 3.30 8.00
58-Ghost Rider 1.00 2.50 6.00
61-70: All Byrne-a; 61-H-T. 62-Ms. Marvel; last 30¢ issue. 63-Iron Fist. 64-Daughters of the Dragon. 65-Capt. Britain (1st U.S. app.). 66-Capt. Britain; 1st app. Arcade. 67-Tigra; Kraven the Hunter app. 68-Man-Thing. 69-Havok (from X-Men). 70-Thor 1.20 3.00
71-74,76-78,80: 71-Falcon. 72-Iron Man. 73-Daredevil. 74-Not Ready for Prime Time Players (Belushi). 76-Dr. Strange. 77-Ms. Marvel. 78-Wonder Man. 80-Dr. Strange/Clea; last 35¢ issue 1.20 3.00
75,79: Byrne-a(p). 75-Power Man; Cage app. 79-Mary Jane Watson as Red Sonja; Clark Kent cameo (1 panel, 3/79) 1.20 3.00
81-85,87,88,90,92-99: 81-Satana. 82-Black Widow. 83-Nick Fury. 84-Shang-Chi. 92-Hawkeye. 93-Werewolf by Night. 94-SpM vs. The Shroud. 95-Mockingbird (intro.); Nick Fury app. 96-Howard the Duck; last 40¢ issue. 97-Spider-Woman/Hulk. 98-Black Widow. 99-Machine Man. 85-Shang-Chi/ Black Widow/Nick Fury. 87-Black Panther. 88-Invisible Girl. 90-Beast .80 2.00
86-Guardians of the Galaxy 1.60 4.00
89-Nightcrawler (from X-Men) 1.20 3.00
91-Ghost Rider 1.00 2.00 5.00
100-(Double-size)-Fantastic Four/Storm/Black Panther; origin/1st app. Karma, one of the New Mutants; origin Storm; X-Men x-over; Miller-c/a(p); Byrne-a (on X-Men app. only) 1.30 3.25 8.00
101-116: 101-Nighthawk(Ditko-a). 102-Doc Samson. 103-Ant-Man. 104-Hulk/ Ka-Zar. 105-Hulk/Powerman/Iron Fist. 106-Capt. America. 107-She-Hulk. 108-Paladin; Dazzler cameo. 109-Dazzler; Paladin app. 110-Iron Man. 111-Devil-Slayer. 112-King Kull; last 50¢ issue. 113-Quasar. 114-Falcon. 115-Thor. 116-Valkyrie 1.50
117-Wolverine-c/story 1.70 5.00 12.00
118-140,142-149: 118-Professor X; Wolverine app. (4 pgs.); X-Men cameo. 119-Gargoyle. 120-Dominic Fortune. 121-Human Torch. 122-Man-Thing. 123-Daredevil. 124-The Beast. 125-Tigra. 126-Hulk & Powerman/Son of Satan. 127-The Watcher. 128-Capt. America; Spider-Man/Capt. America photo-c. 129-The Vision. 130-Scarlet Witch. 131-Frogman. 132-Mr. Fantastic. 133-Fantastic Four. 134-Jack of Hearts. 135-Kitty Pryde; X-Men cameo. 136-Wonder Man. 137-Aunt May/Franklin Richards. 138-Sandman. 139-Nick Fury. 140-Black Widow. 142-Capt. Marvel. 143-Starfox. 144-Moon Knight. 145-Iron Man. 146-Nomad. 147-Human Torch; SpM back to old costume. 148-Thor. 149-Cannonball 1.50
141-Daredevil; SpM/Black Widow app. (Spidey in new black costume; ties w/

Marvel Triple Action #40 © MEG

Marvel Two-In-One #29 © MEG

Mary Marvel #16 © FAW

GD25 FN65 NM94

Amaz. S-M #252 for 1st black costume) 1.40 3.50
150-X-Men ($1.00, double-size); B. Smith-c 1.80 4.50
Annual 1(1976)-SpM/X-Men (early app.) 2.00 6.00 15.00
Annuals 2-7: 2(1979)-SpM/Hulk. 3(1980)-Hulk/Power Man/Machine Man/Iron Fist; Miller-c(p). 4(1981)-SpM/Daredevil/Moon Knight/Power Man/Iron Fist; brief origins of each; Miller-c; Miller scripts on Daredevil. 5(1982)-SpM/The Thing/Scarlet Witch/Dr. Strange/Quasar. 6(1983)-SpM/New Mutants (early app.), Cloak & Dagger. 7(1984)-Alpha Flight; Byrne-c(i) .80 2.00

NOTE: ***Art Adams** c-141p. **Austin** a-79i; c-76i, 79i, 96i, 101i, 112i, 130i. **Bolle** a-9i. **Byrne** a(p)-53-55, 59-70, 75, 79, 100; c-68p, 70p, 72p, 75, 76p, 79p, 129i, 133i. **Colan** a-87p. **Ditko** a-101. **Kane** a(p)-4-6, 13, 14, 16-19, 23; c(p)-4, 13, 14, 17-19, 23, 25, 26, 32-35, 37, 41, 44, 45, 47, 53, 54. **Miller** a-100p; c-95p, 99p, 100p, 102p, 106. **Mooney** a-2i, 7i, 8, 10p, 11p, 16i, 24-31p, 72, 93i, Annual 5i. **Nasser** a-89p; c-101p. **Simonson** c-99i, 148. **Paul Smith** c-131, 132. **Starlin** c-27. **Sutton** a-93p. "H-T" means Human Torch; "SpM" means Spider-Man; "S-M" means Sub-Mariner.*

MARVEL TREASURY EDITION ($1.50/$2.50)
1974; No 2, Dec, 1974 - No. 28, 1981 (100 pgs.; oversized, new-a &-r)
Marvel Comics Group

1-Spectacular Spider-Man; story-r/Marvel Super-Heroes #14; Romita-c/a(r); G. Kane, Ditko-r; Green Goblin/Hulk-r 1.00 2.00 5.00
1-1,000 numbered copies signed by Stan Lee & John Romita on front-c & sold thru mail for $5.00; 1st 1,000 copies off the press 1.70 5.00 12.00
2-4: 2-Fantastic Four-r/F.F. 6,11,48-50(Silver Surfer). 3-The Mighty Thor-r/Thor #125-130. 4-Conan the Barbarian; Barry Smith-c/a(r)/Conan #11 1.00 2.50
5-14,16,17: 5-The Hulk (origin-r/Hulk #3). 6-Dr. Strange. 7-Mighty Avengers. 8-Giant Superhero Holidy Grab-Bag; Spider-Man, Hulk, Nick Fury. 9-Giant; Super-hero Team-up. 10-Thor; r/Thor #154-157. 11-Fantastic Four. 12-Howard the Duck (r/#H. the Duck #1 & G.S. Man-Thing #4,5) plus new Defenders story. 13-Giant Super-Hero Holiday Grab-Bag. 14-The Sensational Spider-Man; r/1st Morbius from Amazing S-M #101,102 plus #100 & r/Not Brand Echh #6. 16-The Defenders (origin) & Valkyrie; r/Defenders #1,4,13,14. 17-The Hulk .80 2.00
15-Conan; B. Smith, Neal Adams-i; r/Conan #24 1.00 2.50
18-The Astonishing Spider-Man; r/Spider-Man's 1st team-ups with Iron Fist, The X-Men, Ghost Rider & Werewolf by Night; inside back-c has photos from 1978 Spider-Man TV show .80 2.00
19-28: 19-Conan the Barbarian. 20-Hulk. 21-Fantastic Four. 22-Spider-Man. 23-Conan. 24-Rampaging Hulk. 25-Spider-Man vs. The Hulk. 26-The Hulk; Wolverine app. 27-Spider-Man. 28-Spider-Man/Superman; (origin of each) 1.60 4.00

NOTE: *Reprints-2, 3, 5, 7-9, 13, 14, 16, 17. **Neal Adams** a(i)-6, 15. **Brunner** a-6, 12; c-6. **Buscema** a-15, 19, 28; c-28. **Colan** a-6r; c-12p. **Ditko** a-1, 6. **Gil Kane** c-16p. **Kirby** a-2, 10, 11; c-7. **Romita** c-1, 5. **B. Smith** a-4, 15, 19; c-4, 19.*

MARVEL TREASURY OF OZ FEATURING THE MARVELOUS LAND OF OZ
1975 ($1.50, oversized) (See MGM's Marvelous...)
Marvel Comics Group

1-Buscema-a; Romita-c .80 2.00

MARVEL TREASURY SPECIAL (Also see 2001: A Space Odyssey)
1974; 1976 ($1.50, oversized, 84 pgs.)
Marvel Comics Group

Vol. 1-Spider-Man, Torch, Sub-Mariner, Avengers "Giant Superhero Holiday Grab-Bag"; Wood, Colan/Everett, plus 2 Kirby-r; reprints Hulk vs. Thing from Fantastic Four #25,26 1.50
Vol. 1-... Featuring Captain America's Bicentennial Battles (6/76)-Kirby-a; B. Smith inks, 11 pgs. 1.50

MARVEL TRIPLE ACTION (See Giant-Size...)
Feb, 1972 - No. 24, Mar, 1975; No. 25, Aug, 1975 - No. 47, Apr, 1979
Marvel Comics Group

1-(25¢ giant, 52 pgs.)-Dr. Doom, Silver Surfer, The Thing begin, end #4 ('66 reprints from Fantastic Four) 1.40 3.50
2-47: 45-r/X-Men #45. 46-r/Avengers #53(X-Men) 1.00

NOTE: *#5-44, 46, 47 reprint Avengers #11 thru ?. #40-r/Avengers #48(1st Black Knight). **Buscema** a(r)-35p, 36p, 38p, 39p, 41, 42, 43p, 44p, 46p, 47p. **Ditko** a-2r; c-47. **Kirby** a(r)-1-4p. **Starlin** c-7. **Tuska** a(r)-40p, 43i, 46i, 47i. #2 through at least #17 are 20¢-c.*

GD25 FN65 NM94

MARVEL TWO-IN-ONE (...Featuring ... #82? on; also see The Thing)
January, 1974 - No. 100, June, 1983
Marvel Comics Group

1-Thing team-ups begin; Man-Thing 4.10 12.40 29.00
2-4: 2-Sub-Mariner; last 20¢ issue. 3-Daredevil. 4-Capt. America 1.80 5.00 11.00
5-Guardians of the Galaxy (9/74, 2nd app.?) 2.70 8.10 19.00
6-Dr. Strange (11/74) 2.40 7.30 17.00
7,9,10 1.20 2.90 7.00
8-Early Ghost Rider app. (3/75) 1.70 5.00 12.00
11-20: 13-Power Man. 14-Son of Satan (early app.). 17-Spider-Man. 18-Last 25¢ issue 1.80 4.50
21-26,28,29,31-40: 29-Master of Kung Fu; Spider-Woman cameo. 39-Vision 1.40 3.50
27-Deathlok 1.00 2.50 6.00
30-2nd full app. Spider-Woman (see Marvel Spotlight #32 for 1st app.) .90 2.30 5.50
41,42,44-49: 42-Capt. America. 45-Capt. Marvel. 46-Thing battles Hulk-c/story 1.50
43,50,53,55-Byrne-a(p). 53-Quasar(7/79, 2nd app.) 1.00 2.50
51-The Beast, Nick Fury, Ms. Marvel; Miller-p 1.20 3.00
52-Moon Knight app. 1.20 3.00
54-Death of Deathlok: Byrne-a 2.00 6.00 14.00
56-60,64-68,70-79,81,82: 60-Intro. Impossible Woman. 68-Angel. 71-1st app. Maelstrom. 75-Avengers (52 pgs.). 76-Iceman 1.00
61-63: 61-Starhawk (from Guardians); "The Coming of Her" storyline begins, ends #63; cover similar to F.F. #67 (Him-c). 62-Moondragon; Thanos & Warlock cameo in flashback; Starhawk app. 63-Warlock?; Warlock revived shortly; Starhawk & Moondragon app. .80 2.00
69-Guardians of the Galaxy 1.60 4.00
80-Ghost Rider 1.00 2.50 6.00
83,84: 83-Sasquatch. 84-Alpha Flight app. .80 2.00
85-99: 90-Spider-Man. 93-Jocasta dies. 96-X-Men-c & cameo 1.00
100-Double size, Byrne scripts 1.50
Annual 1 (1976, 52 pgs.)-Thing/Liberty Legion .80 2.00
Annual 2(1977, 52 pgs.)-Thing/Spider-Man; 2nd death of Thanos; end of Thanos saga; Warlock app.; Starlin-c/a 3.70 11.00 26.00
Annual 3,4 (1978-79, 52 pgs.): 3-Nova. 4-Black Bolt 1.50
Annual 5-7 (1980-82, 52 pgs.): 5-Hulk. 6-1st app. American Eagle. 7-The Thing/Champion; Sasquatch, Colossus app.; X-Men cameo (1 pg.) 1.00

NOTE: ***Austin** c(i)-42, 54, 56, 58, 61, 63, 66. **John Buscema** a-30p, 45; c-30p. **Byrne** (p)-43, 50, 53-55; c-43, 53p, 56p, 98i, 99i. **Gil Kane** a-1p, 2p; c(p)-1-3, 9, 11, 14, 28. **Kirby** c-10, 12, 19p, 20, 25, 27. **Mooney** a-18i, 38i, 90i. **Nasser** a-70p. **Perez** a(p)-56-58, 60, 64, 65; c(p)-32, 33, 42, 50-52, 54, 55, 57, 58, 61-66, 70. **Roussos** a-Annual 1i. **Simonson** c-43i, 97p, Annual 6i. **Starlin** c-6, Annual 1. **Tuska** a-6p.*

MARVEL UNIVERSE (See Official Handbook Of The...)

MARVEL X-MEN COLLECTION, THE
Jan, 1994 - No. 3, Mar, 1994 ($2.95, limited series)
Marvel Comics

1-3-r/X-Men trading cards by Jim Lee 1.20 3.00

MARVIN MOUSE
September, 1957
Atlas Comics (BPC)

1-Everett-c/a; Maneely-a 7.50 22.50 45.00

MARY JANE & SNIFFLES (See 4-Color #402, 474 & Looney Tunes)

MARY MARVEL COMICS (Monte Hale #29 on) (Also see Captain Marvel #18, Marvel Family, Shazam, & Wow Comics)
Dec, 1945 - No. 28, Sept, 1948
Fawcett Publications

1-Captain Marvel introduces Mary on-c; intro/origin Georgia Sivana 100.00 300.00 700.00
2 46.00 140.00 325.00
3,4: 3-New logo 36.00 107.00 250.00
5-8: 8-Bulletgirl x-over in Mary Marvel; X-Mas-c 25.00 75.00 175.00

The Masked Man #12 © Eclipse

The Mask Returns #4 © Mike Richardson

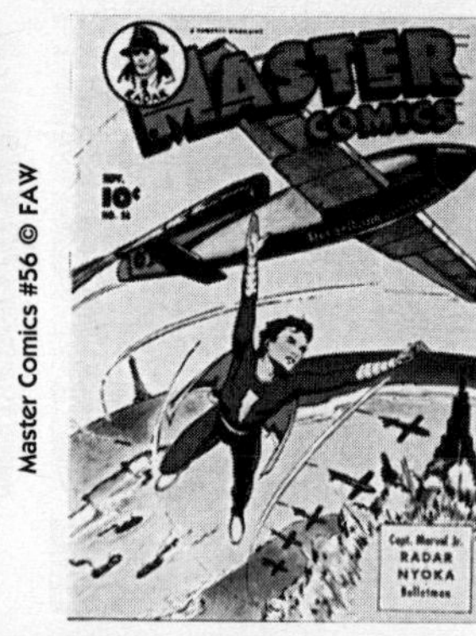

Master Comics #56 © FAW

GD25 FN65 NM94

9,10 22.00 65.00 150.00
11-20 14.00 43.00 100.00
21-28: 28-Western-c 13.00 40.00 90.00

MARY POPPINS (See Movie Comics & Walt Disney Showcase No. 17)

MARY'S GREATEST APOSTLE (St. Louis Grignion de Montfort)
No date (16 pgs.; paper cover)
Catechetical Guild (Topix) (Giveaway)
nn 2.40 6.00 12.00

MARY WORTH (See Harvey Comics Hits #55 & Love Stories of...)
March, 1956 (Also see Romantic Picture Novelettes)
Argo
1 5.35 16.00 32.00

MASK (TV)(DC Comics, 1985 & 1987)(Value: cover or less)

MASK, THE
Aug, 1991 - No. 4, Oct, 1991 ($2.50, 36 pgs., mini-series)
Dark Horse Comics
1-4: 1-1st app. Lt. Kellaway as The Mask 1.00 2.00 5.00
0-(12/91, B&W, 56 pgs.)-r/Mayhem #1-4 1.60 4.00

MASK COMICS
Feb-Mar, 1945 - No. 2, Apr-May, 1945; No. 2, Fall, 1945
Rural Home Publications
1-Classic L. B. Cole Satan-c/a; Palais-a 107.00 321.00 750.00
2-(Scarce)-Classic L. B. Cole Satan-c; Black Rider, The Boy Magician, & The Collector app. 64.00 193.00 450.00
2-(Fall, 1945)-No publ.-same as regular #2; L. B. Cole-c 46.00 140.00 325.00

MASKED BANDIT, THE
1952
Avon Periodicals
nn-Kinstler-a 11.00 32.00 75.00

MASKED MAN, THE (Eclipse)(Value: cover or less)

MASKED MARVEL (See Keen Detective Funnies)
Sept, 1940 - No. 3, Dec, 1940
Centaur Publications
1-The Masked Marvel begins 121.00 365.00 850.00
2,3: 2-Gustavson, Tarpe Mills-a 86.00 257.00 600.00

MASKED RAIDER, THE (Billy The Kid #9 on; Frontier Scout, Daniel Boone #10-13; also see Blue Bird)
June, 1955 - No. 8, July, 1957; No. 14, Aug, 1958 - No. 30, June, 1961
Charlton Comics
1-Masked Raider & Talon the Golden Eagle begin; painted-c 9.15 27.50 55.00
2 4.70 14.00 28.00
3-8: 8-Billy The Kid app. 4.00 11.00 22.00
14,16-30: 22-Rocky Lane app. 3.20 8.00 16.00
15-Williamson-a, 7 pgs. 4.00 11.00 22.00

MASKED RANGER
April, 1954 - No. 9, Aug, 1955
Premier Magazines
1-The Masked Ranger, his horse Streak, & The Crimson Avenger (origin) begin, end #9; Woodbridge/Frazetta-a 25.00 75.00 175.00
2,3 8.35 25.00 50.00
4-8-All Woodbridge-a. 5-Jesse James by Woodbridge. 6-Billy The Kid by Woodbridge. 7-Wild Bill Hickok by Woodbridge. 8-Jim Bowie's Life Story 10.00 30.00 60.00
9-Torres-a; Wyatt Earp by Woodbridge; Says Death of Masked Ranger on-c 10.00 30.00 65.00
NOTE: *Check a-1. **Woodbridge** c/a-1, 4-9.*

MASK OF DR. FU MANCHU, THE (See Dr. Fu Manchu)
1951

GD25 FN65 NM94

Avon Periodicals
1-Sax Rohmer adapt.; Wood-c/a (26 pgs.); Hollingsworth-a 68.00 205.00 475.00

MASK: OFFICIAL MOVIE ADAPTATION, THE
July, 1994 - No. 2, Aug, 1994 ($2.50)
Dark Horse Comics
1,2-Movie adaptation 1.00 2.50

MASK RETURNS, THE
Oct, 1992 - No. 4, Mar, 1993 ($2.50, 36 pgs., mini-series)
Dark Horse Comics
1-4: 1-"Mask" mask c-f. 4-"Walter" mask c-f 1.40 3.50

MASQUE OF THE RED DEATH (See Movie Classics)

MASQUES (J. N. Williamson's...)(Innovation)(Value: cover or less)

MASTER COMICS (Combined with Slam Bang Comics #7 on)
Mar, 1940 - No. 133, Apr, 1953 (No. 1-6: oversized issues)
(#1-3: 15¢, 52 pgs.; #4-6: 10¢, 36 pgs.; #7-Begin 68 pg. issues)
Fawcett Publications

GD25 FN65 VF82 NM94

1-Origin & 1st app. Master Man; The Devil's Dagger, El Carim, Master of Magic, Rick O'Say, Morton Murch, White Rajah, Shipwreck Roberts, Frontier Marshal, Streak Sloan, Mr. Clue begin (all features end #6) 480.00 1440.00 3120.00 4800.00
(Estimated up to 100 total copies exist, 4 in NM/Mint)

GD25 FN65 NM94

2 157.00 471.00 1100.00
3-5 121.00 365.00 850.00
6-Last Master Man 121.00 365.00 850.00
NOTE: *#1-6 rarely found in near mint to mint condition due to large-size format.*
7-(10/40)-Bulletman, Zoro, the Mystery Man (ends #22), Lee Granger, Jungle King, & Buck Jones begin; only app. The War Bird & Mark Swift & the Time Retarder; Zoro, Lee Granger, Jungle King & Mark Swift all continue from Slam Bang; Bulletman moves from Nickel 200.00 600.00 1400.00
8-The Red Gaucho (ends #13), Captain Venture (ends #22) & The Planet Princess begin 107.00 321.00 750.00
9,10: 10-Lee Granger ends 86.00 257.00 600.00
11-Origin & 1st app. Minute-Man (2/41) 193.00 580.00 1350.00
12 100.00 300.00 700.00
13-Origin & 1st app. Bulletgirl; Hitler-c 136.00 407.00 950.00
14-16: 14-Companions Three begins, ends #31 86.00 257.00 600.00
17-20: 17-Raboy-a on Bulletman begins. 20-Captain Marvel cameo app. in Bulletman 82.00 246.00 575.00

GD25 FN65 VF82 NM94

21-(12/41; Scarce)-Captain Marvel & Bulletman team up against Capt. Nazi; origin & 1st app. Capt. Marvel Jr's most famous nemesis Captain Nazi who will cause creation of Capt. Marvel Jr. in Whiz #25. Part I of trilogy origin of Capt. Marvel Jr.; 1st Mac Raboy-c for Fawcett; Capt. Nazi-c 280.00 840.00 1820.00 2800.00
(Estimated up to 110 total copies exist, 6 in NM/Mint)
22-(1/42)-Captain Marvel Jr. moves over from Whiz #25 & teams up with Bulletman against Captain Nazi; part III of trilogy origin of Capt. Marvel Jr. & his 1st cover and adventure 260.00 780.00 1690.00 2600.00
(Estimated up to 135 total copies exist, 7 in NM/Mint)

GD25 FN65 NM94

23-Capt. Marvel Jr. c/stories begin (1st solo story); fights Capt. Nazi by himself 186.00 557.00 1300.00
24,25,29: 29-Hitler & Hirohito-c 74.00 223.00 520.00
26-28,30-Captain Marvel Jr. vs. Capt. Nazi. 30-Flag-c 74.00 223.00 520.00
31,32: 32-Last El Carim & Buck Jones; intro Balbo, the Boy Magician in El Carim story 52.00 156.00 365.00
33-Balbo, the Boy Magician (ends #47), Hopalong Cassidy (ends #49) begins 52.00 156.00 365.00
34-Capt. Marvel Jr. vs. Capt. Nazi-c/story 57.00 171.00 400.00
35 50.00 150.00 350.00

Master Comics #117 © FAW

Master of Kung Fu #15 © MEG

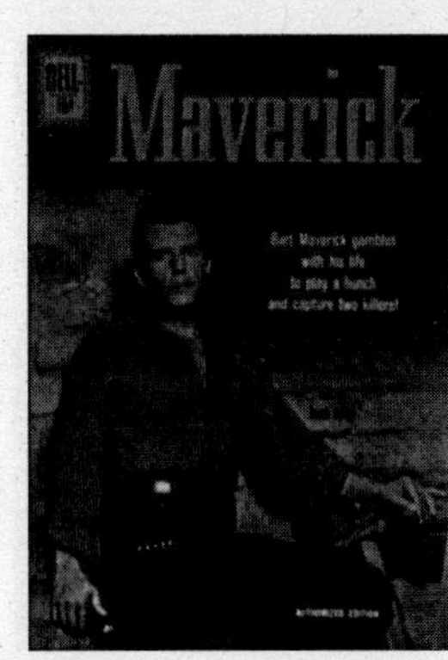

Maverick #19 © Warner Bros.

GD25 FN65 NM94

36-40: 40-Flag-c 46.00 137.00 320.00
41-Bulletman, Capt. Marvel Jr. & Bulletgirl x-over in Minute-Man; only app. Crime Crusaders Club (Capt. Marvel Jr., Minute-Man, Bulletman & Bulletgirl); only team in Fawcett Comics 50.00 150.00 350.00
42-47,49: 47-Hitler becomes Corpl. Hitler Jr. 49-Last Minute-Man 29.00 86.00 200.00
48-Intro. Bulletboy; Capt. Marvel cameo in Minute-Man 34.00 103.00 240.00
50-Intro Radar & Nyoka the Jungle Girl & begin series (5/44); Radar also intro in Captain Marvel #35 (same date); Capt. Marvel x-over in Radar; origin Radar; Capt. Marvel & Capt. Marvel, Jr. introduce Radar on-c 22.00 65.00 150.00
51-58 16.00 48.00 110.00
59-62: Nyoka serial "Terrible Tiara" in all; 61-Capt. Marvel Jr. 1st meets Uncle Marvel 18.00 54.00 125.00
63-80 12.00 36.00 85.00
81,83-87,89-91,95-99: 88-Hopalong Cassidy begins (ends #94). 95-Tom Mix begins (ends #133) 11.00 32.00 75.00
82,88,92-94-Krigstein-a 11.50 34.00 80.00
100 11.00 32.00 75.00
101-106-Last Bulletman 10.00 30.00 65.00
107-132: 132-B&W and color illos in **POP** 9.15 27.50 55.00
133-Bill Battle app. 10.00 30.00 70.00
NOTE: ***Mac Raboy*** *a-15-39, 40 in part, 42, 58; c-21-49, 51, 52, 54, 56, 58, 59. Bulletman c-7-11, 13(half), 15, 18(part), 19, 20, 21(w/Capt. Marvel & Capt. Nazi), 22(w/Capt. Marvel, Jr.). Capt. Marvel, Jr. c-23-133. Master Man c-1-6. Minute Man c-12, 13(half), 14, 16, 17, 18(part).*

MASTER DETECTIVE
1964 (Reprints)
Super Comics
10,17,18: 10,18-Exist? 17-r/Young King Cole #?; McWilliams-r 1.20 3.00 6.00

MASTER OF KUNG FU (Formerly Special Marvel Edition; see Deadly Hands of Kung Fu & Giant-Size...)
No. 17, April, 1974 - No. 125, June, 1983
Marvel Comics Group
17-Starlin-a; intro Black Jack Tarr; 3rd Shang-Chi (ties w/Deadly Hands #1) 2.60 7.70 18.00
18-20: 19-Man-Thing-c/story 1.60 4.00 9.50
21-23,25-30 1.00 2.50 6.00
24-Starlin, Simonson-a 1.20 2.90 7.00
31-99: 33-1st Leiko Wu. 43-Last 25¢ issue 1.20 3.00
100-Double size 1.60 4.00
101-117,119-124 1.00 2.50
118,125-Double size issues 1.40 3.50
Annual 1(4/76)-Iron Fist app. 1.00 2.00 5.00
NOTE: ***Austin*** *c-63i, 74i.* ***Buscema*** *c-44p.* ***Gulacy*** *a(p)-18-20, 22, 25, 29-31, 33-35, 38, 39, 40(p&i), 42-50, 53r(#20); c-51, 55, 64, 67.* ***Gil Kane*** *c(p)-20, 38, 39, 42, 45, 59, 63.* ***Nebres*** *c-73i.* ***Starlin*** *a-17p, 24; c-54.* ***Sutton*** *a-42i. #53 reprints #20.*

MASTER OF KUNG-FU: BLEEDING BLACK
Feb, 1991 ($2.95, 84 pgs.)
Marvel Comics
1-The Return of Shang-chi 1.20 3.00

MASTER OF RAMPLING GATE (Anne Rice's...)(Innovation)(Value: cover or less)

MASTER OF THE WORLD (See 4-Color #1157)

MASTERS OF TERROR (Magazine)
July, 1975 - No. 2, Sept, 1975 (Black & White) (All reprints)
Marvel Comics Group
1-Brunner, Barry Smith-a; Morrow-c; Neal Adams-r(i); Starlin-a(p); Gil Kane-a .70 1.80
2-Reese, Kane, Mayerik-a; Steranko-c 1.20

MASTERS OF THE UNIVERSE (DC, 1982 & 1986-88)(Value: cover or less)

MASTERS OF THE UNIVERSE (Comic Album)
1984 (8-1/2x11"; $2.95; 64 pgs.)
Western Publishing Co.
11362-Based on Mattel toy & cartoon 1.20 3.00

MASTERWORKS SERIES OF GREAT COMIC BOOK ARTISTS, THE
(Sea Gate/DC)(Value: cover or less)

MATT SLADE GUNFIGHTER (Kid Slade Gunfighter #5 on; See Western Gunfighters)
May, 1956 - No. 4, Nov, 1956
Atlas Comics (SPI)
1-Intro Matt & horse Eagle; Williamson/Torres-a 12.00 36.00 85.00
2-Williamson-a 7.50 22.50 45.00
3,4 5.85 17.50 35.00
NOTE: ***Maneely*** *a-1, 3, 4; c-1, 2, 4.* ***Roth*** *a-2-4.* ***Severin*** *a-1, 3, 4.* ***Maneely*** *c/a-1.*

MAUD
1906 (32 pgs. in color; 10x15-1/2") (Cardboard covers)
Frederick A. Stokes Co.
nn-By Fred Opper 25.00 75.00 250.00

MAVERICK (TV)
No. 892, 4/58 - No. 19, 4-6/62 (All have photo-c)
Dell Publishing Co.
4-Color 892 (#1)-James Garner photo-c begin 16.00 48.00 110.00
4-Color 930,945,962,980,1005 (6-8/59): 945-James Garner/Jack Kelly photo-c begin 10.00 30.00 60.00
7 (10-12/59) - 14: Last Garner/Kelly-c 8.35 25.00 50.00
15-18: Jack Kelly/Roger Moore photo-c 8.35 25.00 50.00
19-Jack Kelly photo-c 8.35 25.00 50.00

MAVERICK MARSHAL
Nov, 1958 - No. 7, May, 1960
Charlton Comics
1 4.00 11.00 22.00
2-7 2.40 6.00 12.00

MAVERICKS
Jan, 1994 - Present ($2.50)
Daggar Comics Group
1-($2.75) 1.10 2.75
1-Bronze 1.60 4.00
1-Gold .80 2.10 5.00
1-Silver 1.80 4.25
2-5 1.00 2.50

MAX BRAND (See Silvertip)

MAXIMORTAL, THE (King Hell/Tundra)(Value: cover or less)

MAXX (Also see Darker Image & Primer #5)
Mar, 1993 - Present ($1.95, color)
Image Comics
1-10-Sam Kieth-c/a & scripts. 6-Savage Dragon cameo(1 pg.). 7,8-Pitt-c & story .80 2.00
1-Glow-in-the-dark variant 10.00

MAYA (See Movie Classics)
March, 1968
Gold Key
1 (10218-803)(TV) 1.70 5.00 12.00

MAYHEM
May, 1989 - No. 4, Sept, 1989 ($2.50, B&W, 52 pgs.)
Dark Horse Comics
1- 4-part Stanley Ipkiss/Mask story begins; Mask-c 2.10 6.00 15.00
2-4: 2-Mask 1/2 back-c. 4-Mask-c 1.10 3.00 8.00

MAZE AGENCY, THE (Comico/Innovation)(Value: cover or less)

MAZIE (...& Her Friends) (See Flat-Top, Mortie, Stevie & Tastee-Freez)
1953 - #12, 1954; #13, 12/54 - #22, 9/56; #23, 9/57 - #28, 8/58
Mazie Comics(Magazine Publ.)/Harvey Publ. No. 13-on

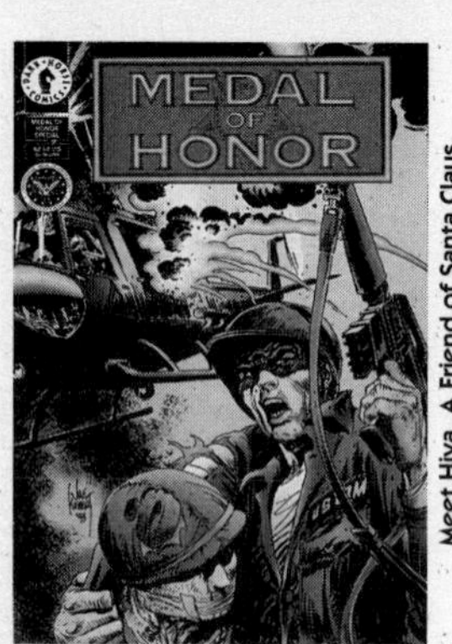

Medal Of Honor #1 © DH

Meet Hiya A Friend of Santa Claus © Sundial Shoe store Giveaway

Megaton Man Meets The Uncategorizable X-Thems #1 © Kitchen Sink

	GD25	FN65	NM94
1-(Teen-age)-Stevie's girl friend	5.85	17.50	35.00
2	3.20	8.00	16.00
3-10	2.40	6.00	12.00
11-28	1.60	4.00	8.00

MAZIE
1950 - No. 7, 1951 (5¢) (5x7-1/4"-miniature)(52 pgs.)
Nation Wide Publishers

1-Teen-age	10.00	30.00	70.00
2-7	5.85	17.50	35.00

MAZINGER (See First Comics Graphic Novel #17)

'MAZING MAN (DC)(Value: cover or less)

McCRORY'S CHRISTMAS BOOK
1955 (36 pgs.; slick cover)
Western Printing Co. (McCrory Stores Corp. giveaway)

nn-Painted-c	3.20	8.00	16.00

McCRORY'S TOYLAND BRINGS YOU SANTA'S PRIVATE EYES
1956 (16 pgs.)
Promotional Publ. Co. (Giveaway)

nn-Has 9 pg. story plus 7 pgs. toy ads	2.40	6.00	12.00

McCRORY'S WONDERFUL CHRISTMAS
1954 (20 pgs.; slick cover)
Promotional Publ. Co. (Giveaway)

nn	3.20	8.00	16.00

McHALE'S NAVY (TV) (See Movie Classics)
May-July, 1963 - No. 3, Nov-Jan, 1963-64 (All have photo-c)
Dell Publishing Co.

1	5.00	15.00	30.00
2,3	4.00	12.00	24.00

McKEEVER & THE COLONEL (TV)
Feb-Apr, 1963 - No. 3, Aug-Oct, 1963
Dell Publishing Co.

1-Photo-c	5.85	17.50	35.00
2,3	4.70	14.00	28.00

McLINTOCK (See Movie Comics)

MD
Apr-May, 1955 - No. 5, Dec-Jan, 1955-56
E. C. Comics

1-Not approved by code	10.00	30.00	70.00
2-5	8.35	25.00	50.00

NOTE: ***Crandall, Evans, Ingels, Orlando** art in all issues; **Craig** c-1-5.*

MECHA (Dark Horse)(Value: cover or less)

MEDAL FOR BOWZER, A
1966 (8 pgs.)
American Visuals

nn-Eisner-c/script	27.00	80.00	185.00

MEDAL OF HONOR COMICS
Spring, 1946
A. S. Curtis

1-War stories	8.35	25.00	50.00

MEDAL OF HONOR SPECIAL
1994 ($2.50)
Dark Horse Comics

1-Kubert-c/a (first story)		1.00	2.50

MEDIA STARR (Innovation)(Value: cover or less)

MEET ANGEL (Formerly Angel & the Ape)
No. 7, Nov-Dec, 1969
National Periodical Publications

	GD25	FN65	NM94
7-Wood-a(i)	1.50	3.75	9.00

MEET CORLISS ARCHER (Radio/Movie)(My Life #4 on)
March, 1948 - No. 3, July, 1948
Fox Features Syndicate

1-(Teen-age)-Feldstein-c/a; headlight-c	37.00	111.00	260.00
2-Feldstein-c only	29.00	86.00	200.00
3-Part Feldstein-c only	22.00	67.00	155.00

NOTE: *No. 1-3 used in Seduction of the Innocent, pg. 39.*

MEET HERCULES (See Three Stooges)

MEET HIYA A FRIEND OF SANTA CLAUS
1949 (18 pgs.?) (paper cover)
Julian J. Proskauer/Sundial Shoe Stores, etc. (Giveaway)

nn	5.00	15.00	30.00

MEET MERTON
Dec, 1953 - No. 4, June, 1954
Toby Press

1-(Teen-age)-Dave Berg-c/a	5.85	17.50	35.00
2-Dave Berg-c/a	4.00	10.00	20.00
3,4-Dave Berg-c/a	3.60	9.00	18.00
I.W. Reprint #9	.80	2.00	4.00
Super Reprint #11('63), 18	.80	2.00	4.00

MEET MISS BLISS (Becomes Stories Of Romance #5 on)
May, 1955 - No. 4, Nov, 1955
Atlas Comics (LMC)

1-Al Hartley-c/a	8.35	25.00	50.00
2-4	5.35	16.00	32.00

MEET MISS PEPPER (Formerly Lucy, The Real Gone Gal)
No. 5, April, 1954 - No. 6, June, 1954
St. John Publishing Co.

5-Kubert/Maurer-a	13.00	40.00	90.00
6-Kubert/Maurer-a; Kubert-c	11.00	32.00	75.00

MEET THE NEW POST GAZETTE SUNDAY FUNNIES
3/12/49 (16 pgs.; paper covers) (7-1/4x10-1/4")
Commercial Comics (insert in newspaper)
Pittsburgh Post Gazette

Dick Tracy by Gould, Gasoline Alley, Terry & the Pirates, Brenda Starr, Buck Rogers by Yager, The Gumps, Peter Rabbit by Fago, Superman, Funnyman by Siegel & Shuster, The Saint, Archie, & others done especially for this book. A fine copy sold at auction in 1985 for $276.00.
Estimated value.... $150 – $300

MEGALITH DEATHWATCH 2000 (Megalith #3 on)
Apr, 1993 - No. 7, Jan, 1994 ($2.50)
Continuity

0-Foil-c; no c-price, giveaway; Adams plot		1.00	2.50
1-3-Bagged w/card: 1-Gatefold-c by Nebres; Adams plot. 2-Fold-out-c; Adams plot. 3-Indestructible-c		1.00	2.50
4-7-Embossed-c: 4-Adams/Nebres-c; Adams part-i. 5-Sienkiewicz-i. 6-Adams part-i. 7-Adams-c(p); Adams plot		1.00	2.50

MEGATON (A super hero)
Nov, 1983; No. 2, Oct, 1985 - No. 8, Aug, 1987 (B&W)
Megaton Publ. (#3: 44 pgs.; #4: 52 pgs.)

1-($2.00, 68 pgs.)-Erik Larsen's 1st pro work; Vanguard by Larsen begins (1st app.), ends #4; 1st app. Megaton, Berzerker, & Ethrian; Guice-c/a(p); Gustovich-a(p) in #1,2	2.30	5.80	14.00
2-($2.00, 68 pgs.)-The Dragon cameo (1 pg.) by Larsen (later The Savage Dragon in Image Comics); Guice-c/a(p)	1.70	4.20	10.00
3-1st full app. Savage Dragon-c/story by Larsen; 1st comic book work by Angel Medina (pin-up)	2.90	8.60	20.00
4-2nd full app. Savage Dragon by Larsen; 4,5-Wildman by Grass Green	2.20	5.40	13.00
5-1st Liefeld published-a (inside f/c, 6/86)	1.00	2.50	6.00
6,7: 6-Larsen-c		1.20	3.00

Melting Pot #1 © Kitchen Sink

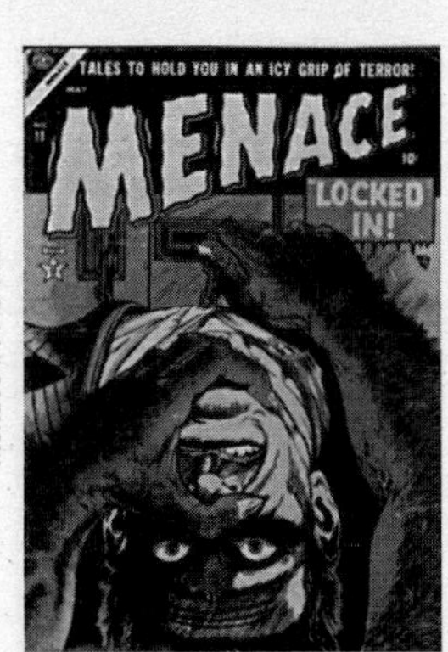

TALES TO HOLD YOU IN AN ICY GRIP OF TERROR!
MENACE
LOCKED IN!

Menace #11 © MEG

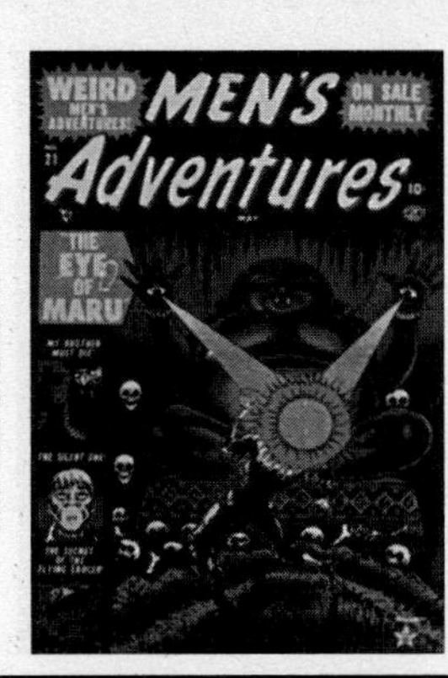

WEIRD
MEN'S Adventures
ON SALE MONTHLY
THE EYE OF MARU

Men's Adventures #21 © MEG

	GD25	FN65	NM94
8-1st Liefeld story-a (7 pg. super hero story) plus 1 pg. Youngblood ad		1.60	4.00
...Explosion (6/87, 16 pg. color giveaway)-1st app. Youngblood by Rob Liefeld (2 pg. spread); shows Megaton heroes	3.60	10.70	25.00
...Holiday Special 1 (1994, $2.95, color, 40 pgs., publ. by Entity Comics)-Gold foil logo; bagged w/Kelley Jones card; Vanguard, Megaton plus shows unpublished-c to 1987 Youngblood #1 by Liefeld/Ordway	1.20	3.00	

NOTE: *Copies of Megaton Explosion were also released in early 1992 all signed by Rob Liefeld and were made available to retailers.*

MEGATON MAN (See Don Simpson's Bizarre Heroes)
Nov, 1984 - No. 10, 1986
Kitchen Sink Enterprises

	GD25	FN65	NM94
1-10		.80	2.00
1-2nd printing (1989)		.80	2.00
...Meets The Uncategorizable X-Thems 1 (4/89, $2.00)		.80	2.00

MEL ALLEN SPORTS COMICS (The Voice of the Yankees)
No. 5, Nov, 1949; No. 6, June, 1950
Standard Comics

	GD25	FN65	NM94
5(#1 on inside)-Tuska-a	14.00	43.00	100.00
6(#2)-Lou Gehrig story	10.00	30.00	70.00

MELTING POT
Dec, 1993 - Present ($2.95, color)
Kitchen Sink Press

	GD25	FN65	NM94
1-3-By Eastman/Talbot/Bisley; Bisley-painted-c		1.20	3.00

MELVIN MONSTER (See Peter, the Little Pest)
Apr-June, 1965 - No. 10, Oct, 1969
Dell Publishing Co.

	GD25	FN65	NM94
1-By John Stanley	14.00	43.00	100.00
2-10-All by Stanley. #10-r/#1	10.00	30.00	70.00

MELVIN THE MONSTER (Dexter The Demon #7)
July, 1956 - No. 6, July, 1957
Atlas Comics (HPC)

	GD25	FN65	NM94
1-Maneely-c/a	9.15	27.50	55.00
2-6: 4-Maneely-c/a	6.35	19.00	38.00

MEMORIES (Epic Comics)(Value: cover or less)

MENACE
March, 1953 - No. 11, May, 1954
Atlas Comics (HPC)

	GD25	FN65	NM94
1-Horror & sci/fi stories begin; Everett-c/a	34.00	103.00	240.00
2-Post-atom bomb disaster by Everett; anti-Communist propaganda/torture scenes; Sinnott sci/fi story "Rocket to the Moon"	22.00	65.00	150.00
3,4,6-Everett-a. 4-Sci/fi story "Escape to the Moon". 6-Romita sci/fi story "Science Fiction"	16.50	50.00	115.00
5-Origin & 1st app. The Zombie by Everett (reprinted in Tales of the Zombie #1)(7/53); 5-Sci/fi story "Rocket Ship"	25.00	75.00	175.00
7,8,10,11: 7-Frankenstein story. 8-End of world story; Heath 3-D art(3 pgs.). 10-H-Bomb panels	13.00	40.00	90.00
9-Everett-a r-in Vampire Tales #1	15.00	45.00	105.00

NOTE: ***Brodsky** c-7, 8, 11. **Colan** a-6; c-9. **Everett** a-1-6, 9; c-1-6. **Heath** a-1-8; c-10. **Katz** a-11. **Maneely** a-3, 5, 7-9. **Powell** a-11. **Romita** a-3, 6, 8, 11. **Shelly** a-10. **Shores** a-7. **Sinnott** a-2, 7. **Tuska** a-1, 2, 5.*

MEN AGAINST CRIME (Formerly Mr. Risk; Hand of Fate #8 on)
No. 3, Feb, 1951 - No. 7, Oct, 1951
Ace Magazines

	GD25	FN65	NM94
3-Mr. Risk app.	6.35	19.00	38.00
4-7: 4-Colan-a; entire book-r as Trapped! #4	4.00	11.00	22.00

MEN, GUNS, & CATTLE (See Classics Illustrated Special Issue)

MEN IN ACTION (Battle Brady #10 on)
April, 1952 - No. 9, Dec, 1952 (War stories)
Atlas Comics (IPS)

	GD25	FN65	NM94
1-Berg, Reinman-a	9.15	27.50	55.00
2	5.00	15.00	30.00
3-6,8,9: 3-Heath-c/a	4.00	11.00	22.00
7-Krigstein-a; Heath-c	6.70	20.00	40.00

NOTE: ***Brodsky** c-1, 4-6. **Maneely** c-5. **Pakula** a-1, 6. **Robinson** c-8. **Shores** c-9.*

MEN IN ACTION
April, 1957 - No. 9, 1958
Ajax/Farrell Publications

	GD25	FN65	NM94
1	5.85	17.50	35.00
2	4.00	10.00	20.00
3-9	3.20	8.00	16.00

MEN INTO SPACE (See 4-Color No. 1083)

MEN OF BATTLE (Also see New Men of Battle)
V1#5, March, 1943 (Hardcover)
Catechetical Guild

	GD25	FN65	NM94
V1#5-Topix reprints	3.00	7.50	15.00

MEN OF COURAGE
1949
Catechetical Guild

	GD25	FN65	NM94
Bound Topix comics-V7#2,4,6,8,10,16,18,20	3.00	7.50	15.00

MEN OF WAR
August, 1977 - No. 26, March, 1980 (#9,10: 44 pgs.)
DC Comics, Inc.

	GD25	FN65	NM94
1-Enemy Ace, Gravedigger (origin #1,2) begin		.80	2.00
2-26: 9-Unknown Soldier app.			1.00

NOTE: ***Chaykin** a-9, 10, 12-14, 19, 20. **Evans** c-25. **Kubert** c-2-23, 24p, 26.*

MEN'S ADVENTURES (Formerly True Adventures)
No. 4, Aug, 1950 - No. 28, July, 1954
Marvel/Atlas Comics (CCC)

	GD25	FN65	NM94
4(#1)(52 pgs.)	17.00	52.00	120.00
5-Flying Saucer story	10.00	30.00	65.00
6-8: 7-Buried alive story. 8-Sci/fic story	8.35	25.00	50.00
9-20: All war format	5.35	16.00	32.00
21,22,24-26: All horror format. 25-Shrunken head-c	7.50	22.50	45.00
23-Crandall-a; Fox-a(i); horror format	9.15	27.50	55.00
27,28-Human Torch & Toro-c/stories; Captain America & Sub-Mariner stories in each (also see Young Men #24-28)	54.00	160.00	375.00

NOTE: ***Ayers** a-27(H. Torch). **Berg** a-15, 16. **Brodsky** c-4-9, 11, 12, 16-18, 24. **Burgos** c-27, 28(Human Torch). **Colan** a-14, 19. **Everett** a-10, 14, 22, 25, 28; c-14, 21-23. **Heath** a-8, 11, 24; c-13, 20, 26. **Lawrence** a-23; 27(Captain America). **Maneely** a-24; c-10, 15. **Mac Pakula** a-15, 25. **Post** a-23. **Powell** a-27(Sub-Mariner). **Reinman** a-11, 12. **Robinson** c-19. **Romita** a-22. **Shores** c-25. **Sinnott** a-21. **Tuska** a-24. Adventure-#4-8; War-#9-20; Weird/Horror-#21-26.*

MEN WHO MOVE THE NATION
(Giveaway) (Black & White)
Publisher unknown

	GD25	FN65	NM94
nn-Neal Adams-a	4.00	10.00	20.00

MEPHISTO VS... (See Silver Surfer #3)
Apr, 1987 - No. 4, July, 1987 ($1.50, mini-series)
Marvel Comics Group

	GD25	FN65	NM94
1-Fantastic Four; Austin-i			1.50
2-4: 2-X-Factor. 3-X-Men. 4-Avengers			1.50

MERC (See Mark Hazzard: Merc)

MERCHANTS OF DEATH (Acme Press (Eclipse))(Value: cover or less)

MERCY
1993 ($5.95, mature readers, 68 pgs.)
DC Comics (Vertigo)

	GD25	FN65	NM94
nn	1.00	2.50	6.00

MERLIN JONES AS THE MONKEY'S UNCLE (See Movie Comics and The Misadventures of... under Movie Comics)

MERRILL'S MARAUDERS (See Movie Classics)

MERRY CHRISTMAS (See A Christmas Adventure, Donald Duck..., Dell Giant #39, &

Metal Men #1 © DC

Metamorpho #10 © DC

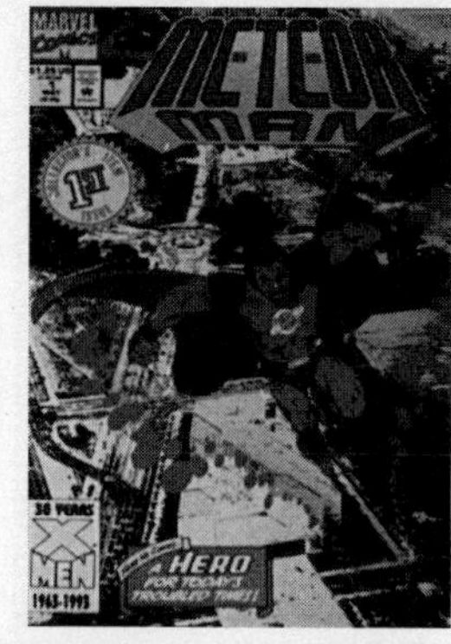

Meteor Man #1 © MEG

	GD25	FN65	NM94

March of Comics #153)

MERRY CHRISTMAS, A
1948 (Giveaway)
K. K. Publications (Child Life Shoes)

nn	4.00	12.00	24.00

MERRY CHRISTMAS
1956 (7-1/4x5-1/4")
K. K. Publications (Blue Bird Shoes Giveaway)

nn	1.80	4.50	9.00

MERRY CHRISTMAS FROM MICKEY MOUSE
1939 (16 pgs.) (Color & B&W)
K. K. Publications (Shoe store giveaway)

nn-Donald Duck & Pluto app.; text with art (Rare); c-reprint/Mickey Mouse Mag. V3#3 (12/37)(Rare)	80.00	240.00	800.00

MERRY CHRISTMAS FROM SEARS TOYLAND
1939 (16 pgs.) (Color)
Sears Roebuck Giveaway

nn-Dick Tracy, Little Orphan Annie, The Gumps, Terry & the Pirates	22.00	65.00	150.00

MERRY COMICS
December, 1945 (No cover price)
Carlton Publishing Co.

nn-Boogeyman app.	13.00	40.00	90.00

MERRY COMICS
1947
Four Star Publications

1	10.00	30.00	60.00

MERRY-GO-ROUND COMICS
1944 (25¢, 132 pgs.); 1946; 9-10/47 - No. 2, 1948
LaSalle Publ. Co./Croyden Publ./Rotary Litho.

nn(1944)(LaSalle)-Funny animal; 29 new features	12.00	36.00	85.00
21	4.70	14.00	28.00
1(1946)(Croyden)-Al Fago-c; funny animal	7.50	22.50	45.00
V1#1,2(1947-48; 52 pgs.)(Rotary Litho. Co. Ltd., Canada); Ken Hultgren-a	5.00	15.00	30.00

MERRY MAILMAN (See Fawcett's Funny Animals #87-89)

MERRY MOUSE (Also see Funny Tunes & Space Comics)
June, 1953 - No. 4, Jan-Feb, 1954
Avon Periodicals

1-1st app.; funny animal; Frank Carin-c/a	5.85	17.50	35.00
2-4	4.00	10.00	20.00

META-4 (First)(Value: cover or less)

METAL MEN (See Brave & the Bold, DC Comics Presents, and Showcase)
4-5/63 - No. 41, 12-1/69-70; No. 42, 2-3/73 - No. 44, 7-8/73; No. 45, 4-5/76 - No. 56, 2-3/78
National Periodical Publications/DC Comics

Showcase #37 (3-4/62)-1st app. Metal Men	59.00	178.00	475.00
Showcase #38 (5-6/62)-2nd app. Metal Men	45.00	135.00	360.00
Showcase #39 (7-8/62)-3rd app. Metal Men	34.00	103.00	275.00
Showcase #40 (9-10/62)-4th app.Metal Men	32.00	96.00	255.00
1-(4-5/63)-5th app. Metal Men	53.00	159.00	370.00
2	17.00	51.00	120.00
3-5	11.00	34.00	80.00
6-10	7.00	21.00	50.00
11-20: 12-Beatles cameo (12/65)	5.00	15.00	35.00
21-26,28-30: 21-Batman, Robin & Flash x-over	3.60	11.00	25.00
27-Origin Metal Men retold	6.50	19.00	45.00
31-41(1968-70): 38-Last 12¢ issue. 41-Last 15¢	2.90	8.60	20.00
42-44(1973)-Reprints	1.65	4.70	11.00
45('76)-49-Simonson-a in all: 48,49-Re-intro Eclipso	1.65	4.70	11.00
50-56: 50-Part-r. 54,55-Green Lantern x-over	1.65	4.70	11.00

NOTE: ***Andru/Esposito** c-1-29. **Aparo** c-53-56. **Giordano** c-45, 46. **Kane** a-30, 31p; c-31. **Simonson** a-45-49; c-47-52. **Staton** a-50-56.*

METAL MEN
Oct, 1993 - No. 4, Jan, 1994 ($1.25, mini-series)
DC Comics

1-($2.50)-Multi-colored foil-c		1.00	2.50
2-4: 2-Origin			1.25

METAMORPHO (See Action Comics #413, Brave & the Bold, 1st Issue Special, & World's Finest #217)
July-Aug, 1965 - No. 17, Mar-Apr, 1968 (All 12¢ issues)
National Periodical Publications

Brave and the Bold #57 (12-1/64-65)-Origin & 1st app. Metamorpho by Ramona Fraden	15.00	45.00	105.00
Brave and the Bold #58 (2-3/65)-2nd app.	7.00	21.00	48.00
1-(7-8/65)-3rd app. Metamorpho	10.00	30.00	70.00
2,3	5.70	17.00	40.00
4-6	3.60	10.70	25.00
7-9	2.90	8.60	20.00
10-Origin & 1st app. Element Girl (1-2/67)	3.60	11.00	25.00
11-17	2.10	6.00	15.00

NOTE: ***Ramona Fraden** a-B&B 57, 58, 1-4. **Orlando** a-5, 6; c-5-9, 11. **Sal Trapani** a-7-16.*

METAMORPHO
Aug, 1993 - No. 4, Nov, 1993 ($1.50, mini-series)
DC Comics

1-4			1.50

METAPHYSIQUE (Norm Breyfogle's...)(Eclipse)(Value: cover or less)

METEOR COMICS
November, 1945
L. L. Baird (Croyden)

1-Captain Wizard, Impossible Man, Race Wilkins app.; origin Baldy Bean, Capt. Wizard's sidekick; bare-breasted mermaids story	24.00	72.00	165.00

METEOR MAN
Aug, 1993 - No. 6, Jan, 1994 ($1.25, limited series)
Marvel Comics

1-6: 1-Polybagged w/button & rap newspaper. 4-Night Thrasher-c/story. 6-Terry Austin-c(i)			1.25

METROPOL (See Ted McKeever's...)

MEZZ: GALACTIC TOUR 2494
May, 1994 ($2.50)
Dark Horse Comics

1		1.00	2.50

MGM'S MARVELOUS WIZARD OF OZ (See Marvel Treasury of Oz)
1975 ($1.50, 84 pgs.; oversize)
Marvel Comics Group/National Periodical Publications

1-Adaptation of MGM's movie; J. Buscema-a		1.60	4.00

M.G.M'S MOUSE MUSKETEERS (Formerly M.G.M.'s The Two Mouseketeers)
No. 670, Jan, 1956 - No. 1290, Mar-May, 1962
Dell Publishing Co.

4-Color 670 (#4)	3.60	9.00	18.00
4-Color 711,728,764	2.80	7.00	14.00
8 (4-6/57) - 21 (3-5/60)	2.40	6.00	12.00
4-Color 1135,1175,1290	2.80	7.00	14.00

M.G.M.'S SPIKE AND TYKE
No. 499, Sept, 1953 - No. 1266, Dec-Feb, 1961-62
Dell Publishing Co.

4-Color 499 (#1)	3.60	9.00	18.00
4-Color 577,638	2.80	7.00	14.00
4(12-2/55-56)-10	2.40	6.00	12.00

Mickey Finn #10 © EAS

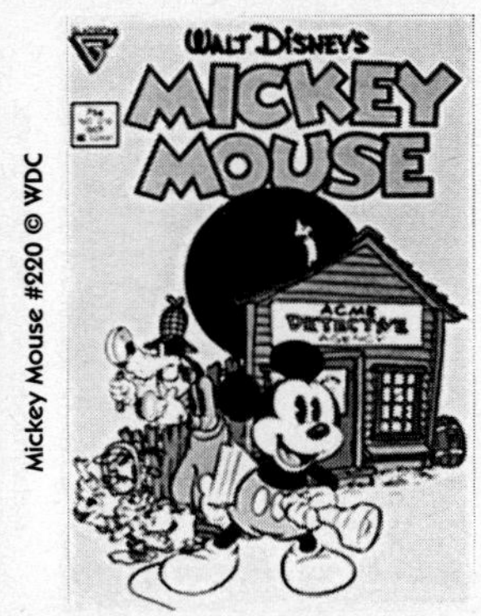

Mickey Mouse #220 © WDC

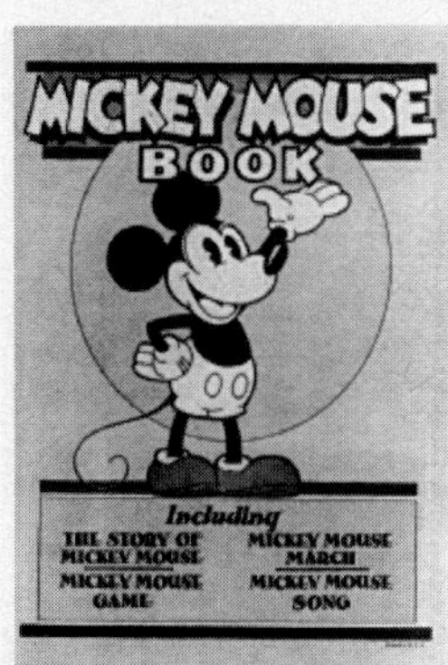

Mickey Mouse Book (1930) © WDC

GD25 FN65 NM94

11-24(12-2/60-61) 2.00 5.00 10.00
4-Color 1266 2.40 6.00 12.00

M.G.M.'S THE TWO MOUSKETEERS (See 4-Color 475, 603, 642)

MICHAELANGELO CHRISTMAS SPECIAL (See Teenage Mutant Ninja Turtles Christmas Special)

MICHAELANGELO, TEENAGE MUTANT NINJA TURTLE
1986 (One shot) ($1.50, B&W)
Mirage Studios
1 1.40 4.00 10.00
1-2nd printing ('89, $1.75)-Reprint plus new-a 1.20 3.00

MICKEY AND DONALD (See Walt Disney's...)

MICKEY AND DONALD IN VACATIONLAND (See Dell Giant No. 47)

MICKEY & THE BEANSTALK (See Story Hour Series)

MICKEY & THE SLEUTH (See Walt Disney Showcase #38, 39, 42)

MICKEY FINN (Also see Big Shot Comics #74 & Feature Funnies)
Nov?, 1942 - V3#2, May, 1952
Eastern Color 1-4/McNaught Synd. #5 on (Columbia)/Headline V3#2
1 24.00 72.00 165.00
2 11.50 34.00 80.00
3-Charlie Chan story 9.15 27.50 55.00
4 7.00 21.00 42.00
5-10 5.00 15.00 30.00
11-15(1949): 12-Sparky Watts app. 4.00 11.00 22.00
V3#1,2(1952) 3.20 87.00 16.00

MICKEY MANTLE (See Baseball's Greatest Heroes #1)**MICKEY MOUSE**

MICKEY MOUSE (See The Best of Walt Disney Comics, Cheerios giveaways, Donald Donald and ..., Dynabrite Comics, 40 Big Pages..., Gladstone Comic Album, Merry Christmas From..., Walt Disney's Mickey and Donald, Walt Disney's Comics & Stories, Walt Disney's..., & Wheaties)

MICKEY MOUSE (...Secret Agent #107-109; Walt Disney's... #148-205?)
(See Dell Giants for annuals)
#16, 1941 - #84, 7-9/62; #85, 11/62 - #218, 7/84; #219, 10/86 - #256, 4/90
Dell Publ. Co./Gold Key #85-204/Whitman #205-218/Gladstone #219 on

GD25 FN65 VF82
4-Color 16(1941)-1st Mickey Mouse comic book; "...vs. the Phantom Blot" by Gottfredson 600.00 1800.00 6000.00
(Estimated up to 200 total copies exist, 5 in VF-NM)

GD25 FN65 NM94
4-Color 27(1943)- "7 Colored Terror" 86.00 257.00 600.00
4-Color 79(1945)-By Carl Barks (1 story) 114.00 343.00 800.00
4-Color 116(1946) 24.00 72.00 165.00
4-Color 141,157(1947) 21.00 63.00 145.00
4-Color 170,181,194('48) 17.00 52.00 120.00
4-Color 214('49),231,248,261 14.00 43.00 100.00
4-Color 268-Reprints/WDC&S #22-24 by Gottfredson ("Surprise Visitor") 14.00 43.00 100.00
4-Color 279,286,296 11.50 34.00 80.00
4-Color 304,313(#1),325(#2),334 9.15 27.50 55.00
4-Color 343,352,362,371,387 7.50 22.50 45.00
4-Color 401,411,427(10-11/52) 5.35 16.00 32.00
4-Color 819-Mickey Mouse in Magicland 4.00 12.00 24.00
4-Color 1057,1151,1246(1959-61)-Album 4.00 10.00 20.00
28(12-1/52-53)-32,34 3.60 9.00 18.00
33-(Exists with 2 dates, 10-11/53 & 12-1/54) 3.60 9.00 18.00
35-50 2.00 6.00 14.00
51-73,75-80 1.70 4.20 10.00
74-Story swipe "The Rare Stamp Search" from 4-Color #422- "The Gilded Man" 2.00 6.00 14.00
81-99: 93,95-titled "Mickey Mouse Club Album" 1.70 4.20 10.00
100-105: Reprint 4-Color #427,194,279,170,343,214 in that order 1.70 5.00 12.00
106-120 1.70 4.20 10.00
121-130 1.20 2.90 7.00
131-146 1.00 2.50 6.00
147,148: 147-Reprints "The Phantom Fires" from WDC&S #200-202.148-Reprints "The Mystery of Lonely Valley" from WDC&S #208-210 1.00 2.50 6.00
149-158 1.60 4.00
159-Reprints "The Sunken City" from WDC&S #205-207 1.00 2.00 5.00
160-170: 162-170-r 1.40 3.50
171-178,180-218: 200-r/Four Color #371 1.50
179-(52 pgs.) 1.50
219-1st Gladstone issue; The Seven Ghosts serial-r begins by Gottfredson 1.60 4.00
220,221 1.20 3.00
222-225: 222-Editor-in Grief strip-r 1.00 2.50
226-230 1.50
231-243,245-254: 240-r/March of Comics #27. 245-r/F.C. #279. 250-r/ F.C. #248 1.00
244 (1/89, $2.95, 100 pgs.)-Squarebound 60th anniversary issue; gives history of Mickey 1.20 3.00
255,256 ($1.95, 68 pgs.) .80 2.00
NOTE: *Reprints #195-197, 198(2/3), 199(1/3), 200-208, 211(1/2), 212, 213, 215(1/3), 216-on.* ***Gottfredson** Mickey Mouse serials in #219-239, 241-244, 246-249, 251-253, 255.*
Album 01-518-210(Dell), 1(10082-309)(9/63-Gold Key) 2.40 6.00 12.00
...& Goofy "Bicep Bungle"(1952, 16 pgs., 3-1/4x7") Fritos giveaway, soft-c (also see Donald Duck & Ludwig Von Drake) 4.70 14.00 28.00
...& Goofy Explore Business(1978) 1.50
...& Goofy Explore Energy(1976-1978, 36 pgs.); Exxon giveaway in color; regular size 1.50
...& Goofy Explore Energy Conservation(1976-1978)-Exxon 1.50
...& Goofy Explore The Universe of Energy(1985, 20 pgs.); Exxon giveaway in color; regular size 1.50
...Club 1(1/64-Gold Key)(TV) 4.00 10.00 20.00
Mini Comic 1(1976)(3-1/4x6-1/2")-Reprints 158 1.50
New Mickey Mouse Club Fun Book 11190 (Golden Press, 1977, $1.95, 224 pgs.) 1.20 3.00
The Perils of Mickey nn (1993, 5-1/4x7-1/4", 16 pgs.)-Nabisco giveaway w/ games, Nabisco coupons & 6 pgs. of stories; Phantom Blot app. 1.00
Surprise Party 1(30037-901, G.K.)(1/69)-40th Anniversary (see Walt Disney Showcase #47) 4.00 10.00 20.00
Surprise Party 1(1979)-r/1969 issue 1.00 2.50

MICKEY MOUSE ADVENTURES
June, 1990 - No. 18, Nov, 1991 ($1.50)
Disney Comics
1-18: 1-Bradbury, Murry-r/M.M. #45,73 plus new-a. 2-Begin all new stories. 8-Byrne-c. 9-Fantasia 50th ann. issue w/new adapt. of movie. 10-r/F.C. #214 1.50

MICKEY MOUSE BOOK
1930 (4 printings, 9"x12", stapled-c, 20 pgs.)
Bibo & Lang

nn-First Disney licensed publication in magazine format, despite "book" used in title. (see first book: Adventures of Mickey Mouse.) Story of how Mickey met Walt and got his name as "originated by Bobette Bibo, age 11 years." Contains music & lyrics to "Mickey Mouse (You Cute Little Feller)," written by Irving Bibo. Minnie, Clarabelle Cow, Horace Horsecollar and a caricature of Walt Disney shaking hands with Mickey Mouse appear. 4/15/30 Mickey strip by Win Smith appears on page 8 and the strip for 4/17/30 appears on the back cover of one of the printings.

NOTE: Most copies are missing pages 9 & 10 which contain a puzzle to be cut out. Ub Iwerks-c

GD25 FN65 VF82 NM94
1st-4th Prints (complete) 800.00 2400.00 5700.00 8000.00
(Estimated up to 75 total copies exist)
1st-4th Printings (pgs. 9&10 cut out, but not missing)

Mickey Mouse Magazine #6 © WDC

Mickey Mouse Magazine V2#1© WDC

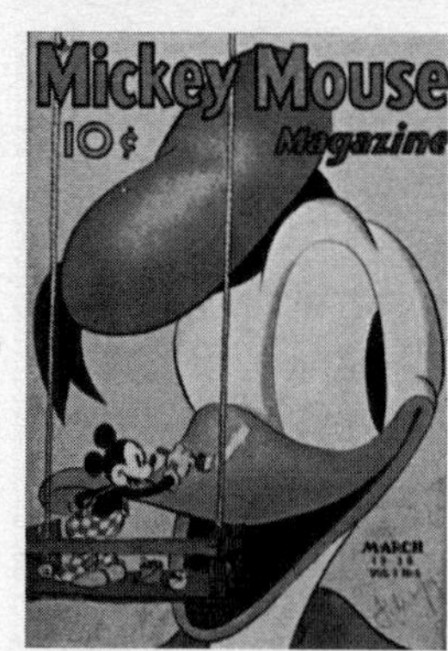

Mickey Mouse Magazine V3#6 © WDC

GD25 FN65 NM94

300.00 900.00 1950.00 3000.00
1st-4th Printings (pgs. 9&10 missing) 200.00 600.00 1300.00 2000.00

MICKEY MOUSE BOOK
ca. 1933-1934 (34 pgs., 10"x8-3/4", cardboard covers)
Whitman Publishing Co.

948-1932 & 1933 Sunday strips in color, printed from the same plates as Mickey Mouse Comic #3 by David McKay, but only pages 5-17 & 32-48 (including all of the "Wolf Barker" continuity) 130.00 385.00 900.00

NOTE: Some copies bound with back cover upside down. Variance doesn't affect value. Same art appears on front and back covers of all copies. Height of Whitman reissue of McKay book trimmed 1/2 inch.

MICKEY MOUSE CLUB MAGAZINE (See Walt Disney...)

MICKEY MOUSE CLUB SPECIAL (See The New Mickey Mouse...)

MICKEY MOUSE COMIC
1931 - No. 4, 1934 (52 Pgs., 10"x9-3/4", cardboard covers (later reprints exist)
David McKay Co.

1(1931)-Reprints Floyd Gottfredson daily strips in black & white from 1930 & 1931, including the famous two week sequence in which Mickey tries to commit suicide 180.00 535.00 1250.00
2(1932)-1st app. of Pluto reprinted from 7/8/31 daily. All pgs. from 1931 130.00 385.00 900.00
3(1933)-Reprints 1932 & 1933 Sunday pages in color, one strip per page, including the "Lair of Wolf Barker" continuity pencilled by Gottfredson and inked by Al Taliaferro &? First app. Mickey's nephews, Morty & Kerdie, one identified by name of Mortimer Fieldmouse, not to be confused with Uncle Mortimer Mouse who is introduced in the Wolf Barker story 180.00 535.00 1250.00
4(1934)-1931 dailies, include the only known reprint of the infamous strip of 2/4/31 where the villainous Kat Nipp snips off the end of Mickey's tail with a pair of scissors 107.00 321.00 750.00

MICKEY MOUSE COMICS DIGEST
1986 - No. 5, 1987 (96 pgs.)
Gladstone Publishing

	GD25	FN65	NM94
1-3 ($1.25)			1.25
4,5 ($1.50)			1.50

MICKEY MOUSE MAGAZINE
V1#1, Jan, 1933 - V1#9, Sept, 1933 (5-1/4x7-1/4")
No. 1-3 published by Kamen-Blair (Kay Kamen, Inc.)
Walt Disney Productions

GD25 FN65 VF82

(Scarce)-Distributed by dairies and leading stores through their local theatres. First few issues had 5¢ listed on cover, later ones had no price.

	GD25	FN65	VF82
V1#1	357.00	1071.00	2500.00
2-9	117.00	350.00	750.00

MICKEY MOUSE IN COLOR
1988 (Deluxe, 13"x17", hardcover, $250.00;
(Trade, 9-7/8"x11-1/2", hardcover, $39.95)
Another Rainbow/Pantheon

Deluxe limited edition of 3,000 copies signed by Floyd Gottfredson and Carl Barks, designated as the "Official Mickey Mouse 60th Anniversary" book. Mickey Sunday and daily reprints, plus Barks "Riddle of the Red Hat" from Four Color #79. Comes with 45 r.p.m. record interview with Gottfredson and Barks. 240 pgs. 36.00 107.00 250.00
Deluxe, limited to 100 copies, as above, but with a unique colored pencil original drawing of Mickey Mouse by Carl Barks. Add value of art to book price. 600.00
Pantheon trade edition, edited down & without Barks, 192 pgs. 5.50 17.00 40.00

MICKEY MOUSE MAGAZINE
V1#1, Nov, 1933 - V2#12, Oct, 1935
Mills giveaways issued by different dairies
Walt Disney Productions

	GD25	FN65	NM94
V1#1	86.00	257.00	600.00
2-12: 2-X-Mas issue	43.00	130.00	300.00
V2#1-12: 2-X-Mas issue. 4-St. Valentine-c	29.00	86.00	200.00

MICKEY MOUSE MAGAZINE (Becomes Walt Disney's Comics & Stories)
(No V3#1, V4#6)
Summer, 1935 (June-Aug, indicia) - V5#12, Sept, 1940
V1#1-5, V3#11,12, V4#1-3 are 44 pgs; V2#3-100 pgs; V5#12-68 pgs; rest are 36 pgs.
K. K. Publ./Western Publishing Co. GD25 FN65 VF82 NM94

V1#1 (Large size, 13-1/4x10-1/4"; 25¢)-Contains puzzles, games, cels, stories & comics of Disney characters. Promotional magazine for Disney cartoon movies and paraphernalia 900.00 2700.00 5850.00 9,000.00
(Estimated up to 100 total copies exist, 3 in NM/Mint)

Note: *Some copies were autographed by the editors & given away with all early one year subscriptions.*

GD25 FN65 VF82

2 (Size change, 11-1/2x8-1/2"; 10/35; 10¢)-High quality paper begins; Messmer-a 121.00 365.00 850.00
3,4: 3-Messmer-a 68.00 205.00 475.00
5-1st Donald Duck solo-c; last 44 pg. & high quality paper issue 79.00 236.00 550.00
6-9: 6-36 pg. issues begin; Donald becomes editor. 8-2nd Donald solo-c. 9-1st Mickey/Minnie-c 64.00 193.00 450.00
10-12, V2#1,2: 11-1st Pluto/Mickey-c; Donald fires himself and appoints Mickey as editor 61.00 182.00 425.00
V2#3-Special 100 pg. Christmas issue (25¢); Messmer-a; Donald becomes editor of Wise Quacks 257.00 771.00 1800.00
4-Mickey Mouse Comics & Roy Ranger (adventure strip) begin; both end V2#9; Messmer-a 54.00 160.00 375.00

GD25 FN65 NM94

5-Ted True (adventure strip, ends V2#9) & Silly Symphony Comics (ends V3#3) begin 43.00 130.00 300.00
6-9: 6-1st solo Minnie-c. 6-9-Mickey Mouse Movies cut-out in each 43.00 130.00 300.00
10-1st full color issue; Mickey Mouse (by Gottfredson; ends V3#12) & Silly Symphony (ends V3#3) full color Sunday-r, Peter The Farm Detective (ends V5#8) & Ole Of The North (ends V3#3) begins 64.00 193.00 450.00
11-13: 12-Hiawatha-c & feature story 43.00 130.00 300.00
V3#2-Big Bad Wolf Halloween-c 50.00 150.00 350.00
3 (12/37)-1st app. Snow White & The Seven Dwarfs (before release of movie)(possibly 1st in print); Mickey X-Mas-c 86.00 260.00 600.00
4 (1/38)-Snow White & The Seven Dwarfs serial begins (on stands before release of movie); Ducky Symphony (ends V3#11) begins 72.00 215.00 500.00
5-1st Snow White & Seven Dwarfs-c (St. Valentine's Day) 93.00 280.00 650.00
6-Snow White serial ends; Lonesome Ghosts app. (2 pp.) 50.00 150.00 350.00
7-Seven Dwarfs Easter-c 49.00 145.00 340.00
8-10: 9-Dopey-c. 10-1st solo Goofy-c 40.00 120.00 280.00
11,12 (44 pgs; 8 more pgs. color added). 11-Mickey the Sheriff serial (ends V4#3) & Donald Duck strip-r (ends V3#12) begin. Color feature on Snow White's Forest Friends 43.00 130.00 300.00
V4#1 (10/38; 44 pgs.)-Brave Little Tailor-c/feature story, nominated for Academy Award; Bobby & Chip by Otto Messmer (ends V4#2) & The Practical Pig (ends V4#2) begin 43.00 130.00 300.00
2 (44 pgs.)-1st Huey, Dewey & Louie-c 43.00 130.00 300.00
3 (12/38, 44 pgs.)-Ferdinand The Bull-c/feature story, Academy Award winner; Mickey Mouse & The Whalers serial begins, ends V4#12 43.00 130.00 300.00
4-Spotty, Mother Pluto strip-r begin, end V4#8 40.00 120.00 280.00
5-St. Valentine's day-c. 1st Pluto solo-c 47.00 141.00 330.00
7 (3/39)-The Ugly Duckling-c/feature story, Academy Award winner 43.00 130.00 300.00
7 (4/39)-Goofy & Wilbur The Grasshopper classic-c/feature story from 1st Goofy solo cartoon movie; Timid Elmer begins, ends V5#5

Micronauts #15 © MEG

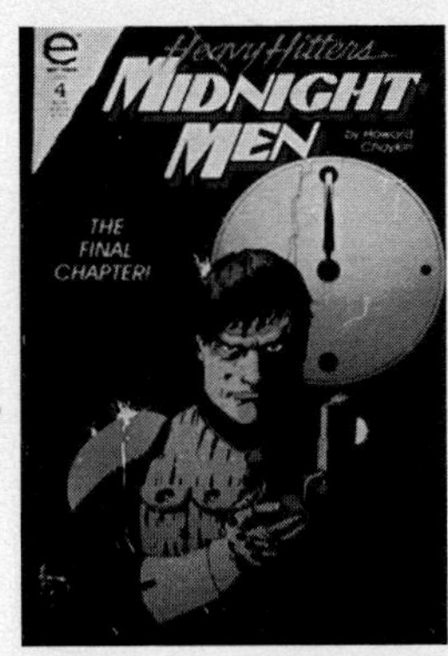

Midnight Men #4 © MEG

Midnight Son Unlimited #6 © MEG

	GD25	FN65	NM94
	43.00	130.00	300.00
8-Big Bad Wolf-c from Practical Pig movie poster; Practical Pig feature story	43.00	130.00	300.00
9-Donald Duck & Mickey Mouse Sunday-r begin; The Pointer feature story, nominated for Academy Award	43.00	130.00	300.00
10-Classic July 4th drum & fife-c; last Donald Sunday-r	54.00	160.00	375.00
11-1st slick-c; last over-sized issue	40.00	120.00	280.00
12 (9/39; format change, 10-1/4x8-1/4")-1st full color, cover to cover issue; Donald's Penguin-c/feature story	48.00	145.00	335.00
V5#1-Black Pete-c; Officer Duck-c/feature story; Autograph Hound feature story; Robinson Crusoe serial begins	48.00	145.00	335.00
2-Goofy-c; 1st app. Pinocchio (cameo)	64.00	195.00	450.00
3 (12/39)-Pinocchio Christmas-c (Before movie release). 1st app. Jiminy Cricket; Pinocchio serial begins	72.00	215.00	500.00
4,5: 5-Jiminy Cricket-c; Pinocchio serial ends; Donald's Dog Laundry feature story	48.00	145.00	335.00
6-Tugboat Mickey feature story; Rip Van Winkle feature begins, ends V5#8	47.00	140.00	325.00
7-2nd Huey, Dewey & Louie-c	47.00	140.00	325.00
8-Last magazine size issue; 2nd solo Pluto-c; Figaro & Cleo feature story	47.00	140.00	325.00
9 (6/40; change to comic book size)-Jiminy Cricket feature story; Donald-c & Sunday-r begin	52.00	155.00	360.00
10-Special Independence Day issue	52.00	155.00	360.00
11-Hawaiian Holiday & Mickey's Trailer feature stories; last 36 pg. issue	52.00	155.00	360.00
12 (Format change)-The transition issue (68 pgs.) becoming a comic book. With only a title change to follow, becomes Walt Disney's Comics & Stories #1 with the next issue	350.00	1070.00	2800.00
V4#1 (Giveaway)	36.00	107.00	250.00

NOTE: ***Otto Messmer**-a is in many issues of the first two-three years. The following story titles and issues have gags created by **Carl Barks:** V4#3(12/38)-'Donald's Better Self' & 'Donald's Golf Game;' V4#4(1/39)-'Donald's Lucky Day;' V4#7(3/39)-'Hockey Champ;' V4#7(4/39)-'Donald's Cousin Gus;' V4#9(6/39)-'Sea Scouts;' V4#12(9/39)-'Donald's Penguin;' V5#9 (6/40)-'Donald's Vacation;' V5#10(7/40)-'Bone Trouble;' V5#12(9/40)-'Window Cleaners.'*

MICKEY MOUSE MARCH OF COMICS
1947 - 1951 (Giveaway)
K. K. Publications

	GD25	FN65	NM94
8(1947)-32 pgs.	71.00	215.00	500.00
27(1948)	50.00	150.00	350.00
45(1949)	39.00	116.00	270.00
60(1950)	35.00	105.00	245.00
74(1951)	29.00	867.00	200.00

MICKEY MOUSE SUMMER FUN (See Dell Giants)

MICKEY MOUSE'S SUMMER VACATION (See Story Hour Series)

MICROBOTS, THE
December, 1971 (One Shot)
Gold Key

	GD25	FN65	NM94
1 (10271-112)	1.20	3.00	7.00

MICRONAUTS
Jan, 1979 - No. 59, Aug, 1984 (Mando paper #53 on)
Marvel Comics Group

	GD25	FN65	NM94
1-Intro/1st app. Baron Karza		.90	2.20
2-5			1.20
6-36,39-59: 7-Man-Thing app. 8-1st app. Capt. Universe (8/79). 9-1st app. Cilicia. 13-1st app. Jasmine. 15-Death of Microtron. 15-17-Fantastic Four app. 17-Death of Jasmine. 20-Ant-Man app. 21-Microverse series begins. 25-Origin Baron Karza. 25-29-Nick Fury app. 27-Death of Biotron. 34,35-Dr. Strange app. 35-Double size; origin Microverse; intro Death Squad. 40-Fantastic Four app. 57-(52 pgs.). 59-Golden painted-c			1.00
37-Nightcrawler app.; X-Men cameo (2 pgs.)		.80	2.00
38-First direct sale		.65	1.60
nn-Reprints #1-3; blank UPC; diamond on top			.40
Annual 1(12/79)-Ditko-c/a		1.00	2.50
Annual 2(10/80)-Ditko-c/a		.80	2.00

NOTE: *#38-on distributed only through comic shops. **N. Adams** c-7i. **Chaykin** a-13-18p. **Ditko** a-39p. **Giffen** a-36p, 37p(part). **Golden** a-1-12p; c-2-7p, 8-23, 24p, 38, 39, 59. **Guice** a-48-58p; c-49-58. **Gil Kane** a-38, 40-45p; c-40-45. **Layton** c-33-37. **Miller** c-31.*

MICRONAUTS (Marvel, 1984-86)(Value: cover or less)

MICRONAUTS SPECIAL EDITION (Marvel)(Value: cover or less)

MIDGET COMICS (Fighting Indian Stories)
Feb, 1950 - No. 2, Apr, 1950 (5-3/8x7-3/8", 68 pgs.)
St. John Publishng Co.

	GD25	FN65	NM94
1-Fighting Indian Stories; Matt Baker-c	10.00	30.00	70.00
2-Tex West, Cowboy Marshal (also in #1)	6.35	19.00	38.00

MIDNIGHT (See Smash Comics #18)

MIDNIGHT
April, 1957 - No. 6, June, 1958
Ajax/Farrell Publ. (Four Star Comic Corp.)

	GD25	FN65	NM94
1-Reprints from Voodoo & Strange Fantasy with some changes	9.15	27.50	55.00
2-6	5.00	15.00	30.00

MIDNIGHT EYE
1991 - No. 6, 1992 ($4.95, color, adults, 44 pgs.)
Viz Premiere Comics

	GD25	FN65	NM94
1-6: Japenese stories translated into English	1.00	2.00	5.00

MIDNIGHT MEN
June, 1993 - No. 4, Sept, 1993 ($1.95, mini-series)
Epic Comics (Marvel)

	GD25	FN65	NM94
1-($2.50)-Embossed-c; Chaykin-c/a & scripts in all		1.00	2.50
2-4		.80	2.00

MIDNIGHT MYSTERY
Jan-Feb, 1961 - No. 7, Oct, 1961
American Comics Group

	GD25	FN65	NM94
1-Sci/Fi story	10.00	30.00	60.00
2-7: 7-Gustavson-a	5.00	15.00	30.00

NOTE: ***Reinman** a-1, 3. **Whitney** a-1, 4-6; c-1-3, 5, 7.*

MIDNIGHT SONS UNLIMITED
Apr, 1993 - Present ($3.95, 68 pgs.)
Marvel Comics (Midnight Sons imprint #4 on)

	GD25	FN65	NM94
1-11: Blaze, Darkhold (by Quesada #1), Ghost Rider, Morbius & Nightstalkers in all. 1-Painted-c. 3-Spider-Man app. 4-Siege of Darkness part 17; new Dr. Strange & new Ghost Rider app.; spot varnish-c		1.60	4.00

MIDNIGHT TALES
Dec, 1972 - No. 18, May, 1976
Charlton Press

	GD25	FN65	NM94
V1#1		1.60	4.00
2-18: 11-14-Newton-a(p)		1.20	3.00
12,17(Modern Comics reprint, 1977)			1.00

NOTE: ***Adkins** a-12i, 13i. **Ditko** a-12. **Howard** (Wood imitator) a-1-15, 17, 18; c-1-18. **Don Newton** a-11-14p. **Staton** a-1, 3-11, 13. **Sutton** a-3-5, 7-10.*

MIGHTY ATOM, THE (...& the Pixies #6) (Formerly The Pixies #1-5)
No. 6, 1949; Nov, 1957 - No. 6, Aug-Sept, 1958
Magazine Enterprises

	GD25	FN65	NM94
6(1949-M.E.)-no month (1st Series)	4.35	13.00	26.00
1-6(2nd Series)-Pixies-r	2.80	7.00	14.00
I.W. Reprint #1(nd)	.40	1.00	2.00
Giveaway(1959, '63, Whitman)-Evans-a	1.60	4.00	8.00
Giveaway ('64r, '65r, '67r, '68r, '73r, '76r)-Evans-r?		.50	1.00

MIGHTY BEAR (Formerly Fun Comics; becomes Unsane #15)
No. 13, Jan, 1954 - No. 14, Mar, 1954; 9/57 - No. 3, 2/58
Star Publ. No. 13,14/Ajax-Farrell (Four Star)

	GD25	FN65	NM94
13,14-L. B. Cole-c	8.35	25.00	50.00

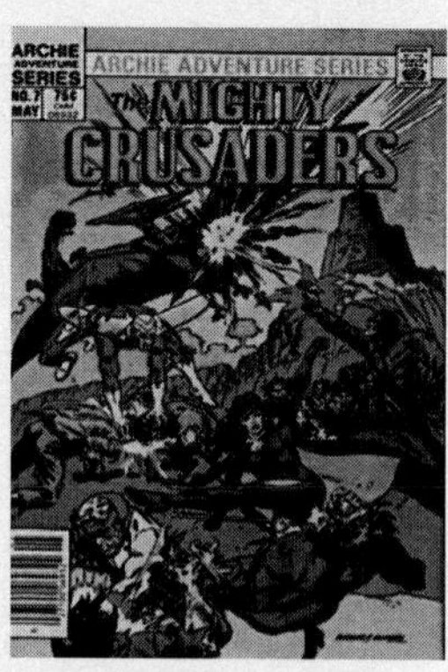

Mighty Crusaders #7 © AP

Mighty Midget Comics: Balbo © Lowe & Co.

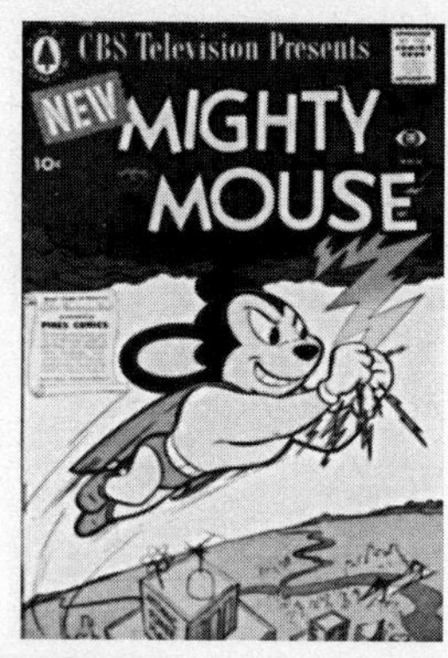

Mighty Mouse #72 © Viacom

GD25 FN65 NM94

1-3('57-58)Four Star; becomes Mighty Ghost #4 — 4.00 10.00 20.00

MIGHTY COMICS (...Presents) (Formerly Flyman)
No. 40, Nov, 1966 - No. 50, Oct, 1967 (All 12¢ issues)
Radio Comics (Archie)

40-Web — 1.90 6.00 13.00
41-50: 41-Shield, Black Hood. 42-Black Hood. 43-Shield, Web & Black Hood. 44-Black Hood, Steel Sterling & The Shield. 45-Shield & Hangman; origin Web retold. 46-Steel Sterling, Web & Black Hood. 47-Black Hood & Mr. Justice. 48-Shield & Hangman; Wizard x-over in Shield. 49-Steel Sterling & Fox; Black Hood x-over in Steel Sterling. 50-Black Hood & Web; Inferno x-over in Web — 1.60 5.00 11.00
NOTE: ***Paul Reinman** a-40-50.*

MIGHTY CRUSADERS, THE (Also see Adventures of the Fly, The Crusaders & Fly Man)
Nov, 1965 - No. 7, Oct, 1966 (All 12¢ issues)
Mighty Comics Group (Radio Comics)

1-Origin The Shield — 4.00 12.00 28.00
2-Origin Comet — 2.15 6.50 15.00
3-Origin Fly-Man — 1.85 5.50 13.00
4-1st S.A. app. Fireball, Inferno & Fox; Firefly, Web, Bob Phantom, Blackjack, Hangman, Zambini, Kardak, Steel Sterling, Mr. Justice, Wizard, Capt. Flag, Jaguar x-over — 2.40 7.25 17.00
5-Intro. Ultra-Men (Fox, Web, Capt. Flag) & Terrific Three (Jaguar, Mr. Justice, Steel Sterling) — 1.85 5.50 13.00
6,7: 7-Steel Sterling feature; origin Fly-Girl — 1.85 5.50 13.00
NOTE: ***Reinman** a-6.*

MIGHTY CRUSADERS, THE (All New Advs. of...#2)
Mar, 1983 - No. 13, Sept, 1985 ($1.00, 36 pgs, Mando paper)
Red Circle Prod./Archie Ent. No. 6 on

1-13: 1-Origin Black Hood, The Fly, Fly Girl, The Shield, The Wizard, The Jaguar, Pvt. Strong & The Web. 2-Mister Midnight begins. 4-Darkling replaces Shield. 5-Origin Jaguar, Shield begins. 7-Untold origin Jaguar — 1.00
NOTE: ***Buckler** a-1-3, 4i, 5p, 7p, 8i, 9i; c-1-10p.*

MIGHTY GHOST (Formerly Mighty Bear #1-3)
No. 4, June, 1958
Ajax/Farrell Publ.

4 — 3.20 8.00 16.00

MIGHTY HERCULES, THE (TV)
July, 1963 - No. 2, Nov, 1963
Gold Key

1,2(10072-307, 10072-311) — 12.00 36.00 85.00

MIGHTY HEROES, THE (TV) (Funny)
Mar, 1967 - No. 4, July, 1967
Dell Publishing Co.

1-Also has a 1957 Heckle & Jeckle-r — 11.00 33.00 78.00
2-4: 4-Has two 1958 Mighty Mouse-r — 8.70 26.00 52.00

MIGHTY HEROES
1987 (B&W, one-shot)
Spotlight Comics

1-Heckle & Jeckle backup — 1.00

MIGHTY MARVEL WESTERN, THE
Oct, 1968 - No. 46, Sept, 1976 (#1-14: 68 pgs.; #15,16: 52 pgs.)
Marvel Comics Group (LMC earlier issues)

1-Begin Kid Colt, Rawhide Kid, Two-Gun Kid-r — 1.30 3.10 7.50
2-10 — 1.30 3.25
11-20 — .90 2.25
21-46: 24-Kid Colt-r end. 25-Matt Slade-r begin. 31-Baker-r. 32-Origin-r/ Rawhide Kid #23; Williamson-r/Kid Slade #7. 37-Williamson, Kirby-r/ Two-Gun Kid 51 — 1.40
NOTE: ***Jack Davis** a(r)-21-24. **Keller** r-1, 22. **Kirby** a(r)-1-3, 6, 9, 12, 14, 16, 26, 29, 32, 36, 41, 43, 44; c-29. **Maneely** a(r)-22. No Matt Slade-#43.*

GD25 FN65 NM94

MIGHTY MIDGET COMICS, THE (Miniature)
No date; circa 1942-1943 (36 pgs.) (Approx. 5x4")
(Black & White & Red) (Sold 2 for 5¢)
Samuel E. Lowe & Co.

Bulletman #11(1943)-r/cover/Bulletman #3 — 10.00 30.00 65.00
Captain Marvel Adventures #11 — 10.00 30.00 65.00

GD25 FN65 –

Captain Marvel #11 (Same as above except for full color ad on back cover; this issue was glued to cover of Captain Marvel #20 and is not found in fine-mint condition) — 225.00 675.00 –

GD25 FN65 NM94

Captain Marvel Jr. #11 (Same-c as Master #27 — 10.00 30.00 65.00

GD25 FN65 –

Captain Marvel Jr. #11 (Same as above except for full color ad on back-c; this issue was glued to cover of Captain Marvel #21 and is not found in fine-mint condition) — 225.00 675.00 –

GD25 FN65 NM94

Golden Arrow #11 — 9.15 27.50 55.00
Ibis the Invincible #11(1942)-Origin; reprints cover to Ibis #1 — 10.00 30.00 65.00
Spy Smasher #11(1942) — 10.00 30.00 65.00
NOTE: *The above books came in a box called "box full of books" and was distributed with other Samuel Lowe puzzles, paper dolls, coloring books, etc. They are not titled Mighty Midget Comics. All have a war bond seal on back cover which is otherwise blank. These books came in a "Mighty Midget" flat cardboard counter display rack.*
Balbo, the Boy Magician #12 — 4.20 12.50 25.00
Bulletman #12 — 9.15 27.50 55.00
Commando Yank #12 — 5.85 17.50 35.00
Dr. Voltz the Human Generator — 4.20 12.50 25.00
Lance O'Casey #12 — 4.20 12.50 25.00
Leatherneck the Marine — 4.20 12.50 25.00
Minute Man #12 — 9.15 27.50 55.00
Mister "Q" — 4.20 12.50 25.00
Mr. Scarlet and Pinky #12 — 7.50 22.50 45.00
Pat Wilton and His Flying Fortress — 4.20 12.50 25.00
The Phantom Eagle #12 — 5.00 15.00 30.00
State Trooper Stops Crime — 4.20 12.50 25.00
Tornado Tom; r-/from Cyclone #1-3; origin — 4.35 13.00 26.00

MIGHTY MOUSE (See Adventures of..., Dell Giant #43, Giant Comics Edition, March of Comics #205, 237, 247, 257, 447, 459, 471, 483, Oxydol-Dreft, Paul Terry's, & Terry-Toons Comics)

MIGHTY MOUSE (1st Series)
Fall, 1946 - No. 4, Summer, 1947
Timely/Marvel Comics (20th Century Fox)

1 — 86.00 257.00 600.00
2 — 43.00 130.00 300.00
3,4 — 30.00 90.00 210.00

MIGHTY MOUSE (2nd Series) (Paul Terry's... #62-71)
Aug, 1947 - No. 67, 11/55; No. 68, 3/56 - No. 83, 6/59
St. John Publishing Co./Pines No. 68 (3/56) on (TV issues #72 on)

5(#1) — 29.00 86.00 200.00
6-10 — 15.00 45.00 105.00
11-19 — 10.00 30.00 60.00
20 (11/50) - 25-(52 pg. editions) — 8.35 25.00 50.00
20-25-(36 pg. editions) — 7.00 21.00 42.00
26-37: 35-Flying saucer-c — 5.85 17.50 35.00
38-45-(100 pgs.) — 13.50 41.00 95.00
46-83: 62-64,67-Painted-c. 82-Infinity-c — 5.35 16.00 32.00
Album 1(10/52, 25¢, 100 pgs., St. John)-Gandy Goose app. — 22.00 67.00 155.00
Album 2,3(11/52 & 12/52, St. John) (100 pgs.) — 17.00 52.00 120.00
Fun Club Magazine 1(Fall, 1957-Pines, 25¢, 100 pgs.) (CBS TV)-Tom Terrific, Heckle & Jeckle, Dinky Duck, Gandy Goose — 13.00 40.00 90.00
Fun Club Magazine 2-6(Winter, 1958-Pines) — 8.35 25.00 50.00
3-D 1-(1st printing-9/53, 25¢)(St. John)-Came w/glasses; stiff covers; says

Mike Grell's Sable #2 © Mike Grell

Military Comics #38 © QUA

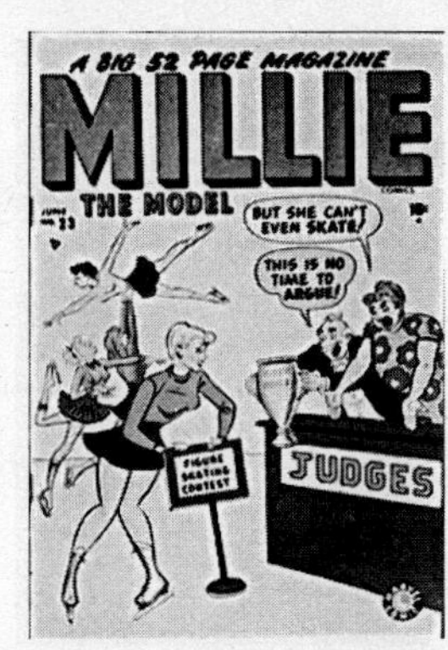

Millie The Model #23 © MEG

	GD25	FN65	NM94
World's First! on-c; 1st 3-D comic	24.00	73.00	170.00
3-D 1-(2nd printing-10/53, 25¢)-Came w/glasses; slick, glossy covers, slightly smaller	22.00	65.00	150.00
3-D 2,3(11/53, 12/53, 25¢)-(St. John)-With glasses	20.00	60.00	140.00

MIGHTY MOUSE (TV)(3rd Series)(Formerly Adventures of Mighty Mouse)
No. 161, Oct, 1964 - No. 172, Oct, 1968
Gold Key/Dell Publishing Co. No. 166-on

161(10/64)-165(9/65)-(Becomes Adventures of... No. 166 on)	3.90	11.60	27.00
166(3/66), 167(6/66)-172	2.90	8.60	20.00

MIGHTY MOUSE (TV)(Spotlight, 1987)(Value: cover or less)

MIGHTY MOUSE (TV)
Oct, 1990 - No. 10, July, 1991 ($1.00)(Based on Sat. cartoon)
Marvel Comics

1-10: 1-Dark Knight-c parody. 2-10: 3-Intro Bat-Bat; Byrne-c. 4,5-Crisis-c/story parodies w/Perez-c. 6-Spider-Man-c parody. 7-Origin Bat-Bat			1.00

MIGHT MOUSE ADVENTURE MAGAZINE
1987 ($2.00, B&W, 52 pgs., magazine size, one-shot)
Spotlight Comics

1-Deputy Dawg, Heckle & Jeckle backup stories		.80	2.00

MIGHTY MOUSE ADVENTURES (Adventures of... #2 on)
November, 1951
St. John Publishing Co.

1	27.00	80.00	185.00

MIGHTY MOUSE ADVENTURE STORIES (Paul Terry's... on-c only)
1953 (50¢, 384 pgs.)
St. John Publishing Co.

nn-Rebound issues	40.00	120.00	280.00

MIGHTY MUTANIMALS (See Teenage Mutant Ninja Turtles Adventures #19)
May, 1991 - No. 3, July, 1991 ($1.00, mini-series)
Apr, 1992 - Present ($1.25)
Archie Comics

1-3: 1-Story cont'd from TMNT Advs. #19			1.00
1-8 (1992): 7-1st app. Merdude			1.25

MIGHTY SAMSON (Also see Gold Key Champion)
7/64 - #20, 11/69; #21, 8/72; #22, 12/73 - #31, 3/76; #32, 8/82
Gold Key (Painted c-1-31)

1-Origin/1st app.; Thorne-a begins	4.60	14.00	32.00
2-5	2.10	6.00	15.00
6-10: 7-Tom Morrow begins, ends #20	1.70	5.00	12.00
11-20	1.70	4.20	10.00
21-32: 21,22,32-r	1.00	2.00	5.00

MIGHTY THOR (See Thor)

MIKE BARNETT, MAN AGAINST CRIME (TV)
Dec, 1951 - No. 6, Oct, 1952
Fawcett Publications

1	10.00	30.00	70.00
2	7.00	21.00	42.00
3,4,6	5.85	17.50	35.00
5- "Market for Morphine" cover/story	7.50	22.50	45.00

MIKE GRELL'S SABLE (First)(Value: cover or less)

MIKE MIST MINUTE MIST-ERIES (See Ms. Tree/Mike Mist in 3-D)
April, 1981 ($1.25, B&W, one-shot)
Eclipse Comics

1			1.25

MIKE SHAYNE PRIVATE EYE
Nov-Jan, 1962 - No. 3, Sept-Nov, 1962
Dell Publishing Co.

	GD25	FN65	NM94
1	3.20	8.00	16.00
2,3	2.00	5.00	10.00

MILITARY COMICS (Becomes Modern Comics #44 on)
Aug, 1941 - No. 43, Oct, 1945
Quality Comics Group

	GD25	FN65	VF82	NM94
1-Origin/1st app. Blackhawk by C. Cuidera (Eisner scripts); Miss America, The Death Patrol by Jack Cole (also #2-7,27-30), & The Blue Tracer by Guardineer; X of the Underground, The Yankee Eagle, Q-Boat & Shot & Shell, Archie Atkins, Loops & Banks by Bud Ernest (Bob Powell)(ends #13) begin	500.00	1500.00	3250.00	5000.00

(Estimated up to 160 total copies exist, 9 in NM/Mint)

	GD25	FN65	NM94
2-Secret War News begins (by McWilliams #2-16); Cole-a; new uniform with yellow circle & hawk's head for Blackhawk	214.00	643.00	1500.00
3-Origin/1st app. Chop Chop	171.00	515.00	1200.00
4	139.00	418.00	975.00
5-The Sniper begins; Miss America in costume #4-7	111.00	332.00	775.00
6-9: 8-X of the Underground begins (ends #13). 9-The Phantom Clipper begins (ends #16)	93.00	280.00	650.00
10-Classic Eisner-c	100.00	300.00	700.00
11-Flag-c	75.00	225.00	525.00
12-Blackhawk by Crandall begins, ends #22	100.00	300.00	700.00
13-15: 14-Private Dogtag begins (ends #83)	71.00	215.00	500.00
16-20: 16-Blue Tracer ends. 17-P.T. Boat begins	61.00	182.00	425.00
21-31: 22-Last Crandall Blackhawk. 23-Shrunken head-c. 27-Death Patrol revived	54.00	162.00	375.00
32-43	46.00	140.00	325.00

NOTE: ***Berg** a-6. **Al Bryant** c-31-34, 38, 40-43. **J. Cole** a-1-3, 27-32. **Crandall** a-12-22; c-13-20. **Cuidera** c-2-9. **Eisner** c-1, 2(part), 9, 10. **Kotsky** c-21-29, 35, 37, 39. **McWilliams** a-2-16. **Powell** a-1-13. **Ward** Blackhawk-30, 31(15 pgs. each); c-30.*

MILITARY WILLY
1907 (14 pgs.; half in color (every other page))
(regular comic book format)(7x9-1/2")(stapled)
J. I. Austen Co.

nn-By F. R. Morgan	22.00	67.00	155.00

MILLENNIUM (DC)(Value: cover or less)

MILLENNIUM INDEX (Independent)(Value: cover or less)

MILLIE, THE LOVABLE MONSTER
Sept-Nov, 1962 - No. 6, Jan, 1973
Dell Publishing Co.

12-523-211, 2(8-10/63)	5.00	15.00	30.00
3(8-10/64)	4.00	11.00	22.00
4(7/72), 5(10/72), 6(1/73)	1.70	5.00	12.00

NOTE: ***Woggon** a-3-6; c-3-6. 4 reprints 1; 5 reprints 2; 6 reprints 3.*

MILLIE THE MODEL (See Comedy Comics, A Date With..., Gay Comics, Joker Comics #28, Life With..., Mad About..., Marvel Mini-Books & Modeling With...)
1945 - No. 207, December, 1973
Marvel/Atlas/Marvel Comics (CnPC #1)(SPI/Male/VPI)

1-Origin	49.00	146.00	340.00
2 (10/46)-Millie becomes The Blonde Phantom to sell Blonde Phantom perfume; a pre-Blonde Phantom app. (see All-Select #11, Fall, 1946)	27.00	81.00	190.00
3-7: 4-7- Willie app. 7-Willie smokes extra strong tobacco	16.00	48.00	110.00
8,10-Kurtzman's "Hey Look". 8-Willie & Rusty app.	16.00	48.00	110.00
9-Powerhouse Pepper by Wolverton, 4 pgs.	19.00	58.00	135.00
11-Kurtzman-a, "Giggles 'n' Grins"	11.50	34.00	80.00
12,15,17-20: 12-Rusty & Hedy Devine app.	9.15	27.50	55.00
13,14,16-Kurtzman's "Hey Look". 13-Hedy Devine app.	10.00	30.00	70.00
21-30	6.70	20.00	40.00
31-60	4.70	14.00	28.00

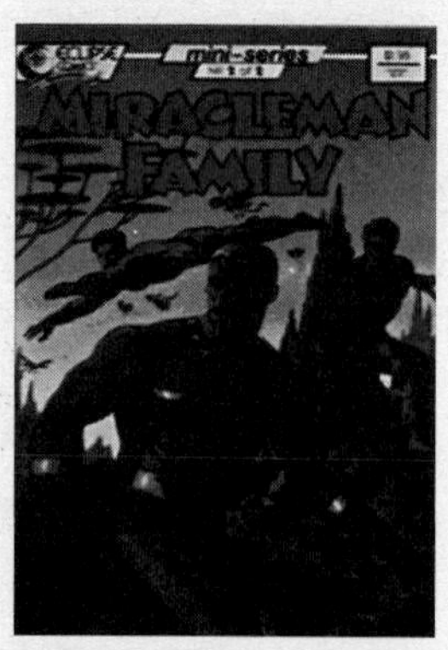

Miracleman Family #2 © Eclipse

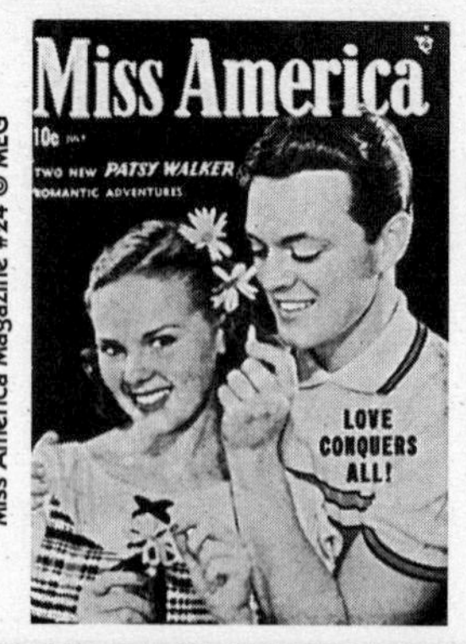

Miss America Magazine #24 © MEG

Miss Fury Comics #2 © MEG

	GD25	FN65	NM94
61-99	4.00	10.00	20.00
100	4.70	14.00	28.00
101-153,155-190: 107-Jack Kirby app. in story	2.80	7.00	14.00
154-New Millie begins (10/67)	4.00	10.00	20.00
191-207: 192-(52 pgs.)	1.60	4.00	8.00
Annual 1(1962)-Early Marvel annual (2nd?)	16.00	48.00	110.00
Annual 2(1963)	12.00	36.00	85.00
Annual 3-5)1964-1966)	9.15	27.50	55.00
Annual 6-10(1967-11/71)	6.35	19.00	38.00
Queen-Size 11(9/74), 12(1975)	4.70	14.00	28.00

NOTE: ***Dan DeCarlo** a-18-93.*

MILLION DOLLAR DIGEST (Richie Rich... #23 on; also see Richie Rich...)
11/86 - No. 7, 11/87; No. 8, 4/88 - No. 34, Nov, 1994 ($1.25/$1.75, digest size)
Harvey Publications

1-8: 8-(68 pgs.) — 1.25
9-34: 9-Begin $1.75-c. 14-May not exist — .70 — 1.75

MILT GROSS FUNNIES (Also see Picture News #1)
Aug, 1947 - No. 2, Sept, 1947
Milt Gross, Inc. (ACG?)

1,2 — 9.15 — 27.50 — 55.00

MILTON THE MONSTER & FEARLESS FLY (TV)
May, 1966
Gold Key

1 (10175-605) — 8.00 — 24.00 — 48.00

MINUTE MAN (See Master Comics & Mighty Midget Comics)
Summer, 1941 - No. 3, Spring, 1942 (68 pgs.)
Fawcett Publications

1 — 114.00 — 343.00 — 800.00
2,3 — 82.00 — 246.00 — 575.00

MINUTE MAN
No date (B&W; 16 pgs.; paper cover blue & red)
Sovereign Service Station giveaway

nn-American history — 1.20 — 3.00 — 6.00

MINUTE MAN ANSWERS THE CALL, THE
1942 (4 pgs.)
By M. C. Gaines (War Bonds giveaway)

nn-Sheldon Moldoff-a — 8.35 — 25.00 — 50.00

MIRACLE COMICS
Feb, 1940 - No. 4, March, 1941
Hillman Periodicals

1-Sky Wizard Master of Space, Dash Dixon, Man of Might, Pinkie Parker, Dusty Doyle, The Kid Cop, K-7, Secret Agent, The Scorpion, & Blandu, Jungle Queen begin; Masked Angel only app. (all 1st app.)
114.00 — 343.00 — 800.00
2 — 60.00 — 180.00 — 420.00
3,4: 3-Bill Colt, the Ghost Rider begins. 4-The Veiled Prophet & Bullet Bob (by Burnley) app. — 54.00 — 160.00 — 375.00

MIRACLEMAN
Aug, 1985 - No. 15, Nov, 1988; No. 16, Dec, 1989 - Present?
Eclipse Comics

1-r/British Marvelman series; Alan Moore scripts in #1-16 — 1.25
1-Gold & Silver editions — .80 — 2.00
2-12: 8-Airboy preview. 9,10-Origin Miracleman. 9-Shows graphic scenes of childbirth — 1.25
13-15-($1.75) — .70 — 1.75
16-18-($1.95): 17-Dave McKean-c begin, end #22; Neil Gaiman scripts in #17-24 — .80 — 2.00
19-24-($2.50); 23,24-B. Smith-c — 1.00 — 2.50
3-D 1 (12/85) — 1.00 — 2.50

MIRACLEMAN: APOCRYPHA (Eclipse)(Value: cover or less)

MIRACLEMAN FAMILY (Eclipse)(Value: cover or less)

MIRACLE OF THE WHITE STALLIONS, THE (See Movie Comics)

MIRACLE SQUAD, THE (Fantagraphics)(Value: cover or less)

MIRACLE SQUAD: BLOOD AND DUST, THE (Apple)(Value: cover or less)

MIRRORWALKER (Now)(Value: cover or less)

MISADVENTURES OF MERLIN JONES, THE (See Movie Comics & Merlin Jones as the Monkey's Uncle under Movie Comics)

MISCHIEVOUS MONKS OF CROCODILE ISLE, THE
1908 (8-1/2x11-1/2"; 4 pgs. in color; 12 pgs.)
J. I. Austen Co., Chicago

nn-By F. R. Morgan; reads longwise — 20.00 — 60.00 — 200.00

MISS AMERICA COMICS (Miss America Magazine #2 on; also see Blonde Phantom & Marvel Mystery Comics)
1944 (One Shot)
Marvel Comics (20CC)

1-2 pgs. pin-ups — 104.00 — 310.00 — 725.00

MISS AMERICA MAGAZINE (Formerly Miss America; Miss America #51 on)
V1#2, Nov, 1944 - No. 93, Nov, 1958
Miss America Publ. Corp./Marvel/Atlas (MAP)

V1#2-Photo-c of teenage girl in Miss America costume; Miss America, Patsy Walker (intro.) comic stories plus movie reviews & stories; intro. Buzz Baxter & Hedy Wolfe; 1 pg. origin Miss America

	GD25	FN65	NM94
	100.00	300.00	700.00
3-5-Miss America & Patsy Walker stories	38.00	115.00	265.00
6-Patsy Walker only	8.35	25.00	50.00
V2#1(4/45)-6(9/45)-Patsy Walker continues	4.35	13.00	26.00
V3#1(10/45)-6(4/46)	4.35	13.00	26.00
V4#1(5/46),2,5(9/46)	4.00	12.00	24.00
V4#3(7/46)-Liz Taylor photo-c	7.50	22.50	45.00
V4#4 (8/46; 68 pgs.)	4.00	11.00	22.00
V4#6 (10/46; 92 pgs.)	4.00	11.00	22.00
V5#1(11/46)-6(4/47), V6#1(5/47)-3(7/47)	4.00	11.00	22.00
V7#1(8/47)-14,16-23(#56, 6/49)	3.60	9.00	18.00
V7#15-All comics	4.00	11.00	22.00
V7#24(#57, 7/49)-Kamen-a (becomes Best Western #58 on?)	3.60	9.00	18.00
V7#25(8/49), 27-44(3/52), VII,nn(5/52)	3.20	8.00	16.00
V7#26(9/49)-All comics	4.00	11.00	22.00
V1,nn(7/52)-V1,nn(1/53)(#46-49)	3.20	8.00	16.00
V7#50(Spring '53), V1#51-V7?#54(7/53)	3.20	8.00	16.00
55-93	3.20	8.00	16.00

NOTE: *Photo-c #1, 4, V2#1, 4, 5, V3#5, V4#3, 4, 6, V7#15, 16, 24, 26, 34, 37, 38. Painted c-3.* ***Powell** a-V7#31.*

MISS BEVERLY HILLS OF HOLLYWOOD (See Adventures of Bob Hope)
Mar-Apr, 1949 - No. 9, July-Aug, 1950 (52 pgs.)
National Periodical Publications

	GD25	FN65	NM94
1 (Meets Alan Ladd)	44.00	133.00	310.00
2-William Holden photo on-c	31.00	94.00	220.00
3-5: 2-9-Part photo-c. 5-Bob Hope photo on-c	27.00	80.00	185.00
6,7,9: 6-Lucille Ball photo on-c	24.00	72.00	165.00
8-Reagan photo on-c	31.00	94.00	220.00

NOTE: *Beverly meets Alan Ladd in #1, Eve Arden #2, Betty Hutton #4, Bob Hope #5.*

MISS CAIRO JONES
1945
Croyden Publishers

1-Bob Oksner daily newspaper-r (1st strip story); lingerie panels
16.00 — 48.00 — 110.00

MISS FURY COMICS (Newspaper strip reprints)
Winter, 1942-43 - No. 8, Winter, 1946 (Published quarterly)
Timely Comics (NPI 1/CmPI 2/MPC 3-8)

1-Origin Miss Fury by Tarpe' Mills (68 pgs.) in costume w/pin-ups

Mission Impossible #1 © Paramount

Mr. and Mrs. J. Evil Scientist #1 © H-B

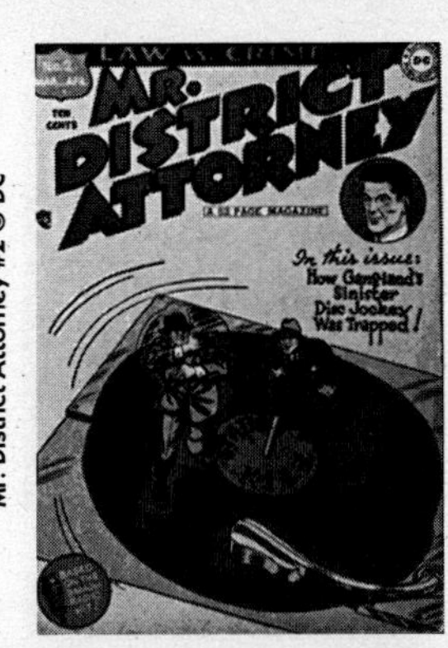

Mr. District Attorney #2 © DC

	GD25	FN65	NM94
	250.00	750.00	1750.00
2-(60 pgs.)-In costume w/pin-ups	114.00	343.00	800.00
3-(60 pgs.)-In costume w/pin-ups; Hitler-c	89.00	268.00	625.00
4-(52 pgs.)-In costume, 2 pgs. w/pin-ups	71.00	215.00	500.00
5-(52 pgs.)-In costume w/pin-ups	68.00	205.00	475.00
6-(52 pgs.)-Not in costume in inside stories, w/pin-ups	60.00	180.00	420.00
7,8-(36 pgs.)-In costume 1 pg. each; no pin-ups	59.00	175.00	410.00

NOTE: *Schomburg c-1, 5, 6.*

MISS FURY
1991 - No. 4, 1991 ($2.50, color, mini-series)
Adventure Comics

	GD25	FN65	NM94
1-4: 1-Origin; granddaughter of original Miss Fury		1.00	2.50
1-Limited ed. ($4.95)	1.00	2.00	5.00

MISSION IMPOSSIBLE (TV)
May, 1967 - No. 4, Oct, 1968; No. 5, Oct, 1969 (All have photo-c)
Dell Publishing Co.

	GD25	FN65	NM94
1	7.00	20.00	46.00
2-5: 5-Reprints #1	5.00	15.00	35.00

MISS LIBERTY (Becomes Liberty Comics)
1945 (MLJ reprints)
Burten Publishing Co.

	GD25	FN65	NM94
1-The Shield & Dusty, The Wizard, & Roy, the Super Boy app.; r/Shield-Wizard #13	23.00	70.00	160.00

MISS MELODY LANE OF BROADWAY (See The Adventures of Bob Hope)
Feb-Mar, 1950 - No. 3, June-July, 1950 (52 pgs.)
National Periodical Publications

	GD25	FN65	NM94
1-Movie stars photos app. on all-c	43.00	130.00	300.00
2,3: 3-Ed Sullivan photo on-c	30.00	90.00	210.00

MISS PEACH
Oct-Dec, 1963; 1969
Dell Publishing Co.

	GD25	FN65	NM94
1-Jack Mendelsohn-a/script	10.00	30.00	60.00
...Tells You How to Grow (1969; 25¢)-Mel Lazarus-a; also given away (36 pgs.)	5.85	17.50	35.00

MISS PEPPER (See Meet Miss Pepper)

MISS SUNBEAM (See Little Miss...)

MISS VICTORY (See Captain Fearless #1,2, Holyoke One-Shot #3, Veri Best Sure Fire & Veri Best Sure Shot Comics)

MISS VICTORY GOLDEN ANNIVERSARY SPECIA (AC)(Value: cover or less)

MISTER AMERICA
Apr, 1994 - No. 2, May, 1994 ($2.95, mini-series)
Endeavor Comics

	GD25	FN65	NM94
1,2		1.20	3.00

MR. & MRS. (Also see Ain't It A Grand and Glorious Feeling?)
1922 (52 & 28 pgs.) (9x9-1/2", cardboard-c)
Whitman Publishing Co.

	GD25	FN65	NM94
nn-By Briggs (B&W, 52 pgs.)	16.50	50.00	115.00
nn-28 pgs.-(9x9-1/2")-Sunday strips-r in color	19.00	58.00	135.00

MR. & MRS. BEANS (See Single Series #11)

MR. & MRS. J. EVIL SCIENTIST (TV)(See The Flintstones & Hanna-Barbera Band Wagon #3)
Nov, 1963 - No. 4, Sept, 1966 (Hanna-Barbera, all 12¢)
Gold Key

	GD25	FN65	NM94
1-From The Flintstones	5.00	15.00	36.00
2-4	3.00	9.00	21.00

MR. ANTHONY'S LOVE CLINIC (Based on radio show)
Nov, 1949 - No. 5, Apr-May, 1950 (52 pgs.)
Hillman Periodicals

	GD25	FN65	NM94
1-Photo-c	9.15	27.50	55.00
2	5.35	16.00	32.00
3-5: 5-Photo-c	4.70	14.00	28.00

MR. BUG GOES TO TOWN (See Cinema Comics Herald)
1941 (52 pgs.)(Giveaway)
K.K. Publications

	GD25	FN65	NM94
nn-Cartoon movie	37.00	110.00	260.00

MR. DISTRICT ATTORNEY (Radio/TV)
Jan-Feb, 1948 - No. 67, Jan-Feb, 1959 (1-23: 52 pgs.)
National Periodical Publications

	GD25	FN65	NM94
1-Howard Purcell c-5-23 (most)	79.00	236.00	550.00
2	31.00	92.00	215.00
3-5	23.00	70.00	160.00
6-10	18.00	54.00	125.00
11-20	14.00	43.00	100.00
21-43: 43-Last pre-code (1-2/55)	11.00	32.00	75.00
44-67	10.00	30.00	60.00

MR. DISTRICT ATTORNEY (See 4-Color #13 & The Funnies #35)

MISTER E (DC)(Value: cover or less)

MISTER ED, THE TALKING HORSE (TV)
Mar-May, 1962 - No. 6, Feb, 1964 (All photo-c; photo back-c: 1-6)
Dell Publishing Co./Gold Key

	GD25	FN65	NM94
4-Color 1295	13.00	40.00	90.00
1(11/62) (Gold Key)-Photo-c	10.00	30.00	60.00
2-6-Photo-c	5.85	17.50	35.00

(See March of Comics #244, 260, 282, 290)

MR. MAGOO (TV) (The Nearsighted..., ...& Gerald McBoing Boing 1954 issues; formerly Gerald McBoing-Boing And ...)
No. 6, Nov-Jan, 1953-54; 5/54 - 3-5/62; 9-11/63 - 3-5/65
Dell Publishing Co.

	GD25	FN65	NM94
6	10.00	30.00	65.00
4-Color 561(5/54),602(11/54)	10.00	30.00	65.00
4-Color 1235(#1, 12-2/62),1305(#2, 3-5/62)	9.15	27.50	55.00
3(9-11/63) - 5	8.35	25.00	50.00
4-Color 1235(12-536-505)(3-5/65)-2nd Printing	5.00	15.00	30.00

MISTER MIRACLE (See Cancelled Comic Cavalcade)
3-4/71 - V4#18, 2-3/74; V5#19, 9/77 - V6#25, 8-9/78; 1987
National Periodical Publications/DC Comics

	GD25	FN65	NM94
1-1st app. Mr. Miracle (#1-3 are 15¢)	2.90	8.60	20.00
2,3	1.70	5.00	12.00
4-8: 4-Boy Commandos-r begin; all 52 pgs.	1.60	4.70	11.00
9,10: 9-Origin Mr. Miracle; Darkseid cameo	1.40	3.50	8.50
11-18: 15-Intro/1st app. Shilo Norman. 18-Barda & Scott Free wed; New Gods app. & Darkseid cameo	1.30	3.00	7.50
19-25 (1977-78)		1.60	4.00
Special 1(1987, $1.25, 52 pgs.)		1.20	3.00

NOTE: ***Austin** a-19i. **Ditko** a-6r. **Golden** a-23-25p; c-25p. **Heath** a-24i, 25i; c-25i. **Kirby** a(p)/c-1-18. **Nasser** a-19i. **Rogers** a-19-22p; c-19, 20p, 21p, 22-24. 4-8 contain **Simon & Kirby** Boy Commandos reprints from Detective 82,76, Boy Commandos 1, 3 & Detective 64 in that order.*

MISTER MIRACLE
Jan, 1989 - No. 28, June, 1991 ($1.00)
DC Comics

	GD25	FN65	NM94
1-28: 13,14-Lobo app. 22-1st new Mr. Miracle w/new costume			1.00

MR. MIRACLE (See Capt. Fearless #1 & Holyoke One-Shot #4)

MR. MONSTER (Doc Stearn... #7 on; See Airboy-Mr. Monster Special, Dark Horse Presents, Super Duper Comics & Vanguard Illustrated #7)
Jan, 1985 - No. 10, June, 1987 ($1.75, color, Baxter paper)
Eclipse Comics

	GD25	FN65	NM94
1-1st story-r from Vanguard Ill. #7(1st app.)	1.00	2.50	5.50
2-Dave Stevens-c		1.20	3.00
3-10: 3-Alan Moore scripts; Wolverton-r/Weird Mysteries #5. 6-Ditko-r/Fan-			

Mr. Monster #10 © Eclipse

Mr. T and the T-Force #1 © NOW

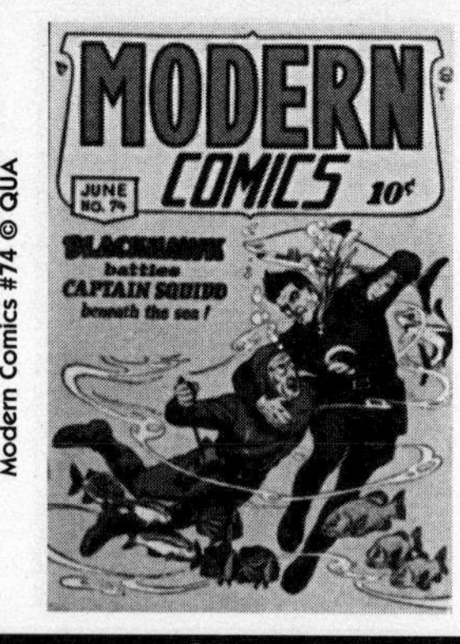

Modern Comics #74 © QUA

GD25 FN65 NM94

tastic Fears #5 plus new Giffen-a 10 6-D issue .80 2.00

MR. MONSTER
Feb, 1988 - No. 8, July, 1991 ($1.75, B&W)
Dark Horse Comics

1-7 .70 1.75
8-($4.95, 60 pgs.)-Origins conclusion 1.00 2.00 5.00

MR. MONSTER ATTACKS! (Tundra)(Value: cover or less)

MR. MONSTER'S SUPER-DUPER SPECIAL
May, 1986 - No. 8, July, 1987
Eclipse Comics

1-(5/86)...3-D High Octane Horror #1 1.20 3.00
1-(5/86)...2-D version, 100 copies 2.30 5.50
2-(8/86)...High Octane Horror #1 .70 1.80
3-(9/86)...True Crime #1 .70 1.80
4-(11/86)...True Crime #2 .70 1.80
5-(1/87)...Hi-Voltage Super Science #1 .70 1.80
6-(3/87)...High Shock Schlock #1 .70 1.80
7-(5/87)...High Shock Schlock #2 .70 1.80
8-(7/87)...Weird Tales Of The Future #1 .70 1.80

MR. MUSCLES (Formerly Blue Beetle #18-21)
No. 22, Mar, 1956; No. 23, Aug, 1956
Charlton Comics

22,23 4.20 12.50 25.00

MISTER MYSTERY (Tales of Horror and Suspense)
Sept, 1951 - No. 19, Oct, 1954
Mr. Publ. (Media Publ.) No. 1-3/SPM Publ./Stanmore (Aragon)

1-Kurtzmanesque horror story 34.00 103.00 240.00
2,3-Kurtzmanesque story. 3-Anti-Wertham edit. 25.00 75.00 175.00
4,6: Bondage-c; 6-Torture 25.00 75.00 175.00
5,8,10 20.00 60.00 140.00
7- "The Brain Bats of Venus" by Wolverton; partially re-used in Weird Tales of the Future #7 61.00 182.00 425.00
9-Nostrand-a 20.00 60.00 140.00
11-Wolverton "Robot Woman" story/Weird Mysteries #2, cut up, rewritten & partially redrawn 36.00 107.00 250.00
12-Classic injury to eye-c 55.00 165.00 385.00
13,14,17,19: 17-Severed heads-c. 19-Reprints 16.00 48.00 110.00
15- "Living Dead" junkie story 16.00 48.00 110.00
16-Bondage-c 16.00 48.00 110.00
18- "Robot Woman" by Wolverton reprinted from Weird Mysteries #2; decapitation, bondage-c 31.00 92.00 215.00

NOTE: *Andru a-1, 2p, 3p.* ***Andru/Esposito*** *c-1-3.* ***Baily*** *c-10-18(most).* ***Mortellaro*** *c-5-7. Bondage c-7. Some issues have graphic dismemberment scenes.*

MR. MYSTIC (See Will Eisner Presents)

MISTER Q (See Mighty Midget Comics & Our Flag Comics #5)

MR. RISK (Formerly All Romances; Men Against Crime #3 on)(Also see Our Flag Comics & Super-Mystery Comics)
No. 7, Oct, 1950 - No. 2, Dec, 1950
Ace Magazines

7,2 5.00 15.00 30.00

MR. SCARLET & PINKY (See Mighty Midget Comics)

MR. T AND THE T-FORCE
June, 1993 - Present ($1.95, color)
Now Comics

1-10-Newsstand editions: 1-7-polybagged with photo trading card in each. 1,2-Neal Adams-c/a(p). 3-Dave Dorman painted-c .80 2.00
1-10-Direct Sale editions polybagged w/line drawn trading cards. 1-Contains gold foil trading card by Neal Adams .80 2.00

MISTER UNIVERSE (Professional wrestler)
July, 1951; No. 2, Oct, 1951 - No. 5, April, 1952
Mr. Publications Media Publ. (Stanmor, Aragon)

GD25 FN65 NM94

1 13.00 40.00 90.00
2- "Jungle That Time Forgot", (24 pg. story); Andru/Esposito-c 10.00 30.00 60.00
3-Marijuana story 10.00 30.00 60.00
4,5- "Goes to War" cover/stories 5.85 17.50 35.00

MISTER X (See Vortex)
6/84 - No. 14, 8/88 ($1.50/$2.25, direct sales, color, coated paper)
V2#1, Apr, 1989 - V2#12, Mar, 1990 ($2.00/$2.50, B&W, newsprint)
Mr. Publications/Vortex Comics

1 1.70 4.00
2 1.00 2.50
3-14: 11-Dave McKean story & art (6 pgs.) .80 2.00
V2#1-11 (Second Coming, $2.00, B&W): 1-Four different covers. 10-Photo-c .80 2.00
V2#12 ($2.50) 1.00 2.50
Return of... ($11.95, graphic novel)-r/1-4 1.70 5.00 12.00
Return of... ($34.95, hardcover limited edition)-r/1-4 5.00 15.00 35.00
Special (no date, 1990? .80 2.00

MISTY (Marvel)(Value: cover or less)

MITZI COMICS (Becomes Mitzi's Boy Friend #2 on)(See All Teen)
Spring, 1948 (One Shot)
Timely Comics

1-Kurtzman's "Hey Look" plus 3 pgs. "Giggles 'n' Grins" 13.00 40.00 90.00

MITZI'S BOY FRIEND (Formerly Mitzi Comics; becomes Mitzi's Romances)
No. 2, June, 1948 - No. 7, April, 1949
Marvel Comics (TCI)

2 6.70 20.00 40.00
3-7 5.35 16.00 32.00

MITZI'S ROMANCES (Formerly Mitzi's Boy Friend)
No. 8, June, 1949 - No. 10, Dec, 1949
Timely/Marvel Comics (TCI)

8-Becomes True Life Tales #8 (10/49) on? 6.70 20.00 40.00
9,10: 10-Painted-c 5.35 16.00 32.00

MOBY DICK (See Feature Presentations #6, Four Color #717, and King Classics)

MOBY DUCK (See Donald Duck #112 & Walt Disney Showcase #2,11)
Oct, 1967 - No. 11, Oct, 1970; No. 12, Jan, 1974 - No. 30, Feb, 1978
Gold Key (Disney)

1 1.70 5.00 12.00
2-5 1.20 2.90 7.00
6-11 1.60 4.00
12-30: 21,30-r .80 2.00

MODEL FUN (With Bobby Benson)
No. 3, Winter, 1954-55 - No. 5, July, 1955
Harle Publications

3-Bobby Benson 5.00 15.00 30.00
4,5-Bobby Benson 3.60 9.00 18.00

MODELING WITH MILLIE (Formerly Life With Millie)
No. 21, Feb, 1963 - No. 54, June, 1967
Atlas/Marvel Comics Group (Male Publ.)

21 7.50 22.50 45.00
22-30 4.70 14.00 28.00
31-54 4.00 11.00 22.00

MODERN COMICS (Formerly Military Comics #1-43)
No. 44, Nov, 1945 - No. 102, Oct, 1950
Quality Comics Group

44-Blackhawk continues 46.00 140.00 325.00
45-52: 49-1st app. Fear, Lady Adventuress 30.00 90.00 210.00
53-Torchy by Ward begins (9/46) 35.00 105.00 245.00
54-60: 55-J. Cole-a 26.00 78.00 180.00

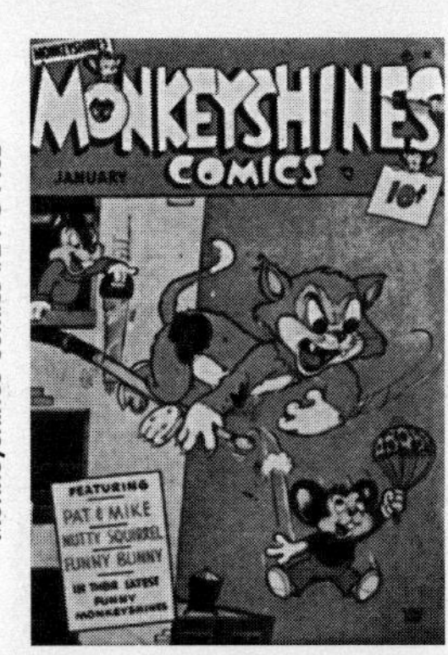

Monkeyshines Comics #24 © ACE

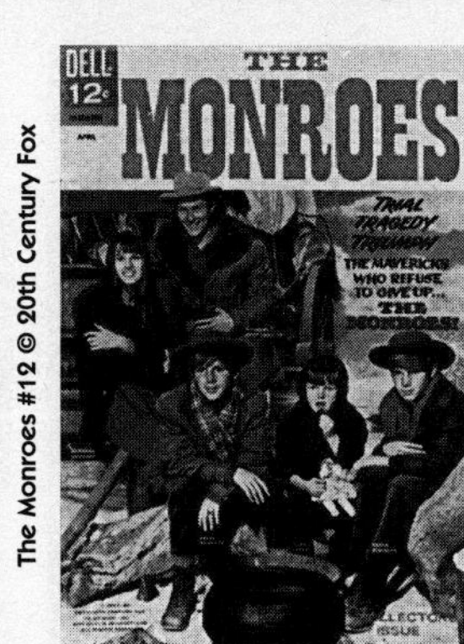

The Monroes #12 © 20th Century Fox

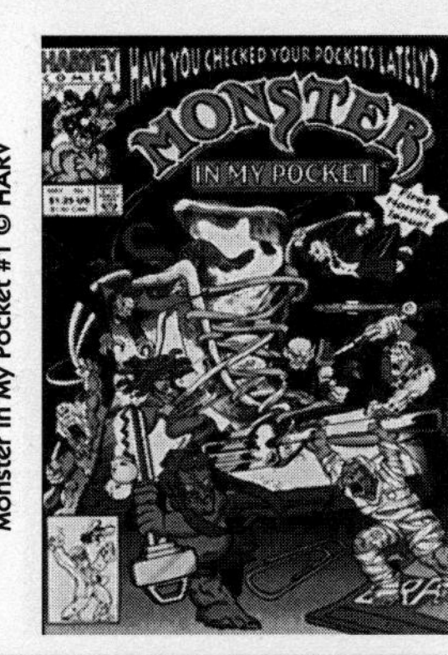

Monster In My Pocket #1 © HARV

GD25 FN65 NM94

61-77,79,80: 73-J. Cole-a 24.00 73.00 170.00
78-1st app. Madame Butterfly 26.00 78.00 180.00
81-99,101: 82,83-One pg. J. Cole-a. 83-The Spirit app.; last 52 pg. issue?
99-Blackhawks on the moon-c/story 24.00 73.00 170.00
100 24.00 73.00 170.00
102-(Scarce)-J. Cole-a; Spirit by Eisner app. 27.00 81.00 190.00

NOTE: ***Al Bryant** c-44-51, 54, 55, 66, 69. **Jack Cole** a-55, 73. **Crandall** Blackhawk-#46, 47, 50, 51, 54, 56, 58-60, 64, 67-70, 73, 74, 76-78, 80-83; c-60-65, 67, 68, 70-95. **Crandall/Cuidera** c-56-59, 96-102. **Gustavson** a-47. **Ward** Blackhawk-#52, 53, 55 (15 pgs. each). Torchy in #53-102; by **Ward** only in #53-89(9/49); by **Gil Fox** #93, 102.*

MODERN LOVE
June-July, 1949 - No. 8, Aug-Sept, 1950
E. C. Comics

1 46.00 140.00 325.00
2-Craig/Feldstein-c 37.00 111.00 260.00
3-Spanking panel 31.00 94.00 220.00
4-6 (Scarce): 4-Bra/panties panels 44.00 133.00 310.00
7,8 34.00 100.00 235.00

NOTE: ***Craig** a-3. **Feldstein** a-in most issues; c-1, 2i, 3-8. **Harrison** a-4. **Iger** a-6-8. **Ingels** a-1, 2, 4-7. **Palais** a-5. **Wood** a-7. **Wood/Harrison** a-5-7. (Canadian reprints known; see Table of Contents.)*

MOD LOVE
1967 (50¢, 36 pgs.)
Western Publishing Co.

1 4.00 10.00 20.00

MODNIKS, THE
Aug, 1967 - No. 2, Aug, 1970
Gold Key

10206-708(#1), 2 1.30 3.25 8.00

MOD SQUAD (TV)
Jan, 1969 - No. 3, Oct, 1969 - No. 8, April, 1971
Dell Publishing Co.

1-Photo-c 3.60 10.70 25.00
2-8: 2-4-Photo-c. 8-Reprints #2 2.00 6.00 14.00

MOD WHEELS
March, 1971 - No. 19, Jan, 1976
Gold Key

1 1.65 4.00 10.00
2-19: 11,15-Extra 16 pgs. ads 1.00 2.00 5.00

MOE & SHMOE COMICS
Spring, 1948 - No. 2, Summer, 1948
O. S. Publ. Co.

1 5.85 17.50 35.00
2 4.20 12.50 25.00

MOEBIUS (Graphic novel)
Oct, 1987 - No. 6, 1988; No. 7, 1990; No. 8, 1991 ($9.95, adults, 8x11")
Epic Comics (Marvel)

1,2,4-6,8: (#2, 2nd printing, $9.95) 1.65 4.00 10.00
3,7: 3-(1st & 2nd printings, $12.95) 1.85 5.50 13.00
0 (1990, $12.95) 1.85 5.50 13.00
Moebius I-Signed & numbered hard-c ($45.95, Graphitti Designs, 1,500 copies printed)-r/#1-3 6.50 20.00 46.00

MOLLY MANTON'S ROMANCES (Romantic Affairs #3)
Sept, 1949 - No. 2, Dec, 1949 (52 pgs.)
Marvel Comics (SePI)

1-Photo-c (becomes Blaze the Wonder Collie #2 (10/49) on? & Molly Manton's Romances #2 9.15 27.50 55.00
2-Titled "Romances of..."; photo-c 5.85 17.50 35.00

MOLLY O'DAY (Super Sleuth)
February, 1945 (1st Avon comic)
Avon Periodicals

1-Molly O'Day, The Enchanted Dagger by Tuska (r/Yankee #1), Capt'n Courage, Corporal Grant app. 34.00 103.00 240.00

MONKEES, THE (TV)(Also see Circus Boy, Groovy, Not Brand Echh #3, Teen-Age Talk, Teen Beam & Teen Beat)
March, 1967 - No. 17, Oct, 1969 (#1-4,6,7,10 have photo-c)
Dell Publishing Co.

1-Photo-c 11.00 32.00 75.00
2-4,6,7,10,12,15: All photo-c 5.40 16.00 38.00
5,8,9,11,13,14,16,17-No photo-c: 17-Reprints #1 3.90 11.60 27.00

MONKEY AND THE BEAR, THE
Sept, 1953 - No. 3, Jan, 1954
Atlas Comics (ZPC)

1-Howie Post-c/a in all; funny animal 5.00 15.00 30.00
2,3 3.60 9.00 18.00

MONKEYSHINES COMICS
Summer, 1944 - No. 27, July, 1949
Ace Periodicals/Publishers Specialists/Current Books/Unity Publ.

1-Funny animal 8.35 25.00 50.00
2-(Aut/44) 4.20 12.50 25.00
3-10: 3-(Win/44) 4.00 10.00 20.00
11-27: 23,24-Fago-c/a 3.60 9.00 18.00

MONKEY SHINES OF MARSELEEN
1909 (11-1/2x17") (28 pgs. in two colors)
Cupples & Leon Co.

nn-By Norman E. Jennett 22.00 65.00 150.00

MONKEY'S UNCLE, THE (See Merlin Jones As... under Movie Comics)

MONOLITH (Comico)(Value: cover or less)

MONROES, THE (TV)
April, 1967
Dell Publishing Co.

1-Photo-c 3.00 7.50 15.00

MONSTER
1953 - No. 2, 1953
Fiction House Magazines

1-Dr. Drew by Grandenetti; reprint from Rangers Comics #48; Whitman-c 29.00 86.00 200.00
2 -Whitman-c 23.00 70.00 160.00

MONSTER CRIME COMICS (Also see Crime Must Stop)
October, 1952 (15¢, 52 pgs.)
Hillman Periodicals

1 (Scarce) 57.00 171.00 400.00

MONSTER HOWLS (Magazine)
December, 1966 (Satire) (35¢, 68 pgs.)
Humor-Vision

1 4.00 11.00 22.00

MONSTER HUNTERS
Aug, 1975 - No. 9, Jan, 1977; No. 10, Oct, 1977 - No. 18, Feb, 1979
Charlton Comics

1,2: 1-Howard-a; Newton-c. 2-Ditko-a 1.00 2.00 5.00
3-13,15-18 .80 2.00
14-Special all-Ditko issue 1.40 3.50
1,2(Modern Comics reprints, 1977) 1.00

NOTE: ***Ditko** a-2, 6, 8, 10, 13-15r, 18r; c-13-15, 18. **Howard** r-13. **Morisi** a-1. **Staton** a-1, 13. **Sutton** a-2, 4; c-2, 4. Reprints in #12-18.*

MONSTER IN MY POCKET (Harvey)(Value: cover or less)

MONSTER MENACE
Dec, 1993 - No. 4, Mar, 1994 ($1.25, mini-series)
Marvel Comics

1-4-Pre-code Atlas horror reprints. 1-Ditko-r. 2-Ditko, Kirby-r; Ditko-c.

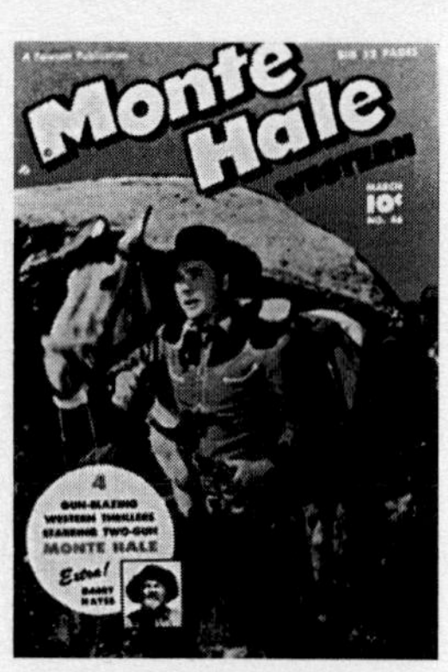

Monte Hale Western #46 © FAW

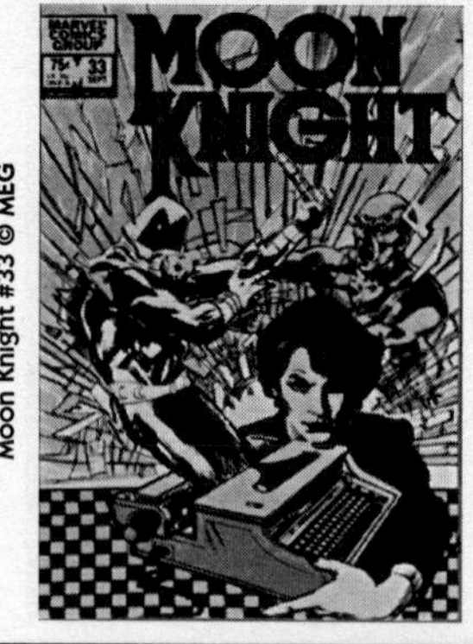

Moon Knight #33 © MEG

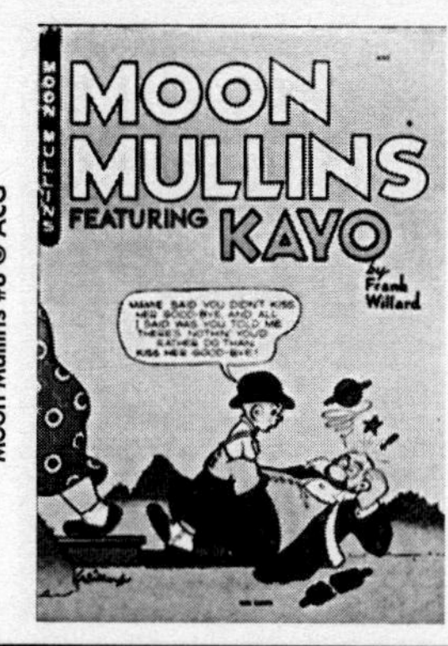

Moon Mullins #8 © ACG

GD25 FN65 NM94

3-Ditko-c/a(r) 1.25

MONSTER OF FRANKENSTEIN (See Frankenstein)

MONSTERS ON THE PROWL (Chamber of Darkness #1-8)
No. 9, 2/71 - No. 27, 11/73; No. 28, 6/74 - No. 30, 10/74
Marvel Comics Group (No. 13,14: 52 pgs.)

9-Barry Smith inks 1.00 2.50 5.50
10-30: 16-(4/72)-2nd app. King Kull; see Creatures on the Loose #10 (3/71); Severin-c 1.20 3.00

NOTE: ***Ditko** r-5, 9, 14, 16. **Kirby** r-10-17, 21, 23, 25, 27, 28, 30; c-9, 25. **Kirby/Ditko** r-14, 17-20, 22, 24, 26, 29. **Reinman** r-5. **Marie/John Severin** a-16(Kull). 9-13, 15 contain one new story. Woodish art by **Reese**-11. King Kull created by Robert E. Howard.*

MONSTERS UNLEASHED (Magazine)
July, 1973 - No. 11, April, 1975; Summer, 1975 (B&W)
Marvel Comics Group

1 1.00 2.70 6.50
2-11: 2-The Frankenstein Monster begins. 3-Neal Adams-c/a; The Man-Thing begins (origin-r). 4-Intro. Satana, the Devil's daughter 7-Williamson-a(r). 8-N. Adams-r. 9-Wendigo app. 10-Origin Tigra 1.60 4.00
Annual 1 (Summer,1975)-Kane-a 1.20 3.00

NOTE: ***Boris** c-2, 6. **Brunner** a-2; c-11. **J. Buscema** a-2p, 4p, 5p. **Colan** a-1, 4r. **Davis** a-3r. **Everett** a-2r. **G. Kane** a-3. **Krigstein** r-4. **Morrow** a-3; c-1. **Perez** a-8. **Ploog** a-6. **Reese** a-1, 2. **Tuska** a-3p. **Wildey** a-1r.*

MONTANA KID, THE (See Kid Montana)

MONTE HALE WESTERN (Movie star; Formerly Mary Marvel #1-28; also see Fawcett Movie Comic, Motion Picture Comics, Picture News #8, Real Western Hero, Six-Gun Heroes, Western Hero & XMas Comics)
No. 29, Oct, 1948 - No. 88, Jan, 1956
Fawcett Publications/Charlton No. 83 on

29-(#1, 52 pgs.)-Photo-c begin, end #82; Monte Hale & his horse Pardner begin 39.00 118.00 275.00
30-(52 pgs.)-Big Bow and Little Arrow begin, end #34; Captain Tootsie by Beck 19.00 57.00 130.00
31-36,38-40-(52 pgs.): 34-Gabby Hayes begins, ends #80. 39-Captain Tootsie by Beck 15.00 45.00 105.00
37,41,45,49-(36 pgs.) 10.00 30.00 65.00
42-44,46-48,50-(52 pgs.): 47-Big Bow & Little Arrow app. 10.00 30.00 70.00
51,52,54-56,58,59-(52 pgs.) 9.15 27.50 55.00
53,57-(36 pgs.): 53-Slim Pickens app. 7.50 22.50 45.00
60-81: 36 pgs. #60-on. 80-Gabby Hayes ends 7.50 22.50 45.00
82-Last Fawcett issue (6/53) 9.15 27.50 55.00
83-1st Charlton issue (2/55); B&W photo back-c begin. Gabby Hayes returns, ends #86 9.15 27.50 55.00
84 (4/55) 7.50 22.50 45.00
85-86 6.70 20.00 40.00
87-Wolverton-r, 1/2 pg. 7.50 22.50 45.00
88-Last issue 7.50 22.50 45.00

NOTE: ***Gil Kane** a-33?, 34? Rocky Lane -1 pg. (Carnation ad)-38, 40, 41, 43, 44, 46, 55.*

MONTY HALL OF THE U.S. MARINES (See With the Marines...)
Aug, 1951 - No. 11, Apr, 1953
Toby Press

1 7.50 22.50 45.00
2 4.70 14.00 28.00
3-5 4.00 12.00 24.00
6-11 4.00 10.00 20.00

NOTE: *Full page pin-ups (Pin-Up Pete) by **Jack Sparling** in #1-9.*

MOON, A GIRL...ROMANCE, A (Becomes Weird Fantasy #13 on; formerly Moon Girl #1-8)
No. 9, Sept-Oct, 1949 - No. 12, Mar-Apr, 1950
E. C. Comics

9-Moon Girl cameo; spanking panel 60.00 180.00 420.00
10,11 45.00 135.00 315.00
12-(Scarce) 63.00 190.00 440.00

NOTE: ***Feldstein, Ingels** art in all. **Feldstein** c-9-12. **Wood/Harrison** a-10-12. Canadian reprints known; see Table of Contents.*

GD25 FN65 NM94

MOON GIRL AND THE PRINCE (#1) (Moon Girl #2-6; Moon Girl Fights Crime #7, 8; becomes A Moon, A Girl, Romance #9 on)(Also see Animal Fables #7 and Happy Houlihans)
Fall, 1947 - No. 8, Summer, 1949
E. C. Comics

1-Origin Moon Girl (see Happy Houlihans #1) 75.00 225.00 525.00
2 41.00 122.00 285.00
3,4: 4-Moon Girl vs. a vampire 34.00 103.00 240.00
5-E.C.'s 1st horror story, "Zombie Terror" 96.00 290.00 675.00
6-8 (Scarce): 7-Origin Star (Moongirl's sidekick) 45.00 135.00 315.00

NOTE: ***Craig** a-2, 5. **Moldoff** a-1-8; c-2-6. **Wheelan's** Fat and Slat app. in #3, 4, 6. #2 & #3 are 52 pgs., #4 on, 36 pgs. Canadian reprints known; (see Table of Contents.)*

MOON KNIGHT (Also see The Hulk, Marc Spector..., Marvel Preview #21, Marvel Spotlight & Werewolf by Night #32)
November, 1980 - No. 38, July, 1984 (Mando paper No. 33 on)
Marvel Comics Group

1-Origin resumed in #4; begin Sienkiewicz-c/a 1.60 4.00
2-34,36-38: 4-Intro Midnight Man. 16-The Thing app. 25-Double size 1.50
35-($1.00, 52 pgs.)-X-men app.; F.F. cameo .80 2.00

NOTE: ***Austin** c-27i, 31i. **Kaluta** c-36-38; back c-35. **Miller** c-9, 12p, 13p, 15?, 27p. **Ploog** back c-35. **Sienkiewicz** a-1-15, 17-20, 22-26, 28-30, 37; c-1-5, 7, 8, 10, 11, 14-26, 28-30, 31p, 33, 34.*

MOON KNIGHT
June, 1985 - No. 6, Dec, 1985
Marvel Comics Group

V2#1-6: 1-Double size; new costume. 6-Painted-c 1.00

MOON KNIGHT: DIVIDED WE FALL
1992 ($4.95, 52 pgs.)
Marvel Comics

nn-Denys Cowan-c/a(p) 1.00 2.00 5.00

MOON KNIGHT SPECIAL
Oct, 1992 ($2.50, 52 pgs.)
Marvel Comics

1-Shang Chi, Master of Kung Fu-c/story 1.00 2.50

MOON KNIGHT SPECIAL EDITION
Nov, 1983 - No. 3, Jan, 1984 ($2.00, mini-series, Baxter paper)
Marvel Comics Group

1-3: Reprints from Hulk mag. by Sienkiewicz 1.50

MOON MULLINS
1927 - 1933 (52 pgs.) (daily B&W strip reprints)
Cupples & Leon Co.

Series 1('27)-By Willard 31.00 94.00 220.00
Series 2('28), Series 3('29), Series 4('30) 19.00 57.00 130.00
Series 5('31), 6('32), 7('33) 16.00 48.00 110.00
Big Book 1('30)-B&W 27.00 80.00 185.00

MOON MULLINS (See Popular Comics, Super Book #3 & Super Comics)
1941 - 1945
Dell Publishing Co.

4-Color 14(1941) 36.00 107.00 250.00
Large Feature Comic 29(1941) 20.00 60.00 200.00
4-Color 31(1943) 19.00 57.00 130.00
4-Color 81(1945) 10.00 30.00 70.00

MOON MULLINS
Dec-Jan, 1947-48 - No. 8, 1949 (52 pgs.)
Michel Publ. (American Comics Group)

1-Alternating Sunday & daily strip-r 15.00 45.00 105.00
2 9.15 27.50 55.00
3-8: 8-...Featuring Kayo on-c 7.00 21.00 42.00

NOTE: ***Milt Gross** a-2-6, 8. **Frank Willard** r-all.*

MOON PILOT (See 4-Color #1313)

MOONSHADOW

Moonshadow #1 © DC

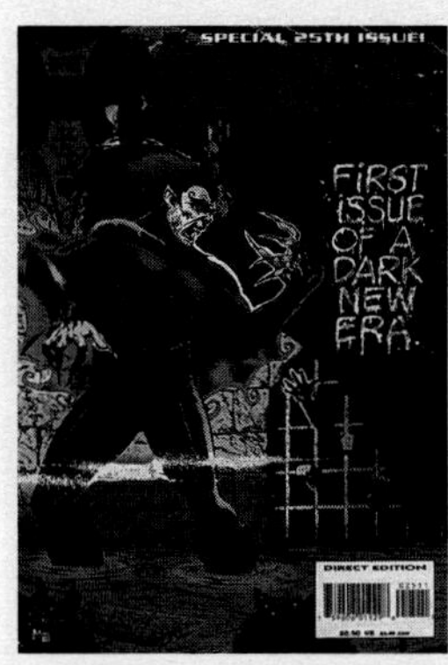

Morbius #25 © MEG

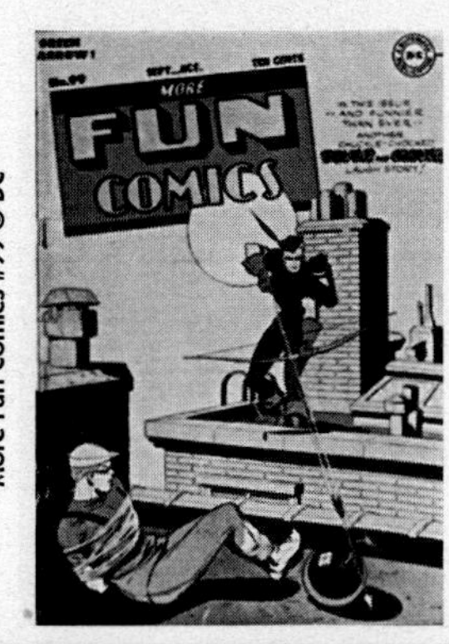

More Fun Comics #99 © DC

GD25 FN65 NM94

May, 1985 - No. 12, Feb, 1987 ($1.50/$1.75)(Adults only)
Epic Comics (Marvel)
1-Origin; 1st fully painted comic book 1.20 3.00
2-12: 11-Origin .80 2.00
Trade paperback (1987?)-reprints 2.00 6.00 14.00
Signed & #'d hard-c ($39.95, 1,200 copies)-r/1-12 5.50 17.00 40.00

MOONSHADOW
Sept, 1994 - Present ($2.25, limited series:12)
DC Comics
1-4 .90 2.25

MOON-SPINNERS, THE (See Movie Comics)

MOPSY (See Pageant of Comics & TV Teens)
Feb, 1948 - No. 19, Sept, 1953
St. John Publ. Co.
1-Part-r; reprints "Some Punkins" by Neher 13.00 40.00 90.00
2 8.35 25.00 50.00
3-10(1953): 8-Lingerie panels 6.35 19.00 38.00
11-19: 19-Lingerie-c 5.00 15.00 30.00
NOTE: *#1, 3-6, 13, 18, 19 have paper dolls.*

MORBIUS REVISITED
Aug, 1993 - No. 5, Dec, 1993 ($1.95, mini-series)
Marvel Comic
1-5-Reprints Fear #27-31 .80 2.00

MORBIUS: THE LIVING VAMPIRE (Also see Amazing Spider-Man #101, 102, Fear #20, Marvel Team-Up #3, 4, Midnight Sons Unl. & Vampire Tales)
Sept, 1992 - Present ($1.75/$1.95)
Marvel Comics (Midnight Sons imprint #16 on)
1-($2.75, 52 pgs.)-Polybagged w/poster; Ghost Rider & Johnny Blaze x-over (part 3 of Rise of the Midnight Sons) 1.80 4.50
2 .90 2.25
3-5: 3,4-Vs. Spider-Man-c/story .70 1.80
6-11,13-20: 15-Ghost Rider app. 16-Spot varnish-c. 16,17-Siege of Darkness parts 5 &13. 18-Deathlok app. .70 1.75
12-($2.25)-Outer-c is a Darkhold envelope made of black parchment w/gold ink; Midnight Massacre x-over .90 2.25
21-24,26-31: 21-Begin $1.95-c; bound-in Spider-Man trading card sheet; S-M app. .80 2.00
25-($2.50, 52 pgs.)-Gold foil logo 1.00 2.50

MORE FUN COMICS (Formerly New Fun Comics #1-6)
No. 7, Jan, 1936 - No. 127, Nov-Dec, 1947 (No. 7,9-11: paper-c)
National Periodical Publications GD25 FN65 VF82
7(1/36)-Oversized, paper-c; 1 pg. Kelly-a 500.00 1500.00 3000.00
(Estimated up to 15 total copies exist, none in NM/Mint)
8(2/36)-Oversized (10x12"), slick-c; 1 pg. Kelly-a 500.00 1500.00 3000.00
9(3-4/36)(Very rare, 1st comic-sized issue)-Last multiple panel-c 667.00 2000.00 4000.00
10,11(7/36): 10-Last Henri Duval by Siegel & Shuster. 11-1st "Calling All Cars" by Siegel & Shuster; new classic logo begins 367.00 1100.00 2200.00
12(8/36)-Slick-c begin 283.00 850.00 1700.00
V2#1(9/36, #13) 235.00 825.00 1650.00
2(10/36, #14)-Dr. Occult in costume (1st in color)(Superman proto-type; 1st DC appearance) continues from The Comics Magazine, ends #17 1333.00 4000.00 8000.00
(Estimated up to 10 total copies exist, none in NM/Mint)
V2#3(11/36, #15), 16(V2#4), 17(V2#5): 16-Cover numbering begins; Xmas-c; last Superman tryout issue 550.00 1650.00 3300.00
18-20(V2#8, 5/37) 200.00 600.00 1200.00
GD25 FN65 NM94
21(V2#9)-24(V2#12, 9/37) 171.00 515.00 1200.00
25(V3#1, 10/37)-27(V3#3, 12/37): 27-Xmas-c 171.00 515.00 1200.00
28-30: 30-1st non-funny cover 171.00 515.00 1200.00
31-35: 32-Last Dr. Occult 150.00 450.00 1050.00
36-40: 36-(10/38)-The Masked Ranger & sidekick Pedro begins; Ginger Snap by Bob Kane (2 pgs.; 1st-a?). 39-Xmas-c 150.00 450.00 1050.00
41-50: 41-Last Masked Ranger 114.00 343.00 800.00
51-The Spectre app. (in costume) in one panel ad at end of Buccaneer story 357.00 1071.00 2500.00
GD25 FN65 VF82 NM94
52-(2/40)-Origin/1st app. The Spectre (in costume splash panel only), part 1 by Bernard Baily (parts 1 & 2 written by Jerry Siegel; Spectre's costume changes color from purple & blue to green & grey; last Wing Brady 3200.00 9600.00 20,800.00 32,000.00
(Estimated up to 60 total copies exist, 3 in NM/Mint)
53-Origin The Spectre (in costume at end of story), part 2; Capt. Desmo begins 2050.00 6150.00 13,325.00 20,500.00
(Estimated up to 60 total copies exist, 3 in NM/Mint)
54-The Spectre in costume; last King Carter 725.00 2175.00 3987.00 5800.00
55-(Scarce, 5/40)-Dr. Fate begins (Intro & 1st app.); last Bulldog Martin 1062.00 3190.00 5845.00 8500.00
(Estimated up to 100 total copies exist, 6 in NM/Mint)
GD25 FN65 NM94
56-60: 56-Congo Bill begins (6/40), 1st app.; 1st Dr. Fate-c (classic), origin continues. 58-Classic Spectre-c 286.00 857.00 2000.00
61-66: 61-Classic Dr. Fate-c. 63-Last St. Bob Neal. 64-Lance Larkin begins. 65-Classic Spectre-c 229.00 685.00 1600.00
GD25 FN65 VF82 NM94
67-(5/41)-Origin (1st) Dr. Fate; last Congo Bill & Biff Bronson (C.B. continues in Action Comics #37 (6/41) 525.00 1575.00 2887.00 4200.00
(Estimated up to 105 total copies exist, 6 in NM/Mint)
GD25 FN65 NM94
68-70: 68-Clip Carson begins. 70-Last Lance Larkin 171.00 515.00 1200.00
GD25 FN65 VF82 NM94
71-Origin & 1st app. Johnny Quick by Mort Wysinger (9/41); sci/fi-c 450.00 1350.00 2475.00 3600.00
(Estimated up to 90 total copies exist, 6 in NM/Mint)
GD25 FN65 NM94
72-Dr. Fate's new helmet; last Sgt. Carey, Sgt. O'Malley & Captain Desmo; German submarine-c (only German war-c) 143.00 430.00 1000.00
GD25 FN65 VF82 NM94
73-Origin & 1st app. Aquaman (11/41) & begins; intro. Green Arrow & Speedy 750.00 2250.00 4125.00 6000.00
(Estimated up to 85 total copies exist, 5 in NM/Mint)
GD25 FN65 NM94
74-2nd Aquaman 171.00 515.00 1200.00
75-80: 76-Last Clip Carson; Johnny Quick (by Meskin #76-97) begins, ends #107. 80-Last large logo 157.00 471.00 1100.00
81-88: 82-1st small logo. 84-Only Japanese war-c. 87-Last Radio Squad 104.00 310.00 725.00
89-Origin Green Arrow & Speedy Team-up 121.00 365.00 850.00
90-99: 91-1st bi-monthly issue. 93-Dover & Clover begin (1st app., 9-10/43). 97-Kubert-a. 98-Last Dr. Fate 71.00 215.00 500.00
100 100.00 300.00 700.00
GD25 FN65 VF82 NM94
101-Origin & 1st app. Superboy (1-2/45)(not by Siegel & Shuster); last Spectre issue 550.00 1650.00 3575.00 5500.00
(Estimated up to 200 total copies exist, 9 in NM/Mint)
GD25 FN65 NM94
102-2nd Superboy 114.00 343.00 800.00
103-3rd Superboy 83.00 250.00 580.00
104-107: 107-Last Johnny Quick & Superboy 70.00 210.00 490.00
108-120: 108-Genius Jones begins (3-4/46; cont'd from Adventure Comics #102) 15.00 45.00 105.00
121-124,126: 121-123,126-Post-c (Jimminy-c) 11.50 34.00 80.00
125-Superman on cover 64.00 193.00 450.00
127-(Scarce)-Post-c/a 24.00 73.00 170.00
NOTE: *All issues are scarce to rare. Cover features: The Spectre-#52-55, 57-60, 62-67. Dr. Fate-#56, 61, 68-76. The Green Arrow & Speedy-#77-85, 88-97, 99, 101 (w/Dover & Clover-#98, 103). Johnny Quick-#86, 87, 100. Dover & Clover-#102, (104, 106 w/Superboy), 107,*

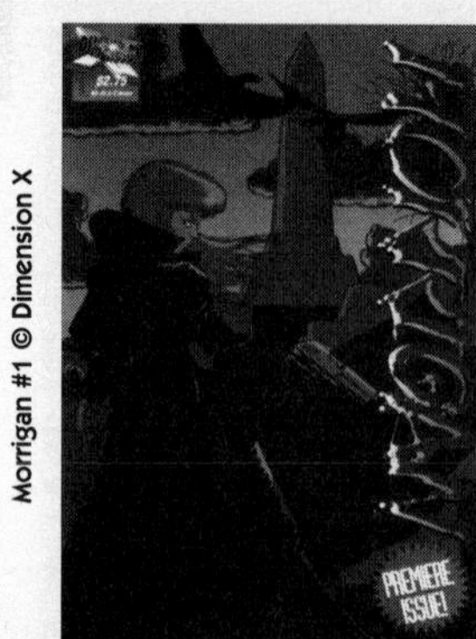

Morrigan #1 © Dimension X

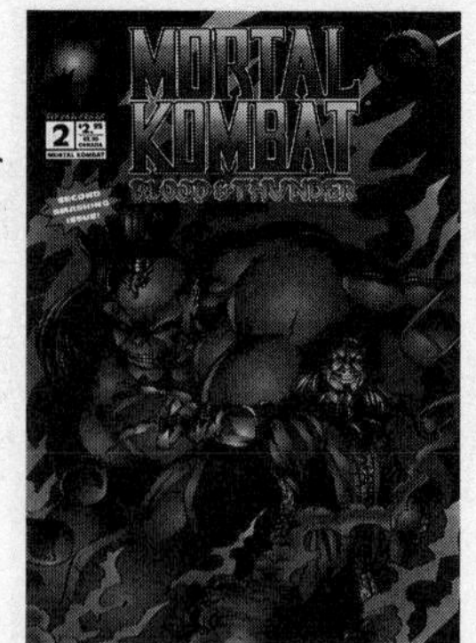

Mortal Kombat #2 © Midway

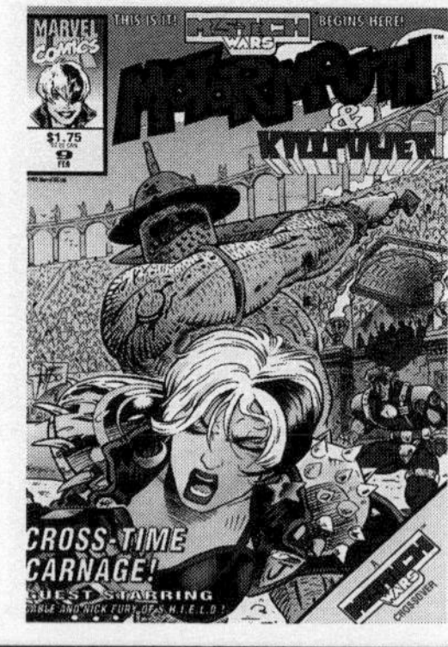

Motormouth #9 © MEG

*108(w/Genius Jones), 110, 112, 114, 117, 119. Genius Jones-#109, 111, 113, 115, 118, 120. **Baily** a-45, 52-on; c-52-55, 57-60, 62-67. **Al Capp** a-45(signed Koppy). **Ellsworth** c-7. **Creig Flessel** c-30, 31, 35-48(most). **Guardineer** c-47, 49, 50. **Kiefer** a-20. **Meskin** c-86, 87, 100? **Moldoff** c-51. **George Papp** c-77-85. **Post** c-121-127. **Vincent Sullivan** c-8-28, 32-34.*

MORE SEYMOUR (See Seymour My Son)
October, 1963
Archie Publications

	GD25	FN65	NM94
1	2.40	6.00	12.00

MORE TRASH FROM MAD (Annual)
1958 - No. 12, 1969
E. C. Comics

	GD25	FN65	NM94
nn(1958)-8 pgs. color Mad reprint from #20	22.00	65.00	150.00
2(1959)-Market Product Labels	14.00	43.00	100.00
3(1960)-Text book covers	13.00	40.00	90.00
4(1961)-Sing Along with Mad booklet	13.00	40.00	90.00
5(1962)-Window Stickers; r/from Mad #39	10.00	30.00	65.00
6(1963)-TV Guise booklet	11.00	32.00	75.00
7(1964)-Alfred E. Neuman commemorative stamps	8.00	24.00	48.00
8(1965)-Life size poster-Alfred E. Neuman	5.85	17.50	35.00
9,10(1966-67)-Mischief Sticker	5.00	15.00	30.00
11(1968)-Campaign poster & bumper sticker	5.00	15.00	30.00
12(1969)-Pocket medals	5.00	15.00	30.00

NOTE: ***Kelly Freas** c-1, 2, 4. **Mingo** c-3, 5-9, 12.*

MORGAN THE PIRATE (See 4-Color #1227)

MORLOCK 2001
Feb, 1975 - No. 3, July, 1975
Atlas/Seaboard Publ.

	GD25	FN65	NM94
1,2: 1-(Super-hero)-Origin & 1st app.			1.00
3-Ditko/Wrightson-a; origin The Midnight Man & The Midnight Men			1.20

MORNINGSTAR SPECIAL (Comico)(Value: cover or less)

MORRIGAN
Aug, 1993 ($2.75, B&W)
Dimension X

	GD25	FN65	NM94
1-Foil stamped-c		1.10	2.75

MORTAL KOMBAT
July, 1994 - Present ($2.95)
Malibu Comics

	GD25	FN65	NM94
1-6: 1-Two variant covers exist		1.20	3.00

MORTIE (Mazie's Friend; also see Flat-Top)
Dec, 1952 - No. 4, June, 1953?
Magazine Publishers

	GD25	FN65	NM94
1	5.00	15.00	30.00
2-4	3.20	8.00	16.00

MORTIGAN GOTH: IMMORTALIS (See Marvel Frontier Comics Unlimited)
Sept, 1993 - No. 4, Mar, 1994 ($1.95, mini-series)
Marvel Comics

	GD25	FN65	NM94
1-($2.95)-Foil-c		1.20	3.00
2-4		.80	2.00

MORT THE DEAD TEENAGER
Nov, 1993 - No. 4, Mar, 1994 ($1.75, mini-series)
Marvel Comics

	GD25	FN65	NM94
1-4		.70	1.75

MORTY MEEKLE (See 4-Color #793)

MOSES & THE TEN COMMANDMENTS (See Dell Giants)

MOTHER GOOSE (See Christmas With Mother Goose & 4-Color #41, 59, 68, 862)

MOTHER OF US ALL
1950? (32 pgs.)
Catechetical Guild Giveaway

	GD25	FN65	NM94
nn	1.60	4.00	8.00

MOTHER TERESA OF CALCUTTA
1984
Marvel Comics Group

	GD25	FN65	NM94
1			1.25

MOTION PICTURE COMICS (See Fawcett Movie Comics)
No. 101, 1950 - No. 114, Jan, 1953 (All-photo-c)
Fawcett Publications

	GD25	FN65	NM94
101- "Vanishing Westerner"; Monte Hale (1950)	27.00	80.00	185.00
102- "Code of the Silver Sage"; Rocky Lane (1/51)	25.00	75.00	175.00
103- "Covered Wagon Raid"; Rocky Lane (3/51)	25.00	75.00	175.00
104- "Vigilante Hideout"; Rocky Lane (5/51)-Book length Powell-a	25.00	75.00	175.00
105- "Red Badge of Courage"; Audie Murphy; Bob Powell-a (7/51)	30.00	90.00	210.00
106- "The Texas Rangers"; George Montgomery (9/51)	25.00	75.00	175.00
107- "Frisco Tornado"; Rocky Lane (11/51)	22.00	67.00	155.00
108- "Mask of the Avenger"; John Derek	15.00	45.00	105.00
109- "Rough Rider of Durango"; Rocky Lane	22.00	67.00	155.00
110- "When Worlds Collide"; George Evans-a (5/52); Williamson & Evans drew themselves in story; (also see Famous Funnies No. 72-88)	74.00	223.00	520.00
111- "The Vanishing Outpost"; Lash LaRue	27.00	81.00	190.00
112- "Brave Warrior"; Jon Hall & Jay Silverheels	13.50	41.00	95.00
113- "Walk East on Beacon"; George Murphy; Shaffenberger-a	10.00	30.00	70.00
114- "Cripple Creek"; George Montgomery (1/53)	11.50	34.00	80.00

MOTION PICTURE FUNNIES WEEKLY (Amazing Man #5 on?)
1939 (36 pgs.)(Giveaway)(Black & White)
No month given; last panel in Sub-Mariner story dated 4/39
(Also see Colossus, Green Giant & Invaders No. 20)
First Funnies, Inc.

	GD25	FN65	NM94
1-Origin & 1st printed app. Sub-Mariner by Bill Everett (8 pgs.); Fred Schwab-c; reprinted in Marvel Mystery #1 with color added over the craft tint which was used to shade the black & white version; Spy Ring, American Ace (reprinted in Marvel Mystery #3) app. (Rare)-only eight (8) known copies,one near mint with white pages, the rest with brown pages.	2600.00	5500.00	11,000.00
Covers only to #2-4 (set)			600.00

NOTE: The only eight known copies (with a ninth suspected) were discovered in 1974 in the estate of the deceased publisher. Covers only to issues No. 2-4 were also found which evidently were printed in advance along with #1. #1 was to be distributed only through motion picture movie houses. However, it is believed that only advanced copies were sent out and the motion picture houses not going for the idea. Possible distribution at local theaters in Boston suspected. The last panel of Sub-Mariner contains a rectangular box with "Continued Next Week" printed in it. When reprinted in Marvel Mystery, the box was left in with lettering omitted.

MOTORBIKE PUPPIES, THE (Dark Zulu Lies)(Value: cover or less)

MOTORHEAD SPECIAL (See Comic's Greatest World)
Mar, 1994 ($3.95, one-shot, 52 pgs.)
Dark Horse Comics

	GD25	FN65	NM94
1-Jae Lee-c; Barb Wire, The Machine & Wolf Gang app.		1.60	4.00

MOTORMOUTH (... & Killpower #7? on)
June, 1992 - No. 13, June, 1993 ($1.75)
Marvel Comics UK

	GD25	FN65	NM94
1-13: 1,2-Nick Fury app. 3-Punisher-c/story. 5,6-Nick Fury & Punisher app. 6-Cable cameo. 7-9-Cable app.		.70	1.80

MOUNTAIN MEN (See Ben Bowie)

MOUSE MUSKETEERS (See M.G.M.'s...)

MOUSE ON THE MOON, THE (See Movie Classics)

MOVIE CLASSICS
Jan, 1963 - Dec, 1969
Dell Publishing Co.

Movie Classics (The Hallelujah Trail) © Mirish-Kappa

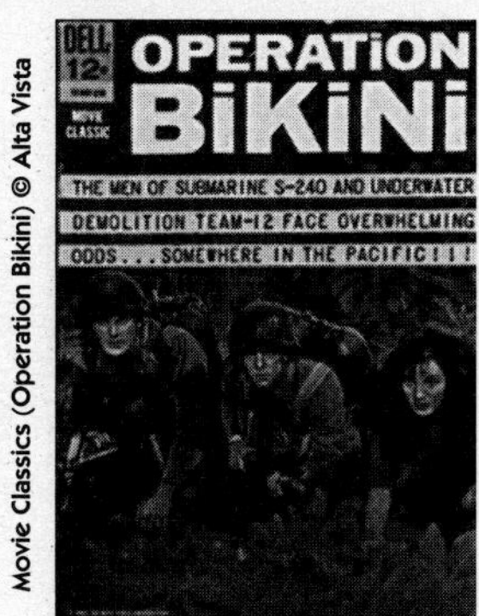

Movie Classics (Operation Bikini) © Alta Vista

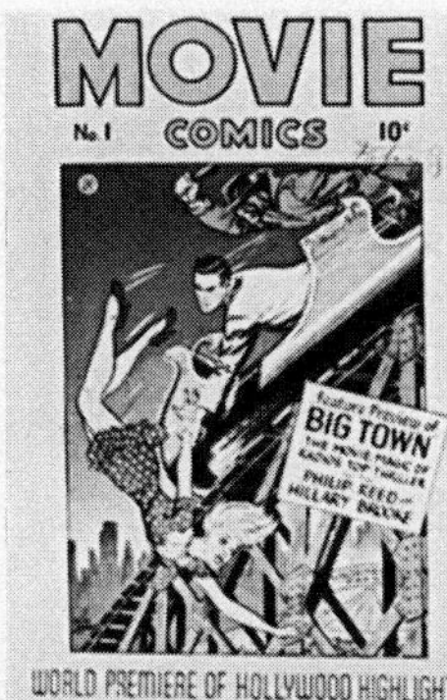

Movie Comics #1 © DC

	GD25	FN65	NM94
(Before 1963, most movie adaptations were part of the 4-Color series)			
(Disney movie adaptations after 1970 are in Walt Disney Showcase)			
Around the World Under the Sea 12-030-612 (12/66)	3.60	9.00	18.00
Bambi 3(4/56)-Disney; r/4-Color #186	4.00	12.00	24.00
Battle of the Bulge 12-056-606 (6/66)	4.00	11.00	22.00
Beach Blanket Bingo 12-058-509	8.35	25.00	50.00
Bon Voyage 01-068-212 (12/62)-Disney; photo-c	4.00	12.00	24.00
Castilian, The 12-110-401	4.00	12.00	24.00
Cat, The 12-109-612 (12/66)	3.20	8.00	16.00
Cheyenne Autumn 12-112-506 (4-6/65)	7.50	22.50	45.00
Circus World, Samuel Bronston's 12-115-411; John Wayne app.; John Wayne photo-c	12.00	36.00	85.00
Countdown 12-150-710 (10/67)-James Caan photo-c	4.00	10.00	20.00
Creature, The 1 (12-142-302) (12-2/62-63)	5.35	16.00	32.00
Creature, The 12-142-410 (10/64)	4.00	10.00	20.00
David Ladd's Life Story 12-173-212 (10-12/62)-Photo-c	10.00	30.00	60.00
Die, Monster, Die 12-175-603 (3/66)-Photo-c	5.85	17.50	35.00
Dirty Dozen 12-180-710 (10/67)	5.35	16.00	32.00
Dr. Who & the Daleks 12-190-612 (12/66)-Peter Cushing photo-c; 1st U.S. app. of Dr. Who	13.50	41.00	95.00
Dracula 12-231-212 (10-12/62)	4.70	14.00	28.00
El Dorado 12-240-710 (10/67)-John Wayne; photo-c	13.50	41.00	95.00
Ensign Pulver 12-257-410 (8-10/64)	4.00	10.00	20.00
Frankenstein 12-283-305 (3-5/63)	4.70	14.00	28.00
Great Race, The 12-299-603 (3/66)-Natallie Wood, Tony Curtis photo-c	5.00	15.00	30.00
Hallelujah Trail, The 12-307-602 (2/66) (Shows 1/66 inside); Burt Lancaster, Lee Remick photo-c	5.85	17.50	35.00
Hatari 12-340-301 (1/63)-John Wayne	10.00	30.00	60.00
Horizontal Lieutenant, The 01-348-210 (10/62)	4.00	10.00	20.00
Incredible Mr. Limpet, The 12-370-408; Don Knotts photo-c	4.70	14.00	28.00
Jack the Giant Killer 12-374-301 (1/63)	10.00	30.00	60.00
Jason & the Argonauts 12-376-310 (8-10/63)-Photo-c	10.00	30.00	70.00
Lancelot & Guinevere 12-416-310 (10/63)	7.50	22.50	50.00
Lawrence 12-426-308 (8/63)-Story of Lawrence of Arabia; movie ad on back-c; not exactly like movie	7.00	21.00	42.00
Lion of Sparta 12-439-301 (1/63)	4.00	10.00	20.00
Mad Monster Party 12-460-801 (9/67)-Based on Kurtzman's screenplay	7.50	22.50	45.00
Magic Sword, The 01-496-209 (9/62)	7.00	21.00	42.00
Masque of the Red Death 12-490-410 (8-10/64)-Vincent Price photo-c	5.85	17.50	35.00
Maya 12-495-612 (12/66)-Clint Walker & Jay North part photo-c	5.35	16.00	32.00
McHale's Navy 12-500-412 (10-12/64)	4.00	11.00	22.00
Merrill's Marauders 12-510-301 (1/63)-Photo-c	4.00	10.00	20.00
Mouse on the Moon, The 12-530-312 (10/12/63)-Photo-c	4.00	11.00	22.00
Mummy, The 12-537-211 (9-11/62) 2 versions with different back-c	5.35	16.00	32.00
Music Man, The 12-538-301 (1/63)	4.00	10.00	20.00
Naked Prey, The 12-545-612 (12/66)-Photo-c	8.00	24.00	48.00
Night of the Grizzly, The 12-558-612 (12/66)-Photo-c	5.00	15.00	30.00
None But the Brave 12-565-506 (4-6/65)	8.00	24.00	48.00
Operation Bikini 12-597-310 (10/63)-Photo-c	4.00	12.00	24.00
Operation Crossbow 12-590-512 (10-12/65)	4.00	12.00	24.00
Prince & the Pauper, The 01-654-207 (5-7/62)-Disney	5.00	15.00	30.00
Raven, The 12-680-309 (9/63)-Vincent Price photo-c	5.85	17.50	35.00
Ring of Bright Water 01-701-910 (10/69) (inside shows #12-701-909)	5.00	15.00	30.00
Runaway, The 12-707-412 (10-12/64)	3.60	9.00	18.00
Santa Claus Conquers the Martians #? (1964)-Photo-c	10.00	30.00	60.00
Santa Claus Conquers the Martians 12-725-603 (3/66, 12¢)-Reprints 1964 issue; photo-c	8.35	25.00	50.00
Another version given away with a Golden Record, SLP 170, nn, no price (3/66)-Complete with record	14.00	43.00	120.00
Six Black Horses 12-750-301 (1/63)-Photo-c	4.00	12.00	24.00
Ski Party 12-743-511 (9-11/65)-Frankie Avalon photo-c	5.85	17.50	35.00
Smoky 12-746-702 (2/67)	3.60	9.00	18.00
Sons of Katie Elder 12-748-511 (9-11/65); John Wayne app.; photo-c	16.00	48.00	110.00
Tales of Terror 12-793-302 (2/63)-Evans-a	4.00	11.00	22.00
Three Stooges Meet Hercules 01-828-208 (8/62)-Photo-c	10.00	30.00	65.00
Tomb of Ligeia 12-830-506 (4-6/65)	4.00	10.00	20.00
Treasure Island 01-845-211 (7-9/62)-Disney; r/4-Color #624	4.00	12.00	24.00
Twice Told Tales (Nathaniel Hawthorne) 12-840-401 (11-1/63-64); Vincent Price photo-c	4.70	14.00	28.00
Two on a Guillotine 12-850-506 (4-6/65)	4.00	10.00	20.00
Valley of Gwangi 01-880-912 (12/69)	10.00	30.00	70.00
War Gods of the Deep 12-900-509 (7-9/65)	4.00	11.00	22.00
War Wagon, The 12-533-709 (9/67); John Wayne app.	11.00	32.00	75.00
Who's Minding the Mint? 12-924-708 (8/67)	4.00	10.00	20.00
Wolfman, The 12-922-308 (6-8/63)	4.00	11.00	22.00
Wolfman, The 1(12-922-410)(8-10/64)-2nd printing; r/#12-922-308	4.00	11.00	22.00
Zulu 12-950-410 (8-10/64)-Photo-c	10.00	30.00	70.00

MOVIE COMICS (See Cinema Comics Herald & Fawcett Movie Comics)

MOVIE COMICS
April, 1939 - No. 6, Sept-Oct, 1939 (Most all photo-c)
National Periodical Publications/Picture Comics

	GD25	FN65	NM94
1- "Gunga Din", "Son of Frankenstein", "The Great Man Votes", "Fisherman's Wharf", & "Scouts to the Rescue" part 1; Wheelan "Minute Movies" begin	271.00	815.00	1900.00
2- "Stagecoach", "The Saint Strikes Back", "King of the Turf","Scouts to the Rescue" part 2, "Arizona Legion", Andy Devine photo-c	171.00	515.00	1200.00
3- "East Side of Heaven", "Mystery in the White Room", "Four Feathers", "Mexican Rose" with Gene Autry, "Spirit of Culver", "Many Secrets", "The Mikado"	136.00	407.00	950.00
4- "Captain Fury", Gene Autry in "Blue Montana Skies", "Streets of N.Y." with Jackie Cooper, "Oregon Trail" part 1 with Johnny Mack Brown, "Big Town Czar" with Barton MacLane, & "Star Reporter" with Warren Hull	107.00	321.00	750.00
5- "The Man in the Iron Mask", "Five Came Back", "Wolf Call", "The Girl & the Gambler", "The House of Fear", "The Family Next Door", "Oregon Trail" part 2	107.00	321.00	750.00
6- "The Phantom Creeps", "Chumps at Oxford", & "The Oregon Trail" part 3; 2nd Robot-c	136.00	407.00	950.00

NOTE: *Above books contain many original movie stills with dialogue from movie scripts. All issues are scarce. 2-Andy Devine photo-c.*

MOVIE COMICS
Dec, 1946 - No. 4, 1947
Fiction House Magazines

	GD25	FN65	NM94
1-Big Town (by Lubbers), Johnny Danger begin; Celardo-a; Mitzi of the Movies by Fran Hopper	39.00	118.00	275.00
2-(2/47)- "White Tie & Tails" with William Bendix; Mitzi of the Movies begins by Matt Baker, ends #4	29.00	86.00	200.00
3-(6/47)-Andy Hardy starring Mickey Rooney	29.00	86.00	200.00
4-Mitzi In Hollywood by Matt Baker; Merton of the Movies with Red Skelton; Yvonne DeCarlo & George Brent in "Slave Girl"	33.00	100.00	230.00

MOVIE COMICS
Oct, 1962 - March, 1972

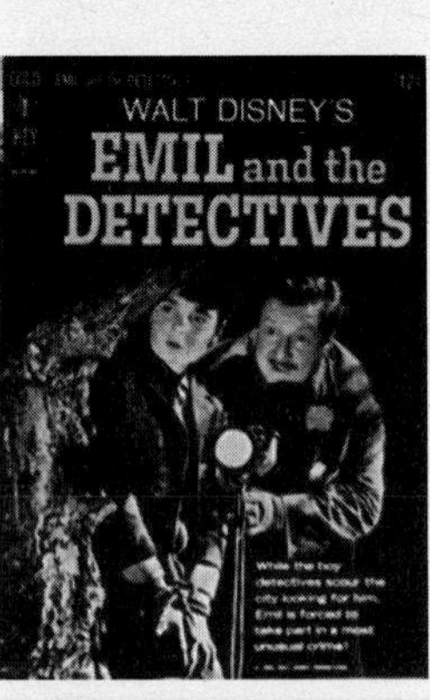

Movie Comics (Emil & the Detectives) © WDC

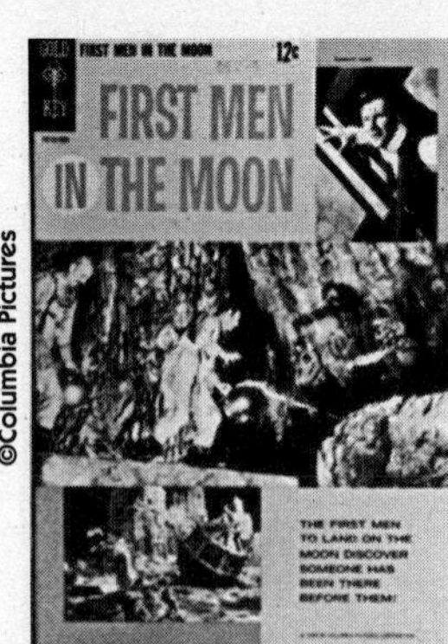

Movie Comics (First Men In The Moon) ©Columbia Pictures

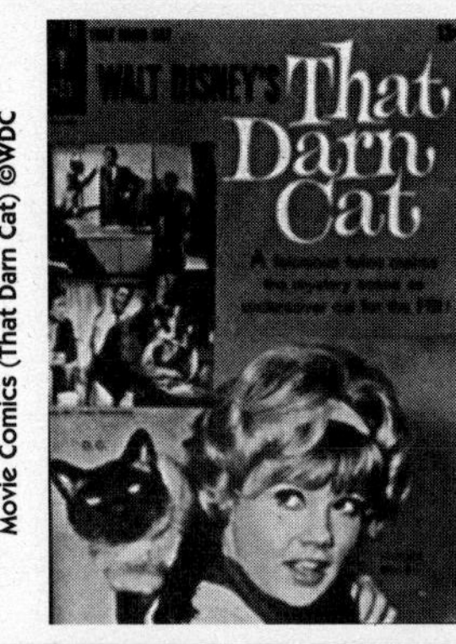

Movie Comics (That Darn Cat) ©WDC

GD25 FN65 NM94

Gold Key/Whitman
Alice in Wonderland 10144-503 (3/65)-Disney; partial reprint of 4-Color #331 4.00 12.00 24.00
Aristocats, The 1 (30045-103)(3/71)-Disney; with pull-out poster (25¢) 8.35 25.00 50.00
Bambi 1 (10087-309)(9/63)-Disney; r/4-C #186 4.00 12.00 24.00
Bambi 2 (10087-607)(7/66)-Disney; r/4-C #186 4.00 10.00 20.00
Beneath the Planet of the Apes 30044-012 (12/70)-with pull-out poster; photo-c 5.35 16.00 32.00
Big Red 10026-211 (11/62)-Disney; photo-c 3.60 9.00 18.00
Big Red 10026-503 (3/65)-Disney; reprints 10026-211; photo-c 3.60 9.00 18.00
Blackbeard's Ghost 10222-806 (6/68)-Disney 4.00 10.00 20.00
Bullwhip Griffin 10181-706 (6/67)-Disney; Manning-a; photo-c 4.70 14.00 28.00
Captain Sindbad 10077-309 (9/63)-Manning-a; photo-c 7.50 22.50 45.00
Chitty Chitty Bang Bang 1 (30038-902)(2/69)-with pull-out poster; Disney; photo-c 6.00 18.00 36.00
Cinderella 10152-508 (8/65)-Disney; r/4-C #786 4.00 10.00 20.00
Darby O'Gill & the Little People 10251-001(1/70)-Disney; reprints 4-Color #1024 (Toth-a); photo-c 6.00 18.00 36.00
Dumbo 1 (10090-310)(10/63)-Disney; r/4-C #668 4.00 10.00 20.00
Emil & the Detectives 10120-502 (2/65)-Disney; photo-c 4.35 13.00 26.00
Escapade in Florence 1 (10043-301)(1/63)-Disney; starring Annette Funicello 10.00 30.00 60.00
Fall of the Roman Empire 10118-407 (7/64); Sophia Loren photo-c 4.00 12.00 24.00
Fantastic Voyage 10178-702 (2/67)-Wood/Adkins-a; photo-c 5.85 17.50 35.00
55 Days at Peking 10081-309 (9/63)-Photo-c 4.00 12.00 24.00
Fighting Prince of Donegal, The 10193-701 (1/67)-Disney 4.00 10.00 20.00
First Men in the Moon 10132-503 (3/65)-Fred Fredericks-a; photo-c 4.00 11.00 22.00
Gay Purr-ee 30017-301(1/63, 84 pgs.) 5.00 15.00 30.00
Gnome Mobile, The 10207-710 (10/67)-Disney 4.35 13.00 26.00
Goodbye, Mr. Chips 10246-006 (6/70)-Peter O'Toole photo-c 4.00 10.00 20.00
Happiest Millionaire, The 10221-804 (4/68)-Disney 3.60 9.00 18.00
Hey There, It's Yogi Bear 10122-409 (9/64)-Hanna-Barbera 5.35 16.00 32.00
Horse Without a Head, The 10109-401 (1/64)-Disney 4.00 10.00 20.00
How the West Was Won 10074-307 (7/63)-Tufts-a 5.00 15.00 30.00
In Search of the Castaways 10048-303 (3/63)-Disney; Hayley Mills photo-c 8.35 25.00 50.00
Jungle Book, The 1 (6022-801)(1/68-Whitman)-Disney; large size (10x13-1/2"); 59¢ 4.35 13.00 26.00
Jungle Book, The 1 (30033-803)(3/68, 68 pgs.)-Disney; same contents as Whitman #1 3.20 8.00 16.00
Jungle Book, The 1 (6/78, $1.00 tabloid) 1.20
Jungle Book (1984)-r/Giant 1.00
Kidnapped 10080-306 (6/63)-Disney; reprints 4-Color #1101; photo-c 3.60 9.00 18.00
King Kong 30036-809(9/68-68 pgs.)-painted-c 4.00 10.00 20.00
King Kong nn-Whitman Treasury($1.00, 68 pgs.,1968), same cover as Gold Key issue 1.20 3.00 6.00
King Kong 11299(#1-786, 10x13-1/4", 68 pgs., $1.00, 1978) 1.00
Lady and the Tramp 10042-301 (1/63)-Disney; r/4-Color #629 4.00 11.00 22.00
Lady and the Tramp 1 (1967-Giant; 25¢)-Disney; reprints part of Dell #1 6.00 18.00 36.00
Lady and the Tramp 2 (10042-203)(3/72)-Disney; r/4-Color #629 2.80 7.00 14.00
Legend of Lobo, The 1 (10059-303)(3/63)-Disney; photo-c

GD25 FN65 NM94

3.60 9.00 18.00
Lt. Robin Crusoe, U.S.N. 10191-610 (10/66)-Disney; Dick Van Dyke photo-c 3.20 8.00 16.00
Lion, The 10035-301 (1/63)-Photo-c 2.80 7.00 14.00
Lord Jim 10156-509 (9/65)-Photo-c 3.60 9.00 18.00
Love Bug, The 10237-906 (6/69)-Disney; Buddy Hackett photo-c 4.00 10.00 20.00
Mary Poppins 10136-501 (1/65)-Disney; photo-c 6.00 18.00 36.00
Mary Poppins 30023-501 (1/65-68 pgs.)-Disney; photo-c 10.00 30.00 60.00
McLintock 10110-403 (3/64); John Wayne app.; John Wayne & Maureen O'Hara photo-c 14.00 43.00 100.00
Merlin Jones as the Monkey's Uncle 10115-510 (10/65)-Disney; Annette Funicello front/back photo-c 6.00 18.00 36.00
Miracle of the White Stallions, The 10065-306 (6/63)-Disney 4.00 11.00 22.00
Misadventures of Merlin Jones, The 10115-405 (5/64)-Disney; Annette Funicello photo front/back-c 6.00 18.00 36.00
Moon-Spinners, The 10124-410 (10/64)-Disney; Haley Mills photo-c 8.35 25.00 50.00
Mutiny on the Bounty 1 (10040-302)(2/63)-Marlon Brando photo-c 4.00 12.00 24.00
Nikki, Wild Dog of the North 10141-412 (12/64)-Disney; reprints 4-Color #1226 3.20 8.00 16.00
Old Yeller 10168-601 (1/66)-Disney; reprints 4-Color #869; photo-c 3.20 8.00 16.00
One Hundred & One Dalmations 1 (10247-002) (2/70)-Disney; reprints 4-Color #1183 4.00 10.00 20.00
Peter Pan 1 (10086-309)(9/63)-Disney; reprints 4-Color #442 4.35 13.00 26.00
Peter Pan 2 (10086-909)(9/69)-Disney; reprints 4-Color #442 3.20 8.00 16.00
Peter Pan 1 ('83)-r/4-Color #442 1.00
P.T. 109 10123-409 (9/64)-John F. Kennedy 5.85 17.50 35.00
Rio Conchos 10143-503(3/65) 5.35 16.00 32.00
Robin Hood 10163-506 (6/65)-Disney; reprints 4-Color #413 4.00 10.00 20.00
Shaggy Dog & the Absent-Minded Professor 30032-708 (8/67-Giant, 68 pgs.) Disney; reprints 4-Color #985,1199 6.00 18.00 36.00
Sleeping Beauty 1 (30042-009)(9/70)-Disney; reprints 4-Color #973; with pull-out poster 5.85 17.50 35.00
Snow White & the Seven Dwarfs 1 (10091-310)(10/63)-Disney; reprints 4-Color #382 4.00 10.00 20.00
Snow White & the Seven Dwarfs 10091-709 (9/67)-Disney; reprints 4-Color #382 3.60 9.00 18.00
Snow White & the Seven Dwarfs 90091-204 (2/84)-Reprints 4-Color #382 1.00
Son of Flubber 1 (10057-304)(4/63)-Disney; sequel to "The Absent-Minded Professor" 4.00 10.00 20.00
Summer Magic 10076-309 (9/63)-Disney; Hayley Mills photo-c; Manning-a 8.35 25.00 50.00
Swiss Family Robinson 10236-904 (4/69)-Disney; reprints 4-Color #1156; photo-c 4.00 10.00 20.00
Sword in the Stone, The 30019-402 (2/64-Giant, 68 pgs.)-Disney (see March of Comics #258 & Wart and the Wizard 6.70 20.00 40.00
That Darn Cat 10171-602 (2/66)-Disney; Hayley Mills photo-c 7.50 22.50 45.00
Those Magnificent Men in Their Flying Machines 10162-510 (10/65); photo-c 4.00 10.00 20.00
Three Stooges in Orbit 30016-211 (11/62-Giant, 32 pgs.)-All photos from movie; stiff-photo-c 11.50 34.00 80.00
Tiger Walks, A 10117-406 (6/64)-Disney; Torres?, Tufts-a; photo-c 6.00 18.00 36.00
Toby Tyler 10142-502 (2/65)-Disney; reprints 4-Color #1092; photo-c 4.00 10.00 20.00
Treasure Island 1 (10200-703)(3/67)-Disney; reprints 4-Color #624; photo-c

Movie Love #8 © FF

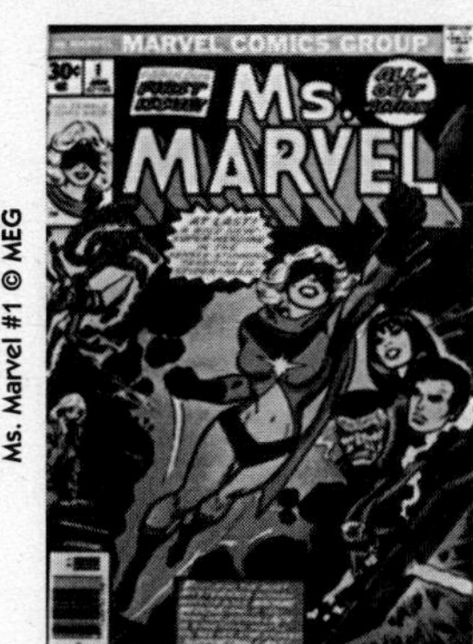

Ms. Marvel #1 © MEG

Ms. Tree Quarterly #3 © DC

	GD25	FN65	NM94
	3.20	8.00	16.00
20,000 Leagues Under the Sea 1 (10095-312)(12/63)-Disney; reprints 4-Color #614	3.20	8.00	16.00
Wonderful Adventures of Pinocchio, The 1 (10089-310)(10/63)-Disney; reprints 4-Color #545 (see Wonderful Advs. of...)	3.20	8.00	16.00
Wonderful Adventures of Pinocchio, The 10089-109 (9/71)-Disney; reprints 4-Color #545	3.20	8.00	16.00
Wonderful World of the Brothers Grimm 1 (10008-210)(10/62)	4.70	14.00	28.00
X, the Man with the X-Ray Eyes 10083-309 (9/63)-Ray Milland photo on-c	8.35	25.00	50.00
Yellow Submarine 35000-902 (2/69-Giant, 68 pgs.)-With pull-out poster; The Beatles cartoon movie	25.00	75.00	175.00
Without poster	7.00	21.00	50.00

MOVIE LOVE (Also see Personal Love)
Feb, 1950 - No. 22, Aug, 1953
Famous Funnies

	GD25	FN65	NM94
1-Dick Powell photo-c; Mickey Rooney on-c	10.00	30.00	60.00
2-Myrna Loy photo-c	5.00	15.00	30.00
3-7,9: 6-Ricardo Montalban photo-c	4.00	12.00	24.00
8-Williamson/Frazetta-a, 6 pgs.	23.00	70.00	160.00
10-Frazetta-a, 6 pgs.	28.00	85.00	200.00
11,14-16: 14-Janet Leigh photo-c	4.00	10.00	20.00
12-Dean Martin & Jerry Lewis photo-c (12/51, pre-dates Advs. of Dean Martin & Jerry Lewis comic)	5.00	15.00	30.00
13-Ronald Reagan photo-c with 1 pg. biog.	15.00	45.00	105.00
17-One pg. Frazetta ad	4.00	11.00	22.00
18-22: 19-John Derek photo-c	4.00	10.00	20.00

NOTE: *Each issue has a full-length movie adaptation with photo covers.*

MOVIE THRILLERS
1949 (Movie adaptation; Burt Lancaster photo-c)
Magazine Enterprises

	GD25	FN65	NM94
1- "Rope of Sand" with Burt Lancaster	23.00	70.00	160.00

MOVIE TOWN ANIMAL ANTICS (Formerly Animal Antics; becomes Raccoon Kids #52 on)
No. 24, Jan-Feb, 1950 - No. 51, July-Aug, 1954
National Periodical Publications

	GD25	FN65	NM94
24-Raccoon Kids continue	10.00	30.00	60.00
25-51	8.35	25.00	50.00

NOTE: ***Sheldon Mayer** a-28-33, 35, 37-41, 43, 44, 47, 49-51.*

MOVIE TUNES COMICS (Formerly Animated...; Frankie No. 4 on)
No. 3, Fall, 1946
Marvel Comics (MgPC)

	GD25	FN65	NM94
3-Super Rabbit, Krazy Krow, Silly Seal & Ziggy Pig	9.15	27.50	55.00

MOWGLI JUNGLE BOOK (See 4-Color #487, 582, 620)

MR. (See Mister)

MS. MARVEL (Also see The Avengers #183)
Jan, 1977 - No. 23, Apr, 1979
Marvel Comics Group

	GD25	FN65	NM94
1-1st app. Ms. Marvel; Scorpion app. in #1,2		1.30	3.25
2-Origin		.90	2.25
3-10: 5-Vision app. 10-Last 30¢ issue		.70	1.80
11-23: 18-Avengers x-over. 19-Capt. Marvel app. 20-New costume. 23-Vance Astro (leader of the Guardians) app.			1.50

NOTE: ***Austin** c-14i, 16i, 17i, 22i. **Buscema** a-1-3p; c(p)-2, 4, 6, 7; 15. **Infantino** a-14p, 19p. **Gil Kane** c-8. **Mooney** a-4-8p, 13p, 15-18p. **Starlin** c-12.*

MS. MYSTIC (Pacific)(Value; cover or less)

MS. MYSTIC
Oct, 1993 - Present ($2.50, color)
Continunity Comics

	GD25	FN65	NM94
V2#1-4: 1-Adams-c(i)/part-i. 2-4-Embossed-c. 2-Nebres part-i. 3-Adams-c(i)/plot. 4-Adams-c(p)/plot		1.00	2.50

MS. MYSTIC DEATHWATCH 2000 (Ms. Mystic #3)
May, 1993 - No. 3, Aug, 1993 ($2.50, color)
Continuity

	GD25	FN65	NM94
1-Bagged w/card; Adams-c & plot		1.00	2.50
2-Bagged w/card; Adams plot		1.00	2.50
3-Bagged w/card; wraparound indestructible-c by Golden/Cory; Adams plot		1.00	2.50

MS. TREE QUARTERLY/SPECIAL (DC)(Value: cover or less)

MS. TREE'S THRILLING DETECTIVE ADVS (Eclipse)(Value: cover or less)

MS. VICTORY SPECIAL(Americomics)(Value: cover or less)

MUGGSY MOUSE (Also see Tick Tock Tales)
1951 - No. 3, 1951; No. 4, 1954 - No. 5, 1954; 1963
Magazine Enterprises

	GD25	FN65	NM94
1(A-1 #33)	5.00	15.00	30.00
2(A-1 #36)-Racist-c	5.85	17.50	35.00
3(A-1 #39), 4(A-1 #95), 5(A-1 #99)	3.20	8.00	16.00
Super Reprint #14(1963)	1.00	2.50	5.00
I.W. Reprint #1,2 (nd)	1.00	2.50	5.00

MUGGY-DOO, BOY CAT
July, 1953 - No. 4, Jan, 1954
Stanhall Publ.

	GD25	FN65	NM94
1-Funny animal; Irving Spector-a	5.85	17.50	35.00
2-4	4.20	12.50	25.00
Super Reprint #12('63), 16('64)	1.00	2.50	5.00

MUMMY, THE (See Universal Presents... under Dell Giants & Movie Classics)

MUMMY ARCHIVES, THE (Millennium)(Value: cover or less)

MUNDEN'S BAR ANNUAL (First)(Value: cover or less)

MUNSTERS, THE (TV)
Jan, 1965 - No. 16, Jan, 1968 (All photo-c)
Gold Key

	GD25	FN65	NM94
1 (10134-501)	20.00	60.00	140.00
2	9.00	28.00	65.00
3-5	7.90	24.00	55.00
6-16	6.90	21.00	48.00

MUPPET BABIES, THE (TV)(Marvel & Harvey)(Value: cover or less)

MUPPETS TAKE MANHATTAN, THE (Marvel)(Value: cover or less)

MURCIELAGA, SHE-BAT
Jan, 1993 - No. 2, 1993 (B&W)
Heroic Publishing

	GD25	FN65	NM94
1-($1.50, 28 pgs.)			1.50
2-($2.95, 36 pgs.)-Coated-c		1.20	3.00

MURDER, INCORPORATED (My Private Life #16 on)
1/48 - No. 15, 12/49; (2 No.9's); 6/50 - No. 3, 8/51
Fox Feature Syndicate

	GD25	FN65	NM94
1 (1st Series); 1,2 have 'For Adults Only' on-c	26.00	78.00	180.00
2-Electrocution story	19.00	57.00	130.00
3-7,9(4/49),10(5/49),11-15	11.00	32.00	70.00
8-Used in **SOTI**, pg. 160	13.00	40.00	90.00
9(3/49)-Possible use in **SOTI**, pg. 145; r/Blue Beetle #56('48)	11.00	32.00	75.00
5(#1, 6/50)(2nd Series)-Formerly My Desire #4	9.15	27.50	55.00
2(8/50)-Morisi-a	7.50	22.50	45.00
3(8/51)-Used in **POP**, pg. 81; Rico-a; lingerie-c/panels	9.15	27.50	55.00

MURDEROUS GANGSTERS
July, 1951; No. 2, Dec, 1951 - No. 4, June, 1952
Avon Periodicals/Realistic No. 3 on

	GD25	FN65	NM94
1-Pretty Boy Floyd, Leggs Diamond; 1 pg. Wood-a	27.00	81.00	190.00
2-Baby-Face Nelson; 1 pg. Wood-a; painted-c	16.50	50.00	115.00

Mutatis #2 © MEG

Mutt & Jeff #108 © Ball Synd.

My Desire #3 © FOX

GD25 FN65 NM94

3-Painted-c 13.00 40.00 90.00
4- "Murder by Needle" drug story; Mort Lawrence-a; Kinstler-c 16.50 50.00 115.00

MURDER TALES (Magazine)
V1#10, Nov, 1970 - V1#11, Jan, 1971 (52 pgs.)
World Famous Publications

V1#10-One pg. Frazetta ad 2.10 6.50 15.00
11-Guardineer-r; bondage-c 1.30 3.25 8.00

MUSHMOUSE AND PUNKIN PUSS (TV)
September, 1965 (Hanna-Barbera)
Gold Key

1 (10153-509) 8.00 24.00 48.00

MUSIC MAN, THE (See Movie Classics)

MUTANT MISADVENTURES OF CLOAK AND DAGGER, THE (Becomes Cloak and Dagger #14 on)
Oct, 1988 - No. 19, Aug, 1991 (#1: $1.25; #2-on: $1.50)
Marvel Comics

1-8,10-18: 1-X-Factor app. 9,10-Painted-c. 12-Dr. Doom app. 14-Begin new direction. 16-18-Spider-Man x-over. 18-Infinity Gauntlet x-over; Thanos cameo; Ghost Rider app. 1.50
9-($2.50, 52 pgs.)-The Avengers x-over 1.00 2.50
19-($2.50, 52 pgs.)-Origin Cloak & Dagger 1.00 2.50
NOTE: ***Austin** a-12i; c(i)-4, 12, 13; scripts-all. **Russell** a-2i. **Williamson** a-14i-16i; c-15i.*

MUTANTS & MISFITS (Silverline)(Value: cover or less)

MUTATIS
1992 - No. 3, 1992 ($2.25, mini-series)
Epic Comics (Marvel)

1-3: Painted-c .90 2.25

MUTINY (Stormy Tales of the Seven Seas)
Oct, 1954 - No. 3, Feb, 1955
Aragon Magazines

1 10.00 30.00 70.00
2,3: 2-Capt. Mutiny. 3-Bondage-c 8.35 25.00 50.00

MUTINY ON THE BOUNTY (See Classics Illustrated #100 & Movie Comics)

MUTT & JEFF (...Cartoon, The)
1910 - No. 5, 1916 (5-3/4x15-1/2") (Hardcover-B&W)
Ball Publications

GD25 FN65 VF82
1(1910)(68 pgs., 50¢) 65.00 195.00 650.00
2,3: 2(1911, 68 pgs.)-Opium den panels; Jeff smokes opium (pipe dreams). 3(1912, 68 pgs.) 50.00 150.00 500.00
4(1915)(68 pgs., 50¢)(Rare) 50.00 150.00 500.00
5(1916)(68 pgs.)(Rare)-Photos of Fisher, 1st pg. 55.00 165.00 550.00
NOTE: *Mutt & Jeff first appeared in newspapers in 1908. Cover variations exist showing Mutt & Jeff reading various newspapers; i.e., The Oregon Journal, The American, and The Detroit News. Reprinting of each issue began soon after publication. No. 5 may not have been reprinted. Values listed include the reprints.*

MUTT & JEFF
No. 6, 1919 - No. 22, 1933? (B&W dailies) (9-1/2x9-1/2"; stiff-c; 52 pgs.)
Cupples & Leon Co.

6-22-By Bud Fisher 30.00 90.00 300.00
NOTE: *Later issues are somewhat rarer.*
nn(1920)-(Advs. of...) 16x11"; 20 pgs.; reprints 1919 Sunday strips 45.00 135.00 450.00
Big Book nn(1926, 144 pgs., hardcovers) 35.00 105.00 350.00
Dust jacket only (rare) 35.00 105.00 350.00
Big Book 1(1928)-Thick book (hardcovers) 35.00 105.00 350.00
Dust jacket only (rare) 35.00 105.00 350.00
Big Book 2(1929)-Thick book (hardcovers) 35.00 105.00 350.00
Dust jacket only (rare) 35.00 105.00 350.00
NOTE: *The Big Books contain three previous issues rebound.*

MUTT & JEFF
1921 (9x15")
Embee Publ. Co.

nn-Sunday strips in color (Rare) 65.00 195.00 650.00

MUTT AND JEFF (See All-American, All-Flash #18, Cicero's Cat, Comic Cavalcade, Famous Feature Stories, The Funnies, Popular & Xmas Comics)
Summer, 1939 (nd) - No. 148, Nov, 1965
All American/National 1-103(6/58)/Dell 104(10/58)-115 (10-12/59)/
Harvey 116(2/60)-148

GD25 FN65 NM94
1(nn)-Lost Wheels 130.00 385.00 900.00
2(nn)-Charging Bull (Summer, 1940, nd; on sale 6/20/40) 71.00 215.00 500.00
3(nn)-Bucking Broncos (Summer, 1941, nd) 50.00 150.00 350.00
4(Winter, '41), 5(Summer, '42) 46.00 140.00 325.00
6-10 22.00 65.00 150.00
11-20: 20-X-Mas-c 14.00 43.00 100.00
21-30 10.00 30.00 70.00
31-50: 32-X-Mas-c 7.50 22.50 45.00
51-75-Last Fisher issue. 53-Last 52 pgs. 5.85 17.50 35.00
76-99,101-103: 76-Last precode issue(1/55) 4.20 12.50 25.00
100 5.00 15.00 30.00
104-148: 117,118,120-131-Richie Rich app. 3.20 8.00 16.00
...Jokes 1-3(8/60-61, Harvey)-84 pgs.; Richie Rich in all; Little Dot in #2,3 4.00 110.00 22.00
...New Jokes 1-4(10/63-11/65, Harvey)-68 pgs.; Richie Rich in #1-3; Stumbo in #1 2.40 6.00 12.00
NOTE: *Most all issues by **Al Smith**. Issues from 1963 on have **Fisher** reprints. Clarification: early issues signed by Fisher are mostly drawn by Smith.*

MY BROTHERS' KEEPER (Spire Christian)(Value: cover or less)

MY CONFESSIONS (My Confession #7&8; formerly Western True Crime; A Spectacular Feature Magazine #11)
No. 7, Aug, 1949 - No. 10, Jan-Feb, 1950
Fox Feature Syndicate

7-Wood-a (10 pgs.) 13.00 40.00 90.00
8-Harrison/Wood-a (19 pgs.) 11.50 34.00 80.00
9,10 5.85 17.50 35.00

MY DATE COMICS (Teen-age)
July, 1947 - V1No.4, Jan, 1948 (2nd Romance comic; see Young Romance)
Hillman Periodicals

1-S&K-c/a 22.00 65.00 150.00
2-4-S&K-c/a; Dan Barry-a 14.00 43.00 100.00

MY DESIRE (Formerly Jo-Jo Comics; becomes Murder, Inc. #5 on)
No. 30, Aug, 1949 - No. 4, April, 1950
Fox Feature Syndicate

30(#1) 9.15 27.50 55.00
31 (#2, 10/49),3(2/50),4 5.85 17.50 35.00
31 (Canadian edition) 4.00 12.00 24.00
32(12/49)-Wood-a 11.50 34.00 80.00

MY DIARY (Becomes My Friend Irma #3 on?)
Dec, 1949 - No. 2, Mar, 1950
Marvel Comics (A Lovers Mag.)

1,2-Photo-c 9.15 27.50 55.00

MY DOG TIGE (Buster Brown's Dog)
1957 (Giveaway)
Buster Brown Shoes

nn 4.00 10.00 20.00

MY EXPERIENCE (Formerly All Top; becomes Judy Canova #23 on)
No. 19, Sept, 1949 - No. 22, Mar, 1950
Fox Feature Syndicate

19-Wood-a 13.50 41.00 95.00
20 5.85 17.50 35.00
21-Wood-a(2) 14.00 43.00 100.00
22-Wood-a (9 pgs.) 11.50 34.00 80.00

My Favorite Martian #1 © Jack Cherton TV

My Greatest Adventure #17 © DC

My Love Affair #1 © FOX

MY FAVORITE MARTIAN (TV)
1/64; No.2, 7/64 - No. 9, 10/66 (No. 1,3-9 have photo-c)
Gold Key

	GD25	FN65	NM94
1-Russ Manning-a	10.00	30.00	72.00
2	5.00	15.00	36.00
3-9	6.00	17.00	40.00

MY FRIEND IRMA (Radio/TV) (Formerly My Diary? and/or Western Life Romances?)
No. 3, June, 1950 - No. 47, Dec, 1954; No. 48, Feb, 1955
Marvel/Atlas Comics (BFP)

	GD25	FN65	NM94
3-Dan DeCarlo-a in all; 52 pgs. begin, end ?	10.00	30.00	60.00
4-Kurtzman-a (10 pgs.)	11.00	32.00	75.00
5- "Egghead Doodle" by Kurtzman (4 pgs.)	9.15	27.50	55.00
6,8-10: 9-paper dolls, 1 pg; Millie app. (5 pgs.)	5.35	16.00	32.00
7-One pg. Kurtzman-a	5.85	17.50	35.00
11-23: 23-One pg. Frazetta-a	4.00	11.00	22.00
24-48	3.20	8.00	16.00

MY GIRL PEARL
4/55 - #4, 10/55; #5, 7/57 - #6, 9/57; #7, 8/60 - #11, ?/61
Atlas Comics

	GD25	FN65	NM94
1-Dan DeCarlo-c/a in #1-6	9.15	27.50	55.00
2	5.00	15.00	30.00
3-6	3.20	8.00	16.00
7-11	2.80	7.00	14.00

MY GREATEST ADVENTURE (Doom Patrol #86 on)
Jan-Feb, 1955 - No. 85, Feb, 1964
National Periodical Publications

	GD25	FN65	NM94
1-Before CCA	93.00	280.00	840.00
2	44.00	133.00	400.00
3-5	28.00	83.00	250.00
6-10: 6-Science fiction format begins	22.00	67.00	200.00
11-15,19	17.00	52.00	155.00
16-18,20,21,28-Kirby-a: 18-Kirby-c	15.00	45.00	135.00
22-27,29,30	10.00	30.00	90.00
31-40	8.00	23.00	70.00
41-61: 58,60,61-Toth-a; Last 10¢ issue	5.50	16.50	50.00
62-79: 77-Toth-a	3.35	10.00	30.00
80-(6/63)-Intro/origin Doom Patrol and begin series; origin & 1st app. Negative Man, Elasti-Girl & S.A. Robotman	36.00	95.00	320.00
81-85: 81,85-Toth-a	13.00	36.00	120.00

NOTE: ***Anderson** a-42. **Cameron** a-24. **Colan** a-77. **Meskin** a-25, 26, 32, 39, 45, 50, 56, 57, 61, 64, 70, 73, 74, 76, 79; c-76. **Moreira** a-11, 12, 15, 17, 20, 23, 25, 27, 37, 40-43, 46, 48, 55-57, 59, 60, 62-65, 67, 69, 70; c-1-4, 7-10. **Roussos** c/a-71-73. **Wildey** a-32.*

MY GREATEST THRILLS IN BASEBALL
Date? (16 pg. Giveaway)
Mission of California

	GD25	FN65	NM94
nn-By Mickey Mantle	46.00	137.00	320.00

MY GREAT LOVE (Becomes Will Rogers Western #5)
Oct, 1949 - No. 4, Apr, 1950
Fox Feature Syndicate

	GD25	FN65	NM94
1	9.15	27.50	55.00
2-4	5.00	15.00	30.00

MY INTIMATE AFFAIR (Inside Crime #3)
Mar, 1950 - No. 2, May, 1950
Fox Feature Syndicate

	GD25	FN65	NM94
1	9.15	27.50	55.00
2	5.00	15.00	30.00

MY LIFE (Formerly Meet Corliss Archer)
No. 4, Sept, 1948 - No. 15, July, 1950
Fox Feature Syndicate

	GD25	FN65	NM94
4-Used in **SOTI**, pg. 39; Kamen/Feldstein-a	23.00	70.00	160.00
5-Kamen-a	11.00	32.00	70.00
6-Kamen/Feldstein-a	11.00	32.00	75.00
7-Wash cover	8.35	25.00	50.00
8,9,11-15	5.00	15.00	30.00
10-Wood-a	11.00	32.00	75.00

MY LITTLE MARGIE (TV)
July, 1954 - No. 54, Nov, 1964
Charlton Comics

	GD25	FN65	NM94
1-Photo front/back-c	20.00	60.00	140.00
2-Photo front/back-c	10.00	30.00	65.00
3-7,10	5.85	17.50	35.00
8,9-Infinity-c	6.35	19.00	38.00
11-14: Part-photo-c (#13, 8/56)	5.00	15.00	30.00
15-19	4.00	11.00	22.00
20-(25¢, 100 pg. issue)	9.15	27.50	55.00
21-38-Last 10¢ issue?	3.60	9.00	18.00
39-53	2.40	6.00	12.00
54-Beatles on cover; lead story spoofs the Beatle haircut craze of the 1960's	12.00	36.00	85.00

NOTE: *Doll cut-outs in 32, 33, 40, 45, 50.*

MY LITTLE MARGIE'S BOY FRIENDS (TV) (Freddy V2#12 on)
Aug, 1955 - No. 11, Apr?, 1958
Charlton Comics

	GD25	FN65	NM94
1-Has several Archie swipes	9.15	27.50	55.00
2	5.85	17.50	35.00
3-11	4.00	11.00	22.00

MY LITTLE MARGIE'S FASHIONS (TV)
Feb, 1959 - No. 5, Nov, 1959
Charlton Comics

	GD25	FN65	NM94
1	9.15	27.50	55.00
2-5	5.85	17.50	35.00

MY LOVE (Becomes Two Gun Western #5 (11/50) on?)
July, 1949 - No. 4, Apr, 1950 (All photo-c)
Marvel Comics (CLDS)

	GD25	FN65	NM94
1	8.35	25.00	50.00
2,3	5.35	16.00	32.00
4-Betty Page photo-c (see Cupid #2)	19.00	57.00	130.00

MY LOVE
Sept, 1969 - No. 39, Mar, 1976
Marvel Comics Group

	GD25	FN65	NM94
1	1.70	5.00	12.00
2-9: 4-6-Colan-a	1.00	2.50	6.00
10-Williamson-r/My Own Romance #71; Kirby-a	1.20	2.90	7.00
11-20: 14-Morrow-c/a; Kirby/Colletta-r		1.60	4.00
21,22,24-39: 38,39-Reprints		1.50	3.00
23-Steranko-r/Our Love Story #5	1.00	2.00	5.00
Special(12/71)	1.00	2.00	5.00

NOTE: ***John Buscema** a-1-7, 10, 22r(2), 24r, 25r, 29r, 34r, 36r, 37r, Spec. (r)(4); c-13, 15, 25, 27, Spec. **Colan** a-16, 22, 24r, 35r, 39r. **Colan/Everett** a-13, 15, 16, 27(r/#13).*

MY LOVE AFFAIR (March of Crime #7 on)
July, 1949 - No. 6, May, 1950
Fox Feature Syndicate

	GD25	FN65	NM94
1	9.15	27.50	55.00
2	5.35	16.00	32.00
3-6-Wood-a. 5-(3/50)-Becomes Love Stories #6	11.00	32.00	75.00

MY LOVE LIFE (Formerly Zegra)
No. 6, June, 1949 - No. 13, Aug, 1950; No. 13, Sept, 1951
Fox Feature Syndicate

	GD25	FN65	NM94
6-Kamenish-a	10.00	30.00	65.00
7-13	5.35	16.00	32.00
13 (9/51)	4.70	14.00	28.00

MY LOVE MEMOIRS (Formerly Women Outlaws; Hunted #13 on)
No. 9, Nov, 1949 - No. 12, May, 1950

My Love Memoirs #11 © FOX

My Personal Problem #1 © AJAX

My Secret Confession #1 © Sterling

Fox Feature Syndicate

	GD25	FN65	NM94
9,11,12-Wood-a	10.00	30.00	70.00
10	5.35	16.00	32.00

MY LOVE SECRET (Formerly Phantom Lady; Animal Crackers #31)
No. 24, June, 1949 - No. 30, June, 1950; No. 53, 1954
Fox Feature Syndicate/M. S. Distr.

	GD25	FN65	NM94
24-Kamen/Feldstein-a	10.00	30.00	65.00
25-Possible caricature of Wood on-c?	5.85	17.50	35.00
26,28-Wood-a	10.00	30.00	70.00
27,29,30: 30-Photo-c	4.70	14.00	28.00
53-(Reprint, M.S. Distr.) 1954? nd given; formerly Western Thrillers; becomes Crimes by Women #54; photo-c	3.60	9.00	18.00

MY LOVE STORY (Hoot Gibson Western #5 on)
Sept, 1949 - No. 4, Mar, 1950
Fox Feature Syndicate

	GD25	FN65	NM94
1	9.15	27.50	55.00
2	5.00	15.00	30.00
3,4-Wood-a	11.00	32.00	75.00

MY LOVE STORY
April, 1956 - No. 9, Aug, 1957
Atlas Comics (GPS)

	GD25	FN65	NM94
1	7.50	22.50	45.00
2	4.00	11.00	22.00
3-Matt Baker-a	4.70	14.00	28.00
4-6,8,9	4.00	10.00	20.00
7-Matt Baker, Toth-a	5.00	15.00	30.00

NOTE: ***Brewster** a-3. **Colletta** a-1(2), 3, 4(2), 5; c-3.*

MY NAME IS CHAOS
1992 - No. 4, 1992 ($4.95, mini-series, 52 pgs.)
DC Comics

	GD25	FN65	NM94
Book 1-4: Tom Veitch scripts; painted-c	1.00	2.00	5.00

MY ONLY LOVE
July, 1975 - No. 9, Nov, 1976
Charlton Comics

	GD25	FN65	NM94
1,2,4-9		1.20	3.00
3-Toth-a		1.60	4.00

MY OWN ROMANCE (Formerly My Romance; Teen-Age Romance #77 on)
No. 4, Mar, 1949 - No. 76, July, 1960
Marvel/Atlas (MjPC/RCM No. 4-59/ZPC No. 60-76)

	GD25	FN65	NM94
4-Photo-c	9.15	27.50	55.00
5-10: 5,6,8-10-Photo-c	4.00	12.00	24.00
11-20: 14-Powell-a	4.00	10.00	20.00
21-42: 42-Last precode (2/55)	3.60	9.00	18.00
43-54,56-60	2.80	7.00	14.00
55-Toth-a	4.35	13.00	26.00
61-70,72-76	2.40	6.00	12.00
71-Williamson-a	4.70	14.00	28.00

NOTE: ***Brewster** a-59. **Colletta** a-45(2), 48, 50, 55, 57(2), 59; c-58i, 59, 61. **Everett** a-25; c-58p. **Morisi** a-18. **Orlando** a-61. **Romita** a-36. **Tuska** a-10.*

MY PAL DIZZY (See Comic Books, Series I)

MY PAST (...Confessions) (Formerly Western Thrillers)
No. 7, Aug, 1949 - No. 11, April, 1950 (Crimes Inc. #12)
Fox Feature Syndicate

	GD25	FN65	NM94
7	8.35	25.00	50.00
8-10	5.00	15.00	30.00
11-Wood-a	10.00	30.00	70.00

MY PERSONAL PROBLEM
11/55; No. 2, 2/56; No. 3, 9/56 - No. 4, 11/56; 10/57 - No. 3, 5/58
Ajax/Farrell/Steinway Comic

	GD25	FN65	NM94
1	5.85	17.50	35.00
2-4	4.00	11.00	22.00
1-3('57-'58)-Steinway	3.60	9.00	18.00

MY PRIVATE LIFE (Formerly Murder, Inc.; becomes Pedro #18)
No. 16, Feb, 1950 - No. 17, April, 1950
Fox Feature Syndicate

	GD25	FN65	NM94
16,17	7.00	21.00	42.00

MYRA NORTH (See The Comics, Crackajack Funnies, 4-Color #3 & Red Ryder)

MY REAL LOVE
No. 5, June, 1952
Standard Comics

	GD25	FN65	NM94
5-Toth-a, 3 pgs.; Tuska, Cardy, Vern Greene-a; photo-c	8.35	25.00	50.00

MY ROMANCE (Becomes My Own Romance #4 on)
Sept, 1948 - No. 3, Jan, 1949
Marvel Comics (RCM)

	GD25	FN65	NM94
1	9.15	27.50	55.00
2,3: 2-Anti-Wertham editorial (11/48)	5.00	15.00	30.00

MY ROMANTIC ADVENTURES (Formerly Romantic Adventures)
No. 68, 8/56 - No. 115, 12/60; No. 116, 7/61 - No. 138, 3/64
American Comics Group

	GD25	FN65	NM94
68	5.00	15.00	30.00
69-85	3.20	8.00	16.00
86-Three pg. Williamson-a (2/58)	4.70	14.00	28.00
87-100	2.40	6.00	12.00
101-138	1.40	3.50	7.00

NOTE: ***Whitney** art in most issues.*

MY SECRET (Becomes Our Secret #4 on)
Aug, 1949 - No. 3, Oct, 1949
Superior Comics, Ltd.

	GD25	FN65	NM94
1	9.15	27.50	55.00
2,3	5.85	17.50	35.00

MY SECRET AFFAIR (Becomes Martin Kane #4)
Dec, 1949 - No. 3, April, 1950
Hero Book (Fox Feature Syndicate)

	GD25	FN65	NM94
1-Harrison/Wood-a (10 pgs.)	11.50	34.00	80.00
2-Wood-a (poor)	8.35	25.00	50.00
3-Wood-a	10.00	30.00	70.00

MY SECRET CONFESSION
September, 1955
Sterling Comics

	GD25	FN65	NM94
1-Sekowsky-a	5.00	15.00	30.00

MY SECRET LIFE (Formerly Western Outlaws; Romeo Tubbs #26 on)
No. 22, July, 1949 - No. 27, May, 1950
Fox Feature Syndicate

	GD25	FN65	NM94
22	6.70	20.00	40.00
23,26-Wood-a, 6 pgs.	10.00	30.00	70.00
24,25,27	4.35	13.00	26.00

NOTE: *The title was changed to Romeo Tubbs after #25 even though #26 & 27 did come out.*

MY SECRET LIFE (Formerly Young Lovers; Sue & Sally Smith #48)
No. 19, Aug, 1957 - No. 47, Sept, 1962
Charlton Comics

	GD25	FN65	NM94
19	2.80	7.00	14.00
20-35	1.40	3.50	7.00
36-47: 44-Last 10¢ issue	1.00	2.50	5.00

MY SECRET MARRIAGE
May, 1953 - No. 24, July, 1956
Superior Comics, Ltd.

	GD25	FN65	NM94
1	7.00	21.00	42.00
2	4.00	10.00	20.00
3-24	2.80	7.00	14.00
I.W. Reprint #9	.80	2.00	4.00

Mys-Tech Wars #1 © MEG

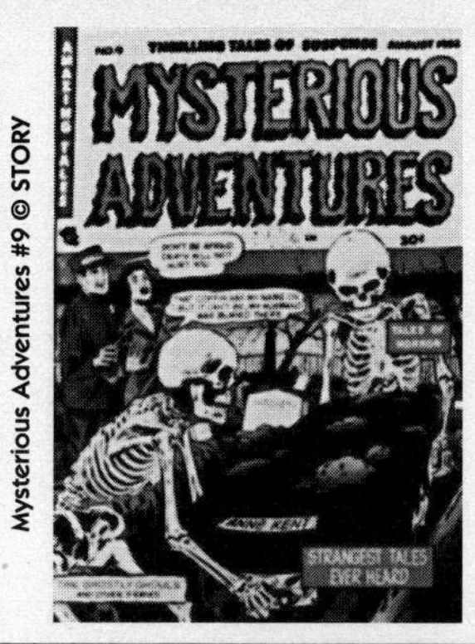

Mysterious Adventures #9 © STORY

Mystery Comics #2 © WHW

NOTE: *Many issues contain* ***Kamenish*** *art.*

MY SECRET ROMANCE (Becomes A Star Presentation #3)
Jan, 1950 - No. 2, March, 1950
Hero Book (Fox Feature Syndicate)

	GD25	FN65	NM94
1-Wood-a	11.00	32.00	75.00
2-Wood-a	10.00	30.00	70.00

MY SECRET STORY (Formerly Captain Kidd #25; Sabu #30 on)
No. 26, Oct, 1949 - No. 29, April, 1950
Fox Feature Syndicate

	GD25	FN65	NM94
26	8.35	25.00	50.00
27-29	5.35	16.00	32.00

MYS-TECH WARS
Mar, 1993 - No. 4, June, 1993 ($1.75, mini-series)
Marvel Comics UK

	GD25	FN65	NM94
1-4: 1-Gatefold-c		.70	1.75

MYSTERIES (...Weird & Strange)
May, 1953 - No. 11, Jan, 1955
Superior/Dynamic Publ. (Randall Publ. Ltd.)

	GD25	FN65	NM94
1	19.00	57.00	130.00
2-A-Bomb blast story	10.00	30.00	65.00
3-9,11	8.35	25.00	50.00
10-Kamenish-c/a reprinted from Strange Mysteries #2; cover is from a panel in Strange Mysteries #2	9.15	27.50	55.00

MYSTERIES OF SCOTLAND YARD (See A-1 Comics #121)

MYSTERIES OF UNEXPLORED WORLDS (See Blue Bird) (Becomes Son of Vulcan V2#49 on)
Aug, 1956; No. 2, Jan, 1957 - No. 48, Sept, 1965
Charlton Comics

	GD25	FN65	NM94
1	23.00	70.00	160.00
2-No Ditko	9.15	27.50	55.00
3,4,8,9-Ditko-a	13.50	41.00	95.00
5,6-Ditko-c/a (all)	16.00	48.00	110.00
7-(2/58, 15¢, 68 pgs.); Ditko-a(4)	16.00	48.00	110.00
10-Ditko-c/a(4)	16.00	48.00	110.00
11-Ditko-c/a(3); signed J. Kotdi	16.00	48.00	110.00
12,19,21-24,26-Ditko-a	11.00	32.00	75.00
13-18,20	4.00	12.00	22.00
25,27-30	2.30	6.90	16.00
31-45	1.65	4.00	10.00
46(5/65)-Son of Vulcan begins (origin/1st app.)	2.40	7.25	17.00
47,48	1.65	4.00	10.00

NOTE: ***Ditko*** *c-3-6, 10, 11, 19, 21-24. Covers to #23 & 24 reprint story panels.*

MYSTERIOUS ADVENTURES
March, 1951 - No. 24, Mar, 1955; No. 25, Aug, 1955
Story Comics

	GD25	FN65	NM94
1-All horror stories	27.00	80.00	185.00
2	13.50	41.00	95.00
3,4,6,10	11.50	34.00	80.00
5-Bondage-c	14.00	43.00	100.00
7-Daggar in eye panel	20.00	60.00	140.00
8-Eyeball story	19.00	57.00	130.00
9-Extreme violence	16.00	48.00	110.00
11-13: 11(12/52)-Used in **SOTI**, pg. 84	16.00	48.00	110.00
14-E.C. Old Witch swipe	12.00	36.00	85.00
15-21: 18-Used in Senate Investigative report, pgs. 5,6; E.C. swipe/TFTC #35; The Coffin-Keeper & Corpse (hosts). 20-Used by Wertham in the Senate hearings. 21-Bondage/beheading-c	19.00	58.00	135.00
22- "Cinderella" parody	13.00	40.00	90.00
23-Disbrow-a (6 pgs.); E.C. swipe "The Mystery Keeper's Tale" (host) and "Mother Ghoul's Nursery Tale"	12.00	36.00	85.00
24,25	10.00	30.00	65.00

NOTE: ***Tothish*** *art by* ***Ross Andru****-#22, 23.* ***Bache*** *a-8.* ***Cameron*** *a-5-7.* ***Harrison*** *a-12.* ***Hollingsworth*** *a-3-8, 12.* ***Schaffenberger*** *a-24, 25.* ***Wildey*** *a-15, 17.*

MYSTERIOUS ISLAND (See 4-Color #1213)

MYSTERIOUS ISLE
Nov-Jan, 1963/64 (Jules Verne)
Dell Publishing Co.

	GD25	FN65	NM94
1	2.40	6.00	12.00

MYSTERIOUS STORIES (Formerly Horror From the Tomb #1)
No. 2, Dec-Jan, 1954-1955 - No. 7, Dec, 1955
Premier Magazines

	GD25	FN65	NM94
2-Woodbridge-c; last pre-code issue	17.00	52.00	120.00
3-Woodbridge-c/a	12.00	36.00	85.00
4-7: 5-Cinderella parody. 6-Woodbridge-c	11.50	34.00	80.00

NOTE: ***Hollingsworth*** *a-2, 4.*

MYSTERIOUS SUSPENSE
October, 1968 (12¢)
Charlton Comics

	GD25	FN65	NM94
1-Return of the Question by Ditko (c/a)	3.60	10.75	25.00

MYSTERIOUS TRAVELER (See Tales of the...)

MYSTERIOUS TRAVELER COMICS (Radio)
Nov, 1948
Trans-World Publications

	GD25	FN65	NM94
1-Powell-c/a(2); Poe adaptation, "Tell Tale Heart"	36.00	109.00	255.00

MYSTERY COMICS
1944 - No. 4, 1944 (No months given)
William H. Wise & Co.

	GD25	FN65	NM94
1-The Magnet, The Silver Knight, Brad Spencer, Wonderman, Dick Devins, King of Futuria, & Zudo the Jungle Boy begin (all 1st app.); Schomburg-c on all	61.00	182.00	425.00
2-Bondage-c	39.00	118.00	275.00
3-Lance Lewis, Space Detective begins (1st app.); Robot-c	32.00	96.00	225.00
4(V2#1 inside)	32.00	96.00	225.00

MYSTERY COMICS DIGEST
March, 1972 - No. 26, Oct, 1975
Gold Key

	GD25	FN65	NM94
1-Ripley's Believe It or Not; reprint of Ripley's #1 origin Ra-Ka-Tep the Mummy; Wood-a	1.00	2.00	5.00
2-Boris Karloff Tales of Mystery; Wood-a; 1st app. Werewolf Count Wulfstein		1.00	2.50
3-Twilight Zone (TV); Crandall, Toth & George Evans-a; 1st app. Tragg & Simbar the Lion Lord; 2 Crandall/Frazetta-r/Twilight Zone #1		1.00	2.50
4-Ripley's Believe It or Not; 1st app. Baron Tibor, the Vampire		.80	2.00
5-Boris Karloff Tales of Mystery; 1st app. Dr. Spektor		.80	2.00
6-Twilight Zone (TV); 1st app. U.S. Marshal Reid & Sir Duane; Evans-r		.80	2.00
7-Ripley's Believe It or Not; origin The Lurker in the Swamp; 1st app. Duroc		1.20	
8-Boris Karloff Tales of Mystery; McWilliams-r; Orlando-r			1.20
9-Twilight Zone (TV); Williamson, Crandall, McWilliams-a; 2nd Tragg app.; Torres, Evans, Heck/Tuska reprints		1.00	2.50
10,13-Ripley's Believe It or Not: 13-Orlando-r			1.00
11,14-Boris Karloff Tales of Mystery. 14-1st app. Xorkon			1.00
12,15-Twilight Zone (TV)			1.00
16,19,22,25-Ripley's Believe It or Not			1.00
17-Boris Karloff Tales of Mystery; Williamson-r; Orlando-r			1.50
18,21,24-Twilight Zone (TV)			1.00
20,23,26-Boris Karloff Tales of Mystery			1.00

NOTE: *Dr. Spektor app.-#5, 10-12, 21. Durak app.-#15. Duroc app.-#14 (later called Durak). King George 1st app.-#8.*

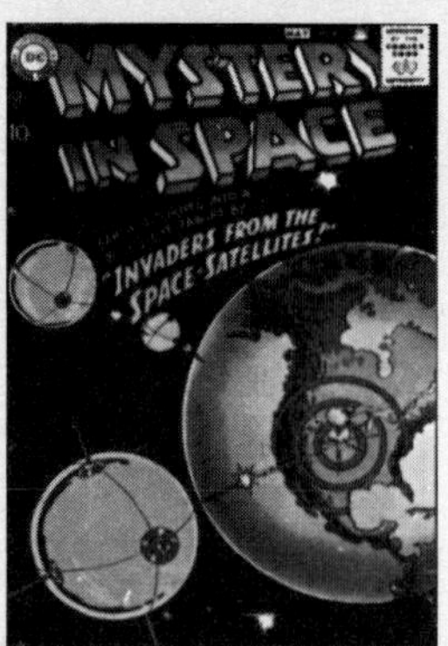

Mystery In Space #43 © DC

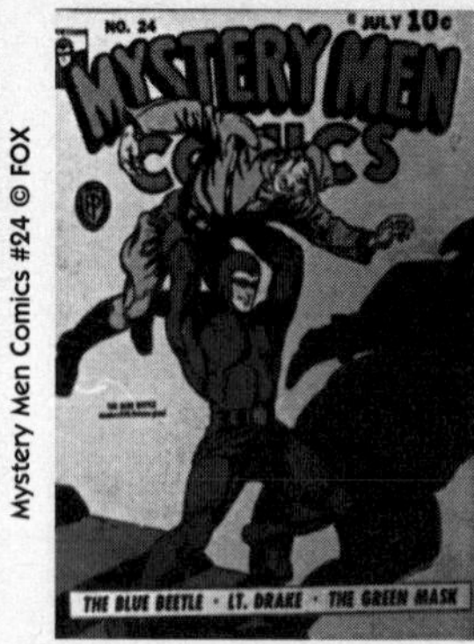

Mystery Men Comics #24 © FOX

Mystery Tales #40 © MEG

GD25 FN65 NM94

MYSTERY IN SPACE
4-5/51 - No. 110, 9/66; No. 111, 9/80 - No. 117, 3/81 (#1-3: 52 pgs.)
National Periodical Publications

1-Frazetta-a, 8 pgs.; Knights of the Galaxy begins, ends #8 257.00 771.00 1800.00
2 100.00 300.00 700.00
3 86.00 257.00 600.00
4,5 68.00 205.00 475.00
6-10: 7-Toth-a 56.00 167.00 390.00
11-15: 13-Toth-a 36.00 109.00 255.00
16-18,20-25: Interplanetary Insurance feature by Infantino in all. 21-1st app. Space Cabbie. 24-Last pre-code issue 34.00 100.00 235.00
19-Virgil Finlay-a 36.00 109.00 255.00
26-40: 26-Space Cabbie feature begins 27.00 81.00 190.00
41-52: 47-Space Cabbie feature ends 21.00 63.00 145.00

GD25 FN65 VF82 NM94
Showcase #17 (11-12/58)-Origin & 1st app. Adam Strange 117.00 350.00 875.00 1400.00

GD25 FN65 NM94
Showcase #18 (1-2/59)-2nd app. Adam Strange 103.00 309.00 825.00
Showcase #19 (3-4/59)-3rd app. Adam Strange 95.00 285.00 950.00

GD25 FN65 VF82 NM94
53-Adam Strange begins (8/59, 10 pg. story) 92.00 275.00 688.00 1100.00

GD25 FN65 NM94
54 37.00 111.00 295.00
55-Grey tone-c 23.00 69.00 185.00
56-60: 59-Kane/Anderson-a 17.00 51.00 135.00
61-71: 61-1st app. Adam Strange foe Ulthoon. 62-1st app. A.S. foe Mortan. 63-Origin Vandor. 66-Star Rovers begin (1st app.). 68-Dust Devils app. 71-Last 10¢ issue 13.00 38.00 100.00
72-74,76-80 8.00 24.00 65.00
75-JLA x-over in Adam Strange (5/62)(sequel to JLA #3) 22.00 66.00 175.00
81-86 5.00 15.00 40.00
87-(11/63)-Adam Strange/Hawkman double feat begins; 3rd Hawkman tryout series 19.00 56.00 150.00
88-Adam Strange & Hawkman stories 15.00 45.00 120.00
89-Adam Strange & Hawkman stories 14.00 41.00 110.00
90-Adam Strange & Hawkman team-up for 1st time (3/64); Hawkman moves to own title next month 17.00 51.00 135.00
91-103: 91-End Infantino art on Adam Strange; double-length Adam Strange story. 92-Space Ranger begins (6/64), ends #103. 92-94,96,98-Space Ranger-c. 94,98-Adam Strange/Space Ranger team-up. 102-Adam Strange ends (no Space Ranger). 103-Origin Ultra, the Multi-Alien; last Space Ranger 2.30 6.90 16.00
104-110: 110-(9/66)-Last 12¢ issue .90 2.30 5.50
V17#111(9/80)-117: 117-Newton-a(3 pgs.) 1.40 3.50

NOTE: ***Anderson*** *a-2, 4, 8-10, 12-17, 19, 45-48, 51, 57, 59i, 61-64, 70, 76, 87-91; c-9, 10, 15-25, 87, 89, 105-108, 110.* ***Aparo*** *a-111.* ***Austin*** *a-112i.* ***Bolland*** *a-115.* ***Craig*** *a-114, 116.* ***Ditko*** *a-111, 114-116.* ***Drucker*** *a-13, 14.* ***Elias*** *a-98, 102, 103.* ***Golden*** *a-113p.* ***Sid Greene*** *a-78, 91.* ***Infantino*** *a-1-8, 11, 14-25, 27-46, 48, 49, 51, 53-91, 103, 117; c-60-86, 88, 90, 91, 105, 107.* ***Gil Kane*** *a-14p, 15p, 18p, 19p, 26p, 29-59p(most), 100-102; c-52, 101.* ***Kubert*** *a-113; c-111-115.* ***Moriera*** *c-27, 28.* ***Rogers*** *a-111.* ***Sekowsky*** *a-52.* ***Simon & Kirby*** *a-4(2 pgs.).* ***Spiegle*** *a-111, 114.* ***Starlin*** *c-116.* ***Sutton*** *a-112.* ***Tuska*** *a-115p, 117p.*

MYSTERY MEN COMICS
Aug, 1939 - No. 31, Feb, 1942
Fox Features Syndicate

1-Intro. & 1st app. The Blue Beetle, The Green Mask, Rex Dexter of Mars by Briefer, Zanzibar by Tuska, Lt. Drake, D-13-Secret Agent by Powell, Chen Chang, Wing Turner, & Captain Denny Scott 300.00 900.00 2100.00
2-Robot & sci/fi-c (2nd Robot-c w/Movie #6) 114.00 343.00 800.00
3 (10/39) 100.00 300.00 700.00
4-Capt. Savage begins (11/39) 91.00 275.00 640.00
5 71.00 214.00 500.00
6-8 60.00 180.00 420.00
9-The Moth begins 52.00 156.00 365.00
10-Wing Turner by Kirby 52.00 156.00 365.00
11-Intro. Domino 39.00 118.00 275.00
12,14-18 37.00 110.00 260.00
13-Intro. Lynx & sidekick Blackie (8/40) 39.00 118.00 275.00
19-Intro. & 1st app. Miss X (ends #21) 39.00 118.00 275.00
20-31: 26-The Wraith begins 33.00 100.00 230.00

NOTE: ***Briefer*** *a-1-15, 20, 24; c-9.* ***Cuidera*** *a-22.* ***Lou Fine*** *c-1-8.* ***Powell*** *a-1-15, 24.* ***Simon*** *c-10-12.* ***Tuska*** *a-1-16, 22, 24, 27. Bondage-c 1, 3, 7, 8, 25, 27-29, 31. Blue Beetle c-7, 8, 10-31. D-13 Secret Agent c-6. Green Mask c-1, 3-5. Rex Dexter of Mars c-2, 9.*

MYSTERY TALES
March, 1952 - No. 54, Aug, 1957
Atlas Comics (20CC)

1-Horror/weird stories in all 46.00 140.00 325.00
2-Krigstein-a 25.00 75.00 175.00
3-10: 6-A-Bomb panel. 10-Story similar to "The Assassin" from Shock SuspenStories 18.00 54.00 125.00
11,13-21: 14-Maneely s/f story. 20-Electric chair issue. 21-Matt Fox-a; decapitation story 13.00 40.00 90.00
12-Matt Fox-a 14.00 43.00 100.00
22-Forte/Matt Fox-c; a(i) 14.00 43.00 100.00
23-26 (2/55)-Last precode issue 11.00 32.00 75.00
27,29-35,37,38,41-43,48,49: 43-Morisi story contains Frazetta art swipes from Untamed Love 10.00 30.00 60.00
28-Jack Katz-a 10.00 30.00 65.00
36,39-Krigstein-a 10.00 30.00 65.00
40,45-Ditko-a (#45 is 3 pgs. only) 10.00 30.00 65.00
44,51-Williamson/Krenkel-a 11.00 32.00 70.00
46-Williamson/Krenkel-a; Crandall text illos 11.00 32.00 70.00
47-Crandall, Ditko, Powell-a 11.00 32.00 70.00
50-Torres, Morrow-a 10.00 30.00 65.00
52,53 8.35 25.00 50.00
54-Crandall, Check-a 10.00 30.00 60.00

NOTE: ***Ayers*** *a-18, 49, 52.* ***Berg*** *a-17, 51.* ***Colan*** *a-1, 3, 18, 35, 43.* ***Colletta*** *a-18.* ***Drucker*** *a-41.* ***Everett*** *a-2, 29, 33, 35, 41; c-8-11, 14, 38, 39, 41, 43, 44, 46, 48-51, 53.* ***Fass*** *a-16.* ***Forte*** *a-21, 22, 45, 46.* ***Matt Fox*** *a-12?, 21, 22; c-22.* ***Heath*** *a-3; c-3, 15, 17, 26.* ***Heck*** *a-25.* ***Kinstler*** *a-15.* ***Mort Lawrence*** *a-26, 32, 34.* ***Maneely*** *a-1, 9, 14, 22; c-12, 23, 24, 27.* ***Mooney*** *a-3, 40.* ***Morisi*** *a-43, 49, 52.* ***Morrow*** *a-50.* ***Orlando*** *a-51.* ***Pakula*** *a-16.* ***Powell*** *a-21, 29, 37, 38, 47.* ***Reinman*** *a-1, 14, 17.* ***Robinson*** *a-7p, 42.* ***Romita*** *a-37.* ***Roussos*** *a-4, 44.* ***R.Q. Sale*** *a-45, 46, 49.* ***Severin*** *c-52.* ***Shores*** *a-17, 45.* ***Tuska*** *a-10, 12, 14.* ***Whitney*** *a-2.* ***Wildey*** *a-37.*

MYSTERY TALES
1964
Super Comics

Super Reprint #16,17('64): 16-r/Tales of Horror #2. 17-r/Eerie #14(Avon) 1.40 3.50 7.00
Super Reprint #18-Kubert-r/Strange Terrors #4 1.40 3.50 7.00

MYSTIC (3rd Series)
March, 1951 - No. 61, Aug, 1957
Marvel/Atlas Comics (CLDS 1/CSI 2-21/OMC 22-35/CSI 35-61)

1-Atom bomb panels; horror/weird stories in all 44.00 133.00 310.00
2 25.00 75.00 175.00
3-Eyes torn out 22.00 65.00 150.00
4- "The Devil Birds" by Wolverton (6 pgs.) 41.00 122.00 285.00
5,7-10 15.00 45.00 105.00
6- "The Eye of Doom" by Wolverton (7 pgs.) 41.00 122.00 285.00
11-20: 16-Bondage/torture c/story 13.00 40.00 90.00
21-25,27-36-Last precode (3/55). 25-E.C. swipe 11.00 32.00 75.00
26-Atomic War, severed head stories 12.00 36.00 85.00
37-51,53-57,61: 57-Story "Trapped in the Ant-Hill" (1957) is very similar to "The Man in the Ant Hill" in TTA #27 10.00 30.00 60.00
52-Wood-a; Crandall-a? 11.00 32.00 75.00
58,59-Krigstein-a 10.00 30.00 65.00
60-Williamson/Mayo-a (4 pgs.) 10.00 30.00 65.00

NOTE: ***Andru*** *a-23, 25.* ***Ayers*** *a-35, 53; c-8.* ***Berg*** *a-49.* ***Cameron*** *a-49, 51.* ***Check*** *a-31, 60.* ***Colan*** *a-3, 7, 12, 21, 37, 60.* ***Colletta*** *a-29.* ***Drucker*** *a-46, 52, 56.* ***Everett*** *a-8, 9, 17, 40, 44, 57; c-13, 18, 21, 42, 47, 49, 51-55, 57-59, 61.* ***Forte*** *a-35, 52, 58.* ***Fox*** *a-24i.* ***Al Hartley*** *a-35.* ***Heath*** *a-10; c-10, 20, 22, 23, 25, 30.* ***Infantino*** *a-12.* ***Kane*** *a-8, 24p.* ***Jack Katz*** *a-31, 33.* ***Mort***

Mystic #53 © MEG

The 'Nam #53 © MEG

Namor, The Sub-Mariner #54 © MEG

GD25 FN65 NM94 | GD25 FN65 NM94

Lawrence a-19, 37. Maneely a-22, 24, 58; c-7, 15, 28, 29, 31. Moldoff a-29. Morisi a-48, 49, 52. Morrow a-51. Orlando a-57, 61. Pakula a-52, 57, 59. Powell a-52, 54-56. Robinson a-5. Romita a-11, 15. R.Q. Sale a-35, 53, 58. Sekowsky a-1, 2, 4, 5. Severin c-56, 60. Tuska a-15. Whitney a-33. Wildey a-28, 30. Ed Win a-17, 20. Canadian reprints known-title 'Startling.'

MYSTICAL TALES
June, 1956 - No. 8, Aug, 1957
Atlas Comics (CCC 1/EPI 2-8)

	GD25	FN65	NM94
1-Everett-c/a	25.00	75.00	175.00
2,4: 2-Berg-a	13.00	40.00	90.00
3,5: 3,4-Crandall-a. 5-Williamson-a (4 pgs.)	13.50	41.00	95.00
6-Torres, Krigstein-a	11.50	34.00	80.00
7-Bolle, Forte, Torres, Orlando-a	11.00	32.00	75.00
8-Krigstein, Check-a	11.50	34.00	80.00

NOTE: Everett a-1; c-1-4, 6, 7. Orlando a-1, 2, 7. Pakula a-3. Powell a-1, 4.

MYSTIC COMICS (1st Series)
March, 1940 - No. 10, Aug, 1942
Timely Comics (TPI 1-5/TCI 8-10)

	GD25	FN65	VF82	NM94
1-Origin The Blue Blaze, The Dynamic Man, & Flexo the Rubber Robot; Zephyr Jones, 3X's & Deep Sea Demon app.; The Magician begins (all 1st app.); c-from Spider pulp V18#1, 6/39	1062.00	3188.00	5844.00	8500.00

(Estimated up to 110 total copies exist, 4 in NM/Mint)

	GD25	FN65	NM94
2-The Invisible Man & Master Mind Excello begin; Space Rangers, Zara of the Jungle, Taxi Taylor app.	279.00	835.00	1950.00
3-Origin Hercules, who last appears in #4	214.00	643.00	1500.00
4-Origin The Thin Man & The Black Widow; Merzak the Mystic app.; last Flexo, Dynamic Man, Invisible Man & Blue Blaze (some issues have date sticker on cover; others have July w/August overprint in silver color); Roosevelt assassination-c	243.00	730.00	1700.00
5-(3/41)-Origin The Black Marvel, The Blazing Skull, The Sub-Earth Man, Super Slave & The Terror; The Moon Man & Black Widow app.; 5-German war-c begin, end #10	235.00	707.00	1650.00
6-(10/41)-Origin The Challenger & The Destroyer (1st app.?; also see All-Winners #2, Fall, 1941)	235.00	707.00	1650.00
7-The Witness begins (12/41, origin & 1st app.); origin Davey & the Demon; last Black Widow; Hitler opens his trunk of terror-c by Simon & Kirby (classic-c)	221.00	665.00	1550.00
8,9: 9-Gary Gaunt app.; last Black Marvel, Mystic & Blazing Skull; Hitler-c	135.00	407.00	950.00
10-Father Time, World of Wonder, & Red Skeleton app.; last Challenger & Terror	135.00	407.00	950.00

NOTE: Gabrielle c-8-10. Kirby/Schomburg c-6. Rico a-9(2). Schomburg a-1-4; c-1-5. Sekowsky a-9. Sekowsky/Klein a-8(Challenger). Bondage c-1, 2, 9.

MYSTIC COMICS (2nd Series)
Oct, 1944 - No. 3, Win, 1944-45; No. 4, Mar, 1945
Timely Comics (ANC)

	GD25	FN65	NM94
1-The Angel, The Destroyer, The Human Torch, Terry Vance the Schoolboy Sleuth, & Tommy Tyme begin	135.00	407.00	950.00
2-(Fall/44)-Last Human Torch & Terry Vance; bondage/hypo-c	75.00	225.00	525.00
3-Last Angel (two stories) & Tommy Tyme	71.00	215.00	500.00
4-The Young Allies-c & app.; Schomburg-c	66.00	200.00	465.00

MY STORY (...True Romances in Pictures #5,6) (Formerly Zago)
No. 5, May, 1949 - No. 12, Aug, 1950
Hero Books (Fox Features Syndicate)

	GD25	FN65	NM94
5-Kamen/Feldstein-a	10.00	30.00	70.00
6-8,11,12: 12-Photo-c	5.00	15.00	30.00
9,10-Wood-a	11.00	32.00	75.00

MY TRUE LOVE (Formerly Western Killers #64; Frank Buck #70 on)
No. 65, July, 1949 - No. 69, March, 1950
Fox Features Syndicate

	GD25	FN65	NM94
65	8.35	25.00	50.00
66-69: 69-Morisi-a	5.85	17.50	35.00

NAIVE INTER-DIMENSIONAL COMMANDO KOALAS (Eclipse)(Value: cover or less)

NAKED PREY, THE (See Movie Classics)

'NAM, THE (See Savage Tales #1, 2nd series)
Dec, 1986 - No. 84, Sept, 1993
Marvel Comics Group

	GD25	FN65	NM94
1-Golden a(p)/c begins, ends #13		1.10	2.75
1 (2nd printing)			1.00
2		.80	2.00
3-7: 7 Golden-a (2 pgs.)			1.50
8-51,54-64: 32-Death R. Kennedy. 58-Silver logo			1.25
52-Frank Castle (The Punisher) app.		1.00	2.50
53-Frank Castle (The Punisher) app.			1.50
52,53-Gold 2nd printings			1.25
65-74,76-84: 65-Heath-c/a; begin $1.75-c. 67-69-Punisher 3 part story. 70-Lomax scripts begin			1.50
75-($2.25, 52 pgs.)		.90	2.25
Trade Paperback 1-r/#1-4		1.80	4.50
Trade Paperback 2-r/#5-8		1.90	4.50

'NAM MAGAZINE, THE (Marvel)(Value: value: cover or less)

NAMORA (See Marvel Mystery Comics #82 & Sub-Mariner Comics)
Fall, 1948 - No. 3, Dec, 1948
Marvel Comics (PrPI)

	GD25	FN65	NM94
1-Sub-Mariner x-over in Namora; Namora by Everett(2), Sub-Mariner by Rico (10 pgs.)	121.00	365.00	850.00
2-The Blonde Phantom & Sub-Mariner story; Everett-a	93.00	280.00	650.00
3-(Scarce)-Sub-Mariner app.; Everett-a	93.00	280.00	650.00

NAMOR, THE SUB-MARINER (See Prince Namor & Sub-Mariner)
Apr, 1990 - Present ($1.00/$1.25/$1.50)
Marvel Comics

	GD25	FN65	NM94
1-Byrne-c/a/scripts in 1-25 (scripts only #26-32)		1.20	3.00
2-5: 5-Iron Man app.			1.50
6-11: 8,10,16-Re-intro Iron Fist (8-cameo only)			1.25
12-($1.50, 52 pgs.)-Re-intro. The Invaders		.70	1.75
13-22: 18-Punisher cameo (1 panel); 21-23,25-Wolverine cameos. 22-Last $1.00-c. 22,23-Iron Fist app.			1.00
23-25: 24-Namor vs. Wolverine			1.25
26-New look for Namor w/new costume; 1st Jae Lee-c/a this title (5/92) & begins	1.30	3.10	7.50
27		1.60	4.00
28-Iron Fist-c/story		1.40	3.50
29,30		.90	2.25
31-36,38-49: 31-Dr. Doom-c/story. 33,34-Iron Fist cameo. 35-New Tiger Shark-c/story. 48-The Thing app.		.60	1.25
37-($2.00)-Aqua holo-grafx foil-c		.80	2.00
50-(1.75, 52 pgs.)-Newsstand edition; w/bound-in S-M trading card sheet (both versions)		.60	1.50
50-(2.95, 52 pgs.)-Collector edition w/foil-c		1.20	3.00
51-61: 51-Begin $1.50-c			1.50
Annual 1 (1991, $2.00, 68 pgs.)-3 pg. origin recap		.80	2.00
Annual 2 (1992, $2.25, 68 pgs.)-Return/Defenders		.90	2.25
Annual 3 (1993, $2.95, 68 pgs.)-Bagged w/card		1.20	3.00
Annual 4 (1994, $2.95, 68 pgs.)-Painted-c		1.20	3.00

NOTE: Jae Lee a-26-30p, 31-37, 38p, 39, 40; c-26-40.

NANCY AND SLUGGO (See Comics On Parade & Sparkle Comics)
No. 16, 1949 - No. 23, 1954
United Features Syndicate

	GD25	FN65	NM94
16(#1)	6.35	19.00	38.00
17-23	4.00	11.00	22.00

NANCY & SLUGGO (Nancy #146-173; formerly Sparkler Comics)
No. 121, Apr, 1955 - No. 192, Oct, 1963
St. John/Dell #146-187/Gold Key #188 on

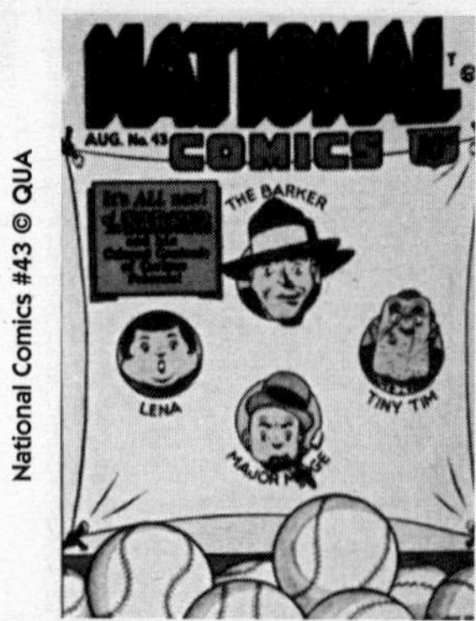

National Comics #43 © QUA

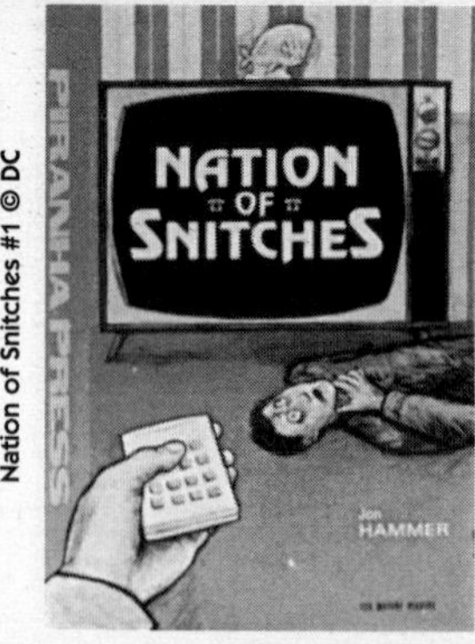

Nation of Snitches #1 © DC

Navy Heroes #1 © Almanac Pub.

	GD25	FN65	NM94
121(4/55)(St. John)	4.70	14.00	28.00
122-145(7/57)(St. John)	4.00	10.00	20.00
146(9/57)-Peanuts begins, ends #192 (Dell)	4.00	12.00	24.00
147-161 (Dell)	3.60	9.00	18.00
162-165,177-180-John Stanley-a	7.00	21.00	42.00
166-176-Oona & Her Haunted House series; Stanley-a	8.00	24.00	48.00
181-187(3-5/62)(Dell)	3.20	8.00	16.00
188(10/62)-192 (Gold Key)	3.20	8.00	16.00
4-Color 1034(9-11/59)-Summer Camp	3.60	9.00	18.00

(See Dell Giant #34, 45 & Dell Giants)

NANNY AND THE PROFESSOR (TV)
Aug, 1970 - No. 2, Oct, 1970 (Photo-c)
Dell Publishing Co.

	GD25	FN65	NM94
1(01-546-008), 2	5.35	16.00	32.00

NAPOLEON (See 4-Color No. 526)

NAPOLEON & SAMANTHA (See Walt Disney Showcase No. 10)

NAPOLEON & UNCLE ELBY (See Clifford McBride's...)
July, 1942 (68 pgs.) (One Shot)
Eastern Color Printing Co.

	GD25	FN65	NM94
1	24.00	72.00	165.00
1945-American Book-Strafford Press (128 pgs.) (8x10-1/2"; B&W reprints; hardcover)	12.00	35.00	70.00

NARRATIVE ILLUSTRATION, THE STORY OF THE COMICS
Summer, 1942 (32 pgs., 7-1/4"x10", B&W w/color inserts)
M.C. Gaines

nn-16pgs. text with illustrations of ancient art, strips and comic covers; 4 pg. WWII War Bond promo, "The Minute Man Answers the Call" color comic drawn by Shelly and a special 8-page color comic insert of "The Story of Saul" from Picture Stories from the Bible #1 or soon to appear in PS #1. Insert has special title page indicating it was No. 10 of a Sunday newspaper supplement insert series that had already run in a New England "Sunday Herald." (very rare; only one known copy.) Estimated value... 1,000.00

NASCAR ADVENTURES (Vortex)(Value: cover or less)

NASCUB ADVENTURES, THE (New Image)(Value: cover or less)

NATHANIEL DUSK (DC)(Value: cover or less)

NATHANIEL DUSK II (DC)(Value: cover or less)

NATIONAL COMICS
July, 1940 - No. 75, Nov, 1949
Quality Comics Group

	GD25	FN65	NM94
1-Uncle Sam begins (1st app.); origin sidekick Buddy by Eisner; origin Wonder Boy & Kid Dixon; Merlin the Magician (ends #45); Cyclone, Kid Patrol, Sally O'Neil Policewoman, Pen Miller (by Klaus Nordling; ends #22), Prop Powers (ends #26), & Paul Bunyan (ends #22) begin	314.00	943.00	2200.00
2	139.00	418.00	975.00
3-Last Eisner Uncle Sam	104.00	310.00	725.00
4-Last Cyclone	82.00	246.00	575.00
5-(11/40)-Quicksilver begins (1st app.)(3rd w/lightning speed?); origin Uncle Sam; bondage-c	96.00	290.00	675.00
6-11: 8-Jack & Jill begins (ends #22). 9-Flag-c	75.00	225.00	525.00
12	54.00	160.00	375.00
13-16-Lou Fine-a	62.00	182.00	435.00
17,19-22: 22-Last Pen Miller (moves to Crack #23)	48.00	145.00	335.00
18-(12/41)-Shows orientals attacking Pearl Harbor; on stands one month before actual event	61.00	182.00	425.00
23-The Unknown & Destroyer 171 begin	52.00	156.00	365.00
24-26,28,30: 26-Wonder Boy ends	38.00	115.00	265.00
27-G-2 the Unknown begins (ends #46)	38.00	115.00	265.00
29-Origin The Unknown	38.00	115.00	265.00
31-33: 33-Chic Carter begins (ends #47)	36.00	107.00	250.00
34-40: 35-Last Kid Patrol. 39-Hitler-c	22.00	65.00	150.00
41-50: 42-The Barker begins (1st app?, 5/44); The Barker covers begin. 48-Origin The Whistler	15.00	45.00	105.00
51-Sally O'Neil by Ward, 8 pgs. (12/45)	19.00	58.00	135.00
52-60	11.50	34.00	80.00
61-67: 67-Format change; Quicksilver app.	10.00	30.00	60.00
68-75: The Barker ends	7.50	22.50	45.00

NOTE: ***Cole*** *Quicksilver-13; Barker-43; c-43, 46, 47, 49-51.* ***Crandall*** *Uncle Sam-11-13 (with* ***Fine****), 25, 26; c-24-26, 30-33, 43.* ***Crandall*** *Paul Bunyan-10-13.* ***Fine*** *Uncle Sam-13 (w/****Crandall****), 17, 18; c-1-14, 16, 18, 21.* ***Gill Fox*** *c-69-74.* ***Guardineer*** *Quicksilver-27, 35.* ***Gustavson*** *Quicksilver-14-26.* ***McWilliams*** *a-23-28, 55, 57. Uncle Sam c-1-41. Barker c-42-75.*

NATIONAL CRUMB, THE (Magazine-Size)
August, 1975 (52 pgs.) (Satire)
Mayfair Publications

	GD25	FN65	NM94
1	1.30	3.25	8.00

NATIONAL VELVET (TV)
May-July, 1961 - No. 2, March, 1963 (All photo-c)
Dell Publishing Co./Gold Key

	GD25	FN65	NM94
4-Color 1195 (#1)	7.50	22.50	45.00
4-Color 1312	4.00	12.00	24.00
01-556-207, 12-556-210 (Dell)	4.00	11.00	22.00
1(12/62), 2(3/63) (Gold Key)	4.00	11.00	22.00

NATION OF SNITCHES
1990 ($4.95, color, 52 pgs.)
Piranha Press (DC)

	GD25	FN65	NM94
nn	1.00	2.00	5.00

NATURE BOY (Formerly Danny Blaze; Li'l Rascal Twins #6 on)
No. 3, March, 1956 - No. 5, Feb, 1957
Charlton Comics

	GD25	FN65	NM94
3-Origin; Blue Beetle story; Buscema-c/a	16.00	49.00	115.00
4,5	13.00	39.00	90.00

NOTE: ***John Buscema*** *a-3, 4p, 5; c-3.* ***Powell*** *a-4.*

NATURE OF THINGS (See 4-Color No. 727, 842)

NAUSICAA OF THE VALLEY OF WIND (Viz)(Value: cover or less)

NAVY ACTION (Sailor Sweeney #12-14)
Aug, 1954 - No. 11, Apr, 1956; No. 15, 1/57 - No. 18, 8/57
Atlas Comics (CDS)

	GD25	FN65	NM94
1-Powell-a	10.00	30.00	65.00
2-Lawrence-a	5.35	16.00	32.00
3-11: 4-Last precode (2/55)	4.00	11.00	22.00
15-18	3.60	9.00	18.00

NOTE: ***Berg*** *a-7, 9.* ***Colan*** *a-8.* ***Drucker*** *a-7, 17.* ***Everett*** *a-3, 7, 16; c-16, 17.* ***Heath*** *c-1, 2, 6.* ***Maneely*** *a-7, 8, 18; c-9, 11.* ***Pakula*** *a-2, 3, 9.* ***Reinman*** *a-17.*

NAVY COMBAT
June, 1955 - No. 20, Oct, 1958
Atlas Comics (MPI)

	GD25	FN65	NM94
1-Torpedo Taylor begins by Don Heck	10.00	30.00	65.00
2	5.35	16.00	32.00
3-10	4.00	11.00	22.00
11,13,15,16,18-20	4.00	10.00	20.00
12-Crandall-a	5.85	17.50	35.00
14-Torres-a	4.35	13.00	26.00
17-Williamson-a, 4 pgs.; Torres-a	4.70	14.00	28.00

NOTE: ***Berg*** *a-10, 11.* ***Colan*** *a-11.* ***Drucker*** *a-7.* ***Everett*** *a-3, 20; c-8 & 9 w/****Tuska****, 10, 13-16.* ***Heck*** *a-11(2).* ***Maneely*** *c-1, 6, 11, 17.* ***Morisi*** *a-8.* ***Pakula*** *a-7.* ***Powell*** *a-20.*

NAVY HEROES
1945
Almanac Publishing Co.

	GD25	FN65	NM94
1-Heavy in propaganda	8.35	25.00	50.00

NAVY: HISTORY & TRADITION
1958 - 1961 (nn) (Giveaway)
Stokes Walesby Co./Dept. of Navy

1772-1778, 1778-1782, 1782-1817, 1817-1865, 1865-1936, 1940-1945

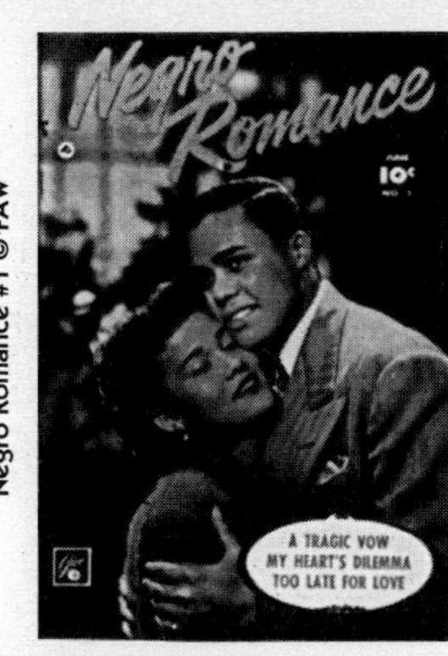

Negro Romance #1 © FAW

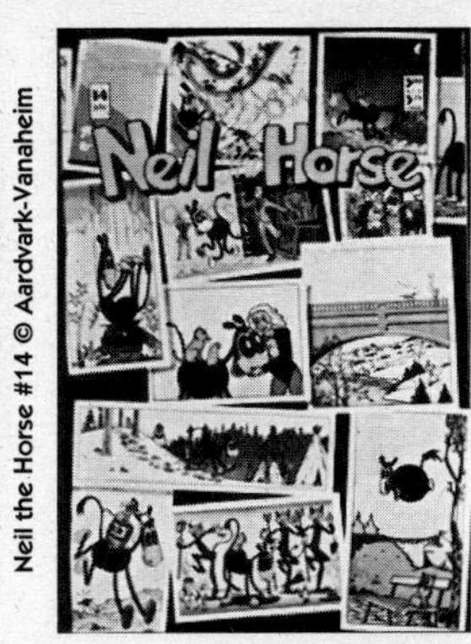

Neil the Horse #14 © Aardvark-Vanaheim

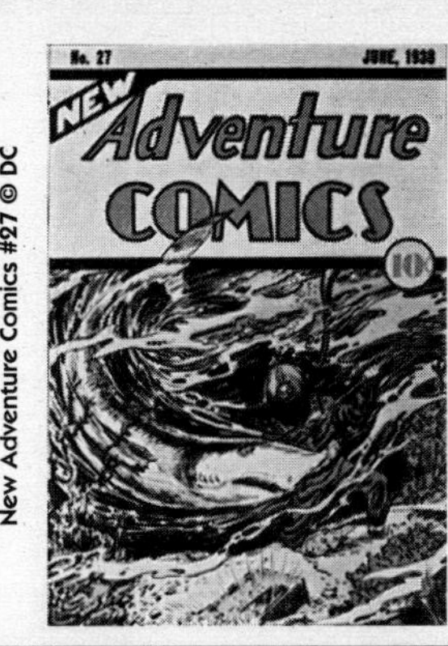

New Adventure Comics #27 © DC

	GD25	FN65	NM94
	4.00	12.00	24.00
1861: Naval Actions of the Civil War: 1865	4.00	12.00	24.00

NAVY PATROL
May, 1955 - No. 4, Nov, 1955
Key Publications

	GD25	FN65	NM94
1	4.70	14.00	28.00
2-4	2.80	7.00	14.00

NAVY TALES
Jan, 1957 - No. 4, July, 1957
Atlas Comics (CDS)

	GD25	FN65	NM94
1-Everett-c; Berg, Powell-a	9.15	27.50	55.00
2-Williamson/Mayo-a(5 pgs); Crandall-a	8.35	25.00	50.00
3,4-Reinman-a; Severin-c. 4-Crandall-a	6.70	20.00	40.00

NOTE: ***Colan** a-4. **Maneely** c-2. **Sinnott** a-4.*

NAVY TASK FORCE
Feb, 1954 - No. 8, April, 1956
Stanmor Publications/Aragon Mag. No. 4-8

	GD25	FN65	NM94
1	5.35	16.00	32.00
2	3.20	8.00	16.00
3-8: #8-r/Navy Patrol #1	2.40	6.00	12.00

NAVY WAR HEROES
Jan, 1964 - No. 7, Mar-Apr, 1965
Charlton Comics

	GD25	FN65	NM94
1	1.60	4.00	8.00
2-7	.60	1.50	3.00

NAZA (Stone Age Warrior)
Nov-Jan, 1963-64 - No. 9, March, 1966
Dell Publishing Co.

	GD25	FN65	NM94
12-555-401 (#1)-Painted-c	2.10	6.40	15.00
2-9: 2-4-Painted-c	1.70	4.20	10.00

NAZZ, THE (DC)(Value: cover or less)

NEBBS, THE
1928 (Daily B&W strip reprints; 52 pgs.)
Cupples & Leon Co.

	GD25	FN65	NM94
nn-By Sol Hess; Carlson-a	14.00	43.00	100.00

NEBBS, THE (Also see Crackajack Funnies)
1941; 1945
Dell Publishing Co./Croydon Publishing Co.

	GD25	FN65	NM94
Large Feature Comic 23(1941)	12.00	36.00	120.00
1(1945, 36 pgs.)-Reprints	10.00	30.00	60.00

NECROMANCER: THE GRAPHIC NOVEL
1989 ($8.95)
Epic Comics (Marvel)

	GD25	FN65	NM94
nn	1.50	3.75	9.00

NECROPOLIS (Fleetway/Quality)(Value: cover or less)

NECROSCOPE (Malibu)(Value: cover or less)

NEGRO (See All-Negro)

NEGRO HEROES (Calling All Girls, Real Heroes, & True Comics reprints)
Spring, 1947 - No. 2, Summer, 1948
Parents' Magazine Institute

	GD25	FN65	NM94
1	47.00	141.00	330.00
2-Jackie Robinson-c/story	54.00	163.00	380.00

NEGRO ROMANCE (Negro Romances #4)
June, 1950 - No. 3, Oct, 1950 (All photo-c)
Fawcett Publications

	GD25	FN65	NM94
1-Evans-a	79.00	235.00	550.00
2,3	64.00	195.00	450.00

NEGRO ROMANCES (Formerly Negro Romance; Romantic Secrets #5 on)
No. 4, May, 1955
Charlton Comics

	GD25	FN65	NM94
4-Reprints Fawcett #2	50.00	150.00	350.00

NEIL GAIMAN'S MR. HERO-THE NEWMATIC MAN
Mar, 1995-Present (1.95'color)
Tekno Comix

	GD25	FN65	NM94
1,2 ; 1-Intro Teknophage; bound-in game piece and trading card	0.40	0.80	2.00

NEIL THE HORSE (Aardvark-Vanaheim/Renegade)(Value: cover or less)

NELLIE THE NURSE (Also see Gay Comics & Joker Comics)
1945 - No. 36, Oct, 1952; 1957
Marvel/Atlas Comics (SPI/LMC)

	GD25	FN65	NM94
1-(1945)	23.00	70.00	160.00
2-(Spring/46)	11.50	34.00	80.00
3,4: 3-New logo (9/46)	9.15	27.50	55.00
5-Kurtzman's "Hey Look" (3); Georgie app.	10.00	30.00	70.00
6-8,10: 7,8-Georgie app. 10-Millie app.	7.50	22.50	45.00
9-Wolverton-a (1 pg.); Mille the Model app.	9.15	27.50	55.00
11,14-16,18-Kurtzman's "Hey Look"	10.00	30.00	60.00
12- "Giggles 'n' Grins" by Kurtzman	8.35	25.00	50.00
13,17,19,20: 17-Annie Oakley app.	6.35	19.00	38.00
21-27,29,30	5.00	15.00	30.00
28-Mr. Nexdoor-r (3 pgs.) by Kurtzman/Rusty #22	5.85	17.50	35.00
31-36: 36-Post-c	4.20	12.50	25.00
1('57)-Leading Mag. (Atlas)-Everett-a, 20 pgs	6.35	19.00	38.00

NELLIE THE NURSE (See 4-Color No. 1304)

NEMESIS THE WARLOCK (Eagle)(Value: cover or less)

NEMESIS THE WARLOCK (Fleetway/Quality)(Value: cover or less)

NEUTRO
January, 1967
Dell Publishing Co.

	GD25	FN65	NM94
1-Jack Sparling-c/a (super hero)	2.40	7.30	17.00

NEVADA (See Zane Grey's Stories of the West #1)

NEVER AGAIN (War stories; becomes Soldier & Marine V2#9)
Aug, 1955 - No. 2, Oct?, 1955; No. 8, July, 1956 (No #3-7)
Charlton Comics

	GD25	FN65	NM94
1	5.85	17.50	35.00
2-(Becomes Fightin' Air Force #3), 8-(Formerly Foxhole?)	4.00	10.00	20.00

NEW ADVENTURE COMICS (Formerly New Comics; becomes Adventure Comics #32 on; V1#12 indicia says NEW COMICS #12)
V1#12, Jan, 1937 - No. 31, Oct, 1938
National Periodical Publications

	GD25	FN65	VF82	NM94
V1#12-Federal Men by Siegel & Shuster continues; Jor-L mentioned; Whitney Ellsworth-c begin, end #14	333.00	1000.00	2000.00	–
V2#1(2/37, #13), V2#2 (#14)	250.00	750.00	1500.00	–

	GD25	FN65	NM94
15(V2#3)-20(V2#8): 15-1st Adventure logo; Creig Flessel-c begin, end #31. 16-1st Shuster-c; 1st non-funny cover. 17-Nadir, Master of Magic begins, ends #30	214.00	643.00	1500.00
21(V2#9),22(V2#10, 2/37): 22-X-Mas-c	186.00	557.00	1300.00
23-31	157.00	471.00	1100.00

NEW ADVENTURE OF WALT DISNEY'S SNOW WHITE AND THE SEVEN DWARFS, A (See Snow White Bendix Giveaway)

NEW ADVENTURES OF CHARLIE CHAN, THE (TV)
May-June, 1958 - No. 6, Mar-Apr, 1959
National Periodical Publications

	GD25	FN65	NM94
1 (Scarce)-Gil Kane/Sid Greene-a in all	46.00	139.00	370.00
2 (Scarce)	31.00	92.00	245.00
3-6 (Scarce)-Greene/Giella-a	25.00	75.00	200.00

NEW ADVENTURES OF CHOLLY AND FLYTRAP: TILL DEATH DO US

New Adventures of Superboy #5 © DC

New Funnies #75 © DELL

New Gods #2 © DC

GD25 FN65 NM94

PART, THE (Epic)(Value: cover or less)

NEW ADVENTURES OF HUCK FINN, THE (TV)
December, 1968 (Hanna-Barbera)
Gold Key

1- "The Curse of Thut"; part photo-c 3.40 8.50 17.00

NEW ADVENTURES OF PETER PAN (Disney)
1953 (36 pgs.; 5x7-1/4") (Admiral giveaway)
Western Publishing Co.

nn 10.00 30.00 60.00

NEW ADVENTURES OF PINOCCHIO (TV)
Oct-Dec, 1962 - No. 3, Sept-Nov, 1963
Dell Publishing Co.

12-562-212(#1) 11.50 34.00 80.00
2,3 8.35 25.00 50.00

NEW ADVENTURES OF ROBIN HOOD (See Robin Hood)

NEW ADVENTURES OF SHERLOCK HOLMES (See 4-Color #1169, 1245)

NEW ADVENTURES OF SPEED RACER
Dec, 1993 - Present ($1.95, color)
Now Comics

1-7 .80 2.00
0-(Premiere)-3-D cover 1.60 4.00

NEW ADVENTURES OF SUPERBOY, THE (Also see Superboy)
Jan, 1980 - No. 54, June, 1984
DC Comics

1-54: 7-Has extra story "The Computers That Saved Metropolis" by Starlin (Radio Shack giveaway w/indicia). 11-Superboy gets new power. 14-Lex Luthor app. 15-Superboy gets new parents. 28-Dial "H" For Hero begins, ends #49. 45-47-1st app. Sunburst. 48-Begin 75¢-c. 50-Legion app. 1.00

NOTE: **Buckler** *a-9p; c-36p.* **Giffen** *a-50; c-50. 40i.* **Gil Kane** *c-32p, 33p, 35, 39, 41-49.* **Miller** *c-51.* **Starlin** *a-7. Krypto back-ups in 17, 22. Superbaby in 11, 14, 19, 24.*

NEW ADVENTURES OF THE PHANTOM BLOT, THE (See The Phantom Blot)

NEW AMERICA (Eclipse)(Value: cover or less)

NEW ARCHIES, THE (TV)
Oct, 1987 - No. 22, May, 1990 (75¢)
Archie Comic Publications

1-16: 3-Xmas issue 1.00
17-22 (.95-$1.00): 21-Xmas issue 1.00

NEW ARCHIES DIGEST (TV)(...Comics Digest Magazine #4?-10; ...Digest Magazine #11 on)
May, 1988 - No. 14, July, 1991 ($1.35/$1.50, digest size, quarterly)
Archie Comics

1-14: 6-Begin $1.50-c 1.50

NEW BOOK OF COMICS (Also see Big Book Of Fun)
1937; No. 2, Spring, 1938 (100 pgs. each) (Reprints)
National Periodical Publ.

GD25 FN65 VF82 NM94

1(Rare)-1st regular size comic annual; 2nd DC annual; contains r/New Comics #1-4 & More Fun #9; r/Federal Men (8 pgs.), Henri Duval (1 pg.), & Dr. Occult in costume (1 pg.) by Siegel & Shuster; Moldoff, Sheldon Mayer (15 pgs.)-a 1333.00 4000.00 8000.00 –
(Estimated up to 50 total copies exist, none in NM/Mint)

GD25 FN65 VF82 NM94

2-Contains-r/More Fun #15 & 16; r/Dr. Occult in costume (a Superman proto-type), & Calling All Cars (4 pgs.) by Siegel & Shuster 700.00 2100.00 4200.00 –

NEW COMICS (New Adventure #12 on)
12/35 - No. 11, 12/36 (No. 1-6: paper cover) (No. 1-5: 84 pgs.)
National Periodical Publ.

GD25 FN65 VF82 NM94

V1#1-Billy the Kid, Sagebrush 'n' Cactus, Jibby Jones, Needles, The Vikings, Sir Loin of Beef, Now-When I Was a Boy, & other 1-2 pg. strips; 2 pgs. Kelly art(1st)-(Gulliver's Travels); Sheldon Mayer-a(1st)(2 2pg. strips); Vincent Sullivan-c(1st) 1500.00 4500.00 9000.00 –
(Estimated up to 50 total copies exist, none in NM/Mint)

2-1st app. Federal Men by Siegel & Shuster & begins (also see The Comics Magazine #2); Mayer, Kelly-a (Rare)(1/36) 583.00 1750.00 3500.00 –

3-6: 3,4-Sheldon Mayer-a which continues in The Comics Magazine #1. 3-Vincent Sullivan-c. 4-Dickens' "A Tale of Two Cities" adaptation begins. 5-Junior Federal Men Club; Kiefer-a. 6- "She" adaptation begins 383.00 1150.00 2300.00 –

7-11: 11-Christmas-c 317.00 950.00 1900.00 –

NOTE: *#1-6 rarely occur in mint condition.* **Whitney Ellsworth** *c-4-11.*

NEW DEFENDERS (See Defenders)

NEW DNAGENTS, THE (Eclipse)(Value: cover or less)(Formerly DNAgents)

NEW FUN COMICS (More Fun #7 on; see Big Book of Fun Comics)
Feb, 1935 - No. 6, Oct, 1935 (10x15", No. 1-4,: slick covers)
(No. 1-5: 36 pgs; 40 pgs. No. 6)
National Periodical Publications

GD25 FN65 VF82 NM94

V1#1 (1st DC comic); 1st app. Oswald The Rabbit; Jack Woods (cowboy) begins 4500.00 13,500.00 27,000.00 –
(Estimated up to 10 total copies exist, 1 in VF/NM)

2(3/35)-(Very Rare) 1667.00 5000.00 10,000.00 –
(Estimated up to 5 total copies exist)

3-5(8/35): 3-Don Drake on the Planet Soro-c/story (sci/fi, 4/35). 5-Soft-c 917.00 2750.00 5500.00 –

6(10/35)-1st Dr. Occult by Siegel & Shuster (Leger & Reuths); last "New Fun" title. "New Comics" #1 begins in Dec. which is reason for title change to More Fun; Henri Duval (ends #10) by Siegel & Shuster begins; paper-c 1583.00 4750.00 9500.00 –
(Estimated up to 10 total copies exist of #3-6)

NEW FUNNIES (The Funnies #1-64; Walter Lantz...#109 on; New TV... #259, 260, 272, 273; TV Funnies #261-271)
No. 65, July, 1942 - No. 288, Mar-Apr, 1962
Dell Publishing Co.

GD25 FN65 NM94

65(#1)-Andy Panda in a world of real people, Raggedy Ann & Andy, Oswald the Rabbit (with Woody Woodpecker x-overs), Li'l Eight Ball & Peter Rabbit begin 61.00 182.00 425.00

66-70: 66-Felix the Cat begins. 67-Billy & Bonnie Bee by Frank Thomas begins. 69-Kelly-a (2 pgs.); The Brownies begin (not by Kelly) 30.00 90.00 210.00

71-75: 72-Kelly illos. 75-Brownies by Kelly? 18.00 54.00 125.00

76-Andy Panda (Carl Barks & Pabian-a); Woody Woodpecker x-over in Oswald ends 100.00 300.00 700.00

77,78: 77-Kelly-c. 78-Andy Panda in a world with real people ends 18.00 54.00 125.00

79-81 13.00 40.00 90.00

82-Brownies by Kelly begins; Homer Pigeon begins 14.00 43.00 100.00

83-85-Brownies by Kelly in ea. 83-X-mas-c. 85-Woody Woodpecker, 1 pg. strip begins 14.00 43.00 100.00

86-90: 87-Woody Woodpecker stories begin 10.00 30.00 60.00

91-99 6.70 20.00 40.00

100 (6/45) 7.50 22.50 45.00

101-110 4.20 12.50 25.00

111-120: 119-X-Mas-c 4.00 10.00 20.00

121-150: 131,143-X-Mas-c 3.20 8.00 16.00

151-200: 155-X-Mas-c. 168-X-Mas-c. 182-Origin & 1st app. Knothead & Splinter. 191-X-Mas-c 2.00 5.00 10.00

201-240 1.60 4.00 8.00

241-288: 270,271-Walter Lantz c-app. 281-1st story swipes/WDC&S #100 1.20 3.00 6.00

NOTE: *Early issues written by* **John Stanley.**

NEW GODS, THE (New Gods #12 on)(See Adventure #459, 1st Issue Special #13 & Super-Team Family)

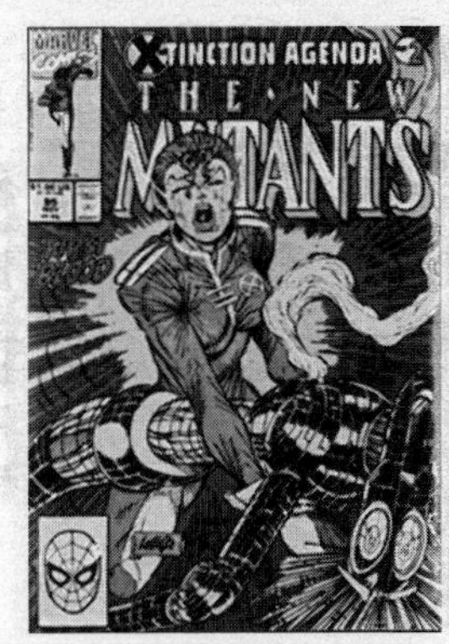

The New Mutants #95 © MEG

New Romances #14 © STD

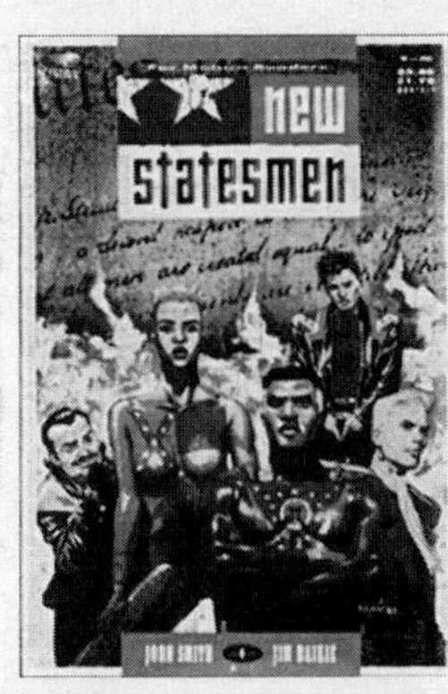

New Statesmen #1 © Fleetway

GD25 FN65 NM94

2-3/71 - V2#11, 10-11/72; V3#12, 7/77 - V3#19, 7-8/78
National Periodical Publications/DC Comics

1-Intro/1st app. Orion; 4th app. Darkseid (cameo; 3 weeks after Forever People #1) (#1-3 are 15¢ issues) 5.00 15.00 36.00
2-Darkseid-c/story (2nd full app., 4-5/71) 2.60 7.70 18.00
3-1st app. Black Racer 2.30 7.00 16.00
4-9: (25¢, 52 pg. giants): 4-Darkseid cameo; origin Manhunter-r. 5,7,8-Young Gods feature. 7-Darkseid app. (2-3/72); origin Orion; 1st origin of all New Gods as a group. 9-1st app. Bug 1.70 5.00 12.00
10,11 1.70 4.20 10.00
12-19: Darkseid storyline w/minor apps. 12-New costume Orion (see 1st Issue Special #13 for 1st new costume). 19-Story continued in Adventure Comics #459,460 1.60 4.00

NOTE: *#4-9(25¢, 52 pgs.) contain Manhunter-r by* ***Simon*** *&* ***Kirby*** *from Adventure #73, 74, 75, 76, 77, 78 with covers in that order.* ***Adkins*** *i-12-14, 17-19.* ***Kirby*** *c/a-1-11p.* ***Newton*** *a(p)-12-14, 16-19.* ***Starlin*** *c-17.* ***Staton*** *c-19p.*

NEW GODS
May, 1984 - No. 6, Nov, 1984 ($2.00, Baxter paper)
DC Comics

1-New Kirby-c; r/New Gods #1,2 .80 2.00
2-6: 6-New art by Kirby .80 2.00

NEW GODS
Feb, 1989 - No. 28, Aug, 1991 ($1.50)
DC Comics

1-28 1.50

NEW GUARDIANS, THE (DC)(Value: cover or less)

NEW HEROIC (See Heroic)

NEW JUSTICE MACHINE, THE (Innovation)(Value: cover or less)

NEW KIDS ON THE BLOCK, THE (Harvey)(Value: cover or less)

NEWLYWEDS
1907; 1917 (cardboard covers)
Saalfield Publ. Co.

...& Their Baby' by McManus; Saalfield, (1907, 13x10", 52 pgs.); daily strips in full color 50.00 150.00 350.00
...& Their Baby's Comic Pictures, The, by McManus, Saalfield, (1917, 14x10", 22 pgs, oblong, cardboard-c); reprints 'Newlyweds' (Baby Snookums stips) mainly from 1916; blue cover; says for painting & crayoning, but some pages in color. (Scarce) 43.00 130.00 300.00

NEWMEN
Apr, 1994 - Present ($1.95, color)
Image Comics

1-5-Matsuda-c/a: 1-Liefeld/Matsuda plot .80 2.00

NEW MEN OF BATTLE, THE
1949 (nn) (Carboard covers)
Catechetical Guild

nn(V8#1-3,5,6)-192 pgs.; contains 5 issues of Topix rebound 4.20 12.50 25.00
nn(V8#7-V8#11)-160 pgs.; contains 5 iss. of Topix 4.20 12.50 25.00

NEW MUTANTS, THE (See Marvel Graphic Novel #4 for 1st app.)
March, 1983 - No. 100, April, 1991
Marvel Comics Group

1 1.00 2.50 6.00
2,3: 3,4-Ties into X-Men #167 1.40 3.50
4-10: 10-1st app. Magma 1.00 2.50
11-17,19,20: 13-Kitty Pryde app. 16-1st app. Warpath (w/out costume); see X-Men #193 .90 2.25
18-Intro. new Warlock 1.20 3.00 7.00
21-Double size; origin new Warlock; newsstand version has cover price written in by Sienkiewicz 1.00 2.00 5.00
22-30: 23-25-Cloak & Dagger app. .90 2.25
31-58: 35-Magneto intro'd as new headmaster. 43-Portacio-i. 50-Double size.
58-Contains pull-out mutant registration form .70 1.75
59-Fall of The Mutants begins, ends #61 1.20 3.00
60-($1.25, 52 pgs.) .90 2.25
61-Fall of The Mutants ends .70 1.75
62,64-72,74-85: 68-Intro Spyder. 76-X-Factor & X-Terminator app. 85-Liefeld-c begin 1.25
63-X-Men & Wolverine clones app.; begin $1.00-c 1.40 3.50
73-($1.50, 52 pgs.) .70 1.75
86-Rob Liefeld-a begins; McFarlane-c(i) swiped from Ditko splash pg.; Cable cameo (last page teaser) 1.40 4.00 10.00
87-1st full app. Cable (3/90) 5.00 15.00 35.00
87-2nd printing; gold metallic ink-c ($1.00) 1.50
88-2nd app. Cable 2.10 6.40 15.00
89-3rd app. Cable 1.40 4.00 10.00
90,91: 90-New costumes. 90,91-Sabretooth app. 1.40 4.00 10.00
92-No Liefeld-a; Liefeld-c 1.60 4.00
93,94-Cable vs. Wolverine 1.40 4.00 10.00
95-97-X-Tinction Agenda x-over. 95-Death of new Warlock. 97-Wolverine & Cable-c, but no app. 1.40 4.00 10.00
95-Gold 2nd printing 1.00 2.50
98-1st app. Deadpool, Gideon & Domino (2/91); 2nd Shatterstar (cameo) 1.40 4.00 10.00
99-1st app. of Feral (of X-Force) 1.20 2.90 7.00
100-($1.50, 52 pgs.)-1st app. X-Force (cameo) 1.20 2.90 7.00
100-Gold 2nd printing 1.20 3.00
100-Silver ink 3rd printing 1.50
Annual 1 (1984) 1.20 3.00
Annual 2 (1986, $1.25) .90 2.25
Annual 3 (1987, $1.25) .70 1.80
Annual 4 (1988, $1.75)-Evolutionary War x-over .80 2.00
Annual 5 (1989, $2.00, 68 pgs.)-Atlantis Attacks; 1st Liefeld-a on New Mutants 2.10 6.00 15.00
Annual 6 (1990, $2.00, 68 pgs.)-1st new costumes by Liefeld (3 pgs.); 1st app. (cameo) Shatterstar (of X-Force) .40 1.00 2.00
Annual 7 (1991, $2.00, 68 pgs.)-Liefeld pin-up only; X-Terminators back-up story; 2nd app. X-Force (continued in New Warriors Annual #1) .40 1.00 2.00
Special 1-Special Edition ('85, 68 pgs.)-Ties in w/X-Men Alpha Flight mini-series; cont'd in X-Men Annual #9; Art Adams/Austin-a 1.00 2.00 5.00
Summer Special 1(Sum/90, $2.95, 84 pgs.) 1.20 3.00

NOTE: ***Art Adams*** *c-38, 39.* ***Austin*** *c-57i.* ***Byrne*** *c/a-75p.* ***Liefeld*** *a-86-91p, 93-96p, 98-100, Annual 5p, 6(3 pgs.); c-85-91p, 92, 93p, 94, 95, 96p, 97-100, Annual 5, 6p.* ***McFarlane*** *c-85-89i, 93i.* ***Portacio*** *a(i)-43.* ***Russell*** *a-48i.* ***Sienkiewicz*** *a-18-31, 35-38i; c-18-31, 35, 37.* ***Simonson*** *c-11p.* ***B. Smith*** *c-36, 40-48.* ***Williamson*** *a(i)-69, 71-73, 78-80, 82, 83; c(i)-69, 72, 73, 78i.*

NEW PEOPLE, THE (TV)
Jan, 1970 - No. 2, May, 1970
Dell Publishing Co.

1,2 1.70 5.00 12.00

NEW ROMANCES
No. 5, May, 1951 - No. 21, Apr?, 1954
Standard Comics

5-Photo-c 8.35 25.00 50.00
6-9: 6-Barbara Bel Geddes, Richard Basehart "Fourteen Hours" photo-c. 7-Ray Milland & Joan Fontaine photo-c. 9-Photo-c from '50s movie 4.20 12.50 25.00
10,14,16,17-Toth-a 5.35 17.50 35.00
11-Toth-a; Liz Taylor, Montgomery Cliff photo-c 10.00 30.00 65.00
12,13,15,18-21 3.60 9.00 18.00

NOTE: ***Celardo*** *a-9.* ***Moreira*** *a-6.* ***Tuska*** *a-7, 20. Photo c-5-16.*

NEW STATESMEN, THE (Fleetway/Quality)(Value: cover or less)

NEWSTRALIA (Innovation)(Value: cover or less)

NEW TALENT SHOWCASE (DC)(Value: cover or less)

NEW TEEN TITANS, THE (See DC Comics Presents 26, Marvel and DC Present & Teen Titans; Tales of the Teen Titans #41 on)

The New Teen Titans #25 © DC

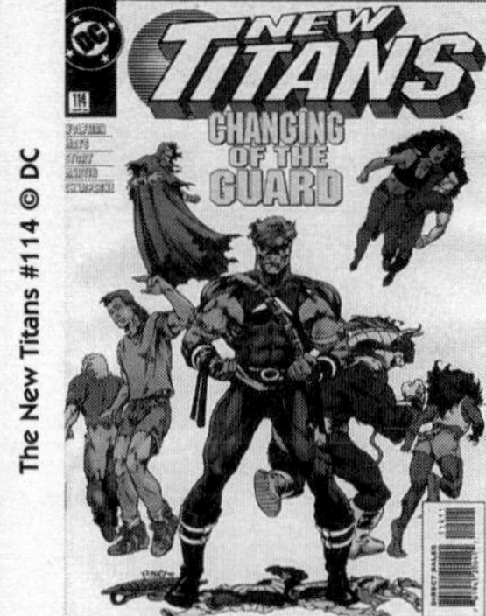

The New Titans #114 © DC

The New Warriors #51 © MEG

GD25 FN65 NM94

November, 1980 - No. 40, March, 1984
DC Comics

1-Robin, Kid Flash, Wonder Girl, The Changeling (1st app.), Starfire, The Raven, Cyborg begin; partial origin 1.65 4.00 10.00
2-1st app. Deathstroke the Terminator 1.90 6.00 13.00
3-9: 3-Origin Starfire; Intro The Fearsome Five. 4-Origin continues; J.L.A. app. 6-Origin Raven. 7-Cyborg origin. 8-Origin Kid Flash retold. 9-Minor cameo Deathstroke on last pg. 1.60 4.00
10-2nd app. Deathstroke the Terminator (see Marvel & DC Present for 3rd app.); origin Changeling retold 1.30 3.30 8.00
11-20: 13-Return of Madame Rouge & Capt. Zahl; Robotman revived. 14-Return of Mento; origin Doom Patrol. 15-Death of Madame Rouge & Capt. Zahl; intro. new Brotherhood of Evil. 16-1st app. Captain Carrot (free 16 pg. preview). 18-Return of Starfire. 19-Hawkman teams-up 1.50
21-30: 21-Intro Night Force in free 16 pg. insert; intro Brother Blood. 23-1st app. Vigilante (not in costume), & Blackfire. 24-Omega Men app. 25-Omega Men cameo; free 16 pg. preview Masters of the Universe. 26-1st app. Terra. 27-Free 16 pg. preview Atari Force. 29-The New Brotherhood of Evil & Speedy app. 30-Terra joins the Titans 1.20
31-33,35-38,40: 37-Batman & The Outsiders x-over. 38-Origin Wonder Girl 1.00
34-4th app. Deathstroke the Terminator 1.40 3.50
39-Last Dick Grayson as Robin; Kid Flash quits .80 2.00
Annual 1(11/82)-Omega Men app. 1.40
Annual V2#2(9/83)-1st app. Vigilante in costume .70 1.75
Annual 3 (See Tales of the Teen Titans Annual #3)
nn(11/83-Keebler Co. Giveaway)-In cooperation with "The President's Drug Awareness Campaign"; came in Presidential envelope w/letter from White House (Nancy Reagan) .60 1.20
nn-(re-issue of above on Mando paper for direct sales market); American Soft Drink Ind. version; I.B.M. Corp. version .50 1.00

NOTE: ***Perez** a-1-4p, 6-34p, 37-40p, Annual 1p, 2p; c-1-12, 13-17p, 18-21, 22p, 23p, 24-37, 38, 39(painted), 40, Annual 1, 2.*

NEW TEEN TITANS, THE (Becomes The New Titans #50 on)
Aug, 1984 - No. 49, Nov, 1988 ($1.25/$1.75; deluxe format)
DC Comics

1-New storyline; Perez-c/a begins 1.70 4.25
2,3: 2-Re-intro Lilith 1.00 2.50
4-10: 5-Death of Trigon. 7-9-Origin Lilith. 8-Intro Kole. 10-Kole joins .70 1.80
11-19: 13,14-Crisis x-over 1.20
20-Robin (Jason Todd) joins; original Teen Titans return .80 2.00
21-49: 37-Begin $1.75-c. 38-Infinity, Inc. x-over. 47-Origin all Titans 1.40
Annual 1 (9/85)-Intro. Vanguard .80 2.00
Annual 2 (8/86; $2.50): Byrne c/a(p); origin Brother Blood; intro new Dr. Light 1.00 2.50
Annual 3 (11/87)-Intro. Danny Chase .80 2.00
Annual 4 ('88, $2.50)-Perez-c .90 2.25

NOTE: ***Orlando** c-33p. **Perez** a-1-5; c-1-6, 19-23, 43. **Steacy** c-47.*

NEW TERRYTOONS (TV)
6-8/60 - No. 8, 3-5/62; 10/62 - No. 54, 1/79
Dell Publishing Co./Gold Key

1(1960-Dell)-Deputy Dawg, Dinky Duck & Hashimoto San begin (1st app. of each) 5.00 15.00 30.00
2-8(1962) 3.60 9.00 18.00
1(30010-210)(10/62-Gold Key, 84 pgs.)-Heckle & Jeckle begins 6.70 20.00 45.00
2(30010-301)-84 pgs. 5.85 17.50 40.00
3-10 2.40 6.00 12.00
11-20 1.20 3.00 6.00
21-30 .60 1.50 3.00
31-54 .40 1.00 2.00

NOTE: *Reprints: #4-12, 38, 40, 47. (See March of Comics #379, 393, 412, 435)*

GD25 FN65 NM94

NEW TESTAMENT STORIES VISUALIZED
1946 - 1947
Standard Publishing Co.

"New Testament Heroes–Acts of Apostles Visualized, Book I"
"New Testament Heroes–Acts of Apostles Visualized, Book II"
"Parables Jesus Told" Set.... 10.00 30.00 65.00

NOTE: *All three are contained in a cardboard case, illustrated on front and info about the set.*

NEW TITANS, THE (Formerly The New Teen Titans)
No. 50, Dec, 1988 - Present ($1.75)
DC Comics

50-Perez-c/a begins; new origin Wonder Girl 1.60 4.00
51-59: 50-55-Painted-c. 55-Nightwing (Dick Grayson) forces Danny Chase to resign; Batman app. in flashback .90 2.25
60-A Lonely Place of Dying Part 2 continues from Batman #440; new Robin tie-in; Timothy Drake app. 1.00 2.50 5.50
61-A Lonely Place of Dying Part 4 1.50 3.75
62-65: Deathstroke the Terminator app. 65-Timothy Drake (Robin) app. 1.90 4.75
66-69,71: 71-(44 pgs.)-10th anniversary issue; Deathstroke cameo 1.00 2.50
70-1st Deathstroke solo cover/story 1.10 2.75
72-79-Deathstroke in all: 74-Intro. Pantha. 79-Terra brought back to life; 1 panel cameo Team Titans (1st app.) 1.10 2.75
80-99,101-111: Deathstroke in #80-84,86. 80-2nd full app. Team Titans. 83, 84-Deathstroke kills his son, Jericho. 85-Team Titans app. 86-Deathstroke vs. Nightwing-c/story; last Deathstroke app. 87-New costume Nightwing. 90-92-Parts 2,5,8 Total Chaos (Team Titans) .70 1.75
100-($3.50, 52 pgs.)-Holo-grafx foil-c 1.40 3.50
112-114: 112-Begin $1.95-c. 114-(9/94) .80 2.00
0,115-119: 0-(10/94) .80 2.00
Annual 5,6 (1989, 1990, $3.50, 68 pgs.) 1.40 3.50
Annual 7 (1991, $3.50, 68 pgs.)-Armaggedon 2001 x-over; 1st full app. Teen (Team) Titans (new group) 1.40 3.50
Annual 8,9 (1992, '93, $3.50, 68 pgs.): 8-Deathstroke app.; Eclipso app. (minor) 1.40 3.50
Annual 10 (1994, $3.50, 68 pgs.)-Elseworlds story 1.40 3.50

NOTE: ***Perez** a-50-55p, 57-60p, 61(layouts); c-50-61, 62-67i, Annual 5i; co-plots-66.*

NEW TV FUNNIES (See New Funnies)

NEW TWO-FISTED TALES, THE
1993 ($4.95, 52 pgs.)
Dark Horse Comics/Byron Preiss

1-Kurtzman-r & new-a 1.00 2.00 5.00

NEW WARRIORS, THE (See Thor #411,412)
July, 1990 - Present ($1.00/$1.25/$1.50)
Marvel Comics

1-Williamson-i; Bagley-c/a(p) in 1-13, Annual 1 2.10 6.40 15.00
1-Gold 2nd printing (7/91) 1.10 2.75
2-Williamson-c/a(i) 1.70 4.20 10.00
3: 1,3-Guice-c(i) 1.10 3.00 6.50
4,5 .90 2.30 5.50
6,7,10: 7-Punisher cameo (last pg.) 1.40 3.50
8,9-Punisher app. 1.00 2.00 5.00
11-14: 14-Darkhawk & Namor x-over .80 2.00
15-19: 17-Fantastic Four & Silver Surfer x-over. 19-Gideon (of X-Force) app.; last $1.00-c 1.25
20-24,26-46: 28-Intro Turbo & Cardinal. 31-Cannonball & Warpath app. 42-Nova vs. Firelord. 46-Photo-c 1.25
25-($2.50, 52 pgs.)-Die-cut cover 1.00 2.50
40-($2.25)-Gold foil collector's edition .90 2.25
47-49,51-56: 47-Begin $1.50-c; bound-in S-M trading card sheet. 52-12 pg. ad insert 1.50
50-($2.95, 52 pgs.)-Glow in the dark-c 1.20 3.00
Annual 1 (1991, $2.00, 68 pgs.)-Origins all members; 3rd app. X-Force (cont'd from New Mutants Annual #7 & cont'd in X-Men Annual #15); x-over before

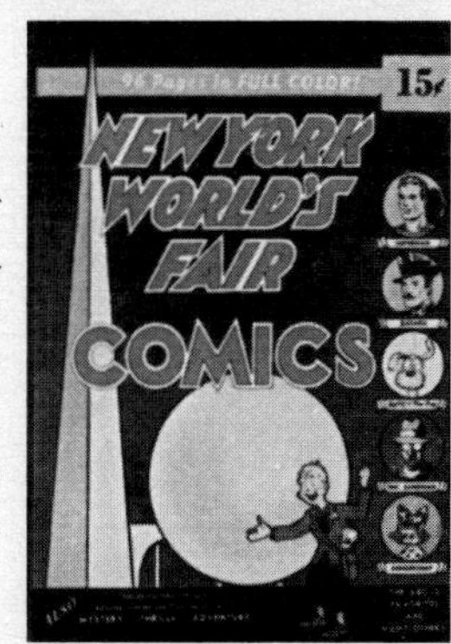

New York Worlds Fair (1939) © DC

Nexus #3 © First

Nick Fury, Agent Of S.HI.E.L.D. #6 (12/89) © MEG

GD25 FN65 NM94

X-Force #1 1.80 4.50
Annual 2 (1992, $2.25, 68 pgs.) .90 2.25
Annual 3 (1993, $2.95, 68 pgs.)-Bagged w/card 1.20 3.00
Annual 4 (1994, $2.95, 68 pgs.) 1.20 3.00

NEW WAVE, THE (Eclipse)(Value: cover or less)

NEW WORLD (See Comic Books, series I)

NEW YORK GIANTS (See Thrilling True Story of the Baseball Giants)

NEW YORK STATE JOINT LEGISLATIVE COMMITTEE TO STUDY THE PUBLICATION OF COMICS, THE
1951, 1955
N.Y. State Legislative Document

This document was referenced by Wertham for **Seduction of the Innocent.** Contains numerous repros from comics showing violence, sadism, torture, and sex.
1955 version (196p, No. 37, 2/23/55)-Sold for $180 in 1986.

NEW YORK WORLD'S FAIR (Also see Big Book of Fun & New Book of Fun)
1939, 1940 (100 pgs.; cardboard covers) (DC's 4th & 5th annuals)
National Periodical Publ.

GD25 FN65 VF82 NM94

1939-Scoop Scanlon, Superman (blond haired Superman on-c), Sandman, Zatara, Slam Bradley, Ginger Snap by Bob Kane begin; 1st published app. The Sandman (see Adventure #40 for his 1st drawn story); Vincent Sullivan-c; cover background by Guardineer 2000.00 6000.00 11,000.00 16,000.00
(Estimated up to 110 total copies exist, 4 in NM/Mint)
1940-Batman, Hourman, Johnny Thunderbolt, Red, White & Blue & Hanko (by Creig Flessel) app.; Superman, Batman & Robin-c (1st time they all appear together); early Robin app.; 1st Burnley-c/a (per Burnley) 1063.00 3188.00 5844.00 8500.00

NOTE: *The 1939 edition was published 4/29/39 and released 4/30/39, the day the fair opened, at 25¢, and was first sold only at the fair. Since all other comics were 10¢, it didn't sell. Remaining copies were advertised beginning in the August issues of most DC comics for 25¢, but soon the price was dropped to 15¢. Everyone that sent a quarter through the mail for it received a free Superman #1 or a #2 to make up the dime difference. 15¢ stickers were placed over the 25¢ price. Four variations on the 15¢ stickers are known. The 1940 edition was published 5/11/40 and was priced at 15¢. It was a precursor to World's Best #1.*

NEW YORK: YEAR ZERO (Eclipse)(Value: cover or less)

NEXT MAN (Comico)(Value: cover or less)

NEXT MEN (See John Byrne's...)

NEXT NEXUS, THE (First)(Value: cover or less)

NEXUS (See First Comics Graphic Novel #4, 19 & The Next Nexus)
June, 1981 - No. 6, Mar, 1984; No. 7, Apr, 1985 - No. 80?, May, 1991
(Direct sale only, 36 pgs.; V2#1('83)-printed on Baxter paper
Capital Comics/First Comics No. 7 on

1-B&W version; mag. size; w/double size poster 1.40 4.00 10.00
1-B&W 1981 limited edition; 500 copies printed and signed; same as above except this version has a 2-pg. poster & a pencil sketch on paperboard by Rude 2.10 6.40 15.00
2-B&W, magazine size 1.00 3.00 6.00
3-B&W, magazine size; contains 33-1/3 rpm record ($2.95 price) 1.40 3.50
V2#1-Color version 1.20 3.00
2-80: 2-Nexus' origin begins. 50-($3.50, 52 pgs.). 73-Begin $2.25-c .80 2.00

NOTE: ***Bissette*** *c-29.* ***Rude*** *c-3(B&W), V2#1-22, 24-27, 33-36, 39-42, 45-48, 50, 58-60; a-1-3, V2#1-7, 8-16p, 18-22p, 24-27p, 33-36p, 39-42p, 45-48p, 50, 58, 59p, 60.* ***Paul Smith*** *a-37, 38, 43, 44, 51-55p; c-37, 38, 43, 44, 51-55.*

NEXUS: ALIEN JUSTICE
Dec, 1992 - No. 3, Feb, 1993 ($3.95, mini-series)
Dark Horse Comics

1-3: Rude-c/a 1.60 4.00

NEXUS FILES (First)(Value: cover or less)

NEXUS LEGENDS (First)(Value: cover or less)

NEXUS THE LIBERATOR (Dark Horse)(Value: cover or less)

NEXUS: THE ORIGIN (Dark Horse)(Value: cover or less)

NFL SUPERPRO (Marvel)(Value: cover or less)

NICKEL COMICS
1938 (Pocket size - 7-1/2x5-1/2")(132 pgs.)
Dell Publishing Co.

1- "Bobby & Chip" by Otto Messmer, Felix the Cat artist. Contains some English reprints 54.00 160.00 375.00

NICKEL COMICS
May, 1940 - No. 8, Aug, 1940 (36 pgs.; Bi-Weekly; 5¢)
Fawcett Publications

1-Origin/1st app. Bulletman 200.00 600.00 1400.00
2 79.00 235.00 550.00
3 68.00 205.00 475.00
4-The Red Gaucho begins 61.00 182.00 425.00
5-8: 8-World's Fair-c; Bulletman moved to Master Comics #7 in October 57.00 171.00 400.00

NOTE: ***Beck*** *c-5-8.* ***Jack Binder*** *c-1-4. Bondage c-5. Bulletman c-1-8.*

NICK FURY, AGENT OF SHIELD (See Fury, Marvel Spotlight #31 & Shield)
6/68 - No. 15, 11/69; No. 16, 11/70 - No. 18, 3/71
Marvel Comics Group

1 6.40 19.00 45.00
2-4: 4-Origin retold 3.40 10.30 24.00
5-Classic-c 4.00 12.00 28.00
6,7: 7-Salvador Dali painting swipe 2.10 6.40 15.00
8-11,13: 9-Hate Monger begins, ends #11. 10-Smith layouts/pencil. 11-Smith-c. 13-1st app. Super-Patriot; last 12¢ issue 1.20 2.90 7.00
12-Smith-c/a 1.50 3.80 9.00
14-Begin 15¢ issues 1.80 4.50
15-1st app. & death of Bullseye-c/story(11/69); Nick Fury shot & killed 3.90 12.00 27.00
16-18-(25¢, 52 pgs.)-r/Str. Tales #135-143 1.00 2.50

NOTE: ***Adkins*** *a-3i.* ***Craig*** *a-10i.* ***Sid Greene*** *a-12i.* ***Kirby*** *a-16-18r.* ***Springer*** *a-4, 6, 7, 8p, 9, 10p, 11; c-8, 9.* ***Steranko*** *a(p)-1-3, 5; c-1-7.*

NICK FURY AGENT OF SHIELD (Also see Strange Tales #135)
Dec, 1983 - No. 2, Jan, 1984 ($2.00, Baxter paper, 52 pgs.)
Marvel Comics Group

1,2-r/Nick Fury #1-4; new Steranko-c .80 2.00

NICK FURY, AGENT OF S.H.I.E.L.D.
Sept, 1989 - No. 47, May, 1993 ($1.50/$1.75)
Marvel Comics

V2#1-26: 10-Capt. America app. 13-Return of The Yellow Claw. 15-Fantastic Four app. 1.50
27-29-Wolverine-c/stories .80 2.00
30-47: 30,31-Deathlok app. 32-Begin $1.75-c. 36-Cage app. 37-Woodgod c/story. 38-41-Flashes back to pre-Shield days after WWII. 44-Capt. America-c/s. 45-Viper-c/s. 46-Gideon x-over .70 1.75

NOTE: ***Alan Grant*** *scripts-11.* ***Guice*** *a(p)-20-23, 25, 26; c-20-28.*

NICK FURY VS. S.H.I.E.L.D.
June, 1988 - No. 6, Nov, 1988 ($3.50, 52 pgs, deluxe format)
Marvel Comics

1-Steranko-c 1.00 2.50 6.00
2-(Low print run) Sienkiewicz-c 1.00 2.50 6.00
3-6 1.20 3.00

NICK HALIDAY (Thrill of the Sea)
May, 1956
Argo

1-Daily & Sunday strip-r by Petree 6.35 19.00 38.00

NIGHT AND THE ENEMY (Graphic Novel)
1988 (8-1/2x11") ($11.95, color, 80 pgs.)
Comico

1-Harlan Ellison scripts/Ken Steacy-c/a; r/Epic Illustrated & new-a

The Night Man #12 © Malibu

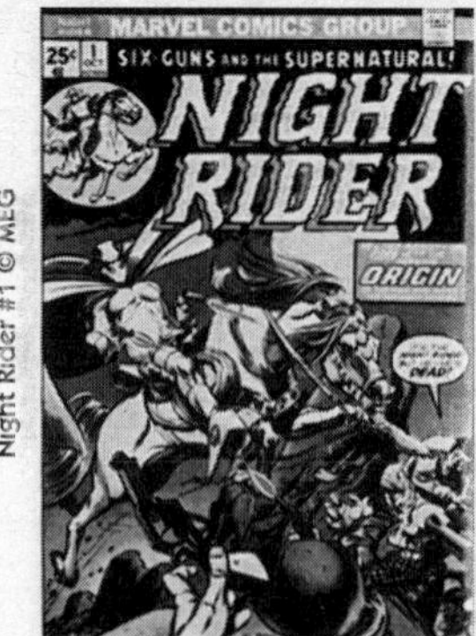

Night Rider #1 © MEG

Nightstalkers #12 © MEG

	GD25	FN65	NM94
(1st and 2nd printings)	1.70	5.00	12.00
1-Limited edition ($39.95)	5.50	17.00	40.00

NIGHT BEFORE CHRISTMAS, THE (See March of Comics No. 152)

NIGHTBREED (See Clive Barker's Nightbreed)

NIGHTCAT (Marvel)(Value: cover or less)

NIGHTCRAWLER
Nov, 1985 - No. 4, Feb, 1986 (Mini-series from X-Men)
Marvel Comics Group

	GD25	FN65	NM94
1-Cockrum-c/a		.90	2.25
2-4			1.50

NIGHT FORCE, THE (See New Teen Titans #21)
Aug, 1982, No. 14, Sept, 1983 (60¢)
DC Comics

	GD25	FN65	NM94
1-14: 13-Origin The Baron. 14-Nudity panels			1.00

NOTE: ***Colan*** *c/a-1-14p.* ***Giordano*** *c-1i, 2i, 4i, 5i, 7i, 12i.*

NIGHT GLIDER
April, 1993 ($2.95, one-shot)
Topps Comics

	GD25	FN65	NM94
1-Polybagged w/Kirbychrome trading card		1.20	3.00

NIGHTINGALE, THE
1948 (14 pgs., 7-1/4x10-1/4", B&W) (10¢)
Henry H. Stansbury Once-Upon-A-Time Press, Inc.

(Very Rare)-Low distribution; distributed to Westchester County & Bronx, N.Y. only; used in **Seduction of the Innocent**, pg. 312,313 as the 1st and only "good" comic book ever published. Ill. by Dong Kingman; 1,500 words of text, printed on high quality paper & no word balloons. Copyright registered 10/22/48, distributed week of 12/5/48. (By Hans Christian Andersen) Estimated value. $200

NIGHT MAN, THE (See Sludge #1)
Oct, 1993 - Present ($1.95)
Malibu Comics (Ultraverse)

	GD25	FN65	NM94
1-($2.50, 48 pgs.)-Rune flip-c/story by B. Smith (3 pgs.)		1.00	2.50
1-Ultra-Limited silver foil-c	1.90	6.00	13.00
2-11: 3-Break-Thru x-over; Freex app. 4-Origin Firearm (2 pgs.) by Chaykin. 6-TNTNT app. 8-1st app. Teknight		.80	2.00

NIGHTMARE
Summer, 1952 - No. 2, Fall, 1952; No. 3,4, 1953 (Painted-c)
Ziff-Davis (Approved Comics)/St. John No. 3,4

	GD25	FN65	NM94
1-1 pg. Kinstler-a; Tuska-a(2)	32.00	96.00	225.00
2-Kinstler-a-Poe's "Pit & the Pendulum"	22.00	67.00	155.00
3-Kinstler-a	19.00	57.00	130.00
4-Exist?	14.00	43.00	100.00

NIGHTMARE (Weird Horrors #1-9) (Amazing Ghost Stories #14 on)
No. 10, Dec, 1953 - No. 13, Aug, 1954
St. John Publishing Co.

	GD25	FN65	NM94
10-Reprints Ziff-Davis Weird Thrillers #2 w/new Kubert-c plus 2 pgs. Kinstler-a; Anderson, Colan & Toth-a	34.00	100.00	235.00
11-Krigstein-a; painted-c; Poe adapt., "Hop Frog"	22.00	67.00	155.00
12-Kubert bondage-c; adaptation of Poe's "The Black Cat"; Cannibalism story	19.00	57.00	130.00
13-Reprints Z-D Weird Thrillers #3 with new cover; Powell-a(2), Tuska-a; Baker-c	14.00	43.00	100.00

NIGHTMARE (Magazine)
Dec, 1970 - No. 23, Feb, 1975 (B&W, 68 pgs.)
Skywald Publishing Corp.

	GD25	FN65	NM94
1-Everett-a	2.60	7.50	18.00
2-5: 4-Decapitation story	1.30	3.25	8.00
6-Kaluta-a; Jeff Jones photo & interview	1.65	4.00	10.00
7,9,10: 9-Wrightson-a	1.20	3.00	7.00
8-Features E. C. movie "Tales From the Crypt"; reprints some E.C. comics panels	1.65	4.00	10.00
11-23: 12-Excessive gore, severed heads. 20-Byrne's 1st artwork (8/74); severed head-c. 21-(1974 Summer Special)-Kaluta-a. 22-Tomb of Horror issue. 23-(1975 Winter Special)	1.00	2.00	5.00
Annual 1(1972)-B. Jones-a	1.20	3.00	7.00
Winter Special 1(1973)	1.20	3.00	7.00
Yearbook nn(1974)	1.00	2.50	6.00

NOTE: ***Adkins*** *a-5.* ***Boris*** *c-2, 3, 5 (#4 is not by Boris).* ***Byrne*** *a-20p.* ***Everett*** *a-4, 5.* ***Jeff Jones*** *a-6, 21r(Psycho #6); c-6.* ***Katz*** *a-5.* ***Reese*** *a-4, 5.* ***Wildey*** *a-5, 6, 21, '74 Yearbook.*

NIGHTMARE (Alex Nino's...)(Innovation)(Value: cover or less)

NIGHTMARE & CASPER (See Harvey Hits #71) (Casper & Nightmare #6 on) (See Casper The Friendly Ghost #19)
Aug, 1963 - No. 5, Aug, 1964 (25¢)
Harvey Publications

	GD25	FN65	NM94
1-All reprints?	6.00	18.00	36.00
2-5: All reprints?	3.60	9.00	18.00

NIGHTMARE ON ELM STREET, A (See Freddy Krueger's...)

NIGHTMARE ON ELM STREET: THE BEGINNING, A (Innovation)(Value: cover or less)

NIGHTMARES (See Do You Believe in Nightmares)

NIGHTMARES (Eclipse)(Value: cover or less)

NIGHTMARES ON ELM STREET (Innovation)(Value: cover or less)

NIGHTMARK: BLOOD & HONOR
1994 - No. 3, 1994 ($2.50, B&W, mini-series)
Alpha Productions

	GD25	FN65	NM94
1,2		1.00	2.50

NIGHTMARK MYSTERY SPECIAL
Jan, 1994 ($2.50, B&W)
Alpha Productions

	GD25	FN65	NM94
1		1.00	2.50

NIGHTMASK (Marvel)(Value: cover or less)

NIGHT MASTER
Feb, 1987 ($1.50, B&W)
Silverwolf

	GD25	FN65	NM94
1-Tim Vigil-c/a			1.50

NIGHT MUSIC (Eclipse)(Value: cover or less)

NIGHT NURSE
Nov, 1972 - No. 4, May, 1973
Marvel Comics Group

	GD25	FN65	NM94
1-4		1.20	3.00

NIGHT OF MYSTERY
1953 (no month) (One Shot)
Avon Periodicals

	GD25	FN65	NM94
nn-1 pg. Kinstler-a, Hollingsworth-c	23.00	70.00	160.00

NIGHT OF THE GRIZZLY, THE (See Movie Classics)

NIGHTRAVEN: THE COLLECTED STORIES
1991 ($9.95, graphic novel)
Marvel Comics UK, Ltd.

	GD25	FN65	NM94
nn-Bolton-r/British Hulk mag.; David Lloyd-c/a	1.65	4.00	10.00

NIGHT RIDER
Oct, 1974 - No. 6, Aug, 1975 (Western)
Marvel Comics Group

	GD25	FN65	NM94
1: 1-6 reprint Ghost Rider #1-6 (#1-origin)		.80	2.00
2-6			1.25

NIGHTSTALKERS (See Midnight Sons Unlimited)
Nov, 1992 - Present ($1.75)
Marvel Comics (Midnight Sons imprint #14 on)

	GD25	FN65	NM94
1-($2.75, 52 pgs.)-Polybagged w/poster; part 5 of Rise of the Midnight Sons storyline; Garney/Palmer-c/a begins; Hannibal King, Blade & Frank Drake begin (see Tomb of Dracula for & Dr. Strange)		1.10	2.75

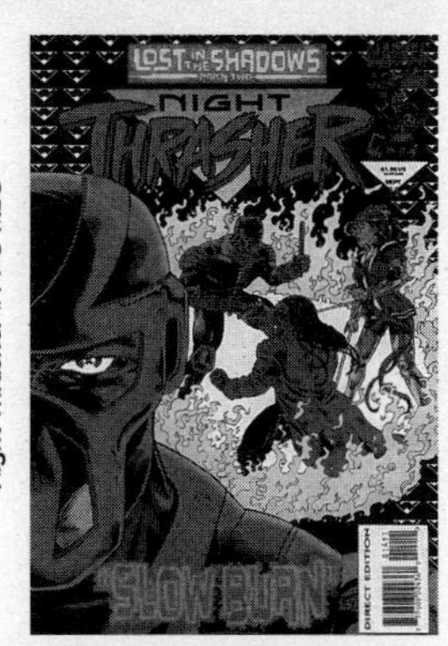

Night Thrasher #14 © MEG

Nomad #18 © MEG

Not Brand Echh #1 © MEG

GD25 FN65 NM94

2-9,11-21: 5-Punisher app. 7-Ghost Rider app. 8,9-Morbius app. 14-Spot varnish-c. 14,15-Siege of Darkness parts 1 & 9 .70 1.75
10-($2.25)-Outer-c is a Darkhold envelope made of black parchment w/gold ink; Midnight Massacre part 1 .90 2.25

NIGHT THRASHER (See The New Warriors)
Aug, 1993 - Present ($1.75/$1.95)
Marvel Comics

1-($2.95, 52 pgs.)-Red holo-grafx foil-c; origin 1.20 3.00
2-9: 2-Intro Tantrum. 3-Gideon (of X-Force) app. .70 1.75
10-22: 10-Begin 1.95-c; bound-in trading card sheet; Iron Man app. .80 2.00

NIGHT THRASHER: FOUR CONTROL
Oct, 1992 - No. 4, Jan, 1993 ($2.00, mini-series)
Marvel Comics

1-Hero from New Warriors .80 2.00
2-4: 2-Intro Tantrum. 3-Gideon (of X-Force) app. .80 2.00

NIGHTVEIL (Americomics)(Value: cover or less)

NIGHT WALKER (Fleetway)(Value: cover or less)

NIGHTWATCH
Apr, 1994 - Present ($1.50)
Marvel Comics

1-($2.95)-Collectors edition; foil-c; Ron Lim-c/a begins; Spider-Man app. 1.20 3.00
1-($1.50)-Regular edition 1.50
2-12: 2-Bound-in S-M trading card sheet; 5,6-Venom-c & app. 7-Cardiac app. 1.50

NIGHTWINGS (See DC Science Fiction Graphic Novel)

NIKKI, WILD DOG OF THE NORTH (See 4-Color 1226 & Movie Comics)

NINE LIVES OF FELIX THE CAT, THE (Harvey)(Value: cover or less)

1963
Apr, 1993 - No. 6, Oct, 1993 ($1.95, color, mini-series)
Image Comics

1-6-Alan Moore scripts; Veitch-a(p) .80 2.00

1984 (Magazine) (1994 #11 on)
June, 1978 - No. 10, Jan, 1980 ($1.50)
Warren Publishing Co.

1-Nino-a in all 1.20 3.00
2-10 .70 1.80

NOTE: ***Alacla** a-1-3, 5i. **Corben** a-1-8; c-1, 2. **Thorne** a-7-10. **Wood** a-1, 2, 5i.*

1994 (Formerly 1984) (Magazine)
No. 11, Feb, 1980 - No. 29, Feb, 1983
Warren Publishing Co.

11-29: 27-The Warhawks return .80 2.00

NOTE: ***Corben** c-26. **Nino** a-11-19, 20(2), 21, 25, 26, 28; c-21. **Redondo** c-20. **Thorne** a-11-14, 17-21, 25, 26, 28, 29.*

NINJA HIGH SCHOOL FEATURING SPEED RACER (Malibu/Now)(Value: cover or less)

NINJA HIGH SCHOOL IN COLOR (Eternity)(Value: cover or less)

NINJA HIGH SCHOOL: THE PROM FORMULA (Eternity)(Value: cover or less)

NINJAK (See Bloodshot #6, 7 & Deathmate)
Feb, 1994 - Present ($2.25, color)
Valiant

1-($3.50)-Chromium-c; Quesada-c/a(p) in #1-3 1.40 3.50
2-14: 3-Batman, Spawn & Random (from X-Factor) app. as costumes at party (cameo). 4-w/bound-in trading card. 5,6-X-O app .90 2.25

NINTENDO COMICS SYSTEM (Valiant)(Value: cover or less)

NIPPY'S POP
1917 (Sunday strip reprints-B&W) (10-1/2x13-1/2")
The Saalfield Publishing Co.

GD25 FN65 NM94

nn-32 pgs. 14.00 43.00 100.00

NOAH'S ARK (Spire Christian)(Value: cover or less)

NO ESCAPE
June, 1994 - No. 3, Aug, 1994 ($1.50)
Marvel Comics

1-3-Based on movie 1.50

NOMAD (See Captain America #180)
Nov, 1990 - No. 4, Feb, 1991 ($1.50, limited series)
Marvel Comics

1-4: 1,4-Captain America app. 1.50

NOMAD
V2#1, May, 1992 - No. 25, May, 1994 ($1.75)
Marvel Comics

V2#1-($2.00)-Has gatefold-c w/map/wanted poster 1.20 3.00
2-5: 4-Deadpool x-over. 5-Punisher vs. Nomad-c/story .70 1.80
6-25: 6-Punisher & Daredevil-c/story cont'd in Punisher War Journal #48. 7-Gambit-c/story. 10-Red Wolf app. 21-Man-Thing-c/story. 25-Bound-in trading card sheet .70 1.75

NOMAN (See Thunder Agents)
Nov, 1966 - No. 2, March, 1967 (25¢, 68 pgs.)
Tower Comics

1-Wood/Williamson-c; Lightning begins; Dynamo cameo; Kane-a(p) & Whitney-a 5.00 16.00 38.00
2-Wood-c only; Dynamo x-over; Whitney-a 3.90 11.60 27.00

NONE BUT THE BRAVE (See Movie Classics)

NOODNIK COMICS (See Pinky the Egghead)
Dec, 1953; No. 2, Feb, 1954 - No. 5, Aug, 1954
Comic Media/Mystery/Biltmore

3-D(1953, 25¢; Comic Media)(#1)-Came w/glasses 27.00 80.00 185.00
2-5 4.70 14.00 28.00

NORMALMAN (See Cerebus the Aardvark #55, 56)
Jan, 1984 - No. 12, Dec, 1985 ($1.70/$2.00)
Aardvark-Vanaheim/Renegade Press #6 on

1-5 ($1.70, color)-Jim Valentino-c/a in all .70 1.70
6-12 ($2.00, B&W): 10-Cerebus cameo; Sim-a (2 pgs.) .80 2.00
...3-D 1 (Annual, 1986, $2.25) .90 2.25

NORMALMAN-MEGATON MAN SPECIAL
Aug, 1994 ($2.50, color)
Image Comics

1 1.00 2.50

NORTH AVENUE IRREGULARS (See Walt Disney Showcase #49)

NORTHSTAR
Apr, 1994 - No. 4, July, 1994 ($1.75, mini-series)
Marvel Comics

1-4-Character from Alpha Flight .70 1.75

NORTH TO ALASKA (See 4-Color No. 1155)

NORTHWEST MOUNTIES (Also see Approved Comics #12)
Oct, 1948 - No. 4, July, 1949
Jubilee Publications/St. John

1-Rose of the Yukon by Matt Baker; Walter Johnson-a; Lubbers-c 25.00 75.00 175.00
2-Baker-a; Lubbers-c. Ventrilo app. 18.00 54.00 125.00
3-Bondage-c, Baker-a; Sky Chief, K-9 app. 19.00 57.00 130.00
4-Baker-c/a(2 pgs.); Blue Monk & The Desperado app. 19.00 57.00 130.00

NOSFERATU (Dark Horse)(Value: cover or less)

NOSFERATU, PLAGUE OF TERROR (Millennium)(Value: cover or less)

NO SLEEP 'TIL DAWN (See 4-Color #831)

Nova #9 © MEG

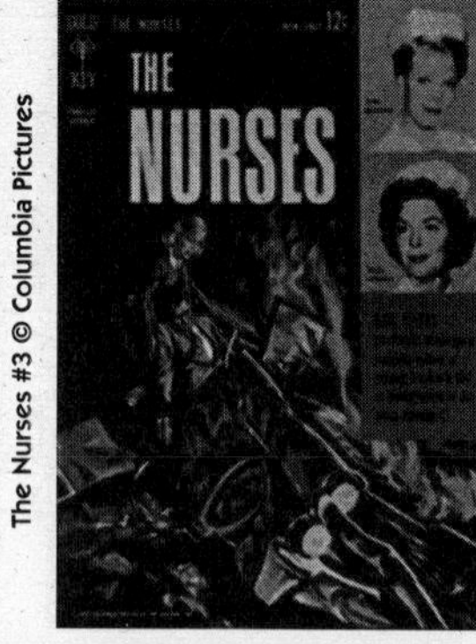

The Nurses #3 © Columbia Pictures

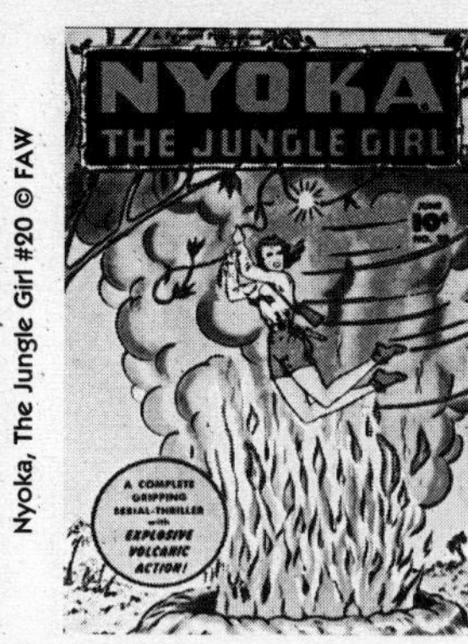

Nyoka, The Jungle Girl #20 © FAW

GD25 FN65 NM94

NOT BRAND ECHH (Brand Echh #1-4; See Crazy, 1973)
Aug, 1967 - No. 13, May, 1969 (No. 9-13: 25¢, 68 pgs.)
Marvel Comics Group (LMC)

1: 1-8 are 12¢ issues 3.90 12.00 27.00
2-4: 3-Origin Thor, Hulk & Capt. America; Monkees, Alfred E. Neuman cameo. 4-X-Men app. 2.00 6.00 14.00
5-8: 5-Origin/intro. Forbush Man. 7-Origin Fantastical-4 & Stuporman. 8-Beatles cameo; X-Men satire 2.00 6.00 14.00
9-13-All Giants. 9-Beatles cameo. 10-All-r; The Old Witch, Crypt Keeper & Vault Keeper cameos. 12,13-Beatles cameo 2.10 6.00 15.00

NOTE: ***Colan** a(p)-4, 5, 8, 9, 13. **Everett** a-1i. **Kirby** a(p)-1, 3, 5-7, 10r; c-1p. **J. Severin** a-1; c-3, 6-8, 11. **M. Severin** a-1-13; c-2, 9, 10, 12, 13. **Sutton** a-3, 4, 5i, 6i, 8, 9, 10r, 11-13; c-5. Archie satire in #9. Avengers satire in #8, 12.*

NOTHING CAN STOP THE JUGGERNAUT (Marvel)(Value: cover or less)

NO TIME FOR SERGEANTS (TV)
No. 914, July, 1958; Feb-Apr, 1965 - No. 3, Aug-Oct, 1965
Dell Publishing Co.

4-Color 914 (Movie)-Toth-a; Andy Griffith photo-c 10.00 30.00 65.00
1(2-4/65)-3 (TV): Photo-c 4.70 14.00 28.00

NOVA (The Man Called... No. 22-25)(See New Warriors)
Sept, 1976 - No. 25, May, 1979
Marvel Comics Group

1-Origin/1st app. Nova 1.10 2.70 6.50
2-11: 4-Thor x-over 1.30 3.25
12-Spider-Man x-over 1.00 2.00 5.00
13-25: 13-Intro Crime-Buster. 14-Last 30¢ issue. 18-Yellow Claw app. 19-Wally West (Kid Flash) cameo .70 1.80

NOTE: ***Austin** c-21i, 23i. **John Buscema** a(p)-1-3, 8, 21; c-1p, 2, 15. **Infantino** a(p)-15-20, 22-25; c-17-20, 21p, 23p, 24p. **Kirby** c-4p, 5, 7. **Nebres** c-25i. **Simonson** a-23i.*

NOVA
Jan, 1994 - Present ($1.75/$1.95)(Started as 4-part mini-series)
Marvel Comics

1-($2.95, 52 pgs.)-Collector's Edition w/gold foil-c; new costume for Nova 1.20 3.00
1-($2.25, 52 pgs.)-Newsstand Edition w/o foil-c .90 2.25
2-4: 3-Spider-Man-c/story. 5-Stan Lee app. .70 1.75
5-16: 5-Begin 1.95-c; bound-in card sheet .40 1.00 2.00

NOW AGE ILLUSTRATED (See Pendulum Illustrated Classics)

NTH MAN THE ULTIMATE NINJA (See Marvel Comics Presents 25)
Aug, 1989 - No. 16, Sept, 1990 ($1.00)
Marvel Comics

1-7,9-16-Ninja mercenary 1.00
8-Dale Keown's 1st Marvel work (1/90, pencils) 1.80 4.50

NUCLEUS (Also see Cerebus)
May, 1979 ($1.50, B&W, adult fanzine)
Heiro-Graphic Publications

1-Contains "Demonhorn" by Dave Sim; early app. of Cerebus The Aardvark (4 pg. story) 4.00 12.00 28.00

NUKLA
Oct-Dec, 1965 - No. 4, Sept, 1966
Dell Publishing Co.

1-Origin & 1st app. Nukla (super hero) 3.00 9.40 22.00
2,3 1.70 5.00 12.00
4-Ditko-a, c(p) 3.10 9.00 22.00

NURSE BETSY CRANE (Formerly Teen Secret Diary)
V2#12, Aug, 1961 - V2#27, Mar, 1964 (See Soap Opera Romances)
Charlton Comics

V2#12-27 .80 2.00 4.00

NURSE HELEN GRANT (See The Romances of...)

NURSE LINDA LARK (See Linda Lark)

GD25 FN65 NM94

NURSERY RHYMES
No. 10, July-Aug, 1951 - No. 2, Winter, 1951 (Painted-c)
Ziff-Davis Publ. Co. (Approved Comics)

10 (#1), 2: 10-Howie Post-a 10.00 30.00 65.00

NURSES, THE (TV)
April, 1963 - No. 3, Oct, 1963 (Photo-c: #1,2)
Gold Key

1 3.60 9.00 18.00
2,3 2.40 6.00 12.00

NUTS! (Satire)
March, 1954 - No. 5, Nov, 1954
Premiere Comics Group

1-Hollingsworth-a 19.00 58.00 135.00
2,4,5: 5-Capt. Marvel parody 13.00 40.00 90.00
3-Drug "reefers" mentioned 13.50 41.00 95.00

NUTS (Magazine) (Satire)
Feb, 1958 - No. 2, April, 1958
Health Knowledge

1 6.70 20.00 40.00
2 5.00 15.00 30.00

NUTS & JOLTS (See Large Feature Comic #22)

NUTSY SQUIRREL (Formerly Hollywood Funny Folks)(See Comic Cavalcade)
#61, 9-10/54 - #69, 1-2/56; #70, 8-9/56 - #71, 10-11/56; #72, 11/57
National Periodical Publications

61-Mayer-a; Grossman-a in all 10.00 30.00 70.00
62-72: Mayer a-62,65,67-72 7.50 22.50 45.00

NUTTY COMICS
Winter, 1946 (Funny animal)
Fawcett Publications

1-Capt. Kidd story; 1 pg. Wolverton-a 10.00 30.00 70.00

NUTTY COMICS
1945 - No. 8, June-July, 1947
Home Comics (Harvey Publications)

nn-Helpful Hank, Bozo Bear & others (funny animal) 5.85 17.50 35.00
2-4 4.00 11.00 22.00
5-8: 5-Rags Rabbit begins(1st app.); infinity-c 3.60 9.00 18.00

NUTTY LIFE (Formerly Krazy Life #1; becomes Wotalife Comics #3 on)
No. 2, Summer, 1946
Fox Features Syndicate

2 7.00 21.00 42.00

NYOKA, THE JUNGLE GIRL (Formerly Jungle Girl; see The Further Adventures of..., Master Comics #50 & XMas Comics)
No. 2, Winter, 1945 - No. 77, June, 1953 (Movie serial)
Fawcett Publications

2 43.00 130.00 300.00
3 25.00 75.00 175.00
4,5 21.00 63.00 145.00
6-10 14.00 43.00 100.00
11,13,14,16-18-Krigstein-a: 17-Sam Spade ad by Lou Fine 14.00 43.00 100.00
12,15,19,20 12.00 36.00 85.00
21-30: 25-Clayton Moore photo-c? 8.35 25.00 50.00
31-40 6.70 20.00 40.00
41-50 5.00 15.00 30.00
51-60 4.00 12.00 24.00
61-77 4.00 10.00 20.00

NOTE: *Photo-c from movies 25, 30-70, 72, 75-77. Bondage c-4, 5, 7, 8, 14, 24.*

NYOKA, THE JUNGLE GIRL (Formerly Zoo Funnies; Space Adventures #23 on)
No. 14, Nov, 1955 - No. 22, Nov, 1957

Offcastes #2 © MEG

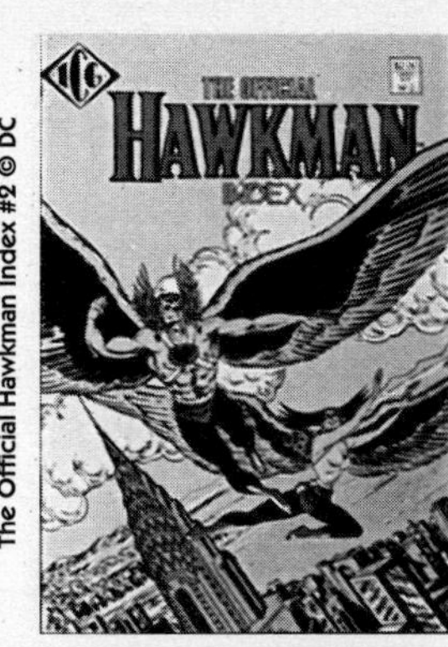

The Official Hawkman Index #2 © DC

Oh My Goddess #1 © DH

	GD25	FN65	NM94

Charlton Comics

14	6.70	20.00	40.00
15-22	5.00	15.00	30.00

OAKLAND PRESS FUNNYBOOK, THE
9/17/78 - 4/13/80 (16 pgs.) (Weekly)
Full color in comic book form; changes to tabloid size 4/20/80-on
The Oakland Press

Contains Tarzan by Manning, Marmaduke, Bugs Bunny, etc. (low distribution); 9/23/79 - 4/13/80 contain Buck Rogers by Gray Morrow & Jim Lawrence — .65 1.60

OAKY DOAKS (See Famous Funnies #190)
July, 1942 (One Shot)
Eastern Color Printing Co.

1	23.00	70.00	160.00

OBIE
1953 (6¢)
Store Comics

1	.80	2.00	4.00

OBNOXIO THE CLOWN
April, 1983 (One Shot) (Character from Crazy Magazine)
Marvel Comics Group

1-Vs. the X-Men			1.00

OCCULT FILES OF DR. SPEKTOR, THE
Apr, 1973 - No. 24, Feb, 1977; No. 25, May, 1982 (Painted-c #1-24)
Gold Key/Whitman No. 25

1-1st app. Lakota; Baron Tibor begins	1.50	3.80	9.00
2-5		1.80	4.50
6-10: 8-Dracula app.		1.30	3.25
11-13,15-25: 11-1st app. Spektor as Werewolf. 25-Reprints		1.00	2.50
14-Dr. Solar app.	1.20	2.90	7.00
9(Modern Comics reprint, 1977)		.70	1.75

NOTE: *Also see Dan Curtis, Golden Comics Digest 33, Gold Key Spotlight, Mystery Comics Digest 5, & Spine Tingling Tales.*

ODELL'S ADVENTURES IN 3-D (See Adventures in 3-D)

OFFCASTES (Epic Comics)(Value: cover or less)

OFFICIAL CRISIS ON INFINITE EARTHS INDEX, THE (Eclipse)(Value: cover or less)

OFFICIAL CRISIS ON INFINITE EARTHS CROSSOVER INDEX, THE (Eclipse)(Value: cover or less)

OFFICIAL DOOM PATROL INDEX, THE (Eclipse)(Value: cover or less)

OFFICIAL HANDBOOK OF THE CONAN UNIVERSE (See Handbook of...)

OFFICIAL HANDBOOK OF THE MARVEL UNIVERSE, THE
Jan, 1983 - No. 15, May, 1984
Marvel Comics Group

1-Lists Marvel heroes & villains (letter A)		1.60	4.00
2 (B-C)		1.20	3.00
3-5: 3-(C-D). 4-(D-G). 5-(H-J)		1.10	2.75
6-9: 6-(K-L). 7-(M). 8-(N-P); Punisher-c. 9-(Q-S)		.90	2.25
10-15: 10-(S). 11-(S-U). 12-(V-Z); Wolverine-c. 13,14-Book of the Dead. 15-Weaponry catalogue		.80	2.00

NOTE: ***Byrne** c/a(p)-1-14; c-15p. **Grell** a-9. **Layton** a-2, 5, 7. **Miller** a-2, 3. **Nebres** a-3, 4, 8. **Simonson** a-11. **Paul Smith** a-1-3, 6, 7, 9, 10, 12. **Starlin** a-7. **Steranko** a-8p.*

OFFICIAL HANDBOOK OF THE MARVEL UNIVERSE, THE
Dec, 1985 - No. 20, Feb, 1988 ($1.50 cover; maxi-series)
Marvel Comics Group

V2#1-Byrne-c		1.30	3.25
2-5: 2,3-Byrne-c		1.00	2.50
6-10		.80	2.00
11-20		.60	1.50
Trade paperback Vol. 1-10 ($6.95)	1.20	3.00	7.00

OFFICIAL HANDBOOK OF THE MARVEL UNIVERSE, THE
July, 1989 - No. 8, Mid-Dec, 1990 ($1.50, mini-series, 52 pgs.)
Marvel Comics

V3#1-8: 1-McFarlane-a(2 pgs.)			1.25

OFFICIAL HAWKMAN INDEX, THE (Independent)(Value: cover or less)

OFFICIAL JUSTICE LEAGUE OF AMERICA INDEX, THE (Independent)(Value: cover or less)

OFFICIAL LEGION OF SUPER-HEROES INDEX, THE (Independent)(Value: cover or less)

OFFICIAL MARVEL INDEX TO MARVEL TEAM-UP (Marvel)(Value: cover or less)

OFFICIAL MARVEL INDEX TO THE AMAZING SPIDER-MAN (Marvel)(Value: cover or less)

OFFICIAL MARVEL INDEX TO THE AVENGERS, THE
V2#1, Oct, 1994 - Present ($1.95)
Marvel Comics

V2#1		.80	2.00

OFFICIAL MARVEL INDEX TO THE FANTASTIC FOUR (Marvel)(Value: cover or less)

OFFICIAL MARVEL INDEX TO THE X-MEN, THE
V2#1, Apr, 1994 - Present ($1.95)
Marvel Comics

V2#1-5: 1-Covers X-Men #1-51. 2-Covers #52-122,Special #1,2,Giant-Size #1,2. 3-Byrne-c; covers #123-177, Annuals 3-7, Spec. Ed. #1. 4-Covers Uncanny X-Men #178-234, Annuals 8-12. 5-Covers #235-287, Annuals 13-15		.80	2.00

OFFICIAL SOUPY SALES COMIC (See Soupy Sales)

OFFICIAL TEEN TITANS INDEX, THE (Eclipse)(Value: cover or less)

OFFICIAL TRUE CRIME CASES (Formerly Sub-Mariner #23; All-True Crime Cases #26 on)
No. 24, Fall, 1947 - No. 25, Winter, 1947-48
Marvel Comics (OCI)

24(#1)-Burgos-a; Syd Shores-c	14.00	43.00	100.00
25-Syd Shores-c; Kurtzman's "Hey Look"	11.50	34.00	80.00

OF SUCH IS THE KINGDOM
1955 (36 pgs., 15¢)
George A. Pflaum

nn-Reprints from 1951 Treasure Chest	2.00	5.00	10.00

O.G. WHIZ (See Gold Key Spotlight #10)
2/71 - No. 6, 5/72; No. 7, 5/78 - No. 11, 1/79 (No. 7: 52 pgs.)
Gold Key

1,2-John Stanley scripts	7.00	21.00	50.00
3-6(1972)	3.60	10.75	25.00
7-11(1978-79)-Part-r: 9-Tubby app.	1.20	3.00	7.00

OH, BROTHER! (Teen Comedy)
Jan, 1953 - No. 5, Oct, 1953
Stanhall Publ.

1-By Bill Williams	5.00	15.00	30.00
2-5	3.60	9.00	18.00

OH MY GODDESS!
Aug, 1994 - Present ($2.50, B&W, limited series:6)
Dark Horse Comics

1-4		1.00	2.50

OH SKIN-NAY!
1913 (8-1/2x13")
P.F. Volland & Co.

nn-The Days Of Real Sport by Briggs	19.00	57.00	130.00

OH SUSANNA (See 4-Color #1105)

O.K. Comics #2 © UFS

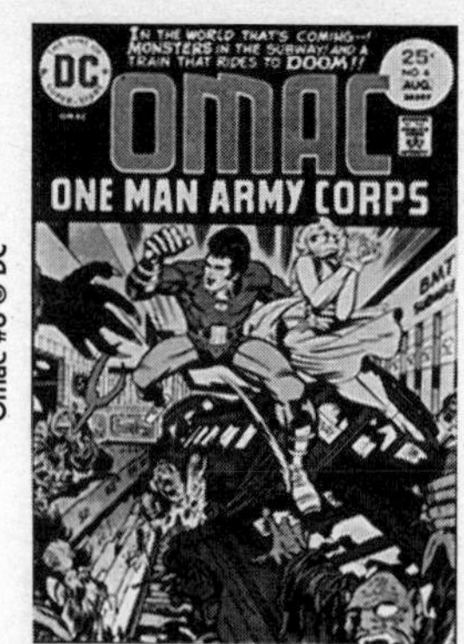

Omac #6 © DC

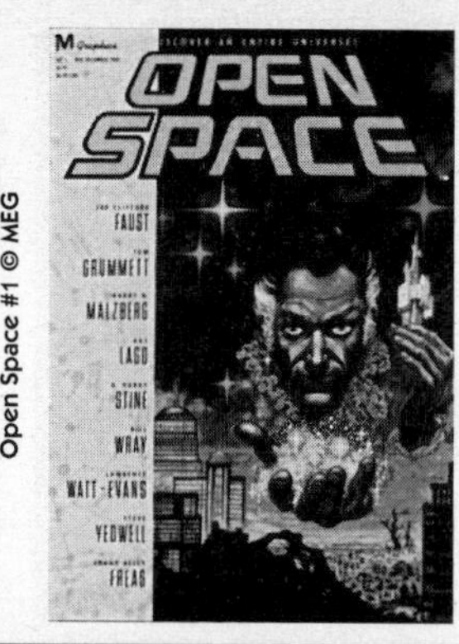

Open Space #1 © MEG

GD25 FN65 NM94

OKAY COMICS
July, 1940
United Features Syndicate

1-Captain & the Kids & Hawkshaw the Detective reprints 33.00 100.00 230.00

OK COMICS
July, 1940 - No. 2, Oct, 1940
United Features Syndicate

1-Little Giant, Phantom Knight, Sunset Smith, & The Teller Twins begin 50.00 150.00 350.00
2 (Rare)-Origin Mister Mist 50.00 150.00 350.00

OKLAHOMA KID
June, 1957 - No. 4, 1958
Ajax/Farrell Publ.

1 7.50 22.50 45.00
2-4 4.20 12.50 25.00

OKLAHOMAN, THE (See 4-Color #820)

OLD GLORY COMICS
1944 (Giveaway)
Chesapeake & Ohio Railway

nn-Capt. Fearless reprint 4.70 14.00 28.00

OLD IRONSIDES (See 4-Color #874)

OLD YELLER (See 4-Color #869, Movie Comics, and Walt Disney Showcase #25)

OLYMPIANS, THE (Epic)(Value: cover or less)

OMAC (One Man Army; ...Corps. #4 on; also see Kamandi #59 & Warlord)
Sept-Oct, 1974 - No. 8, Nov-Dec, 1975
National Periodical Publications

1-Origin 1.10 2.70 6.50
2-8: 8-2 pg. Neal Adams ad 1.50 3.75

NOTE: ***Kirby** a-1-8p; c-1-7p. **Kubert** c-8. See Cancelled Comic Cavalcade.*

OMAC: ONE MAN ARMY CORPS
1991 - No. 4, 1991 ($3.95, B&W, mini-series, mature readers, 52 pgs.)
DC Comics

Book One - Four: John Byrne-c/a & scripts 1.60 4.00

O'MALLEY AND THE ALLEY CATS
April, 1971 - No. 9, Jan, 1974 (Disney)
Gold Key

1 2.00 6.00 14.00
2-9 1.50 3.80 9.00

OMEGA ELITE (Blackthorne)(Value: cover or less)

OMEGA MEN, THE (See Green Lantern #141)
Dec, 1982 - No. 38, May, 1986 ($1.00/$1.50; Baxter paper)
DC Comics

1 1.50
2,4,6-8,11-18,21-36,38: 2-Origin Broot. 7-Origin The Citadel. 26,27-Alan Moore scripts. 30-Intro new Primus. 31-Crisis x-over. 34,35-Teen Titans x-over 1.00
3-1st app. Lobo (5 pgs.)(6/83); Lobo-c 1.30 3.10 7.50
5,9-2nd & 3rd app. Lobo (cameo, 2 pgs. each) 1.20 3.00
10-1st full Lobo story 1.30 3.10 7.50
19-Lobo cameo 1.50
20-2nd full Lobo story 1.70 4.25
37-1st solo Lobo story (8 pg. back-up by Giffen) 1.00 2.50
Annual 1(11/84, 52 pgs.), 2(11/85) 1.50

NOTE: ***Giffen** c/a-1-6p. **Morrow** a-24r. **Nino** c/a-16, 21.*

OMEGA THE UNKNOWN
March, 1976 - No. 10, Oct, 1977
Marvel Comics Group

1-1st app. Omega 1.20 3.00
2-7,10: 2-Hulk-c/story. 3-Electro-c/story .70 1.80
8-1st app. 2nd Foolkiller (Greg Salinger), 1 panel only (cameo) 1.10 2.75
9-1st full app. 2nd Foolkiller 1.40 3.50

NOTE: ***Kane** c(p)-3, 5, 8, 9. **Mooney** a-1-3, 4p, 5, 6p, 7, 8i, 9, 10.*

OMEN
1989 - No. 3? ($2.00, B&W, adult)
Northstar Publishing

1-Tim Vigil-c/a in all 1.20 3.00 7.00
1-2nd printing .80 2.00
2,3 .90 2.25

OMNI MEN (Blackthorne)(Value: cover or less)

ONE (Pacific)(Value: cover or less)

ONE, THE (Epic)(Value: cover or less)

ONE-ARM SWORDSMAN, THE (Victory)(Value: cover or less)

ONE HUNDRED AND ONE DALMATIANS (See 4-Color #1183, Cartoon Tales, Movie Comics, and Walt Disney Showcase #9, 51)

101 DALMATIONS
1991 (Color, graphic novel, 52 pgs.)
Disney Comics

nn-($4.95, direct sale)-r/movie adaptation & more 1.00 2.00 5.00
1-($2.95, newsstand edition) 1.20 3.00

100 PAGES OF COMICS
1937 (Stiff covers; square binding)
Dell Publishing Co.

101(Found on back cover)-Alley Oop, Wash Tubbs, Capt. Easy, Og Son of Fire, Apple Mary, Tom Mix, Dan Dunn, Tailspin Tommy, Doctor Doom 129.00 385.00 900.00

100 PAGE SUPER SPECTACULAR (See DC 100 Page...)

ONE MILE UP (Eclipse)(Value: cover or less)

$1,000,000 DUCK (See Walt Disney Showcase #5)

ONE MILLION YEARS AGO (Tor #2 on)
September, 1953
St. John Publishing Co.

1-Origin & 1st app. Tor; Kubert-c/a; Kubert photo inside front cover 16.00 48.00 110.00

ONE SHOT (See 4-Color...)

1001 HOURS OF FUN (See Large Feature Comic #13)

ON STAGE (See 4-Color #1336)

ON THE AIR
1947 (Giveaway) (paper cover)
NBC Network Comic

nn-(Rare) 20.00 60.00 140.00

ON THE DOUBLE (See 4-Color #1232)

ON THE LINKS
December, 1926 (48 pgs.) (9x10")
Associated Feature Service

nn-Daily strip-r 13.00 40.00 90.00

ON THE ROAD WITH ANDRAE CROUCH (Spire Christian)(Value: cover or less)

ON THE SPOT (Pretty Boy Floyd...)
Fall, 1948
Fawcett Publications

nn-Pretty Boy Floyd photo on-c; bondage-c 22.00 65.00 150.00

ONYX OVERLORD
Oct, 1992 - No. 4, Jan, 1993 ($2.75, mini-series)
Epic Comics (Marvel)

1-4: Moebius scripts 1.10 2.75

The Original Ghost Rider Rides Again! #1 © MEG

Our Army At War #97 © DC

Our Army At War #101 © DC

	GD25	FN65	NM94

OPEN SPACE (Marvel)(Value: cover or less)

OPERATION BIKINI (See Movie Classics)

OPERATION BUCHAREST (See The Crusaders)

OPERATION CROSSBOW (See Movie Classics)

OPERATION PERIL
Oct-Nov, 1950 - No. 16, Apr-May, 1953 (#1-5: 52 pgs.)
American Comics Group (Michel Publ.)

	GD25	FN65	NM94
1-Time Travelers, Danny Danger (by Leonard Starr) & Typhoon Tyler (by Ogden Whitney) begin	25.00	75.00	175.00
2	14.00	43.00	100.00
3-5: 3-Horror story. 5-Sci/fi-c/story	13.00	40.00	90.00
6-12-Last Time Travelers. 6,8,9-Sci/fi-c	11.00	32.00	75.00
13-16: All war format	5.35	16.00	32.00

NOTE: ***Starr** a-2, 5. **Whitney** a-1, 2, 5-10, 12; c-1, 3, 5, 8, 9.*

ORAL ROBERTS' TRUE STORIES (Junior Partners #120 on)
1956 (no month) - No. 119, 7/59 (15¢)(No #102: 25¢)
TelePix Publ. (Oral Roberts' Evangelistic Assoc./Healing Waters)

	GD25	FN65	NM94
V1#1(1956)-(Not code approved)- "The Miracle Touch"	16.00	48.00	110.00
102-(Only issue approved by code, 10/56)	10.00	30.00	65.00
103-119: 115-(114 on inside)	6.70	20.00	40.00

NOTE: *Also see Happiness & Healing For You.*

ORANGE BIRD, THE
No date (1980) (36 pgs.; in color; slick cover)
Walt Disney Educational Media Co.

	GD25	FN65	NM94
nn-Included with educational kit on foods			1.00
...in Nutrition Adventures nn (1980)			.60
...and the Nutrition Know-How Revue nn (1983)			.60

ORBIT (Eclipse)(Value: cover or less)

ORIENTAL HEROES (Jademan)(Value: cover or less)

ORIGINAL ASTRO BOY, THE (Now)(Value: cover or less)(Also see Astro Boy)

ORIGINAL BLACK CAT, THE (Recollections)(Value: cover or less)

ORIGINAL DICK TRACY, THE (Gladstone)(Value: cover or less)

ORIGINAL E-MAN AND MICHAEL MAUSER, THE (First)(Value: cover or less)

ORIGINAL GHOST RIDER, THE
July, 1992 - No. 20, Feb, 1994 ($1.75)
Marvel Comics

	GD25	FN65	NM94
1-20: 1-7-r/Marvel Spotlight #5-11 by Ploog w/new-c. 3-New Phantom Rider (former Night Rider) back-ups begin by Ayers. 4-Quesada-c(p). 8-Ploog-c. 8,9-r/Ghost Rider #1,2. 10-r/Marvel Spotlight #12. 11-18,20-r/Ghost Rider #3-12. 19-r/Marvel Two-in-One #8		.70	1.75

ORIGINAL GHOST RIDER RIDES AGAIN, THE
July, 1991 - No. 7, Jan, 1992, ($1.50, mini-series, 52 pgs.)
Marvel Comics

	GD25	FN65	NM94
1-Reprints Ghost Rider #68(origin),69 w/covers			1.50
2-7: Reprints G.R. #70-81 w/covers			1.50

ORIGINAL NEXUS GRAPHIC NOVEL (See First Comics Graphic Novel #19)

ORIGINAL SHIELD, THE
April, 1984 - No. 4, Oct, 1984
Archie Enterprises, Inc.

	GD25	FN65	NM94
1-4: 1,2-Origin Shield; Ayers p-1-4, Nebres c-1,2			1.00

ORIGINAL SWAMP THING SAGA, THE (See DC Special Series #2, 14, 17, 20)

ORIGIN OF THE DEFIANT UNIVERSE, THE
Feb, 1994 ($1.50, color, 20 pgs.)
Defiant Comics

	GD25	FN65	NM94
1-Weiss-c			1.50

OSCAR COMICS (Formerly Funny Tunes; Awful...#11 & 12)
(Also see Cindy Comics)
No. 24, Spring, 1947 - No. 10, Apr, 1949; No. 13, Oct, 1949
Marvel Comics

	GD25	FN65	NM94
24(#1, Spring, 1947)	10.00	30.00	65.00
25(#2, Sum, 1947)-Wolverton-a plus Kurtzman's "Hey Look"	11.50	34.00	80.00
26(#3)-Same as regular #3 except #26 was printed over in black ink with #3 appearing on-c below the over print	7.50	22.50	45.00
3-9,13: 8-Margie app.	7.50	22.50	45.00
10-Kurtzman's "Hey Look"	9.15	27.50	55.00

OSWALD THE RABBIT (Also see New Fun Comics #1)
No. 21, 1943 - No. 1268, 12-2/61-62 (Walter Lantz)
Dell Publishing Co.

	GD25	FN65	NM94
4-Color 21(1943)	50.00	150.00	350.00
4-Color 39(1943)	35.00	105.00	245.00
4-Color 67(1944)	17.00	52.00	120.00
4-Color 102(1946)-Kelly-a, 1 pg.	15.00	45.00	105.00
4-Color 143,183	9.15	27.50	55.00
4-Color 225,273	5.85	17.50	35.00
4-Color 315,388	4.00	11.00	22.00
4-Color 458,507,549,593	3.60	9.00	18.00
4-Color 623,697,792,894,979,1268	2.80	7.00	14.00

OSWALD THE RABBIT (See The Funnies, March of Comics #7, 38, 53, 67, 81, 95, 111, 126, 141, 156, 171, 186, New Funnies & Super Book #8, 20)

OUR ARMY AT WAR (Becomes Sgt. Rock #302 on; also see Army At War)
Aug, 1952 - No. 301, Feb, 1977
National Periodical Publications

	GD25	FN65	NM94
1	114.00	343.00	800.00
2	57.00	171.00	400.00
3,4: 4-Krigstein-a	43.00	130.00	300.00
5-7	32.00	96.00	225.00
8-11,14-Krigstein-a	32.00	96.00	225.00
12,15-20	24.00	73.00	170.00
13-Krigstein-c/a; flag-c	27.00	81.00	190.00
21-31: Last precode (2/55)	17.00	52.00	120.00
32-40	15.00	45.00	105.00
41-60	12.00	36.00	85.00
61-70	11.00	32.00	75.00
71-80	10.00	30.00	65.00
81-1st Sgt. Rock app. (4/59) by Andru & Esposito in Easy Co. story	123.00	368.00	1225.00
82-Sgt. Rock cameo in Easy Co. story (6 panels)	38.00	113.00	300.00
83-1st Kubert Sgt. Rock (6/59)	50.00	150.00	500.00
84,86-90	17.00	51.00	135.00
85-Origin & 1st app. Ice Cream Soldier	19.00	56.00	150.00
91-All Sgt. Rock issue	39.00	117.00	350.00
92-100: 95-1st app. Bulldozer; 1st app. Zack	9.00	28.00	85.00
101-120: 101-1st app. Buster. 111-1st app. Wee Willie & Sunny. 113-1st app. Wildman & Jackie Johnson. 115-Rock revealed as orphan; 1st x-over Mlle Marie. 118-Sunny dies	6.00	17.00	45.00
121-127,129-150: 126-1st app. Canary. 139-1st app. Little Sure Shot. 140-All Sgt. Rock issue	3.00	9.00	25.00
128-Training & origin Sgt. Rock	16.00	47.00	125.00
151-Intro. Enemy Ace by Kubert (2/65)	19.00	56.00	150.00
152,154,156,157,159-163,165-170: 157-2 pg. pin-up. 162,163-Viking Prince x-over in Sgt. Rock	3.00	8.00	22.00
153-2nd app. Enemy Ace (4/65)	8.00	24.00	65.00
155-3rd app. Enemy Ace (6/65)(see Showcase)	4.00	11.00	28.00
158-Origin & 1st app. Iron Major(9/65), formerly Iron Captain	3.00	9.00	25.00
164-Giant G-19	4.00	13.00	35.00
171-176,178-181	1.90	5.60	13.00
177-(80 pg. Giant G-32)	3.60	11.00	25.00
182,183,186-Neal Adams-a. 186-Origin retold	2.10	6.00	15.00

184,185,187-189,191-199: 184-Wee Willie dies. 189-Intro. The Teen-age

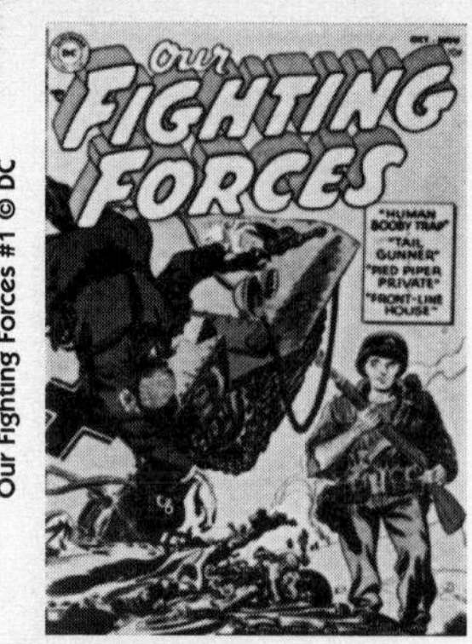

Our Fighting Forces #1 © DC

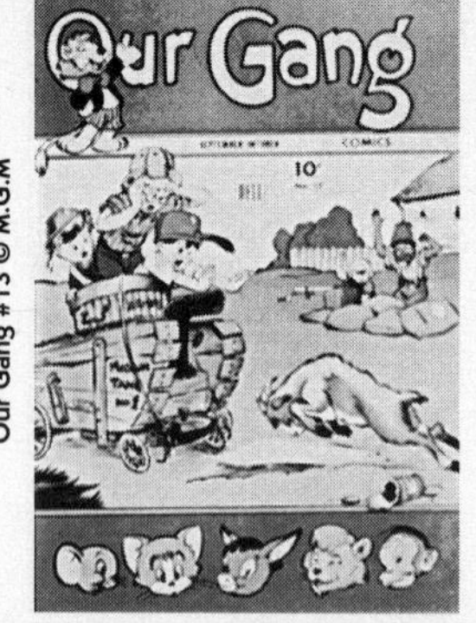

Our Gang #13 © M.G.M

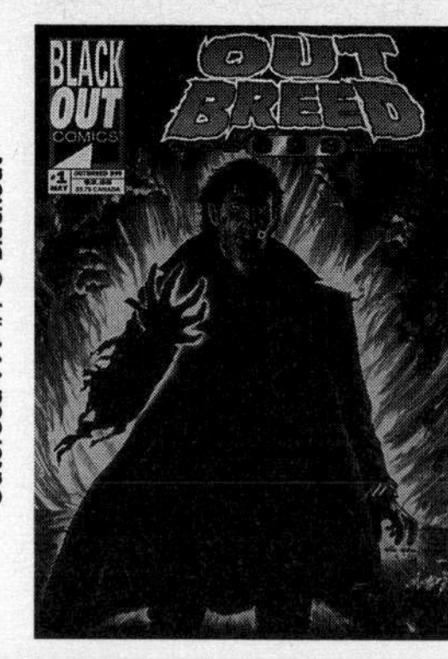

Outbreed 999 #1 © Blackout

	GD25	FN65	NM94
Underground Fighters of Unit 3	1.70	4.20	10.00
190-(80 pg. Giant G-44)	2.30	7.00	16.00
200-12 pg. Rock story told in verse; Evans-a	1.70	5.00	12.00
201-Krigstein-r/#14	1.30	3.00	8.00
202,204-215: 204,205-All reprints; no Sgt. Rock	1.00	3.00	6.00
203-(80 pg. Giant G-56)-All-r, Sgt. Rock story	1.60	4.00	9.50
216,229-(80 pg. Giants G-68, G-80): 216-Has G-58 on-c by mistake	1.40	3.50	8.50
217-228,230-239,241	1.00	2.00	5.00
240-Neal Adams-a	1.10	2.70	6.50
242-(50¢ issue DC-9)-Kubert-c	1.10	2.70	6.50
243-301: 244-N. Adams-a? 270,275-(100 pgs.). 280-(68 pgs.)-200th app. Sgt. Rock; reprints Our Army at War #81,83	1.00	2.00	5.00

NOTE ***Alcala** a-251. **Drucker** a-27, 67, 68, 79, 82, 83, 96, 164, 177, 203, 212, 243r, 244, 269r, 275r, 280r. **Evans** a-165-175, 200, 266, 269, 270, 274, 276, 278, 280. **Glanzman** a-218, 220, 222, 223, 225, 227, 230-232, 238, 240, 241, 244, 247, 248, 256-259, 261, 265-267, 271, 282, 283, 298. **Grandenetti** c-91. **Grell** a-287. **Heath** a-50, 164, & most 176-281. **Kubert** a-38, 59, 67, 68 & most issues from 83-165, 233, 267, 275, 300; c-84, 280. **Maurer** a-233, 237, 239, 240, 45, 280, 284, 288, 290, 291, 295. **Severin** a-236, 252, 265, 267, 269r, 272. **Toth** a-235, 241, 254. **Wildey** a-283-285, 287p. **Wood** a-249.*

OUR FIGHTING FORCES
Oct-Nov, 1954 - No. 181, Sept-Oct, 1978
National Periodical Publications/DC Comics

	GD25	FN65	NM94
1-Grandenetti-c/a	48.00	143.00	475.00
2	27.00	80.00	240.00
3-Kubert-c; last precode issue (3/55)	24.00	73.00	220.00
4,5	17.00	52.00	155.00
6-9	14.00	43.00	130.00
10-Wood-a	16.00	47.00	140.00
11-20: 20-Grey tone-c (4/57)	11.00	33.00	100.00
21-30	8.00	24.00	65.00
31-40	9.00	26.00	60.00
41-Unknown Soldier tryout	10.00	30.00	70.00
42-44	7.00	21.00	50.00
45-Gunner & Sarge begin, end #94	24.00	71.00	165.00
46	11.00	32.00	75.00
47	7.00	22.00	52.00
48,50	5.00	15.00	36.00
49-1st Pooch	9.00	26.00	60.00
51-64: 51-Grey tone-c. 64-Last 10¢ issue	4.30	12.90	30.00
65-70	3.00	9.00	21.00
71-80: 71-Grey tone-c	1.90	5.60	13.00
81-90	1.70	5.00	12.00
91-100: 95-Devil-Dog begins, ends 98. 99-Capt. Hunter begins, ends #106	1.30	3.30	8.00
101-181: 106-Hunters Hellcats begin. 116-Mlle. Marie app. 121-Intro. Heller. 123-Losers (Capt. Storm, Gunner & Sarge, Johnny Cloud) begin by Kirby. 134,146-Toth-a	1.00	2.50	6.00

NOTE: ***N. Adams** c-147. **Drucker** a-28, 37, 39, 42-44, 49, 53, 133r. **Evans** a-149, 164-174, 177-181. **Glanzman** a-125-128, 132, 134, 138-141, 143, 144. **Heath** a-2, 16, 18, 28, 41, 44, 49, 114, 135-138r; c-51. **Kirby** a-151-162p; c-152-159. **Kubert** c/a in many issues. **Maurer** a-135. **Redondo** a-166. **Severin** a-123-130, 131i, 132-150.*

OUR FIGHTING MEN IN ACTION (See Men In Action)

OUR FLAG COMICS
Aug, 1941 - No. 5, April, 1942
Ace Magazines

	GD25	FN65	NM94
1-Captain Victory, The Unknown Soldier (intro.) & The Three Cheers begin	157.00	471.00	1100.00
2-Origin The Flag (patriotic hero); 1st app?	86.00	257.00	600.00
3-5: 5-Intro & 1st app. Mr. Risk	71.00	215.00	500.00

NOTE: ***Anderson** a-1, 4. **Mooney** a-1, 2; c-2.*

OUR GANG COMICS (With Tom & Jerry #39-59; becomes Tom & Jerry #60 on; based on film characters)
Sept-Oct, 1942 - No. 59, June, 1949
Dell Publishing Co.

	GD25	FN65	NM94
1-Our Gang & Barney Bear by Kelly, Tom & Jerry, Pete Smith, Flip & Dip, The Milky Way begin (all 1st app.)	86.00	257.00	600.00
2-Benny Burro begins (#2 by Kelly)	43.00	130.00	300.00
3-5	29.00	86.00	200.00
6-Bumbazine & Albert only app. by Kelly	43.00	130.00	300.00
7-No Kelly story	22.00	65.00	150.00
8-Benny Burro begins by Barks	57.00	171.00	400.00
9-Barks-a(2): Benny Burro & Happy Hound; no Kelly story	50.00	150.00	350.00
10-Benny Burro by Barks	36.00	107.00	250.00
11-1st Barney Bear & Benny Burro by Barks (5-6/44); Happy Hound by Barks	50.00	150.00	350.00
12-20	22.00	65.00	150.00
21-30: 30-X-Mas-c	14.00	43.00	100.00
31-36-Last Barks issue	11.00	32.00	75.00
37-40	5.85	17.50	35.00
41-50	4.00	11.00	22.00
51-57	3.60	9.00	18.00
58,59-No Kelly art or Our Gang stories	3.00	7.50	15.00

NOTE: ***Barks** art in part only. **Barks** did not write Barney Bear stories #30-34. (See March of Comics #3, 26). Early issues have photo back-c.*

OUR LADY OF FATIMA
3/11/55 (15¢) (36 pgs.)
Catechetical Guild Educational Society

	GD25	FN65	NM94
395	3.00	7.50	15.00

OUR LOVE (True Secrets #3 on? or Romantic Affairs #3 on?)
Sept, 1949 - No. 2, Jan, 1950
Marvel Comics (SPC)

	GD25	FN65	NM94
1-Photo-c	9.15	27.50	55.00
2-Photo-c	5.35	16.00	32.00

OUR LOVE STORY
Oct, 1969 - No. 38, Feb, 1976
Marvel Comics Group

	GD25	FN65	NM94
1	1.60	4.00	8.00
2-4,6-13	.80	2.00	4.00
5-Steranko-a	2.40	6.00	12.00
14-New story by Gary Fredrich & Tarpe' Mills	1.00	2.50	5.00
15-38: 27-Colan/Everett-a(r?); Kirby/Colletta-r	.40	1.00	2.00

NOTE: ***J. Buscema** a-1-3, 5-7, 9, 13r, 16r, 19r(2), 21r, 22r(2), 23r, 34r, 35r; c-11, 13, 16, 22, 23, 24, 27, 35. **Colan** a-3-6, 21r(#6), 22r, 23r(#3), 24r(#4), 27; c-19. **Katz** a-17. **Weiss** a-16, 17, 29r(#17).*

OUR MISS BROOKS (See 4-Color #751)

OUR SECRET (Exciting Love Stories)(Formerly My Secret)
No. 4, Nov, 1949 - No. 8, Jun, 1950
Superior Comics Ltd.

	GD25	FN65	NM94
4-Kamen-a; spanking scene	10.00	30.00	60.00
5,6,8	6.70	20.00	40.00
7-Contains 9 pg. story intended for unpublished Ellery Queen #5; lingerie panels	7.50	22.50	45.00

OUTBREED 999
May, 1994 ($2.95, color)
Blackout Comics

	GD25	FN65	NM94
1		1.20	3.00

OUTBURSTS OF EVERETT TRUE
1921 (32 pgs.) (B&W)
Saalfield Publ. Co.

	GD25	FN65	NM94
1907 (2-panel strips reprint)	14.00	43.00	100.00

OUTCASTS (DC)(Value: cover or less)

OUTER LIMITS, THE (TV)
Jan-Mar, 1964 - No. 18, Oct, 1969 (All painted-c)
Dell Publishing Co.

	GD25	FN65	NM94
1	6.60	20.00	46.00
2	3.60	10.70	25.00

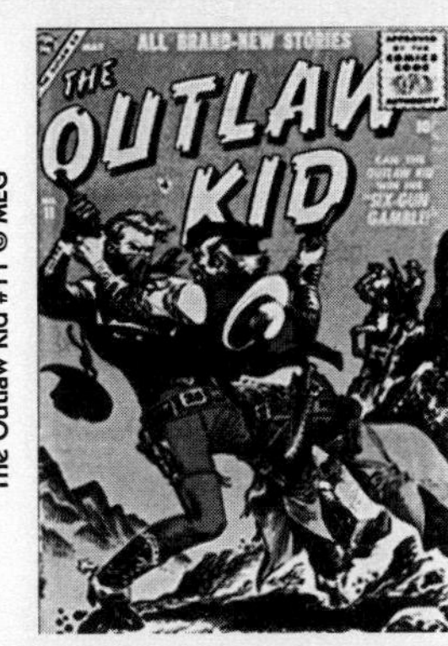

The Outlaw Kid #11 © MEG

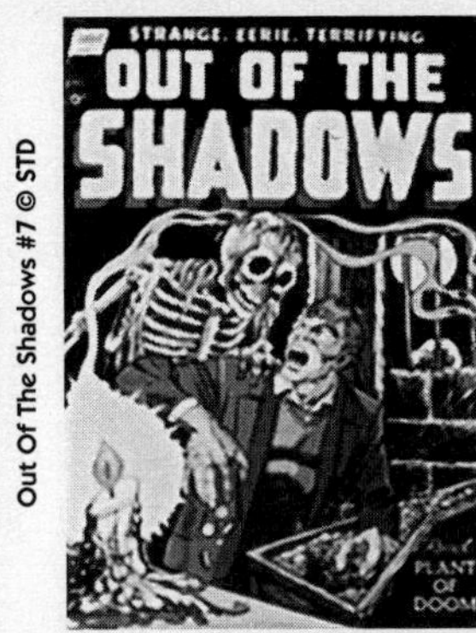

Out Of The Shadows #7 © STD

Out Of The Vortex #11 © DH

GD25 FN65 NM94

3-10 2.40 7.30 17.00
11-18: 17-Reprints #1. 18-r/#2 2.00 6.00 14.00

OUTER SPACE (Formerly This Magazine Is Haunted, 2nd Series)
No. 17, May, 1958 - No. 25, Dec, 1959; Nov, 1968
Charlton Comics

17-Williamson/Wood style art; not by them (Sid Check?) 10.00 30.00 60.00
18-20-Ditko-a 12.00 36.00 85.00
21-25: 21-Ditko-c 8.35 25.00 50.00
V2#1(11/68)-Ditko-a, Boyette-c 4.20 12.50 25.00

OUTER SPACE BABES, THE
Feb, 1994 ($2.95, color)
Silhouette Studios

V3#1 1.20 3.00

OUTLANDERS (Dark Horse)(Value: cover or less)

OUTLAW (See Return of the...)

OUTLAW FIGHTERS
Aug, 1954 - No. 5, April, 1955
Atlas Comics (IPC)

1-Tuska-a 9.15 27.50 55.00
2-5: 5-Heath-c/a, 7 pgs. 5.85 17.50 35.00
NOTE: **Heath** c/a-5. **Maneely** c-2. **Pakula** a-2. **Reinman** a-2. **Tuska** a-1, 2.

OUTLAW KID, THE (1st Series; see Wild Western)
Sept, 1954 - No. 19, Sept, 1957
Atlas Comics (CCC No. 1-11/EPI No. 12-29)

1-Origin; The Outlaw Kid & his horse Thunder begin; Black Rider app. 16.00 48.00 110.00
2-Black Rider app. 9.15 27.50 55.00
3-7,9: 3-Wildey-a(3) 8.35 25.00 50.00
8-Williamson/Woodbridge-a, 4 pgs. 6.70 20.00 40.00
10-Williamson-a 7.00 21.00 42.00
11-17,19: 13-Baker text illo. 15-Williamson text illo (unsigned) 4.70 14.00 28.00
18-Williamson/Mayo-a 5.85 17.50 35.00
NOTE: **Berg** a-4, 7, 13. **Maneely** c-1-3, 5-8, 11-13, 15, 16, 18. **Pakula** a-3. **Severin** c-10, 17, 19. **Shores** a-1. **Wildey** a-1(3), 2-8, 10, 11, 12(4), 13(4), 15-19(4 each); c-4.

OUTLAW KID, THE (2nd Series)
Aug, 1970 - No. 30, Oct, 1975
Marvel Comics Group

1,2-Reprints; 1-Orlando-r, Wildey-r(3) 1.00 2.00 5.00
3,9-Williamson-a(r) 1.10 2.75
4-8: 8-Double size; Crandall-r .80 2.00
10-30: 10-Origin; new-a in #10-16. 27-Origin-r/#10 .70 1.80
NOTE: **Ayers** a-10, 27r. **Berg** a-7, 25r. **Everett** a-2(2 pgs.). **Gil Kane** c-10, 11, 15, 27r, 28. **Roussos** a-10i, 27i(r). **Severin** c-1, 9, 20, 25. **Wildey** r-1-4, 6-9, 19-22, 25, 26. **Williamson** a-28r. **Woodbridge/Williamson** a-9r.

OUTLAWS
Feb-Mar, 1948 - No. 9, June-July, 1949
D. S. Publishing Co.

1-Violent & suggestive stories 17.00 52.00 120.00
2-Ingels-a 17.00 52.00 120.00
3,5,6: 3-Not Frazetta. 5-Sky Sheriff by Good app. 6-McWilliams-a 8.35 25.00 50.00
4-Orlando-a 10.00 30.00 60.00
7,8-Ingels-a in each 13.00 40.00 90.00
9-(Scarce)-Frazetta-a (7 pgs.) 32.00 96.00 225.00
NOTE: *Another #3 was printed in Canada with* **Frazetta** *art "Prairie Jinx," 7 pgs.*

OUTLAWS, THE (Formerly Western Crime Cases)
No. 10, May, 1952 - No. 13, Sept, 1953; No. 14, April, 1954
Star Publishing Co.

10-L. B. Cole-c 7.50 22.50 45.00
11-14-L. B. Cole-c. 14-Reprints Western Thrillers #4 (Fox) w/new L.B. Cole-c; Kamen, Feldstein-r 5.85 17.50 35.00

OUTLAWS, THE (DC)(Value: cover or less)

OUTLAWS OF THE WEST (Formerly Cody of the Pony Express #10)
No. 11, 7/57 - No. 81, 5/70; No. 82, 7/79 - No. 88, 4/80
Charlton Comics

11 6.70 20.00 40.00
12,13,15-17,19,20 4.00 10.00 20.00
14-(68 pgs., 2/58) 4.00 12.00 24.00
18-Ditko-a 8.00 24.00 48.00
21-30 2.80 7.00 14.00
31-50 1.60 4.00 8.00
51-70: 54-Kid Montana app. 64-Captain Doom begins (1st app.) 1.00 2.00 5.00
71-81: 73-Origin & 1st app. The Sharp Shooter, last app. #74. 75-Last Capt. Doom. 80,81-Ditko-a 1.20 3.00
82-88 1.50
64,79(Modern Comics-r, 1977, '78) 1.00

OUTLAWS OF THE WILD WEST
1952 (25¢, 132 pgs.) (4 rebound comics)
Avon Periodicals

1-Wood back-c; Kubert-a (3 Jesse James-r) 22.00 65.00 150.00

OUT OF SANTA'S BAG (See March of Comics #10)

OUT OF THE NIGHT (The Hooded Horseman #18 on)
Feb-Mar, 1952 - No. 17, Oct-Nov, 1954
American Comics Group (Creston/Scope)

1-Williamson/LeDoux-a (9 pgs.) 39.00 118.00 275.00
2-Williamson-a (5 pgs.) 33.00 100.00 230.00
3,5-10: 9-Sci/Fic story 13.50 41.00 95.00
4-Williamson-a (7 pgs.) 29.00 86.00 200.00
11-17: 13-Nostrand-a? 17-E.C. Wood swipe 11.00 32.00 75.00
NOTE: **Landau** a-14, 16, 17. **Shelly** a-12.

OUT OF THE PAST A CLUE TO THE FUTURE
1946? (16 pgs.) (paper cover)
E. C. Comics (Public Affairs Comm.)

nn-Based on public affairs pamphlet "What Foreign Trade Means to You" 19.00 57.00 130.00

OUT OF THE SHADOWS
No. 5, July, 1952 - No. 14, Aug, 1954
Standard Comics/Visual Editions

5-Toth-p; Moreira, Tuska-a; Roussos-c 24.00 72.00 165.00
6-Toth/Celardo-a; Katz-a(2) 17.00 52.00 120.00
7-Jack Katz-c/a(2) 12.00 36.00 85.00
8,10: 8-Katz shrunken head-c. 10-Sekowsky-a 10.00 30.00 60.00
9-Crandall-a(2) 12.00 36.00 85.00
11-Toth-a, 2 pgs.; Katz-a; Andru-c 12.00 36.00 85.00
12-Toth/Peppe-a(2); Katz-a 17.00 52.00 120.00
13-Cannabalism story; Sekowsky-a; Roussos-c 13.50 41.00 95.00
14-Toth-a 13.50 41.00 95.00

OUT OF THE VORTEX (Comics' Greatest World:... #1-4)
Oct., 1993 - Present ($2.00)
Dark Horse Comics

1-17: 1-Foil logo. 4-Dorman-c(p). 6-Hero Zero x-over .80 2.00

OUT OF THIS WORLD
June, 1950 (One Shot)
Avon Periodicals

1-Kubert-a(2) (one reprinted/Eerie #1, 1947) plus Crom the Barbarian by Giunta (origin); Fawcette-c 48.00 145.00 335.00

OUT OF THIS WORLD
Aug, 1956 - No. 16, Dec, 1959
Charlton Comics

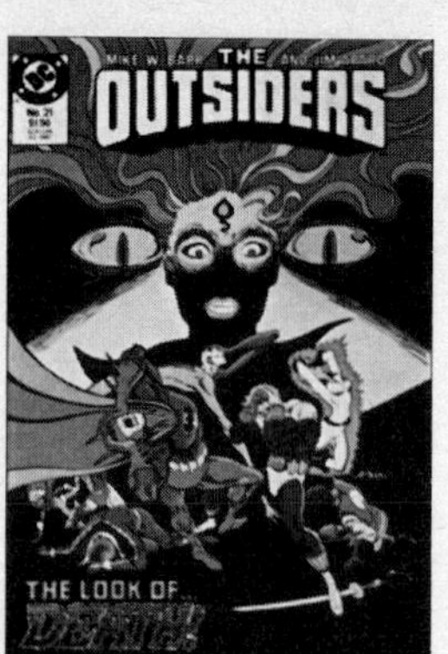

The Outsiders #21 © DC

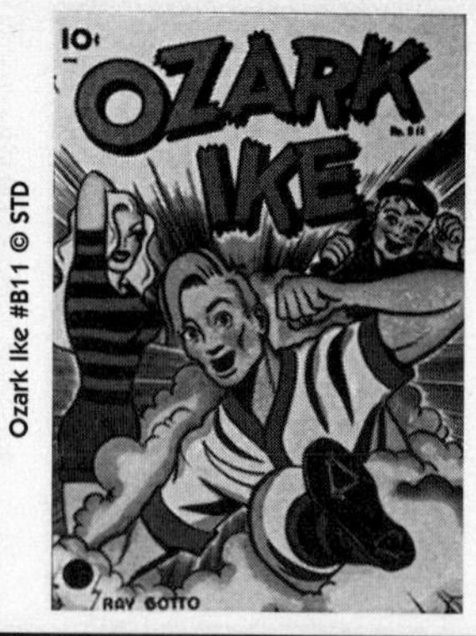

Ozark Ike #B11 © STD

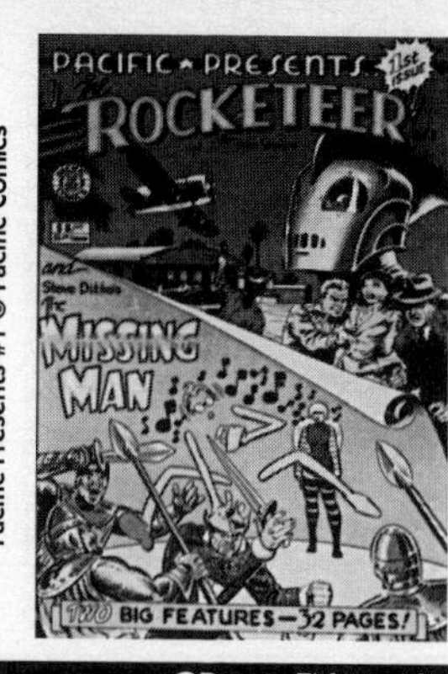

Pacific Presents #1 © Pacific Comics

	GD25	FN65	NM94
1	14.00	43.00	100.00
2	9.15	27.50	55.00
3-6-Ditko-a(4) each	18.00	54.00	125.00
7-(2/58, 15¢, 68 pgs.)-Ditko-c/a(4)	18.00	54.00	125.00
8-(5/58, 15¢, 68 pgs.)-Ditko-a(2)	14.00	43.00	100.00
9-12,16-Ditko-a	13.00	40.00	90.00
13-15	5.85	17.50	35.00

NOTE: ***Ditko** c-3-7, 11, 12, 16. **Reinman** a-10.*

OUT OUR WAY WITH WORRY WART (See 4-Color No. 680)

OUTPOSTS (Blackthorne)(Value: cover or less)

OUTSIDERS, THE (DC)(Value: cover or less)

OUTSIDERS
Nov, 1993 - Present ($1.75)
DC Comics

	GD25	FN65	NM94
1-Alpha; Travis Charest-c		.70	1.75
1-Omega; Travis Charest-c		.70	1.75
2-9: 5-Atomic Knight app. 8-New Batman-c/story		.70	1.75
10,11: 10-Begin $1.95-c. 11-(9/94)-Zero Hour		.80	2.00
0,12-16: 0-(10/94)		.80	2.00

OUTSTANDING AMERICAN WAR HEROES
1944 (16 pgs.) (paper cover)
The Parents' Institute

	GD25	FN65	NM94
nn-Reprints from True Comics	4.00	10.00	20.00

OVERSEAS COMICS (Also see G.I. Comics & Jeep Comics)
1944 - No. 105?, 1946 (7-1/4x10-1/4"; 16 pgs. in color)
Giveaway (Distributed to U.S. armed forces)

	GD25	FN65	NM94
23-105-Bringing Up Father (by McManus), Popeye, Joe Palooka, Dick Tracy, Superman, Gasoline Alley, Buz Sawyer, Li'l Abner, Blondie, Terry & the Pirates, Out Our Way	4.00	10.50	21.00

OWL, THE (See Crackajack Funnies #25 & Popular Comics #72)
April, 1967; No. 2, April, 1968
Gold Key

	GD25	FN65	NM94
1,2-Written by Jerry Siegel; '40s super hero	3.00	9.00	21.00

OXYDOL-DREFT
1950 (Set of 6 pocket-size giveaways; distributed through the mail as a set)
Oxydol-Dreft (Scarce)

	GD25	FN65	NM94
1-3: 1-Li'l Abner. 2-Daisy Mae. 3-Shmoo	10.00	30.00	60.00
4-John Wayne; Williamson/Frazetta-c from John Wayne #3	13.00	40.00	90.00
5-Archie	10.00	30.00	60.00
6-Terrytoons Mighty Mouse	10.00	30.00	60.00

NOTE: *Set is worth more with original envelope.*

OZ (See First Comics Graphic Novel, Marvel Treaury Of Oz & MGM's Marvelous...)

OZARK IKE
Feb, 1948; Nov, 1948 - No. 24, Dec, 1951; No. 25, Sept, 1952
Dell Publishing Co./Standard Comics B11 on

	GD25	FN65	NM94
4-Color 180(1948-Dell)	10.00	30.00	60.00
B11, B12, 13-15	7.50	22.50	45.00
16-25	5.35	16.00	32.00

OZ SQUAD
1992 - No. 3, 1992 ($2.50, B&W); No. 4, 1994 ($2.75, B&W)
Brave New Worlds/Patchwork Press (No. 4)

	GD25	FN65	NM94
1-3		1.00	2.50
4		1.10	2.75

OZ-WONDERLAND WARS, THE
Jan, 1986 - No. 3, March, 1986 (Mini-series)
DC Comics

	GD25	FN65	NM94
1-3	.40	1.00	2.00

OZZIE & BABS (TV Teens #14 on)
Dec, 1947 - No. 13, Fall, 1949
Fawcett Publications

	GD25	FN65	NM94
1-Teen-age	7.50	22.50	45.00
2	4.00	11.00	22.00
3-13	3.60	9.00	18.00

OZZIE & HARRIET (See The Adventures of...)

PACIFIC COMICS GRAPHIC NOVEL (See Image Graphic Novel)

PACIFIC PRESENTS (Also see Starslayer #2, 3)
Oct, 1982 - No. 2, Apr, 1983; No. 3, Mar, 1984 - No. 4, June, 1984
Pacific Comics

	GD25	FN65	NM94
1-Chapter 3 of The Rocketeer; Stevens-c/a	1.00	2.50	6.00
2-Chapter 4 of The Rocketeer (4th app.); nudity; Stevens-c/a		1.60	4.00
3,4: 3-1st app. Vanity		.80	2.00

NOTE: ***Conrad** a-3, 4; c-3. **Ditko** a-1-3; c-1(1/2). **Dave Stevens** a-1, 2; c-1(1/2), 2.*

PACT, THE
Feb, 1994 - No. 3, June, 1994 ($1.95, color, limited series)
Image Comics

	GD25	FN65	NM94
1-3-Valentino co-scripts & layouts		.80	2.00

PADRE OF THE POOR
nd (Giveaway) (16 pgs.; paper cover)
Catechetical Guild

	GD25	FN65	NM94
nn	2.00	5.00	10.00

PAGEANT OF COMICS (See Jane Arden & Mopsy)
Sept, 1947 - No. 2, Oct, 1947
Archer St. John

	GD25	FN65	NM94
1-Mopsy strip-r	6.70	20.00	40.00
2-Jane Arden strip-r	6.70	20.00	40.00

PANCHO VILLA
1950
Avon Periodicals

	GD25	FN65	NM94
nn-Kinstler-c	16.00	48.00	110.00

PANHANDLE PETE AND JENNIFER (TV) (See Gene Autry #20)
July, 1951 - No. 3, Nov, 1951
J. Charles Laue Publishing Co.

	GD25	FN65	NM94
1	7.50	22.50	45.00
2,3	5.00	15.00	30.00

PANIC (Companion to Mad)
Feb-Mar, 1954 - No. 12, Dec-Jan, 1955-56
E. C. Comics (Tiny Tot Comics)

	GD25	FN65	NM94
1-Used in Senate Investigation hearings; Elder draws entire E. C. staff; Santa Claus & Mickey Spillane parody	19.00	58.00	135.00
2	10.00	30.00	65.00
3,4: 3-Senate Subcommittee parody; Davis draws Gaines, Feldstein & Kelly, 1 pg.; Old King Cole smokes marijuana. 4-Infinity-c; John Wayne parody	9.15	27.50	55.00
5-11: 8-Last pre-code issue (5/55). 9-Superman, Smilin' Jack & Dick Tracy app. on-c; has photo of Walter Winchell on-c	7.50	22.50	45.00
12 (Low distribution; thousands were destroyed)	10.00	30.00	65.00

NOTE: ***Davis** a-1-12; c-12. **Elder** a-1-12. **Feldstein** c-1-3, 5. **Kamen** a-1. **Orlando** a-1-9. **Wolverton** c-4, panel-3. **Wood** a-2-9, 11, 12.*

PANIC (Magazine) (Satire)
July, 1958 - No. 6, July, 1959; V2#10, Dec, 1965 - V2#12, 1966
Panic Publications

	GD25	FN65	NM94
1	8.35	25.00	50.00
2-6	4.20	12.50	25.00
V2#10-12: Reprints earlier issues	3.60	9.00	18.00

NOTE: ***Davis** a-3(2 pgs.), 4, 5, 10; c-10. **Elder** a-5. **Powell** a-V2#10, 11. **Torres** a-1-5. **Tuska** a-V2#11.*

PARADAX (Eclipse & Vortex)(Value: cover or less)

PARADE (See Hanna-Barbera...)

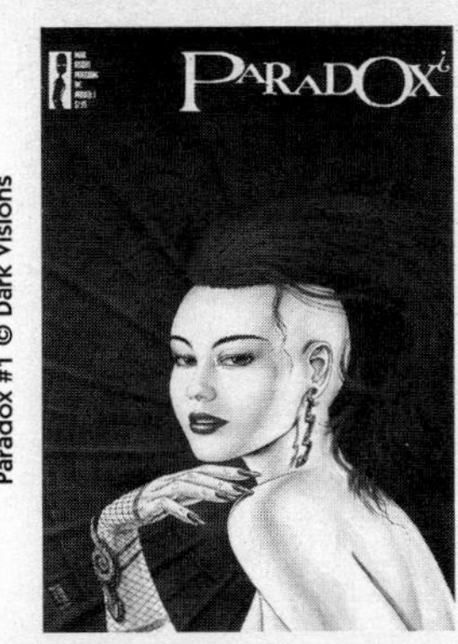

Paradox #1 © Dark Visions

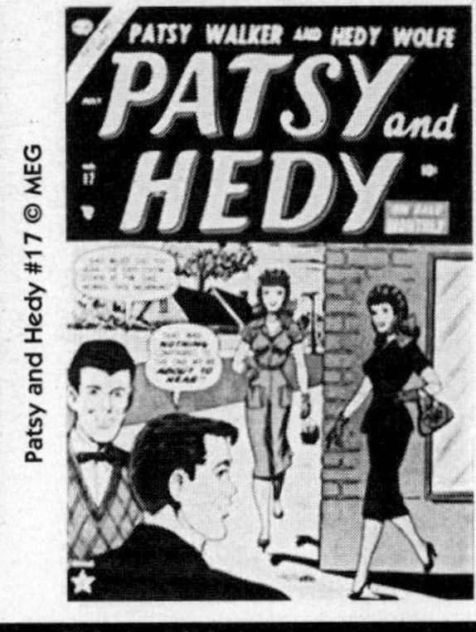

Patsy and Hedy #17 © MEG

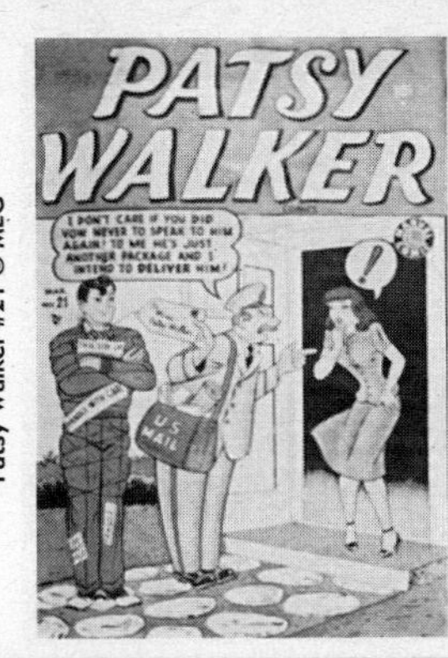

Patsy Walker #21 © MEG

GD25 FN65 NM94

PARADE COMICS (Frisky Animals on Parade #2 on)
Sept, 1957
Ajax/Farrell Publ. (World Famous Publ.)

1 4.20 12.50 25.00

NOTE: *Cover title: Frisky Animals on Parade.*

PARADE OF PLEASURE
1954 (192 pgs.) (Hardback book)
Derric Verschoyle Ltd., London, England

By Geoffrey Wagner. Contains section devoted to the censorship of American comic books with illustrations in color and black and white. (Also see **Seduction of the Innocent**). Distributed in USA by Library Publishers, N. Y. 36.00 107.00 250.00
with dust jacket.... 59.00 178.00 415.00

PARADOX
June, 1994 - Present ($2.95, B&W, mature)
Dark Visions Publishing

1,2 1.20 3.00

PARAMOUNT ANIMATED COMICS (See Harvey Comics Hits #60, 62)
Feb, 1953 - No. 22, July, 1956
Harvey Publications

1-Baby Huey, Herman & Katnip, Buzzy the Crow begin 14.00 43.00 100.00
2 9.15 27.50 55.00
3-6 7.00 21.00 42.00
7-Baby Huey becomes permanent cover feature; cover title becomes Baby Huey with #9 14.00 43.00 100.00
8-10: 9-Infinity-c 6.70 20.00 40.00
11-22 4.70 14.00 28.00

PARANOIA (Adventure)(Value: cover or less)

PARENT TRAP, THE (See 4-Color #1210)

PARODY
Mar, 1977 - No. 3, Aug, 1977 (B&W humor magazine)
Armour Publishing

1-3 .80 2.00

PAROLE BREAKERS
Dec, 1951 - No. 3, July, 1952
Avon Periodicals/Realistic #2 on

1(#2 on inside)-r-c/Avon paperback #283 (painted) 25.00 75.00 175.00
2-Kubert-a; r-c/Avon paperback #114 (photo-c) 17.00 52.00 120.00
3-Kinstler-c 16.50 50.00 115.00

PARTRIDGE FAMILY, THE (TV)(Also see David Cassidy)
March, 1971 - No. 21, Dec, 1973
Charlton Comics

1 2.00 6.00 14.00
2-4,6-21 1.20 3.00 7.00
5-Partridge Family Summer Special (52 pgs.); The Shadow, Lone Ranger, Charlie McCarthy, Flash Gordon, Hopalong Cassidy, Gene Autry & others app. 2.40 7.25 17.00

PARTS UNKNOWN
July, 1992 - No. 4, Oct, 1992 ($2.50, B&W, mini-series, mature readers)
Eclipse Comics/FX

1-4: All contain FX gaming cards 1.00 2.50

PASSION, THE
No. 394, 1955
Catechetical Guild

394 2.80 7.00 14.00

PAT BOONE (TV)(Also see Superman's Girlfriend Lois Lane #9)
Sept-Oct, 1959 - No. 5, May-Jun, 1960 (All have photo-c)
National Periodical Publications

1 36.00 107.00 250.00
2-5: 3-Fabian, Connie Francis & Paul Anka photos on-c. 4-Previews "Journey To The Center Of The Earth". 4-Johnny Mathis & Bobbie Darin photos on-c. 5-Dick Clark & Frankie Avalon photos on-c 27.00 81.00 190.00

PATCHES
Mar-Apr, 1945 - No. 11, Nov, 1947
Rural Home/Patches Publ. (Orbit)

1-L. B. Cole-c 16.00 48.00 110.00
2 9.15 27.50 55.00
3-11: 5-Danny Kaye-c/story; L.B. Cole-c. 6-Henry Aldrich story. 7-Hopalong Cassidy-c/story. 8-Smiley Burnette-c/s (6/47); pre-dates Smiley Burnette #1. 9-Mr. District Attorney story (radio). Leav/Keigstein-a (16 pgs.). 9-11-Leav-c. 10-Jack Carson (radio) c/story; Leav-c. 11-Red Skelton story 8.35 25.00 50.00

PATHWAYS TO FANTASY
July, 1984
Pacific Comics

1-Barry Smith-c/a; Jeff Jones-a (4 pgs.) 1.50

PATORUZU (See Adventures of...)

PATSY & HEDY (Teenage)(Also see Hedy Wolfe)
Feb, 1952 - No. 110, Feb, 1967
Atlas Comics/Marvel (GPI/Male)

1-Patsy Walker & Hedy Wolfe; Al Jaffee-c 13.00 40.00 90.00
2 7.50 22.50 45.00
3-10: 3,8-Al Jaffee-c 5.85 17.50 35.00
11-20 4.00 12.00 24.00
21-40 3.60 9.00 18.00
41-60 2.40 6.00 12.00
61-110: 88-Lingerie panel 1.60 4.00 8.00
Annual 1(1963)-Early Marvel annual 6.35 19.00 38.00

PATSY & HER PALS (Teenage)
May, 1953 - No. 29, Aug, 1957
Atlas Comics (PPI)

1-Patsy Walker 10.00 30.00 70.00
2 6.35 19.00 38.00
3-10 4.70 14.00 28.00
11-29: 24-Everett-c 4.00 10.00 20.00

PATSY WALKER (See All Teen, A Date With Patsy, Girls' Life, Miss America Magazine, Patsy & Hedy, Patsy & Her Pals & Teen Comics)
1945 (no month) - No. 124, Dec, 1965
Marvel/Atlas Comics (BPC)

1-Teenage 38.00 115.00 265.00
2 17.00 52.00 120.00
3-10: 5-Injury-to-eye-c; spanking panel 11.50 34.00 80.00
11,12,15,16,18 9.15 27.50 55.00
13,14,17,19-22-Kurtzman's "Hey Look" 10.00 30.00 65.00
23,24 6.70 20.00 40.00
25-Rusty by Kurtzman; painted-c 10.00 30.00 65.00
26-29,31: 26-31: 52 pgs. 5.00 15.00 30.00
30(52 pgs.)-Egghead Doodle by Kurtzman (1 pg.) 7.50 22.50 45.00
32-57: Last precode (3/55) 4.00 10.00 20.00
58-80 3.20 8.00 16.00
81-99: 92,98-Millie x-over 2.40 6.00 12.00
100 2.80 7.00 14.00
101-124 1.60 4.00 8.00
Fashion Parade 1(1966, 68 pgs.) 5.85 17.50 35.00

NOTE: *Painted c-25-28. Anti-Wertham editorial in #21. Georgie app. in #8, 11. Millie app. in #10, 92, 98. Mitzi app. in #11. Rusty app. in #12, 25. Willie app. in #12.* ***Al Jaffee*** *c-57, 58.*

PAT THE BRAT (Adventures of Pipsqueak #34 on)
June, 1953; Summer, 1955 - No. 4, 5/56; No. 15, 7/56 - No. 33, 7/59
Archie Publications (Radio)

nn(6/53) 10.00 30.00 65.00

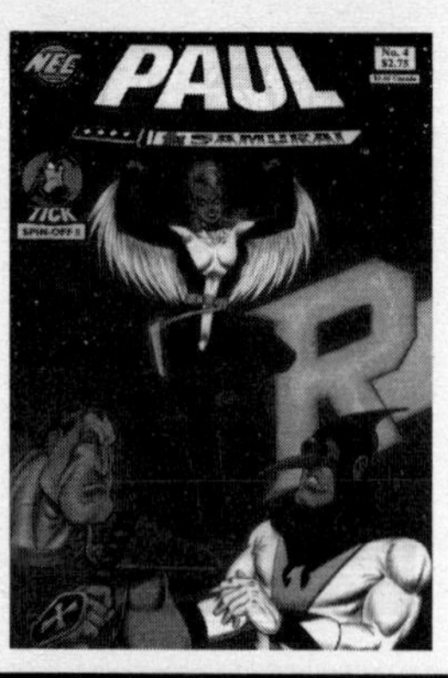

Paul the Samurai #1 © Ben Edlund

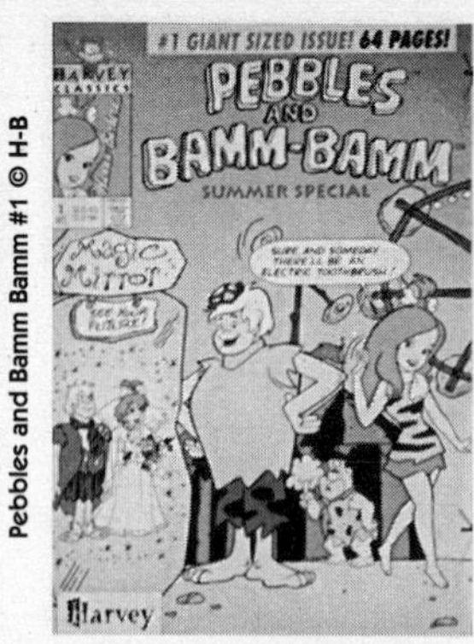

Pebbles and Bamm Bamm #1 © H-B

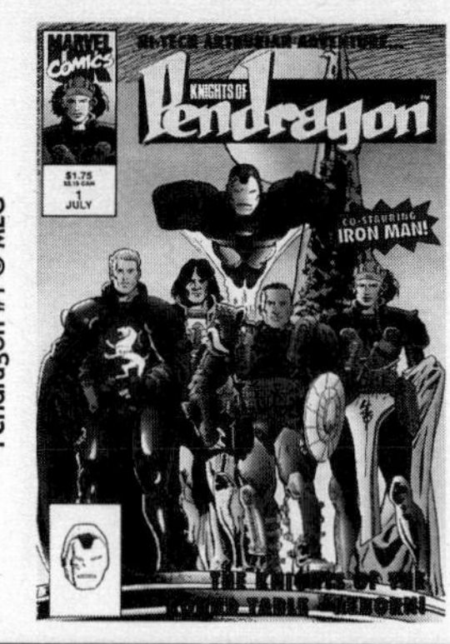

Pendragon #1 © MEG

	GD25	FN65	NM94
1(Summer, 1955)	7.00	21.00	42.00
2-4-(5/56) (#5-14 not published)	4.00	12.00	24.00
15-(7/56)-33	2.80	7.00	14.00

PAT THE BRAT COMICS DIGEST MAGAZINE
October, 1980
Archie Publications

	GD25	FN65	NM94
1			1.50

PATTY POWERS (Formerly Della Vision #3)
No. 4, Oct, 1955 - No. 7, Oct, 1956
Atlas Comics

	GD25	FN65	NM94
4	5.85	17.50	35.00
5-7	4.00	10.00	20.00

PAT WILTON (See Mighty Midget Comics)

PAUL (Spire Christian)(Value: cover or less)

PAULINE PERIL (See The Close Shaves of...)

PAUL REVERE'S RIDE (See 4-Color #822 & Walt Disney Showcase #34)

PAUL TERRY'S ADVENTURES OF MIGHTY MOUSE (See Adventures of...)

PAUL TERRY'S COMICS (Formerly Terry-Toons Comics; becomes Adventures of Mighty Mouse No. 126 on)
No. 85, Mar, 1951 - No. 125, May, 1955
St. John Publishing Co.

	GD25	FN65	NM94
85,86-Same as Terry-Toons #85, & 86 with only a title change; published at same time?; Mighty Mouse, Heckle & Jeckle & Gandy Goose continue from Terry-Toons	9.15	27.50	55.00
87-99	5.35	16.00	32.00
100	7.00	21.00	42.00
101-104,107-125: 121,122,125-Painted-c	5.00	15.00	30.00
105,106-Giant Comics Edition (25¢, 100 pgs.) (9/53 & ?). 105-Little Roquefort-c/story	13.00	40.00	90.00

PAUL TERRY'S HOW TO DRAW FUNNY CARTOONS
1940's (14 pgs.) (Black & White)
Terrytoons, Inc. (Giveaway)

	GD25	FN65	NM94
nn-Heckle & Jeckle, Mighty Mouse, etc.	11.00	32.00	75.00

PAUL TERRY'S MIGHTY MOUSE (See Mighty Mouse)

PAUL TERRY'S MIGHTY MOUSE ADVENTURE STORIES (See Mighty Mouse Adventure Stories)

PAUL THE SAMURAI (See The Tick #4)
July, 1992 - No. 6, July, 1993 ($2.75, B&W)
New England Comics

	GD25	FN65	NM94
1		1.20	3.00
2-6		1.10	2.75

PAWNEE BILL
Feb, 1951 - No. 3, July, 1951
Story Comics (Youthful Magazines?)

	GD25	FN65	NM94
1-Bat Masterson, Wyatt Earp app.	9.15	27.50	55.00
2,3: 3-Origin Golden Warrior; Cameron-a	5.35	16.00	32.00

PAY-OFF (This Is the..., ...Crime, ...Detective Stories)
July-Aug, 1948 - No. 5, Mar-Apr, 1949 (52 pgs.)
D. S. Publishing Co.

	GD25	FN65	NM94
1-True Crime Cases #1,2	14.00	43.00	100.00
2	10.00	30.00	60.00
3-5-Thrilling Detective Stories	8.35	25.00	50.00

PEACEMAKER, THE (Also see Fightin' Five)
V3#1, Mar, 1967 - No. 5, Nov, 1967 (All 12¢ cover price)
Charlton Comics

	GD25	FN65	NM94
1-Fightin' Five begins	2.30	6.90	16.00
2,3,5	1.50	3.80	9.00
4-Origin The Peacemaker	2.30	6.90	16.00
1,2(Modern Comics reprint, 1978)			1.00

PEACEMAKER (DC)(Value: cover or less)(Also see Crisis On Infinite Earths)

PEANUTS (Charlie Brown) (See Fritzi Ritz, Nancy & Sluggo, Tip Top, Tip Topper & United Comics)
1953-54; No. 878, 2/58 - No. 13, 5-7/62; 5/63 - No. 4, 2/64
Dell Publishing Co./Gold Key

	GD25	FN65	NM94
1(1953-54)-Reprints United Features' Strange As It Seems, Willie, Ferdnand	11.00	32.00	75.00
4-Color 878(#1)	14.00	43.00	100.00
4-Color 969,1015('59)	10.00	30.00	70.00
4(2-4/60)	8.35	25.00	50.00
5-13	5.35	16.00	32.00
1(Gold Key, 5/63)	8.70	26.00	52.00
2-4	6.20	18.50	37.00

PEBBLES & BAMM BAMM (TV) (See Cave Kids #7, 12)
Jan, 1972 - No. 36, Dec, 1976 (Hanna-Barbera)
Charlton Comics

	GD25	FN65	NM94
1-From the Flintstones	4.30	12.90	30.00
2-10	2.10	6.50	15.00
11-36	1.50	3.80	9.00

PEBBLES & BAMM BAMM (TV)
Nov, 1993 - No. 3, Mar, 1994 ($1.50) (Hanna-Barbera)
Harvey Comics

	GD25	FN65	NM94
V2#1-3		.90	2.25
...Giant Size 1 (10/93, $2.25, 68 pgs.)("Summer Special" on-c)		.90	2.25

PEBBLES FLINTSTONE (TV) (See The Flintstones #11)
Sept, 1963 (Hanna-Barbera)
Gold Key

	GD25	FN65	NM94
1 (10088-309)-Early Pebbles app.	8.00	24.00	55.00

PECKS BAD BOY
1906 - 1908 (Strip reprints) (11-1/4x15-3/4")
Thompson of Chicago (by Walt McDougal)

	GD25	FN65	NM94
...& Cousin Cynthia(1907)-In color	28.00	85.00	280.00
...& His Chums (1908)-Hardcover; in full color; 16 pgs.	28.00	85.00	280.00
Advs. of...And His Country Cousins (1906)-In color, 18 pgs., oblong	28.00	85.00	280.00
Advs. of...in Pictures (1908)-In color; Stanton & Van V. Liet Co.	28.00	85.00	280.00

PEDRO (Formerly My Private Life #17; also see Romeo Tubbs)
No. 18, June, 1950 - No. 2, Aug, 1950?
Fox Features Syndicate

	GD25	FN65	NM94
18(#1)-Wood-c/a(p)	16.00	48.00	110.00
2-Wood-a?	11.50	34.00	80.00

PEE-WEE PIXIES (See The Pixies)

PELLEAS AND MELISANDE (See Night Music #4, 5)

PENALTY (See Crime Must Pay the...)

PENDRAGON (Knights of... #5 on; also see Knights of...)
July, 1992 - No. 15, Sept, 1993 ($1.75)
Marvel Comics UK, Ltd.

	GD25	FN65	NM94
1-15: 1-4-Iron Man app. 6-8-Spider-Man app.		.70	1.75

PENDULUM ILLUSTRATED BIOGRAPHIES
1979 (B&W)
Pendulum Press
19-355x-George Washington/Thomas Jefferson, 19-3495-Charles Lindbergh/Amelia Earhart, 19-3509-Harry Houdini/Walt Disney, 19-3517-Davy Crockett/Daniel Boone-Redondo-a, 19-3525-Elvis Presley/Beatles, 19-3533-Benjamin Franklin/Martin Luther King Jr, 19-3541-Abraham Lincoln/Franklin D. Roosevelt, 19-3568-Marie Curie/Albert Einstein-Redondo-a, 19-3576-Thomas Edison/Alexander Graham Bell-Redondo-a, 19-3584-Vince Lombardi/Pele, 19-3592-Babe Ruth/Jackie Robinson, 19-3606-Jim Thorpe/Althea Gibson

	GD25	FN65	NM94
Softback		1.50	
Hardback		4.50	

Penthouse Comix #3 © Penthouse Int.

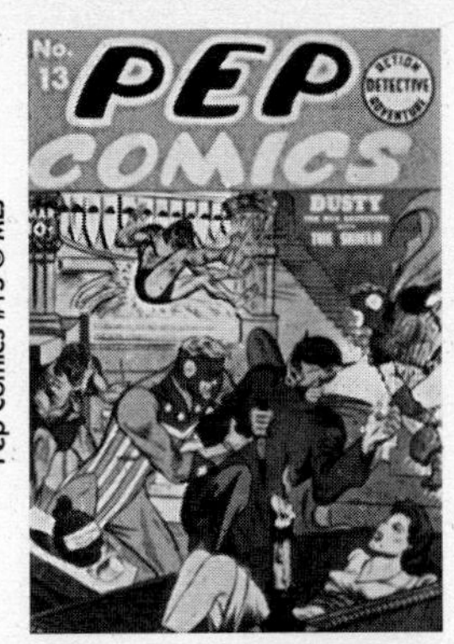

Pep Comics #13 © MLJ

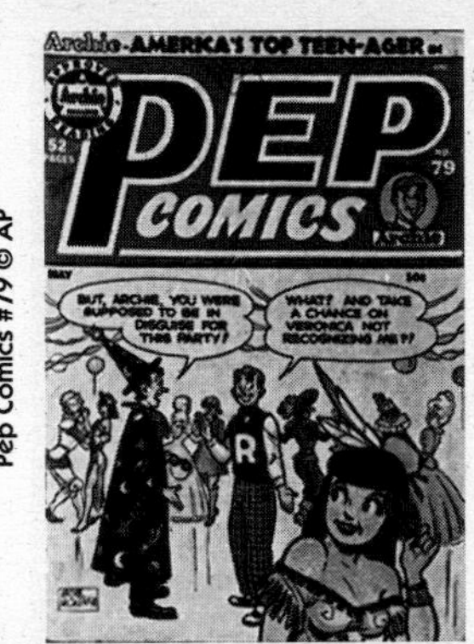

Pep Comics #79 © AP

GD25 FN65 NM94

NOTE: *Above books still available from publisher.*

PENDULUM ILLUSTRATED CLASSICS (Now Age Illustrated)
1973 - 1978 (75¢, 62pp, B&W, 5-3/8x8") (Also see Marvel Classics)
Pendulum Press

64-100x(1973)-Dracula-Redondo art, 64-131x-The Invisible Man-Nino art, 64-0968-Dr. Jekyll and Mr. Hyde-Redondo art, 64-1005-Black Beauty, 64-1010-Call of the Wild, 64-1020-Frankenstein, 64-1025-Hucklebury Finn, 64-1030-Moby Dick-Nino-a, 64-1040-Red Badge of Courage, 64-1045-The Time Machine-Nino-a, 64-1050-Tom Sawyer, 64-1055-Twenty Thousand Leagues Under the Sea, 64-1069-Treasure Island, 64-1328(1974)-Kidnapped, 64-1336-Three Musketeers-Nino art, 64-1344-A Tale of Two Cities, 64-1352-Journey to the Center of the Earth, 64-1360-The War of the Worlds-Nino-a, 64-1379-The Greatest Advs. of Sherlock Holmes-Redondo art, 64-1387-Mysterious Island, 64-1395-Hunchback of Notre Dame, 64-1409-Helen Keller-story of my life, 64-1417-Scarlet Letter, 64-1425-Gulliver's Travels, 64-2618(1977)-Around the World in Eighty Days, 64-2626-Captains Courageous, 64-2634-Connecticut Yankee, 64-2642-The Hound of the Baskervilles, 64-2650-The House of Seven Gables, 64-2669-Jane Eyre, 64-2677-The Last of the Mohicans, 64-2685-The Best of O'Henry, 64-2693-The Best of Poe-Redondo-a, 64-2707-Two Years Before the Mast, 64-2715-White Fang, 64-2723-Wuthering Heights, 64-3126(1978)-Ben Hur-Redondo art, 64-3134-A Christmas Carol, 64-3142-The Food of the Gods, 64-3150-Ivanhoe, 64-3169-The Man in the Iron Mask, 64-3177-The Prince and the Pauper, 64-3185-The Prisoner of Zenda, 64-3193-The Return of the Native, 64-3207-Robinson Crusoe, 64-3215-The Scarlet Pimpernel, 64-3223-The Sea Wolf, 64-3231-The Swiss Family Robinson, 64-3851-Billy Budd, 64-386x-Crime and Punishment, 64-3878-Don Quixote, 64-3886-Great Expectations, 64-3894-Heidi, 64-3908-The Iliad, 64-3916-Lord Jim, 64-3924-The Mutiny on Board H.M.S. Bounty, 64-3932-The Odyssey, 64-3940-Oliver Twist, 64-3959-Pride and Prejudice, 64-3967-The Turn of the Screw

Softback		1.45
Hardback		4.50

NOTE: *All of the above books can be ordered from the publisher; some were reprinted as Marvel Classic Comics #1-12. In 1972 there was another brief series of 12 titles which contained Classics Ill. artwork. They were entitled* ***Now Age Books*** *Illustrated, but can be easily distinguished from later series by the small Classics Illustrated logo at the top of the front cover. The format is the same as the later series. The 48 pg. C.I. art was stretched out to make 62 pgs. After Twin Circle Publ. terminated the Classics Ill. series in 1971, they made a one year contract with Pendulum Press to print these twelve titles of C.I. art. Pendulum was unhappy with the contract, and at the end of 1972 began their own art series, utilizing the talents of the Filipino artist group. One detail which makes this rather confusing is that when they redid the art in 1973, they gave it the same identifying no. as the 1972 series. All 12 of the 1972 C.I. editions have new covers, taken from internal art panels. In spite of their recent age, all of the 1972 C.I. series are very rare. Mint copies would fetch at least $50. Here is a list of the 1972 series, with C.I. title no. counterpart:*

64-1005 (CI#60-A2) 64-1010 (CI#91) 64-1015 (Cl-Jr #503) 64-1020 (CI#26)
64-1025 (CI#19-A2) 64-1030 (CI#5-A2) 64-1035 (CI#169) 64-1040 (CI#98)
64-1045 (CI#133) 64-1050 (CI#50-A2) 64-1055 (CI#47) 64-1060 (CI-Jr#535)

PENDULUM ILLUSTRATED ORIGINALS
1979 (In color)
Pendulum Press

94-4254-Solarman: The Beginning		.65	1.60

PENDULUM'S ILLUSTRATED STORIES
1990 - No. 72, 1990? (No cover price ($4.95), color, squarebound, 68 pgs.)
Pendulum Press

1-72: Reprints Pendulum Ill. Classics series	1.00	2.00	5.00

PENNY
1947 - No. 6, Sept-Oct, 1949 (Newspaper reprints)
Avon Comics

1-Photo & biography of creator	9.15	27.50	55.00
2-5	5.00	15.00	30.00
6-Perry Como photo on-c	5.85	17.50	35.00

PENTHOUSE COMIX
1994 - Present ($4.95, color, bimonthly, adult magazine)
General Media International

1	1.00	2.50	6.00
2-6	1.00	2.00	5.00

PEP COMICS (See Archie Giant Series #576, 589, 601, 614, 624)
Jan, 1940 - No. 411, Mar, 1989
MLJ Magazines/Archie Publications No. 56 (3/46) on

	GD25	FN65	VF82	NM94
1-Intro. The Shield by Irving Novick (1st patriotic hero); origin & 1st app. The Comet by Jack Cole, The Queen of Diamonds & Kayo Ward; The Rocket, The Press Guardian (The Falcon #1 only), Sergeant Boyle, Fu Chang, & Bentley of of Scotland Yard; Robot-c; Shield-c begin	629.00	1885.00	3142.00	4400.00

(Estimated up to 150 total copies exist, 7 in NM/Mint)

	GD25	FN65	NM94
2-Origin The Rocket	136.00	407.00	950.00
3	107.00	321.00	750.00
4-Wizard cameo	86.00	257.00	600.00
5-Wizard cameo in Shield story	86.00	257.00	600.00
6-10: 8-Last Cole Comet; no Cole-a in #6,7	64.00	193.00	450.00
11-Dusty, Shield's sidekick begins (1st app.); last Press Guardian, Fu Chang	71.00	215.00	500.00
12-Origin & 1st app. Fireball (2/41); last Rocket & Queen of Diamonds; Danny in Wonderland begins	89.00	268.00	625.00
13-15	57.00	171.00	400.00
16-Origin Madam Satan; blood drainage-c	89.00	268.00	625.00
17-Origin/1st app. The Hangman (7/41); death of The Comet; Comet is revealed as Hangman's brother	200.00	600.00	1400.00
18-21: 20-Last Fireball. 21-Last Madam Satan	55.00	165.00	385.00

	GD25	FN65	VF82	NM94
22-Intro. & 1st app. Archie, Betty, & Jughead(12/41); (also see Jackpot)	625.00	1875.00	3440.00	5000.00

(Estimated up to 150 total copies exist, 7 in NM/Mint)

	GD25	FN65	NM94
23	93.00	280.00	650.00
24,25: 24-Coach Kleets app. (unnamed until Archie #94); bondage/torture-c. 25-1st app. Archie's jalopy; 1st skinny Mr. Weatherbee prototype	82.00	246.00	575.00
26-1st app. Veronica Lodge (4/42)	107.00	321.00	750.00
27-30: 29-Origin Shield retold; 30-Capt. Commando begins; bondage/torture-c; 1st Miss Grundy (definitive version); see Jackpot #4	63.00	190.00	440.00
31-35: 31-MLJ offices & artists are visited in Sgt. Boyle story; 1st app. Mr. Lodge. 32-Shield dons new costume. 34-Bondage/Hypo-c. 33-Pre-Moose tryout (see Jughead #1)	50.00	150.00	350.00
36-1st Archie-c (2/43) w/Shield & Hangman	86.00	257.00	600.00
37-40	37.00	111.00	260.00
41-50: 41-Archie-c begin. 47-Last Hangman issue; infinity-c. 48-Black Hood begins (5/44); ends #51,59,60	27.00	80.00	185.00
51-60: 52-Suzie begins. 56-Last Capt. Commando. 59-Black Hood not in costume; spanking & lingerie panels; Archie dresses as his aunt; Suzie ends. 60-Katy Keene begins(3/47), ends #154	19.00	57.00	130.00
61-65-Last Shield. 62-1st app. Li'l Jinx (7/47)	15.00	45.00	105.00
66-80: 66-G-Man Club becomes Archie Club (2/48); Nevada Jones by Bill Woggon. 78-1st app. Dilton	10.00	30.00	65.00
81-99	7.50	22.50	45.00
100	10.00	30.00	65.00
101-130	4.00	12.00	24.00
131-149	2.80	7.00	14.00
150-160-Super-heroes app. in each (see note). 150 (10/61?)-2nd or 3rd app. The Jaguar? 152-157-Sci/Fi-c. 157-Li'l Jinx story	3.20	8.00	16.00
161-167,169-200	1.00	2.50	6.00
168-Jaguar app.	1.20	3.00	7.00
201-260		1.20	3.00
261-411: 383-Marvelous Maureen begins (Sci/fi). 393-Thunderbunny begins. 400-Story featuring Archie staff (DeCarlo-a)			1.00

NOTE: ***Biro*** *a-2, 4, 5.* ***Jack Cole*** *a-1-5, 8.* ***Al Fagaly*** *c-55-72.* ***Fuje*** *a-39, 45, 47; c-34.* ***Meskin*** *a-2, 4, 5, 11(2).* ***Montana*** *c-30, 32, 33, 36, 73-87(most).* ***Novick*** *c-1-28, 29(w/****Schomburg****), 31i.* ***Harry Sahle*** *c-35, 39-50.* ***Schomburg*** *c-38.* ***Bob Wood*** *a-2, 4-6, 11. The Fly app. in 151, 154, 160. Flygirl app. in 153, 155, 156, 158. Jaguar app. in 150, 152, 157, 159, 168. Katy Keene by* ***Bill Woggon*** *in many later issues. Bondage c-7, 12, 13, 15, 18, 21, 31, 32. Cover features: Shield #1-16; Shield/Hangman #17-27, 29-41; Hangman #28. Archie #36, 41-on.*

PEPE (See 4-Color #1194)

PERCY & FERDIE
1921 (52 pgs.) (B&W dailies, 10x10", cardboard-c)
Cupples & Leon Co.

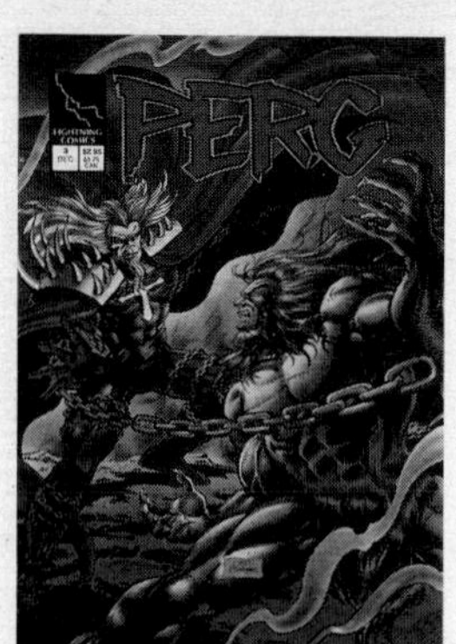

Perg #3 © Joseph A. Zyskowski

Personal Love #28 © FF

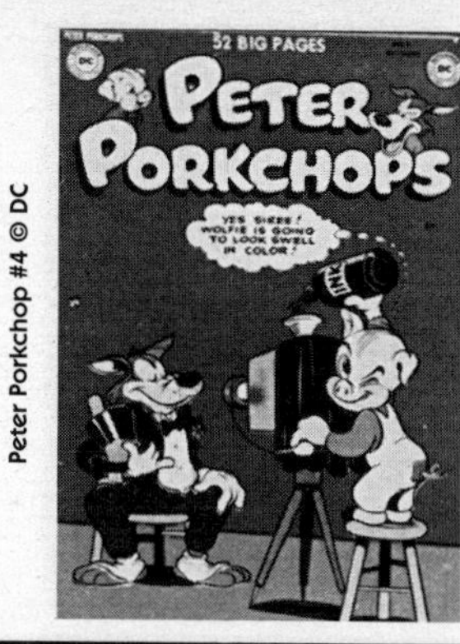

Peter Porkchop #4 © DC

	GD25	FN65	NM94
nn-By H. A. MacGill	13.50	41.00	95.00

PERFECT CRIME, THE
Oct, 1949 - No. 33, May, 1953 (#2-12, 52 pgs.)
Cross Publications

	GD25	FN65	NM94
1-Powell-a(2)	16.00	48.00	110.00
2 (4/50)	10.00	30.00	60.00
3-10: 7-Steve Duncan begins, ends #30	8.35	25.00	50.00
11-Used in **SOTI**, pg. 159	10.00	30.00	60.00
12-14	6.70	20.00	40.00
15- "The Most Terrible Menace" 2 pg. drug editorial	7.50	22.50	45.00
16,17,19-25,27-29,31-33	5.00	15.00	30.00
18-Drug cover, heroin drug propaganda story, plus 2 pg. anti-drug editorial	11.00	32.00	75.00
26-Drug-c with hypodermic; drug propaganda story	11.50	34.00	80.00
30-Strangulation cover	12.00	36.00	85.00

NOTE: *Powell a-No. 1, 2, 4. **Wildey** a-1, 5. Bondage c-11.*

PERFECT LOVE
#10, 8-9/51 (cover date; 5-6/51 indicia date); #2, 10-11/51 - #10, 12/53
Ziff-Davis(Approved Comics)/St. John No. 9 on

	GD25	FN65	NM94
10(#1)(8-9/51)-Painted-c	11.00	32.00	75.00
2(10-11/51)	8.35	25.00	50.00
3,5-7: 3-Painted-c. 5-Photo-c	5.85	17.50	35.00
4,8 (Fall, 1952)-Kinstler-a; last Z-D issue	6.35	19.00	38.00
9,10 (10/53, 12/53, St. John): 9-Painted-c. 10-Photo-c	5.35	16.00	32.00

PERG
Oct, 1993 - Present ($2.95, color)
Lightning Comics

	GD25	FN65	NM94
1-($3.50)-Flip-c is glow-in-the-dark by Saltares		1.40	3.50
1-Platinum Edition	1.30	3.00	8.00
2-8: 4-Origin Perg		1.20	3.00
2,3-Platinum Edition		1.80	4.50
4-Platinum Edition		1.30	3.25
7-Blue & Pink cover versions		1.20	3.00

PERRI (See 4-Color #847)

PERRY MASON (See Feature Books #49, 50)

PERRY MASON MYSTERY MAGAZINE (TV)
June-Aug, 1964 - No. 2, Oct-Dec, 1964
Dell Publishing Co.

	GD25	FN65	NM94
1,2: 2-Raymond Burr photo-c	4.00	11.00	22.00

PERSONAL LOVE (Also see Movie Love)
Jan, 1950 - No. 33, June, 1955
Famous Funnies

	GD25	FN65	NM94
1	11.00	32.00	75.00
2-Kathryn Grayson & Mario Lanza photo-c	6.35	19.00	38.00
3-7,10: 10-Loretta Young & Joseph Cotton photo-c	4.70	14.00	28.00
8,9: 8-Esther Williams photo-c	5.00	15.00	30.00
11-Toth-a; Glenn Ford & Gene Tierney photo-c	8.35	25.00	50.00
12,16,17-One pg. Frazetta each. 17-Rock Hudson & Yvonne DeCarlo photo-c	4.70	14.00	28.00
13-15,18-23: 14-Kirk Douglas photo-c. 15,22-Dale Robertson photo-c. 18-Gregory Peck/Susan Hayworth photo-c. 19-Anthony Quinn photo-c. 20-Robert Wagner photo-c. 23-Rhonda Fleming-c	4.00	12.00	24.00
24,27,28-Frazetta-a in each (8,8&6 pgs.). 27-Rhonda Fleming & Fernando Lamas photo-c. 28,30-Mitzi Gaynor photo-c	24.00	73.00	170.00
25-Frazetta-a (tribute to Betty Page, 7 pg. story); Tyrone Power/Terry Moore photo-c from "King of the Khyber Rifles"	24.00	73.00	170.00
26,29,30,33: 29-Charlton Heston photo-c.	4.00	11.00	22.00
31-Marlon Brando & Jean Simmons photo-c; last pre-code (2/55)	5.85	17.50	35.00
32-Classic Frazetta-a (8 pgs.); Kirk Douglas & Bella Darvi photo-c	39.00	116.00	270.00

NOTE: *All have photo-c. Many feature movie stars. **Everett** a-5, 9, 10, 24.*

PERSONAL LOVE (Going Steady V3#3 on)
V1#1, Sept, 1957 - V3#2, Nov-Dec, 1959
Prize Publ. (Headline)

	GD25	FN65	NM94
V1#1	5.35	16.00	32.00
2	3.60	9.00	18.00
3-6(7-8/58)	3.20	8.00	16.00
V2#1(9-10/58)-V2#6(7-8/59)	2.80	7.00	14.00
V3#1-Wood?/Orlando-a	4.00	10.00	20.00
2	2.40	6.00	12.00

PETER CANNON - THUNDERBOLT (Also see Thunderbolt)
Sept, 1992 - No. 12, Aug, 1993 ($1.25)(See Crisis on Infinite Earths)
DC Comics

	GD25	FN65	NM94
1-12			1.25

PETER COTTONTAIL
Jan, 1954; Feb, 1954 - No. 2, Mar, 1954 (Says 3/53 in error)
Key Publications

	GD25	FN65	NM94
1(1/54)-Not 3-D	5.35	16.00	32.00
1(2/54)-(3-D, 25¢)-Came w/glasses; written by Bruce Hamilton	17.00	52.00	120.00
2-Reprints 3-D #1 but not in 3-D	4.35	13.00	26.00

PETER GUNN (See 4-Color #1087)

PETER PAN (See 4-Color #442, 446, 926, Hook, Movie Classics & Comics, New Adventures of... & Walt Disney Showcase #36)

PETER PAN
1991 ($5.95, graphic novel, 68 pgs.)(Celebrates release of video)
Disney Comics

	GD25	FN65	NM94
nn-r/Peter Pan Treasure Chest from 1953	1.00	2.50	6.00

PETER PANDA
Aug-Sept, 1953 - No. 31, Aug-Sept, 1958
National Periodical Publications

	GD25	FN65	NM94
1-Grossman-c/a in all	31.00	94.00	220.00
2	14.00	43.00	100.00
3-10	11.00	32.00	70.00
11-31	7.50	22.50	45.00

PETER PAN: THE RETURN TO NEVER-NEVER LAND (Adventure)(Value: cover or less)

PETER PAN TREASURE CHEST (See Dell Giants)

PETER PARKER (See The Spectacular Spider-Man)

PETER PAT (See Single Series #8)

PETER PAUL'S 4 IN 1 JUMBO COMIC BOOK
No date (1953)
Capitol Stories (Charlton)

	GD25	FN65	NM94
1-Contains 4 comics bound; Space Adventures, Space Western, Crime & Justice, Racket Squad in Action	29.00	86.00	200.00

PETER PENNY AND HIS MAGIC DOLLAR
1947 (16 pgs.; paper cover; regular size)
American Bankers Association, N. Y. (Giveaway)

	GD25	FN65	NM94
nn-(Scarce)-Used in **SOTI**, pg. 310, 311	12.00	36.00	85.00
Diff. version (7-1/4x11")-redrawn, 16 pgs., paper-c	8.35	25.00	50.00

PETER PIG
No. 5, May, 1953 - No. 6, Aug, 1953
Standard Comics

	GD25	FN65	NM94
5,6	4.00	10.00	20.00

PETER PORKCHOPS (See Leading Comics #23)
11-12/49 - No. 61, 9-11/59; No. 62, 10-12/60 (1-11: 52 pgs.)
National Periodical Publications

	GD25	FN65	NM94
1	31.00	94.00	220.00
2	16.00	48.00	110.00
3-10: 6- "Peter Rockets to Mars!" c/story	11.00	32.00	75.00

Peter Rabbit Comics #4 © AVON

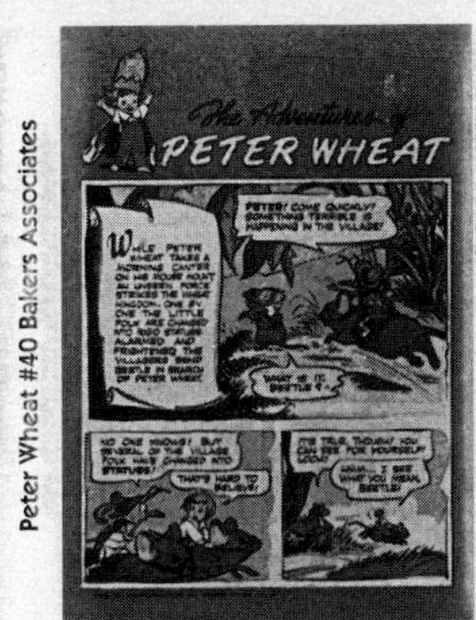

Peter Wheat #40 Bakers Associates

The Phantom #68 © CC

	GD25	FN65	NM94
11-30	9.15	27.50	55.00
31-62	7.50	22.50	45.00

NOTE: ***Otto Feur*** *a-all.* ***Sheldon Mayer*** *a-30-38, 40-44, 46-52, 61.*

PETER PORKER, THE SPECTACULAR SPIDER-HAM
May, 1985 - No. 17, Sept, 1987 (Also see Marvel Tails)
Star Comics (Marvel)

	GD25	FN65	NM94
1-Michael Golden-c		.80	2.00
2-17: 12-Origin/1st app. Bizarro Phil. 13-Halloween issue			1.00

NOTE: *Back-up features: 2-X-Bugs. 3-Iron Mouse. 4-Croctor Strange. 5-Thrr, Dog of Thunder.*

PETER POTAMUS (TV)
January, 1965 (Hanna-Barbera)
Gold Key

	GD25	FN65	NM94
1	7.00	21.00	42.00

PETER RABBIT (See Large Feature Comic #1, New Funnies #65 & Space Comics)

PETER RABBIT
1922 - 1923 (9-1/4x6-1/4") (paper cover)
John H. Eggers Co. The House of Little Books Publishers

B1-B4-(Rare)-(Set of 4 books which came in a cardboard box)-Each book reprints half of a Sunday page per page and contains 8 B&W and 2 color pages; by Harrison Cady

	GD25	FN65	NM94
each....	40.00	120.00	270.00
Box only	50.00	150.00	350.00

PETER RABBIT (Adventures of...; New Advs. of... #9 on)(Also see Funny Tunes & Space Comics)
1947 - No. 34, Aug-Sept, 1956
Avon Periodicals

	GD25	FN65	NM94
1(1947)-Reprints 1943-44 Sunday strips; contains a biography & drawing of Cady	29.00	86.00	200.00
2 (4/48)	22.00	65.00	150.00
3 ('48) - 6(7/49)-Last Cady issue	19.00	58.00	135.00
7-10(1950-8/51): 9-New logo	4.70	14.00	28.00
11(11/51)-34('56)-Avon's character	3.60	9.00	18.00
...Easter Parade (1952, 25¢, 132 pgs.)	12.00	36.00	85.00
...Jumbo Book (1954-Giant Size, 25¢)-Jesse James by Kinstler (6 pgs.); space ship-c	18.00	54.00	125.00

PETER RABBIT
1958
Fago Magazine Co.

	GD25	FN65	NM94
1	5.85	17.50	35.00

PETER RABBIT 3-D (Eternity)(Value: cover or less)

PETER, THE LITTLE PEST (#4 titled Petey)
Nov, 1969 - No. 4, May, 1970
Marvel Comics Group

	GD25	FN65	NM94
1	1.30	3.25	8.00
2-4-r-Dexter the Demon & Melvin the Monster	1.00	2.00	5.00

PETER WHEAT (The Adventures of...)
1948 - 1956? (16 pgs. in color) (paper covers)
Bakers Associates Giveaway

	GD25	FN65	NM94
nn(No.1)-States on last page, end of 1st Adventure of...; Kelly-a	29.00	86.00	200.00
nn(4 issues)-Kelly-a	19.00	57.00	130.00
6-10-All Kelly-a	13.00	40.00	90.00
11-20-All Kelly-a	11.00	32.00	75.00
21-35-All Kelly-a	10.00	30.00	60.00
36-66	6.70	20.00	40.00
...Artist's Workbook ('54, digest size)	6.70	20.00	40.00
...Four-In-One Fun Pack (Vol. 2, '54), oblong, comics w/puzzles	8.35	25.00	50.00
...Fun Book ('52, 32 pgs., paper-c, B&W & color, 8-1/2x10-3/4")-Contains cut-outs, puzzles, games, magic & pages to color	10.00	30.00	70.00

NOTE: ***Al Hubbard*** *art #36 on; written by Del Connell.*

PETER WHEAT NEWS
1948 - No. 30, 1950 (4 pgs. in color)
Bakers Associates

	GD25	FN65	NM94
Vol. 1-All have 2 pgs. Peter Wheat by Kelly	24.00	72.00	165.00
2-10	14.00	43.00	100.00
11-20	8.35	25.00	50.00
21-30	5.35	16.00	32.00

NOTE: *Early issues have no date &* ***Kelly*** *art.*

PETE'S DRAGON (See Walt Disney Showcase #43)

PETE THE PANIC
November, 1955
Stanmor Publications

	GD25	FN65	NM94
nn-Code approved	3.20	8.00	16.00

PETEY (See Peter, the Little Pest)

PETTICOAT JUNCTION (TV)
Oct-Dec, 1964 - No. 5, Oct-Dec, 1965 (#1-3, 5 have photo-c)
Dell Publishing Co.

	GD25	FN65	NM94
1	8.35	25.00	50.00
2-5	5.85	17.50	35.00

PETUNIA (See 4-Color #463)

PHANTASMO (See The Funnies #45 and Large Feature Comic #18)

PHANTOM, THE
1939 - 1949
David McKay Publishing Co.

	GD25	FN65	NM94
Feature Books 20	55.00	165.00	550.00
Feature Books 22	45.00	135.00	450.00
Feature Books 39	43.00	130.00	300.00
Feature Books 53,56,57	31.00	94.00	220.00

PHANTOM, THE (See Ace Comics, Defenders Of The Earth, Eat Right to Work and Win, Future Comics, Harvey Comics Hits #51,56, Harvey Hits #1, 6, 12, 15, 26, 36, 44, 48, & King Comics)

PHANTOM, THE (nn 29-Published overseas only) (Also see Comics Reading Library)
Nov, 1962 - No. 17, July, 1966; No. 18, Sept, 1966 - No. 28, Dec, 1967; No. 30, Feb, 1969 - No. 74, Jan, 1977
Gold Key (#1-17)/King (#18-28)/Charlton (#30 on)

	GD25	FN65	NM94
1-Manning-a	9.00	28.00	65.00
2-King, Queen & Jack begins, ends #11	4.90	15.00	34.00
3-10	3.90	12.00	27.00
11-17: 12-Track Hunter begins	3.10	9.00	22.00
18-Flash Gordon begins; Wood-a	3.40	10.00	24.00
19,20-Flash Gordon ends (both by Gil Kane)	2.40	7.30	17.00
21-24,26,27: 21-Mandrake begins. 20,24-Girl Phantom app. 26-Brick Bradford app.	2.40	7.30	17.00
25-Jeff Jones-a(4 pgs.); 1 pg. Williamson ad	2.40	7.30	17.00
28(nn)-Brick Bradford app.	2.00	6.00	14.00
30-40: 36,39-Ditko-a	1.70	5.00	12.00
41-66: 46-Intro. The Piranha. 62-Bolle-c	1.50	3.80	9.00
67-71,73-Newton-c/a: 67-Origin retold	1.00	2.50	6.00
72,74: 74-Newton flag-c; Newton-a	1.00	2.50	6.00

NOTE: ***Aparo*** *a-31-34, 36-38; c-31-38, 60, 61. Painted c-1-17.*

PHANTOM, THE
May, 1988 - No. 4, Aug, 1988 ($1.25, mini-series)
DC Comics

	GD25	FN65	NM94
1-4: Orlando-c/a in all			1.25

PHANTOM, THE
Mar, 1989 - No. 13, Mar, 1990 ($1.50)
DC Comics

	GD25	FN65	NM94
1-13: 1-Brief origin			1.50

PHANTOM, THE
1992 - Present? ($2.25, color)

Phantom Lady #17 © FOX

Phantom Witch Doctor #1 © AVON

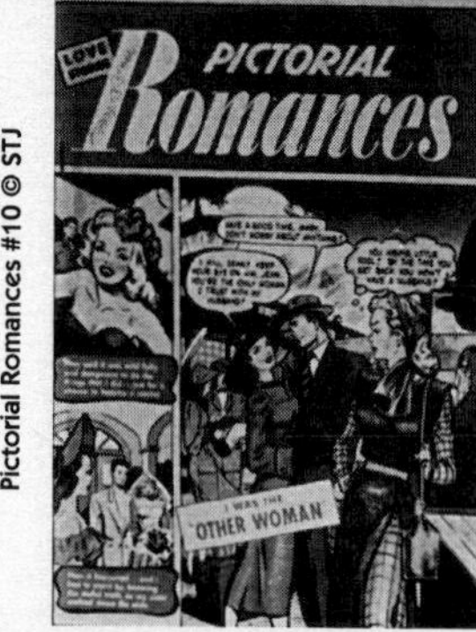

Pictorial Romances #10 © STJ

GD25 FN65 NM94

Wolf Publishing
1-8 .90 2.25

PHANTOM BLOT, THE (#1 titled New Adventures of...)
Oct, 1964 - No. 7, Nov, 1966 (Disney)
Gold Key
1 (Meets The Beagle Boys) 5.85 17.50 35.00
2-1st Super Goof 4.00 10.00 20.00
3-7 3.00 7.50 15.00

PHANTOM EAGLE (See Mighty Midget, Marvel Super Heroes #16 & Wow #6)

PHANTOM FORCE
Dec, 1993 - No. 2, 1994 (Color, limited series)
Image Comics
1-($2.50)-Polybagged w/trading card; Kirby Liefeld-c; Kirby plots/Pencils with inks by Liefeld, McFarlane, Jim Lee, Silvestri, Larsen, Williams, Ordway & Miki 1.00 2.50
2-($3.50)-Kirby-a(p); Kirby/Larson-c 1.40 3.50

PHANTOM FORCE
No. 0, Mar, 1994 - Present ($2.50, color)
Genesis West
0-Kirby/Jim Lee-c; Kirby-p pgs. 1,5,24-29 1.10 2.75
3-7: 3-(5/94)-Kirby/McFarlane-c 4-(5/94)-Kirby-c(p). 5-(6/94) 1.10 2.75

PHANTOM LADY (1st Series) (My Love Secret #24 on) (Also see All Top, Daring Adventures, Freedom Fighters, Jungle Thrills, & Wonder Boy)
No. 13, Aug, 1947 - No. 23 April, 1949
Fox Features Syndicate
13(#1)-Phantom Lady by Matt Baker begins (1st app.); The Blue Beetle story 179.00 535.00 1250.00
14(#2) 118.00 355.00 825.00
15-P.L. injected with experimental drug 93.00 280.00 650.00
16-Negligee-c, panels; true crime stories begin 93.00 280.00 650.00
17-Classic bondage cover; used in **SOTI**, illo "Sexual stimulation by combining 'headlights' with the sadist's dream of tying up a woman" 214.00 643.00 1500.00
18,19 86.00 257.00 600.00
20-23: 23-Bondage-c 71.00 215.00 500.00
NOTE: ***Matt Baker** a-in all; c-13, 15-21. **Kamen** a-22, 23.*

PHANTOM LADY (2nd Series) (See Terrific Comics) (Formerly Linda)
V1#5, Dec-Jan, 1954/1955 - No. 4, June, 1955
Ajax/Farrell Publ.
V1#5(#1)-By Matt Baker 50.00 150.00 350.00
V1#2-Last pre-code 41.00 124.00 290.00
3,4-Red Rocket. 3-Heroin story 34.00 100.00 235.00

PHANTOM PLANET, THE (See 4-Color No. 1234)

PHANTOM STRANGER, THE (1st Series)(See Saga of Swamp Thing)
Aug-Sept, 1952 - No. 6, June-July, 1953
National Periodical Publications
1(Scarce)-1st app. 129.00 385.00 900.00
2 (Scarce) 86.00 257.00 600.00
3-6 (Scarce) 79.00 235.00 550.00

PHANTOM STRANGER, THE (2nd Series) (See Showcase #80)
May-June, 1969 - No. 41, Feb-Mar, 1976
National Periodical Publications
1-2nd S.A. app. P. Stranger; only 12¢ issue 6.60 20.00 46.00
2,3 2.30 6.90 16.00
4-1st new look Phantom Stranger; N. Adams-a 2.70 8.10 19.00
5-7 1.70 5.00 12.00
8-14: 14-Last 15¢ issue 1.40 3.50 8.50
15-19: All 25¢ giants (52 pgs.) 2.30 5.50
20-41: 20-Dark Circle begins, ends #24. 23-Spawn of Frankenstein begins by Kaluta; series ends #30. 26-Book-length story featuring Ph. Stranger, Dr. 13 & Spawn/Frankenstein. 31-The Black Orchid begins (6-7/74). 33-Deadman-c/story. 34-Last 20¢ issue (#35 on are 25¢). 39-41-Deadman app. 1.80 4.50
NOTE: ***N. Adams** a-4; c-3-19. **Aparo** a-7-26; c-20-24, 33-41. **B. Bailey** a-27-30. **DeZuniga** a-14-16, 19-22, 31, 34. **Grell** a-33. **Kaluta** a-23-25; c-26. **Meskin** r-15, 16, 18. **Redondo** a-32, 35, 36. **Sparling** a-20. **Starr** a-17r. **Toth** a-15r. Black Orchid by **Carrilo**-38-41. Dr. 13 solo in-13, 18, 19, 20, 21, 34. Frankenstein by **Kaluta**-23-25; by **Baily**-27-30. No Black Orchid-33, 34, 37.*

PHANTOM STRANGER (See Justice League of America #103)
Oct, 1987 - No. 4, Jan, 1988 (75¢, mini-series)
DC Comics
1-Mignola/Russell-c/a & Eclipso app. in all 1.60
2-4: 3,4-Eclipso-c 1.10

PHANTOM WITCH DOCTOR (Also see Durango Kid #8 & Eerie #8)
1952
Avon Periodicals
1-Kinstler-c/a (7 pgs.) 31.00 94.00 220.00

PHANTOM ZONE, THE (See Adventure #283 & Superboy #100, 104)
January, 1982 - No. 4, April, 1982
DC Comics
1-Superman app. in all 1.10
2-4: Batman, Green Lantern app. 1.35
NOTE: ***Colan** a-1-4p; c-1-4p. **Giordano** c-1-4i.*

PHAZE (Eclipse)(Value: cover or less)

PHIL RIZZUTO (Baseball Hero)(See Sport Thrills, Accepted reprint)
1951 (New York Yankees)
Fawcett Publications
nn-Photo-c 49.00 146.00 340.00

PHOENIX
Jan, 1975 - No. 4, Oct, 1975
Atlas/Seaboard Publ.
1-Origin 1.20
2-4: 3-Origin & only app. The Dark Avenger. 4-New origin/costume The Protector (formerly Phoenix) 1.00
NOTE: ***Infantino** appears in #1, 2. **Austin** a-3i. **Thorne** c-3.*

PHOENIX (...The Untold Story)
April, 1984 ($2.00, One shot)
Marvel Comics Group
1-Byrne/Austin-r/X-Men #137 with original unpublished ending 1.80 4.50

PICNIC PARTY (See Dell Giants)

PICTORIAL CONFESSIONS (Pictorial Romances #4 on)
Sept, 1949 - No. 3, Dec, 1949
St. John Publishing Co.
1-Baker-c/a(3) 14.00 43.00 100.00
2-Baker-a; photo-c 10.00 30.00 60.00
3-Kubert, Baker-a; part Kubert-c 10.00 30.00 60.00

PICTORIAL LOVE STORIES (Formerly Tim McCoy)
No. 22, Oct, 1949 - No. 26, July, 1950
Charlton Comics
22-26-All have "Me-Dan Cupid" 10.00 30.00 70.00

PICTORIAL LOVE STORIES
October, 1952
St. John Publishing Co.
1-Baker-c/a 13.00 40.00 90.00

PICTORIAL ROMANCES (Formerly Pictorial Confessions)
No. 4, Jan, 1950; No. 5, Jan, 1951 - No. 24, Mar, 1954
St. John Publishing Co.
4-All Baker; photo-c 13.00 40.00 90.00
5,10-All Matt Baker issues 10.00 30.00 65.00
6-9,12,13,15,16-Baker-c, 2-3 stories 7.50 22.50 45.00
11-Baker-c/a(3); Kubert-r/Hollywood Confessions 1 8.35 25.00 50.00

Picture Parade #2 © GIL

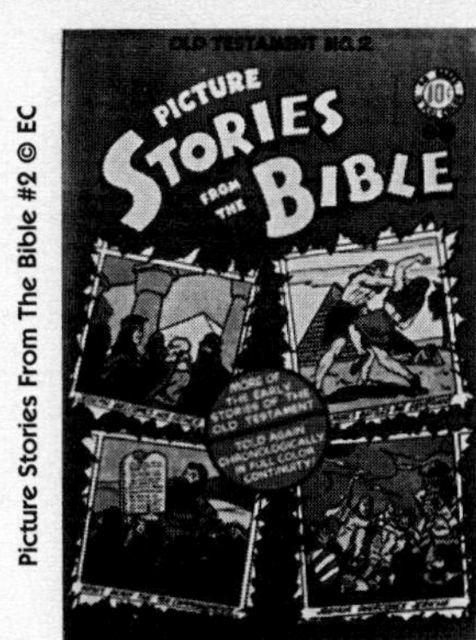

Picture Stories From The Bible #2 © EC

Pinhead & Foodini #1 © FAW

	GD25	FN65	NM94
14,21-24-Baker-c/a each	5.85	17.50	35.00
17-20(7/53)-25¢, 100 pgs. each; Baker-c/a	13.50	41.00	95.00

NOTE: ***Matt Baker*** *art in most issues.* ***Estrada*** *a-19(2).*

PICTURE NEWS
Jan, 1946 - No. 10, Jan-Feb, 1947
Lafayette Street Corp.

	GD25	FN65	NM94
1-Milt Gross begins, ends No. 6; 4 pg. Kirby-a; A-Bomb-c/story	25.00	75.00	175.00
2-Atomic explosion panels; Frank Sinatra/Perry Como story	11.50	34.00	80.00
3-Atomic explosion panels; Frank Sinatra, June Allyson, Benny Goodman stories	10.00	30.00	70.00
4-Atomic explosion panels; "Caesar and Cleopatra" movie adapt. w/Claude Raines & Vivian Leigh; Jackie Robinson story	11.50	34.00	80.00
5-7: 5-Hank Greenberg story. 6-Joe Louis-c/story	8.35	25.00	50.00
8-Monte Hale story (9-10/46; 1st?)	10.00	30.00	65.00
9-A-Bomb story; "Crooked Mile" movie adaptation; Joe DiMaggio story	10.00	30.00	65.00
10-Dick Quick; A-Bomb story; Krigstein, Gross-a	10.00	30.00	65.00

PICTURE PARADE (Picture Progress #5 on)
Sept, 1953 - V1#4, Dec, 1953 (28 pgs.)
Gilberton Company (Also see A Christmas Adventure)

	GD25	FN65	NM94
V1#1-Andy's Atomic Adventures; A-bomb blast-c; (Teachers version distributed to schools exists)	11.50	34.00	80.00
2-Around the World with the United Nations	9.15	27.50	55.00
3-Adventures of the Lost One(The American Indian), 4-A Christmas Adventure (r-under same title in 1969)	9.15	27.50	55.00

PICTURE PROGRESS (Formerly Picture Parade)
V1#5, Jan, 1954 - V3#2, Oct, 1955 (28-36 pgs.)
Gilberton Corp.

	GD25	FN65	NM94
V1#5-9,V2#1-9: 5-News in Review 1953. 6-The Birth of America. 7-The Four Seasons. 8-Paul Revere's Ride. 9-The Hawaiian Islands(5/54). V2#1-The Story of Flight(9/54). 2-Vote for Crazy River(The Meaning of Elections). 3-Louis Pasteur. 4-The Star Spangled Banner. 5-News in Review 1954. 6-Alaska: The Great Land. 7-Life in the Circus. 8-The Time of the Cave Man. 9-Summer Fun(5/55)	4.20	12.50	25.00
V3#1,2: 1-The Man Who Discovered America. 2-The Lewis & Clark Expedition	4.20	12.50	25.00

PICTURE SCOPE JUNGLE ADVENTURES (See Jungle Thrills)

PICTURE STORIES FROM AMERICAN HISTORY
1945 - No. 4, Sum, 1947 (#1,2: 10¢, 56 pgs.; #3,4: 15¢, 52 pgs.)
National/All-American/E. C. Comics

	GD25	FN65	NM94
1	19.00	57.00	130.00
2-4	14.00	43.00	100.00

PICTURE STORIES FROM SCIENCE
Spring, 1947 - No. 2, Fall, 1947
E.C. Comics

	GD25	FN65	NM94
1,2: 1-(15¢). 2-(10¢)	19.00	57.00	130.00

PICTURE STORIES FROM THE BIBLE (See Narrative Illustration, the Story of the Comics by M.C. Gaines)
1942 - No. 4, Fall, 1943; 1944-46
National/All-American/E.C. Comics

	GD25	FN65	NM94
1-4('42-Fall, '43)-Old Testament (DC)	17.00	52.00	120.00
Complete Old Testament Edition, (12/43-DC, 50¢, 232 pgs.);-1st printing; contains #1-4; 2nd - 8th (1/47) printings exist; later printings by E.C.	22.00	65.00	150.00
Complete Old Testament Edition (1945-publ. by Bible Pictures Ltd.)-232 pgs., hardbound, in color with dust jacket	22.00	65.00	150.00

NOTE: *Both Old and New Testaments published in England by Bible Pictures Ltd. in hardback, 1943, in color, 376 pgs. (2 vols.: O.T. 232 pgs. & N.T. 144 pgs.), and were also published by Scarf Press in 1979 (Old Test., $9.95) and in 1980 (New Test., $7.95)*

	GD25	FN65	NM94
1-3(New Test.; 1944-46, DC)-52 pgs. ea.	13.00	40.00	90.00
The Complete Life of Christ Edition (1945, 25¢, 96 pgs.)-Contains #1&2 of the New Testament Edition	17.00	52.00	120.00
1,2(Old Testament-r in comic book form)(E.C., 1946; 52 pgs.)	13.00	40.00	90.00
1(DC),2(AA),3(EC)(New Testament-r in comic book form)(E.C., 1946; 52 pgs.)	13.00	40.00	90.00
Complete New Testament Edition (1946-E.C., 50¢, 144 pgs.)-Contains #1-3	17.00	52.00	120.00

NOTE: *Another British series entitled* ***The Bible Illustrated*** *from 1947 has recently been discovered, with the same internal artwork. This eight edition series (5-OT, 3-NT) is of particular interest to Classics Ill. collectors because it exactly copied the C.I. logo format. The British publisher was Thorpe & Porter, who in 1951 began publishing the British Classics Ill. series. All editions of The Bible Ill. have new British painted covers. While this market is still new, and not all editions have as yet been found, current market value is about the same as the first U.S. editions of Picture Stories From The Bible.*

PICTURE STORIES FROM WORLD HISTORY
Spring, 1947 - No. 2, Summer, 1947 (52, 48 pgs.)
E.C. Comics

	GD25	FN65	NM94
1,2: 1-(15¢). 2-(10¢)	19.00	57.00	130.00

PINHEAD
Dec, 1993 - Present ($2.50)
Epic Comics (Marvel)

	GD25	FN65	NM94
1-($2.95)-Embossed foil-c by Kelley Jones; Intro Pinhead & Disciples (Snakeoil, Hangman, Fan Dancer & Dixie)		1.20	3.00
2-9		1.00	2.50

PINHEAD & FOODINI (TV)(Also see Foodini & Jingle Dingle Christmas...)
July, 1951 - No. 4, Jan, 1952 (Early TV comic)
Fawcett Publications

	GD25	FN65	NM94
1-(52 pgs.)-Photo-c; based on TV puppet show	24.00	72.00	165.00
2-Photo-c	11.00	32.00	75.00
3,4: 3-Photo-c	9.15	27.50	55.00

PINHEAD VS. MARSHALL LAW (Law in Hell)
Nov, 1993 - No. 2, Dec, 1993 ($2.95, limited series)
Epic Comics (Marvel)

	GD25	FN65	NM94
1,2: 1-Embossed red foil-c. 2-Embossed silver foil-c		1.20	3.00

PINK LAFFIN
1922 (9x12")(Strip-r)
Whitman Publishing Co.

	GD25	FN65	NM94
...the Lighter Side of Life, ...He Tells 'Em, ...and His Family, ...Knockouts; Ray Gleason-a (All rare) each...	14.00	43.00	100.00

PINK PANTHER, THE (TV)(See The Inspector & Kite Fun Book)
April, 1971 - No. 87, 1984
Gold Key

	GD25	FN65	NM94
1-The Inspector begins	2.40	7.30	17.00
2-10	1.40	3.50	8.50
11-30: Warren Tufts-a #16-on	1.10	2.70	6.50
31-60		1.50	3.75
61-87		1.20	3.00
Mini-comic No. 1(1976)(3-1/4x6-1/2")		.80	2.00

NOTE: *Pink Panther began as a movie cartoon. (See Golden Comics Digest #38, 45 and March of Comics #376, 384, 390, 409, 418, 429, 441, 449, 461, 473, 486); #37, 72, 80-85 contain reprints.*

PINK PANTHER SUPER SPECIAL (TV)
Oct, 1993 ($2.25, 68 pgs.)
Harvey Comics

	GD25	FN65	NM94
V2#1-The Inspector & Wendy Witch stories also		.90	2.25

PINK PANTHER, THE
Nov, 1993 - No. 9, July, 1994 ($1.50)
Harvey Comics

	GD25	FN65	NM94
V2#1-9			1.50

PINKY LEE (See Adventures of...)

PINKY THE EGGHEAD

Pioneer West Romances #3 © FH

Piracy #5 © EC

Planet Comics #7 © FH

GD25 FN65 NM94

1963 (Reprints from Noodnik)
I.W./Super Comics

I.W. Reprint #1,2(nd) 1.00 2.00 5.00
Super Reprint #14 1.00 2.00 5.00

PINOCCHIO (See 4-Color #92, 252, 545, 1203, Mickey Mouse Mag. V5#3, Movie Comics under Wonderful Advs. of..., New Advs. of..., Thrilling Comics #2, Walt Disney Showcase, Walt Disney's..., Wonderful Advs. of..., & World's Greatest Stories #2)

PINOCCHIO
1940 (10 pgs.; linen-like paper)
Montgomery Ward Co. (Giveaway)

nn 14.00 43.00 100.00

PINOCCHIO AND THE EMPEROR OF THE NIGHT (Marvel)(Value: cover or less)

PINOCCHIO LEARNS ABOUT KITES (See Kite Fun Book)

PIN-UP PETE (Also see Great Lover Romances & Monty Hall...)
1952
Toby Press

1-Jack Sparling pin-ups 12.00 36.00 85.00

PIONEER MARSHAL (See Fawcett Movie Comics)

PIONEER PICTURE STORIES
Dec, 1941 - No. 9, Dec, 1943
Street & Smith Publications

1-The Legless Air Ace begins 20.00 60.00 140.00
2 -True life story of Errol Flynn 10.00 30.00 70.00
3-9 9.15 27.50 55.00

PIONEER WEST ROMANCES (Firehair #1,2,7-11)
No. 3, Spring, 1950 - No. 6, Winter, 1950-51
Fiction House Magazines

3-(52 pgs.)-Firehair continues 13.00 40.00 90.00
4-6 13.00 40.00 90.00

PIPSQUEAK (See The Adventures of...)

PIRACY
Oct-Nov, 1954 - No. 7, Oct-Nov, 1955
E. C. Comics

1-Williamson/Torres-a 22.00 65.00 150.00
2-Williamson/Torres-a 14.00 43.00 100.00
3-7 11.50 34.00 80.00

NOTE: ***Crandall*** *a-in all; c-2-4.* ***Davis*** *a-1, 2, 6.* ***Evans*** *a-3-7; c-7.* ***Ingels*** *a-3-7.* ***Krigstein*** *a-3-5, 7; c-5, 6.* ***Wood*** *a-1, 2; c-1.*

PIRANA (See The Phantom #46 & Thrill-O-Rama #2, 3)

PIRATE CORPS, THE (Eternity)(Value: cover or less)

PIRATE OF THE GULF, THE (See Superior Stories #2)

PIRATES COMICS
Feb-Mar, 1950 - No. 4, Aug-Sept, 1950 (All 52 pgs.)
Hillman Periodicals

1 16.00 48.00 110.00
2-Dave Berg-a 11.50 34.00 80.00
3,4-Berg-a 11.00 32.00 75.00

PIRATES OF DARK WATER, THE (TV)(Marvel)(Value: cover or less)

P.I.'S: MICHAEL MAUSER AND MS. TREE, THE (First)(Value: cover or less)

PITT, THE (Marvel)(Value: cover or less)(Also see The Draft & The War)

PITT (See Youngblood #4)
Jan, 1993 - Present ($1.95, color, intended as 4-part mini-series)
Image Comics

1-Dale Keown-c/a. 1-1st app. The Pitt 1.20 3.00
2-5: Dale Keown-c/a .80 2.00

PIUS XII MAN OF PEACE
No date (12 pgs.; 5-1/2x8-1/2") (B&W)
Catechetical Guild Giveawaynn 4.00 10.50 21.00

GD25 FN65 NM94

PIXIE & DIXIE & MR. JINKS (TV)(See Jinks, Pixie, and Dixie & Whitman Comic Books)
July-Sept, 1960 - Feb, 1963 (Hanna-Barbera)
Dell Publishing Co./Gold Key

4-Color 1112 7.50 22.50 45.00
4-Color 1196,1264 5.85 17.50 35.00
01-631-207 (Dell, 7/62), 1(2/63-Gold Key) 5.85 17.50 35.00

PIXIE PUZZLE ROCKET TO ADVENTURELAND
November, 1952
Avon Periodicals

1 10.00 30.00 65.00

PIXIES, THE (Advs. of...)(The Mighty Atom and ...#6 on)(See A-1 Comics #16)
Winter, 1946 - No. 4, Fall?, 1947; No. 5, 1948
Magazine Enterprises

1-Mighty Atom 5.85 17.50 35.00
2-5-Mighty Atom 3.60 9.00 18.00
I.W. Reprint #1(1958), 8-(Pee-Wee Pixies), 10-I.W. on cover, Super on inside 1.40 3.50 7.00

PLANET COMICS
1/40 - No. 62, 9/49; No. 63, Wint, 1949-50; No. 64, Spring, 1950; No. 65, 1951(nd); No. 66-68, 1952(nd); No. 69, Wint, 1952-53; No. 70-72, 1953(nd); No. 73, Winter, 1953-54
Fiction House Magazines

	GD25	FN65	VF82	NM94
1-Origin Auro, Lord of Jupiter by Briefer (ends #61); Flint Baker & The Red Comet begin; Eisner/Fine-c	813.00	2438.00	4470.00	6500.00

(Estimated up to 160 total copies exist, 10 in NM/Mint)

	GD25	FN65	NM94
2-Lou Fine-c (Scarce)	314.00	943.00	2200.00
3-Eisner-c	243.00	730.00	1700.00
4-Gale Allen and the Girl Squadron begins	207.00	621.00	1450.00
5,6-(Scarce): 5-Eisner/Fine-c	193.00	580.00	1350.00
7-12: 8-Robot-c. 12-The Star Pirate begins	150.00	450.00	1050.00
13-14: 13-Reff Ryan begins	118.00	354.00	825.00
15-(Scarce)-Mars, God of War begins (11/41); see Jumbo Comics #31 for 1st app.	229.00	685.00	1600.00
16-20,22	112.00	336.00	785.00
21-The Lost World & Hunt Bowman begin	114.00	343.00	800.00
23-26: 26-Space Rangers begin (9/43), end #71	104.00	310.00	725.00
27-30	82.00	246.00	575.00
31-35: 33-Origin Star Pirates Wonder Boots, reprinted in #52. 35-Mysta of the Moon begins, ends #62	69.00	208.00	485.00
36-45: 38-1st Mysta of the Moon-c. 41-New origin of "Auro, Lord of Jupiter". 42-Last Gale Allen. 43-Futura begins	62.00	186.00	435.00
46-60: 48-Robot-c. 53-Used in **SOTI**, pg. 32	51.00	154.00	360.00
61-68,70: 61-Last 68 pg. issue. 64,70-Robot-c. 65-70-All partial-r of earlier issues. 70-r/stories from #41	34.00	103.00	240.00
69-Used in **POP**, pgs. 101,102	34.00	103.00	240.00
71-73-No series stories. 71-Space Rangers strip	27.00	80.00	185.00
I.W. Reprint #1(nd)-r/#70; cover-r from Attack on Planet Mars	5.85	17.50	35.00
I.W. Reprint #8 (r/#72), 9-r/#73	5.85	17.50	35.00

NOTE: ***Anderson*** *a-33-38, 40-51 (Star Pirate).* ***Matt Baker*** *a-53-59 (Mysta of the Moon).* ***Celardo*** *c-12.* ***Bill Discount*** *a-71 (Space Rangers).* ***Elias*** *c-70.* ***Evans*** *a-46-49 (Auro, Lord of Jupiter), 50-64 (Lost World).* ***Fine*** *c-2, 5.* ***Hopper*** *a-31, 35 (Gale Allen), 41, 42, 48, 49 (Mysta of the Moon).* ***Ingels*** *a-24-31 (Lost World), 56-61 (Auro, Lord of Jupiter).* ***Lubbers*** *a-44-47 (Space Rangers); c-40, 41.* ***Moriera*** *a-43, 44 (Mysta of the Moon.* ***Renee*** *a-40-49 (Lost World); c-33, 35, 39.* ***Tuska*** *a-30 (Star Pirate).* ***M. Whitman*** *a-50-52 (Mysta of the Moon), 53-58 (Star Pirate); c-71-73.* ***Starr*** *a-59.* ***Zolnerwich*** *c-10. 13-25. Bondage c-53.*

PLANET COMICS
Apr, 1988 - No. 3? (2.00, color; B&W #3)
Blackthorne Publishing

1-3: New stories. 1-Dave Stevens-c .80 2.00

PLANET OF THE APES (Magazine) (Also see Adventures on the... & Power Record Comics)

Planet of Vampires #1 © Atlas/Seaboard

Plastic Man #11 © DC

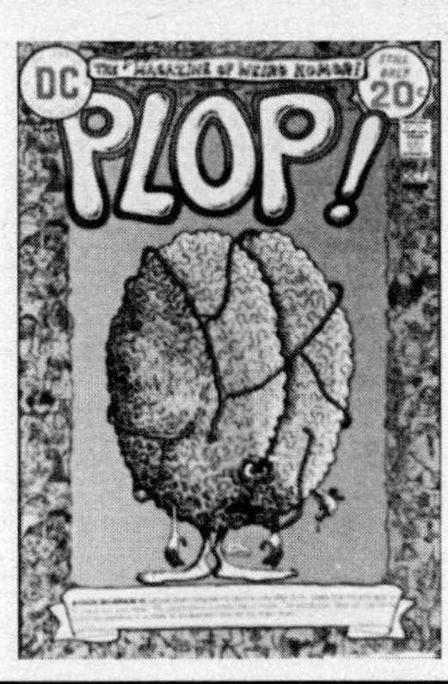

Plop! #7 © DC

Aug, 1974 - No. 29, Feb, 1977 (B&W) (Based on movies)
Marvel Comics Group

	GD25	FN65	NM94
1-Ploog-a	1.00	2.50	5.50
2-Ploog-a		1.10	2.75
3-10		.80	2.00
11-20			1.50
21-29			1.00

NOTE: ***Alcala*** *a-7-11, 17-22, 24.* ***Ploog*** *a-1-4, 6, 8, 11, 13, 14, 19.* ***Sutton*** *a-11, 12, 15, 17, 19, 20, 23, 24, 29.* ***Tuska*** *a-1-6.*

PLANET OF THE APES
Apr, 1990 - No. 24, 1992 ($2.50, B&W)
Adventure Comics

	GD25	FN65	NM94
1-New movie tie-in; comes w/outer-c (3 colors)	1.00	2.50	5.50
1-Limited serial numbered edition ($5.00)	1.00	2.00	5.00
1-2nd printing (no outer-c, $2.50)		1.00	2.50
2-24		1.00	2.50
Annual 1 ($3.50)		1.40	3.50
...Urchak's Folly 1-4 ($2.50, mini-series)		1.00	2.50

PLANET OF VAMPIRES
Feb, 1975 - No. 3, July, 1975
Seaboard Publications (Atlas)

	GD25	FN65	NM94
1-Neal Adams-c(i); 1st Broderick c/a(p)			1.50
2,3: 2-Neal Adams-c. 3-Heath-c/a			1.00

PLANET TERRY (Marvel)(Value: cover or less)

PLASM (See Warriors of Plasm)
June, 1993 (Color)
Defiant Comics

	GD25	FN65	NM94
0-Came bound into Diamond Previews V3#6 (6/93); price is for complete Previews with comic still attached		1.60	4.00
0-Comic only removed from Previews		1.20	3.00

PLASMER
Nov, 1993 - No. 4, Feb, 1994 ($1.95, mini-series)
Marvel Comics UK

	GD25	FN65	NM94
1-($2.50)-Polybagged w/4 trading cards		1.00	2.50
2-4: Capt. America & Silver Surfer app.		.80	2.00

PLASTIC FORKS (Marvel)(Value: cover or less)

PLASTIC MAN (Also see Police Comics & Smash Comics #17)
Sum, 1943 - No. 64, Nov, 1956
Vital Publ. No. 1,2/Quality Comics No. 3 on

	GD25	FN65	NM94
nn(#1)- "In The Game of Death"; Jack Cole-c/a begins; ends-#64?	271.00	815.00	1900.00
nn(#2, 2/44)- "The Gay Nineties Nightmare"	135.00	407.00	950.00
3 (Spr, '46)	86.00	257.00	600.00
4 (Sum, '46)	71.00	215.00	500.00
5 (Aut, '46)	61.00	182.00	425.00
6-10	46.00	140.00	325.00
11-20	43.00	130.00	300.00
21-30: 26-Last non-r issue?	34.00	100.00	235.00
31-40: 40-Used in POP, pg. 91	27.00	80.00	185.00
41-64: 53-Last precode issue. 54-Robot-c	20.00	60.00	140.00
Super Reprint 11,16,18: 11('63)-r/#16. 16-r/#18; Cole-a. 18('64)-Spirit-r by Eisner from Police #95	5.35	16.00	32.00

NOTE: ***Cole*** *r-44, 49, 56, 58, 59 at least.* ***Cuidera*** *c-32-64i.*

PLASTIC MAN (See DC Special #15 & House of Mystery #160)
11-12/66 - No. 10, 5-6/68; V4#11, 2-3/76 - No. 20, 10-11/77
National Periodical Publications/DC Comics

	GD25	FN65	NM94
1-Real 1st app. Silver Age Plastic Man (House of Mystery #160 is actually tryout); Gil Kane-c/a; 12¢ issues begin	6.90	21.00	48.00
2-5: 4-Infantino-c; Mortimer-a	3.30	10.00	23.00
6-10('68): 7-G.A. Plastic Man & Woozy Winks (1st S.A. app.) app.; origin retold. 10-Sparling-a; last 12¢ issue	1.70	5.00	12.00
V4#11('76)-20: 11-20-Fraden-p. 17-Origin retold		1.40	3.50

PLASTIC MAN (DC, 1988-89)(Value: cover or less)

PLASTRON CAFE
Dec, 1992 - 1993 ($2.25, B&W)
Mirage Studios

	GD25	FN65	NM94
1-4: 1-Teenage Mutant Ninja Turtles app.; Kelly Freas-c. 2-Hildebrandt painted-c. 4-Spaced & Alien Fire stories		.90	2.25

PLAYFUL LITTLE AUDREY (TV)(Also see Little Audrey #25)
6/57 - No. 110, 11/73; No. 111, 8/74 - No. 121, 4/76
Harvey Publications

	GD25	FN65	NM94
1	17.00	52.00	120.00
2	10.00	30.00	60.00
3-5	7.50	22.50	45.00
6-10	5.00	15.00	30.00
11-20	3.20	8.00	16.00
21-40	2.40	6.00	12.00
41-60	1.80	4.50	9.00
61-80	1.20	2.90	7.00
81-99		1.60	4.00
100: 52 pg. Giant	1.20	3.00	7.00
101-103: 52 pg. Giants	1.00	2.50	6.00
104-121		1.20	3.00
...In 3-D (Spring, 1988, $2.25, Blackthorne #66)		.90	2.25

PLOP! (Also see The Best of DC #60)
Sept-Oct, 1973 - No. 24, Nov-Dec, 1976
National Periodical Publications

	GD25	FN65	NM94
1-20: Sergio Aragones-a. 1,5-Wrightson-a	1.00	2.00	5.00
21,22,24 (52 pgs.)		1.80	4.50
23-No Aragones-a (52 pgs.)		.70	1.80

NOTE: ***Alcala*** *a-1-3.* ***Anderson*** *a-5.* ***Aragones*** *a-1-22, 24.* ***Ditko*** *a-16p.* ***Evans*** *a-1.* ***Mayer*** *a-1.* ***Orlando*** *a-21, 22; c-21.* ***Sekowsky*** *a-5, 6p.* ***Toth*** *a-11.* ***Wolverton*** *r-4, 22-24(1 pg.ea.); c-1-12, 14, 17, 18.* ***Wood*** *a-14, 16i, 18-24; c-13, 15, 16, 19.*

PLUTO (See Cheerios Premiums, Four Color #537, Mickey Mouse Magazine, Walt Disney Showcase #4, 7, 13, 20, 23, 33 & Wheaties)
No. 7, 1942; No. 429, 10/52 - No. 1248, 11-1/61-62 (Walt Disney)
Dell Publishing Co.

	GD25	FN65	NM94
Large Feature Comic 7(1942)-Written by Carl Barks, Jack Hannah, & Nick George (Barks' 1st comic book work)	90.00	270.00	900.00
4-Color 429 (#1)	10.00	30.00	60.00
4-Color 509	6.70	20.00	40.00
4-Color 595,654,736,853	4.00	12.00	30.00
4-Color 941,1039,1143,1248	4.00	10.00	20.00

POCAHONTAS
1941 - No. 2, 1942
Pocahontas Fuel Company (Coal)

	GD25	FN65	NM94
nn(#1), 2	10.00	30.00	65.00

POCKET COMICS (Becomes Super Duper #5?; also see Double Up)
Aug, 1941 - No. 4, Jan, 1942 (Pocket size; 100 pgs.)
Harvey Publications (1st Harvey comic)

	GD25	FN65	NM94
1-Origin & 1st app. The Black Cat, Cadet Blakey the Spirit of '76, The Red Blazer, The Phantom, Sphinx, & The Zebra; Phantom Ranger, British Agent #99, Spin Hawkins, Satan, Lord of Evil begin (1st app. of each); Simon-c/a in #1-3	66.00	200.00	465.00
2-Black Cat on-c #2-4	43.00	130.00	300.00
3,4	34.00	100.00	235.00

POGO PARADE (See Dell Giants)

POGO POSSUM (Also see Animal Comics & Special Delivery)
No. 105, 4/46 - No. 148, 5/47; 10-12/49 - No. 16, 4-6/54
Dell Publishing Co.

	GD25	FN65	NM94
4-Color 105(1946)-Kelly-c/a	75.00	220.00	515.00
4-Color 148-Kelly-c/a	68.00	205.00	475.00
1-(10-12/49)-Kelly-c/a in all	57.00	171.00	400.00
2	43.00	130.00	300.00

Police Academy #3 © Warner Bros.

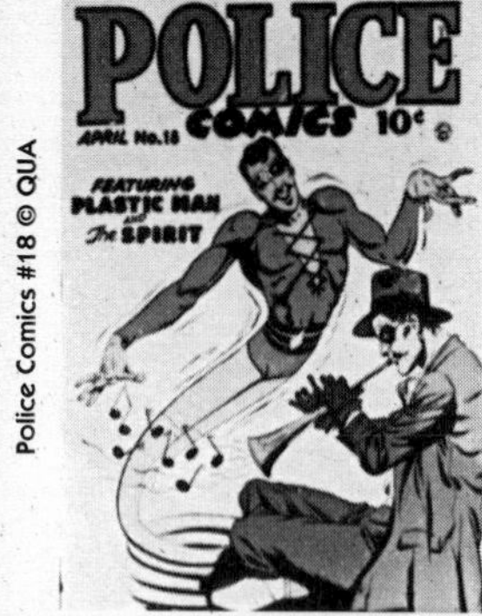

Police Comics #18 © QUA

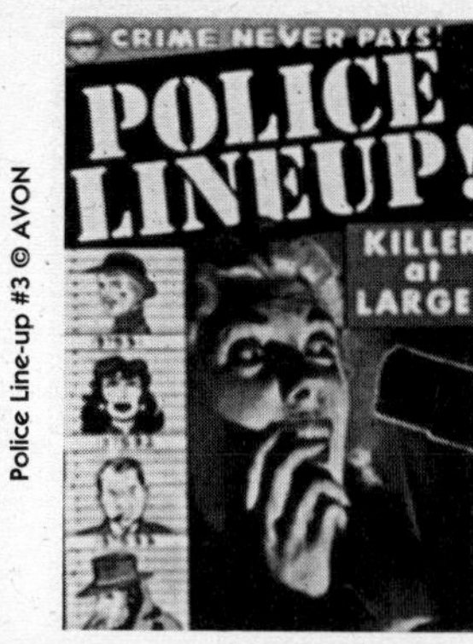

Police Line-up #3 © AVON

	GD25	FN65	NM94
3-5	29.00	86.00	200.00
6-10: 10-Infinity-c	24.00	73.00	170.00
11-16: 11-X-Mas-c	19.00	58.00	135.00

NOTE: *#1-4, 9-13: 52 pgs.; #5-8, 14-16: 36 pgs.*

POINT BLANK (Eclipse)(Value: cover or less)

POLICE ACADEMY (TV)(Marvel)(Value: cover or less)

POLICE ACTION
Jan, 1954 - No. 7, Nov, 1954
Atlas News Co.

	GD25	FN65	NM94
1-Violent-a by Robert Q. Sale	11.50	34.00	80.00
2	6.70	20.00	40.00
3-7: 7-Powell-a	5.85	17.50	35.00

NOTE: ***Ayers** a-4, 5. **Colan** a-1. **Forte** a-1, 2. **Mort Lawrence** a-5. **Maneely** a-3; c-1, 5. **Reinman** a-6, 7.*

POLICE ACTION
Feb, 1975 - No. 3, June, 1975
Atlas/Seaboard Publ.

1-3: 1-Lomax, N.Y.P.D., Luke Malone begin; McWilliams-a. 2-Origin Luke Malone, Manhunter 1.00

NOTE: ***Ploog** art in all. **Sekowsky/McWilliams** a-1-3. **Thorne** c-3.*

POLICE AGAINST CRIME
April, 1954 - No. 9, Aug, 1955
Premiere Magazines

	GD25	FN65	NM94
1-Disbrow-a; extreme violence (man's face slashed with knife); Hollingsworth-a	13.00	40.00	90.00
2-Hollingsworth-a	8.35	25.00	50.00
3-9	6.70	20.00	40.00

POLICE BADGE #479 (Formerly Spy Thrillers #1-4)
No. 5, Sept, 1955
Atlas Comics (PrPI)

	GD25	FN65	NM94
5-Maneely-c/a (6 pgs.)	6.70	20.00	40.00

POLICE CASE BOOK (See Giant Comics Editions)

POLICE CASES (See Authentic... & Record Book of...)

POLICE COMICS
Aug, 1941 - No. 127, Oct, 1953
Quality Comics Group (Comic Magazines)

	GD25	FN65	NM94
1-Origin/1st app. Plastic Man by Jack Cole (r-in DC Special #15), The Human Bomb by Gustavson, & No. 711; intro. Chic Carter by Eisner, The Firebrand by Reed Crandall, The Mouthpiece by Guardineer, Phantom Lady, & The Sword; Firebrand-c 1-4	486.00	1457.00	3400.00
2-Plastic Man smuggles opium	229.00	685.00	1600.00
3	157.00	471.00	1100.00
4	150.00	450.00	1050.00
5-Plastic Man-c begin; Plastic Man forced to smoke marijuana; Plastic Man covers begin, end #102	136.00	407.00	950.00
6,7	129.00	386.00	900.00
8-Manhunter begins (origin/1st app.) (3/42)	157.00	471.00	1100.00
9,10	114.00	343.00	800.00
11-The Spirit strip reprints begin by Eisner (origin-strip #1); 1st comic book app. The Spirit & 1st cover app. (9/42)	179.00	535.00	1250.00
12-Intro. Ebony	114.00	343.00	800.00
13-Intro. Woozy Winks; last Firebrand	114.00	343.00	800.00
14-19: 15-Last No. 711; Destiny begins	75.00	225.00	525.00
20-The Raven x-over in Phantom Lady; features Jack Cole himself	75.00	225.00	525.00
21,22: 21-Raven & Spider Widow x-over in Phantom Lady (cameo in #22)	64.00	193.00	450.00
23-30: 23-Last Phantom Lady. 24-26-Flatfoot Burns by Kurtzman in all	57.00	171.00	400.00
31-41: 37-1st app. Candy by Sahle & begins (12/44). 41-Last Spirit-r by Eisner	40.00	120.00	280.00
42,43-Spirit-r by Eisner/Fine	33.00	100.00	230.00
44-Fine Spirit-r begin, end #88,90,92	29.00	86.00	200.00
45-50: 50-(#50 on-c, #49 on inside, 1/46)	29.00	86.00	200.00
51-60: 58-Last Human Bomb	24.00	72.00	165.00
61-88: 63-(Some issues have #65 printed on cover, but #63 on inside) Kurtzman-a, 6 pgs.	18.00	54.00	125.00
89,91,93-No Spirit stories	16.50	50.00	115.00
90,92-Spirit by Fine	19.00	58.00	135.00
94-99,101,102: Spirit by Eisner in all; 101-Last Manhunter. 102-Last Spirit & Plastic Man by Jack Cole	24.00	72.00	165.00
100	29.00	86.00	200.00
103-Content change to crime; Ken Shannon & T-Man begin (1st app. of each, 12/50)	15.00	45.00	105.00
104-111,114-127: Crandall-a most issues (not in 104,105,122,125-127). 109-Atomic bomb story	11.50	34.00	80.00
112-Crandall-a	11.50	34.00	80.00
113-Crandall-c/a(2), 9 pgs. each	12.00	36.00	85.00

NOTE: *Most Spirit stories signed by Eisner are not by him; all are reprints. **Cole** c-17, 19-21, 24-26, 28-31, 36-38, 40-42, 45-48, 65-68, 69, 73, 75. **Crandall** Firebrand-1-8. Spirit by **Eisner** 1-41, 94-102; by **Eisner/Fine**-42, 43; by **Fine**-44-88, 90, 92. 103, 109. **Al Bryant** c-33, 34. **Cole** c-17-32, 35-102(most). **Crandall** c-13, 14. **Crandall/Cuidera** c-105-127. **Eisner** c-4i. **Gill Fox** c-1-3, 4p, 5-12, 15. Bondage c-103, 109, 125.*

POLICE LINE-UP
Aug, 1951 - No. 4, July, 1952 (Painted-c #1-3)
Avon Periodicals/Realistic Comics #3,4

	GD25	FN65	NM94
1-Wood-a, 1 pg. plus part-c; spanking panel-r/Saint #5	24.00	72.00	165.00
2-Classic story "The Religious Murder Cult", drugs, perversion; r/Saint #5; c-r/Avon paperback #329	18.00	54.00	125.00
3-Kubert-a(r?)/part-c; Kinstler-a (inside-c only)	12.00	36.00	85.00
4	12.00	36.00	85.00

POLICE THRILLS
1954
Ajax/Farrell Publications

	GD25	FN65	NM94
1-Exist?	6.70	20.00	40.00

POLICE TRAP (Public Defender In Action #7 on)
8-9/54 - No. 4, 2-3/55; No. 5, 7/55 - No. 6, 9/55
Mainline No. 1-4/Charlton No. 5,6

	GD25	FN65	NM94
1-S&K covers-all issues; Meskin-a; Kirby scripts	14.00	43.00	100.00
2-4	10.00	30.00	60.00
5,6-S&K-c/a	13.00	40.00	90.00

POLICE TRAP
No. 11, 1963; No. 16-18, 1964
Super Comics

	GD25	FN65	NM94
Reprint #11,16-18: 11-r/Police Trap #3. 16-r/Justice Traps the Guilty #? 17-r/Inside Crime #3	1.40	3.50	7.00

POLL PARROT
Poll Parrot Shoe Store/International Shoe
1950 - No. 4, 1951; No. 2, 1959 - No. 16, 1962
K. K. Publications (Giveaway)

	GD25	FN65	NM94
1 ('50)-Howdy Doody; small size	11.50	34.00	80.00
2-4('51)-Howdy Doody	10.00	30.00	60.00
2('59)-16('62): 2-The Secret of Crumbley Castle. 5-Bandit Busters. 7-The Make-Believe Mummy. 8-Mixed Up Mission('60). 10-The Frightful Flight. 11-Showdown at Sunup. 12-Maniac at Mubu Island. 13-...and the Runaway Genie. 14-Bully for You. 15-Trapped In Tall Timber. 16-...& the Rajah's Ruby('62)	3.00	7.50	15.00

POLLY & HER PALS (See Comic Monthly #1)

POLLYANNA (See 4-Color #1129)

POLLY PIGTAILS (Girls' Fun & Fashion Magazine #44 on)
Jan, 1946 - V4#43, Oct-Nov, 1949
Parents' Magazine Institute/Polly Pigtails

	GD25	FN65	NM94
1-Infinity-c; photo-c	9.15	27.50	55.00

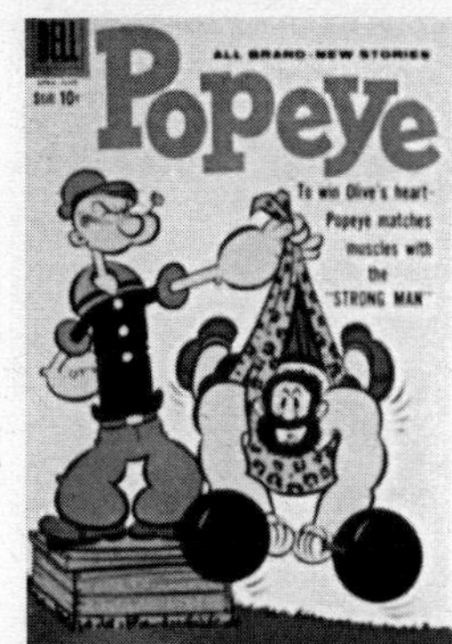

Popeye #48 (Dell) © KING

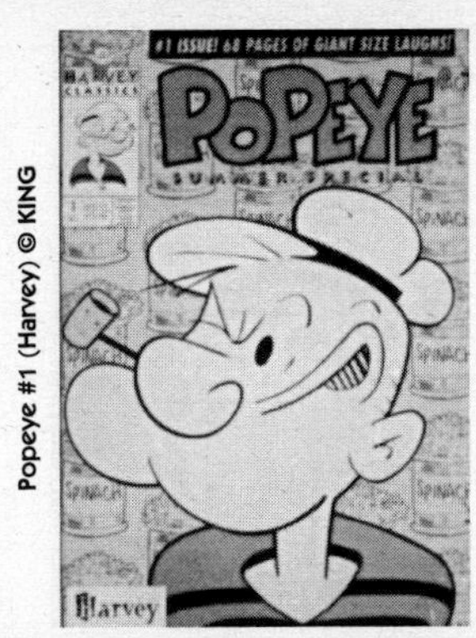

Popeye #1 (Harvey) © KING

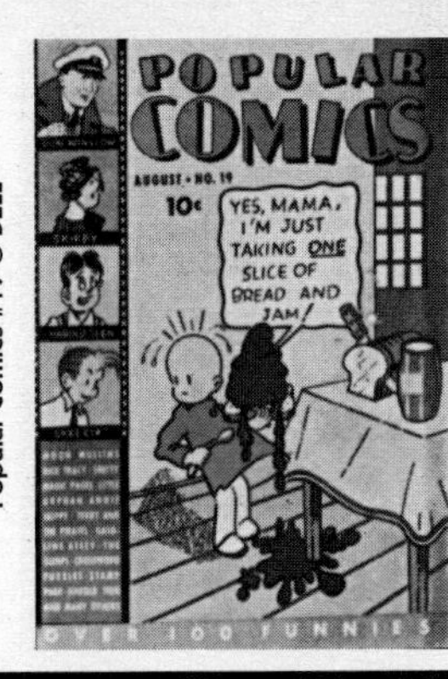

Popular Comics #19 © DELL

	GD25	FN65	NM94
2-Photo-c	4.70	14.00	28.00
3-5: 3,4-Photo-c	4.00	10.00	20.00
6-10: 7-Photo-c	3.20	8.00	16.00
11-30: 22-Photo-c	2.40	6.00	12.00
31-43	2.00	5.00	10.00

PONY EXPRESS (See Four Color #942)

PONYTAIL
7-9/62 - No. 12, 10-12/65; No. 13, 11/69 - No. 20, 1/71
Dell Publishing Co./Charlton No. 13 on

	GD25	FN65	NM94
12-641-209(#1)	2.00	5.00	10.00
2-12	1.20	3.00	6.00
13-20	.80	2.00	4.00

POP COMICS
1955 (36 pgs.; 5x7"; in color) (7¢)
Modern Store Publ.

	GD25	FN65	NM94
1-Funny animal	.80	2.00	4.00

POPEYE (See Comic Album #7, 11, 15, Comics Reading Libraries, Eat Right to Work and Win, Giant Comic Album, King Comics, Kite Fun Book, Magic Comics, March of Comics #37, 52, 66, 80, 96, 117, 134, 148, 157, 169, 194, 246, 264, 274, 294, 453, 465, 477 & Wow Comics, 1st series)

POPEYE (See Thimble Theatre)
1935 (25¢; 52 pgs.; B&W) (By Segar)
David McKay Publications

	GD25	FN65	NM94
1-Daily strip serial reprints- "The Gold Mine Thieves"	50.00	150.00	500.00
2-Daily strip-r	40.00	120.00	400.00

NOTE: *Popeye first entered Thimble Theatre in 1929.*

POPEYE
1937 - 1939 (All by Segar)
David McKay Publications

	GD25	FN65	NM94
Feature Books nn (100 pgs.) (Very Rare)	500.00	1500.00	5000.00
Feature Books 2 (52 pgs.)	55.00	165.00	550.00
Feature Books 3 (100 pgs.)-r/nn issue with a new-c	50.00	150.00	500.00
Feature Books 5,10 (76 pgs.)	45.00	135.00	450.00
Feature Books 14 (76 pgs.) (Scarce)	55.00	165.00	550.00

POPEYE (Strip reprints through 4-Color #70)
1941 - 1947; #1, 2-4/48 - #65, 7-9/62; #66, 10/62 - #80, 5/66; #81, 8/66 - #92, 12/67; #94, 2/69 - #138, 1/77; #139, 5/78 - #171, 7/84 (no #93,160,161)
Dell #1-65/Gold Key #66-80/King #81-92/Charlton #94-138/Gold Key #139-155/ Whitman #156 on

	GD25	FN65	NM94
Large Feature Comic 24('41)-Half by Segar	40.00	120.00	400.00
4-Color 25('41)-by Segar	71.00	215.00	500.00
Large Feature Comic 10('43)	35.00	105.00	350.00
4-Color 17('43),26('43)-by Segar	57.00	171.00	400.00
4-Color 43('44)	33.00	100.00	230.00
4-Color 70('45)-Title: ...& Wimpy	27.00	81.00	190.00
4-Color 113('46-original strips begin),127,145('47),168	14.00	43.00	100.00
1(2-4/48)(Dell)-All new stories continue	33.00	100.00	230.00
2	17.00	52.00	120.00
3-10: 5-Popeye on moon w/rocket-c	14.00	43.00	100.00
11-20	12.00	36.00	85.00
21-40	10.00	30.00	65.00
41-45,47-50	7.00	21.00	42.00
46-Origin Swee' Pee	10.00	30.00	60.00
51-60	6.35	19.00	38.00
61-65 (Last Dell issue)	5.00	15.00	30.00
66,67-Both 84 pgs. (Gold Key)	8.00	24.00	48.00
68-80	4.00	10.00	20.00
81-92,94-100	2.00	6.00	14.00
101-130	1.60	3.80	9.00
131-159,162-171: 144-50th Anniversary issue	1.00	2.50	6.00
Bold Detergent giveaway (Same as regular issue #94)		1.60	4.00

NOTE: *Reprints-#145, 147, 149, 151, 153, 155, 157, 163-68(1/3), 170.*

POPEYE
1972 - 1974 (36 pgs. in color)
Charlton (King Features) (Giveaway)

	GD25	FN65	NM94
E-1 to E-15 (Educational comics)		.80	2.00
nn-Popeye Gettin' Better Grades-4 pgs. used as intro. to above giveaways (in color)		.80	2.00

POPEYE
Nov, 1993 - No. 7, Aug, 1994 ($1.50)
Harvey Comics

	GD25	FN65	NM94
V2#1-7			1.50
...Summer Special V2#1-(10/93, $2.25, 68 pgs.)-Sagendorf-r & others		.90	2.25

POPEYE CARTOON BOOK
1934 (40 pgs. with cover)(8-1/2x13")(cardboard covers)
The Saalfield Publ. Co.

	GD25	FN65	NM94
2095-(Rare)-1933 strip reprints in color by Segar; each page contains a vertical half of a Sunday strip, so the continuity reads row by row completely across each double page spread. If each page is read by itself, the continuity makes no sense. Each double page spread reprints one complete Sunday page (from 1933)	100.00	300.00	1000.00
12 Page Version	50.00	150.00	500.00

POPEYE SPECIAL (Ocean)(Value: cover or less)

POPPLES (TV, movie)(Marvel)(Value: cover or less)

POPPO OF THE POPCORN THEATRE
10/29/55 - No. 13, 1956 (Published weekly)
Fuller Publishing Co. (Publishers Weekly)

	GD25	FN65	NM94
1	6.70	20.00	40.00
2-5	4.00	12.00	24.00
6-13	3.60	9.00	18.00

NOTE: *By **Charles Biro.** 10¢ cover, given away by supermarkets such as IGA.*

POP-POP COMICS
No date (Circa 1945) (52 pgs.)
R. B. Leffingwell Co.

	GD25	FN65	NM94
1-Funny animal	7.50	22.50	45.00

POPSICLE PETE FUN BOOK (See All-American Comics #6)
1947, 1948
Joe Lowe Corp.

	GD25	FN65	NM94
nn-36 pgs. in color; Sammy 'n' Claras, The King Who Couldn't Sleep & Popsicle Pete stories, games, cut-outs	9.15	27.50	55.00
Adventure Book ('48)-Has Classics ad with checklist to HRN #343 (Great Expectations #43)	7.50	22.50	45.00

POPULAR COMICS
Feb, 1936 - No. 145, July-Sept, 1948
Dell Publishing Co.

	GD25	FN65	VF82
1-Dick Tracy (1st comic book app.), Little Orphan Annie, Terry & the Pirates, Gasoline Alley, Don Winslow (1st app.), Harold Teen, Little Joe, Skippy, Moon Mullins, Mutt & Jeff, Tailspin Tommy, Smitty, Smokey Stover, Winnie Winkle & The Gumps begin (all strip-r)	400.00	1200.00	2400.00
(Estimated up to 90 total copies exist, 4 in NM/Mint)			
2	142.00	425.00	850.00
3	108.00	325.00	650.00
4,5: 5-Tom Mix begins	85.00	255.00	510.00
6-10: 8,9-Scribbly, Reglar Fellers app.	67.00	200.00	400.00
	GD25	**FN65**	**NM94**
11-20: 12-X-Mas-c	50.00	150.00	350.00
21-27: 27-Last Terry & the Pirates, Little Orphan Annie, & Dick Tracy	36.00	107.00	250.00
28-37: 28-Gene Autry app. 31,32-Tim McCoy app. 35-Christmas-c; Tex Ritter app.	31.00	92.00	215.00
38-43-Tarzan in text only. 38-(4/39)-Gang Busters (radio, 2nd app.) & Zane Grey's Tex Thorne begins? 43-1st non-funny-c?	34.00	103.00	240.00

Popular Romance #20 © BP/STD

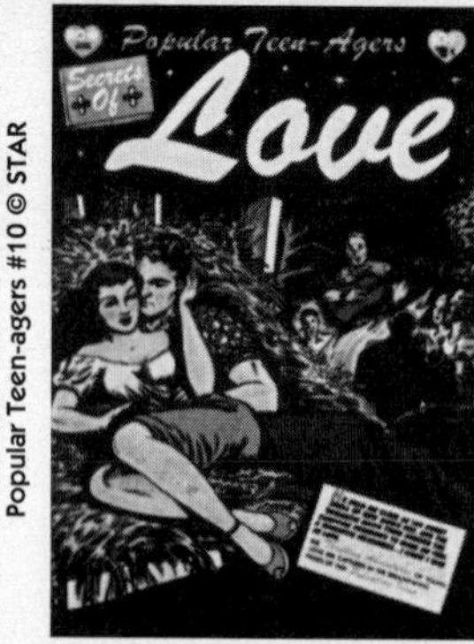

Popular Teen-agers #10 © STAR

Power & Glory #1A © Howard Chaykin

	GD25	FN65	NM94
44,45: 45-Hurricane Kid-c	24.00	72.00	165.00
46-Origin/1st app. Martan, the Marvel Man(12/39)	34.00	103.00	240.00
47-50	22.00	67.00	155.00
51-Origin The Voice (The Invisible Detective) strip begins (5/40)	24.00	73.00	170.00
52-59: 55-End of World story	18.00	54.00	125.00
60-Origin/1st app. Professor Supermind and Son (2/41)	19.00	57.00	130.00
61-71: 63-Smilin' Jack begins	15.00	45.00	105.00
72-The Owl & Terry & the Pirates begin (2/42); Smokey Stover reprints begin	29.00	86.00	200.00
73-75	19.00	57.00	130.00
76-78-Capt. Midnight in all	25.00	75.00	175.00
79-85-Last Owl	16.50	50.00	115.00
86-99: 98-Felix the Cat, Smokey Stover-r begin	13.00	40.00	90.00
100	14.00	43.00	100.00
101-130	9.15	27.50	55.00
131-145: 142-Last Terry & the Pirates	8.35	25.00	50.00

NOTE: *Martan, the Marvel Man c-47-49, 52, 57-59. Professor Supermind c-60-63, 64(1/2), 65, 66. The Voice c-53.*

POPULAR FAIRY TALES (See March of Comics #6, 18)

POPULAR ROMANCE
No. 5, Dec, 1949 - No. 29, July, 1954
Better-Standard Publications

	GD25	FN65	NM94
5	5.85	17.50	35.00
6-9: 7-Palais-a; lingerie panels	4.00	11.00	22.00
10-Wood-a (2 pgs.)	5.85	17.50	35.00
11,12,14-16,18-21,28,29	3.60	9.00	18.00
13,17-Severin/Elder-a (3&8 pgs.)	4.00	11.00	22.00
22-27-Toth-a	7.50	22.50	45.00

NOTE: *All have photo-c.* ***Tuska*** *art in most issues.*

POPULAR TEEN-AGERS (Secrets of Love) (School Day Romances #1-4)
No. 5, Sept, 1950 - No. 23, Nov, 1954
Star Publications

	GD25	FN65	NM94
5-Toni Gay, Midge Martin & Eve Adams continue from School Day Romances; Ginger Bunn (formerly Ginger Snapp & becomes Honey Bunn #6 on) begins; all features end #8	16.00	48.00	110.00
6-8 (7/51)-Honey Bunn begins; all have L. B. Cole-c; 6-Negligee panels	13.00	40.00	90.00
9-(...Romances; 1st romance issue, 10/51)	7.50	22.50	45.00
10-(...Secrets of Love thru #23)	7.50	22.50	45.00
11,16,18,19,22,23	5.85	17.50	35.00
12,13,17,20,21-Disbrow-a	6.70	20.00	40.00
14-Harrison/Wood-a; 2 spanking scenes	12.00	36.00	85.00
15-Wood?, Disbrow-a	10.00	30.00	65.00
Accepted Reprint 5,6 (nd); L.B. Cole-c	4.00	10.00	20.00

NOTE: *All have* ***L. B. Cole*** *covers.*

PORE LI'L MOSE
1902 (30 pgs.; 10-1/2x15"; in full color)
New York Herald Publ. by Grand Union Tea
Cupples & Leon Co.

	GD25	FN65	NM94
nn-By R. F. Outcault; 1 pg. strips about early Negroes	71.00	215.00	500.00

PORKY PIG (See Bugs Bunny &..., Kite Fun Book, Looney Tunes, March of Comics #42, 57, 71, 89, 99, 113, 130, 143, 164, 175, 192, 209, 218, 367, and Super Book #6, 18, 30)

PORKY PIG (...& Bugs Bunny #40-69)
No. 16, 1942 - No. 81, Mar-Apr, 1962; Jan, 1965 - No. 109, July, 1984
Dell Publishing Co./Gold Key No. 1-93/Whitman No. 94 on

	GD25	FN65	NM94
4-Color 16(#1, 1942)	71.00	215.00	500.00
4-Color 48(1944)-Carl Barks-a	100.00	300.00	700.00
4-Color 78(1945)	24.00	72.00	165.00
4-Color 112(7/46)	14.00	43.00	100.00
4-Color 156,182,191('49)	10.00	30.00	70.00
4-Color 226,241('49),260,271,277,284,295	8.35	25.00	50.00
4-Color 303,311,322,330: 322-Sci/fi-c/story	5.85	17.50	35.00
4-Color 342,351,360,370,385,399,410,426	4.00	12.00	24.00
25 (11-12/52)-30	3.20	8.00	16.00
31-50	1.80	4.50	9.00
51-81(3-4/62)	1.20	3.00	6.00
1(1/65-Gold Key)(2nd Series)	2.00	5.00	10.00
2,4,5-r/4-Color 226,284 & 271 in that order	1.00	2.00	5.00
3,6-10		1.20	3.00
11-50			1.50
51-109			1.00

NOTE: *Reprints-#1-8, 9-35(2/3); 36-46, 58, 67, 69-74, 76, 78, 102-109(1/3-1/2).*

PORKY'S BOOK OF TRICKS
1942 (48 pgs.) (8-1/2x5-1/2")
K. K. Publications (Giveaway)

	GD25	FN65	NM94
nn-7 pg. comic story, text stories, plus games & puzzles (scarce)	39.00	116.00	270.00

PORTIA PRINZ OF THE GLAMAZONS (Eclipse)(Value: cover or less)

POST GAZETTE (See Meet the New...)

POWDER RIVER RUSTLERS (See Fawcett Movie Comics)

POWER & GLORY
Feb, 1994 - No. 4, May, 1994 ($2.50, mini-series, mature)
Malibu comics (Bravura imprint)

	GD25	FN65	NM94
1A, 1B-By Howard Chaykin; w/Bravura stamp		1.00	2.50
1-($2.95)-Newsstand ed. polybagged w/children's warning on bag; Howard Chaykin-c/a begin		1.20	3.00
2-4-Contains Bravura stamp		1.00	2.50

POWER COMICS
1944 - No. 4, 1945
Holyoke Publ. Co./Narrative Publ.

	GD25	FN65	NM94
1-L. B. Cole-c	71.00	215.00	500.00
2-Hitler, Hirohito-c (scarce)	71.00	215.00	500.00
3-Classic L.B. Cole-c; Dr. Mephisto begins?	71.00	215.00	500.00
4-L.B. Cole-c; Miss Espionage app. #3,4; Leav-a	57.00	171.00	400.00

POWER COMICS
1977 - No. 5, Dec, 1977 (B&W)
Power Comics Co.

	GD25	FN65	NM94
1- "A Boy And His Aardvark" by Dave Sim; first Dave Sim aardvark (not Cerebus)	1.20	3.00	7.50
1-Reprint (3/77, black-c)		1.60	4.00
2-Cobalt Blue by Gustovich		.80	2.00
3-5: 3-Nightwitch. 4-Northern Light. 5-Bluebird		.80	2.00

POWER COMICS (Eclipse)(Value: cover or less)

POWER FACTOR (Wonder & Innovation)(Value: cover or less)

POWER GIRL (DC)(Value: cover or less)(See All-Star 58, Infinity, Inc., Showcase #97-99)

POWERHOUSE PEPPER COMICS (See Gay Comics, Joker Comics & Tessie the Typist)
No. 1, 1943; No. 2, May, 1948 - No. 5, Nov, 1948
Marvel Comics (20CC)

	GD25	FN65	NM94
1-(60 pgs.)-Wolverton-a in all; c-2,3	114.00	345.00	800.00
2	64.00	195.00	450.00
3,4	57.00	171.00	400.00
5-(Scarce)	71.00	215.00	500.00

POWER LINE (Marvel)(Value: cover or less)

POWER LORDS (DC)(Value: cover or less)

POWER MAN (Formerly Hero for Hire; ...& Iron Fist #68 on; see Cage & Giant-Size...)
No. 17, Feb, 1974 - No. 125, Sept, 1986
Marvel Comics Group

	GD25	FN65	NM94
17-Luke Cage continues; Iron Man app.	1.40	4.30	10.00
18-20: 18-Last 20¢ issue	.80	2.10	5.00

Power Pack #62 © MEG

Predator: Big Game #4 © 20th Century Fox

Predator: Invaders From The Fourth Dimension #1 © 20th Century Fox

GD25 FN65 NM94

21-31: 31-Part Neal Adams-i 1.20 3.00
32-47: 34-Last 25¢ issue. 36-r/Hero For Hire #12. 41-1st app. Thunderbolt. 45-Starlin-c. .90 2.25
48-50-Byrne-a(p); 48-Power Man/Iron Fist 1st meet. 50-Iron Fist joins Cage .90 2.25
51-56,58-60: 58-Intro El Aguila 1.25
57-New X-Men app. (6/79) 1.50 3.75
61-65,67-77,79-83,85-124: 75-Double size. 77-Daredevil app. 87-Moon Knight app. 90-Unus app. 109-The Reaper app. 100-Double size; origin K'un L'un 1.00
66-2nd app. Sabretooth (see Iron Fist #14) 3.20 8.00 20.00
78-3rd app. Sabretooth (cameo under cloak) 1.50 3.75 9.00
84-4th app. Sabretooth 1.50 3.75 9.00
125-Double size; death of Iron Fist .80 2.00
Annual 1(1976)-Punisher cameo in flashback 1.20 3.00

NOTE: ***Austin*** *c-102i.* ***Byrne*** *a-48-50; c-102, 104, 106, 107, 112-116.* ***Kane*** *c(p)-24, 25, 28, 48.* ***Miller*** *a-68, 76(2 pgs.); c-66-68, 70-74, 80i.* ***Mooney*** *a-38i, 53i, 55i.* ***Nebres*** *a-76p.* ***Nino*** *a-42i, 43i.* ***Perez*** *a-27.* ***B. Smith*** *a-47i.* ***Tuska*** *a(p)-17, 20, 24, 26, 28, 29, 36, 47. Painted c-75, 100.*

POWER OF STRONGMAN, THE (AC)(Value: cover or less)

POWER OF THE ATOM (DC)(Value: cover or less)(See Secret Origins #29)

POWER PACHYDERMS (Marvel)(Value: cover or less)

POWER PACK
Aug, 1984 - No. 62, Feb, 1991
Marvel Comics Group

1-($1.00, 52 pgs.)-Origin & 1st app. Power Pack .80 2.00
2-18,20-26,28,30-45,47-62 1.00
19-(52 pgs.)-Cloak & Dagger, Wolverine app. 1.00 2.50 6.00
27-Mutant massacre; Wolverine & Sabretooth app. 1.10 2.70 6.50
29-Spider-Man & Hobgoblin app. .80 2.00
46-Punisher app. 1.20 3.00
...Holiday Special 1 (2/92, $2.25, 68 pgs.) 1.00

NOTE: ***Austin*** *scripts-53.* ***Morrow*** *a-51.* ***Spiegle*** *a-55i.* ***Williamson*** *a(i)-43, 50, 52.*

POWER RECORD COMICS
1974 - 1978 ($1.49, 7x10" comics, 20 pgs. with 45 R.P.M. record)
Marvel Comics/Power Records

PR10-Spider-Man-r/from #124,125; Man-Wolf app. PR11-Hulk-r. PR12-Captain America-r/#168. PR13-Fantastic Four-r/#126. PR14-Frankenstein-Ploog-r/#1. PR15-Tomb of Dracula-Colan-r/#2. PR16-Man-Thing-Ploog-r/#5. PR17-Werewolf By Night-Ploog-r/Marvel Spotlight #2. PR18-Planet of the Apes-r. PR19-Escape From the Planet of the Apes-r. PR20-Beneath the Planet of the Apes-r. PR21-Battle for the Planet of the Apes-r. PR24-Spider-Man II-New-a begins. PR25-Star Trek "Passage to Moauv". PR26-Star Trek "Crier in Emptiness." PR27-Batman "Stacked Cards"; N. Adams-a(p). PR28-Superman "Alien Creatures". PR29-Space: 1999 "Breakaway". PR30-Batman; N. Adams-r/Det.(7 pgs.). PR31-Conan-N. Adams-a; reprinted in Conan #116. PR32-Space: 1999 "Return to the Beginning". PR33-Superman-G.A. origin, Buckler-a(p). PR34-Superman. PR35-Wonder Woman-Buckler-a(p). PR36-Holo-Man. PR37-Robin Hood. PR39-Huckleberry Finn. PR40-Davy Crockett. PR41-Robinson Crusoe. PR42-20,000 Leagues Under the Sea. PR46-Star Trek "The Robot Masters". PR47-Little Women
With record; each... 1.60 4.70 11.00

POW MAGAZINE (Bob Sproul's) (Satire Magazine)
Aug, 1966 - No. 3, Feb, 1967 (30¢)
Humor-Vision

1-3: 2-Jones-a. 3-Wrightson-a 4.00 10.00 20.00

PRAIRIE MOON AND OTHER STORIES (Dark Horse)(Value: cover or less)

PREDATOR (Also see Aliens Vs. ..., Batman vs. ..., Dark Horse Comics, & Dark Horse Presents)
June, 1989 - No. 4, Mar, 1990 ($2.25, mini-series)
Dark Horse Comics

1-Based on movie; 1st app. Predator 3.30 9.90 23.00
1-2nd printing 1.80 4.50
2 1.40 4.00 10.00
3 1.30 3.10 7.50
4 1.80 4.50
Trade paperback (1990, $12.95)-r/#1-4 1.85 5.50 13.00

PREDATOR: BAD BLOOD
Dec, 1993 - No. 4, 1994 ($2.50, mini-series)
Dark Horse Comics

1-4 1.00 2.50

PREDATOR: BIG GAME
Mar, 1991 - No. 4, June, 1991 ($2.50, mini-series)
Dark Horse Comics

1: 1-3-Contain 2 Dark Horse trading cards 1.20 3.00
2-4 1.10 2.75

PREDATOR BLOODY SANDS OF TIME
Feb, 1992 - No. 2, Feb, 1992 ($2.50, mini-series)
Dark Horse Comics

1,2-Dan Barry-c/a(p)/scripts 1.00 2.50

PREDATOR COLD WAR
Sept, 1991 - No. 4, Dec, 1991 ($2.50, mini-series)
Dark Horse Comics

1-4: All have painted-c 1.00 2.50

PREDATOR: INVADERS FROM THE FOURTH DIMENSION
July, 1994 ($3.95, 52 pgs.)
Dark Horse Comics

1 1.60 4.00

PREDATOR: RACE WAR (See Dark Horse Presents #67)
Feb, 1993 - No. 4, Oct, 1993 ($2.50, color, mini-series)
Dark Horse Comics

1-4-Dorman painted-c #1-4 1.00 2.50
0-(4/93) 1.00 2.50

PREDATOR 2
Feb, 1991 - No. 2, June, 1991 ($2.50, color, mini-series)
Dark Horse Comics

1-Adapts movie; 2 trading cards inside; photo-c 1.00 2.50
2-Photo-c; w/2 trading cards inside 1.00 2.50

PREDATOR VS. MAGNUS ROBOT FIGHTER
Oct, 1992 - No. 2, 1993 ($2.95)
Dark Horse/Valiant

1 (Regular)-Barry Smith-c; Lee Weeks-a in both 1.10 2.70 6.50
1 (Platinum edition, 11/92)-Barry Smith-c 30.00
2-Contains 2 bound-in trading cards; Barry Smith-c .80 2.10 5.00

PREHISTORIC WORLD (See Classics Illustrated Special Issue)

PREMIERE (See Charlton Premiere)

PRESTO KID, THE (See Red Mask)

PRETTY BOY FLOYD (See On the Spot)

PREZ (See Cancelled Comic Cavalcade & Supergirl #10)
Aug-Sept, 1973 - No. 4, Feb-Mar, 1974
National Periodical Publications

1-4: 1-Origin; Joe Simon scripts 1.00

PRICE, THE (See Eclipse Graphic Album Series)

PRIDE AND THE PASSION, THE (See 4-Color #824)

PRIDE OF THE YANKEES, THE (See Real Heroes & Sport Comics)
1949 (The Life of Lou Gehrig)
Magazine Enterprises

nn-Photo-c; Ogden Whitney-a 61.00 182.00 425.00

PRIMAL (Dark Horse)(Value: cover or less)

PRIMAL FORCE
No. 0, Oct, 1994 - Present ($1.95)
DC Comics

0-6: Red Tornado, Golem, Jack O'Lantern, Meridian & Silver Dragon .80 2.00

PRIMAL MAN (See The Crusaders)

Prime #10 © Malibu

Prize Comics #25 © PRIZE

Prize Comics Western #74 © PRIZE

GD25 FN65 NM94

PRIME (See Flood Relief)
June, 1993 - Present ($1.95)
Malibu Comics (Ultraverse)

1-1st app. Prime; has coupon for Ultraverse Premiere #0 — 1.90 4.50
1-With coupon missing — .60 1.50
1-Full cover holographic edition; 1st of kind w/Hardcase #1 & Strangers #1 — 3.60 11.00 25.00
1-Ultra 5,000 edition w/silver ink-c — 1.40 4.20 10.00
2-Polybagged w/card & coupon for U. Premiere #0 — 1.00 2.00 5.00
3,4-Prototype app. 4-Direct sale w/o card — .90 2.25
4-($2.50)-Newsstand ed. polybagged w/card — 1.00 2.50
5-($2.50, 48 pgs.)-Rune flip-c/story part B by Barry Smith; see Sludge #1 for 1st app. Rune; 3-pg. Night Man preview — 1.00 2.50
6-11,14-18: 6-Bill & Chelsea Clinton app. 7-Break-Thru x-over. 8-Mantra app.; 2-pg. origin Freex by Simonson. 10-Firearm app. — .80 2.00
12-(3.50, 68 pgs.)-Flip book w/Ultraverse Premiere #3; silver foil logo — .80 2.00
13-($2.95, 52 pgs.)-Variant covers — 1.20 3.00
... Time: A Prime Collection (1994, $9.95)-r/1-4 — 1.65 4.00 10.00

PRIMER (Comico...)
Oct (no month), 1982 - No. 6, Feb, 1984 (B&W)
Comico

1 (52 pgs.) — 1.20 3.00
2-1st app. Grendel & Argent by Wagner — 2.90 8.60 20.00
3,4 — .80 2.00
5-1st Sam Kieth art in comics ('83) & 1st The Maxx — 1.00 2.00 5.00
6-Intro & 1st app. Evangeline — 1.40 3.50

PRIMUS (TV)
Feb, 1972 - No. 7, Oct, 1972
Charlton Comics

1-Staton-a in all — 1.30 3.25 8.00
2-7: 6-Drug propaganda story — 1.00 2.00 5.00

PRINCE: ALTER EGO (Piranha)(Value: cover or less)

PRINCE AND THE NEW POWER GENERATION (Piranha/DC)(Value: cover or less)

PRINCE AND THE PAUPER, THE (Disney)(Value: cover or less)

PRINCE NAMOR, THE SUB-MARINER (Marvel)(Value: cover or less)(Also see Namor ...)

PRINCE NIGHTMARE (Aaaargh)(Value: cover or less)

PRINCE VALIANT (See Ace Comics, Comics Reading Libraries, Feature Books #26, Four Color #567, 650, 699, 719, 788, 849, 900 & King Comics #146, 147)

PRINCE VANDAL
Nov, 1993 - Present ($2.50, color)
Triumphant Comics

1-6: 1,2-Triumphant Unleashed x-over — 1.00 2.50

PRIORITY: WHITE HEAT (AC)(Value: cover or less)

PRISCILLA'S POP (See 4-Color #569, 630, 704, 799)

PRISON BARS (See Behind...)

PRISON BREAK!
1951 (Sept) - No. 5, Sept, 1952 (Painted c-3)
Avon Periodicals/Realistic No. 3 on

1-Wood-c & 1 pg.; has-r/Saint #7 retitled Michael Strong Private Eye — 25.00 75.00 175.00
2-Wood-c; Kubert-a; Kinstler inside front-c — 18.00 54.00 125.00
3-Orlando, Check-a; c-/Avon paperback 179 — 15.00 45.00 105.00
4,5: 4-Kinstler-c & inside f/c; Lawrence, Lazarus-a. 5-Kinstler-c; Infantino-a — 13.50 41.00 95.00

PRISONER, THE (TV)
1988 - No. 4, 1989 ($3.50, squarebound, mini-series)
DC Comics

GD25 FN65 NM94

1-4 (Books a-d) — 1.40 3.50

PRISON RIOT
1952
Avon Periodicals

1-Marijuana Murders-1 pg. text; Kinstler-c — 17.00 52.00 120.00

PRISON TO PRAISE
1974 (35¢)
Logos International

nn-True Story of Merlin R. Carothers — 1.00

PRIVATE BUCK (See Large Feature Comic #12 & 21)

PRIVATEERS (Vanguard)(Value: cover or less)

PRIVATE EYE (Cover title: Rocky Jorden...#6-8)
Jan, 1951 - No. 8, March, 1952
Atlas Comics (MCI)

1-Cover title: Crime Cases... #1-5 — 12.00 36.00 85.00
2,3-Tuska c/a(3) — 8.35 25.00 50.00
4-8 — 6.70 20.00 40.00

NOTE: ***Henkel*** a-6(3), 7; c-7. ***Sinnott*** a-6.

PRIVATE EYE (See Mike Shayne...)

PRIVATE SECRETARY
Dec-Feb, 1962-63 - No. 2, Mar-May, 1963
Dell Publishing Co.

1,2 — 2.00 5.00 10.00

PRIVATE STRONG (See The Double Life of...)

PRIZE COMICS (...Western #69 on) (Also see Treasure Comics)
March, 1940 - No. 68, Feb-Mar, 1948
Prize Publications

1-Origin Power Nelson, The Futureman & Jupiter, Master Magician; Ted O'Neil, Secret Agent M-11, Jaxon of the Jungle, Bucky Brady & Storm Curtis begin (1st app. of each) — 164.00 493.00 1150.00
2-The Black Owl begins (1st app.) — 71.00 215.00 500.00
3,4: 4-Robot-c — 57.00 171.00 400.00
5,6: Dr. Dekkar, Master of Monsters app. in each — 50.00 150.00 350.00
7-(Scarce)-Black Owl by S&K; origin/1st app. Dr. Frost & Frankenstein; The Green Lama, Capt. Gallant, The Great Voodini & Twist Turner begin; 1st app. The Green Lama (12/40) — 129.00 385.00 900.00
8,9-Black Owl & Ted O'Neil by S&K — 64.00 193.00 450.00
10-12,14-20: 11-Origin Bulldog Denny. 16-Spike Mason begins — 50.00 150.00 350.00
13-Yank & Doodle begin (8/41, origin/1st app.) — 57.00 171.00 400.00
21-24 — 39.00 118.00 275.00
25-30 — 21.00 63.00 145.00
31-33 — 17.00 52.00 120.00
34-Origin Airmale, Yank & Doodle; The Black Owl joins army, Yank & Doodle's father assumes Black Owl's role — 21.00 63.00 145.00
35-36,38-40: 35-Flying Fist & Bingo begin — 14.00 43.00 100.00
37-Intro. Stampy, Airmale's sidekick; Hitler-c — 15.00 45.00 105.00
41-50: 45-Yank & Doodle learn Black Owl's I.D. (their father). 48-Prince Ra begins — 10.00 30.00 70.00
51-62,64,67,68: 53-Transvestism story. 55-No Frankenstein. 57-X-Mas-c. 64-Black Owl retires — 10.00 30.00 60.00
63-Simon & Kirby c/a — 11.00 32.00 75.00
65,66-Frankenstein-c by Briefer — 10.00 30.00 65.00

NOTE: ***Briefer*** a 7-on; c-65, 66. ***J. Binder*** a-16; c-21-29. ***Guardineer*** a-62. ***Kiefer*** c-62. ***Palais*** c-68. ***Simon & Kirby*** c-63, 75, 83.

PRIZE COMICS WESTERN (Formerly Prize Comics #1-68)
No. 69(V7#2), Apr-May, 1948 - No. 119, Nov-Dec, 1956
Prize Publications (Feature) (No. 69-84: 52 pgs.)

69(V7#2) — 11.50 34.00 80.00
70-75: 74-Kurtzman-a (8 pgs.) — 10.00 30.00 60.00
76-Randolph Scott photo-c; "Canadian Pacific" movie adaptation

Propellerman #5 © DH

Prophet #2 © Rob Liefeld

Psi-Lords #2 © Voyager Comm.

GD25 FN65 NM94

11.00 32.00 75.00
77-Photo-c; Severin/Elder, Mart Bailey-a; "Streets of Laredo" movie adaptation 10.00 30.00 65.00
78-Photo-c; S&K-a, 10 pgs.; Severin, Mart Bailey-a; "Bullet Code", & "Roughshod" movie adaptations 13.50 41.00 95.00
79-Photo-c; Kurtzman-a, 8 pgs.; Severin/Elder, Severin, Mart Bailey-a; "Stage To Chino" movie adaptation w/George O'Brien 13.50 41.00 95.00
80,81-Photo-c; Severin/Elder-a(2) 10.00 30.00 70.00
82-Photo-c; 1st app. The Preacher by Mart Bailey; Severin/Elder-a(3) 10.00 30.00 70.00
83,84 9.15 27.50 55.00
85-1st app. American Eagle by John Severin & begins (V9#6, 1-2/51) 19.00 57.00 130.00
86,92,101-105 10.00 30.00 60.00
87-91,93-99,110,111-Severin/Elder-a(2-3) each 10.00 30.00 65.00
100 11.00 32.00 75.00
106-108,112 7.50 22.50 45.00
109-Severin/Williamson-a 10.00 30.00 65.00
113-Williamson/Severin-a(2)/Frazetta? 10.00 30.00 70.00
114-119: Drifter series in all; by Mort Meskin #114-118 5.35 16.00 32.00

NOTE: *Fass a-81.* ***Severin & Elder*** *c-84-99.* ***Severin*** *a-72, 75, 77-79, 83-86, 96, 97, 100-105; c-100-109(most), 110-119.* ***Simon & Kirby*** *c-75, 83.*

PRIZE MYSTERY
May, 1955 - No. 3, Sept, 1955
Key Publications

1 5.85 17.50 35.00
2,3 4.20 12.50 25.00

PROFESSIONAL FOOTBALL (See Charlton Sport Library)

PROFESSOR COFFIN
No. 19, Oct, 1985 - No. 21, Feb, 1986
Charlton Comics

19-21: Wayne Howard-a(r) 1.00

PROFESSOR OM (Innovation)(Value: cover or less)

PROJECT A-KO
Mar, 1994 - Present ($2.95)
Malibu Comics

1-4-Based on anime film 1.20 3.00

PROJECT: HERO (Vanguard)(Value: cover or less)

PROPELLERMAN
Jan, 1993 - No. 8, Mar, 1994 ($2.95, limited series)
Dark Horse Comics

1-8: 2,4,8-Contain 2 trading cards 1.20 3.00

PROPHET (See Youngblood #2)
Oct, 1993 - Present ($1.95, color)
Image Comics

1-($2.50)-Liefeld/Panosian-c/a; 1st app. Mary McCormick; Liefeld scripts in 1-4; #1-3 contain coupons for Prophet #0 1.10 2.75
1-Gold foil embossed-c edition rationed to dealers 5.00
2-4: 2-Liefeld-c(p). 3-1st app. Judas. 4-1st app. Omen; Black and White Pt. 3 by Thibert .80 2.00
4-Alternate-c by Stephen Platt 1.50 3.00 7.50
5,6-Platt-c/a .80 2.00
0-(7/94, $2.50)-San Diego Comic Con ed., 2200 copies 1.00 2.50

PROTECTORS (Also see The Ferret)
Sept, 1992 - No. 20, May, 1994 ($1.95-$2.50/$2.25/$2.50)
Malibu Comics

1-12 ($2.50, direct sale)-With poster & diff-c: 1-Origin; has 3/4 outer-c 1.00 2.50
1-12 ($1.95, newsstand)-Without poster .80 2.00
13-16 ($2.25): 13-Polybagged w/Skycap .90 2.25
17-20: 17-Begin $2.50-c 1.00 2.50

PROTOTYPE (See Flood Relief)
Aug, 1993 - Present ($1.95)
Malibu Comics (Ultraverse)

1,2 .80 2.00
1-Ultra Limited silver foil-c 1.40 4.20 10.00
3-($2.50, 48 pgs.)-Rune flip-c/story by B. Smith (3 pgs.) 1.00 2.50
4-12: 4-Intro Wrath. 5-Break-Thru & Strangers x-over. 6-Arena cameo. 7,8-Arena-c/story. 12-(7/94) .80 2.00
0,13-17: 0-(8/94, $2.50, 44 pgs.) 1.00 2.50

PROWLER (Eclipse)(Value: cover or less)(Also see Revenge of the...)

PROWLER, THE
Nov, 1994 ($1.75)
Marvel Comics

1-Spider-Man app. .70 1.75

PROWLER IN "WHITE ZOMBIE", THE (Eclipse)(Value: cover or less)

PRUDENCE & CAUTION
May, 1994 - No. 2, June, 1994 ($2.50, color)(Also Spanish versions)
Defiant Comics

1-($3.50, 52 pgs.) 1.40 3.50
2-($2.50) 1.00 2.50

PSI-FORCE (Marvel)(Value: cover or less)

PSI-JUDGE ANDERSON (Fleetway/Quality)(Value: cover or less)

PSI-LORDS
Sept, 1994 - Present ($2.25, color)
Valiant

1-($3.50)-Chromium wraparound-c 1.40 3.50
2-4: 3-Chaos Effect Epsilon Pt. 2 .90 2.25

PSYCHO (Magazine)
Jan, 1971 - No. 24, Mar, 1975 (68 pgs.; B&W) (No #22?)
Skywald Publishing Corp.

1-All reprints 1.65 4.00 10.00
2-Origin & 1st app. The Heap, & Frankenstein series by Adkins 1.20 3.00 7.00
3-24: 13-Cannabalism. 18-Injury to eye-c. 20-Severed Head-c. 24-1975 Winter Special 1.60 4.00
Annual 1(1972) 1.00 2.50 6.00
Fall Special(1974)-Reese, Wildey-a(r) 1.60 4.00
Winter Special 1 (1975)-Dave Sim scripts 1.60 4.00
Yearbook(1974-nn) 1.60 4.00

NOTE: ***Boris*** *c-3, 5.* ***Buckler*** *a-4, 5.* ***Everett*** *a-3-6.* ***Jeff Jones*** *a-6, 7, 9; c-12.* ***Kaluta*** *a-13.* ***Katz/Buckler*** *a-3.* ***Morrow*** *a-1.* ***Reese*** *a-5.* ***Sutton*** *a-3.* ***Wildey*** *a-5.*

PSYCHO, THE (DC)(Value: cover or less)

PSYCHO (Alfred Hitchcock's...)(Innovation)(Value: cover or less)(Adapts movie)

PSYCHOANALYSIS
Mar-Apr, 1955 - No. 4, Sept-Oct, 1955
E. C. Comics

1-All Kamen-c/a; not approved by code 13.00 40.00 90.00
2-4-Kamen-c/a in all 10.00 30.00 70.00

PSYCHOBLAST (First)(Value: cover or less)

PSYCHONAUTS
Oct, 1993 - No. 4, Jan, 1994 ($4.95, mini-series)
Epic Comics (Marvel)

1-4: American/Japanese co-produced comic 1.00 2.00 5.00

P.T. 109 (See Movie Comics)

PUBLIC DEFENDER IN ACTION (Formerly Police Trap)
No. 7, Mar, 1956 - No. 12, Oct, 1957
Charlton Comics

7 6.70 20.00 40.00
8-12 4.20 12.50 25.00

Punch Comics #1 © CHES

Punisher #94 © MEG

Punisher: No Escape © MEG

	GD25	FN65	NM94

PUBLIC ENEMIES
1948 - No. 9, June-July, 1949
D. S. Publishing Co.

	GD25	FN65	NM94
1-True Crime Stories	12.00	36.00	85.00
2-Used in **SOTI**, pg. 95	13.00	40.00	90.00
3-5: 5-Arrival date of 10/1/48	9.15	27.50	55.00
6,8,9	7.50	22.50	45.00
7-McWilliams-a; injury to eye panel	9.15	27.50	55.00

PUDGY PIG
Sept, 1958 - No. 2, Nov, 1958
Charlton Comics

	GD25	FN65	NM94
1,2	3.20	8.00	16.00

PUMA BLUES (Aardvark-Vanaheim)(Value: cover or less)

PUMPKINHEAD: THE RITES OF EXORCISM
1993 - No. 2, 1993 ($2.50, mini-series)
Dark Horse Comics

	GD25	FN65	NM94
1,2-Based on movie; painted-c by McManus		1.00	2.50

PUNCH & JUDY COMICS
1944; No. 2, Fall, 1944 - V3#2, 12/47; V3#3, 6/51 - V3#9, 12/51
Hillman Periodicals

	GD25	FN65	NM94
V1#1-(60 pgs.)	14.00	43.00	100.00
2	8.35	25.00	50.00
3-12(7/46)	5.85	17.50	35.00
V2#1(8/49),3-9	4.00	11.00	22.00
V2#2,10-12, V3#1-Kirby-a(2) each	15.00	45.00	105.00
V3#2-Kirby-a	13.00	40.00	90.00
3-9	4.00	10.00	20.00

PUNCH COMICS
12/41; #2, 2/42; #9, 7/44 - #19, 10/46; #20, 7/47 - #23, 1/48
Harry 'A' Chesler

	GD25	FN65	NM94
1-Mr. E, The Sky Chief, Hale the Magician, Kitty Kelly begin	75.00	225.00	525.00
2-Captain Glory app.	41.00	124.00	290.00
9-Rocketman & Rocket Girl & The Master Key begin	29.00	86.00	200.00
10-Sky Chief app.; J. Cole-a; Master Key-r/Scoop #3	22.00	65.00	150.00
11-Origin Master Key-r/Scoop #1; Sky Chief, Little Nemo app.; Jack Cole-a; Fineish art by Sultan	22.00	65.00	150.00
12-Rocket Boy & Capt. Glory app; Skull-c	22.00	65.00	150.00
13-17,19: 13-Cover has list of 4 Chesler artists' names on tombstone	19.00	58.00	135.00
18-Bondage-c; hypodermic panels	22.00	65.00	150.00
20-Unique cover with bare-breasted women	37.00	111.00	260.00
21-Hypo needle story	19.00	58.00	135.00
22,23-Little Nemo-not by McCay. 22-Intro Baxter (teenage)	16.50	50.00	115.00

PUNCHY AND THE BLACK CROW
No. 10, Oct, 1985 - No. 12, Feb, 1986
Charlton Comics

	GD25	FN65	NM94
10-12: Al Fago funny animal-r			1.00

PUNISHER (See Amazing Spider-Man #129, Blood and Glory, Captain America #241, Classic Punisher, Daredevil #182-184, 257, Daredevil and the..., Ghost Rider V2#5, 6, Marc Spector #8 & 9, Marvel Preview #2, Marvel Super Action, Marvel Tales, Power Pack #46, Spectacular Spider-Man #81-83, 140, 141, 143 & new Strange Tales #13 & 14)

PUNISHER
Jan, 1986 - No. 5, May, 1986 (Mini-series)
Marvel Comics Group

	GD25	FN65	NM94
1-Double size	5.00	15.00	35.00
2	3.00	7.70	18.00
3-Has 2 diff. cover prices, 75¢ & 95¢(w/UPC)	1.40	4.00	10.00
4,5	1.30	3.00	8.00
Trade Paperback (1988)-r/#1-5	1.65	4.70	11.00

PUNISHER
July, 1987 - Present
Marvel Comics Group

	GD25	FN65	NM94
V2#1	3.00	7.70	18.00
2	1.40	4.00	10.00
3-5	1.00	3.00	6.00
6,7: 7-Last 75¢ issue	.90	2.30	5.50
8-Portacio/Williams-c/a begins, ends #18	1.20	2.90	7.00
9-Scarcer, low distribution	1.40	3.50	8.50
10-Daredevil app.; ties in w/Daredevil #257	2.70	8.00	19.00
11-15: 13-18-Kingpin app.	1.00	2.00	5.00
16-20: 19-Stroman-c/a. 20-Portacio-c(p)		1.40	3.50
21-24,26-30: 24-1st app. Shadowmasters		.70	1.75
25-($1.50, 52 pgs.)-Shadowmasters app.		1.10	2.75
31-40		.65	1.60
41-49 ($1.25)			1.00
50-($1.50, 52 pgs.)			1.50
51-59: 57-Photo-c; came with outer-c (newsstand ed. w/o outer-c). 59-Punisher is severely cut & has skin grafts (has black skin); last $1.00-c			1.00
60-74,76-85,87-89: 60-Begin $1.25-c. 60-62-Luke Cage app. 62-Punisher back to white skin. 68-Tarantula-c/story. 85-Prequel to Suicide Run Pt. 0. 87,88-Suicide Run Pt. 6 & 9			1.00
75-($2.75, 52 pgs.)-Embossed silver foil-c		1.10	2.75
86-($2.95, 52 pgs.)-Embossed & foil stamped-c; Suicide Run part 3		1.20	3.00
90-101: 90-Begin 1.50-c; bound-in card sheet			1.50
Annual 1 (1988)-Evolutionary War x-over	1.30	4.00	9.00
Annual 2 (1989, $2.00, 68 pgs.)-Atlantis Attacks x-over; Jim Lee-a(p) (back-up story, 6 pgs.); Moon Knight app.		1.80	4.50
Annual 3,4 ('90, '91, $2.00, 68 pgs.): 4-Golden-c(p)		.80	2.00
Annual 5 (1992, $2.25, 68 pgs.)		.90	2.25
Annual 6 (1993, $2.95, 68 pgs.)-Bagged w/card		1.20	3.00
Annual 7 (1994, $2.95)-Rapido app.		1.20	3.00
...: A Man Named Frank (1994, $6.95, TPB)	1.20	2.90	7.00
...and Wolverine in African Saga nn (1989, $5.95, 52 pgs.)-Reprints Punisher War Journal #6 & 7; Jim Lee-c/a(r)	1.00	2.00	5.00
Back to School Special 1 (11/92, $2.95, 68 pgs.)		1.20	3.00
Back to School Special 2 (10/93, $2.95, 68 pgs.)		1.20	3.00
Back to School Special 3 (10/94, $2.95)		1.20	3.00
.../Batman: Deadly Knights (10/94, $4.95)	1.00	2.00	5.00
...Bloodlines nn (1991, $5.95, 68 pgs.)	1.00	2.50	6.00
...: Die Hard in the Big Easy nn ('92, $4.95, 52 pgs.)	1.00	2.00	5.00
...G-Force nn (1992, $4.95, 52 pgs.)-Painted-c	1.00	2.00	5.00
...Holiday Special 1 (1/93, $2.95, 52 pgs.)-Foil-c		1.20	3.00
...Holiday Special 2 (1/94, $2.95, 68 pgs.)		1.20	3.00
...Invades the 'Nam: Final Invasion nn (2/94, $6.95)-J. Kubert-c & chapter break art; reprints The 'Nam #52,53,67-69	1.20	2.90	7.00
...Meets Archie (8/94, $3.95, 52 pgs.)-Die cut-c; no ads; same contents as Archie Meets The Punisher		1.60	4.00
...Movie Special 1 (6/90, $5.95, 68 pgs.)	1.00	2.50	6.00
...: No Escape nn (1990, $4.95, 52 pgs.)-New-a	1.00	2.50	6.00
...The Prize nn (1990, $4.95, 68 pgs.)-New-a	1.00	2.00	5.00
Summer Special 1 (8/91, $2.95, 52 pgs.)-No ads		1.20	3.00
Summer Special 2 (8/92, $2.50, 52 pgs.)-Bisley painted-c; Austin-a(i)		1.00	2.50
Summer Special 3 (8/93, $2.50, 52 pgs.)-No ads		1.00	2.50
Summer Special 4 (7/94, $2.95, 52 pgs.)		1.20	3.00

NOTE: **Austin** *c(i)-47, 48.* **Cowan** *c-39.* **Heath** *a-26, 27, 89, 90; c-26, 27.* **Quesada** *c-56p.* **Sienkiewicz** *c-Back to School 1.* **Stroman** *a-76p(9 pgs.).* **Williamson** *a(i)-25, 61, 62, 64-70, 74, Annual 5; c(i)-62, 65-68.*

PUNISHER AND WOLVERINE: DAMAGING EVIDENCE (See Wolverine and...)

PUNISHER ARMORY, THE
7/90 ($1.50); No. 2, 6/91; No. 3, 4/92 - Present ($1.75/$2.00)

The Punisher Magazine #4 © MEG

The Punisher War Journal #70 © MEG

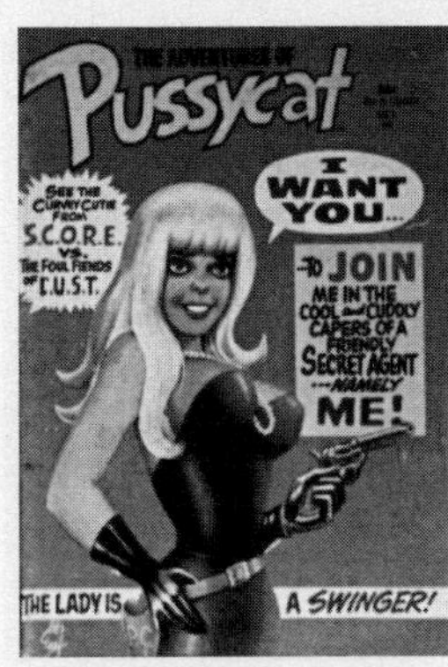

Pussycat #1 © MEG

GD25 FN65 NM94

Marvel Comics
1($1.50)-r/weapons pgs. from War Journal; Jim Lee-c 1.40 3.50
2 ($1.75)-Jim Lee-c .80 2.00
3-13 ($2.00): All new material. 3-Jusko painted-c .80 2.00

PUNISHER MAGAZINE, THE
Oct, 1989 - No. 16, Nov, 1990 ($2.25, B&W, Magazine, 52 pgs.)
Marvel Comics
1-3: 1-r/Punisher #1('86). 2,3-r/Punisher 2-5 .90 2.25
4-16: 4-7-r/Punisher V2#1-8. 4-Chiodo-c. 8-r/Punisher #10 & Daredevil #257; Portacio & Lee-r. 14-r/Punisher War Journal #1,2 w/new Lee-c. 16-r/Punisher W. J. #3,8 .90 2.25
NOTE: ***Chiodo** painted c-4, 7, 16. **Jusko** painted c-6, 8. **Jim Lee** r-8, 14-16; c-14. **Portacio/Williams** r-7-12.*

PUNISHER MOVIE COMIC
Nov, 1989 - No. 3, Dec, 1989 ($1.00, mini-series)
Marvel Comics
1-3: Movie adaptation 1.25
1 (1989, $4.95, squarebound)-contains #1-3 1.00 2.00 5.00

PUNISHER: ORIGIN OF MICRO CHIP, THE
July, 1993 - No. 2, Aug, 1993 ($1.75, mini-series)
Marvel Comics
1,2 .70 1.75

PUNISHER: P.O.V.
1991 - No. 4, 1991 ($4.95, mini-series, 52 pgs.)
Marvel Comics
1-4: Starlin scripts & Wrightson painted-c/a in all. 2-Nick Fury app. 1.00 2.00 5.00

PUNISHER: THE GHOSTS OF INNOCENTS
Jan, 1993 - No. 2, Jan, 1993 ($5.95, 52 pgs.)
Marvel Comics
1,2-Starlin scripts 1.00 2.50 6.00

PUNISHER 2099 (See Punisher War Journal #50)
Feb, 1993 - Present ($1.25/$1.50)
Marvel Comics
1-($1.75)-Foil stamped-c .90 2.25
1-($1.75)-Second printing .70 1.75
2-15: 13-Spider-Man 2099 x-over; Ron Lim-c(p) 1.25
16-27: 16-Begin $1.50-c; bound-in card sheet 1.50

PUNISHER WAR JOURNAL, THE
Nov, 1988 - Present ($1.50/$1.75/$1.95)
Marvel Comics
1-Origin The Punisher; Jim Lee-c/a begins; Matt Murdock cameo; 1st Lee-a on Punisher 2.10 6.40 15.00
2-Daredevil x-over 1.30 3.90 9.00
3-5: 3-Daredevil x-over 1.20 2.90 7.00
6-Two part Wolverine story begins 2.00 6.00 14.00
7-Wolverine-c, story ends 1.20 2.90 7.00
8-10 1.00 1.80 4.50
11,12,17-19: 19-Last Jim Lee-c/a 1.40 3.50
13-16,20-22: No Jim Lee-a. 13-Lee-c only. 13-15-Heath-i. 14,15-Spider-Man x-over .70 1.75
23-28,31-49,51-60,62,63,65: 23-Begin $1.75-c. 31-Andy & Joe Kubert art. 36-Photo-c. 47,48-Nomad/Daredevil-c/stories; see Nomad. 57,58-Daredevil & Ghost Rider-c/stories. 62,63-Suicide Run Pt. 4 & 7 1.50
29,30-Ghost Rider app. .70 1.75
50-($2.95, 52 pgs.)-Preview of Punisher 2099 (1st app.); embossed-c 1.20 3.00
61-($2.95, 52 pgs.)-Embossed foil-c; Suicide Run Pt. 1 1.20 3.00
64-($2.95, 52 pgs.)-Die-cut-c; Suicide Run Pt. 10 1.20 3.00
64-($2.25, 52 pgs.)-Regular cover edition .90 2.25
66-77: 66-Begin 1.95-c; bound-in card sheet .80 2.00
NOTE: ***Jusko** painted c-31, 32. **Jim Lee** a(p)-1-13, 17-19; c-1-15, 17, 18, 19p. Painted c-40.*

PUNISHER: WAR ZONE, THE
Mar, 1992 - Present ($1.75/$1.95)
Marvel Comics
1-($2.25, 40 pgs.)-Die cut-c; Romita, Jr.-c/a begins .90 2.25
2 .80 2.00
3-22,24,26: 8-Last Romita, Jr.-c/a. 19-Wolverine app. 24-Suicide Run Pt. 5 .70 1.75
23-($2.95, 52 pgs.)-Enbossed foil-c; Suicide Run part 2; Buscema part-p 1.20 3.00
25-($2.25, 52 pgs.)-Suicide Run part 8; painted-c .90 2.25
27-39: 27-Begin 1.95-c; bound-in card sheet .80 2.00
Annual 1 (1993, $2.95, 68 pgs.)-Bagged w/card; John Buscema-a 1.20 3.00
Annual 2 (1994, $2.95, 68 pgs.) 1.20 3.00

PUPPET COMICS
Spring, 1946 - No. 2, Summer, 1946
George W. Dougherty Co.
1,2-Funny animal 7.50 22.50 45.00

PUPPET MASTER 2: CHILDREN OF THE PUPPET MASTER (Eternity)(Value: cover or less)

PUPPETOONS (See George Pal's...)

PURE OIL COMICS (Also see Salerno Carnival of Comics, 24 Pages of Comics, & Vicks Comics)
Late 1930's (24 pgs.; regular size) (Paper cover)
Pure Oil Giveaway
nn-Contains 1-2 pg. strips; i.e., Hairbreadth Harry, Skyroads, Buck Rogers by Calkins & Yager, Olly of the Movies, Napoleon, S'Matter Pop, etc. 32.00 95.00 225.00
Also a 16 pg. 1938 giveaway w/Buck Rogers 29.00 85.00 200.00

PURGE
Aug, 1993 ($1.95, color, limited series intended)
ANIA/U.P. Comics
1 .80 2.00

PURPLE CLAW, THE (Also see Tales of Horror)
Jan, 1953 - No. 3, May, 1953
Minoan Publishing Co./Toby Press
1-Origin; horror/weird stories in all 18.00 54.00 125.00
2,3: 1-3 r-in Tales of Horror #9-11 12.00 36.00 85.00
I.W. Reprint #8-Reprints #1 2.40 6.00 12.00

PUSSYCAT (Magazine)
Oct, 1968 (B&W reprints from Men's magazines)
Marvel Comics Group
1-(Scarce)-Ward, Everett, Wood-a; Everett-c 17.00 52.00 120.00

PUZZLE FUN COMICS (Also see Jingle Jangle)
Spring, 1946 - No. 2, Summer, 1946 (52 pgs.)
George W. Dougherty Co.
1-Gustavson-a 16.00 48.00 110.00
2 11.50 34.00 80.00
NOTE: *#1 & 2('46) each contain a **George Carlson** cover plus a 6 pg. story "Alec in Fumbleland"; also many puzzles in each.*

QUACK!
July, 1976 - No. 6, 1977? ($1.25, B&W)
Star Reach Productions
1-Brunner-c/a on Duckaneer (Howard the Duck clone); Dave Stevens, Gilbert, Shaw-a 1.70 4.25
1-2nd printing (10/76) 1.50
2,4-6: 2-Newton the Rabbit Wonder by Aragones/Leialoha; Gilbert, Shaw-a; Leialoha-c. 6-Brunner-a (Duckeneer); Gilbert-a .80 2.00
3-The Beavers by Dave Sim begin, end #5; Gilbert, Shaw-a; Sim/Leialoha-c 1.60 4.00

QUADRANT

Quantum Leap #1 © Universal City Studios

The Question Quarterly #1 © DC

Quick-Draw McGraw #6 © H-B

1983 - No. 8, 1986 (B&W, nudity, adults)
Quadrant Publications

1-Peter Hsu-c/a in all 1.30 3.00 8.00
2 1.20 3.00
3-8 .75 1.90

QUAKER OATS (Also see Cap'n Crunch)
1965 (Giveaway) (2-1/2x5-1/2") (16 pgs.)
Quaker Oats Co.

"Plenty of Glutton", starring Quake & Quisp; "Lava Come-Back", "Kite Tale", "A Witch in Time" .60 1.50 3.00

QUANTUM LEAP (TV) (See A Nightmare on Elm Street)
Sept, 1991 - No. 12, June?, 1993 ($2.50, color, painted-c)
Innovation Publishing

1-12: Based on TV show; all have painted-c. 8-Has photo gallery 1.00 2.50
Special Edition 1 (10/92)-r/#1 w/8 extra pgs. of photos & articles 1.00 2.50
Time and Space Special 1 (#13) ($2.95)-Foil logo 1.20 3.00

QUASAR (See Avengers #302, Captain America #217, Incredible Hulk #234, Marvel Team-Up #113 & Marvel Two-in-One #53)
Oct, 1989 - Present ($1.00/$1.25) (Direct sale #17 on)
Marvel Comics

1-Origin; formerly Marvel Boy/Marvel Man .80 2.00
2-5: 3-Human Torch app. 1.50
6-Venom cameo (2 pgs.) .80 2.00
7-Cosmic Spidey app. 1.00 2.50
8-15,18-24: 11-Excalibur x-over. 14-McFarlane-c. 20-Fantastic Four app. 23-Ghost Rider x-over 1.20
16-($1.50, 52 pgs.) 1.50
17-Flash parody (Buried Alien) .80 2.00
25-($1.50, 52 pgs.)-New costume Quasar 1.50
26-Infinity Guantlet x-over; Thanos-c/story .80 2.00
27-Infinity Guantlet x-over 1.50
28-30: 30-Thanos cameo in flashback; last $1.00-c 1.00
31-49,51-65: 31-Begin $1.25-c; D.P. 7 guest stars. 38-40-Infinity War x-overs. 38-Battles Warlock. 39-Thanos-c & cameo. 40-Thanos app. 42-Punisher-c/story. 53-Warlock & Moondragon app. 58-w/bound-in card sheet .60 1.25
50-($2.95, 52 pgs.)-Holo-grafx foil-c; Silver Surfer, Man-Thing, Ren & Stimpy app. 1.20 3.00
Special #1-3 ($1.25, newsstand)-Same as #32-34 1.25

QUEEN OF THE DAMNED, THE (Anne Rice's...)(Innovation)(Value: cover or less)

QUEEN OF THE WEST, DALE EVANS (TV)(See Dale Evans Comics & Western Roundup under Dell Giants)
No. 479, 7/53 - No. 22, 1-3/59 (All photo-c; photo back c-4-8, 15)
Dell Publishing Co.

4-Color 479(#1, '53) 14.00 43.00 100.00
4-Color 528(#2, '54) 10.00 30.00 60.00
3(4-6/54)-Toth-a 10.00 30.00 65.00
4-Toth, Manning-a 10.00 30.00 65.00
5-10-Manning-a. 5-Marsh-a 7.50 22.50 45.00
11,19,21-No Manning 21-Tufts-a 5.35 16.00 32.00
12-18,20,22-Manning-a 6.70 20.00 40.00

QUENTIN DURWARD (See 4-Color #672)

QUESTAR ILLUSTRATED SCIENCE FICTION CLASSICS
1977 (224 pgs.) ($1.95)
Golden Press

11197-Stories by Asimov, Sturgeon, Silverberg & Niven; Starstream-r 1.20 3.00

QUEST FOR DREAMS LOST (Also see Word Warriors)
July 4, 1987 ($2.00, B&W, 52 pgs.)(Proceeds donated to help illiteracy)
Literacy Volunteers of Chicago

1-Teenage Mutant Ninja Turtles by Eastman/Laird, Trollords, Silent Invasion, The Realm, Wordsmith, Reacto Man, Eb'nn, Aniverse 1.00 2.50

QUESTION, THE (See Americomics, Blue Beetle (1967), Charlton Bullseye & Mysterious Suspense)

QUESTION, THE (DC)(Value: cover or less)

QUESTION, THE (Also see Blue Beetle & Mysterious Suspense)
Feb, 1987 - No. 36, Mar, 1990 ($1.50)
DC Comics

1-36 1.50
Annual 1 (1988, $2.50) 1.00 2.50
Annual 2 (1989, $3.50) 1.40 3.50

QUESTION QUARTERLY, THE (DC)(Value: cover or less)

QUESTPROBE
8/84; No. 2, 1/85; No. 3, 11/85 - No. 4, 12/85 (Limited series)
Marvel Comics Group

1-4: 1-The Hulk app. by Romita. 2-Spider-Man; Mooney-a(i). 3-Human Torch & Thing 1.00

QUICK-DRAW McGRAW (TV) (Hanna-Barbera)(See Whitman Comic Books)
No. 1040, 12-2/59-60 - No. 11, 7-9/62; No. 12, 11/62; No. 13, 2/63; No. 14, 4/63; No. 15, 6/69 (1st show aired 9/29/59)
Dell Publishing Co./Gold Key No. 12 on

4-Color 1040(#1) 11.30 34.00 68.00
2(4-6/60)-6: 2-Augie Doggie & Snooper & Blabber stories (8 pgs. each); pre-dates both of their #1 issues. 4-Augie Doggie & Snooper & Blabber stories. 5-Early Snagglepuss app.; last 10¢ issue 7.30 22.00 44.00
7-11 5.30 16.00 32.00
12,13-Title change to ...Fun-Type Roundup (84pgs.) 8.00 23.00 60.00
14,15 4.70 14.00 28.00

QUICK-DRAW McGRAW (TV)(See Spotlight #2)
Nov, 1970 - No. 8, Jan, 1972 (Hanna-Barbera)
Charlton Comics

1 4.40 13.00 31.00
2-8 2.30 6.90 16.00

QUICK-TRIGGER WESTERN (...Action #12; Cowboy Action #5-11)
No. 12, May, 1956 - No. 19, Sept, 1957
Atlas Comics (ACI No. 12/WPI No. 13-19)

12-Baker-a 10.00 30.00 60.00
13-Williamson-a, 5 pgs. 10.00 30.00 65.00
14-Everett, Crandall, Torres-a; Heath-c 8.35 25.00 55.00
15-Torres, Crandall-a 7.50 22.50 45.00
16-Orlando, Kirby-a 6.70 20.00 40.00
17,18: 18-Baker-a 6.70 20.00 40.00
19 5.00 15.00 30.00

NOTE: ***Ayers*** *a-17.* ***Colan*** *a-16.* ***Maneely*** *a-15, 17; c-15, 18.* ***Morrow*** *a-18.* ***Powell*** *a-14.* ***Severin*** *a-19; c-12, 13, 16, 17, 19.* ***Shores*** *a-16.* ***Tuska*** *a-17.*

QUINCY (See Comics Reading Libraries)

Q-UNIT
Dec, 1993 - Present ($2.95, color)
Harris Comics

1-($2.95)-Polybagged w/trading card version 1.2 1.20 3.00

RABID
1994 ($5.95, B&W)
FantaCo Enterprises

1 1.00 2.50 6.00

RACCOON KIDS, THE (Formerly Movietown Animal Antics)
No. 52, Sept-Oct, 1954 - No. 64, Nov, 1957
National Periodical Publications (Arleigh No. 63,64)

52-Doodles Duck by Mayer 11.50 34.00 80.00
53-64: 53-62-Doodles Duck by Mayer 9.15 27.50 55.00

RACE FOR THE MOON

Radioactive Man #412 (4th iss.)

Raggedy Ann and Andy #20 © DELL

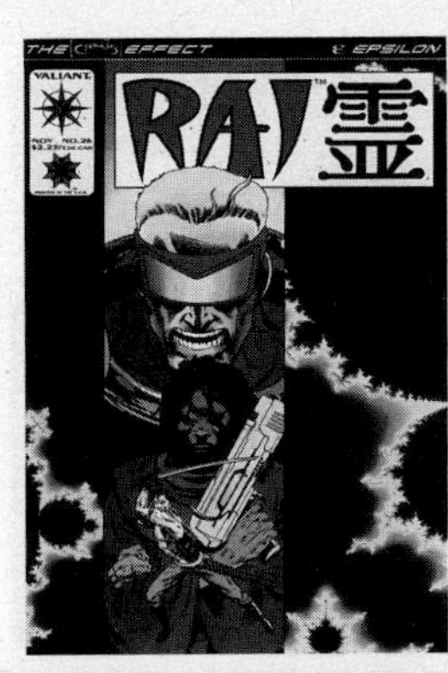

Rai #26 © Voyager Comm.

GD25 FN65 NM94

March, 1958 - No. 3, Nov, 1958
Harvey Publications

1-Powell-a(5); 1/2-pg. S&K-a; cover redrawn from Galaxy Science Fiction pulp (5/53) 10.00 30.00 65.00
2-Kirby/Williamson-c(r)/a(3); Kirby-p 7 more stories 19.00 57.00 130.00
3-Kirby/Williamson-c/a(4); Kirby-p 6 more stories 19.00 58.00 135.00

RACE OF SCORPIONS (Dark Horse)(Value: cover or less)

RACER-X (Now)(Value: cover or less)

RACK & PAIN
Mar, 1994 - No. 4, June, 1994 ($2.50, mini-series)
Dark Horse Comics

1-4: 1-Greg Capullo-c 1.00 2.50

RACKET SQUAD IN ACTION
May-June, 1952 - No. 29, March, 1958
Capitol Stories/Charlton Comics

1 17.00 52.00 120.00
2-4 9.15 27.50 55.00
5-Dr. Neff, Ghost Breaker app; headlights-c 11.50 34.00 80.00
6-Dr. Neff, Ghost Breaker app. 9.15 27.50 55.00
7-10: 10-Explosion-c 7.50 22.50 45.00
11-Ditko-c/a 16.50 50.00 115.00
12-Ditko explosion-c (classic); Shuster-a(2) 29.00 86.00 200.00
13-Shuster-c(p)/a; acid in woman's face 10.00 30.00 60.00
14-Marijuana story "Shakedown" 8.35 25.00 50.00
15-28 5.85 17.50 35.00
29-(15¢, 68 pgs.) 6.70 20.00 40.00

RADIANT LOVE (Formerly Daring Love #1)
No. 2, Dec, 1953 - No. 6, Aug, 1954
Gilmor Magazines

2 4.70 14.00 28.00
3-6 3.20 8.00 16.00

RADICAL DREAMER
No. 0, May, 1994 - Present ($1.75?, color)
Blackball Comics

0,1-($1.99)-Poster format .80 2.00

RADIOACTIVE MAN (Simpson's TV show)
1993 - No. 6, 1994 ($1.95/$2.25, color, limited series)
Bongo Comics

1-($2.95)-Glow-in-the-dark-c; bound-in jumbo poster; origin Radioactive Man; (cover dated Nov. 1952) 1.30 3.25
2-Says #88 on-c & inside & dated May 1962; cover parody of Atlas Kirby monster-c; Superior Squad app.; origin Fallout Boy .80 2.00
3-($1.95)-Cover "dated" Aug 1972 #216 .80 2.00
4-($2.25)-Cover "dated" Oct 1980 #412; w/trading card .90 2.25
5-($2.25)-Cover "dated" Jan 1986 #679; w/trading card .90 2.25
6-($2.25)-Cover "dated" #1000 .90 2.25

RAGAMUFFINS (Eclipse)(Value: cover or less)

RAGGEDY ANN AND ANDY (See Dell Giants, March of Comics #23 & New Funnies)
No. 5, 1942 - No. 533, 2/54; 10-12/64 - No. 4, 3/66
Dell Publishing Co.

4-Color 5(1942) 50.00 150.00 350.00
4-Color 23(1943) 37.00 111.00 260.00
4-Color 45(1943) 30.00 90.00 210.00
4-Color 72(1945) 25.00 75.00 175.00
1(6/46)-Billy & Bonnie Bee by Frank Thomas 25.00 75.00 175.00
2,3: 3-Egbert Elephant by Dan Noonan begins 13.00 40.00 90.00
4-Kelly-a, 16 pgs. 13.50 41.00 95.00
5-10: 7-Little Black Sambo, Black Mumbo & Black Jumbo only app; Christmas-c 10.00 30.00 70.00
11-21: 21-Alice In Wonderland cover/story 10.00 30.00 60.00
22-27,29-39(8/49), 4-Color 262(1/50): 34-"...In Candyland" 7.00 21.00 42.00
28-Kelly-c 7.50 22.50 45.00
4-Color 306,354,380,452,533 5.35 16.00 32.00
1(10-12/64-Dell) 3.60 9.00 18.00
2,3(10-12/65), 4(3/66) 1.80 4.50 9.00

NOTE: ***Kelly** art ("Animal Mother Goose")-#1-34, 36, 37; c-28. Peterkin Pottle by **John Stanley** in 32-38.*

RAGGEDY ANN AND ANDY
Dec, 1971 - No. 6, Sept, 1973
Gold Key

1 1.30 3.25 8.00
2-6 1.60 4.00

RAGGEDY ANN & THE CAMEL WITH THE WRINKLED KNEES (See Dell Jr. Treasury #8)

RAGMAN (See Batman Family #20, The Brave & The Bold #196 & Cancelled Comic Cavalcade)
Aug-Sept, 1976 - No. 5, June-July, 1977
National Periodical Publications/DC Comics No. 5

1-Origin & 1st app. 1.30 3.25
2-5: 2-Origin ends; Kubert-c. 4-Drug use story 1.50

NOTE: ***Kubert** a-4, 5; c-1-5. **Redondo** studios a-1-4.*

RAGMAN (2nd series)
Oct, 1991 - No. 8, May, 1992 ($1.50, mini-series)
DC Comics

1-Giffen plots/breakdowns 1.10 2.75
2-8: 3-Origin. 8-Batman-c/story 1.50

RAGMAN: CRY OF THE DEAD
Aug, 1993 - No. 6, Jan, 1994 ($1.75, mini-series)
DC Comics

1-6: Joe Kubert-c .70 1.75

RAGS RABBIT (Formerly Babe Ruth Sports #10 or Little Max #10?; also see Harvey Hits #2, Harvey Wiseguys & Tastee Freez)
No. 11, June, 1951 - No. 18, March, 1954 (Written & drawn for little folks)
Harvey Publications

11-(See Nutty Comics #5 for 1st app.) 2.80 7.00 14.00
12-18 2.40 6.00 12.00

RAI (Rai and the Future Force #9 on; see Magnus #5-8)
Mar, 1992 - No. 0, Nov, 1992; No. 9, May, 1993 - Present ($1.95/$2.25, color)
Valiant

1-Valiant's 1st original character 2.00 6.40 15.00
2 1.40 4.30 10.00
3 3.10 9.00 22.00
4-Low print run; last $1.95-c 3.60 11.00 25.00
5-8: 6,7-Unity x-overs. 7-Death of Rai 1.20 3.60 8.50
0-(11/92)-Origin/1st app. new Rai (Rising Spirit) & 1st full app. & partial origin Bloodshot; also see Eternal Warrior #4; tells future of all characters 1.30 3.00 8.00
9-($2.50)-Gatefold-c; story cont'd from Magnus #24; Magnus, Eternal Warrior & X-O app. 1.00 2.50
10-27: 15-Manowar Armor app. 17-19-Magnus x-over. 21-1st app. The Starwatchers (cameo); bound-in trading card. 22-Death of Rai. 26-Chaos Effect Epsilon Pt. 3 .90 2.25

NOTE: ***Layton** c-2i, 9i. **Miller** c-6. **Simonson** c-7.*

RAIDERS OF THE LOST ARK
Sept, 1981 - No. 3, Nov, 1981 (Movie adaptation)
Marvel Comics Group

1-r/Marvel Comics Super Special #18 1.50
2,3 1.00

NOTE: ***Buscema** a(p)-1-3; c(p)-1. **Simonson** a-3i; scripts-1-3.*

RAINBOW BRITE AND THE STAR STEALER (DC)(Value: cover or less)

Ramm #1 © Megaton Comics

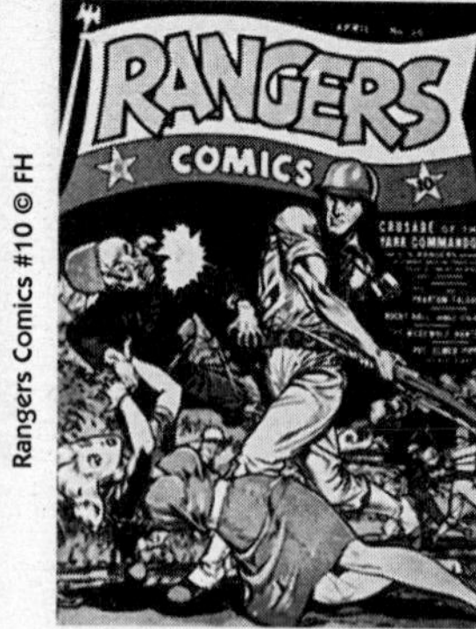

Rangers Comics #10 © FH

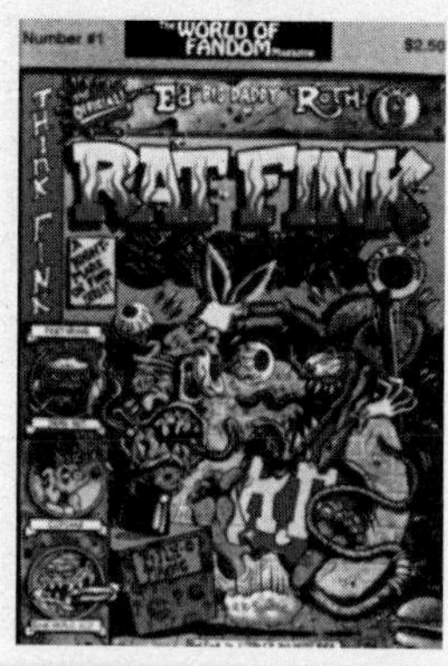

Ratfink #1 © Canrom

GD25 FN65 NM94

RALPH KINER, HOME RUN KING
1950 (Pittsburgh Pirates)
Fawcett Publications

	GD25	FN65	NM94
nn-Photo-c; life story	43.00	130.00	300.00

RALPH SNART ADVENTURES
June, 1986 - V2#9, 1987; V3#1 - #26, Feb, 1991; V4#1, 1992 - #4, 1992
Now Comics

	GD25	FN65	NM94
1-($1.00, B&W)			1.00
2,3			1.25
V2#1 (11/86, B&W) - 9			1.50
V3#1 (9/88, $1.75)-Color series begins		.70	1.75
2-23,25,26		.70	1.75
24-($2.50)-3-D issue		1.00	2.50
V4#1-4-Direct sale versions w/cards		1.00	2.50
V4#1-4-Newsstand versions w/random cards		.80	2.00
Book 1	1.30	3.30	8.00
3-D Special (11/92, $3.50)-Complete 12-card set w/3-D glasses		1.40	3.50

RAMAR OF THE JUNGLE (TV)
1954 (no month); No. 2, Sept, 1955 - No. 5, Sept, 1956
Toby Press No. 1/Charlton No. 2 on

	GD25	FN65	NM94
1-Jon Hall photo-c; last pre-code issue	11.50	34.00	80.00
2-5: 2-Jon Hall photo-c	10.00	30.00	60.00

RAMM
May, 1987 - No. 2, Sept, 1987 ($1.50, B&W)
Megaton Comics

	GD25	FN65	NM94
1,2-Both have 1 pg. Youngblood ad by Liefeld			1.50

RAMPAGING HULK (The Hulk #10 on; see Marvel Treasury Edition)
Jan, 1977 - No. 10, Aug, 1978 ($1.00, B&W magazine)(#10 is in color)
Marvel Comics Group

	GD25	FN65	NM94
1-Bloodstone featured		1.60	4.00
2-Old X-Men app; origin old & new X-Men in text w/Cockrum illos	1.30	3.10	7.50
3-10: 9-Thor vs. Hulk battle; Shanna the She-Devil story. 10-Color issue		.80	2.00

NOTE: ***Alcala** a-1-3i, 5i, 8i. **Buscema** a-1. **Giffen** a-4. **Nino** a-4i. **Simonson** a-1-3p. **Starlin** a-4(w/**Nino**), 7; c-4, 5, 7.*

RANDOLPH SCOTT (Movie star)(See Crack Western #67, Prize Comics Western #76, Western Hearts #8, Western Love #1 & Western Winners #7)

RANGE BUSTERS
Sept, 1950 - No. 8, 1951
Fox Features Syndicate

	GD25	FN65	NM94
1	10.00	30.00	70.00
2	7.50	22.50	45.00
3-8	6.35	19.00	38.00

RANGE BUSTERS (Formerly Cowboy Love?; Wyatt Earp, Frontier Marshall #11 on)
No. 8, May, 1955 - No. 10, Sept, 1955
Charlton Comics

	GD25	FN65	NM94
8	5.00	15.00	30.00
9,10	3.60	9.00	18.00

RANGELAND LOVE
Dec, 1949 - No. 2, Mar, 1950 (52 pgs.)
Atlas Comics (CDS)

	GD25	FN65	NM94
1-Robert Taylor & Arlene Dahl photo-c	10.00	30.00	70.00
2-Photo-c	10.00	30.00	60.00

RANGER, THE (See 4-Color #255)

RANGE RIDER (See The Flying A's...)

RANGE RIDER, THE (See 4-Color #404)

RANGE ROMANCES
Dec, 1949 - No. 5, Aug, 1950 (#5: 52 pgs.)
Comic Magazines (Quality Comics)

	GD25	FN65	NM94
1-Gustavson-c/a	16.50	50.00	115.00
2-Crandall-c/a; "spanking" scene	20.00	60.00	140.00
3-Crandall, Gustavson-a; photo-c	13.00	40.00	90.00
4-Crandall-a; photo-c	11.00	32.00	75.00
5-Gustavson-a; Crandall-a(p); photo-c	11.50	34.00	80.00

RANGERS COMICS (...of Freedom #1-7)
10/41 - No. 67, 10/52; No. 68, Fall, 1952; No. 69, Winter, 1952-53
Fiction House Magazines (Flying stories)

	GD25	FN65	NM94
1-Intro. Ranger Girl & The Rangers of Freedom; ends #7, cover app. only #5	132.00	396.00	925.00
2	57.00	171.00	400.00
3	50.00	150.00	350.00
4,5	45.00	135.00	315.00
6-10: 8-U.S. Rangers begin	37.00	111.00	260.00
11,12-Commando Rangers app.	34.00	100.00	235.00
13-Commando Ranger begins-not same as Commando Rangers	33.00	100.00	230.00
14-20	25.00	75.00	175.00
21-Intro/origin Firehair (begins, 2/45)	29.00	86.00	200.00
22-30: 23-Kazanda begins, ends #28. 28-Tiger Man begins (origin/1st app., 4/46), ends #46. 30-Crusoe Island begins, ends #40	19.00	58.00	135.00
31-40: 33-Hypodermic panels	16.00	48.00	110.00
41-46: 41-Last Werewolf Hunter	12.00	36.00	85.00
47-56- "Eisnerish" Dr. Drew by Grandenetti. 48-Last Glory Forbes. 53-Last 52 pg. issue. 55-Last Sky Rangers	13.00	40.00	90.00
57-60-Straight Dr. Drew by Grandenetti	10.00	30.00	70.00
61,62,64-66: 64-Suicide Smith begins	10.00	30.00	60.00
63-Used in **POP**, pgs. 85, 99	10.00	30.00	60.00
67-69: 67-Space Rangers begin, end #69	10.00	30.00	60.00

NOTE: *Bondage, discipline covers, lingerie panels are common. Crusoe Island by **Larsen**-#30-36. Firehair by **Lubbers**-#30-49. Glory Forbes by **Baker**-#36-45, 47; by **Whitman**-#34, 35. I Confess in #41-53. Jan of the Jungle in #42-58. King of the Congo in #49-53. Tiger Man by **Celardo**-#30-39. **M. Anderson** a-30? **Baker** a-36-38, 42, 44. **John Celardo** a-34, 36-39. **Lee Elias** a-21-28. **Evans** a-19, 38-46, 48-52. **Hopper** a-25, 26. **Ingels** a-13-16. **Larsen** a-34. **Bob Lubbers** a-30-38, 40-44; c-40-45. **Moreira** a-41-47. **Tuska** a-16, 17, 19, 22. **M. Whitman** c-61-66. **Zolnerwich** c-1-17.*

RANGO (TV)
August, 1967
Dell Publishing Co.

	GD25	FN65	NM94
1-Tim Conway photo-c	3.20	8.00	16.00

RANMA 1/2 (Viz)(Value: cover or less)

RAPHAEL (See Teenage Mutant Ninja Turtles)
1985 (One shot, $1.50, B&W w/2 color cover, 7-1/2x11")
Mirage Studios

	GD25	FN65	NM94
1-1st Turtles one-shot spin-off; contains 1st drawing of the Turtles as a group from 1983	1.65	4.00	10.00
1-2nd printing (11/87); new-c & 8 pgs. art		1.60	4.00

RASCALS IN PARADISE
Aug, 1994 - No. 3, Dec, 1994 ($3.95, limited series, magazine size)
Dark Horse Comics

	GD25	FN65	NM94
1-3-Jim Silke-a/story		1.60	4.00

RATFINK (See Frantic & Zany)
October, 1964
Canrom, Inc.

	GD25	FN65	NM94
1-Woodbridge-a	4.00	12.00	24.00

RAT PATROL, THE (TV)
March, 1967 - No. 5, Nov, 1967; No. 6, Oct, 1969
Dell Publishing Co.

	GD25	FN65	NM94
1-Christopher George photo-c	6.00	18.00	36.00
2	4.30	13.00	26.00

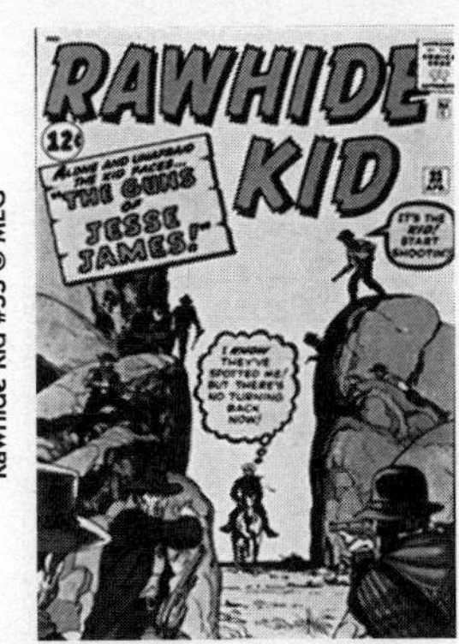

Rawhide Kid #33 © MEG

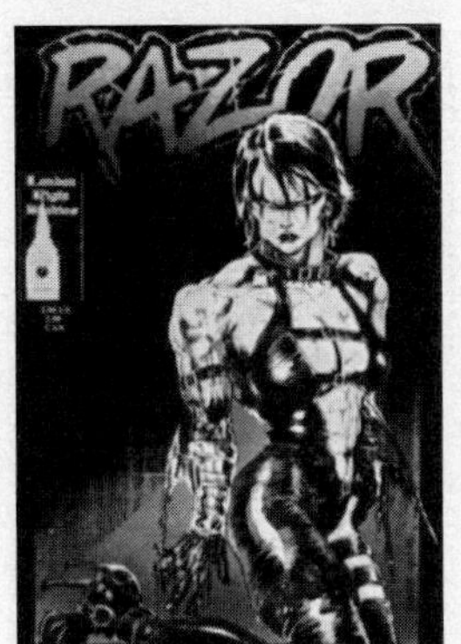

Razor #2 © Everett Hartsoe

Real Clue Crime Stories V2 #8 © HILL

GD25 FN65 NM94

3-6: 3-6-Photo-c 3.20 10.00 19.00

RAVAGE 2099 (See Marvel Comics Presents #117)
Dec, 1992 - Present ($1.25/$1.50)
Marvel Comics

1-($1.75)-Gold foil stamped-c; Stan Lee scripts 1.00 2.50
1-($1.75)-2nd printing .70 1.75
2,3 .80 2.00
4-17: 5-Last Ryan-c. 6-Last Ryan-a. 14-Punisher 2099 x-over. 15-Ron Lim-c(p) 1.25
18-30: 18-Begin $1.50-c; bound-in card sheet 1.50

RAVEN, THE (See Movie Classics)

RAVEN (Renaissance)(Value: cover or less)

RAVENS AND RAINBOWS (Pacific)(Value: cover or less)

RAWHIDE (TV)
Sept-Nov, 1959 - June-Aug, 1962; July, 1963 - No. 2, Jan, 1964
Dell Publishing Co./Gold Key

4-Color 1028 (#1) 24.00 70.00 165.00
4-Color 1097,1160,1202,1261,1269 16.00 48.00 110.00
01-684-208(8/62-Dell) 14.00 43.00 100.00
1(10071-307, G.K.), 2-(12¢) 12.00 36.00 85.00
NOTE: *All have Clint Eastwood photo-c.* **Tufts** *a-1028.*

RAWHIDE KID
3/55 - No. 16, 9/57; No. 17, 8/60 - No. 151, 5/79
Atlas/Marvel Comics (CnPC No. 1-16/AMI No. 17-30)

1-Rawhide Kid, his horse Apache & sidekick Randy begin; Wyatt Earp app.; #1 was not code approved; Maneely splash pg. 57.00 171.00 400.00
2 23.00 70.00 160.00
3-5 14.00 43.00 100.00
6-10: 7-Williamson-a (4 pgs.) 11.50 34.00 80.00
11-16: 16-Torres-a 10.00 30.00 65.00
17-Origin by Jack Kirby 15.00 45.00 105.00
18-22,24-30: 22-Monster-c/story by Kirby/Ayers 8.35 25.00 50.00
23-Origin retold by Jack Kirby 13.00 40.00 90.00
31,32,36-44,46: 38-Red Raven-c/story; Kirby-c (2/64). 40-Two-Gun Kid x-over. 42-1st Larry Lieber issue. 46-Toth-a 6.70 20.00 40.00
33-35-Davis-a. 35-Intro & death of The Raven 7.50 22.50 45.00
45-Origin retold 7.50 22.50 45.00
47-70: 50-Kid Colt x-over. 64-Kid Colt story. 66-Two-Gun Kid story. 67-Kid Colt story 4.00 10.00 20.00
71-86: 79-Williamson-a(r). 86-Origin-r; Williamson-r/Ringo Kid #13 (4 pgs.) 2.40 6.00 12.00
87-99 1.60 4.00 8.00
100-Origin retold & expanded 1.70 5.00 12.00
101-151: 115-Last new story 1.00 2.50 6.00
Special 1(9/71, 25¢, 68 pgs.)-All Kirby/Ayers-r 1.30 3.25 8.00
NOTE: **Ayers** *a-13, 14, 16.* **Colan** *a-5, 35, 37; c-145p, 148p, 149p.* **Davis** *a-125r.* **Everett** *a-54i, 65, 66, 88, 96i, 148i(r).* **Gulacy** *c-147.* **Heath** *c-4.* **G. Kane** *c-101, 144.* **Keller** *a-5, 144r.* **Kirby** *a-17-32, 34, 42, 43, 84, 86, 92, 109r, 112r, 137r, Spec. 1; c-17-35, 37, 38, 40, 41, 43-47, 137r.* **Maneely** *c-1, 2, 5, 6, 14.* **Morisi** *a-13.* **Morrow/Williamson** *r-111.* **Roussos** *r-146i, 147i, 149-151i.* **Severin** *a-16; c-8, 13.* **Torres** *a-99r.* **Tuska** *a-14.* **Wildey** *r-146-151(Outlaw Kid).* **Williamson** *r-79, 86, 95.*

RAWHIDE KID (Marvel)(Value: cover or less)

RAY, THE (See Freedom Fighters & Smash Comics #14)
Feb, 1992 - No. 6, July, 1992 ($1.00, mini-series)
DC Comics

1-Sienkiewicz-c; Joe Quesada-a(p) in 1-5 .80 2.10 5.00
2 1.20 3.00
3: 3-6-Quesada-c(p) 1.00 2.50
4-6: 6-Quesada layouts only 1.50
...In a Blaze of Power (1994, $12.95)-r/1-6 w/new Quesada-c 1.90 5.60 13.00

RAY, THE
May, 1994 - Present ($1.75/$1.95)
DC Comics

1-3: 1,2-Quesada-c(p); Superboy app. .70 1.75
1-($2.95)-Collectors Edition w/different Quesada-c; embossed foil-c 1.20 3.00
4,5: 4-Begin $1.95-c. 5-(9/94) .80 2.00
0,6-11: 0-(10/94) .80 2.00

RAY BRADBURY COMICS
Feb, 1993 - Present ($2.95, color)
Topps Comics

1-5-Polybagged w/3 trading cards each. 1-All dinosaur issue; Corben-a; Williamson/Torres/Krenkel-r/Weird Science-Fantasy #25. 2-All dinosaur issue; Steacy painted-c; Stout-a 1.20 3.00
...Special Edition 1 (1994, $2.95)_The Illustrated Man 1.20 3.00
...Trilogy of Terror V3#1 (5/94, $2.50) 1.00 2.50
...Martian Chronicles V4#1 (6/94, $2.50)-Steranko-c 1.00 2.50

RAZOR
May, 1992 - Present ($3.95, B&W, mature)
London Night Studios

0-(5/92, $3.95)-Direct market 1.30 3.30 8.00
1-(8/92, $2.50)-Fathom Press 1.00 2.00 5.00
1-2nd printing 1.20 3.00
2-($2.95)-J. O'Barr-c 1.20 3.00
2-Limited editions in red & blue 1.30 3.30 8.00
2-Platinum; no price on cover 1.30 3.30 8.00
3-($3.95)-Jim Balent-c 1.70 4.25
3-w/poster insert 1.90 4.75
4-Vigil-c 1.60 4.00
4-w/poster insert 1.80 4.50
5-Linsner-c 1.00 2.50 6.00
5-Platinum 1.30 3.10 7.50
6-10 1.60 4.00
Annual 1 (1993, $2.95-1st app. Shi 2.10 6.40 15.00
Annual 1-Gold (1200 printed) 2.90 8.60 20.00
.../Dark Angel: The Final Nail 1(Boneyard Press),2(LNS) (Both 6/94, $2.95)
.../Shi Special 1 (7/94, $3.00) 1.20 3.00
...: The Suffering 1 ($2.95) 1.20 3.00
...: The Suffering 1Platinum 1.30 3.10 7.50

RAZORLINE
Sept, 1993 (75¢)
Marvel Comics

1-Clive Barker super-heroes: Ectokid, Hokum & Hex, Hyperkind & Saint Sinner (all 1st app.) 1.00

REAL ADVENTURE COMICS (Action Adventure #2 on)
April, 1955
Gillmor Magazines

1 4.00 10.00 20.00

REAL CLUE CRIME STORIES (Formerly Clue Comics)
V2#4, June, 1947 - V8#3, May, 1953
Hillman Periodicals

V2#4(#1)-S&K c/a(3); Dan Barry-a 27.00 81.00 190.00
5-7-S&K c/a(3-4). 7-Iron Lady app. 21.00 63.00 145.00
8-12 6.35 19.00 38.00
V3#1-8,10-12, V4#1-3,5-8,11,12 4.70 14.00 28.00
V3#9-Used in **SOTI**, pg. 102 8.35 25.00 50.00
V4#4-S&K-a 8.35 25.00 50.00
V4#9,10-Krigstein-a 7.50 22.50 45.00
V5#1-5,7,8,10,12 4.20 12.50 25.00
6,9,11-Krigstein-a 7.00 21.00 42.00
V6#1-5,8,9,11 4.00 10.00 20.00
6,7,10,12-Krigstein-a. 10-Bondage-c 7.00 21.00 42.00
V7#1-3,5-11, V8#1-3: V7#6-1 pg. Frazetta ad "Prayer" - 1st app.? 4.00 10.00 20.00
4,12-Krigstein-a 7.00 21.00 42.00

Real Fact Comics #8 © DC

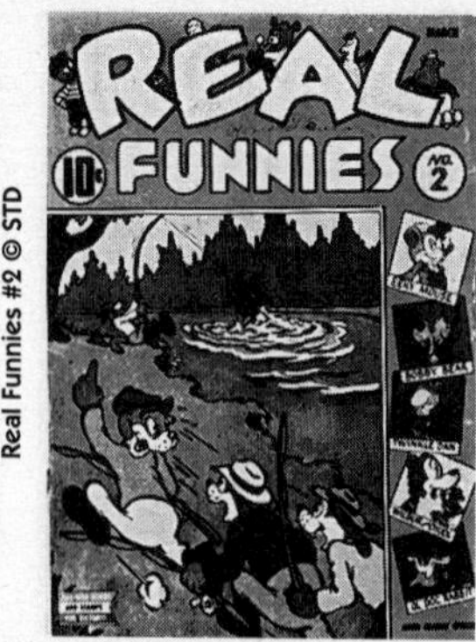

Real Funnies #2 © STD

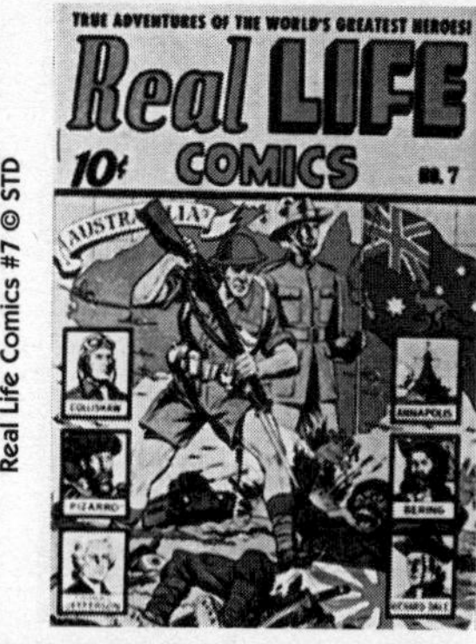

Real Life Comics #7 © STD

GD25 FN65 NM94

NOTE: **Barry** a-9, 10; c-V2#8. **Briefer** a-V6#6. **Fuje** a- V2#7(2), 8, 11. **Infantino** a-V2#8; c-V2#11. **Lawrence** a-V3#8, V5#7. **Powell** a-V4#11, 12. V5#4, 5, 7 are 68 pgs.

REAL EXPERIENCES (Formerly Tiny Tessie)
No. 25, January, 1950
Atlas Comics (20CC)

	GD25	FN65	NM94
25-Virginia Mayo photo-c from movie "Red Light"	4.20	12.50	25.00

REAL FACT COMICS
Mar-Apr, 1946 - No. 21, July-Aug, 1949
National Periodical Publications

	GD25	FN65	NM94
1-S&K-c/a; Harry Houdini story; Just Imagine begins (not by Finlay); Fred Ray-a	46.00	140.00	325.00
2-S&K-a; Rin-Tin-Tin & P. T. Barnum stories	32.00	96.00	225.00
3-H.G. Wells, Lon Chaney stories; 1st DC letter column	24.00	72.00	165.00
4-Virgil Finlay-a on 'Just Imagine' begins, ends #12 (2 pgs. each); Jimmy Stewart & Jack London stories; Joe DiMaggio 1 pg. biography	31.00	92.00	215.00
5-Batman/Robin-c taken from cover of Batman #9; 5 pg. story about creation of Batman & Robin; Tom Mix story	136.00	407.00	950.00
6-Origin & 1st app. Tommy Tomorrow by Finlay (1-2/47); Flag-c; 1st writing by Harlan Ellison (letter column, non-professional); "First Man to Reach Mars" epic-c/story	96.00	290.00	675.00
7-(No. 6 on inside)-Roussos-a; D. Fairbanks sty.	13.00	40.00	90.00
8-2nd app. Tommy Tomorrow by Finlay (5-6/47)	50.00	150.00	350.00
9-S&K-a; Glenn Miller, Indianapolis 500 stories	24.00	72.00	165.00
10-Vigilante by Meskin (based on movie serial); 4 pg. Finlay s/f story	22.00	65.00	150.00
11,12: 11-Annie Oakley, G-Men stories; Kinstler-a	13.00	40.00	90.00
13-Dale Evans and Tommy Tomorrow-c/stories	45.00	135.00	315.00
14,17,18: 14-Will Rogers story	11.50	34.00	80.00
15-Nuclear explosion part-c ("Last War on Earth" story); Clyde Beatty story	13.00	40.00	90.00
16-Tommy Tomorrow app.; 1st Planeteers?	41.00	125.00	290.00
19-Sir Arthur Conan Doyle story	11.50	34.00	80.00
20-Kubert-a, 4 pgs; Daniel Boone story	15.00	45.00	105.00
21-Kubert-a, 2 pgs; Kit Carson story	11.50	34.00	80.00

NOTE: **Barry** c-16. **Virgil Finlay** c-6, 8. **Meskin** c-10. **Roussos** a-1-4, 6.

REAL FUN OF DRIVING!!, THE
1965, 1967 (Regular size)
Chrysler Corp.

	GD25	FN65	NM94
nn-Shaffenberger-a (12 pgs.)	1.00	2.50	5.00

REAL FUNNIES
Jan, 1943 - No. 3, June, 1943
Nedor Publishing Co.

	GD25	FN65	NM94
1-Funny animal, humor; Black Terrier app. (clone of The Black Terror)	22.00	65.00	150.00
2,3	11.00	32.00	75.00

REAL GHOSTBUSTERS, THE (Now)(Value: cover or less)(Also see Slimer)

REAL HEROES COMICS
Sept, 1941 - No. 16, Oct, 1946
Parents' Magazine Institute

	GD25	FN65	NM94
1-Roosevelt-c/story	23.00	70.00	160.00
2-J. Edgar Hoover-c/story	10.00	30.00	65.00
3-5,7-10: 4-Churchill, Roosevelt stories	8.35	25.00	50.00
6-Lou Gehrig-c/story	12.00	36.00	85.00
11-16: 13-Kiefer-a	5.00	15.00	30.00

REAL HIT
1944 (Savings Bond premium)
Fox Features Publications

	GD25	FN65	NM94
1-Blue Beetle-r	12.00	36.00	85.00

NOTE: *Two versions exist, with and without covers. The coverless version has the title, No. 1 and price printed at top of splash page.*

REALISTIC ROMANCES
July-Aug, 1951 - No. 17, Aug-Sept, 1954 (No #9-14)
Realistic Comics/Avon Periodicals

	GD25	FN65	NM94
1-Kinstler-a; c-/Avon paperback #211	12.00	36.00	85.00
2	7.00	21.00	42.00
3,4	5.35	16.00	32.00
5,8-Kinstler-a	5.85	17.50	35.00
6-c-/Diversey Prize Novels #6; Kinstler-a	6.70	20.00	40.00
7-Evans-a?; c-/Avon paperback #360	6.70	20.00	40.00
15,17: 17-Kinstler-c	5.00	15.00	30.00
16-Kinstler marijuana story-r/Romantic Love #6	6.70	20.00	40.00
I.W. Reprint #1,8,9		1.50	3.00

NOTE: **Astarita** a-2-4, 7, 8, 17. Photo c-1, 2. Painted c-3, 4.

REAL LIFE COMICS
Sept, 1941 - No. 59, Sept, 1952
Nedor/Better/Standard Publ./Pictorial Magazine No. 13

	GD25	FN65	NM94
1-Uncle Sam-c/story; Daniel Boone story	29.00	86.00	200.00
2	13.50	41.00	95.00
3-Hitler cover	22.00	65.00	150.00
4,5: 4-Story of American flag "Old Glory"	10.00	30.00	65.00
6-10: 6-Wild Bill Hickok story	10.00	30.00	60.00
11-20: 17-Albert Einstein story	7.50	22.50	45.00
21-23,25,26,28-30: 29-A-Bomb story	5.85	17.50	35.00
24-Story of Baseball (Babe Ruth)	10.00	30.00	65.00
27-Schomburg A-Bomb-c; story of A-Bomb	10.00	30.00	65.00
31-33,35,36,42-44,48,49: 49-Baseball issue	4.70	14.00	28.00
34,37-41,45-47: 34-Jimmy Stewart story. 37-Story of motion pictures; Bing Crosby story. 38-Jane Froman story. 39- "1,000,000 A.D." story. 40-Bob Feller story. 41-Jimmie Foxx story; "Home Run" Baker story. 45-Story of Olympic games; Burl Ives & Kit Carson story. 46-Douglas Fairbanks Jr. & Sr. story. 47-George Gershwin story	5.00	15.00	35.00
50-Frazetta-a (5 pgs.)	16.50	50.00	115.00
51-Jules Verne "Journey to the Moon" by Evans	11.00	32.00	75.00
52-Frazetta-a (4 pgs.); Severin/Elder-a(2); Evans-a	16.50	50.00	115.00
53-57-Severin/Elder-a. 54-Bat Masterson-c/story	9.15	27.50	55.00
58-Severin/Elder-a(2)	10.00	30.00	60.00
59-1 pg. Frazetta; Severin/Elder-a	8.35	25.00	50.00

NOTE: *Some issues had two titles.* **Guardineer** a-40(2), 44. **Meskin** a-52. **Roussos** a-50. **Schomburg** c-1, 2, 4, 5, 7, 11, 13-21, 23, 24, 26, 28, 30-32, 34-40, 42, 44-47, 55. **Tuska** a-53. Photo-c 5, 6.

REAL LIFE SECRETS (Real Secrets #2 on)
Sept, 1949 (One shot)
Ace Periodicals

	GD25	FN65	NM94
1-Painted-c	6.70	20.00	40.00

REAL LIFE STORY OF FESS PARKER (Magazine)
1955
Dell Publishing Co.

	GD25	FN65	NM94
1	11.50	34.00	80.00

REAL LIFE TALES OF SUSPENSE (See Suspense)

REAL LOVE (Formerly Hap Hazard)
No. 25, April, 1949 - No. 76, Nov, 1956
Ace Periodicals (A. A. Wyn)

	GD25	FN65	NM94
25	8.35	25.00	50.00
26	4.20	12.50	25.00
27-L. B. Cole-a	5.85	17.50	35.00
28-35	3.60	9.00	18.00
36-66: 66-Last pre-code (2/55)	3.00	7.50	15.00
67-76	2.00	5.00	10.00

NOTE: Photo c-50-76. Painted c-46.

REALM, THE
Feb, 1986 - No. 20? ($1.50/$1.95/$2.50, B&W)
Arrow Comics/WeeBee Comics #13/Caliber Press #14 on

	GD25	FN65	NM94
1		1.60	4.00

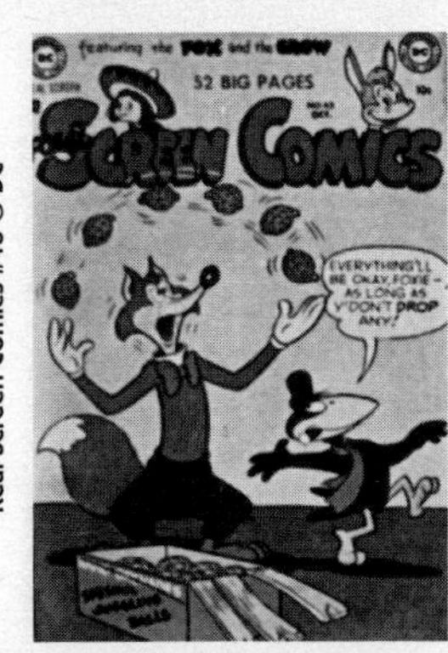

Real Screen Comics #43 © DC

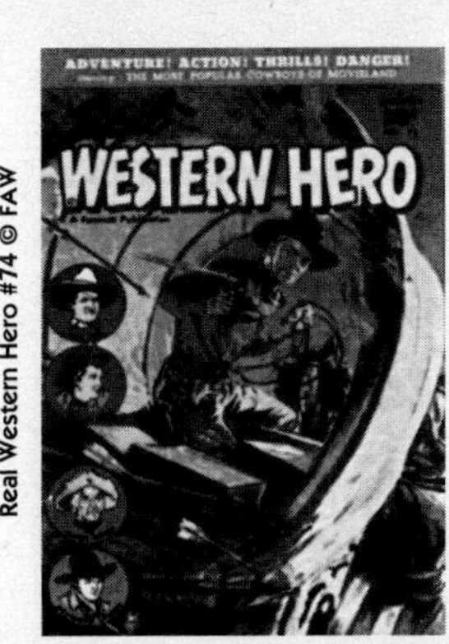

Real Western Hero #74 © FAW

Red Circle Comics #4 © Enwil

	GD25	FN65	NM94
2		.80	2.00
3,5-16: 13-Begin $1.95-c			1.25
4-1st app. Deadworld (9/86)	2.15	6.50	15.00
17-20: 17-Begin $2.50-c		1.00	2.50
Book 1 ($4.95, B&W)	1.00	2.00	5.00

REAL McCOYS, THE (TV)
No. 1071, 1-3/60 - 5-7/1962 (All have Walter Brennan photo-c)
Dell Publishing Co.

4-Color 1071,1134-Toth-a in both	11.50	34.00	80.00
4-Color 1193,1265	10.00	30.00	60.00
01-689-207 (5-7/62)	9.15	27.50	55.00

REAL SCREEN COMICS (#1 titled Real Screen Funnies; TV Screen Cartoons #129-138)
Spring, 1945 - No. 128, May-June, 1959 (#1-40: 52 pgs.)
National Periodical Publications

1-The Fox & the Crow, Flippity & Flop, Tito & His Burrito begin	90.00	270.00	630.00
2	45.00	135.00	315.00
3-5	28.00	84.00	195.00
6-10 (2-3/47)	19.00	57.00	130.00
11-20 (10-11/48): 13-The Crow x-over in Flippity & Flop	14.00	43.00	100.00
21-30 (6-7/50)	10.00	30.00	70.00
31-50	10.00	30.00	60.00
51-99	7.50	22.50	45.00
100	8.35	25.00	50.00
101-128	5.35	16.00	32.00

REAL SECRETS (Formerly Real Life Secrets)
No. 2, Nov, 1950 - No. 5, May, 1950
Ace Periodicals

2-Painted-c	6.35	19.00	38.00
3-5: 3-Photo-c	4.00	11.00	22.00

REAL SPORTS COMICS (All Sports Comics #2 on)
Oct-Nov, 1948 (52 pgs.)
Hillman Periodicals

1-Powell-a (12 pgs.)	27.00	81.00	190.00

REAL WAR STORIES
July, 1987; No. 2, Jan, 1991 ($2.00, color, 52 pgs.)
Eclipse Comics

1-Bolland-a(p), Bissette-a, Totleben-a(i); Alan Moore scripts (2nd printing exists, 2/88)		.80	2.00
2-($4.95)	1.00	2.00	5.00

REAL WESTERN HERO (Formerly Wow #1-69; Western Hero #76 on)
No. 70, Sept, 1948 - No. 75, Feb, 1949 (All 52 pgs.)
Fawcett Publications

70(#1)-Tom Mix, Monte Hale, Hopalong Cassidy, Young Falcon begin	27.00	81.00	190.00
71-75: 71-Gabby Hayes begins. 71,72-Captain Tootsie by Beck. 75-Big Bow and Little Arrow app.	17.00	52.00	120.00

NOTE: *Painted/photo c-70-73; painted c-74, 75.*

REAL WEST ROMANCES
4-5/49 - V1#6, 3/50; V2#1, Apr-May, 1950 (All 52 pgs. & photo-c)
Crestwood Publishing Co./Prize Publ.

V1#1-S&K-a(p)	14.00	43.00	100.00
2-Spanking panel	11.50	34.00	80.00
3-Kirby-a(p) only	8.35	25.00	50.00
4-S&K-a; Whip Wilson, Reno Browne photo-c	13.00	40.00	90.00
5-Audie Murphy, Gale Storm photo-c; S&K-a	11.50	34.00	80.00
6-Produced by S&K, no S&K-a; Robert Preston & Cathy Downs photo-c	10.00	30.00	60.00
V2#1-Kirby-a(p)	7.50	22.50	45.00

NOTE: ***Meskin** a-V1#5, 6. **Severin/Elder** a-V1#3-6, V2#1. **Meskin** a-V1#6. **Leonard Starr** a-1-3. Photo-c V1#1-6, V2#1.*

RE-ANIMATOR IN FULL COLOR
Oct, 1991 - No. 3, 1992 ($2.95, color, mini-series)
Adventure Comics

1-3: Adapts horror movie. 1-Dorman painted-c		1.20	3.00

REAP THE WILD WIND (See Cinema Comics Herald)

REBEL, THE (See 4-Color #1076, 1138, 1207, 1262)

R.E.B.E.L.S. '94
No. 0, Oct, 1994 - Present ($1.95)
DC Comics

0-6		.80	2.00

RECORD BOOK OF FAMOUS POLICE CASES
1949 (25¢, 132 pgs.)
St. John Publishing Co.

nn-Kubert-a(3); r/Son of Sinbad; Baker-c	27.00	80.00	185.00

RED ARROW
May-June, 1951 - No. 3, Oct, 1951
P. L. Publishing Co.

1	7.50	22.50	45.00
2,3	5.85	17.50	35.00

RED BALL COMIC BOOK
1947 (Red Ball Shoes giveaway)
Parents' Magazine Institute

nn-Reprints from True Comics	2.40	6.00	12.00

RED BAND COMICS
Feb, 1945 - No. 4, May, 1945
Enwil Associates

1	20.00	60.00	140.00
2-Origin Bogeyman & Santanas	16.50	50.00	115.00
3,4-Captain Wizard app. in both (1st app.); each has identical contents/cover	14.00	43.00	100.00

REDBLADE
Apr, 1993 - No. 3, July, 1993 ($2.50, mini-series)
Dark Horse Comics

1-3: 1-Double gatefold-c		1.00	2.50

RED CIRCLE COMICS
Jan, 1945 - No. 4, April, 1945
Rural Home Publications (Enwil)

1-The Prankster & Red Riot begin	20.00	60.00	140.00
2-Starr-a; The Judge (costumed hero) app.	16.00	48.00	110.00
3,4-Starr-c/a. 3-The Prankster not in costume	12.00	36.00	85.00
4-(Dated 4/45)-Leftover covers to #4 were later restapled over early 1950s coverless comics; variations in the coverless comics used are endless; Woman Outlaws, Dorothy Lamour, Crime Does Not Pay, Sabu, Diary Loves, Love Confessions & Young Love V3#3 known	10.00	30.00	60.00

RED CIRCLE SORCERY (Chilling Adventures in Sorcery #1-5)
No. 6, Apr, 1974 - No. 11, Feb, 1975 (All 25¢ issues)
Red Circle Productions (Archie)

6-11: 8-Only app. The Cobra. 10-Wood-a(i)			1.50

NOTE: ***Chaykin** a-6, 10. **B. Jones** a-7(w/**Wrightson**, **Kaluta**, **J. Jones**). **McWilliams** a-10(2 & 3 pgs.). **Mooney** a-11p. **Morrow** a-6-8, 9(text illos), 10, 11i; c-6-11. **Thorne** a-8, 10. **Toth** a-8, 9.*

REDDEVIL (AC)(Value: cover or less)

RED DOG (See Night Music #7)

RED DRAGON COMICS (1st Series) (Formerly Trail Blazers; see Super Magician V5#7, 8)
No. 5, Jan, 1943 - No. 9, Jan, 1944
Street & Smith Publications

5-Origin Red Rover, the Crimson Crimebuster; Rex King, Man of Adventure, Captain Jack Commando, & The Minute Man begin; text origin Red Dragon;

Red Mask #49 © ME

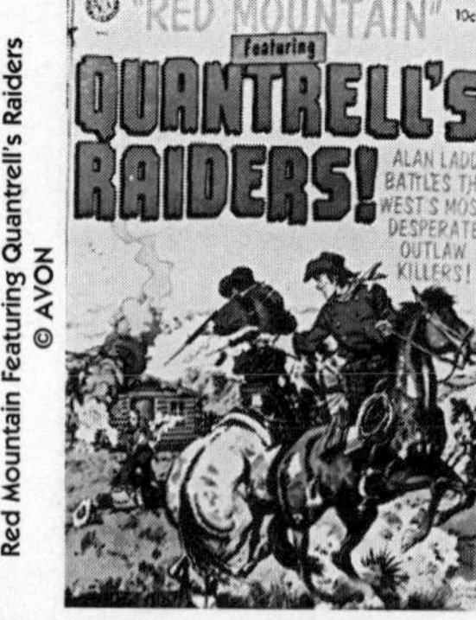

Red Mountain Featuring Quantrell's Raiders © AVON

Red Ryder Comics #11 © DELL

GD25 FN65 NM94

Binder-c 57.00 171.00 400.00
6-Origin The Black Crusader & Red Dragon (3/43); 1st story app. Red Dragon & 1st cover 86.00 257.00 600.00
7-Classic-c 57.00 171.00 400.00
8-The Red Knight app. 43.00 130.00 300.00
9-Origin Chuck Magnon, Immortal Man 43.00 130.00 300.00

RED DRAGON COMICS (2nd Series)(See Super Magician V2#8)
Nov, 1947 - No. 6, Jan, 1949; No. 7, July, 1949
Street & Smith Publications

1-Red Dragon begins; Elliman, Nigel app.; Edd Cartier-c/a 61.00 185.00 430.00
2-Cartier-c 48.00 145.00 335.00
3-1st app. Dr. Neff Ghost Breaker by Powell; Elliman, Nigel app. 41.00 122.00 285.00
4-Cartier c/a 54.00 162.00 375.00
5-7 31.00 92.00 215.00
NOTE: ***Maneely** a-5, 7. **Powell** a-2-7; c-3, 5, 7.*

REDDY GOOSE
No #, 1958?; No. 2, Jan, 1959 - No. 16, July, 1962 (Giveaway)
International Shoe Co. (Western Printing)

nn (#1) 6.70 20.00 40.00
2-16 4.00 10.50 21.00

REDDY KILOWATT (5¢) (Also see Story of Edison)
1946 - No. 2, 1947; 1956 - 1960 (no month) (16 pgs.; paper cover)
Educational Comics (E. C.)

nn-Reddy Made Magic (1946, 5¢) 12.00 35.00 70.00
nn-Reddy Made Magic (1958) 5.35 16.00 32.00
2-Edison, the Man Who Changed the World (3/4" smaller than #1) (1947, 5¢) 12.00 35.00 70.00
...Comic Book 2 (1954)- "Light's Diamond Jubilee" 6.70 20.00 40.00
...Comic Book 2 (1958, 16 pgs.)- "Wizard of Light" 5.35 16.00 32.00
...Comic Book 3 (1956, 8 pgs.)- "The Space Kite"; Orlando story; regular size 5.35 16.00 32.00
...Comic Book 3 (1960, 8 pgs.)- "The Space Kite"; Orlando story; regular size 4.70 14.00 28.00
NOTE: *Several copies surfaced in 1979.*

REDDY MADE MAGIC
1956, 1958 (16 pgs.) (paper cover)
Educational Comics (E. C.)

1-Reddy Kilowatt-r (splash panel changed) 8.00 24.00 48.00
1 (1958 edition) 5.00 15.00 30.00

RED EAGLE (See Feature Books #16)

REDEYE (See Comics Reading Libraries)

RED FOX (Formerly Manhunt! #1-14; also see Extra Comics)
No. 15, 1954
Magazine Enterprises

15(A-1 #108)-Undercover Girl story; L.B. Cole-c/a (Red Fox); r-from Manhunt; Powell-a 11.00 32.00 75.00

RED GOOSE COMIC SELECTIONS (See Comic Selections)

RED HAWK (See A-1 Comics #90, Bobby Benson's... #14-16 & Straight Arrow #2)

RED ICEBERG, THE
1960 (10¢) (16 pgs.) (Communist propaganda)
Impact Publ. (Catechetical Guild)

nn-(Rare)- 'We The People' back-c 37.00 110.00 240.00
2nd version- 'Impact Press' back-c 43.00 130.00 280.00
NOTE: *This book was the Guild's last anti-communist propaganda book and had very limited circulation. 3 - 4 copies surfaced in 1979 from the defunct publisher's files. Other copies do turn up.*

RED MASK (Formerly Tim Holt; see Best Comics, Blazing Six-Guns)
No. 42, 6-7/1954 - No. 53, 5/56; No. 54, 9/57
Magazine Enterprises No. 42-53/Sussex No. 54 (M.E. on-c)

GD25 FN65 NM94

42-Ghost Rider by Ayers continues, ends #50; Black Phantom continues; 3-D effect c/stories begin 16.00 48.00 110.00
43-3-D effect-c/stories 14.00 43.00 100.00
44-50: 3-D effect stories only. 47-Last pre-code issue. 50-Last Ghost Rider 13.00 40.00 90.00
51-The Presto Kid begins by Ayers (1st app.); Presto Kid-c begins, ends #54; last 3-D effect story 13.00 40.00 90.00
52-Origin The Presto Kid 13.00 40.00 90.00
53,54-Last Black Phantom 10.00 30.00 65.00
I.W. Reprint #1 (r-/#52). 2 (nd, r/#51 w/diff.-c). 3, 8 (nd; Kinstler-c); 8-r/Red Mask #52 2.40 6.00 12.00
NOTE: ***Ayers** art on Ghost Rider & Presto Kid. **Bolle** art in all (Red Mask); c-43, 44, 49. **Guardineer** a-52. Black Phantom in #42-44, 47-50, 53, 54.*

REDMASK OF THE RIO GRANDE (AC)(Value: cover or less)

RED MOUNTAIN FEATURING QUANTRELL'S RAIDERS
1952 (Movie) (Also see Jesse James #28)
Avon Periodicals

nn-Alan Ladd; Kinstler-c/a 19.00 57.00 130.00

"RED" RABBIT COMICS
Jan, 1947 - No. 22, Aug-Sept, 1951
Dearfield Comic/J. Charles Laue Publ. Co.

1 9.15 27.50 55.00
2 5.00 15.00 30.00
3-10 4.00 11.00 22.00
11-17,19-22 3.60 9.00 18.00
18-Flying Saucer-c (1/51) 4.70 14.00 28.00

RED RAVEN COMICS (Human Torch #2 on; also see X-Men #44)
August, 1940 (Also see Sub-Mariner #26, 2nd series)
Timely Comics

GD25 FN65 VF82 NM94

1-Origin & 1st app. Red Raven; Comet Pierce & Mercury by Kirby, The Human Top & The Eternal Brain; intro. Magar, the Mystic & only app.; Kirby-c (his 1st signed work) 938.00 2813.00 5156.00 7500.00
(Estimated up to 50 total copies exist, 6 in NM/Mint)

RED RYDER COMICS (Hi Spot #2)(Movies, radio)(See Crackajack Funnies)
9/40; No. 3, 8/41 - No. 5, 12/41; No. 6, 4/42 - No. 151, 4-6/57
Hawley Publ. No. 1-5/Dell Publishing Co.(K.K.) No. 6 on

GD25 FN65 NM94

1-Red Ryder, his horse Thunder, Little Beaver & his horse Papoose strip reprints begin by Fred Harman; 1st meeting of Red & Little Beaver; Harman line-drawn-c #1-85 129.00 385.00 900.00
3-(Scarce)-Alley Oop, King of the Royal Mtd., Capt. Easy, Freckles & His Friends, Myra North, Dan Dunn strip-r begin 86.00 257.00 600.00
4,5 43.00 130.00 300.00
6-1st Dell issue (4/42) 43.00 130.00 300.00
7-10 36.00 107.00 250.00
11-20 27.00 80.00 185.00
21-32-Last Alley Oop, Dan Dunn, Capt. Easy, Freckles 17.00 52.00 120.00
33-40 (52 pgs.) 10.00 30.00 70.00
41 (52 pgs.)-Rocky Lane photo back-c; photo back-c begin, end #57 11.00 32.00 75.00
42-46 (52 pgs.): 46-Last Red Ryder strip-r 10.00 30.00 60.00
47-53 (52 pgs.): 47-New stories on Red Ryder begin. 49,52-Harmon photo back-c 8.35 25.00 50.00
54-57 (36 pgs.) 6.70 20.00 40.00
58-73 (36 pgs.): 59-Harmon photo back-c. 73-Last King of the Royal Mtd; strip-r by Jim Gary 6.70 20.00 40.00
74-85,93 (52 pgs.)-Harman line-drawn-c 6.70 20.00 40.00
86-92 (52 pgs.)-Harman painted-c 6.70 20.00 40.00
94-96 (36 pgs.)-Harman painted-c 5.00 15.00 30.00
97,98,107,108 (36 pgs.)-Harman line-drawn-c 5.00 15.00 30.00
99,101-106 (36 pgs.)-Jim Bannon Photo-c 5.00 15.00 30.00
100 (36 pgs.)-Bannon photo-c 5.85 17.50 35.00
109-118 (52 pgs.)-Harman line-drawn-c 4.00 12.00 24.00

Red Seal Comics #21 © SUPR

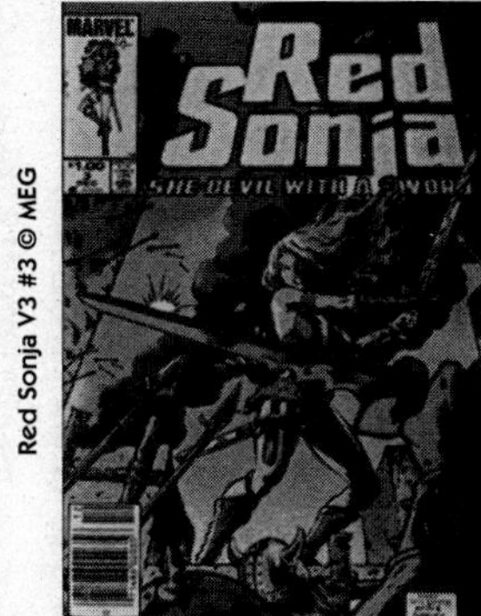
Red Sonja V3 #3 © MEG

Red Warrior #1 © MEG

GD25 FN65 NM94

119-129 (52 pgs.): 119-Painted-c begin, not by Harman, end #151
4.00 11.00 22.00
130-144 (#130 on have 36 pgs.) 4.00 10.00 20.00
145-148: 145-Title change to Red Ryder Ranch Magazine with photos
3.20 8.00 16.00
149-151: 149-Title changed to Red Ryder Ranch Comics
3.20 8.00 16.00
4-Color 916 (7/58) 4.00 10.00 20.00
Buster Brown Shoes Giveaway (1941, color, soft-c, 32 pgs.)
24.00 72.00 165.00
Red Ryder Super Book Of Comics 10 (1944; paper-c; 32 pgs.; blank back-c)-Magic Morro app. 24.00 72.00 165.00
Red Ryder Victory Patrol-nn(1944, 32 pgs.)-r-/#43,44; comic has a paper-c & is stapled inside a triple cardboard fold-out-c; contains membership card, decoder, map of R.R. home range, etc. Herky app. (Langendorf Bread give-away; sub-titled 'Super Book of Comics')(Rare) 300.00 900.00 2800.00
Wells Lamont Corp. giveaway (1950)-16 pgs. in color; regular size; paper-c; 1941-r 22.00 65.00 150.00
NOTE: ***Fred Harman** a-1-99; c-1-98, 107-118. Don Red Barry, Allan Rocky Lane, Wild Bill Elliott & Jim Bannon starred as Red Ryder in the movies. Robert Blake starred as Little Beaver.*

RED RYDER PAINT BOOK
1941 (148 pgs.) (8-1/2x11-1/2")
Whitman Publishing Co.

nn-Reprints 1940 daily strips 22.00 65.00 150.00

RED SEAL COMICS (Formerly Carnival Comics, and/or Spotlight Comics?)
No. 14, 10/45 - No. 18, 10/46; No. 19, 6/47 - No. 22, 12/47
Harry 'A' Chesler/Superior Publ. No. 19 on

14-The Black Dwarf begins (continued from Spotlight?); Little Nemo app; bondage/hypo-c; Tuska-a 38.00 115.00 265.00
15-Torture story; funny-c 29.00 86.00 200.00
16-Used in **SOTI**, pg. 181, illo "Outside the forbidden pages of de Sade, you find draining a girl's blood only in children's comics;" drug club story r-later in Crime Reporter #1; Veiled Avenger & Barry Kuda app; Tuska-a; funny-c
39.00 118.00 275.00
17-Lady Satan, Yankee Girl & Sky Chief app; Tuska-a
24.00 73.00 170.00
18,20-Lady Satan & Sky Chief app. 24.00 73.00 170.00
19-No Black Dwarf (on-c only); Zor, El Tigre app. 18.00 54.00 125.00
21-Lady Satan & Black Dwarf app. 18.00 54.00 125.00
22-Zor, Rocketman app. (68 pgs.) 18.00 54.00 125.00

REDSKIN (Thrilling Indian Stories)(Famous Western Badmen #13 on)
Sept, 1950 - No. 12, Oct, 1952
Youthful Magazines

1-Walter Johnson-a (7 pgs.) 10.00 30.00 60.00
2 7.00 21.00 42.00
3-12: 3-Daniel Boone story. 6-Geronimo story 5.85 17.50 35.00
NOTE: ***Walter Johnson** c-3, 4. **Palais** a-11. **Wildey** a-5, 11. Bondage c-6, 12.*

RED SONJA (Also see Conan #23, Kull & The Barbarians, Marvel Feature & Savage Sword Of Conan #1)
1/77 - No. 15, 5/79; V1#1, 2/83 - V2#2, 3/83; V3#1, 8/83 - V3#4, 2/84; V3#5, 1/85 - V3#13, 1986
Marvel Comics Group

1-Created by Robert E. Howard 1.30 3.25
2-5: 5-Last 30¢ issue .80 2.00
6-15, V1#1,V2#2: 14-Last 35¢ issue 1.00
V3#1-4 ($1.00, 52 pgs.) 1.20
5-13 (65-75¢) 1.00
NOTE: ***Brunner** c-12-14. **J. Buscema** a(p)-12, 13, 15; c-V#1. **Nebres** a-V3#3i(part). **N. Redondo** a-8i, V3#2i, 3i. **Simonson** a-V3#1. **Thorne** c/a-1-11.*

RED SONJA: THE MOVIE (Marvel)(Value: cover or less)

RED TORNADO (DC)(Value: cover or less)(See All-American #20 & Justice League of America #64)

RED WARRIOR
Jan, 1951 - No. 6, Dec, 1951
Marvel/Atlas Comics (TCI)

1-Red Warrior & his horse White Wing; Tuska-a 11.50 34.00 80.00
2-Tuska-c 8.35 25.00 50.00
3-6: 4-Origin White Wing. 6-Maneely-c 6.70 20.00 40.00

RED WOLF (See Avengers #80 & Marvel Spotlight #1)
May, 1972 - No. 9, Sept, 1973
Marvel Comics Group

1-(Western hero); Gil Kane/Severin-c; Shores-a 1.50 3.75
2-9: 2-Kane-c; Shores-a. 6-Tuska-r in back-up. 7-Red Wolf as super hero begins. 9-Origin sidekick, Lobo (wolf) .80 2.00

REESE'S PIECES (Eclipse)(Value: cover or less)

REFORM SCHOOL GIRL!
1951
Realistic Comics

nn-Used in **SOTI**, pg. 358, & cover ill. with caption "Comic books are supposed to be like fairy tales" 86.00 257.00 600.00
(Prices vary widely on this book)
NOTE: *The cover and title originated from a digest-sized book published by Diversey Publishing Co. of Chicago in 1948. The original book "House of Fury", Doubleday, came out in 1941. The girl's real name which appears on the cover of the digest and comic is Marty Collins, Canadian model and ice skating star who posed for this special color photograph for the Diversey novel.*

REGENTS ILLUSTRATED CLASSICS
1981 (Plus more recent reprintings)
(48 pgs., b&w-a with 14 pgs. of teaching helps)
Prentice Hall Regents, Englewood Cliffs, NJ 07632
NOTE: *This series contains Classics Ill. art, and was produced from the same illegal source as **Cassette Books.** But when Twin Circle sued to stop the sale of the Cassette Books, they decided to permit this series to continue. This series was produced as a teaching aid. The 20 title series is divided into four levels based upon number of basic words used therein. There is also a teacher's manual for each level. All of the titles are still available from the publisher for about $5 each retail. The number to call for mail order purchases is (201)767-5937. Almost all of the issues have new covers taken from some interior art panel. Here is a list of the series by Regents ident. no. and the Classics Ill. counterpart.*

16770(CI#24-A2)18333(CI#3-A2)21668(CI#13-A2)32224(CI#21)33051(CI#26)
35788(CI#84)37153(CI#16)44460(CI#19-A2)44808(CI#18-A2)52395(CI#4-A2)
58627(CI#5-A2)60067(CI#30)68405(CI#23-A1)70302(CI#29)78192(CI#7-A2)
78193(CI#10-A2)79679(CI#85)92046(CI#1-A2)93062(CI#64)93512(CI#25)

REGGIE (Formerly Archie's Rival...; Reggie & Me #19 on)
No. 15, Sept, 1963 - No. 18, Nov, 1965
Archie Publications

15(9/63), 16(10/64) 6.35 19.00 38.00
17(8/65), 18(11/65) 6.35 19.00 38.00
NOTE: *Cover title No. 15 & 16 is Archie's Rival Reggie.*

REGGIE AND ME (Formerly Reggie)
No. 19, Aug, 1966 - No. 126, Sept, 1980 (No. 50-68: 52 pgs.)
Archie Publications

19-Evilheart app. 3.20 8.00 16.00
20-23-Evilheart app.; with Pureheart #22 1.60 4.00 8.00
24-40 1.00 2.50
41-60 1.50
61-126 1.00

REGGIE'S JOKES (See Reggie's Wise Guy Jokes)

REGGIE'S REVENGE!
Spring, 1994 - Present ($2.00, color, 52 pgs.)(Published semi-annually)
Archie Comic Publications, Inc.

1,2: 1-Bound-in pull-out poster .80 2.00

REGGIE'S WISE GUY JOKES
Aug, 1968 - No. 60, Jan, 1982 (#5-28 are Giants)
Archie Publications

1 2.00 6.00 14.00
2-4 1.00 2.50 6.00
5-10 1.20 3.00
11-28 1.50

The Ren & Stimpy Show #23 © Nickelodeon

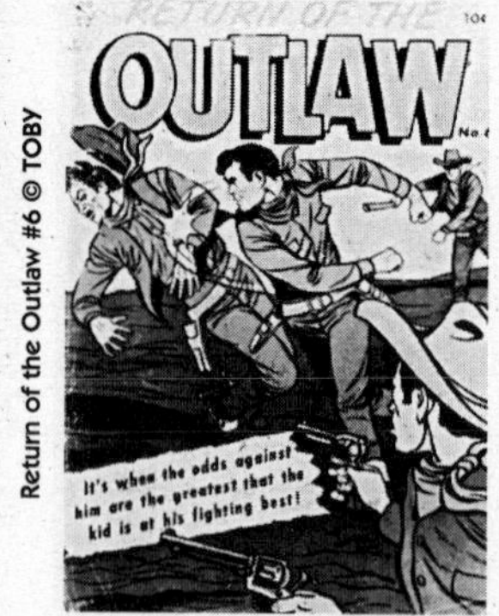

Return of the Outlaw #6 © TOBY

Rex Allen Comics #4 © DELL

	GD25	FN65	NM94
29-60			1.00

REGISTERED NURSE
Summer, 1963
Charlton Comics

	GD25	FN65	NM94
1-r/Nurse Betsy Crane & Cynthia Doyle	1.00	2.50	5.00

REG'LAR FELLERS (See All-American Comics, Popular Comics & Treasure Box of Famous Comics)
1921 - 1929
Cupples & Leon Co./MS Publishng Co.

	GD25	FN65	NM94
1(1921)-52 pgs. B&W dailies (Cupples & Leon, 10x10")	16.00	48.00	110.00
1925, 48 pgs. B&W dailies (MS Publ.)	16.00	48.00	110.00
Softcover (1929, nn, 36 pgs.)	16.00	48.00	110.00
Hardcover (1929, 96 pgs.)-B&W reprints	17.00	52.00	120.00

REG'LAR FELLERS
No. 5, Nov, 1947 - No. 6, Mar, 1948
Visual Editions (Standard)

	GD25	FN65	NM94
5,6	6.70	20.00	40.00

REG'LAR FELLERS HEROIC (See Heroic Comics)

REID FLEMING, WORLD'S TOUGHEST MILKMAN (Eclipse)(Value: cover or less)

RELUCTANT DRAGON, THE (See 4-Color #13)

REMEMBER PEARL HARBOR
1942 (68 pgs.) (Illustrated story of the battle)
Street & Smith Publications

	GD25	FN65	NM94
nn-Uncle Sam-c; Jack Binder-a	34.00	103.00	240.00

REN & STIMPY SHOW, THE (TV)
Dec, 1992 - Present ($1.75/$1.95)
Marvel Comics

	GD25	FN65	NM94
1-($2.25)-Polybagged w/scratch & sniff Ren or Stimpy air fowler (equal amounts of each were made)	2.10	6.40	15.00
1-2nd printing; different dialogue on-c		.90	2.25
1-3rd printing; yet different dialogue on-c		.90	2.25
2	1.40	4.30	10.00
3		1.90	4.75
4-6: 4-Muddy Mudskipper back-up. 5-Bill Wray painted-c. 6-Spider-Man vs. Powered Toast Man		1.70	4.25
7-17: 12-1st solo back-up story w/Tank & Brenner		.70	1.75
18-29: 18-Begin $1.95-c; Powered Toast Man app.		.80	2.00
...Don't Try This at Home (3/94, 12.95, TPB)-r/#9-12	1.85	5.50	13.00
...Pick of the Litter nn (1993, 12.95, TPB)-r/#1-4	1.85	5.50	13.00
...Running Joke nn (1993, $12.95, TPB)-r/#1-4 plus new-a	1.85	5.50	13.00
...Special: Powered Toast Man 1 (4/94, 2.95, 52 pgs.)		1.20	3.00
...Special 2 (7/94, 2.95, 52 pgs.)		1.20	3.00
...Special 3 (10/94, 2.95, 52 pgs.)-Choose adventure		1.20	3.00
...Tastes Like Chicken nn (11/93,$12.95,TPB)-r/5-8	1.85	5.50	13.00
...Your Pals (1994, $12.95, TPB)-r/13-16	1.90	5.60	13.00

RENFIELD
1994 - Present ($2.95, B&W, limited series:5)
Caliber Press

	GD25	FN65	NM94
1		1.20	3.00

RENO BROWNE, HOLLYWOOD'S GREATEST COWGIRL (Formerly Margie Comics; Apache Kid #53 on; also see Western Hearts, Western Life Romances & Western Love)
No. 50, April, 1950 - No. 52, Sept, 1950 (52 pgs.)
Marvel Comics (MPC)

	GD25	FN65	NM94
50-Reno Browne photo-c on all	22.00	65.00	150.00
51,52	19.00	58.00	135.00

REPTILICUS (Becomes Reptisaurus #3 on)
Aug, 1961 - No. 2, Oct, 1961
Charlton Comics

	GD25	FN65	NM94
1 (Movie)	11.00	33.00	78.00
2	7.00	22.00	52.00

REPTISAURUS (Reptilicus #1,2)
V2#3, Jan, 1962 - No. 8, Dec, 1962; Summer, 1963
Charlton Comics

	GD25	FN65	NM94
V2#3-8: 8-Montes/Bache-c/a	4.30	13.00	30.00
Special Edition 1 (Summer, 1963)	3.90	11.60	27.00

REQUIEM FOR DRACULA
Feb, 1993 ($2.00, 52 pgs.)
Marvel Comics

	GD25	FN65	NM94
nn-r/Tomb of Dracula #69,70 by Gene Colan		.80	2.00

RESCUERS, THE (See Walt Disney Showcase #40)

RESCUERS DOWN UNDER (Disney)(Value: cover or less)

RESTLESS GUN (See 4-Color #934, 986, 1045, 1089, 1146)

RETURN FROM WITCH MOUNTAIN (See Walt Disney Showcase #44)

RETURN OF GORGO, THE (Formerly Gorgo's Revenge)
No. 2, Aug, 1963; No. 3, Fall, 1964 (#2 is last 10¢ issue; #3 is 12¢)
Charlton Comics

	GD25	FN65	NM94
2,3-Ditko-c/a; based on M.G.M. movie	6.30	19.00	44.00

RETURN OF KONGA, THE (Konga's Revenge #2 on)
1962
Charlton Comics

	GD25	FN65	NM94
nn	6.30	19.00	44.00

RETURN OF MEGATON MAN (Kitchen Sink)(Value: cover or less)

RETURN OF THE OUTLAW
Feb, 1953 - No. 11, 1955
Toby Press (Minoan)

	GD25	FN65	NM94
1-Billy the Kid	7.50	22.50	45.00
2	4.20	12.50	25.00
3-11	4.00	10.00	20.00

REVEALING LOVE STORIES (See Fox Giants)

REVEALING ROMANCES
Sept, 1949 - No. 6, Aug, 1950
Ace Magazines

	GD25	FN65	NM94
1	5.85	17.50	35.00
2	4.00	10.00	20.00
3-6	3.20	8.00	16.00

REVELATIONS (Eclipse)(Value: cover or less)

REVENGE OF THE PROWLER (Eclipse)(Value: cover or less)

REVENGERS FEATURING ARMOR AND SILVER STREAK, THE (Continuity)(Value: cover or less)(Becomes Armor #4 on)

REVENGERS FEATURING MEGALITH (Continuity)(Value: cover or less)

REVENGERS SPECIAL (Continuity)(Value: cover or less)

REX ALLEN COMICS (Movie star)(Also see 4-Color #877 & Western Roundup under Dell Giants)
No. 316, Feb, 1951 - No. 31, Dec-Feb, 1958-59 (All-photo-c)
Dell Publishing Co.

	GD25	FN65	NM94
4-Color 316(#1)(52 pgs.)-Rex Allen & his horse Koko begin; Marsh-a	17.00	52.00	120.00
2 (9-11/51, 36 pgs.)	10.00	30.00	60.00
3-10	7.50	22.50	45.00
11-20	5.85	17.50	35.00
21-23,25-31	5.35	16.00	32.00
24-Toth-a	6.35	19.00	38.00

NOTE: ***Manning** a-20, 27-30. Photo back-c F.C. #316, 2-12, 20, 21.*

REX DEXTER OF MARS (See Mystery Men Comics)
Fall, 1940 (68 pgs.)
Fox Features Syndicate

Richard Dragon Kung-Fu Fighter #1 © DC

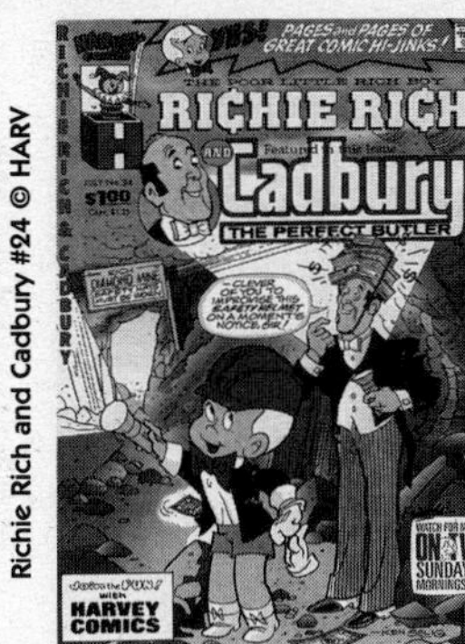

Richie Rich and Cadbury #24 © HARV

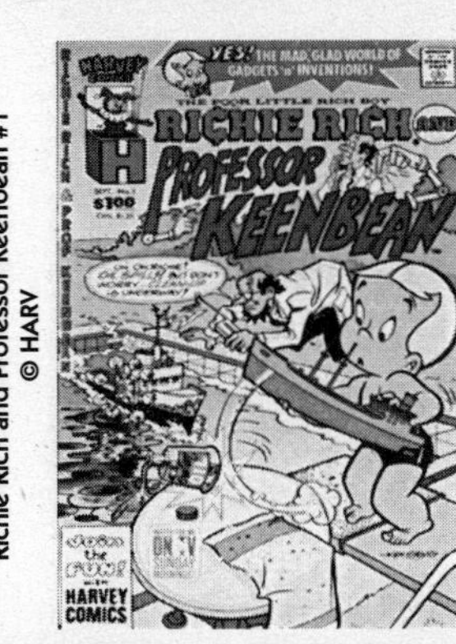

Richie Rich and Professor Keenbean #1 © HARV

	GD25	FN65	NM94
1-Rex Dexter, Patty O'Day, & Zanzibar (Tuska-a) app.; Briefer-c/a	136.00	407.00	950.00

REX HART (Formerly Blaze Carson; Whip Wilson #9 on)
No. 6, Aug, 1949 - No. 8, Feb, 1950 (All photo-c)
Timely/Marvel Comics (USA)

	GD25	FN65	NM94
6-Rex Hart & his horse Warrior begin; Black Rider app; Captain Tootsie by Beck	20.00	60.00	140.00
7,8: 18 pg. Thriller in each. 8-Blaze the Wonder Collie app. in text	14.00	43.00	100.00

REX MORGAN, M.D. (Also see Harvey Comics Library)
Dec, 1955 - No. 3, Apr?, 1956
Argo Publ.

	GD25	FN65	NM94
1-r/Rex Morgan daily newspaper strips & daily panel-r of "These Women" by D'Alessio & "Timeout" by Jeff Keate	9.15	27.50	55.00
2,3	6.70	20.00	40.00

REX THE WONDER DOG (See The Adventures of...)

RHUBARB, THE MILLIONAIRE CAT (See 4-Color #423, 466, 563)

RIBIT! (Comico)(Value: cover or less)

RIBTICKLER (Also see Fox Giants)
1945 - No. 9, Aug, 1947; 1957; 1959
Fox Feature Synd./Green Publ. (1957)/Norlen (1959)

	GD25	FN65	NM94
1-Funny animal	10.00	30.00	70.00
2-(1946)	5.85	17.50	35.00
3-9: 3,7-Cosmo Cat app.	4.20	12.50	25.00
3,7,8 (Green Publ.-1957)	2.80	7.00	14.00
3,7,8 (Norlen Mag.-1959)	2.80	7.00	14.00

RICHARD DRAGON, KUNG-FU FIGHTER (See Brave & the Bold)
Apr-May, 1975 - No. 18, Nov-Dec, 1977 (1-4 are based on novel)
National Periodical Publications/DC Comics

	GD25	FN65	NM94
1,2: 1-Based on novel. 2-Starlin/Weiss-a			1.60
3-18: 3-Kirby-a(p). 4-8-Wood inks			1.00

RICHARD THE LION-HEARTED (See Ideal a Classical Comic)

RICHIE RICH (See Harvey Collectors Comics, Harvey Hits, Little Dot, Little Lotta, Little Sad Sack, Million Dollar Digest, Mutt & Jeff, Super Richie, and 3-D Dolly)

RICHIE RICH (...the Poor Little Rich Boy) (See Harvey Hits #3, 9)
Nov, 1960 - #218, Oct, 1982; #219, Oct, 1986 - #254, Jan, 1991
Harvey Publications

	GD25	FN65	NM94
1-(See Little Dot for 1st app.)	97.00	291.00	680.00
2	49.00	145.00	340.00
3-5	27.00	81.00	190.00
6-10: 8-Christmas-c	16.50	50.00	115.00
11-20	10.00	30.00	60.00
21-40	6.70	20.00	40.00
41-60: 56-1st app. Super Richie. 59-Buck, prototype of Dollar the Dog	4.00	11.00	22.00
61-80: 65-1st app. Dollar the Dog. 71-Nixon & Robert Kennedy caricatures	2.40	6.00	12.00
81-99	1.20	3.00	8.00
100(12/70)-1st app. Irona the robot maid	2.40	6.00	12.00
101-111,117-120	1.00	2.50	6.00
112-116: All 52 pg. Giants	1.20	3.00	7.00
121-140: 137-1st app. Mr. Cheepers		1.60	4.00
141-160: 145-Infinity-c		1.30	3.25
161-180		.85	2.10
181-254: 210-Stone-Age Riches app. 237-Last original material		.65	1.60

RICHIE RICH (2nd series)(Harvey)(Value: cover or less)

RICHIE RICH ADVENTURE DIGEST MAGAZINE (Harvey)(Value: cover or less)

RICHIE RICH AND... (Harvey)(Value: cover or less)

RICHIE RICH AND BILLY BELLHOPS
October, 1977 (One Shot) (52 pgs.)
Harvey Publications

	GD25	FN65	NM94
1		1.20	3.00

RICHIE RICH AND CADBURY
10/77; #2, 9/78 - #23, 7/82; #24, 7/90 - #29, 1/91 (1-10: 52pgs.)
Harvey Publications

	GD25	FN65	NM94
1	1.00	2.00	5.00
2-5		.80	2.00
6-29: 24-Begin $1.00-c			1.00

RICHIE RICH AND CASPER
Aug, 1974 - No. 45, Sept, 1982
Harvey Publications

	GD25	FN65	NM94
1	1.30	3.25	8.00
2-5		1.60	4.00
6-10: 10-Xmas-c		.80	2.00
11-20			1.50
21-40: 22-Xmas-c			1.20
41-45			1.00

RICHIE RICH AND DOLLAR THE DOG (See Richie Rich #65)
Sept, 1977 - No. 24, Aug, 1982 (#1-10: 52 pgs.)
Harvey Publications

	GD25	FN65	NM94
1		1.60	4.00
2-10		.80	2.00
11-24			1.00

RICHIE RICH AND DOT
October, 1974 (One Shot)
Harvey Publications

	GD25	FN65	NM94
1	1.00	2.50	6.00

RICHIE RICH AND GLORIA
Sept, 1977 - No. 25, Sept, 1982 (#1-11: 52 pgs.)
Harvey Publications

	GD25	FN65	NM94
1		1.60	4.00
2-5		.80	2.00
6-25			1.00

RICHIE RICH AND HIS GIRLFRIENDS
April, 1979 - No. 16, Dec, 1982
Harvey Publications

	GD25	FN65	NM94
1-(52 pg. Giant)		1.20	3.00
2-(52 pg. Giant)		1.00	2.40
3-10		.80	2.00
11-16			1.00

RICHIE RICH AND HIS MEAN COUSIN REGGIE
April, 1979 - No. 3, 1980 (50¢) (#1,2: 52 pgs.)
Harvey Publications

	GD25	FN65	NM94
1		1.80	2.00
2-3: (#4 was advertised, but never released)			1.50

RICHIE RICH AND JACKIE JOKERS (Also see Jackie Jokers)
Nov, 1973 - No. 48, Dec, 1982
Harvey Publications

	GD25	FN65	NM94
1: 52 pg. Giant; contains material from unpublished Jackie Jokers #5	2.60	7.50	18.00
2,3-(52 pg. Giants). 2-R.R. & Jackie 1st meet	1.50	3.75	9.00
4,5	1.00	2.50	6.00
6-10		1.60	4.00
11-20: 11-1st app. Kool Katz		1.20	3.00
21-40: 26-Star Wars parody			1.50
41-48			1.00

RICHIE RICH AND PROFESSOR KEENBEAN
Sept, 1990 - No. 2, Nov, 1990 ($1.00)
Harvey Comics

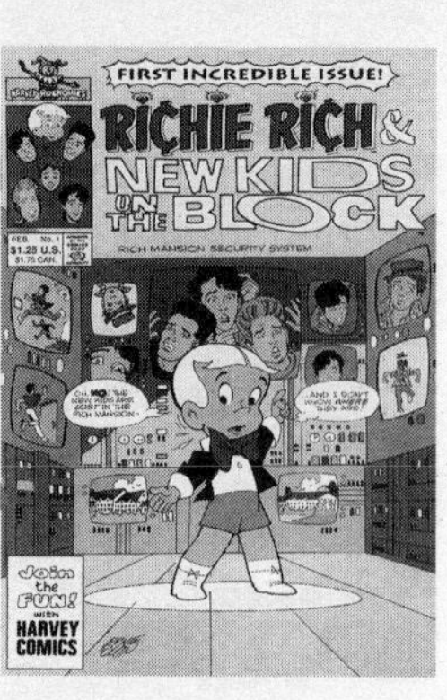

Richie Rich & New Kids on The Block #1 © HARV

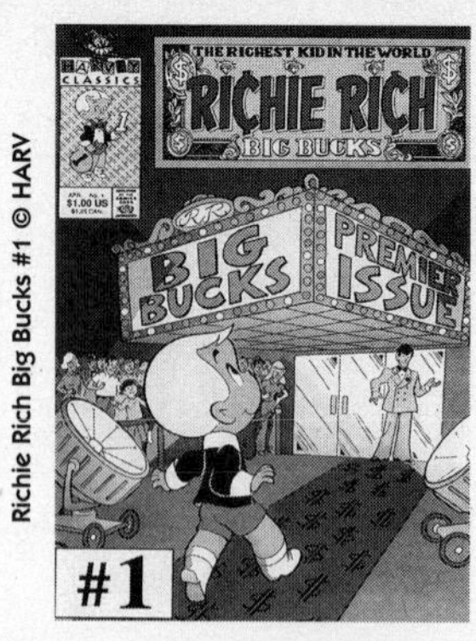

Richie Rich Big Bucks #1 © HARV

Richie Rich Giant Size #1 © HARV

	GD25	FN65	NM94
1,2			1.00

RICHIE RICH AND THE NEW KIDS ON THE BLOCK (Harvey)(Value: cover or less)

RICHIE RICH AND TIMMY TIME
Sept, 1977 (50¢) (One Shot) (52 pgs.)
Harvey Publications

	GD25	FN65	NM94
1		1.20	3.00

RICHIE RICH BANK BOOKS
Oct, 1972 - No. 59, Sept, 1982
Harvey Publications

	GD25	FN65	NM94
1	3.20	8.00	20.00
2-5	1.65	4.00	10.00
6-10	1.00	2.50	6.00
11-20: 18-Super Richie app.		1.60	4.00
21-30		1.20	3.00
31-40		.80	2.00
41-59			1.00

RICHIE RICH BEST OF THE YEARS
Oct, 1977 - No. 6, June, 1980 (Digest, 128 pgs.)
Harvey Publications

	GD25	FN65	NM94
1(10/77)-Reprints, #2(10/78)-Reprints, #3(6/79, 75¢)		.80	2.00
4-6(11/79-6/80, 95¢)			1.00

RICHIE RICH BIG BUCKS (Harvey)(Value: cover or less)

RICHIE RICH BILLIONS
Oct, 1974 - No. 48, Oct, 1982 (#1-33: 52 pgs.)
Harvey Publications

	GD25	FN65	NM94
1	2.00	6.00	14.00
2-5	1.20	3.00	7.00
6-10	1.00	2.00	5.00
11-20		1.20	3.00
21-33		.80	2.00
34-48: 35-Onion app.			1.00

RICHIE RICH CASH
Sept, 1974 - No. 47, Aug, 1982
Harvey Publications

	GD25	FN65	NM94
1-1st app. Dr. N-R-Gee	2.00	6.00	14.00
2-5	1.20	3.00	7.00
6-10		1.60	4.00
11-20		1.20	3.00
21-30		.80	2.00
31-47: 33-Dr. Blemish app.			1.00

RICHIE RICH CASH MONEY
May, 1992 - No. 2, Aug, 1992 ($1.25)
Harvey Comics

	GD25	FN65	NM94
1,2			1.25

RICHIE RICH, CASPER & WENDY NATIONAL LEAGUE
June, 1976 (52 pgs.)
Harvey Publications

	GD25	FN65	NM94
1 (Released-3/76 with 6/76 date)		1.20	3.00
1 (6/76)-2nd version w/San Francisco Giants & KTVU 2 logos; has "Compliments of Giants and Straw Hat Pizza" on-c		1.20	3.00

RICHIE RICH COLLECTORS COMICS (See Harvey Collectors Comics)

RICHIE RICH DIAMONDS
Aug, 1972 - No. 59, Aug, 1982 (#1, 23-45: 52 pgs.)
Harvey Publications

	GD25	FN65	NM94
1-(52 pg. Giant)	3.60	10.75	25.00
2-5	1.65	4.00	10.00
6-10	1.00	2.50	6.00
11-22		1.60	4.00
23-30		1.20	3.00
31-45: 39-Origin Little Dot			1.50
46-50			1.20
51-59			1.00

RICHIE RICH DIGEST (Harvey)(Value: cover or less)

RICHIE RICH DIGEST STORIES (Harvey)(Value: cover or less)

RICHIE RICH DIGEST WINNERS (Harvey)(Value: cover or less)

RICHIE RICH DOLLARS & CENTS
Aug, 1963 - No. 109, Aug, 1982 (#1-43: 68 pgs.; 44-60, 71-94: 52 pgs.)
Harvey Publications

	GD25	FN65	NM94
1: (#1-64 are all reprint issues)	14.00	43.00	100.00
2	7.50	22.50	45.00
3-5: 5-r/1st app. of R.R. from Little Dot #1	4.70	14.00	28.00
6-10	3.60	9.00	18.00
11-20	2.80	7.00	14.00
21-30: 25-1st app. Nurse Jenny	1.80	4.50	9.00
31-43: 43-Last 68 pg. issue	1.00	2.50	6.00
44-60: All 52 pgs.		1.60	4.00
61-70		1.00	2.50
71-94: All 52 pgs.			1.50
95-109: 100-Anniversary issue			1.00

RICHIE RICH FORTUNES
Sept, 1971 - No. 63, July, 1982 (#1-15: 52 pgs.)
Harvey Publications

	GD25	FN65	NM94
1	3.60	10.75	25.00
2-5	1.65	4.00	10.00
6-10	1.20	3.00	6.00
11-15: 11-1st app. The Onion	1.00	2.00	5.00
16-30		1.20	3.00
31-40			1.50
41-63: 62-Onion app.			1.00

RICHIE RICH GEMS
Sept, 1974 - No. 43, Sept, 1982
Harvey Publications

	GD25	FN65	NM94
1	2.00	6.00	14.00
2-5	1.20	3.00	7.00
6-10		1.60	4.00
11-20		1.00	2.50
21-30			1.50
31-43: 36-Dr. Blemish, Onion app. 38-1st app. Stone-Age Riches			1.00

RICHIE RICH GIANT SIZE
Oct, 1992 - No. 2? ($2.25, 68 pgs.)
Harvey Comics

	GD25	FN65	NM94
V2#1,2-Richie Rich, Little Audrey & Melvin, Little Dot & Little Lotta stories		.90	2.25

RICHIE RICH GOLD AND SILVER
Sept, 1975 - No. 42, Oct, 1982 (#1-27: 52 pgs.)
Harvey Publications

	GD25	FN65	NM94
1	1.65	4.00	10.00
2-5	1.00	2.00	5.00
6-10		.80	2.00
11-27			1.50
28-42: 34-Stone-Age Riches app.			1.00

RICHIE RICH GOLD NUGGETS DIGEST (Harvey)(Value: cover or less)

RICHIE RICH HOLIDAY DIGEST MAGAZINE (...Digest #4)
Jan, 1980 - #3, Jan, 1982; #4, 3/88; #5, 2/89 (Published annually)
Harvey Publications

	GD25	FN65	NM94
1-3: All X-Mas-c			1.00
4-(3/88, $1.25), 5-(2/89, $1.75)			1.25

RICHIE RICH INVENTIONS
Oct, 1977 - No. 26, Oct, 1982 (#1-11: 52 pgs.)
Harvey Publications

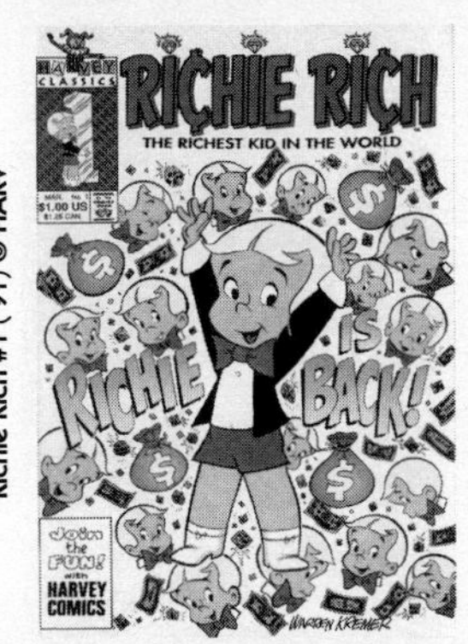

Richie Rich #1 ('91) © HARV

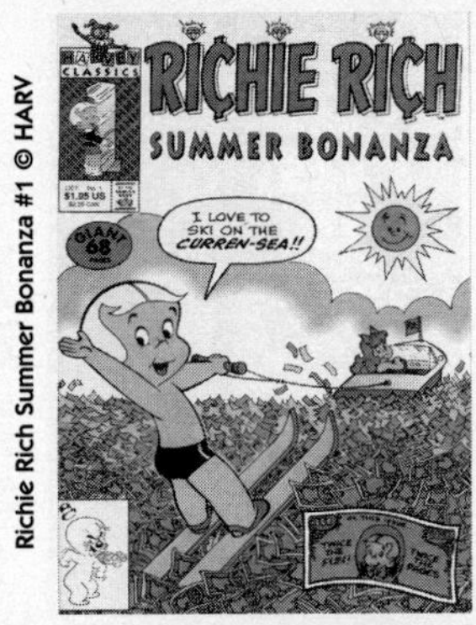

Richie Rich Summer Bonanza #1 © HARV

Rick Geary's Wonders & Oddities © Rick Geary

	GD25	FN65	NM94
1	1.00	2.00	5.00
2-5		1.00	2.50
6-11			1.50
12-26			1.00

RICHIE RICH JACKPOTS
Oct, 1972 - No. 58, Aug, 1982 (#41-43: 52 pgs.)
Harvey Publications

	GD25	FN65	NM94
1	3.60	10.75	25.00
2-5	1.70	5.00	12.00
6-10	1.20	3.00	7.00
11-20: 16-Super Richie app.		1.60	4.00
21-30		1.20	3.00
31-40,44-50: 37-Caricatures of Frank Sinatra, Dean Martin, Sammy Davis, Jr. 45-Dr. Blemish app.		.80	2.00
41-43 (52 pgs.)		1.20	3.00
51-58			1.50

RICHIE RICH MILLION DOLLAR DIGEST (...Magazine #?-on)(Also see Million Dollar Digest)
October, 1980 - No. 10, Oct, 1982 ($1.50)
Harvey Publications

	GD25	FN65	NM94
1-10			1.50

RICHIE RICH MILLIONS
9/61; #2, 9/62 - #113, 10/82 (#1-48: 68 pgs.; 49-64, 85-97: 52 pgs.)
Harvey Publications

	GD25	FN65	NM94
1: (#1-5 are all reprint issues)	16.00	48.00	110.00
2	9.15	27.50	55.00
3-10: (All other giants are new & reprints)	7.50	22.50	45.00
11-20	4.20	12.50	25.00
21-30	2.80	7.00	14.00
31-48: 48-Last 68 pg. Giant	1.80	4.50	9.00
49-64: 52 pg. Giants	1.00	2.50	6.00
65-74: 68-1st Super Richie-c (11/74). 74-1st app. Mr. Woody; Super Richie app.		1.20	3.00
75-94: 52 pg. Giants		1.40	3.50
95-100			1.50
101-113			1.00

RICHIE RICH MONEY WORLD
Sept, 1972 - No. 59, Sept, 1982
Harvey Publications

	GD25	FN65	NM94
1-(52 pg. Giant)-1st app. Mayda Munny	3.60	10.75	25.00
2-5: 2-Super Richie app.	1.65	4.00	10.00
6-10: 9,10-Richie Rich mistakenly named Little Lotta on covers	1.00	2.00	5.00
11-20: 16,20-Dr. N-R-Gee		1.20	3.00
21-30		.80	2.00
31-50			1.50
51-59			1.00
...Digest 1 (2/91, $1.75) - 8 (12/93, $1.75)		.70	1.75

RICHIE RICH PROFITS
Oct, 1974 - No. 47, Sept, 1982
Harvey Publications

	GD25	FN65	NM94
1	2.30	6.75	16.00
2-5	1.30	3.25	8.00
6-10: 10-Origin of Dr. N-R-Gee		1.60	4.00
11-20: 15-Christmas-c		1.20	3.00
21-30			1.50
31-47			1.00

RICHIE RICH RELICS (Harvey)(Value: cover or less)

RICHIE RICH RICHES
July, 1972 - No. 59, Aug, 1982 (#1, 2, 41-45: 52 pgs.)
Harvey Publications

	GD25	FN65	NM94
1-(52 pg. Giant)	2.60	7.50	18.00
2-(52 pg. Giant)	1.50	3.75	9.00
3-5	1.20	3.00	7.00
6-10		1.60	4.00
11-20: 17-Super Richie app. (3/75)		1.20	3.00
21-40			1.50
41-45: 52 pg. Giants		.80	2.00
46-59: 56-Dr. Blemish app.			1.00

RICHIE RICH SUCCESS STORIES
Nov, 1964 - No. 105, Sept, 1982 (#1-38: 68 pgs., 39-55, 67-90: 52 pgs.)
Harvey Publications

	GD25	FN65	NM94
1	14.00	43.00	100.00
2-5	7.50	22.50	45.00
6-10	4.20	12.50	25.00
11-30: 27-1st Penny Van Dough (8/69)	2.80	7.00	14.00
31-38: 38-Last 68 pg. Giant	1.80	4.50	9.00
39-55-(52 pgs.): 44-Super Richie app.	1.20	2.90	7.00
56-66		1.80	4.50
67-90: 52 pgs. (Early issues are reprints)		.80	2.00
91-105: 91-Onion app. 101-Dr. Blemish app.			1.50

RICHIE RICH SUMMER BONANZA (Harvey)(Value: cover or less)

RICHIE RICH TREASURE CHEST DIGEST (...Magazine #3)
Apr, 1982 - No. 3, Aug, 1982 (95¢, Digest Mag.)(#4 advertised but not publ.)
Harvey Publications

	GD25	FN65	NM94
1-3			1.50

RICHIE RICH VACATION DIGEST
Oct, 1992 ($1.75, digest size)
Harvey Comics

	GD25	FN65	NM94
1		.70	1.75

RICHIE RICH VACATIONS DIGEST
11/77; No. 2, 10/78 - No. 7, 10/81; No. 8, 8/82; No. 9, 10/82 (Digest, 132 pgs.)
Harvey Publications

	GD25	FN65	NM94
1-Reprints		.80	2.00
2-9			1.50

RICHIE RICH VAULT OF MYSTERY
Nov, 1974 - No. 47, Sept, 1982
Harvey Publications

	GD25	FN65	NM94
1	1.65	4.00	10.00
2-10	1.00	2.00	5.00
11-20		1.20	3.00
21-30		.80	2.00
31-47			1.00

RICHIE RICH ZILLIONZ
Oct, 1976 - No. 33, Sept, 1982 (#1-4: 68 pgs.; #5-18: 52 pgs.)
Harvey Publications

	GD25	FN65	NM94
1	1.65	4.00	10.00
2-4: 4-Last 68 pg. Giant	1.00	2.00	5.00
5-10		1.20	3.00
11-18: 18-Last 52 pg. Giant			1.50
19-33			1.00

RICK GEARY'S WONDERS AND ODDITIES (Dark Horse)(Value: cover or less)

RICKY
No. 5, September, 1953
Standard Comics (Visual Editions)

	GD25	FN65	NM94
5-Teenage humor	4.00	10.00	20.00

RICKY NELSON (TV)(See Sweethearts V2#42)
No. 956, Dec, 1958 - No. 1192, June, 1961 (All photo-c)
Dell Publishing Co.

	GD25	FN65	NM94
4-Color 956,998	23.00	70.00	160.00
4-Color 1115,1192-Manning-a	18.00	54.00	125.00

RIDER, THE (Frontier Trail #6; also see Blazing Sixguns I.W. Reprint #10, 11)

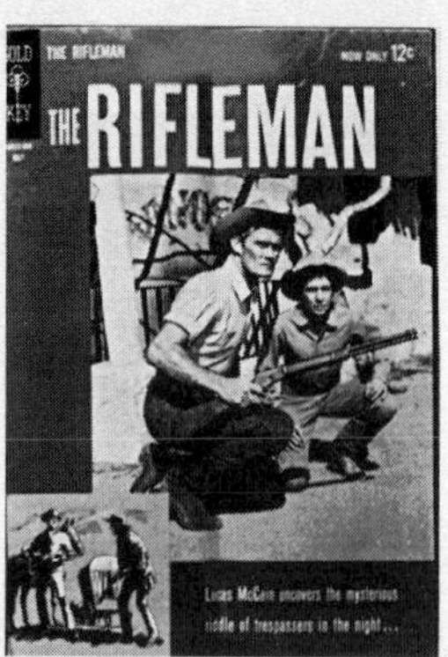

The Rifleman #5 © DELL

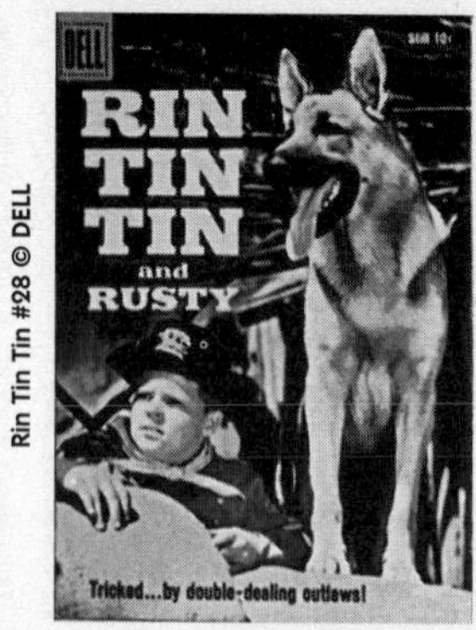

Rin Tin Tin #28 © DELL

Rip Hunter: Time Master #10 © DC

March, 1957 - No. 5, 1958
Ajax/Farrell Publ. (Four Star Comic Corp.)

	GD25	FN65	NM94
1-Swift Arrow, Lone Rider begin	7.50	22.50	45.00
2-5	4.70	14.00	28.00

RIFLEMAN, THE (TV)
No. 1009, 7-9/59 - No. 12, 7-9/62; No. 13, 11/62 - No. 20, 10/64
Dell Publ. Co./Gold Key No. 13 on

	GD25	FN65	NM94
4-Color 1009 (#1)	17.00	52.00	120.00
2 (1-3/60)	10.00	30.00	70.00
3-Toth-a (4 pgs.)	11.00	32.00	75.00
4,5,7-10	10.00	30.00	60.00
6-Toth-a (4 pgs.)	10.00	30.00	65.00
11-20	8.35	25.00	50.00

NOTE: ***Warren Tufts** a-2-9. All have Chuck Connors photo-c. Photo back c-13-15.*

RIMA, THE JUNGLE GIRL
Apr-May, 1974 - No. 7, Apr-May, 1975
National Periodical Publications

	GD25	FN65	NM94
1-Origin, part 1 (#1-5: 20¢; 6,7: 25¢)		.80	2.00
2-4-Origin, parts 2-4			1.00
5-7: 7-Origin & only app. Space Marshal			1.00

NOTE: ***Kubert** c-1-7. **Nino** a-1-5. **Redondo** a-1-6.*

RING OF BRIGHT WATER (See Movie Classics)

RING OF THE NIBELUNG, THE (DC)(Value: cover or less)

RINGO KID, THE (2nd Series)
Jan, 1970 - No. 23, Nov, 1973; No. 24, Nov, 1975 - No. 30, Nov, 1976
Marvel Comics Group

	GD25	FN65	NM94
1-Williamson-a r-from #10, 1956		1.70	4.25
2-30: 13-Wildey-r. 20-Williamson-r/#1		.80	2.00

RINGO KID WESTERN, THE (See Wild Western & Western Trails)
Aug, 1954 - No. 21, Sept, 1957 (1st series)
Atlas Comics (HPC)/Marvel Comics

	GD25	FN65	NM94
1-Origin; The Ringo Kid begins	20.00	60.00	140.00
2-Black Rider app.; origin/1st app. Ringo's Horse Arab	10.00	30.00	70.00
3-5	7.50	22.50	45.00
6-8-Severin-a(3) each	8.35	25.00	50.00
9,11,12,14-21: 12-Orlando-a (4 pgs.)	5.35	16.00	32.00
10,13-Williamson-a (4 pgs.)	6.70	20.00	40.00

NOTE: ***Berg** a-8. **Maneely** a-1-5, 15, 16(text illos only), 17(4), 18, 20, 21; c-1-6, 8, 13, 15-18, 20. **J. Severin** c-10, 11. **Sinnott** a-1. **Wildey** a-16-18.*

RIN TIN TIN (See March of Comics #163,180,195)

RIN TIN TIN (TV) (...& Rusty #21 on; see Western Roundup under Dell Giants)
Nov, 1952 - No. 38, May-July, 1961; Nov, 1963 (All Photo-c)
Dell Publishing Co./Gold Key

	GD25	FN65	NM94
4-Color 434 (#1)	19.00	58.00	135.00
4-Color 476,523	10.00	30.00	65.00
4(3-5/54)-10	8.35	25.00	50.00
11-20	7.00	21.00	42.00
21-38	5.85	17.50	35.00
... & Rusty 1 (11/63-Gold Key)	7.50	22.50	45.00

RIO (Comico)(Value: cover or less)(Also see Eclipse Monthly)

RIO AT BAY (Dark Horse)(Value: cover or less)

RIO BRAVO (See 4-Color #1018)

RIO CONCHOS (See Movie Comics)

RIOT (Satire)
Apr, 1954 - No. 3, Aug, 1954; No. 4, Feb, 1956 - No. 6, June, 1956
Atlas Comics (ACI No. 1-5/WPI No. 6)

	GD25	FN65	NM94
1-Russ Heath-a	18.00	54.00	125.00
2-Li'l Abner satire by Post	13.50	41.00	95.00
3-Last precode (8/54)	11.50	34.00	80.00
4-Infinity-c; Marilyn Monroe "7 Year Itch" movie satire; Mad Rip-off ads	16.50	50.00	115.00
5-Marilyn Monroe, John Wayne parody; part photo-c	17.00	52.00	120.00
6-Lorna of the Jungle satire by Everett; Dennis the Menace satire-c/story; part photo-c	11.00	32.00	75.00

NOTE: ***Berg** a-3. **Burgos** c-1, 2. **Colan** a-1. **Everett** a-1, 4, 6. **Heath** a-1. **Maneely** a-1, 2, 4-6; c-3, 4, 6. **Post** a-1-4. **Reinman** a-2. **Severin** a-4-6.*

RIOT GEAR
Sept, 1993 - Present ($2.50, color, serially numbered comics)
Triumphant Comics

	GD25	FN65	NM94
1-11: 1-2nd app. Riot Gear. 2-1st app. Rabin. 3,4-Triumphant Unleashed x-over. 3-1st app. Surzar. 4-Death of Captain Tich		1.00	2.50
...Violent Past 1,2: 1-(2/94, 2.50)		1.00	2.50

R.I.P. (TSR)(Value: cover or less)

RIPCORD (See 4-Color #1294)

RIP HUNTER TIME MASTER (See Showcase #20, 21, 25, 26 & Time Masters)
Mar-Apr, 1961 - No. 29, Nov-Dec, 1965
National Periodical Publications

	GD25	FN65	NM94
Showcase #20 (5-6/59)-Origin & 1st app. Rip Hunter; Moriera-a	61.00	180.00	550.00
Showcase #21 (7-8/59)-2nd app. Rip Hunter; Sekowsky-c/a	36.00	108.00	325.00
Showcase #25,26 (3-4/60, 5-6/60)-3rd & 4th app. Rip Hunter by Kubert	26.00	79.00	210.00
1-(3-4/61)	49.00	148.00	345.00
2	24.00	71.00	165.00
3-5: 5-Last 10¢ issue	14.00	40.00	100.00
6,7-Toth-a in each	11.00	33.00	78.00
8-15	8.00	24.00	56.00
16-20	6.40	19.00	45.00
21-29: 29-Gil Kane-c	5.00	15.00	36.00

RIP IN TIME (Fantagor)(Value: cover or less)

RIP KIRBY (See Feature Books #51, 54, Harvey Comics Hits #57, & Street Comix)

RIPLEY'S BELIEVE IT OR NOT! (See Ace Comics, All-American Comics, Mystery Comics Digest #1, 4, 7, 10, 13, 16, 19, 22, 25)

RIPLEY'S BELIEVE IT OR NOT!
Sept, 1953 - No. 4, March, 1954
Harvey Publications

	GD25	FN65	NM94
1-Powell-a	10.00	30.00	60.00
2-4	6.70	20.00	40.00
J. C. Penney giveaway (1948)	6.70	20.00	40.00

RIPLEY'S BELIEVE IT OR NOT! (Formerly ...True War Stories)
No. 4, April, 1967 - No. 94, Feb, 1980
Gold Key

	GD25	FN65	NM94
4-Photo-c; McWilliams-a	4.00	11.00	22.00
5-Subtitled "True War Stories"; Evans-a; 1st Jeff Jones-a in comics? (2 pgs.)	2.80	7.00	14.00
6-10: 6-McWilliams-a. 10-Evans-a(2)	2.80	7.00	14.00
11-20: 15-Evans-a	1.80	4.50	10.00
21-30	1.20	2.90	7.00
31-38,40-60		1.60	4.00
39-Crandall-a	1.00	2.00	5.00
61-94: 74,77-83-(52 pgs.)		1.20	3.00
Story Digest Mag. 1(6/70)-4-3/4x6-1/2"	1.20	3.00	7.00

NOTE: ***Evanish** art by **Luiz Dominguez** #22-25, 27, 30, 31, 40. **Jeff Jones** a-5(2 pgs.). **McWilliams** a-65, 66, 70, 89. **Orlando** a-8. **Sparling** c-68. Reprints-74, 77-84, 87 (part); 91, 93 (all). **Williamson, Wood** a-80r/#1.*

RIPLEY'S BELIEVE IT OR NOT! TRUE GHOST STORIES (Becomes ...True War Stories) (See Dan Curtis)
June, 1965 - No. 2, Oct, 1966
Gold Key

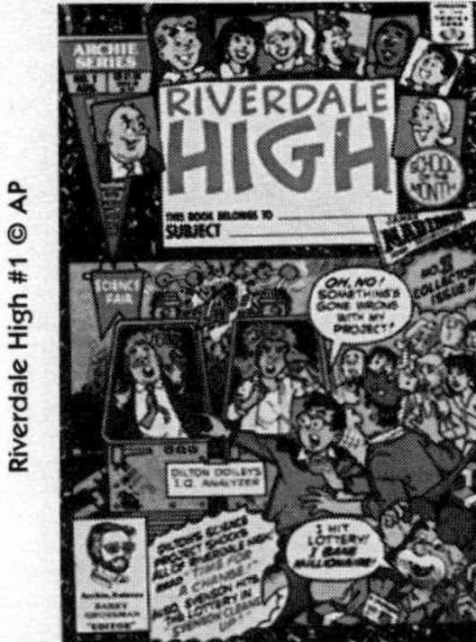

Riverdale High #1 © AP

Robin #8 © DC

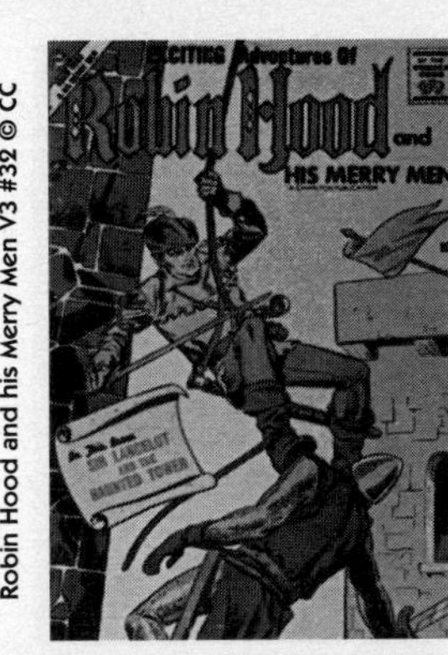

Robin Hood and his Merry Men V3 #32 © CC

	GD25	FN65	NM94
1-Williamson, Wood & Evans-a; photo-c	5.35	16.00	32.00
2-Orlando, McWilliams-a; photo-c	4.00	10.00	20.00
Mini-Comic 1(1976-3-1/4x6-1/2")			1.50
11186(1977)-Golden Press; ($1.95, 224 pgs.)-All-r		1.20	3.00
11401(3/79)-Golden Press; ($1.00, 96 pgs.)-All-r			1.50

RIPLEY'S BELIEVE IT OR NOT! TRUE WAR STORIES (Formerly ...True Ghost Stories; becomes Ripley's Believe It or Not! #4 on)
Nov, 1966
Gold Key

	GD25	FN65	NM94
1(#3)-No Williamson-a	4.00	11.00	22.00

RIPLEY'S BELIEVE IT OR NOT! TRUE WEIRD
June, 1966 - No. 2, Aug, 1966 (B&W Magazine)
Ripley Enterprises

	GD25	FN65	NM94
1,2-Comic stories & text	1.20	3.00	6.00

RIVERDALE HIGH (Archie's... #7,8)
Aug, 1990 - No. 8, Oct, 1991 ($1.00, bi-monthly)
Archie Comics

	GD25	FN65	NM94
1-8			1.00

RIVETS (See 4-Color #518)

RIVETS (A dog)
Jan, 1956 - No. 3, May, 1956
Argo Publ.

	GD25	FN65	NM94
1-Reprints Sunday & daily newspaper strips	4.00	11.00	22.00
2,3	2.80	7.00	14.00

ROACHMILL
Dec, 1986 - No. 6, Oct, 1987 ($1.75, B&W)
Blackthorne Publ.

	GD25	FN65	NM94
1-6		.70	1.75

ROACHMILL
May, 1988 - No. 10, Dec, 1990 ($1.75, B&W)
Dark Horse Comics

	GD25	FN65	NM94
1-10: 10-Contains trading cards		.70	1.75

ROAD RUNNER (See Beep Beep, the...)

ROADWAYS
May, 1994 ($2.75, B&W, limited series)
Cult Press

	GD25	FN65	NM94
1		1.10	2.75

ROARIN' RICK'S RARE BIT FIENDS
July, 1994 ($2.95, B&W, mature)
King Hell Press

	GD25	FN65	NM94
1-R. Veitch		1.20	3.00

ROBERT E. HOWARD'S CONAN THE BARBARIAN (Marvel)(Value: cover or less)

ROBIN (See Aurora, Detective Comics #38, New Teen Titans, Robin II, Robin III, Robin 3000, Star Spangled Comics #65 & Teen Titans)

ROBIN (See Batman #457)
Jan, 1991 - No. 5, May, 1991 ($1.00, mini-series)
DC Comics

	GD25	FN65	NM94
1-Free poster by N. Adams; Bolland-c on all	1.00	2.00	5.00
1-2nd & 3rd printings (without poster)			1.25
2			1.25
2-2nd printing			1.00
3-5			1.50
Annual 1,2 (1992-93, $2.50, 68 pgs.): 1-Grant/Wagner scripts; Sam Kieth-c. 2-Intro Razorsharp; Jim Balen-c(p)		1.00	2.50

ROBIN (See Detective #668)
Nov, 1993 - Present ($1.50)
DC Comics

	GD25	FN65	NM94
1-($2.95)-Collector's edition w/foil embossed-c; 1st app. Robin's car, The Redbird; Azrael as Batman app.		1.20	3.00
1-10-Regular editions: 3-5-The Spoiler app. 6-The Huntress-c/story cont'd from Showcase '94 #5. 7-Knightquest: The Conclusion w/new Batman vs. Bruce Wayne. 8-KnightsEnd Pt. 5. 9-KnightsEnd Aftermath; Batman-c & app. 10-(9/94)-Zero Hour			1.50
0,11-16: 0-(10/94). 11-(11/94)			1.50
Annual 3 (1994, $2.95)-Elseworlds story		1.20	3.00

ROBIN: A HERO REBORN
1991 ($4.95, squarebound, trade paperback)
DC Comics

	GD25	FN65	NM94
nn-r/Batman #455-457 & Robin #1-5; Bolland-c	1.00	2.00	5.00

ROBIN HOOD (See The Advs. of..., Brave and the Bold, Four Color #413, 669, King Classics, Movie Comics & Power Record Comics)

ROBIN HOOD (...& His Merry Men, The Illustrated Story of...) (See Classic Comics #7 & Classics Giveaways, 12/44)

ROBIN HOOD (New Adventures of...)
1952 (36 pgs.) (5x7-1/4")
Walt Disney Productions (Flour giveaways)

	GD25	FN65	NM94
"New Adventures of Robin Hood", "Ghosts of Waylea Castle", & "The Miller's Ransom" each....	4.00	11.00	22.00

ROBIN HOOD (Adventures of... #7, 8)
No. 52, Nov, 1955 - No. 6, June, 1957
Magazine Enterprises (Sussex Publ. Co.)

	GD25	FN65	NM94
52 (#1)-Origin Robin Hood & Sir Gallant of the Round Table	11.00	32.00	75.00
53 (#2), 3-6: 6-Richard Greene photo-c (TV)	9.15	27.50	55.00
I.W. Reprint #1,2,9: 1-r/#3. 2-r/#4. 9-r/#52 (1963)	2.00	5.00	10.00
Super Reprint #10,15: 10-r/#53. 15-r/#5	2.00	5.00	10.00
Super Reprint #11,17(1964)-Both exist?	2.00	5.00	10.00

NOTE: ***Bolle** a-in all; c-52. **Powell** a-6.*

ROBIN HOOD (Not Disney)
May-July, 1963 (One shot)
Dell Publishing Co.

	GD25	FN65	NM94
1	3.20	8.00	16.00

ROBIN HOOD
1973 (Disney) (8-1/2x11"; cardboard covers) ($1.50, 52 pgs.)
Western Publishing Co.

	GD25	FN65	NM94
96151- "Robin Hood", based on movie, 96152- "The Mystery of Sherwood Forest", 96153- "In King Richard's Service", 96154- "The Wizard's Ring" each....		1.60	4.00

ROBIN HOOD
July, 1991 - No. 3, 1991 ($2.50, color, mini-series)
Eclipse Comics

	GD25	FN65	NM94
1-3: Timothy Truman layouts		1.00	2.50

ROBIN HOOD AND HIS MERRY MEN (Formerly Danger & Adventure)
No. 28, April, 1956 - No. 38, Aug, 1958
Charlton Comics

	GD25	FN65	NM94
28	6.70	20.00	40.00
29-37	5.00	15.00	30.00
38-Ditko-a (5 pgs.); Rocke-c	10.00	30.00	70.00

ROBIN HOOD'S FRONTIER DAYS (...Western Tales, Adventures of... #1)
No date (Circa 1955) 20 pgs., slick-c (Seven issues?)
Shoe Store Giveaway (Robin Hood Stores)

	GD25	FN65	NM94
nn	4.20	12.50	25.00
nn-Issues with Crandall-a	7.50	22.50	45.00

ROBIN HOOD TALES (Published by National Periodical #7 on)
Feb, 1956 - No. 6, Nov-Dec, 1956
Quality Comics Group (Comic Magazines)

	GD25	FN65	NM94
1-All have Baker/Cuidera-c	20.00	60.00	140.00
2-5-Matt Baker-a	20.00	60.00	140.00
6-Baker-a	14.00	43.00	100.00

Robo Cop #2 © Orion Pictures

Robo Cop II (Movie) © Orion Pictures

Robotech: The Macross Saga #4 © Comico

	GD25	FN65	NM94
Frontier Days giveaway (1956)	5.85	17.50	35.00

ROBIN HOOD TALES (Cont'd from Quality series)(See Brave & the Bold #5)
No. 7, Jan-Feb, 1957 - No. 14, Mar-Apr, 1958
National Periodical Publications

	GD25	FN65	NM94
7-All have Andru/Esposito-c	27.00	81.00	190.00
8-14	22.00	67.00	155.00

ROBINSON CRUSOE (See King Classics & Power Record Comics)
Nov-Jan, 1963-64
Dell Publishing Co.

	GD25	FN65	NM94
1	1.60	4.00	8.00

ROBIN II (The Joker's Wild)
Oct, 1991 - No. 4, Dec, 1991 ($1.50, mini-series)
DC Comics

	GD25	FN65	NM94
1-(Direct sale, $1.50)-With 4 different-c; same hologram on each			1.50
1-(Newsstand, $1.00)-No hologram; 1 version			1.00
1-Collector's set ($10.00)-Contains all 5 versions bagged with hologram trading card inside	1.65	4.00	10.00
2-(Direct sale, $1.50)-With 3 different-c			1.50
2-4-(Newsstand, $1.00)-1 version of each			1.00
2-Collector's set ($8.00)-Contains all 4 versions bagged with hologram trading card inside	1.30	3.25	8.00
3-(Direct sale, $1.50)-With 2 different-c			1.50
3-Collector's set ($6.00)-Contains all 3 versions bagged with hologram trading card inside	1.00	2.50	6.00
4-(Direct sale, $1.50)-Only one version			1.50
4-Collector's set ($4.00)-Contains both versions bagged with Bat-Signal hologram trading card		1.60	4.00
Multi-pack (All four issues w/hologram sticker)		1.60	4.00
Deluxe Complete Set ($30.00)-Contains all 14 versions of #1-4 plus a new hologram trading card; numbered & limited to 25,000; comes with slipcase & 2 acid free backing boards	4.30	13.00	30.00

ROBIN III: CRY OF THE HUNTRESS
Dec, 1992 - No. 6, Mar, 1993 (Color, mini-series)
DC Comics

	GD25	FN65	NM94
1-6 ($2.50, collector's ed.)-Polybagged w/movement enhanced-c plus mini-poster of newsstand-c by Zeck		1.00	2.50
1-6 ($1.25, newsstand ed.): All have Zeck-c			1.25

ROBIN 3000
1992 - No. 2, 1992 ($4.95, mini-series, 52 pgs.)
DC Comics

	GD25	FN65	NM94
1,2-Foil logo; Elseworlds storyline; Russell-c/a	1.00	2.00	5.00

ROBOCOP
Oct, 1987 ($2.00, B&W, magazine, one-shot)
Marvel Comics

	GD25	FN65	NM94
1-Movie adaptation		.80	2.00

ROBOCOP (Also see Dark Horse Comics)
March, 1990 - No. 23, Jan, 1992 ($1.50)
Marvel Comics

	GD25	FN65	NM94
1-Based on movie	1.00	2.00	5.00
2		1.40	3.50
3-6		1.00	2.50
7-23			1.50
nn (7/90, $4.95, color, 52 pgs.)-r/B&W magazine in color; adapts 1st movie		1.80	4.50

ROBOCOP: MORTAL COILS
Sept, 1993 - No. 4, Dec, 1993 ($2.50, color, mini-series)
Dark Horse Comics

	GD25	FN65	NM94
1-4: 1,2-Cago painted-c		1.00	2.50

ROBOCOP: PRIME SUSPECT
Oct, 1992 - No. 4, Jan, 1993 ($2.50, color, mini-series)
Dark Horse Comics

	GD25	FN65	NM94
1-4: 1,3-Nelson painted-c. 2,4-Bolton painted-c		1.00	2.50

ROBOCOP: ROULETTE
Dec, 1993 - No. 4, 1994 ($2.50, color, mini-series)
Dark Horse Comics

	GD25	FN65	NM94
1-4: 1,3-Nelson painted-c. 2,4-Bolton painted-c		1.00	2.50

ROBOCOP 2
Aug, 1990 ($2.25, B&W, magazine, 68 pgs.)
Marvel Comics

	GD25	FN65	NM94
1-Adapts movie sequel		.90	2.25

ROBOCOP 2
Aug, 1990; Late Aug, 1990 - #3, Late Sept, 1990 ($1.00, mini-series)
Marvel Comics

	GD25	FN65	NM94
nn-(8/90, $4.95, color, 68 pgs.)-Same contents as B&W magazine	1.00	2.00	5.00
1: #1-3 reprint no number issue		1.20	3.00
2,3: 2-Guice-c(i)			1.50

ROBOCOP 3
July, 1993 - No. 3, Nov, 1993 ($2.50, color, mini-series)
Dark Horse Comics

	GD25	FN65	NM94
1-3: Nelson painted-c; Nguyen-a(p)		1.00	2.50

ROBOCOP VERSUS THE TERMINATOR
Sept, 1992 - No. 4, 1992 (Dec.) ($2.50, color, mini-series)
Dark Horse Comics

	GD25	FN65	NM94
1-4: Miller scripts & Simonson-c/a in all		1.00	2.50
1-Platinum Edition			13.00

NOTE: *All contain a different Robocop cardboard cut-out stand-up.*

ROBO-HUNTER (Eagle)(Value: cover or less)(Also see Sam Slade...)

R.O.B.O.T. BATTALION 2050 (Eclipse)(Value: cover or less)

ROBOT COMICS (Renegade)(Value: cover or less)

ROBOTECH DEFENDERS
Mar, 1985 - No. 2, Apr, 1985 (Mini-series)
DC Comics

	GD25	FN65	NM94
1,2			1.00

ROBOTECH IN 3-D (Comico)(Value: cover or less)

ROBOTECH MASTERS (TV)
July, 1985 - No. 23, Apr, 1988 ($1.50, color)
Comico

	GD25	FN65	NM94
1		1.00	2.50
2-23		.65	1.60

ROBOTECH SPECIAL (Comico)(Value: cover or less)

ROBOTECH THE GRAPHIC NOVEL (Comico)(Value: cover or less)

ROBOTECH: THE MACROSS SAGA (TV)(Formerly Macross)
No. 2, Feb, 1985 - No. 36, Feb, 1989 ($1.50, color)
Comico

	GD25	FN65	NM94
2		1.20	3.00
3-10		.80	2.00
11-34: 12,17-Ken Steacy painted-c. 26-Begin $1.75-c		.70	1.75
35,36-($1.95)		.80	2.00

ROBOTECH: THE NEW GENERATION
July, 1985 - No. 25, July, 1988 (Color)
Comico

	GD25	FN65	NM94
1-25			1.50

ROBOTECH II: THE SENTINELS SWIMSUIT SPECTACULAR (Eternity)(Value: cover or less)

ROBOTIX (Marvel)(Value: cover or less)

ROBOTMEN OF THE LOST PLANET (Also see Space Thrillers)

The Rocketeer (The Movie) © Dave Stevens

Rock & Roll Comics #18 © Revolutionary

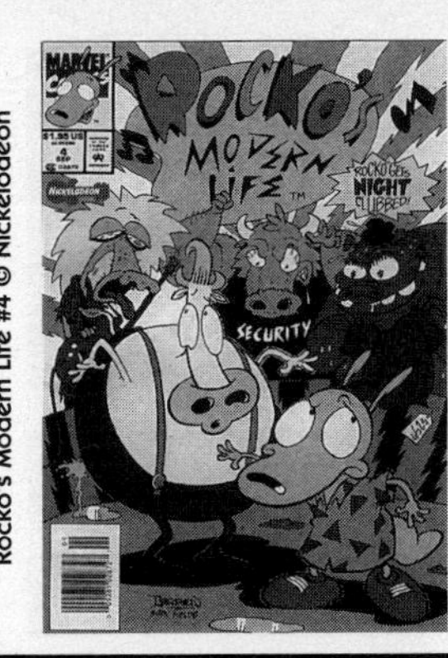

Rocko's Modern Life #4 © Nickelodeon

	GD25	FN65	NM94
1952 (Also see Strange Worlds #19)			
Avon Periodicals			
1-McCann-a (3 pgs.); Fawcette-a	75.00	225.00	525.00

ROB ROY (See 4-Color #544)

ROCK AND ROLLO (Formerly TV Teens)
V2#14, Oct, 1957 - No. 19, Sept, 1958
Charlton Comics

	GD25	FN65	NM94
V2#14-19	4.00	10.00	20.00

ROCKET COMICS
Mar, 1940 - No. 3, May, 1940
Hillman Periodicals

	GD25	FN65	NM94
1-Rocket Riley, Red Roberts the Electro Man (origin), The Phantom Ranger, The Steel Shark, The Defender, Buzzard Barnes and his Sky Devils, Lefty Larson, & The Defender, the Man with a Thousand Faces begin (1st app. of each); all have Rocket Riley-c	157.00	471.00	1100.00
2,3	82.00	246.00	575.00

ROCKETEER, THE (See Eclipse Graphic Album Series, Pacific Presents & Starslayer)

ROCKETEER ADVENTURE MAGAZINE, THE
July, 1988 ($2.00, color); No. 2, July, 1989 ($2.75, color)
Comico

	GD25	FN65	NM94
1-($2.00)-Dave Stevens-c/a in all; Kaluta back-up-a	1.00	2.00	5.00
2-($2.75)-Stevens/Dorman painted-c		1.20	3.00

ROCKETEER SPECIAL EDITION, THE
Nov, 1984 ($1.50, color, Baxter paper)(Chapter 5 of Rocketeer serial)
Eclipse Comics

	GD25	FN65	NM94
1-Stevens-c/a; Kaluta back-c; pin-ups inside	1.50	4.00	9.00

ROCKETEER: THE OFFICIAL MOVIE ADAPTATION, THE
1991
W. D. Publications (Disney)

	GD25	FN65	NM94
nn-($5.95, 68 pgs.)-Squarebound deluxe edition	1.00	2.50	6.00
nn-($2.95, 68 pgs.)-Stapled regular edition		1.20	3.00
...3-D Comic Book (1991, $7.98, 52 pgs.)	1.30	3.30	8.00

ROCKET KELLY (See The Bouncer, Green Mask #10); becomes Li'l Pan #6)
1944; Fall, 1945 - No. 5, Oct-Nov, 1946
Fox Feature Syndicate

	GD25	FN65	NM94
nn (1944)	18.00	54.00	125.00
1	18.00	54.00	125.00
2-The Puppeteer app. (costumed hero)	13.00	40.00	90.00
3-5: 5-(#5 on cover, #4 inside)	11.50	34.00	80.00

ROCKETMAN (Strange Fantasy #2 on) (See Hello Pal & Scoop Comics)
June, 1952 (Strange Stories of the Future)
Ajax/Farrell Publications

	GD25	FN65	NM94
1-Rocketman & Cosmo	26.00	78.00	180.00

ROCKET MAN: KING OF THE ROCKET MEN (Innovation)(Value: cover or less)

ROCKET RACCOON (Marvel)(Value: cover or less)

ROCKET RANGER (Adventure)(Value: cover or less)

ROCKETS AND RANGE RIDERS
May, 1957 (16 pgs., soft-c) (Giveaway)
Richfield Oil Corp.

	GD25	FN65	NM94
nn-Toth-a	14.00	43.00	100.00

ROCKET SHIP X
September, 1951; 1952
Fox Features Syndicate

	GD25	FN65	NM94
1	43.00	130.00	300.00
1952 (nn, nd, no publ.)-Edited 1951-c	29.00	86.00	200.00

ROCKET TO ADVENTURE LAND (See Pixie Puzzle...)

ROCKET TO THE MOON
1951
Avon Periodicals

	GD25	FN65	NM94
nn-Orlando-c/a; adapts Otis Aldebert Kline's "Maza of the Moon"	75.00	225.00	525.00

ROCK FANTASY COMICS
Dec, 1989 - No. 16?, 1991 ($2.25/$3.00, B&W)(No cover price)
Rock Fantasy Comics

	GD25	FN65	NM94
1-Pink Floyd part 1		1.60	4.00
1-2nd printing ($3.00-c)		1.20	3.00
2,3: 2-Rolling Stones #1. 3-Led Zeppelin #1		1.20	3.00
2,3: 2nd printings ($3.00-c, 1/90 & 2/90)		1.20	3.00
4-Stevie Nicks Not published			
5-Monstrosities of Rock #1; photo back-c		1.00	2.50
5-2nd printing ($3.00, 3/90 indicia, 2/90-c)		1.20	3.00
6-15,17,18: 6-Guns n' Roses #1 (1st & 2nd printings, 3/90)-Begin $3.00-c. 7-Sex Pistols #1. 8-Alice Cooper; not published. 9-Van Halen #1; photo back-c. 10-Kiss #1; photo back-c. 11-Jimi Hendrix #1; wraparound-c		1.20	3.00
16-($5.00, 68 pgs.)-The Great Gig in the Sky(Floyd)	1.00	2.00	5.00

ROCK HAPPENING (Harvey Pop Comics:...)(See Bunny)
Sept, 1969 - No. 2, Nov, 1969
Harvey Publications

	GD25	FN65	NM94
1,2: Featuring Bunny	3.60	9.00	18.00

ROCK N' ROLL COMICS
June, 1989 - Present ($1.50/$1.95, B&W; color #15 on)
Revolutionary Comics

	GD25	FN65	NM94
1-Guns N' Roses	1.65	4.00	10.00
1-2nd thru 6th printings			1.50
1-7th printing (full color w/new-c/a; $1.95)		.80	2.00
2-Metallica	1.00	2.00	5.00
2-2nd thru 6th printings (6th in color)			1.50
3-Bon Jovi (no reprints)		1.00	2.50
4-8,10-64: 4-Motley Crue(2nd printing only, 1st destroyed). 5-Def Leppard (2 printings). 6-Rolling Stones(4 printings). 7-The Who(3 printings). 8-Skid Row; not published. 10-Warrant/Whitesnake(2 printings; 1st has 2 diff.-c). 11-Aerosmith (2 printings?). 12-New Kids on the Block(2 printings). 12-3rd printing; rewritten & titled NKOTB Hate Book. 13-Led Zeppelin. 14-Sex Pistols. 15-Poison; 1st color issue. 16-Van Halen. 17-Madonna. 18-Alice Cooper. 19-Public Enemy/2 Live Crew. 20-Queensryche/Tesla. 21-Prince? 22-AC/DC; begin $2.50-c. 23-Living Colour. 24-Anthrax		1.00	2.50
9-Kiss		1.60	4.00
9-2nd & 3rd printings		.80	2.00

NOTE: *Most issues were reprinted except #3. Later reprints are in color. #8 was not released.*

ROCKO'S MODERN LIFE (TV)
June, 1994 - Present ($1.95) (Nickelodeon cartoon)
Marvel Comics

	GD25	FN65	NM94
1-11		.80	2.00

ROCKY AND HIS FIENDISH FRIENDS (TV)(Bullwinkle)
Oct, 1962 - No. 5, Sept, 1963 (Jay Ward)
Gold Key

	GD25	FN65	NM94
1 (25¢, 84 pgs.)	20.00	69.00	170.00
2,3 (25¢, 84 pgs.)	13.00	41.00	105.00
4,5 (Regular size, 12¢)	9.00	28.00	70.00

ROCKY AND HIS FRIENDS (See 4-Color #1128, 1152, 1166, 1208, 1275, 1311, Kite Fun Book and March of Comics #216)

ROCKY HORROR PICTURE SHOW THE COMIC BOOK, THE
July, 1990 - No. 3, 1990 ($2.95, color, mini-series, 52 pgs.)(Photo-c #1)
Caliber Press

	GD25	FN65	NM94
1-Adapts cult film plus photos, etc.		1.80	4.50
1-2nd printing		1.20	3.00
2,3		1.40	3.50
...Collection ($4.95)	1.00	2.00	5.00

ROCKY JONES SPACE RANGER (See Space Adventures #15-18)

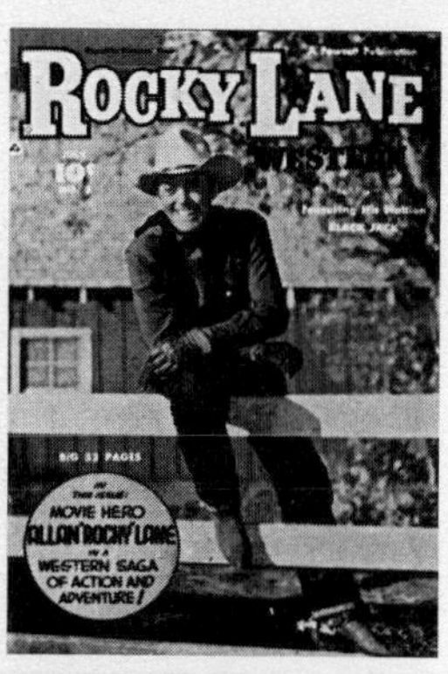

Rocky Lane Western #3 © FAW

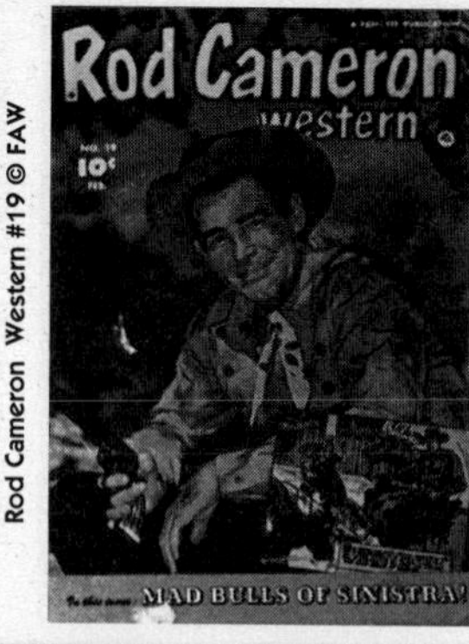

Rod Cameron Western #19 © FAW

Rom #57 © MEG

ROCKY JORDEN PRIVATE EYE (See Private Eye)

ROCKY LANE WESTERN (Allan Rocky Lane starred in Republic movies & TV (for a short time as Allan Lane, Red Ryder & Rocky Lane) (See Black Jack Fawcett Movie Comics, Motion Picture Comics & Six-Gun Heroes)
May, 1949 - No. 87, Nov, 1959
Fawcett Publications/Charlton No. 56 on

	GD25	FN65	NM94
1 (36 pgs.)-Rocky, his stallion Black Jack, & Slim Pickens begin; photo-c begin, end #57; photo back-c	79.00	235.00	550.00
2 (36 pgs.)-Last photo back-c	32.00	96.00	225.00
3-5 (52 pgs.): 4-Captain Tootsie by Beck	22.00	65.00	150.00
6,10 (36 pgs.): 10-Complete western novelette "Badman's Reward"	17.00	52.00	120.00
7-9 (52 pgs.)	19.00	57.00	130.00
11-13,15-17 (52 pgs.): 15-Black Jack's Hitching Post begins, ends #25	13.50	41.00	95.00
14,18 (36 pgs.)	11.00	32.00	75.00
19-21,23,24 (52 pgs.): 20-Last Slim Pickens. 21-Dee Dickens begins, ends #55,57,65-68	11.00	32.00	75.00
22,25-28,30 (36 pgs. begin)	10.00	30.00	70.00
29-Classic complete novel "The Land of Missing Men" with hidden land of ancient temple ruins (r-in #65)	13.50	41.00	95.00
31-40	10.00	30.00	65.00
41-54	9.15	27.50	55.00
55-Last Fawcett issue (1/54)	10.00	30.00	60.00
56-1st Charlton issue (2/54)-Photo-c	12.00	36.00	85.00
57,60-Photo-c	9.15	27.50	55.00
58,59,61-64: 59-61-Young Falcon app. 64-Slim Pickens app.	6.35	19.00	38.00
65-r/#29, "The Land of Missing Men"	7.50	22.50	45.00
66-68: Reprints #30,31,32	6.35	19.00	38.00
69-78,80-86	6.35	19.00	38.00
79-Giant Edition (68 pgs.)	7.00	22.50	45.00
87-Last issue	7.00	21.00	42.00

NOTE: *Complete novels in #10, 14, 18, 22, 25, 30-32, 36, 38, 39, 49. Captain Tootsie in #4, 12, 20. Big Bow and Little Arrow in #11, 28, 63. Black Jack's Hitching Post in #15-25, 64, 73.*

ROCKY LANE WESTERN (AC)(Value: cover or less)

ROD CAMERON WESTERN (Movie star)
Feb, 1950 - No. 20, April, 1953
Fawcett Publications

	GD25	FN65	NM94
1-Rod Cameron, his horse War Paint, & Sam The Sheriff begin; photo front/back-c begin	49.00	146.00	340.00
2	22.00	65.00	150.00
3-Novel length story "The Mystery of the Seven Cities of Cibola"	19.00	57.00	130.00
4-10: 9-Last photo back-c	15.00	45.00	105.00
11-19	11.50	34.00	80.00
20-Last issue & photo-c	12.00	36.00	85.00

NOTE: *Novel length stories in No. 1-8, 12-14.*

RODEO RYAN (See A-1 Comics #8)

ROGAN GOSH
1994 ($6.95)
DC Comics (Vertigo)

	GD25	FN65	NM94
nn-Peter Milligan scripts	1.20	3.00	7.00

ROGER BEAN, R. G. (Regular Guy)
1915 - No. 5, 1917 (34 pgs.; B&W; 4-3/4x16"; cardboard covers)
(No. 1 & 4 bound on side, No. 3 bound at top)
The Indiana News Co.

	GD25	FN65	NM94
1-By Chic Jackson (48 pgs.)	13.00	40.00	90.00
2-5	10.00	30.00	65.00

ROGER DODGER (Also in Exciting Comics #57 on)
No. 5, Aug, 1952
Standard Comics

	GD25	FN65	NM94
5-Teen-age	4.00	10.00	20.00

ROGER RABBIT (Also see Marvel Graphic Novel)
June, 1990 - No. 18, Nov, 1991 ($1.50)
Disney Comics

	GD25	FN65	NM94
1-All new stories		1.80	4.00
2,3		.80	2.00
4-18			1.50
In 3-D 1 (1992, $2.50)-Sold at Wal-Mart?; w/glasses		1.00	2.50

ROGER RABBIT'S TOONTOWN
Aug, 1991 - No. 5, Dec, 1991 ($1.50)
Disney Comics

	GD25	FN65	NM94
1-5			1.50

ROG 2000 (Pacific & Fantagraphics)(Value: cover or less)

ROGUE TROOPER (Fleetway/Quality)(Value: cover or less)

ROGUE TROOPER: THE FINAL WARRIOR (Quality)(Value: cover or less)

ROLY POLY COMIC BOOK
1945 - No. 15, 1946 (MLJ reprints)
Green Publishing Co.

	GD25	FN65	NM94
1-Red Rube & Steel Sterling begin; Sahle-c	23.00	70.00	160.00
6-The Blue Circle & The Steel Fist app.	11.50	34.00	80.00
10-Origin Red Rube retold; Steel Sterling story (Zip #41)	11.00	32.00	75.00
11,12,14: The Black Hood app. in each. 14-Decapitation-c	11.50	34.00	80.00
15-The Blue Circle & The Steel Fist app.; cover exact swipe from Fox Blue Beetle #1	26.00	78.00	180.00

ROM
December, 1979 - No. 75, Feb, 1986
Marvel Comics Group

	GD25	FN65	NM94
1-Based on a Parker Bros. toy; origin/1st app.		1.00	2.50
2-5			1.20
6-16: 13-Saga of the Space Knights begins			1.00
17,18-X-Men app.		1.00	2.50
19-24,26-30: 19-X-Men cameo. 24-F.F. cameo; Skrulls, Nova & The New Champions app. 26,27-Galactus app.			1.00
25-Double size			1.20
31-75: 31,32-Brother of Evil Mutants app. 32-X-Men cameo. 34,35-Sub-Mariner app. 41,42-Dr. Strange app. 50-Skrulls app. (52 pgs.). 56,57-Alpha Flight app. 58,59-Ant-Man app. 65-West Coast Avengers & Beta Ray Bill app. 65,66-X-Men app.			1.00
Annual 1,4: 1(1982, 52 pgs.). 4(1985, 52 pgs.)			1.20
Annual 2,3: 2(1983, 52 pgs.). 3(1984, 52 pgs.)			1.00

NOTE: ***Austin** c-3i, 18i, 61i. **Byrne** a-74i; c-56, 57, 74. **Ditko** a-59-75p. **Golden** c-7-12, 19. **Guice** a-61i; c-55, 58, 60p, 70p. **Layton** a-59i, 72i; c-15, 59i, 69. **Miller** c-2p?, 3p, 17p, 18p. **Russell** a(i)-64, 65, 67, 69, 71, 75; c-64, 65i, 66, 71i, 75. **Severin** c-41p. **Sienkiewicz** a-53i; c-46, 47, 52-54, 68, 71p, Annual 2. **P. Smith** c-59p. **Starlin** c-67.*

ROMANCE (See True Stories of...)

ROMANCE AND CONFESSION STORIES (See Giant Comics Edition)
No date (1949) (25¢, 100 pgs.)
St. John Publishing Co.

	GD25	FN65	NM94
1-Baker-c/a; remaindered St. John love comics	27.00	80.00	185.00

ROMANCE DIARY
December, 1949 - No. 2, March, 1950
Marvel Comics (CDS)(CLDS)

	GD25	FN65	NM94
1,2	9.15	27.50	55.00

ROMANCE OF FLYING, THE (See Feature Books #33)

ROMANCES OF MOLLY MANTON (See Molly Manton)

ROMANCES OF NURSE HELEN GRANT, THE
August, 1957
Atlas Comics (VPI)

	GD25	FN65	NM94
1	4.20	12.50	25.00

Romantic Adventures #32 © ACG

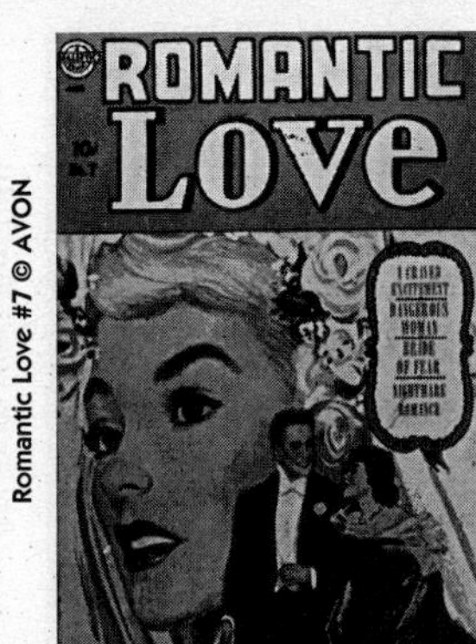

Romantic Love #7 © AVON

Romantic Secrets #34 © CC

GD25 FN65 NM94

ROMANCES OF THE WEST (Becomes Romantic Affairs #3?)
Nov, 1949 - No. 2, Mar, 1950 (52 pgs.)
Marvel Comics (SPC)

1-Movie photo-c of Yvonne DeCarlo & Howard Duff (Calamity Jane & Sam Bass) 14.00 43.00 100.00
2-Photo-c 10.00 30.00 70.00

ROMANCE STORIES OF TRUE LOVE (Formerly Love Problems & Advice)
No. 45, 5/57 - No. 50, 3/58; No. 51, 9/58 - No. 52, 11/58
Harvey Publications

45-51: 45,46,48-50-Powell-a 2.40 6.00 12.00
52-Matt Baker-a 4.00 12.00 24.00

ROMANCE TALES (Formerly Western Winners #6?)
No. 7, Oct, 1949 - No. 9, March, 1950 (7,8: photo-c)
Marvel Comics (CDS)

7 8.35 25.00 50.00
8,9: 8-Everett-a 5.85 17.50 35.00

ROMANCE TRAIL
July-Aug, 1949 - No. 6, May-June, 1950 (All photo-c & 52 pgs.)
National Periodical Publications

1-Kinstler, Toth-a; Jimmy Wakely photo-c 43.00 130.00 300.00
2-Kinstler-a; Jim Bannon photo-c 22.00 65.00 150.00
3-Photo-c; Kinstler, Toth-a 24.00 72.00 165.00
4-Photo-c; Toth-a 17.00 52.00 120.00
5,6-Photo-c 14.00 43.00 100.00

ROMAN HOLIDAYS, THE (TV)
Feb, 1973 - No. 4, Nov, 1973 (Hanna-Barbera)
Gold Key

1 1.90 6.00 13.00
2-4 1.70 4.20 10.00

ROMANTIC ADVENTURES (My... #49-67, covers only)
Mar-Apr, 1949 - No. 67, July, 1956 (Becomes My... #68 on)
American Comics Group (B&I Publ. Co.)

1 10.00 30.00 70.00
2 5.85 17.50 35.00
3-10 4.00 11.00 22.00
11-20 (4/52) 3.60 9.00 18.00
21-45,49,51,52: 52-Last Pre-code (2/55) 2.80 7.00 14.00
46-48-3-D effect-c/stories (TrueVision) 7.50 22.50 45.00
50-Classic cover/story "Love of A Lunatic" 5.85 17.50 35.00
53-67 2.00 5.00 10.00
NOTE: *#1-23, 52 pgs.* ***Shelly*** *a-40. Whitney c/art in many issues.*

ROMANTIC AFFAIRS (Formerly Molly Manton's Romances #2 and/or Romances of the West #2 and/or Our Love #2?)
No. 3, March, 1950
Marvel Comics (SPC)

3-Photo-c from Molly Manton's Romances #2 5.35 16.00 32.00

ROMANTIC CONFESSIONS
Oct, 1949 - V3#1, April-May, 1953
Hillman Periodicals

V1#1-McWilliams-a 10.00 30.00 60.00
2-Briefer-a; negligee panels 5.85 17.50 35.00
3-12 4.00 11.00 22.00
V2#1,2,4-8,10-12: 2-McWilliams-a 3.60 9.00 18.00
3-Krigstein-a 6.35 19.00 38.00
9-One pg. Frazetta ad 3.60 9.00 18.00
V3#1 3.60 9.00 18.00

ROMANTIC HEARTS
Mar, 1951 - No. 10, Oct, 1952; July, 1953 - No. 12, July, 1955
Story Comics/Master/Merit Pubs.

1(3/51) (1st Series) 9.15 27.50 55.00
2 4.70 14.00 28.00
3-10: Cameron-a 4.00 11.00 22.00
1(7/53) (2nd Series)-Some say #11 on-c 5.35 16.00 32.00
2 4.00 10.00 20.00
3-12 3.20 8.00 16.00

ROMANTIC LOVE
9-10/49 - #3, 1-2/50; #4, 2-3/51 - #13, 10/52; #20, 3-4/54 - #23, 9-10/54
Avon Periodicals/Realistic (No #14-19)

1-c-/Avon paperback #252 15.00 45.00 105.00
2-5: 3-c-/paperback Novel Library #12. 4-c-/paperback Diversey Prize Novel #5. 5-c-/paperback Novel Library #34 10.00 30.00 60.00
6- "Thrill Crazy" marijuana story; c-/Avon paperback #207; Kinstler-a 11.00 32.00 75.00
7,8: 8-Astarita-a(2) 9.15 27.50 55.00
9-12: 9-c-/paperback Novel Library #41; Kinstler-a. 10-c-/Avon paperback #212. 11-c-/paperback Novel Library #17; Kinstler-a. 12-c-/paperback Novel Library #13 10.00 30.00 60.00
13,21,22: 22-Kinstler-c 9.15 27.50 55.00
20-Kinstler-c/a 9.15 27.50 55.00
23-Kinstler-c 6.70 20.00 40.00
nn(1-3/53)(Realistic-r) 5.85 17.50 35.00
NOTE: ***Astarita*** *a-7, 10, 11, 21. Painted c-1-3, 5, 7-11, 13. Photo c-4, 6.*

ROMANTIC LOVE
No. 4, June, 1950
Quality Comics Group

4 (6/50)(Exist?) 4.20 12.50 25.00
I.W. Reprint #2,3,8 1.50 3.00

ROMANTIC MARRIAGE (Cinderella Love #25 on)
#1-3 (1950, no months); #4, 5-6/51 - #17, 9/52; #18, 9/53 - #24, 9/54
Ziff-Davis/St. John No. 18 on (#1-8: 52 pgs.)

1-Photo-c 11.50 34.00 80.00
2-Painted-c; Anderson-a (also #15) 7.50 22.50 45.00
3-9: 3,4,8,9-Painted-c; 5-7-Photo-c 5.85 17.50 35.00
10-Unusual format; front-c is a painted-c; back-c is a photo-c complete with logo, price, etc. 10.00 30.00 70.00
11-17 13-Photo-c. 17-(9/52)-Last Z-D issue 5.00 15.00 30.00
18-22,24: 20-Photo-c 5.00 15.00 30.00
23-Baker-c 5.35 16.00 32.00

ROMANTIC PICTURE NOVELETTES
1946
Magazine Enterprises

1-Mary Worth-r; Creig Flessel-c 11.00 32.00 75.00

ROMANTIC SECRETS (Becomes Time For Love)
Sept, 1949 - No. 39, 4/53; No. 5, 10/55 - No. 52, 11/64 (#1-5: photo-c)
Fawcett/Charlton Comics No. 5 (10/55) on

1-(52 pg. issues begin, end #?) 10.00 30.00 65.00
2,3 5.85 17.50 35.00
4,9-Evans-a 6.70 20.00 40.00
5-8,10 4.00 11.00 22.00
11-23 4.00 10.00 20.00
24-Evans-a 5.00 15.00 30.00
25-39('53) 3.20 8.00 16.00
5 (Charlton, 2nd series)(10/55, formerly Negro Romances #4) 5.35 16.00 32.00
6-10 3.20 8.00 16.00
11-20 1.60 4.00 8.00
21-35: Last 10¢ issue? 1.00 2.50 5.00
36-52('64) .60 1.50 3.00
NOTE: ***Bailey*** *a-20.* ***Powell*** *a(1st series)-5, 7, 10, 12, 16, 17, 20, 26, 29, 33, 34, 36, 37.* ***Sekowsky*** *a-26. Photo c(1st series)-1-5, 16, 25, 27, 33.* ***Swayze*** *a(1st series)-16, 18, 19, 23, 26-28, 31, 32, 39.*

ROMANTIC STORY (Cowboy Love #28 on)
11/49 - #22, Sum, 1953; #23, 5/54 - #27, 12/54; #28, 8/55 - #130, 11/73
Fawcett/Charlton Comics No. 23 on

Ronin #6 © DC

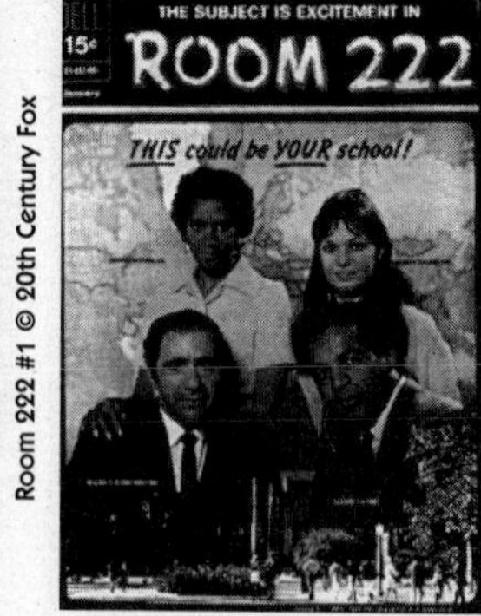

Room 222 #1 © 20th Century Fox

Roy Rogers Comics #26 © DELL

	GD25	FN65	NM94
1-Photo-c begin, end #24; 52 pgs. begins	10.00	30.00	70.00
2	5.85	17.50	35.00
3-5	5.00	15.00	30.00
6-14	4.00	11.00	22.00
15-Evans-a	5.00	15.00	30.00
16-22(Sum, '53; last Fawcett issue). 21-Toth-a?	3.20	8.00	16.00
23-39: 26,29-Wood swipes	3.20	8.00	16.00
40-(100 pgs.)	5.00	15.00	30.00
41-50	2.60	6.50	13.00
51-80: 57-Hypo needle story	1.00	2.50	7.00
81-100		1.20	3.00
101-130		.80	2.00

NOTE: ***Jim Aparo** a-94.* ***Powell** a-7, 8, 16, 20, 30.* ***Marcus Swayze** a-2, 12, 20, 32.*

ROMANTIC THRILLS (See Fox Giants)

ROMANTIC WESTERN
Winter, 1949 - No. 3, June, 1950 (All Photo-c)
Fawcett Publications

	GD25	FN65	NM94
1	12.00	36.00	85.00
2-(Spr/50)-Williamson, McWilliams-a	13.50	41.00	95.00
3	10.00	30.00	65.00

ROMEO TUBBS (...That Lovable Teenager; formerly My Secret Life)
No. 26, 5/50 - No. 28, 7/50; No. 1, 1950; No. 27, 12/52
Fox Feature Syndicate/Green Publ. Co. No. 27

	GD25	FN65	NM94
26-Teen-age	8.35	25.00	50.00
27-Contains Pedro on inside; Wood-a	11.00	32.00	75.00
28, 1	6.70	20.00	40.00

RONALD McDONALD (TV)
Sept, 1970 - No. 4, March, 1971
Charlton Press (King Features Synd.)

	GD25	FN65	NM94
1	1.00	2.00	5.00
2-4		1.20	3.00

RONIN
July, 1983 - No. 6, Aug, 1984 ($2.50, mini-series, 52 pgs.)
DC Comics

	GD25	FN65	NM94
1-Miller script, c/a in all		1.60	4.00
2-5		1.20	3.00
6-Scarcer; has fold-out poster		2.50	6.00
Trade paperback (1987, $12.95)-Reprints #1-6	1.85	5.50	13.00

ROOK (See Eerie Magazine & Warren Presents: The Rook)
November, 1979 - No. 14, April, 1982
Warren Publications

	GD25	FN65	NM94
1-Nino-a			1.50
2-14: 3,4-Toth-a			1.00

ROOKIE COP (Formerly Crime and Justice?)
No. 27, Nov, 1955 - No. 33, Aug, 1957
Charlton Comics

	GD25	FN65	NM94
27	6.70	20.00	40.00
28-33	4.20	12.50	25.00

ROOM 222 (TV)
Jan, 1970; No. 2, May, 1970 - No. 4, Jan, 1971
Dell Publishing Co.

	GD25	FN65	NM94
1	5.00	15.00	36.00
2-4: 2,4-Photo-c. 3-Marijuana story. 4 r/#1	3.00	9.00	21.00

ROOTIE KAZOOTIE (TV)(See 3-D-ell)
No. 415, Aug, 1952 - No. 6, Oct-Dec, 1954
Dell Publishing Co.

	GD25	FN65	NM94
4-Color 415 (#1)	11.00	32.00	75.00
4-Color 459,502(#2,3)	8.35	25.00	50.00
4(4-6/54)-6	8.35	25.00	50.00

ROOTS OF THE SWAMPTHING (DC)(Value: cover or less)

ROUND THE WORLD GIFT
No date (mid 1940's) (4 pgs.)
National War Fund (Giveaway)

	GD25	FN65	NM94
nn	11.50	34.00	80.00

ROUNDUP (...Western Crime Stories)
July-Aug, 1948 - No. 5, Mar-Apr, 1949 (All 52 pgs.)
D. S. Publishing Co.

	GD25	FN65	NM94
1-Kiefer-a	13.00	40.00	90.00
2-Marijuana drug mention story	10.00	30.00	60.00
3-5	8.35	25.00	50.00

ROYAL ROY (Marvel)(Value: cover or less)

ROY CAMPANELLA, BASEBALL HERO
1950 (Brooklyn Dodgers)
Fawcett Publications

	GD25	FN65	NM94
nn-Photo-c; life story	46.00	138.00	320.00

ROY ROGERS (See March of Comics #17, 35, 47, 62, 68, 73, 77, 86, 91, 100, 105, 116, 121, 131, 136, 146, 151, 161, 167, 176, 191, 206, 221, 236, 250)

ROY ROGERS AND TRIGGER
April, 1967
Gold Key

	GD25	FN65	NM94
1-Photo-c; reprints	4.70	14.00	28.00

ROY ROGERS COMICS (See Western Roundup under Dell Giants)
No. 38, 4/44 - No. 177, 12/47 (#38-166: 52 pgs.)
Dell Publishing Co.

	GD25	FN65	NM94
4-Color 38 (1944)-49 pg. story; photo front/back-c on all 4-Color issues (1st western comic with photo-c)	100.00	300.00	700.00
4-Color 63 (1945)-Color photos on all four-c	47.00	141.00	330.00
4-Color 86,95 (1945)	34.00	100.00	235.00
4-Color 109 (1946)	27.00	80.00	185.00
4-Color 117,124,137,144	19.00	57.00	130.00
4-Color 153,160,166: 166-48 pg. story	16.00	48.00	110.00
4-Color 177 (36 pgs.)-32 pg. story	16.00	48.00	110.00

ROY ROGERS COMICS (...& Trigger #92(8/55)-on)(Roy starred in Republic movies, radio & TV) (Singing cowboy) (Also see Dale Evans, It Really Happened #8, Queen of the West Dale Evans, & Roy Rogers' Trigger)
Jan, 1948 - No. 145, Sept-Oct, 1961 (#1-19: 36 pgs.)
Dell Publishing Co.

	GD25	FN65	NM94
1-Roy, his horse Trigger, & Chuck Wagon Charley's Tales begin; photo-c begin, end #145	57.00	171.00	400.00
2	26.00	78.00	180.00
3-5	19.00	58.00	135.00
6-10	14.00	43.00	100.00
11-19: 19-Chuck Wagon Charley's Tales ends	10.00	30.00	70.00
20 (52 pgs.)-Trigger feature begins, ends #46	10.00	30.00	70.00
21-30 (52 pgs.)	10.00	30.00	60.00
31-46 (52 pgs.): 37-X-Mas-c	7.50	22.50	45.00
47-56 (36 pgs.): 47-Chuck Wagon Charley's Tales returns, ends #133. 49-X-mas-c. 55-Last photo back-c	5.85	17.50	35.00
57 (52 pgs.)-Heroin drug propaganda story	6.70	20.00	40.00
58-70 (52 pgs.): 61-X-Mas-c	5.35	16.00	32.00
71-80 (52 pgs.): 73-X-Mas-c	4.70	14.00	28.00
81-91 (36 pgs. #81-on): 85-X-Mas-c	4.00	11.00	22.00
92-99,101-110,112-118: 92-Title changed to Roy Rogers and Trigger (8/55)	4.00	11.00	22.00
100-Trigger feature returns, ends #133?	5.85	17.50	35.00
111,119-124-Toth-a	6.35	19.00	38.00
125-131: 125-Toth-a (1 pg.)	4.70	14.00	28.00
132-144-Manning-a. 138,144-Dale Evans featured	5.00	15.00	30.00
145-Last issue	6.35	19.00	38.00
...& the Man From Dodge City (Dodge giveaway, 16 pgs., 1954)-Frontier, Inc. (5x7-1/4")	11.00	32.00	75.00

Official Roy Rogers Riders Club Comics (1952; 16 pgs., reg. size, paper-c)

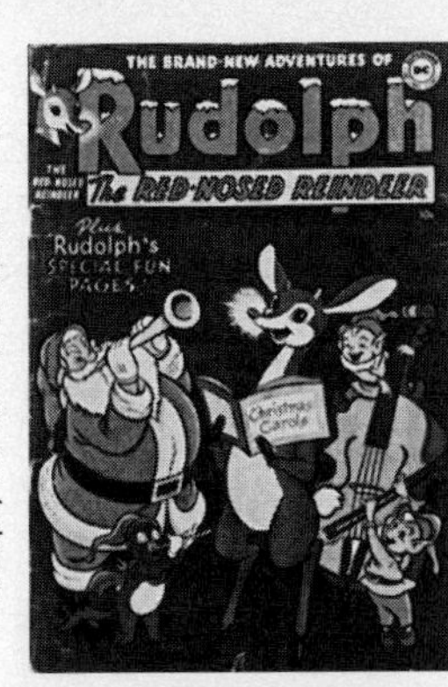

Rudolph, The Red Nosed Reindeer © DC

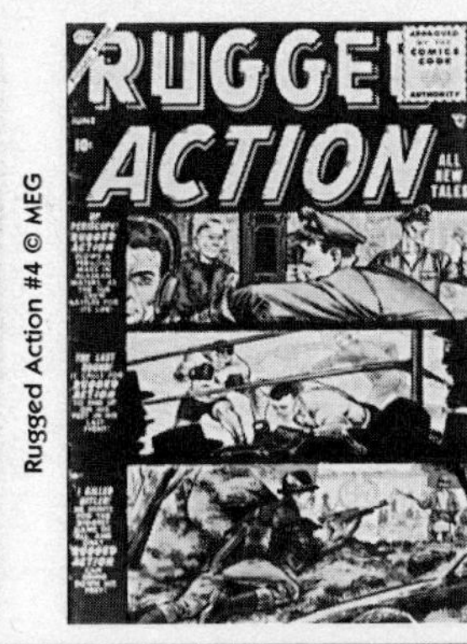

Rugged Action #4 © MEG

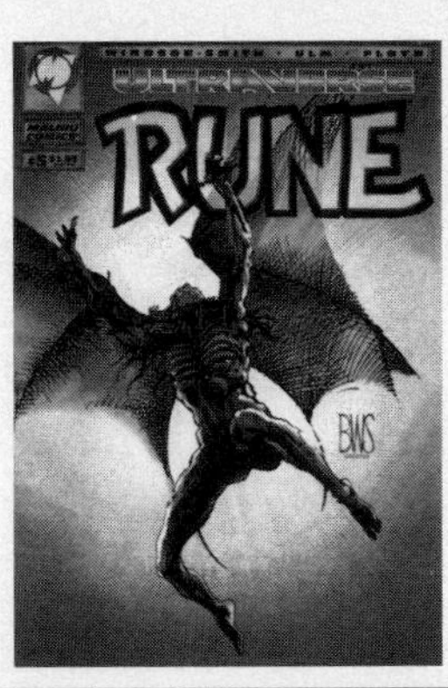

Rune #5 © BWS

12.00 36.00 85.00
NOTE: ***Buscema*** *a-74-108(2 stories each).* ***Manning*** *a-123, 124, 132-144.* ***Marsh*** *a-110. Photo back-c No. 1-9, 11-35, 38-55.*

ROY ROGERS' TRIGGER (TV)
No. 329, May, 1951 - No. 17, June-Aug, 1955
Dell Publishing Co.

	GD25	FN65	NM94
4-Color 329 (#1)-Painted-c	11.00	32.00	75.00
2 (9-11/51)-Photo-c	10.00	30.00	70.00
3-5: 3-Painted-c begin, end #17, most by S. Savitt	4.00	10.00	20.00
6-17: Title merges with Roy Rogers after #17	3.00	7.50	15.00

ROY ROGERS WESTERN CLASSICS (AC)(Value: cover or less)

RUDOLPH, THE RED NOSED REINDEER (See Limited Collectors' Edition #20, 24, 33, 42, 50)

RUDOLPH, THE RED-NOSED REINDEER
1939 (2,400,000 copies printed); Dec, 1951
Montgomery Ward (Giveaway)

	GD25	FN65	NM94
Paper cover - 1st app. in print; written by Robert May; ill. by Denver Gillen	10.00	30.00	70.00
Hardcover version	14.00	43.00	100.00
1951 Edition (Has 1939 date)-36 pgs., slick-c printed in red & brown; pulp interior printed in four mixed-ink colors: red, green, blue & brown	6.70	20.00	40.00
1951 Edition with red-spiral promotional booklet printed on high quality stock, 8-1/2"x11", in red & brown, 25 pages composed of 4 fold outs, single sheets and the Rudolph comic book inserted (rare)	50.00	150.00	350.00

RUDOLPH, THE RED-NOSED REINDEER
1950 - No. 13?, Winter, 1962-63 (Issues are not numbered)
National Periodical Publications

	GD25	FN65	NM94
1950 issue (#1); Grossman-c/a begins	11.50	34.00	80.00
1951-54 issues (4 total)	8.35	25.00	50.00
1955-62 issues (8 total)	5.35	16.00	32.00

NOTE: *The 1962-63 issue is 84 pages. 13 total issues published. Has games & puzzles also.*

RUFF AND REDDY (TV)
No. 937, 9/58 - No. 12, 1-3/62 (Hanna-Barbera)(#9 on: 15¢)
Dell Publishing Co.

	GD25	FN65	NM94
4-Color 937(#1)(1st Hanna-Barbera comic book)	12.00	36.00	85.00
4-Color 981,1038	9.15	27.50	55.00
4(1-3/60)-12: 8-Last 10¢ issue	6.70	20.00	40.00

RUGGED ACTION (Strange Stories of Suspense #5 on)
Dec, 1954 - No. 4, June, 1955
Atlas Comics (CSI)

	GD25	FN65	NM94
1-Brodsky-c	8.35	25.00	50.00
2-4: 2-Last precode (2/55)	5.35	16.00	32.00

NOTE: ***Ayers*** *a-2, 3.* ***Maneely*** *c-2, 3.* ***Severin*** *a-2.*

RULAH JUNGLE GODDESS (Formerly Zoot; I Loved #28 on) (Also see All Top Comics & Terrors of the Jungle)
No. 17, Aug, 1948 - No. 27, June, 1949
Fox Features Syndicate

	GD25	FN65	NM94
17	55.00	165.00	385.00
18-Classic girl-fight interior splash	41.00	124.00	290.00
19,20	39.00	116.00	270.00
21-Used in **SOTI**, pg. 388,389	41.00	124.00	290.00
22-Used in **SOTI**, pg. 22,23	39.00	116.00	270.00
23-27	29.00	86.00	200.00

NOTE: ***Kamen*** *c-17-19, 21, 22.*

RUNAWAY, THE (See Movie Classics)

RUN BABY RUN
1974 (39¢)
Logos International

	GD25	FN65	NM94
nn-By Tony Tallarico from Nicky Cruz's book			1.00

RUN, BUDDY, RUN (TV)
June, 1967 (Photo-c)
Gold Key

	GD25	FN65	NM94
1 (10204-706)	3.00	7.50	15.00

RUNE (See Sludge & all other Ultraverse titles for previews)
1994 - Present ($1.95, color)
Malibu Comics (Ultraverse)

	GD25	FN65	NM94
1,2,4-Barry Windsor-Smith-c/a/stories begin		.80	2.00
1-Ultra 5000 Limited silver foil edition	1.40	4.20	10.00
0-Obtained by sending coupons from 11 comics; came w/Solution #0, poster, temporary tattoo, card	1.70	4.20	10.00
3-(3/94, $3.50, 68 pgs.)-Flip book w/Ultraverse Premiere #1		1.40	3.50
1-(1/94)-"Ashcan" edition flip book w/Wrath #1			1.00

RUST
7/87 - No. 15, 11/88; V2#1, 2/89 - No. 7, 1989 ($1.50/$1.75, color)
Now Comics

	GD25	FN65	NM94
1-3 ($1.50)			1.50
4-11,13-15, V2#1-7 ($1.75)		.70	1.75
12-(8/88, $1.75)-5 pg. preview of The Terminator (1st app.)	1.30	3.25	8.00

RUST (Adventure, 1992)(Value: cover or less)

RUSTY, BOY DETECTIVE
Mar-April, 1955 - No. 5, Nov, 1955
Good Comics/Lev Gleason

	GD25	FN65	NM94
1-Bob Wood, Carl Hubbell-a begins	6.70	20.00	40.00
2-5	4.20	12.50	25.00

RUSTY COMICS (Formerly Kid Movie Comics; Rusty and Her Family #21, 22; The Kelleys #23 on; see Millie The Model)
No. 12, Apr, 1947 - No. 22, Sept, 1949
Marvel Comics (HPC)

	GD25	FN65	NM94
12-Mitzi app.	11.00	32.00	75.00
13	7.50	22.50	45.00
14-Wolverton's Powerhouse Pepper (4 pgs.) plus Kurtzman's "Hey Look"	12.00	36.00	85.00
15-17-Kurtzman's "Hey Look"	10.00	30.00	70.00
18,19	5.35	16.00	32.00
20-Kurtzman-a (5 pgs.)	10.00	30.00	70.00
21,22-Kurtzman-a (17 & 22 pgs.)	13.50	41.00	95.00

RUSTY DUGAN (See Holyoke One-Shot #2)

RUSTY RILEY (See 4-Color #418, 451, 486, 554)

SAARI ("The Jungle Goddess")
November, 1951
P. L. Publishing Co.

	GD25	FN65	NM94
1	27.00	81.00	190.00

SABLE (First)(Value: cover or less)(Formerly Jon Sable, Freelance; also see Mike Grell's...)

SABRE (Eclipse)(Value: cover or less)(Also see Eclipse Graphic Album Series)

SABRETOOTH (See Iron Fist, Power Man, X-Factor #10 & X-Men)
Aug, 1993 - No. 4, Nov, 1993 ($2.95, mini-series, coated paper)
Marvel Comics

	GD25	FN65	NM94
1-4: 1-Die-cut-c. 3-Wolverine app.		1.20	3.00

SABRETOOTH CLASSIC
May, 1994 - Present ($1.50)
Marvel Comics

	GD25	FN65	NM94
1-12: 1-3-r/Power Man & Iron Fist #66,78,84. 4-r/Spec. S-M #116			1.50

SABRINA'S CHRISTMAS MAGIC (See Archie Giant Series Magazine #196, 207, 220, 231, 243, 455, 467, 479, 491, 503, 515)

SABRINA'S HALLOWEEN SPOOOKTACULAR
1993 - Present ($2.00, 52 pgs., published annually)
Archie Publications

	GD25	FN65	NM94
1-Neon orange ink-c; bound-in poster		.80	2.00

Saddle Justice #4 © EC

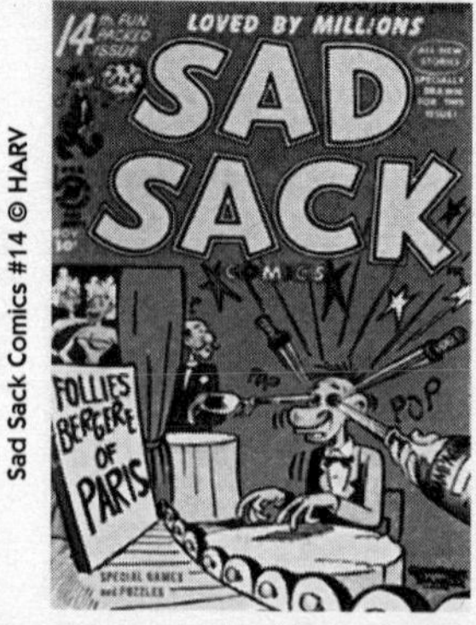

Sad Sack Comics #14 © HARV

Sad Sack Laugh Special #6 © HARV

SABRINA, THE TEEN-AGE WITCH (TV)(See Archie Giant Series 544, Archie's Madhouse 22, Archie's TV..., Chilling Advs. In Sorcery)
April, 1971 - No. 77, Jan, 1983 (Giants No. 1-17)
Archie Publications

	GD25	FN65	NM94
1	5.00	15.00	35.00
2	2.30	6.75	16.00
3-5: 3,4-Archie's Group x-over	1.30	3.25	8.00
6-10	1.00	2.00	5.00
11-20		1.20	3.00
21-77		.80	2.00

SABU, "ELEPHANT BOY" (Movie; formerly My Secret Story)
No. 30, June, 1950 - No. 2, Aug, 1950
Fox Features Syndicate

	GD25	FN65	NM94
30(#1)-Wood-a; photo-c from movie	16.00	48.00	110.00
2-Photo-c from movie; Kamen-a	11.00	32.00	75.00

SACHS & VIOLENS
Nov, 1993 - No. 4, July, 1994 ($2.25, color, mini-series, adult)
Epic Comics (Marvel)

	GD25	FN65	NM94
1-($2.75)-Embossed-c w/bound-in trading card		1.10	2.75
1-($3.50)-Platinum edition (1 for each 10 ordered)			8.00
2-4-Perez-c/a; bound-in trading card: 2-(5/94)		.90	2.25

SACRAMENTS, THE
October, 1955 (25¢)
Catechetical Guild Educational Society

	GD25	FN65	NM94
304	2.40	6.00	12.00

SACRED AND THE PROFANE, THE (See Eclipse Graphic Album Series #9 & Epic Illustrated #20)

SAD CASE OF WAITING ROOM WILLIE, THE
1950? (nd) (14 pgs. in color; paper covers; regular size)
American Visuals Corp. (For Baltimore Medical Society)

	GD25	FN65	NM94
nn-By Will Eisner (Rare)	43.00	130.00	300.00

SADDLE JUSTICE (Happy Houlihans #1,2; Saddle Romances #9 on)
No. 3, Spring, 1948 - No. 8, Sept-Oct, 1949
E. C. Comics

	GD25	FN65	NM94
3-The 1st E.C. by Bill Gaines to break away from M. C. Gaines' old Educational Comics format. Craig, Feldstein, H. C. Kiefer, & Stan Asch-a; mentioned in Love and Death	36.00	107.00	250.00
4-1st Graham Ingels-a for E.C.	36.00	107.00	250.00
5-8-Ingels-a in all	33.00	100.00	230.00

NOTE: ***Craig** and **Feldstein** art in most issues. Canadian reprints known; see Table of Contents. **Craig** c-3, 4. **Ingels** c-5-8. #4 contains a biography of **Craig**.*

SADDLE ROMANCES (Saddle Justice #3-8; Weird Science #12 on)
No. 9, Nov-Dec, 1949 - No. 11, Mar-Apr, 1950
E. C. Comics

	GD25	FN65	NM94
9-Ingels-c/a	36.00	107.00	250.00
10-Wood's 1st work at E. C.; Ingels-a; Feldstein-c	38.00	115.00	265.00
11-Ingels-a; Feldstein-c	36.00	107.00	250.00

NOTE: *Canadian reprints known; see Table of Contents. **Wood/Harrison** a-10, 11.*

SADIE SACK (See Harvey Hits #93)

SAD SACK AND THE SARGE
Sept, 1957 - No. 155, June, 1982
Harvey Publications

	GD25	FN65	NM94
1	11.50	34.00	80.00
2	5.35	16.00	32.00
3-10	4.35	13.00	26.00
11-20	3.60	9.00	18.00
21-30	2.40	6.00	12.00
31-50	1.40	3.50	7.00
51-90,97-100		1.40	3.50
91-96: All 52 pg. Giants		1.80	4.50
101-155		.90	2.25

SAD SACK COMICS (See Harvey Collector's Comics #16, Little Sad Sack, Tastee Freez Comics #4 & True Comics #55)
Sept, 1949 - No. 287, Oct, 1982; No. 288, 1992 - Present
Harvey Publications/Lorne-Harvey Publications (Recollections) #288 On

	GD25	FN65	NM94
1-Infinity-c; Little Dot begins (1st app.); civilian issues begin, end #21; based on comic strip	39.00	118.00	275.00
2-Flying Fool by Powell	19.00	57.00	130.00
3	11.00	32.00	75.00
4-10	9.15	27.50	55.00
11-21	6.35	19.00	38.00
22-("Back In The Army Again" on covers #22-36); "The Specialist" story about Sad Sack's return to Army	4.00	11.00	22.00
23-50	2.80	7.00	14.00
51-100: 62-"The Specialist" reprinted	1.70	4.20	10.00
101-150	1.00	2.00	5.00
151-222		1.20	3.00
223-228 (25¢ Giants, 52 pgs.)		1.40	3.50
229-287: 286,287 had limited distribution		.90	2.25
288,289 ($2.75, 1992): 289-50th anniversary issue		1.10	2.75
290-293 ($1.00, 1993, B&W)			1.00
3-D 1 (1/54, 25¢)-Came with 2 pairs of glasses; titled "Harvey 3-D Hits"	19.00	58.00	135.00
Armed Forces Complimentary copies, HD #1-40 (1957-1962)	1.20	3.00	6.00
...At Home for the Holidays 1 (1993, no-c price)-Publ. by Lorne-Harvey' X-Mas issue		.80	2.00

NOTE: *The Sad Sack Comics comic book was a spin-off from a Sunday Newspaper strip launched through John Wheeler's Bell Syndicate. The previous Sunday page and the first 21 comics depicted the Sad Sack in civvies. Unpopularity caused the Sunday page to be discontinued in the early '50s. Meanwhile Sad Sack returned to the Army, by popular demand, in issue No. 22, remaining there ever since. Incidentally, relatively few of the first 21 issues were ever collected and remain scarce due to this.*

SAD SACK FUN AROUND THE WORLD
1974 (no month)
Harvey Publications

	GD25	FN65	NM94
1-About Great Britain		1.60	4.00

SAD SACK GOES HOME
1951 (16 pgs. in color, no cover price)
Harvey Publications

	GD25	FN65	NM94
nn-By George Baker	6.70	20.00	40.00

SAD SACK LAUGH SPECIAL
Winter, 1958-59 - No. 93, Feb, 1977 (#1-60: 68 pgs.; #61-76: 52 pgs.)
Harvey Publications

	GD25	FN65	NM94
1-Giant 25¢ issues begin	9.15	27.50	55.00
2	4.70	14.00	28.00
3-10	4.00	10.00	20.00
11-30	2.40	6.00	12.00
31-60: 31-1st app. Hi-Fi Tweeter. 60-Last 68 pg. Giant	1.20	2.90	7.00
61-76-(All 52 pg. issues)	1.00	2.00	5.00
77-93		1.20	3.00

SAD SACK NAVY, GOBS 'N' GALS
Aug, 1972 - No. 8, Oct, 1973
Harvey Publications

	GD25	FN65	NM94
1: 52 pg. Giant	1.00	2.50	6.00
2-8		1.40	3.50

SAD SACK'S ARMY LIFE (See Harvey Hits #8, 17, 22, 28, 32, 39, 43, 47, 51, 55, 58, 61, 64, 67, 70)

SAD SACK'S ARMY LIFE (...Parade #1-57, ...Today #58 on)
Oct, 1963 - No. 60, Nov, 1975; No. 61, May, 1976
Harvey Publications

	GD25	FN65	NM94
1-(68 pg. issues begin)	5.85	17.50	35.00
2-10	3.60	9.00	18.00

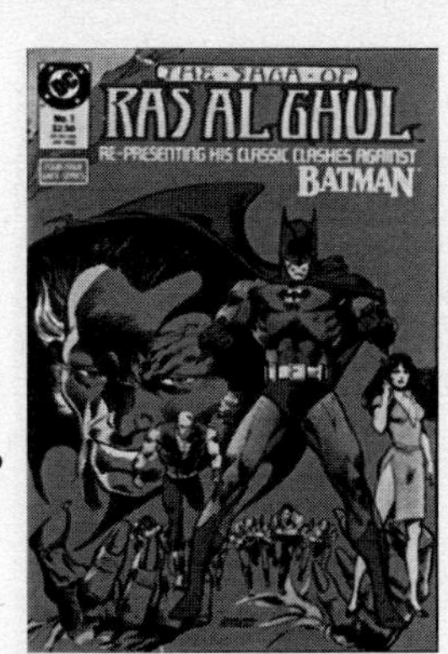

The Saga of Ra's Al Ghul #1 © DC

The Saga Of The Original Human Torch #2 © MEG

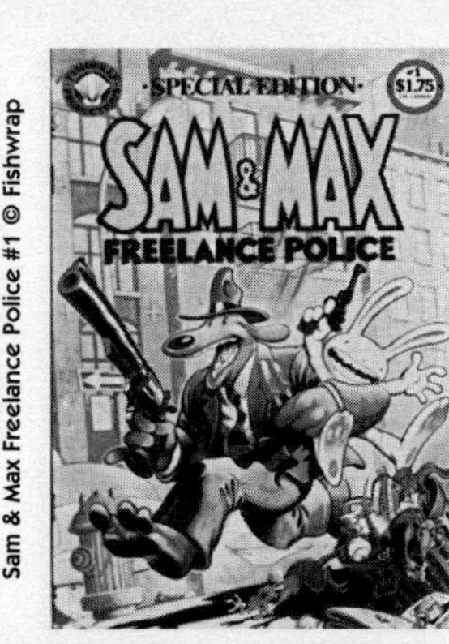

Sam & Max Freelance Police #1 © Fishwrap

	GD25	FN65	NM94
11-20	1.80	4.50	9.00
21-34: Last 68 pg. issue	1.00	2.50	6.00
35-51: All 52 pgs.		1.20	3.00
52-61		.80	2.00

SAD SACK'S FUNNY FRIENDS (See Harvey Hits #75)
Dec, 1955 - No. 75, Oct, 1969
Harvey Publications

	GD25	FN65	NM94
1	9.15	27.50	55.00
2-10	4.70	14.00	28.00
11-20	2.60	6.50	13.00
21-30	1.20	3.00	6.00
31-75		1.60	4.00

SAD SACK'S MUTTSY (See Harvey Hits #74, 77, 80, 82, 84, 87, 89, 92, 96, 99, 102, 105, 108, 111, 113, 115, 117, 119, 121)

SAD SACK USA (...Vacation #8)
Nov, 1972 - No. 7, Nov, 1973; No. 8, Oct, 1974
Harvey Publications

	GD25	FN65	NM94
1	1.00	2.00	5.00
2-8		1.00	2.50

SAD SACK WITH SARGE & SADIE
Sept, 1972 - No. 8, Nov, 1973
Harvey Publications

	GD25	FN65	NM94
1-(52 pg. Giant)	1.00	2.00	5.00
2-8		1.00	2.50

SAD SAD SACK WORLD
Oct, 1964 - No. 46, Dec, 1973 (#1-31: 68 pgs.; #32-38: 52 pgs.)
Harvey Publications

	GD25	FN65	NM94
1	3.60	9.00	18.00
2-10	1.80	4.50	9.00
11-31: 31-Last 68 pg. issue	1.40	3.50	7.00
32-38-(All 52 pgs)		1.60	4.00
39-46		1.00	2.50

SAFEST PLACE IN THE WORLD, THE
1993 ($2.50, color, one-shot)
Dark Horse Comics

	GD25	FN65	NM94
1-By Steve Ditko (c/a/scripts)		1.00	2.50

SAGA OF BIG RED, THE
Sept, 1976 ($1.25) (In color)
Omaha World-Herald

	GD25	FN65	NM94
nn-by Win Mumma; story of the Nebraska Cornhuskers (sports)		.80	2.00

SAGA OF CRYSTAR, CRYSTAL WARRIOR, THE (Marvel)(Value: cover or less)

SAGA OF RA'S AL GHUL, THE (DC)(Value: cover or less)

SAGA OF RA'S AL GHUL, THE
Jan, 1988 - No. 4, Apr, 1988 ($2.50, mini-series)
DC Comics

	GD25	FN65	NM94
1-4-r/N. Adams Batman		1.00	2.50

SAGA OF THE SWAMP THING, THE (See Swamp Thing)

SAGA OF THE ORIGINAL HUMAN TORCH
Apr, 1990 - No. 4, July, 1990 ($1.50, limited series)
Marvel Comics

	GD25	FN65	NM94
1-4: 1-Origin; Buckler-c/a(p). 3-Hitler-c			1.50

SAGA OF THE SUB-MARINER, THE
Nov, 1988 - No. 12, Oct, 1989 ($1.25/$1.50 #5 on)
Marvel Comics

	GD25	FN65	NM94
1-12: 9-Original X-Men app.			1.50

SAILOR ON THE SEA OF FATE (See First Comics Graphic Novel #11)

SAILOR SWEENEY (Navy Action #1-11, 15 on)
No. 12, July, 1956 - No. 14, Nov, 1956
Atlas Comics (CDS)

	GD25	FN65	NM94
12-14: 12-Shores-a. 13-Severin-c	6.35	19.00	38.00

SAINT, THE (Also see Movie Comics(DC) #2 & Silver Streak #18)
Aug, 1947 - No. 12, Mar, 1952
Avon Periodicals

	GD25	FN65	NM94
1-Kamen bondage-c/a	50.00	150.00	350.00
2	26.00	78.00	180.00
3,4: 4-Lingerie panels	20.00	60.00	140.00
5-Spanking panel	26.00	78.00	180.00
6-Miss Fury app. by Tarpe Mills (14 pgs.)	33.00	100.00	230.00
7-c-/Avon paperback #118	18.00	54.00	125.00
8,9(12/50): Saint strip-r in #8-12; 9-Kinstler-c	14.00	43.00	100.00
10-Wood-a, 1 pg; c-/Avon paperback #289	14.00	43.00	100.00
11	10.00	30.00	70.00
12-c-/Avon paperback #123	13.00	404.00	90.00

NOTE: *Lucky Dale, Girl Detective in #1,2,4,6.* ***Hollingsworth*** *a-4, 6. Painted-c 7, 8, 10-12.*

ST. GEORGE (Marvel)(Value: cover or less)

SAINT SINNER (See Razorline)
Oct, 1993 - Present ($1.75)
Marvel Comics

	GD25	FN65	NM94
1-($2.50)-Foil embossed-c; by Clive Barker		1.00	2.50
2-9: 5-Ectokid x-over		.70	1.75

ST. SWITHIN'S DAY (Trident)(Value: cover or less)

SALERNO CARNIVAL OF COMICS (Also see Pure Oil Comics, 24 Pages of Comics, & Vicks Comics)
Late 1930s (16 pgs.) (paper cover) (Giveaway)
Salerno Cookie Co.

	GD25	FN65	NM94
nn-Color reprints of Calkins' Buck Rogers & Skyroads, plus other strips from Famous Funnies	43.00	130.00	300.00

SALOME' (See Night Music #6)

SAM & MAX FREELANCE POLICE (Marvel)(Value: cover or less)

SAM AND MAX, FREELANCE POLICE SPECIAL (Comico)(Value: cover or less)

SAM & MAX FREELANCE POLICE SPECIAL COLOR COLLECTION (Marvel)(Value: cover or less)

SAM HILL PRIVATE EYE
1950 - No. 7, 1951
Close-Up (Archie)

	GD25	FN65	NM94
1	10.00	30.00	70.00
2	6.70	20.00	40.00
3-7	5.85	17.50	35.00

SAM SLADE ROBOHUNTER (Quality)(Value: cover or less)

SAMSON (1st Series) (Captain Aero #7 on; see Big 3 Comics)
Fall, 1940 - No. 6, Sept, 1941 (See Fantastic Comics)
Fox Features Syndicate

	GD25	FN65	NM94
1-Samson begins, ends #6; Powell-a, signed 'Rensie;' Wing Turner by Tuska app; Fine-c?	121.00	365.00	850.00
2-Dr. Fung by Powell; Fine-c?	54.00	160.00	375.00
3-Navy Jones app.; Joe Simon-c	45.00	135.00	315.00
4-Yarko the Great, Master Magician begins	39.00	116.00	270.00
5,6: 6-Origin The Topper	29.00	86.00	200.00

SAMSON (2nd Series) (Formerly Fantastic Comics #10, 11)
No. 12, April, 1955 - No. 14, Aug, 1955
Ajax/Farrell Publications (Four Star)

	GD25	FN65	NM94
12-Wonder Boy	17.00	52.00	120.00
13,14: 13-Wonder Boy, Rocket Man	13.00	40.00	90.00

SAMSON (See Mighty Samson)

SAMSON & DELILAH (See A Spectacular Feature Magazine)

SAMUEL BRONSTON'S CIRCUS WORLD (See Circus World under Movie Comics)

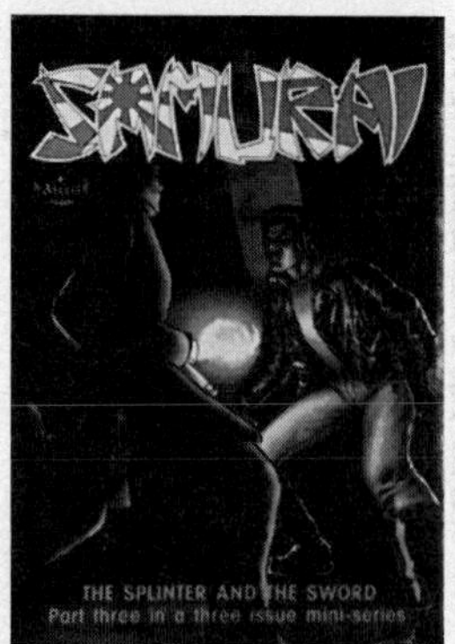

Samurai V2 #3 © Aircel

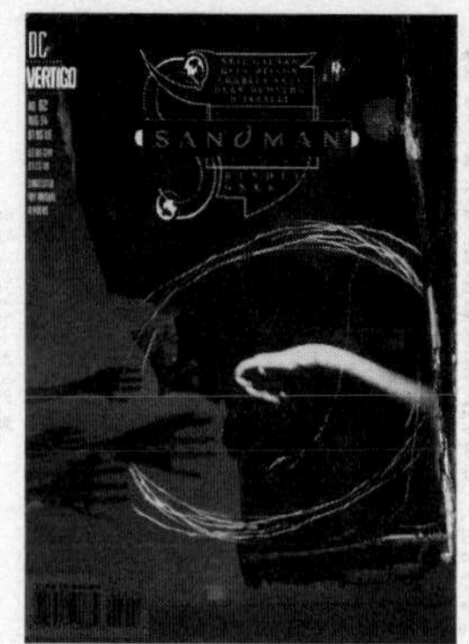

Sandman #62 © DC

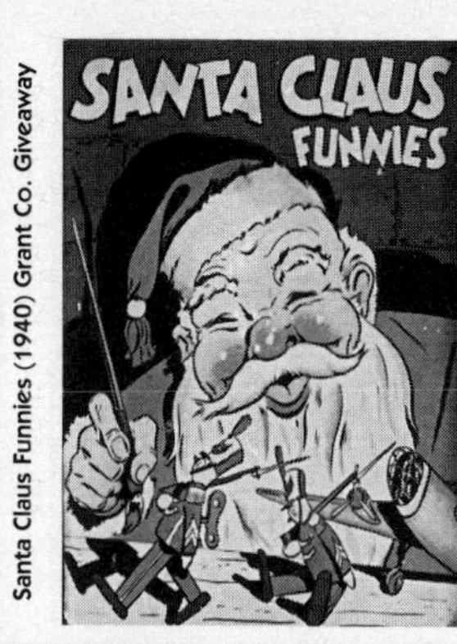

Santa Claus Funnies (1940) Grant Co. Giveaway

GD25 FN65 NM94

SAMURAI (Also see Eclipse Graphic Album Series #14)
1985 - No. 22, 1988? ($1.70, B&W)
Aircel Publications

1 — 1.40 3.50
1-2nd & 3rd printings — .70 1.70
2-12,17-22 — .70 1.70
2-2nd printing — .70 1.70
13-Dale Keown's 1st published artwork (1987) — 1.20 2.90 7.00
14-16-Dale Keown-a — 1.00 2.00 5.00

SAMURAI CAT (Marvel)(Value: cover or less)

SAMUREE
May, 1993 - Present ($2.50, color)
Continuity Comics

V2#1-4-Embossed-c: 2,4-Adams plot, Nebres-i. 3-Nino-c(i) — 1.00 2.50

SANCTUARY (Viz)(Value: cover or less)

SANDMAN, THE (See Adventure Comics #40, New York World's Fair & World's Finest #3)
Winter, 1974; No. 2, Apr-May, 1975 - No. 6, Dec-Jan, 1975-76
National Periodical Publications

1-1st app. new Sandman; Kirby-a; Joe Simon scripts (last S&K collaboration) — 1.30 3.25 8.00
2-6: 6-Kirby/Wood-c/a — 1.70 4.25
NOTE: ***Kirby** a-1p, 4-6p; c-1-5, 6p.*

SANDMAN (See Books of Magic, Vertigo Jam & Vertigo Preview)
Jan, 1989 - Present ($1.50/$1.75, mature readers)
DC Comics (Vertigo imprint #47 on)

1 ($2.00, 52 pgs.)-1st app. new Sandman; Neil Gaiman scripts begin; Sam Kieth-a(p) in #1-5 — 11.00 32.00 75.00
2-Cain & Abel app. (from HOM & HOS) — 5.70 17.00 40.00
3-5: 3-John Constantine app. — 5.00 15.00 35.00
6,7 — 4.00 10.70 25.00
8-Regular ed. has Jeanette Kahn publishorial & American Cancer Society ad w/no indicia on inside front-c; Death-c/story (1st app.) — 7.00 21.00 50.00
8-Limited ed. (600+ copies?); has Karen Berger editorial and next issue teaser on inside covers (has indicia) — 26.00 80.00 185.00
9-13: 10-Has explaination about #8 mixup; has bound-in Shocker movie poster — 2.00 6.00 14.00
14-($2.50, 52 pgs.)-Bound-in Nightbreed fold-out — 2.10 6.00 15.00
15-20: 16-Photo-c. 17,18-Kelley Jones-a. 19-Vess-a — 1.40 3.50 8.50
18-Error version w/1st 3 panels on pg. 1 in blue ink — 1.30 3.30 8.00
19-Error version w/switched pgs. (no 2 pg. spread) — 1.30 3.30 8.00
21-27: Seasons of Mist storyline. 22-World Without End preview. 24-Kelley Jones/Russell-a — 1.20 2.90 7.00
28-30 — 1.00 2.00 5.00
31-35,37-48: 38-40,57-Photo-c. 41,44-50,57-Metallic ink on-c. 48-Cerebus appears as a doll — 1.20 3.00
36-($2.50, 52 pgs.) — 1.80 4.50
49,51-53,55: 49-Begin $1.95-c — 1.10 2.75
50-($2.95, 52 pgs.)-Black-c w/metallic ink by McKean; Russell-a; McFarlane pin-up — 1.50 3.75
50-($2.95)-Signed & limited (5,000) Treasury Edition with sketch of Neil Gaiman — 2.00 5.00 12.00
54-Re-intro Prez; Death app.; Belushi, Nixon cameos — 1.60 4.00
56-69 — .80 2.00
Annual 1 (10/94, $3.95) — 1.60 4.00
... nn (1990, $12.95, 296 pgs., TPB)-r/#8-16 — 1.85 5.50 13.00
...: A Gallery of Dreams ($2.95)-Intro by N. Gaiman — 1.20 3.00
Special 1 (1991, $3.50, 68 pgs.)-Glow-in-the-dark-c — 1.20 2.90 7.00

SANDMAN MYSTERY THEATRE
Apr, 1993 - Present ($1.95, mature)
DC Comics (Vertigo)

1-26: 1-Matt Wagner scripts begin. 5-Neon ink logo — .80 2.00
Annual 1 (10/94, $3.95, 68 pgs.) — 1.60 4.00

SANDS OF THE SOUTH PACIFIC
January, 1953
Toby Press

1 — 13.00 40.00 90.00

SANTA AND HIS REINDEER (See March of Comics #166)

SANTA AND POLLYANNA PLAY THE GLAD GAME
Aug, 1960 (16 pgs.) (Disney giveaway)
Sales Promotion

nn — 2.40 6.00 12.00

SANTA AND THE ANGEL (See Dell Junior Treasury #7 & Four Color #259)

SANTA & THE BUCCANEERS
1959
Promotional Publ. Co. (Giveaway)

nn-Reprints 1952 Santa & the Pirates — 1.80 4.50 9.00

SANTA & THE CHRISTMAS CHICKADEE
1974 (20 pgs.)
Murphy's (Giveaway)

nn — 1.00 2.00 5.00

SANTA & THE PIRATES
1952
Promotional Publ. Co. (Giveaway)

nn-Marv Levy-c/a — 1.80 4.50 9.00

SANTA AT THE ZOO (See 4-Color #259)

SANTA CLAUS AROUND THE WORLD (See March of Comics #241)

SANTA CLAUS CONQUERS THE MARTIANS (See Movie Classics)

SANTA CLAUS FUNNIES (Also see The Little Fir Tree)
nd; 1940 (Color & B&W; 8x10"; 12 pgs., heavy paper)
W. T. Grant Co./Whitman Publishing (Giveaway)

nn-(2 versions) — 10.00 30.00 65.00

SANTA CLAUS FUNNIES (Also see Dell Giants)
Dec?, 1942 - No. 1274, Dec, 1961
Dell Publishing Co.

nn(#1)(1942)-Kelly-a — 39.00 118.00 275.00
2(12/43)-Kelly-a — 25.00 75.00 175.00
4-Color 61(1944)-Kelly-a — 24.00 72.00 165.00
4-Color 91(1945)-Kelly-a — 19.00 57.00 130.00
4-Color 128('46),175('47)-Kelly-a — 14.00 43.00 100.00
4-Color 205,254-Kelly-a — 13.00 40.00 90.00
4-Color 302,361 — 4.00 12.00 24.00
4-Color 525,607,666,756,867 — 4.00 11.00 22.00
4-Color 958,1063,1154,1274 — 4.00 10.00 20.00
NOTE: *Most issues contain only one Kelly story.*

SANTA CLAUS PARADE
1951; No. 2, Dec, 1952; No. 3, Jan, 1955 (25¢)
Ziff-Davis (Approved Comics)/St. John Publishing Co.

nn(1951-Ziff-Davis)-116 pgs. (Xmas Special 1,2) — 20.00 60.00 140.00
2(12/52-Ziff-Davis)-100 pgs.; Dave Berg-a — 15.00 45.00 105.00
V1#3(1/55-St. John)-100 pgs.; reprints-c/#1 — 13.00 40.00 90.00

SANTA CLAUS' WORKSHOP (See March of Comics #50, 168)

SANTA IS COMING (See March of Comics #197)

SANTA IS HERE (See March of Comics #49)

SANTA ON THE JOLLY ROGER
1965
Promotional Publ. Co. (Giveaway)

nn-Marv Levy-c/a — .80 2.00 4.00

SANTA! SANTA!

Santa's Gift Book (1944)

Santa's New Story Book, Campbell (Giveaway)

Satan's Sx: Hellspawn 3# © Topps

GD25 FN65 NM94

1974 (20 pgs.)
R. Jackson (Montgomery Ward giveaway)
nn 1.20 3.00

SANTA'S BUSY CORNER (See March of Comics #31)

SANTA'S CANDY KITCHEN (See March of Comics #14)

SANTA'S CHRISTMAS BOOK (See March of Comics #123)

SANTA'S CHRISTMAS COMICS
December, 1952 (100 pgs.)
Standard Comics (Best Books)
nn-Supermouse, Dizzy Duck, Happy Rabbit, etc. 13.00 40.00 90.00

SANTA'S CHRISTMAS COMIC VARIETY SHOW
1943 (24 pgs.)
Sears Roebuck & Co.
Contains puzzles & new comics of Dick Tracy, Little Orphan Annie, Moon Mullins, Terry & the Pirates, etc. 14.00 43.00 100.00

SANTA'S CHRISTMAS LIST (See March of Comics #255)

SANTA'S CHRISTMAS TIME STORIES
nd (Late 1940s) (16 pgs.; paper cover)
Premium Sales, Inc. (Giveaway)
nn 4.00 11.00 22.00

SANTA'S CIRCUS
1964 (Half-size)
Promotional Publ. Co. (Giveaway)
nn-Marv Levy-c/a 1.20 3.00 6.00

SANTA'S FUN BOOK
1951, 1952 (Regular size, 16 pgs., paper-c)
Promotional Publ. Co. (Murphy's giveaway)
nn 2.40 6.00 12.00

SANTA'S GIFT BOOK
No date (16 pgs.)
No Publisher
nn-Puzzles, games only 2.40 6.00 12.00

SANTA'S HELPERS (See March of Comics #64, 106, 198)

SANTA'S LITTLE HELPERS (See March of Comics #270)

SANTA'S NEW STORY BOOK
1949 (16 pgs.; paper cover)
Wallace Hamilton Campbell (Giveaway)
nn 4.70 14.00 28.00

SANTA'S REAL STORY BOOK
1948, 1952 (16 pgs.)
Wallace Hamilton Campbell/W. W. Orris (Giveaway)
nn 4.35 13.00 26.00

SANTA'S RIDE
1959
W. T. Grant Co. (Giveaway)
nn 2.40 6.00 12.00

SANTA'S RODEO
1964 (Half-size)
Promotional Publ. Co. (Giveaway)
nn-Marv Levy-a 1.00 2.00 5.00

SANTA'S SECRETS
1951, 1952? (16 pgs.; paper cover)
Sam B. Anson Christmas giveaway
nn-Has games, stories & pictures to color 2.80 7.00 14.00

SANTA'S SHOW (See March of Comics #311)

SANTA'S SLEIGH (See March of Comics #298)

GD25 FN65 NM94

SANTA'S STORIES
1953 (Regular size; paper cover)
K. K. Publications (Klines Dept. Store)
nn-Kelly-a 14.00 43.00 100.00
nn-Another version (1953, glossy-c, half-size, 7-1/4x5-1/4")-Kelly-a 10.00 30.00 70.00

SANTA'S SURPRISE (See March of Comics #13)

SANTA'S SURPRISE
1947 (36 pgs.; slick cover)
K. K. Publications (Giveaway)
nn 4.20 12.50 25.00

SANTA'S TINKER TOTS
1958
Charlton Comics
1-Based on "The Tinker Tots Keep Christmas" 2.40 6.00 12.00

SANTA'S TOYLAND (See March of Comics #242)

SANTA'S TOYS (See March of Comics #12)

SANTA'S TOYTOWN FUN BOOK
1953
Promotional Publ. Co. (Giveaway)
nn-Marv Levy-c 1.40 3.50 7.00

SANTA'S VISIT (See March of Comics #283)

SANTIAGO (See 4-Color #723)

SARGE SNORKEL (Beetle Bailey)
Oct, 1973 - No. 17, Dec, 1976
Charlton Comics
1 1.00 2.00 5.00
2-17 .80 2.00

SARGE STEEL (Becomes Secret Agent #9 on; also see Judomaster)
Dec, 1964 - No. 8, Mar-Apr, 1966 (All 12¢ issues)
Charlton Comics
1-Origin & 1st app. 1.70 5.00 12.00
2-5,7,8 1.00 2.50 6.00
6-2nd app. Judomaster 1.40 3.50 8.50

SATAN'S SIX
Apr, 1993 - No. 4, July, 1993 ($2.95, mini-series)
Topps Comics
1-Polybagged w/Kirbychrome trading card; Kirby/McFarlane-c plus 8 pgs. Kirby-a(p); has coupon for Kirbychrome ed. of Secret City Saga #0 1.20 3.00
2-4-Polybagged w/3 cards. 4-Teenagents preview 1.20 3.00

SATAN'S SIX: HELLSPAWN
June, 1994 - No. 3, July, 1994 ($2.50, limited series)
Topps Comics
1-3: 1-(6/94)-Indicia incorrectly shows "Vol 1 #2". 2-(6/94) 1.00 2.50

SAVAGE COMBAT TALES
Feb, 1975 - No. 3, July, 1975
Atlas/Seaboard Publ.
1-3: 1-Sgt. Stryker's Death Squad begins (origin). 2-Only app. Warhawk 1.00

NOTE: ***McWilliams** a-1-3; c-1. **Sparling** a-1, 3. **Toth** a-2.*

SAVAGE DRAGON, THE (See Megaton #3 & 4)
July, 1992 - No. 3, Dec, 1992 ($1.95, color, mini-series)
Image Comics
1-Erik Larsen-c/a/scripts & bound-in poster in all; 4 cover color variations w/4 different posters 1.20 2.90 7.00
2-Intro Super Patriot-c/story (10/92) 1.60 4.00
3-Contains coupon for Image Comics #0 1.30 3.25

Savage Dragon #11 © Eric Larson

The Savage She Hulk #2 © MEG

Savage Tales #4 © MEG

GD25 FN65 NM94

3-With coupon missing .80 2.00
...Vs. Savage Megaton Man 1 (3/93, $1.95)-Larsen & Simpson-c/a .80 2.00

SAVAGE DRAGON, THE
June, 1993 - Present ($1.95, color)
Image Comics

1,3-7-Erik Larsen-c/a/scripts. 3-Mighty Man back-up story w/Austin-i. 4-Flip book w/Ricochet. 5-Mighty Man flip-c & back-up plus poster. 6-Jae Lee poster. 7-Vanguard poster .90 2.25
2-($2.95, 52 pgs.)-Teenage Mutant Ninja Turtles-c/story; flip book features Vanguard #0 (see Megaton for 1st app.) 1.30 3.25
8-12: 8-Deadly Duo poster by Larsen .80 2.00

SAVAGE DRAGON/TEENAGE MUTANT NINJA TURTLES CROSSOVER
Sept, 1993 ($2.75, color)
Mirage Studios

1-Erik Larsen-c(i) only 1.10 2.75

SAVAGE HENRY (Vortex)(Value: cover or less)

SAVAGE RAIDS OF GERONIMO (See Geronimo #4)

SAVAGE RANGE (See 4-Color #807)

SAVAGE RETURN OF DRACULA
1992 ($2.00, 52 pgs.)
Marvel Comics

1-r/Tomb of Dracula #1,2 by Gene Colan .80 2.00

SAVAGE SHE-HULK, THE (See The Avengers, Marvel Graphic Novel #18 & The Sensational She-Hulk)
Feb, 1980 - No. 25, Feb, 1982
Marvel Comics Group

1-Origin & 1st app. She-Hulk 1.00 2.50 6.00
2-10 1.10 2.75
11-25: 25-(52 pgs.) .90 2.25
NOTE: ***Austin*** *a-25i; c-23i-25i.* ***J. Buscema*** *a-1p; c-1, 2p.* ***Golden*** *c-8-11.*

SAVAGE SWORD OF CONAN (The... #41 on; ...The Barbarian #175 on)
Aug, 1974 - Present ($1.00/$1.25/$2.25, B&W magazine)(Mature readers)
Marvel Comics Group

1-Smith-r; J. Buscema/N. Adams/Krenkel-a; origin Blackmark by Gil Kane (part 1, ends #3); Blackmark's 1st app. in magazine form-r/from paperback) & Red Sonja (3rd app.) 11.00 33.00 78.00
2-Neal Adams-c; Chaykin/N. Adams-a 5.00 15.00 35.00
3-Severin/B. Smith-a; N. Adams-a 2.90 8.60 20.00
4-Neal Adams/Kane-a(r) 2.10 6.40 15.00
5-10: 5-Jeff Jones frontispiece (r) 1.70 5.00 12.00
11-20 1.50 3.80 9.00
21-50: 34-3 pg. preview of Conan newspaper strip. 35-Cover similar to Savage Tales #1. 45-Red Sonja returns; begin $1.25-c 1.30 3.00 8.00
51-100: 63-Toth frontispiece. 65-Kane-a w/Chaykin/Miller/Simonson/Sherman finishes. 70-Article on movie. 83-Red Sonja-r by Neal Adams from #1 1.00 2.00 5.00
101-176: 163-Begin $2.25-c. 169-King Kull story. 171-Soloman Kane by Williamson (i). 172-Red Sonja story 1.40 3.50
177-231: 179,187,192-Red Sonja app. 190-193-4 part King Kull story. 196, 202-King Kull story. 200-New Buscema-a; Robert E. Howard app. with Conan in story. 204-60th anniversary (1932-92). 211-Rafael Kayanan's 1st Conan-a. 214-Sequel to Red Nails by Robert E. Howard .90 2.25
Special 1(1975, B&W)-B. Smith-r/Conan #10,13 1.30 3.25 8.00
NOTE: ***N. Adams*** *a-14p, 60, 83p(r).* ***Alcala*** *a-2 ,4, 7, 12, 15-20, 23, 24, 28, 59, 67, 69, 75, 76i, 80i, 82i, 83i, 89, 180i, 184i, 187i, 189i, 216p.* ***Austin*** *a-78i.* ***Boris*** *painted c-1, 4, 5, 7, 9, 10, 12, 15.* ***Brunner*** *a-30; c-8, 30.* ***Buscema*** *a-1-5, 7, 10-12, 15-24, 26-28, 31, 32, 36-43, 45, 47-58p, 60-67p, 70, 71-74p, 76-81p, 87-96p, 98, 99-101p, 190-204p; painted c-40.* ***Chaykin*** *c-31.* ***Chiodo*** *painted c-71, 76, 79, 81, 84, 85, 178.* ***Conrad*** *c-215, 217.* ***Corben*** *a-4, 16, 29.* ***Finlay*** *a-16.* ***Golden*** *a-98, 101; c-98, 101, 105, 106, 117, 124, 150.* ***Kaluta*** *a-11, 18; c-3, 91, 93.* ***Gil Kane*** *a-2, 3, 8, 13r, 29, 47, 64, 65, 67, 85p, 86p.* ***Rafael Kayanan*** *a-211-213, 215, 217.* ***Krenkel*** *a-9, 11, 14, 16, 24.* ***Morrow*** *a-7.* ***Nebres*** *a-93i, 101i, 107, 114.* ***Newton*** *a-6.* ***Nino*** *c/a-6.* ***Redondo*** *painted c-48-50, 52, 56, 57, 85i, 90, 96i.* ***Marie & John Severin*** *a-Special 1.* ***Simonson*** *a-7, 8, 12, 15-17.* ***Barry Smith*** *a-7, 16, 24, 82r, Special 1r.* ***Starlin*** *c-26.* ***Toth*** *a-64.*

GD25 FN65 NM94

Williamson *a(i)-162, 171, 186. No. 8 , 10 & 16 contain a Robert E. Howard Conan adaptation.*

SAVAGE TALES (...Featuring Conan #4 on)(Magazine)
May, 1971; No. 2, 10/73; No. 3, 2/74 - No. 12, Summer, 1975 (B&W)
Marvel Comics Group

1-Origin/1st app. The Man-Thing by Morrow; Conan the Barbarian by Barry Smith (1st Conan x-over outside his own title); Femizons by Romita-r/in #3; Ka-Zar story by Buscema 19.00 58.00 135.00
2-B. Smith, Brunner, Morrow, Williamson-a; Wrightson King Kull reprint/ Creatures on the Loose #10 6.00 19.00 45.00
3-B. Smith, Brunner, Steranko, Williamson-a 4.30 12.90 30.00
4,5-N. Adams-c; last Conan (Smith-r/#4) plus Kane/N. Adams-a. 5-Brak the Barbarian begins, ends #8 2.90 8.60 20.00
6-Ka-Zar begins; Williamson-r; N. Adams-c 1.10 2.70 6.50
7-N. Adams-i 1.00 2.00 5.00
8-Shanna, the She-Devil app. thru #10; Williamson-r 1.80 4.50
9,11 1.40 3.50
10-Neal Adams-a(i), Williamson-r 1.80 4.50
...Featuring Ka-Zar Annual 1 (Summer, '75, B&W)(#12 on inside)-Ka-Zar origin by G. Kane; B. Smith-r/Astonishing Tales .90 2.30 5.50
NOTE: ***Boris*** *c-7, 10.* ***Buscema*** *a-5r, 6p, 8p; c-2.* ***Colan*** *a-1p.* ***Fabian*** *c-8.* ***Golden*** *a-1, 4; c-1.* ***Heath*** *a-10p, 11p.* ***Kaluta*** *c-9.* ***Maneely*** *r-2, 4(The Crusader in both).* ***Morrow*** *a-1, 2, Annual 1.* ***Reese*** *a-2.* ***Severin*** *a-1-7.* ***Starlin*** *a-5. Robert E. Howard adaptations-1-4.*

SAVAGE TALES (Magazine size)
Nov, 1985 - No. 9, Mar, 1987 ($1.50, B&W, mature readers)
Marvel Comics Group

1-1st app. The Nam; Golden, Morrow-a 1.00 2.00 5.00
2-9: 2,7-Morrow-a. 4-2nd Nam story; Golden-a 1.50

SAVED BY THE BELL (Harvey)(Value: cover or less)

SCAMP (Walt Disney)(See Walt Disney's Comics & Stories #204)
No. 703, 5/56 - No. 1204, 8-10/61; 11/67 - No. 45, 1/79
Dell Publishing Co./Gold Key

4-Color 703(#1) 10.00 30.00 60.00
4-Color 777,806('57),833 7.50 22.50 45.00
5(3-5/58)-10(6-8/59) 5.85 17.50 35.00
11-16(12-2/60-61) 4.00 10.00 20.00
4-Color 1204(1961) 4.00 10.00 20.00
1(12/67-Gold Key)-Reprints begin 3.60 9.00 18.00
2(3/69)-10 1.70 4.20 10.00
11-20 1.30 3.25 8.00
21-45 1.00 2.50 6.00
NOTE: *New stories-#20(in part), 22-25, 27, 29-31, 34, 36-40, 42-45. New covers-#11, 12, 14, 15, 17-25, 27, 29-31, 34, 36-38.*

SCARAB
Nov, 1993 - No. 8, June, 1994 ($1.95, limited series)
DC Comics (Vertigo)

1-8-Glenn Fabry painted-c: 1-Silver ink-c. 2-Phantom Stranger app. .80 2.00

SCAR FACE (See The Crusaders)

SCARECROW OF ROMNEY MARSH, THE (See W. Disney Showcase #53)
April, 1964 - No. 3, Oct, 1965 (Disney TV Show)
Gold Key

10112-404 (#1) 4.00 10.00 20.00
2,3 3.00 7.50 15.00

SCARLET O'NEIL (See Harvey Comics Hits #59 & Invisible...)

SCARLETT
Jan, 1993 - No. 14, Feb, 1994 ($1.75)
DC Comics

1-($2.95) 1.20 3.00
2-14 .70 1.75

SCARLET WITCH (See Avengers #16, Vision &... & X-Men #4)
Jan, 1994 - No. 4, Apr, 1994 ($1.75, mini-series)
Marvel Comics

Scary Tales #1 © CC

Science Comics #2 © Export Pub. Ent.

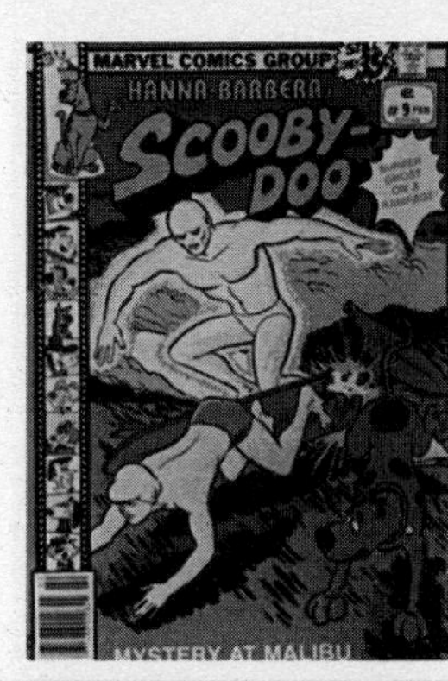

Scooby Doo #9 © H-B

GD25 FN65 NM94

1-4 .70 1.75

SCARY TALES
8/75 - #9, 1/77; #10, 9/77 - #20, 6/79; #21, 8/80 - #46, 10/84
Charlton Comics

1-Origin/1st app. Countess Von Bludd, not in #2 1.20 3.00
2-11: 3-Sutton painted-c 1.50
12-36,39,46-All reprints 1.50
37,38,40-45-New-a. 38-Mr. Jigsaw app. 1.50
1(Modern Comics reprint, 1977) 1.00

NOTE: ***Adkins** a-31i; c-31i. **Ditko** a-3, 5, 7, 8(2), 11, 12, 14-16r, 18(3)r, 19r, 21r, 30r, 32, 39r; c-5, 11, 14, 18, 30, 32. **Newton** a-31p; c-31p. **Powell** a-18r. **Staton** a-1(2 pgs.), 4, 20r; c-1, 20. **Sutton** a-9; c-4, 9.*

SCAVENGERS (Quality)(Value: cover or less)

SCAVENGERS
1993(nd, July) - Present ($2.50, color, serially numbered)
Triumphant Comics

1-9: 5,6-Triumphant Unleashed x-over. 9-(3/94) 1.00 2.50
0-Retail edition (3/94, &2.50, 36 pgs.) 1.00 2.50
0-Giveaway edition (3/94, 20 pgs.) 1.00 2.50
0-Coupon redemption edition 1.00 2.50
10,11: 10-(4/94) 1.00 2.50

SCHOOL DAY ROMANCES (...of Teen-Agers #4; Popular Teen-Agers #5 on)
Nov-Dec, 1949 - No. 4, May-June, 1950 (Teenage)
Star Publications

1-Toni Gayle (later Toni Gay), Ginger Snapp, Midge Martin & Eve Adams begin 13.00 40.00 90.00
2,3: 3-Jane Powell photo on-c & true life story 10.00 30.00 60.00
4-Ronald Reagan photo on-c; L.B. Cole-c 16.00 48.00 110.00

NOTE: *All have **L. B. Cole** covers.*

SCHWINN BICYCLE BOOK (...Bike Thrills, 1959)
1949; 1952; 1959 (10¢)
Schwinn Bicycle Co.

1949 4.00 10.50 21.00
1952-Believe It or Not type facts; comic format; 36 pgs. 2.00 5.00 10.00
1959 1.60 4.00 8.00

SCIENCE COMICS (1st Series)
Feb, 1940 - No. 8, Sept, 1940
Fox Features Syndicate

1-Origin Dynamo (1st app., called Electro in #1), The Eagle (1st app.), & Navy Jones; Marga, The Panther Woman (1st app.), Cosmic Carson & Perisphere Payne, Dr. Doom begin; bondage/hypo-c; Electro-c 257.00 771.00 1800.00
2: 2,3-Dynamo-c 107.00 321.00 750.00
3,4: 4-Kirby-a; Cosmic Carson-c 93.00 280.00 650.00
5-8: 5,8-Eagle-c. 6,7-Dynamo-c 69.00 205.00 480.00

NOTE: *Cosmic Carson by **Tuska**-#1-3; by **Kirby**-#4. **Lou Fine** c-1-3 only.*

SCIENCE COMICS (2nd Series)
January, 1946 - No. 5, 1946
Humor Publications (Ace Magazines?)

1-Palais-c/a in #1-3; A-Bomb-c 10.00 30.00 65.00
2 5.00 15.00 30.00
3-Feldstein-a (6 pgs.) 10.00 30.00 65.00
4,5: 4-Palais-c 4.20 12.50 25.00

SCIENCE COMICS
May, 1947 (8 pgs. in color)
Ziff-Davis Publ. Co.

nn-Could be ordered by mail for 10¢; like the nn Amazing Adventures (1950) & Boy Cowboy (1950); used to test the market 30.00 90.00 210.00

SCIENCE COMICS (True Science Illustrated)
March, 1951
Export Publication Ent., Toronto, Canada
Distr. in U.S. by Kable News Co.

1-Science Adventure stories plus some true science features; man on moon story 6.70 20.00 40.00

SCIENCE FICTION SPACE ADVENTURES (See Space Adventures)

SCOOBY DOO (TV)(...Where are you? #1-16,26; ...Mystery Comics #17-25, 27 on)(See March Of Comics #356, 368, 382, 391)
March, 1970 - No. 30, Feb, 1975 (Hanna-Barbera)
Gold Key

1 4.30 13.00 30.00
2-5 2.60 7.70 18.00
6-10 2.10 6.00 15.00
11-20: 11-Tufts-a 1.50 3.80 9.00
21-30 .90 2.30 5.50

SCOOBY DOO (TV)
April, 1975 - No. 11, Dec, 1976 (Hanna-Barbera)
Charlton Comics

1 2.30 6.90 16.00
2-5 1.10 2.70 6.50
6-11 .90 2.30 5.50

SCOOBY-DOO (TV)
Oct, 1977 - No. 9, Feb, 1979 (Hanna-Barbera)
Marvel Comics Group

1-Dyno-Mutt begins 1.20 3.00
2-9 1.50

SCOOBY-DOO (TV)
Sept, 1992 - No. 3, May, 1993 ($1.25)
Harvey Comics

V2#1,2 1.25
...Big Book 1,2 (11/92, 4/93, $1.95, 52 pgs.) .80 2.00
...Giant Size 1,2 (10/92, 3/93, $2.25, 68 pgs.) .90 2.25

SCOOP COMICS (Becomes Yankee Comics #4-7, a digest sized cartoon book not listed in this guide; becomes Snap #9)
November, 1941 - No. 3, Mar, 1943; No. 8, 1944
Harry 'A' Chesler (Holyoke)

1-Intro. Rocketman & Rocketgirl & begins; origin The Master Key & begins; Dan Hastings begins; Charles Sultan-c/a 69.00 205.00 480.00
2-Rocket Boy begins; injury to eye story (reprinted in Spotlight #3) 41.00 122.00 285.00
3-Injury to eye story-r from #2; Rocket Boy 36.00 107.00 250.00
8-Formerly Yankee Comics; becomes Snap 24.00 73.00 170.00

SCOOTER (See Swing With...)

SCOOTER COMICS
April, 1946
Rucker Publ. Ltd. (Canadian)

1-Teen-age/funny animal 7.00 21.00 42.00

SCORCHED EARTH (Tundra)(Value: cover or less)

SCORE, THE (Piranha)(Value: cover or less)

SCORPIAN AVENGING SPIRIT OF THE ARAPAHOES
July, 1993 - Present ($2.50, B&W)
Annruel Studios

0,1-Silver-c,1-Gold-c,2 1.00 2.50

SCORPION
Feb, 1975 - No. 3, July, 1975
Atlas/Seaboard Publ.

1-Intro.; bondage-c by Chaykin 1.20
2,3: 2-Wrightson-a; Kaluta, Simonson assists(p) 1.00

NOTE: ***Chaykin** a-1, 2; c-1. **Mooney** a-3i.*

SCORPION CORPS
Nov, 1993 - Present ($2.75/$2.50, color)

Scout #7 © Timothy Truman

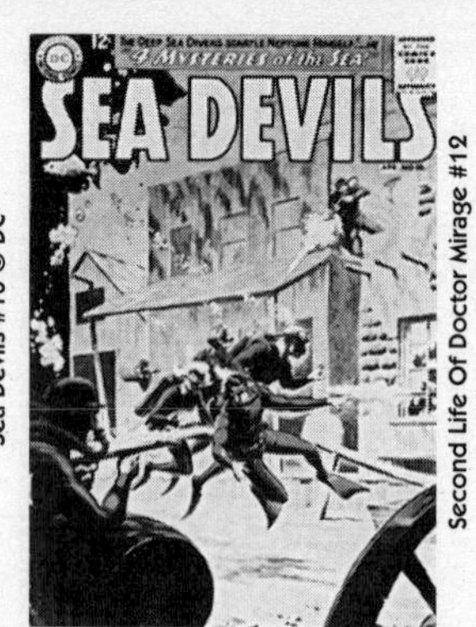

Sea Devils #10 © DC

Second Life Of Doctor Mirage #12 © Voyager Comm.

GD25 FN65 NM94

Dagger Comics Group
1,2-($2.75): 1-Intro Angel Dust, Shellcase, Tork, Feedback & Magnon 1.10 2.75
2-Bronze 1.10 2.75
2-Gold 1.20 3.00
2-Silver 1.30 3.25
3-7-($2.50) 1.00 2.50

SCORPIO ROSE (Eclipse)(Value: cover or less)

SCOTLAND YARD (Inspector Farnsworth of...) (Texas Rangers in Action #5 on?)
June, 1955 - No. 4, March, 1956
Charlton Comics Group
1-Tothish-a 10.00 30.00 70.00
2-4: 2-Tothish-a 8.35 25.00 50.00

SCOUT (Eclipse)(Value: cover or less)

SCOUT: WAR SHAMAN (Eclipse)(Value: cover or less)(Formerly Scout)

SCREAM (...Comics) (Andy Comics #20 on)
Autumn, 1944 - No. 19, April, 1948
Humor Publications/Current Books(Ace Magazines)
1-Teenage humor 11.50 34.00 80.00
2 6.70 20.00 40.00
3-15: 11-Racist humor (Indians) 5.35 16.00 32.00
16-Intro. Lily-Belle 5.35 16.00 32.00
17,19 4.00 12.00 24.00
18-Hypo needle story 5.35 16.00 33.00

SCREAM (Magazine)
Aug, 1973 - No. 11, Feb, 1975 (68 pgs.) (B&W)
Skywald Publishing Corp.
1 1.50 3.80 9.00
2-5: 2-Origin Lady Satan. 3 (12/73)-#3 found on pg. 22 1.00 2.00 5.00
6-11: 6-Origin The Victims. 9-Severed head-c. 11- "Mr. Poe and the Raven" story 1.20 3.00

SCRIBBLY (See All-American Comics, Buzzy, The Funnies, Leave It To Binky & Popular Comics)
8-9/48 - No. 13, 8-9/50; No. 14, 10-11/51 - No. 15, 12-1/51-52
National Periodical Publications
1-Sheldon Mayer-c/a in all; 52 pgs. begin 89.00 268.00 625.00
2 56.00 167.00 390.00
3-5 45.00 135.00 315.00
6-10 34.00 100.00 235.00
11-15: 13-Last 52 pgs. 29.00 86.00 200.00

SCUD: THE DISPOSABLE ASSASSIN
Feb, 1994 - Present ($2.95, B&W)
Fireman Press
1-3 1.20 3.00

SEA DEVILS (See Limited Collectors' Edition #39,45, & Showcase #27-29)
Sept-Oct, 1961 - No. 35, May-June, 1967
National Periodical Publications
Showcase #27 (7-8/60)-1st app. Sea Devils; Russ Heath-c/a begins, ends #10; grey tone-c begin, end #5 68.00 204.00 545.00
Showcase #28 (9-10/60)-2nd app. Sea Devils 39.00 118.00 315.00
Showcase #29 (11-12/60)-3rd app. Sea Devils 40.00 120.00 320.00
1-(9-10/61) 40.00 130.00 350.00
2-Last 10¢ issue 20.00 60.00 160.00
3-Begin 12¢ issues thru #35 16.00 50.00 110.00
4,5 15.00 45.00 105.00
6-10 8.00 24.00 55.00
11,12,14-20 5.70 17.00 40.00
13-Kubert, Colan-a; Joe Kubert app. in story 6.00 18.00 42.00
21-35: 22-Intro. International Sea Devils; origin & 1st app. Capt. X & Man Fish 3.90 12.00 27.00

GD25 FN65 NM94

NOTE: ***Heath** a-B&B 27-29, 1-10; c-B&B 27-29, 1-10, 14-16. **Moldoff** a-16i.*

SEADRAGON (Elite)(Value: cover or less)

SEA HOUND, THE (Captain Silver's Log Of The...)
1945 (no month) - No. 2, Sept-Oct, 1945
Avon Periodicals
nn (#1) 10.00 30.00 70.00
2 8.35 25.00 50.00

SEA HOUND, THE (Radio)
No. 3, July, 1949 - No. 4, Sept, 1949
Capt. Silver Syndicate
3,4 6.70 20.00 40.00

SEA HUNT (TV)
No. 928, 8/58 - No. 1041, 10-12/59; No. 4, 1-3/60 - No. 13, 4-6/62
Dell Publishing Co. (All have Lloyd Bridges photo-c)
4-Color 928(#1) 13.00 40.00 90.00
4-Color 994(#2), 4-13: Manning-a #4-6,8-11,13 9.15 27.50 55.00
4-Color 1041(#3)-Toth-a 10.00 30.00 65.00

SEAQUEST (TV)
Mar, 1994 ($2.25, color)
Nemesis Comics
1-Has 2 diff-c stocks (slick & cardboard); Alcala-i .90 2.25

SEARCH FOR LOVE
Feb-Mar, 1950 - No. 2, Apr-May, 1950 (52 pgs.)
American Comics Group
1 8.35 25.00 50.00
2,3(6-7/50): 3-Exist? 5.00 15.00 30.00

SEARCHERS (See 4-Color #709)

SEARS (See Merry Christmas From...)

SEASON'S GREETINGS
1935 (6-1/4x5-1/4") (32 pgs. in color)
Hallmark (King Features)
nn-Cover features Mickey Mouse, Popeye, Jiggs & Skippy. "The Night Before Christmas" told one panel per page, each panel by a famous artist featuring their character. Art by Alex Raymond, Gottfredson, Swinnerton, Segar, Chic Young, Milt Gross, Sullivan (Messmer), Herriman, McManus, Percy Crosby & others (22 artists in all)
Estimated value... 400.00

SEBASTION (Disney Comics)(Value: cover or less)

SEBASTION O
May, 1993 - No. 3, July, 1993 ($1.95, mini-series)
DC Comics (Vertigo)
1-3-Grant Morrison scripts .80 2.00

SECOND LIFE OF DOCTOR MIRAGE, THE (See Shadowman #16)
Nov, 1993 - Present ($2.50, color)
Valiant
1-19: 1-With bound-in poster. 5-Shadowman x-over. 7-Bound-in trading card 1.00 2.50
1-Gold ink logo edition; no price on-c 5.50

SECRET AGENT (Formerly Sarge Steel)
V2#9, Oct, 1966; V2#10, Oct, 1967
Charlton Comics
V2#9-Sarge Steel part-r begins 1.40 3.50 8.50
10-Tiffany Sinn, CIA app. (from Career Girl Romances #39); Aparo-a 1.70 4.25

SECRET AGENT (TV)
Nov, 1966; No. 2, Jan, 1968
Gold Key

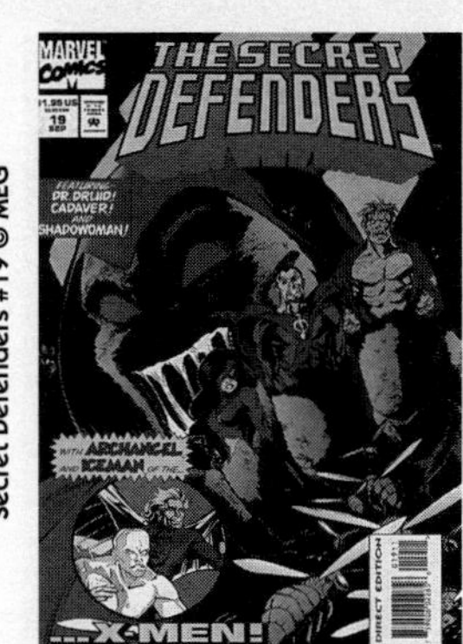

Secret Defenders #19 © MEG

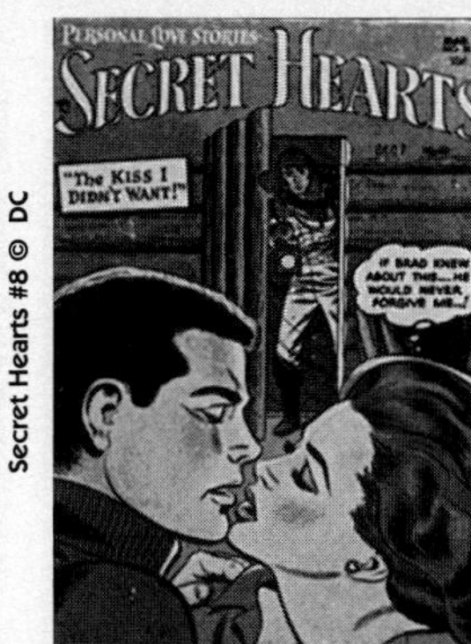

Secret Hearts #8 © DC

Secret Origins #7 © DC

	GD25	FN65	NM94
1-Photo-c	10.00	30.00	70.00
2-Photo-c	7.00	21.00	48.00

SECRET AGENT X-9 (See Flash Gordon #4 by King)
1934 (Book 1: 84 pgs.; Book 2: 124 pgs.) (8x7-1/2")
David McKay Publications

	GD25	FN65	NM94
Book 1-Contains reprints of the first 13 weeks of the strip by Alex Raymond; complete except for 2 dailies	39.00	118.00	275.00
Book 2-Contains reprints immediately following contents of Book 1, for 20 weeks by Alex Raymond; complete except for two dailies. Note: Raymond mis-dated the last five strips from 6/34, and while the dating sequence is confusing, the continuity is correct	34.00	100.00	235.00

SECRET AGENT X-9 (See Feature Books #8 & Magic Comics)

SECRET AGENT Z-2 (See Holyoke One-Shot No. 7)

SECRET CITY SAGA (See Jack Kirby's Secret City Saga)

SECRET DEFENDERS (Also see The Defenders & Fantastic Four #374)
Mar, 1993 - Present ($1.75)
Marvel Comics

	GD25	FN65	NM94
1-($2.50)-Red foil stamped-c; Dr. Strange, Nomad, Wolverine, Spider Woman & Darkhawk begin		1.10	2.75
2-11,13,14: 9-New team w/Silver Surfer, Thunderstrike, Dr. Strange & War Machine. 13-Thanos replaces Dr. Strange as leader		.70	1.75
12-($2.50)-Prismatic foil-c		1.00	2.50
15-27: 15-Begin $1.95-c.; bound-in card sheet. 18-Giant Man & Iron Fist app.		.80	2.00

SECRET DIARY OF EERIE ADVENTURES
1953 (One Shot) (25¢ giant; 100 pgs.)
Avon Periodicals

	GD25	FN65	NM94
nn-(Rare)-Kubert-a; Hollingsworth-c; Sid Check back-c	107.00	321.00	750.00

SECRET HEARTS
9-10/49 - No. 6, 7-8/50; No. 7, 12-1/51-52 - No. 153, 7/71 (All 52 pgs.)
National Periodical Publications (Beverly)(Arleigh No. 50-113)

	GD25	FN65	NM94
1-Kinstler-a; photo-c begin, end #6	38.00	115.00	265.00
2-Toth-a (1 pg.); Kinstler-a	18.00	54.00	125.00
3,6 (1950)	16.00	48.00	110.00
4,5-Toth-a	16.50	50.00	115.00
7(12-1/51-52) (Rare)	16.50	50.00	115.00
8-10 (1952)	10.00	30.00	70.00
11-20	10.00	30.00	60.00
21-26: 26-Last precode (2-3/55)	8.35	25.00	50.00
27-40	5.85	17.50	35.00
41-50	4.00	12.00	24.00
51-60	4.00	10.00	20.00
61-75: 75-Last 10¢ issue	3.20	8.00	16.00
76-109	2.40	6.00	12.00
110- "Reach for Happiness" serial begins, ends #138	1.50	3.80	9.00
111-119,121-126,128-133,135-138-140	1.00	2.50	6.00
120,134-Neal Adams-c	1.30	3.25	8.00
127 (4/68)-Beatles cameo	1.50	3.80	9.00
141,142- "20 Miles to Heartbreak", Chapter 2 & 3 (see Young Love for Chapters 1 & 4); Toth, Colletta-a	1.00	2.50	6.00
143-148,150-153: 144-Morrow-a. 153-Kirby-i	1.00	2.50	6.00
149-Toth-a	1.20	2.90	7.00

SECRET ISLAND OF OZ, THE (See First Comics Graphic Novel)

SECRET LOVE (See Fox Giants & Sinister House of...)

SECRET LOVE
12/55 - No. 3, 8/56; 4/57 - No. 5, 2/58; No. 6, 6/58
Ajax-Farrell/Four Star Comic Corp. No. 2 on

	GD25	FN65	NM94
1(12/55-Ajax, 1st series)	5.85	17.50	35.00
2,3	4.00	11.00	22.00
1(4/57-Ajax, 2nd series)	4.70	14.00	28.00
2-6: 5-Bakerish-a	3.60	9.00	18.00

SECRET LOVES
Nov, 1949 - No. 6, Sept, 1950 (#5: photo-c)
Comic Magazines/Quality Comics Group

	GD25	FN65	NM94
1-Ward-c	13.00	40.00	90.00
2-Ward-c	11.50	34.00	80.00
3-Crandall-a	9.15	27.50	55.00
4,6	5.85	17.50	35.00
5-Suggestive art "Boom Town Babe"	8.00	24.00	48.00

SECRET LOVE STORIES (See Fox Giants)

SECRET MISSIONS (Admiral Zacharia's...)
February, 1950
St. John Publishing Co.

	GD25	FN65	NM94
1-Joe Kubert-c; stories of U.S. foreign agents	12.00	36.00	85.00

SECRET MYSTERIES (Formerly Crime Mysteries & Crime Smashers)
No. 16, Nov, 1954 - No. 19, July, 1955
Ribage/Merit Publications No. 17 on

	GD25	FN65	NM94
16-Horror, Palais-a; Myron Fass-c	12.00	36.00	85.00
17-19-Horror. 17-Fass-c; mis-dated 3/54?	8.35	25.00	50.00

SECRET ORIGINS (See 80 Page Giant #8)
Aug-Oct, 1961 (Annual) (Reprints)
National Periodical Publications

	GD25	FN65	NM94
1-Origin Adam Strange (Showcase #17), Green Lantern (Green Lantern #1), Challengers (partial-r/Showcase #6, 6 pgs. Kirby-a), J'onn J'onzz (Det. #225), The Flash (Showcase #4), Green Arrow (1 pg. text), Superman-Batman team (W. Finest #94), Wonder Woman (Wonder Woman #105)	27.00	81.00	325.00

SECRET ORIGINS
Feb-Mar, 1973 - No. 6, Jan-Feb, 1974; No. 7, Oct-Nov, 1974 (All 20¢ issues)
National Periodical Publications (All origin reprints)

	GD25	FN65	NM94
1-Superman(r/1 pg. origin/Action #1, 1st time since G.A.), Batman(Det. #33), Ghost(Flash #88), The Flash(Showcase #4)	2.00	5.00	12.00
2-4: 2-Green Lantern & The Atom(Showcase #22 & 34), Supergirl(Action #252). 3-Wonder Woman(W.W. #1), Wildcat(Sensation #1). 4-Vigilante (Action #42) by Meskin, Kid Eternity(Hit #25)	.90	2.30	5.50
5-7: 5-The Spectre by Baily(More Fun #52,53). 6-Blackhawk(Military #1) & Legion of Super-Heroes(Superboy #147). 7-Robin(Detective #38), Aquaman (More Fun #73)		1.70	4.25

NOTE: ***Infantino*** *a-1.* ***Kane*** *a-2.* ***Kubert*** *a-1.*

SECRET ORIGINS
4/86 - No. 50, 8/90 (All origins)(52 pgs. #6 on)(#27 on: $1.50)
DC Comics

	GD25	FN65	NM94
1-Origin Superman		1.60	4.00
2-Blue Beetle		1.20	3.00
3-5: 3-Shazam. 4-Firestorm. 5-Crimson Avenger		1.00	2.50
6-Halo/G.A. Batman		1.80	4.50
7-12,14-26: 7-Green Lantern(Guy Gardner)/G.A. Sandman. 8-Shadow Lass/ Doll Man. 9-G.A. Flash/Skyman. 10-Phantom Stranger w/Alan Moore scripts; Legends spin-off. 11-G.A. Hawkman/Power Girl. 12-Challengers of Unknown/ G.A. Fury (2nd modern app.). 14-Suicide Squad; Legends spin-off. 15-Spectre/Deadman. 16-G.A. Hourman/Warlord. 17-Adam Strange/Dr. Occult. 18-G.A. Gr. Lantern/The Creeper. 19-Uncle Sam/The Guardian. 20-Batgirl/ G.A. Dr. Mid-Nite. 21-Jonah Hex/Black Condor. 22-Manhunters. 23-Floronic Man/Guardians of the Universe. 24-Blue Devil/Dr. Fate. 25-LSH/Atom. 26-Black Lightning/Miss America		1.00	2.50
13-Origin Nightwing; Johnny Thunder app.		1.80	4.50

27-38,40-44: 27-Zatara/Zatanna. 28-Midnight/Nightshade. 29-Power of the Atom/Mr. America; new 3 pg. Red Tornado story by Mayer (last app. of Scribbly, 8/88). 30-Plastic Man/Elongated Man. 31-JSA. 32-JLA. 33-35-JLI. 36-Green Lantern/Poison Ivy. 37-Legion Of Substitute Heroes/Doctor Light. 38-Green Arrow/Speedy; Grell scripts. 40-All Ape issue. 41-Rogues Gallery of Flash. 42-Phantom Girl/Grim Ghost. 43-Original Hawk & Dove/

Secret Society Of Super-Villians #1 © DC

Secrets Of Haunted House #30 © DC

Secret Weapons #14 © Voyager Comm.

GD25 FN65 NM94

Cave Carson/Chris KL-99. 44-Batman app.; story based on Det. #40 .80 2.00
39-Animal Man-c/story continued in Animal Man #10; Grant Morrison scripts; Batman app. 1.80 4.50
45-49: 45-Blackhawk/El Diablo. 46-JLA/LSH/New Titans. 47-LSH. 48-Ambush Bug/Stanley & His Monster/Rex the Wonder Dog/Trigger Twins. 49-Newsboy Legion/Silent Knight/brief origin Bouncing Boy .70 1.75
50-($3.95, 100 pgs.)-Batman & Robin in text, Flash of Two Worlds, Johnny Thunder, Dolphin, Black Canary & Space Museum 1.70 4.25
Annual 1 (8/87)-Capt. Comet/Doom Patrol .90 2.25
Annual 2 ('88, $2.00)-Origin Flash II & Flash III .90 2.25
Annual 3 ('89, $2.95, 84 pgs.)-Teen Titans; 1st app. new Flamebird who replaces original Bat-Girl 1.30 3.25
Special 1 (10/89, $2.00)-Batman villains: Penguin, Riddler, & Two-Face; Bolland-c; Sam Kieth-a; Neil Gaiman scripts(2) 1.20 3.00
NOTE: ***Art Adams*** *a-33i(part).* ***M. Anderson*** *8, 19, 21; c-19(part).* ***Bolland*** *c-7.* ***Byrne*** *c/a-Annual 1.* ***Colan*** *c/a-5p.* ***Forte*** *a-37.* ***Giffen*** *a-18p, 44p, 48.* ***Kaluta*** *c-39.* ***Gil Kane*** *a-2, 28; c-2p.* ***Kirby*** *c-19(part).* ***Mayer*** *a-29.* ***Morrow*** *a-21.* ***Orlando*** *a-10.* ***Perez*** *a-50i; c- Annual 3.* ***Rogers*** *a-6p.* ***Russell*** *a-27i.* ***Staton*** *a-36, 50p.* ***Steacy*** *a-35.* ***Tuska*** *a-4p, 9p.*

SECRET ORIGINS OF SUPER-HEROES (See DC Special Series #10, 19)

SECRET ORIGINS OF THE WORLD'S GREATEST SUPER-HEROES
1989 ($4.95, 148 pgs.)
DC Comics

nn-r/origin Batman, Superman, JLA .90 2.30 5.50

SECRET ROMANCE
Oct, 1968 - No. 41, Nov, 1976; No. 42, Mar, 1979 - No. 48, Feb, 1980
Charlton Comics

1-Begin 12¢ issues, ends #? 1.60 4.00 8.00
2-10: 9-Reese-a .80 2.00 4.00
11-48 .40 1.00 2.00
NOTE: *Beyond the Stars app.-No. 9, 11, 12, 14.*

SECRET ROMANCES (Exciting Love Stories)
April 1951 - No. 27, July, 1955
Superior Publications Ltd.

1 9.15 27.50 55.00
2 5.00 15.00 30.00
3-10 4.00 12.00 24.00
11-13,15-18,20-27 3.60 9.00 18.00
14,19-Lingerie panels 4.00 12.00 24.00

SECRET SERVICE (See Kent Blake of the...)

SECRET SIX (See Action Comics Weekly)
Apr-May, 1968 - No. 7, Apr-May, 1969 (12¢)
National Periodical Publications

1-Origin/1st app. 5.00 15.00 35.00
2-7 2.90 9.00 20.00

SECRET SOCIETY OF SUPER-VILLAINS
May-June, 1976 - No. 15, June-July, 1978
National Periodical Publications/DC Comics

1-Origin; JLA cameo & Capt. Cold app. 1.-0 2.50
2-5: 2-Re-intro/origin Capt. Comet; Green Lantern x-over. 5-Green Lantern, Hawkman x-over; Darkseid app. .80 2.00
6-15: 9,10-Creeper x-over. 11-Capt. Comet; Orlando-i. 15-G.A. Atom, Dr. Midnite, & JSA app. 1.50

SECRET SOCIETY OF SUPER-VILLAINS SPECIAL (See DC Special Series #6)

SECRETS OF HAUNTED HOUSE
4-5/75 - #5, 12-1/75-76; #6, 6-7/77 - #14, 10-11/78; #15, 8/79 - #46, 3/82
National Periodical Publications/DC Comics

1 1.30 3.25
2-10 .90 2.25
11-46: 31-Mr. E series begins, ends #41 1.50
NOTE: ***Aragones*** *a-1.* ***Bissette*** *a-46.* ***Buckler*** *c-32-40p.* ***Ditko*** *a-9, 12, 41, 45.* ***Golden*** *a-10.* ***Howard*** *a-13i.* ***Kaluta*** *c-8, 10, 11, 14, 16, 29.* ***Kubert*** *c-41, 42.* ***Sheldon Mayer*** *a-43p.* ***McWilliams*** *a-35.* ***Nasser*** *a-24.* ***Newton*** *a-30p.* ***Nino*** *a-1, 13, 19.* ***Orlando*** *c-13, 30, 43, 45i.* ***N. Redondo*** *a-4, 5, 29.* ***Rogers*** *c-26.* ***Spiegle*** *a-31-41.* ***Wrightson*** *c-5, 44.*

SECRETS OF HAUNTED HOUSE SPECIAL (See DC Special Series #12)

SECRETS OF LIFE (See 4-Color #749)

SECRETS OF LOVE (See Popular Teen-Agers...)

SECRETS OF LOVE AND MARRIAGE
V2#1, Aug, 1956 - V2#25, June, 1961
Charlton Comics

V2#1 3.60 9.00 18.00
V2#2-6 2.00 5.00 10.00
V2#7-9-(All 68 pgs.) 1.60 4.00 8.00
10-25 1.20 3.00 6.00

SECRETS OF MAGIC (See Wisco)

SECRETS OF SINISTER HOUSE (Sinister House of Secret Love #1-4)
No. 5, June-July, 1972 - No. 18, June-July, 1974
National Periodical Publications

5-9: 5-(52 pgs.). 7-Redondo-a 1.00 2.50
10-Neal Adams-a(i) 1.00 2.50 6.00
11-18: 15-Redondo-a. 17-Barry-a; early Chaykin 1 pg. strip .70 1.80
NOTE: ***Alcala*** *a-6, 13, 14.* ***Kaluta*** *c-6, 7.* ***Nino*** *a-8, 11-13. Ambrose Bierce adapt.-#14.*

SECRETS OF THE LEGION OF SUPER-HEROES
Jan, 1981 - No. 3, March, 1981 (Mini-series)
DC Comics

1-3: 1-Origin of the Legion. 2-Retells origins of Brainiac 5, Shrinking Violet, Sun-Boy, Bouncing Boy, Ultra-Boy, Matter-Eater Lad, Mon-El, Karate Kid, & Dream Girl 1.00

SECRETS OF TRUE LOVE
February, 1958
St. John Publishing Co.

1 4.00 10.00 20.00

SECRETS OF YOUNG BRIDES
No. 5, Sept, 1957 - No. 44, Oct, 1964; July, 1975 - No. 9, Nov, 1976
Charlton Comics

5 4.00 11.00 22.00
6-10: 8-Negligee panel 2.40 6.00 12.00
11-20 1.80 4.50 9.00
21-30: Last 10¢ issue? 1.00 2.50 6.00
31-44 1.20 3.00
1-9 (2nd series) 1.50

SECRET SQUIRREL (TV)(See Kite Fun Book)
October, 1966 (Hanna-Barbera, 12¢)
Gold Key

1 10.00 28.00 75.00

SECRET STORY ROMANCES (Becomes True Tales of Love)
Nov, 1953 - No. 21, Mar, 1956
Atlas Comics (TCI)

1-Everett-a; Jay Scott Pike-c 9.15 27.50 55.00
2 4.70 14.00 28.00
3-11: 11-Last pre-code (2/55) 4.00 11.00 22.00
12-21 3.60 9.00 18.00
NOTE: ***Colletta*** *a-10, 14, 15, 17, 21; c-10, 14, 17.*

SECRET VOICE, THE (See Great American Comics Presents...)

SECRET WARS II (Also see Marvel Super Heroes...)
July, 1985 - No. 9, Mar, 1986 (Maxi-series)
Marvel Comics Group

1-9: 2-1st app. Boom Boom. 2,8,9-X-Men app. 5,8,9-Spider-Man app. 9-(75¢, 52 pgs.) 1.00

SECRET WEAPONS
Sept, 1993 - Present ($2.25, color)
Valiant

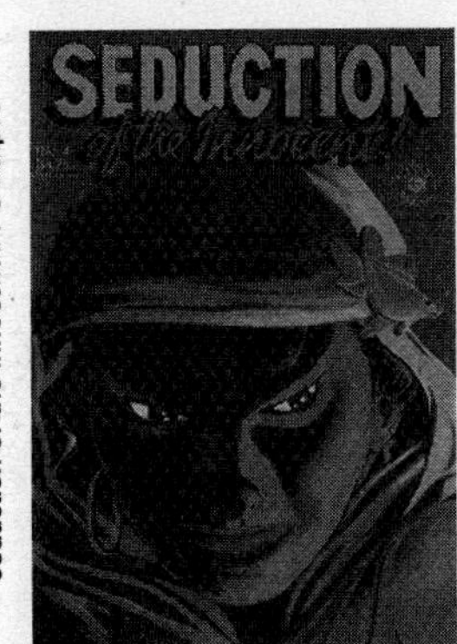

Seduction of the Innocent #4 © Eclipse

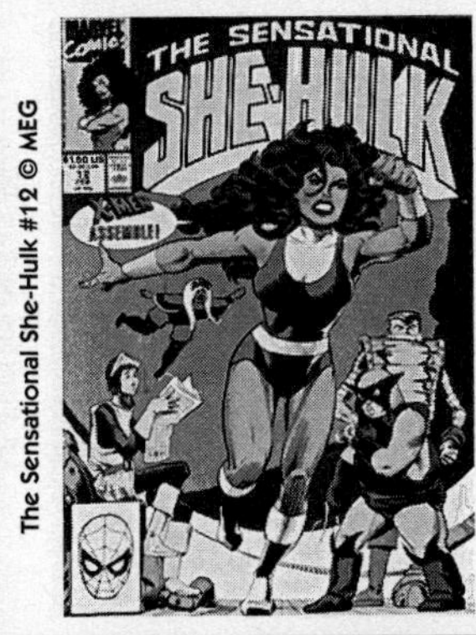

The Sensational She-Hulk #12 © MEG

Sensation Comics #15 © DC

GD25 FN65 NM94 GD25 FN65 NM94

1-10,12-16: 3-Reese-a(i). 5-Ninjak app. 9-Bound-in trading card. 12-Bloodshot app. .90 2.25
11-($2.50)-Enclosed in manilla envelope; Sep on envelope, Aug on-c; Blootshot app. 1.00 2.50

SECTAURS (Marvel)(Value: cover or less)

SEDUCTION OF THE INNOCENT (Also see New York State Joint Legislative Committee to Study...)
1953, 1954 (400 pgs.) (Hardback, $4.00)(Written by Fredric Wertham, M.D.)
Rinehart & Co., Inc., N. Y. (Also printed in Canada by Clarke, Irwin & Co. Ltd., Toronto)

(1st Version)-with bibliographical note intact (pages 399 & 400)(several copies got out before the comic publishers forced the removal of this page) 40.00 120.00 270.00
Dust jacket only 30.00 90.00 200.00
(2nd Version)-without bibliographical note 15.00 45.00 100.00
Dust jacket only 11.00 32.00 75.00
(3rd Version)-Published in England by Kennikat Press, 1954, 399 pgs. has bibliographical page 10.00 30.00 60.00
1972 r-/of 3rd version; 400 pgs. w/bibliography page; Kennikat Press 4.00 12.00 24.00

NOTE: *Material from this book appeared in the November, 1953(Vol.70, pp50-53,214) issue of the* ***Ladies' Home Journal*** *under the title "What Parents Don't Know About Comic Books". With the release of this book, Dr. Wertham reveals seven years of research attempting to link juvenile delinquency to comic books. Many illustrations showing excessive violence, sex, sadism, and torture are shown. This book was used at the Kefauver Senate hearings which led to the Comics Code Authority. Because of the influence this book had on the comic in dustry and the collector's interest in it, we feel this listing is justified. Also see* ***Parade of Pleasure.***

SEDUCTION OF THE INNOCENT! (Eclipse)(Value: cover or less)

SEEKER
Apr, 1994 - Present ($2.50, color)
Sky Comics

1 1.00 2.50

SELECT DETECTIVE (Exciting New Mystery Cases)
Aug-Sept, 1948 - No. 3, Dec-Jan, 1948-49
D. S. Publishing Co.

1-Matt Baker-a 13.00 40.00 90.00
2-Baker, McWilliams-a 10.00 30.00 65.00
3 9.15 27.50 55.00

SEMPER FI (Marvel)(Value: cover or less)

SENSATIONAL POLICE CASES (Becomes Captain Steve Savage, 2nd series)
1952; 1954 - No. 4, July-Aug, 1954
Avon Periodicals

nn-(1952, 25¢, 100 pgs.)-Kubert-a?; Check, Larsen, Lawrence & McCann-a; Kinstler-c 27.00 81.00 190.00
1 (1954)-Exists? 10.00 30.00 65.00
2-4: 2-Kirbyish-a (3-4/54). 4-Reprint/Saint #5 8.35 25.00 50.00
I.W. Reprint #5-(1963?, nd)-Reprints Prison Break #5(1952-Realistic); Infantino-a 2.80 7.00 14.00

SENSATIONAL SHE-HULK, THE (She-Hulk #21-23; see Savage She-Hulk)
V2#1, 5/89 - No. 60, Feb, 1994 ($1.50/$1.75, deluxe format)
Marvel Comics

V2#1-Byrne-c/a(p)/scripts begin, end #8 1.40 3.50
2-8: 3-Spidey. 4-Reintro G.A. Blonde Phantom .90 2.25
9-49,51-60: 14-17-Howard the Duck app. 21-23-Return of the Blonde Phantom. 22-All Winners Squad app. 25-Thor app. 26-Excalibur app.; Guice-c. 29-Wolverine app. (3 pgs.). 30-Hobgoblin-c & cameo. 31-Byrne-c/a/scripts begin again. 35-Last $1.50-c. 37-Wolverine/Punisher/Spidey-c, but no app. 39-Thing app. 56-War Zone app.; Hulk cameo. 57-Vs. Hulk-c/story. 58-Electro-c/story. 59-Jack O'Lantern app. .80 1.90
50-($2.95, 52 pgs.)-Embossed green foil-c; Byrne app.; last Byrne-c/a; Austin, Chaykin, Simonson-a; Miller-a(2 pgs.) 1.30 3.25

NOTE: ***Dale Keown*** *a(p)-13, 15-22.*

SENSATIONAL SHE-HULK IN CEREMONY, THE (Marvel)(Value: cover or less)

SENSATIONAL SPIDER-MAN (Marvel)(Value: cover or less)

SENSATION COMICS (Sensation Mystery #110 on)
Jan, 1942 - No. 109, May-June, 1952
National Per. Publ./All-American

	GD25	FN65	VF82	NM94
1-Origin Mr. Terrific(1st app.), Wildcat(1st app.), The Gray Ghost, & Little Boy Blue; Wonder Woman(cont'd from All Star #8), The Black Pirate begin; intro. Justice & Fair Play Club	900.00	2700.00	5850.00	9000.00

(Estimated up to 150 total copies exist, 7 in NM/Mint)

1-Reprint, Oversize 13-1/2x10". WARNING: This comic is an exact duplicate reprint of the original except for its size. DC published it in 1974 with a second cover titling it as a Famous First Edition. There have been many reported cases of the outer cover being removed and the interior sold as the original edition. The reprint with the new outer cover removed is practically worthless. See Famous First Edition for value.

	GD25	FN65	NM94
2-Etta Candy begins	271.00	815.00	1900.00
3-W. Woman gets secretary's job	143.00	430.00	1000.00
4-1st app. Stretch Skinner in Wildcat	121.00	365.00	850.00
5-Intro. Justin, Black Pirate's son	93.00	280.00	650.00
6-Origin/1st app. Wonder Woman's magic lasso	96.00	287.00	670.00
7-10	77.00	231.00	540.00
11,12,14-20	68.00	205.00	475.00
13-Hitler, Tojo, Mussolini-c (as bowling pins)	77.00	231.00	540.00
21-30	51.00	154.00	360.00
31-33	39.00	116.00	270.00
34-Sargon, the Sorcerer begins (10/44), ends #36; begins again #52	40.00	120.00	280.00
35-40: 38-X-Mas-c	33.00	100.00	230.00
41-50: 43-The Whip app.	29.00	86.00	200.00
51-60: 51-Last Black Pirate. 56,57-Sargon by Kubert	25.00	75.00	175.00
61-67,69-80: 63-Last Mr. Terrific. 66-Wildcat by Kubert	25.00	75.00	175.00
68-Origin & 1st app.Huntress (8/47)	27.00	81.00	190.00
81-Used in **SOTI**, pg. 33,34; Krigstein-a	27.00	81.00	190.00
82-90: 83-Last Sargon. 86-The Atom app. 90-Last Wildcat	19.00	57.00	130.00
91-Streak begins by Alex Toth	19.00	58.00	135.00
92,93: 92-Toth-a (2 pgs.)	20.00	60.00	140.00
94-1st all girl issue	27.00	80.00	185.00
95-99,101-106: 95-Unmasking of Wonder Woman-c/story. 99-1st app. Astra, Girl of the Future, ends #106. 103-Robot-c. 105-Last 52 pgs. 106-Wonder Woman ends	27.00	80.00	185.00
100-(11-12/50)	36.00	110.00	255.00
107-(Scarce, 1-2/52)-1st mystery issue; Johnny Peril by Toth(p), 8 pgs. & begins; continues from Danger Trail #5 (3-4/51)(see Comic Cavalcade #15 for 1st app.)	43.00	130.00	300.00
108-(Scarce)-Johnny Peril by Toth(p)	36.00	110.00	255.00
109-(Scarce)-Johnny Peril by Toth(p)	43.00	130.00	300.00

NOTE: ***Krigstein*** *a-(Wildcat)-81, 83, 84.* ***Moldoff*** *Black Pirate-1-25; Black Pirate not in 34-36, 43-48.* ***Oskner*** *c(i)-89-91, 94-106. Wonder Woman by* ***H. G. Peter***, *all issues except #8, 17-19, 21; c-4-7, 9-18, 20-88, 92, 93.* ***Toth*** *a-91, 98; c-107. Wonder Woman c-1-106.*

SENSATION MYSTERY (Formerly Sensation Comics #1-109)
No. 110, July-Aug, 1952 - No. 116, July-Aug, 1953
National Periodical Publications

110-Johnny Peril continues 25.00 75.00 175.00
111-116-Johnny Peril in all. 116-M. Anderson-a 25.00 75.00 175.00

NOTE: ***M. Anderson*** *c-110.* ***Colan*** *a-114p.* ***Giunta*** *a-112.* ***G. Kane*** *c(p)-108, 109, 111-115.*

SENTINELS OF JUSTICE, THE (See Americomics & Captain Paragon &...)

SENTRY SPECIAL
1991 ($2.75, color)(Hero Alliance spin-off)
Innovation Publishing

1-Lost in Space preview (3 pgs.) 1.10 2.75

SERAPHIM (Innovation)(Value: cover or less)

SERGEANT BARNEY BARKER (Becomes G. I. Tales #4 on)
Aug, 1956 - No. 3, Dec, 1956

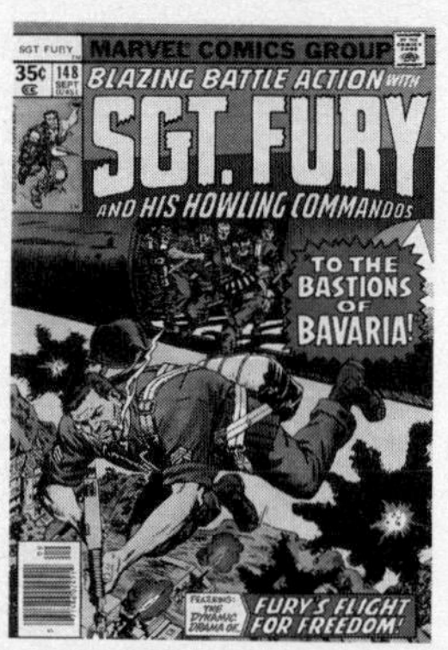

Sgt. Fury #148 © MEG

Sergent Preston of the Yukon #6 © DELL

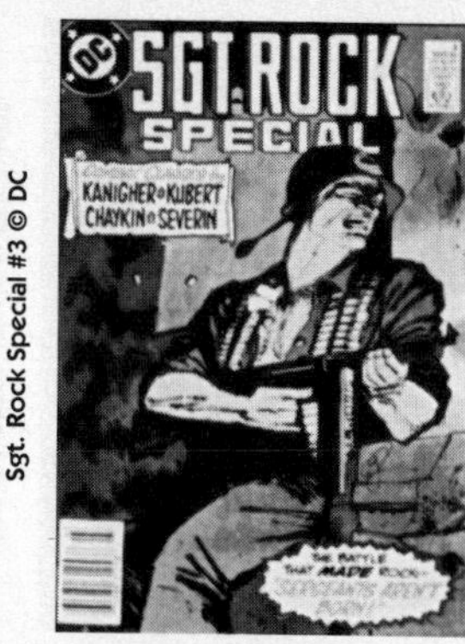

Sgt. Rock Special #3 © DC

GD25 FN65 NM94

Atlas Comics (MCI)
1-Severin-c/a(4) 12.00 36.00 85.00
2,3: 2-Severin-c/a(4). 3-Severin-c/a(5) 10.00 30.00 65.00

SERGEANT BILKO (Phil Silvers Starring as...) (TV)
May-June, 1957 - No. 18, Mar-Apr, 1960
National Periodical Publications
1-All have Bob Oskner-c 57.00 171.00 400.00
2 31.00 95.00 220.00
3-5 25.00 75.00 175.00
6-18: 11,12,15,17-Photo-c 20.00 60.00 140.00

SGT. BILKO'S PVT. DOBERMAN (TV)
June-July, 1958 - No. 11, Feb-Mar, 1960
National Periodical Publications
1-Bob Oskner c-1-4,7,11 34.00 103.00 240.00
2 20.00 60.00 140.00
3-5: 5-Photo-c 15.00 45.00 105.00
6-11: 6,9-Photo-c 11.00 32.00 75.00

SGT. DICK CARTER OF THE U.S. BORDER PATROL (See Holyoke One-Shot)

SGT. FURY (& His Howling Commandos)(See Fury & Special Marvel Edition)
May, 1963 - No. 167, Dec, 1981
Marvel Comics Group (BPC earlier issues)
1-1st app. Sgt. Nick Fury (becomes agent of Shield in Strange Tales #135); Kirby/Ayers-c/a; 1st Dum-Dum Dugan & the Howlers 70.00 200.00 650.00
2-Kirby-a 28.00 84.00 225.00
3-5: 3-Reed Richards x-over. 4-Death of Junior Juniper. 5-1st Baron Strucker app.; Kirby-a 15.00 45.00 120.00
6-10: 8-Baron Zemo, 1st Percival Pinkerton app. 9-Hitler-c & app. 10-1st app. Capt. Savage (the Skipper)(9/64) 10.00 30.00 80.00
11,12,14-20: 14-1st Blitz Squad. 18-Death of Pamela Hawley 7.00 21.00 50.00
13-Captain America & Bucky app.(12/64); 2nd solo Capt. America x-over outside The Avengers; Kirby-a 21.00 64.00 170.00
21-30: 25-Red Skull app. 27-1st app. Eric Koenig; origin Fury's eye patch 5.00 15.00 35.00
31-50: 34-Origin Howling Commandos. 35-Eric Koenig joins Howlers. 43-Bob Hope, Glen Miller app. 44-Flashback on Howlers 1st mission 2.90 8.60 20.00
51-60 2.30 7.00 16.00
61-80: 64-Capt. Savage & Raiders x-over. 76-Fury's Father app. in WWI story 2.00 6.00 14.00
81-100: 98-Deadly Dozen x-over. 100-Capt. America, Fantastic 4 cameos; Stan Lee, Martin Goodman & others app. 1.70 4.20 10.00
101-120: 101-Origin retold 1.10 2.70 6.50
121-130: 121-123-r/#19-21 .90 2.30 5.50
131-150 1.60 4.00
151-167: 167-Reprints (from 1963) 1.40 3.50
Annual 1(1965, 25¢, 72 pgs.)-r/#4,5 & new-a 13.00 39.00 90.00
Special 2(1966) 5.70 17.00 40.00
Special 3(1967) 4.00 10.70 25.00
Special 4(1968) 2.50 6.30 15.00
Special 5-7(1969-11/71) 1.40 4.00 8.50
NOTE: ***Ayers*** *a-8.* ***Ditko*** *a-15i.* ***Gil Kane*** *c-37, 96.* ***Kirby*** *a-1-7, 13p, 167p(r). Special 5; c-1-20, 25, 167p.* ***Severin*** *a-44-46, 48, 162, 164; inks-49-79, Special 4, 6; c-4i, 5, 6, 44, 46, 110, 149i, 155i, 162-166.* ***Sutton*** *a-57p. Reprints in #80, 82, 85, 87, 89, 91, 93, 95, 99, 101, 103, 105, 107, 109, 111, 121-123, 145-155, 167.*

SGT. FURY AND HIS HOWLING DEFENDERS (See The Defenders #147)

SERGEANT PRESTON OF THE YUKON (TV)
No. 344, Aug, 1951 - No. 29, Nov-Jan, 1958-59
Dell Publishing Co.
4-Color 344(#1)-Sergeant Preston & his dog Yukon King begin; painted-c begin, end #18 12.00 36.00 85.00
4-Color 373,397,419('52) 7.50 22.50 45.00
5(11-1/52-53)-10(2-4/54) 5.35 16.00 32.00
11,12,14-17 4.70 14.00 28.00
13-Origin Sgt. Preston 5.35 16.00 32.00
18-Origin Yukon King; last painted-c 5.35 16.00 32.00
19-29: All photo-c 6.35 19.00 38.00

SERGEANT PRESTON OF THE YUKON
1956 (4 comic booklets) (Soft-c, 16 pgs., 7x2-1/2" & 5x2-1/2")
Giveaways with Quaker Cereals
"How He Found Yukon King", "The Case That Made Him A Sergeant", "How Yukon King Saved Him From The Wolves", "How He Became A Mountie" each... 5.35 16.00 32.00

SGT. ROCK (Formerly Our Army at War; see Brave & the Bold #52)
No. 302, March, 1977 - No. 422, July, 1988 (See G.I. Combat #108)
National Periodical Publications/DC Comics
302 1.70 4.20 10.00
303-310 1.30 3.30 8.00
311-320: 318-Reprints 1.00 2.00 5.00
321-350 1.60 4.00
351-422: 422-1st Joe, Adam, Andy Kubert-a team .90 2.25
Annual 2-4: 2(1982)-Formerly Sgt. Rock's Prize Battle Tales #1. 3(1983). 4(1984) 1.20 3.00
NOTE: ***Estrada*** *a-322, 327, 331, 336, 337, 341, 342i.* ***Glanzman*** *a-384, 421.* ***Kubert*** *a-302, 303, 305r, 306, 328, 351, 356, 368, 373, 422; c-317, 318r, 319-323, 325-333-on, Annual 2, 3.* ***Severin*** *a-347.* ***Spiegle*** *a-382, Annual 2, 3.* ***Thorne*** *a-384.* ***Toth*** *a-385r.* ***Wildey*** *a-307, 311, 313, 314.*

SGT. ROCK SPECIAL (Sgt. Rock #14 on; see DC Special Series #3)
Oct, 1988 - No. 21, Feb, 1992; No. 1, 1992 ($2.00, quarterly, 52 pgs.)
DC Comics
1 1.10 2.75
2-8,10-21: All-r; 5-r/1st Sgt. Rock/Our Army at War #81. 7-Tomahawk-r by Thorne. 10-All Rock issue. 11-r/1st Haunted Tank story. 12-All Kubert issue; begins monthly. 13-Dinosaur story by Heath(r). 14-Enemy Ace-r (22 pgs.) by Adams/Kubert. 15-Enemy Ace (22 pgs.) by Kubert. 16-Iron Major-c/story. 16,17-Enemy Ace-r. 19-r/Batman/Sgt. Rock team-up/B&B #108 by Aparo .90 2.25
9-Enemy Ace-r by Kubert 1.10 2.75
1 (1992, $2.95, 68 pgs.)-Simonson-c; unpubbed Kubert-a; Glanzman, Russell, Pratt, & Wagner-a 1.30 3.25
NOTE: ***Neal Adams*** *r-1, 8, 14p.* ***Chaykin*** *r-3, 9(2pgs.); c-3.* ***Drucker*** *r-6.* ***Glanzman*** *r-20.* ***Heath*** *r-5, 9-13, 16, 19, 21.* ***Krigstein*** *r-4, 8.* ***Kubert*** *r-1-17, 20, 21; c-1p, 2, 8, 14-21.* ***Miller*** *r-6p.* ***Severin*** *r-3, 6, 10.* ***Simonson*** *r-2, 4; c-4.* ***Thorne*** *r-7.* ***Toth*** *r-2, 8, 11.* ***Wood*** *r-4.*

SGT. ROCK SPECTACULAR (See DC Special Series #13)

SGT. ROCK'S PRIZE BATTLE TALES (Becomes Sgt. Rock Annual #2 on; see DC Special Series #18 & 80 Page Giant #7)
Winter, 1964 (One Shot) (Giant - 80 pgs.)
National Periodical Publications
1-Kubert, Heath-r; new Kubert-c 23.00 69.00 160.00

SGT. STRYKER'S DEATH SQUAD (See Savage Combat Tales)

SERGIO ARAGONES' GROO THE WANDERER (See Groo...)

SEVEN BLOCK (Marvel)(Value: cover or less)

SEVEN DEAD MEN (See Complete Mystery #1)

SEVEN DWARFS (See 4-Color #227, 382)

SEVEN SAMUROID, THE (See Image Graphic Novel)

SEVEN SEAS COMICS
Apr, 1946 - No. 6, 1947 (no month)
Universal Phoenix Features/Leader No. 6
1-South Sea Girl by Matt Baker, Capt. Cutlass begin; Tugboat Tessie by Baker app. 46.00 137.00 320.00
2 41.00 122.00 285.00
3-6: 3-Six pg. Feldstein-a 37.00 111.00 260.00
NOTE: ***Baker*** *a-1-6; c-3-6.*

1776 (See Charlton Classic Library)

Shade: The Changing Man #48 © DC

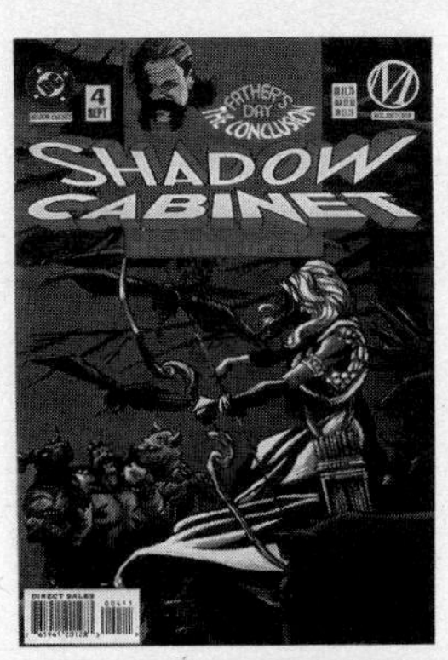

Shadow Cabinet # © DC

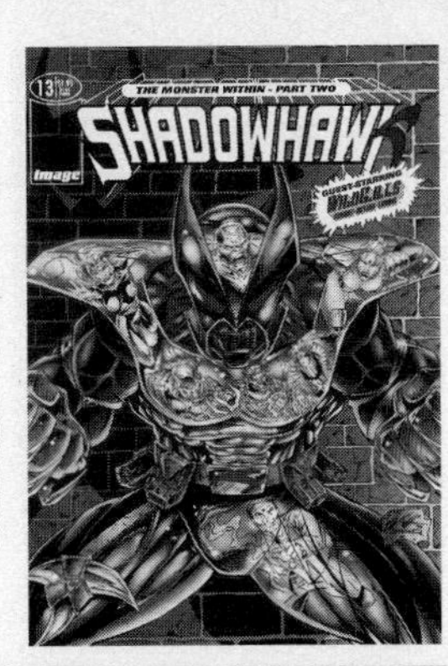

Shadowhawk #13 © Jim Valentino

GD25 FN65 NM94 | GD25 FN65 NM94

7TH VOYAGE OF SINBAD, THE (See 4-Color #944)

77 SUNSET STRIP (TV)
No. 1066, Jan-Mar, 1960 - No. 2, Feb, 1963 (All photo-c)
Dell Publ. Co./Gold Key

4-Color 1066-Toth-a 12.00 36.00 85.00
4-Color 1106,1159-Toth-a 10.00 30.00 65.00
4-Color 1211,1263,1291, 01-742-209(7-9/62)-Manning-a in all 10.00 30.00 60.00
1(11/62-G.K.), 2-Manning-a in each 10.00 30.00 60.00

77TH BENGAL LANCERS, THE (See 4-Color #791)

SEX, LIES AND MUTUAL FUNDS OF THE YUPPIES FROM HELL
(Marvel)(Value: cover or less)(Also see Yuppies From Hell)

SEYMOUR, MY SON (See More Seymour)
September, 1963
Archie Publications (Radio Comics)

1 4.00 11.00 22.00

SHADE, THE CHANGING MAN (See Cancelled Comic Cavalcade)
June-July, 1977 - No. 8, Aug-Sept, 1978
National Periodical Publications/DC Comics

1-1st app. Shade; Ditko-c/a in all 1.90 4.75
2-8 1.20 3.00

SHADE, THE CHANGING MAN (2nd series) (Also see Suicide Squad #16)
July, 1990 - Present ($1.50/$1.75, mature readers)
DC Comics (Vertigo imprint #33 on)

1-($2.50, 52 pgs.)-Peter Milligan scripts in all 1.00 2.50
2-16: 6-Preview of World Without End .70 1.75
17-40: 17-Begin $1.75-c. 33-Metallic ink on-c. .70 1.75
41-49,51-59: 41-Begin $1.95-c. 42-44-John Constantine 3 part story .80 2.00
50-($2.95, 52 pgs.) 1.20 3.00

SHADO: SONG OF THE DRAGON (See Green Arrow #63-66)
1992 - No. 4, 1992 ($4.95, mini-series, 52 pgs.)
DC Comics

Book One - Four: Grell scripts; Morrow-a(i) 1.00 2.00 5.00

SHADOW, THE
Aug, 1964 - No. 8, Sept, 1965 (All 12¢)
Archie Comics (Radio Comics)

1-Jerrry Siegel scripts in all; Shadow (pulp char.)-c 4.00 12.00 28.00
2-8: 2-App. in super-hero costume on-c only; Reinman-a(backup). 3-Superhero begins; Reinman-a (book-length novel). 3,4,6,7-The Fly 1 pg. strips. 4-8-Reinman-a. 5-8-Jerry Siegel scripts. 7-Shield app. 2.60 7.70 18.00

SHADOW, THE
Oct-Nov, 1973 - No. 12, Aug-Sept, 1975
National Periodical Publications

1-Kaluta-a begins 3.30 10.00 23.00
2 1.90 6.00 13.00
3-Kaluta/Wrightson-a 2.40 7.30 17.00
4,6-Kaluta-a ends. 4-Chaykin, Wrightson part-i 1.60 5.00 11.00
5,7-12: 11-The Avenger (pulp character) x-over 1.10 2.70 6.50

NOTE: ***Craig*** *a-10.* ***Cruz*** *a-10-12.* ***Kaluta*** *a-1, 2, 3p, 4, 6; c-1-4, 6, 10-12.* ***Kubert*** *c-9.* ***Robbins*** *a-5, 7-9; c-5, 7, 8.*

SHADOW, THE (DC, 1986 & 1987 series)(Value: cover or less)

SHADOW, THE
May, 1986 - No. 4, Aug, 1986 (Mini-series)
DC Comics

1-4: Howard Chaykin art in all 1.50
Blood & Judgement ($12.95)-r/1-4 1.90 6.00 13.00

SHADOW, THE
Aug, 1987 - No. 19, Jan, 1989 ($1.50)
DC Comics

1-19 1.50
Annual 1 (12/87, $2.25), Annual 2 (1988) .90 2.25

SHADOW, THE
June, 1994 - No. 2, July, 1994 ($2.50)
Dark Horse Comics

1,2-Adaptation from Universal Pictures film .90 2.25

SHADOW CABINET
Jan, 1994 - Present ($1.75)
DC Comics (Milestone)

0-($2.50, 52 pgs.)-Silver ink-c; Simonson-c 1.00 2.50
1-9: 1-Byrne-c .70 1.75

SHADOW COMICS (Pulp, radio)
March, 1940 - V9#5, Aug-Sept, 1949
Street & Smith Publications

NOTE: *The Shadow first appeared on radio in 1929 and was featured in pulps beginning in April, 1931, written by Walter Gibson. The early covers of this series were reprinted from the pulp covers.*

V1#1-Shadow, Doc Savage, Bill Barnes, Nick Carter (radio), Frank Merriwell, Iron Munro, the Astonishing Man begin 371.00 1115.00 2600.00
2-The Avenger begins, ends #6; Capt. Fury only app. 121.00 365.00 850.00
3(nn-5/40)-Norgil the Magician app.; cover is exact swipe of Shadow pulp from 1/33 93.00 280.00 650.00
4,5: 4-The Three Musketeers begins, ends #8. 5-Doc Savage ends 79.00 236.00 550.00
6,8,9: 9-Norgil the Magician app. 64.00 193.00 450.00
7-Origin/1st app. The Hooded Wasp & Wasplet (11/40); series ends V3#8; Hooded Wasp/Wasplet app. on-c thru #9 69.00 208.00 485.00
10-Origin The Iron Ghost, ends #11; The Dead End Kids begins, ends #14 64.00 193.00 450.00
11-Origin Hooded Wasp & Wasplet retold 64.00 193.00 450.00
12-Dead End Kids app. 51.00 154.00 360.00
V2#1,2(11/41): 2-Dead End Kids story 46.00 139.00 325.00
3-Origin & 1st app. Supersnipe (3/42); series begins; Little Nemo story 64.00 193.00 450.00
4,5: 4,8-Little Nemo story 43.00 130.00 300.00
6-9: 6-Blackstone the Magician story 40.00 120.00 280.00
10-12: 10-Supersnipe app. 40.00 120.00 280.00
V3#1-12: 10-Doc Savage begins, not in V5#5, V6#10-12, V8#4 37.00 111.00 260.00
V4#1-12 34.00 103.00 240.00
V5#1-12 31.00 94.00 220.00
V6#1-11: 9-Intro. Shadow, Jr. (12/46) 28.00 84.00 195.00
12-Powell-c/a; atom bomb panels 31.00 94.00 220.00
V7#1,2,5,7-9,12: 2,5-Shadow, Jr. app.; Powell-a 31.00 94.00 220.00
3,6,11-Powell-c/a 34.00 103.00 240.00
4-Powell-c/a; Atom bomb panels 37.00 111.00 260.00
10(1/48)-Flying Saucer-c/story (2nd of this theme; see The Spirit 9/28/47); Powell-c/a 43.00 130.00 300.00
V8#1-12-Powell-a. 8-Powell Spider-c/a 34.00 103.00 240.00
V9#1,5-Powell-a 31.00 94.00 220.00
2-4-Powell-c/a 34.00 103.00 240.00

NOTE: ***Binder*** *c-V3#1.* ***Powell*** *art in most issues beginning V6#12. Painted c-1-6.*

SHADOW EMPIRES: FAITH CONQUERS
Aug, 1994 - No. 4, Nov, 1994 ($2.95, limited series)
Dark Horse Comics

1-4 1.20 3.00

SHADOWHAWK (See Images of Shadowhawk & Youngblood #2)
Aug, 1992 - No. 4, Mar, 1993 ($1.95, color, mini-series)
Image Comics

1-($2.50)-Embossed silver foil stamped-c; Valentino/Liefeld-c; Valentino-c/a/scripts in all; has coupon for Image #0 1.65 4.00 10.00
1-With coupon missing 1.20 3.00
1-($1.95)-Newsstand version w/o foil stamp .90 2.25

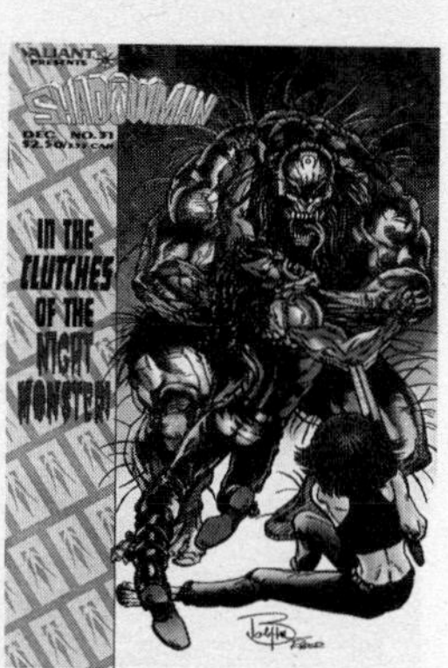

Shadowman #31 © Voyager Comm.

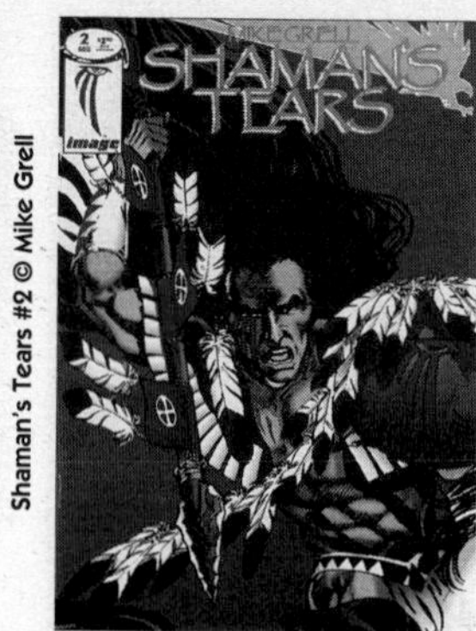

Shaman's Tears #2 © Mike Grell

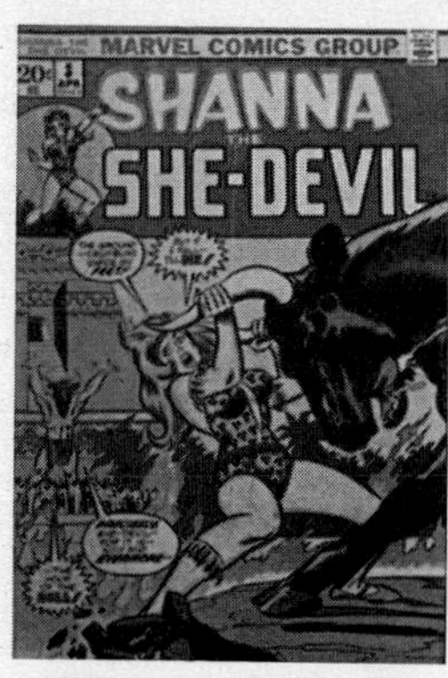

Shana The She-Devil #3 © MEG

GD25 FN65 NM94

2-Shadowhawk poster w/McFarlane-i; brief Spawn app.; wraparound-c w/silver ink highlights 1.00 2.50
3-($2.50)-Glow-in-the-dark-c 1.00 2.50
4-($1.95)-Savage Dragon-c/story; Valentino/Larsen-c .80 2.00

SHADOWHAWK II
May, 1993 - No. 3, Aug, 1993 (Color, mini-series)
Image Comics

1-($3.50)-Die-cut mirricard-c 1.40 3.50
2-($1.95)-Foil embossed logo; reveals identity .80 2.00
3-($2.95)-Pop-up-c w/Pact ashcan insert 1.20 3.00

SHADOWHAWK III
Nov, 1993 - No. 4, Mar, 1994 ($1.95, color, mini-series);
No. 5, Aug, 1994 - Present ($1.95, color)
Image Comics

V3#1-4: 1-Gold foil & red foil stamped-c variations; intro Valentine. 2-(52 pgs.)-Shadowhawk contracts HIV virus; U.S. Male by M. Anderson(p) in free 16 pg. insert .80 2.00
5,6: 5-Pull-out poster. 6-w/ShadowBone pull-out poster; WildC.A.T.s app. .80 2.00
Shadowhawk Gallery 1 (4/94, $1.95, color) .80 2.00

SHADOW: IN THE COILS OF LEVIATHON
Oct, 1993 - No. 4, Apr, 1994 ($2.50, mini-series)
Dark Horse Comics

1-4-Kaluta-c & part script; bound-in poster(#1-Kaluta) 1.20 3.00

SHADOWLINE SAGA: CRITICAL MASS, A (Marvel)(Value: cover or less)

SHADOWMAN (See X-O Manowar #4)
May, 1992 - Present ($2.50, color)
Valiant

1-Partial origin 1.70 5.10 12.00
2-5: 3-1st app. Sousa the Soul Eater .90 3.00 6.00
6,7 .90 2.50
8-1st app. Master Darque .80 2.10 5.00
9,10 1.00 2.50
11-15,17-32: 15-Minor Turok app. 17,18-Archer & Armstrong x-over. 19-Aerosmith-c/story. 23-Dr. Mirage x-over. 24-(4/94). 25-Bound-in trading card. 29-Chaos Effect 1.00 2.50
16-1st app. Dr. Mirage (8/93) 1.60 3.75
0-($2.50, 4/94)-Regular edition 1.00 2.50
0-($3.50)-Wraparound chromium-c edition 1.40 3.50

SHADOWMASTERS (Marvel)(Value: cover or less)

SHADOW OF THE BATMAN
Dec, 1985 - No. 5, Apr, 1986 ($1.75, mini-series)
DC Comics

1-Detective-r (all have wraparound-c) 1.00 2.00 5.00
2,3,5: 3-Penguin-c & cameo. 5-Clayface app. 1.20 3.00
4-Joker-c/story 1.60 4.00

NOTE: **Austin** *a(new)-2i, 3i; r-2-4i.* **Rogers** *a(new)-1, 2p, 3p, 4, 5; r-1-5p; c-1-5.*

SHADOW OF THE TORTURER, THE (Innovation)(Value: cover or less)

SHADOW PLAY (Whitman)(Value: cover or less)

SHADOW RIDERS
June, 1993 - No. 4, Sept, 1993 ($1.75, mini-series)
Marvel Comics UK, Ltd.

1-($2.50)-Embossed-c; Cable-c/story 1.00 2.50
2-4-Cable app. 2-Ghost Rider app. .70 1.75

SHADOWS FROM BEYOND (Formerly Unusual Tales)
V2#50, October, 1966
Charlton Comics

V2#50-Ditko-c 1.00 2.50 6.00

SHADOW STRIKES!, THE (DC)(Value: cover or less)

SHADOW WAR OF HAWKMAN (DC)(Value: cover or less)

GD25 FN65 NM94

SHAGGY DOG & THE ABSENT-MINDED PROFESSOR (See 4-Color #985, Movie Comics & Walt Disney Showcase #46)

SHALOMAN
Aug, 1988 - Present (B&W)
Al Wiesner

V1#1-9 .70 1.75
V2#1 .80 2.00
2-4 1.00 2.50
5 (Color)-Shows Vol 2, No. 4 in indicia 1.20 3.00

SHAMAN'S TEARS
May, 1993 - No. 2, Aug, 1993 ($2.50, color)
Image Comics

1,2: 1-Embossed red foil stamped-c; Mike Grell-c/a & scripts in all. 2-Cover unfolds into poster (8/93-c, 7/93 inside) 1.00 2.50

SHANNA, THE SHE-DEVIL (See Savage Tales #8)
Dec, 1972 - No. 5, Aug, 1973 (All are 20¢ issues)
Marvel Comics Group

1-1st app. Shanna; Steranko-c; Tuska-a(p) 1.90 4.75
2-Steranko-c; heroin drug story 1.00 2.50
3-5 .70 1.80

SHARDS
Apr, 1994 - Present ($2.50, B&W, limited series:6)
Ascension Comics

1-Flip-c 1.00 2.50

SHARK FIGHTERS, THE (See 4-Color No. 762)

SHARP COMICS (Slightly large size)
Winter, 1945-46 - V1#2, Spring, 1946 (52 pgs.)
H. C. Blackerby

V1#1-Origin Dick Royce Planetarian 29.00 86.00 200.00
2-Origin The Pioneer; Michael Morgan, Dick Royce, Sir Gallagher, Planetarian, Steve Hagen, Weeny and Pop app. 27.00 80.00 185.00

SHARPY FOX (See Comic Capers & Funny Frolics)
1958; 1963
I. W. Enterprises/Super Comics

1,2-I.W. Reprint (1958) 1.20 3.00 6.00
14-Super Reprint (1963) 1.20 3.00 6.00

SHATTER (First Comics, all issues)(Value: cover or less)

SHAZAM (See Giant Comics to Color & Limited Collectors' Edition)

SHAZAM! (TV)(See World's Finest #253)
Feb, 1973 - No. 35, May-June, 1978
National Periodical Publications/DC Comics

1-1st revival of original Captain Marvel since G.A. (origin retold), by Beck; Captain Marvel Jr. & Mary Marvel x-over 1.00 2.00 5.00
2-35: 2,6-Infinity photo-c. 2-Re-intro Mr. Mind & Tawney. 4-Origin retold. 5-Capt. Marvel Jr. origin retold. 8-(100 pgs.)-r/Capt. Marvel Jr. by Raboy; origin/C.M. #80; origin Mary Marvel/C.M. #18; origin Mr. Tawny/C.M. #79. 10-Last C.C. Beck issue. 11-Shaffenberger-a begins. 12-17-(All 100 pgs.). 15-Lex Luthor x-over. 25-1st app. Isis. 30-1st DC app. 3 Lt. Marvels. 31-1st DC app. Minuteman. 34-Origin Capt. Nazi & Capt. Marvel Jr. retold 1.00 2.50

NOTE: *Reprints in #1-8, 10, 12-17, 21-24.* **Beck** *a-1-10, 12-17r, 21-24r; c-1, 3-9.* **Nasser** *c-35p.* **Newton** *a-35p.* **Raboy** *a-5r, 8r, 17r.* **Shaffenberger** *a-11, 14-20, 25, 26, 27p, 28, 29-31p, 33i, 35i; c-20, 22, 23, 25, 26i, 27i, 28-33.*

SHAZAM: THE NEW BEGINNING
Apr, 1987 - No. 4, July, 1987 (Mini-series; Legends spin-off)
DC Comics

1-4: 1-New origin & 1st modern app. Captain Marvel; Marvel Family cameo. 2-4-Sivana & Black Adam app. 1.00

SHEA THEATRE COMICS (Also see Theatre Comics)
No date (1940's) (32 pgs.)

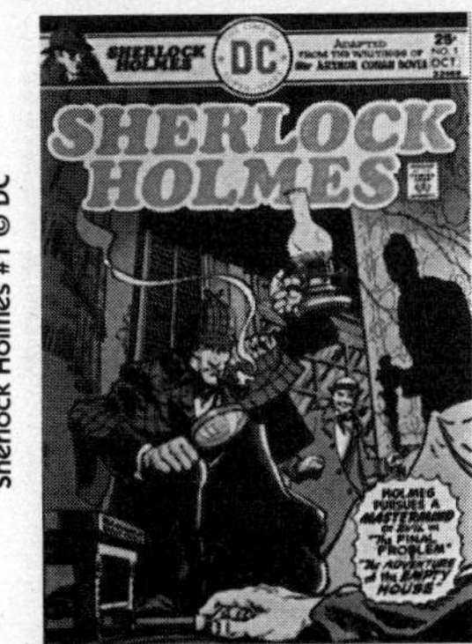

Sherlock Holmes #1 © DC

Shield-Wizard Comics #2 © AP

Shi: Way of the Warrior #2 © William Tucci

GD25 FN65 NM94

Shea Theatre
nn-Contains Rocket Comics; MLJ cover in one color 7.50 22.50 45.00

SHE-BAT (See Murcielaga, She-Bat & Valeria the She-Bat)

SHEENA (Marvel)(Value: cover or less)

SHEENA, QUEEN OF THE JUNGLE (See Jerry Iger's Classic..., Jumbo Comics, & 3-D Sheena)
Spring, 1942; No. 2, Wint, 1942-43; No. 3, Spring, 1943; No. 4, Fall, 1948; No. 5, Sum, 1949; No. 6, Spring, 1950; No. 7-10, 1950(nd); No. 11, Spring, 1951 - No. 18, Winter, 1952-53 (#1-3: 68 pgs.; #4-7: 52 pgs.)
Fiction House Magazines

1-Sheena begins 157.00 471.00 1100.00
2 (Winter, 1942-43) 82.00 246.00 575.00
3 (Spring, 1943) 61.00 182.00 425.00
4,5 (Fall, 1948, Sum, 1949): 4-New logo; cover swipe from Jumbo #20
38.00 115.00 265.00
6,7 (Spring, 1950, 1950) 31.00 94.00 220.00
8-10(1950 - Win/50, 36 pgs.) 30.00 90.00 210.00
11-18: 15-Cover swipe from Jumbo #43. 18-Used in **POP**, pg. 98
24.00 73.00 170.00
I.W. Reprint #9-r/#18; c-r/White Princess #3 5.00 15.00 30.00
NOTE: ***Baker** c-5-10? **Whitman** c-11-18(most).*

SHEENA 3-D SPECIAL (Blackthorne)(Value: cover or less)

SHE-HULK (See The Savage She-Hulk & The Sensational She-Hulk)

SHERIFF BOB DIXON'S CHUCK WAGON (TV) (See Wild Bill Hickok #22)
November, 1950
Avon Periodicals

1-Kinstler-c/a(3) 10.00 30.00 65.00

SHERIFF OF COCHISE, THE
1957 (16 pgs.) (TV Show)
Mobil Giveaway

nn-Shaffenberger-a 2.40 6.00 12.00

SHERIFF OF TOMBSTONE
Nov, 1958 - No. 17, Sept, 1961
Charlton Comics

V1#1-Giordano-c; Severin-a 8.35 25.00 50.00
2 4.70 14.00 28.00
3-17 3.60 9.00 18.00

SHERLOCK HOLMES (See 4-Color #1169,1245, Marvel Preview & Spectacular Stories)

SHERLOCK HOLMES (All New Baffling Adventures of...)(Young Eagle #3 on?)
Oct, 1955 - No. 2, Mar, 1956
Charlton Comics

1-Dr. Neff, Ghost Breaker app. 33.00 100.00 230.00
2 29.00 86.00 200.00

SHERLOCK HOLMES (Also see The Joker)
Sept-Oct, 1975
National Periodical Publications

1-Cruz-a; Simonson-c 1.50

SHERRY THE SHOWGIRL (Showgirls #4)
July, 1956 - No. 3, Dec, 1956; No. 5, Apr, 1957 - No. 7, Aug, 1957
Atlas Comics

1-Dan DeCarlo-c/a in all 9.15 27.50 55.00
2 5.85 17.50 35.00
3,5-7 4.70 14.00 28.00

SHE'S JOSIE (See Josie)

S.H.I.E.L.D. (Nick Fury & His Agents of...) (Also see Nick Fury)
Feb, 1973 - No. 5, Oct, 1973 (All 20¢ issues)
Marvel Comics Group

1-Steranko-c 1.00 2.00 5.00
2-5: 2-Steranko flag-c. 1-5 all contain-r from Str. Tales #146-155. 3-5-are cover-r; 3-Kirby/Steranko-c(r). 4-Steranko-c(r) 1.00 2.50
NOTE: ***Buscema** a-3p(r). **Kirby** layouts 1-5; c-3 (w/**Steranko**). **Steranko** a-3r, 4r(2).*

SHIELD, THE (Becomes Shield-Steel Sterling #3; #1 titled Lancelot Strong; also see Advs. of the Fly, Double Life of Private Strong, Fly Man, Mighty Comics, The Mighty Crusaders, The Original... & Pep Comics #1)
June, 1983 - No. 2, Aug, 1983
Archie Enterprises, Inc.

1,2: Steel Sterling app. 1.00

SHIELD-STEEL STERLING (Formerly The Shield)
No. 3, Dec, 1983 (Becomes Steel Sterling No. 4)
Archie Enterprises, Inc.

3-Nino-a 1.00

SHIELD WIZARD COMICS (Also see Pep Comics & Top-Notch Comics)
Summer, 1940 - No. 13, Spring, 1944
MLJ Magazines

1-(V1#5 on inside)-Origin The Shield by Irving Novick & The Wizard by Ed Ashe, Jr; Flag-c 257.00 771.00 1800.00
2-(Winter/40)-Origin The Shield retold; Wizard's sidekick, Roy the Super Boy begins (see Top-Notch #8 for 1st app.) 107.00 321.00 750.00
3,4 71.00 215.00 500.00
5-Dusty, the Boy Detective begins 68.00 205.00 475.00
6-8: 6-Roy the Super Boy begins. 7-Shield dons new costume (Summer, 1942); S & K-c? 61.00 182.00 425.00
9-13: 13-Bondage-c 54.00 161.00 375.00
NOTE: ***Bob Montana** c-13. **Novick** c-1-6,8-11. **Harry Sahle** c-12.*

SHINING KNIGHT (See Adventure Comics #66)

SHIP AHOY
November, 1944 (52 pgs.)
Spotlight Publishers

1-L. B. Cole-c 10.00 30.00 65.00

SHIPWRECKED! (Disney)(Value: cover or less)

SHI: THE WAY OF THE WARRIOR (See Razor Annual #1 for 1st app.)
Mar, 1994 - Present ($2.50, color)
Crusade Comics

1 1.40 3.50 8.50
1-Commemorative ed., B&W, new-c; given out at 1994 San Diego Comic Con
1.00
2 1.00 2.50

SHMOO (See Al Capp's... & Washable Jones &...)

SHOCK (Magazine)
May, 1969 - V3#4, Sept, 1971 (B&W)(Reprints from horror comics)
Stanley Publications

V1#1-Cover-r/Weird Tales of the Future #7 by Bernard Baily; r/Weird Chills #1
3.10 9.00 22.00
2-Wolverton-r/Weird Mysteries 5; r-Weird Mysteries #7 used in **SOTI**; cover reprints cover to Weird Chills #1 2.60 7.70 18.00
3,5,6 1.70 5.00 12.00
4-Harrison/Williamson-r/Forbid. Worlds #6 2.00 6.00 14.00
V2#2, V1#8, V2#4-6, V3#1-4: V2#4-Cover swipe from Weird Mysteries #6
1.70 5.00 12.00
NOTE: ***Disbrow** r-V2#4; Bondage c-V1#4, V2#6, V3#1.*

SHOCK DETECTIVE CASES (Formerly Crime Fighting Detective)
(Becomes Spook Detective Cases No. 22)
No. 20, Sept, 1952 - No. 21, Nov, 1952
Star Publications

20,21-L.B. Cole-c; based on true crime cases 10.00 30.00 60.00
NOTE: ***Palais** a-20. No. 21-Fox-r.*

SHOCK ILLUSTRATED (...Adult Crime Stories; Magazine format)
Sept-Oct, 1955 - No. 3, Spring, 1956 (Adult Entertainment on-c #1,2)(All 25¢)
E. C. Comics

Shocking Mystery Cases #53 © STAR

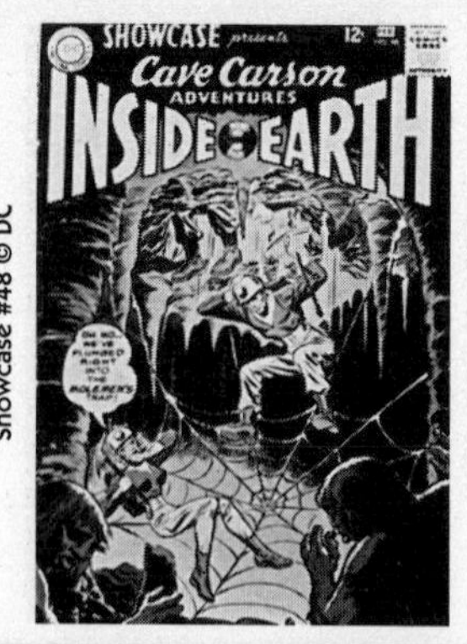

Showcase #48 © DC

Showcase #51 © DC

GD25 FN65 NM94

1-All by Kamen; drugs, prostitution, wife swapping 4.70 14.00 28.00
2-Williamson-a redrawn from Crime SuspenStories #13 plus Ingels, Crandall, Evans & part Torres-i; painted-c 5.85 17.50 35.00
3-Only 100 known copies bound & given away at E.C. office; Crandall, Evans-a; painted-c; shows May, 1956 on-c 100.00 300.00 700.00

SHOCKING MYSTERY CASES (Formerly Thrilling Crime Cases)
No. 50, Sept, 1952 - No. 60, Oct, 1954 (All crime reprints?)
Star Publications

50-Disbrow "Frankenstein" story 20.00 60.00 140.00
51-Disbrow-a 10.00 30.00 70.00
52-55,57-60 10.00 30.00 60.00
56-Drug use story 10.00 30.00 65.00
NOTE: *L. B. Cole covers on all; a-60(2 pgs.). Hollingsworth a-52. Morisi a-55.*

SHOCKING TALES DIGEST MAGAZINE
Oct, 1981 (95¢)
Harvey Publications

1-1957-58-r; Powell, Kirby, Nostrand-a .80 2.00

SHOCK SUSPENSTORIES
Feb-Mar, 1952 - No. 18, Dec-Jan, 1954-55
E. C. Comics

1-Classic Feldstein electrocution-c 66.00 197.00 460.00
2 38.00 115.00 265.00
3,4: 4-Used in **SOTI**, pg. 387,388 25.00 75.00 175.00
5-Hanging-c 24.00 72.00 165.00
6,7: 6-Classic bondage-c. 7-Classic face melting-c 30.00 90.00 210.00
8-Williamson-a 25.00 75.00 175.00
9-11: 9-Injury to eye panel. 10-Junkie story 21.00 63.00 145.00
12- "The Monkey" classic junkie cover/story; anti-drug propaganda issue 24.00 73.00 170.00
13-Frazetta's only solo story for E.C., 7 pgs. 30.00 90.00 210.00
14-Used in Senate Investigation hearings 16.00 48.00 110.00
15-Used in 1954 Reader's Digest article, "For the Kiddies to Read"; Bill Gaines stars in prose story "The EC Caper" 16.00 48.00 110.00
16- "Red Dupe" editorial; rape story 14.00 43.00 100.00
17,18 14.00 43.00 100.00
NOTE: *Ray Bradbury adaptations-1, 7, 9. Craig a-11; c-11. Crandall a-9-13, 15-18. Davis a-1-5. Evans a-7, 8, 14-18; c-16-18. Feldstein c-1, 7-9, 12. Ingels a-1, 2, 6. Kamen a-in all; c-10, 13, 15. Krigstein a-14, 18. Orlando a-1, 3-7, 9, 10, 12, 16, 17. Wood a-2-15; c-2-6, 14.*

SHOCK SUSPENSTORIES
Sept, 1992 - Present ($1.50/$2.00, color, quarterly)
Russ Cochran

1,2-r/#1,2 above with original-c 1.50
3-7-($2.00)-r/#3-7 above with original-c .80 2.00

SHOGUN WARRIORS
Feb, 1979 - No. 20, Sept, 1980 (Based on Mattel toys)
Marvel Comics Group (1-3: 35¢; 4-19: 40¢; 20: 50¢)

1-Raydeen, Combatra, & Dangard Ace begin .80 2.00
2-20: 11-Austin-c. 12-Simonson-c. 19,20-FF x-over 1.50

SHOOK UP (Magazine) (Satire)
November, 1958
Dodsworth Publ. Co.

V1#1 3.60 9.00 18.00

SHORT RIBS (See 4-Color #1333)

SHORT STORY COMICS (See Hello Pal,...)

SHORTY SHINER (The Five-Foot Fighter in the Ten Gallon Hat)
June, 1956 - No. 3, Oct, 1956
Dandy Magazine (Charles Biro)

1 4.70 14.00 28.00
2,3 3.60 9.00 18.00

SHOTGUN SLADE (See 4-Color #1111)

SHOWCASE (See Cancelled Comic Cavalcade & New Talent...)

GD25 FN65 NM94

3-4/56 - No. 93, 9/70; No. 94, 8-9/77 - No. 104, 9/78
National Per. Publ./DC Comics

GD25 FN65 VF82 NM94
1-Fire Fighters; w/Fireman Farrell 210.00 630.00 1365.00 2100.00

GD25 FN65 NM94
2-King of the Wild; Kubert-a (animal stories) 75.00 225.00 600.00
3-The Frogmen by Russ Heath; Heath greytone-c (early DC example, 7-8/56) 69.00 206.00 550.00

GD25 FN65 VF82 NM94
4-Origin/1st app. The Flash (1st DC Silver Age hero, Sept-Oct, 1956) & The Turtle; Kubert-a; r/in Secret Origins #1 ('61 & '73); Flash shown reading G.A. Flash #13; Infantino/Kubert-c 1400.00 4200.00 12,600.00 21,000.00

GD25 FN65 NM94
5-Manhunters 89.00 268.00 715.00

GD25 FN65 VF82 NM94
6-Origin/1st app. Challengers of the Unknown by Kirby, partly r/in Secret Origins #1 & Challengers #64,65 (1st Silver Age super-hero team & 1st original concept S.A. series)(1-2/56) 160.00 480.00 1440.00 2400.00

GD25 FN65 NM94
7-Challengers of the Unknown by Kirby (2nd app.) reprinted in Challengers of the Unknown #75 108.00 325.00 1300.00

GD25 FN65 VF82 NM94
8-The Flash (5-6/57, 2nd app.); origin & 1st app. Capt. Cold 975.00 2925.00 5850.00 –
9-Lois Lane (Pre-#1, 7-8/57) (1st Showcase character to win own series) Superman app. on-c 500.00 1500.00 2750.00 –

GD25 FN65 NM94
10-Lois Lane; Jor-el cameo; Superman app. on-c 142.00 425.00 1700.00
11-Challengers of the Unknown by Kirby (3rd) 115.00 345.00 1150.00
12-Challengers of the Unknown by Kirby (4th) 100.00 300.00 1200.00
13-The Flash (3rd app.); origin Mr. Element 270.00 810.00 2700.00
14-The Flash (4th app.); origin Dr. Alchemy, former Mr. Element 292.00 875.00 3500.00

GD25 FN65 VF82 NM94
15-Space Ranger (7-8/58, 1st app.) 77.00 230.00 690.00 1150.00

GD25 FN65 NM94
16-Space Ranger (9-10/58, 2nd app.) 65.00 195.00 650.00

GD25 FN65 VF82 NM94
17-Adventures on Other Worlds; origin/1st app. Adam Strange (11-12/58) 117.00 350.00 875.00 1400.00
18-Adventures on Other Worlds (2nd A. Strange) 103.00 309.00 825.00
19-Adam Strange; 1st Adam Strange logo 95.00 285.00 950.00
20-Rip Hunter; origin & 1st app. (5-6/59); Moriera-a 61.00 180.00 550.00
21-Rip Hunter (7-8/59, 2nd app.); Sekowsky-c/a 36.00 108.00 325.00

GD25 FN65 VF82 NM94
22-Origin & 1st app. Silver Age Green Lantern by Gil Kane (9-10/59); reprinted in Secret Origins #2 325.00 975.00 2437.00 3900.00
23-Green Lantern (3-4.60, 2nd app.); nuclear explosion-c 144.00 433.00 867.00 1300.00
24-Green Lantern (1-2/60, 3rd app.) 147.00 442.00 883.00 1325.00

GD25 FN65 NM94
25,26-Rip Hunter by Kubert. 25-Grey tone-c 26.00 79.00 210.00
27-Sea Devils (7-8/60, 1st app.); Heath-c/a 68.00 204.00 545.00
28-Sea Devils (9-10/60, 2nd app.); Heath-c/a 39.00 118.00 315.00
29-Sea Devils; Heath-c/a; grey tone c-27-29 40.00 120.00 320.00
30-Origin Silver Age Aquaman (1-2/61) (see Adventure #260 for 1st S.A. origin) 54.00 162.00 540.00
31,32-Aquaman 30.00 90.00 300.00
33-Aquaman 36.00 108.00 360.00

GD25 FN65 VF82 NM94
34-Origin & 1st app. Silver Age Atom by Kane & Anderson (9-10/61); reprinted in Secret Origins #2 117.00 350.00 700.00 1050.00

GD25 FN65 NM94
35-The Atom by Gil Kane (2nd); last 10¢ issue 96.00 289.00 675.00
36-The Atom by Gil Kane (1-2/62, 3rd app.) 71.00 214.00 500.00
37-Metal Men (3-4/62, 1st app.) 59.00 178.00 475.00
38-Metal Men (5-6/62, 2nd app.) 45.00 135.00 360.00

Showcase #98 © DC

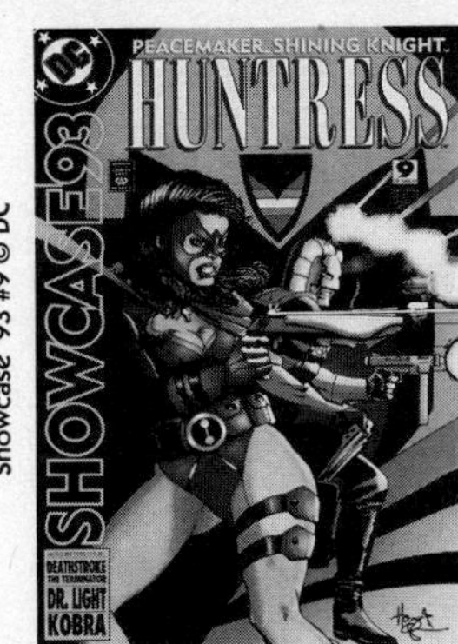

Showcase '93 #9 © DC

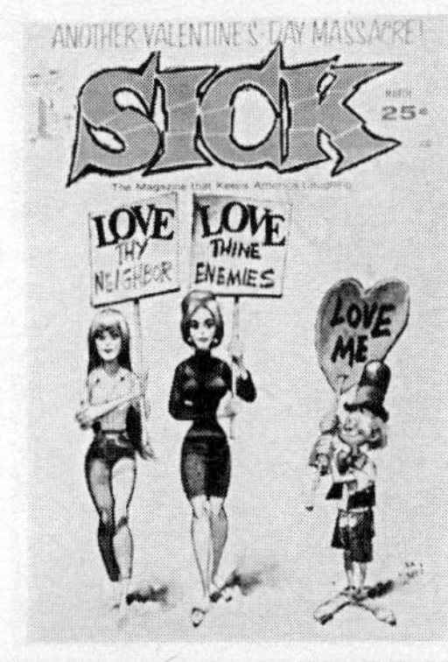

Sick #35 © CC

GD25 FN65 NM94

39-Metal Men (7-8/62, 3rd app.) 34.00 103.00 275.00
40-Metal Men (9-10/62, 4th app.) 32.00 96.00 255.00
41,42-Tommy Tomorrow (parts 1 & 2). 42-Origin 16.00 47.00 125.00
43-Dr. No (James Bond); Nodel-a; originally published as British Classics Illustrated #158A & as #6 in a European Detective series, all with diff. painted-c. This Showcase #43 version is actually censored, deleting all racial skin color and dialogue thought to be racially demeaning (1st DC S.A. movie adaptation)(based on Ian Fleming novel & movie) 39.00 118.00 315.00
44-Tommy Tomorrow 10.00 30.00 80.00
45-Sgt. Rock (7-8/63); pre-dates B&B #52; origin retold; Heath-c 20.00 60.00 160.00
46,47-Tommy Tomorrow 8.00 24.00 65.00
48,49-Cave Carson (3rd tryout series; see B&B) 5.00 15.00 45.00
50,51-I Spy (Danger Trail-r by Infantino), King Farady story (#50 has new 4 pg. story) 4.00 13.00 40.00
52-Cave Carson 4.00 12.00 35.00
53,54-G.I. Joe (11-12/64, 1-2/65); Heath-a 5.00 15.00 45.00
55-Dr. Fate & Hourman (3-4/65); origin of each in text; 1st solo app. G.A. Green Lantern in Silver Age (pre-dates Gr. Lantern #40); 1st S.A. app. Solomon Grundy 20.00 60.00 180.00
56-Dr. Fate & Hourman 6.00 18.00 55.00
57-Enemy Ace by Kubert (7-8/65, 4th app. after Our Army at War #155) 12.00 40.00 85.00
58-Enemy Ace by Kubert (5th app.) 10.00 30.00 80.00
59-Teen Titans (11-12/65, 3rd app.) 8.00 25.00 75.00
60-1st Silver Age app. The Spectre; Anderson-a (1-2/66); origin in text 24.00 71.00 165.00
61-The Spectre by Anderson (2nd app.) 14.00 41.00 95.00
62-Origin & 1st app. Inferior Five (5-6/66) 6.00 18.00 55.00
63,65-Inferior Five. 65-X-Men parody (11-12/66) 4.00 10.50 28.00
64-The Spectre by Anderson (3rd app.) 13.00 39.00 90.00
66,67-B'wana Beast 2.00 6.00 14.00
68,69,71-Maniaks 2.00 6.00 14.00
70-Binky (9-10/67)-Tryout issue 2.00 6.00 14.00
72-Top Gun (Johnny Thunder-r)-Toth-a 2.00 6.00 14.00
73-Origin/1st app. Creeper; Ditko-c/a (3-4/68) 10.00 30.00 90.00
74-Intro/1st app. Anthro; Post-c/a (5/68) 6.00 18.00 55.00
75-Origin/1st app. Hawk & the Dove; Ditko-c/a 8.00 23.00 75.00
76-1st app. Bat Lash (8/68) 4.00 11.00 35.00
77-1st app. Angel & The Ape (9/68) 4.00 11.00 35.00
78-1st app. Jonny Double (11/68) 2.30 7.00 16.00
79-1st app. Dolphin (12/68); Aqualad origin-r 3.00 8.00 28.00
80-1st S.A. app. Phantom Stranger (1/69); Neal Adams-c 1.90 6.00 13.00
81-Windy & Willy 1.90 6.00 12.00
82-1st app. Nightmaster (5/69) by Grandenetti & Giordano; Kubert-c 4.00 13.00 42.00
83,84-Nightmaster by Wrightson w/Jones/Kaluta ink assist in each; Kubert-c. 83-Last 12¢ issue 84-Origin retold; begin 15¢ 4.00 11.00 38.00
85-87-Firehair; Kubert-a 1.80 5.00 11.00
88-90-Jason's Quest: 90-Manhunter 2070 app. 1.00 2.50 6.00
91-93-Manhunter 2070: 92-Origin 1.00 2.50 6.00
94-Intro/origin new Doom Patrol & Robotman 1.30 3.00 7.50
95,96-The Doom Patrol. 95-Origin Celsius 1.80 4.50
97-99-Power Girl; origin-97,98; JSA cameos 1.80 4.50
100-(52 pgs.)-Most Showcase characters featured 1.80 4.50
101-103-Hawkman; Adam Strange x-over 1.80 4.50
104-(52 pgs.)-O.S.S. Spies at War 1.80 4.50

NOTE: ***Anderson*** *a-22-24i, 34-36i, 55, 56, 60, 61, 64, 101-103i; c-50i, 51i, 55, 56, 60, 61, 64.* ***Aparo*** *c-94-96.* ***Boring*** *c-10.* ***Estrada*** *a-104.* ***Fraden*** *c(p)-30, 31, 33.* ***Heath*** *c-3, 27-29.* ***Infantino*** *c/a(p)-4, 8, 13, 14; c-50p, 51p.* ***Gil Kane*** *a-22-24p, 34-36p; c-17-19, 22-24p(w/ Giella), 31.* ***Kane/Anderson*** *c-34-36.* ***Kirby*** *c-11, 12.* ***Kirby/Stein*** *c-6, 7.* ***Kubert*** *a-2, 4i, 25, 26, 45, 53, 54, 72; c-25, 26, 53, 54, 57, 58, 82-87, 101-104; c-2, 4i.* ***Moriera*** *c-5.* ***Orlando*** *a-62p, 63p, 97i; c-62, 63, 97i.* ***Sekowsky*** *a-65p.* ***Sparling*** *a-78.* ***Staton*** *a-94, 95-99p, 100; c-97-100p.*

SHOWCASE 93
Jan, 1993 - No. 12, Dec, 1993 ($1.95, limited series, 52 pgs.)
DC Comics

1-12: 1-Begin 4 part Catwoman story & 6 part Blue Devil story; begin Cyborg story; Art Adams/Austin-c. 2-Maguire/Austin-c; Flash by Travis Charest (p) begins; Bolland-c. 6-Azrael in Bat-costume (2 pgs.). 7,8-Knightfall parts 13 & 14. 6-10-Deathstroke app. (6,10-cameo). 9,10-Austin-i. 10-Azrael as Batman in new costume app.; Gulacy-c. 11-Perez-c. 12-Creeper app.; Alan Grant scripts .80 2.00

SHOWCASE 94
Jan, 1994 - No. 12, Dec, 1994 ($1.95, limited series, 52 pgs.)
DC Comics

1-12: 1,2-Joker & Gunfire 2 part stories. 1-New Gods. 4-Riddler story. 5-Huntress-c/story w/app. new Batman. 6-Huntress-c/story w/app. Robin; Atom story .80 2.00

NOTE: ***Alan Grant*** *scripts-3, 4.* ***Mignola*** *c-3.* ***Nebres*** *a(i)-2.* ***Simonson*** *c-5.*

SHOWGIRLS (Formerly Sherry the Showgirl #3)
No. 4, 2/57; June, 1957 - No. 2, Aug, 1957
Atlas Comics (MPC No. 2)

4-Dan DeCarlo-c/a begins 6.70 20.00 40.00
1-Millie, Sherry, Chili, Pearl & Hazel begin 8.35 25.00 50.00
2 6.35 19.00 38.00

SHROUD, THE (See Super-Villain Team-Up #5)
Mar, 1994 - No. 4, June, 1994 ($1.75, mini-series)
Marvel Comics

1-4: 1,2,4-Spider-Man & Scorpion app. .70 1.75

SHROUD OF MYSTERY (Whitman)(Value: cover or less)

SICK (Sick Special #131) (Magazine) (Satire)
Aug, 1960 - No. 131, Feb, 1980
Feature Publ./Headline Publ./Crestwood Publ. Co./Hewfred Publ./ Pyramid Comm./Charlton Publ. No. 109 (4/76) on

V1#1-Jack Paar photo on-c; Torres-a 14.00 43.00 100.00
2-5-Torres-a in all 8.35 25.00 50.00
6 5.35 16.00 32.00
V2#1-8(#7-14) 4.35 13.00 26.00
V3#1-8(#15-22) 4.00 10.00 20.00
V4#1-5(#23-27) 3.20 8.00 16.00
28-32,34-40: 29-Beatles-c by Jack Davis 2.00 5.00 10.00
33-Ringo Starr photo-c & spoof on "A Hard Day's Night"; inside-c has Beatles photos 4.00 12.00 24.00
41-131: 45 has #44 on-c & #45 on inside. 70-John & Yoko-c. 128-Superman-c/movie parody. 131-Superman parody 1.00 2.50 6.00
Annual 1969, 1970, 1971 2.15 6.50 15.00
Annual 2-4(1980) 1.20 3.00 7.00
Big Sick Laff-in (1968)-w/psychedelic posters 3.60 9.00 18.00
Birthday Annual (1967)-3 pg. Huckleberry Fink fold out 3.60 9.00 18.00
7th Annual Yearbook (1967)-Davis-c, 2 pg. glossy poster insert 3.60 9.00 18.00
Special 2 (1978) 1.00 2.00 5.00
Yearbook 14(1974), 15(1975, 84 pgs.) 1.00 2.50 6.00

NOTE: ***Davis*** *a-42, 87; c-22, 23, 25, 29, 31, 32.* ***Powell*** *a-7, 31, 57.* ***Simon*** *a-1-3, 10, 41, 42, 87, 99; c-1, 47, 57, 59, 69, 91, 95-97, 99, 100, 102, 107, 112.* ***Torres*** *a-1-3, 29, 31, 47, 49.* ***Tuska*** *a-14, 41-43. Civil War Blackouts-23, 24. #42 has biography of Bob Powell.*

SIDESHOW
1949 (One Shot)
Avon Periodicals

1-(Rare)-Similar to Bachelor's Diary 19.00 58.00 135.00

SIEGEL AND SHUSTER: DATELINE 1930s (Eclipse)(Value: cover or less)

SILENT INVASION, THE (Renegade)(Value: cover or less)

SILENT MOBIUS (Viz)(Value: cover or less)

SILK HAT HARRY'S DIVORCE SUIT
1912 (5-3/4x15-1/2") (B&W)
M. A. Donoghue & Co.

Newspaper reprints by Tad (Thomas Dorgan) 13.00 40.00 90.00

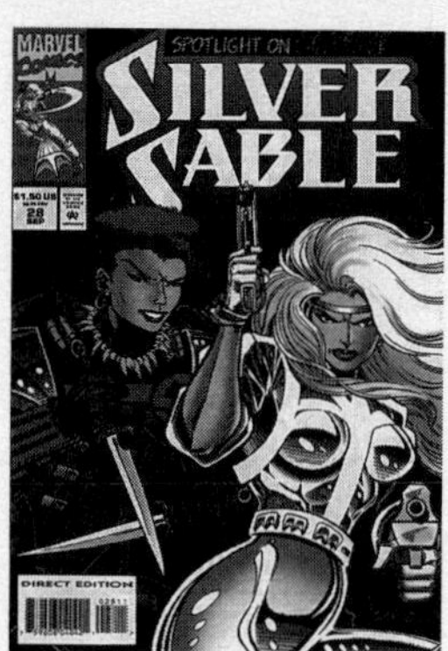

Silver Sable #28 © MEG

Silver Streak Comics #20 © Newsbook

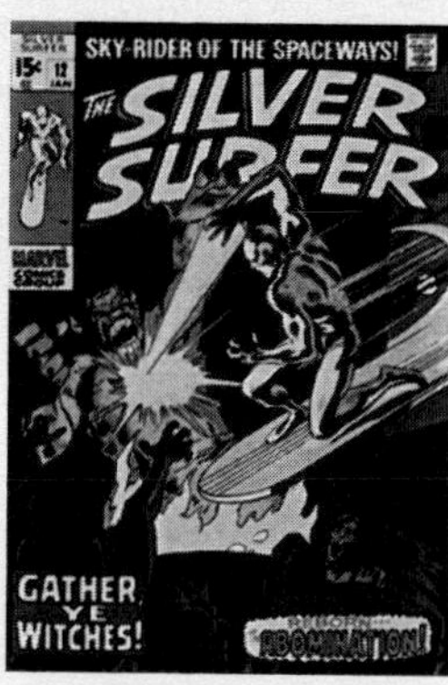

Silver Surfer #12 © MEG

GD25 FN65 NM94

SILLY PILLY (See Frank Luther's...)

SILLY SYMPHONIES (See Dell Giants)

SILLY TUNES
Fall, 1945 - No. 7, June, 1947
Timely Comics

1-Silly Seal, Ziggy Pig begin 13.00 40.00 90.00
2-(2/46) 8.35 25.00 50.00
3-7: 6-New logo 6.70 20.00 40.00

SILVER (See Lone Ranger's Famous Horse...)

SILVERBACK (Comico)(Value: cover or less)

SILVERBLADE (DC)(Value: cover or less)

SILVERHAWKS (Marvel)(Value: cover or less)

SILVERHEELS (Pacific)(Value: cover or less)

SILVER KID WESTERN
Oct, 1954 - No. 5, July?, 1955
Key/Stanmor Publications

1 7.50 22.50 45.00
2 4.00 11.00 22.00
3-5 4.00 10.00 20.00
I.W. Reprint #1,2-Severin-c: 1-r/#? 2-r/#1 1.20 3.00 6.00

SILVER SABLE AND THE WILD PACK (See Amazing Spider-Man #265)
June, 1992 - Present ($1.25)
Marvel Comics

1-($2.00)-Embossed & foil stamped-c; Spider-Man app. 1.20 3.00
2-4: 4,5-Dr. Doom-c/story .70 1.75
5-23: 6,7-Deathlok-c/story. 9-Origin Silver Sable. 10-Punisher-c/s. 15-Capt. America-c/s. 16,17-Intruders app. 18,19-Venom-c/s. 19-Siege of Darkness x-over. 23-Daredevil (in new costume) & Deadpool app. 1.25
24,26-37: 24-Begin $1.50-c; bound-in card sheet 1.50
25-($2.00, 52 pgs.)-Li'l Sylvie backup story .80 2.00

SILVER STAR (Pacific)(Value: cover or less)(See Jack Kirby's...)

SILVER STAR (Also see Jack Kirby's...)
Feb, 1983 - No. Jan, 1984 ($1.00, color)
Pacific Comics

1-6: 1-1st app. Last of the Viking Heroes. 1-5-Kirby-c/a. 2-Ditko-a 1.00

SILVER STREAK COMICS (Crime Does Not Pay #22 on)
Dec, 1939 - No. 21, May, 1942; No. 22-24, 1946 (Silver logo-#1-5)
Your Guide Publs. No. 1-7/New Friday Publs. No. 8-17/Comic House Publ./Newsbook Publ.

GD25 FN65 VF82 NM94

1-(Scarce)-Intro The Claw by Cole (r-/in Daredevil #21), Red Reeves, Boy Magician, & Captain Fearless; The Wasp, Mister Midnight begin; Spirit Man app. Silver metallic-c begin, end #5; Claw c-1,2,6-8 650.00 1950.00 4225.00 6500.00
(Estimated up to 100 total copies exist, 6 in NM/Mint)

GD25 FN65 NM94

2-The Claw by Cole; Simon-c/a 286.00 857.00 2000.00
3-1st app. & origin Silver Streak (2nd with lightning speed); Dickie Dean the Boy Inventor, Lance Hale, Ace Powers, Bill Wayne, & The Planet Patrol begin 236.00 707.00 1650.00
4-Sky Wolf begins; Silver Streak by Jack Cole (new costume); 1st app. Jackie, Lance Hale's sidekick 107.00 321.00 750.00
5-Jack Cole c/a(2) 121.00 364.00 850.00

GD25 FN65 VF82 NM94

6-(Scarce, 9/40)-Origin & 1st app. Daredevil (blue & yellow costume) by Jack Binder; The Claw returns; classic Cole Claw-c 813.00 2438.00 4469.00 6500.00
7-Claw vs. Daredevil (new costume-blue & red) by Jack Cole & 3 other Cole stories (38 pgs.) 571.00 1715.00 2858.00 4000.00
(#6, 7-Estimated up to 120 total copies of each exist, 7-10 in NM/Mint)

GD25 FN65 NM94

8-Claw vs. Daredevil by Cole; last Cole Silver Streak 171.00 515.00 1200.00
9-Claw vs. Daredevil by Cole 132.00 396.00 925.00
10-Origin & 1st app. Captain Battle (5/41); Claw vs. Daredevil by Cole; Robot-c 107.00 321.00 750.00
11-Intro. Mercury by Bob Wood, Silver Streak's sidekick; conclusion Claw vs. Daredevil by Rico; in 'Presto Martin,' 2nd pg., newspaper says 'Roussos does it again' 75.00 225.00 525.00
12-14: 13-Origin Thun-Dohr 61.00 182.00 425.00
15-17-Last Daredevil issue. 16-Hitler-c 57.00 171.00 400.00
18-The Saint begins (2/42, 1st app.) by Leslie Charteris (see Movie Comics #2 by DC); The Saint-c 50.00 150.00 350.00
19-21(1942): 20,21 have Wolverton's Scoop Scuttle. 21-Hitler app. in strip on cover 36.00 107.00 250.00
22,24(1946)-Reprints 22.00 65.00 150.00
23-Reprints?; bondage-c 22.00 65.00 150.00
nn(11/46)(Newsbook Publ.)-R-/S.S. story from #4-7 plus 2 Captain Fearless stories, all in color; bondage/torture-c 38.00 115.00 265.00

NOTE: ***Binder*** *c-3, 4, 13-15, 17.* ***Jack Cole*** *a-(Daredevil)-#6-10, (Dickie Dean)-#3-10, (Pirate Prince)-#7, (Silver Streak)-#4-8, nn; c-5 (Silver Streak), 6 (Claw), 7, 8 (Daredevil).* ***Everett*** *Red Reed begins #20.* ***Guardineer*** *a-#8-13.* ***Don Rico*** *a-11-17 (Daredevil); c-11, 12, 16.* ***Simon*** *a-3 (Silver Streak).* ***Bob Wood*** *a-9 (Silver Streak); c-9, 10. Captain Battle c-11, 13-15, 17. Claw c-#1, 2, 6-8. Daredevil c-7, 8, 12. Dickie Dean c-19. Ned of the Navy c-20 (war). The Saint c-18. Silver Streak c-5, 9, 10, 16, 23.*

SILVER SURFER (See Fantastic Four, Fantasy Masterpieces V2#1, Marvel Graphic Novel, Marvel Presents #8, Marvel's Greatest Comics & Tales To Astonish #92)

SILVER SURFER, THE
Aug, 1968 - No. 18, Sept, 1970; June, 1982 (No. 1-7: 25¢, 68 pgs.)
Marvel Comics Group

1-More detailed origin by John Buscema (p); The Watcher back-up stories begin (origin), end #7 49.00 146.00 390.00
2 19.00 56.00 150.00
3-1st app. Mephisto 16.00 47.00 125.00
4-Low distribution; Thor & Loki app. 47.00 141.00 375.00
5-7-Last giant size. 5-The Stranger app.; Fantastic Four app. 6-Brunner inks. 7-(8/69)-1st app. Frankenstein's monster (cameo) 9.00 28.00 75.00
8-10: 8-18-(15¢ issues) 7.00 21.00 55.00
11-13,15-18: 15-Silver Surfer vs. Human Torch; Fantastic Four app. 17-Nick Fury app. 18-Vs. The Inhumans; Kirby-c/a 5.00 16.00 42.00
14-Spider-Man x-over 8.00 24.00 64.00
V2#1 (6/82, 52 pgs.)-Byrne-c/a 1.50 3.75 9.00

NOTE: ***Adkins*** *a-8-15i.* ***Brunner*** *a-6i.* ***J. Buscema*** *a-1-17p.* ***Colan*** *a-1-3p.* ***Reinman*** *a-1-4i. #1-14 were reprinted in Fantasy Masterpieces V2#1-14.*

SILVER SURFER (See Marvel Graphic Novel #38)
V3#1, July, 1987 - Present
Marvel Comics Group

V3#1-Double size ($1.25) 1.20 2.90 7.00
2 1.20 3.00
3-10 .80 2.00
11-14 .70 1.75
15-Ron Lim-c/a begins (9/88) 1.20 2.90 7.00
16,17 1.80 4.25
18-20 1.20 3.00
21-24,26-30,33,40-43 .70 1.80
25,31 ($1.50, 52 pgs.): 25-Skrulls app. .80 2.00
32,39-No Ron Lim-c/a. 39-Alan Grant scripts 1.50
34-Thanos returns (cameo); Starlin scripts begin 1.70 4.20 10.00
35-1st full Thanos app. in Silver Surfer (3/90); reintro Drax the Destroyer on last pg. (cameo) 1.70 5.00 12.00
36-Recaps history of Thanos; Capt. Marvel & Warlock app. in recap 1.00 2.50 6.00
37-1st full app. Drax the Destroyer; Drax-c 1.80 4.50
38-Silver Surfer battles Thanos 1.20 3.00 7.00
44,45,49-Thanos stories (c-44,45) 1.00 2.50
46,47: 46-Return of Adam Warlock (2/91); re-intro Gamora & Pip the Troll. 47-Warlock battles Drax .90 2.30 5.50

Silver Surfer V3 #96 © MEG

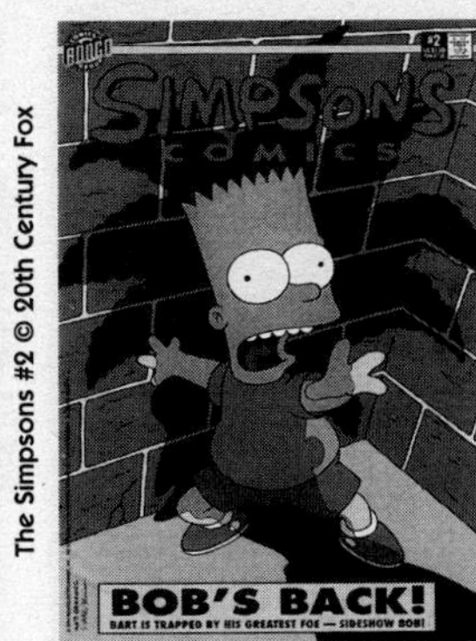

The Simpsons #2 © 20th Century Fox

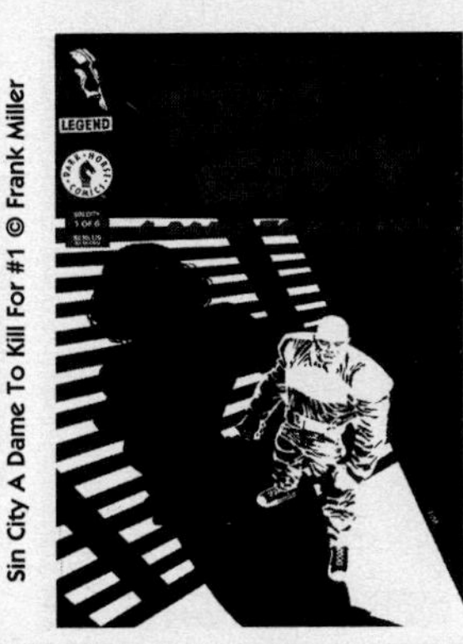

Sin City A Dame To Kill For #1 © Frank Miller

GD25 FN65 NM94

48-Last Starlin scripts (also #50) .80 1.90
50-($1.50, 52 pgs.)-Embossed & silver foil-c; Silver Surfer has brief battle w/Thanos; story cont'd in Infinity Gauntlet #1 1.10 3.00 6.50
50-2nd & 3rd printings .90 2.25
51-53: Infinity Gauntlet x-over 1.00 2.50
54-57: Infinity Gauntlet x-overs. 54-Rhino app. 55,56-Thanos-c & app. 57-Thanos-c & cameo .80 2.00
58,59-Infinity Guantlet x-overs; 58-Ron Lim-c only. 59-Thanos battles Silver Surfer-c/story; Thanos joins 1.30 3.25
60-66: 61-Last $1.00-c. 63-Capt. Marvel app. 1.50
67-69-Infinity War x-overs .80 2.00
70-74,76-81,83-91: 76-78-Jack of Hearts-c/s. 83-85-Infinity Crusade x-over; 83,84-Thanos cameo. 85-Storm, Wonder Man x-over. 86-Thor-c/s. 87-Dr. Strange & Warlock app. 88-Thanos-c/s .60 1.25
75-($2.50, 52 pgs.)-Embossed foil-c; Lim-c/a .70 1.75 3.50
82-($1.75, 52 pgs.) .35 .90 1.75
92-103: 92-Begin $1.50-c; bound-in card sheet. 95-FF app. 96-Hulk & FF app. 97-Terrax & Nova app. 1.50
Annual 1 (1988, $1.75)-Evolutionary War app.; 1st Ron Lim-a on Silver Surfer (20 pg. back-up story & pin-ups) 1.00 2.50 6.00
Annual 2-4 (1989-91, $2.00, 68 pgs.): 2-Atlantis Attacks. 4-3 pg. origin story; Silver Surfer battles Guardians of the Galaxy 1.00 2.50
Annual 5 (1992, $2.25, 68 pgs.)-Return of the Defenders, part 3; Lim-c/a (3 pgs. of pin-ups only) 1.00 2.50
Annual 6 (1993, $2.95, 68 pgs.)-Polybagged w/trading card; 1st app. Legacy; card is by Lim/Austin 1.20 3.00
Annual 7 (1994, $2.95) 1.20 3.00
Graphic Novel (Hardcover, $14.95) 2.10 6.00 15.00
Graphic Novel (The Enslavers, $16.95) 2.40 7.00 17.00
...: The First Coming of Galactus nn (11/92, $5.95, 68 pgs.)-Reprints Fantastic Four #48-50 with new Lim-c 1.00 2.50 6.00
NOTE: ***Austin** c(i)-71, 73, 74, 76, 79. **Cully Hamner** a-83p. **Ron Lim** a(p)-15-31, 33-38, 40-55, (56, 57-part-p), 60-65, 73-82; c(p)-15-31, 32-38, 40-84, 86-92, Annual 5, 6. **M. Rogers** a-1-10, 12, 19, 21; c-1-12, 21.*

SILVER SURFER, THE
Dec, 1988 - No. 2, Jan, 1989 ($1.00, limited series)
Epic Comics (Marvel)
1,2: By Stan Lee (scripts) & Moebius (art) 1.00 2.50

SILVER SURFER VS. DRACULA
Feb, 1994 ($1.75, one-shot)
Marvel Comics
1-r/Tomb of Dracula #50; Everett Vampire-r/Venus #19; Howard the Duck back-up by Brunner; Lim-c(p) .70 1.75

SILVER SURFER/WARLOCK: RESURRECTION
Mar, 1993 - No. 4, June, 1993 ($2.50, mini-series)
Marvel Comics
1-4: Starlin-c/a & scripts 1.00 2.50

SILVERTIP (Max Brand)
No. 491, Aug, 1953 - No. 898, May, 1958
Dell Publishing Co.
4-Color 491 (#1) 10.00 30.00 60.00
4-Color 572,608,637,667,731,789,898-Kinstler-a; all painted-c 5.35 16.00 32.00
4-Color 835 4.70 14.00 28.00

SIMPSONS COMICS (See Bartman, Itchy & Scratchy & Radioactive Man)
1993 - Present ($1.95, color)
Bongo Comics Group
1-($2.25)-FF#1-c swipe; pull-out poster; flip book 1.10 2.75
2,3-($1.95): 2-Patty & Selma on flip side. 3-Krusty, Agent of K.L.O.W.N. flip-c/story .80 2.00
4-($2.25)-Infinity-c; flip-c of Busman #1; w/trading card .90 2.25
5-Wraparound-c w/trading card .90 2.25

SIMPSONS COMICS AND STORIES
1993 ($2.95, color, one-shot)
Welsh Publishing Group
1-(Direct Sale)-Polybagged w/Bartman poster 1.20 3.00
1-(Newsstand Edition)-Without poster 1.20 3.00

SIMULATORS, THE (Neatly Chiseled Features)(Value: cover or less)

SINBAD, JR (TV Cartoon)
Sept-Nov, 1965 - No. 3, May, 1966
Dell Publishing Co.
1 3.00 7.50 15.00
2,3 2.00 5.00 10.00

SINDBAD (See Capt. Sindbad under Movie Comics, and Fantastic Voyages of Sindbad)

SIN CITY: A DAME TO KILL FOR (See Dark Horse Presents)
Nov, 1993 - No. 6, May, 1994 ($2.95, B&W, limited series)
Dark Horse Comics (Legend imprint)
1-6: Frank Miller-c/a/scripts & lettering 1.20 3.00

SINGING GUNS (See Fawcett Movie Comics)

SINGLE SERIES (Comics on Parade #30 on)(Also see John Hix...)
1938 - No. 28, 1942 (All 68 pgs.)
United Features Syndicate
1-Captain and the Kids (#1) 71.00 215.00 500.00
2-Broncho Bill (1939) (#1) 38.00 114.00 265.00
3-Ella Cinders (1939) 32.00 96.00 225.00
4-Li'l Abner (1939) (#1) 57.00 170.00 400.00
5-Fritzi Ritz (#1) 24.00 72.00 165.00
6-Jim Hardy by Dick Moores (#1) 31.00 94.00 220.00
7-Frankie Doodle 24.00 72.00 165.00
8-Peter Pat (On sale 7/14/39) 24.00 72.00 165.00
9-Strange As It Seems 24.00 72.00 165.00
10-Little Mary Mixup 24.00 72.00 165.00
11-Mr. and Mrs. Beans 24.00 72.00 165.00
12-Joe Jinks 22.00 65.00 150.00
13-Looy Dot Dope 22.00 65.00 150.00
14-Billy Make Believe 22.00 65.00 150.00
15-How It Began (1939) 24.00 72.00 165.00
16-Illustrated Gags (1940)-Has ad for Captain and the Kids #1 reprint listed below 12.00 36.00 85.00
17-Danny Dingle 17.00 52.00 120.00
18-Li'l Abner (#2 on-c) 50.00 150.00 350.00
19-Broncho Bill (#2 on-c) 31.00 94.00 220.00
20-Tarzan by Hal Foster 100.00 300.00 700.00
21-Ella Cinders (#2 on-c; on sale 3/19/40) 28.00 84.00 195.00
22-Iron Vic 23.00 70.00 160.00
23-Tailspin Tommy by Hal Forrest (#1) 26.00 78.00 180.00
24-Alice in Wonderland (#1) 34.00 103.00 240.00
25-Abbie and Slats 27.00 81.00 190.00
26-Little Mary Mixup (#2 on-c, 1940) 24.00 72.00 165.00
27-Jim Hardy by Dick Moores (1942) 24.00 73.00 170.00
28-Ella Cinders and Abbie and Slats (1942) 24.00 72.00 165.00
1-Captain and the Kids (1939 reprint)-2nd Edition 39.00 118.00 275.00
1-Fritzi Ritz (1939 reprint)-2nd edition 19.00 57.00 130.00
NOTE: *Some issues given away at the 1939-40 New York World's Fair (#6).*

SINISTER HOUSE OF SECRET LOVE, THE (Becomes Secrets of Sinister House No. 5 on)
Oct-Nov, 1971 - No. 4, Apr-May, 1972 (52 pgs.)
National Periodical Publications
1 1.30 3.25
2-4: 2-Jeff Jones-c. 3-Toth-a (36 pgs.) 1.10 2.75

SIR CHARLES BARKLEY AND THE REFEREE MURDERS
1993 ($9.95, color, 8-1/2" x 11", 52 pgs.)
Hamilton Comics
nn-Photo-c; Sports fantasy comic book fiction (uses real names of NBA super stars). Scipt by Alan Dean Foster, art by Joe Stanton. Comes with bound-in

Six From Sirius #1 © MEG

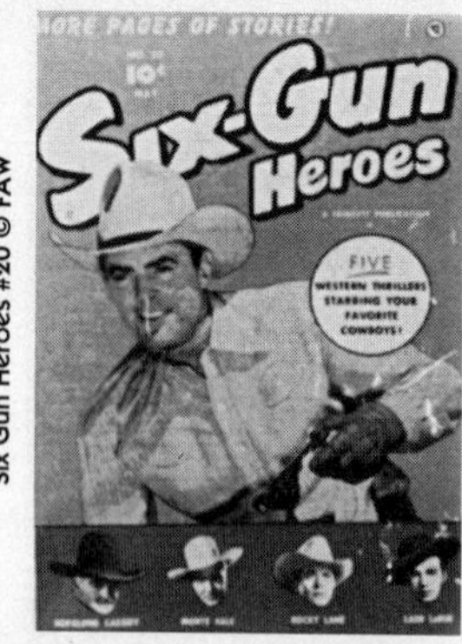

Six Gun Heroes #20 © FAW

Skull The Slayer #3 © MEG

GD25 FN65 NM94

sheet of 35 gummed "Moods of Charles Barkley" stamps. Photo/story on Barkley 2.00 5.00 10.00
Special Edition of 100 copies for charity signed on an affixed book plate by Barkley, Foster & Stanton 150.00
Ashcan edition given away to dealers, distributors & promoters (low distribution). Four pages in color, balance of story in b&w 3.00 9.00 20.00

SIR LANCELOT (See 4-Color #606, 775)

SIR WALTER RALEIGH (See 4-Color #644)

SISTERHOOD OF STEEL (Marvel)(Value: cover or less)

6 BLACK HORSES (See Movie Classics)

SIX FROM SIRIUS (Marvel, series I & II)(Value: cover or less)

SIX-GUN HEROES
March, 1950 - No. 23, Nov, 1953 (Photo-c #1-23)
Fawcett Publications

1-Rocky Lane, Hopalong Cassidy, Smiley Burnette begin (same date as Smiley Burnette #1) 39.00 120.00 275.00
2 22.00 65.00 150.00
3-5 13.50 41.00 95.00
6-15: 6-Lash LaRue begins 10.00 30.00 75.00
16-22: 17-Last Smiley Burnette. 18-Monte Hale begins 10.00 30.00 65.00
23-Last Fawcett issue 10.00 30.00 70.00

NOTE: *Hopalong Cassidy photo c-1-3. Monte Hale photo c-18. Rocky Lane photo c-4, 5, 7, 9, 11, 13, 15, 17, 20, 21, 23. Lash LaRue photo c-6, 8, 10, 12, 14, 16, 19, 22.*

SIX-GUN HEROES (Continued from Fawcett; Gunmasters #84 on)
No. 24, Jan, 1954 - No. 83, Mar-Apr, 1965 (All Vol. 4)(See Blue Bird)
Charlton Comics

24-Lash LaRue, Hopalong Cassidy, Rocky Lane & Tex Ritter begin; photo-c 14.00 43.00 100.00
25 8.35 25.00 50.00
26-30: 26-Rod Cameron story. 28-Tom Mix begins? 6.70 20.00 40.00
31-40: 38-Jingles & Wild Bill Hickok (TV) 5.35 16.00 32.00
41-46,48,50 5.00 15.00 30.00
47-Williamson-a, 2 pgs; Torres-a 5.85 17.50 35.00
49-Williamson-a (5 pgs.) 5.85 17.50 35.00
51-56,58-60: 58-Gunmaster app. 4.00 10.00 20.00
57-Origin & 1st app. Gunmaster 4.20 12.50 25.00
61-70: 62-Origin Gunmaster 2.80 7.00 14.00
71-83: 76-Gunmaster begins 2.40 6.00 12.00

SIXGUN RANCH (See 4-Color #580)

SIX-GUN WESTERN
Jan, 1957 - No. 4, July, 1957
Atlas Comics (CDS)

1-Crandall-a; two Williamson text illos 13.00 40.00 90.00
2,3-Williamson-a in both 10.00 30.00 70.00
4-Woodbridge-a 6.70 20.00 40.00

NOTE: ***Ayers** a-2, 3. **Maneely** a-1; c-2, 3. **Orlando** a-2. **Pakula** a-2. **Powell** a-3. **Romita** a-1, 4. **Severin** c-1, 4. **Shores** a-2.*

SIX MILLION DOLLAR MAN, THE (TV)
6/76 - No. 4, 12/76; No. 5, 10/77; No. 6, 2/78 - No. 9, 6/78
Charlton Comics

1-Staton-c/a; Lee Majors photo on-c 1.20
2-9: 2-Neal Adams-c; Staton-a 1.00

SIX MILLION DOLLAR MAN, THE (TV)(Magazine)
July, 1976 - No. 7, Nov, 1977 (B&W)
Charlton Comics

1-Neal Adams-c/a 1.20
2-Neal Adams-c 1.20
3-7: 3-N. Adams part inks; Chaykin-a 1.20

666 THE MARK OF THE BEAST (Fleetway/Quality)(Value: cover or less)

SKATEMAN (Pacific)(Value: cover or less)

GD25 FN65 NM94

SKATING SKILLS
1957 (36 & 12 pgs.; 5x7", two versions) (10¢)
Custom Comics, Inc./Chicago Roller Skates

nn-Resembles old ACG cover plus interior art 1.00 2.50 5.00

SKEEZIX (Also see Gasoline Alley)
1925 - 1928 (Strip reprints) (soft covers) (pictures & text)
Reilly & Lee Co.

...and Uncle Walt (1924)-Origin 12.00 36.00 120.00
...and Pal (1925) 10.00 30.00 100.00
...at the Circus (1926) 10.00 30.00 100.00
...& Uncle Walt (1927) 10.00 30.00 100.00
...Out West (1928) 10.00 30.00 100.00
Hardback Editions... 16.00 48.00 160.00

SKELETON HAND (...In Secrets of the Supernatural)
Sept-Oct, 1952 - No. 6, July-Aug, 1953
American Comics Group (B&M Dist. Co.)

1 26.00 78.00 180.00
2 17.00 52.00 120.00
3-6 14.00 43.00 100.00

SKIN GRAFT: THE ADVENTURES OF A TATTOOED MAN
July, 1993 - No. 4, Oct, 1993 ($2.50, mini-series, adult)
DC Comics (Vertigo)

1-4 1.00 2.50

SKI PARTY (See Movie Classics)

SKIPPY
Circa 1920s (10x8", 16 pgs., color/B&W cartoons)
No publisher listed

nn-By Percy Crosby 67.00 200.00 465.00

SKIPPY'S OWN BOOK OF COMICS (See Popular Comics)
1934 (52 pgs.) (Giveaway)(Strip reprints)
No publisher listed

	GD25	FN65	VF82	NM94
nn-(Rare)-By Percy Crosby	500.00	1500.00	3250.00	5000.00

(Estimated up to 40 total copies exist, 2 in NM/Mint)

Published by Max C. Gaines for Phillip's Dental Magnesia to be advertised on the Skippy Radio Show and given away with the purchase of a tube of Phillip's Tooth Paste. This is the first four-color comic book of reprints about one character.

SKREEMER (DC)(Value: cover or less)

SKULL & BONES
1992 - No. 3, 1992 ($4.95, mini-series, 52 pgs.)
DC Comics

	GD25	FN65	NM94
Book 1-3: 1-1st app.	1.00	2.00	5.00

SKULL, THE SLAYER
August, 1975 - No. 8, Nov, 1976 (All 20¢/25¢ issues)
Marvel Comics Group

1-Origin & 1st app.; Gil Kane-c .70 1.70
2-8: 2-Gil Kane-c. 8-Kirby-c 1.20

SKY BLAZERS (CBS Radio)
Sept, 1940 - No. 2, Nov, 1940
Hawley Publications

1-Sky Pirates, Ace Archer, Flying Aces begin 33.00 100.00 230.00
2 27.00 81.00 190.00

SKY GAL (AC Comics)(Value: cover or less)

SKY KING "RUNAWAY TRAIN" (TV)
1964 (16 pgs.) (regular size)
National Biscuit Co.

nn 3.60 9.00 18.00

SKYMAN (See Big Shot Comics & Sparky Watts)
Fall?, 1941 - No. 2, 1941; No. 3, 1948 - No. 4, 1948
Columbia Comics Group

Sleepwalker #2 © MEG

Sludge #7 © Malibu

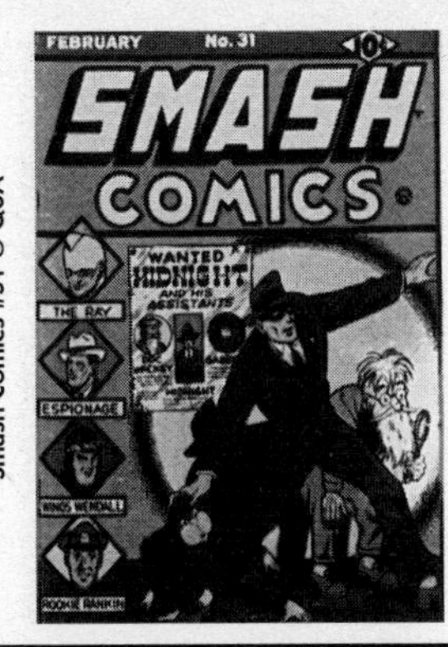

Smash Comics #31 © QUA

GD25 FN65 NM94

1-Origin Skyman, The Face, Sparky Watts app.; Whitney-c/a; 3rd story-r from Big Shot #1; Whitney c-1-4 61.00 182.00 425.00
2 (1941)-Yankee Doodle 34.00 103.00 240.00
3,4 (1948) 23.00 70.00 160.00

SKY PILOT
No. 10, 1950(nd) - No. 11, Apr-May, 1951 (Saunders painted-c)
Ziff-Davis Publ. Co.
10,11-Frank Borth-a 10.00 30.00 60.00

SKY RANGER (See Johnny Law...)

SKYROCKET
1944
Harry 'A' Chesler
nn-Alias the Dragon, Dr. Vampire, Skyrocket & The Desperado app. 18.00 54.00 125.00

SKY SHERIFF (Breeze Lawson...) (Also see Exposed & Outlaws)
Summer, 1948
D. S. Publishing Co.
1-Edmond Good-c/a 9.15 27.50 55.00

SKY WOLF (Eclipse Comics)(Value: cover or less)(Also see Airboy)

SLACKER COMICS
Aug, 1994 - Present ($2.95, B&W, quarterly)
Slave Labor Graphics
1 1.20 3.00

SLAINE, THE BERSERKER (Quality)(Value: cover or less)

SLAM BANG COMICS (Western Desperado #8)
March, 1940 - No. 7, Sept, 1940 (Combined with Master Comics #7)
Fawcett Publications
1-Diamond Jack, Mark Swift & The Time Retarder, Lee Granger, Jungle King begin & continue in Master 107.00 321.00 750.00
2 50.00 150.00 350.00
3-Classic-c 64.00 193.00 450.00
4-7: 6-Intro Zoro, the Mystery Man (also in #7). 7-Bondage-c 46.00 140.00 325.00

SLAM BANG COMICS
No. 9, No date
Post Cereal Giveaway
9-Dynamic Man, Echo, Mr. E, Yankee Boy app. 3.60 9.00 18.00

SLAPSTICK
Nov, 1992 - No. 4, Feb, 1993 ($1.25, mini-series)
Marvel Comics
1-4: Fry/Austin-c/a. 4-Ghost Rider, D.D., F.F. app. 1.25

SLAPSTICK COMICS
nd (1946?) (36 pgs.)
Comic Magazines Distributors
nn-Firetop feature; Post-a(2) 14.00 43.00 100.00

SLASH-D DOUBLECROSS
1950 (132 pgs.) (pocket size)
St. John Publishing Co.
nn-Western comics 14.00 43.00 100.00

SLASH MARAUD (DC)(Value: cover or less)

SLAUGHTERMAN (Comico)(Value: cover or less)

SLAVE GIRL COMICS (See Malu... & White Princess of the Jungle #2)
Feb, 1949 - No. 2, Apr, 1949 (52 pgs.)
Avon Periodicals/Eternity Comics (1989)
1-Larsen-c/a 57.00 171.00 400.00
2-Larsen-a 45.00 135.00 315.00
1 (3/89, $2.25, B&W, 44 pgs., Eternity)-r/#1 .90 2.25

SLEDGE HAMMER (TV)(Marvel)(Value: cover or less)

GD25 FN65 NM94

SLEEPING BEAUTY (See Dell Giants, 4-Color #973, 984 & Movie Comics)

SLEEPWALKER
June, 1991 - No. 33, Feb, 1994 ($1.00/$1.25)
Marvel Comics
1-1st app. Sleepwalker 1.50
2-5: 4-Williamson-i. 5-Spider-Man-c/story 1.50
6-10: 7-Infinity Gauntlet x-over. 8-Vs. Deathlok-c/story 1.50
11-18,20-24,26-33: 11-Ghost Rider-c/story. 12-Quesada-c/a(p) 14-Intro Spectra. 15-F.F.-c/story. 17-Darkhawk & Spider-Man x-over. 18-Infinity War x-over; Quesada/Williamson-c. 20,21-Sam Kieth-c. 21,22-Hobgoblin app. 1.25
19-($2.00)-Die-cut Sleepwalker mask cover .80 2.00
25-($2.95, 52 pgs.)-Holo-grafx foil-c; origin 1.20 3.00
Holiday Special 1 (1/93, $2.00, 52 pgs.)-Quesada-c(p) .80 2.00

SLEEZE BROTHERS, THE (Marvel)(Value: cover or less)

SLICK CHICK COMICS
1947(nd) - No. 3, 1947(nd)
Leader Enterprises
1-Teenage humor 9.15 27.50 55.00
2,3 6.70 20.00 40.00

SLIMER! (TV) (Now)(Value: cover or less)

SLIM MORGAN (See Wisco)

SLUDGE
Oct, 1993 - Present ($1.95, color)
Malibu Comics (Ultraverse)
1-($2.50, 48 pgs.)-Intro/1st app. Sludge; Rune flip-c/story Pt. 1(1st app., 3 pgs.) by Barry Smith; The Night Man app. (3 pg. preview); The Mighty Magnor 1 pg strip begins by Aragones (cont. in other titles) 1.00 2.50
1-Ultra 5000 Limited silver foil 2.10 6.40 15.00
2-11: 3-Break-Thru x-over. 4-2 pg. Mantra origin. 8-Bloodstorm app. .80 2.00

SLUGGER (Little Wise Guys Starring...)
April, 1956
Lev Gleason Publications
1-Biro-c 4.20 12.50 25.00

SMASH COMICS (Becomes Lady Luck #86 on)
Aug, 1939 - No. 85, Oct, 1949
Quality Comics Group
1-Origin Hugh Hazard & His Iron Man, Bozo the Robot, Espionage, Starring Black X by Eisner, & Hooded Justice (Invisible Justice #2 on); Chic Carter & Wings Wendall begin; 1st Robot on the cover of a comic book (Bozo) 143.00 430.00 1000.00
2-The Lone Star Rider app; Invisible Hood gains power of invisibility 57.00 171.00 400.00
3-Captain Cook & Eisner's John Law begin 36.00 107.00 275.00
4,5: 4-Flash Fulton begins 30.00 90.00 250.00
6-12: 12-One pg. Fine-a 31.00 92.00 215.00
13-Magno begins (8/40); last Eisner issue; The Ray app. in full page ad; The Purple Trio begins 32.00 96.00 225.00
14-Intro. The Ray (9/40) by Lou Fine & others 157.00 471.00 1100.00
15,16: 16-The Scarlet Seal begins 76.00 230.00 535.00
17-Wun Cloo becomes plastic super-hero by Jack Cole (9-months before Plastic Man) 76.00 230.00 535.00
18-Midnight by Jack Cole begins (origin & 1st app., 1/41) 89.00 268.00 625.00
19-22: Last Fine Ray; The Jester begins-#22 55.00 165.00 385.00
23,24: 24-The Sword app.; last Chic Carter; Wings Wendall dons new costume #24,25 46.00 137.00 320.00
25-Origin/1st app. Wildfire; Rookie Rankin begins 55.00 165.00 385.00
26-30: 28-Midnight-c begin, end #85 43.00 130.00 300.00
31,32,34: Ray by Rudy Palais; also #33 34.00 100.00 235.00
33-Origin The Marksman 43.00 130.00 300.00

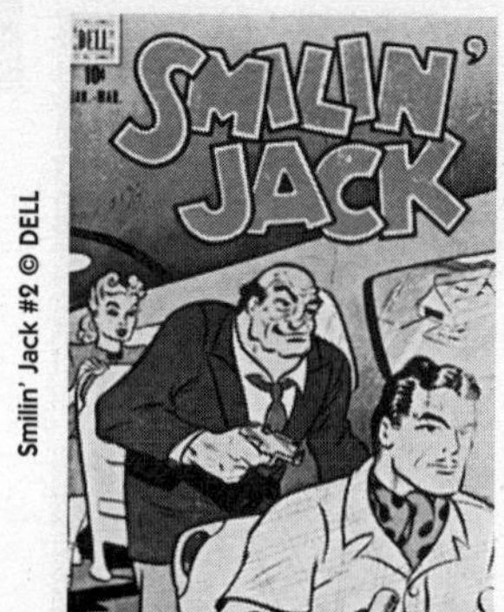

Smilin' Jack #2 © DELL

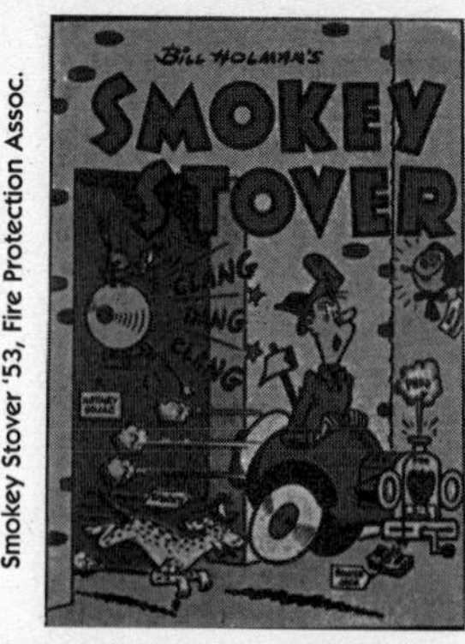

Smokey Stover '53, Fire Protection Assoc.

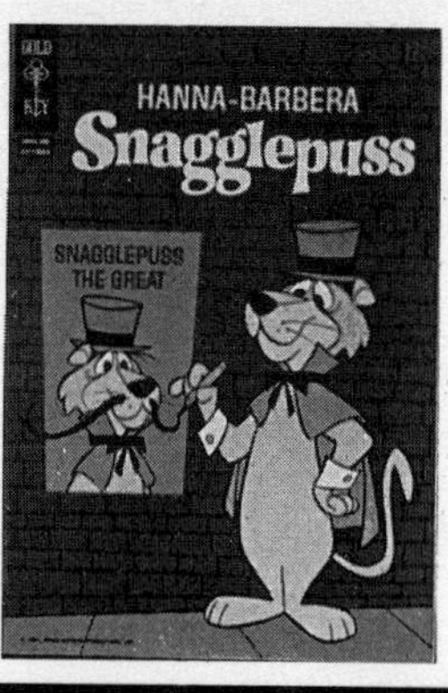

Snagglepuss #4 © H-B

	GD25	FN65	NM94
35-37	34.00	100.00	235.00
38-The Yankee Eagle begins; last Midnight by Jack Cole	34.00	100.00	235.00
39,40-Last Ray issue	30.00	90.00	210.00
41,43-50	15.00	45.00	105.00
42-Lady Luck begins by Klaus Nordling	18.00	54.00	125.00
51-60	12.00	36.00	85.00
61-70	11.00	32.00	75.00
71-85: 79-Midnight battles the Men from Mars-c/s	10.00	30.00	70.00

NOTE: ***Al Bryant*** *c-54, 63-68.* ***Cole*** *a-17-38, 68, 69, 72, 73, 78, 80, 83, 85; c-38, 60-62, 69-84.* ***Crandall*** *a-(Ray)-23-29, 35-38; c-36, 39, 40, 42-44, 46.* ***Fine*** *a(Ray)-14, 15, 16(w/**Tuska**), 17-22.* ***Fox*** *c-24-35.* ***Fuje*** *Ray-30.* ***Gil Fox*** *a-6-7, 9, 11-13.* ***Guardineer*** *a-(The Marksman)-39-?, 49, 52.* ***Gustavson*** *a-4-7, 9, 11-13 (The Jester)-22-46; (Magno)-13-21; (Midnight)-39(Cole inks), 49, 52, 63-65.* ***Kotzky*** *a-(Espionage)-33-38; c-45, 47-53.* ***Nordling*** *a-49, 52, 63-65.* ***Powell*** *a-11, 12, (Abdul the Arab)-13-24.Black X c-2, 6, 9, 11, 13, 16. Bozo the Robot c-1, 3, 5, 8, 10, 12, 14, 18, 20, 22, 24, 26. Midnight c-28-85. The Ray c-15, 17, 19, 21, 23, 25, 27. Wings Wendall c-4, 7.*

SMASH HIT SPORTS COMICS
V2#1, Jan, 1949
Essankay Publications

	GD25	FN65	NM94
V2#1-L.B. Cole-c/a	16.00	48.00	110.00

S'MATTER POP?
1917 (44 pgs.; B&W; 10x14"; cardboard covers)
Saalfield Publ. Co.

	GD25	FN65	NM94
nn-By Charlie Payne; in full color; pages printed on one side	27.00	81.00	190.00

SMILE COMICS (Also see Gay Comics, Tickle, & Whee)
1955 (52 pgs.; 5x7-1/4") (7¢)
Modern Store Publ.

	GD25	FN65	NM94
1	.60	1.50	3.00

SMILEY BURNETTE WESTERN (Also see Patches #8 & Six-Gun Heroes)
March, 1950 - No. 4, Oct, 1950 (All photo front & back-c)
Fawcett Publications

	GD25	FN65	NM94
1-Red Eagle begins	39.00	116.00	270.00
2-4	26.00	78.00	180.00

SMILIN' JACK (See Famous Feature Stories, Popular Comics, Super Book #1, 2, 7, 19 & Super Comics)
No. 5, 1940 - No. 8, Oct-Dec, 1949
Dell Publishing Co.

	GD25	FN65	NM94
4-Color 5	63.00	190.00	440.00
4-Color 10 (1940)	57.00	170.00	400.00
Large Feature Comic 12,14,25 (1941)	40.00	120.00	400.00
4-Color 4 (1942)	47.00	141.00	330.00
4-Color 14 (1943)	37.00	111.00	260.00
4-Color 36,58 (1943-44)	24.00	72.00	165.00
4-Color 80 (1945)	17.00	52.00	120.00
4-Color 149 (1947)	11.50	34.00	80.00
1 (1-3/48)	11.50	34.00	80.00
2	6.70	20.00	40.00
3-8 (10-12/49)	4.70	14.00	28.00
Popped Wheat Giveaway (1947)-1938 strip reprints; 16 pgs. in full color	.95	2.40	4.80
Shoe Store Giveaway-1938 strip reprints; 16 pgs.	4.00	11.00	22.00
Sparked Wheat Giveaway (1942)-16 pgs. in full color	4.00	11.00	22.00

SMILING SPOOK SPUNKY (See Spunky)

SMITTY (See Treasure Box of Famous Comics)
1928 - 1933 (B&W newspaper strip reprints)
(cardboard covers; 9-1/2x9-1/2", 52 pgs.; 7x8-1/4", 36 pgs.)
Cupples & Leon Co.

	GD25	FN65	NM94
1928-(96 pgs. 7x8-3/4")	17.00	50.00	120.00
1928-(Softcover, 36 pgs., nn)	18.00	54.00	125.00
1929-At the Ball Game, 1930-The Flying Office Boy, 1931-The Jockey, 1932-In the North Woods each...	12.00	36.00	85.00
1933-At Military School	12.00	36.00	85.00
Mid-1930s issue-(36 pgs.; 7x8-3/4")-Reprint of 1928 Treasure Box issue	10.00	30.00	70.00
Hardback Editions-(100 pgs., 7x8-1/4")-With dust jacket each...	24.00	73.00	170.00

SMITTY (See Popular Comics, Super Book #2, 4 & Super Comics)
No. 11, 1940 - No. 7, Aug-Oct, 1949; No. 909, Apr, 1958
Dell Publishing Co.

	GD25	FN65	NM94
4-Color 11 (1940)	38.00	115.00	265.00
Large Feature Comic 26 (1941)	20.00	60.00	200.00
4-Color 6 (1942)	22.00	65.00	150.00
4-Color 32 (1943)	17.00	52.00	120.00
4-Color 65 (1945)	13.00	40.00	90.00
4-Color 99 (1946)	11.50	34.00	80.00
4-Color 138 (1947)	10.00	30.00	65.00
1 (2-4/48)	10.00	30.00	65.00
2-(5-7/48)	5.35	16.00	32.00
3,4: 3-(8-10/48), 4-(11-1/48-49)	4.00	11.00	22.00
5-7, 4-Color 909 (4/58)	3.60	9.00	18.00

SMOKEY BEAR (TV) (See March Of Comics #234, 362, 372, 383, 407)
Feb, 1970 - No. 13, Mar, 1973
Gold Key

	GD25	FN65	NM94
1	1.00	2.50	6.00
2-13		1.20	3.00

SMOKEY STOVER (See Popular Comics, Super Book #5, 17, 29 & Super Comics)
No. 7, 1942 - No. 827, Aug, 1957
Dell Publishing Co.

	GD25	FN65	NM94
4-Color 7 (1942)-Reprints	34.00	103.00	240.00
4-Color 35 (1943)	17.00	52.00	120.00
4-Color 64 (1944)	13.00	40.00	90.00
4-Color 229 (1949)	5.35	16.00	32.00
4-Color 730,827	4.00	10.00	20.00
General Motors giveaway (1953)	4.35	13.00	26.00
National Fire Protection giveaway(1953 & 1954)-16 pgs., paper-c	4.35	13.00	26.00

SMOKEY THE BEAR (See Forest Fire for 1st app.)
No. 653, 10/55 - No. 1214, 8/61 (See March of Comics #234)
Dell Publishing Co.

	GD25	FN65	NM94
4-Color 653 (#1)	10.00	30.00	60.00
4-Color 708,754,818,932	5.00	15.00	30.00
4-Color 1016,1119,1214	4.00	11.00	22.00
True Story of..., The('59)-U.S. Forest Service giveaway-Publ. by Western Printing Co. (reprinted in 1964 & 1969)-Reprints 1st 16 pgs. of 4-Color 932	2.80	7.00	14.00

SMOKY (See Movie Classics)

SMURFS (TV)(Marvel)(Value: cover or less)

SNAFU (Magazine)
Nov, 1955 - V2#2, Mar, 1956 (B&W)
Atlas Comics (RCM)

	GD25	FN65	NM94
V1#1-Heath/Severin-a; Everett, Maneely-a	10.00	30.00	60.00
V2#1,2-Severin-a	8.35	25.00	50.00

SNAGGLEPUSS (TV)(See Hanna-Barbera Band Wagon #3, Quick-Draw McGraw & Spotlight #4)
Oct, 1962 - No. 4, Sept, 1963 (Hanna-Barbera)
Gold Key

	GD25	FN65	NM94
1	9.20	27.50	55.00
2-4	5.80	17.50	35.00

SNAP (Formerly Scoop #8; becomes Jest #10,11 & Komik Pages #10)
No. 9, 1944
Harry 'A' Chesler

	GD25	FN65	NM94
9-Manhunter, The Voice	11.50	34.00	80.00

Solor #33 © Voyager Comm.

Solitaire #5 © Malibu

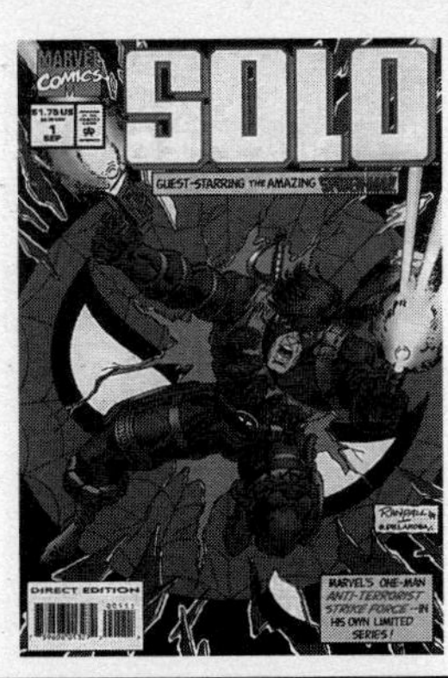

Solo #1 © MEG

SNAPPY COMICS
1945
Cima Publ. Co. (Prize Publ.)

	GD25	FN65	NM94
1-Airmale app.; 9 pg. Sorcerer's Apprentice adapt; Kiefer-a	17.00	52.00	120.00

SNARKY PARKER (See Life With...)

SNIFFY THE PUP
No. 5, Nov, 1949 - No. 18, Sept, 1953
Standard Publications (Animated Cartoons)

	GD25	FN65	NM94
5-Two Frazetta text illos	8.35	25.00	50.00
6-10	3.60	9.00	18.00
11-18	2.80	7.00	14.00

SNOOPER AND BLABBER DETECTIVES (TV) (See Whitman Comic Books)
Nov, 1962 - No. 3, May, 1963 (Hanna-Barbera)
Gold Key

	GD25	FN65	NM94
1	9.20	27.50	55.00
2,3	6.70	20.00	40.00

SNOW FOR CHRISTMAS
1957 (16 pgs.) (Giveaway)
W. T. Grant Co.

	GD25	FN65	NM94
nn	3.00	7.50	15.00

SNOW WHITE (See Christmas With..., 4-Color #49, 227, 382, Mickey Mouse Magazine, & Movie Comics)

SNOW WHITE AND THE SEVEN DWARFS
1952 (32 pgs.; 5x7-1/4", soft-c) (Disney)
Bendix Washing Machines

	GD25	FN65	NM94
nn	11.00	32.00	75.00

SNOW WHITE AND THE SEVEN DWARFS
1957 (Small size)
Promotional Publ. Co.

	GD25	FN65	NM94
nn	4.00	10.50	21.00

SNOW WHITE AND THE SEVEN DWARFS
1958 (16 pgs, 5x7-1/4", soft-c) (Disney premium)
Western Printing Co.

	GD25	FN65	NM94
nn- "Mystery of the Missing Magic"	6.70	20.00	40.00

SNOW WHITE AND THE SEVEN DWARFS
April, 1982 (60¢)
Whitman Publications

	GD25	FN65	NM94
nn-r/Four Color #49		1.20	3.00

SNOW WHITE AND THE SEVEN DWARFS GOLDEN ANNIVERSARY
Fall, 1987 ($2.95, magazine size, 52 pgs.)
Gladstone Publishing

	GD25	FN65	NM94
1-Contains poster	1.30	3.25	8.00

SNOW WHITE AND THE 7 DWARFS IN "MILKY WAY"
1955 (16 pgs., soft-c, 5x7-1/4") (Disney premium)
American Dairy Association

	GD25	FN65	NM94
nn	11.00	32.00	75.00

SOAP OPERA LOVE
Feb, 1983 - No. 3, June, 1983
Charlton Comics

	GD25	FN65	NM94
1-3			1.00

SOAP OPERA ROMANCES
July, 1982 - No. 5, March, 1983
Charlton Comics

	GD25	FN65	NM94
1-5-Nurse Betsy Crane-r			1.00

SOJOURN ($1.50)
Sept, 1977 - No. 2, 1978 (Full tabloid size) (Color & B&W)
White Cliffs Publ. Co.

	GD25	FN65	NM94
1-Tor by Kubert, Eagle by Severin, E. V. Race, Private Investigator by Doug Wildey, T. C. Mars by Aragones begin plus other strips		.65	1.60
2		.65	1.60

SOLAR (...Man of the Atom; also see Doctor Solar)
Sept, 1991 - Present ($1.75/$1.95, color, 44 pgs.)
Valiant

	GD25	FN65	NM94
1-Layton-i on Solar; Barry Windsor-Smith-c/a	1.90	5.60	13.00
2-Layton-i on Solar, Smith-a	1.70	4.20	10.00
3-1st app. Harada (11/91)	2.00	6.40	15.00
4	1.70	5.10	12.00
5-7: 7-vs. X-O Armor; last $1.95-c	1.70	4.20	10.00
8,9: 8-Begin $2.25-c	1.70	4.20	10.00
10-(6/92, $3.95)-1st app. Eternal Warrior (6 pgs.); black embossed-c; origin & 1st app. Geoff McHenry (Geomancer)	4.00	13.00	30.00
10-2nd printing ($3.95)		1.60	4.00
11-1st full app. Eternal Warrior	.90	2.30	5.50
12,13,15: 12,13-Unity x-overs. 15-2nd Dr. Eclipse		1.20	3.00
14-1st app. Fred Bender (becomes Dr. Eclipse)	1.70	4.20	10.00
16-40: 17-X-O Manowar app. 23-Solar splits. 29-1st Valiant Vision book. 33-Valiant Vision; bound-in trading card		.90	2.25
0-($9.95, TPB)-Alpha and Omega r/origin story; polybagged w/poster	1.70	4.00	10.00

NOTE: *#1-10 all have free 8 pg. insert "Alpha and Omega" which is a 10 chapter Solar origin story. All 10 centerfolds can pieced together to show climax of story.* ***Ditko*** *a-11p, 14p.* ***Layton*** *a-1-3i; c-2i, 11i, 17i, 25i.* ***Miller*** *c-12.* ***Quesada*** *c-17p, 20-23p, 29p.* ***Simonson*** *c-13.* ***B. Smith*** *a-1-10; c-1, 3, 5, 7, 19i.* ***Thibert*** *c-22i, 23i.*

SOLARMAN (Marvel)(Value: cover or less)

SOLDIER & MARINE COMICS (Fightin' Army #16 on)
No. 11, Dec, 1954 - No. 15, Aug, 1955; V2#9, Dec, 1956
Charlton Comics (Toby Press of Conn. V1#11)

	GD25	FN65	NM94
V1#11 (12/54)-Bob Powell-a	4.20	12.50	25.00
V1#12(2/55)-15: 12-Photo-c	3.00	7.50	15.00
V2#9(Formerly Never Again; Jerry Drummer V2#10 on)	3.00	7.50	15.00

SOLDIER COMICS
Jan, 1952 - No. 11, Sept, 1953
Fawcett Publications

	GD25	FN65	NM94
1	8.35	25.00	50.00
2	4.20	12.50	25.00
3-5	4.00	10.00	20.00
6-11: 8-Illo. in **POP**	3.20	8.00	16.00

SOLDIERS OF FORTUNE
Mar-Apr, 1951 - No. 13, Feb-Mar, 1953
American Comics Group (Creston Publ. Corp.)

	GD25	FN65	NM94
1-Capt. Crossbones by Shelly, Ace Carter, Lance Larson begin	16.00	48.00	110.00
2	10.00	30.00	65.00
3-10: 6-Bondage-c	9.15	27.50	55.00
11-13 (War format)	4.00	11.00	22.00

NOTE: ***Shelly*** *a-1-3, 5.* ***Whitney*** *a-6, 8-11, 13; c-1-3, 5, 6.*

SOLDIERS OF FREEDOM (Americomics)(Value: cover or less)

SOLITAIRE
Nov, 1993 - Present ($1.95, color)
Malibu Comics (Ultraverse)

	GD25	FN65	NM94
1-($2.50)-Collector's edition bagged w/playing card		1.00	2.50
1-12: 1-Regular edition w/o playing card. 2,4-Break-Thru x-over. 3-2 pg. origin The Night Man. 4-Gatefold-c. 5-Two pg. origin the Strangers		.80	2.00

SOLO
Sept, 1994 - Present ($1.75, limited series)
Marvel Comics

	GD25	FN65	NM94
1-4-Spider-Man app.		.70	1.75

SOLO AVENGERS (Marvel)(Value: cover or less)

The Solution #9 © Malibu

Son Of Satan #2 © MEG

Space Adventures V3 #29 © CC

GD25 FN65 NM94

SOLOMON AND SHEBA (See 4-Color #1070)

SOLOMON KANE (Marvel)(Value: cover or less)

SOLUTION, THE
Sept, 1993 - Present ($1.95, color)
Malibu Comics (Ultraverse)

1,3-13: 1-Intro Meathook, Deathdance, Black Tiger, Tech. 4-Break-Thru x-over; gatefold-c. 5-2 pg. origin The Strangers. 11-Brereton-c — .80 — 2.00
1-($2.50)-Newsstand ed. polybagged w/trading card — 1.00 — 2.50
1-Ultra 5000 Limited silver foil — 1.40 — 4.20 — 10.00
0-Obtained w/Rune #0 by sending coupons from 11 comics — 1.00 — 3.00 — 7.50
2-($2.50, 48 pgs.)-Rune flip-c/story by B. Smith; The Mighty Magnor 1 pg. strip by Aragones — 1.00 — 2.50

SOMERSET HOLMES (Pacific/Eclipse)(Value: cover or less)

SONG OF THE SOUTH (See Brer Rabbit & 4-Color #693)

SONIC DISRUPTORS (DC)(Value: cover or less)

SONIC HEDGEHOG (TV, video game)
Feb, 1993 - No. 3, May, 1993 ($1.25, mini-series)
July, 1993 - Present ($1.25)
Archie Comics

0(2/93),1-3: Shaw-a(p) & covers — 1.25
1-11: 8-Neon ink-c — 1.25

SONIC THE HEDGEHOG (Archie)(Value: cover or less)

SON OF AMBUSH BUG (DC)(Value: cover or less)

SON OF BLACK BEAUTY (See 4-Color #510, 566)

SON OF CELLULOID (Eclipse)(Value: cover or less)

SON OF FLUBBER (See Movie Comics)

SON OF MUTANT WORLD (Fantagor)(Value: cover or less)

SON OF SATAN (Also see Ghost Rider #1 & Marvel Spotlight #12)
Dec, 1975 - No. 8, Feb, 1977 (All 25$ issues)
Marvel Comics Group

1-Mooney-a; Kane-c(p), Starlin splash(p) — 1.50 — 3.80 — 9.00
2-8: 2-Origin The Possessor. 5-Russell-p. 8-Heath-a — 1.00 — 2.00 — 5.00

SON OF SINBAD (Also see Abbott & Costello & Daring Adventures)
February, 1950
St. John Publishing Co.

1-Kubert-c/a — 30.00 — 90.00 — 210.00

SON OF TOMAHAWK (See Tomahawk)

SON OF VULCAN (Formerly Mysteries of Unexplored Worlds #1-48; Thunderbolt V3#51 on)
V2#49, Nov, 1965 - V2#50, Jan, 1966
Charlton Comics

V2#49,50: 50-Roy Thomas scripts (1st pro work) — 2.00 — 5.00 — 12.00

SON OF YUPPIES FROM HELL (Marvel)(Value: cover or less)(See Yuppies From Hell)

SONS OF KATIE ELDER (See Movie Classics)

SORCERY (See Chilling Adventures in... & Red Circle...)

SORORITY SECRETS
July, 1954
Toby Press

1 — 5.35 — 16.00 — 32.00

SOULQUEST (Innovation)(Value: cover or less)

SOUPY SALES COMIC BOOK (TV)(The Official...)
1965
Archie Publications

1 — 10.00 — 30.00 — 70.00

SOUTHERN KNIGHTS, THE (See Crusaders #1)

GD25 FN65 NM94

1983 - No. 34? (B&W)
Guild Publ/Fictioneer Books

2-Magazine size — 1.50
3-34 — 1.50
Dread Halloween Special 1 — .90 — 2.25
Special 1 (Spring, 1989, $2.25) — .90 — 2.25
Graphic Novels #1-4 — 1.00 — 2.00 — 5.00

SOVIET SUPER SOLDIERS (Marvel)(Value: cover or less)

SPACE ACE (Also see Manhunt!)
No. 5, 1952
Magazine Enterprises

5(A-1 #61)-Guardineer-a — 34.00 — 103.00 — 240.00

SPACE ACTION
June, 1952 - No. 3, Oct, 1952
Ace Magazines (Junior Books)

1-Cameron-a in all (1 story) — 50.00 — 150.00 — 350.00
2,3 — 39.00 — 118.00 — 275.00

SPACE ADVENTURES (War At Sea #22 on)
7/52 - No. 21, 8/56; No. 23, 5/58 - No. 59, 11/64; V3#60, 10/67; V1#2, 7/68 - V1#8, 7/69; No. 9, 5/78 - No. 13, 3/79
Capitol Stories/Charlton Comics

1 — 33.00 — 100.00 — 230.00
2 — 16.00 — 48.00 — 110.00
3-5: 4,6-Flying saucer-c/stories — 12.00 — 36.00 — 85.00
6-9: 7-Sex change story "Transformation" — 11.00 — 32.00 — 75.00
10,11-Ditko-c/a; 11-Two Ditko stories — 29.00 — 86.00 — 200.00
12-Ditko-c (classic) — 34.00 — 101.00 — 235.00
13-(Fox-r, 10-11/54); Blue Beetle-c/story — 11.50 — 34.00 — 80.00
14-Blue Beetle-c/story; Fox-r (12-1/54-55, last pre-code) — 11.00 — 32.00 — 75.00
15,17,18-Rocky Jones-c/s.(TV); 15-Part photo-c — 11.50 — 34.00 — 80.00
16-Krigstein-a; Rocky Jones-c/story (TV) — 14.00 — 43.00 — 100.00
19 — 10.00 — 30.00 — 60.00
20-Reprints Fawcett's "Destination Moon" — 19.00 — 58.00 — 135.00
21-(8/56) (no #22)(Becomes War At Sea) — 10.00 — 30.00 — 60.00
23-(5/58; formerly Nyoka, The Jungle Girl)-Reprints Fawcett's "Destination Moon" — 16.00 — 48.00 — 110.00
24,25,31,32-Ditko-a. 24-Severin-a(signed "LePoer") — 12.00 — 36.00 — 85.00
26,27-Ditko-a(4) each. 26,28-Flying saucer-c — 13.50 — 41.00 — 95.00
28-30 — 5.35 — 16.00 — 32.00
33-Origin/1st app. Capt. Atom by Ditko (3/60) — 28.00 — 84.00 — 225.00
34-40,42-All Captain Atom by Ditko — 11.00 — 34.00 — 90.00
41,43-59: 44-1st app. Mercury Man; also in #45 — 2.00 — 6.00 — 17.00
V3#60(#1, 10/67)-Origin & 1st app. Paul Mann & The Saucers From the Future — 3.00 — 9.40 — 22.00
2-8(1968-69)-2,5,6,8-Ditko-a; 2,4-Aparo-c/a — 1.60 — 4.00 — 9.50
9-13(1978-79)-Capt. Atom-r/Space Adventures by Ditko; 9-Reprints origin/1st app. Capt. Atom from #33 — .80 — 2.00

NOTE: ***Aparo** a-V3#60. c-V3#8. **Ditko** c-12, 31-42. **Giordano** c-3, 4, 7-9, 18p. **Krigstein** c-15. **Shuster** a-11. Issues 13 & 14 have Blue Beetle logos; #15-18 have Rocky Jones logos.*

SPACE ARK (AC)(Value: cover or less)

SPACE BUSTERS
Spring, 1952 - No. 2, Fall, 1952 (Painted covers by Norman Saunders)
Ziff-Davis Publ. Co.

1-Krigstein-a(3) — 54.00 — 160.00 — 375.00
2-Kinstler-a(2 pgs.) — 43.00 — 130.00 — 300.00

NOTE: ***Anderson** a-2. Bondage c-2.*

SPACE CADET (See Tom Corbett,...)

SPACE COMICS (Formerly Funny Tunes)
No. 4, Mar-Apr, 1954 - No. 5, May-June, 1954
Avon Periodicals

4,5-Space Mouse, Peter Rabbit, Super Pup (formerly Spotty the Pup), &

Spaced #12 © Eclipse

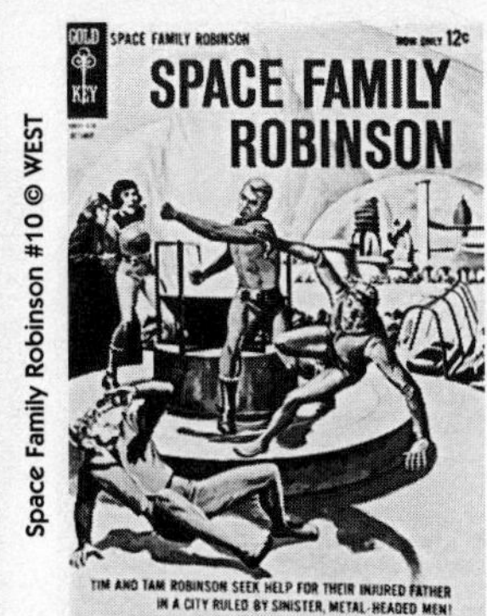

Space Family Robinson #10 © WEST

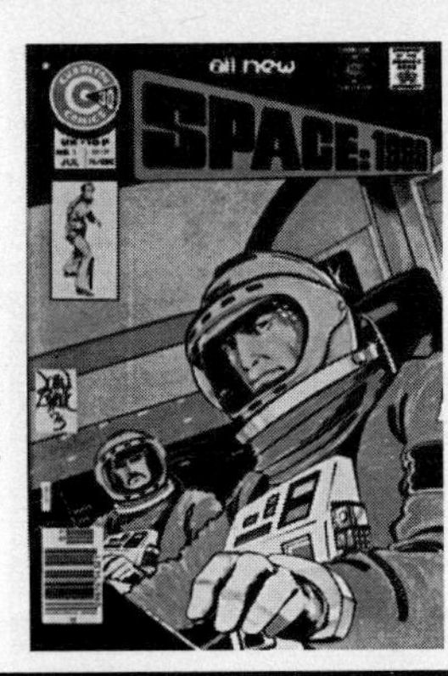

Space: 1999 #5 © CC

	GD25	FN65	NM94
Merry Mouse continue from Funny Tunes	5.00	15.00	30.00
I.W. Reprint #8 (nd)-Space Mouse-r	1.20	3.00	6.00

SPACED
1982 - No. 13, 1988 ($1.25/$1.50, B&W, quarterly)
Anthony Smith Publ. #1,2/Unbridled Ambition/Eclipse Comics #10 on

	GD25	FN65	NM94
1-($1.25-c)	3.00	8.60	20.00
2-($1.25-c)	2.00	5.60	13.00
3,4: 3-Begin $1.50-c	1.10	3.00	6.50
5,6		1.20	3.00
7-13			1.50
Special Edition (1983, Mimeo)	1.00	2.50	6.00

SPACE DETECTIVE
July, 1951 - No. 4, July, 1952
Avon Periodicals

	GD25	FN65	NM94
1-Rod Hathway, Space Detective begins, ends #4; Wood-c/a(3)-23 pgs.; "Opium Smugglers of Venus" drug story; Lucky Dale-r/Saint #4	79.00	236.00	550.00
2-Tales from the Shadow Squad story; Wood/Orlando-c; Wood inside layouts; "Slave Ship of Saturn" story	50.00	150.00	350.00
3-Kinstler-c	27.00	81.00	190.00
4-Kinstlerish-a by McCann	27.00	81.00	190.00
I.W. Reprint #1(Reprints #2), 8(Reprints cover #1 & part Famous Funnies #191)	4.00	10.00	20.00
I.W. Reprint #9-Exist?	4.00	10.00	20.00

SPACE EXPLORER (See March of Comics #202)

SPACE FAMILY ROBINSON (TV)(...Lost in Space #15-37, ...Lost in Space On Space Station One #38 on)(See Gold Key Champion)
Dec, 1962 - No. 36, Oct, 1969; No. 37, 10/73 - No. 54, 11/78; No. 55, 3/81 - No. 59, 5/82 (All painted covers)
Gold Key

	GD25	FN65	NM94
1-(Low distribution); Spiegle-a in all	24.00	71.00	190.00
2(3/63)-Family becomes lost in space	10.00	30.00	80.00
3-10: 6-Captain Venture back-up stories begin	5.00	16.00	42.00
11-20: 14-(10/65). 15-Title change (1/66)	4.00	11.00	28.00
21-36: 28-Last 12¢ issue. 36-Captain Venture ends	2.00	7.00	18.00
37-48: 37-Origin retold		1.50	3.75
49-59: Reprints #49,50,55-59		.90	2.25

NOTE: *The TV show first aired on 9/15/65. Title changed after TV show debuted.*

SPACE FAMILY ROBINSON (See March of Comics #320, 328, 352, 404, 414)

SPACE GHOST (TV) (Also see Golden Comics Digest #2 & Hanna-Barbera Super TV Heroes #3-7)
March, 1967 (Hanna-Barbera) (TV debut was 9/10/66)
Gold Key

	GD25	FN65	NM94
1 (10199-703)-Spiegle-a	25.00	75.00	250.00

SPACE GHOST (TV)(Comico)(Value: cover or less)

SPACE GIANTS, THE
1979 (One shot, $1.00, B&W, TV)
FBN Publications

	GD25	FN65	NM94
1-Based on Japanese TV series		1.60	4.00

SPACEHAWK (Dark Horse)(Value: cover or less)

SPACE KAT-ETS (...in 3-D)
Dec, 1953 (25¢, came w/glasses)
Power Publishing Co.

	GD25	FN65	NM94
1	25.00	75.00	175.00

SPACEMAN (Speed Carter...)
Sept, 1953 - No. 6, July, 1954
Atlas Comics (CnPC)

	GD25	FN65	NM94
1-Grey tone-c	46.00	139.00	325.00
2	29.00	86.00	200.00
3-6: 4-A-Bomb explosion-c	25.00	75.00	175.00

NOTE: ***Everett** c-1, 3. **Heath** a-1. **Maneely** a-1(3), 2(4), 3(3), 4-6; c-5, 6. **Romita** a-1. **Sekowsky** c-4. **Sekowsky/Abel** a-4(3). **Tuska** a-5(3).*

SPACE MAN
No. 1253, 1-3/62 - No. 8, 3-5/64; No. 9, 7/72 - No. 10, 10/72
Dell Publishing Co.

	GD25	FN65	NM94
4-Color 1253 (#1)(1-3/62)	8.35	25.00	50.00
2,3	4.20	12.50	25.00
4-8	3.60	9.00	18.00
9,10: 9-Reprints #1253. 10-Reprints #2	1.20	3.00	6.00

SPACE MOUSE (Also see Funny Tunes & Space Comics)
April, 1953 - No. 5, Apr-May, 1954
Avon Periodicals

	GD25	FN65	NM94
1	7.50	22.50	45.00
2	5.00	15.00	30.00
3-5	4.00	10.00	20.00

SPACE MOUSE (Walter Lantz...#1; see Comic Album #17)
No. 1132, Aug-Oct, 1960 - No. 5, Nov, 1963 (Walter Lantz)
Dell Publishing Co./Gold Key

	GD25	FN65	NM94
4-Color 1132,1244	4.70	14.00	28.00
1(11/62)(G.K.)	4.00	12.00	24.00
2-5	3.60	9.00	18.00

SPACE MYSTERIES
1964 (Reprints)
I.W. Enterprises

	GD25	FN65	NM94
1-r/Journey Into Unknown Worlds #4 w/new-c	1.60	4.00	8.00
8,9: 9-r/Planet Comics #73	1.80	4.50	9.00

SPACE: 1999 (TV) (Also see Power Record Comics)
Nov, 1975 - No. 7, Nov, 1976
Charlton Comics

	GD25	FN65	NM94
1-Origin Moonbase Alpha; Staton-c/a		1.40	3.50
2,7: 2-Staton-a		1.00	2.50
3-6: All Byrne-a; c-3,5,6		1.80	4.50

SPACE: 1999 (TV)(Magazine)
Nov, 1975 - No. 8, Nov, 1976 (B&W) (#7 shows #6 on inside)
Charlton Comics

	GD25	FN65	NM94
1-Origin Moonbase Alpha; Morrow-c/a		1.40	3.50
2,3-Morrow-c/a		1.00	2.50
4-8: 4-6-Morrow-c. 5,8-Morrow-a		.80	2.00

SPACE PATROL (TV)
Summer, 1952 - No. 2, Oct-Nov, 1952 (Painted-c by Norman Saunders)
Ziff-Davis Publishing Co. (Approved Comics)

	GD25	FN65	NM94
1-Krigstein-a	63.00	190.00	440.00
2-Krigstein-a(3)	49.00	146.00	340.00
...'s Special Mission (8 pgs., B&W, Giveaway)	55.00	165.00	385.00

SPACE PIRATES (See Archie Giant Series #533)

SPACE RANGER (See Mystery in Space #92, Showcase #15 & Tales of the Unexpected)

SPACE SQUADRON (In the Days of the Rockets)(Becomes Space Worlds #6)
June, 1951 - No. 5, Feb, 1952
Marvel/Atlas Comics (ACI)

	GD25	FN65	NM94
1-Space team; Brodsky c-1,5	46.00	139.00	325.00
2: Tuska c-2-4	41.00	122.00	285.00
3-5: 3-Capt. Jet Dixon by Tuska(3). 4-Weird advs. begin	32.00	96.00	225.00

SPACE THRILLERS
1954 (25¢ Giant)
Avon Periodicals

	GD25	FN65	NM94
nn-(Scarce)-Robotmen of the Lost Planet; contains 3 rebound comics of The Saint & Strange Worlds. Contents could vary	79.00	236.00	550.00

SPACE TRIP TO THE MOON (See Space Adventures #23)

SPACE USAGI

Space War #16 © CC

Sparkler Comics #15 © UFS

Sparkling Stars #5 © HOKE

June, 1992 - No. 3, 1992 ($2.00, B&W, mini-series)
Nov, 1993 - Present ($2.75, color)
Mirage Studios

	GD25	FN65	NM94
1-3: Usagi Yojimbo by Stan Sakai		.80	2.00
V2#1-3		1.10	2.75

SPACE WAR (Fightin' Five #28 on)
Oct, 1959 - No. 27, Mar, 1964; No. 28, Mar, 1978 - No. 34, 3/79
Charlton Comics

	GD25	FN65	NM94
V1#1-Giordano-c begin, end #3	12.00	36.00	85.00
2,3	6.00	18.00	42.00
4-6,8,10-Ditko-c/a	12.00	36.00	85.00
7,9,11-15: Last 10¢ issue?	3.00	9.40	22.00
16-27	2.70	8.00	19.00
28,29,33,34-Ditko-c/a(r)	4.70	14.00	33.00
30-Ditko-c/a(r); Staton, Sutton/Wood-a	5.00	15.00	35.00
31-Ditko-c/a(3); same-c as Strange Suspense Stories #2 (1968); atom blast-c	5.30	16.00	37.00
32-r/Charlton Premiere V2#2; Sutton-a		1.20	3.00

SPACE WESTERN (Formerly Cowboy Western Comics; becomes Cowboy Western Comics #46 on)
No. 40, Oct, 1952 - No. 45, Aug, 1953
Charlton Comics (Capitol Stories)

	GD25	FN65	NM94
40-Intro Spurs Jackson & His Space Vigilantes; flying saucer story	39.00	118.00	275.00
41,43-45: 41-Flying saucer-c. 45-Hitler app.	30.00	90.00	210.00
42-Atom bomb explosion-c	32.00	96.00	225.00

SPACE WORLDS (Formerly Space Squadron #1-5)
No. 6, April, 1952
Atlas Comics (Male)

	GD25	FN65	NM94
6-Sol Brodsky-c	29.00	86.00	200.00

SPANKY & ALFALFA & THE LITTLE RASCALS (See The Little Rascals)

SPANNER'S GALAXY (DC)(Value: cover or less)

SPARKIE, RADIO PIXIE (Radio)(Becomes Big Jon & Sparkie #4)
Winter, 1951 - No. 3, July-Aug, 1952 (Painted-c)(Sparkie #2,3; #1?)
Ziff-Davis Publ. Co.

	GD25	FN65	NM94
1-Based on children's radio program	16.00	48.00	110.00
2,3: 3-Big Jon and Sparkie on-c only	11.50	34.00	80.00

SPARKLE COMICS
Oct-Nov, 1948 - No. 33, Dec-Jan, 1953-54 (#1-3: 52 pgs.)
United Features Syndicate

	GD25	FN65	NM94
1-Li'l Abner, Nancy, Captain & the Kids, Ella Cinders	10.00	30.00	70.00
2	5.85	17.50	35.00
3-10	4.20	12.50	25.00
11-20	4.00	11.00	22.00
21-33	3.20	8.00	16.00

SPARKLE PLENTY (See 4-Color #215 & Harvey Comics Library #2)

SPARKLER COMICS (1st Series)
July, 1940 - No. 2, 1940
United Feature Comic Group

	GD25	FN65	NM94
1-Jim Hardy	27.00	81.00	190.00
2-Frankie Doodle	22.00	65.00	150.00

SPARKLER COMICS (2nd Series)(Nancy & Sluggo #121 on)(Cover title becomes Nancy and Sluggo #101? on)
July, 1941 - No. 120, Jan, 1955
United Features Syndicate

	GD25	FN65	NM94
1-Origin 1st app. Sparkman; Tarzan (by Hogarth in all issues), Captain & the Kids, Ella Cinders, Danny Dingle, Dynamite Dunn, Nancy, Abbie & Slats, Broncho Bill, Frankie Doodle, begin; Sparkman c-1-9,11,12; Hap Hopper c-10,13	143.00	430.00	1000.00
2	55.00	165.00	385.00
3,4	46.00	139.00	325.00
5-10: 9-Sparkman's new costume	41.00	122.00	285.00
11-13,15-20: 12-Sparkman's new costume (color change). 19-1st Race Riley and the Commandos plus-c	31.00	94.00	220.00
14-Tarzan-c by Hogarth	34.00	103.00	240.00
21,25,28,31,34,37,39-Tarzan-c by Hogarth	31.00	92.00	215.00
22-24,26,27,29,30: 22-Race Riley & the Commandos strips begin, ends #44	24.00	73.00	170.00
32,33,35,36,38,40	13.50	41.00	95.00
41,43,45,46,48,49	10.00	30.00	65.00
42,44,47,50-Tarzan-c (42,47,50 by Hogarth)	17.00	52.00	120.00
51,52,54-70: 57-Li'l Abner begins (not in #58); Fearless Fosdick app. in #58	9.15	27.50	55.00
53-Tarzan-c by Hogarth	15.00	45.00	105.00
71-80	5.85	17.50	35.00
81,82,84-90: 85-Li'l Abner ends. 86-Lingerie panels	5.00	15.00	30.00
83-Tarzan-c	9.15	27.50	55.00
91-96,98-99	5.00	15.00	30.00
97-Origin Casey Ruggles by Warren Tufts	10.00	30.00	65.00
100	6.70	20.00	40.00
101-107,109-112,114-120	4.00	11.00	22.00
108,113-Toth-a	7.50	22.50	45.00

SPARKLING LOVE
June, 1950; 1953
Avon Periodicals/Realistic (1953)

	GD25	FN65	NM94
1(Avon)-Kubert-a; photo-c	14.00	43.00	100.00
nn(1953)-Reprint; Kubert-a	6.35	19.00	38.00

SPARKLING STARS
June, 1944 - No. 33, March, 1948
Holyoke Publishing Co.

	GD25	FN65	NM94
1-Hell's Angels, FBI, Boxie Weaver, Petey & Pop, & Ali Baba begin	11.00	32.00	75.00
2-Speed Spaulding story	7.50	22.50	45.00
3-Actual FBI case photos & war photos	5.35	16.00	32.00
4-10: 7-X-Mas-c	4.70	14.00	28.00
11-19: 13-Origin/1st app. Jungo the Man-Beast-c/s	4.00	12.00	24.00
20-Intro Fangs the Wolf Boy	4.70	14.00	28.00
21-29,32,33: 29-Bondage-c	4.00	12.00	24.00
31-Sid Greene-a	4.70	14.00	28.00

SPARK MAN (See Sparkler Comics)
1945 (One Shot) (36 pgs.)
Frances M. McQueeny

	GD25	FN65	NM94
1-Origin Spark Man r/Sparkler #1-3; female torture story; cover redrawn from Sparkler #1	22.00	65.00	150.00

SPARKY WATTS (Also see Big Shot Comics & Columbia Comics)
Nov?, 1942 - No. 10, 1949
Columbia Comic Corp.

	GD25	FN65	NM94
1(1942)-Skyman & The Face app; Hitler-c	30.00	90.00	210.00
2(1943)	14.00	43.00	100.00
3(1944)	11.50	34.00	80.00
4(1944)-Origin	11.00	32.00	75.00
5(1947)-Skyman app.; Boody Rogers-c/a	10.00	30.00	60.00
6,7,9,10: 6(1947),10(1949)	6.70	20.00	40.00
8(1948)-Surrealistic-c	9.15	27.50	55.00

NOTE: ***Boody Rogers*** *c-1-8.*

SPARTACUS (See 4-Color #1139)

SPAWN (Also see Batman/Spawn: War Devil)
May, 1992 - Present ($1.95, color, mature readers)
Image Comics

	GD25	FN65	NM94
1-1st app. Spawn; McFarlane-c/a begins; McFarlane/Steacy-c	1.70	4.00	10.00
2-1st app. Violator; McFarlane/Steacy-c	1.30	3.00	8.00
3-Violator app.	1.20	2.90	7.00

Spawn #24 © Todd McFarlane

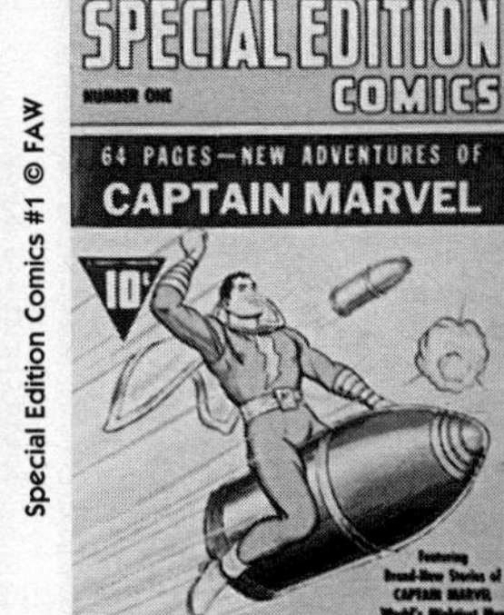

Special Edition Comics #1 © FAW

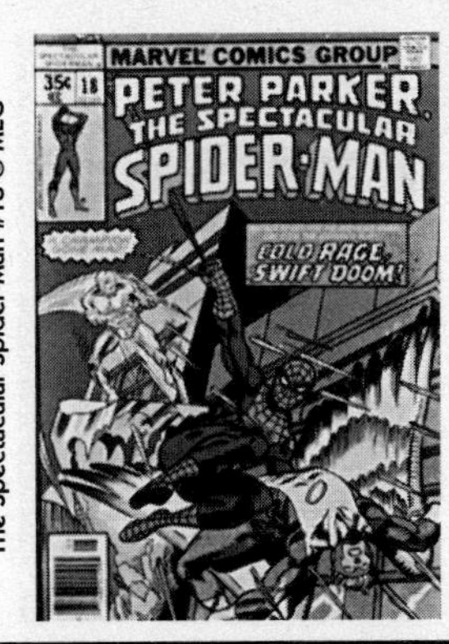

The Spectacular Spider-Man #18 © MEG

	GD25	FN65	NM94
4-Has coupon for Image Comics #0-Alan Moore scripts w/Miller poster; Violator app.	1.50	3.80	9.00
4-With coupon missing		.80	2.00
4-Newsstand edition w/o poster or coupon	1.00	2.00	5.00
5-Cerebus cameo (1 pg.) as stuffed animal	1.00	2.00	5.00
6-18,21-28: 7-Spawn Mobile poster. 8-Miller poster; Alan Moore scripts. 9-Neil Gaiman scripts; Jim Lee poster. 10-Cerebus app.; Dave Sim scripts. 11-Miller scripts; Darrow poster. 12-Bloodwulf poster by Liefeld. 14,15-Violator app. 16-18-Morrison scripts; Capullo-c/a(p). 21,23,24-McFarlane-a/stories		.80	2.00
...-Batman (1994, $3.95)-Miller scripts; McFarlane-a		1.60	4.00

NOTE: ***Capullo*** *a-16p; c-16p.* ***McFarlane*** *a-1-15; c-1-15p.* ***Thibert*** *a-16i(part). Posters come with issues 1-4, 7-9, 11, 12.*

SPECIAL AGENT (Steve Saunders...)(Also see True Comics #68)
Dec, 1947 - No. 8, Sept, 1949 (Based on true FBI cases)
Parents' Magazine Institute (Commended Comics No. 2)

	GD25	FN65	NM94
1-J. Edgar Hoover photo on-c	9.15	27.50	55.00
2	4.70	14.00	28.00
3-8	4.00	11.00	22.00

SPECIAL COLLECTORS' EDITION
Dec, 1975 (No month given) (10-1/4x13-1/2")
Marvel Comics Group

	GD25	FN65	NM94
1-Kung Fu, Iron Fist (early), Sons of the Tiger		1.30	3.25

SPECIAL COMICS (Becomes Hangman #2 on)
Winter, 1941-42
MLJ Magazines

	GD25	FN65	NM94
1-Origin The Boy Buddies (Shield & Wizard x-over); death of The Comet; origin The Hangman retold; Hangman-c	164.00	493.00	1150.00

SPECIAL DELIVERY
1951 (32 pgs.; B&W)
Post Hall Synd. (Giveaway)

nn-Origin of Pogo, Swamp, etc.; 2 pg. biog. on Walt Kelly
(One copy sold in 1980 for $150.00)

SPECIAL EDITION (See Gorgo and Reptisaurus)

SPECIAL EDITION (U. S. Navy Giveaways)
1944 - 1945 (Regular comic format with wording simplified, 52 pgs.)
National Periodical Publications

	GD25	FN65	NM94
1-Action (1944)-Reprints Action #80	82.00	245.00	490.00
2-Action (1944)-Reprints Action #81	82.00	245.00	490.00
3-Superman (1944)-Reprints Superman #33	82.00	245.00	490.00
4-Detective (1944)-Reprints Detective #97	87.00	262.00	525.00
5-Superman (1945)-Reprints Superman #34	82.00	245.00	490.00
6-Action (1945)-Reprints Action #84	82.00	245.00	490.00

NOTE: ***Wayne Boring*** *c-1, 2, 6.* ***Dick Sprang*** *c-4.*

SPECIAL EDITION COMICS
1940 (August) (One Shot, 68 pgs.)
Fawcett Publications

	GD25	FN65	VF82	NM94
1-1st book devoted entirely to Captain Marvel; C.C. Beck-c/a; only app. of Capt. Marvel with belt buckle; Capt. Marvel appears with button-down flap; 1st story (came out before Captain Marvel #1)	600.00	1800.00	3900.00	6000.00

(Estimated up to 150 total copies exist, 7 in NM/Mint)

NOTE: *Prices vary widely on this book. Since this book is all Captain Marvel stories, it is actually a pre-Captain Marvel #1. There is speculation that this book almost became* ***Captain Marvel*** *#1. After* ***Special Edition*** *was published, there was an editor change at Fawcett. The new editor commissioned Kirby to do a nn* ***Captain Marvel*** *book early in 1941. This book was followed by a 2nd book several months later. This 2nd book was advertised as a #3 (making Special Edition the #1, & the nn issue the #2). However, the 2nd book did come out as a #2.*

SPECIAL EDITION: SPIDER-MAN VS. THE HULK (See listing under The Amazing Spider-Man)

SPECIAL EDITION X-MEN
Feb, 1983 (One Shot) ($2.00, Baxter paper)
Marvel Comics Group

	GD25	FN65	NM94
1-r/Giant-Size X-Men #1 plus one new story	1.85	5.50	13.00

SPECIAL MARVEL EDITION (Master of Kung Fu #17 on)
Jan, 1971 - No. 16, Feb, 1974 (#1-4: 25¢, 68 pgs.; #5-16: 20¢, regular ed.)
Marvel Comics Group

	GD25	FN65	NM94
1-Thor-r by Kirby; 68 pgs.	1.10	2.70	6.50
2-4: Thor-r by Kirby; 68 pg. Giant		1.90	4.75
5-14: Sgt. Fury-r; 11-r/Sgt. Fury #13 (Capt. America)		1.60	4.00
15-Master of Kung Fu (Shang-Chi) begins (1st app., 12/73); Starlin-a; origin/1st app. Nayland Smith & Dr. Petric	6.00	17.00	39.00
16-1st app. Midnight; Starlin-a (2nd Shang-Chi)	3.90	11.60	27.00

SPECIAL MISSIONS (See G.I. Joe...)

SPECIAL WAR SERIES (Attack V4#3 on?)
Aug, 1965 - No. 4, Nov, 1965
Charlton Comics

	GD25	FN65	NM94
V4#1-D-Day (also see D-Day listing)	1.50	3.80	9.00
2-Attack!	1.10	2.70	6.50
3-War & Attack (also see War & Attack)	1.10	2.70	6.50
4-Judomaster (intro/1st app.; see Sarge Steel)	3.60	10.70	25.00

SPECTACULAR ADVENTURES (See Adventures)

SPECTACULAR FEATURE MAGAZINE, A (Formerly My Confessions) (Spectacular Features Magazine #12)
No. 11, April, 1950
Fox Feature Syndicate

	GD25	FN65	NM94
11 (#1)-Samson and Delilah	19.00	57.00	130.00

SPECTACULAR FEATURES MAGAZINE (Formerly A Spectacular Feature Magazine)
No. 12, June, 1950 - No. 3, Aug, 1950
Fox Feature Syndicate

	GD25	FN65	NM94
12 (#2)-Iwo Jima; photo flag-c	19.00	57.00	130.00
3-True Crime Cases From Police Files	13.00	40.00	90.00

SPECTACULAR SPIDER-MAN, THE (See Marvel Special Edition and Marvel Treasury Edition)

SPECTACULAR SPIDER-MAN, THE (Magazine)
July, 1968 - No. 2, Nov, 1968 (35¢)
Marvel Comics Group

	GD25	FN65	NM94
1-(B&W)-Romita/Mooney 52 pg. story plus updated origin story with Everett-a(i)	8.60	26.00	60.00
2-(Color)-Green Goblin-c & 58 pg. story; Romita painted-c (story reprinted in King Size Spider-Man #9); Romita/Mooney-a	11.00	34.00	80.00

SPECTACULAR SPIDER-MAN, THE (Peter Parker...#54-132, 134)
Dec, 1976 - Present
Marvel Comics Group

	GD25	FN65	NM94
1-Origin recap in text; return of Tarantula	6.90	21.00	48.00
2-Kraven the Hunter app.	2.90	8.60	20.00
3-5: 3-Intro Lightmaster. 4-Vulture app.	1.90	6.00	13.00
6-8-Morbius app.; 6-r/Marvel Team-Up #3 w/Morbius	2.90	8.60	20.00
9-20: 9,10-White Tiger app. 11-Last 30¢-c. 17,18-Angel & Iceman app. (from Champions); Ghost Rider cameo in flashback	1.10	2.70	6.50
21,24-26: 21-Scorpion app. 26-Daredevil app.	.90	2.30	5.50
22,23-Moon Knight app.	1.70	4.20	10.00
27-Miller's 1st art on Daredevil (2/79); also see Captain America #235	2.10	6.40	15.00
28-Miller Daredevil (p)	1.60	4.70	11.00
29-55,57,59: 33-Origin Iguana. 38-Morbius app.	1.00	2.00	5.00
56-2nd app. Jack O'Lantern (Macendale) & 1st Spidey/Jack O'Lantern battle (7/81)	1.50	3.80	9.00
58-Byrne-a(p)	.90	2.30	5.50
60-Double size; origin retold with new facts revealed	1.00	2.00	5.00
61-63,65-68,71-74: 65-Kraven the Hunter app.		1.40	3.50

The Spectacular Spider-Man #87 © MEG

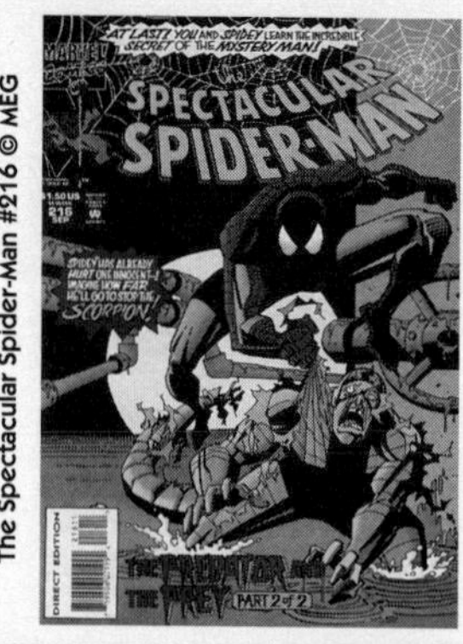

The Spectacular Spider-Man #216 © MEG

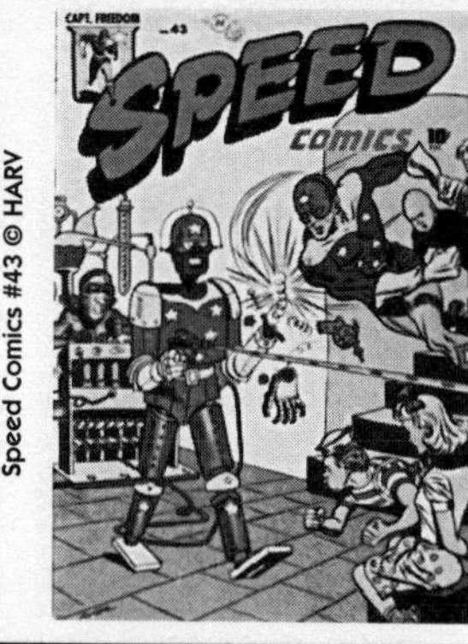

Speed Comics #43 © HARV

GD25 FN65 NM94

64-1st app. Cloak & Dagger (3/82) 2.00 6.00 14.00
69,70-Cloak & Dagger app. 1.60 4.70 11.00
75-Double size 1.00 2.00 5.00
76-80: 78,79-Punisher cameo 1.40 3.50
81,82-Punisher, Cloak & Dagger app. 1.90 6.00 13.00
83-Origin Punisher retold (10/83) 2.30 6.90 16.00
84,86-99: 90-Spider-man's new black costume, last panel(ties w/Amazing Spider-Man #252 & Marvel Team-Up #141 for 1st app.). 94-96-Cloak & Dagger app. 98-Intro The Spot 1.60 4.00
85-Hobgoblin (Ned Leeds) app. (12/83); gains powers of original Green Goblin (see Amazing Spider-Man #238) 4.10 12.40 29.00
100-(3/85)-Double size 1.00 2.00 5.00
101-115,117,118,120-129: 107-110-Death of Jean DeWolff. 111-Secret Wars II tie-in. 128-Black Cat new costume 1.40 3.50
116,119-Sabretooth-c/story 1.10 2.70 6.50
130-Hobgoblin app. 1.00 2.00 5.00
131-Six part Kraven tie-in 1.20 2.90 7.00
132-Kraven tie-in 1.00 2.50 6.00
133-139: 138-1st full app. Tombstone (origin #139) .90 2.25
140-Punisher cameo app. 1.30 3.25
141-Punisher app. 1.20 2.90 7.00
142,143-Punisher app. 1.80 4.50
144-146,148-157: 151-Tombstone returns .90 2.25
147-1st app. new Hobgoblin (Macendale) in 1 pg. cameo; continued in Web of Spider-Man #48 3.40 10.30 24.00
158-Spider-Man gets new powers (1st Cosmic Spidey, continued in Web of Spider-Man #59) 2.00 6.00 14.00
159-Cosmic Spider-Man app. 1.50 3.80 9.00
160-170: 161-163-Hobgoblin app. 168-170-Avengers x-over. 169-1st app. The Outlaws .80 2.00
171-184: 180,181,183,184-Green Goblin app. 1.50
185-188,190-199: 197-199-Original X-Men-c/story 1.40
189-($2.95, 52 pgs.)-Silver hologram on-c; battles Green Goblin; origin Spidey retold; Vess poster w/Spidey & Hobgoblin 1.50 3.80 9.00
189-(2nd printing)-Gold hologram on-c 1.10 2.75
195-(Deluxe ed.)-Polybagged w/audio cassette 1.20 3.00
200-($2.95)-Holo-grafx foil-c; Green Goblin-c/story 1.20 3.00
201-211: 203-Maximum Carnage x-over. 204-Begin 4 part death of Tombstone story. 207,208-The Shroud-c/story. 208-Siege of Darkness x-over (#207 is a tie-in). 209-Black Cat back-up 1.40
212-222: 212-Begin $1.50-c; bound-in card sheet. 215,216-Scorpion app. 217-Power & Responsibility Pt. 4 1.50
213-Collectors ed. polybagged w/16 pg. preview & animation cel; foil-c; 1st meeting Spidey & Typhoid Mary 1.20 3.00
213-Version polybagged w/Gamepro #7; no-c date, price 1.50
219-($2.95)-Deluxe edition foil-c; flip book 1.20 3.00
Annual 1 (1979)-Doc Octopus-c & 46 pg. story 1.00 2.50 6.00
Annual 2 (1980)-Origin/1st app. Rapier 1.80 4.50
Annual 3-7: 3(1981)-Last Man-Wolf. 4(1984). 5(1985). 6(10/86). 7(1987) 1.40 3.50
Annual 8 (1988, $1.75)-Evolutionary War x-over; Daydreamer returns Gwen Stacy "clone" back to real self (not Gwen Stacy) 1.60 4.00
Annual 9 (1989, $2.00, 68 pgs.)-Atlantis Attacks 1.20 3.00
Annual 10 (1990, $2.00, 68 pgs.)-McFarlane-a 1.00 2.50
Annual 11 (1991, $2.00, 68 pgs.)-Iron Man app. .80 2.00
Annual 12 (1992, $2.25, 68 pgs.)-Venom solo story cont'd from Amazing Spider-Man Annual #26 .90 2.25
Annual 13 (1993, $2.95, 68 pgs.)-Polybagged w/trading card; John Romita, Sr. back-up-a 1.20 3.00
Annual 14 (1994, $2.95) 1.20 3.00

NOTE: ***Austin*** *c-21i, Annual 11i.* ***Byrne*** *c(p)-17, 43, 58, 101, 102.* ***Giffen*** *a-120p.* ***Hembeck*** *c/a-86p.* ***Larsen*** *c-Annual 11p.* ***Miller*** *c-46p, 48p, 50, 51p, 52p, 54p, 55, 56p, 57, 60.* ***Mooney*** *a-7i, 11i, 21p, 23p, 25p, 26p, 29-34p, 36p, 37p, 39i, 41, 42i, 49p, 50i, 51i, 53p, 54-57i, 59-66i, 68i, 71i, 73-79i, 81-83i, 85i, 87-99i, 102i, 125p, Annual 1i, 2p.* ***Nasser*** *c-37p.* ***Perez*** *c-10.* ***Simonson*** *c-54i.*

SPECTACULAR STORIES MAGAZINE (Formerly A Star Presentation)
No. 4, July, 1950 - No. 3, Sept, 1950
Fox Feature Sydicate (Hero Books)
4-Sherlock Holmes (true crime stories) 25.00 75.00 175.00
3-The St. Valentine's Day Massacre (true crime) 16.00 48.00 110.00

SPECTRE, THE (See Adventure Comics #431, More Fun & Showcase)
Nov-Dec, 1967 - No. 10, May-June, 1969 (All 12¢)
National Periodical Publications
Showcase #60 (1-2/66)-1st Silver Age app. The Spectre; Murphy Anderson-a; origin in text 24.00 71.00 165.00
Showcase #61 (3-4/66,)-2nd app. The Spectre by Murphy Anderson 14.00 41.00 95.00
Showcase #64 (9010/66)-3rd app. by Anderson 13.00 39.00 90.00
Brave and the Bold #72 (6-7/67)-4th app. Spectre 3.10 9.40 22.00
1-(11-12/67)-Anderson-c/a 10.00 30.00 70.00
2-5-Neal Adams-c/a; 3-Wildcat x-over 6.40 19.00 45.00
6-8,10: 6-8-Anderson inks. 7-Hourman app. 2.90 8.60 20.00
9-Wrightson-a 3.00 9.40 22.00

SPECTRE, THE (DC 1987-'89)(Value: cover or less)

SPECTRE, THE (Also see Brave and the Bold #72, 75, 116, 180, 199)
Dec, 1992 - Present ($1.75)
DC Comics
1-($1.95)-Glow-in-the-dark-c; Mandrake-a begins 1.20 3.00
2-7,9-12,14-20: 10-Kaluta-c. 11-Hildebrandt painted-c. 16-Aparo/K. Jones-a. 20-Sienkiewicz-c .70 1.75
8,13-($2.50)-Glow-in-the-dark-c 1.00 2.50
21,22: 21-Begin $1.95-c. 22-(9/94)-Superman-c & app. .80 2.00
0,23-29: 0-(10/94). 23-(11/94) .80 2.00

SPEEDBALL (See Amazing Spider-Man Annual #12, Marvel Super-Heroes & The New Warriors)
Sept, 1988(10/88-inside) - No. 11, July, 1989 (75¢)
Marvel Comics
1-11: Ditko/Guice a-1-4, c-1; Ditko a-1-10; c-1-11p 1.00

SPEED BUGGY (TV)(Also see Fun-In #12, 15)
July, 1975 - No. 9, Nov, 1976 (Hanna-Barbera)
Charlton Comics
1 1.20 3.00
2-9 .70 1.75

SPEED CARTER SPACEMAN (See Spaceman)

SPEED COMICS (New Speed)(Also see Double Up)
10/39 - #11, 8/40; #12, 3/41 - #44, 1-2/47 (#14-16: pocket size, 100 pgs.)
Brookwood Publ./Speed Publ./Harvey Publications No. 14 on
1-Origin & 1st app. Shock Gibson; Ted Parrish, the Man with 1000 Faces begins; Powell-a; becomes Champion #2 on? 143.00 430.00 1000.00
2-Powell-a 64.00 193.00 450.00
3 39.00 118.00 275.00
4,5: 4-Powell-a? 34.00 103.00 240.00
6-11: 7-Mars Mason begins, ends #11 31.00 92.00 215.00
12 (3/41; shows #11 in indicia)-The Wasp begins; Major Colt app. (Capt. Colt #12) 34.00 100.00 235.00
13-Intro. Captain Freedom & Young Defenders; Girl Commandos, Pat Parker (costumed heroine), War Nurse begins; Major Colt app. 41.00 122.00 285.00
14-16 (100 pg. pocket size, 1941): 14-2nd Harvey comic (See Pocket); Shock Gibson dons new costume. 15-Pat Parker dons costume, last in costume #23; no Girl Commandos 33.00 100.00 230.00
17-Black Cat begins (4/42, early app.; see Pocket #1); origin Black Cat-r/ Pocket #1; not in #40,41 50.00 150.00 350.00
18-20 29.00 86.00 200.00
21,22,25-30: 26-Flag-c 24.00 73.00 170.00
23-Origin Girl Commandos 34.00 103.00 240.00
24-Pat Parker team-up with Girl Commandos 25.00 75.00 175.00
31-44: 31-Hitler & Hirohito-c. 38-Flag-c 22.00 65.00 150.00

NOTE: ***Al Avison*** *c-14-16, 30, 43.* ***Briefer*** *a-6, 7.* ***Jon Henri*** *(Kirbyesque) c-17-20.* ***Kubert*** *a-7-*

Spellbound #13 © MEG

Spider-Man #4 © MEG

Spider-Man #50 © MEG

GD25 FN65 NM94

11(Mars Mason), 37, 38, 42-44. ***Kirby/Caseneuve*** *c-21-23.* ***Palais*** *c-37, 39-42.* ***Powell*** *a-1, 2, 4-7, 28, 31, 44.* ***Schomburg*** *c-31-36.* ***Tuska*** *a-3, 6, 7. Bondage c-18, 35. Captain Freedom c-16-24, 25(part), 26-44(w/Black Cat #27, 29, 31, 32-40). Shock Gibson c-1-15.*

SPEED DEMONS (Formerly Frank Merriwell at Yale #1-4?; Submarine Attack #11 on)
No. 5, Feb, 1957 - No. 10, 1958
Charlton Comics

5-10 2.40 6.00 12.00

SPEED RACER (Also see The New Adventures of...)
July, 1987 - No. 38, Nov, 1990 ($1.75, color)
Now Comics

1-38 .80 1.90
1-2nd printing .70 1.80
Special 1 (1988, $2.00) .80 2.00
Special 2 (1988, $3.50) 1.40 3.50

SPEED RACER FEATURING NINJA HIGH SCHOOL
Aug, 1993 - No. 2, 1993 ($2.50, color, mini-series)
Now Comics

1,2: 1-Polybagged w/card. 2-Exists? 1.00 2.50

SPEED RACER: RETURN OF THE GRX
Mar, 1994 - No. 2, Apr, 1994 ($1.95, color, limited series)
Now Comics

1,2 .80 2.00

SPEED SMITH THE HOT ROD KING (Also see Hot Rod King)
Spring, 1952
Ziff-Davis Publishing Co.

1-Saunders painted-c 14.00 43.00 100.00

SPEEDY GONZALES (See 4-Color #1084)

SPEEDY RABBIT (See Television Puppet Show)
nd (1953); 1963
Realistic/I. W. Enterprises/Super Comics

nn (1953)-Realistic Reprint? 1.80 4.50 9.00
I.W. Reprint #1 (2 versions w/diff. c/stories exist) .80 2.00 4.00
Super Reprint #14(1963) .80 2.00 4.00

SPELLBINDERS (Quality)(Value: cover or less)

SPELLBOUND (See The Crusaders)

SPELLBOUND (Tales to Hold You... #1, Stories to Hold You...)
Mar, 1952 - #23, June, 1954; #24, Oct, 1955 - #34, June, 1957
Atlas Comics (ACI 1-15/Male 16-23/BPC 24-34)

1-Horror/weird stories in all 39.00 118.00 275.00
2-Edgar A. Poe app. 19.00 58.00 135.00
3-5: 3-Whitney-a; cannibalism story 17.00 52.00 120.00
6-Krigstein-a 17.00 52.00 120.00
7-10: 8-Ayers-a 13.00 40.00 90.00
11-16,18-20: 14-Ed Win-a 11.00 32.00 75.00
17-Krigstein-a 11.50 34.00 80.00
21-23: 23-Last precode (6/54) 10.00 30.00 65.00
24-28,30,31,34: 25-Orlando-a 9.15 27.50 55.00
29-Ditko-a (4 pgs.) 10.00 30.00 65.00
32,33-Torres-a 10.00 30.00 60.00

NOTE: ***Brodsky*** *a-5; c-1, 5-7, 10, 11, 13, 15, 25-27, 32.* ***Colan*** *a-17.* ***Everett*** *a-2, 5, 7, 10, 16, 28, 31; c-2, 8, 9, 14, 17-19, 28, 30.* ***Forgione/Abel*** *a-29.* ***Forte/Fox*** *a-16.* ***Al Hartley*** *a-2.* ***Heath*** *a-2, 4, 8, 9, 12, 14, 16; c-3, 4, 12, 16, 20, 21.* ***Infantino*** *a-15.* ***Keller*** *a-5.* ***Kida*** *a-2, 14.* ***Maneely*** *a-7, 14, 27; c-24, 29, 31.* ***Mooney*** *a-5, 13, 18.* ***Mac Pakula*** *a-22, 32.* ***Post*** *a-8.* ***Powell*** *a-19, 20, 32.* ***Robinson*** *a-1.* ***Romita*** *a-24, 26, 27.* ***R.Q. Sale*** *a-29.* ***Sekowsky*** *a-5.* ***Severin*** *c-29.* ***Sinnott*** *a-8, 16, 17.*

SPELLBOUND (Marvel, 1988)(Value: cover or less)

SPELLJAMMER (DC)(Value: cover or less)

SPENCER SPOOK (Formerly Giggle Comics; see Adventures of...)
No. 100, Mar-Apr, 1955 - No. 101, May-June, 1955
American Comics Group

100,101 4.70 14.00 28.00

SPIDER, THE
1991 - Book 3, 1991 ($4.95, color, 52 pgs.)
Eclipse Books

Book 1-3-Truman-c/a 1.00 2.00 5.00

SPIDER-MAN (See Amazing..., Giant-Size..., Marvel Tales, Marvel Team-Up, Spectacular..., Spidey Super Stories, Venom, & Web Of...)

SPIDER-MAN
Aug, 1990 - Present ($1.75)
Marvel Comics

1-Silver edition, direct sale only (unbagged) 1.00 2.00 5.00
1-Silver bagged edition; direct sale, no price on comic, but $2.00 on plastic bag (125,000 print run) 2.00 6.40 15.00
1-Regular edition w/Spidey face in UPC area (unbagged); green-c 1.60 4.00
1-Regular bagged edition w/Spidey face in UPC area; green cover (125,000) 1.20 4.00 8.50
1-Newsstand bagged w/UPC code 1.70 4.25
1-Gold edition, 2nd printing (unbagged) with Spider-Man in box (400,000-450,000) 1.60 4.00
1-Gold 2nd printing w/UPC code; sold in Wal-Mart; not scarce 1.20 3.00
1-Platinum ed. mailed to retailers only (10,000 print run); has new McFarlane-a & editorial material instead of ads; stiff-c, no cover price 225.00
2-McFarlane-c/a/scripts continue 1.70 4.00
3-5 1.00 2.50
6,7-Ghost Rider & Hobgoblin app. 1.90 4.50
8-Wolverine cameo; Wolverine storyline begins 1.00 2.50
9-12: 12-Wolverine storyline ends 1.00 2.50
13-Spidey's black costume returns; Morbius app. 1.00 2.00 5.00
14,15: 14-Morbius app. 15-Erik Larsen-c/a; Beast c/s .80 2.00
16-X-Force-c/story w/Liefeld assists; continues in X-Force #4; reads sideways; last McFarlane issue 1.00 2.50
17-Thanos-c/story; Leonardi/Williamson-c/a 1.00 2.50
18-23,25: 13,14-Spidey in black costume. 18-Ghost Rider-c/story. 18-23-Sinister Six storyline w/Erik Larsen-c/a/scripts. 19-Hulk & Hobgoblin-c & app. 20-22-Deathlok app. 22,23-Ghost Rider, Hulk, Hobgoblin app. 23-Wrap-around gatefold-c. 24-Infinity War x-over w/Demogoblin & Hobgoblin-c/story .70 1.75
24-Demogoblin dons new costume & battles Hobgoblin-c/story .40 1.00 2.00
26-($3.50, 52 pgs.)-Silver hologram on-c w/gatefold poster by Ron Lim; Spidey retells his origin .70 1.75 3.50
26-2nd printing; gold hologram on-c .70 1.75 3.50
27-45: 32-34-Punisher-c/story. 37-Maximum Carnage x-over. 39,40-Electro-c/s (cameo #38). 41-43-Iron Fist-c/stories w/Jae Lee-c/a. 42-Intro Platoon. 44-Hobgoblin app. .65 1.60
46-49,51-56: 46-Begin $1.95-c; bound-in card sheet. 51-Power & Responsibility Pt. 3 .80 2.00
46-($2.95)-Polybagged; silver ink-c w/16 pg. preview of cartoon series & animation style print; bound-in trading card sheet 1.20 3.00
50-($2.50)-Newsstand edition 1.00 2.50
50-($3.95)-Collectors edition w/holographic-c .80 1.60 4.00
51-($2.95)-Deluxe edition foil-c; flip book 1.20 3.00
...: Carnage nn (6/93, $6.95, TPB)-r/Amazing S-M #344,345,359-363; spot varnish-c 1.20 3.00 7.00
.../Dr. Strange: "The Way to Dusty Death" nn (1992, $6.95, 68 pgs.) 1.20 3.00 7.00
Special Edition 1 (12/92-c, 11/92 inside)-The Trial of Venom; ordered thru mail with $5.00 donation or more to UNICEF; embossed metallic ink; came bagged w/bound-in poster; Daredevil app. 1.65 4.00 10.00
...Vs. Venom nn (1990, $8.95, TPB)-r/Amaz. S-M #300,315-317 w/new McFarlane-c 1.50 3.80 9.00

NOTE: ***Erik Larsen*** *c/a-15, 18-23.* ***M. Rogers/Keith Williams*** *c/a-27, 28.*

SPIDER-MAN AND DAREDEVIL

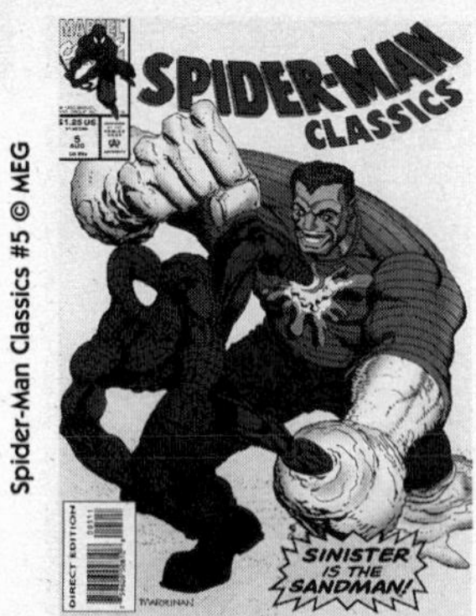

Spider-Man Classics #5 © MEG

Spider-Man 2099 Annual #1 © MEG

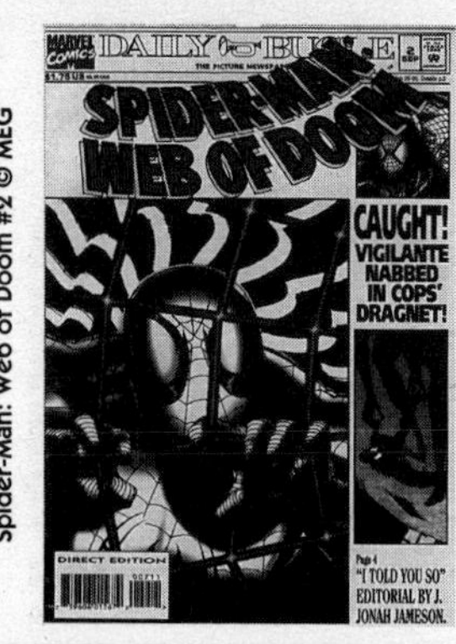

Spider-Man: Web of Doom #2 © MEG

GD25 FN65 NM94

March, 1984 ($2.00, one-shot, deluxe paper)
Marvel Comics Group

1-r/Spectacular Spider-Man #26-28 by Miller 1.30 3.25

SPIDER-MAN AND HIS AMAZING FRIENDS
Dec, 1981 (One shot) (See Marvel Action Universe)
Marvel Comics Group

1-Adapted from NBC TV cartoon show; Green Goblin-c/story; 1st Spidey, Firestar, Iceman team-up; Spiegle-p 1.30 3.25

SPIDER-MAN AND THE INCREDIBLE HULK (See listing under Amazing...)

SPIDER-MAN AND X-FACTOR
May, 1994 - No. 3, July, 1994 ($1.95, limited series)
Marvel Comics

1-3 .80 2.00

SPIDER-MAN CLASSICS
Apr, 1993 - Present ($1.25)
Marvel Comics

1-21: 1-r/Amaz. Fantasy #15 & Strange Tales #115. 2-16-r/Amaz. Spider-Man #1-15. 6-Austin-c(i) 1.25
15-($2.95)-Polybagged w/16 pg. insert & animation style print; r/Amazing S-M #14 (1st Green Goblin) 1.20 3.00

SPIDER-MAN COMICS MAGAZINE
Jan, 1987 - No. 13, 1988 ($1.50, Digest-size)
Marvel Comics Group

1-13-Reprints 1.50

SPIDER-MAN MAGAZINE
Mar, 1994 - Present ($1.95, color, magazine)
Marvel Comics

1-Contains 4 S-M promo cards & 4 X-Men Ultra Fleer cards; Spider-Man story by Romita, Sr.; X-Men story; puzzles & games .80 2.00
2-5: 2-Doc Octopus & X-Men stories .80 2.00

SPIDER-MAN MEGAZINE
Oct, 1994 - Present ($2.95, 100 pgs.)
Marvel Comics

1-6: 1-r/ASM #16,224,225, Marvel Team-Up #1 1.20 3.00

SPIDER-MAN: THE ARACHNIS PROJECT
Aug, 1994 - No. 6, Jan, 1995 ($1.75, limited series)
Marvel Comics

1-6-Venom, Styx, Stone & Jury app. .70 1.75

SPIDER-MAN: THE MUTANT AGENDA
No. 0, Feb, 1994; Mar, 1994 - No. 3, May, 1994 ($1.75, mini-series)
Marvel Comics

0-(2/94, $1.25, 52 pgs.)-Crosses over w/newspaper strip; has empty pages to paste in newspaper strips; gives origin of Spidey 1.25
1-3: Beast & Hobgoblin app. 1-X-Men app. .70 1.75

SPIDER-MAN SAGA (Marvel)(Value: cover or less)

SPIDER-MAN 2099 (See Amazing Spider-Man #365)
Nov, 1992 - Present ($1.25)
Marvel Comics

1-($1.75, stiff-c)-Red foil stamped-c; begins origin of Miguel O'Hara (Spider-Man 2099); Leonardi/Williamson-c/a begins 1.30 3.25
1-2nd printing ($1.75) .70 1.75
2-Origin continued, ends #3 1.10 2.75
3,4: 4-Doom 2099 app. .80 2.00
5-18: 13-Extra 16 pg. insert on Midnight Sons 1.25
19-24,26-30: 19-Begin $1.50-c; bound-in trading card sheet 1.50
25-($2.25, 52 pgs.)-Newsstand edition .90 2.25
25-($2.95, 52 pgs.)-Deluxe edition w/embossed foil-c 1.20 3.00
Annual 1 (1994, $2.95, 68 pgs.) 1.20 3.00
NOTE: ***Ron Lim*** *a(p)-18; c(p)-13, 16, 18.* ***Leonardi/Williamson*** *a-1-13, 15-17, 19, 20; c-1-12, 15, 17, 19, 20.*

GD25 FN65 NM94

SPIDER-MAN UNLIMITED
May, 1993 - Present ($3.95, quarterly, 68 pgs.)
Marvel Comics

1-10: 1-Begin Maximum Carnage storyline, ends #2; Ron Lim-c/a(p) in #1-6. 1-Carnage-c/s. 2-Venom & Carnage-c/s 1.60 4.00

SPIDER-MAN VS. DRACULA
Jan, 1994 ($1.75, 52 pgs.)
Marvel Comics

1-r/Giant-Size Spider-Man #1 plus new Matt Fox-a .70 1.75

SPIDER-MAN VS. WOLVERINE
Feb, 1987 (One-shot); V2#1, 1990 (Both have 68 pgs.)
Marvel Comics Group

1-Williamson-c/a(i); intro Charlemagne; death of Ned Leeds (old Hobgoblin) 3.00 8.00 18.00
V2#1 (1990, $4.95)-Reprints #1 (2/87) 1.00 2.00 5.00

SPIDER-MAN: WEB OF DOOM
Aug, 1994 - No. 3, Oct, 1994 ($1.75, limited series)
Marvel Comics

1-3 .70 1.75

SPIDER REIGN OF THE VAMPIRE KING, THE (Also see The Spider)
1992 - No. 3, 1992 ($4.95, color, coated stock, mini-series, 52 pgs.)
Eclipse Books

Book One - Three: Truman scripts & painted-c 1.00 2.00 5.00

SPIDER'S WEB, THE (See G-8 and His Battle Aces)

SPIDER-WOMAN (Also see The Avengers #240, Marvel Spotlight #32, Marvel Super Heroes Secret Wars #7 & Marvel Two-In-One #29)
April, 1978 - No. 50, June, 1983 (New logo #47 on)
Marvel Comics Group

1-New complete origin & mask added 1.70 4.25
2-36,39-49: 6,19-Werewolf by Night-c/stories. 13,15-The Shroud-c/s. 20,28,29-Spider-Man app. 46-Kingpin app. 49-Tigra-c/story .60 1.60
37,38-X-Men x-over; 37-1st app. Siryn of X-Force; origin retold 1.30 3.25
50-(52 pgs.)-Death of Spider-Woman; photo-c 1.30 3.25
NOTE: ***Austin*** *a-37i.* ***Byrne*** *c-26p.* ***Layton*** *c-19.* ***Miller*** *c-32p.*

SPIDER-WOMAN
Nov, 1993 - No. 4, Feb, 1994 ($1.75, mini-series)
Marvel Comics

V2#1-4: 1,2-Origin; U.S. Agent app. .70 1.75

SPIDEY SUPER STORIES (Spider-Man)
Oct, 1974 - No. 57, Mar, 1982 (35¢) (no ads)
Marvel/Children's TV Workshop

1-Origin (stories simplified) 1.20 3.00
2-12: 2-Kraven. 6-Iceman .80 2.00
13-38,40-44,46-57: 31-Moondragon-c/story; Dr. Doom app. 33-Hulk. 34-Sub-Mariner. 38-F.F. 44-Vision. 56-Battles Jack O'Lantern-c/story (exactly one year after 1st app. in Machine Man #19) .80 1.90
39-Thanos-c/story 1.10 2.75
45-Silver Surfer & Dr. Doom app. 1.10 2.75

SPIKE AND TYKE (See M.G.M.'s...)

SPIN & MARTY (TV) (Walt Disney's)(See Walt Disney Showcase #32)
No. 714, June, 1956 - No. 1082, Mar-May, 1960 (All photo-c)
Dell Publishing Co. (Mickey Mouse Club)

4-Color 714 (#1) 11.50 34.00 80.00
4-Color 767,808 (#2,3) 10.00 30.00 60.00
4-Color 826 (#4)-Annette Funicello photo-c 26.00 78.00 180.00
5(3-5/58) - 9(6-8/59) 8.35 25.00 50.00
4-Color 1026,1082 8.35 25.00 50.00

SPINE-TINGLING TALES (Doctor Spektor Presents...)
May, 1975 - No. 4, Jan, 1976 (All 25¢ issues)

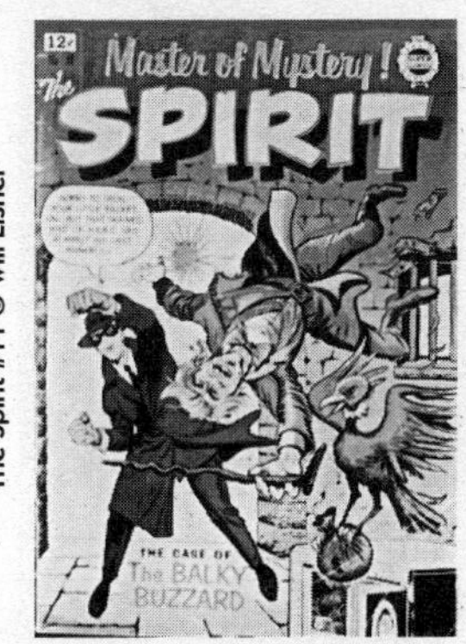

The Spirit #11 © Will Eisner

The Spirit 3/12/50 © Will Eisner

The Spirit #8 © Will Eisner

Gold Key

	GD25	FN65	NM94
1-4: 1-1st Tragg-r/Mystery Comics Digest #3. 2-Origin Ra-Ka-Tep-r/Mystery Comics Digest #1; Dr. Spektor #12. 3-All Durak-r issue; 4-Baron Tibor's 1st app.-r/Mystery Comics Digest #4; painted-c			1.00

SPIRAL PATH, THE (Eclipse)(Value: cover or less)

SPIRAL ZONE
Feb, 1988 - No. 4, May, 1988 ($1.00, mini-series)
DC Comics

	GD25	FN65	NM94
1-4-Based on Tonka toys			1.00

SPIRIT, THE (Weekly Comic Book)
6/2/40 - 10/5/52 (16 pgs.; 8 pgs.) (no cover) (in color)
(Distributed through various newspapers and other sources)
Will Eisner
NOTE: **Eisner** script, pencils/inks for the most part from 6/2/40-4/26/42; a few stories assisted by Jack Cole, Fine, Powell and Kotsky.

	GD25	FN65	NM94
6/2/40(#1)-Origin/1st app. The Spirit; reprinted in Police #11; Lady Luck (Brenda Banks)(1st app.) by Chuck Mazoujian & Mr. Mystic (1st. app.) by S. R. (Bob) Powell begin	60.00	180.00	420.00
6/9/40(#2)	26.00	78.00	180.00
6/16/40(#3)-Black Queen app. in Spirit	17.00	51.00	110.00
6/23/40(#4)-Mr. Mystic receives magical necklace	13.00	40.00	90.00
6/30/40(#5)	13.00	40.00	90.00
7/7/40(#6)-Black Queen app. in Spirit	13.00	40.00	90.00
7/14/40(#7)-8/4/40(#10)	10.00	30.50	70.00
8/11/40-9/22/40	9.00	27.00	62.00
9/29/40-Ellen drops engagement with Homer Creep	8.00	24.00	56.00
10/6/40-11/3/40	8.00	24.00	56.00
11/10/40-The Black Queen app.	8.00	24.00	56.00
11/17/40, 11/24/40	8.00	24.00	56.00
12/1/40-Ellen spanking by Spirit on cover & inside; Eisner-1st 3 pgs., J. Cole rest	11.50	34.00	80.00
12/8/40-3/9/41	5.70	17.00	40.00
3/16/41-Intro. & 1st app. Silk Satin	10.00	30.00	70.00
3/23/41-6/1/41: 5/11/41-Last Lady Luck by Mazoujian; 5/18/41-Lady Luck by Nick Viscardi begins, ends 2/22/42	5.70	17.00	40.00
6/8/41-2nd app. Satin; Spirit learns Satin is also a British agent	8.50	25.50	60.00
6/15/41-1st app. Twilight	7.00	21.00	50.00
6/22/41-Hitler app. in Spirit	5.00	15.00	35.00
6/29/41-1/25/42,2/8/42	5.00	15.00	35.00
2/1/42-1st app. Duchess	7.00	21.00	50.00
2/15/42-4/26/42-Lady Luck by Klaus Nordling begins 3/1/42	5.00	15.00	35.00
5/3/42-8/16/42-Eisner/Fine/Quality staff assists on Spirit	4.00	12.00	24.00
8/23/42-Satin cover splash; Spirit by Eisner/Fine although signed by Fine	8.00	24.00	56.00
8/30/42,9/27/42-10/11/42,10/25/42-11/8/42-Eisner/Fine/Quality staff assists on Spirit	4.00	12.00	24.00
9/6/42-9/20/42,10/18/42-Fine/Belfi art on Spirit; scripts by Manly Wade Wellman	2.75	8.00	16.00
11/15/42-12/6/42,12/20/42,12/27/42,1/17/43-4/18/43,5/9/43-8/8/43-Wellman/Woolfolk scripts, Fine pencils, Quality staff inks	2.75	8.00	16.00
12/13/42,1/3/43,1/10/43,4/25/43,5/2/43-Eisner scripts/layouts; Fine pencils, Quality staff inks	3.35	10.00	20.00
8/15/43-Eisner script/layout; pencils/inks by Quality staff; Jack Cole-a	2.00	6.00	12.00
8/22/43-12/12/43-Wellman/Woolfolk scripts, Fine pencils, Quality staff inks; Mr. Mystic by Guardineer-10/10/43-10/24/43	2.00	6.00	12.00
12/19/43-8/13/44-Wellman/Woolfolk/Jack Cole scripts; Cole, Fine & Robin King-a; Last Mr. Mystic-5/14/44	1.70	5.00	10.00
8/20/44-12/16/45-Wellman/Woolfolk scripts; Fine art with unknown staff assists	1.70	5.00	10.00

NOTE: *Scripts/layouts by Eisner, or Eisner/Nordling, Eisner/Mercer or Spranger/Eisner; inks by Eisner or Eisner/Spranger in issues 12/23/45-2/2/47.*

	GD25	FN65	NM94
12/23/45-1/6/46: 12/23/45-Christmas-c	3.50	10.50	24.00
1/13/46-Origin Spirit retold	5.00	15.00	35.00
1/20/46-1st postwar Satin app.	4.50	14.00	32.00
1/27/46-3/10/46: 3/3/46-Last Lady Luck by Nordling	3.50	10.50	24.00
3/17/46-Intro. & 1st app. Nylon	4.50	14.00	32.00
3/24/46,3/31/46,4/14/46	3.50	10.50	24.00
4/7/46-2nd app. Nylon	4.00	12.00	28.00
4/21/46-Intro. & 1st app. Mr. Carrion & His Pet Buzzard Julia	5.00	15.00	35.00
4/28/46-5/12/46,5/26/46-6/30/46: Lady Luck by Fred Schwab in issues 5/5/46-11/3/46	3.50	10.50	24.00
5/19/46-2nd app. Mr. Carrion	4.00	12.00	28.00
7/7/46-Intro. & 1st app. Dulcet Tone & Skinny	5.00	15.00	35.00
7/14/46-9/29/46	3.50	10.50	24.00
10/6/46-Intro. & 1st app. P'Gell	5.70	17.00	40.00
10/13/46-11/3/46,11/16/46-11/24/46	3.50	10.50	24.00
11/10/46-2nd app. P'Gell	4.00	12.00	28.00
12/1/46-3rd app. P'Gell	3.70	11.00	26.00
12/8/46-2/2/47	3.00	9.00	21.00

NOTE: *Scripts, pencils/inks by Eisner except where noted in issues 2/9/47-12/19/48.*

	GD25	FN65	NM94
2/9/47-7/6/47: 6/8/47-Eisner self satire	3.00	9.00	21.00
7/13/47- "Hansel & Gretel" fairy tales	4.50	14.00	32.00
7/20/47-Li'L Abner, Daddy Warbucks, Dick Tracy, Fearless Fosdick parody; A-Bomb blast-c	4.50	14.00	32.00
7/27/47-9/14/47	3.00	9.00	21.00
9/21/47-Pearl Harbor flashback	3.00	9.00	21.00
9/28/47-1st mention of Flying Saucers in comics-3 months after 1st sighting in Idaho on 6/25/47	6.50	19.00	45.00
10/5/47- "Cinderella" fairy tales	4.50	14.00	32.00
10/12/47-11/30/47	3.00	9.00	21.00
12/7/47-Intro. & 1st app. Powder Pouf	5.00	15.00	35.00
12/14/47-12/28/47	3.00	9.00	21.00
1/4/48-2nd app. Powder Pouf	4.00	12.00	28.00
1/11/48-1st app. Sparrow Fallon; Powder Pouf app.	4.00	12.00	28.00
1/18/48-He-Man ad cover; satire issue	4.00	12.00	28.00
1/25/48-Intro. & 1st app. Castanet	4.50	14.00	32.00
2/1/48-2nd app. Castanet	3.50	10.50	24.00
2/8/48-3/7/48	3.00	9.00	21.00
3/14/48-Only app. Kretchma	3.50	10.50	24.00
3/21/48,3/28/48,4/11/48-4/25/48	3.00	9.00	21.00
4/4/48-Only app. Wild Rice	3.50	10.50	24.00
5/2/48-2nd app. Sparrow	3.00	9.00	21.00
5/9/48-6/27/48,7/11/48,7/18/48: 6/13/48-Television issue	3.00	9.00	21.00
7/4/48-Spirit by Andre Le Blanc	2.00	6.00	14.00
7/25/48-Ambrose Bierce's "The Thing" adaptation classic by Eisner/Grandenetti	6.50	19.00	45.00
8/1/48-8/15/48,8/29/48-9/12/48	3.00	9.00	21.00
8/22/48-Poe's "Fall of the House of Usher" classic by Eisner/Grandenetti	6.50	19.00	45.00
9/19/48-Only app. Lorelei	3.70	11.00	26.00
9/26/48-10/31/48	3.00	9.00	21.00
11/7/48-Only app. Plaster of Paris	4.00	12.00	28.00
11/14/48-12/19/48	3.00	9.00	21.00

NOTE: *Scripts by Eisner or Feiffer or Eisner/Feiffer or Nordling. Art by Eisner with backgrounds by Eisner, Grandenetti, Le Blanc, Stallman, Nordling, Dixon and/or others in issues 12/26/48-4/1/51 except where noted.*

	GD25	FN65	NM94
12/26/48-Reprints some covers of 1948 with flashbacks	3.00	9.00	21.00
1/2/49-1/16/49	3.00	9.00	21.00
1/23/49,1/30/49-1st & 2nd app. Thorne	4.00	12.00	28.00
2/6/49-8/14/49	3.00	9.00	21.00
8/21/49,8/28/49-1st & 2nd app. Monica Veto	4.00	12.00	28.00
9/4/49,9/11/49	3.00	9.00	21.00
9/18/49-Love comic cover; has gag love comic ads on inside	4.30	13.00	30.00
9/25/49-Only app. Ice	3.70	11.00	26.00

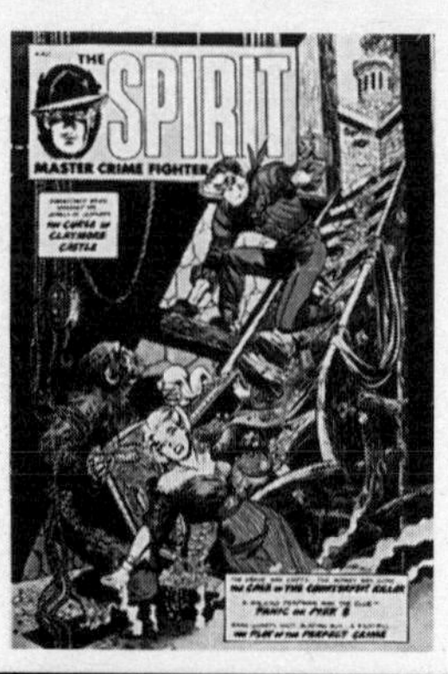

The Spirit #1(FH) © Will Eisner

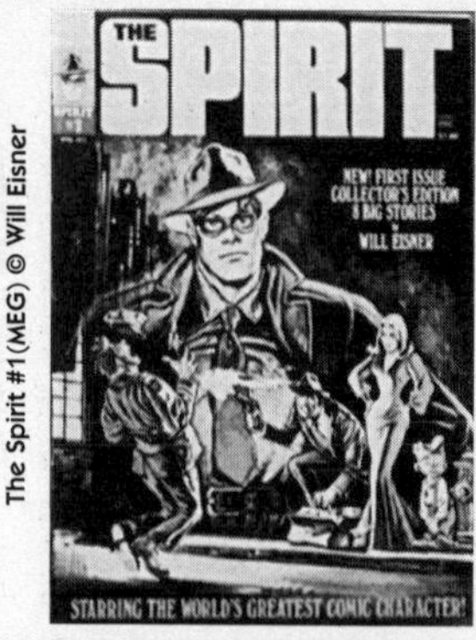

The Spirit #1(MEG) © Will Eisner

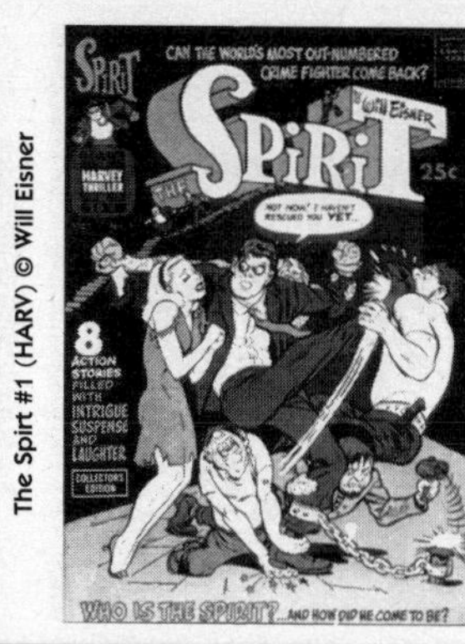

The Spirit #1 (HARV) © Will Eisner

	GD25	FN65	NM94
10/2/49,10/9/49-Autumn News appears & dies in 10/9 issue	3.70	11.00	26.00
10/16/49-11/27/49,12/18/49,12/25/49	3.00	9.00	21.00
12/4/49,12/11/49-1st & 2nd app. Flaxen	4.00	12.00	24.00
1/1/50-Flashbacks to all of the Spirit girls-Thorne, Ellen, Satin, & Monica	5.00	15.00	35.00
1/8/50-Intro. & 1st app. Sand Saref	7.00	21.00	50.00
1/15/50-2nd app. Saref	5.00	15.00	35.00
1/22/50-2/5/50	3.00	9.00	21.00
2/12/50-Roller Derby issue	3.50	10.50	24.00
2/19/50-Half Dead Mr. Lox - Classic horror	3.70	11.00	26.00
2/26/50-4/23/50,5/14/50,5/28/50,7/23/50-9/3/50	3.00	9.00	21.00
4/30/50-Script/art by Le Blanc with Eisner framing	1.70	5.00	10.00
5/7/50,6/4/50-7/16/50-Abe Kanegson-a	1.70	5.00	10.00
5/21/50-Script by Feiffer/Eisner, art by Blaisdell, Eisner framing	1.70	5.00	10.00
9/10/50-P'Gell returns	4.00	12.00	28.00
9/17/50-1/7/51	3.00	9.00	21.00
1/14/51-Life Magazine cover; brief biography of Comm. Dolan, Sand Saref, Silk Satin, P'Gell, Sammy & Willum, Darling O'Shea, & Mr. Carrion & His Pet Buzzard Julia, with pin-ups by Eisner	3.70	11.00	26.00
1/21/51,2/4/51-4/1/51	3.00	9.00	21.00
1/28/51- "The Meanest Man in the World" classic by Eisner	3.70	11.00	26.00
4/8/51-7/29/51,8/12/51-Last Eisner issue	3.00	9.00	21.00
8/5/51,8/19/51-7/20/52-Not Eisner	1.70	5.00	10.00
7/27/52-(Rare)-Denny Colt in Outer Space by Wally Wood; 7 pg. S/F story of E.C. vintage	32.00	95.00	225.00
8/3/52-(Rare)- "Mission...The Moon" by Wood	32.00	95.00	225.00
8/10/52-(Rare)- "A DP On The Moon" by Wood	32.00	95.00	225.00
8/17/52-(Rare)- "Heart" by Wood/Eisner	27.00	81.00	190.00
8/24/52-(Rare)- "Rescue" by Wood	32.00	95.00	225.00
8/31/52-(Rare)- "The Last Man" by Wood	32.00	95.00	225.00
9/7/52-(Rare)- "The Man in The Moon" by Wood	32.00	95.00	225.00
9/14/52-(Rare)-Eisner/Wenzel-a	6.50	19.00	45.00
9/21/52-(Rare)- "Denny Colt, Alias The Spirit/Space Report" by Eisner/Wenzel	11.50	34.00	80.00
9/28/52-(Rare)- "Return From The Moon" by Wood	32.00	95.00	225.00
10/5/52-(Rare)- "The Last Story" by Eisner	11.50	34.00	80.00

Large Tabloid pages from 1946 on (Eisner) - Price 30 percent over listed prices.

NOTE: *Spirit sections came out in both large and small format. Some newspapers went to the 8-pg. format months before others. Some printed the pages so they cannot be folded into a small comic book section; these are worth less. (Also see Three Comics & Spiritman).*

SPIRIT, THE (1st Series)(Also see Police Comics #11)
1944 - No. 22, Aug, 1950
Quality Comics Group (Vital)

	GD25	FN65	NM94
nn(#1)- "Wanted Dead or Alive"	57.00	171.00	400.00
nn(#2)- "Crime Doesn't Pay"	34.00	103.00	240.00
nn(#3)- "Murder Runs Wild"	27.00	80.00	185.00
4,5: 4-Flatfoot Burns begins, ends #22. 5-Wertham app.	20.00	60.00	140.00
6-10	17.00	52.00	120.00
11	16.00	48.00	110.00
12-17-Eisner-c. 19-Honeybun app.	26.00	78.00	180.00
18-21-Strip-r by Eisner; Eisner-c	36.00	107.00	250.00
22-Used by N.Y. Legis. Comm; classic Eisner-c	49.00	146.00	340.00
Super Reprint #11-r/Quality Spirit #19 by Eisner	3.60	9.00	18.00
Super Reprint #12-r/Spirit #17 by Fine; Simon-c	3.20	8.00	16.00

SPIRIT, THE (2nd Series)
Spring, 1952 - No. 5, 1954
Fiction House Magazines

	GD25	FN65	NM94
1-Not Eisner	27.00	81.00	190.00
2-Eisner-c/a(2)	28.00	84.00	195.00
3-Eisner/Grandenetti-c	19.00	57.00	130.00
4-Eisner/Grandenetti-c; Eisner-a	22.00	65.00	150.00
5-Eisner-c/a(4)	27.00	81.00	190.00

SPIRIT, THE
Oct, 1966 - No. 2, Mar, 1967 (Giant Size, 25¢, 68 pgs.)
Harvey Publications

	GD25	FN65	NM94
1-Eisner-r plus 9 new pgs.(origin Denny Colt, Take 3, plus 2 filler pgs.) (#3 was advertised, but never published)	5.00	15.00	35.00
2-Eisner-r plus 9 new pgs.(origin of the Octopus)	5.00	15.00	35.00

SPIRIT, THE (Underground)
Jan, 1973 - No. 2, Sept, 1973 (Black & White)
Kitchen Sink Enterprises (Krupp Comics)

	GD25	FN65	NM94
1-New Eisner-c & 4 pgs. new Eisner-a plus-r (titled Crime Convention)	1.30	3.25	8.00
2-New Eisner-c & 4 pgs. new Eisner-a plus-r (titled Meets P'Gell)	1.65	4.00	10.00

SPIRIT, THE (Magazine)
4/74 - No. 16, 10/76; No. 17, Winter, 1977 - No. 41, 6/83 (B&W w/color)
Warren Publ. Co./Krupp Comic Works No. 17 on

	GD25	FN65	NM94
1-Eisner-r begin	1.00	2.00	5.00
2-5		1.20	3.00
6-9,11-16: 7-All Ebony issue. 8-Female Foes issue. 12-X-Mas issue. 16-Giant Summer Special ($1.50)		.90	2.40
10-Giant Summer Special ($1.50)-Origin		1.10	2.80
17,18(8/78): 17-Lady Luck-r. 20-Outer Space-r			1.20
19-21-New Eisner-a. 20,21-Wood-r (#21-r/A DP on the Moon by Wood)			1.20
22,23-Wood-r (#22-r/Mission the Moon by Wood)			1.20
24-29,31-35: 28-r/last story (10/5/52)			1.20
30-(7/81)-Special Spirit Jam issue w/Caniff, Corben, Bolland, Byrne, Miller, Kurtzman, Rogers, Sienkiewicz-a & 40 others			1.50
36-Begin Spirit Section-r; r/1st story (6/2/40) in color; new Eisner-c/a (18 pgs.)($2.95)		1.20	3.00
37-41: 37-r/2nd story in color plus 18 pgs. new Eisner-a. 38-41: r/3rd - 6th stories in color. 41-Lady Luck Mr. Mystic in color		1.20	3.00
Special 1(1975)-All Eisner-a		.70	1.80

NOTE: *Covers pencilled/inked by* **Eisner** *only #1-9,12-16; painted by Eisner & Ken Kelly #10 & 11; painted by Eisner #17-up; one color story reprinted in #1-10.* **Austin** *a-30i.* **Byrne** *a-30p.* **Miller** *a-30p.*

SPIRIT, THE (See Will Eisner's 3-D Classics Featuring...)
Oct, 1983 - No. 87, Jan, 1992 (Baxter paper) ($2.00)
Kitchen Sink Enterprises

	GD25	FN65	NM94
1-4: 1-Origin-r/12/23/45 Spirit Section. 2-r/sections 1/20/46-2/10/46. 3-r/2/17/46-3/10/46. 4-r/3/17/46-4/7/46		.90	2.25
5-11 ($2.95 cover): 11-Last color issue		.90	2.25
12-87 ($1.95/$2.00, B&W): 54-r/section 2/19/50. 85-87-Reprint the Outer Space Spirit stories by Wood. 86-r/A DP on the Moon by Wood from 1952		.90	2.25

SPIRIT: THE ORIGIN YEARS
May, 1992 - Present ($2.95, B&W, high quality paper)
Kitchen Sink Press

	GD25	FN65	NM94
1-4: 1-r/sections 6/2/40(origin)-6/23/40 (all 1940s)		1.20	3.00

SPIRITMAN (Also see Three Comics)
No date (1944) (10¢)
(Triangle Sales Co. ad on back cover)
No publisher listed

	GD25	FN65	NM94
1-Three 16pg. Spirit sections bound together, (1944, 10¢, 52 pgs.)	16.00	48.00	110.00
2-Two Spirit sections (3/26/44, 4/2/44) bound together; by Lou Fine	13.00	40.00	90.00

SPIRIT WORLD (Magazine)
Fall, 1971 (Black & White)
National Periodical Publications

	GD25	FN65	NM94
1-Kirby-a; Neal Adams-c	1.00	2.50	6.00

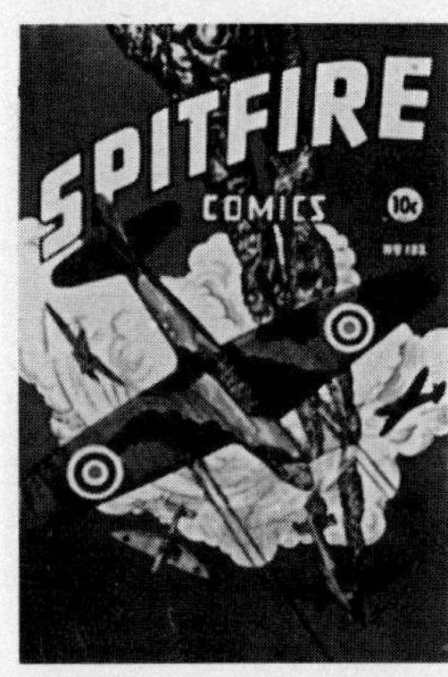

Spitfire Comics #132 © EP

Spook #22 © STAR

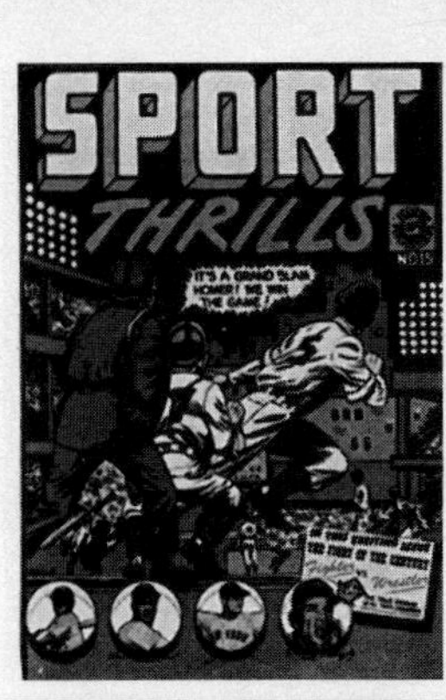

Sport Thrills #15 © STAR

GD25 FN65 NM94 | GD25 FN65 NM94

SPITFIRE
No. 132, 1944 (Aug) - No. 133, 1945 (Female undercover agent)
Malverne Herald (Elliot)(J. R. Mahon)
132,133: Both have Classics Gift Box ads on b/c with checklist to #20 — 14.00 43.00 100.00

SPITFIRE AND THE TROUBLESHOOTERS (Marvel)(Value: cover or less)

SPITFIRE COMICS (Also see Double Up)
Aug, 1941 - No. 2, Oct, 1941 (Pocket size; 100 pgs.)
Harvey Publications
1-Origin The Clown, The Fly-Man, The Spitfire & The Magician From Bagdad — 42.00 126.00 295.00
2 — 37.00 111.00 260.00

SPLITTING IMAGE
Mar, 1993 - No. 2, 1993 ($1.95, color)
Image Comics
1,2-Simpson-c/a; parody comic — .80 2.00

SPOOF
Oct, 1970; No. 2, Nov, 1972 - No. 5, May, 1973
Marvel Comics Group
1-Infinity-c; Dark Shadows-c & parody — 1.80 4.50
2-5: 3-Beatles, Osmond's, Jackson 5, David Cassidy, Nixon & Agnew-c. 5-Rod Serling, Woody Allen, Ted Kennedy-c — 1.00 2.50

SPOOK (Formerly Shock Detective Cases)
No. 22, Jan, 1953 - No. 30, Oct, 1954
Star Publications
22-Sgt. Spook-r; acid in face story; hanging-c — 16.50 50.00 115.00
23,25,27: 27-Two Sgt. Spook-r — 10.00 30.00 70.00
24-Used in **SOTI**, pgs. 182,183-r/Inside Crime #2; Transvestism story — 12.00 36.00 85.00
26-Disbrow-a — 11.00 32.00 75.00
28,29-Rulah app. 29-Jo-Jo app. — 11.00 32.00 75.00
30-Disbrow-c/a(2); only Star-c — 11.00 32.00 75.00
NOTE: ***L. B. Cole** covers-all issues; a-28(1 pg.). **Disbrow** a-26(2), 28, 29(2), 30(2); No. 30 r/Blue Bolt Weird Tales #114.*

SPOOK COMICS
1946
Baily Publications/Star
1-Mr. Lucifer story — 19.00 57.00 130.00

SPOOKY (The Tuff Little Ghost; see Casper The Friendly Ghost)
11/55 - 139, 11/73; No. 140, 7/74 - No. 155, 3/77; No. 156, 12/77 - No. 158, 4/78; No. 159, 9/78; No. 160, 10/79; No. 161, 9/80
Harvey Publications
1-Nightmare begins (see Casper #19) — 27.00 80.00 185.00
2 — 13.00 40.00 90.00
3-10(1956-57) — 7.50 22.50 45.00
11-20(1957-58) — 4.00 11.00 22.00
21-40(1958-59) — 2.80 7.00 14.00
41-60 — 1.80 4.50 9.00
61-80 — 1.20 2.90 7.00
81-120 — 1.60 4.00
121-126,133-140 — .90 2.25
127-132: All 52 pg. Giants — 1.40 3.50
141-161 — .65 1.60

SPOOKY
Nov, 1991 - No. 4, Sept, 1992 ($1.00/$1.25)
Harvey Comics
1-4: 3-Begin $1.25-c — 1.25
...Digest 1-3 (10/92, 6/93, 10/93, $1.75, 100 pgs.)-Casper, Wendy, etc. — .70 1.75

SPOOKY HAUNTED HOUSE
Oct, 1972 - No. 15, Feb, 1975
Harvey Publications
1 — 1.70 5.00 12.00
2-5 — 1.00 2.50 6.00
6-10 — 1.20 3.00
11-15 — 1.50

SPOOKY MYSTERIES
No date (1946) (10¢)
Your Guide Publ. Co.
1-Mr. Spooky, Super Snooper, Pinky, Girl Detective app. — 11.50 34.00 80.00

SPOOKY SPOOKTOWN
9/61; No. 2, 9/62 - No. 52, 12/73; No. 53, 10/74 - No. 66, Dec, 1976
Harvey Publications
1-Casper, Spooky; 68 pgs. begin — 11.00 32.00 75.00
2 — 6.35 19.00 38.00
3-5 — 4.70 14.00 28.00
6-10 — 3.60 9.00 18.00
11-20 — 2.40 6.00 12.00
21-39: 39-Last 68 pg. issue — 1.00 2.50 6.00
40-45: All 52 pgs. — 1.20 3.00
46-66: 61-Hot Stuff/Spooky team-up story — .80 2.00

SPORT COMICS (Becomes True Sport Picture Stories #5 on)
Oct, 1940(No mo.) - No. 4, Nov, 1941
Street & Smith Publications
1-Life story of Lou Gehrig — 39.00 118.00 275.00
2 — 19.00 58.00 135.00
3,4 — 17.00 52.00 120.00

SPORT LIBRARY (See Charlton Sport Library)

SPORTS ACTION (Formerly Sport Stars)
No. 2, Feb, 1950 - No. 14, Sept, 1952
Marvel/Atlas Comics (ACI No. 2,3/SAI No. 4-14)
2-Powell painted-c; George Gipp life story — 23.00 70.00 160.00
3-Everett-a — 14.00 43.00 100.00
4-11,14: Weiss-a — 13.00 40.00 90.00
12,13: 12-Everett-c. 13-Krigstein-a — 14.00 43.00 100.00
NOTE: *Title may have changed after No. 3, to Crime Must Lose No. 4 on, due to publisher change. **Sol Brodsky** c-4-7, 13, 14. **Maneely** c-3, 8-11.*

SPORT STARS
Feb-Mar, 1946 - No. 4, Aug-Sept, 1946 (Half comic, half photo magazine)
Parents' Magazine Institute (Sport Stars)
1- "How Tarzan Got That Way" story of Johnny Weissmuller — 27.00 80.00 185.00
2-Baseball greats — 17.00 52.00 120.00
3,4 — 14.00 43.00 100.00

SPORT STARS (Becomes Sports Action #2 on)
Nov, 1949 (52 pgs.)
Marvel Comics (ACI)
1-Knute Rockne; painted-c — 25.00 75.00 175.00

SPORT THRILLS (Formerly Dick Cole; becomes Jungle thrills #16)
No. 11, Nov, 1950 - No. 15, Nov, 1951
Star Publications
11-Dick Cole begins, ends #13?; Ted Williams & Ty Cobb life stories — 13.00 40.00 90.00
12-Joe DiMaggio, Phil Rizzuto stories & photos on-c; L.B. Cole-c/a — 10.00 30.00 65.00
13-15-All L. B. Cole-c. 13-Jackie Robinson, Pee Wee Reese stories & photo on-c. 14-Johnny Weissmuler life story — 10.00 30.00 65.00
Accepted Reprint #11 (#15 on-c, nd); L.B. Cole-c — 4.00 12.00 24.00
Accepted Reprint #12 (nd); L.B. Cole-c; Joe DiMaggio & Phil Rizzuto life stories-r/#12 — 4.00 12.00 24.00

SPOTLIGHT (TV)

Spy-Hunters #5 © ACG

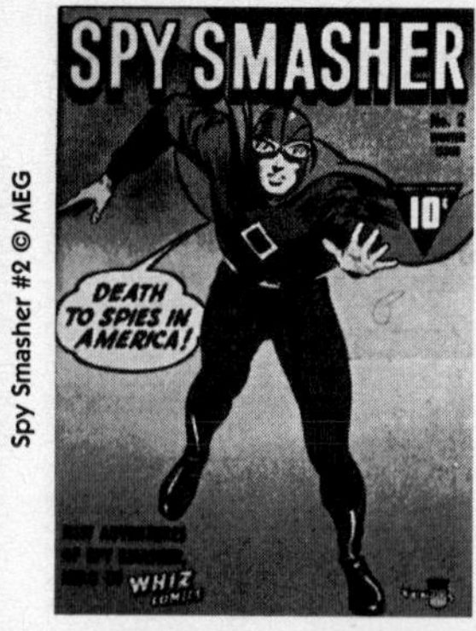

Spy Smasher #2 © MEG

Squalor #1 © First

Sept, 1978 - No. 4, Mar, 1979 (Hanna-Barbera)
Marvel Comics Group

	GD25	FN65	NM94
1-4: 1-Huckleberry Hound, Yogi Bear; Shaw-a. 2-Quick Draw McGraw, Augie Doggie, Snooper & Blabber. 3-The Jetsons, Yakky Doodle. 4-Magilla Gorilla, Snagglepuss		.80	2.00

SPOTLIGHT COMICS (Becomes Red Seal Comics #14 on?)
Nov, 1944 - No. 3, 1945
Harry 'A' Chesler (Our Army, Inc.)

	GD25	FN65	NM94
1-The Black Dwarf (cont'd in Red Seal?), The Veiled Avenger, & Barry Kuda begin; Tuska-c	39.00	118.00	275.00
2	34.00	101.00	235.00
3-Injury to eye story (reprinted from Scoop #3)	35.00	105.00	245.00

SPOTTY THE PUP (Becomes Super Pup #4, see Television Puppet Show)
No. 2, Oct-Nov, 1953 - No. 3, Dec-Jan, 1953-54 (Also see Funny Tunes)
Avon Periodicals/Realistic Comics

	GD25	FN65	NM94
2,3	4.00	11.00	22.00
nn (1953, Realistic-r)	2.40	6.00	12.00

SPUNKY (...Junior Cowboy)(...Comics #2 on)
April, 1949 - No. 7, Nov, 1951
Standard Comics

	GD25	FN65	NM94
1,2-Text illos by Frazetta	6.70	20.00	40.00
3-7	4.00	10.00	20.00

SPUNKY THE SMILING SPOOK
Aug, 1957 - No. 4, May, 1958
Ajax/Farrell (World Famous Comics/Four Star Comic Corp.)

	GD25	FN65	NM94
1-Reprints from Frisky Fables	5.85	17.50	35.00
2-4	4.00	10.00	20.00

SPY AND COUNTERSPY (Becomes Spy Hunters #3 on)
Aug-Sept, 1949 - No. 2, Oct-Nov, 1949 (52 pgs.)
American Comics Group

	GD25	FN65	NM94
1-Origin, 1st app. Jonathan Kent, Counterspy	13.50	41.00	95.00
2	10.00	30.00	65.00

SPY CASES (Formerly The Kellys)
No. 26, Sept, 1950 - No. 19, Oct, 1953
Marvel/Atlas Comics (Hercules Publ.)

	GD25	FN65	NM94
26 (#1)	13.00	40.00	90.00
27(#2),28(#3, 2/51): 27-Everett-a; bondage-c	9.15	27.50	55.00
4(4/51) - 7,9,10	6.70	20.00	40.00
8-A-Bomb-c/story	8.35	25.00	50.00
11-19: 10-14-War format	5.35	16.00	32.00

NOTE: ***Sol Brodsky*** *c-1-5, 8, 9, 11-14, 17, 18.* ***Maneely*** *a-8; c-7, 10.* ***Tuska*** *a-7.*

SPY FIGHTERS
March, 1951 - No. 15, July, 1953 (Cases from official records)
Marvel/Atlas Comics (CSI)

	GD25	FN65	NM94
1-Clark Mason begins; Tuska-a; Brodsky-c	13.50	41.00	95.00
2-Tuska-a	8.00	24.00	48.00
3-13: 3-5-Brodsky-c. 7-Heath-c	6.70	20.00	40.00
14,15-Pakula-a(3), Ed Win-a. 15-Brodsky-c	7.00	21.00	42.00

SPY-HUNTERS (Formerly Spy & Counterspy)
No. 3, Dec-Jan, 1949-50 - No. 24, June-July, 1953 (#3-14: 52 pgs.)
American Comics Group

	GD25	FN65	NM94
3-Jonathan Kent continues, ends #10	13.50	41.00	95.00
4-10: 4,8,10-Starr-a	9.15	27.50	55.00
11-15,17-22,24: 18-War-c begin. 21-War-c/stories begin	6.70	20.00	40.00
16-Williamson-a (9 pgs.)	10.00	30.00	70.00
23-Graphic torture, injury to eye panel	12.00	36.00	85.00

NOTE: ***Drucker*** *a-12.* ***Whitney*** *a-many issues; c-7, 8, 10-12, 15, 16.*

SPYKE (Epic Comics)(Value: cover or less)

SPYMAN (Top Secret Adventures on cover)
Sept, 1966 - No. 3, Feb, 1967 (12¢ issues)
Harvey Publications (Illustrated Humor)

	GD25	FN65	NM94
1-Steranko-a(p)-1st pro work; 1 pg. Neal Adams ad; Tuska-c/a, Crandall-a(i)	3.90	11.60	27.00
2,3: Simon-c. 2-Steranko-a(p)	2.90	8.60	20.00

SPY SMASHER (See Mighty Midget, Whiz & XMas Comics)
Fall, 1941 - No. 11, Feb, 1943 (Also see Crime Smasher)
Fawcett Publications

	GD25	FN65	NM94
1-Spy Smasher begins; silver metallic-c	243.00	730.00	1700.00
2-Raboy-c	111.00	332.00	775.00
3,4: 3-Bondage-c	81.00	242.00	565.00
5-7: Raboy-a; 6-Raboy-c/a. 7-Part photo-c(movie)	76.00	227.00	530.00
8-11: 9-Hitler, Tojo, Mussolini-c. 10-Hitler-c	61.00	182.00	425.00
Well Known Comics (1944, 12 pgs., 8-1/2x10-1/2"), paper-c, glued binding, printed in green; Bestmaid/Samuel Lowe giveaway	17.00	50.00	100.00

SPY THRILLERS (Police Badge No. 479 #5)
Nov, 1954 - No. 4, May, 1955
Atlas Comics (PrPI)

	GD25	FN65	NM94
1-Brodsky c-1,2	11.50	34.00	80.00
2-Last precode (1/55)	7.50	22.50	45.00
3,4	5.85	17.50	35.00

SQUADRON SUPREME (Marvel)(Value: cover or less)

SQUADRON SUPREME
Aug, 1985 - No. 12, Aug, 1986 (Maxi-series)
Marvel Comics Group

	GD25	FN65	NM94
1-Double size			1.50
2-12			1.00

SQUALOR (First)(Value: cover or less)

SQUEEKS
Oct, 1953 - No. 5, June, 1954
Lev Gleason Publications

	GD25	FN65	NM94
1-Funny animal; Biro-c	5.35	16.00	32.00
2-Biro-c	3.60	9.00	18.00
3-5: 3-Biro-c	3.00	7.50	15.00

STAINLESS STEEL RAT (Eagle)(Value: cover or less)

STALKER
June-July, 1975 - No. 4, Dec-Jan, 1975-76
National Periodical Publications

	GD25	FN65	NM94
1-Origin & 1st app; Ditko/Wood-c/a		1.40	3.50
2-4-Ditko/Wood-c/a		1.00	2.50

STALKERS (Marvel)(Value: cover or less)(Also see Epic)

STAMP COMICS (Stamps... on-c; Thrilling Adventures In...#8)
Oct, 1951 - No. 7, Oct, 1952 (No. 1: 15¢)
Youthful Magazines/Stamp Comics, Inc.

	GD25	FN65	NM94
1-('Stamps' on indicia No. 1)	24.00	72.00	165.00
2	13.00	40.00	90.00
3-6: 3,4-Kiefer, Wildey-a	11.50	34.00	80.00
7-Roy Krenkel (4 pgs.)	14.00	43.00	100.00

NOTE: *Promotes stamp collecting; gives stories behind various commemorative stamps. No. 2, 10¢ printed over 15¢ c-price.* ***Kiefer*** *a-1-7.* ***Kirkel*** *a-1-6.* ***Napoli*** *a-2-7.* ***Palais*** *a-2-4, 7.*

STANLEY & HIS MONSTER (Formerly The Fox & the Crow)
No. 109, Apr-May, 1968 - No. 112, Oct-Nov, 1968
National Periodical Publications

	GD25	FN65	NM94
109-112	2.00	5.00	12.00

STANLEY & HIS MONSTER
Feb, 1993 - No. 4, May, 1993 ($1.50, mini-series)
DC Comics

	GD25	FN65	NM94
1-4			1.50

Star Comics V2 #1 © CHES

Starfire #3 © DC

Starman #4 © DC

GD25 FN65 NM94 GD25 FN65 NM94

STAN SHAW'S BEAUTY & THE BEAST (Dark Horse)(Value: cover or less)

STAN SHAW'S BEAUTY & THE BEAST
Nov, 1993 ($4.95, color, one-shot)
Dark Horse Comics

	GD25	FN65	NM94
1	1.00	2.00	5.00

STARBLAST
Jan, 1994 - No. 4, Apr, 1994 ($1.75, mini-series)
Marvel Comics

	GD25	FN65	NM94
1-($2.00, 52 pgs.)-Nova, Quasar, Black Bolt; painted-c		.80	2.00
2-4		.70	1.75

STAR BLAZERS (Comico, 1987 & 1989)(Value: cover or less)

STAR BRAND (Marvel)(Value: cover or less)

STARCHILD
1992 - Present ($2.25/$2.50, B&W)
Tailspin Press

	GD25	FN65	NM94
1,2-(1992)		.90	2.25
0-(4/93)-Illos by Chadwick, Eisner, Sim, M. Wagner; $2.50-c begins		1.00	2.50
3-10: 3-(7/93). 4-(11/93). 6-(2/94)		1.00	2.50

STAR COMICS
Feb, 1937 - V2#7 (No. 23), Aug, 1939 (#1-6: large size)
Ultem Publ. (Harry `A' Chesler)/Centaur Publications

	GD25	FN65	NM94
V1#1-Dan Hastings (s/f) begins	107.00	321.00	750.00
2	54.00	160.00	375.00
3-6 (#6, 9/37): 4,5-Little Nemo-c/stories	49.00	146.00	340.00
7-9: 8-Severed head centerspread; Impy & Little Nemo by Winsor McCay Jr, Popeye app. by Bob Wood; Mickey Mouse & Popeye app. as toys in Santa's bag on-c; X-Mas-c	43.00	130.00	300.00
10 (1st Centaur; 3/38)-Impy by Winsor McCay Jr; Don Marlow by Guardineer begins	61.00	182.00	425.00
11-1st Jack Cole comic-a, 1 pg. (4/38)	43.00	130.00	300.00
12-15: 12-Riders of the Golden West begins; Little Nemo app. 15-Speed Silvers by Gustavson & The Last Pirate by Burgos begins	39.00	118.00	275.00
16 (12/38)-The Phantom Rider & his horse Thunder begins, ends V2#6	39.00	118.00	275.00
V2#1(#17, 2/39)-Phantom Rider-c (only non-funny-c)	39.00	118.00	275.00
2-7(#18-23): 2-Diana Deane by Tarpe Mills app. 3-Drama of Hollywood by Mills begins. 7-Jungle Queen app.	35.00	105.00	245.00

NOTE: ***Biro** c-6, 9, 10. **Burgos** a-15, 16, V2#1-7. **Ken Ernst** a-10, 12, 14. **Filchock** c-15, 18, 22. **Gill Fox** c-14, 19. **Guardineer** a-6, 8-14. **Gustavson** a-13-16, V2#1-7. **Winsor McCay** c-4, 5. **Tarpe Mills** a-15, V2#1-7. **Schwab** c-20, 23. **Bob Wood** a-10, 12, 13; c-7, 8.*

STAR COMICS MAGAZINE (Marvel)(Value: cover or less)

S.T.A.R. CORPS
Nov, 1993 - No. 6, Apr, 1994 ($1.50, limited series)
DC Comics

	GD25	FN65	NM94
1-6: 1,2-Austin-c(i). 1-Superman app.			1.50

STAR FEATURE COMICS
1963
I. W. Enterprises

	GD25	FN65	NM94
Reprint #9-Stunt-Man Stetson-r/Feat. Comics #141	1.00	2.50	5.00

STARFIRE (See New Teen Titans & Teen Titans #18)
Aug-Sept, 1976 - No. 8, Oct-Nov, 1977
National Periodical Publications/DC Comics

	GD25	FN65	NM94
1-Origin (CCA stamp fell off cover art; so it was approved by code)		.70	1.80
2-8			1.30

STAR HUNTERS (See DC Super Stars #16)
Oct-Nov, 1977 - No. 7, Oct-Nov, 1978
National Periodical Publications/DC Comics

	GD25	FN65	NM94
1-7: 1-Newton-a(p). 7-Giant			1.10

NOTE: ***Buckler** a-4-7p; c-1-7p. **Layton** a-1-5i; c-1-6i. **Nasser** a-3p. **Sutton** a-6i.*

STARJAMMERS (See X-Men Spotlight on Starjammers)

STARK TERROR (Magazine)
Dec, 1970 - No. 5, Aug, 1971 (52 pgs.) (B&W)
Stanley Publications

	GD25	FN65	NM94
1-Bondage, torture-c	3.00	7.50	15.00
2-4 (Gillmor/Aragon-r)	1.60	4.00	8.00
5 (ACG-r)	1.40	3.50	7.00

STARLET O'HARA IN HOLLYWOOD (Teen-age) (Also see Cookie)
Dec, 1948 - No. 4, Sept, 1949
Standard Comics

	GD25	FN65	NM94
1-Owen Fitzgerald-a in all	13.00	40.00	90.00
2	10.00	30.00	65.00
3,4	9.15	27.50	55.00

STAR-LORD THE SPECIAL EDITION (Also see Marvel Comics Super Special #10, Marvel Premiere & Preview & Marvel Spotlight V2#6,7)
Feb, 1982 (One Shot) (Direct sale, 1st Baxter paper comic)
Marvel Comics Group

	GD25	FN65	NM94
1-Byrne/Austin-a; Austin-c, Golden-a(p); 8 pgs. of new-a; Dr. Who story; 1st deluxe format comic	.90	2.30	5.50

STARMAN (See Adventure #467, Brave & the Bold, 1st Issue Special, Justice League & Showcase)
Oct, 1988 - No. 45, Apr, 1992 ($1.00)
DC Comics

	GD25	FN65	NM94
1-27,29-45: 1-Origin. 4-Intro The Power Elite. 9,10,34-Batman app. 14-Superman app. 17-Power Girl app. 26,27-G.A. Starman app. 38-War of the Gods x-over. 42-Lobo cameo. 42-45-Eclipso-c/stories (#43,44 with Lobo)			1.10
28-Starman disguised as Superman; leads into Superman #50		.90	2.25

STARMAN
No. 0, Oct, 1994 - Present ($1.95)
DC Comics

	GD25	FN65	NM94
0-6		.80	2.00

STARMASTERS (Americomics)(Value: cover or less)

STAR PRESENTATION, A (Formerly My Secret Romance #1,2; Spectacular Stories #4 on) (Also see This Is Suspense)
No. 3, May, 1950
Fox Features Syndicate (Hero Books)

	GD25	FN65	NM94
3-Dr. Jekyll & Mr. Hyde by Wood & Harrison (reprinted in Startling Terror Tales #10); "The Repulsing Dwarf" by Wood; Wood-c	39.00	118.00	275.00

STAR QUEST COMIX (Warren Presents... on cover)
October, 1978
Warren Publications

	GD25	FN65	NM94
1-Corben, Maroto, Neary-a			1.00

STAR RAIDERS (See DC Graphic Novel #1)

STAR RANGER (Cowboy Comics #13 on)
Feb, 1937 - No. 12, May, 1938 (Large size: No. 1-6)
Ultem Publ./Centaur Publications

	GD25	FN65	NM94
1-(1st Western comic)-Ace & Deuce, Air Plunder; Creig Flessel-a	114.00	343.00	800.00
2	50.00	150.00	350.00
3-6	43.00	130.00	300.00
7-9: 8-Christmas-c	39.00	116.00	270.00
V2#10 (1st Centaur; 3/38)	61.00	182.00	425.00
11,12	46.00	139.00	325.00

NOTE: ***J. Cole** a-10, 12; c-12. **Ken Ernst** a-11. **Gill Fox** a-8(illo), 9, 10. **Guardineer** a-1, 3, 6, 7, 8(illos), 9, 10, 12. **Gustavson** a-8-10, 12. **Fred Schwab** c-2-11. **Bob Wood** a-8-10.*

STAR RANGER FUNNIES (Formerly Cowboy Comics)

Star Slammers #1 © Walter Simonson

Star Spangled Comics #30 © DC

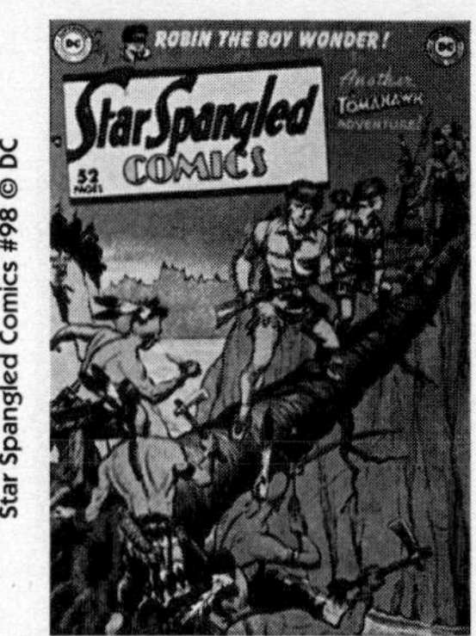

Star Spangled Comics #98 © DC

GD25 FN65 NM94 GD25 FN65 NM94

V1#15, Oct, 1938 - V2#5, Oct, 1939
Centaur Publications

V1#15-Eisner, Gustavson-a 71.00 215.00 500.00
V2#1 (1/39) 50.00 150.00 350.00
2-5: 2-Night Hawk by Gustavson. 4-Kit Carson app.
43.00 130.00 300.00

NOTE: ***Jack Cole*** *a-V2#1, 3; c-V2#1.* ***Filchock*** *c-V2#2, 3.* ***Guardineer*** *a-V2#3.* ***Gustavson*** *a-V2#2.* ***Pinajian*** *c/a-V2#5.*

STAR REACH CLASSICS (Eclipse)(Value: cover or less)

STARR FLAGG, UNDERCOVER GIRL (See Undercover...)

STARRIORS (Marvel)(Value: cover or less)

STARS AND STRIPES COMICS
No. 2, May, 1941 - No. 6, Dec, 1941
Centaur Publications

2(#1)-The Shark, The Iron Skull, A-Man, The Amazing Man, Mighty Man, Minimidget begin; The Voice & Dash Dartwell, the Human Meteor, Reef Kinkaid app.; Gustavson Flag-c 164.00 493.00 1150.00
3-Origin Dr. Synthe; The Black Panther app. 100.00 300.00 700.00
4-Origin/1st app. The Stars and Stripes; injury to eye-c
86.00 257.00 600.00
5(#5 on cover & inside) 63.00 190.00 440.00
5(#6)-(#5 on cover, #6 on inside) 63.00 190.00 440.00

NOTE: ***Gustavson*** *c/a-3.* ***Myron Strauss*** *c-4, 5(#5), 5(#6).*

STAR SLAMMERS
May, 1994 - No. 5, Jan, 1995 ($2.50, mini-series, mature)
Malibu Comics

1-5: W. Simonson-a/stories; contain Bravura stamps 1.00 2.50

STARSLAYER
Feb, 1982 - No. 6, Apr, 1983; No. 7, Aug, 1983 - No. 34, Nov, 1985
Pacific Comics/First Comics No. 7 on

1-Origin & 1st app.; excessive blood & gore; 1 pg. Rocketeer cameo which continues in #2 1.30 3.25
2-Origin/1st full app. the Rocketeer (4/82) by Dave Stevens (Chapter 1 of Rocketeer saga; see Pacific Presents #1,2) 1.90 6.00 13.00
3-Chapter 2 of Rocketeer saga by Stevens 1.30 3.00 7.50
4 .90 2.25
5-2nd app. Groo the Wanderer by Aragones 1.20 2.90 7.00
6,7: 7-Grell-a ends .90 2.25
8-34: 10-1st app. Grimjack (11/83, ends #17). 18-Starslayer meets Grimjack. 20-The Black Flame begins (9/84, 1st app.), ends #33. 27-Book length Black Flame story 1.25

NOTE: ***Grell*** *a-1-7; c-1-8.* ***Stevens*** *back c-2, 3.* ***Sutton*** *a-17p, 20-22p, 24-27p, 29-33p.*

STAR SPANGLED COMICS (Star Spangled War Stories #131 on)
Oct, 1941 - No. 130, July, 1952
National Periodical Publications

1-Origin/1st app. Tarantula; Captain X of the R.A.F., Star Spangled Kid (see Action #40), Armstrong of the Army begin; Robot-c
314.00 943.00 2200.00
2 114.00 343.00 800.00
3-5 71.00 214.00 500.00
6-Last Armstrong/Army; Penniless Palmer begins 46.00 139.00 325.00

GD25 FN65 VF82 NM94

7-(4/42)-Origin/1st app. The Guardian by S&K, & Robotman (by Paul Cassidy & created by Siegel);The Newsboy Legion (1st app.), Robotman & TNT begin; last Captain X 525.00 1575.00 2887.00 4200.00
(Estimated up to 100 total copies exist, 5 in NM/Mint)

GD25 FN65 NM94

8-Origin TNT & Dan the Dyna-Mite 164.00 493.00 1150.00
9,10 143.00 430.00 1000.00
11-17 107.00 321.00 750.00
18-Origin Star Spangled Kid 132.00 396.00 925.00
19-Last Tarantula 105.00 315.00 735.00
20-Liberty Belle begins (5/43) 105.00 315.00 735.00
21-29-Last S&K issue; 23-Last TNT. 25-Robotman by Jimmy Thompson begins. 29-Intro Robbie the Robotdog 84.00 250.00 585.00
30-40: 31-S&K-c 41.00 124.00 290.00
41-50: 41,49,51-Kirby-c 37.00 111.00 260.00
51-64: Last Newsboy Legion & The Guardian; last Liberty Belle? #53 by S&K
37.00 111.00 260.00
65-Robin begins with cover app. (2/47); Batman cameo in 1 panel; Robin-c begin, end #95 121.00 364.00 850.00
66-Batman cameo in Robin story 77.00 231.00 540.00
67,68,70-80: 72-Burnley Robin-c 61.00 182.00 425.00
69-Origin/1st app. Tomahawk by F. Ray (6/47) 93.00 280.00 650.00
81-Origin Merry, Girl of 1000 Gimmicks in Star Spangled Kid story
46.00 139.00 325.00
82,85: 82-Last Robotman? 46.00 139.00 325.00
83-Tomahawk enters the lost valley, a land of dinosaurs; Capt. Compass begins, ends #130 46.00 139.00 325.00
84,87 (Rare): 87-Batman cameo in Robin 69.00 206.00 480.00
86-Batman cameo in Robin story; last Star Spangled Kid
51.00 154.00 360.00
88(1/49)-94: Batman-c/stories in all. 91-Federal Men begin, end #93. 94-Manhunters Around the World begin, end #121 56.00 167.00 390.00
95-Batman story; last Robin-c 50.00 150.00 350.00
96,98-Batman cameo in Robin stories. 96-1st Tomahawk-c (also #97-121)
34.00 103.00 240.00
97,99 28.00 84.00 195.00
100 36.00 107.00 250.00
101-109,118,119,121: 121-Last Tomahawk-c 27.00 80.00 185.00
110,111,120-Batman cameo in Robin stories. 120-Last 52 pg. issue
28.00 84.00 195.00
112-Batman & Robin story 31.00 92.00 215.00
113-Frazetta-a (10 pgs.) 39.00 116.00 270.00
114-Retells Robin's origin (3/51); Batman & Robin story
38.00 115.00 265.00
115,117-Batman app. in Robin stories 29.00 86.00 200.00
116-Flag-c 28.00 84.00 195.00
122-(11/51)-Ghost Breaker-c/stories begin (origin/1st app.), ends #130 (Ghost Breaker covers #122-130) 28.00 84.00 195.00
123-126,128,129 20.00 60.00 140.00
127-Batman cameo 22.00 65.00 150.00
130-Batman cameo in Robin story 24.00 72.00 165.00

NOTE: *Most all issues after #29 signed by Simon & Kirby are not by them.* ***Bill Ely*** *c-122-130.* ***Mortimer*** *c-65-74(most), 76-95(most).* ***Fred Ray*** *c-96-106, 109, 110, 112, 113, 115-120.* ***S&K*** *c-7-31, 33, 34, 36, 37, 39, 40, 48, 49, 50-54, 56-58.* ***Hal Sherman*** *c-1-6.* ***Dick Sprang*** *c-75.*

STAR SPANGLED KID (See Action #40, Leading Comics & Star Spangled Comics)

STAR SPANGLED WAR STORIES (Formerly Star Spangled Comics #1-130; Becomes The Unknown Soldier #205 on) (See Showcase)
No. 131, 8/52 - No. 133, 10/52; No. 3, 11/52 - No. 204, 2-3/77
National Periodical Publications

131(#1) 72.00 216.00 575.00
132 53.00 159.00 425.00
133-Used in **POP**, pg. 94 50.00 150.00 400.00
3-6: 4-Devil Dog Dugan app. 6-Evans-a 25.00 75.00 200.00
7-10 19.00 58.00 155.00
11-20 17.00 51.00 135.00
21-30: 30-Last precode (2/55) 14.00 43.00 115.00
31-33,35-40 10.00 31.00 72.00
34-Krigstein-a 11.00 33.00 78.00
41-50: 45-1st DC grey tone-c (5/56) 9.00 28.00 65.00
51-83: 67-Easy Co. story without Sgt. Rock 7.00 20.00 46.00
84-Origin Mlle. Marie 14.00 41.00 95.00
85-89-Mlle. Marie in all 7.40 22.00 52.00
90-1st dinosaur issue-c/story (4-5/60) 27.00 80.00 240.00
91,93-No dinosaur stories 5.00 15.00 36.00
92,94-99: All dinosaur-c/s. 94-(12/60)- "Ghost Ace" story; Baron Von Richter as The Enemy Ace (pre-dates Our Army... #151) 14.00 41.00 95.00
100-Dinosaur-c/story 16.00 49.00 115.00

Star Spangled War Stories #73 © DC

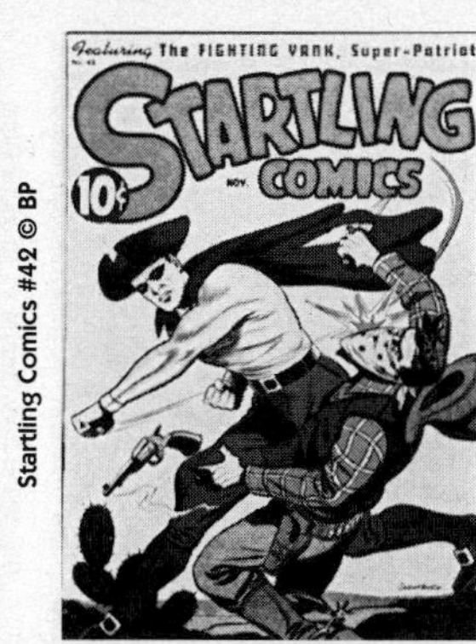

Startling Comics #42 © BP

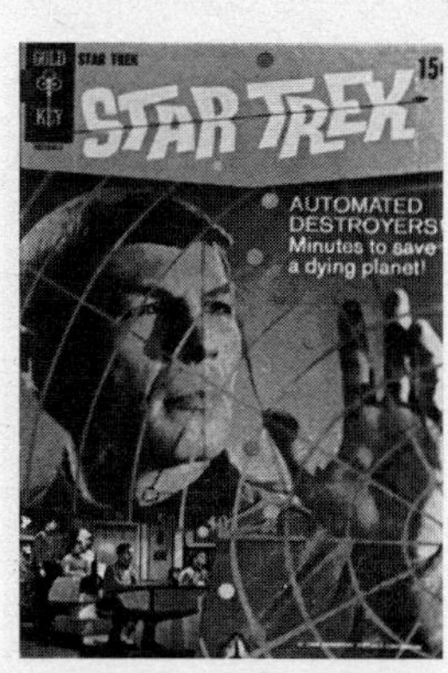

Star Trek #3 (Gold Key) © Paramount

	GD25	FN65	NM94
101-115: All dinosaur issues	9.00	28.00	65.00
116-125,127-133,135-137-Last dinosaur story; Heath Birdman-#129,131	8.00	24.00	55.00
126-No dinosaur story	4.00	13.00	30.00
134-Dinosaur story; Neal Adams-a	10.00	30.00	70.00
138-New Enemy Ace-c/stories begin by Joe Kubert (4-5/68), end #150 (also see Our Army at War #151 & Showcase #57)	9.00	26.00	60.00
139-Origin Enemy Ace (7/68)	6.40	19.00	45.00
140-143,145: 145-Last 12¢ issue (6-7/69)	5.00	14.10	33.00
144-Neal Adams/Kubert-a	4.00	12.00	28.00
146-Enemy Ace-c only	2.40	7.30	17.00
147,148-New Enemy Ace stories	3.10	9.40	22.00
149,150-Last new Enemy Ace by Kubert. Viking Prince by Kubert	2.40	7.30	17.00
151-1st Unknown Soldier (6-7/70); Enemy Ace-r begin (from Our Army at War, Showcase & SSWS); end #161	4.70	14.10	33.00
152,153,155-Enemy Ace reprints	1.70	5.10	12.00
154-Origin Unknown Soldier	3.60	11.00	25.00
156-1st Battle Album	1.70	4.20	10.00
157-161: 157-Sgt. Rock x-over in Unknown Soldier story. 161-Last Enemy Ace reprint	1.20	2.90	7.00
162-204: 181-183-Enemy Ace vs. Balloon Buster serial app. 200-Enemy Ace app.		1.60	4.00

NOTE: ***Chaykin** a-167. **Drucker** a-59, 61, 64, 66, 67, 73-84. **Estrada** a-149. **John Giunta** a-72. **Glanzman** a-167, 171, 172, 174. **Heath** a-122, 132, 133; c-67, 122, 132-134. **Kaluta** a-197i; c-167. **G. Kane** a-169. **Kubert** a-6-163(most later issues), 200. **Maurer** a-160, 165. **Severin** a-65, 162. **S&K** c-7-31, 33, 34, 37, 40. **Simonson** a-170, 172, 174, 180. **Sutton** a-168. **Thorne** a-183. **Toth** a-164. **Wildey** a-161. Suicide Squad in 110, 116-118, 120, 121, 127.*

STARSTREAM (Whitman)(Value: cover or less)

STARSTRUCK (Marvel & Dark Horse)(Value: cover or less)

STAR STUDDED
1945 (25¢, 132 pgs.); 1945 (196 pgs.)
Cambridge House/Superior Publishers

	GD25	FN65	NM94
nn-Captain Combat by Giunta, Ghost Woman, Commandette, & Red Rogue app.; Infantino-a	19.00	58.00	135.00
nn-The Cadet, Edison Bell, Hoot Gibson, Jungle Lil (196 pgs.); copies vary; Blue Beetle in some	16.00	48.00	110.00

STAR TEAM
1977 (20 pgs.) (6-1/2x5")
Marvel Comics Group (Ideal Toy Giveaway)

	GD25	FN65	NM94
nn			1.00

STARTLING COMICS
June, 1940 - No. 53, May, 1948
Better Publications (Nedor)

	GD25	FN65	NM94
1-Origin Captain Future-Man Of Tomorrow, Mystico (By Eisner/Fine), The Wonder Man; The Masked Rider & his horse Pinto begins; Masked Rider formerly in pulps; drug use story	129.00	385.00	900.00
2 -Don Davis, Espionage Ace begins	51.00	154.00	360.00
3	41.00	122.00	285.00
4	32.00	96.00	225.00
5-9	25.00	75.00	175.00
10-The Fighting Yank begins (9/41, origin/1st app.)	157.00	471.00	1100.00
11-2nd app. Fighting Yank	43.00	130.00	300.00
12-15: 12-Hitler, Hirohito, Mussolini-c	30.00	90.00	210.00
16-Origin The Four Comrades; not in #32,35	36.00	107.00	250.00
17-Last Masked Rider & Mystico	25.00	75.00	175.00
18-Pyroman begins (12/42, origin)(also see America's Best Comics #3 for 1st app., 11/42)	57.00	171.00	400.00
19	24.00	72.00	165.00
20-The Oracle begins (3/43); not in #26,28,33,34	24.00	72.00	165.00
21-Origin The Ape, Oracle's enemy	23.00	70.00	160.00
22-33	22.00	65.00	150.00
34-Origin The Scarab & only app.	23.00	70.00	160.00
35-Hypodermic syringe attacks Fighting Yank in drug story	23.00	70.00	160.00
36-43: 36-Last Four Comrades. 38-Bondage/torture-c. 40-Last Capt. Future & Oracle. 41-Front Page Peggy begins; A-Bomb-c. 43-Last Pyroman	22.00	65.00	150.00
44-Lance Lewis, Space Detective begins; Ingels-c; sci/fi-c begin	32.00	96.00	225.00
45-Tygra begins (intro/origin, 5/47); Ingels-c/a (splash pg. & inside f/c B&W ad	32.00	96.00	225.00
46-Ingels-c/a	32.00	96.00	225.00
47,48,50-53: 50,51-Sea-Eagle app.	25.00	75.00	175.00
49-Classic Schomburg Robot-c; last Fighting Yank	64.00	193.00	450.00

NOTE: ***Ingels** a-44, 45; c-44, 45, 46(wash). **Schomburg (Xela)** c-21-43; 47-53 (airbrush). **Tuska** c-45? Bondage c-16, 21, 37, 46-49. Captain Future c-1-9, 13, 14. Fighting Yank c-10-12, 15-17, 21, 22, 24, 26, 28, 30, 32, 34, 36, 38, 40, 42. Pyroman c-18-20, 23, 25, 27, 29, 31, 33, 35, 37, 39, 41, 43.*

STARTLING TERROR TALES
No. 10, May, 1952 - No. 14, Feb, 1953; No. 4, Apr, 1953 - No. 11, 1954
Star Publications

	GD25	FN65	NM94
10-(1st Series)-Wood/Harrison-a (r/A Star Presentation #3) Disbrow/Cole-c; becomes 4 different titles after #10; becomes Confessions of Love #11 on, The Horrors #11 on, Terrifying Tales #11 on, Terrors of the Jungle #11 on & continues w/Startling Terror #11	36.00	107.00	250.00
11-(#1a, 8/52)-L. B. Cole Spider-c; r-Fox's "A Feature Presentation" #5	20.00	60.00	140.00
12(#1b),14(#3)	10.00	30.00	60.00
13(#2)-Jo-Jo-r; Disbrow-a	10.00	30.00	65.00
4-7,9,11(1953-54) (2nd Series): 11-New logo	9.15	27.50	55.00
8-Spanking scene-r/Crimes By Women #14	10.00	30.00	60.00
10-Disbrow-a	10.00	30.00	60.00

NOTE: ***L. B. Cole** covers-all issues. **Palais** a-V2#8r, V2#11r.*

STAR TREK (TV) (See Dan Curtis Giveaways, Dynabrite Comics & Power Record Comics)
7/67; No. 2, 6/68; No. 3, 12/68; No. 4, 6/69 - No. 61, 3/79
Gold Key

	GD25	FN65	NM94
1-Photo-c begin, end #9	56.00	167.00	390.00
2	29.00	86.00	200.00
3-5	24.00	71.00	165.00
6-9	19.00	56.00	130.00
10-20	10.00	30.00	70.00
21-30	7.00	21.00	50.00
31-40	5.00	15.00	35.00
41-61: 52-Drug propaganda story	3.00	9.00	22.00
...the Enterprise Logs nn (8/76)-Golden Press, ($1.95, 224 pgs.)-r/#1-8 plus 7 pgs. by McWilliams (#11185)-Photo-c	1.50	3.75	9.00
...the Enterprise Logs Vol. 2 ('76)-r/#9-17 (#11187)-Photo-c	1.30	3.25	8.00
...the Enterprise Logs Vol. 3 ('77)-r/#18-26 (#11188); McWilliams-a (4 pgs.)-Photo-c	1.20	3.00	7.00
Star Trek Vol. 4 (Winter '77)-Reprints #27,28,30-34,36,38 (#11189) plus 3 pgs. new art	1.20	3.00	7.00

NOTE: ***McWilliams** a-38, 40-44, 46-61. #29 reprints #1; #35 reprints #4; #37 reprints #5; #45 reprints #7. The tabloids all have photo covers and blank inside covers. Painted covers #10-44, 46-59.*

STAR TREK
April, 1980 - No. 18, Feb, 1982
Marvel Comics Group

	GD25	FN65	NM94
1: 1-3-r/Marvel Super Special; movie adapt.	1.00	2.00	5.00
2-18: 5-Miller-c		1.40	3.50

NOTE: ***Austin** c-18i. **Buscema** a-13. **Gil Kane** a-15. **Nasser** c/a-7. **Simonson** c-17.*

STAR TREK (Also see Who's Who In Star Trek)
Feb, 1984 - No. 56, Nov, 1988 (Mando paper, 75¢)
DC Comics

	GD25	FN65	NM94
1-Sutton-a(p) begins	1.60	5.00	11.00
2-5	1.20	2.90	7.00

Star Trek: Deep Space Nine #3 © Paramount

Star Trek: The Nexct Generation #4 © Paramount

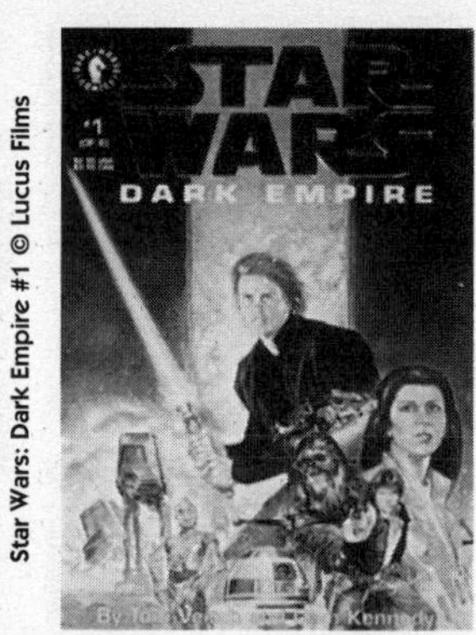

Star Wars: Dark Empire #1 © Lucus Films

	GD25	FN65	NM94
6-10: 7-Origin Saavik	.90	2.30	5.50
11-20: 19-Walter Koenig story		1.50	3.75
21-32		1.10	2.75
33-($1.25, 52 pgs.)-20th anniversary issue		1.60	4.00
34-49: 37-Painted-c. 49-Begin $1.00-c		.80	2.00
50-($1.50, 52 pgs.)		1.20	3.00
51-56			1.50
Annual 1-3: 1(1985). 2(1986). 3(1988, $1.50)		1.20	3.00

NOTE: *Morrow a-28, 35, 36, 56.* ***Orlando*** *c-8i.* ***Perez*** *c-1-3.* ***Spiegle*** *a-19.* ***Starlin*** *c-24, 25.* ***Sutton*** *a-1-6p, 8-18p, 20-27p, 29p, 31-34p, 39-52p, 55p; c-4-6p, 8-22p, 46p.*

STAR TREK
Oct, 1989 - Present ($1.50/$1.75/$1.95)
DC Comics

	GD25	FN65	NM94
1-Capt. Kirk and crew	1.30	3.00	7.50
2,3		1.40	3.50
4-23,25-30: 10-12-The Trial of James T. Kirk. 21-Begin $1.75-c		1.00	2.50
24-($2.95, 68 pgs.)-40 pg. epic w/pin-ups		1.30	3.25
31-49,51-60		.70	1.75
50-($3.50, 68 pgs.)-Painted-c		1.40	3.50
61-71: 61-Begin $1.95-c		.80	2.00
Annual 1,2('90, '91, $2.95, 68 pgs.): 1-Morrow-a		1.20	3.00
Annual 3,4 ('92,93, $3.50, 68 pgs.): 3-Painted-c		1.40	3.50
Annual 5 (1994, $3.95)		1.60	4.00
Special 1 (1994, $3.50, 68 pgs.)		1.40	3.50

STAR TREK: DEEP SPACE NINE (TV)
Aug, 1993 - Present ($2.50)
Malibu Comics

	GD25	FN65	NM94
1-Direct Sale Edition w/line drawn-c		1.00	2.50
1-Newsstand Edition with photo-c		1.00	2.50
2-20: 2-Polybagged w/trading card. 9-4 pg. prelude to Hearts & Minds		1.00	2.50

STAR TREK: DEEP SPACE NINE HEARTS AND MINDS
June, 1994 - No. 4, Sept, 1994 ($2.50, limited series)
Mailbu Comics

	GD25	FN65	NM94
1-4		1.00	2.50
1-Holographic-c	1.20	3.00	7.00

STAR TREK MOVIE SPECIAL
1984 (June) - No. 2, 1987 ($1.50, 68 pgs); No. 1, 1989 ($2.00, 52 pgs.)
DC Comics

	GD25	FN65	NM94
nn-(#1)-Adapts Star Trek III; Sutton-p (68 pgs.)			1.50
2-Adapts Star Trek IV; Sutton-a (68 pgs.)			1.50
1 (1989)-Adapts Star Trek V; painted-c		.80	2.00

STAR TREK VI: THE UNDISCOVERED COUNTRY
1992 (Movie adaptation)
DC Comics

	GD25	FN65	NM94
1-($2.95, regular edition, 68 pgs.)		1.20	3.00
nn-($5.95, prestige edition)-Has photos of movie not included in regular edition; painted-c by Palmer; photo back-c	1.00	2.50	6.00

STAR TREK - THE MODALA IMPERATIVE
Late July, 1991 - No. 4, Late Sept, 1991 ($1.75, mini-series)
DC Comics

	GD25	FN65	NM94
1		1.00	2.50
2-4		.80	2.00

STAR TREK: THE NEXT GENERATION (TV)
Feb, 1988 - No. 6, July, 1988 (Mini series, based on TV show)
DC Comics

	GD25	FN65	NM94
1 ($1.50, 52 pgs.)-Sienkiewicz painted-c	1.70	5.10	12.00
2-6 ($1.00)	1.20	2.90	7.00

STAR TREK: THE NEXT GENERATION (TV)
Oct, 1989 - Present ($1.50/$1.75/$1.95)
DC Comics

	GD25	FN65	NM94
1-Capt. Picard and crew from TV show	1.80	4.60	11.00
2,3	1.30	3.00	7.50
4,5	1.00	2.00	5.00
6-10		1.40	3.50
11-23,25-30: 21-Begin $1.75-c		.90	2.25
24-($2.50, 52 pgs.)		1.00	2.50
31-49,51-60		.70	1.75
50-($3.50, 68 pgs.)-Painted-c		1.40	3.50
61-70: 61-Begins $1.95-c		.80	2.00
Annual 1 (1990, $2.95, 68 pgs.)		1.40	3.50
Annual 2-4 (1991-93, $3.50, 68 pgs.)		1.60	4.00
Special 1 (1993, $3.50, 68 pgs.)-Contains 3 stories		1.40	3.50
...Special 2 (Sum/94, $3.95, 68 pgs.)		1.60	4.00
...The Series Finale (1994, $3.95, 68 pgs.)		1.60	4.00

STAR TREK: THE NEXT GENERATION - THE MODALA IMPERATIVE
Early Sept, 1991 - No. 4, Late Oct, 1991 ($1.75, mini-series)
DC Comics

	GD25	FN65	NM94
1		1.00	2.50
2-4		.80	2.00

STAR WARS (Movie) (See Classic..., Contemporary Motivators, Dark Horse Comics, The Droids, The Ewoks, Marvel Movie Showcase, Marvel Special Ed.)
July, 1977 - No. 107, Sept, 1986
Marvel Comics Group

	GD25	FN65	NM94
1-(Regular 30¢ edition)-Price in square w/UPC code; #1-6 adapt first movie	3.00	9.40	22.00
1-(35¢ cover; limited distribution - 1500 copies?)- Price in square w/UPC code (see note below)	54.00	161.00	375.00
2-6: 2-4-30¢ issues. 4-Battle with Darth Vader. 6-Dave Stevens-i	1.20	2.90	7.00
2-4-35¢ with UPC code; not reprints	1.20	2.90	7.00
7-10		1.60	4.00
11-20		1.00	2.50
21-38		.80	2.00
39-44-The Empire Strikes Back-r by Al Williamson in all		.90	2.25
45-107: 92,100-($1.00, 52 pgs.)			1.00
1-9-Reprints; has "reprint" in upper lefthand corner of cover or on inside or price and number inside a diamond with no date or UPC on cover; 30¢ and 35¢ issues published			1.00
Annual 1 (12/79, 52 pgs.)-Simonson-c		.80	2.00
Annual 2 (11/82, 52 pgs.), 3(12/83, 52 pgs.)			1.20

NOTE: *The rare 35¢ edition has the cover price in a square box, and the UPC box in the lower left hand corner has the UPC code lines running through it.* ***Austin*** *c-11-15i, 21i, 38; c-12-15i, 21i.* ***Byrne*** *c-13p.* ***Chaykin*** *a-1-10p; c-1.* ***Golden*** *c/a-38.* ***Miller*** *c-47p.* ***Nebres*** *c/a-Annual 2i.* ***Portacio*** *a-107i.* ***Sienkiewicz*** *c-92i, 98.* ***Simonson*** *a-16p, 49p, 51-63p, 65p, 66p; c-16, 49-51, 52p, 53-62, Annual 1.* ***Steacy*** *painted a-105i, 106i; c-105.* ***Williamson*** *a-39-44p, 50p, 98; c-39, 40, 41-44p. Painted c-81, 87, 92, 95, 98, 100, 105.*

STAR WARS: DARK EMPIRE
Dec, 1991 - No. 6, Oct, 1992 ($2.95, limited series)
Dark Horse Comics

	GD25	FN65	NM94
1-All have Dorman painted-c	3.60	10.70	25.00
1-2nd printing		1.20	3.00
2-Low print run	4.00	12.00	29.00
2,3-2nd printings		1.20	3.00
3	1.20	2.90	7.00
4	1.00	2.00	5.00
5,6		1.40	3.50
Gold Embossed Set (#1-6)-With gold embossed foil logo (price is for set)	10.00	30.00	70.00
Platinum Embossed Set (#1-6)			150.00
... (4/93, $16.95, TPB)	2.40	7.00	17.00

STARS WARS: DROIDS (See Dark Horse Comics #17-19)
Apr, 1994 - No. 6, Sept, 1994 ($2.50, limited series)
Dark Horse Comics

	GD25	FN65	NM94
1-($2.95)-Embossed-c		1.20	3.00
2-($2.25)		.90	2.25

S.T.A.T. #1 © Majestic

Steed and Mrs. Peel #1 © Eclipse

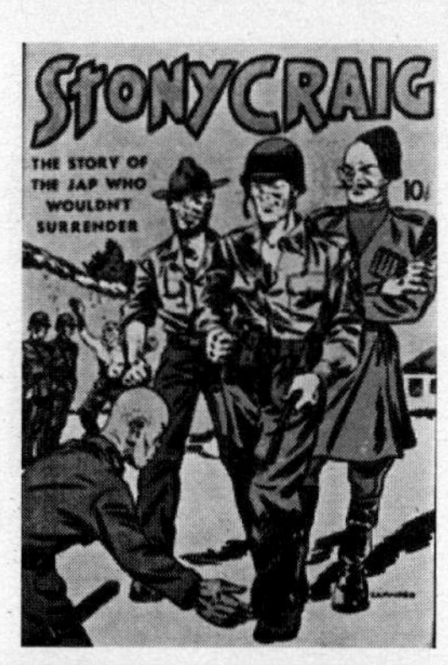

Stony Craig © Pentagon Publishing

GD25 FN65 NM94

3-6 1.00 2.50

STAR WARS: RETURN OF THE JEDI
Oct, 1983 - No. 4, Jan, 1984 (Mini-series, movie adaptation)
Marvel Comics Group

1-4-Williamson-p in all; r/Marvel Super Special #27 1.00
Oversized issue (1983, $2.95, 10-3/4x8-1/4", 68 pgs., cardboard-c)-Reprints above 4 issues 1.20 3.00

STAR WARS: TALES OF THE JEDI (See Dark Horse Comics #7)
Oct, 1993 - No. 5, Feb, 1994 ($2.50, limited series)
Dark Horse Comics

1-5: All have Dave Dorman painted-c. 3-r/Dark Horse Comics #7-9 w/new coloring & some panels redrawn 1.00 2.50
1-5-Gold foil embossed logo; limited # printed-7500 2.00 5.10 12.00

STAR WARS: TALES OF THE JEDI-THE FREEDOM NADD UPRISING
Aug, 1994 - No. 2, Nov, 1994 ($2.50, limited series)
Dark Horse Comics

1,2 1.00 2.50

S.T.A.T.
Dec, 1993 ($2.25, color)
Majestic Entertainment

1 .90 2.25

STATIC (Charlton)(Value: cover or less)

STATIC
June, 1993 - Present ($1.50/$1.75)
DC Comics (Milestone)

1-($2.95)-Collector's Edition; polybagged w/poster & trading card & backing board (direct sale only 1.20 3.00
1-13: 2-Origin. 8-Shadow War; Simonson silver ink-c 1.50
14-($2.50, 52 pgs.)-Worlds Collide Pt. 14 1.00 2.50
15-22: 15-Begin $1.75-c .70 1.75

STEALTH SQUAD
Sept, 1993 ($2.50, color, mini-series intended)
Petra Comics

1-Super hero team 1.00 2.50

STEED AND MRS. PEEL (TV)(Eclipse)(Value: cover or less)

STEEL
Feb, 1994 - Present ($1.50)
DC Comics

1-8: 1-From Reign of the Superman storyline. 6,7-Worlds Collide Pt. 5 & 12. 8-(9/94) 1.50
0,9-14: 0-(10/94). 9-(11/94) 1.50
Annual 1 (1994, $2.95)-Elseworlds story 1.20 3.00

STEELGRIP STARKEY (Epic)(Value: cover or less)

STEEL STERLING (Formerly Shield-Steel Sterling; see Blue Ribbon, Jackpot, Mighty Comics, Mighty Crusaders, Roly Poly & Zip Comics)
No. 4, Jan, 1984 - No. 7, July, 1984
Archie Enterprises, Inc.

4-7: 6-McWilliams-a 1.00

STEEL, THE INDESTRUCTIBLE MAN (See All-Star Squadron #8)
March, 1978 - No. 5, Oct-Nov, 1978
DC Comics

1 1.20
2-5: 5-Giant 1.00

STEELTOWN ROCKERS (Marvel)(Value: cover or less)

STEVE CANYON (See 4-Color #519, 578, 641, 737, 804, 939, 1033, and Harvey Comics Hits #52)

STEVE CANYON
1959 (96 pgs.; no text; 6-3/4x9"; hardcover)(B&W inside)
Grosset & Dunlap

100100-Reprints 2 stories from strip (1953, 1957) 4.20 12.50 25.00
100100 (softcover edition) 4.00 10.00 20.00

STEVE CANYON COMICS
Feb, 1948 - No. 6, Dec, 1948 (Strip reprints) (No. 4,5: 52pgs.)
Harvey Publications

1-Origin; has biog of Milton Caniff; Powell-a, 2 pgs.; Caniff-a 19.00 57.00 130.00
2-Caniff, Powell-a in #2-6 12.00 36.00 85.00
3-6: 6-Intro Madame Lynx-c/story 11.00 32.00 75.00
Dept. Store giveaway #3(6/48, 36pp) 10.00 30.00 70.00
...'s Secret Mission (1951, 16 pgs., Armed Forces giveaway); Caniff-a 10.00 30.00 65.00
Strictly for the Smart Birds (1951, 16 pgs.)-Information Comics Div. (Harvey) Premium 9.35 28.00 56.00

STEVE CANYON IN 3-D
June, 1986 ($2.25, one-shot)
Kitchen Sink Press

1-Contains unpublished story from 1954 .90 2.25

STEVE DONOVAN, WESTERN MARSHAL (TV)
No. 675, Feb, 1956 - No. 880, Feb, 1958 (All photo-c)
Dell Publishing Co.

4-Color 675-Kinstler-a 8.35 25.00 50.00
4-Color 768-Kinstler-a 6.70 20.00 40.00
4-Color 880 4.70 14.00 28.00

STEVE ROPER
April, 1948 - No. 5, Dec, 1948
Famous Funnies

1-Contains 1944 daily newspaper-r 10.00 30.00 60.00
2 5.35 16.00 32.00
3-5 4.35 13.00 26.00

STEVE SAUNDERS SPECIAL AGENT (See Special Agent)

STEVE SAVAGE (See Captain...)

STEVE ZODIAC & THE FIRE BALL XL-5 (TV)
January, 1964
Gold Key

10108-401 (#1) 8.35 25.00 50.00

STEVIE (Mazie's boy friend)(Also see Flat-Top, Mazie & Mortie)
Nov, 1952 - No. 6, April, 1954
Mazie (Magazine Publ.)

1-Teenage humor; Stevie, Mortie & Mazie begin 5.35 16.00 32.00
2-6 4.00 10.00 20.00

STEVIE MAZIE'S BOY FRIEND (See Harvey Hits #5)

STEWART THE RAT (See Eclipse Graphic Album Series)

ST. GEORGE (See listing under Saint...)

STIGG'S INFERNO (Vortex/Eclipse)(Value: cover or less)

STING OF THE GREEN HORNET (See The Green Hornet)
June, 1992 - No. 4, 1992 ($2.50, color, mini-series)
Now Comics

1-4: Butler-c/a 1.00 2.50
1-4 ($2.75)-Collectors Ed.; polybagged w/poster 1.10 2.75

STONEY BURKE (TV)
June-Aug, 1963 - No. 2, Sept-Nov, 1963
Dell Publishing Co.

1,2-Jack Lord photo covers 2.40 6.00 12.00

STONY CRAIG
1946 (No #)
Pentagon Publishing Co.

nn-Reprints Bell Syndicate's "Sgt. Stony Craig" newspaper strips

Stories by Famous Authors #12 © Seaboard

Stormwatch #25 © Jim Lee

Straight Arrow #13 © ME

GD25 FN65 NM94

5.35 16.00 32.00

STORIES BY FAMOUS AUTHORS ILLUSTRATED (Fast Fiction #1-5)
No. 6, Aug, 1950 - No. 13, March, 1951
Seaboard Publ./Famous Authors Ill.

1-Scarlet Pimpernel-Baroness Orczy 27.00 80.00 185.00
2-Capt. Blood-Raphael Sabatini 27.00 80.00 185.00
3-She, by Haggard 33.00 100.00 230.00
4-The 39 Steps-John Buchan 17.00 52.00 120.00
5-Beau Geste-P. C. Wren 18.00 54.00 125.00

NOTE: *The above five issues are exact reprints of Fast Fiction #1-5 except for the title change and new Kiefer covers on #1 and 2. Kiefer c(r)-3-5. The above 5 issues were released before Famous Authors #6.*

6-Macbeth, by Shakespeare; Kiefer art (8/50); used in **SOTI**, pg. 22,143; Kiefer-c; 36 pgs. 21.00 63.00 145.00
7-The Window; Kiefer-c/a; 52 pgs. 16.50 50.00 115.00
8-Hamlet, by Shakespeare; Kiefer-c/a; 36 pgs. 21.00 63.00 145.00
9-Nicholas Nickleby, by Dickens; G. Schrotter-a; 52 pgs. 17.00 52.00 120.00
10-Romeo & Juliet, by Shakespeare; Kiefer-c/a; 36 pgs. 17.00 52.00 120.00
11-Ben-Hur; Schrotter-a; 52 pgs. 18.00 54.00 125.00
12-La Svengali; Schrotter-a; 36 pgs. 18.00 54.00 125.00
13-Scaramouche; Kiefer-c/a; 36 pgs. 18.00 54.00 125.00

NOTE: *Artwork was prepared/advertised for #14, The Red Badge Of Courage. Gilberton bought out Famous Authors, Ltd. and used that story as C.I. #98. Famous Authors, Ltd. then published the Classics Junior series. The Famous Authors titles were published as part of the regular Classics Ill. Series in Brazil starting in 1952.*

STORIES OF CHRISTMAS
1942 (32 pgs.; paper cover) (Giveaway)
K. K. Publications

nn-Adaptation of "A Christmas Carol"; Kelly story "The Fir Tree"; Infinity-c 33.00 100.00 230.00

STORIES OF ROMANCE (Formerly Meet Miss Bliss)
No. 5, Mar, 1956 - No. 13, Aug, 1957
Atlas Comics (LMC)

5-Baker-a? 5.85 17.50 35.00
6-13: 11-Baker, Romita-a; Colletta-c/a 4.00 10.00 20.00

NOTE: ***Ann Brewster** a-13. **Colletta** a-9(2), 11; c-5, 11.*

STORMQUEST
Nov, 1994 - Present ($1.95, color)
Caliber Press

1,2 .80 2.00

STORMWATCH
May, 1993 - Present ($1.95, color)
Image Comics

1-8: 1-Jim Lee-c & part scripts; Lee plots in all. 1-3 contain coupon for limited edition Stormwatch trading card #00 by Lee. 3-1st app. Backlash (cameo) .80 2.00
0-($2.50)-Polybagged w/card; 1st full app. Backlash 1.00 2.50
9-(4/94, $2.50)-Intro Defile 1.00 2.50
25-(6/94, June 1995 on-c, $2.50) 1.00 2.50
10-(6/94), 11,12-Both (8/94) .80 2.00
10-Alternate Portacio-c, see Deathblow #5 .80 2.00
Special 1 (1/94, $3.50, 52 pgs.) 1.40 3.50
...Sourcebook 1 (1/94, $2.50) 1.00 2.50

STORMWATCHER (Eclipse)(Value: cover or less)

STORMY (See 4-Color #537)

STORY HOUR SERIES (Disney)
1948, 1949; 1951-1953 (36 pgs., paper-c) (4-1/2x6-1/4")
Given away with subscription to Walt Disney's Comics & Stories
Whitman Publishing Co.

nn(1948)-Mickey Mouse and the Boy Thursday 10.00 30.00 70.00
nn(1948)-Mickey Mouse the Miracle Master 10.00 30.00 70.00
nn(1948)-Minnie Mouse and Antique Chair 10.00 30.00 70.00
nn(1949)-The Three Orphan Kittens(B&W & color) 5.85 17.50 35.00
nn(1949)-Danny-The Little Black Lamb 5.85 17.50 35.00
800(1948)-Donald Duck in "Bringing Up the Boys" 11.50 34.00 80.00
1953 edition 7.50 22.50 45.00
801(1948)-Mickey Mouse's Summer Vacation 8.35 25.00 50.00
1951, 1952 editions 4.00 11.00 22.00
802(1948)-Bugs Bunny's Adventures 6.70 20.00 40.00
803(1948)-Bongo 4.70 14.00 28.00
804(1948)-Mickey and the Beanstalk 6.70 20.00 40.00
805-15(1949)-Andy Panda and His Friends 5.00 15.00 30.00
806-15(1949)-Tom and Jerry 5.35 16.00 32.00
808-15(1949)-Johnny Appleseed 4.70 14.00 28.00
1948, 1949 Hard Cover Edition of each.... $2.00 - $3.00 more.

STORY OF EDISON, THE
1956 (16 pgs.) (Reddy Killowatt)
Educational Comics

nn-Reprint of Reddy Kilowatt #2(1947) 5.00 15.00 30.00

STORY OF HARRY S. TRUMAN, THE
1948 (16 pgs.) (In color, regular size)(Soft-c)
Democratic National Committee (Giveaway)

nn-Gives biography on career of Truman; used in **SOTI**, pg. 311 10.00 30.00 70.00

STORY OF JESUS (See Classics Illustrated Special Issue)

STORY OF MANKIND, THE (See 4-Color #851)

STORY OF MARTHA WAYNE, THE
April, 1956
Argo Publ.

1-Newspaper strip-r 4.00 11.00 22.00

STORY OF RUTH, THE (See 4-Color #1144)

STORY OF THE COMMANDOS, THE (Combined Operations)
1943 (15¢, 68 pgs.; B&W)
Long Island Independent (Distr. by Gilberton)

nn-All text (no comics); photos & illustrations; ad for Classic Comics on back cover (Rare) 24.00 72.00 165.00

STORY OF THE GLOOMY BUNNY, THE (See March of Comics #9)

STRAIGHT ARROW (Radio)(See Best of the West & Great Western)
Feb-Mar, 1950 - No. 55, Mar, 1956 (All 36 pgs.)
Magazine Enterprises

1-Straight Arrow (alias Steve Adams) & his palomino Fury begin; 1st mention of Sundown Valley & the Secret Cave 31.00 94.00 220.00
2-Red Hawk begins (1st app?) by Powell (origin), ends #55 16.00 48.00 110.00
3-Frazetta-c 21.00 63.00 145.00
4,5: 4-Secret Cave-c 10.00 30.00 65.00
6-10 9.15 27.50 55.00
11-Classic story "The Valley of Time", with an ancient civilization made of gold 10.00 30.00 60.00
12-19 7.50 22.50 45.00
20-Origin Straight Arrow's Shield 10.00 30.00 65.00
21-Origin Fury 10.00 30.00 70.00
22-Frazetta-c 14.00 43.00 100.00
23,25-30: 25-Secret Cave-c. 28-Red Hawk meets The Vikings 6.70 20.00 40.00
24-Classic story "The Dragons of Doom!" with prehistoric pteradactyls 8.35 25.00 50.00
31-38: 36-Red Hawk drug story by Powell 5.35 16.00 32.00
39-Classic story "The Canyon Beast", with a dinosaur egg hatching a Tyranosaurus Rex 7.50 22.50 45.00
40-Classic story "Secret of The Spanish Specters", with Conquistadors' lost treasure 7.50 22.50 45.00
41,42,44-54: 45-Secret Cave-c 4.35 13.00 26.00

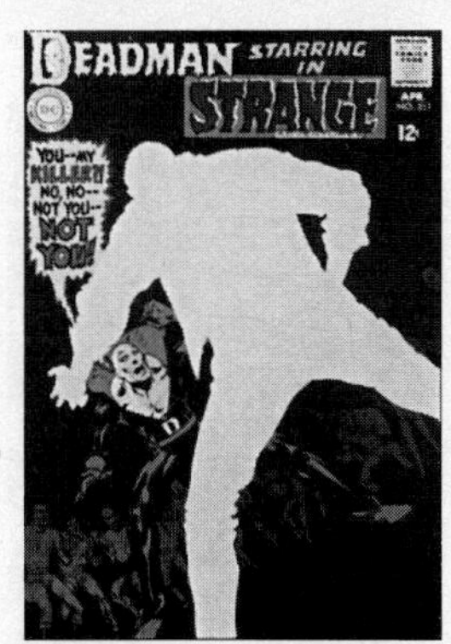

Strange Adventures #211 © DC

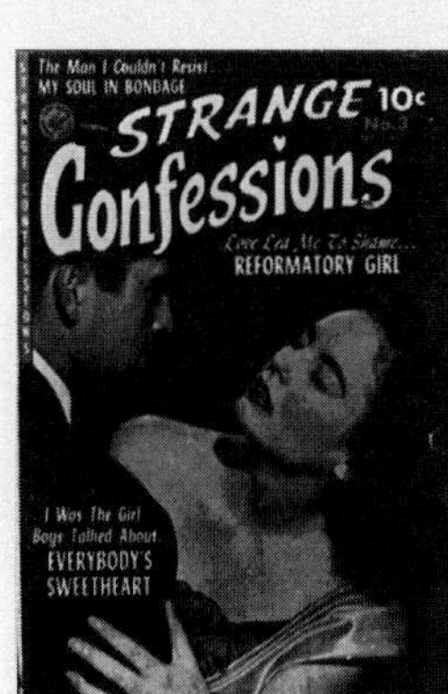

Strange Confessions #3 © Z-D

Strange Fantasy #3 © AJAX

	GD25	FN65	NM94
43-Intro & 1st app. Blaze, S. Arrow's Warrior dog	6.70	20.00	40.00
55-Last issue	7.50	22.50	45.00

NOTE: *Fred Meagher a 1-55; c-1, 2, 4-21, 23-55. Powell a 2-55. Whitney a-1. Many issues advertise the radio premiums associated with Straight Arrow.*

STRAIGHT ARROW'S FURY (See A-1 Comics #119)

STRANGE (Tales You'll Never Forget)
March, 1957 - No. 6, May, 1958
Ajax-Farrell Publ. (Four Star Comic Corp.)

	GD25	FN65	NM94
1	10.00	30.00	70.00
2-Censored r/Haunted Thrills	5.85	17.50	35.00
3-6	5.00	15.00	30.00

STRANGE ADVENTURES
Aug-Sept, 1950 - No. 244, Oct-Nov, 1973 (No. 1-12: 52 pgs.)
National Periodical Publications

	GD25	FN65	NM94
1-Adaptation of "Destination Moon"; preview of movie w/photo-c from movie (also see Fawcett Movie Comic #2); adapt. of Edmond Hamilton's "Chris KL-99" in #1-3; Darwin Jones begins	250.00	750.00	1750.00
2	114.00	343.00	800.00
3,4	71.00	214.00	500.00
5-8,10: 7-Origin Kris KL-99	66.00	200.00	465.00
9-Captain Comet begins (c/s)(6/51, intro/origin)	139.00	418.00	975.00
11-20: 12,13,17,18-Toth-a	45.00	135.00	315.00
21-30: 28-Atomic explosion panel. 30-Robot-c	35.00	105.00	245.00
31,34-38	31.00	92.00	215.00
32,33-Krigstein-a	32.00	96.00	225.00
39-Ill. in **SOTI** "Treating police contemptuously" (top right)	39.00	118.00	275.00
40-49-Last Capt. Comet; not in 45,47,48	29.00	86.00	200.00
50-53-Last precode issue (2/55)	22.00	67.00	155.00
54-70	13.00	38.00	100.00
71-99	8.00	24.00	65.00
100	11.40	34.00	80.00
101-110: 104-Space Museum begins by Sekowsky	7.00	21.00	50.00
111-116,118,119: 114-Star Hawkins begins, ends #185; Heath-a in Wood E.C. style	6.40	19.00	45.00
117-Origin/1st app. Atomic Knights (6/60)	38.00	113.00	375.00
120-2nd app. Atomic Knights	17.00	50.00	165.00
121,122,124,125,127,128,130,131,133,134: 124-Intro/origin Faceless Creature. 134-Last 10¢ issue	5.40	16.30	38.00
123,126-3rd & 4th app. Atomic Knights	9.00	27.00	90.00
129,132,135,138,141,144,147-Atomic Knights app. 144-Only Atomic Knights cover (by Murphy Anderson)	6.00	17.00	50.00
136,137,139,140,142,143,145,146,148,149,151,152,154,155,157-159	3.60	10.70	25.00
150,153,156,160: Atomic Knights in each. 153-2nd app. Faceless Creature; atomic explosion-c (6/63). 159-Star Rovers app.; Gil Kane/Anderson-a. 160-Last Atomic Knights	5.00	15.00	35.00
161-179: 161-Last Space Museum. 163-Star Rovers app. 170-Infinity-c. 177-Intro/origin Immortal Man	2.10	6.00	15.00
180-Origin/1st app. Animal Man	27.00	81.00	180.00
181-183,185-189: 187-Intro/origin The Enchantress	1.40	3.50	8.50
184-2nd app. Animal Man by Gil Kane	16.00	48.00	110.00
190-1st app. Animal Man in costume	19.00	58.00	135.00
191-194,196-200,202-204	1.00	2.50	6.00
195-1st full app. Animal Man	11.00	32.00	75.00
201-Last Animal Man; 2nd full app.	5.50	17.00	40.00
205-Intro/origin Deadman by Infantino (10/67) & begin series, ends #216	6.50	19.00	45.00
206-Neal Adams-a begins	5.00	15.00	35.00
207-210	3.60	10.70	25.00
211-216: 211-Space Museum-r. 216-(1-2/69)-Deadman story finally concludes in Brave & the Bold #86 (10-11/69); secret message panel by Neal Adams (pg. 13); tribute to Steranko	2.90	8.60	20.00
217-221,223-231: 217-r/origin & 1st app. Adam Strange from Showcase #17, begin-r; Atomic Knights-r begin. 218-Last 12¢ issue. 225-Last 15¢ issue. 226, 227-New Adam Strange text story w/illos by Anderson (8,6 pgs.). 226-236-(68-52 pgs.). 231-Last Atomic Knights reprint	.90	2.30	5.50
222-New Adam Strange story; Kane/Anderson-a	1.70	4.20	10.00
232-244		1.40	3.50

NOTE: *Neal Adams a-206-216; c-207-216, 228, 235. Anderson a-8-52, 94, 96, 99, 115, 117, 119-163, 217r, 218r, 222, 223-225r, 226, 242i(r); c-18, 19, 21, 23, 24, 27, 30, 32-44(most); c/r-157i, 190i, 217-224, 228-231, 233, 235-239, 241-243. Ditko a-188, 189. Drucker a-42, 43, 45. Elias a-212. Finlay a-2, 3, 6, 7, 210r, 229r. Giunta a-237r. Heath a-116. Infantino a-10-101, 106-151, 154, 157-163, 180, 190, 218-221r, 223-244p(r); c-50; c(r)-190p, 197, 199-211, 218-221, 223-244. Kaluta c-238, 240. Gil Kane a-8-116, 124, 125, 130, 138, 146-157, 173-186, 204r, 222r, 227-231r; c(p)-11-17, 25, 154, 157. Kubert a-55(2 pgs.), 226; c-219, 220, 225-227, 232, 234. Moriera c-26, 28, 29, 71. Morrow c-230. Mortimer c-8. Powell a-4. Sekowsky a-71p, 97-162p, 217p(r), 218p(r); c-206, 217-219r. Simon & Kirby a-2r (2 pgs) Sparling a-201. Toth a-8, 12, 13, 17-19. Wood a-154i. Atomic Knights in #117, 120, 123, 126, 129, 132, 135, 138, 141, 144, 147, 150, 153, 156, 160. Atomic Knights reprints by Anderson in 217-221, 223-231. Chris KL99 in 1-3, 5, 7, 9, 11, 15. Capt. Comet covers-9-14, 17-19, 24, 26, 27, 32-44.*

STRANGE AS IT SEEMS (See Famous Funnies-A Carnival of Comics, Feature Funnies #1, The John Hix Scrap Book & Peanuts)

STRANGE AS IT SEEMS
1932 (64 pgs.; B&W; square binding)
Blue-Star Publishing Co.

	GD25	FN65	NM94
1-Newspaper-r	19.00	57.00	130.00

NOTE: *Published with and without No. 1 and price on cover.*

	GD25	FN65	NM94
Ex-Lax giveaway(1936, B&W, 24 pgs., 5x7")-McNaught Synd.	3.60	9.00	18.00

STRANGE AS IT SEEMS
1939
United Features Syndicate

	GD25	FN65	NM94
Single Series 9, 1, 2	24.00	72.00	165.00

STRANGE ATTRACTORS
1993 ($2.50, B&W)
RetroGraphix

	GD25	FN65	NM94
1-(5/93), 2-(8/93), 3-(11/93), 4-(2/94)		1.00	2.50

STRANGE COMBAT TALES
Oct, 1993 - No. 4, Jan, 1994 ($2.50, mini-series)
Epic Comics (Marvel)

	GD25	FN65	NM94
1-4		1.00	2.50

STRANGE CONFESSIONS
Jan-Mar (Spring on-c), 1952 - No. 4, Fall, 1952 (All have photo-c)
Ziff-Davis Publ. Co. (Approved)

	GD25	FN65	NM94
1(Scarce)-Kinstler-a	29.00	86.00	200.00
2(Scarce, 7-8/52)	20.00	60.00	140.00
3(Scarce, 9-10/52)-#3 on-c, #2 on inside; Reformatory girl story; photo-c	20.00	60.00	140.00
4(Scarce)-Reformatory girl story	20.00	60.00	140.00

STRANGE DAYS (Eclipse)(Value: cover or less)

STRANGE FANTASY (Eerie Tales of Suspense!)(Formerly Rocketman #1)
Aug, 1952 - No. 14, Oct-Nov, 1954
Ajax-Farrell

	GD25	FN65	NM94
2(#1, 8/52)-Jungle Princess story; Kamenish-a; reprinted from Ellery Queen #1	20.00	60.00	140.00
2(10/52)-No Black Cat or Rulah; Bakerish, Kamenish-a; hypo/meathook-c	16.50	50.00	115.00
3-Rulah story, called Pulah	16.00	48.00	110.00
4-Rocket Man app. (2/53)	13.50	41.00	95.00
5,6,8,10,12,14	10.00	30.00	70.00
7-Madam Satan/Slave story	13.50	41.00	95.00
9(w/Black Cat), 9(w/Boy's Ranch; S&K-a)(A rebinding of Harvey interiors; not publ. by Ajax)	12.00	36.00	85.00
9-Regular issue	10.00	30.00	70.00
11-Jungle story	11.00	32.00	75.00
13-Bondage-c; Rulah (Kolah) story	13.50	41.00	95.00

STRANGE GALAXY (Magazine)
V1#8, Feb, 1971 - No. 11, Aug, 1971 (B&W)

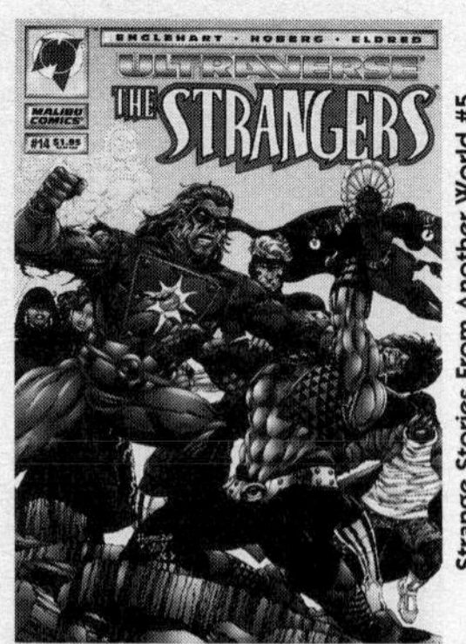

The Strangers #14 © Malibu

Strange Stories From Another World #5 © FAW

Strange Suspence Stories #62 © CC

GD25 FN65 NM94

Eerie Publications
V1#8-Reprints-c/Fantastic V19#3 (2/70) (a pulp) 1.70 5.00 12.00
9-11 1.30 3.25 8.00

STRANGE JOURNEY
Sept, 1957 - No. 4, June, 1958 (Farrell reprints)
America's Best (Steinway Publ.) (Ajax/Farrell)
1 11.50 34.00 80.00
2-4: 2-Flying saucer-c 8.35 25.00 50.00

STRANGE LOVE (See Fox Giants)

STRANGE MYSTERIES
Sept, 1951 - No. 21, Jan, 1955
Superior/Dynamic Publications
1-Kamenish-a & horror stories begin 31.00 94.00 220.00
2 17.00 52.00 120.00
3-5 13.00 40.00 90.00
6-8 11.50 34.00 80.00
9-Bondage 3-D effect-c 16.00 48.00 110.00
10-Used in **SOTI**, pg. 181 11.00 32.00 75.00
11-18 10.00 30.00 65.00
19-r/Journey Into Fear #1; cover is a splash from one story; Baker-r(2) 11.00 32.00 75.00
20,21-Reprints; 20-r/#1 with new-c 8.35 25.00 50.00

STRANGE MYSTERIES
1963 - 1964
I. W. Enterprises/Super Comics
I.W. Reprint #9; Rulah-r/Spook #28 2.40 6.00 12.00
Super Reprint #10-12,15-17(1963-64): 10,11-r/Strange #2,1. 12-r/Tales of Horror #5 (3/53) less-c. 15-r/Dark Mysteries #23. 16-r/The Dead Who Walk. 17-r/Dark Mysteries #22 2.40 6.00 12.00
Super Reprint #18-r/Witchcraft #1; Kubert-a 2.40 6.00 12.00

STRANGE PLANETS
1958; 1963-64
I. W. Enterprises/Super Comics
I.W. Reprint #1(nd)-Reprints E. C. Incredible S/F #30 plus-c/Strange Worlds #3 6.70 20.00 40.00
I.W. Reprint #8-r/? Exist? 3.60 9.00 18.00
I.W. Reprint #9-Orlando/Wood-r/Strange Worlds #4; cover-r from Flying Saucers #1 10.00 30.00 60.00
Super Reprint #10-Wood-r (22 pg.) from Space Detective #1; cover-r/Attack on Planet Mars 9.15 27.50 55.00
Super Reprint #11-Wood-r (25 pg.) from An Earthman on Venus 11.00 32.00 75.00
Super Reprint #12-Orlando-r/Rocket to the Moon 9.15 27.50 55.00
Super Reprint #15-Reprints Journey Into Unknown Worlds #8; Heath, Colan-r 3.60 9.00 18.00
Super Reprint #16-Reprints Avon's Strange Worlds #6; Kinstler, Check-a 4.00 11.00 22.00
Super Reprint #17-r/? 2.00 5.00 10.00
Super Reprint #18-r/Great Exploits #1 (Daring Adventures #6); Space Busters, Explorer Joe, The Son of Robin Hood; Krigstein-a 3.60 9.00 18.00

STRANGERS, THE
June, 1993 - Present ($1.95, color)
Malibu Comics (Ultraverse)
1-4,6-12,14-19: 1-1st app. The Strangers; has coupon for Ultraverse Premiere #0; 1st app. the Night Man (not in costume). 2-Polybagged w/trading card. 7-Break-Thru x-over. 8-2 pg. origin Solution. 12-Silver foil logo; wraparound-c .80 2.00
1-With coupon missing 1.50
1-Full cover holographic edition, 1st of kind w/Hardcase #1 & Prime #1 3.60 11.00 25.00
1-Ultra 5000 limited silver foil 1.40 4.20 10.00
4-($2.50)-Newsstand edition bagged w/card 1.00 2.50

GD25 FN65 NM94

5-($2.50, 52 pgs.)-Rune flip-c/story by B. Smith (3 pgs.); The Mighty Magnor 1 pg. strip by Aragones; 3-pg. Night Man preview 1.00 2.50
13-($3.50, 68 pgs.)-Mantra app.; flip book w/Ultraverse Premiere #4 1.40 3.50

STRANGE SPORTS STORIES (See Brave & the Bold, DC Special, and DC Super Stars #10)
Sept-Oct, 1973 - No. 6, July-Aug, 1974
National Periodical Publications
Brave and the Bold #45-49 (12-1/62-63 - 8-9/63)-Strange Sports Stories by Infantino 6.40 19.00 45.00
1 1.30 3.25 8.00
2-6: 3-Swan/Anderson-a 1.00 2.00 5.00

STRANGE STORIES FROM ANOTHER WORLD (Unknown World #1)
No. 2, Aug, 1952 - No. 5, Feb, 1953
Fawcett Publications
2-Saunders painted-c 29.00 86.00 200.00
3-5-Saunders painted-c 22.00 65.00 150.00

STRANGE STORIES OF SUSPENSE (Rugged Action #1-4)
No. 5, Oct, 1955 - No. 16, Aug, 1957
Atlas Comics (CSI)
5(#1) 20.00 60.00 140.00
6,9 11.50 34.00 80.00
7-E. C. swipe cover/Vault of Horror #32 12.00 36.00 85.00
8-Morrow/Williamson-a; Pakula-a 12.00 36.00 85.00
10-Crandall, Torres, Meskin-a 12.00 36.00 85.00
11-13: 12-Torres, Pakula-a. 13-E.C. art swipes 10.00 30.00 60.00
14-16: 14-Williamson/Mayo-a. 15-Krigstein-a. 16-Fox, Powell-a 10.00 30.00 65.00

NOTE: ***Everett** a-6, 7, 13; c-8, 9, 11-14. **Heath** a-5. **Maneely** c-5. **Morisi** a-11. **Morrow** a-13. **Powell** a-8. **Severin** c-7. **Wildey** a-14.*

STRANGE STORY (Also see Front Page)
June-July, 1946 (52 pgs.)
Harvey Publications
1-The Man in Black Called Fate by Powell 17.00 52.00 120.00

STRANGE SUSPENSE STORIES (Lawbreakers Suspense Stories #10-15; This Is Suspense #23-26; Captain Atom V1#78 on)
6/52 - No. 5, 2/53; No. 16, 1/54 - No. 22, 11/54; No. 27, 10/55 - No. 77, 10/65; V3#1, 10/67 - V1#9, 9/69
Fawcett Publications/Charlton Comics No. 16 on
1-(Fawcett)-Powell, Sekowsky-a 46.00 140.00 325.00
2-George Evans horror story 29.00 86.00 200.00
3-5 (2/53)-George Evans horror stories 24.00 73.00 170.00
16(1-2/54)-Formerly Lawbreakers S.S. 14.00 43.00 100.00
17,21: 21-Shuster-a 11.00 32.00 75.00
18-E.C. swipe/HOF 7; Ditko-c/a(2) 20.00 60.00 140.00
19-Ditko electric chair-c; Ditko-a 25.00 75.00 175.00
20-Ditko-c/a(2) 19.00 58.00 135.00
22(11/54)-Ditko-c, Shuster-a; last pre-code issue; becomes This Is Suspense 16.50 50.00 115.00
27(10/55)-(Formerly This Is Suspense #26) 7.50 22.50 45.00
28-30,38 5.35 16.00 32.00
31-33,35,37,40-Ditko-c/a(2-3 each) 11.50 34.00 80.00
34-Story of ruthless business man, Wm. B. Gaines; Ditko-c/a 24.00 72.00 165.00
36-(15¢, 68 pgs.); Ditko-a(4) 12.00 36.00 85.00
39,41,52,53-Ditko-a 10.00 30.00 70.00
42-44,46,49,54-60 4.20 12.50 25.00
45,47,48,50,51-Ditko-c/a 10.00 30.00 60.00
61-74 2.00 5.00 10.00
75(6/65)-Reprints origin/1st app. Captain Atom by Ditko from Space Advs. #33; r/Severin-a/Space Advs. #24 (75-77: 12¢ issues) 11.00 30.00 80.00
76,77-Captain Atom-r by Ditko/Space Advs. 4.30 12.90 30.00
V3#1(10/67)-4: All 12¢ issues 1.70 4.20 10.00

Strange Tales #35 © MEG

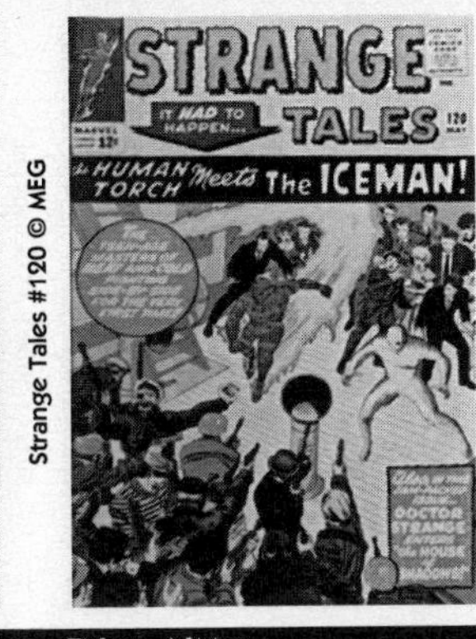

Strange Tales #120 © MEG

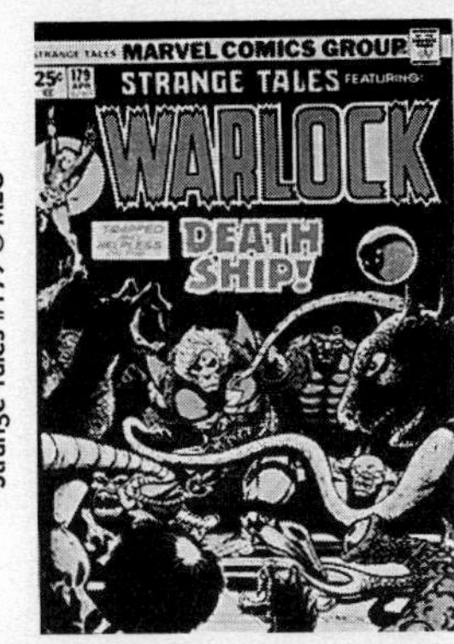

Strange Tales #179 © MEG

GD25 FN65 NM94

V1#2-9: All 12¢ issues. 2-Ditko-c/a; atom bomb-c .90 2.30 5.50
NOTE: ***Alascia** a-19. **Aparo** a-60, V3#1, 2, 4; c-V1#4, 8. **Baily** a-1-3; c-2, 5. **Evans** c-3, 4. **Giordana** c-16, 17p, 24p, 25p. **Montes/Bache** c-66. **Powell** a-4. **Shuster** a-19, 21. **Marcus Swayze** a-27.*

STRANGE TALES (...Featuring Warlock #178-181; Doctor Strange #169 on)
June, 1951 - #168, May, 1968; #169, Sept, 1973 - #188, Nov, 1976
Atlas (CCPC #1-67/ZPC #68-79/VPI #80-85)/Marvel #86(7/61) on

	GD25	FN65	NM94
1-Horror/weird stories begin	168.00	503.00	1675.00
2	69.00	206.00	550.00
3,5: 3-Atom bomb panels	50.00	150.00	400.00
4-Cosmic eyeball story "The Evil Eye"	55.00	165.00	440.00
6-9: 6-Heath-c/a	38.00	110.00	300.00
10-Krigstein-a	40.00	120.00	320.00
11-14,16-20	21.00	64.00	170.00
15-Krigstein-a	23.00	68.00	180.00
21,23-27,29-34: 27-Atom bomb panels. 33-Davis-a. 34-Last pre-code issue (2/55)	18.00	53.00	140.00
22-Krigstein, Forte/Fox-a	18.00	54.00	145.00
28-Jack Katz story used in Senate Investigation report, pgs. 7 & 169	19.00	56.00	150.00
35-41,43,44: 37-Vampire story by Colan	14.00	41.00	110.00
42,45,59,61-Krigstein-a; #61 (2/58)	14.00	43.00	115.00
46-57,60: 53,56-Crandall-a. 60-(8/57)	11.00	34.00	90.00
58,64-Williamson-a in each, with Mayo-#58	12.00	36.00	95.00
62,63,65,66: 62-Torres-a. 66-Crandall-a	9.00	28.00	85.00
67-Prototype ish. (Quicksilver)	13.00	40.00	120.00
68,71,72,74,77,80: Ditko/Kirby-a in #67-80	11.00	33.00	100.00
69-Prototype ish. (Prof. X)	17.00	50.00	150.00
70-Prototype ish. (Giant Man)	17.00	50.00	150.00
73-Prototype ish. (Ant-Man)	17.00	50.00	150.00
75-Prototype ish. (Iron Man)	17.00	50.00	150.00
76-Prototype ish. (Human Torch)	17.00	50.00	150.00
78-Prototype ish. (Ant-Man)	17.00	50.00	150.00
79-Prototype ish. (Dr. Strange) (12/60)	17.00	50.00	150.00
81-83,85-88,90,91-Ditko/Kirby-a in all: 90-(11/61)-Atom bomb blast panel	9.00	28.00	85.00
84-Prototype ish. (Magneto)(5/61); has powers like Magneto of X-Men over two years later; Ditko/Kirby-a	15.00	50.00	135.00
89-1st app. Fin Fang Foom (10/61) by Kirby	31.00	92.00	275.00
92-Prototype ish. (Ancient One); last 10¢ issue	11.00	33.00	100.00
93,95,96,98-100: Kirby-a	9.00	27.00	80.00
94-Prototype ish. (The Thing); Kirby-a	10.00	30.00	90.00
97-1st app. Aunt May & Uncle Ben by Ditko (6/62), before Amazing Fantasy #15; Kirby-a	24.00	73.00	220.00

	GD25	FN65	VF82	NM94
101-Human Torch begins by Kirby (10/62); origin recap Fantastic Four & Human Torch; H. Torch-c begin	69.00	208.00	416.00	625.00

	GD25	FN65	NM94
102-1st app. Wizard	31.00	94.00	250.00
103-105: 104-1st app. Trapster. 105-2nd Wizard	23.00	69.00	185.00
106,108,109: 106-Fantastic Four guests (3/63)	16.00	49.00	130.00
107-(4/63)-Human Torch/Sub-Mariner battle; 4th S.A. Sub-Mariner app. & 1st x-over outside of Fantastic Four	19.00	56.00	150.00

	GD25	FN65	VF82	NM94
110-(7/63)-Intro Doctor Strange, Ancient One & Wong by Ditko	82.00	245.00	490.00	735.00

	GD25	FN65	NM94
111-2nd Dr. Strange	31.00	94.00	250.00
112,113	10.00	30.00	80.00
114-Acrobat disguised as Captain America, 1st app. since the G.A.; intro. & 1st app. Victoria Bentley; 3rd Dr. Strange app. & begin series (11/63)	29.00	88.00	265.00
115-Origin Dr. Strange; Human Torch vs. Sandman (Spidey villain; 2nd app. & brief origin); early Spider-Man x-over, 12/63	40.00	120.00	360.00
116-(1/64)-Human Torch battles The Thing; 1st Thing x-over	10.00	30.00	80.00
117,118,120: 120-1st Iceman x-over (from X-Men)	7.00	21.00	55.00
119-Spider-Man x-over (2 pg. cameo)	10.00	30.00	80.00
121,122,124,126-134: Thing/Torch team-up in 121-134. 126-Intro Clea. 128-Quicksilver & Scarlet Witch app. (1/65). 130-The Beatles cameo. 134-Last Human Torch; The Watcher-c/story; Wood-a(i)	6.40	19.00	45.00
123-1st app. The Beetle (see Amazing Spider-Man #21 for next app.); 1st Thor x-over (8/64); Loki app.	7.00	21.00	50.00
125-Torch & Thing battle Sub-Mariner (10/64)	6.40	19.00	45.00
135-Col. (formerly Sgt.) Nick Fury becomes Nick Fury Agent of Shield (origin/1st app.) by Kirby (8/65); series begins	9.00	27.00	80.00
136-147,149: 138-Intro Eternity. 145-Begins alternating-c features w/Nick Fury (odd #'s) & Dr. Strange (even #'s). 146-Last Ditko Dr. Strange who is in consecutive stories since #113. 146-Only Ditko Dr. Strange-c this title. 147-Dr. Strange (by Everett #147-152) continues thru #168, then Dr. Strange #169	4.30	12.90	30.00
148-Origin Ancient One	7.00	17.00	55.00
150(11/66)-John Buscema's 1st work at Marvel	4.30	12.90	30.00
151-Kirby/Steranko-c/a; 1st Marvel work by Steranko	5.70	17.00	40.00
152,153-Kirby/Steranko-a	4.30	12.90	30.00
154-158-Steranko-a/script	4.30	12.90	30.00
159-Origin Nick Fury retold; Intro Val; Captain America-c/story; Steranko-a	4.90	15.00	34.00
160-162-Steranko-a/scripts; Capt. America app.	4.00	12.00	28.00
163-166,168-Steranko-a(p). 168-Last Nick Fury (gets own book next month) & last Dr. Strange who also gets own book	4.00	12.00	28.00
167-Steranko pen/script; classic flag-c	5.40	16.00	38.00
169-177: 169-1st app. Brother Voodoo(origin in 169,170) & begin series, ends #173. 174-Origin Golem. 177-Brunner-c		1.40	3.50
178-(2/75)-Warlock by Starlin begins; origin Warlock & Him retold; 1st app. Magus; Starlin-c/a & scripts in 178-181 (all before Warlock #9)	2.90	8.60	20.00
179-181-All Warlock. 179-Intro/1st app. Pip the Troll. 180-Intro Gamora. 181-(8/75)-Warlock story continued in Warlock #9	1.60	4.00	9.50
182-188		1.00	2.50
Annual 1(1962)-Reprints from Strange Tales #73,76,78, Tales of Suspense #7,9, Tales to Astonish #1,6,7, & Journey Into Mystery #53,55,59; (1st Marvel annual?)	40.00	120.00	360.00
Annual 2(7/63)-Reprints from Strange Tales #67, Strange Worlds (Atlas) #1-3, World of Fantasy #16; new Human Torch vs. Spider-Man story by Kirby/Ditko (1st Spidey x-over; tied for 6th app. with Amazing Spider-Man #5); Kirby-c	47.00	142.00	425.00

NOTE: ***Briefer** a-17. **Burgos** a-123p. **J. Buscema** a-174p. **Colan** a-11, 20, 37, 53, 169-173p, 188p. **Davis** c-71. **Ditko** a-46, 50, 67-122, 123-125p, 126-146, 175r, 182-188r; c-51, 93, 115, 121, 146. **Everett** a-4, 21, 40-42, 73, 147-152, 164i; c-8, 10, 11, 13, 15, 24, 45, 49-54, 56, 58, 60, 61, 63, 148, 150, 152, 158i. **Forte** a-27, 43, 50, 53, 54, 60. **Heath** a-6; c-6, 18-20. **Kamen** a-45. **G. Kane** c-170-173, 182p. **Kirby** Human Torch-101-105, 108, 109, 114, 120; Nick Fury-135p, 141-143p; (Layouts)-135-153; other **Kirby** a-67-100p; c-68-70, 72-74, 76-92, 94, 95, 101-114, 116-123, 125-130, 132-135, 136p, 138-145, 147, 149, 151p. **Kirby/Ayers** c-101-106, 108-110. **Kirby/Ditko** a-80, 88, 121; c-75, 93, 97, 100. . **Lawrence** a-29. **Leiber/ Fox** a-110, 111, 113. **Maneely** a-3, 37, 42; c-33, 40. **Moldoff** a-20. **Mooney** a-174i. **Morisi** a-53, 56. **Morrow** a-54. **Orlando** a-41, 44, 46, 49, 52. **Powell** a-42, 44, 49, 54, 130-134p; c-131p. **Reinman** a-11, 50, 74, 88, 91, 95, 104, 106, 112i, 124-127i. **Robinson** a-17. **Romita** c-169. **Roussos** c-201i. **R.Q. Sale** a-56; c-16. **Sekowski** a-3, 11. **Severin** a(i)-136-138; c-137. **Starlin** a-178, 179, 180p, 181p; c-178-180, 181p. **Steranko** a-151-161, 162-168p; c-151i, 153, 155, 157, 159, 161, 163, 165, 167. **Torres** a-53, 62. **Tuska** a-14, 166p. **Whitney** a-149. **Wildey** a-42, 56. **Woodbridge** a-59. Fantastic Four cameos #101-134. Jack Katz app.-26.*

STRANGE TALES
Apr, 1987 - No. 19, Oct, 1988
Marvel Comics Group

V2#1-19 1.00

STRANGE TALES OF THE UNUSUAL
Dec, 1955 - No. 11, Aug, 1957
Atlas Comics (ACI No. 1-4/WPI No. 5-11)

	GD25	FN65	NM94
1-Powell-a	26.00	78.00	180.00
2	13.00	40.00	90.00
3-Williamson-a (4 pgs.)	13.50	41.00	95.00
4,6,8,11	10.00	30.00	60.00

Strange Worlds #3 © MEG

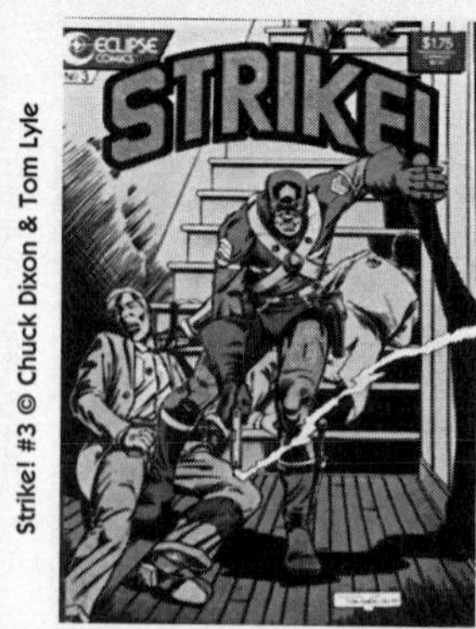

Strike! #3 © Chuck Dixon & Tom Lyle

Street Fighter II #3 © Capcom

GD25 FN65 NM94

5-Crandall, Ditko-a 13.00 40.00 90.00
7,9: 7-Kirby, Orlando-a. 9-Krigstein-a 10.00 30.00 70.00
10-Torres, Morrow-a 10.00 30.00 60.00

NOTE: ***Baily** a-6. **Brodsky** c-2-4. **Everett** a-2, 6; c-6, 9, 11. **Heck** a-1. **Maneely** c-1. **Orlando** a-7. **Pakula** a-10. **Romita** a-1. **R.Q. Sale** a-3. **Wildey** a-3.*

STRANGE TERRORS
June, 1952 - No. 7, Mar, 1953
St. John Publishing Co.

1-Bondage-c; Zombies spelled Zoombies on-c; Fineesque-a 26.00 78.00 180.00
2 15.00 45.00 105.00
3-Kubert-a; painted-c 19.00 58.00 135.00
4-Kubert-a (reprinted in Mystery Tales #18); Ekgren painted-c; Fineesque-a; Jerry Iger caricature 26.00 78.00 180.00
5-Kubert-a; painted-c 19.00 57.00 130.00
6-Giant (25¢, 100 pgs.)(1/53); bondage-c 26.00 78.00 180.00
7-Giant (25¢, 100 pgs.); Kubert-c/a 30.00 90.00 210.00

NOTE: ***Cameron** a-6, 7. **Morisi** a-6.*

STRANGE WORLD OF YOUR DREAMS
Aug, 1952 - No. 4, Jan-Feb, 1953
Prize Publications

1-Simon & Kirby-a 43.00 130.00 300.00
2,3-Simon & Kirby-a. 2-Meskin-a 34.00 103.00 240.00
4-S&K-c; Meskin-a 27.00 81.00 190.00

STRANGE WORLDS (#18 continued from Avon's Eerie #1-17)
11/50 - No. 9, 11/52; No. 18, 10-11/54 - No. 22, 9-10/55 (No #11-17)
Avon Periodicals

1-Kenton of the Star Patrol by Kubert (r/Eerie #1 from 1947); Crom the Barbarian by John Giunta 57.00 171.00 400.00
2-Wood-a; Crom the Barbarian by Giunta; Dara of the Vikings app.; used in **SOTI**, pg. 112; injury to eye panel 54.00 160.00 375.00
3-Wood/Orlando-a (Kenton), Wood/Williamson/Frazetta/Krenkel/Orlando-a (7 pgs.); Malu Slave Girl Princess app.; Kinstler-c 107.00 321.00 750.00
4-Wood-c/a (Kenton); Orlando-a; origin The Enchanted Daggar; Sultan-a 49.00 146.00 340.00
5-Orlando/Wood-a (Kenton); Wood-c 49.00 146.00 275.00
6-Kinstler-a(2); Orlando/Wood-c; Check-a 27.00 80.00 185.00
7-Fawcette & Becker/Alascia-a 19.00 58.00 135.00
8-Kubert, Kinstler, Hollingsworth & Lazarus-a; Lazarus Robot-c 22.00 67.00 155.00
9-Kinstler, Fawcette, Alascia-a 19.00 58.00 135.00
18-(Formerly Eerie #17)-Reprints "Attack on Planet Mars" by Kubert 19.00 58.00 135.00
19-r/Avon's "Robotmen of the Lost Planet"; last pre-code issue; Robot-c 19.00 58.00 135.00
20-War-c/story; Wood-c(r)/U.S. Paratroops #1 5.85 17.50 35.00
21,22-War-c/stories. 22-New logo 4.70 14.00 28.00
I.W. Reprint #5-Kinstler-a(r)/Avon's #9 2.40 6.00 12.00

STRANGE WORLDS
Dec, 1958 - No. 5, Aug, 1959
Marvel Comics (MPI No. 1,2/Male No. 3,5)

1-Kirby & Ditko-a; flying saucer issue 34.00 101.00 335.00
2-Ditko-c/a 21.00 62.00 205.00
3-Kirby-a(2) 17.00 50.00 165.00
4-Williamson-a 16.00 47.00 155.00
5-Ditko-a 14.00 41.00 135.00

NOTE: ***Buscema** a-3, 4. **Ditko** a-1-5; c-2.. **Heck** a-2. **Kirby** a-1, 3. **Kirby/Brodsky** c-1, 3-5.*

STRAWBERRY SHORTCAKE (Marvel)(Value: cover or less)

STRAY TOASTERS (Marvel)(Value: cover or less)

STREET COMIX (50¢)
1973 (36 pgs.; B&W) (20,000 print run)
Street Enterprises/King Features

GD25 FN65 NM94

1-Rip Kirby 1.00
2-Flash Gordon 1.20

STREETFIGHTER (Ocean)(Value: cover or less)

STREET FIGHTER
Sept, 1993 - No. 3, Nov, 1993 ($2.95)
Malibu Comics

1-3: 3-Includes poster; Ferret x-over 1.20 3.00

STREET FIGHTER II
Apr, 1994 - No. 8, Nov, 1994 ($2.95, color, limited series)
Tokuma Comics (Viz)

1-8 1.20 3.00

STREET POET RAY (Blackthorne)(Value: cover or less)

STREETS
1993 - No. 3, 1993 ($4.95, limited series, 52 pgs.)
DC Comics

Book 1-3-Estes painted-c 1.00 2.00 5.00

STRICTLY PRIVATE (You're in the Army Now)
July, 1942 (#1 on sale 6/15/42)
Eastern Color Printing Co.

1,2-Private Peter Plink. 2-Says 128 pgs. on-c 17.00 52.00 120.00

STRIKE! (Eclipse)(Value: cover or less)

STRIKE FORCE AMERICA (Comico)(Value: cover or less)(See The Elementals V2#16)

STRIKEFORCE: MORITURI (Marvel, 1986 & 1989 titles)(Value: cover or less)

STRIKER (Viz)(Value: cover or less)

STRONG MAN (Also see Complimentary Comics & Power of...)
Mar-Apr, 1955 - No. 4, Sept-Oct, 1955
Magazine Enterprises

1(A-1 #130)-Powell-c/a 16.00 48.00 110.00
2-4: (A-1 #132,134,139)-Powell-a. 2-Powell-c 13.00 40.00 90.00

STRONTIUM DOG (Eagle & Quality)(Value: cover or less)

STRYFE'S STRIKE FILE
Jan, 1993 ($1.75, no ads)
Marvel Comics

1-Stroman, Capullo, Andy Kubert, Brandon Peterson-a; silver metallic ink-c; X-Men tie-in to X-Cutioner's Song .70 1.75
1-Gold metallic ink 2nd printing .70 1.75

STUMBO THE GIANT (See Harvey Hits #49, 54, 57, 60, 63, 66, 69, 72, 78, 88 & Hot Stuff #2)

STUMBO TINYTOWN
Oct, 1963 - No. 13, Nov, 1966 (All 25¢ giants)
Harvey Publications

1-Stumbo, Hot Stuff & others begin 13.00 40.00 90.00
2 7.50 22.50 45.00
3-5 5.00 15.00 30.00
6-13 4.00 12.00 24.00

STUNTMAN COMICS (Also see Thrills Of Tomorrow)
Apr-May, 1946 - No. 2, June-July, 1946; No. 3, Oct-Nov, 1946
Harvey Publications

1-Origin Stuntman by S&K reprinted in Black Cat #9; S&K-c 76.00 230.00 535.00
2-S&K-c/a; The Duke of Broadway story 51.00 154.00 360.00
3-Small size (5-1/2x8-1/2"; B&W; 32 pgs.); distributed to mail subscribers only; S&K-a; Kid Adonis by S&K reprinted in Green Hornet #37
Estimated value... $250.00-$400.00
(Also see All-New #15, Boy Explorers #2, Flash Gordon #5 & Thrills of Tomorrow)

STUPID HEROES
Sept, 1993 ($2.75, color)
Mirage Studios

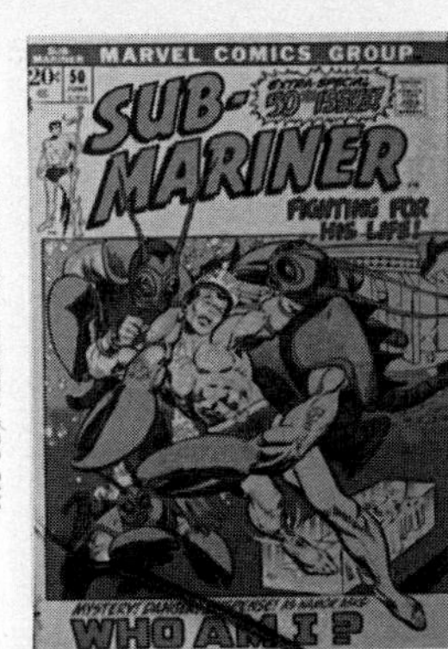

The Sub-Mariner #50 © MEG

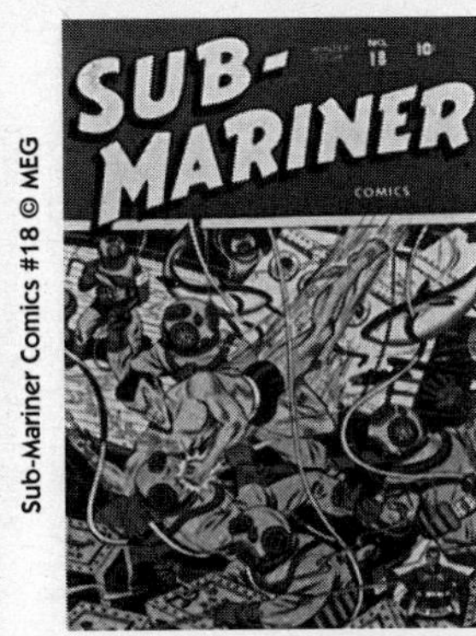

Sub-Mariner Comics #18 © MEG

Subspecies #1 © Full Moon Ent.

GD25 FN65 NM94 | GD25 FN65 NM94

1-Laird-c/a & scripts; 2 trading cards bound in 1.10 2.75

STYGMATA
1994 - Present ($2.95, color)
Entity Comics
0-Foil-c 1.20 3.00
1-Foil-c 1.20 3.00

SUBMARINE ATTACK (Formerly Speed Demons)
No. 11, May, 1958 - No. 54, Feb-Mar, 1966
Charlton Comics
11 3.60 9.00 18.00
12-20 2.40 6.00 12.00
21-54 1.80 4.50 9.00
NOTE: *Glanzman c/a-25. Montes/Bache a-38, 40, 41.*

SUB-MARINER (See All-Select, All-Winners, Blonde Phantom, Daring, The Defenders, Fantastic Four #4, Human Torch, The Invaders, Iron Man &..., Marvel Mystery, Marvel Spotlight #27, Men's Adventures, Motion Picture Funnies Weekly, Namora, Namor, The..., Prince Namor, The Sub-Mariner, Saga Of The..., Tales to Astonish #70 & 2nd series, USA & Young Men)

SUB-MARINER, THE (2nd Series)(Sub-Mariner #31 on)
May, 1968 - No. 72, Sept, 1974 (No. 43: 52 pgs.)
Marvel Comics Group
1-Origin Sub-Mariner; story continued from Iron Man & Sub-Mariner #1
18.00 54.00 125.00
2-Triton app. 7.00 21.00 50.00
3-10: 5-1st Tiger Shark (9/68). 6-Tiger Shark-c & 2nd app., cont'd from #5. 7-Photo-c. 8-Sub-Mariner vs. Thing. 9-1st app. Serpent Crown (origin in #10 & 12) 4.30 13.00 30.00
11-13,15: 15-Last 12¢ issue 3.20 8.00 20.00
14-Sub-Mariner vs. G.A. Human Torch; death of Toro (1st modern app. & only app. Toro, 6/69) 5.00 15.00 35.00
16-20: 19-1st Sting Ray (11/69); Stan Lee, Romita, Heck, Thomas, Everett & Kirby cameos. 20-Dr. Doom app. 1.70 5.00 12.00
21-33,36-40: 22-Dr. Strange x-over. 25-Origin Atlantis. 30-Capt. Marvel x-over. 37-Death of Lady Dorma. 38-Origin retold. 40-Spider-Man x-over
1.25 3.00 7.50
34,35-Prelude to 1st Defenders story. 34-Hulk & Silver Surfer x-over. 35-Namor/Hulk/Silver Surfer team-up to battle The Avengers-c/story (3/71); hints at teaming up again 2.40 7.30 17.00
41-49,51-72: 42-Last 15¢ issue. 44,45-Sub-Mariner vs. H. Torch. 47,48-Dr. Doom app. 49-Cosmic Cube story. 59-1st battle with Thor. 61-Last artwork by Everett; 1st 4 pgs. completed by Mortimer; pgs. 5-20 by Mooney. 62-1st Tales of Atlantis, ends 66. 64-Hitler cameo. 67-New costume; F.F. x-over. 69-Spider-Man x-over (6 panels) 1.00 2.00 5.00
50-1st app. Nita, Namor's niece (later Namorita in New Warriors)
1.20 2.90 7.00
Special 1,2: 1(1/71)-r/Tales to Astonish #70-73. 2(1/72)-r/T.T.A. #74-76; Everett-a 1.20 2.90 7.00
NOTE: ***Bolle** a-67i. **Buscema** a(p)-1-8, 20, 24. **Colan** a(p)-10, 11, 40, 43, 46-49, Special 1, 2; c(p)-10, 11, 40. **Craig** a-17i, 19-23i. **Everett** a-45r, 50-55, 57, 58, 59-61(plot), 63(plot); c-47, 48i, 55, 57-59i, 61, Spec. 2. **G. Kane** c(p)-42-52, 58, 66, 70, 71. **Mooney** a-24i, 25i, 32-35i, 39i, 42i, 44i, 45i, 60i, 61i, 65p, 66p, 68i. Severin c/a-38i. **Starlin** c-59p. **Tuska** a-41p, 42p, 69-71p. **Wrightson** a-36i. #53, 54-r/stories Sub-Mariner Comics #41 & 39.*

SUB-MARINER COMICS (1st Series) (The Sub-Mariner #1, 2, 33-42)(Official True Crime Cases #24 on; Amazing Mysteries #32 on; Best Love #33 on)
Spring, 1941 - No. 23, Sum, 1947; No. 24, Wint, 1947 - No. 31, 4/49; No. 32, 7/49; No. 33, 4/54 - No. 42, 10/55
Timely/Marvel Comics (TCI 1-7/SePI 8/MPI 9-32/Atlas Comics (CCC 33-42))
GD25 FN65 VF82 NM94
1-The Sub-Mariner by Everett & The Angel begin
1100.00 3300.00 7150.00 11,000.00
(Estimated up to 190 total copies exist, 8 in NM/Mint)
GD25 FN65 NM94
2-Everett-a 357.00 1071.00 2500.00
3-Churchill assassination-c; 40 pg. Sub-Mariner story
279.00 835.00 1950.00
4-Everett-a, 40 pgs.; 1 pg. Wolverton-a 229.00 685.00 1600.00
5: 5,8-Gabrielle/Klein-c 157.00 471.00 1100.00
6-10: 9-Wolverton-a, 3 pgs.; flag-c 121.00 364.00 850.00
11-15 86.00 257.00 600.00
16-20 77.00 231.00 540.00
21-Last Angel; Everett-a 66.00 200.00 465.00
22-Young Allies app. 66.00 200.00 465.00
23-The Human Torch, Namora x-over (Sum/47); 2nd app. Namora after Marvel Mystery #82 66.00 200.00 465.00
24-Namora x-over (3rd app.) 66.00 200.00 465.00
25-The Blonde Phantom begins (Spr/48), ends No. 31; Kurtzman-a; Namora x-over; last quarterly issue 76.00 230.00 535.00
26-28: 28-Namora cover; Everett-a 66.00 200.00 465.00
29-31 (4/49): 29-The Human Torch app. 31-Capt. America app.
66.00 200.00 465.00
32 (7/49, Scarce)-Origin Sub-Mariner 114.00 343.00 800.00
33 (4/54)-Origin Sub-Mariner; The Human Torch app.; Namora x-over in Sub-Mariner #33-42 59.00 178.00 415.00
34,35-Human Torch in each 48.00 140.00 335.00
36,37,39-41: 36,39-41-Namora app. 48.00 140.00 335.00
38-Origin Sub-Mariner's wings; Namora app.; last pre-code (2/55)
57.00 171.00 400.00
42-Last issue 58.00 174.00 405.00
NOTE: *Angel by **Gustavson**-#1, 8. **Brodsky** c-34-36, 42. **Everett** a-1-4, 22-24, 26-42; c-32, 33, 40. **Maneely** a-38; c-37, 39-41. **Rico** c-27-31. **Schomburg** c-1-4, 6, 8-18, 20. **Sekowsky** c-24. 25, 26(w/**Rico**). **Shores** c-21-23, 38. Bondage c-13, 22, 24, 25, 34.*

SUBSPECIES
May, 1991 - No. 4, Aug, 1991 ($2.50, color, mini-series)
Eternity Comics
1-4: New stories based on horror movie 1.00 2.50

SUBURBAN SHE-DEVILS (Marvel)(Value: cover or less)

SUE & SALLY SMITH (Formerly My Secret Life)
V2#48, Nov, 1962 - No. 54, Nov, 1963 (Flying Nurses)
Charlton Comics
V2#48 1.20 3.00 6.00
49-54 .80 2.00 4.00

SUGAR & SPIKE (Also see The Best of DC & DC Silver Age Classics)
Apr-May, 1956 - No. 98, Oct-Nov, 1971
National Periodical Publications
1 (Scarce) 80.00 240.00 800.00
2 42.00 127.00 380.00
3-5: 3-Letter column begins 37.00 110.00 330.00
6-10 21.00 63.00 190.00
11-20 19.00 58.00 175.00
21-29,31-40: 26-Christmas-c 13.00 39.00 90.00
30-Scribbly & Scribbly, Jr. x-over 14.00 40.00 100.00
41-60 8.00 24.00 55.00
61-80: 69-1st app. Tornado-Tot-c/story. 72-Origin & 1st app. Bernie the Brain
5.00 15.00 35.00
81-98: 84-Bernie the Brain apps. as Superman in 1 panel (9/69). 85-(68 pgs.); r-#72. 96-(68 pgs.). 97,98-(52 pgs.) 3.60 10.70 25.00
NOTE: *All written and drawn by **Sheldon Mayer**.*

SUGAR BEAR
No date, circa 1975? (16 pgs.) (2-1/2x4-1/2")
Post Cereal Giveaway
"The Almost Take Over of the Post Office", "The Race Across the Atlantic", "The Zoo Goes Wild" each... 1.00

SUGAR BOWL COMICS (Teen-age)
May, 1948 - No. 5, Jan, 1949
Famous Funnies
1-Toth-c/a 11.00 32.00 75.00
2,4,5 4.70 14.00 28.00
3-Toth-a 9.15 27.50 55.00

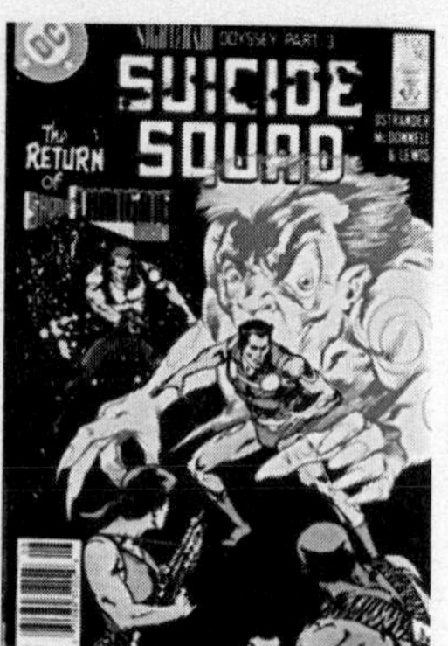

Suicide Squad #16 © DC

Sun Girl #2 © MEG

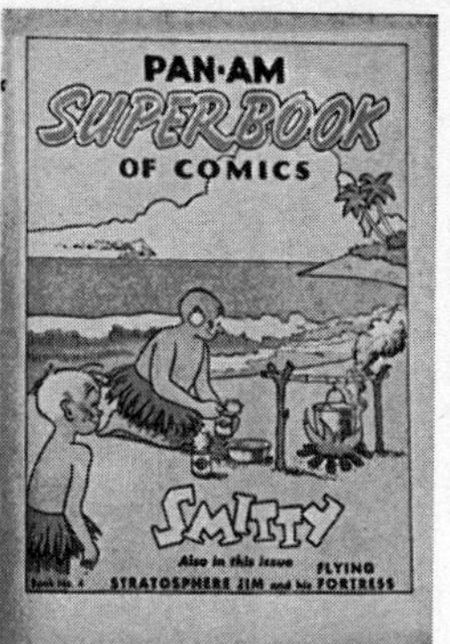

Super Book Of Comics #4 © WEST

GD25 FN65 NM94

SUGARFOOT (See 4-Color #907, 992, 1059, 1098, 1147, 1209)

SUICIDE SQUAD (DC)(Value: cover or less)(See Brave & the Bold and Doom Patrol & Suicide Squad)

SUMMER FUN (See Dell Giants)

SUMMER FUN (Formerly Li'l Genius; Holiday Surprise #55)
No. 54, Oct, 1966 (Giant)
Charlton Comics

	GD25	FN65	NM94
54	1.60	4.00	8.00

SUMMER FUN (Disney, 1991)(Value: cover or less)

SUMMER LOVE (Formerly Brides in Love?)
V2#46, Oct, 1965; V2#47, Oct, 1966; V2#48, Nov, 1968
Charlton Comics

	GD25	FN65	NM94
V2#46-Beatles-c/story	8.35	25.00	50.00
47-Beatles story	8.35	25.00	50.00
48	.80	2.00	4.00

SUMMER MAGIC (See Movie Comics)

SUNDANCE (See 4-Color #1126)

SUNDANCE KID (Also see Blazing Six-Guns)
June, 1971 - No. 3, Sept, 1971 (52 pgs.)
Skywald Publications

	GD25	FN65	NM94
1-Durango Kid; Two Kirby Bullseye-r		1.20	3.00
2-Swift Arrow, Durango Kid, Bullseye by S&K; Meskin plus 1 pg. origin		.80	2.00
3-Durango Kid, Billy the Kid, Red Hawk-r			1.50

SUNDAY FUNNIES
1950
Harvey Publications

	GD25	FN65	NM94
1	3.00	7.50	15.00

SUN DEVILS (DC)(Value: cover or less)

SUN FUN KOMIKS
1939 (15¢; black, white & red)
Sun Publications

	GD25	FN65	NM94
1-Satire on comics	22.00	65.00	150.00

SUN GIRL (See The Human Torch & Marvel Mystery Comics #88)
Aug, 1948 - No. 3, Dec, 1948
Marvel Comics (CCC)

	GD25	FN65	NM94
1-Sun Girl begins; Miss America app.	93.00	280.00	650.00
2,3: 2-The Blonde Phantom begins	74.00	220.00	515.00

SUNNY, AMERICA'S SWEETHEART (Formerly Cosmo Cat #1-10)
No. 11, Dec, 1947 - No. 14, June, 1948
Fox Features Syndicate

	GD25	FN65	NM94
11-Feldstein-c/a	45.00	135.00	315.00
12-14-Feldstein-c/a; 14-Lingerie panels	36.00	110.00	255.00
I.W. Reprint #8-Feldstein-a; r/Fox issue	10.00	30.00	65.00

SUN-RUNNERS (Pacific/Eclipse/Amazing)(Value: cover or less)

SUNSET CARSON (Also see Cowboy Western)
Feb, 1951 - No. 4, 1951 (No month) (Sunset Carson photo on-c of each)
Charlton Comics

	GD25	FN65	NM94
1-Photo/retouched-c (Scarce, all issues)	68.00	205.00	475.00
2-Kit Carson story; adapts "Kansas Raiders" w/Brian Donlevy, Audie Murphy & Margaret Chapman	54.00	160.00	375.00
3,4	41.00	124.00	290.00

SUPER ANIMALS PRESENTS PIDGY & THE MAGIC GLASSES
Dec, 1953 (25¢, came w/glasses)
Star Publications

	GD25	FN65	NM94
1-(3-D Comics)-L. B. Cole-c	34.00	103.00	240.00

SUPER BOOK OF COMICS
nd (1943?) (32 pgs., soft-c) (Pan-Am/Gilmore Oil/Kelloggs premiums)
Western Publishing Co.

	GD25	FN65	NM94
nn-Dick Tracy (Gilmore)-Magic Morro app.	39.00	118.00	275.00
1-Dick Tracy & The Smuggling Ring; Stratosphere Jim app. (Rare) (Pan-Am)	32.00	96.00	225.00
1-Smilin' Jack, Magic Morro (Pan-Am)	10.00	30.00	65.00
2-Smilin' Jack, Stratosphere Jim (Pan-Am)	10.00	30.00	65.00
2-Smitty, Magic Morro (Pan-Am)	10.00	30.00	65.00
3-Captain Midnight, Magic Morro (Pan-Am)	14.00	43.00	100.00
3-Moon Mullins?	9.15	27.50	55.00
4-Red Ryder, Magic Morro (Pan-Am)	9.15	27.50	55.00
4-Smitty, Stratosphere Jim (Pan-Am)	9.15	27.50	55.00
5-Don Winslow, Magic Morro (Gilmore)	9.15	27.50	55.00
5-Don Winslow, Stratosphere Jim (Pan-Am)	9.15	27.50	55.00
5-Terry & the Pirates	14.00	43.00	100.00
6-Don Winslow, Stratosphere Jim (Pan-Am)-McWilliams-a	10.00	30.00	65.00
6-King of the Royal Mounted, Magic Morro (Pan-Am)	10.00	30.00	65.00
7-Dick Tracy, Magic Morro (Pan-Am)	16.00	48.00	110.00
7-Little Orphan Annie	10.00	30.00	65.00
8-Dick Tracy, Stratosphere Jim (Pan-Am)	14.00	43.00	110.00
8-Dan Dunn, Magic Morro (Pan-Am)	10.00	30.00	65.00
9-Terry & the Pirates, Magic Morro (Pan-Am)	13.00	40.00	90.00
10-Red Ryder, Magic Morro (Pan-Am)	9.15	27.50	55.00

SUPER-BOOK OF COMICS
(Omar Bread & Hancock Oil Co. giveaways)
1944 - No. 30, 1947 (Omar); 1947 - 1948 (Hancock) (16 pgs.)
Western Publishing Co.

Note: The Hancock issues are all exact reprints of the earlier Omar issues. The issue numbers were removed in some of the reprints.

	GD25	FN65	NM94
1-Dick Tracy (Omar, 1944)	19.00	57.00	130.00
1-Dick Tracy (Hancock, 1947)	14.00	43.00	100.00
2-Bugs Bunny (Omar, 1944)	6.70	20.00	40.00
2-Bugs Bunny (Hancock, 1947)	5.00	15.00	30.00
3-Terry & the Pirates (Omar, 1944)	11.00	32.00	75.00
3-Terry & the Pirates (Hancock, 1947)	10.00	30.00	65.00
4-Andy Panda (Omar, 1944)	6.70	20.00	40.00
4-Andy Panda (Hancock, 1947)	5.00	15.00	30.00
5-Smokey Stover (Omar, 1945)	5.00	15.00	30.00
5-Smokey Stover (Hancock, 1947)	4.00	10.00	20.00
6-Porky Pig (Omar, 1945)	6.70	20.00	40.00
6-Porky Pig (Hancock, 1947)	5.00	15.00	30.00
7-Smilin' Jack (Omar, 1945)	6.70	20.00	40.00
7-Smilin' Jack (Hancock, 1947)	5.00	15.00	30.00
8-Oswald the Rabbit (Omar, 1945)	5.00	15.00	30.00
8-Oswald the Rabbit (Hancock, 1947)	4.00	10.00	20.00
9-Alley Oop (Omar, 1945)	11.50	34.00	80.00
9-Alley Oop (Hancock, 1947)	10.00	30.00	70.00
10-Elmer Fudd (Omar, 1945)	5.00	15.00	30.00
10-Elmer Fudd (Hancock, 1947)	4.00	10.00	20.00
11-Little Orphan Annie (Omar, 1945)	7.50	22.50	45.00
11-Little Orphan Annie (Hancock, 1947)	5.35	16.00	32.00
12-Woody Woodpecker (Omar, 1945)	5.00	15.00	30.00
12-Woody Woodpecker (Hancock, 1947)	4.00	10.00	20.00
13-Dick Tracy (Omar, 1945)	11.50	34.00	80.00
13-Dick Tracy (Hancock, 1947)	10.00	30.00	70.00
14-Bugs Bunny (Omar, 1945)	5.00	15.00	30.00
14-Bugs Bunny (Hancock, 1947)	4.00	10.00	20.00
15-Andy Panda (Omar, 1945)	4.35	13.00	26.00
15-Andy Panda (Hancock, 1947)	4.00	10.00	20.00
16-Terry & the Pirates (Omar, 1945)	10.00	30.00	70.00
16-Terry & the Pirates (Hancock, 1947)	9.15	27.50	55.00
17-Smokey Stover (Omar, 1946)	5.00	15.00	30.00
17-Smokey Stover (Hancock, 1948?)	4.00	10.00	20.00
18-Porky Pig (Omar, 1946)	4.35	13.00	26.00

Superboy #12 © DC

Superboy #131 © DC

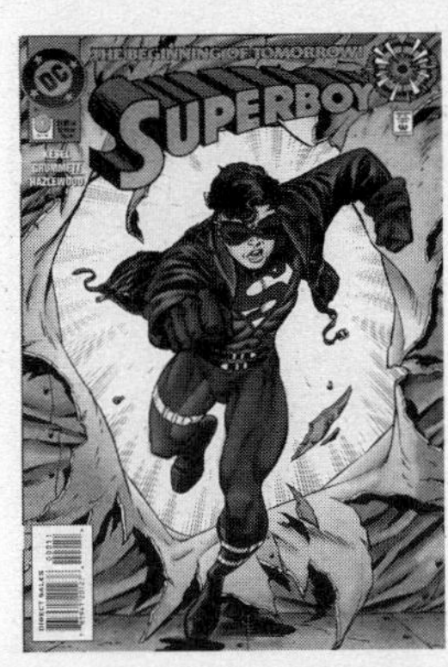

Superboy #0 © DC

	GD25	FN65	NM94
18-Porky Pig (Hancock, 1948?)	4.00	10.00	20.00
19-Smilin' Jack (Omar, 1946)	5.00	15.00	30.00
nn-Smilin' Jack (Hancock, 1948)	4.00	10.00	20.00
20-Oswald the Rabbit (Omar, 1946)	4.35	13.00	26.00
nn-Oswald the Rabbit (Hancock, 1948)	4.00	10.00	20.00
21-Gasoline Alley (Omar, 1946)	7.50	22.50	45.00
nn-Gasoline Alley (Hancock, 1948)	5.35	16.00	32.00
22-Elmer Fudd (Omar, 1946)	4.35	13.00	26.00
nn-Elmer Fudd (Hancock, 1948)	4.00	10.00	20.00
23-Little Orphan Annie (Omar, 1946)	6.70	20.00	40.00
nn-Little Orphan Annie (Hancock, 1948)	5.00	15.00	30.00
24-Woody Woodpecker (Omar, 1946)	4.35	13.00	26.00
nn-Woody Woodpecker (Hancock, 1948)	4.00	10.00	20.00
25-Dick Tracy (Omar, 1946)	10.00	30.00	70.00
nn-Dick Tracy (Hancock, 1948)	9.15	27.50	55.00
26-Bugs Bunny (Omar, 1946))	4.35	13.00	26.00
nn-Bugs Bunny (Hancock, 1948)	4.00	10.00	20.00
27-Andy Panda (Omar, 1946)	4.35	13.00	26.00
27-Andy Panda (Hancock, 1948)	4.00	10.00	20.00
28-Terry & the Pirates (Omar, 1946)	10.00	30.00	70.00
28-Terry & the Pirates (Hancock, 1948)	9.15	27.50	55.00
29-Smokey Stover (Omar, 1947)	4.35	13.00	26.00
29-Smokey Stover (Hancock, 1948)	4.00	10.00	20.00
30-Porky Pig (Omar, 1947)	4.35	13.00	26.00
30-Porky Pig (Hancock, 1948)	4.00	10.00	20.00
nn-Bugs Bunny (Hancock, 1948)-Does not match any Omar book	4.00	10.00	20.00

SUPERBOY (See Adventure, Aurora, DC Comics Presents, DC 100 Page Super Spectacular #15, DC Super Stars, 80 Page Giant #10, More Fun Comics, The New Advs. of... & Superman Family #191)

SUPERBOY (...& the Legion of Super-Heroes with #231)(Becomes The Legion of Super-Heroes No. 259 on)
Mar-Apr, 1949 - No. 258, Dec, 1979 (#1-16: 52 pgs.)
National Periodical Publications/DC Comics

	GD25	FN65	VF82	NM94
1-Superman cover	450.00	1350.00	2925.00	4500.00

(Estimated up to 275 total copies exist, 15 in NM/Mint)

	GD25	FN65	NM94
2-Used in **SOTI**, pg. 35-36,226	150.00	450.00	1050.00
3	114.00	343.00	800.00
4,5: 5-1st pre-Supergirl tryout (c/story, 11-12/49)	79.00	235.00	550.00
6-10: 8-1st Superbaby. 10-1st app. Lana Lang	68.00	205.00	475.00
11-15	52.00	156.00	365.00
16-20	36.00	107.00	250.00
21-26,28-30: 21-Lana Lang app.	27.00	81.00	190.00
27-Low distribution	29.00	88.00	205.00
31-38: 38-Last pre-code issue (1/55)	20.00	60.00	140.00
39-48,50 (7/56)	12.00	37.00	110.00
49 (6/56)-1st app. Metallo (Jor-El's robot)	16.00	47.00	140.00
51-60	9.00	28.00	85.00
61-67	8.00	23.00	70.00
68-Origin/1st app. original Bizarro (10-11/58)	43.00	130.00	390.00
69-77,79: 75-Spanking-c. 76-1st Supermonkey. 77-Pre-Pete Ross tryout	6.00	18.00	55.00
78-Origin Mr. Mxyzptlk & Superboy's costume	11.00	33.00	100.00
80-1st meeting Superboy/Supergirl (4/60)	10.00	30.00	90.00
81,83-85,87,88: 83-Origin/1st app. Kryptonite Kid	5.00	15.00	45.00
82-1st Bizarro Krypto	5.00	15.00	46.00
86-(1/61)-4th Legion app; Intro Pete Ross	10.00	30.00	90.00
89-(6/61)-1st app. Mon-el; 2nd Phantom Zone	20.00	60.00	180.00
90-92: 90-Pete Ross learns Superboy's I.D. 92-Last 10¢ issue	5.00	15.00	45.00
93-10th Legion app.(12/61); Chameleon Boy app.	4.50	15.00	35.00
94-97,99	3.00	9.40	22.00
98-(7/62)-18th Legion app; origin & 1st app. Ultra Boy; Pete Ross joins Legion	4.70	14.00	33.00
100-(10/62)-Ultra Boy app; 1st app. Phantom Zone villains, Dr. Xadu & Erndine. 2 pg. map of Krypton; origin Superboy retold; r-cover of Superman #1	20.00	60.00	140.00
101-120: 104-Origin Phantom Zone. 115-Atomic bomb-c. 117-Legion app.	1.90	5.60	13.00
121-128: 124-(10/65)-1st app. Insect Queen (Lana Lang). 125-Legion cameo. 126-Origin Krypto the Super Dog retold with new facts	1.40	4.00	8.50
129-(80-pg. Giant G-22)-Reprints origin Mon-el	1.60	4.70	11.00
130-137,139,140: 131-Legion statues cameo in Dog Legionnaires story. 132-1st app. Supremo. 133-Superboy meets Robin	1.00	2.00	5.00
138 (80-pg. Giant G-35)	1.60	4.70	11.00
141-146,148-155,157-164,166-173,175,176: 145-Superboy's parents regain their youth. 171-1st app. Aquaboy? 172,173,176-Legion app.; 172-Origin Yango (Super Ape). 176-Partial photo-c		1.50	3.75
147(6/68)-Giant G-47; 1st origin of L.S.H. (Saturn Girl, Lightning Lad, Cosmic Boy); origin Legion of Super-Pets-r/Adv. #293?	1.60	4.00	9.50
156,165,174 (Giants G-59,71,83): 165-r/1st app. Krypto the Superdog from Adventure Comics #210	1.30	3.10	7.50
177-184,186,187 (All 52 pgs.): 184-Origin Dial H for Hero-r		1.40	3.50
185-DC 100 Pg. Super Spectacular #12; Legion-c/story; Teen Titans, Kid Eternity(r/Hit #46), Star Spangled Kid-r(S.S. 55)	1.00	2.00	5.00
188-196: 188-Origin Karkan. 191-Origin Sunboy retold; Legion app. 193-Chameleon Boy & Shrinking Violet get new costumes. 195-1st app. Erg/Wildfire; Phantom Girl gets new costume. 196-Last Superboy solo story		.90	2.25
197-Legion series begins; Lightning Lad's new costume	1.00	2.50	6.00
198,199: 198-Element Lad & Princess Projectra get new costumes		1.00	2.50
200-Bouncing Boy & Duo Damsel marry; J'onn J'onzz cameo	1.00	2.00	5.00
201,204,206,207,209: 201-Re-intro Erg as Wildfire. 204-Supergirl resigns from Legion. 206-Ferro Lad & Invisible Kid app. 209-Karate Kid gets new costume		1.10	2.75
202,205-(100 pgs.): 202-Light Lass gets new costume; Mike Grell's 1st comic work-i (5-6/74)		1.30	3.25
203-Invisible Kid dies		1.50	3.75
208,210: 208-(68 pgs.). 210-Origin Karate Kid		1.30	3.25
211-220: 212-Matter-Eater Lad resigns. 216-1st app. Tyroc who joins Legion in #218		1.00	2.50
221-249: 226-Intro. Dawnstar. 228-Death of Chemical King. 240-Origin Dawnstar. 242-(52 pgs.). 243-Legion of Substitute Heroes app. 243-245-(44 pgs.)		.80	1.90
250-258: 253-Intro Blok. 257-Return of Bouncing Boy & Duo Damsel by Ditko		.80	1.90
Annual 1(Sum/64, 84 pgs.)-Origin Krypto-r	10.00	30.00	110.00
Spectacular 1(1980, Giant)-Distr. through comic stores; mostly-r		.80	1.90

NOTE: **Neal Adams** *c-143, 145, 146, 148-155, 157-161, 163, 164, 166-168, 172, 173, 175, 176, 178.* **M. Anderson** *a-245i.* **Ditko** *a-257p.* **Grell** *a-202i, 203-219, 220-224p, 235p; c-207-232, 235, 236p, 237, 239p, 240p, 243p, 246, 258.* **Nasser** *a(p)-222, 225, 226, 230, 231, 233, 236.* **Simonson** *a-237p.* **Starlin** *a(p)-239, 250, 251; c-238.* **Staton** *a-227p, 243-249p, 252-258p; c-247-251p.* **Swan/Moldoff** *c-109.* **Tuska** *a-172, 173, 176, 183, 235p.* **Wood** *inks-153-155, 157-161. Legion app.-172, 173, 176, 177, 183, 184, 188, 190, 191, 193, 195.*

SUPERBOY (TV)(DC, 1990-'91)(Value: cover or less)

SUPERBOY (3rd series)
Feb, 1994 - Present ($1.50)
DC Comics

	GD25	FN65	NM94
1-8-Metropolis Kid from Reign of the Supermen: 6,7-Worlds Collide Pt. 3 & 8. 8-(9/94)-Zero Hour			1.50
0-(10/94)			1.50
9-14: 9-(11/94)-King Shark app.			1.50
Annual 1 (1994, $2.95, 68 pgs.)-Elseworlds story, Pt. 2 of The Super Seven (see Adventures Of Superman Annual #6)		1.20	3.00

SUPER BRAT

Super-Brat #7 © TOBY

Super Comics #85 © DELL

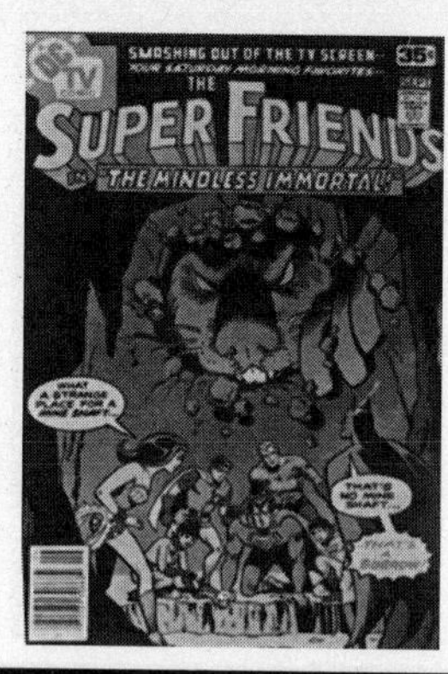

Super Friends #213 © DC

	GD25	FN65	NM94

January, 1954 - No. 4, July, 1954
Toby Press

	GD25	FN65	NM94
1	4.20	12.50	25.00
2-4: 4-Li'l Teevy by Mel Lazarus	3.00	7.50	15.00
I.W. Reprint #1,2,3,7,8('58)	.60	1.50	3.00
I.W. (Super) Reprint #10('63)	.60	1.50	3.00

SUPERCAR (TV)
Nov, 1962 - No. 4, Aug, 1963 (All painted covers)
Gold Key

	GD25	FN65	NM94
1	24.00	71.00	165.00
2,3	12.00	36.00	85.00
4	18.00	54.00	125.00

SUPER CAT (Formerly Frisky Animals; also see Animal Crackers)
No. 56, Nov, 1953 - No. 58, May, 1954; Sept, 1957 - No. 4, May, 1958
Star Publications #56-58/Ajax/Farrell Publ. (Four Star Comic Corp.)

	GD25	FN65	NM94
56-58-L.B. Cole-c on all	10.00	30.00	65.00
1(1957-Ajax)- "The Adventures of..."	5.85	17.50	35.00
2-4	4.00	11.00	22.00

SUPER CIRCUS (TV)
January, 1951 - No. 5, Sept, 1951 (Mary Hartline)
Cross Publishing Co.

	GD25	FN65	NM94
1-(52 pgs.)-Cast photos on-c	9.15	27.50	55.00
2-Cast photos on-c	7.00	21.00	42.00
3-5	5.35	16.00	32.00

SUPER CIRCUS (TV)
No. 542, March, 1954 - No. 694, Mar, 1956 (Featuring Mary Hartline)
Dell Publishing Co.

	GD25	FN65	NM94
4-Color 542,592,694: Mary Hartline photo-c	5.85	17.50	35.00

SUPER COMICS
May, 1938 - No. 121, Feb-Mar, 1949
Dell Publishing Co.

	GD25	FN65	NM94
1-Terry & The Pirates, The Gumps, Dick Tracy, Little Orphan Annie, Little Joe, Gasoline Alley, Smilin' Jack, Smokey Stover, Smitty, Tiny Tim, Moon Mullins, Harold Teen, Winnie Winkle begin	150.00	450.00	1050.00
2	66.00	197.00	460.00
3	57.00	171.00	400.00
4,5: 4-Dick Tracy-c; also #8-10,17,26(part),31	49.00	146.00	340.00
6-10	37.00	111.00	260.00
11-20: 20-Smilin' Jack-c (also #29,32)	30.00	90.00	210.00
21-29: 21-Magic Morro begins (origin & 1st app., 2/40). 22,27-Ken Ernst-c (also #25?); Magic Morro c-22,25,27,34	27.00	80.00	185.00
30- "Sea Hawk" movie adaptation-c/story with Errol Flynn	27.00	80.00	185.00
31-40: 34-Ken Ernst-c. 35-Dick Tracy-c begin	22.00	65.00	150.00
41-50: 41-Intro Lightning Jim. 43-Terry & The Pirates ends	16.50	50.00	115.00
51-60	13.00	40.00	90.00
61-70: 62-Flag-c. 65-Brenda Starr-r begin? 67-X-Mas-c	11.50	34.00	80.00
71-80	10.00	30.00	65.00
81-99	8.35	25.00	50.00
100	10.00	30.00	65.00
101-115-Last Dick Tracy (moves to own title)	6.35	19.00	38.00
116,118-All Smokey Stover	5.35	16.00	32.00
117-All Gasoline Alley	5.35	16.00	32.00
119-121-Terry & The Pirates app. in all	5.35	16.00	32.00

SUPER COPS, THE (Red Circle)(Value: cover or less)

SUPER COPS (Now)(Value: cover or less)

SUPER CRACKED (See Cracked)

SUPER DC GIANT (25-50¢, all 68-52 pg. Giants)
No. 13, 9-10/70 - No. 26, 7-8/71; V3#27, Summer, 1976 (No #1-12)
National Periodical Publications

	GD25	FN65	NM94
S-13-Binky		1.60	4.00
S-14-Top Guns of the West; Kubert-c; Trigger Twins, Johnny Thunder, Wyoming Kid-r; Moreira-r (9-10/70)		1.60	4.00
S-15-Western Comics; Kubert-c; Pow Wow Smith, Vigilante, Buffalo Bill-r; new Gil Kane-a (9-10/70)	1.00	2.00	5.00
S-16-Best of the Brave & the Bold; Batman-r & Metamorpho origin-r from Brave & the Bold	1.00	2.00	5.00
S-17-Love 1970		1.40	3.50
S-18-Three Mouseketeers; Dizzy Dog, Doodles Duck, Bo Bunny-r; Sheldon Mayer-a		1.60	4.00
S-19-Jerry Lewis; no Neal Adams-a		1.60	4.00
S-20-House of Mystery; N. Adams-c; Kirby-r(3)		1.60	4.00
S-21-Love 1971		1.20	3.00
S-22-Top Guns of the West		1.40	3.50
S-23-The Unexpected		1.20	3.00
S-24-Supergirl		1.20	3.00
S-25-Challengers of the Unknown; all Kirby/Wood-r		1.60	4.00
S-26-Aquaman (1971)		1.60	4.00
27-Strange Flying Saucers Adventures (Sum, 1976)		1.20	3.00

NOTE: ***Sid Greene** r-27p(2), **Heath** r-27. **G. Kane** a-14r(2), 15, 27r(p). **Kubert** r-16.*

SUPER-DOOPER COMICS
1946 - No. 8, 1946 (10¢, 32 pgs., paper cover)(#1-4 exist?)
Able Manufacturing Co.

	GD25	FN65	NM94
1-The Clock, Gangbuster app.	12.00	36.00	85.00
2	8.35	25.00	50.00
3,4,6	6.70	20.00	40.00
5,7-Capt. Freedom & Shock Gibson	8.35	25.00	50.00
8-Shock Gibson, Sam Hill	8.35	25.00	50.00

SUPER DUCK COMICS (The Cockeyed Wonder) (See Jolly Jingles)
Fall, 1944 - No. 94, Dec, 1960 (Also see Laugh #24)(#1-5 are quarterly)
MLJ Mag. No. 1-4(9/45)/Close-Up No. 5 on (Archie)

	GD25	FN65	NM94
1-Origin; Hitler & Hirohito-c	36.00	107.00	250.00
2-Bill Vigoda-c	17.00	52.00	120.00
3-5: 4-20-Al Fagaly-c (most)	12.00	36.00	85.00
6-10	10.00	30.00	65.00
11-20	8.35	25.00	50.00
21,23-40	6.70	20.00	40.00
22-Used in **SOTI**, pg. 35,307,308	7.50	22.50	45.00
41-60	5.00	15.00	30.00
61-94	4.00	10.00	20.00

SUPER DUPER (Formerly Pocket Comics #1-4?)
No. 5, 1941 - No. 11, 1941
Harvey Publications

	GD25	FN65	NM94
5-Captain Freedom & Shock Gibson app.	22.00	65.00	150.00
8,11	11.50	34.00	80.00

SUPER DUPER COMICS (Formerly Latest Comics?)
No. 3, May-June, 1947
F. E. Howard Publ.

	GD25	FN65	NM94
3-1st app. Mr. Monster	7.50	22.50	45.00

SUPER FRIENDS (TV) (Also see Best of DC & Limited Collectors' Edition)
Nov, 1976 - No. 47, Aug, 1981 (#14 is 44 pgs.)
National Periodical Publications/DC Comics

	GD25	FN65	NM94
1-Superman, Batman, Robin, Wonder Woman, Aquaman, Atom, Wendy, Marvin & Wonder Dog begin (1st Super Friends)		1.00	2.50
2-47: 2-Penguin-c/story. 7-1st app. Wonder Twins, & The Seraph; Batgirl x-over. 8-1st app. Jack O'Lantern. 9-1st app. Icemaiden. 13-1st app. Dr. Mist. 14-Origin Wonder Twins. 25-1st app. Fire & Green Fury. 28-Bizarro app. 31-Black Orchid app. 36,43-Plastic Man app. 47-Origin Fire & Green Fury		.80	2.00
...Special 1 (1981, giveaway, no ads, no code or price)-r/Super Friends #19 & 36		.70	1.80

NOTE: ***Estrada** a-1p, 2p. **Orlando** a-1p. **Staton** a-43, 45.*

Supergirl #4 © DC

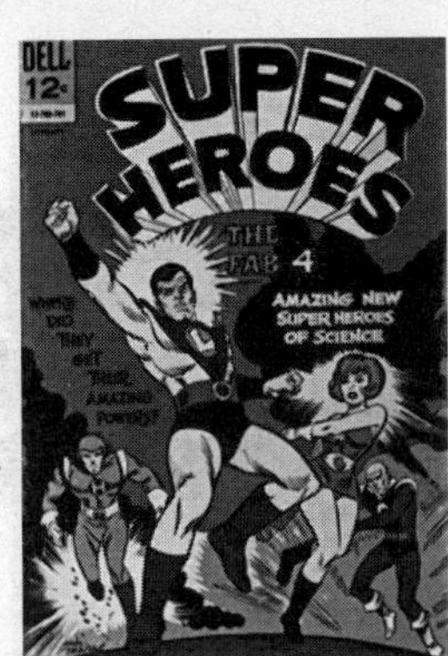

Super Heroes #1 © DELL

Superman #15 © DC

GD25 FN65 NM94

SUPER FUN
January, 1956 (By A.W. Nugent)
Gillmor Magazines

1-Comics, puzzles, cut-outs by A.W. Nugent 2.40 6.00 12.00

SUPER FUNNIES (...Western Funnies #3,4)
Dec, 1953 - No. 4, Sept, 1954
Superior Comics Publishers Ltd. (Canada)

1-(3-D, 10¢)-...Presents Dopey Duck; make your own 3-D glasses cut-out inside front-c; did not come w/glasses 33.00 100.00 230.00
2-Horror & crime satire 7.50 22.50 45.00
3-Phantom Ranger-c/s; Geronimo, Billy the Kid app. 4.20 12.50 25.00
4-Phantom Ranger-c/story 4.20 12.50 25.00

SUPERGEAR COMICS
1976 (4 pgs. in color) (slick paper)
Jacobs Corp. (Giveaway)

nn-(Rare)-Superman, Lois Lane; Steve Lombard app. (500 copies printed, over half destroyed?) 1.00 2.50 6.00

SUPERGIRL (See Action, Adventure #281, Brave & the Bold, Crisis on Infinite Earths #7, Daring New Advs. of..., Super DC Giant, Superman Family, & Super-Team Family)

SUPERGIRL
Nov, 1972 - No. 9, Dec-Jan, 1973-74; No. 10, Sept-Oct, 1974
National Periodical Publications

1-1st solo title; Zatanna begins, ends #5 1.10 2.75
2-10: 5-Zatanna origin-r. 8-JLA x-over; Batman cameo .70 1.80
NOTE: *Zatanna in #1-5, 7(Guest); Prez app. in #10. #1-10 are 20¢ issues.*

SUPERGIRL (Formerly Daring New Adventures of...)
No. 14, Dec, 1983 - No. 23, Sept, 1984
DC Comics

14-23: 16-Ambush Bug app. 20-JLA & New Teen Titans app. 1.00
...Movie Special (1985)-Adapts movie; Morrow-a; photo back-c 1.20
Giveaway ('84, '86 Baxter, nn)(American Honda/U.S. Dept. Transportation)-Torres-c/a 1.20

SUPERGIRL
Feb, 1994 - No. 4, May, 1994 ($1.50, mini-series)
DC Comics

1-4: Guice-a(i) 1.50

SUPERGIRL/LEX LUTHOR SPECIAL (Supergirl and Team Luthor on-c)
1993 ($2.50, 68 pgs.)
DC Comics

1-Pin-ups by Byrne & Thibert also 1.00 2.50

SUPER GOOF (Walt Disney) (See Dynabrite & The Phantom Blot)
Oct, 1965 - No. 74, 1982
Gold Key No. 1-57/Whitman No. 58 on

1 3.60 9.00 20.00
2-5 2.00 5.00 10.00
6-10 1.60 4.00 8.00
11-20 1.20 3.00 6.00
21-30 1.20 3.00
31-50 .80 2.00
51-74 1.00
NOTE: *Reprints in #16, 24, 28, 29, 37, 38, 43, 45, 46, 54(1/2), 56-58, 65(1/2), 72(r-#2).*

SUPER GREEN BERET (Tod Holton...)
April, 1967 - No. 2, June, 1967 (25¢, 68 pgs.)
Lightning Comics (Milson Publ. Co.)

1,2 3.60 9.00 18.00

SUPER HEROES (See Giant-Size... & Marvel...)

SUPER HEROES
Jan, 1967 - No. 4, June, 1967
Dell Publishing Co.

1-Origin & 1st app. Fab 4 2.90 9.00 20.00
2-4 1.70 5.10 12.00

SUPER-HEROES BATTLE SUPER-GORILLAS (See DC Special #16)
Winter, 1976 (One Shot, 52 pgs.; all reprints)
National Periodical Publications

1-Superman, Batman, Flash stories; Infantino-a(p) 1.25

SUPER HEROES PUZZLES AND GAMES
1979 (32 pgs.) (regular size)
General Mills Giveaway (Marvel Comics Group)

nn-Four 2-pg. origin stories of Spider-Man, Captain America, The Hulk, & Spider-Woman 1.80 4.50

SUPER HEROES VERSUS SUPER VILLAINS
July, 1966 (no month given)(68 pgs.)
Archie Publications (Radio Comics)

1-Flyman, Black Hood, Web, Shield-r; Reinman-a 5.00 15.00 35.00

SUPERICHIE (Formerly Super Richie)
No. 5, Oct, 1976 - No. 18, Jan, 1979 (52 pgs. giants)
Harvey Publications

5-18: 5-Origin/1st app. new costumes for Rippy & Crashman 1.00

SUPERIOR STORIES
May-June, 1955 - No. 4, Nov-Dec, 1955
Nesbit Publishing Co.

1-The Invisible Man by H.G. Wells 12.00 36.00 85.00
2-The Pirate of the Gulf by J.H. Ingrahams 7.50 22.50 45.00
3-Wreck of the Grosvenor by William Clark Russell 7.50 22.50 45.00
4-The Texas Rangers by O'Henry 7.50 22.50 45.00
NOTE: ***Morisi** c/a in all. Kiwanis stories in #3 & 4. #4 has photo of Gene Autry on-c.*

SUPER MAGIC (Super Magician Comics #2 on)
May, 1941
Street & Smith Publications

V1#1-Blackstone the Magician-c/story; origin/1st app. Rex King (Black Fury); Charles Sultan-c; Blackstone-c begin 86.00 257.00 600.00

SUPER MAGICIAN COMICS (Super Magic #1)
No. 2, Sept, 1941 - V5#8, Feb-Mar, 1947
Street & Smith Publications

V1#2-Blackstone the Magician continues; Rex King, Man of Adventure app. 34.00 103.00 240.00
3-Tao-Anwar, Boy Magician begins 23.00 70.00 160.00
4-Origin Transo 19.00 58.00 135.00
5-7,9-12: 11-Supersnipe app. 19.00 58.00 135.00
8-Abbott & Costello story (1st app?, 11/42) 21.00 63.00 145.00
V2#1-The Shadow app. 25.00 75.00 175.00
2-12: 5-Origin Tigerman. 8-Red Dragon begins 10.00 30.00 70.00
V3#1-12: 5-Origin Mr. Twilight 10.00 30.00 70.00
V4#1-12: 11-Nigel Elliman begins 10.00 30.00 60.00
V5#1-6 10.00 30.00 60.00
7,8-Red Dragon by Edd Cartier-c/a 23.00 70.00 160.00
NOTE: ***Jack Binder** c-1-14(most). Red Dragon c-V5#7, 8.*

SUPERMAN (See Action Comics, Advs. of..., All-New Coll. Ed., All-Star Comics, Best of DC DC, Brave & the Bold, Cosmic Odyssey, DC Comics Presents, Heroes Against Hunger, Krypton Chronicles, Limited Coll. Ed., Man of Steel, Phantom Zone, Power Record Comics, Special Edition, Steel, Super Friends, Superman: The Man of Steel, Taylor's Christmas Tabloid, Three-Dimension Advs., World Of Krypton, World Of Metropolis, World Of Smallville & World's Finest)

SUPERMAN (Becomes Adventures of...#424 on)
Summer, 1939 - No. 423, Sept, 1986 (#1-5 are quarterly)
National Periodical Publications/DC Comics

GD25 FN65 VF82 NM94

1(nn)-1st four Action stories reprinted; origin Superman by Siegel & Shuster; has a new 2 pg. origin plus 4 pgs. omitted in Action story; see The Comics Magazine #1 & More Fun #14-17 for Superman proto-type app.; cover r/splash page from Action #10; 1st pin-up Superman on back-c - 1st pin-up in comics 8,000.00 24,000.00 52,000.00 80,000.00
(Estimated up to 190 total copies exist, 3 in NM/Mint)

Superman #90 © DC

Superman #208 © DC

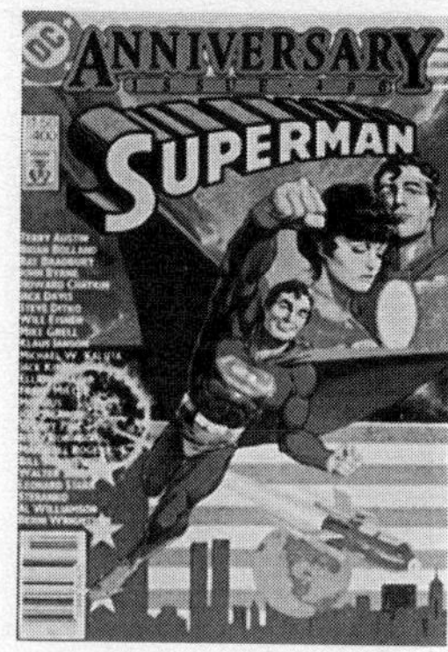

Superman #400 © DC

GD25 FN65 NM94

1-Reprint, Oversize 13-1/2x10". **WARNING**: This comic is an exact duplicate reprint of the original except for its size. DC published it in 1978 with a second cover titling it as a Famous First Edition. There have been many reported cases of the outer cover being removed and the interior sold as the original edition. The reprint with the new outer cover removed is practically worthless. See Famous First Edition for value.

	GD25	FN65	NM94
2-All daily strip-r; full pg. ad for N.Y. World's Fair	929.00	2786.00	6500.00
3-2nd story-r from Action #5; 3rd story-r from Action #6	607.00	1820.00	4250.00
4-2nd mention of Daily Planet (Spr/40); also see Action #23; 2nd & 3rd app. Luthor (red-headed; also see Action #23)	457.00	1371.00	3200.00
5-4th Luthor app. (red hair)	314.00	943.00	2200.00
6,7: 6-1st splash pg. in a Superman comic. 7-1st Perry White? (11-12/40)	250.00	750.00	1750.00
8-10: 10-5th app. Luthor (1st bald Luthor, 5-6/41)	214.00	642.00	1500.00
11-13,15: 13-Jimmy Olsen & Luthor app.	150.00	450.00	1050.00
14-Patriotic Shield-c by Fred Ray	229.00	685.00	1600.00
16-20: 16-1st Lois Lane-c this title (5-6/42); 2nd Lois-c after Action #29. 17-Hitler, Hirohito-c	129.00	386.00	900.00
21-23,25: 25-Clark Kent's only military service; Fred Ray's only super-hero story	100.00	300.00	700.00
24-Jack Burnley flag-c	121.00	365.00	850.00
26-29: 27,29-31-Lois Lane-c. 28-Lois Lane Girl Reporter series begins, ends #40,42	93.00	280.00	650.00
28-Overseas edition for Armed Forces; same as reg. #28	93.00	280.00	650.00
30-Origin & 1st app. Mr. Mxyztplk (9-10/44)(pronounced "Mix-it-plk") in comic books; name later became Mxyzptlk ("Mix-yez-pit-l-ick"); the character was inspired by a combination of the name of Al Capp's Joe Blyfstyk (the little man with the black cloud over his head) & the devilish antics of Bugs Bunny; he 1st app. in newspapers 3/7/44	143.00	430.00	1000.00
31-40: 33-(3-4/45)-3rd app. Mxyztplk. 35,36-Lois Lane-c. 38-Atomic bomb story (1-2/46); delayed because of gov't cencorship; Superman shown reading Batman #32 on cover	82.00	246.00	575.00
41-50: 42-Lois Lane-c. 45-Lois Lane as Superwoman (see Action #60 for 1st app.). 46-(5-6/47)-1st app. Superboy this title? 48-1st time Superman travels thru time	61.00	182.00	425.00
51,52: 51-Lois Lane-c	49.00	146.00	340.00
53-Origin Superman retold; 10th anniversary ('48)	200.00	600.00	1400.00
54,56-60: 58-Intro Tiny Trix	51.00	154.00	360.00
55-Used in **SOTI**, pg. 33	54.00	163.00	380.00
61-Origin Superman retold; origin Green Kryptonite (1st Kryptonite story); Superman returns to Krypton for 1st time & sees his parents for 1st time since infancy, discovers he's not earth man	100.00	300.00	700.00
62-65,67-70: 62-Orson Welles-c/story. 65-1st Krypton Foes: Mala, K120, & U-Ban. 67-Perry Como-c/story. 68-1st Luthor-c this title (see Action Comics)	50.00	150.00	350.00
66-2nd Superbaby story	50.00	150.00	350.00
71-75: 74-2nd Luthor-c this title. 75-Some have #74 on-c	46.00	140.00	325.00
72-Giveaway(9-10/51)-(Rare)-Price blackened out; came with banner wrapped around book; without banner	56.00	170.00	395.00
72-Giveaway with banner	75.00	225.00	525.00
76-Batman x-over; Superman & Batman learn each other's I.D. for the 1st time (5-6/52)(also see World's Finest #71)	135.00	407.00	950.00
77-81: 78-Last 52 pg. issue. 81-Used in **POP**, pg. 88	45.00	135.00	315.00
82-87,89,90	40.00	120.00	280.00
88-Prankster, Toyman & Luthor team-up	41.00	124.00	290.00
91-95: 95-Last precode issue (2/55)	36.00	110.00	255.00
96-99: 96-Mr. Mxyztplk-c/story	24.00	73.00	220.00

	GD25	FN65	VF82	NM94
100 (9-10/55)-Shows cover to #1 on-c	120.00	360.00	780.00	1200.00

	GD25	FN65	NM94
101-110	24.00	71.00	190.00
111-120	21.00	62.00	165.00
121-130: 123-Pre-Supergirl tryout-c/story (8/58). 127-Origin/1st app. Titano. 128-Red Kryptonite used (4/59). 129-Intro/origin Lori Lemaris, The Mermaid	18.00	53.00	140.00
131-139: 139-Lori Lemaris app.; "Untold Story of Red Kryptonite" back-up story	13.00	39.00	105.00
140-1st Blue Kryptonite & Bizarro Supergirl; origin Bizarro Jr. #1	14.00	43.00	115.00
141-145,148: 142-2nd Batman x-over	10.00	30.00	80.00
146-(7/61)-Superman's life story; back-up hints at Earth II	13.00	38.00	100.00
147(8/61)-7th Legion app; 1st app. Legion of Super-Villains; 1st app. Adult Legion; swipes-c to Adv. #247	11.00	34.00	90.00
149(11/61)-9th Legion app. (cameo); "The Death of Superman" imaginary story; last 10¢ issue	10.00	30.00	80.00
150-162: 152(4/62)-15th Legion app. 155-(8/62)-19th Legion app; Lightning Man & Cosmic Man, & Adult Legion app. 156,162-Legion app. 157-Gold Kryptonite used (see Adv. 299); Mon-el app.; Lightning Lad cameo (11/62). 158-1st app. Flamebird & Nightwing & Nor-Kan of Kandor (12/62). 161-1st told death of Ma and Pa Kent	5.00	15.00	35.00
161-2nd printing (1987, $1.25)-New DC logo; sold thru So Much Fun Toy Stores (cover title: Superman Classic)		.90	2.25
163-166,168-180: 166-XMas-c. 168-All Luthor issue; JFK tribute/memorial. 169-Bizarro Invasion of Earth-c/story; last Sally Selwyn. 170-Pres. Kennedy story is finally published after delay from #169 due to assassination. 172,173-Legion cameos. 174-Super-Mxyzptlk; Bizarro app.	4.00	12.00	28.00
167-New origin Brainiac & Brainiac 5; intro Tixarla (later Luthor's wife)	8.00	24.00	55.00
181,182,184-186,188-192,194-196,198,200: 181-1st 2965 story/series. 189-Origin/destruction of Krypton II	2.90	8.60	20.00
183,187,193,197 (Giants G-18,G-23,G-31,G-36)	3.60	10.70	25.00
199-1st Superman/Flash race (8/67): also see Flash #175 & World's Finest #198,199 (r-in Limited Coll. Ed. #48)	21.00	64.00	150.00
201,203-206,208-211,213-216,218-221,223-226,228-231: 213-Brainiac-5 app.	1.80	5.00	11.00
202 (80-pg. Giant G-42)-All Bizarro issue	2.30	6.90	16.00
207,212,217,222,239 (Giants G-48,G-54,G-60,G-66,G-84): 207-Legion app.; 30th anniversary Superman (6/68)	2.30	6.90	16.00
227,232(Giants, G-72,G-78)-All Krypton issues	2.30	6.90	16.00
233-238: 233-2nd app. Morgan Edge; Clark Kent switches from newspaper reporter to TV newscaster; all Kryptonite on earth destroyed	1.80	5.00	11.00
240-Kaluta-a	1.00	2.50	6.00
241-244 (All 52 pgs.): 243-G.A.-r/#38	1.00	2.30	5.50
245-DC 100 Pg. Super Spectacular #7; Air Wave, Kid Eternity, Hawkman-r; Atom-r/Atom #3	1.00	2.90	7.00
246-248,250,251,253 (All 52 pgs.): 246-G.A.-r/#40. 248-World of Krypton story. 251-G.A.-r/#45. 253-Finlay-a, 2 pgs., G.A.-r/#1	1.00	1.90	4.75
249,254-Neal Adams-a. 249-(52 pgs.); origin & 1st app. Terra-Man by Neal Adams (inks)	1.40	4.00	8.50
252-DC 100 Pg. Super Spectacular #13; Ray(r/Smash #17), Black Condor, (r/Crack #18), Hawkman(r/Flash #24); Starman-r/Adv. #67; Dr. Fate & Spectre-r/More Fun #57; N. Adams-c	1.30	3.30	8.00
255-271,273-277,279-283: 263-Photo-c. 264-1st app. Steve Lombard. 276-Intro Capt. Thunder. 279-Batman, Batgirl app.		1.00	2.50
272,278,284-All 100 pgs. G.A.-r in all. 272-r/2nd app. Mr. Mxyztplk from Action #80	1.00	2.00	5.00
285-299: 289-Partial photo-c. 292-Origin Lex Luthor retold		1.00	2.50
300-Retells origin (6/76)	1.00	2.70	6.50
301-399: 301,320-Solomon Grundy app. 323-Intro. Atomic Skull. 327-329-(44 pgs.). 330-More facts revealed about I. D. 338-The bottled city of Kandor enlarged. 344-Frankenstein & Dracula app. 353-Brief origin. 354,355,357-Superman 2020 stories (354-Debut of Superman III). 356-World of Krypton story (also #360,367,375). 366-Fan letter by Todd McFarlane. 372-Superman 2021 story. 376-Free 16 pg. preview Daring New Advs. of Supergirl. 377-Free 16 pg. preview Masters of the Universe		.90	2.25
400 (10/84, $1.50, 68 pgs.)-Many top artists featured; Chaykin painted cover, Miller back-c	1.00	2.00	5.00

401-410,412-422: 405-Super-Batman story. 408-Nuclear Holocaust-c/story.

Superman (2nd Series) #41 © DC

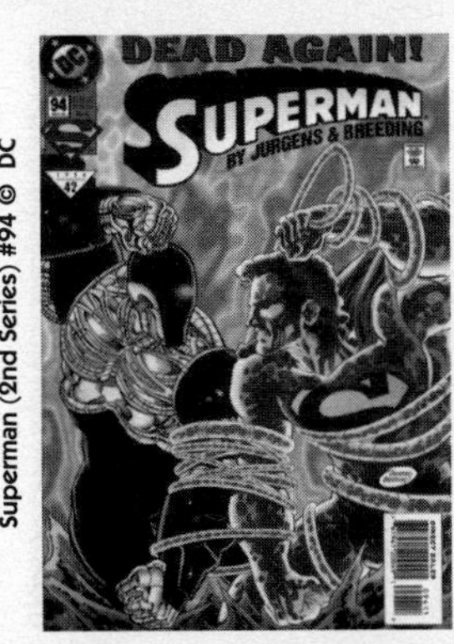

Superman (2nd Series) #94 © DC

Superman and the Great Cleveland Fire © DC

GD25 FN65 NM94

414,415-Crisis x-over. 422-Horror-c .90 2.25
411-Special Julius Schwartz tribute issue .90 2.25
423-Alan Moore scripts; Perez-a(i); last Earth I Superman story, cont'd in Action #583 1.40 4.00 8.50
Annual 1(10/60, 84 pgs.)-Reprints 1st Supergirl story/Action #252; r/Lois Lane #1; Krypto-r (1st Silver Age DC annual) 58.00 173.00 575.00
Annual 2(Wint, 1960-61)-Super-villain issue; Brainiac, Titano, Metallo, Bizarro origin-r 31.00 92.00 275.00
Annual 3(Sum, 1961)-Strange Lives of Superman 25.00 75.00 200.00
Annual 4(Wint, 1961-62)-11th Legion app; 1st Legion origins (text & pictures); advs. in time, space & on alien worlds 21.00 64.00 170.00
Annual 5(Sum, 1962)-All Krypton issue 19.00 58.00 135.00
Annual 6(Wint, 1962-63)-Legion-r/Adv. #247 17.00 51.00 120.00
Annual 7(Sum, 1963)-Origin-r/Superman-Batman team/Adv. 275; r/1955 Superman dailies 13.00 39.00 90.00
Annual 8(Wint, 1963-64)-All origins issue 11.00 32.00 75.00
Annual 9(8/64)-Was advertised but came out as 80 Page Giant #1 instead
Annual 9(1983)-Toth/Austin-a 1.00 2.50 6.00
Annuals 10-12: 10(1984, $1.25)-M. Anderson inks. 11(1985)-Moore scripts. 12(1986)-Bolland-c 1.00 2.00 5.00
...IV Movie Special (1987, $2.00, one-shot)-Movie adaptation; Heck-a .80 2.00
Special 1(1983)-G. Kane-c/a; contains German-r 1.00 2.00 5.00
Special 2,3(1984, 1985, $1.25, 52 pgs.) 1.00 2.00 5.00
The Amazing World of Superman "Official Metropolis Edition" (1973, $2.00, 14x10-1/2")-Origin retold; Wood-r(i) from Superboy #153,161 1.60 4.00 8.00
Kelloggs Giveaway-(2/3 normal size, 1954)-r-two stories/Superman #55 30.00 90.00 200.00
...Meets the Quik Bunny (1987, Nestles Quik premium, 36 pgs.) 1.00
...Movie Special-(9/83)-Adaptation of Superman III; other versions exist with store logos on bottom 1/3 of-c 1.00
Pizza Hut Premiums (12/77)-Exact reprints of 1950s comics except for paid ads (set of 6 exist?); Vol. 1-r#97 (#113-r also known) 1.50
Radio Shack Giveaway-36 pgs. (7/80) "The Computers That Saved Metropolis", Starlin/Giordano-a; advertising insert in Action #509, New Advs. of Superboy #7, Legion of Super-Heroes #265, & House of Mystery #282. (All comics were 68 pgs.) Cover of inserts printed on newsprint. Giveaway contains 4 extra pgs. of Radio Shack advertising that inserts do not 1.50
Radio Shack Giveaway-(7/81) "Victory by Computer" 1.50
Radio Shack Giveaway-(7/82) "Computer Masters of Metropolis" 1.00
11195 (2/79, $1.95, 224 pgs.)-Golden Press 1.00 2.40

*NOTE: **N. Adams** a-249i, 254p; c-204-208, 210, 212-215, 219, 231, 233-237, 240-243, 249-252, 254, 263, 307, 308, 313, 314, 317. **Adkins** a-323i. **Austin** c-368i. **Wayne Boring** art-late 1940's to early 1960's. **Buckler** a(p)-352, 363, 364, 369; c(p)-324-327, 356, 363, 368, 369, 373, 376, 378. **Burnley** a-252r; c-19-25, 30, 33, 34, 35p, 38p, 39p, 45p. **Fine** a-252r. **Gil Kane** a-272r, 367, 372, 375, Special 2; c-374p, 375p, 377, 381, 382, 384-390, 392, Annual 9. **Joe Kubert** c-216. **Morrow** a-238. **Perez** c-364p. **Fred Ray** a-25; c-6, 8-18. **Starlin** c-355. **Staton** a-354i, 355i. **Swan/Moldoff** c-149. **Williamson** a(i)-408-410, 412-416; c-408i, 409i. **Wrightson** a-400, 416.*

SUPERMAN (2nd series)
Jan, 1987 - Present (.75/$1.00/$1.25)
DC Comics

1-Byrne-c/a begins; intro new Metallo 1.10 2.75
2-8,10: 3-Legends x-over; Darkseid-c & app. 7-Origin/1st app. Rampage. 8-Legion app. .70 1.80
9-Joker-c 1.40 3.50
11-49,51,52,54-56,58-67: 11-1st new Mr. Mxyzptlk. 12-Lori Lemaris revived. 13-1st app. Toyman. 13,14-Millennium x-over. 20-Doom Patrol app.; Supergirl revived in cameo. 21-Supergirl-c/story; 1st app. Matrix who becomes new Supergirl. 31-Mr. Mxyzptlk app. 37-Newsboy Legion app. 41-Lobo app. 44-Batman storyline, part 1. 45-Free extra 8 pgs. 54-Newsboy Legion story. 63-Aquaman x-over. 67-Last $1.00-c .70 1.80
50-($1.50, 52 pgs.)-Clark Kent proposes to Lois 1.70 4.25
50-2nd printing .65 1.60
53-Clark reveals i.d. to Lois cont'd from Action #662 1.20 3.00
53-2nd printing 1.50
57-($1.75, 52 pgs.) .70 1.75
68-72: 65,66,68-Deathstroke-c/stories. 70-Superman & Robin team-up 1.50
73-Doomsday cameo 1.70 4.25
74-Doomsday battle issue, part 2, cont'd from Justice League #69 1.00 2.50 6.00
73,74-2nd printings .70 1.80
75-($2.50)-Collector's Ed.; Doomsday, part 6; death of Superman; polybagged w/poster of funeral, obituary from Daily Planet, postage stamp & armband premiums (direct sale only) 2.10 6.00 15.00
75-Direct sale copy (no upc code, 1st print) 1.50 3.75
75-Direct sale copy (no upc code, 2nd print) 1.25
75-Direct sale copy (no upc code, 3rd, 4th prints) 1.25
75-Newsstand copy w/upc code 1.40 3.50
75-Platinum Edition; given away to retailers 110.00
76,77-Funeral for a friend parts 4 & 8 .90 2.25
78-($1.95)-Collector's Edition with die-cut outer-c & bound-in mini poster; Doomsday cameo .90 2.25
78-($1.50)-Newsstand Edition w/poster and different-c; Doomsday-c & cameo .70 1.80
79-81,83-89: 83-Funeral for a Friend epilogue; new Batman (Azrael) cameo. 87,88-Bizarro-c/story .70 1.80
82-($3.50)-Collector's Edition w/all chromium-c; real Superman revealed; Green Lantern x-over from G.L. #46; no ads 1.40 3.50
82-($2.00, 44 pgs.)-Regular Edition w/different-c .80 2.00
90-93: 93-(9/94)-Zero Hour 1.50
0-(10/94) 1.50
94-99: 94-(11/94) 1.50
Annual 1,2: 1 (1987)-No Byrne-a. 2 (1988)-Byrne-a; Newsboy Legion; return of the Guardian 1.50
Annual 3 (1991, $2.00, 68 pgs.)-Armageddon 2001 x-over; Batman app.; Austin-c(i) & part inks .80 2.00
Annual 3-2nd & 3rd printings; 3rd has silver ink .80 2.00
Annual 4 (1992, $2.50, 68 pgs.)-Eclipso app. 1.00 2.50
Annual 5 (1993, $2.50, 68 pgs.) 1.00 2.50
Annual 6 (1994, $2.95, 68 pgs.)-Elseworlds story 1.20 3.00
The Death of Superman trade paperback nn (1993, $4.95)-Reprints Man of Steel #17-19, Superman #73-75, Advs. of Superman #496,497, Action #683,684 & Justice League #69 2.00 5.00
The Death of Superman, 2nd & 3rd printings 2.00 5.00
The Death of Superman Platinum Edition 15.00
Special 1 (1992, $3.50, 68 pgs.)-Simonson-c/a 1.40 3.50
Superman Gallery, The 1 (1993, $2.95)-Poster-a 1.20 3.00
...: The Legacy of Superman #1 (3/93, $2.50, one-shot, 68 pgs.)-Art Adams-c; Simonson-a 1.00 2.50
...: Time and Time Again (1994, $7.50)-Reprints 1.30 3.10 7.50
...: Under a Yellow Sun nn (1994, $5.95, 68 pgs.)-A Novel by Clark Kent; embossed-c 1.00 2.50 6.00
Daily News Magazine Presents DC Comics' Superman nn-(1987, 8 pgs.)-Supplement to New York Daily News; Perez-c/a 1.00

*NOTE: **Austin** a(i)-1-3. **Byrne** a-1-16p, 17, 19-21p, 22; c-1-17, 20-22; scripts-1-22. **Guice** c/a-64. **Kirby** c-37p. **Joe Quesada** c-Annual 4. **Russell** c/a-23i. **Simonson** c-69i. #19-21 2nd printings sold in multi-packs.*

SUPERMAN AND THE GREAT CLEVELAND FIRE (Giveaway)
1948 (4 pgs., no cover)(Hospital Fund)
National Periodical Publications

nn-In full color 50.00 150.00 350.00

SUPERMAN/DOOMSDAY: HUNTER/PREY
1994 - No. 3, 1994 ($4.95, limited series, 52 pgs.)
DC Comics

1-3 1.00 2.00 5.00

SUPERMAN FAMILY, THE (Formerly Superman's Pal Jimmy Olsen)
No. 164, Apr-May, 1974 - No. 222, Sept, 1982
National Periodical Publications/DC Comics

164-Jimmy Olsen, Supergirl, Lois Lane begin .70 1.80
165-176 (100-68 pgs.) 1.50

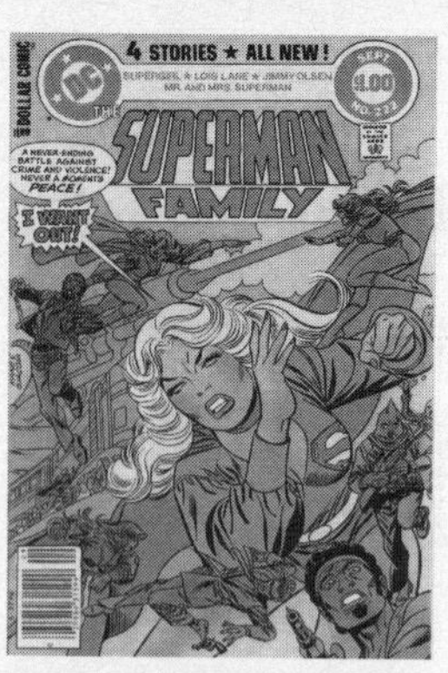

The Superman Family #222 © DC

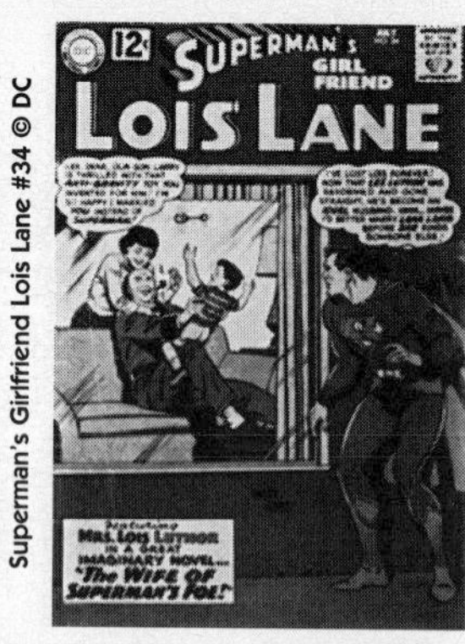

Superman's Girlfriend Lois Lane #34 © DC

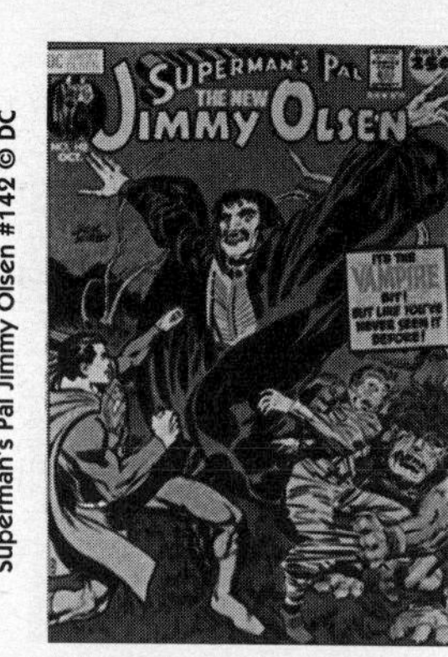

Superman's Pal Jimmy Olsen #142 © DC

GD25 FN65 NM94

177-181 (52 pgs.) 1.40
182,194: Marshall Rogers-a in each. 182-$1.00 issues begin; Krypto begins, ends #192 .90 2.25
183-193,195-222: 183-Nightwing-Flamebird begins, ends #194. 189-Brainiac 5, Mon-el app. 191-Superboy begins, ends #198. 200-Book length story. 211-Earth II Batman & Catwoman marry 1.25

NOTE: ***N. Adams*** *c-182-185.* ***Anderson*** *a-186i.* ***Buckler*** *c(p)-190, 191, 209, 210, 215, 217, 220.* ***Jones*** *a-191-193.* ***Gil Kane*** *c(p)-221, 222.* ***Mortimer*** *a(p)-191-193, 199, 201-222.* ***Orlando*** *a(i)-186, 187.* ***Rogers*** *a-182, 194.* ***Staton*** *a-191-194, 196p.* ***Tuska*** *a(p)-203, 207-209.*

SUPERMAN FOR EARTH
1991 ($4.95, 52 pgs.)(Printed on recycled paper)
DC Comics

nn-Ordway wraparound-c 1.00 2.00 5.00

SUPERMAN (Miniature)
1942; 1955 - 1956 (3 issues; no #'s; 32 pgs.)
The pages are numbered in the 1st issue: 1-32; 2nd: 1A-32A, and 3rd: 1B-32B
National Periodical Publications

No date-Py-Co-Pay Tooth Powder giveaway (8 pgs.; circa 1942) 82.00 245.00 575.00
1-The Superman Time Capsule (Kellogg's Sugar Smacks)(1955) 50.00 150.00 350.00
1A-Duel in Space (1955) 38.00 115.00 265.00
1B-The Super Show of Metropolis (also #1-32, no B)(1955) 38.00 115.00 265.00

NOTE: *Numbering variations exist. Each title could have any combination-#1, 1A, or 1B.*

SUPERMAN RECORD COMIC
1966 (Golden Records)
National Periodical Publications

(with record)-Record reads origin of Superman from comic; came with iron-on patch, decoder, membership card & button; comic-r/Superman #125,146 12.00 36.00 85.00
Comic only 5.00 15.00 35.00

SUPERMAN'S BUDDY (Costume Comic)
1954 (4 pgs.) (One Shot) (Came in box w/costume; slick-paper/c)
National Periodical Publications

1-(Rare)-w/box & costume 130.00 385.00 900.00
Comic only 57.00 171.00 400.00
1-(1958 edition)-Printed in 2 colors 14.00 43.00 100.00

SUPERMAN'S CHRISTMAS ADVENTURE
1940, 1944 (16 pgs.) (Giveaway)
Distributed by Nehi drinks, Bailey Store, Ivey-Keith Co., Kennedy's Boys Shop, Macy's Store, Boston Store
National Periodical Publications

1(1940)-Burnley-a; F. Ray-c/r from Superman #6 314.00 943.00 2200.00
nn(1944) w/Santa Claus & X-mas tree-c 94.00 283.00 660.00
nn(1944) w/Candy cane & Superman-c 81.00 242.00 565.00

SUPERMAN SCRAPBOOK (Has blank pages; contains no comics)

SUPERMAN'S GIRLFRIEND LOIS LANE (See Action Comics #1, 80 Page Giant #3, 14, Lois Lane, Showcase #9, 10, Superman #28 & Superman Family)

SUPERMAN'S GIRLFRIEND LOIS LANE
Mar-Apr, 1958 - No. 136, Jan-Feb, 1974; No. 137, Sept-Oct, 1974
National Periodical Publ.

	GD25	FN65	VF82	NM94
Showcase #9 (7-8/57)-Lois Lane (pre #1); 1st Showcase character to win own series	500.00	1500.00	2750.00	–
		GD25	FN65	NM94
Showcase #10 (9-10/57)-Jor-el cameo		142.00	425.00	1700.00
	GD25	FN65	VF82	NM94
1-(3-4/58)	148.00	443.00	780.00	1475.00
		GD25	FN65	NM94
2		61.00	184.00	490.00
3		44.00	131.00	350.00

GD25 FN65 NM94

4,5 30.00 90.00 240.00
6-10: 9-Pat Boone-c/story 21.00 62.00 165.00
11-20: 12-(10/59)-Aquaman app. 14-Supergirl x-over; Batman app? 11.00 34.00 80.00
21-29: 23-1st app. Lena Thorul, Lex Luthor's sister. 27-Bizarro-c/story. 29-Aquaman, Batman, Green Arrow cameo; last 10¢ issue 8.00 25.00 58.00
30-32,34-49: 47-Legion app. 4.00 12.00 28.00
33(5/62)-Mon-el app. 4.70 14.00 33.00
50(7/64)-Triplicate Girl, Phantom Girl & Shrinking Violet app. 3.00 10.30 24.00
51-55,57-67,69: 59-Jor-el app.; Batman back-up sty 2.30 7.00 16.00
56-Saturn Girl app. 2.40 7.30 17.00
68-(Giant G-26) 4.00 12.90 30.00
70-Penguin & Catwoman app. (1st S.A. Catwoman, 11/66; also see Detective #369 for 3rd app.); Batman & Robin cameo 13.00 36.00 90.00
71-Catwoman story cont'd from #70 (2nd app.); see Detective #369 for 3rd app. 8.60 25.80 60.00
72,73,75,76,78 1.50 3.80 9.00
74-1st Bizarro Flash (5/67); JLA cameo 2.60 7.70 18.00
77-(Giant G-39) 2.10 6.40 15.00
79-Neal Adams-c begin, end #95,108 1.00 2.50 6.00
80-85,87-94: 89-Batman x-over; all N. Adams-c. 93-Wonder Woman-c/story 1.00 2.00 5.00
86,95: (Giants G-51,G-63)-Both have Neal Adams-c. 95-Wonder Woman x-over 1.60 4.70 11.00
96-103,105-111: 105-Origin/1st app. The Rose & the Thorn. 108-Neal Adams-c. 111-Morrow-a 1.80 4.50
104,113-(Giants G-75,87): 113-Kubert-a (previously unpublished G.A. story) 1.80 4.60 11.00
112,114-123 (52 pgs.): 122-G.A. Lois Lane-r/Superman #30. 123-G.A. Batman-r/Batman #35 (w/Catwoman) 1.00 2.00 5.00
124-137: 130-Last Rose & the Thorn. 132-New Zatanna story. 136-Wonder Woman x-over 1.10 2.75
Annual 1(Sum, 1962)-r/L. Lane #12; Aquaman app. 13.00 38.00 125.00
Annual 2(Sum, 1963) 7.00 20.00 68.00

NOTE: ***Buckler*** *a-117-121p.* ***Curt Swan (or Kurt Schaffenberger)*** *a-1-50(most); c(p)-1-15.*

SUPERMAN'S PAL JIMMY OLSEN (Superman Family #164 on)
(See Action Comics #6 for 1st app. & 80 Page Giant)
Sept-Oct, 1954 - No. 163, Feb-Mar, 1974
National Periodical Publ.

	GD25	FN65	VF82	NM94
1	205.00	615.00	1332.00	2050.00
		GD25	FN65	NM94
2		89.00	267.00	800.00
3-Last pre-code issue		52.00	155.00	465.00
4,5		34.00	103.00	310.00
6-10		25.00	75.00	225.00
11-20		17.00	50.00	150.00
21-30: 29-1st app. Krypto in Jimmy Olsen		12.00	36.00	85.00

31-40: 31-Origin & 1st app.Elastic Lad (Jimmy Olsen). 33-One pg. biography of Jack Larson (TV Jimmy Olsen). 36-Intro Lucy Lane. 37-2nd app. Elastic Lad & 1st cover app. 9.00 28.00 65.00
41-50: 41-1st J.O. Robot. 48-Intro/origin Superman Emergency Squad 6.00 19.00 50.00
51-56: 56-Last 10¢ issue 5.00 15.00 40.00
57-62,64-70: 57-Olsen marries Supergirl. 62-Mon-el & Elastic Lad app. but not as Legionnaires. 70-Element Lad app. 1.70 5.00 12.00
63(9/62)-Legion of Super-Villains app. 1.90 6.00 13.00
71,74,75,78,80-84,86,89,90: 86-Jimmy Olsen Robot becomes Congorilla 1.50 3.80 9.00
72(10/63)-Legion app; Elastic Lad (Olsen) joins 1.80 5.00 11.00
73-Ultra Boy app. 1.80 5.00 11.00
76,85-Legion app. 1.80 5.00 11.00
77,79: 77-Olsen with Colossal Boy's powers & costume; origin Titano retold. 79-(9/64)-Titled The Red-headed Beatle of 1000 B.C. 1.50 3.80 9.00

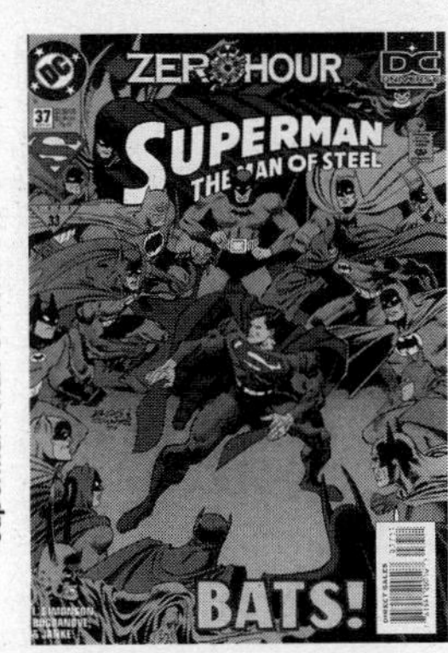

Superman: Man Of Steel #37 © DC

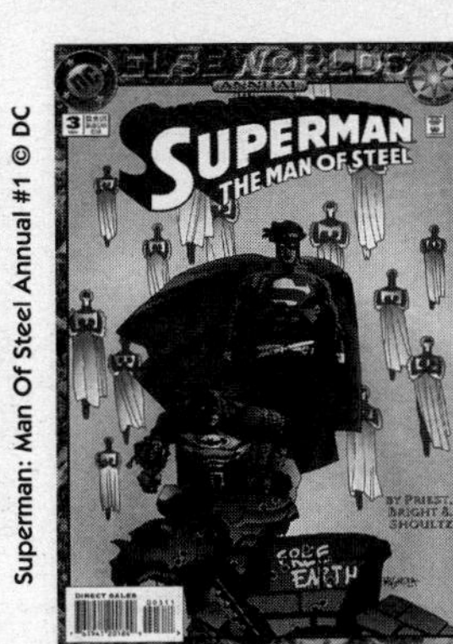

Superman: Man Of Steel Annual #1 © DC

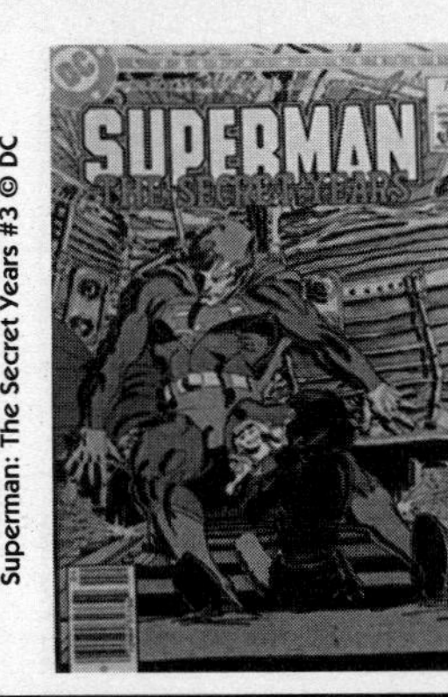

Superman: The Secret Years #3 © DC

GD25 FN65 NM94

87-Legion of Super-Villains app. 1.80 5.00 11.00
88-Star Boy app. 1.50 3.80 9.00
91-94,96-99: 99-Olsen w/powers & costumes of Lightning Lad, Sun Boy & Star Boy 1.10 2.70 6.50
95,104 (Giants G-25,G-38) 2.30 7.00 16.00
100-Legion cameo 1.30 3.00 8.00
101-103,105-112,114-121,123-130,132: 106-Legion app. 110-Infinity-c. 117-Batman & Legion cameo 1.60 4.00
113,122,131,140 (Giants G-50,G-62,G-74,G-86): 113-Unpublished G.A. Kubert-a (2 pgs.) 1.70 3.40 8.50
133-Re-intro Newsboy Legion & begins by Kirby; 1st app. Morgan Edge in 1 panel cameo (10/70) 1.10 2.70 6.50
134-1st app. Darkseid (1 panel, 12/70) 1.30 3.10 7.50
135-139,141-163: 135-2nd app. Darkseid (1 pg. cameo; see New Gods & Forever People); G.A. Guardian app. 136-Origin new Guardian. 138-Partial photo-c. 139-Last 15¢ issue. 141-Photo-c; Newsboy Legion-r by S&K begin; full pg. self-portrait Kirby; Don Rickles cameo. 141-150-(25¢, 52 pgs.). 149, 150-G.A. Plastic Man-r in both; last 52 pg. issue. 150-Newsboy Legion app. 1.60 4.00

NOTE: *Issues #141-148 contain **Simon & Kirby** Newsboy Legion reprints from Star Spangled #7, 8, 9, 10, 11, 12, 13, 14 in that order. **N. Adams** c-109-112, 115, 117, 118, 120, 121, 132, 134-136, 147, 148. **Kirby** a-133-139p, 141-148p; c-133, 137, 139, 142, 145p. **Kirby/N. Adams** c-137, 138, 141-144, 146. **Curt Swan** c-1-14(most).*

SUPERMAN SPECTACULAR (Also see DC Special Series #5)
1982 (Magazine size)(Square binding)
DC Comics
1 .80 2.00

SUPERMAN: SPEEDING BULLETS
1993 ($4.95, one-shot, 52 pgs.)
DC Comics
1-Elseworlds storyline 1.00 2.00 5.00

SUPERMAN: THE EARTH STEALERS
1988 ($2.95, one-shot, 52 pgs, prestige format)
DC Comics
1-Byrne scripts; painted-c 1.40 3.50
1-2nd printing 1.20 3.00

SUPERMAN: THE MAN OF STEEL (Also see The Man of Steel)
July, 1991 - Present ($1.00/$1.25)
DC Comics
1-($1.75, 52 pgs.)-Painted-c .80 2.00
2-10: 3-War of the Gods x-over. 5-Reads sideways. 10-Last $1.00-c 1.10
11-16: 14-Superman & Robin team-up 1.25
17-1st app. Doomsday (cameo) 1.40 3.50
17-2nd printing 1.25
18-1st full app. Doomsday 1.60 4.70 11.00
18-2nd & 3rd printings 1.25
19-Doomsday battle issue (c/story) 1.00 2.50
20,21-Funeral for a Friend .80 2.00
22-($1.95)-Collector's Edition w/die-cut outer-c & bound-in poster; Steel-c/story .40 1.00 2.00
22-($1.50)-Newsstand Ed. w/poster & different-c 1.50
23-37: 23-Begin $1.50-c. 30-Regular edition. 32-Bizarro-c/story. 35,36-Worlds Collide Pt. 1 & 10. 37-(9/94)-Zero Hour 1.50
30-($2.50)-Collector's Edition; polybagged with Superman & Lobo vinyl clings that stick to wraparound-c; Lobo-c/story 1.00 2.50
0-(10/94) 1.50
38-44: 38-(11/94) 1.50
Annual 1,2 (1992-93, $2.50, 68 pgs.): 1-Eclipso app.; Joe Quesada-c(p). 2-Intro Edge 1.00 2.50
Annual 3 (1994, $2.95, 68 pgs.)-Elseworlds story; Mignola-c; Batman app. 1.20 3.00

SUPERMAN: THE SECRET YEARS
Feb, 1985 - No. 4, May, 1985 (Mini-series)
DC Comics
1-Miller-c on all 1.50
2-4 1.00

SUPERMAN 3-D (See Three-Dimension Adventures)

SUPERMAN-TIM (Becomes Tim)
Aug, 1942 - May, 1950 (Half size) (B&W Giveaway w/2 color covers)
Superman-Tim Stores/National Periodical Publications
8/42(#1) 71.00 215.00 525.00
2/43(#2)-Two pg. Superman illo 31.00 94.00 220.00
3/43, 6/43, 8/43, 9/43(#6)-Two pg. Superman illo 24.00 72.00 165.00
3/44, 2/45, 11/49 issues-Two pg. Superman illos 16.00 48.00 110.00
10/43, 12/43, 2/44-no Superman 15.00 45.00 105.00
4/44-1/45, 3/45, 4/45, 4/46, 5/46, 6/46, 7/46, 8/46 issues-no Superman 13.50 41.00 95.00
9/46-1st stamp album issue (worth more if complete with Superman stamps) 34.00 103.00 240.00
10/46-1st Superman story 24.00 72.00 165.00
11/46, 12/46, 1/47, 2/47, 3/47, 4/47, 5/47-8/47 issues-Superman story in each; 2/47-Infinity-c 24.00 72.00 165.00
9/47-Stamp album issue & Superman story 31.00 94.00 220.00
10/47, 11/47, 12/47-Superman stories 24.00 72.00 165.00
1/48, 2/48, 6/48, 8/48, 10/48, 11/48, 2/49-10/49 issues-no Superman 17.00 52.00 120.00
9/48-Stamp album issue 19.00 57.00 130.00
12/49-5/50 Superman stories 22.00 65.00 150.00

NOTE: *16 pgs. through 9/47; 8 pgs. 10/47 on? The stamp album issues (3) may contain Superman stamps that were made to glue in these books. Books with the stamps in cluded would be worth more, and the value would depend upon completeness of the album. There is no stamp album in the 9/49 issue.*

SUPERMAN VS. THE AMAZING SPIDER-MAN (Also see Marvel Treasury Edition No. 28)
1976 (100 pgs.) ($2.00) (Over-sized)
National Periodical Publications/Marvel Comics Group
1-Andru/Giordano-a .90 2.25
1-2nd printing; 5000 numbered copies signed by Stan Lee & Carmine Infantino on front cover & sold through mail 2.30 6.90 16.00

SUPERMAN WORKBOOK
1945 (One Shot) (68 pgs; reprints) (B&W)
National Periodical Publ./Juvenile Group Foundation
nn-Cover-r/Superman #14 114.00 343.00 800.00

SUPER MARIO BROS. (Also see Adventures of the...)
1990 - No. 5?, 1991 ($1.95, color, slick-c)
V2#1, 1991 - No. 5, 1991 ($1.50, color)
Valiant Comics
1-5: 1-Wildman-a .80 2.00
V2#1-5 1.50
Special Edition 1 (1990, $1.95)-Wildman-a .80 2.00

SUPERMOUSE (...the Big Cheese; see Coo Coo Comics)
Dec, 1948 - No. 34, Sept, 1955; No. 35, Apr, 1956 - No. 45, Fall, 1958
Standard Comics/Pines No. 35 on (Literary Ent.)
1-Frazetta text illos (3) 22.00 65.00 150.00
2-Frazetta text illos 11.00 32.00 75.00
3,5,6-Text illos by Frazetta in all 10.00 30.00 60.00
4-Two pg. text illos by Frazetta 10.00 30.00 65.00
7-10 4.20 12.50 25.00
11-20: 13-Racist humor (Indians) 4.00 10.00 20.00
21-45 2.80 7.00 14.00
1-Summer Holiday issue (Summer, 1957, 25¢, 100 pgs.)-Pines 10.00 30.00 60.00
2-Giant Summer issue (Summer, 1958, 25¢, 100 pgs.)-Pines; has games, puzzles & stories 7.50 22.50 45.00

SUPER-MYSTERY COMICS
July, 1940 - V8#6, July, 1949

Super-Mystery Comics V4 #3 © ACE

Supernatural Thrillers #7 © MEG

Super-Villian Team-up #4 © MEG

GD25 FN65 NM94

Ace Magazines (Periodical House)

V1#1-Magno, the Magnetic Man & Vulcan begins (1st app.); Q-13, Corp. Flint, & Sky Smith begin 121.00 365.00 850.00
2 60.00 180.00 425.00
3-The Black Spider begins (1st app.) 54.00 160.00 375.00
4-Origin Davy 41.00 124.00 290.00
5-Intro. The Clown & begin series (12/40) 41.00 124.00 290.00
6(2/41) 36.00 107.00 250.00
V2#1(4/41)-Origin Buckskin 36.00 107.00 250.00
2-6(2/42): 6-Vulcan begins again 32.00 96.00 225.00
V3#1(4/42),2: 1-Black Ace begins 29.00 86.00 200.00
3-Intro. The Lancer; Dr. Nemesis & The Sword begin; Kurtzman-c/a(2) (Mr. Risk & Paul Revere Jr.); Robot-c 39.00 118.00 275.00
4-Kurtzman-c/a 31.00 94.00 220.00
5-Kurtzman-a(2); L.B. Cole-a; Mr. Risk app. 34.00 100.00 235.00
6(10/43)-Mr. Risk app.; Kurtzman's Paul Revere Jr.; L.B. Cole-a 34.00 100.00 235.00
V4#1(1/44)-L.B. Cole-a 26.00 78.00 180.00
2-6(4/45): 2,5,6-Mr. Risk app. 20.00 60.00 140.00
V5#1(7/45)-6 17.00 52.00 120.00
V6#1-6: 3-Torture story. 4-Last Magno. Mr. Risk app. in #2,4-6. 6-New logo 14.00 43.00 100.00
V7#1-6, V8#1-4,6 14.00 43.00 100.00
V8#5-Meskin, Tuska, Sid Greene-a 16.00 48.00 110.00

NOTE: ***Sid Greene*** *a-V7#4.* ***Mooney*** *c-V1#5, 6, V2#1-6.* ***Palais*** *a-V5#3, 4; c-V4#6-V5#4, V6#2, V8#4. Bondage c-V2#5, 6, V3#2, 5. Magno c-V1#1-V3#6, V4#2-V5#5, V6#2. The Sword c-V4#1, 6(w/Magno).*

SUPERNATURAL THRILLERS
Dec, 1972 - No. 6, Nov, 1973; No. 7, July, 1974 - No. 15, Oct, 1975
Marvel Comics Group

1-3: 1-It!; Sturgeon adaptation. 2-The Invisible Man; H.G. Wells adapt. 3-The Valley of the Worm; R.E. Howard adapt. 1.10 2.75
4-15: 4-Dr. Jekyll & Mr. Hyde; R.L. Stevenson adapt. 5-1st app. The Living Mummy. 6-The Headless Horseman; last 20¢ issue. 7-The Living Mummy begins 1.00 2.50

NOTE: ***Brunner*** *c-11.* ***Buckler*** *a-5p.* ***Ditko*** *a-8r, 9r.* ***G. Kane*** *a-3p; c-3, 9p, 15p.* ***Mayerik*** *a-2p, 7, 8, 9p, 10p, 11.* ***McWilliams*** *a-14i.* ***Mortimer*** *a-4.* ***Steranko*** *c-1, 2.* ***Sutton*** *a-15.* ***Tuska*** *a-6p.*

SUPERPATRIOT (Also see Freak Force & Savage Dragon #2)
July, 1993 - No. 4, Dec, 1993 ($1.95, color, mini-series)
Image Comics

1-4: D. Johnson-c/a; Larsen scripts; Giffen plots .80 2.00

SUPER POWERS
7/84 - No. 5, 11/84; 9/85 - No. 6, 2/86; 9/86 - No. 4, 12/86
DC Comics

1 (7/84, 1st series)-Joker/Penguin-c/story; Batman app. 1.30
2-5: 1-5-Kirby-c; 5-Kirby-c/a 1.20
1 (9/85, 2nd series)-Kirby-c/a in all; Capt. Marvel & Firestorm join; Batman cameo; Darkseid storyline in #1-6 1.40
2-6: 4-Batman cameo. 5,6-Batman app. 1.40
1-4 (1986, 3rd series): 1-Cyborg joins; 1st app. Samurai from Super Friends TV show. 1-4-Batman cameos; Darkseid storyline in #1-4 1.20

SUPER PUP (Formerly Spotty The Pup) (See Space Comics)
No. 4, Mar-Apr, 1954 - No. 5, 1954
Avon Periodicals

4,5: 5-Robot-c 4.00 10.00 20.00

SUPER RABBIT (See All Surprise, Animated Movie Tunes, Comedy Comics, Comic Capers, Ideal Comics, It's A Duck's Life, Movie Tunes & Wisco)
Fall, 1944 - No. 14, Nov, 1948
Timely Comics (CmPI)

1-Hitler & Hirohito-c; Ziggy Pig & Silly begin? 54.00 160.00 375.00
2 27.00 81.00 190.00
3-5 17.00 52.00 120.00
6-Origin 19.00 58.00 135.00

GD25 FN65 NM94

7-10: 9-Infinity-c 11.00 32.00 75.00
11-Kurtzman's "Hey Look" 12.00 36.00 85.00
12-14 10.00 30.00 70.00
I.W. Reprint #1,2('58),7,10('63) 1.80 4.50 9.00

SUPER RICHIE (Superichie #5 on) (See Richie Rich Millions #68)
Sept, 1975 - No. 4, Mar, 1976 (All 52 pg. Giants)
Harvey Publications

1 1.20 3.00
2-4 .80 2.00

SUPERSNIPE COMICS (Formerly Army & Navy #1-5)
V1#6, Oct, 1942 - V5#1, Aug-Sept, 1949 (See Shadow Comics V2#3)
Street & Smith Publications

V1#6-Rex King - Man of Adventure (costumed hero, see Super Magic/ Magician) by Jack Binder begins; Supersnipe by George Marcoux continues from Army & Navy #5; Bill Ward-a 61.00 182.00 425.00
7,8,10-12: 8-Hitler, Tojo, Mussolini in Hell with Devil-c. 11-Little Nemo app. 38.00 114.00 265.00
9-Doc Savage x-over in Supersnipe; Hitler-c 50.00 150.00 350.00
V2#1-12: 1-Huck Finn by Clare Dwiggins begins, ends V3#5 26.00 78.00 180.00
V3#1-12: 8-Bobby Crusoe by Dwiggins begins, ends V3#12. 9-X-Mas-c 22.00 66.00 155.00
V4#1-12, V5#1: V4#10-X-Mas-c 16.50 50.00 115.00

NOTE: ***George Marcoux*** *c-V1#6-V3#4. Doc Savage app. in some issues.*

SUPER SOLDIERS
Apr, 1993 - No. 8, Nov, 1993 ($1.75)
Marvel Comics UK

1-($2.50)-Embossed silver foil logo 1.00 2.50
2-8: 5-Capt. America app. 6-Origin; Nick Fury app.; neon ink-c .70 1.75

SUPERSPOOK (Formerly Frisky Animals on Parade)
No. 4, June, 1958
Ajax/Farrell Publications

4 4.00 11.00 22.00

SUPER SPY (See Wham Comics)
Oct, 1940 - No. 2, Nov, 1940 (Reprints)
Centaur Publications

1-Origin The Sparkler 114.00 343.00 800.00
2-The Inner Circle, Dean Denton, Tim Blain, The Drew Ghost, The Night Hawk by Gustavson, & S.S. Swanson by Glanz app. 71.00 214.00 500.00

SUPER STAR HOLIDAY SPECIAL (See DC Special Series #21)

SUPER-TEAM FAMILY
10-11/75 - No. 15, 3-4/78 (#1-4: 68 pgs.; #5 on: 52 pgs.)
National Periodical Publications/DC Comics

1-Reprints by Neal Adams & Kane/Wood .90 2.25
2,3-New stories .60 1.60
4-7-Reprints; 4-G.A. JSA-r & Superman/Batman/Robin-r from World's Finest 1.10
8-10-New Challengers of the Unknown stories .90 2.25
11-15-New stories 1.30

NOTE: ***Neal Adams*** *r-1-3.* ***Brunner*** *c-3.* ***Buckler*** *c-8p.* ***Tuska*** *a-7r.* ***Wood*** *a-1i(r), 3.*

SUPER TV HEROES (See Hanna-Barbera...)

SUPER-VILLAIN CLASSICS
May, 1983
Marvel Comics Group

1-Galactus - The Origin 1.00

SUPER-VILLAIN TEAM-UP (See Fantastic Four #6 & Giant-Size...)
8/75 - No. 14, 10/77; No. 15, 11/78; No. 16, 5/79; No. 17, 6/80
Marvel Comics Group

1-Sub-Mariner & Dr. Doom begin, end #10 1.00 2.00 5.00
2-17: 5-1st app. The Shroud. 6-F.F., Shroud app. 7-Origin Shroud. 9-Avengers

Suspence #6 © MEG

Suzie #76 © AP

Swamp Thing #14 © DC

GD25 FN65 NM94

app. 11-15-Dr. Doom & Red Skull app. 1.00 2.50
NOTE: ***Buckler** c-4p, 5p, 7p. **Buscema** c-1. **Byrne/Austin** c-14. **Evans** a-1p, 3p. **Everett** a-1p. **Giffen** a-8p, 13p; c-13p. **Kane** c-2p, 9p. **Mooney** a-4i. **Starlin** c-6. **Tuska** r-1p, 15p. **Wood** r-15p.*

SUPER WESTERN COMICS (Also see Buffalo Bill)
Aug, 1950 - No. 4, Mar, 1951
Youthful Magazines

1-Buffalo Bill begins; Wyatt Earp, Calamity Jane & Sam Slade app; Powell-c/a 9.15 27.50 55.00
2-4 5.35 16.00 32.00

SUPER WESTERN FUNNIES (See Super Funnies)

SUPERWORLD COMICS
April, 1940 - No. 3, Aug, 1940 (All have 68 pgs.)
Hugo Gernsback (Komos Publ.)

1-Origin & 1st app. Hip Knox, Super Hypnotist; Mitey Powers & Buzz Allen, the Invisible Avenger, Little Nemo begin; cover by Frank R. Paul (all have sci/fi-c)(Scarce) 314.00 943.00 2200.00
2-Marvo 1-2 Go+, the Super Boy of the Year 2680 (1st app.); Paul-c (Scarce) 185.00 557.00 1300.00
3 (Scarce) 136.00 407.00 950.00

SUPREME (See Youngblood #3)
Nov, 1992 - Present ($1.95, color, created by Rob Liefeld)
Image Comics

V2#1-Embossed foil logo; Liefeld-a(i) & scripts 1.40 3.50
1-Gold Edition 20.00
2-(3/93)-Liefeld co-plots & inks; 1st app. Grizlock .80 2.00
3-12,25,13-19: 3-Intro Bloodstrike; 1st app. Khrome. 5-1st app. Thor. 6-The Starguard cameo. 7-1st full app. The Starguard. 10-Black and White part 1 (1st app.) by Art Thibert (2 pgs. ea. installment). 11-Coupon #4 for Extreme Prejudice #0; Black and White part 7 by Thibert. 12-(4/94). 25-(5/94). 13,14-(6/94) .80 2.00
NOTE: ***Rob Liefeld** a(i)-1, 2; co-plots-2-4; scripts-1, 5, 6. **Platt** c-12, 25. **Thibert** c(i)-7-9.*

SURE-FIRE COMICS (Lightning Comics #4 on)
June, 1940 - No. 4, Oct, 1940 (Two No. 3's)
Ace Magazines

V1#1-Origin Flash Lightning & begins; X-The Phantom Fed, Ace McCoy, Buck Steele, Marvo the Magician, The Raven, Whiz Wilson (Time Traveler) begin (all 1st app.); Flash Lightning c-1-4 100.00 300.00 700.00
2 56.00 167.00 390.00
3(9/40) 46.00 139.00 325.00
3(#4)(10/40)-nn on-c, #3 on inside 46.00 139.00 325.00

SURF 'N' WHEELS
Nov, 1969 - No. 6, Sept, 1970
Charlton Comics

1 1.70 4.20 10.00
2-6 1.20 2.90 7.00

SURGE (Eclipse)(Value: cover or less)

SURPRISE ADVENTURES (Formerly Tormented)
No. 3, Mar, 1955 - No. 5, July, 1955
Sterling Comic Group

3-5: 3,5-Sekowsky-a 4.20 12.50 25.00

SUSIE Q. SMITH (See Four Color #323, 377, 453, 553)

SUSPENSE (Radio/TV issues #1-11; Real Life Tales of... #1-4) (Amazing Detective Cases #3 on?)
Dec, 1949 - No. 29, Apr, 1953 (#1-8,17-23: 52 pgs.)
Marvel/Atlas Comics (CnPC No. 1-10/BFP No. 11-29)

1-Powell-a; Peter Lorre, Sidney Greenstreet photo-c from Hammett's "The Verdict" 39.00 118.00 275.00
2-Crime stories; Dennis O'Keefe & Gale Storm photo-c from Universal movie "Abandoned" 19.00 58.00 135.00
3-Change to horror 20.00 60.00 140.00

GD25 FN65 NM94

4,7-10 14.00 43.00 100.00
5-Krigstein, Tuska, Everett-a 16.00 48.00 110.00
6-Tuska, Everett, Morisi-a 14.00 43.00 100.00
11-17,19,20: 14-Hypo-c; A-Bomb panels 11.50 34.00 80.00
18,22-Krigstein-a 13.50 41.00 95.00
21,23,26-29 10.00 30.00 65.00
24-Tuska-a 10.00 30.00 70.00
25-Electric chair-c/story 13.50 41.00 95.00
NOTE: ***Ayers** a-20. **Briefer** a-5, 7, 27. **Brodsky** c-4, 6-9, 11, 16, 17, 25. **Colan** a-8(2), 9. **Everett** a-5, 6(2), 19, 23, 28; c-21-23, 26. **Fuje** a-29. **Heath** a-5, 6, 8, 10, 12, 14; c-14, 19, 24. **Maneely** a-12, 23, 24, 28, 29; c-5, 6p, 10, 13, 15, 18. **Mooney** a-24, 28. **Morisi** a-6, 12. **Palais** a-10. **Rico** a-7-9. **Robinson** a-29. **Romita** a-20(2), 25. **Sekowsky** a-11, 13, 14. **Sinnott** a-23, 25. **Tuska** a-5, 6(2), 12; c-12. **Whitney** a-15, 16, 22. **Ed Win** a-27.*

SUSPENSE COMICS
Dec, 1943 - No. 12, Sept, 1946
Continental Magazines

1-The Grey Mask begins; bondage/torture-c; L. B. Cole-a (7 pgs.) 143.00 430.00 1000.00
2-Intro. The Mask; Rico, Giunta, L. B. Cole-a (7 pgs.) 100.00 300.00 700.00
3-L.B. Cole-a; classic Schomburg-c 286.00 857.00 2000.00
4-6: 5-L. B. Cole-c begin 71.00 214.00 500.00
7,9,10,12: 9-L.B. Cole eyeball-c 64.00 193.00 450.00
8-Classic L. B. Cole spider-c 143.00 430.00 1000.00
11-Classic Devil-c 129.00 385.00 900.00
NOTE: ***L. B. Cole** c-5-12. **Fuje** a-8. **Larsen** a-11. **Palais** a-10, 11. Bondage c-1, 3, 4.*

SUSPENSE DETECTIVE
June, 1952 - No. 5, Mar, 1953
Fawcett Publications

1-Evans-a (11 pgs); Baily-c/a 25.00 75.00 175.00
2-Evans-a (10 pgs.) 16.00 48.00 110.00
3-5 12.00 36.00 85.00
NOTE: ***Baily** a-4, 5; c-1-3. **Sekowsky** a-2, 4, 5; c-5.*

SUSPENSE STORIES (See Strange Suspense Stories)

SUZIE COMICS (Formerly Laugh Comix; see Laugh Comics, Liberty Comics #10, Pep Comics & Top-Notch Comics #28)
No. 49, Spring, 1945 - No. 100, Aug, 1954
Close-Up No. 49,50/MLJ Mag./Archie No. 51 on

49-Ginger begins 19.00 57.00 130.00
50-55: 54-Transvestism story 11.50 34.00 80.00
56-Katy Keene begins by Woggon 11.00 32.00 75.00
57-65 9.15 27.50 55.00
66-80 8.35 25.00 50.00
81-100: 88-Used in **POP**, pgs. 76,77; Bill Woggon draws himself in story.
100-Last Katy Keene 7.00 21.00 42.00
NOTE: ***Al Fagaly** c-49-67. Katy Keene app. in 53-82, 85-100.*

SWAMP FOX, THE (See 4-Color #1179 & Walt Disney Presents #2)

SWAMP FOX, THE
1960 (14 pgs, small size) (Canada Dry Premiums)
Walt Disney Productions

Titles: (A)-Tory Masquerade, (B)-Rindau Rampage, (C)-Turnabout Tactics; each came in paper sleeve, books 1,2 & 3;
Set with sleeves 5.00 15.00 30.00
Comic only 1.80 4.50 9.00

SWAMP THING (See Brave & the Bold, Challengers of the Unknown #82, DC Comics Presents #8 & 85, DC Special Series #2, 14, 17, 20, House of Secrets #92, Limited Collectors' Edition C-59, & Roots of the...)

SWAMP THING
Oct-Nov, 1972 - No. 24, Aug-Sept, 1976
National Periodical Publications/DC Comics

1-Wrightson-c/a begins; origin 9.00 26.00 60.00
2-1st app. Patchwork Man (1 panel cameo) 5.00 15.00 35.00
3-1st full app. Patchwork Man 2.90 8.60 20.00
4-6,8-10: 10-Last Wrightson issue 2.30 7.00 16.00

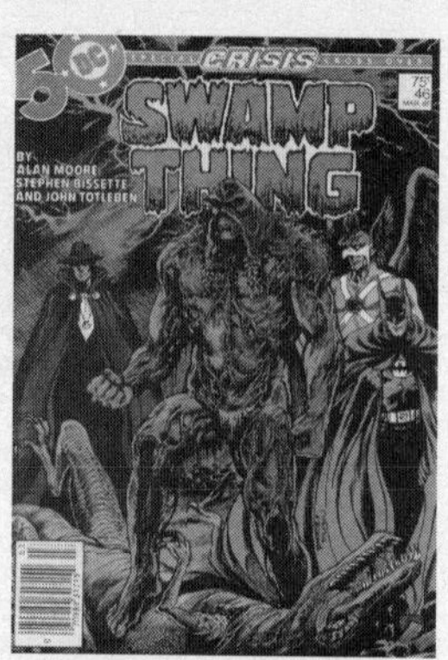

Swamp Thing #46 © DC

Swamp Thing #147 (2nd) © DC

Sweetheart Diary V2 #8 © FAW

	GD25	FN65	NM94
7-Batman-c/story	2.40	7.30	17.00
11-24-Redondo-a. 13-Origin retold (1 pg.). 23-Swamp Thing reverts back to Dr. Holland. 23,24-New logo		1.60	4.00

NOTE: ***J. Jones** a-9i(assist). **Kaluta** a-9i. **Redondo** c-12-19, 21. **Wrightson** issues (#1-10) reprinted in DC Special Series #2, 14, 17, 20 & Roots of the Swampthing.*

SWAMP THING (Saga Of The... #1-38,42-45)
May, 1982 - Present (Later issues for mature readers; #86 on: $1.50)
DC Comics (Vertigo imprint #129 on)

	GD25	FN65	NM94
1-Origin retold; Phantom Stranger series begins; ends #13; Yeates-c/a begins		.80	2.00
2-15: 2-Photo-c from movie			1.40
16-19: Bissette-a. 13-Last Yeates-a		1.00	2.50
20-1st Alan Moore issue	3.00	9.00	21.00
21-New origin	2.60	7.70	18.00
22-25: 24-JLA x-over; Last Yeates-c	1.20	2.90	7.00
26-30		1.80	4.50
31-33: 33-r/1st app. from House of Secrets #92		1.20	3.00
34	1.70	4.20	10.00
35,36		1.00	2.50
37-1st app. John Constantine (Hellblazer)(6/85)	1.60	4.70	11.00
38-40: John Constantine app.		1.80	4.50
41-45: 44-Batman cameo. 44-51-John Constantine app		.80	2.00
46-51: 46-Crisis x-over; Batman cameo. 50-($1.25, 52 pgs.)-Deadman, Dr. Fate, Demon		.70	1.75
52-Arkham Asylum-c/story; Joker-c/cameo		1.60	4.00
53-($1.25, 52 pgs.)-Arkham Asylum; Batman-c/story	1.00	2.00	5.00
54-64: 58-Spectre preview. 64-Last Moore issue		.70	1.75
65-83,85-99,101-124,126-130: 65-Direct only begins. 66-Batman & Arkham Asylum story. 70,76-John Constantine x-over; 76-X-over w/Hellblazer #9. 79-Super-man-c/story. 85-Jonah Hex app. 102-Preview of World Without End. 116-Photo-c. 129-Metallic ink on-c		.80	2.00
84-Sandman cameo		1.40	3.50
100 ($2.50, 52 pgs.)		1.10	2.75
125-($2.95, 52 pgs.)-20th anniversary issue		1.20	3.00
131-152: 131-Begin $1.95-c. 140-New direction & Morrison scripts begin		.80	2.00
Annual 1(1982, $1.00)-Movie Adapt.; painted-c			1.00
Annual 2(1985)-Alan Moore scripts, Bissette-a(p)		1.20	3.00
Annual 3(1987, $2.00)-New format; Bolland-c		.80	2.00
Annual 4(1988, $2.00)-Batman-c/story		1.20	3.00
Annual 5(1989, $2.95, 68 pgs.)-Batman cameo; re-intro Brother Power (Geek), 1st app. since 1968		1.20	3.00
Annual 6(1991, $2.95, 68 pgs.)		1.20	3.00
Annual 7(1993, $3.95)-Children's Crusade		1.60	4.00
Saga of the Swamp Thing (1987, $10.95)-r/#21-27	1.65	4.70	11.00
2nd printing (1989, $12.95)	1.85	5.50	13.00
...Love and Death (1990, $17.95)-r/#28-34 & Annual #2; Totleben painted-c	2.60	7.50	18.00

NOTE: ***Bissette** a(p)-16-19, 21-27, 29, 30, 34-36, 39-42, 44, 46, 50, 64; c-17i, 24-32p, 35-37p, 40p, 44p, 46-50p, 51-58, 61, 62, 63p. **Kaluta** c/a-74. **Spiegle** a-1-3, 6. **Sutton** a-98p. **Totleben** a(i)-10, 16-27, 29, 31, 34-40, 42, 44, 46, 48, 50, 53, 55i; c-25-32i, 33, 35-40i, 42i, 44i, 46-50i, 53, 55i, 59p, 64, 65, 68, 73, 76, 80, 82, 84, 89, 91-100, Annual 4, 5. **Vess** painted c-121, 129-139, Annual 7. **Williamson** 86i. **Wrightson** a-18i(r), 33r. John Constantine appears in #44-51, 65-67, 70-74, 76, 77, 114, 115.*

SWAT MALONE (America's Home Run King)
Sept, 1955
Swat Malone Enterprises

	GD25	FN65	NM94
V1#1-Hy Fleishman-a	7.50	22.50	45.00

SWEENEY (Formerly Buz Sawyer)
No. 4, June, 1949 - No. 5, Sept, 1949
Standard Comics

	GD25	FN65	NM94
4,5: 5-Crane-a	6.70	20.00	40.00

SWEE'PEA (See 4-Color #219)

SWEETHEART DIARY (Cynthia Doyle #66-on)
Wint, 1949; #2, Spr, 1950; #3, 6/50 - #5, 10/50; #6, 1951(nd); #7, 9/51 - #14, 1/53; #32, 10/55; #33, 4/56 - #65, 8/62 (#1-14: photo-c)
Fawcett Publications/Charlton Comics No. 32 on

	GD25	FN65	NM94
1	10.00	30.00	70.00
2	5.85	17.50	35.00
3,4-Wood-a	11.00	32.00	75.00
5-10: 8-Bailey-a	5.00	15.00	30.00
11-14: 13-Swayze-a. 14-Last Fawcett issue	3.60	9.00	18.00
32 (10/55; 1st Charlton issue)(Formerly Cowboy Love #31)	4.00	11.00	22.00
33-40: 34-Swayze-a	2.40	6.00	12.00
41-60	1.40	3.50	7.00
61-65		1.75	3.50

SWEETHEARTS (Formerly Captain Midnight)
#68, 10/48 - #121, 5/53; #122, 3/54; V2#23, 5/54 - #137, 12/73
Fawcett Publications/Charlton No. 122 on

	GD25	FN65	NM94
68-Photo-c begin	11.00	32.00	75.00
69-80	4.00	12.00	24.00
81-84,86-93,95-99,105	3.60	9.00	18.00
85,94,103,110,117-George Evans-a	5.00	15.00	30.00
100	4.00	11.00	22.00
101,107-Powell-a	4.00	10.00	20.00
102,104,106,108,109,112-116,118,121	2.80	7.00	14.00
111-1 pg. Ronald Reagan biography	5.00	15.00	30.00
119-Marilyn Monroe & Richard Widmark photo-c (1/54?); also appears in story; part Wood-a	29.00	86.00	200.00
120-Atom Bomb story	7.50	22.50	45.00
122-(1st Charlton? 3/54)-Marijuana story	5.85	17.50	35.00
V2#23 (5/54)-28: 28-Last precode issue (2/55)	2.80	7.00	14.00
29-39,41,43-45,47-50	1.80	4.50	9.00
40-Photo-c; Tommy Sands story	3.60	9.00	18.00
42-Ricky Nelson photo-c/story	7.50	22.50	45.00
46-Jimmy Rodgers photo-c/story	3.60	9.00	18.00
51-60	1.80	4.50	9.00
61-80	1.00	2.50	6.00
81-100		1.20	3.00
101-110		.80	2.00
111-137			1.50

NOTE: *Photo c-68-121(Fawcett), 40, 42, 46(Charlton). **Swayze** a(Fawcett)-70-118(most).*

SWEETHEART SCANDALS (See Fox Giants)

SWEETIE PIE (See 4-Color #1185, 1241)

SWEETIE PIE
Dec, 1955 - No. 15, Fall, 1957
Ajax-Farrell/Pines (Literary Ent.)

	GD25	FN65	NM94
1-By Nadine Seltzer	4.70	14.00	28.00
2 (5/56; last Ajax?)	3.20	8.00	16.00
3-15 (#3-10, exist?)	2.00	5.00	10.00

SWEET LOVE
Sept, 1949 - No. 5, May, 1950 (All photo-c)
Home Comics (Harvey)

	GD25	FN65	NM94
1	5.35	16.00	32.00
2	4.00	10.00	20.00
3,4: 3-Powell-a	3.20	8.00	16.00
5-Kamen, Powell-a	4.35	13.00	26.00

SWEET ROMANCE
October, 1968
Charlton Comics

	GD25	FN65	NM94
1		1.60	4.00

SWEET SIXTEEN (...Comics and Stories for Girls)
Aug-Sept, 1946 - No. 13, Jan, 1948 (All have movie stars photos on covers)
Parents' Magazine Institute

	GD25	FN65	NM94
1-Van Johnson's life story; Dorothy Dare, Queen of Hollywood Stunt Artists begins (in all issues); part photo-c	13.00	40.00	90.00

Swift Arrow #1 © AJAX

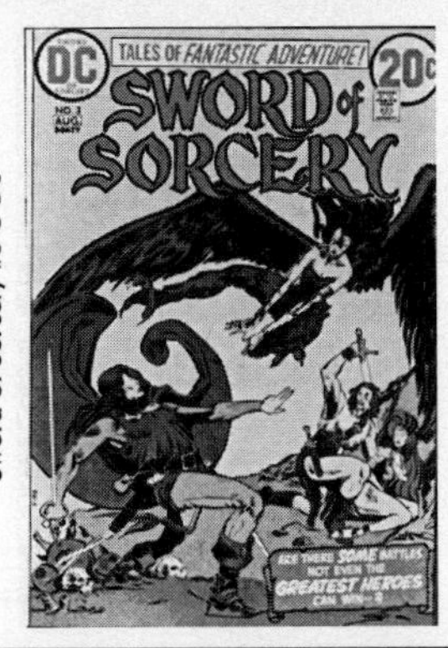

Sword of Sorcery #3 © DC

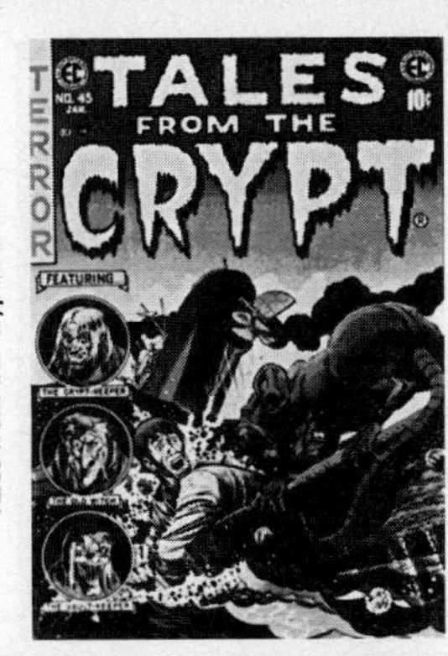

Tales from the Crypt #45 © EC

GD25 FN65 NM94

2-Jane Powell, Roddy McDowall "Holiday in Mexico" photo on-c; Alan Ladd story 10.00 30.00 60.00
3-6,8-11: 4-Elizabeth Taylor photo on-c. 5-Ann Francis photo on-c; Gregory Peck story. 6-Dick Haymes story. 8-Shirley Jones photo on-c. 10-Jean Simmons photo on-c; James Stewart story 7.50 22.50 45.00
7-Ronald Reagan's life story 14.00 43.00 100.00
12-Bob Cummings, Vic Damone story 7.50 22.50 45.00
13-Robert Mitchum's life story 9.15 27.50 55.00

SWEET XVI (Marvel)(Value: cover or less)

SWIFT ARROW (Also see Lone Rider & The Rider)
Feb-Mar, 1954 - No. 5, Oct-Nov, 1954; Apr, 1957 - No. 3, Sept, 1957
Ajax/Farrell Publications

1(1954) (1st Series) 10.00 30.00 60.00
2 5.85 17.50 35.00
3-5: 5-Lone Rider story 4.35 13.00 26.00
1 (2nd Series) (Swift Arrow's Gunfighters #4) 4.70 14.00 28.00
2,3: 2-Lone Rider begins 4.00 10.00 20.00

SWIFT ARROW'S GUNFIGHTERS (Formerly Swift Arrow)
No. 4, Nov, 1957
Ajax/Farrell Publ. (Four Star Comic Corp.)

4 4.70 14.00 28.00

SWIFTSURE (Harrier)(Value: cover or less)

SWING WITH SCOOTER
June-July, 1966 - No. 35, Aug-Sept, 1971; No. 36, Oct-Nov, 1972
National Periodical Publications

1 3.60 9.00 18.00
2-10: 9-Alfred E. Newman swipe in last panel 2.00 5.00 10.00
11-20 1.60 4.00 8.00
21-36: 33-Interview with David Cassidy. 34-Interview with Ron Ely (Doc Savage) 1.00 2.50 6.00
NOTE: ***Orlando*** *a-1-11; c-1-11, 13. #20, 33, 34: 68 pgs.; #35: 52 pgs.*

SWISS FAMILY ROBINSON (See 4-Color #1156, King Classics & Movie Comics)

SWORD & THE DRAGON, THE (See 4-Color #1118)

SWORD & THE ROSE, THE (See 4-Color #505, 682)

SWORD IN THE STONE, THE (See March of Comics #258 & Movie Comics & Wart and the Wizard)

SWORD OF SORCERY
Feb-Mar, 1973 - No. 5, Nov-Dec, 1973 (All 20¢ issues)
National Periodical Publications

1-Leiber Fafhrd & The Grey Mouser; Chaykin/Neal Adams (Crusty Bunkers) art; Kaluta-c 1.60 4.00
2-Wrightson-c(i); Neal Adams-a(i) 1.00 2.50
3-5: 3-Wrightson-i(5 pgs.). 5-Starlin-a(p); Conan cameo .80 2.00
NOTE: ***Chaykin*** *a-1-4p; c-2p, 3-5.* ***Kaluta*** *a-3i.* ***Simonson*** *a-3i, 4i, 5p; c-5.*

SWORD OF THE ATOM (DC)(Value: cover or less)

SWORDS OF TEXAS (Eclipse)(Value: cover or less)

SWORDS OF THE SWASHBUCKLERS (Marvel)(Value: cover or less)

SYPHONS
May, 1994 - No. 3, 1994 ($2.50, color, limited series)
Now Comics

V2#1,2: 1-Stardancer, Knightfire, Raze & Brigade begin 1.00 2.50

TAFFY COMICS
Mar-Apr, 1945 - No. 12, 1948
Rural Home/Orbit Publ.

1-L.B. Cole-c; origin & 1st app. of Wiggles The Wonderworm plus 7 chapter WWII funny animal adventures 16.00 48.00 110.00
2-L.B. Cole-c; Wiggles-c/stories in #1-4 10.00 30.00 65.00
3,4,6-12: 6-Perry Como-c/story. 7-Duke Ellington, 2 pgs. 8-Glenn Ford-c/story. 9-Lon McCallister part photo-c & story. 10-Mort Leav-c. 11-Mickey Rooney-c/story 6.70 20.00 40.00

GD25 FN65 NM94

5-L.B. Cole-c; Van Johnson-c/story 8.35 25.00 50.00

TAILGUNNER JO (DC)(Value: cover or less)

TAILSPIN
November, 1944
Spotlight Publishers

nn-Firebird app.; L.B. Cole-c 11.50 34.00 80.00

TAILSPIN TOMMY STORY & PICTURE BOOK
No. 266, 1931? (nd) (Color strip reprints; 10-1/2x10")
McLoughlin Bros.

266-By Forrest 20.00 60.00 120.00

TAILSPIN TOMMY (Also see Famous Feature Stories & The Funnies)
1932 (100 pgs., hardcover)
Cupples & Leon Co.

nn-(Rare)-B&W strip reprints from 1930 by Hal Forrest & Glenn Claffin 27.00 81.00 190.00

TAILSPIN TOMMY (Also see Popular Comics)
1940; 1946
United Features Syndicate/Service Publ. Co.

Single Series 23(1940) 26.00 78.00 180.00
Best Seller (nd, 1946)-Service Publ. Co. 11.00 32.00 75.00

TALENT SHOWCASE (See New Talent Showcase)

TALES CALCULATED TO DRIVE YOU BATS
Nov, 1961 - No. 7, Nov, 1962; 1966 (Satire)
Archie Publications

1-Only 10¢ issue; has cut-out Werewolf mask (price includes mask) 8.00 24.00 55.00
2-Begin 12¢ issues 4.60 14.00 32.00
3-6 3.00 9.00 21.00
7-Storyline change 2.60 7.70 18.00
1(1966, 25¢, 44 pgs.)-r/#1 3.30 9.90 23.00

TALES FROM THE ANIVERSE (Arrow)(Value: cover or less)

TALES FROM THE CRYPT (Formerly The Crypt Of Terror; see Three Dimensional...)
No. 20, Oct-Nov, 1950 - No. 46, Feb-Mar, 1955
E.C. Comics

20-See Crime Patrol #15 for 1st Crypt Keeper 104.00 310.00 725.00
21-Kurtzman-r/Haunt of Fear #15(#1) 82.00 246.00 575.00
22-Moon Girl costume at costume party, one panel 66.00 200.00 465.00
23-25: 24-E. A. Poe adaptation 50.00 150.00 350.00
26-30 41.00 124.00 290.00
31-Williamson-a(1st at E.C.); B&W and color illos. in **POP**; Kamen draws himself, Gaines & Feldstein; Ingels, Craig & Davis draw themselves in his story 44.00 133.00 310.00
32,35-39: 38-Censored-c 33.00 100.00 230.00
33-Origin The Crypt Keeper 57.00 171.00 400.00
34-Used in **POP**, pg. 83; lingerie panels 33.00 100.00 230.00
40-Used in Senate hearings & in Hartford Cournat anti-comics editorials-1954 33.00 100.00 230.00
41-45: 45-2 pgs. showing E.C. staff 31.00 94.00 220.00
46-Low distribution; pre-advertised cover for unpublished 4th horror title "Crypt of Terror" used on this book 38.00 114.00 265.00
NOTE: ***Ray Bradbury*** *adaptations-34, 36.* ***Craig*** *a-20, 22-24; c-20.* ***Crandall*** *a-38, 44.* ***Davis*** *a-24-46; c-29-46.* ***Elder*** *a-37, 38.* ***Evans*** *a-32-34, 36, 40, 41, 43, 46.* ***Feldstein*** *a-20-23; c-21-25, 28. Ingels a-in all.* ***Kamen*** *a-20, 22, 25, 27-31, 33-36, 39, 41-45.* ***Krigstein*** *a-40, 42, 45.* ***Kurtzman*** *a-21.* ***Orlando*** *a-27-30, 35, 37, 39, 41-45.* ***Wood*** *a-21, 24, 25; c-26, 27. Canadian reprints known; see Table of Contents.*

TALES FROM THE CRYPT (Magazine)
No. 10, July, 1968 (35¢, B&W)
Eerie Publications

10-Contains Farrell reprints from 1950s 3.20 8.00 16.00

TALES FROM THE CRYPT

Tales of Evil #1 © MEG

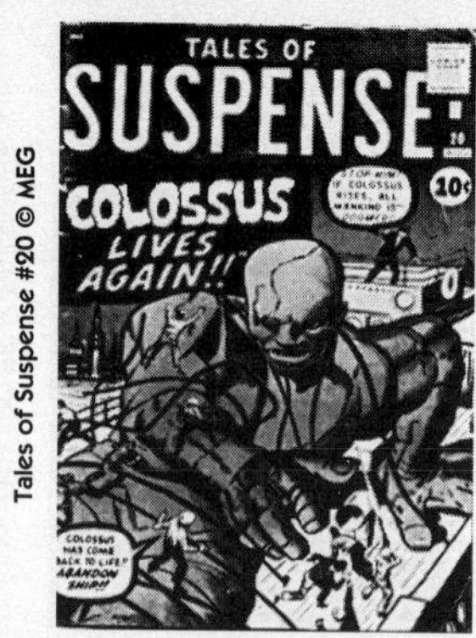

Tales of Suspense #20 © MEG

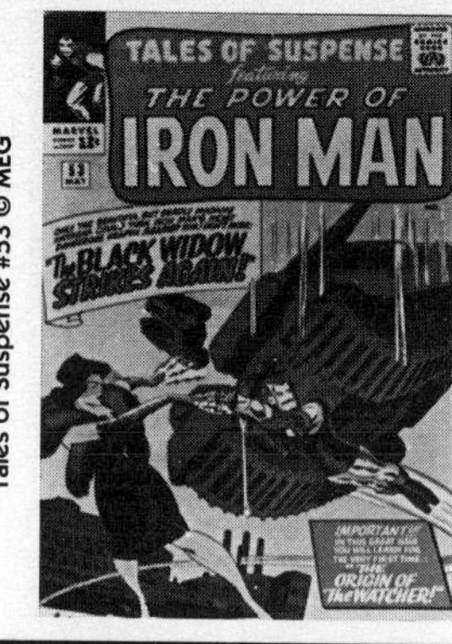

Tales of Suspense #53 © MEG

GD25 FN65 NM94

July, 1990 - No. 6, May, 1991 ($1.95, 68 pgs.)(#4 on: $2.00)
Gladstone Publishing

1-r/TFTC #33 & Crime S.S. #17; Davis-c(r) .80 2.00
2-6: 2,3,5,6-Davis-c(r). 4-Craig-c(r) .80 2.00

TALES FROM THE CRYPT (Cochran, large size)(Value: cover or less)

TALES FROM THE CRYPT
Sept, 1992 - Present ($1.50, color)
Russ Cochran

1-4-r/Crypt of Terror #17-19, TFTC #20 w/original-c 1.50
5-7 ($2.00)-r/TFTC #21-23 w/original-c .80 2.00

TALES FROM THE GREAT BOOK
Feb, 1955 - No. 4, Jan, 1956
Famous Funnies

1-Story of Samson; John Lehti-a in all 5.35 16.00 32.00
2-4: 2-Joshua. 3-Joash the Boy King. 4-David 3.60 9.00 18.00

TALES FROM THE HEART OF AFRICA (Marvel)(Value: cover or less)

TALES FROM THE TOMB (Also see Dell Giants)
Oct, 1962 (25¢ giant)
Dell Publishing Co.

GD FN VF NM
1(02-810-210)-All stories written by John Stanley
10.50 32.00 75.00 160.00

TALES FROM THE TOMB (Magazine)
V1#6, July, 1969 - V7#1, Feb, 1975 (52 pgs.)
Eerie Publications

V1#6-8 2.85 8.00 20.00
V2#1-3,5,6: 6-Rulah-r 1.70 5.00 12.00
4-LSD story-r/Weird V3#5 1.70 5.00 12.00
V3#1-Rulah-r 1.70 5.00 12.00
2-6('70),V4#1-5('72),V5#1-6('73),V6#1-6('74),V7#1('75)
1.60 3.80 9.00

TALES OF ASGARD
Oct, 1968 (25¢, 68 pgs.); Feb, 1984 ($1.25, 52 pgs.)
Marvel Comics Group

1-Reprints Tales of Asgard (Thor) back-up stories from Journey into Mystery #97-106; new Kirby-c 3.60 10.75 25.00
V2#1 (2/84)-Thor-r; Simonson-c 1.00

TALES OF DEMON DICK & BUNKER BILL
1934 (78 pgs; 5x10-1/2"; B&W)(hardcover)
Whitman Publishing Co.

793-By Dick Spencer 16.00 48.00 110.00

TALES OF EVIL
Feb, 1975 - No. 3, July, 1975 (All 25¢ issues)
Atlas/Seaboard Publ.

1-3: 2-Intro. The Bog Beast; Sparling-a. 3-Origin The Man-Monster; Buckler-a(p) 1.00
NOTE: ***Grandenetti*** *a-1, 2.* ***Lieber*** *c-1.* ***Sekowsky*** *a-1.* ***Sutton*** *a-2.* ***Thorne*** *c-2.*

TALES OF GHOST CASTLE
May-June, 1975 - No. 3, Sept-Oct, 1975 (All 25¢ issues)
National Periodical Publications

1-3: 1,3-Redondo-a. 2-Nino-a 1.00

TALES OF G.I. JOE (Marvel)(Value: cover or less)

TALES OF HORROR
June, 1952 - No. 13, Oct, 1954
Toby Press/Minoan Publ. Corp.

1 21.00 63.00 145.00
2-Torture scenes 16.00 48.00 110.00
3-8,13 10.00 30.00 65.00
9-11-Reprints Purple Claw #1-3 10.00 30.00 70.00
12-Myron Fass-c/a; torture scenes 11.00 32.00 75.00

GD25 FN65 NM94

NOTE: ***Andru*** *a-5.* ***Baily*** *a-5.* ***Myron Fass*** *a-2, 3, 12; c-1-3, 12.* ***Hollingsworth*** *a-2.* ***Sparling*** *a-6, 9; c-9.*

TALES OF JUSTICE
No. 53, May, 1955 - No. 67, Aug, 1957
Atlas Comics(MjMC No. 53-66/Male No. 67)

53 10.00 30.00 70.00
54-57: 54-Powell-a 7.50 22.50 45.00
58,59-Krigstein-a 9.15 27.50 55.00
60-63,65: 60-Powell-a 5.85 17.50 35.00
64,67-Crandall-a 7.50 22.50 45.00
66-Torres, Orlando-a 7.50 22.50 45.00
NOTE: ***Everett*** *a-53, 60.* ***Orlando*** *a-65, 66.* ***Severin*** *a-64; c-58, 60, 65.* ***Wildey*** *a-64, 67.*

TALES OF ORDINARY MADNESS (Dark Horse)(Value: cover or less)

TALES OF SUSPENSE (Becomes Captain America #100 on)
Jan, 1959 - No. 99, March, 1968
Atlas (WPI No. 1,2/Male No. 3-12/VPI No. 13-18)/Marvel No. 19 on

1-Williamson-a (5 pgs.); Heck-c; #1-4 have sci/fi-c 110.00 330.00 1100.00
2,3: 3-Flying saucer-c/story 43.00 128.00 385.00
4-Williamson-a (4 pgs.); Kirby/Everett-c/a 39.00 118.00 355.00
5,6,8,10: 5-Kirby monster-c begin 26.00 77.00 230.00
7-Prototype ish. (Lava Man) 33.00 99.00 265.00
9-Prototype ish. (Iron Man) 36.00 107.00 285.00
11-15,17-20: 12-Crandall-a. 13-Elektro-c/story. 14-Intro/1st app. Colossus-c/sty. 20-Colossus-c/story (2nd app.) 21.00 62.00 165.00
16-1st Metallo-c/story (4/61, Iron Man prototype) 28.00 83.00 220.00
21-25: 25-Last 10¢ issue 15.00 45.00 120.00
26,27,29,30,33,34,36-38: 33-(9/62)-Hulk 1st x-over cameo (picture on wall)
14.00 43.00 115.00
28-Prototype ish. (Stone Men) 15.00 45.00 120.00
31-Prototype ish. (Dr. Doom) 16.00 49.00 130.00
32-Prototype ish. (Dr. Strange)(8/62)-Sazzik The Sorcerer app.; "The Man and the Beehive" story, 1 month before TTA #35 (2nd Antman), came out after "The Man in the Ant Hill" in TTA #27 (1/62) (1st Antman)-Characters from both stories were tested to see which got best fan response
16.00 49.00 130.00
35-Prototype ish. (The Watcher) 15.00 45.00 120.00

GD25 FN65 VF82 NM94
39 (3/63)-Origin/1st app. Iron Man & begin series; 1st Iron Man story has Kirby layouts 333.00 1000.00 2000.00 3000.00

GD25 FN65 NM94
40-2nd app. Iron Man (in new armor) 119.00 358.00 1075.00
41-3rd app. Iron Man; Dr. Strange (villain) app. 78.00 234.00 545.00
42-45: 45-Intro. & 1st app. Happy & Pepper 34.00 103.00 240.00
46,47: 46-1st app. Crimson Dynamo 21.00 64.00 150.00
48-New Iron Man armor by Ditko 26.00 77.00 180.00
49-1st X-Men x-over (same date as X-Men #3, 1/64); also 1st Avengers x-over (w/o Captain America); 1st Tales of the Watcher back-up story & begins (2nd app. Watcher; see F.F. #13) 18.00 54.00 125.00
50-1st app. Mandarin 13.00 39.00 90.00
51-1st Scarecrow 11.00 33.00 78.00
52-1st app. The Black Widow (4/64) 15.00 45.00 105.00
53-Origin The Watcher; 2nd Black Widow app. 13.00 39.00 90.00
54-56: 56-1st app. Unicorn; 4th Avengers x-over 8.00 25.00 58.00
57-Origin/1st app. Hawkeye (9/64) 18.00 54.00 125.00
58-Captain America battles Iron Man (10/64)-Classic-c; 2nd Kraven app. (Cap's 1st app. in this title) 31.00 94.00 220.00
59-Iron Man plus Captain America double feature begins (11/64); 1st S.A. Captain America solo story; intro Jarvis, Avenger's butler; classic-c
31.00 94.00 220.00
60-2nd app. Hawkeye (#64 is 3rd app.) 14.00 40.00 100.00
61,62,64: 62-Origin Mandarin (2/65) 8.00 25.00 58.00
63-1st Silver Age origin Captain America (3/65) 22.00 66.00 155.00
65,66-G.A. Red Skull in WWII stories: 65-1st Silver-Age Red Skull (5/65). 66-Origin Red Skull 143.00 40.00 100.00
67-78,81-98: 69-1st app. Titanium Man. 70-Begin alternating-c features w/Capt.

Tales of Terror Annual (1952) © EC

Tales of the Legion #318 © DC

Tales of the Mysterious Traveler #13 © CC

GD25 FN65 NM94

America (even #'s) & Iron Man (odd #'s). 75-1st app. Agent 13 later named Sharon Carter. 76-Intro Batroc & Sharon Carter, Agent 13 of Shield. 78-Col. Nick Fury app. 81-Intro the Adaptoid by Kirby (also in #82-84). 88-Mole Man app. in Iron Man story. 92-1st Nick Fury x-over (cameo, as Agent of Shield, 8/67). 94-Intro Modok. 95-Capt. America's i.d. revealed. 98-1st app. new Zemo (son?) in cameo (#99 is 1st full app.) 6.40 19.00 45.00

79-Begin 3 part Iron Man Sub-Mariner battle story; Sub-mariner-c & cameo; 1st app. Cosmic Cube; 1st modern Red Skull 7.00 21.00 50.00

80-Iron Man battles Sub-Mariner story cont'd in Tales to Astonish #82 8.00 24.00 55.00

99-Captain America story cont'd in Captain America #100; Iron Man story cont'd in Iron Man & Sub-Mariner #1 9.00 26.00 60.00

NOTE: ***J. Buscema*** *a-1; c-3.* ***Colan*** *a-39, 73-99p; c(p)-73, 75, 77, 79, 81, 83, 85-87, 89, 91, 93, 95, 97, 99.* ***Craig*** *a-73-83i(as Gary Michaels), 99i.* ***Crandall*** *a-12.* ***Davis*** *a-38.* ***Ditko*** *a-1-15, 17-44, 46, 47-49p; c-2, 10i, 13i, 23i.* ***Kirby/Ditko*** *a-7; c-10, 13, 22, 28, 34.* ***Everett*** *a-8.* ***Forte*** *a-5, 9.* ***Heath*** *a-2, 10.* ***Gil Kane*** *a-88p, 89-91; c-88, 89-91p.* ***Kirby*** *a(p)-2-4, 6-35, 40, 41, 43, 59-75, 77-86, 92-99; layouts-69-75, 77; c(p)4-28(most), 29-56, 58-72, 74, 76, 78, 80, 82, 84, 86, 92, 94, 96, 98.* ***Leiber/Fox*** *a-42, 43, 45, 51.* ***Reinman*** *a-26, 44i, 49i, 52i, 53i.* ***Tuska*** *a-58, 70-74.* ***Wood*** *c/a-71i.*

TALES OF SWORD & SORCERY (See Dagar)

TALES OF TERROR
1952 (no month)
Toby Press Publications

1-Fawcette-c; Ravielli-a 11.50 34.00 80.00

NOTE: *This title was cancelled due to similarity to the E.C. title.*

TALES OF TERROR (See Movie Classics)

TALES OF TERROR (Magazine)
Summer, 1964
Eerie Publications

1 3.60 9.00 18.00

TALES OF TERROR (Eclipse)(Value: cover or less)

TALES OF TERROR ANNUAL
1951 - No. 3, 1953 (25¢, 132 pgs., 16 stories each)
E.C. Comics

	GD25	FN65	VF82
nn(1951)(Scarce)-Feldstein infinity-c	371.00	1115.00	2600.00
(Estimated up to 35 total copies exist, 3 in NM/Mint)			
	GD25	**FN65**	**NM94**
2(1952)-Feldstein-c	158.00	475.00	1100.00
3(1953)-Feldstein bondage/torture-c	118.00	354.00	825.00

NOTE: *No. 1 contains three horror and one science fiction comic which came out in 1950. No. 2 contains a horror, crime, and science fiction book which generally had cover dates in 1951, and No. 3 had horror, crime, and shock books that generally appeared in 1952. All E.C. annuals contain four complete books that did not sell on the stands which were rebound in the annual format, minus the covers, and sold from the E.C. office and on the stands in key cities. The contents of each annual may vary in the same year. Crypt Keeper, Vault Keeper, Old Witch app. on all-c.*

TALES OF TERROR ILLUSTRATED (See Terror Illustrated)

TALES OF TEXAS JOHN SLAUGHTER (See 4-Color #997)

TALES OF THE BEANWORLD
Feb, 1985 - No. 19, 1991; No. 20, 1993 - Present ($1.50/$2.00, B&W)
Beanworld Press/Eclipse Comics

	FN65	NM94
1	1.70	4.25
2-19	.90	2.25
20 ($2.50)	1.00	2.50
21 ($2.95)	1.20	3.00

TALES OF THE GREEN BERET
Jan, 1967 - No. 5, Oct, 1969
Dell Publishing Co.

	GD25	FN65	NM94
1-Glanzman-a in 1-4 & 5r	3.00	7.50	15.00
2-5: 5-Reprints #1	1.80	4.50	9.00

TALES OF THE GREEN HORNET
Sept, 1990 - No. 2, 1990 ($1.75, color); V3#1, Sept, 1992 - No. 3, Nov, 1992
Now Comics

1,2 1.75

GD25 FN65 NM94

V3#1 ($2.75)-Polybagged w/hologram trading card 1.10 2.75
V3#2,3 ($2.50) 1.00 2.50

TALES OF THE GREEN LANTERN CORPS (DC)(Value: cover or less)(See Green Lantern #107)

TALES OF THE GREEN LANTERN CORPS
May, 1981 - No. 3, July, 1981 (Mini-series)
DC Comics

1-3: 1-Origin of G.L. & the Guardians 1.40
Annual 1 (1/85)-Gil Kane-c/a .60 1.60

TALES OF THE INVISIBLE SCARLET O'NEIL (See Harvey Comics Hits #59)

TALES OF THE KILLERS (Magazine)
V1#10, Dec, 1970 - V1#11, Feb, 1971 (B&W, 52 pgs.)
World Famous Periodicals

	GD25	FN65	NM94
V1#10-One pg. Frazetta	2.15	6.50	15.00
11	1.65	4.00	10.00

TALES OF THE LEGION (Formerly Legion of Super-Heroes)
No. 314, Aug, 1984 - No. 354, Dec, 1987
DC Comics

314-354: 321-Reprints begin 1.25
Annual 4,5 (1986, 1987)-Formerly LSH Annual 1.40

TALES OF THE MARINES (Formerly Devil-Dog Dugan #1-3)
No. 4, Feb, 1957 (Marines At War #5 on)
Atlas Comics (OPI)

4-Powell-a; Severin-c 4.00 11.00 22.00

TALES OF THE MYSTERIOUS TRAVELER (See Mysterious...)
Aug, 1956 - No. 13, June, 1959; V2#14, Oct, 1985 - No. 15, Dec, 1985
Charlton Comics

	GD25	FN65	NM94
1-No Ditko-a; Giordano/Alascia-c	29.00	86.00	200.00
2-Ditko-a(1)	27.00	80.00	190.00
3-Ditko-c/a(1)	24.00	73.00	170.00
4-6-Ditko-c/a(3-4 stories each)	27.00	80.00	210.00
7-9-Ditko-a(1-2 each). 8-Rocke-c	24.00	73.00	170.00
10,11-Ditko-c/a(3-4 each)	27.00	81.00	190.00
12,13	10.00	30.00	70.00
V2#14,15 (1985)-Ditko-c/a			1.00

TALES OF THE NEW TEEN TITANS
June, 1982 - No. 4, Sept, 1982 (Mini-series)
DC Comics

1-4 1.00

TALES OF THE PONY EXPRESS (See 4-Color #829, 942)

TALES OF THE SUN RUNNERS (Sirius)(Value: cover or less)

TALES OF THE TEENAGE MUTANT NINJA TURTLES
May, 1987 - No. 7, Aug (Apr-c), 1989 (B&W, $1.50)(See Teenage Mutant...)
Mirage Studios

1 1.80 4.50
2-7: Title merges w/Teenage Mutant Ninja... 1.00 2.50

TALES OF THE TEEN TITANS (Formerly The New Teen Titans)
No. 41, April, 1984 - No. 91, July, 1988 (75¢)
DC Comics

41,45-59: 46-Aqualad & Aquagirl join. 50-Double size; app. Betty Kane (Batgirl) out of costume. 52-1st app. Azrael in cameo (not same as newer character). 53-1st full app. Azrael; Deathstroke cameo (1 panel). 54,55-Deathstroke-c/stories. 56-Intro Jinx. 57-Neutron app. 59-r/DC Comics Presents #26 1.00

42-44: The Judas Contract part 1-3 with Deathstroke the Terminator in all; concludes in Annual #3. 44-Dick Grayson becomes Nightwing (3rd to be Nightwing) & joins Titans; Jericho (Deathstroke's son) joins; origin Deathstroke 1.40 3.50 8.50

60-91-r/New Teen Titans Baxter series. 68-B. Smith-c. 70-Origin Kole. 83-91 are $1.00 cover 1.00

Tales of the Unexpected #31 © DC

Tales to Astonish #17 © DC

Tales to Astonish V2 #2 © DC

Annual 3(1984, $1.25)-Part 4 of The Judas Contract; Deathstroke-c/story; Death of Terra; indicia says Teen Titans Annual; formerly New Teen Titans Annual #1,2 1.20 3.00
Annual 4,5: 4-(1986, $1.25)-Reprints. 5-(1987) 1.25

TALES OF THE TEXAS RANGERS (See Jace Pearson...)

TALES OF THE UNEXPECTED (Becomes The Unexpected #105 on)(See Adventure #75, Super DC Giant)
Feb-Mar, 1956 - No. 104, Dec-Jan, 1967-68
National Periodical Publications

	GD25	FN65	NM94
1	79.00	237.00	790.00
2	45.00	135.00	360.00
3-5	31.00	94.00	250.00
6-10	23.00	69.00	185.00
11,14,19,20	13.00	39.00	105.00
12,13,15-18,21-24: All have Kirby-a. 15,17-Grey tone-c. 16-Character named 'Thor' with a magic hammer by Kirby (8/57, not like later Thor)	17.00	51.00	135.00
25-30	13.00	38.00	100.00
31-39	10.00	30.00	80.00

	GD25	FN65	VF82	NM94
Showcase #15 (7-8/58)-1st app. Space Ranger	77.00	230.00	690.00	1150.00

	GD25	FN65	NM94
Showcase #16 (9-10/58)-2nd Space Ranger	65.00	195.00	650.00

	GD25	FN65	VF82	NM94
40-Space Ranger begins (8/59, 3rd app.), ends #82	70.00	210.00	455.00	700.00

	GD25	FN65	NM94
41,42-Space Ranger stories	28.00	83.00	220.00
43-1st Space Ranger-c this title; grey tone-c	54.00	162.00	540.00
44-46	21.00	64.00	150.00
47-50	15.00	45.00	105.00
51-60: 54-Dinosaur-c/story	13.00	39.00	90.00
61-67: 67-Last 10¢ issue	10.00	30.00	70.00
68-82: 82-Last Space Ranger	5.00	15.00	35.00
83-100: 91-1st Automan (also in #94,97)	4.00	10.70	25.00
101-104	2.90	8.60	20.00

NOTE: ***Neal Adams*** *c-104.* ***Anderson*** *a-50.* ***Brown*** *a-50-82(Space Ranger); c-19, 40, & many Space Ranger-c.* ***Cameron*** *a-24, 27, 29; c-24.* ***Heath*** *a-49.* ***Bob Kane*** *a-24, 48.* ***Kirby*** *a-12, 13, 15-18, 21-24; c-13, 18, 22.* ***Meskin*** *a-15, 18, 26, 27, 35, 66.* ***Moreira*** *a-16, 20, 29, 38, 44, 62, 71; c-38.* ***Roussos*** *c-10.* ***Wildey*** *a-31.*

TALES OF THE WEST (See 3-D...)

TALES OF THE WIZARD OF OZ (See 4-Color #1308)

TALES OF THE ZOMBIE (Magazine)
Aug, 1973 - No. 10, Mar, 1975 (75¢, B&W)
Marvel Comics Group

	GD25	FN65	NM94
V1#1-Reprint/Menace #5; origin	2.15	6.50	15.00
2,3: 2-Everett biography & memorial	1.30	3.25	8.00
V2#1(#4)-Photos & text of James Bond movie "Live & Let Die"	1.30	3.25	8.00
5-10: 8-Kaluta-a	1.30	3.25	8.00
Annual 1(Summer,'75)(#11)-B&W; Everett, Buscema-a	1.00	2.00	5.00

NOTE: ***Alcala*** *a-7-9.* ***Boris*** *c-1-4.* ***Colan*** *a-2r, 6.* ***Heath*** *a-5r.* ***Reese*** *a-2.* ***Tuska*** *a-2r.*

TALES OF THUNDER (Deluxe)(Value: cover or less)

TALES OF VOODOO (Magazine)
V1#11, Nov, 1968 - V7#6, Nov, 1974
Eerie Publications

	GD25	FN65	NM94
V1#11	3.20	8.00	20.00
V2#1(3/69)-V2#4(9/69)	1.70	5.00	12.00
V3#1-6('70): 4- "Claws of the Cat" redrawn from Climax #1	1.65	4.00	10.00
V4#1-6('71), V5#1-6('72), V6#1-6('73), V7#1-6('74)	1.65	4.00	10.00
Annual 1	1.65	4.00	10.00

NOTE: *Bondage-c-V1#10, V2#4, V3#4.*

TALES OF WELLS FARGO (See 4-Color #876, 968, 1023,1075, 1113, 1167, 1215, & Western Roundup under Dell Giants)

TALESPIN (Also see Cartoon Tales & Disney's Talespin Limited Series)
June, 1991 - No. 7, Dec, 1991 ($1.50)
Disney Comics

1-7 1.50

TALES TO ASTONISH (Becomes The Incredible Hulk #102 on)
Jan, 1959 - No. 101, March, 1968
Atlas (MAP No. 1/ZPC No. 2-14/VPI No. 15-21/Marvel No. 22 on

	GD25	FN65	NM94
1-Jack Davis-a; #1-4 have sci/fi-c	110.00	330.00	1100.00
2-Ditko flying saucer-c (Martians)	50.00	150.00	450.00
3,4	34.00	103.00	310.00
5-Prototype ish. (Stone Men); Williamson-a (4 pgs.); Kirby monster-c begin	37.00	110.00	330.00
6,8-10	27.00	80.00	240.00
7-Prototype ish. (Toad Men)	28.00	83.00	250.00
11-14,17-20: 13-Swipes story from Menace #8	21.00	64.00	170.00
15-Prototype ish. (Electro)	24.00	73.00	195.00
16-Prototype ish. (Stone Men)	24.00	73.00	195.00
21-26,28-34: 21-(7/61)-Hulk prototype?	16.00	47.00	125.00

	GD25	FN65	VF82	NM94
27-1st Ant-Man app. (1/62); last 10¢ issue (see Strange Tales #73,78 & Tales of Suspense #32)	217.00	650.00	1625.00	2600.00
35-(9/62)-2nd app. Ant-Man, 1st in costume; begin series & Ant-Man-c	125.00	375.00	812.00	1250.00

	GD25	FN65	NM94
36-3rd app. Ant-Man	51.00	152.00	455.00
37-40: 38-1st app. Egghead	32.00	96.00	225.00
41-43	21.00	64.00	150.00
44-Origin & 1st app. The Wasp (6/63)	26.00	77.00	180.00
45-48	16.00	49.00	115.00
49-Ant-Man becomes Giant Man (11/63)	20.00	60.00	140.00
50-56,58: 50-Origin/1st app. Human Top (alias Whirlwind). 52-Origin/1st app. Black Knight (2/64). 53-Origin Colossus	11.00	34.00	80.00
57-Early Spider-Man app. (7/64)	14.00	40.00	100.00
59-Giant Man vs. Hulk feature story (9/64); Hulk's 1st app. this title	17.00	51.00	120.00
60-Giant Man & Hulk double feature begins	20.00	60.00	140.00
61-69: 61-All Ditko issue. 62-1st app./origin The Leader; new Wasp costume. 65-New Giant Man costume. 68-New Human Top costume. 69-Last Giant Man	8.00	24.00	55.00
70-Sub-Mariner & Incredible Hulk begins (8/65)	11.00	32.00	75.00
71-81,83-91,94-99: 72-Begin alternating-c features w/Sub-Mariner (even #'s) & Hulk (odd #'s). 79-Hulk vs. Hercules-c/story. 81-1st app. Boomerang. 90-1st app. The Abomination. 97-X-Men cameo (brief)	5.70	17.00	40.00
82-Iron Man battles Sub-Mariner (1st Iron Man x-over outside The Avengers & TOS); story cont'd from Tales of Suspense #80	8.00	24.00	55.00
92-1st Silver Surfer x-over (outside of Fantastic Four, 6/67); 1 panel cameo only	6.90	21.00	48.00
93-Hulk battles Silver Surfer-c/story (1st full x-over)	8.00	23.00	54.00
100-Hulk battles Sub-Mariner full-length story	6.90	21.00	48.00
101-Hulk story cont'd in Incredible Hulk #102; Sub-Mariner story continued in Iron Man & Sub-Mariner #1	9.00	28.00	65.00

NOTE: ***Ayers*** *c(i)-9-12, 16, 18, 19.* ***Berg*** *a-1.* ***Burgos*** *a-62-64p.* ***Buscema*** *a-85-87p.* ***Colan*** *a(p)-70-76, 78-82, 84, 85, 101; c(p)-71-76, 78, 80, 82, 84, 86, 88, 90.* ***Ditko*** *a-1, 3-48, 50i, 60-67p; c-2, 7i, 8i, 14i, 17i.* ***Everett*** *a-78, 79i, 80-84, 85-90i, 94i, 95, 96; c(i)-79-81, 83, 86, 88.* ***Forte*** *a-6.* ***Kane*** *a-76, 88-91; c-89, 91.* ***Kirby*** *a(p)-1, 5-34-40, 44, 49-51, 68-70, 82, 83; layouts-71-84; c(p)-1, 3-48, 50-70, 72, 73, 75, 77, 78, 79, 81, 85, 90.* ***Kirby/Ditko*** *a-7, 8, 12, 13, 50; c-7, 8, 10, 13.* ***Leiber/Fox*** *a-47, 48, 50, 51.* ***Powell*** *a-65-69p, 73, 74.* ***Reinman*** *a-6, 36, 45, 46, 54i, 56-60i.*

TALES TO ASTONISH (2nd Series)
Dec, 1979 - No. 14, Jan, 1981
Marvel Comics Group

V1#1-Reprints Sub-Mariner #1 by Buscema 1.50
2-14: Reprints Sub-Mariner #2-14 1.30

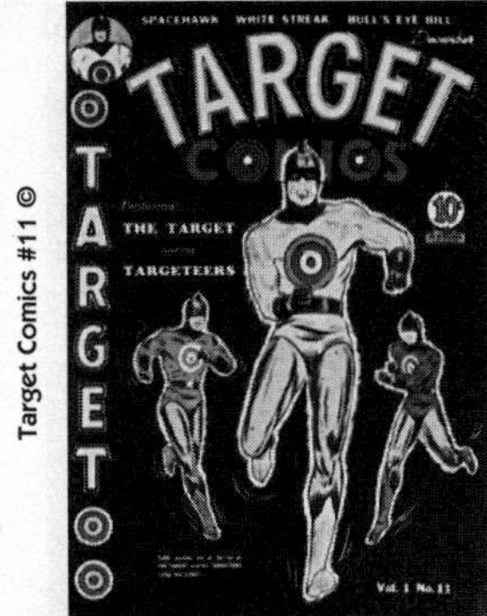

Target Comics #11 ©

Targitt #2 © MEG

Tarzan #10 (Dell) © ERB

GD25 FN65 NM94

TALES TO HOLD YOU SPELLBOUND (See Spellbound)

TALKING KOMICS
1947 (20 pgs.) (Slick covers)
Belda Record & Publ. Co.

Each comic contained a record that followed the story - much like the Golden Record sets. Known titles: Chirpy Cricket, Lonesome Octopus, Sleepy Santa, Grumpy Shark, Flying Turtle, Happy Grasshopper
with records... 1.60 4.00 8.00

TALLY-HO COMICS
December, 1944
Swappers Quarterly (Baily Publ. Co.)

nn-Frazetta's 1st work as Giunta's assistant; Man in Black horror story; violence; Giunta-c 25.00 75.00 175.00

TALOS OF THE WILDERNESS SEA (DC)(Value: cover or less)

TALULLAH (See Comic Books Series I)

TAMMY, TELL ME TRUE (See 4-Color #1233)

TANK GIRL (Dark Horse)(Value: cover or less)

TAPPING THE VEIN (Eclipse)(Value: cover or less)

TARANTULA (See Weird Suspense)

TARGET: AIRBOY (Eclipse)(Value: cover or less)

TARGET COMICS (...Western Romances #106 on)
Feb, 1940 - V10#3 (#105), Aug-Sept, 1949
Funnies, Inc./Novelty Publications/Star Publications

V1#1-Origin & 1st app. Manowar, The White Streak by Burgos, & Bulls-Eye Bill by Everett; City Editor (ends #5), High Grass Twins by Jack Cole (ends #4), T-Men by Joe Simon(ends #9), Rip Rory (ends #4), Fantastic Feature Films by Tarpe Mills (ends #39), & Calling 2-R (ends #14) begin; marijuana use story 286.00 857.00 2000.00
2 121.00 364.00 850.00
3,4 89.00 268.00 625.00
5-Origin The White Streak in text; Space Hawk by Wolverton begins (6/40) (see Blue Bolt & Circus) 243.00 730.00 1700.00
6-The Chameleon by Everett begins (7/40, 1st app.); White Streak origin cont'd. in text; early mention of comic collecting in letter column; 1st letter column in comics? (7/40) 109.00 325.00 760.00
7-Wolverton Spacehawk-c/story (Scarce) 286.00 857.00 2000.00
8,9,12: 12-(1/41) 89.00 268.00 625.00
10-Intro/1st app. The Target (11/40); Simon-c 121.00 364.00 850.00
11-Origin The Target & The Targeteers 114.00 343.00 800.00
V2#1-Target by Bob Wood; Uncle Sam flag-c 61.00 182.00 425.00
2-Ten part Treasure Island serial begins; Harold Delay-a; reprinted in Catholic Comics V3#1-10 (see Key Comics #5) 55.00 165.00 375.00
3-5: 4-Kit Carter, The Cadet begins 42.00 125.00 295.00
6-9: Red Seal with White Streak in #6-10 42.00 125.00 295.00
10-Classic-c 50.00 150.00 350.00
11,12: 12-10-part Last of the Mohicans serial begins; Delay-a 42.00 125.00 295.00
V3#1-10: 8-Flag-c; 6-part Gulliver Travels serial begins; Delay-a. 10-Last Wolverton issue 42.00 125.00 295.00
11,12 10.00 30.00 60.00
V4#1-12: 6-Targetoons by Wolverton (1 pg.). 8-X-Mas-c 7.50 22.50 45.00
V5#1-8 6.70 20.00 40.00
V6#1-10, V7#1-12 5.85 17.50 35.00
V8#1,3-5,8,9,11,12 5.00 15.00 30.00
2,6,7-Krigstein-a 6.35 19.00 38.00
10-L.B. Cole-c 13.00 40.00 90.00
V9#1,4,6,8,10,12, V10#2,3-L.B. Cole-c 13.00 40.00 90.00
V9#2,3,5,7,9,11, V10#1 5.00 15.00 30.00

NOTE: ***Certa*** *c-V8#9, 11, 12, V9#5, 9, 11, V10#1.* ***Jack Cole*** *a-1-8.* ***Everett*** *a-1-9; c(signed Blake)-1, 2.* ***Al Fago*** *c-V6#8.* ***Sid Greene*** *c-V2#9, 12, V3#3.* ***Walter Johnson*** *c-V5#6, V6#4.* ***Tarpe Mills*** *a-1-4, 6, 8, 11, V3#1.* ***Rico*** *a-V7#4, 10, V8#5, 6, V9#3; c-V7#6, 8, 10, V8#2, 4, 6, 7.* ***Simon*** *a-1, 2.* ***Bob Wood*** *c-V2#2, 3, 5, 6.*

GD25 FN65 NM94

TARGET: THE CORRUPTORS (TV)
No. 1306, Mar-May, 1962 - No. 3, Oct-Dec, 1962 (All have photo-c)
Dell Publishing Co.

4-Color 1306(#1), #2,3 5.00 15.00 30.00

TARGET WESTERN ROMANCES (Formerly Target Comics; becomes Flaming Western Romances #3)
No. 106, Oct-Nov, 1949 - No. 107, Dec-Jan, 1949-50
Star Publications

106(#1)-Silhouette nudity panel; L.B. Cole-c 19.00 58.00 135.00
107(#2)-L.B. Cole-c; lingerie panels 16.00 48.00 110.00

TARGITT
March, 1975 - No. 3, July, 1975
Atlas/Seaboard Publ.

1-3: 1-Origin; Nostrand-a in all. 2-1st in costume 1.00

TARZAN (See Aurora, Comics on Parade, Crackajack, DC 100-Page Super Spec., Famous Feature Stories #1, Golden Comics Digest #4, 9, Jeep Comics #1-29, Jungle Tales of..., Limited Collectors' Edition, Popular, Sparkler, Sport Stars #1, Tip Top & Top Comics)

TARZAN
No. 5, 1939 - No. 161, Aug, 1947
Dell Publishing Co./United Features Syndicate

Large Feature Comic 5('39)-(Scarce)-By Hal Foster; reprints 1st dailies from 1929 90.00 270.00 900.00
Single Series 20(:40)-By Hal Foster 100.00 300.00 700.00
4-Color 134(2/47)-Marsh-c/a 64.00 193.00 450.00
4-Color 161(8/47)-Marsh-c/a 55.00 165.00 385.00

TARZAN (...of the Apes #138 on)
1-2/48 - No. 131, 7-8/62; No. 132, 11/62 - No. 206, 2/72
Dell Publishing Co./Gold Key No. 132 on

1-Jesse Marsh-a begins 100.00 300.00 700.00
2 55.00 165.00 385.00
3-5 41.00 124.00 290.00
6-10: 6-1st Tantor the Elephant. 7-1st Valley of the Monsters 32.00 96.00 225.00
11-15: 11-Two Against the Jungle begins, ends #24. 13-Lex Barker photo-c begin 27.00 80.00 185.00
16-20 21.00 63.00 145.00
21-24,26-30 16.00 48.00 110.00
25-1st "Brothers of the Spear" episode; series ends #156,160,161,196-206 19.00 58.00 135.00
31-40 10.00 30.00 65.00
41-54: Last Barker photo-c 7.00 21.00 50.00
55-60: 56-Eight pg. Boy story 5.50 16.00 38.00
61,62,64-70 4.30 13.00 30.00
63-Two Tarzan stories, 1 by Manning 4.60 13.70 32.00
71-79 3.40 10.00 24.00
80-99: 80-Gordon Scott photo-c begin 3.70 11.00 26.00
100 4.60 13.70 32.00
101-109 3.10 9.00 22.00
110 (Scarce)-Last photo-c 4.00 12.00 28.00
111-120 2.60 7.70 18.00
121-131: Last Dell issue 2.00 6.00 14.00
132-154: 132-1st Gold Key issue. 139-(12/63)-1st app. Korak (Boy); leaves Tarzan & gets own book 1/64 1.60 4.70 11.00
155-Origin Tarzan 3.00 8.00 16.00
156-161: 157-Banlu, Dog of the Arande begins, ends #159, 195. 169-Leopard Girl app. 1.30 3.00 7.50
162,165,168,171 (TV)-Ron Ely photo covers 1.90 6.00 13.00
163,164,166,167,169,170: 169-Leopard Girl app. 1.20 2.90 7.00
172-199,201-206: 178-Tarzan origin-r/#155; Leopard Girl app., also in #179, 190-193 1.20 2.40 6.00
200 (Scarce) 1.20 2.90 7.00
Story Digest 1-(6/70, G.K.) 1.20 2.90 7.00

NOTE: *#162, 165, 168, 171 are TV issues. #1-153 all have* ***Marsh*** *art on Tarzan. #154-161, 163, 164, 166, 167, 172-177 all have* ***Manning*** *art on Tarzan. #178, 202 have* ***Manning*** *Tarzan*

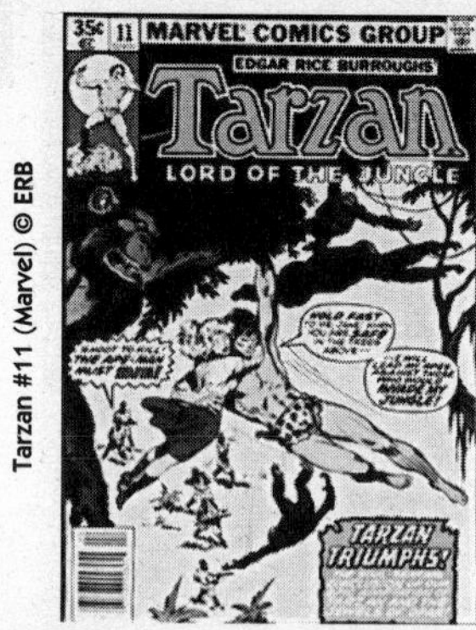

Tarzan #11 (Marvel) © ERB

The Tarzan Family #62 © ERB

Team America #11 © MEG

GD25 FN65 NM94

*reprints. No "Brothers of the Spear" in #1-24, 157-159, 162-195. #39-126, 128-156 all have **Russ Manning** art on "Brothers of the Spear". #196-201, 203-205 all have **Manning** B.O.T.S. reprints; #25-38, 127 all have Jesse **Marsh** art on B.O.T.S. #206 has a Marsh B.O.T.S. reprint. **Gollub** c-8-12. **Marsh** c-1-7. **Doug Wildey** a-162, 179-187. Many issues have front and back photo covers.*

TARZAN (Continuation of Gold Key series)
No. 207, April, 1972 - No. 258, Feb, 1977
National Periodical Publications

207-Origin Tarzan by Joe Kubert, part 1; John Carter begins (origin); 52 pg. issues thru #209 — 1.70 3.40 8.50
208,209: 208-210-Parts 2-4 of origin. 209-Last John Carter — .90 2.30 5.50
210-229,231-258: 210-Kubert-a. 211-Hogarth, Kubert-a. 212-214: Adaptations from "Jungle Tales of Tarzan". 213-Beyond the Farthest Star begins, ends #218. 215-218,224,225-All by Kubert. 215-part Foster-r. 219-223: Adapts "The Return of Tarzan" by Kubert. 226-Manning-a. 231-234-(All 100 pgs.)-Adapts "Tarzan and the Lion Man"; Rex, the Wonder Dog r-#232, 233. 235-(100 pgs.)-Last Kubert issue. 238-(68 pgs.). 240-243 adapts "Tarzan & the Castaways". 250-256 adapts "Tarzan the Untamed." 252,253-r/#213 — 1.60 4.00
230-DC 100 Page Super Spectacular; Kubert, Kaluta-a(p); Korak begins, ends #234; Carson of Venus app. — 1.80 4.50
Comic Digest 1-(Fall, 1972, 50¢, 160 pgs.)(DC)-Digest size; Kubert-c; Manning-a — 1.80 4.50

*NOTE: **Anderson** a-207, 209, 217, 218. **Chaykin** a-216. **Finlay** a(r)-212. **Foster** strip-r #207-209, 211, 212, 221. **Heath** a-230i. **G. Kane** a(r)-232p, 233p. **Kubert** a-207-225, 227-235, 257r, 258r; c-207-249, 253. **Lopez** a-250-255p; c-250p, 251, 252, 254. **Manning** strip-r 230-235, 238. **Morrow** a-208. **Nino** a-231-234. **Sparling** a-230, 231. **Starr** a-233r.*

TARZAN
June, 1977 - No. 29, Oct, 1979
Marvel Comics Group

1 — .80 2.00
2-29: 2-Origin by John Buscema — 1.50
Annual 1-3: 1-(1977). 2-(1978). 3-(1979) — 1.50

*NOTE: **N. Adams** c-11i, 12i. **Alcala** a-9i, 10i; c-8i, 9i. **Buckler** c-25-27p, Annual 3p. **John Buscema** a-1-3, 4-18p, Annual 1; c-1-7, 8p, 9p, 10, 11p, 12p, 13, 14-19p, 21p, 22, 23p, 24p, 28p, Annual 1. **Mooney** a-22i. **Nebres** a-22i. **Russell** a-29i.*

TARZAN BOOK (The Illustrated...)
1929 (80 pgs.)(7x9")
Grosset & Dunlap

1(Rare)-Contains 1st B&W Tarzan newspaper comics from 1929. Cloth reinforced spine & dust jacket (50¢); Foster-c
with dust jacket... — 57.00 170.00 400.00
without dust jacket... — 25.00 75.00 175.00
2nd Printing(1934, 25¢, 76 pgs.)-4 Foster pgs. dropped; paper spine, circle in lower right cover with 25¢ price. The 25¢ is barely visible on some copies — 15.00 45.00 105.00
1967-House of Greystoke reprint-7x10", using the complete 300 illustrations/text from the 1929 edition minus the original indicia, foreword, etc. Initial version bound in gold paper & sold for $5.00. Officially titled **Burroughs Biblophile #2**. A very few additional copies were bound in heavier blue paper.
Gold binding... — 3.60 9.00 18.00
Blue binding... — 4.00 12.00 24.00

TARZAN FAMILY, THE (Formerly Korak, Son of Tarzan)
No. 60, Nov-Dec, 1975 - No. 66, Nov-Dec, 1976
(#60-62: 68 pgs.; #63 on: 52 pgs.)
National Periodical Publications

60-66: 60-Korak begins; Kaluta-r — 1.00

*NOTE: Carson of Venus-r 60-65. New John Carter-62-64, 65r, 66r. New Korak-60-66. Pellucidar feature-66. Foster strip r-60(9/4/32-10/16/32), 62(6/29/32-7/31/32), 63(10/11/31-12/13/31). **Kaluta** Carson of Venus-60-65. **Kubert** a-61, 64; c-60-64. **Manning** strip-r 60-62, 64. **Morrow** a-66r.*

TARZAN KING OF THE JUNGLE (See Dell Giant #37, 51)

TARZAN, LORD OF THE JUNGLE
Sept, 1965 (Giant)(soft paper cover)(25¢)
Gold Key

1-Marsh-r — 6.00 18.00 42.00

TARZAN: LOVE, LIES AND THE LOST CITY (See Tarzan the Warrior)
Aug. 10, 1992 - No. 3, Sept, 1992 ($2.50, color, mini-series)
Malibu Comics

1-($3.95, 68 pgs.)-Flip book format; Simonson & Wagner scripts — 1.60 4.00
2,3-No Simonson or Wagner scripts — 1.00 2.50

TARZAN MARCH OF COMICS (See March of Comics #82, 98, 114, 125, 144, 155, 172, 185, 204, 223, 240, 252, 262, 272, 286, 300, 332, 342, 354, 366)

TARZAN OF THE APES
1934? (Hardcover, 68 pgs., 4x12")
Metropolitan Newspaper Service

1-Strip reprints — 16.00 48.00 110.00

TARZAN OF THE APES (Marvel)(Value: cover or less)

TARZAN OF THE APES TO COLOR
No. 988, 1933 (24 pgs.)(10-3/4x15-1/4")(Coloring book)
Saalfield Publishing Co.

988-(Very Rare)-Contains 1929 daily reprints with some new art by Hal Foster. Two panels blown up large on each page with one at the top of opposing pages on every other double-page spread. Believed to be the only time these panels appeared in color. Most color panels are reproduced a second time in b&w to be colored — 150.00 450.00 1000.00

TARZAN'S JUNGLE ANNUAL (See Dell Giants)

TARZAN'S JUNGLE WORLD (See Dell Giant #25)

TARZAN THE WARRIOR (Also see Tarzan: Love, Lies and the Lost City)
March 19, 1992 - No. 5, 1992 ($2.50, color, mini-series)
Malibu Comics

1-5: 1-Bisley painted pack-c (flip book format-c) — 1.00 2.50
1-2nd printing w/o flip-c by Bisley — 1.00 2.50

TASMANIAN DEVIL & HIS TASTY FRIENDS
November, 1962 (12¢)
Gold Key

1-Bugs Bunny & Elmer Fudd x-over — 6.00 18.00 75.00

TASTEE-FREEZ COMICS
1957 (36 pgs.)(10¢ value on-c)(6 different issues given away)
Harvey Comics

1,3: 1-Little Dot. 3-Casper — 5.35 16.00 32.00
2,4,5: 2-Rags Rabbit. 4-Sad Sack. 5-Mazie — 4.00 10.00 20.00
6-Dick Tracy — 5.35 16.00 32.00

TAYLOR'S CHRISTMAS TABLOID
Mid 1930s, Cleveland, Ohio
Dept. Store Giveaway (Tabloid size; in color)

nn-(Very Rare)-Among the earliest pro work of Siegel & Shuster; one full color page called "The Battle in the Stratosphere", with a pre-Superman look; Shuster art thoughout. (Only 1 known copy)
Estimated value... — 2400.00

TEAM AMERICA (See Captain America #269)
June, 1982 - No. 12, May, 1983
Marvel Comics Group

1-Origin; Ideal Toy motorcycle characters — 1.20
2-10: 9-Iron man app. — 1.00
11-Ghost Rider app. — 1.00 2.00 5.00
12-Double size — .80 2.00

TEAM ANARCHY
Oct, 1993 - Present ($2.50, color)
Dagger Comics

1-($2.75)-Red foil logo; intro Team Anarchy — 1.10 2.75
1-Platinum — 1.10 2.75

Team 7 #1 © Aegis Ent. Inc.

Team Youngblood #14 © Rob Liefeld

Teen-Age Diary Secrets #6 © STJ

2-8 1.00 2.50
3-Bronze 1.10 2.75
3-Gold 1.40 3.50
3-Silver 1.00 2.50

TEAM HELIX
Jan, 1993 - No. 4, Apr, 1993 ($1.75, mini-series)
Marvel Comics
1-4: Teen Super Group. 1,2-Wolverine app. .70 1.75

Team 7
Oct, 1994-Present (2.50,color)
Image Comics Inc.
1-Two variant-c 0.50 1.00 2.50

TEAM TITANS (See Deathstroke & New Titans Annual #7)
Sept, 1992 - No. 24, Sept, 1994 ($1.75/$1.95)
DC Comics
1-Five different #1s exist w/origins in 1st half & the same 2nd story in each: Kilowat, Mirage, Nightrider w/Netzer/Perez-a, Redwing, & Terra w/part Perez-p; part 3 of Total Chaos .90 2.25
2-Total Chaos, part 6 .80 2.00
3-21: 11-Metallik app. .70 1.75
22-24: 22-Begin $1.95-c. 24-Zero Hour .80 2.00
Annual 1 (1993, $3.50, 68 pgs.) 1.40 3.50
Annual 2 (1994, $3.50, 68 pgs.)-Elseworlds story 1.40 3.50

TEAM YANKEE (First)(Value: cover or less)

TEAM YOUNGBLOOD (Also see Youngblood)
Sept, 1993 - Present ($1.95/$2.50, color, on-going series)
Image Comics (Extreme Studios)
1-9-Liefeld scripts in all: 1,2,4-6,8-Thibert-c(i). 1-1st app. Dutch & Masada. 3-Spawn cameo. 5-1st app. Lynx. 7,8-Coupons 1 & 4 for Extreme Prejudice #0; Black and White Pt. 4 & 8 by Thibert. 8-Coupon #4 for E. P. #0. 9-Liefeld wraparound-c(p)/a(p) on Pt. I .80 2.00
10-14: 10-Begin $2.50-c; Liefeld-c(p) 1.00 2.50

TEDDY ROOSEVELT & HIS ROUGH RIDERS (See Real Heroes #1)
1950
Avon Periodicals
1-Kinstler-c; Palais-a; Flag-c 13.00 40.00 90.00

TEDDY ROOSEVELT ROUGH RIDER (See Battlefield #22 & Classics Illustrated Special Issue)

TED MCKEEVER'S METROPOL (Epic, 1991 & 1992)(Value: cover or less)

TEE AND VEE CROSLEY IN TELEVISION LAND COMICS
(Also see Crosley's House of Fun)
1951 (52 pgs.; 8x11"; paper cover; in color)
Crosley Division, Avco Mfg. Corp. (Giveaway)
Many stories, puzzles, cut-outs, games, etc. 4.70 14.00 28.00

TEENA
No. 11, 1948 - No. 15, 1948; No. 20, Aug, 1949 - No. 22, Oct, 1950
Magazine Enterprises/Standard Comics No. 20 on
A-1 #11-Teen-age 6.35 19.00 38.00
A-1 #12, 15 5.35 16.00 32.00
20-22 (Standard) 3.60 9.00 18.00

TEEN-AGE BRIDES (True Bride's Experiences #8 on)
Aug, 1953 - No. 7, Aug, 1954
Harvey/Home Comics
1-Powell-a 6.35 19.00 38.00
2-Powell-a 4.00 12.00 24.00
3-7: 3,6-Powell-a 4.00 10.00 20.00

TEEN-AGE CONFESSIONS (See Teen Confessions)

TEEN-AGE CONFIDENTIAL CONFESSIONS
July, 1960 - No. 22, 1964
Charlton Comics
1 4.00 10.00 20.00
2-10 2.00 5.00 10.00
11-22 1.20 3.00 6.00

TEEN-AGE DIARY SECRETS (Formerly Blue Ribbon Comics; becomes Diary Secrets #10 on)
No. 4, 9/49; nn (#5), 9/49 - No. 7, 11/49; No. 8, 2/50; No. 9, 8/50
St. John Publishing Co.
4(9/49)-Oversized; part mag., part comic 16.00 48.00 110.00
nn(#5),6,8: 6,8-Photo-c; Baker-a(2-3) in each 11.00 32.00 75.00
7,9-Digest size 12.00 36.00 85.00

TEEN-AGE DOPE SLAVES (See Harvey Comics Library #1)

TEENAGE HOTRODDERS (Top Eliminator #25 on; see Blue Bird)
April, 1963 - No. 24, July, 1967
Charlton Comics
1 4.00 11.00 22.00
2-10 2.40 6.00 12.00
11-24 1.80 4.50 9.00

TEEN-AGE LOVE (See Fox Giants)

TEEN-AGE LOVE (Formerly Intimate)
V2#4, July, 1958 - No. 96, Dec, 1973
Charlton Comics
V2#4 3.60 9.00 18.00
5-9 2.00 5.00 10.00
10(9/59)-20 1.60 4.00 8.00
21-35 1.00 2.50 6.00
36-70 1.20 3.00
71-96: 61&62-Jonnie Love begins (origin) 1.20

TEENAGE MUTANT NINJA TURTLES (Also see Anything Goes, Donatello, First Comics Graphic Novel, Gobbledygook, Grimjack #26, Leonardo, Michaelangelo, Raphael & Tales Of The...)
1984 - No. 62, Aug, 1993 ($1.50/$1.75, B&W; all 44-52 pgs.)
Mirage Studios
1-1st printing (3000 copies)-Only printing to have ad for Gobbledygook #1 & 2; Shredder app. (#1-4: 7-1/2x11") 33.00 99.00 230.00
1-2nd printing (6/84)(15,000 copies) 3.60 11.00 25.00
1-3rd printing (2/85)(36,000 copies) 1.30 4.00 9.00
1-4th printing, new-c (50,000 copies) 1.10 3.00 6.50
1-5th printing, new-c (8/88-c, 11/88 inside) .80 2.00
1-Counterfeit. **Note**: Most counterfeit copies have a half inch wide white streak or scratch marks across the center of back cover. Black part of cover is a bluish black instead of a deep black. Inside paper is very white & inside cover is bright white. These counterfeit the 1st printings (no value).
2-1st printing (1984; 15,000 copies) 9.00 28.00 65.00
2-2nd printing 1.30 3.30 8.00
2-3rd printing; new Corben-c/a (2/85) 1.10 2.75
2-Counterfeit with glossy cover stock (no value).
3-1st printing (1985, 44 pgs.) 3.60 10.70 25.00
3-Variant, 500 copies, given away in NYC. Has 'Laird's Photo' in white rather than light blue 11.00 32.00 75.00
3-2nd printing; contains new back-up story 1.10 2.75
4-1st printing (1985, 44 pgs.) 1.60 4.70 11.00
4-2nd printing (5/87) .70 1.75
5-Fugitoid begins, ends #7; 1st full color-c (1985) 1.50 4.00 9.00
5-2nd printing (11/87) .70 1.75
6-1st printing (1986) 1.25 3.00 7.50
6-2nd printing (4/88-c, 5/88 inside) .70 1.75
7-4 pg. Eastman/Corben color insert; 1st color TMNT (1986, $1.75-c); Bade Biker back-up story 1.25 3.00 7.50
7-2nd printing (1/89) w/o color insert .70 1.75
8-Cerebus-c/story with Dave Sim-a (1986) 1.00 2.50 5.50
9,10: 9 (9/86)-Rip In Time by Corben 1.90 4.75
11-15 1.30 3.25

Teenage Mutant Ninja Turtles Adventures #4

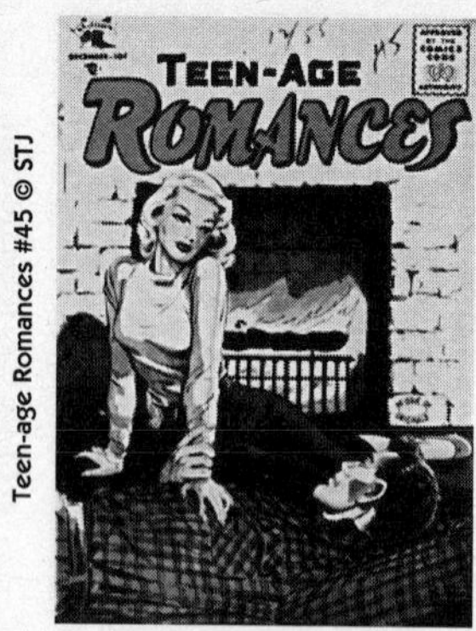

Teen-age Romances #45 © STJ

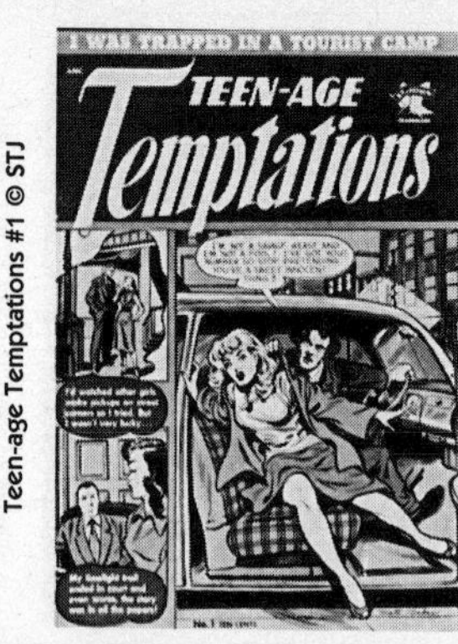

Teen-age Temptations #1 © STJ

16-18: 18-Mark Bode'-a 1.10 2.75
18-2nd printing ($2.25, color, 44 pgs.)-New-c .70 1.80
19-51: 19-Begin $1.75-c. 24-26-Veitch-c/a. 35-Begin $2.00-c. 50-Features pin-ups by Larsen, McFarlane, Simonson, etc. .70 1.80
32-2nd printing ($2.75, 52 pgs., full color) 1.00 2.50
52-62: 52-Begin $2.25-c .90 2.25
Book 1,2($1.50, B&W): 2-Corben-c 1.50
...Christmas Special 1 (12/90, $1.75, B&W, 52 pgs.)-Cover title: Michaelangelo Christmas Special; r/Michaelangelo one-shot plus new Raphael story .70 1.75
...Special (The Maltese Turtle) nn (1/93, $2.95, color, 44 pgs.) 1.20 3.00
...Special: "Times" Pipeline nn (9/92, $2.95, color, 44 pgs.)-Mark Bode-c/a 1.20 3.00
Hard-c ($100)-r/#1-10 plus one-shots w/dust jackets - limited to 1000 w/letter of authenticity 14.00 43.00 100.00
Soft-c ($40)-r/#1-10 6.70 20.00 40.00

TEENAGE MUTANT NINJA TURTLES
V2#1, Oct, 1993 - Present ($2.75, color)
Mirage Studios

1-6: 1-Wraparound-c 1.10 2.75

TEENAGE MUTANT NINJA TURTLES ADVENTURES (TV)
8/88 - No. 3, 12/88; 3/89 - Present ($1.00/$1.25/$1.50)
Archie Comics

1-Adapts TV cartoon; not by Eastman/Laird 1.20 3.00
2,3 (Mini-series) .80 2.00
1 (2nd on going series) 1.00 2.50
2-5: 5-Begins original stories not based on TV .80 2.00
1-11: 2nd printings 1.00
6-49,51-58: 14-Simpson-a(p). 19-1st Mighty Mutanimals (also in #20, 51-54). 20-Begin $1.25-c. 22-Gene Colan-c/a 1.25
50-($1.50)-Poster by Eastman/Laird 1.50
59-61,63-68: 59-Begin $1.50-c 1.50
62-($1.75)-w/poster 1.75
nn (1990, $5.95)-Movie adaptation 1.00 2.50 6.00
nn (Spring, 1991, $2.50, 68 pgs.)-(Meet Archie) 1.00 2.50
nn (Sum, 1991, $2.50, 68 pgs.)-(Movie II)-Adapts movie sequel 1.00 2.50
...Meet the Conservation Corps 1 (1992, $2.50, 68 pgs.) 1.00 2.50
...III The Movie: The Turtles are Back...In Time (1993, $2.50, 68 pgs.) 1.00 2.50
...Special 1 (Sum/92, $2.50, 68 pgs.)-Bill Wray-c 1.00 2.50
...Special 4 (Spr/93, $2.50, 68 pgs.) 1.00 2.50
...Special 5 (Sum/93, $2.50, 68 pgs.) 1.00 2.50
...Giant Size Special 6 (Fall/93, $1.95, 52 pgs.) .80 2.00
...Special 7,8 (Win/93, Spr/94, $1.95, 52 pgs.) .80 2.00
...Special 9 (Sum/94, $1.95, 52 pgs.)-Jeff Smith-c .80 2.00
...Special 10 (Fall/94, $2.00, 52 pgs.) .80 2.00
NOTE: *There are 2nd printings of #1-11 w/B&W inside covers. Originals are color.*

TEENAGE MUTANT NINJA TURTLES CLASSICS DIGEST (TV)
Aug, 1993 - Present ($1.75)
Archie Comics

1-6-Reprints TMNT Advs. .70 1.75

TEENAGE MUTANT NINJA TURTLES/FLAMING CARROT CROSSOVER
Nov, 1993 - No. 4, Feb, 1994 ($2.75, color, mini-series)
Mirage Publishing

1-4-Bob Burden story 1.10 2.75

TEENAGE MUTANT NINJA TURTLES PRESENTS: APRIL O'NEIL
Mar, 1993 - No. 3, June, 1993 ($1.25, mini-series)
Archie Comics

1-3 .60 1.25

TEENAGE MUTANT NINJA TURTLES PRESENTS: DONATELLO AND LEATHERHEAD
July, 1993 - No. 3, Sept, 1993 ($1.25, mini-series)
Archie Comics

1-3 .60 1.25

TEENAGE MUTANT NINJA TURTLES PRESENTS: MERDUDE
Oct, 1993 - No. 3, Dec, 1993 ($1.25, mini-series)
Archie Comics

1-3-See Mighty Mutanimals #7 for 1st app. Merdude .60 1.25

TEEN-AGE ROMANCE (Formerly My Own Romance)
No. 77, Sept, 1960 - No. 86, March, 1962
Marvel Comics (ZPC)

77-86 2.80 7.00 14.00

TEEN-AGE ROMANCES
Jan, 1949 - No. 45, Dec, 1955
St. John Publ. co. (Approved Comics)

1-Baker-c/a(1) 22.00 65.00 150.00
2-Baker-c/a 11.50 34.00 80.00
3-Baker-c/a(3); spanking panel 12.00 36.00 85.00
4,5,7,8-Photo-c; Baker-a(2-3) each 10.00 30.00 65.00
6-Slightly large size; photo-c; part magazine; Baker-a (10/49) 10.00 30.00 70.00
9-Baker-c/a; Kubert-a 12.00 36.00 85.00
10-12,20-Baker-c/a(2-3) each 10.00 30.00 60.00
13-19,21,22-Complete issues by Baker 12.00 36.00 85.00
23-25-Baker-c/a(2-3) each 8.35 25.00 50.00
26,27,33,34,36-42-Baker-a. 38-Suggestive-c. 42-r/Cinderella Love #9; Last pre-code (3/55) 5.35 16.00 32.00
28-30-No Baker-a 3.20 8.00 16.00
31-Baker-c 4.00 10.00 20.00
32-Baker-c/a (1 pg.) 4.00 10.00 20.00
35-Baker-c/a (16 pgs.) 4.70 14.00 28.00
43-45-Baker-a 4.00 11.00 22.00

TEEN-AGE TALK
1964
I.W. Enterprises

Reprint #1-Monkees photo-c 1.80 4.50 9.00
Reprint #5,8,9 .60 1.50 3.00

TEEN-AGE TEMPTATIONS (Going Steady #10 on)(See True Love Pictorial)
Oct, 1952 - No. 9, Aug, 1954
St. John Publishing co.

1-Baker-c/a; has story "Reform School Girl" by Estrada 24.00 73.00 170.00
2-Baker-c 9.15 27.50 55.00
3-7,9-Baker-c/a 11.50 34.00 80.00
8-Teenagers smoke reefers; Baker-c/a 12.00 36.00 85.00
NOTE: ***Estrada** a-1, 3-5.*

TEEN BEAM (Formerly Teen Beat #1)
No. 2, Jan-Feb, 1968
National Periodical Publications

2-Orlando, Drucker-a(r); Monkees photo-c 2.10 6.40 15.00

TEEN BEAT (Becomes Teen Beam #2)
Nov-Dec, 1967
National Periodical Publications

1-Photos & text only; Monkees photo-c 3.00 9.40 22.00

TEEN COMICS (Formerly All Teen; Journey Into Unknown Worlds #36 on)
No. 21, April, 1947 - No. 35, May, 1950
Marvel comics (WFP)

21-Kurtzman's "Hey Look"; Patsy Walker, Cindy (1st app.?), Georgie, Margie app.; Syd Shores-a begins, end #23 9.15 27.50 55.00
22,23,25,27,29,31-35: 22-(6/47)-Becomes Hedy Devine #22 (8/47) on? 5.85 17.50 35.00
24,26,28,30-Kurtzman's "Hey Look" 9.15 27.50 55.00

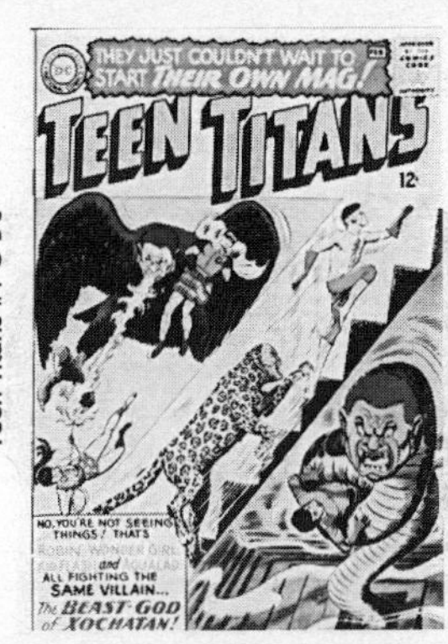

Teen Titans #1 © DC

Tegra Jungle Empress #1 © FOX

Tell it to the Marines #12 © TOBY

GD25 FN65 NM94

TEEN CONFESSIONS
Aug, 1959 - No. 97, Nov, 1976
Charlton Comics
1 7.00 21.00 42.00
2 4.00 10.00 21.00
3-10 3.00 7.50 15.00
11-30 1.80 4.50 9.00
31-Beatles-c 7.50 22.50 45.00
32-36,38-55 1.00 2.50 5.00
37 (1/66)-Beatles Fan Club story; Beatles-c 7.50 22.50 45.00
56-58,60-97: 89,90-Newton-c .50 1.00
59-Kaluta's 1st pro work? (12/69) 1.00 2.50 5.00

TEENIE WEENIES, THE (America's Favorite Kiddie Comic)
No. 10, 1950 - No. 11, Apr-May, 1951 (Newspaper reprints)
Ziff-Davis Publishing Co.
10,11-Painted-c 12.00 36.00 85.00

TEEN-IN (Tippy Teen)
Summer, 1968 - No. 4, Fall, 1969
Tower Comics
nn(#1, Summer, 1968), nn(#2, Spring, 1969),3,4 3.00 7.50 15.00

TEEN LIFE (Formerly Young Life)
No. 3, Winter, 1945 - No. 5, Fall, 1945 (Teenage magazine)
New Age/Quality Comics Group
3-June Allyson photo on-c & story 7.50 22.50 45.00
4-Duke Ellington photo on-c & story 6.35 19.00 38.00
5-Van Johnson, Woody Herman & Jackie Robinson articles; Van Johnson & Woody Herman photos on-c 8.35 25.00 50.00

TEEN ROMANCES
1964
Super Comics
10,11,15-17-Reprints .60 1.50 3.00

TEEN SECRET DIARY (Nurse Betsy Crane #12 on)
Oct, 1959 - No. 11, June, 1961; No. 1, 1972
Charlton Comics
1 4.00 10.00 20.00
2 2.00 5.00 10.00
3-11 1.20 3.00 6.00
1 (1972) .40 1.00 2.00

TEEN TALK (See Teen)

TEEN TITANS (See Brave & the Bold, DC Super-Stars #1, Marvel & DC Present, New Teen Titans, New Titans, Official...Index and Showcase)
1-2/66 - No. 43, 1-2/73; No. 44, 11/76 - No. 53, 2/78
National Periodical Publications/DC Comics
Brave and the Bold #54 (6-7/64)-Origin & 1st app. Teen Titans; Kid Flash, Robin & Aqualad begin 29.00 86.00 200.00
Brave and the Bold #60 (6-7/65)-2nd app. Teen Titans; 1st app. new Wonder Girl (Donna Troy), who joins Titans 9.70 29.00 68.00
Showcase #59 (11-12/65)-3rd app. Teen Titans 8.00 25.00 75.00
1-(1-2/66)-Titans join Peace Corps; Batman, Flash, Aquaman, Wonder Woman cameos 22.00 66.00 155.00
2 11.00 32.00 75.00
3-5: 4-Speedy app. 5.40 16.00 38.00
6-10: 6-Doom Patrol app.; Beast Boy x-over; readers polled on him joining Titans 4.30 12.90 30.00
11-19: 11-Speedy app. 13-X-Mas-c. 18-1st app. Starfire (11-12/68). 19-Wood-i; Speedy begins as regular 2.90 8.60 20.00
20-22: All Neal Adams-a. 21-Hawk & Dove app.; last 12¢ issue. 22-Origin Wonder Girl 3.30 10.00 23.00
23-30: 23-Wonder Girl dons new costume. 25-Flash, Aquaman, Batman, Green Arrow, Green Lantern, Superman, & Hawk & Dove guests; 1st app. Lilith who joins T.T. West in #50. 29-Hawk & Dove & Ocean Master app. 30-Aquagirl app. 1.70 5.10 12.00
31-43: 31-Hawk & Dove app. 36,37-Superboy-r. 38-Green Arrow/Speedy-r; Aquaman/Aqualad story. 39-Hawk & Dove-r. (36-39: 52 pgs.) 1.30 3.00 8.00
44,45,47,49,51,52: 44-Mal becomes the Guardian 1.80 4.50
46-Joker's daughter begins (see Batman Family) 1.70 4.20 10.00
48-Intro Bumblebee; Joker's daughter becomes Harlequin 1.70 4.20 10.00
50-1st revival original Bat-Girl; intro. Teen Titans West 1.50 3.80 9.00
53-Origin retold 1.00 2.00 5.00
NOTE: *Aparo a-36. Buckler c-46-53. Cardy c-1-16. Kane a(p)-19, 22-24, 39r. Tuska a(p)-31, 36, 38, 39. DC Super-Stars #1 (3/76) was released before #44.*

TEEN TITANS SPOTLIGHT (DC)(Value: cover or less)

TEEN TITANS SPOTLIGHT
Aug, 1986 - No. 21, Apr, 1988
DC Comics
1-21 1.10

TEEPEE TIM (...Heap Funny Indian Boy)(Formerly Ha Ha Comics)
No. 100, Feb-Mar, 1955 - No. 102, June-July, 1955
American Comics Group
100-102 3.00 7.50 15.00

TEGRA JUNGLE EMPRESS (Zegra Jungle Empress #2 on)
August, 1948
Fox Features Syndicate
1-Blue Beetle, Rocket Kelly app.; used in **SOTI**, pg. 31 31.00 92.00 215.00

TEKWORLD (William Shatner's... on-c only)
Sept, 1992 - Present ($1.75)
Epic comics (Marvel)
1-Based on Shatner's novel, TekWar, set in L.A. in the year 2120 1.00 2.50
2-27 .70 1.75

TELEVISION (See TV)

TELEVISION COMICS
No. 5, Feb, 1950 - No. 8, Nov, 1950
Standard Comics (Animated Cartoons)
5-1st app. Willy Nilly 7.50 22.50 45.00
6-8: 6 has #2 on inside 5.35 16.00 32.00

TELEVISION PUPPET SHOW (See Spotty the Pup)
1950 - No. 2, Nov, 1950
Avon Periodicals
1,2: 1st app. Speedy Rabbit, Spotty The Pup 11.50 34.00 80.00

TELEVISION TEENS MOPSY (See TV Teens)

TELL IT TO THE MARINES
Mar, 1952 - No. 15, July, 1955
Toby Press Publications
1-Lover O'Leary and His Liberty Belles (with pin-ups), ends #6; Spike & Bat begin, end #6 11.50 34.00 80.00
2-Madame Cobra-c/story 7.00 21.00 42.00
3-5 5.00 15.00 30.00
6-12,14,15: 7-9,14,15-Photo-c 4.00 10.00 20.00
13-John Wayne photo-c 8.35 25.00 50.00
I.W. Reprint #1,9: 1-Exist? 9-r/#1 above 2.00 4.00
Super Reprint #16(1964)-r/#4 above 2.00 4.00

TEMPUS FUGITIVE (DC)(Value: cover or less)

TEN COMMANDMENTS (See Moses & the... and Classics Illustrated Special)

TENDER LOVE STORIES
Feb, 1971 - No. 4, July, 1971 (All 25¢, 52 pgs.)
Skywald Publ. Corp.
1-4 .60 1.50 3.00

Terminator #1 © Cinema 84

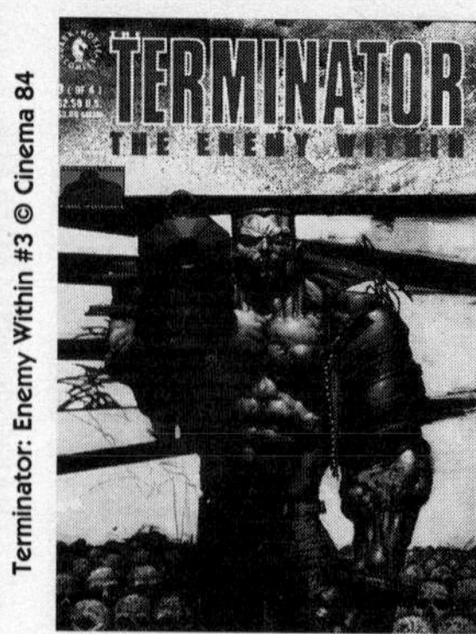

Terminator: Enemy Within #3 © Cinema 84

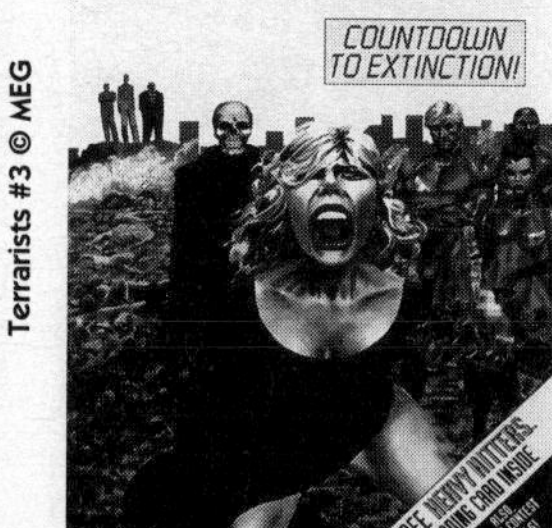

COUNTDOWN TO EXTINCTION!
FREE HEAVY HITTERS TRADING CARD INSIDE

Terrarists #3 © MEG

GD25 FN65 NM94

TENDER ROMANCE (Ideal Romance #3 on)
Dec, 1953 - No. 2, Feb, 1954
Key Publications (Gilmour Magazines)

1-Headlight & lingerie panels; B. Baily-c 10.00 30.00 65.00
2-Bernard Baily-c 5.85 17.50 35.00

TENNESSEE JED (Radio)
nd (1945) (16 pgs.; paper cover; regular size; giveaway)
Fox Syndicate? (Wm. C. Popper & Co.)

nn 12.00 36.00 85.00

TENNIS (...For Speed, Stamina, Strength, Skill)
1956 (16 pgs.; soft cover; 10¢)
Tennis Educational Foundation

Book 1-Endorsed by Gene Tunney, Ralph Kiner, etc. showing how tennis has helped them 4.00 12.00 24.00

TENSE SUSPENSE
Dec, 1958 - No. 2, Feb, 1959
Fago Publications

1,2 5.35 16.00 32.00

TEN STORY LOVE (Formerly a pulp magazine with same title)
V29#3, June-July, 1951 - V36#5(#209), Sept, 1956 (#3-6: 52 pgs.)
Ace Periodicals

V29#3(#177)-Part comic, part text; painted-c 7.50 22.50 45.00
4-6(1/52) 4.00 11.00 22.00
V30#1(3/52)-6(1/53) 3.60 9.00 18.00
V31#1(2/53),V32#2(4/53)-6(12/53) 2.80 7.00 14.00
V33#1(1/54)-3(5#54, #195), V34#4(7/54, #196)-6(10/54, #198) 2.80 7.00 14.00
V35#1(12/54, #199)-3(4/55, #201)-Last precode 2.00 5.00 10.00
V35#4-6(9/55, #201-204), V36#1(11/55, #205)-3, 5(9/56, #209) 1.80 4.50 9.00
V36#4-L.B. Cole-a 4.00 10.00 20.00

TEN WHO DARED (See 4-Color #1178)

TERMINATOR, THE (See Robocop vs. ... & Rust #12 for 1st app.)
Sept, 1988 - No. 17, 1989 ($1.75, color, Baxter paper)
Now Comics

1-Based on movie 2.00 6.90 16.00
2 1.10 3.00 8.00
3-5 1.80 4.50
6-10 1.70 4.25
11,13-17 .80 2.00
12 ($2.95, 52 pgs.)-Intro. John Connor 1.20 3.00
Trade paperback (1989, $9.95) 1.65 4.00 10.00

TERMINATOR, THE
Aug, 1990 - No. 4, Nov, 1990 ($2.50, color, mini-series)
Dark Horse Comics

1-Set 39 years later than the movie 1.70 4.25
2-4 1.00 2.50

TERMINATOR: ALL MY FUTURES PAST, THE
V3#1, Aug, 1990 - V3#2, Sept, 1990 ($1.75, color, mini-series)
Now Comics

V3#1,2 .70 1.75

TERMINATOR: ENDGAME, THE
Sept, 1992 - No. 3, Nov, 1992 ($2.50, color, mini-series)
Dark Horse Comics

1-3: Guice-a(p); painted-c 1.00 2.50

TERMINATOR: HUNTERS AND KILLERS, THE
Mar, 1992 - No. 3, May, 1992 ($2.50, color, mini-series)
Dark Horse Comics

1-3 1.00 2.50

GD25 FN65 NM94

TERMINATOR: ONE SHOT, THE
July, 1991 ($5.95, color, 56 pgs.)
Dark Horse Comics

nn-Matt Wagner-a; contains stiff pop-up inside 2.50 6.00

TERMINATOR: SECONDARY OBJECTIVES, THE
July, 1991 - No. 4, Oct, 1991 ($2.50, color, mini-series)
Dark Horse Comics

1-Gulacy-c/a(p) in all 1.00 2.50
2-4 1.00 2.50

TERMINATOR: THE BURNING EARTH, THE
V2#1, Mar, 1990 - V2#5, July, 1990 ($1.75, color, mini-series)
Now Comics

V2#1-5 .70 1.75
Trade paperback (1990, $9.95)-Reprints V2#1-5 1.65 4.00 10.00

TERMINATOR: THE ENEMY WITHIN, THE
Nov, 1991 - No. 4, Feb, 1992 ($2.50, color, mini-series)
Dark Horse Comics

1-4: All have Simon Bisley painted-c 1.00 2.50

TERMINATOR 2: JUDGEMENT DAY
Early Sept, 1991 - No. 3, Early Oct, 1991 ($1.00, mini-series)
Marvel Comics

1-3: Based on movie sequel; 1-3-Same as nn issues 1.00
nn (1991, $4.95, squarebound, 68 pgs.)-Photo-c 1.00 2.00 5.00
nn (1991, $2.25, B&W, magazine, 68 pgs.) .90 2.25

TERRAFORMERS (Wonder)(Value: cover or less)

TERRANAUTS (Epic)(Value: cover or less)

TERRARISTS (Fantasy General)(Value: cover or less)

TERRARISTS
Nov, 1993 - No. 4, Feb, 1994 ($2.50, mini-series)
Epic Comics (Marvel)

1-4-Bound-in trading cards in all 1.00 2.50

TERRIFIC COMICS (Also see Suspense Comics)
Jan, 1944 - No. 6, Nov, 1944
Continental Magazines

1-Kid Terrific; opium story 129.00 385.00 900.00
2-1st app. The Boomerang by L.B. Cole & Ed Wheelan's "Comics" McCormick, called the world's #1 comic book fan begins 100.00 300.00 700.00
3-Diana becomes Boomerang's costumed aide 86.00 257.00 600.00
4-Classic war-c 100.00 300.00 700.00
5-The Reckoner begins; Boomerang & Diana by L.B. Cole; Schomburg bondage-c 100.00 300.00 700.00
6-L.B. Cole-c/a 86.00 257.00 600.00

NOTE: ***L.B. Cole** a-1, 2(2), 3-6. **Fuje** a-5, 6. **Rico** a-2; c-1. **Schomburg** c-2, 5.*

TERRIFIC COMICS (Formerly Horrific; Wonder Boy #17 on)
No. 14, Dec, 1954; No. 16, Mar, 1955 (No #15)
Mystery Publ.(Comic Media)/(Ajax/Farrell)

14-Art swipe/Advs. into the Unknown #37; injury-to-eye-c; pg. 2, panel 5 swiped from Phantom Stranger #4; surrealistic Palais-a; Human Cross story 14.00 43.00 100.00
16-Wonder Boy-c/story (last pre-code) 10.00 30.00 70.00

TERRIFYING TALES (Formerly Startling Terror Tales #10)
No. 11, Jan, 1953 - No. 15, Apr, 1954
Star Publications

11-Used in **POP**, pgs. 99,100; all Jo-Jo-r 28.00 84.00 195.00
12-Reprints Jo-Jo #19 entirely; L.B. Cole splash 23.00 707.00 160.00
13-All Rulah-r; classic devil-c 29.00 86.00 200.00
14-All Rulah reprints 24.00 72.00 165.00
15-Rulah, Zago-r; used in **SOTI**-r/Rulah #22 24.00 72.00 165.00

NOTE: *All issues have **L.B. Cole** covers; bondage covers-No. 12-14.*

TERROR ILLUSTRATED (Adult Tales of...)

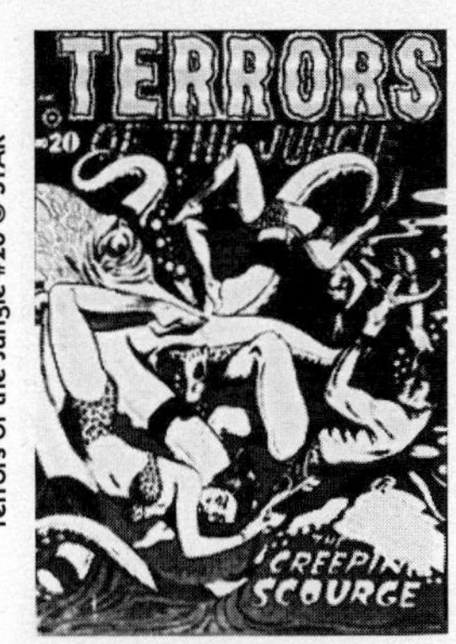

Terrors of the Jungle #20 © STAR

Terry and the Pirates #47 © DELL

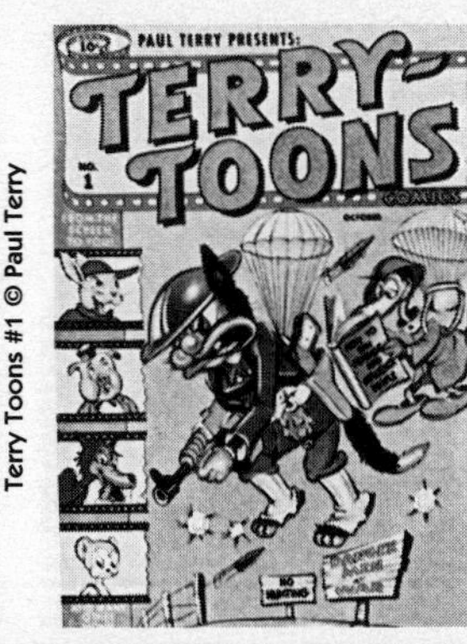

Terry Toons #1 © Paul Terry

GD25 FN65 NM94 | GD25 FN65 NM94

Nov-Dec, 1955 - No. 2, Spring (April on-c), 1956 (Magazine, 25¢)
E.C. Comics

	GD25	FN65	NM94
1-Adult Entertainment on-c	10.00	30.00	60.00
2-Charles Sultan-a	8.35	25.00	50.00

NOTE: ***Craig, Evans, Ingels, Orlando*** *art in each.* ***Crandall*** *c-1, 2.*

TERROR INC. (See A Shadowline Saga #3)
July, 1992 - No. 13, July, 1993 ($1.75)
Marvel Comics

	GD25	FN65	NM94
1-13: 6,7-Punisher-c/story. 9,10-Wolverine-c/story. 13-Ghost Rider app.		.70	1.75

TERRORS OF THE JUNGLE (Formerly Jungle Thrills)
No. 17, 5/52 - No. 21, 2/53; No. 4, 4/53 - No. 10, 9/54
Star Publications

	GD25	FN65	NM94
17-Reprints Rulah #21, used in **SOTI**; L.B. Cole bondage-c	27.00	81.00	190.00
18-Jo-Jo-r	17.00	52.00	120.00
19,20(1952)-Jo-Jo-r; Disbrow-a	16.00	48.00	110.00
21-Jungle Jo, Tangi-r; used in **POP**, pg. 100 & color illos.; shrunken heads on-c	19.00	57.00	130.00
4-10: All Disbrow-a. 5-Jo-Jo-r. 8-Rulah, Jo-Jo-r. 9-Jo-Jo-r; Disbrow-a; Tangi by Orlando10-Rulah-r	16.00	48.00	110.00

NOTE: ***L.B. Cole*** *c-all; bondage c-17, 19, 21, 5, 7.*

TERROR TALES (See Beware Terror Tales)

TERROR TALES (Magazine)
V1#7, 1969 - V6#6, Dec, 1974; V7#1, Apr, 1976 - V10, 1979?
(V1-V6: 52 pgs.; V7 on: 68 pgs.)
Eerie Publications

	GD25	FN65	NM94
V1#7	2.85	8.00	20.00
V1#8-11('69): 9-Bondage-c	1.70	5.00	12.00
V2#1-6('70), V3#1-6('71), V4#1-7('72), V5#1-6('73), V6#1-6('74)	1.50	3.80	9.00
V7#1,4(no V7#2), V8#1-3('77), V9, V10	1.50	3.80	9.00
V7#3-LSD story-r/Weird V3#5	1.50	3.80	9.00

TERRY AND THE PIRATES (See Famous Feature Stories, Merry Christmas From Sears Toyland, Popular Comics, Super Book #3,5,9,16,28, & Super Comics)

TERRY AND THE PIRATES
1939 - 1953 (By Milton Caniff)
Dell Publishing Co.

	GD25	FN65	NM94
Large Feature Comic 2(1939)	50.00	150.00	500.00
Large Feature Comic 6(1939)-r/1936 dailies	50.00	150.00	500.00
4-Color 9(1940)	63.00	190.00	440.00
Large Feature Comic 27('41), 6('42)	40.00	120.00	400.00
4-Color 44('43)	43.00	130.00	300.00
4-Color 101('45)	29.00	86.00	200.00
Buster Brown Shoes giveaway(1938)-32 pgs.; in color	27.00	80.00	185.00
Canada Dry Premiums-Books #1-3(1953, 36 pgs.; 2x5")-Harvey	12.00	36.00	85.00
Family Album(1942)	16.00	48.00	110.00
Gambles Giveaway (1938, 16 pgs.)	7.50	22.50	45.00
Gillmore Giveaway (1938, 24 pgs.)	8.35	25.00	50.00
Popped Wheat Giveaway(1938)-Strip reprints in full color; Caniff-a	1.00	2.50	5.00
Shoe Store giveaway (Weatherbird)(1938, 16 pgs., soft-c)(2-diff.)	7.50	22.50	45.00
Sparked Wheat Giveaway(1942, 16 pgs.)-In color	7.50	22.50	45.00

TERRY AND THE PIRATES
1941 (16 pgs.; regular size)(shipped folded in the mail)
Libby's Radio Premiu

	GD	FN	VF
"Adventure of the Ruby of Genghis Khan" - Each pg. is a puzzle that must be completed to read the story	171.00	514.00	1200.00

TERRY AND THE PIRATES (Formerly Boy Explorers; Long John Silver & the Pirates #30 on) (Daily strip-r) (Two #26's)
No. 3, 4/47 - No. 26, 4/51; No. 26, 6/55 - No. 28, 10/55
Harvey Publications/Charlton No. 26-28

	GD	FN	NM
3(#1)-Boy Explorers by S&K; Terry & the Pirates begin by Caniff; 1st app. The Dragon Lady	30.00	90.00	210.00
4-S&K Boy Explorers	16.00	48.00	110.00
5-11: 11-Man in Black app. by Powell	9.15	27.50	55.00
12-20: 16-Girl threatened with red hot poker	7.50	22.50	45.00
21-26(4/51)-Last Caniff issue & last pre-code issue	6.70	20.00	40.00
26-28('55)(Formerly This Is Suspense)-No Caniff-a	5.00	15.00	30.00

NOTE: ***Powell*** *a (Tommy Tween)-5-10, 12, 14; 15-17(1/2 to 2 pgs. each).*

TERRY BEARS COMICS (TerryToons, The... #4)
June, 1952 - No. 3, Mar, 1953
St. John Publishing Co.

	GD25	FN65	NM94
1-By Paul Terry	5.00	15.00	30.00
2,3	4.00	12.00	24.00

TERRY-TOONS ALBUM (See Giant Comics Edition)

TERRY-TOONS COMICS (1st Series) (Becomes Paul Terry's Comics #85 on; later issues titled "Paul Terry's...")
Oct, 1942 - No. 86, May, 1951
Timely/Marvel No. 1-59 (8/47)(Becomes Best Western No. 58 on?, Marvel)/ St. John No. 60 (9/47) on

	GD25	FN65	NM94
1 (Scarce)-Features characters that 1st app. on movie screen; Gandy Goose & Sourpuss begin; war-c; Gandy Goose c-1-37	104.00	311.00	725.00
2	47.00	141.00	330.00
3-5	31.00	94.00	220.00
6-10: 7-Hitler, Hirohito, Mussolini-c	24.00	72.00	165.00
11-20	14.00	43.00	100.00
21-37	10.00	30.00	70.00
38-Mighty Mouse begins (1st app., 11/45); Mighty Mouse-c begin, end #86; Gandy, Sourpuss welcome Mighty Mouse on-c	94.00	283.00	660.00
39-2nd app. Mighty Mouse	25.00	75.00	175.00
40-49: 43-Infinity-c	12.00	36.00	85.00
50-1st app. Heckle & Jeckle (11/46)	29.00	86.00	200.00
51-60: 55-Infinity-c. 60-(9/47)-Atomic explosion panel; 1st St. John issue	10.00	30.00	60.00
61-84	7.50	22.00	45.00
85,86-Same book as Paul Terry's Comics #85,86 with only a title change; published at same time?	7.50	22.00	45.00

TERRY-TOONS COMICS (2nd Series)
June, 1952 - No. 9, Nov, 1953; 1957; 1958
St. John Publishing Co./Pines

	GD25	FN65	NM94
1-Gandy Goose & Sourpuss begin by Paul Terry	11.50	34.00	80.00
2	6.70	20.00	40.00
3-9	5.85	17.50	35.00
Giant Summer Fun Book 101,102-(Sum, 1957, Sum, 1958, 25¢, Pines)(TV) CBS Television Presents...; Tom Terrific, Mighty Mouse, Heckle & Jeckle Gandy Goose app.	10.00	30.00	60.00

TERRYTOONS, THE TERRY BEARS (Formerly Terry Bears Comics)
No. 4, Summer, 1958 (CBS Television Presents...)
Pines Comics

	GD25	FN65	NM94
4	4.00	10.00	20.00

TESSIE THE TYPIST (Tiny Tessie #24; see Comedy Comics, Gay Comics & Joker Comics)
Summer, 1944 - No. 23, Aug, 1949
Timely/Marvel Comics (20CC)

	GD25	FN65	NM94
1-Doc Rockblock & others by Wolverton	39.00	118.00	275.00
2-Wolverton's Powerhouse Pepper	24.00	72.00	165.00
3-(3/45)-No Wolverton	8.35	25.00	50.00
4,5,7,8-Wolverton-a. 4-(Fall/45)	14.00	43.00	100.00
6-Kurtzman's "Hey Look", 2 pgs. Wolverton-a	15.00	45.00	105.00
9-Wolverton's Powerhouse Pepper (8 pgs.) & 1 pg. Kurtzman's "Hey Look"	18.00	54.00	125.00

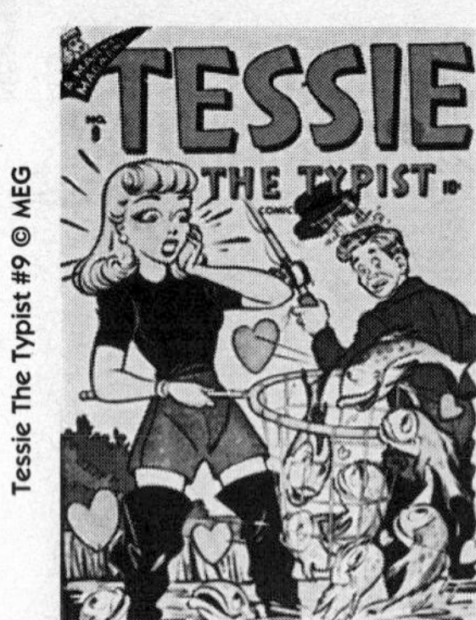

Tessie The Typist #9 © MEG

Texas Kid #10 © MEG

Tex Ritter Western #11 © FAW

GD25 FN65 NM94 GD25 FN65 NM94

10-Wolverton's Powerhouse Pepper (4 pgs.) 16.50 50.00 115.00
11-Wolverton's Powerhouse Pepper (8 pgs.) 18.00 54.00 125.00
12-Wolverton's Powerhouse Pepper (4 pgs.) & 1 pg. Kurtzman's "Hey Look" 16.50 50.00 115.00
13-Wolverton's Powerhouse Pepper (4 pgs.) 16.00 48.00 110.00
14-Wolverton's Dr. Whackyhack (1 pg.); 1-1/2 pgs. Kurtzman's "Hey Look" 12.00 36.00 85.00
15-Kurtzman's "Hey Look" (3 pgs.) & 3 pgs. Giggles 'n' Grins 13.00 40.00 90.00
16-18-Kurtzman's "Hey Look" (?, 2 & 1 pg.) 9.15 27.50 55.00
19-Annie Oakley story (8 pgs.) 7.50 22.50 45.00
20-23: 20-Anti-Wertham editorial (2/49) 6.70 20.00 40.00
NOTE: *Lana app.-21. Millie The Model app.-13, 15, 17, 21. Rusty app.-10, 11, 13, 15, 17.*

TEXAN, THE (Fightin' Marines #15 on; Fightin' Texan #16 on)
Aug, 1948 - No. 15, Oct, 1951
St. John Publishing Co.

1-Buckskin Belle 11.00 32.00 75.00
2 6.35 19.00 38.00
3,10: 10-Oversized issue 5.35 16.00 32.00
4,5,7,15-Baker-c/a 10.00 30.00 60.00
6,9-Baker-c 6.35 19.00 38.00
8,11,13,14-Baker-c/a(2-3) each 10.00 30.00 60.00
12-All Matt Baker-c/a; Peyote story 11.00 32.00 75.00
NOTE: ***Matt Baker** c-4-9, 11-15. **Larsen** a-4-6, 8-10, 15. **Tuska** a-1, 2, 7-9.*

TEXAN, THE (See 4-Color #1027, 1096)

TEXAS JOHN SLAUGHTER (See 4-Color #997, 1181 & Walt Disney Presents #2)

TEXAS KID (See Two-Gun Western, Wild Western)
Jan, 1951 - No. 10, July, 1952
Marvel/Atlas Comics (LMC)

1-Origin; Texas Kid (alias Lance Temple) & his horse Thunder begin; Tuska-a 14.00 43.00 100.00
2 9.15 27.50 55.00
3-10 7.50 22.50 45.00
NOTE: ***Maneely** a-1-4; c-1, 3, 5-10.*

TEXAS RANGERS, THE (See Jace Pearson of... and Superior Stories #4)

TEXAS RANGERS IN ACTION (Formerly Captain Gallant or Scotland Yard?)
No. 5, July, 1956 - No. 79, Aug, 1970 (See Blue Bird Comics)
Charlton Comics

5 5.85 17.50 35.00
6,7,9,10 4.00 10.00 20.00
8-Ditko-a (signed) 5.00 15.00 30.00
11-Williamson-a(5&8 pgs.); Torres/Williamson-a (5 pgs.) 6.35 19.00 38.00
12,14-20 2.80 7.00 14.00
13-Williamson-a (5 pgs); Torres, Morisi-a 5.00 15.00 30.00
21-30: 31-Last 10¢ issue? 2.40 6.00 12.00
31-59 1.80 4.50 9.00
60-Riley's Rangers begin 1.00 2.50 6.00
61-70: 65-1st app. The Man Called Loco, origin in #67 1.60 4.00
71-79 .80 2.00
76(Modern Comics-r, 1977) 1.00

TEXAS SLIM (See A-1 Comics #2-8,10)

TEX DAWSON, GUN-SLINGER (Gunslinger #2 on)
January, 1973 (20¢)(Also see Western Kid, 1st series)
Marvel Comics Group

1-Steranko-c; Williamson-r (4 pgs.); Tex Dawson-r by Romita(3) from 1955; Tuska-r 1.50

TEX FARNUM (See Wisco)

TEX FARRELL (...Pride of the Wild West)
Mar-Apr, 1948
D. S. Publishing Co.

1-Tex Farrell & his horse Lightning; Shelly-c 10.00 30.00 65.00

TEX GRANGER (Formerly Calling All Boys; see True Comics)
No. 18, June, 1948 - No. 24, Sept, 1949
Parents' Magazine Institute/Commended

18-Tex Granger & his horse Bullet begin 8.35 25.00 50.00
19 6.70 20.00 40.00
20-24: 22-Wild Bill Hickok story. 23-Vs. Billy the Kid 5.00 15.00 30.00

TEX MORGAN (See Blaze Carson and Wild Western)
Aug, 1948 - No. 9, Feb, 1950
Marvel Comics (CCC)

1-Tex Morgan, his horse Lightning & sidekick Lobo begin 19.00 58.00 135.00
2 12.00 36.00 85.00
3-6: 3,4-Arizona Annie app. 10.00 30.00 60.00
7-9: All photo-c. 7-Captain Tootsie by Beck. 8-18 pg. story "The Terror of Rimrock Valley"; Diablo app. 13.00 40.00 90.00
NOTE: *Tex Taylor app.-6, 7, 9. **Brodsky** c-6. **Syd Shores** c-2, 5.*

TEX RITTER WESTERN (Movie star; singing cowboy; see Six-Gun Heroes and Western Hero)
Oct, 1950 - No. 46, May, 1959 (Photo-c: 1-21)
Fawcett No. 1-20 (1/54)/Charlton No. 21 on

1-Tex Ritter, his stallion White Flash & dog Fury begin; photo front/back-c begin 55.00 165.00 385.00
2 24.00 72.00 165.00
3-5: 5-Last photo back-c 19.00 58.00 135.00
6-10 16.00 48.00 110.00
11-19 10.00 30.00 70.00
20-Last Fawcett issue (1/54) 11.50 34.00 80.00
21-1st Charlton issue; photo-c (3/54) 13.00 40.00 90.00
22-B&W photo back-c begin, end #32 9.15 27.50 55.00
23-30: 23-25-Young Falcon app. 7.50 22.50 45.00
31-38,40-45 6.35 19.00 38.00
39-Williamson-a; Whitman-c (1/58) 8.35 25.00 50.00
46-Last issue 7.50 22.50 45.00

TEX TAYLOR (...The Fighting Cowboy on-c #1, 2)(See Blaze Carson, Kid Colt, Tex Morgan, Wild West, Wild Western, & Wisco)
Sept, 1948 - No. 9, March, 1950
Marvel Comics (HPC)

1-Tex Taylor & his horse Fury begin 19.00 58.00 135.00
2 11.50 34.00 80.00
3 10.00 30.00 70.00
4-6: All photo-c. 4-Anti-Wertham editorial. 5,6-Blaze Carson app. 11.50 34.00 85.00
7-Photo-c; 18 pg. Movie-Length Thriller "Trapped in Time's Lost Land!" with sabre toothed tigers, dinosaurs; Diablo app. 13.50 41.00 95.00
8-Photo-c; 18 pg. Movie-Length Thriller "The Mystery of Devil-Tree Plateau!" with dwarf horses, dwarf people & a lost miniature Inca type village; Diablo app. 13.50 41.00 95.00
9-Photo-c; 18 pg. Movie-Length Thriller "Guns Along the Border!" Captain Tootsie by Schreiber; Nimo the Mountain Lion app. 13.50 41.00 95.00
NOTE: ***Syd Shores** c-1-3.*

THANE OF BAGARTH (Also see Hercules, 1967 series)
No. 24, Oct, 1985 - No. 25, Dec, 1985
Charlton Comics

24,25 1.00

THANOS QUEST, THE (See Capt. Marvel #25, Infinity Gauntlet, Iron Man #55, Logan's Run, Marvel Feature #12, Silver Surfer #34 & Warlock #9)
1990 - No. 2, 1990 ($4.95, squarebound, 52 pgs.)
Marvel Comics

1-Both have Starlin scripts & covers 1.30 3.00 7.50
2 1.00 3.00 6.00
1,2-2nd printings ($4.95) 1.00 2.00 5.00

The Thing! #9 © CC

Thing #36 © MEG

The Thing From Another World #4 © DH

GD25 FN65 NM94

THAT CHEMICAL REFLEX
1994 ($2.50, B&W, adult)
CFD Productions

1-Dan Brereton-a — 1.00 2.50

THAT DARN CAT (See Movie Comics & Walt Disney Showcase #19)

THAT'S MY POP! GOES NUTS FOR FAIR
1939 (76 pgs.) (B&W)
Bystander Press

nn-by Milt Gross — 20.00 60.00 140.00

THAT THE WORLD MAY BELIEVE
No date (16 pgs.) (Graymoor Friars distr.)
Catechetical Guild Giveaway

nn — 1.60 4.00 8.00

THAT WILKIN BOY (Meet Bingo...)
Jan, 1969 - No. 52, Oct, 1982
Archie Publications

1 — 3.00 7.50 15.00
2-10 — 1.60 4.00 8.00
11-26: 12-26-Giants — 1.00 2.00 5.00
27-52 — .80 2.00

T.H.E. CAT (TV)
Mar, 1967 - No. 4, Oct, 1967 (All have photo-c)
Dell Publishing Co.

1 — 2.90 9.00 20.00
2-4 — 2.00 6.00 14.00

THERE'S A NEW WORLD COMING (Spire Christian)(Value: cover or less)

THEY ALL KISSED THE BRIDE (See Cinema Comics Herald)

THEY RING THE BELL
1946
Fox Feature Syndicate

1 — 10.00 30.00 65.00

THIEF OF BAGHDAD (See 4-Color #1229)

THIMBLE THEATRE STARRING POPEYE
1931 - No. 2, 1932 (25¢, B&W, 52 pgs.)(Rare)
Sonnet Publishing Co.

1-Daily strip serial-r in both by Segar — 80.00 240.00 800.00
2 — 70.00 210.00 700.00

NOTE: *The very first Popeye reprint book. Popeye first entered Thimble Theatre in 1929.*

THIMK (Magazine) (Satire)
May, 1958 - No. 6, May, 1959
Counterpoint

1 — 5.35 16.00 32.00
2-6 — 4.00 10.00 20.00

THING!, THE (Blue Beetle #18 on)
Feb, 1952 - No. 17, Nov, 1954
Song Hits No. 1,2/Capitol Stories/Charlton

1-Weird/horror stories in all; shrunken head-c — 50.00 150.00 350.00
2,3 — 36.00 107.00 250.00
4-6,8,10: 5-Severed head-c; headlights — 27.00 80.00 185.00
7-Injury to eye-c & inside panel; E.C. swipes from Vault of Horror #28 — 43.00 130.00 300.00
9-Used in **SOTI**, pg. 388 & illo "Stomping on the face is a form of brutality which modern children learn early" — 49.00 148.00 345.00
11-Necronomicon story; Hansel & Gretel parody; Injury-to-eye panel; Check-a — 39.00 118.00 275.00
12- "Cinderella" parody; Ditko-c/a; lingerie panels — 52.00 156.00 365.00
13,15-Ditko-c/a(3 & 5); 13-Ditko E.C. swipe/Haunt of Fear #15(#1) "House of Horror" — 52.00 156.00 365.00
14-Extreme violence/torture; Rumpelstiltskin story; Ditko-c/a(4) — 52.00 156.00 365.00
16-Injury to eye panel — 33.00 100.00 230.00
17-Ditko-c; classic parody "Through the Looking Glass"; Powell-r/Beware Terror Tales #1 & recolored — 44.00 133.00 310.00

NOTE: *Excessive violence, severed heads, injury to eye are common No. 5 on.* ***Al Fago*** *c-4.* ***Forgione*** *c-1i, 2, 6, 8, 9.* ***Palais*** *c-16. All* ***Ditko*** *issues #14, 15.*

THING, THE (See Fantastic Four, Marvel Fanfare, Marvel Feature #11, 12 & Marvel Two-In-One)
July, 1983 - No. 36, June, 1986
Marvel Comics Group

1-Life story of Ben Grimm; Byrne scripts begin — .90 2.25
2-36: 5-Spider-Man, She-Hulk app. — 1.30

NOTE: ***Byrne*** *a-2i, 7; c-1, 7, 36i; scripts-1-13, 19-22.* ***Sienkiewicz*** *c-13i.*

THING, THE (From Another World)
1991 - No. 2, 1992 ($2.95, color, mini-series, stiff-c)
Dark Horse Comics

1,2-Based on Universal movie; painted-c/a — 1.20 3.00

THING FROM ANOTHER WORLD: CLIMATE OF FEAR, THE
July, 1992 - No. 4, Dec, 1992 ($2.50, color, mini-series)
Dark Horse Comics

1-4: Painted-c — 1.00 2.50

THING FROM ANOTHER WORLD: ETERNAL VOWS
Dec, 1993 - No. 4, 1994 ($2.50, color, mini-series)
Dark Horse Comics

1-4-Gulacy-c/a — 1.00 2.50

THIRD WORLD WAR (Fleetway)(Value: cover or less)

THIRTEEN (...Going on 18)
11-1/61-62 - No. 25, 12/67; No. 26, 7/69 - No. 29, 1/71
Dell Publishing Co.

1 — 5.85 17.50 35.00
2-10 — 4.70 14.00 28.00
11-29: 26-29-r — 3.20 8.00 20.00

NOTE: ***John Stanley*** *script-No. 3-29; art?*

13: ASSASSIN (TSR)(Value: cover or less)

THIRTY SECONDS OVER TOKYO (See American Library)

THIS IS SUSPENSE! (Formerly Strange Suspense Stories; Strange Suspense Stories #27 on)
No. 23, Feb, 1955 - No. 26, Aug, 1955
Charlton Comics

23-Wood-a(r)/A Star Presentation #3 "Dr. Jekyll & Mr. Hyde"; last pre-code issue — 16.00 48.00 110.00
24-Censored Fawcett-r; Evans-a (r/This Magazine Is Haunted #1) — 10.00 30.00 60.00
25,26: 26-Marcus Swayze-a — 6.70 20.00 40.00

THIS IS THE PAYOFF (See Pay-Off)

THIS IS WAR
No. 5, July, 1952 - No. 9, May, 1953
Standard Comics

5-Toth-a — 10.00 30.00 60.00
6,9-Toth-a — 8.35 25.00 50.00
7,8: 8-Ross Andru-c — 3.60 9.00 18.00

THIS IS YOUR LIFE, DONALD DUCK (See 4-Color #1109)

THIS MAGAZINE IS CRAZY (Crazy #? on)
V3#2, July, 1957 - V4#8, Feb, 1959 (25¢, magazine, 68 pgs.)
Charlton Publ. (Humor Magazines)

V3#2-V4#7: V4#5-Russian Sputnik-c parody — 4.00 12.00 24.00
V4#8-Davis-a (8 pgs.) — 5.35 16.00 32.00

THIS MAGAZINE IS HAUNTED (Danger and Adventure #22 on)
Oct, 1951 - No. 14, 12/53; No. 15, 2/54 - V3#21, Nov, 1954
Fawcett Publications/Charlton No. 15(2/54) on

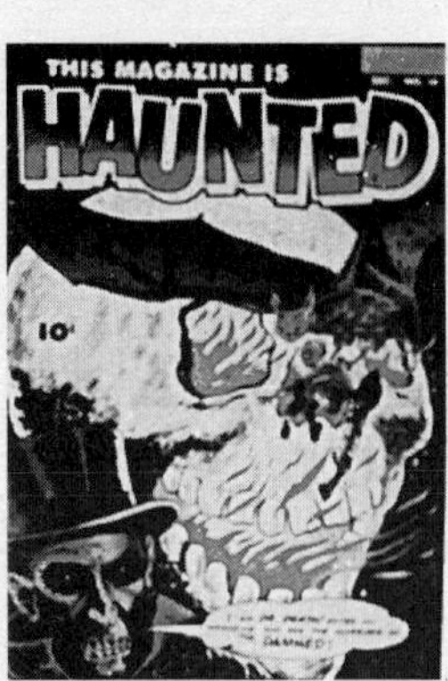

This Magazine Is Haunted #14 © FAW

Thor #277 © MEG

Thor #478 © MEG

GD25 FN65 NM94

1-Evans-a(i?); Dr. Death as host begins 36.00 107.00 250.00
2,5-Evans-a 25.00 75.00 175.00
3,4: 3-Vampire-c/story 13.00 40.00 90.00
6-9,11,12,14 10.00 30.00 70.00
10-Severed head-c 16.50 50.00 115.00
13-Severed head-c/story 16.00 48.00 110.00
15,20: 15-Dick Giordano-c. 20-Cover is swiped from panel in The Thing #16 10.00 30.00 60.00
16,19-Ditko-c. 19-Injury-to-eye panel; story-r/#1 19.00 57.00 130.00
17-Ditko-c/a(4); blood drainage story 24.00 72.00 165.00
18-Ditko-c/a(1 story); E.C. swipe/Haunt of Fear #5; injury-to-eye panel; reprints "Caretaker of the Dead" from Beware Terror Tales & recolored 20.00 60.00 140.00
21-Ditko-c, Evans-a 17.00 52.00 120.00

NOTE: *Baily a-1, 3, 4, 21r/#1.* ***Moldoff*** *c/a-1-13.* ***Powell*** *a-3-5, 11, 12, 17.* ***Shuster*** *a-18-20. Issues 19-21 have reprints which have been recolored from This Magazine is Haunted #1.*

THIS MAGAZINE IS HAUNTED (2nd Series) (Formerly Zaza the Mystic; Outer Space #17 on)
V2#12, July, 1957 - V2#16, April, 1958
Charlton Comics

V2#12-14-Ditko-c/a in all 20.00 60.00 140.00
15-No Ditko-c/a 4.00 12.00 24.00
16-Ditko-a 13.50 41.00 95.00

THIS MAGAZINE IS WILD (See Wild)

THIS WAS YOUR LIFE (Chick)(Value: cover or less)

THOR (See Avengers #1, Giant-Size..., Marvel Collectors Item Classics, Marvel Graphic Novel #33, Marvel Preview, Marvel Spectacular, Marvel Treasury Edition, Special Marvel Edition & Tales of Asgard)

THOR (Formerly Journey Into Mystery)(The Mighty Thor #413 on)
March, 1966 - Present
Marvel Comics Group

126-Thor continues (#125-130 Thor vs. Hercules) 12.00 36.00 95.00
127-133,135-140: 127-1st app. Pluto 5.00 16.00 42.00
134-Intro High Evolutionary 7.00 20.00 54.00
141-157,159,160: 146-Inhumans begin (early app.), end #151 (see Fantastic Four #45 for 1st app.). 146,147-Origin The Inhumans. 148,149-Origin Black Bolt in each. 149-Origin Medusa, Crystal, Maximus, Gorgon, Kornak 4.00 11.00 28.00
158-Origin-r/#83; 158,159-Origin Dr. Blake (Thor) 7.00 22.00 58.00
161,167,170-179: 179-Last Kirby issue 2.00 7.00 18.00
162,168,169-Origin Galactus; Kirby-a 4.00 11.00 30.00
163,164-2nd & 3th brief cameo Warlock (Him) 3.00 8.00 20.00
165-1st full app. Warlock (Him) (6/69, see Fantastic Four #67); last 12¢ issue; Kirby-a 6.00 17.00 44.00
166-2nd full app. Warlock (Him); battles Thor 5.00 15.00 39.00
180,181-Neal Adams-a 2.00 5.00 12.00
182-192,194-200 1.00 2.50 6.00
193-(25¢, 52 pgs.); Silver Surfer x-over 4.00 12.00 32.00
201-250: 225-Intro. Firelord 1.60 4.00
251-280: 271-Iron Man x-over. 274-Death of Balder the Brave 1.20 3.00
281-299: 294-Origin Asgard & Odin 1.00 2.50
300-(12/80)-End of Asgard; origin of Odin & The Destroyer 1.00 2.50 6.00
301-336: 316-Iron Man x-over .80 1.90
337-Simonson-c/a begins, ends #382; Beta Ray Bill becomes new Thor 1.00 2.50 6.00
338-Two variants exist, 60¢ & 75¢ cover price 1.40 3.50
339,340: 340-Donald Blake returns as Thor .80 1.90
341-373,375-381,383: 341-Clark Kent & Lois Lane cameo. 373-X-Factor tie-in 1.40
374-Mutant Massacre; X-Factor app. 1.50 3.80 9.00
382-($1.25)-Anniversary issue; last Simonson-a 1.00 2.50
384-Intro. new Thor .90 2.25
385-399,401-410,413-428: 385-Hulk x-over. 391-Spider-Man x-over; 1st Eric Masterson. 395-Intro Earth Force. 408-Eric Masterson becomes Thor. 427, 428-Excalibur x-over 1.25
400-($1.75, 68 pgs.)-Origin Loki 1.00 2.50
411-Intro New Warriors (apps. in costume in last panel); Juggernaut-c/story 1.30 3.25
412-1st full app. New Warriors (Marvel Boy, Kid Nova, Namorita, Night Thrasher, Firestar & Speedball) 2.70 8.00 19.00
429,430-Ghost Rider x-over 1.30 3.25
431,434-443: 434-Capt. America x-over. 437-Thor vs. Quasar; Hercules app.; Tales of Asgard back-up stories begin. 443-Dr. Strange & Silver Surfer x-over; last $1.00-c 1.50
432-($1.50, 52 pgs.)-Thor's 300th app. (vs. Loki); reprints origin & 1st app. from Journey into Mystery #83 1.30 3.25
433-Intro new Thor 1.00 2.50 5.50
444-449,451-473: 448-Spider-Man-c/story. 455,456-Dr. Strange back-up. 457-Old Thor returns (3 pgs.). 459-Intro Thunderstrike. 460-Starlin scripts begin. 465-Super Skrull app. 466-Drax app. 469,470-Infinity Watch x-over. 472-Intro the Godlings 1.50
450-($2.50, 68 pgs.)-Flip-book format; r/story JIM #87 (1st Loki) plus-c plus a gallery of past-c; gatefold-c 1.20 3.00
474,476-485: 474-Begin $1.50-c; bound-in trading card sheet 1.50
475-($2.00, 52 pgs.)-Regular edition .80 2.00
475-($2.50, 52 pgs.)-Collectors edition w/foil embossed-c 1.00 2.50
Special 2(9/66)-See Journey Into Mystery for 1st annual 5.30 16.00 42.00
King Size Special 3(1/71) 1.50 3.80 9.00
Special 4(12/71)-r/Thor #131,132 & JIM #113 1.50 3.80 9.00
Annual 5-8: 5(11/76). 6(10/77)-Guardians of the Galaxy app. 7(1978). 8(1979)-Thor vs. Zeus-c/story 1.20 2.90 7.00
Annual 9-12: 9('81). 10('82). 11('83). 12('84) 1.40 3.50
Annual 13-16: 13(1985). 14('89, $2.00, 68 pgs.)-Atlantis Attacks. 15('90, $2.00, 68 pgs.). 16('91, $2.00, 68 pgs.)-3 pg. origin; Guardians of the Galaxy x-over .80 2.00
Annual 17 (1992, $2.25, 68 pgs.) .90 2.25
Annual 18 (1993, $2.95, 68 pgs.)-Polybagged w/card 1.20 3.00
Annual 19 (1994, $2.95, 68 pgs.) 1.20 3.00
...Alone Against the Celestials nn (6/92, $5.95)-r/Thor #387-389 1.00 2.50 6.00

NOTE: ***Neal Adams*** *a-180,181; c-179-181.* ***Austin*** *a-342i, 346i; c-312i.* ***Buscema*** *a(p)-178, 182-213, 215-226, 231-238, 241-253, 254r, 256-259, 272-278, 283-285, 370, Annual 6, 8, 11i; c(p)-175, 182-196, 198-200, 202-204, 206, 211, 212, 215, 219, 221, 226, 256, 259, 261, 262, 272-278, 283, 289, 370, Annual 6.* ***Everett*** *a(i)-143, 170-175; c(i)-171, 172, 174, 176, 241.* ***Gil Kane*** *a-318p; c(p)-201, 205, 207-210, 216, 220, 222, 223, 231, 233-240, 242, 243, 318.* ***Kirby*** *a(p)-126-177, 179, 194r, 254r; c(p)-126-169, 171-174, 176-178, 249-253, 255, 257, 258, Annual 5, Special 1-4.* ***Mooney*** *a(i)-201, 204, 214-216, 218, 322i, 324i, 325i, 327i.* ***Sienkiewicz*** *c-332, 333, 335.* ***Simonson*** *a-260-271p, 337-354, 357-367, 380, Annual 7p; c-260, 263-271, 337-355, 357-369, 371, 373-382, Annual 7.* ***Starlin*** *c-213.*

THOR CORPS
Sept, 1993 - No. 4, Dec, 1993 ($1.75, mini-series)
Marvel Comics

1-4: 1-Invaders cameo. 2-Invaders app. 3-Spider-Man 2099, Rawhide Kid, Two-Gun Kid & Kid Colt app. 4-Painted-c .70 1.75

THOSE MAGNIFICENT MEN IN THEIR FLYING MACHINES (See Movie Comics)

THREE CABALLEROS (See 4-Color #71)

THREE CHIPMUNKS, THE (See 4-Color #1042)

THREE COMICS (Also see Spiritman)
1944 (10¢, 52 pgs.) (2 different covers exist)
The Penny King Co.

1,3,4-Lady Luck, Mr. Mystic, The Spirit app. (3 Spirit sections bound together); Lou Fine-a 18.00 54.00 125.00

NOTE: *No. 1 contains Spirit Sections 4/9/44 - 4/23/44, and No. 4 is also from 4/44.*

3-D (NOTE: The prices of all the 3-D comics listed include glasses. Deduct 40-50 percent if glasses are missing, and reduce slightly if glasses are loose.)

3-D ACTION
Jan, 1954 (Oversized, 15¢)(2 pairs of glasses included)

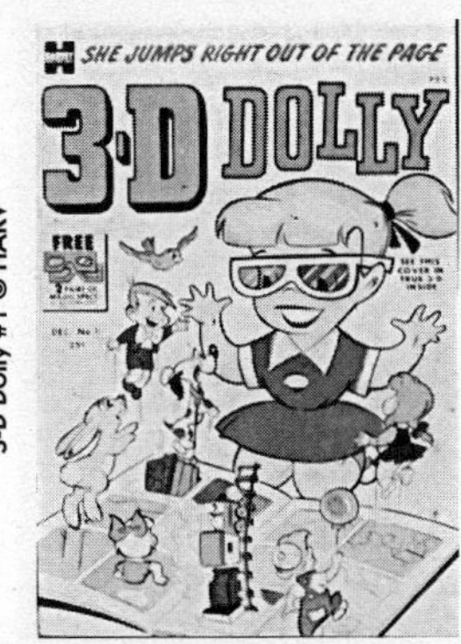

SHE JUMPS RIGHT OUT OF THE PAGE
3-D DOLLY
FREE

3-D Dolly #1 © HARV

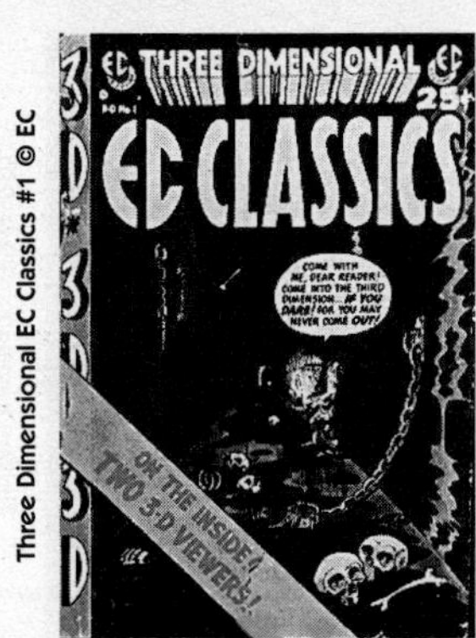

Three Dimensional EC Classics #1 © EC

ONLY 15¢
3-D
TALES OF THE WEST
ONLY 15¢

3-D Tales of the West #1 © MEG

GD25 FN65 NM94

Atlas Comics (ACI)
1-Battle Brady; Sol Brodsky-c 35.00 105.00 245.00

3-D ADVENTURE COMICS (Stats)(Value: cover or less)

3-D ALIEN TERROR (Eclipse)(Value: cover or less)

3-D ANIMAL FUN (See Animal Fun)

3-D BATMAN (Also see Batman 3-D)
1953 (Reprinted in 1966)
National Periodical Publications
1953-(25¢)-Reprints Batman #42 & 48 (Penguin-c/story); Tommy Tomorrow app.; came with pair of 3-D Bat glasses 93.00 278.00 740.00
1966-Tommy Tomorrow app.; Penguin-c/story(r); has inside-c photos of Batman & Robin from TV show (50¢) 34.00 103.00 240.00

3-D CIRCUS
1953 (25¢, came w/glasses)
Fiction House Magazines (Real Adventures Publ.)
1 35.00 105.00 245.00

3-D COMICS (See Mighty Mouse, Tor and Western Fighters)

3-D DOLLY
December, 1953 (25¢, came with 2 pairs of glasses)
Harvey Publications
1-Richie Rich story redrawn from his 1st app. in Little Dot #1; shows cover in 3-D on inside 22.00 65.00 150.00

3-D-ELL
1953 - No. 3, 1953 (3-D comics) (25¢, came w/glasses?)
Dell Publishing Co.
1,2-Rootie Kazootie 37.00 111.00 260.00
3-Flukey Luke 34.00 103.00 240.00

3-D EXOTIC BEAUTIES (3-D Zone)(Value: cover or less)

3-D FEATURES PRESENTS JET PUP
Oct-Dec (Winter on-c), 1953 (25¢, came w/glasses)
Dimensions Publications
1-Irving Spector-a(2) 35.00 105.00 245.00

3-D FUNNY MOVIES
1953 (25¢, came w/glasses)
Comic Media
1-Bugsey Bear & Paddy Pelican 35.00 105.00 245.00

THREE-DIMENSION ADVENTURES (Superman)
1953 (25¢, large size, came w/glasses)
National Periodical Publications
nn-Origin Superman (new art) 94.00 281.00 750.00

THREE DIMENSIONAL ALIEN WORLDS (Pacific)(Value: cover or less)

THREE DIMENSIONAL DNAGENTS (See New DNAgents)

THREE DIMENSIONAL E. C. CLASSICS (Three Dimensional Tales From the Crypt No. 2)
Spring, 1954 (Prices include glasses; came with 2 pair)
E. C. Comics
1-Stories by Wood (Mad #3), Krigstein (W.S. #7), Evans (F.C. #13), & Ingels (CSS #5); Kurtzman-c (rare in high grade due to unstable paper) 66.00 195.00 525.00
NOTE: *Stories redrawn to 3-D format. Original stories not necessarily by artists listed. CSS: Crime SuspenStories; F.C.: Frontline Combat; W.S.: Weird Science.*

THREE DIMENSIONAL TALES FROM THE CRYPT (Formerly Three Dimensional E. C. Classics)(Cover title: ...From the Crypt of Terror)
No. 2, Spring, 1954 (Prices include glasses; came with 2 pair)
E. C. Comics
2-Davis (TFTC #25), Elder (VOH #14), Craig (TFTC #24), & Orlando (TFTC #22) stories; Feldstein-c (rare in high grade due to unstable paper) 66.00 195.00 525.00
NOTE: *Stories redrawn to 3-D format. Original stories not necessarily by artists listed. TFTC: Tales From the Crypt; VOH: Vault of Horror.*

3-D LOVE
December, 1953 (25¢, came w/glasses)
Steriographic Publ. (Mikeross Publ.)
1 35.00 105.00 245.00

3-D NOODNICK (See Noodnick)

3-D ROMANCE
January, 1954 (25¢, came w/glasses)
Steriographic Publ. (Mikeross Publ.)
1 35.00 105.00 245.00

3-D SHEENA, JUNGLE QUEEN (Also see Sheena 3-D)
1953 (25¢, came w/glasses)
Fiction House Magazines
1-Maurice Whitman-c 64.00 190.00 445.00

3-D SUBSTANCE (3-D Zone)(Value: cover or less)

3-D TALES OF THE WEST
Jan, 1954 (Oversized) (15¢, came with 2 pair of glasses)
Atlas Comics (CPS)
1 (3-D)-Sol Brodsky-c 37.00 111.00 260.00

3-D THREE STOOGES (Eclipse)(Value: cover or less)

3-D WHACK (See Whack)

3-D ZONE, THE (3-D Zone)(Value: cover or less)

3 FUNMAKERS, THE
1908 (64 pgs.) (10x15")
Stokes and Company
nn-Maude, Katzenjammer Kids, Happy Hooligan (1904-06 Sunday strip reprints in color) 40.00 120.00 400.00

3 LITTLE PIGS (See 4-Color #218)

3 LITTLE PIGS, THE (See Walt Disney Showcase #15 & 21)
May, 1964; No. 2, Sept, 1968 (Walt Disney)
Gold Key
1-Reprints 4-Color #218 4.00 10.00 20.00
2 2.40 6.00 12.00

THREE MOUSEKETEERS, THE (1st Series)(See Funny Stuff #1)
3-4/56 - No. 24, 9-10/59; No. 25, 8-9/60 - No. 26, 10-12/60
National Periodical Publications
1 20.00 60.00 140.00
2 10.00 30.00 70.00
3-10: 6,8-Grey tone-c 9.15 27.50 55.00
11-26: 24-Cover says 11/59, inside says 9-10/59 7.50 22.50 45.00
NOTE: ***Rube Grossman** a-1-26. **Sheldon Mayer** a-1-8; c-1-7.*

THREE MOUSEKETEERS, THE (2nd Series) (See Super DC Giant)
May-June, 1970 - No. 7, May-June, 1971 (#5-7: 68 pgs.)
National Periodical Publications
1-Mayer-r in all 1.70 5.00 12.00
2-7: 5-Dodo & the Frog, Bo Bunny & Doodles Duck begin 1.20 2.90 7.00

THREE MUSKETEERS, THE (See Disney's The Three Musketeers)

THREE NURSES (Confidential Diary #12-17; Career Girl Romances #24 on)
V3#18, May, 1963 - V3#23, Mar, 1964
Charlton Comics
V3#18-23 1.00 2.00 5.00

THREE RASCALS
1958; 1963
I. W. Enterprises
I.W. Reprint #1,2,10: 1-(Says Super Comics on inside)-(M.E.'s Clubhouse Rascals). #2-(1958). 10-(1963)-r/#1 .80 2.00 4.00

The Three Stooges #9 © Norman Maurer Prod.

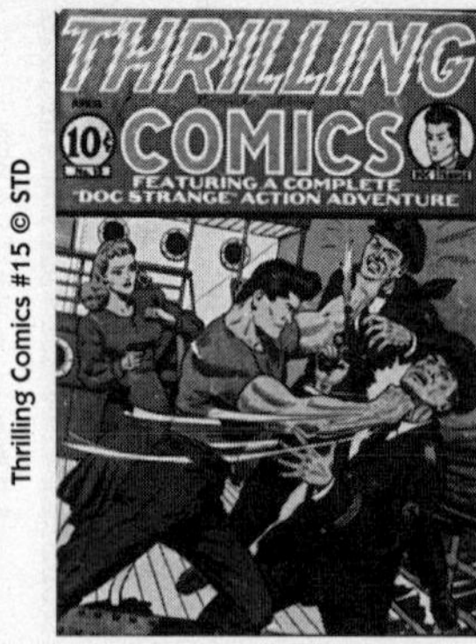

THRILLING
10¢
COMICS
FEATURING A COMPLETE "DOC STRANGE" ACTION ADVENTURE

Thrilling Comics #15 © STD

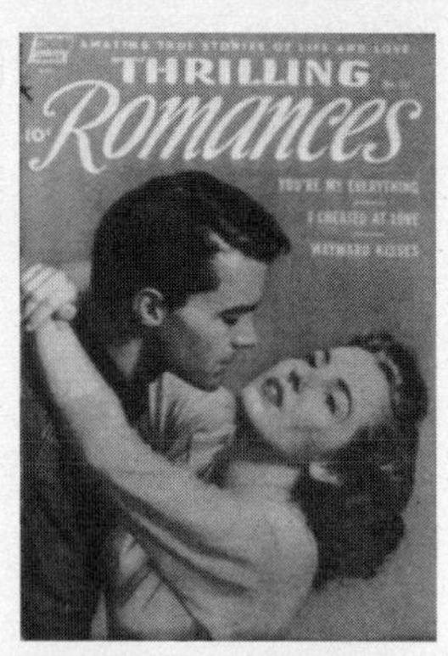

Thrilling Romances #20 © STD

GD25 FN65 NM94

THREE RING COMICS
March, 1945
Spotlight Publishers
1-Funny animal 10.00 30.00 70.00

THREE RING COMICS (Also see Captain Wizard & Meteor Comics)
April, 1946
Century Publications
1-Prankster-c; Captain Wizard, Impossible Man, Race Wilkins, King O'Leary, & Dr. Mercy app. 22.00 65.00 150.00

THREE ROCKETEERS (See Blast-Off)

THREE STOOGES (See Comic Album #18, The Little Stooges, March of Comics #232, 248, 268, 280, 292, 304, 316, 336, 373, Movie Classics & Comics & 3-D Three Stooges)

THREE STOOGES
Feb, 1949 - No. 2, May, 1949; Sept, 1953 - No. 7, Oct, 1954
Jubilee No. 1,2/St. John No. 1 (9/53) on
1-(Scarce, 1949)-Kubert-a; infinity-c 82.00 246.00 575.00
2-(Scarce)-Kubert, Maurer-a 64.00 193.00 450.00
1(9/53)-Hollywood Stunt Girl by Kubert (7 pgs.) 54.00 160.00 375.00
2(3-D, 10/53, 25¢)-Came w/glasses; Stunt Girl story by Kubert 39.00 118.00 275.00
3(3-D, 11/53, 25¢)-Came w/glasses; has 3-D-c 39.00 118.00 275.00
4(3/54)-7(10/54): 4-1st app. Li'l Stooge? 30.00 90.00 210.00
NOTE: *All issues have* ***Kubert-Maurer*** *art &* ***Maurer*** *covers. 6, 7-Partial photo-c.*

THREE STOOGES
No. 1043, Oct-Dec, 1959 - No. 55, June, 1972
Dell Publishing Co./Gold Key No. 10 (10/62) on
4-Color 1043 (#1) 19.00 58.00 135.00
4-Color 1078,1127,1170,1187 10.00 30.00 70.00
6(9-11/61) - 10: 6-Professor Putter begins; ends #16 10.00 30.00 60.00
11-14,16-20: 17-The Little Monsters begin (5/64)(1st app.?) 7.50 22.50 45.00
15-Go Around the World in a Daze (movie scenes) 9.15 27.50 55.00
21,23-30 6.70 20.00 40.00
22-Movie scenes from "The Outlaws Is Coming" 7.50 22.50 45.00
31-55 5.85 17.50 35.00
NOTE: *All Four Colors, 6-50, 52-55 have photo-c.*

THREE STOOGES IN 3-D, THE (Eternity)(Value: cover or less)

3 WORLDS OF GULLIVER (See 4-Color #1158)

THRILL COMICS (See Flash Comics, Fawcett)

THRILLER (DC)(Value: cover or less)

THRILLING ADVENTURES IN STAMPS COMICS (Formerly Stamp Comics)
V1#8, Jan, 1953 (25¢, 100 pgs.)
Stamp Comics, Inc. (Very Rare)
V1#8-Harrison, Wildey, Kiefer, Napoli-a 57.00 171.00 400.00

THRILLING ADVENTURE STORIES (See Tigerman)
Feb, 1975 - No. 2, Aug, 1975 (B&W, 68 pgs.)
Atlas/Seaboard Publ.
1,2: 1-Tigerman, Kromag the Killer begin; Heath, Thorne-a. 2-Heath, Toth, Severin, Simonson-a; Neal Adams-c 1.00 2.40

THRILLING COMICS
Feb, 1940 - No. 80, April, 1951
Better Publ./Nedor/Standard Comics
1-Origin & 1st app. Dr. Strange (37 pgs.), ends #?; Nickie Norton of the Secret Service begins 121.00 365.00 850.00
2-The Rio Kid, The Woman in Red, Pinocchio begins 50.00 150.00 350.00
3-The Ghost & Lone Eagle begin 41.00 122.00 285.00
4-10: 5-Dr. Strange changed to Doc Strange 30.00 90.00 210.00
11-18,20 27.00 80.00 185.00
19-Origin & 1st app. The American Crusader (8/41), ends #39,41 35.00 105.00 245.00
21-30: 24-Intro. Mike, Doc Strange's sidekick (1/42). 29-Last Rio Kid 24.00 72.00 165.00
31-40: 36-Commando Cubs begin (7/43, 1st app.) 19.00 57.00 130.00
41,44-Hitler-c 19.00 57.00 130.00
42,43,45-52: 52-The Ghost ends 14.00 43.00 100.00
53-The Phantom Detective begins; The Cavalier app.; no Commando Cubs 14.00 43.00 100.00
54-The Cavalier app.; no Commando Cubs 14.00 43.00 100.00
55-Lone Eagle ends 14.00 43.00 100.00
56-Princess Pantha begins (10/46, 1st app.) 25.00 75.00 175.00
57-66: 61-Ingels-a; The Lone Eagle app. 65-Last Phantom Detective & Commando Cubs. 66-Frazetta text illo 20.00 60.00 140.00
67,70-73: Frazetta-a(5-7 pgs.) in each. 72-Sea Eagle app.; Buck Ranger, Cowboy Detective begins 24.00 73.00 170.00
68,69-Frazetta-a(2), 8 & 6 pgs.; 9 & 7 pgs. 26.00 78.00 180.00
74-Last Princess Pantha; Tara app. 12.00 36.00 85.00
75-78: 75-All western format begins 8.35 25.00 50.00
79-Krigstein-a 10.00 30.00 60.00
80-Severin & Elder, Celardo, Moreira-a 10.00 30.00 60.00
NOTE: *Bondage c-5, 9, 13, 20, 22, 27-30, 38, 41, 52, 54, 70.* ***Kinstler*** *a-45.* ***Leo Morey*** *a-7.* ***Schomburg (Xela)*** *c-7, 9-19, 36-80 (airbrush 62-71).* ***Tuska*** *a-62, 63. Woman in Red not in #19, 23, 31-33, 39-45. No. 45 exists as a Canadian reprint but numbered #48. No. 72 exists as a Canadian reprint with no* ***Frazetta*** *story. American Crusader c-20-24. Buck Ranger c-72-80. Commando Cubs c-37, 39, 41, 43, 45, 47, 49, 51. Doc Strange c-1-19, 25-36, 38, 40, 42, 44, 46, 48, 50, 52-57, 59. Princess Pantha c-58, 60-71.*

THRILLING CRIME CASES (Formerly 4Most; becomes Shocking Mystery Cases #50 on)
No. 41, June-July, 1950 - No. 49, 1952
Star Publications
41 10.00 30.00 70.00
42-45-Chameleon story (Fox-r) 10.00 30.00 60.00
46-48: 47-Used in **POP**, pg. 84 9.15 27.50 55.00
49-Classic L. B. Cole-c 19.00 57.00 130.00
NOTE: ***L. B. Cole*** *c-all; a-43p, 45p, 46p, 49(2 pgs.).* ***Disbrow*** *a-48.* ***Hollingsworth*** *a-48.*

THRILLING ROMANCES
No. 5, Dec, 1949 - No. 26, June, 1954
Standard Comics
5 8.35 25.00 50.00
6,8 4.00 11.00 22.00
7-Severin/Elder-a (7 pgs.) 5.35 16.00 32.00
9,10-Severin/Elder-a; photo-c 5.00 15.00 30.00
11,14-21,26: 14-Gene Tierney & Danny Kaye photo-c from movie "On the Riviera". 15-Tony Martin/Janet Leigh photo-c 3.60 9.00 18.00
12-Wood-a (2 pgs.) 7.50 22.50 45.00
13-Severin-a 4.35 13.00 26.00
22-25-Toth-a 5.85 17.50 35.00
NOTE: *All photo-c.* ***Celardo*** *a-9, 16.* ***Colletta*** *a-23, 24(2).* ***Toth*** *text illos-19.* ***Tuska*** *a-9.*

THRILLING SCIENCE TALES (AC)(Value: cover or less)

THRILLING TRUE STORY OF THE BASEBALL...
1952 (Photo-c, each)
Fawcett Publications
...Giants-photo-c; has Willie Mays rookie photo-biography; Willie Mays, Eddie Stanky & others photos on-c 55.00 165.00 385.00
...Yankees-photo-c; Yogi Berra, Joe DiMaggio, Mickey Mantle & others photos on-c 49.00 148.00 345.00

THRILLOGY (Pacific)(Value: cover or less)

THRILL-O-RAMA
Oct, 1965 - No. 3, Dec, 1966
Harvey Publications (Fun Films)
1-Fate (Man in Black) by Powell app.; Doug Wildey-a(2); Simon-c 1.70 4.20 10.00
2-Pirana begins (see Phantom #46); Williamson 2 pgs.; Fate (Man in Black)

Thrill- o -Rama #2 © HARV

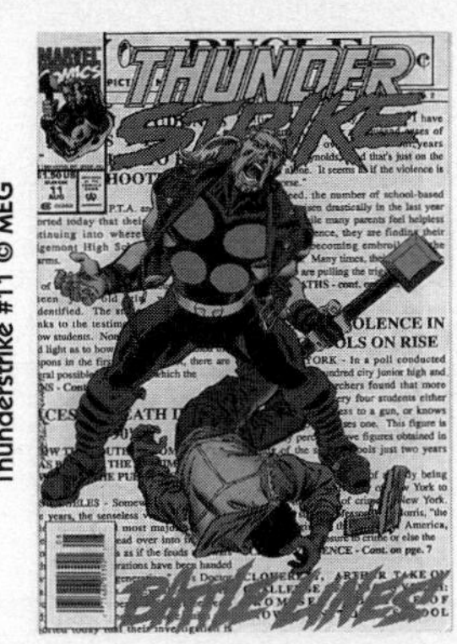

Thunderstrike #11 © MEG

The Tick: Karma Tornado #5 © Ben Edlund

GD25 FN65 NM94

app.; Tuska/Simon-c 1.70 4.20 10.00
3-Fate (Man in Black) app.; Sparling-c 1.10 2.70 6.50

THRILLS OF TOMORROW (Formerly Tomb of Terror)
No. 17, Oct, 1954 - No. 20, April, 1955
Harvey Publications

17-Powell-a (horror); r/Witches Tales #7 7.50 22.50 45.00
18-Powell-a (horror); r/Tomb of Terror #1 5.85 17.50 35.00
19,20-Stuntman-c/stories by S&K (r/from Stuntman #1 & 2); 19 has origin & is last pre-code (2/55) 20.00 60.00 140.00
NOTE: ***Kirby** c-19, 20. **Palais** a-17. **Simon** c-18?*

THROBBING LOVE (See Fox Giants)

THROUGH GATES OF SPLENDOR (Spire Christian)(Value: cover or less)

THUMPER (Disney)(Also see 4-Color #19 & 243)
1942 (50 cents, 32pgs., hardcover book, 7"x8-1/2" w/dust jacket)
Grosset & Dunlap
nn-Given away (along with a copy of Bambi) for a $2.00, 2-year subscription to WDC&S in 1942. (Xmas offer). Book only 14.00 43.00 100.00
Dust jacket only 8.35 25.00 50.00

THUMP'N GUTS (Kitchen Sink)(Value: cover or less)

THUN'DA (...King of the Congo)
1952 - No. 6, 1953
Magazine Enterprises

1(A-1 #47)-Origin; Frazetta c/a; only comic done entirely by Frazetta; all Thun'da stories, no Cave Girl 90.00 270.00 630.00
2(A-1 #56)-Powell-c/a begins, ends #6; Intro/1st app. Cave Girl in filler strip (also app. in 3-6) 14.00 43.00 100.00
3(A-1 #73), 4(A-1 #78) 10.00 30.00 70.00
5(A-1 #83), 6(A-1 #86) 10.00 30.00 65.00

THUN'DA TALES (See Frank Frazetta's...)

THUNDER AGENTS (See Dynamo, Noman & Tales Of Thunder)
11/65 - No. 17, 12/67; No. 18, 9/68, No. 19, 11/68, No. 20, 11/69
(No. 1-16: 68 pgs.; No. 17 on: 52 pgs.)(All are 25¢)
Tower Comics

1-Origin & 1st app. Dynamo, Noman, Menthor, & The Thunder Squad; 1st app. The Iron Maiden 12.00 36.00 85.00
2-Death of Egghead; A-bomb blast panel 7.00 21.00 50.00
3-5: 4-Guy Gilbert becomes Lightning who joins Thunder Squad; Iron Maiden app. 4.60 14.00 32.00
6-10: 7-Death of Menthor. 8-Origin & 1st app. The Raven 2.90 8.60 20.00
11-15: 13-Undersea Agent app.; no Raven story 2.30 5.80 14.00
16-19 1.70 4.20 10.00
20-Special Collectors Edition; all reprints 1.00 2.00 5.00
NOTE: ***Crandall** a-1, 4p, 5p, 18, 20r; c-18. **Ditko** a-6, 7p, 12p, 13?, 14p, 16, 18. **Giunta** a-6. **Kane** a-1, 5p, 6p?, 14, 16p; c-14, 15. **Reinman** a-13. **Sekowsky** a-6. **Tuska** a-1p, 7, 8, 10, 13-17, 19. **Whitney** a-9p, 10, 13, 15, 17, 18; c-17. **Wood** a-1-11, 15(w/**Ditko**-12, 18), (inks-#9, 13, 14, 16, 17), 19i, 20r; c-1-8, 9i, 10-13(#10 w/**Williamson**(p)), 16.*

T.H.U.N.D.E.R. AGENTS (See Blue Ribbon Comics, Hall of Fame Featuring the..., JCP Features & Wally Wood's...)
May, 1983 - No. 2, Jan, 1984
JC Comics (Archie Publications)

1,2-New material .80 2.00

THUNDER BIRDS (See Cinema Comics Herald)

THUNDERBOLT (See The Atomic...)

THUNDERBOLT (Peter Cannon...; see Crisis on Infinite Earths & Peter...)
Jan, 1966; No. 51, Mar-Apr, 1966 - No. 60, Nov, 1967
Charlton Comics

1-Origin & 1st app. Thunderbolt 1.40 3.50 8.50
51-(Formerly Son of Vulcan #50) 1.00 2.00 5.00
52-59: 54-Sentinels begin. 59-Last Thunderbolt & Sentinels (back-up story) 1.30 3.25
60-Prankster app. 1.00 2.00 5.00
57,58 ('77)-Modern Comics-r 1.00
NOTE: ***Aparo** a-60. **Morisi** a-1, 51-56, 58; c-1, 51-56, 58, 59.*

THUNDERBUNNY (Red Circle)(Value: cover or less)(Also see Blue Ribbon Comics #13, Charlton Bullseye & Pep Comics #393)

THUNDERCATS (TV)(Star/Marvel)(Value: cover or less)

THUNDER MOUNTAIN (See 4-Color #246)

THUNDERSTRIKE (See Thor #459)
June, 1993 - Present ($1.25)
Marvel Comics

1-($2.95, 52 pgs.)-Holo-grafx lightning patterned foil-c; Bloodaxe returns 1.20 3.00
2-7: 2-Juggernaut-c/s. 4-Capt. America app. 4-6-Spider-Man app. 1.25
8-16: 8-Begin $1.50-c; bound-in trading card sheet 1.50
Marvel Double Feature...Thunderstrike/Code Blue #13 ($2.50)-Same as Thunderstrike #13 w/Code Blue flip book 1.00 2.50

TICK, THE (Also see The Chroma-Tick)
June, 1988 - No. 12, May, 1993 ($1.75/$1.95/$2.25; B&W, over-sized)
New England Comics Press

Special Edition 1-1st comic book app. serially numbered & limited to 5,000 copies 5.40 16.00 38.00
Special Edition 2-Serially numbered and limited to 3000 copies 4.30 13.00 30.00
1-Reprints Special Ed. 1 w/minor changes 4.30 13.00 30.00
1-2nd printing 1.60 4.00
1-3rd printing ($1.95, 6/89) .80 2.00
1-4th printing ($2.25) .90 2.25
1-5th printing ($2.75) 1.10 2.75
2-Reprints Special Ed. 2 w/minor changes 2.40 7.30 17.00
2-2nd printing ($1.95) 1.20 3.00
2-3rd & 4th printings ($2.25) .90 2.25
2-5th printing ($2.75) 1.10 2.75
3-5 ($1.95): 4-1st app. Paul the Samurai 1.80 4.50
3-2nd & 3rd printings ($2.25) .90 2.25
3-4th printing ($2.75) 1.10 2.75
4-2nd printing ($2.25) .90 2.25
4-3rd - 5th printings ($2.75) .10 2.75
6-8 ($2.25) .90 2.25
5-8-2nd printings ($2.75) 1.10 2.75
6-3rd printing ($2.75) 1.10 2.75
8-Variant with no logo, price, issue number or company logos 1.80 5.00 11.00
9-12 ($2.75) .10 2.75
The Tick's Giant Circus of the Mighty 1,2: 1-(Summer, 1992, $2.75, B&W, magazine size) .10 2.75

TICK'S GIANT CIRCUS OF THE MIGHTY, THE
Summer, 1992 - No. 3, Fall, 1993 ($2.75, B&W)
New England Comics

1-(A-O). 2-(P-Z). 3-1993 Update 1.10 2.75

TICK KARMA TORNADO, THE
Oct, 1993 - Present ($2.75, color)
New England Comics Press

1-($3.25) 1.30 3.25
2-8 1.10 2.75

TICKLE COMICS (Also see Gay, Smile, & Whee Comics)
1955 (7¢, 52 pgs.) (5x7-1/4")
Modern Store Publ.

1 .50 1.25 2.50

TICK TOCK TALES
Jan, 1946 - V3#33, Jan-Feb, 1951
Magazine Enterprises

Tillie The Toiler 1925 © Cupples & Leon

Timecop #2 © Mark Verheiden

Time Walker #1 © Voyager Comm

	GD25	FN65	NM94
1-Koko & Kola begin	10.00	30.00	60.00
2	5.00	15.00	30.00
3-10	4.00	12.00	24.00
11-33: 19-Flag-c. 23-Muggsy Mouse, The Pixies & Tom-Tom the Jungle Boy app. 25-The Pixies & Tom-Tom app.	3.20	8.00	16.00

TIGER (Also see Comics Reading Libraries)
March, 1970 - No. 6, Jan, 1971 (15¢)
Charlton Press (King Features)

	GD25	FN65	NM94
1	1.00	2.00	5.00
2-6		1.20	3.00

TIGER BOY (See Unearthly Spectaculars)

TIGER GIRL
September, 1968 (15¢)
Gold Key

	GD25	FN65	NM94
1(10227-809)-Sparling-c/a; Jerry Siegel scripts	3.00	9.40	22.00

TIGERMAN (Also see Thrilling Adventure Stories)
April, 1975 - No. 3, Sept, 1975 (All 25¢ issues)
Seaboard Periodicals (Atlas)

	GD25	FN65	NM94
1-3: 2,3-Ditko-p in each			1.00

TIGER WALKS, A (See Movie Comics)

TIGRESS, THE
Aug, 1992 - Present (B&W)
Hero Graphics

	GD25	FN65	NM94
1-($3.50)-Tigress vs. Flare		1.40	3.50
2-5- ($2.95)		1.20	3.00
6-(6/93, $3.95, 44 pgs.)		1.60	4.00

TILLIE THE TOILER
1925 - No. 8, 1933 (52 pgs.) (B&W daily strip reprints)
Cupples & Leon Co.

	GD25	FN65	NM94
nn (#1)	13.00	40.00	130.00
2-8	10.00	30.00	100.00

NOTE: *First strip appearance was January, 1921.*

TILLIE THE TOILER (See Comic Monthly)
No. 15, 1941 - No. 237, July, 1949
Dell Publishing Co.

	GD25	FN65	NM94
4-Color 15(1941)	36.00	107.00	250.00
Large Feature Comic 30(1941)	18.00	54.00	180.00
4-Color 8(1942)	22.00	65.00	150.00
4-Color 22(1943)	17.00	52.00	120.00
4-Color 55(1944)	13.00	40.00	90.00
4-Color 89(1945)	13.00	40.00	90.00
4-Color 106('45),132('46): 132-New stories begin	10.00	30.00	65.00
4-Color 150,176,184	9.15	27.50	55.00
4-Color 195,213,237	6.35	19.00	38.00

TILLY AND TED-TINKERTOTLAND
1945 (Giveaway) (20 pgs.)
W. T. Grant Co.

	GD25	FN65	NM94
nn-Christmas comic	5.35	16.00	32.00

TIM (Formerly Superman-Tim; becomes Gene Autry-Tim)
June, 1950 - Oct, 1950 (Half-size, B&W)
Tim Stores

	GD25	FN65	NM94
4 issues; 6/50, 9/50, 10/50 known	6.35	19.00	38.00

TIMBER WOLF (See Action Comics #372, & Legion of Super-Heroes)
Nov, 1992 - No. 5, Mar, 1993 ($1.25, mini-series)
DC Comics

	GD25	FN65	NM94
1-5			1.25

TIME BANDITS (Marvel)(Value: cover or less)

TIME BEAVERS (See First Comics Graphic Novel #2)

TIMECOP
Sept, 1994 - No. 2, Nov, 1994 ($2.50, limited series)
Dark Horse Comics

	GD25	FN65	NM94
1,2-Movie adaptation		1.00	2.50

TIME FOR LOVE (Formerly Romantic Secrets)
V2#53, Oct, 1966; Oct, 1967 - No. 47, May, 1976
Charlton Comics

	GD25	FN65	NM94
V2#53(10/66), 1(10/67), 2(12/67)-20		1.60	4.00
21-47: 30-(10/72)-Full-length portrait of David Cassidy		.80	2.00

TIME KILLERS (Fleetway/Quality)(Value: cover or less)

TIMELESS TOPIX (See Topix)

TIME MACHINE, THE (See 4-Color #1085)

TIME MASTERS (DC)(Value: cover or less)

TIMESPIRITS (Marvel)(Value: cover or less)

TIME TUNNEL, THE (TV)
Feb, 1967 - No. 2, July, 1967 (12¢ issues)
Gold Key

	GD25	FN65	NM94
1,2-Photo back-c	4.30	13.00	30.00

TIME TWISTERS (Quality)(Value: cover or less)

TIME 2: THE EPIPHANY (See First Comics Graphic Novel #9)

TIMEWALKER
Jan, 1994 - Present ($2.50, color)
Valiant Comics

	GD25	FN65	NM94
1,2		1.00	2.50

TIME WARP (DC)(Value: cover or less)(See The Unexpected #210)

TIME WARRIORS THE BEGINNING (Fantasy General)(Value: cover or less)

TIME WARRIOR/WEB-MAN (Blazing Comics)(Value: cover or less)

TIM HOLT (Movie star) (Becomes Red Mask #42 on; also see Crack Western #72, & Great Western)
1948 - No. 41, April-May, 1954 (All 36 pgs.)
Magazine Enterprises

	GD25	FN65	NM94
1-(A-1 #14)-Line drawn-c w/Tim Holt photo on-c; Tim Holt, His horse Lightning & sidekick Chito begin	46.00	139.00	325.00
2-(A-1 #17)(9-10/48)-Photo-c begin, end #18	27.00	80.00	185.00
3-(A-1 #19)-Photo back-c	19.00	58.00	135.00
4(1-2/49),5: 5-Photo front/back-c	16.00	48.00	110.00
6-(5/49)-1st app. The Calico Kid (alias Rex Fury), his horse Ebony & Sidekick Sing-Song (begin series); photo back-c	22.00	65.00	150.00
7-10: 7-Calico Kid by Ayers. 8-Calico Kid by Guardineer (r-in/Great Western #10). 9-Map of Tim's Home Range	12.00	36.00	85.00
11-The Calico Kid becomes The Ghost Rider (origin & 1st app.) by Dick Ayers (r-in/Great Western I.W. #8); his horse Spectre & sidekick Sing-Song begin series	31.00	94.00	220.00
12-16,18-Last photo-c	10.00	30.00	65.00
17-Frazetta Ghost Rider-c	27.00	80.00	185.00
19,22,24: 19-Last Tim Holt-c; Bolle line-drawn-c begin; Tim Holt photo on covers #19-28,30-41	9.15	27.50	55.00
20-Tim Holt becomes Redmask (origin); begin series; Redmask-c #20-on	11.50	34.00	80.00
21-Frazetta Ghost Rider/Redmask-c	23.00	70.00	160.00
23-Frazetta Redmask-c	19.00	57.00	130.00
25-1st app. Black Phantom	14.00	43.00	100.00
26-30: 28-Wild Bill Hickok, Bat Masterson team up with Redmask. 29-B&W photo-c	7.50	22.50	45.00
31-33-Ghost Rider ends	6.70	20.00	40.00
34-Tales of the Ghost Rider begins (horror)-Classic "The Flower Women" & "Hard Boiled Harry!"	8.35	25.00	50.00
35-Last Tales of the Ghost Rider	7.50	22.50	45.00
36-The Ghost Rider returns, ends #41; liquid hallucinogenic drug story	8.35	25.00	50.00

37-Ghost Rider classic "To Touch Is to Die!", about Inca treasure

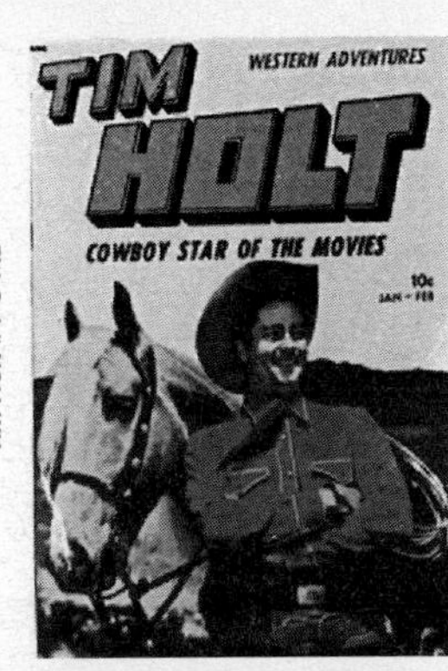

Tim Holt #4 © ME

Tim Tyler Cowboy #11 © STD

Tiny Tot Comics #10 © DELL

GD25 FN65 NM94

8.35 25.00 50.00
38-The Black Phantom begins (not in #39); classic Ghost Rider "The Phantom Guns of Feather Gap!" 8.35 25.00 50.00
39-41: All 3-D effect c/stories 10.00 30.00 70.00
NOTE: ***Dick Ayers*** *a-7, 9-41.* ***Bolle*** *a-1-41; c-19, 20, 22, 24-28, 30-41.*

TIM IN SPACE (Formerly Gene Autry Tim; becomes Tim Tomorrow)
1950 (1/2 size giveaway) (B&W)
Tim Stores
nn 4.00 10.00 20.00

TIM McCOY (Formerly Zoo Funnies; Pictorial Love Stories #22 on)
No. 16, Oct, 1948 - No. 21, Aug, 1949 (Western Movie Stories)
Charlton Comics
16-John Wayne, Montgomery Clift app. in "Red River"; photo back-c 36.00 107.00 250.00
17-21: 17-Allan "Rocky" Lane guest stars. 18-Rod Cameron guest stars. 19-Whip Wilson, Andy Clyde guest star; Jesse James story. 20-Jimmy Wakely guest stars. 21-Johnny Mack Brown guest stars 30.00 90.00 210.00

TIM McCOY, POLICE CAR 17
No. 674, 1934 (32 pgs.) (11x14-3/4") (B&W) (Like Feature Books)
Whitman Publishing Co.
674-1933 movie ill. 19.00 58.00 135.00

TIMMY (See 4-Color #715, 823, 923, 1022)

TIMMY THE TIMID GHOST (Formerly Win-A-Prize?; see Blue Bird)
No. 3, 2/56 - No. 44, 10/64; No. 45, 9/66; 10/67 - No. 23, 7/71; V4#24, 9/85 - No. 26, 1/86
Charlton Comics
3(1956) (1st Series) 6.70 20.00 40.00
4,5 4.00 10.00 20.00
6-10 2.40 6.00 12.00
11,12(4/58,10/58)(100 pgs.) 4.35 13.00 26.00
13-20 2.00 5.00 10.00
21-45(1966) 1.00 2.50 6.00
1(10/67, 2nd series) 1.00 2.50 6.00
2-23 1.00 2.50
24-26 (1985-86): Fago-r 1.10

TIM TOMORROW (Formerly Tim In Space)
8/51, 9/51, 10/51, Christmas, 1951 (5x7-3/4")
Tim Stores
nn-Prof. Fumble & Captain Kit Comet in all 4.00 11.00 22.00

TIM TYLER (See Harvey Comics Hits #54)

TIM TYLER (Also see Comics Reading Libraries)
1942
Better Publications
1 10.00 30.00 65.00

TIM TYLER COWBOY
No. 11, Nov, 1948 - No. 18, 1950
Standard Comics (King Features Synd.)
11-By Lyman Young 6.70 20.00 40.00
12-18: 13-15-Full length western adventures 4.70 14.00 28.00

TINKER BELL (See 4-Color #896, 982, & Walt Disney Showcase #37)

TINY FOLKS FUNNIES (See 4-Color #60)

TINY TESSIE (Tessie #1-23; Real Experiences #25)
No. 24, Oct, 1949 (52 pgs.)
Marvel Comics (20CC)
24 5.85 17.50 35.00

TINY TIM (Also see Super Comics)
No. 4, 1941 - No. 235, July, 1949
Dell Publishing Co.
Large Feature Comic 4('41) 26.00 78.00 260.00
4-Color 20(1941) 31.00 94.00 220.00
4-Color 42(1943) 17.00 52.00 120.00
4-Color 235 5.85 17.50 35.00

TINY TOT COMICS
Mar, 1946 - No. 10, Nov-Dec, 1947 (For younger readers)
E. C. Comics
1(nn)-52 pg. issues begin, end #4 23.00 70.00 160.00
2 (5/46) 16.00 48.00 110.00
3-10: 10-Christmas-c 13.00 40.00 90.00

TINY TOT FUNNIES (Formerly Family Funnies; becomes Junior Funnies)
No. 9, June, 1951
Harvey Publ. (King Features Synd.)
9-Flash Gordon, Mandrake, Dagwood, Daisy, etc. 4.20 12.50 25.00

TINY TOTS COMICS
1943 (Not reprints)
Dell Publishing Co.
1-Kelly-a(2); fairy tales 34.00 103.00 240.00

TIPPY & CAP STUBBS (See 4-Color #210, 242 & Popular Comics)

TIPPY'S FRIENDS GO-GO & ANIMAL
July, 1966 - No. 15, Oct, 1969 (25¢)
Tower Comics
1 3.60 9.00 18.00
2-5,7,9-15: 12-15 titled "Tippy's Friend Go-Go" 2.40 6.00 12.00
6-The Monkees photo-c 5.00 15.00 30.00
8-Beatles app. on front/back-c 7.50 22.50 45.00

TIPPY TEEN (See Vicki)
Nov, 1965 - No. 27, Feb, 1970 (25¢)
Tower Comics
1 2.15 6.50 15.00
2-27: 5-1 pg. Beatles pin-up. 16-Twiggy photo-c 1.30 3.25 8.00
Special Collectors' Editions nn-(1969, 25¢) 1.30 3.25 8.00

TIPPY TERRY
1963
Super/I. W. Enterprises
Super Reprint #14('63)-Little Grouchy reprints .80 2.00 4.00
I.W. Reprint #1 (nd) .80 2.00 4.00

TIP TOP COMICS
4/36 - No. 210, 1957; No. 211, 11-1/57-58 - No. 225, 5-7/61
United Features #1-187/St. John #188-210/Dell Publishing Co. #211 on

GD25 FN65 VF82 NM94
1-Tarzan by Hal Foster, Li'l Abner, Broncho Bill, Fritzi Ritz, Ella Cinders, Capt. & The Kids begin; strip-r (1st comic book app. of each) 571.00 1715.00 2860.00 4000.00
(Estimated up to 80 total copies exist, 4 in NM/Mint)

GD25 FN65 VF82
2 138.00 412.00 825.00
3 113.00 338.00 675.00
4 78.00 233.00 465.00
5-10: 7-Photo & biography of Edgar Rice Burroughs. 8-Christmas-c 65.00 195.00 390.00

GD25 FN65 NM94
11-20: 11-Has Tarzan pin-up. 20-Christmas-c 45.00 135.00 315.00
21-31,33-35,37-40 34.00 100.00 235.00
32,36: 32-1st published Jack Davis-a (cartoon). 36-Kurtzman panel (1st published comic work) 36.00 110.00 255.00
41-Reprints 1st Tarzan Sunday 34.00 100.00 235.00
42-50: 43-Mort Walker panel 31.00 94.00 220.00
51-53 26.00 78.00 180.00
54-Origin Mirror Man & Triple Terror, also featured on cover 34.00 100.00 235.00
55,56,58,60: Last Tarzan by Foster 20.00 60.00 140.00
57,59,61,62-Tarzan by Hogarth 26.00 78.00 180.00

Tip Top Comics #26 © UFS

T- Man #3 © QUA

Tomahawk #1 © DC

GD25 FN65 NM94

63-80: 65,67-70,72-74,77,78-No Tarzan 13.00 40.00 90.00
81-90 11.50 34.00 80.00
91-99 10.00 30.00 60.00
100 10.00 30.00 70.00
101-140: 110-Gordo story. 111-Li'l Abner app. 118, 132-No Tarzan. 137-Sadie Hawkins Day story 6.70 20.00 40.00
141-170: 145,151-Gordo stories. 157-Last Li'l Abner; lingerie panels 4.70 14.00 28.00
171-188-Tarzan reprints by B. Lubbers in all. 177-Peanuts by Schulz begins?; no Peanuts in #178,179,181-183 5.00 15.00 30.00
189-225 4.00 10.00 20.00
Bound Volumes (Very Rare) sold at 1939 World's Fair; bound by publisher in pictorial comic boards (also see Comics on Parade)
Bound issues 1-12 214.00 643.00 1500.00
Bound issues 13-24 143.00 430.00 1000.00
Bound issues 25-36 121.00 365.00 850.00
NOTE: *Tarzan covers-#1(part), 2(part), 3, 9, 11, 13, 16, 18, 21, 24, 27, 30, 32-34, 36, 37, 39, 41, 43, 45, 47, 50, 52 (all worth 10-20 percent more). Tarzan by* ***Foster****-#1-40, 44-50; by* ***Rex Maxon****-#41-43; by* ***Burne Hogarth****-#57, 59, 62.*

TIP TOPPER COMICS
Oct-Nov, 1949 - No. 28, 1954
United Features Syndicate
1-Li'l Abner, Abbie & Slats 8.35 25.00 50.00
2 5.00 15.00 30.00
3-5: 5-Fearless Fosdick app. 4.20 12.50 25.00
6-10: 6-Fearless Fosdick app. 4.00 11.00 22.00
11-25: 17-22,24,26-Peanuts app. (2 pgs.) 3.20 8.00 16.00
26-28-Twin Earths 4.35 13.00 26.00
NOTE: *Many lingerie panels in Fritzi Ritz stories.*

TITAN SPECIAL
June, 1994 ($3.95, color)
Dark Horse Comics
1-($3.95, 52 pgs.) 1.60 4.00

TITANS SELL-OUT SPECIAL
Nov, 1992 ($3.50, 52 pgs.)
DC Comics
1-Fold-out Nightwing poster; 1st Teeny Titans 1.40 3.50

T-MAN (Also see Police Comics #103)
Sept, 1951 - No. 38, Dec, 1956
Quality Comics Group
1-Pete Trask, T-Man begins; Jack Cole-a 25.00 75.00 175.00
2-Crandall-c 13.00 40.00 90.00
3,6-8: All Crandall-c 11.50 34.00 80.00
4,5-Crandall-c/a each 12.00 36.00 85.00
9,10-Crandall-c 10.00 30.00 70.00
11-Used in **POP**, pg. 95 & color illo. 8.35 25.00 50.00
12-19,21,22-26: 21- "The Return of Mussolini" c/story. 24-Last pre-code issue (4/55). 25-Not Crandall-a 6.70 20.00 40.00
20-H-Bomb explosion-c/story 10.00 30.00 60.00
27-38 5.85 17.50 35.00
NOTE: *Anti-communist stories common.* ***Crandall*** *c-2-10p.* ***Cuidera*** *c(i)-1-38. Bondage c-15.*

TMNT MUTANT UNIVERSE SOURCEBOOK
1992 - Present ($1.95, 52 pgs.)(Lists characters from A-Z)
Archie Comics
1-3: 3-New characters; fold-out poster .80 2.00

TNT COMICS
Feb, 1946 (36 pgs.)
Charles Publishing Co.
1-Yellowjacket app. 17.00 52.00 120.00

TOBY TYLER (See 4-Color #1092 and Movie Comics)

TODAY'S BRIDES
Nov, 1955; No. 2, Feb, 1956; No. 3, Sept, 1956; No. 4, Nov, 1956
Ajax/Farrell Publishing Co.
1 5.00 15.00 30.00
2-4 3.60 9.00 18.00

TODAY'S ROMANCE
No. 5, March, 1952 - No. 8, Sept, 1952 (All photo-c?)
Standard Comics
5-Photo-c 5.00 15.00 30.00
6-Photo-c; Toth-a 5.35 16.00 32.00
7,8 3.20 8.00 16.00

TOKA (Jungle King)
Aug-Oct, 1964 - No. 10, Jan, 1967 (Painted-c #1,2)
Dell Publishing Co.
1 2.10 6.00 15.00
2 1.30 3.00 8.00
3-10 1.10 2.70 6.50

TOMAHAWK (Son of... on-c of #131-140; see Star Spangled Comics #69 & World's Finest Comics #65)
Sept-Oct, 1950 - No. 140, May-June, 1972
National Periodical Publications
1-Tomahawk & boy sidekick Dan Hunter begin by Fred Ray 105.00 315.00 735.00
2-Frazetta/Williamson-a (4 pgs.) 50.00 150.00 350.00
3-5 34.00 103.00 240.00
6-10: 7-Last 52 pg. issue 24.00 73.00 170.00
11-20 16.50 50.00 115.00
21-27,30: 30-Last precode (2/55) 12.00 36.00 85.00
28-1st app. Lord Shilling (arch-foe) 14.00 43.00 100.00
29-Frazetta-r/Jimmy Wakely #3 (3 pgs.) 19.00 57.00 130.00
31-40 11.50 34.00 80.00
41-50 10.00 30.00 65.00
51-56,58-60 7.50 22.50 45.00
57-Frazetta-r/Jimmy Wakely #6 (3 pgs.) 10.00 30.00 70.00
61-77: 77-Last 10¢ issue 5.85 17.50 35.00
78-85: 81-1st app. Miss Liberty. 83-Origin Tomahawk's Rangers 4.20 12.50 25.00
86-100: 96-Origin/1st app. The Hood, alias Lady Shilling 2.00 6.00 14.00
101-110: 107-Origin/1st app. Thunder-Man 1.50 3.80 9.00
111-130,132-138,140 1.00 2.00 5.00
131-Frazetta-r/Jimmy Wakely #7 (3 pgs.); origin Firehair retold 1.00 2.50 6.00
139-Frazetta-r/Star Spangled #113 1.60 4.00
NOTE: ***Neal Adams*** *c-116-119, 121, 123-130.* ***Fred Ray*** *c-1, 2, 8, 11, 30, 34, 35, 40-43, 45, 46, 82. Firehair by* ***Kubert****-131-134, 136.* ***Maurer*** *a-138.* ***Severin*** *a-135.* ***Starr*** *a-5.* ***Thorne*** *a-137, 140.*

TOM AND JERRY (See Comic Album #4, 8, 12, Dell Giant #21, Dell Giants, Four Color #193, Golden Comics Digest #1, 5, 8, 13, 15, 18, 22, 25, 28, 35, Kite fun Book & March of Comics #21, 46, 61, 70, 88, 103, 119, 128, 145, 154, 173, 190, 207, 224, 281, 295, 305, 321, 333, 345, 361, 365, 388, 400, 444, 451, 463, 480)

TOM AND JERRY (...Comics, early issues) (M.G.M.)
(Formerly Our Gang No. 1-59) (See Dell Giants for annuals)
No. 193, 6/48; No. 60, 7/49 - No. 212, 7-9/62; No. 213, 11/62 - No. 291, 2/75; No. 292, 3/77 - No. 342, 5/82 - No. 344, 1982?
Dell Publishing Co./Gold Key No. 213-327/Whitman No. 328 on
4-Color 193 (#1)-Titled "M.G.M. Presents..." 14.00 43.00 100.00
60-Barney Bear, Benny Burro cont. from Our Gang 8.35 25.00 50.00
61 7.50 22.50 45.00
62-70: 66-X-Mas-c 5.85 17.50 35.00
71-80: 77,90-X-Mas-c 4.35 13.00 26.00
81-99: 81-Spike & Tyke begin? 84-Droopy begins? 4.00 11.00 22.00
100 4.00 12.00 24.00
101-120 3.60 9.00 18.00
121-140: 126-X-Mas-c 3.20 8.00 16.00
141-160 2.40 6.00 12.00

Tom & Jerry Comics #94 © M.G.M.

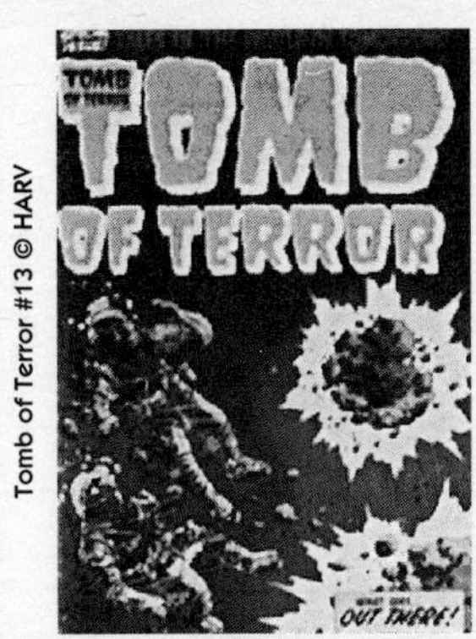

Tomb of Terror #13 © HARV

Tom Mix Western #27 © FAW

	GD25	FN65	NM94
161-200	2.00	5.00	10.00
201-212(7-9/62)(Last Dell issue)	1.60	4.00	8.00
213,214-(84 pgs.)-Titled "...Funhouse"	4.35	13.00	26.00
215-240: 215-Titled "...Funhouse"	1.20	2.90	7.00
241-270	1.00	2.50	6.00
271-300: 286- "Tom & Jerry"		1.20	3.00
301-344			1.50
Mouse From T.R.A.P. 1(7/66)-Giant, G. K.	4.35	13.00	26.00
Summer Fun 1(7/67, 68 pgs.)(Gold Key)-Reprints Barks' Droopy from Summer Fun #1	4.35	13.00	26.00

NOTE: *#60-87, 98-121, 268, 277, 289, 302 are 52 pgs.. Reprints-#225, 241, 245, 247, 252, 254, 266, 268, 270, 292-327, 329-342, 344.*

TOM & JERRY (Harvey)(Value: cover or less)

TOM & JERRY ADVENTURES (Harvey)(Value: cover or less)

TOM & JERRY AND FRIENDS (Harvey)(Value: cover or less)

TOM & JERRY BIG BOOK (Harvey)(Value: cover or less)

TOM & JERRY GIANT SIZE (Harvey)(Value: cover or less)

TOMB OF DARKNESS (Formerly Beware)
No. 9, July, 1974 - No. 23, Nov, 1976
Marvel Comics Group

	GD25	FN65	NM94
9-23: 15,19-Ditko-r. 17-Woodbridge-r/Astonishing #62; Powell-r. 20-Everett Venus-r/Venus #19. 22-r/Venus #19. 23-Everett-r			1.50

TOMB OF DRACULA (See Giant-Size Dracula, Dracula Lives, Nightstalkers, Power Record Comics & Requiem for Dracula)
April, 1972 - No. 70, Aug, 1979
Marvel Comics Group

	GD25	FN65	NM94
1-1st app. Dracula & Frank Drake; Colan-p in all	9.00	27.00	62.00
2	5.40	16.00	38.00
3-5: 3-Intro. Dr. Rachel Van Helsing & Inspector Chelm	3.60	11.00	25.00
6-10: 10-1st app. Blade the Vampire Slayer	2.70	8.10	19.00
11-20: 12-Brunner-c(p). 13-Origin Blade	1.70	5.10	12.00
21-40: 25-1st app. & origin Hannibal King	1.50	3.80	9.00
41-49,51-60	1.00	2.50	6.00
50-Silver Surfer app.	1.50	3.80	9.00
61-70: 70-Double size	1.00	2.00	5.00

NOTE: ***N. Adams** c-1, 6. **Colan** a-1-70p; c(p)-8, 38-42, 44-56, 58-70. **Wrightson** c-43.*

TOMB OF DRACULA, THE (Magazine)
Oct, 1979 - No. 6, Aug, 1980 (B&W)
Marvel Comics Group

	GD25	FN65	NM94
1,4-6		1.50	3.75
2,3: 2-Ditko-a (36 pgs.). 3-Miller-a(2 pg. sketch)		1.90	4.75

NOTE: ***Buscema** a-4p, 5p. **Chaykin** c-5, 6. **Colan** a(p)-1, 3-6. **Miller** a-3. **Romita** a-2p.*

TOMB OF DRACULA
1991 - No. 4, 1992 ($4.95, squarebound, mini-series, 52 pgs.)
Epic Comics (Marvel)

	GD25	FN65	NM94
Book 1-4: Colan/Williamson-a; Colan painted-c	1.00	2.00	5.00

TOMB OF LEGEIA (See Movie Classics)

TOMB OF TERROR (Thrills of Tomorrow #17 on)
June, 1952 - No. 16, July, 1954
Harvey Publications

	GD25	FN65	NM94
1	17.00	52.00	120.00
2	10.00	30.00	65.00
3-Bondage-c; atomic disaster story	11.00	32.00	75.00
4-12: 4-Heart ripped out. 8-12-Nostrand-a	10.00	30.00	65.00
13,14-Special S/F issues. 14-Check-a	12.00	36.00	85.00
15-S/F issue; c-shows head exploding	16.00	48.00	110.00
16-Special S/F issue; Nostrand-a	12.00	36.00	85.00

NOTE: ***Edd Cartier** a-13? **Elias** c-2, 5-16. **Kremer** a-1, 7; c-1. **Nostrand** a-8-12, 15r 16. **Palais** a-2, 3, 5-7. **Powell** a-1, 3, 5, 9-16. **Sparling** a-12, 13, 15.*

TOMBSTONE TERRITORY (See 4-Color #1123)

TOM CAT (Formerly Bo; Atom The Cat #9 on)
No. 4, Apr, 1956 - No. 8, July, 1957
Charlton Comics

	GD25	FN65	NM94
4-Al Fago-c/a	5.00	15.00	30.00
5-8	4.00	10.00	20.00

TOM CORBETT, SPACE CADET (TV)
No. 378, Jan-Feb, 1952 - No. 11, Sept-Nov, 1954 (All painted covers)
Dell Publishing Co.

	GD25	FN65	NM94
4-Color 378 (#1)-McWilliams-a	17.00	52.00	120.00
4-Color 400,421-McWilliams-a	10.00	30.00	70.00
4(11-1/53) - 11	7.50	22.50	45.00

TOM CORBETT SPACE CADET (See March of Comics #102)

TOM CORBETT SPACE CADET (TV)
V2#1, May-June, 1955 - V2#3, Sept-Oct, 1955
Prize Publications

	GD25	FN65	NM94
V2#1	20.00	60.00	140.00
2,3-Meskin-c	17.00	52.00	120.00

TOM, DICK & HARRIET (See Gold Key Spotlight)

TOM LANDRY AND THE DALLAS COWBOYS (Spire Christiain)(Value: cover or less)

TOM MIX (...Commandos Comics #10-12)
Sept, 1940 - No. 12, Nov, 1942 (36 pgs.); 1983 (One-shot)
Given away for two Ralston box-tops; 1983 came in cereal box
Ralston-Purina Co.

	GD25	FN65	NM94
1-Origin (life) Tom Mix; Fred Meagher-a	214.00	643.00	1500.00
2	71.00	215.00	500.00
3-9	50.00	150.00	350.00
10-12: 10-Origin Tom Mix Commando Unit; Speed O'Dare begins; Japanese sub-c. 12-Sci/fi-c	41.00	122.00	285.00
1983- "Taking of Grizzly Grebb", Toth-a; 16 pg. miniature	1.20	3.00	6.00

TOM MIX WESTERN (Movie, radio star) (Also see The Comics, Crackajack Funnies, Master Comics, 100 Pages Of Comics, Popular Comics, Real Western Hero, Six Gun Heroes, Western Hero & XMas Comics)
Jan, 1948 - No. 61, May, 1953 (1-17: 52 pgs.)
Fawcett Publications

	GD25	FN65	NM94
1 (Photo-c, 52 pgs.)-Tom Mix & his horse Tony begin; Tumbleweed Jr. begins, ends #52,54,55	79.00	235.00	550.00
2 (Photo-c)	36.00	107.00	250.00
3-5 (Painted/photo-c): 5-Billy the Kid & Oscar app.	27.00	81.00	190.00
6,7 (Painted/photo-c)	22.00	67.00	155.00
8-Kinstler tempera-c	22.00	67.00	155.00
9,10 (Painted/photo-c)-Used in **SOTI**, pgs. 323-25	20.00	60.00	140.00
11-Kinstler oil-c	19.00	57.00	130.00
12 (Painted/photo-c)	16.00	48.00	110.00
13-17 (Painted-c, 52 pgs.)	16.00	48.00	110.00
18,22 (Painted-c, 36 pgs.)	13.50	41.00	95.00
19 (Photo-c, 52 pgs.)	14.00	43.00	100.00
20,21,23 (Painted-c, 52 pgs.)	11.50	34.00	80.00
24,25,27-29 (52 pgs.): 24-Photo-c begin, end #61. 29-Slim Pickens app.	11.50	34.00	80.00
26,30 (36 pgs.)	11.00	32.00	75.00
31-33,35-37,39,40,42 (52 pgs.): 39-Red Eagle app.	10.00	30.00	70.00
34,38 (36 pgs. begin)	10.00	30.00	60.00
41,43-60: 57-(9/52)-Dope smuggling story	7.50	22.50	45.00
61-Last issue	9.15	27.50	55.00

NOTE: *Photo-c from 1930s Tom Mix movies (he died in 1940). Many issues contain ads for Tom Mix, Rocky Lane, Space Patrol and other premiums. Captain Tootsie by **C.C. Beck** in #6-11, 20.*

TOM MIX WESTERN
1988 - No. 2, 1989? ($2.95, B&W w/16 pgs. color, 44 pgs.)
AC Comics

	GD25	FN65	NM94
1-Tom Mix-r/Master #124,128,131,102 plus Billy the Kid-r by Severin; photo front/back/inside-c		1.20	3.00

Tomorrow Knights #5 © Epic

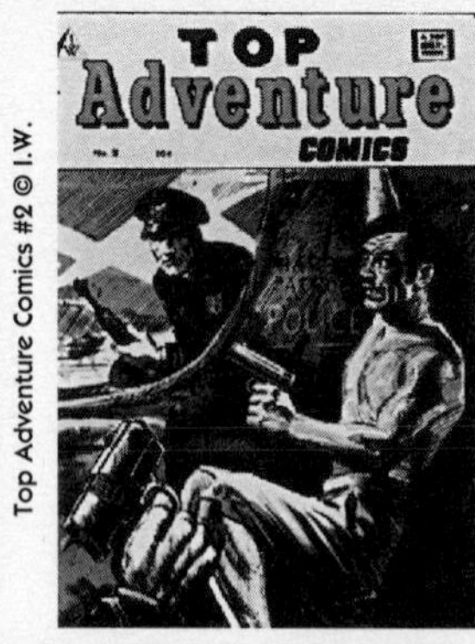

Top Adventure Comics #2 © I.W.

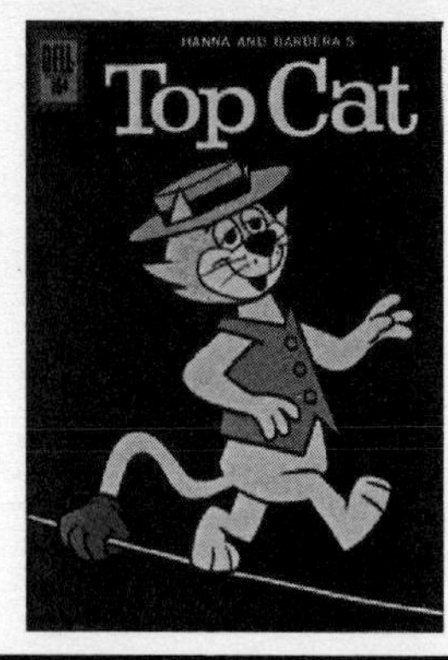

Top Cat #2 © H-B

GD25 FN65 NM94

2-($2.50, B&W)-Gabby Hayes-r; photo covers 1.00 2.50
...Holiday Album 1 (1990, $3.50, B&W, one-shot, 44 pgs.)-Contains photos & 1950s Tom Mix-r; photo inside-c 1.40 3.50

TOMMY OF THE BIG TOP (Thrilling Circus Adventures)
No. 10, Sept, 1948 - No. 12, Mar, 1949
King Features Syndicate/Standard Comics

10-By John Lehti 4.20 12.50 25.00
11,12 3.00 7.50 15.00

TOMMY TOMORROW (See Action Comics #127, Real Fact #6 & World's Finest #102)

TOMORROW KNIGHTS (Marvel)(Value: cover or less)

TOMORROW KNIGHTS
June, 1990 - No. 6, Mar, 1991 ($1.50)
Epic Comics (Marvel)

1-($1.95, 52 pgs.) .80 2.00
2-6 1.50

TOM SAWYER (See Adventures of... & Famous Stories)

TOM SAWYER & HUCK FINN
1925 (52 pgs.) (10-3/4x10") (stiff covers)
Stoll & Edwards Co.

nn-By Dwiggins; reprints 1923, 1924 Sunday strips in color 15.00 45.00 150.00

TOM SAWYER COMICS
1951? (Paper cover)
Giveaway

nn-Contains a coverless Hopalong Cassidy from 1951; other combinations possible 1.60 4.00 8.00

TOM SKINNER-UP FROM HARLEM (See Up From Harlem)

TOM TERRIFIC! (TV)(See Mighty Mouse Fun Club Magazine #1)
Summer, 1957 - No. 6, Fall, 1958 (See Terry Toons Giant Summer Fun Book)
Pines Comics (Paul Terry)

1-1st app.?; CBS Television Presents... 16.00 48.00 110.00
2-6 11.50 34.00 80.00

TOM THUMB (See 4-Color #972)

TOM-TOM, THE JUNGLE BOY (See A-1 Comics & Tick Tock Tales)
1947 - No. 3, 1947; Nov, 1957 - No. 3, Mar, 1958
Magazine Enterprises

1-Funny animal 5.85 17.50 40.00
2,3(1947): 3-Christmas issue 4.20 12.50 28.00
Tom-Tom & Itchi the Monk 1(11/57) - 3(3/58) 2.40 6.00 12.00
I.W. Reprint No. 1,2,8,10 .80 2.00 4.00

TONKA (See 4-Color #966)

TONTO (See The Lone Ranger's Companion...)

TONY TRENT (The Face #1,2)
No. 3, 1948 - No. 4, 1949
Big Shot/Columbia Comics Group

3,4: 3-The Face app. by Mart Bailey 10.00 30.00 70.00

TOODLES, THE (The Toodle Twins with #1)
No. 10, July-Aug, 1951; Mar, 1956 (Newspaper-r)
Ziff-Davis (Approved Comics)/Argo

10-Painted-c, some newspaper-r by The Baers 6.70 20.00 40.00
...Twins 1(Argo, 3/56)-Reprints by The Baers 4.70 14.00 28.00

TOONERVILLE TROLLEY
1921 (Daily strip reprints) (B&W) (52 pgs.)
Cupples & Leon Co.

1-By Fontaine Fox 25.00 75.00 250.00

TOOTS & CASPER (See Large Feature Comic #5)

TOP ADVENTURE COMICS
1964 (Reprints)
I. W. Enterprises

1-r/High Adv. (Explorer Joe #2); Krigstein-r 2.40 6.00 12.00
2-Black Dwarf-r/Red Seal #22; Kinstler-c 2.40 6.00 12.00

TOP CAT (TV) (Hanna-Barbera)(See Kite Fun Book)
12-2/61-62 - No. 3, 6-8/62; No. 4, 10/62 - No. 31, 9/70
Dell Publishing Co./Gold Key No. 4 on

1 (TV show debuted 9/27/61) 14.00 40.00 100.00
2 8.30 25.00 50.00
3-5: 3-Last 15¢ issue. 4-Begin 12¢ issues; 1st app. Yakky Doodle in 1 pg. strip. 5-1st app. Touche' Turtle 5.50 16.50 33.00
6-10 4.00 11.00 22.00
11-20 3.00 8.50 17.00
21-31: 21,24,25,29-Reprints 2.00 5.50 11.00
NOTE: *Augie Doggie back up stories in #1-4.*

TOP CAT (TV) (Hanna-Barbera)(See TV Stars #4)
Nov, 1970 - No. 20, Nov, 1973
Charlton Comics

1 3.70 11.10 26.00
2-10 2.30 6.90 16.00
11-20 1.70 4.00 10.00
NOTE: *#8 (1/72) went on sale late in 1972 between #14 and #15 with the 1/73 issues.*

TOP COMICS
July, 1967 (All reprints)
K. K. Publications/Gold Key

nn-The Gnome-Mobile (Disney-movie) 1.60 4.00 8.00
1-Beagle Boys (#7), Beep Beep the Road Runner (#5), Bugs Bunny, Chip 'n' Dale, Daffy Duck (#50), Flipper, Huckleberry Hound, Huey, Dewey & Louie, Junior Woodchucks, Lassie, The Little Monsters (#71), Moby Duck, Porky Pig (has Gold Key label - says Top Comics on inside), Scamp, Super Goof, Tarzan of the Apes (#169), Three Stooges (#35), Tom & Jerry Top Cat (#21), Tweety & Sylvester (#7), Walt Disney C&S (#322), Woody Woodpecker, Yogi Bear, Zorro (r/G.K. Zorro #7 w/Toth-a; says 2nd printing) known; each character given own book 1.60 4.00 8.00
1-Uncle Scrooge (#70) 2.40 6.00 12.00
1-Donald Duck (not Barks), Mickey Mouse 2.00 5.00 10.00
1-Flintstones 4.20 12.50 25.00
1-The Jetsons 5.85 17.50 35.00
2-Bugs Bunny, Daffy Duck, Donald Duck (not Barks), Mickey Mouse (#114), Porky Pig, Super Goof, Three Stooges, Tom & Jerry, Tweety & Sylvester, Uncle Scrooge (#71)-Barks-c, Walt Disney's C&S (r/#325), Woody Woodpecker, Yogi Bear (#30), Zorro (r/#8; Toth-a) 1.60 4.00 8.00
2-Snow White & 7 Dwarfs(6/67)(1944-r) 2.00 5.00 10.00
3-Donald Duck 1.80 4.50 9.00
3-Uncle Scrooge (#72) 2.00 6.00 12.00
3,4-The Flintstones 4.20 12.50 25.00
3-Mickey Mouse (r/#115), Tom & Jerry, Woody Woodpecker, Yogi Bear 1.60 4.00 8.00
4-Mickey Mouse, Woody Woodpecker 1.60 4.00 8.00
NOTE: *Each book in this series is identical to its counterpart except for cover, and came out at same time. The number in parentheses is the original issue it contains.*

TOP DETECTIVE COMICS
1964 (Reprints)
I. W. Enterprises

9-r/Young King Cole #14; Dr. Drew (not Grandenetti) 1.60 4.00 8.00

TOP DOG (See Star Comics Magazine, 75¢)
Apr, 1985 - No. 14, June, 1987 (Children's book)
Star Comics (Marvel)

1-14: 10-Peter Parker & J. Jonah Jameson cameo 1.00

TOP ELIMINATOR (Teenage Hotrodders #1-24; Drag 'n' Wheels #30 on)
No. 25, Sept, 1967 - No. 29, July, 1968
Charlton Comics

Topix V10 #10 © CGE

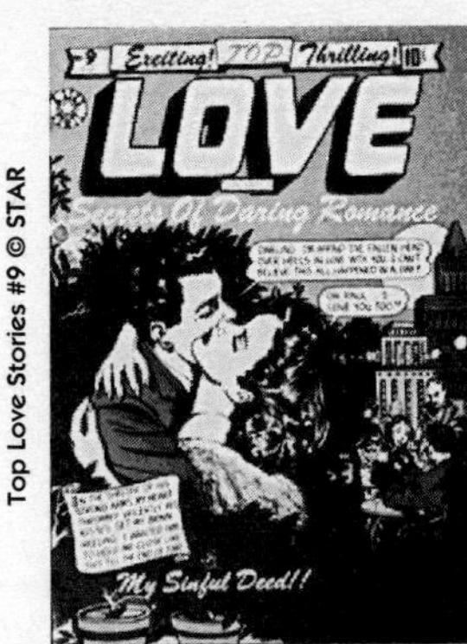

Top Love Stories #9 © STAR

Top-Notch #21 © MLJ

	GD25	FN65	NM94
25-29	1.40	3.50	7.00

TOP FLIGHT COMICS
1947; July, 1949
Four Star Publications/St. John Publishing Co.

	GD25	FN65	NM94
1(1947)	7.50	22.50	45.00
1(7/49, St. John)-Hector the Inspector; funny animal	5.85	17.50	35.00

TOP GUN (See 4-Color #927 & Showcase #72)

TOP GUNS OF THE WEST (See Super DC Giant)

TOPIX (...Comics) (Timeless Topix-early issues) (Also see Men of Battle, Men of Courage & Treasure Chest)(V1-V5#1,V7#1-20-paper-c)
11/42 - V10#15, 1/28/52 (Weekly - later issues)
Catechetical Guild Educational Society

	GD25	FN65	NM94
V1#1(8 pgs.,8x11")	13.00	40.00	90.00
2,3(8 pgs.,8x11")	9.15	27.50	55.00
4-8(16 pgs.,8x11")	6.70	20.00	40.00
V2#1-10(16 pgs.,8x11"): V2#8-Pope Pius XII	4.70	14.00	28.00
V3#1-10(16 pgs.,8x11")	4.70	14.00	28.00
V4#1-10	4.20	12.50	25.00
V5#1(10/46,52 pgs.)-9,12-15(12/47): 13-Shows V5#4	3.60	9.00	18.00
10,11-Life of Christ editions	5.00	15.00	30.00
V6#1-14	2.40	6.00	12.00
V7#1(9/1/48)-20(6/15/49), 32 pgs.	2.40	6.00	12.00
V8#1(9/19/49)-3,5-11,13-30(5/15/50)	2.40	6.00	12.00
4-Dagwood Splits the Atom(10/10/49)-Magazine format	3.60	9.00	18.00
12-Ingels-a	5.35	16.00	32.00
V9#1(9/25/50)-11,13-30(5/14/51)	2.00	5.00	10.00
12-Special 36 pg. Xmas issue, text illos format	2.40	6.00	12.00
V10#1(10/1/51)-15: 14-Hollingsworth-a	2.00	5.00	10.00

TOP JUNGLE COMICS
1964 (Reprint)
I. W. Enterprises

	GD25	FN65	NM94
1(nd)-Reprints White Princess of the Jungle #3, minus cover	2.40	6.00	12.00

TOP LOVE STORIES (Formerly Gasoline Alley #2)
No. 3, 5/51 - No. 19, 3/54
Star Publications

	GD25	FN65	NM94
3(#1)	10.00	30.00	60.00
4,5,7-9	7.50	22.50	45.00
6-Wood-a	11.50	34.00	80.00
10-16,18,19-Disbrow-a	7.50	22.50	45.00
17-Wood art (Fox-r)	9.15	27.50	55.00

NOTE: *All have **L. B. Cole** covers.*

TOP-NOTCH COMICS (...Laugh #28-45; Laugh Comix #46 on)
Dec, 1939 - No. 45, June, 1944
MLJ Magazines

	GD25	FN65	NM94
1-Origin/1st app. The Wizard; Kardak the Mystic Magician, Swift of the Secret Service (ends #3), Air Patrol, The Westpointer, Manhunters (by J. Cole), Mystic (ends #2) & Scott Rand (ends #3) begin; Wizard covers begin, end #8	371.00	1115.00	2600.00
2-Dick Storm (ends #8), Stacy Knight M.D. (ends #4) begin; Jack Cole-a	136.00	407.00	950.00
3-Bob Phantom, Scott Rand on Mars begin; J. Cole-a	107.00	320.00	750.00
4-Origin/1st app. Streak Chandler on Mars; Moore of the Mounted only app.; J. Cole-a	86.00	257.00	600.00
5-Flag-c; origin/1st app. Galahad; Shanghai Sheridan begins (ends #8); Shield cameo; Novick-a	86.00	257.00	600.00
6-Meskin-a	71.00	215.00	500.00
7-The Shield x-over in Wizard; The Wizard dons new costume	86.00	257.00	600.00
8-Origin/1st app. The Firefly & Roy, the Super Boy (9/40, 2nd costumed boy hero after Robin?; also see Toro in Human Torch #1 (Fall/40)	93.00	280.00	650.00
9-Origin & 1st app. The Black Hood; 1st Black Hood-c & logo (10/40); Fran Frazier begins	329.00	985.00	2300.00
10	107.00	321.00	750.00
11-20	57.00	171.00	400.00
21-30: 23-26-Roy app. 24-No Wizard. 25-Last Bob Phantom. 27-Last Firefly. 28-Suzie, Pokey Oakey begin. 29-Last Kardak	46.00	140.00	325.00
31-44: 33-Dotty & Ditto by Woggon begins (2/43, 1st app.). 44-Black Hood series ends	27.00	81.00	190.00
45-Last issue	29.00	86.00	200.00

NOTE: ***J. Binder** a-1-3. **Meskin** a-2, 3, 6, 15. **Bob Montana** a-30; c-28-31. **Harry Sahle** c-42-45. **Woggon** a-33-40, 42. Bondage c-17, 19. Black Hood also appeared on radio in 1944. Black Hood app. on c-9-34, 41-44. Roy the Super Boy app. on c-8, 9, 11-27. The Wizard app. on c-1-8, 11-13, 15-22, 24, 25, 27. Pokey Oakey app. on c-28-43. Suzie app. on c-44-on.*

TOPPER & NEIL (See 4-Color #859)

TOPPS COMICS
1947
Four Star Publications

	GD25	FN65	NM94
1-L. B. Cole-c	10.00	30.00	70.00

TOPPS COMICS PRESENTS
No. 0, 1993 (Giveaway, B&W, 36 pgs.)
Topps Comics

	GD25	FN65	NM94
0-Dracula vs. Zorro, Teenagents, Silver Star, & Bill the Galactic Hero stories			1.00

TOPS
July, 1949 - No. 2, Sept, 1949 (25¢, 68 pgs.) (10-1/4x13-1/4")
(Large size-magazine format; for the adult reader)
Tops Magazine, Inc. (Lev Gleason)

	GD25	FN65	NM94
1 (Rare)-Story by Dashiell Hammett; Crandall/Lubbers, Tuska, Dan Barry, Fuje-a; Biro painted-c	86.00	257.00	600.00
2 (Rare)-Crandall/Lubbers, Biro, Kida, Fuje, Guardineer-a	79.00	235.00	550.00

TOPS COMICS
1944 (132 pgs.) (10¢)
Consolidated Book Publishers

	GD25	FN65	NM94
2000-(Color-c, inside in red shade & some in full color)-Ace Kelly by Rick Yager, Black Orchid, Don on the Farm, Dinky Dinkerton (Rare)	22.00	65.00	150.00

NOTE: *This book is printed in such a way that when the staple is removed, the strips on the left side of the book correspond with the same strips on the right side. Therefore, if strips are removed from the book, each strip can be folded into a complete comic section of its own.*

TOPS COMICS (See Tops in Humor)
1944 (Small size, 32 pgs.) (7-1/4x5")
Consolidated Book (Lev Gleason)

	GD25	FN65	NM94
2001-The Jack of Spades (costumed hero)	11.50	34.00	80.00
2002-Rip Raider	7.50	22.50	45.00
2003-Red Birch (gag cartoons)	1.80	4.50	9.00

TOP SECRET
January, 1952
Hillman Publ.

	GD25	FN65	NM94
1	13.00	40.00	90.00

TOP SECRET ADVENTURES (See Spyman)

TOP SECRETS (...of the F.B.I.)
Nov, 1947 - No. 10, July-Aug, 1949
Street & Smith Publications

	GD25	FN65	NM94
1-Powell-c/a	23.00	70.00	160.00
2-Powell-c/a	16.50	50.00	115.00
3-6,8-10-Powell-a	13.50	41.00	95.00
7-Used in **SOTI**, pg. 90 & illo. "How to hurt people"; used by N.Y. Legis. Comm.; Powell-c/a	22.00	65.00	150.00

NOTE: ***Powell** c-1-3, 5-10.*

Tor #2 © STJ

Torchy #4 © QUA

Total Eclipse #3 © Eclipse

GD25 FN65 NM94

TOPS IN ADVENTURE
Fall, 1952 (25¢, 132 pgs.)
Ziff-Davis Publishing Co.

1-Crusader from Mars, The Hawk, Football Thrills, He-Man; Powell-a; painted-c 34.00 100.00 235.00

TOPS IN HUMOR (See Tops Comics?)
1944 (Small size) (7-1/4x5")
Consolidated Book Publ. (Lev Gleason)

2001(#1)-Origin The Jack of Spades, Ace Kelly by Rick Yager, Black Orchid (female crime fighter) app. 13.00 40.00 90.00
2 8.35 25.00 50.00

TOP SPOT COMICS
1945
Top Spot Publ. Co.

1-The Menace, Duke of Darkness app. 19.00 57.00 130.00

TOPSY-TURVY
April, 1945
R. B. Leffingwell Publ.

1-1st app. Cookie 7.50 22.50 45.00

TOR (Prehistoric Life on Earth) (Formerly One Million Years Ago)
No. 2, Oct, 1953; No. 3, May, 1954 - No. 5, Oct, 1954
St. John Publishing Co.

3-D 2(10/53)-Kubert-c/a 10.00 30.00 70.00
3-D 2(10/53)-Oversized, otherwise same contents 10.00 30.00 60.00
3-D 2(11/53)-Kubert-c/a; has 3-D cover 10.00 30.00 60.00
3-5-Kubert-c/a: 3-Danny Dreams by Toth; Kubert 1 pg. story (w/self portrait) 10.00 30.00 70.00

NOTE: *The two October 3-D's have same contents and* ***Powell*** *art; the October & November issues are titled 3-D Comics. All 3-D issues are 25¢ and came with 3-D glasses.*

TOR (See Sojourn)
May-June, 1975 - No. 6, Mar-Apr, 1976
National Periodical Publications

1-6: 1-New origin by Kubert. 2-Origin-r/St. John #1 1.00

NOTE: ***Kubert*** *a-1, 2-6r; c-1-6.* ***Toth*** *a(p)-3r.*

TOR (3-D)(Eclipse)(Value: cover or less)

TOR
June, 1993 - No. 4, 1993 ($5.95, mini-series)
Epic Comics (Marvel)

1-4: Joe Kubert-a & story 1.00 2.50 6.00

TORCHY (...Blonde Bombshell) (See Dollman, Military, & Modern)
Nov, 1949 - No. 6, Sept, 1950
Quality Comics Group

1-Bill Ward-c, Gil Fox-a 86.00 257.00 600.00
2,3-Fox-c/a 40.00 122.00 285.00
4-Fox-c/a(3), Ward-a (9 pgs.) 52.00 156.00 365.00
5,6-Ward-c/a, 9 pgs; Fox-a(3) each 62.00 186.00 435.00
Super Reprint #16(1964)-r/#4 with new-c 7.50 22.50 45.00

TO RIVERDALE AND BACK AGAIN (Archie Comics Presents...)
1990 ($2.50, 68 pgs.)
Archie Comics

nn-Byrne-c, Colan-a(p); adapts NBC TV movie 1.00 2.50

TORMENTED, THE (Becomes Surprise Adventures #3 on)
July, 1954 - No. 2, Sept, 1954
Sterling Comics

1,2-Weird/horror stories 11.50 34.00 80.00

TORNADO TOM (See Mighty Midget Comics)

TOTAL ECLIPSE (Eclipse)(Value: cover or less)

TOTAL ECLIPSE: THE SERAPHIM OBJECTIVE (Eclipse)(Value: cover or less)

TOTAL RECALL (DC)(Value: cover or less)

GD25 FN65 NM94

TOTAL WAR (M.A.R.S. Patrol #3 on)
July, 1965 - No. 2, Oct, 1965 (Painted covers)
Gold Key

1,2-Wood-a in each 4.60 13.70 32.00

TOUGH KID SQUAD COMICS
March, 1942
Timely Comics (TCI)

GD25 FN65 VF82 NM94
1-(Scarce)-Origin & 1st app.The Human Top & The Tough Kid Squad; The Flying Flame app. 650.00 1950.00 3575.00 5200.00
(Estimated up to 100 total copies exist, 6 in NM/Mint)

TOWER OF SHADOWS (Creatures on the Loose #10 on)
Sept, 1969 - No. 9, Jan, 1971
Marvel Comics Group

GD25 FN65 NM94
1-Steranko, Craig-a(p) 3.00 9.90 23.00
2-Neal Adams-a 2.00 5.50 11.00
3-Barry Smith, Tuska-a 2.00 5.50 11.00
4-Marie Severin-c 1.30 3.00 8.00
5,7-B. Smith(p), Wood-a. 5-Wood draws himself (1st pg., 1st panel) 1.70 4.20 10.00
6,8: Wood-a; 8-Wrightson-c 1.30 3.00 8.00
9-Wrightson-c; Roy Thomas app. 1.20 2.90 7.00
Special 1(12/71)-Neal Adams-a 1.20 2.90 7.00

NOTE: ***J. Buscema*** *a-1p, 2p, Special 1r.* ***Colan*** *a-3p, 6p, Special 1.* ***J. Craig*** *a(r)-1p.* ***Ditko*** *a-6, 8, 9r, Special 1.* ***Everett*** *a-9(i)r; c-5i.* ***Kirby*** *a-9(p)r.* ***Severin*** *c-5p, 6.* ***Steranko*** *a-1p.* ***Tuska*** *a-3.* ***Wood*** *a-5-8. Issues 1-9 contain new stories with some pre-Marvel age reprints in 6-9.* ***H. P. Lovecraft*** *adaptation-9.*

TOWN & COUNTRY
May, 1940
Publisher?

nn-Origin The Falcon 33.00 100.00 230.00

TOWN THAT FORGOT SANTA, THE
1961 (24 pgs.) (Giveaway)
W. T. Grant Co.

nn 2.80 7.00 14.00

TOXIC AVENGER (Marvel)(Value: cover or less)

TOXIC CRUSADERS (TV)
May, 1992 - No. 8, Dec, 1992 ($1.25)
Marvel Comics

1-3-Sam Kieth-c; based on USA network cartoon 1.50
4-8: 8-Kieth-c(i) 1.25

TOYBOY (Continuity)(Value: cover or less)

TOYLAND COMICS
Jan, 1947 - No. 2, Mar, 1947; No. 3, July, 1947 - No. 4, 1947
Fiction House Magazines

1-Wizard of the Moon begins 17.00 52.00 120.00
2-4: 2,3-Bob Lubbers-c. 3-Tuska-a 10.00 30.00 70.00
148 pg. issue 19.00 57.00 130.00

NOTE: *All above contain strips by* ***Al Walker.***

TOY TOWN COMICS
1945 - No. 7, May, 1947
Toytown/Orbit Publ./B. Antin/Swapper Quarterly

1-Mertie Mouse; L. B. Cole-c/a; funny animal 15.00 45.00 105.00
2-L. B. Cole-a 10.00 30.00 70.00
3-7-L. B. Cole-a. 5-Wiggles the Wonderworm-c 10.00 30.00 60.00

TRAGG AND THE SKY GODS (See Gold Key Spotlight, Mystery Comics Digest #3,9 & Spine Tingling Tales)
June, 1975 - No. 8, Feb, 1977; No. 9, May, 1982 (Painted-c #3-8)
Gold Key/Whitman No. 9

1-Origin .80 2.00
2-9: 4-Sabre-Fang app. 8-Ostellon app.; 9-r/#1 1.00

NOTE: ***Santos*** *a-1, 2, 9r; c-3-7.* ***Spiegel*** *a-3-8.*

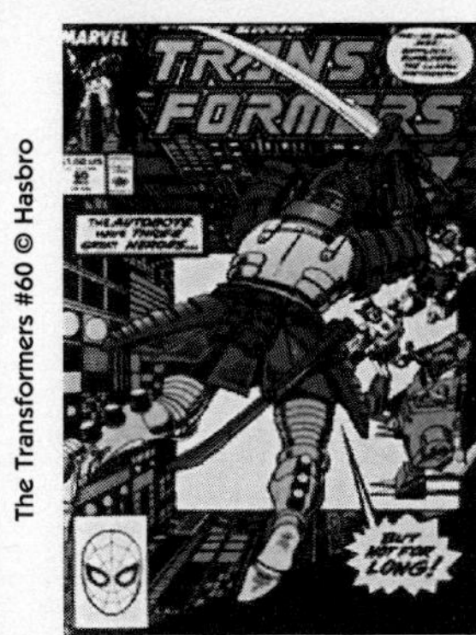

The Transformers #60 © Hasbro

Trapped #1 © HARV

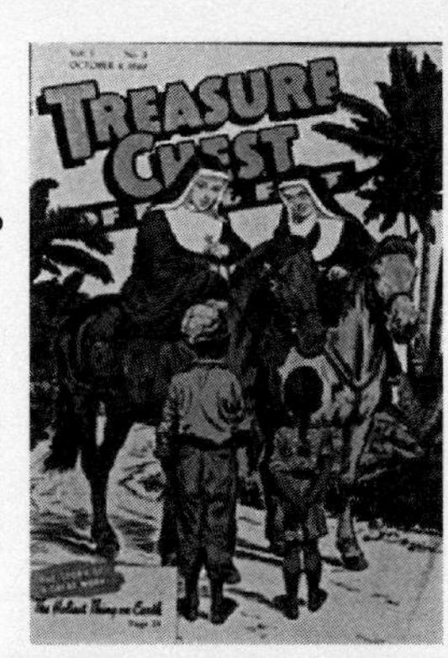

Treasure Chest V5 #3 © George Pflaum

GD25 FN65 NM94

TRAIL BLAZERS (Red Dragon #5 on)
1941; No. 2, Apr, 1942 - No. 4, Oct, 1942 (True stories of American heroes)
Street & Smith Publications

1-Life story of Jack Dempsey & Wright Brothers 24.00 73.00 170.00
2-Brooklyn Dodgers-c/story; Ben Franklin story 14.00 43.00 100.00
3,4: 3-Fred Allen, Red Barber, Yankees stories 132.00 40.00 90.00

TRAIL COLT (Also see Extra Comics & Manhunt!)
1949 - No. 2, 1949
Magazine Enterprises

nn(A-1 #24)-7 pg. Frazetta-a r-in Manhunt #13; Undercover Girl app.; The Red Fox by L. B. Cole; Ingels-c; Whitney-a (Scarce) 30.00 90.00 210.00
2(A-1 #26)-Undercover Girl; Ingels-c; L. B. Cole-a (6 pgs.) 24.00 73.00 170.00

TRANCERS (Eternity)(Value: cover or less)

TRANSFORMERS, THE (TV)(Marvel, all titles)(Value: cover or less)(See G.I. Joe and...)

TRANSFORMERS: GENERATION 2
Nov, 1993 - No. 12, Oct, 1994 ($1.75)
Marvel Comics

1-($2.95, 68 pgs.)-Collector's ed. w/bi-fold metallic-c 1.20 3.00
1-11: 1-Newsstand edition (68 pgs.) .70 1.75
12-($2.25, 52 pgs.) .90 2.25

TRANSMUTATION OF IKE GARUDA, THE (Marvel)(Value: cover or less)

TRAPMAN
June, 1994 - Present ($2.95, color, limited series:12, quarterly)
Phantom Comics

1,2 1.20 3.00

TRAPPED
1951 (Giveaway) (16 pgs.) (soft cover)
Harvey Publications (Columbia University Press)

nn-Drug education comic (30,000 printed?) distributed to schools.; mentioned in **SOTI**, pgs. 256,350 2.40 6.00 12.00
NOTE: *Many copies surfaced in 1979 causing a setback in price; beware of trimmed edges, because many copies have a brittle edge.*

TRAPPED!
Oct, 1954 - No. 5, June?, 1955
Periodical House Magazines (Ace)

1 (All reprints) 7.50 22.50 45.00
2-5: 4-r/Men Against Crime #4 in its entirety 4.70 14.00 28.00
NOTE: ***Colan** a-1, 4. **Sekowsky** a-1.*

TRASH (Trash)(Value: cover or less)

TRAVELS OF HAPPY HOOLIGAN, THE
1906 (10-1/4x15-3/4", 32 pgs., cardboard covers)
Frederick A. Stokes Co.

nn-Contains reprints from 1905 40.00 120.00 280.00

TRAVELS OF JAIMIE McPHEETERS, THE (TV)
December, 1963
Gold Key

1-Kurt Russell photo on-c plus photo back-c 4.00 10.00 20.00

TREASURE BOX OF FAMOUS COMICS
Mid 1930's (36 pgs.) (6-7/8x8-1/2") (paper covers)(Boxed set of 5 books)
Cupples & Leon Co.

Little Orphan Annie (1926)-Softcover 17.00 52.00 120.00
Hardcover 29.00 86.00 200.00
Reg'lar Fellers (1928)-Softcover 13.00 40.00 90.00
Hardcover 22.00 65.00 150.00
Smitty (1928)-Softcover 13.00 40.00 90.00
Hardcover 22.00 65.00 150.00
Harold Teen (1931)-Softcover 13.00 40.00 90.00
Hardcover 22.00 65.00 150.00
How Dick Tracy & Dick Tracy Jr. Caught The Racketeers (1933)
Softcover 22.00 65.00 150.00
Hardcover 36.00 107.00 250.00
Softcover set of five books in box 114.00 343.00 800.00
Box only 43.00 130.00 300.00
NOTE: *Dates shown are copyright dates; all books actually came out in 1934 or later. The softcovers are abbreviated versions of the hardcover editions.*

TREASURE CHEST (Catholic Guild; also see Topix)
3/12/46 - V27#8, July, 1972 (Educational comics)
George A. Pflaum (not publ. during Summer)

V1#1 16.00 48.00 110.00
2-6 (5/21/46): 5-Dr. Styx app. by Baily 7.50 22.50 45.00
V2#1-20 (9/3/46-5/27/47) 5.00 15.00 30.00
V3#1-5,7-20 (1st slick cover) 4.00 11.00 22.00
V3#6-Jules Verne's "Voyage to the Moon" 5.85 17.50 35.00
V4#1-20 (9/9/48-5/31/49) 3.60 9.00 18.00
V5#1-20 (9/6/49-5/31/50) 2.80 7.00 14.00
V6#1-20 (9/14/50-5/31/51) 2.80 7.00 14.00
V7#1-20 (9/13/51-6/5/52) 2.00 5.00 10.00
V8#1-20 (9/11/52-6/4/53) 2.00 5.00 10.00
V9#1-20 ('53-'54) 1.60 4.00 8.00
V10#1-20 ('54-'55) 1.60 4.00 8.00
V11('55-'56), V12('56-'57) 1.40 3.50 7.00
V13#1,3-5,7,9-V17#1 ('57-'63) 1.20 3.00 6.00
V13#2,6,8-Ingels-a 5.35 16.00 32.00
V17#2- "This Godless Communism" series begins(not in odd #'d issues); cover shows hammer & sickle over Statue of Liberty; 8 pg. Crandall-a of family life under communism 13.00 40.00 90.00
V17#3,5,7,9,11,13,15,17,19 .80 2.00 4.00
V17#4,6,14- "This Godless Communism" stories 10.00 30.00 60.00
V17#8-Shows red octopus encompassing Earth, firing squad; 8 pgs. Crandall-a 10.00 30.00 70.00
V17#10- "This Godless Communism" - how Stalin came to power, part I; Crandall-a 10.00 30.00 65.00
V17#12-Stalin in WWII, forced labor, death by exhaustion; Crandall-a 10.00 30.00 65.00
V17#16-Kruschev takes over; de-Stalinization 10.00 30.00 65.00
V17#18-Kruschev's control; murder of revolters, brainwash, space race by Crandall 10.00 30.00 65.00
V17#20-End of series; Kruschev-people are puppets, firing squads hammer & sickle over Statue of Liberty, snake around communist manifesto by Crandall 10.00 30.00 65.00
V18#1-20, V19#11-20, V20#1-20(1964-65): V18#11-Crandall draws himself & 13 other artists on cover .80 2.00 4.00
V18#5- "What About Red China?" - describes how communists took over China 4.70 1[illegible].00 28.00
V19#1-10- "Red Victim" anti-communist series in all 4.70 14.00 28.00
V21-V25(1965-70)-(two V24#5's 11/7/68 & 11/21/68) (no V24#6) .60 1.50 3.00
V26, V27#1-8 (V26,27-68 pgs.) .40 1.00 2.00
Summer Edition V1#1-6('66), V2#1-6('67) .40 1.00 2.00
NOTE: ***Anderson** a-V18#13. **Borth** a-V7#10-19 (serial), V8#8-17 (serial), V9#1-10 (serial), V13#2, 6, 11, V14-V25 (except V22#1-3, 11-13), Summer Ed. V1#3-6. **Crandall** a-V16#7, 9, 12, 14, 16-18, 20; V17#1, 2, 4-6, 10, 12, 14, 16-18, 20; V18#1, 2, 3(2 pg.), 7, 9-20; V19#4, 11, 13, 16, 19, 20; V20#1, 2, 4, 6, 8-10, 12, 14-16, 18, 20; V21#1-5, 8-11, 13, 16-18; V22#3, 7, 9-11, 14; V23#3, 6, 9, 16, 18; V24#7, 8, 10, 13, 16; V25#8, 16; V27#1-7r, 8r(2 pg.), Summer Ed. V1#3-5, V2#3; c-V16#7, V18#2(part), 7, 11, V19#4, 19, 20, V20#15, V21#5, 9, V22#3, 7, 9, 11, V23#9, 16, V24#13, 16, V25#8, Summer Ed. V1#2 (back c-V1#2-5). **Powell** a-V10#11. V19#11, 15, V10#13, V13#6, 8 all have wraparound covers. All the above Crandall issues should be priced by condition from $4-8.00 in mint unless already priced.*

TREASURE CHEST OF THE WORLD'S BEST COMICS
1945 (500 pgs.) (hardcover)
Superior, Toronto, Canada

Contains Blue Beetle, Captain Combat, John Wayne, Dynamic Man, Nemo, Li'l Abner; contents can vary - represents random binding of extra books; Capt. America on-c 71.00 215.00 500.00

TREASURE COMICS

Treasure Comics #3 © PRIZE

Tribe #3 © Axis

Troll II #1 © Rob Liefeld

GD25 FN65 NM94

No date (1943) (50¢, 324 pgs.; cardboard covers)
Prize Publications? (no publisher listed)

1-(Rare)-Contains rebound Prize Comics #7-11 from 1942 (blank inside-c) 185.00 557.00 1300.00

TREASURE COMICS
June-July, 1945 - No. 12, Fall, 1947
Prize Publications (American Boys' Comics)

1-Paul Bunyan & Marco Polo begin; Highwayman & Carrot Topp only app.; Kiefer-a 20.00 60.00 140.00
2-Arabian Knight, Gorilla King, Dr. Styx begin 10.00 30.00 70.00
3,4,9,12: 9-Kiefer-a 8.35 25.00 50.00
5-Marco Polo-c; Krigstein-a 13.00 40.00 90.00
6,11-Krigstein-a; 11-Krigstein-c 11.00 32.00 75.00
7,8-Frazetta-a (5 pgs. each). 7-Capt. Kidd Jr. app. 25.00 75.00 175.00
10-Simon & Kirby-c/a 18.00 54.00 125.00
NOTE: ***Barry** a-9-11; c-12. **Kiefer** a-3, 5, 7; c-2, 6, 7. **Roussos** a-11.*

TREASURE ISLAND (See Classics Illustrated #64, Doc Savage Comics #1, 4-Color #624, King Classics, Movie Classics & Movie Comics)

TREASURY OF COMICS
1947; No. 2, July, 1947 - No. 4, Sept, 1947; No. 5, Jan, 1948
St. John Publishing Co.

nn(#1)-Abbie an' Slats (nn on-c, #1 on inside) 13.00 40.00 90.00
2-Jim Hardy Comics; featuring Windy & Paddles 10.00 30.00 65.00
3-Bill Bumlin 7.50 22.50 45.00
4-Abbie an' Slats 10.00 30.00 65.00
5-Jim Hardy Comics #1 10.00 30.00 65.00

TREASURY OF COMICS
Mar, 1948 - No. 5, 1948 (Reg. size); 1948-1950 (Over 500 pgs., $1.00)
St. John Publishing Co.

1 16.50 50.00 115.00
2(#2 on-c, #1 on inside) 10.00 30.00 65.00
3-5 9.15 27.50 55.00
1-(1948, 500 pgs., hard-c)-Abbie & Slats, Abbott & Costello, Casper, Little Annie Rooney, Little Audrey, Jim Hardy, Ella Cinders (16 books bound together) (Rare) 107.00 321.00 750.00
1(1949, 500 pgs.)-Same format as above 107.00 321.00 750.00
1(1950, 500 pgs.)-Same format as above; different-c; (also see Little Audrey Yearbook) (Rare) 107.00 321.00 750.00

TREASURY OF DOGS, A (See Dell Giants)

TREASURY OF HORSES, A (See Dell Giants)

TREKKER (Dark Horse)(Value: cover or less)

TRENCHER (See Blackball Comics)
May, 1993 - No. 4, Oct, 1993 ($1.95, color)
Image Comics

1-4: By Keith Giffen. 3-Supreme-c/story .80 2.00

TRIALS OF LULU AND LEANDER, THE
1906 (32 pgs. in color) (10x16")
William A. Stokes Co.
nn-By F. M. Howarth 25.00 75.00 175.00

TRIB COMIC BOOK, THE
Sept. 24, 1977 - Vol.2, #10, Mar. 11, 1978 (8-1/2"x11")(Weekly, 24 pgs., color)
Winnipeg Tribune

1-Color pages (Sunday strips)-Spiderman, Asterix, Disney's Scamp, Wizard of Id, Doonesbury, Inside Woody Allen, Mary Worth, & others (similar to Spirit sections) 1.70 5.00 12.00
2-up 1.30 3.25 8.00

TRIBE (See Wildcats #4)
April, 1993 ($2.50, color)
Image Comics

1-By Johnson & Stroman; gold foil & embossed on black-c 1.00 2.50
1-Ivory Edition; gold foil & embossed on white-c; available only through the creators ($2.50) 4.00

GD25 FN65 NM94

TRIBE
V1#2, Sept, 1993 - V1#3, 1994 ($1.95, color)
Axis Comics

V1#2,3-By Johnson & Stroman .80 2.00

TRIGGER (See Roy Rogers'...)

TRIGGER TWINS
Mar-Apr, 1973 (One Shot, 20¢ issue)
National Periodical Publications

1-Trigger Twins & Pow Wow Smith-r/All-Star Western #94,103 & Western Comics #81; Infantino-r(p) 1.20 3.00

TRINITY (See DC Universe: Trinity)

TRIPLE GIANT COMICS (See Archie All-Star Specials under Archie Comics)

TRIPLE THREAT
Winter, 1945
Special Action/Holyoke/Gerona Publ.

1-Duke of Darkness, King O'Leary 11.00 32.00 75.00

TRIP WITH SANTA ON CHRISTMAS EVE, A
No date (Early 1950s) (16 pgs.; full color; paper cover)
Rockford Dry Goods Co. (Giveaway)

nn 3.20 8.00 16.00

TRIUMPHANT UNLEASHED
No. 0, Nov, 1993 - No. 1, Nov, 1993 ($2.50, color)
Triumphant Comics

0-Serially numbered 1.00 2.50
0-Red logo 1.00 2.50
0-White logo (no cover price; giveaway) 1.00 2.50
1-Cover is negative & reverse of #0-c 1.00 2.50

TROLL
Dec, 1993 ($2.50, color, one-shot, 44 pgs.)
Image Comics (Extreme Studios)

1-Liefeld scripts; Matsuda-c/a(p) 1.00 2.50

TROLL II
July, 1994 ($3.95, color, one-shot)
Image Comics

1 1.60 4.00

TROLLORDS (Comico & Apple)(Value: cover or less)

TROLL: ONCE A HERO
Aug, 1994 ($2.50, color, one-shot)
Image Comics

1 1.00 2.50

TROLL PATROL
Jan, 1993 ($1.95, 52 pgs.)
Harvey Comics

1 .80 2.00

TROUBLE SHOOTERS, THE (See 4-Color #1108)

TROUBLE WITH GIRLS, THE (Malibu/Eternity/Epic)(Value: cover or less)

TRUE ADVENTURES (Formerly True Western)(Men's Adventures #4 on)
No. 3, May, 1950 (52 pgs.)
Marvel Comics (CCC)

3-Powell, Sekowsky-a; Brodsky-c 11.00 32.00 75.00

TRUE ANIMAL PICTURE STORIES
Winter, 1947 - No. 2, Spr-Summer, 1947
True Comics Press

1,2 7.00 21.00 42.00

TRUE AVIATION PICTURE STORIES (Becomes Aviation Adventures & Model Building #16 on)

True Aviation Picture Stories #4 © PMI

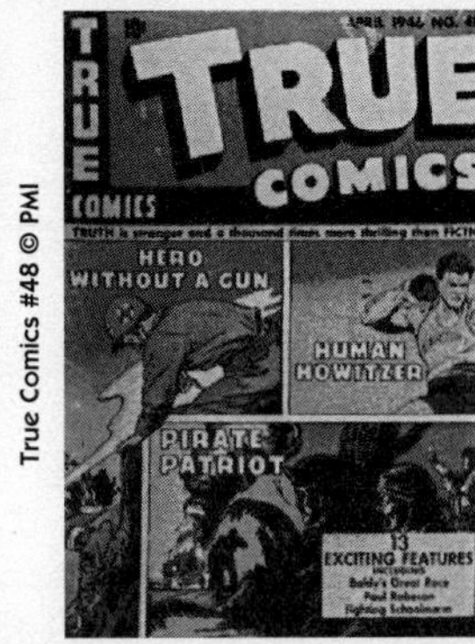

True Comics #48 © PMI

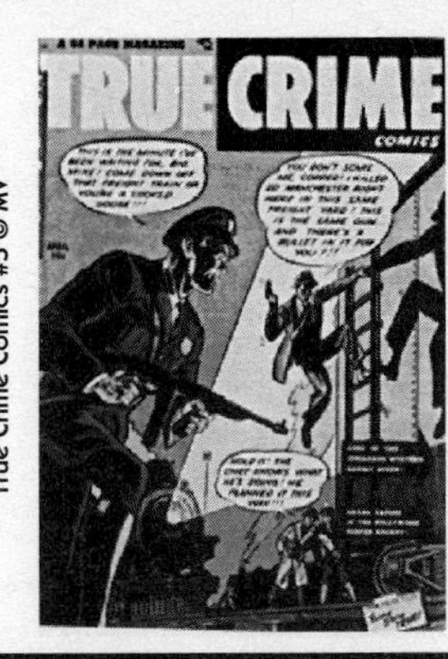

True Crime Comics #5 © MV

GD25 FN65 NM94

1942; No. 2, Jan-Feb, 1943 - No. 15, Sept-Oct, 1946
Parents' Magazine Institute

1-(#1 & 2 titled ...Aviation Comics Digest)(not digest size) 11.00 32.00 75.00
2 7.00 21.00 42.00
3-14: 3-10-Plane photos on-c. 11,13-Photo-c 5.85 17.50 35.00
15-(Titled "True Aviation Adventures & Model Building") 5.00 15.00 30.00

TRUE BRIDE'S EXPERIENCES (Formerly Teen-Age Brides)
(True Bride-To-Be Romances No. 17 on)
No. 8, Oct, 1954 - No. 16, Feb, 1956
True Love (Harvey Publications)

8 4.70 14.00 28.00
9,10: 10-Last pre-code (2/55) 3.20 8.00 16.00
11-15 2.40 6.00 12.00
16-Spanking panels (3) 4.00 12.00 24.00
NOTE: ***Powell** a-8-10, 12, 13.*

TRUE BRIDE-TO-BE ROMANCES (Formerly True Bride's Experiences)
No. 17, Apr, 1956 - No. 30, Nov, 1958
Home Comics/True Love (Harvey)

17-S&K-c, Powell-a 5.85 17.50 35.00
18-20,22,25-28,30 2.80 7.00 14.00
21,23,24,29-Powell-a. 29-Baker-a (1 pg.) 3.60 9.00 18.00

TRUE COMICS (Also see Outstanding American War Heroes)
April, 1941 - No. 84, Aug, 1950
True Comics/Parents' Magazine Press

1-Marathon run story; life story Winston Churchill 25.00 75.00 175.00
2-Red Cross story; Everett-a 13.00 40.00 90.00
3-Baseball Hall of Fame story 14.00 43.00 100.00
4,5: 4-Story of American flag "Old Glory". 5-Life story of Joe Louis 11.00 32.00 75.00
6-Baseball World Series story 13.50 41.00 95.00
7-10: 7-Buffalo Bill story. 10,11-Teddy Roosevelt 8.35 25.00 50.00
11-16,18-20: 11-Thomas Edison, Douglas MacArthur stories. 13-Harry Houdini story. 14-Charlie McCarthy story. 15-Flag-c; Bob Feller story. 18-Story of America begins, ends #26. 19-Eisenhower-c/s 7.50 22.50 45.00
17-Brooklyn Dodgers story 9.15 27.50 55.00
21-30: 24-Marco Polo story 6.35 19.00 38.00
31-Red Grange "Galloping Ghost" story 4.70 14.00 28.00
32-46: 39-FDR story. 46-George Gershwin story 4.00 12.00 24.00
47-Atomic bomb issue (c/story, 3/46) 8.35 25.00 50.00
48-66: 55-(12/46)-1st app. Sad Sack by Baker (1/2 pg.). 58-Jim Jeffries (boxer) story; Harry Houdini story. 59-Bob Hope story. 60-Speedway Speed Demon-c/story. 66-Will Rogers-c/story 4.00 11.00 22.00
67-1st oversized issue (12/47); Steve Saunders, Special Agent begins 5.35 16.00 32.00
68-72,74-79: 68-70,72,74-78-Features True FBI advs. 69-Jack Benny story. 71-Joe DiMaggio-c/story. 72-Jackie Robinson story. 74-Amos 'n' Andy story. 78-Stan Musial-c/story 4.00 11.00 22.00
73-Walt Disney's life story 5.35 16.00 32.00
80-84 (Scarce)-All distr. to subscribers through mail only; paper-c. 80-Rocket trip to the moon story. 81-Red Grange story 16.00 48.00 110.00
(Prices vary widely on issues 80-84)
NOTE: ***Bob Kane** a-7. **Palais** a-80. **Powell** c/a-80. #80-84 have soft covers and combined with Tex Granger, Jack Armstrong, and Calling All Kids. #68-78 featured true FBI adventures.*

TRUE COMICS AND ADVENTURE STORIES
1965 (Giant) (25¢)
Parents' Magazine Institute

1,2: 1-Fighting Hero of Viet Nam; LBJ on-c 1.40 3.50 7.00

TRUE COMPLETE MYSTERY (Formerly Complete Mystery)
No. 5, April, 1949 - No. 8, Oct, 1949
Marvel Comics (PrPI)

5 16.00 48.00 110.00
6-8: 6-8-Photo-c 13.00 40.00 90.00

TRUE CONFIDENCES
1949 (Fall) - No. 4, June, 1950 (All photo-c)
Fawcett Publications

1-Has ad for Fawcett Love Adventures #1, but publ. as Love Memoirs #1 as Marvel published the title first; Swayze-a 11.00 32.00 75.00
2-4: 3-Swayze-a. 4-Powell-a 7.50 22.50 45.00

TRUE CRIME CASES (...From Official Police Files)
1944 (25¢, 100 pg. Giant)
St. John Publishing Co.

nn-Matt Baker-c 27.00 80.00 185.00

TRUE CRIME COMICS (Also see Complete Book of...)
No. 2, May, 1947; No. 3, July-Aug, 1948 - No. 6, June-July, 1949;
V2#1, Aug-Sept, 1949 (52 pgs.)
Magazine Village

2-Jack Cole-c/a; used in **SOTI**, pgs. 81,82 plus illo. "A sample of the injury-to-eye motif" & illo. "Dragging living people to death"; used in **POP**, pg. 105; "Murder, Morphine and Me" classic drug propaganda story used by N.Y. Legis. Comm. 93.00 280.00 650.00
3-Classic Cole-c/a; drug story with hypo, opium den & withdrawing addict 66.00 197.00 460.00
4-Jack Cole-c/a; c-taken from a story panel in #3; r-(2) **SOTI** & **POP** stories/#2 59.00 178.00 415.00
5-Jack Cole-c, has same-c blurbs w/diff-c (but similar) to #3; Marijuana racket story 36.00 107.00 250.00
6-Reprints #4 plus-c w/different coloring on-c 19.00 57.00 130.00
V2#1-Used in **SOTI**, pgs. 81,82 & illo. "Dragging living people to death"; Toth, Wood (3 pgs.), Roussos-a; Cole-r from #2 50.00 150.00 350.00
NOTE: *V2#1 was reprinted in Canada as V2#9 (12/49); same-c & contents minus Wood-a.*

TRUE GHOST STORIES (See Ripley's...)

TRUE LIFE ROMANCES (...Romance on cover)
Dec, 1955 - No. 3, Aug, 1956
Ajax/Farrell Publications

1 7.50 22.50 45.00
2 4.20 12.50 25.00
3-Disbrow-a 5.00 15.00 30.00

TRUE LIFE SECRETS
Mar-April, 1951 - No. 28, Sept, 1955; No. 29, Jan, 1956
Romantic Love Stories/Charlton

1-Photo-c begin, end #3? 9.15 27.50 55.00
2 4.70 14.00 28.00
3-19 4.00 11.00 22.00
20-29: 25-Last precode(3/55) 3.60 9.00 18.00

TRUE LIFE TALES (Formerly Mitzi's Romances #8?)
No. 8, Oct, 1949 - No. 2, Jan, 1950 (52 pgs.)
Marvel Comics (CCC)

8(#1, 10/49), 2-Both have photo-c 6.70 20.00 40.00

TRUE LOVE (Eclipse)(Value: cover or less)

TRUE LOVE CONFESSIONS
May, 1954 - No. 11, Jan, 1956
Premier Magazines

1-Marijuana story 7.50 22.50 45.00
2 4.00 11.00 22.00
3-11 3.60 9.00 18.00

TRUE LOVE PICTORIAL
1952 - No. 11, Aug, 1954
St. John Publishing Co.

1-Only photo-c 10.00 30.00 70.00
2-Baker-c 6.35 19.00 38.00
3-5(All 25¢, 100 pgs.): 5-(4/53)-Formerly Teen-Age Temptations; Kubert-a

True Love Pictorial #6 © STJ

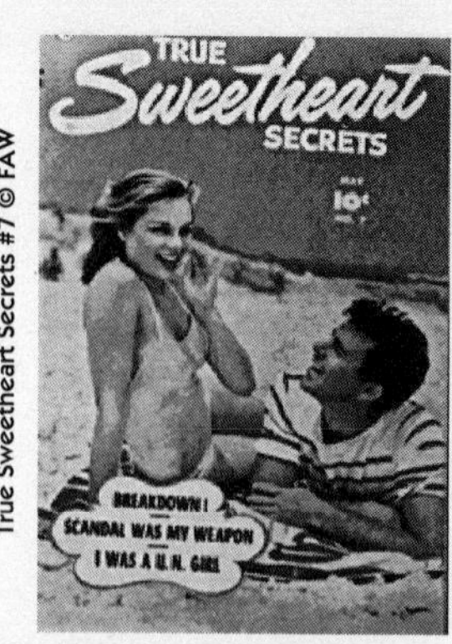

True Sweetheart Secrets #7 © FAW

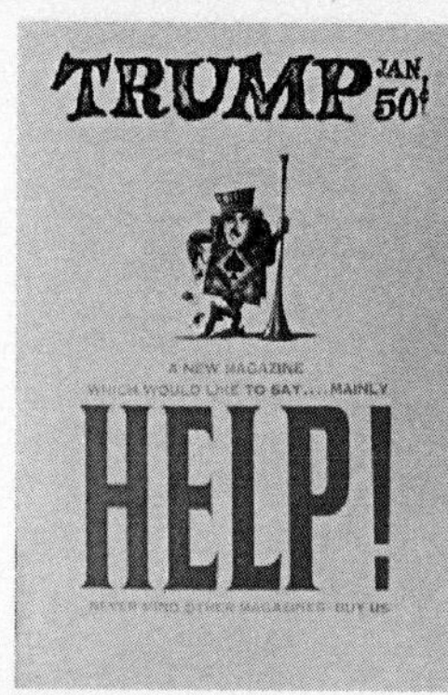

Trump #1 © HMH

	GD25	FN65	NM94
in #3,5; Baker-a in #3-5	20.00	60.00	140.00
6,7-Baker-c/a	10.00	30.00	65.00
8,10,11-Baker-c/a	10.00	30.00	60.00
9-Baker-c	7.50	22.50	45.00

TRUE MOVIE AND TELEVISION (Part teenage magazine)
Aug, 1950 - No. 3, Nov, 1950; No. 4, Mar, 1951 (52 pgs.) (1-3: 10¢)
Toby Press

	GD25	FN65	NM94
1-Elizabeth Taylor photo-c; Gene Autry, Shirley Temple, Li'l Abner app.	30.00	90.00	210.00
2-(9/50)-Janet Leigh/Liz Taylor/Ava Gardner & others photo-c; Frazetta John Wayne illo from J.Wayne Adv. Comics #2 (4/50)	23.00	70.00	160.00
3-June Allyson photo-c; Montgomery Cliff, Esther Williams, Andrews Sisters app; Li'l Abner featured; Sadie Hawkins' Day	20.00	60.00	140.00
4-Jane Powell photo-c (15¢)	10.00	30.00	60.00

NOTE: *16 pgs. in color, rest movie material in black & white.*

TRUE SECRETS (Formerly Our Love?)
No. 3, Mar, 1950; No. 4, Feb, 1951 - No. 40, Sept, 1956
Marvel (IPS)/Atlas Comics (MPI) #4 on

	GD25	FN65	NM94
3 (52 pgs.)(IPS one-shot)	9.15	27.50	55.00
4,5,7-10	4.70	14.00	28.00
6,22-Everett-a	5.85	17.50	35.00
11-20	4.00	11.00	22.00
21,23-28: 28-Last pre-code (2/55)	3.20	8.00	16.00
29-40: 24-Colletta-c. 34,36-Colletta-a	2.80	7.00	14.00

TRUE SPORT PICTURE STORIES (Formerly Sport Comics)
V1#5, Feb, 1942 - V5#2, July-Aug, 1949
Street & Smith Publications

	GD25	FN65	NM94
V1#5-Joe DiMaggio-c/story	22.00	67.00	155.00
6-12 (1942-43): 12-Jack Dempsey story	12.00	36.00	85.00
V2#1-12 (1944-45): 7-Stan Musial-c/story; photo story of the New York Yankees	10.00	30.00	70.00
V3#1-12 (1946-47): 7-Joe DiMaggio, Stan Musial, Bob Feller & others back from the armed service story. 8-Billy Conn vs. Joe Louis-c/story	10.00	30.00	60.00
V4#1-12 (1948-49), V5#1,2	9.15	27.50	55.00

NOTE: ***Powell** a-V3#10, V4#1-4, 6-8, 10-12; V5#1, 2; c-V3#11, V4#3-7, 9-12. **Ravielli** c-V5#2.*

TRUE STORIES OF ROMANCE
Jan, 1950 - No. 3, May, 1950 (All photo-c)
Fawcett Publications

	GD25	FN65	NM94
1	9.15	27.50	55.00
2,3: 3-Marcus Swayze-a	6.35	19.00	38.00

TRUE STORY OF JESSE JAMES, THE (See 4-Color #757)

TRUE SWEETHEART SECRETS
5/50; No. 2, 7/50; No. 3, 1951(nd); No. 4, 9/51 - No. 11, 1/53
Fawcett Publications (All photo-c)

	GD25	FN65	NM94
1-Photo-c; Debbie Reynolds?	10.00	30.00	60.00
2-Wood-a (11 pgs.)	12.00	36.00	85.00
3-11: 4,5-Powell-a. 8-Marcus Swayze-a	5.85	17.50	35.00

TRUE TALES OF LOVE (Formerly Secret Story Romances)
No. 22, April, 1956 - No. 31, Sept, 1957
Atlas Comics (TCI)

	GD25	FN65	NM94
22	5.00	15.00	30.00
23-31-Colletta-a in most: 25-Everett-a; Colletta-a	3.00	7.50	15.00

TRUE TALES OF ROMANCE
No. 4, June, 1950
Fawcett Publications

	GD25	FN65	NM94
4-Photo-c	5.35	16.00	32.00

TRUE 3-D
Dec, 1953 - No. 2, Feb, 1954 (25¢)(Both came with 2 pair of glasses)
Harvey Publications

	GD25	FN65	NM94
1-Nostrand, Powell-a	6.70	20.00	40.00
2-Powell-a	10.00	30.00	70.00

NOTE: *Many copies of #1 surfaced in 1984.*

TRUE-TO-LIFE ROMANCES (Formerly Guns Against Gangsters)
#8, 11-12/49; #9, 1-2/50; #3, 4/50 - #5, 9/50; #6, 1/51 - #23, 10/54
Star Publications

	GD25	FN65	NM94
8(#1, 1949)	11.00	32.00	75.00
9(#2),4-10	9.15	27.50	55.00
3-Janet Leigh/Glenn Ford photo on-c plus true life story of each	10.00	30.00	65.00
11,22,23	7.50	22.50	45.00
12-14,17-21-Disbrow-a	10.00	30.00	60.00
15,16-Wood & Disbrow-a in each	11.00	32.00	75.00

NOTE: ***Kamen** a-13. **Kamen/Feldstein** a-14. All have **L.B. Cole** covers.*

TRUE WAR EXPERIENCES
Aug, 1952 - No. 4, Dec, 1952
Harvey Publications

	GD25	FN65	NM94
1	6.70	20.00	40.00
2-4	4.00	10.00	20.00

TRUE WAR ROMANCES (Becomes Exotic Romances #22 on)
Sept, 1952 - No. 21, June, 1955
Quality Comics Group

	GD25	FN65	NM94
1-Photo-c	9.15	27.50	55.00
2	4.70	14.00	28.00
3-10: 9-Whitney-a	4.00	10.00	20.00
11-21: 20-Last precode (4/55). 14-Whitney-a	3.20	8.00	16.00

TRUE WAR STORIES (See Ripley's...)

TRUE WESTERN (True Adventures #3)
Dec, 1949 - No. 2, March, 1950
Marvel Comics (MMC)

	GD25	FN65	NM94
1-Photo-c; Billy The Kid story	11.50	34.00	80.00
2: Alan Ladd photo-c	16.00	48.00	110.00

TRUE WEST ROMANCE
No. 21, 1952
Quality Comics Group

	GD25	FN65	NM94
21 (Exist?)	4.00	10.00	20.00

TRUMP (Magazine format)
Jan, 1957 - No. 2, Mar, 1957 (50¢)
HMH Publishing Co.

	GD25	FN65	NM94
1-Harvey Kurtzman satire	17.00	52.00	120.00
2-Harvey Kurtzman satire	14.00	43.00	100.00

NOTE: ***Davis, Elder, Heath, Jaffee** art-#1,2; **Wood** a-1. Article by Mel Brooks in #2.*

TRUMPETS WEST (See 4-Color #875)

TRUTH ABOUT CRIME (See Fox Giants)

TRUTH ABOUT MOTHER GOOSE (See 4-Color #862)

TRUTH BEHIND THE TRIAL OF CARDINAL MINDSZENTY, THE (See Cardinal Mindszenty)

TRUTHFUL LOVE (Formerly Youthful Love)
No. 2, July, 1950
Youthful Magazines

	GD25	FN65	NM94
2-Ingrid Bergman's true life story	5.85	17.50	35.00

TRY-OUT WINNER BOOK (Marvel)(Value: cover or less)

TSR WORLDS (DC)(Value: cover or less)

TUBBY (See Marge's...)

TUFF GHOSTS STARRING SPOOKY
July, 1962 - No. 39, Nov, 1970; No. 40, Sept, 1971 - No. 43, Oct, 1972
Harvey Publications

	GD25	FN65	NM94
1-12¢ issues begin	8.35	25.00	50.00
2-5	4.20	12.50	25.00
6-10	3.00	7.50	15.00

Turok, Dinosaur Hunter #15 © Votager Comm.

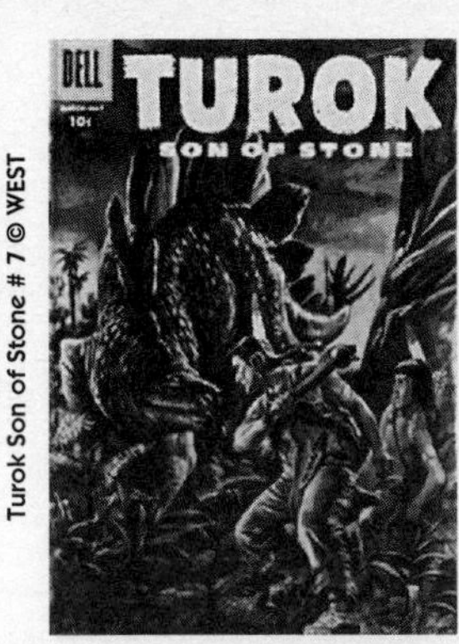

Turok Son of Stone # 7 © WEST

Tweety And Slvester #7 © Warner Bros.

	GD25	FN65	NM94
11-20	2.00	5.00	10.00
21-30: 29-Hot Stuff/Spooky team-up story	1.20	2.90	7.00
31-39,43		1.40	3.50
40-42: 52 pg. Giants		1.60	4.00

TUFFY
No. 5, July, 1949 - No. 9, Oct, 1950
Standard Comics

	GD25	FN65	NM94
5-All by Sid Hoff	4.00	12.00	24.00
6-9	2.80	7.00	14.00

TUFFY TURTLE
No date
I. W. Enterprises

	GD25	FN65	NM94
1-Reprint	.80	2.00	4.00

TUROK, DINOSAUR HUNTER (See Magnus Robot Fighter #12)
June, 1993 - Present ($2.50, color)
Valiant

	GD25	FN65	NM94
1-($3.50)-Chromium & foil-c		1.40	3.50
1-Gold foil-c variant			15.00
2-21: 4-Andar app. 5-Death of Andar. 7-9-Truman/Glanzman-a. 11-Bound-in trading card. 16-Chaos Effect		1.00	2.50
...Yearbook 1 (1994, $3.95, 52 pgs.)		1.60	4.00

TUROK, SON OF STONE (See Dan Curtis, Golden Comics Digest #31 & March of Comics #378, 399, 408)
No. 596, 12/54 - No. 29, 9/62; No. 30, 12/62 - No. 91, 7/74; No. 92, 9/74 - No. 125, 1/80; No. 126, 3/81 - No. 130, 4/82
Dell Publ. Co. #1-29(9/62)/Gold Key #30(12/62)-85(7/73)/Gold Key or Whitman #86(9/73)-125(1/80)/Whitman #126(3/81) on

	GD25	FN65	NM94
4-Color 596 (12/54)(#1)-1st app./origin Turok & Andar; dinosaur-c	75.00	225.00	525.00
4-Color 656 (10/55)(#2)-1st mention of Lanok	45.00	135.00	315.00
3(3-5/56)-5: 3-Cave men	30.00	90.00	210.00
6-10: 8-Dinosaur of the deep	19.00	58.00	135.00
11-20: 17-Prehistoric Pygmies	11.00	34.00	80.00
21-30: 30-33-Painted back-c pin-ups	8.00	24.00	55.00
31-40: 31-Drug use story	6.30	19.00	44.00
41-50	4.70	14.00	33.00
51-60: 58-Flying Saucer c/story	4.00	12.00	28.00
61-70: 62-12 & 15¢-c. 63-Only line drawn-c	3.10	9.00	22.00
71-84: 84-Origin & 1st app. Hutec	2.30	5.80	14.00
85-130:93-r-c/#19 w/changes. 94-r-c/#28 w/changes. 97-r-c/#31 w/changes. 98-r/#58 w/o spaceship & spacemen on-c. 99-r-c/#52 w/changes. 114,115-(52 pgs.)	1.40	3.50	8.50
Giant 1(30031-611) (11/66)-Slick-c; r/#10-12 & 16 plus cover to #11	11.00	34.00	80.00
Giant 1-Same as above but with paper-c	13.00	39.00	90.00

NOTE: *Most painted-c; line-drawn #63 & 130.* ***Alberto Gioletti*** *a-24-27, 30-119, 123; painted-c No. 30-129.* ***Sparling*** *a-117, 120-130. Reprints-#36, 54, 57, 75, 112, 114(1/3), 115(1/3), 118, 121, 125, 127(1/3), 128, 129(1/3), 130(1/3), Giant 1. Cover r-93, 94, 97-99, 126(all different from original covers.*

TURTLE SOUP
Sept, 1987 ($2.00, B&W, one shot, 76 pgs.)
Mirage Studios

	GD25	FN65	NM94
1-Featuring Teenage Mutant Ninja Turtles		1.40	3.50

TURTLE SOUP (Mirage, 1991-92)(Value: cover or less)

TV CASPER & COMPANY
Aug, 1963 - No. 46, April, 1974 (25¢ Giants)
Harvey Publications

	GD25	FN65	NM94
1: 68 pg. Giants begin; Casper, Little Audrey, Baby Huey, Herman & Catnip, Buzzy the Crow begin	9.15	27.50	55.00
2-5	4.20	12.50	25.00
6-10	3.00	7.50	15.00
11-20	1.70	4.20	10.00
21-31: 31-Last 68 pg. issue	1.20	2.90	7.00
32-46: All 52 pgs.		1.60	4.00

NOTE: *Many issues contain reprints.*

TV FUNDAY FUNNIES (See Famous TV...)

TV FUNNIES (See New Funnies)

TV FUNTIME (See Little Audrey)

TV LAUGHOUT (See Archie's...)

TV SCREEN CARTOONS (Formerly Real Screen)
No. 129, July-Aug, 1959 - No. 138, Jan-Feb, 1961
National Periodical Publications

	GD25	FN65	NM94
129-138 (Scarce)	9.15	27.50	55.00

TV STARS (TV)
Aug, 1978 - No. 4, Feb, 1979 (Hanna-Barbera)
Marvel Comics Group

	GD25	FN65	NM94
1-Great Grape Ape app.	1.00	2.50	5.50
2,4: 4-Top Cat app.		1.00	2.50
3-Toth-c/a; Dave Stevens inks		1.80	4.50

TV TEENS (Formerly Ozzie & Babs; Rock and Rollo #14 on)
V1#14, Feb, 1954 - V2#13, July, 1956
Charlton Comics

	GD25	FN65	NM94
V1#14 (#1)-Ozzie & Babs	6.70	20.00	40.00
15 (#2)	4.00	10.00	20.00
V2#3(6/54) - 6-Don Winslow	4.00	11.00	22.00
7-13-Mopsy. 8(7/55)	4.00	10.00	20.00

TWEETY AND SYLVESTER (1st Series)
No. 406, June, 1952 - No. 37, June-Aug, 1962
Dell Publishing Co.

	GD25	FN65	NM94
4-Color 406 (#1)-1st app.?	7.50	22.50	45.00
4-Color 489,524	4.00	11.00	22.00
4 (3-5/54) - 20	2.80	7.00	14.00
21-37	1.60	4.00	8.00

(See March of Comics #421, 433, 445, 457, 469, 481)

TWEETY AND SYLVESTER (2nd Series)(See Kite Fun Book)
Nov, 1963; No. 2, Nov, 1965 - No. 121, July, 1984
Gold Key No. 1-102/Whitman No. 103 on

	GD25	FN65	NM94
1	3.00	7.50	15.00
2-10	1.40	3.50	7.00
11-30		1.60	4.00
31-70		.80	2.00
71-121: 99,119-r(1/3)			1.00
Mini Comic No. 1(1976, 3-1/4x6-1/2")			1.00

12 O'CLOCK HIGH (TV)
Jan-Mar, 1965 - No. 2, Apr-June, 1965 (Photo-c)
Dell Publishing Co.

	GD25	FN65	NM94
1,2	4.30	13.00	30.00

24 PAGES OF COMICS (No title) (Also see Pure Oil Comics, Salerno Carnival of Comics, & Vicks Comics)
Late 1930s
Giveaway by various outlets including Sears

	GD25	FN65	NM94
nn-Contains strip reprints-Buck Rogers, Napoleon, Sky Roads, War on Crime	29.00	86.00	200.00

2099 UNLIMITED
Sept, 1993 - Present ($3.95, 68 pgs.)
Marvel Comics

	GD25	FN65	NM94
1-8: 1-1st app. Hulk 2099 & begins. 1-3-Spider-Man 2099 app.		1.60	4.00

20,000 LEAGUES UNDER THE SEA (See 4-Color #614, King Classics, Movie Comics & Power Record Comics)

TWICE TOLD TALES (See Movie Classics)

TWILIGHT (DC)(Value: cover or less)

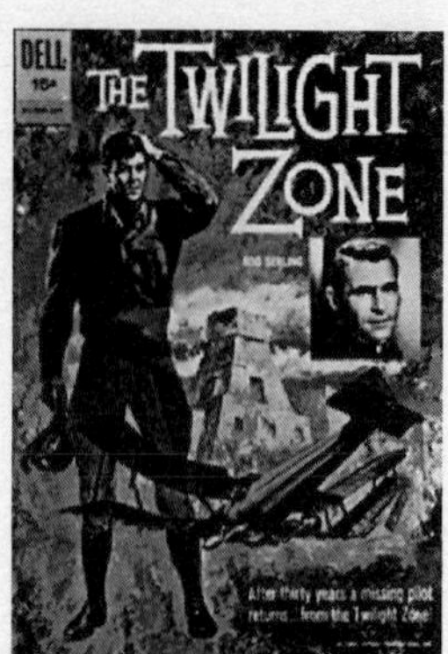

The Twilight Zone #01860-207 © CBS

Two-Fisted Tales #19 © EC

Two-Gun Kid #19 © MEG

TWILIGHT AVENGER, THE (Elite)(Value: cover or less)

TWILIGHT MAN (First)(Value: cover or less)

TWILIGHT ZONE, THE (TV) (See Dan Curtis)
No. 1173, 3-5/61 - No. 91, 4/79; No. 92, 5/82
Dell Publishing Co./Gold Key/Whitman No. 92

	GD25	FN65	NM94
4-Color 1173 (#1)-Crandall/Evans-c/a	19.00	58.00	135.00
4-Color 1288-Crandall/Evans-c/a	11.00	34.00	80.00
01-860-207 (5-7/62-Dell, 15¢)	8.00	24.00	55.00
12-860-210 on-c; 01-860-210 on inside(8-10/62-Dell)-Evans-c/a (3 stories)	8.00	24.00	55.00
1(11/62-Gold Key)-Crandall/Frazetta-a (10 & 11 pgs.); Evans-a	9.30	28.00	65.00
2	6.30	19.00	44.00
3-11: 3(11 pgs.),4(10 pgs.),9-Toth-a	4.00	12.00	28.00
12-15: 12-Williamson-a. 13,15-Crandall-a. 14-Orlando/Crandall/Torres-a	3.00	9.40	22.00
16-20	2.10	6.00	15.00
21-27: 21-Crandall-a(r). 25-Evans/Crandall-a(r); Toth-r/#4. 26-Flying Saucer-c/story; Crandall, Evans-a(r). 27-Evans-r(2)	1.60	5.00	11.00
28-32: 32-Evans-a(r)	.90	2.30	5.50
33-51: 43-Celardo-a. 51-Williamson-a		1.80	4.50
52-70		.90	2.25
71-92: 71-Reprint. 83,84-(52 pgs.). 92-r/#1		.60	1.60
Mini Comic #1(1976, 3-1/4x6-1/2")		.60	1.60

NOTE: ***Bolle*** *a-13(w/****McWilliams****), 50, 55, 57, 59, 77, 78, 80, 83, 84.* ***McWilliams*** *a-59, 78, 80, 82, 84.* ***Miller*** *a-84, 85.* ***Orlando*** *a-15, 19, 20, 22, 23.* ***Sekowsky*** *a-3.* ***Simonson*** *a-50, 54, 55, 83r.* ***Weiss*** *a-39, 79r(#39). (See Mystery Comics Digest 3, 6, 9, 12, 15, 18, 21, 24). Reprints-26(1/3), 71, 73, 79, 83, 84, 86, 92. Painted c-1-91.*

TWILIGHT ZONE, THE (TV)
Nov, 1990 ($2.95, color)
Oct, 1991; V2#1, Nov, 1991 - No. 14? 1992 ($1.95, color)
V3#1, 1993 - No. 4, 1993 ($2.50, color)
Now Comics

	GD25	FN65	NM94
1-(11/90, $2.95, 52 pgs.)-Direct sale edition; Neal Adams-a, Sienkiewicz-c; Harlan Ellison scripts	1.10	2.70	6.50
1-(11/90, $1.75)-Newsstand ed. w/N. Adams-c		.90	2.25
1-Prestige Format (10/91, $4.95)-Reprints above with extra Harlan Ellison short story	1.00	2.00	5.00
1-Collector's Edition (10/91, $2.50)-None-code approved and polybagged; reprints 11/90 issue; gold logo	1.50	3.75	9.00
1-Reprint ($2.50)-r/direct sale 11/90 version		1.00	2.50
1-Reprint ($2.50)-r/newsstand 11/90 version		1.00	2.50
V2#1-Direct sale & newsstand ed. w/different-c		.80	2.00
V2#2-8,10-14		.80	2.00
V2#9-($2.95)-3-D Special; polybagged w/glasses & hologram on-c		1.20	3.00
V2#9-($4.95)-Prestige Edition; contains 2 extra stories & a different hologram on-c; polybagged w/glasses	1.00	2.00	5.00
V3#1-4		1.00	2.50
Anniversary Special 1 (1992, $2.50)		1.00	2.50
Annual 1 (4/93, $2.50)-No ads		1.00	2.50

TWINKLE COMICS
May, 1945
Spotlight Publishers

	GD25	FN65	NM94
1	14.00	43.00	100.00

TWIST, THE
July-September, 1962
Dell Publishing Co.

	GD25	FN65	NM94
01-864-209-Painted-c	4.70	14.00	28.00

TWISTED TALES (Pacific)(Value: cover or less)

TWISTED TALES
Nov, 1982 - No. 10, Dec, 1984
Pacific Comics/Independent Comics Group

	GD25	FN65	NM94
1-10			1.50

TWO BIT THE WACKY WOODPECKER (See Wacky...)
1951 - No. 3, May, 1953
Toby Press

	GD25	FN65	NM94
1	5.85	17.50	35.00
2,3	3.60	9.00	18.00

TWO FACES OF COMMUNISM (Also see Double Talk)
1961 (36 pgs.; paper cover) (Giveaway)
Christian Anti-Communism Crusade, Houston, Texas

	GD25	FN65	NM94
nn	11.00	32.00	75.00

TWO-FISTED TALES (Formerly Haunt of Fear #15-17)
No. 18, Nov-Dec, 1950 - No. 41, Feb-Mar, 1955
E. C. Comics

	GD25	FN65	NM94
18(#1)-Kurtzman-c	79.00	235.00	550.00
19-Kurtzman-c	57.00	171.00	400.00
20-Kurtzman-c	35.00	105.00	245.00
21,22-Kurtzman-c	26.00	78.00	180.00
23-25-Kurtzman-c	20.00	60.00	140.00
26-35: 33- "Atom Bomb" by Wood	14.00	43.00	100.00
36-41	10.00	30.00	70.00
Two-Fisted Annual (1952, 25¢, 132 pgs.)	70.00	210.00	490.00
Two-Fisted Annual (1953, 25¢, 132 pgs.)	52.00	156.00	365.00

NOTE: ***Berg*** *a-29.* ***Colan*** *a-39p.* ***Craig*** *a-18, 19, 32.* ***Crandall*** *a-35, 36.* ***Davis*** *a-20-36, 40; c-30, 34, 35, 41, Annual 2.* ***Evans*** *a-34, 40, 41; c-40.* ***Feldstein*** *a-18.* ***Krigstein*** *a-41.* ***Kubert*** *a-32, 33.* ***Kurtzman*** *a-18-25; c-18-29, 31, Annual 1.* ***Severin*** *a-26, 28, 29, 31, 34-41 (No. 37-39 are all-****Severin*** *issues); c-36-39.* ***Severin/Elder*** *a-19-29, 31, 33, 36.* ***Wood*** *a-18-28, 30-35, 41; c-32, 33. Special issues: #26 (ChanJin Reservoir), 31 (Civil War), 35 (Civil War). Canadian reprints known; see Table of Contents. #25-Davis biog. #27-Wood biog. #28-Kurtzman biog.*

TWO-FISTED TALES
Oct, 1992 - Present ($1.50, color)
Russ Cochran

	GD25	FN65	NM94
1-4: 1-4r/Two-Fisted Tales #18-21 w/original-c			1.50

TWO-GUN KID (Also see All Western Winners, Best Western, Black Rider, Blaze Carson, Kid Colt, Western Winners, Wild West, & Wild Western)
3/48(No mo.) - No. 10, 11/49; No. 11, 12/53 - No. 59, 4/61; No. 60, 11/62 - No. 92, 3/68; No. 93, 7/70 - No. 136, 4/77
Marvel/Atlas (MCI No. 1-10/HPC No. 11-59/Marvel No. 60 on)

	GD25	FN65	NM94
1-Two-Gun Kid & his horse Cyclone begin; The Sheriff begins	71.00	214.00	500.00
2	30.00	90.00	210.00
3,4: 3-Annie Oakley app.	23.00	70.00	160.00
5-Pre-Black Rider app. (Wint. 48/49); spanking panel; Anti-Wertham editorial (1st?)	29.00	86.00	200.00
6-10(11/49): 8-Blaze Carson app. 9-Black Rider app.	19.00	58.00	135.00
11(12/53)-Black Rider app.; explains how Kid Colt became an outlaw	14.00	43.00	100.00
12-Black Rider app.	14.00	43.00	100.00
13-20: 13-1st to have Atlas globe on-c. 14-Opium story	11.00	32.00	75.00
21-24,26-29	10.00	30.00	65.00
25,30: 25-Williamson-a (5 pgs.). 30-Williamson/Torres-a (4 pgs.)	10.00	30.00	70.00
31-33,35,37-40	7.50	22.50	45.00
34-Crandall-a	8.35	25.00	50.00
36,41,42,48-Origin in all	8.35	25.00	50.00
43,44,47	5.85	17.50	35.00
45,46-Davis-a	6.70	20.00	40.00
49,50,52,55,57-Severin-a(2) in each	5.00	15.00	30.00
51-Williamson-a (5 pgs.)	6.70	20.00	40.00
53,54-Severin-a(3) in each	5.85	17.50	35.00
56,59: 59-Last 10¢ issue (4/61)	3.60	9.00	18.00
58,60-New origin. 58-Kirby/Ayers-c/a "The Monster of Hidden Valley" cover/story (Kirby monster-c)	3.60	9.00	18.00

2001: A Space Odyssey #5 ©

Ultraforce #1 © Malibu

Uncanny Tales #8 © MEG

GD25 FN65 NM94

61-80: 64-Intro. Boom-Boom 1.80 4.50 9.00
81-92: 92-Last new story; last 12¢ issue .80 2.00 4.00
93-100,102-136 .30 .75 1.50
101-Origin retold/#58 .60 1.50 3.00
NOTE: ***Ayers*** *a-26, 27.* ***Davis*** *c-45-47.* ***Drucker*** *a-23.* ***Everett*** *a-82, 91.* ***Fuje*** *a-13.* ***Heath*** *a-3(2), 4(3), 5(2), 7; c-13, 21, 23, 53.* ***Keller*** *a-16, 19, 28.* ***Kirby*** *a-54, 55, 57-62, 75-77, 90, 95, 101, 119, 120, 129; c-10, 52, 54-65, 67-72, 74-76, 116.* ***Maneely*** *a-20; c-11, 12, 16, 19, 20, 25-28, 35, 49.* ***Powell*** *a-38, 102, 104.* ***Severin*** *a-9, 29, 51, 55, 57, 99r(3); c-9, 51, 99.* ***Shores*** *c-1-8, 11.* ***Tuska*** *a-11, 12.* ***Whitney*** *a-87, 89-91, 98-113, 124, 129; c-87, 89, 91, 113.* ***Wildey*** *a-21.* ***Williamson*** *a-110r. Kid Colt in #13, 14, 16-21.*

TWO GUN WESTERN (1st Series) (Formerly Casey Crime Photographer #1-4? or My Love #1-4?)
No. 5, Nov, 1950 - No. 14, June, 1952
Marvel/Atlas Comics (MPC)

5-The Apache Kid (Intro & origin) & his horse Nightwind begin by Buscema
17.00 52.00 120.00
6-10: 8-Kid Colt, The Texas Kid & his horse Thunder begin?
11.50 34.00 80.00
11-14: 13-Black Rider app. 10.00 30.00 60.00
NOTE: ***Maneely*** *a-6, 7, 9; c-6, 11-13.* ***Morrow*** *a-9.* ***Romita*** *a-8.* ***Wildey*** *a-8.*

2-GUN WESTERN (2nd Series) (Formerly Billy Buckskin #1-3; Two-Gun Western #5 on)
No. 4, May, 1956
Atlas Comics (MgPC)

4-Colan, Ditko, Severin, Sinnott-a; Maneely-c 11.00 32.00 75.00

TWO-GUN WESTERN (Formerly 2-Gun Western)
No. 5, July, 1956 - No. 12, Sept, 1957
Atlas Comics (MgPC)

5-Return of the Gun-Hawk-c/story; Black Rider app. 10.00 30.00 60.00
6,7 6.70 20.00 40.00
8,10,12-Crandall-a 8.35 25.00 50.00
9,11-Williamson-a in both (5 pgs. each) 8.35 25.00 50.00
NOTE: ***Ayers*** *a-9.* ***Colan*** *a-5.* ***Everett*** *c-12.* ***Forgione*** *a-5, 6.* ***Kirby*** *a-12.* ***Maneely*** *a-6, 8, 12; c-5, 6, 8, 11.* ***Morrow*** *a-9, 10.* ***Powell*** *a-7, 11.* ***Severin*** *c-10.* ***Sinnott*** *a-5.* ***Wildey*** *a-9.*

TWO MOUSEKETEERS, THE (See 4-Color #475, 603, 642 under M.G.M.'s...; becomes M.G.M.'s Mouse Musketeers)

TWO ON A GUILLOTINE (See Movie Classics)

2000 A.D. MONTHLY/PRESENTS (Eagle/Quality)(Value: cover or less)

2000 AD SHOWCASE (Quality)(Value: cover or less)

2001, A SPACE ODYSSEY (Marvel, Treasury Special & '76 series)(Value: cover or less)

2001 NIGHTS (Viz)(Value: cover or less)

2010 (Marvel)(Value: cover or less)

UFO & ALIEN COMIX
Jan, 1978 (One Shot)
Warren Publishing Co.

nn-Toth, Severin-a(r) 1.00 2.50

UFO & OUTER SPACE (Formerly UFO Flying Saucers)
No. 14, June, 1978 - No. 25, Feb, 1980 (All painted covers)
Gold Key

14-Reprints UFO Flying Saucers #3 1.00 2.50
15,16-Reprints 1.50
17-20-New material .80 2.00
21-25: 23-McWilliams-a. 24-(3 pg.-r). 25-Reprints UFO Flying Saucers #2 w/cover 1.50

UFO ENCOUNTERS
May, 1978 (228 pgs.) ($1.95)
Western Publishing Co.

11192-Reprints UFO Flying Saucers 1.60 4.00
11404-Vol.1 (128 pgs.)-See UFO Mysteries for Vol.2 .80 2.00

UFO FLYING SAUCERS (UFO & Outer Space #14 on)
Oct, 1968 - No. 13, Jan, 1977 (No. 2 on, 36 pgs.)
Gold Key

1(30035-810) (68 pgs.) 2.15 6.50 15.00
2(11/70), 3(11/72), 4(11/74) 1.30 3.25 8.00
5(2/75)-13: Bolle-a #4 on 1.00 2.00 5.00

UFO MYSTERIES
1978 (96 pgs.) ($1.00) (Reprints)
Western Publishing Co.

11400($1.00, 96 pgs.) .80 2.00
11404(Vol.2)-Cont'd from UFO Encounters, pgs. 129-224 .80 2.00

ULTRACYBERNETIC DOLPHINDROIDS, THE
Dec, 1993 - Present ($2.50, color, mini-series)
Polestar Comics

1 1.00 2.50

ULTRAFORCE
Aug, 1994 - Present ($1.95, color)
Malibu Comics

1-($2.50, 44 pgs.)-Bound-in trading card; team consisting of Prime, Prototype, Hardcase, Pixx, Ghoul, Contrary & Topaz 1.00 2.50

ULTRA KLUTZ (Onward)(Value: cover or less)

ULTRAMAN
Mar, 1994 - Present ($1.75/1.95, color)
Nemesis Comics

-1,1-($2.25)-Collector's edition. -1-Foil-c. 1-Special 3/4 wraparound-c
.90 2.25
-1,1-($1.75)-Newsstand edition .70 1.75
2-4: 3-Begin $1.95-c .80 2.00

ULTRAVERSE ORIGINS
Jan, 1994 (99¢)
Malibu Comics

1-Gatefold-c; 2 pg. origins all characters 1.00
1-Newsstand edition; different-c, no gatefold 1.00

UNBIRTHDAY PARTY WITH ALICE IN WONDERLAND (See 4-Color #341)

ULTRAVERSE PREMIERE
1994
Malibu Comics

0-Ordered thru mail w/coupons 2.10 5.00

UNCANNY TALES
June, 1952 - No. 56, Sept, 1957
Atlas Comics (PrPI/PPI)

1-Heath-a; horror/weird stories begin 48.00 145.00 335.00
2 24.00 73.00 170.00
3-5 21.00 63.00 145.00
6-Wolvertonish-a by Matt Fox 21.00 63.00 145.00
7-10: 8-Atom bomb story; Tothish-a (by Sekowsky?). 9-Crandall-a
18.00 54.00 125.00
11-20: 17-Atom bomb panels; anti-communist story; Hitler story. 19-Krenkel-a
14.00 43.00 100.00
21-27: 25-Nostrand-a? 12.00 36.00 85.00
28-Last precode issue (1/55); Kubert-a; #1-28 contain 2-3 sci/fi stories each
13.00 40.00 90.00
29-41,43-49,51,52: 52-Oldest? Iron Man prototype (2/57)
9.15 27.50 55.00
42,54,56-Krigstein-a 10.00 30.00 65.00
50,53,55-Torres-a 9.15 27.50 55.00
NOTE: ***Andru*** *a-15, 27.* ***Ayers*** *a-22.* ***Bailey*** *a-51.* ***Briefer*** *a-19, 20.* ***Brodsky*** *c-1, 3, 4, 6, 8, 12-16, 19.* ***Brodsky/Everett*** *c-9.* ***Cameron*** *a-47.* ***Colan*** *a-11, 16, 17, 52.* ***Drucker*** *a-37, 42, 45.* ***Everett*** *a-2, 9, 12, 32, 36, 39, 48; c-7, 11, 17, 39, 41, 50, 52, 53.* ***Fass*** *a-9, 10, 15, 24. Forte a-18, 27, 34, 52, 53.* ***Heath*** *a-13, 14; c-5, 10, 18.* ***Keller*** *a-3.* ***Lawrence*** *a-14, 17, 19, 23, 27, 28, 35.* ***Maneely*** *a-4, 8, 10, 16, 29, 35; c-2, 22, 26, 33, 38.* ***Moldoff*** *a-23.* ***Morisi*** *a-48, 52.* ***Morrow*** *a-46, 51.* ***Orlando*** *a-49, 50, 53.* ***Powell*** *a-12, 18, 34, 36, 38, 43, 50, 56.* ***Robinson*** *a-3, 13.* ***Reinman*** *a-12.* ***Romita*** *a-10.* ***Roussos*** *a-8.* ***Sale*** *a-47, 53; c-20.* ***Sekowsky*** *a-25.* ***Sinnott*** *a-15, 52.* ***Torres*** *a-53.* ***Tothish****-a by* ***Andru****-27.* ***Wildey*** *a-22, 48.*

The Uncanny X-Men #148 © MEG

The Uncanny X-Men #153 © MEG

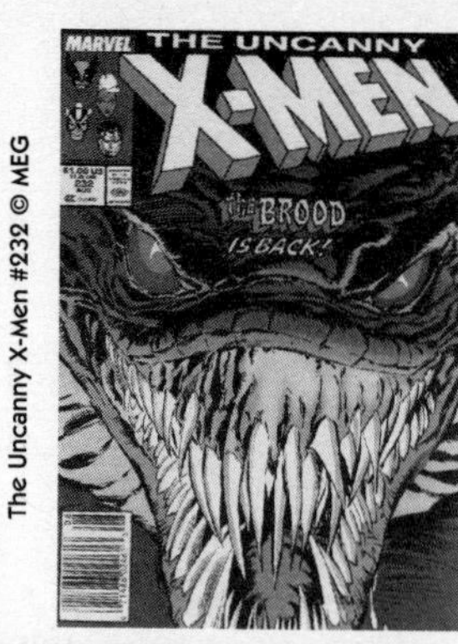

The Uncanny X-Men #232 © MEG

GD25 FN65 NM94

UNCANNY TALES
Dec, 1973 - No. 12, Oct, 1975
Marvel Comics Group

1-12: 1-Crandall-r/Uncanny Tales #9('50s) 1.00 2.50
NOTE: *Ditko* reprints-#4, 6-8, 10-12.

UNCANNY X-MEN, THE (The X-Men #1-93; X-Men #94-141; The Uncanny X-Men on-c only #114-141; The Uncanny X-Men #142 on)
Sept, 1963 - No. 66, Mar, 1970; No. 67, Dec, 1970 - Present
Marvel Comics Group

GD25 FN65 VF82 NM94

1-Origin/1st app. X-Men (Angel, Beast, Cyclops, Iceman & Marvel Girl); 1st app. Magneto & Professor X 360.00 1067.00 2133.00 3200.00

GD25 FN65 NM94

2-1st app. The Vanisher 125.00 375.00 1125.00
3-1st app. The Blob (1/64) 55.00 165.00 495.00
4-1st Quick Silver & Scarlet Witch & Brotherhood of the Evil Mutants (3/64); 1st app. Toad; 2nd app. Magneto 44.00 133.00 400.00
5-Magneto & Evil Mutants-c/story 33.00 98.00 295.00
6-10: 6-Sub-Mariner app. 7-Magneto app. 8-1st Unus the Untouchable. 9-Early Avengers app. (1/65); 1st Lucifer. 10-1st S.A. app. Ka-Zar & Zabu the sabertooth (3/65) 23.00 70.00 210.00
11,13-15: 11-1st app. The Stranger. 14-1st app. Sentinels. 15-Origin Beast 21.00 64.00 170.00
12-Origin Prof. X; Origin/1st app. Juggernaut 23.00 69.00 185.00
16-20: 19-1st app. The Mimic (4/66) 10.00 29.00 78.00
21-27,29,30: 27-Re-enter The Mimic (r-in #75); Spider-Man cameo 9.00 28.00 65.00
28-1st app. The Banshee (1/67)(r-in #76) 12.00 36.00 85.00
31-34,36,37,39,40: 34-Adkins-c/a. 39-New costumes 6.40 19.00 45.00
35-Spider-Man x-over (8/67)(r-in #83); 1st app. Changeling 10.00 30.00 70.00
38-Origins of the X-Men series begins, ends #57 9.00 28.00 65.00
41-49: 42-Death of Prof. X (Changeling disguised as). 44-1st S.A. app. G.A. Red Raven. 49-Steranko-c; 1st Polaris 5.70 17.00 40.00
50,51-Steranko-c/a 6.30 19.00 44.00
52 4.00 12.00 28.00
53-Barry Smith-c/a (his 1st comic book work) 6.30 19.00 44.00
54,55-B. Smith-c. 54-1st app. Alex Summers who later becomes Havok. 55-Summers discovers he has mutant powers 5.40 16.00 38.00
56,57,59-63,65-Neal Adams-a(p). 56-Intro Havok without costume. 65-Return of Professor X 5.40 16.00 38.00
58-1st app. Havok in costume; N. Adams-a(p) 9.00 26.00 60.00
64-1st app. Sunfire 6.30 19.00 44.00
66-Last new story w/original X-Men; battles Hulk 4.00 12.00 29.00
67-70,72: (52 pgs.). 67-Reprints begin, end #93 2.70 8.10 19.00
71,73-93: 71-Last 15¢ issue. 73-86-r/#25-38 w/new-c. 83-Spider-Man-c/story. 87-93-r/#39-45 with covers 2.10 6.00 15.00
94 (8/75)-New X-Men begin (see Giant-Size X-Men for 1st app.); Colossus, Nightcrawler, Thunderbird, Storm, Wolverine, & Banshee join; Angel, Marvel Girl, & Iceman resign 29.00 87.00 290.00
94-Variant w/Mark Jewelers pull-out ad 29.00 87.00 290.00
95-Death of Thunderbird 8.00 24.00 55.00
96-99: 98,99-25¢ & 30¢ versions exist 6.30 19.00 44.00
100-Old vs. New X-Men; part origin Phoenix; last 25¢ issue (8/76) 7.00 21.00 48.00
101-Phoenix origin concludes 5.40 16.00 38.00
102-107: 102-Origin Storm. 104-1st app. Starjammers (brief cameo); Magneto-c/story. 106-Old vs. New X-Men; 30¢ & 35¢ issues exist. 107-1st full app. Starjammers; last 30¢ issue 2.70 8.10 19.00
108-Byrne-a begins (see Marvel Team-Up #53) 5.40 16.00 38.00
109-1st app. Weapon Alpha (becomes Vindicator) 4.70 14.00 33.00
110,111: 110-Phoenix joins 2.70 8.10 19.00
112-119: 117-Origin Professor X 2.30 7.00 16.00
120-1st app. Alpha Flight (cameo), story line begins (4/79); 1st app. Vindicator (formerly Weapon Alpha); last 35¢ issue 5.00 15.00 35.00

GD25 FN65 NM94

121-1st full Alpha Flight story 5.40 16.00 38.00
122-128: 123-Spider-Man x-over. 124-Colossus becomes Proletarian 2.10 6.40 15.00
129-Intro Kitty Pryde (1/80); last Banshee; Dark Phoenix saga begins 2.30 7.00 16.00
130-1st app. The Dazzler by Byrne (2/80) 2.40 7.30 17.00
131-135: 131-Dazzler app. 132-1st White Queen. 133-Wolverine app. 134-Phoenix becomes Dark Phoenix 1.70 5.10 12.00
136,138: 138-Dazzler app.; Cyclops leaves 1.70 4.20 10.00
137-Giant; death of Phoenix 1.90 6.00 13.00
139-Alpha Flight app.; Kitty Pryde joins; new costume for Wolverine 3.40 10.30 24.00
140-Alpha Flight app. 3.00 9.40 22.00
141-Intro Future X-Men & The New Brotherhood of Evil Mutants; 1st app. Rachel (Phoenix II); death of Frank Richards 3.40 10.30 24.00
142-Rachel app.; deaths of Wolverine, Storm & Colossus 2.70 8.10 19.00
143-Last Byrne issue 1.50 3.80 9.00
144-150: 144-Man-Thing app. 145-Old X-Men app. 148-Spider-Woman, Dazzler app. 150-Double size 1.30 3.00 7.50
151-157,159-161,163,164: 161-Origin Magneto. 163-Origin Binary. 164-1st app. Binary as Carol Danvers 1.00 2.00 5.00
158-1st app. Rogue in X-Men (6/82, see Avengers Annual #10) 1.00 2.50 6.00
162-Wolverine solo story 1.70 4.20 10.00
165-Paul Smith-c/a begins, ends #175 1.30 3.00 8.00
166-Double size; Paul Smith-a 1.10 2.70 6.50
167-170: 167-New Mutants app. (3/83); same date as New Mutants #1; 1st meeting w/X-Men; ties into N.M. #3,4; Starjammers app.; contains skin "Tattooz" decals. 168-1st app. Madelyne Pryor (last pg. cameo) in X-Men (see Avengers Annual #10) .90 2.30 5.50
171-Rogue joins X-Men; Simonson-c/a 1.40 3.50 8.50
172-174: 172,173-Two part Wolverine solo story. 173-Two cover variations, blue & black. 174-Phoenix cameo 1.00 2.00 5.00
175-(52 pgs.)-Anniversary issue; Phoenix returns 1.00 2.50 6.00
176-185: 181-Sunfire app. 182-Rogue solo story. 184-1st app. Forge (8/84) 1.60 4.00
186-Double-size; Barry Smith/Austin-a 1.00 2.00 5.00
187-192,194-199: 190,191-Spider-Man & Avengers x-over. 195-Power Pack x-over 1.60 4.00
193-Double size; 100th app. New X-Men; 1st app. Warpath in costume (see New Mutants #16) 1.00 2.50 6.00
200-(12/85, $1.25, 52 pgs.) 1.70 4.20 10.00
201-(1/86)-1st app. Cable? (as baby Nathan; see X-Factor #1); 1st Whilce Portacio-c/a(i) on X-Men (guest artist) 3.60 10.70 25.00
202-204,206-209: 204-Nightcrawler solo story; 2nd Portacio-a(i) on X-Men. 207-Wolverine/Phoenix story 1.00 2.50 6.00
205-Wolverine solo story by Barry Smith 2.40 7.30 17.00
210,211-Mutant Massacre begins 2.90 9.00 20.00
212,213-Wolverine vs. Sabretooth (Mutant Mass.) 5.00 15.00 35.00
214-221,223,224: 219-Havok joins (7/87); brief app. Sabretooth 1.00 2.00 5.00
222-Wolverine battles Sabretooth-c/story 2.40 7.30 17.00
225-227: Fall Of The Mutants. 226-Double size 1.50 3.80 9.00
228-239,241: 229-$1.00 begin 1.00 2.00 5.00
240-Sabretooth app. 1.00 2.50 6.00
242-Double size, X-Factor app., Inferno tie-in 1.00 2.00 5.00
243,245-247: 245-Rob Liefeld-a(p) 1.60 4.00
244-1st app. Jubilee 1.50 3.80 9.00
248-1st Jim Lee art on X-Men (1989) 4.70 14.00 33.00
248-2nd printing (1992, $1.25) 1.25
249-252: 252-Lee-c 1.00 2.50
253-255: 253-All new X-Men begin. 254-Lee-c 1.80 4.50
256,257-Jim Lee-c/a begins 1.70 5.10 12.00
258-Wolverine solo story; Lee-c/a 2.00 6.00 14.00
259-Silvestri-c/a; no Lee-a 1.00 2.50 6.00

The Uncanny X-Men #274 © MEG

The Uncanny X-Men #317 © MEG

The Uncanny X-Men Annual #18 © MEG

GD25 FN65 NM94

260-265-No Lee-a. 260,261,264-Lee-c 1.00 2.50
266-1st full app. Gambit (see Ann. #14)-No Lee-a 4.10 12.40 29.00
267-Jim Lee-c/a resumes; 2nd full Gambit app. 2.00 6.00 14.00
268-Capt. America, Black Widow & Wolverine team-up; Lee-a 3.30 9.90 23.00
269-Lee-a 1.00 2.90 7.00
270-X-Tinction Agenda begins 1.70 5.10 12.00
270-Gold 2nd printing 1.60 4.00
271,272-X-Tinction Agenda 1.30 3.00 8.00
273-New Mutants (Cable) & X-Factor x-over; Golden, Byrne & Lee part pencils 1.20 2.90 7.00
274 1.00 2.50 6.00
275-($1.50, 52 pgs.)-Tri-fold-c by Jim Lee (p); Prof. X 1.20 2.90 7.00
275-Gold 2nd printing 1.00 2.50
276-280: 277-Last Lee-c/a. 280-X-Factor x-over .70 1.80
281-(10/91)-New team begins (Storm, Archangel, Colossus, Iceman & Marvel Girl); Whilce Portacio-c/a begins; Byrne scripts begin; wraparound-c (white logo) 1.10 2.70 6.50
281-2nd printing with red metallic ink logo w/o UPC box ($1.00-c); does not say 2nd printing inside 1.10
282-1st app. Bishop (cover & 1 pg. cameo) 1.10 2.70 6.50
282-Gold ink 2nd printing ($1.00-c) 1.00
283-1st full app. Bishop (12/91) 1.70 4.20 10.00
284-293,297-299: 284-Last $1.00-c. 286,287-Lee plots. 287-Bishop joins team. 288-Lee/Portacio plots. 290-Last Portacio-c/a. 294-Brandon Peterson-a(p) begins (#292 is 1st Peterson-c) 1.25
294-296 ($1.50)-Polybagged w/trading card in each; X-Cutioner's Song x-overs; all have Peterson/Austin-c/a .80 2.00
300-($3.95, 68 pgs.)-Holo-grafx foil-c; Magneto app. 1.60 4.00
301-303,305-309,311 1.25
304-($3.95, 68 pgs.)-Wraparound-c with Magneto hologram on-c; 30th anniversary issue; Jae Lee-a (4 pgs.) 1.60 4.00
310-($1.95)-Bound-in trading card sheet .80 2.00
312-321: 312-Begin $1.50-c; bound-in card sheet 1.50
316,317-($2.95)-Foil enhanced editions 1.20 3.00
318-322-($1.95)-Deluxe editions .80 2.00
Special 1(12/70)-Kirby-c/a; origin The Stranger 6.40 19.00 45.00
Special 2(11/71) 5.70 17.00 40.00
Annual 3(1979, 52 pgs.)-New story; Miller/Austin-c; Wolverine still in old yellow costume 2.40 7.30 17.00
Annual 4(1980, 52 pgs.)-Dr. Strange guest stars 1.30 3.00 7.50
Annual 5(1981, 52 pgs.) 1.00 2.50 6.00
Annual 6(1982, 52 pgs.)-Dracula app. 1.00 2.00 5.00
Annual 7,8: 7-(1983, 52 pgs.). 8-(1984, 52 pgs.) 1.00 2.00 5.00
Annual 9(1985)-New Mutants x-over cont'd from New Mutants Special Ed. #1; Art Adams-a 1.85 5.50 13.00
Annual 10(1986)-Art Adams-a 1.65 4.70 11.00
Annual 11(1987) 1.20 3.00
Annual 12(1988, $1.75)-Evolutionary War; A.Adams-a(p) 1.60 4.00
Annual 13(1989, $2.00, 68 pgs.)-Atlantis Attacks 1.20 3.00
Annual 14(1990, $2.00, 68 pgs.)-1st app. Gambit (minor app., 5 pgs.); Fantastic Four, New Mutants (Cable) & X-Factor x-over; Arthur Adams-c/a(p) 1.30 3.25 8.00
Annual 15 (1991, $2.00, 68 pgs.)-4 pg. origin; New Mutants x-over; 4 pg. Wolverine solo back-up story; 4th app. X-Force cont'd from New Warriors Annual #1 1.60 4.00
Annual 16 (1992, $2.25, 68 pgs.)-Jae Lee-c/a(p)(2) .90 2.25
Annual 17 (1993, $2.95, 68 pgs.)-Bagged w/card 1.20 3.00
Annual 18 (1994, $2.95, 68 pgs.) 1.20 3.00
...-The Dark Phoenix Saga (1990, $12.95) 1.90 5.60 13.00

NOTE: **Art Adams** *a-Annual 9, 10p, 12p, 14p; c-218p.* **Neal Adams** *a-56-63p, 65p; c-56-63.* **Adkins** *a-34, 35p; c-31, 34, 35.* **Austin** *a-108i, 109i, 111-117i, 119-143i, 186i, 204i, 228i, 294-297i, Annual 3i, 7i, 9i, 13; c-109-111i, 114-122i, 123, 124-141i, 142, 143, 196i, 204i, 228i, 294-297i, Annual 3i.* **J. Buscema** *c-42, 43, 45.* **Buscema/Tuska** *a-45.* **Byrne** *a(p)-108, 109, 111-143, 273; c(p)-113-116, 127, 129, 131-141.* **Capullo** *c-14.* **Ditko** *r-86, 89-91, 93.* **Everett** *c-73.* **Golden** *a-273, Annual 7p.* **Guice** *a-216p, 217p.* **G. Kane** *c(p)-33, 74-76, 79, 80, 94, 95.* **Kirby** *a(p)-1-17 (#12-17, 67r-layouts); c(p)-1-17, 25, 30 (18, 26-parts).* **Layton** *a-105i; c-112i, 113i.* **Jim Lee** *a(p)-248, 256-258, 267-277; c(p)-252, 254, 256-261, 264, 267, 270, 275-277, 286.* **Perez** *a-Annual 3p; c(p)-112, 128, Annual 3.* **Peterson** *a(p)-294-300, 304(part); c(p)-294-299.* **Whilce Portacio** *a(p)-281-286, 289, 290; a(i)-267; c-281-285p, 289p, 290; c(i)-267.* **Romita, Jr.** *a-300; c-300.* **Roussos** *a-84i.* **Simonson** *a-171p; c-171, 217.* **B. Smith** *a-53, 186p, 198p, 205, 214; c-53-55, 186p, 198, 205, 212, 214, 216.* **Paul Smith** *a(p)-165-170, 172-175, 278; c-165-170, 172-175, 278.* **Sparling** *a-78p.* **Steranko** *a-50p, 51p; c-49-51.* **Sutton** *a-106i.* **Art Thibert** *a(i)-281-286; c(i)-281, 282, 284, 285.* **Toth** *a-12p, 67p(r).* **Tuska** *a-40-42i, 43-46p, 88i(r); c-39-41, 77p, 78p.* **Williamson** *a-202i, 203i, 211i; c-202i, 203i, 206i.* **Wood** *c-14i.*

UNCANNY X-MEN AND THE NEW TEEN TITANS (See Marvel and DC Present...)

UNCANNY X-MEN AT THE STATE FAIR OF TEXAS, THE
1983 (36 pgs.)(One-Shot)
Marvel Comics Group
nn-Supplement to the Dallas Times Herald 3.20 8.00 20.00

UNCANNY X-MEN IN DAYS OF FUTURE PAST, THE
1989 ($3.95, squarebound, 52 pgs.)
Marvel Comics
nn-Byrne/Austin-r (2 stories); Guice-c(p) 1.60 4.00

UNCENSORED MOUSE, THE
Apr, 1989 - No. 2, Apr, 1989 ($1.95, B&W)(Came sealed in plastic bag)
Eternity Comics
1-Early Gottfredson strip-r in each 1.60 4.00
2-Both contain racial stereotyping & violence 1.00 2.50 6.00
NOTE: *Both issues contain unauthorized reprints. Series was cancelled.* **Win Smith** *r-1, 2.*

UNCLE CHARLIE'S FABLES
Jan, 1952 - No. 5, Sept, 1952 (All have Biro painted-c)
Lev Gleason Publications
1-Norman Maurer-a; has Biro's picture 9.15 27.50 55.00
2-Fuje-a; Biro photo 6.35 19.00 38.00
3-5 5.00 15.00 30.00

UNCLE DONALD & HIS NEPHEWS DUDE RANCH (See Dell Giant #52)

UNCLE DONALD & HIS NEPHEWS FAMILY FUN (See Dell Giant #38)

UNCLE JOE'S FUNNIES
1938 (B&W)
Centaur Publications
1-Games, puzzles & magic tricks, some interior art; Bill Everett-c 30.00 90.00 210.00

UNCLE MILTY (TV)
Dec, 1950 - No. 4, July, 1951 (52 pgs.)(Early TV comic)
Victoria Publications/True Cross
1-Milton Berle photo on-c of #1,2 39.00 118.00 275.00
2 22.00 65.00 150.00
3,4 18.00 54.00 125.00

UNCLE REMUS & HIS TALES OF BRER RABBIT (See 4-Color #129, 208, 693)

UNCLE SAM QUARTERLY (Blackhawk #9 on)(See Freedom Fighters)
Autumn, 1941 - No. 8, Fall, 1943 (Also see National Comics)
Quality Comics Group
1-Origin Uncle Sam; Fine/Eisner-c, chapter headings, 2 pgs. by Eisner; (2 versions: dark cover, no price; light cover with price sticker); Jack Cole-a 214.00 643.00 1500.00
2-Cameos by The Ray, Black Condor, Quicksilver, The Red Bee, Alias the Spider, Hercules & Neon the Unknown; Eisner, Fine-c/a 86.00 257.00 600.00
3-Tuska-c/a; Eisner-a(2) 64.00 193.00 450.00
4 57.00 171.00 400.00
5-8: 7-Hitler, Mussolini & Tojo-c 46.00 139.00 325.00
NOTE: **Kotzky** *(or* **Tuska***) a-3-8.*

UNCLE SAM'S CHRISTMAS STORY
1958
Promotional Publ. Co. (Giveaway)
nn-Reprints 1956 Christmas USA 2.40 6.00 12.00

UNCLE SCROOGE (Disney) (Becomes Walt Disney's... #210 on) (See Cartoon Tales, Dell Giants #33, 55, Disney Comic Album, Donald and Scrooge,

Uncle Scrooge #4 © WDC

Undercover Girl #6 © ME

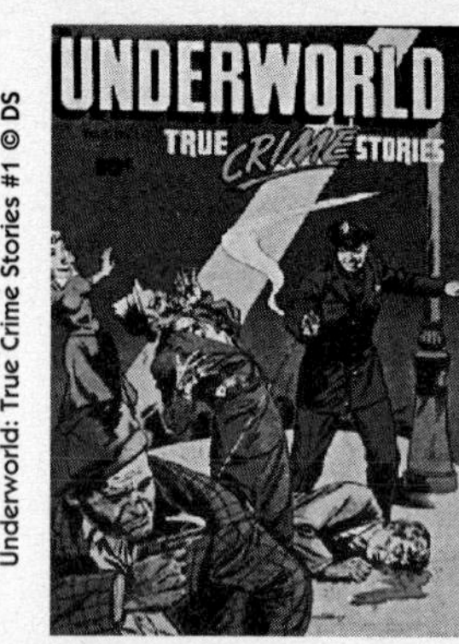

Underworld: True Crime Stories #1 © DS

GD25 FN65 NM94

Dynabrite, Four Color #178, Gladstone Comic Album, Walt Disney's Comics & Stories #98, Walt Disney's ...)
No. 386, 3/52 - No. 39, 8-10/62; No. 40, 12/62 - No. 209, 1984
Dell #1-39/Gold Key #40-173/Whitman #174-209

4-Color 386(#1)-in "Only a Poor Old Man" by Carl Barks; r-in Uncle Scrooge & Donald Duck #1('65) & The Best of Walt Disney Comics (1974) — 100.00 300.00 700.00
1-(1986)-Reprints F.C. #386; given away with lithograph "Dam Disaster at Money Lake" & as a subscription offer giveaway to Gladstone subscribers — 2.60 7.70 18.00
4-Color 456(#2)-in "Back to the Klondike" by Carl Barks; r-in Best of U.S. & D.D. #1('66) & Gladstone C.A. #4 — 57.00 171.00 400.00
4-Color 495(#3)-r-in #105 — 43.00 130.00 300.00
4(12-2/53-54)-r-in Gladstone Comic Album #11 — 36.00 107.00 250.00
5-r-in Gladstone Special #2 & W.D. Digest #1 — 29.00 86.00 200.00
6-r-in U.S. #106,165,233 & Best of U.S. & D.D. #1('66) — 25.00 75.00 175.00
7-The Seven Cities of Cibola by Barks; r-in #217 & Best of D.D. & U.S. #2 ('67) — 22.00 65.00 150.00
8-10: 8-r-in #111,222. 9-r-in #104,214. 10-r-in #67 — 17.00 52.00 120.00
11-20: 11-r-in #237. 17-r-in #215. 19-r-in Gladstone C.A. #1. 20-r-in #213 — 15.00 45.00 105.00
21-30: 24-X-Mas-c. 26-r-in #211 — 13.00 40.00 90.00
31-35,37-40: 34-r-in #228. 40-X-Mas-c — 11.00 32.00 75.00
36-1st app. Magica De Spell; Number one dime 1st identified by name — 13.00 40.00 90.00
41-60: 48-Magica De Spell-c/story (3/64). 49-Sci/fi-c. 51-Beagle Boys-c/story (8/64) — 10.00 30.00 60.00
61-63,66,68-70:70-Last Barks issue w/original story — 8.35 25.00 50.00
64-Barks Vietnam War story "Treasure of Marco Polo" banned for reprints by Disney since the 1970s because of its third world revolutionary war theme — 14.00 43.00 100.00
67,71-73: 67,72,73-Barks-r. 71-Barks script only — 8.35 25.00 50.00
74-84: 74-Barks-r(1pg.). 75-81,83-Not by Barks. 82,84-Barks-r begin — 5.85 17.50 35.00
85-110 — 4.30 13.00 30.00
111-141,143-152,154-157 — 2.30 6.90 16.00
142-Reprints 4-Color #456 with-c — 2.85 8.00 20.00
153,158,162-164,166,168-170,178,180: No Barks — 1.00 2.50 6.00
159-160,165,167,172-176-Barks-a — 1.30 3.25 8.00
161(r/#14), 171(r/#11), 177(r/#16), 179(r/#9), 183(r/#6)-Barks-r — 1.00 2.00 8.00
181(r/4-Color #495), 195(r/4-Color #386) — 1.30 3.25 8.00
182,186,191-194,197-202,204-206: No Barks — 1.00 2.00 5.00
184,185,187,188-Barks-a — 1.00 2.50 6.00
189(r/#5), 190(r/#4), 196(r/#13), 203(r/#12), 207(r/#93,92), 208(r/U.S. #18), 209(r/U.S. #21)-Barks-r — 1.00 2.50 6.00
Uncle Scrooge & Money(G.K.)-Barks-r/from WDC&S #130 (3/67) — 5.00 15.00 30.00
Mini Comic #1(1976)(3-1/4x6-1/2")-r/U.S. #115; Barks-c — 1.00
NOTE: *Barks c-4-Color 386, 456, 495, #4-37, 39, 40, 43-71.*

UNCLE SCROOGE & DONALD DUCK
June, 1965 (25¢, paper cover)
Gold Key
1-Reprint of 4-Color #386(#1) & lead story from 4-Color #29 — 10.00 30.00 60.00

UNCLE SCROOGE COMICS DIGEST
Dec, 1986 - No. 5, Aug, 1987 ($1.25, Digest-size)
Gladstone Publishing
1-5 — 1.25

UNCLE SCROOGE GOES TO DISNEYLAND (See Dell Giants)
Aug, 1985 ($2.50)
Gladstone Publishing Ltd.
1-Reprints Dell Giant w/new-c by Mel Crawford, based on old cover — 1.00 2.50
...Comics Digest 1 ($1.50, digest size) — 1.50

UNCLE SCROOGE IN COLOR
1987 ($29.95, Hardcover, 9-1/4"X12-1/4", 96 Pgs.)
Gladstone Publishing
nn-Reprints "Christmas on Bear Mountain" from Four Color 178 by Barks; Uncle Scrooge's Christmas Carol (published as Donald Duck & the Christmas Carol, A Little Golden Book), reproduced from the original art as adapted by Norman McGary from pencils by Barks; and Uncle Scrooge the Lemonade King, reproduced from the original art, plus Barks' original pencils — 8.35 25.00 50.00
nn-Slipcase edition of 750, signed by Barks, issued at $79.95 — 45.00 135.00 300.00

UNCLE SCROOGE THE LEMONADE KING
1960 (A Top Top Tales Book, 32 pgs., color, 6-3/8"x7-5/8")
Whitman Publishing Co.
2465-Storybook pencilled by Carl Barks, finished art adapted by Norman McGary — 60.00 180.00 400.00

UNCLE WIGGILY (See 4-Color #179, 221, 276, 320, 349, 391, 428, 503, 543, & March of Comics #19)

UNDERCOVER GIRL (Starr Flagg) (See Extra Comics & Manhunt!)
No. 5, 1952 - No. 7, 1954
Magazine Enterprises
5(#1)(A-1 #62)-Fallon of the F.B.I. in all — 27.00 81.00 190.00
6(A-1 #98), 7(A-1 #118)-All have Starr Flagg — 25.00 75.00 175.00
NOTE: *Powell c-6, 7. Whitney a-5-7.*

UNDERDOG (TV)(See Kite Fun Book, March of Comics #426, 438, 467, 479)
July, 1970 - No. 10, Jan, 1972; Mar, 1975 - No. 23, Feb, 1979
Charlton Comics/Gold Key
1 (1st series, Charlton)-1st app. Underdog — 5.40 16.00 38.00
2-10 — 2.90 8.60 20.00
1 (2nd series, Gold Key) — 3.40 10.30 24.00
2-10 — 1.60 4.70 11.00
11-23: 13-1st app. Shack of Solitude — 1.30 3.00 8.00

UNDERDOG (Spotlight)(Value: cover or less)

UNDERDOG SUMMER SPECIAL (TV)
Oct, 1993 ($2.25, 68 pgs.)
Harvey Comics
1 — .90 2.25

UNDERSEA AGENT
Jan, 1966 - No. 6, Mar, 1967 (25¢, 68 pgs.)
Tower Comics
1-Davy Jones, Undersea Agent begins — 5.50 17.00 40.00
2-6: 2-Jones gains magnetic powers. 5-Origin & 1st app. of Merman. 6-Kane/Wood-c(r) — 3.70 11.00 26.00
NOTE: *Gil Kane a-3-6; c-4, 5. Moldoff a-2i.*

UNDERSEA FIGHTING COMMANDOS (See Fighting Undersea...)
1964
I.W. Enterprises
I.W. Reprint #1,2('64): 1-r/#? 2-r/#1; Severin-c — 1.40 3.50 7.00

UNDERWATER CITY, THE (See 4-Color #1328)

UNDERWORLD (...True Crime Stories)
Feb-Mar, 1948 - No. 9, June-July, 1949 (52 pgs.)
D. S. Publishing Co.
1-Moldoff (Shelly)-c; excessive violence — 26.00 78.00 180.00
2-Moldoff (Shelly)-c; Ma Barker story used in **SOTI**, pg. 95; female electrocution panel; lingerie art — 27.00 80.00 185.00
3-McWilliams-c/a; extreme violence, mutilation — 22.00 65.00 150.00
4-Used in Love and Death by Legman; Ingels-a — 16.00 48.00 110.00
5-Ingels-a — 12.00 36.00 85.00
6-9: 8-Ravielli-a — 10.00 30.00 65.00

The Unexpected #186 © DC

Union #0 © Rob Liefeld

Universal Soldier #3 © Carolco Pict

GD25 FN65 NM94

UNDERWORLD (DC)(Value: cover or less)

UNDERWORLD CRIME
June, 1952 - No. 9, Oct, 1953
Fawcett Publications

1 19.00 57.00 130.00
2 11.00 32.00 75.00
3-6,8,9 (8,9-exist?) 10.00 30.00 65.00
7-(6/53)-Bondage/torture-c 16.00 48.00 110.00

UNDERWORLD STORY, THE
1950 (Movie)
Avon Periodicals

nn-(Scarce)-Ravielli-c 19.00 57.00 130.00

UNEARTHLY SPECTACULARS
Oct, 1965 - No. 3, Mar, 1967 (#1: 12¢; #2,3: 25¢ giants)
Harvey Publications

1-Tiger Boy; Simon-c 1.90 5.60 13.00
2-Jack Q. Frost, Tiger Boy & Three Rocketeers app.; Williamson, Wood, Kane-a; r-1 story/Thrill-O-Rama #2 3.00 9.40 22.00
3-Jack Q. Frost app.; Williamson/Crandall-a; r-from Alarming Advs. #1, 1962 3.00 9.40 22.00

NOTE: ***Crandall** a-3r. **G. Kane** a-2. **Orlando** a-3. **Simon, Sparling, Wood** c-2. **Simon/Kirby** a-3r. **Torres** a-1?. **Wildey** a-1(3). **Williamson** a-2, 3r. **Wood** a-2(2).*

UNEXPECTED, THE (Formerly Tales of the...)
No. 105, Feb-Mar, 1968 - No. 222, May, 1982
National Periodical Publications/DC Comics

105-Begin 12¢ cover price 2.00 6.00 14.00
106-113: 113-Last 12¢ issue (6-7/69) 1.70 4.20 10.00
114,115,117,118,120,122-127 1.00 2.50 6.00
116,119,121,128-Wrightson-a 1.30 3.00 8.00
129-162: 132-136-(52 pgs.). 157-162-(100 pgs.) 1.10 3.00
163-188: 187,188-(44 pgs.) .60 1.60
189,190,192-195 ($1.00, 68 pgs.): 189 on are combined with House of Secrets & The Witching Hour .80 2.00
191-Rogers-a(p) ($1.00, 68 pgs.) 1.20 3.00
196-221: 200-Return of Johnny Peril by Tuska. 205-213-Johnny Peril app. 210-Time Warp story 1.40

NOTE: ***Neal Adams** c-110, 112-118, 121, 124. **J. Craig** a-195. **Ditko** a-189, 221p, 222p; c-222. **Drucker** a-107r, 132r. **Giffen** a-219, 222. **Kaluta** c-203, 212. **Kirby** a-127r, 162. **Kubert** c-204, 214-216, 219-221. **Mayer** a-217p, 220, 221p. **Moldoff** a-136r. **Moreira** a-133. **Mortimer** a-212p. **Newton** a-204p. **Orlando** a-202; c-191. **Perez** a-217p. **Redondo** a-155, 166, 195. **Reese** a-145. **Sparling** a-107, 205-209p, 212p. **Spiegle** a-217. **Starlin** c-198. **Toth** a-126r, 127r. **Tuska** a-127, 132, 134, 136, 139, 152, 180, 200p. **Wildey** a-128r, 193. **Wood** a-122i, 133i, 137i, 138i. **Wrightson** a-161r(2 pgs.). Johnny Peril in #106-114, 116, 117, 200, 205-213.*

UNEXPECTED ANNUAL, THE (See DC Special Series #4)

UNIDENTIFIED FLYING ODDBALL (See Walt Disney Showcase #52)

UNION
June, 1993 - No. 0, July, 1994 ($1.95, color)
Image Comics

1-($2.50)-Embossed foil-c; Texeira-c/a in all 1.00 2.50
1-($1.95)-Newsstand edition w/o foil-c .80 2.00
2-4 .80 2.00
0-(7/94, $2.50) 1.00 2.50
0-Alternate Portacio-c, see Deathblow #5 1.00 2.50

UNITED COMICS (Formerly Fritzi Ritz #7; has Fritzi Ritz logo)
Aug, 1940; No. 8, 1950 - No. 26, Jan-Feb, 1953
United Features Syndicate

1(68 pgs.)-Fritzi Ritz & Phil Fumble 17.00 52.00 120.00
8-Fritzi Ritz, Abbie & Slats 4.00 110.00 22.00
9-26: 20-Strange As It Seems; Russell Patterson Cheesecake-a. 22,25-Peanuts app. 3.60 9.00 18.00

NOTE: *Abbie & Slats reprinted from Tip Top.*

UNITED NATIONS, THE (See Classics Illustrated Special Issue)

UNITED STATES AIR FORCE PRESENTS: THE HIDDEN CREW
1964 (36 pgs.) (Full color)
U.S. Air Force

nn-Shaffenberger-a .80 2.00 4.00

UNITED STATES FIGHTING AIR FORCE (Also see U.S. Fighting Air Force)
Sept, 1952 - No. 29, Oct, 1956
Superior Comics Ltd.

1 6.70 20.00 40.00
2 4.00 10.00 20.00
3-10 2.40 65.00 12.00
11-29 1.80 4.50 9.00

UNITED STATES MARINES
1943 - No. 4, 1944; No. 5, 1952 - No. 8, 1952; No. 7 - No. 11, 1953
William H. Wise/Life's Romances Publ. Co./Magazine Enterprises #5-8/Toby Press #7-11

nn-Mart Bailey-a 7.50 22.50 45.00
2-Bailey-a; Tojo-c 5.35 16.00 32.00
3,4: 3-Tojo-c 4.70 14.00 28.00
5(A-1 #55)-Bailey-a, 6(A-1 #60), 7(A-1 #68), 8(A-1 #72) 4.00 12.00 24.00
7-11 (Toby) 2.40 6.00 12.00

NOTE: ***Powell** a-5-7.*

UNITY
No. 0, Aug, 1992 - No. 1, 1992 (Color, free, both limited, 20 pgs.)
Valiant

0-(Blue)-Prequel to Unity x-overs in all Valiant titles; free to everone that bought all 8 titles that month; B. Smith-c/a 1.20 3.00 7.00
0-Red logo; sames above, but w/red logo (5,000) 7.00 21.00 50.00
0-Gold variant 4.00 11.00 25.00
1-(?/92)-Epilogue to unity x-overs; 1 copy available for every 8 Unity books ordered by dealers. B. Smith-c/a 1.20 3.00 7.00
1-(Gold)-Promotional copy 8.00 24.00 55.00
1-(Platinum)-Promo copy; scarcer 9.00 28.00 65.00

UNIVERSAL MONSTERS: ...
1993 - Present ($4.95/$5.95, 52 pgs.)(All adapt original movies)
Dark Horse Comics

...: Frankenstein nn-($3.95)-Painted-c/a 1.60 4.00
...: Dracula nn-($4.95) 1.00 2.00 5.00
...: The Mummy nn-($4.95)-Painted-c 1.00 2.00 5.00
...: Creature From the Black Lagoon nn-($4.95)-Art Adams/Austin-c/a 1.00 2.00 5.00

UNIVERSAL PRESENTS DRACULA-THE MUMMY & OTHER STORIES (Also see Dell Giants)
Sept-Nov, 1963 (84 pgs.)(one shot)
Dell Publishing Co.

GD FN VF NM
02-530-311-r/Dracula 12-231-212, The Mummy 12-437-211 & part of Ghost Stories No. 1 13.00 39.00 91.00 195.00

UNIVERSAL SOLDIER
Sept, 1992 - No. 3, Nov, 1992 (Color, mini-series, based on movie)
Now Comics

1-3 ($2.50, direct sale ed.)-Polybagged, mature readers. 1-Hologram on-c; all direct sale editions have painted-c 1.00 2.50
1-3 ($1.95, newsstand ed.)-Rewritten & redrawn code approved version; all newsstand editions have photo-c .80 2.00

UNIVERSAL SOLDIER (Fleetway Editions, Ltd.)(Value: cover or less)

UNKEPT PROMISE
1949 (24 pgs.)
Legion of Truth (Giveaway)

nn-Anti-alcohol 6.70 20.00 40.00

UNKNOWN MAN, THE
1951 (Movie)
Avon Periodicals

Unknown Worlds #6 © ACG

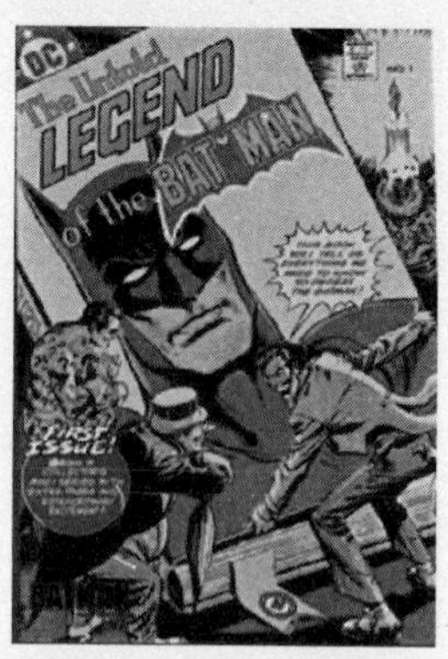

Untold Legends of Batman #1 © DC

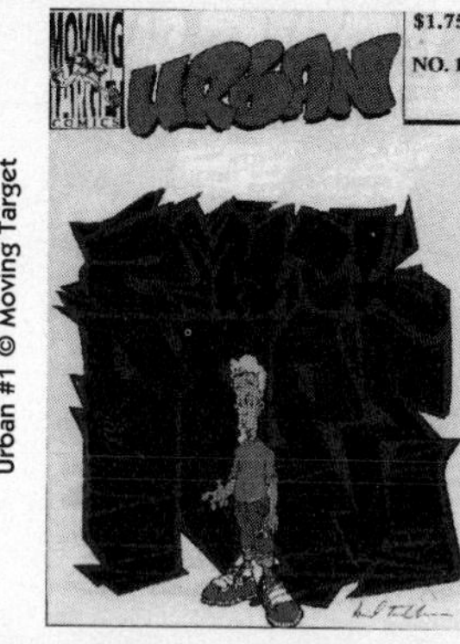

Urban #1 © Moving Target

GD25 FN65 NM94

nn-Kinstler-c 19.00 58.00 135.00

UNKNOWN SOLDIER (Formerly Star-Spangled War Stories)
No. 205, Apr-May, 1977 - No. 268, Oct, 1982
National Periodical Publications/DC Comics

205-268: 219-221-(44 pgs.). 248,249-Origin. 251-Enemy Ace begins. 268-Death of Unknown Soldier .70 1.70

NOTE: ***Chaykin** a-234. **Evans** a-265-267; c-235. **Kubert** c-Most. **Miller** a-219p. **Severin** a-251-253, 260, 261, 265-267. **Simonson** a-254-256. **Spiegle** a-258, 259, 262-264.*

UNKNOWN SOLDIER, THE (DC)(Value: cover or less)(See Brave & the Bold #146)

UNKNOWN WORLD (Strange Stories From Another World #2 on)
June, 1952
Fawcett Publications

1-Norman Saunders painted-c 24.00 73.00 170.00

UNKNOWN WORLDS (See Journey Into...)

UNKNOWN WORLDS
Aug, 1960 - No. 57, Aug, 1967
American Comics Group/Best Synd. Features

1-Schaffenberger-c 13.00 38.00 115.00
2-5: 2-Dinosaur-c/story 7.00 20.00 60.00
6-11: 9-Dinosaur-c/story. 11-Last 10¢ issue 5.00 15.00 45.00
12-19: 12-Begin 12¢ issues?; ends #57 4.00 11.00 33.00
20-Herbie cameo (12-1/62-63) 4.00 13.00 38.00
21-35 2.00 7.00 22.00
36- "The People vs. Hendricks" by Craig; most popular ACG story ever 3.00 9.00 27.00
37-46 2.00 7.00 20.00
47-Williamson-a r-from Adventures Into the Unknown #96, 3 pgs.; Craig-a 2.00 7.00 22.00
48-57: 53-Frankenstein app. 2.00 6.00 17.00

NOTE: ***Ditko** a-49, 50p, 54. **Forte** a-3, 6, 11. **Landau** a-56(2). **Reinman** a-3, 9, 13, 20, 22, 23, 36, 38, 54. **Whitney** c/a-most issues. John Force, Magic Agent app.-35, 36, 48, 50, 52, 54, 56.*

UNKNOWN WORLDS OF FRANK BRUNNER (Eclipse)(Value: cover or less)

UNKNOWN WORLDS OF SCIENCE FICTION
Jan, 1975 - No. 6, Nov, 1975; 1976 (B&W Magazine) ($1.00)
Marvel Comics Group

1-Williamson/Krenkel/Torres/Frazetta-r/Witzend #1, Neal Adams-r/Phase 1; Brunner & Kaluta-r; Freas/Romita-c 1.60 4.00
2-6: 5-Kaluta text illos 1.20 3.00
Special 1(1976,100 pgs.)-Newton painted-c 1.20 3.00

NOTE: ***Brunner** a-2; c-4, 6. **Buscema** a-Special 1p. **Chaykin** a-5. **Colan** a(p)-1, 3, 5, 6. **Corben** a-4. **Kaluta** a-2, Special 1(ext illos); c-2. **Morrow** a-3, 5. **Nino** a-3, 6, Special 1. **Perez** a-2, 3. Ray Bradbury interview in #1.*

UNSANE (Formerly Mighty Bear #13, 14? or The Outlaws #10-14?)
No. 15, June, 1954
Star Publications

15-Disbrow-a(2); L. B. Cole-c 20.00 60.00 140.00

UNSEEN, THE
No. 5, 1952 - No. 15, July, 1954
Visual Editions/Standard Comics

5-Horror stories in all; Toth-a 19.00 57.00 130.00
6,7,9,10-Jack Katz-a 12.00 36.00 85.00
8,11,13,14 10.00 30.00 60.00
12,15-Toth-a. 12-Tuska-a 12.00 36.00 85.00

NOTE: ***Nick Cardy** c-12. **Fawcette** a-13, 14. **Sekowsky** a-7, 8(2), 10, 13, 15.*

UNTAMED
June, 1993 - No. 3, Aug, 1993 ($1.95, mini-series)
Epic Comics (Marvel)

1-($2.50)-Embossed-c 1.00 2.50
2,3 .80 2.00

UNTAMED LOVE (Also see Frank Frazetta's Untamed Love)
Jan, 1950 - No. 5, Sept, 1950
Quality Comics Group (Comic Magazines)

GD25 FN65 NM94

1-Ward-c, Gustavson-a 16.00 48.00 110.00
2,4: 2-5-Photo-c 10.00 30.00 65.00
3,5-Gustavson-a 10.00 30.00 70.00

UNTOLD LEGEND OF THE BATMAN, THE
July, 1980 - No. 3, Sept, 1980 (Mini-series)
DC Comics

1-Origin; Joker-c; Byrne's 1st work at DC 1.60 4.00
2,3 1.20 3.00
1-3: Batman cereal premiums (1989, 28 pgs., 6X9"); 1st & 2nd printings known .80 2.00

NOTE: ***Aparo** a-1i, 2, 3. **Byrne** a-1p.*

UNTOLD ORIGIN OF THE FEMFORCE, THE (AC)(Value: cover or less)

UNTOUCHABLES, THE (TV)
No. 1237, 10-12/61 - No. 4, 8-10/62 (All have Robert Stack photo-c)
Dell Publishing Co.

4-Color 1237,1286 16.00 48.00 110.00
01-879-207, 12-879-210(01879-210 on inside) 10.00 30.00 65.00
Topps Bubblegum premiums-2-1/2x4-1/2", 8 pgs. (3 diff. issues) "The Organization, Jamaica Ginger, The Otto Frick Story (drug), 3000 Suspects, The Antidote, Mexican Stakeout, Little Egypt, Purple Gang, Bugs Moran Story, & Lily Dallas Story" 2.80 7.00 14.00

UNUSUAL TALES (Blue Beetle & Shadows From Beyond #50 on)
Nov, 1955 - No. 49, Mar-Apr, 1965
Charlton Comics

1 14.00 40.00 115.00
2 7.00 21.00 55.00
3-5 4.00 12.00 33.00
6-Ditko-c only 6.00 17.00 44.00
7,8-Ditko-c/a 12.00 36.00 95.00
9-Ditko-c/a (20 pgs.) 13.00 38.00 100.00
10-Ditko-c/a(4) 15.00 43.00 120.00
11-(3/58, 68 pgs.)-Ditko-a(4) 14.00 41.00 110.00
12,14-Ditko-a 9.00 28.00 75.00
13,16-20 3.00 10.00 26.00
15-Ditko-c/a 9.00 27.00 72.00
21,24,28 2.00 7.00 18.00
22,23,25-27,29-Ditko-a 6.00 18.00 48.00
30-49 2.00 6.00 16.00

NOTE: ***Colan** a-11. **Ditko** c-22, 23, 25-27, 31(part).*

UP FROM HARLEM (Spire Christian)(Value: cover or less)

UP-TO-DATE COMICS
No date (1938) (36 pgs.; B&W cover) (10¢)
King Features Syndicate

nn-Popeye & Henry cover; The Phantom, Jungle Jim & Flash Gordon by Raymond, The Katzenjammer Kids, Curley Harper & others 20.00 60.00 140.00

(Variations to above contents exist.)

UP YOUR NOSE AND OUT YOUR EAR (Magazine)
April, 1972 - No. 2, June, 1972 (52 pgs.) (Satire)
Klevart Enterprises

V1#1,2 1.20 3.00

URBAN
1994 ($1.75, B&W)
Moving Target Entertainment

1 1.75

URTH 4 (Continuity)(Value: cover or less)

USA COMICS
Aug, 1941 - No. 17, Fall, 1945
Timely Comics (USA)

GD25 FN65 VF82 NM94

1-Origin Major Liberty (called Mr. Liberty #1), Rockman by Wolverton, & The Whizzer by Avison; The Defender with sidekick Rusty & Jack Frost begin;

U.S. Agent #1 © MEG

U.S. 1 #8 © MEG

V #3 © DC

GD25 FN65 NM94 | GD25 FN65 NM94

The Young Avenger only app.; S&K-c plus 1 pg. art
687.00 2063.00 3781.00 5500.00
(Estimated up to 145 total copies exist, 7 in NM/Mint)

GD25 FN65 NM94

2-Origin Captain Terror & The Vagabond; last Wolverton Rockman
257.00 771.00 1800.00
3-No Whizzer 200.00 600.00 1400.00
4-Last Rockman, Major Liberty, Defender, Jack Frost, & Capt. Terror; Corporal Dix app. 157.00 471.00 1100.00
5-Origin American Avenger & Roko the Amazing; The Blue Blade, The Black Widow & Victory Boys, Gypo the Gypsy Giant & Hills of Horror only app.; Sergeant Dix begins; no Whizzer; Hitler, Mussolini & Tojo-c
129.00 385.00 900.00
6-Captain America (ends #17), The Destroyer, Jap Buster Johnson, Jeep Jones begin; Terror Squad only app. 171.00 515.00 1200.00
7-Captain Daring, Disk-Eyes the Detective by Wolverton app.; origin & only app. Marvel Boy (3/43); Secret Stamp begins; no Whizzer, Sergeant Dix
150.00 450.00 1050.00
8-10: 9-Last Secret Stamp. 10-The Thunderbird only app.
107.00 321.00 750.00
11,12: 11-No Jeep Jones 93.00 280.00 650.00
13-17: 13-No Whizzer; Jeep Jones ends. 15-No Destroyer; Jap Buster Johnson ends 68.00 205.00 475.00

NOTE: ***Brodsky*** *c-14.* ***Gabrielle*** *c-4, 8.* ***Schomburg*** *c-6-8, 10, 12, 13, 15-17.* ***Shores*** *a-1, 4; c-9, 11.* ***Ed Win*** *a-4. Cover features: 1-The Defender; 2, 3-Captain Terror; 4-Major Liberty; 5-Victory Boys; 6-17-Captain America & Bucky.*

U.S. AGENT (See Jeff Jordan...)

U.S. AGENT (See Captain America #354)
June, 1993 - No. 4, Sept, 1993 ($1.75, mini-series)
Marvel Comics
1-4 .70 1.75

USAGI YOJIMBO (See Albedo, Doomsday Squad #3 & Space Usagi)
July, 1987 - No. 36? ($2.00, B&W)
Fantagraphics Books
1 1.70 4.25
1,8,10-2nd printings .80 2.00
2-9,11-28: 11-Aragones-a .90 2.25
10-Leonardo app. (TMNT) 1.60 4.00
29-36: 29-Begin $2.25-c .90 2.25
Color Special 1 (11/89, $2.95, 68 pgs.)-new & r 1.20 3.00
Summer Special 1 (1986, B&W, $2.75)-r/early Albedo issues
1.40 3.50 8.50

USAGI YOJIMBO
Mar, 1993 - Present ($2.75, Color)
Mirage Studios
V2#1-9: 1-Teenage Mutant Ninja Turtles app. 1.10 2.75

U.S. AIR FORCE COMICS (Army Attack #38 on)
Oct, 1958 - No. 37, Mar-Apr, 1965
Charlton Comics
1 5.00 15.00 30.00
2 3.00 7.50 15.00
3-10 2.00 5.00 10.00
11-20 1.40 3.50 7.00
21-37 .80 2.00 4.00

NOTE: ***Glanzman*** *c/a-9, 10, 12.* ***Montes/Bache*** *a-33.*

USA IS READY
1941 (68 pgs.) (One Shot)
Dell Publishing Co.
1-War propaganda 29.00 90.00 200.00

U.S. BORDER PATROL COMICS (Sgt. Dick Carter of the...) (See Holyoke One Shot)

U.S. FIGHTING AIR FORCE (Also see United States Fighting Air Force)
No date (1960s?)
I. W. Enterprises
1,9(nd): 1-r/United States Fighting...#?. 9-r/#1 .60 1.50 3.00

U.S. FIGHTING MEN
1963 - 1964 (Reprints)
Super Comics
10-r/With the U.S. Paratroops #4(Avon) 1.20 3.00 6.00
11,12,15-18: 11-r/Monty Hall #10. 12,16,17,18-r/U.S. Fighting Air Force #10,3,?&? 15-r/Man Comics #11 .80 2.00 4.00

U.S. JONES (Also see Wonderworld Comics #28)
Nov, 1941 - No. 2, Jan, 1942
Fox Features Syndicate
1-U.S. Jones & The Topper begin; Nazi-c 86.00 257.00 600.00
2-Nazi-c 68.00 205.00 475.00

U.S. MARINES
Fall, 1964 (One shot, 12¢)
Charlton Comics
1 1.00 2.50 5.00

U.S. MARINES IN ACTION!
Aug, 1952 - No. 3, Dec, 1952
Avon Periodicals
1-Louis Ravielli-c/a 5.85 17.50 35.00
2,3: 3-Kinstler-c 4.00 12.00 22.00

U.S. 1 (Marvel)(Value: cover or less)

U.S. PARATROOPS (See With the...)

U.S. PARATROOPS
1964?
I. W. Enterprises
1,8: 1-r/With the U.S. Paratroops #1; Wood-c. 8-r/With the U.S. Paratroops #6; Kinstler-c 1.20 3.00 6.00

U.S. TANK COMMANDOS
June, 1952 - No. 4, March, 1953
Avon Periodicals
1-Kinstler-c 6.70 20.00 40.00
2-4: Kinstler-c 4.20 12.50 25.00
I.W. Reprint #1,8: 1-r/#1. 8-r/#3 1.20 3.00 6.00

NOTE: ***Kinstler*** *a-I.W. #1; c-1-4, I.W. #1, 8.*

"V" (TV)(DC)(Value: cover or less)

VACATION COMICS (See A-1 Comics #16)

VACATION DIGEST (Harvey)(Value: cover or less)

VACATION IN DISNEYLAND (Also see Dell Giants)
Aug-Oct, 1959; May, 1965 (Walt Disney)
Dell Publishing Co./Gold Key (1965)
4-Color 1025-Barks-a 22.00 65.00 150.00
1(30024-508)(G.K., 5/65, 25¢)-r/Dell Giant #30 & cover to #1 ('58); celebrates Disneyland's 10th anniversary 4.00 12.00 24.00

VACATION PARADE (See Dell Giants)

VALERIA THE SHE BAT (Also see Comics Debut #1)
May, 1993 - Present (Color)
Continuity Comics
1-Premium; glow-in-the-dark-c; N. Adams-a/scripts; given as gift to retailers
5.70 17.00 40.00
5-(11/93)-Embossed-c; N. Adams-a/scripts 1.00 2.50

NOTE: *Due to lack of continuity, #2-4 do not exist.*

VALKYRIE (Eclipse, 1987 & 1988)(Value: cover or less)

VALLEY OF THE DINOSAURS (TV)
April, 1975 - No. 11, Dec, 1976 (Hanna-Barbara)
Charlton Comics
1 1.20 3.00
2-11: 3-Byrne text illos (early work, 7/75) 1.50

Valor #21 © DC

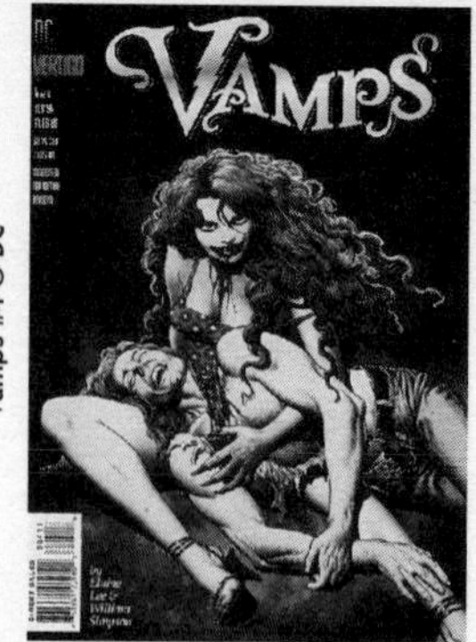

Vamps #4 © DC

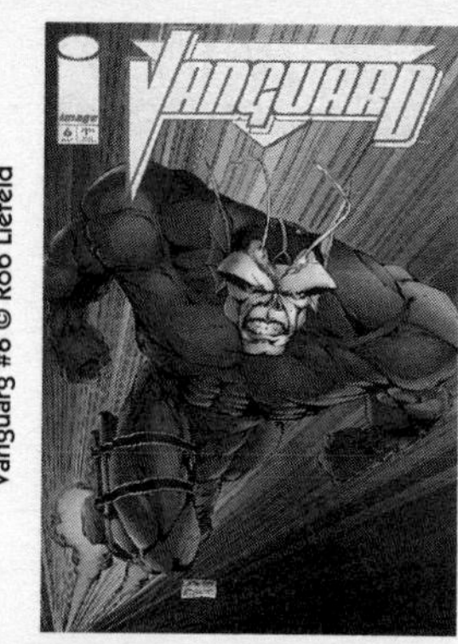

Vanguarg #6 © Rob Liefeld

	GD25	FN65	NM94

VALLEY OF GWANGI (See Movie Classics)

VALOR
Mar-Apr, 1955 - No. 5, Nov-Dec, 1955
E. C. Comics

	GD25	FN65	NM94
1-Williamson/Torres-a; Wood-c/a	23.00	70.00	160.00
2-Williamson-c/a; Wood-a	20.00	60.00	140.00
3,4: 3-Williamson, Crandall-a. 4-Wood-c	14.00	43.00	100.00
5-Wood-c/a; Williamson/Evans-a	13.00	40.00	90.00

NOTE: ***Crandall** a-3, 4. **Ingels** a-1, 2, 4, 5. **Krigstein** a-1-5. **Orlando** a-3, 4; c-3. **Wood** a-1, 2, 5; c-1, 4, 5.*

VALOR
Nov, 1992 - No. 23, Sept, 1994 ($1.25)
DC Comics

	GD25	FN65	NM94
1-12: 1-Eclipso the Darkness Within aftermath. 2-Vs. Supergirl. 4-Vs. Lobo. 12-Lobo cameo			1.25
13-22: 13-Begin $1.50-c. 14-Legionnaires, JLA app. 17-Austin-c(i); death of Valor. 18-22-Build-up to Zero Hour			1.50
23-Last issue-Zero Hour		.70	1.75

VALOR THUNDERSTAR AND HIS FIREFLIES (Now)(Value: cover or less)

VAMPIRE LESTAT, THE
Jan, 1990 - No. 12, 1991 ($2.50, painted color, mini-series)
Innovation Publishing

	GD25	FN65	NM94
1-Adapts novel; Bolton painted-c on all	4.10	12.40	29.00
1-2nd printing (has UPC code, 1st prints don't)		1.20	3.00
1-3rd & 4th printings		1.00	2.50
2-1st printing	1.70	5.10	12.00
2-2nd & 3rd printings		1.00	2.50
3-5	1.10	2.70	6.50
3-6,9-2nd printings		1.00	2.50
6-12		1.70	4.25

VAMPIRELLA (Magazine)(See Warren Presents)
Sept, 1969 - No. 112, Feb, 1983; No. 113, Jan, 1988? (B&W)
Warren Publishing Co./Harris Publications #113

	GD25	FN65	NM94
1-Intro. Vampirella	29.00	86.00	200.00
2-Amazonia series begins, ends #12	11.40	34.00	80.00
3 (Low distribution)	32.00	96.00	225.00
4-7	6.00	18.00	42.00
8-Vampi begins by Tom Sutton as serious strip (early issues-gag line)	5.40	16.00	38.00
9-Barry Smith-a; Boris-c	6.00	17.00	40.00
10-No Vampi story	2.90	9.00	20.00
11-15: 11-Origin & 1st app. Pendragon. 12-Vampi by Gonzales begins	4.00	12.00	28.00
16-18,20-25: 17-Tomb of the Gods begins, ends #22. 25-Begin partial color issues	2.40	7.30	17.00
19 (1973 Annual)	3.00	9.90	23.00
26,28-36,38-40: 30-Intro. Pantha; Corben-a(color). 31-Origin Luana, the Beast Girl. 33-Pantha ends	1.70	4.20	10.00
27 (1974 Annual)	1.70	5.10	12.00
37 (1975 Annual)	1.70	4.20	10.00
41-45,47-50: 50-Spirit cameo by Eisner	.90	2.30	5.50
46-Origin retold (10/75)	.90	2.30	5.50
51-99: 93-Cassandra St. Knight begins, ends #103; new Pantha series begins, ends 108		1.60	4.00
100 (96 pg. r-special)-Origin reprinted		1.70	4.25
101-110,112: 108-Torpedo series by Toth begins		1.00	2.50
111-Giant Collector's Edition ($2.50)		1.10	2.75
113 (1988)		.80	2.00
Annual 1(1972)-New origin Vampirella by Gonzales; reprints by Neal Adams (from #1), Wood (from #9)	16.00	49.00	115.00
Special 1 (1977; large-square bound)	1.70	4.20	10.00

NOTE: ***Neal Adams** a-1, 10p, 19p(r/#10). **Alcala** a-90, 93i. **Bode'/Todd** c-3. **Bode'/Jones** c-4. **Boris** c-9. **Brunner** a-10, 12(1 pg.). **Corben** a-30, 31, 33, 54. **Crandall** a-1, 19(r/#1). **Frazetta** c-1, 5, 7, 11, 31. **Heath** a-76-78, 83. **Jones** a-5, 9, 12, 27, 32, 33(2 pg.), 34, 50i, 83r. **Nino** a-59i, 61i, 67, 76, 85, 90. **Ploog** a-14. **Barry Smith** a-9. **Starlin** a-78. **Sutton** a-11. **Toth** a-90i, 108, 110. **Wood** a-9, 10, 12, 19(r/#12), 27r; c-9. **Wrightson** a-33(w/**Jones**), 63r. All reprint issues-37, 74, 83, 87, 91, 105, 107, 109, 111. Annuals from 1973 on are included in regular numbering. Later annuals are same format as regular issues.*

VAMPIRELLA (Also see Vengeance of...)
Nov, 1992 - No. 5, Nov, 1993 ($2.95, color)
Harris Publications

	GD25	FN65	NM94
1-Jim Balent inks in #1-3; Adam Hughes c-1-3	3.10	9.40	22.00
1-2nd printing		1.20	3.00
2	3.60	10.70	25.00
3-5: 5-Brereton painted-c		1.70	4.25
Trade paperback nn (10/93, $5.95)-r/#1-4; Jusko-c	1.00	2.50	6.00

NOTE: *Issues 1-5 contain certificates for free **Dave Stevens** Vampirella poster.*

VAMPIRELLA: MORNING IN AMERICA
1991 - No. 4, 1992 ($3.95, B&W, mini-series, 52 pgs.)
Harris Publications/Dark Horse Comics

	GD25	FN65	NM94
1: All have Kaluta painted covers	1.00	2.00	5.00
2-4		1.60	4.00

VAMPIRE TALES (Magazine)
Aug, 1973 - No. 11, June, 1975 (B&W) (75¢)
Marvel Comics Group

	GD25	FN65	NM94
1-Morbius, the Living Vampire begins by Pablo Marcos (1st solo Morbius series & 5th Morbius app.)	3.00	9.40	22.00
2-Intro. Satana; Steranko-r	1.30	3.00	8.00
3,4,6-11: 3-Satana app. 6-1st Lilith app. 8-Blade app. (see Tomb of Dracula)		1.60	4.00
5-Origin Morbius	1.30	3.00	7.50
Annual 1(10/75)-Heath-r/#9		1.20	3.00

NOTE: ***Alcala** a-6, 8, 9i. **Boris** c-4, 6. **Chaykin** a-7. **Everett** a-1r. **Gulacy** a-7p. **Heath** a-9. **Infantino** a-3r. **Gil Kane** a-4, 5r.*

VAMPS
Aug, 1994 - No. 6, Jan, 1995 ($1.95, limited series, mature)
DC Comics

	GD25	FN65	NM94
1-6		.80	2.00

VANGUARD (...Outpost: Earth) (See Megaton)
1987 ($1.50, color)
Megaton Comics

	GD25	FN65	NM94
1-Erik Larsen-c(p)		1.20	3.00

VANGUARD (See Savage Dragon #2)
Oct, 1993 - Present ($1.95, color)
Image Comics

	GD25	FN65	NM94
1-6: 1-Wraparound gatefold-c; Erik Larsen back-up-a; Supreme x-over. 3-(12/93)-Indicia says December 1994. 4-Berzerker back-up. 5-Angel Medina-a(p)		.80	2.00

VANGUARD ILLUSTRATED
Nov, 1983 - No. 11, Oct, 1984 (Color, Baxter paper)
Pacific Comics

	GD25	FN65	NM94
1-6,8-11: 1,7-Nudity scenes. 2-1st app. Stargrazers (see Legends of the Stargrazers; Dave Stevens-c			1.50
7-1st app. Mr. Monster (r-in Mr. Monster #1)	1.00	2.00	5.00

NOTE: ***Evans** a-7. **Kaluta** c-5, 7p. **Perez** a-6; c-6. **Rude** a-1-4; c-4. **Williamson** c-3.*

VANITY (Pacific)(Value: cover or less)

VARIETY COMICS (The Spice of Comics)
1944 - No. 2, 1945; No. 3, 1946 - No. 5, 1946?
Rural Home Publications/Croyden Publ. Co.

	GD25	FN65	NM94
1-Origin Captain Valiant	13.00	40.00	90.00
2-Captain Valiant	7.50	22.50	45.00
3(1946-Croyden)-Captain Valiant	6.70	20.00	40.00
4,5-Exist?	5.85	17.50	35.00

Vault of Evil #2 © MEG

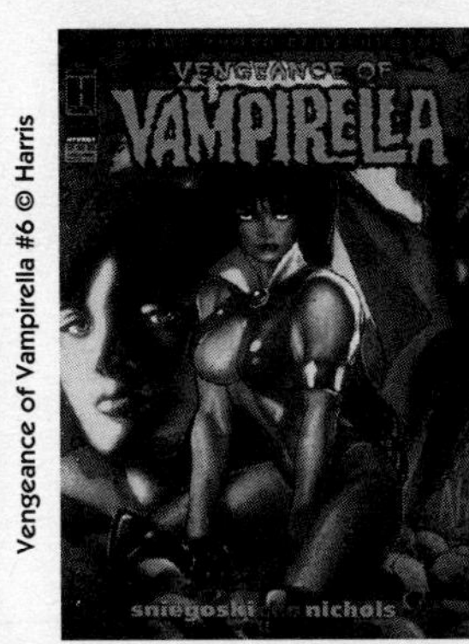

Vengeance of Vampirella #6 © Harris

Venom: Nights of Vengeance #2 © MEG

GD25 FN65 NM94

VARIETY COMICS (See Fox Giants)

VARIOGENESIS
June, 1994 ($3.50, color)
Dagger Comics Group

0 — 1.40 — 3.50

VARSITY
1945
Parents' Magazine Institute

1 — 5.35 — 16.00 — 32.00

VAUDEVILLE AND OTHER THINGS
1900 (10-1/2x13") (in color) (18+ pgs.)
Isaac H. Blandiard Co.

nn-By Bunny — 34.00 — 102.00 — 340.00

VAULT OF EVIL
Feb, 1973 - No. 23, Nov, 1975
Marvel Comics Group

1 (1950s reprints begin) — 1.20 — 3.00
2-23: 3,4-Brunner-c — .70 — 1.75

*NOTE: **Ditko** a-14r, 15r, 20-22r. **Drucker** a-10r(Mystic #52), 13r(Uncanny Tales #42). **Everett** a-11r(Menace #2), 13r(Menace #4); c-10. **Heath** a-5r. **Krigstein** a-20r(Uncanny Tales #54). **Reinman** r-1. **Tuska** a-6r.*

VAULT OF HORROR (Formerly War Against Crime #1-11)
No. 12, Apr-May, 1950 - No. 40, Dec-Jan, 1954-55
E. C. Comics

12 (Scarce) — 350.00 — 1050.00 — 2800.00
13-Morphine story — 88.00 — 265.00 — 615.00
14 — 81.00 — 242.00 — 565.00
15- "Terror in the Swamp" is same story w/minor changes as "The Thing in the Swamp" from Haunt of Fear #15 — 66.00 — 197.00 — 460.00
16 — 48.00 — 145.00 — 335.00
17-19 — 37.00 — 111.00 — 260.00
20-25: 22-Frankenstein-c & adaptation. 23-Used in **POP**, pg. 84; Davis-a(2). 24-Craig biography — 30.00 — 90.00 — 210.00
26-B&W & color illos in **POP** — 30.00 — 90.00 — 210.00
27-35: 30-Dismemberment-c. 31-Ray Bradbury biog. 32-Censored-c. 35-X-Mas-c — 22.00 — 65.00 — 150.00
36- "Pipe Dream" classic opium addict story by Krigstein; "Twin Bill" cited in articles by T.E. Murphy, Wertham — 22.00 — 65.00 — 150.00
37-1st app. Drusilla, a Vampirella look alike; Williamson-a — 22.00 — 65.00 — 150.00
38-39: 39-Bondage-c — 18.00 — 54.00 — 125.00
40-Low distribution — 22.00 — 65.00 — 150.00

*NOTE: **Craig** art in all but No. 13 & 33; c-12-40. **Crandall** a-33, 34, 39. **Davis** a-17-38. **Evans** a-27, 28, 30, 32, 33. **Feldstein** a-12-16. **Ingels** a-13-20, 22-40. **Kamen** a-15-22, 25, 29, 35. **Krigstein** a-36, 38-40. **Kurtzman** a-12, 13. **Orlando** a-24, 31, 40. **Wood** a-12-14. #22, 29 & 31 have Ray Bradbury adaptations. #16 & 17 have H. P. Lovecraft adaptations.*

VAULT OF HORROR, THE
Aug, 1990 - No. 6, June, 1991 ($1.95, 68 pgs.)(#4 on: $2.00)
Gladstone Publishing

1-Craig-c(r); all contain EC reprints — 1.50 — 3.75
2-6: 2,4-6-Craig-c(r). 3-Ingels-c(r) — .80 — 2.00

VAULT OF HORROR
Sept, 1991 - No. 5, May, 1992? ($2.00, color)
Oct, 1992 - Present ($1.50, color)
Russ Cochran

1-5: E.C reprints — .80 — 2.00
1-4: 1-4r/VOH #12-15 w/original-c — 1.50

V...-COMICS (Morse code for "V" - 3 dots, 1 dash)
Jan, 1942 - No. 2, Mar-Apr, 1942
Fox Features Syndicate

1-Origin V-Man & the Boys; The Banshee & The Black Fury, The Queen of Evil, & V-Agents begin; Nazi-c — 86.00 — 257.00 — 600.00
2-Nazi bondage/torture-c — 71.00 — 215.00 — 500.00

VECTOR (Now)(Value: cover or less)

VEGAS KNIGHTS
1989 ($1.95, color)
Pioneer Comics

1 — .80 — 2.00

VENGEANCE OF VAMPIRELLA
Apr, 1994 - Present ($2.95, color)
Harris Comics

1-($3.50)-Quesada/Palmiotti "bloodfoil" wraparound-c — 1.70 — 4.50 — 10.00
1-2nd printing; blue foil-c — 1.40 — 3.50
2-9 — 1.40 — 3.50

VENGEANCE SQUAD
July, 1975 - No. 6, May, 1976 (#1-3 are 25¢ issues)
Charlton Comics

1-Mike Mauser, Private Eye begins by Staton — .80 — 2.00
2-6: Morisi-a in all — .60 — 1.60
5,6(Modern Comics-r, 1977) — 1.40

VENGER ROBO (Viz)(Value: cover or less)

VENOM: FUNERAL PYRE
Aug, 1993 - No. 3, Oct, 1993 ($2.95, limited series)
Marvel Comics

1-3: 1-Holo-grafx foil-c; Punisher app. in all — 1.20 — 3.00

VENOM: LETHAL PROTECTOR (Also see Amazing Spider-Man #298 & Marvel Comics Presents)
Feb, 1993 - No. 6, July, 1993 ($2.95, limited series)
Marvel Comics

1-Red holo-grafx foil-c; Bagley-c/a in all — 1.00 — 2.00 — 5.00
1-Gold variant sold to retailers — 20.00
2-6: Spider-Man app. in all — 1.20 — 3.00

VENOM: NIGHTS OF VENGEANCE
Aug, 1994 - No. 4, Nov, 1994 ($2.95, limited series)
Marvel Comics

1-4: 1-Red foil-c — 1.20 — 3.00

VENOM: THE ENEMY WITHIN
Feb, 1994 - No. 3, Apr, 1994 ($2.95, limited series)
Marvel Comics

1-3-Demogoblin & Morbius app.: 1-Glow-in-the-dark-c — 1.20 — 3.00

VENOM: THE MACE
May, 1994 - No. 3, July, 1994 ($2.95, limited series)
Marvel Comics

1-3: 1-Embossed-c — 1.20 — 3.00

VENOM: THE MADNESS
Nov, 1993 - No. 3, Jan, 1994 ($2.95, limited series)
Marvel Comics

1-3: Kelley Jones-c/a(p). 1-Embossed-c; Juggernaut app. — 1.20 — 3.00

VENTURE (AC)(Value: cover or less)

VENUS (See Marvel Spotlight #2 & Weird Wonder Tales)
August, 1948 - No. 19, April, 1952 (Also see Marvel Mystery #91)
Marvel/Atlas Comics (CMC 1-9/LCC 10-19)

1-Venus & Hedy Devine begin; 1st app. Venus; Kurtzman's "Hey Look" — 86.00 — 257.00 — 600.00
2 — 46.00 — 140.00 — 325.00
3,5 — 40.00 — 120.00 — 280.00
4-Kurtzman's "Hey Look" — 41.00 — 125.00 — 290.00
6-9: 6-Loki app. 7,8-Painted-c. 9-Begin 52 pgs.; book-length feature "Whom the Gods Destroy!" — 38.00 — 115.00 — 265.00
10-S/F-horror issues begin (7/50) — 41.00 — 125.00 — 290.00
11-S/F end of the world (11/50) — 49.00 — 146.00 — 340.00

Venus Wars II #9 © DH

Veronica #41 © AP

Victory #1 © Jack Kirby

12-Colan-a 34.00 100.00 235.00
13-19-Venus by Everett, 2-3 stories each; covers-#13,15-19; 14-Everett part cover (Venus). 17-Bondage-c 51.00 154.00 360.00

NOTE: ***Berg*** *s/f story-13.* ***Everett*** *c-13, 14(part; Venus only), 15-19.* ***Heath*** *s/f story-11.* ***Maneely*** *s/f story-10(3pg.), 16.* ***Morisi*** *a-19.* ***Syd Shores*** *c-6.*

VENUS WARS, THE (Dark Horse)(Value: cover or less)

VENUS WARS II, THE (Dark Horse)(Value: cover or less)

VERI BEST SURE FIRE COMICS
No date (circa 1945) (Reprints Holyoke One-Shots)
Holyoke Publishing Co.

1-Captain Aero, Alias X, Miss Victory, Commandos of the Devil Dogs, Red Cross, Hammerhead Hawley, Capt. Aero's Sky Scouts, Flagman app.; same-c as Veri Best Sure Shot #1 23.00 70.00 160.00

VERI BEST SURE SHOT COMICS
No date (circa 1945) (Reprints Holyoke One-Shots)
Holyoke Publishing Co.

1-Capt. Aero, Miss Victory by Quinlan, Alias X, The Red Cross, Flagman, Commandos of the Devil Dogs, Hammerhead Hawley, Capt. Aero's Sky Scouts; same-c as Veri Best Sure Fire #1 23.00 70.00 160.00

VERONICA (Also see Archie's Girls, Betty &...)
April, 1989 - Present (75 & 95¢)
Archie Comics

1-30: 1,2-(75¢). 3-30 (95¢-$1.00) 1.00
21-45: 21-Begin $1.25-c. 34-Neon ink-c 1.25

VERONICA'S PASSPORT DIGEST MAGAZINE (Becomes Veronica's Digest Magazine #3 on)
Nov, 1992 - Present ($1.50, digest size)
Archie Comics

1-5 1.50

VERONICA'S SUMMER SPECIAL (See Archie Giant Series Magazine #615, 625)

VERSION (Dark Horse)(Value: cover or less)

VERTIGO JAM
Aug, 1993 ($3.95, 68 pgs.)(Painted-c by Fabry)
DC Comics (Vertigo)

1-Sandman by Neil Gaiman, Hellblazer, Animal Man, Doom Patrol, Swamp Thing, Kid Eternity & Shade the Changing Man 1.60 4.00

VERTIGO PREVIEW
1992 (75¢, 36 pgs.)
DC Comics (Vertigo)

1-Vertigo previews; Sandman by Neil Gaiman 1.00

VERTIGO VISIONS
June, 1993 - Present (68 pgs.)
DC Comics (Vertigo)

The Geek 1 (6/93, $3.95) 1.60 4.00
The Phantom Stranger 1 (10/93, $3.50) 1.40 3.50
Dr. Occult 1 (7/94, $3.95) 1.60 4.00

VERY BEST OF DENNIS THE MENACE, THE
July, 1979 - No. 2, Apr, 1980 (132 pgs., Digest, 95¢, $1.00)
Fawcett Publications

1,2-Reprints .80 2.00

VERY BEST OF DENNIS THE MENACE, THE
April, 1982 - No. 3, Aug, 1982 ($1.25, digest size)
Marvel Comics Group

1-3-Reprints 1.25

NOTE: ***Hank Ketcham*** *c-all. A few thousand of #1 & 2 were printed with DC emblem.*

V FOR VENDETTA
Sept, 1988 - No. 10, May, 1989 ($2.00, maxi-series)
DC Comics

1-10: Alan Moore scripts in all .80 2.00

GD25 FN65 NM94

Trade paperback (1990, $14.95) 2.10 6.00 15.00

VIC BRIDGES FAZERS SKETCHBOOK AND FACT FILE (AC)(Value: cover or less)

VIC FLINT (Crime Buster...)(See Authentic Police Cases #10-14 & Fugitives From Justice #2)
August, 1948 - No. 5, April, 1949 (Newspaper reprints; NEA Service)
St. John Publishing Co.

1 9.15 27.50 55.00
2 5.85 17.50 35.00
3-5 4.70 14.00 28.00

VIC FLINT (Crime Buster...)
Feb, 1956 - No. 2, May, 1956 (Newspaper reprints)
Argo Publ.

1,2 5.35 16.00 32.00

VIC JORDAN (Also see Big Shot Comics #32)
April, 1945
Civil Service Publ.

1-1944 daily newspaper-r 10.00 30.00 65.00

VICKI (Humor)
Feb, 1975 - No. 4, Aug, 1975 (No. 1,2: 68 pgs.)
Atlas/Seaboard Publ.

1-Reprints Tippy Teen 1.20 3.00
2-4 .65 1.60

VICKI VALENTINE (Renegade)(Value: cover or less)

VICKS COMICS (Also see Pure Oil Comics, Salerno Carnival of Comics & 24 Pages of Comics)
nd (circa 1938) (68 pgs. in color) (Giveaway)
Eastern Color Printing Co. (Vicks Chemical Co.)

nn-Famous Funnies-r (before #40); contains 5 pgs. Buck Rogers (4 pgs. from F.F. #15, & 1 pg. from #16) Joe Palooka, Napoleon, etc. app. 60.00 180.00 425.00
nn-16 loose, untrimmed page giveaway; paper-c; r/Famous Funnies #14; Buck Rogers, Joe Palooka app. 23.00 70.00 160.00

VICKY
Oct, 1948 - No. 5, June, 1949
Ace Magazine

nn(10/48)-Teenage humor 4.20 12.50 25.00
4(12/48), nn(2/49), 4(4/49), 5(6/49): 5-Dotty app. 4.00 10.00 20.00

VIC TORRY & HIS FLYING SAUCER (Also see Mr. Monster's...#5)
1950 (One Shot)
Fawcett Publications

nn-Book-length saucer story by Powell; photo/painted-c 43.00 130.00 300.00

VICTORY
June, 1994 - Present ($2.50, limited series:5)
Topps Comics

1 1.00 2.50

VICTORY COMICS
Aug, 1941 - No. 4, Dec, 1941 (#1 by Funnies, Inc.)
Hillman Periodicals

1-The Conqueror by Bill Everett, The Crusader, & Bomber Burns begin; Conqueror's origin in text; Everett-c 185.00 557.00 1300.00
2-Everett-c/a 86.00 257.00 600.00
3,4 61.00 182.00 425.00

VIC VERITY MAGAZINE
1945; No. 2, Jan?, 1947 - No. 7, Sept, 1946 (A comic book)
Vic Verity Publications

1-C. C. Beck-c/a 11.50 34.00 80.00
2-Beck-c 7.00 21.00 42.00

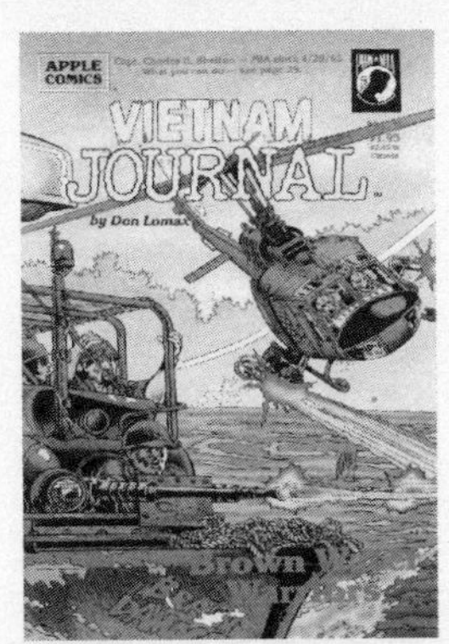

Vietnam Journal #9 © Don Lomax

Violator #2 © Todd McFarlane

Viper #2 © DC

	GD25	FN65	NM94
3-7: 6-Beck-a. 7-Beck-c	5.85	17.50	35.00

VIDEO JACK (Marvel)(Value: cover or less)

VIETNAM JOURNAL
Nov, 1987 - No. 11, July, 1989 ($1.75/$1.95, B&W)
Apple Comics

	GD25	FN65	NM94
1-Don Lomax-c/a/scripts in all		.80	2.00
1-2nd print		.80	2.00
2-11: 10,11-$2.00/$2.25-c		.80	2.00
...: Indian Country Vol. 1 (1990, $12.95)-r/#1-4 plus one new story	1.85	5.50	13.00

VIETNAM JOURNAL: VALLEY OF DEATH
June, 1994 - Present ($2.75, B&W, limited series:2)
Apple Comics

	GD25	FN65	NM94
1-By Don Lomax		1.10	2.75

VIGILANTE, THE (DC)(Value: cover or less)(Also see Action Comics #42, Justice League of America #78, Leading Comics, New Teen Titans #23 & World's Finest #244)

VIGILANTES, THE (See 4-Color #839)

VIKINGS, THE (See 4-Color #910)

VILLAINS AND VIGILANTES (Eclipse)(Value: cover or less)

VINTAGE MAGNUS (...Robot Fighter)
Jan, 1992 - No. 4, Apr, 1992 ($2.25, color, mini-series)
Valiant

	GD25	FN65	NM94
1-Layton-c; r/origin from Magnus R.F. #22	1.00	2.00	5.00
2-4		1.20	3.00

VIOLATOR (Also see Spawn #2)
May, 1994 - Present ($1.95, color)
Image Comics

	GD25	FN65	NM94
1-3-Alan Moore scripts: 1,2-Bart Sears-c(p)/a(p)		.80	2.00

VIPER
Aug, 1994 - No. 4, Nov, 1994 ($1.95, limited series)
DC Comics

	GD25	FN65	NM94
1-4-Adaptation of television show		.80	2.00

VIRGINIAN, THE (TV)
June, 1963
Gold Key

	GD25	FN65	NM94
1(10060-306)-Part photo-c of James Drury plus photo back-c	4.70	14.00	28.00

VIRUS
1993 - No. 4, 1993 ($2.50, color, mini-series)
Dark Horse Comics

	GD25	FN65	NM94
1-4: Ploog-c		1.00	2.50

VISION, THE
Nov, 1994 - Present ($1.75)
Marvel Comics

	GD25	FN65	NM94
1-3		.70	1.75

VISION AND THE SCARLET WITCH, THE (Marvel, 1982 & 1985)(Value: cover or less)

VISIONARIES (Marvel)(Value: cover or less)

VISIONS
1979 - No. 5, 1983 (B&W, fanzine)
Vision Publications

	GD25	FN65	NM94
1-Flaming Carrot begins(1st app?); N. Adams-c	7.00	21.00	50.00
2-N. Adams, Rogers-a; Gulacy back-c; signed & numbered to 2000	3.60	11.00	25.00
3-Williamson-c(p); Steranko back-c	1.30	4.00	9.00
4-Flaming Carrot-c & info.	2.00	6.00	14.00
5-1 pg. Flaming Carrot	1.10	2.70	6.50

NOTE: *After #4, Visions became an annual publication of The Atlanta Fantasy Fair.*

VOID INDIGO (Marvel)(Value: cover or less)

VOLTRON (TV)(Modern)(Value: cover or less)

VOODA (Jungle Princess) (Formerly Voodoo)
No. 20, April, 1955 - No. 22, Aug, 1955
Ajax-Farrell (Four Star Publications)

	GD25	FN65	NM94
20-Baker-c/a (r/Seven Seas #6)	18.00	54.00	125.00
21,22-Baker-a plus Kamen/Baker story, Kimbo Boy of Jungle, & Baker-c (p) in all. 22-Censored Jo-Jo-r (name Powaa)	16.00	48.00	110.00

NOTE: *#20-22 each contain one heavily censored-r of South Sea Girl by **Baker** from Seven Seas Comics with name changed to Vooda. #20-r/Seven Seas #6; #21-r/#4; #22-4/#3.*

VOODOO (Weird Fantastic Tales) (Vooda #20 on)
May, 1952 - No. 19, Jan-Feb, 1955
Ajax-Farrell (Four Star Publ.)

	GD25	FN65	NM94
1-South Sea Girl-r by Baker	30.00	90.00	210.00
2-Rulah story-r plus South Sea Girl from Seven Seas #2 by Baker (name changed from Alani to El'nee)	24.00	72.00	165.00
3-Bakerish-a; man stabbed in face	17.00	52.00	120.00
4,8-Baker-r. 8-Severed head panels	17.00	52.00	120.00
5-7,9,10: 5-Nazi death camp story (flaying alive). 6-Severed head panels	13.00	40.00	90.00
11-14,16-18: 14-Zombies take over America. 16-Post nuclear world story. 17-Electric chair panels	11.00	32.00	75.00
15-Opium drug story-r/Ellery Queen #3	12.00	36.00	85.00
19-Bondage-c; Baker-r(2)/Seven Seas #5 w/minor changes & #1, heavily modified; last pre-code; contents & covers chane to jungle theme	14.00	43.00	100.00
Annual 1(1952, 25¢, 100 pgs.)-Baker-a	37.00	111.00	260.00

VOODOO (See Tales of...)

VORTEX
Nov, 1982 - No. 15, 1988(No month) ($1.50/$1.75, B&W)
Vortex Publs.

	GD25	FN65	NM94
1 ($1.95)-Peter Hsu-a; Ken Steacy-c; nudity	1.50	4.00	9.00
2-1st app. Mister X (on-c only)		1.20	3.00
3		1.00	2.50
4-15: 12-Sam Kieth-a		.70	1.80

VORTEX
1991 - No. 2? ($2.50, color, limited series)
Comico

	GD25	FN65	NM94
1,2: Heroes from The Elementals		1.00	2.50

VOYAGE TO THE BOTTOM OF THE SEA (TV)
No. 1230, Sept-Nov, 1961; Dec, 1964 - #16, Apr, 1970 (Painted covers)
Dell Publishing Co./Gold Key

	GD25	FN65	NM94
4-Color 1230(Movie-1961)	10.00	30.00	60.00
10133-412(#1, 12/64)(Gold Key)	6.70	20.00	40.00
2(7/65) - 5: Photo back-c, 1-5	4.70	14.00	28.00
6-14	4.00	10.00	20.00
15,16-Reprints	2.80	7.00	14.00

VOYAGE TO THE DEEP
Sept-Nov, 1962 - No. 4, Nov-Jan, 1964 (Painted-c)
Dell Publishing Co.

	GD25	FN65	NM94
1	5.35	16.00	32.00
2-4	4.00	10.00	20.00

WACKO
Sept, 1980 - No. 3, Oct, 1981 (B&W magazine, 84 pgs.)
Ideal Publ. Corp.

	GD25	FN65	NM94
1-3		.80	2.00

WACKY ADVENTURES OF CRACKY (Also see Gold Key Spotlight)
Dec, 1972 - No. 12, Sept, 1975
Gold Key

	GD25	FN65	NM94
1	1.50	3.75	9.00
2		1.60	4.00

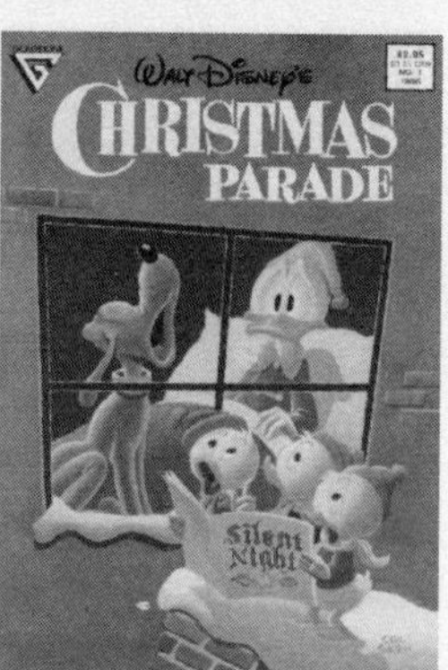

Walt Disney's Christmas Parade #1 © WDC

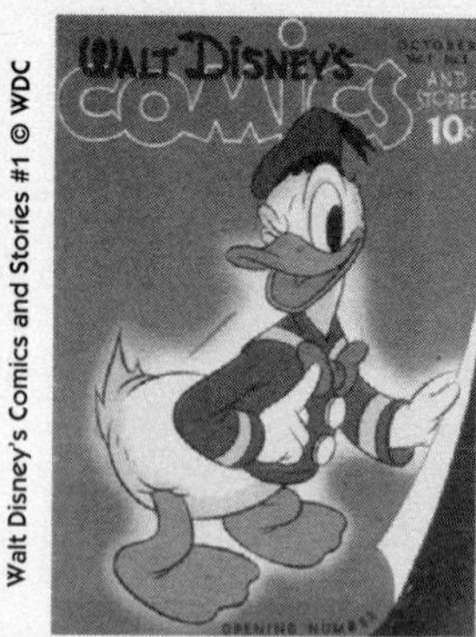

Walt Disney's Comics and Stories #1 © WDC

Walt Disney's Comics and Stories #3 © WDC

	GD25	FN65	NM94
3-12		.80	2.00

(See March of Comics #405, 424, 436, 448)

WACKY DUCK (...Comics #3-6; formerly Dopey Duck; Justice Comics #7 on) (See Film Funnies)
No. 3, Fall, 1946 - No. 6, Summer, 1947; Aug, 1948 - No. 2, Oct, 1948
Marvel Comics (NPP)

	GD25	FN65	NM94
3	11.50	34.00	80.00
4-Infinity-c	14.00	43.00	100.00
5,6(1947)-Becomes Justice comics	10.00	30.00	70.00
1,2(1948)	7.50	22.50	45.00
I.W. Reprint #1,2,7('58)	1.00	2.50	5.00
Super Reprint #10(I.W. on-c, Super-inside)	1.00	2.50	5.00

WACKY QUACKY (See Wisco)

WACKY RACES (TV)
Aug, 1969 - No. 7, Apr, 1972 (Hanna-Barbera)
Gold Key

	GD25	FN65	NM94
1	2.15	6.50	15.00
2-7	1.30	3.25	8.00

WACKY SQUIRREL (Also see Dark Horse Presents)
Oct, 1987 - No. 4, 1988 ($1.75, B&W)
Dark Horse Comics

	GD25	FN65	NM94
1-4: 4-Superman parody		.70	1.75
Halloween Adventure Special 1 (1987, $2.00)		.80	2.00
Summer Fun Special 1 (1988, $2.00)		.80	2.00

WACKY WITCH (Also see Gold Key Spotlight)
March, 1971 - No. 21, Dec, 1975
Gold Key

	GD25	FN65	NM94
1	2.15	6.50	15.00
2	1.30	3.25	8.00
3-10	1.00	2.00	5.00
11-21		1.20	3.00

(See March of Comics #374, 398, 410, 422, 434, 446, 458, 470, 482)

WACKY WOODPECKER (See Two Bit the...)
1958; 1963
I. W. Enterprises/Super Comics

	GD25	FN65	NM94
I.W. Reprint #1,2,7(nd-reprints Two Bit...)	.80	2.00	4.00
Super Reprint #10('63)	.80	2.00	4.00

WAGON TRAIN (1st Series) (TV) (See Western Roundup under Dell Giants)
No. 895, Mar, 1958 - No. 13, Apr-June, 1962 (All photo-c)
Dell Publishing Co.

	GD25	FN65	NM94
4-Color 895 (#1)	10.00	30.00	70.00
4-Color 971(#2),1019(#3)	6.35	19.00	38.00
4(1-3/60),6-13	5.00	15.00	30.00
5-Toth-a	5.35	16.00	32.00

WAGON TRAIN (2nd Series)(TV)
Jan, 1964 - No. 4, Oct, 1964 (All front & back photo-c)
Gold Key

	GD25	FN65	NM94
1-Tufts-a in all	4.20	12.50	25.00
2-4	3.60	9.00	18.00

WAITING ROOM WILLIE (See Sad Case of...)

WALLY (Teen-age)
Dec, 1962 - No. 4, Sept, 1963
Gold Key

	GD25	FN65	NM94
1	3.00	7.50	15.00
2-4	1.60	4.00	8.00

WALLY THE WIZARD (Marvel)(Value: cover or less)

WALLY WOOD'S T.H.U.N.D.E.R. AGENTS (Deluxe)(Value: cover or less)

WALT DISNEY CHRISTMAS PARADE (Also see Christmas Parade)
Winter, 1977 (224 pgs.) (cardboard covers, $1.95)
Whitman Publishing Co. (Golden Press)

	GD25	FN65	NM94
11191-Barks-r/Christmas in Disneyland #1, Dell Christmas Parade #9 & Dell Giant #53		1.00	2.40

WALT DISNEY COMICS DIGEST
June, 1968 - No. 57, Feb, 1976 (50¢) (Digest size)
Gold Key

	GD25	FN65	NM94
1-Reprints Uncle Scrooge #5; 192 pgs.	5.00	15.00	35.00
2-4-Barks-r	2.85	8.00	20.00
5-Daisy Duck by Barks (8 pgs.); last published story by Barks (art only) plus 21 pg. Scrooge-r by Barks	5.50	17.00	40.00
6-13-All Barks-r	2.10	6.50	15.00
14,15	1.30	3.25	8.00
16-Reprints Donald Duck #26 by Barks	2.10	6.50	15.00
17-20-Barks-r	1.70	5.00	12.00
21-31,33,35-37-Barks-r; 24-Toth Zorro	1.70	4.20	10.00
32,41,45,47-49	1.00	2.50	6.00
34-Reprints 4-Color #318	1.70	4.20	10.00
38-Reprints Christmas in Disneyland #1	1.70	4.20	10.00
39-Two Barks-r/WDC&S #272, 4-Color #1073 plus Toth Zorro-r	1.70	4.20	10.00
40-Mickey Mouse-r by Gottfredson	1.20	2.90	7.00
42,43-Barks-r	1.20	2.90	7.00
44-(Has Gold Key emblem, 50¢)-Reprints 1st story of 4-Color #29,256,275,282	2.85	8.00	20.00
44-Republished in 1976 by Whitman; not identical to original; a bit smaller, blank back-c, 69¢	1.30	3.25	8.00
46,50,52-Barks-r. 52-Barks-r/WDC&S #161,132	1.00	2.50	6.00
51-Reprints 4-Color #71	1.70	4.20	10.00
53-55: 53-Reprints Dell Giant #30. 54-Reprints Donald Duck Beach Party #2. 55-Reprints Dell Giant #49	1.00	2.00	5.00
56-r/Uncle Scrooge #32 (Barks)	1.20	2.90	7.00
57-r/Mickey Mouse Almanac('57) & two Barks stories	1.00	2.50	6.00

NOTE: *#1-10, 196 pgs.; #11-41, 164 pgs.; #42 on, 132 pgs. Old issues were being reprinted & distributed by Whitman in 1976.*

WALT DISNEY PRESENTS (TV)
No. 997, June-Aug, 1959 - No. 6, Dec-Feb, 1960-61 (All photo-c)
Dell Publishing Co.

	GD25	FN65	NM94
4-Color 997 (#1)	8.35	25.00	50.00
2(12-2/60)-The Swamp Fox(origin), Elfego Baca, Texas John Slaughter (Disney TV show) begin	5.85	17.50	35.00
3-6: 5-Swamp Fox by Warren Tufts	5.00	15.00	30.00

WALT DISNEY'S CHRISTMAS PARADE (Also see Christmas Parade)
Winter, 1988; No. 2, Winter, 1989 ($2.95, 100 pgs.)
Gladstone

	GD25	FN65	NM94
1,2: 1-Barks-r/painted-c. 2-Barks-r		1.20	3.00

WALT DISNEY'S COMICS AND STORIES (Cont. of Mickey Mouse Magazine) (#1-30 contain Donald Duck newspaper reprints) (Titled "Comics And Stories" #264 to #?; titled "Walt Disney's Comics And Stories" #511 on)
10/40 - #263, 8/62; #264, 10/62 - #510, 1984; #511, 10/86 - Present
Dell Publishing Co./Gold Key #264-473/Whitman #474-510/Gladstone #511-547(4/90)/Disney Comics #548(6/90)-#585/Gladstone #586(8/93) on

NOTE: The whole number can always be found at the bottom of the title page in the lower left-hand or right hand panel.

	GD25	FN65	VF82	NM94
1(V1#1-c; V2#1-indicia)-Donald Duck strip-r by Al Taliaferro & Gottfredson's Mickey Mouse begin	1000.00	3000.00	6500.00	10,000.00

(Estimated up to 245 total copies exist, 12 in NM/Mint)

	GD25	FN65	NM94
2	400.00	1200.00	4000.00
3	170.00	505.00	1350.00
4-X-Mas-c	120.00	356.00	950.00

4-Special promotional, complimentary issue; cover same except one corner was blanked out & boxed in to identify the giveaway (not a paste-over). This special pressing was probably sent out to former subscribers to Mickey Mouse Mag. whose subscriptions had expired. (Very rare-5 known copies)

Walt Disney's Comics and Stories #69 © WDC

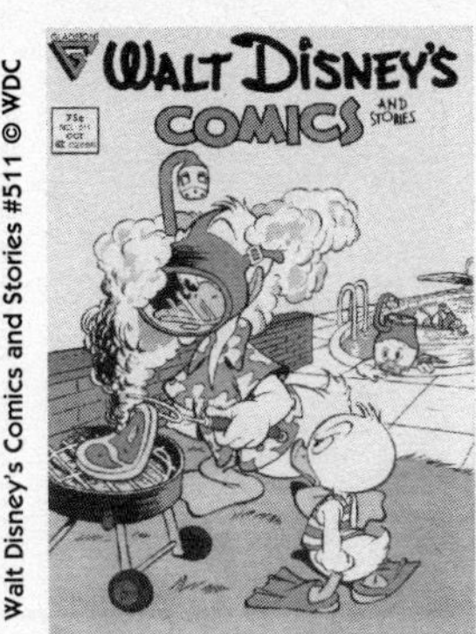

Walt Disney's Comics and Stories #511 © WDC

Walt Disney's Comics and Stories #523 © WDC

GD25 FN65 NM94

188.00 563.00 1500.00
5-Goofy-c 94.00 281.00 750.00
6-10: 8-Only Clarabelle Cow-c 75.00 225.00 600.00
11-14: 11-1st Huey, Dewey & Louie-c this title (See Mickey Mouse Magazine V4#2 for 1st-c ever 66.00 200.00 530.00
15-17: 15-The 3 Little Kittens (17 pgs.). 16-The 3 Little Pigs (29 pgs.); X-Mas-c. 17-The Ugly Duckling (4 pgs.) 59.00 178.00 475.00
18-21 50.00 150.00 400.00
22-30: 22-Flag-c 44.00 131.00 350.00
31-New Donald Duck stories by Carl Barks begin; see Four Color #9 for first Barks Donald Duck 275.00 825.00 2200.00
32-Barks-a 125.00 375.00 1000.00
33-Barks-a; infinity-c 88.00 263.00 700.00
34-Gremlins by Walt Kelly begin, end #41; Barks-a 75.00 225.00 600.00
35,36-Barks-a 66.00 200.00 530.00
37-Donald Duck by Jack Hannah 33.00 100.00 265.00
38-40-Barks-a. 39-X-Mas-c. 40,41-Gremlins by Kelly; no Barks-a? 47.00 140.00 375.00
41-50-Barks-a. 43-Seven Dwarfs-c app. (4/44) 38.00 112.00 300.00
51-60-Barks-a. 51-X-Mas-c. 52-Li'l Bad Wolf begins, ends #203 (not in #55). 58-Kelly flag-c 25.00 75.00 200.00
61-70: Barks-a. 61-Dumbo story. 63,64-Pinocchio stories. 63-Cover swipe from New Funnies #94. 64-X-Mas-c. 65-Pluto story. 66-Infinity-c. 67,68-Mickey Mouse Sunday-r by Bill Wright 22.00 65.00 175.00
71-80: Barks-a. 75-77-Brer Rabbit stories, no Mickey Mouse. 76-X-Mas-c 16.00 48.00 125.00
81-87,89,90: Barks-a. 82-Goofy-c. 82-84-Bongo stories. 86-90-Goofy & Agnes app. 89-Chip 'n' Dale story 14.00 41.00 110.00
88-1st app. Gladstone Gander by Barks (1/48) 18.00 53.00 140.00
91-97,99: Barks-a. 95-1st WDC&S Barks-c. 96-No Mickey Mouse; Little Toot begins, ends #97. 99-X-Mas-c 11.00 32.00 90.00
98-1st Uncle Scrooge app. in WDC&S (11/48) 25.00 75.00 200.00
100-(1/49)-Barks-a 15.00 45.00 120.00
101-110-Barks-a. 107-Taliaferro-c; Donald acquires super powers 10.00 30.00 80.00
111,114,117-All Barks 9.00 27.00 70.00
112-Drug (ether) issue (Donald Duck) 9.00 27.00 70.00
113,115,116,118-123: No Barks. 116-Dumbo x-over. 121-Grandma Duck begins, ends #168; not in #135,142,146,155 4.00 12.00 32.00
124,126-130-All Barks. 124-X-Mas-c 7.50 22.50 60.00
125-1st app. Junior Woodchucks (2/51); Barks-a 11.00 32.00 90.00
131,133,135-139-All Barks 7.50 22.50 60.00
132-Barks-a(2) (D. Duck & Grandma Duck) 8.00 24.00 65.00
134-Intro. & 1st app. The Beagle Boys (11/51) 16.00 48.00 125.00
140-1st app. Gyro Gearloose by Barks (5/52) 16.00 48.00 125.00
141-150-All Barks. 143-Little Hiawatha begins, ends #151,159 5.00 15.00 40.00
151-170-All Barks 4.25 13.00 35.00
171-199-All Barks 4.00 11.00 30.00
200 5.00 15.00 40.00
201-240: All Barks. 204-Chip 'n' Dale & Scamp begin 4.00 11.00 30.00
241-283: Barks-a. 241-Dumbo x-over. 247-Gyro Gearloose begins, ends #274. 256-Ludwig Von Drake begins, ends #274 3.00 9.00 24.00
284,285,287,290,295,296,309-311-Not by Barks 1.50 4.50 12.00
286,288,289,291-294,297,298,308-All Barks stories; 293-Grandma Duck's Farm Friends. 297-Gyro Gearloose. 298-Daisy Duck's Diary-r 2.00 6.00 16.00
299-307-All contain early Barks-r (#43-117). 305-Gyro Gearloose 2.25 6.75 18.00
312-Last Barks issue with original story 2.25 6.75 18.00
313-315,317-327,329-334,336-341 1.50 4.50 12.00
316-Last issue published during life of Walt Disney 1.50 4.50 12.00
328,335,342-350-Barks-r 1.50 4.50 12.00
351-360-With posters inside; Barks reprints (2 versions of each with & without posters)-without posters... 1.50 4.50 12.00
351-360-With posters... 2.25 6.75 18.00

GD25 FN65 NM94

361-400-Barks-r 1.50 4.50 12.00
401-429-Barks-r 1.50 4.50 12.00
430,433,437,438,441,444,445,466,506-No Barks 1.00 2.50 6.00
431,432,434-436,439,440,442,443-Barks-r 1.00 2.50 6.00
446-465,467-505,507-510: All Barks-r. 494-r/WDC&S #98 1.00 2.00 5.00
511-Wuzzles by Disney studio (1st by Gladstone) .90 2.30 5.50
512 1.20 3.00
513-520: 518-Infinity-c .70 1.80
521-545: 522-r/1st app. Huey, Dewey & Louie from D. Duck Sunday page. 535-546-Barks-r. 541-545-($1.50, 52 pgs.) .65 1.60
546,547-($1.95, 68 pgs.): 546-Kelly-r. 547-Rosa-a .90 2.25
548-($1.50, 6/90)-1st Disney issue; New-a; no M. Mouse .70 1.75
549,551-570,572,573,577-579,581,584 ($1.50): 549-Barks-r begin. 551-r/1 story from F.C. #29. 556,578-r/Mickey Mouse Cheerios Premium by Dick Moores. 570-Valentine issue; has Mickey/Minnie centerfold .65 1.60
550 ($2.25, 52 pgs.)-Donald Duck by Barks; previously only printed in The Netherlands (1st time in U.S.); also r/Chip 'n Dale & Scamp from #204 1.00 2.50
571-($2.95, 68 pgs)-r/Donald Duck's Atomic Bomb by Barks from 1947 Cheerios premium 1.60 4.00
574-576,580,582,583 ($2.95, 68 pgs.): 574-r/1st Pinocchio Sunday strip (1939-40). 580-r/Donald Duck's 1st app. from Silly Symphony strip 12/16/34 by Taliaferro. 582,583-r/Mickey Mouse on Sky Island from WDC&S #1,2 1.30 3.25
585-($2.50, 52 pgs.)-r/#140; Barks-r 1.30 3.25
586,587: 586-Gladstone issues begin again .70 1.75
588-599 1.50

NOTE: *(#1-38, 68 pgs.; #39-42, 60 pgs.; #43-57, 61-134, 143-168, 446, 447, 52 pgs.; #58-60, 135-142, 169-540, 36 pgs.)*

NOTE: ***Barks** art in all issues #31 on, except where noted; c-95, 96, 104, 108, 109, 130-172, 174-178, 183, 198-200, 204, 206-209, 212-216, 218, 220, 226, 228-233, 235-238, 240-243, 247, 250, 253, 256, 260, 261, 276-283, 288-292, 295-298, 301, 303, 304, 306, 307, 309, 310, 313-316, 319, 321, 322, 324, 326, 328, 329, 331, 332, 334, 341, 342, 350, 351, 540(never before published), 546r, 557-586r(most). **Kelly** r-546, 547, 582, 583; covers(most)-34-94, 97-103, 105, 106, 110-123, 537r, 538r, 541r, 543r, 544r. Walt Disney's Comics & Stories featured Mickey Mouse serials which were in practically every issue from #1 through #394. The titles of the serials, along with the issues they are in, are listed in previous editions of this price guide. **Floyd Gottfredson** Mickey Mouse serials in issues #1-14, 18-66, 69-74, 78-100, 128, 562, 563, 567-572, 575, 580-present plus "Mickey Mouse in a Warplant" (3 pgs.), and "Pluto Catches a Nazi Spy" (4 pgs.) in #62; "Mystery Next Door", #93; "Sunken Treasure", #94; "Aunt Marissa", #95; "Gangland", #98; "Thanksgiving Dinner", #99; and "The Talking Dog", #100. Mickey Mouse by **Paul Murry** #152 on except 155-57 (**Dick Moore**), 327-29 (**Tony Strobl**), 348-50 (**Jack Manning**). **Don Rosa** story/a-523, 524, 526, 528, 531, 547. **Al Taliaferro** Silly Symphonies in #5-"Three Little Pigs"; #13-"Birds of a Feather"; #14-"The Boarding School Mystery"; #15-"Cookieland" and "Three Little Kittens"; #16-"The Practical Pig"; #17-"The Ugly Duckling"; "The Wise Little Hen" in #580; and "Ambrose the Robber Kitten"; #19-"Penguin Isle"; and "Bucky Bug" in #20-23, 25, 26, 28 (one continuous story from 1932-34; first 2 pgs. not Taliaferro). **Gottfredson** strip r-562, 563, 568-572, 581, 585, 586, 590. **Taliaferro** strip r-584, 580.*

WALT DISNEY'S COMICS & STORIES
1943 (36 pgs.) (Dept. store Xmas giveaway)
Walt Disney Productions

nn-X-Mas-c with Donald & the Boys 47.00 141.00 330.00

WALT DISNEY'S COMICS & STORIES
1942-1963 known (4 pgs. in color, slick paper, 7-1/3"x10-1/4")
(folded horizontally once or twice as mailers)
K.K. Publications (Xmas subscription offer)

1942 mailer-r/Kelly cover to WDC&S 25; 2-year subscription + two Grosset & Dunlap hardcover books (32-pages each), of Bambi and of Thumper, offered for $2.00; came in an illustrated C&S envelope with an enclosed postage paid envelope (Rare) Mailer only 22.00 65.00 150.00
with envelopes 30.00 90.00 200.00
1949 mailer-A rare Barks item: Same WDC&S cover as 1942 mailer, but with art changed so that newphew is handing teacher Donald a comic book rather than an apple, as originally drawn by Kelly. The tiny, 7/8"x1-1/4" cover shown was a rejected cover by Barks that was intended for C&S 110, but was redrawn by Kelly for C&S 111. The original art has been lost and this is its only app. (Rare) 40.00 120.00 270.00

Walt Disney's Donald and Mickey #23 © WDC

Walt Disney's Donald Duck #253 © WDC

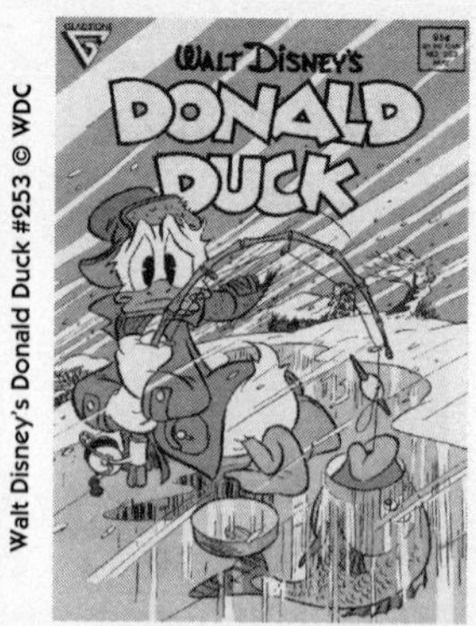

Walt Disney's Junior Woodchucks #1 © WDC

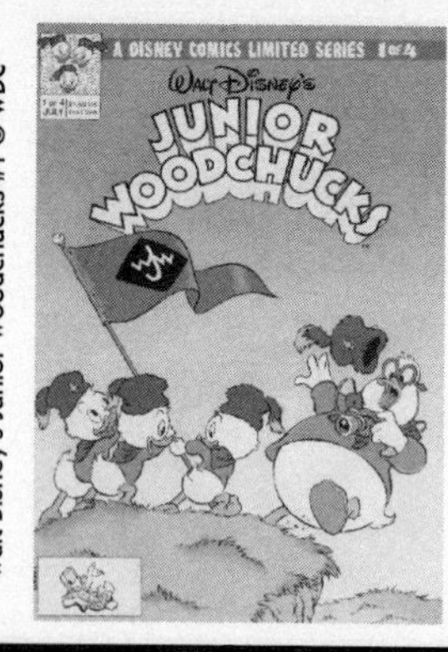

GD25 FN65 NM94

1950 mailer-P.1 r/Kelly cover to Dell Xmas Parade 1 (without title); p.2 r/Kelly cover to C&S 101 (w/o title), but with the art altered to show Donald reading C&S 122 (by Kelly); hardcover book, "Donald Duck in Bringing Up the Boys" given with a $1.00 one-year subscription; P.4 r/full Kelly Xmas cover to C&S 99 (Rare) 14.00 43.00 100.00

1953 mailer-P.1 r/cover Dell Xmas Parade 4 (w/o title); insides offer "Donald Duck Full Speed Ahead," a 28-page, color, 5-5/8"x6-5/8" book, not of the Story Hour series; P.4 r/full Barks C&S 148 cover (Rare) 10.00 30.00 60.00

1963 mailer-Pgs. 1,2 & 4 r/GK Xmas art; P.3 r/a 1963 C&S cover (Scarce) 5.00 15.00 35.00

NOTE: It is assumed a different mailer was printed each Xmas for at least twenty years. A 1952 mailer is known.

WALT DISNEY'S COMICS DIGEST
Dec, 1986 - No. 7, Sept, 1987
Gladstone

1-7 1.25

WALT DISNEY'S DONALD AND MICKEY (Formerly Walt Disney's Mickey and Donald)
No. 19, Sept, 1993 - Present ($1.50)(36 & 68 pgs.)
Gladstone (Bruce Hamilton Company)

19,21-24,26-30-New & reprints. 19-Murry-r. 19,21,23,24-Barks-r. 22-Barks "Omelet" story r/WDC&S #146 1.20 3.00
20,25-($2.95, 68 pgs.): 20-Barks, Gottfredson-r 1.20 3.00

WALT DISNEY'S DONALD DUCK ADVENTURES (D.D. Adv. #1-3)
Nov, 1987-No. 20, Apr, 1990 (1st series); No. 21, Aug, 1993-Present (3rd series)
Gladstone

1 1.00 2.00 5.50
2-r/F.C. #308 .90 2.25
3,4,6,7,9-11,13,15-18: 3-r/F.C. #223. 4-r/F.C. #62. 9-r/F.C. #159. 16-r/F.C. #291; Rosa-c. 18-r/F.C. #318; Rosa-c .80 2.00
5,8-Don Rosa-a .90 2.20
12($1.50, 52pgs)-Rosa-c/a w/Barks poster 1.20 3.00
14-r/F.C. #29, "Mummy's Ring" 1.00 2.50
19 ($1.95, 68 pgs.)-Barks-r/F.C. #199 .80 2.00
20 ($1.95, 68 pgs.)-Barks-r/F.C. #189 & cover-r .80 2.00
21,22: 21-r/D.D. #46. 22-r/F.C. #282 1.80
23-27,29-33 1.50
28-($2.95, 68 pgs.)-r/FC #199, "Sheriff of Bullet Valley" 1.20 3.00

NOTE: ***Barks** a-1-22r, 28r; c-10r, 14r, 20r.* ***Rosa** a-5, 8, 12; c-13, 16-18, 21, 23.*

WALT DISNEY'S DONALD DUCK ADVENTURES (2nd series)
June, 1990 - No. 38, July, 1993 ($1.50)
Disney Comics

1-Rosa-a & scripts 1.20 3.00
2-42: 2,3-Barks-r & new-a. 4,5-New-a? 9-r/F.C. #178 by Barks. 11-Mad #1 cover parody. 14-Barks-r. 21-r/FC #203 by Barks. 22-Rosa-a (10 pgs.) & scripts. 24-Rosa-a & scripts. 26-r/March of Comics #41 by Barks. 29-r/MOC #20 by Barks. 37-Rosa-a; Barks-r. 34-Rosa-c/a 1.50

NOTE: ***Barks** r-4, 9(F.C. #178), 14(D.D. #45), 27, 38.*

WALT DISNEY SHOWCASE
Oct, 1970 - No. 54, Jan, 1980 (No. 44-48: 68pgs., 49-54: 52pgs.)
Gold Key

1-Boatniks (Movie)-Photo-c 2.60 7.70 18.00
2-Moby Duck 1.70 4.20 10.00
3,4,7: 3-Bongo & Lumpjaw-r. 4,7-Pluto-r 1.30 3.25 8.00
5-$1,000,000 Duck (Movie)-Photo-c 1.70 5.00 12.00
6-Bedknobs & Broomsticks (Movie) 1.70 5.00 12.00
8-Daisy & Donald 1.30 3.25 8.00
9-101 Dalmatians (cartoon feat.); r/F.C. #1183 1.70 4.20 10.00
10-Napoleon & Samantha (Movie)-Photo-c 1.70 5.00 12.00
11-Moby Duck-r 1.20 2.90 7.00
12-Dumbo-r/Four Color #668 1.30 3.25 8.00
13-Pluto-r 1.20 2.90 7.00
14-World's Greatest Athlete (Movie)-Photo-c 1.70 5.00 12.00
15-3 Little Pigs-r 1.30 3.25 8.00
16-Aristocats (cartoon feature); r/Aristocats #1 1.70 5.00 12.00
17-Mary Poppins; r/M.P. #10136-501-Photo-c 1.70 5.00 12.00
18-Gyro Gearloose; Barks-r/F.C. #1047,1184 2.60 7.70 18.00
19-That Darn Cat; r/That Darn Cat #10171-602-Hayley Mills photo-c 1.70 5.00 12.00
20,23-Pluto-r 1.30 3.25 8.00
21-Li'l Bad Wolf & The Three Little Pigs 1.20 2.90 7.00
22-Unbirthday Party with Alice in Wonderland; r/Four Color #341 1.70 4.20 10.00
24-26: 24-Herbie Rides Again (Movie); sequel to "The Love Bug"; photo-c. 25-Old Yeller (Movie); r/F.C. #869; Photo-c. 26-Lt. Robin Crusoe USN (Movie); r/Lt. Robin Crusoe USN #10191-601; photo-c 1.30 3.25 8.00
27-Island at the Top of the World (Movie)-Photo-c 1.70 4.20 10.00
28-Brer Rabbit, Bucky Bug-r/WDC&S #58 1.30 3.25 8.00
29-Escape to Witch Mountain (Movie)-Photo-c 1.70 4.20 10.00
30-Magica De Spell; Barks-r/Uncle Scrooge #36 & WDC&S #258 3.10 9.00 22.00
31-Bambi (cartoon feature); r/Four Color #186 1.70 4.20 10.00
32-Spin & Marty-r/F.C. #1026; Mickey Mouse Club (TV)-Photo-c 1.70 5.00 12.00
33-39: 33-Pluto-r/F.C. #1143. 34-Paul Revere's Ride with Johnny Tremain (TV); r/F.C. #822. 35-Goofy-r/F.C. #952. 36-Peter Pan-r/F.C. #442. 37-Tinker Bell & Jiminy Cricket-r/F.C. #982,989. 38,39-Mickey & the Sleuth, Parts 1 & 2 1.00 2.50 6.00
40-The Rescuers (cartoon feature) 1.20 2.90 7.00
41-Herbie Goes to Monte Carlo (Movie); sequel to "Herbie Rides Again"; photo-c 1.30 3.25 8.00
42-Mickey & the Sleuth 1.00 2.50 6.00
43-Pete's Dragon (Movie)-Photo-c 1.70 4.20 10.00
44-Return From Witch Mountain (new) & In Search of the Castaways-r (Movies)-Photo-c; 68 pg. giants begin 1.70 4.20 10.00
45-The Jungle Book (Movie); r/#30033-803 1.70 4.20 10.00
46-The Cat From Outer Space (Movie)(new), & The Shaggy Dog (Movie)-r/F.C. #985; photo-c 1.20 2.90 7.00
47-Mickey Mouse Surprise Party-r 1.20 2.90 7.00
48-The Wonderful Advs. of Pinocchio-r/F.C. #1203; last 68 pg. issue 1.20 2.90 7.00
49-54: 49-North Avenue Irregulars (Movie); Zorro-r/Zorro #11; 52 pgs. begin; photo-c. 50-Bedknobs & Broomsticks-r/#6; Mooncussers-r/World of Adv. #1; photo-c. 51-101 Dalmatians-r. 52-Unidentified Flying Oddball (Movie); r/Picnic Party #8; photo-c. 53-The Scarecrow-r (TV). 54-The Black Hole (Movie)-Photo-c (predates Black Hole #1) 1.00 2.00 5.00

WALT DISNEY'S JUNIOR WOODCHUCKS LIMITED SERIES
July, 1991 - No. 4, Oct, 1991 ($1.50, limited series; new & reprint-a)
W. D. Publications (Disney)

1-4: 1-The Beagle Boys app.; Barks-r 1.50

WALT DISNEY'S MAGAZINE (TV)(Formerly Walt Disney's Mickey Mouse Club Magazine) (50¢) (Bi-monthly)
V2#4, June, 1957 - V4#6, Oct, 1959
Western Publishing Co.

V2#4-Stories & articles on the Mouseketeers, Zorro, & Goofy and other Disney characters & people 6.70 20.00 40.00
V2#5, V2#6(10/57) 5.00 15.00 30.00
V3#1(12/57), V3#3-6(10/58) 4.00 12.00 24.00
V3#2-Annette Funicello photo-c 11.50 34.00 80.00
V4#1(12/58) - V4#2-4,6(10/59) 4.00 12.00 24.00
V4#5-Annette Funicello photo-c, w/ 2-photo articles 11.50 34.00 80.00

NOTE: *V2#4-V3#6 were 11-1/2x8-1/2", 48 pgs.; V4#1 on were 10x8", 52 pgs. (Peak circulation of 400,000).*

WALT DISNEY'S MERRY CHRISTMAS (See Dell Giant #39)

WALT DISNEY'S MICKEY AND DONALD(M & D #1,2)(Becomes Walt Disney's Donald & Mickey #19 on)
Mar, 1988 - No. 18, May, 1990 (95¢)

Walt Disney's Sebastian #1 © WDC

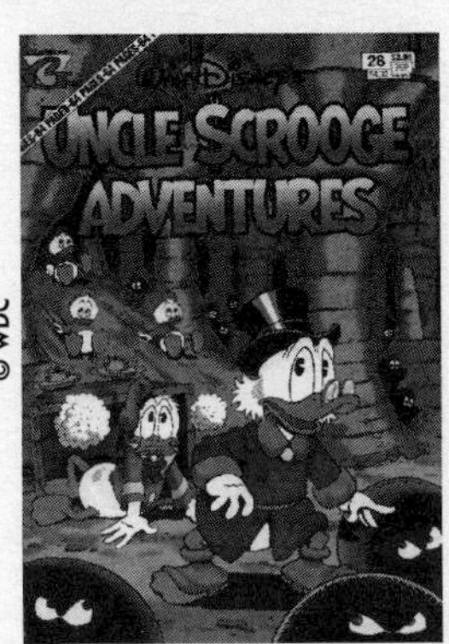

Walt Disney's Uncle Scrooge Adventures #28 © WDC

The Wanderers #10 © DC

GD25 FN65 NM94

Gladstone

1-Don Rosa-a; r/1949 Firestone giveaway 1.60 4.00
2 1.00 2.50
3-Infinity-c .80 2.00
4-8: Barks-r 1.20
9-15: 9-r/1948 Firestone giveaway; X-Mas-c 1.00
16 ($1.50, 52 pgs.)-r/FC #157 1.50
17,18 ($1.95, 68 pgs.): 17-Barks M.M.-r/FC #79 plus Barks D.D.-r; Rosa-a; X-Mas-c. 18-Kelly-c(r); Barks-r .80 2.00

NOTE: ***Barks** reprints in 1-15, 17, 18. **Kelly** c-13r, 14 (r/Walt Disney's C&S #58), 18r.*

WALT DISNEY'S MICKEY MOUSE CLUB MAGAZINE (TV)(Becomes Walt Disney's Magazine) (Quarterly)
Winter, 1956 - V2#3, April, 1957 (11-1/2x8-1/2") (48 pgs.)
Western Publishing Co.

V1#1 14.00 43.00 100.00
2-4 8.35 25.00 50.00
V2#1-3 6.70 20.00 40.00
Annual(1956)-Two different issues; ($1.50-Whitman); 120 pgs., cardboard covers, 11-3/4x8-3/4"; reprints 16.00 48.00 110.00
Annual(1957)-Same as above 14.00 43.00 100.00

WALT DISNEY'S PINOCCHIO SPECIAL (Gladstone)(Value: cover or less)

WALT DISNEY'S SEBASTIAN (See Sebastian)

WALT DISNEY'S SPRING FEVER (Disney)(Value: cover or less)

WALT DISNEY'S THE JUNGLE BOOK (Disney)(Value: cover or less)

WALT DISNEY'S UNCLE SCROOGE (Formerly Uncle Scrooge #1-209)
No. 210, 10/86 - No. 242, 4/90; No. 243, 6/90 - Present
Gladstone #210-242/Disney Comics #243-280/Gladstone #281 on

210-1st Gladstone issue; r/WDC&S #134 (1st Beagle Boys) 1.00 2.50 6.00
211-218: 217-r/U.S. #7(Seven Cities of Cibola) 1.00 2.50
219-Son Of The Sun by Rosa 2.00 6.00 14.00
220-Don Rosa story/a 1.60 4.00
221-230: 224-Rosa-c/a. 226,227-Rosa-a .80 2.00
231-240: 235-Rosa story/art .60 1.60
241-($1.95, 68 pgs.)-Rosa finishes over Barks-r .90 2.25
242-($1.95, 68 pgs.)-Barks-r; Rosa-a(1 pg.) .90 2.25
243-249,251-284-($1.50): 243-1st by Disney Comics; new-a begins. 261-263-Don Rosa-c/a. 274-All Barks issue. 275-Contains poster by Rosa. 281-Gladstone issues start again. 283-r/WDC&S #98 .70 1.80
250-($2.25, 52 pgs.)-Barks-r; wraparound-c 1.00 2.50
285-The Life and Times of Scrooge McDuck Pt. 1; Rosa-c/a/scripts 1.00 2.00 5.00
286-292-The Life and Times of Scrooge McDuck Pt. 2-8; Rosa-c/a/scripts .70 1.75

NOTE: ***Barks** r-210-218, 220-223, 224(2pg.), 225-234, 236-242, 245, 246, 250-253, 255, 256, 258, 261(2 pg.), 265, 267, 268, 272-284; c(r)-210, 212, 221, 228, 229, 232, 233, 284. **Rosa** a-219, 220, 224, 226, 227, 235, 261-263, 268, 275-277, 285-289; c-219, 224, 231, 261-263, 276, 278-281, 285-289; scripts-219, 220, 224, 235, 261-263, 268, 276, 285-289.*

WALT DISNEY'S UNCLE SCROOGE ADVENTURES (U. Scrooge Advs. #1-3)
Nov, 1987 - No. 21, May, 1990; No. 22, Sept, 1993 - Present
Gladstone Publishing

1-Barks-r begin 1.20 2.90 7.00
2-5: 5-Rosa-c/a .80 2.00
6-19: 9,14-Rosa-a. 10-r/U.S. #18(all Barks) 1.50
20,21 ($1.95, 68 pgs.) 20-Rosa-c/a. 21-Rosa-a 1.00 2.50
22 ($1.50)-Rosa-c; r/U.S. #26 .80 1.90
23-($2.95, 68 pgs.)-Vs. The Phantom Blot-r/P.B. #3; Barks-r; painted-c 1.40 3.50
24-26,29-33 ($1.50): 23-Painted-c(c-r/U.S. Goes to Disneyland). 25-r/U.S. #21 1.50
27-Guardians of the Lost Library - Rosa-c/a/story; origin of Junior Woodchuck Guidebook .90 2.25
28-($2.95, 68 pgs.)-r/U.S. #13 w/restored missing panels 1.20 3.00

NOTE: ***Barks** r-1-4, 6-8, 10-13, 15-21, 23, 24; c(r)-15, 16, 17, 21. **Rosa** a-5, 9, 14, 20, 21, 27; c-5, 13, 14, 17(finishes), 20, 22, 24, 25, 27, 28; scripts-5, 9, 14, 27.*

WALT DISNEY'S WHEATIES PREMIUMS (See Wheaties)

WALTER LANTZ ANDY PANDA (Also see Andy Panda)
Aug, 1973 - No. 23, Jan, 1978 (Walter Lantz)
Gold Key

1-Reprints 1.00 2.00 5.00
2-10-All reprints .80 2.00
11-23: 15,17-19,22-Reprints 1.50

WALT KELLY'S...
Dec, 1987; April, 1988 ($1.75/$2.50, color, Baxter)
Eclipse Comics

...Christmas Classics 1 (12/87, $1.75)-Kelly-r/Peter Wheat & Santa Claus Funnies .70 1.75
...Springtime Tales 1 (4/88, $2.50)-Kelly-r 1.00 2.50

WALTONS, THE (See Kite Fun Book)

WALT SCOTT'S CHRISTMAS STORIES (See 4-Color #959, 1062)

WAMBI, JUNGLE BOY (See Jungle Comics)
Spring, 1942; No. 2, Wint, 1942-43; No. 3, Spring, 1943; No. 4, Fall, 1948; No. 5, Sum, 1949; No. 6, Spring, 1950; No. 7-10, 1950(nd); No. 11, Spring, 1951 - No. 18, Winter, 1952-53 (#1-3: 68 pgs.)
Fiction House Magazines

1-Wambi, the Jungle Boy begins 52.00 156.00 365.00
2 (1942)-Kiefer-c 27.00 81.00 190.00
3 (1943)-Kiefer-c/a 19.00 58.00 135.00
4 (1948)-Origin in text 13.00 40.00 90.00
5 (Fall, 1949, 36 pgs.)-Kiefer-c/a 11.00 32.00 75.00
6-10: 7-(52 pgs.)-New logo 10.00 30.00 65.00
11-18 7.50 22.50 45.00
I.W. Reprint #8('64)-r/#12 with new-c 2.40 6.00 12.00

NOTE: ***Alex Blum** c-8. **Kiefer** c-1-5. **Whitman** c-11-18.*

WANDERERS (DC)(Value: cover or less)(See Adventure Comics #375, 376)

WANTED COMICS
No. 9, Sept-Oct, 1947 - No. 53, April, 1953 (#9-33: 52 pgs.)
Toytown Publications/Patches/Orbit Publ.

9-True crime cases; radio's Mr. D. A. app. 11.00 32.00 75.00
10,11: 10-Giunta-a; radio's Mr. D. A. app. 7.50 22.50 45.00
12-Used in **SOTI**, pg. 277 8.35 25.00 50.00
13-Heroin drug propaganda story 7.50 22.50 45.00
14-Marijuana drug mention story (2 pgs.) 5.85 17.50 35.00
15-17,19,20 4.70 14.00 28.00
18-Marijuana story, "Satan's Cigarettes"; r-in #45 & retitled 13.00 40.00 90.00
21,22: 21-Krigstein-a. 22-Extreme violence 6.35 19.00 38.00
23,25-34,36-38,40-44,46-48,53 4.00 10.00 20.00
24-Krigstein-a; "The Dope King", marijuana mention story 6.70 20.00 40.00
35-Used in **SOTI**, pg. 160 5.85 17.50 35.00
39-Drug propaganda story "The Horror Weed" 9.15 27.50 55.00
45-Marijuana story from #18 5.35 16.00 32.00
49-Has unstable pink-c that fades easily; rare in mint condition 4.20 12.50 25.00
50-Has unstable pink-c like #49; surrealist-c by Buscema; horror stories 8.35 25.00 50.00
51- "Holiday of Horror" junkie story; drug-c 5.85 17.50 35.00
52-Classic "Cult of Killers" opium use story 5.85 17.50 35.00

NOTE: ***Buscema** c-50, 51. **Lawrence** and **Leav** c/a most issues. **Syd Shores** c/a-48; c-37. Issues 9-46 have wanted criminals with their descriptions & drawn picture on cover.*

WANTED: DEAD OR ALIVE (See 4-Color #1102,1164)

WANTED, THE WORLD'S MOST DANGEROUS VILLAINS (See DC Special)
July-Aug, 1972 - No. 9, Aug-Sept, 1973 (All reprints & 20¢ issues)
National Periodical Publications

1-Batman, Green Lantern (story r-from G.L. #1), & Green Arrow

War Action #4 © MEG

War Birds #2 © FH

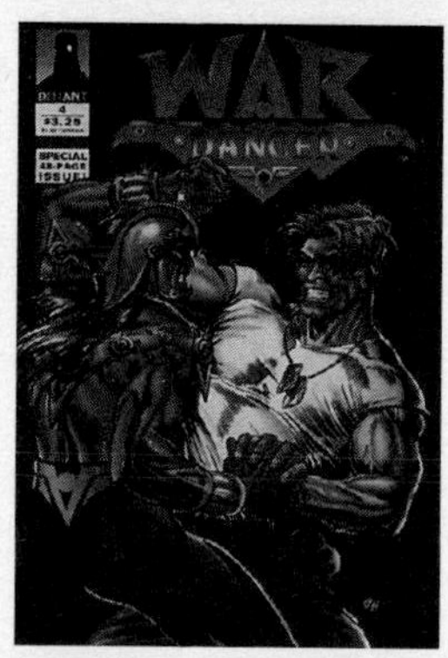

Wardancer #4 © EEP

	GD25	FN65	NM94
		1.70	4.25
2-Batman/Joker/Penguin-c/story r-from Batman #25; plus Flash story (r-from Flash #121)	1.10	2.70	6.50
3-9: 3-Dr. Fate(r/More Fun #65), Hawkman(r/Flash #100), & Vigilante(r/Action #69). 4-Gr. Lantern(r/All-American #61) & Kid Eternity(r/Kid Eternity #15). 5-Dollman/Green Lantern. 6-Burnley Starman; Wildcat/Sargon. 7-Johnny Quick(r/More fun #76), Hawkman(r/Flash #90), Hourman by Baily(r/Adv. #72). 8-Dr. Fate/Flash(r/Flash #114). 9-S&K Sandman/Superman		.90	2.25

NOTE: ***Kane*** *r-1, 5.* ***Kubert*** *r-3i, 6, 7.* ***Meskin*** *r-3, 7.* ***Reinman*** *r-4, 6.*

WAR
July, 1975 - No. 9, Nov, 1976; No. 10, Sept, 1978 - No. 49?, 1984
Charlton Comics

	GD25	FN65	NM94
1-49: 47-Reprints			1.00
7,9(Modern Comics-r, 1977)			1.00

WAR, THE (Marvel)(Value: cover or less)

WAR ACTION (Korean War)
April, 1952 - No. 14, June, 1953
Atlas Comics (CPS)

	GD25	FN65	NM94
1	11.00	32.00	75.00
2	6.70	20.00	40.00
3-10,14: 7-Pakula-a	4.70	14.00	28.00
11-13-Krigstein-a	7.00	21.00	42.00

NOTE: ***Brodsky*** *c-1-4.* ***Heath*** *a-1; c-7, 14.* ***Keller*** *a-6.* ***Maneely*** *a-1.* ***Tuska*** *a-2, 8.*

WAR ADVENTURES
Jan, 1952 - No. 13, Feb, 1953
Atlas Comics (HPC)

	GD25	FN65	NM94
1-Tuska-a	10.00	30.00	65.00
2	5.85	17.50	35.00
3-7,9-13: 3-Pakula-a. 7-Maneely-c	4.20	12.50	25.00
8-Krigstein-a	7.00	21.00	42.00

NOTE: ***Brodsky*** *c-1-3, 6, 8, 11, 12.* ***Heath*** *a-5, 7, 10; c-4, 5, 9, 13.* ***Robinson*** *a-3; c-10.*

WAR ADVENTURES ON THE BATTLEFIELD (See Battlefield)

WAR AGAINST CRIME! (Becomes Vault of Horror #12 on)
Spring, 1948 - No. 11, Feb-Mar, 1950
E. C. Comics

	GD25	FN65	NM94
1-Real Stories From Police Records on-c #1-9	54.00	160.00	375.00
2,3	29.00	86.00	200.00
4-9	27.00	81.00	190.00
10-1st Vault Keeper app. & 1st Vault of Horror	164.00	493.00	1150.00
11-2nd Vault Keeper app.; 1st horror-c	100.00	300.00	700.00

NOTE: *All have* ***Johnny Craig*** *covers.* ***Feldstein*** *a-4, 7-9.* ***Harrison/Wood*** *a-11.* ***Ingels*** *a-1, 2, 8.* ***Palais*** *a-8. Changes to horror with #10.*

WAR AND ATTACK (Also see Special War Series #3)
Fall, 1964; V2#54, June, 1966 - V2#63, Dec, 1967
Charlton Comics

	GD25	FN65	NM94
1-Wood-a	3.00	7.50	15.00
V2#54(6/66)-#63 (Formerly Fightin' Air Force)	1.40	3.50	7.00

NOTE: ***Montes/Bache*** *a-55, 56, 60, 63.*

WAR AT SEA (Formerly Space Adventures)
No. 22, Nov, 1957 - No. 42, June, 1961
Charlton Comics

	GD25	FN65	NM94
22	4.00	10.00	20.00
23-30	2.00	5.00	10.00
31-42	1.40	3.50	7.00

WAR BATTLES
Feb, 1952 - No. 9, Dec, 1953
Harvey Publications

	GD25	FN65	NM94
1-Powell-a; Elias-c	7.50	22.50	45.00
2-Powell-a	4.70	14.00	28.00
3-5,7-9: 3,7-Powell-a	4.00	10.00	20.00
6-Nostrand-a	5.00	15.00	30.00

GD25 FN65 NM94

WAR BIRDS
1952(nd) - No. 3, Winter, 1952-53
Fiction House Magazines

	GD25	FN65	NM94
1	10.00	30.00	70.00
2,3	7.00	21.00	42.00

WAR COMBAT (Becomes Combat Casey #6 on)
March, 1952 - No. 5, Nov, 1952
Atlas Comics (LBI No. 1/SAI No. 2-5)

	GD25	FN65	NM94
1	9.15	27.50	55.00
2	5.00	15.00	30.00
3-5	4.00	11.00	22.00

NOTE: ***Berg*** *a-2, 4, 5.* ***Brodsky*** *c-1, 2, 4, 5.* ***Henkel*** *a-5.* ***Maneely*** *a-1, 4; c-3.*

WAR COMICS (War Stories #5 on)(See Key Ring Comics)
May, 1940 (No mo. given) - No. 4, Sept, 1941?
Dell Publishing Co.

	GD25	FN65	NM94
1-Sikandur the Robot Master, Sky Hawk, Scoop Mason, War Correspondent begin; McWilliams-c; 1st war comic	43.00	130.00	300.00
2-Origin Greg Gilday (5/41)	24.00	73.00	170.00
3-Joan becomes Greg Gilday's aide	16.00	48.00	110.00
4-Origin Night Devils	19.00	56.00	130.00

WAR COMICS
Dec, 1950 - No. 49, Sept, 1957
Marvel/Atlas (USA No. 1-41/JPI No. 42-49)

	GD25	FN65	NM94
1	14.00	43.00	100.00
2	8.35	25.00	50.00
3-10	5.85	17.50	35.00
11-20: 11-Flame thrower w/burning bodies on-c	4.20	12.50	25.00
21,23-32: 26-Valley Forge story. 32-Last precode issue (2/55)	4.00	11.00	22.00
22-Krigstein-a	7.50	22.50	45.00
33-37,39-42,44,45,47,48	4.00	11.00	22.00
38-Kubert/Moskowitz-a	5.85	17.50	35.00
43,49-Torres-a. 43-Severin/Elder E.C. swipe from Two-Fisted Tales #31	5.35	16.00	32.00
46-Crandall-a	5.85	17.50	35.00

NOTE: ***Colan*** *a-4, 36, 48, 49.* ***Drucker*** *a-37, 43, 48.* ***Everett*** *a-17.* ***Heath*** *a-7-9, 16, 19, 25, 36; c-11, 16, 19, 25, 26, 29-31, 36.* ***G. Kane*** *a-19.* ***Lawrence*** *a-36.* ***Maneely*** *a-7, 9; c-6, 27, 37.* ***Orlando*** *a-42, 48.* ***Pakula*** *a-26.* ***Ravielli*** *a-27.* ***Reinman*** *a-26.* ***Robinson*** *a-15; c-13.* ***Severin*** *a-26, 27; c-48.*

WAR DANCER (Also see Doctor Chaos #2)
Feb, 1994 - Present ($2.50, color)
Defiant

	GD25	FN65	NM94
1-3,5,6: 1-Intro War Dancer; Weiss-c(p) begin. 1-3-Weiss-a(p)		1.00	2.50
4-($3.25, 52 pgs.)		1.30	3.25

WAR DOGS OF THE U.S. ARMY
1952
Avon Periodicals

	GD25	FN65	NM94
1-Kinstler-c/a	10.00	30.00	65.00

WARFRONT
9/51 - #35, 11/58; #36, 10/65; #37, 9/66 - #38, 12/66; #39, 2/67
Harvey Publications

	GD25	FN65	NM94
1-Korean War	8.35	25.00	50.00
2	4.20	12.50	25.00
3-10	3.60	9.00	18.00
11,12,14,16-20	2.80	7.00	14.00
13,15,22-Nostrand-a	5.35	16.00	32.00
21,23-27,29,31-33,35	2.40	6.00	12.00
28,30,34-Kirby-c	4.35	13.00	26.00
36-Dynamite Joe begins, ends #39; Williamson-a	3.20	8.00	16.00
37-Wood-a (17 pgs.)	4.00	10.00	20.00
38,39-Wood-a, 2-3 pgs.; Lone Tiger app.	2.40	6.00	12.00

NOTE: ***Powell*** *a-1-6, 9-11, 14, 17, 20, 23, 25-28, 30, 31, 34, 36.* ***Powell/Nostrand*** *a-12, 13, 15.*

Warheads #1 © MEG

Warlock #32 © MEG

Warlord #69 © DC

GD25 FN65 NM94

Simon c-36?, 38.

WAR FURY
Sept, 1952 - No. 4, March, 1953
Comic Media/Harwell (Allen Hardy Associates)

1-Heck-c/a in all; Palais-a; bullet hole in forehead-c; all issues are very violent 6.70 20.00 40.00
2-4: 4-Morisi-a 4.20 12.50 25.00

WAR GODS OF THE DEEP (See Movie Classics)

WARHAWKS (TSR)(Value: cover or less)

WARHEADS
June, 1992 - No. 14, Aug, 1993 ($1.75, color)
Marvel Comics UK

1-Wolverine-c/story; indicia says #2 by mistake 1.10 2.75
2-14: 2-Nick Fury app. 3-Iron Man-c/story. 4,5-X-Force. 5-Liger vs. Cable. 6,7-Death's Head II app. (#6 is cameo) .70 1.75

WARHEADS: BLACK DAWN (Epic)(Value: cover or less)

WAR HEROES (See Marine War Heroes)

WAR HEROES
7-9/42 (no month); No. 2, 10-12/42 - No. 10, 10-12/44; No. 11, 3/45
Dell Publishing Co. (Published quarterly)

1-General Douglas MacArthur-c 19.00 57.00 130.00
2 10.00 30.00 65.00
3,5: 3-Pro-Russian back-c 7.50 22.50 45.00
4-Disney's Gremlins app. 13.50 41.00 95.00
6-11: 6-Tothish-a by Discount 6.70 20.00 40.00
NOTE: *No. 1 was to be released in July, but was delayed. Painted c-4, 6-9.*

WAR HEROES
May, 1952 - No. 8, April, 1953
Ace Magazines

1 7.50 22.50 45.00
2-Lou Cameron-a 4.70 14.00 28.00
3-8: 6,7-Cameron-a 4.00 10.00 20.00

WAR HEROES (Also see Blue Bird Comics)
Feb, 1963 - No. 27, Nov, 1967
Charlton Comics

1 3.00 7.50 15.00
2-10: 2-John F. Kennedy story 1.60 4.00 8.00
11-27: 27-1st Devils Brigade by Glanzman 1.00 2.50 5.00
NOTE: ***Montes/Bache** a-3-7, 21, 25, 27; c-3-7.*

WAR IS HELL
Jan, 1973 - No. 15, Oct, 1975
Marvel Comics Group

1-Williamson-a(r), 5 pgs.; Ayers-a 1.50
2-15: 2-9-All reprints 1.00
NOTE: ***Bolle** a-3r. **Powell** a-1. **Woodbridge** a-1. Sgt. Fury reprints-7, 8.*

WARLOCK (The Power of...)(Also see Fantastic Four #66, 67, Incredible Hulk #178, Infinity Crusade, Infinity Gauntlet, Infinity War, Marvel Premiere #1, Silver Surfer V3#46, Strange Tales #178-181 & Thor #165)
Aug, 1972 - No. 8, Oct, 1973; No. 9, Oct, 1975 - No. 15, Nov, 1976
Marvel Comics Group

1-Origin by Kane 3.30 9.90 23.00
2,3 1.40 4.00 10.00
4-8: 4-Death of Eddie Roberts 1.30 3.10 7.50
9-Starlin's 2nd Thanos saga begins, ends #15; new costume Warlock; Thanos cameo only; story cont'd from Strange Tales #178-181; Starlin-c/a in #9-15 1.50 4.00 9.00
10-Origin Thanos & Gamora; recaps events from Capt. Marvel #25-34. Thanos vs.The Magus-c/story 4.30 13.00 30.00
11-Thanos app.; Warlock dies 3.60 11.00 25.00
12-14: 14-Origin Star Thief; last 25¢ issue 1.70 4.00 10.00
15-Thanos-c/story 3.00 9.00 21.00

NOTE: ***Buscema** a-2p; c-8p. **G. Kane** a-1p, 3-5p; c-1p, 2, 3, 4p, 5p, 7p. **Starlin** a-9-14p, 15; c-9, 10, 11p, 12p, 13-15. **Sutton** a-1-8i.*

WARLOCK (...Special Edition on-c)
Dec, 1982 - No. 6, May, 1983 ($2.00, 52 pgs.) (slick paper)
Marvel Comics Group

1-6: 1-Warlock-r/Strange Tales #178-180. 2-r/Str. Tales #180,181 & Warlock #9. 3-r/Warlock #10-12(Thanos origin recap). 4-r/Warlock #12-15. 5-r/Warlock #15, Marvel Team-Up #55 & Avengers Ann. #7. 6-r/2nd half Avengers Annual #7 & Marvel Two-in-One Annual #2 1.10 3.00 6.50
Special Edition #1(12/83) .90 2.25
NOTE: ***Byrne** a-5r. **Starlin** a-1-6r; c-1-6(new). Direct sale only.*

WARLOCK
V2#1, May, 1992 - No. 6, Oct, 1992 ($2.50, limited series)
Marvel Comics

V2#1-6: 1-Reprints 1982 reprint series w/Thanos 1.00 2.50

WARLOCK AND THE INFINITY WATCH
Feb, 1992 - Present ($1.75)(Sequel to Infinity Gauntlet)
Marvel Comics

1-Starlin scripts begin; brief origin recap Warlock 1.50 3.75
2-Reintro Moondragon 1.30 3.25
3 .90 2.25
4-24,26: 7-Reintro The Magus; Moondragon app.; Thanos cameo on last 2 pgs. 8,9-Thanos battles Gamora-c/story. 8-Magus & Moondragon app. 10-Thanos-c/story; Magus app. 13-Hulk x-over. 21-Drax vs. Thor .70 1.75
25-($2.95, 52 pgs.)-Die-cut & embossed double-c; Thor & Thanos app. 1.20 3.00
28-39: 28-Begin $1.95-c; bound-in card sheet .80 2.00
NOTE: ***Austin** c/a-1-4i, 7i. **Leonardi** a(p)-3, 4. **Medina** c/a(p)-1, 2, 5; 6, 9, 10, 14, 15, 20. **Williams** a(i)-8, 12, 13, 16-19.*

WARLOCK CHRONICLES
June, 1993 - No. 8, Feb, 1994 ($2.00, limited series)
Marvel Comics

1-($2.95)-Holo-grafx foil & embossed-c; origin retold; Starlin scripts begin; Keith Williams-a(i) in all 1.20 3.00
2-8: 3-Thanos & Mephisto-c/story. 4-Vs. Magus-c/s. 8-Contains free 16 pg. Razorline insert .80 2.00

WARLOCK 5 (Aircel)(Value: cover or less)

WARLORD (See 1st Issue Special)
1-2/76; No.2, 3-4/76; No.3, 10-11/76 - No. 133, Wint, 1988-89
National Periodical Publications/DC Comics #123 on

1-Story cont'd. from 1st Issue Special #8 2.00 6.00 14.00
2-Intro. Machiste 1.20 2.90 7.00
3-5 1.00 2.00 5.00
6-10: 6-Intro Mariah. 7-Origin Machiste. 9-Dons new costume 1.60 4.00
11-20: 11-Origin-r. 12-Intro Aton. 15-Tara returns; Warlord has son 1.20 3.00
21-40: 27-New facts about origin. 28-1st app. Wizard World. 32-Intro Shakira. 37,38-Origin Omac by Starlin. 38-Intro Jennifer Morgan, Warlord's daughter. 39-Omac ends. 40-Warlord gets new costume .80 2.00
41-47,49-52: 42-47-Omac back-up series. 49-Claw The Unconquered app. 50-Death of Aton. 51-Reprints #1 1.25
48-(52 pgs.)-1st app. Arak; contains free 14 pg. Arak Son of Thunder; Claw The Unconquered app. .80 2.00
53-130,132: 55-Arion Lord of Atlantis begins, ends #62. 63-The Barren Earth begins; free 16pg. Masters of the Universe preview. 91-Origin w/new facts. 114,115-Legends x-over. 100-($1.25, 52 pgs.). 125-Death of Tara 1.30
131-1st DC work by Rob Liefeld (9/88) 1.20 3.00
133-($1.50, 52 pgs.) 1.50
Remco Toy Giveaway (2-3/4x4") 1.00
Annual 1(1982)-Grell-c, a(p) .80 2.00

War Machine #6 © MEG

Warstrike #4 © Malibu

Watchmen #12 © DC

	GD25	FN65	NM94
Annual 2-6: 2('83). 3('84). 4('85). 5('86). 6('87)			1.00

NOTE: ***Grell** a-1-15, 16-50p, 51r, 52p, 59p, Annual 1p; c-1-70, 100-104, 112, 116, 117, Annual 1, 5. **Wayne Howard** a-64i. **Starlin** a-37-39p.*

WARLORD
Jan, 1992 - No. 6, June, 1992 ($1.75, mini-series)
DC Comics

	GD25	FN65	NM94
1-6: Grell=c & scripts in all		.70	1.75

WARLORDS (See DC Graphic Novel #2)

WAR MAN
Nov, 1993 - No. 2, Dec, 1993 ($2.50, limited series)
Epic Comics (Marvel)

	GD25	FN65	NM94
1,2		1.00	2.50

WAR MACHINE (Also see Iron Man #281,282 & Marvel Comics Presents #152)
Apr, 1994 - Present ($1.50)
Marvel Comics

	GD25	FN65	NM94
"Ashcan" edition (nd, 75¢, B&W, 16 pgs.)			.75
1-($2.00, 52 pgs.)-Newsstand edition; Cable app.		.80	2.00
1-($2.95, 52 pgs.)-Collectors ed.; embossed foil-c		1.20	3.00
2-14: 2-Bound-in trading card sheet; Cable app. 2,3-Deathlok app.			1.50
8-($2.95)-Polybagged w/16 pg. Marvel Action Hour preview & acetate print		1.20	3.00

WAR OF THE GODS (DC)(Value: cover or less)

WARP (First)(Value: cover or less)

WARPED (Empire/Solson)(Value: cover or less)

WARPATH (Indians on the...)
Nov, 1954 - No. 3, April, 1955
Key Publications/Stanmor

	GD25	FN65	NM94
1	8.35	25.00	50.00
2,3	5.00	15.00	30.00

WARP GRAPHICS ANNUAL (WaRP)(Value: cover or less)

WARREN PRESENTS
Jan, 1979 - No. 14, Nov, 1981
Warren Publications

	GD25	FN65	NM94
1-14-Eerie, Creepy, & Vampirella-r		.80	2.00
...The Rook 1 (5/79)-r/Eerie #82-85		.80	2.00

WAR REPORT
Sept, 1952 - No. 5, May, 1953
Ajax/Farrell Publications (Excellent Publ.)

	GD25	FN65	NM94
1	7.50	22.50	45.00
2	4.20	12.50	25.00
3-5: 4-Used in **POP**, pg. 94	4.00	10.00	20.00

WARRIOR COMICS
1945 (1930s DC reprints)
H.C. Blackerby

	GD25	FN65	NM94
1-Wing Brady, The Iron Man, Mark Markon	12.00	36.00	85.00

WARRIORS OF PLASM (Also see Plasm)
Aug, 1993 - Present ($2.95/$2.50, color)
Defiant Comics

	GD25	FN65	NM94
1-4-Lapham-c/a: 1-1st app. Glory. 4-Bound-in fold-out poster		1.20	3.00
5-7,10-13: 5-Begin $2.50-c		1.00	2.50
8,9 ($2.75, 44 pgs.)		1.10	2.75
...The Collected Edition (2/94, $9.95)-r/Plasm #0, WOP #1-4 & Splatterball	1.70	4.20	10.00

WAR ROMANCES (See True...)

WAR SHIPS
1942 (36 pgs.)(Similar to Large Feature Comics)
Dell Publishing Co.

	GD25	FN65	NM94
nn-Cover by McWilliams; contains photos & drawings of U.S. war ships	11.00	32.00	75.00

WAR STORIES (Formerly War Comics)
No. 5, 1942(nd); No. 6, Aug-Oct, 1942 - No. 8, Feb-Apr, 1943
Dell Publishing Co.

	GD25	FN65	NM94
5-Origin The Whistler	19.00	57.00	130.00
6-8: 6-8-Night Devils app. 8-Painted-c	14.00	43.00	100.00

WAR STORIES (Korea)
Sept, 1952 - No. 5, May, 1953
Ajax/Farrell Publications (Excellent Publ.)

	GD25	FN65	NM94
1	6.70	20.00	40.00
2	4.00	11.00	22.00
3-5	3.60	9.00	18.00

WAR STORIES (See Star Spangled...)

WARSTRIKE
May, 1994 - Present ($1.95)
Malibu Comics (Ultraverse)

	GD25	FN65	NM94
1-9: 1-Simonson-c		.80	2.00
1-Ultra 5000 Limited silver foil	2.50	6.30	15.00

WART AND THE WIZARD (See The Sword & the Stone under Movie Comics)
Feb, 1964 (Walt Disney)(Characters from Sword in the Stone movie)
Gold Key

	GD25	FN65	NM94
1 (10102-402)	3.00	7.50	15.00

WARTIME ROMANCES
July, 1951 - No. 18, Nov, 1953
St. John Publishing Co.

	GD25	FN65	NM94
1-All Baker-c/a	16.00	48.00	110.00
2-All Baker-c/a	10.00	30.00	65.00
3,4-All Baker-c/a	9.15	27.50	55.00
5-8-Baker-c/a(2-3) each	8.35	25.00	50.00
9-12,16,18-Baker-c/a each	6.00	18.00	36.00
13-15,17-Baker-c only	4.00	12.00	24.00

WAR VICTORY ADVENTURES (#1 titled War Victory Comics)
Summer, 1942 - No. 3, Winter, 1943-44 (5¢)
U.S. Treasury Dept./War Victory/Harvey Publ.

	GD25	FN65	NM94
1-(Promotion of Savings Bonds)-Featuring America's greatest comic art by top syndicated cartoonists; Blondie, Joe Palooka, Green Hornet, Dick Tracy, Superman, Gumps, etc.; (36 pgs.); all profits were contributed to U.S.O. & Army/Navy relief funds	28.00	84.00	195.00
2-Battle of Stalingrad story; Powell-a (8/43); flag-c	13.50	41.00	95.00
3-Capt. Red Cross-c & text only; Powell-a	12.00	36.00	85.00

WAR WAGON, THE (See Movie Classics)

WAR WINGS
October, 1968
Charlton Comics

	GD25	FN65	NM94
1		1.60	4.00

WARWORLD! (Dark Horse)(Value: cover or less)

WASHABLE JONES AND THE SHMOO (Also see Al Capp's Shmoo)
June, 1953
Toby Press

	GD25	FN65	NM94
1- "Super-Shmoo"	14.00	43.00	100.00

WASH TUBBS (See The Comics, Crackajack Funnies & 4-Color #11, 28, 53)

WASTELAND (DC)(Value: cover or less)

WATCHMEN
Sept, 1986 - No. 12, Oct, 1987 (12 issue maxi-series)
DC Comics

	GD25	FN65	NM94
1-Alan Moore scripts in all		1.50	3.75
2-12		1.10	2.75

WATCH OUT FOR BIG TALK

World Championship Wrestling #11 © WCW

The Web #14 © DC

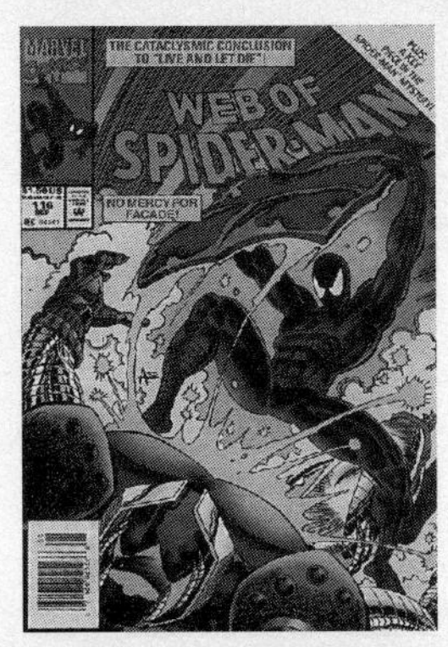

Web of Spider-Man #116 © MEG

GD25 FN65 NM94

950
iveaway
n-Dan Barry-a (about crooked politicians) 4.00 12.00 24.00

/ATER BIRDS AND THE OLYMPIC ELK (See 4-Color #700)

/CW WORLD CHAMPIONSHIP WRESTLING (Marvel)(Value: cover or less)

/EAPON X
.pr, 1994 ($12.95, one-shot)
Iarvel Comics
ın-r/Marvel Comics Presents #72-84 1.90 6.00 13.00

VEASEL PATROL SPECIAL, THE (Eclipse)(Value: cover or less)

/EATHER-BIRD (See Comics From..., Dick Tracy, Free Comics to You... & 'erry and the Pirates)
958 - No. 16, July, 1962 (Shoe store giveaway)
ıternational Shoe Co./Western Printing Co.
1 3.60 9.00 18.00
2-16 1.80 4.50 9.00
IOTE: *The numbers are located in the lower bottom panel, pg. 1. All feature a character called Veather-Bird.*

/EATHER BIRD COMICS (See Comics From Weather Bird)
957 (Giveaway)
Veather Bird Shoes
ın-Contains a comic bound with new cover. Several combinations possible; contents determines price (40 - 60 percent of contents).

/EAVEWORLD (Epic)(Value: cover or less)

/EB, THE (Also see Mighty Comics & Mighty Crusaders)
Sept, 1991 - No. 14, Oct, 1992 ($1.00, color)
mpact Comics (DC)
1-14: 5-The Fly x-over 9-Trading card inside 1.00
Annual 1 (1992, $2.50, 68 pgs.)-With Trading card 1.00 2.50
IOTE: ***Gil Kane** c-5, 9, 10, 12-14. **Bill Wray** a(i)-1-9, 10(part).*

/EB OF EVIL
Nov, 1952 - No. 21, Dec, 1954
Comic Magazines/Quality Comics Group
1-Used in **SOTI**, pg. 388. Jack Cole-a; morphine use story 34.00 100.00 235.00
2-4,6,7: 2,3-Jack Cole-a. 4,6,7-Jack Cole-c/a 21.00 63.00 145.00
5-Electrocution-c/story; Jack Cole-c/a 25.00 75.00 175.00
8-11-Jack Cole-a 17.00 52.00 120.00
12,13,15,16,19-21 10.00 30.00 60.00
14-Part Crandall-c; Old Witch swipe 10.00 30.00 65.00
17-Opium drug propaganda story 10.00 30.00 60.00
18-Acid-in-face story 11.00 32.00 75.00
IOTE: ***Jack Cole** a(2 each)-2, 6, 8, 9. **Cuidera** c-1-21i. **Ravielli** a-13.*

/EB OF HORROR (Magazine)
Dec, 1969 - No. 3, Apr, 1970
Major Magazines
1-Jeff Jones painted-c; Wrightson-a 5.35 16.00 32.00
2-Jones painted-c; Wrightson-a(2), Kaluta-a 4.00 11.00 22.00
3-Wrightson-c/a (1st published-c); Brunner, Kaluta, Bruce Jones-a 4.00 11.00 22.00

/EB OF MYSTERY
Feb, 1951 - No. 29, Sept, 1955
Ace Magazines (A. A. Wyn)
1 25.00 75.00 175.00
2-Bakerish-a 15.00 45.00 105.00
3-10: 4-Colan-a 13.00 40.00 90.00
11-18,20-26: 12-John Chilly's 1st cover art. 13-Surrealistic-c. 20-r/The Beyond #1 11.50 34.00 80.00
19-Reprints Challenge of the Unknown #6 used in N.Y. Legislative Committee 11.50 34.00 80.00
27-Bakerish-a(r/The Beyond #2); last pre-code ish 11.00 32.00 75.00
28,29: 28-All-r 9.15 27.50 55.00
NOTE: *This series was to appear as "Creepy Stories", but title was changed before publication. **Cameron** a-6, 8, 11-13, 17-20, 22, 24, 25, 27; c-8, 13, 17. **Palais** a-28r. **Sekowsky** a-1-3, 7, 8, 11, 14, 21, 29. **Tothish** a-by **Bill Discount** #16. 29-all-r, 19-28-partial-r.*

GD25 FN65 NM94

WEB OF SPIDER-MAN
Apr, 1985 - Present
Marvel Comics Group
1-Painted-c (5th app. black costume?) 4.30 13.00 30.00
2,3 1.40 3.50 8.50
4-8: 7-Hulk x-over; Wolverine splash 1.10 2.70 6.50
9-13: 10-Dominic Fortune guest stars; painted-c .90 2.30 5.50
14-28: 18-1st app. Venom (behind the scenes, 9/86). 19-Intro Humbug & Solo 1.00 2.00 5.00
29-Wolverine, new Hobgoblin (Macendale) app. 2.30 6.90 16.00
30-Origin recap The Rose & Hobgoblin I (entire book is flashback story); Punisher & Wolverine cameo 2.10 6.00 15.00
31,32-Six part Kraven storyline begins 1.70 4.20 10.00
33-37,39-47,49: 36-1st app. Tombstone (cameo) 1.10 2.75
38-Hobgoblin app.; begin $1.00-c 1.30 3.00 7.50
48-Origin Hobgoblin II(Demogoblin) cont'd from Spectacular Spider-Man #147; Kingpin app. 3.60 11.00 25.00
50-($1.50, 52 pgs.) 1.00 2.50
51-58 .80 2.00
59-Cosmic Spidey cont'd from Spect. Spider-Man 1.65 4.00 10.00
60-65,68-85,87-89,91-94: 69,70-Hulk x-over. 74-76-Austin-c(i). 76-Fantastic Four x-over. 78-Cloak & Dagger app. 81-Origin/1st app. Bloodshed. 84-Begin 6 part Rose & Hobgoblin II storyline; last $1.00-c. 93-Gives brief history of Hobgoblin. 93,94-Hobgoblin (Macendale) Reborn-c/story, parts 1,2; Moon Knight app. 94-Venom cameo .80 2.00
66,67-Green Goblin (Norman Osborn) app. as a super-hero 1.20 3.00
86-Demon leaves Hobgoblin; 1st Demogoblin 1.20 3.00
90-($2.95, 52 pgs.)-Polybagged w/silver hologram-c, gatefold poster showing Spider-Man & Spider-Man 2099 (Williamson-i) .80 2.10 5.00
90-2nd printing; gold hologram-c 1.20 3.00
95-Begin 4 part x-over w/Spirits of Venom w/Ghost Rider/Blaze/Spidey vs. Venom & Demogoblin (cont'd in Ghost Rider/Blaze #5,6) 1.30 3.25
96-99,101-106: 96-Spirits of Venom part 3; painted-c. 101,103-Maximum Carnage x-over. 103-Venom & Carnage app. 104-106-Nightwatch back-up stories .70 1.80
100-($2.95, 52 pgs.)-Holo-grafx foil-c; intro new Spider-Armor 1.30 3.25
107-111: 107-Intro Sandstorm; Sand & Quicksand app. 1.25
112-124: 112-Begin $1.50-c; bound-in trading card sheet. 113-Gambit & Black Cat app. 117-Flip book; Power & Responsibility Pt. 1. 118-1st solo clone story; Venom app 1.50
113-($2.95)-Collector's ed. polybagged w/foil-c; 16 pg. preview of Spider-Man cartoon & animation cel 1.20 3.00
117-($2.95)-Collector's edition; foil-c; flip book 1.20 3.00
Annual 1 (1985) 1.20 3.00
Annual 2 (1986)-New Mutants; Art Adams-a 1.30 3.00 8.00
Annual 3 (1987) 1.20 3.00
Annual 4 (1988, $1.75)-Evolutionary War x-over 1.40 3.50
Annual 5 (1989, $2.00, 68 pgs.)-Atlantis Attacks; Captain Universe by Ditko (p) & Silver Sable stories; F.F. app. 1.10 2.75
Annual 6 ('90, $2.00, 68 pgs.)-Punisher back-up plus Capt. Universe by Ditko; G. Kane-a 1.10 2.75
Annual 7 (1991, $2.00, 68 pgs.)-Origins of Hobgoblin I, Hobgoblin II, Green Goblin I & II & Venom; Larsen/Austin-c 1.10 2.75
Annual 8 (1992, $2.25, 68 pgs.)-Part 3 of Venom story; New Warriors x-over; Black Cat back-up story 1.10 2.75
Annual 9 (1993, $2.95, 68 pgs.)-Bagged w/card 1.30 3.25
Annual 10 (1994, $2.95, 68 pgs.) 1.20 3.00

WEDDING BELLS
Feb, 1954 - No. 19, Nov, 1956
Quality Comics Group

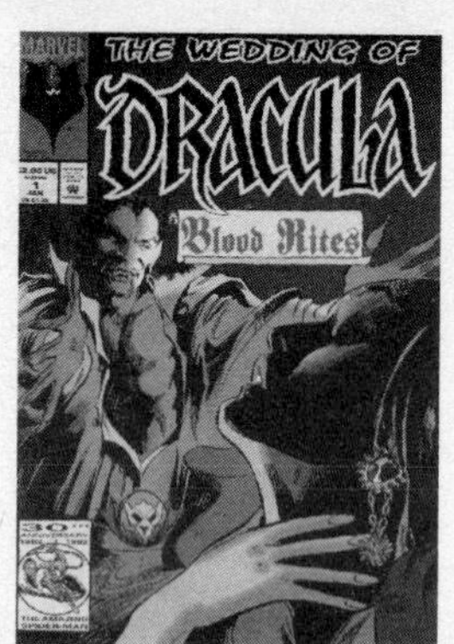

The Wedding of Dracula #1 © MEG

The Weird #3 © DC

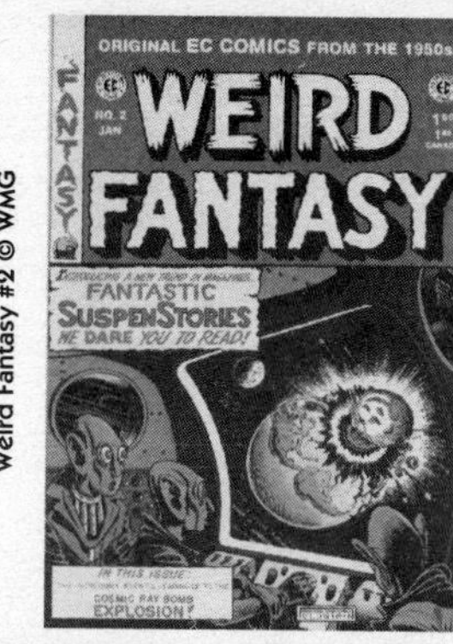

Weird Fantasy #2 © WMG

GD25 FN65 NM94

1-Whitney-a 10.00 30.00 65.00
2 5.85 17.50 35.00
3-9: 8-Last precode (4/55) 4.00 11.00 22.00
10-Ward-a (9 pgs.) 8.35 25.00 50.00
11-14,17 3.00 7.50 15.00
15-Baker-c 3.60 9.00 18.00
16-Baker-c/a 4.35 13.00 26.00
18,19-Baker-a each 4.00 11.00 22.00

WEDDING OF DRACULA
Jan, 1993 ($2.00, 52 pgs.)
Marvel Comics

1-Reprints Tomb of Dracula #30,45,46 .80 2.00

WEEKENDER, THE (Illustrated...)
V1#3, Sept, 1945 - V1#4, Nov, 1945; V2#1, Jan, 1946 (52 pgs.)
Rucker Publ. Co.

V1#3,4: 3-Super hero-c. 4-Same-c as Punch Comics #10 (9/44); r/Hale the Magician (7 pgs.) & r/Mr. E (8 pgs.-Lou Fine? or Gustavson?) plus 3 humor strips & many B&W photos & r/newspaper articles plus cheesecake photos of Hollywood stars 11.50 34.00 80.00
V2#1-36 pgs. comics, 16 in newspaper format with photos; partial Dynamic Comics reprints; 4 pgs. of cels from the Disney film Pinocchio; Little Nemo story by Winsor McCay, Jr.; Jack Cole-a; same-c as Dynamic #11 14.00 43.00 100.00

WEEKLY COMIC MAGAZINE
May 12, 1940 (16 pgs.) (Full Color) (Others exist without super-heroes)
Fox Publications

(1st Version)-8 pg. Blue Beetle story, 7 pg. Patty O'Day story; two copies known to exist. Estimated value... $500.00
(2nd Version)-7 two-pg. adventures of Blue Beetle, Patty O'Day, Yarko, Dr. Fung, Green Mask, Spark Stevens, & Rex Dexter; one copy known to exist. Estimated value... $400.00

Discovered with business papers, letters and exploitation material promoting **Weekly Comic Magazine** for use by newspapers in the same manner of **The Spirit** weeklies. Interesting note: these are dated three weeks before the first Spirit comic. Letters indicate that samples may have been sent to a few newspapers. These sections were actually 15-1/2x22" pages which will fold down to an approximate 8x10" comic booklet. Other various comic sections were found with the above, but were more like the Sunday comic sections in format.

WEIRD (Magazine)
V1#10, 1/66 - V8#6, 12/74; V9#1, 1/75 - V11#4, Dec, 1978
(V1-V8: 52 pgs.; V9 on: 68 pgs.)
Eerie Publications

V1#10(#1)-Intro. Morris the Caretaker of Weird (ends V2#10); Burgos-a 3.25 9.50 22.00
11,12 1.70 5.00 12.00
V2#1-4(10/67), V3#1(1/68), V2#6(4/68)-V2#7,9,10(12/68), V3#1(2/69)-V3#4 1.70 5.00 12.00
V2#8-r/Ditko's 1st story/Fantastic Fears #5 2.60 7.70 18.00
5(12/69)-Rulah reprint; "Rulah" changed to "Pulah", LSD story reprinted in Horror Tales V4#4, Tales From the Tomb V2#4, & Terror Tales V7#3 1.70 5.00 12.00
V4#1-6('70), V5#1-6('71), V6#1-7('72), V7#1-7('73), V8#1-6('74), V9#1-4 (1/75-'76)(no V9#1), V10#1-3('77), V11#1-4 1.70 5.00 12.00

NOTE: *V9#4 (12/76) has a cover swipe from Horror Tales V5#1 (2/73).*

WEIRD, THE (DC)(Value: cover or less)

WEIRD ADVENTURES
May-June, 1951 - No. 3, Sept-Oct, 1951
P. L. Publishing Co. (Canada)

1- "The She-Wolf Killer" by Matt Baker (6 pgs.) 26.00 78.00 180.00
2-Bondage/hypodermic panel 20.00 60.00 140.00
3-Male bondage/torture-c; severed head story 19.00 57.00 130.00

WEIRD ADVENTURES
No. 10, July-Aug, 1951
Ziff-Davis Publishing Co.

GD25 FN65 NM94

10-Painted-c 20.00 60.00 140.00

WEIRD CHILLS
July, 1954 - No. 3, Nov, 1954
Key Publications

1-Wolverton-r/Weird Mysteries No. 4; blood transfusion-c by Baily 37.00 111.00 260.00
2-Extremely violent injury to eye-c by Baily; Hitler story 36.00 107.00 250.00
3-Bondage E.C. swipe-c by Baily 21.00 63.00 145.00

WEIRD COMICS
April, 1940 - No. 20, Jan, 1942
Fox Features Syndicate

1-The Birdman, Thor, God of Thunder (ends #5), The Sorceress of Zoom, Blast Bennett, Typhon, Voodoo Man, & Dr. Mortal begin; Lou Fine bondage-c 229.00 685.00 1600.00
2-Lou Fine-c 93.00 280.00 650.00
3,4: 3-Simon-c. 4-Torture-c 68.00 205.00 475.00
5-Intro. Dart & sidekick Ace (8/40) (ends #20); bondage/hypo-c 70.00 210.00 490.00
6,7-Dynamite Thor app. in each. 6-Super hero covers begin 62.00 186.00 435.00
8-Dynamo, the Eagle (11/40, early app.; see Science #1) & sidekick Buddy & Marga, the Panther Woman begin 62.00 186.00 435.00
9,10: 10-Navy Jones app. 54.00 160.00 375.00
11-20: 16-Flag-c. 17-Origin The Black Rider. 20-Origin The Rapier; Swoop Curtis app; Churchill & Hitler-c 41.00 124.00 290.00

NOTE *Cover features: Sorceress of Zoom-4; Dr. Mortal-5; Dart & Ace-6-13, 15; Eagle-14, 16-20.*

WEIRD FANTASY (Formerly A Moon, A Girl, Romance; becomes Weird Science-Fantasy #23 on)
No. 13, May-June, 1950 - No. 22, Nov-Dec, 1953
E. C. Comics

13(#1) (1950) 110.00 332.00 775.00
14-Necronomicon story; cosmic ray bomb explosion-c 61.00 182.00 425.00
15,16: 16-Used in **SOTI**, pg. 144 50.00 150.00 350.00
17 (1951) 43.00 130.00 300.00
6-10: 6-Robot-c 31.00 92.00 215.00
11-13 (1952): 12-E.C. artists cameo. 13-Anti-Wertham "Cosmic Correspondence" 24.00 72.00 165.00
14-Frazetta/Williamson(1st team-up at E.C.)/Krenkel-a (7 pgs.); Orlando draws E.C. staff; "Cosmic Ray Bomb Explosion" by Feldstein stars Gaines & Feldstein 39.00 116.00 270.00
15-Williamson/Evans-a(3), 4,3,&7 pgs. 26.00 78.00 180.00
16-19-Williamson/Krenkel-a in all. 18-Williamson/Feldstein-c 24.00 73.00 170.00
20-Frazetta/Williamson-a (7 pgs.) 26.00 78.00 180.00
21-Frazetta/Williamson-c & Williamson/Krenkel-a 39.00 116.00 270.00
22-Bradbury adaptation 18.00 54.00 125.00

NOTE: ***Ray Bradbury*** *adaptations-13, 17-20, 22.* ***Crandall*** *a-22.* ***Elder*** *a-17.* ***Feldstein*** *a-13(#1)-8; c-13(#1)-18 (#18 w/****Williamson****), 20.* ***Harrison/Wood*** *a-13.* ***Kamen*** *a-13(#1)-16, 18-22.* ***Krigstein*** *a-22.* ***Kurtzman*** *a-13(#1)-17(#5), 6.* ***Orlando*** *a-9-22 (2 stories in #16); c-19, 22.* ***Severin/Elder*** *a-18-21.* ***Wood*** *a-13(#1)-14, 17(2 stories ea. in #10-13). Ray Bradbury adaptations in #17-19, 22. Canadian reprints exist; see Table of Contents.*

WEIRD FANTASY
Oct, 1992 - Present ($1.50, color)
Russ Cochran

1,2-r/Weird Fantasy #13,14(#1,2); Feldstein-c 1.50
3-5-r/Weird Fantasy #15-17(#3-5) .80 2.00

WEIRD HORRORS (Nightmare #10 on)
June, 1952 - No. 9, Oct, 1953
St. John Publishing Co.

1-Tuska-a 25.00 75.00 175.00
2,3: 3-Hashish story 13.00 40.00 90.00
4,5 12.00 36.00 85.00

Weird Mystery Tales #2 © DC

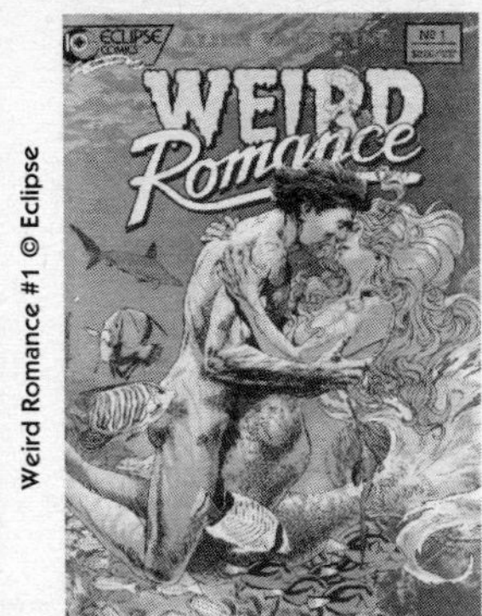

Weird Romance #1 © Eclipse

Weird Suspense #3 © Seaboard

GD25 FN65 NM94 GD25 FN65 NM94

6-Ekgren-c; atomic bomb story 22.00 67.00 155.00
7-Ekgren-c; Kubert, Cameron-a 25.00 75.00 175.00
8,9-Kubert-c/a 17.00 52.00 120.00
NOTE: ***Cameron** a-7, 9. **Finesque** a-1-5. **Forgione** a-6. **Morisi** a-3. Bondage c-8.*

WEIRD MYSTERIES
Oct, 1952 - No. 12, Sept, 1954
Gillmore Publications

1-Partial Wolverton-c swiped from splash page "Flight to the Future" in Weird Tales of the Future #2; "Eternity" has an Ingels swipe 38.00 115.00 265.00
2- "Robot Woman" by Wolverton; Bernard Baily-c reprinted in Mister Mystery #18; acid in face panel 55.00 165.00 385.00
3,6: Both have decapitation-c 25.00 75.00 175.00
4- "The Man Who Never Smiled" (3 pgs.) by Wolverton; B. Baily skull-c 48.00 145.00 335.00
5-Wolverton story "Swamp Monster" (6 pgs.) 48.00 145.00 335.00
7-Used in **SOTI**, illo "Indeed", illo "Sex and blood" 41.00 122.00 285.00
8-Wolverton-c panel-r/#5; used in a '54 Readers Digest anti-comics article by T. E. Murphy entitled "For the Kiddies to Read" 24.00 73.00 170.00
9-Excessive violence, gore & torture 23.00 70.00 160.00
10-Silhouetted nudity panel 21.00 63.00 145.00
11,12: 12-r/Mr. Mystery #8(2), Weird Mysteries #3 & Weird Tales of the Future #6 17.00 52.00 120.00
NOTE: ***Baily** c-2-12. Anti-Wertham column in #5. #1-12 all have 'The Ghoul Teacher' (host).*

WEIRD MYSTERIES (Magazine)
Mar-Apr, 1959 (68 pgs.) (35¢) (B&W)
Pastime Publications

1-Torres-a; E. C. swipe from Tales From the Crypt #46 by Tuska "The Ragman" 4.70 14.00 28.00

WEIRD MYSTERY TALES (See DC 100 Page Super Spectacular)

WEIRD MYSTERY TALES (See Cancelled Comic Cavalcade)
July-Aug, 1972 - No. 24, Nov, 1975
National Periodical Publications

1-Kirby-a; Wrightson splash pg. 1.00 3.00 6.00
2-24: 21-Wrightson-c 1.10 2.75
NOTE: ***Alcala** a-5, 10, 13, 14. **Aparo** c-4. **Bailey** a-8. **Bolle** a-8?. **Howard** a-4. **Kaluta** a-4, 24; c-1. **G. Kane** a-10. **Kirby** a-1, 2p, 3p. **Nino** a-5, 6, 9, 13, 16, 21. **Redondo** a-9, 17. **Sparling** c-6. **Starlin** a-3?, 4. **Wood** a-23.*

WEIRD ROMANCE (Eclipse)(Value: cover or less)

WEIRD SCIENCE (Formerly Saddle Romances) (Becomes Weird Science-Fantasy #23 on)
No. 12, May-June, 1950 - No. 22, Nov-Dec, 1953
E. C. Comics

12(#1) (1950) 114.00 343.00 800.00
13 64.00 193.00 450.00
14,15 (1950): 14-Robot-c 56.00 167.00 390.00
5-10: 5-Atomic explosion-c 36.00 107.00 250.00
11-14 (1952): 12- "Dream of Doom" stars Gaines & E.C. artists 24.00 73.00 170.00
15-18-Williamson/Krenkel-a in each; 15-Williamson-a. 17-Used in **POP**, pgs. 81,82. 18-Bill Gaines doll app. in story 27.00 81.00 190.00
19,20-Williamson/Frazetta-a (7 pgs. each). 19-Used in **SOTI**, illo "A young girl on her wedding night stabs her sleeping husband to death with a hatpin..." 36.00 109.00 255.00
21-Williamson/Frazetta-a (6 pgs.); Wood draws E.C. staff; Gaines & Feldstein app. in story 36.00 109.00 255.00
22-Williamson/Frazetta/Krenkel/Krigstein-a (8 pgs.); Wood draws himself in his story (last pg. & panel) 36.00 109.00 255.00
NOTE: ***Elder** a-14, 19. **Evans** a-22. **Feldstein** a-12(#1)-8; c-12(#1)-8, 11. **Ingels** a-15. **Kamen** a-12(#1)-13, 15-18, 20, 21. **Kurtzman** a-12(#1)-7. **Orlando** a-10-22. **Wood** a-12(#1), 13(#2), 5-22 (#9, 10, 12, 13 all have 2 **Wood** stories); c-9, 10, 12-22. Canadian reprints exist; see Table of Contents. Ray Bradbury adaptations in #17-20.*

WEIRD SCIENCE
Sept, 1990 - No. 4, Mar, 1991 ($1.95, 68 pgs.)(#3 on: $2.00)
Gladstone Publishing

1-Wood-c(r); all reprints in each .80 2.00
2-4: 2-4-Wood-c(r) .80 2.00

WEIRD SCIENCE
Sept, 1992 - Present ($1.50/$2.00, color)
Russ Cochran

1,2-r/Weird Science #12,13(#1,2) w/original-c 1.50
3-7 ($2.00): r/#14,15(#3,4),5-7 w/original-c .80 2.00

WEIRD SCIENCE-FANTASY (Formerly Weird Science & Weird Fantasy) (Becomes Incredible Science Fiction #30)
No. 23 Mar, 1954 - No. 29, May-June, 1955 (#23,24: 15¢)
E. C. Comics

23-Williamson, Wood-a; Bradbury adaptation 27.00 80.00 185.00
24-Williamson & Wood-a; Harlan Ellison's 1st professional story, "Upheaval!", later adapted into a short story as "Mealtime", and then into a TV episode of Voyage to the Bottom of the Sea as "The Price of Doom" 27.00 80.00 185.00
25-Williamson-c; Williamson/Torres/Krenkel-a plus Wood-a; Bradbury adaptation; cover price back to 10¢ 30.00 90.00 210.00
26-Flying Saucer Report; Wood, Crandall-a 25.00 75.00 175.00
27-Adam Link/I Robot series begins? 27.00 80.00 185.00
28-Williamson/Krenkel/Torres-a; Wood-a 29.00 86.00 200.00
29-Frazetta-c; Williamson/Krenkel & Wood-a; last pre-code issue; new logo 48.00 145.00 335.00
NOTE: ***Crandall** a-26, 27, 29. **Evans** a-26. **Feldstein** c-24, 26, 28. **Kamen** a-27, 28. **Krigstein** a-23-25. **Orlando** a-in all. **Wood** a-in all; c-23, 27. The cover to #29 was originally intended for Famous Funnies #217 (Buck Rogers), but was rejected.*

WEIRD SCIENCE-FANTASY
Nov, 1992 - Present ($1.50/$2.00, color)
Russ Cochran

1,2-r/Weird Science-Fantasy #23,24 1.50
3-5: r/#25-27 .80 2.00

WEIRD SCIENCE-FANTASY ANNUAL
1952, 1953 (Sold thru the E. C. office & on the stands in some major cities) (25¢, 132 pgs.)
E. C. Comics

1952-Feldstein-c 157.00 471.00 1100.00
1953-Feldstein-c 91.00 272.00 635.00
NOTE: *The 1952 annual contains books cover-dated in 1951 & 1952, and the 1953 annual from 1952 & 1953. Contents of each annual may vary in same year.*

WEIRD SUSPENSE
Feb, 1975 - No. 3, July, 1975
Atlas/Seaboard Publ.

1-3: 1-Tarantula begins. 3-Buckler-c 1.00

WEIRD SUSPENSE STORIES (Canadian reprint of Crime SuspenStories #1-3; see Table of Contents)

WEIRD TALES ILLUSTRATED
1992 - No. 2, 1992 ($2.95, color, high quality paper)
Millennium Publications

1,2-Bolton painted-c. 1-Adapts E.A. Poe & Harlan Ellison stories. 2-E.A. Poe & H.P. Lovecraft adaptations 1.20 3.00
1-($4.95, 52 pgs.)-Deluxe edition w/Tim Vigil-a not in regular #1; stiff-c; Bolton painted-c 1.00 2.00 5.00

WEIRD TALES OF THE FUTURE
March, 1952 - No. 8, July-Aug, 1953
S.P.M. Publ. No. 1-4/Aragon Publ. No. 5-8

1-Andru-a(2); Wolverton partial-c 44.00 133.00 310.00
2,3-Wolverton-c/a(3) each. 2- "Jumpin Jupiter" satire by Wolverton begins, ends #5 71.00 215.00 500.00
4- "Jumpin Jupiter" satire & "The Man From the Moon" by Wolverton; partial Wolverton-c 41.00 124.00 290.00
5-Wolverton-c/a(2); "Jumpin Jupiter" satire 71.00 215.00 500.00

Weird War Tales #104 © DC

Weird Western Tales #53 © DC

Weird Wonder Tales #14 © MEG

GD25 FN65 NM94

6-Bernard Baily-c 27.00 81.00 190.00
7- "The Mind Movers" from the art to Wolverton's "Brain Bats of Venus" from Mr. Mystery #7 which was cut apart, pasted up, partially redrawn, and rewritten by Harry Kantor, the editor; Baily-c 41.00 122.00 285.00
8-Reprints Weird Mysteries #1(10/52) minus cover; gory cover showing heart ripped out by B. Baily 26.00 78.00 180.00

WEIRD TALES OF THE MACABRE (Magazine)
Jan, 1975 - No. 2, Mar, 1975 (B&W) (75¢)
Atlas/Seaboard Publ.

1-Jeff Jones painted-c .80 2.00
2-Boris Vallejo painted-c; Severin-a .65 1.60

WEIRD TERROR (Also see Horrific)
Sept, 1952 - No. 13, Sept, 1954
Allen Hardy Associates (Comic Media)

1- "Portrait of Death", adapted from Lovecraft's "Pickman's Model"; lingerie panels, Hitler story 23.00 70.00 160.00
2-Text on Marquis DeSade, Torture, Demonology, & St. Elmo's Fire 16.00 48.00 110.00
3-Extreme violence, whipping, torture; article on sin eating, dowsing 16.00 48.00 110.00
4-Dismemberment, decapitation, article on human flesh for sale, Devil, whipping 19.00 58.00 135.00
5-Article on body snatching, mutilation; cannibalism story 14.00 43.00 100.00
6-Dismemberment, decapitation, man hit by lightning 19.00 57.00 130.00
7,9,10 13.00 40.00 90.00
8-Decapitation story; Ambrose Bierce adapt. 17.00 52.00 120.00
11-End of the world story with atomic blast panels; Tothish-a by Bill Discount 17.00 52.00 120.00
12-Discount-a 11.50 34.00 80.00
13-Severed head panels 13.00 40.00 90.00

NOTE: ***Don Heck*** *a-most issues; c-1-13.* ***Landau*** *a-6.* ***Morisi*** *a-2-5, 7, 9, 12.* ***Palais*** *a-1, 5, 6, 8(2), 10, 12.* ***Powell*** *a-10.* ***Ravielli*** *a-11, 20.*

WEIRD THRILLERS
Sept-Oct, 1951 - No. 5, Oct-Nov, 1952 (#2-5: painted-c)
Ziff-Davis Publ. Co. (Approved Comics)

1-Rondo Hatton photo-c 34.00 100.00 235.00
2-Toth, Anderson, Colan-a 25.00 75.00 175.00
3-Two Powell, Tuska-a; classic-c 24.00 72.00 165.00
4-Kubert, Tuska-a 21.00 63.00 145.00
5-Powell-a 19.00 57.00 130.00

NOTE: ***M. Anderson*** *a-2, 3.* ***Roussos*** *a-4. #2, 3 reprinted in Nightmare #10 & 13; #4, 5 reprinted in Amazing Ghost Stories #16 & #15.*

WEIRD WAR TALES
Sept-Oct, 1971 - No. 124, June, 1983 (#1-5: 52 pgs.)
National Periodical Publications/DC Comics

1-Kubert-a in #1-4,7; c-1-7 .90 2.00 5.50
2,3-Drucker-a: 2-Crandall-a. 3-Heath-a 1.80 4.50
4-7,9,10: 5,6,10-Toth-a. 5,7-Heath-a 1.40 3.50
8-Neal Adams-c/a(i) .90 2.00 5.50
11-50: 36-(68 pgs.)-Crandall & Kubert-r/#2; Heath-r/#3. 36,38-Kubert-c .90 2.25
51-124: 93-Intro/origin Creature Commandos. 101-Intro/origin G.I. Robot .70 1.75
64,68-Frank Miller-a 1.00 2.50

WEIRD WESTERN TALES (Formerly All-Star Western)
No. 12, June-July, 1972 - No. 70, Aug, 1980
National Periodical Publications/DC Comics

12-(52 pgs.)-3rd app. Jonah Hex; Bat Lash, Pow Wow Smith reprints; El Diablo by Neal Adams/Wrightson 2.10 6.00 15.00
13-Jonah Hex-c (1st?) & 4th app.; Neal Adams-a 1.70 4.00 10.00
14,29: 14-Toth-a. 29-Origin Jonah Hex 1.20 3.00 7.00
15-Neal Adams-c/a; no Jonah Hex 1.20 3.00 7.00
16,17,19-28,30-38: Jonah Hex in all. 38-Last Jonah Hex 1.10 2.75
18-1st all Jonah Hex issue (7-8/73) & begins .90 2.00 5.50
39-70: 39-Origin/1st app. Scalphunter & begins. 64-Bat Lash-c/story .80 2.00

NOTE: ***Evans*** *inks-39-48; c-39i, 40, 47.* ***G. Kane*** *a-15.* ***Kubert*** *c-12, 33.* ***Starlin*** *c-44, 45.* ***Wildey*** *a-26. 48 & 49 are 44 pgs..*

WEIRD WONDER TALES
Dec, 1973 - No. 22, May, 1977
Marvel Comics Group

1-Wolverton-r/Mystic #6 (Eye of Doom) 1.00 2.50
2-22: 16-18-Venus-r by Everett from Venus #19,18 & 17. 19-22-Dr. Druid (Droom)-r .80 2.00

NOTE: *All 1950s & early 1960s reprints.* ***Check*** *r-1.* ***Colan*** *r-17.* ***Ditko*** *r-4, 5, 10-13, 19-21.* ***Drucker*** *r-12, 20.* ***Everett*** *r-3(Spellbound #16), 6(Astonishing #10), 9(Adv. Into Mystery #5).* ***Kirby*** *r-6, 11, 13, 16-22; c-17, 19, 20.* ***Krigstein*** *r-19.* ***Kubert*** *r-22.* ***Maneely*** *r-8.* ***Mooney*** *r-7p.* ***Powell*** *r-3, 7.* ***Torres*** *r-7.* ***Wildey*** *r-2, 7.*

WEIRD WORLDS (See Adventures Into...)

WEIRD WORLDS (Magazine)
V1#10(12/70), V2#1(2/71) - No. 4, Aug, 1971 (52 pgs.)
Eerie Publications

V1#10 1.70 5.00 12.00
V2#1-4 1.70 4.20 10.00

WEIRD WORLDS
Aug-Sept, 1972 - No. 9, Jan-Feb, 1974; No. 10, Oct-Nov, 1974 (All 20¢ issues)
National Periodical Publications

1-Edgar Rice Burrough's John Carter Warlord of Mars & David Innes begin (1st DC app.); Kubert-c 1.80 4.50
2-7: 7-Last John Carter 1.00 2.50
8-10: 8-Iron Wolf begins by Chaykin (1st app.) .70 1.75

NOTE: ***Neal Adams*** *a-2i, 3i. John Carter by* ***Andersonin*** *#1-3.* ***Chaykin*** *c-7, 8.* ***Kaluta*** *a-4; c-4-6, 10.* ***Orlando*** *a-4i; c-2, 3.* ***Wrightson*** *a-2i.*

WELCOME BACK, KOTTER (TV) (See Limited Collectors' Edition #57)
Nov, 1976 - No. 10, Mar-Apr, 1978
National Periodical Publications/DC Comics

1-Sparling-a(p) .80 2.00
2-10: 3-Estrada-a 1.00

WELCOME SANTA (See March of Comics #63,183)

WELLS FARGO (See Tales of...)

WENDY AND THE NEW KIDS ON THE BLOCK (Harvey)(Value: cover or less)

WENDY DIGEST (Harvey)(Value: cover or less)

WENDY PARKER COMICS
July, 1953 - No. 8, July, 1954
Atlas Comics (OMC)

1 8.35 25.00 50.00
2 4.70 14.00 28.00
3-8 4.00 11.00 22.00

WENDY, THE GOOD LITTLE WITCH (TV)
8/60 - #82, 11/73; #83, 8/74 - #93, 4/76; #94, 9/90 - #97, 12/90
Harvey Publications

1-Wendy & Casper the Friendly Ghost begins 14.00 43.00 100.00
2 7.50 22.50 45.00
3-5 5.85 17.50 35.00
6-10 4.20 12.50 25.00
11-20 3.00 7.50 15.00
21-30 2.00 5.00 10.00
31-50 1.00 2.50 6.00
51-69 1.00 2.00 5.00
70-74: All 52 pg. Giants 1.00 2.50 6.00
75-93 .80 2.00
94-97 (1990, $1.00-c): 94-Has #194 on-c 1.00
(See Casper the Friendly Ghost #20 & Harvey Hits #7, 16, 21, 23, 27, 30, 33)

Wendy: The Good Little Witch #1(2nd series) © HARV

West Coast Avengers Ann. #4 © MEG

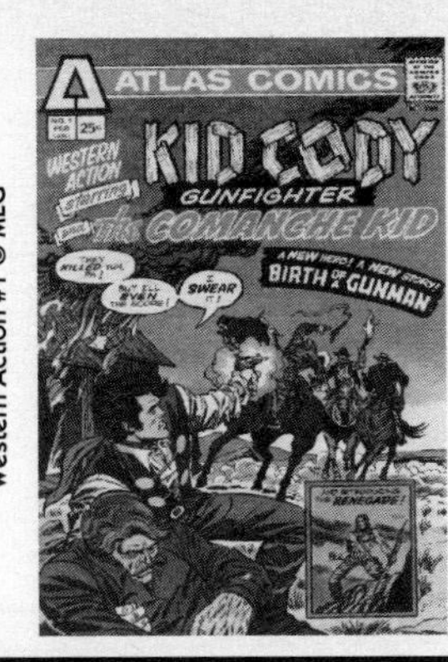

Western Action #1 © MEG

GD25 FN65 NM94

WENDY THE GOOD LITTLE WITCH (2nd series)
Apr, 1991 - No. 15, Aug, 1994 ($1.00/$1.25 #7-11/$1.50 #12-15)
Harvey Comics

1-15-Reprints Wendy & Casper stories. 12-Bunny app. 1.00

WENDY WITCH WORLD
10/61; No. 2, 9/62 - No. 52, 12/73; No. 53, 9/74
Harvey Publications

1-(25¢, 68 pg. Giants begin) 10.00 30.00 60.00
2-5 4.70 14.00 28.00
6-10 3.60 9.00 18.00
11-20 2.00 5.00 10.00
21-30 1.00 2.50 6.00
31-39: 39-Last 68 pg. issue 1.00 2.00 5.00
40-45: 52 pg. issues 1.40 3.50
46-53 .90 2.25

WEREWOLF (Super Hero) (Also see Dracula & Frankenstein)
Dec, 1966 - No. 3, April, 1967
Dell Publishing Co.

1-1st app. .90 2.00 5.50
2,3 1.30 3.25

WEREWOLF BY NIGHT (See Giant-Size..., Marvel Spotlight #2-4 & Power Record Comics)
Sept, 1972 - No. 43, Mar, 1977
Marvel Comics Group

1-Ploog-a cont'd. from Marvel Spotlight #4 5.60 17.00 39.00
2 2.70 8.10 19.00
3-5 1.90 6.00 13.00
6-10 1.70 4.20 10.00
11-20: 15-New origin Werewolf; Dracula-c/story cont'd from Tomb of Dracula #18 1.40 3.50 8.50
21-31 1.00 2.50 6.00
32-Origin & 1st app. Moon Knight (8/75) 8.00 24.00 55.00
33-2nd app. Moon Knight 4.60 14.00 32.00
34-36,38-43: 35-Starlin/Wrightson-c 1.60 4.00
37-Moon Knight app; part Wrightson-c 1.30 3.00 8.00

NOTE: ***Bolle** a-6i. **G. Kane** a-11p, 12p; c-21, 22, 24-30, 34p. **Mooney** a-7i. **Ploog** 1-4p, 5, 6p, 7p, 13-16p; c-5-8, 13-16. **Reinman** a-8i. **Sutton** a(i)-9, 11, 16, 35.*

WEREWOLVES & VAMPIRES (Magazine)
1962 (One Shot)
Charlton Comics

1 6.35 19.00 38.00

WEST COAST AVENGERS
Sept, 1984 - No. 4, Dec, 1984 (Mini-series; Mando paper)
Marvel Comics Group

1-Origin & 1st app. W.C. Avengers; Hawkeye, Iron Man, Mockingbird & Tigra 1.10 2.75
2-4 1.50

WEST COAST AVENGERS (Becomes Avengers West Coast #48 on)
Oct, 1985 - No. 47, Aug, 1989 (On-going series)
Marvel Comics Group

V2#1 1.20 3.00
2-10 .80 2.00
11-20 1.50
21-41 1.00
42-Byrne-a(p)/scripts begin .90 2.20
43-47: 46,46-Byrne-c. 46-1st app. Great Lakes Avengers 1.10
Annual 1 (1986) .90 2.20
Annual 2 (1987) .80 2.00
Annual 3 (1988, $1.75)-Evolutionary War app. 1.10 2.75
Annual V2#4 (1989, $2.00, 68 pgs.)-Atlantis Attacks; Byrne/Austin-a .90 2.20
Annual V2#5,6 (1990, 1991, $2.00, 68 pgs.) .80 2.00
Annual V2#7 (1992, $2.25, 68 pgs.)-Darkhawk app. .90 2.25

WESTERN ACTION
No. 7, 1964
I. W. Enterprises

7-Reprints Cow Puncher #? by Avon .80 2.00 4.00

WESTERN ACTION
February, 1975
Atlas/Seaboard Publ.

1-Kid Cody by Wildey & The Comanche Kid stories; intro. The Renegade 1.00

WESTERN ACTION THRILLERS
April, 1937 (10¢, 100 pgs.)(Square binding)
Dell Publishers

1-Buffalo Bill, The Texas Kid, Laramie Joe, Two-Gun Thompson, & Wild West Bill app. 64.00 193.00 450.00

WESTERN ADVENTURES COMICS (Western Love Trails #7 on)
Oct, 1948 - No. 6, Aug, 1949
Ace Magazines

nn(#1)-Sheriff Sal, The Cross-Draw Kid, Sam Bass begin 15.00 45.00 105.00
nn(#2)(12/48) 9.15 27.50 55.00
nn(#3)(2/49)-Used in **SOTI**, pgs. 30,31 10.00 30.00 60.00
4-6 7.00 21.00 42.00

WESTERN BANDITS
1952 (Painted-c)
Avon Periodicals

1-Butch Cassidy, The Daltons by Larsen; Kinstler-a; c-part-r/paperback Avon Western Novel #1 11.00 32.00 75.00

WESTERN BANDIT TRAILS (See Approved Comics)
Jan, 1949 - No. 3, July, 1949
St. John Publishing Co.

1-Tuska-a; Baker-c; Blue Monk, Ventrilo app. 14.00 43.00 100.00
2-Baker-c 10.00 30.00 70.00
3-Baker-c/a; Tuska-a 12.00 36.00 85.00

WESTERN COMICS (See Super DC Giant #15)
Jan-Feb, 1948 - No. 85, Jan-Feb, 1961 (1-27: 52pgs.)
National Periodical Publications

1-Wyoming Kid & his horse Racer, The Vigilante in "Jesse James Rides Again" (Meskin-a), Cowboy Marshal, Rodeo Rick begin 63.00 190.00 440.00
2 30.00 90.00 210.00
3,4-Last Vigilante 25.00 75.00 175.00
5-Nighthawk & his horse Nightwind begin (not in #6); Captain Tootsie by Beck 22.00 65.00 150.00
6,7,9,10 17.00 52.00 120.00
8-Origin Wyoming Kid; 2 pg. pin-ups of rodeo queens 24.00 72.00 165.00
11-20 14.00 43.00 100.00
21-40: 24-Starr-a. 27-Last 52 pgs. 28-Flag-c 10.00 30.00 70.00
41-49: Last precode issue (2/55). 43-Pow Wow Smith begins, ends #85 10.00 30.00 65.00
50-60 10.00 30.00 60.00
61-85-Last Wyoming Kid. 77-Origin Matt Savage Trail Boss. 82-1st app. Fleetfoot, Pow Wow's girlfriend 7.50 22.50 45.00

NOTE: ***G. Kane, Infantino** art in most. **Meskin** a-1-4. **Moreira** a-28-39. **Post** a-3-5.*

WESTERN CRIME BUSTERS
Sept, 1950 - No. 10, Mar-Apr, 1952
Trojan Magazines

1-Six-Gun Smith, Wilma West, K-Bar-Kate, & Fighting Bob Dale begin; headlight-a 23.00 70.00 160.00
2 11.50 34.00 80.00
3-5: 3-Myron Fass-c 10.00 30.00 70.00

Westerner #16 © Toytown

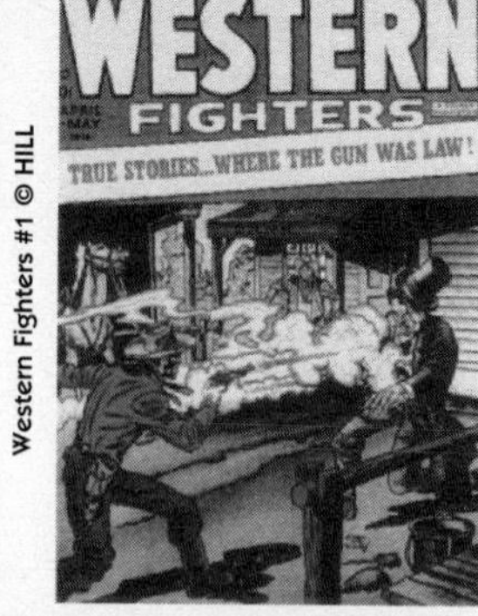

Western Fighters #1 © HILL

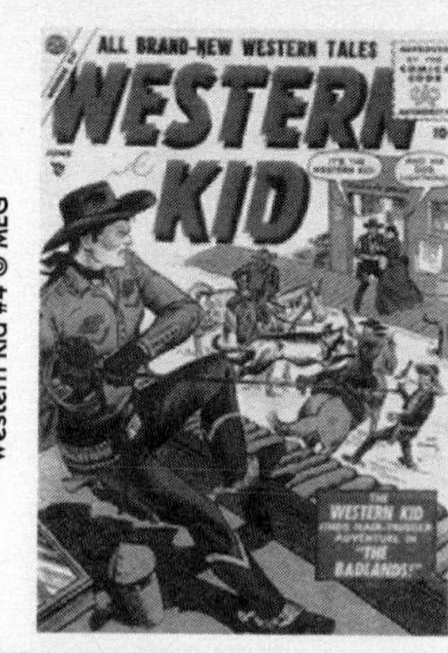

Western Kid #4 © MEG

GD25 FN65 NM94

6-Wood-a 23.00 70.00 160.00
7-Six-Gun Smith by Wood 23.00 70.00 160.00
8 10.00 30.00 70.00
9-Tex Gordon & Wilma West by Wood; Lariat Lucy app. 23.00 70.00 160.00
10-Wood-a 22.00 65.00 150.00

WESTERN CRIME CASES (Formerly Indian Warriors #7,8; becomes The Outlaws #10 on)
No. 9, Dec, 1951
Star Publications

9-White Rider & Super Horse; L. B. Cole-c 8.35 25.00 50.00

WESTERN DESPERADO COMICS (Formerly Slam Bang Comics)
No. 8, 1940 (Oct.?)
Fawcett Publications

8-(Rare) 54.00 160.00 375.00

WESTERNER, THE (Wild Bill Pecos)
No. 14, June, 1948 - No. 41, Dec, 1951 (#14-31: 52 pgs.)
"Wanted" Comic Group/Toytown/Patches

14 10.00 30.00 60.00
15-17,19-21: 19-Meskin-a 4.70 14.00 28.00
18,22-25-Krigstein-a 8.35 25.00 50.00
26(4/50)-Origin & 1st app. Calamity Kate, series ends #32; Krigstein-a 10.00 30.00 60.00
27-Krigstein-a(2) 10.00 30.00 65.00
28-41: 33-Quest app. 37-Lobo, the Wolf Boy begins 4.00 11.00 22.00
NOTE: ***Mort Lawrence** a-20-27, 29, 37, 39; c-19, 22-24, 26, 27. **Leav** c-14-18, 20, 31. **Syd Shores** a-39; c-34, 35, 37-41.*

WESTERNER, THE
1964
Super Comics

Super Reprint 15-17: 15-r/Oklahoma Kid #? 16-r/Crack West. #65; Severin-c; Crandall-r. 17-r/Blazing Western #2; Severin-c .80 2.00 4.00

WESTERN FIGHTERS
Apr-May, 1948 - V4#7, Mar-Apr, 1953 (#1-V3#2: 52 pgs.)
Hillman Periodicals/Star Publ.

V1#1-Simon & Kirby-c 24.00 72.00 165.00
2-Kirby-a(p)? 9.15 27.50 55.00
3-Fuje-c 7.50 22.50 45.00
4-Krigstein, Ingels, Fuje-a 9.15 27.50 55.00
5,6,8,9,12 5.35 16.00 32.00
7,10-Krigstein-a 9.15 27.50 55.00
11-Williamson/Frazetta-a 20.00 60.00 140.00
V2#1-Krigstein-a 9.15 27.50 55.00
2-12: 4-Berg-a 4.00 11.00 22.00
V3#1-11 4.00 10.00 20.00
12-Krigstein-a 8.35 25.00 50.00
V4#1,4-7 4.00 10.00 20.00
2,3-Krigstein-a 8.35 25.00 50.00
3-D 1(12/53, 25¢, Star Publ.)-Came w/glasses; L. B. Cole-c 27.00 81.00 190.00
NOTE: ***Kinstlerish** a-V2#6, 8, 9, 12; V3#2, 5-7, 11, 12; V4#1(plus cover). **McWilliams** a-11. **Powell** a-V2#2. **Reinman** a-1-12, V4#3. **Rowich** c-5, 6i. **Starr** a-5.*

WESTERN FRONTIER
Apr-May, 1951 - No. 7, 1952
P. L. Publishers

1 9.15 27.50 55.00
2 5.35 16.00 32.00
3-7 4.00 11.00 22.00

WESTERN GUNFIGHTERS (1st Series) (Apache Kid #11-19)
No. 20, June, 1956 - No. 27, Aug, 1957
Atlas Comics (CPS)

20 9.15 27.50 55.00
21-Crandall-a 9.15 27.50 55.00
22-Wood & Powell-a 13.00 40.00 90.00
23,24: 23-Williamson-a. 24-Toth-a 9.15 27.50 55.00
25-27 6.70 20.00 40.00
NOTE: ***Berg** a-20. **Colan** a-20, 27. **Crandall** a-21. **Heath** a-25. **Maneely** a-24, 25; c-22, 23, 25. **Morisi** a-24. **Pakula** a-23. **Severin** c-20, 27. **Woodbridge** a-27.*

WESTERN GUNFIGHTERS (2nd Series)
Aug, 1970 - No. 33, Nov, 1975 (#1-6: 25¢, 68 pgs.; #7: 52 pgs.)
Marvel Comics Group

1-Ghost Rider begins; Fort Rango, Renegades & Gunhawk app. 1.00 2.00 5.00
2-33: 2-Origin Nightwind (Apache Kid's horse). 7-Origin Ghost Rider retold. 10-Origin Black Rider. 12-Origin Matt Slade 1.20 3.00
NOTE: ***Baker** r-2, 3. **Colan** r-2. **Drucker** r-3. **Everett** a-6i. **G. Kane** c-29, 31. **Kirby** a-1p(r), 10, 11. **Kubert** r-2. **Maneely** r-2, 10. **Morrow** r-29. **Severin** c-10. **Barry Smith** a-4. **Steranko** c-14. **Sutton** a-1, 2i, 3, 4. **Torres** r-26('57). **Wildey** r-8, 9. **Williamson** r-2, 18. **Woodbridge** r-27('57). Renegades in #4, 5; Ghost Rider in #1-7.*

WESTERN HEARTS
Dec, 1949 - No. 10, Mar, 1952 (All photo-c)
Standard Comics

1-Severin-a; Whip Wilson & Reno Browne photo-c 13.50 41.00 95.00
2-Beverly Tyler & Jerome Courtland photo-c from movie "Palomino"; Williamson/Frazetta-a (2 pgs.) 14.00 43.00 100.00
3-Rex Allen photo-c 7.50 22.50 45.00
4-7,10-Severin & Elder, Al Carreno-a. 5-Ray Milland & Hedy Lamarr photo-c from movie "Copper Canyon". 6-Fred MacMurray & Irene Dunn photo-c from movie "Never a Dull Moment". 7-Jock Mahoney photo-c. 10-Bill Williams & Jane Nigh photo-c 7.50 22.50 45.00
8-Randolph Scott & Janis Carter photo-c from "Santa Fe"; Severin & Elder-a 8.35 25.00 50.00
9-Whip Wilson & Reno Browne photo-c; Severin & Elder-a 10.00 30.00 60.00

WESTERN HERO (Wow Comics #1-69; Real Western Hero #70-75)
No. 76, Mar, 1949 - No. 112, Mar, 1952
Fawcett Publications

76(#1, 52 pgs.)-Tom Mix, Hopalong Cassidy, Monte Hale, Gabby Hayes, Young Falcon (ends #78,80), & Big Bow and Little Arrow (ends #102,105) begin; painted-c begin 23.00 70.00 160.00
77 (52 pgs.) 12.00 36.00 85.00
78,80-82 (52 pgs.): 81-Capt. Tootsie by Beck 12.00 36.00 85.00
79,83 (36 pgs.): 83-Last painted-c 10.00 30.00 70.00
84-86,88-90 (52 pgs.): 84-Photo-c begin, end #112. 86-Last Hopalong Cassidy 10.00 30.00 75.00
87,91,95,99 (36 pgs.): 87-Bill Boyd begins, ends #95 10.00 30.00 65.00
92-94,96-98,101 (52 pgs.): 96-Tex Ritter begins. 101-Red Eagle app. 10.00 30.00 70.00
100 (52 pgs.) 10.00 30.00 75.00
102-111: 102-Begin 36 pg. issues 10.00 30.00 65.00
112-Last issue 10.00 30.00 70.00
NOTE: *1/2 to 1 pg. Rocky Lane (Carnation) in 80-83, 86, 88, 97. Photo covers feature Hopalong Cassidy #84, 86, 89; Tom Mix #85, 87, 90, 92, 94, 97; Monte Hale #88, 91, 93, 95, 98, 100, 104, 107, 110; Tex Ritter #96, 99, 101, 105, 108, 111; Gabby Hayes #103.*

WESTERN KID (1st Series)
Dec, 1954 - No. 17, Aug, 1957
Atlas Comics (CPC)

1-Origin; The Western Kid (Tex Dawson), his stallion Whirlwind & dog Lightning begin 13.00 40.00 90.00
2 (2/55)-Last pre-code 7.50 22.50 45.00
3-8 6.70 20.00 40.00
9,10-Williamson-a in both (4 pgs. each) 7.50 22.50 45.00
11-17 4.70 14.00 28.00
NOTE: ***Ayers** a-6, 7. **Maneely** c-2-7, 10, 14. **Romita** a-1-17; c-1, 12. **Severin** c-17.*

WESTERN KID, THE (2nd Series)
Dec, 1971 - No. 5, Aug, 1972 (All 20¢ issues)

Western Killers #64 © FOX

Western Love #2 © Prize

Western Outlaws #21 © MEG

	GD25	FN65	NM94

Marvel Comics Group

1-Reprints; Romita-c/a(3)		1.30	3.25
2-5: 2-Romita-a; Severin-c. 3-Williamson-r. 4-Everett-r		.90	2.25

WESTERN KILLERS
nn, July?, 1948; No. 60, Sept, 1948 - No. 64, May, 1949; No. 6, July, 1949
Fox Features Syndicate

nn(#59?)(nd, F&J Trading Co.)-Range Busters; formerly Blue Beetle #57?	12.00	36.00	85.00
60 (#1, 9/48)-Extreme violence; lingerie panel	16.00	48.00	110.00
61-64, 6: 61-Jack Cole, Starr-a	11.00	32.00	75.00

WESTERN LIFE ROMANCES (My Friend Irma #3 on?)
Dec, 1949 - No. 2, Mar, 1950 (52 pgs.)
Marvel Comics (IPP)

1-Whip Wilson & Reno Browne photo-c	13.00	40.00	90.00
2-Audie Murphy & Gale Storm photo-c; spanking scene	10.00	30.00	70.00

WESTERN LOVE
July-Aug, 1949 - No. 5, Mar-Apr, 1950 (All photo-c & 52 pgs.)
Prize Publications

1-S&K-a; Randolph Scott photo-c from movie "Canadian Pacific" (see Prize Comics #76)	17.00	52.00	120.00
2,5-S&K-a: 2-Whip Wilson & Reno Browne photo-c. 5-Dale Robertson photo-c	14.00	43.00	100.00
3,4: 3-Reno Browne? photo-c	10.00	30.00	65.00

NOTE: ***Meskin*** & ***Severin/Elder*** *a-2-5.*

WESTERN LOVE TRAILS (Formerly Western Adventures)
No. 7, Nov, 1949 - No. 9, Mar, 1950
Ace Magazines (A. A. Wyn)

7	9.15	27.50	55.00
8,9	6.70	20.00	40.00

WESTERN MARSHAL (See Steve Donovan... & Ernest Haycox's 4-Color 534, 591, 613, 640 & [based on Haycox's "Trailtown"])

WESTERN OUTLAWS (Junior Comics #9-16; My Secret Life #22 on)
No. 17, Sept, 1948 - No. 21, May, 1949
Fox Features Syndicate

17-Kamen-a; Iger shop-a in all; 1 pg. "Death and the Devil Pills" r-in Ghostly Weird #122	17.00	52.00	120.00
18-21	11.00	32.00	75.00

WESTERN OUTLAWS
Feb, 1954 - No. 21, Aug, 1957
Atlas Comics (ACI No. 1-14/WPI No. 15-21)

1-Heath, Powell-a; Maneely hanging-c	13.50	41.00	95.00
2	8.35	25.00	50.00
3-10: 7-Violent-a by R.Q. Sale	6.35	19.00	38.00
11,14-Williamson-a in both (6 pgs. each)	7.50	22.50	45.00
12,18,20,21: Severin covers	5.35	16.00	32.00
13-Baker-a	5.85	17.50	35.00
15-Torres-a	6.35	19.00	38.00
16-Williamson text illo	4.70	14.00	28.00
17,19-Crandall-a. 17-Williamson text illo	6.35	19.00	38.00

NOTE: ***Ayers*** *a-7, 10, 18, 20.* ***Bolle*** *a-21.* ***Colan*** *a-5, 10, 11, 17.* ***Drucker*** *a-11.* ***Everett*** *a-9, 10.* ***Heath*** *a-1; c-3, 4, 8, 16.* ***Kubert*** *a-9p.* ***Maneely*** *a-13, 16, 17, 19; c-1, 5, 7, 9, 10, 12, 13.* ***Morisi*** *a-18.* ***Powell*** *a-3, 16.* ***Romita*** *a-7, 13.* ***Severin*** *a-8, 16, 19; c-17, 18, 20, 21.* ***Tuska*** *a-6, 15.*

WESTERN OUTLAWS & SHERIFFS (Formerly Best Western)
No. 60, Dec, 1949 - No. 73, June, 1952
Marvel/Atlas Comics (IPC)

60 (52 pgs.)	16.00	48.00	110.00
61-65: 61-Photo-c	13.00	40.00	90.00
66,68-72: 66-Story contains 5 hangings	10.00	30.00	60.00
67-Cannibalism story	12.00	34.00	80.00
73-Black Rider story; Everett-c	10.00	30.00	65.00

NOTE: ***Maneely*** *a-62, 67; c-62, 69-73.* ***Robinson*** *a-68.* ***Sinnott*** *a-70.* ***Tuska*** *a-69-71.*

WESTERN PICTURE STORIES (1st Western comic)
Feb, 1937 - No. 4, June, 1937
Comics Magazine Company

1-Will Eisner-a	121.00	365.00	850.00
2-Will Eisner-a	79.00	235.00	550.00
3,4: 3-Eisner-a. 4-Caveman Cowboy story	64.00	193.00	450.00

WESTERN PICTURE STORIES (See Giant Comics Edition #6, 11)

WESTERN ROMANCES (See Target...)

WESTERN ROUGH RIDERS
Nov, 1954 - No. 4, May, 1955
Gillmor Magazines No. 1,4 (Stanmor Publications)

1	5.85	17.50	35.00
2-4	4.00	11.00	22.00

WESTERN ROUNDUP (See Dell Giants & Fox Giants)

WESTERN TALES (Formerly Witches...)
No. 31, Oct, 1955 - No. 33, July-Sept, 1956
Harvey Publications

31,32-All S&K-a; Davy Crockett app. in each	11.50	34.00	80.00
33-S&K-a; Jim Bowie app.	11.50	34.00	80.00

NOTE: *#32 & 33 contain Boy's Ranch reprints.* ***Kirby*** *c-31.*

WESTERN TALES OF BLACK RIDER (Formerly Black Rider; Gunsmoke Western #32 on)
No. 28, May, 1955 - No. 31, Nov, 1955
Atlas Comics (CPS)

28 (#1): The Spider (a villain) dies	11.50	34.00	80.00
29-31	9.15	27.50	55.00

NOTE: ***Lawrence*** *a-30.* ***Maneely*** *c-28-30.* ***Severin*** *a-28.* ***Shores*** *c-31.*

WESTERN TEAM-UP
November, 1973 (20¢)
Marvel Comics Group

1-Origin & 1st app. The Dakota Kid; Rawhide Kid-r; Gunsmoke Kid-r by Jack Davis		.70	1.80

WESTERN THRILLERS (My Past Confessions #7 on)
Aug, 1948 - No. 6, June, 1949; No. 52, 1954?
Fox Features Syndicate/M.S. Distr. No. 52

1- "Velvet Rose" (Kamenish-a); "Two-Gun Sal", "Striker Sisters" (all women outlaws issue); Brodsky-c	30.00	90.00	210.00
2	10.00	30.00	75.00
3,6	10.00	30.00	65.00
4,5-Bakerish-a; 5-Butch Cassidy app.	11.50	34.00	80.00
52-(Reprint, M.S. Dist.)-1954? No date given (becomes My Love Secret #53)	5.00	15.00	30.00

WESTERN THRILLERS (Cowboy Action #5 on)
Nov, 1954 - No. 4, Feb, 1955 (All-r/Western Outlaws & Sheriffs)
Atlas Comics (ACI)

1	10.00	30.00	70.00
2-4	6.70	20.00	40.00

NOTE: ***Heath*** *c-3.* ***Maneely*** *a-1; c-2.* ***Powell*** *a-4.* ***Robinson*** *a-4.* ***Romita*** *c-4.* ***Tuska*** *a-2.*

WESTERN TRAILS (Ringo Kid Starring in...)
May, 1957 - No. 2, July, 1957
Atlas Comics (SAI)

1-Ringo Kid app.; Severin-c	8.35	25.00	50.00
2-Severin-c	5.85	17.50	35.00

NOTE: ***Bolle*** *a-1, 2.* ***Maneely*** *a-1, 2.* ***Severin*** *c-1, 2.*

WESTERN TRUE CRIME (Becomes My Confessions)
No. 15, Aug, 1948 - No. 6, June, 1949
Fox Features Syndicate

15(#1)-Kamenish-a; formerly Zoot #14 (5/48)?	15.00	45.00	105.00
16(#2)-Kamenish-a; headlight panels, violence	11.50	34.00	80.00
3,5,6	8.35	25.00	50.00

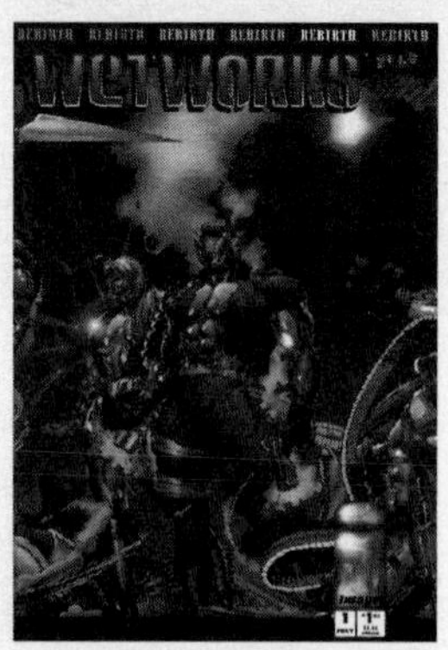
Wetworks #1 © Aegis Ent. Inc.

What If #65 © MEG

What The--? #8 © MEG

GD25 FN65 NM94

4-Johnny Craig-a 12.00 36.00 85.00

WESTERN WINNERS (Formerly All-Western Winners; becomes Black Rider #8 on & Romance Tales #7 on?)
No. 5, June, 1949 - No. 7, Dec, 1949
Marvel Comics (CDS)

5-Two-Gun Kid, Kid Colt, Black Rider; Shores-c 24.00 72.00 165.00
6-Two-Gun Kid, Black Rider, Heath Kid Colt story; Captain Tootsie by C.C. Beck 19.00 58.00 135.00
7-Randolph Scott Photo-c w/true stories about the West 19.00 58.00 135.00

WEST OF THE PECOS (See 4-Color #222)

WESTWARD HO, THE WAGONS (See 4-Color #738)

WETWORKS (See WILDC.A.T.S: Covert Action Teams #2)
June, 1994 - Present ($1.95, color)
Image Comics

1-5: 1-"July" on-c; gatefold wraparound-c; Portacio/Williams-c/a 1.30 3.25
2-Alternate Portacio-c, see Deathblow #5 .90 2.25

WHACK (Satire)
Oct, 1953 - No. 3, May, 1954
St. John Publishing Co. (Jubilee Publ.)

1-(3-D, 25¢)-Kubert-a; Maurer-c; came w/glasses 23.00 70.00 160.00
2,3-Kubert-a in each. 2-Bing Crosby on-c; Mighty Mouse & Steve Canyon parodies. 3-Li'l Orphan Annie parody; Maurer-c 12.00 36.00 85.00

WHACKY (See Wacky)

WHAM COMICS (See Super Spy)
Nov, 1940 - No. 2, Dec, 1940
Centaur Publications

1-The Sparkler, The Phantom Rider, Craig Carter and his Magic Ring, Detecto, Copper Slug, Speed Silvers by Gustavson, Speed Centaur & Jon Linton (s/f) begin 104.00 310.00 725.00
2-Origin Blue Fire & Solarman; The Buzzard app. 75.00 225.00 525.00

WHAM-O GIANT COMICS
April, 1967 (Newspaper size) (One Shot) (Full Color, 98¢)
Wham-O Mfg. Co. (Six issue subscription was advertised)

1-Radian & Goody Bumpkin by Wood; 1 pg. Stanley-a; Fine, Tufts-a; flying saucer reports; wraparound-c 5.00 15.00 35.00

WHAT DO YOU KNOW ABOUT THIS COMICS SEAL OF APPROVAL?
nd (1955) (4 pgs.; color; slick paper-c)
No publisher listed (DC Comics Giveaway)

nn-(Rare) 54.00 160.00 375.00

WHAT IF? (What If? Featuring... #13 & #?-33)(1st series)
Feb, 1977 - No. 47, Oct, 1984; June, 1988 (All 52 pgs.)
Marvel Comics Group

1-Brief origin Spider-Man, Fantastic Four 2.40 7.30 17.00
2-Origin The Hulk retold 1.60 4.70 11.00
3-5: 3-Avengers. 4-Invaders. 5-Capt. America 1.20 2.90 7.00
6-10: 8-Daredevil; Spidey parody. 9-Origins Venus, Marvel Boy, Human Robot, 3-D Man. 11-Marvel Bullpen as F. F. 1.00 2.50 6.00
11,12 1.00 2.00 5.00
13-Conan app.; John Buscema-c/a(p) 1.20 2.90 7.00
14-16 1.80 4.50
17-Ghost Rider & Son of Satan app. 1.30 3.00 8.00
18-26,29: 18-Begin 75¢-c; Dr. Strange. 19-Spider-Man. 22-Origin Dr. Doom retold 1.70 4.25
27-X-Men app.; Miller-c 1.70 5.10 12.00
28-Daredevil by Miller; Ghost Rider app. 1.70 5.10 12.00
30-"What If...Spider-Man's Clone Had Lived?" 1.10 3.00 6.50
31-Begin $1.00-c; featuring Wolverine & the Hulk; X-Men app.; death of Hulk, Wolverine & Magneto 2.15 6.50 15.00
32-47: 32,36-Byrne-a. 34-Marvel crew each draw themselves. 35-What if Elektra had lived?; Miller/Austin-a. 37-Old X-Men & Silver Surfer app.
39-Thor battles Conan 1.10 2.75
Special 1 ($1.50, 6/88)-Iron Man, F.F., Thor app. .80 2.00

NOTE: ***Austin** a-27p, 32i, 34, 35i; c-35i, 36i.* ***J. Buscema** a-13p, 15p; c-10, 13p, 23p.* ***Byrne** a-32i, 36; c-36p.* ***Colan** a-21p; c-17p, 18p, 21p.* ***Ditko** a-35, Special 1.* ***Golden** c-29, 40-42.* ***Guice** a-40p.* ***Gil Kane** a-3p, 24p; c(p)-2-4, 7, 8.* ***Kirby** a-11p; c-9p, 11p.* ***Layton** a-32i, 33i; c-30, 32p, 33i, 34.* ***Miller** a-28p, 32i, 35p; c-27, 28p.* ***Mooney** a-8i, 30i.* ***Perez** a-15p.* ***Robbins** a-4p.* ***Simonson** a-15p, 32i.* ***Starlin** a-32i.* ***Stevens** a-8, 16i(part).* ***Sutton** a-2i, 18p, 28.* ***Tuska** a-5p.* ***Weiss** a-37p.*

WHAT IF...? (2nd series)
V2#1, July, 1989 - Present ($1.25/$1.50)
Marvel Comics

V2#1-...The Avengers Had Lost the Evol. War 1.90 4.75
2-5: 2-Daredevil, Punisher app. 1.10 2.75
6-X-Men app. 1.60 4.00
7-Wolverine app.; Liefeld-c/a(1st on Wolvie?) 1.00 2.50 5.50
8,11: 11-Fantastic Four app.; McFarlane-c(i) .90 2.25
9,12-X-Men 1.20 3.00
10-Punisher 1.20 3.00
13-15,17-21,23,27-29: 13-Prof. X; Jim Lee-c. 14-Capt. Marvel; Lim/Austin-c. 15-F.F.; Capullo-c/a(p). 17-Spider-Man/Kraven. 18-F.F. 19-Vision. 20,21-Spider-Man. 23-X-Men. 27-Namor/F.F. 28,29-Capt. America. 29-Swipes cover to Avengers #4 1.50
16-Wolverine battles Conan; Red Sonja app.; X-Men cameo 1.80 4.50
22-Silver Surfer by Lim/Austin-c/a 1.20 3.00
24-Wolverine; Punisher app. 1.10 2.75
25-($1.50, 52 pgs.)-Wolverine app. 1.20 3.00
26-Punisher app. .80 2.00
30-($1.75, 52 pgs.)-Sue Richards/F.F. .70 1.75
31-40: 31-Cosmic Spider-Man & Venom app.; Hobgoblin cameo. 32,33-Phoenix; X-Men app. 35-Fantastic Five (w/Spidey). 36-Avengers vs. Guardians of the Galaxy. 37-Wolverine; Thibert-c(i). 38-Thor; Rogers-p (part). 40-Storm; X-Men app. 1.50
41-($1.75, 52 pgs.)-Avengers vs. Galactus .70 1.75
42-49,51-60: 42-Spider-Man. 43-Wolverine. 44-Venom/Punisher. 45-Ghost Rider. 46-Cable. 47-Magneto. 49-Infinity Gauntlet w/Silver Surfer & Thanos. 52-Dr. Doom. 54-Death's Head. 57-Punisher as Shield. 58-"What if Punisher Had Killed Spider-Man" w/cover similar to Amazing S-M #129. 59-...Wolverine led Alpha Flight. 60-X-Men Wedding Album 1.25
50-($2.95, 52 pgs.)-Foil embossed-c; "What If Hulk Had Killed Wolverine" 1.20 3.00
61-70: 61-Begin $1.50-c; bound-in card sheet; Spider-Man 1.50

WHAT'S BEHIND THESE HEADLINES
1948 (16 pgs.)
William C. Popper Co.

nn-Comic insert "The Plot to Steal the World" 4.00 10.00 20.00

'WHAT'S NEW? - THE COLLECTED ADVENTURES OF PHIL & DIXIE'
Oct, 1991 - No. 2, 1991? ($5.95, mostly color, squarebound, 52 pgs.)
Palliard Press

1,2-By Phil Foglio 1.00 2.50 6.00

WHAT THE- -?!
Aug, 1988 - Present ($1.25/$1.50, semi-annually #5 on)
Marvel Comics

1-All contain parodies 1.00 2.50
2,4,5: 5-Punisher/Wolverine parody; Jim Lee-a 1.50
3-X-Men parody; Todd McFarlane-a 1.20 3.00
6-25: 6-($1.00)-Punisher, Wolverine, Alpha Flight. 9-Wolverine. 16-EC back-c parody. 17-Wolverine/Punisher parody. 18-Star Trek parody w/Wolverine. 19-Punisher, Wolverine, Ghost Rider. 21-Weapon X parody. 22-Punisher/Wolverine parody 1.25
26-Fall Special ($2.50, 68 pgs.)-Spider-Ham 2099-c/story; origin Silver Surfer; Hulk & Doomsday parody .90 2.50
Summer Special 1 (1993, $2.50)-X-Men parody .90 2.50

NOTE: ***Austin** a-6i.* ***Byrne** a-2, 6, 10; c-2, 6-8, 10, 12, 13.* ***Golden** a-22.* ***Dale Keown** a-8p(8*

Whirlwind Comics #2 © Nita

Whisper #14 © First

White Pincess of the Jungle #3 © AVON

GD25 FN65 NM94

*pgs.). **McFarlane** a-3. **Rogers** c-15i, 16p. **Severin** a-2. **Staton** a-21p. **Williamson** a-2i.*

WHEATIES (Premiums) (32 titles)
1950 & 1951 (32 pgs.) (Pocket size)
Walt Disney Productions

(Set A-1 to A-8, 1950)
A-1-Mickey Mouse & the Disappearing Island, A-2-Grandma Duck, Homespun Detective, A-3-Donald Duck & the Haunted Jewels, A-4-Donald Duck & the Giant Ape, A-5-Mickey Mouse, Roving Reporter, A-6-Li'l Bad Wolf, Forest Ranger, A-7-Goofy, Tightrope Acrobat, A-8-Pluto & the Bogus Money each... 4.20 12.50 25.00

(Set B-1 to B-8, 1950)
B-1-Mickey Mouse & the Pharoah's Curse, B-2-Pluto, Canine Cowpoke, B-3-Donald Duck & the Buccaneers, B-4-Mickey Mouse & the Mystery Sea Monster, B-5-Li'l Bad Wolf in the Hollow Tree Hideout, B-6-Donald Duck, Trail Blazer, B-7-Goofy & the Gangsters, B-8 Donald Duck, Klondike Kid each... 4.20 12.50 25.00

(Set C-1 to C-8, 1951)
C-1-Donald Duck & the Inca Idol, C-2-Mickey Mouse & the Magic Mountain, C-3-Li'l Bad Wolf, Fire Fighter, C-4-Gus & Jaq Save the Ship, C-5-Donald Duck in the Lost Lakes, C-6-Mickey Mouse & the Stagecoach Bandits, C-7-Goofy, Big Game Hunter, C-8-Donald Duck Deep-Sea Diver each... 4.00 10.00 20.00

(Set D-1 to D-8, 1951)
D-1-Donald Duck in Indian Country, D-2-Mickey Mouse and the Abandoned Mine, D-3-Pluto & the Mysterious Package, D-4-Bre'r Rabbit's Sunken Treasure, D-5-Donald Duck, Mighty Mystic, D-6-Mickey Mouse & the Medicine Man, D-7-Li'l Bad Wolf and the Secret of the Woods, D-8-Minnie Mouse, Girl Explorer each... 4.00 10.00 20.00

NOTE: Some copies lack the Wheaties ad.

WHEE COMICS (Also see Gay, Smile & Tickle Comics)
1955 (7¢, 52 pgs.) (5x7-1/4")
Modern Store Publications

1-Funny animal .80 2.00 4.00

WHEELIE AND THE CHOPPER BUNCH (TV)
July, 1975 - No. 7, July, 1976 (Hanna-Barbera)
Charlton Comics

1,2: 1-Byrne text illo (see Nightmare for 1st art); Staton-a. 2-Byrne-c/a.
2,3-Mike Zeck text illos 1.30 3.00 8.00
3-7-Staton-a. 3-Byrne-c/a 1.70 4.25

WHEN KNIGHTHOOD WAS IN FLOWER (See 4-Color #505, 682)

WHEN SCHOOL IS OUT (See Wisco)

WHERE CREATURES ROAM
July, 1970 - No. 8, Sept, 1971
Marvel Comics Group

1-Kirby/Ayers-r 1.00 2.00 5.00
2-8-Kirby-r 1.00 2.50

*NOTE: **Ditko** r-1, 2, 4, 6, 7. All contain pre super-hero reprints.*

WHERE MONSTERS DWELL
Jan, 1970 - No. 38, Oct, 1975
Marvel Comics Group

1-Kirby/Ditko-r; all contain pre super-hero-r 1.00 2.00 5.00
2-10,12: 4-Crandall-a(r). 12-Giant issue 1.00 2.50
11,13-37: 18,20-Starlin-c .70 1.75
38-Williamson-r/World of Suspense #3 .90 2.25

*NOTE: **Ditko** a(r)-4, 8, 10, 12, 17-19, 23-25, 37. **Reinman** a-4r. **Severin** c-15.*

WHERE'S HUDDLES? (TV) (See Fun-In #9)
Jan, 1971 - No. 3, Dec, 1971 (Hanna-Barbera)
Gold Key

1 1.40 3.50 8.50
2,3: 3-r/most #1 1.00 2.00 5.00

WHIP WILSON (Movie star) (Formerly Rex Hart; Gunhawk #12 on; see Western Hearts, Western Life Romances, Western Love)
No. 9, April, 1950 - No. 11, Sept, 1950 (#9,10: 52 pgs.; #11: 36 pgs.)
Marvel Comics

9-Photo-c; Whip Wilson & his horse Bullet begin; origin Bullet; issue #23 listed on splash page; cover changed to #9 41.00 125.00 290.00
10,11-Photo-c 27.00 81.00 190.00
I.W. Reprint #1(1964)-Kinstler-c; r-Marvel #11 2.80 7.00 14.00

WHIRLWIND COMICS (Also see Cyclone Comics)
June, 1940 - No. 3, Sept, 1940
Nita Publication

1-Cyclone begins (origin/1st app.); Cyclone-c 75.00 225.00 525.00
2,3-Cyclone-c 57.00 171.00 400.00

WHIRLYBIRDS (See 4-Color #1124, 1216)

WHISPER (Capital & First)(Value: cover or less)

WHITE CHIEF OF THE PAWNEE INDIANS
1951
Avon Periodicals

nn-Kit West app.; Kinstler-c 11.00 32.00 75.00

WHITE EAGLE INDIAN CHIEF (See Indian Chief)

WHITE FANG (Disney, movie adapt.)(Value: cover or less)

WHITE INDIAN
No. 11, July, 1953 - No. 15, 1954
Magazine Enterprises

11(A-1 94), 12(A-1 101), 13(A-1 104)-Frazetta-r(Dan Brand) in all from Durango Kid. 11-Powell-c 17.00 52.00 120.00
14(A-1 117), 15(A-1 135)-Check-a; Torres-a-#15 9.15 27.50 55.00

NOTE: #11 contains reprints from Durango Kid #1-4; #12 from #5, 9, 10, 11; #13 from #7, 12, 13, 16. #14 & 15 contain all new stories.

WHITE PRINCESS OF THE JUNGLE (Also see Jungle Adventures & Top Jungle Comics)
July, 1951 - No. 5, Nov, 1952
Avon Periodicals

1-Origin of White Princess (Taanda) & Capt'n Courage (r); Kinstler-c 29.00 86.00 200.00
2-Reprints origin of Malu, Slave Girl Princess from Avon's Slave Girl Comics #1 w/Malu changed to Zora; Kinstler-c/a(2) 24.00 72.00 165.00
3-Origin Blue Gorilla; Kinstler-c/a 18.00 54.00 125.00
4-Jack Barnum, White Hunter app.; r/Sheena #9 16.00 48.00 110.00
5-Blue Gorilla by McCann?; Kinstler inside-c; Fawcette/Alascia-a(3) 16.00 48.00 110.00

WHITE RIDER AND SUPER HORSE (Formerly Humdinger V2#2; Indian Warriors #7 on; also see Blue Bolt #1, 4Most & Western Crime Cases)
1950 - No. 6, Mar, 1951
Novelty-Star Publications/Accepted Publ.

1: 1-3-Exist? 10.00 30.00 60.00
2,3 7.50 22.50 45.00
4-6-Adapts "The Last of the Mohicans". 4-(9/50)-Says #11 on inside 7.50 22.50 45.00
Accepted Reprint #5(r/#5),6 (nd); L.B. Cole-c 4.70 14.00 28.00

*NOTE: All have **L. B. Cole** covers.*

WHITE WILDERNESS (See 4-Color #943)

WHITMAN COMIC BOOK, A
Sept., 1962 (136 pgs.; 7-3/4x5-3/4; hardcover) (B&W)
Whitman Publishing Co.

1-4,6-8: 1-Yogi Bear. 2-Huckleberry Hound. 3-Flintstones. 4-Snooper & Blabber Fearless Detectives/Quick Draw McGraw of the Wild West. 6-Mr. Jinks and Pixie & Dixie. 7-Augie Doggie & Loopy de Loop. 8-Bugs Bunny-r from #47,51,53,54 & 55 1.00 3.00 7.00
5-Donald Duck-reprints most of WDC&S #209-213. Includes 5 Barks stories, 1 complete Mickey Mouse serial by Paul Murry & 1 Mickey Mouse serial missing the 1st episode 10.00 30.00 70.00

Who Dunnit? #1 © Eclipse

Who's Who in Star Trek #1 © Paramount

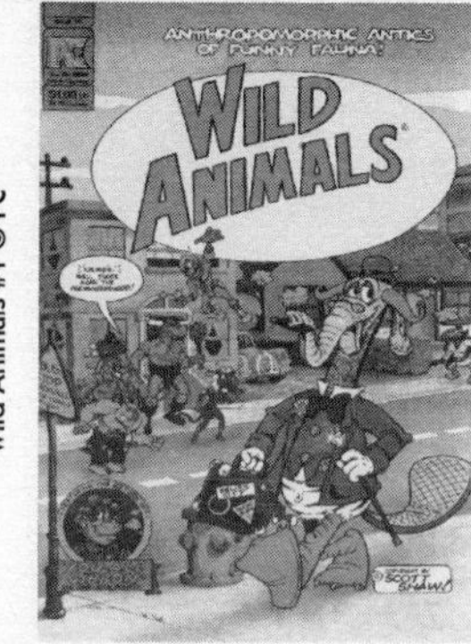

Wild Animals #1 © PC

NOTE: *Hanna-Barbera #1-6(TV), original stories. Dell reprints-#7, 8.*

WHIZ COMICS (Formerly Flash Comics & Thrill Comics #1)
No. 2, Feb, 1940 - No. 155, June, 1953
Fawcett Publications

	GD25	FN65	VF82	NM94
1-(nn on cover, #2 inside)-Origin & 1st newsstand app. Captain Marvel (formerly Captain Thunder) by C. C. Beck (created by Bill Parker), Spy Smasher, Golden Arrow, Ibis the Invincible, Dan Dare, Scoop Smith, Sivana, & Lance O'Casey begin	4,600.00	13,800.00	29,900.00	46,000.00

(Estimated up to 100 total copies exist, 3 in NM/Mint)
(The only Mint copy sold in 1990 for $74,000 cash/trade)

1-Reprint, oversize 13-1/2x10". **WARNING**: This comic is an exact duplicate reprint (except for dropping "Gangway for Captain Marvel" from-c) of the original except for its size. DC published it in 1974 with a second cover titling it as a Famous First Edition. There have been many reported cases of the outer cover being removed and the interior sold as the original edition. The reprint with the new outer cover removed is practically worthless. See Famous First Edition for value.

	GD25	FN65	NM94
2-(3/40, nn on cover, #3 inside); cover to Flash #1 redrawn, pg. 12, panel 4; Spy Smasher reveals I.D. to Eve	400.00	1200.00	2800.00
3-(4/40, #3 on-c, #4 inside)-1st app. Beautia	257.00	771.00	1800.00
4-(5/40, #4 on cover, #5 inside)-Brief origin Capt. Marvel retold	214.00	643.00	1500.00
5-Captain Marvel wears button-down flap on splash page only	171.00	515.00	1200.00
6-10: 7-Dr. Voodoo begins (by Raboy-#9-22)	129.00	386.00	900.00
11-14: 12-Capt. Marvel does not wear cape	93.00	280.00	650.00
15-Origin Sivana; Dr. Voodoo by Raboy	109.00	328.00	765.00
16-18-Spy Smasher battles Captain Marvel	109.00	328.00	765.00
19,20	66.00	200.00	465.00
21-Origin & 1st app. Lt. Marvels	71.00	215.00	500.00
22-24: 23-Only Dr. Voodoo by Tuska	55.00	165.00	385.00
25-(12/41)-Captain Nazi jumps from Master Comics #21 to take on Capt. Marvel solo after being beaten by Capt. Marvel/Bulletman team, causing the creation of Capt. Marvel Jr.; 1st app./origin of Capt. Marvel Jr. (part II of trilogy origin); Captain Marvel sends Jr. back to Master #22 to aid Bulletman against Capt. Nazi; origin Old Shazam in text	343.00	1030.00	2400.00
26-30	48.00	145.00	335.00
31,32: 32-1st app. The Trolls; Hitler/Mussolini satire by Beck	41.00	122.00	285.00
33-Spy Smasher, Captain Marvel x-over on cover and inside	46.00	140.00	325.00
34,36-40: 37-The Trolls app. by Swayze	33.00	100.00	230.00
35-Captain Marvel & Spy Smasher-c	38.00	115.00	265.00
41-50: 43-Spy Smasher, Ibis, Golden Arrow x-over in Capt. Marvel. 44-Flag-c. 47-Origin recap (1 pg.)	23.00	70.00	160.00
51-60: 52-Capt. Marvel x-over in Ibis. 57-Spy Smasher, Golden Arrow, Ibis cameo	20.00	60.00	140.00
61-70	18.00	54.00	125.00
71,77-80	16.00	48.00	110.00
72-76-Two Captain Marvel stories in each; 76-Spy Smasher becomes Crime Smasher	16.50	50.00	115.00
81-99: 86-Captain Marvel battles Sivana Family. 91-Infinity-c	16.00	48.00	110.00
100-(8/48)-Anniversary issue	19.00	58.00	135.00
101-106: 102-Commando Yank app. 106-Bulletman app.	16.00	48.00	110.00
107-152: 107-White House photo-c. 108-Brooklyn Bridge photo-c. 112-Photo-c 139-Infinity-c. 140-Flag-c. 142-Used in **POP**, pg. 89	16.00	48.00	110.00
153-155-(Scarce):154,155-1st/2nd Dr. Death stories	19.00	58.00	135.00
Wheaties Giveaway(1946, Miniature, 6-1/2x8-1/4", 32 pgs.); all copies were taped at each corner to a box of Wheaties and are never found in fine or mint condition; "Capt. Marvel & the Water Thieves", plus Golden Arrow, Ibis, Crime Smasher stories	66.00	250.00	–

NOTE: ***Krigstein** Golden Arrow-No. 75, 78, 91, 95, 96, 98-100. **M.Swayze** a-37, 38, 59; c-38. **Schaffenberger** c-138-158(most). **Wolverton** 1/2 pg. "Culture Corner"-No. 65-67, 68(2 1/2 pgs), 70-85, 87-96, 98-100, 102-109, 112-121, 123, 125, 126, 128-131, 133, 134, 136, 142, 143, 146.*

WHODUNIT
Aug-Sept, 1948 - No. 3, Dec-Jan, 1948-49 (#1,2: 52 pgs.)
D.S. Publishing Co.

	GD25	FN65	NM94
1-Baker-a (7 pgs.)	11.50	34.00	80.00
2,3	8.35	25.00	50.00

WHODUNNIT? (Eclipse)(Value: cover or less)

WHO FRAMED ROGER RABBIT (See Marvel Graphic Novel)

WHO IS NEXT?
No. 5, January, 1953
Standard Comics

	GD25	FN65	NM94
5-Toth, Sekowsky, Andru-a	13.00	40.00	90.00

WHO'S MINDING THE MINT? (See Movie Classics)

WHO'S WHO IN STAR TREK
Mar, 1987 - #2, Apr, 1987 ($1.50)
DC Comics

	GD25	FN65	NM94
1,2		1.90	4.75

WHO'S WHO IN THE LEGION OF SUPER-HEROES (DC)(Value: cover or less)

WHO'S WHO: THE DEFINITIVE DIRECTORY OF THE DC UNIVERSE (DC)(Value: cover or less)

WHO'S WHO UPDATE '87 (DC)(Value: cover or less)

WHO'S WHO UPDATE '88 (DC)Value: cover or less)

WILBUR COMICS (Teen-age) (Also see Laugh Comics, Laugh Comix, Liberty Comics #10 & Zip Comics)
Sum', 1944 - No. 87, 11/59; No. 88, 9/63; No. 89, 10/64; No. 90, 10/65
(No. 1-46: 52 pgs.)(#1-11 are quarterly)
MLJ Magazines/Archie Publ. No. 8, Spring, 1946 on

	GD25	FN65	NM94
1	38.00	115.00	265.00
2(Fall, 1944)	19.00	58.00	135.00
3,4(Wint, '44-45; Spr, '45)	14.00	43.00	100.00
5-1st app. Katy Keene (Sum, '45) & begin series; Wilbur story same as Archie story in Archie #1 except Wilbur replaces Archie	49.00	146.00	340.00
6-10: 10-(Fall, 1946)	14.00	43.00	100.00
11-20	10.00	30.00	60.00
21-30: 30-(4/50)	6.35	19.00	38.00
31-50	4.20	12.50	25.00
51-70	3.60	9.00	18.00
71-90: 88-Last 10¢ issue (9/63)	1.80	4.50	9.00

NOTE: *Katy Keene in No. 5-56, 58-69. **Al Fagaly** c-6-9, 12-24 at least. **Vigoda** c-2.*

WILD
Feb, 1954 - No. 5, Aug, 1954
Atlas Comics (IPC)

	GD25	FN65	NM94
1	16.00	48.00	110.00
2	10.00	30.00	70.00
3-5	9.15	27.50	55.00

NOTE: ***Berg** a-5; c-4. **Burgos** c-3. **Colan** a-4. **Everett** a-1-3. **Heath** a-2, 3, 5. **Maneely** a-1-3, 5; c-1, 5. **Post** a-2, 5. **Ed Win** a-1, 3.*

WILD (This Magazine Is...) (Magazine)
Jan, 1968 - No. 3, 1968 (52 pgs.) (Satire)
Dell Publishing Co.

	GD25	FN65	NM94
1-3	1.00	2.50	6.00

WILD ANIMALS (Pacific)(Value: cover or less)

WILD BILL ELLIOTT (Also see Western Roundup under Dell Giants)
No. 278, 5/50 - No. 643, 7/55 (No #11,12) (All photo-c)
Dell Publishing Co.

	GD25	FN65	NM94
4-Color 278(#1, 52pgs.)-Titled "Bill Elliott"; Bill & his horse Stormy begin; photo front/back-c begin	13.00	40.00	90.00
2 (11/50), 3 (52 pgs.)	7.50	22.50	45.00
4-10(10-12/52)	5.85	17.50	35.00
4-Color 472(6/53),520(12/53)-Last photo back-c	5.85	17.50	35.00
13(4-6/54) - 17(4-6/55)	4.70	14.00	28.00

Wildcats Trilogy #3 ©Aegis Ent. Inc.

Wild Dog #3 © DC

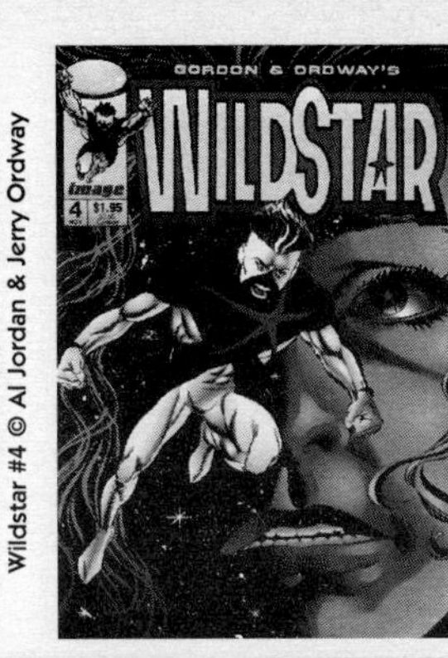

Wildstar #4 © Al Jordan & Jerry Ordway

GD25 FN65 NM94

4-Color 643 (7/55) 4.70 14.00 28.00

WILD BILL HICKOK (Also see Blazing Sixguns)
Sept-Oct, 1949 - No. 28, May-June, 1956
Avon Periodicals

1-Ingels-c 14.00 43.00 100.00
2-Painted-c; Kit West app. 7.50 22.50 45.00
3-5-Painted-c (4-Cover by Howard Winfield) 4.20 12.50 25.00
6-10,12: 8-10-Painted-c. 12-Kinsler-c? 4.20 12.50 25.00
11,13,14-Kinstler-c/a (#11-c & inside-f/c art only) 4.70 14.00 28.00
15,17,18,20: 20-Kit West by Larsen 3.60 9.00 18.00
16-Kamen-a; r-3 stories/King of the Badmen of Deadwood
4.00 12.00 24.00
19-Meskin-a 3.60 9.00 18.00
21-Reprints 2 stories/Chief Crazy Horse 3.60 9.00 18.00
22-McCann-a?; r/Sheriff Bob Dixon's... 3.60 9.00 18.00
23-27: 23-Kinstler-c. 24-27-Kinstler-c/a(r) (24,25-r?) 4.00 11.00 22.00
28-Kinstler-c/a (new); r-/Last of the Comanches 4.00 11.00 22.00
I.W. Reprint #1-r/#2; Kinstler-c 1.00 2.50 5.00
Super Reprint #10-12: 10-r/#18. 11-r/#?. 12-r/#8 1.00 2.50 5.00
NOTE: *#23, 25 contain numerous editing deletions in both art and script due to code.* ***Kinstler*** *c-6, 7, 11-14, 17, 18, 20-22, 24-28.* ***Howard Larsen*** *a-1, 2, 4, 5, 6(3), 7-9, 11, 12, 17, 18, 20-24, 26.* ***Meskin*** *a-7.* ***Reinman*** *a-6, 17.*

WILD BILL HICKOK AND JINGLES (TV)(Formerly Cowboy Western)
No. 68, Aug, 1958 - No. 75, Dec, 1959 (Also see Blue Bird)
Charlton Comics

68,69-Williamson-a (all are 10¢ issues) 8.35 25.00 50.00
70-Two pgs. Williamson-a 5.35 16.00 32.00
71-75 (#76, exist?) 4.00 10.00 20.00

WILD BILL PECOS WESTERN (AC)(Value: cover or less)

WILD BOY OF THE CONGO (Also see Approved Comics)
No. 10, 2-3/51 - No. 12, 8-9/51; No. 4, 10-11/51 - No. 15, 6/55
Ziff-Davis No. 10-12,4-8/St. John No. 9 on

10(#1)(2-3/51)-Origin; bondage-c by Saunders (painted); used in **SOTI**, pg. 189; painted-c begin, end #9 13.00 40.00 90.00
11(4-5/51),12(8-9/51)-Norman Saunders painted-c 8.35 25.00 50.00
4(10-11/51)-Saunders painted bondage-c 8.35 25.00 50.00
5(Winter,'51)-Saunders painted-c 7.00 21.00 42.00
6,8,9(10/53),10: 6-Saunders-c. 8,9-Painted-c 7.00 21.00 42.00
7(8-9/52)-Kinstler-a 8.35 25.00 50.00
11-13-Baker-c. 11-r/#7 w/new Baker-c; Kinstler-a (2 pgs.)
8.35 25.00 50.00
14(4/55)-Baker-c; r-#12('51) 8.35 25.00 50.00
15(6/55) 5.85 17.50 35.00

WILD CARDS (Marvel)(Value: cover or less)

WILDCAT (See Sensation Comics #1)

WILDC.A.T.S: COVERT ACTION TEAMS
Aug, 1992 - No. 4, Mar, 1993; No. 5, Nov, 1993 - Present ($1.95/$2.50, color)
Image Comics

1-1st app.; Jim Lee/Williams-c/a & Lee scripts begin; contains 2 trading cards (another version has different cards inside) 1.00 2.50 6.00
1-All gold foil signed edition 40.00
1-All gold foil unsigned edition 10.00
1-Newsstand edition w/o cards .80 2.00
2-($2.50)-Prism foil stamped-c; contains coupon for Image Comics #0 & 4 pg. preview to Portacio's Wetworks (back-up) 1.90 4.75
2-With coupon missing .80 2.00
2-Direct sale misprint w/o foil-c .80 2.00
2-Newsstand ed., no prism or coupon .80 2.00
3-Lee/Liefeld-c (1/93-c, 12/92 inside) .80 2.00
4-($2.50)-Polybagged w/Topps trading card; 1st app. Tribe by Johnson & Stroman; Youngblood cameo 1.00 2.50
5-7-Jim Lee/Williams-c/a; Lee script .80 2.00
8-18: 8-Begin $2.50-c; X-Men's Jean Grey & Scott Summers cameos
1.00 2.50
11-Alternate Portacio-c, see Deathblow #5 1.00 2.50
...Sourcebook 1 (9/93, $2.50)-Foil embossed-c 1.00 2.50
...Sourcebook 1-($1.95)-Newsstand ed. w/o foil embossed-c .80 2.00
...Special 1 (11/93, $3.50, 52 pgs.)-Charest/Williams-c/a 1.40 3.50
Trade paperback (1993, $9.95)-r/#1-4; bagged w/#0 1.65 4.00 10.00

WILDC.A.T.S TRILOGY
June, 1993 - No. 3, Dec, 1993 ($1.95, color, mini-series)
Image Comics

1-($2.50)-Multi-color foil-c; Jae Lee-c/a in all 1.00 2.50
1-($1.95)-Newsstand ed. w/o foil-c .80 2.00
2,3-($1.95)-Jae Lee-c/a .80 2.00

WILD DOG (DC)(Value: cover or less)

WILD FRONTIER (Cheyenne Kid #8 on)
Oct, 1955 - No. 7, April, 1957
Charlton Comics

1-Davy Crockett 6.35 19.00 38.00
2-6-Davy Crockett in all 4.00 11.00 22.00
7-Origin & 1st app. Cheyenne Kid 4.00 11.00 22.00

WILD KINGDOM (TV)
1965 (Giveaway) (regular size) (16 pgs., slick-c)
Western Printing Co.

nn-Mutual of Omaha's... 2.40 6.00 12.00

WILDSTAR: SKY ZERO
Mar, 1993 - No. 4, Nov, 1993 ($1.95, color, mini-series)
Image Comics

1-($2.50)-Embossed-c w/silver ink; Ordway-c/a in all 1.00 2.50
1-($1.95)-Newsstand ed. w/silver ink-c, not embossed .80 2.00
1-Gold variant 20.00
2-4 .80 2.00

WILDTHING
Apr, 1993 - No. 7, Oct, 1993 ($1.75, color)
Marvel Comics UK

1-($2.50)-Embossed-c; Venom & Carnage cameo 1.00 2.50
2-7: 2-Spider-Man & Venom. 6-Mysterio app. .70 1.75

WILD WEST (Wild Western #3 on)
Spring, 1948 - No. 2, July, 1948
Marvel Comics (WFP)

1-Two-Gun Kid, Arizona Annie, & Tex Taylor begin; Shores-c
18.00 54.00 125.00
2-Captain Tootsie by Beck; Shores-c 16.00 48.00 110.00

WILD WEST (Black Fury #1-57)
V2#58, November, 1966
Charlton Comics

V2#58 .80 2.00

WILD WEST C.O.W.-BOYS OF MOO MESA (TV)
Dec, 1992 - No. 3, Feb, 1993; Mar, 1993 - No. 3, July, 1993 ($1.25)
Archie Comics

1-3 (Mini-series) 1.25
1-3 1.25

WILD WESTERN (Formerly Wild West #1,2)
No. 3, 9/48 - No. 57, 9/57 (3-11: 52 pgs; 12-on: 36 pgs)
Marvel/Atlas Comics (WFP)

3(#1)-Tex Morgan begins; Two-Gun Kid, Tex Taylor, & Arizona Annie continue from Wild West 20.00 60.00 140.00
4-Last Arizona Annie; Captain Tootsie by Beck; Kid Colt app.
13.50 41.00 95.00
5-2nd app. Black Rider (1/49); Blaze Carson, Captain Tootsie (by Beck) app.
16.00 48.00 110.00
6-8: 6-Blaze Carson app; anti-Wertham editorial 10.00 30.00 70.00

Will Eisner's Mr. Mystic #1 © Will Eisner

Will to Power #2 © DH

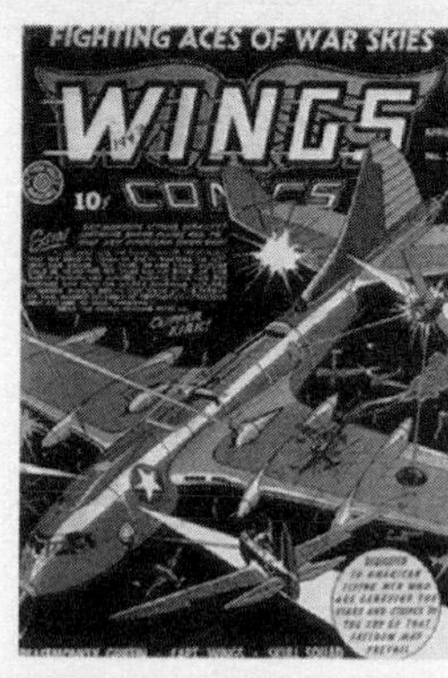

Wings #32 © FH

GD25 FN65 NM94

9-Photo-c; Black Rider begins, ends #19 13.50 41.00 95.00
10-Charles Starrett photo-c 16.00 48.00 110.00
11-(Last 52 pg. issue) 10.00 30.00 65.00
12-14,16-19: All Black Rider-c/stories. 12-14-The Prairie Kid & his horse Fury app. 9.15 27.50 55.00
15-Red Larabee, Gunhawk (origin), his horse Blaze, & Apache Kid begin, end #22; Black Rider-c/story 10.00 30.00 60.00
20-29: 20-Kid Colt-c begin. 24-Has 2 Kid Colt stories. 26-1st app. The Ringo Kid? (2/53); 4 pg. story 8.35 25.00 50.00
30-Katz-a 8.35 25.00 50.00
31-40 5.85 17.50 35.00
41-47,49-51,53,57 4.35 13.00 26.00
48-Williamson/Torres-a (4 pgs); Drucker-a 7.50 22.50 45.00
52-Crandall-a 7.50 22.50 45.00
54,55-Williamson-a in both (5 & 4 pgs.), #54 with Mayo plus 2 text illos 7.00 21.00 42.00
56-Baker-a? 4.35 13.00 26.00

NOTE: *Annie Oakley in #46, 47. Apache Kid in #15-22, 39. Arizona Kid in #21, 23. Arrowhead in #34-39. Black Rider in #5, 9-19, 33-44. Fighting Texan in #17. Kid Colt in #4-6, 9-11, 20-47, 52, 54-56. Outlaw Kid in #43. Red Hawkins in #13, 14. Ringo Kid in #26, 39, 41, 43, 44, 46, 47, 50, 52-56. Tex Morgan in #3, 4, 6, 9, 11. Tex Taylor in #3-6, 9, 11. Texas Kid in #23-25. Two-Gun Kid in #3-6, 9, 11, 12, 33-39, 41. Wyatt Earp in #47.* **Ayers** *a-41, 42.* **Berg** *a-26; c-24.* **Colan** *a-49.* **Forte** *a-28, 30.* **Al Hartley** *a-16.* **Heath** *a-4, 5, 8; c-34, 44.* **Keller** *a-24, 26(2), 29-40, 44-46, 48, 52.* **Maneely** *a-10, 12, 15, 16, 28, 35, 38, 40-45; c-18-22, 33, 35, 36, 38, 39, 41, 42, 45.* **Morisi** *a-23, 52.* **Pakula** *a-42, 52.* **Powell** *a-51.* **Romita** *a-24(2).* **Severin** *a-46, 47; c-48.* **Shores** *a-3, 5, 30, 31, 33, 35, 36, 38, 41; c-3-5.* **Sinnott** *a-34-39.* **Wildey** *a-43. Bondage c-19.*

WILD WESTERN ACTION (Also see The Bravados)
March, 1971 - No. 3, June, 1971 (Reprints, 25¢, 52 pgs.)
Skywald Publishing Corp.

1-Durango Kid, Straight Arrow-r; with all references to "Straight" in story relettered to "Swift"; Bravados begin; Shores-a (new) .80 2.00
2-Billy Nevada, Durango Kid 1.50
3-Red Mask, Durango Kid 1.50

WILD WESTERN ROUNDUP
Oct, 1957; 1960-'61
Red Top/Decker Publications/I. W. Enterprises

1(1957)-Kid Cowboy-r 2.80 7.00 14.00
I.W. Reprint #1('60-61)-r/#1 by Red Top 1.00 2.50 5.00

WILD WEST RODEO
1953 (15¢)
Star Publications

1-A comic book coloring book with regular full color cover & B&W inside 4.00 10.00 20.00

WILD WILD WEST, THE (TV)
June, 1966 - No. 7, Oct, 1969 (Robert Conrad photo-c; 1,2-Photo back-c)
Gold Key

1,2-McWilliams-a 7.00 22.00 52.00
3-7 5.10 15.00 36.00

WILD, WILD WEST, THE (TV)(Millennium)(Value: cover or less)

WILKIN BOY (See That...)

WILL EISNER PRESENTS (Eclipse)(Value: cover or less)

WILL EISNER'S 3-D CLASSICS FEATURING THE SPIRIT (Kitchen Sink)(Value: cover or less)

WILLIE COMICS (Formerly Ideal #1-4; Crime Cases #24 on; Li'l Willie #20 & 21) (See Gay Comics, Laugh, Millie The Model & Wisco)
#5, Fall, 1946 - #19, 4/49; #22, 1/50 - #23, 5/50 (No #20 & 21)
Marvel Comics (MgPC)

5(#1)-George, Margie, Nellie the Nurse & Willie begin 11.50 34.00 80.00
6,8,9 6.70 20.00 40.00
7(1),10,11-Kurtzman's "Hey Look" 8.35 25.00 50.00
12,14-18,22,23 5.00 15.00 30.00
13,19-Kurtzman's "Hey Look" (#19 is last by Kurtzman?) 7.50 22.50 45.00

NOTE: *Cindy app. in #17. Jeanie app. in #17. Little Lizzie app. in #22.*

WILLIE MAYS (See The Amazing...)

WILLIE THE PENGUIN
April, 1951 - No. 6, April, 1952
Standard Comics

1-Funny animal 5.00 15.00 30.00
2-6 3.60 9.00 18.00

WILLIE THE WISE-GUY (Also see Cartoon Kids)
Sept, 1957
Atlas Comics (NPP)

1-Kida, Maneely-a 5.35 16.00 32.00

WILLIE WESTINGHOUSE EDISON SMITH THE BOY INVENTOR
1906 (36 pgs. in color) (10x16")
William A. Stokes Co.

nn-By Frank Crane 32.00 96.00 225.00

WILLOW (Marvel)(Value: cover or less)

WILL ROGERS WESTERN (Formerly My Great Love #1-4; see Blazing & True Comics #66)
No. 5, June, 1950 - No. 2, Aug, 1950
Fox Features Syndicate

5(#1),2: Photo-c 23.00 70.00 160.00

WILL TO POWER
June, 1994 - Present ($1.00, color, 20 pgs., weekly)
Dark Horse Comics

1-19: 1-3-Bart Sears-c 1.00

WILL-YUM (See 4-Color #676, 765, 902)

WIN A PRIZE COMICS (Timmy The Timid Ghost #3 on?)
Feb, 1955 - No. 2, Apr, 1955
Charlton Comics

V1#1-S&K-a; Poe adapt; E.C. War swipe 52.00 156.00 365.00
2-S&K-a 36.00 107.00 250.00

WINDY & WILLY
May-June, 1969 - No. 4, Nov-Dec, 1969
National Periodical Publications

1-4: r/Dobie Gillis with some art changes 1.60 4.00

WINGS COMICS
9/40 - No. 109, 9/49; No. 110, Wint, 1949-50; No. 111, Spring, 1950; No. 112, 1950(nd); No. 113 - No. 115, 1950(nd); No. 116, 1952(nd); No. 117, Fall, 1952 - No. 122, Wint, 1953-54; No. 123 - No. 124, 1954(nd)
Fiction House Magazines

1-Skull Squad, Clipper Kirk, Suicide Smith, Jane Martin, War Nurse, Phantom Falcons, Greasemonkey Griffin, Parachute Patrol & Powder Burns begin 136.00 407.00 950.00
2 61.00 182.00 425.00
3-5 45.00 135.00 315.00
6-10 39.00 118.00 275.00
11-15 34.00 103.00 240.00
16-Origin & 1st app. Captain Wings & begin series 39.00 116.00 270.00
17-20 27.00 81.00 190.00
21-30 24.00 73.00 170.00
31-40 18.00 54.00 125.00
41-50 15.00 45.00 105.00
51-60: 60-Last Skull Squad 13.50 41.00 95.00
61-67: 66-Ghost Patrol begins (becomes Ghost Squadron #71 on), ends #112? 13.50 41.00 95.00
68,69: 68-Clipper Kirk becomes The Phantom Falcon-origin, Part 1; part 2 in #69 13.50 41.00 95.00
70-72: 70-1st app. The Phantom Falcon in costume, origin-Part 3; Capt. Wings battles Col. Kamikaze in all 11.00 32.00 75.00

Winter World #3 © Eclipse

Wireheads #1 © Fleetway

Witchcraft #3 © DC

GD25 FN65 NM94 | GD25 FN65 NM94

73-99: 80-Phantom Falcon by Larsen. 99-King of the Congo begins? 11.00 32.00 75.00
100-(12/48) 11.50 34.00 80.00
101-124: 111-Last Jane Martin. 112-Flying Saucer-c/story (1950). 115-Used in **POP**, pg. 89 10.00 30.00 65.00

NOTE: *Bondage covers are common. Captain Wings battles Sky Hag-#75, 76; ...Mr. Atlantis-#85-92; ...Mr. Pupin(Red Agent)-#98-103. Capt. Wings by* ***Elias****-#52-64, 68, 69; by* ***Lubbers****-#29-32, 70-111; by* ***Renee****-#33-46.* ***Evans*** *a-85-106, 108-111(Jane Martin); text illos-72-84.* ***Larsen*** *a-52, 59, 64, 73-77. Jane Martin by* ***Fran Hopper****-#68-84; Suicide Smith by* ***John Celardo****-#72, 74, 76, 80-104; by* ***Hollingsworth****-#68-70, 105-109, 111; Ghost Squadron by* ***Astarita****-#67-79; by* ***Maurice Whitman****-#80-111. King of the Congo by* ***Moreira****-#99, 100. Skull Squad by* ***M. Baker****-#52-60; Clipper Kirk by* ***Baker****-#60, 61; by* ***Colan****-#53; by* ***Ingels****-(some issues?). Phantom Falcon by* ***Larsen****-#73-84.* ***Elias*** *c-58-72.* ***Fawcette*** *c-3-12, 16, 17, 19, 22-33.* ***Lubbers*** *c-74-109.* ***Tuska*** *a-5.* ***Whitman*** *c-110-124.* ***Zolnerwich*** *c-15, 21.*

WINGS OF THE EAGLES, THE (See 4-Color #790)

WINKY DINK (Adventures of...)
No. 75, March, 1957 (One Shot)
Pines Comics

75-Marv Levy-c/a 4.00 11.00 22.00

WINKY DINK (See 4-Color #663)

WINNIE-THE-POOH (Also see Dynabrite Comics)
January, 1977 - No. 33, 1984 (Walt Disney)
(Winnie-The-Pooh began as Edward Bear in 1926 by Milne)
Gold Key No. 1-17/Whitman No. 18 on

1-New art 1.50
2-33: 5,12-33-New material 1.00

WINNIE WINKLE
1930 - No. 4, 1933 (52 pgs.) (B&W daily strip reprints)
Cupples & Leon Co.

1 17.00 52.00 120.00
2-4 11.00 32.00 75.00

WINNIE WINKLE (See Popular Comics & Super Comics)
1941 - No. 7, Sept-Nov, 1949
Dell Publishing Co.

Large Feature Comic 2 (1941) 14.00 42.00 140.00
4-Color 94 (1945) 13.00 40.00 90.00
4-Color 174 8.35 25.00 50.00
1(3-5/48)-Contains daily & Sunday newspaper-r from 1939-1941 7.50 22.50 45.00
2 (6-8/48) 4.70 14.00 28.00
3-7 3.60 9.00 18.00

WINTERWORLD (Eclipse)(Value: cover or less)

WIREHEADS (Fleetway/Quality)(Value: cover or less)

WISCO/KLARER COMIC BOOK (Miniature)
1948 - 1964 (24 pgs.) (3-1/2x6-3/4")
Marvel Comics/Vital Publications/Fawcett Publications

Given away by Wisco "99" Service Stations, Carnation Malted Milk, Klarer Health Wieners, Fleers Dubble Bubble Gum, Rodeo All-Meat Wieners, Perfect Potato Chips, & others; see ad in Tom Mix #21

Blackstone & the Gold Medal Mystery (1948) 4.35 13.00 26.00
Blackstone "Solves the Sealed Vault Mystery" (1950) 4.35 13.00 26.00
Blaze Carson in "The Sheriff Shoots It Out" (1950) 4.35 13.00 26.00
Captain Marvel & Billy's Big Game (r/Capt. Marvel Adv. #76) 29.00 85.00 200.00
(Prices vary widely on this book)
China Boy in "A Trip to the Zoo" #10 (1948) 1.60 4.00 8.00
Indoors-Outdoors Game Book 1.60 4.00 8.00
Jim Solar Space Sheriff in "Battle for Mars", "Between Two Worlds", "Conquers Outer Space", "The Creatures on the Comet", "Defeats the Moon Missile Men", "Encounter Creatures on Comet", "Meet the Jupiter Jumpers", "Meets the Man From Mars", "On Traffic Duty", "Outlaws of the Spaceways", "Pirates of the Planet X", "Protects Space Lanes", "Raiders From the Sun", "Ring Around Saturn", "Robots of Rhea", "The Sky Ruby", "Spacetts of the Sky", "Spidermen of Venus", "Trouble on Mercury" 3.60 9.00 18.00
Johnny Starboard & the Underseas Pirates (1948) 3.00 7.50 15.00
Kid Colt in "He Lived by His Guns" (1950) 5.85 17.50 35.00
Little Aspirin as "Crook Catcher" #2 (1950) 1.60 4.00 8.00
Little Aspirin in "Naughty But Nice" #6 (1950) 1.60 4.00 8.00
Return of the Black Phantom (not M.E. character)(Roy Dare)(1948) 2.40 6.00 12.00
Secrets of Magic 2.00 5.00 10.00
Slim Morgan "Brings Justice to Mesa City" #3 2.00 5.00 10.00
Super Rabbit(1950)-Cuts Red Tape, Stops Crime Wave! 5.00 15.00 30.00
Tex Farnum, Frontiersman (1948) 2.40 6.00 12.00
Tex Taylor in "Draw or Die, Cowpoke!" (1950) 4.20 12.50 25.00
Tex Taylor in "An Exciting Adventure at the Gold Mine" (1950) 4.20 12.50 25.00
Wacky Quacky in "All-Aboard" 1.20 3.00 6.00
When School Is Out 1.20 3.00 6.00
Willie in a "Comic-Comic Book Fall" #1 1.60 4.00 8.00
Wonder Duck "An Adventure at the Rodeo of the Fearless Quacker!" (1950) 3.00 7.50 15.00

Rare uncut version of three; includes Capt. Marvel, Tex Farnum, Black Phantom Estimated value... $300.00

WISE GUYS (See Harvey...)

WISE LITTLE HEN, THE
1935 (c.1934)(48 pgs.); 1937 (Story book)
David McKay Publ./Whitman

nn-(1935 edition w/dust jacket)(48 pgs. with color, 8-3/4x9-3/4") -Debut of Donald Duck (see Advs. of Mickey Mouse); Donald app. on cover with Wise Little Hen & Practical Pig; painted cover; same artist as the B&W's from Silly Symphony Cartoon, The Wise Little Hen (1934) (McKay)
Book only 43.00 130.00 300.00
Dust jacket only 29.00 86.00 200.00
888(1937)(9-1/2x13", 12 pgs.)(Whitman) Donald Duck app. 22.00 65.00 150.00

WITCHCRAFT (See Strange Mysteries, Super Reprint #18)
Mar-Apr, 1952 - No. 6, Mar, 1953
Avon Periodicals

1-Kubert-a; 1 pg. Check-a 41.00 122.00 285.00
2-Kubert & Check-a 29.00 86.00 200.00
3,6: 3-Lawrence-a; Kinstler inside-c 19.00 58.00 135.00
4-People cooked alive c/story 24.00 72.00 165.00
5-Kelly Freas painted-c 27.00 81.00 190.00

NOTE: ***Hollingsworth*** *a-4-6; c-4, 6.* ***McCann*** *a-3?*

WITCHCRAFT
June, 1994 - No. 3, Aug, 1994 ($2.95, limited series)
DC Comics (Vertigo)

1-3-Kaluta-c 1.20 3.00
1-Platinum edition 20.00

WITCHES TALES (Witches Western Tales #29,30)
Jan, 1951 - No. 28, Dec, 1954 (date misprinted as 4/55)
Witches Tales/Harvey Publications

1-Powell-a (1 pg.) 25.00 75.00 175.00
2-Eye injury panel 12.00 36.00 85.00
3-7,9,10 9.15 27.50 55.00
8-Eye injury panels 10.00 30.00 65.00
11-13,15,16: 12-Acid in face story 8.35 25.00 50.00
14,17-Powell/Nostrand-a. 17-Atomic disaster story 10.00 30.00 65.00
18-Nostrand-a; E.C. swipe/Shock S.S. 10.00 30.00 65.00
19-Nostrand-a; E.C. swipe/ "Glutton"; Devil-c 10.00 30.00 65.00
20-24-Nostrand-a. 21-E.C. swipe; rape story. 23-Wood E.C. swipes/Two-Fisted Tales #34 10.00 30.00 65.00
25-Nostrand-a; E.C. swipe/Mad Barber; decapitation-c 10.00 30.00 65.00

Witching Hour #84 © DC

Wolff & Byrd Counselors Of The Macabre #2 © Batton Lash

Wolverine #86 © MEG

GD25 FN65 NM94

26-28: 27-r/#6 with diff.-c. 28-r/#8 with diff.-c 7.50 22.50 45.00
NOTE: *Check a-24.* ***Elias*** *c-8, 10, 16-27.* ***Kremer*** *a-18; c-25.* ***Nostrand*** *a-17-25; 14, 17(w/Powell).* ***Palais*** *a-1, 2, 4(2), 5(2), 7-9, 12, 14, 15, 17.* ***Powell*** *a-3-7, 10, 11, 19-27. Bondage-c 1, 3, 5, 6, 8, 9.*

WITCHES TALES (Magazine)
V1#7, July, 1969 - V7#1, Feb, 1975 (52 pgs.) (B&W)
Eerie Publications

V1#7(7/69) - 9(11/69) 2.30 6.90 16.00
V2#1-6('70), V3#1-6('71) 1.70 5.00 12.00
V4#1-6('72), V5#1-6('73), V6#1-6('74), V7#1 1.70 4.20 10.00
NOTE: *Ajax/Farrell reprints in early issues.*

WITCHES' WESTERN TALES (Formerly Witches Tales)(Western Tales #31on)
No. 29, Feb, 1955 - No. 30, April, 1955
Harvey Publications

29,30-Featuring Clay Duncan & Boys' Ranch; S&K-r/from Boys' Ranch including-c. 29-Last pre-code 12.00 36.00 85.00

WITCHING HOUR (The ... later issues)
Feb-Mar, 1969 - No. 85, Oct, 1978
National Periodical Publications/DC Comics

1-Toth-a, plus Neal Adams-a (2 pgs.) 2.60 7.70 18.00
2,6: 6-Toth-a 1.70 4.20 10.00
3,5-Wrightson-a; Toth-p. 3-Last 12¢ issue 1.30 3.00 7.50
4,7,9-12: Toth-a in all 1.00 2.50 6.00
8-Toth, Neal Adams-a 1.20 2.90 7.00
13-Neal Adams-c/a, 2pgs. 1.70 4.25
14-Williamson/Garzon, Jones-a; N. Adams-c 1.70 4.25
15-20 .90 2.25
21-85: 38-(100 pgs.). 84-(44 pgs.) 1.10
NOTE: *Combined with The Unexpected with #189.* ***Neal Adams*** *c-7-11, 13, 14.* ***Alcala*** *a-24, 27, 33, 41, 43.* ***Anderson*** *a-9, 38.* ***Cardy*** *c-4, 5.* ***Kaluta*** *a-7.* ***Kane*** *a-12p.* ***Morrow*** *a-10, 13, 15, 16.* ***Nino*** *a-31, 40, 45, 47.* ***Redondo*** *a-20, 23, 24, 34, 65; c-53.* ***Reese*** *a-23.* ***Sparling*** *a-1.* ***Toth*** *a-1, 3-12, 38r.* ***Tuska*** *a-11, 12.* ***Wood*** *a-15.*

WITHIN OUR REACH (Star Reach)(Value: cover or less)

WITH THE MARINES ON THE BATTLEFRONTS OF THE WORLD
1953 (no month) - No. 2, March, 1954 (Photo covers)
Toby Press

1-John Wayne story 21.00 63.00 145.00
2-Monty Hall in #1,2 5.00 15.00 30.00

WITH THE U.S. PARATROOPS BEHIND ENEMY LINES (Also see U.S. Paratroops...; #2-6 titled U.S. Paratroops...)
1951 - No. 6, Dec, 1952
Avon Periodicals

1-Wood-c & inside f/c 11.50 34.00 80.00
2-Kinstler-c & inside f/c only 6.70 20.00 40.00
3-6: 6-Kinstler-c & inside f/c only 5.35 16.00 32.00
NOTE: ***Kinstler*** *c-2, 4-6.*

WITNESS, THE (Also see Amazing Mysteries, Captain America #71, Ideal #4, Marvel Mystery #92 & Mystic #7)
Sept, 1948
Marvel Comics (MjMe)

1(Scarce)-Rico-c? 81.00 242.00 565.00

WITTY COMICS
1945 - No. 7, 1945
Irwin H. Rubin Publ./Chicago Nite Life News No. 2

1-The Pioneer, Junior Patrol; war-c 11.00 32.00 75.00
2-The Pioneer, Junior Patrol 7.50 22.50 45.00
3-7-Skyhawk 6.35 19.00 38.00

WIZARD OF FOURTH STREET, THE (Dark Horse)(Value: cover or less)

WIZARD OF OZ (See Classics Illustrated Jr. 535, Dell Jr. Treasury No. 5, First Comics Graphic Novel, 4-Color No. 1308, Marvelous..., & Marvel Treasury of Oz)

WOLFF & BYRD, COUNSELORS OF THE MACABRE
May, 1994 - Present ($2.50, B&W)
Exhibit A Press

1,2 1.00 2.50

GD25 FN65 NM94

WOLF GAL (See Al Capp's...)

WOLFMAN, THE (See Movie Classics)

WOLFPACK (Marvel)(Value: cover or less)

WOLVERINE (See Alpha Flight, Daredevil #196, 249, Ghost Rider; Wolverine; Punisher, Havok &..., Incredible Hulk #180, Incredible Hulk &..., Kitty Pryde And..., Marvel Comics Presents, Power Pack, Punisher and..., Spider-Man vs... & X-Men #94)

WOLVERINE
Sept, 1982 - No. 4, Dec, 1982 (Mini-series)
Marvel Comics Group

1-Frank Miller-c/a(p) in all 4.30 13.00 30.00
2,3 2.90 8.60 20.00
4 3.30 9.90 23.00
TPB 1(7/87, $4.95)-Reprints #1-4 with new Miller-c 1.30 3.10 7.50
TPB nn-2nd printing ($9.95)-r/#1-4 1.65 4.00 10.00

WOLVERINE
Nov, 1988 - Present ($1.50/$1.75, Baxter paper)
Marvel Comics

1-Buscema a-1-16, c-1-10; Williamson a(i)-1,4-8 3.30 10.00 23.00
2 1.70 5.10 12.00
3-5: 4-Barry Smith back-c 1.30 3.00 8.00
6-9: 6-McFarlane back-c. 7,8-Hulk app. 1.30 3.10 7.50
10-1st battle with Sabretooth (before Wolverine had his claws) 3.60 10.75 25.00
11-16: 11-New costume 1.00 2.50 6.00
17-20: 17-Byrne-c/a(p) begins, ends #23 1.60 4.00
21-30: 24,25,27-Jim Lee-c. 26-Begin $1.75-c 1.20 3.00
31-40,44,47 .80 2.00
41-Sabretooth claims to be Wolverine's father; Cable cameo 1.10 3.00 6.50
41-Gold 2nd printing ($1.75) .65 1.60
42-Sabretooth, Cable & Nick Fury app.; Sabretooth proven not to be Wolverine's father .90 1.80 4.50
42-Gold ink 2nd printing ($1.75) .70 1.75
43-Sabretooth cameo (2 panels); saga ends 1.60 4.00
45,46-Sabretooth-c/stories 1.40 3.50
48,49-Sabretooth app. 48-Begin 3 part Weapon X sequel 1.00 2.50
50-($2.50, 64 pgs.)-Die cut-c; Wolverine back to old yellow costume; Forge, Cyclops, Jubilee, Jean Grey & Nick Fury app. .80 1.60 4.00
51-74,76-80: 51-Sabretooth-c & app. 54-Shatterstar(from X-Force) app. 55-Gambit, Jubilee, Sunfire-c/story. 55-57,73-Gambit app. 58,59-Terror, Inc. x-over. 60-64-Sabre-tooth storyline (60,62,64-c) .70 1.75
75-($3.95, 68 pgs.)-Wolverine hologram on-c 1.00 2.00 5.00
81-84,86,88-91: 81-Begin $1.95-c; bound-in card sheet .80 2.00
85-($2.50)-Newsstand edition 1.00 2.50
85-($3.50)-Collectors edition 1.40 3.50
87,88-($1.95)-Deluxe edition .80 2.00
87-($1.50)-Regular edition 1.50
Annual nn (1990, $4.50, squarebound, 52 pgs.)-The Jungle Adventure; Simonson scripts; Mignola-c/a 1.80 4.50
Annual 2 (12/90, $4.95, squarebound, 52 pgs.)-Bloodlust 1.00 2.00 5.00
Annual nn (#3, 8/91, $5.95, 68 pgs.)-Rahne of Terror; Cable & The New Mutants app.; Andy Kubert-c/a (2nd print exists) 1.00 2.50 6.00
...Battles the Incredible Hulk nn (1989, $4.95, squarebound, 52 pg.)-r/Incredible Hulk #180,181 1.00 2.00 5.00
...: Blood Hungry nn (1993, $6.95, 68 pgs.)-Kieth-r/Marvel Comics Presents #85-92 w/ new Kieth-c 1.20 3.00 7.00
...: Bloody Choices nn (1993, $7.95, 68 pgs.)-r/Graphic Novel; Nick Fury app. 1.30 3.25 8.00
...: Global Jeopardy 1 (12/93, $2.95, one-shot)-Embossed-c; Sub-Mariner, Zabu, Ka-Zar, Shanna & Wolverine app.; produced in cooperation with World Wildlife Fund 1.20 3.00

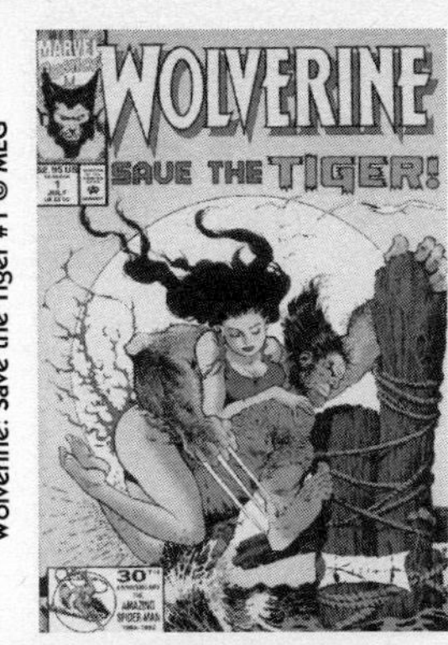

Wolverine: Save the Tiger #1 © MEG

Wolverine and the Punisher #1 © MEG

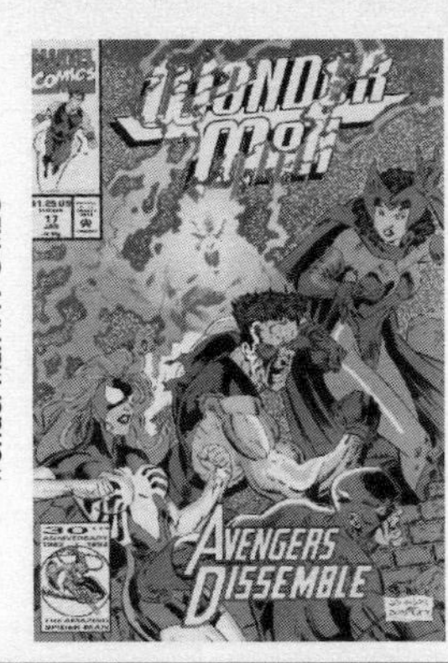

Wonder Man #17 © MEG

GD25 FN65 NM94

...: Inner Fury nn (1992, $5.95, 52 pgs.)-Sienkiewicz-c/a 1.00 2.50 6.00
...: Save the Tiger 1 (7/92, $2.95, 84 pgs.)-Reprints Wolverine stories from Marvel Comics Presents #1-10 w/new Kieth-c 1.20 3.00
...Typhoid's Kiss (6/94, $6.95)-r/Wolverine stories from Marvel Comics Presents #109-116 1.20 2.90 7.00
...Evilution (9/94, $5.95) 1.00 2.50 6.00

NOTE: *Austin c-3i. Bolton c(back)-5. Buscema 25, 27p. Byrne a-17-22p, 23; c-1(back), 17-22, 23p. Colan a-24. Andy Kubert c/a-51. Jim Lee c-24, 25, 27. Silvestri a(p)-31-43, 45, 46, 48-50, 52, 53, 55-57; c-31-42p, 43, 45p, 46p, 48, 49p, 50p, 52p, 53p, 55-57p. Stroman a-44p; c-60p. Williamson a-3i; c(i)-1, 3-6.*

WOLVERINE AND THE PUNISHER: DAMAGING EVIDENCE
Oct, 1993 - No. 3, Dec, 1993 ($2.00, mini-series)
Marvel Comics

1-3: 2,3-Indicia says "The Punisher and Wolverine..." .80 2.00

WOLVERINE SAGA
Sept, 1989 - No. 4, Mid-Dec, 1989 ($3.95, mini-series, 52 pgs.)
Marvel Comics

1-Gives history; Liefeld/Austin-c (front & back) 1.00 2.00 5.00
2-4: 2-Romita, Jr./Austin-c. 4-Kaluta-c 1.60 4.00

WOMAN OF THE PROMISE, THE
1950 (General Distr.) (32 pgs.) (paper cover)
Catechetical Guild

nn 3.00 7.50 15.00

WOMEN IN LOVE (A Feature Presentation #5)
Aug, 1949 - No. 4, Feb, 1950
Fox Features Synd./Hero Books

1 15.00 45.00 105.00
2-Kamen/Feldstein-c 11.50 34.00 80.00
3 8.35 25.00 50.00
4-Wood-a 11.00 32.00 75.00

WOMEN IN LOVE (Thrilling Romances for Adults)
Winter, 1952 (25¢, 100 pgs.)
Ziff-Davis Publishing Co.

nn-(Scarce)-Kinstler-a; painted-c 34.00 103.00 240.00

WOMEN OUTLAWS (My Love Memories #9 on)(Also see Red Circle)
July, 1948 - No. 8, Sept, 1949
Fox Features Syndicate

1-Used in **SOTI**, illo "Giving children an image of American womanhood"; negligee panels 39.00 118.00 275.00
2-Spanking panel 34.00 103.00 240.00
3-Kamenish-a 31.00 94.00 220.00
4-8 23.00 70.00 160.00
nn(nd)-Contains Cody of the Pony Express; same cover as #7 17.00 52.00 120.00

WOMEN TO LOVE
No date (1953)
Realistic

nn-(Scarce)-Reprints Complete Romance #1; c-/Avon paperback #165 25.00 75.00 175.00

WONDER BOY (Formerly Terrific Comics) (See Blue Bolt, Bomber Comics & Samson)
No. 17, May, 1955 - No. 18, July, 1955 (Code approved)
Ajax/Farrell Publ.

17-Phantom Lady app. Bakerish-c/a 20.00 60.00 140.00
18-Phantom Lady app. 19.00 57.00 130.00

NOTE: *Phantom Lady not by Matt Baker.*

WONDER COMICS (Wonderworld #3 on)
May, 1939 - No. 2, June, 1939 (68 pgs.)
Fox Features Syndicate

GD25 FN65 VF82 NM94

1-(Scarce)-Wonder Man only app. by Will Eisner; Dr. Fung (by Powell), K-51 begins; Bob Kane-a; Eisner-c 725.00 2175.00 3987.00 5800.00
(Estimated up to 70 total copies exist, 3 in NM/Mint)

GD25 FN65 NM94

2-(Scarce)-Yarko the Great, Master Magician (see Samson) by Eisner begins; 'Spark' Stevens by Bob Kane, Patty O'Day, Tex Mason app. Lou Fine's 1st-c; Fine-a (2 pgs.); Yarko-c (Wonder Man-c #1) 300.00 900.00 2100.00

WONDER COMICS
May, 1944 - No. 20, Oct, 1948
Great/Nedor/Better Publications

1-The Grim Reaper & Spectro, the Mind Reader begin; Hitler/Hirohito bondage-c 61.00 182.00 425.00
2-Origin The Grim Reaper; Super Sleuths begin, end #8,17 36.00 107.00 250.00
3-5 31.00 92.00 215.00
6-10: 6-Flag-c. 8-Last Spectro. 9-Wonderman begins 26.00 78.00 180.00
11-14: 11-Dick Devens, King of Futuria begins, ends #14. 11,12-Ingels-c & splash pg. 29.00 86.00 200.00
15-Tara begins (origin), ends #20 34.00 103.00 240.00
16,18: 16-Spectro app.; last Grim Reaper. 18-The Silver Knight begins 29.00 86.00 200.00
17-Wonderman with Frazetta panels; Jill Trent with all Frazetta inks 31.00 94.00 220.00
19-Frazetta panels 29.00 86.00 200.00
20-Most of Silver Knight by Frazetta 34.00 103.00 240.00

NOTE: *Ingels c-11, 12. Roussos a-19. Schomburg (Xela) c-1-10; (airbrush)-13-20. Bondage c-12, 13, 15. Cover features: Grim Reaper #1-8; Wonder Man #9-15; Tara #16-20.*

WONDER DUCK (See Wisco)
Sept, 1949 - No. 3, Mar, 1950
Marvel Comics (CDS)

1-Funny animal 10.00 30.00 70.00
2,3 8.35 25.00 50.00

WONDERFUL ADVENTURES OF PINOCCHIO, THE (See Movie Comics & Walt Disney Showcase #48)
No. 3, April, 1982 (Walt Disney)
Whitman Publishing Co.

3-(Continuation of Movie Comics?); r/FC #92 1.20 3.00

WONDERFUL WORLD OF DUCKS (See Golden Picture Story Book)
1975
Colgate Palmolive Co.

1-Mostly-r 1.00

WONDERFUL WORLD OF THE BROTHERS GRIMM (See Movie Comics)

WONDERLAND COMICS
Summer, 1945 - No. 9, Feb-Mar, 1947
Feature Publications/Prize

1-Alex in Wonderland begins; Howard Post-c 8.35 25.00 50.00
2-Howard Post-c/a(2) 5.00 15.00 30.00
3-9: 3,4-Post-c 4.00 10.00 20.00

WONDER MAN (Marvel, 1986 & 1991)(Value: cover or less)(See The Avengers #9, 151)

WONDERS OF ALADDIN, THE (See 4-Color #1255)

WONDER WOMAN (See Adventure Comics #459, All-Star Comics, Brave & the Bold, DC Comics Presents, Justice League of America, Legend of..., Power Record Comics, Sensation Comics, Super Friends and World's Finest Comics #244)

WONDER WOMAN
Summer, 1942 - No. 329, Feb, 1986
National Periodical Publications/All-American Publ./DC Comics

GD25 FN65 VF82 NM94

1-Origin Wonder Woman retold (more detailed than All-Star #8); H. G. Peter-c/a begins 1000.00 3000.00 5500.00 8000.00
(Estimated up to 150 total copies exist, 8 in NM/Mint)
1-Reprint, Oversize 13-1/2x10". **WARNING:** This comic is an exact reprint of the original except for its size. DC published it in 1974 with a second cover titling it as a Famous First

Wonder Woman #247 © DC

Wonder Woman #86 (2nd series) © DC

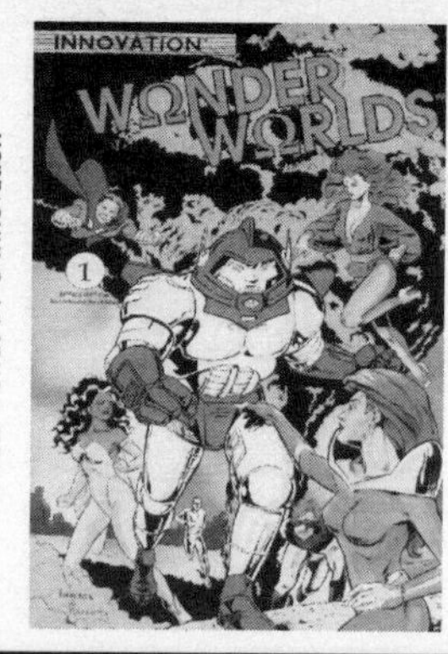

Wonder Worlds #1 © Innovation

Edition. There have been many reported cases of the outer cover being removed and the interior sold as the original edition. The reprint with the new outer cover removed is practically worthless. See Famous First Edition for value.

	GD25	FN65	NM94
2-Origin/1st app. Mars; Duke of Deception app.	200.00	600.00	1400.00
3	129.00	385.00	900.00
4,5: 5-1st Dr. Psycho app.	100.00	300.00	700.00
6-10: 6-1st Cheetah app. 10-Invasion from Saturn	82.00	246.00	575.00
11-20	61.00	182.00	425.00
21-30: 23-Story from Wonder Woman's childhood	52.00	156.00	365.00
31-40: 38-Last H.G. Peter-c	39.00	116.00	270.00
41-44,46-49: 49-Used in **SOTI**, pgs. 234,236; last 52 pg. issue	27.00	81.00	190.00
45-Origin retold	54.00	160.00	375.00
50-(44 pgs.)-Used in **POP**, pg. 97	25.00	75.00	175.00
51-60: 60-New logo	19.00	57.00	130.00
61-72: 62-Origin of W.W. i.d. 64-Story about 3-D movies. 70-1st Angle Man app. 72-Last pre-code (2/55)	16.50	50.00	115.00
73-90: 80-Origin The Invisible Plane. 89-Flying saucer-c/story	11.00	34.00	90.00
91-94,96,97,99: 97-Last H. G. Peter-a	7.00	21.00	55.00
95-A-Bomb-c	8.00	23.00	60.00
98-New origin & new art team (Andru & Esposito) begin (5/58); origin W.W. id w/new facts	8.00	24.00	65.00
100-(8/58)	10.00	29.00	78.00
101-104,106-110: 107-1st advs. of Wonder Girl; 1st Merboy; tells how Wonder Woman won her costume	6.00	19.00	50.00
105-(Scarce, 4/59)-W. W.'s secret origin; W. W. appears as girl (no costume yet) (called Wonder Girl - see DC Super-Stars #1)	28.00	83.00	250.00
111-120	5.00	14.00	38.00
121-126: 122-1st app. Wonder Tot. 124-1st app. Wonder Woman Family. 126-Last 10¢ issue	3.00	9.00	23.00
127-130: 128-Origin The Invisible Plane retold. 129-2nd app. Wonder Woman Family (#133 is 3rd app.)	2.00	5.00	12.00
131-150: 132-Flying saucer-c	1.30	3.00	8.00
151-155,157,158,160-170 (1967): 151-Wonder Girl solo issue	1.20	2.90	7.00
156-(8/65)-Early mention of a comic book shop & comic collecting; mentions DCs selling for $100 a copy	1.20	2.90	7.00
159-Origin retold (1/66); 1st S.A. origin?	1.30	3.00	8.00
171-178	1.00	2.00	5.00
179-195: 179-Wears no costume to issue #203. 180-Death of Steve Trevor. 195-Wood inks		1.60	4.00
196 (52 pgs.)-Origin-r/All-Star #8 (6 out of 9 pgs.)		1.80	4.50
197,198 (52 pgs.)-Reprints		1.80	4.50
199,200 (5-6/72)-Jeff Jones-c; 52 pgs.	.90	2.30	5.50
201-210: 201,202-Catwoman app. 204-Return to old costume; death of I Ching. 202-Fafhrd & The Grey Mouser debut		.70	1.75
211-230,233-240: 211,214-(100 pgs.). 212-The Cavalier app. 217-(68 pgs.). 220-N. Adams assist. 223-Steve Trevor revived as Steve Howard & learns W.W.'s I.D. 228-Both Wonder Women team up & new World War II stories begin, end #243. 237-Origin retold. 243-Both W. Women team-up again			1.10
231,232-JSA guest star		.70	1.75
241-266,269-280,284-286: 241-Intro Bouncer. 247-249-(44 pgs.). 248-Steve Trevor Howard dies. 249-Hawkgirl app. 250-Origin/1st app. Orana, the new W. Woman. 251-Orana dies. 269-Last Wood a(i) for DC? (7/80). 271-Huntress & 3rd Life of Steve Trevor begin			1.10
267,268-Re-intro Animal Man (5/80 & 6/80)	2.40	7.30	17.00
281-283: Joker covers & stories in Huntress back-ups		1.30	3.25
287-New Teen Titans x-over		.70	1.70
288-299,301-328: 288-New costume & logo. 291-293-Three part epic with Super-Heroines			1.10
300-($1.50, 76 pgs.)-Anniv. iss.; Giffen-a; New Teen Titans, JLA & G.A. Wonder Woman app.; 1st app. Lyta Trevor who becomes Fury in All-Star Squadron #25; W.W. & Steve Trevor revealed as married		.70	1.70
329-Double size		.70	1.70
Pizza Hut Giveaways (12/77)-Reprints #60,62			1.00

NOTE: ***Andru/Esposito*** *c-66-160(most).* ***Colan*** *a-288-305p; c-288-290p.* ***Giffen*** *a-300p.* ***Grell*** *c-217.* ***Kaluta*** *c-297.* ***Gil Kane*** *c-294p, 303-305, 307, 312, 314.* ***Miller*** *c-298p.* ***Morrow*** *c-233.* ***Nasser*** *a-232p; c-231p, 232p.* ***Bob Oskner*** *c(i)-39-65(most).* ***Perez*** *c-283p, 284p.* ***Spiegle*** *a-312.* ***Staton*** *a(p)-241, 271-287, 289, 290, 294-299; c(p)-241, 245, 246. Huntress back-up stories 271-287, 289, 290, 294-299, 301-321.*

WONDER WOMAN
Feb, 1987 - Present (.75/$1.00/$1.25)
DC Comics

	GD25	FN65	NM94
1-New origin; Perez-c/a begins		1.20	3.00
2-20: 8-Origin Cheetah. 12,13-Millennium x-over. 18,26-Free 16 pg. story			1.25
21-49,51-62: 24-Last Perez-a; scripts continue thru #62. 60-Vs. Lobo; last Perez-c. 62-Last $1.00-c			1.00
50-($1.50, 52 pgs.)-New Titans, Justice League			1.50
63-81: 63-New direction & Bolland-c begin; Deathstroke story continued from Wonder Woman Special #1			1.25
82-90: 82-Begin $1.50-c. 88-Superman-c & app. 90-(9/94)			1.50
0,91-96: 0-(10/94). 91-(11/94)			1.50
Annual 1,2: 1 ('88, $1.50)-Art Adams-a(p&i). 2 ('89, $2.00, 68 pgs.)-All women artists issue; Perez-c(i)		.80	2.00
Annual 3 (1992, $2.50, 68 pgs.)-Quesada-c(p)		1.00	2.50
Special 1 (1992, $1.75, 52 pgs.)-Deathstroke-c/story continued in Wonder Woman #63		.80	2.00

WONDER WOMAN SPECTACULAR (See DC Special Series #9)

WONDER WORKER OF PERU
No date (16 pgs.) (B&W) (5x7")
Catechetical Guild (Giveaway)

	GD25	FN65	NM94
nn	3.60	9.00	18.00

WONDERWORLD COMICS (Formerly Wonder Comics)
No. 3, July, 1939 - No. 33, Jan, 1942
Fox Features Syndicate

	GD25	FN65	NM94
3-Intro The Flame by Fine; Dr. Fung (Powell-a), K-51 (Powell-a?), & Yarko the Great, Master Magician (Eisner-a) continues; Eisner/Fine-c	300.00	900.00	2100.00
4	100.00	300.00	700.00
5-10	86.00	257.00	600.00
11-Origin The Flame	107.00	321.00	750.00
12-20: 13-Dr. Fung ends	54.00	160.00	375.00
21-Origin The Black Lion & Cub	50.00	150.00	350.00
22-27: 22,25-Dr. Fung app.	38.00	115.00	265.00
28-Origin & 1st app. U.S. Jones (8/41); Lu-Nar, the Moon Man begins	52.00	156.00	365.00
29,31-33: 32-Hitler-c	32.00	96.00	225.00
30-Origin Flame Girl	62.00	186.00	435.00

NOTE: *Spies at War by* ***Eisner*** *in #13, 17. Yarko by* ***Eisner*** *in #3-11.* ***Eisner*** *text illos-3.* ***Lou Fine*** *a-3-11; c-3-13, 15; text illos-4.* ***Nordling*** *a-4-14.* ***Powell*** *a-3-12.* ***Tuska*** *a-5-9. Bondage-c 14, 15, 28, 31, 32. Cover features: The Flame-#3, 5-31; U.S. Jones-#32, 33.*

WONDERWORLDS
1992 ($3.50, color, squarebound, 100 pgs.)
Innovation Publishing

	GD25	FN65	NM94
1-Rebound super-hero comics, contents may vary; Hero Alliance, Terraformers, etc.		1.40	3.50

WOODSY OWL (See March of Comics #395)
Nov, 1973 - No. 10, Feb, 1976
Gold Key

	GD25	FN65	NM94
1		1.60	4.00
2-10		.80	2.00

WOODY WOODPECKER (Walter Lantz... #73 on?)(See Dell Giants for annuals) (Also see The Funnies, Jolly Jingles, Kite Fun Book, New Funnies)
No. 169, 10/47 - No. 72, 5-7/62; No. 73, 10/62 - No. 201, 4/84 (nn 192)
Dell Publishing Co./Gold Key No. 73-187/Whitman No. 188 on

	GD25	FN65	NM94
4-Color 169-Drug turns Woody into a Mr. Hyde	16.00	48.00	110.00

Woody Woodpecker Adventures #1 © Walter Lantz Prod.

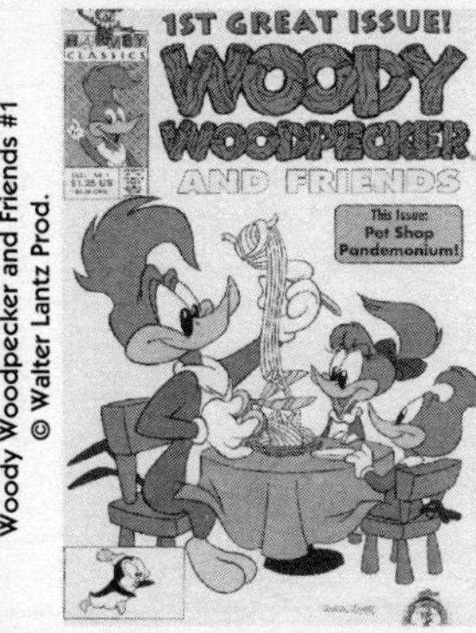

Woody Woodpecker and Friends #1 © Walter Lantz Prod.

World of Archie #8 © AP

	GD25	FN65	NM94
4-Color 188	11.50	34.00	80.00
4-Color 202,232,249,264,288	7.50	22.50	45.00
4-Color 305,336,350	4.70	14.00	28.00
4-Color 364,374,390,405,416,431('52)	4.00	11.00	22.00
16 (12-1/52-53) - 30('55)	2.80	7.00	14.00
31-50	2.40	6.00	12.00
51-72 (Last Dell)	1.80	4.50	9.00
73-75 (Giants, 84 pgs., Gold Key)	3.75	11.25	30.00
76-80	1.80	4.50	9.00
81-100	1.00	2.50	6.00
101-120		1.80	4.50
121-191,193-201 (No #192)		.80	2.00
Christmas Parade 1(11/68-Giant)(G.K.)	4.00	10.00	20.00
Clover Stamp-Newspaper Boy Contest('56)-9 pg. story-(Giveaway)	3.60	9.00	18.00
In Chevrolet Wonderland(1954-Giveaway)(Western Publ.)-20 pgs., full story line; Chilly Willy app.	8.35	25.00	50.00
...Meets Scotty McTape(1953-Scotch Tape giveaway)-16 pgs., full size	7.50	22.50	45.00
Summer Fun 1(6/66-G.K.)(84 pgs.)	3.75	11.25	30.00

NOTE: *15¢ editions exist. Reprints-No. 92, 102, 103, 105, 106, 124, 125, 152, 153, 157, 162, 165, 194(1/3)-200(1/3).*

WOODY WOODPECKER (See Comic Album #5,9,13, Dell Giant #24, 40, 54, Dell Giants, The Funnies, Golden Comics Digest #1, 3, 5, 8, 15, 16, 20, 24, 32, 37, 44, March of Comics #16, 34, 85, 93, 109, 124, 139, 158, 177, 184, 203, 222, 239, 249, 261, 420, 454, 466, 478, New Funnies & Super Book #12, 24)

WOODY WOODPECKER (Harvey)(Value: cover or less)

WOODY WOODPECKER ADVENTURES (Harvey)(Value: cover or less)

WOODY WOODPECKER AND FRIENDS (Harvey)(Value: cover or less)

WOOLWORTH'S CHRISTMAS STORY BOOK
1952 - 1954 (16 pgs., paper-c) (See Jolly Christmas Book)
Promotional Publ. Co.(Western Printing Co.)

	GD25	FN65	NM94
nn	4.00	11.00	22.00

NOTE: *1952 issue-Marv Levy c/a.*

WOOLWORTH'S HAPPY TIME CHRISTMAS BOOK
1952 (Christmas giveaway, 36 pgs.)
F. W. Woolworth Co.(Whitman Publ. Co.)

	GD25	FN65	NM94
nn	4.00	11.00	22.00

WORD WARRIORS (Also see Quest for Dreams Lost)
1987 ($1.50, B&W)(Proceeds donated to help illiteracy)
Literacy Volunteers of Chicago

	GD25	FN65	NM94
1-Jon Sable by Grell, Ms. Tree, Streetwolf; Chaykin-c			1.50

WORLD AROUND US, THE (Illustrated Story of...)
Sept, 1958 - No. 36, Oct, 1961 (25¢)
Gilberton Publishers (Classics Illustrated)

	GD25	FN65	NM94
1-Dogs; Evans-a	4.70	14.00	28.00
2-4: 2-Indians; Check-a. 3-Horses; L. B. Cole-c. 4-Railroads; L. B. Cole-a (5 pgs.)	4.70	14.00	28.00
5-Space; Ingels-a	6.35	19.00	38.00
6-The F.B.I.; Disbrow, Evans, Ingels-a	5.00	15.00	30.00
7-Pirates; Disbrow, Ingels, Kinstler-a	5.85	17.50	35.00
8-Flight; Evans, Ingels, Crandall-a	5.00	15.00	30.00
9-Army; Disbrow, Ingels, Orlando-a	4.70	14.00	28.00
10-13: 10-Navy; Disbrow, Kinstler-a. 11-Marine Corps. 12-Coast Guard; Ingels-a (9 pgs.). 13-Air Force; L.B. Cole-c	4.00	12.00	24.00
14-French Revolution; Crandall, Evans, Kinstler-a	6.70	20.00	40.00
15-Prehistoric Animals; Al Williamson-a, 6 & 10 pgs. plus Morrow-a	7.00	21.00	42.00
16-18: 16-Crusades; Kinstler-a. 17-Festivals; Evans, Crandall-a. 18-Great Scientists; Crandall, Evans, Torres, Williamson, Morrow-a	5.35	16.00	32.00
19-Jungle; Crandall, Williamson, Morrow-a	7.00	21.00	42.00
20-Communications; Crandall, Evans, Torres-a	7.50	22.50	45.00
21-American Presidents; Crandall/Evans, Morrow-a	5.85	17.50	35.00
22-Boating; Morrow-a	4.00	11.00	22.00
23-Great Explorers; Crandall, Evans-a	4.70	14.00	28.00
24-Ghosts; Morrow, Evans-a	5.85	17.50	35.00
25-Magic; Evans, Morrow-a	5.85	17.50	35.00
26-The Civil War	7.00	21.00	42.00
27-Mountains (High Advs.); Crandall/Evans, Morrow, Torres-a	5.85	17.50	35.00
28-Whaling; Crandall, Evans, Morrow, Torres, Wildey-a; L.B. Cole-c	5.00	15.00	30.00
29-Vikings; Crandall, Evans, Torres, Morrow-a	6.35	19.00	38.00
30-Undersea Adventure; Crandall/Evans, Kirby, Morrow, Torres-a	7.00	21.00	42.00
31-Hunting; Crandall/Evans, Ingels, Kinstler, Kirby-a	5.00	15.00	30.00
32,33: 32-For Gold & Glory; Morrow, Kirby, Crandall, Evans-a. 33-Famous Teens; Torres, Crandall, Evans-a	5.35	16.00	32.00
34-36: 34-Fishing; Crandall/Evans-a. 35-Spies; Kirby, Morrow?, Evans-a. 36-Fight for Life (Medicine); Kirby-a	4.70	14.00	28.00

NOTE: See Classics Illustrated Special Edition. Another *World Around Us* issue entitled *The Sea* had been prepared in 1962 but was never published in the U.S. It was published in the British/European *World Around Us* series. Those series then continued with seven additional WAU titles not in the U.S. series.

WORLD FAMOUS HEROES MAGAZINE
Oct, 1941 - No. 4, Apr, 1942 (A comic book)
Comic Corp. of America (Centaur)

	GD25	FN65	NM94
1-Gustavson-c; Lubbers, Glanzman-a; Davy Crockett, Paul Revere, Lewis & Clark, John Paul Jones stories; Flag-c	79.00	235.00	550.00
2-Lou Gehrig life story; Lubbers-a	39.00	118.00	275.00
3,4-Lubbers-a. 4-Wild Bill Hickok story; 2 pg. Marlene Dietrich story	33.00	100.00	230.00

WORLD FAMOUS STORIES
1945
Croyden Publishers

	GD25	FN65	NM94
1-Ali Baba, Hansel & Gretel, Rip Van Winkle, Mid-Summer Night's Dream	10.00	30.00	60.00

WORLD IS HIS PARISH, THE
1953 (15¢)
George A. Pflaum

	GD25	FN65	NM94
nn-The story of Pope Pius XII	4.00	11.00	22.00

WORLD OF ADVENTURE (Walt Disney's...)(TV)
April, 1963 - No. 3, Oct, 1963 (All 12¢)
Gold Key

	GD25	FN65	NM94
1-3-Disney TV characters; Savage Sam, Johnny Shiloh, Capt. Nemo, The Mooncussers	1.20	3.00	6.00

WORLD OF ARCHIE, THE (See Archie Giant Series Mag. #148, 151, 156, 160, 165, 171, 177, 182, 188, 193, 200, 208, 213, 225, 232, 237, 244, 249, 456, 461, 468, 473, 480, 485, 492, 497, 504, 509, 516, 521, 532, 543, 554, 565, 574, 587, 599, 612, 627)

WORLD OF ARCHIE
Aug, 1992 - Present ($1.25)
Archie Comics

	GD25	FN65	NM94
1-14: 9-Neon ink-c			1.25

WORLD OF FANTASY
May, 1956 - No. 19, Aug, 1959
Atlas Comics (CPC No. 1-15/ZPC No. 16-19)

	GD25	FN65	NM94
1	24.00	73.00	170.00
2-Williamson-a (4 pgs.)	16.00	48.00	110.00
3-Sid Check, Roussos-a	11.50	34.00	80.00
4-7	10.00	30.00	70.00
8-Matt Fox, Orlando, Berg-a	11.50	34.00	80.00
9-Krigstein-a	10.00	30.00	70.00
10,12-15	9.15	27.50	55.00
11-Torres-a	10.00	30.00	60.00
16-Williamson-a (4 pgs.); Ditko, Kirby-a	11.50	34.00	80.00

World of Krypton #1 © DC

Worlds Collide #1 © DC

World's Finest #2 © DC

GD25 FN65 NM94

17-19-Ditko, Kirby-a 11.50 34.00 80.00

NOTE: ***Ayers*** *a-3.* ***B. Baily*** *a-4.* ***Berg*** *a-5, 6, 8.* ***Brodsky*** *c-3.* ***Check*** *a-3.* ***Ditko*** *a-17, 19.* ***Everett*** *a-2; c-4-7, 9, 12, 13.* ***Forte*** *a-4.* ***Infantino*** *a-14.* ***Kirby*** *c-15, 17-19.* ***Krigstein*** *a-9.* ***Maneely*** *c-2, 14.* ***Mooney*** *a-14.* ***Morrow*** *a-7.* ***Orlando*** *a-8, 13, 14.* ***Pakula*** *a-9.* ***Powell*** *a-4, 6.* ***R.Q. Sale*** *a-3, 9.* ***Severin*** *c-1.*

WORLD OF GIANT COMICS, THE (See Archie All-Star Specials under Archie Comics)

WORLD OF GINGER FOX, THE (Comico)(Value: cover or less)

WORLD OF JUGHEAD, THE (See Archie Giant Series Mag. #9, 14, 19, 24, 30, 136, 143, 149, 152, 157, 161, 166, 172, 178, 183, 189, 194, 202, 209, 215, 227, 233, 239, 245, 251, 457, 463, 469, 475, 481, 487, 493, 499, 505, 511, 517, 523, 531, 542, 553, 564, 577, 590, 602)

WORLD OF KRYPTON, THE (World of...#3; see Superman #248)
7/79 - No. 3, 9/79; 12/87 - No. 4, 3/88 (Both are mini-series)
DC Comics, Inc.

1-3 (1979, 40¢; 1st comic book mini-series): 1-Jor-El marries Lara. 3-Baby Superman sent to Earth; Krypton explodes; Mon-el app. 1.00
1-4 (75¢)-Byrne scripts; Byrne/Simonson-c 1.00

WORLD OF METROPOLIS (DC)(Value: cover or less)

WORLD OF MYSTERY
June, 1956 - No. 7, July, 1957
Atlas Comics (GPI)

1-Torres, Orlando-a; Powell-a? 24.00 73.00 170.00
2-Woodish-a 10.00 30.00 65.00
3-Torres, Davis, Ditko-a 11.50 34.00 80.00
4-Pakula, Powell-a 12.00 36.00 85.00
5,7: 5-Orlando-a 10.00 30.00 60.00
6-Williamson/Mayo-a (4 pgs.); Ditko-a; Crandall text illo 12.00 36.00 85.00

NOTE: ***Brodsky*** *c-2.* ***Colan*** *a-7.* ***Everett*** *c-1, 3.* ***Pakula*** *a-4, 6.* ***Romita*** *a-2.* ***Severin*** *c-7.*

WORLD OF SMALLVILLE (DC)(Value: cover or less)

WORLD OF SUSPENSE
April, 1956 - No. 8, July, 1957
Atlas News Co.

1 22.00 67.00 155.00
2-Ditko-a (4 pgs.) 11.50 34.00 80.00
3,7-Williamson-a in both (4 pgs. each); #7-with Mayo 11.50 34.00 80.00
4-6,8 10.00 30.00 60.00

NOTE: ***Berg*** *a-6.* ***Cameron*** *a-2.* ***Ditko*** *a-2.* ***Drucker*** *a-1.* ***Everett*** *a-1, 5; c-6.* ***Heck*** *a-5.* ***Maneely*** *a-1; c-1-3.* ***Orlando*** *a-5.* ***Powell*** *a-6.* ***Reinman*** *a-4.* ***Roussos*** *a-6.* ***Shores*** *a-1.*

WORLD OF WHEELS (Formerly Dragstrip Hotrodders)
No. 17, Oct, 1967 - No. 32, June, 1970
Charlton Comics

17-20-Features Ken King 1.30 3.25 8.00
21-32-Features Ken King 1.00 2.00 5.00
Modern Comics Reprint 23(1978) .80 2.00

WORLD OF WOOD (Eclipse)(Value: cover or less)

WORLD'S BEST COMICS (World's Finest Comics #2 on)
Spring, 1941 (Cardboard-c)(DC's 6th annual format comic)
National Per. Publications (100 pgs.) GD25 FN65 VF82 NM94

1-The Batman, Superman, Crimson Avenger, Johnny Thunder, The King, Young Dr. Davis, Zatara, Lando, Man of Magic, & Red, White & Blue begin; Superman, Batman & Robin covers begin (inside-c is blank); Fred Ray-c; 15¢ cover price 1125.00 3375.00 6187.00 9000.00
(Estimated up to 185 total copies exist, 6 in NM/Mint)

WORLDS BEYOND (Stories of Weird Adventure)(Worlds of Fear #2 on)
Nov, 1951
Fawcett Publications GD25 FN65 NM94

1-Powell, Bailey-a; Moldoff-c 22.00 65.00 150.00

WORLDS COLLIDE
July, 1994 ($2.50)
DC Comics

GD25 FN65 NM94

1-($2.50, 52 pgs.) 1.00 2.50
1-($3.95, 52 pgs.)-Polybagged w/vinyl clings 1.60 4.00

WORLD'S FAIR COMICS (See New York...)

WORLD'S FINEST (DC, 1990)(Value: cover or less)(Also see Legends of the...)

WORLD'S FINEST COMICS (Formerly World's Best Comics #1)
No. 2, Sum, 1941 - No. 323, Jan, 1986 (#2-9 have 100 pgs.)
National Periodical Publ./DC Comics (#1-17 have cardboard covers)

2 (100 pgs.)-Superman, Batman & Robin covers continue from World's Best; (cover price 15¢ #2-70) 371.00 1115.00 2600.00
3-The Sandman begins; last Johnny Thunder; origin & 1st app. The Scarecrow 271.00 815.00 1900.00
4-Hop Harrigan app.; last Young Dr. Davis 200.00 600.00 1400.00
5-Intro. TNT & Dan the Dyna-Mite; last King & Crimson Avenger 200.00 600.00 1400.00
6-Star Spangled Kid begins (Sum/42); Aquaman app.; S&K Sandman with Sandy in new costume begins, ends #7 140.00 422.00 985.00
7-Green Arrow begins (Fall/42); last Lando, King, & Red, White & Blue; S&K art 140.00 422.00 985.00
8-Boy Commandos begin (by Simon(p) #12) 121.00 365.00 850.00
9-Batman cameo in Star Spangled Kid; S&K-a; last 100 pg. issue; Hitler, Mussolini, Tojo-c 132.00 396.00 925.00
10-S&K-a; 76 pg. issues begin 114.00 343.00 800.00
11-17-Last cardboard cover issue 96.00 288.00 750.00
18-20: 18-Paper covers begin; last Star Spangled Kid. 20-Last quarterly issue 83.00 250.00 650.00
21-30: 21-Begin bi-monthly. 30-Johnny Everyman app. 58.00 175.00 475.00
31-40: 33-35-Tomahawk app. 50.00 150.00 400.00
41-50: 41-Boy Commandos end. 42-Intro The Wyoming Kid & begins (9-10/49), ends #63. 43-Full Steam Foley begins, ends #48. 48-Last square binding. 49-Tom Sparks, Boy Inventor begins 40.00 120.00 300.00
51-60: 51-Zatara ends. 54-Last 76 pg. issue. 59-Manhunters Around the World begins (7-8/52), ends #62 40.00 120.00 300.00
61-64: 61-Joker story. 63-Capt. Compass app. 18.00 54.00 140.00
65-Origin Superman; Tomahawk begins (7-8/53), ends #101 48.00 145.00 360.00
66-70-(15¢ issues, scarce)-Last 15¢, 68pg. issue 37.00 110.00 285.00
71-(10¢ issue, scarce)-Superman & Batman begin as team (7-8/54); were in separate stories until now; Superman & Batman exchange identities; 10¢ issues begin 60.00 180.00 600.00
72-(10¢ issue, scarce) 47.00 140.00 420.00
73-(10¢ issue, scarce) 51.00 152.00 455.00
74-Last pre-code issue 40.00 120.00 360.00
75-(1st code approved, 3-4/55) 37.00 110.00 330.00
76-80: 77-Superman loses powers & Batman obtains them this issue only 29.00 86.00 230.00
81-90: 88-1st Joker/Luthor team-up. 89-2nd Batmen of All Nations (aka Club of Heroes). 90-Batwoman's 1st app. in World's Finest (10/57, 3rd app. anywhere) plus-c app. 23.00 68.00 180.00
91-93,95-99: 96-99-Kirby Green Arrow 15.00 45.00 120.00
94-Origin Superman/Batman team retold 50.00 150.00 400.00
100 (3/59) 28.00 84.00 225.00
101-110: 102-Tommy Tomorrow begins, ends #124 10.00 31.00 82.00
111-121: 111-1st app. The Clock King. 113-Intro. Miss Arrowette in Green Arrow; 1st Bat-Mite/Mr. Mxyzptlk team-up (11/60). 121-Last 10¢ issue 8.00 23.00 62.00
122-128,130-142: 123-2nd Bat-Mite/Mr. Mxyzptlk team-up (2/62). 125-Aquaman begins (5/62), ends #139 (Aquaman #1 is dated 1-2/62). 135-Last Dick Sprang story. 140-Last Green Arrow; last Clayface until Action #443. 142-Origin The Composite Superman (villain); Legion app. 3.90 12.00 27.00
129-Joker/Luthor team-up-c/story 5.00 16.00 38.00
143-150: 143-1st Mailbag 2.40 7.30 17.00
151-155,157-160: 154-1st Super Sons story; last Batwoman in costume until Batman Family #10. 157-2nd Super Sons story; last app. Kathy Kane (Bat-

World's Finest Comics #323 © DC

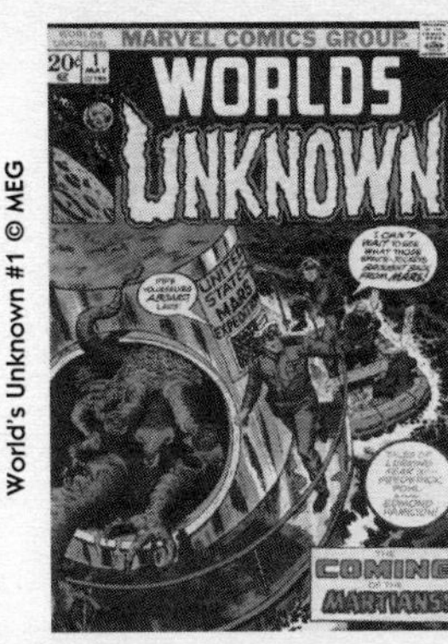

World's Unknown #1 © MEG

World Without End #1 © DC

GD25 FN65 NM94

woman) until Batman Family #10 2.00 6.00 14.00
156-1st Bizarro Batman; Joker-c/story 9.00 26.00 60.00
161,170 (80-Pg. Giants G-28,G-40) 2.60 8.00 18.00
162-165,167-169,171-174: 168,172-Adult Legion app. 169-3rd app. new Batgirl (9/67)(cover and 1 panel cameo) 1.70 4.20 10.00
166-Joker-c/story 2.00 6.00 14.00
175,176-Neal Adams-a; both reprint J'onn J'onzz origin/Detective #225,226 1.70 5.10 12.00
177-Joker/Luthor team-up-c/story 1.70 5.10 12.00
178,180-187: 182-Silent Knight-r/Brave & Bold #6. 186-Johnny Quick-r. 187-Green Arrow origin-r/Adv. #256 1.10 2.20 5.50
179,188 (80-Pg. Giants G-52,G-64): 179-r/#94 1.40 3.50 8.50
189-196: 190-193-Robin-r .90 1.70 4.25
197-(80 Pg. Giant G-76) 1.30 3.10 7.50
198,199-3rd Superman/Flash race (see Flash #175 & Superman #199) 7.00 21.00 55.00
200-205: 204-Last 15¢ issue. 205-(52 pgs.)-Shining Knight-r (6 pgs.) by Frazetta/Adv. #153; Teen Titans x-over 1.20 3.00
206 (80-Pg. Giant G-88) 1.70 4.25
207-248: 207-212-(25¢, 52 pgs.). 208-Origin Robotman-r/Det. #138. 215-Intro. Batman Jr. & Superman Jr. 217-Metamorpho begins, ends #220; Batman/Superman team-ups begin. 223-228-(100 pgs.). 223-N. Adams-r. 223-Deadman origin. 226-N. Adams, S&K, Toth-r; Manhunter part origin-r/Det. #225,226. 227-Deadman app. 229-r/origin Superman-Batman team. 242-Super Sons. 244-Green Arrow, Black Canary, Wonder Woman, Vigilante begin; $1.00, 84 pg. issues begin. 246-Death of Stuff in Vigilante; origin Vigilante retold. 248-Last Vigilante 1.70 4.25
249-The Creeper begins by Ditko, ends #255 1.10 2.20 5.50
250-270,272-299: 250-The Creeper origin retold by Ditko. 252-Last 84 pg. issue. 253-Capt. Marvel begins; 68 pgs. begin, end #265. 255-Last Creeper. 256-Hawkman begins. 257-Black Lightning begins. 263-Super Sons. 266-282-(52 pgs.). 264-Clay Face app. 267-Challengers of the Unknown app. 268-Capt. Marvel Jr. origin retold. 274-Zatanna begins. 279, 280-Capt. Marvel Jr. & Kid Eternity learn they are brothers. 284-Legion app. .90 2.25
271-Origin Superman/Batman team retold 1.00 2.50
300-($1.25, 52pgs.)-Justice League of America, New Teen Titans & The Outsiders app.; Perez-a (3 pgs.) 1.30 3.25
301-323: 304-Origin Null and Void. 309,319-Free 16 pg. story in each (309-Flash Force 2000, 319-Mask preview) .80 2.00
Giveaway (c. 1944-45, 8 pgs., in color, paper-c)-Johnny Everyman-r/World's Finest 13.00 40.00 90.00
Giveaway (c. 1949, 8 pgs., in color, paper-c)- "Make Way For Youth" r/World's Finest; based on film of same name 10.00 30.00 70.00

NOTE: ***Neal Adams** a-230ir; c-174-176, 178-180, 182, 183, 185, 186, 199-205, 208-211, 244-246, 258. **Austin** a-244-246i. **Burnley** a-8, 10; c-7-9, 11-14, 15p?, 16-18p, 20-31p. **Colan** a-274p, 297, 299. **Ditko** a-249-255. **Giffen** a-322; c-284p, 322. **G. Kane** a-38, 174r, 282, 283; c-281, 282, 289. **Kirby** a-187. **Kubert** Zatara-40-44. **Miller** c-285p. **Mooney** c-134. **Morrow** a-245-248. **Mortimer** c-16-21, 26-71. **Nasser** a(p)-244-246, 259, 260. **Newton** a-253-281p. **Orlando** a-224r. **Perez** a-300i; c-271, 276, 277p, 278p. **Fred Ray** c-1-5. **Fred Ray/Robinson** c-13-16. **Robinson** a-2, 9, 13-15; c-6. **Rogers** a-259p. **Roussos** a-212r. **Simonson** c-291. **Spiegle** a-275-278, 284. **Staton** a-262p, 273p. **Swan/Moldoff** c-126. **Swan/Mortimer** c-79-82. **Toth** a-228r. **Tuska** a-230r, 250p, 252p, 254p, 257p, 283p, 284p, 308p. Boy Commandos by **Infantino** #39-41.*

(Also see 80 Page Giant #15)

WORLD'S FINEST COMICS DIGEST (See DC Special Series #23)

WORLD'S GREATEST ATHLETE (See Walt Disney Showcase #14)

WORLD'S GREATEST SONGS
Sept, 1954
Atlas Comics (Male)

1-(Scarce)-Heath & Harry Anderson-a; Eddie Fisher life story plus-c; gives lyrics to Frank Sinatra song "Young at Heart" 25.00 75.00 175.00

WORLD'S GREATEST STORIES
Jan, 1949 - No. 2, May, 1949
Jubilee Publications

1-Alice in Wonderland; Lewis Carroll adapt. 17.00 52.00 120.00
2-Pinocchio 16.00 48.00 110.00

WORLD'S GREATEST SUPER HEROES
1977 (3-3/4x3-3/4") (24 pgs. in color) (Giveaway)
DC Comics (Nutra Comics) (Child Vitamins, Inc.)

nn-Batman & Robin app.; health tips .80 2.00

WORLDS OF FEAR (Stories of Weird Adventure)(Formerly Worlds Beyond #1)
V1#2, Jan, 1952 - V2#10, June, 1953
Fawcett Publications

V1#2 23.00 70.00 160.00
3-Evans-a 17.00 52.00 120.00
4-6(9/52) 15.00 45.00 105.00
V2#7-9 13.50 41.00 95.00
10-Saunders painted-c; man with no eyes surrounded by eyeballs-c plus eyes ripped out story 25.00 75.00 175.00

NOTE: ***Moldoff** c-2-8. **Powell** a-2, 4, 5. **Sekowsky** a-4, 5.*

WORLDS UNKNOWN
May, 1973 - No. 8, Aug, 1974
Marvel Comics Group

1-r/from Astonishing #54; Torres, Reese-a 1.30 3.25
2-8 .90 2.25

NOTE: ***Adkins/Mooney** a-5. **Buscema** c/a-4p. **W. Howard** c/a-3i. **Kane** a(p)-1,2; c(p)-5, 6, 8. **Sutton** a-2. **Tuska** a(p)-7, 8; c-7p. No. 7, 8 has Golden Voyage of Sinbad movie adaptation.*

WORLD WAR STORIES
Apr-June, 1965 - No. 3, Dec, 1965
Dell Publishing Co.

1-Glanzman-a in all 4.00 11.00 22.00
2,3 2.40 6.00 12.00

WORLD WAR II (See Classics Illustrated Special Issue)

WORLD WAR III
Mar, 1953 - No. 2, May, 1953
Ace Periodicals

1-(Scarce)-Atomic bomb blast-c 44.00 133.00 310.00
2-Used in **POP**, pg. 78 & B&W & color illos; Cameron-a 39.00 118.00 275.00

WORLD WITHOUT END (DC)(Value: cover or less)

WORLD WRESTLING FEDERATION BATTLEMANIA
1991 - No. 5?, 1991 ($2.50, color, magazine size, 68 pgs.)
Valiant

1-5: 5-Includes 2 free pull-out posters 1.00 2.50

WORST FROM MAD, THE (Annual)
1958 - No. 12, 1969 (Each annual cover is reprinted from the cover of the Mad issues being reprinted)
E. C. Comics

nn(1958)-Bonus; record labels & travel stickers; 1st Mad annual; r/Mad #29-34 30.00 90.00 210.00
2(1959)-Bonus is small 33-1/3 rpm record entitled "Meet the Staff of Mad"; r/Mad #35-40 36.00 107.00 250.00
3(1960)-Has 20x30" campaign poster "Alfred E. Neuman for President"; r/Mad #41-46 20.00 60.00 140.00
4(1961)-Sunday comics section; r/Mad #47-54 20.00 60.00 140.00
5(1962)-Has 33-1/3 record; r/Mad #55-62 30.00 90.00 210.00
6(1963)-Has 33-1/3 record; r/Mad #63-70 32.00 96.00 225.00
7(1964)-Mad protest signs; r/Mad #71-76 12.00 36.00 85.00
8(1965)-Build a Mad Zeppelin 13.50 41.00 95.00
9(1966)-33-1/3 rpm record 22.00 65.00 150.00
10(1967)-Mad bumper sticker 8.00 24.00 48.00
11(1968)-Mad cover window stickers 8.00 24.00 48.00
12(1969)-Mad picture postcards; Orlando-a 8.00 24.00 48.00

NOTE: *Covers: **Bob Clarke**-#8. **Mingo**-#7, 9-12.*

WOTALIFE COMICS (Formerly Nutty Life #2; Phantom Lady #13 on)
No. 3, Aug-Sept, 1946 - No. 12, July, 1947; 1959

Wrath #1 © Malibu

X #4 © DH

Xenya #1 © Sanctuary Press

	GD25	FN65	NM94

Fox Features Syndicate/Norlen Mag.

	GD25	FN65	NM94
3-Cosmo Cat, Li'l Pan, others begin	8.35	25.00	50.00
4-12-Cosmo Cat, Li'l Pan in all	5.00	15.00	30.00
1(1959-Norlen)-Atomic Rabbit, Atomic Mouse; reprints cover to #6; reprints entire book?	4.70	14.00	28.00

WOTALIFE COMICS
1957 - No. 5, 1957
Green Publications

	GD25	FN65	NM94
1	4.00	10.00	20.00
2-5	3.00	7.50	15.00

WOW COMICS
July, 1936 - No. 4, Nov, 1936 (52 pgs., magazine size)
Henle Publishing Co.

	GD25	FN65	NM94
1-Buck Jones in "The Phantom Rider" (1st app. in comics), Fu Manchu; Capt. Scott Dalton begins; Eisner-a; Briefer-c	200.00	600.00	1400.00
2-Ken Maynard, Fu Manchu, Popeye by Segar plus article on Popeye; Eisner-a	129.00	385.00	900.00
3-Eisner-c/a(3); Popeye by Segar, Fu Manchu, Hiram Hick by Bob Kane, Space Limited app.; Jimmy Dempsey talks about Popeye's punch; Bob Ripley Believe it or Not begins; Briefer-a	129.00	385.00	900.00
4-Flash Gordon by Raymond, Mandrake, Popeye by Segar, Tillie The Toiler, Fu Manchu, Hiram Hick by Bob Kane; Eisner-a(3); Briefer-c/a	171.00	515.00	1200.00

WOW COMICS (Real Western Hero #70 on)(See XMas Comics)
Winter, 1940-41; No. 2, Summer, 1941 - No. 69, Fall, 1948
Fawcett Publications

	GD25	FN65	VF82	NM94
nn(#1)-Origin Mr. Scarlet by S&K; Atom Blake, Boy Wizard, Jim Dolan, & Rick O'Shay begin; Diamond Jack, The White Rajah, & Shipwreck Roberts, only app.; 1st mention of Gotham City in comics; the cover was printed on unstable paper stock and is rarely found in fine or mint condition; blank inside-c; bondage-c by Beck	1000.00	3000.00	6500.00	10,000.00

(Estimated up to 100 total copies exist, 3 in NM/Mint)

	GD25	FN65	NM94
2 (Scarce)-The Hunchback begins	129.00	385.00	900.00
3 (Fall, 1941)	71.00	215.00	500.00
4-Origin & 1st app. Pinky	76.00	230.00	535.00
5	52.00	156.00	365.00
6-Origin & 1st app. The Phantom Eagle (7/15/42); Commando Yank begins	45.00	135.00	315.00
7,8,10: 10-Swayze-c/a on Mary Marvel	40.00	120.00	280.00
9 (1/6/43)-Capt. Marvel, Capt. Marvel Jr., Shazam app.; Scarlet & Pinky x-over; Mary Marvel-c/stories begin (cameo #9)	79.00	235.00	550.00
11-17,19,20: 15-Flag-c	27.00	81.00	190.00
18-1st app. Uncle Marvel (10/43); infinity-c	34.00	100.00	235.00
21-30: 28-Pinky x-over in Mary Marvel	16.00	48.00	110.00
31-40: 32-68-Phantom Eagle by Swayze	11.00	32.00	75.00
41-50	10.00	30.00	65.00
51-58: Last Mary Marvel	10.00	30.00	60.00
59-69: 59-Ozzie (teenage) begins. 62-Flying Saucer gag-c (1/48). 65-69-Tom Mix stories (cont'd in Real Western Hero)	8.35	25.00	50.00

NOTE: *Cover features: Mr. Scarlet-#1-5; Commando Yank-#6, 7, (w/Mr. Scarlet #8); Mary Marvel-#9-56, (w/Commando Yank-#46-50), (w/Mr. Scarlet & Commando Yank-#51), (w/Mr. Scarlet & Pinky #53), (w/Phantom Eagle #54, 56), (w/Commando Yank & Phantom Eagle #58); Ozzie-#59-69.*

WRATH (Also see Prototype #4)
Jan, 1994 - Present ($1.95, color)
Malibu Comics

	GD25	FN65	NM94
1-9: 2-Mantra x-over. 3-Intro/1st app. Slayer. 4,5-Freex app.		.80	2.00
1-Ultra 5000 Limited silver foil	1.40	4.20	10.00
Giant Size 1 ($2.50, 44 pgs.)		1.00	2.50

WRATH OF THE SPECTRE, THE
May, 1988 - No. 4, Aug, 1988 ($2.50, mini-series)
DC Comics

	GD25	FN65	NM94
1-4: Aparo-r/Adventure #431-440		1.00	2.50

WRECK OF GROSVENOR (See Superior Stories #3)

WRINGLE WRANGLE (See 4-Color #821)

WULF THE BARBARIAN
Feb, 1975 - No. 4, Sept, 1975
Atlas/Seaboard Publ.

	GD25	FN65	NM94
1-4: 1-Origin. 2-Intro. Berithe the Swordswoman; Neal Adams, Wood, Reese-a assists			1.00

WYATT EARP
Nov, 1955 - #29, June, 1960; #30, Oct, 1972 - #34, June, 1973
Atlas Comics/Marvel No. 23 on (IPC)

	GD25	FN65	NM94
1	14.00	43.00	100.00
2-Williamson-a (4 pgs.)	9.15	27.50	55.00
3-6,8-11: 3-Black Bart app. 8-Wild Bill Hickok app.	7.50	22.50	45.00
7,12-Williamson-a, 4 pgs. ea.; #12 with Mayo	7.50	22.50	45.00
13-20: 17-1st app. Wyatt's deputy, Grizzly Grant	5.85	17.50	35.00
21-Davis-c	4.70	14.00	28.00
22-24,26-29: 22-Ringo Kid app. 23-Kid From Texas app. 29-Last 10¢ issue	4.00	10.00	20.00
25-Davis-a	4.00	11.00	22.00
30-Williamson-r (1972)		.80	2.00
31-34-Reprints. 32-Torres-a(r)			1.00

NOTE: ***Ayers** a-8, 10(2), 17, 20(4). **Berg** a-9. **Everett** c-6. **Kirby** c-25, 29. **Maneely** a-1; c-1-4, 8, 12, 17, 20. **Maurer** a-2(2), 3(4), 4(4), 8(4). **Severin** a-4, 9(4), 10; c-2, 9, 10, 14. **Wildey** a-5, 17, 24, 28.*

WYATT EARP (TV) (Hugh O'Brian Famous Marshal)
No. 860, Nov, 1957 - No. 13, Dec-Feb, 1960-61 (Hugh O'Brian photo-c)
Dell Publishing Co.

	GD25	FN65	NM94
4-Color 860 (#1)-Manning-a	12.00	36.00	85.00
4-Color 890,921(6/58)-All Manning-a	8.35	25.00	50.00
4 (9-11/58) - 12-Manning-a. 5-Photo back-c	5.85	17.50	35.00
13-Toth-a	6.70	20.00	40.00

WYATT EARP FRONTIER MARSHAL (Formerly Range Busters)
No. 12, Jan, 1956 - No. 72, Dec, 1967 (Also see Blue Bird)
Charlton Comics

	GD25	FN65	NM94
12	5.85	17.50	35.00
13-19	3.60	9.00	18.00
20-(68 pgs.)-Williamson-a(4), 8,5,5,& 7 pgs.	7.50	22.50	45.00
21-30	2.40	6.00	12.00
31-50: 31-Crandall-r	1.60	4.00	8.00
51-72	1.00	2.00	5.00

X (Comics' Greatest World: X #1 only) (Also see Comics' Greatest World & Dark Horse Comics #8)
Feb, 1994 - Present ($2.00)
Dark Horse Comics

	GD25	FN65	NM94
1-11: 3-Pit Bulls x-over		.80	2.00
.../Hero Illustrated Special #2 (6/94, $1.00, 20 pgs.)			1.00
...: One Shot to the Head (1994, $2.50, 36 pgs.)-Miller-c		1.00	2.50

XANADU COLOR SPECIAL (Eclipse)(Value: cover or less)

XENOBROOD
No. 0, Oct, 1994 - Present ($1.50)
DC Comics

	GD25	FN65	NM94
0,1-6: 0-Indicia says "Xenobroods"			1.50

XENON (Eclipse)(Value: cover or less)

XENOTECH
Sept, 1993 - Present ($2.75, color)
Mirage Studios

	GD25	FN65	NM94
1,2-Bound with 2 trading cards		1.10	2.75

XENOZOIC TALES (Kitchen Sink)(Value: cover or less)

XENYA

X-Factor #106 © MEG

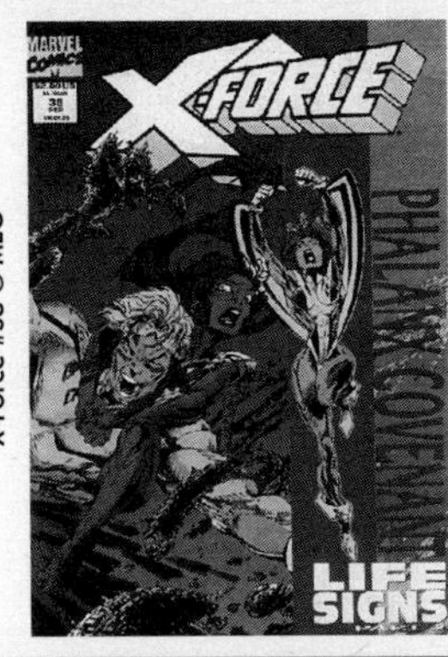

X-Force #38 © MEG

Ximos: Violent Past #1 © Triumphant

GD25 FN65 NM94 | GD25 FN65 NM94

Apr, 1994 - Present ($2.95, color)
Sanctuary Press
1-Hildebrandt-c; intro Xenya 1.20 3.00

X-FACTOR (Also see The Avengers #263, Fantastic Four #286)
Feb, 1986 - Present
Marvel Comics Group
1-($1.25, 52 pgs)-Story recaps 1st app. from Avengers #263; story cont'd from F.F. #286; return of original X-Men (now X-Factor); Guice/Layton-a; Baby Nathan app. (2nd after X-Men #201) 1.70 4.20 10.00
2,3 1.00 2.00 5.00
4,5: 5-1st app. Apocalypse (2-pg. cameo) .90 1.80 4.50
6-10: 6-1st full app. Apocalypse. 10-Sabretooth app. (11/86, 3 pgs.) cont'd in X-Men #212; 1st app. in an X-men comic book 1.40 3.50
11-20: 13-Baby Nathan app. in flashback. 15-Intro wingless Angel 1.10 2.75
21-23: 23-1st app. Archangel (2 pg. cameo) .90 2.25
24-1st full app. Archangel (now in Uncanny X-Men); Fall Of The Mutants begins; origin Apocalypse 1.90 5.60 13.00
25,26: Fall Of The Mutants; 26-New outfits 1.60 4.00
27-30 .80 2.00
31-37,39,41-49: 35-Origin Cyclops 1.50
38,50-($1.50, 52 pgs.): 50-Liefeld/McFarlane-c .80 2.00
40-Rob Liefeld-c/a (4/89, 1st at Marvel?) 1.00 2.50 6.00
51-53-Sabretooth app. 52-Liefeld-c(p) 1.00 2.00 5.00
54-59: 54-Intro Crimson; Silvestri-c/a(p) 1.00
60-X-Tinction Agenda x-over; New Mutants (w/Cable) x-over in #60-62; Wolverine in #62 1.30 3.25 8.00
60-Gold ink 2nd printing 1.00 2.50
61,62-X-Tinction Agenda. 62-Jim Lee-c 1.00 2.50 6.00
63-Portacio/Thibert-c/a(p) begins, ends #69 1.00 2.50 6.00
64-67,69,70: 65-68-Lee co-plots. 65-The Apocalypse Files begins, ends #68. 66,67-Baby Nathan app. 67-Inhumans app. 69,70-X-Men (w/Wolverine) x-over .80 2.00
68-Baby Nathan is sent into future to save his life 1.00 2.00 5.00
71-New team begins (Havok, Polaris, Wolfsbane & Madrox); Stroman-c/a begins 1.00 2.50 6.00
71-2nd printing ($1.25) 1.25
72-74: 74-Last $1.00-c 1.50
75-($1.75, 52 pgs.) .70 1.75
76-83,87-91,93-99,101: 77-Cannonball (of X-Force) app. 87-Quesada-c/a(p) begins, ends #92. 88-1st app. Random 1.25
84-86 ($1.50)-Polybagged with trading card in each; X-Cutioner's Song x-overs. 84-86-Jae Lee-a(p). 85,86-Jae Lee-c .80 2.00
92-($3.50, 68 pgs.)-Wraparound-c by Quesada w/Havok hologram on-c; begin X-Men 30th anniversary issues; Quesada-c/a .70 1.75 3.50
92-2nd printing .70 1.75 3.50
100-($2.95, 52 pgs.)-Embossed foil-c; death of Multiple Man 1.20 3.00
100-($1.75, 52 pgs.)-Regular edition .70 1.75
102-105,107-114: 102-Begin $1.50-c; bound-in card sheet 1.50
106-($2.00)-Newsstand edition .80 2.00
106-($2.95)-Collectors edition 1.20 3.00
108,109-($1.95)-Deluxe edition .80 2.00
Annual 1-6: 1-(10/86). 2-(10/87). 3-(1988, $1.75)-Evolutionary War x-over. 4-(1989, $2.00, 68 pgs.)-Atlantis Attacks; Byrne/Simonson-a; Byrne-c, 5-(1990, $2.00, 68 pgs.)-Fantastic Four, New Mutants x-over; Keown 2 pg. pin-up. 6-(1991, $2.00, 68 pgs.)-New Warriors app.; 5th app. X-Force cont'd from X-Men Annual #15 1.00 2.50
Annual 7 (1992, $2.25, 68 pgs.)-1st Quesada-a(p) on X-Factor plus-c(p) .90 2.25
Annual 8 (1993, $2.95, 68 pgs.)-Bagged w/trading card 1.20 3.00
Annual 9 (1994, $2.95, 68 pgs.)-Austin-a(i) 1.20 3.00
...Prisoner of Love nn (1990, $4.95, 52 pgs.)-Starlin scripts; Guice-a 1.00 2.00 5.00
NOTE: ***Art Adams** a-41p, 42p. **Buckler** a-50p. **Liefeld** a-40; c-40, 50i, 52p. **McFarlane** c-50i. **Brandon Peterson** a-78p(part). **Whilce Portacio** c/a(p)-63-69. **Quesada** c(p)-78, 79, 82. **Simonson** c/a-10, 11, 13-15, 17-19, 21, 23-31, 33, 34, 36-39; c-16. **Paul Smith** a-44-48; c-43.
Stroman a(p)-71-75, 77, 78(part), 80, 81; c(p)-71-77, 80, 81, 84.*

X-FORCE (Also see The New Mutants #100 & 1992 X-Men Annuals)
Aug, 1991 - Present ($1.00/$1.25)
Marvel Comics
1-($1.50, 52 pgs.)-Polybagged with 1 of 5 diff. Marvel Universe trading cards inside (1 each); 6th app. of X-Force; Liefeld-c/a begins 1.20 3.00
1-1st printing with Cable trading card inside 1.00 2.00 5.00
1-2nd printing; metallic ink-c (no bag or card) 1.50
2,3: 2-Deadpool-c/story. 3-New Brotherhood of Evil Mutants app. .80 2.00
4-Spider-Man x-over; cont'd from Spider-Man #16; reads sideways 1.10 2.75
5-10: 6-Last $1.00-c. 7,9-Weapon X back-ups. 10-Weapon X full-length story (part 3). 11-1st Weapon Prime (cameo); Deadpool-c/story 1.50
11-15,19-24,26-33: 15-Cable leaves X-Force 1.25
16-18-($1.50)-Polybagged w/trading card in each; X-Cutioner's Song x-overs .80 2.00
25-($3.50, 52 pgs.)-Wraparound-c w/Cable hologram on-c; Cable returns 1.40 3.50
34-37,39-45: 34-Begin $150-c; bound-in card sheet 1.50
38-($2.00)-Newsstand edition .80 2.00
38-($2.95)-Collectors edition 1.20 3.00
Annual 1 (1992, $2.25, 68 pgs.)-1st Greg Capullo-a(p) on X-Force .90 2.25
Annual 2 (1993, $2.95, 68 pgs.)-Polybagged w/trading card; intro X-Treme & Neurtap 1.20 3.00
Annual 3 (1994, $2.95) 1.20 3.00
...And Spider-Man: Sabotage nn (11/92, $6.95)-Reprints X-Force #3,4 & Spider-Man #16 1.20 3.00 7.00
NOTE: ***Capullo** a(p)-15-25, Annual 1; c(p)-14-27. **Rob Liefeld** a-1-7, 9p; c-1-9, 11p; plots-1-12. **Mignola** a-8p.*

XIMOS: VIOLENT PAST
Mar, 1994 - No. 2, Mar, 1994 ($2.50, color, limited series)
Triumphant Comics
1,2 1.10 2.75

XMAS COMICS
12?/1941 - No. 2, 12?/1942 (50¢, 324 pgs.)
No. 3, 12?/1943 - No. 7, 12?/1947 (25¢, 132 pgs.)
Fawcett Publications GD25 FN65 VF82 NM94
1-Contains Whiz #21, Capt. Marvel #3, Bulletman #2, Wow #3, & Master #18; Raboy back-c. Not rebound, remaindered comics; printed at same time as originals 210.00 630.00 1365.00 2100.00
(Estimated up to 110 total copies exist, 5 in NM/Mint)
GD25 FN65 NM94
2-Capt. Marvel, Bulletman, Spy Smasher 70.00 210.00 700.00
3-7-Funny animals (Hoppy, Billy the Kid & Oscar) 30.00 90.00 300.00

XMAS COMICS
No. 4, Dec, 1949 - No. 7, Dec, 1952 (50¢, 196 pgs.)
Fawcett Publications
4-Contains Whiz, Master, Tom Mix, Captain Marvel, Nyoka, Capt. Video, Bob Colt, Monte Hale, Hot Rod Comics, & Battle Stories. Not rebound, remaindered comics; printed at the same time as originals 30.00 90.00 300.00
5-7-Same as above. 7-Bill Boyd app.; stocking on cover is made of green felt (novelty cover) 25.00 75.00 250.00

XMAS FUNNIES
No date (Paper cover) (36 pgs.?)
Kinney Shoes (Giveaway)
Contains 1933 color strip-r; Mutt & Jeff, etc. 31.00 94.00 220.00

X-MEN, THE (See Adventures of Cyclops and Phoenix, Amazing Adventures, Capt. America #172, Classic X-Men, Giant-Size..., Heroes For Hope..., Kitty Pryde &..., Marvel & DC Present,

X-Men #36 © MEG

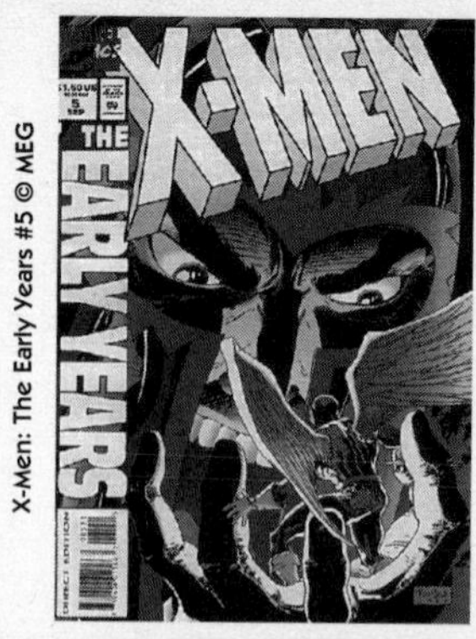

X-Men: The Early Years #5 © MEG

X-Men 2099 #12 © MEG

GD25 FN65 NM94

Marvel Collector's Edition:..., Marvel Fanfare, Marvel Graphic Novel, Marvel Super Heroes, Marvel Team-up, Marvel Triple Action, The Marvel X-Men Collection, Nightcrawler, Official Marvel Index To..., Special Edition..., The Uncanny..., X-Factor, X-Terminators)

X-MEN (2nd series)
Oct, 1991 - Present ($1.00/$1.25)
Marvel Comics

1-($1.50, 52 pgs.)-Jim Lee-c/a begins; new team begins (Cyclops, Beast, Wolverine, Gambit, Psylocke & Rogue); new Uncanny X-Men & Magneto app.; cover 1a-Beast & Storm-c .80 2.00
1-b-Colossus & Gambit-c .80 2.00
1-c-Wolverine & Cyclops-c .80 2.00
1-d-Magneto-c .80 2.00
1-e-($3.95)-Double gate-fold-c consisting of all four covers from 1a-d by Jim Lee; contains all pin-ups from #1a-d plus inside-c foldout poster; no ads; printed on coated stock 1.00 2.50 5.50
2,3,5,7: 5-Byrne scripts 1.60 4.00
4-Wolverine back to old yellow costume (same date as Wolverine #50); last $1.00-c 1.60 4.00
6-Sabretooth-c/story 1.60 4.00
8-Gambit vs. Bishop-c/story; last Lee-a; Ghost Rider cameo cont'd in Ghost Rider #26 1.60 4.00
9-Wolverine vs. Ghost Rider; cont'd/G.R. #26 1.60 4.00
10-Return of Longshot 1.60 4.00
11-13,17-24,26-29,31: 12,13-Art Thibert-c/a. 28,29-Sabretooth app. .60 1.25
11-Silver ink 2nd printing; came with X-Men board game 2.00 6.40 15.00
14-16-($1.50)-Polybagged with trading card in each; X-Cutioner's Song x-overs; 14-Andy Kubert-c/a begins .80 2.00
25-($3.50, 52 pgs.)-Wraparound-c with Gambit hologram on-c; Magneto storyline 1.80 4.50
25-30th anniversary issue w/B&W-c with Magneto in color & Magneto hologram & no price on-c 20.00
30-($1.95)-Wedding issue w/bound-in trading card sheet .80 2.00
32-43: 32-Begin $1.50-c; bound-in card sheet. 33-Gambit & Sabretooth-c & story 1.50
36,37-($2.95)-Collectors editions 1.20 3.00
38-Deluxe edition .80 2.00
Annual 1 (1992, $2.25, 68 pgs.)-Lee-c & layouts .90 2.25
Annual 2 (1993, $2.95, 68 pgs.)-Bagged w/card 1.20 3.00
Annual 3 (1994, $2.95) 1.20 3.00
...Premium Edition #1 (1993)-Cover says "Toys 'R' Us Limited Edition X-Men" 1.50
...Ashcan #1 1.00

NOTE: ***Jim Lee*** *a-1-11p; c-1-6p, 7, 8, 9p, 10, 11p.* ***Art Thibert*** *a-6-9i, 12, 13; c-6i, 12, 13.*

X-MEN ADVENTURES (TV)
Nov, 1992 - No. 15, Jan, 1994 ($1.25)
Marvel Comics

1-Wolverine, Cyclops, Jubilee, Rogue, Gambit 1.00 2.00 5.00
2-5: 3-Magneto-c/story 1.40 3.50
6-10: 6-Sabretooth-c/s. 7-Cable-c/s. 10-Archangel guest star .80 2.00
11-14: 11-Cable-c/s 1.25
15-($1.75, 52 pgs.) .70 1.75

X-MEN ADVENTURES II (TV)
Feb, 1994 - Present ($1.25)(Based on 2nd TV season)
Marvel Comics

1-8: 4-Bound-in trading card sheet. 5-Alpha Flight app. 1.25
9-14: 9-Begin $1.50-c 1.50
...Captive Hearts/Slave Island (TPB, $4.95)-r/X-Men Adventures #5-8 1.00 2.00 5.00

X-MEN/ALPHA FLIGHT
Dec, 1985 - No. 2, Dec, 1985 ($1.50, mini-series)
Marvel Comics Group

1,2: 1-Intro The Berserkers; Paul Smith-a 1.20 3.00

X-MEN AND THE MICRONAUTS, THE
Jan, 1984 - No. 4, April, 1984 (Mini-series)
Marvel Comics Group

1-4: Guice-c/a(p) in all 1.50

X-MEN CLASSIC (Formerly Classic X-Men)
No. 46, Apr, 1990 - Present ($1.25)
Marvel Comics

46-69,71-78,80-89,91-96,98,99: Reprints from X-Men. 54-($1.25, 52 pgs.). 57, 60-63,65-Russell-c(i); 62-r/X-Men #158(Rogue). 66-r/#162(Wolverine). 69-Begins-r of Paul Smith issues (#165 on) 1.25
70,79,90,97-($1.75, 52 pgs.): 70-r/X-Men #166. 90-r/#186 .70 1.75
100-106-($1.50) 1.50

X-MEN CLASSICS
Dec, 1983 - No. 3, Feb, 1984 ($2.00; Baxter paper)
Marvel Comics Group

1-3: X-Men-r by Neal Adams 1.20 3.00

X-MEN SPOTLIGHT ON... STARJAMMERS (Also see X-Men #104)
1990 - No. 2, 1990 ($4.50, 52 pgs.)
Marvel Comics

1,2-Starjammers 1.80 4.50

X-MEN SURVIVAL GUIDE TO THE MANSION
Aug, 1993 ($6.95)
Marvel Comics

1-Spiral bound 1.20 3.00 7.00

X-MEN: THE EARLY YEARS
May, 1994 - Present ($1.50)
Marvel Comics

1-13-r/X-Men #1-8 w/new-c 1.50

X-MEN: THE WEDDING ALBUM
1994 ($2.95, magazine size, one-shot)
Marvel Comics

1-Wedding of Scott Summers & Jean Grey 1.20 3.00

X-MEN 2099
Oct, 1993 - Present ($1.25/$1.50)
Marvel Comics

1-($1.75)-Foil-c; Ron Lim/Adam Kubert-a begins .70 1.75
1-2nd printing ($1.75) .70 1.75
1-Gold edition (15,000 made); sold thru Diamond for $19.40 2.85 8.00 20.00
2-7: 3-Death of Tina; Lim-c/a(p) in #1-8 1.25
8-19: 8-Begin $1.50-c; bound-in trading card sheet 1.50

X-MEN UNLIMITED
1993 - Present ($3.95, 68 pgs.)
Marvel Comics

1-8: 2-More detailed origin Magneto. 3-Sabretooth-c/s 1.60 4.00

X-MEN VS. DRACULA
Dec, 1993 ($1.75)
Marvel Comics

1-r/X-Men Annual #6; Austin-c(i) .70 1.75

X-MEN VS. THE AVENGERS, THE
Apr, 1987 - No. 4, July, 1987 ($1.50, mini-series, Baxter paper)
Marvel Comics Group

1 1.40 3.50
2-4 1.00 2.50

X-O MANOWAR
Feb, 1992 - Present ($1.95/$2.25, color, high quality)
Valiant

X-O Man of War #32 © Voyager Comm.

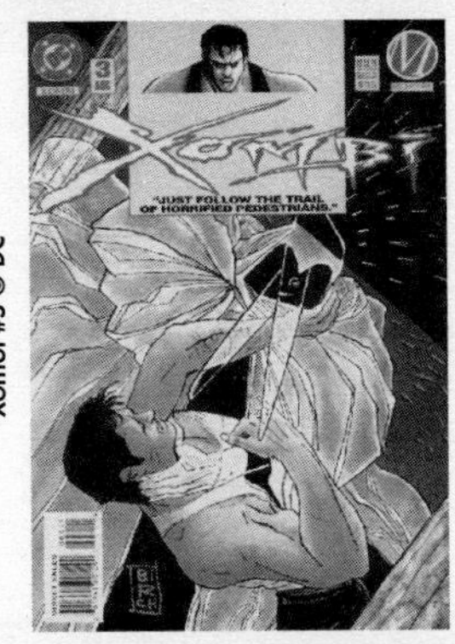

Xombi #3 © DC

The Yellow Kid #1

GD25 FN65 NM94

1-Barry Windsor-Smith/Layton-a; partial origin 2.90 9.00 20.00
2-B. Smith/Layton-c; Layton part inks 2.10 6.40 15.00
3-Layton-c(i) 1.40 4.30 10.00
4-1st app. Shadowman (cameo) 2.60 8.00 18.00
5,6: 5-B. Smith-c; last $1.95-c. 6-Ditko-a(p) .90 2.30 5.50
7,8-Unity x-overs. 7-Miller-c. 8-Simonson-c 1.00 3.00 6.00
9-13: 12-1st app. Randy Calder 1.40 3.50
14,15-Turok-c/stories .80 1.60 4.00
15-Hot pink logo variant; came with Ultra Pro Rigid Comic Sleeves box; no price on cover 1.30 3.00 8.00
16-24,26-38: 20-Serial number contest insert. 27-29-Turok x-over. 28-Bound-in trading card. 30-Solar app.; 1st app. of "new good skin." 33-Chaos Effect Delta Pt. 3 .90 2.25
25-($3.50)-Has 16 pg. Armorines #0 bound-in w/origin 1.40 3.50
0-(8/93, $3.50)-Wraparound embossed chromium-c by Quesada; Solar app.; origin X-O Manowar 1.40 3.50
0-Gold variant 3.00 8.60 20.00
Retribution trade paperback nn (1993, $9.95)-Polybagged with copy of X-O Database #1 inside 1.65 4.00 10.00

NOTE: ***Layton** a-1i, 2i(part); c-1, 2i, 3i, 6i, 21i. **Reese** a-4i(part); c-26i.*

XOMBI
Jan, 1994 - Present ($1.75)
DC Comics (Milestone)

0-($1.95)-Shadow War x-over; Simonson silver ink varnish-c .80 2.00
1-9: 1-John Byrne-c .70 1.75

X-TERMINATORS
Oct, 1988 - No. 4, Jan, 1989 ($1.00, mini-series)
Marvel Comics

1-1st app.; X-Men/X-Factor tie-in; Williamson-i 1.20 3.00
2 .70 1.75
3,4 1.25

X, THE MAN WITH THE X-RAY EYES (See Movie Comics)

X-VENTURE
July, 1947 - No. 2, Nov, 1947 (Super heroes)
Victory Magazines Corp.

1-Atom Wizard, Mystery Shadow, Lester Trumble begin 57.00 171.00 400.00
2 36.00 107.00 250.00

XYR (See Eclipse Graphic Album Series #21)

YAK YAK (See 4-Color #1186, 1348)

YAKKY DOODLE & CHOPPER (TV) (Also see Spotlight #3 & Top Cat #4)
Dec, 1962 (Hanna-Barbera)
Gold Key

1 5.50 17.00 33.00

YALTA TO KOREA (Also see Korea My Home)
1952 (8 pgs.) (Giveaway) (Paper cover)
M. Phillip Corp. (Republican National Committee)

nn-Anti-communist propaganda book 16.50 50.00 115.00

YANG (See House of Yang)
Nov, 1973 - No. 13, May, 1976; V14#14, Sept, 1985 - No. 17, Jan, 1986
Charlton Comics

1-Origin 1.60 4.00
2-13(1976) .80 2.00
14-17(1986) 1.00
3,10,11(Modern Comics-r, 1977) 1.00

YANKEE COMICS
Sept, 1941 - No. 4, Mar, 1942
Harry 'A' Chesler

1-Origin The Echo, The Enchanted Dagger, Yankee Doodle Jones, The Firebrand, & The Scarlet Sentry; Black Satan app.; Yankee Doodle Jones app. on all covers 69.00 208.00 485.00
2-Origin Johnny Rebel; Major Victory app.; Barry Kuda begins 43.00 129.00 300.00
3,4 36.00 107.00 250.00
4 (nd, 1940s; 7-1/4x5", 68 pgs, distr. to the service)-Foxy Grandpa, Tom, Dick & Harry, Impy, Ace & Deuce, Dot & Dash, Ima Slooth by Jack Cole (Remington Morse publ.) 1.70 5.00 12.00

YANKS IN BATTLE
Sept, 1956 - No. 4, Dec, 1956; 1963
Quality Comics Group

1-Cuidera-c(i) 6.70 20.00 40.00
2-4: Cuidera-c(i) 4.00 11.00 22.00
I.W. Reprint #3(1963)-r/#?; exist? 1.00 2.50 5.00

YARDBIRDS, THE (G. I. Joe's Sidekicks)
Summer, 1952
Ziff-Davis Publishing Co.

1-By Bob Oskner 7.50 22.50 45.00

YARNS OF YELLOWSTONE
1972 (36 pgs.) (50¢)
World Color Press

nn-Illustrated by Bill Chapman 1.00 2.00 5.00

YELLOW CLAW (Also see Giant Size Master of Kung Fu)
Oct, 1956 - No. 4, April, 1957
Atlas Comics (MjMC)

1-Origin by Joe Maneely 42.00 125.00 415.00
2-Kirby-a 31.00 92.00 305.00
3,4-Kirby-a; 4-Kirby/Severin-a 28.00 84.00 280.00

NOTE: ***Everett** c-3. **Maneely** c-1. **Reinman** a-2i, 3. **Severin** c-2, 4.*

YELLOWJACKET COMICS (Jack in the Box #11 on)(See TNT Comics)
Sept, 1944 - No. 10, June, 1946
E. Levy/Frank Comunale/Charlton

1-Intro & origin Yellowjacket; Diana, the Huntress begins; E.A. Poe's "The Black Cat" adaptation 39.00 115.00 270.00
2-Yellowjacket-c begin, end #10 21.00 63.00 145.00
3,5 19.00 57.00 130.00
4-E.A. Poe's "Fall of the House Of Usher" adaptation; Palais-a 20.00 60.00 140.00
6-10: 1,3,4,6-10-Have stories narrated by old witch in "Tales of Terror" 17.00 52.00 120.00

YELLOW KID, THE (Magazine)
1897 - #6, June 5, 1897 (5¢)(B&W)(color covers)
Howard Ainslee & Co., N.Y.

1-Outcault Yellow kid on-c only #1-6 400.00 1200.00 -
2 200.00 600.00 -
3-6 (#5, 5/22/97) 135.00 400.00 -

NOTE: Richard Outcault's Yellow Kid from the Hearst New York American represents the very first comic strip in America. Eventually the first prototype comic books appeared reprinting these early strips. This magazine is listed here due to historical importance and is not a comic book.

YELLOW KID IN MCFADDEN'S FLATS, THE
1897 (50¢, 5 1/2x7 1/2", B&W, squarebound)
G. W. Dillingham Company, New York

nn-The first "comic" book?; E. W. Townsend narrative w/R. F. Outcault Sunday comic page art-r & some original drawings 835.00 2500.00

YELLOWSTONE KELLY (See 4-Color #1056)

YELLOW SUBMARINE (See Movie Comics)

YIN FEI THE CHINESE NINJA (Leung)(Value: cover dor less)

YOGI BEAR (See Dell Giant #41, Golden Comics Digest, Kite Fun Book, March of Comics #253, 265, 279, 291, 309, 319, 337, 344, Movie Comics under "Hey There It's..." & Whitman Comic Books)

YOGI BEAR (TV) (Hanna-Barbera) (See Four Color #990)
No. 1067, 12-2/59-60 - No. 9, 7-9/62; No. 10, 10/62 - No. 42, 10/70
Dell Publishing Co./Gold Key No. 10 on

Yogi Bear #9 © H-B

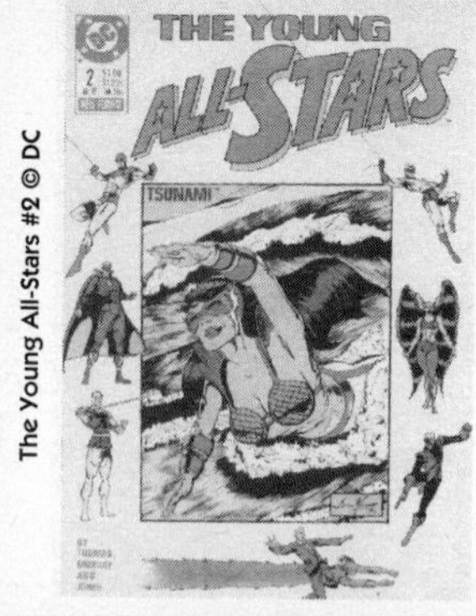

The Young All-Stars #2 © DC

Youngblood Yearbook #1 © Rob Liefeld

GD25 FN65 NM94

4-Color 1067 (#1)-TV show debuted 1/30/61 11.50 34.00 80.00
4-Color 1104,1162 (5-7/61) 8.35 25.00 50.00
4(8-9/61) - 6(12-1/61-62) 5.85 17.50 35.00
4-Color 1271(11/61) 5.85 17.50 35.00
4-Color 1349(1/62)-Photo-c 10.00 30.00 70.00
7(2-3/62) - 9(7-9/62)-Last Dell 5.85 17.50 35.00
10(10/62-G.K.), 11(1/63)-titled "Yogi Bear Jellystone Jollies" (80 pgs.); 11-X-Mas-c 5.00 15.00 40.00
12(4/63), 14-20 4.00 12.00 24.00
13(7/63, 68 pgs.)-Surprise Party 5.85 17.50 35.00
21-30 3.20 8.00 16.00
31-42 2.00 5.00 10.00
Giveaway ('84, '86)-City of Los Angeles, "Creative First Aid" & "Earthquake Preparedness for Children" .80 2.00

YOGI BEAR (TV)
Nov, 1970 - No. 35, Jan, 1976 (Hanna-Barbera)
Charlton Comics

1 3.25 9.50 22.00
2-6,8-10 1.70 5.00 12.00
7-Summer Fun (Giant, 52 pgs.) 2.30 6.75 16.00
11-35: 28-31-partial-r 1.30 3.25 8.00

YOGI BEAR (TV)(See The Flintstones, 3rd series & Spotlight #1)
Nov, 1977 - No. 9, Mar, 1979 (Hanna-Barbera)
Marvel Comics Group

1-Flintstones begin .80 2.00
2-9 1.00

YOGI BEAR (TV)
Sept, 1992 - No. 6, Mar, 1994 ($1.25/$1.50) (Hanna-Barbera)
Harvey Comics

V2#1-4 1.25
5,6: 5-Begin $1.50-c 1.50
...Big Book V2#1,2 ($1.95, 52 pgs): 1-(11/92). 2-(3/93) .80 2.00
...Giant Size V2#1,2 ($2.25, 68 pgs.): 1-(10/92). 2-(4/93) .90 2.25

YOGI BEAR'S EASTER PARADE (See The Funtastic World of Hanna-Barbera #2)

YOGI BERRA (Baseball hero)
1951 (Yankee catcher)
Fawcett Publications

nn-Photo-c 52.00 156.00 365.00

YOSEMITE SAM (...& Bugs Bunny)
Dec, 1970 - No. 81, Feb, 1984
Gold Key/Whitman

1 1.70 5.00 12.00
2-10 1.00 2.00 5.00
11-30 1.20 3.00
31-81: 81-(1/3-r) .80 2.00
(See March of Comics #363, 380, 392)

YOUNG ALLIES COMICS (All-Winners #21; see Kid Komics #2)
Summer, 1941 - No. 20, Oct, 1946
Timely Comics (USA 1-7/NPI 8,9/YAI 10-20)

GD25 FN65 VF82 NM94
1-Origin/1st app. The Young Allies (Bucky, Toro, others); 1st meeting of Captain America & Human Torch; Red Skull-c & app.; S&K-c/splash; Hitler-c 620.00 1860.00 4030.00 6200.00
(Estimated up to 165 total copies exist, 9 in NM/Mint)

GD25 FN65 NM94
2-(Winter, 1941)-Captain America & Human Torch app.; Simon & Kirby-c 200.00 600.00 1400.00
3-Fathertime, Captain America & Human Torch app.; Remember Pearl Harbor issue (Spring, 1942); Stan Lee scripts; Vs. Japs-c/full-length story 164.00 493.00 1150.00
4-The Vagabond & Red Skull, Capt. America, Human Torch app. Classic Red Skull-c 200.00 600.00 1400.00

GD25 FN65 NM94

5-Captain America & Human Torch app. 86.00 257.00 600.00
6-10: 9-Hitler, Tojo, Mussolini-c. 10-Origin Tommy Tyme & Clock of Ages; ends #19 68.00 205.00 475.00
11-20: 12-Classic decapitation story 54.00 160.00 375.00
NOTE: ***Brodsky*** *c-15.* ***Gabrielle*** *a-3; c-3, 4.* ***S&K*** *c-1, 2.* ***Schomburg*** *c-5-14, 16-19.* ***Shores*** *c-20.*

YOUNG ALL-STARS (DC)(Value: cover or less)

YOUNGBLOOD (See Brigade #4, Megaton Explosion & Team Youngblood)
Apr, 1992 - No. 4, Feb, 1993 ($2.50, color, mini-series);
No. 6, June, 1994 (No #5) - Present ($3.50, color, on-going series)
Image Comics

1-Liefeld-c/a/scripts in all; flip book format with 2 trading cards; 1st Image comic book published 1.10 2.70 6.50
1-2nd printing 1.00 2.50
2-(JUN-c, July 1992 indicia)-1st app. Shadowhawk in solo back-up story; 2 trading cards inside; flip book format; 1st app. Prophet, Kirby, Berzerkers, Darkthorn 1.60 4.00
2-2nd printing (1.95) .80 2.00
3-(OCT-c, August 1992 indicia)-Contains 2 trading cards inside (flip book); 1st app. Supreme in back-up story; 1st app. Showdown 1.00 2.50
0-(12/92, $1.95)-Contains 2 trading cards; 2 cover variations exist, green or beige logo; w/Image #0 coupon .80 2.00
4-(2/93)-Glow-in-the-dark-c w/2 trading cards; 2nd app. Dale Keown's The Pitt; Bloodstrike app. 1.00 2.50
6-($3.50, 52 pgs.)-Wraparound-c 1.40 3.50
7-9: 7-Liefeld-c(p)/a(p)/story 1.00 2.50
...Battlezone 1 (MAY-c, 4/93 inside, $1.95)-Arsenal book; Liefeld-c(p) .80 2.00
...Battlezone 2 (7/94, $2.95)-Wraparound-c 1.20 3.00
...Yearbook 1 (7/93, $2.50)-Fold out panel; 1st app. Tyrax & Kanan 1.00 2.50

YOUNGBLOOD: STRIKEFILE
Apr, 1993 - Present ($2.50/$2.95, color, began as mini-series)
Image Comics

1-($1.95)-Flip book w/Jae Lee-c/a & Liefeld-c/a in #1-3; 1st app. The Allies, Giger, & Glory .80 2.00
2-4-($2.50): 3-Thibert-i asisst. 4-Liefeld-c(p); no Lee-a 1.00 2.50
5,6: 5-Begin $2.95-c; Liefeld-c(p) 1.20 3.00

YOUNG BRIDES (True Love Secrets)
Sept-Oct, 1952 - No. 30, Nov-Dec, 1956 (Photo-c: 1-4)
Feature/Prize Publications

V1#1-Simon & Kirby-a 16.00 48.00 110.00
2-S&K-a 9.15 27.50 55.00
3-6-S&K-a 8.35 25.00 50.00
V2#1,3-7,10-12 (#7-18)-S&K-a 7.50 22.50 45.00
2,8,9-No S&K-a 3.20 8.00 16.00
V3#1-3(#19-21)-Last precode (3-4/55) 2.80 7.00 14.00
4,6(#22,24), V4#1,3(#25,27) 2.00 5.00 10.00
V3#5(#23)-Meskin-c 3.20 8.00 16.00
V4#2(#26)-All S&K issue 7.00 21.00 42.00
V4#4(#28)-S&K-a 5.85 17.50 35.00
V4#5,6(#29,30) 4.00 10.00 20.00

YOUNG DEATH (Fleetway/Quality)(Value: cover or less)

YOUNG DR. MASTERS (See The Adventures of Young Dr. Masters)

YOUNG DOCTORS, THE
January, 1963 - No. 6, Nov, 1963
Charlton Comics

V1#1 1.20 3.00 6.00
2-6 .60 1.50 3.00

YOUNG EAGLE
12/50 - No. 10, 6/52; No. 3, 7/56 - No. 5, 4/57 (Photo-c: 1-10)
Fawcett Publications/Charlton

The Young Indiana Jones Chronicals #1 © Lucus Films

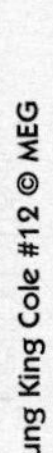
Young King Cole #12 © MEG

Young Men #12 © MEG

GD25 FN65 NM94

1-Intro Young Eagle 12.00 36.00 85.00
2-Complete picture novelette "The Mystery of Thunder Canyon"
7.00 21.00 42.00
3-9 5.85 17.50 35.00
10-Origin Thunder, Young Eagle's Horse 4.35 13.00 26.00
3-5(Charlton)-Formerly Sherlock Holmes? 3.60 9.00 18.00

YOUNG HEARTS
Nov, 1949 - No. 2, Feb, 1950
Marvel Comics (SPC)

1-Photo-c 8.35 25.00 50.00
2-Colleen Townsend photo-c from movie 5.35 16.00 32.00

YOUNG HEARTS IN LOVE
1964
Super Comics

17,18: 17-r/Young Love V5#6 (4-5/62) 1.00 2.50 5.00

YOUNG HEROES (Formerly Forbidden Worlds #34)
No. 35, Feb-Mar, 1955 - No. 37, June-July, 1955
American Comics Group (Titan)

35-37-Frontier Scout 6.70 20.00 40.00

YOUNG INDIANA JONES CHRONICLES, THE
Feb, 1992 - Present ($2.50)
Dark Horse Comics

1-15: Dan Barry scripts in all 1.00 2.50

NOTE: ***Dan Barry*** *a(p)-1, 2, 5, 6, 10; c-1-10.* ***Morrow*** *a-3, 4, 5p, 6p.* ***Springer*** *a-1i, 2i.*

YOUNG INDIANA JONES CHRONICLES, THE
1992 - Present ($3.95, squarebound, 68 pgs.)
Hollywood Comics (Disney)

1-3: 1-r/YIJC #1,2 by D. Horse. 2-r/#3,4. 3-r/#5,6 1.60 4.00

YOUNG KING COLE (...Detective Tales)(Becomes Criminals on the Run)
Fall, 1945 - V3#12, July, 1948
Premium Group/Novelty Press

V1#1-Toni Gayle begins 13.50 41.00 120.00
2 10.00 30.00 60.00
3-4 8.35 25.00 50.00
V2#1-7(8-9/46-7/47): 6,7-Certa-c 5.85 17.50 35.00
V3#1,3-6,8,9,12: 3-Certa-c. 5-McWilliams-c/a. 8,9-Harmon-c
5.00 15.00 30.00
2-L.B. Cole-a; Certa-c 6.70 20.00 40.00
7-L.B. Cole-c/a 8.35 25.00 50.00
10,11-L.B. Cole-c 7.50 22.50 45.00

YOUNG LAWYERS, THE (TV)
Jan, 1971 - No. 2, April, 1971
Dell Publishing co.

1,2 1.70 5.00 12.00

YOUNG LIFE (Teen Life #3 on)
Summer, 1945 - No. 2, Fall, 1945
New Age Publ./Quality Comics Group

1-Skip Homeier, Louis Prima stories 10.00 30.00 60.00
2-Frank Sinatra photo on-c plus story 10.00 30.00 60.00

YOUNG LOVE (Sister title to Young Romance)
2-3/49 - No. 73, 12-1/56-57; V3#5, 2-3/60 - V7#1, 6-7/63
Prize(Feature)Publ.(Crestwood)

V1#1-S&K-c/a(2) 26.00 78.00 180.00
2-Photo-c begin; S&K-a 12.00 36.00 85.00
3-S&K-a 10.00 30.00 65.00
4-5-Minor S&K-a 6.70 20.00 40.00
V2#1(#7)-S&K-a(2) 10.00 30.00 65.00
2-5(#8-11)-Minor S&K-a 5.00 15.00 30.00
6,8(#12,14)-S&K-c only. 14-S&K 1 pg. art 7.50 22.50 45.00
7,9-12(#13,15-18)-S&K-c/a 10.00 30.00 65.00
V3#1-4(#19-22)-S&K-c/a 8.35 25.00 50.00
5-7,9-12(#23-25,27-30)-Photo-c resume; S&K-a 6.70 20.00 40.00
8(#26)-No S&K-a 3.60 9.00 18.00
V4#1,6(#31,36)-S&K-a 6.70 20.00 40.00
2-5,7-12(#32-35,37-42)-Minor S&K-a 5.00 15.00 30.00
V5#1-12(#43-54), V6#1-9(#55-63)-Last precode; S&K-a in some
3.60 9.00 18.00
V6#10-12(#64-66) 2.80 7.00 14.00
V7#1-7(#67-73) 2.00 5.00 10.00
V3#5(2-3/60),6(4-5/60)(Formerly All For Love) 1.60 4.00 8.00
V4#1(6-7/60)-6(4-5/61) 1.40 3.50 7.00
V5#1(6-7/61)-6(4-5/62) 1.40 3.50 7.00
V6#1(6-7/62)-6(4-5/63), V7#1 1.20 3.00 6.00

NOTE: ***Meskin*** *a-14(2), 27, 42.* ***Powell*** *a-V4#6.* ***Severin/Elder*** *a-V1#3. S&K art not in #53, 57, 58, 61, 63-65. Photo c-V3#5-V5#11.*

YOUNG LOVE
#39, 9-10/63 - #120, Wint./75-76; #121, 10/76 - #126, 7/77
National Periodical Publ.(Arleigh Publ. Corp #49-60)/DC Comics

39 4.00 10.00 20.00
40-50 2.40 6.00 12.00
51-70: 64-Simon & Kirby-a 1.80 4.50 9.00
71,72,74-77,80 1.00 2.50 6.00
73,78,79-Toth-a 1.20 3.00
81-126: 107-114-(100 pgs.): 107-DC 100 Pg. Super Spect. 1.50

NOTE: ***Bolle*** *a-117.* ***Colan*** *a-107r.* ***Nasser*** *a-123, 124.* ***Orlando*** *a-122.* ***Simonson*** *c-125.* ***Toth*** *a-73, 78, 79, 122-125r.* ***Wood*** *a-109r(4 pgs.).*

YOUNG LOVER ROMANCES (Formerly & becomes Great Lover...)
No. 4, June, 1952 - No. 5, Aug, 1952
Toby Press

4,5-Photo-c 4.00 11.00 22.00

YOUNG LOVERS (My Secret Life #19 on)(Formerly Brenda Starr?)
No. 16, July, 1956 - No. 18, May, 1957
Charlton Comics

16,17('56): 16-Marcus Swayze-a 4.00 10.00 20.00
18-Elvis Presley picture-c, text story (biography)(Scarce)
43.00 130.00 300.00

YOUNG MARRIAGE
June, 1950
Fawcett Publications

1-Powell-a; photo-c 9.15 27.50 55.00

YOUNG MEN (Formerly Cowboy Romances)(...on the Battlefield #12-20 (4/53); ...In Action #21)
No. 4, 6/50 - No. 11, 10/51; No. 12, 12/51 - No. 28, 6/54
Marvel/Atlas Comics (IPC)

4-(52 pgs.) 11.50 34.00 80.00
5-11 7.50 22.50 45.00
12-23: 12-20-War format. 21-23-Hot Rod issues starring Flash Foster
6.70 20.00 40.00
24-(12/53)-Origin Captain America, Human Torch, & Sub-Mariner which are revived thru #28; Red Skull app. 50.00 150.00 500.00
25-28: 25-Romita-c/a (see Men's Advs.) 38.00 113.00 375.00

NOTE: ***Berg*** *a-7, 14, 17, 18, 20; c-17?* ***Brodsky*** *c-4-9, 13, 14, 16, 17, 21-25.* ***Burgos*** *c-26-28.* ***Colan*** *a-14, 15.* ***Everett*** *a-18-20.* ***Heath*** *a-13, 14.* ***Maneely*** *c-10, 12, 15.* ***Pakula*** *a-14, 15.* ***Robinson*** *c-18. Captain America by* ***Romita****-#24?, 25, 26?, 27, 28. Human Torch by* ***Burgos****-#25, 27, 28. Sub-Mariner by* ***Everett****-#24-28.*

YOUNG REBELS, THE (TV)
January, 1971
Dell Publishing Co.

1-Photo-c 1.65 4.00 10.00

YOUNG ROMANCE COMICS (The 1st romance comic)
Sept-Oct, 1947 - V16#4, June-July, 1963 (#1-33: 52 pgs.)
Prize/Headline (Feature Publ.) (Crestwood)

V1#1-S&K-c/a(2) 27.00 81.00 190.00

Young Zen Intergalactic Ninja #1 © Zen Comics

Zago, Jungle Princess #2 © FOX

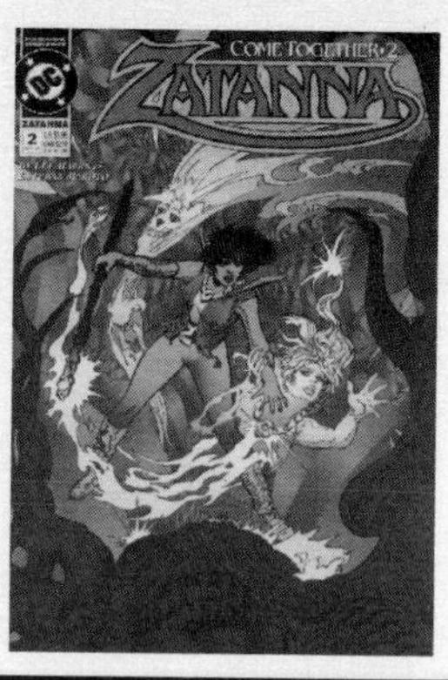
Zatanna #2 © DC

2-S&K-c/a(2-3) 16.00 48.00 110.00
3-6-S&K-c/a(2-3) each 13.00 40.00 90.00
V2#1-6(#7-12)-S&K-c/a(2-3) each 11.50 34.00 80.00
V3#1-3(#13-15): V3#1-Photo-c begin; S&K-a 9.15 27.50 55.00
4-12(#16-24)-Photo-c; S&K-a 9.15 27.50 55.00
V4#1-11(#25-35)-S&K-a 8.35 25.00 50.00
12(#36)-S&K, Toth-a 10.00 30.00 65.00
V5#1-12(#37-48), V6#4-12(#52-60)-S&K-a 8.35 25.00 50.00
V6#1-3(#49-51)-No S&K-a 4.00 11.00 22.00
V7#1-11(#61-71)-S&K-a in most 7.50 22.50 45.00
V7#12(#72), V8#1-3(#73-75)-Last precode (12-1/54-55)-No S&K-a 2.80 7.00 14.00
V8#4(#76, 4-5/55), 5(#77)-No S&K-a 2.40 6.00 12.00
V8#6-8(#78-80, 12-1/55-56)-S&K-a 4.70 14.00 28.00
V9#3,5,6(#81, 2-3/56, 83,84)-S&K-a 4.70 14.00 28.00
4, V10#1(#82,85)-All S&K-a 5.85 17.50 35.00
V10#2-6(#86-90, 10-11/57)-S&K-a 4.70 14.00 28.00
V11#1,2,5,6(#91,92,95,96)-S&K-a 4.70 14.00 28.00
3,4(#93,94), V12#2,4,5(#98,100,101)-No S&K 2.00 5.00 10.00
V12#1,3,6(#97,99,102)-S&K-a 4.70 14.00 28.00
V13#1(#103)-Powell-a; S&K's last-a for Crestwood 4.70 14.00 28.00
2-6(#104-108) 1.40 3.50 7.00
V14#1-6, V15#1-6, V16#1-4(#109-124) 1.20 3.00 6.00

NOTE: ***Meskin** a-16, 24(2), 33, 47, 50. **Robinson/Meskin** a-6. **Leonard Starr** a-11. Photo c-13-32, 34-65. Issues 1-3 say "Designed for the More **Adult** Readers of **Comics**" on cover.*

YOUNG ROMANCE COMICS (Continued from Prize series)
No. 125, Aug-Sept, 1963 - No. 208, Nov-Dec, 1975
National Periodical Publ.(Arleigh Publ. Corp. No. 127)

125 4.00 12.00 24.00
126-162: 154-Neal Adams-c 2.40 6.00 12.00
163,164-Toth-a 1.60 4.00 8.00
165-196: 170-Michell from Young Love ends; Lily Martin, the Swinger begins 1.20 3.00
197-208: 197-204-(100 pgs.) 1.20 3.00

YOUNG ZEN INTERGALACTIC NINJA (Also see Zen...)
1993 - No. 3, 1994 ($2.95, B&W)
Entity Comics

1-($3.50)-Polybagged w/Sam Kieth chromium trading card; gold foil logo 1.40 3.50
2,3-($2.95)-Gold foil logo 1.20 3.00

YOUR DREAMS (See Strange World of...)

YOUR TRIP TO NEWSPAPERLAND
June, 1955 (12 pgs.; 14x11-1/2")
Philadelphia Evening Bulletin (Printed by Harvey Press)

nn-Joe Palooka takes kids on tour through newspaper 4.00 11.00 22.00

YOUR UNITED STATES
1946
Lloyd Jacquet Studios

nn-Used in **SOTI**, pg. 309,310; Sid Greene-a 19.00 58.00 135.00

YOUTHFUL HEARTS (Daring Confessions #4 on)
May, 1952 - No. 3, Sept, 1952
Youthful Magazines

1-"Monkey on Her Back" swipes E.C. drug story/Shock SuspenStories #12; Frankie Laine photo on-c; Doug Wildey-a in all 15.00 45.00 105.00
2,3: 2-Vic Damone photo on-c. 3-Johnny Raye photo on-c 11.00 32.00 75.00

YOUTHFUL LOVE (Truthful Love #2)
May, 1950
Youthful Magazines

1 7.50 22.50 45.00

YOUTHFUL ROMANCES
8-9/49 - No. 5, 4/50; No. 6, 2/51; No. 7, 5/51 - #14, 10/52; #15, 1/53 - #18, 7/53; #5, 9/53 - #8, 5/54
Pix-Parade #1-14/Ribage #15 on

1-(1st series)-Titled Youthful Love-Romances 14.00 43.00 100.00
2-Walter Johnson c-1-4 9.15 27.50 55.00
3-5 7.50 22.50 45.00
6,7,9-14(10/52, Pix-Parade; becomes Daring Love #15); 7-Tony Martin photo on-c 5.85 17.50 35.00
8-Wood-c 11.50 34.00 80.00
15-18 (Ribage)-All have photos on-c 4.70 14.00 28.00
5(9/53, Ribage)-Les Paul photo on-c w/stories 4.00 10.00 20.00
6,7(#7, 2/54), 8(5/54)-All have photo on-c w/stories; 6-Bobby Wayne. 7-Tony Martin. 8-Gordon McCrae 3.60 9.00 18.00

YUPPIES FROM HELL (Marvel)(Value: cover or less)(See Sex, Lies, &..., Son of...)

ZAGO, JUNGLE PRINCE (My Story #5 on)
Sept, 1948 - No. 4, March, 1949
Fox Features Syndicate

1-Blue Beetle app.; partial-r/Atomic #4 (Toni Luck) 32.00 96.00 225.00
2,3-Kamen-a 23.00 70.00 160.00
4-Baker-c 20.00 60.00 140.00

ZANE GREY'S STORIES OF THE WEST
No. 197, 9/48 - No. 996, 5-7/59; 11/64 (All painted-c)
Dell Publishing Co./Gold Key 11/64

4-Color 197(#1)(9/48) 13.00 40.00 90.00
4-Color 222,230,236('49) 8.35 25.00 50.00
4-Color 246,255,270,301,314,333,346 5.35 16.00 32.00
4-Color 357,372,395,412,433,449,467,484 4.70 14.00 28.00
4-Color 511-Kinstler-a 5.00 15.00 30.00
4-Color 532,555,583,604,616,632(5/55) 4.70 14.00 28.00
27(9-11/55) - 39(9-11/58) 4.00 11.00 22.00
4-Color 996(5-7/59) 4.00 11.00 22.00
10131-411-(11/64-G.K.)-Nevada; r/4-Color #996 2.80 7.00 14.00

ZANY (Magazine)(Satire)(See Frantic & Ratfink)
Sept, 1958 - No. 4, May, 1959
Candor Publ. Co.

1-Bill Everett-c 7.50 22.50 45.00
2-4: 4-Everett-c 4.70 14.00 28.00

ZATANNA (Also see Adv. Comics #413, JLA #161, Supergirl #1, World's Finest Comics #274)
July, 1993 - No. 4, Oct, 1993 ($1.95, mini-series)
DC Comics

1-4 .80 2.00

ZATANNA SPECIAL (DC)(Value: cover or less)

ZAZA, THE MYSTIC (Formerly Charlie Chan; This Magazine Is Haunted V2#12 on)
No. 10, April, 1956 - No. 11, Sept, 1956
Charlton Comics

10,11 8.35 25.00 50.00

ZEGRA JUNGLE EMPRESS (Formerly Tegra)(My Love Life #6 on)
No. 2, Oct, 1948 - No. 5, April, 1949
Fox Features Syndicate

2 34.00 100.00 235.00
3-5 25.00 75.00 175.00

ZEN, INTERGALACTIC NINJA (Also see Young Zen...)
Sept, 1992 - Present ($1.25, color)(Formerly a B&W comic by Zen Comics)
Zen Comics/Archie Comics

1-4: 1-Origin Zen; contains mini-poster 1.25

ZEN, INTERGALACTIC NINJA
No. 0, June-July, 1993 - No. 3, 1994 ($2.95, B&W, mini-series)
Entity Comics

Zero Hour: Crisis in Time #4(1st iss.) © DC

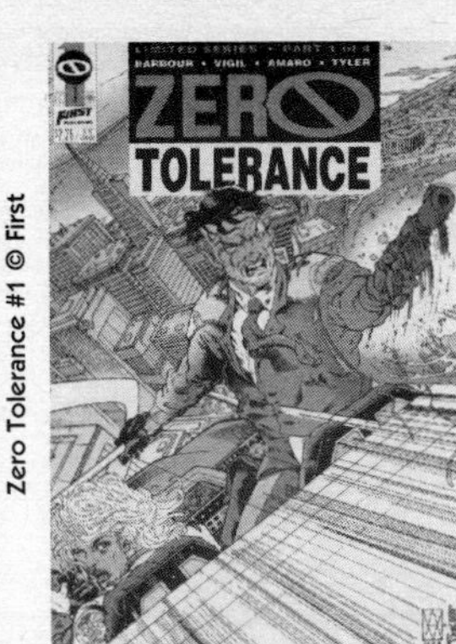

Zero Tolerance #1 © First

Zone Continuum #1 © Bruce Zick

	GD25	FN65	NM94
0-Gold foil stamped-c; photo-c of Zen model		1.20	3.00
1-3-Gold foil stamped-c; Bill Maus-c/a		1.20	3.00
0-(1993, $3.50, color)-Chromium-c by Jae Lee		1.40	3.50

ZEN INTERGALACTIC NINJA: APRIL FOOL'S SPECIAL
1994 ($2.50, B&W)
Parody Press

	GD25	FN65	NM94
1-w/flip story of Renn Intergalactic Chihuahua		1.00	2.50

ZEN INTERGALACTIC NINJA COLOR
1994 - Present ($2.25, color)
Entity Comics

	GD25	FN65	NM94
1-($3.95)-Chromium die cut-c		1.60	4.00
1-($2.25)		.90	2.25
0-($2.25)-Newsstand; Jae Lee-c; r/...All New Color Special #0		.90	2.25
2-($2.50)-Flip book format		1.00	2.50
2-($3.50)-Flip book format; polybagged w/chromium trading card		1.40	3.50
3,4-($2.50)		1.00	2.50

ZEN INTERGALACTIC NINJA MILESTONE
1994 - No. 3, 1994 ($2.95, color, limited series)
Entity Comics

	GD25	FN65	NM94
1-3-Gold foil logo; r/Defend the Earth		1.20	3.00

ZEN INTERGALATIC NINJA SPRING SPECTACULAR
1994 ($2.95, B&W)
Entity Comics

	GD25	FN65	NM94
1-Gold foil logo		1.20	3.00

ZEN INTERGALACTIC NINJA STARQUEST
1994 - Present ($2.95, B&W)
Entity Comics

	GD25	FN65	NM94
1-3-Gold foil logo		1.20	3.00

ZEN, INTERGALACTIC NINJA: THE HUNTED
1993 - No. 3, 1994 ($2.95, B&W, mini-series)
Entity Comics

	GD25	FN65	NM94
1-3-($2.95)-Newsstand Edition; foil logo		1.20	3.00
1-($3.50)-Polybagged w/chromium card by Kieth; foil logo		1.40	3.50

ZERO HOUR: CRISIS IN TIME
No. 4(#1), Sept, 1994 - No. 0(#5), Oct, 1994 ($1.50, limited series)
DC Comics

	GD25	FN65	NM94
4(#1)-0(#5)			1.50
"Ashcan"-(1994, free, B&W, 8 pgs.)			.50

ZERO PATROL, THE (Continuity)(Value: cover or less)

ZERO TOLERANCE
Oct, 1990 - No. 4, Jan, 1991 ($2.25, color, limited series)
First Comics

	GD25	FN65	NM94
1-4: Tim Vigil-c/a(p) (his 1st color mini-series)		.90	2.25

ZIGGY PIG-SILLY SEAL COMICS (See Animal Fun, Animated Movie-Tunes, Comic Capers, Krazy Komics, Silly Tunes & Super Rabbit)
Fall, 1944 - No. 6, Fall, 1946
Timely Comics (CmPL)

	GD25	FN65	NM94
1-Vs. the Japs	16.00	48.00	110.00
2	9.15	27.50	55.00
3-5	7.50	22.50	45.00
6-Infinity-c	10.00	30.00	60.00
I.W. Reprint #1(1958)-r/Krazy Komics	1.20	3.00	6.00
I.W. Reprint #2,7,8	1.00	2.50	5.00

ZIP COMICS
Feb, 1940 - No. 47, Summer, 1944 (#1-7?: 68 pgs.)
MLJ Magazines

	GD25	FN65	NM94
1-Origin Kalathar the Giant Man, The Scarlet Avenger, & Steel Sterling; Mr. Satan (by Edd Ashe), Nevada Jones (masked hero) & Zambini, the Miracle Man, War Eagle, Captain Valor begins	286.00	857.00	2000.00
2-Nevada Jones adds mask & horse Blaze	121.00	365.00	850.00
3	86.00	257.00	600.00
4,5	69.00	208.00	485.00
6-9: 9-Last Kalathar & Mr. Satan	59.00	175.00	410.00
10-Inferno, the Flame Breather begins, ends #13	64.00	193.00	450.00
11,12: 11-Inferno without costume	51.00	154.00	360.00
13-17,19: 17-Last Scarlet Avenger	51.00	154.00	360.00
18-Wilbur begins (9/41, 1st app.)	56.00	167.00	390.00
20-Origin & 1st app. Black Jack (11/41); Hitler-c	75.00	225.00	525.00
21-26: 25-Last Nevada Jones. 26-Black Witch begins; last Captain Valor	47.00	141.00	330.00
27-Intro. Web (7/42) plus-c app.	75.00	225.00	525.00
28-Origin Web	75.00	225.00	525.00
29,30: 29-The Hyena app.	38.00	115.00	265.00
31-38: 34-1st Applejack app. 35-Last Zambini, Black Jack. 38-Last Web issue	31.00	92.00	215.00
39-Red Rube begins (origin, 8/43)	31.00	92.00	215.00
40-47: 45-Wilbur ends	24.00	72.00	165.00

NOTE: *Biro a-5, 9, 17; c-3-17.* ***Meskin*** *a-1-3, 5-7, 9, 10, 12, 13, 15, 16 at least.* ***Montana*** *c-29, 30, 32-35.* ***Novick*** *c-18-28, 31.* ***Sahle*** *c-37, 38, 40-46. Bondage c-8, 9, 33, 34. Cover features: Steel Sterling-1-43, 47; (w/Blackjack-20-27 & Web-27-35), 28-39; (w/Red Rube-40-43); Red Rube-44-47.*

ZIP-JET (Hero)
Feb, 1953 - No. 2, Apr-May, 1953
St. John Publishing Co.

	GD25	FN65	NM94
1,2-Rocketman-r from Punch Comics; #1-c from splash in Punch #10	34.00	103.00	240.00

ZIPPY THE CHIMP (CBS TV Presents...)
No. 50, March, 1957; No. 51, Aug, 1957
Pines (Literary Ent.)

	GD25	FN65	NM94
50,51	4.70	14.00	28.00

ZODY, THE MOD ROB
July, 1970
Gold Key

	GD25	FN65	NM94
1	1.20	3.00	7.00

ZOMBIE 3-D (3-D Zone)(Value: cover or less)

ZONE (Dark Horse)(Value: cover or less)

ZONE CONTINUM, THE
1994 ($2.95, B&W)
Caliber Press

	GD25	FN65	NM94
1		1.20	3.00

ZOO ANIMALS
No. 8, 1954 (15¢, 36 pgs.)
Star Publications

	GD25	FN65	NM94
8-(B&W for coloring)	4.00	10.00	20.00

ZOO FUNNIES (Tim McCoy #16 on)
Nov, 1945 - No. 15, 1947
Charlton Comics/Children Comics Publ.

	GD25	FN65	NM94
101(#1)(11/45, 1st Charlton comic book)-Funny animal; Al Fago-c	13.00	40.00	90.00
2(12/45, 52 pgs.)	7.50	22.50	45.00
3-5	5.85	17.50	35.00
6-15: 8-Diana the Huntress app.	4.00	12.00	24.00

ZOO FUNNIES (Becomes Nyoka, The Jungle Girl #14 on?)
July, 1953 - No. 13, Sept, 1955; Dec, 1984
Capitol Stories/Charlton Comics

	GD25	FN65	NM94
1-1st app.? Timothy The Ghost; Fago-c/a	7.50	22.50	45.00
2	4.20	12.50	25.00
3-7 (8/46)	4.00	10.00	20.00
8-13-Nyoka app.	5.85	17.50	35.00
1(1984)			1.00

ZOONIVERSE (Eclipse)(Value: cover or less)

ZOO PARADE (See 4-Color #662)

ZOOM COMICS
December, 1945 (One Shot)
Carlton Publishing Co.

	GD25	FN65	NM94
nn-Dr. Mercy, Satannas, from Red Band Comics; Capt. Milksop origin retold	29.00	86.00	200.00

ZOOT (Rulah Jungle Goddess #17 on)
nd (1946) - No. 16, July, 1948 (Two #13s & 14s)
Fox Features Syndicate

	GD25	FN65	NM94
nn-Funny animal only	12.00	36.00	85.00
2-The Jaguar app.	11.00	32.00	75.00
3(Fall, 1946) - 6-Funny animals & teen-age	6.70	20.00	40.00
7-(6/47)-Rulah, Jungle Goddess begins (origin & 1st app.)	54.00	160.00	375.00
8-10	41.00	122.00	285.00
11-Kamen bondage-c	43.00	130.00	300.00
12-Injury-to-eye panels, torture scene	26.00	78.00	180.00
13(2/48)	26.00	78.00	180.00
14(3/48)-Used in **SOTI**, pg. 104, "One picture showing a girl nailed by her wrists to trees with blood flowing from the wounds, might be taken straight from an ill. ed. of the Marquis deSade"	33.00	100.00	230.00
13(4/48),14(5/48)-Becomes Western True Crime #15 on?	26.00	78.00	180.00
15,16	26.00	78.00	180.00

ZORRO (Walt Disney with #882)(TV)(See Eclipse Graphic Album)
May, 1949 - No. 15, Sept-Nov, 1961 (Photo-c 882 on)
Dell Publishing Co.
(Zorro first appeared in a pulp story Aug 19, 1919 - 1994 was 75th anniversary)

	GD25	FN65	NM94
4-Color 228 (#1)	24.00	72.00	165.00
4-Color 425,617,732	14.00	43.00	100.00
4-Color 497,538,574-Kinstler-a	15.00	45.00	105.00
4-Color 882-Photo-c begin; Toth-a	22.00	65.00	150.00
4-Color 920,933,960,976-Toth-a in all	14.00	43.00	100.00
4-Color 1003('59)-Toth-a	14.00	43.00	100.00
4-Color 1037-Annette Funicello photo-c	18.00	54.00	125.00
8(12-2/59-60)	10.00	30.00	65.00
9,12-Toth-a. 12-Last 10¢ issue	10.00	30.00	70.00
10,11,13-15-Last photo-c	9.15	27.50	55.00

NOTE: ***Warren Tufts** a-4-Color 1037, 8, 9, 10, 13.*

ZORRO (Walt Disney)(TV)
Jan, 1966 - No. 9, March, 1968 (All photo-c)
Gold Key

	GD25	FN65	NM94
1-Toth-a	8.35	25.00	50.00
2,4,5,7-9-Toth-a. 5-r/F.C. #1003 by Toth	5.00	15.00	30.00
3,6-Tufts-a	4.20	12.50	25.00

NOTE: *#1-9 are reprinted from Dell issues. **Tufts** a-3, 4. #1-r/F.C. #882. #2-r/F.C. #960. #3-r/#12-c & #8 inside. #4-r/#9-c & insides. #6-r/#11(all); #7-r/#14-c. #8-r/F.C. #933 inside & back-c & #976-c. #9-r/F.C. #920.*

ZORRO (TV)
Dec, 1990 - No. 12, Nov, 1991 ($1.00)
Marvel Comics

	GD25	FN65	NM94
1-12: Based on new TV show. 12-Toth-c			1.00

ZORRO
Nov, 1993 - Present ($2.50)
Topps Comics

	GD25	FN65	NM94
0-(11/93, $1.00, 20 pgs.)-Painted-c; collector's ed.			1.00
1-8,10-14: 1-Miller-c. 3-Lady Rawhide-c by Adam Hughes. 3,7,8-Lady Rawhide app. 4-Mike Grell-c. 6-Mignola-c. 7-Lady Rawhide-c by Gulacy. 8-Perez-c		1.00	2.50
9-($2.95)-Lady Rawhide-c & app.		1.20	3.00

ZOT! (Eclipse)(Value: cover or less)

Z-2 COMICS (Secret Agent...)(See Holyoke One-Shot #7)

ZULU (See Movie Classics)

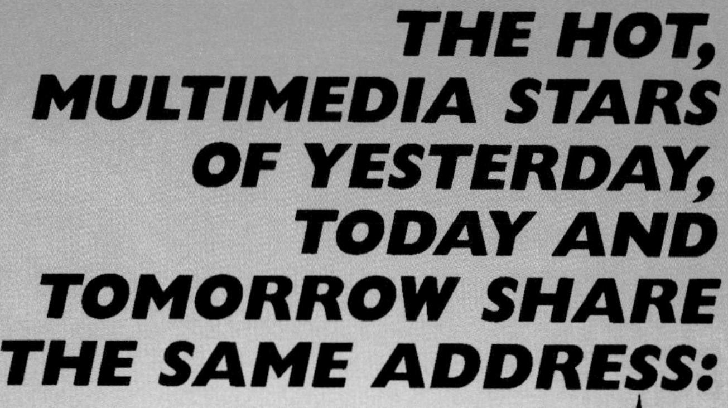
THE HOT,
MULTIMEDIA STARS
OF YESTERDAY,
TODAY AND
TOMORROW SHARE
THE SAME ADDRESS:

Comics On Parade #29 © UFS

Daring Comics #9 © MEG

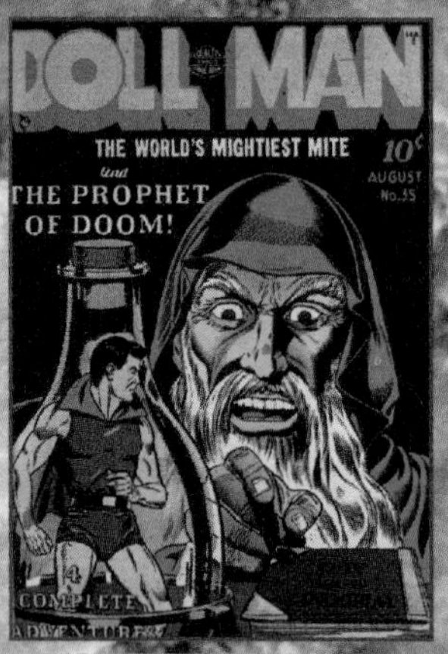

Doll Man #35 © QUA

TALES OF FANTASY AND SUSPENSE!
JAN-FEB
10¢
No.14
EERIE
MASTER of the DEAD!

Eerie #14 © AVON

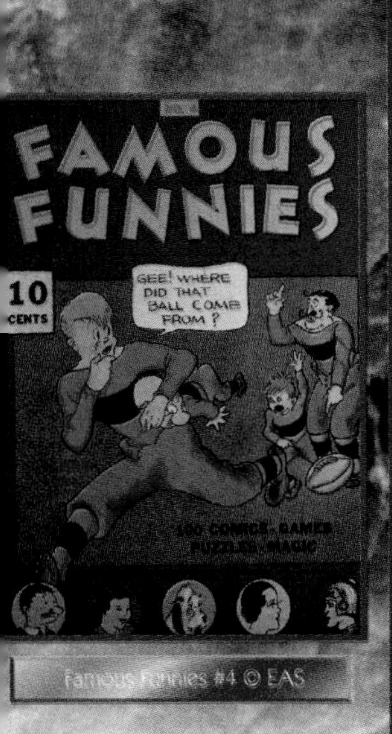

Famous Funnies #4 © EAS

Feature Book #5 © KING

Fight Comics #2 © FH

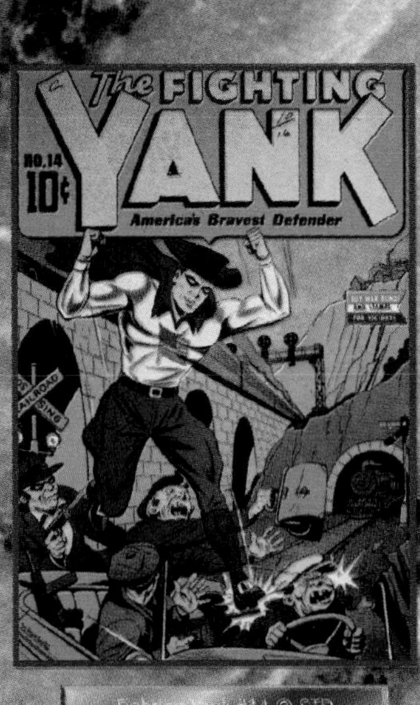

Fighting Yank #14 © STD

Flaming Love #6 © QUA

Flash Comics #2 © DC

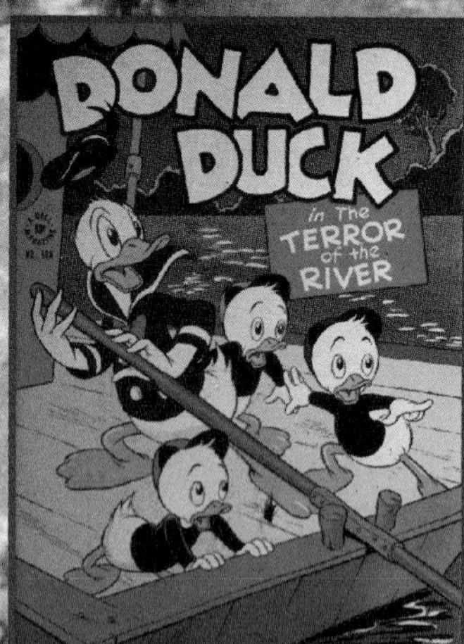

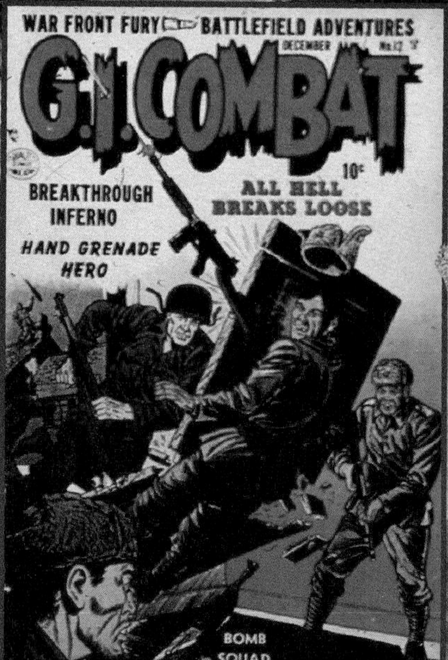

Four Color #108 © WDC

G.I. Combat #12 © DC

MARVEL
METAL
CYCLOPS

Hangman #4 © MLF

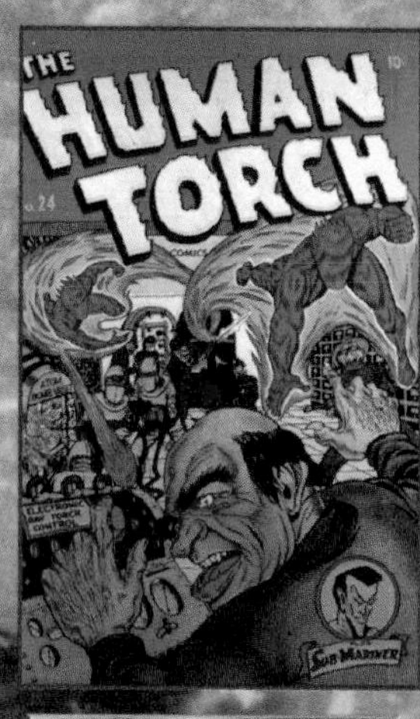

Human Torch #24 © MEG

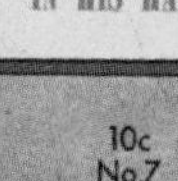

Intimate Confessions #7 © Realistic

Journey Into Mystery #16 © MEG

Journey Into Unknown Worlds #17 © MEG

Jumbo Comics #15 © FH

Jungle Comics #71 © FH

The Killers #1 © ME

Leading Comics #7 © DC

Lone Ranger #7 © Lone Ranger

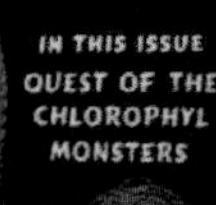

Lost Worlds #1 © STD

Looney Tunes #1 © Warner Bros.

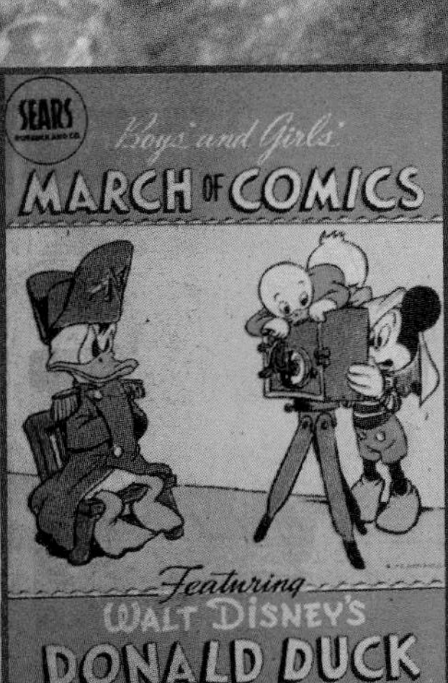

March Of Comics #4 © WDC

The Marvel Family #29 © FAW

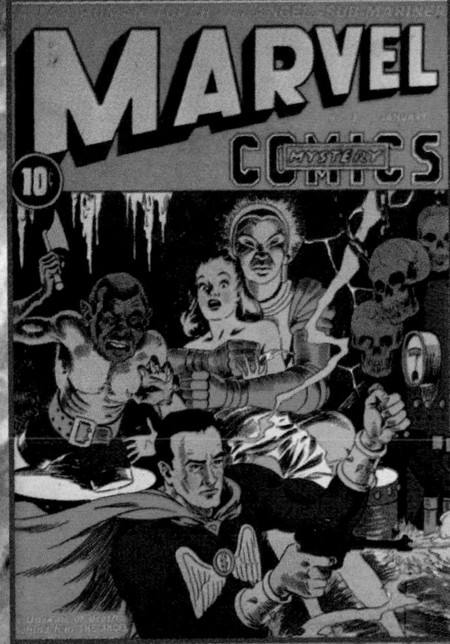

Marvel Mystery Comics #3 © MEG

Marvel Tales #123 © MEG

Master Comics #8 © FAW

Mickey Mouse Magazine #1 © WDC

Miss Fury #1 © MEG

More Fun Comics #68 © DC

My Secret Story #29 © FOX

OVERSTREET INDIAN ARROWHEAD PRICE GUIDE!!

THE FOURTH EDITION IS DUE TO BE RELEASED IN THE SUMMER OF '95!

- Over 5,000 actual size illustrations, many in full color!
- Tips on grading and evaluating projectile points!
- Clearly defined grading definitions!
- Information on pricing your collection!
- How to locate the best sites!
- How to buy authentic relics!
- A Complete chronology of early man!

The Guide That Makes You An Expert!

Available at your favorite comic shop or book store in the Summer of '95!

Mysteries #7 © Superior

Our Army At War #9 © DC

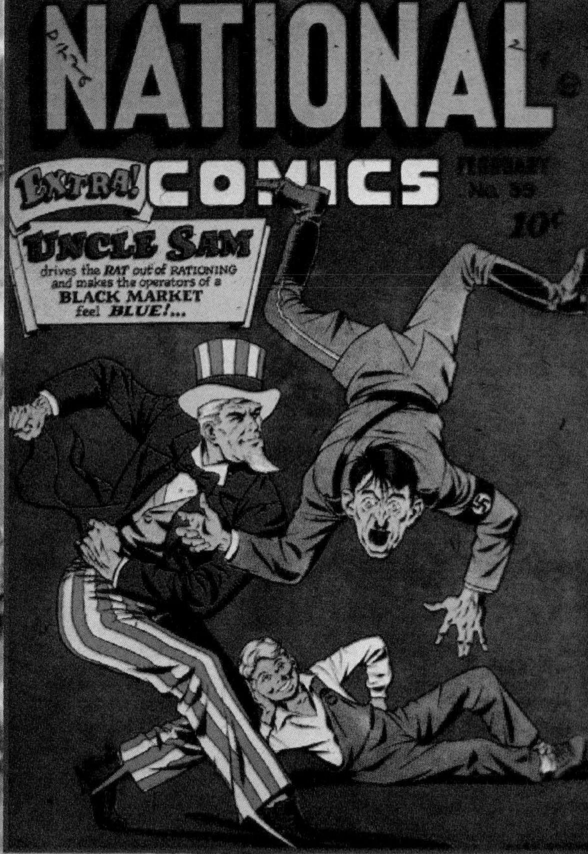

National Comics #39 © QUA

Power Comics #3 © HOLY

Roy Rogers Comics #1 © Roy Rogers

Showcase #9 © DC

Seven Seas Comics #1 © Universal Phoenix

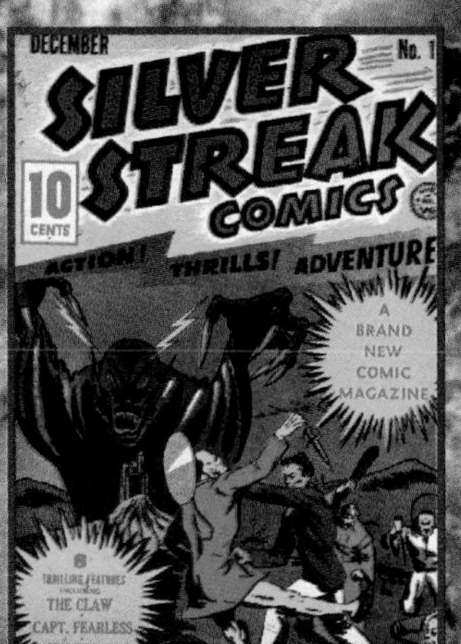

Silver Streak #1 © LEV

Space Adventures #17 © CC

Star Spangled War Stories #4 © DC

Spy Smasher #6 © FAW

Sub-Mariner #9 © MEG

Strange Tales #15 © MEG

Superman #11 © DC

Suspense Comics #3 © Continental

Tales To Astonish #17 © MEG

Target Comics V3#2 © NOVP

TV FOR COMIC COLLECTORS

From Overstreet & Threshold Home Video!

Featuring interviews, cameos, and commentary from an all-star lineup:

Murphy Anderson
Carl Barks
Dan Barry
Bill Cole
Peter David
Will Eisner
Harlan Ellison
Danny Fuchs
Bill Gaines
Steve Geppi
Bruce Hamilton
Russ Heath
Roger Hill
Gil Kane
Jack Kirby
Stan Lee
Paul Levitz
Todd McFarlane
Shelly Moldoff
Marty Nodell
Paul Norris
Bob Overstreet
Chris Pedrin
Robert Rogovin
Julius Schwartz
Jim Shooter
Jeff Smith
Dick Sprang
Vincent Sullivan
Jerry Weist

and many, many more!

THE OVERSTREET WORLD OF COMIC BOOKS

one hour video is now available at your favorite comic store! Suggested retail price: $19.95! Pick one up today!

USA #1 © MEG

Turok #3 © Western Publ.

Uncle Scrooge #4 © WDC

Voodoo #1 © Ajax

Walt Disney's Comics & Stories V3/#1 © WDC

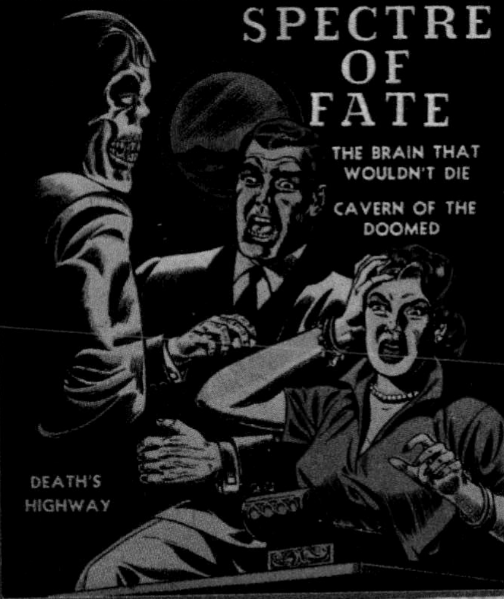

Web Of Evil #10 © QUA

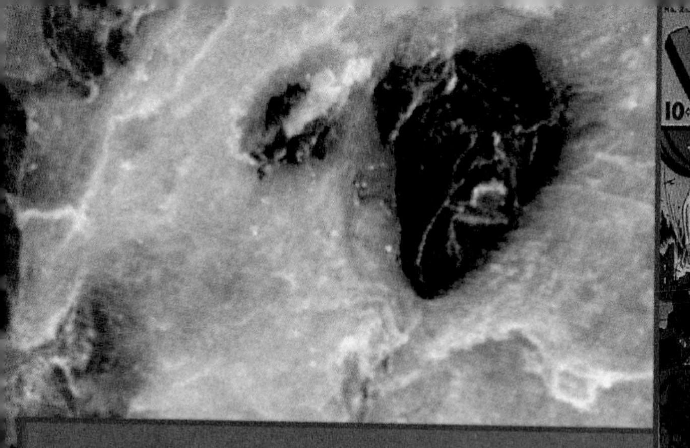

Wonder Comics #2 © BP

Western Crime-Busters #4 © Trojan

World's Best Comics #1 © DC

Wow Comics #58 © FAW

Yellowjacket #1 © F. Comunale

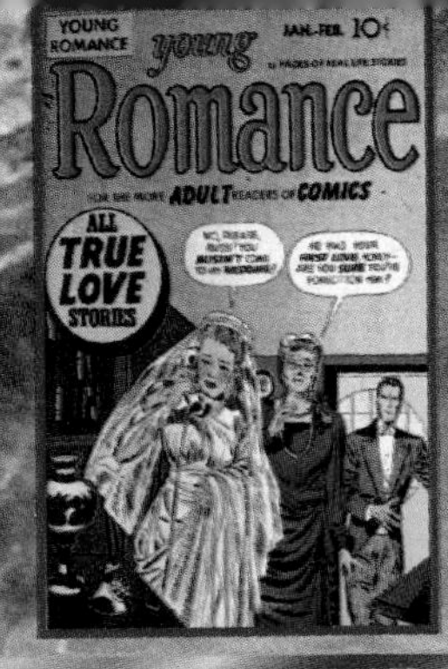

Young Romance #3 © PRIZE

Zoot #12 © FOX

Jim Hanley's Universe sucks less

A shocking admission: Jim Hanley's Universe is the worst place to buy comic books, except for the others

By Jim Hanley

Lets face it, all comic book stores are pretty awful.

It's not that their owners are all unprincipled louts, (though some are) it's just that running a comics store takes some rather specialized skills. You have to know site selection, financial control, merchandising, bookkeeping, inventory control, advertising design, advertising placement, and personnel management (to say nothing of being familiar with the business end of a vacuum cleaner.)

It also helps to know what Scott McCloud calls the "Vocabulary of rcomics." After all, if you can't tell good comics from bad, you'll have a hard time ordering ones that your customers will buy. These skills take a long time and much trial and error to learn and they don't come cheap.

Customer service

This brings me to the biggest hurdle for the store owner: customer service. I don't mean old saws like "the customer is always right." I'm talking about simple courtesies like trying to making sure that every customer gets his or her comics even if it means looking in the bottom box or giving up your personal copy. Things like calling another store to find that missing issue or the right T-shirt size. These are things that most of our competitors don't seem to understand.

We suck less

Of course, we do lots of dumb things too. What sets us apart from everyone else is the fact that we admit our service sometimes sucks. And we work to correct it. I've found that customers will forgive almost any goofy thing we do as long as we do three things:

- Say we're sorry
- Mean it
- Fix the problem
- Not do it again

(Um, that was four things, wasn't it? I'm sorry. I won't do that again.)

Who needs Jim Hanley's Universe?

One of the most important lessons that I've ever learned is that comic book readers don't need to spend their money at Jim Hanley's Universe. Other stores carry the same comics we do. We all get them on the same day at almost the same time. So we have to keep trying to get better to keep our customers happy (quite aside from attracting those of you who don't shop with us yet). After all, it's your money.

Do I have to move?

Well, if you want to shop every week in our fairly clean, not too disorganized, marginally well stocked stores, it does help to live nearby. But I don't think this sales pitch will convince many comics fans to uproot their families and move to New York (or New Jersey.)

Luckily, we have recently decided to bring the same miserable level of service that New Yorkers have come to tolerate to the comic fans around the world, so now you can deal with our mail order department, no matter what comic book store has disappointed you in the past. Send for a free catalogue. If we don't lose your letter, we'll eventually send you one.

My parents would be so proud.

Jim Hanley
Figurehead †

† For all the good that does me.

Staten Island & Mail Orders
350 New Dorp Lane
Staten Isl., NY 10306
(718) 351-6299

Midtown
126 West 32nd St
(near Penn Station)
New York, NY 10001
(212) 268-7088

Downtown
166 Chambers St
(at Greenwich St)
New York, NY 10007
(212) 349-2930

New Jersey
Route 1 & Ford Ave
near Vintage Vinyl
Fords, NJ 08863
(908) 417-5744

HEROES
CONVENTION
CHARLOTTE

REDBEARD'S BOOK DEN
A BOOK DEN BOOK
RARE and SCARCE COMICS,
COLLECTORS CARDS
BOUGHT/SOLD/TRADED
"Undergrounds too"
NO COLLECTION TOO LARGE OR SMALL!
LB Cole
REDBEARD'S BOOK DEN
P.O. BOX 217
Crystal Bay, NV. 89402-0217
PH:(702) 831-4848
Fax (702) 831-4483

Let's give something back to someone who has given us so much. Let's give Jack Kirby something as simple as a little credit!

Please join me in signing your name to the letter below, or write your own letter to Terry Stewart, President of Marvel Comics.

Terry Stewart, President
Marvel Comics Company
387 Park Avenue South
New York, NY 10016 USA

Dear Terry,

Count me among the fans of Marvel Comics who feel that Jack Kirby deserves a little credit for helping to create the Marvel Universe. Without the creative teamwork of Stan Lee and Jack Kirby I might never have known a world filled with the Fantastic Four, The Silver Surfer, The X-Men, The Avengers, Thor, Sgt. Fury, or the Hulk. On these titles and with other characters developed by Stan and Jack, I ask that you place the by-line "Created by Stan Lee and Jack Kirby." This would serve as a long overdue tribute to the genius of their teamwork. Just as Jerry Siegel and Joe Shuster will always be formally identified as the creators of Superman, I would like to see Jack Kirby and Stan Lee afforded a similar tribute for their many contributions to the Marvel Universe.

Sincerely,

____

Note: This ad copy was prepared prior to Jack's death. For more information regarding this letter writing campaign, please contact:
Dr. Mark Miller
6466 S.W. Barnes Rd.
Portland, OR 97221 USA

We are paying 60% of guide for the following:

Adventure (32-267)
Adv. of Bob Hope (1-50)
Adv. of Jerry Lewis (1-50)
Adv. of Ozzie & Harriet
All American
All Flash
All New
All Top (8-18)
Blackhawk (9-110)
Blue Beetle (47-57)
Captain America (1st)

Flash (1st)
Hit (1-20)
House of Mystery (1-50)
House of Secrets (1-25)
Leading (1-14)
Legend of Dan'l Boone
Mary Marvel
Military
Movie Comics (D.C.)
My Greatest Adventure (1-50)

Mystery Men
National (1-23)
New Book of Comics
Phantom Stranger
Science (Fox)
Shadow (Fox)
Showcase (1-30)
Speed (1-20)
Superman (1-125)
Superman's Pal (1-30)

We are paying 55% of guide for the following:

Airboy
Air Fighters
All Select
All Star
All Winners
Amazing Spiderman (1-20)
America's Greatest
Blonde Phamtom
Brave & the Bold (1-30)
Brenda Starr (1-12)
Bulletman
Captain Marvel
Captain Marvel Jr.
Captain Midnight
Catman
Challengers of the Unknown (1-10)
Classics Comics (1st 1-20)

Comic Cavalcade (1-29)
Crash
Daredevil (1st 1-20)
Daring Mystery
Dollman
Fantastic
Fantastic Four (1-20)
Frontier Fighters
Green Hornet (1-20)
Human Torch
Ibis
John Wayne
JO-JO (7-29)
Journey into Mystery (1-85)
Jungle (1-10)
Kid Komics
Lash Larue (1-46)
Marvel Family

Marvel Mystery
Master
Miss Fury
Modern
More Fun (52-107)
Mystery In Space (1-90)
Mystic (1st)
Nickel
Pep (1-40)
Phamtom Lady
Planet
Pogo Possum
Police (1-20)
Rangers (1-20)
Rulah
Saint
Sensation
Shield Wizard

Silver Streak (1-17)
Smash
Spy Smasher
Star Spangled
Strange Adventure (1-120)
Strange Tales (1-100)
Sub-Mariner (1st)
Superboy (1-50)
Tomahawk (1-30)
Top-Notch
U.S.A.
W.D. Comics & Stories (1-40)
Weird Comics
Whiz
World's Finest (1-110)
Young Allies
Zip (1-39)
Zoot (7-16)

We are also paying 50-75% of guide for many other titles. Comics must be properly graded and complete. Please send your listing of comics for sale or your list of comics you wish to purchase. We are also dealing heavily in Sci-Fi material plus thousands of Marvels, D.C.'s Western, Funny Material and Much More! Please Send one dollar for our current retail listing of comics in stock. Will Travel for Large Collections or if you're passing through the area call for an appointment.

CBG Customer Service Award — 1986

JAMES F. PAYETTE
RARE BOOKS AND COMICS
P.O. BOX 750, BETHLEHEM, NH 03574
(603) 869-2097 Fax (603) 869-3475

WORLDWIDE MAIL ORDER SERVICE

DAVID T. ALEXANDER

P.O. BOX 273086
TAMPA, FLORIDA 33618
(813) 968-1805
FAX (813) 264-6226

OUR AMAZING CATALOGS ARE LOADED WITH ITEMS TO SERVE **ALL** OF YOUR COLLECTING NEEDS! OUR 17 NEW CATALOGS FOR 1995 ARE CHOCK **FULL** OF **HUNDREDS** OF **THOUSANDS** OF **RARE COMICS, BOOKS, PULPS, POSTERS, MAGS, PRINTS, ART — YOU NAME IT!!**

WE HAVE BEEN DEALING IN COMICS SINCE THE 60's. THE VARIETY AND DEPTH OF **OUR INVENTORY IS SECOND TO NONE.** WE HAVE OPENED A LARGE NUMBER OF COMIC BOOK STORES THROUGHOUT THE UNITED STATES DURING THE PAST 25 YEARS, AND CAN NOW **OFFER THIS SERVICE TO YOU —**

WANT TO OWN A COMIC BOOK BUSINESS?

EARN BIG $ AND HAVE A **GREAT TIME** IN ONE OF AMERICA'S FASTEST GROWING INDUSTRIES

BECOME AN AFFILIATE STORE —
— WITH ONE OF THE FOLLOWING:

SPECIAL
MAIL ORDER BUSINESS START UP PACKAGE includes catalog, mailing list, inventory, etc!
ONLY $1995.00
CALL TODAY FOR DETAILS!!!

★ **THE MEGA STORE** **$100,000—**
BECOME A POWER IN THE COMIC BOOK AND COLLECTABLE INDUSTRY — AT THIS LEVEL YOUR STORE WILL HAVE A MASSIVE INVENTORY (APPROX. 125,000 ITEMS), INTERNATIONAL ADVERTISING AND WORLD-WIDE PROMINENCE.

★ **COMPLETE STORE** **$35,000—**
YOU GET: SITE LOCATION, STORE DESIGN, FIXTURES, TRAINING, INVENTORY *(55% OFF RETAIL VALUE)* — COMPREHENSIVE CROSS SECTION OF MARVEL, D.C., POSTERS, BACK ISSUES, NEW MERCHANDISE, COLLECTORS ITEMS —— AND MORE — THIS PACKAGE COULD BE A FULL TIME OCCUPATION OR EMPLOYEE OPERATED!

★ **SMALL STORE / MAIL ORDER BUSINESS** **$12,500—**
YOU GET: SITE LOCATION, FIXTURES, TRAINING, AND INVENTORY *(52% OFF RETAIL VALUE)* — AN EXCELLENT WAY FOR THE PART TIMER TO BEGIN!!

★ **COMBINATION PACKAGES —** WE WILL **TAILOR MAKE** A BUSINESS TO SUIT YOUR NEEDS AND FINANCES!!

★ ALL BUSINESS PACKAGES GET INVENTORY AT 50% OFF!!

IF YOU WANT TO BE YOUR **OWN BOSS** AND **EARN BIG $$,** THIS COULD BE THE **OPPORTUNITY** FOR YOU!!—**SEND $5°° FOR COMPLETE DETAILS.**

BUYING BUYING BUYING

CURRENTLY NEEDED: SENSATION, DARING MYSTERY, ALL WINNERS, EXCITING, THRILLING, BLACK TERROR, STARTLING, BATMAN, CAPTAIN AMERICA, MORE FUN, GREEN HORNET, GREEN MASK, SILVER STREAK, PHANTOM LADY, ACTION, ALL TOP, CRASH, CATMAN, MARVEL MYSTERY, HIT, AMERICA'S BEST, MILITARY, ALL NEW, SCIENCE, SPEED, ROCKET, MISS FURY, DETECTIVE, SHADOW, MYSTIC, DOC SAVAGE, PLANET, JUNGLE, TUROK, HUMAN TORCH...**AND MANY MORE!**

THINKING OF SELLING? I AM ACTIVELY PURCHASING GOLDEN AGE AND PRE-1969 COMIC BOOKS, BIG LITTLE BOOKS, PULP MAGAZINES, AND ORIGINAL ART. I WILL PAY YOU TOP PRICES FOR QUALITY MATERIAL. I AM EASY TO DEAL WITH. QUICK, CONFIDENTIAL TRANSACTIONS. ANY QUANTITY, ANY CONDITION, ANY TIME.

LARGE COLLECTIONS OR ACCUMULATIONS OUR SPECIALTY

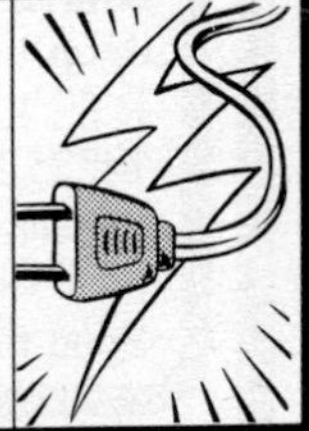

Many retailers know us only as
COMICS On Call
1 800 654-HERO
but most retailers also know us as...
Cards On Call!
The largest inventory of collector cards in the industry
- just a phone call away - all at incredible prices!
Games On Call!
A huge inventory of Adventure/RP games,
miniatures, dice and supplies - all at competitive discounts!
Toys On Call!
A vast inventory of action figures (including products
from Toy Biz, Kenner & Playmates) vehicles, models &
family games, all just a toll-free call away!
Call 1-800-654-HERO today for our stock listings
and free newsletter, or to place an order!
(if busy 201-927-4447, or fax to 201-927-4551/4171)
Free shipping on all comics orders over $100
HWDC
Comics On Call is a division of Heroes World Distribution Co.
961 Rte. 10 East, Randolph, NJ 07869

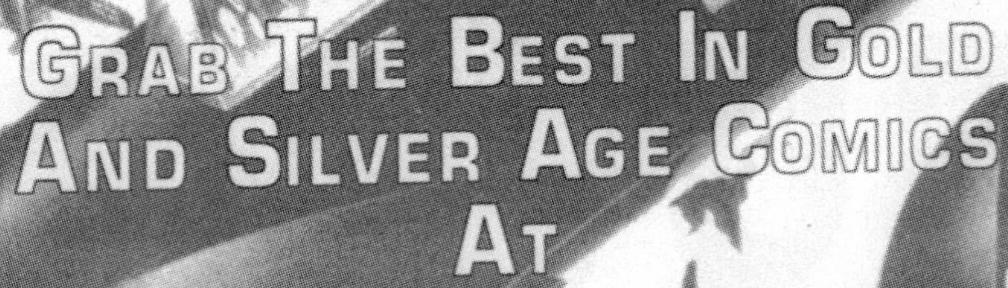
GRAB THE BEST IN GOLD
AND SILVER AGE COMICS
AT

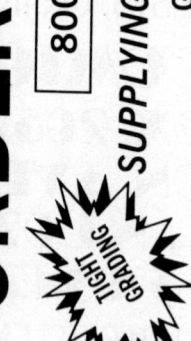

CONTINUED ON NEXT PAGE

CONTINUED ON NEXT PAGE ▶▶▶

CBG Customer Service Award - 1991
PHILIP M. LEVINE AND SONS
RARE AND ESOTERIC BOOKS
P. O. Box 246
Three Bridges, NJ 08887
Phone (908) 788-0532
FAX (908) 788-1028
Customer Service Award Toy Shop 1991
ON
SEND US ALL OF YOUR PRE-
1975 COMIC BOOKS TODA
We will make you an immediate cas offer. If we don't buy your books, we will pay the "book rate postage" both ways. We are always buying and selling comics, giveaway comics, Big Little books, old paperbacks, MAD memorabilia, Seduction of the Innocent and related censorship material, radio premiums, early crime magazines, "Cardboard Age" comics, antediluvian comics and related material, pulps, Catechetical Guild comics and related material, Golden Age comics, Silver Age comics, old toys and Gum Cards. We have the largest inventory of old "TV Guides" in North America. Send us your name & address today to get on our mailing list.
You can come and see us at all the Atlantique City shows, all New York area collectible shows and all Wex-Rex shows, Chicago Comic Con, Motor City Comic Cons, Allentown Pennsylvania Paper Fairs and the San Diego Comic Con.
Don't forget to send us your books. We have been buying and selling comic books for 40 years.
SEND US YOUR WANT LIST TODAY!

EEP?
SHUFFLE ON DOWN TO
THE AMERICAN COMIC BOOK COMPANY
IN FABULOUS
LONG BEACH, CA 90807
©1977 BY SCOTT SHAW!

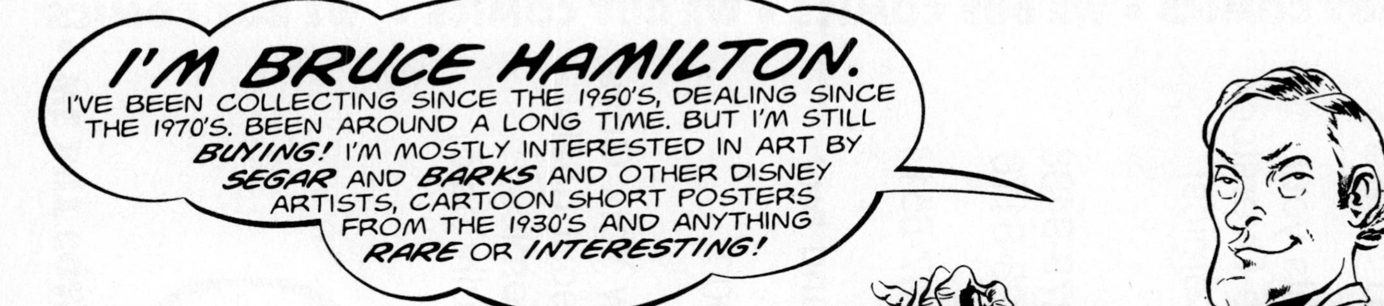
I'M BRUCE HAMILTON.
I'VE BEEN COLLECTING SINCE THE 1950'S, DEALING SINCE THE 1970'S. BEEN AROUND A LONG TIME. BUT I'M STILL BUYING! I'M MOSTLY INTERESTED IN ART BY SEGAR AND BARKS AND OTHER DISNEY ARTISTS, CARTOON SHORT POSTERS FROM THE 1930'S AND ANYTHING RARE OR INTERESTING!
BRUCE HAMILTON
P.O. BOX 4235
PRESCOTT, ARIZONA 86302
PHONE: (602) 776-1300
FAX: (602) 445-7536
Newton 72

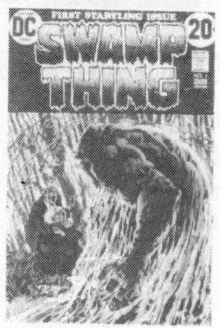

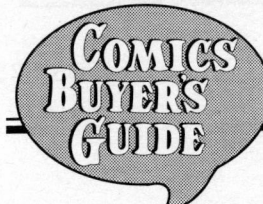

COMICBOOK WANTS

I am a collector looking for a "few good books". Among my wants are:

LITTLE DETECTIVE FUNNIES: 2,3 (Will pay 3x Guide)

DO THESE BOOKS EXIST?

LITTLE GIANT COMICS: 4 (Will pay 2x Guide)
KEEN COMICS #1
AMAZING MYSTERY FUNNIES 1/2 (Fine or better)
MYSTERY MEN COMICS: 7,8,10 (also any number Mile High or Larson)
BIG BOOK OF FUN COMICS
SCIENCE COMICS: 5,6,7,8 (VF or better)
WEIRD COMICS: 2,3 (VF or better) and higher numbers
WHIRLWIND COMICS: 3 (also any number Mile High)
WONDERWORLD COMICS: 11,21,22,24,29,31

Also seeking Mile High or Larson copies of issues 4,5,7,8,9,11,15 and higher numbers.

TARGET COMICS: 2,8,9 (F+ or better)
NATIONAL COMICS 24 - Mile High or Larson preferred
ACTION COMICS 2,23
FANTASTIC COMICS 17 and up- Mile High or Larson preferred
MASTER COMICS 5,6
HOORAY COMICS 1
CHAMPION/CHAMP COMICS 10,13,15,16,17,21,22 Mile High or Larson perferred

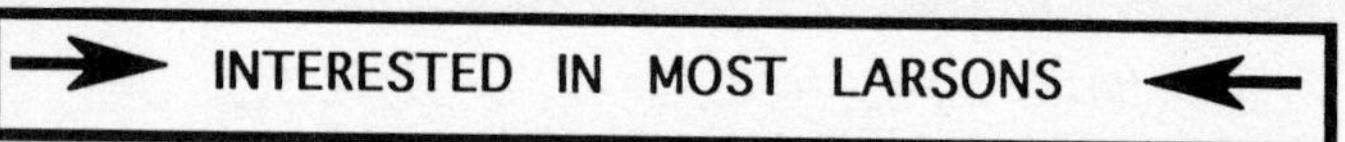

CONTACT: JON BERK c/o GORDON, MUIR 203-525-5361
10 COLOMBUS BLVD.
HARTFORD, CONN. 06106

COMIC MAN AUCTIONS

SECRET IDENTITY
RANDY KESSELRING

COMIC MAN IS ACTIVELY SEEKING CONSIGNMENTS FOR OUR UPCOMING AUCTIONS. **OUR AUCTIONS FEATURE SOME OF THE RAREST MOST DESIRABLE COMIC BOOKS AND ORIGINAL ART.** MANY ITEMS ARE CONSIGNED BY THE ORIGINAL OWNERS. PLEASE CALL TO BE PLACED ON OUR MAILING LIST.

AND.....

IF YOU HAVE ITEMS TO SELL, CONTACT US! WE OFFER:

- LOW COMMISSIONS
- FAST TURNAROUND
- HIGHER PRICES REALIZED THAN OTHER MAJOR AUCTION HOUSES

Lot #1 - **Jumbo #1**. The (rare) over-sized first issue, featuring Sheena, Queen of the Jungle. This book is listed as "Scarce" by Overstreet and is seldom offered for sale. This book is 100% complete with paper in the range of 7-8 owl. Tape on spine due to wear. Good .... **Min Bid $500.00**

Lot #2 - **Superman #1.** At the last San Diego show there were virtually no copies offered for sale. In Christie's October sale there wasn't a copy. We are pleased to offer a complete solid copy with slight restoration. Pages are tan (owl 6) but not brittle. This book is much nicer than copies offered by dealers at San Diego '93 for $7-8,000.00. Good + ...**Min. Bid $6,000.00**

Lot #3 - **New Comics #9** - Scarce early (pre-hero) DC book appears Fine +, but has a diagonal crease over corner. We are calling it a VG/F ... **Min. Bid $500.00**

Lot #5 - **New Fun #2** - Rare, Rare, Rare are the only 3 words I can think of to describe this book. Overstreet estimates only 5 known copies. This copy comes from a recently discovered collection which has not seen daylight for over 30 years. This copy is unrestored and has surprisingly supple paper, owl is approx. 6. Only catch is that the back cover is missing. Still a great opportunity to obtain a copy of the rarest of the rare. Fair ....**Min. Bid $500.00**

Lot #7 - **More Fun #7** - Rare 1st issue (1/36). Overstreet estimates only 15 known copies. When was the last time you had a chance to buy a copy? This book is complete. However, spine has tape, and there is some chipping along edge. Paper quality is good, and book is very restorable. Good cond. owl 6.5 .... **Min. Bid $400.00**

Lot #8 - **More Fun #21** - Scarce Pre-Hero DC, this is a solid copy with some light tape on the spine, owl is approx. 5-6. Good .... **Min. bid $85.00**

PLEASE CALL US ON OUR TOLL-FREE NUMBER TO DISCUSS YOUR HOLDINGS. WE AUCTION:

- COMICS (Min. Value $100)
- ORIGINAL ART
- TOYS, PREMIUMS, ANIMATION, ETC.
- SPORTS MEMORABILIA, CARDS, ETC.

1-800-866-1882

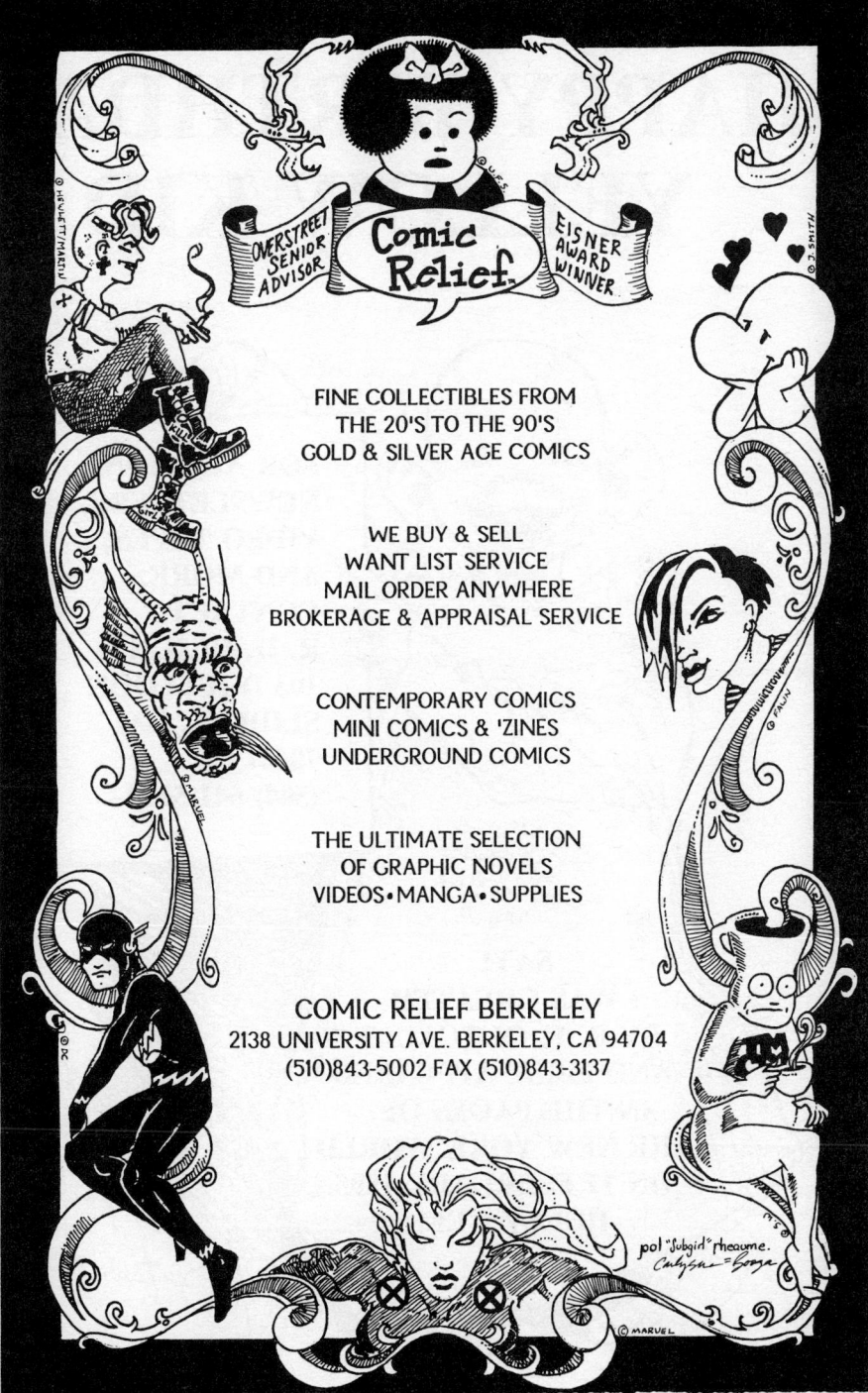

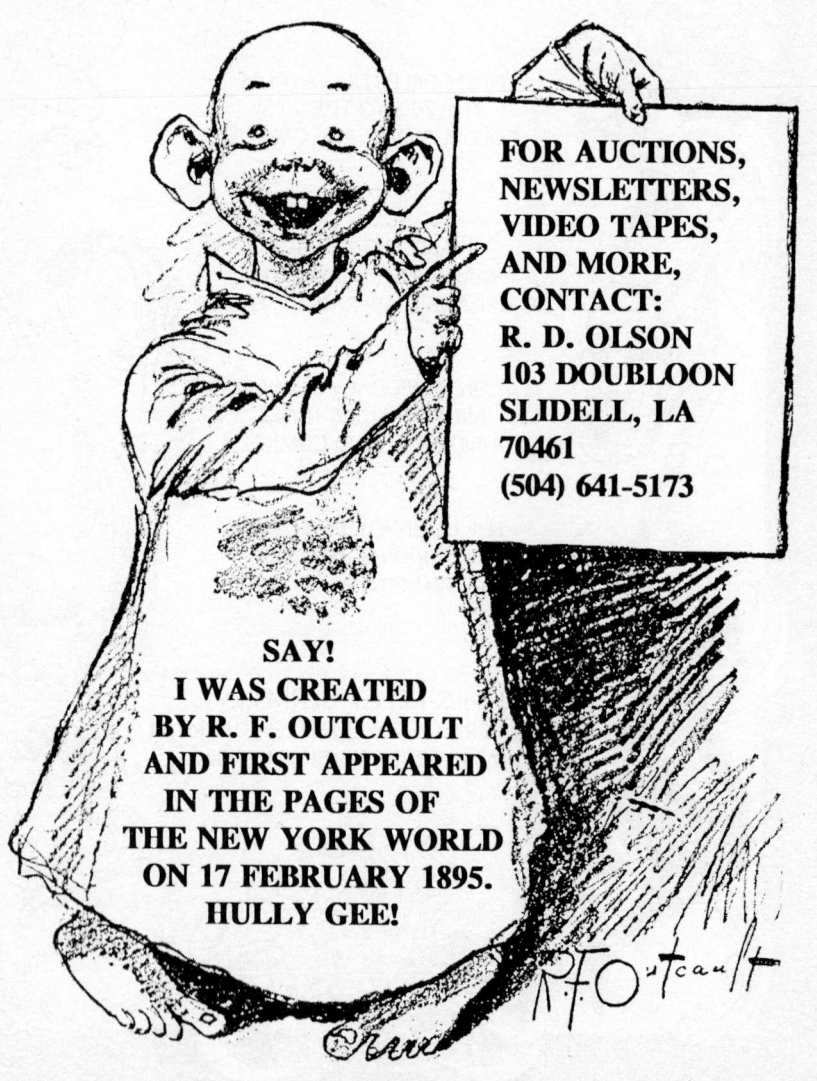

CLASSIFIED ADVERTISING

Canadian dealer is looking for10¢, 12¢ comics and all Classic Illustrated. Will value your collection in U.S. dollars. Our cash offers are quite high because we pay premium price for average comic which make up the majority of collections. Looking for books- send $2.00 for our current list. Will travel to view collections.
David Rowlandson - 705-789-1187
"An Eye for Comics"
4 Morgan Heights
Huntsville, Ontario, Canada P0A 1K0

WANTED! Anything by or about HOWARD CHAYKIN, especially obscure and unusual material and not just comic book. Also wanted: syndicated work by FRAZETTA, and live tapes and printed collectibles relating to RANDY CALIFORNIA/SPIRIT. Write me: TIM BARNES, 103 Tredworth Rd. Gloucester, Glos. GL1 4QU ENGLAND. Seventh Glorious Year!

SEND $1.00 FOR GIANT 1995 "NUMBER ONE PLUS" COMIC CATALOG. EARLY BATMAN, SUPERMAN, GOLDEN AGE, SILVER AGE, MARVELS; BIG LITTLE BOOKS, SUNDAY COMIC PAGES & MUCH MORE! SPECIAL MOVIE SALES: SEND $1.00 FOR "1995 MOVIE CATALOG" OF VINTAGE MOVIE ITEMS TO PRESENT. WRITE: HAL VERB, P.O. BOX 421815 SAN FRANCISCO, CA. 94142-1815

COMIC COLLECTORS. Learn how to get cash from your collection and at the same time, buy or trade for any comic you've ever wanted. It's almost too easy! Send $5.00 and LSASE to JOHN LEE P.O. Box 459 WAYNE, MI 48184-5.

BEATLES!!! BEATLES!!! BEATLES!!!

I want items on the Beatles like toys, dolls, Yellow Submarine items, movie items, concert stubs, etc. Monkees & Circus Boy items also wanted. Rick Rann, Box 877 Oak Park, IL 60303

COMIC COLLECTORS. Send LSASE to LEE ENTERPRISES, P.O.Box 459 Wayne, MI 48184-4 for a free list of 1940's to present comics. Good deals and satisfaction is guaranteed.

$*$*SUPERMAN COLLECTIBLE WANTED!*$*$

BUYING ALL SUPERMAN ITEMS FROM 1938-1966: TOYS, GAMES, FIGURES, BUTTONS, RINGS, PREMIUMS, ADV. MATERIALS...ANYTHING!!!! DANNY FUCHS, 209-80p 18th AVE., BAYSIDE, NY 11360. 718-225-9030 FAX: 718-225-3688.

"AMERICA'S FOREMOST SUPERMAN COLLECTOR"

Newer comics at 50% O.P.G. (G.A. 75% & up). Send a SASE plus 25¢ per list. Request lists desired. Comic Book•BLB•N.P. Comic Strip•Pulp•Paperbacks•Movie TV Items•Old Life, Look, Post, Misc. Magazines. Above also bought. Glenn Rauch, 3500 Manila Dr. Westerville, OH 43081

Carl Bark's Surviving Comic Book Art $24.95 + shipping. Matti Eronen, P.O. Box 295, FIN-00151 Helsinki, Finland, Fax+358-0-542 202. More details from: John Nichols, (804) 696-2925, FAX (804) 696-1675.

POGO books, comics, artwork, animation, figurines, pins, Peter Wheat and other non-Pogo Kelly collectibles, obscure items. List $2. Extensive Search, 51 Squaw Rock, Danielson, CT. 06239 (203) 774-1203.

FREE Comics catalogue. LOW PRICES. Golden-Silver Age, Marvels, DC's, Disneys. All Kinds. I like to TRADE too. Money Back Guarantee. SPECIAL BONUS WITH PURCHASE. Send an EXTRA1st class stamp to DAVE YARUSS, 7916 BLUE LAKE DR, SAN DIEGO, CALIF. 92119. WANTED: Disney Animation Art.

ORIGINAL ART WANTED!

Batman, Metamorpho, Doom Patrol, Metal Men and other 1960s art. Looking for Gahan Wilson original art: "Nuts", "Sunday Funnies", Playboy, etc. Original art from Beatle & Monkees related comic book issues wanted. Beatles cartoon & Yellow Sub cels wanted. Rick Rann, Box 877, Oak Park, IL 60303.

ORIGINAL ART WANTED.

PLASTIC MODEL KITS-SELL/BUY/TRADE: FROM/OF COMICS, TV, MOVIES, SCIENCE FICTION, MISSILES, SPACE, FIGURES, ETC. FREE CATALOG OF HUNDREDS! JOHN F. GREEN INC., 1821 W. JACARANDA, FULLERTON. CA 92633 (714) 526-5467/(800) 807-4759.

SELLING AND BUYING 1920's-1970's

Comic books (much scarce), Sunday Comic Pages and sections (lots), BLB'S S, S-F, related paper collectibles. Catalog $1 (Air $2) 416-222-5808 anytime! My 25th year in OPG. KEN MITCHELL 710 CONACHER DRIVE, WILLOWDALE, ONTARIO. M2M 3N6 CANADA

$400,000 SEARCH!!!

OLD COMIC BOOKS WANTED!! 1933-1976

Very serious buyer. Generally paying 40-80% of guide. Send lists or call Rick Semowich, 56 John Smith Rd. Binghamton, NY 13901. Phone:(607) 648-4025.

HEAVY METAL artwork, cels, posters, collectibles and obscurities. Free information. Also, STAR TREK animation. SASE for information. Extensive Search, 51 Squaw Rock, Danielson, CT. 06239. (203) 774-1203.

COMIC BOOKS FOR SALE

ONE OF THE WORLD'S LARGEST CATALOGUES SELLING GOLDEN AGE, DC, MARVEL, DELL AND CLASSICS ILLUSTRATED COMICS PLUS BIG LITTLE BOOKS, SUNDAY PAGES, ORIGINAL ART. WE SUPPLY CANADIAN COLLECTORS AND COMIC STORES WITH ALL SIZES AND TYPES OF PLASTIC BAGS, ACID FREE BOXES AND BACKING BOARDS, ETC. SEND $2.00 FOR CATALOGUE.

COMIC BOOKS WANTED

HIGHEST PRICES PAID FOR COMIC BOOKS, BIG LITTLE BOOKS, NEWSPAPER COMICS BEFORE 1965. NO COLLECTION TOO LARGE OR SMALL. 40 YEARS EXPERIENCE AS A COLLECTOR AND DEALER. CONTACT US BEFORE SELLING.

INTERNATIONAL COMIC BOOK COMPANY
CALVIN AND ELEANOR SLOBODIAN
74 WATERLOO CRESCENT,
BRANDON, MANITOBA, CANADA R7B3W7
PHONE (204) 728-4337.

---

100 Different fine to Near Mint Comic Books! for $39.95 or 50 Different for $24.95 plus $3.95 shipping. SEND TO: John Kressig 1412 Thomas Pl.-Dubuque, IA 52001-2160

Buying Classics Illustrated and Classic Comics-Call or write Phil Gaudino, 84-19 106 St., Richmond Hill, NY 11418-718-847-6850

X MARKS THE SPOT!

YOU HAVE FOUND COMIC TREASURES!

WANTED: Comics from 1940-1970. Friendly, fast, professional service. No collection too large or too small. Please send your list to COMIC TREASURES, P.O. BOX 17036, DEPT A, IRVINE CA 92713-7036 or call & leave message at (714) 452-1724.

SELLING: Golden Age to Modern Age. Strict grading & great service! Send for a FREE catalog to the address listed above.

WANTED-Star Wars Toys, dolls, plates, bed items, watches, etc. Also G.I. Joe, Raiders, 007, Uncle, Thunderbirds. Fireball XL5, 1999, Supercar, Capt. Action, Superman, Munsters, Shogun W., Add. Family & all TV, Movie etc. D. Wilson, 14 Berryman St, North Ryde NSW Australia.

COMICS & THINGS FOR SALE!

Low prices & great packaging. Send SASE Jim Dallmeier 9047 Aero Dr., Pico Rivera, CA 90660

"HARRYHAUSENS'S WORLD"

Tribute, limited color poster 22" X 27" Signed by artist. Over 40 monsters! Only 2,000 printed. $25 U.S.A. & $28 Foreign orders. Jim Dallmeier 9047 Aero Dr. Pico Rivera CA 90660

ATTENTION OLD-TIME FANS: Don't miss THE GOLDEN AGE OF COMIC FANDOM, the first authoritative book-length history of Comic Fandom (1947-1974). Many illustrations & photos. Limited Collector's Edition! Send $11.95 + $2.50 P&H to Bill Schelly, 3032 N.E. 130th St., Seattle, WA. 98125

Comic Books Thousands available. 1947-1993. Send SASE to D.E. Kerksiek P.O. Box 231, Stover, Mo. 65078 (314) 377-4133.

MAGAZINE PAINTINGS-ILLUSTRATIONS

Original art for cover paintings & illustrations from pulp magazines: detective, mystery, science-fiction, paperback books, men's magazines, comic books, sunday funnies, children's books, movie posters, pinup calendars. BUY-SELL-TRADE. Send photo/price. Tim Issacson, 1002 Clinton, Oak Park, IL.
60304 (708)383-5646.
ORIGINAL ART WANTED.

MONKEY HOUSE COMICS

Is always buying pre-1965 comic books, especially: Atlas, Timely, DC, and precode horror. Please call or write for my offer before you sell for less. Send for my free list and include your wants. We have thousands of books for sale, all fully guaranteed. Buy with confidence!

MONKEY HOUSE COMICS
David C. Cummings
28 Hawthorne Cir.
Peabody, MA 01960
(508) 532-2448 4-9pm EST

Affordable Silver and Golden Age Comics. Send SASE to: Comicbook Hotline Inc., P.O. Box 8230, North Bergen, NJ 07047 (201) 656-3228. Call after 8 P.M. We also buy.

SALE: Early GLADSTONE Disney '86-'88. Barks, Rosa, Gottfredson, Murry, etc. New condition, reasonably priced. Descriptive list: C. Vesce, Box 223. Wanaque NJ 07465. SSAE appreciated.

E.K. WONG, 4282 10th Ave., Port Alberni, BC

QUICK REFERENCE LISTS

The following lists were compiled to give our readers more detailed information about their favorite comic books. We invite your criticism, comments, and suggestions for omitted entries.

1ST APPEARANCE

A-Man the Amazing Man - Amazing-Man Comics #5, 9/39
Adam Strange - Showcase #17, 11-12/58
Adult Legion - Superman #147, 8/61
Agent Liberty - Superman #60 (2nd Series), 10/91
Air Man - (Hawkman imitator) Keen Detective Funnies #23, 8/40
Air Wave - Detective Comics #60, 2/42
Air Wave II - Green Lantern #100, 1/78
Airboy - Air Fighters Comics V1#2, 11/42
Airwave I - Detective Comics #60, 2/42
Alex Summers - (becomes Havok) X-Men #54, 3/69
Alfred - Batman #16 4-5/43; (1st skinny Alfred) Detective Comics #83, 1/44
Alice Cooper - Marvel Premiere #50, 10/79
Alicia Masters - Fantastic Four #8, 11/62
Aliens - Aliens #1 May '88; Magnus, Robot Fighter #1, 2/63
Alley Oop - Funnies #1, 10/36
Alpha Flight - X-Men #120, 4/78
Amazing Man - All Star Squadron #23, 7/83
American Ace - (1st newsstand app.) Marvel Mystery Comics #2, 12/39
American Crusader - Thrilling Comics #19, 8/41
American Eagle - Marvel Two-In-One Annual #6, 1981; (1st published app.) Motion Picture Funnies Weekly #1, 1939
Ancient One - Strange Tales #110, 7/63
Andy Panda - Crackajack Funnies #39, 9/41
Angel - Marvel Comics #1, 10-11/39
Angel (now Archangel) - X-Men #1, 9/63
Angel & the Ape - Showcase #77, 9/68
Animal Man - (in costume) Strange Adventures #190, 7/66; (no costume) Strange Adventures #180, 9/65; (re-intro) Wonder Woman #267, 5/80
Ant-Man - (costume) Tales to Astonish #35, 9/62; (new) Marvel Premiere #47, 4/79; (no costume) Tales to Astonish #27, 1/62; (re-intro) Avengers #46, 11/67
Anthro - Showcase #74, 5/68
Apache Kid - Two Gun Western #5,11/50
Ape, The - Startling Comics #21, 5/43
Aqua-Girl - Aquaman #33, 5-6/67
Aquababy - Aquaman #23, 9-10/65
Aquaboy - Superboy #171
Aquagirl - (try out, not same as other) Adventure Comics #266, 11/59
Aquagirl - Aquaman #33, 5-6/67
Aqualad - Adventure Comics #269, 2/60
Aquarian (Wundarr) - Adventure Into Fear #17, '73
Aquaman - More Fun Comics #73, 11/41;
Arak - Warlord #48, 8/81
Archangel - (cameo) (formerly Angel) X-Factor #23, 12/87; (full app.) X-Factor #24, 1/88
Archie Andrews - Pep Comics #22, 12/41
Arion - Warlord #55
Arrow - Funny Pages V2#10, 9/38
Arthur Stacy - Amazing Spider-Man #93, 2/71
Asbestos Lady - Captain America Comics #63, 7/47
Astro Boy - Astro Boy #1, 8/65
Atom - All-American Comics #19, 10/40; (S.A.) Showcase #34, 9-10/61
Atoman - Atoman #1, 2/46
Atomaster - Comic Books #1, 1950
Atomic Mouse - Atomic Mouse #1, 3/53
Atomic Rabbit - Atomic Rabbit #1, 8/55
Atomic Thunderbolt - Atomic Thunderbolt #1, 2/46
Aunt May - Amazing Fantasy #15, 8-9/62; (prototype) Strange Tales #92, 6/62
Aurora - X-Men #120
Avenger - Shadow Comics #2, 4/40
Azrael - (cameo) Tales of the Teen Titans #52, 4/85; (full app.) Tales of the Teen Titans #53, 5/85
Baby Huey - Casper, the Friendly Ghost #1, 9/49; (1st Harvey app.) Harvey Comics Hits #60, 9/52
Badger - Badger #1, 12/83
Balbo, the Boy Magician - Master Comics #32, 11/42
Bamm Bamm - (Flintstones) Flintstones #16, 1/64
Barker - National Comics #42, 5/44
Barney Bear - Our Gang Comics #1, 9-10/42
Baron Strucker - Sgt. Fury #5, 1/64
Bat Lash - Showcase #76, 8/68
Bat-Girl - Batman #139, 4/61; (new) Detective #359, 1/67
Batgirl - Detective Comics #359, 1/67
Batman - Detective Comics #27, May '39; (new look w/new costume) Detective Comics #327, 5/64
Batman, Jr. - World's Finest Comics #215, 10/72
Batmite - Detective Comics #267, 5/59
Batwoman - Detective Comics #233, 7/56; (1st modern app. G.A. Batwoman) Brave and the Bold #182, 1/82; (new) Detective Comics #624, 12/90; (re-intro) Batman Family #10, 3-4/77
Beast - X-Men #1, 9/63; (new) (1st in mutated form) Amazing Adventures #11, 3/72
Beast Boy - (becomes Changeling) Doom Patrol #99, 11/65
Belit - Giant-Size Conan #1, 9/74
Bennett Brant - Amazing Spider-Man #11, 4/64
Bernie the Brain - Sugar & Spike #72, ?, '68
Berserkers, The - X-Men/Alpha Flight #1, 12/85
Betty - Pep Comics #22, 12/41
Betty Brant - Amazing Spider-Man #4, 9/63
Bill Barnes - (Air Ace) Shadow Comics #1, 3/40
Binary - (formerly Ms. Marvel) X-Men #164, 12/82
Birdman, The - Weird Comics #1, 4/40
Bishop - (cameo) X-Men #282, 11/91; (full app.) X-Men #283, 12/91
Bizarro Jimmy Olsen - Adventure Comics #287, 8/61
Bizarro Lana Lang - Adventure Comics #292, 1/62
Bizarro Lois Lane - Action Comics #255, 8/59
Bizarro Lucy Lane - Adventure Comics #292, 1/62
Bizarro Marilyn Monroe - Adventure Comics #294, 3/62
Bizarro Perry White - Adventure Comics #287, 8/61
Bizarro President Kennedy - Adventure Comics #294, 3/62
Black Bolt - (1st full app.) Fantastic Four #46, 1/66 (cameo) (from Inhumans) Fantastic Four #45, 12/65
Black Canary - Flash Comics #86, 8/47; (Silver Age) Justice League of America #74; (1st modern app.) Detective Comics #554, 9/85; (1st solo story) Flash Comics #92, 2/48
Black Cat - Pocket Comics #1, 8/41
Black Cobra - Captain Flight Comics #8 ?, '46
Black Condor - Crack Comics #1, 5/40
Black Dwarf - Spotlight Comics #1, 11/44
Black Flame - Starslayer #20 9/84; Action Comics #304, 9/63
Black Fury - Fantastic Comics #18, 5/41
Black Goliath - Black Goliath #1, 2/76
BlackHawk - Military Comics #1, 8/41
Black Hood - Top-Notch Comics #9, 10/40; (S.A.) Adventures of the Fly #7, 7/60
Black Jack - Zip Comics #20, 11/41
Black Knight - Black Knight #1, 5/55
Black Knight - Tales to Astonish #52, 2/64
Black Knight II - Avengers #48, 1/68
Black Lightning - Black Lightning #1, 4/77
Black Marvel - Mystic Comics #5, 3/41
Black Orchid - Adventure Comics #428, 6-7/73; (new) Black Orchid #1, 12/88
Black Owl - Prize Comics #2, 4/40
Black Panther - Stars & Stripes #3, 7/41
Black Panther - Fantastic Four #52, 7/66
Black Phantom - Tim Holt #25, 9/51
Black Pirate - Sensation Comics #1, 1/42
Black Rider - All Western Winners #2, Win '48-49
Black Spider - Super-Mystery Comics V1#3, 10/40
Black Terror - Exciting Comics #9, 5/41

Black Widow - Mystic Comics #4, 7-8/40
Black Widow - Tales of Suspense #52, 4/64
Blackie the Hawk - Blackhawk #75, 4/54
Blackie the Hawk - (re-intro) Blackhawk #108, 1/57
Blade the Vampire Slayer - Tomb of Dracula #10, ?/73?
Blok - (Legion) Superboy #253, 7/79
Blonde Phantom - All-Select Comics #11, Fall '46; (re-intro) Sensational She-Hulk #4, 8/89
Blondie - Ace Comics #1, 4/37
Bloodshot - (cameo) Eternal Warrior #4, 11/92; (1st full app.) Rai #0, 11/92
Bloodstone - Marvel Presents #1, 10/75
Blue Beetle - (G.A.) Mystery Men Comics #1, 8/39; (Charlton) Blue Beetle #18, 2/55; (Ted Kord) Captain Atom #83, 11/66; (1st DC app.) Crisis on Infinite Earths #1, 4/85
Blue Blade - USA Comics #5, Sum '42
Blue Blaze - Mystic Comics #1, 3/40
Blue Bolt - Blue Bolt #1, 6/40
Blue Circle - Blue Circle Comics #1, 6/44
Blue Devil - Fury of Firestorm #24, 6/84
Blue Streak - Crash Comics #1, 5/40
Bo Bunny - Funny Stuff #70, 1-2?/53
Bobby Benson - Bobby Benson's B-Bar-B Riders #1, 5-6/50
Boboes - Marvel Mystery Comics #32, 6/42
Bomba - Bomba, the Jungle Boy #1, 9-10/67
Bombshell - Boy Comics #3, 4/42
Booster Gold - Booster Gold #1, 2/86
Bouncer - Bouncer nn, 1944
Bouncing Boy - (Legion) Action Comics #276, 5/61
Boy Commandos - Detective Comics #64, 6/42
Bozo the Robot - Smash Comics #1, 8/39
Braniac 5 - Action Comics #276, 5/61
Brick Bradford - King Comics #1, 4/36
Broncho Bill - Tip Top Comics #1, 4/36
Brother Power - Brother Power, the Geek #1, 9-10/68; (re-intro) Saga of Swamp Thing Annual #5, 1989
Buck Rogers - (in comics) Famous Funnies #3, 9/34
Buckskin - Super Mystery V2#1, 4/41
Bucky - (Captain America's sidekick) Captain America Comics #1, 3/41;(Silver Age) Avengers #4, 3/64;
Bugs Bunny - Looney Tunes & Merrie Melodies #1, 1941
Bullet - Amazing Mystery Funnies V3#1, 1/40
Bulletboy - Master Comics #48, 3/44
Bulletman - Nickel Comics #1, 5/40
Bumblebee - Teen Titans (1st series) #48, 1977
Buzzy - All Funny Comics #1, Win '43-44
Buzzy the Crow - Harvey Comics Hits #60, 9/52
B'Wanna Beast - Showcase #66
Cable - (1st full app.) New Mutants #87, 3/90; (cameo) New Mutants #86, 2/90
Cain - (House of Mystery host) House of Mystery #176, 10/67
Calico Kid - (becomes Ghost Rider) Tim Holt #6, 5/49
Camilla - Jungle Comics #1, 1/40
Candy - Police Comics #37, 12/44
Captain & the Kids - Famous Comics Cartoon Books #1200, 1934; Tip Top Comics #1, 4/36
Captain Action - Captain Action & Action Boy nn, 1967
Captain Aero - Captain Aero Comics V1#7, 12/41
Captain America - Captain America Comics #1, 3/41; (Silver Age) Strange Tales #114, 11/63; (Acrobat disguised as) Avengers #4, 3/64; (fomerly Super Patriot) Captain America #333, 9/87; (new) Captain America #181, 1/75; (new) (formerly Nomad) Captain America #183, 3/75
Captain Atom - (1st DC app.) Crisis on Infinite Earths #6, 9/85; (new) Captain Atom #84, 1/67; (new) Captain Atom #1 3/87; (S.A.) Space Adventures #33, 3/60
Captain Battle - Silver Streak Comics #10, 5/41
Captain Britain - Captain Britain #1, 3/87; (1st U.S. app.) Marvel Team-Up #65, 1/78
Captain Comet - Strange Adventures #9, 6/51; (re-intro) Secret Society of Super-Villains #2, 7-8/76
Captain Commando - Pep Comics #30, 8/42
Captain Courageous - Banner Comics #3, 9/41
Captain Daring - Buccaneers #19, 1/50; Daring Mystery Comics #7, 4/41
Captain Desmo - Adventure Comics #32, 11/38
Captain Easy - Funnies #1, 10/36; Famous Comics Cartoon Books #1202, 1934
Captain Fearless - Silver Streak Comics #1, 12/39
Captain Fight - Fight Comics #16, 12/41
Captain Flag - Blue Ribbon Comics #16, 9/41
Captain Flash - Captain Flash #1, 11/54
Captain Freedom - Speed Comics #13, 5/41
Captain Future - Man of Tomorrow - Startling Comics #1, 6/40
Captain George Stacy - Amazing Spider-Man #56, 1/68
Captain Marvel (Shazam) - Whiz Comics #1, 2/40; (M.F.Enterprises) Captain Marvel #1, 4/66; (modern) Shazam: the New Beginning #1, 4/87; (new) Legends #1, 11/86; (re-intro) Shazam! #1, 2/73
Captain Marvel (female) - Amazing Spider-Man Annual #16, 1982
Captain Marvel of the Kree - Marvel Super-Heroes #12, 12/67
Captain Marvel, Jr. - Whiz Comics #25, 12/41
Captain Midnight - Funnies #57, 7/41
Captain Savage - Mystery Men Comics #4, 11/39
Captain Storm - Captain Storm #1, 5-6/64
Captain Strong - Action Comics #421, 3/73
Captain Terror - U.S.A. #2, 11/41
Captain Terry Thunder - Jungle Comics #1, 1/40
Captain Thunder - Flash Comics (Fawcett) #1, 1/40
Captain Thunder - Superman #276, ? '74
Captain Triumph - Crack Comics #27, 1/43
Captain Universe - Micronauts #8, 8/79
Captain Victory - Our Flag Comics #1, 8/41
Captain Wizard - Red Band Comics #3, ? '45
Captain Wonder - Kid Komics #1, 2/43
Captain Yank - Big Shot Comics #29, 11/42
Casper the Friendly Ghost - (1st Harvey app.) Harvey Comics Hits #60, 9/52; Casper #1, 9/49
Cat - The Cat #1, 11/72
Cat Girl - Adventures of the Fly #9, 11/60
Catman - Crash Comics #5, 11/40
Cave Carson - Brave and the Bold #31, 8-9/60
Cerebus - Cerebus the Aardvark #1, 12/77
Challenger - Mystic Comics #6, 10/41
Chameleon - Target Comics V1#6, 7/40
Chameleon Boy - (Legion) Action Comics #267, 8/60
Champ - Champion Comics #2, 12/39
Changeling - (formerly Beast Boy) New Teen Titans #1, 11/80; (X-Men) X-Men #35, 8/67
Charlie Chan - Feature Comics #23, 8/39
Charlie-27 - Marvel Super Heroes #18, 1/69
Checkmate - Action Comics #598, 3/88
Chemical King - (Legion) Adventure Comics #371, 8/68
Chlorophyll Kid - (Legion) Adventure Comics #306, 2/63
Chop Chop - (Blackhawk's sidekick) Military Comics #3, 10/41
Chuck - (Black Fury's aide) Fantastic Comics #18, 5/41
Cisco Kid - Cisco Kid Comics #1, Win '44
Claw the Unconquered - Claw the Unconquered #1, 5-6/75
Clea - Strange Tales #126, 11/64
Cletus Kasady - (1st full app.) Amazing Spider-Man #345, 3/91; (cameo; becomes Carnage) Amazing Spider-Man #344, 2/91
Clip Carson - More Fun Comics #68, 6/41
Cloak - (Spy Master) Big Shot Comics #1, 5/40
Cloak & Dagger - Spec. Spider-Man #64, 3/82
Clock - Crack Comics #1, 5/40
Clock - Funny Pages V1#6, 11/36
Clown - Super-Mystery Comics V1#5, 12/40
Clown - Spitfire Comics #1, 8/41
Cobra Kid - (Black Cobra's sidekick) Captain Flight Comics #8, ? '46
Colossal Boy - (Legion) Action Comics #267, 8/60
Colossus - Tales of Suspense #14, 2/61; Giant-Size X-Men #1, Sum '75
Combat Kelly - Combat Kelly #1, 11/51; (new) Combat Kelly #1, 6/72
Comet - Pep Comics #1, 1/40; (re-intro) Comet #1, 10/83; (S.A.) Advent. of the Fly #30, 10/64
Commando Yank - Wow Comics #6, 7/15/42
Commissioner Gordon - Detective Comics #27, 5/39
Conan, the Barbarian - (1st in comics) Conan, the Barbarian #1, 10/70
Concrete - Dark Horse Presents #1, 7/86
Congo Bill - More Fun Comics #56, 6/40

Congorilla - Action Comics #248, 1/59
Conqueror, The - Victory Comics #1, 8/41
Cookie - Topsy-Turvy #1, 4/45
Corporal Collins - Blue Ribbon Comics #2, 12/39
Cosmic Boy - (Legion) Adventure Comics #247, 4/58
Cosmo Cat - All Top Comics #1, 1945
Cosmo Mann - Bang-Up Comics #1, 12/41
Cosmo, the Phantom of Disguise - Detective Comics #1, 3/37
Cotton Carver - Adventure Comics #50, 5/40
Cougar - The Cougar #1, 4/75
Creeper - Showcase #73, 3-4/67
Crimebuster - Boy Comics #3, 4/42
Crimson Avenger - Detective Comics #20, 10/38
Crusader - Aquaman #56, 3-4/71; (formerly old Marvel Boy) Fantastic Four #164, 11/75
Crypt Keeper - Crime Patrol #15, 12-1/49-50
Crystal - Fantastic Four #45, 12/65
Cyborg - (New Teen Titans) DC Comics Presents #26, 10/80
Cyclone - Whirlwind Comics #1, 6/40
Cyclops - X-Men #1, 9/63
Cyclotronic Man - Black Lightning #4, 7/77
D-Man - Captain America #328, 4/86
Daffy Duck - Looney Tunes & Merrie Melodies #1, 1941
Daimon Hellstrom - (1st full app.) Ghost Rider #2, 10/73; (cameo) (Son of Satan) Ghost Rider #1, 9/73
Daisy Duck - (back cover only) Large Feature Comic #16, 6/41
Dale Daring - Adventure Comics #32, 11/38
Dan Hastings - Star Comics #1, 2/37
Danny Chase - New Teen Titans Annual #3, 1987
Daredevil - Silver Streak Comics #6, 9/40 (blue & yellow costume)
Daredevil - Daredevil #1, 4/64
Darkhawk - Darkhawk #1, 3/91
Darklon the Mystic - Eerie #79, 11/76
Dart & sidekick Ace - Weird Comics #5, 8/40
David - (Samson's aide) Fantastic Comics #10, 9/40
Dawnstar - (Legion) Superboy #226, 4/77
Dazzler - X-Men #130, 2/80
Deadman - Strange Adventures #205, 10/67
Deadpool - New Mutants #98, 2/91
Death - Sandman #8, 1990
Death's Head - (new) (1 pg. strip on back-c) Dragon's Claws #3, 9/88; (new) (1st full app.) Dragon's Claws #5, 11?/88
Deathlok the Demolisher - Astonishing Tales #25, 8/74
Deathstroke the Terminator - New Teen Titans #2, 12/80; (1st solo story) New Titans #70, 10/90
Demon - Demon #1, 8-9/72
Dennis the Menace - Dennis the Menace #1, 8/53
Deputy Dawg - New Terrytoons #1, 6-8/60
Destroyer, The - USA Comics #6, 12/42
Destroyer - Invaders #16, 5/77; Mystic Comics #6, 10/41
Destroyer Duck - Destroyer Duck #1, 1982
Destructor - The Destructor #1, 2/75
Dev-Em, the Knave from Krypton - Adventure Comics #287, 8/61
Devil-Slayer - Marvel Spotlight #33, 4/77
Dial "H" for Hero - (Robby Reed) House of Mystery #156, 11-12/65
Dick Cole - Blue Bolt #1, 6/40
Dick Tracy - (1st comic book app.) Popular Comics #1, 2/36
Dixie Dugan - Feature Funnies #1, 10/37
Doc Samson - Incredible Hulk #141, 7/71
Doc Savage - (1st in comics) Shadow Comics #1, 3/40; (pulp-1st app.) 3/33
Doc Strong - Blue Ribbon Comics #4, 6/40
Doctor Fate - (female) Doctor Fate #25, 2/91
Doctor Midnight - (new) Infinity, Inc. #21, 12/85
Doctor Solar - Doctor Solar #1, 10/62; (1st in costume) Doctor Solar #5, ? '63
Doctor Strange - Strange Tales #110, 7/63
Dodo & the Frog - Funny Stuff #18, 2/47
Doiby Dickles - (Green Lantern's side-kick) All-American Comics #27, 6/41
Doll Man - Feature Comics #27, 12/39
Dolphin - (of Forgotten Heroes) Showcase #79, 12/68
Dominic Fortune - Marvel Preview #2, 1975; (1st color app.) Marvel Premiere #56, 10/80; (new) Iron Man #213, 12/86
Domino - New Mutants #98, 2/91
Donald Duck - The Wise Little Hen, 1934
Don Winslow - Popular Comics #1, 2/36
Doodles Duck - Dodo & the Frog #80, 9-10/54
Dotty & Ditto - Top-Notch Comics #33, 2/43
Dr. Fate - More Fun Comics #55, 5/40; (Silver Age) Justice League of America #21
Dr. Hypno - Amazing-Man Comics #14, 7/40
Dr. Mid-Nite - (1st story app.) All-American Comics #25, 4/41; (text only) All-American Comics #24, 3/41
Dr. Mystic - (Superman prototype) Comics Magazine #1, 5/36
Dr. Neff, Ghost Breaker - Red Dragon Comics #3, 5/48
Dr. Occult - New Fun Comics #6, 10/35; (1st in color & 1st DC app.) More Fun Comics #14, 10/36
Dr. Specktor - Mystery Comics Digest #5, ? '72?
Dr. Strange - Thrilling Comics #1, 2/40
Dr. Strange - Strange Tales #110, 7/63
Dr. Who - Marvel Premiere #57, 12/80
Dracula - Tomb of Dracula #1, 4/72; Dracula #2, 11/66
Dragon - (1st full app.) Megaton #3, 2/86; (cameo)(later Savage Dragon) Megaton #2, 10/85
Drax the Destroyer - Iron Man #55, 2/73
Dreadstar - Epic Illustrated #15, 12/82
Dream Girl - (Legion) Adventure Comics #317, 2/64
Duo Damsel - (Legion)(formerly Triplicate Girl) Adventure Comics #341, 2/66
Duplicate Boy - Adventure Comics #324
Dusty - (Shield's sidekick) Pep Comics #11, 1/41
Dynamic Man - Mystic Comics #1, 3/40
Dynamite Thor - Blue Beetle #6, 3-4/41
Dynamo - Thunder Agents #1, 11/65; (Electro #1 only) Science Comics #1, 2/40
Dynamo, The Eagle - Weird Comics #8, 11/40
Eagle - Science Comics #1, 2/40
Ebony - Police Comics #12, 10/42
Echo, The - All-New Comics #1, 1/43
Eclipso - House of Secrets #61, 7-8/63
Eddie Brock - (becomes Venom) Amazing Spider-Man #298, 3/88
Egbert - Egbert #1, Spr '46
El Diablo - All Star Western #2, 10-11/70
Elasti-Girl - My Greatest Adventure #80, 6/63
Elastic Lad - (Jimmy Olsen) Superman's Pal Jimmy Olsen #31, ?/62
Electro, the Marvel of the Age - Marvel Mystery Comics #4, 2/40
Elektra - Daredevil #168, ? /81?
Element Girl - Metamorpho #10, 1-2/67
Element Lad - (Legion) Adventure Comics #307, 4/63
Elfquest - Fantasty Quarterly #1, Spr '78
Ella Cinders - Famous Comics Cartoon Books #1203, 1934; Tip Top Comics #1, 4/36
Ellery Queen - (1st app. in comics) Crackajack Funnies #23, 5/40
Elmer Fudd - Looney Tunes & Merrie Melodies #1, 1941
Elongated Man - Flash #112, 4-5/60
E-Man - E-Man #1, 10/73
Enchantress - Journey Into Mystery #103, 4/64
Enemy Ace - Our Army at War #151, 2/65
Erg - (becomes Wildfire) Superboy #198,? '73?
Eternal Warrior - (cameo) Solar #10, 6/92; (full app.) Solar #11, 7/92
Evangeline - Primer #6, 2/84
Everyman - Captain America #267, 3/82
Face - (Tony Trent) Big Shot Comics #1, 5/40
Faceless Creature - Strange Adv. #124, 1/61
Falcon - Pep Comics #1, 1/40
Falcon - Captain America #117, 9/69; Daring Mystery Comics #5, 6/40
Fantomah, Mystery Woman - Jungle Comics #1, 1/40
Fatman - Fatman the Human Flying Saucer #1, 4/67
Fearless Flint, the Flint Man - Famous Funnies #89, 12/42
Feral - (of X-Force) New Mutants #99, 3/91
Ferret - Man of War #2, 1/42
Ferret, Mystery Detective - Marvel Mystery Comics #4, 2/40
Ferris - (becomes Star Sapphire) Showcase #22, 9-10/59
Ferro Lad - (Legion) Adventure Comics #346, 7/66
Fiery Mask - Daring Mystery Comics #1, 1/40
Fighting American - Fighting American #1, 4-5/54
Fighting Yank - Startling Comics #10, 9/41
Fin - Daring Mystery Comics #7, 4/41
Fin Fang Foom - Strange Tales #89, 10/61

Fire - Super Friends #25
Fireball - Pep Comics #12, 2/41; (S.A.) Mighty Crusaders #4, 5?/66
Firebrand - Police Comics #1, 8/41
Firefist - Blue Beetle #1, 6/86
Firefly - Top-Notch Comics #8, 9/40
Firehair - Rangers Comics #21, 2/45
Firehawk - Fury of Firestorm #17, 10/83
Fire Lad - Adventure Comics #306, 2/63
Firelord - Thor #225, 7/74
FireStar - X-Men #193, 4/85
Firestorm - Firestorm,the Nuclear Man #1, 3/78; (new) Firestorm, the Nuclear Man Annual #5, 10/87
Flag, The - Our Flag Comics #2, 10/41
Flame, The - Wonderworld Comics #3, 7/39
Flamebird - (Jimmy Olsen as) Superman #158, 12/62; (new) Secret Origins Annual #3, 1989
Flaming Carrot - Visions #1, 1979
Flash - Flash Comics #1, 1/40; (G.A.) (1st app. in S.A.) Flash #123, 9/61
Flash - Showcase #4, 9-10/56
Flash Gordon - King Comics #1, 4/36
Flash Lightning - (becomes Lash Lightning) Sure-Fire Comics #1, 6/40
Flash Rabbit - All Top Comics #1, 1945
Flexo the Rubber Man - Mystic Comics #1, 3/40
Flintstones - Dell Giant #48, 7/61
Fly - Double Life of Private Strong #1, 6/59
Fly Girl - (1st in costume) Adventures of the Fly #14, 9?/61; (w/o costume) Adventures of the Fly #13, 7?/61
Fly-Man, The - Spitfire Comics #1, 8/41
Forbush Man - Not Brand Echh #5, 12/67
Forge - (X-Force) X-Men #184, 8/84
Fox - Blue Ribbon Comics #4, 6/40; (new) Black Hood #11, 11/92
Frankenstein - Prize Comics #7, 12/40; Frankenstein #2, 9/66
Frankenstein's monster - (cameo) Silver Surfer #7, 8/69
Freckles & His Friends - Famous Comics Cartoon Books #1204, 1934
Fred Bender - (becomes Dr. Eclipse) Solar #14, 10/92
Freezum - Blue Bolt V2#5, 10/41
Fritzi Ritz - Tip Top Comics #1, 4/36
Fu Manchu - (1st in Detective) Detective Comics #17, 7/38; (1st cvr.) Det. #1, 3/37
G. I. Robot - Weird War Tales #101, 7/81
Gambit - (cameo) X-Men Annual #14, 1990; (full app.) X-Men #266, 8/90
Gandy Goose - Terry-Toons Comics #1, 10/42
Gangbuster - Adventures of Superman #434, 11/87
Gargoyle - Defenders #94, 4/80
Gary Concord - (Ultra Man) All-American Comics #8, 11/39
Genius Jones - All Funny Comics #1, Win '43-44
Gentleman Ghost - Atom & Hawkman #43, 6-7/69
Ghost Breaker - Star Spangled Comics #122, 11/51
Ghost Patrol - Flash Comics #29, 5/42
Ghost Patrol - Wings #66, 2/46
Ghost Rider - (formerly Calico Kid) Tim Holt #11, ?/49
Ghost Rider - (western) Ghost Rider #1, 2/67; (Johnny Blaze) Marvel Spotlight #5, 8/72; (new-Daniel Ketch) Ghost Rider V2#1, 5/90
Giant-Man - (formerly Ant-Man) Tales to Astonish #49, 11/63
Gideon - New Mutants #98, 2/91
Gladstone Gander - Walt Disney's Comics and Stories #88, 1/48
Glory Grant - Amazing Spider-Man #140, 1/75
Gnort - Justice League International #10
God Of Thunder, The - Weird Comics #1, 4/40
Godiva - New Teen Titans Annual #3, 11/87
Golden Arrow - Whiz Comics #1, 2/40
Golden Dragon - Adventure Comics #32, 11/38
Golden Girl - Golden Lad #5, 6/46
Golden Gladiator - Brave and the Bold #1, 8-9/55
Golden Gorilla - Action Comics #224, 1/57
Golden Lad - Golden Lad #1, 7/45
Golem - Strange Tales #174, 2/74
Goliath - (formerly Giant-Man) Avengers #28, 5/66 (formerly Hawkeye) Avengers #63, 4/69
Grandma Duck - Donald and Mickey Merry Christmas nn, 1945
Gray Ghost - Sensation Comics #1, 1/42
Great Gazoo - (Flintstones) Flintstones #34
Green Arrow - More Fun Comics #73, 11/41
Green Falcon - Blue Ribbon Comics #4, 6/40
Green Flame - Super Friends #42, 3/81
Green Fury - (formerly Green Flame) Infinity, Inc. #32, 11/86
Green Hornet - (1st in comics) Green Hornet Comics #1, 12/40; (Silver Age) Green Hornet #1, 2/67
Green Lama - Prize Comics #7, 12/40
Green Lantern - All-American Comics #16, 7/40; (S.A.) Showcase #22, 9-10/59
Green Mask - Mystery Men Comics #1, 8/39
Green Turtle - Blazing Comics #1, 6/44
Grendel - Primer #2, 2/83
Grey Mask - Suspense Comics #1, 12/43
Grimjack - Starslayer #10, 11/83
Grim Reaper, The - Wonder Comics #1, 5/44
Groo the Wanderer - Destroyer Duck #1, 1982
Gruesomes - (Flintstones) Flintstones #24
Guardian - Star Spangled Comics #7, 4/42; (formerly Vindicator) Alpha Flight #2, 9/83
Guardian Angel - (formerly Hop Harrigan) All-American Comics #25, 4/41
Guardsman I - Iron Man #43, 11?/71?
Guardsman II - Iron Man #96, 3/77
Gunner & Sarge - All-American Men of War #57, ? '58?; Our Fighting Forces #45, 5/59
Guy Gardner - (later a Green Lantern) Green Lantern #59, 3/68; (1st app. as a Green Lantern) Green Lantern #116, 5/79
Gwen Stacy - Amazing Spider-Man #31, 12/65
Gyro Gearloose - Walt Disney's Comics and Stories #140, 5/52
Halo - Blue Beetle #24, 8/43
Hangman - Pep Comics #17, 7/41
Hangman - (re-intro) Comet #6, 12/91; (S.A.) Fly Man #33, 9/65
Happy Houlihans - Blackstone, the Magician Detective #1, Fall '47
Harada - Solar #3, 11/91
Harbinger - Harbinger #1, 1/92
Harlequin - (Joker's Daughter) Teen Titans #48, '77
Harry Osborn - (later becomes Green Goblin II) Amazing Spider-Man #31, 12/65
Harvey Bullock - Batman #361, 7/83
Havok - (no costume) X-Men #56, 5/69; (with costume) X-Men #58, 7/69
Hawk & Dove - Showcase #75, 7-8/67
Hawkeye - Tales of Suspense #57, 9/64; (formerly Goliath) Avengers #98, 4/72
Hawkgirl - (formerly Shiera Sanders) All Star Comics #5, 6-7/41; (Silver Age) Brave & the Bold #34, 2-3/61
Hawkman - Flash Comics #1, 1/40; (S.A.) Brave and the Bold #34, 2-3/61; (modern) Hawkworld: Book #1, 1989
Heap - Air Fighters Comics V1#3, 12/42
Heckle & Jeckle - Terry-Toons Comics #50, 11/46
Hedy Devine - Hedy Devine Comics #22, 8/47
Hedy Wolfe - Miss America Magazine #2, 11/44
Heimdall - Journey Into Mystery #85, 10/62
Hellblazer - (John Constantine) Saga of Swamp Thing #37, 6/85
Hellcat - Avengers #144, 2/76
Her - (formerly Paragon) Marvel Two-In-One #61, 3/80
Herbie - Forbidden Worlds #73, ? '59?
Hercules - Blue Ribbon Comics #4, 6/40; Incredible Hulk #3, 9/62; Hit Comics #1 7/40; Mystic Comics #3, 6/40
Herman & Catnip - Harvey Comics Hits #60, 9/52
High Evolutionary - Thor #134, 11/66
Him - (Warlock) (cameo) Fantastic Four #67, 10/67 (Warlock) (full app.) Thor #165, 6/69
Hocus & Pocus - Action Comics #83, 4/45
Hooded Horseman - Blazing West #14, 11-12/50
Hooded Wasp - Shadow Comics #7, 11/40
Hop Harrigan - All-American Comics #1, 4/39
Hoppy the Marvel Bunny - Fawcett's Funny Animals #1, 12/42
Hourman - Adventure Comics #48, 3/40; (1st app. in S.A.) Justice League of America #21, 8/63
Hourman - (new) Infinity, Inc. #21, 12/85
Howard the Duck - Fear #19, 12/73
Huey, Dewey and Louie - Donald Duck nn (bubble pipe cover)
Hulk - (green skin) Incredible Hulk #2, 7/62; (grey skin) Incredible Hulk #1, 5/62; (new) Incredible Hulk #377, 1/91; (re-intro with grey skin) Incredible Hulk #324, 10/86
Hulk 2099 - 2099 Unlimited #1, 9/93
Human Target - Action Comics #419, 1/73
Human Top - Red Raven Comics #1,

8/40; Tough Kid Squad #1, 3/42
Human Torch - Marvel Comics #1, 10-11/39; (Johnny Storm) Fantastic Four #1, 11/61; (re-intro G.A.) Avengers West Coast #50, 9?/89
Humphrey - Joe Palooka #15, 12/47
Hunchback, The - Wow Comics #2, Spr, 1941
Huntress - (G.A.) Sensation Comics #68, 8/47; (1st S.A. app. of G.A. Huntress) Brave and the Bold #62, 10-11/65; (modern) All Star Comics #69, 11-12/77
Hurricane - Captain America Comics #1, 3/41
Hydroman - Heroic Comics #1, 8/40
Hyper, the Phenomenal - Hyper Mystery Comics #1, 5/40
Ibis the Invincible - Whiz Comics #1, 2/40
Ice - Super Friends #9
Ice Cream Soldier - Our Army at War #85, 8/59
Iceman - X-Men #1, 9/63
Imp - Captain America Comics #12, 3/42
Impossible Man - Fantastic Four #11, 2/63; (re-intro) Fantastic Four #176, 11/76
Impossible Woman - Marvel Two-In-One #60, 2/80
Inferno - (S.A.) Mighty Crusaders #4, 5?/66
Inferno, the Flame Breather - Zip Comics #10, 1/41
Insect Queen - (Lana Lang) (Legion) Superboy #124, 10/65
Invisible Girl - (Sue Storm) Fantastic Four #1, 11/61
Invisible Kid - (Legion) Action Comics #267, 8/60 (new) Legion of Super-Heroes Annual #1, 1982
Invisible Scarlett O'Neil - Famous Funnies #81, 4/42
Iron Fist - Marvel Premiere #15, 5/74; (re-intro, cameo) Namor, the Sub-Mariner #8, 11/90; (re-intro, full app.) Namor, the Sub-Mariner #10, 1/91
Iron Major - Our Army at War #158, 9/65
Iron Man - (Tony Starks) Tales of Suspense #39, 3/63; (new armor) Tales of Suspense #40, 4/63; (new) (Jim Rhodes) Iron Man #231, 6/88
Iron Wolf - Weird Worlds #8, 11-12/73
Isis - Shazam! #25, ? '76
Jack Monroe - (1st full app.) Captain America #154, 10/72; (cameo) Captain America #153, 9/72
Jack of Hearts - Deadly Hands of Kung-Fu #22, 4?/76; (1st solo book) Marvel Premiere #44, 10/78
Jack Q. Frost - Unearthly Spectaculars #1, 10/65
Jack Woods - Adventure Comics #39, 1/39
Jaguar - Adventures of the Jaguar #1, 9/61
Jarella (Hulk's love) - The Incredible Hulk #140, 6/71
Jason Bard - (becomes Robin) Detective Comics #392, 10/69
Jason Todd - Batman #357, 3/83; (1st in Robin costume) Batman #366, 12/83
Jean DeWolf - Marvel Team Up #48, 8/76
Jester - Smash Comics #22, 5/41
Jigsaw - Jigsaw #1, 9/66
Jiminy Cricket - Mickey Mouse Magazine V5#3, 12/39
Jimmy "Minuteman" Martin - Adventure Comics #53, 8/40
Jimmy Martin as Hourman's aide - Adventure Comics #71, 2/42
Jimmy Olsen - Action Comics #6, 11/38; (new) Man of Steel #2, 10/86
Jo-Jo, Congo King - Jo-Jo Comics #7, 7/47
Joe Palooka - Joe Palooka nn, 1933; (1st in comic book format) Feature Funnies #1, 10/37
Joe Robertson - Amazing Spider-Man #52, 9/67
John Carter of Mars - Funnies #30, 4/39
John Carter, Warlord of Mars - Weird Worlds #1, 8-9/72
John Connor - Terminator #12, ?/89
John Constantine - (Hellblazer) Saga of Swamp Thing #37, 6/85
John Force - (Magic Agent) Magic Agent #1, 1-2/62
John Jameson - Amazing Spider-Man #1, 3/63
John Law - Smash Comics #3, 10/39
John Stewart - (later a Green Lantern) Green Lantern #87, 12-1/71-72
Jonah Hex - All Star Western #10, 2-3/72
Johnny Blaze - (re-intro) Ghost Rider V2#10, 2/91; (Ghost Rider) Marvel Spotlight #5, 8/72
Johnny Cloud - All-American Men of War #82
Johnny Dynamite - Dynamite #3, 9/53
Johnny Peril - Comic Cavalcade #15, 6-7/46
Johnny Quick - More Fun Comics #71, 9/41
Johnny Thunder - All-American Comics #100, 8/48; Flash Comics #1, 1/40; (1st S.A. app.) Flash #137, ?/63
Jon Linton - Amazing Mystery Funnies V2#11, 11/39
Jonah Hex - All Star Western #10, 2-3/72
J'onn J'onzz (See Martian Manhunter)
Jonni Thunder - (Thunderbolt) Jonni Thunder #1, 2/85
Jonny Double - Showcase #78, 11/68
Jordan Brothers - Green Lantern #9, 11-12/61
Jose Delgado - (becomes Gangbuster) Adventures of Superman #432, 9/87
Jubilee - X-Men #244, 2?/89
Judomaster - Special War Series V4#4, 11/65; (1st DC app.) Crisis on Infinite Earths #6, 9/85
Jughead Jones - Pep Comics #22, 12/41
Julie Madison - Detective Comics #31, 9/39
Jungle Jim - Ace Comics #1, 4/37
Junior Woodchucks - Walt Disney's Comics and Stories #125, 2/51
Kaanga, Lord of the Jungle - Jungle Comics #1, 1/40
Kamandi - Kamandi, the Last Boy on Earth #1, 10-11/72
Karate Kid - (Legion) Adventure Comics #346, 7/66
Karma - (New Mutants) Marvel Team-Up #100, 12/80
Katy Keene - Wilbur Comics #5, Sum '45
Kazar the Great - Marvel Comics #1, 10-11/39; (Silver Age) X-men #10, 6/64
Ken Shannon - Police Comics #103, 12/50
Kid Eternity - Hit Comics #25, 12/42
Kid Flash - (later becomes Flash) Flash #110, 12-1/59-60
Killer Frost I - Firestorm, the Nuclear Man #3, 6-7/78
King Kull - Creatures on the Loose #10, 3/71
Kit - (Black Cat's sidekick) Black Cat Comics #28, 4/51
Kitty Pryde - (Ariel) (X-Men) X-Men #129, 1/80
Kobra - Kobra #1, 2-3/76
Kole - (New Teen Titan) New Teen Titans #8, 5?/85
Kong the Untamed - Kong the Untamed #1, 6-7/75
Kraven - (War of the Worlds) Amazing Adventures #18, 5/73
Krazy Kat - Ace Comics #1, 4/37
Krypto - Adventure Comics #210, 3/55
Kryptonite (Blue) - Superman #128, 4/59
Kryptonite (Gold) - Superman #140, 4/60
Kryptonite (Red) - Adventure #299, 8/62
Kryptonite Kid - Superboy #83, ?/60
Lady Blackhawk - Blackhawk #133, 2/58
Lady Luck - Spirit nn, 6/2/40
Lana Lang - (becomes Insect Queen) Superboy #10, 9-10/50
Lance Hale - Silver Streak Comics #3, 3/40
Lance O'Casey - Whiz Comics #1, 2/40
Lancer - Super-Mystery Comics V3#3, 1/43
Lash Lightning - (formerly Flash Lightning) Lightning Comics V2#2, 8/41
Lassie - Adventures of Lassie nn, ?/49
Lemonade Kid - Bobby Benson's B-Bar-B
Riders #15, 6/50
Leopard Girl - Jungle Action #1, 10/54
Li'l Abner - Tip Top Comics #1, 4/36
Li'l Jinx - Pep Comics #62, 7/47
Liberator - Exciting Comics #15, 12/41
Liberty Belle - Star Spangled #20, 5/43
Light Lass - (formerly Lightning Lass) Adventure Comics #317, 2/64
Lightning - Thunder Agents #4, 4/66
Lightning - (cover only) Jumbo Comics #14, 4/40; (1st story app.) Jumbo Comics #15, 5/40
Lightning Boy - (Legion) Adventure Comics #247, 4/58
Lightning Girl - Lightning Comics V3#1, 6/42
Lightning Lad - (formerly Lightning Boy) Adventure Comics #267, 12/59
Lightning Lass - (Legion) Adventure Comics #308, 5/63
Lilith - Vampire Tales #6, ?/74; (Dracula's daughter) Giant-Size Chillers #1, 6/74; (re-intro) New Teen Titans #2, 9/84; (Teen Titans) Teen Titans #25, 1-2/70
Little Audrey - LIttle Audrey #1, 4/48
Little Dot - Sad Sack Comics #1, 9/49
Little Dynamite - Boy Comics #6, 10/42
Little Lotta - LIttle Dot #1, 9/53
Little Lulu - Marge's Little Lulu 4-Color #74, 6/45; (as text illo) King Comics #46, 2/40
Little Max - Joe Palooka #27, 12/48
Little Orphan Annie - Popular Comics #1, 2/36
Little Wise Guys - Daredevil Comics #13, 10/42
LIving Mummy - Supernatural Thrillers #5,
8/73

Liz Allen - Amazing Spider-Man #4, 9/63
Lobo - (1st full story) Omega Men #10, 1/84; (1st solo story, back-up) Omega Men #37, 4/86; (cameo) Omega Men #3, 6/83
Lockheed - X-Men #166, 2/83
Lois Lane - Action Comics #1, 6/38; (new) Man of Steel #2, 10/86
Lois Lane as Superwoman - Action Comics #60, 5/43
Lone Warrior - Banner Comics #3, 9/41
Longshot - Longshot #1, 9/85
Lori Lemaris the Mermaid - Superman #129, 5/59
Lt. Marvels - Whiz Comics #21, 9/41
Lucy Lane - Superman's Pal Jimmy Olsen #36, ?/62
Luke Cage - (Hero for Hire) Hero For Hire #1, 6/72
Lynx & sidekick Blackie - Mystery Men Comics #13, 8/40
Mad Hatter - Mad Hatter #1, 1-2/46
Madame Satan - Pep Comics #16, 6/41
Madame Web - Amazing Spider-Man #210, 11/80
Madelyne Pryor - (of X-Men) Avengers Annual #10, 1981
Madrox - Giant-Size Fantastic Four #4, 2/75
Mage - (re-intro) Grendel #16, 1/88
Magic Morro - Super Comics #21, 2/40
Magician from Mars - Amazing-Man Comics #7, 11/39
Magicman - Forbidden Worlds #125
Magma - New Mutants #10, 12/83
Magno the Magnetic Man & Davey - Super-Mystery Comics V1#1, 7/40
Magnus, Robot Fighter - Magnus, Robot
Fighter #1, 2/63
Major Mynah - Atom #37, 6-7/68
Man Bat - Detective #400, 6/70
Man in Black - Front Page Comic Book #1, 1945
Man of War - Man of War #1, 11/41
Manowar - Target Comics #1, 2/40
Man-Thing - Savage Tales #1, 5/71; (1st full story) Fear #15, 8/73
Mandrake the Magician - King Comics #1, 4/36
Manhunter - Police Comics #8, 3/42; (1st in new costume) Detective Comics #437, 10-11/73; (Paul Kirk) Adventure Comics #58, 1/41; (new) Adventure Comics #73, 4/42
Mantis - Avengers #112, 6/73
Margie - Comedy Comics #34, Fall '46
Mark Merlin - House of Secrets #23, 8/59
Marshal Law - Marshal Law #1, 10/87
Martan, the Marvel Man - Popular Comics #46, 12/39
Martian Manhunter - (J'onn J'onzz) Detective Comics #225, 11/55; (re-intro) Justice League of America #228, 7/84
Marvel Boy - (1st & only app.) Daring Mystery Comics #6, 9/40
Marvel Girl - (becomes Phoenix) X-Men #1, 9/63
Marvel Man - (later Quasar) Captain America #217, 1/78
Mary Jane & Sniffles - Looney Tunes & Merrie Melodies #1, 1941
Mary Jane Watson - (1st mention) Amazing Spider-Man #15, 8/64; (cameo, face not shown) Amazing Spider-Man #25, 6/65; (cameo, face shown) Amazing Spider-Man #42, 11/66; (cameo, not shown) Amazing Spider-Man #38, 7/66; (re-intro) Amazing Spider-Man #243, 8/83
Mary Marvel - Captain Marvel Adventures
#18, 12/42
Mask, The - Exciting Comics #1, 4/40
Mask, The - Suspense Comics #2, 1944
Masked Marvel - Keen Detective Funnies V2#7, 7/39
Masked Raider - Marvel Comics #1, 10-11/39
Master Key - Scoop Comics #1, 11/41
Master Man - Master Comics #1, 3/40
Master of Kung-Fu - (Shang-Chi) Special
Marvel Edition #15, 12/73
Matter Eater Lad - (Legion) Adventure Comics #303, 12/62
Maximillian O'Leary - (Sargon's aide) All-
American Comics #70, 1-2/46
Maya - Atom #1, 6-7/62
Megaton - Megaton #1, 11/83
Menthor - Thunder Agents #1, 11/65
Mento - (non-member) Doom Patrol #91, 11/64
Mentor - Iron Man #55, 2/73
Mera - Aquaman #11, 9-10/63
Merboy - Wonder Woman #107
Mercury - (Silver Streak's sidekick) Silver Streak Comics #11, 6/41
Mercury Man - Space Adventures #44, ?/61?
Metal Men - Showcase #37, 3-4/62
Metallo - (Jor-El's robot) Superboy #49, 6/56
Metamorpho - Brave and the Bold #57, 12-1/64-65
Mickey Finn - (1st comic book app.) Feature Funnies #1, 10/37
Mickey Mouse - Mickey Mouse Book nn, '30
Midnight - Smash Comics #18, 1/41
Mighty Girl - Adventure Comics #453, 9-10/77
Mighty Mouse - Terry-Toons Comics #38, 11/45
Mighty Samson - Mighty Samson #1, 7/64
Millie the Model - Gay Comics #1, 3/44
Milton Berle - Uncle Milty #1, 12/50
Minnie Mouse - Mickey Mouse Book nn, 1930
Minute Man - Master Comics #11, 2/41
Minuteman - (re-intro) Shazam! #31, 9-10/77
Miss Arrowette - World's Finest #113, 4/60
Miss America - (modern) Giant-Size Avengers #1, 8/74
Miss Masque - Exciting Comics #51, 9/46; America's Best Comics #23, 9/47
Miss Patriot - Marvel Mystery Comics #50, 12/43
Miss Victory - Captain Fearless Comics #1, 8/41
Mister Miracle - Mister Miracle #1, 3-4/71
Mister X - (on cover only) Vortex #2
Moby Duck - Donald Duck #112
Mockingbird - Marvel Team-Up #95, 7/80
Modred the Mystic - Marvel Chillers #1, 10/75
Molly O'Day - Molly O'Day #1, 2/45
Mon-El - (Legion) Superboy #89, 6/61
Monarch Starstalker - Marvel Premiere #32, 10/76
Moon Girl - Happy Houlihans #1, Fall '47; Moon Girl and the Prince #1, Fall '47
Moon Knight - Werewolf by Night #32, 8/75; (1st solo book) Marvel Spotlight #28, 6/76
Moondragon - Iron Man #54, 1/73; (re-intro) Warlock and the Infinity Watch #2, 3/92
Morbius - Amaz. Spider-Man #101, 10/71
Morgan Edge - (cameo) Superman's Pal Jimmy Olsen #133, 10/70
Morlock 2001 - Morlock 2001 #1, 2/75
Morty and Ferdie - (Mickey Mouse's nephews) Mickey Mouse #3, 1933
Moth Man - Mystery Men Comics #9, 4/40
Mr. America - (formerly Tex Thompson) Action Comics #33, 2/41
Mr. Fantastic - (Reed Richards) Fantastic Four #1, 11/61
Mr. Justice - Blue Ribbon Comics #9, 2/41
Mr. Miracle - Captain Fearless Comics #1, 8/41
Mr. Monster - Super Duper Comics #3, 5-6/47; (new) Vanguard Illustrated #7, 5/84
Mr. Mystic - Spirit nn, 6/2/40
Mr. Satan - Zip Comics #1, 2/40
Mr. Scarlet - Wow Comics #1, Win '40-41
Mr. Tawny - Captain Marvel #79, 12/47; (Silver Age) Shazam! #2, 4/73
Mr. Terrific - Sensation Comics #1, 1/42; (1st app. in S.A.) Justice League of America #37, 8?/65
Ms. Marvel - (becomes Binary) Ms. Marvel #1, 1/77
Ms. Victory - Femforce Special #1, Fall '84; (new) Femforce #25
Mutt & Jeff- (1st in comic book format) Funnies #1, 10/36
Mutt & Jeff - Mutt & Jeff #1, 1910
Mystery Men of Mars - All-American Comics #1, 4/39
Nam - Savage Tales #1, 11/85
Namora - Marvel Mystery Comics #82, 5/47
Ned Leeds - (later becomes Hobgoblin)
Amazing Spider-Man #18, 11/64
Negative Man - My Greatest Adventure #80, 6/63
Neil the Horse - Charlton Bullseye #2, 8?/81
Nemesis - Adventures into the Unknown #154, ?/66?
Nemesis Kid - (Legion) Adventure Comics #346, 7/66
Neon the Unknown - Hit Comics #1, 7/40
Neuman, Alfred E. - (cover only, fake ad) Mad #21, 3/55
Nevada Jones - Zip Comics #1, 2/40
New Gods - New Gods #1, 2-3/71
Nick Fury - (formerly Sgt. Fury) Strange Tales #135, 8/65
Night Hawk - All-New Comics #1, 1/43
Nightcrawler - Giant-Size X-Men #1, Sum '75
Nightgirl - Adventure Comics #306, 11/63

Nighthawk - Avengers #71, 12/69
Nightmare - (Casper's horse) Casper, the Friendly Ghost #19, 4/54
Nightmaster - Showcase #82, 5/69
Nightshade - Amazing-Man Comics #24,
10/41; Captain Atom #82, 9/66; (1st DC app.) Crisis on Infinite Earths #6, 9/85
Night Thrasher - Thor #412
Nightwing - (Dick Grayson) Tales of the Teen Titans #44, 7/84; (Superman as) Superman #158, 12/62; (Van-Zee) Superman Family #183, 5-6/77
Nita - (later Namorita in New Warriors) Sub-Mariner #50
Nomad - (formerly Steve Rogers) Captain America #180, 12/74
Noman - Thunder Agents #1, 11/65
Norman Osborn - (Green Goblin I) Amazing Spider-Man #37, 6/66
Nova - Nova #1, 9/76
Nth Man - Marvel Comics Presents #25, ?/89
Nukla - Nukla #1, 10-12/65
Nutsy Squirrel - Funny Folks #1, 4-5/46
Nyoka, the Jungle Girl - Master Comics #50, 5/44
Ocean Master - Aquaman #25, 1-2/66
Odin - (1st full app.) Journey Into Myst. #86, 11/62; (cameo) Journey Into Mystery #85,10/62
Omac - Omac #1, 9-10/74
Omega - Omega the Unknown #1, 3/76
Oracle, The - Startling Comics #20, 2/43
Orion - (New Gods) New Gods #1, 2-3/71; (of New Gods) (1st new costume) First Issue Special #13, 4/76
Oswald the Rabbit - New Fun Comics #1, 2/35
Outlaw Kid - Outlaw Kid #1, 9/54
Owl - Crackajack Funnies #25, 7/40
Pantha - (New Titan) New Titans #74, 3/91
Paragon - (becomes Her) Incredible Hulk Annual #6, 1977
Pat Parker - (in costume) Speed Comics #15, 11/41; (no costume) Speed Comics #13, 5/41
Pat, Patsy & Pete - Looney Tunes & Merrie Melodies #1, 1941
Patchwork Man - (cameo) Swamp Thing #2, 12-1/72-73; (full app.) Swamp Thing #3, 2-3/73
Patriot - Marvel Mystery Comics #21, 7/41; (modern age) Marvel Premiere #29, 4/76
Patsy Walker - Miss America Magazine #2, 11/44
Peacemaker - Fightin' Five V2#40, ?/66; (1st DC app.) Crisis on Infinite Earths #6, 9/85
Pebbles - (Flintstones) Flintstones #11, 6/63
Perry White - Superman #7, 11-12/40
Pete Ross - (Legion) Superboy #86, 1/61; (tryout only) Superboy #77, 9?/59
Peter Parker's parents - Amazing Spider-Man Special #5, 11/68; (re-intro) Amazing Spider-Man #365, 8/92
Peter Porkchops - Leading Comics #23, 2-3/47
Phantasmo, Master of the World - Funnies #45, 7/40
Phantom - Ace Comics #11, 2/38
Phantom Eagle - (S.A.) Marvel Super-Heroes #16, 9/68; (G.A.) Wow Comics #6, 7/42
Phantom Falcon - Wings #68, 4/46
Phantom Girl - (Legion) Action Comics #276, 5/61
Phantom Lady - Police Comics #1, 8/41
Phantom Lady - Phantom Lady #13, 8/47
Phantom of the Fair - Amazing Mystery Funnies V2#7, 7/39
Phantom Rider - Star Comics #16, 12/38
Phantom Stranger - Phantom Stranger #1, 5-6/69
Phoenix - (formerly Marvel Girl) X-Men #101, 10/76
Phoenix II - (Rachel) X-Men #141, 1/81
Pinocchio - (cameo) Mickey Mouse Mag.V5#2, 11/39; (full app.) Mickey Mouse Magazine V5#3, 12/39
Pip the Troll - Strange Tales #179, 4/75
Plastic Man - Police Comics #1, 8/41; (S.A. tryout) House of Mystery #160, 7/66; (S.A.) Plastic Man #1, 11-12/66
Pluto - Thor #127, 4/66
Pluto - (Disney) Mickey Mouse #2, 1932
Pogo - Animal Comics #1, 12-1/41-42
Polar Boy - Adventure #306, 11/63
Polaris - (X-Men) X-Men #44, 5/68
Popsicle Pete - All-American Comics #6, 9/39
Porky Pig - Looney Tunes & Merrie Melodies #1, '41
Pow Wow Smith - Detective Comics #151, 9/49
Power Girl - All Star Comics #58, 1-2/76
Power Man - (Rip Regan) Fight Comics #3, 3/40
Power Nelson the Future Man - Prize Comics #1, 3/40
Powerhouse Pepper - Joker Comics #1, 4/42
Predator - Predator #1, 6/89
Presto Kid - Red Mask #51, 9/55
Prince Ra-Man - (formerly Mark Merlin) House of Secrets #73, 7-8/65
Prince Valiant - Ace Comics #26, 5/39
Princess Pantha - Thrilling Comics #56, 10/46
Princess Projectra - (Legion) Adventure Comics #346, 7/66
Professor Supermind & Son - Popular Comics #60, 2/41
Professor Warren - Amazing Spider-Man #31, 12/65
Professor X - X-Men #1, 9/63
Psylocke - New Mutants Annual #2, 10/86
Punisher - Amaz. Spider-Man #129, 2/74
Punisher 2099 - Punisher War Journal #50, 1/93
Pureheart the Powerful - Archie as Pureheart the Powerful #1, 9/66
Purple Mask - Daring Mystery Comics #3, 4/40
Pyroman - America's Best Comics #3, 11/42; Startling Comics #18, 12/42
Quantum Queen - Adventure Comics #375, 12/68
Quasar - (formerly Marvel Man) Incredible Hulk #234, Apr '79; (re-intro) Avengers #302, 4/89
Question - Captain Atom #83, 11/66; (1st DC app.) Crisis on Infinite Earths #6, 9/85
Quicksilver - National Comics #5, 11/40; X-Men #4, 3/64
Quislet - (Legion) Legion of Super-Heroes #14, 9/85
Quisp - Aquaman #1, 1-2/62
Rachel - (Pheonix II) X-Men #141, 1/81
Radar - Captain Marvel Adventures #35, 5/44; Master Comics #50, 5/44
Rage - Avengers #326, 11/90
Ragman - Ragman #1, 8-9/76
Rags Rabbit - Nutty Comics #5, ?/46
Rai - Magnus Robot Fighter #5, 10/91; (new) Rai #0, 11/92
Rainbow Boy - Heroic Comics #14, 9/42
Randy Robertson - Amazing Spider-Man #67, 12/68
Ravage 2099 - Marvel Comics Presents #117, '92
Raven, The - Sure-Fire Comics #1, 6/40
Raven - Thunder Agents #8, 9?/66; (New Teen Titans) DC Comics Presents #26, 10/80
Rawhide Kid - Rawhide Kid #1, 3/55
Ray - Smash Comics #14, 9/40
Ray O'Light - All-New Comics #1, 1/43
Red Bee - Hit Comics #1, 7/40
Red Blazer - Pocket Comics #1, 8/41; All-
New Comics #6, 1/44
Red Demon - Black Cat Comics #4, 2-3/47
Red Dragon - (1st story app.) Red Dragon Comics #6, 3/43; (text app. only) Red Dragon Comics #5, 1/43
Red Guardian - Avengers #43, 8/67; (new) Defenders #3, 5/76
Red Hawk - Blazing Comics #1, 6/44
Red Hawk - Straight Arrow #2, 4-5/50
Red Mask - Best Comics #1, 11/39
Red Raven - Red Raven Comics #1, 8/40; (1st modern app. G.A. Red Raven) X-Men #44, 5/69
Red Rocket - Captain Flight Comics #5, 11/44
Red Rube - Zip Comics #39, 8/43
Red Ryder - (1st app. in comics, strip-r) Crackajack Funnies #9, 3/39
Red Sonja - (1st full app.) Conan, the Barbarian #24, 3/73; (cameo) Conan #23, 2/73
Red Tornado - (formerly Ma Hunkle) All-
American Comics #20, 11/40; (S.A.) Justice League of America #64, 8/68
Red White & Blue - All-American Comics #1, 4/39
Red Wolf - Avengers #80, 9/70; (1st solo book) Marvel Spotlight #1, 11/71
Reflecto - (Legion) Legion of Super-Heroes #277, 7/81
Rex Dexter of Mars - Mystery Men Comics #1, 8/39
Rex King - Supersnipe #6, 10/42
Rex The Wonder Dog - Rex the Wonder Dog #1, 1-2/52
Richie Rich - LIttle Dot #1, 9/53
Richy the Amazing Boy - Blue Ribbon Comics #1, 11/39
Rip Hunter - Showcase #20, 5-6/59
Robby Reed - (Dial "H" for Hero) House of Mystery #156, 11-12/65
Robin - (1st app. in S.A.) Justice League of America #55, ?/67; (Batman's side kick) Detective Comics #38, 4/40; (Jason Todd) Batman #368, 2/84; (Carrie Kelly) Batman: The Dark Knight #2, 4/86; (Timothy Drake) Batman #442 (1st), #457 (official) 12/90
Robin Hood - (DC) Brave and the Bold

#5, 4-4/56
Robocop - Robocop #1, 10/87
Robotman - Star Spangled Comics #7, 4/42; (new) Showcase #94, Aug-Sept '77; (S.A.) My Greatest Adventure #80, 6/63
Rocket Girl - Hello Pal Comics #1, 1/43
Rocket Man - Hello Pal Comics #1, 1/43
Rocketeer - (cameo) Starslayer #1, 2/82; (full app.) Starslayer #2, 4/82
Rocketgirl - Scoop Comics #1, 11/41
Rocketman - Scoop Comics #1, 11/41
Rocky X of the Rocketeers - Boy Comics #80
Rogue - (of X-Men) Avengers Annual #10, 1981 (see X-Men #158)
Roh Kar, the Man Hunter from Mars - Batman #78, 8-9/53
Rom - Rom #1, 12/79
Rond Vidar - (Universo's son, Legion) Adventure Comics #349, 10/66
Rose And The Thorn - Superman's Girlfriend Lois Lane #105, 1968
Roy Raymond - Detective Comics #153, 11/49
Roy the Super Boy - Top-Notch Comics #8, 9/40
Rudolph the Red Nosed Reindeer - Rudolph the Red Nosed Reindeer nn, 1939
Ruff and Reddy - Four Color #937, 9/58
Rulah, Jungle Goddess - Zoot #7, 6/47
Rusty & His Pals - Adventure Comics #32, 11/38
Sabre - Eclipse Graphic Album Series #1, 10/78
Sabrina the Teen-age Witch - Archie's Madhouse #22, 10/62
Sad Sack - True Comics #55, 12/46
Saint, The - Silver Streak Comics #18, 2/42
Samson - Fantastic Comics #1, 12/39
Sandman - (1st published app.) New York World's Fair nn, 1939; (1st app. in S.A.) Justice League of America #46, 8/66; (1st conceived story) Adventure Comics #40, 7/39; (modern) Sandman (2nd Series) #1, 1/89
Sandy the Golden Boy - Adventure Comics #69, 12/41
Sarge Steel - Sarge Steel #1, 12/64
Sargon The Sorcerer - All American Comics #26, 5/41
Sasquatch - X-Men #120
Satana - Vampire Tales #2, ?/73
Saturn Girl - Adventure Comics #247, 4/58
Scalphunter - Weird Western Tales #39, 3-4/77
Scarlet Avenger - Zip Comics #1, 2/40
Scarlet Witch - X-Men #4, 3/64
Scorpion - Scorpion #1, 2/75
Scribbly - Funnies #2, 11/36
Sensor Girl - (Legion) Legion of Super-Heroes #14, 9/85
Sergeant Spook - Blue Bolt #1, 6/40
Sgt. Bilko - Sgt. Bilko #1, 5-6/57
Sgt. Fury - (becomes Nick Fury of Shield) Sgt. Fury #1, 5/63
Sgt. Rock - Our Army at War #81, 4/59
Sgt. Rock by Kubert - Our Army at War #83, 6/59
Shade the Changing Man - Shade #1, 6-7/77
Shadow - (1st in comics) Shadow Comics #1, 3/40; (DC) The Shadow #1, 10-11/73
Shadowcat - X-Men #129
Shadow Lass - (Legion) Adventure Comics #365, 2/68
Shadow, Jr. - Shadow Comics V6#9, 12/46
Shadowhawk - Youngblood #2, 6/92
Shadowman - Shadowman #1, 5/92; (cameo) X-O Manowar #4, 5/92
Shang-Chi - (Master of Kung-Fu) Special Marvel Edition #15, 12/73
Shanna, the She-Devil - Shanna, the She-Devil #1, 12/72
Shakira - Warlord #32
Sharon Carter - Tales of Suspense #76 (formerly Agent 13), 1966
Shatterstar - (of X-Force) (cameo) New Mutants Annual #6, 1990
Shazam (Captain Marvel) - Shazam #1, 2/73
She-Bat - Detective Comics #424, 6?/72
She-Hulk - Savage She-Hulk #1, 2/80
Sheena - Jumbo Comics #1, 9/38
Sherlock Holmes - Classic Comics #33, 1/47
Shield - Pep Comics #1, 1/40; (S.A.) Adventures of the Fly #8, 9/60
Shiera Sanders - (later becomes Hawkgirl) Flash Comics #1, 1/40
Shining Knight - Adventure Comics #66, 9/41
Shock Gibson - Speed Comics #1, 10/39
Shrinking Violet - (Legion) Action Comics #276, 5/61
Sif - Journey Into Mystery #102, 3/64
Silent Knight - Brave and the Bold #1, 8-9/55
Silly Seal - Krazy Komics #1, 7/42
Silver Fox - Blue Ribbon Comics #2, 12/39
Silver Knight - Wonder Comics #18, 6/48
Silver Sable - Amazing Spider-Man #265, 6/85
Silver Streak - Silver Streak Comics #3, 3/40
Silver Surfer - Fantastic Four #48, 3/66
Siryn - (of X-Force) Spider-Woman #37, 4/81
Skippy - Skippy's Own Book Of Comics, 1934
Skull the Slayer - Skull, the Slayer #1, 8/75
Sky Wizard - Miracle Comics #1, 2/40
Skyman - Big Shot Comics #1, 5/40; (formerly Star Spangled Kid) Infinity, Inc. #31, 10/86
Skywolf - Air Fighters Comics V1#2, 11/42
Slam Bradley - Detective Comics #1, 3/37
Sleepwalker - Sleepwalker #1, 6/91
Snapper Carr - Brave and the Bold #28, 2-3/60
Snow White & the Seven Dwarfs - Mickey Mouse Magazine V3#3, 12/37
Socko Strong - Adventure Comics #40, 7/39
Solomon Kane - (1st color app.) Marvel Premiere #33, 12/76
Son Of Satan (Daimon Hellstrom) - (cameo) Ghost Rider #1, 9/73; (full app.) #2, 10/73
Son of Vulcan - Mysteries of Unexplored Worlds #46, 5/65
Space Ace - Manhunt! #1, 10/47
Space Cabbie - Mystery In Space #21, 8-9/54
Space Museum - Strange Adventures #104, 5/59
Space Ranger - Showcase #15, 7-8/58
Sparkler, The - Super Spy #1, 10/40
Sparkman - Sparkler Comics #1, 7/41
Sparky - (Blue Beetle's sidekick) Blue Beetle #14, 9/42; (Red Blazer's side kick) All-New Comics #6, 1/44
Sparky Watts - Big Shot Comics #14, 6/41
Spawn - Spawn #1, 5/92
Spectre - (1st full app. in costume) More Fun Comics #54, 4/40; (in costume splash panel) More Fun Comics #52, 2/40; (S.A.) Showcase #60, 1-2/66; (in costume in one panel ad) More Fun Comics #51, 1/40
Speed Centaur - Amazing Mystery Funnies V2#8, 8/39
Speed Saunders - Detective Comics #1, 3/37
Speed Spaulding - Famous Funnies #72, 7/40
Speedball - Amazing Spider-Man Annual #22, '88
Speedboy - (Fighting America's side kick) Fighting American #1, 4-5/54
Speedy - (Green Arrow's sidekick) More Fun Comics #73, 11/41
Spencer Smythe - Amazing Spider-Man #25, 6/65
Spider-Man - Amazing Fantasy #15, 8-9/62; (cosmic) Spectacular Spider-Man #158, 12/89
Spider-Man - (black costume) Amazing Spider-Man #252, 5/84
Spider-Man 2099 - Amazing Spider-Man #365, 8/92
Spider-Woman - Marvel Spotlight #32, 2/77; (new) Marvel Super Heroes Secret Wars #7, 11/84
Spirit - Spirit nn, 6/40; (1st comic book app.) Police Comics #11, 9/42
Spooky - Casper, the Friendly Ghost #10, 6/53
Spy Smasher - Whiz Comics #1, 2/40
Stalker - Stalker #1, 6-7/75
Stanley & His Monster - Fox and the Crow #95, 12-1?/65-66
Starboy - (Legion) Adventure Comics #282, 3/61
Starfire - (Teen Titans) Teen Titans #18, 11-12/68; (new) (New Teen Titans) DC Comics Presents #26, 10/80
Starfox - Iron Man #55, 2/73
Starhawk - (1st full app.) Defenders #28, 10/75; (cameo) Defenders #27, 9/75; (re-intro) Guardians of the Galaxy #22, 3/92
Star-Lord - Marvel Preview #4, 11/75
Starman - Adventure Comics #61, 4/41; (1st app. in S.A.) Justice League of America #29, 8/64; (new) First Issue Special #12, 3/76
Star Sapphire - All-Flash #32, 12-1/47-48; (formerly Ferris) Green Lantern #16, 10/62; (re-intro, 1st full app.) Green Lantern #191, 8/85; (re-intro, cameo) Green Lantern #191, 8/85
Starslayer - Starslayer #1, 2/82
Star Spangled Kid - Action Comics #40, 9/41
Stars and Stripes - Stars and Stripes Comics #4, 9/41
Star Spangled Kid - Star Spangled

Comics #1, 10/41
Steel Fist - Blue Circle Comics #1, 6/44
Steel Sterling - Zip Comics #1, 2/40; (Silver Age) Fly Man #39, 9/66
Steel the Indestructable Man - Steel #1, 3/78; (re-intro) All Star Squadron #8, 4/82
Steve Conrad Adventurer - Adventure Comics #47, 2/40
Stone Boy - Adventure Comics #306, 2/63
Storm - Giant-Size X-Men #1, Sum '75
Stormy Foster, the Great Defender - Hit Comics #18, 12/41
Straight Arrow - Straight Arrow #1, 2-3/50
Stranger - X-Men #11, 5/65
Stratosphere Jim - Crackajack Funnies #18, 12/39
Stripesy - Action Comics #40, 9/41
Strongman - Crash Comics #1, 5/40
Stuff - (Vigilante sidekick) Action Comics #45, 2/42
Stumbo the Giant - Hot Stuff, the Little Devil #2, 12/57
Stuntman - Stuntman #1, 4-5/46
Stuntman Stetson - Feature Comics #140, 11/49
Sub-Mariner - (1st newsstand app.) Marvel Comics #1, 10-11/39; (1st published app.?) Motion Pic.Funnies Weekly #1, 1939; (Silver Age) Fantastic Four #4, 5/62; (new) Namor, the Sub-Mariner #26, 5/92
Sub-Zero Man - Blue Bolt #1, 6/40
SunBoy - (Legion) Action Comics #276, 5/61
Sunfire - (X-Men) X-Men #64, 1/70
Super American - Fight Comics #15, 10/41
Superbaby - Superboy #8, 5-6/50
Superboy - More Fun Comics #101, 1-2/45
Super Cat - Animal Crackers #1, 1946
Super Duck - Jolly Jingles #10, Sum '43; (re-intro) Laugh #24, ?/90
Supergirl - Action Comics #252, 5/59; (re-intro) Action Comics #674, 2/92; (tryout only) Superboy #5, 11-12/49
Super Goof - Phantom Blot #2, ?/65
Super Mouse - Coo Coo Comics #1, 10/42
Super Patriot - Nick Fury Agent of Shield #13, 6?/69; (new) Captain America #323, 11/86
Super Rabbit - Comedy Comics #14, 3/43
Super Richie - Richie Rich Millions #68, 11/74
Superichie - Superichie #5, 10/76
Superkatt - Giggle #9, 6/44
Superman - Action Comics #1, 6/38
Superman, Jr. - World's Finest Comics #215, 10/72
Supersnipe - Shadow Comics V2#3, 3/42
Superwoman - DC Comics Presents Annual #2, 7/83
Supreme - Youngblood #3, 10/92
Swamp Thing - House of Secrets #92, 6-7/71
Swift Deer - (J. Thunder's sidekick) All-American Western #113, 4-5/50
Sword - Captain Courageous Comics #6, 3/42; Super-Mystery Comics V3#3, 1/43
T-Man - Police Comics #103, 12/50
Tailspin Tommy - Tailspin Tommy Story & Picture Book #266, 1931; (1st in comic book format) Funnies #1, 10/36
Tank Killer - G. I. Combat #67, 12?/58
Tarantula - All-Star Comics #1, 10/41
Target - Target Comics V1#10, 11/40
Targitt - (in costume) Targitt #2, 6/75; (no costume) Targitt #1, 3/75
Tarzan - Tarzan Book #1, 1929; (1st comic book app.) Tip Top Comics #1, 4/36
Teenage Mutant Ninja Turtles - Teenage Mutant Ninja Turtles #1, 1984
Tellus - (Legion) Legion of Super-Heroes #14, 9/85
Terminator - Rust #12, 8/88
Terra - (New Teen Titan) New Teen Titans #26, 12/82
Terra-Man - Superman #249, 12/71
Terry & The Pirates - Popular Comics #1, 2/36
Tessie the Typist - Joker Comics #2, 6/42
Tex Thompson - (becomes Mr. America) Action Comics #1, 6/38
Thing - (Ben Grimm) Fantastic Four #1, 11/61
Thongor - Creatures On The Loose #22, 1973
Thor - (Beta Ray Bill) Thor #337, 11/83; (Dargo) Thor #384, 10/87; (Donald Blake) Journey Into Mystery #83, 8/62; (Eric Masterson) Thor #433, 6/91
Thorndike - (becomes Hourman's aide) Adventure Comics #74, 5/42
Three Lt. Marvels - Whiz # 21, 9/41; (re-intro) Shazam! #30, 7-8/77
Three-D Man - Marvel Premiere #35, 4/77
Thunderbird - Giant-Size X-Men #1, Sum '75
Thunderbolt - Power Man #41, 10/76; (1st DC app.) Crisis on Infinite Earths #6, 9/85; (Jonni Thunder) Jonni Thunder #1, 2/85; (Peter Cannon) Thunderbolt #1, 1/66
Thunderbunny - Charlton Bullseye #6, 12?/81
Thunderstrike - (Eric Masterson) Thor #459, 2/93
Tick - Tick #1, 6/88
Tiger Girl - Fight Comics #32, 6/44
Tigra - Startling Comics #45, 5/47
Tigra - (formerly The Cat) Giant-Size Creatures #1, 5/75
Tim - (Black Terror's sidekick) Exciting Comics #9, 5/41
Timber Wolf - (Legion) Adventure Comics #327, 12/64
Timothy Drake - Batman #436, 8/89; (1st in Robin costume) Batman #442, 1990
Timothy the Ghost - Zoo Funnies #1, 7/53
TNT & Dan the Dyna-Mite - World's Finest Comics #5, Spr '42
Todd Hunter - Adventure Comics #32, 11/38
Tom & Jerry - Our Gang Comics #1, 9-10/42
Tom Brent - Adventure Comics #32, 11/38
Tom Mix - The Comics #1, 3/37
Tomahawk - Star Spangled Comics #69, 6/47
Tommy the Amazing Kid - Amazing-Man Comics #23, 8/41
Tommy Tomorrow - Real Fact Comics #6, 1-2/47
Tony Trent - (The Face) Big Shot Comics #1, 5/40
Tor - One Million Years Ago #1, 9/53
Torchy - Doll Man Quarterly #8, Spr '46
Toro - (Human Torch's sidekick) Human Torch #2(#1), Fall '40; (modern) Sub-Mariner #14, 6/69
Torpedo - (new) Daredevil #126, 9/75
Tragg - Mystery Comics Digest #3, ?/72
Trail Colt - Manhunt! #8, 5/48
Triplicate Girl - (Legion) Action Comics #276, 5/61
Tubby - King Comics #46, 2/40; Marge's Little Lulu Four Color #74, ? '45
Tuk the Cave Boy - Captain America Comics #1, 3/41
Turbo - New Warriors #28, 10/92
Turok - Turok Four Color #596, 12/54; (re-intro in Valiant Universe) Magnus Robot Fighter #12, 5/92
Two Gun Kid - Two Gun Kid #1, 3/48
Ty-Gor, Son of the Tiger - Blue Ribbon Comics #4, 6/40
Tygra - Startling Comics #45, 5/47
Tyroc - (Legion) Superboy #216
U.S. Agent - Captain America #354, 6/89
Ultra Boy - (Legion) Superboy #98, 7/62
Ultra Man - (Gary Concord) All-American Comics #8, 11/9
Uncle Ben - Amazing Fantasy #15, 8-9/62
Uncle Marvel - Captain Marvel Adventures #43, 2/45, Wow Comics #18, 10/43
Uncle Sam - National Comics #1, 7/40
Uncle Scrooge - Donald Duck 4-Color #178, 12/47
Underdog - Underdog #1, 7/70
Union Jack I - Invaders #7, 7/76
Union Jack II - Invaders #20, 9/77
Union Jack III - Captain America #254, 2/81
Unknown Soldier - Star Spangled War Stories #151, 6-7/70
Untouchables - Four Color 1237, 10-12/61
Usagi Yojimbo - Albedo #1, 4/85
U.S. Jones - Wonderworld #28, 8/41
Val - Strange Tales #159, 8/67
V-Man - Big-3 #7, 1/42; V...- Comics #1, 1/42
Valkyrie - Air Fighters Comics V2#2,11/43
Vampirella - Vampirella #1, 9/69
Vanessa - (Kingpin's wife) Amazing Spider-Man #83, 4/70
Vanguard - New Teen Titans Annual #1, 1985; Iron Man #109, Apr '78; Megaton #1, 11/83
Vault Keeper - War Against Crime #10, 12-1/49-50
Veiled Avenger - Spotlight Comics #1, 11/44
Venus - Venus #1, 8/48
Veronica Lodge - Pep Comics #26, 4/42
Vicki Vale - Batman #45, 2-3/48
Victoria Bentley - Strange Tales #114, 11/63
Victory Boys - USA Comics #5, Sum '42
Vigilante - Action Comics #42, 11/41; (female) (1st full app.) Deathstroke: the Terminator #10, 5/92; (female) (cameo) Deathstroke: the Terminator #9, 4/92; (modern, in costume) New

Teen Titans Annual #2, 1985; (modern, not in costume) New Teen Titans #23, 9/82; (S.A.) Justice League of America #78, 5?/70

Viking Prince - Brave and the Bold #1, 8-9/55

Vindicator - (formerly Weapon Alpha) (becomes Guardian) X-Men #120, 4/79

Vision - (G.A.) Marvel Mystery Comics #13, 11/40; (S.A.) Avengers #57, 10/68

Vixen - Action Comics #521, 7/81

Voice, The - Popular Comics #51, 5/40

Voltage, Man of Lightning - Fat & Slat #1, Sum '47

Vulcan - Super-Mystery Comics V1#1, 7/40

Wagon Train - Four Color #895, 3/58

Wambi, Jungle Boy - Jungle Comics #1, 1/40

Warlock - (Him) (cameo) Fantastic Four #67, 10/67; (Him) (full app.) Thor #165, 6/69; (new) New Mutants #18, 8/84; (re-intro) Silver Surfer #46, 2/91

Warlord - First Issue Special #8, 11/75

Warpath - (with costume) X-Men #193, 5/85; (without costume) New Mutants #16, 6/84

Wash Tubbs - Famous Comics Cartoon Books #1202, 1934

Wasp, The - Speed Comics #12, 3/41

Wasp - Tales to Astonish #44, 6/63

Wasplet - (Hooded Wasp's sidekick) Shadow Comics #7, 11/40

Watcher - Fantastic Four #13, 4/63

Waverider - Armageddon 2001 #1, 5/91

Weapon Alpha - (becomes Vindicator) X-Men #109, 2/78

Web - Zip Comics #27, 7/42; (S.A.) Fly Man #36, 3/66

Wendigo - Incredible Hulk #162, 4/73

Wendy the Good Little Witch - Casper, the Friendly Ghost #20, ?/54

Werewolf - Werewolf #1, 12/66

Werewolf by Night - Marvel Spotlight #2, 1?/72

Whirlybats - Detective Comics #257, 7/58

White Rider & Super Horse - Blue Bolt #1, 6/40

White Streak - Target Comics V1#1, 2/40

White Tiger - Deadly Hands of Kung-Fu #19, 1?/76

White Witch - (Legion) Adventure Comics #351, 12/66

Whizzer, The - USA Comics #1, 8/41; (modern) Giant-Size Avengers #1, 8/74

Whizzer McGee - (Phantasmo's sidekick) Funnies #45, 7/40

Wiggles the Wonderworm - Taffy Comics #1, 3/45

Wilbur - Zip Comics #18, 9/41

Wild Bill Elliott - Four Color #278, 5/50

Wildcat - Sensation Comics #1, 1/42; (S.A.) Brave and the Bold #62, 10-11/65

Wildfire - (formerly Erg) Superboy #201, '74

Will O' the Wisp - Amazing Spider-Man #167, 4/77

Willie - Gay Comics #1, Mar '44

Winky, Blinky & Noddy - All-Flash #5, Sum '42

Witch Hazel - Marge's Little Lulu #39, 9/51

Witness - Mystic Comics #7, 12/40

Wizard - Top-Notch Comics #1, 12/39; (S.A.) Fly Man #33, 9/65

Wizard - Strange Tales #102, 11/62

Wolverine - (1st full app.) Incredible Hulk #181, 11/74; (cameo) Incredible Hulk #180, 10/74

Wonder Boy - Blue Bolt #1, 6/40; National Comics #1, 7/40

Wonder Boy - Bomber Comics #1, 3/44

Wonder Duck - Wonder Duck #1, 9/49

Wonder Girl - Wonder Woman #107, 7/61; (new) (Teen Titan) Brave and the Bold #60, 6-7/65

Wonder Man - Startling Comics #1, 6/40

Wonderman - Wonder Comics #9, 1945

Wonder Man - Avengers #9, 10/64; Wonder Comics #1, 5/39; (re-intro) Avengers #151, 9/76

Wonder Tot - Wonder Woman #122

Wonder Woman - All Star Comics #8, 12-1/41-42; (Orana) Wonder Woman #250, 12/78

Wonder Woman Family - Wonder Woman #124, 12/62

Wonderman - (Brad Spencer) Mystery Comics #1, 1944

Wong - Strange Tales #110, 7/63

Woodgod - Marvel Premiere #31, 8/76

Woody Woodpecker - Funnies #64, 5/42

Woozy Winks - Police Comics #13, 11/42

X-O Manowar - X-O Manowar #1, 2/92

X-Terminators - X-Terminators #1, 10/88

Yank and Doodle - Prize Comics #13, 8/41

Yankee Doodle Jones - Yankee Comics #1, 9/41

Yarko the Great, Master Magician - Wonder Comics #2, 6/39

Yellow Claw - Yellow Claw #1, 10/56

Yellowjacket - Yellowjacket #1, 9/44

Yellowjacket - Avengers #59, 12/68; (formerly Goliath) Avengers #63, 4/69

Zanzibar - Mystery Men Comics #1, 8/39

Zardi, the Eternal Man - Amazing-Man Comics #11, 4/40

Zatanna - Hawkman #4, 10-11/64

Zatara - Action Comics #1, 6/38

Zebra - All-New Comics #7, 3/44; Pocket Comics #1, 8/41

Zegra, Jungle Empress - Zegra #2, 10/48

Ziggy Pig - Krazy Komics #1, 7/42

Zombie - Menace #5, 7/53

Zorro - Zorro Four Color #228, 5/49

Yogi Bear - Four Color #1067, 12-2/59-60

Yosemite Sam - Yosemite Sam #1, 12/70

1ST APPEARANCE: VILLAIN

Abomination - Tales to Astonish #90, 4/67

Abra Kadabra - Flash #128, 2?/62

Absorbing Man - Journey Into Mystery #114, 3/65

Amazo The Android - Brave & The Bold #30, 6-7/60

Angle Man - Wonder Woman #70, 11/54

Annihilus - Fantastic Four Annual #6, 11/68

Apocalypse - (cameo) X-Factor #5, 6/86; (full app.) X-Factor #6, 7/86

Arcade - Marvel Team-Up #66, 2/78

Atomic Skull - Superman #323, 5/78

Attuma - Fantastic Four #33, 12/64

Bane - Batman: Vengeance of Bane Special #1, '92

Banshee - X-Men #28, 1/67

Baron Blood - Invaders #7, 7/76

Baron Mordo - Strange Tales #111, 8/63

Baron Strucker - Sgt. Fury #5, 1963

Baron Zemo - Captain America #276

Batmite - Detective #267, 5/59

Batroc - Tales of Suspense #76, 4/66

Beetle - Strange Tales #123, 8/64

Bengal - Daredevil #258, 9/88

Beyonder - Marvel Two-In-One #63, 1986

Big Man - Amazing Spider-Man #10, 3/64

Bizarro - Superboy #68, 10-11/56

Bizarro Batman - World's Finest Comics #156

Bizarro Flash - Superman's Girlfriend Lois Lane #74, 5/67

Bizarro Krypto - Superboy #82, ?/60

Bizarro Lana Lang - Adventure Comics #292, 1/62

Bizarro Lucy Lane -Adventure Comics #292, 1/62

Bizarro Lex Luthor - Adventure Comics #293, 2/62

Bizarro Lois Lane - Action Comics #255, 8/59

Bizarro Mxyzptlk - Adventure Comics #286, 7/61

Bizarro Supergirl - Superman #140, 10/60

Bizarro Titano - Adventure Comics #295, 4/62

Black Cat - Amazing Spider-Man #194, 7/79

Black Mask - Batman #386, 8/85

Blackout - Ghost Rider #2, 6/90

Black Racer - New Gods #3, 6-7/71

Black Spider - Detective Comics #463

Blastarr - Fantastic Four #62, 5/67

Blizzard - Iron Man #86, ?/76?

Blob - X-Men #3, 1/64

Blockbuster - Detective Comics #345, 11/65

Boomerang - Tales to Astonish #81, 7/66

Brain Storm - Justice League of America #32, 12/64

Brain Wave - All Star Comics #15, 2-3/43

Brainiac - Action Comics #242, 7/58; (modern) Adventures of Superman #438, 2/88

Brainwasher - (Kingpin) Amazing Spider-Man #59, 4/68

Brother Blood - New Teen Titans #21, 7/82

Brother Voodoo - Strange Tales #169, 9/73

Bullet - Daredevil #250, 12/88

Bullseye - Nick Fury Agent of Shield #15, 11/69

Calypso - Amazing Spider-Man #209, 10/80

Captain Boomerang - Flash #117, 12/60

Captain Cold - Showcase #8, 5-6/57

Captain Fear - Adventure Comics #425, 12-1/72-73

Captain Nazi - Master Comics #21, 12/41

Cardinal - New Warriors #28, 10/92
Carnage - (1st full app.) Amazing Spider-Man #361, 4/92; (cameo) Amazing Spider-Man #360, 3/92
Carrion - Spectacular Spider-Man #25, 12/78
Cat-Man - Detective Comics #311, 1/63
Catwoman - (1st in costume) Batman #3, Fall '40; (1st time called Catwoman) Batman #2, Sum '40; (modern, Selina Kyle) Batman #404, 2/87; (new costume w/o cat-head mask) Batman #35, 5-6/46; (new) Detective Comics #624, 12/90; (S.A.) Superman's Girlfriend Lois Lane #70, 11/66; (The Cat) Batman #1, Spr '40
Cavalier - Detective Comics #81, 11/43
Chameleon - Amazing Spider-Man #1, 3/63
Changeling - X-Men #35, 8/67
Cheetah - Wonder Woman #6, Fall '43; (new) (cameo) Wonder Woman #274, 12/80; (new) (full app.) Wonder Woman #275, 1/81
Chronos - Atom #3, 10-11/62
Chunk - Flash #9, 2/88
Claw - Silver Streak Comics #1, 12/39
Clayface I - (Basil Karlo) Detective Comics #40, 6/40
Clayface II - (Matt Hagen) Detective Comics #298, 12/61
Clayface III - (Preston Payne) Detective Comics #478, 7-8/78
Clock King - World's Finest Comics #111, 8/60
Clown - Flash #270, 2/79
Cobra (see Human Cobra)
Colonel Computron - Flash #304, 12/81
Composite Superman - World's Finest #142
Computo - Adventure Comics #340, 1/66
Constrictor - Incredible Hulk #212, 6/77
Copperhead - Daredevil #124, 6?/75
Crime Master - Amazing Spider-Man #26, 7/65
Crimson Dynamo - (Anton Vanko) Tales of Suspense #46, 10/63
Crimson Dynamo II - (Boris Turgenov) Tales of Suspense #52, 4/64
Crimson Dynamo III - (Alex Nevsky) Iron Man #21, 3/78
Crimson Dynamo IV - (Yuri Petrovich) Champions #8, 10/76
Crimson Dynamo V - (Dimitri Bukharin) Iron Man #109, 4/78
Cyclone - Amazing Spider-Man #143, 4/75
Dark Phoenix - X-Men #134
Darkseid - (1st full app.) Forever People #1, 2-3/71; (cameo) Superman's Pal Jimmy Olsen #134, 12/70
Deadshot - Batman #59, 6-7/50; (1st modern app.) Detective Comics #474, 11-12/77
Death's Head - Daredevil #56, 9/69
Deathstalker - (formerly Death's Head) Daredevil #114, 7/?/74
Demogoblin - Web of Spider-Man #86, 3/92
Despero - Justice League of America #1, 10-11/60
Destroyer - Journey Into Mystery #118, 7/65
Diablo - Fantastic Four #30, 9/64
Doctor Destiny - Justice League of America #5, 6-7/61
Doctor Doom - Fantastic Four #5, 6/62
Doctor Light I - Justice League of America #12, 6/62
Doctor Light II - Crisis on Infinite Earths #4, 6/85
Doctor Octopus - Amazing Spider-Man #3, 6/63
Doctor Polaris - Green Lantern #21, 6/63
Doctor Regulus - Adventure Comics #348, 9/66
Doom 2099 - Marvel Comics Presents #118, '92
Doomsday - (cameo) Superman: The Man of Steel #17, 11/92; (full app.) Superman: The Man of Steel #18, 12/92
Dormammu - Strange Tales #126, 11/64
Dr. Death - (modern) Batman #345, 3/82
Dr. Doom - Fantastic Four #5, 6/62
Dr. Double X - Detective Comics #261, 11/58
Dr Light - Justice League of America #12, '62
Dr. Octopus - Amazing Spider-Man #3, 5/63
Dr. Phosphorous - Detective Comics #469
Dr. Psycho - Wonder Woman #5, 6-7/43
Dr. Spectro - Captain Atom #78, 12/65; (new) Captain Atom #6, 8/87; (1st DC app.) Crisis on Infinite Earths #9, 12/85
Dragon Man - Fantastic Four #35, 2/65
Drax the Destroyer - (re-intro) (cameo) Silver Surfer #35, 3/90; (re-intro) (full app.) Silver Surfer #37, 5/90
Dreadknight - Iron Man #101, 8/77
Dragon Man - Fantastic Four #35, 2/65
Dummy - (Vigilante villain) Leading Comics #1, Win '41-42
Electro - Amazing Spider-Man #9, 2/64
Enchantress - Journey Into Mystery #103, 4/64
Enchantress - Strange Adventures #187
Enforcer - Ghost Rider #22, ?/77
Evil Star - Green Lantern #37, 7/65
Exterminator - (becomes Death-Stalker) Daredevil #39, 4/68
Fatal Five - Adventure Comics #352, 1/67
Fatman - Batman #113, 2/58
Felix Faust - Justice League of America #10, 3/62
Fiddler - All-Flash #32, 12-1/47-48
Fin Fang Foom - Strange Tales #89, 10/61
Firelord - Thor #225
Foolkiller - (1st) Man-Thing #3, 3/74
Foolkiller II - (Greg Salinger) (cameo) Omega the Unknown #8, 5/77; (Greg Salinger) (full app.) Omega the Unknown #9, 7/77
Galactus - Fantastic Four #48, 3/66
Gambler - Green Lantern #12, Sum '44
Gamora - Strange Tales #180, 6/75; (re-intro) Silver Surfer #46, 2/91
Gentleman Ghost - (modern) Batman #310, 4/79
Gibbon - Amazing Spider-Man #110, 7/72
Gladiator - Daredevil #18, 7/66
Golden Glider - Flash #250, 6/77
Gorgon - Fantastic Four #44, 11/65
Gorilla Grodd, the Super Gorilla - Flash #106, 4-5/59
Green Goblin I - (Norman Osborn) Amazing Spider-Man #14, 7/64
Green Goblin II - (Harry Osborn) Amazing Spider-Man #136, 9/74
Grey Gargoyle - Journey Into Mystery #107, 8/64
Grim Reaper - Avengers #52, 5/68
Grizzly - Amazing Spider-Man #139, 12/74
Hammerhead - Amazing Spider-Man #113, 10/72
Harlequin - All-American Comics #89, 9/47
Hate Monger - Fantastic Four #21, 12/63
Havoc - (not in costume) X-Men #56; (in costume) #58
Heat Wave - Flash #140, 6/63
Hector Hammond - Green Lantern #5, 3-4/61
Hela - Journey Into Mystery #102, 3/64
High Evolutionary - Thor #134, 11/66
Hobgoblin - (new) (Macendale) Spectacular Spider-Man #147, 2/89
Hobgoblin I - (Ned Leeds) Amazing Spider-Man #238, 3/83
Hobgoblin II - (Macendale/Jack O'Lantern) Amazing Spider-Man #289, 6/87
Hugo Strange - (1st modern app.) Detective Comics #470, 3-4/77
Human Cobra - Journey Into Mystery #98, 11/63
Human Top - (Whirlwind) Tales to Astonish #50, 12/63
Humbug - Web of Spider-Man #19, 10/86
Hydro Man - Amazing Spider-Man #212, 12/81
Hyena - Firestorm #4, 8-9/78
Icicle - All-American Comics #90, 10/47
Insect Queen - (Lana Lang) Superboy #124, 10/65
Iron Jaw - Boy Comics #3, 4/42
Jack O'Lantern - (Macendale) Machine Man #19, 2/81; (new) Captain America #396, 1/92
Jackal - Amazing Spider-Man #129, 2/74
Jester - Daredevil #42 ,7/68
Jigsaw - Amazing Spider-Man #188, 1/79
Joker - Batman #1, Spr '40
Joker's Daughter - Batman Family #6, 7-8/76
Juggernaut - X-Men #12, 7/65
Kang - Avengers #8, 9/64
Kanjar Ro - Justice League of America #3, 2-3/61
Key, The - Justice League of America #41, 12/65
Killer Croc - Batman #357, 3/83
Killer Shark - Blackhawk #50, 3/52
Kingpin - Amazing Spider-Man #50, 7/67
Klaw - Fantastic Four #53, 8/66
Kraven the Hunter - Amazing Spider-Man #15, 8/64
Kurgo - Fantastic Four #7, 10/62
Leader - Tales to Astonish #62, 12/64
Legion of Super Villains - Superman #147, 8/61
Lex Luthor - (bald) Superman #10, 5-6/41; (new) Man of Steel #4, 12/86; (red hair) Action Comics #23, 5/40; (Silver Age) Adventure Comics #271, 4/60
Lightmaster - Spectacular Spider-Man #3, 2/77
Living Monolith - X-Men #56

Lizard - Amazing Spider-Man #6, 11/63
Loki - Journey Into Mystery #85, 10/62
Looter - Amazing Spider-Man #36, 5/66
Lord Shilling - (Tomahawk foe) Tomahawk #28, 11/54
Lunatik - (1st full app.) Defenders #56, 2/78; (cameo) Defenders #53, 11/77
Mad Hatter - Batman #49, 10-11/48; Detective Comics #230, 4/56
Mad Thinker - Fantastic Four #15, 6/63
Madame Medusa - Fantastic Four #36, 3/65
Maelstrom - Marvel Two-In-One #71, 1/81
Magica de Spell-Uncle Scrooge #36, 12/62
Magneto - X-Men #1, 9/63
Magpie - (new) Man of Steel #3, 11/86
Magus - Strange Tales #178, 2/75; (re-intro) Warlock and the Infinity Watch #7, 8/92
Malevolence - (Mephisto's daughter) Guardians of the Galaxy #7, 12/90
Man-Ape - Avengers #62
Man-Bat - Detective Comics #400, 6/70
Man-Wolf - Amazing Spider-Man #124, 9/73
Mandarin - Tales of Suspense #50, 2/64
Manhunters - 1st Issue Special #5, 8/75
Mephisto - Silver Surfer #3, 12/68
Metallo (Jor-El's robot) - (1st app.) Superboy #49, 6/56; (new) Superman #310, 4/77; (new) Superman #1, 1/87; (re-intro) Action Comics #252, 5/59; (re-intro, 3rd app.) Adventure Comics #276, 9/60
Microwave Man - Action Comics #487, 9/78
Mime - Batman #412, 10/87
Mimic - X-Men #19, 4/66
Mirror Master - Flash #105, 2-3/59
Mist - Adventure Comics #67, 10/41
Mister Element - Showcase #13, 3-4/58
Mister Sinister - X-Men #221
Modok - Tales of Suspense #94, 10/67
Modred the Mystic - (re-intro) Darkhold #3, 12/92
Mole Man- Fantastic Four #1, 11/61
Molecule Man - Fantastic Four #20, 11/63
Molten Man - Amazing Spider-Man #28, 9/65
Morbius the Living Vampire - Amazing Spider-Man #101, 10/71
Mordru - Adventure Comics #369, 6/68
Mortan - (Adam Strange foe) Mystery In Space #62
Mr. Atom - Captain Marvel Adventures #78, 11/47
Mr. Baffle - Detective Comics #63, 5/42
Mr. Hyde - Journey Into Mystery #99,12/63
Mr. Mind - Captain Marvel Adventures #22, 3/43; (re-intro) Shazam! #2, 4/73
Mr. Mxyzptlk - Superman #131, 8/59; (new) Superman #11, 11/87; Superman #30, 10/44
Mr. Tawny - Captain Marvel Adventures #79, 12/47
Multi-Man - Challengers of the Unknown #14, 12-1/59-60
Mysterio - Amazing Spider-Man #13, 6/64
Nightmare - Strange Tales #110, 7/63
Nightshade - Captain America #164, 8/73
Nitro - Captain Marvel #34, 9/74
Ocean Master - Aquaman #29
Outsider - Detective Comics #334, 12/64
Owl - Daredevil #3, 8/64
Paladin - Daredevil #150, 2/78
Parasite - Action Comics #340, 9/66; Fury of Firestorm #58, 1987
Peg-leg Pete - Mickey Mouse #3, 1933
Penguin - Detective Comics #58, 12/41; (S.A.) Batman #155, 4/63
Pied Piper - Flash #106, 4-5/59
Pieface - Green Lantern #2, 9-10/60
Plant-Master - Atom #1, 6-7/62
Plunderer - Daredevil #12, 1/66
Poison Ivy - Batman #181, ?/66
Porcupine - Tales To Astonish #48, 10/63
Prankster - Action Comics #51, 8/42
Princess Python - Amazing Spider-Man #22, 3/65
Professor Amos Fortune - Justice League of America #6, 8-9/61
Professor Zoom - Flash #139, ?/63
Prowler - Amazing Spider-Man #78, 11/69
Psycho Pirate - All Star Comics #23, Win '44-45
Psycho-Man - Fantastic Four Annual #5, 11/67
Puma - Amazing Spider-Man #256, 9/84
Punisher - Amazing Spider-Man #129, 2/74
Puppet Master - Batman #3, Fall '40; Fantastic Four #8, 11/62
Rainbow Raider - Flash #286, 6/80
Rama-Tut - Fantastic Four #19, 10/63
Rampage - Superman #7, 7/87
Rancor - (1st full app.) Guardians of the Galaxy #9, 2/91; (cameo) (descendant of Wolverine) Guardians of the Galaxy #8, 1/91
Ras Al Ghul - Batman #232, 7/71
Reaper - Batman #237, 12/71
Red Ghost - Fantastic Four #13, 4/63
Red Skull - Captain America Comics #1, 3/41; (S.A.) Tales of Suspense #65, 5/65
Rhino - Amazing Spider-Man #41, 10/66
Riddler - Detective Comics #140, 10/48; (S.A.) Batman #171, 5/65
Ringmaster - Incredible Hulk #3, 9/62
Rose - Amazing Spider-Man #253, 6/84
Rose and the Thorn - Flash Comics #89, 11/47; (new) Superman's Girlfriend Lois Lane #105
Saber-Tooth - Flash #291, 11/80
Sabretooth - Iron Fist #14, 8/77
Sandman - Amazing Spider-Man #4, 9/63
Sandstorm - Web of Spider-Man #107, 12/93
Sargon - (re-intro) Flash #186, 8?/69
Sargon the Sorcerer - (1st story app.) All-American Comics #26, 5/41; (text only) All-American Comics #24, 3/41
Sauron - X-Men #60
Scarecrow - Tales of Suspense #51, 3/64; World's Finest Comics #3, Fall '41; Dead of Night #11, 8/75; (S.A.) Batman #189, ? '67?
Schemer - Amazing Spider-Man #83, 4/70
Scorpion - Amazing Spider-Man #20, 1/65
Serpent Crown - Sub-Mariner #9, 1/69
Sha-Shan - Amazing Spider-Man #108, 5/72
Shade - (modern) Flash #298, 6/81
Shadow Thief - Brave and the Bold #36, 6-7/61
Shaper - Incredible Hulk #155, 9/72
Shark - Amazing-Man Comics #6, 10/39; Green Lantern #24, 10/63
Shocker - Amazing Spider-Man #46, 3/67
Shotgun - Daredevil #272, 9?/89
Shroud - Super-Villain Team-Up #5, 4/76
Signalman - Batman #112, 12/57; (S.A.) Detective Comics #466
Silvermane - Amazing Spider-Man #73, 6/69
Silver Samurai - Daredevil #111, 6/74
Sinestro - Green Lantern #7, 7-8/61
Sivana - Whiz Comics #1, 2/40
Sivana, Jr. - Captain Marvel Adventures #52, 1/46
Sky Pirate - Green Lantern #27, 8-9/47
Solarr - Captain America #160, 4/73
Solo - Web of Spider-Man #19, 10/86
Solomon Grundy - All-American Comics #61, 11/44; (S.A.) Showcase #55, 3-4/65
Sonar - Green Lantern #14, 7/62
Sorcerer - Alpha Flight #71, 5/89
Speed McGee - Flash #5, 10/87
Spirit of Vengeance - (futuristic Ghost Rider) Guardians of the Galaxy #13, 6/91
Spyder - New Mutants #68, 10/88
Star Thief - Warlock #14, 10/76
Stilt-Man - Daredevil #8, 6/65
Sting Ray - Sub-Mariner #19, 11/69
Stranger - X-Men #11, 5/65
Sub-Mariner - (S.A) Fantastic Four #4, 5/62
Sunburst - New Adventures of Superboy #45, 9/83
Super Skrull - Fantastic Four #18, 9/63
Supremo - Superboy #132, ?/66
Swordsman - Avengers #19, 8/65
Tantrum - Night Thrasher: Four Control #2, 11/92
Tarantula - Amazing Spider-Man #134, 7/74
Taskmaster - Avengers #119, 1/80
Tattooed Man - Green Lantern #23, 9?/63
Terra-Man - Superman #249, 4/72
Terrax - Fantastic Four #211, 10/79
Terrible Tinkerer - Amazing Spider-Man #2, 5/63
Thanos - Iron Man #55, 2/73; (re-intro) (cameo) Silver Surfer #34, 2/90; (re-intro) (full app.) Silver Surfer #35, 3/.90
Thinker - All-Flash #12, Fall '43
Thundra - Fantastic Four #129, 12/72
Tiger Shark - (new) Namor, the Sub-Mariner #35, 2/93; (S.A.) Sub-Mariner #5, 9/68
Time Trapper - Adventure Comics #321, 6/64
Titanium Man - Tales of Suspense #69, 9/65
Titano - Superman #127, 2/59
Toad - X-Men #4, 3/64
Tombstone - Web of Spider-Man #36, 3/88; (full app.) Spectacular Spider-Man #138, 5/88
Top - Flash #122, 6-7?/61
Torpedo - Daredevil #126, 8?/75
Toyman - Action Comics #64, 9/43; (new) Superman #13, 1/88; (S.A.)

Action Comics #432, 2/74
Trapster - Strange Tales #104, 1/63
Trauma - Incredible Hulk #394, 6/92
Trickster - Flash #113, 6-7/60
Turtle - Showcase #4, 9-10/56
Tweedledum & Tweedledee - Detective Comics #74, 4/43
Two-Face - Detective Comics #66, 8/42; (S.A) Batman #234, 9/71
Typhoid Mary - Daredevil #254, 5/88
Ulik - Thor #137
Ultron - Avengers #54
Ulthoon - (Adam Strange foe) Mystery In Space #61,
Umar - Strange Tales #150, 11/66
Unicorn - Tales of Suspense #56, 8/64
Universo - Adventure Comics #349, 10/66
Unus the Untouchable - X-Men #8, 11/64
U. S. Jones - Wonderworld Comics #28, 8/41
Vandall Savage - Green Lantern #10 ,Win '43; (S.A.) Flash #137, ?/63
Vanisher - X-Men #2, 11/63
Venom - (1st full app.) Amazing Spider-Man #300, 5/88; (cameo w/costume) Amazing Spider-Man #298; (cameo, no costume), #299, 4/88
Vindicator - X-Men #109, 5/78
Viper - Captain America #110, 2/69
Vulture - Amazing Spider-Man #2, 5/63
Warpath - X-Men #193, 5/85
Watcher - Fantastic Four #13, 4/63
Weapon Omega - Alpha Flight #102, 11/81
Weather Wizard - Flash #110, 12-1/59-60
Whirlwind - (Human Top) Tales to Astonish #50, 12/63
White Queen - X-Men #132, 4/80
Wizard - Strange Tales #102, 11/62
Zemo - Avengers #6, 7/64
Zzzax - Incredible Hulk #166, 8/73

1ST APPEARANCE: GROUP

Adult Legion - Superman #147, 8/61
All Star Squadron - Justice League of America #193, 8/81
All Winners Squad - All Winners Comics #19, Fall, 1946
Alpha Flight -(cameo) X-Men #120, 4/79; (full app.) X-Men #121, 5/79
Atari Force - New Teen Titans #27, 1/83
Atomic Knights - Strange Adventures #117, 6/60
Avengers - Avengers #1, 9/63
Avengers new line up - Avengers #16, 5/65; Avengers #150, 8/76; Avengers #181, 3/79; Avengers #211, 9/81
Avengers West Coast - West Coast Avengers #1, 9/84
Big-3 - (Blue Beetle/Flame/Samson) Big-3 #1, Fall, 1940
Bizarro Legionnaires - Adventure Comics #329, 2/65
Boy Commandos - Detective Comics #64, 6/42
Brainiac 5 - Action Comics #276, 5/61
Challengers of the Unknown - Showcase #6, 1-2/57
Champions - Champions #1, 10/75
Creature Commandos - Weird War Tales #93, 11/80
Damage Control - Marvel Comics Presents #19, 5/89
Darkstars - Dark Stars #1, 10/92
Defenders - Marvel Feature #1, 12/71; (new) Defenders #125, 11/83; (prelude) Sub-Mariner #34, 2/71
Doom Patrol - My Greatest Adventure #80, 6/63; (new) Showcase #94, 8-9/77
Easy Company - Our Army At War #81, 4/59
Elementals, The - Justice Machine Annual #1, 1/84
Eternals - Eternals #1, 7/76
Excalibur - Excalibur Special Edition nn, 1987
Explorers - Boy Explorers #1, 5-6/46
Fab 4 - Super Heroes #1, 1/67
Fantastic Four - Fantastic Four #1, 11/61; (1st in costumes) Fantastic Four #3, 3/62; (new team) Fantastic Four #306, 9/87
Federal Men - New Comics #2, 1/36
Femforce - Femforce Special #1, Fall, 1984
Fightin' Five - Fightin' Five V2#28, 7/64
Forever People - Forever People #1, 2-3/71
Freedom Fighters - Justice League of America #107, 1975
Frightful Four - Fantastic Four #36, 10/64
Future X-Men - X-Men #141, 1/81
Ghost Patrol - Flash Comics #29, 5/42
Girl Commandos - Speed Comics #13, 4/41
Great Lakes Avengers - West Coast Avengers #46, 7/89
Green Lantern Corp. - Green Lantern #130
Guardians of the Galaxy - Marvel Super-Heroes #18, 1/69; (1st solo book) Marvel Presents #3, 2/76
Guardians of the Universe - Green Lantern #1, 7-8/60
H.A.R.D. Corps - Harbinger #10, 10/92
Inferior Five - Showcase #62, 5-6/66
Infinity, Inc. - All Star Squadron #25, 9/83
Inhumans - Fantastic Four #45, 12/65
Injustice Society Of The World - All Star Comics #37, 10-11/47
Intergalactic Vigilante Squadron - Adventure Comics #237, 6/57
International Sea Devils - Sea Devils #22, 3-4/66
Invaders - Avengers #71, 12/69; (re-intro) Namor, the Sub-Mariner #12, 3/91
Justice League Europe - Justice League International #24, 2/89; (new) Justice League Spectacular #1, 1992
Justice League International - (new) Justice League Spectacular #1, 1992
Justice League of America - Brave and the Bold #28, 2-3/60; Legends #6, 4/87; (new team) Justice League of America Annual #2, 1984
Justice Society of America - All Star Comics #3, Win, '40-41; (1st S.A. cameo) Flash #137, ?/63
Kiss - (1st full app.) Howard the Duck #13, 6/77; (cameo) Howard the Duck #12, 3/77
Knights of the Galaxy - Mystery In Space #1, 4-5/51
Legion of Monsters - (Ghost Rider, Man-Thing, Morbius, Werewolf) Marvel Premiere #28, 1975
Legion of Substitute Heroes - Adventure Comics #306, 3/63
Legion of Super Heroes - Adventure Comics #247, 4/58
Legion Of Super Pets - Adventure Comics #293, 2/62
Liberators - Avengers #83, 12/70
Liberty Legion - Marvel Premiere #29, 1975
Losers - (Storm/Gunner/Sarge/J. Cloud) G. I. Combat #138, 10-11/69
Lt. Marvels - Whiz Comics #21, 9/41
Marvel Family - Captain Marvel Adventures #18, 12/42
Masters Of Evil - Avengers #6, 2/64
Masters of the Universe - New Teen Titans #25, 11/82
Mercenaries - G.I. Combat #244, 1982
Metal Men - Showcase #37, 3-4/62
Mighty Crusaders - Mighty Crusaders #1, 11/65
New Gods - New Gods #1, 2-3/71
New Mutants - Marvel Graphic Novel #4, 1982
New Teen Titans - DC Comics Presents #26, 10/80
New Warriors - (cameo) Thor #411, 12/89; (full app.) Thor #412, 12/89
Newsboy Legion - Star Spangled Comics #7, 4/42; (re-intro) Superman's Pal Jimmy Olsen #133, 10/70
Next Men - Dark Horse Presents #54, 9/91
Night Force - New Teen Titans #21, 7/82
Omega Men - Green Lantern #141, 6/81
Our Gang - Our Gang Comics #1, 9-10/42
Outsiders - Brave and the Bold #200, 7/83
Planeteers - Real Fact Comics #16, 9-10/48
Power Elite - Starman #4, Win '88
Power Pack - Power Pack #1, 8/84
Sea Devils - Showcase #27, 7-8/60
Secret Six - Secret Six #1, 4-5/68; (re-intro) Action Comics #601, 6/88
Sentinels - X-Men #14, 11/65
Seven Soldiers of Victory - Leading Comics #1, Wint, '41-42
Shadowmaster - Punisher #24, ?/89
S.H.I.E.L.D. - Nick Fury Agent of Shield #1, 6/68
Stargazers - Vanguard III. #2, 12/83
Starjammers - (cameo) X-Men #104, 4/77; (full app.) X-Men #107, 10/77
Star Rovers - Mystery In Space #66, 1961

Stargrazers - Vanguard Illustrated #2, 12/83
Suicide Squad - Brave and the Bold #25, 8-9/59; (new) Legends #3, 1/87
Super Friends - Super Friends #1, 11/76
Team America - Captain America #269, 5/82
Team Titans - (Teen Titans) New Titans Annual #7, 1991
Teenage Mutant Ninja Turtles - Gobbledygook #1, 1984
Teen Titans - Brave and the Bold #54, 6-7/64; (re-intro.) DC Super Stars #1, 3/76
Terrific Three - (Jaguar, Mr. Justice, Steel Sterling) Mighty Crusaders #5, 9/66
Three Mouseketeers - Funny Stuff #1, Sum '44
Thunder Agents - Thunder Agents #1, 11/65
Tiger Squadron - Blue Beetle #20, 4/43
Toxic Crusaders - Toxic Crusaders #1, 5/92
Tough Kid Squad - Tough Kid Squad #1, 3/42
Transformers - Transformers #1, 9/84
Tribe - WILDC.A.T.s: Covert Action Teams #4, 3/93
Ultra-Men - (Fox, Web, Capt. Flag) Mighty Crusaders #5, 9/66
Wanderers - Adventure Comics #375, 12/68
Warlords - **West Coast Avengers** - West Coast Avengers #1, 9/84
Wildcats - WILDC.A.T.s: Covert Action Teams #1, 8/92
X-Factor - Avengers #263, 1/86; (new team) X-Factor #71, 10/91
X-Force - (cameo) New Mutants #100, 4/91
X-Men - X-Men #1, 9/63; X-Men #1, 10/91; (new team) X-Men #253, 1989; (new team) X-Men #281, 10/91; (new) Giant-Size X-Men #1, Sum, '75
X-Terminators - X-Terminators #1, 10/88
Young Allies - Young Allies #1, Sum '41
Youngblood - (1 pg. ad) Megaton #8, 8/87; (2pgs.) Megaton Explosion nn, 6/87

1ST APPEARANCE: VILLAIN GROUP

Beagle Boys - Walt Disney's Comics and Stories #134, 11/51
Blue Trinity - Flash #7, 12/87
Brotherhood of Evil - (new) New Teen Titans #15, 1/82
Brotherhood of Evil Mutants - X-Men #4, 3/64; (new) X-Men #141, 1/81
Citadel - Green Lantern #136, 1/81
Enforcers - Amazing Spider-Man #10, 3/64
Fearsome Five - New Teen Titans #3, 1/81
Frightful Four - (Sandman/Wizard/P.P. Pete) Fantastic Four #36, 3/65
Injustice Society - All Star Comics #37, 10-11/47
Krypton Foes - Superman #65, 7-8/50
Legion of Super-Villains - Superman #147, 8/61
Masters of Evil - Avengers #6, 7/64; (new) Avengers #54, 7/68
Phantom Zone Villains (Dr. Zadu & Emdine) - Superboy #100, 10/62
Royal Flush Gang - Justice League of America #43, ?/66; (new) Justice League of America #203, 6/82
Secret Society of Super-Villains - Secret Society of Super-Villains #1, 5-6/76
Sinister Six - Amazing Spider-Man Annual #1, 1964
Skrulls - Fantastic Four #2, 1/62
Toad Men - Incredible Hulk #2, 7/62

1ST CROSS-OVERS

Ant-Man - Fantastic Four #16, 7/63
Avengers - Tales of Suspense #49, 1/64
Capt. America - (outside of Avengers) Sgt. Fury #13
Conan - Savage Tales #1, 5/71
Daredevil - Amazing Spider-Man #16, 9/64
Doctor Strange - Fantastic Four #27, 6/64
Fantastic Four - Amazing Spider-Man #1, 3/63
Hulk - Fantastic Four #12, 3/63
G.A. Green Lantern x-over in S.A. - Showcase #55, 3-4/65
Iceman - Strange Tales #120, 5/64
Iron Man - (x-over outside Avengers) Tales to Astonish #82, 8/66
Magneto - Journey Into Mystery #109, 10/64
Nick Fury - (as agent of Shield) Tales of Suspense #92, 8/67
S.A. Captain America - Sgt. Fury #13, 12/64
Sgt. Fury - Fantastic Four #21, 12/63
Silver Surfer - (cameo) Tales to Astonish #92, 6/67; (full app.) Tales to Astonish #93, 7/67
Spider-Man - Strange Tales Annual #2, 7/63
Sub-Mariner - (outside Fantastic Four) Strange Tales #107, (4/63)
Thing - Strange Tales #116, 1/64
Thor - Strange Tales #123, 8/64
X-Men - Tales of Suspense #49, 1/64

1ST SUPERPETS

Bat-Hound - Batman #92, 6/55
Captain Carrot - New Teen Titans #16, 2/82
Comet - (Superhorse) Adventure Comics #293, 2/62
Cosmo - (Challengers Spacepet) Challengers of the Unknown #18, 9-10/60
Krypto the Super Dog - Adventure Comics #210, 3/55
Legion of Super Pets - Adventure Comics #293, 2/62
Rang-A-Tang the Wonder Dog - Blue Ribbon Comics #1, 11/39
Streak the Wonder Dog - Green Lantern #30, 2-3/48
Streaky the Super Cat - Action Comics #261, 2/60
Supermonkey - Superboy #76, 8?/59
Wolf - (Boy Commandos mascot) Boy Commandos #34, 7-8/49

1ST OF A PUBLISHER

Ace Magazines - Sure-Fire #1, 6/40
American Comics Group - Giggle #1 & Ha Ha #1, 10/43
Atlas Comics - All Winners #11, Wint. '43/44
Avon Comics -Molly O'Day #1, 2/45
Better Publications (Standard) - Best Comics #1, 11/39
Bilbara Publishing Co. - Cyclone #1, 6/40
Brookwood Publications - Speed Comics #1, 10/39
Carlton Publishing Co. - Zoom Comics #1, 12/45
Catechetical Guild - Topix #1, 11/42
Centaur Publications -Funny Pages V2#6, 3/38; Funny Picture Stories V2#6, 3/38; Star Comics #10, 3/38; Star Ranger V2#10, 3/38
Charlton Comics -Zoo Funnies #1, 11/45
Columbia Comics Group - Big Shot #1, 5/40
Comico - Primer #1, 10/82
Comics Magazine - Comics Magazine #1, 5/36
Dark Horse - Dark Horse Presents #1, 7/86
David McKay Publ. - King Comics #1, 4/36
DC Comics - New Fun Comics #1, 2/35
Defiant Comics - Warriors Of Plasm #1, 8/93
Dell Publishing Co. - Popular Comics #1, 2/36
Eastern Color - Funnies On Parade nn, 1933
Elliot Publications - Double Comics,

1940

Fawcett Publications - Whiz Comics #2 (#1), 2/40

Fiction House - Jumbo Comics #1, 9/38

Flying Cadet - Flying Cadet #1, 1/43

Fox Features Syndicate - Wonder Comics #1, 5/39

Funnies, Inc. - Motion Picture Funnies Weekly #1, 1939

Gilberton Publ. - Classic Comics #1, 10/41

Gladstone - Disneyland Birthday Party, 8/85; Uncle Scrooge Goes To Disneyland, 8/85

Globe Syndicate - Circus Comics #1, 6/38

Great Publications - Great Comics #1, 11/41

Harry 'A' Chesler - Star Comics #1, 2/37

Harvey Comics - Pocket Comics #1, 8/41

Hawley Publications - Captain Easy nn, 1939

Hillman Periodicals - Miracle Comics #1, 2/40

Holyoke (Continental) - Crash Comics #1, 5/40

Hugo Gernsback - Superworld #1, 4/40

Hyper Publications - Hyper Mystery #1, 5/40

Image Comics - Youngblood #1, 4/92

K.K. Publications - Mickey Mouse Magazine #1, Sum, 1935

Lev Gleason - Silver Streak #1, 12/39

Mirage Studios - Gobbledygook #1, no month '84

MLJ Magazines - Blue Ribbon Comics #1, 11/39

Nita Publications - Whirlwind Comics #1, 6/40

Novelty Publications - Target Comics #1, 6/40

Parents' Magazine Institute - True Comics #1, 4/41

Prize Publications - Prize Comics #1, 3/40

Progressive Publishers - Feature Comics #21, 6/39

Quality Comics Group - Feature Comics #21, 6/39

Ralston-Purina Co. - Tom Mix #1, 9/40

Standard Comics (Better Publ.) - Best Comics #1, 11/39

Street and Smith Publications - Shadow Comics #1, 3/40

Sun Publications - Colossus Comics #1, 3/40

Timely Comics - Marvel Mystery #1, 11/39

United Features Syndicate - Tip Top Comics #1, 4/36

Valiant Comics - (hero) Magnus Robot Fighter, 5/91

Warren all comics magazine - Creepy #1, no month '64

Whitman Publishing Co. - Mammoth Comics #1, 1937

Will Eisner - Spirit #1, 6/2/40

William H. Wise - Columbia Comics #1, 1943

1ST PROTOTYPE

Some of today's popular super hero characters were developed from or after earlier forms or prototypes. These prototype characters sometimes were introduced to test new ideas and concepts which later developed into full fledged super heros, or old material sometimes would inspire new characters. Below is a list of all known prototypes. The Marvel/Atlas issues have been verified by Stan Lee, Steve Ditko and Jack Kirby.

Ancient One - Strange Tales #92, 1/62

Ant-Man - Strange Tales #73, 2/60; Strange Tales #78, 11/60

Aunt May - Strange Tales #97, 6/62

Doctor Doom - Tales of Suspense #31, 7/62

Doctor Strange - Journey Into Mystery #78, 3/62; Strange Tales #79, 12/60; Tales of Suspense #32, 8/62

Electro - Tales To Astonish #15, 1/61

Giant-Man - Strange Tales #70, 8/59

Hulk - Journey Into Mystery #62, 11/60; Journey Into Mystery #66, 3/61

Human Torch - Strange Tales #76, 8/60

Iron Man - Strange Tales #75, 6/60; Tales of Suspense #9, 5/60; Tales of Suspense #16, 4/61

Kamandi - Alarming Tales #1, 9/57

Lava Men - Tales of Suspense #7, 1/60

Magneto - Strange Tales #84, 5/61

Mr. Hyde - Journey Into Mystery #79, 4/62

Professor X - Amazing Adult Fantasy #14, 7/62; Strange Tales #69, 6/59

Quicksilver - Strange Tales #67, 2/59

Red Tornado - House Of Mystery #155, 9-10/65

Sandman - Journey Into Mystery #70, 7/61

Savage Dragon - Marvel Comics Presents #50, 1990

Spider-Man - Journey Into Mystery #73, 10/61

Stone Men - Tales of Suspense #28, 4/62; Tales to Astonish #5, 9/59; Tales to Astonish #16, 2/61

Superman - (Dr. Mystic) Comics Magazine #1, 5/36; More Fun Comics #14, 10/36; New Book of Comics #2, Spr '38

Toad Men - Tales to Astonish #7, 1/60

Uncle Ben - Strange Tales #97, 6/62

Watcher - Tales of Suspense #35, 11/62

DIRECTORY OF COMIC AND NOSTALGIA SHOPS
(PAID ADVERTISING STORE LISTINGS)

You can have your store listed here for very reasonable rates. Send for details and deadline for next year's Guide. The following list of stores have paid to be included in this list. We cannot assume any responsibility in your dealings with these shops. This list is provided for your information only. When planning your trips, it would be advisable to make appointments in advance. Remember, to get your shop included in the next edition, **write for rates.** Items stocked by these shops are listed just after the telephone numbers and are coded as follows:

(a) Golden Age Comics
(b) Silver Age Comics
(c) New Comics, magazines
(d) Pulps
(e) Paperbacks
(f) Big Little Books
(g) Magazines (old)
(h) Books (old)
(i) Movie Posters, Lobby Cards
(j) Original Art
(k) Toys (old)
(l) Records (old)
(m) Trading Cards
(n) Underground Comics
(o) Video Tapes
(p) Premiums
(q) Comic Related Posters
(r) Comic Supplies
(s) Role Playing Games
(t) Star Trek Items
(u) Dr. Who Items
(v) Japanimation Items

ALABAMA

Wizard's Comics
324 N. Court
Florence AL 35630
PH: (205) 766-6821 (a-c,q-u)

Sincere Comics
4667 Airport Blvd
Mobile AL 36608
PH: (205) 342-2603
(a-c,e,m,p,q,r,s,u)

ARIZONA

Greg's Comics
2722 S Alma School Rd #8
Mesa AZ 85210
PH: (602) 752-1881 (a-c,k,m,q-s)

Atomic Comics East
1318 West Southern #1
Mesa AZ 85202
PH: (602) 649-0807 (a-c,g,k,m-u)

All About Books & Comics I
517 E Camelback
Phoenix AZ 85012
PH: (602) 277-0757
(a-c,e,g,h,i,k,l,m,n,p-u)

All About Books & Comics West II
4208 W Dunlap
Phoenix AZ 85051
PH: (602) 435-0410
(a-c,g,i,k,l,m,n,p-u)

All About Books & Comics III
13835 N Tatum Blvd.
Phoenix AZ 85032
PH: (602) 494-1976 (b,c,g,m,p-u)

Atomic Comics West
3029 West Peoria #A
Phoenix AZ 85029
PH: (602) 395-1066 (a-c,g,k,m-u)

Key Comics
PO Box 3855
Scottsdale AZ 85271-3855
PH: (602) 949-8499 (a-c,j)

All About Books & Comics IV
810 S. Ash
Tempe AZ 85281
PH: (602) 858-9447 (b,c,g,m,n,p-u)

ARKANSAS

Alpha Books & Comics
708 Garrison Ave
Fort Smith AR 72901
PH: (501) 785-5642
(a-c,e,g,h,m,n,p,q,r,u)

Alternate Worlds (A & E)
4501 Central Ave Suite 144
(Hot Springs Mall)
Hot Springs AR 71913
PH: (501) 525-8999 (a-c,m,o,q,r-u)

Comic Book Store
9307 Treasure Hill
Little Rock AR 72227
PH: (501) 227-9777
(a-c,e,g,k,m,p,q,r,s,u)

Pie-Eyes
8001 Geyer Springs Rd
Little Rock, AR 72209
PH: (501) 568-1414 (a-c,e-i,k,m-s),

Collector's Edition Comics
3217 John F. Kennedy Blvd.
North Little Rock AR 72116
PH: (501) 791-4222
(a-c,e,g,k,m,p,q,r,s,u)

CALIFORNIA

Heroes
24 E Campbell Ave
Campbell CA 95008
PH: (408) 378-3667
(a-g,j,k,m,o-s,u)

Crush Comics & Cards
2869 Castro Valley Blvd
Castro Valley CA 94546
PH: (510) 581-4779 (a-c,g,k,m,p,q,s,u)

Comics Unlimited
11900 South Street
Cerritos CA 90703
PH: (310) 403-1521
(b,c,g,k,l,m,p,q,s,u)

Collectors Ink
932-A W. 8th Avenue
Chico CA 95926
PH: (916) 345-0958 (a-c,g,k,l,m,n,p-u)

Comic Bookie
415 W. Foothill Blvd #318
Claremont CA 91711
PH: (909) 399-0228
(b,c,g,k,l,m,n,p,q,s,t,u)

Superior Comics
1970 Newport Blvd
Costa Mesa CA 92627
PH: (714) 631-3933
(a-c,f,g,j,k,m,n,p,q,r,u)

Flying Colors Comics & Other Cool Stuff
2980 Treat Blvd
Concord CA 94518
PH: (510) 825-5410 (a-c,m,p,q,s,u)

High Quality Comics
(mail order only)
1106 2nd Suite 110
Encinitas CA 92024
PH: (619) 723-7269 (b,c,g,j,n)

Comic Gallery
322-J W. El Norte Parkway
Escondido CA 92026
PH: (619) 745-5660
(b,c,m,n,p,q,r,s,u)

Comicmania!
124 W. Commonwealth
Fullerton CA 92632
PH: (714) 992-6649
(a-c,f,g,h,i,j,k,m,n,o,p,q,r,s,u)

Geoffrey's Comics
15530 Crenshaw Blvd
Gardena CA 90249
PH: (310) 538-3198 (a-c,l,n,q,u)

Comics Unlimited
12913 Harbor Blvd.
Garden Grove CA 92640
PH: (714) 638-2040
(a-c,g,k,l,m,p,q,s,u)

Shooting Star Comics & Games
618 E Colorado Blvd. Unit #C
Glendale CA 91205
PH: (818) 502-1535
(b,c,g,k,l,m,n,p,q,r,u)

Bud Plant Comic Art
P.O. Box 1689-P4
Grass Valley CA 95945
PH: (916) 273-2166 (h,n,p,q)

Clay's Comics
1018 "B" Street
Hayward CA 94541
PH: (510) 733-9633
(c,k,l,m,p,q,r,s,u)

Treasures of Youth
1201 "C" Street
Hayward CA 94541
PH: (510) 888-9675 (a,b,d,m,q,s,u)

Dave's Action Comics
4145 Norse Way
Long Beach CA 90808
PH: (310) 429-2762
(b,c,e,j,k,m,o,p,q,s,u)

Another World
1615 Colorado Blvd
Los Angeles CA 90041
PH: (213) 257-7757
(a-c,d,f,g,h,m,s,t,u)

Cheap Comics
527 N Fairfax Ave.
Los Angeles CA 90036
PH: (213) 655-9323
(a-c,g,k,m,p,q,u)

Collector's Arena
2724 Griffith Park Blvd
Los Angeles CA 90027
PH: (213) 660-2228 (c,k,m,p,q)

Comic Cats
2531 Sawtelle Blvd #104
Los Angeles CA 90064
PH: (818) 348- 0133 (a-u)

Golden Apple Comics
7711 Melrose Avenue
Los Angeles CA 90046
PH: 213-658-6047
(a-c,e,l,m,n,p,q,t)

Golden Apple Comics
8934 West Pico Blvd
Los Angeles CA 90034
PH: (310) 274-2008 (c,l,m,n,p,r,u)

Meltdown Comics & Collectibles
7511 Sunset Blvd
Los Angeles CA 90046
PH: (213) 851-7223
(b,c,g,i,j,k,l-s,u)

Pacific Comic Exchange, Inc.
(by appointment only)
P.O. Box 34849
Los Angeles CA 90034
PH: (310) 836-7234 (PCEI) (a,b)

Comic Dreams
231 W. Yosemite Ave
Manteca CA 95336
PH: (209) 823-7393 (c,m,p,q,r,s,u)

Brians Books
73 N. Milpitas Blvd
Milpitas CA 95035
PH: (408) 942-6903
(a-c,g,m,p,q,s,u)

The Dragon's Treasure
35149 Newark Blvd. #A
Newark CA 94560
PH: (510) 796-6154
(b,c,g,m,p,q,r,u)

Ninth Nebula
The Comic Book Store
11517 Burbank Blvd.
North Hollywood CA 91601
PH: (818) 509-2968
(a-c,e,g-j,l-n,p-u)

Golden Apple Comics
8962 Reseda Blvd.
Northridge CA 91324
PH: (818) 993-7804
(a-c,e,l-n,p,q,u)

Dr Comics & Mr Games
4014 Piedmont Ave.
Oakland, CA 94611
PH: (510) 601-7800
(a-c,k,m,n,p,q-s,u)

Clubhouse Comics
422 W. 'B' St.
Ontario, CA 91762
PH: (909) 988-2240 (a-c,e,g-k,m,n,q,s)

Freedonia Funnyworks
350 S. Tustin Ave
Orange CA 92666
PH: (714) 639-5830
(a-c,g,h-k,m,q,s,u)

Lee's Comics
3783 El Camino Real
Palo Alto CA 94306
PH: (800) 201-4LEE
(a-c,g,m,n,p-r,u)

Neverland Comics & Games
248 Golf Club Road
Pleasant Hill CA 94523
PH: (510) 682-1891
(c,e,k,l,m,p,q,r,s,u)

A-1 Comics
5800 Madison Ave. "W"
Sacramento CA 95841
PH: (916) 331-9203
(a-c,d-f,g,i-k,m,p,r,s,u)

Comic Gallery
4224 Balboa Ave
San Diego CA 92117
PH: (619) 483-4853
(b,c,m,n,p,q-s,u)

Comic Gallery
9460-G Mira Mesa Blvd
San Diego CA 92126
PH: (619) 578-9444
(b,c,m,n,p,q-s,u)

San Diego Comics & Collectibles
6937 El Cajon Blvd
San Diego CA 92115
PH: (619) 698-1177 (a-c,k,m)

Amazing Adventures
3800 Noriega St.
San Fransisco CA 94122
PH: (415) 661-1344 (a-c,k,m,n)

The Comic & Card Outpost
1349 Taraval Street
Between 23 & 24th Ave.
San Francisco CA 94116
PH:(415) 753-8515
(b,c,e,k,m,p,q,s)

Comics And Da-Kind
1643 & 1653 Noriega St
San Francisco CA 94122
PH: (415) 753-3037 (a-c,g,k,m,p,s,u)

The Funny Papers
5957 Geary Blvd at 24th Ave
San Francisco CA 94121
PH: (415) 752-1914 (a-e,g-m,o-u)

Lee's Comics
2222 S El Camino Real
San Mateo CA 94403
PH: (415) 571-1489
(a-c,g,m,n,p,q,r,u)

San Mateo Comics & Original Art
106 South B Street
San Mateo CA 94401
PH: (415) 344-1536
(a-c,d,j,k,m,o,p,r,s,u)

Brians Books
2767 El Camino
Santa Clara CA 95051
PH: (408) 985-7481
(a-c,g,m,p,q,s,u)

Atlantis Fantasyworld
1020 Cedar Street
Santa Cruz CA 95060
PH: (408) 426-0158
(b,c,g,i,k,m,n,p,q,r,s,u)

Clubhouse Comics & Cards
714 Soquel Ave
Santa Cruz CA 95062
PH: (408) 423 9768
(a-c,j,k,l,m,n,q,s,u)

Cool City Comics
1632 Ocean Park
Santa Monica CA 90405
PH: (310) 396 7005 (b,c,i,j,k,p,s)

Hi De Ho Comics & Fantasy
525 Santa Monica Blvd.
Santa Monica CA 90401
PH: (310) 394-2820 (a-n, p-u)

Mega City Comics
2955 J-2 Cochran St
Simi Valley CA 93065
PH: (805) 583-3027
(b,c,e,g,i,j,k,m,n,p,q,r,s,u)

Hi De Ho Comics & Fantasy
1720 N Moorpark Rd
Thousand Oaks CA 91360
PH: (805) 495-1705 (a-n,p-u)

Silver City Comics
4671 Torrance Blvd.
Torrance CA 90503
PH: (310) 542-8034
(a-c,i,m,o,q-t,u)

Neverland Comics & Games
3365 Sonoma Blvd #20
Vallejo CA 94590
PH: (800) 936- MAGIC
(c,e,k,l-n,p-s,u)

Ralph's Comic Corner
2377 E Main Street
Ventura CA 93003
PH: (805) 653-2732 (a-f,m,n,p-s,u)

Comics+
12353 F10 Mariposa Rd
Victorville CA 92392
PH: (619) 245-6753
(b,c,e,g,k,m,n,p-s,u)

Comics Unlimited
16344 Beach Blvd.
Westminister CA 92683
PH:(714) 841-6646
(a-c,g,k,l,m,p-s,u)

Pegasus Hobbies
6554 Greenleaf
Whittier CA 90601
PH:(310) 907-4663
(a-c,g,k,m,q,r,s,u)

COLORADO

Castaway Comics
648 Peoria St
Aurora CO 80011
PH: (303) 341-1958
(a-c,g,j,k,m,n,p,q,s)

Marshak's House of Fantasy
1240 W. Elizabeth
Ft. Collins CO 80521
PH: (303) 224-3599 (c,l,m,p,q,r,s,u)

CONNECTICUT

Outer Limits Comic Shop
Rt 37-52 1/2 Pembroke Road
Danbury CT 06811
PH: (203) 746-1068 (a-c,m,n,p,q)

Collector's Dream
20 Prospect Street
Moosup CT 06354
PH: (203) 564-8857 (a-e,g,n,p-s)

FLORIDA

Emerald City Too Comics & Collectibles
2475-L (12) McMullen Booth Road
Clearwater FL 34619
PH: (813) 797-0664 (a-c,g,k,m,o-u)

Comic City
7128 Sterling Rd
Davie FL 33024
PH: (305) 433-1780 (b,c,k,m,q)

Tropic Comics East
5439 N Federal Hwy
Ft Lauderdale FL 33308
PH: (305) 351-0001
(a-d,g,j,n,p,q,u)

The Dragon's Lair
628 North Ingraham Ave
Lakeland FL 33801
PH: (813) 682-0448 (b,c,i,m,r,s)

Captain Comix & Cards Inc.
905 US 1
Lake Park FL 33403
PH: (407) 842-6649
(c-e,g-k,m-p,q,s,u)

Phil's Comic Shoppe
6350 W Atlantic Blvd.
Margate FL 33063
PH: (305) 977-6947 (a-c,j,k,m,q)

Comic Warehouse Inc
1029 Airport Rd #B6
Naples FL 33942
PH: (813) 643-1020
(a-c,e,g,j,k,m,p,q,r,s,u)

Starbase K-7
829 Sand Lake Rd
Orlando FL 32809
PH: (407) 240-7989
(a-c,e,g,i-m,p-u)

Bay Hill Comics & Used Book Exchange
7657 Turkey Lake Rd
Orlando FL 32819
PH: (407) 363-0040
(b,c,e,g,m,o,p,s)

Sincere Comics
3300 N Pace Blvd.
Pensacola FL 32505
PH: (904) 432-1352
(a-c,e,f,m,p-s,u)

Tropic Comics
313 S. State Rd 7
Plantation FL 33317
PH: (305) 587-8878 (a-g,i-n,o-q,u)

Tropic Comics South, Inc.
742 NE 16th St
N Miami Beach FL 33162
PH: (305) 940-8700
(a-d,g,j,n,p,q,u)

Emerald City Comics & Collectables, Inc.
9249 Seminole Blvd
Seminole FL 34642
PH: (813) 398-2665 (a-c,g,k,m-u)

SMRC Comics
5745 Sunset Drive
South Miami FL 33143
PH: (305) 665-4020 (a,b,q)

Comic & Gaming Exchange
8432 W Oakland Pk Blvd
Sunrise FL 33351
PH: (305) 742-0777 (b-e,g,k,m-u)

Tropic Comics North, Inc.
1018 21st Street US1
Vero Beach FL 32960
PH: (407) 562-8501 (a-c,g,j,n,p-r)

GEORGIA

Oxford Comics Inc.
2395 Peachtree Road N.E.
Atlanta GA 30305
PH: (404) 233-8682
(a-c,g,k,m,n,p,r-u)

Oxford Comics at Buckhead
360 Pharr Road NE
Atlanta GA 30305
PH: (404) 262-3278
(b,c,g,k,m,n,p,r-u)

Comic Company
1058 Mistletoe Road
Decatur GA 30033
PH: (404) 248-9846 (a-c,g,m,n,p,q)

Showcase Comics
5920 Roswell Rd #D204
Sandy Springs GA 30328
PH: (404) 255-5170 (a-c,i,k,m,q,u)

Odin's Cosmic Bookshelf
Killian Hill Crossing
4760 Hwy 29, Ste A-1
Lilburn GA 30247
PH: (404) 923-0123
(a-c,e,g,h,m,o-s,u)

White Books & Comics
Great New York Flea Market
I-75 Exit 142 West
Ringgold GA
PH: (706) 820-1449 (a,b,e,g,h,q)

Odin's Cosmic Bookshelf
Stone Mountain Festival
1825 Rockbridge Rd SW
Stone Mountain GA 30087
PH: (404) 413-0123
(a-c,g,k,m,o-s,u)

HAWAII

Compleat Comics Company
1728 Kaahumanu Avenue
Wailuku HI 96793
PH: (808) 242-5875 (b,c,m,n,p-s)

IDAHO

New Mythology Comics & Science Fiction
1725 Broadway
Boise ID 83706
PH: (208) 344-6744 (a-c,e,m,n,p-s)

ILLINOIS

Graham Crackers Comics LTD
369 W Army Trail Rd
Bloomingdale IL 60108
PH: (708) 894-8810
(c,g,k,m,p,q,r,u)

Graham Crackers Comics LTD
120 N Bolingbrook Dr
Bolingbrook IL 60440
PH: (708) 739-6810
(c,g,k,m,p,q,r,t,u)

Joe Sarno's Comic Kingdom
5941 W. Irving Park Road
Chicago IL 60634
PH: (312) 545-2231 (a-c,d,j,m,q)

Larry's Comic Book Store
1219 W. Devon Ave
Chicago IL 60660
PH: (312) 274-1832 (a-c,t,u)

Larry Laws
(Appointment Only)
831 Cornelia
Chicago IL 60657-1734
PH: (312) 477-9247 (e,g,h,m,o)

Yesterday
1143 West Addison St.
Chicago, IL 60613
PH: (312) 248-8087
(a,b,d-g,l-n,q,s)

The Paper Escape
205 W First St
Dixon IL 61021
PH: (815) 284-7567 (c,e,m,p,r,s)

Graham Crackers Comics LTD
3230 S. Main Street
Downers Grove IL 60515
PH: (708) 852-1810
(c,g,k,m,p,q,r,u)

GEM Comics
156 N York Rd
Elmhurst IL 60126
PH: (708) 833-8787
(b,c,g,k,m,p,q,r)

Action Comics & Games
1637 Waukegan Rd
Glenview IL 60025
PH: (708) 724-1111
(b,c,g,k,m,p-r,u)

Graham Crackers Comics LTD
5 E. Chicago Ave
Naperville IL 60540
PH: (708) 355-4310
(a-d,f,g,k,m,n,p-s,u)

Tomorrow Is Yesterday
5600 N. 2nd Street
Rockford IL 61111
PH: (815) 633-0330 (a-n,p-u)

Comic Heaven
110 N Chicago Street
Rossville IL 60963
PH: (217) 748-6210 (a-c,k,m,o,p,q)

Graham Crackers Comics LTD
108 E. Main Street
St Charles IL 60174
PH: (708) 584-0610
(c,g,k,m,p,q,r,u)

Unicorn Comics & Cards
216 S Villa Avenue
Villa Park, IL 60181
PH: (708) 279-5777
(a-e,g,h,j,l-n,p-r)

Thumbs Up Comics & Cards
1788 W Hintz Rd
Wheeling IL 60090
PH: (708) 670-1309 (b,c,j,k,m,p,q)

INDIANA

The Book Broker
2127 S. Weinbach Ave
Evansville IN 47714
PH: (812) 479-5647
(a-c,e-i,l,m,n,p-u)

Books Comics and Things
5950 W Jefferson Blvd
Fort Wayne IN 46804
PH: (219) 436-0159
(a-c,m,p,q,r,s,t)

Books Comics and Things
2212 Maplecrest Rd
Fort Wayne IN 46815
PH: (219) 749-4045
(a-c,m,p,q,r,s,t)

Comic Carnival
6265 N Carrollton Ave
Indianapolis IN 46220
PH: (317) 253-8882 (a-j,l-t)

Comic Carnival
7311 U.S. 31 South
Indinapolis IN 46227
PH: (317) 889-8899 (a-j,l-t)

Comic Carnival
5002 S Madison Ave
Indianapolis IN 46227
PH: (317) 787-3773 (a-j,l-t)

Comic Carnival
3837 N. High School Rd
Indianapolis IN 46254
PH: (317) 293-4386 (a-j,l-t)

Comic Carnival
9729 E Washington St
Indianapolis IN 46229
PH: (317) 898-5010 (a-j,l-t)

Galactic Greg's
1407 E Lincolnway
Valparaiso IN 46383
PH: (219) 464-0119 (a-c,m,n,q-t)

IOWA

Oak Leaf Comics
1926 Valley Park Dr
Cedar Falls IA 50613
PH: (319) 277 1835 (b,c,k,m,n,p-u)

Comic World & Sports Cards
1626 Central Ave
Dubuque IA 52001
PH: (319) 557-1897
(a-c,e,g,m,p-u)

Oak Leaf Comics
23-5th SW
Mason City IA 50401
PH: (515) 424-0333 (a-c,f,k-s,u)

KANSAS

Kwality Comics
1111 Massachusetts
Lawrence KS 66044
PH: (913) 843-7239 (a-c,e,g,i,m-u)

Prairie Dog Comics Main Store
7130 W Maple
Wichita KS 67207
PH: (316) 942-3456 (a-u)

KENTUCKY

Pac-Rat's, Inc.
1051 Bryant Way
Bowling Green KY 42103
PH: (502) 782-8092 (a-c,g,l,m,p-s)

Comic Book World Inc
7130 Turfway Rd
Florence KY 41042
PH: (606) 371-9562 (a-c,m,p,q,r,s)

Comic Book World Inc.
6905 Shepherdsville Rd
Louisville KY 40219
PH: (502) 964-5500 (a-c,m,p,q,r,s)

LOUISIANA

B.T. & W.D. Giles
P.O. Box 271
Keithville LA 71047
PH: (318) 925-6654 (a,b,d-f,h,l)

More Fun Comics
8200 Oak Street
New Orleans LA 70118
PH: (504) 865-1800 (a-c,g,m,n,p,q)

MAINE

Top Shelf Coins and Comics
34 Main Street
Bangor ME 04401
PH: (207) 947-4939 (a-c,m,q)

Moonshadow Comics
357 Maine Mall Rd
South Portland ME 04106
PH: (207) 772-4605
(a-c,g,i,m,n,q-u)

MARYLAND

Comic Book Kingdom, Inc.
4307 Harford Rd
PO Box 3679
Baltimore MD 21214-3679
PH: (410) 426-4529 (a-c,f,g,m,q)

Geppi's Comic World
1722 North Rolling Road
Baltimore MD 21244
PH: (410) 298-1758 (a-c,f)

Geppi's Comic World
Harbor Place
301 Light Street Pavilion
Baltimore MD 21202
PH: (410) 547-0910 (a-c,f)

Big Planet Comics
4908 Fairmont Ave
Bethesda MD 20814
PH: (301) 654-6856 (b,c,n,p,q)

Alternate Worlds
Yorktowne Plaza
72 Cranbrook Rd
Cockeysville MD 21030
PH: (410) 666-3290
(b,c,g,k,m,n,p-u),

The Closet of Comics
7315 Baltimore Avenue
College Park MD 20740
PH: (301) 699-0498
(b,c,d,l,m,n,p,q)

Comics To Astonish
9400 Snowden River Parkway
Columbia MD 21045
PH: (410) 381-2732
(a-c,j,k,m,p,q,r)

The Dugout Cards & Comics
9200 Baltimore Nat'l Pike
Ellicott City MD 21042
PH: (410) 461-8664 (c,k,m,q,s)

Comic Classics
203 E. Main Street
Frostburg MD 21532
PH: (301) 689-1823 (a-c,m,n,p,q,s)

Collectors World
235 Muddy Branch Rd
Gaithersburg MD 20878
PH: (301) 840-9729
(a-c,k,m,n,p,s,u)

Collectors World
612 Quince Orchard Rd
Gaithersburg MD 20878
PH:(301) 840-0520 (a-c,k,m,n,p,s,u)

Comic Classics
365 Main Street
Laurel MD 20707
PH: (301) 490-9811
(410) 792-4744
(a-c,k,m,n,p,q,s,t,u)

Zenith Comics & Collectibles
18200 Georgia Ave
Olney MD 20832
PH: (301) 774-1345 (a-c,j-s,u)

Adventure Comics
1055 Rockville Pike
Rockville MD 20852
PH: (301) 251-2888 (a-c,j,p,q)

Geppi's Comic World
Silver Spring
8317 Fenton Street
Silver Spring MD 20910
PH: (301) 588-2546 (a-c,f)

MASSACHUSETTS

New England Comics
131 Harvard Avenue
Allston MA 02134
PH: (617) 783-1848
(a-c,e,g,k-n,p-u)

New England Comics
1840 Centre Street
West Roxbury
Boston MA 02132
PH: (617) 325-1848
(a-c,e,g,k-n,p-u)

New England Comics
748 Crescent Street
East Crossing Plaza
Brockton MA 02402
PH: (508) 559-5068
(a-c,e,g,k-n,p-u)

New England Comcis
316 Harvard Street
Coolidge Corner
Brookline MA 02146
PH: (617) 566-0115
(a-c,e,g,k-n,p-u)

New England Comics
12 B Eliot Street
Harvard Square
Cambridge, MA 02138
PH: (617) 354-5352
(a-c,e,g,k-n,p-u)

The Harvey Collection
1794 Bridge Street
12 Bridgewood Plaza (Rt. 38)
Dracut MA 01826
PH: (508) 452-6966 (a,b,e,g,h,l)

That's Entertainment
387 Main St
Fitchburg MA 01420
PH: (508) 342-8607 (a-u)

Bop City Comics
Rt 9 Marshalls Mall
Framingham MA 01701
PH: (508) 872-2317 (a-u)

Jams Comic Connection
435 King Street (Rt 110/2A)
Littleton MA 01460
PH: (508) 486-1099
(c,e,g,k,m,p,q,r,s)

New England Comics
Malden Center
12A Pleasant Street
Malden MA 02148
PH: (617) 322-2404
(a-c,e,g,k-n,p-u)

New England Comics
732 Washington Street
Norwood Center
Norwood MA 02062
PH: (617) 769-4552
(a-c,e,g,k-n,p-u)

Outer Limits Limited
377 Court Street
Rt 3A Cordage Park, Bldg. 3
N. Plymouth MA 02360
PH: (508) 747-2550 (b,c,g,m,q,s)

Newbury Comics
240 Andover St
Peabody MA 01960
PH: (508) 531-9713
(c,e,g,i,j-n,p,q,s)

New England Comics
11 Court Street
Plymouth Center
Plymouth MA 02360
PH: (508) 746-8797
(a-c,e,g,k-n,p-u)

New England Comics
1511 Hancock Street
Quincy Center
Quincy MA 02169
PH: (617) 770-1848
(a-c,e,g,k-n,p-u)

Newbury Comics
551 Boston Turnpike
Shrewsbury MA 01545
PH: (508) 845-3391
(c,e,g,i,j-n,p,q,s)

The Outer Limits
463 Moody Street
Waltham MA 02154
PH: (617) 891-0444 (a-u)

Bookstore & Restaurant, Inc.
Box 502 Kendrick Ave
Wellfleet MA 02667
PH: (508) 349-2101 (a-c,d,e,f,g,h,i)

Stan's Toy Chest
8 West Main Street
Westboro MA 01581
PH: (508) 366-5091
(a-c,d-k,m,o-q,s)

New England Comics
1840 Centre Street
West Roxbury MA 02132
PH: (617) 325-1848
(a-c,e,g,k-n,p-u)

That's Entertainment
244 Park Avenue
Worcester MA 01609
PH: (508) 755-4207 (a-u)

MICHIGAN

Tom & Terry Comics
508 Lafayette Ave
Bay City MI 48708
PH: (517) 895-5525
(b,c,e,g,i,k,l,m,p,r,s,t)

Comics North
108 E State Street
Cheboygan MI 49721-1752
PH: (616) 627-3740 (b,c,p,q,r,s)

Campus Comics
541 E Grand River
E. Lansing MI 48823
PH: (517) 351-4513 (b,c,r)

Curious Book
307 E Grand River
E. Lansing MI 48823
PH: (517) 332-0112 (d-k,m,o,s,u)

Curious Comic Shop
210 M.A.C. Ave
E. Lansing MI 48823
PH: (517)-332-0222 (a-c,l-u)

Amazing Book Store, Inc.
3718 Richfield Rd
Flint MI 48506
PH: (810) 736-3025 (b,e,q)

Tardy's Collector's Corner, Inc
2009 Eastern Ave. SE
Grand Rapids MI 49507
PH: (616) 247-7828 (a-c,g,m,n,p,q)

Argos Book Shop
1405 Robinson Rd SE
Grand Rapids MI 49506
PH: (616) 454-0111 (a-k,o-u)

Coy's Comics
301 S Hamilton
Saginaw MI 48602
PH: (517) 790-1810
(a-c,f,g,k,l,m-s,u)

Galaxy Comics
3069 Bay Plaza
Saginaw MI 48604
PH: (517) 799-6334
(a-c,k,m,n,p,q,s)

MINNESOTA

John Mlachnik
(Appointment Only)
P.O. Box 69
Chisholm MN 55719
PH: (218) 254-3763 (a,b)

Nostalgia Zone
3149 1/2 Hennepin Ave S
Minneapolis MN 55408
PH: (612) 822-2806
(a,b,d-n,p,q,r,t)

Midway Book & Comic
1579 University Ave (at Snelling)
St Paul MN 55104
PH: (612) 644-7605 (a-h,n,p,q)

MISSOURI

The Collector's Cove
5507 Lake Avenue
Saint Joseph MO 64504
PH: (816) 238-8166 (b,c,k,m,p,q,s)

MO's Comics & Stories
4573 Gravois
St Louis MO 63116
PH: (314) 353-9500 (a-c,f,o,q,s)

MONTANA

The Book Exchange
3100 Harrison Ave
Butte Plaza Mall
Butte MT 59701
PH: (406) 494-7788 (c,e,h,q)

The Book Exchange
2335 Brooks St
Tremper's Shopping Ctr
Missoula MT 59801
PH: (406) 728-6342 (c,e,h,q,r)

NEBRASKA

Just Comics, Inc.
11814 S 25th St
Omaha NE 68123
PH: (402) 292-3337
(b,c,k,m,p,q,s,u)

NEVADA

Fandom's Comicworld & Gallery
2001 East Second Street
Reno NV 89502
PH: (702) 786-6663
(a-c,i,j,m,p,q,u)

Fandom's Comicworld & Gallery
669 N McCarran
Sparks NV 89431
PH: (702) 358-7977 (a-c,j,m,p,r,s)

NEW HAMPSHIRE

James F. Payette
P.O. Box 750
Bethlehem MH 03574
PH: (603) 869-2097 (a,b,d-h)

Dover Cards and Comics
11 Main Street
Dover NH 03820-3811
PH: (603) 749-6862
(a-c,g,m,n,p,q,r,u)

Comic Store
643 Elm Street
Manchester NH 03101
PH: (603) 668-6705
(a-c,g,j,k,l,m,n,p-u)

Comic Store
300 Main Street
Nashua NH 03060
PH: (603) 881-4855
(a-c,g,j,k,l,m,n,p-u)

NEW JERSEY

The Hobby Shop
Route 34 Strathmore S/C
Aberdeen NJ 07747
PH: (908) 583-0505 (a-c,k,m,q,r,s)

Comic Plus
Laurel Square, Hwy 70 & 88
Brick NJ 08723
PH: (908) 206-1070
(a-c,g,h,k,m,p,q)

Legends
2E-13 Deptford Mall
300 N Almonesson Rd
Deptford NJ 08096
PH: (609) 845-8055

Comic Collectibles
PO Box 536
East Brunswick NJ 08816
PH: (908) 238-9023

Thunder Road Sportscards and Comics
1973 North Olden Ave
Ewing NJ 08618
PH: (609) 771-1055 (a,b,k,m,q)

Jim Hanley's Universe
A&P Shopping Center
Rt. 1 & Ford Ave.
Fords NJ 08863
PH: (908) 417-5744
(a-c,g,m,n,p-u)

A Time Lost.....And Found
310 E Evesham Rd
Glendora NJ 08029
PH: (609) 939-1909
(a-e,g,k,m,n,p,q-t)

Star Spangled Comics
353 Rte 22 (At Green Brook Rd)
Green Brook NJ 08812
PH: (908) 356-8338
(a-c,g,j,m,p,q,r,u)

Dreamer's Comics
229 Main Street
Hackettstown NJ 07840
PH: (908) 850-5255 (a-c,k,l,m,p,q)

Thunder Road Sportscards and Comics
1637 Route 33
Hamilton Square NJ 08690
PH: (609) 587-5353 (a,b,k,m,q)

The Comic Book Shop
Lake Side Shopping Center
Route 15 South
Lake Hopatcong NJ 07849
PH: (201) 663-4440 (b,c,e,m,p,r)

Comics Plus
Middletown Plaza
1383 Hwy 35
Middletown NJ 07748
PH: (908) 706-0102
(a-c,g,h,k,m,p,q)

Montclair Book Center
221 Glenridge Ave
Montclair NJ 07042
PH: (201) 783-3630 (a-h,m,n,p-t)

Fat Jack's Comicrypt
521 White Horse Pike
Oaklyn NJ 08107
PH: (609) 858-3877 (a-c,m,n,p-t)

MC Comics Inc
54 Old Matawan Rd
Old Bridge NJ 08857
PH: (908) 238-5969
(a-c,g,k,m,n,p,q,s)

Passaic Book Center, Inc.
594-96 Main Ave Dept FP5
Passaic NJ 07055
PH: (201) 778-6646 (a-u)

Mr. Collector
327 Union Blvd
Totowa NJ 07512
PH: (201) 595-0900 (a-c,m,q)

Legends
F7 Cumberland Mall
Vineland NJ 08360
PH: (609) 825-0300

Comics Plus
Ocean Plaza Hwy 35
& Sunset Ave
Wanamassa NJ 07712
PH: (908) 922-3308
(a-c,g,h,k,m,p,q)

Comic Museum
790 Woodlane Road
Westampton NJ 08060
PH: (609) 261-0996
(a-c,e,m,n,p,q,t,u)

JHV Associates
(Appointment Only)
PO Box 317
Woodbury Heights, NJ 08097
PH: (609) 845-4010 (a,b,d)

NEW MEXICO

Bruce's Comics
2432 Cerrillos Rd
Santa Fe NM 87505
PH: (505) 474-0494
(a-i,m,n,p,q,r,s,u)

NEW YORK

Fantaco Enterprises, Inc.
21 Central Ave
Albany NY 12210
PH: (518) 463-1400 (c,l-n,q,r,u)

Long Island Comics
1675 Sunrise Hwy
Bay Shore L.I. NY 11706
PH: (516) 665-4342 (Afternoons)
(b,c,e,g,q)

Comic Shop At Pinocchio
1814 McDonald Ave
Brooklyn NY 11223
PH: (718) 645-2573 (b,c,g,k,m,q,s)

Wow-Comics
642 Pelham Pkwy South
Bronx NY 10462
PH: (718) 829-0461 (a-c,k,m,q-s)

Heroes on the Half Shelf
93 West Main St
East Islip NY 11730
PH: (516) 224-7360 (c,m,p,q,r)

Comics & Hobbies
156 Mamaroneck Ave
Mamaroneck NY 10543
PH: (914) 698-9473 (c,h,m,q,r)

Comics Plus
Sangertown Square Mall
New Hartford NY 13413
PH: (315) 724-3370
(a-c,g,k,m,n,p,q,r,s,u)

Action Comics
1724 2nd Ave
New York NY 10128
PH: (212) 534-0096
(a-c,g,k,m,p,q,r,s)

Funny Business Comics Ltd.
660 B Amsterdam Ave
(92nd Street)
New York City NY 10025
PH: (212) 799-9477 (b,c,m,n)

Big Apple Comic
2489 Broadway (92/93 St.)
New York, NY 10025
PH: (201) 585-2765 (a-d,j,m,n,q)

Alex's MVP Cards & Comics
256 E 89th St
New York, NY 10128
PH: (212) 831-2273 (a-c,j,k,m,p,q)

Jerry Ohlinger's Movie Material Store, Inc.
242 West 14 Street
New York, NY 10011
PH: (212) 989-0869 (i)

Jim Hanley's Universe
166 Chambers Street
New York, NY 10007
PH: (212) 349-2930
(a-c,g,m,n,p-u)

Jim Hanley's Universe
126 West 32nd Street
New York, NY 10001
PH: (212) 268-7088
(a-c,g,m,n,p-u)

Manhattan Comics & Cards
228 W 23rd Street
New York, NY 10011
PH: (212) 243-9349 (a-c,g,j-n,q,u)

Fantastic Planet
24 Oak Street
Plattsburgh, NY 12901
PH: (518) 563-2946
(a-c,e,g,m,p-u)

Dragons Den
Poughkeepsie Plaza Mall Rt 9
Poughkeepsie, NY 12601
PH: (914) 471-1401

Iron Vic Comics
1 Raymond Ave
Poughkeepsie NY 12603
PH: (914) 473-8365 (a-d,g,j,m,n,q)

Empire® Comics
1176 Mt Hope Ave
Rochester NY 14620
PH: (716) 442-0371
(a-c,f,h,k,q-s,m,u)

Empire® Comics
375 Stone Rd
Rochester NY 14616
PH: (716) 663-6877
(a-c,f,h,k,q-s,m,u)

Alien World Inc.
322 Sunrise Highway
Rockville Centre NY 11570
PH: (516) 536-8151
(b,c,g,h,k,m,p,r)

One if by Cards, Two if by Comics, Inc.
1107 Central Ave
Scarsdale NY 10583
PH: (914) 725-2225 (b,c,j,k,m,q)

Jim Hanley's Universe
350 New Dorp Lane
Staten Island, NY 10306
PH: (718) 351-6299
(a-c,g,m,n,p-u)

Krypton Comics of Staten Island, Inc.
2143 Hylan Boulevard
Staten Island NY 10306
PH: (718) 667-7695 (b,c,k,m,p,q,r)

Twilight Book & Game Emporium, Inc.
Carousel Center
Syracuse NY 13290
PH: (315) 466-1601
(c,e,g,k,m,q,r,s,t)

Twilight Book & Game Emporium, Inc.
1401 N. Salina St
Syracuse NY 13208
PH: (315) 471-3139
(a-c,e,g,k,m,n,p-u)

Aquilonia Comics
412 Fulton St
Troy NY 12180
PH: (518) 271-1069
(a-c,e,g,m,n,p,q,s,t)

Ravenswood, Inc.
263 Genesee Street
Utica NY 13501
PH: (315) 735-3699
(a-c,g,m,p,q,r,s,t)

Collector's Comics
3247 Sunrise Hwy
Wantagh NY 11793
PH: (516) 783-8700
(a-c,e,g,m,n,p,r,u)

NORTH CAROLINA

Super Giant Comics
273-A Tunnel Road
Asheville NC 28805
PH: (704) 253-6188
(a-e,g,h,j,l-n,q,r)

Heroes Aren't Hard to Find
Corner Central Ave & the Plaza
PO Box 9181
Charlotte NC 28299
PH: (704) 375-7462
(a-c,g,j,k,l,m,n,p,s,u)

Heroes Are Here
208 S Berkeley Blvd
Goldsboro NC 27534
PH: (919) 751-3131 (a-c,m,p,q)

Heroes Are Here, Too
116 E Fifth St
Greenville NC 27834
PH: (919) 757-0948 (a-c,m,p,q)

The Nostalgia Newsstand
919 Dickinsen Ave
Greenville NC 27834
PH: (919) 758-6909 (b,c,e,n,p,q)

Comic X-Press
240 Newton Road
Fayetteville NC 27618
PH: (919) 676-1210
(a-c,j,m,p,q,r,u)

Comic X-Press
3802 Sycamore Dairy Rd
Fayetteville NC 28314
PH: (910) 867-3080
(a-c,j,m,p,r,q,u)

Acme Comics
3808-C High Point Rd
Greensboro NC 27407
PH: (910) 855-0217
(a-c,j,m,n,p,q,s,u)

Acme Comics
2150 Lawndale Dr
Greensboro NC 27408
PH: (910) 574-2263
(a-c,m,n,p,q,s,u)

Parts Unknown The Comic Book Store
The Cotton Mill Square, 801
Merritt Dr
Greensboro NC 27407
PH: (910) 294-0091 (a-c,g,p,q)

Tales Resold
3936 Atlantic Ave
Raleigh NC 27604
PH: (919) 878-8551
(a-c,d,e,g,h,j,p,q)

Booktrader Comics
121 Country Club Rd
Rocky Mount NC 27804
PH: (919) 443-3993 (e)

Comics & Cards Unlimited
506 Waynesville Plaza
Waynesville NC 28786
PH: (704) 456-8787
(a-c,g,k,l,m,q,r)

Acme Comics
1201 Silas Creek Parkway
Winston-Salem NC 27103
PH: (910) 777-0290
(a-c,m,n,p,q,s,u)

Heroes Aren't Hard to Find
Silas Creek Shopping Ctr
3234 Silas Creek Parkway
Winston-Salem NC 27103
PH: (919) 765-4370 (a-c,g,j-l,p-s,u)

Rays Comics And Collectibles
12201-6 Hickory Tree Crossing
Shopping Center
Winston-Salem NC 27127
PH: (910) 764-2055 (a-u)

NORTH DAKOTA

Barry's Collector's Corner
City Center Mall
Grand Forks, ND 58201
PH: (701) 772-2518
(a-c,f,g,i,k,m,n,q-s)

Tom's Coin Stamp Gem Baseball & Comic Shop
#2 1st Street SW
Minot ND 58701
PH: (701) 852-4522 (a-q,s,u)

OHIO

Kenmore Komics And Games
1020 Kenmore Blvd
Akron OH 44314
PH: (216) 745-5530
(b,c,m,p,q,r,s,t,u)

Dark Star III Books & Comics
1273 N Fairfield Rd
Beavercreek OH 45432
PH: (513) 427-3213
(b,c,e,h,m,p-q,s-u)

Comic Book World Inc.
4016 Harrison Ave
Cincinnati OH 45211
PH: (513) 661-6300 (a-c,m,p,q-s)

Comic Central
7185 Beechmont Avenue
Cincinnati OH 45230
513-231-4800 (a-c,k,m,p,q,u)

Collectors Warehouse Inc.
5437 Pearl Road
Cleveland OH 44129
PH: (216) 842-2896 (a-j,k-n,p-s)

Bookery Fantasy & Comics
35 N Broad St
Fairborn OH 45324
PH: (513) 879-1408 (c,e,g,j-u)

Bookery Fantasy SA/GA
37 N Broad St
Fairborn OH 45324
PH: (513) 878-0144 (a,b,d-f,h,i)

Dark Star II Books & Comics
1410 W. Dorothy Lane
Kettering OH 45409
PH: (513) 293-7307
(b,c,e,h,m,p-q,s-u)

Bookie Parlor
2778 Wilmington Pike
Kettering OH 45419
PH: (513) 293-2243 (a-c,g,m,p,q,s)

Monarch Cards & Comics
4400 Heatherdowns -
Colonial Village Plaza
Toledo OH 43614
PH: (419) 382-1451 (c,g,k,m,p,q,s)

Dark Star Books & Comics
237 Xeniz Ave
Yellow Springs OH 45387
PH: (513) 767-9400
(a-c,e-h,m,n,p-q,s-u)

Funnie Farm Bookstore
328 N Dixie Dr
Vandalia OH 45377
PH: (513) 898-2794 (a-c,m,p,q,r)

OKLAHOMA

Planet Comics
918 W Main
Norman OK 73069
PH: (405) 329-9695
(b,c,e,g,k,l,m,n,p-u)

New World Comics & Games
2203 W. Main #10
Norman OK 73069
PH: (405) 321-7445
(a-c,g,i,m,n,p-u)

New World Comics & Games
6219 N Meridian
Oklahoma City OK 73112
PH: (405) 721-7634
(a-c,g,i,m,n,p-u)

New World Comics & Games
4420 SE 44th St
Oklahoma City OK 73157
PH: (405) 677-2559
(a-c,g,i,m,n,p-u)

Comic Empire of Tulsa
3122 S Mingo
Tulsa OK 74146
PH: (918) 664-5808 (a-c,m,n,p,q)

Want List Comics
(Appointment Only)
PO Box 701932
Tulsa OK 74170-1932
PH: (918) 299-0440 (a,b,f,h-k,m)

Starbase 21
2130 S Sheridan Rd
Tulsa OK 74129
PH: (918) 838-3388
(a-c,e,g,j,l,m,p-u)

OREGON

Rictor's Comic Heaven
1110 NW Van Buren
Corvallis OR 97330
PH: (503) 757-7376 (a-c,g,m,n,p,q)

Emerald City Comics
770 E 13th
Eugene OR 97401
PH: (503) 345-2568
(c,e,m,p,q,r,s,u)

Nostalgia Collectibles
527 Willamette
Eugene OR 97401
PH: (503) 484-9202 (a-g,i-n,p,q,r,t)

Beyond Comics
322 East Main
Medford OR 97501
PH: (503) 779-9543 (a-c,m,q,r,p)

Heroes Haven
627 SE Jackson Street
Roseburg OR 97470
PH: (503) 673-5004 (a-c,m,p,q,r,s)

PENNSYLVANIA

Cap's Comic Cavalcade
1894 Catasauqua Rd
Allentown PA 18103
PH: (610) 264-5540 (a-c,g,k-u)

Dreamscape Comics
310 West Broad Street
Bethlehem PA 18018
PH: (215) 867-1178 (a-c,m,n,p-r)

Showcase Comics I
874 W Lancaster Ave
Bryn Mawr PA 19010
PH: (610) 527-6236
(a-c,g,m,n,q,r,s,t,u)

Comix Connection/Camp Hill
604 Camp Hill Mall
Camp Hill PA 17011
PH: (800) 730-0994
(a-c,g,k,m,n,p,q,r,u)

Time Tunnel Collectibles
1001 Castle Shannon Blvd
Castle Shannon PA 15234-1803
PH: (412) 531-8833 (a-c,g,j,m,p,q)

New Dimension Comics
20550 Route 19- Piazza Plaza
Cranberry Township PA
16066-7520
PH: (412) 776-0433 (a-c,m,q,r,s)

Adventures In Comics
3279 W. Liberty Ave
Dormont PA 15216
PH: (412) 531-5644 (a-c,g,k,m,p-u)

Dreamscape Comics
25th Street Shopping Center
Easton PA 18042
PH: (215) 250-9818 (a-c,m,n,p-r)

Swallow A Slug Comics
4 Center Square
Elizabethtown PA 17022
PH: (717) 361-7198
(a,b,c,k,m,n,o,q)

Golden Unicorn Comics
860 Alter St
Hazleton PA 18201
PH: (717) 455-4645
(b,c,g,m,n,p,q,r)

Puff N' Stuff
703 Lowry Ave
Jeannette PA 15644
PH: (412) 523-8444 (c,k,m,q,u)

Captain Blue Hen Comics & Cards
1800 Lincoln Hwy East
Lancaster PA 17602
PH: (717) 397-8011
(a-i,k,m,p,q,r,s,u)

The Comic Store
2481 Lincoln Hwy E
Lancaster PA 17602
PH: (717) 397-8636 (c,g,m,p,q,r,s)

The Comic Store
28 McGovern Ave
Lancaster PA 17602
PH: (717) 397-8737
(a-c,d,g,m,n,p,q,r,s,u)

Hobbies & Heroes
332 Main Street
Latrobe PA 15650
PH: (412) 539-1101 (b,c,g,q,r,s)

Yukon Cards and Comics
Rte 209 and Market Street
Lykens PA 17048
PH: (717) 453-9904 (b,c,g,m,q,s)

Showcase Comics II
Granite Run Mall, Rte 1
Media PA 19063
PH: (610) 891-9229
(a-c,g,m,n,q,r,s,t,u)

Fat Jack's Comicrypt II
7598 Haverford Ave (rear)
Philadelphia PA 19151
PH: (215) 473-6333
(a-c,g,m,n,p,q,u)

Fat Jack's Comicrypt III
5506 North 5th St
Philadelphia PA 19120
PH: (215) 924-8210
(a-c,g,m,n,p,q,u)

Fat Jack's Comicrypt I
2006 Sansom St
Philadelphia PA 19103
PH: (215) 963-0788
(a-c,g,m,n,p,q,u)

Showcase Comics III
424 South Street
Philadelphia PA 19147
PH: (215) 625-9613
(a-c,g,m,n,q,r,s,t,u)

Crown Antiques and Collectables
2200 Murray
Pittsburgh PA 15217
PH: (412) 422-7995 (a-m,o,s)

Duncan Comics, Books, and Accessories
1047 Perry Highway
Pittsburgh (North Hills) PA 15237
PH: (412) 635-0886
(b,c,d,e,g,h,k,l,m,p,q)

Eide's Entertainment
1111 Penn Ave
Pittsburgh PA 15222
PH: (412) 261-0900 (a-q,s-u)

Legends
2600 Plymouth Meeting Mall
Plymouth Meeting PA 19462
PH: (610) 828-5848
(a-c,g,k,m,n,p,q,r,s,u)

Legends
3009 Willow Grove Mall
Willow Grove PA 19090
PH: (215) 657-6141
(a-c,g,j,k,m,n,p,q,r,s,u)

Comic Store West
351 Loucks Rd
York PA 17404
PH: (717) 845-9198
(b,c,m,n,p,q-s,u)

Comix Connection / York
1201 Carlisle Rd
(Rt 74 at US 30)
York PA 17404
PH: (717) 843-6516
(a-c,g,k,m,n,p,q,r,u)

RHODE ISLAND

The Annex
314 Broadway
Newport RI 02840
PH: (401) 847-4607
(b,c,k,m,n,q,r,s,u)

Fantasy Zone Comics
7610 Post Road
North Kingstown RI 02852
PH: (401) 294-6044 (b,c,g,m,p,q,r)

Video Hut & Comics
462 Central Ave
Pawtucket RI 02861
PH: (401) 724-0440 (c,g,i,k,l,m,p,q)

Newbury Comics
1500 Bald Hill Rd
Warwick RI 02886
PH: (401) 821-3170
(c,e,g,i,j-n,p,q,s)

Time Capsule Comics
2737 Post Road
Warwick RI 02886
PH: (401) 732-8007 (a-c,g,j-o,q-s)

SOUTH CAROLINA

Zapp Comic
3464 Cinema Center
Anderson SC 29621
PH: (803) 261-3578 (a-c,g,j,l,n,q)

Book Exchange
1219 Savannah Hwy
Charleston SC 29407
PH: (803) 556-5051 (a-c,h,q)

Heroes Aren't Hard to Find
1415- A Laurens Rd
Greenville SC 29607
PH: (803) 235-3488
(a-c,g,j-n,p-s,u)

Heroes Aren't Hard to Find
Westgate Mall I-26 & US 29
Spartanburg SC 29301
PH: (803) 574-1713
(a-c,g,j-n,p-s,u)

TENNESSEE

Big D's Cards & Comics
1062 North Washington
Cookeville TN 38501
PH: (615) 528-6070 (b,c,g,k,m,q)

Outer Limits Comics
116 Watson Glen
Franklin TN 37064
PH: (615) 790-2392 (a-c,k,m,p,q,s)

Comics Universe
1869 Hwy 45 By-Pass
Jackson TN 38305
PH: (901) 664-9131
(a-c,j,m,p,q,r,s)

Collectors World
10820 Kingston Pike
Knoxville TN 37922
PH: (615) 675-6830 (a-m,o-u)

The Great Escape
111-B Gallatin Road North
Madison TN 37115
PH: (615) 865-8052 (a-c,g,k-m,p-s)

Comics & Collectibles
4730 Poplar Ave #2
Memphis TN 38117
PH: (901) 683-7171
(a-c,m,n,p,q,r,u)

Collectors World
1511 East Main St
Murfreesboro TN 37130
PH: (615) 895-1120 (a-m,o-u)

Collectors World
5751 Nolensville Rd
Nashville TN 37211
PH: (615) 333-9458 (a-m,o-u)

Comics & Cards
4825 Trousdale Dr
Nashville TN 37220
PH: (615) 834-9913 (a-m,o-u)

The Great Escape
1925 Broadway
Nashville TN 37203
PH: (615) 327-0646 (a-u)

Walt's Paperback Books
2604 Franklin Rd
Nashville TN 37204
PH: (615) 298-2506 (b,c,e,l,m,q)

TEXAS

Lone Star Comics Books & Games
504 East Abram St
Arlington TX 76010
PH: (817) Metro 265-0491
(a-c,e,g,k,m,p-t,u)

Lone Star Comics Books & Games
3415 South Cooper St., #141
Arlington TX 76015
PH: (817) 557-5252
(a-c,e,g,k,m,p-t,u)

Austin Books
5002 N Lamar
Austin TX 78751
PH: (512) 454-4197
(b,c,e,g,i,k,m,n,p,q,r,s)

Lone Star Comics Books & Games
11661 Preston Forest Village
Dallas TX 75230
PH: (214) 373-0934
(a-c,e,g,k,m,p-t,u)

Remember When Comics & Movie Material
2431 Valwood Pkwy
Dallas TX 75234
PH: (214) 243-3439
(a-c,g,i,j,m,p,q,s,t)

Good Time Charlies
114 W Knox
Ennis TX 75119
PH: (214) 875-9737
(a-c,e,g,h,k,l,m,o,p,q,s,u)

Lone Star Comics Books & Games
6312 Hulen Bend Blvd
Ft Worth TX 76132
PH: (817) 346-7773
(a-c,e,g,k,m,p-t,u)

Einstein's Comics, Games, And Art
1540 Northwest Highway
Garland TX 75041
PH: (214) 270-7878 (c,p,q,r,c)

Bedrock City Comic Co
2204-D FM 1960 W
Houston TX 77090
PH: (713) 444-9763 (a-d,f,g,k,m-u)

Bedrock City Comic Co
6521 Westheimer
Houston TX 77057
PH: (713) 780-0675 (a-d,f,g,k,m-u)

L. King Collectables
3001 Fondren, Suite E
Houson TX 77063
PH: (713) 782-2273 (c,k,m,q,r,s)

Third Planet Sci-Fi Super Store
2718 Southwest Freeway
Houston TX 77098
PH: (713) 528-1067 (a-u)

Lone Star Comics Books & Games
931 Melbourne
Hurst TX 76053
PH: (817) 595-4375
(a-c,e,g,k,m,p-t,u)

Lone Star Comics Books & Games
2550 N Beltline Rd
Irving TX 75062
PH: (817) 659-0317
(a-c,e,g,k,m,p-t,u)

Lone Star Comics Books & Games
3600 Gus Thomasson, Suite 107
Mesquite TX 75150
PH: (214) 681-2040
(a-c,e,g,k,m,p-t,u)

Ka-Boom Comics N' Stuf'
2011 W Spring Creek Pkwy #900
Plano TX 75023
PH: (214) 517-6864
(b,c,g,k,m,p,q,r,s)

Lone Star Comics Books

& Games
1900 Preston Rd #345
Plano TX 75093
PH: (214) 985-1953
(a-c,e,g,k,m,p-t,u)

Ground Zero Comics
1700 SSE Loop 323, Suite 302
Tyler TX 75701
PH: (903) 566-1185
(c,e,g,l,m,p,q,r,s,u)

Bankston's Cards & Comics
1321 S Valley Mills Dr
Waco Tx 76711
PH: (817) 755-0070 (b,c,e,k,m,q,s)

UTAH

Comics Utah #1
258 East 100 South
Salt Lake City UT 84118
PH: (800) 927-5075
(a-c,e,m,p,q,r,s)

Comics Utah #2
2750 West 5400 South
Salt Lake City UT 84111
PH: (801) 966-8581
(a-c,e,m,p,q,r,s)

VERMONT

Earth Prime Comics
154 Church Street
Burlington VT 05401
PH: (802) 863-3666
(a-c,k,m,n,p,q,r,s)

VIRGINIA

Comic and Card Collectorama
2008 Mt Vernon Ave
Alexandria VA (Greater D.C. Area)
22301
PH: (703) 548-3466
(a,b,e,f,m,p,q,s,t)

Fantasia Comics
1325 B West Main Street
Charlottesville VA 22903
PH: (804) 971-1029
(b,c,g,m,n,q,r,s)

Fantasia Comcis
1691 Seminole Trail
Charlottesville VA 22901
PH: (804) 974-7512
(b,c,g,m,n,p,q,r,s)

Trilogy Shop #3
3916-A6 Portsmouth Blvd
Chesapeake VA 23321
PH: (804) 488-6578 (c,m,p-s)

Zeno's Books
1112 Sparrow Rd
Chesapeake VA 23325
PH: (804) 420-2344 (a-j,m,r,t)

Geppi's Comic World
1606 Crystal Square Arcade
Crystal City Underground
Arlington VA 22202
PH: (703) 413-0618 (a-c,f)

Hole In the Wall Books
905 West Broad Street
Falls Church VA 22046
PH: (703) 536-2511
(b-e,g,h,l,n,q-u)

Marie's Books & Things
1701 Princess Anne Street
Fredericksburg VA 22401-1344
PH: (703) 373-5196
(a-c,e,f,g,h,p,s)

Benders Books & Cards
22 South Mallory St
Hampton VA 23663
PH: (804) 723-3741 (a-j,m-u)

Cosmic Bookstore
10953 Lute Ct
Manassas VA 22110
PH: (703) 330-8573
(b-e,g,h,j,l,q-u)

World's Best
9817 Jefferson Ave
Newport News VA 23605
PH: (804) 595-9005
(b,c,g,i,k,l,m,n,p,q,r,s,u)

Trilogy Shop #2
700 E Little Creek Rd
Norfolk VA 23518
PH: (804) 587-2540 (c,e,m,p-u)

Dave's Comics
7019 Three Chopt Rd
Richmond VA 23226
PH: (804) 282-1211
(b,c,g,m,p,q,r,s,u)

Nostalgia Plus
1601 Willow Lawn Dr
Richmond VA 23230
PH: (804) 282-5532 (a-c,g,m,n,p,q)

Stories
5065 and 5067 Forest Hill Ave
Richmond VA 23225
PH: (804) 231-4213
(b,c,e,g,h,k,m,n,p,q,s,u)

B & D Comic Shop
802 Elm Ave., SW
Roanoke VA 24016
PH: (703) 342-6642
(b,c,e,g,k,l,m,p,q,r,s)

Big Planet Comics
426 Maple Ave East
Vienna VA 22180
PH: (703) 242-9412 (b,c,p,q,m)

Comics & Things
4406 Holland Rd
Va. Beach VA 23452
PH: (804) 486-5870
(a-e,g,h,i,k,l,m,p,q,r,s,u)

Trilogy Shop #1
5773 Princess Anne Rd
Va Beach VA 23462
PH: (804) 490-2205
(a-c,e,g,i,k,m,p-u)

Trilogy Shop #4
857 S Lynnhaven Rd
Va Beach VA 23452
PH: (804) 468-0412 (c,m,p-s)

WASHINGTON

Quiet Corner
Paperback Exchange
2100 N National Ave
Chehalis WA 98532
PH: (206) 748-4792
(b,c,e,g,k,m,p,q,r,s)

Book Rack & Comic Shop
1481 N. Midway Blvd
Oak Harbor WA 98277
PH: (206) 675-6705 (c,e,m,p,q,r)

Comic Dungeon
1622 1/2 N 45th St
Seattle WA 98103
PH: (206) 545-8373
(a,b,c,f,g,k,m,n,o,p,q,s)

The Comic Character Shop
Old Firehouse Antique Mall
110 Alaskan Way South
Seattle WA 98104
PH: (206) 283-0532 (b,h,i,j,k,p)

Golden Age Collectables, Ltd.

1501 Pike Place Market
401 Lower Level
Seattle WA 98101
PH: (206) 622-9799
(a-g,i-k,m-o,q-v)

Rocket Comics
8544 Greenwood N.
Seattle, WA 98103
PH: (206) 784-7300 (a-c,k,m,p)

Aces High Comics
14602 NE Fourth Plain Rd,
Unit B
Vancouver WA 98682
PH: (360) 254-7678 (a-c,g,m,n,p,q)

Digital Heroes
13 Boyer Ave
Walla Walla WA 99362
PH: (509) 525-0380 (b,c,k,m,p,q-u)

Galaxy Comics
1720 5th Street, Suite D
Wenatchee WA 98801
PH: (509) 663-4330 (b,c,m,p,q,r)

Games Plus
17612 - 140th Ave. NE
Woodinville, WA 98072
PH: (206) 485-7295 (c,e,g,m,p,q,r)

WEST VIRGINIA

Comic Castle
314 Neville St
Beckley WV 25801
PH: (304) 253-1974
(b,c,k,m,n,o,p,q,r)

C & C Comics
318 Winfield Rd
St Albans WV 25177
PH: (304) 727-5207 (b,c,m,n,p,q,s)

WISCONSIN

Westfield's Comics, Etc.
Loehmann's Plaza
17125E W Bluemound Rd
Brookfield WI 53005
PH: (414) 821-0242
(b,c,g,k,l,m,p,q,r,s,t,u)

Capital City Comics
1910 Monroe Street
Madison, WI 53711
PH: (608) 251-8445

20th Century Books
108 King St
Madison WI 53703
PH: (608) 251-6226
(c,e,h,m,n,q,s-u)

Westfield's Comics, Etc.
676 S Whitney Way
Madison WI 53711
PH: (608) 277-1280
(b,c,g,k,l,m,p,q-u)

Capital City Comics
2565 N. Downer Ave.
Milwaukee, WI 53211
PH: (414) 332-8199

The Mill
1405 Hwy 47 South
PO Box 1456
Woodruff WI 54568-1456
PH: (715) 356-5468 (a,b,e,h,k,q)

CALGARY/ALBERTA

Another Dimension Comics
324-10 St NW
Calgary Alberta CD T2N 1V8
PH: (403) 283-7078
(a-c,e,g,k,m,n,p,q-s,u)

Another Dimension Comics
Chinook Centre, 6455 Macleod
Trail S
Calgary Alberta CD
PH: (403) 255-2588
(b,c,e,g,k,m,p,q-s)

Another Dimension Comics
4625 Varsity Dr NW
Calgary Alberta CD T2A 0Z9
PH: (403) 288-1802
(b,c,e,g,k,m,p,q,s)

Another Dimension Comics
2640-52 St NE
Calgary Alberta CD T1Y 3R6
PH: (403) 293-1272
(b,c,e,g,k,m,p,q,r,s)

QUEBEC

Heroes Comic Laval
1116 Cure LaBelle
Chomedey Laval
Quebec CD H7V 2V5
PH: (514) 686-9155 (a-e,m,q-t,u)

Komico Inc.
4210 Decarie
Montreal Quebec CD H4A 3K3
PH: (514) 489-4009 (a-c,g,n,p,q)

Premiere Issue
27 "A" D'Auteuil
(Vieux-Quebec)
Quebec CD G1R 4B9
PH: (418) 692-3985 (a-e,g,i,m,p,q,r,s)

BRITISH COLUMBIA

Page After Page
1771 Harvey Ave
Kelowna, BC CD V1Y 6G4
PH: (604) 860-6554 (b,c,e,q,r)

Teds Paperback & Comics
269 Leon Ave
Kelowna, BC CD V1Y 6T1
PH: (604) 763-1258 (a-c,e,q)

Golden Age Collectables
830 Granville St
Vancouver, BC CD V3Z 1K3
PH: (604) 683-2819 (a-d,f,i,j,n,o)

MANITOBA

The Collector's Slave
156 Imperial Ave
Winnipeg, Manitoba CD
R2M 0K8
PH: (204) 237-4428
(b,c,e-g,k-n,p-r,t,u)

HONG KONG

Clark's Comics
Shop 204, 2/F.,
Causeway Bay Centre
15-23 Sugar St., Hong Kong
PH: (852) 28907718

FRANCE

Dangereuses Visions-Comics Megastore
81 Rue De La Monnaie
59800 Lille France
PH: 33 20 06 51 51
(b,c,g,k,l,m,n,p,q,s,u)

NETHERLANDS

Haagse Stripshop
Wacenstraat 133
2512 AT The Hague
Netherlands
PH: 31-703634115
(c,e,j,k,l,m,n,p,q,s,u)

ADVERTISERS DIRECTORY

ADVERTISERS DIRECTORY (Cont'd)